# All Music Guide to Electronica

## THE DEFINITIVE GUIDE

## TO ELECTRONIC MUSIC

Edited by

Vladimir Bogdanov

Chris Woodstra

Stephen Thomas Erlewine

John Bush

### All Media Guide

All Media Guide has created the world's largest and most comprehensive information databases for music, videos, DVDs, and video games. With coverage of both in-print and out-of-print titles, the massive AMG archive includes reviews, plot synopses, biographies, ratings, images, titles, credits, essays, and thousands of descriptive categories. All content is original, written expressly for AMG by a worldwide network of professional staff and freelance writers specializing in music, movies, and games. The AMG databases—All Music Guide®, All Movie Guide®, and All Game Guide™—are licensed by major retailers and Internet content sites and are available to the public through its websites (www.allmusic.com, www.allmovie.com, www.allgame.com) and through its series of books: *All Music Guide*, *All Music Guide to Rock*, *All Music Guide to Country*, *All Music Guide to Jazz*, *All Music Guide to Blues*, and *All Music Guide to Electronica*.

**All Media Guide, 301 E. Liberty Street, Suite 400, Ann Arbor, MI 48104**
T: 734/887-5600 F: 734/827-2492
contact@allmusic.com

Published by Backbeat Books
600 Harrison Street, San Francisco, CA 94105
www.backbeatbooks.com
Email: books@musicplayer.com
An imprint of Music Player Network
United Entertainment Media, Inc.
Publishers of MusicPlayer.com

©2001 AEC One Stop Group, Inc., MusicPlayer.com, United Entertainment Media. All rights reserved. No part of this work covered by copyrights hereon may be reproduced or copied in any manner whatsoever without the written permission of ALL MEDIA GUIDE. Unauthorized duplication is a violation of law. **AMG**™ and **All Music Guide**® are trademarks of AEC One Stop, Inc.

Distributed to the book trade in the U.S and Canada by Publishers Group West 1700 Fourth Street, Berkeley, CA 94710
Distributed to the music trade in the U.S. and Canada by Hal Leonard Publishing P.O. Box 13819, Milwaukee, WI 53213

Cover Design: Wagner Design, Ann Arbor, Michigan
Text Composition by Graphic Composition, Inc., Athens, Georgia

Library of Congress Cataloging-in-Publication Data
All music guide to electronica : the definitive guide to electronic music / edited by Vladimir Bogdanov ... [et al.].
    p. cm.
  Includes discographies and index.
  ISBN 0-87930-628-9 (alk. paper)
   1. Underground dance music—Bio-bibliography.  2. Underground dance music—Discography.  3. Underground dance music—Reviews.
  I. Bogdanov, Vladimir, 1965-

ML102.U53 A55 2001
781.64—dc21

2001025514

Printed in the United States of America
01 02 03 04 05  5 4 3 2 1

# Contents

How to Use this Book .................................................. iv
Contributors ........................................................... v
Introduction .......................................................... vi
Brief Style Descriptions ............................................. vii

## Biographies & Reviews

A ................................................................... 1
B .................................................................. 35
C .................................................................. 77
D ................................................................. 113
E ................................................................. 159
F ................................................................. 177
G ................................................................. 206
H ................................................................. 228
I ................................................................. 253
J ................................................................. 266
K ................................................................. 277
L ................................................................. 290
M ................................................................. 307
N ................................................................. 352
O ................................................................. 366
P ................................................................. 381
Q ................................................................. 421
R ................................................................. 422
S ................................................................. 437
T ................................................................. 502
U ................................................................. 531
V ................................................................. 541
W ................................................................. 550
X ................................................................. 563
Y ................................................................. 564
Z ................................................................. 568
Various Artists ................................................... 571

## Style Essays & Maps

House ............................................................. 629
Techno ............................................................ 631
Electronica ....................................................... 634
Jungle/Drum'n'bass ................................................ 636
Trance ............................................................ 638
Trip-Hop .......................................................... 640
Ambient ........................................................... 642
Electro ........................................................... 644
Garage ............................................................ 645
Hardcore Techno ................................................... 646
Acid Jazz ......................................................... 647
British Dance Culture ............................................. 649
Essential Recordings .............................................. 649

## Resources and References

Book Reviews ...................................................... 653
Label Descriptions ................................................ 657
Mail-Order Stores ................................................. 664
Index ............................................................. 666

# How to Use This Book

ARTIST NAME  (Alternate name in parentheses).

VITAL STATISTICS  For groups, **f.** indicates date and place of formation; **db.** indicates date disbanded. For individual performers date and place of birth (**b.**) and death (**d.**), if known, are given.

PERFORMER(S) / STYLE  Indicates a group, musician, DJ, or producer, followed by the styles of music associated with the performer or group.

BIOGRAPHY  A quick view of the artist's life and musical career. For major performers, proportionately longer biographies are provided.

ALBUM REVIEWS  These are the albums selected by our editors and contributors.

KEY TO SYMBOLS  ● ☆ ★

● ★ FIRST PURCHASE  Albums marked with either a filled circle or a filled star should be your first purchase. This is where to begin to find out if you like this particular artist. These albums are representative of the best this artist has to offer. If you don't like these picks, chances are this artist is not for you. In the case of an artist who has a number of distinct periods, you will find an essential pick marked for each period. Albums are listed chronologically when possible.

☆ ESSENTIAL RECORDINGS  Albums marked with a star should be part of any good collection of the genre. Often, these are also a good first purchase (filled star). By hearing these albums, you can get a good overview of the entire genre. These are must-hear and must-have recordings. You can't go wrong with them.

ALBUM TITLE  The name of the album is listed in bold as it appears on the original when possible. Very long titles have been abbreviated, or repeated in full as part of the comment, where needed.

DATE  The year of an album's first recording or release, if known.

RECORD LABEL  Record labels indicate the current (or most recent) release of this recording. Label numbers are not included because they change frequently.

ALBUM RATINGS:  ✦ TO ✦✦✦✦✦  In addition to the stars and circles used to distinguish exceptional noteworthy albums, as explained above, all albums are rated on a scale from one to five diamonds.

REVIEWERS  The name of each review's author are given at the end of the review.

## Mouse on Mars
**f.** 1993, Düsseldorf, Germany
*Group / Experimental Ambient, Experimental Techno, Electronica, Electro-Techno, Ambient Techno, Post-Rock/Experimental, IDM*

German post-techno duo Mouse on Mars are among a growing number of electronic music groups dabbling in complex, heavily hybridized forms that include everything from ambient, techno, and dub to rock, jazz, and jungle. The combined efforts of Andi Toma and Jan St. Werner (of Cologne and Düsseldorf, respectively), MoM formed in 1993, reportedly after Werner and Toma met at a death metal concert. Working from Werner's studio, the pair fused an admiration for the early experiments of Kraut-rock outfits like Can, Neu!, Kluster, and Kraftwerk into an off-beat update including influences from the burgeoning German techno and ambient scenes. A demo of material found its way to London-based guitar-ambient group Seefeel, who passed it on to the offices of their label, Too Pure. MOM's first single, "Frosch," was released by the label soon after, and was also included on the debut album, *Vulvaland*. Immediately hailed for its beguiling, inventive edge that seemed to resist all efforts at easy "schublade" (an even less flattering approximation of the English "pigeonhole"), *Vulvaland* was reissued in 1995 by (oddly) Rick Rubin's American Recordings label, who also released their follow-up, *Iaora Tahiti*, soon after. More upbeat and varied than their debut, the album made some inroads into the American marketplace, but the group's somewhat challenging complexity and steadfast refusal to pander make widespread popularity unlikely. They returned in 1997 with three different releases—the EP *Cache Coeur Naif*, the LP *Autoditacker*, and the vinyl-only *Instrumentals*. Another vinyl-only release (*Glam*) appeared in 1998, and was followed a year later by the "official" follow-up to *Autoditacker*, *Niun Niggung*. Although remixes are rare, the group have been appearing with increasing frequency on compilations of experimental electronic music, including Volume's popular *Trance Europe Express* series. They were also prominently featured on a pair of tribute albums—*Folds and Rhizomes*, and *In Memoriam*—dedicated to French poststructuralist philosopher Gilles Deleuze. Werner also records as half of the duo Microstoria (with Oval's Markus Popp) and solo as Lithops. —*Sean Cooper*

**Vulvaland** / 1994 / Too Pure/American ✦✦✦✦
A wibbly, barely digital match of ambient texturology with experimental strains of techno, dub, and krautrock. While the flip relies too heavily on four-on-the-floor ambient house cliches, the A-side is a prize, cultivating a weird, electronics-based avant-pop vibe as successful as it is unique. —*Sean Cooper*

★ **Iaora Tahiti** / Oct. 3, 1995 / Too Pure/American ✦✦✦✦✦
More upbeat and with far greater detail than the debut, *Iaora Tahiti* proves Werner and Toma haven't stood still. The pair's fondness for all things lo-fi follows them here, but just as evident is a depth and punch lacking in their earlier material. Jungle-style programming pops up on the first single, "Bib," as well as elements of dub, funk, industrial, film soundtracks, and musique concrète. Their finest work to date. —*Sean Cooper*

☆ **Autoditacker** / Aug. 18, 1997 / Thrill Jockey ✦✦✦✦✦
*Autoditacker* finds Mouse on Mars continuing to grow and improve, adding textures and detail to their dense, electronic soundscapes without compromising their sound. They still are indebted to Kraut-rock and dub, but they continue to add new sounds and styles to their music, including long ambient stretches and flirtations with drum'n'bass. There are no silent moments on *Autoditacker*—every inch of the tape is filled with rhythms, keyboards, and electronic squiggles. Each listen reveals new layers of the group's arrangements, and the shifting instrumentation and themes recall the best adventurous jazz in terms of unpredictability. It's another stunning record in a distinguished, inventive catalog. —*Stephen Thomas Erlewine*

# Contributors

**All Music Guide to Electronica**

**Editors**
Vladimir Bogdanov, President
Chris Woodstra, Vice President of Content Development
Stephen Thomas Erlewine, Director of Content, Pop Music
John Bush, Senior Editor, Pop Music

**AMG Pop Editors**
Al Campbell
Steve Huey
Zac Johnson
Joslyn Lane
Heather Phares
Diana Potts
Stacia Proefrock
Sean Westergaard
MacKenzie Wilson

**Contributors**
Nitsuh Abebe
Aric Laurence Allen
Rick Anderson
Jason Ankeny
Aaron Badgley
Jason Birchmeier
Vladimir Bogdanov
Myles Boisen
John Book
Rob Bowman
Michael Breece
Scott Bultman
Jeff Burger
Nick Burton
John Bush
Bryan Buss
Becky Byrkit
Dean Carlson
Bil Carpenter
Troy Carpenter
Sean Carruthers
Bill Cassel
Evan Cater
Rick Clark
Jonathan Cohen
Matt Conaway
Sean Cooper
William Cooper
Jason Damas
Mike DaRonco
Michael P. Dawson
Tom Demalon
Donna DiChario
Charlotte Dillon
Jim Dorsch
John Dougan
Bruce Eder
Iotis Erlewine
Stephen Thomas Erlewine
Alan Esher
John Floyd
Paul Fucito
Michael Gallucci
James A. Gardner
Chris Genzel
Marc Gilman
Richard S. Ginell
Dan Gizzi
Ryan Randall Goble
Adam Greenberg
Matthew Greenwald
Jason Gross
Craig Harris
Kelvin Hayes
Alex Henderson
Matthew Hilburn
Ed Hogan
Steve Huey
Ken Hunt
David Jehnzen
Michael Jourdan
Jason Kane
Julian Katz
Jason Kaufman
Theo Kavadias
Andy Kellman
Nick Kemper
David Kent-Abbott
Brian Kirby
Linda Kohanov
Steve Kurutz
Joshua Landau
Sanz Lashley
Joslyn Layne
Jonathan Lewis
Craig Lytle
Marc van der Pol
Greg Matherly
Derrick Mathis
Steven McDonald
Kembrew McLeod
Ted Mills
Brian Musich
Michael G. Nastos
Brett Neely
Jim Newsom
Alex Ogg
Pat Padua
Roch Parisien
Chris Parker
Archie Patterson
John Patterson
Heather Phares
Richard Pierson
Diana Potts
Jim Powers
Greg Prato
Stacia Proefrock
Ned Raggett
William Ruhlmann
Amy Schroeder
Thomas Schulte
Tim Sheridan
Craig Robert Smith
David Ross Smith
Carlos Souffront
Leo Stanley
Roger Steffens
Peter Stepek
Freddy Stidean
Denise Sullivan
Stanton Swihart
Sara Sytsma
David Szatmary
Bob Tarte
William Tilland
"Blue" Gene Tyranny
Richie Unterberger
John Vallier
Michael Waynick
Jonathan Widran
William I. Lengeman III
MacKenzie Wilson
Christopher Witt
Chris Woodstra
Carol Wright
Ron Wynn
Scott Yanow
Curtis Zimmermann

**AMG Technical Editors**
Jonathan Ball
George Davis
Sharkey La Donk
Heather Humphries
Lee (Jack) Isles
Andy Kellman
Don Kline
Tim Sendra
Rob Theakston
Chris True

**AMG Copy Editors**
Jason Birchmeier
Kerri Covey
Elizabeth Erlewine
Margaret Erlewine
Benjamin Goldstein
Jennifer Jones
David Lynch
Karen Paik
Stephanie Somerville

# Introduction

Electronic dance has been the music of the future for so long, it's often difficult to consider its context in the past. A relentless forward drive is the prime motivator for electronic dance music, and has been ever since its emergence in the aggressive, mechanistic house and techno productions that shot out of Chicago and Detroit in the mid-'80s. Of course, the mere mention of origins reveals that electronic dance does indeed have a history behind it, just as jazz and rock (or any number of dance musics that later developed beyond their sources) exposed deep musical roots to general audiences only after being recognized as important styles of music around the world.

When the history of electronic dance music *is* discussed, the preferred method of study is a chronological timeline, usually beginning in the '70s with two important developments, the rigid German synthesizer pop of Kraftwerk and the hedonistic funk of disco. As the story goes, these two styles—the relentlessly technical vs. the irresistibly sensual, polar opposites at first blush—spawned house and techno in the '80s, at which point the music went overground (especially in Britain and Europe) and added subtler, more listener-oriented production techniques just before arriving on time for rock critics and major labels to take notice during the late '90s.

It should, however, be obvious that—as is true with most styles of music—the development of electronic dance is much more complex than most would like to think. Looking back to the European introduction of Indonesian gong music at the Paris Exhibition of 1889, Luigi Russolo's concepts regarding the presence of noise in music, and history's first brush with electric instruments near the beginning of the twentieth century, there are literally thousands of innovators involved in the progression of electronic music, from respected academic composers to eccentric visionaries of all persuasions.

As such, the electronic dance music which emerged in the '80s and '90s directly benefited from developments already set forth decades before, by the ranks of post-classical composers who inserted increasingly mechanical percussion and chance operations into their scores; university professors and fringe audio-scientists who spent hours assembling cut-and-paste symphonies with tape machines long before samplers were invented; Jamaican dub wizards who pioneered the aesthetic of studio-as-instrument to produce the very first remixes (or versions) on the B-sides of reggae singles; the hundreds of disco and hip-hop DJs who provided seamless dance mixes using two turntables, a mixer and a crate of vinyl—all these and many more contributed greatly to the development of dance, electronic, and experimental music.

With that long and winding road in mind, *The All Music Guide to Electronica* includes all the house, techno, and electronica names that should be in any history of the music, plus in-depth looks at the artists who both inspired them and contributed to the music's development. So, if fans of Aphex Twin, Masters at Work, Model 500, Prodigy, the Chemical Brothers, or Squarepusher wish to pursue the roots of innovation in the music of Tod Dockstader, the Salsoul Orchestra, Parliament, Lee "Scratch" Perry, Public Enemy, or Weather Report, they're more than welcome. Since this book is a reflection of the extensively hyper-linked *All Music Guide* web site, it includes all the artists listeners would expect to see—plus many they may only become interested in later. In fact, the variety often reveals a cozy sense of kinship between artists rarely grouped or discussed together. Consider Cabaret Voltaire, John Cage, Cajmere, Can, and Cappella, a series of artists appearing within a few pages of this book, each possessing far greater conceptual relations to its neighbors than fans might realize.

But truly understanding the myriad artists, labels, and styles grouped within the electronica umbrella has long been the province of only a select group of people. By going to clubs to hear their favorite DJs and searching through specialty shops for all manner of out-of-print records and mixtapes, they've discovered great music in a wide variety of styles. For many others, though (usually older audiences accustomed to rock or traditional pop), electronic dance music remains alien and difficult to understand, due to differences both conceptual and stylistic as well as the apparent musical ones.

First and most obviously, electronic dance is simply not suited best for typical listening sources, from commercial radio to home stereos. Certainly, the music's focus is radically different: building grooves from the beats up for later intepretation by DJs, and only occasionally adapting mainstream conventions like pop songwriting or rock album statements. And the fact that those musical fusions and dilutions are often more familiar to the traditional minds at media outlets (major labels, radio stations, music magazines) often creates misconceptions about what the music truly is about. There's also a staggering variety of musical styles and artists grouped (rightly or wrongly) under one banner, from disco-centric house producers like Armand Van Helden to experimental electronics crews like Finland's Pan Sonic. Also, the clandestine atmosphere surrounding music often played at extra-legal events, and the sense of record-collector one-upmanship that comes from hyped records being pressed in very limited quantities, often makes for snobbish atmospheres. Even the producers themselves encourage the confusion, assuming different guises for their releases and recording for many labels. More so than almost any other current style, electronic dance and experimental music are very difficult genres to understand and appreciate on their own terms.

In view of those problems, *The All Music Guide to Electronica* is not only the most comprehensive guide to the music ever published, it's also the most easy to use. Since this book is geared to many different levels of knowledge, it's an equally engaging tool whether you're dipping your feet in the water for the first time or a longtime fan and collector (or anywhere between). This book sets forth to explain the sounds and styles of electronic and experimental dance music, rate works by the increasingly large number of artists contained within the umbrella, and help listeners find more music based on styles they're already interested in. Before the main artist section is a brief list of styles and descriptions for dealing with all the varying sounds of electronic and experimental music. For those who wish to know more, the back of the book includes extended essays and album recommendations for major styles like house, techno, trance, trip-hop, jungle, electro, and more. Also included are book reviews and even a section listing the best web sites for online mail-order—just in case listeners want to pick up the latest single on Planet E Records but live nowhere near Record Time in Detroit. Enjoy!

# Brief Style Descriptions

## Acid House

The style of dance that exploded American house music around the world, **Acid House** first appeared in the mid-'80s in the work of Chicago producers like DJ Pierre, Adonis, Farley Jackmaster Funk, and Phuture (the latter of whom coined the term in their classic single, "Acid Trax"). Mixing elements of the house music that was already up and running in Chicago (as well as New York) with the squelchy sounds and deep bassline of the Roland TB-303 synthesizer, *acid house* was strictly a Chicago phenomenon until stacks of singles began to cross the Atlantic, arriving in the hands of eager young Brits. The sound jelled in small warehouse parties held in London in 1986-87, and then went overground during 1988's infamous Summer of Love, when thousands of clubgoers traveled to the hinterlands for the massive events later known as raves. *Acid house* hit the British pop charts quite quickly, with M/A/R/R/S, S'Express, and Technotronic landing huge hits before the dawn of the '90s. By that time, the *acid house* phenomenon had largely passed in England and was replaced by rave music. New-school US producers from Cajmere to Armand Van Helden to Felix Da Housecat kept the sound alive and well during the '90s.

## Acid Jazz

The music played by a generation raised on jazz as well as funk and hip-hop, **Acid Jazz** used elements of all three; its existence as a percussion-heavy, primarily live music placed it closer to jazz and Afro-Cuban than any other dance style, but its insistence on keeping the groove allied it with funk, hip-hop, and dance music. The term itself first appeared in 1988 as both an American record label and the title of an English compilation series that reissued jazz-funk music from the '70s, called "rare groove" by the Brits during a major mid-'80s resurgence. A variety of *acid jazz* artists emerged during the late '80s and early '90s: live bands such as Stereo MC's, James Taylor Quartet, the Brand New Heavies, Groove Collective, Galliano, and Jamiroquai, as well as studio projects like Palm Skin Productions, Mondo Grosso, Outside, and United Future Organization.

## Acid Techno

When the squelch of mid-'80s acid house music was given time to sink into the minds of impressionable youths, they became quite influenced by the sound. Many who began to make music in the early '90s applied the sound to harder techno instead of the warm sounds of classic Chicago house. Quite similar to early German trance, **Acid Techno** includes the earlier recordings of Aphex Twin, Plastikman, and Dave Clarke, among others.

## Alternative Rap

**Alternative Rap** refers to hip-hop groups that refuse to conform to any of the traditional stereotypes of rap, such as gangsta, funk, bass, hardcore, and party rap. Instead, they blur genres, drawing equally from funk and pop/rock, as well as jazz, soul, reggae, and even folk. Though Arrested Development and the Fugees managed to cross over into the mainstream, most *alternative rap* groups are embraced primarily by alternative rock fans, not hip-hop or pop audiences.

## Ambient

**Ambient** music evolved from the experimental electronic music of '70s synth-based artists like Brian Eno and Kraftwerk, and the trance-like techno dance music of the '80s. *Ambient* is a spacious, electronic music that is concerned with sonic texture, not songwriting or composing. It's frequently repetitive and it all sounds the same to the casual listener, even though there are quite significant differences between the artists. *Ambient* became a popular cult music in the early '90s, thanks to ambient techno artists like the Orb and Aphex Twin.

## Ambient Breakbeat

**Ambient Breakbeat** refers to a narrow subgenre of electronic acts with less energy than the trip-hop or funky breaks, but with a pronounced hip-hop influence to their music. Some of the more downtempo works on British labels like Mo'Wax and Ninja Tune paved the way for New York's DJ Wally (of the Liquid Sky Records brigade) and British artists such as Req, each good examples of the style.

## Ambient Dub

Coined by the Beyond label for its compilation series of the same name, **Ambient Dub** has since been generalized by artists, critics, and audiences alike to refer to any form of rhythmic, usually beat-oriented ambient using the tastes, textures, and techniques of Jamaican dub-style production (e.g. reverb, emphasis on bass and percussion, heavy use of effects). Although the term has fallen out of favor due to the fevered intermingling of styles characteristic of post-rave electronica, it remains useful in demarcating the denser, more electronic applications of dub from the more hip-hop derived styles of downtempo, atmospheric beat music. Artists include the Orb, Higher Intelligence Agency, Sub Dub, Techno Animal, Automaton, and Solar Quest.

## Ambient House

An early categorical marker used to distinguish newer wave ambient artists such as the Orb, the KLF, Irresistible Force, Future Sound of London, and Orbital, **Ambient House** was often applied indiscriminately to designate dance music not necessarily just for dancing. In its more rigorous application, *ambient house* implied music appropriating certain primary elements of acid house music—mid-tempo, four-on-the-floor beats; synth pads and strings; soaring vocal samples—used in a dreamier, more atmospheric fashion. It's since been replaced (or rather, some would argue, complicated) by a barrage of more specific terms and is rarely used.

## Ambient Pop

**Ambient Pop** combines elements of the two distinct styles which lend the blissed-out genre its name—while the music possesses a shape and form common to conventional pop, its electronic textures and atmospheres mirror the hypnotic, meditative qualities of ambient. The mesmerizing lock-groove melodies of Kraut-rock are a clear influence as well, although *ambient pop* is typically much less abrasive. Essentially an extension of the dream pop that emerged in the wake of the shoegazer movement, it's set apart from its antecedents by its absorption of contemporary electronic idioms, including sampling, although for the most part live instruments continue to define the sound.

## Ambient Techno

A rarefied, more specific reorientation of ambient house, **Ambient Techno** is usually applied to artists such as B12, early Aphex Twin, the Black Dog, Higher Intelligence Agency, and Biosphere. It distinguished artists who combined the melodic and rhythmic approaches of techno and electro—use of 808 and 909 drum machines; well-produced, thin-sounding electronics; minor-key melodies and alien-sounding samples and sounds—with the soaring, layered, aquatic atmospheres of beatless and experimental ambient. Most often associated with labels such as Apollo, GPR, Warp, and Beyond, the terminology morphed into "intelligent techno" after Warp released its *Artificial*

*Intelligence* series (although the music's stylistic references remained largely unchanged).

## Bass Music

Springing from the fertile dance scenes in Miami (freestyle) and Detroit (electro) during the mid-'80s, **Bass Music** brought the funky-breaks aesthetic of the '70s into the digital age with drum-machine frequencies capable of pulverizing the vast majority of unsuspecting car or club speakers. Early Miami pioneers like 2 Live Crew and DJ Magic Mike pushed the style into its distinctive booty obsession, and Detroit figures like DJ Assault, DJ Godfather, and DJ Bone melded it with techno to create an increasingly fast-paced music. *Bass music* even flirted with the charts during the early '90s, as 95 South's "Whoot (There It Is)" and 69 Boyz' "Tootsee Roll" both hit the charts and went multi-platinum.

## Big Beat

Rescuing the electronica community from a near fall off the edge of its experimental fringe, **Big Beat** emerged in the mid-'90s as the next wave of big dumb dance music. Regional pockets around the world had emphasized the "less intelligent" side of dance music as early as 1994, in reaction to the growing coterie of chin-stroking intellectuals attached to the drum'n'bass and experimental movements. *Big beat* as a distinct movement finally coalesced in 1995-96 around two British labels: Brighton's Skint and London's Wall of Sound. The former—home to releases by Fatboy Slim, Bentley Rhythm Ace, and Lo-Fidelity Allstars—deserves more honors for innovation and quality, though Wall of Sound was founded slightly earlier and released great singles by Propellerheads, Wiseguys, and Les Rythmes Digitales. *Big beat* soon proved very popular in America as well, and artists attached to City of Angels Records (the Crystal Method, Überzone, Lunatic Calm, Front BC) gained a higher profile thanks to like-minded Brits. Other than Fatboy Slim, the other superstar artists of *big beat* were the Chemical Brothers and Prodigy, two groups who predated the style (and assisted its birth). Both the Chemical Brothers and Prodigy were never tight fits either, given productions that often reflected the more intelligent edge of trip-hop, and rarely broke into the mindless arena of true *big beat*.

The sound of *big beat*, a rather shameless fusion of old-school party breakbeats with appropriately off-the-wall samples, was reminiscent of house music's sampladelic phase of the late '80s as well as old-school rap and its penchant for silly samples and irresistible breaks. Though the sample programming and overall production was leaps and bounds beyond its predecessors, *big beat* was nevertheless criticized for dumbing down the electronica wave of the late '90s. Even while recordings by the Chemical Brothers, Prodigy, and Fatboy Slim hit the American charts and earned positive reviews—granted, from rock critics—worldwide, many dance fans rejected the style wholesale for being too reliant on gimmicky production values and played-out samples. *Big beat* lasted a surprisingly long time, given the restraints of a style reliant on the patience of listeners who've heard the same break dozens of times, as well as the patience of DJs to hunt local thrift stores to find interesting samples on old instructional records.

## Dance-Pop

An outgrowth of disco, **Dance-Pop** featured a pounding club beat framing simple, catchy melodies closer to fully-formed songs than pure dance music. It's primarily the medium of producers, who write the songs and construct the tracks, picking an appropriate vocalist to sing the song. These dance divas become stars, but frequently the artistic vision is the producer's. Naturally, there are some major exceptions—Madonna and Janet Jackson have had control over the sound and direction of their records—but *dance-pop* is music that is about image, not substance.

## Dark Ambient

Brian Eno's original vision of ambient music as unobtrusive musical wallpaper, later fused with warm house rhythms and given playful qualities by the Orb in the '90s, found its opposite in the style known as **Dark Ambient**. Populated by a wide assortment of personalities—ranging from aging industrial and metal experimentalists (Scorn's Mick Harris, Current 93's David Tibet, Nurse with Wound's Steven Stapleton) to electronic boffins (Kim Cascone/PGR, Psychick Warriors Ov Gaia), Japanese noise artists (K.K. Null, Merzbow), and latter-day indie rockers (Main, Bark Psychosis)—*dark ambient* features toned-down or entirely missing beats with unsettling passages of keyboards, eerie samples, and treated guitar effects. Like most styles related in some way to electronic/dance music of the '90s, it's a very nebulous term; many artists enter or leave the style with each successive release.

## Detroit Techno

Early **Detroit Techno** is characterized by, alternately, a dark, detached, mechanistic vibe and a smooth, bright, soulful feel (the latter deriving in part from the Motown legacy and the stock-in-trade between early techno and the Chicago-style house developing simultaneously to the southwest). While essentially designed as dance music meant to uplift, the stark, melancholy edge of early tracks by Cybotron, Model 500, Rhythm Is Rhythm, and Reese also spoke to Detroit's economic collapse in the late '70s following the city's prosperous heyday as the focal point of the American automobile industry.

The music's oft-copied ruddy production and stripped-down aesthetic were largely a function of the limited technology available to the early innovators (records were often mastered from two-track onto cassette). The increasingly sophisticated arrangements of contemporary techno (on through to hardcore and jungle), conversely, has much to do with the growth and increasing affordability of MIDI-encoded equipment and desktop digital audio. Second- and third-wave *Detroit techno*, too, has gained considerably in production, although artists such as Derrick May, Juan Atkins, and Kenny Larkin have sought to combine the peerless sheen of the digital arena with the compositional minimalism of their Detroit origins.

No longer simply contained within the 313 area code, *Detroit techno* has become a global phenomenon (partly as a result of the more widespread acclaim many of the original Detroit artists have found in other countries), buoyed by the fact that many of the classic early tracks remain in print (available through Submerge). Detroit's third wave began re-exploring the aesthetic commitment of the music's early period, with hard-hitting beats (Underground Resistance, Jeff Mills), soulful grooves (Kenny Larkin, Stacey Pullen), and a renewed interest in techno's breakbeat roots (Aux 88, Drexciya, "Mad" Mike, Dopplereffekt).

## Disco

**Disco** marked the dawn of dance-based popular music. Growing out of the increasingly groove-oriented sound of early '70s and funk, *disco* emphasized the beat above anything else, even the singer and the song. *Disco* was named after discotheques, clubs that played nothing but music for dancing. Most of the discotheques were gay clubs in New York, and the DJs in these clubs specifically picked soul and funk records that had a strong, heavy groove. After being played in the *disco*, the records began receiving radio play and respectable sales. Soon, record companies and producers were cutting records created specifically for discos. Naturally, these records also had strong pop hooks, so they could have crossover success. *Disco* albums frequently didn't have many tracks—they had a handful of long songs that kept the beat going. Similarly, the singles were issued on 12" records, which allowed for extended remixes. DJs could mix these tracks together, matching the beats on each song since they were marked with how fast they were in terms of beats per minute. In no time, the insistent, pounding *disco* beat dominated the pop chart, and everyone cut a *disco* record, from rockers like the Rolling Stones and Rod Stewart to pop acts like the Bee Gees and new wave artists like Blondie. There were *disco* artists that became stars—Donna Summer, Chic, the Village People, and KC & the Sunshine Band were brand names—but the music was primarily a producer's medium, since they created the tracks and wrote the songs. *Disco* lost momentum as the '70s became the '80s, but it didn't die—it mutated into a variety of different dance-based genres, ranging from dance-pop and hip-hop to house and techno.

## Downbeat

**Downbeat** is a quite generic term sometimes used to replace ambient house and ambient techno, considering that the amount and complexity of electronic listening music described under the "ambient" umbrella had made the terms practically useless by the mid-'90s. It often implies the use of moderate breakbeats instead of the steady four-four beats of most ambient house or ambient techno. The style also breaches territory claimed by trip-hop, ambient techno, and electro-techno. In its widest possible definition, *downbeat* is any form of electronic music created for the living room instead of the dance floor.

## Dream-Pop

**Dream Pop** is an atmospheric subgenre of alternative rock that relies on sonic textures as much as melody. *Dream pop* often features breathy vocals and processed, echo-laden guitars and synthesizers. Though the Cocteau Twins, with their indecipherable vocals and languid soundscapes, are frequently seen as the leaders of *dream pop*, the genre has more stylistic diversity than their slow, electronic textures. *Dream pop* also encompasses the post-Velvet Underground guitar rock of Galaxie 500, as well as the loud, shimmering feedback of My Bloody Valentine. It is all tied together by a reliance on sonic texture, both in terms of instruments and vocals.

## Dub

**Dub** derives its name from the practice of dubbing instrumental, rhythm-oriented versions of reggae songs onto the B-sides of 45 rpm singles, which evolved into a legitimate and accepted style of its own as those re-recordings became forums for engineers to experiment with the possibilities of their mixing consoles. The practice of re-recording reggae tracks without vocals dated back to 1967, when DJs found that dancehall crowds and partygoers greatly enjoyed being given the opportunity to sing the lyrics themselves. Around 1969, some DJs began talking, or "toasting," over these instrumentals (known as "versions"), frequently reinterpreting the already familiar original lyrics. The most important early DJ was U-Roy, who became renowned for his ability to improvise dialogues with the recorded singers; U-Roy ran the sound system owned by engineer King Tubby, who mixed all of the instrumental tracks over which his DJ toasted. Eventually, Tubby began to experiment with remixing the instrumental tracks, bringing up the level of the rhythm section, dropping out most or all of the vocals, and adding new effects like reverb and echo. The results were seen by many reggae fans as stripping the music down to its purest essence. 45-rpm singles with *dub* versions on the B-sides became ubiquitous, and King Tubby's credit on the back soon became a drawing card in and of itself. Full fledged *dub* albums began to appear in 1973, with many highlights stemming from Tubby's mixes for producers Bunny Lee and Augustus Pablo (the latter of whom also played the haunting melodica, which became one of *dub's* signature added elements); other key early producers included the minimalistic Keith Hudson and the colorful, elaborate Lee "Scratch" Perry. By 1976, *dub's* popularity in Jamaica was second only to Rastafarian roots reggae, and the sound had also found acceptance the UK (thanks largely to the Island label), where roots reggae artists like Burning Spear and Black Uhuru became just as well-known for their forays into *dub*. The Mad Professor and the experimental Adrian Sherwood helped Britain's *dub* scene remain vital in the '80s, but in spite of skilled newcomers like Scientist, Prince Jammy, and Mikey Dread, Jamaican popular taste had by then shifted to DJ toasters and lyrical improvisers, which led to the prominence of dancehall and ragga. The downtempo atmospherics and bass- and rhythm-heavy textures of *dub* had a lasting influence outside of reggae, beginning with Public Image Ltd.'s 1979 *Metal Box/Second Edition* album; during the '90s, *dub* was frequently incorporated into the melting-pot eclecticism of underground avant-garde rock, and Britain's thriving electronica/drum'n'bass scene owed a great deal to *dub's* mixing and production techniques.

## Electro

Blending '70s funk with the emerging hip-hop culture and synthesizer technology of the early '80s produced the style known as **Electro**. But what seemed to be a brief fad for the public—no more than two or three hits, including Afrikaa Bambaataa's "Planet Rock" and Grandmaster Flash's "The Message," neither of which made the pop Top 40—was in fact a fertile testing ground for innovators who later diverged into radically different territory, including Dr. Dre (who worked with the World Class Wreckin' Cru) and techno godfather Juan Atkins (with Cybotron). *Electro* also provided an intriguing new direction for one of the style's prime influences. Herbie Hancock, whose 1973 Headhunters album proved a large fusion hit, came storming back in 1983 with the *electro* single "Rockit." Despite its successes (documented in full on Rhino's four-disc *Electric Funk* set), the style was quickly eclipsed by the mid-'80s rise of hip-hop music built around samples (often from rock records) rather than musical synthesizers. Nevertheless, many techno and dance artists continued harking back to the sound, and a full-fledged *electro* revival emerged in Detroit and Britain during the mid-'90s.

## Electro-Acoustic

**Electro-Acoustic** music thrives in more unfamiliar territory; the styles that emerge are often dictated by the technology itself. Rather than sampling or synthesizing acoustic sounds to electronically replicate them, these composers tend to mutate the original timbres, sometimes to an unrecognizable state. True artists in the genre also create their own sounds (as opposed to using the preset sounds that come with modern synthesizers). In progressive *electro-acoustic* music, the electronics play an equal if not greater part in the overall concept. Acoustic instruments performed in real time are usually processed through reverb, harmonizing, and so on, which adds an entirely new dimension to the player's technique. At best, this music opens up new worlds of listening, thinking, and feeling. At worst, progressive electronic artists worship technology for its own sake, relinquishing the heart and soul of true artistic expression.

## Electro-Techno

Influenced by the early-'80s phenomenon of electro-funk but also reliant upon Detroit techno and elements of ambient house, *Electro-Techno* emerged in the mid-'90s when a full-fledged electro flashback hit London clubs, complete with body-rocking robots and vocoder-distorted vocals, inspired by original electro classics like Afrikaa Bambaataa's "Planet Rock." The actual fad—spearheaded by Clear Records and led by artists like Jedi Knights, Tusken Raiders, and Gescom (masks for Global Communication, µ-Ziq, and Autechre, respectively)—was quick in passing, but it inspired some excellent music during the latter half of the '90s, including the work of England's Skam Records, Sweden's Dot Records and, closer to the original sources, Detroit's Drexciya and AUX 88.

## Electronic

**Electronic** is a broad designation that could be construed to cover many different styles of music—after all, *electronic* instrumentation has become commonplace, and much dance-oriented music from the late '80s on is primarily, often exclusively, *electronic*. However, in this case, it refers mostly to *electronic music* as it took shape early on, when artists were still exploring the unique possibilities of electronically generated sound, as well as more recent music strongly indebted to those initial experiments. Avant-garde composers had long been fascinated with the ways technology could be used to produce previously unheard textures and combinations of sounds. French composer Edgard Varèse was a pioneer in this field, building his own *electronic* instruments as early as the 1920s and experimenting with tape loops during the '50s. Varèse's work was hugely influential on American avant-gardist John Cage and German composer Karlheinz Stockhausen, both of whom greatly expanded the compositional structures in which *electronic* devices could be incorporated. But *electronic music* didn't really begin to enter the wider consciousness until around the '70s, when sequencers and synthesizers became more affordable and easier to obtain. Wendy Carlos' 1968 *Switched-On Bach* album, a selection of Bach pieces performed on the Moog synthesizer, had ignited tremendous public attention, and Stockhausen's teachings had begun to inspire a burgeoning experimental music scene in Germany. Kraut-rock groups such as Can and Neu! integrated synthesizers and tape manipulations into their rabid experimentalism, but the two most important *electronic* artists to emerge from the scene were Kraftwerk and Tangerine Dream. Kraftwerk pioneered the concept of pop music performed exclusively on synthesizers, and their robotic, mechanical, hypnotic style had a tremendous impact on nearly all electronic pop produced in the remainder of the 20th century. Tangerine Dream, meanwhile, was indebted to minimalist classical composition, crafting an atmospheric, slowly shifting, trance-inducing sound that helped invent the genre known as space music. Other crucial figures included Klaus Schulze, who explored a droning variation on space music that was even more trancelike than Tangerine Dream, and Brian Eno, whose inventive production and experiments with electronics in a pop context eventually gave way to his creation of ambient music, which aimed to blend thoroughly into its environment and often relied heavily on synthesizers. Ambient and space music helped give rise to new age, which emphasized the peaceful, soothing, and meditative qualities of those influences while adding greater melodicism; the progressive electronic branch of new age crafted a more dramatic, lushly orchestrated style that broke with *electronic music's* roots in minimalism. Synth-pop, techno, and its artier companion electronica all owed a great deal to the basic innovations of early *electronic* artists as well.

## Electronica

A suitably vague term used to describe the emergence of electronic dance music increasingly geared to listening instead of strictly dancing, **Electronica** was first used in the title of a series of compilations (actually called *New Electronica*) spotlighting original sources of Detroit techno such as Juan Atkins and Underground Resistance alongside European artists who had gained much from the Motor City's futuristic vision for techno. The word was later appropriated by the American press as an easy catch-all for practically any young artist using electronic equipment and/or instruments, but *electronica* serves to describe techno-based music that can be used for home listening as well as on the dance floor (since many *electronica* artists are club DJs as well).

## Euro-Dance

**Euro-Dance** refers to a specific style of club/dance music produced on the European continent during the '80s and '90s. *Euro-dance* is generally informed by disco, hi-NRG, and house music, and performed entirely in the recording studio on synthesizers and drum machines; the producers are much more responsible for the finished product than the singers. Like its close relative Euro-pop, it's usually simple, lightweight, and catchy, with fluffy, repetitive lyrics that don't require much translation among listeners who speak different languages. The main difference between *Euro-dance* and Euro-pop is the exclusive and pronounced dance-club orientation of the former; while Euro-pop is frequently informed by dance music, it doesn't have to be, and when it is, it doesn't always fit into dance-club playlists. Most *Euro-dance* artists concentrate on crafting hit singles, with album releases almost an afterthought.

## Experimental Dub

Thousands of miles away from sunny Jamaica, a loose collective of Berlin producers jump-started the style of music known as **Experimental Dub**. If the scene was centered at all, it occurred at Hard Wax Records, a record store as well as a tight distribution company that was home to several of the style's crucial labels (Basic Channel, Chain Reaction, Imbalance) and producers (Maurizio, Mark Ernestus, Porter Ricks, Pole, Monolake). Indebted to Chicago acid house and minimalist Detroit techno figures like Jeff Mills, Rob Hood, and Plastikman, *experimental dub* was rather easily characterized; the sound usually focused on a mix of crackling, murky atmospheres that sounded almost subaquatic, with a mid-tempo beat and strong, clanging percussion. The similarities to classic Jamaican dub producers King Tubby and Lee "Scratch" Perry were indirect at best, but the term worked well for identifying the signature sound of many of Germany's best experimental producers. Other than the Basic Channel camp, *experimental dub*'s most important figures were Mike Ink (aka Wolfgang Voigt) and Thomas Brinkmann. Ink, a longtime Berlin producer responsible for more than a half-dozen aliases and labels, did most of his important work on the Profan and Studio 1 labels. Brinkmann, a comparative newcomer to the style, earned praise for his remixes of material by Ink and Plastikman. *Experimental dub,* in turn, inspired several major techno figures (including Plastikman and Mills) by the late '90s, and its influence was even seen in American indie-rock and post-rock.

## Experimental Electro

With the revival of the classic electro style, dubbed the neo-electro movement, came a wave of **Experimental Electro** artists with more abstract agendas, still influenced by the sound of the streets but with more curious minds when it came to noodling around in the studio. Names such as Freeform and Bisk characterized the style.

## Experimental Rock

As the name suggests, **Experimental Rock** is music pushing the envelope of the form, far removed from the classic pop sensibilities of before. Typically, *experimental rock* is the diametric opposite of standard "verse-chorus-verse" music. Because the whole point is to liberate and innovate, no hard and fast rules apply, but distinguishing characteristics include improvisational performances, avant-garde influences, odd instrumentation, opaque lyrics (or no lyrics at all), strange compositional structures and rhythms, and an underlying rejection of commercial aspirations.

## Experimental Techno

The field of electronic dance music has limitless possibilities for experimentation, so **Experimental Techno** has a similarly wide range of styles—from the disc-error clicks and scratches of European experimenters Oval and Pan sonic to the off-kilter effects (but straight-ahead rhythms) of Cristian Vogel, Neil Landstrumm, and Si Begg. *Experimental techno* can also include soundscape terrorists such as Twisted Science, Nonplace Urban Field, and Atom Heart; digital-age punks like Alec Empire; and former industrial stalwarts under new guises, such as Scorn, Download, or Techno Animal. Any artist wishing to take electronic dance places it's never been can be characterized as experimental, and for better or worse, that includes a large cast.

## Freestyle

Often growing in tandem with contemporary styles like electro and house, **Freestyle** emerged in the twin Latin capitals of New York City and Miami during the early '80s. *Freestyle* classics like "I Wonder If I Take You Home" by Lisa Lisa & Cult Jam, "Let the Music Play" by Shannon, and "Party Your Body" by Stevie B relied on angular, synthesized beats similar to electro and early house, but also emphasized the romantic themes of classic R&B and disco. The fusion of mechanical and sensual proved ready for crossover during the period, and both Shannon and Lisa Lisa hit the Top 40 during 1984-85. *Freestyle* also dovetailed nicely with the rise of dance-pop during the mid-'80s—Madonna's early producer and remixer, John Benitez (aka Jellybean), was also active in the *freestyle* community. By the end of the decade, a number of artists—Exposé, Brenda K. Starr, Trinere, the Cover Girls, India, and Stevie B—followed them into the pop or R&B charts. Even after popular success waned in the late '80s, though, *freestyle* moved to the underground as a vital stream of modern dance music alongside house, techno, and bass music. Similar to mainstream house, *freestyle* artists are usually (though by no means exclusively) either female vocalists or male producers. Newer figures like Lil Suzy, George Lamond, Angelique, Johnny O, and others became big stars in the *freestyle* community.

## Funky Breaks

An amalgam of trance, hip-hop, and jungle, **Funky Breaks** became one of the most widely heard styles in electronic music thanks to its popularity as the sound of choice for those wishing to make some noise on pop charts and television commercials during the late '90s. Pioneered by the Chemical Brothers plus James Lavelle's epic-stature Mo'Wax Records stable, *funky breaks* really came into the fore in 1997, the year music-industry experts predicted would finally break the new electronica in the mainstream. Of the artists picked to spearhead the revolution, almost all—the Prodigy, Death in Vegas, the Crystal Method, Propellerheads—had that sound. That's also a significant reason why the electronica revolution failed, at least commercially, since the highly-touted acts all sounded similar.

## Gabba

Most popular in the Netherlands and Scotland, **Gabba** is the hardest form of hardcore techno, frequently exceeding speeds of over 200 BPM. Popular DJs and producers like Paul Elstak and the Mover categorized gabba's early evolution from German trance and British rave. By the mid-'90s, the music had acquired some rather unsavory connotations with neo-fascism and the skinhead movement, though much of the scene was free from it. Surprisingly, *gabba* made a rather successful attempt at the Dutch pop charts, with Elstak producing several hits. Many producers and fans proclaimed him a sell-out, and soon there appeared a divide in the scene between the hardcore and the *really* hardcore.

## Garage

Named for what is arguably the birthplace of house music, the Paradise Garage in New York, **Garage** is the dance style closest in spirit and execution to the original disco music of the '70s. Favoring synthesizer runs and gospel vocals similar to house music but with production values even more polished and shimmering than house, *garage* has a very soulful, organic feel. Though the style was most popular in New Jersey in the '80s, the mainstream of British dance clubs championed the style throughout the '90s as well.

## Goa Trance

Named after a region on the coast of southwestern India famed as a clubbing and drugging paradise ever since the '60s, **Goa Trance** broke away from the Teutonic bent of European trance during the early '90s and carried the torch for trance during the rest of the decade. The presence of LSD on the *Goa* scene—instead of the ubiquitous club drug Ecstasy—translated the music into an appropriately psychedelic version of trance that embraced the mystical properties of Indian music and culture. Traditional Indian instruments such as the sitar and sarod (or electronic near-equivalents) often made appearances in the music, pushed along by the driving, hypnotic sequencer music that trance had always been known for. The style is considerably less turntable-oriented than other electronic dance styles, especially since vinyl tends to melt in the heat (DATs are often used instead). As a consequence, *Goa* had comparatively few DJs to recommend it worldwide until the late '90s. Labels like Dragonfly, Blue Room Released, Flying Rhino, Platipus, and Paul Oakenfold's Perfecto Fluoro became important sources for the sound. Oakenfold, Britain's most popular DJ, finally gave *Goa trance* the cache it had lacked in the past by caning it on the radio and in clubs across the country. The British sound system known as Return to the Source also brought *Goa trance* to the mainstream hordes, releasing three volumes in a compilation series of the best trance music on the scene.

## Happy Hardcore

Gradually evolving from the English rave scene of the late '80s and early '90s, **Happy Hardcore** featured many of the same elements that characterized rave: impossibly high beats per minute, similarly fast synthesizer/piano runs, and vocal samples altered to make the most soulful diva sound like a warbling chipmunk. The jungle/drum'n'bass movement had also emerged from rave, but the two scenes split and grew quite anathemic. The positive vibes of *happy hardcore* were criticized by most clubgoers as music for the drugged-out youth, but just as the hardcore-into-jungle scene found favor with critics later in the decade, a certain amount of respect for *happy hardcore* appeared as well. The work of combination DJ/producers such as Slipmatt, Hixxy & Sharkey, Force & Styles, and DJ Dougal produced innumerable compilations, as well as the inevitable solo production LPs.

## Hardcore Techno

The fastest, most abrasive form of dance music currently available at any one time, **Hardcore Techno** was, by the mid-'90s, the province of a startlingly wide array of producers, including breakbeat junglists, industrial trancesters, digital-era punks, and cartoonish ravers. The style originally emerged from Great Britain's 1988 Summer of Love; though the original soundtrack to those warehouse parties was influenced by the relatively mid-tempo rhythms of Chicago acid house, increased drug intake caused many ravers to embrace quicker rhythms and altogether more frenetic forms of music. Many DJs indulged their listeners by speeding up house records originally intended for 33-rpm play, and producers carried the torch by sampling the same records for their releases. During 1991-92, hardcore/rave music had hit the legitimate airwaves as well, led by hits like SL2's "On a Ragga Tip", T-99's "Anasthasia," and RTS' "Poing."

The resulting major-label feeding frenzy produced heavy coverage for lightweight novelty fare like "Go Speed Go" by Alpha Team, "Sesame's Treat" by Smart E's, and "James Brown Is Dead" by L.A. Style. By 1993, British producers like Rob Playford, 4 Hero, and Omni Trio began leading hardcore techno into the breakbeat territory that would later become known as jungle, even as the Teutonic end of hardcore morphed into harder trance and gabba.

During the mid-'90s, most ravers had grown out of the dance scene or simply tired of the sound; though the original hardcore/rave sound had spread to much of the British hinterlands as well as continental Europe, most Londoners favored progressive house or the emerging ambient techno. The simultaneous lack of critical coverage but wide spread of the sound—into the north of England and Scotland as well as the continental centers of Germany and the Netherlands—served to introduce a variety of underground styles, from the digital hardcore of Germany's Alec Empire to English happy hardcore. In fact, the term had practically become a dinosaur by the end of the decade.

## Hi-NRG

**Hi-NRG** is a fast variation of disco that evolved in the '80s. Driven by a fast drum machine and synthesizers, *Hi-NRG* was essentially a dance-oriented music with only slight hints of pop. There would be a few hooks—generally sung by disembodied vocalists wailing in the background—but the emphasis of the music, like most dance music, was in the beat. *Hi-NRG* was a predecessor to techno and house, which drew from its beats in decidedly different ways. House had a funkier, soulful rhythm, while techno expanded with the mechanical beats of *Hi-NRG*.

## House

**House** music grew out of the post-disco dance club culture of the early '80s. After disco became popular, certain urban DJs—particularly those in gay communities—altered the music to make it less pop-oriented. The beat became more mechanical and the bass grooves became deeper, while elements of electronic synth-pop, Latin soul, dub reggae, rap, and jazz were grafted over the music's insistent, unvarying four-four beat. Frequently, the music was purely instrumental and when there were vocalists, they were faceless female divas that often sang wordless melodies. By the late '80s, *house* had broken out of underground clubs in cities like Chicago, New York, and London, and had begun making inroads on the pop charts, particularly in England and Europe but later in America under the guise of artists like C+C Music Factory and Madonna. At the same time, *house* was breaking into the pop charts; it fragmented into a number of subgenres, including hip-house, ambient house, and most significantly, acid house (a subgenre of house with the instantly recognizable squelch of Roland's TB-303 bass-line generator). During the '90s, *house* ceased to be cutting-edge music, yet it remained popular in clubs throughout Europe and America. At the end of the decade, a new wave of progressive house artists including Daft Punk, Basement Jaxx, and House of 909 brought the music back to critical quarters with praised full-length works.

## IDM

A loaded term meant to distinguish electronic music of the '90s and later that's equally comfortable on the dancefloor as in the living room, **IDM (Intelligent Dance Music)** eventually acquired a good deal of negative publicity, not least among the legion of dance producers and fans whose exclusion from the community prompted the question of whether they produced stupid dance music. Born in the late '80s, the sound grew out of a fusion between the hard-edged dance music heard on the main floor at raves and larger club events, and the more downtempo music of the nearby chill-out rooms. DJs like Mixmaster Morris and Dr. Alex Paterson blended Chicago house, softer synth-pop/new wave, and ambient/environmental music, prompting a wave of producers inspired by a variety of sources. (Many DJs and producers were also reacting against the increasingly chart-leaning slant of British dance music during those years, exemplified by novelty hits like "Pump Up the Jam" by Technotronic and "Sesame's Treat" by Smart E's.) The premiere *IDM* label, Sheffield's Warp Records, proved home to the best in the sound—in fact, the seminal Warp compilation Artificial Intelligence alone introduced listeners worldwide to a half-dozen of the style's most crucial artists: Aphex Twin, the Orb, Plastikman, Autechre, Black Dog Productions, and B12. Other labels—Rising High, GPR, R&S, Rephlex, Fat Cat, Astralwerks—released quality *IDM* as well, though by the mid-'90s much of the electronica produced for headphone consumption had diverged either toward the path of more experimentation or more beat orientation. With no centered, commercial scene to speak of, North America became a far more hospitable clime to *IDM*, and by the end of the '90s, dozens of solid labels had opened for business, including Drop Beat, Isophlux, Suction, Schematic, and Cytrax. Despite frequent attempts to rename the style (Warp's "electronic listening music" and Aphex Twin's "braindance" were two choices), *IDM* continued to be the *de facto* way for fans to describe their occasionally undescribable favorites.

## Industrial

**Industrial** music was a dissonant, abrasive style of music that grew out of the tape-music and electronic experiments of the mid-'70s bands Cabaret Voltaire and Throbbing Gristle (the term was coined from the latter's label, Industrial Records). The music was largely electronic, distorted, and rather avant-garde for rock circles. By the mid-'80s, *industrial* dance bands Ministry, Front 242, Nitzer Ebb, and Skinny Puppy had evolved from the original template. During the next decade, *industrial* went overground and became a new kind of heavy-metal courtesy of crossover groups like Nine Inch Nails, White Zombie, and Marilyn Manson.

## Industrial Dance

During the '80s, industrial music progressed from being an obscure, experimentalist style to a position where it was quite popular and straight-ahead for a growing audience unenthused by limp-wristed alternative music as well as cock rock and heavy metal. Early distinguished by the term "electronic body music," several artists, such as Front 242, Nitzer Ebb, Skinny Puppy, and Ministry gained significant airplay in clubs. By the '90s, industrial had split along a guitar/electronics divide, with the latter usually carrying on the tradition of electronic body music. America's Cleopatra Records featured the most **Industrial Dance** acts, including Leætherstrip, Spahn Ranch, and Die Krupps.

## Jungle/Drum'n'bass

Based almost entirely in England, **Jungle** (also known as drum'n'bass) is a permutation of hardcore techno that emerged in the early '90s. *Jungle* is the most rhythmically complex of all forms of techno, relying on extremely fast polyrhythms and breakbeats. Usually, it's entirely instrumental—it is among the hardest of all hardcore techno, consisting of nothing but fast drum machines and deep bass. As its name implies, *jungle* does have more overt reggae, dub, and R&B influences than most hardcore—and that is why some critics claimed that the music was the sound of black techno musicians and DJs reclaiming it from the white musicians and DJs who dominated the hardcore scene. Nevertheless, *jungle* never slows down to develop a groove—it just speeds along. Like most techno genres, *jungle* is primarily a singles genre designed for a small, dedicated audience, although the crossover success of Goldie and his 1995 debut *Timeless* suggested a broader appeal and more musical possibilities than other forms of techno. Dozens of respected artists followed in their wake, fusing breakbeats with influences lifted from jazz, film music, ambient, and trip-hop.

## Kraut-Rock

**Kraut-Rock** refers to the legions of German bands of the early '70s that expanded the sonic possibilities of art and progressive rock. Instead of following in the direction of their British and American counterparts, who were moving toward jazz and classical-based compositions and concept albums, the German bands became more mechanical and electronic. Working with early synthesizers and splicing together seemingly unconnected reels of tape, bands like Faust, Can, and Neu! created a droning, pulsating sound that owed more to the avant-garde than to rock 'n' roll. Although the bands didn't make much of an impact while they were active in the '70s, their music anticipated much post-punk of the early '80s, particularly industrial rock. *Kraut-rock* also came into vogue in the '90s, when groups like Stereolab and Tortoise began incorporating the hypnotic rhythms and electronic experiments of the German art-rock bands into their own, vaguely avant-garde indie-rock.

## Madchester

**Madchester** was the dominant force in British rock during the late '80s and early '90s. A fusion of acid house dance rhythms and melodic pop, *Madchester* was distinguished by its loping beats, psychedelic flourishes, and hooky choruses. While the song structures were familiar, the arrangements and attitude were modern, and even the retro-pop touches—namely the jangling guitars, swirling organs, and sharp pop sense—functioned as postmodern collages. There were two approaches to this collage, as evidenced by the Stone Roses and Happy Mondays. The Roses were a traditional guitar-pop band, and their songs were straight-ahead pop tunes, bolstered by baggy beats; it was modernized '60s pop. Happy Mondays cut and pasted like rappers sampled, taking choruses from the Beatles and LaBelle and putting them into the context of darkly psychedelic dance. Despite their different approaches, both bands shared a love for acid-house music and culture, as well as the hometown of Manchester, England. As the group's popularity grew, the British press tagged the two groups—as well as similarly-minded bands like the Charlatans [UK] and Inspiral Carpets—"Madchester" after a Happy Mondays song. (It was also known as "baggy," since the bands wore baggy clothing). *Madchester* was enormously popular for several years in the UK before fading, largely because the Roses and the Mondays fell prey to laziness and drug abuse, respectively. The genre never made much impact in America outside of alternative circles, but *Madchester's* offspring—bands like Oasis, Pulp, and Blur that were heavily influenced by the collision of contemporary and classic pop—became international stars in the mid-'90s.

## Minimalism

One of the main innovations in the contemporary classical field, **Minimalism** has also influenced new age composers and electronic producers alike, particularly in progressive electronic styles where sequencers play an important role. Generally, this music is characterized by a strong and relentless pulse, the insistent repetition of short melodic fragments, and harmonies that change over long periods of time. A trio of '60s figures, LaMonte Young, Terry Riley, and Steve Reich, did the most to pioneer the field, though Philip Glass had the most success with the style during the '70s.

## Neo-Electro

For several months in 1995, British clubs were afire with the sights and sounds of robots, body-poppers, and a revival of America's early-'80s electro movement. Though much of the attention was given to the old-school masters (Afrika Bambaataa, the Egyptian Lover, Newcleus), much of the influence for the electro revival had come from more recent sounds. Detroit acts such as Drexciya, Underground Resistance, and Ectomorph had begun looking back to electro, and Drexciya's multi-volume series of 1994 EPs were much-heard on the other side of the Atlantic. In Britain, Clear Records headed the revival hot-list, with singles from Jedi Knights, Tusken Raiders, Plaid, and Gescom (almost all were aliases for more well-known dance acts including Global Communication, µ-Ziq, and Autechre). Though the electro revival didn't last long as a British club trend, good records continued to be released (especially by Clear), and other labels, such as Skam, Musik Aus Strom, and Dot, progressed beyond the sound to create intelligent new music with heavy electro influences.

## Newbeat

A rather brief phenomenon (even for the style-a-minute world of dance music), **Newbeat** emerged late in the '80s as a mid-tempo derivation of acid house. Influenced as well by Detroit techno and Euro-dance, *newbeat* was centered in Belgium, where labels such as R&S and Antler-Subway—home of the *newbeat* anthem "I Sit on Acid" by Lords of Acid—characterized the style with acid synth leanings, but more pop-friendly approaches to dance. The blazing success of the KLF during 1990-91 sustained *newbeat* for awhile, but after their exit from the music industry, the style faded quickly. While both Antler-Subway and Lords of Acid later moved on to a self-parodying approach to acid house, R&S became a respected name in the dance industry, focusing mostly on trance and ambient techno.

## Noise

Sludgy, abrasive, and punishing, **Noise** is everything its name promises, expanding on the music's capacity for sonic assault while almost entirely rejecting the role of melody and songcraft. From the ear-splitting, teeth-rattling attack of Japan's Merzbow to the thick, grinding intensity of Amphetamine Reptile-label bands like Tar and Vertigo, it's dark, brutal music that pushes rock to its furthest extremes. By the end of the '90s, a resurgence in the use of sine waves—originally explored by musique concrète artists in the '50s—became increasingly frequent among *noise* artists such as Otomo Yoshihide.

## Noise Pop

**Noise Pop** is just that—pop music wrapped in barbed-wire kisses of feedback, dissonance, and abrasion. It occupies the halfway point between bubblegum and the avant-garde, a collision between conventional pop songcraft and the sonic assault of white noise—guitars veer out of control but somehow the melody pushes forward, and the tension between the two opposing forces frequently makes for fascinating listening.

## Nu Breaks

A hard-edged dance style developed late in the '90s with the convergence of techno and drum'n'bass as well as a few elements of the earlier rave scenes, **Nu Breaks** was led by artists and DJs including Brits Adam Freeland, Dylan Rhymes, Beber, Freq Nasty, and Rennie Pilgrem plus a bare few Americans like BT. From drum'n'bass the style borrowed two-step breakbeats and chilling effects, from techno its smooth flow and machine percussion, and from early-'90s rave/hardcore some of the crowd-pleasing bells and whistles (figuratively as well as literally) that in some cases had not been heard for years. Freeland was probably the best-known of the *nu breaks* crew (especially since most producers concentrated on singles output), as rock-steady mix sets like Coastal Breaks and Tectonics earned acclaim with dance fans around the world.

## Old School Rap

**Old School Rap** is the style of the very first rap artists who emerged from New York City in the late '70s and early '80s. *Old school* is easily identified by its relatively simple raps—most lines take up approximately equal amounts of time, and the rhythms of the language rarely twisted around the beats of the song. The cadences usually fell squarely on the beat, and when they didn't, they wouldn't stray for long, returning to the original pattern for quick resolution. The emphasis was not on lyrical technique, but simply on good times—aside from the socially conscious material of Grandmaster Flash, which greatly expanded rap's horizons, most *old school rap* had the fun, playful flavor of the block parties and dances at which it was born. In keeping with the laidback, communal good vibes, *old school rap* seemed to have more room and appreciation for female MCs, although none achieved the higher profile of Grandmaster Flash & the Furious Five or the Sugarhill Gang. Some *old school* songs were performed over disco or funk-style tracks, while others featured synthesized backing (this latter type of music, either with or without raps, was known as electro). *Old school rap*'s recorded history begins with two 1979 singles, Fatback's "King Tim III" and the Sugarhill Gang's "Rapper's Delight," although the movement had been taking shape for almost a decade prior. Sugarhill Records quickly became *the* center for *old school rap*, dominating the market until Run-D.M.C. upped the ante for technique and hardcore urban toughness in 1983-84. Their sound and style soon took over the rap world, making *old school*'s party orientation and '70s funk influences seem outdated. When compared with the more complex rhythms and rhyme schemes of modern-day rap—or even the hip-hop that was being produced less than ten years after "Rapper's Delight"—*old school rap* can sound dated and a little unadventurous. However, the best *old school* tracks retain their liveliness as great party music no matter what the era, holding up surprisingly well considering all that's happened since.

## Post-Rock/Experimental

**Post-Rock** was an experimental, avant-garde movement that emerged in the mid-'90s. Most *post-rock* was droning and hypnotic, drawing from ambient, free-form jazz, avant-garde, and electronic music more than rock. The majority of *post-rock* groups were like Tortoise, a Chicago-based band with a rotating lineup. Tortoise viewed their music not as songs, but as ever-changing compositions that they improvised nightly. Most *post-rock* groups were defiantly anti-mainstream and anti-indie-rock in the vein of Tortoise. However, there were certain groups—like Stereolab—that essentially worked in a pop and indie-rock format, only touching on the experimental and avant-garde tendencies of most post-rockers. Thrill Jockey's reissue of albums by European experimental names like Mouse on Mars and Oval led to the birth of a transatlantic scene, of sorts, with Germans more focused on electronic music while most Americans preferred rock-oriented setups.

## Progressive House

House music had reached the mainstream by the late '80s (more so in Britain than anywhere else), and while several early house hits were by genuine pioneers, they were later overwhelmed by the novelty acts and one-hit wonders dominating the charts around the turn of the decade. As well, ambient, techno, and trance made gains early in the '90s as electronic styles with both street cred and a group of young artists making intelligent music. A generation of house producers soon emerged, weaned on the first wave of house and anxious to reapply the more soulful elements of the music. With a balance of sublime techno and a house sound more focused on New York garage than Chicago acid house, groups like Leftfield, the Drum Club, Spooky, and Faithless hit the dance charts (and occasionally Britain's singles charts). Though critically acclaimed full-lengths were never quite as important as devastating club tracks, several **Progressive House** LPs were stellar works, including Leftfield's *Leftism*, Spooky's *Gargantuan*, and the Drum Club's *Everything Is Now*. By the mid-'90s, the innovations of *progressive house* had become the mainstream of house music around the world.

## Rave

**Rave** is more of an event than a genre of music. *Raves* were underground parties where acid house and hardcore records were played and large quantities of drugs—particularly ecstasy—were consumed. Most of the music played at *raves* had a psychedelic quality, even before drugs became a major element of the scene. DJs played at the *raves*, mixing stacks of house and techno singles; the DJs, not the recording artists themselves, became the most recognizable names in the scene. *Raves* were primarily an English phenomenon during the late '80s and early '90s. They were conducted in large venues, particularly abandoned warehouses and open fields. Eventually, the British government became concerned that *raves* were a dangerous, antisocial phenomenon that had to be shut down, but the parties never disappeared, especially since word of the events were usually passed through word of mouth and handmade fliers. In the States, *raves* began to make some inroads in the early '90s, but they never gained a large audience, even by underground standards. Throughout the '90s, bands that were directly influenced by *rave* culture—particularly "baggy" bands like the Stone Roses, Happy Mondays, and Charlatans; Brit-pop acts like Pulp and Oasis; and techno artists like the Prodigy—made their way into the mainstream, and the culture continued to capture the attention of British youth into the late '90s.

## Shibuya-Kei

The Japanese pop phenomenon known as **Shibuya-Kei** exploded forth from the ultra-trendy Shibuya shopping district of west Tokyo, an area home to some of the most fashionable and best-stocked record and clothing stores in the world. *Shibuya-kei*—literally, "Shibuya style"—was the name given to the like-minded pop musicians who emerged from this consumer culture, a group of young Japanese weaned on a steady and amazingly eclectic diet of Western pop exports; the result was an unprecedented collision of sights and sounds, with trailblazing acts like Pizzicato 5 drawing on disparate influences ranging from the lush lounge-pop of Burt Bacharach to the rhythms and energy of urban hip-hop. In its purest form, *shibuya-kei* is classic Western pop refracted through the looking glass of modern Eastern society—music cut up, pasted together, and spit out in new and exciting ways. *Shibuya-kei* is also pop music at its cutest: it's a view to a world where the sweetness and simplicity of the girl-group era never ended but simply evolved, never out of step with the times but always true to its roots as well—the Lolita complex so pervasive throughout Japanese culture informs much of this music, and its youthful innocence is the key to much of its endearing charm.

## Shoegazing

**Shoegazing** is a genre of late '80s and early '90s British indie-rock, named after the bands' motionless performing style, where they stood on stage and stared at the floor while they played. But *shoegazing* wasn't about visuals—it was about pure sound. The sound of the music was overwhelmingly loud, with long, droning riffs, waves of distortion, and cascades of feedback. Vocals and melodies disappeared into the walls of guitars, creating a wash of sound where no instrument was distinguishable from the other. Most *shoegazing* groups worked off the template My Bloody Valentine established with their early EPs and their first full-length album, *Isn't Anything*, but Dinosaur Jr., the Jesus & Mary Chain, and the Cocteau Twins were also major influences. Bands that followed—most notably Ride, Lush, Chapterhouse, and the Boo Radleys—added their own stylistic flourishes. Ride veered close to '60s psychedelia, while Lush alternated between straight pop and the dream pop of the Cocteau Twins. None of the *shoegazers* were dynamic performers or interesting interviews, which prevented them from breaking through into the crucial US market. In 1992—after the groups had dominated the British music press and indie charts for about three years—the *shoegazing* groups were swept aside by the twin tides of American grunge and Suede, the band to initiate the wave of Brit-pop that ruled British music during the mid-'90s. Some *shoegazers* broke up within a few years (Chapterhouse, Ride), while other groups—such as the Boo Radleys and Lush—evolved with the times and were able to sustain careers into the late '90s.

## Space-Rock

Once used as a tag to describe '70s-era acts like Hawkwind, in more recent years the term **Space-Rock** has come to embody a new generation of heady, hypnotic bands with aspirations of cosmic transcendence. Arguably the first and most prominent of the new *space-rock* groups was Britain's Spacemen 3, whose famous "Taking drugs to make music to take drugs to" credo subsequently influenced most, if not all, of the like-minded bands in their wake; indeed, the music of the genre is typically narcotic, defined by washes of heavily reverbed guitar, minimalist drumming, and gentle, languid vocals.

## Speed Garage

Revving up the sweet sound of garage techno by adding ragga vocals, rewinds, and DJ scratching along with occasional drum'n'bass rhythms, **Speed Garage** hit the London clubscene in 1996, gaining momentum from its Sunday-night status as a good end-of-the-week comedown to supplant jungle/drum'n'bass as the hotly tipped dance style of the late '90s. Influenced by American producers like Todd Edwards and Armand Van Helden, *speed garage* grew with European acts such as the Dream Team, Double 99, Boris Dlugosch, and the Tuff Jam crew.

## Tech-House

**Tech-House** is used to describe a variety of rangy, mostly European producers who culled many of the rhythms and effects of acid and progressive house yet with a clean, simplistic production style suggestive of Detroit and British techno. The style came to cover a wide variety of names including Herbert, Daniel Ibbotson, Terry Lee Brown Jr., Funk D'Void, and Ian O'Brien, among others.

## Techno

**Techno** had its roots in the electronic house music made in Detroit in the mid-'80s. Where house still had explicit connection to disco even when it was entirely mechanical, *techno* was strictly electronic music, designed for a small, specific audience. The first *techno* producers and DJs—Kevin Saunderson, Juan Atkins, and Derrick May, among others—emphasized the electronic, synthesized beats of electro-funk artists like Afrika Bambaataa and synth-rock units like Kraftwerk. In the United States, *techno* was strictly an underground phenomenon, but in England, it broke into the mainstream in the late '80s. In the early '90s, *techno* began to fragment into a number of subgenres, including hardcore, ambient, and jungle. In hardcore techno, the beats-per-minute on each record were sped up to ridiculous, undanceable levels—it was designed to alienate a broad audience. Ambient took the opposite direction, slowing the beats down and relying on watery electronic textures—it was used as come-down music, when ravers and club-goers needed a break from acid house and hardcore techno. Jungle was nearly as aggressive as hardcore, combining driving *techno* beats with breakbeats and dancehall reggae—essentially. All subgenres of *techno* were initially designed to be played in clubs, where they would be mixed by DJs. Consequently, most of the music was available on 12" singles or various-artists compilations, where the songs could run for a long time, providing the DJ with a lot of material to mix into his set. In the mid-'90s, a new breed of *techno* artists—most notably ambient acts like the Orb and Aphex Twin, but also harder-edged artists like the Prodigy and Goldie—began constructing albums that didn't consist of raw beats intended for mixing. Not surprisingly, these artists—particularly the Prodigy—became the first recognizable stars in *techno*.

## Trance

Breaking out of the German techno and hardcore scene of the early '90s, **Trance** emphasized brief synthesizer lines repeated endlessly throughout tracks, with only the addition of minimal rhythmic changes and occasional synthesizer atmospherics to distinguish them—in effect putting listeners into a trance that approached those of religious origin. Despite waning interest in the sound during the mid-'90s, *trance* made a big comeback later in the decade, even supplanting house as the most popular dance music of choice around the globe.

Inspired by acid house and Detroit techno, *trance* coalesced with the opening of R&S Records in Ghent, Belgium and Harthouse/Eye Q Records in Frankfurt, Germany. R&S defined the sound early on with singles like "Energy Flash" by Joey Beltram, "The Ravesignal" by CJ Bolland, and others by Robert Leiner, Sun Electric, and Aphex Twin. Harthouse, begun in 1992 by Sven Väth with Heinz Roth & Matthias Hoffman, made the most impact on the sound of *trance* with Hardfloor's minimal epic "Hardtrance Acperience" and Väth's own "L'Esperanza," plus releases by Arpeggiators, Spicelab, and Barbarella. Artists like Väth, Bolland, Leiner, and many others made the transition to the full-length realm, though without much of an impact on the wider music world.

Despite a long nascent period when it appeared *trance* had disappeared, replaced by breakbeat dance (trip-hop and jungle), the style's increasing impact on Britain's dance scene finally crested in the late '90s. The classic German sound had changed somewhat though, and the term "progressive" trance gained favor to describe influences from the smoother end of house and Euro dance. By 1998, most of the country's best-known DJs—Paul Oakenfold, Pete Tong, Tony De Vit, Danny Rampling, Sasha, Judge Jules—were playing *trance* in Britain's superclubs. Even America turned on to the sound (eventually), led by its own cast of excellent DJs, including Christopher Lawrence and Kimball Collins.

## Tribal House

By the early '90s, house music had undergone several fusions with other styles, creating ambient house, hip-house and, when the four-on-the-floor punch was blended with polyrhythmic percussion, **Tribal House**. The style covers a bit of ground, from the mainstream leanings of Frankie Bones and Ultra Naté to the electro-hippie sensibilities of Banco de Gaia, Loop Guru, and Eat Static (all denizens of the UK's Planet Dog Records).

## Trip-Hop

Yet another in a long line of plastic placeholders to attach itself to one arm or another of the UK post-acid house dance scene's rapidly mutating experimental underground, **Trip-Hop** was coined by the English music press in an attempt to characterize a new style of downtempo, jazz-, funk-, and soul-inflected experimental breakbeat music which began to emerge around in 1993 in association with labels such as Mo'Wax, Ninja Tune, Cup of Tea, and Wall of Sound. Similar to (though largely vocal-less) American hip-hop in its use of sampled drum breaks, typically more experimental, and infused with a high index of ambient-leaning and apparently psychotropic atmospherics (hence "trip"), the term quickly caught on to describe everything from Portishead and Tricky, to DJ Shadow and U.N.K.L.E., to Coldcut, Wagon Christ, and Depth Charge—much to the chagrin of many of these musicians, who saw their music largely as an extension of hip-hop proper, not a gimmicky offshoot. One of the first commercially significant hybrids of dance-based listening music to crossover to a more mainstream audience, *trip-hop* full-length releases routinely topped indie charts in the UK and, in artists such as Shadow, Tricky, Morcheeba, the Sneaker Pimps, and Massive Attack, account for a substantial portion of the first wave of "electronica" acts to reach Stateside audiences.

# A

## Acen (Acen Razvi)

*Producer / Rave*

Author of two club hits and one of the few rave artists privileged enough to even record an LP, Acen Razvi produced tracks with dense breakbeats and all matter of sampled, sped-up vocalists, from rude-boy chatters and divas to Jim Morrison. Released on the hardcore label Production House, "Trip II the Moon" also sampled James Bond's *You Only Live Twice* and hit the British Top 40 in 1992; "Close Your Eyes" also charted. Soon after the release of 1993's *75 Minutes* album, however, Acen had practically disappeared. He resurfaced two years later, recording for the new-school electro label Clear Records as Spacepimp. By the late '90s, Acen had also re-appeared on F-111 with singles like "116.7" and "Cylon." —*John Bush*

● **75 Minutes** / 1993 / Profile ♦♦

The only album released (so far) by Acen is a period piece, solid in its own right but including far too many versions of the same singles for its own good. Multiple remixes of "Trip II the Moon" and "Close Your Eyes" can be expected, but no less than half of the album's twelve tracks are versions of what was (probably) going to be the next single, "Window in the Sky." That leaves space for two "album" tracks, both of which prove that the best place to hear Acen is on a hardcore compilation. —*John Bush*

## John Acquaviva

b. Nov. 19, 1963, Apulia, Italy

*Producer, DJ / Tech-House, Detroit Techno, Club/Dance, Techno, House*

John Acquaviva is known primarily through his association with, and recordings for, +8 Records, the label he founded with Richie Hawtin (aka Plastikman). Acquaviva is also one of the most prized techno DJs around the globe, as well as a multi-label entrepreneur—he helms Probe and Definitive Records in addition to +8. While growing up in London, Ontario, Acquaviva became a music lover and started DJing in 1980. He gradually accumulated a small bedroom studio of equipment to produce music similar to the Chicago and Detroit records he enjoyed, when he met Richie Hawtin in 1989.

Hawtin was a DJ with a wish to produce as well, so the two began recording together. Their first single, "Elements of Tone" by States of Mind, became the first release on +8 Records. When later releases—by Acquaviva and Hawtin plus Kenny Larkin, Mark Gage and Jochem Paap (aka Speedy J)—pushed +8's pedigree into the stratosphere during 1991-92, Acquaviva and Hawtin formed Probe and Definitive to spread the wealth. Eventually, Acquaviva took over Definitive, pushing the label closer to his vision for progressive tech-house with releases by Ian Pooley, Clemens Neufeld, and David Alvarado. His DJing quickly entered the world-class level as well, encompassing an incredibly wide range of music—from straightahead techno, Chicago house and disco to Michael Jackson and Brazilian pop. His first mix album, *Transmissions, Vol. 1*, was released in 1996. Two years later, Acquaviva shared the Studio !K7 mix album *X-Mix, Vol. 3: Enter Digital Reality* with Hawtin and released his second solo jaunt, *From Saturday to Sunday Mix*. *Cream CD 1999* followed. —*John Bush*

**Transmissions, Vol. 1** / Oct. 29, 1996 / Virgin Music Canada ♦♦♦♦

Acquaviva's debut remix album is a slamming tech-house set featuring Ian Pooley, Terrence Parker, L.A. Williams, LFO and Plastikman, among others. —*John Bush*

● **From Saturday to Sunday Mix** / Jun. 2, 1998 / Florida ♦♦♦♦

Acquaviva mixes a range of tech-house on this two-disc set, including Metro Dade and the Kooky Scientist alongside Jedi Knights, DJ Duke, Kevin Yost, Omegaman and Groove Culture. —*John Bush*

**Skills** / Oct. 13, 1998 / Studio !K7 ♦♦♦♦

The first volume in a new series from Studio !K7 focuses on Acquaviva's live mixing skills with a batch of dance classics, including tracks by Phuture, Fingers Inc., Nightmares on Wax and X-Press 2, as well as more contemporary selections by Ian Pooley, Laurent Garnier and Salt City Orchestra. —*John Bush*

## Adamski (Adam Tinley)

b. 1968

*Producer / Club/Dance, Acid House*

Born in the late '60s, Adamski (born Adam Tinley) appeared to have reached the perfect age for recording twenty years later, square in the middle of Britain's acid-house boom. In fact, he had made his chart debut a decade earlier with the adolescent punk band the Stupid Babies. (The group, which also included his five-year-old brother Dominic on vocals, hit number three on the indie charts with "Baby Sitters" and even recorded a radio session for John Peel.) Also a member of the post-punk hip hop band Diskord Datkord during the mid-'80s, Tinley became interested in house music by the end of the decade. After meeting Chicagoan Jimi Polo, Adamski was introduced to many major figures in house including Marshall Jefferson and Adonis. He learned the basics of the sequencer from Polo as well, and began playing live at warehouse parties and raves around London.

He signed with MCA by the end of the decade and debuted with "N-R-G," a No. 12 hit in the UK. (He was later forced to turn over some royalties due to a dispute with lawyers, who contended that the track hoisted a TV commercial melody.) His subsequent single, "Killer," wisely forestalled the (recognizable) samples and hit number one—though thanks may also be due to its vocalist, Seal. His debut album *Liveandirect* made a bit of an impression, with mixes of both "N-R-G" and "Killer" to recommend itself, and his late 1990 single "The Space Jungle" hit the Top Ten as well. As was far from surprising with the British rave movement however, Adamski disappeared from the charts after 1992, when his third album *Naughty* was released. Six years later, he resurfaced on ZTT with *Adamski's Thing*. —*John Bush*

● **Liveandirect** / Jul. 10, 1990 / MCA ♦♦♦♦

*Liveandirect* is by no means the worst rave crossover LP released during the late '80s and early '90s, but it has dated just as badly as its contemporaries. Though Adamski's pop singles "N-R-G" and "Killer" still have an inkling of the freshness they must have possessed back in 1989, other album tracks (like "Magik Sound" and "Rap You Into Sound") display little sense of how full-lengths are supposed to flow. —*John Bush*

**Dr. Adamski's Musical Pharmacy** / 1991 / MCA ♦♦

**Naughty** / 1992 / MCA ♦♦

**Adamski's Thing** / Oct. 26, 1998 / Uptown/Universal ♦♦♦

Adamski returned in 1998 with an album quite distinct from its predecessors, for several reasons. First, it's a true collaboration, with American house diva Gerideau, instead of the multiple vocalists on 1992's *Naughty*, and therefore lacks the somewhat scattered qualities of previous Adamski LPs. Second, *Adamski's Thing* reflects the producer's maturity (after raising his daughter), and is much closer to straight-ahead house (with a heavy Ibizan influence) than rave or hardcore. The singles "Intravenous Venus" and "One of the People" (with added vocals by his daughter) are quite solid, but overall *Adamski's Thing* sacrifices the energy of earlier Adamski recordings for a mainstream sound which leans uncomfortably close to blandness. —*John Bush*

## Barry Adamson

b. Jun. 1, 1958
*Vocals, Bass, Producer / Alternative Dance, Alternative Pop/Rock*

Barry Adamson's work as a bassist for Magazine and Nick Cave's Bad Seeds gave little indication of the complex, cinematic works he has composed as a solo artist. After leaving the Bad Seeds in 1987, Adamson decided to follow the path of film composers like John Barry, Ennio Morricone, and Bernard Herrmann, whose work had intrigued him since childhood. His first full-length album, 1989's *Moss Side Story* (he had released one previous EP in 1988), was a tour de force blending post-punk, industrial, spy guitar, and various classic movie composer quotes into a seamless 54-minute soundtrack to an ominous film noir that didn't exist. This recording led to Adamson's work on soundtracks for actual films in the early '90s, including *Delusion*, *Gas Food Lodging*, and *Shuttle Cock*. Adamson also continued to compose quasi-cinematic recordings for imaginary films like 1996's *Oedipus Shmoedipus*, although none has matched the sustained excitement of *Moss Side Story*. *As Above, So Below* followed in 1998, and a best-of compilation titled *The Murky World of Barry Adamson* appeared a year after that. —*Richie Unterberger*

● **Moss Side Story** / 1989 / Mute ◆◆◆◆

Adamson's first full-length album is still unequivocally his best. Elements of rock, voices from news reports, blood-curdling wordless female vocals (courtesy of experimental/punk diva Diamanda Galas), lounge keyboards, and swirling funereal ambient music are interwoven on this taut and compelling, almost continuous imaginary "soundtrack." The result is a sinister and edgy soundscape that's as gripping as any black-and-white thriller. The CD adds three bonus cuts, including Adamson's updates of "The Man With The Golden Arm" and "Alfred Hitchcock Presents." —*Richie Unterberger*

**Delusion** / 1991 / Mute ◆◆

It's perhaps unsurprising that Adamson's eclectic compositional talent doesn't work nearly as well when he has to wed his vision to an actual film. This soundtrack for an obscure 1991 movie contains plenty of interesting bits, elements, and pieces—somber Spanish guitar, haunting orchestral passages, *Phantom of the Opera* organ phrases, manic Latin music, and a too-brief, ominous update of the 1963 British instrumental hit "Diamonds." The problem is that it doesn't ebb and flow into a sum greater than its parts. In fact, the jarring bits of dialogue (which are meaningless without the context of the film) are often downright annoying, and make the sum substantially less than whatever whole it may have formed. —*Richie Unterberger*

**Soul Murder** / 1992 / Mute ◆◆◆

Equally as ambitious as *Moss Side Story*, but this doesn't come off nearly as well. Apparently constructed to evoke similar underworld soundscapes, too much of this is built around simple, sparse (sometimes electronic) riffs. The production lacks force and density, and the pieces don't flow into each other with the cohesion that he's demonstrated in other work. Nifty bits of haunting orchestral ambience and lounge jazz keyboards remain, and it does hit a groove at times, especially with the goofy French pop song (with childish vocals) "Un Petit Miracle" and the brutal ska treatment of the James Bond theme. —*Richie Unterberger*

**The Negro Inside Me** / Oct. 19, 1993 / Mute ◆◆

Something of a holding pattern. On this six-song EP, Adamson extrapolates from contemporary black dance beats, samples his American publicist's answering machine message and Jane Birkin's hit "Je T'Aime," and throws in lounge jazz piano bits and more. The pieces aren't that striking, and one gets the sense that he's tossing out some ideas to play with in the interim between full-length scores/albums. —*Richie Unterberger*

**Oedipus Shmoedipus** / Aug. 7, 1996 / Mute ◆◆◆◆

After some releases with more of a pop, beat-heavy feel, Adamson moves back—sort of—into the land of noirish soundtrack. Unlike *Moss Side Story*, it's not really a soundtrack with repeated themes and motifs. A lot of pieces establish soundtrack-like moods, but the flow never builds up a momentum of its own. As individual soundscapes, though, the tracks (largely instrumental) are reasonably impressive, whether it's burlesque-type fare, a takeoff on Miles Davis, or lounge jazz. If noir is what you want, "It's Business As Usual" is especially creepy, with its neurotic answering machine messages nearly buried under waves of disquieting sounds; achieving a similar effect, in an entirely different manner, is "Vermillion Kisses," a fairytale narrative with a morbid ending. Nick Cave adds a guest vocal to (and co-writes) "The Sweetest Embrace"; Pulp's Jarvis Cocker can be heard (and co-writes) another cut. Adamson's skill in layering and devising unusual sound textures still qualifies him as one of experimental rock's more imaginative composers and producers. But on the more rock-oriented pieces, he's using too many of those damn beat-boxes for his own good. —*Richie Unterberger*

**As Above, So Below** / Jun. 23, 1998 / Mute ◆◆◆◆

A vague concept record littered with recurring images of heaven and hell, *As Above, So Below* spotlights Barry Adamson at his most defiantly eclectic; co-produced by Flood, the album moves breathlessly from pop to jazz to blues to avant-stylings, juxtaposing swing numbers like "Jazz Devil" with ballads like "Can't Get Loose." Adamson's sheer creative recklessness alone makes it worth a listen. —*Jason Ankeny*

**The Murky World of Barry Adamson** / May 18, 1999 / Mute ◆◆◆

*The Murky World of Barry Adamson* collects the best of the former Bad Seed's solo recordings. Adamson's moody, filmic songs mix sex and menace with impenetrable cool, especially on "The Vibes Ain't Nothing but the Vibes" and "Something Wicked This Way Comes," both from his 1996 album *Oedipus Schmoedipus*. Along with selected tracks from every album from *Moss Side Story* to *As Above, So Below*, *The Murky World of Barry Adamson* also includes three previously unreleased tracks: "Walk the Last Mile," "Mitch & Andy" and "Saturn in the Summertime." *Murky World* is a delectable sampler of Adamson's dark musical talents. —*Heather Phares*

## Add N To (X)

f. 1994, London, England
*Group / Electronica, Post-Rock/Experimental*

Name-checking a diverse cast of progenitors including Varèse, Xenakis and Robert Moog as well as Can and Stereolab, Add N to (X) are electro-historians of a sort, collectors of vintage synthesizer technology and fierce propagators of the man-machine aesthetic (the cover of their second album features member Ann Shenton on the operating table with a synthesizer either being inserted or taken out of her organ cavity). The trio formed when Shenton met Barry Smith in 1993; both were fans of vintage synth and the proto-electronica crafted in the '60s and '70s by such luminaries as Wendy Carlos, Pierre Henry and even Roxy Music. After becoming Add N to (X) one year later, Shenton and Smith recruited theremin expert Steven Claydon plus an organic rhythm section for their live show, consisting of Stereolab's Andy Ramsay on drums and Rob Hallam from the High Llamas. After the debut Add N to (X) album *Vero Electronics* was released in 1996 on Blow Up, the group toured America, where their propulsive live show earned more comparisons to Suicide than an ostensibly sympathetic group like Tortoise. *On the Wires of Our Nerves* appeared in 1998 and *Avant Hard* followed in April of 1999. The following year they released *Add Insult to Injury*, which saw the group move in a more accessible, pop direction. —*John Bush*

**Vero Electronics** / Jan. 29, 1996 / Blow Up ◆◆◆

**On the Wires of Our Nerves** / May 19, 1998 / Mute ◆◆◆◆

Truth be told, at least at this point in the trio's career, Add N to (X) isn't all that. They're good, but great? *On the Wires* lands a convincing "maybe" at best to that question, raising another one along the way—namely, what happens when a certain style of futurism finally becomes a retro style that can be slotted alongside everything from rockabilly to medieval folk chanting? Arguably Kraftwerk, obvious mentors to a lot of what's going on here, were equally as retro in their day, which was part of the appeal—harking back, in a quietly emotional way, to a certain outdated 1920s/1930s vision of the future long since gone while at the same time forecasting where forthcoming musics would end up. To Add N to (X)'s further credit, they're not a one-note tribute band like Komputer or Kraftwelt, bringing in some of the rougher electronic sides of Kraut-rock as much as they do early avant noisesters like Cabaret Voltaire. Add to that a great visual sense—the grotesque album cover is a wonderful blend of the sterile and visceral, its own sick joke—and there should be much more on this album than there is. But there isn't. For all the hollow drum machine sounds (and at-times real drumming, which underlays the best songs here), analog synth loops and tweaks, odd Vocoder interjections and other things besides which should make Add N to (X) a welcome alternative to Yet Another Rock Band, the sense here is that the three recorded some jam sessions, thought that would suffice, and then left the studio. Praise doesn't belong to a band just for being there and using certain instruments—thankfully, though, the trio would find a better way in its immediate future than what's on display through *On the Wires*. —*Ned Raggett*

- **Avant Hard** / Apr. 20, 1999 / Mute ♦♦♦♦

Add N to (X)'s third album, *Avant Hard*, combines the noisy, analog aesthetic of their previous works with an increasingly sophisticated, structured approach. Though the group's overdriven, menacing synth sound prevails on songs like "Robot New York" and "Buckminster Fuller," unexpected touches like the operatic vocals on "Fyuz" and the go-go guitars on "Skills" provide a welcome contrast and round out the band's sonic palette.

*Avant Hard* finds Add N to (X) expanding their emotional range as well. The album begins with theoretical pieces like the aptly-named "Barry 7's Contraption" and segues into a brace of filmic songs like the horror-show creepiness of "Steve's Going to Teach Himself Who's Boss" to the robo-porn soundtrack that is "Metal Fingers In My Body." "Revenge of the Black Regent" and "Ann's Eveready Equestrian" take this trend toward drama and build it to near-Wagnerian heights, blending synths, strings, choral voices and sound effects into symphonies of urban decay.

Finally, *Avant Hard* ends on a relatively gentle note, with a pair of songs— "Oh Yeah Oh No" and "Machine is Bored With Love"—that explore Add N to (X)'s softer, even poignant side. "Machine" is based on samples from the early-'70s experimental band Egg, adding to a long list of musical pioneers— including Joe Meek, Suicide, Kraftwerk and Bruce Haack—that the group borrows from and updates. With analog savvy and rock attitude, *Avant Hard* reveals itself as one of Add N to (X)'s finest moments. —*Heather Phares*

**Add Insult to Injury** / Oct. 17, 2000 / Mute ♦♦♦♦

Add N to (X)'s *Add Insult to Injury* should come with the disclaimer "no analog synths were hurt in the making of this album." The trio made an art of abusing their instruments on albums like *Vero Electronics*, *On the Wires of Our Nerves*, and especially 1999's brilliant *Avant Hard*. Their songs used to be virtually steeped in the blood of tweaked vintage synths, but on their fourth full-length they show a surprising streak of humanity toward their equipment, and the result is a curiously subdued, somewhat inhibited-sounding work.

*Add Insult to Injury*'s division of labor is also curious. Of the album's 12 songs, eight were written and performed by Ann Shenton, Steven Claydon, and High Llamas' drummer Rob Allum, while four were written by Barry 7 and feature contributions from keyboardist/mixer/arranger Dean Honer and drummer Ross Orton. It's almost like two different groups operating under the same name, and certainly gives the album a less-than-cohesive feel. Most of Shenton and Claydon's songs, such as the opening track "Adding N To (X)" and "You Must Create," put textures ahead of melodies or song structures, making them sound a bit like cuts off of old synth reference albums, though the fuzzed-out "Brothel Charge," the sleekly menacing "Kingdom of Shades," and "Hit for Cheese"—an S&M-tinged synth-punk duet between Shenton and a robot—are standout tracks.

Perhaps it's because he contributed fewer songs, but Barry 7's tracks are more focused and accessible. The excellent "Monster Bobby" is a stomping chant sung by soccer hooligan androids or a robotic Gary Glitter, while the fizzy synth-pop of the single "Plug Me In" is as streamlined and cute as an iMac. "Incinerator No. 1"'s pounding sludge recalls a bit of *On the Wires of Our Nerves*' beautifully ugly noise, and "The Regent Is Dead" completes the trilogy of songs that began on that album. Though it doesn't quite reach the sinister heights of *Avant Hard*'s "Revenge of the Black Regent," "The Regent Is Dead" does manage to be elegiac and martial all at once, mixing a synth choir with theremins and a snare-driven beat.

Though it never quite strikes the perfect balance between pop and experimentation, *Add Insult to Injury* reaffirms that Add N to (X) are still a step ahead of most other vintage synth-based groups, even though it can't help but feel like a small step backward after *Avant Hard*'s synapse-frying creativity and energy. Hopefully, on their next album the band will get back to what they do best: sacrificing their keyboards in the name of art. —*Heather Phares*

## Adonis (Adonis Smith)

b. Jan. 4, 196?, Chicago, IL
*Producer / Club/Dance, Acid House, House*

Despite his formal training and lack of clubbing experience, Adonis made waves on the dancefloor when he recorded several of the best Chicago house singles of the '80s, including "No Way Back," "Do It Properly" and "We're Rockin' Down the House." Born on Chicago's west side, he became interested in contemporary jazz—which he studied at the American Conservatory of Music—but also listened to '70s funk like Parliament, Funkadelic and Earth, Wind & Fire.

After hanging out with a neighbor's R&B group for awhile, he was called on to play bass and eventually joined as a full-time member. He gigged with several different bands during the early '80s (including one with Larry Heard, the only other major house producer not previously involved with Chicago's clubscene) and gradually became more interested in the keyboard player's synthesizers than his own bass guitar. A friend introduced him to house music via Jesse Saunders' "On and On"; after feeling a drive to make better-produced music than what he had heard, Adonis began recording.

Despite his musical education, early singles like "No Way Back" and "We're Rockin' Down the House" weren't any more melodic than most house records around. In fact, they were less so, with pounding basslines and minimalistic rhythms that made waves in the clubs and became classics of the Chicago house explosion. Record-label trouble forced Adonis to semi-retire from recording before he could gain any kind of major contract, but he continued to produce and remix on an independent basis into the '90s. In 1993, he and two other house legends (Farley Jackmaster Funk and Chip E) entered the studio and recorded material as Black Balls. —*John Bush*

- **No Way Back [Single]** / 1986 / Trax ♦♦♦♦

Adonis' first single for Trax was his peak for the label, though it's best found now on Chicago compilations. It's an aggressive, throbbing acid-house jacker that's arguably heavier on the electro influences than house. The intoned chorus of "too far gone/ain't no way back" is a much-sampled tagline. —*John Bush*

**We're Rockin' Down the House/Girls Out on the Floor [Single]** / 1987 / Trax ♦♦♦

## Adrenalin Junkies

*Group / Industrial-Dance, Industrial*

An electronica act perfectly in line with the philosophy of extreme noise and metal propagated by the grindcore enthusiasts at Earache Records, Adrenalin Junkies were formed by guitarist/vocalist Chad and programmer/vocalist Miss Chief. Led by their breakout single "Outcry," the duo debuted with *Electro Tribe* in late 1999. —*John Bush*

- **Electro Tribe** / Jan. 25, 2000 / Earache ♦

Informed, slightly pessimistic listeners will have no trouble seeing exactly where the shouting breakbeat hardcore group Adrenalin Junkies is coming from. Released a few years after the electronica boom led by the Chemical Brothers, *Electro Tribe* recycles dance-metal conventions from the late '90s, courtesy of influences like Prodigy and Atari Teenage Riot (ATR's Alec Empire could easily attempt legal action for their inclusion of a track called "Digital Hardcore"). However, the programming is nowhere near the league of Liam Howlett or Alec Empire, leaving an act like the personality-driven Adrenalin Junkies out in the cold. —*John Bush*

## Adult

f. 1998, Detroit, MI
*Group / Electro-Techno, Detroit Techno*

Trying to figure out who is who in the Detroit electro scene can be a never-ending mystery that only the most determined will ever unravel. The mysterious duo behind Adult first revealed themselves on vinyl in 1998 with the *Dispassionate Furniture* record and released another record that same year under the pseudonym Plasma Co. titled *Modern Romantics*, which appeared on the Koln-based Electrecord label. But it was the *Dispassionate Furniture* record on Detroit's Ersatz Audio label that instantly drew attention to this mysterious duo, who referred to themselves on the record as Vulpine and Kuperus (most likely Jack Vulpine of Le Car and Nicola Kuperus, the woman responsible for the label's trademark surreal imagery). This record strayed a bit from earlier Ersatz Audio releases with its integration of vocals into the signature style of raw analog synth and old school drum machine-driven electro. Furthermore, the duo based the music around the motif of furniture and one's sometimes frustrating ability to secure comfort. In other words, something weird was going on. Adult then followed up this release shortly afterwards in 1999 with the *Entertainment* EP on Ersatz Audio, yet another vocal electro record featuring the noteworthy song "Human Wreck." By this second release, it was clear that Adult had already developed a style based not only around their intricate collage of retro electro sounds but also around the almost punk-like attitude of their raw, robotic vocals and the confident yet undeniably odd lyrics. In this same year, Adult built upon their presence by remixing Ectomorph's "The Haunting" for Intuit-Solar's *Comin' From tha D* series of records and contributed the song "Lost Love" to the *Oral-Olio* compilation on Ersatz Audio. By 2000, the duo behind Adult had made a name for themselves as one of the more intriguing artists in Detroit, releasing the *New-Phonies* EP on Rotterdam's Clone label and remixing G.D. Luxxe's "I'm Always Busy" for another Detroit-area label, Interdimensional Transmissions. Furthermore, Adult has also focused their efforts on live performances in some of the more techno-friendly areas of Northern Europe and, most notably, at the high-profile *Detroit Electronic Music Festival* in May 2000. —*Jason Birchmeier*

- **Entertainment [Single]** / 1999 / Ersatz Audio ♦♦♦♦

The Ersatz Audio camp—particularly Adult—takes a perverse and bit insane look at modern pop culture for its inspiration. For example, the way the words "adult" and "entertainment" combine to evoke particular ideas serves as a bit of a metaphor for the collective's music. It's not so much the sounds in the songs—which are a collage of classic analog sounds that have become a staple of the schemas about the early '80s video game and synth-pop movements—but rather the way Adult integrates android-sounding vocals to their electro, instantly setting them apart from most of their peers. Drexciya sprinkled in the occasional vocals but never made it a key part of their art as Adult did. In a way, one can see Adult as moving the electro genre forward to a more evolved state beyond merely a soundtrack for dancing to a valid style of futuristic pop music; all the elements are there: catchy choruses, lyrically charged verses, instrumental bridges, tangential analog gear solos, and concise song structuring. The four songs here all stay true to this aesthetic and arguably can be considered the collective's most realized record yet. —*Jason Birchmeier*

**Dispassionate Furniture (I'm Sitting In) [Single]** / Mar. 1, 1999 / Ersatz Audio ♦♦♦

Don't think Adult is a little weird? Then check out this record to understand why this characteristic sometimes gets attributed to the Detroit duo of Vulpine and Kuperus. Of course, weird isn't necessarily a bad thing, and in the case of this particular record, the underlying sense of weirdness gives this record the personality it needs to surpass the status of merely an above-average electro record to the status of a true eyebrow-raising release deserving recognition. The motif may be subtle, but it is there: furniture. Yes, furniture. Kraftwerk wrote songs about the "Autobahn" and their "Pocket Computer," Juan Atkins wrote songs about "Cosmic Cars" and "No UFO's," and now Adult has written songs about "Dispassionate Furniture" and "Lack of Comfort." What impresses one most besides the amazingly creative beats is the fact that Adult manages to toy with such a pop culture item as furniture without making it sound overly kitschy. Of course, without such effective beats, captivating synth riffs, and the many complimentary layers of sound operating simultaneously, their lyrics would sound more than a bit silly. Don't think of this music as programmed loops of sound being tweaked but rather the precise mathematical construction of a collage that includes everything from old-school synths and dusty drum machine percussion to robotic spoken word poetry and stream-of-consciousness furniture motifs. —*Jason Birchmeier*

## The Advent

f. 1993, London, England
*Group / Detroit Techno, Club/Dance, Techno*

Longtime advocates of sonic terrorism even before banding together as the Advent in 1993, Cisco Ferreira and Colin McBean's assault on conventional techno flourished in part because of abundant glimpses into related styles, from electro and trance to progressive house. Soon after leaving school, Ferreira began working as an engineer at Jack Trax Records, a job which enabled him to glimpse first-hand the work of such auteurs as Derrick May and Marshall Jefferson. He began recording in 1988 with C.J. Bolland as Space Opera (eventually releasing four singles for R&S Records) and also recorded the first single for Fragile ("Why Don't You Answer" as himself) before meeting McBean, a top DJ who had worked with Keith Franklin of Bang the Party as the DJ team KCC.

The pair began recording together in 1990; their first activity was an engineering job for Fade to Black (aka Jay Denham), but later they debuted on vinyl with their first single, recorded for inclusion on a sampler by Network Records. The official debut of the Advent came in 1994, just after Ferreira signed to Internal Records (also the home of Orbital). He convinced McBean to join him in the recording of a series of crucially limited singles, then the debut Advent album *Elements of Life* in late 1995. Critics championed the duo's energetic update of original techno renegades like Derrick May and Kevin Saunderson, and the Advent followed with the remix album *Shaded Elementz* one year later. Their second proper album *A New Beginning* appeared in 1997, though Internal Records dropped the duo soon after its release. After transferring to the Metalbox division of Northwest/BMG, the Advent returned later that year with *Kombination Phunk*, which alternated remixes with several original productions. In 1999, McBean left, citing his reluctance to continue touring, though he continued to record under his solo alias, G Flame and Mr. G. —*John Bush*

- **Elements of Life** / Oct. 1995 / Internal ♦♦♦♦

It's a bit of a surprise that Cisco Ferreira and Colin McBean could weave aggressive Detroit techno, acid, electro and ambient into such a beguiling, trademarked sound after the styles had been around for over a decade, but the hard-school electronics of this double-disc debut Advent album proved that techno could have a staying power far beyond its original conception. Of the 16 strong tracks, highlights are hard to choose though the renegade cosmic-electro of "Spaceism" and "Farencounters" shine a bit brighter than the rest. —*John Bush*

**Shaded Elementz** / Sep. 2, 1996 / London ♦♦♦

The *Elements of Life* remix album includes eight tracks by some of the Advent's most sympathetic peers, including Luke Slater, Surgeon, Damon Wild, Joey Beltram and Cari Lekebusch. There's no less than three remixes of "It One Jah," but *Shaded Elementz* is another excellent addition to the Advent's catalogue. —*John Bush*

**A New Beginning** / Apr. 28, 1997 / ffrr ♦♦♦♦

As the title suggests, the Advent's second proper album moves on from the electro/acid feel of their early EPs and debut full-length. Instead, *New Beginning* is a set of sleek techno movers with intense beats and off-kilter percussion fills to build on the minimalist techno slant. Most of the twelve tracks on *New Beginning* were written strictly by Cisco Ferreira. —*John Bush*

**Kombination Phunk** / Nov. 24, 1997 / Metalbox ♦♦♦

The duo's first album for Metalbox/BMG combined remixes of Advent-ized material by Dopplereffekt, Joey Beltram and Surgeon, plus original productions like "Elektra Fix" and "C-On." The sound is good throughout, covering their usual blend of the harsher side of techno and electro, but some of the duo's own productions sound remarkably similar to other non-remixed originals before Advent got hold of them. —*John Bush*

## Adventures in Stereo

f. 1994
*Group / Indie Pop, Alternative Pop/Rock*

The sampling project Adventures in Stereo formed from the ashes of the short-lived 4AD label band Spirea X, which included vocalist Judith Boyle and former Primal Scream member Jim Beattie. The duo formed Adventures in Stereo in the mid-'90s with Simon Dine, who created the group's music—girl group-inspired miniatures reminiscent of the work of Stereolab or Broadcast—solely on an Akai sampler, constructing songs from obscure and unrecognizable loops. After issuing two acclaimed EPs, the band's history became convoluted: Dine split from the group, but both parties kept working under the AIS name. In 1997, early recordings and unreleased material were released on a self-titled LP on Scotland's Creeping Bent label, while a similarly-packaged collection of Dine's subsequent work was issued a short time later, also under the title *Adventures in Stereo* and on the Underground Sounds imprint. The Boyle/Beattie unit returned in 1998 with *Alternative Stereo Sounds*. Their second US release *Monomania* followed two years later. —*Jason Ankeny*

- **Adventures in Stereo [Creeping Bent]** / 1997 / Creeping Bent ♦♦♦♦

The first Adventures in Stereo album (not to be confused with another, similarly-packaged self-titled set on the Underground Sounds label) collects the early EPs which won the group a cult following on both sides of the Atlantic. Drawing in equal parts from Phil Spector's girl-group masterpieces and Stereolab's cut-and-paste Moog symphonies, AIS constructs minimalist pop gems, charming miniatures assembled from remnants of long-forgotten records from the collection of sampler extraordinaire Simon Dine; highlights like "Underground Sound," "Summer High" and "Airline," frosted with the gauzy vocals of Judith Boyle, are lost in time between the AM radio of the '60s and the experimental music of the '90s. —*Jason Ankeny*

**Adventures in Stereo [Underground Sounds]** / 1997 / Underground Sounds ♦♦♦

**Alternative Stereo Sounds** / 1998 / Creeping Bent ♦♦♦

**Monomania** / Jul. 4, 2000 / Bobsled ♦♦♦♦

The Scottish duo Adventures In Stereo is a pop band full of heartfelt lyrics swirling on top of '60s wonderlust, for tweaked harmonies and nostalgia haven't frolicked so freely since the melodic beauty of Lush and Saint Etienne. Ex-Primal Scream founder Jim Beattie and birdlike songstress Judith Boyle mold shiny stylings found on their second release, *Monomania*.

Boyle may not be Petula Clark, but her sweet vocal moods are so angelic—songs like "International" and "Ghosts" are old fashioned tunes that could have withstood the days of '60s pop melodrama. "This Day" is jaunty with Boyle's shoegazing chorus chiming along quick rhythms. "Birds" twinges with Blur-like bass drops and percussion shimmies and shakes. There isn't any wanking off on a guitar or raunchy frontman snarling. Adventures In Stereo is too kind. —*MacKenzie Wilson*

## Aerial M (David Pajo)

*Drums, Guitar, Producer / Experimental Rock, Indie Rock, Post-Rock/ Experimental, Instrumental Rock*

Aerial M was the alias of multi-instrumentalist David Pajo, a seminal figure in the development of the post-rock aesthetic whose tenures in bands including Slint and Tortoise set the stage for some of the most innovative and influential music of recent decades. He first surfaced in 1985 playing guitar in the legendary Louisville, Kentucky teen thrash band Squirrel Bait; following their 1987 break-up, Pajo joined Slint, a band whose revolutionary instrumental sound continues to resonate throughout the American underground scene. Slint proved short-lived as well, however, and after their 1991 dissolution he joined the Palace Brothers, appearing on their early recordings; from there Pajo relocated to England, where he spent over a year studying at Norwich Arts College. Upon his return to the US he rejoined the Palace Brothers, additionally playing guitar in the For Carnation and drumming in King Kong. Most important, however, was his tenure as one of two bassists in Tortoise, which began in 1996 with the landmark *Millions Now Living Will Never Die;* Pajo soon left the group, however, to focus on Aerial M, a solo project which he debuted with the single "Safeless." "Vol de Nuit," one half of a split single recorded with Monade, followed in late 1996, trailed a year later by Aerial M's self-titled debut LP, issued on the Drag City label. *Post-Global Music* followed in 1999. —*Jason Ankeny*

• **As Performed By ...** / Aug. 26, 1997 / Drag City ♦♦♦♦

David Pajo is a perfect example of the spiderweb-like lineage present in Louisville's and Chicago's new rock scenes. A founding member of legendary Louisville noise-instrumentalists, Slint, and main contributor to Tortoise's last two albums, Pajo has quietly collaborated on some of the most affecting music of the decade. Under the moniker Aerial M, Pajo has fashioned here seven beautiful instrumentals that reference but only slightly resemble his earlier work with Slint or Tortoise. Instead, *As Performed By...*, on which Pajo plays all the instruments, is a study in breathtaking melodies and simple, effective songwriting. "Dazed and Awake" accurately describes the feel of the album's opener, enveloping one's head with bright guitar work and understated dynamics. The six-minute "Aass" leaves behind the bottom-end boom that is Tortoise's trademark, allowing the song to spread through warm and longing double-guitar repetition. "Skrag Theme" would approximate a Slint melody if it were played with the amplifiers on "3," while the loops and effects on "Compassion Form" recall both the experimentation of Tortoise and the textures of *Directions in Music*. *As Performed By...* is an unassumingly gorgeous debut worthy of the same level of praise awarded to Pajo's past compositions. —*Jonathan Cohen*

**M Is ... [Single]** / Dec. 9, 1997 / Drag City ♦♦♦♦

*M Is...* is essential for its inclusion of "Wedding Song No. 3," a David Pajo creation upon which an entire remix album was later based. More rousing than most songs under the Aerial M moniker, the track's contrapuntal guitar lines regularly meet in the center for some old-fashioned major-key riffing. In line with Pajo's attention to dynamic, the song retreats into softer, percussion-less territory before reprising the main section again. Quite excellent. "Mountains Have Ears" is a bit out of left-field, a kitchen-sink melange of flute samples and finger-picked guitars on top of gurgling electronic beats. —*Jonathan Cohen*

**Post-Global Music** / Jan. 26, 1999 / Drag City ♦♦♦

On this remix album, David Pajo (ex-Slint, Tortoise) offers up his Aerial M project to the cutting boards of Flacco, Tied & Tickled Trio, DJ Your Food, and Bundy K. Brown. All four tracks are based around Aerial M's "Wedding Song No. 3," but a number of the band's other songs pop up on the record in some form. Flacco comes up with a Tortoise-y treatment, laying chugging percussion behind the song's major-key guitar melody. Tied & Tickled obliterate the original version of the track with a hyperactive saxophone and the sounds of an orchestra warming up. DJ Your Food builds his mix on the original track's "bridge," treating it with tranced-out, far-off effects (think Brown's *Directions in Music* record) and mind-melding beats. But it's Brown's 18-minute epic that covers the most ground. He best captures the spirit of the disc when he introduces the solemn riff from M's "Aass" and obscures its appearance like so many funhouse mirrors. *Post-Global Music* makes for an interesting, if not entirely on-target, addition to the Aerial M discography. —*Jonathan Cohen*

**October [EP]** / Feb. 3, 1999 / Drag City ♦♦

Here's where things get a bit confusing in the Aerial M discography. Although this EP is titled *October*, one of its two songs ("Vivea") served as the title for a previous release (yet, was not included therein). The song in question premiered during the band's 1998 European tour and doesn't stray far from familiar Aerial M territory: understated percussion, gently zooming bass and a repeated guitar melody. The simple prettiness of "Vivea" (un-intrusive synth and piano textures are a nice touch) warrants its eight-minute running time. "Last Caress," originally recorded by Glenn Danzig (!), gets revamped from a hardcore assault into a backporch, acoustic treatment (complete with chirping crickets) that helps mask lines like, "I killed your baby today/I raped your momma today." To say the least, an interesting choice for the first Aerial M recording with vocals. —*Jonathan Cohen*

## Aerial Service Area

f. 1994

*Group / Ambient Techno*

Aerial Service Area is an on-again-off-again collaboration involving ambient/electronic composers Victor Sol and Niko Heyduck. The pair have released two full-length albums through Pete Namlook's Fax label under the name, both of which number among the finest of the already impressive (to say nothing of extensive) Frankfurt-based imprint's titles. Combining bits of work compiled (both apart and together) over the course of nearly a decade, they are also some of the more enduring examples of minimal experimental electronic music to advance from ambient's post-rave crop.

Victor Sol is a Barcelona-based producer whose list of credits includes collaborative works with Atom Heart, Charles Gate, and Dandy Jack; Heyduck has also worked with Atom Heart (most notably on +N's 1996 album, *Built*, along with Sol and Dandy Jack). The pair began releasing music as Aerial Service Area in 1995, debuting the project with an hour-plus-long collection of deep, beatless ambient. Within a matter of only months, a second CD, *150 G Space Weight*, appeared, again featuring a minimal, beatless stride of subtly shifting electronic textures. The project has remained in remission ever since, although a number of other solo and collaborative projects have appeared, including Sol's solo debut for Rather Interesting, *Paranoid*. —*Sean Cooper*

• **Aerial Service Area** / Apr. 1995 / Fax ♦♦♦♦

"ETI Encoding," the first track from Victor Sol and Niko Heyduck's collaborative Fax debut, consists of little more than a modulating tone paired eventually (about five minutes into it, in fact) with a similarly modulating harmonic. Somehow, this minimal setup manages to be both engaging and provocative, an uncanny effect which sets the tone for the whole of this remarkable album. Though subsequent tracks feature a wider palette of sounds, *Aerial Service Area*'s beauty lies in its calm economy, similar to the best of Pete Namlook's or Vidna Obmana's solo works. The album also features Atom Heart's Uwe Schmidt on three tracks. —*Sean Cooper*

**150 G Space Weight** / Aug. 1995 / Fax ♦♦♦

Like its predecessor, this is deep chill of an introspective bent, with a somewhat less pervasive structural presence. Sol and Heyduck construct mini-mantras (nine in all) of thick, warm electronics which echo off one another in surprisingly (given how little is actually happening at any given moment) beautiful combinations. —*Sean Cooper*

## Afro-Mystik

f. San Francisco, CA
*Group / Club/Dance, House*

Afro-Mystik's sound is as eclectic as its group members. Hailing from the San Francisco Bay Area, this collection of musicians blends hip-hop, jungle, jazz and samba rhythms to produce a downtempo, soothing blend of mixed beats and lyrics. Chris Smith, aka DJ Fluid, takes the helm on production, with Liana Young and Ismail Azim lending vocals and rhymes. Mr. Bungle's Trevor Dunn is on bass, while Simone White (Disposable Heroes of Hip-hoprisy and Omar Sosa) are on drums and Carlos Araiza takes care of percussion. In 1999 Afro-Mystik released their first CD, *Future Tropic* on Om Records. The label is notorious for its support of Bay Area producers and DJs such as Mark Farina and Soulstice. —*Diana Potts*

- **Future Tropic** / Oct. 19, 1999 / Om ✦✦
There's absolutely no reason why this music should be boring. Here's how it's described on the back cover: "primitive, itchy, Afro-Brazilian, hypo-electronic [sic] beatscapes, consciousness-altering, cerebral-bending [sic], poetic lyricism, the soul of Afro-Latin rhythm meets futuristic techno-funk." Sounds great, right? And at the beginning of each of the album's 13 tracks, you think it's going to pan out—the grooves are complex, funky, and engaging. But then you keep listening, and nothing happens. "Samba de Rua" bounces along on a warm bed of Brazilian percussion, the mix spiced up with vocal samples and the odd whistle or flute, but there's no harmonic movement and no significant change in texture for almost five minutes; when the beat finally breaks down into a spare drum-and-keyboards groove, it stays that way until a flute solo gets tacked onto it, and that's it until the track ends, having wasted eight minutes of your life on about two minutes' worth of ideas. "Shoplift the Future" features a fun hip-hop adaptation of the Garden of Eden story, and the harp lick that weaves through the laidback funk of "Move It Out" is a very nice touch. But what makes "Move It Out" worth listening to for six and a half minutes is the singing; when Afro-Mystic gets back to instrumentals, your mind starts wandering again and you find yourself getting annoyed—"Are they still stuck on that lick?" This album's worth plundering for ideas, but few listeners will want to sit all the way through it. —*Rick Anderson*

## Age (Thomas P. Heckmann)

*Producer / Experimental Techno, Club/Dance, Techno*

Working under many labels and twice as many pseudonyms, Thomas P. Heckmann has kept true to traditional techno methods and resources. Heckmann was one of the first in his native land of Germany to explore a style of techno that is comparable with early Underground Resistance and +8 recordings. Thomas' tracks are strong with sounds that originate from the 303 and use of the four/four rhythm. His most well known contributions come from working with, his own label, Trope Records, Force Inc. and his releases under the names Drax and Age. He has also recorded under the names Exit 100, Skydiver, Spectral Emotions and Purple Plejade—to name a few.

Heckmann started tinkering with techno when he was 11 years old, finding a niche with the second generation acid techno style. He was lead there by his fondness for early KLF and 808 State. Heckmann's first recording, *Liquid*, came some years later and was under the name Exit 100 and for a new Frankfurt label named Force Inc. The 1992 release brought a lot of attention to the still young Heckmann, landing him a deal to have Liquid licensed to Daniel Miller's English label, Mute Records. It gained him high marks from *Melody Maker Magazine* and reached No. 20 on the 1992 French independent charts. Shortly thereafter, using the name Age, Heckmann released *Trope*. The song was a hit, and is considered a staple in the trance techno fan diet.

In the early '90s Heckmann left Force Inc. and ventured over to Labworks Records in Germany under the name Spectral Emotions. There he collaborated with label mate Hoschi to do a release for the Holland based label, Djax-Up-Beats, under the name Purple Plejade. The same year, a collection of his releases as Age were pulled together for 1993's *Early Sessions and Outtakes*. In 1993 Heckmann also released his last single as Exit 100, entitled *Circuits*. With the death of Exit 100, came the birth of Heckmann's label, Trope

Records and another music personality, Drax. Its with his own label that Heckmann would release his applauded *Amphetamine*, which put Heckmann back on the 1994 French charts at number 20, under the Drax moniker. That year, Heckmann started another label, Acid Fucker Unite (AFU), which was more focused on the die-hard acid techno sound. On AFU, Thomas recorded as Silent Breed and Electro Nation. He put on the Age mask again in 1994 for *The Orion Years*. Going into the late nineties Heckmann further proved his dislike for crediting his own name by adding the alias's, TPH, 8-bit Science, Stromkland, and Metric System, to his recording roster.

After a four year separation, Heckmann returned to Force Inc. as Age for the appropriately titled 1997 single, *Return to the Force* and the album *Isolation* (1998). In 1998 Heckmann started a series called *Welt In Scherben* (World in Fragments). A year later, he released the third installment in the series, a 12", that combined Thomas' traditional use of far out space sounds, the 303 and hard, German dancefloor rhythms. In 1999 Heckmann took a break from the aliases and used his real name for two full-length CDs, *Raum*, and the fifth volume of the obscure *Welt in Scherben*, in May and October, respectively. —*Diana Potts*

- **Isolation** / Mar. 23, 1998 / Force Inc. ✦✦✦
Thomas P. Heckmann's first LP for Force Inc as Age is a solid album of tightly produced yet surprisingly lush techno. Tracks like "Near Dark," "The Burning Building," "In the Beginning," and the title track are rigid and heavy on the beat but given an array of subtle production tweaks and experiments. It's the inimical sound of a techno producer who'd been around for almost a decade, mastering his craft and still testing the waters of hard electronic dance that's as commandingly danceable as it is listenable. —*John Bush*

**Orion Years** / Dec. 14, 1999 / Force Inc. ✦✦✦

## Aim (Andy Turner)

*Producer / Trip-Hop, Club/Dance*

Aim's Andy Turner is a cinematic British trip-hop producer who retains close ties to the rap influences of his youth. The son of a jazz musician, Turner began his music career in 1989 as a rap DJ. He began recording as well and signed to the Grand Central label after meeting label head Mark Rae at a record store. Turner made his Aim debut with 1995's *Pacific Northwest EP* and followed with tracks from a few Grand Central compilations as well as another EP, *Soul Dive*. In 1999, he released his album debut, *Cold Water Music*. Turner has also remixed Ian Brown, St. Etienne, the Charlatans UK, Raissa, and Mucho Macho. —*John Bush*

- **Cold Water Music** / Oct. 11, 1999 / Grand Central ✦✦✦✦
From the traditionalist artwork and cover, liner notes, and the intro (a hazy, spoken-word track reminiscent of Lee Hazlewood), listeners can easily be forgiven for expecting an electronica/rock crossover album on the order of Air or Groove Armada. Instead, Aim's *Cold Water Music* is a jazzy, beat-heavy project that's just a few steps removed from straight-ahead hip-hop. Producer Andy Turner, a self-confessed beathead, cycles between jazz-rap and alternative, wall-of-sound influences to bedrock his productions. Turner also gets props for drafting three excellent rappers—Q'n'C, YZ, and AG—to add vocals, resulting in several tracks that evoke the heyday of rap's Golden Age, but are also tough enough to survive even on modern mainstream rap radio. Though half of the standard songs are vocal tracks, Turner also shines on the instrumentals, constructing a paranoid beat symphony on "Demonique" with shrieking strings and an extended vocal sample from some forgotten B-movie. —*John Bush*

## Air Liquide

f. 1991, Cologne, Germany
*Group / Electronica, Electro-Techno, Ambient Techno, Techno*

Not to be confused with the international chemical company of the same name, the Cologne-based duo of Cem Oral and Ingmar Koch (who go by the names Jammin' Unit and Walker, respectively) have been making hard-hitting experimental acid and techno as Air Liquide since the early '90s. Recording first for their own Structure label group before signing with Rising High in 1993, the pair currently record for the New York-based Smile Communications, as well as in various side projects for labels such as DJ Ungle Fever, Anodyne, Blue Angel, and Oral's own Pharma imprint. Although the pair have dabbled in everything from beatless ambient to back-breaking, nosebleed gabber, the bulk of their material has clustered around dirty, mid-tempo acid and breakbeat techno, with the focus on thick 303 lines and simple, minimal phrases. They've also increasingly moved to a more hip-hop-infused brand of caustic electro, with tracks appearing on Rising High's *Further Self-Evident Truths* label compilations and the Coldcut *Journeys by DJ* mixed CD.

Koch got his start in the music industry on the far side of the integrity line, pumping out assembly-line house and hip-hop for the German Hype! and Technoline labels, before the latter went bankrupt in the early '90s. He then headed for university, studying electronic composition and attempting to break the bad habits he'd picked up in mainstream production. It was then that Koch met Oral, a member of the same German underground scene that included J. Burger, Mike Ink, and Biochip C.'s Martin Damm. Together the group consolidated their efforts toward assembling the influential Structure label group, which included the Structure, Monotone, Blue, and DJ Ungle Fever imprints. With releases running the spectrum from ambient, house, and techno to acid and hardcore, Koch and Oral's work together began to coalesce into a coherent sound reflecting shared influences such as Chicago acid, early New York hip-hop, and '70s prog experimentalists such as Neu! and Can.

Soon after Structure dissolved into the various labels and projects of its key participants, Walker and Jammin' Unit signed the Air Liquide name to the English Rising High label, through which they released a number of well-received full- and EP-length albums, including *Liquid Air*, *Nephology*, and *Weather Machine*. The pair also recorded for Smile. Walker continued to release material on his own Pharma label, as well as through DJ Ungle Fever, Analog, and others. Oral released several solo albums as Jammin' Unit, for Rising High and Blue Planet. —*Sean Cooper*

**Nephology** / 1993 / Rising High ♦♦♦

● **The Increased Difficulty of Concentration** / Oct. 25, 1994 / Sm:)e ♦♦♦♦
A sprawling 2-CD compilation of tunes roughly separable into either ambient or experimental acid/techno. Although a bit simplistic at times, the material's as good as anything the duo released through Rising High, proving the move to Smile hasn't shaken their sound. Also in evidence is an increased predilection for breaks, which has continued to grow since this set's release. —*Sean Cooper*

**Black** / Oct. 24, 1995 / Sm:)e ♦♦
The flip side of *Red* in the color series is a mail-order-only compilation of unreleased tracks including more downtempo material, plus a Soul Slinger remix of "Nephology" and a live track from the 1994 *Love Parade*. —*John Bush*

**Red** / Oct. 24, 1995 / Sm:)e ♦♦♦♦
Seemingly more of a compilation than anything else — almost half the tracks have remixing credits from the likes of Vapourspace and Jammin' Unit (which admittedly just means half the band remixing itself!) — *Red* still holds together surprisingly well as an album-length collection of Air Liquide's clinically aggressive techno, mixing both sheen and electronic dirt together quite well. Even more impressive is how it's held up over the accelerated life-cycles of modern dance-based music — unlike many releases aiming to be clearly of their time first and foremost, *Red* sounds like it just wants to be damn good, period. "If There Was No Gravity" betrays the origins of the album more than anything else — the slightly drifty, slightly dippy whispering about mythology and the like is very post-ambient chill circa 1994, when the original song appeared. Jammin' Unit's remix plays up a squalling bass loop, while adding all sorts of creepy, subtle loops during the instrumental breaks, making the song more than the sum of its parts. "Interactive Warlords" sets the general tone of *Red* right from the start, both perfectly propulsive and with a just-soft-enough side balancing out rough bursts and clicks not that far removed from the Aphex Twin's fascination with technical aggro. Titling one track "Tanz Der Lemminge II" is a nice nod to Kraut-rock's Amon Düül II, though the crisp techno beat of the DJ Hell/Tom remix is not exactly something you'd hear on *Wolf City* or *Yeti*. As for the Vapourspace remix, while it's not on the level of Mark Gage's own highlights like "Gravitational Arch of Ten," his take on "Theme From Robot Wars — System Engaged" does have a nice slow build to it. With a dollop of prescience added for effect ("MP3," titled after the then-new format but years before it became the record companies' boogeyman), *Red* is worth looking into if one gets the chance. —*Ned Raggett*

**Sonic Weather Machine** / May 27, 1996 / Rising High ♦♦

## Air

f. 1995, Paris, France
*Group / Indie Pop, Ambient-Pop, Electronica, Club/Dance, Alternative Pop/Rock*

More apt to cite stately rock paragons Burt Bacharach and Brian Wilson as their inspirations than Derrick May or Aphex Twin, the French duo Air gained inclusion into the late-'90s electronica surge due chiefly to the labels their recordings appeared on, not the actual music they produced. Their sound, a variant of the classic disco sound coaxed into a relaxing prozac vision of the late '70s, looked back to a variety of phenomena from the period — synthesizer maestros Tomita, Jean-Michel Jarre and Vangelis, new wave music of the non-spikey variety, and obscure Italian film soundtracks. Despite gaining quick entrance into the dance community (through releases for Source and Mo'Wax), Air's 1998 debut album *Moon Safari* charted a light — well, airy — course along soundscapes composed with melody lines by Moog and Rhodes, not Roland and Yamaha. The presence of several female vocalists, an equipment list whose number of pieces stretched into the dozens and a baroque tuba solo on one track; all of this conspired to make Air more of a happening in the living room than the dancefloor.

Though Nicolas Godin and Jean-Benoît Dunckel both grew up in Versailles, the two didn't meet until they began studying at the same college. Dunckel, who had studied at the Conservatoire in Paris, played in an alternative band named Orange. One of Dunckel's bandmates, Alex Gopher, introduced Godin into the lineup. While Gopher himself departed (later to record for the Solid label), Dunckel and Godin continued on, becoming Air by 1995. During 1996-97, the duo released singles on Britain's Mo'Wax ("Modular") and the domestic Source label ("Casanova 70," "Le Soleil Est Prés de Moi"). Though Air often evinced the same '60s Continental charm as Dimitri from Paris — due no doubt to the influence of Serge Gainsbourg — the duo had little in common musically with other acts (Daft Punk), in the wave of French electronica lapping at the shores of Britain and America during 1997. That same year, Air remixed Depeche Mode and Neneh Cherry, and joined French *musique concrète* popster Jean-Jacques Perrey for a track on the Source compilation *Sourcelab 3*. Signed to Virgin, Air released their debut album *Moon Safari* in early 1998. The singles "Sexy Boy" and "Kelly Watch the Stars" became moderate hits in Britain, and earned airplay on MTV. Later that year, Godin and Dunckel mounted an ambitious tour throughout Europe and America, though they had originally decided to forego live appearances. Their early singles were collected in 1999 under the title *Premiers Symptomes;* the duo's soundtrack to the Sofia Coppola film *The Virgin Suicides* followed in early 2000. —*John Bush*

★ **Moon Safari** / Jan. 19, 1998 / Caroline ♦♦♦♦♦
A cavalcade of analog synthesizers, organs, electric pianos and processed voices populate *Moon Safari*, a thoroughly appealing, otherworldly debut album from Air. Where most of their dance contemporaries push the boundaries of trip-hop or jungle, Air blends Euro-dance with new wave. Any futuristic element on their album feels strangely outdated, since they're borrowed from the early '80s, which gives their music an odd, out-of-time feeling. The waves of gurgling synths beneath the spacious, colorful chords and melodies give the impression that the music is floating in space. For all the atmospherics and layers of synths, there's a distinct pop sense to *Moon Safari* that makes it accessible and damn near irresistible. —*Stephen Thomas Erlewine*

**Premiers Symptomes [EP]** / Feb. 9, 1998 / Source ♦♦♦♦

**Virgin Suicides [Original Soundtrack]** / Feb. 29, 2000 / Astralwerks ♦♦♦
Two years after the arrival of their debut album, the French twosome Air returned, not with a proper sophomore LP, but with *The Virgin Suicides*, a full soundtrack to the directing debut of Sophia Coppola. Only one track, "Playground Love," has vocals, and that comes from an outsider (Gordon Tracks) who sounds more like the Auteurs' Luke Haines than Beth Hirsch, the only real vocalist employed previously. The trademarked Air sound is for the most part unchanged; as on *Moon Safari*, producers Godin and Dunckel rely on contemplative electronic mood-music in a minor key, heavy on the analog synth and organ yet with plenty of traditional textures (guitar, brass, strings, live-sounding drums) in keeping with lounge music and space-pop from the '60s and '70s. And though all the music here is as meticulously detailed as the tracks on *Moon Safari*, the soundtrack cultivates an atmosphere more in league with traditional scoring — instead of focusing on pop songs in an electronic context, Air constructed these tracks as mere soundbytes, simple

themes with little embellishment on the basic ideas. Of course, that's perfectly in keeping with the secondary role soundtracks should play to truly serve the movies for which they're composed. Listeners eager for a second dose of the exquisite electronic pop found on *Moon Safari* will be pleased with much of *The Virgin Suicides*, but will probably have to wait until Air's proper follow-up to find more evidence of their greatness. —*John Bush*

## Akasha

f. 1994, Brixton, London, England
*Group / Big Beat, Electronica, Trip-Hop, Club/Dance*
Equally admired by jazz fans and drum'n'bass DJs, Charles James Casey and Damian John Hand recorded several of the most diverse EPs for the nominally trip-hop/big-beat Wall of Sound Records. Based in Brixton, the duo debuted in early 1995 with the EP *Jazadelica*, the third release on Wall of Sound. The EP earned much praise, earning Akasha a spot at 1995's *Glastonbury Festival*. There, Casey and Hand unveiled their onstage incarnation, a nine-piece band with several accomplished musicians. In 1998 they released two remix EPs, and a year later the full-length album, *Cinematique* followed. —*John Bush*

● **Cinematique** / Oct. 11, 1999 / Wall of Sound ♦♦
Akasha's first album for Wall of Sound balances some great trip-hop productions ("The Blues, Part One" and "Sweet Child of Mine" with Neneh Cherry) with a few tracks of meandering jazz-fusion. Many of the songs fall flat, leaving Akasha with a full-length that works barely half the time. —*John Bush*

**Cinematique: The Remixes** / Oct. 25, 1999 / Wall of Sound ♦♦

## Alio Die (Stefano Musso)

*Producer / Experimental Ambient, Ambient Techno, Electro-Acoustic, Ambient*
Since the late '80s, Stefano Musso has recorded deep, evocative experimental ambient and electro-acoustic soundscapes under the name Alio Die. Combining sweeping electronics with found sound and acoustical treatments which have echoed through the recent works of composers such as Robert Rich, Tetsu Inoue, and Brian Williams, Musso has assembled a rich and varied collection of recordings for such labels as Projekt, Timebase, Fathom, and his own Hic Sunt Leones label. Based in Milan, Musso studied art and electronic composition there, founding Alio Die in 1989 as a live performance act, and eventually self-releasing a debut, *Under an Holy Ritual*, in 1992. Enthusiastically received in his home country, *Holy Ritual* expanded Musso's international presence significantly in 1993 when it was licensed by the popular US-based gothic/darkwave label Projekt. The connection brought a crossover audience to Musso's music, and—together with artists such as Asmus Tietchens, Vidna Obmana, Coil, and A Produce—helped ready ears for such mid-'90s dark ambient/isolationist outfits as Lull, Final, Download, and Lustmord. Musso subsequently released three additional solo albums, including the first full-length—*Suspended Feathers*—issued by the celebrated, limited-run Amplexus label. A shadowy, cavernous, intensely detailed fusion of acoustical elements, step-and-repeat sample treatments, sparse, echoing percussion, and deep, atmospheric sound design, *Suspended Feathers* presented Musso at his very best, playing ambient's static tendencies off of shifting melodic and textural passages that suggest movement without sacrificing the music's vague, entropic formlessness. In addition to full-length and compilation appearances, Musso has contributed to releases by Vidna Obmana and Steve Roach, and teamed up with Robert Rich in 1996 to record the full-length work *Fissures* for Stephen Hill's Fathom label. Another collaborative effort, *Echo Passage* with Vidna Obmana, followed in 2000. —*Sean Cooper*

**Under an Holy Ritual** / 1990 / Projekt ♦♦♦♦
Using sparse instrumentation and heavily processed sound effects, Alio Die submerges listeners into a world of nocturnal reverberations, dripping catacombs and "things that go bump in the night." Fans of O Yuki Conjugate will find commonality with Alio Die's concepts, though the focus is more on atmospherics and less on percussive dynamics. Both appear to imbibe from the same cup of mind-altering elixir. —*Backroads Music/Heartbeats*

**The Door of Possibilities** / 1995 / Hic Sunt Leones ♦♦♦
Stefano Musso and Darren Tate both contributed several tracks to this 1995 album of ambient/industrial space rock. —*John Bush*

● **Suspended Feathers** / 1995 / Aqua/Amplexus ♦♦♦♦
The first full-length release on the Italian Amplexus imprint—an extremely limited-run "music and design" label/project—Alio Die's *Suspended Feathers* is easily his most accomplished work to date. A flawless, organic blend of textured acoustical elements, deep, meditative drones, field recordings, and all methods of sampler microscopy, the album combines shifting, programmatic textural composing with more dimensional aspects which, in addition to their emotional depth, give Musso's pieces a sense of space and movement. Quite simply some of the most enveloping, affecting "pure" ambient you're ever likely to hear; a pity, given how hard the album is to track down. —*Sean Cooper*

## Dot Allison

*Vocals / Trip-Hop, Alternative Pop/Rock*
Scottish singer/songwriter Dot Allison first made a name for herself with One Dove, an early '90s group that blended dance and dream-pop elements on their first and only album, 1993's *Morning Dove White*. After One Dove disbanded in the mid '90s, Allison disappeared from pop music until 1999, when a string of singles, concert appearances and collaborations with artists like Arab Strap and Death In Vegas heralded her debut full-length *Afterglow*. —*Heather Phares*

● **Afterglow** / Aug. 24, 1999 / Arista ♦♦♦♦
Former One Dove frontwoman Dot Allison returns after an extended absence with her solo debut, *Afterglow*. She continues in the same vein as her former band, and certainly manages to live up to the high musical standards of that trip-pop act. Allison co-produced the album, and also plays guitar and keyboards and handles programming chores. *Afterglow* is a strong, dreamy effort that envelops the listener immediately. "Tomorrow Never Comes" is sparse and heartbreaking, while "Close Your Eyes" has a light dance feel and a radio-ready hook. "In Winter Still," with its strings and piano, could have come from a Cocteau Twins record. Allison delivers a pair of stellar pieces in the absolutely gorgeous "Did I Imagine You?" (co-written with Hal David) and the haunting "Message Personnel." —*Tom Demalon*

## Marc Almond

b. Jul. 9, 1959, Southport, England
*Vocals / New Romantic, New Wave, Synth-Pop, Dance-Pop*
After disbanding Soft Cell, vocalist Marc Almond pursued a solo career that followed the same vaguely sleazy, electronic dance-pop his former group had made popular. Almond's strength was never his personality—his voice tends to waver around the notes instead of hitting them—it was the atmosphere he created with the synths and drum machines. Underneath all of the electronics and disco rhythms, Almond hearkened back to the days of cabaret singers, updating it with that sound for dance clubs of the '80s.

Before he properly started a solo career, Marc Almond formed Marc and the Mambas, a loose congregation that featured Matt Johnson of The The and Annie Hogan. *Untitled* (1983), the group's first album, featured covers of Lou Reed, Syd Barrett, and Jacques Brel; throughout his career, Almond would cover the songs of Brel, which he had learned from the records of Scott Walker. Like Walker, Almond used Brel's heavily orchestrated compositions and social ruminations as a starting point, both musically and lyrically—Almond added a self-conscious element of camp with his Euro-disco and occasionally sleazy lyrics. *Torment and Toreros* (1983), Marc and the Mambas' second album, explored this path in more detail than *Untitled*, only to an orchestral background. After its release, the group broke up.

Almond formed the backing group the Willing Sinners in 1984, releasing *Vermin in Ermine* in 1984. Almond began to hit his stride with this album, which fulfilled most of his campy cabaret fantasies. *Stories of Johnny*, released the following year, was more cohesive, spawning a British hit with the title song. Even though he maintained a cult following in England and various parts of Europe, his records were not being released in the US.

In 1987, Almond released *Mother Fist...and Her Five Daughters*, his first proper solo album and his bleakest work to date; a compilation, *Singles 1984-1987*, appeared the same year. *Stars We Are*, released the following year, was a brighter, more welcoming album that revived his commercial career. In addition to a duet with Nico on "Your Kisses Burn," Almond duetted with Gene Pitney on Pitney's own "Something's Gotten Hold of My Heart," which became a number one single. *Stars We Are* also became his first album released in the US since Soft Cell.

Almond followed the success of *The Stars We Are* in 1990 with the pet project *Jacques*, a collection of Brel songs. That same year, he released *Enchanted*, which was more successful than *Jacques*, yet it didn't reach the heights of *Stars We Are*. In 1991, he released *The Tenement Symphony* and in 1993, a live album entitled *Twelve Years of Tears* appeared. Two years later, *Treasure Box* was released, and Almond returned in 1999 with *Open All Night*. —*Stephen Thomas Erlewine*

**Torment and Toreros** / 1983 / Some Bizarre ♦♦
If there's any acid test for being a Almond fanatic, it would have to be *Torment*, originally a double album and still the longest thing he's yet released. It isn't so much length as it is subject matter, though informed by his consistent bitterness with the industry as experienced via the soon-to-implode Soft Cell, the sheer self-loathing and unrestrained anger have never been paralleled by any of his other releases. Matched by an expanded Mambas lineup, including a string quartet featuring rock journeyman Martin McCarrick in one of his earliest appearances, Almond swings from slow weepers over lost innocence, sexual and otherwise, to frantic explosions of lyrical bile. Though often great, once you hit "Catch a Falling Star" and its snarling, obscenity-laden take on fame, clearly the unexpected pop star of "Tainted Love" has absented himself. Some of his most effective moments appear through the collection [benefiting from co-production by Flood, one of the English producer's first major efforts], including another Brel cover, "The Bulls," the frenetic and aptly titled "A Million Manias," and a lovely take on Peter Hammill's "Vision." However, it's the worst possible starting point for a new fan and definitely only one for the truly obsessive. —*Ned Raggett*

**Untitled** / 1983 / Some Bizarre ♦♦
For his debut solo album, *Untitled*, Marc Almond formed a hodgepodge band called the Mambas—the most prominent collaborators were Matt Johnson and Annie Hogan—and made a conscious departure from Soft Cell. There are some touches of synth-pop here and there, but for the most part the record is considerably more ambitious, covering torch songs, tortured balladry in the vein of Scott Walker, covers of the Velvet Underground and Syd Barrett, and straight pop. It doesn't ever add up to anything cohesive, but the parts are intriguing. —*Stephen Thomas Erlewine*

**Vermin in Ermine** / 1984 / Some Bizarre ♦♦♦
With the wracked final days of Soft Cell behind him, Almond gleefully threw himself into a full-time solo career with a splash; while a chunk of bile still clearly remains—the portentous "Ugly Head" sounds as much personal therapy as it does grinding semi-big band blues—a much more musically upbeat angle dominates, especially on the lush, winning single "The Boy Who Came Back." Allied with producer Mike Hedges, already riding high from his work with the Cure and Siouxsie and the Banshees, and with a newly stable backing band, The Willing Sinners, featuring Hogan, McCarrick and bassist Billy McGee at the core, Almond lets go over an interestingly varied palette of music, from the shimmering and sharp "Tenderness is a Weakness" to the percussion-heavy "Split Lip." Now freely continuing the classic Soft Cell lyrical vibe of passion in the city's darker, more secret corners—the titles "Shining Sinners" and "Gutter Hearts" almost say it all! Almond's in fine voice throughout. A lengthy release—the CD version runs a full 75 minutes with some extra B-sides attached—but a good one. —*Ned Raggett*

**Stories of Johnny** / 1985 / Some Bizarre ♦♦♦♦
Making his first label jump since signing to Mercury in the early Soft Cell days, *Stories* continues the drive towards a brighter commercial sound, with Hedges once again producing and the Sinners line-up in perfect sync and well-versed in everything from lush Eurodisco to nightclub jazz and smouldering ballads (add some extra credit for the solid work of album guest Martin Ditchum on "all kinds of percussion"). The troika of brilliant singles from the album's first half makes the album a keeper alone: the tender title track [written about a young friend of Almond who ODed], a sassy remake of Mel Torme's "The House is Haunted," and "Love Letter," where electronics resurface to a degree not seen since Soft Cell's collapse. However, there's plenty of other fine delights throughout, such as the solid rocker "The Flesh is Willing" and the snarling "Contempt," not to mention "I Who Never," a soaring breakup number, and "My Candle Burns," another in the fine series of understatedly intense Almond love/obsession songs. Fans of Marc at his harsher will find this perhaps a bit too smooth at points, but as a balance of killer hooks, great music and Almond's ever-improving singing, this is a winner through and through. —*Ned Raggett*

**A Woman's Story** / 1986 / Virgin ♦♦♦♦
Great screaming melodrama as Almond does his best to prove that he's the best possible cabaret performer that no one will put on a cabaret stage. Depending on the mood you happen to be, this collection can either be taken seriously or as a tongue-in-cheek celebration of some great over-the-top material (which even applies to Peter Hammill's "Just Good Friends"). Almond's frenetic cover of "The Heel" alone should raise this mini-album to classic status. —*Steven McDonald*

**Mother Fist... and Her Five Daughters** / 1987 / Some Bizarre ♦♦♦♦
Following up both *Stories* and his fine covers EP *A Woman's Story*, Almond took a turn for the more challenging on *Mother Fist*, to be rewarded with the loss of his contract and a search for a new label home. Quite why that should have happened is all the more surprising when upon listening it becomes clear that *Mother Fist* was and still is the best Almond album of original material to date. With Hedges once again producing and the Willing Sinners still producing instrumental magic—the great work of Hogan on keyboards, McCarrick on cello and accordion and McGee on bass and orchestrations simply can't be overstated here—Almond created a generally sparer and more theatrical album that embraces classic European cabaret to wonderful effect, more so than any American or English 'rock' album since Bowie's *Aladdin Sane* or Lou Reed's *Berlin*. The wonderful, cheeky swing of the opening title track—an unashamed, Truman Capote-inspired ode to masturbation—moves to the pulsing, piano-and-bass driven lover's lament "There is a Bed," followed by the supremely drugged out and sleazy "Saint Judy" [as in Garland], each track showcasing Almond with a different but equally accomplished vocal approach. *Mother Fist* keeps going from strength to strength as the album progresses, almost a series of short stories come to life exploring hustlers, burnt-out boxers, romantic dreams and desires; its centerpiece, the wonderful "Mr. Sad," shifts from a solo vocal with electric guitar to a full orchestral blast perfectly. All this and two great should-have-been hit singles, "Melancholy Rose" and the pulsing "Ruby Red," as well! An all-around triumph. —*Ned Raggett*

● **Singles: 1984-1987** / 1987 / Some Bizarre ♦♦♦♦
A classic "act leaves the label, repackage the singles" move, collecting every single from the *Vermin in Ermine* days through *Mother Fist*, with the one added bonus being the title track to his covers EP, an attractive version of the Judy Garland song "A Woman's Story." Not really necessary for the heavy-duty fan, but as an introduction to Almond's mid-to-late eighties work, it's fine enough. Still, the sole emphasis on his most commercial moments, lacking the context of his many striking album moments from that era, results in an unavoidably skewed picture of what he was up to at the time. —*Ned Raggett*

**Stars We Are** / 1988 / Capitol ♦♦♦♦
Another year and another label for Almond, along with a newly stripped down band, La Magia, with Willing Sinner vets Hogan, McGee and Steve Humphreys on drums. Even more so than *Stories of Johnny*, this is Almond with an eye and ear on making a commercial record while still being himself, and the result is much better than expected. Bob Kraushaar's production feels much more lighter and brighter in general than Mike Hedges' past efforts, and the songwriting often matches it—the sprightly opening title track, followed by the tenderly passionate "These My Dreams Are Yours," makes for what had to be the most upbeat start to a Almond album yet! Similar moments crop up throughout the record, including "Bitter Sweet," with a killer sweeping chorus, the sparkling, slightly jazzy "The Very Last Pearl," which gives pulsing nightlife one of its best makeovers ever, and a triumphant, everything and the kitchen sink version of Gene Pitney's "Something's Gotten Hold of My Heart," replaced on later versions of the album with the UK-chart-topping duet with Pitney himself. That said, it's still a Marc album through and through—the lighter songs still have his sweet purr in the vocals [and Hogan's keyboards and instrumental arrangements remain uniformly excellent], while moodier and expectedly dramatic numbers still turn up in abundance. The forceful duet with Nico, "Your Kisses Burn," calls to mind prime Lee and Nancy, with masses of strings to boot; elsewhere, "The Sensualist" acts as his clearest statement yet on the many erotic joys life has to offer. Perhaps most surprisingly of all, "Tears Run Rings," his most overtly political number to date, became a minor US hit. —*Ned Raggett*

**Enchanted** / 1990 / Capitol ♦♦
A slightly fallow period for Almond's more high-profile releases began with *Enchanted*, an ultimately flawed attempt to build on his more mainstream

success with *The Stars We Are*. Crucially, keyboardist and co-songwriter Hogan, who had been Almond's longest musical partner ever, starting with the first solo record in 1982, had departed, while La Magia ceased to exist as a musical entity. McGee remained to provide orchestral arrangements, which give the album some zest, while the subject matter is still Almond's own, tales of "Waifs and Strays," a "Toreador In the Rain," and "Orpheus in Red Velvet." This said, the album ends up as just too anonymous to truly succeed—Bob Kraushaar's production this time out seems much more concerned at creating slick-Euro-pop as opposed to the distinct blend of styles that Marc usually pursues. There are a couple of solid winners nonetheless, like the perversely jaunty "Death's Diary" and "A Lover Spurned," a dramatic tale of vengeance from the other woman. Regardless, this is possibly Marc's most disappointing release overall. —*Ned Raggett*

**Memorabilia** / 1991 / Mercury ♦♦♦♦
*Memorabilia* is a fine, but far from perfect, overview of Marc Almond's entire career, from Soft Cell to his solo recordings. Concentrating primarily on accessible, pop-oriented material, the collection overlooks some of his most ambitious material, but that makes the record a good introduction for the curious. However, they should be forewarned that Almond recut the vocals for three Soft Cell songs, including the hit "Tainted Love" and the title track, for this compilation, thereby lessening the value of the record in the eyes of most casual fans, since these are not the familiar versions. —*Stephen Thomas Erlewine*

**Tenement Symphony** / Oct. 29, 1991 / Sire ♦♦♦
Almond's newest label jump resulted in what looked like an ideal creation on paper—two songs produced and cowritten by the Grid, the techno duo featuring Marc's Soft Cell collaborator Dave Ball, three more songs worked on with sole surviving Willing Sinner/La Magia member, keyboardist/orchestrator Billy McGee, and a mini-song cycle, the Tenement Symphony itself, produced by uber-studio wizard Trevor Horn. But did it work? Much like *Enchanted*, there's a little too much of Almond getting lost in rote synthdisco for comfort at points. But there are enough pluses to outweigh the minuses—the opening "Meet Me in My Dream," one of the Grid collaborations, is a beautiful start, equal to "The Stars We Are," while the Symphony itself, though perhaps taking itself a bit too seriously as a conceit, has three solid singles to its credit—a completely over-the-top [but what else to expect from Trevor Horn?] version of Jacques Brel's "Jacky," the concluding "My Hand Over My Heart," another sweep of the heartstrings dance ballad, and the surprise UK hit single of the bunch, the gentle and [for Horn] understated "The Days of Pearly Spencer," another sixties cover given the Almond treatment to good effect. —*Ned Raggett*

**Twelve Years of Tears** / May 25, 1993 / Sire ♦♦♦♦
While Almond's tours during the early nineties had mostly consisted of performances backed only by the piano of Martin Watkins—both dramatic and admittedly cost-effective!—a lengthy mega-splash of a retrospective evening at London's Royal Albert Hall was staged in late 1992, consisting of three hours, costume changes galore, dancers, fireworks, the lot. *Twelve Years*, a full 75 minutes worth of highlights, does a mostly fantastic job of showcasing what on balance sounds like Almond's ultimate performance for all sides of his talented musical personality. Mostly, not totally—*Tenement*'s "Champagne" has Almond a bit more flat on the vocals than usual, while the *Enchanted* selections, though nice enough, just don't stand up well next to the other performances. And what performances those are! Besides full band versions of expected Soft Cell hits like "Bedsitter" and even "Tainted Love" itself, as well as solo smashes like "Something's Gotten Hold of My Heart" and "Jacky," Marc uses a featured section accompanied only by pianist Martin to sing two of *Mother Fist*'s best numbers, "Mr. Sad" and "There Is a Bed," a haunting, spare version of Soft Cell's lament "Youth," another solid version of Brel's "If You Go Away" and, to top it all off, a lovely, heartfelt version of Charles Aznavour's sympathetic, wry portrait of a transvestite, "What Makes a Man a Man." With an amazing eight-minute take of Soft Cell's break-up ballad "Say Hello Wave Goodbye" wrapping everything up with a full orchestra, backup singers, guitars and Marc singing at his bravura best, *Twelve Years* shines. —*Ned Raggett*

**Violent Silence/Flesh Volcano** / 1997 / Some Bizarre UK/Thirsty Ear ♦♦♦
Collecting two at-the-time incredibly out-of-print mid-'80s EPs, this disc's spine reads as being a full partnership between Almond and Foetus, a semi-regular collaborator for Almond's solo career during its first few years. However, only the first three songs represent that actual pairing, being the original *Flesh Volcano* tracks from 1986. It's essentially nothing more or less than Foetus at his most industrial and clattering with Almond at his most theatrically pained and howling—great if you want it, but not as earth-shattering as you might hope. The real winners are the *Violent Silence* tracks, which were recorded by Almond and his core Willing Sinners line-up of Hogan, McCarrick and McGee in 1984. Inspired by and dedicated to French extreme sensualist/philosopher George Bataille, the songs capture Almond in perfectly poised moods; you can almost taste the incense and smell the leather on such masterful tunes of total love/hate obsession as "Healthy as Hate" and "Body Unknown." The Willing Sinners' music is deceptively gentle and low-key, making the lyrics of dominance and eroticism all the more striking. A mixed release in the end, but one with its solid charms. —*Ned Raggett*

**Flesh Volcano/Slut** / Feb. 10, 1998 / Thirsty Ear ♦♦♦
*Flesh Volcano/Slut* combines Marc Almond's two collaborations with Jim "Foetus" Thirlwell. While both musicians share a fascination with the seamy side of urban life, they're not musically compatible, since Foetus favors noise and Almond favors camp. There isn't really a middle ground between these two extremes, and the attempt to find that common ground is pretty much intolerable. —*Stephen Thomas Erlewine*

**Live in Concert** / Oct. 6, 1998 / Thirsty Ear ♦♦
A belated [and probably exploitative] CD release of the soundtrack of a videotape filmed in December 1987, this album should be more successful than it is. The Willing Sinners had shrunk to a new core trio, La Magia, but key members Hogan and McGee were still on board and in fine form. Meanwhile, coming off the brilliant *Mother Fist* album, Almond also debuted a number of great tracks from future releases including the title track of *The Stars We Are*, songs from his two French tribute albums, and his chart-topping remake of Gene Pitney's "Something's Got a Hold of My Heart." The big problem, simply, is the recording itself—while not indifferent bootleg quality per se, something like this should sound a heck of a lot more powerful and crisp than it is! The end result is a semi-muddy disappointment, though hearing some Almond/audience banter is always a kick. Still, though, fans of his Virgin label years deserve much better. —*Ned Raggett*

**Open All Night** / Aug. 17, 1999 / Import ♦♦♦♦
This is the album that Marc Almond has been trying to make since leaving Soft Cell. He has managed to fuse together all of his influences: pop, disco, dance, electronic, R&B and cabaret all thrown into the mix to produce this incredibly diverse and entertaining album. Perhaps it was the freedom of recording and releasing the CD as a semi-independent release. It was initially to be released in 1998 on the British label Echo, and in fact the first single release from the album, "Black Kiss," was released on that label. Echo released Almond from his contract and he decided to go the independent route; for him, this was a good move. He has produced a very original work that still falls into the Marc Almond mold. Although fans will love this CD, it is accessible enough to attract new listeners as well. Almond has surrounded himself with very talented guests on this album, including Siouxsie Sioux (of Siouxsie and the Banshees and the Creatures), who duets with Almond on the brilliant "Threat of Love." Song topics are the usual for Almond (death, sleaze, love, lust and the like) but what makes this album so interesting is the music: beautiful, well-crafted melodies with heavy dance beats. Not an easy task, but he does it very well. Almond is very talented and a great deal deeper than he has been given credit for. This is a great example of just how creative he is when given the artistic freedom. [*Open All Night* is also available in an import release.] —*Aaron Badgley*

## The Aloof

f. 1990

*Group / Electronica, Trip-Hop, Club/Dance, Techno*

Unlike many bands who started out playing more or less straight-ahead rock but in the late '90s began to assimilate electronic elements, the Aloof was formed as a strictly dance squad and only later added a vocalist and employed tighter song structures. The band began in 1990 when DJ Dean Thatcher and producer Jagz Kooner (also a member of Andrew Weatherall's Sabres of Paradise) issued the single "Never Get out of the Boat" on a limited white-label pressing, but was only officially launched when ffrr Records gave the single a proper release. By the following year, the duo added vocalist Ricky Barrow and programmer Gary Burns (also with the Sabres) and recorded several singles for Cowboy Records. While playing live PAs at nightclubs around Great Britain, the Aloof grew disgusted with the burnt-out house scene and decided to become a true live band. Adding drummer Richard Thair (later with Red Snapper) in 1993, the expanded quintet set up their own label, Flaw Records, and released *Cover the Crime* in 1994. The album became popular on British indie charts, and earned the Aloof a contract with East West, which reissued the LP in 1995 and also released their second album *Sinking* one year later. The group played several festivals during the summer of 1996, opened for Leftfield and watched their single "One Night Stand" reach the British Top 30 late that year. The album *Seeking Pleasure* followed in 1998, though the group was dropped from East West after weak sales and a shake-up in the label's dance division. Kooner left soon after, and the Aloof moved to Screaming Target Records for 1999's *This Constant Chase for Thrills*. —*John Bush*

**Cover the Crime** / 1995 / East West ♦♦♦♦
The debut Aloof album filters a heavy dub influence through the darkside of post-rave techno. The group's stated emphasis on live performance comes through on several of the more freestyle tracks, and *Cover the Crime* is a clever, wide-ranging album. —*John Bush*

● **Sinking** / May 27, 1996 / East West ♦♦♦♦
Not quite as dark as the premiere Aloof LP, *Sinking* adds a contemplative earthiness gained from the blues and film music, especially on "Wish You Were Here" (not a Floyd cover), while the orchestral flair of closing track "The Last Stand" show the Aloof working through a variety of inspirations with a surplus of good ideas to back them up. —*John Bush*

**Seeking Pleasure** / Aug. 31, 1998 / East West ♦♦♦

**This Constant Chase for Thrills** / Oct. 4, 1999 / Screaming Target ♦♦♦
Less claustrophobic than their final album for East West, *This Constant Chase for Thrills* is an atmospheric production that cycles through downtempo house, dub, and earthy trip-hop, with vocalist Ricky Barrow stretching his urban-bluesman impression. Compared to previous Aloof albums, the differences aren't major—the team is still writing the same kind of tortured tracks ("Infatuated," "Tearing Up Inside") that they always have. It appears that making an album free from the pressure of major-label politics, however, has resulted in a breath of fresh air, four LPs down the road. —*John Bush*

## Alpha
f. 1996, Bristol, England
*Group / Electronica, Trip-Hop*

The duo of Corin Dingley and Andy Jenks formed Alpha after working on such projects as Statik Sound System and the Sugarboat. The duo are inspired by film soundtracks and the songwriting of Jimmy Webb with the same intensity that Massive Attack give to hip-hop and dub. Both collectives, however, are from Bristol and recruit vocalists to bring their downtempo, beat-heavy compositions to life. Alpha was signed to Massive Attack's Melankolic Records in 1997; that same year, they released their debut album *Come from Heaven*. The *Pepper* EP followed in 1998. —*John Bush*

● **Come from Heaven** / Sep. 23, 1997 / Caroline ♦♦♦
While Massive Attack wisely didn't have a complete clone of theirs be the first act on their Melankolic label, Alpha still clearly follows in the footsteps of the Bristol masters. The same sense of smoky late-night blues and vibes, subtle tension and weird beauty abound, but while Massive cranks up the ominous paranoia, Alpha favors a softer, driftier approach, a touch more user-friendly but as a result a bit less distinct. For what it is, though, *Heaven* is quite fine, a gently queasy blend of sounds and styles that manages to be tasteful and downright romantic without being airbrushed soul. Opening track "My Things" sets the tone cleverly, blending an orchestral sample from a Percy Faith take on Bacharach and David's "The April Fools" into a layered wash of keyboards and soft pulses that is at once easy listening and slightly off. Bacharach/David interpretations are actually a touchstone throughout the album, being sampled on at least four different tracks. The Shara Nelson equivalent for the album is Wendy Stubbs, who has a fine contralto that purrs around about half the album's songs, including "Rain" and the wittily entitled "Nyquil." At points the production gives her a distinct Beth Gibbons flavor as well, "Slim" being especially noticeable on this front. On the Horace Andy side of things, Martin Barnard has a soft, higher vocal range than most; it is at once soothing and quietly entrancing, a good choice for the songs he works on, including "Sometime Later" and "Back," the latter of which intriguingly mixes both another Bacharach/David sample and a snippet of Sylvia Plath reading her poetry into the music. When the duo fully stretches its collage/sampling muscles, as on the title track, it can be quite breathtaking, a careful balance between chaos and atmospherics. *Heaven* makes for a fine start to Alpha's career—definitely a band to watch for. —*Ned Raggett*

**Pepper: Remixes & Rarities [EP]** / Aug. 25, 1998 / Caroline ♦♦
For those who found *Come from Heaven*, Alpha's debut album, just a bit too consistently downtempo, this remix EP offers a thoroughly enjoyable remedy: remixes, most of them resolutely funky and upbeat, and a few rare tracks that contrast with them nicely. "With" comes in a politely funky hip-hop remix courtesy of the Underdog, while "Hazeldub (MoreRockersPeaceAndLoveMix)" is a drum'n'bass setting that manages to be both frenetic and wispily lovely at the same time. "Honey" is an instrumental based too entirely on a single breakbeat, but it segues nicely into the illbient prettiness of Tim Simenon's remix of "Sometime Later." There are some great vocals from Helen White on "Slim," which also features a thunderous drum sample in a nice juxtaposition. Frankly, this album is far superior to the band's debut—varied in tone and texture, melodically attractive, by turns booty-shaking and bliss-inducing. —*Rick Anderson*

## Alter Ego
f. 1992
*Group / Ambient Techno, Techno*

Releasing arguably the first album of "listening techno" in Germany (the 1994 self-titled debut) and building on the style with subsequent releases, Roman Flügel and Jörn Elling-Wuttke are the exception that proves the rule in boom-boom dominated Deutschland. Better known and revered in England, where dance-based electronic music of a home-listening stripe has been the norm for nearly a decade, Alter Ego have also managed to influenced countrymen and labelmates such as Hardfloor and Yokota to move away from Germany's increasingly commercial trance/techno scene and into headier, more experimental climes. The pair signed to Sven Väth's trance-dominated Harthouse label in 1993, after releasing a self-titled full-length on their own Klang Elektronics (under the name Acid Jesus) which caught Väth's attention. Flügel was a jazz drummer prior to his work with Wuttke, and the pair met in the late '80s as a result of the snowballing German trance scene. They began producing tracks in the studio Wuttke was piecing together, and had an immediate hit as Acid Jesus with their first single, "Move My Body."

By the time they'd signed with Harthouse, however, Flügel and Wuttke were no longer interested in pursuing the club side of dance-based electronic music. Turned off by the German trance and techno scenes' steady commercialization, Flügel and Wuttke sought to innovate German techno out of redundancy by diversifying. Originally slated for release on Harthouse ambient sublabel Recycle or Die, *Alter Ego* got a main label release instead, and together with the subsequent *Decoding the Hacker Myth*, succeeded in slowing the pace of German techno and adding a cachet of new influences (UK ambient techno outfits such as B12 and the Black Dog, hip-hop and electro, jazz and soul). *Decoding the Hacker Myth* was reissued in 1996, coupled with a bonus disc of remixes by the likes of Luke Slater, Two Lone Swordsmen, and Matt "Dr. Rockit" Herbert's Wishmountain project. Flügel has also released an EP and full-length as Ro70 on David Moufang's Source label, and both Flügel and Wuttke continue to release tracks under such side-project pseudonyms as Sensorama, Primitive Painter, and Eight Miles High for Ladomat, R&S, and Klang. They also worked on production for Väth's *Contact* LP. —*Sean Cooper*

**Alter Ego** / 1994 / Harthouse/Eye Q ♦♦♦
An atypical release from Harthouse, this self-titled album mixes slowed-down trance and elements of soul. The result is not unlike a Teutonic version of Massive Attack. —*John Bush*

● **Decoding the Hacker Myth** / Feb. 20, 1996 / Harthouse/Eye Q ♦♦♦♦
This German collective works with what could be best described as "listening techno"—electronica designed not for dancing, but for laidback home listening. This means that each track is organized more like a song, with enough movement to keep things from becoming repetitive; on songs like "Brom," they drop out most of the beats in favor of a sort of organized ambiance. The majority of the album is pleasant in a beepy and bubbly sort of way, and very organic-sounding—a bit like Spring Heel Jack without the breakbeats. Excellent electronica for home use. —*Nitsuh Abebe*

## Altern-8

f. 1989, Stafford, England, db. 1993
*Group / Rave, Club/Dance*

Altern-8 was a verging-on-the-cartoonish rave outfit that pushed their singles into the British charts with promotional theatrics borrowed from the KLF and attention-getting chemical-warfare uniforms from head to toe. Originally formed by Mark Archer and Chris Peat as a side-gig from their Nexus 21 project, Altern-8 debuted with two EPs, 1990's *Overload* and the following year's *Evapor 8*. The singles "Activ 8 (Come with Me)" and "Evapor 8" both nicked the rave-hungry Top Ten during late 1991 and early 1992, thanks in part to a variety of group-sponsored, press-publicized half-truths—the duo's reliance on drug-enhancing chemicals like Vicks Vapo-Rub, their nasty habit of spiking audience-distributed pastries with Ecstasy, even their candidacy in the General Elections. The mini-LP *Full On—Mask Hysteria* followed later in 1992, and Altern-8 even managed a brief American contract (two EPs on Capitol, *Infiltr-8 America* and *Brutal-8-E*) before breaking up in 1993. Archer later appeared in Slo-Moshun with Danny Taurus. *—John Bush*

- **Full On—Mask Hysteria** / 1992 / Network ♦♦♦♦
The title only accentuates the (intentional?) humorous aspects of Altern 8, but the music isn't half bad for the period. *Full On—Mask Hysteria* doesn't include much more than versions of their charting singles, but then again, 75 minutes of 1991-era mainstream rave would be too much for most listeners. *—John Bush*

## Amon Düül

f. 1968, Munich, Germany, **db.** 1981
*Group / Kraut-Rock, Prog-Rock/Art Rock*

One of the first active Kraut-rock units, Amon Düül grew out of a multi-media artist commune in Munich that mixed radical political criticism with a unique vision of free-form improvisation tied to American psychedelic rock, especially compared to the avant-garde inclinations of other space-rock units like Tangerine Dream and Cluster. Such open-ended and non-musical origins made the later activity of the group quite confusing, as a quartet of (slightly) more musically inclined members branched out in 1969 as Amon Düül II. Meanwhile, the original Amon Düül continued releasing albums, most of which had actually been recorded during a mammoth jam session by the entire conglomeration in 1969. Though Amon Düül ceased recording material by 1972, frequent reissues during the decade—and the resumption of the Amon Düül name by several Amon Düül II alumni in the '80s—resulted in still more confusion. Listeners unfamiliar with the lineup of every Amon Düül-related release can content themselves with the fact that the main line of the group began with Amon Düül in the late '60s and moved to Amon Düül II for the '70s recordings.

When originally founded in 1968 however, the group was more of an alternative-living commune project than actual recording artists. Wishing to bring their vision of hippie living to a worldwide audience, the collective named themselves Amon Düül (Amon being an Egyptian sun god, Düül a character from Turkish fiction) and recorded hours of material during what is reportedly one mammoth recording session from early 1969. Even before the release of the self-titled Amon Düül debut that year, several members—led by vocalist Renate Knaup-Kroaetenschwanz (aka Renate Knaup), guitarist Chris Karrer, bassist John (Johannes) Weinzierl, drummer Peter Leopold and organist Falk U. Rogner—had broken away from the original group to form Amon Düül II. That group released its own debut album *Phallus Dei* in 1969. While three additional albums credited to Amon Düül appeared in 1970 and 1971 (*Collapsing/Singvögel Rückwärts & Co., Paradieswärts Düül* and *Disaster*), they were actually comprised of additional recordings from 1969 sessions.

By 1971, it was clear that Amon Düül II was the major unit of the axis. Still, lineups were barely stable enough to credit the same group with all of the work released under the Amon Düül II banner. Members came and went during the early '70s—the only constants were Karrer and Weinzierl—and Amon Düül II gradually progressed away from the acid-improv style of their first recordings to embrace a more pop-oriented approach to progressive rock on 1973's *Vive La Trance* and the following year's *Hijack*, which saw many old members returning to the fold. Two new additions, Stefan Zauner and Klaus Ebert, added a keyboard-dominated quasi-disco sound to 1976's *Pyragony*, and the duo's sound soon dominated the crumbling Amon Düül II lineup. Both Knaup and Weinzierl left the group by 1978 (to play with, respectively, Popol Vuh and Embryo), and Amon Düül II finally halted one year after.

Just two years later, however, Amon Düül II reunited with most of the original lineup to record another album, *Vortex*. That same year, Weinzierl moved to Wales to begin a British version of the band with old bandmate Dave Anderson. What should have been billed Amon Düül III was, however, simply christened Amon Düül. The release of four albums during the '80s (including *Hawk Meets Penguin, Meetings with Menmachines* and *Die Losung*) confused even adept listeners, while Amon Düül II appeared to be finished. *—John Bush*

**Phallus Dei** / 1969 / Repertoire ♦♦♦♦
"Kanaan" starts the album wonderfully, a melange of rumbling rock power, strings and sitars, Lothar Meid's almost Bowie-ish vocals with Renate Knaup's wordless chanting in the background, that's just as intoxicating many years after its first appearance as it was upon release. The slightly jazzy concluding minute avoids sounding forced, blending in beautifully with the song's general flow. "Dem Guten, Schoenen, Wahren" takes a truly wacked-out turn, with Meid's bizarre falsetto coming to the fore, swooping around the main melodies without regard for them in yelps and chants, while the music chugs along in what almost sounds like a beer-hall singalong at points, taking a more haunting, beautiful turn at others (the heavily produced violins are an especially spooky touch). "Luzifers Ghilom" brings out the psych-folk origins of the band a bit more with Shrat's bongos, while the rest of the band pulls off a nicely heroic rock piece that never sounds too inflated or stupid, with appropriately nutty vocal breaks and interjections along the way—the sublime and the ridiculous never sounded so good together. "Henriette Krotenschwanz" ends the first side with a brief choral military march (if you will). The title track takes up the remainder of the album, a complex piece which never loses a sense of fun while always staying musically compelling. After a quiet start, the opening minutes consist of a variety of drones and noises constantly brought up and down in the mix, leading to a full band performance that builds and skips along with restrained fuzz power. Everything builds to a sudden climax halfway through, where all the members play a series of melodies in unison, while drums pound in the background. After a quick violin solo, everything settles into a fine percussion jam, with the full band kicking in shortly thereafter. With Karrer's crazed vocals showing where Mark E. Smith got some good ideas from, *Phallus* gets the Düül II career off to a flying start. *—Ned Raggett*

**Psychedelic Underground** / 1969 / Repertoire ♦♦♦♦
Some albums just have the perfect name, and Amon Düül's debut nails that to a T. Obscure upon release and obscure even now, for all the cult appeal, *Underground* is music at its most experimental and relentlessly uncommercial, using late-'60s inspirations as a launching ground for what came to be described as Kraut-rock. Psych-folk was another common term, one which applies just fine to much of the music here, feeling like an enthusiastic medieval festival gone just out of control enough, and with electricity to boot. Taken from a jam session from the previous year, but treated with many studio effects that enhance the strangeness of the collection, *Underground* rocks to its own weird beat. Opening track "Ein Wunderhubsches Madchen Traumt von Sandosa" captures what sounds like a great experience for everyone involved, a 17-minute composition heavy on the drums and percussion, with a basic, chugging guitar riff in one channel and chanting, call-and-response vocals located throughout the mix. At one point the jam is faded out in favor of piano parts, train noises and the like, only to be brought back in again just as strongly, before finally fading into the gentler "Kaskados Minnelied," a mix of acoustic and electric guitars, along with a stringed instrument of some sort, that favors drones as much as it does soft riffs. The tracks on the second side have the same understandable vibe, but some are sparer in comparison, as with the keening strummed guitar/vocal combination "Im Garten Sandosa" and "Mama Düül und Ihre Sauerkrautband spielt auf," which is mostly clattering percussion in one stereo channel! You could say the sound quality isn't the best, but given the year of recording and the prevelance of lo-fi production approaches in more recent years, it doesn't sound that bad at all. *—Ned Raggett*

**Yeti** / 1970 / Repertoire ♦♦♦♦
The double-album *Yeti* defines the term *space rock* with a full-throttle voyage into the realms of supersonic guitars and keyboards. Highlights like the extended "Soap Shop Rock" suite, "She Came Through the Chimney" and "Archangels Thunderbird" fuse psychedelic and progressive elements to mind-blowing perfection. *—Archie Patterson*

### Collapsing/Singvögel Rückwärts & Co. / 1970 / Metronome ♦♦♦

The second Amon Düül album bore marked similarities to the first for very good reason—it too consisted of tracks recorded at the 1968 jam session which ended up being the bulk of the group's released work. Instead of longer tracks, *Collapsing* instead consisted of snippets or songs that were the length of more conventional pop recordings, while sounding nothing like said recordings at all. The same sense of "instantaneous taping and damn the fidelity" is here as well, though at times things are much crisper than might be expected, as the piercing two-note guitar riff on "Booster" demonstrates. Though the album is also apparently credited to a mysterious outfit called *Singvogel Ruckwarts*, of whom nothing appears to be known (a song is named after them, which actually has a clear introduction and plenty of post-production touches like backwards instruments and jarring edits), this sounds like Amon Düül straight up. Percussion here is even rougher than on *Psychedelic Underground*, feeling much more stripped-down and basic, while vocals are even more unintelligible or wordless (on "Bass, Gestrichen," only a low moaning is heard amongst the clatter, while the impossible-to-interpret grunts and wails on "Krawall" are weirdly fascinating). Evidence of later studio tweaking appears here as on *Underground*, with the muffled classical fanfare sampled to introduce "Tusch F. F." and the repeated vinyl skip-loop on "Lua-Lua-He" being two examples among several. "Nachrichten Aus Cannabistan" has one of the funnier such moments, when, 30 seconds in, the stomping rhythm is audibly slowed down as if a vinyl player were stopped, to be replaced by another drum pattern fading up in the mix. Very strange and interesting stuff, with a unique flavor to it that may never be recaptured. —*Ned Raggett*

### Para Dieswärts Düül / 1970 / Ohr ♦♦♦

Surprisingly, the third Amon Düül album wasn't recorded at the jam session which produced the band's other major releases; even more surprisingly, *Paradieswarts* sounded next to nothing like the other three. Out went the rough and ready drumming, stomping and chanting; in went an extremely delicate sense of expansive songwriting, retaining the predilection for length (the shortest of the album's three songs was almost eight minutes long) but otherwise aiming at a new kind of tastefulness. This said, a completely radical reinvention this isn't; while the first track, the sidelong "Love Is Peace," has plenty of stuff none of the other albums did (intelligible lyrics in English no less, soft guitar melodies, low-key flutes and more), that sense of simple rhythms and riffs repeated and slightly changed and altered over the course of the song predominates nonetheless. The song has a solid, sweet groove to it, becoming a sing-along in the chorus almost in spite of itself; a slightly wigged-out midsection, with flange and echo, soon dissipates into acoustic fingerpicking and strumming rather than completely going nuts. "Snow Your Thirst and Open Your Mouth" approaches the other albums a bit more closely as well, in sounding like it could easily be a jam (the percussion especially sounds like a cousin to the freakouts elsewhere), although it's far more restrained overall. "Paramechanische Welt" closes the record with a folky acoustic guitar, droning strings, and piano strum that moves along well, even without percussion until halfway through; it makes for a lovely conclusion to a surprising record. The CD reissue from 1997 adds on the tracks from the group's only 7" single; "Eternal Flow" is a minimal guitar melody with soft lead and backing vocals that's quite haunting, while "Paramechanical World" is a gentle stunner, with wistfully mournful singing and quietly emotional guitar music in a combination which Hood would rediscover nearly three decades later. —*Ned Raggett*

### Tanz der Lemminge / 1971 / Mantra ♦♦♦♦

There aren't many double art-rock albums from the early '70s that have stood the test of time, but then again, there aren't many albums like *Tanz*, and there certainly aren't many groups like Amon Düül II. While exact agreement over which of their classic albums is the absolute standout may never be reached, in terms of ambition combined with good musicianship and good humor both, *Tanz*, the group's third album, is probably the best candidate still. The musical emphasis is more on expansive arrangements and a generally gentler, acoustic or soft electric vibe; the brain-melting guitar from *Yeti* isn't as prominent on *Tanz*, for example, aside from the odd freakout here and there. You will find lengthy songs divided up into various movements, but with titles like "Dehypnotized Toothpaste" and "Overheated Tiara," po-faced seriousness is left at the door. The music isn't always wacky per se, but knowing that the group can laugh at itself is a great benefit. The first three tracks each take up a side of vinyl on the original release, and all are quite marvelous. "Syntelman's March of the Roaring Seventies" works through a variety of acoustic parts, steering away from folksiness for a more abstract, almost playfully classical sense of space and arrangement, before concluding with a brief jam. "Restless Skylight-Transistor Child" is more fragmented, switching between aggressive (and aggressively weird) and subtle passages. One part features Meid and Knaup singing over an arrangement of guitars, synths and mock choirs that's particularly fine, and quite trippy to boot. "Chamsin Soundtrack" exchanges variety for a slow sense of mystery and menace, with instruments weaving in and out of the mix while never losing the central feel of the song. Three briefer songs close out the record, a nice way to get in some quick grooves at the end. —*Ned Raggett*

### Disaster / 1971 / BASF ♦♦♦♦

Like the first two albums, *Disaster* comes from the same 1968 jam session, which if nothing else shows that the phrase "burst of creativity" can have a very real equivalent. As with the previous two releases, the emphasis is on open-ended, percussion-heavy, choppy-guitared songs with random, often wordless chanting, with rough sound being the general order of the day. Compared to the other two, *Disaster* has a slightly more "live" feeling, with less evidence of later studio additions or tweaks. It's a touch calmer as well, though nowhere near as sweet as *Paradieswaerts Düül* turned out to be. Exactly how planned this release was is up to question—it appeared after the band had broken up, and its two-LP original format speaks of a serious clearing out of the vaults. Regardless, there are some definite winners here; *Disaster* could even be considered the logical conclusion of the band's "try anything and see what works" ethic. Opening song "Drum Things (Erschalgzuegtes)" is very much a classic lengthy jam in the style of *Psychedelic*'s "Ein Wunderhubsches," with what sound like fingerbells providing a notable percussion element along with the pounding drums, especially at the end. Numerous other longer tracks like "Somnium (Trauma)" (which ends with some great drum work) and "Chaoticolor (Entsext)" make up the bulk of the album's length, most settling on a key riff and grooving away on it just fine, with slight alterations appearing as each piece progresses. Some of the shorter numbers are as close as the group ever got to catchy pop; one sprightly number, a Beatles semi-revamp barely a minute long before petering out, has the perfect title "Yea Yea Yea (Zerbeatelt)." Unfairly trashed over the years, *Disaster* is just like the band that made it—wonderful, weird and wiggy. —*Ned Raggett*

### Carnival in Babylon / 1972 / Mantra ♦♦♦

Amon Düül II's follow-up to their landmark double-LP set *Tanz der Lemminge* features a musical approach less experimental than previous recordings, but nonetheless distinctive and broad-reaching in its sphere of influences. The almost epic tack of the earlier works has been pared down here, but full-forward, guitar-heavy tracks like "C.I.D. in Uruk," "Ballad of the Shimmering Sands" and "Kronwinkl 12" use disparate folk and hard rock elements cannily. The band moves the music with a majestic sweep punctuated by the snaky guitar work of Chris Karrer and John Weinzierl. —*Nick Burton*

### Wolf City / 1972 / A&M ♦♦♦♦

Amon Düül II's fifth studio album is a more conventional recording than most, though there's still a lot of the involved experimenting and dark undercurrent which sets the band apart from the mainstream, along with the off-kilter hooks and odd humor which saved from being lumped alongside more serious (and less easy to take seriously) prog-rock outfits. After the lengthy explorations of *Tanz Der Lemminge*, *Wolf City* seems targeted to an extent at a commercial English-speaking audience, perhaps reflective of their increased status in the United Kingdom, if not in America. Regardless, opening song "Surrounded by the Stars," the longest track on the album at just under eight minutes, is also one of the band's best, with strong vocals from Knaup, a dramatic building verse (complete with mock choir), an equally dramatic violin-accompanied instrumental break, and a catchy chorus leading to a fun little freakout. Knaup actually takes the lead vocals more often this time out and turns in some lovely performances, as on the beautiful, perhaps slightly precious "Green Bubble Raincoated Man," with a great full-band performance grows from a nice restraint to a slam-bang, epic rockout. Meid gets his moments in as well, his sometimes straightforward, sometimes not-so-much vocals adding to the overall effect as before. The one full instrumental, "Wie Der Wind," is excellent, with guest Indian musicians adding extra instrumentation to an intoxicating, spacious performance. While *Wolf City* generally sounds like a tight band playing things live or near-live, there are some equally gripping moments clearly resulting from studio work, like the strange loop opening the title track (percussion, guitar?). Concluding with the groovy good-time "Sleepwalker's Timeless Bridge," including some fantastic e-bow guitar work, *Wolf City* works the balance between art and accessibility and does so with resounding success. —*Ned Raggett*

**Viva La Trance** / 1973 / Mantra ♦♦♦
Amon Düül II's extraordinary 1973 album finds the influential German art rock band working surprisingly well in a short song format while still stamping their music with their unique sound. "Fly United," "Trap" and "Ladies Mimikry" show diverse styles of pop and rock running happily into each other with memorably quirky results. The instrumentation here is as quirky as ever—perhaps even more than usual, with Chris Karrer's violin and sax playing now in the fore. The melodies are often shimmering. Unfortunately the band never again sustained the excellence displayed here after this album. —*Nick Burton*

**Live in London** / 1974 / United Artists ♦♦
A curious release in the Amon Düül II catalog—originally it appeared only in Britain, and then as an astonishingly cheap budget release!—*Live in London* is, unsurprisingly, exactly what it says it is. Recorded near the end of 1972, it features the full band lineup performing songs mostly from *Yeti* and *Tanz Der Lemminge* for a quite enthusiastic crowd (if prog-rock bands performed for a bunch of stoned hippies, one would never know that from the cheers throughout). The group pours on the energy in turn; while they aren't simply playing at full blast throughout, the song selection and inspired performances are the mark of a band able to cut it just as well live as in studio. Whether it was a conscious decision on the band's part to focus mostly on the rockers as opposed to the drifters is up for grabs, but it works; even the spacier numbers, like the aptly titled "Improvisations," consisting mostly of buried feedback and burbling keyboard intrusions, still have a good power to them. The heavy groove of "Eye Shaking King" is one standout to note; it's such a great take that swaying and gentle headbanging seems like the only natural things to do, while Karrer's fiery midsong guitar solo is one of his best performances. Two lengthy *Tanz* tracks, "Syntelman's" and "Restless Skylight," appear in abbreviated forms, gaining in a more direct performance what they lose in length, while Knaup and Meid share vocals throughout to further reshape the songs for the live venue, a nice and successful change from the album cuts. Closing on a fine medley of "Riding on a Cloud" and "Paralyzed Paradise," with some more excellent mindfuck guitar on the latter (only a couple of minutes worth, but just enough), *Live in London* is worth scrounging around for. A 2000 UK CD reissue includes bonus tracks, but they appear to just be remixes of album cuts. —*Ned Raggett*

**Anthology (Best of 1970-Viva)** / 1987 / Castle ♦♦♦♦

● **Best of Amon Düül II 1969-1974** / Jan. 21, 1997 / Purple Pyramid ♦♦♦♦
The only side of the continually frustrating Cleopatra label that makes any sense at all, the reissue subsidiary Purple Pyramid continued its commitment to quality archival Kraut-rock with *The Best of Amon Düül II 1969-1974*, a collection that charts the best moments from the best period of one of the most fascinating (and often bewildering) German groups of the '70s. Included are tracks from several of Amon Düül II's best LPs: from *Yeti* comes "Soap Shop Rock" and "Pale Gallery"; from *Tanz der Lemminge* comes "A Short Stop at the Transylvanian Brain-Surgery" and "Stumbling over Melted Moonlight"; and from *Wolf City* there's "Surrounded by the Stars," "Deutsch Népal" and the title track. Though Amon Düül II's albums of the period are necessary for fans of the group, this makes not only a perfect introduction for new listeners but also a handy summation of what made the band great. —*John Bush*

## Amorphous Androgynous
f. 1992, London, England
*Group / Ambient Techno, IDM*
One year before Garry Cobain and Brian Dougans released *Lifeforms*, their breakthrough album as Future Sound of London, the duo recorded *Tales of Ephidrena* as Amorphous Androgynous. Charting an intriguing fusion of industrial techno with the free-form organic passages that would become the norm in ambient techno several years later, *Tales of Ephidrena* was the first hint of what was to become the trademark sound of FSOL. [See Also: Future Sound of London] —*John Bush*

● **Tales of Ephidrena** / 1993 / Astralwerks ♦♦♦♦
Named in displaced reference to a form of speed popular with late-night studio hounds, *Ephidrina* is probably the nearest the group have come to an even compromise between their ambient and dance pretensions, trading equally between lush, contemplative textures and upbeat, simplistic rhythmic structures. Enjoyable but by no means essential. —*Sean Cooper*

## Laurie Anderson (Laura Phillips Anderson)
b. Jun. 5, 1947, Chicago, IL
*Vocals, Violin, Songwriter / Multimedia, Experimental Rock, Experimental*
After briefly entering the mainstream pop radar in 1981 with her lone hit "O Superman," Laurie Anderson enjoyed a public visibility greater than virtually any other avant-garde figure of her era. Her infrequent forays into rock aside, Anderson nevertheless remained firmly grounded within the realm of performance art, her ambitious multimedia projects encompassing not only music but also film, mime, visual projections, dance, and—most importantly—spoken and written language, the cornerstone of all of her work. Born in Chicago on June 5, 1947, she studied violin as a teen; relocating to New York City at age 20, she later attended Barnard College, graduating with a B.A. in art history in 1969. After earning an M.F.A. in sculpture from Columbia University in 1972, Anderson taught art history and Egyptian architecture at City College; she mounted her first public performances a year later.

By 1976, Anderson was regularly mounting performances in museums, concert halls and art festivals throughout North America and Europe; claiming to base all of her projects on the power of words and language, her work also emphasized visual imagery and cutting-edge technology, with pieces like 1980's "Born, Never Asked" written for both orchestra and electronics. A year later Anderson recorded "O, Superman" for the tiny New York label 110 Records; an eleven-minute single built around electronic drones and featuring opaque lyrics half-spoken and half-sung (in a voice sometimes electronically treated), this most unlikely hit became a smash in Britain, where it reached the number two spot on the national pop charts. Warner Bros. soon signed Anderson to record a full-length LP, and in 1982 she issued *Big Science*, a work drawn from a much larger project, the seven-hour multi-media performance *United States*.

With 1984's *Mister Heartbreak*, Anderson produced her most overtly pop-oriented work, teaming with artists including Peter Gabriel and Adrian Belew; the end result even reached the American Top 100. That same year she also issued *United States Live*, a recorded document of the complete performance spread across a five-LP set. Anderson's next project, *Home of the Brave*, was a concert film; a year later, she also scored the Jonathan Demme/Spaulding Gray film *Swimming to Cambodia*. A proper studio album, *Strange Angels*, did not follow until 1989; the next several years were devoted to performance tours, including 1990's "Empty Places," 1991's "Voices from the Beyond" and 1993's "Stoires from the Nerve Bible." In 1994, Anderson teamed with producer Brian Eno for *Bright Red*, also featuring her boyfriend Lou Reed; the following year she released the LP *The Ugly One with Jewels* as well as *Puppet Motel*, a CD-ROM confirming her ongoing interest in the latest technology. —*Jason Ankeny*

**You're the Guy I Want to Share My Money With** / 1981 / Giorno Poetry Systems ♦♦
Experimental music and cutting-edge spoken word recordings from Anderson, William Burroughs and John Giorno, three of the foremost practitioners of these genres. Each artist is featured on one side of this double-LP and then each contribute a short track to side four. —*William I. Lengeman III*

● **Big Science** / 1982 / Warner Brothers ♦♦♦♦
*Big Science* is essentially a chunk of the more elaborate and difficult four-part multi-media performance piece *United States Live*. But, that said, *Big Science* never sounds like a portion, it is in fact a meal in itself. The music is moody and minimalistic, and Anderson's wry observations are perspicacious, smartalecky and, at times, laugh-out-loud funny. There have been numerous artists attempting work like this since *Big Science*; few, however, equal Anderson's panache. Not your average pop record. Oh yeah, "O Superman" is here in all its glory. —*John Dougan*

**Mister Heartbreak** / 1984 / Warner Brothers ♦♦♦♦
A more pop-oriented record (there are songs here and musicians like Adrian

Belew and Peter Gabriel), Anderson displays a functional singing voice that graces such wonderful songs as "Sharkey's Day" and "Excellent Birds" (a duet with Gabriel). More accessible than *Big Science*, but in some ways a record indicating that while she may not be a musician herself, Anderson certainly knows how to pick them, work with them, and challenge them. A thoroughly wonderful record. —*John Dougan*

**United States Live** / 1984 / Warner Brothers ♦♦♦
Once her popularity seemed assured, Warner Bros. felt safe releasing this five-record set (since reissued on four CDs) comprising *United States*' entire four-and-a-half hours. It's not the first place I'd recommend going to hear Anderson's work, but for those so inclined it's well worth the effort. Although live performances of *United States* included film segments that ran during some of her monologues, *United States* is about communication and how we interpret and use language. It's a bit pretentious, a tad long-winded, and its size makes it unwieldy to listen to in one sitting, but this is an important work loaded with enough insight, wit and humanity to make relistening and re-evaluating worthwhile. —*John Dougan*

**Home of the Brave** / 1986 / Warner Brothers ♦♦♦
The soundtrack to Anderson's film, containing both older songs, such as "Sharkey's Night," and new material, notably "Language Is A Virus." It suffers by being shortened for album length and missing the visual element, but is still enjoyable. —*William Ruhlmann*

**Strange Angels** / Oct. 1989 / Warner Brothers ♦♦♦♦
Purists may disagree, but I think *Strange Angels* is Anderson's most stunning work. It may be due to its nearly giddy selection of pop songs (including the supremely ecstatic "Babydoll"), but here Anderson sounds supremely confident—as a pop singer/songwriter. Rather than weighing down her songs with avant-gardisms, *Strange Angels* positively luxuriates in this conflation of the avant-garde and the popular. Hence, there is a relentless joyfulness that imbues this record, but never sacrifices intelligence one iota. A brilliantly conceived record, *Strange Angels* offers the best of both worlds to the benighted and aficionados. —*John Dougan*

**Bright Red** / Oct. 25, 1994 / Warner Brothers ♦♦
Almost six years after *Strange Angels*, Anderson's follow-up was the dark and foreboding *Bright Red*. A slight disappointment, Brian Eno's production heightens the almost amorphous quality of the material, which succeeds in fits and starts. Still, there are moments like "Speechless" and "Poison" that are as gripping as anything she's ever recorded. As with any artist this interesting, Anderson's prodigious talents are on display; you'll simply have to dig a little deeper for them to be revealed. —*John Dougan*

**The Ugly One with the Jewels and Other Stories** / Mar. 14, 1995 / Warner Brothers ♦♦♦♦
On her later albums, Laurie Anderson had moved from her earlier spoken word-plus-effects style to a more overtly musical approach, with less effective results. *The Ugly One With The Jewels*, a recording of a live performance of readings from her book *Stories From The Nerve Bible*, returned her to speaking instead of singing, and it was her best album since *Big Science*. The 18 stories reflected Anderson's extensive travels, including forays into the Third World and to convents, although she made Los Angeles and Houston sound just as exotic. In fact, telling her stories over sounds from birds to guitars to electronic beeps, she seemed an anthropologist from another world, always finding the natives friendly but strange. And she didn't fail to recognize that she could appear just as odd to them: "The Ugly One With The Jewels" was a name used by one of her subjects to describe her. —*William Ruhlmann*

**Talk Normal: The Laurie Anderson Anthology** / Oct. 17, 2000 / Rhino ♦♦♦
*Talk Normal: The Laurie Anderson Anthology* gathers 35 career highlights that range from Anderson's most performance art-oriented material to her poppiest moments. Leading off with "O Superman (For Massenet)," her unlikely 1982 hit, the first disc pares down *Big Science*—itself a distillation of her four-hour piece *United States*—to its starkest and most hypnotic tracks, including "From the Air," "Born, Never Asked," and the title track. "Sharkey's Day," "Excellent Birds," and "Langue D'Amour," all from the more melodic, emotional *Mister Heartbreak*, close out disc one, along with more pieces from *United States*, including "Walk the Dog," "Cartoon Song," and "Lighting Out for the Territories." Similarly, the second disc picks highlights from the *Home of the Brave* soundtrack—"Smoke Rings" and "Language Is a Virus" chief among them—and includes six tracks from her most melodic, song-structured album, *Strange Angels*. "Coolsville," "The Day the Devil," and the title track work especially well outside of the album's context and mix nicely with *Bright Red* tracks like "Speak My Language" and "In Our Sleep." The anthology closes with a sampling of *The Ugly One With the Jewels*' vignettes, including "The Night Flight From Houston," "The Rotowhirl," and "The End of the World." Though the anthology distills Anderson's work so much that it tends to blur the character of her individual albums, *Talk Normal* still presents most of the nuances in Anderson's distant yet open, ironic yet emotional style. For new listeners who want a bigger, more representative picture of Anderson's work than *Big Science* provides, *Talk Normal* is a good starting point. —*Heather Phares*

## Horace Andy (Horace Hinds)

b. Feb. 19, 1951, Kingston, Jamaica
*Vocals / Smooth Reggae, Roots Reggae, Lovers Rock*

Although he has one of the most distinctive voices in reggae music, Horace Andy, despite considerable exposure in the early '90s as a guest vocalist with British trip-hoppers Massive Attack, is venerated primarily by hardcore reggae aficionados. And while he's not as well-known as other talented Jamaican vocalists such as Winston (Burning Spear) Rodney, Culture's Joseph Hill, or Toots Hibbert, he is worthy of inclusion in the pantheon.

Born Horace Hinds in Kingston, Jamaica in 1951, Andy came on the reggae scene as part of the second generation of great singers who were following in the footsteps of seminal reggae vocalists such as Ken Boothe, John Holt, and Delroy Wilson. What separated Andy from that group and virtually all Jamaican male vocalists of the early '70s (a notable exception being Junior Murvin) was his clear, powerful, high tenor voice. With the ability to shift from sultry croon to full-throated wail (not unlike, say, Al Green), as well as his delicately impeccable phrasing, Andy could be positively stunning. By the age of 21 he was already a music-scene veteran, having cut the hit records "Skylarking," "The Love of a Woman," and "I Found Someone" among others. In the early '70s he was one of the most in-demand vocalists on the island, recording great sides for Bunny Lee; the relationship that would last for nearly the rest of the decade and account for some of Andy's best recorded work.

After leaving Bunny Lee, Andy went to work with New York producer Everton DaSilva. Unlike Lee, who tended to be a tad autocratic when it came to recording, DaSilva gave Andy the latitude needed to craft his own records. It was a great idea, leading to the recording of Andy's signature work, *In the Light* (with a companion dub LP) in 1977. Andy's vocals seemed to soar higher than ever before and the band, which included such Jamaican luminaries as Augustus Pablo and Horsemouth Wallace, never sounded better. A highly prized piece of music to those deeply into reggae, *In the Light* was not a huge seller and by the mid-'80s was extremely difficult to find.

Andy continued recording through the '80s, working with producers such as Lloyd Barnes (aka Bullwackie) and the enigmatic Tappa Zukie, but he remained an obscure figure, an immensely talented singer that mostly went unheard by pop and rock audiences. That changed in 1990 when Andy was asked to contribute vocals to Massive Attack's brilliant debut *Blue Lines*. Ecstatic with the results, the band asked him back for 1994's *Protection* (which also featured another haunting vocalist, Tracey Thorn) as well as 1998's *Mezzanine*. Andy continued to make solo records, including a tribute LP to Bob Marley, and in 1995 the British label Blood & Fire reissued both *In the Light* and *In the Light Dub* on one disc. He hardly became a household name, but by the late '90s much of Horace Andy's great work became quite easily available. —*John Dougan*

● **In the Light/In the Light Dub** / 1995 / Blood & Fire ♦♦♦♦
The difference between an essential reggae reissue and a craven ripoff usually comes down to two things: sound and packaging. This two-for-one reissue of Horace Andy's *In the Light* album (which includes dub mixes of all the original album's songs) is a classic example of the Blood & Fire label's loving devotion to both sonic and cosmetic detail. The sound is phenomenal—modern ears jaded by years of direct-from-vinyl remastering will be stunned by the clarity, definition and sonic depth of these recordings. Andy himself is at the top of his form through most of the album, though not on all tracks; he'd have done better to leave the lover's rock stuff for someone else, and "Do You Love My Music" and "Fever" are far from essential. But he's at his best on such cultural roots excursions as "Leave Rasta" and "In the Light," and in that

genre he has few peers. His all-star backing band includes Leroy Sibbles, Horsemouth Wallace and even Augustus Pablo on keyboards. Solidly recommended overall, with minor reservations. —*Rick Anderson*

**Good Vibes (1975-1979)** / Jul. 1, 1997 / Blood & Fire ♦♦♦♦
Horace Andy, an enormously popular reggae singer in the '70s, has enjoyed a resurgence of popularity in the late '90s, due in part to his extensive work with the British band Massive Attack. This has led, thankfully, to massive reissues of his earlier work, of which this is one of the better examples. Each of the ten tracks is presented in "discomix" style—the normal, vocal version comes first, and then segues seamlessly into the dub version. Those who have found his recent solo work under the aegis of Mad Professor to be a bit bloodless and overproduced will find this collection of '70s singles refreshing. It starts out slow, with a disappointing piece of meta-reggae—reggae songs about how wonderful reggae is are rarely revelatory—but things pick up quickly with "Serious Thing" and the inevitable "Skylarking," and the momentum stays strong up to the end. Andy's high, almost girlish voice and weird vibrato may be an acquired taste for some, but he's worth the effort. —*Rick Anderson*

**Mr. Bassie** / 1998 / Heartbeat ♦♦♦♦
Horace Andy possesses one of the truly immortal voices of reggae—a reedy tenor that cuts effortlessly through the mix and has influenced countless other reggae singers. He began recording as a teenager, and his voice and delivery have actually changed little since those early days, when he was cranking out hits for producer Clement "Coxsone" Dodd at the great Studio One label. Though never a real household name, in recent years he's made something of a comeback with several good solo albums and guest appearances with the British group Massive Attack. *Mr. Bassie* collects fourteen tracks from Andy's early-'70s heyday, all recorded under the aegis of Coxsone Dodd with the backing of Kingston's finest studio bands. There are many standout tunes, including cover versions of soul classics like "Ain't No Sunshine" and "Oh Lord, Why Lord," and he delivers a rendition of Paul Simon's rock-steady composition "Mother and Child Reunion" that, while faithful to the original in terms of style and arrangement, leaves Simon's original vocal in the dust. Several collections of Horace Andy singles have come out recently on various labels, but this is one of the best. —*Rick Anderson*

**Living in the Flood** / Feb. 29, 2000 / Astralwerks ♦♦♦♦
Horace Andy is one of the true living legends of reggae, a great falsetto singer whose earliest work established a roots reggae foundation upon which numerous other singers would later build, and who has managed to continue to make vital and influential music throughout the '90s and into the 21st century, largely thanks to his collaborations with the British trip-hop band Massive Attack. It's Massive Attack's Melankolic label that has given Andy a place to hang his hat, first with the career overview *Skylarking*, and now with an outstanding album of all-new material. The sound here is strictly roots, with real drums and horns (inexplicably, there are no musician credits), old-fashioned reggae grooves and cultural lyrics. Andy is singing as beautifully as ever (on every track except "True Love," which finds him painfully off pitch), and on such highlight tracks as "Juggling" and the epochal "Living in the Flood," you'd swear he was still in his 20s. (The US version of this album includes a Mad Professor remix of "After All," and there is a hidden track embedded in the program after it.) —*Rick Anderson*

## Dave Angel (David Gooden)

b. May 13, 1966, Chelsea, London, England
*Producer, DJ / Club/Dance, Techno*

A child of the London acid-house explosion, British-born DJ and producer Dave Angel makes Detroit-styled techno with strong jazz and soul influences. One of the first artists of international renown to take Motor City futurism to a major-label level, Angel (born Dave Gooden) signed with Island's Blunted sublabel in 1996 and recorded his debut longform release, *Tales of the Unexpected*. Previously, Angel released EPs through the Black Market, Love, Apollo, and R&S labels, as well as his own Rotation label, which was established following a string of charting hits in the early '90s, including the "Nightmare Mix" for pop group Eurythmics' "Sweet Dreams (Are Made of This)." The son of a jazz musician, Angel's roots are in bebop and modern jazz (as both a fanatic and a radio jockey) as much as in the Detroit-styled techno he is more often known for. Although he lived the common inner-city experience of crime and drugs, Angel glommed onto the burgeoning acid house scene in the late '80s after a series of jail sentences and the death of his father. Self-taught as both a producer and musician, Angel drew heavily in style and mood from original Detroit luminaries such as Juan Atkins, Derrick May, and Eddie Fowlkes. A DJ of renown, Angel's following (both on the decks and on wax) has been strongest in Germany, where the hardcore, trance, and techno scenes regularly attract audiences far in excess of the house-centered UK and American scenes. His second album *Globetrotting* gained release on 4th & Broadway in 1997. Released from his Island deal the following year, Angel returned with two EPs, a two-disc mix album (*39 Flavours of Tech Funk*), and a second mix release via the *X-Mix* series. —*Sean Cooper*

**Tales of the Unexpected** / Feb. 1996 / Blunted ♦♦♦♦
Angel's debut album is an exquisite piece of British techno, as tight as anything out of Detroit but also reliant on sampladelic house and soul. Though tracks like "Timeless," "Scatman" and "Bump" lack the immediate punch of his early R&S singles, dividends are paid far down the line as Angel proves himself a master of the ultra-sublime club track which rewards additional listens. —*John Bush*

● **Classics** / May 27, 1996 / R&S ♦♦♦♦
Including the majority of the contents from four singles Dave Angel recorded for R&S Records (and subsidiaries) during 1992-93, *Classics* distills the early career of one of the best straightahead British techno producers. Never as consciously "intelligent" as Warp acts like the Black Dog and B12, Angel navigated the divide between techno for head and heart with apparent ease, balancing his hard-hitting percussion attack with moody effects and a sense of atmosphere. Many of his best productions are on this collection, including "Bounce Back," "Jungle Love," "Free Flow" and "Brother from Jazz." In total, the individual moments on *Classics* rival Angel's later album productions. —*John Bush*

**Globetrotting** / 1997 / 4th & Broadway ♦♦♦♦
Acquiescing only slightly to the rise of earthy breakbeats within British dance music, Dave Angel turns in another collection of club burners that reveal additional highlights on the home stereo. The blunted samples used to introduce the album would have worked better on a trip-hop LP, but jet-setting selections like "Tokyo Stealth Fighter," "Chicago Emerald City" and "Sensor Zurich" prove that Angel hadn't lost his edge. —*John Bush*

**39 Flavours of Tech Funk** / 1998 / React ♦♦♦♦
An epic journey through techno and tech-house, Dave Angel's double-disc mix album on React includes (count 'em) 39 tracks of bracing techno-trance, a stellar DJ production. With no comedowns and few breaks, Angel sticks to pummeling techno-funk courtesy of his favorite producers—there are no less than five tracks by Olav Basoski (and three of them in a row), four by Mark Seven, three by Ian Pooley and three by Nico Awtsventin plus Angel's own remixes of tracks by Mark NRG, Kamaflarge, and Warped 69. Despite the glut of similar-sounding mix albums on the market, *39 Flavours of Tech Funk* is, truly, in a league of its own. —*John Bush*

## Animals on Wheels (Andy Coleman)

b. Cambridge, England
*Producer / Drill'N'Bass, Electronica, Jungle/Drum'N'Bass*

"Drill'n'bass" outfit Animals on Wheels was the first signing to UK beatfreak label Ninja Tune from the Bovinyl imprint, run by Cambridge-based Andy Coleman. Coleman is also the principle behind AOW, whose humorous brand of jazzy, hyperdriven breakbeat fracture is comparable to that of Aphex Twin, Plug, and Squarepusher, among others. (The curious name derives, reportedly, from a friend of Coleman's who claims the largest collection of the like-named tchotchkes.) Coleman issued a trio of twelves on his own label, as well as a handful of compilation tracks, before releasing his debut for Ninja Tune, the full-length *Designs and Mistakes*, in 1997. A trendy blend of dimestore jazz samples, mile-a-minute breaks, and fizzy downtempo weirdness, the album probably missed the cheeky jungle curve by about six months, although it earned Coleman a wider audience for his music than the comparatively short reach of Bovinyl allowed. *Nuvo I Cadira* followed in 1999. —*Sean Cooper*

● **Designs & Mistakes** / Nov. 10, 1997 / Ninja Tune ♦♦♦♦
*Designs and Mistakes* is a thricewise cross between sloppy, jazz-driven drill'n'bass, Aphex-y distorto jungle, and druggy downtempo head music, each managed competently, but none managing to completely obscure the

numbers from which their colors seem to derive. An unfortunate victim of electronica's version of Moore's law, the album's already a bit stale by the time the wrapper's off. Good for a mindless listen, but better passed over for something a little less contrived. —*Sean Cooper*

## Anti Pop Consortium

*Group / Underground Rap, Hardcore Rap*
At the height of hip-hop and gangsta rap's rise to mainstream consciousness in the '90s, the poetic foursome of Anti Pop Consortium formed in 1997 to challenge monotonous commercial rap forces. Priest, Beans, M. Sayyid, and the savvy elixir of E. Blaize played NYC's lyrical urban underground, mixing staccato-style theatrical rhyming that reflected childhood events, eventually teaming with the newly launched multi-cultural hip-hop label, 75 Ark. Anti Pop Consortium kicks excess rap violence to the curb on their 2000 debut, *The Tragic Epilogue*, in an effort to redefine the art of turntablism, DJ culture, and the state of urban hip-hop. —*MacKenzie Wilson*

- Tragic Epilogue / Feb. 22, 2000 / 75 Ark ◆◆◆◆
The tongue-tripping raps, obtuse science-fiction metaphors, and excellent minor-key productions on *Tragic Epilogue* immediately recall Kool Keith's *Doctor Octagon*, the 1996 LP that energized the rap underground. Still, Anti Pop Consortium never come across as derivative; the raps (mostly by Beans, High Priest, and Sayyid) are steadily inventive and on a similar high plane as the best non-mainstream rappers out there (Kool Keith, Jurassic 5, Mos Def). Though all of the best tracks ("Nude Paper," "Laundry," "9.99," "Your World Is Flat") come on the first side, and the second doesn't really compete, Anti Pop Consortium's debut is well-produced and well-performed. —*John Bush*

## Aphex Twin (Richard D. James)

**b.** Aug. 18, 1971
*Producer / Drill'N'Bass, Experimental Jungle, Experimental Techno, Electronica, Ambient Techno, Acid Techno, Trance, Techno, IDM*
Exploring the experimental possibilities inherent in acid and ambience, the two major influences on home-listening techno during the late '80s, Richard D. James' recordings as Aphex Twin brought him more critical praise than any other electronic artist during the '90s. Though his first major single "Didgeridoo" was a piece of acid thrash designed to tire dancers during his DJ sets, ambient stylists and critics later took him under their wing for *Selected Ambient Works 85-92*, a sublime touchstone in the field of ambient techno. James' reaction to the exposure portrayed an artist unwilling to become either pigeonholed or categorizable. His second Aphex Twin album, *Selected Ambient Works, Vol. 2*, was so minimal as to be barely conscious—in what appeared to be an elaborate joke on the electronic community. Follow-ups showed James gradually returning to his hardcore and acid roots, even while his stated desire to crash the British Top Ten (and perform on *Top of the Pops*) resulted in a series of cartoonish pop songs whose twisted genius was near-masked by their many absurdities. His iconoclastic behavior surprisingly aligned with MTV audiences turned on to end-of-the-millennium nihilist-pop along the lines of Marilyn Manson and Nine Inch Nails.

James began taking apart electronics gear as a teenager growing up in Cornwall, England. (If the title *Selected Ambient Works 85-92* is to be believed, it contains recordings made at the age of 14.) Inspired by acid-house in the late '80s, James began DJing raves around Cornwall. His first release was the *Analogue Bubblebath* EP, recorded with Tom Middleton and released on the Mighty Force label in September 1991. Middleton left later that year to form Global Communication, after which James recorded a second volume in the *Analogue Bubblebath* series. This EP (the first to include "Digeridoo") got some airplay on the London pirate radio-station Kiss FM, and prompted Belgium's R&S Records to sign him early the following year. A re-recording of "Digeridoo" made number 55 in the British charts just after its April 1992 release date, and James followed with the *Xylem Tube* EP in June. He also co-formed (with Grant Wilson-Claridge) his own Rephlex label around that time, releasing a series of singles as Caustic Window during 1992-93. Available in cruelly limited editions, most of the recordings continued the cold acid precision of "Digeridoo"—though several expressed humor and fragility barely dreamed of in the hardcore/rave scene to that point.

The climate for "intelligent" techno had begun to warm in the early '90s, though. The Orb had proved the commercial viability of ambient house with their chart-topping "Blue Room" single, and R&S scrambled to find useful material from its own artists. In November 1992, James acquiesced with *Selected Ambient Works 85-92*, consisting mostly of home material recorded during the past few years. Simply stated, it was a masterpiece of ambient techno, the genre's second work of brilliance after The Orb's *Adventures Beyond the Ultraworld*. As his star began to shine, several bands approached him to remix their work, and he complied, with mostly unrecognizable reworkings of tracks by St. Etienne, the Cure, Jesus Jones, Meat Beat Manifesto and Curve.

Early in 1993, Richard James signed to Warp Records, the influential British label that virtually introduced the concept of futuristic "electronic listening music" with a series of albums (sub-titled *Artificial Intelligence*) by ambient techno pioneers Black Dog, Autechre, B12, and FUSE (aka Richie Hawtin) among others. James' release in the series, titled *Surfing on Sine Waves*, was recorded as Polygon Window and released in January 1993. The album charted a course between the raw muscle of James' nose-bleed techno and the understated minimalism of *Selected Ambient Works*. A deal between Warp and TVT gave *Surfing on Sine Waves* an American release (James' first) by the summer. A second album was released that year, *Analogue Bubblebath 3*, for Rephlex. Recorded as AFX, the LP renounced any debt to ambient music and was the most bracing work yet in the Aphex Twin canon. On a tour of America with Orbital and Moby later that year, James clung to the head-banging material, to the detriment of his mostly unreplaceable gear. He later cut down on his live-performance schedule.

In December of 1993, the new single "On" resulted in James' highest chart placing, a number 32 spot on the British charts. The two-part single included remixes by old pal Tom Middleton (as Reload) and future Rephlex star μ-Ziq. Despite James' appearance on the pop charts, his following album *Selected Ambient Works, Vol. 2* appeared to be a joke on the ambient techno community. So minimal as to be barely conscious, the quadruple-album left most of the beats behind, with only tape loops of unsettling ambient noise remaining. The album mostly struck out with critics, but hit No. 11 on the British charts and earned James a major-label American contract with Sire soon after. During 1994, he worked on the ever-growing Rephlex stable, signing μ-Ziq (Michael Paradinas), Kosmik Kommando (Mike Dred), and Kinesthesia/Cylob (Chris Jeffs) to the label. In August 1994, he released the fourth *Analogue Bubblebath*, this one a five-track EP.

The year 1995 began with the January release of *Classics*, a compilation of his early R&S singles. Two months later, James released the single "Ventolin," a harsh, appropriately wheezing ode to the asthma drug on which he relied. *I Care Because You Do* followed in April, pairing his hardcore experimentalism with more symphonic ambient material, aligned with the work of many post-classical composers—including Philip Glass, who arranged an orchestral version of the album's "Icct Hedral" on the August 1995 single, "Donkey Rhubarb."

Later that year, the *Hangable Auto Bulb* EP replaced *Analogue Bubblebath 3* as Aphex Twin's most brutal, uncompromising release—a fusion of experimental music and jungle being explored at the same time on releases by Plug and Squarepusher. In July 1996, Rephlex released the long-awaited collaboration between Richard James and Michael Paradinas (μ-Ziq). The album, *Expert Knob Twiddlers* (credited to Mike & Rich) watered down the experimentalism of Aphex Twin with μ-Ziq's easy-listening electro-funk. The fourth proper Aphex Twin album, November 1996's *Richard D. James Album*, continued his forays into acid-jungle and experimental music. Retaining the experimental edge, but with a stated wish to make the British pop charts, James' next two releases, 1997's *Come to Daddy* EP and 1999's *Windowlicker* EP, were acid storms of industrial drum'n'bass. The accompanying videos, both directed by Chris Cunningham, featured the bodies of small children and models (respectively) dancing around, all with special-effects-created Aphex Twin faces grinning maniacally. James released nothing during the year 2000, but did record the score to *Flex*, a short Chris Cunningham film exhibited as part of the Apocalypse exhibition at London's Royal Academy. [See Also: Polygon Window] —*John Bush*

Analogue Bubblebath III / 1992 / Rephlex ◆◆◆
His first full-length release, this long out-of-print album features James's early brand of techno, indebted to acid and trance but still of a distorted quality all its own. No song titles are provided on the CD version (which comes in a slimline case with only a sticker on the front), but the LP version (en-

closed in a brown paper bag) lists long decimals as the titles. *Analogue Bubblebath III* was re-released by Rephlex in late 1997, but again as a limited-edition issue. —*John Bush*

★ **Selected Ambient Works 85-92** / 1993 / R&S ♦♦♦♦♦
*Selected Ambient Works* is a desperately sparse album: thin percussion and several haunted-synth lines are the only components on most songs, and Richard D. James added only one vocal sample on the entire album ("We are the music makers, and we are the dreamers of dreams"). Also, the sound quality is relatively poor; it was recorded direct to cassette tape and reportedly suffered a mangling job by a cat. All this belies the status of *Selected Ambient Works* as a watershed of ambient music. It reveals no influences and sounds unlike anything that preceded it, due in large part to the effects James managed to wrangle from his supply of home-manufactured contraptions. —*John Bush*

☆ **Selected Ambient Works, Vol. 2** / Apr. 1994 / Sire ♦♦♦♦♦
*Selected Ambient Works, Vol. 2* is a more difficult and challenging album than the Aphex Twin's previous collection. The music is all texture; there are only the faintest traces of beats and forward movement. Instead, all of these untitled tracks are long, unsettling electronic soundscapes, alternately quiet and confrontational; although most of the music is rather subdued, it is never easy listening. While some listeners may find this double-disc album dull (both discs run over 70 minutes), many listeners will be intrigued and fascinated by the intricately detailed music of the Aphex Twin. —*Stephen Thomas Erlewine*

**Classics** / 1995 / R&S ♦♦♦
Given Richard D. James' popularity, R&S Records of Belgium decided to combine two singles recorded for the label, half of another single, two remixes, and a live track for the *Classics* album. At 13 tracks and 74 minutes, it's a good compilation of his early dark techno. —*John Bush*

**I Care Because You Do** / Apr. 25, 1995 / Sire ♦♦♦♦
James' most consistent work, *I Care Because You Do* fuses his earlier hardcore techno days with the smooth rhythm and atmosphere of his ambient work, often on the same song. "Ventolin" is one of the harshest singles ever recorded; the orchestrated closer "Next Heap With" is the highlight of the album. —*John Bush*

**51/13 Aphex Singles Collection** / 1996 / WEA Japan/Sire/Warp ♦♦
This Australian disc basically collects tracks from two Warp singles ("Ventolin," "Donkey Rhubarb") released by Aphex Twin during 1995. Besides the memorable A-sides, there are four remixes of "Ventolin" and the Philip Glass orchestration of "Icct Hedral." It's not quite the greatest hits compendium that Aphex Twin needs, but it works well for trainspotting fans. —*John Bush*

☆ **Richard D. James Album** / Nov. 4, 1996 / Elektra ♦♦♦♦♦
Perhaps inspired by the experimental drum'n'bass being created by Squarepusher (a recent signee to his Rephlex label), Richard D. James' third major-label album as Aphex Twin was his first to work with jungle—though, to his credit, he had released the breakbeat EP *Hangable Auto Bulb* almost a year earlier. Contemporaries Orbital and Underworld were beginning to incorporate moderate use of drum'n'bass in their work as well, but this album was more extreme than virtually all jungle being made at the time. The beats are jackhammer quick and even more jarring considering what is—for the most part—laid over the top: the same fragile, slow-moving melodies that characterized Aphex Twin's earlier ambient works. Most overtly disturbing is "Milkman," the first straightahead vocal track from Aphex Twin; the song is a childlike ode that gradually deteriorates into a bizarre fantasy concerning the milkman's wife. With all the Aphex Twin's curious idiosyncracies, though, *Richard D. James Album* is a very listenable record and a worthy follow-up to *I Care Because You Do*. [The American issue features the English EP "Girl/Boy."] —*John Bush*

**Come to Daddy [EP]** / Oct. 6, 1997 / Sire ♦♦♦♦
*Come to Daddy* has been interpreted by some as Richard D. James' sly sendup of the Prodigy's massive hit "Firestarter." If that's the case, it only goes to show how clever the Aphex Twin really is. Built around an intense drum loop and a deliriously demented, booming voice yelling "Come to Daddy!," the track could be the biggest sonic assault James has ever constructed, and even with the underlying menace, it remains one of his most accessible and memorable songs. The EP is filled out with several "Come to Daddy" remixes that reveal subtleties in the main track, plus a few tracks like "Flim" that show Aphex still capable of the gorgeous, fragile melodies of his early ambient work. —*Stephen Thomas Erlewine*

**Windowlicker [Single]** / Mar. 23, 1999 / Sire ♦♦♦
An extension of its satiric predecessor, "Windowlicker" focuses on eerie lounge-porn music (with a video to match) instead of the thrashcore of "Come to Daddy." Later Aphex trademarks like hyper-breakbeat drum programs and heavily tweaked voices are in full effect, though the cloying melody could make longtime fans run for the toilet (or fall off the couch laughing). Of the two unpronounceable B-sides, one includes more breakbeat thrash, while the other looks back to *Selected Ambient Works* territory with a toybox melody that's only potentially disturbing. The enhanced single also included the video of the title track, directed by Chris Cunningham, and possibly even more disturbing than "Come to Daddy." —*John Bush*

## Aphrodite (Gavin King)
*Producer, DJ / Jungle/Drum'N'Bass, Club/Dance*
Aphrodite's Gavin King is one of the reigning, well, *kings* of jump-up style jungle, a sparse, high-energy offshoot of drum'n'bass designed for maximum dancefloor impact. With tracks propelled by simple, rolling drum loops, huge, warbling basslines, and loads of chopped-up hip-hop and ragga samples, King's releases as Aphrodite, Alladin, and Amazon II (a side project with producer Tony B.) began ruling dance floors in 1995 after top DJs such as Hype and Zinc began playing the socks off them. Although many of Aphrodite's earlier tracks were deep in a ragga style, his late-1995 and 1996 releases began bridging the gap between ragga's gimmicky, sample-heavy refrains and jump-up's more spry stepping. His discography is cluttered with chart-topping jump-up tracks, including "King of the Beats," "Woman That Rolls," "Mash Up Your," and "Dub Moods." Releasing most of his tracks on his own Aphrodite Recordings label, King also hooked up with DJ/producer Mickey Finn in 1996 to record a number of tracks (including "Bad Ass" and "Big Time") for release on the joint-established imprint Urban Takeover. He's also rumored to be the man behind any number of white label-only bootleg jungle versions, including mixes of "Mission: Impossible," "No Diggity," and the Luniz' "I Got Five on It," in addition to legitimate remix work for such artists as Dub War and Nine Inch Nails. The 1997 CD compilation *Aphrodite Recordings* is the best, most comprehensive introduction to his work, while his self-titled 1999 American debut collected old tracks and a few new remixes. King has also appeared at the helm of several mix albums, including *Full Force* and *Takeover Bid: Round One*. —*Sean Cooper*

● **Aphrodite Recordings** / Aug. 25, 1997 / Aphrodite ♦♦♦♦
A compendium of sorts for the mighty Aphrodite, aka Gavin King, whose various ragga and jump-up tracks have scaled the high points of most jungle DJs' sets at one point or another throughout the mid-'90s. *Aphrodite Recordings* gives a sense of the largeness, although, as usual with jump-up, these tracks don't sound nearly as interesting outside of a club. Anthems such as "King of the Beats," "Woman That Rolls," "Style from the Darkside," and "Spice," as well as a few lesser rinsed (occasionally for good reason) cuts. In addition to King's solo tracks as Aphrodite, the CD also features cuts by Amazon II (his ragga project with Tony B.) and Alladin (featuring King with producer QED). —*Sean Cooper*

**Takeover Bid: Round One** / Sep. 22, 1998 / Moonshine Music ♦♦♦♦
The first volume in the *Takeover Bid* series (manned by Mickey Finn on round two) includes an unsurprising clutch of tracks by Aphrodite himself ("Underworld," "Wikki Wikki Plate," "Rising Quince," "Bomber Style"), though none are major anthems. The other selections—by Click 'N Cycle, DJ Tee Bee, even a remix of a Prodigy track—aren't stellar, King's mixing saves the day and makes *Takeover Bid: Round One* a solid jump-up album. —*John Bush*

**Aphrodite** / Oct. 26, 1999 / Gee Street ♦♦♦♦
The American debut from Gavin King is a reworked version of the 1997 singles collection released in Britain as *Aphrodite Recordings*. Included are a few special remixes of some of his best-known productions, "Spice (Even Spicier)," "Music's Hypnotising (Re-Charged)," and "Style from the Dark Side '99", plus new tracks and a few untouched classics. Though the instantly recognizable Aphrodite production style—one minute of excellent mid-tempo hip-hop breaks, then your average jump-up anthem complete with a quivering bassline and not much else—isn't suited to a track-after-track collection,

just getting original classics like "King of the Beats," "Summer Breeze," and "Woman That Rolls" makes it all worthwhile. —*John Bush*

## Apollo 440

f. 1990, Liverpool, England
*Group / Electronica, Club/Dance, Techno*

A '90s dance act unafraid to throw a growing variety of styles (and samples) into the mix, Apollo 440 hit the British Top Ten in 1997 by sampling Van Halen for the single "Ain't Talkin' Bout Dub," and big-band drummer Gene Krupa for "Krupa." The group was formed in 1991 by Howard Gray (a former studio engineer), his brother Trevor, classically trained on the piano, and their Liverpool schoolmate Noko, formerly the guitarist in Howard Devoto's Luxuria. The group was initially influenced by Britain's acid-house explosion, and worked as remixers (sometimes under the name Stealthsonic Orchestra) for U2, EMF, and Shabba Ranks before making the leap to actual recording. The single "Astral America" appeared on the group's own Stealth Sonic Records in 1993, followed by club hits like "(Don't Fear) The Reaper" and "Krupa," both of which used an often formulaic hook borrowed from obvious musical classics of the past. Apollo 440's debut album, *Millennium Fever*, appeared in 1995, followed two years later by *Electro Glide in Blue*. The group resurfaced in early 2000 with *Getting High on Your Own Supply*. —*John Bush*

**Millenium Fever** / 1995 / Sony ♦♦♦
Besides the forging techno-pop of tracks like "Astral America" and "(Don't Fear) the Reaper," Apollo 440's debut album has several more epic-length tracks, like "Liquid Cool" and "Rumble/Spirit of America." —*John Bush*

● **Electro Glide in Blue** / Mar. 3, 1997 / Stealth/Sony ♦♦♦♦
A more satisfying album than their previous Sony effort, *Electro Glide in Blue* sees Apollo 440 moving closer to straightahead techno and away from commercial pop, a good move considering the electronic atmosphere of the times. Whether it's the Sony Playstation video-game track "Rapid Racer" or an incredibly well-done duet with former Associates vocalist Billy Mackenzie on "Pain in Any Language," Apollo 440 proves they're no strangers to the dancefloor. —*John Bush*

**Getting High on Your Own Supply** / Sep. 6, 1999 / Stealth Sonic ♦♦♦♦
No need to worry about Apollo 440 turning intelligent in the wake of electronica's growing experimental leanings. Their third album overall, *Getting High on Your Own Supply* is a ride through sampladelic breakbeat that's just as mad as 1997's *Electro Glide in Blue*. Seemingly oblivious that even their youngest listeners could spot their samples, Apollo 440 pillage Led Zeppelin and Status Quo (among others), blending styles from trance, ska, hip-hop, dub, and disco with a tossed-off feel that's quite charming. From the breakout single "Stop the Rock" to the unabashed, old-school silliness of "Cold Rock the Mic" and a remix of last year's "Lost in Space" theme which fuses black metal with jungle breakbeats, *Getting High on Your Own Supply* is another dumb but infectious party album to file alongside Fatboy Slim's *You've Come a Long Way, Baby*. —*John Bush*

## Appliance

f. 1996, Exeter, Devon, England
*Group / Experimental Rock, Indie Rock, Post-Rock/Experimental, Kraut-Rock*

Exeter, England-based post-rock trio Appliance was formed by guitarist/vocalist James Brooks, bassist Stuart Christie, and drummer David Ireland, schoolmates whose earliest music sprung from their mutual admiration of bands like Spacemen 3 and Joy Division. Upon completing their recorded debut "Weightless Conditions" for an improvisational compilation on the M.T.B. label, Christie left the group to focus on his solo project Harmony 400, with bassist Michael Parker tapped as his replacement. Honing their own contemplative, minimalist sound over the course of the EP trilogy *Organised Sound, Into Your Home* and *Time and Space* (released between July 1997 and July 1998 on the trio's own Surveillance.com label), Appliance signed to the Mute label in early 1999, soon issuing the single "Food Music"; the full-length *Manual* followed that fall. An EP named *Six Modular Pieces* was released in mid-2000. —*Jason Ankeny*

● **Manual** / Oct. 19, 1999 / Mute ♦♦♦♦
Part of the post-rock/neo-Kraut/retro-electronic revival of the late '90s, UK trio Appliance deftly sidesteps the sometimes overbearing seriousness of those tags with a warm glow to their music, as wonderfully captured on their debut *Manual*. Perhaps unsurprisingly given their home at Mute Records, Appliance calls to mind kings of electronic music Kraftwerk, but in the *Autobahn/Radioactivity* sense of gentle melancholy rather than the frigid propulsion of *Trans-Europe Express*. An even stronger touchstone is the powerful beat and equally striking ambient drift of Neu!, whose motorik percussion gets clearly referenced on "Food Music." Stereolab is a likely touchstone for the band as well, but Appliance is clever enough not to clone too much, changing the opening guitar chime of "Pre-Rocket Science" to a crisp funk wah-wah after the opening notes. Lead bandmember James Brooks delivers his lyrics flatly, not quite in a spoken word approach but only just singing them, relying on understatement to get his sometimes bemusing, sometimes creepy images across. Together he and bandmates David Ireland and Michael Parker use an astounding range of instruments (at least 50 are listed in the liner notes) to create songs that stand out; they are striking not because of their flowery complexity but due to their obsessive, trancy drive, whether on the rock-of-the-gods surge of "Throwing a Curve Ball" or on the slow-building concluding crunch of "Pacifica," or on more restrained brain fryers like the amusingly-titled "Heroes of Telemark." Appliance aren't above a wry wit as well, titling one strong, chug-trance number "Enjoy Your Nutrition," while branding others tracks with such names as "Hot Pursuit" and perhaps the all-too-appropriate "Soyuz." Though the connections to the past are strong, the trio brings out the best in their influences; while they haven't quite made a distinct mark of their own yet, the three do have a great start under their belt already. —*Ned Raggett*

**Six Modular Pieces [EP]** / Jul. 18, 2000 / Mute ♦♦
This six-track EP of audio furniture comprises a few lo-fi garage numbers with layers of textured guitars, bleep effects, and vintage synthesizers. Occasionally, the electronics are difficult to spot beneath the dense, wall-of-sound guitar effects, but Appliance contributes some solid ideas in the vein of post-rock retro-electro. —*John Bush*

## Aquasky

f. 1993, Bournemouth, Dorset, England
*Group / Electronica, Jungle/Drum'N'Bass, Club/Dance, Nu Breaks*

Originally from Bournemouth but later transplanted to London, Kieron Bailey, Brent Newitt and Dave Wallace come from a generation of junglists with neither a strict focus on breakbeats nor even a fusion of jungle with various other styles (hip-hop, reggae, jazz, etc.). The trio's recordings as Aquasky have encompassed a range of styles, some with the pristine jazzy feel of LTJ Bukem productions, others for Moving Shadow that hark back to the original hardcore spirit of drum'n'bass, and still others with a hip-hop base—and vocals from actual rappers, including Big Shug from Gang Starr.

The three were all school-chums from an early age, though their paths eventually separated; Bailey played drums for a variety of metal and funk bands, Newitt grew into an electro/hip-hop fan and break-dancer, and Wallace became a production tech-head influenced by Kraftwerk and the Art of Noise. All three were producing tracks (Bailey as Jazziac Sunflowers, Newitt as Artinis, Wallace as an engineer for both) when they decided to reunite in 1993 under the umbrella of Britain's drum'n'bass movement. Naming themselves Aquasky, the trio recorded a full dozen singles from 1993 to 1996—for Moving Shadow, Reinforced, Black on Black, Blue Bazique and their own Aqua Records—then provided a remix for the Art of Noise's *Drum & Bass Collection*. The mini-LP *Orange Dust* emerged in 1997, followed by their full-length debut *Bodyshock* two years later. Besides their alias recordings as Soul Motive and Skindivers, Wallace has also recorded as himself for Moving Shadow and All Good Vinyl. —*John Bush*

**Orange Dust** / Jul. 14, 1997 / Aqua ♦♦♦
Aquasky, much heralded for fusing a variety of styles to breakbeats, sticks mostly to polished jazzy jungle on their mini-LP for Passengers. Aside from the down-tempo hip-hop numbers "Rough" and "Raw Skillz" (with rapping by Gang Starr, Big Shug, and Kwam), the music is good, but a bit too straightahead. —*John Bush*

● **Bodyshock** / Mar. 29, 1999 / Moving Shadow ♦♦♦♦
Aquasky's first full-length is a double-disc set that appends the trio's distinctive brand of darkside breakbeat mayhem to all kinds of dance-related styles from rave to soul, dub to electro, and old-school to techno. It's quite a feat in itself, charting so many different styles yet remaining true to their jungle roots, as the wibbly bassline and neurological-warfare effects on tracks "Suspekt Device" and "Battlestar" illustrate. "Supernova" even features a bit of scratching, turntablist style, by Outkastz on the Cut. —*John Bush*

## AR Kane

f. 1986, London, England, db. 1995
*Group / Dream Pop, Alternative Dance, Alternative Pop/Rock*

Arguably the most criminally underrecognized band of their era, the British duo AR Kane anticipated virtually all of the key musical breakthroughs of the '90s a decade before the fact, with the roots of everything from shoegazing to trip-hop to ambient dub—even those of post-rock—lying in their dreamy, oceanic sound. Formed in London in 1986, AR Kane was essentially the partnership of Alex Ayuli and Rudi Tambala; hailed in the press as "the black Jesus and Mary Chain" upon debuting the following year on One Little Indian with the single "When You're Sad," they moved to 4AD later in 1987 to release the follow-up EP *Lollita*, an impressively eclectic blend of gorgeous dream-pop bliss and nightmarish squalls of feedback produced by the Cocteau Twins' Robin Guthrie.

While at 4AD, label chief Ivo Watts-Russell suggested that Ayuli and Tambala team with roster mates Martyn and Steven Young of Colourbox, champion mixer Chris "C.J." Mackintosh and London DJ Dave Dorrell to record a single fusing the rhythms and beats of classic soul recordings with state-of-the-art electronics and production. Dubbing the collaboration M/A/R/R/S, the resulting single, "Pump Up the Volume"—a breakthrough effort heralding sampling's gradual absorption from hip-hop into dance music and ultimately the pop mainstream—soon topped the British charts, the first 4AD release ever to accomplish the feat. Plans for a M/A/R/R/S follow-up never materialized, however, and AR Kane again picked up stakes, moving on to Rough Trade to begin work on their much-anticipated full-length debut.

The resulting album, 1988's *69*, fulfilled all the promise of AR Kane's earlier work and more; cosmic yet funky, its liquid grooves immersed in waves of ecstatic noise, the record's mastery of atmosphere and mood—in tandem with its nearly formless songs—establish it as a clear antecedent not only of the nascent shoegazer sound but also much of the underground dance music to emerge in the years to follow. The duo's double-LP follow-up, 1989's *i*, was even more impressive in its scope, breathlessly veering from melodic dance-pop to eerie drone-rock to epic dub mosaics. And then... nothing: only three years later did the next AR Kane LP, *Americana*—a handful of new tracks combined with past highlights—appear on the Luaka Bop label. By the time of a proper follow-up, 1994's *New Clear Child*, the moment had clearly passed. —*Jason Ankeny*

**69** / 1988 / Rough Trade ♦♦♦♦

With both early EPs and the M/A/R/R/S smash success behind them, AR Kane found themselves more than ready to go ahead with a full album in 1988, and did so wonderfully. It's safe to say that the start of the opening track alone, "Crazy Blue," resembles little else recorded that year or any other one—a few plucked guitar notes, a sudden jazzy scat-vamp by singer Rudi with his truly unique voice, then a more direct poppish strum, the woozy line, "Ooooh... everything's gone crazy now," followed by a series of intense reverbed chime sounds and bongo-like percussion. From there on in, things take a turn for the strangely captivating in song after song. Never simply poppy nor completely arty, and definitely not just the Jesus and Mary Chain/Cocteau Twins fusion most claimed they were (admittedly song titles like "Spermwhale Trip Over" and "Baby Milk Snatcher" easily led to the description!), AR Kane here feel playful, mysterious and inventive all at once, impossible to truly pin down. The best one-two punch on the record comes from "Sulliday," with buried, measured percussion and evocative drones, and "Dizzy," featuring a mesmerizing call-and-response by Rudi with himself, veering between more gentle, direct vocals and echoed shouts, eerily foretelling much of what Tricky would similarly do years later. An unfairly long-lost classic. —*Ned Raggett*

• **i** / 1989 / Rough Trade ♦♦♦♦

In retrospect, *i* now seems like a crystal ball prophesying virtually every major musical development of the '90s; from the shimmering techno of "A Love from Outer Space" to the liquid dub of "What's All This Then?," from the alien drone-pop of "Conundrum" to the sinister shoegazer miasma of "Supervixens"—it's all here, an underground road map for countless bands to follow. Breathtaking in its scope and positively epic in its ambitions, the album is loosely organized into four sonic suites containing four tracks each, broken up by a series of wild-card noise interludes; the music shifts and mutates constantly, growing progressively deeper and darker with each passing song. Largely overlooked upon its original release, *i* is still an underappreciated masterpiece, but it's inconceivable to imagine that electronica and post-rock could ever have blossomed without it. —*Jason Ankeny*

**Remixes [EP]** / 1990 / Rough Trade ♦♦♦

Nowhere near the level of unadulterated brilliance of 1989's *i*, this collection of exactly what it says it is—remixes from said record—still provides some interesting revisions of a number of AR Kane's most accessible songs. No "Supervixens" or "Down" here, but two versions of "Crack Up," along with other generally dance-friendly numbers like "Miles Apart" and "Love From Outer Space," do surface. The duo themselves remix three of the tracks, while long-time collaborator/producer Robin Guthrie does the honors with the rest. Generally, the remixes make everything a little more lighter and uncluttered—the temptation is to say everything was aimed at a radio audience, yet this being AR Kane, even at their most direct things can never be quite so broadcast-ready! Still, "Miles Apart" has much more of a sharp feel to it this out, while "Sugarwings"—already a gentle strum of a soul weeper on *i*—becomes yet more gentle and relaxed as a result. Fun if you find it, but you need to find *i* a lot more quickly! —*Ned Raggett*

**Americana** / Jan. 28, 1992 / Luaka Bop ♦♦♦♦

If nothing else, David Byrne deserves commendation for putting this out; Rough Trade's collapse the previous year left AR Kane even more obscure than before, so having some major label pull didn't hurt! While just a compilation of various tracks from their Rough Trade career, *Americana* remains much better than nothing. However, both *69* and *i* are so complete and best heard as albums than the slightly scattershot arrangement of selected tracks feels a bit odd as a result. Regardless, many of the band's most striking moments, such as "Supervixens," "A Love From Outer Space," "And I Say," and "The Madonna is With Child," appear, along with some rarities to boot. Then-new track "Water" is more slight than the usual fare, though the acoustic guitar-driven "Green Hazed Daze," from an early single, wears its Cocteauness on its sleeve strongly. The real keeper, though, is "Up," from another single—an endlessly building slow beauty of a track driven by eight repeated notes, more echo and reverb than thought possible and a quietly exultant Rudi lyric. Not a bad place to start if you can't find anything else. —*Ned Raggett*

**New Clear Child** / 1994 / Third Stone ♦♦

What proved to be the final AR Kane release also, unfortunately, turned out the least fascinating of their three studio albums. Whether it was the lengthy time away from the studio, its split recording sessions at London and San Francisco or simply a lack of spark on the part of the band, *New Clear Child* simply doesn't cut the mustard compared to the stellar heights of the band's past work. Certainly, fine moments exist nonetheless—the opening "Deep Blue Breath," accompanied by a children's choir and driven by a solid funk underpinning as well as string shadings, promises much, and Rudi's voice remains beguiling and seductive throughout as ever. Still, *New Clear Child* even at its most inspired, such as the closing, oddly-structured "Sea Like A Child" and the semi-acoustic meander of "Surf Motel," doesn't have that sense of awe and shrouded, powerful mystery which characterized *sixty-nine* or the full, sweeping command of genres of *i*, sounding too crisp, too clean, and frankly just a little too commercially anonymous smooth jazz at too many points. While still astounding compared to thousands of less-inspired albums, *New Clear Child* leaves you wishing. —*Ned Raggett*

## Archive

f. 1994, South London, England
*Group / Trip-Hop, Club/Dance*

The trip-hop project Archive was formed by Darius Keeler and Danny Griffiths, who originally met in 1990. The pair released a few singles on their own Swam label, worked with Genaside II, and formed Archive in 1994. Signed to Island, Keeler and Griffiths released their debut *Londinium* in 1997. After splitting briefly, the two re-formed and released their second album *Take My Head* on Independiente in 1999. —*John Bush*

• **Londinium** / Sep. 23, 1996 / Island ♦♦♦

The debut album from the rather mysterious (though major-label-backed) project Archive, *Londinium* sounds like R&B on Prozac: trip-hop with evocative, gauzy synth textures (some from soul samples) girded by simplistic yet effective downbeat techno. There's either a sweet-voiced female or an abstract rapper (sometimes both) on almost every cut, and plenty of organic instruments added to the mix as well; lending a hand with the guitar work on four tracks is Underworld's Rick Smith. (Archive even samples Underworld's

"MMM Skyscraper I Love You" elsewhere.) Despite an admirable production job and some enviably deep grooves, *Londinium* is just a tad too consciously stylish for its own good. —*John Bush*

### Arcon 2 (Leon Mar)

*Producer / Experimental Jungle, Jungle/Drum'N'Bass, Club/Dance*

Best known for his alternately jazzy and uplifting drum'n'bass and extreme, focused darkcore, Leon Mar (aka Fink, Noel Ram, Oil, and Arcon 2) has been producing dance tracks for the better part of a decade. At first little known in the jungle community (though his roots, like many of jungle proper's biggest names, lay firmly in hardcore), Mar rode a fast track to notoriety through a string of acclaimed releases for 4Hero's noted Reinforced label, recording such tracks as "Liquid Earth," "Silent Running," and "The Beckoning" under his own name and as Arcon 2. Mar was also included on the tough-as-nails Reinforced compilation, *Above the Law* next to such noted artists as Goldie, L Double, and Dillinja. Although Mar's earlier Reinforced material, as well as a scattering of tracks and remixes for Echo Drop and Selector mined a softer, more fusion-fueled vibe, Mar's work since "The Beckoning" (also Reinforced's first CD-EP) has tended toward the dark'n'hard, with thick, warbling bass set against snapping breaks and ominous atmospheres. Released toward the end of 1996, "The Beckoning" in particular cemented Mar's name as One to Watch in the 9-7, and subsequent work (including a jaw-dropping remix for Neotropic's Riz Maslen on her *15 Levels* EP, as well as a pair of mixes on the Future Sound of London's "We Have Explosive" maxi and the first non-FSOL release on the latter's Electronic Brain Violence label) proved as much; Mar nailed a recording deal with Warner Bros. in 1997 and released his self-titled first album later that year. —*Sean Cooper*

**The Beckoning/Skyland [Single]** / Dec. 2, 1996 / Reinforced ♦♦♦

Mar's fourth Arcon 2 release for Reinforced (and the label's first CD single!) isn't quite techstep, although the track's humming bassline and warping breaks suggest an affinity with artists such as Dom & Roland, DJ Trace, and the more progressive end of Goldie's discography. The track's bleakness, however, gave Mar big ups amongst the darkcore set, and deservedly so. —*Sean Cooper*

• **Arcon 2** / Nov. 3, 1997 / Reinforced ♦♦♦♦

Leon Mar's debut full-length is a solid, if somewhat monochromatic, collection of the dark, brooding, heavily syncopated drum'n'bass he helped develop along with artists such as Ed Rush, Dom & Roland, Source Direct, and Origin Unknown. One of the style's watermarks, "The Beckoning," is included here, but the two years that separate that track from most of the rest of *Arcon 2* do not appear to have been spent on R&D; most of the newer tracks do little to up the ante beyond adding a few instrumental embellishments (bits of guitar, flute, and muddy synth) or slowing the pace a bit (via the obligatory downtempo cuts). Listenable and among the better jungle full-lengths, but still a ways off from essential. —*Sean Cooper*

### Arkarna

f. 1994, London, England
*Group / Electronica, Alternative Dance, Club/Dance*

The techno-pop trio Arkarna was led by vocalist and programmer Ollie Jacobs, whose musical career began when he was a teenager working at his father's London recording studio, Rollover, where he handled engineering and production duties on projects for Dreadzone, Deep Forest, Leftfield, and others. Jacobs formed Arkarna with guitarist James Barnett, a onetime member of Lunarci, and guitarist Lalo Creme, the son of 10cc alum Lol Creme. Despite signing to WEA in 1995, the trio did not issue their debut single "House on Fire" until mid-1997, when it also appeared on the soundtrack to the big-budget flop *Batman and Robin;* their first LP, *Fresh Meat*, appeared a few months later. —*Jason Ankeny*

• **Fresh Meat** / Aug. 11, 1997 / Fume/Reprise ♦♦

Arkarna is one of many post-techno rock bands that attempt to fuse techno with rock 'n' roll, but instead of sounding anything like their contemporaries Prodigy, Radiohead, Chemical Brothers and DJ Shadow, they sound like descendants of Jesus Jones. There are hooks on the group's debut, *Fresh Meat*, but they are simple and repetitive, and the rhythm tracks lack complexity, while lead vocalist James Barnett's voice is almost annoyingly thin; the single "House on Fire" actually displays them at their worst instead of their best. A few cuts, such as "Eat Me," suggest that the group has the capability of making bright, melodic dance-pop, but there aren't enough similar moments to make *Fresh Meat* worthwhile. —*Stephen Thomas Erlewine*

### Armando (Armando Gallop)

b. Feb. 12, 1970, Chicago, IL, d. Dec. 17, 1996
*Producer, DJ / Club/Dance, Acid House, House*

An early acid-house pioneer while still in his teens, Armando contributed several classics to the Chicago canon during the mid-'80s, including "Land of Confusion" and "100% of Dissin' You." Born on Chicago's south side to Cuban immigrants, he was a star on the baseball field until spinal meningitis forced him out of the sport. To fill his time, he began spinning records and was organizing his own parties at the age of 16. One year later he was on the radio as well, substituting for Farley Keith on Chicago's biggest dance show, the Hot Mix 5.

Already one of the Windy City's hottest DJs around the time he received his driver's license, Armando formed Warehouse Records with Mike Dunn, just in time for his first big releases, 1988's "151" and "Land of Confusion." The latter single blew up in Chicago and quickly crossed the Atlantic, just in time for Britain's acid-house explosion. The following year Armando was on the leading edge of a return to the underground minimalist style typified by his own previous acid club-hits. He provided production on classic Warehouse tracks by Ron Trent ("Altered States"), DJ Rush ("Child Play"), and Robert Armani ("Circus Bells"), and delivered as well with another of his own club smashes, "100% of Dissin' U."

Though he worked on an album for Mike Dunn in 1993, Armando did little actual production during the early '90s, focusing instead on a residency at the seminal nightclub the Warehouse from 1992 through 1994. After working on A&R at one of the prime third-wave Chicago labels, Felix Da Housecat's Radikal Fear, he began recording again with the Radikal Fear singles "Transaxual" and "Radikal Bitch," both of which made Armando a big house favorite yet again, and the Dutch label Djax-Up-Beats licensed much of the Warehouse Records discography for release (with new-school European producers like Hardfloor and Edge of Motion providing fresh remixes for the B-sides). Armando returned the favor, recording singles for European labels including Labwerks, IDM, STR and Djax plus Americans Jive and Dance Mania. In mid-1996, after more than ten years of production, Armando finally recorded his debut album, *One World One Future*. He also appeared alongside Mike Dunn, Felix Da Housecat, DJ Sneak and Roy Davis, Jr., on the Radikal Fear LP *The Chicago All Stars*, but died of leukemia less than two months after its release. —*John Bush*

• **One World One Future** / May 13, 1996 / Play It Again Sam ♦♦♦♦

Armando's only full-length is squarely Chicago acid-house without a whiff of a sellout. Including his recent singles "Transaxual" and "Radikal Bitch," plus mixes by Cajmere and Mike Dunn, *One World One Future* manages to invigorate the 303 and 808 lines Armando had been using for over a decade with organic instruments and tight basslines. —*John Bush*

### Army of Lovers

f. 1987, Sweden
*Group / Euro-Dance, Euro-Pop*

The flamboyant multi-cultural Swedish dance-pop group Army of Lovers formed in 1987, the brainchild of composer and producer Alexander Bard. Five years earlier Bard first emerged as a member of the short-lived trio Baard, best known for the single "Life in a Goldfish Bowl." In 1985—in drag, no less—he led Barbie, a band also comprising hairdresser Jean-Pierre Barda (alias Farouk), Yazmina Chantal, and model Camilla Henemark (a.k.a. Katanga); two years later, Bard, Barda and Henemark (now performing under the name La Camilla) founded Army of Lovers, taking the name in honor of the '70s cult movie *Armee der Liebenden*.

With the aid of designer and stylist Camilla Thulin, the group created an outrageously campy image, their wardrobe drawing heavily on religious imagery while also referencing history and folklore. Army of Lovers debuted in 1988 with the single "When the Night Is Cold," followed by the more dance-minded "Love Me Like a Loaded Gun." After scoring a 1989 hit with "Supernatural," the following year they issued their debut LP *Disco Extravaganza* (issued in the US as *Army of Lovers*). 1991's *Massive Luxury Overdose*, recorded with producer Anders Wollbeck, was their breakthrough; in tandem with a pair of lurid videos, the singles "Crucified" and "Obsession" became club hits, and the group became major stars in their native Scandanavia and throughout Eastern Europe.

In the wake of the record's success, however, La Camilla was fired and replaced by model and school teacher Michaela Dornonville de la Cour, who debuted on the single "Judgment Day." After recording music for the soundtrack to the film *Ha Ett Underbart Liv,* Army of Lovers recruited former phone-sex operator Dominika Peczynski and released 1993's *The Gods of Earth and Heaven;* the single "Israelism" became the subject of considerable controversy when it was accused of mocking Jewish culture, but ironically rose to the number one spot on the Israeli pop charts. After 1994's *Glory Glamour and Gold,* de la Cour exited, paving the way for the return of La Camilla prior to the release of the 1996 *Les Greatest Hits.* With Army of Lovers on hiatus, Bard formed a new group, Vacuum, and issued 1997's *The Plutonium Cathedral;* La Camilla, meanwhile, mounted a solo career. —*Jason Ankeny*

### Army of Lovers / Aug. 13, 1991 / Giant ♦♦♦

The portentous intro song "Birds of Prey" sounds like something that could have been poached by Marilyn Manson in later years. Here, though, the massive electronic bombast is strictly for campy fun rather than making any sort of serious statement—Army of Lovers in a nutshell, and bless them for it. Its self-titled release fuses Eurodisco's pulse and sheen (and at points the all-important string swirls, as "Ride the Bullet" merrily shows) with gay abandon in all senses of the word. The Army doesn't quite hit the heights that Deee-Lite served up with its own delicious debut *World Clique,* from the same year, but comes awfully close. Earlier hits "Supernatural" and "Love Me Like a Loaded Gun" appear with a slew of similarly minded songs (great titles abound—some standouts: "Mondo Trasho" and "I Am the Amazon"). Bard's deliciously creamy and politely sleazy vocals and sense of style give the whole thing an outre but perfect elegance, while Barda and La Camilla round out things with their own presence as well. If not as distinct in terms of singing and performance compared to other dance divas, they still lend a lovely *joie de vivre* to Bard's tales of laser sex and dance explosions. Due credit has to also go to Magnus Frykberg, who cowrote nearly everything with Bard and whose synth work blends the all-important beat with a consistent lushness in sound. The Army aren't afraid to play around with house, hip-hop and various worldbeat percussion styles, adding just that little bit more to all the goings-on. Quirky samples sneak in at points as well, from *The Andy Griffith Show*'s whistled theme to the "ooga-chuckas" from "Hooked on a Feeling." Add to that such delectabilities as the French vocals on "Scorpio Rising" and random theremin noises, and the Army begins its mission in full effect. —*Ned Raggett*

### Massive Luxury Overdose / Mar. 17, 1992 / Giant ♦♦♦♦

Some album titles do nail it, and this is one of the prime candidates. From the near-cartoonishly foppish front cover photo, with the three members primed with necklaces, silk kaftans, airbrushing and more, to nearly everything on the actual disc, *Overdose* is just that. The most memorable number remains the band's biggest hit single, "Crucified," a totally over-the-top disco anthem on all fronts that takes ABBA's winning combination of memorable hooks and harmonies as inspiration and slathers a load of glitter and make-up over the whole thing. Having ultracampy lyrical asides like "I cry, I pray, mon dieu" doesn't hurt the sheer giddiness at work, and neither do the "I'm crucified like my saviour" chorus, church organ and twangy Duane Eddy guitar. The Army's merry series of blasphemies kicks along throughout the album, with such numbers as the half-twinky, half-ominous "Candyman Messiah" and "Say Goodbye to Babylon" taking religious imagery and tweaking it for all it's worth. New singer De La Cour does a fine job in La Camilla's shoes, though the latter pops up on a song or two throughout the album. The fondness for ritzy sci-fi scenarios still runs riot, as song titles like "Dynasty of Planet Chromada," "The Particle Song" and "Walking With a Zombie" make clear, while the same sticky-sweet combination of upbeat anthems and try-anything-at-least-once musical touches gets even more amped up here. Andreas Wollbeck rather than Frykberg is the main outside collaborator with Bard here, but the change isn't a notable one in comparison to the previous album, except for a general tendency towards big songs with bigger choruses. At points the Army ends up sounding like a clipped and discoed B-52s (check out "We Stand United"), but in general it's just them inhabiting their own little corner of dancefloor paradise, fripperies and all. —*Ned Raggett*

### Gods of Earth and Heaven / Jun. 1, 1993 / Alex ♦♦♦♦

Along with the controversial hit "Israelism," Army of Lovers' third LP *The Gods of Earth and Heaven* features the singles "La Plage de Saint Tropez" and "I Am." —*Jason Ankeny*

### • Les Greatest Hits / 1995 / Ils International ♦♦♦♦

*Les Greatest Hits* remains the best introduction to Army of Lovers' music; along with the singles "Supernatural," "Crucified," "Obsession" and "Israelism," it also features the new tracks "Give My Life," "Venus and Mars" and "Requiem." —*Jason Ankeny*

## Arovane (Uwe Zahn)

b. 1965, Hameln, Germany
*Producer / Experimental Techno, Electro-Techno, IDM*

Berlin's Uwe Zahn released his first tracks as the *Arovane* EP on the Din label, which also released the first of German dub minimalist Stefan Betke's work as Pole. Stylistically, Arovane's work hearkens back to the insular melodic electro of early Autechre, combining interesting, highly syncopated machine box rhythms with warm, delicate synth textures that evoke a gauzy, somewhat nostalgic mood contrasted by the sharpness of the rhythms. Indeed, while Autechre's *Amber* has become a touchpoint of sorts for a whole new generation of laptop do-it-yourselfers whose music rarely rises above tribute, Zahn's Arovane work is a legitimate extension of an aesthetic left largely unfinished, and is some of the most interesting and accomplished music of its kind. Fans of Ae, Funkstorung, Higher Intelligence Agency, and Phoenecia take note. After the *Arovane* EP, two additional EPs for Din (*Icol Diston, AMX*) preceded the release of Arovane's LP debut, *Atol Scrap.* Later that year, *Tides* appeared on City Centre Offices. —*Sean Cooper*

### Arovane [EP] / 1998 / Din ♦♦♦♦

Four tracks of wonderfully affecting melodic downtempo electro recalling the less fidgety works of Autechre and Funkstörung. Arovane's melodic instincts are among the sharpest in the post-techno underground, and his ability to weave layer upon layer of watery synth through complex, multipart rhythms is often breathtaking. An excellent debut. —*Sean Cooper*

### Icol Diston [EP] / 1999 / Din ♦♦♦♦

Arovane's second EP is a bit more uptempo than the first, and the arrangements are less complex . But the emotive deepness that characterized Uwe Zahn's debut EP is here in full, proving he's capable of warm, engaging music in a variety of styles and moods. —*Sean Cooper*

### Atol Scrap / Jan. 25, 2000 / Din ♦♦♦♦

*Atol Scrap* features a full hour of some of the most intriguing electronic listening music recorded during the late '90s. Uwe Zahn's productions balance two competing sides of electronics with apparent ease. On one side, the warm and inviting; on the other, the relentlessly technical and complex. There've been plenty of producers who've excelled at either heavily processed rhythms *or* haunted melodies (think Autechre and Boards of Canada, respectively), but *Atol Scrap* documents the emergence of that rare artist who displays astonishing skills at both. Zahn flashes his Berlin credentials with the calm, faraway ambience of "Scapen Te," similar to Chain Reaction producers like Monolake, Pole, and Porter Ricks. On several tracks ("Norvum," "Revart Amx"), though, he experiments with complex rhythms, revealing ties to the growing crowd of DSP (digital signal processing) artists led by Autechre and Oval. In a way listeners could hardly have imagined, Arovane has it both ways and doesn't cave to either side. —*John Bush*

### • Tides / 2000 / Din ♦♦♦♦

In a time when debut films, plays, or novels are seen as the sole make-or-break factor in an artist's career, one should still never underestimate a creative force that truly doesn't come into its own until at least the second time around. This is why Arovane's *Tides* should be a testament to waiting to see how something develops rather than letting it all fade away too soon. It is— surprisingly—a lovely, lilting album of electronic class. Few people could have predicted the quantum leap of quality between the debut and this release. As soon as the first track—"Theme"—begins, one knows things are different: a harpsichord trills over waves of big, slow beats, a languid pace lives on yet with a progression that keeps it breathing, and everything sounds, well, correct. True, where Arovane seemed much too eager to ape idols such as Aphex Twin or Autechre in 1999's debut *Atol Scrap,* the goal here seems to be to take a different tack: try and outdo Boards of Canada. Where Boards of Canada excelled was in the endlessly fascinating dynamic between gorgeous melodies and absolutely huge basslines. In *Tides,* Arovane seems to have taken such a delightful premise and carried it through from a new vantage point. So you get the ambient thumps of songs like "A Secret" (with enough high swishes to leave you wanting more), the rumbling, slow breaks of songs like "The Storm" (with a layering of melodies that demands to be appreciated), or even the subtle crescendo of songs like "Epilogue." Indeed, if Arovane's debut was trying to be magnetic with piddling about, this follow-up is just hypnotic due to good old fashioned songwriting. Again, it's true that one shouldn't underestimate second albums. *Tides* might not capture that sheer dynamic exquisiteness of a release like *Music Has the Right to Children*, yet its ideals are often just as splendorous. Surprisingly short, sweet, and not too many bloops and bleeps. This is just about everything that minimalist electronic musicians should try and emulate. *Tides* is beautiful work. —*Dean Carlson*

## The Art of Noise

f. Jan. 1984, London, England
*Group / Experimental Rock, New Wave, Synth-Pop*

Anne Dudley, Gary Langan, and Paul Morley were members of producer Trevor Horn's in-house studio band in the early '80s before they formed Art of Noise, a techno pop group whose music was an amalgam of studio gimmickry, tape splicing, and synthesized beats. The Art of Noise took material from a variety of sources: hip-hop, rock, jazz, R&B, traditional pop, found sounds, and noise all worked their way into the group's distinctly postmodern soundscapes.

Dudley was the center of the group, having arranged and produced material for Frankie Goes to Hollywood, ABC, and Paul McCartney before forming the Art of Noise. The trio signed with Trevor Horn's ZTT label, releasing their first EP, *Into Battle with the Art of Noise*, in 1983. The following year, the group released the full-length *(Who's Afraid Of?) The Art of Noise!*, which featured the hit single "Close (To the Edit)."

After "Close (To the Edit)," the group parted ways with Horn and ZTT, releasing *In Visible Silence* in 1986; the album included the UK Top Ten hit "Peter Gunn," which featured Duane Eddy on guitar. *Re-works of the Art of Noise*, an album of remixes and live tracks, was released that same year. *In No Sense? Nonsense!*, released in 1987, saw the band experimenting with orchestras and choirs, as well as horns and rock bands. The next year, the Art of Noise released a greatest-hits collection, *The Best of the Art of Noise*, which featured their collaboration with Tom Jones on Prince's "Kiss."

*Below the Waste* (1990) captured the band experimenting with world music; it received a lukewarm critical and commercial reception. The following year, a low-key remix album directed by Killing Joke's Youth called *The Ambient Collection* appeared. Later in the year, the Art of Noise broke up. Dudley eventually worked with Killing Joke's Jaz Coleman and Phil Collins. Horn and Dudley reunited in 1999 for a new album, *The Seduction of Claude Debussy*. —*Stephen Thomas Erlewine*

### Art of Noise / 1983 / ZTT/Island ♦♦♦

The Art of Noise debuted with this long, ten-track EP (also called *The Art of Noise*), dominated by tracks like "Beat Box" (#1 dance/disco), a collage of steady bass drum beats and sound effects. No use looking for embedded meaning; this was surface sound all the way. If you wanted, you could dance to it, but its real function may have been as a new kind of background music. —*William Ruhlmann*

### Into Battle with the Art of Noise [EP] / 1983 / ZTT/Island ♦♦♦

The title says it all, because Art of Noise were probably one of the most combative bands around at the time, tackling preconceptions of what music is and how to write it, and combining modern technology and avant-garde techniques to create stunning new fusions. The impact of early tracks can still be felt today, and even if something like "Moments in Love" seems like nothing but an easy instrumental, the unnerving, ominous midsection breaks the orchestrated mood until a sudden flourish of harps returns everything back to a now-uncertain calm. The remainder of the EP's tracks are quick and almost fragmentary but show the group having fun with touches and approaches that would be brought to bear elsewhere: the orchestral stabs and ominous flow of "Donna," the brutal percussion stomp of "Flesh in Armour," and the cut-up revamp of the Andrews Sisters and "The Army Now." One listen to *Into Battle with the Art of Noise* and some of the influences in industrial, hip-hop, techno, and pop become clearer. —*Ned Raggett*

### (Who's Afraid Of?) The Art of Noise! / 1984 / ZTT/Island ♦♦♦♦

Art of Noise's first full album consolidated the future shock of the earlier EPs and singles in one entertaining and often frightening and screwed up package. Rarely has something aiming for modern pop status also sought to destroy and disturb so effectively. The most legendary song is still "Close (To the Edit)," benefiting not merely from the innovative video but from its strong funk groove and nutty sense of humor in the mostly lyricless vocals, not to mention the "Hey!" vocal hook the Prodigy would sample for "Firestarter." Its close cousin, the title track, brilliantly blends a nagging bass synth, echoed drum, and percussion fills, and constantly shifting vocal cut-ups, random noises, and strange melodies. They're just two highlights on this prescient release, though. Part of the thrill of *Who's Afraid* is the sense of juxtaposition and playing around, something still not very common in music and even less so in the pop music genre. The blunt political protest of "A Time for Fear (Who's Afraid)" and the more abstract "How to Kill," achieved via appropriate sampling, slams right up against the rough beat sonics and serene orchestration. If such material had appeared on Rephlex or even DHR in the mid- to late '90s, few would have been surprised. Things aren't all dour and gloomy, though; "Beat Box" captures heavy grooves from said source with quirky vocal bits and soft vibes. Patented Trevor Horn orchestral stabs surface throughout, while Anne Dudley's knack for gentler shadings and dramatic arrangements also comes through clearly, something that would surface ever more strongly in her freelance production career. The full ten-minute version of "Moments in Love" is perhaps her triumph here, a seemingly pretty instrumental turned increasingly strange. —*Ned Raggett*

### In Visible Silence / 1986 / China/Chrysalis ♦♦♦

AON hit their stride with the release of this record, while showing their colors in the choices of material—while the usual offbeat AON elements were present, so was "Peter Gunn," with Duane Eddy guesting on guitar. Another AON hit, "Legs," was present, as was the original version of "Paranoimia," enhanced in its single versions by the addition of routines from Max Headroom performed by Matt Frewer, who would later play the digital ding-a-ling on a short-lived TV series. The Frewer versions replaced the original on some pressings, including the original CD, but the original version has since been restored, with both Frewer versions now confined to best-of collections. —*Steven McDonald*

### Daft / 1987 / Import ♦♦

The place for Art of Noise neophytes to start, *Daft* collects *(Who's Afraid Of?) The Art of Noise!* and *Into Battle with the Art of Noise*, along with two reworkings of "Moments in Love" from the original UK release of that song, to make a fantastic hour's worth of music. If anything, a single or two aside, *Daft* beats out the official *Best Of* compilation by a mile. Having aged superbly with time, AON's early works sound all the more advanced and of-the-moment, a testament especially to Trevor Horn's excellent production and Anne Dudley's gripping arrangements. Further entertainment comes from the liner notes, which aren't merely state-of-the-art 1984 album design but an apparently barbed attack on the further incarnation of the band from one Otto Flake. The exact seriousness of this is up to the reader. As for the "Moments in Love" versions, both are gentler and elegant than the already lush original, and none the worse for that, though "(Three Fingers Of) Love" does have rather disconcerting sound effects added to it. —*Ned Raggett*

### ● The Best of the Art of Noise / 1988 / China ♦♦♦♦

All of the Art of Noise's best tracks are here, including "Close (To the Edit)," "Legacy," and a cover of Prince's "Kiss" with Tom Jones on lead vocals. —*Stephen Thomas Erlewine*

### The Drum & Bass Collection / Oct. 14, 1996 / Discovery ♦♦♦

The third in a series of reworkings of Art of Noise hits like "Peter Gunn" and "Kiss" focuses on drum-and-bass remixes characterized by lightning-fast break beats and moody sonic textures. Among the remixers are Doc Scott, Lemon D and Jay Majik of the Metalheadz label. —*Jason Ankeny*

### Fon Mixes / Jan. 14, 1997 / Discovery ♦♦

The Prodigy, LFO, Youth, and 808 State's Graham Massey are among the featured artists on this collection of rave mixes created at Sheffield, England's Fon Studios. —*Jason Ankeny*

### The Seduction of Claude Debussy / Jun. 15, 1999 / ZTT/Universal ♦♦

More than ten years after the Art of Noise left Trevor Horn's ZTT label to record on their own, original members Anne Dudley and Paul Morley reunited with Horn plus 10cc's Lol Creme to record another LP, organized around the work of French modernist composer Claude Debussy. With a guest list including John Hurt as well as Rakim, the album charts the artistic use of sampled breakbeats—pioneered by the Art of Noise themselves—with nods to '80s hip-hop plus their '90s equivalent, drum'n'bass. Though the Art of Noise doesn't sound quite as brash as they did in their '80s prime, *The Seduction of Claude Debussy* is an interesting showcase of what made the group great. —*Keith Farley*

## Artificial Material (Adam Lee Miller)
*Producer / Electro-Techno, Detroit Techno*

Artificial Material is the solo project of Adam Lee Miller, a founding member of Detroit electro/new wavers Le Car. Also the man behind the Ersatz Audio and Monoplaza imprints, Miller's solo AM material has appeared in a pretty even split between his own label and the Cologne-based electro imprint Electrecord (with the tracks "Foreign Motel" and "Wireless Intercom" both making it onto Studio !K7's *Electrecord 2000* compilation). In addition to the label's debut release, Miller's second AM release for his own label was a four-track split 12" with Electrecord's Third Electric; entitled "Duologue," the EP's two AM tracks are quite representative, pairing thin, minimal electronics with pronounced, new wave-derived two-beat rhythms and bouncy, exaggerated analog basslines. Miller's musical roots unsurprisingly reflect this connection; although he grew up on the same brand of Detroit techno and electro as contemporaries like AUX 88 and Will Web, his passion lay primarily with first-wave European electro-pop innovators such as Visage, Soft Cell, the Normal, and John Foxx. Miller studied art history and remains active in painting. He formed Ersatz Audio and Monoplaza with fellow Le Car members Ian R. Clark and Robert Salzmann in 1995, after tiring of waiting for the numerous European labels interested in releasing their work to actually follow through on licensing; a self-titled Artificial Material album appeared later that year, followed in 1997 by *Duologue*. —*Sean Cooper*

**Artificial Material** / 1995 / Ersatz Audio ♦♦

● **Duologue [Single]** / Jul. 28, 1997 / Ersatz Audio ♦♦♦
"Duologue" is a 4-track split single with Ersatz Audio's own Artificial Material and Cologne-based neo-electro duo Third Electric. The AM side is uptempo two-beat new wave/electro fusion at its best, with quirky, oddly musical electronics and thin, clunky rhythms. 3E's half is typically outstanding, as well, with one deep, ambient-ish downtempo number and one bizarro uptempo snarefest submerged in a pool of reverb. —*Sean Cooper*

## As One (Kirk Degiorgio)
*Producer / Jazz-House, Electronica, Ambient Techno, Club/Dance, Techno, IDM*

As One's Kirk Degiorgio is one of the lesser recognized key players in the UK techno underground. While his visionary fusions of Detroit soul and cold, crystalline tech on records such as *Reflections* and *Celestial Soul* have earned him a strong reputation as a producer, Degiorgio has been as influential on the label front, with his Applied Rhythmic Technologies (A.R.T.) and more recent Op-Art imprints contributing greatly to the birth and continuing vitality of the UK experimental techno/electronica scenes often more closely associated with and credited to labels such as Rephlex and Warp. Formed in 1991, A.R.T. released early tracks from Black Dog, B12/Redcell/Stasis, and Neuropolitique, and helped bring wider attention to a core of UK artists working in a vein inspired by (but not simply reducible to) the music's Detroit originators. Although the label has gained wider acknowledgment through co-release projects with names such as Rephlex, B12, and New Electronica (with two label comps titled *Objets d'Art* released on the latter), A.R.T. remains something of a connoisseur's choice, with limited releases that tend to disappear soon after they're released. Degiorgio slowed A.R.T.'s already leisurely release schedule in 1996, establishing Op-Art as a more artist-oriented label geared toward wider exposure.

With his own material, Degiorgio has released records through A.R.T. and R&S (as Future/Past), as well as New Electronica and future funk Rephlex breakaway Clear (under his As One guise). Degiorgio's music dwells most often on his split affinity for Carl Craig/Derrick May-style Detroit gear and an ongoing commitment to the mid-'70s experimental jazz and funk fusions of Herbie Hancock and Miles Davis. The latter influence is less evident on his earlier A.R.T. and New Electronica records (such as *Reflections* and *Celestial Soul*), which tend to stick to a comparatively more conservative dancefloor framework, but his late-'90s R&S and Clear material moved progressively to the fringes of techno/jazz fusion, particularly in the increasingly bold keyboard work. His debut Clear release, *The Message in Herbie's Shirts* (a tribute to Hancock, whose artistic evolution, Degiorgio somewhat facetiously claims, can be traced through the styles of shirt worn on the sleeves of his records), though hardly characteristic of the label, became one of its strongest, most consistent releases. After compiling his complete Clear material on the CD collection *In with Their ARPs and Moogs and Jazz and Things*, Degiorgio closed out an active 1997 with the release of his first album for Mo'Wax, *Planetary Folklore*. —*Sean Cooper*

**Reflections** / Oct. 1994 / New Electronica ♦♦♦♦
As on other notable Brit-techno debut LPs from *Bytes* to *Electro-Soma*, the first As One album distills the influences of a very Detroit-styled attendance on moody melodies and intricate percussion programming. Tracks like "Mihara" and "Asa Nisi Masa" use an assortment of fragile effects and synth lines to bely the complex, phased rhythm patterns bubbling underneath. The first fruits of Degiorgio's worldbeat bent are visible with song titles including "Dance of the Uighurs" and "Moon Over the Moab." —*John Bush*

**Celestial Soul** / 1995 / New Electronica ♦♦
Kirk Degiorgio's second album recorded under As One moves farther away from the techno-soul of his debut, using harder beats and a wider range of styles. —*John Bush*

**The Message in Herbie's Shirts [EP]** / May 27, 1996 / Clear ♦♦♦
Herbie being Herbie Hancock, Kirk Degiorgio's main influence and the subject here of a humorous correlation of fashion and aesthetic epoch. While Degiorgio's music probably won't be drawing any V.S.O.P. heads to his side of the techno/jazz divide any time soon, the record does fill in aspects of Degiorgio's stylistic impetus perhaps lacking on earlier albums such as the dark, somewhat spacey *Celestial Soul*. Mostly techno here, of course, but with a funked-up, jazzy edge and occasional breakbeat selection combining a range of sounds and styles with a straying, blustery flair. —*Sean Cooper*

**The Art of Prophecy** / Feb. 10, 1997 / PIAS ♦♦♦
The last album of metallic Detroit-style techno before Degiorgio departed for a trip through electro-jazz-funk, *The Art of Prophecy* hardly lacks for dense percussion on tracks like "Relentless," "Theme from Op-Art" and "The Hideout." —*John Bush*

**In with Their ARPs and Moogs and Jazz and Things** / May 26, 1997 / Clear ♦♦♦♦
*In with Their ARPs* is only half the distinct album it appears; it actually repeats the whole of As One's 1995 Clear LP, *The Message in Herbie's Shirts*, and adds a quartet of new tracks which improve on that album's somewhat spotty complexion. Like the preceding album, the new tracks still cluster around a sturdy combo of soul, jazz, and funk influences, but the results are smoother and less gimmicky, as if Digiorgio finally stopped paying attention to the label it was coming out on (Clear's rep for quirky playground gear is by now well-known) and focused instead on the music. —*Sean Cooper*

★ **Planetary Folklore** / Nov. 3, 1997 / Mo'Wax ♦♦♦♦♦
*Planetary Folklore* is a sparkling synthesis of Degiorgio's percussion-heavy early Detroit material with the exploratory Afro-grooves of Herbie Hancock's *Mwandishi* period and contemporary work by Pharoah Sanders. The title track and "The Path of Most Resistance" make deft use of some hair-triggered percussion samples, while "Amalia's Mode" and "Libran Legacy" are solid summations of Degiorgio's inspiration from the early-'70s intersection of free jazz and electronics. —*John Bush*

## Ash Ra Tempel
f. 1970, Berlin, Germany
*Group / Experimental Rock, Space-Rock, Kraut-Rock, Prog-Rock/Art Rock*

Along with Tangerine Dream, Ash Ra Tempel (later Ashra) was one of the first bands to convert the trippier side of late-'60s psychedelia into the *kosmische* rock of the '70s. Most Ash Ra titles were solely the work of Manuel Göttsching, plus any other additional players who happened to be around during the recording of his ten albums. Göttsching trained in classical guitar and studied improvisational music plus electronics at school. In 1970, he formed Ash Ra Tempel with no less than Klaus Schulze (fresh from a brief stint in Tangerine Dream) and Hartmut Enke. After a self-titled album in 1971, Schulze left for a solo career; Göttsching continued on with a variety of band-members and guests, including Timothy Leary on 1973's *Seven Up* (and Schulze again, for *Join Inn*).

By 1975, Göttsching had released his first solo album (*Inventions for Electric Guitar*) and though *Ashra* returned the following year, the next two records by the "group" were Göttsching-only albums, the brilliant *New Age of Earth* in 1976 and *Blackouts* one year later. For the '80s, most Ashra LPs were band-setting albums (with the assistance of guitarist Lutz Ulbrich and drummer Harald Grosskopf) while Göttsching solo records (like the landmark *E2-E4*) were, truly, solo records. He also reunited with Schulze to work on Alphaville's 1989 LP, *The Breathtaking Blue*. [See Also: Manuel Göttsching] *—John Bush*

### Ash Ra Tempel / 1971 / Ohr ♦♦♦

In light of the '90s post-rock scene and the often clear links back to Krautrock of all stripes, Ash Ra Tempel's monster debut album stands as being both astonishingly prescient and just flat out good, a logical extension of the space-jam-freakout ethos into rarified realms. Featuring the original trio of Enke, Gottsching and Schulze, *Ash Ra Tempel* consists of only two side-long tracks, both of which are gripping examples of technical ability mixed with rock power. If more progressive music was like it, there wouldn't be as many continuing complaints about that genre as a whole. "Amboss" contains the more upfront explosions of sound, though it mixes in restraint as much as crunch. Starting with Gottsching's extended guitar notes and Schulze's cymbals, it begins with a slow, ominous build that is equally haunting, as mysterious as the cryptic artwork of temples and figures found on the inside. Quick, rumbling drums slowly fade up some minutes in, with more crashing guitar mixing in with the previous tones, creating a disorienting drone experience. The active jam then takes over the rest of the song at the point, the three going off just as they want to (Gottsching's soloing in particular is fantastic) before all coming back together for an explosive, shuddering series of climaxes. "Traummaschine," in marked contrast, is a quieter affair, with Gottsching's deep drones setting and continuing the tone throughout. Fading in bit by bit, the guitars are accompanied by equally mesmerizing keyboards from Schulze, creating something that calls to mind everything from Eno's ambient works to Lull's doom-laden soundscapes and, after more distinct guitar pluckings start to surface, Flying Saucer Attack's rural psychedelia. Halfway through, soft percussion blends with the music to create a gentle but persistent intensity, cue for a series of shifts between calmer and more active sections, but all kept more restrained than on "Amboss." *—Ned Raggett*

### Schwingungen / 1972 / Ohr ♦♦♦♦

An otherworldly fusion of space music, blues-rock and free jazz, *Schwingungen* begins with two extended jams that trade some bluesy solos and fuzz guitars plus the tremulous vocals of Göttsching himself. Side two is an entirely different proposition, beginning with a spare vibes/electronics duet that gradually works into a deep cosmic-rock jam. Göttsching and the band appear to be still exploring their late-'60s influences (Cream, Hendrix, Pink Floyd) but are already embarked on a *kosmische* journey unlike any other band. *—John Bush*

### Join Inn / 1973 / Ohr ♦♦♦

Ash Ra became a working power-trio for *Join Inn*, with Göttsching on guitar, Hartmut Enke on bass and space-rock hero Klaus Schulze on drums, organ and synth. The title of the A-side ("Freak 'N' Roll") sums up the music quite well, while the B-side "Jenseits" is a prescient *kosmische* jam with occasional voicings from Rosi Mueller. *—John Bush*

### Seven-Up / 1973 / Komische ♦♦

Even with the presence of special guest Timothy Leary, *Seven Up* sticks to its predecessor's penchant for bizarre bluesy psychedelia on the first side while the second takes off into the deepest realms of space-rock. Fans of Leary may be a bit surprised, since he's but one of the five voices sprinkled throughout the album, and sounds more like a poor man's Eric Burdon than an acid visionary might on tracks like "Right Hand Lover," "Downtown" and "Power Drive." Side two consists of three drawn-out space jams that conclude with a rushing of air quite close to a vacuum cleaner. Except for the last bit, *Seven Up* is not quite the meeting of minds that acid and Kraut fans expected. *—John Bush*

### Starring Rosi / 1973 / Komische ♦♦♦

Including more vocals (from guest Rosi Mueller) than any early Ash Ra LP, *Starring Rosi* spans guitar-virtuoso experimental rock on "Laughter Loving," fairy-tale acoustic pop on "Day Dream," and *kosmische* philosophy on "Interplay of Forces." Though it smacks of a school lesson (with Göttsching showing off his skills in a number of different styles), the album holds together surprisingly well. *—John Bush*

### ● New Age of Earth / 1976 / Virgin ♦♦♦♦

The title was more prophetic than most—though *Earth* thankfully isn't quite so bathetic as any number of releases on Windham Hill, by this point Gottsching was well into his electronic phase, the jam freakouts of the earliest albums replaced by a clean, crisp electronic bed. Unlike the rigorous pulse of fellow Kraut-rock pioneers Kraftwerk, though, Gottsching generally favored a more consciously playful and simply beautiful approach, aiming to create pleasant music to just enjoy and relax to. If not as serious and avant-garde as other artists, Gottsching was still coming up with the goods, so quite why his later albums have been generally ignored in comparison remains a mystery. Opening track "Sunrain" sounds like it could soundtrack a narrativeless documentary on just that, or at least some sequence of nature photography; bright and sparkling, the synths and drum machines blend together nicely. "Ocean of Tenderness" has a similar sense of film accompaniment, being a gentle, minimal flow of keyboard shading, electronic chirps deep in the mix, and a soft lead melody that carefully unwinds throughout the lengthy track, with a low-key bass pulse appearing a few minutes in as contrast. "Deep Distance" lives up to the title nicely, combining sweetly spaced-out drones with minimal percussion that sounds like raindrops as much as anything else as lead melodies slowly come to the fore. "Nightdust," which takes up the original second side of the album, captures the original psych-jam feeling of Ash Ra Tempel more than anything else. A lengthy Gottsching guitar solo, heavily processed and extremely trebly, begins the piece over a series of soft synth shadings, leading to a marvelous composition with chilly, spectral keyboards and, later, deep electronic pulses and more straightforward guitar. It's a spectacular performance, showing that even on his own Gottsching's fire was still present, though aimed in other directions. *—Ned Raggett*

### Blackouts / 1977 / Virgin ♦♦♦♦

For *Blackouts*, Gottsching tied series of rather unobtrusive sequencer trance to either multiple, interlocking guitar lines (as on the brilliant opener "77 Slightly Delayed") or to his flighty solos, reminiscent of similarly spacey work by Steve Hillage. *—John Bush*

### Correlations / 1979 / Virgin ♦♦♦

With the addition of guitarist Lutz Ulbrich and drummer Harald Grosskopf, Ashra became a full-fledged band for the first time in several years. No surprise, then, that tracks like "Ice Train" and "Club Cannibal" are quite rock-oriented even with Göttsching's continued reliance on an assortment of synthesizers. *Correlations* still has some fine moments, though they're more tied to proto-synth-pop than the space music of past Ashra classics. *—John Bush*

### Join Inn/Starring Rosi / Jul. 7, 1998 / Cleopatra ♦♦

### Schwingungen/Seven-Up / Jul. 14, 1998 / Cleopatra ♦♦♦♦

## Asian Dub Foundation

f. 1993, Farringdon, England
*Group / Electronica, Club/Dance, Alternative Pop/Rock*

Asian Dub Foundation formed in 1993 as an outgrowth of the documentary *Identical Beat*, a film shot at London's Farringdon Community Music House, the site of a series of summer workshops designed to teach Asian children the essentials of music technology. In charge of the workshops were tutor Aniruddha Das and youth worker John Pandit, also a noted DJ; with one of their students, a 15-year-old Bengali rapper named Deedar Zaman, they soon formed a sound system which they called the Asian Dub Foundation. After each adopted an alias—bassist/tabla player Das became Dr. Das, Pandit became Pandit G, and Zaman became Master D—they gradually evolved into a working band with the 1994 addition of former Higher Intelligence Agency guitarist Steve Chandra Savale, an innovative performer known for tuning his strings to one note like a sitar, turning up the distortion unit and playing his instrument with a knife, earning him the knickname "Chandrasonic." Emerging in the midst of considerable anti-Asian violence throughout Britain, the Foundation's early demos landed them a contract with Nation Records, and they recorded their debut EP *Conscious* in 1994.

Channeling influences ranging from punk to ambient music to Bengali folk songs, Asian Dub Foundation quickly gained a strong fanbase not only among clubgoers but also among the anti-fascist movement, who applauded the group's vocal stand against racism. After earning a reputation as standout live performers, the band—which now included dancer Bubble-E and second DJ Sun-J—won widespread acclaim for the 1995 single "Rebel Warrior." Their first full-length effort, *Facts and Fictions*, followed later that same year, and in 1998 Asian Dub Foundation returned with *Rafi's Revenge*. *Community Music* appeared in mid-2000. *—Jason Ankeny*

**Facts and Fictions** / 1995 / Nation ♦♦♦
Asian Dub Foundation's album debut finds the band with their chops fully intact, even at this early date. Dr. Das' rapping flow is speedy and intricate, though continually inflected in the same ways (very reminiscent of Rage Against the Machine's Zack de la Rocha). The production and programming, by Steve Chandrasonic and Dr. Das, is the real highlight here, incorporating traditional Indian percussion and instruments, but constantly name-checking contemporary dance styles like bhangra and ragga jungle. The haunting vocals that open "Rebel Warrior" make it a highlight, while Chandra's deep drum programs provide continual thrills. —*John Bush*

● **Rafi's Revenge** / Nov. 3, 1998 / PolyGram ♦♦♦♦
Much of the really interesting music coming out of England in the late '90s is being produced by members of what has come to be called the Asian Underground—a dancehall aristocracy of mostly South Asian DJs, producers, dub artists and instrumentalists who seem bent on completely transforming the UK dance-music scene into a welter of wildly various and pan-ethnic influences: bhangra, dub, ragga, funk, speed-rap and metal, even surf guitar and classical Hindustani music all get thrown into the stew, and the result is thick, spicy and delicious. On this release from Asian Dub Foundation, that vision is realized in tracks that blend Indian percussion with reggae basslines and jungle breakbeats, as on the head-banging "Buzzin'," or which combine a straight one-drop reggae beat with Indian keyboard and pop vocal samples, as on "Black White." The singing is paradigmatic: vocalist Deeder sings and shouts in an accent divided in equal parts between Cockney, Indian and Jamaican. This is an exhausting but exhilarating album, and its depth and complexity of texture keeps revealing new surprises with repeated listenings. —*Rick Anderson*

**R.A.F.I.** / Jul. 25, 2000 / Virgin ♦♦
On *R.A.F.I.*, the Asian Dub Foundation further refine their sound, honing their blend of miscellaneous styles—ragga, jungle, dub, rock, hip-hop, rap—to a consistent aesthetic characterizing each of the songs and the album as a whole. Yet with this new-found consistency, part of the experimental ideology that fueled their breakthrough album, *Rafi's Revenge*, has been polished in favor of the evolved sound. If this album is less daring with its application of influence, it also benefits from this very lack of daringness by staying true to a common sound: fractured drum'n'bass rhythms, deep dub basslines, dancehall reggae rapping, revolutionary ideology, and rock accessibility. This album won't lead anyone to call them the next Rage Against the Machine, but it will satisfy anyone with a hunger for the group's truly patented sound. —*Jason Birchmeier*

## Astral Projection
f. 1994, Israel
*Group / Goa Trance, Trance, Club/Dance*
The psychedelic trance outfit Astral Projection have gained respect and sales as one of the best in their field despite their base in Israel, far afield from the European dance mainstream. The group evolved from a production partnership involving childhood friends Avi Nissim and Lior Perlmutter, each of whom were DJs in Israel's dance/industrial scene of the late '80s before beginning their production careers in 1989. One year later, "Monster Mania" (recorded as SFX) became a club hit after being released on Belgium's Music Man label. The duo spent time living in New York running their own X-Rave, but returned to Israel by 1994. Nissim and Perlmutter founded another label named Outmosphere, which became Trust in Trance by 1995.
Initially, the label was strictly a compilation-oriented venture; also in 1995, the pair issued the first volume in an ongoing series (*Trust in Trance: Psychedelic Vibes*) that featured many of their own productions—including the first as Astral Projection. The second in the series did well on the Israeli charts, while the third volume broke them in Europe as well, earning re-release on the British trance label TIP (it appeared as the single-artist album *Trust in Trance* as Astral Projection). Nissim and Perlmutter soon jettisoned the compilation concept and released their first true Astral Projection album, *Dancing Galaxy*. It became one of the best-selling trance albums in history after its release in 1997. *Another World* followed in 1999 and *Astral Scene* the following year. Nissim and Perlmutter also reissued their early SFX recordings on *The Unreleased Tracks 89-94* and released a DJ album, *In the Mix*. —*John Bush*

**Trust in Trance** / Apr. 29, 1996 / TIP ♦♦♦

**Dancing Galaxy** / Oct. 20, 1997 / Transient ♦♦♦♦
The climax of Astral Projection's search for intelligent trance, *Dancing Galaxy* offers wave after wave of exquisitely produced acid lines on tracks like "No One Ever Dreams," "Soundform" and the title track. The Japanese release includes a bonus 3" CD single. —*John Bush*

**The Unreleased Tracks 89-94** / Aug. 24, 1998 / Trust in Trance Israel ♦♦♦
A basic trainer for those interested in Astral Projection's origins in the techno/trance artists SFX, *Unreleased Tracks 89-94* is most likely unnecessary for casual fans. —*John Bush*

● **Another World** / Mar. 29, 1999 / Transient ♦♦♦♦
This is quite possibly the best Goa you'll ever hear. Astral Projection, the trance duo based in Israel, returned for *Another World* with more cuts and beats than ever. If it's trance, Goa, or psytrance that the listener wants, this is by all means the best buy. Every track on the album is fast, long, hopping, and spews forth the complex sound that's the trademark of Astral Projection. The songs range from a slower breakbeat type of sound on "Still on Mars," presumably the sequel to their earlier "Life on Mars," to purely computerized techno-esque trills on "Visions of Nasca" to what seems to be black box recordings on "Searching for UFOs." The songs form a coherent whole, though, which is important, as the album appears to be primarily for usage in the midst of a rave or some such item. Listeners may think that the songs sound similar, but that's partially intentional. One of the great marks of an electronica album of any sort, be it pure techno, Goa, breakbeats, etc., is that it makes for a good party album, which means that it must never, ever slow down. This is exactly what Astral Projection is good at, and it shows on *Another World*. True Goa fans should check out Astral Projection's first album, *Dancing Galaxy* first, but definitely give *Another World* a few times through the CD player. —*Adam Greenberg*

## Astralasia
f. 1989
*Group / Ambient Dub, Trance, Club/Dance*
The mysterious ambient dub and tribal house unit known as Astralasia fits in with other British electro-hippie mystics such as Eat Static, Banco de Gaia and frequent collaborators Suns of Arqa. After a self-titled debut album on the miniscule Fungus label, Astralasia moved to the Magick Eye label, which issued as its first release the band's follow-up, 1992's *The Politics of Ecstasy*. Three albums down the road, Astralasia released the compilation *Astralogy*, and then signed an American deal with the industrial label Cleopatra, which issued *The Space Between* in late 1996 and then two albums in 1997: *Seven Pointed Star* and *Seven by Seven*. One year later, Astralasia released their eighth album in as many years, *White Bird*. —*John Bush*

**Astralasia** / 1990 / Fungus ♦♦

**The Politics of Ecstasy** / 1992 / Magik Eye ♦♦

**Pitched Up at the Edge of Reality** / 1993 / Magick Eye ♦♦

**Astralogy** / 1995 / Magik Eye ♦♦♦
Though the early tracks on this Astralasia collection (spanning 1991 to 1995) are rather bland examples of ambient techno-trance, *Astralogy* also presents the group hitting their stride with later highpoints like "Hashishin," "Mother Durga" and "Sul-E-Stomp" (recorded with Suns of Arqa). It's the best single Astralasia release available, even if it does stop before their American contract with Cleopatra. —*John Bush*

● **The Space Between** / Sep. 10, 1996 / Cleopatra ♦♦♦♦
Astralasia offer a bit more variation on their form than usual for *The Space Between*, including the Indian breakbeat odyssey of "Sully's Trip," mainstream house on "Apple of Durgha's Eyes," and mid-tempo trance on "Madam." —*John Bush*

**The Seven Pointed Star** / Nov. 4, 1996 / Cleopatra ♦♦♦
The nine tracks of aggressive interstellar trance on *The Seven Pointed Star* make for an intense, though hardly varying, journey through the stars. Highlights include "Four Moons," "Whirlpool-Kaos" and the title track. —*John Bush*

**White Bird** / Jun. 8, 1998 / Cleopatra ♦♦♦
*White Bird* finds Astralasia's take on psychedelic trance developing somewhat from previous releases. Though the effects and vocal samples on "Special World" and "One Fine Day" sound quite familiar, there's also some beat magic to recommend these songs. —*John Bush*

## Atari Teenage Riot
f. 1992, Berlin, Germany
*Group / Gabba, Hardcore Techno, Club/Dance*

Berlin hardcore dissenters Atari Teenage Riot are among a new generation of German techno artists (also including ATR's Alec Empire, EC80R, Speed Freak, DJ Bleed, etc.) seeking to reconnect music with political radicalism through ever more challenging, experimental hybrids, engaging everything from speed metal and acid to jungle and hardcore punk. Formed in 1992 by Empire, Hanin Elias, and Carl Crack, ATR's controversial first single, "Hunting for Nazis," was released by German techno stronghold Force Inc. that same year (Force Inc. owner Achim Szepanski is also known for his commitment to political radicalism). Since then the group has released a string of singles and full-lengths, all of them instantly recognizable for their brash, noisy fusions of brittle, 200+ bpm breaks, massive guitar riffs, and a good deal of shouting. Similar in motivation to Detroit's Underground Resistance or industrial dance group Consolidated, ATR have professed a concern with a general conservative shift in the Western political climate (particularly in Germany after the collapse of communism in Russia and Eastern Europe) and for the development of new, overtly political forms of youth culture by way of response.

Somewhat surprisingly, the group's early singles landed them a recording deal with UK major Phonogram in 1993, through whom they released a number of singles before skipping out on their contract (the label reportedly wanted more straight-ahead, commercial techno from the group). Using their Phonogram advance for the full-length album they never delivered, ATR formed Digital Hardcore Recordings (DHR) in 1994, the imprint under which they would release most of their subsequent material to date, including the full-lengths *Delete Yourself* and *The Future of War*, plus a number of singles and EPs. DHR has also expanded to include a number of up-and-coming German artists—including EC80R and Shizuo—with similar political leanings, and signed a domestic licensing deal with Beastie Boys label Grand Royal in 1996. Partly as a result of that deal and partly through the increasing popularity of ATR member Alec Empire (who's released a number of solo full-lengths and singles through Force Inc., Chrome, Mille Plateaux, and Riot Beats, as well as DHR), ATR have become one of the first new-school European techno artists to achieve success in America, with alternative radio and MTV picking up on the group in late 1996 and the release early the following year of an American compilation collecting tracks from the first two albums. Their third album *60 Second Wipe Out* appeared in 1999 on Elektra. —*Sean Cooper*

**Delete Yourself** / Mar. 1996 / DHR/Grand Royal ♦♦♦
Although *Delete Yourself* is a raucous, blustery advance of punk vigor—full of pissed-off shouting and loud, angry guitars—its backbone of gabber-core techno, sputtering, overdriven breakbeats, and sampled, scud-attack speed metal riffs means nailing the album down to any one style is an exercise in futility. Somewhat frail and ridiculous upon repeat listenings, the album is similar in tone perhaps to some late-'80s New York and Washington DC hardcore, lessening amazement that Atari Teenage Riot was given a contract by the Beastie Boys imprint Grand Royal in 1997. —*Sean Cooper*

**The Future of War** / Mar. 17, 1997 / Digital Hardcore ♦♦

● **Burn, Berlin, Burn** / Apr. 22, 1997 / Grand Royal ♦♦♦♦
This American compilation of the group's first two import-only albums—including five tracks from 1995's *Delete Yourself* and nine from 1997's *The Future of War*—offers a fair selection of songs, including the extreme noise terror of "Deutschland (Has Gotta Die)" and "Into the Riot." If there is one drawback, it's that *Burn, Berlin, Burn* lacks the coherence and flow of Atari Teenage Riot's proper albums. Still, in lieu of forking over $50 for the imports, it's a much wiser purchase. —*John Bush*

**60 Second Wipe Out** / May 11, 1999 / Elektra ♦♦
It would be silly to expect some sort of crossover or sell-out on Atari Teenage Riot's major-label debut, *60 Second Wipe Out*. Instead, the group that introduced distorted breakbeat thrash to American/alternative audiences returned with an album of much the same. There is no lack of anarchist politics and hands-in-the-air shoutalongs, whose lyrics are pretty aptly summed up by the titles "Death of a President D.I.Y.!," "By Any Means Necessary" and "Revolution Action" (the latter was released as a trailer single, perhaps intentionally, on the same day the German legislature met in Berlin's Reichstag for the first time in over 50 years). Frontman Alec Empire's computer-thrash productions haven't taken any giant leaps in the two years since the previous ATR LP, though he does add bridges to a few songs, including the marathon five minutes of "Western Decay." Still, *60 Second Wipe Out* has all of the ingredients fans could expect from their favorite anarcho-hardcore-electronica group. —*John Bush*

## Juan Atkins
b. Sep. 12, 1962, Detroit, MI
*Producer, DJ / Detroit Techno, Club/Dance, Techno*

At the dawn of the '80s, Juan Atkins began recording what stands as perhaps the most influential body of work in the field of techno. Exploring his vision of a futuristic music which welded the more cosmic side of Parliament funk with rigid computer synth-pop embodied by Kraftwerk and the techno-futurist possibilities described by sociologist Alvin Toffler (author of *The Third Wave* and *Future Shock*), Atkins blurred his name behind aliases such as Cybotron, Model 500 and Infiniti—all, except for Cybotron, comprised solely of himself—to release many classics of sublime Detroit techno. And though it's often difficult (and misleading) to pick the precise genesis for any style of music, the easiest choice for techno is an Atkins release, the 1982 electro track "Clear," recorded by Atkins and Rick Davis as Cybotron. He soon left the progressively album-oriented Cybotron to begin working alone, and released his most seminal material from 1985 to 1989 as Model 500. And while fellow Detroit legends Kevin Saunderson and Derrick May were known for their erratic output during the following decade, Atkins recorded much more during the '90s than he had during the '80s, soaking up new rhythmic elements from contemporary dance music but keeping his unerring, instantly recognizable sense of melody intact throughout. As the electronic scene began looking back to the past to find musical innovators, Atkins was a name much-discussed and -anthologized, hailed as the godfather of techno.

Born in Detroit in 1962 (the son of a concert promoter), Juan Atkins began playing bass as a teenager and then moved on to keyboards and synthesizers, after being turned on to their use in Parliament records. Two local DJs, Ken Collier and the Electrifyin' Mojo, first introduced Atkins to a wide range of other synthesizer-driven bands—Kraftwerk, Telex, Gary Numan, Prince, the B-52's—in the late '70s. Atkins then turned on two friends he had met (initially through his younger brother) while attending Belleville Junior High School, Derrick May and Kevin Saunderson. He also bought his first synthesizer, a Korg MS10, and began recording with cassette decks and a mixer for overdubs.

Hoping to learn more about the burgeoning field of musical electronics after high-school graduation, Atkins studied at Washtenaw County Community College in nearby Ypsilanti; there he met Rick Davis, a Vietnam War veteran, synthesizer expert and fellow Electrifyin' Mojo devotee—Davis had even released an experimental record used by Mojo to open his radio show. The two began recording as Cybotron and released their first single, "Alleys of Your Mind," in 1981 on their own Deep Space Records. The clever balance of urban groove and synthesizer futurism signaled the new electro wave in black music; though crossover success for electro was quite limited, it went on to become one of the most influential styles for the new electronic music of the next decade.

"Alleys of Your Mind" got immediate play from Electrifyin' Mojo and became a big local hit, even though most listeners had no idea it was recorded in Detroit, or America for that matter. The 1982 single "Cosmic Cars" also did well, and Cybotron recorded their debut album, *Enter*. Then the group signed a deal with Fantasy Records to reissue the album. One track, "Clear," was a quasi-instrumental which set the blueprint for what would later be called techno. Instead of merely reworking elements of Kraftwerk into a hip-hop context (which proved the basis for many electro tracks), "Clear" was a balanced fusion of techno-pop and club music. Unfortunately, competing visions for the future of the group forced him to leave the group by 1983. Davis and new member Jon 5 argued to pursue a musical direction closer to rock 'n' roll, while Atkins wanted to continue in the vein of "Clear." (Cybotron carried on in the direction proposed by Davis, and was promptly forgotten.)

Juan Atkins had no trouble staying busy during the mid-'80s. He continued working with the music collective Deep Space Soundworks which he, May and Saunderson had founded in 1981 to provide a club-based forum for their music. Later, the Deep Space family founded their own club, the Music Institute, in the heart of downtown Detroit. It soon became the hub of the Motor City's growing underground family, a place where May, Atkins and Saunderson DJed along with fellow pioneers like Eddie "Flashin'" Fowlkes and Blake Baxter. The club invigorated the fractured sense of community in Detroit, and inspired second-wave technocrats like Carl Craig, Stacey Pullen, Kenny Larkin and Richie Hawtin (Plastikman).

Of course, Atkins continued recording during this time, and the period from 1985 to 1987 proved to be his most influential period. He founded his own label, Metroplex Records, in 1985 and recorded his first single as Model 500, "No UFOs." Derrick May, who was living in Chicago at the time, invited Atkins over and told him to bring his records. The duo sold thousands of copies, and "No UFO's" soon became a hit with Chicago mix shows like the Hot Mix Five. Later Metroplex singles like "Night Drive," "Interference" and "The Chase" also sold well and set the template for Detroit techno; moody and sublime machine music, inspired by the drone of automated factories and trips down the I-96 freeway late at night.

By 1988, Britain had caught up with the advanced music coming from Chicago and Detroit; soon Atkins, May and Saunderson made their first trip (of hundreds) across the Atlantic, in Atkins' case before thousands of people at one of the open-air raves typical of England's Summer of Love. Acts like 808 State, A Guy Called Gerald, LFO, and Black Dog began due in large part to the influence of Atkins, and the man himself was invited to remix current pop acts like Fine Young Cannibals, Seal, Tom Tom Club, the Beloved, and the Style Council. Though dance music in Great Britain shifted its course radically from 1989 to 1991 (to the burgeoning, cartoonish sounds of rave and hardcore), others in Europe were quick to take up the cause of championing Detroit's techno elite. First, the Belgian R&S Records began releasing stellar work by a cast of techno inheritors including New Yorker Joey Beltram and Europeans C.J. Bolland and Speedy J. By 1993, Berlin's Tresor Records had picked up the baton as well, issuing American projects by second-wave Detroit producers Underground Resistance (as X-101), Jeff Mills, Blake Baxter, and Eddie Fowlkes.

Atkins visited the label's studio in 1993 and worked with 3MB, the in-house production team of Thomas Fehlmann and Moritz Von Oswald (both of whom were to go on to better things, in Sun Electric and Basic Channel/Maurizio, respectively). He returned to Berlin several years later to begin recording what was, surprisingly, his first album since the days of Cybotron. Finally, in mid-1995, R&S released the debut Model 500 album, *Deep Space*; more importantly, the label also released *Classics*, a crucial compilation of Model 500's best Metroplex singles output. Another retrospective, Tresor's *Infiniti Collection*, traced Atkins' work as Infiniti, recorded from 1991 to 1994 for a variety of labels including Metroplex and Chicago's Radikal Fear.

Several years passed before he released any additional material, but it came with a rush during 1998-99. First in September 1998, Tresor released an album of new Infiniti recordings named *Skynet*. One month later, the American label Wax Trax! released a Juan Atkins mix album. Finally, in early 1999, the second full Model 500 album *Mind and Body* was released on R&S Records. [See Also: Model 500, Infiniti, Cybotron] —*John Bush*

**Magic Tracks: Deep Detroit, Vol. 2** / Nov. 10, 1993 / Pow Wow ♦♦♦♦
Atkins selects tracks from his own Metroplex Records to steer the listener through a course in classic Detroit techno, with tracks by Scan 7, Infiniti and Eddie "Flashin'" Fowlkes as well as new-school electro acts like Drexciya on his 1993 featured album for Pow Wow. —*John Bush*

• **Wax Trax! Mastermix, Vol. 1** / Oct. 20, 1998 / TVT ♦♦♦♦
Who else but the techno godfather could sum up the music's history efficiently in less than an hour? Beginning with two Detroit classics (his own "No UFOs" and Derrick May's "Nude Photo"), Atkins plays connect-the-dots through garage and early house (Blaze, Martin Circus), minimalist techno (Rob Hood, Walt J) and the music's growing experimentalism during the mid-'90s (courtesy of Maurizio and his own Infiniti project). The mixing is much more raw than on a live Atkins date, perhaps a reaction to the dozens of seamless (read: overdubbed) mix albums already on the market. In any case, *Wax Trax! Mastermix* is an excellent trip through the annals of Detroit techno. —*John Bush*

## Natacha Atlas
*Vocals / Ambient Dub, Club/Dance*
North African and Arabian music is given a modern, dance-inspiring, twist by Brussels-born and Washington, D.C.-based vocalist Natacha Atlas. A former singer for technopop band, Transglobal Underground, and an occasional collaborator of Jah Wobble, Atlas has continued to explore the fusion of her musical roots with western electronic, dance music. While "Option" magazine explained, "(Atlas) has a beautiful voice, which sounds curiously like a blend between traditional Middle Eastern singers and Elizabeth Fraser of the Cocteau Twins", "The Wire" wrote, "buoyed by her devotional calling and the chatter of programmed beats, she swoops, glides and goes reaching for the heavens in a way that needs no translation," "CMJ New Music" praised her for having "explored the far reaches of the ethnotechno spectrum".

The daughter of an English mother and a Sephardic Jew father, Atlas grew up in a Moroccan suburb of Brussels and was heavily influenced by the Arabic culture. In addition to learning to speak French, Spanish and Arabic, Atlas was trained in the traditional techniques of raq sharki or belly dancing. Moving to England as a teen, Atlas quickly attracted attention as the first Arabic rock singer in Northampton.

Dividing her time between England and Brussels, Atlas sang in Arabic and Turkish clubs and appeared briefly with a Belgian salsa band, Mandanga. In the early '90s, Atlas became involved with England's alternative rock scene, appearing on Loca!'s single, "Timbal," Apache Indian's single, "Arranged Marriage," and Jah Wobble's album, *Rising Above Bedlam*, which included five songs she had co-written. Accepting an invitation to join Transglobal Underground, as lead singer and belly dancer, Atlas was featured on the band's albums, *Dream Of 100 Nations* and *International Times*. Atlas continued to work with Wobble, as well, co-writing and singing on three tunes from Wobble's album, *Take Me To God*, in 1994. Atlas' debut solo album, *Diaspora*, released in 1995, featured accompaniment by Tunisian singer-songwriter Walid Rouissi and Egyptian composer and oud player Essam Rashad. *Halim* followed in 1997 and *Gedada* in 1999. Atlas worked with soundtrack composer David Arnold on the score of the Kurt Russell film, *Stargate*. In 2000 she released a collection of remixes of her life's work thus far. —*Craig Harris*

**Diaspora** / 1995 / Nation ♦♦♦
Even in the increasingly multicultural western musical landscape of the '90s, Natacha Atlas has more right than most to claim multiculturalism. The half-Jewish Egyptian-Palestinian diva is fluent in four languages and, besides her training in classical singing, she trained in the raq shari, the art of belly dancing. Her toasting has also been an integral element in the success of UK trance-techno group Transglobal Underground, and on her debut album, she continues and extends all those aspects of her personality. *Diaspora* comes up with a heady mix of traditional Arabic music and sprinkeled techno beats that is so trance-inducing that it wouldn't go unnoticed on the dancefloor eventhough the songs are mysterious, hard to get your head around, and completely exotic. Atlas spreads her gorgeous, serpentine voice over each song like the spell of a snake charmer, and the results are mesmerizing. Despite the foreign tongue, the songs are dripping with passion whether they are concerned with love and seduction, spirituality, ancient history, or the blood feud between Arabs and Jews, and never is the music less than accessible, albeit an accessibility that the listener has to work to acquire because it is so grounded in the Middle East. Although *Diaspora* is a lush, captivating album, it does not entirely detached itself from the sound of Transglobal Underground. Since Atlas enlists some of her Transglobal Underground bandmates, the album is still more of an extension of that band than a wholly individual sound. But on the evidence of engrossing, haunting compositions such as "Yalla Chant" and "Duden," as well as Atlas' otherworldly pipes, that individuality could not be long in coming. —*Stanton Swihart*

**Halim** / May 12, 1997 / Nation ♦♦
Atlas' second solo record—for some strange reason never released in America, where the first and third were—continues in her vein of excellent Arabic singing combined with a wide variety of musical traditions, modern and ancient. Working with four distinct cowriting/production groups this time around, including her collaborators in Transglobal Underground in one group and, in another, Killing Joke mainman Jaz Coleman (pursuing his other interest in orchestrations), Atlas again creates an intoxicating series of love songs, all sung in Arabic but with lyrical snippets printed in English. Perhaps unsurprisingly, the most technological and dancefloor-friendly numbers are done with the Transglobal crowd, who work on about half the album's tracks. "Moustahil" and "Amulet" both feature shuffling dance beats and loops along with a number of performers on such instruments as oud and dharabuka, plus energetic backing vocals from duo Sawt El Atlas. Coleman's tracks, "Enogoom Wil Amar" and "Andeel," equally deserve notice for Atlas' vocals

and his own striking, lush arrangements, while her collaboration with Egyptian musician/orchestra leader Essam Rashad, "Ya Albi Ehda," is a beauty in the vein of older Arabic popular music. No matter who's working with her performing what, though, it's Atlas' show all the way, her singing shimmering out with all the beauty one could ever want in a vocalist. —*Ned Raggett*

● **Gedida** / Mar. 9, 1999 / Beggars Banquet ✦✦✦✦
Natacha Atlas' third album greatly expands upon the promise of her earlier work—on *Gedida*, her fusion of Arabic musical traditions and contemporary dance beats really jells, eliminating the more gimmicky dimensions of earlier records to strike a fascinating balance between old and new. While tracks like "Kifaya" and "Ezzay" magnify the cinematic aspirations of past efforts, *Gedida* also takes a number of fascinating left turns—a cover of Françoise Hardy's "Mon Amie la Rose" is hauntingly beautiful, while on the closing "One Brief Moment" Atlas delivers her first English-language vocal, a move one hopes will bring this unique artist the wider audience she deserves. —*Raymond McKinney*

**The Remix Collection** / Sep. 19, 2000 / Beggars Banquet ✦✦
Polyglot chanteuse Natacha Atlas has always been open to multiple cultural influences, so a remix collection by producers as varied as Talvin Singh, Youth, and DJ Spooky is a natural. And the results are as good as one would expect: Singh takes Atlas to the Asian underground with a bhangrafied drum'n'bass mix of "Duden" (a track which DJ Spooky deconstructs in a funkier and dubbier manner later in the program), while Banco de Gaia gets clubby on "Yalla Chant" and the Bullitnuts turn "Bastet" into a journey to the center of ambient trip-hop. No one gets funkier than Youth, though, whose mid-tempo arrangement of "Yalla Chant" incorporates found-sound samples, virtuoso scratching, and readings from Hindu cosmology into a chugging, wailing cosmic blowup. For the source material to most of this program, pick up Atlas' solo album *Halim* and Transglobal Underground's *Psychic Karaoke*. —*Rick Anderson*

## Atom Heart (Uwe Schmidt)

*Producer / Experimental Techno, Electronica, Electro-Jazz, Ambient Techno, Trance, Club/Dance, House*

Composer and designer Uwe Schmidt is one of experimental electronic music's most prolific and prodigious post-techno experimentalists. Issuing a flood of material under a variety of pseudonyms (from singles and compilation tracks to scads of EPs and full-lengths) and maintaining an almost daunting album-a-month release schedule through his own Rather Interesting label, Schmidt's discography has expanded into the hundreds despite the fact he's only been actively recording for just over a decade. Although his first instrument was a drumkit, Schmidt became fascinated with the possibilities of analog electronics early on, trading his set for a drum machine and borrowing a four-track and some keyboards from friends. His earliest tracks were dance music-focused—primarily hardcore techno, acid, and trance—but by the mid-'90s his sound had departed from the monochromaticism of typical dancefloor fare into dense, complex, multi-layered sound constructions not easily reducible to any one genre. Incorporating elements of techno, acid, ambient, jazz, funk, electro, '60s exotica, and psychedelic rock, Schmidt's current work, though highly rhythmic, is hardly classifiable as dance music at all, lying at the intersection of a sort of future-anterior auteurism and tongue-in-cheek experimentalism unique in contemporary electronica.

Although prolific since his first singles as I, Atomu Shinzo, Bi-Face, and Mike McCoy, Atom Heart began stepping up his production in the early to mid-'90s in association with the noted trance and ambient label Fax, also based in Frankfurt. Through a number of solo and collaborative outings with Tetsu Inoue and label-head Pete Namlook, Schmidt helped to formulate the melodic hard trance and techno sounds associated with the Frankfurt scene, and also had the opportunity to dabble in other forms of electronic experimentation, particularly ambient (to which Fax almost wholly shifted its focus). He released a handful of Fax titles during this period—including *Orange*, *Datacide*, *Softcore*, and *Coeur Atomique*—before Namlook established the Rather Interesting label as a subsidiary of Fax dedicated to Atom Heart-related projects. Although he continues to release material under other names as well (most notably as Lassigue Bendthaus and the Lisa Carbon Trio), his focus remained on Rather Interesting, releasing a somewhat bewildering (given the consistent quality) CD every month and forging a sophisticated, singular aesthetic. Although each title was limited to a 1000-copy pressing, many of them are among the most accomplished, original examples of post-techno experimental electronic music available, utilizing complex split-channel effects and integrated melodic and rhythmic shifts with an iterative, almost mathematical (though never simply derived) eclecticism. During 1999 and 2000, Schmidt earned a higher profile among American listeners with the release of several projects, beginning with Flanger's *Templates* (recorded with Bernd Friedman of Nonplace Urban Field) on the Ninja Tune sublabel Ntone. In 2000, two covers albums—*Pop Artificielle* as Ib and *El Baile Aleman* as Señor Coconut y su Conjunto—gained a comparatively wide release. The former, distributed through Shadow, featured synth-pop covers of pop hits including Donovan's "Sunshine Superman" and David Bowie's "Ashes to Ashes"; the latter, an Emperor Norton release, focused on Kraftwerk songs, performed by Heart's Latin alias Señor Coconut. Schmidt has also, with less frequency, given his hand to remixing, working over tracks from the likes of Prong, Pankow, the Swamp Zombies, and Resistance D. [See Also: Señor Coconut] —*Sean Cooper*

**Coeur Atomique** / 1993 / Fax ✦✦✦✦
Dance-based listening music, more experimental than his earlier trance and techno twelves, but still nowhere near the sophistication of his Rather Interesting work. —*Sean Cooper*

**Datacide II** / 1993 / Fax ✦✦✦✦
The second release in his series of collaborations with Tetsu Inoue (the first appeared on Frankfurt's POD label, which released most of Schmidt's early 12" work). Mostly ambient, with beats bubbling up here and there through dense fields of texture and drone. —*Sean Cooper*

**Dots** / 1994 / Rather Interesting ✦✦✦✦
Where much strictly ambient music goes for the thick, warm soundscapes of analog keyboards and effects, *Dots* is rigidly digital in its approach, culminating in what Schmidt describes on the sleeve as a sort of futuristic elevator music. Fits oddly into the overall RI catalog, but nonetheless represents a strong component in his evolving aesthetic. —*Sean Cooper*

**Softcore** / 1994 / Fax ✦✦✦
Although quite a bit more angular and crude than his Rather Interesting material, *Softcore's* meditations on rhythm and texture stretch the limits of the mixing desk in engaging, often fascinating ways. If later Atom Heart releases such as *BASS* and *Machine Paisley* point to an ever more complex digital desktop aesthetic, *Softcore* is analog almost to a fault, with Schmidt's ideas occasionally outstripping his ability to conceal the technique behind them. —*Sean Cooper*

**Bass** / 1995 / Rather Interesting ✦✦✦
Basically *Silver Sound* part two, though with a warmer, more ambient feel. —*Sean Cooper*

**Mu** / 1995 / Rather Interesting ✦✦✦✦
A dazzling, almost fractally complex collaborative effort with Tetsu Inoue. Material ranges from slow, droning ambient and twittering, experimental electronic, to alternately down-tempo and crunching, breakbeat ambient techno. Uniformly brilliant and easily his finest to date. —*Sean Cooper*

**Real Intelligence** / 1995 / Rather Interesting ✦✦✦✦
A nice, compact introduction to the RI label, released after its first year in operation. Collects top-line tracks from the first nine RI releases, and adds two new cuts (a limited edition 2xLP adds a third, "Housing"). The cover and title take pot shots at the Warp label's *(Artificial Intelligence)* compilations, distancing Schmidt's work from the by-then maligned "intelligent techno" tag. —*Sean Cooper*

**Semiacoustic Nature** / 1995 / Rather Interesting ✦✦✦✦
Schmidt's first real move toward combining, in as balanced a ratio as possible, the various strains of experimentation constituting his previous work. The push toward complex rhythmic programming begun in his previous RI releases is more fully developed here, though with more restrain and intricacy. —*Sean Cooper*

**Silver Sound 60** / 1995 / Rather Interesting ✦✦✦✦
Best described as environmental lounge electro, Schmidt incorporates elements of exotica and jungle in these dense, exquisitely detailed tracks. *Silver Sound 60* also signals a shift in Schmidt's material toward a wilder, more schizophrenic approach to composition and a less derived overall sound. —*Sean Cooper*

**VSVN** / 1995 / Rather Interesting ♦♦♦
Short for "very synthetic virtual noise" (with a cover modeled on the NASA logo), this quirky collection of post-industrial electronica is, for lack of a better term, extremely weird, playing mind-bending games with channel separation and twisting ambient, electro, techno, and psychedelia into odd, not always successful combinations. Also released as a double-LP. —*Sean Cooper*

**Apart** / 1996 / Recent Programmings ♦♦♦♦
More jazzy electro-madness, this time a bit more dancefloor-friendly and with an overall less choppy, schizophrenic feel. Along with three cuts mixed, matched, and redone by Atom Heart himself, Ian Pooley and Matthew Herbert get their digs in on the flip. Released on the relatively new Recent Programmings label (a subsidiary of Semaphore), *Apart* is perhaps most notable for its format, since—apart from a smattering of compilation tracks and his first label compilation *Real Intelligence*—little of this corner of Schmidt's artistic palette has been committed to vinyl. DJs should delight at its availability. —*Sean Cooper*

**Brown** / 1996 / Rather Interesting ♦♦♦
Slated for a mid-1996 release, Atom Heart's solo *Brown* album didn't actually hit US stores until October, since shipments of the release were held up and subsequently lost in customs due to the lack of information on the packaging (the sleeve and tray card are simply chocolate brown, with the title printed on the spine). Finally arriving months late following a repress, the album sounds a bit dated in terms of Atom Heart's overall oeuvre, playing in an ambient-electro-jazz vein similar to earlier works such as *Silver Sound 60* and *BASS*. A nice listen, but by no means essential. —*Sean Cooper*

**Hat** / 1996 / Rather Interesting ♦♦♦♦
A three-way collaboration with Tetsu Inoue and Haruomi Hosono (Yellow Magic Orchestra), yielding yet another benchmark of intricate, almost unclassifiable experimental electronic. Elements of ambient, electro, jazz, techno, and post-classical remain, but the result is undeniably Atom Heart. —*Sean Cooper*

**Machine Paisley** / 1996 / Rather Interesting ♦♦♦♦
Very similar to his Lisa Carbon Trio work, although the album bears the unmistakable stamp of a Rather Interesting release in its diverse detail and tempi and sparkling production. Harder-edged and with a brasher humor. —*Sean Cooper*

● **Digital Superimposing** / 1997 / Side Effects ♦♦♦♦
Like previous all-ambient works by Atom Heart's Uwe Schmidt, his release as Superficial Depth for Brian "Lustmord" Williams' Side Effects label is a programmatic piece best heard from start to finish (a notion intimated in its single-index mastering). Introduced via deep drones and working with almost painful sloth through bassy pulses, sparse electronic rhythms, and low lying melodies through the course of its nearly 70 minutes, the album is magnificent in its subtlety and restraint. Although its simplicity, slightly dark edge, and lack of discernible movement may put off fans of Atom Heart's normally densely rhythmic work (as well as of ambient's lighter, more melodic side), the album more than compensates the long haul. —*Sean Cooper*

**Fonosandwich** / 1997 / Rather Interesting ♦♦♦
A bit of a hodgepodge assortment of Atom Heart cuts, sounding too much like a compilation of tracks which didn't quite make it onto previous RI releases (one can almost pinpoint the albums they might originally have been recorded for!). A few tracks rise above the backward-glance ("Tandoori Club," "Eat My Chillie"), but the overall impression is of aural leftovers. A pleasant listen, but by no means up to the level of aplomb and innovation of previous RI releases. —*Sean Cooper*

**Señor Coconut** / May 19, 1997 / Rather Interesting ♦♦♦
Atom Heart's first release since moving his studios to Santiago, Chile plummets off the deep end of Latin jazz/electronic funk weirdness hinted at in earlier releases such as *Trio de Janeiro* and *Polyester*. Similar in some respects to Latin/lounge plunderphonic collageworks such as Tipsy's *Trip Tease* or Sukia's *Contacto Especial*, *Señor Coconut* adapts percussion, piano, and horn samples to warped, mutant offshoots of mambo, samba, and rumba rhythms, combining the resultant blur with the sort of intricately humorous digital electro-funk that runs through much of his recent work. Strange stuff that would later spark a full-blown alias from Schmidt with 1999's *El Baile Aleman*. —*Sean Cooper*

**Schnittstelle** / 1998 / Rather Interesting ♦♦♦♦
Following a pair of inexplicably ho-hum recordings, Atom Heart's *Schnittstelle* is something of a return to form. Elements of improvisational electronics remain, but Schmidt is back at the concept block with much of this one, constructing tracks from cracks and creases in the digital recording process (the title is German, loosely, for "the point at which something is cut"). Hard disk crashes, data corruption, tracking error, and digital noise and distortion are just a few of the methods applied, making of *Schnittstelle* something akin to the output of experimental digital abusers such as Farmers Manual, Mika Vainio, and Christian Fennesz. The album is far more varied than those comparisons suggest, however, and is among the very finest of Atom Heart's lengthy discography. —*Sean Cooper*

## Attica Blues

*Group / Electronica, Trip-Hop, Club/Dance*
f. 1994, London, England
While the roster on England's much-hyped trip-hop label Mo'Wax is packed to the gills with bedroom boffins turned recording artists, Attica Blues is the closest it comes to having an actual band. The pancultural collective began life in 1994 when producers D'Afro (born Charlie Williams) and Tony Nwachukwu first met up. D'Afro had previously founded London's Urban Poets Society collective, but the duo later became Attica Blues for their continuing studio experiments. While trying to sell some Japanese hip-hop records, D'Afro met up with Mo'Wax founder James Lavelle and was offered a spot on the label. The duo began recording their first single alone but when a local student, the Egyptian-born Roba El-Essawy, visited the studio during the recording for their debut single, D'Afro and Nwachukwu decided to add her to the group. Attica Blues released their first two EPs *Vibes, Scribes 'N Dusty 45s* and *Blueprint* in 1995, and followed with two more during 1996-97. Mo'Wax issued their self-titled debut album in September 1997. D'Afro and Nwachukwu have also worked as remixers for Flora Purim and Sneaker Pimps as well as labelmates U.N.K.L.E., DJ Krush and Adriana Evans. —*John Bush*

● **Attica Blues** / Sep. 8, 1997 / Mo'Wax ♦♦♦♦
Attica Blues' debut album is a downbeat excursion through jazzy trip-hop with the embellishment of dark strings and several rather sly basslines to move things along. Although the production is impeccable, Roba El-Essawy's vocals tend toward a narrow range. All in all, the album is a qualified success. —*John Bush*

## Aube (Akifumi Nakajima)

*Producer / Experimental Ambient, Noise, Experimental*
Akifumi Nakajima's Aube project has amassed a lengthy discography, most entries realizing the maximum capacity for audio variation from a minimum of sampled input (in many cases, a single sound source). Influenced by space rock and musique concrète, Nakajima began recording in 1980 but released nothing until a decade later, when he produced music for an art installation given by a group of friends. Since the installation involved water, he decided to use appropriately watery sounds for the music. Nakajima's first Aube release came in 1991, when the Japanese noise label Vanilla released his cassette LP *Hydrophobia*. Quite a few more water-related recordings followed, and Nakajima soon began branching out by using varied sources such as field recordings, the hum from fluorescent lamps, human voices, brain waves, heartbeats, even pages being ripped from a Bible. He has recorded for Staalplaat, Manifold, Charnel Music, Pure, Iris Light and the Grand Rapids-based upstart Elsie & Jack Records. Nakajima also operates a cassette-only label named G.R.O.S.S. that has released several albums of Aube material. In 1999 the album *Evocation* was added and a year later Aube closely released, *Richochentrance* and *Blood Brain Barrier*, respectively. —*John Bush*

**Cardiac Strain** / 1997 / Alien8 ♦♦♦
While Akifumi Nakajima of Aube not only creates a rather diverse selection of noise works (generally he gravitates more toward ambient than full-blast harsh noise), he also uses some very unique sound sources. This release, as the name implies, is created solely from the human heartbeat, although one wouldn't guess it at first. Distinct heartbeat sounds are heard, but much of the album distorts and twists these sounds beyond recognition. *Cardiac Strain* is among his noisiest albums. A typical track starts off barely audible until Nakajima either shocks the listener with an ear-shattering burst of rhythmic noise, or until the track eases into things and culminates in a point of pure chaos. Either way, this is a great album, considered by many to be one of his best. —*Marc van der Pol*

*Mort Aux Vaches: Still Contemplation* / Mar. 31, 1998 / Staalplaat ♦♦♦♦
- **Pages from the Book** / May 26, 1998 / Elsie & Jack ♦♦♦♦
Another single-sound-source recording—this time for the standout Elsie & Jack label—finds Aube shredding a Bible to create his catalog of sound samples. While the source material is less frequently recognized than on past Aube releases, the results are just as stunning. Limited copies include an actual page from the Bible used for sampling. —*John Bush*

## Autechre

f. 1991, Sheffield, Yorkshire
*Group / Experimental Techno, Electronica, Electro-Techno, Ambient Techno, IDM*

Like the Orb, Aphex Twin, and µ-Ziq, Autechre are about as close to being techno superstars as the tenets of the genre and the limitations of its audience will allow. Through a series of full-length works and a smattering of EPs on Warp, Clear, and their own Skam label, the group have consistently garnered the praise of press and public alike. Unlike many of their more club-bound colleagues, however, Autechre's Sean Booth and Rob Brown have roots planted firmly in American electro, and though the more mood-based, sharply digital texture of their update may seem to speak otherwise, it was through early twelves like Egyptian Lover's "Egypt, Egypt," Grandmaster Flash's "Scorpio," and "Pretty" Tony Butler's "Get Some" that their combined aesthetic began to form.

Booth and Brown met through a mutual friend, trading junked-up pause-button mixtapes of their favorite singles back and forth. Happening onto some bargain-basement analog gear through questionable circumstances, the pair began experimenting with their own music before they were out of high school. After some disastrous experiences with a few small labels, the pair sent a tape off to Warp Records, whose early releases by Sweet Exorcist, Nightmares on Wax, and B12 were announcing a new age in UK-based techno (and one that Autechre would become a key component in). Releasing a handful of early singles through the label, Autechre's first stabs were collected on their debut full-length, *Incunabula*, as well as the 10" box-set remix EP *Basscadet*. Subsequent albums would reach a wider audience through stateside reissue, first on Wax Trax!/TVT and later on Nothing, the label managed by Nine Inch Nails' Trent Reznor. Although stylistically rooted, affectations for the ponderous extend beyond their name and track titles ("C/Pach," "Bronchusevenmx24") with the basic premise of their approach being music without a whole lot of stylistic baggage.

In addition to Autechre, Booth and Brown have released material as Gescom on their own Skam imprint and through the Clear label, most notably *The Sounds of Machines Our Parents Used* EP on the latter. The group have also provided a number of memorable remixes (often times more memorable than their original material) for artists including Palmskin Productions, Slowly, Mike Ink, DJ Food, Scorn, Skinny Puppy, Tortoise, Phoenecia, and Various Artists. [See Also: Gescom] —*Sean Cooper*

**Basscadet [EP]** / 1993 / Warp ♦♦♦
A collection of remixes of tracks deriving from *Incunabula*, released on vinyl as a box set of 10"s. —*Sean Cooper*

☆ **Incunabula** / 1993 / Wax Trax! ♦♦♦♦♦
Although Autechre's debut release doesn't totally display the full experimentation which would dominate their future albums and singles, it is still striking nonetheless, as proof that the early comparisons to fellow Sheffield denizens Cabaret Voltaire weren't just misguided hype. Lumped in with the "intelligent dance music" semi-genre popular at the time, Autechre doesn't hit the same levels as Orbital or labelmate Aphex Twin, but *Incunabula* still stands out as being both good dancefloor material and equally pleasant listening, and not simply new-age hash with a backbeat. "Kalpol Introl" sets the overall mood for the rest of the record, with a sharp blend of minimal but effective beats and bass combined with a variety of keyboard textures and understated melodies. "Bike" ratchets the pace even more, reliant on crisp drum-machine patterns and careful arrangements to create something equally at home either in Detroit or on the autobahn. From there *Incunabula* follows the same general tone; tracks often experiment with ghostly keyboard backing and mostly clinical beats combined with odd, individual touches. Notable examples of this are the quirky organ sounds and vocal fragments on "Autriche" and the warning siren keyboards matched with notably more slamming percussion on "Doctrine." "Basscadet" is the album's undisputed winner at combining avant-garde touches with club underpinnings, armed with a sparkling, clanging, mid-song break and a relentless, mechanistic rhythm not a million miles away from the contemporaneous work of Seefeel, who remixed the track for a single release shortly thereafter. Despite the relative sameness in the basic arrangements of tracks covering the better portion of the album—a few song subtractions wouldn't have hurt the 75-minute length any—*Incunabula* still stands out as a better effort than many other UK techno albums of the early '90s. —*Ned Raggett*

☆ **Amber** / 1994 / Warp ♦♦♦♦♦
In small but noticeable ways on this, their sophomore release, Autechre begin to break from the clean, if at times obvious, artistic techno from their debut record, and reach instead toward something far more distinct. Sean Booth and Rob Brown weren't quite there yet, but their self-production is even more accomplished than before, and their instincts to steer away from overly polite electronic dance music come ever more to the fore at various points throughout *Amber*. "Foil" begins the album with a distinctly spooky feel to it, with droning keyboards playing out over a series of spare percussion patterns; the heavy echo and crumbling, lo-fi bass feel of the track reduces its straightforward danceability, creating an ominous introduction to the album. "Silverside" at once strips things down to a more minimal approach. A string synth section plays out over first gently thudding then more pounding beats. Then a more off-kilter section with distorted vocal samples and sounds provides part of the melodic accompaniment and rhythm. "Glitch" has a nice roiling rumble to it; it isn't as fragmented as later releases, but veers a little more closely to the edge in comparison to earlier songs. "Piezo" is also worth noting, with uplifting synths balancing out a very quirky, almost intrusive series of rhythms, while "Yulquen" eschews beats entirely for a slightly disturbing though still beautiful track which rivals prime Aphex Twin. For all this, *Amber* does suffer a similarity to *Incunabula*, in that a couple of tracks could be removed with no problem, while tracks like "Montreal" and "Slip" continue the basic *Incunabula* formula without noticeable change. Even so, things are clearly starting to gel a little more here than on previous releases; the great leap forward becomes all the more logical in retrospect. —*Ned Raggett*

**Anti- [EP]** / 1994 / Warp ♦♦
Booth and Brown get political with this EP dedicated to the fight against the UK Criminal Justice Bill (which passed into law in 1995) outlawing the public performance of "repetitive beat" music. Autechre's answer, located within, is a track composed entirely of non-repeating rhythmic figures. A novelty item at best. —*Sean Cooper*

**Anvil Vapre [EP]** / 1995 / Warp ♦♦♦
Beginning with looped blasts of static used as rhythm, before charging headlong into a pummeling industrial-strength breakbeat, "Second Bad Vilbel" kicks off *Anvil Vapre* with fire. This album is another definite milestone in Autechre's transformation from an intelligent, dance music group to a much more interesting beast. The use of low rumblings, haunting song breaks and drones, and generally user-unfriendly textures establishes clear connections to the Throbbing Gristle/Cabaret Voltaire school of protean noisemaking, while the sharp, spot-on percussion slams—at times suddenly shifting tempos—still make everything danceable in unexpected ways. "Second Scepe" is calmer in comparison, building up the rhythm, in part, from a series of abbreviated vocal samples and a minimal keyboard bassline. "Second Scout" has a good, deep, funky, techno feel to it, with squelching bass and echoing synths that sound like Derrick May pursuing his George Clinton fascination to another level. "Second Peng" concludes the release on another high note, carefully building and combining a variety of rhythms, keyboard loops, and background sounds to create an excellent, slow pounder of a track. —*Ned Raggett*

★ **Tri Repetae++** / 1995 / Warp ♦♦♦♦♦
Starting with the snarling, slow machine-funk of "Dael," *Tri Repetae* fully confirms Autechre's evolution into electronic noise kings. If not as immediately experimental as the fractured work by the likes of Merzbow, *Tri* expertly harnesses the need for a beat to perfectly balance out the resolutely fierce, crunching samples and busy arrangements, turning from being inspired by Aphex Twin to being equally inspiring in itself. "Rotar" does a particularly fine job on this front, with high-pitched sounds against low, distorted bass blasts—and this only forms part of the percussion arrangement. If anything, Gary Numan is also an unstated but prime influence in "Eutow" and "Clipper"; among other tracks, these contain key elements that sound exactly like the ominous, acoustic Moog siren tones which filled out many of his early

songs (the descending chord hook in the latter, increasingly revamped as the song progresses, is especially compelling in context). The basic combination of soft melody and harsh beats are here as well, coming fully to the fore and resulting in such fine songs as the synth-string/organ wheeze laden "Leterel" and the quirky, sweet "Gnit." Nearly every track has a particular edge or element to it, making it eminently listenable and distinct. "Stud," for all of its macho connotations, actually takes a gentler path than most of the album's tunes, with a flowing synth wash at the center of a stripped-down but sharp digital-drum punch; by the end of the song, the synth loops float freely in an uneasy, ambient wave. With the drowsy pulse of "Overand" and the echoing beats of "Radio" (perhaps not so ironically, the most straightforward of the album's songs) to close things out, *Tri* stands as a varied, accomplished album, clear evidence of Autechre's unique genius around sound. American releases of this album include a bonus disc compiling the *Anvil Vapre* and *Garbage* EPs. —*Ned Raggett*

### Garbage [EP] / Feb. 27, 1995 / Warp ♦♦♦♦

Considered by many to be a key turning point in Autechre's career, *Garbage* definitely showcases the duo with a musical and technical reach rooted in their earliest releases, but only beginning to fully flower here. While the clinical performance style and soft melodies for which the band were initially known remain, their production and arrangement increasingly embraced unfamiliar, more aggressive approaches. The nearly quarter-hour long "Garbagemx36" showcases this combination well; then-typical techno sounds such as chirping birds are worked into an elaborately conceived rhythm combination that, while still serviceable for the dancefloor, has much more going on in it than most such tunes, concluding on a lovely string-synth passage. "Piobrnx19" takes a stranger turn, with more subtly odd keyboard sounds and squeaks over a curious, hollow rhythm that sets the basis for the central, minimal synth melody. With its sparse rhythm track and melody, "Bronchusevenmx24" exercises Autechre's fascination with Aphex Twin, but does so nicely. "Vletrmix21" ends the EP on a soaring, stunning note, with an inspiring, skyward-bound melodic loop that veers between growing ever more majestic and then calming down again, worthy of comparison to Nine Inch Nails' surprisingly powerful and tender instrumental "A Warm Place." —*Ned Raggett*

### Chiastic Slide / Feb. 24, 1997 / Warp ♦♦♦♦

After *Tri Repetae++*, the stunning leap forward with which Autechre astounded the techno world, the duo's fourth proper album came as a disappointment to many. The waves of polar static and mechanic clicks which distinguished *Tri Repetae* make *Chiastic Slide* little more than a variation on a form. Even worse, the album has too few ideas for its near-70-minute length, and the duo seem content with short loops being repeated and repeated over again for up to ten minutes on a single track. Though several songs are on a par with *Tri Repetae*—and that's being generous—*Chiastic Slide* just can't compare with Autechre's earlier work. —*John Bush*

### Cichli Suite [EP] / Aug. 25, 1997 / Warp ♦♦♦

Five versions of the track from Ae's *Chiastic Slide*, and none approaching "sickly" in much sense of the word. Autechre remixing themselves is always an interesting proposition, as their remixes very often exceed their original work by leaps. The tracks here scale a certain height, but only occasionally pick the lock of aimless repetition that tends to hamper the best of their material. Ae's skill for bizarre sound fabrication is showcased in particular on "Charachi" and the stunning downtempo electro brooder "Krib." —*Sean Cooper*

### LP5 / Oct. 13, 1998 / Nothing ♦♦♦♦

Autechre creates a fascinating sonic world on their fifth album release, where electronic pulses and blips are used to create fantastic textural waves. Members Sean Booth and Rob Brown prove they've become masters of programming throughout, issuing a more than suitable follow-up to their critically praised 1995 release *Tri Repetae++* (1997's *Chiastic Slide* wasn't considered a true follow-up by the band). Although it may be hard to take for those uninitiated into Autechre's unique style (it's hard to detect melodies upon first listen), you'll discover something new with each repeated listen. Since all the songs are cut from the same sonic cloth, the album is best when listened to in its entirety, but the tracks "Acroyear2," "Rae," and "Fold4, Wrap5" are definite highlights. Although not for everyone, Autechre's self-titled release should be admired, since it's not comparable to anything past or present. Uncompromisingly cutting-edge. —*Greg Prato*

### Peel Sessions [EP] / Feb. 8, 1999 / Nothing ♦♦♦

Recorded in late 1995, this three-song release nicely showcases Autechre's talent for mixing quiet hooks with aggressive, experimental production. "Milk DX" starts with the shuffling, stuttering mechanical rhythms for which the duo became ever more known, with off-kilter and unexpected sound stabs leaping in and around the gentle melody and a curious, unintelligible vocal line which fades after a few minutes. "Inhake 2" lays down an even more frazzled rhythm, partially composed of half-seconds of static and hiss as well as electro-robot vocals, as a bed for another simple, soft keyboard part. "Drone" has a punchy drum start, but four minutes in, it begins to match its title with a series of distorted, heavily produced drones and sounds, while constantly changing loop frequencies come to the fore. *Peel Sessions* is not their best release, but it is still quite noteworthy. —*Ned Raggett*

### EP7 / Jun. 22, 1999 / Nothing ♦♦♦♦

Less than a year after a vaunted full-length, Autechre return with an hour-long EP that, given the artistic and sonic departures inside, could easily have made it *LP6* instead of *EP7*. Sean Booth and Rob Brown's insistence on coaxing only the most spidery and alien bits of percussion from their PC audio software is in full effect, as on 1998's *LP5*, but the duo appear to have pulled back a bit from the yawing edge of abstract sonic manipulation. The paper-thin *Selected Ambient Works* melodies are back, with everything from steel drums (on "Maphive 6.1") to cheesy organ noodlings (on "Pir") As such, it's a more affecting (and effective) release—not quite as futuristic or distinctive as *LP5* but a bit more fun to listen to. —*John Bush*

## Autocreation

f. 1994
*Group / Ambient Techno, Trip-Hop*

Autocreation formed in 1994 as the trio of Kevin Hector, Tara Patterson, and Mark Van Hoen (the latter of whom also records as Locust for R&S ambient sublabel Apollo). Originally recording as Sine Bubble, Autocreation are a somewhat dancefloor-friendly blend of ambient, techno, and hip-hop-esque breakbeat, and have released two singles (on Template and Op-Art) and a full-length album (on former Orb-owned ambient label Inter-Modo), as well as performing remixes for Seefeel ("Plainsong"), As One ("Mihon"), and Wallstar ("Gurnigan"). Following the release of the *Mettle* full-length, Van Hoen left the group to focus on his solo work, with Patterson and Hector continuing on with the name, releasing the *Sauce* EP on their own Template label and contributing an original track, "Justice Loop," to the second installment of Volume's *Trans-Europe Express* compilation series. The following year also brought the release of "Caught Short," a three-track minimalist breakbeat meditation released by Kirk DeGiorgio's celebrated Op-Art label (the title track was also included on the Op-Art label compilation *Objets d'ART III*). Although Autocreation remain a duo project, both Patterson and Hector have continued to work in sporadic combination with Van Hoen (both live and in the studio), with Hector contributing most recently to the latter's *Last Flowers From the Darkness* LP (Touch, 1997). Hector also records under the name Shanq, although to date his output under that name has included only one remix (Locust's "Your Selfish Ways" single, released by Apollo in 1997). Patterson and Hector plan a revival of their Template label in 1997, with several releases scheduled to appear. —*Sean Cooper*

### Autocreation [Single] / 1996 / Op-Art ♦♦♦♦

The group's debut 12" for Kirk De Giorgio's noted Op-Art label (and their first without the involvement of Mark Van Hoen, who left in '96 to pursue his solo work with R&S and Touch) is an appropriately abstract affair, with crisp, thunderous breaks set against a sparse backdrop of looping guitar samples and minimal electronics. While all of the tracks suggest a circuitous engagement with drum'n'bass, the flip side's "Youngster" goes full-throttle into splintering breaks and bouncing bass. A nice, somewhat cerebral collection. —*Sean Cooper*

### ● Mettle / 1996 / Inter-Modo ♦♦♦♦

Recorded at Mark Van Hoen's studio, The Enclosure, *Mettle* retains much the same feel as Van Hoen's solo material as Locust: dark, brooding, and with an almost tribal air. Of course, Autocreation also adds the contributions of Tara Patterson and Kevin Hector, registered mostly in terms of the breadth of sounds and a sense of movement and progression (which Van Hoen's often looping atmospheres tend to lack). —*Sean Cooper*

### Sauce [Single] / 1996 / Template ♦♦

Two tracks of resolutely danceable, acid-y techno. Unlike most of the rest of Autocreation's work, save for its sparseness and forceful focus. —*Sean Cooper*

## The Automator (Dan Nakamura)
*Producer, DJ / Club/Dance, Hip-Hop*

Dan "The Automator" Nakamura is a San Francisco-based hip-hop producer whose work with "Kool" Keith Thornton on the latter's Dr. Octagon project shot him to unlikely acclaim in 1996. A lo-fi fusion of hip-hop beats and bizarre atmospherics on par with some of the weirder exports from the UK trip-hop scene, *Dr. Octagon* was released by the tiny Bulk Recordings label and achieved a level of overground success increasingly rare in hip-hop's pop-monopolized marketplace. Propelled by Thornton's pornographic rhymes and mind-bending meter, the record owed its success in equal measure to Nakamura's inventive production, which wed loping, downtempo rhythms with, by turns, weeping violins, space-born bleeps and wiggles, and heavy metal guitar riffs. Not Nakamura's freshman effort by a long shot, the two had actually worked together (with Thornton appearing as Sinister 6000) on Nakamura's debut Automator release, the *A Better Tomorrow* EP, appearing on SF's Ubiquity label in early 1996. Nakamura's studio, the Glue Factory, has also served as the workshop for recordings by Mo'Wax's DJ Shadow and for various artists on the latter's Solesides label (most notably on Latyrx's *The Debut*).

Automator's other mix and production credits include Primal Scream, the Eels, Cornershop, DJ Krush, and side-projects with former De La Soul producer Prince Paul and Dust Brother Mike Simpson. In mid-2000, Automator released *A Much Better Tomorrow* on the hip-hop oriented label 75 Ark. —*Sean Cooper*

**A Better Tomorrow [EP]** / Apr. 15, 1996 / Ubiquity ♦♦♦♦
Producer Dan "The Automator" Nakamura's solo debut for San Francisco acid jazz imprint Ubiquity is not quite as notable a deviation from standard-fare hip-hop/acid jazz production as the just-released Dr. Octagon album, which would eventually earn Nakamura his rep. Still a few notches above the typical, however, with several of the tracks featuring Octagon collaborator "Kool" Keith Thornton (under the name Sinister 6000). —*Sean Cooper*

• **A Much Better Tomorrow** / Jul. 18, 2000 / 75 Ark ♦♦♦♦
Even more optimistic for the future after the passage of three years, Dan Nakamura expanded his *Better Tomorrow* EP out to a full-length with the addition of a host of tracks recorded around the same time. Sinister 6000 (aka Kool Keith) freestyles over half of the tracks, rehearsing for the duo's collaboration later that year on the *Dr. Octagon* LP. Except for the occasional eerie cinema sample though, the sound is decidedly different from *Dr. Octagon*. Suitably, these tracks are drum heavy and more reliant on the Automator's production/DJ skills, with Keith spending much less time on the mic. The straight-out instrumentals and studio project tracks don't compare quite as well though, sounding a bit aimless without at least an occasional rap in front of them. Two other rappers make appearances, Neph the Madman on "Wiling" and Poet on the solid "Buck Buck," while Kool Keith's "King of NY" fondly recalls the Beasties' *Paul's Boutique*. —*John Bush*

## AUX 88
f. 1993, Detroit, MI
*Group / Techno-Bass, Electro-Techno, Detroit Techno, Club/Dance, Techno*

Since forming in 1993, Detroit-based electro-techno group AUX 88 have spearheaded a '90s-style rewrite of the breakbeat electro-funk of the early Motor City sound. Often referred to as techno bass, the style integrates elements of early Detroit and New York electro, Miami-born bass music, and the dark, gritty analog edge of Detroit techno, AUX's releases (mostly through the similarly styled Direct Beat label) are typically uptempo, bass-heavy party rockers in line with Detroit classics such as "Cosmic Cars," "Party Race," and "Play It Cool," but with a dark edge similar to "Clear" and "Technicolor." Responding to the wholesale export of the music following its popularity in Europe in the mid- to late-'80s, AUX see themselves filling the cultural gap left by the mainstream absorption of the first few generations of Detroit techno. Rather than simply carry a hometown techno torch, however, AUX have returned to the roots of the music in the electronic breakbeat, and—along with artists like Will Web, Mike Banks, and Drexciya—have found themselves on the front lines of a full-on electro revival.

Originally consisting of producer Tommy Hamilton and DJ Keith "K-1" Tucker, AUX 88 grew out of youths spent infatuated with the futuristic beat music of Kraftwerk and Cybotron. Hamilton and William "BJ" Smith (who would join the group full-time in 1995, following Tucker's departure), spent their after-school childhood knocking out acoustic approximations of tunes like "Clear" and "Numbers" on second-hand bass and drums. Practicing for hours on end to nail the precise timing of electro's machine beats, Smith finally traded his bicycle for a cheap Casio keyboard and began making tracks. While continuing to work with Smith, Hamilton teamed up with Keith Tucker (a longtime Detroit electro and techno DJ) to form AUX 88, and began releasing records in 1994. The group's debut, "Bass Magnetic," met with instant success, and subsequent releases like "My AUX Mind" and "AUX Quadrant" combined with releases from Underground Resistance, Drexciya, and Will Web in announcing a street-level renaissance of Detroit electro. (Many of the group's best early cuts are collected on the CD-only *AUX 88 Meets Alien FM*, released by Submerge in 1995.)

Tucker left AUX 88 in 1995 to pursue a solo career as DJ K-1 (his "K-1 Agenda" was released by Direct Beat in 1996), and the group remained in the care of Smith and Hamilton (until Smith left as well in 1998). The pair released a single, "Break It Down," and contributed a track to Direct Beat's *Experience Da Bass II* compilation EP in 1996 before dropping AUX's first serious long-player, *Is It Man or Machine?* that same year. While distance has meant AUX has been pretty absent from most accounts of a European electro revival (centered, superficially, around labels such as Clear and Warp, and more interestingly around Overdrive, Panic Trax, Anodyne, and Pharma), *Is It Man or Machine?* has found an avid audience in Europe as well. At home, AUX have made a name for themselves as one of the few American techno groups who play live on a regular basis; they're joined on stage by Direct Beat's DJ Dijital, who, as with early hip-hop DJs, cuts up the group's beats in real time, adding manic scratching and noisy drop-ins over sequenced rhythms, basslines, and synth patches. The first AUX 88 LP to be recorded by Hamilton alone was 1998's *Xeo-Genetic*. One year later, the mix album *Electro Boogie* followed on Studio !K7. —*Sean Cooper*

**88 FM** / 1995 / 430 West/Direct Beat ♦♦♦
Collects several tracks from earlier 12"s and adds a few new cuts. DJs will be frustrated trying to track the vinyl down (there is none), but the best cuts derive from classic AUX EPs such as "AUX Quadrant," "Direct Drive," and "My AUX Mind," all of which remain in print. —*Sean Cooper*

**Electro/Techno [Single]** / 1996 / Direct Beat ♦♦♦
Deep, hard-hitting Detroit electro reminiscent of Cybotron and Channel One material such as "Clear" and "Technicolor." The sound is clearer than those early four-track masterpieces, but the deep bass and sweeping filter glissandos pay clear tribute. —*Sean Cooper*

• **Is It Man or Machine?** / Nov. 25, 1996 / Direct Beat ♦♦♦♦
AUX's proper debut is start-to-finish Detroit-style techno bass as expected. Like much Direct Beat material, *Machine* suffers for its throwback ghetto/booty focus, but nobody does the style better than AUX. The CD-version collects many of the duo's early singles, such as "Electrotechno" and "Bass Magnetic." —*Sean Cooper*

**Xeo-Genetic** / Oct. 12, 1998 / Direct Beat ♦♦
*Xeo-Genetic* showcases AUX 88 mastermind Tom Hamilton's sincere attempt to channel the DJ-orientated sounds of electro into the conceptual confines of a full-length album. This is no easy task; the quick tempos, limited palette, and syncopated rhythms of Hamilton's brand of electro don't make ideal listening music. Despite the challenge, Hamilton succeeds to a certain extent in his mission to seam together a total of 20 tracks. Songs such as "Play It Loud" and "Computer Speaks" represent the sort of energized ass shakers one would expect from any artist on the Detroit-based Direct Beat label. Their funky drum-machine rhythms, bleeping riffs, and Kraftwerk-like motifs define for many the ideal sound of electro. Of course, an entire album of dancefloor anthems would be little more than a DJ mix album similar to DJ Di'jital's *Techno Bass 2: The Prototype Mix*; instead, Hamilton inserts some down-tempo electro songs such as "I Need to Find Myself" and "Rise of the Phoenix" that craft moods more than they incite dancing. In addition, short sketches similar to those found on many rap albums appear every few songs. Looking at the array of different songs on the album, the dancefloor anthems such as "Play It Loud" stand out as the album's highlights. The down-tempo songs sound good and should hold the interest of anyone attracted to the electro side of techno. Unfortunately, the sketches detract from *Xeo-Genetic*'s overall appeal; they may bring personality and a sense of motif to album, but

they also sound silly at times. For example, "Hydro Spin" has a reporter going to visit a futuristic club to interview Hamilton, bringing a sense of lowbrow sci-fi kitsch to an otherwise album of serious music. In sum, *Xeo-Genetic* attempts what few have accomplished by constructing a conceptual electro album that is ultimately hampered by the often homogeneous sounds of Hamilton's music and a few embarrassing non-musical moments. —*Jason Birchmeier*

**Electro Boogie** / Oct. 19, 1999 / Studio !K7 ♦♦♦♦
Even given the consistently high quality of mix albums released by Studio !K7 (including volumes by Dave Clarke, Depth Charge, Richie Hawtin, and Kevin Saunderson), AUX 88's volume in the label's *Electro Boogie* series hits some pretty high peaks. Shot through with the fast-paced, aggressive breakbeat electro-techno that AUX 88 produces (and mixes) better than almost anyone, *Electro Boogie* veers from future-shock electro (Dopplereffekt's "Superior Race," Drexciya's "Bubble Metropolis") to booty techno (X-Ile's "I Wanna," DJ Assault's "Shake It Baby") and still finds time to drop a few all-time classics (Underground Resistance's "The Final Frontier," the Unknown DJ's "Basstronic," DJ Good Groove's "Rock It"). Half of the tracks—and most of the highlights—come from the duo's affiliated label, Direct Beat (home to Di'jital, X-Ile, Posatronix, Microknox, DJ K1), and all but two tracks come from Detroit labels. Unlike the occasionally history-lesson feel of past volumes, this one is more than just a time capsule; it's a living, breathing document of the thriving electro scene in Detroit. —*John Bush*

## David Axelrod

**b.** Apr. 17, 1936, Los Angeles, CA
*Producer / Obscuro, Psychedelic Pop, Baroque Pop, Jazz-Funk*
A Grammy award-winning producer for Capitol Records who helmed dozens of great jazz, funk, and soul records during the '60s and '70s (by everyone from Stan Kenton to Lou Rawls to the Electric Prunes to Cannonball Adderley), David Axelrod also forged a distinctive musical style while recording several of the most eccentric albums of the '70s. His sound, as immediately recognizable as it is sparse, combined cavernous, heavily mic'ed drums with baroque orchestration (just a step away from overblown) and ahead-of-his-time themes ranging from the environment to heightened mental awareness.

Born in Los Angeles in 1936, Axelrod learned about arrangement and production largely on his own. He began working as a staff producer for the cool jazz labels Specialty and Contemporary, and led a pair of 1959 LPs— *Free for All* by Frank Rosolino and *The Fox* by Harold Land—that developed an earthy response to the trademarked light, airy sound of West Coast jazz.

By the mid-'60s, Axelrod had grown famous in soul and jazz circles for his excellent site recording at concerts, including two of the finest live albums of the era, Lou Rawls' *Live!* and Cannonball Adderley's *Mercy, Mercy, Mercy! Live at 'The Club.'* Both artists tapped him for studio work as well, and Rawls especially benefited by scoring no less than five pop hits during 1966-67. Capitol rewarded one of its most successful producers just one year later, releasing Axelrod's solo debut, *Song of Innocence*. Based on the visionary, mystical poetry of William Blake (as was its follow-up *Songs of Experience*), the album sounded like nothing else from its era, with melodramatic strings tied to heavy, echoed breakbeats—often supplied by session-drummer supremo Earl Palmer. After *Songs of Experience*, Axelrod turned his attention to the growing plight of the environment with 1970's *Earth Rot*.

Even aside from his burgeoning solo career, Axelrod stayed busy as a producer during the '70s; he recorded several Cannonball Adderley LPs plus works by Gene Ammons and Joe Williams. After 1980's *Marchin'*, however,

he took an extended hiatus from recording. Axelrod returned in 1993 with *Requiem: The Holocaust* on Capitol's Liberty subsidiary, and recorded a surprising tribute to roots music (*The Big Country*) two years later. After several big names in the dance community (including DJ Shadow) began sampling Axelrod grooves in the mid-'90s, Stateside released the retrospective *1968 to 1970: An Axelrod Anthology* in 1999. Album reissues appeared the following year, and Axelrod even recorded a remix of "Rabbit in the Headlights," originally by the DJ Shadow project UNKLE. —*John Bush*

**Song of Innocence** / 1968 / Capitol ♦♦♦♦
**Songs of Experience** / 1969 / Capitol ♦♦♦
**Earth Rot** / 1970 / Capitol ♦♦♦♦

● **1968 to 1970: An Axelrod Anthology** / 1999 / Stateside ♦♦♦♦
Confounding dozens of vinyl-philes who'd paid hundreds of dollars for the original LPs, *1968 to 1970: An Axelrod Anthology* compiles 11 tracks from the first (and best) three albums released by David Axelrod, including the two-volume series devoted to William Blake (*Song of Innocence, Songs of Experience*) and the 1970 ecological nightmare, *Earth Rot*. Alongside those tracks are seven of Axelrod's best productions, for soul singers like Lou Rawls (the Buffalo Springfield's "For What It's Worth") and Letta as well as Cannonball Adderley and the psychedelic mystics known as the Electric Prunes. The solo Axelrod tracks are dreadfully spare, usually just cavernous drum pattern and occasional orchestral texture, but the songs have an odd power that grows over time. Overall, *1968 to 1970: An Axelrod Anthology* is quite preferable to spending collectors' prices for the originals. —*John Bush*

## A:xus (Austin Bascom)

**b.** Toronto, Ontario, Canada
*Producer / Jazz-House, Club/Dance, House*
Though most of his productions have appeared on Chicago labels, producer/DJ Austin Bascom is actually based in Toronto. Soaking up a variety of sounds in Canada's metropolitan hub, Bascom was influenced by not only house and techno but electro, soul, acid jazz, and hip-hop. He began releasing his material in 1995, and created a reputation for lush underground house with club favorites (recorded as Abacus) for two of Chicago's best-loved dance labels, Guidance and 83 West. In 1999, his first A:xus production, the atmospheric samba-house cut "Baghdad Cafe (Callin' U)," became yet another prize for DJs and club fans alike. In early 2000, the full-length *Soundtrack for Life* became the first single-artist full-length released by Guidance. —*John Bush*

● **Soundtrack for Life** / Feb. 29, 2000 / Guidance Recordings ♦♦♦♦
Bascom's focus on alternately earthy and atmospheric house belies the tremendously precise production sense on display for his first full-length. Though he's closest in sound to house and the more danceable end of '90s acid jazz (Faze Action, Beanfield, A Forest Mighty Black), Bascom's fusion of the impeccably produced, the thematically complex, and the musically diverse also places him as an inheritor of Detroit techno. As such, excellent Motor City producers like Derrick May and Carl Craig are the links to a jazz-funk-lite number like "Baghdad Cafe (Calllin' U)," the electro tributes "My Planet Rocks" and "Synchronicity," and the interstellar techno-jazz meditation "Jupiter." The vocal tracks, with contributions from Naomi N'Sembi and Rosina, are well-spaced and not overly indulgent (occasionally a problem on dance albums). Strong, clever production skills and a feel for musical variety that never sounds forced gives *Soundtrack for Life* a solid base that extends its attraction beyond repeated listenings. —*John Bush*

# B

## B12
f. 1989, London, England
*Group / Electronica, Ambient Techno, Club/Dance, Techno, IDM*

One of only a handful of British techno acts ostensibly pursuing a legacy of British techno firmly rooted in its Detroit pre-history, B12 are also (perhaps resultingly) one of the few British techno acts also hailed by the Motor City's aesthetic elite. Notoriously shy of the music press, the London-based duo of Mike Golding and Steve Rutter have quietly made their contribution to post-rave techno by updating Detroit's signature optimistic/dystopian futurism for a digital age, constructing tracks of glinting, heavily syncopated electro-techno with a strong base in melody and mood. A relatively young project, the group have made an impact despite a comparatively conservative release schedule. They issued their first handful of untitled 12"s — attributed to a loosely structured catalog of pseudonyms like Redcell, Musicology, and CStasis — on their own B12 label, and were immediately hailed alongside UK techno acts like LFO, the Black Dog, Sweet Exorcist, and Tricky Disco as heralding something of a new age of post-acid house techno-based electronic music. Included on the Warp label's somewhat disastrously titled *Artificial Intelligence* compilations (the pair signed with Warp in 1992), Golding and Rutter were also (somewhat unfairly) pegged as the sort of likewise artful noodlers what the term "intelligent techno" has since come to signify. Their Warp debut in 1993 assembled the best of their early years, and the group followed the release with a three-year hiatus before releasing the like-sounding *Time Tourist* in 1996. Outside of their relationship with Warp, the group keep all other B12-related music-dealings in-house — including distribution — which means their records can be somewhat hard to find. Their two albums for Warp were reissued in the US by Wax Trax!/TVT. — *Sean Cooper*

★ **Electro-Soma** / 1993 / Wax Trax! ♦♦♦♦♦

A retrospective of sorts, *Electro-Soma* collects the cream of the group's early singles on their own B12 label, including brazen entries from Stasis, Musicology, and Redcell. The CD version adds four tracks. — *Sean Cooper*

**Time Tourists** / Apr. 1996 / Wax Trax! ♦♦♦♦

A slick, arresting slate of ambient-leaning electro-techno with a strong Detroit feel. Again split between the group's many ongoing projects, the tracks vary from four-on-the-floor club movers to after-hours chill-bound breakbeat tracks and funky, almost jazz-oriented electro. — *Sean Cooper*

## Howie B (Howard Bernstein)
b. Glasgow, Scotland
*Mixing, Engineer, Producer / Ambient Techno, Trip-Hop*

Howie B. was a popular London-based DJ and nascent studio hand prior to his move into full-time recording and production in the early '90s. Born in Glasgow, his association with Bristol club faves like Soul II Soul and Massive Attack fueled his aesthetic on a fusion of soul, hip-hop, house, jazz, and funk, first hazarded on early collaborative projects like Dobie and Nomad Soul. B set up his own label, Pussyfoot, in 1994, already having released tracks under his own name and Olde Scottish through noted outbound hip-hop imprints, 2Kool and Mo'Wax, and a small-but-steady stream of material moving hip-hop instrumentals a step beyond the experimental, joined Bernstein with beat junkies like DJ Shadow, U.N.K.L.E., Portishead, and Coldcut at the forefront of a UK breakbeat renaissance. Although his genre-spanning work with Skylab on 1994's *#1* brought his talents for organized chaos before a wider audience, it was ultimately his role in the production chair (for such artists as Tricky, Björk, and eventually U2), that landed him the multi-album recording deal with Polydor which yielded LPs including 1996's *Music for Babies*, 1997's *Turn the Dark Off*, and 1999's *Snatch*. — *Sean Cooper*

**Music for Babies** / Aug. 6, 1996 / Island Independent ♦♦♦♦

As a member of Skylab, U2's *Passengers* project, and a producer for Björk, Howie B has made the most of available technology, and his debut solo album is no different. *Music for Babies* is a laidback trip-hop adventure featuring some effects previously unheard anywhere. The watery, understated percussion suits the title well — the effect must be close to what music sounds like from inside the womb (and indeed, Howie's wife gave birth during the recording). The album flows too slowly for comfort, though: the first song contains five minutes of rather labored effects before the second track, "Cry," starts things off with a downtempo beat; the track's cool high-pitched scratch effects then distort and fly off into canine frequencies at regular intervals. "How to Suckie" has a trance-state mood (complete with muted trumpet and vibraphone) that conjures up the abstract feeling of Pharoah Sanders' late-'60s ethno-jazz recordings. Though *Music for Babies* is one step ahead of most fill-in-the-dots trip-hop, its sleepy mood is a bit too infantile. — *John Bush*

**Turn the Dark Off** / Jul. 28, 1997 / PolyGram ♦♦♦♦

Working with U2 on their 1997 *Pop* album gave Howie B a better sense of what keeps listeners awake, and the improvement is obvious on his second solo album. *Turn the Dark Off* fits in with the crop of contemporary big-beat maestros, like the Chemical Brothers, Prodigy, Bentley Rhythm Ace, and David Holmes. Though it doesn't quite outdistance the pack (blame the lack of energy on some leftover atmospherics from *Music for Babies*), the album still contains enough of Howie B's studio tweaks to make it worthwhile, especially on the unfortunately titled "Buttmeat" and the single "Angels Go Bald Too." — *John Bush*

● **Snatch** / Mar. 16, 1999 / Palm Pictures ♦♦♦♦

From the languished trip-hop of *Music for Babies* to the sublime big-beat on *Turn the Dark Off*, Howie B has excelled at rewiring the latest thing in electronica. In doing so, he displays not only his stellar production skills but also his ear for unheard beats and overall knack for creating excellent headphone music. To this extent, *Snatch* is a similar record. The jumping-off point for this, however, is the increasingly experimentalist slant of electronic music during the late '90s, displayed by the slipped-disc sample minimalism of artists such as Autechre, Panasonic and Mouse on Mars. The opener, "Gallway," takes a few minutes of static electricity to launch into its muted beat attack, while the sub-bass depth on "Cook for You" is practically off the charts. "Trust" blends a few phlegmatic effects reminiscent of Mouse on Mars, with glazed-eye minimalism of the Philip Glass variety, and a melodica sample perhaps gleaned from his trip to Jamaica (the results of which appeared on *Sly & Robbie Stripped to the Bone by Howie B*, released less than a month before). Of course, a month's working vacation in Kingston is going to result in radically different music than spending time in the new-experimentalist center of Cologne, but *Snatch* successfully fuses the earthier side of dub and trip-hop with abstract electronics. It's by far his best album yet. — *John Bush*

## John B. (John B. Williams)
b. 1977, Maidenhead, London, England
*Producer / Jungle/Drum'N'Bass, Club/Dance*

Among the youngest of the new-school drum'n'bass innovators, John B. has amassed an impressive discography in the short few years he's been producing jungle. With track credits scattered among the cream of the underground crop — including Formation, New Identity, Shoebox, and Grooverider's Prototype imprint — John B. has gradually come to the fore as a producer of sharp, tough-to-nail-down tracks that bridge many styles at once. At the same time, he incorporates elements of jazz and funk, electro and techno, and hard- and tech-leaning darkside in brisk, challenging tunes. Born John B. Williams in London's Maidenhead, he began producing in his early teens. Working from a second-hand studio his father helped him piece together, Williams released a few mostly forgettable techno tracks before widening his scope to include the burgeoning drum'n'bass sound. Collecting a few tunes onto a demo, Williams sent his tracks to a more or less random collection of producers and labels, including Goldie and DJ SS's New Identity label, and received encouragement from both (as well as a licensing deal from SS; his "Jazz Sessions 1" appeared on New Identity's label compilation *Jazz and Bass*). He then released the "Sight Beyond"/"Fermat's Theorem" 12" (on New Identity), as well as the "Cooper" single (as IC1 on the 5HQ label). Williams gained a higher profile gig with his appearance on Grooverider's *The Prototype Years* compilation. "Secrets," one of the triple-pack's many exclusives, was a high-point among high-points, and more than held its own next to killers from the likes of Ed Rush, Dillinja, Boymerang, and Dominic Angus (aka Dom & Roland). "Slamfunk", subsequently released on Formation, was the first single from his debut full-length *Visions*, released in early 1998. One year later, *Catalyst* appeared on his own Beta Recordings. —*Sean Cooper*

**Slamfunk [Single]** / Apr. 28, 1997 / Formation ♦♦♦♦
John B.'s debut 12" for Formation, proved to be a calling card for his forthcoming full-length release. The title track is the keeper here, treading dark techstep territory, his knack for subtle jazz phrasing adding a less gimmicky edge to otherwise hissing darkness. The track's strong point, though, is (as usual) the beatwork: "Slamfunk" absolutely swarms with shards of a dozen different breaks, cycling about in frenzied recombination amongst pointed bass throbs and chaotic atmospheres. The flip is a less interesting minimal tech roller similar to Boymerang's "Still." —*Sean Cooper*

• **Visions** / Feb. 24, 1998 / Sm:)e ♦♦♦♦
John B's debut album, a two-disc set subtitled "Organic" and "Synthetic," leaves few trails untaken. The 19-year-old junglist maintains a somewhat jazzy vibe on the Organic disc (with several tracks virtually identical to mainstream hard bop), but explores the fine lines of trance and darkstep with occasional downtempo passages on the second disc. The result is an album which alternates graceful productions in a well-heeled form with outer-edge drum'n'bass experiments. —*John Bush*

**Catalyst** / Sep. 20, 1999 / Beta Recordings ♦♦♦♦
While John B's first album balanced one disc of jazzy drum'n'bass with another featuring his harder tech-step productions, *Catalyst* mashes light and dark together. The album is definitely weighted toward the dark side though, with brilliant effects on drum'n'bass stormers like "Gollum" and "Double J" (the latter with chatting from MC Justiyc). Of the lighter tracks, "Progress" and "Imagine" have a bit of soul flavoring, while "Simulated Sax" is only slightly better than the title indicates. If the results of *Catalyst* are any judge, then John B. should chuck his jazz inclinations and head for the sound of the future. CD copies include a second disc with the tracks from the first in mixed form. —*John Bush*

## Mark B

*Producer / Underground Rap, Ambient Breakbeat, Hip-Hop*
Mark B is just one of the excellent DJ/producers on Jazz Fudge Recordings, the label most closely associated with Britain-by-way-of-Russia's DJ Vadim. Compared to the usual run of scratch-happy turntablists in underground rap, Mark is much more reliant on drum-machine dinosaurs and samplers. He began recording for Jazz Fudge in 1995, and produced a couple of tracks for Vadim's 1996 debut *U.S.S.R. Repertoire (The Theory of Verticality)*. Mark B released his first album, *Underworld Connection*, the following year and he collaborated with rapper Blade for 1998's excellent *Hitmen for Hire* LP. In 1999, he teamed up with Taskforce for the album *New Mic Order*. Mark B also contributed to the OM compilation *Deeper Concentration, Vol. 2*. —*John Bush*

**Underworld Connection** / Jul. 21, 1997 / Jazz Fudge ♦♦
Recorded for DJ Vadim's stellar label Jazz Fudge, *Underworld Connection* contains all the usual abstract hip-hop clichés: shrieking '50s strings, '60s spy music, and '70s funk with incredibly obscure spoken-word bits. Fortunately, Mark B has a way with his studio gear, and he tweaks the mix until it becomes quite a unique work. —*John Bush*

• **Hitmen for Hire** / Apr. 13, 1998 / Jazz Fudge ♦♦♦♦
Instead of delving farther into abstract hip-hop, Mark B teamed up with the rapper Blade for his second album. The collaboration works quite well, as Blade and B (plus Mr. Thing from Scratch Perverts on scratching) construct a dense underground rap album that fortunately never moves too far into beat headspace. From the scratchy old samples on "Intense Preparations" (featuring Lewis Parker) to the 808 bump of "Use Your Head," Mark B displays his considerable production skills, and Blade matches him with verbal dexterity. As could be expected, there are a couple of instrumentals that get a bit bland, and (for better or worse) there are many sophomoric samples. Any way you dice it though, *Hitmen for Hire* is an excellent hip-hop album. —*John Bush*

## Baby Ford (Peter Ford)

*Producer / Club/Dance, Techno, Acid House*
Peter Ford is one of the most recognizable names in current dancefloor techno and was one of the founders of the UK acid house scene. He's released records under a slew of pseudonyms, including Casino Classix, El Mal, Solcyc, Simprini Risin', and his most frequent, Baby Ford. His early work—heavily influenced by the late-'80s acid house sound, as well as Chicago producers such as Marshall Jefferson, Ron Trent, Armando, and Larry Heard—appeared primarily through the Rhythm King label, and included classic cuts such as "Oochy Koochy," "Children of the Revolution," and "Fetish." Material has also appeared on Sire, Source, and Insumision/Transglobal. He's released four full-length albums to date, including the debut *Fordtrax* (a staple of most techno DJs) and 1997's *Headphoneasyrider*, one of his more listener-friendly albums. His recent work has appeared mostly through Trelik and Ifach—two of the UK's most highly regarded experimental techno labels, and both of which Ford has a hand in managing (Trelik together with Eon's Ian Loveday; Ifach with Mark Broom). He's also collaborated with Ian Loveday on a number of projects (including Minimal Man), both for Trelik and for William Orbit's Guerrilla label. Less active as a remixer, Ford has reconfigured tracks for Stefan Robbers' Florence project and pop techno group S'Express, among others. —*Sean Cooper*

**Oooh, The World of Baby Ford** / 1989 / Sire ♦♦♦
Very stylized dance music, with some rock and pop links, is the formula popularized by Baby Ford. This 1989 release has clever, at times annoyingly cute vocals, intricate, layered production, and the kind of omnipresent beats and effects that are both a hallmark and a problem for '90s dance fare. —*Ron Wynn*

**B-Ford 9** / Jun. 30, 1992 / Sire ♦♦♦
While not as perfectly thrilling as *Oooh*, *B Ford 9* still definitely has its moments of invigorating house/techno heaven given a fine combination of dirt and sheen. Its biggest problem is that the opening numbers are the strongest, rendering it another in the long line of dance albums that fail to maintain strength over length. This said, opening numbers are fantastic. "RU486" kicks it all off with a stiff beat and all the expected elements of 1992 UK electronics—siren/bass rumbles, trebly melody line, and so forth—but all fused together just right, with a perfectly nagging hook that constantly repeats and buries samples and cries. "Fetish," a co-production with fellow early-'90s dance figure Eon, continues the winning streak even more effectively—a brutal burst of sound that sounds like the pissed-off cousin of 808 State's "Cubik" or Joey Beltram's "Energy Flash." Stuttered rhythm loops that sound like inhalation, abbreviated vocal samples, and that "stadium house" feeling à la KLF certainly don't hurt. "Move-On" adds Ford's oddly winsome vocal to a fine combination of synth-string heaven and sped-up funk drum-loop fun (it's not jungle, but that was already in the air). "In Your Blood," mixed by C. J. Bolland, takes a more minimal approach that builds and ebbs as it goes: more acid house, synth squelches, and hollow percussion loops that seek nothing more than to demand your presence on the dance floor—and after all, sometimes that's all you need. After that, things start to get less compelling, though there are some fun moments, such as the roughly campy "Sashay Around the Fuzzbox," and the slow funk crawl of "20, Park Drive." A number of remixes and alternate takes round out this uneven but still interesting disc. —*Ned Raggett*

• **Headphoneasyrider** / Apr. 14, 1997 / Blackmarket ♦♦♦♦
Though still on the straight-ahead side of techno experiments, *Headphone*'s crisp, delicate breaks and smooth electronics are a bit of a gear-change from earlier, more acid- and hardcore-tinged records such as *Fordtrax* and *Fetish*. This is easily Ford's most listenable outing to date. —*Sean Cooper*

## Baby Mammoth

f. 1995, Hull, England
*Group / Ambient Techno, Trip-Hop*

Amidst heavy competition, Baby Mammoth is the Pork label's most prolific act, packing in five full LPs of blunted instrumental hip-hop between their debut in late 1996 and the end of the decade. Like other Pork acts such as Fila Brazillia and Solid Doctor, the duo of Mark Blissenden and Andrew Burdall specialize in earthy breaks and ambient atmospheres, and are more slanted to the instrumental edge of acid jazz than other producer-based trip-hop acts. The pair first met Pork label-head Dave Brennand and associate Steve Cobby (aka Fila Brazillia) at a club in Hull, where both band and label are based. The relationship blossomed with the release of Baby Mammoth's debut, *10,000 Years Beneath the Street* in 1996. Blissenden and Burdall released two albums the following year (as well as an EP and single). Baby Mammoth settled down to a more languid release schedule with one LP release each year in 1998 (*Another Day at the Orifice*), 1999 (*Swimming*) and 2000 (*Motion Without Pain*). —*John Bush*

**10,000 Years Beneath the Street** / Sep. 2, 1996 / Pork ♦♦

**Bridging Two Worlds** / Feb. 24, 1997 / Pork ♦♦♦♦

**One . . . Two . . . Freak** / Aug. 11, 1997 / Pork ♦♦♦♦
Baby Mammoth hit their stride with this second album of ambient-groove genius. Although "Skidding on All Fours" adds a bit of skittery drum'n'bass, and two tracks ("Additive," "Warm Air Rising") have some vaguely electro leanings, the great majority of tracks on *One . . . Two . . . Freak* are simply excellent fusion-inspired productions. —*John Bush*

**Another Day at the Orifice** / May 12, 1998 / Pork ♦♦♦
The Mammoth's third album comes complete with a very unpunny Pork-like title that also functions as a dig at the duo's continuing trip through downbeat hip-hop. And though the recipe here is indeed a bit of laidback-breakbeat-by-numbers, the duo reach a bit deeper on several tracks. The mid-tempo acid-psych line in "I'm Not Joking," the lazy ambient wash that drives "Delta's Young Champion," the Oriental lilt of "100% Polyester"—all these make *Another Day at the Orifice* another solid addition to Baby Mammoth's Porkography. —*John Bush*

● **Swimming** / Apr. 5, 1999 / Pork ♦♦♦♦
*Swimming* augments the duo's tried-and-true vision of earthy trip-hop with live musicians from around their hometown of Hull, making for a much more immediate record than others in the Baby Mammoth discography. Guitarist Tom Harland's jazz riffs lend a bit of energy to "Quick Kick," while others like "Long Stroke" and "Smoke" also benefit from experienced programming. —*John Bush*

## The Baby Namboos

f. Manchester, England
*Group / Trip-Hop, Club/Dance*

The trip-hop group Baby Namboos consists of programmer/songwriter Mike Porter, vocalists Claude Williams, Leo Coleing and Aurora Borealis, drummer Mad-dog and bassist Julian Brooke. Porter began the band in 1998, when he went to New York City to visit his cousin Tricky, who encouraged his musical explorations. Soon after, Porter and his friend Coleing began recording in a Manchester studio, adding band members along the way. Tricky continued to provide guidance and encouragement, performed on a few tracks, and released the Baby Namboos' debut album *Ancoats 2 Zambia* on his own Durban Poison imprint. —*Heather Phares*

● **Ancoats 2 Zambia** / Oct. 12, 1999 / Palm ♦♦♦♦
On their debut album *Ancoats 2 Zambia*, the Baby Namboos mix elements of trip-hop, dub, and rap into songs like "Hard Times," "Provoked," and the title track, which showcase the group's three vocalists and atmospheric yet direct approach. Given the album's shuffling beats and hypnotic vocals, it's not surprising that the Baby Namboos are related to—and share a label with—Tricky, who also performs on the title track, "Provoked," and "Persist to Reminisce." A strong, engaging debut, *Ancoats 2 Zambia* exemplifies Durban Poison's style without sounding too derivative of the label's best-known artist. —*Heather Phares*

## Bad Boy Bill

*DJ / Club/Dance, House*

Hard-house DJ Bad Boy Bill was born and raised in Chicago, and began mixing records at the age of 14. An avid fan of Chicago radio station WBMX's Hot Mix Five mixing team, Bill landed his big break when none other than Farley Jackmaster Funk gave him his first broadcast gig; he went on to emerge as one of the hottest turntablists on the Windy City scene, and in 1988 took top honors in the Midwest division of DMC's Battle DJ competition. Bad Boy Bill went on to spin records throughout the world, even maintaining a long-term DJ residency in Germany in addition to hosting "Street Mix," a top-rated weekly radio mix show on Chicago's WBBM. He also founded his own label, International House Records; and through its Mix Connection Multimedia Inc. subdivision issued a series of mix tapes, the ongoing *Bangin the Box* series. Utilizing up to fifty records—a reflection of his hip-hop background—where most DJs would use only ten, Bad Boy Bill gained a great reputation for playing fast and loose with the mix, rarely pausing to rest on his laurels. Along with the *Bangin the Box* series, he's issued several volumes in a four-turntable battle series (with Richard "Humpty" Vission) titled *The House Connection*. In May of 2000 the bangin' series continued with the release of *Bangin in London*. —*Jason Ankeny*

**Bangin the Box, Vol. 2** / Oct. 29, 1996 / Mixed Connections ♦♦

● **Bangin the Box, Vol. 3** / Apr. 21, 1998 / Mixed Connections ♦♦♦♦
The third volume in the *Bangin the Box* series is, like the others, a frenetic hands-on mix of Hi-NRG house that defies listeners not to dance. Spinning through 45 tracks in just an hour, Bad Boy Bill culls pounding productions from the growing dance Diaspora—Ralphi Rosario ("Take Me Up"), Angel Alanis ("Hardcore," "Pimp Player"), Plastikman ("Spastik"), Byron Stingily ("Get Up"), CZR ("Chicago Southside"), Armand Van Helden ("Ultrafunkula"), Richard F ("Crack That Whip"), DJ Bam Bam ("Baby Werk")—and bends each track to his will with turntable spin backs and added effects. As with other mixes that just never stops peaking, it can occasionally grow exhausting, but *Bangin the Box, Vol. 3* is an exhilarating set of hard mainstream dance. —*John Bush*

**Bangin the Box, Vol. 4** / Aug. 31, 1999 / Mixed Connections ♦♦♦

**Bangin in London** / May 2, 2000 / Master Dancetones ♦♦♦♦
Taking his quintessentially American style of cut-up mixing overseas, Bad Boy Bill fortunately didn't tinker with the mix too much, preferring instead to concentrate on the usual extroverted, pumping tracks from favorites like Angel Alanis ("Chi's Revenge," "La Musica," "Funk Master") and Armand Van Helden ("Necessary Evil"). He does toss a few bones to the London audience courtesy of more internationally focused club hits—Moby's "Body Rock," Groove Armada's "I See You Baby," Novy Vs. Eniac's "Pumping"—but there's absolutely no comedown or compromise to Bad Boy Bill's mix on *Bangin in London*. —*John Bush*

## Arthur Baker

b. Apr. 22, 1955, Boston, MA
*Drums, Remixing, Producer / Electro, Club/Dance, Hip-Hop*

Arthur Baker was among the most visible and widely-imitated of the early hip-hop producers, masterminding breakthrough experiments with tape edits and synthetic beats before crossing over to introduce the art of remixing into the pop mainstream. He began his career as a club DJ in Boston, and landed his first production work at Emergency Records, debuting with Northend's "Happy Days." After relocating to New York in 1979, Baker quickly immersed himself in the nascent hip-hop scene; there he was recruited by the Salsoul label to helm a session for Joe Bataan which yielded the rap novelty "Rap-O-Clap-O." His stay in the Big Apple largely unsuccessful, he returned to Boston, producing a handful of singles which went nowhere, among them Glory's "Can You Guess What Groove This Is?"

A move back to New York followed, at which time Baker joined the staff of Tommy Boy Records, where he teamed with co-producer Shep Pettibone to record Afrika Bambaataa's groundbreaking 1982 single "Jazzy Sensation" (a remake of Gwen McCrae's "Funky Sensation"). Assuming sole production control, Baker next reunited with Bambaataa for the classic "Planet Rock," a watershed in hip-hop's early evolution. A wholly-synthesized record inspired by Kraftwerk's *Trans-Europe Express*, its programmed beats left an indelible imprint on the music released in its wake. Baker's success at Tommy Boy led to the formation of his own label, Streetwise Records; after helming underground club hits for Rockers Revenge, Nairobi and Citispeak, he signed a then-unknown New Edition, issuing the teen vocal group's debut single "Candy Girl" in 1982.

Baker's gradual absorption into the pop mainstream continued in 1983, when the cutting-edge British dance group New Order contacted him to produce their single "Confusion"; the record became an immediate club classic, even scraping into the American R&B charts. Remixes of the track also helped pioneer the remix aesthetic throughout the rock mainstream; soon Baker was producing material for Naked Eyes, Face to Face, Diana Ross, Jeff Beck and others. In 1989, he also assembled artists including Al Green, ABC and Jimmy Somerville to record the all-star LP *Merge*, credited to Arthur Baker and the Backbeat Disciples. After a follow-up, 1991's *Give in to the Rhythm*, he returned to production, albeit no longer exerting the same kind of influence as in the decade prior. —*Jason Ankeny*

● **Merge** / Sep. 1989 / A&M ♦♦♦♦
By the time Arthur Baker got around to making an album under his own name in 1989 (or as "Arthur Baker and the Backbeat Disciples," at any rate), he had a lot of favors to call in, having spent most of the '80s remixing music for half of the pop music community. But even on his own tracks, he remained a remixer and producer, creating sparkling dance grooves and having such guests as Al Green, Martin Fry of ABC, Jimmy Somerville, and Andy McClosky of Orchestral Manoeuvres in the Dark, among others, sing over them. The result set toes tapping (although the album was surprisingly eclectic, not hardcore dance music by any means), but it was hard to identify as the work of a particular artist. Nevertheless, individual cuts stood out: Green's "The Message Is Love" got into the R&B charts, and along with "It's Your Time" were UK hits. The album, however, failed to take off, and Baker left A&M. —*William Ruhlmann*

**Give in to the Rhythm** / Sep. 1991 / RCA ♦♦♦
Once again Arthur Baker creates a state-of-the-art dance album that comes off, with its six different vocalists (including Al Green, Lee John, Adele Bertei, and Tata Vega), sounding like a various artists compilation. The tracks are constructed for maximum dance floor efficiency (plus a few concessions to rap), and the singers are suitably emphatic. The clubs were impressed, and individual songs—"IOU," featuring Nikeeta (a remake of an early Baker production), and the soulful "Leave the Guns at Home," with Green—slipped into the pop and R&B charts. But Baker still doesn't add up as a name recording artist and may be better off back behind the mixing desk. —*William Ruhlmann*

## Ballistic Brothers

**f.** 1993, London, England
*Group / Jazz-House, Progressive House, Club/Dance, House*
The Ballistic Brothers are something of a quintessential London post-acid house outfit. Combining the production talents of some of the most popular figures on the progressive house and acid jazz scenes (Ashley Beedle of Black Science Orchestra, Dave Hill of Nuphonic Records, and house-tech duo Rocky and Diesel), the Ballistics pursue a hip-hop/house/jazz/soul crossover that tends to spell "party" no matter where it's played. Releasing most of their initial material on London club staple Junior Boys Own (including their 1994 debut *London Hooligan Soul*), the group established the Soundboy label in 1996 to release the follow-up, *Rude System*. The album's semantic-cum-stylistic switch came via Dave Hill's trip to Jamaica just prior to recording the album, an inspiration that also led the group to pursue a remix project (similar to Mad Professor's take on Massive Attack's 1995 album *Protection*) at Bob Marley's Kingston studio. Group members' individual projects also include X-Press 2, Free Soul, Low Pressing Records, Blacker, Ill Sun Records, Yellow Sox, and the Uschi Classen band. —*Sean Cooper*

**London Hooligan Soul** / 1994 / Junior Boys Own ♦♦♦

● **Rude System** / Jul. 21, 1997 / Soundboy ♦♦♦♦
A rather more listenable LP than the Brothers' first, *Rude System* acknowledges big beat and deep house, but for the most part sticks to the sound of the '70s, pulling in funk lines and a disco vibe for tracks like "Tuning Up" and "Streets Are Real." The Balearic moods on several tracks indicate the wide range of influences by the quartet, specifically the garage tilt of Rocky & Diesel, as well as Ashley Beedle's jazzier inclinations. —*John Bush*

## Afrika Bambaataa (Kevin Donovan)

**b.** Apr. 10, 1960, New York City, NY [South Bronx]
*Vocals, Producer, DJ / Old School Rap, Electro, Club/Dance, Urban, Hip-Hop*
A seminal Bronx DJ during the '70s, Afrika Bambaataa ascended to godfather status with "Planet Rock," the 1982 hip-hop classic which blended the beats of hip-hop with techno-pop futurism inspired by German pioneers Kraftwerk. Even before he began recording in 1980, Bambaataa was hip-hop's foremost DJ, an organizer and promoter of the large block parties during the mid-to-late-'70s which presaged the rise of rap. After the success of "Planet Rock," he recorded electro-oriented rap only sparingly, concentrating instead on fusion—exemplified by his singles with ex-Sex Pistol John Lydon and fellow godfather James Brown. Bambaataa had moved to the background by the late '80s (as far as hip-hop was concerned), but the rise of his Zulu Nation collective—including De La Soul, Queen Latifah, A Tribe Called Quest, and the Jungle Brothers—found him once more being tipped as one of rap's founding fathers.

Born Kevin Donovan in the Bronx on April 10, 1960, Afrika Bambaataa Aasim took his name from a 19th-century Zulu chief. Beginning in 1977, Bambaataa began organizing block parties and break-dancing competitions around the Bronx. His excellent turntable techniques led many to proclaim him the best DJ in the business (though Grandmaster Flash and DJ Kool Herc were more innovative), and his record debut—as a producer—came in 1980 with Soul Sonic Force's "Zulu Nation Throwdown." The single was a rallying cry for the Zulu Nation, a group of like-minded Afrocentric musicians which only gained fame in the late '80s but had influenced the rise of hip-hop crews throughout the decade.

Aside from more production credits on several later singles during 1980-81, Afrika Bambaataa didn't become an actual recording artist until 1982. He signed with Tommy Boy Records and released his first single, "Jazzy Sensation," early that year. "Planet Rock" followed in June and quickly exploded. Recorded with the help of producer/dancefloor authority Arthur Baker and assimilating the melody of Kraftwerk's "Trans-Europe Express," the single hit number four on the R&B charts (but missed the pop Top 40) and joined the Sugarhill Gang's "Rapper's Delight" as one of the early classics of hip-hop. (Grandmaster Flash's "The Message" followed just three months later.) In the single's wake came dozens of electro groups and recordings, though none touched the quality of "Planet Rock"—except, perhaps, Bambaataa's own follow-up, "Looking for the Perfect Beat." Out of those electro groups came several predominant dance styles of the '80s and '90s: Detroit techno, Miami bass, and, to a more limited extent, Chicago house.

Freed somewhat by his new-found popularity, Afrika Bambaataa began branching out in 1984, recording "Unity" with help from James Brown, and "World Destruction" with John Lydon (as Time Zone). That same year, Bambaataa delivered an album debut of sorts, *Shango Funk Theology*, recorded as Shango with Material personnel Bill Laswell and Michael Beinhorn. A virtually LP-length single titled "Funk You!" appeared in 1985, after which Bambaataa recorded his proper album debut, *Beware (The Funk Is Everywhere)*. He left Tommy Boy in 1986 after an album compilation of "Planet Rock" mixes, and signed with Capitol. The first album release for the label was 1988's *The Light*, recorded as Afrika Bambaataa & the Family, which included contributions from George Clinton, UB40, Bootsy Collins, and Boy George. Three years later, Bambaataa's third album *1990-2000: Decade of Darkness* was released on Capitol, coinciding with his career retrospective *Time Zone*, released on his own Planet Rock Records. The new millennium also brought the release of *Hydraulic Funk* on Strictly Hype. —*John Bush*

**Looking for the Perfect Beat** / Dec. 1982 / Tommy Boy ♦♦♦♦
Producer Arthur Baker proved the real star on this seminal 1982 album, adding what were then state-of-the-art studio effects and mixing gimmicks to balance often repetitive rhythms. This was a milestone record, despite what sounded like limited rap skills by '90s standards. —*Ron Wynn*

**Beware (The Funk Is Everywhere)** / 1986 / Tommy Boy ♦♦♦♦
Another stunning assortment of singles are included, with heavier beats, thicker rhythms, and a blistering cover of The MC5's "Kick Out the Jams." —*John Floyd*

★ **Planet Rock—The Album** / 1986 / Tommy Boy ♦♦♦♦♦
All the important early 12"s from 1982-1984 are here, including "Planet Rock" and "Looking for the Perfect Beat," plus three previously unreleased tracks. (Recorded with Soulsonic Force) —*John Floyd*

**The Light** / 1988 / EMI America ♦♦
Diverse personalities and styles are the hook for this 1988 album, which isn't a Bambaataa project, but a group effort with some Bambaataa involvement. The guest list ranges from Boy George to George Clinton, Yellowman, UB40, and Bootsy Collins, with Bambaataa offering a brief, rather formulaic rap on UB40's "Reckless" and "Shout It Out." This was a mildly entertaining effort, but so varied that there was no cohesion or unified focus. —*Ron Wynn*

**1990-2000: The Decade of Darkness** / Jun. 1991 / EMI America ♦♦♦
After several lackluster albums, Bambaataa came back with a record that explored modern-day dance trends without losing his signature sound. Fueled by righteous social commentary throughout the songs, the record showed that he wasn't creatively spent. It wasn't as innovative as his groundbreaking singles from the early '80s, but it was far from being an embarrassment. —*Stephen Thomas Erlewine*

**Don't Stop... Planet Rock (The Remix EP)** / 1992 / Tommy Boy ♦♦
An updated EP takes the by-now-ancient "Planet Rock" beat and runs it through the '90s hip-hop production machine. The results aren't all that successful, even though the sound is now contemporary. But its hook was old-school, as was its charm. The newer version lacks bite. —*Ron Wynn*

**Zulu Groove** / Nov. 18, 1997 / Hudson Vandam ♦♦
Originally released on Celluloid, *Zulu Groove* continues to explore electro-funk and hip-hop. Bambaataa is assisted here by his Zulu Nation collective. —*Steve Huey*

## Banco de Gaia (Toby Marks)

*Producer / Ambient Techno, Ambient Dub, Club/Dance*
Inspired to enter the field of electronic music by Britain's acid house explosion of the late '80s, Toby Marks took quite a different spin on electronica with his recordings as Banco de Gaia. Marks introduced elements of Eastern and Arabic music, sampled similarly exotic sources, and tied the whole to ambient dub rhythms. Marks began releasing cassette-only albums in the early '90s, distributed through a network of clubs and artists known as Planet Dog. When Planet Dog became a record label as well (later the home of Eat Static and Timeshard), Banco de Gaia debuted on disc with the *Desert Wind* EP, released in November 1993. Early the following year, Marks released his first album, *Maya*. For 1995's *Last Train to Lhasa*, Marks concerned himself with the plight of occupied Tibet. The following year brought a rare concert recording, *Live at Glastonbury*, with *Big Men Cry* appearing in 1997; *The Magical Sounds of Banco de Gaia* followed two years later. In late 2000, Marks returned with *Igizeh* through Six Degrees Records. —*John Bush*

**Maya** / Feb. 1994 / MAM ♦♦
The debut full-length *Maya* helped establish Banco de Gaia as one of the first and best eco-ambient units of the early '90s. —*AMG*

**Last Train to Lhasa** / 1995 / Palanet Dog Bark ♦♦♦♦
This double-disc concept album concerns the commercial invasion of Tibet by Chinese merchants hoping to overrun the peaceful country. Despite some watered-down beats, Toby Marks weaves Eastern-rhythms and futuristic synth quite well over both uptempo and ambient tracks. —*John Bush*

**Live at Glastonbury** / Jul. 29, 1996 / Mammoth ♦♦♦
*Live at Glastonbury* captures Banco de Gaia's performance at the 1995 Glastonbury festival, where he ran through many of his most familiar songs—such as "Maya" and "Heliopolis"—often giving them radically new arrangements. Since the album isn't just a straight live set, it is of interest to more listeners than the usual live record. In fact, the album is one of the most convincing statements of purpose Toby Marks has yet released, since it captures most facets of his complex musical personality. —*Stephen Thomas Erlewine*

● **Big Men Cry** / Jul. 7, 1997 / Mammoth ♦♦♦♦
Toby Marks began to move away from the preconceptions of a Banco de Gaia project with 1997's *Big Men Cry*. While it has the ambient dub bent of his previous work, the album expands to include tribal drumming and a lot of live instrumentation, organized and tweaked to perfection by Marks' mature studio capabilities. —*John Bush*

**The Magical Sounds of Banco de Gaia** / May 18, 1999 / Six Degrees ♦♦♦♦
Toby Marks continues the focus on global rhythms and atmospheric melodies for *The Magical Sounds of Banco de Gaia*, though the presence of a few big beats in the mix signifies a wish for some Fatboy Slim-sized crossover. —*John Bush*

## Bandulu

f. 1992, London, England
*Group / Electronica, Ambient Techno, Club/Dance, Techno*
The North London trio of Jamie Bissmire, John O'Connell, and Lucien Thompson make hard-nosed, militant street-grit techno under the names Thunderground, New Adult, Sons of the Subway, Space DJz, and, most often, Bandulu. (The name is a term used in rasta patois for a bandit or criminal.) The group recorded primarily for noted techno imprint Infonet (which has also featured releases from the Black Dog and Global Communication aegis Reload, among others) before signing to Sony subsidiary Blanco y Negro in 1995, where the group's hard-edged sound has shown no sign of relenting. Bandulu have earned props from techno purists just as they've taken the music's clarion call of innovation in a variety of previously unexplored directions—fusing a Detroit-styled ruddiness with elements of dub, jazz, and electro, the latter culled from the trio's youth spent skateboarding, breakdancing, and graffiti writing in the North London area of Muswell Hill. Although earlier singles (such as "Guidance" and "Internal Oceanz") mined similar "armchair" territory as less obviously dancefloor-bound artists—such as Richard Kirk, the Black Dog, and (some) Tony Thorpe—the group's sound has gotten noticeably more aggressive with each release, fusing fast, thick breaks and pummeling beats with the darker sides of acid and hardcore. Bandulu continue to be in demand as remixers, and have also blossomed as a live act, even touring in support of their 1996 LP, *Cornerstone*. —*Sean Cooper*

● **Guidance** / 1993 / Infonet ♦♦♦♦
Bandulu's first album is their closest to British listening techno acts like Black Dog and B12. Highlights "Messenger," "Earth 6," and "Pacekeeper" push an aggressive rhythmic tone, though the melodies are quite fragile. One track, "Better Nation," features a Carl Craig remix. —*John Bush*

**Antimatters** / 1994 / Infonet ♦♦♦
Moving into dub territory from the more tranced-out effects of their debut, Bandulu again come up with scattered moments of genius. Despite the presence of a few dead-weight tracks, *Antimatters* is a worthy follow-up to their debut. —*John Bush*

**Cornerstone** / Apr. 22, 1996 / Blanco Y Negro ♦♦♦

## Bang the Party

f. 1987, London, England, **db.** 1990
*Group / Club/Dance, Acid House, House*
One of the first British dance acts to get airplay on American dancefloors, Bang the Party was formed by Kid Batchelor and Keith Franklin. Batchelor had been playing rare-groove funk and soul with schoolmate Jazzie B (later of Soul II Soul) since the mid-'80s. He later hooked up with Franklin as Bang the Party to record several of the earliest British acid-house tracks: "Jacque's Theme" and "Release Your Body." Much respect was coming from America, and "Release Your Body" even earned a re-release on Derrick May's Transmat Records (with a Mayday Mix to boot). "Bang Bang You're Mine" was another early club classic that skirted the British charts, spawning the duo's only LP, 1990's *Back to Prison*. Though Bang the Party didn't last long, Batchelor continued to DJ at well-known venues, and Franklin later appeared (briefly) in KCC with the Advent's Colin McBean. —*John Bush*

● **Release Your Body [Single]** / 1987 / Transmat ♦♦♦♦
The Transmat reissue of Bang the Party's best-known single includes two mixes each by Kid Batchelor and Derrick May. —*John Bush*

**Back to Prison** / 1990 / Warrior Dance ♦♦♦♦

## Mad Mike Banks

*Producer / Neo-Electro, Electro-Techno, Detroit Techno, Club/Dance*
New school Detroit techno mainstay "Mad" Mike Banks has been an indelible force in the Motor City underground for nearly a decade. As a founding member of Underground Resistance, he's contributed to the '90s renaissance of Detroit techno that has rebuilt the stripped-down hardness of the music from its historic roots (and shuttled artists such as Kenny Larkin, Drexciya, and Jeff Mills to acclaim in the process). He's also reunited American urban dance music with an element of political immediacy and social commentary unseen since the early days of hip-hop (and previously never a big part of techno in anything other than an implicit sense). Forming UR in the late '80s as an uncompromisingly independent outlet for music imbued with a critical—and at times oppositional—edge, Banks, together with partners Jeff Mills and Robert Hood (both of whom, together with Banks, defined the early UR catalog), Banks has built UR into an internationally recognized and respected name. Although Mills and Hood left UR in 1992 to pursue DJ and production opportunities elsewhere, Banks has stuck it out with UR—rebuilding the roster with artists such as Drexciya and Sean Deason, and continuing to record solo under the UR name.

Musically, Banks' roots lie in the early Detroit techno and Chicago house of the mid-'80s, particularly with artists such as Derrick May, Juan Atkins, and Marshall Jefferson—as well as with the experimental synth-pop of Kraftwerk, Gary Numan, and Yellow Magic Orchestra. Banks was a part of the vocal house/garage crew Members of the House, and produced a series of 12"s with the group before defecting in the late '80s to form UR with Banks (who he met through the latter's radio show) and Hood. Through that connection, Banks' music took on shades of acid and industrial, with a harder, more driving feel. More recently, Banks' style has gotten darker and more syncopated, with some releases recalling the early electro of Cybotron and Channel One, exemplified in tracks like "Clear" and "Technicolor." [See Also: Underground Resistance] —*Sean Cooper*

- **Electric Soul [Single]** / 1996 / Direct Beat ♦♦♦♦
"Mad" Mike steps away from UR for a moment to drop one of his strongest breakbeat outings to date. Three-quarters of this Direct Beat four-tracker feature uptempo electro-funk in the "Technicolor"/"Cosmic Cars" vein, with deep, grueling bass, and Atkins-style whispered voice-over (on "X2"). Among DB's finest, most bristling releases. —*Sean Cooper*

## Baraki

*Producer / Drill'N'Bass, Experimental Techno, Electronica, Trip-Hop*
The Japanese producer known as Baraki makes rich, beat-heavy electronica heavy on ideas and cross-genre pollination. A fan of music from an early age, the Kyoto-based musician learned to play guitar, bass, reeds, and synth; he even accompanied Mixmaster Morris on saxophone during the British DJ's live shows, and contributed to the acclaimed Japanese animé *Memories*. He first contributed to the London-based Worm Interface label with a track on the compilation *Alt.Frequencies, Vol. 2: Disco Moonlight*, then released his first album, *Colony Laspberry*, in 1999. —*John Bush*

- **Colony Laspberry** / Jun. 21, 1999 / Worm Interface ♦♦♦
Though *Colony Laspberry* includes all the drill'n'bass frenzy that anyone should expect from the Worm Interface label, Baraki goes the subgenre one better by creating an album as intriguing and well-produced as it is schizophrenic. From cut'n'paste big-beat to environmental ambience to zany drum'n'bass, the album skips across the post-rave landscape, never tarrying long before moving on to yet another musical touchstone. The opener "Rock 'n Job," is a great example, trading the sounds of a quintessentially Japanese version of atmospheric house synthesizer (reminiscent of video games and animé films) with shards of distorted beats and frequently hyperactive rhythm programs. Fortunately, Baraki has the production talents necessary to rein in all this musical madness and come out with a cohesive work. —*John Bush*

## Bark Psychosis

f. 1986, Snaresbrook, England, db. 1994
*Group / Experimental Ambient, Post-Rock/Experimental, Experimental, Alternative Pop/Rock*
Despite a relatively small recorded output and little media recognition, Bark Psychosis was one of the most innovative artists of their era. From rather uninspired origins as a teenaged Napalm Death cover band, the British quartet evolved by leaps and bounds—moving from moody, lush pop to ambient soundscapes, to taut, atmospheric experimental music. Their work was so revolutionary, and so impossible to define, that noted critic Simon Reynolds even found it necessary to invent a new sub-genre—"post-rock"—simply to categorize their vision.

Bark Psychosis was founded in 1986 while its members were attending school in Snaresbrook, England. At the time of their formation, the average age of the group—vocalist Graham Sutton, bassist John Ling, drummer Mark Simnott and keyboardist Daniel Gish—was just 14-years-old. Drawing inspiration everywhere from Joy Division, Swans, and Sonic Youth to Five Star and early Level 42, the quartet only began taking music seriously after Sutton and Ling's graduation, and soon started composing original material. Upon signing to the tiny Cheree label, they debuted in 1988 with a flexi-disc release titled "Clawhammer."

In 1989, Bark Psychosis resurfaced with their first proper single, "All Different Things"; the gauzy 1990 follow-up, "Nothing Feels," was an early breakthrough: a haunting, sophisticated record backed with the equally stunning "I Know." Issued the following year, the *Manman* EP continued their remarkable growth, reflecting Sutton's increasingly fascination with techno and the possibilties of synthesziers, programming, and sampling—while setting the stage for the 1992 landmark *Scum*, an ominous, 21-minute improvisational ambient masterpiece recorded live in a Stratford church.

At the peak of their powers, Bark Psychosis entered the studio in November 1992 to begin work on *Hex*, their long-awaited full-length debut. In sum, the LP took over a year to complete, pushing the group to the brink of emotional and financial collapse: after a major fall-out with Ling, a virtually penniless Gish exited during the summer of 1993 to find steadier work, forcing the remaining trio to complete the album's centerpiece "Big Shot" without him. Upon the record's completion, a tour was planned in support of the single, "A Street Scene," but then Ling exited as well; Gish agreed to return in Ling's absence, but only to play live dates.

Although *Hex* received massive critical acclaim—Reynolds' review of the album marked the first mention of the post-rock label, a tag later attached to similarly uncategorizable bands like Tortoise—Bark Psychosis was essentially dissolved, even though Sutton and Simnett subsequently recorded one final single, the techno-inspired "Blue." After a farewell appearance at Russia's Electronic Music Festival, the group officially disbanded; two posthumous retrospectives, 1994's *Independency* and 1997's *Game Over*, were their final full-length releases. In the wake of Bark Psychosis' demise, Sutton plunged fully into the realm of drum'n'bass, recording under the name Boymerang. —*Jason Ankeny*

- ★ **Hex** / 1994 / Plan 9/Caroline ♦♦♦♦♦
A masterpiece of unrivaled beauty and complexity, Bark Psychosis' *Hex* channels the experimentation of the group's prior singles into a more controlled setting. A series of atmospheric set pieces, the songs find a common ground between accepted musical formulas and avant innovation—at first glance, tracks like "Big Shot" and "Eyes & Smiles" appear tightly structured, yet they avoid the dynamics of conventional songcraft like choruses and solos with remarkable dexterity. Similarly, both "The Loom" and "Fingerspit" are too melodic and finely-honed to pass as mere ambient soundscapes, leaving the record best ascribed to a force not unlike alchemy. *Hex* begins with base musical materials, but transforms them into something mysterious, haunting and breathtakingly visionary. —*Jason Ankeny*

- **Blue [Single]** / Apr. 1994 / Circa ♦♦♦
Bark Psychosis' final single, recorded only with members Graham Sutton and Mark Simnott, is a radical departure from the experimental atmospherics of the group's previous material. Closer in spirit to Sutton's subsequent drum'n'bass work as Boymerang, "Blue" earns points for its adventurous move into dance music territory, but is too much lacking in a distinct identity to rank with the band's strongest work. Rounding out the set are "Hex," a head-on collision between noise abrasion and ambient beauty, and "Big Shot (Alice's Chesire Cat Mix)," an LP track retooled by A.R. Kane's Rudy Tambala. —*Jason Ankeny*

- **Independency** / Jul. 1994 / 3rd Stone ♦♦♦♦
Collecting a series of singles first issued between 1989 and 1992, *Independency* charts Bark Psychosis' extraordinary period of evolution prior to the creation of their lone studio LP, *Hex*. Opening with the delicate "I Know," the set grows by leaps and bounds, expanding in complexity and innovation over the course of tracks like "Manman" and "Tooled Up," before culminating in the 21-minute improvisational ambient opus "Scum"—which is perhaps the band's definitive moment. An invaluable document. —*Jason Ankeny*

- **Game Over** / Aug. 5, 1997 / 3rd Stone ♦♦♦♦
*Game Over* is a schizophrenic epitaph to Bark Psychosis' too-short career, collecting a handful of non-LP tracks (including the single "Blue," and the previously unreleased "Murder City," a live "Pendulum Man," and a cover of Wire's "Three Girl Rhumba") along with a number of cuts from both the *Hex* LP and the *Independency* compilation. While not the place for new fans to begin, the set is essential for completists, and does include some of the group's finest moments, including "A Street Scene" and the epic "Scum." —*Jason Ankeny*

## Basement Jaxx

f. 1994, London, England
*Group / Progressive House, Club/Dance, House*
The production duo of Simon Ratcliffe and Felix Buxton released several of Britain's most respected and enjoyable progressive house anthems of the '90s from their base in South London. Before they met (at a Thames riverboat party organized by Buxton), Ratcliffe grooved to the deep Latin funk of War

and George Duke, while Buxton was turned on to Chicago house. The pair formed Atlantic Jaxx Records in 1994, and were undoubtedly honored to count among fans of their first release none other than DJ legend and Basement Jaxx influence, Tony Humphries (who played "Da Underground" from the EP on his New York mixshow consistently during 1994-95). For their second release, Ratcliffe and Buxton recruited vocalist Corrina Josephs, who later practically became a member of the team herself.

The 1995 single "Samba Magic" was picked up for distribution by Virgin, and in time, Basement Jaxx was drawing praise as one of the top house production units from all corners of the American and British house community. The pair spent much of 1996 working on remixes (for the Pet Shop Boys, Roger Sanchez and Lil' Mo Yin Yang among others), then released a third Basement Jaxx EP. One track from the EP, "Flylife," became a Top 20 hit in England after being re-released by Multiply in mid-1997—and the single proved one of the most popular anthems of the year on the worldwide club-scene. Late that year, Ratcliffe and Buxton released a compilation of their most crucial Atlantic Jaxx sides. After being courted by several major labels, Basement Jaxx signed to the independent XL Recordings (also home to Prodigy) and readied their debut full-length *Remedy* for a 1999 release. —*John Bush*

**Summer Daze [EP]** / 1995 / Atlantic Jaxx ♦♦♦
The *Summer Daze EP* includes four tracks of jumped-up house with great nods to Latin and funk. "I'm Thru With You" features vocals from Corrina Joseph. —*John Bush*

**Basement Jaxx Present Atlantic Jaxx: A Compilation** / Nov. 10, 1997 / Atlantic Jaxx ♦♦♦♦
*Atlantic Jaxx* collects the best tracks released by Basement Jaxx from 1994 through 1997 (many previously vinyl-only), including obvious favorites "Flylife" and "Samba Magic," as well as older cuts such as the epic string mix of "Be Free." —*John Bush*

★ **Remedy** / Aug. 3, 1999 / XL Recordings ♦♦♦♦♦
The duo's long-awaited debut album is one of the most assured, propulsive full-lengths the dance world had seen since Daft Punk's *Homework*. A set of incredibly diverse tracks, *Remedy* is indebted to the raw American house of Todd Terry and Masters at Work, and even shares the NuYoricans' penchant for Latin vibes (especially on the horn-driven "Bingo Bango," and the opener "Rendez-Vu," which trades a bit of salsa wiggle with infectious vocoderized disco). True, Ratcliffe and Buxton do sound more like an American production team than a pair of Brixton boys would—they get props (and vocal appearances) from several of the best American house producers including DJ Sneak, Erick Morillo, and Benji Candelario. "U Can't Stop Me" is an R&B production that could probably have gotten airplay in major rap markets across the US. Elsewhere, Buxton and Ratcliffe chew up and spit out mutated versions of hip-hop, ragga, Latin, R&B, soul, and garage—the varied sound that defined the worldwide house scene of the late '90s. —*John Bush*

## Basic Channel

f. 1993, Berlin, Germany
*Group / Minimal Techno, Experimental Dub, Experimental Techno, Electronica, Ambient Techno*

Basic Channel has become synonymous with a brand of stripped-down, ultra-minimal techno almost devoid of musical substance or intent. Both artist and label, Basic Channel was established by Berlin-based producers Mark Ernestus and Moritz Von Oswald (aka Maurizio) in 1993, and the pair have unhurriedly developed a slim but adored catalog of releases under such names as Cyrus, Phylyps, q1.1, Quadrant, Octagon, and Radiance—working a single-minded concept of nearly featureless machine music ("nearly," of course, being the key to the music's success). Like many German techno artists and labels (Tresor, Studio 1, Mike Ink), Basic Channel harbors a reverence for early Chicago acid and house and first-wave Detroit techno, the latter of which is particularly manifested in Mark and Moritz's ultraconservatism (with respect to rhythm and composition). Releasing under a dozen 12"s since their inception (a few of them, however, nearing album length), Basic Channel issued their first CD-release in 1996 (the group otherwise remain staunch vinyl addicts—they even assembled their own pressing facility). Titled simply *Basic Channel*, the disc was a continuously mixed taster of their 12" releases, which continue to trickle out at a rate of only a few per year. Basic Channel is one in a network of artists and labels—which also includes Thomas Koner/Porter Ricks, the Chain Reaction label (more avant experimental techno), M (Moritz's personal label and home to his Maurizio releases), the Main Street label (pop house), and Imbalance (a CD-only experimental music label). —*Sean Cooper*

**Lyot Remix/Phylyps Trak Remix [Single]** / 1993 / Basic Channel ♦♦♦♦
Berlin's Basic Channel collective released this untitled record baring only the circular and barely legible Basic Channel logo, containing two new versions of Basic Channel's *Phylyps Trak* and Vainqueur's *Lyot*. The "Phylyps Trak Remix" takes the same sounds and motifs found on that record and reworks them, creating a less dense (yet equally as banging) version of this hard techno classic. The flip side, "Lyot Remix," steals the original track's melodic hook, distorts it with layers of fuzz, and then loops it endlessly while an aquatic soundtrack of reverb-drenched spontaneous echoes flows fluidly overtop. In addition, some barely audible synth tones and hissing static wash through the disorientating song. The juxtaposing moods of these two songs—teeth-grinding power and opium-hazed sleepiness—make for a wonderful addition to the Basic Channel series, giving listeners a taste of the Berlin label's two different flavors and previewing the "Lyot Remix"-like sound of the succeeding *Radiance* record. —*Jason Birchmeier*

**Phylyps Trak [Single]** / 1993 / Basic Channel ♦♦♦
Where the *Enforcement* record stressed hypnotizing qualities over dancefloor friendliness, this second Basic Channel record applies the same formula to pounding bass beats, and the result is three variations on a potent style of minimal techno. There are essentially four elements to this record that loop in a distorted, fractured manner with relentlessness: the underlying low-frequency pounding of compressed bass beats, the barely noticeable yet inescapable rhythm of syncopated high-hat percussion, the non-linear flow of a mid-range-frequency riff, and the modulating distortion of alien high-frequency sound streams. While this formula may sound obvious, its application is pure genius. Rather than merely set the loops and slowly fade them in and out of one another, Basic Channel forever tweaks the sounds, leaving only the high-hat percussion as a constant. Even when the high-frequency riffs and sound streams aren't appearing and disappearing, they are twisting, modulating, oscillating, altering, mutating, and doing whatever else imaginable. —*Jason Birchmeier*

**Octagon/Octaedre [Single]** / 1994 / Basic Channel ♦♦♦♦
Perhaps no Basic Channel record better captures the Berlin label's array of different styles on one record. On both the "Octagon" side and the "Octaedre" side, one can hear the many sounds brought together to slightly different results. The forward-moving, choppy mechanical percussion of the *Phylyps Trak* records combines with the fat warmth of the Quadrant dub bass beats to form the rhythm track for each record. The Basic Channel camp then adds the strange hallucinogenic tone alterations from the Cyrus records along with the filtered aquatic noises from the *Radiance* record to bring personality to the intricate rhythm. By merging each of these unique motifs together into one giant compound, Basic Channel has created a monstrous record loaded with hard percussion, throbbing bass, trippy high-end sounds, and twisting minimal repetition to disorientate even the most stable listeners. Spin "Octagon" for a cognitive journey and save "Octaedre" for intense moments. —*Jason Birchmeier*

**Phylyps Trak II [Single]** / 1994 / Basic Channel ♦♦
The second *Phylyps Trak* record in the Basic Channel series of records offers two additional variations on the sound motifs explored on the original and its successive remix. Once again, the Berlin collective take some sharp metallic percussion and assemble an intricate rhythm foundation with little space and plenty of momentum. This forward-moving rhythm is then amplified with some muted, hollow-sounding bass kicks on the thunderous, uptempo side and some heavily altered, high-frequency industrial sounds on the minimal side. This second *Phylyps Trak* record reaches more epic proportions, lasting upwards to ten minutes on each side. Not quite as inventive or harsh as the first record, this sequel does take the sound to more minimal extremes, resulting in a sense of dizzying repetition that seems to never end its disorienting loops. —*Jason Birchmeier*

**Q 1.1 [Single]** / 1994 / Basic Channel ♦♦♦
Similar to the preceding *Phylyps Trak* record and the succeeding *Radiance* record, Basic Channel's *Q 1.1* offers multiple variations of a particular motif. The featured motif on this record involves steady, pumping dub basslines and some dark, mechanical, dusty drum machine percussion. This works prima-

rily because of the record's pristine clarity—making the dub basslines sound tangibly warm and the percussion sound more robotic than it perhaps should. To top things off, some classic techno synth appears periodically to further bolster this record's range of unique sounds. In sum, it's rather amazing to listen as this Berlin collective creatively rework the same sounds in such different ways, inciting a broad palette of emotive responses while always remaining true to dancefloor aesthetic. These compositions aren't nearly as epic as most residing within the collective's canon, but it's almost refreshing to hear songs that don't necessarily challenge one's patience. —*Jason Birchmeier*

**Radiance [EP]** / 1994 / Basic Channel ♦♦♦♦
Of the few Basic Channel records ever put on vinyl, *Radiance* stands alone as the most sedate, disorientating journey in the canon. One side of the record contains almost no bass frequencies or percussion, instead twinkling with phasing loops of sequenced tones to establish a surreal listening experience. The flip side of the record integrates an ultra-deep, dub bassline for a similar set of the twinkling high-end sounds. *Radiance* embodies the concept of ambience, functioning as music capable of drawing one into a strange aural environment (for approximately 15 minutes on each side of the record) until the needle reaches the innermost groove of silent static. Titled well, this song indeed radiates a tranquil mood of sonic bliss in a way that only the more subdued releases by the Chain Reaction camp have come close to duplicating: the transcendental derivation of dark, calm beauty from dated sound equipment. —*Jason Birchmeier*

★ **Basic Channel** / Dec. 2, 1996 / Basic Channel ♦♦♦♦♦
*Basic Channel* collects material from the Basic Channel, Maurizio, and Chain Reaction label family founded by Moritz Von Oswald and Mark Ernestus. The compilation contains edited 12" single versions of tracks by artists like Cyrus, Phylyps, Quadrant, Octagon, Radiance, and Q 1.1. —*Steve Huey*

## Bass Junkie (Phil Klein)

*Producer / Party Rap, Bass Music*
UK-based producer Phil Klein releases Miami bass-inflected new school electro under his Bass Junkie aegis. Appearing most recently on the Breakin' Records label and on his own Parallax imprint, Klein's Bass Junkie material draws liberally from classics of electro-funk and bass music—from Freestyle's "It's Automatic" and Unknown DJ's "808 Beats" to Maggotron's "Planet of Bass"—combining truckloads of samples with crisp, uptempo rhythms and, naturally, the deepest of bone-rattling bass. Although his discography includes a number of tracks released as Battle Systems, I.B.M., and Cybernet Systems, Klein's most popular work to date has been his Bass Junkie material, most likely via its association with the Breakin' Records label (associated with Rephlex Records recording artist DMX Krew). Following a pair of Bass Junkie releases for his own Parallax label, Klein began releasing records through Breakin' in 1997 with the *Unknown Funk* EP. An additional EP (*In Bass No One Can Hear You Scream*) and an LP (*Bass Junkie*) appeared through Breakin' in 1998. Klein's affection for bass music has also stretched into a long-running collaboration with one of the genre's most acclaimed early innovators, Scott Weiser, a.k.a. Miami-based Dynamix II. Bass Junkie and Cybernet Systems tracks have appeared on a number of Dynamix compilations, with the label also issuing a full-length CD of Klein's Bass Junkie material in 1996. *Bass Time Continuum* followed three years later. Additionally, Klein and Weiser share a writing credit on the title track to Klein's *Borg* EP (1996, Panic Trax), and on several releases as I.B.M. —*Sean Cooper*

**A Bass Odyssey [EP]** / 1996 / Parallax ♦♦♦
As the title implies, these four tracks have at least one thing in common: bass—deep and rumbling. The influence of Miami freestyle and bass music producers (such as Tony Butler and Maggotron) on Klein's hybrid electro-funk comes closest to the surface on tracks such as "Energy Flow;" but as with his other Bass Junkie material, he doesn't simply let it rest there, combining old-school sample collage with heavier, new-breed syncopation, and subtle acid lines. Good stuff. —*Sean Cooper*

**Bass, Below & Beyond [EP]** / 1997 / Parallax ♦♦♦♦
Klein's most equitable pairing of old-school electro bass with a new school sensibility to date, each track is a snapshot of the music's current legacy. From the megamix-y "Program The 808" (with shards of the Unknown DJ's "808 Beats" and "Sweat") to the digital mash-up of Kraftwerk and Uncle Jamm's Army (on "Computer Control" and "Automatic Bass") this four-tracker has one for each occasion. Less of a novelty record than the previous *Bass Odyssey* EP. —*Sean Cooper*

**I, Borg [EP]** / 1997 / Battle Trax ♦♦♦♦
Four hardcore-leaning remixes of Klein's stonkin' Dynamix II collaboration, "We Are Borg" (from his 1995 Panic Trax twelve, "The Borg EP"). The mixes are pretty repetitive, and none of them hit with quite the intensity of the original, but Klein's shifting focus from version to version on the various rhythmic elements of the original (the brittle, sprangy snares; the deep, Miami-style bass) is competent and inventive. —*Sean Cooper*

● **Bass Junkie** / 1998 / Breakin' ♦♦♦♦
A mixture of material old and new, some previously available only through Klein's limited-run Parallax imprint. Kinetic, speaker-melting electro-bass, as expected. —*Sean Cooper*

## Bassomatic

*Group / House*
The acid house-pop band Bassomatic formed when *Strange Cargo* producer and Guerilla label-boss William Orbit recruited vocalist Sharon Musgrave for a new project. Led by the Top Ten British hit "Fascinating Rhythm," Bassomatic released their only album, *Set the Controls for the Heart of the Bass*, in 1990. —*John Bush*

● **Set the Controls for the Heart of the Bass** / 1990 / Virgin ♦♦
Arriving after the twin explosions of acid house and Madchester in the UK, *Set the Controls* was inspired much more by the former. Orbit's career defines peripatetic, but much like Norman "Fatboy Slim" Cook (whose Beats International project also made a big British splash at the same time), here he made his own mark before achieving an even greater fame later, for other reasons. The strongest stretch of the album consists of the opening three tracks. "In the Realm of the Senses" combines Musgrave's fine dance diva chops and Orbit's ear for crisp modern Euro disco and techno. If anything, the track is also a homage to the glorious "Supernature" by Cerrone, with vocodered vocal bits and an astronaut feel similar to a more poppy-sounding Orb. The title track is an amusing and commanding revamp of Pink Floyd's own sci-fi zone-out, "Set the Controls for the Heart of the Sun," playing up the space imagery and sounds—right down to the concluding *Star Trek* dialogue snippet—while hitting the beat with a crisp, clinical sharpness. The chorus of female voices chanting adds to the effect. "Fascinating Rhythm" takes everything even higher; a deserved UK Top Ten hit single, its shuffling hip-hop beat is more in line with baggy groups like the Happy Mondays. Otherwise, Musgrave's sleek main vocals, MC Inna One Step's solid dancehall turn in the break, and Orbit's perfect combination of music, production, and beat are all their own. Things get a bit nondescript at this point, but there are some good points: the harmonica and electro-vocal fusion on "Zombie Mantra" and the sampling of a melodramatic English movie on "Wicked Love" both add to their respective songs. Concluding remixes of "In the Realm of the Senses" and "Fascinating Rhythm" end *Set the Controls* on a reasonable high. —*Ned Raggett*

## Blake Baxter

*Producer, DJ / Detroit Techno, Club/Dance, Techno*
Perhaps the most underrated figure of Detroit techno's first wave, Blake Baxter began recording in the mid-'80s before Motor City mainstays like Derrick May and Kevin Saunderson. Presaging the influence of erotic house during the late '80s, Baxter was inspired by the sexual soul of Barry White and Prince, as well as cosmic funk machines like Parliament and Funkadelic. He released his first single on the seminal Chicago house label DJ International, and recorded several classics for Saunderson's KMS Records. By the '90s he had cultivated his connection with Detroit's techno subversives Underground Resistance, for whom he served as a guiding light.

With the Detroit scene on the rise after the release of his DJ International and KMS material, Baxter ducked the hype centered around the crucial compilation *Techno: The New Dance Sound of Detroit* (though his productions figured prominently on it), and moved to the obscure Incognito label. Seminal releases *Sexuality, the Crimes of the Heart* EP, and his 1990 debut album *The Underground Lives* signalled a newly independent-minded producer, spending much time in Berlin during the early '90s. The extended stay yielded several releases, including the Logic singles "Brothers Gonna Work

It Out"—later sampled by the Chemical Brothers—and a 1992 album titled *The Project*. He also recorded with Orlando Voorn as the Ghetto Brothers. Back in Detroit, he recorded "Prince of Techno" for Underground Resistance and set up his own labels, Mix Records and Phat Joint (the latter focusing more on hip-hop). In 1995, Baxter released a retrospective on Disko B entitled *The Vault*. Two years later, *The H Factor (Hurricane Melt)* followed, also on Disko B. The mix album *A Decade Underground* appeared in 1998. —*John Bush*

**Dream Sequence** / 1992 / Tresor ✦✦
Even though the second release in the deep and highly influential Tresor catalog may not stand today as one of the most enduring albums of the early techno era, it provides some valuable insight into the roots of the mid-'90s techno movement in Berlin. By the end of the '90s, Blake Baxter's name didn't have nearly the same recognition as Derrick May, Jeff Mills, or Underground Resistance's. At the beginning of the '90s though, the artist sometimes known as "The Prince of Techno" was an important member of the Detroit techno camp that had first innovated the genre's sound, appearing alongside May and Kevin Saunderson on the monolithic compilation *Techno: The New Dance Sound of Detroit*. Dream Sequence marked Baxter's move to Berlin where he found a new home, joining forces with the men of the *Hardwax* store and the *Tresor* club. The eight songs on this album were recorded in November of 1991 by Baxter, John Klimek, Moritz von Oswald, and Thomas Fehlmann. The results are mixed and inconsistent. Songs such as "Dark Basse" and "The Warning" illustrate the dark sound of early techno that would later creep into the succeeding Tresor releases and also into England's drum'n'bass movement. Songs like "Ghost" and "Laser 101" use the sort of siren sounds found on records such as X-101's *Sonic Destroyer*, and are now thought of as early '90s rave anthems. Two interesting mixes of "One Mo Time" also showcase Baxter's interest in writing a traditional style of dance-pop with vocals. Of these eight songs, the dark-feeling techno songs with sirens and vocal samples remain the most interesting. The record itself isn't very exceptional, and hasn't aged as well as May or Saunderson's work; it does feature some of von Oswald's and Fehlmann's early work, foreshadowing the style of techno that would soon appear in Berlin 1992. —*Jason Birchmeier*

● **The Vault** / 1995 / Disko B ✦✦✦✦
Though Detroit DJ Baxter recorded this album over a six-year span, it still sounds quite fluid. *The Vault* is heavy on the smooth techno-soul, but harder beats do appear. —*John Bush*

**The H Factor (Hurricane Melt)** / Jun. 16, 1997 / Disko B ✦✦✦
Though the cover details blaxploitation funk, Blake Baxter's second album for Disko B runs through several tracks of intense acid-storm techno yet also detours into rather vague house tracks. —*John Bush*

**Globus Mix, Vol. 2: A Decade Underground** / Sep. 29, 1998 / Tresor ✦✦✦✦
The second in a series of house mixes based around the more mainstream Globus club (upstairs from *Tresor*), *A Decade Underground* features Baxter working his way through Detroit classics by the man himself and K-Hand plus Markey, Disco Freaks, Basic Bastard, and even one from Junior Vasquez. —*John Bush*

## François Bayle
b. Apr. 27, 1932, Tamatave, Madagascar
*Composer / Musique Concrète, Electronic*
Electroacoustic innovator François Bayle was born in Tamatave, Madagascar on April 27, 1932. A pupil of Stockhausen, Messiaen, and Pousseur, in 1960 he joined the Groupe de Recherches Musicales (GRM). Studying under musique concrète pioneer Pierre Schaeffer, he concurrently served as a public relations assistant. By 1964, Bayle was named Director of the GRM, and three years later he completed his first major electronic composition, *Espaces Inhabitables*; his major breakthrough was the 1974 development of the Acousmonium, which consisted of 80 assorted loudspeakers designed for tape playback. Unlike many of his contemporaries, Bayle grew increasingly prolific over time, and many of his later pieces are considered among his finest, notable for their evocative, even poetic, construction of sound. Beginning with 1980's *Erosphere* and continuing with key works including 1983's *Son Vitesse-Lumiere* and the following year's *Aeroformes*, Bayle also began experimenting with computer technology, remaining on the cutting edge throughout his long career. —*Jason Ankeny*

**L'Experience Acoustique** / Ina GRM ✦✦✦✦
● **Vibrations Composées/Grande Polyphonie** / Ina GRM ✦✦✦✦

## BBC Radiophonic Workshop
f. 1958, Maida Vale, England
*Group / Film Music*
For decades the BBC Radiophonic Workshop has produced the majority of incidental electronic music broadcast over British airwaves, their adherence to cutting-edge technology pioneering countless creative innovations. The department was formed in 1956, when senior studio manager Desmond Briscoe and music studio manager Daphne Oram agreed upon the need "for something other than normal orchestral incidental music"; a year later the Radiophonics staff produced one of their first experimental radio productions, "Private Dreams and Public Nightmares," and in 1958 they were awarded their own studios at the BBC's Maida Vale facility, complete with a budget of £2,000. The first popular television series to feature a Radiophonics soundtrack, *Quatermass and the Pit*, premiered soon after; before long the crew was responsible for scoring over 150 programs a year, the majority of them for TV.

In 1963, the Radiophonics Workshop's Ron Grainer outlined his ideas for the theme to a new science fiction series being developed for television. A few weeks later the completed track was produced by Delia Derbyshire, the end result—the title theme for the cult classic *Doctor Who*—becoming perhaps the most popular piece in the BBC oeuvre. (Grainer also went on to author much of the incidental music heard in the groundbreaking series *The Prisoner*.) In 1964, John Read combined flute and bass with electronic sounds, the first time musicians were employed in tandem with machines; now a BBC trademark, it's a convention that still remains in place today. Still, the electronic resources at the Radiophonics staff's disposal were fairly primitive throughout much of the '60s, consisting primarily of sine and square waves as well as white noise; only at the end of the decade did they acquire their first Moog and VCS3 synthesizers.

By the mid-'70s, the Radiophonics arsenal also included a Roland Vocoder, its disembodied vocal textures first used by Malcolm Clarke in an award-winning adaptation of Ray Bradbury's *And There Shall Come Soft Rains*. In 1977, Paddy Kingsland introduced polyphonic synths on his theme for Radio 4's *PM* show, and three years later he was the first to use a Fairlight CMI in his score for a TV adaptation of *The Hitch-Hiker's Guide to the Galaxy*. By 1985, all of the Radiophonics studios were equipped with samplers, with Apple Macs installed a year later; by the end of the decade, a totally automated studio was up and running, complete with MIDI routing, and by the '90s, hard-disk recording and sequencing were the norm. Throughout its long existence the Radiophonics Workshop also released a number of albums, many sampled endlessly by contemporary electronica acts. —*Jason Ankeny*

● **Doctor Who: The Music** / 1983 / BBC ✦✦✦
Assorted versions of the title music, plus music from episodes taped between 1971 and 1982. A lot of electronic material, and a fair bit of experimental work that would not be out of place in a university sound lab. It's quite intriguing for fans of the series as well as those interested in the development of electronic music. —*Steven McDonald*

## BBE
f. 1996
*Group / Trance, Club/Dance*
Inspired equally by trance and new age music, the dream-house unit BBE was formed in 1996 by producers Bruno Sanchioni, Bruno Quartier and Emmanuel Top. The trio of French techno experts came together with a debut single, "Seven Days in One Week," which became a hit at clubs from Ibiza to London, and ascended into the Top Five of the British charts. Though Quartier left immediately after the single's success, Sanchioni and Top's follow-up "Flash" also hit the Top Five, alongside similar tunes by Sash! and Robert Miles in a wave of chart-bound dream-house. ZYX Records issued the compilation *Early Works* in 1997, and BBE released their debut album *Games* one year later. Top also has a solo career, with productions on NovaMute and Le Petit Prince. —*John Bush*

● **Games** / Feb. 16, 1998 / Positiva ✦✦
BBE are quite good at what they do—that is, rather melodramatic German trance which sounds about five years out of date and just a bit *too* influenced by excessives like Rick Wakeman and ELO. Several tracks on *Games* break these boundaries—"Aquatic Nebular" and "Le Nouveaux Monde" acknowl-

edge the dance scene's present tense by working in breakbeats and jazzy drum'n'bass—but the predominant sounds are a tad old-school. —*John Bush*

## Beanfield

f. 1994, Munich, Germany
*Group / Trip-Hop, Club/Dance, House*

Beanfield are a trio of German musician/producers allied with the excellent groove label Compost Recordings. The group reside among a generation of dance acts like Faze Action, Fila Brazillia, and A Forest Mighty Black (the latter are close compadres) who balance their status in the electronic community by producing extraordinarily organic sounds, inspired by earthy '70s sounds from funk to Latin and Brazilian jazz to disco. Beanfield formed around keyboard player Tobias Meggle and bassist Jan Krause (formerly with the acid jazz unit Poets of Rhythm), along with Compost label-boss Michael Reinboth. All three played heavy parts in the recording and production of the first few Compost records (circa 1995), by A Forest Mighty Black, Knowtoryus, and Fauna Flash. Beanfield's first single, 1995's "Charles," earned heavy rotation on Gilles Peterson's BBC radio show and gained airplay in the world's more laid-back clubs. The band released their self-titled debut album in 1997, followed by two volumes in a series of remix EPs. Earning even more praise from DJs and critics, *Human Patterns* followed in 1999. —*John Bush*

**Beanfield** / Nov. 10, 1997 / Streetbeat ♦♦♦

• **Human Patterns** / Dec. 7, 1999 / Compost ♦♦♦
As an intriguing blend of organic and synthetic that ends up sounding surprisingly close to their late-'70s inspirations (Brazilian jazz, Afro-beat, fusion, funk), *Human Patterns* is a near match for *Moving Cities* by the similar electronic act Faze Action. Both are excellent albums that just miss true brilliance because they sound *too* familiar, too faithful to their original influences to make for inspiring listening. The instrumentals work better than the two vocal tracks, with rhythmic percussion and Krause's deep-end basslines leading the way through "Abstractions," "Scavenger Hunt," and "Corso." —*John Bush*

## Beastie Boys

f. 1979, New York, NY
*Group / Old School Rap, Alternative Rap, Hardcore Punk, Alternative Pop/Rock, Hip-Hop*

As the first White rap group of any importance, the Beastie Boys received the scorn of critics and strident hip-hop musicians, who accused them of cultural pirating—especially since they began as a hardcore punk group in 1981. But the Beasties weren't pirating—they treated rap as part of a post-punk musical underground, where the do-it-yourself aesthetics of hip-hop and punk weren't that far apart. Of course, the exaggerated B-boy and frat boy parodies of their unexpected hit debut album *Licensed to Ill* didn't help their cause. For much of the mid-'80s, the Beastie Boys were considered macho clowns, and while their ambitious, Dust Brothers-produced second album *Paul's Boutique* dismissed that theory, it was ignored by both the public and the press at the time. In retrospect, it was one of the first albums to predict the genre-bending, self-referential pop kaleidoscope of '90s pop. The Beasties refined their eclectic approach with 1992's *Check Your Head*, where they played their own instruments. *Check Your Head* brought the Beasties back to the top of the charts. Within a few years, they were considered one of the most influential and ambitious groups of the '90s, cultivating a musical community not only through their music, but with their record label Grand Royal and their magazine of the same name.

It was remarkable turn of events for a group that demonstrated no significant musical talent on their first records. All three members of the Beastie Boys—Mike D (b. Mike Diamond, November 20, 1966), MCA (b. Adam Yauch, August 5, 1965), and Ad-Rock (b. Adam Horovitz, October 31, 1967)—came from wealthy middle-class Jewish families in New York and had become involved in the city's punk underground when they were teenagers in the early '80s. Diamond and Yauch formed the Beastie Boys with drummer Kate Schellenbach and guitarist John Berry in 1981, and the group began playing underground clubs around New York. The following year, the Beasties released the 7" EP *Polly Wog Stew* on the indie Rat Cage, which received little attention. That year, the band met Horovitz, who had formed the hardcore group The Young and the Useless. By early 1983, Schellenbach and Berry had left the group—they would later join Luscious Jackson and Thwig, respectively—and Horovitz had joined the Beasties. The revamped group released the rap record "Cookie Puss" as a 12" single later in 1983. Based on a prank phone call the group made to Carvel Ice Cream, the single became an underground hit in New York; by early 1984, they had abandoned punk and turned their attention to rap.

In 1984, the Beasties joined forces with producer Rick Rubin, a heavy metal and hip-hop fan who had recently founded Def Jam Records with fellow New York University student, Russell Simmons. Def Jam officially signed the Beastie Boys in 1985, and that year they had a hit single from the soundtrack to *Krush Groove* with "She's on It"—a rap track that sampled AC/DC's "Back in Black," and suggested the approach of the group's forthcoming debut album. The Beasties received their first significant national exposure later in 1985, when they opened for Madonna on her *Virgin Tour*. The trio taunted the audience with profanity and were generally poorly received. One other major tour followed, opening for Run-D.M.C.'s ill-fated "Raisin' Hell" trek, before *License to Ill* was released late in 1986. An amalgam of street beats, metal riffs, B-boy jokes and satire, *License to Ill* was interpreted as a mindless, obnoxious party record by many critics and conservative action groups—but that didn't stop the album from becoming the fastest-selling debut in Columbia Records' history, moving over 750,000 copies in its first six weeks. Much of that success was due to the single "Fight for Your Right (To Party)," which became a massive crossover success. In fact, *License to Ill* became the biggest-selling rap album of the '80s, which generated much criticism for certain hip-hop fans who believed that the Beasties were merely cultural pirates. On the other side of the coin, the group was being attacked from the right, who claimed their lyrics were violent and sexist and that their concerts—which featured female audience members dancing in go-go cages and a giant inflatable penis, similar to what the Stones used in their mid-'70s concerts—caused even more outrage. Throughout their 1987 tour, they were plagued with arrests and lawsuits, and were accused of inciting crime.

While much of the Beasties' exaggeratedly obnoxious behavior started out as a joke, it became a self-parody by the end of 1987, so it wasn't a surprise that the group decided to revamp their sound and image during the next two years. During 1988, they became involved in a bitter lawsuit with Def Jam and Rick Rubin, who claimed he was responsible for the group's success and threatened to release outtakes as their second album. The group finally broke away by the end of the year; they relocated to California, where they signed with Capitol Records. While in California, they met the production team the Dust Brothers, who convinced the duo to use their prospective debut album as the basis for the Beasties' second album, *Paul's Boutique*. Densely layered with interweaving samples and pop culture references, the retro-funk-psychedelia of *Paul's Boutique* was entirely different than *License to Ill*, and many observers weren't quite sure what to make of it. Several publications gave it rave reviews, but when it failed to produce a single bigger than the No. 36 "Hey Ladies," it was quickly forgotten.

Despite its poor commercial performance, *Paul's Boutique* gained a cult following, and its cut-and-paste sample techniques would later be hailed as visionary—especially after the Dust Brothers altered the approach for Beck's acclaimed 1996 album, *Odelay*. Still, the record was declared a disaster in the early '90s, but that didn't prevent the Beasties from building their own studio and founding their own record label, Grand Royal, for their next record, *Check Your Head*. Alternating between old school hip-hop, raw amateurish funk and hardcore punk, *Check Your Head* was less accomplished than *Paul's Boutique*, yet it was just as diverse. Furthermore, the burgeoning cult around the Beasties made the album a surprise Top 10 hit upon its spring 1992 release. "Jimmy James," "Pass the Mic," and "So Whatcha Want" were bigger hits on college and alternative rock radio than they were on rap radio, and the group suddenly became hip again. Early in 1994, they collected their early punk recordings on the compilation *Some Old Bullshit*, which was followed in June by their fourth album, *Ill Communication*. Essentially an extension of *Check Your Head*, the record debuted at No. 1, and the singles "Sabotage" and "Sure Shot" helped send it to double-platinum status. During the summer of 1994, they co-headlined the fourth Lollapalooza festival with Smashing Pumpkins. That same year, Grand Royal became a full-fledged record label as it released Luscious Jackson's acclaimed debut album, *Natural Ingredients*. The Beasties' *Grand Royal* magazine was also launched that year.

Over the next few years, the Beasties remained quiet as they concentrated on political causes and their record label. In 1996, they released the hardcore EP *Aglio E Olio* and the instrumental soul-jazz and funk collection, *The In Sound from Way Out*. Also that year, Adam Yauch organized a two-day festival to raise awareness and money about Tibet's plight against the Chinese government; the festival went on to become an annual event. The Beastie Boys' long-awaited fifth LP, *Hello Nasty*, finally appeared during the summer of 1998. —*Stephen Thomas Erlewine*

**Licensed to Ill** / 1986 / Def Jam ♦♦♦♦
The impact of this album in 1987 was about as subtle as a brick through a window. It was the first hip-hop album to sell four million copies, and the first album from a White rap group. From the opening kick of John Bonham's drums (taken from "When the Levee Breaks"), the Beasties proceed to steal from every record they can get their hands on and rhyme about an absurd array of macho fantasies. Sure, it's obnoxious—but it's an act, and an insanely humorous one at that; no other rappers brag about being thrown out of White Castle, drinking Budweiser, or having "more rhymes than Phyllis Diller." Even if some of it sounds dated today, the sheer force of the music and whiny rhymes still make this worth hearing. —*Stephen Thomas Erlewine*

▲ **Paul's Boutique** / Jul. 1989 / Capitol ♦♦♦♦♦
Endlessly complex and relentlessly innovative, *Paul's Boutique* is the Beastie Boys' masterpiece. It's very dense, with samples from nearly every genre of music, and has clever, literate, absurd lyrics dropping references from Jack Kerouac to *Dragnet; Paul's Boutique* is a virtual catalog of pop culture, deeply rooted in the '70s. As rappers, the Beasties have grown immeasurably, writing lyrics that are both smart-assed and smart. Musically, the album is much richer than *Licensed to Ill*, covering everything from funk and pop to country and hip-hop, with several layers of samples and beats on each track. *Paul's Boutique* is a brilliant, visionary album, and hasn't aged a day since its release. —*Stephen Thomas Erlewine*

**Check Your Head** / Apr. 21, 1992 / Capitol ♦♦♦♦
*Check Your Head* returned the Beastie Boys to the spotlight, although in the most unlikely manner possible. Refashioning themselves as a loose and gritty groove band, the Beasties picked up their instruments again and made an album of dirty Stax and New Orleans funk, tripped-out reggae, hard hip-hop, blistering hardcore punk, and scores of pop culture references and jokes. In its own way, *Check Your Head* is as trailblazing as *Paul's Boutique*. With its inspired amateurishness, it acknowledges no boundaries or limitations, creating a post-post-punk world where Eddie Harris, Bob Dylan, Cheap Trick, Groove Holmes, Spoonie Gee, and Biz Markie exist together as one music. And, strange as it may sound, it works. —*Stephen Thomas Erlewine*

**Ill Communication** / May 23, 1994 / Grand Royal ♦♦♦♦
More of a refinement and restatement of *Check Your Head* than a bold departure, *Ill Communication* still finds the Beastie Boys in prime form, adding more elements of jazz to their dense, surrealistic sound. From the scores of wah-wah guitars to the short hardcore punk songs, *Ill Communication* is firmly entrenched in '70s worship without sounding recycled. It may offer the same thing as *Check Your Head*, but *Ill Communication* never sounds formulaic or tired. —*Stephen Thomas Erlewine*

**The In Sound from Way Out** / Apr. 2, 1996 / Grand Royal/Capitol ♦♦♦
Originally released through the Beasties' French fan club, *The In Sound from Way Out* is a collection of the group's funky instrumentals from *Check Your Head* and *Ill Communication*, with a couple of new tracks thrown in. The Beasties have a flair for loose, gritty funk and soul-jazz; the stuttering, greasy keyboards of Money Mark give the music an extra edge—he helps make the music sound as authentic as anything from the early '70s. Fans of the band's dynamic wordplay might find *The In Sound From Way Out* a disappointment, but anyone that grooved on the wildly eclectic fusions of *Check Your Head* and *Ill Communication* will find the album endlessly enjoyable. —*Stephen Thomas Erlewine*

**Hello Nasty** / Jul. 14, 1998 / Grand Royal/Capitol ♦♦♦♦
Loaded with analog synthesizers, old drum machines, call-and-response vocals, freestyle rhyming, futuristic sound effects, and virtuoso turntable scratching, *Hello Nasty*, the Beastie Boys' fifth album, is a head-spinning listen—and one that doesn't entirely reveal its secrets upon first play. Since the success of *Check Your Head*, the Beasties have been notorious for their dense, multi-layered explosions, but *Hello Nasty* is their first record since to build on the multi-ethnic junk culture breakthrough of *Check Your Head*—instead of merely replicating it, as *Ill Communication* did. Moving from electro-funk breakdowns to Latin-soul jams to spacy pop, *Hello Nasty* covers as much ground as *Check Your Head* or *Ill Communication*, but the flow is natural, like *Paul's Boutique*, even if the finish is retro-stylized. Hiring DJ Mixmaster Mike (one of the Invisibl Skratch Piklz) as their new man behind the turntable turns out to be a masterstroke. Mixmaster Mike and the Beasties create a sound that strongly recalls the spare electronic funk of the early '80s, but they've spiked it with the samples and postmodern absurdist wit that have become their trademark. On the surface, *Hello Nasty* doesn't appear as dense as *Paul's Boutique* (their first venture into sonic collages) nor does it have a single as grabbing as "Sabotage," but given time, little details emerge and each song forms its own identity. A few stray from the course and the ending is a little anticlimactic, but that doesn't erase the riches of *Hello Nasty*, the old-school kick of "Super Disco Breakin'" and "The Move," Adam Yauch's crooning on "I Don't Know," Brooke Williams' guest vocal on "Dedication," Lee "Scratch" Perry's cameo (the righteous "Putting Shame in Your Game"), and the recurring video game samples, to name just a few. Sonic adventures are rarely this exciting. This alone makes *Hello Nasty* noteworthy, but what makes it remarkable is how it proves that it's possible to look to the future by looking to the past. There's no question that *Hello Nasty* is saturated in old-school sounds and styles, but by reviving the future-shock rock of the early '80s, the Beasties have shrewdly set themselves up for the new millenium. —*Stephen Thomas Erlewine*

## The Beatmasters

f. 1986, London, England
*Group / Club/Dance, Urban, R&B, House*
One of the most successful British writing and producing teams of the late '80s, the Beatmasters were Richard Walmsley, Amanda Glanfield and Paul Carter, the latter pair veterans of the commercial jingle industry. Most famous for their work with Betty Boo, for whom they helmed the smash "Hey DJ, I Can't Dance (To the Music You're Playing)," the Beatmasters also crafted Top 20 hits in tandem with the Cookie Crew ("Rok Da House"), Yazz ("Stand Up for Your Love Rights"), Merlin MC ("Who's in the House") and P.P. Arnold ("Burn It Up"). Additionally, the trio also issued a pair of LPs: 1989's *Anywayawanna* and 1991's *Life and Soul*. They later produced and remixed material for Erasure, Pet Shop Boys and Marc Almond. —*Jason Ankeny*

● **Anywayawanna** / Oct. 16, 1990 / Rhythm King ♦♦♦♦
A kinetic journey through sampledelic house indebted more to its New York axis than Chicago, *Anywayawanna* includes no less than five of the Beatmasters' biggest hits including "Who's in the House," "Hey DJ," "Burn It Up," "Warm Love," and "Rok Da House." Beyond that, it's a great production with none of the wide-open gaps and overly raw grooves that characterize most British house of the day. —*Keith Farley*

## Beats International

f. 1989, Brighton, England, **db.** 1991
*Group / Club/Dance, Acid House, Dance-Pop*
After the 1988 demise of the superb British pop group the Housemartins, Brighton-born bassist Norman Cook returned to his first love, DJing, and became one of the English music scene's most successful remixers. In 1989 he launched a solo recording career with the single "Won't Talk About It," featuring the falsetto vocals of Billy Bragg. The record became a major dance hit, and after a follow-up, "For Spacious Lies," Cook formed Beats International, a loose confederation of studio musicians including vocalists Linda Layton and Lester Noel, rapper MC Wildski, and keyboardist Andy Boucher.

Beats International's 1990 debut single, "Dub Be Good to Me"—a cover of the SOS Band's "Just Be Good to Me" incorporating the bassline of the Clash's "The Guns of Brixton"—topped the UK charts, becoming an international club smash. After another hit, the soul/jazz/worldbeat cocktail "Burundi Blues," the group issued their sample-heavy debut LP *Let Them Eat Bingo*, which debuted in the Top 20 of the British charts. Although Cook had become even more highly sought as a remixer, teaming with artists ranging from Aztec Camera to the Jungle Brothers, he reconvened Beats International in 1991 for *Excursion on the Version*, an exploration of dub and reggae rhythms. When the album failed to repeat the success of its predecessor, Cook disbanded the group to focus on his new unit, Freak Power. [See Also: Fatboy Slim] —*Jason Ankeny*

● **Let Them Eat Bingo** / Apr. 1990 / Elektra ♦♦♦
Though the raft of early-'90s sampladelic British house sensations never weathered the age very well, *Let Them Eat Bingo* still holds its own with a bit more focus on the music, courtesy of inspiration-pointers like "Burundi Blues," "Tribute to King Tubby," and the Top Ten hits "Dub Be Good to Me" and "Won't Talk About It." —*John Bush*

**Excursion on the Version** / 1991 / PolyGram ♦♦
"Everybody get off your feet/And rock to this brand new beat" are the first words you hear on Beats International's second album, and the joke is that there's nothing "brand new" here—not the beats or anything else. Like most disk jockeys, Norman Cook has no problem with commandeering whatever copyrights take his fantasy, so don't be surprised when the chorus to "Echo Chamber," for example, cops part of Steve Miller's "Fly Like an Eagle." Actually, the music on this album isn't as explicitly derivative as that on the group's debut, *Let Them Eat Bingo*, but it's all generally derivative, especially of all-purpose ska and reggae grooves. —*William Ruhlmann*

## Beatsystem (Derek Pierce)

*Producer / Electro, Experimental, Ambient*
UK experimental ambient producer Derek Pierce records for the Nottingham-based Em:t label under the name Beatsystem. Although in the early '90s Pierce released a number of tracks on Em:t's long-running dance-oriented parent, T:me Recordings—even scoring a minor hit in 1990's "Walk on the Wild Side" (released by 4th & B'way)—his more recent work has strayed from the rhythmic origins of his chosen namesake. Beginning in 1995, Pierce's music began to diverge into more esoteric territory, and subsequent work has integrated the more abstract elements of rhythmic electronica with thin digital drones, found sounds, and alternately lush and heavily treated samples (including acoustic guitar, voice, and binaural field recordings). Pierce's full-length debut, *2297*, was released by Em:t in 1997, and drew extensively from the areas of ambient overlap and more academically minded electro-acoustic and minimalist post-classical—often including overt reference to the work of John Cage, Steve Reich, and INA-GRM mentors such as Pierre Schaeffer and Pierre Henry. *2297* is both Pierce's most complete musical statement to date and among the finest releases in the Em:t catalog. —*Sean Cooper*

- **2297** / 1997 / Em:t ♦♦♦♦
Although T:me offshoot Em:t Recordings rapidly earned a reputation for diverse, uniformly high-quality releases from the likes of Woob, Gas, Russell Mills, Carl Stone, and others, few of the Nottingham-based label's releases are as relentless and demanding as this. Beatsystem's debut for Em:t, *2297*, is heavy on digital signal processing, and moves through several styles of electronic music—many of them brazenly abstract—over the course of its 50-plus minutes. From deep, emotive electro-acoustic ambient and electronica to the starkest of minimalist post-classical, digital cut-up, and academic computer music, Pierce renders each with remarkable economy, inventiveness, and skill. —*Sean Cooper*

## Beaver & Krause

f. 1968, San Francisco, CA, db. 1975
*Group / Space Age Pop, Contemporary Instrumental, Electronic*
Composers and synth players Paul Beaver and Bernie Krause were among the most high-profile electronic music acts of the late '60s, recording a series of LPs distinguished not only by their groundbreaking studio advances but also by the presence of notables including Gerry Mulligan and Mike Bloomfield. Krause was a onetime member of the legendary folk group the Weavers—was working as a staff producer at Elektra Records when he met Beaver, a former jazz musician. Under the name Beaver & Krause, they began assembling electronic pieces employing spoken-word passages, acoustic instruments, tape loops and improvisational techniques, debuting in 1968 with *The Nonesuch Guide to Electronic Music*. After 1969's *Ragnarok Electric Funk*, the duo issued *In a Wild Sanctuary* a year later; 1971's *Gandharva*—recorded live in San Francisco's Grace Cathedral and featuring cameos from Mulligan and Bloomfield as well as Bud Shank and Ronnie Montrose—was the most popular of their releases. After 1972's *All Good Men*, Beaver recorded the solo LP *Perchance to Dream;* sadly, it was his final work—he suffered a fatal heart attack on January 16, 1975 at the age of 49. Krause later resurfaced as a noted expert in environmental sound recording. —*Jason Ankeny*

- **In a Wild Sanctuary/Gandharva** / 1994 / Warner Brothers ♦♦♦♦
Beaver & Krause's fascination with electronics did little to temper their enthusiasm for blues-rock, classical, gospel and jazz—each of which were used for selected tracks on these two radical albums reissued by Warner Archives in 1994. The first veers from spiky computer-pop to *Switched-On Bach* classical interpretations, evocative space music to soul-jazz numbers complete with Hammond organ, plus a bout of tribal percussion with a South-seas melody on "People's Park." The partly live album *Gandharva* is more of the same, except for the final five tracks, which were recorded live at Grace Cathedral. The Moog is the star of the show on several tracks, and while a few reeds do enter, it's all part of the same mood (for once on the LP). Taken together, *In a Wild Sanctuary* and *Gandharva* are two of the wildest LPs to come from the electronics boom of the early '70s. —*John Bush*

## Beck (Beck Hansen)

b. Jul. 8, 1970, Los Angeles, CA
*Vocals, Guitar, Producer / Alternative Dance, Indie Rock, Lo-Fi, Club/Dance, Alternative Pop/Rock, Singer/Songwriter*
With his portastudio, keyboard, drum machine, and guitar, singer/songwriter Beck (b. Beck Hansen) created music that celebrated the junk culture of the '90s. Beck's music drew from hip-hop, folk, experimental rock, psychedelia, pop, and rock 'n' roll, recycling everything into a colorful, messy and willfully diverse brand of post-modern rock, filled with warped, satiric imagery and clumsy poetry. With all of his rootless eclecticism, Beck is distinctly a product of the '90s: all of his influences were processed through television and records, not real-life experiences. But that trashy, disposable quality is what makes his music unique.

Beck came to national attention in early 1994, when his folky hip-hop single "Loser" began to receive airplay on alternative rock stations across America. Originally released independently on a Californian label in late 1993, the single became a club hit and quickly spread to underground and alternative radio stations. Beck became the center of a major-label bidding war, and he eventually signed with DGC Records. Beck released his debut album, *Mellow Gold*, in early 1994; it received rave reviews and became a gold record as "Loser" climbed into the Top Ten. Beck's contract with DGC allowed him to release records that he and the company deemed as uncommercial on indie labels. Consequently, the singer/songwriter released two new records by the summer of 1994, which were both recorded roughly around the same time as *Mellow Gold*. *Stereopathetic Soul Manure* was a noisy, more experimental album than his debut and was released on Flipside Records; *One Foot in the Grave* accentuated his folk roots and was released on K Records. Neither album sold on the level of *Mellow Gold*, but they did sell respectably.

As he prepared his second album for DGC, Beck toured with Lollapalooza Five in the summer of 1995. Beck's second major-label album, *Odelay*, finally appeared in the summer of 1996, and it was released to overwhelmingly positive reviews. Throughout 1996, word-of-mouth began to spread on *Odelay*, earning Album of the Year status from most major critic's polls, and even more surprisingly, it received several Grammy Nominations (including Album of the Year). Originally slated for release on indie label Bong Load, *Mutations* instead became *Odelay*'s "unofficial" follow-up when it was released on DGC in the autumn of 1998; the soul-influenced *Midnite Vultures* followed a year later. —*Stephen Thomas Erlewine*

**Mellow Gold** / Mar. 1994 / DGC ♦♦♦♦
From its kaleidoscopic array of junk-culture musical styles to its assured, surrealistic wordplay, Beck's debut album *Mellow Gold* is a stunner. Throughout the record, Beck plays as if there are no divisions between musical genres, freely blending rock, rap, folk, psychedelia, and country. Although his inspired sense of humor occasionally plays like he's a smirking, irony-addled hipster, his music is never kitschy, and his wordplay is constantly inspired. Since *Mellow Gold* was pieced together from home-recorded tapes, it lacks a coherent production, functioning more as a stylistic sampler—there are the stoner raps of "Loser" and "Beercan," the urban folk of "Pay No Mind (Snoozer)," the mock-industrial onslaught of "Motherf—er," the garagey "F—in with My Head," the trancy acoustic "Blackhole," and gently sardonic folk-rock of "Nitemare Hippy Girl." It's a dizzying demonstration of musical skills, yet it's all tied together by a simple yet clever sense of songcraft and a truly original lyrical viewpoint, one that's basic yet as colorful as free verse. By blending boundaries so thoroughly and intoxicatingly, *Mellow Gold* established a new vein of alternative rock, one fueled by ideas instead of attitude. —*Stephen Thomas Erlewine*

**Stereopathetic Soul Manure** / Apr. 1994 / Flipside ♦♦
Within months of the release *Mellow Gold*, Beck released his second album, *Stereopathetic Soul Manure*, a schizophrenic collection of lo-fi recordings spanning 1988 to 1993. Much of the music on the album draws from the noisy, experimental post-punk of Sonic Youth and the dirty, primitive junk-rock of Pussy Galore; his absurdist sense of humor surfaces only rarely, and

only in the guise of such sophomoric cuts as "Jagermeister Pie" and "Satan Gave Me a Taco," while his sense of songcraft is inaudible. Essentially, the record was both a palate-cleanser, one designed to scare away the "Loser" fans, and a bid for indie credibility, since the music on *Stereopathetic* is equally uncompromising and unlistenable as Sonic Youth or their many imitators at their most extreme. —*Stephen Thomas Erlewine*

• **Odelay** / Jun. 18, 1996 / DGC ✦✦✦✦
Beck's debut, *Mellow Gold*, was a glorious sampler of different musical styles, careening from lo-fi hip-hop to folk, moving back through garage rock and arty noise. It was an impressive album, but the parts didn't necessarily stick together. The two albums that followed *Mellow Gold* within months—*Stereopathetic Soul Manure* and *One Foot in the Grave*—were specialist releases that disproved the idea that Beck was simply a one-hit wonder. But *Odelay*, the much-delayed proper follow-up to *Mellow Gold*, proves the depth and scope of his talents. *Odelay* fuses the disparate strands of Beck's music—folk, country, hip-hop, rock 'n' roll, blues, jazz, easy listening, rap, pop—into one dense sonic collage. Songs frequently morph from one genre to another, albeit seemingly unrelated genres—bursts of noise give way to country songs with hip-hop beats, easy listening melodies transform into a weird fusion of pop, jazz and cinematic strings; it's genre-defying music that refuses to see boundaries. All of the songs on *Odelay* are rooted in simple forms—whether it's blues ("Devil's Haircut"), country ("Lord Only Knows," "Sissyneck"), soul ("Hotwax"), folk ("Ramshackle"), or rap ("High 5 [Rock the Catskills]," "Where It's At")—but they twist the conventions of the genre. "Where It's At" is peppered with soul, jazz, funk and rap references, while "Novacane" slams from indie rock to funk and back to white noise. With the aid of the Dust Brothers, Beck has created a dense, endlessly intriguing album overflowing with ideas. Furthermore, it's an album that completely ignores the static, nihilistic trends of the American alternative/independent underground, creating a fluid, creative, and startlingly original work. —*Stephen Thomas Erlewine*

**Midnite Vultures** / Nov. 16, 1999 / Interscope ✦✦✦
Throughout the publicity tour for 1998's *Mutations*, Beck, his publicists, and his label emphasized that this was *not* the proper follow-up to *Odelay*, the 1996 album that cemented Beck's status as a wild, post-post-punk visionary. He was still toiling away on that record, planning to drop it in 1999. By passing off the muted, haunting psychedelic folk-rock, blues, and tropicalia of *Mutations* as a stopgap, Beck set expectations high for this *Odelay* follow-up, especially when word began circulating that Beth Orton, Kool Keith, Johnny Marr, and the Dust Brothers had all contributed to the album. Reportedly, over 40 tracks were recorded for the album, 11 of which (plus the inevitable hidden bonus track) were selected for *Midnite Vultures*. Ironically, in its final incarnation, *Midnite Vultures* doesn't feel at all like a sequel to *Odelay*—it's a genre exercise, like *Mutations*. This time around, Beck has decided to delve into soul, funk, and hip-hop, touching on everything from Stax/Volt to No Limit but using Prince as his home base. He's eschewed samples, more or less, but not the aesthetic. Even when a song is reminiscent of a particular style, whether it's electro-funk or a slow jam, it's assembled in unpredictable ways, with layers of synths, guitars, rhythm loops, horns, and sundry sounds meshing in strange, exciting ways. As it kicks off with the uptempo Stax salute "Sexx Laws," it's hard not to get caught up in the; "Nicotine & Gravy" brilliantly blends funky soul with '80s electro, carrying on the vibe expertly, as does the party jam "Mixed Bizness"; the full-on electro workout "Get Real Paid," is an intoxicating number that sounds like a *Black Album* reject. So far, so good—the songs are tight, catchy, and memorable, and the production is dense. Then "Hollywood Freaks" comes on. Though easily as immaculately produced as anything else on the album, the self-conscious gangsta goof is singularly irritating, not least because of Beck's affected voice. The song is the first on *Midnite Vultures* to feel like a parody, and it's such an awkward, misguided shift in tone that it colors the rest of the album. Songs that sounded like tributes now sound like send-ups, allusions that once seemed affectionate feel a little snide, and the whole thing comes off as, well, a little jive. It's not that the music is bad. *Midnite Vultures* is filled with wonderful little quirks, like the steel guitar break in "Sexx Laws" or the layered backing vocals on "Nicotine & Gravy." Ultimately, what prevents the album from being an unqualified success is the sneaking suspicion that for all the ingenuity, it's all a hipster joke. Humor has always been a big part of Beck's music, but it was gloriously absurd, never elitist. Here, it's possible to see the smirk on his face as he sings "step inside my Hyundai," "make all the lesbians scream," "we're on the good ship ménage à trois," and "Jockin' my Mercedes/ Probably have my baby/ Shop at Old Navy," all of which are a long way from "drive-by body-pierce" (from "Loser") or even "her left eye is lazy" (from "Nicotine & Gravy"). It's likely that all this smug smirkiness was intended to enhance a record that was intended simply as a good-time party album, but it actually undercuts the joy that the music generates. And that's why *Midnite Vultures* is so problematic. Musically, Beck is at the top of his game, with about half of the record ranking among his best, but the self-satisfied tone of the record keeps it at a distance. It's possible to create funny, involving, clever, postmodern party music—the Beastie Boys do it with every record, and Ween has absorbed the absurd spirit of Prince more than most would like to admit—but *Midnite Vultures* misses the mark. And that's especially frustrating because Beck himself has hit that very target before, with both *Mellow Gold* and *Odelay*. —*Stephen Thomas Erlewine*

### Bedouin Ascent (Kingsuk Biswas)

*Producer / Experimental Jungle, Experimental Techno, Electronica, Ambient Techno, Electro*

One of the most obscure artists of the UK experimental/intelligent techno scene (particularly given his output), Bedouin Ascent's Kingsuk Biswas (likely yet another pseudonym) is an impressive force of influence in the areas of overlap between the more ponderous extents of ambient, electro, techno, and drum'n'bass. Recording originally for Rising High before that label shut doors in early 1996, Biswas' early 12"s and debut LP, *Science, Art & Ritual*, were set more squarely in the experimental ambient/techno camp. As the UK underground music scenes tended ever increasingly toward entropy, however, Bedouin Ascent's music has followed suit, shifting to leadership status after 1995's astounding *Music for Particles* LP—as well as remixes for the Rising High Collective, Tortoise, Slack Dog, and others. Generally employing a heavily syncopated method of downtempo drum'n'bass with crisp, shattering snares set in complex patterns and deep, extended bass drones, Biswas often pairs sampled percussion with more typical 808 and 909 drum sounds, recalling the lino-square jaunts of Man Parrish and Cybotron, as well the experimental junglists such as Plug, Witchman, and Squarepusher. Biswas is also one of only a handful of artists who have succeed in fusing elements from these disparate genres in a fashion wholly irreducible to any single category. In addition to his Rising High releases, Biswas has also issued material through the Leaf, Lo, and Blue Angel labels, as well as collaborated with Justin Broadrick and Kevin Martin of Techno Animal, and electro-acoustician Jim O'Rourke. —*Sean Cooper*

• **Science, Art, and Ritual** / 1993 / Rising High ✦✦✦✦
Long after its release, Kingsuk Biswas' first album-length release remains some of his most interesting and innovative work. Combining deep, enthralling melodies with intricate textural arrangements and some of the more complex rhythms of the post-techno lot (compare to the Black Dog and Atom Heart), *Science, Art, and Ritual* is a classic of ambient techno and remains fresh-sounding years after its release. —*Sean Cooper*

**Music for Particles** / 1995 / Rising High ✦✦✦

### B.E.F. (British Electric Foundation)

f. 1980, Sheffield, Yorkshire, England
*Group / New Wave, Synth-Pop*

The production arm of early synth-popsters Heaven 17 and occasionally a recording entity in its own right, B.E.F. (British Electric Foundation) was formed by Martyn Ware and Ian Craig Marsh just after their exit from the original lineup of the Human League. Ware and Marsh had formed the Human League in 1977 as a completely electronic synthesizer band. After adding vocalist Philip Oakey and Adrian Wright, the group released the seminal 1978 single "Being Boiled" and two LPs, 1979's *Reproduction* and the following year's *Travelogue*. Late in 1980 however, both Ware and Marsh left the band over disagreements about its musical direction. Eager to avoid repeating the mistakes they felt the Human League were making (and would continue to make), the pair incorporated British Electric Foundation as a production team instead of a band.

During 1980 and 1981, B.E.F. released two instrumental mini-LPs, *Music for Stowaways* and *Music for Listening To* (both had several tracks in common). The only track on either release with any vocals (and those quite low in the mix) was "Groove Thang," which featured Glenn Gregory, a friend of the duo and a fellow Sheffield resident. By 1981, the three had formed

Heaven 17, remade "Groove Thang" into a more vocal-led track named "(We Don't Need This) Fascist Groove Thang" and stormed the British charts—even though the single was banned by the BBC.

Though Heaven 17's success appeared to circumvent the necessity of B.E.F. as actual recording artists, Ware and Marsh returned in 1982 with the first proper B.E.F. full-length, *Music of Quality and Distinction, Vol. 1*. The LP featured synth-pop covers of soul standards with vocal contributions from Tina Turner, Gary Glitter, Sandie Shaw, Billy Mackenzie and Gregory himself. One year later, Heaven 17 really hit the big time with the single "Temptation" and their second album, *The Luxury Gap*. Ware and Marsh decided to work on Heaven 17 full-time, retiring B.E.F. with the exception of production credits on Heaven 17 LPs.

During the increasingly long breaks between Heaven 17 albums, Martyn Ware began contributing to outside projects. He worked on production for Tina Turner's 1984 breakthrough *Private Dancer* and Terence Trent D'Arby's *Introducing the Hardline According to Terence Trent D'Arby*. By 1988, Heaven 17 had officially broken up. Even so, it was three more years before Ware and Marsh returned with another B.E.F. album, *Music of Quality and Distinction, Vol. 2*. Much less focused on synthesizers than any previous Heaven 17 or B.E.F. material, it featured vocals by Turner and D'Arby as well as Chaka Khan, Mavis Staples and Billy Preston. The two *Music of Quality and Distinction* albums remained unreleased in America, though Virgin reissued an expanded *Music for Listening To* in 1997. —*John Bush*

- **Music for Listening To** / 1981 / Virgin ♦♦♦♦
One of the few synth-pop records of the era—instrumental or otherwise—that attempted to develop the universe of possibilities inherent in the form, *Music for Listening To* spans percussion-heavy sequencer trance, free-floating ambience, and minimalist proto-techno as well as more recognizable synth-funk (notably, the original version of Heaven 17's "Groove Thang"). It's not even a matter of sounding dated; *Music for Listening To* sounds decades ahead of its time and could easily be taken for music produced 20 years later. —*John Bush*

**Music of Quality and Distinction, Vol. 1** / 1982 / Virgin ♦♦♦
Though there are many interesting tracks, *Music of Quality and Distinction, Vol. 1* is quite a scattered album, including synthesizer updates of pop classics as well as a few straight-ahead takes with bizarre vocals. Several of the covers turn out quite well, including Tina Turner's "Ball of Confusion," Glenn Gregory's "Wichita Lineman," and Billy Mackenzie's "The Secret Life of Arabia" (from Bowie's *Heroes*). Paula Yates' tiny voice gives "These Boots Are Made for Walking" a painful lack of aggression, and Mackenzie's rendition of Roy Orbison's "It's Over" turns heartache into hysteria. Most of the songs are familiar, so listeners will at least be able to hum along with Bernadette Nolan's "You Keep Me Hanging On" and Gary Glitter's "Suspicious Minds." —*John Bush*

## Si Begg

*Producer / Experimental Techno, Electronica, Downbeat, Jungle/Drum'N'Bass, Club/Dance, Techno*
London-based experimentalist Si (Simon) Begg is a member of the notorious Cabbage Head artist collective, formed in 1990 in the Midlands town of Leamington Spa, and also including noted dance producers Cristian Vogel and Tim Wright (of Germ). With the exception of a few cassette-only releases as a member of Cabbage Head, he's only been actively releasing music since 1995, Begg's discography (as Cabbageboy, Bigfoot, and Buckfunk 3000, as well as under his own name) has quickly grown to nearly a dozen titles strong, with EPs appearing on such labels as Tresor, Ntone, Eukatech, Language, and Chrome. A restless, often ruthless experimenter with little respect for boundaries, Begg's recorded work (particularly under his Cabbageboy guise) toys incessantly with the conventions of ambient, techno, and drum'n'bass, the results often deviating so sharply from classification that they're simply lost on the listener. His releases (like those of compatriots Vogel, Wright, and Dave Clarke) have nonetheless garnered considerable praise from the continental European techno underground, leading to releases on a number of that scene's most popular and respected labels (including Tresor, Mille Plateaux, and MP subsidiary Chrome). Begg's reputation continues to grow at home as well, with a pair of releases on Ninja Tune subsidiary Ntone—bringing new, less techno-oriented ears to his awkward, esoteric methods.

Weaned from his teens on a range of progressive music—from prog rock and metal to electro and free jazz—Begg joined Cabbage Head upon being introduced to Cristian Vogel by a mutual friend. After releasing a few cassette projects and hosting a few live events, Vogel and Begg formed the Mosquito label to release dancefloor music with a high quotient of weirdness. Although he released no work of his own through Mosquito, Begg used the time and experience to assemble a studio (now located in Harrow, in northwest London) and focus on A&R and label management, experience he's since applied to a label of his own, Noodles (launched at the top of 1997). Begg moved to London in the mid-'90s, hooking up with Coldcut's Jonathon Moore and Matt Black through the local music scene. He released his first EP as Cabbageboy, *Sausage Doctor*, on the pair's Ntone label in '95, following it up with an additional EP, *Planets*, the following year. Begg's connection to Vogel also helped land him a 12" on the somewhat exclusive, extremely selective Tresor label, as well as compilation tracks for Force Inc., K7, Kickin', and Mille Plateaux. Begg's Buckfunk 3000 tracks have also appeared through Moody Boy Tony Thorpe's Crammed subsidiary Language, with the label issuing his debut EP toward the end of 1996. The 1997 Buckfunk 3000 LP *First Class Ticket to Telos* was followed by a Si Begg full-length for Caipirinha, 1998's *Commuter World*. [See Also: Buckfunk 3000, Cabbageboy] —*Sean Cooper*

**Nothing Is True Zen Say [Single]** / Sep. 16, 1996 / Chrome ♦♦♦♦
Begg's debut for experimental newcomer Chrome is somewhat similar to label releases by Alec Empire and Low Frequency Band, featuring heavily chopped up, slightly distorting breakbeats and spurts of electronic texture and noise. And like most Chrome releases, *Zen's* stylistic footing depends in large part on the speed its played at. A break's a break, however, and the games Begg plays with sampled beats are inventive and fascinating. —*Sean Cooper*

**Opus [EP]** / Nov. 11, 1996 / Tresor ♦♦♦

- **Commuter World** / Aug. 25, 1998 / Caipirinha ♦♦♦♦
A quasi-concept album organized around a day in the life of a commuter from northwest London, Begg's first for Caipirinha is an invisible soundtrack with quite a few good bits but a distinct lack of direction throughout and a feel that not much is going on between the musical tracks. There are a few great productions here, though not as many (or as good) as his first LP, *First Class Ticket to Telos* (recorded as Buckfunk 3000). Still, titles like "Delays on the Met Line" and "Walk Home Through the Shoe Box Estate" are quite humorous—at least for those who don't have to deal with the actual scenarios. —*John Bush*

## Dan Bell

**b.** Sep. 9, 1967, Sacramento, CA
*Producer, DJ / Minimal Techno, Detroit Techno, Club/Dance, Techno*
Dan Bell has been a top minimalist Detroit producer from his beginnings as a critical member of Richie Hawtin's Plus 8 Records to his recording of an all-time classic, 1994's "Losing Control" (as DBX) to the foundation of his own Seventh City and Accelerate labels. Born in Sacramento, he grew up near Detroit and was influenced by the sound of techno on Motor City radio during the '80s. Bell began DJing, bought recording equipment, and entered the production world with a job at a recording studio while attending Niagara College near Toronto. Though the work was mostly for hip-hop groups, Bell of ten worked overtime and produced his own tracks.

He had a few productions of his own by 1991, when he moved back to Detroit and met Richie Hawtin. Bell joined Hawtin's new Plus 8 label, and produced several of the imprint's famed early singles ("Technarchy," "Cabaret Seven"), recording with Hawtin and John Acquaviva as Cybersonik. His back-to-basics approach to hard minimalistic techno fit in well with Hawtin's aesthetic. After leaving Plus 8 to form his own Accelerate Records in 1992, Bell began recording as DBX. Singles like "Blip," "Flying Saucer," and "Electric Shock" became hot with DJs from Chicago as well as Detroit. In 1994, Peacefrog released two DBX EPs ("Alien," "Losing Control"). Though "Losing Control" became one of the biggest underground smashes of the decade, Bell's move into the distribution game (by rejuvenating Seventh City as a record distributor) took away valuable production time. Even while the venture soon became one of the main worldwide distributors for Detroit techno, it grew so successful that Bell was forced to put his recording career on hold. He was back on wax by 1996, recording for DS and Klang Electron, as well as Accelerate. Unfortunately, Seventh City distribution folded, and in 1998 Bell returned his concentration to production with the single "Subterranean/The Wild Life/Beserk." Two years later he followed with a mix CD, *The Button Down Mind of Daniel Bell*, released on Tresor Records.—*John Bush*

- **Losing Control [EP]** / 1994 / Peacefrog ♦♦♦♦
Bell's most crucial recording and an undeniable techno classic, DBX's *Losing Control* EP was released on Peacefrog in Britain and, later, Bell's own Accelerate in America. Reminiscent of prime jacking house as well as the darkside of UK hardcore techno circa early '90s, the track works around a monotone voice repeating the title, as a relentless beat pummels the track in a remarkably effective manner, despite its simplicity. —*John Bush*

**Alien [EP]** / 1994 / Klang Electronik ♦♦♦

**The Button Down Mind of Daniel Bell** / Apr. 25, 2000 / EFA ♦♦♦♦
As the DJ mix CD phenomenon slowly becomes a progressively more lucrative phenomenon, there is an even greater need for records such as this. Rather than laying down the sort of anthem-filled, peak-hour sets so common on mix CDs, Dan Bell drops a mid-tempo set with enough funk to keep the energy level high but enough relaxed tempos to warrant repeated listens at any time of the day. His track selection tends to drift toward the quirkier side of mid-tempo house tracks in the vein of Herbert and some of Bell's more down-tempo material. The mix begins with calm tracks from the esteemed Klang and Playhouse labels before moving into some equally interesting arrangements by, most notably, Herbert and Thomas Brinkmann. This first half of the mix isn't that joyous and isn't that funky, but rather a bit odd—not in a negative way, though—as these tracks do their best to make house sound fresh by experimenting with funky yet somewhat jarring rhythms. Beginning with Herbert's dub remix of "Das Bisschen Besser," the set moves from questionable weirdness to sheer brilliance. The quirkiness remains, but the final few tracks bring soul and uplifting vibes, along with some welcome vocals. After the album's peak, Nick Holder's "Feeling Sad," Bell begins a slow decline that hits its most eroded moment during Round Four's "Found a Way," before concluding on a feel-good note with Shake's "Detroit State of Mind." This set will probably change your view of Bell—often associated with hard minimal techno—and, above all, illustrates exactly how to piece together a funky, while at the same time engaging, down-tempo mix more likely to induce dancing than yawning. —*Jason Birchmeier*

## The Beloved
f. 1985, Cambridge, England
*Group / Alternative Dance, Club/Dance, Alternative Pop/Rock*
Originally a quartet whose sound drew inspiration from psychedelia, The Beloved found its greatest success as a rave-influenced dance-pop duo. Throughout its fluid existence, the guiding force behind the group remained vocalist Jon Marsh, who formed the band Journey Through at Cambridge University with Guy Gousden and Tim Havard. With the addition of guitarist Steve Waddington a year later, the group renamed itself The Beloved, and gradually evolved into a moody dance outfit not dissimilar to New Order.
In 1986, the Beloved issued their first single, "This Means War"; a series of releases (including the EP *Happy Now*, the double A-sided single "Surprise Me"/"Heavy Dancing," and the 1987 LP *Where It Is*) followed, but none garnered any significant critical or commercial success. Consequently, Gousden and Havard exited in 1988, at much the same time Marsh and Waddington were falling under the sway of London's burgeoning rave community. After first re-emerging with the ambient-styled single "The Sun Rising," The Beloved then scored an international hit with "Hello," a bubbling techno exercise which name-checked many of the group's influences.
In 1990, the duo issued a pair of albums, *Happiness* and *Blissed Out* (a remix of its sister release), which achieved significant success both in and out of clubs. A long layoff followed however, and when the Beloved returned in 1993 with *Conscience*, Waddington had been ousted in favor of Marsh's wife Helena, resulting in a more pop-oriented flavor. After another three-year absence, they released *X*, a foray back into club culture. —*Jason Ankeny*

**Blissed Out** / 1990 / East West ♦♦♦

- **Happiness** / Mar. 1990 / Atlantic ♦♦♦♦
*Happiness*, the Beloved's debut album, collects their four major hits—"Hello," "The Sun Rising," "Love Takes Me Higher," and "Time After Time"—and sprinkles in a few more club-oriented album tracks to fill out the LP. The post-rave synth-popsters are a bit too heavily tied to the heady days of ABC and Erasure, but *Happiness* suits its title with a set of undeniably pleasant dance-pop. —*John Bush*

**Conscience** / 1993 / Atlantic ♦♦♦
*Conscience*, on which the Beloved consists of vocalist/producer Jon Marsh and co-songwriter/producer Helena Marsh (replacing guitarist Steve Waddington), suggests that the success of *Happiness* was a fluke. In the synth-pop sweepstakes, the Marshes are no competition for the Pet Shop Boys or Erasure, turning out bland, light dance tracks topped by Jon's uninvolved singing of light, upbeat lyrics. —*William Ruhlmann*

## Joey Beltram
b. Nov. 6, 1971, Queens, NY
*Producer, DJ / Minimal Techno, Trance, Club/Dance, Techno*
With a number of legendary tracks such as "Mentasm" and "Energy Flash" to his name, New York-based DJ and producer Joey Beltram is widely acknowledged as a leading innovator in Belgian-style acid and techno. Although his roots as a DJ lie in Chicago house (he still focuses on the style when he spins at home), Beltram's relentless club tracks were highpoints of late-'80s/early-'90s pre-breakbeat hardcore techno, and remain on many DJs' top ten lists as genre- and period-defining examples of post-Detroit European dance music. Born and raised in Queens, Beltram began DJing at a young age, spinning New York and Chicago-style house in his bedroom before moving into production and solo work. By the age of 18, Beltram was recording for Detroit techno staple Transmat and working on tracks with Mundo Muzique and Richie Hawtin for the latter's Plus 8 imprint.
After Beltram released "Energy Flash" on Transmat in 1988, the track was also picked up by R&S, launching his music into a Belgian association which remains to this day. He followed up the reissue with a single for the label in 1992, "Mentasm," a classic of "hoover"-style techno, so-named for its blaring, vacuum-cleaner synth noises and slamming beat. The track was embraced by Belgian techno/hardbeat fans and DJs alike, catapulting Beltram to widespread acclaim. Although Beltram remains best known for his techno work, he by no means confines himself to that style, also dabbling in house and ambient, as evidenced by his eyebrow-raising *Aonox* LP released by the San Francisco experimental label Visible in 1994. He was back to hard minimalistic acid with 1995's *Places* (for Berlin's Tresor) and 1996's *Close Grind* (released on NovaMute as Jb3). Beltram's abundant mixing skills are displayed on the Logic collection *Joey Beltram Live* as well as *The Sound of 2 AM* on Moonshine. —*Sean Cooper*

**Aonox** / 1994 / Visible ♦♦♦♦
A departure to say the least, *Aonox*'s subtle, ambient soundscapes are a far-cry from the banging acid and techno normally associated with the Beltram name. Although the beats remain throughout, the album's focus is on melody and texture, with songs building and unfolding slowly. —*Sean Cooper*

**Mixmag Live!, Vol. 6** / 1995 / Mixmag ♦♦♦♦
Joey Beltram and Mike E-Bloc & Danny Hi-Brid mixed this sixth volume (cassette only) in *Mixmag*'s series of DJ compilations. —*John Bush*

**Places** / Aug. 1995 / Logic ♦♦♦♦
On *Places*, Beltram proved that his take on hard, acid-washed techno remained one of the most original in the field, years after his first innovational singles for R&S. Using minimal patches of acid-stab synthesizer and densely clustered percussion for the tracks "Instant" and "Metro," Beltram forces listeners to play connect the dots. While it often doesn't make much sense at first, repeated listenings reveal layers of intriguing grooves behind the repetition. Swiftly out of print after its first release, *Places* was reissued by Tresor in 1997. —*John Bush*

★ **Classics** / 1996 / R&S ♦♦♦♦♦
Suitably titled, R&S' Beltram collects his finest work for the Belgian label, compiling hardcore mainstays such as "Energy Flash," "My Sound," and "Mentasm." Although it leaves off some crucial cuts by dint of label affiliation, much of Beltram's most significant early work first appeared on R&S, making this CD/LP a perfect introduction to his influential sound. —*Sean Cooper*

**Close Grind** / Dec. 10, 1996 / Nova Mute ♦♦♦♦
Along with the previous year's *Places, Close Grind* reaffirmed Joey Beltram's standing at the head of the headstrong pack; it's a strong collection of minimalist grooves and off-kilter rhythms overlaid with acid noise, and it sounds quite original. —*Steve Huey*

**The Sound of 2 AM** / Jun. 1, 1999 / Moonshine Music ♦♦
For the most part, the eternally famous producer of the life-changing song "Energy Flash" lays down a 17-track hard house set that only occasionally

heads into techno territory. Of course, just because Beltram spins hard house doesn't mean that this is a bad mix; on the contrary, the producer sounds mighty impressive in terms of mixing and keeps the mix jumping with energy and momentum. But it is when he does drop the occasional techno track—such as Christian Smith and John Selway's "Weather" or the Advent's "Sketch 1"—the set reaches it zenith of intensity. The house tracks work fine as high-energy dancefloor material, but when the music hardens and gets dizzying during the techno tracks, one remembers how Beltram initially achieved his fame. The concluding rush of his own monolithic Tresor anthem, "Ballpark," reminds listeners of the problem with this album. There is nothing wrong with Beltram's choice to spin house, but it's unfortunate that he doesn't focus more on the style of aggressive, industrial-flavored techno that he tends to produce so well. —*Jason Birchmeier*

## John Beltran

*Producer / Detroit Techno, Ambient Techno, Club/Dance*

A producer's credentials for recording Detroit-styled techno don't come much better than John Beltran's. Based in nearby Lansing, Beltran worked with Derrick May (as Indio) and released several records on Carl Craig's Retro-Active label (as Open House, with Mark Wilson). And his ear for melody—gained from a healthy enjoyment of world and new age music—has given his productions enough of a bite to be featured by such home-listening-slanted labels as Peacefrog and Dot (as Placid Angles). After releasing singles for American labels Fragmented and Centrifugal during the early '90s, he recorded his debut album *Earth & Nightfall* for R&S Records in 1995.

The production on *Earth & Nightfall* was much more melodic than the usual R&S releases (or for that matter, the usual Detroit producer). One year later, Beltran's *10 Days of Blue* LP for Peacefrog arguably bettered its predecessor. For 1997, Beltran re-upped his Placid Angles guise for an EP on the Swedish new-school electro imprint Dot, then followed with a Placid Angles full-length release, *The Cry* (also on Peacefrog). Late in the year, Beltran released his fourth album, *Moving Through Here*, for the Apollo offshoot of R&S Records. In 1999, Beltran released a self-titled album on Transmat as part of the production trio Indio. [See Also: Indio] —*John Bush*

**Earth and Nightfall** / 1995 / R&S ♦♦♦♦

● **Ten Days of Blue** / Aug. 5, 1996 / Peacefrog ♦♦♦♦
John Beltran's first album for Peacefrog tweaks the blueprint of Detroit techno with a collection of fragile melodies and synthesizer textures worthy of a Derrick May classic, but with more finely wrought percussion. The melancholy beauty of such tracks as "Collage of Dreams" make *Ten Days of Blue* an LP supremely chilled and ready to serve. —*John Bush*

**Moving Through Here** / Nov. 24, 1997 / Apollo ♦♦♦
Something of a shock after his previous albums for Peacefrog (one as himself, and one recorded as Placid Angles), John Beltran's 1997 LP for Apollo/R&S alternates the same cool ambient techno found on his Peacefrog output with more hardcore tracks including the presence of odd female vocals. Though several tracks work for the most part—particularly the breakbeat beauty of "Eden"—the curious balance between up-to-the-minute productions and a very dated sound makes *Moving Through Here* a difficult listen. —*John Bush*

## Bentley Rhythm Ace

f. 1995, Birmingham, England

*Group / Big Beat, Trip-Hop, Club/Dance*

Based in Birmingham, Bentley Rhythm Ace are Mike Stokes (aka Michael Barrywhoosh) and ex-Pop Will Eat Itself bassist Richard Marsh (aka Barry Island). The group formed in 1995 after Marsh was introduced to Stokes at a house party of a mutual friend where Stokes was DJing. Discovering a shared love for screwball novelty records and offbeat groove tunes, the pair met up afterwards to see if they couldn't make a go of a studio collaboration. To date, they've released two EPs and a long-player for Brighton's big-beat Skint label, attracting wide acclaim for their energetic, irreverent blend of hip-hop, funk, and the bizarre lounge, jazz, and exotica records that initially brought them together. The duo's head-scratcher of a name derives from their weekend habit—also commemorated on their first Skint twelve, "This Is Carbootechnodiscobooto"—of rare vinyl shopping at the ubiquitous car-trunk junk sales in their Midlands home. A good deal of the flavor of their material comes from their knack for fusing the fruits of those dusty weekend jaunts with tight, infectious rhythms and engaging arrangements. Following the release of their Skint debut, Stokes and Marsh took up a monthly residency at Heavenly's Sunday Social club (where the Chemical Brothers got their start), and their instant popularity has meant they've been something of a critic's darling ever sense. Their self-titled debut LP was released by Skint in 1997, and featured remixed versions of a few early tracks together with a number of new cuts. The pair have also cultivated something of a devoted club following through their campy live performances, which often involve strange and unusual costumes and props (probably originating from the same car boots as their records). —*Sean Cooper*

● **Bentley Rhythm Ace** / May 12, 1997 / Astralwerks ♦♦♦♦
The UK-based 'big beat' hype was merely a catch-all term for a bunch of characters who liked their funk beats loud and their techno slamming. It's pretty much hip-hop, sampling everything under the sun, and spiced with modern dance music—as everyone from the Chemical Brothers to Bentley Rhythm Ace would happily admit—which is one reason why BRA's self-titled debut is such fun. Perfectly slotting alongside UK labelmates like Fatboy Slim and Lo-Fidelity All-Stars, BRA go merrily nuts with their self-described 'carboottechnodisco' sound, packing their record with injokes of a very English bent (the songtitles alone are proof—"Midlander (There Can Only Be One)," "Mind That Gap," "On Her Majesty's Secret Whistle"). Flecks of the clever weave of pop-culture influences such as Pop Will Eat Itself are unsurprisingly brought to bear on its best records, but BRA is very much its own beast, sacrificing singing for sheer sonic ral-de-rah. BRA also have a good sense of the rave-based crowds they mostly played for; the building rise of songs like "Run on the Spot" and "Spacehopper" are perfectly suited for dancefloor heights. Heaven knows the original release context of much of the strange stuff sampled and chopped; combined with an unerring beat sense, it results in merry insanity. Many tracks have a skittishly low-key feel to them—less pounding but no less giddily off. "Mind That Gap" takes a basic techno pulse and throws in everything from military snare to early synth goofiness, while "Whoosh" has a quirky main keyboard line that is at once naggingly annoying and perfectly suited for funky breakbeats in the mix. At base, BRA's debut is a perfect party album—throw it on, have a good time, and enjoy the extra fun touches while you're re at it. —*Ned Raggett*

## Luciano Berio

b. Oct. 24, 1925, Oneglia, Italy

*Composer / Atonal, Electronic*

A major force in the development of postwar-era experimental music, avant-garde composer and theorist Luciano Berio brought a sense of lyricism and personal expression to even the most complex techniques of electronic and aleatoric music. His modernist approach lent itself to a variety of idioms while incorporating resources including folk traditions, choreography, mime, and acrobatics. Born into a musical family on October 24, 1925 in Oneglia, Italy, Berio studied composition and conducting at Milan's Conservatorio di Musica Giuseppe Verdi. In 1952 he travelled to the US to study under the influential composer Luigi Dallapiccola. A year later, he composed his first major work, *Chamber Music for Mezzo-Soprano, Clarinet, Cello, & Harp (After James Joyce)*. Upon returning to Milan in 1954, he teamed with another famed Italian composer, Bruno Maderna, to found the Studio di Fonologia Musicale. Under Berio's direction, it emerged among the top electronic music centers in Europe.

While heading the studio, Berio began pursuing a means of reconciling electronic music with musique concrète; concurrently, he and Maderna also co-founded the avant-garde journal *Incontri Musicali*. In 1958, Berio completed his breakthrough electro-acoustic piece *Thema/Omaggio a Joyce*, which manipulated a sound source of a reading from *Ulysses; Allez-Hop*, inspired by a Calvino text, followed a year later. In 1960, he relocated to America, where over the next dozen years he taught at Mills College, Harvard, and the Juilliard School. During this period Berio became increasingly fascinated by rock and folk music, increasingly incorporating elements of both into his own work. Indeed, Berio's major works of the era—*Visage, Passagio, Folk Songs, Laborintus II* and the *Sequenza* series among them—seem to draw upon virtually every major Western musical tradition, with an increasing emphasis on electronic media and tape.

Berio's other primary focus was the voice, primarily that of his longtime wife and muse Cathy Berberian, the mezzo-soprano who gave the debut performances of Seventies-era works including a revised *Folk Songs*; other key compositions of the period were *Opera, Linea, Points on the Curve to Find, Cries of London, Il Retorno Degli Snovidenia* and *Coro*. The head of the electro-acoustic department of ICRAM in Paris until 1980, in 1987 Berio founded the Tempo Reale research institute in Milan. With the aforementioned Italo Calvino, he also collaborated on projects including *La Vera Storia* and *Un Re in Ascolto*. His latter-day compositions included the Biblically-influenced *Ofanim, Canticum Novissimi Testamenti I and II* and *Rendering*. The occasion of Berio's 70th birthday in 1995 brought with it not only a number of musical celebrations, but also new recordings of many of his greatest pieces. —*Jason Ankeny*

- **Coro for 40 Voices and 40 Instruments (1976)** / 1991 / Deutsche Grammaphon ◆◆◆◆
Performed by the Cologne Symphony Orchestra and Chorus conducted by the composer, *Coro* is Berio's masterpiece in his romantic-pointillism style. —*"Blue" Gene Tyranny*

## Justin Berkovi

b. 1974, Watford, England
*Producer / Minimal Techno, Electronica, Club/Dance, Techno*
British techno don Justin Berkovi's productions offer just as much to advocates of pounding minimalism as to fans of the emotional ambient wing of techno. Born in Watford (though he spent part of his childhood in Luxembourg as well), Berkovi grew up with synth-pop and hip-hop. After experimenting with electronics and tape loops while still at school, he began focusing on music after graduating from Sussex University in 1996. His first major releases came on Sativae and Cristian Vogel's Mosquito label, and he soon earned notice with singles for dancefloor-experimentalist imprints like DJAX and Force Inc. By 1998, he'd founded his own label, Predicaments, and recorded his first LP, *Charm Hostel*. One year later, *After the Night* was released. —*John Bush*

**Charm Hostel** / May 18, 1998 / Force Inc ◆◆◆
Experimental yet human, Justin Berkovi's *Charm Hostel* is a collection of minimalist techno and house that rewards repeated listenings. —*Steve Huey*

- **After the Night** / May 31, 1999 / Force Inc ◆◆◆◆
Berkovi's second full album for Force Inc is a delicious slice of down-tempo techno and electro. From elegant, listening-slanted tracks like "Exit," "Carine," and "Bad Proximity" to the nightmarish electro of "Bitch Mechanique," "Scare," and "The Juice," Berkovi offers a shadowy, nocturnal twist on the skewed experimental techno of Cristian Vogel and rave/hardcore clichés from the early '90s. Except for a few tracks of (comparatively) straight-ahead techno that sound a bit bland in comparison, *After the Night* is an excellent album of late-night techno to file alongside music-to-drive-by masterpieces like Carl Craig's *Landcruising* or Morgan Geist's *The Driving Memoirs*. —*John Bush*

## The Beta Band

f. 1997, Edinburgh, Scotland
*Group / Experimental Dub, Electronica, Neo-Electro, Trip-Hop, Alternative Pop/Rock*
Their sound veering from post-grunge balladry to funk and ambient breakbeat to Madchester acid-house, the Beta Band emerged on the British scene as (nominally) a pop group with few similarities to any other act going. Formed around three friends originally from Edinburgh—vocalist Stephen Mason, drummer Robin Jones and DJ/sampler John Maclean—the group later added bassist Richard Greentree. Scant months after forming, the Beta Band gained a formidable ally in gaining exposure: manager Brian Cannon, the designer responsible for virtually every Oasis sleeve released to that point. The group's first EP, 1997's *Champion Versions*, featured mixing by the Verve's Nick McCabe. Two additional EPs followed in early 1998, *The Patty Patty Sound* and *Los Amigos del Beta Bandidos*. After collecting all three EPs on an album, the Beta Band began recording for their proper debut, a self-titled effort released in 1999. —*John Bush*

- **The 3 E.P.'s** / Sep. 28, 1998 / Regal ◆◆◆◆
This grouping of the Beta Band's first recordings—three EPs, four tracks each—is a collection of practically indescribabe songs. In fact, many of the tracks are only nominally pop songs; the group ranges from Kraut and avant-rock musings to heavy funk and hip-hop without the forced feeling that it's being done for the sake of critics. —*John Bush*

**The Beta Band** / Jun. 15, 1999 / Astralwerks ◆◆◆◆
Though dismissed by the group themselves as "fucking awful" and "the worst record made this year," the Beta Band's self-titled album otherwise defies simple criticism—seemingly infinite in its sonic complexities, it's an album of remarkable density and detail, a brashly schizophrenic freak-out which weaves its way throughout the history of rock'n'roll. Pop, blues, folk, psychedelia, hip-hop—they're all here, sometimes even colliding within the same song. The disc somehow sounds almost completely different with each successive listen, consistently revealing new layers and possibilities. It constantly runs the risk of collapsing into complete self-indulgence, but in its own way, the Beta Band's genius is their wanton disregard for niceties like verses, choruses, and melodies; rejecting musical theory in favor of the chaos theory, the album's neither a masterpiece nor a mess, but both. —*Jason Ankeny*

## Adam Beyer

b. 1976
*Producer, DJ / Minimal Techno, Club/Dance, Techno*
Part of the surprisingly fertile Swedish techno scene led by the pornophile savants at Svek Records, producer and DJ Adam Beyer concentrates on percussion to a large degree for his appropriately named Drumcodes imprint. Begun in mid-1996, the label released a dozen records during the next two years, half by Beyer himself, with others featuring Cari Lekebusch, Oliver Ho and Thomas Krome. Beyer's first album, *Decoded*, was released on Planet Rhythm in late 1996, and the remix album *Recoded* followed one year later. Another label run by Beyer, Code Red, has released productions by himself, Lekebusch, Krome and Joel Mull. As well, he has recorded for Svek as Concealed Project. —*John Bush*

- **Decoded** / Nov. 18, 1996 / Planet Rhythm ◆◆◆◆
After over a dozen in his Drumcodes series of singles, Beyer dropped a full-length of his trademarked bangin' techno, heavy on the off-kilter effects and percussion. —*Keith Farley*

**Recoded: The Remix Album** / Sep. 22, 1997 / Planet Rhythm ◆◆◆
A four-pack of remixes from Beyer's first full-length release include a host of sympathetic sources—Thomas Krome, Marco Carola, Oliver Ho, the Advent, Abstract Soul, and Zzino Vs. Accelerator. —*Keith Farley*

## Big Audio Dynamite

f. 1984, London, England
*Group / Alternative Dance, Alternative Pop/Rock*
After Mick Jones was fired from the Clash in 1983, he formed Big Audio Dynamite (B.A.D.) one year later with video artist Don Letts (effects and vocals), Greg Roberts (drums), Dan Donovan (keyboards), and Leo "E-Zee Kill" Williams (bass). B.A.D. debuted with the single "The Bottom Line" in September 1985. The group followed the more experimental funk elements of the Clash's *Combat Rock*, adding samplers, dance tracks, and found sounds to Jones' concise pop songwriting. Jones suffered from a near-fatal bout of pneumonia in 1988, but bounced back with 1989's *Megatop Phoenix*. After that record, the band split apart at the end of 1989. Jones added Gary Stonadge (bass/vocals), Chris Kavanagh (drums/vocals), and Nick Hawkins (guitar/vocals) to form Big Audio Dynamite II; Letts, Williams, and Roberts formed Screaming Target; and Donovan joined the Sisters of Mercy. Releasing *The Globe*, the first full-length album with the new lineup in 1991, B.A.D. II experienced their greatest success yet with the American Top 40 hit single "Rush." In 1994, the band's name was truncated to Big Audio, and the album *Higher Power* was released.

After *Higher Power*, Big Audio parted ways with Epic Records, signing with Radioactive in early 1995 and releasing *Punk* later that year. —*Stephen Thomas Erlewine and William Ruhlmann*

**This Is Big Audio Dynamite** / Oct. 1985 / Columbia ◆◆◆
Since Mick Jones was the more melodic, pop force in The Clash, it was a surprise that the band he formed (after being kicked out of that group) was such an unusual mix of synthesized drumming and spoken-word tape inserts. Beneath all the gimmicky sounds (and perhaps accentuated by them) were Jones' often winning songs, among which were the UK Top 40 hits "EMC2" and "Medicine Show." —*William Ruhlmann*

**No. 10, Upping St.** / Oct. 1986 / Columbia ◆◆◆◆
Temporarily reuniting with his former Clash partner Joe Strummer (who co-produced this album and co-wrote five songs), Mick Jones expands on the formula of the debut with Big Audio Dynamite's second album. *No. 10, Upping*

*Street* features better songs that meld samples, found sounds, dance rhythms, and elements of hip-hop more completely and effectively than those on the first record. "C'mon Every Beatbox" and "V. Thirteen" made the UK singles chart. "Badrock City," added to the album after its initial release, made the US R&B singles chart. —*Stephen Thomas Erlewine and William Ruhlmann*

**Tighten Up, Vol. 88** / Jun. 1988 / Columbia ♦♦
Mick Jones tightens the rather free-form structures of the previous B.A.D. albums on *Tighten Up, Vol. '88*. While he was aiming for a greater commercial success, the result was only partially successful; the best tracks didn't work as singles, and the singles didn't have the creative spark that marks the best of B.A.D.'s music. "Just Play Music!" made the UK singles chart. —*Stephen Thomas Erlewine*

**Megatop Phoenix** / Sep. 1989 / Columbia ♦♦♦
On *Megatop Phoenix*, Jones delves further into a dance-influenced, cut-and-paste approach to pop music that manages to capture all of the inventiveness of late-'80s dance music without losing sight of the melodies that have always been his strength. —*Stephen Thomas Erlewine*

**The Globe** / Aug. 1991 / Columbia ♦♦♦♦
Although the second incarnation of Big Audio Dynamite doesn't sound all that different from the first, Mick Jones' songwriting and concepts are reinvigorated on *The Globe*, making it one of the best B.A.D. albums. It also ranked as their most commercially successful in the US, where "Rush" hit the Top 40, with the title track also charting. —*Stephen Thomas Erlewine*

**Higher Power** / Nov. 8, 1994 / Columbia ♦
Nine years and six albums on, Big Audio's formula of Mick Jones-penned pop tunes, hip-hop beats, and odd found sounds was beginning to sound worn. As indicated on such tracks as "Looking for a Song" and "Harrow Road," carrying on seemed to have become something of a burden for Jones, who increasingly turned to '60s-derived guitar riffs and simple pop melodies. The rhythm section remained too far down in the mix to induce dancing, and the tape inserts—well, Jones was still no Pink Floyd. Obviously, by whatever name they chose, Big Audio needed to rethink their approach. —*William Ruhlmann*

**F-Punk** / Jun. 20, 1995 / Radioactive ♦♦
For his first album for Radioactive, Mick Jones changed the name of his group back to Big Audio Dynamite and delivered *Punk*. While the name was a retreat back to B.A.D.'s most creative and exciting days of the '80s, the music on *F-Punk* simply reiterated all of the ideas of their last few albums—which means that it stated the same themes as their previous records. Far from being "punk," with all its classic rock references and allusions to the glory days of 1977, the album sounds tied to the past. —*Stephen Thomas Erlewine*

● **Planet BAD: Greatest Hits** / Sep. 12, 1995 / Columbia ♦♦♦♦
Big Audio Dynamite's albums have always been fairly inconsistent affairs, which makes *Greatest Hits* such a worthwhile purchase. Collecting 15 songs from their six albums at Columbia (when they were alternately called B.A.D. and B.A.D. II) the album contains hits like "Globe" and "Rush," as well as album tracks and college radio hits. —*Stephen Thomas Erlewine*

**Super Hits** / May 4, 1999 / Sony ♦♦♦
Like many conceptual bands, Big Audio Dynamite were primarily an album-based group, turning out records that had a consistent sound and theme. The problem was that Mick Jones had too many ideas. Each B.A.D. record was teeming with intriguing sounds that only made sense on a handful of tracks—in other words, they were an album band most listenable in small doses. That made them easier to anthologize than the average album-rock band, as the enjoyable hits collection *Planet BAD* proved. *Super Hits*, a budget-line comp that concentrates on their Columbia recordings, is nearly as entertaining as the full-fledged hits package, since it contains nearly all of their biggest hits, including "The Bottom Line," "C'Mon Every Beatbox," "Rush," "E equals MC2," "Contact," "Medicine Show," and "The Globe"—everything except "Free," really. Hardcore fans will naturally prefer the full-fledged albums, and some will like the more extensive hits package, but *Super Hits* will satisfy the needs of most casual listeners, especially those on a budget. —*Stephen Thomas Erlewine*

## Big Bud

*Producer / Jungle/Drum'N'Bass, Club/Dance*
A supremely stoked jungle producer who's recorded exclusively for LTJ Bukem's Good Looking/Looking Good stable, Big Bud concentrates on the usual fusion-soaked reveries of breakbeat drum'n'bass. He debuted with a few twelves ("Blue 52," "Emotionography," "State of Mind") for Good Looking; and he earned appearances on the Bukem compilations *Earth 3* and *Logical Progression 3*. Though Big Bud was in danger of being washed away by the hordes of similar (though not as solid) producers attached to Bukem, the release of the single-artist full-length *Infinity + Infinity* in 1999 (a rarity for GL/LG) appeared to push Big Bud ahead of the pack. —*John Bush*

● **Infinity + Infinity** / Sep. 28, 1999 / Good Looking ♦♦♦♦
A rare non-compilation album released on Good Looking, Big Bud's debut goes the route of smooth fusion breaks, as light and airy as anything else released on LTJ Bukem's stable of labels (Good Looking, Looking Good, Earth, etc.). O'Reilly's pinpoint drum programming and ear for excellent effects add a degree of edginess to the album, making it one of the best full-lengths—compilation or otherwise—ever released on a Bukem label. —*John Bush*

## Bigod 20

f. 1988, Brussels, Belgium, db. 1994
*Group / Alternative Pop/Rock*
The late-'80s intersection of industrial EBM (electronic body music) and acid house proved strong in the careers of Psychic TV and Front 242 as well as Bigod 20, the acid house project of longtime EBM producer Talla 2XLC. A trio comprising Talla plus producer Jallokin and later vocalist Zip Campisi, the group debuted in 1988 with a pair of club hits, "Body to Body" and "America"—the latter with additional songwriting credits by Richard 23 and Patrick Codenys of Front 242. Trouble with their label forced a hiatus of over two years, but when the major label Sire Records came calling in 1992, Bigod 20 signed an American deal. The first single under the contract was "The Bog," with 242 vocalist Jean Luc DeMeyer. The duo added Zip Campisi to sing on their debut album *Steel Works*, released later that year. By 1994's *Supercute* however, Talla 2XLC had left for what could loosely be termed a solo career, recording on his own for Polygram, Suck Me Plasma and Cleopatra. —*John Bush*

● **Steel Works** / Oct. 6, 1992 / Sire ♦♦♦
The first Bigod 20 album is bland industrial dance and acid house with just a few elements of more Germanic trance. New member Zip Campisi lends his low-voiced, industrial campness to a few vocal tracks ("On the Run," "Wild at Heart") but the EBM-slanted production of Talla 2XLC is the focus throughout. —*Keith Farley*

**Supercute** / 1994 / Sire/Warner Brothers ♦♦
*Supercute* attempts a bit of artist develoment for Bigod 20, with detours into S&M acid-house (in the vein of Lords of Acid) on "Are You Horny Yet?" and "Slavery Is Guaranteed." The album is still quite similar to its predecessor, cycling through sampled acid-house with not much of a flair for creativity or track production. —*Keith Farley*

## Biochip C (Martin Damm)

*Producer / Electro-Techno, Techno*
Biochip C's Martin Damm is a Frankfurt-based solo artists working in the experimental techno, acid, and electro veins, issuing 12" and full-length releases through such institutions of dancefloor exploration as Force Inc., Mille Plateaux, Monotone, Analog, and his own Anodyne label. Although the lion's share of that work has appeared under the Biochip name, he also splits a good deal of focus between two other projects—Speed Freak (experimental techno and gabber), Phase IV (hardcore), Search & Destroy (gabber), and Subsonic 808 (house). He's also recorded as R.I.C. and Steel for Force Inc. subsidiary Mille Plateaux, combining the complex rhythmic base of his other, harder-edged releases with ambient and industrial elements. Damm was influenced early on by the Chicago acid scene associated with artists such as Robert Armani, DJ Pierre, Armando, and Marshall Jefferson and labels such as Chicago Traxx and Drop Bass Network (the latter through which Damm has released material as Speed Freak), and much of his work utilizes the signature acid warble of the 303. During 1995-96, Damm became one of the few experimental dancefloor artists working in breakbeat forms of acid and techno, with a strong electro influence in evidence on EPs for Force Inc ("Kaori"), Analog ("Tres Amigos en Acid"), and Anodyne ("Moldiver," "Musik Ohne Eire"). The full album *Breakdown* appeared in late 1998. —*Sean Cooper*

**Kaori [EP]** / 1995 / Force Inc ♦♦♦♦
*Kaori* is a scorching, out-of-the-blue five-tracker featuring some of the most focused, full-formed German electro this side of Kraftwerk. Although Biochip

and Steel releases before and since have utilized elements of electronic breakbeat, *Kaori* condenses and synthesizes the best components of American acid and freestyle electro (including the killer Beat Club break lifted for "Pause"), combining them with a harder, darker edge and subtle, bizarre filter textures—some of the best new-school electro to be found. —*Sean Cooper*

● **Drop Me [Single]** / 1996 / Force Inc ♦♦♦♦
Call this four-tracker *"Kaori Pt. 2,"* as Damm follows his earlier Force Inc. twelve with another fat slab of electro gear in the uptempo new-school mode. Once again pillaging the Beat Club's "Security" (though with a distinctive twist) for the mega-mix-esque "Steal It And Deal It," Biochip gives the rest of this EP the overview treatment, moving from style to style—breakbeat acid, dark electro, and humorous, downtempo distorto-breaks à la Chicks With Dicks tracks—exploring the various possibilities open to mid-'90s electronic breakbeat. Top to bottom quality. —*Sean Cooper*

**Los Amigos en Electro [EP]** / 1996 / Anodyne ♦♦♦
Not really a "versus" album in the proper sense, *Amigos* is more of a co-release, with a twelve piece featuring various shades of electro via Martin "Biochip" Damm and Freddy Fresh. Biochip's tracks mix the more straight ahead electro gear of his Force Inc singles with the distorto breakbeat of previous Anodyne twelves. Fresh's funk is a bit thinner, with the beat disappearing altogether from a couple of the tracks. A fine collection of new school club gear overall, though not as useful for home listening. —*Sean Cooper*

**Moldiver [EP]** / 1996 / Anodyne ♦♦♦
Two sides exploring vastly different styles, from intricate (if somewhat flat-sounding) electro-acid and house-y techno, to harsh, mid-tempo industrial breakbeat similar to Damm's work as Steel and Chicks With Dicks. Good but uneven. —*Sean Cooper*

**Musik Ohne Eire [EP]** / 1996 / Anodyne ♦♦♦
Some of Damm's most bizarre combinations come out on his Anodyne work, and "Musik Ohne Eire" (recorded, reportedly, with a mystery guest under the name Chicks With Dicks) is among the weirdest. Five tracks with no single unifying theme, "Musik" moves through harsh ambient-ish breaks à la Aphex Twin and Mike Paradinas, melancholy downtempo hip-hop, and a goofy brand of mid-tempo electro which draws on cheesy West Coast jazz and MOR soul-funk for influence. —*Sean Cooper*

**Breakdown** / Oct. 12, 1998 / Force Inc ♦♦♦♦
*Breakdown* is a 14-track collection of what sounds surprisingly like party music for hardcore techno, gabba, and breakbeat fans, with the electronic-dance equivalent of three chords and a cloud of dust on tracks "I Declare War," "Sleepless in Osaka," and "Bio's Theme." —*Keith Farley*

## Biosphere (Geir Jenssen)
b. Tromso, Norway
*Producer / Ambient House, Electronica, Ambient Techno*

Biosphere's Geir Jenssen hails from Tromso, Norway, a city 500 miles into the Arctic Circle. A founding member of quasi-new age Norwegian trio Bel Canto, Jenssen recorded a pair of albums with the group for the Belgian Crammed label before departing to record solo. First as Bleep, then as Biosphere. He released a number of Bleep singles through the late '90s on Crammed subsidiary SSR, as well as the full-length *The North Pole by Submarine*, issued in 1990 and an acknowledged precursor of what became known as ambient techno. Fusing elements of composition derived from environmental experimentalists such as Brian Eno, Jon Hassell, and Walter Carlos with the rhythmic backbone of urban dance styles such as techno and acid-house, ambient techno's popularity would grow with the popularity of artists such as the KLF, Irresistible Force, Higher Intelligence Agency—and of course Biosphere. Jenssen's first material under that name, the full-length *Microgravity*, appeared in 1991 on the Norwegian Origo Sound label, and was picked up for international release by R&S subsidiary Apollo the following year. In 1993, in addition to scoring the Norwegian film *Evige Stjerner (Eternal Stars)* and working for a multimedia installation, Jenssen collaborated with German ambient composer Pete Namlook on the Fax release *The Fires of Ork* (reissued the following year by Apollo). Jenssen returned to Biosphere in 1994 with a second full-length record, *Patashnik*, and a subsequent live tour the success of which landed one of Jenssen's tracks ("Novelty Waves") in a Levi's commercial. In 1995, Jenssen collaborated with Higher Intelligence Agency's Bobby Bird, performing the live improvisational piece "Polar Frequencies," released by Apollo in 1996. The Biosphere releases *Substrata* and *Insomnia* followed in 1997; *Cirque* appeared three years later. —*Sean Cooper*

★ **Microgravity** / 1992 / Apollo ♦♦♦♦♦
Jenssen's fascination with science-fiction in general (specifically, space) powers his debut album for the R&S wing, Apollo. Welding eerie samples to house rhythms, *Microgravity* has a sinister quality that's refreshing compared to much ambient house of the early '90s. —*John Bush*

**Patashnik** / 1994 / Apollo ♦♦♦♦
One reason why Jenssen's work stands out from the flood of early-'90s ambient/techno releases is his strong sense of the quirkily creepy—not in an Aphex Twin mode, but in his own particular way. The contrasting samples of a child quaveringly saying "We had a dream last night," followed by a rougher sample saying "We had the same dream," gives opening number "Phantasm" an unsettling feeling. Intensified by the on the one hand pretty, on the other disturbing music, buried synth strings and a soft pulse are accentuated by clattering noises deep in the mix—kicking off the striking *Patashnik* very well. Though not as openly dark as acts like Lull, for instance, Biosphere still has an edge which isn't just melancholic, it's downright ominous. There's the slow crawl of "Startoucher," with its buried vocal snippets and deep bass drone, the blend of the space signal atmospheres of "Mir" into the low, brooding intro to "The Shield." Not everything is so shadowy, though; *Patashnik* is primarily a "relax and chill" listening experience, but not without gentle high points. "Novelty Waves," which became a crossover single in some quarters, has a good dancefloor sharpness even as Jenssen slyly sneaks in odd drones and samples through the mix. The opening snippet's "extraterrestrial disc jockey" on "SETI Project" is good for a smile, and is a sharp lead-in to a fast rhythm track. Mostly though, things continue on a deliciously unnerving pace throughout—gentle enough to go down easy, but still just off enough to ensure you can't call this new age folderol for the rave generation. —*Ned Raggett*

**Insomnia** / 1997 / Origo Sound ♦♦♦♦
Geir Jenssen's score for Erik Skjoldbjaerg's acclaimed 1997 film, *Insomnia*, was also released on CD by the Norwegian label Origo Sound (home to Jenssen's earlier Bel Canto recordings and a snatch of recent Biosphere reissues). As with other of Jenssen's latest releases (*Substrata, Polar Sequences*), his *Insomnia* score (here separated into 17 separate tracks, most between two and five minutes) is tense, indolent stuff. The pressure is diminished somewhat by the brevity of the tracks, but those looking for the conceptual breadth typical of his non-cinematic works will be somewhat disappointed (although, to be sure, such expectations ignore the fact that *Insomnia* is, after all, a film score). The above caveat noted, this is beautiful work. —*Sean Cooper*

**Substrata** / 1997 / All Saints ♦♦♦♦
*Substrata* (released, oddly, on the new age-heavy All Saints label) was the first full-length solo work released by Biosphere's Geir Jenssen following a three-year period of silence. The album was the first of three to appear almost simultaneously, however—the other two being the soundtrack to the psychological thriller *Insomnia*, on the Norwegian Origo Sound label, as well as his third Apollo album—proving he'd hardly been in hibernation. Interestingly, while many ambient artists have moved increasingly toward the integration of percussion and rhythmic sequencing, *Substrata* finds Jenssen almost completely abandoning the rhythmic elements of earlier works such as *Patashnik* and "Novelty Waves." Instead, he focuses on dark, subtly melodic, often piercingly melancholic soundscapes that flow seamlessly from one to the next. The album recalls the more abstract moments of Global Communication's ambient works, as well as the glacial expanses of Jenssen's 1996 collaboration with Higher Intelligence Agency, *Polar Sequences*, and is quite easily among his most accomplished, satisfying works to date. —*Sean Cooper*

**Cirque** / Jun. 13, 2000 / Touch ♦♦♦♦
Unsurprisingly, the geography-oriented ambience of Geir Jenssen's Biosphere project proves a tight fit with Touch, the label launched by former travelogue writer Jon Wozencroft. *Cirque* collects 11 short Biosphere pieces, each evocative of a photo included in an accompanying booklet. Though the subjects range throughout Europe (from New Year's Eve on London's South Bank to a rocky meadow near Jenssen's native Tromsö, Norway, to rural Hampshire to a mountain on Crete), the music sticks mostly to either soft,

textured rhythms—if Jenssen were a drummer, he'd be using his whisks—or deep dub/techno with soothing synthesizers over-arching most of the work. One of the highlights, "Black Lamb & Grey Falcon" is ambience of a dark, crackly nature with the melancholy repetition of a guitar and whispers of light classical music in the background. It's difficult to tell whether Jenssen incorporated field recordings into *Cirque*, and if there are any present, they're in heavily processed form; except for a few vocal samples, there's no explicit environmental feel. In keeping with much Biosphere material, *Cirque* owns a sense of grandeur and quiet beauty that once again reinforces Jenssen's immense talent in creating evocative electronic music. —*John Bush*

## Bisk (Naohiro Fujikawa)
*Producer / Experimental Techno, Electronica, Electro-Jazz*

One of only a handful of Japanese experimental techno artists to gain exposure outside of Japan, Naohiro Fujikawa's fractured electronica under the name Bisk is also among the most interesting and innovative post-techno hybrids to appear in the last several years. A native of Hyogo, Fujikawa was barely into his 20s when his debut CD, *Time*, was released by Belgian label Sub Rosa in 1996. Sounding literally years ahead of its time, *Time* was a future-shock of sampler orchestration, the splintering remains of ambient, jazz, techno, hip-hop, electro, and experimental noise/musique concrète recombined into forms both fascinating and bewildering. Fujikawa's only other releases previous to *Time* were on small-run, largely Japan-only compilations (Trip Trap Records' *Floating on the 1st Floor* being the most notable); released under his own name, these tracks were far more derivative than his subsequent material as Bisk. Following *Time*, Fujikawa contributed a track to Bill Laswell's *Oscillations Remix* CD/LP before Sub Rosa issued a second full-length CD, *Strange or Funny-Haha?*, in 1997. Another essential collection of sample-based chaos unlike most other happenings in contemporary electronica, *Strange* sets a standard of quality even higher than its predecessor, and further argued for Fujikawa's status as one of the most important and original new voices in experimental post-techno. The somewhat less impressive *Ticklish Matters* appeared on Sub Rosa in 1998, along with a remix for American hip-hop group East Flatbush Project (included on the *Tried by 12* remix album, co-released by Ninja Tune and Chocolate Industries in December 1998). In addition to his CDs, a trio of exclusive Bisk tracks can be found on Sub Rosa's excellent 1998 compilation, *Water and Architecture*, alongside selections by Seefeel, former Tortoise bassist Bundy Brown and (most appropriately) Uwe "Atom Heart" Schmidt, one of the few artists to whom Fujikawa's work owes a clear debt. —*Sean Cooper*

**Time** / 1996 / Sub Rosa ++++

Japanese composer Naohiro Fujikawa lets fancy run wild on this bewildering collection of jazzed-up electro-techno. Recalling at times the complicated rhythmic experiments of German genre-abusers Atom Heart and Elfish Echo, Fujikawa's approach is almost orchestral in its complexity, with tracks evolving and mutating constantly. Although the jazzier elements present themselves in the more obvious form of samples and instrumental passages, the album is also extremely improvisational in tone, escaping the mechanical feel characteristic of much experimental electronica. —*Sean Cooper*

● **Strange or Funny-Haha?** / Jun. 23, 1997 / Sub Rosa ++++

Bisk's second full-length album for Sub Rosa is both strange and funny-haha; strange in its almost unprecedented fusion of vagued-out electronica (electro, experimental hip-hop, left-field drum'n'bass) with everything from manic bop and Zorn-esque post-free-jazz to avant-gardist loop'n'splice tape massacre and digital sound collage. And funny-haha? Well, for much the same reason, Fujikawa's extreme methods of genre-obliterating abstraction are so warped and smeared that sometimes the only possible response is to shake your head and laugh. However, like its predecessor, *Time*, *Strange* lurks in shadows, its restless buzz approximating the paranoid fidget of a schizophrenic slap-fighting a radio dial. An amazing, exciting, wonderfully esoteric glimpse at one of electronic music's many possible futures. —*Sean Cooper*

**Ticklish Matters** / Nov. 2, 1998 / Sub Rosa ++++

The least groundbreaking of Bisk's albums to date, *Ticklish Matters* is still pretty weird. The title might refer to the preponderance of piano samples, or even to the fits of giggling Bisk's bizarre juxtapositions might inspire. Either way, *Ticklish Matters* contains the same complex, scissored-to-ribbons sample orchestrations of his past work, though it backs a bit off of the almost formless texture-clustering of *Strange or Funny-Haha?* and leaves behind much of the dance music references of *Time*. It's probably the most listenable Bisk record to date, but it's also the least enthralling. —*Sean Cooper*

## Bizarre Inc
f. 1990, Stafford, England
*Group / Club/Dance, Acid House*

The British acid-house outfit Bizarre Inc was primarily the vehicle of DJs Andrew Meecham, Dean Meredith, and Carl Turner; Altern 8's Mark Archer was also a founding member, with vocalists Angie Brown and Yvonne Yanni later signing on as well. Formed in the Stafford area, Bizarre Inc made an immediate impact with its 1991 debut single "Playing with Knives," a massive club hit which topped the UK dance charts; "X-Static," "Plutonic" and "Raise Me" followed prior to the release of their 1992 debut LP *Energique*. A subsequent single, "I'm Gonna Get You," hit the American pop charts in 1993. Bizarre Inc then disappeared from the club scene for several years, causing barely a ripple upon resurfacing in 1996 with *Surprise* and in 1999 with the single "Playing with Knives." —*Jason Ankeny*

● **Energique** / Oct. 20, 1992 / Columbia ++++

Looked at from the perspective of future years, Bizarre Inc's debut album was such a fun, varied album that it seems impossible that it never achieved wider notice. Given the tendency toward neo-ambient on the one hand and the incipient hardcore/jungle underground on the other, *Energique* found itself lost between two camps when it came to modern electronic dance. The trio's kicky, funky house/techno stylings connect perfectly though; audiences enjoying the likes of Basement Jaxx won't have anything to complain about here. The group's two big single hits are unsurprisingly among the highlights. "Playing with Knives (Quadrant Mix)" has a wonderful squelching lead hook, leading into the mid-song shift to vocals and piano effortlessly. The two elements trade off for the rest of the songs, mixing tradition and futurism just right, a blend also explored on songs like the Sterling Void-sampling "Plutonic" and "Agroovin." "I'm Gonna Get You (Original Flavour Mix)" is the other noted smash, with great diva vocals from Angie Brown (one of her earliest star turns) and a simple but still sweeping string section reminiscent of disco's orchestrations at their best. Brown does another good vocal turn on the similarly-arranged "Took My Love." Eon helps on mixing a good chunk of the album, including the two opening cuts. "Raise Me (Ascension Mix)," a great get-your-body-moving starter, has a simple, effective hook and a fine sense of up and down dynamics, while "X-Static (Adult Mix)" is a lower-key number that still keeps everything going. Things get a touch carbon-copy towards the end where a little more variety couldn't have hurt, but "Delicious Minds" is a nice way to wrap things up nonetheless. Light in tone, a bit like a more carefree early Orbital in sound, it concludes *Energique* well. —*Ned Raggett*

**Surprise** / Jun. 24, 1996 / Mercury +++

## Björk (Björk Guðmundsdóttir)
b. Nov. 21, 1965, Reykjavik, Iceland
*Vocals, Keyboards, Producer / Electronica, Alternative Dance, Trip-Hop, Club/Dance, Alternative Pop/Rock*

Björk first came to prominence as one of the lead vocalists of the avant-pop Icelandic sextet the Sugarcubes, but when she launched a solo career after the group's 1992 demise, she quickly eclipsed her old band's popularity. Instead of following in the Sugarcubes' arty guitar-rock pretentions, Björk immersed herself in dance and club culture, working with many of the biggest names in the genre, including Nellee Hooper, Underworld, and Tricky. *Debut*, her first solo effort (except for an Icelandic-only smash released when she was just eleven years old) not only established her new artistic direction, but it became an international hit, making her one of the '90s most unlikely stars.

Though the title of *Debut* implied that it was Björk's first-ever solo project, she had actually been a professional vocalist since she was a child. When she was in elementary school in Reykjavik, she studied classical piano and, eventually, her teachers submitted a tape of her singing Tina Charles' "I Love to Love" to Iceland's Radio One. After "I Love to Love" was aired, a record label called Falkkin offered Björk a record contract. At the age of 11, her eponymous first album was released; the record contained covers of several pop songs, including the Beatles' "Fool on the Hill," and boasted artwork from her mother and guitar work from her stepfather. *Björk* became a hit within Iceland and was not released in any other country.

Björk's musical tastes were changed by the punk revolution of the late '70s.

In 1979, she formed a post-punk group called Exodus and in the following year, she sang in Jam 80. In 1981, Björk and Exodus bassist Jakob Magnusson formed Tappi Tikarrass, which released an EP, *Bitid Fast I Vitid*, on Spor; it was followed by the full-length *Miranda* in 1983. Following Tappi Takarrass, she formed the goth-tinged post-punk group KUKL with Einar Orn Benediktsson. KUKL released two albums, *The Eye* (1984) and *Holidays in Europe* (1986), on Crass Records before the band metamorphisized into the Sugarcubes in the summer of 1986.

The Sugarcubes became one of the rare Icelandic bands to break out of their native country when their debut album, *Life's Too Good*, became a British and American hit in 1988. For the next four years, the group maintained a successful cult following in the UK and the US, while they were stars within Iceland. During 1990, Björk recorded a set of jazz standards and originals with an Icelandic be-bop group called Trio Gudmundar Ingolfssonar. The album, *Gling-Glo*, was released only in Iceland. By 1992, tensions between Björk and Einar had grown substantially, which resulted in the band splitting.

Following the breakup of the group, Björk moved to London, where she began pursuing a dance-oriented solo career. The previous year, she had sung on 808 State's "Ooops," which sparked her interest in club and house music. Björk struck up a working relationship with Nellee Hooper, a producer who had formerly worked with Soul II Soul and Massive Attack. The first result of their partnership was "Human Behaviour," which was released in June of 1993. "Human Behaviour" became a Top 40 hit in the UK, setting the stage for the surprising number three debut of the full-length album, *Debut*. Throughout 1993, Björk had hit UK singles—including "Venus as a Boy," "Big Time Sensuality," and the non-LP "Play Dead," a collaboration with David Arnold taken from the film *Young Americans*—as well as modern rock radio hits in the US and in both countries, she earned rave reviews. At the end of the year, NME magazine named *Debut* the album of the year, while she won International Female Solo Artist and Newcomer at the BRIT Awards; *Debut* went gold in the US, and platinum in the UK.

During 1994, Björk was relatively quiet, as she recorded her second album with Nellee Hooper, Tricky, 808 State's Graham Massey, and Howie B of Mo'Wax Records. She also released a remix EP, co-wrote the title track for Madonna's *Bedtime Stories*, and performed on "MTV Unplugged" that same year. "Army of Me," the first single from Björk's forthcoming album, was released as a teaser single in the spring of 1995; it debuted at No. 10 in the UK and became a moderate alternative rock hit in the US. *Post*, her second album, was released in June of 1995 to positive reviews; it peaked at No. 2 in the UK and No. 32 in the US. *Post* matched its predecessor in terms of sales and praise, going gold in the US and helping her earn her second BRIT Award for Best International Female Artist. *Post* yielded the British hit singles "Isobel" (No. 23), "It's Oh So Quiet" (No. 4), and "Hyperballad" (No. 8), yet her singles failed to make much headway on American radio or MTV. Late in 1996, Björk released *Telegram*, an album comprised of radical remixes of the entire *Post* album; *Telegram* was released in America in January of 1997. *Homogenic*, her most experimental studio effort to date, followed later that same year and spawned many remix releases in the next few years to follow. In the spring of 2000, she was named Best Actress by jurors at the Cannes Film Festival for her work in Lars von Trier's Palme d'Or-winning *Dancer in the Dark*. *Selmasongs*, her score for the film, reunited Björk with her *Homogenic* collaborator Mark Bell and arrived in the fall of 2000, just in time for *Dancer in the Dark's* US release. —*Stephen Thomas Erlewine*

☆ **Debut** / Jul. 1993 / Elektra ♦♦♦♦♦

Björk's first album since the breakup of the Sugarcubes outshines any of her old group's albums. Covering everything from dance-pop and club music to jazzy torch songs, *Debut* reveals Björk as a fine songwriter, capable of writing wrenching ("Like Someone in Love") and intoxicating pop songs ("There's More to Life Than This"). Throughout the record, Björk's thin voice shows a surprising amount of versatility. *Debut* is one of the strongest, most musically varied and consistent dance records of the '90s. —*Stephen Thomas Erlewine*

**The Best Mixes from the Debut (For All the People Who Don't Buy White Labels)** / Sep. 1994 / One Little Indian ♦♦♦

The title may be lengthy, but it's also perfectly accurate; this release serves as a fine catch-all of the earliest remixes done for Björk. Compared to the explosion of mixes and alternate takes that would surface on later singles, the mere six mixes totally forty-one minutes here seem paltry. The quality level, thankfully, remains quite high (quite happily, Mick Hucknall's mix of "Venus as a Boy" has been ignored). It starts with the definite highlight, Underworld's radical revamp of "Human Behavior." A twelve-minute long masterpiece, it replaces the shuffling stutter of the original's percussion with a combination of crisp disco pulse and a fast-paced funk loop, with other quirky keyboard bits and spoken samples floating in and out of the mix. Björk's vocals remain intact, but otherwise this is pretty much Underworld's showcase, and a fine one. The addition of piano at the end adds to the unexpected charm and power of the mix. The remaining mixes are split between avant-techno trio Black Dog and remixer extraordinaire Andy Weatherall, more specifically his Sabres of Paradise project. The Sabres' "Endorphin" mix of "One Day" is a chilled, stoned slice of loveliness, light piano and dub-touched echoes matching the slow beat and Björk's slightly reverb-treated vocals. A faster-paced mix of the same track, the "Springs Eternal" take, has some good, crisp electronic percussion but isn't as strong, while a version of "Come to Me" feeds Björk's vocals through heavy reverb and echo over a quiet series of beats. Black Dog's mix of "Come to Me" has echoes of Muslimgauze's Arabic/techno fusion to it, a nice touch, while their take on "The Anchor Song" has a nicely strange, second-long loop of something and a totally a capella mid-song vocal break that works wonders. —*Ned Raggett*

**Post** / Jun. 13, 1995 / Elektra ♦♦♦♦

*Debut* was a worldwide success, raising the expectations for Björk's second album, *Post*. Björk doesn't depart from the innovations of *Debut*, she refines them, pushing the jazz/dance fusions into different territories, like the big-band explosions of "It's Oh So Quiet" and the trancey "Possibly Maybe." While it's more subtle and not quite as infectious as *Debut*, the album is more accomplished and varied, switching from the menacing "Army of Me" to the graceful "Isobel" without seeming incoherent. —*Stephen Thomas Erlewine*

**Telegram** / Nov. 25, 1996 / Elektra ♦♦♦♦

In theory, *Telegram* is a remixed album of all the songs from *Post*, but the arrangements are so different, it might as well be another record entirely. Björk has re-recorded several of her vocals, handing the original backing tracks to a variety of producers and musicians—everyone from Dillinja to the Brodsky Quartet. While *Telegram* provides some of the most challenging listening yet heard on a Björk album, it is essentially because the new arrangements are radical—in terms of electronic dance music, the actual music and remixes are far from radical. Still, *Telegram* works as an excellent introduction to techno for alternative-pop fans unsure of where to begin exploring. —*Stephen Thomas Erlewine*

★ **Homogenic** / Sep. 22, 1997 / Elektra/Asylum ♦♦♦♦♦

With its icy, experimental sonic textures, the remix album *Telegram* pointed the way toward *Homogenic*, Björk's most adventurous and successful album to date. Where *Debut* and *Post* had bright melodic sensibilities, *Homogenic* is insular and complex, daring the listener to accept it on its own terms. It's dark and introspective, built around swirling, atonal string quartets and jittery electronic rhythms. *Homogenic* is a genuine fusion of chamber music and techno, pushing forward into new sonic territory, yet what gives it weight is the emotional fragility of the songs. Björk has never been so naked and brutally honest with her lyrics, and they are married to music that perfectly conveys the tortured, conflicted sentiments of the songs. There's none of the happy, club-oriented dance-pop of *Debut* on *Homogenic*, and very few of the songs mirror that album's sunny melodicism; indeed, there's little pop on the album at all. Instead, Björk assimilates the sprawling eclecticism of *Post* and *Telegram*, turning in a record that is deeply adventurous and richly rewarding. —*Stephen Thomas Erlewine*

**Volumen [Video]** / Jan. 26, 1999 / Elektra ♦♦♦♦

Björk's video retrospective *Volumen* gathers 14 of her groundbreaking clips, ranging from "Play Dead," featured in the film *Young Americans*, to videos for her 1997 album *Homogenic*. From Sophie Muller and Stephane Sednaoui's dreamlike, quirky videos for "Venus As a Boy," "Big Time Sensuality," and "Possibly Maybe," to striking artistic and technical achievements like Paul White's "Hunter" (which morphs Björk into a cyber-polar bear) the collection presents virtually every side of her abundant creativity. Spumco's silly and suggestive animated clip for "I Miss You," and Spike Jonze's exuberant mini-musical for "It's Oh So Quiet," are also highlights of a collection that is virtually all highlights, but Björk's most successful and representative video collaborations are with Michel Gondry. Interestingly, they're also the most diverse, spanning surreal fairytales like "Human Behaviour" and "Army of Me," to more lyrical pieces like the dreamy, black-and-white "Isobel," the distinctly Icelandic-looking love letter to Björk's homeland, "Joga," and the striking, circular "Bachelorette." Simply put, *Volumen* is a thrillingly creative collection of sound and music from one of the '90s best, most distinctive artists. Though it's unfortunate that two of Björk's best videos—"All Is Full of Love" and "Alarm Call"—are missing from *Volumen*, and the DVD lacks extras such as Electronic Press Kits or a discography (though it does include weblinks), it's still an impressive body of work that devoted Björk fans should own. —*Heather Phares*

**Selmasongs** / Sep. 19, 2000 / Elektra/Asylum ♦♦♦♦
*Selmasongs: Music From the Motion Picture Soundtrack Dancer in the Dark* is, and is not, a Björk album. While it's filled with childlike wonder, rampant creativity, startling emotional leaps, and breathtaking vocals and arrangements—all *de rigeur* for Björk's work—it doesn't hold as much of the wide-ranging playfulness that permeates all of her albums, even 1997's relatively dark *Homogenic*. Instead, the album presents Björk as Selma, her character from Lars VonTrier's *Dancer in the Dark:* a Czech factory worker who is going blind but finds hope and refuge in the musicals she watches at the theater. (VonTrier was inspired to work with Björk after seeing Spike Jonze's musical-inspired video for "It's Oh So Quiet.") Here, she acts through the music she composed, performed, and produced. Selma's unsinkable optimism and tragic end are telegraphed through songs that range from the irrepressible, cartoonish "Cvalda" to the sad, starry lullaby "Scatterheart."

*Selmasongs*' best tracks blend these extremes into poignant, inventive expressions of Björk's talent and Selma's daydreams and suffering. "In the Musicals" shows how easy it is for Selma to slip into one of her Technicolor reveries: "There is always someone to catch me," Björk sighs as clouds of strings, harps, and xylophones rise up to meet her. "New World" reprises the simultaneously hopeful and ominous melody of "Overture," adding striking vocals and shuffling, industrial beats that reflect Selma's life in the factory—as well as Björk's distinctive style. The song is a remarkable update of *West Side Story*'s "Somewhere" and other tragic, yet uplifting, themes from musicals.

Indeed, *Selmasongs* also succeeds as a fairly straightforward soundtrack, sketching in details of Selma's story without revealing everything: her stunted romance with a nice but slow co-worker is captured in "I've Seen It All," a duet with Thom Yorke, while the tense "107 Steps" takes the listener to the very end of her journey. With conductor/arranger Vincent Mendoza and her longtime collaborators Mark "Spike" Stent and Mark Bell, Björk has crafted an album that is both intimate and theatrical, innovative, but tied to tradition. Though *Selmasongs* paints a portrait of a woman losing her sight, it maintains Björk's unique vision perfectly. —*Heather Phares*

## Black Box

f. 1988
*Group / Club/Dance, Pop/Rock, House, Dance-Pop*
Leaders of the Italian house music movement of the late '80s, Black Box was primarily comprised of club DJ Daniele Davoli, computer whiz Mirko Limoni, and classical clarinetist Valerio Semplici—a trio of studio musicians known collectively as the Groove Groove Melody production team. Acclaimed among the most successful producers in all of Italian dance music, Groove Groove Melody helmed dozens of singles each year at their peak. In 1989 they teamed with singer and model Katrin (born Catherine Quinol) as Black Box, debuting with the single "Ride on Time." Not only was the record a huge hit at home, but it soon crossed over into the British pop charts, landing at the number one spot for six consecutive weeks—despite the controversy which erupted in the wake of the discovery that it included uncredited samples of Loleatta Holloway's disco single "Love Sensation." A series of Black Box hits followed, among them "I Don't Know Anybody Else" (a Top Ten smash in the US as well) and "Everybody Everybody," which featured vocals by Martha Wash; the group's debut LP, 1990's *Dreamland*, was also a success. They returned in 1991 with "Strike It Up," another American Top Ten entry, as well as the *Mixed Up!* collection. Additionally, the Groove Groove Melody team scored with material recorded under a variety of other aliases, among them Starlight ("Numero Uno") and Mixmaster ("Grand Piano"). After a long hiatus, Black Box returned in 1996 with the album *Positive Attitude*, which went largely unnoticed. —*Jason Ankeny*

**Dreamland** / May 1990 / RCA ♦♦♦♦
Conventional wisdom has it that disco died with the '70s when in fact, it has remained a sometimes dynamic, sometimes bloodless idiom in the '80s and '90s. Unquestionably, one of the finest examples of '90s disco (or "dance music") is Black Box's *Dreamland*, which reminds one that although glossy production and danceability can be assets, and gutsy, heartfelt vocals make the best disco stand out. The real star of *Dreamland* is Martha Wash, whose full-bodied, gospel-influenced belting on "Everybody, Everybody," "Strike It Up," "I Don't Know Anybody Else," and other dancefloor smashes is on a par with the best '70s disco/soul of such divas as Gloria Gaynor, Linda Clifford and Loleatta Holloway (who puts in a superb guest appearance on "Ride on Time"). For all its cutting-edge hip-hop and house-music appeal, *Dreamland* has strong soul-music roots—a fact that Wash is, no doubt, well aware. —*Alex Henderson*

**Not Anyone [Single]** / 1995 / Groove Groove Melody ♦♦♦
Almost five years after their last success, Black Box returned in 1995 with a new vocalist (Charvoni) and a new single, recorded for Groove Groove Melody. —*John Bush*

● **Strike It Up: The Best of Black Box** / Apr. 14, 1998 / BMG Special Products ♦♦♦♦
Black Box's house hits from the late '80s and '90s are well served by the *Strike It Up* collection, which includes all of the group's best-known dancefloor favorites. In addition to the title cut, the set also features "Ride on Time," "I Don't Know Anybody Else," and "Everybody Everybody"—really, it's all everyone but the hardiest Black Box fans will want so far removed from the group's heyday. —*Jason Ankeny*

## The Black Dog

f. 1989, London, England
*Group / Electronica, Electro-Techno, Ambient Techno, Club/Dance, Techno, IDM*
Taking their name from a British euphemism for imminent doom, the Black Dog (also appearing variously as Black Dog Productions, Balil, Xeper, and Plaid, among others) formed in the early '90s as the trio of Ken Downie, Ed Handley, and Andy Turner. Forging a challenging, relentless combination of early techno, electro, and hip-hop with a penchant for odd time signatures, high-tech atmospherics, and Egyptian iconography, the group immediately distinguished itself from the scores of disposable techno musicians covering familiar ground in the post-rave UK. Something of a closet phenomenon attracting the devotion of DJs who nonetheless refused to play their complicated brew for fear of being booed off the decks, the Black Dog were immediately placed in the emerging "intelligent techno" category upon the release of their full-length debut, *Bytes*. A largely UK-media constituted phrase meant to peg music involving dance music compositional styles nonetheless intended for home listening, the term has since taken hold and is often applied to group's like Autechre, Aphex Twin, µ-Ziq, and As One. As Plaid, Ed Handley and Andy Turner had already released a handful of material (including an album) prior to meeting Downie, but their time spent in BDP was their most productive up to that point. In addition to the Dog's inclusion on the perhaps more high-profile *Artificial Intelligence* compilations on Warp and remixes for the likes of Björk, Blondie, U.N.K.L.E., and Ned's Atomic Dustbin, the group also released several full-length works as a group before Handley and Turner defected in 1995 to refocus on Plaid full-time. The pair released an EP on the Clear label in mid-1995 and two years later, issued their first full-length record, *Not for Threes*, on Warp. Downie continued with the Black Dog name, releasing the full-length *Music for Adverts (and short films)* in 1996. In 1989 the EP *Age of Slack* was released, and followed a year later with various versions of the single *Babylon*. —*Sean Cooper*

★ **Bytes** / Mar. 15, 1992 / Warp ♦♦♦♦♦
BDP's full-length debut was a sprawling deviation from techno-as-throwaway-dancefloor-fare, weaving surprisingly engaging melodic and harmonic passages around complex rhythmic patterns and diverse, somewhat ambient atmospherics. Although all of the material was previously released in 12" or EP form, it holds up surprisingly well as a unified, coherent whole. With B12's *Electro-Soma* and Autechre's *Incunabula*, one of the first and finest blasts in the European "intelligent techno" movement. —*Sean Cooper*

**Temple of Transparent Balls** / 1993 / GPR ♦♦♦
Black Dog's proper debut (this time for the GPR label), *Temple of Transparent Balls* includes probably the group's most well-known single track, "Cost II," released on 12" simultaneously with the album. —*Sean Cooper*

**Parallel** / 1995 / GPR ♦♦♦
A pre-*Bytes* collection of odd tracks released after the group had already parted. Some quality material, but without the integrated feel of their other full-length works. —*Sean Cooper*

☆ **Spanners** / Apr. 25, 1995 / East West ♦♦♦♦♦
The last release under the group name before the trio splintered, *Spanners* is a great full-packed CD of modern electronic music. The band draws on everything from dub to avant-garde experimentalism to create a varied, intoxicating collection. Funk samples are twisted and played with, rather than lovingly reused, lyrics eschewed for obscure or unintelligible samples at most, generally straightforward dancefloor tracks still sound slightly hesitant or off. Even from the first song, "Raxmus," it's not too surprising that this appeared on Warp Records; the blend of shuffling yet crisp beats, ambient tones, and other sonic touches and tweaks practically could have been tailormade as a calling card for the label. Certainly there's a healthy sense of playfulness and obscurity that won't surprise fans of labelmate Aphex Twin—neither will song titles like "Psil-Coysin" and "Nommo." The highlights are many, most often achieving a solid combination of dancefloor-friendliness and unexpected sonic trickery. "Chase the Manhattan" may have a cringeworthy pun of a title, but the brisk funk/world percussion beat, soothing synth washes, and distorted electronic bass stabs all come together wonderfully. "Further Harm" shifts a number of times during its length, sometimes playing around with rough beats low in the mix and at other points serving up a variety of keyboard melodies interspersed with brief vocals. Other numbers of note include "Pot Noodle," with what sounds like a soft acoustic guitar or a keyboard programmed to sound like one playing a lazy, relaxed melody under the main loop; also noteworthy is the echoing, minimal percussion breaks and squelchy electro-inspired tones of "Frisbee Skip." A series of brief bridge tracks entitled "Bolt" (ie, "Bolt1," "Bolt2," etc.) crop up throughout *Spanners*, mostly following their own curious logic as they slide from one track to the next. —*Ned Raggett*

**Music for Adverts (and Short Films)** / Jul. 15, 1996 / Warp ♦♦♦♦
With a cover thumbing its nose at Brian Eno's similarly titled series of albums from the '70s, and song titles ranging in reference from bad Hollywood films to washing powders, it would seem the Black Dog is engaged in a bit of a musical piss-take. Nothing of the sort, actually, as lone Dog Ken Downie's first solo work since the departure of partners Ed Handley and Andy Turner is a serious, often wistful collection of post-rave electronica, incorporating elements of techno, ambient, hip-hop, jungle, and jazz. Although lacking somewhat in complexity, Downie more than makes up for it in focus and emotional content. —*Sean Cooper*

**Peel Session [EP]** / 1999 / Warp ♦♦♦♦
The five-track *Peel Session* EP, recorded in January 1995, includes only one song ("Psycosyin," remixed slightly) from the final collective Black Dog LP, *Spanners* (released four months later). The other four songs are rather sinister-sounding fourth-world electro productions, similar in mood to much of *Spanners* though in many cases surprisingly superior. "Rise Up" and "Simperton" are the highlights. —*John Bush*

## Black Grape

f. 1993, Manchester, England, **db.** Jul. 1998
*Group / British Rap, Alternative Dance, Brit-pop, Alternative Pop/Rock*
After the Happy Mondays disbanded in 1992, most observers would have guessed that the group's leader, vocalist Shaun Ryder, would succumb to the myriad of drug addictions that hastened the breakup of the group. Instead of dying, Ryder recouped his strengths and came back with a new band, Black Grape, in the summer of 1995. Black Grape was embraced by both the British public and press, making Shaun Ryder one of the more unexpected comebacks in rock 'n' roll history.

Ryder formed Black Grape in 1993, recruiting ex-Happy Monday Bez (dancing, percussion), rappers Kermit (b. Paul Leveridge) and Jed from the Ruthless Rap Assassins, and ex-Paris Angels guitarist Wags. Black Grape began recording demos only weeks after the implosion of the Happy Mondays. Over the course of recording and writing *It's Great When You're Straight*, Ryder recruited a number of musicians, most notably producer and bassist Danny Saber, keyboardist/producer Stephen Lironi, and former Bluebells and Smiths guitarist Gary Gannon. Black Grape's debut album was recorded over a period of seven weeks in late 1994 and early 1995; after it was completed, the band signed with Radioactive Records. The group's first single, "Reverend Black Grape," entered the Top Ten upon its release. The group's debut album, *It's Great When You're Straight... Yeah*, was released in August of 1995. The album entered the UK charts at No. 1.

"In the Name of the Father" and "Kelly's Heroes" followed "Reverend Black Grape" into the Top 20 later in 1995. Toward the end of the year, Kermit suffered a severe case of septicemia, a form of blood poisoning caused by bad water (which he drank while in Mexico). Although he came close to death—bits of his heart and liver were flaking off—he had recovered by the spring of 1996. Black Grape were prepared to head to America early in 1996 when the group were denied entry into the country due to their prior drug convictions. After a couple of months, their passports were cleared and the band was admitted into the US. Due to his illness, Kermit had to miss the tour; his spot was filled by Psycho, who became a permanent member of the band after the completion of the tour. Before Black Grape launched their US tour in spring of 1996, Bez left the band due to financial disagreements with the record company.

In May 1996, Black Grape returned with the single "Fat Neck," which entered the UK charts in the Top Ten; the song featured former Smiths member Johnny Marr on guitar. A month after the release of "Fat Neck," the group released their football anthem "England's Irie," which was recorded with Joe Strummer. Like "Fat Neck" before it, "England's Irie" became a Top Ten hit. *Stupid Stupid Stupid* followed in 1997. —*Stephen Thomas Erlewine*

● **It's Great When You're Straight... Yeah** / Oct. 10, 1995 / Radioactive ♦♦♦♦
When the Happy Mondays fell apart in 1992, most observers assumed that Shaun Ryder would never recover from his numerous drug addictions. No one could have predicted that he would return to the top of the charts three years later, relatively fit and healthy, with a new band that fulfilled all of the promises of his old group. Black Grape are what the Happy Mondays always were, only better. Leaving behind the stiff musicianship that plagued even the best Mondays records, Black Grape's debut *It's Great When You're Straight... Yeah* is a surreal, funky, profane, and perversely joyous album, overflowing with casual eclecticism and giddy humor. Working with a band that is looser and grittier than the Mondays, Ryder sounds reinvigorated, creating bizzare rhymes that tie together junk culture, drug lingo, literary references, and utter nonsense. Ryder's lyrics have always been free-wheelingly impenetrable, but now he's working with Kermit, a rapper that is the equal of his skills. Even better, the music has deep grooves and catchy pop hooks that come straight out of left field. From the blaring harmonica of the triumphant "Reverend Black Grape" and the trippy sitars of "In the Name of the Father" to the seedy, rolling "Shake Your Money" and the stinging guitars of "Tramazi Parti," *It's Great* is filled with music that goes in unconventional directions without ever sounding forced. Not only is *It's Great When You're Straight* a triumphant return for Shaun Ryder and his sidekick Bez, it's the first album they have ever recorded that justifies all of the hype. —*Stephen Thomas Erlewine*

**Stupid, Stupid, Stupid** / Nov. 1997 / Radioactive ♦♦♦
Arriving out of nowhere, Black Grape's debut, *It's Great When You're Straight... Yeah*, was a complete surprise—a post-acid-house party record that delivered on all of the Happy Mondays' promise. It was a kinetic, exciting record that disregarded boundaries between rap, house, rock, soul and pop—it was the culmination of what Shaun Ryder began with *Pills N Thrills N Bellyaches*. *It's Great* was greeted warmly by critics and fans, which meant that the group's second album, *Stupid, Stupid, Stupid*, was eagerly anticipated. Perhaps nothing could live up to the expectations of hardcore fans, but *Stupid, Stupid, Stupid* fails to deliver in a variety of ways. Essentially, it plays like *It's Great*, Pt. 2, only without its predecessor's infectious beats, mammoth hooks, and surreal humor. There's a heavier soul influence this time around ("Lonely" is a straight cover of Frederick Knight's 1972 hit "I've Been Lonely for So Long"), but it doesn't sit well with Ryder's thuggish rasp, and that's one of the problems about the album—the vocals and music don't match. Apart from the dynamite opening trilogy of "Get Higher," "Squeaky," and "Marbles," Ryder and Kermit don't sound integrated with the music. Instead, they sound as if they're rapping over pre-existing backing tracks, which aren't as funky or inventive as those from *It's Great*. Perhaps *Stupid, Stupid, Stupid* would sound intoxicating if you're intoxicated, but such stimulation shouldn't be necessary—the music should be intoxicating enough on its own. —*Stephen Thomas Erlewine*

## Black Jazz Chronicles (Ashley Beedle)

*Producer / Jazz-House, Progressive House, Club/Dance*
Years after making his name as part of the Ballistic Brothers and X-Press 2 (plus virtually all of Black Science Orchestra), Ashley Beedle began recording a proper solo project in 1997. With the help of Marden Hill's Chris Bemand,

Beedle released two EPs as Black Jazz Chronicles for Nuphonic Records. The following year brought the project's debut full-length, *Future Ju-Ju*. [See Also: Black Science Orchestra] —*John Bush*

- **Future Ju-Ju** / Feb. 16, 1998 / Nuphonic ♦♦♦♦
The actual solo debut for Ashley Beedle is a fusion of Afrocentric jazz textures and tribal-disco rhythms with science-fiction mythology gained from equal parts Sun Ra and Juan Atkins. It's perhaps the least danceable album his name has been attached to, though much like the contemporary work of Kirk Degiorgio's As One (the vastly similar *Planetary Folklore* was released two months earlier), *Future Ju-Ju* sees Beedle expanding his stylistic reference points to encompass the dancefloor, not leave it behind. —*John Bush*

## Black Science Orchestra

f. 1992, London, England
*Group / Jazz-House, Progressive House, Club/Dance, House*
Ashley Beedle was one of the most efficient in a cast of British producers who rewired American disco during the late '90s with much of the same energy and flair Derrick May used when looking to foreigners like Kraftwerk for his techno blueprint. His work in the Ballistic Brothers, X-Press 2, and Rising Sunz, plus his day-job productions as Black Science Orchestra and Black Jazz Chronicles married the possibilities of the '70s to rare-groove and deep house.

Beedle was born in Hemel Hempstead in 1962. He began DJing during the acid-house explosion of the late '80s, but was turned on to disco as well when he heard Norman Jay DJing obscure tracks on the pirate station Kiss FM. After he joined long-time friend Rob Mello and John Howard as Black Science Orchestra, the trio reworked the Trammps' "Where Were You (When the Lights Went Out)?" into their debut single "Where Were You," released on Junior Boy's Own. House godfather Frankie Knuckles began spinning the record, as well as the second BSO offering "Strong" (recorded with Linsey Edwards replacing Mello). Beedle recruited engineer Marc Woolford and keyboard player Uschi Classen for the third single, "New Jersey Deep," and watched the record become a classic (selected by Knuckles and the Masters at Work team for use in their DJ sets).

Beedle teamed up with Dave Hill and Rocky & Diesel to form the Ballistic Brothers and released one of 1994's hottest LPs, *London Hooligan Soul*. He was back with Black Science Orchestra that same year, now just Beedle and Woolford. Though troubles with sample clearance delayed the album almost two years (the duo eventually drafted session musicians and vocalists instead), Beedle kept busy with the formation of the disco-rave project X-Press 2, this time including himself and Rocky & Diesel. The trio released singles for Radikal-Q and Junior Boy's Own but hit the jackpot with a track called "The Sound" It spent weeks at the top of the American dance charts. Later that year, the debut Black Science Orchestra LP, *Walter's Room*, was released on Junior Boy's Own.

Instead of continuing with Black Science Orchestra, Ashley Beedle reunited with Hill and Rocky & Diesel for a second Ballistic Brothers LP, *Rude System*. Beedle also released two proper solo EPs during 1997, both recorded as Black Jazz Chronicles. The following year brought a BJC album, *Future Ju-Ju*, the most well-integrated fusion of disco, jazz and techno of his varied career. Beedle is an in-demand DJ and also runs three labels: Soundboy Entertainment, Afroart, and Ill Sun. [See Also: Black Jazz Chronicles] —*John Bush*

- **Walter's Room** / Jul. 22, 1996 / Junior Boys Own ♦♦♦♦
Ashley Beedle rewires the original American disco template for a set of updated grooves more reminiscent of Philadelphia International than Strictly Rhythm (even the title is a reference to one of the original disco DJs and remixers, Walter Gibbons). Tracks like "Downtown Science" and "Save Us (The Jam)" find a common ground between house and its '70s forebear, with strings, vibes, and keyboards adding to the earthy atmosphere. —*John Bush*

## Black Tape for a Blue Girl

f. 1986
*Group / Goth Rock, Contemporary Instrumental*
Black Tape for a Blue Girl's ethereal, mournful sound virtually defined the darkwave aesthetic of their label Projekt Records, a company owned and operated by the group's founder, composer and keyboardist Sam Rosenthal. Formed in 1983, Projekt was originally envisioned as an outlet for Rosenthal's solo electronic music. Upon relocating to California three years later, his music adopted a warmer, deeply personal sound heralded by the formation of Black Tape for a Blue Girl, which debuted in 1986 with *The Rope*.

Where subsequent efforts including 1987's *Mesmerized by the Sirens* and its 1989 follow-up *Ashes in the Brittle Air* drew heavily on ambient soundscapes, the group—a revolving ensemble of performers that, in addition to Rosenthal, also at times included vocalists Oscar Herrera and Lucian Casselman, violinist Vicki Richards, clarinetist Richard Watson, and cellist Mera Roberts—expanded into increasingly dense electronic textures over the course of records like 1991's *A Chaos of Desire* and 1993's *This Lush Garden Within*. After a three-year hiatus, Black Tape for a Blue Girl resurfaced in 1996 with the EP *The First Pain to Linger*, a disc packaged with a novel authored by Rosenthal; the full-length epic *Remnants of a Deeper Purity* appeared that same year, followed in 1998 by *As One Aflame Laid Bare by Desire. Before the Buildings Fell* appeared in early 2000. —*Jason Ankeny*

- **Ashes in the Brittle Air** / 1989 / Projekt ♦♦♦
Black Tape's third full album takes the band to a new level of grace. While bandleader Rosenthal's work remains generally consistent—ambient soundscapes mingled with low-key rock mood pieces, backing Rosenthal's varying studies of romantic obsession and fragmentation—the various performances here are more involving than ever. Herrera and Kenny-Smith return as the major vocalists, along with Rosenthal himself on 'slight vocals' and electronics; a bevy of other guest performances flesh out the album as a whole, from guitars to clarinet and violin. The opening title track proves to be the best Black Tape song up to that point, starting with a gentle wash of electronics suddenly punctuated by a tribal percussion hit—wonderfully echoed and layered for atmosphere—and Kenny-Smith's delicate take on the lyrics. Herrera himself gets to shine in the very next number, "Across A Thousand Blades," one of the more overtly goth-rock numbers Black Tape has recorded, with a pulsing rhythm, Cure/Banshees-like guitar and fretless bass adding to Herrera's anguished performance. The rest of the album doesn't quite match up to such an excellent beginning, but as a consistent collection of songs and performances, *Ashes* is never anything less that tastefully atmospheric, and often more than that, a perfect soundtrack to a late night. —*Ned Raggett*

- **A Chaos of Desire** / 1990 / Projekt ♦♦♦♦
In many ways the sister release to *Ashes*, down to the similar cover art and the parallel sources of inspiration (the Paula thanked in *Ashes*' liner notes for "caring inspiration" here gets credit for "destroying my faith"), *Chaos* ratchets up the lyrical intensity even more strongly than before. Given how intense Rosenthal generally is with words, this may seem a hard task, but one listen to the lengthy, majestic album centerpiece "The Hypocrite is Me" will confirm it. Herrera delivers a lyric of deep self-loathing with command, while the music backing him is an intense series of rumbling electronic tones matched at the end by a great, gently reverbed violin solo from guest performer Vicki Richards. Another number of note is "Tear Love From My Mind," a piano-driven piece that provides a gentle showcase for Julianna Towns, the main female vocalist on the album, who has a slightly wider range than Kenny-Smith, but generally provides the same haunting singing approach to Black Tape's material. Herrera gets another excellent moment for himself with "Pandora's Box," a slightly rockier number for the album, but not by much. As is par for the course with Black Tape records, many guest performers appear throughout, including Black Watch violinist/singer J'anna Jacoby, providing only strings, and longtime Rosenthal collaborator Pat Ogl singing and playing guitar on "How Can You Forget Love?," a quietly stately, simpler number that also is one of the more memorable. —*Ned Raggett*

- **Remnants of a Deeper Purity** / Jun. 7, 1996 / Projekt ♦♦♦♦
For the first time since the earliest recordings, Rosenthal assembles and employs a set combination of musicians throughout a Black Tape album—with Herrera and Casselman returning on vocals and other instruments, along with longtime associate Vicki Richards on violin and Mera Roberts on cello. The end result succeeds like no other Black Tape release before, the logical extension of Rosenthal's musical and lyrical foci into a lengthy, commanding and beautiful experience. Using the two-string players throughout with his electronics in a carefully blended effort, punching up the general orchestral heft of his music to new heights, Rosenthal's work this time hits a consistently rich vein; the connections to rock music have never been so tenuous, and to progressive and electronic efforts so strong. Two of Herrera's performances deserve special notice: "With My Sorrows," ending with a captivating quick take on an old Spanish poem, and "For You Will Burn Your Wings Upon the Sun," a nearly thirty-minute piece with Herrera's brief vocal section providing the central punch of the track. But Casselman steals the show with the final track, "I Have No More

Answers"—a simply perfect mix of strings, vast-sounding electronic atmospherics, and piano with Casselman's lovely voice singing an especially touching Rosenthal lyric, it is Black Tape's finest song yet. —*Ned Raggett*

**This Lush Garden Within** / Jun. 10, 1997 / Projekt ♦♦♦
The general Black Tape ethic—dark mood music informed by orchestral and synthesized atmospherics—has often drawn comparison to This Mortal Coil, but *Garden* is the album which most resembles the efforts by the noted UK studio project. As This Mortal Coil did with the 4AD label roster, here Black Tape draws in a wide number of Projekt labelmates, including Padraic Ogl of Thanatos, Mike Vanportfleet of Lycia, and Ryan Lum of Love Spirals Downwards. Here Black Tape also resembles TMC by doing reinterpretive cover versions, in this case a not-bad take on Laurie Anderson's "Gravity's Angel," with vocals by Susan Jennings, the album's cover model and general inspiration (Rosenthal detailed their relationship in a separate self-published book that if nothing else demonstrates that his straight prose can be as extreme in its emotional detail as his songs). As a whole, *Garden* is something of a catchall effort; it doesn't quite achieve the unity earlier Black Tape albums have, and the various performances almost feel more like a compilation at points than a unified product. This said, Herrera and new singer Lucian Casselman (possessed of a warm set of pipes, possibly the best female singer Rosenthal has yet worked with) acquit themselves well, while Rosenthal's ear for lengthy electronic performance pieces still holds up. Of the guest performances, Ogl's spare take on the title track is especially worth noticing. —*Ned Raggett*

**As One Aflame Laid Bare by Desire** / Jan. 12, 1999 / Projekt ♦♦♦♦
For this album, Casselman is out and *A Chaos of Desire*-era vocalist Towns returns. While the lineup returns to the more collective sense of performances from past albums, core performers Rosenthal and Herrera—along with flautist Lisa Feuer(who adds a fine new dimension to the general instrumental approach)—still have Richards on violin on various tracks Roberts only plays on one song while guests perform oboe, harpsichord, and other instruments. In comparison to the marvelous *Remnants of a Deeper Beauty, As One Aflame Laid Bare by Desire* lacks a little something. The trademark lushness of performance and instrumentation remains, and both Herrera and Towns, as well as Rosenthal, discharge their vocal duties as well as always (aside from the opening title track, which Rosenthal sings somewhat awkwardly). Still, too many pieces veer toward the tastefully anonymous at points, while the lyrical focus on Marcel Duchamp's work "The Bride Stripped Bare," though intriguing, almost turns the album into a running essay rather than a series of songs. This said, there is still a number of strong, focused pieces, including the *Apollo*-era Eno evocative "The Apotheosis" and "Russia" (which quotes the same Prokofiev line as Sting's "Russians," but much less obnoxiously). "The Green Box," meanwhile, contains the classic sense of brooding electronic menace and beauty, heightened by Richards' violin, which has so often defined Black Tape's most successful work. —*Ned Raggett*

## Blame (Conrad Shafie)
*Producer, DJ / Jungle/Drum'N'Bass, Club/Dance*
During 1996, LTJ Bukem began to show up on lists of the most-favored names in electronica, due in part to his serene vision for atmospheric drum'n'bass; one year later, his right-hand man and label-mate Blame began to be name-checked as well. Influenced by the Bukem track "Music," Blame and his early partner Justice began producing hardcore breakbeat tracks by 1990. By far the most popular early Blame single was "2 Bad Mice Take You," a spot-on fusion of decaying rave chords and stacks of breakbeats. The single, co-produced with Moving Shadow label-boss Rob Playford, became one of the best-known hardcore tunes of the early '90s. (Perhaps belying the extent of Playford's involvement, it was appropriated for release on the *Kaotic Chemistry* LP by his own 2 Bad Mice project.)

By that time, Blame's own productions had shifted to the more reflective timbres of jazzy jungle. He recorded several singles for Bukem's Good Looking label, and formed (with Justice) Modern Urban Jazz Records. After Bukem hosted and mixed the first volume in his label-retrospective series *Logical Progression*, he passed the baton to Blame for *Logical Progression, Level 2* in 1997. Blame also collaborated on one of the best jungle LPs of the year: the pristine, slightly jazzy *Emotions with Intellect*, recorded as Icons with Justice. In 1998, Blame hosted the first volume in a new Good Looking series, *Progression Sessions*, with tracks by Intense, Seba, Artemis and Bukem himself. [See Also: Icons] —*John Bush*

● **Progression Sessions** / Aug. 17, 1998 / Good Looking ♦♦♦
*Progression Sessions* is the second Good Looking collection helmed by Blame (after 1997's *Logical Progression, Level 2*). Intended to have a live flavor somewhat missing from the wealth of earlier Bukem compilations, the album features several crucial drum'n'bass/jazz crossovers, accomplishing its club-centric mission to good effect. —*John Bush*

## Blancmange
f. Jan. 1979, UK, db. 1986
*Group / New Wave, Electronic*
Blancmange was a British duo made up of two synthesizer players, Neil Arthur (b.1958) and Stephen Luscombe (b.1954). After being in previous groups, they founded Blancmange in January 1979 to record the song "Sad Day." Their UK Top 40 debut album, 1982's *Happy Families*, contained the Top Ten UK hits "Living on the Ceiling" and "Blind Vision." Their second album, 1984's *Mange Tout*, hit the UK Top Ten and contained their third UK Top Ten single, "Don't Tell Me." Their UK Top 40 singles included "Waves" (1983), "That's Love, That It Is" (1983), the ABBA cover song "The Day Before You Came" (1984), and "What's Your Problem?" (1985). Following the commercial failure of their third album, 1985's *Believe You Me*, Blancmange split in 1986, and Luscombe joined the West India Company. —*William Ruhlmann*

**Happy Families** / 1982 / Island ♦♦♦♦
Blancmange's first album, 1982's *Happy Families*, yielded the minor radio hit "Living on the Ceiling," which also received a good deal of attention from early MTV. Though *Happy Families* can accurately be described as techno-pop, it's techno-pop with a modicum of taste and sophistication, putting it more in the ballpark of genre pioneers like OMD and Yazoo than of annoying '80s anachronisms like Kajagoogoo or EBN-OZN. Neil Arthur's lyrics are interesting enough to reward close listening, and his Bowie-esque voice, while somewhat limited, serves the material well. The sound of *Happy Families* is built largely around synthesizers, played by Arthur and partner Stephen Luscombe. The duo have a knack for catchy basslines and drum programming, on top of which they strategically deploy guitars, Eastern instrumentation, and female backing vocals. Particular highlights include "I Can't Explain" (not the Who song), "Feel Me," "Sad Day," and "God's Kitchen." —*Bill Cassel*

**Mange Tout** / 1984 / Sire ♦♦♦
*Mange Tout*, Blancmange's follow-up to *Happy Families*, appeared in 1984. Typical of many second albums, the production is a little glossier, the sound a little less fresh. On *Mange Tout*, Arthur and Luscombe stick to the pattern they established on their debut, alternating catchy, sequencer-heavy pop with down-tempo ballads. Sitar and tabla flavorings continue to play a significant role, as does co-conspirator David Rhodes' guitar. Also typical of many sophomore efforts, *Mange Tout* at times runs short of material. While the singles "Don't Tell Me" and "Blind Vision" are nigh irresistible, the similar "That's Love That It Is" gets to be a bit much. And though the B-side boasts the nifty a cappella "See the Train" and the pleasing (if disturbingly Thompson Twins-like) "My Baby," a couple of the songs carry the stench of filler. The album's closer—a synth-heavy, nearly eight-minute take on Abba's "The Day Before You Came"—isn't terrible, just inexplicable. —*Bill Cassel*

● **Believe You Me** / 1985 / Sire ♦♦♦♦
Having suffered somewhat of a sophomore jinx with *Mange Tout*, Blancmange wisely adjusted their approach for their third release. *Believe You Me* is leaner, subtler, and more organic, without straying too far from their established sound. The Eastern instrumentation is de-emphasized in favor of more string and woodwind sounds. Neil Arthur's vocals are stronger, and his and Stephen Luscombe's songwriting is more focused. The result might best be described as "mature techno-pop," and perhaps predictably, it failed to find an audience, especially in the US. Blancmange disbanded not long after. With this in mind, it's not hard to find a vein of regret running throughout *Believe You Me:* Song titles include "Lose Your Love," "No Wonder They Never Made It Back!" and "Why Don't They Leave Things Alone?," the loveliest, saddest ballad Blancmange ever recorded. Even the poppier tracks, like "22339" and "Believe," are driven by an undercurrent of apprehension. *Believe You Me* wraps up with a couple of bittersweet instrumentals, bringing Blancmange's recording career to a close on a peaceful note. —*Bill Cassel*

## Blaze

f. 1984, Newark, NJ

*Group / Jazz-House, Garage, Club/Dance, House*

The New Jersey production team known as Blaze authored a number of deep house anthems from the '80s and '90s—including "If You Should Need a Friend" and "Lovelee Dae" under their own name, "Hideaway" by De'lacy, and "My Desire" by Amira. Signed to a contract with Motown (ostensibly for their R&B/pop crossover potential) in 1989, the trio of Josh Milan, Kevin Hedge, and Chris Herbert issued one solid album for the label before embarking on a career short on LPs but long on stellar productions for a variety of artists. The production wing of Blaze, namely Milan and Hedge (the latter a former gospel singer), began as early favorites on the New York/New Jersey garage scene of the mid-'80s. The pair, both DJs and fans of Tony Humphries' sets at the Newark club Zanzibar, began producing in 1984 and made a name for themselves two years later with a pair of garage classics, "If You Should Need a Friend" and "Whatcha Gonna Do" (with vocals by Colonel Abrams). Remixes and additional production for British synth-popsters ABC led to a recording contract with Motown in 1989. With semi-permanent vocalist Chris Herbert added to the lineup, Blaze released their debut album *25 Years Later* in 1990. Though the single "So Special" did well in the clubs, it wasn't quite the crossover Motown expected and the group was dropped.

Though the major labels had enough of crossover house music by the early '90s, there was still a major independent market for the music. Milan and Hedge continued to produce and record, both separately and together, during the decade. In 1994, they wrote and produced the British Top Ten hit "Hideaway" by De'Lacy. Three years later, Blaze added Tee Alford and returned with another club hit ("Lovelee Dae") and their second full-length, *Basic Blaze* (recorded for the UK-based Slip'N'Slide label). A Blaze retrospective appeared in 1999. — *John Bush*

● **25 Years Later** / Aug. 7, 1990 / Motown ♦♦♦♦

The New Jersey trio's '90 debut album for Maze. Blaze's roster featured vocalist Chris Herbert, keyboardist Josh Milan, and drummer Kevin Hedge, who came together in the '80s doing a good blend of gospel-tinged soul and East Coast dance. They got some attention on the single "So Special," and also the cuts "Get Up" and "Lover Man." They never really hit it big, but did have potential. — *Ron Wynn*

**Basic Blaze** / Aug. 18, 1997 / Slip 'N' Slide ♦♦♦

Blaze's second LP, released more than seven years after their Motown debut, finds the duo of Joshua Milan and Kevin Hedge elaborating on the same garage and deep house concepts of their first—though with more maturity and the production techniques learned from remixing Babyface and Donald D during the early '90s. — *John Bush*

**The Many Colours of Blaze** / Mar. 1, 1999 / Slip 'N' Slide ♦♦♦♦

Yes, this Blaze retrospective does cover most of the group's club hits of the '90s (including "My Beat" and "Seasons of Love"), but unfortunately it leaves off the collective's seminal tunes from the late '80s. — *John Bush*

## The Blue Nile

f. 1981, Glasgow, Scotland

*Group / Dream Pop, Pop/Rock, Folk-Rock*

The Scottish folk-ambient band the Blue Nile has enjoyed a mystique contrived by its inaccessibility and the infrequency of its recordings, but it has also made a series of critically acclaimed discs. The group was formed by three Glasgow natives who graduated from university there: singer/songwriter/guitarist Paul Buchanan, bassist Robert Bell, and keyboardist Paul Joseph Moore. Engineer Callum Malcolm and drummer Nigel Thomas have worked with the trio consistently, to the point of being considered secondary bandmembers. (*The Blue Nile* is the title of Alan Moorehead's 1962 sequel to *The White Nile*, the two books making up a history of the Nile River.) They recorded their own single, "I Love This Life," which was distributed by Robert Stigwood's RSO Records just before the company closed its doors. They were then signed by Linn Products, which released their debut album, *A Walk Across the Rooftops*, in 1984 (A&M handled it in the US). Since the company was small and the band did not tour, the album took some time to find its audience, though it briefly reached the UK charts and led to high expectations for a second album. This came in 1989 with *Hats*, which reached the British Top 20, throwing off three chart singles, "The Downtown Lights," "Headlights on the Parade," and "Saturday Night." The album also made the lower reaches of the American charts as the Blue Nile embarked on its first tour, a 30-date journey taking place in the British Isles and the US. In the ensuing years, the band members switched record labels, signing to Warner Bros., and contributed to recordings by Robbie Robertson and Julian Lennon. They finally emerged with their third album, *Peace at Last*, in June 1996. Another critically acclaimed release, it placed in the UK Top 20, but failed to chart in the US. — *William Ruhlmann*

**Walk Across the Rooftops** / May 1984 / A&M ♦♦♦♦

The Blue Nile's debut LP is an oblique, supremely enigmatic work which immediately establishes the Glaswegian trio as a force to be reckoned with; while *A Walk Across the Rooftops* doesn't iron all the wrinkles out of the group's spaciously atmospheric sound. Its thoughtful and original use of electronic textures nevertheless makes for compelling listening—an experience furthered by Paul Buchanan's keen sense of compositional dynamics on such highlights as "Tinseltown in the Rain" and "Stay." — *Jason Ankeny*

● **Hats** / Oct. 1989 / A&M ♦♦♦♦

Five long years in the making, the Blue Nile's stellar *Hats* was well worth the wait. Sweeping and majestic, it's a triumph of personal vision over the cold, remote calculations of technology. While created almost solely without benefit of live instruments, it is nevertheless an immensely warm and human album. Paul Buchanan's plaintive vocals and poignant songs are uncommonly moving, and his deployment of lush synth washes and electronic percussion is never gratuitous, each song instead crafted with painterly precision. Impressionistic and shimmering, tracks like "The Downtown Lights" and "From a Late Night Train" are perfectly evocative of their titles: rich in romantic atmosphere and detail, they conjure a nocturnal fantasy world lit by neon and shrouded in fog, leaving *Hats* an intensely cinematic experience as well as a masterpiece of musical obsession. — *Jason Ankeny*

**Peace at Last** / Jul. 1996 / Warner Brothers ♦♦♦

The members of the Blue Nile seem to have taken seriously all those articles and reviews about what audiophiles and technicians they are. This time around they've spent a half-dozen years concocting an album that sounds like they made at least some of it in their living rooms rather than their space-age studio. They achieve the appearance of simplicity and humanity by foregrounding either an acoustic guitar or piano on most tracks, by restraining other instrumentation, by making their synthesizers sound like strings most of the time, and by using real strings on occasion—all of which makes for appropriate settings for Paul Buchanan's songs of domestic contentment. "Happiness," "Sentimental Man," "Holy Love": the titles tell the story, though they don't reveal the underlying fear that it will all go bust ("Now that I've found peace at last," Buchanan sings to open up the album, "tell me, Jesus, will it last?"). Nor do they explain why a guy who keeps insisting that he's happy sounds so mournful. Buchanan belongs to the Bono/Peter Gabriel school of throaty emotiveness, in which sudden, arbitrary ascensions toward the falsetto signal fits of otherwise unacknowledged passion (or maybe just a sneeze coming on). In Buchanan, the singing style and the loose structure of the songs make his protestations of tranquility unconvincing. That may be what he intends, especially since they lend an implied depth to what is the Blue Nile's lightest effort yet. — *William Ruhlmann*

## Boards of Canada

f. Scotland

*Group / Electronica, Ambient Techno, IDM*

Boards of Canada is the duo of Mike Sandison (b. July 14, 1971) and Marcus Eoin (b. May 27, 1973). Based on the northern coast of Scotland, the group got their start on acclaimed experimental electronica label Skam in 1996 after recording an obscene number of tracks and pressing the best of them up as a miniscule-run 12", *Twoism*, a eight-track promo EP the group sent to labels in lieu of a demonstration tape. The pair's first official release appeared on Skam toward the middle of 1996, and was quickly hailed as among the label's finest releases to date. Titled *Hi Scores*, the EP is an engaging mix of simple, infectious three-part synth melodies, subtle hip-hop and electro references, and alternately tense and relaxing beatwork endlessly repeated in shifting combinations (à la Autechre, Bochum Welt, and Cylob). Almost a mini-LP at six tracks and nearly half an hour in length, the debut was followed in late 1996 by a series of live gigs opening for Plaid and Autechre, as well as compilation tracks for Uvm and Skam/Musik Aus Strom side project label Mask (under the name Hellinterface). Further releases for Skam, Mask, and 4th World in-house label Ampoule were scheduled, and in 1998 Boards of Canada issued *Music Has the Right to Children*. — *Sean Cooper*

**Hi Scores [EP]** / Dec. 9, 1996 / Skam ✦✦✦✦
Like Autechre and Bochum Welt, Boards of Canada draw heavily from both new wave and electro in appreciable measures that, when recombined in the context of the group's tugging beats and simple-but-effective songwriting, end up sounding like way more than either. *Hi Scores* is a near-perfect six-tracker of gorgeous, building ambient electro and looping downtempo electronic breakbeat that are as pleasing to the ears as they are head-bucking funky. —*Sean Cooper*

★ **Music Has the Right to Children** / Apr. 20, 1998 / Warp ✦✦✦✦✦
Although Boards of Canada's blueprint for electronic listening music—aching electro-synth with mid-tempo hip-hop beats and occasional light scratching—isn't quite a revolution in and of itself, *Music Has the Right to Children* is an amazing LP. Similar to the early work of Autechre and Aphex Twin, the duo is one of the few European artists which can match their American precursors with regard to a sense of spirit in otherwise electronic music. This is pure machine soul, reminiscent of some forgotten Japanese animation soundtrack or a rusting Commodore 64 just about to give up the ghost. Alternating broadly sketched works with minute-long vignettes (the latter of which comprise several of the best tracks on the album), *Music Has the Right to Children* is one of the best electronic releases of 1998. —*John Bush*

## Bochum Welt (Gianluigi Di Costanzo)

*Producer / Experimental Techno, Electronica, Ambient Techno, Techno, IDM*
Italian electro/techno composer Gianluigi Di Costanzo is the name behind the Milan-based Bochum Welt, whose smattering of atmospheric acid and electro releases have been quick in establishing him as an artist at the edge of post-rave experimental electronica. Inspired by the '70s Dusseldorf scene through such figures as Ralf Hutter and Florian Schneider (both of Kraftwerk), as well as artists such as Brian Eno and Ryuichi Sakamoto, Di Costanzo released his first work as Bochum Welt on the Italian Trance Communications label starting in 1994, at the age of 21. Focusing mostly on acid and more typical floorbang techno, Di Costanzo worked as often on atmospheric electro and ambient, little of which saw release until many years later (most notably on the *Phial EP*). Though Italy is hardly a stronghold of techno experimentation, Di Costanzo's early Trance twelves, as well as a collaboration with labelmates Zenith, attracted the attention of Aphex Twin Richard James, whose Rephlex imprint reissued several tracks from the Bochum Welt back-catalog as the *Scharlach Eingang* EP in 1995. Di Costanzo followed up his Rephlex debut the following year with a full-length for the label, *Module 2*. *Desktop Robotics* followed in 1997, trailed two years later by *Martians and Spaceships*. He has also released material through his own label, Kromode, and the Swiss Axodya label. —*Sean Cooper*

**Les Dances D'Ete [EP]** / 1994 / Kromode ✦✦✦
Gianluigi Di Costanzo's finest body of work predates his comparatively higher-profile material on the UK-based Rephlex label by a few years. Released on the tiny Italian Kromode, early BW 12" and 10" releases (of which "Les Dances D'Ete" is one) were unsoiled by the Aphex affectations that tend to overwhelm his more recent work—the preschool melodies, the retro fixation, the overall off-the-cuff-ness. Though hard to track down, "Les Dances D'Ete," presents Di Costanzo's more serious side, pairing intricate rhythms with brooding, at times sorrowful melodies and ambient atmospheres. —*Sean Cooper*

**Scharlach Eingang [EP]** / 1994 / Rephlex ✦✦
Rephlex's reissue of material culled from the somewhat obscure Trance Communications singles, ruddy, sweeping ambient electro with a dark, somewhat broody edge: the fidelity leaves much to be desired, but the material is top-notch, with Di Costanzo's thick, evocative melodies almost burying spare, funky beats. The label reads 45 RPM, but for armchair listening, 33 is advised. —*Sean Cooper*

**Phial [EP]** / 1995 / Axodya ✦✦
This jam-packed eight-tracker collects many of Di Costanzo's earlier, more experimental tracks, and is split evenly between mid- to down-tempo ambient electro and bloody-nose breakbeat acid. The range makes for somewhat disjointed continuous listening, but it's quality stuff nonetheless, with production clarity and compositional authority a definite cut above the Trance and Rephlex EPs. —*Sean Cooper*

● **Module 2** / Sep. 2, 1996 / Rephlex ✦✦✦✦
A brighter, if somewhat flat-sounding excavation of the ambient-electro aesthetic explored on the "Scharlach Eingang" EP. Treading the middle-ground between the plodding motorway tracks of early Kraftwerk and the harder lino breaks of the neo-electro crowd, little of the material sounds as fleshed out or dynamic as his earlier work, although tracks such as "Radiopropulsive" and "Paph" are excellent. —*Sean Cooper*

**Desktop Robotics [Single]** / Jun. 16, 1997 / Rephlex ✦✦✦✦
Bochum Welt's 1997 EP for Rephlex was accompanied by bonuses all around: on the CD side, *Desktop Robotics* was fitted with a freeware version of Pac-Man for Macintosh, with an original BW soundtrack; on the vinyl side, the EP was released as a double 12", featuring a "special bonus token with extra lives" (a three-track EP, including the soundtrack from the video game). The music? Oh, well there's some of that, too. *Desktop Robotics* proper is a five-tracker of delightful, upbeat melodic electro-pop; electronics-born new wave without the cheesy vocals and bad guitar playing. The good track/bad track ratio is better than with previous Rephlex releases, but *Desktop Robotics* finds Costanzo still a bit shy of his stride. —*Sean Cooper*

**Feelings on a Screen [EP]** / Jul. 7, 1997 / Rephlex ✦✦
Following the excellent *Desktop Robotics* double EP by only a week, Bochum Welt's "Feelings on a Screen" is not surprisingly made of similar materials: vague, plastic-sounding rhythms, smiling, bouncy melodies, and warm, slingshot basslines. Di Costanzo's new-wave past bubbles a bit too close to the surface here, however. His passing fascination for thin, playschool beats suffering under the weight of unfortunately cringe-worthy early-'80s DM/New Order references that aren't even that funny, really. —*Sean Cooper*

## Bola (Darrell Fitton)

*Producer / Electronica, Electro-Techno, IDM*
Manchester's Bola is Darrell Fitton, whose 1995 debut 12" for Skam under that name helped shoot the now-collectible label to underground notoriety. Although the first of Fitton's released tracks appeared on the Warp label's *Artificial Intelligence II* compilation in 1995 and displayed the same style of chrome-dipped melodic techno adhered to by many Warp artists, his subsequent Bola material focused in on a heartier, less accessible aesthetic. His self-titled Skam EP combined vaguely funk-fueled rhythms with harsh, austere synth textures and almost industrial-grade distortion. With the exception of compilation tracks for Silent Records' US-released *Skampilation*, the Skam-V/Vm collaboration *061*, and the mostly obscure *Mask* series (a joint venture between Skam and Munich's Musik aus Strom), three years separated Fitton's debut from his next proper release; "Aguilla" was an extremely limited-run three-track 7" released by Skam in 1998. Two months following appeared *Soup*, Fitton's long-awaited LP debut. An impressive synthesis of the machine-beat ambiance of post-techno with warm, wistful analog soul, *Soup* sounded familiar more than dated, and served as an impressive summing up of the formal qualities of dance music utterly uninterested in the dance floor. In addition to his Bola releases, Fitton loaned his production chops to the first 12" by Warp artists Autechre under their Gescom guise, and is rumored to serve as Skam's in-house engineer. —*Sean Cooper*

**Aguilla [Single]** / 1996 / Skam ✦✦✦
Apart from the gorgeous title cut (also included on the LP it preceded, *Soup*), this three-track single of otherwise recycled ideas isn't worth much. —*Sean Cooper*

**Bola [EP]** / Aug. 1996 / Skam ✦✦✦✦
Although Skam's entire catalog is often spoken of with awe, it's only with this EP that the label begins resembling the claims made about it. Worth picking up for the lead track ("Forcasa 3") alone, the whole of *Bola* is notable for the new sounds and structures it brought to post-Warp underground electronica—sweeping, multilayered melodies, odd time signatures, relentless rhythms, and diverse emotional content. —*Sean Cooper*

● **Soup** / Nov. 23, 1998 / Skam ✦✦✦✦
Three years in the coming, Darrell Fitton's debut Bola LP is a varied, engaging listen. The tracks mostly follow the style of heavily machinic, wistfully melodic post-techno first explored by Warp label artists (such as Black Dog, Autechre, and Aphex Twin) but as evident are the influence of artists such as Tangerine Dream, Skinny Puppy, and Vangelis (the ten-minute closing cut, "Whoblo," sounds like the soundtrack to a pornographic *Blade Runner*). *Soup* includes the best moments of Fitton's two previous Bola releases, the *Bola* EP ("Forcasa 3") and the "Aguilla" 7" (the title cut). —*Sean Cooper*

## CJ Bolland (Christopher Jay Bolland)
b. Jun. 18, 1971, Stockton-On-Tees, England
*Producer, DJ / Electronica, Trance, Club/Dance, Techno*

Born in Yorkshire in 1971 but transplanted to Belgium when he was only three, CJ Bolland received an early education in dance music; his parents ran a club in Antwerp, and his mother DJed there. He grew up listening to the synthesizer music of several eras—from Jean-Michel Jarre to Front 242 and the Neon Judgement—but began devoting most of his time to house and techno by the late '80s. Bolland began producing in 1988, when a drummer friend gave him access to the right gear, and his tracks were soon heard on several Belgian pirate radio stations. He then sent demos to several labels, and finally heard back from R&S Records.

CJ Bolland's first production for R&S, the Project's "Do That Dance," jump-started his career, and he soon saw releases from his projects Pulse, Space Opera (with the Advent's Cisco Ferreira), Cee-Jay, Ravesignal, and Sonic Solution. His 1992 *Ravesignal 3* EP (specifically, the track "Horsepower") made Bolland one of the hottest names in the new global dance community.

Bolland made his album debut soon after, with *The 4th Sign*. His 1993-94 schedule also included production work for Mundo Muzique, Dave Angel, and Joey Beltram, as well as remixing for Orbital, Prodigy, Sven Väth, Westbam, Tori Amos, and Baby Ford, among others. His second album, *Electronic Highway*, was released in 1995, after which Bolland signed a mammoth five-album deal with Internal Records. The first fruits of the contract, *The Analogue Theatre*, were released in late 1996 to critical praise and dance-chart success, thanks to the excitable single "Sugar Is Sweeter." —*John Bush*

**4th Sign** / 1992 / R&S ♦♦

*4th Sign*, CJ Bolland's full-length debut for R&S, is notably—and refreshingly—free of his previous singles successes for the label. Instead of padding out the LP with a few of the club hits he'd recorded during his four-plus years on R&S, Bolland uses the opportunity to explore new methods and construct an album of tracks that work together as well as apart. True, there's not that much different here musically; it's a nine-track course through much of the same hard techno and pummeling trance he'd been known for. But the effects programming is inventive and just a bit leftfield for the dancefloor (at least circa 1992), and Bolland ranges from sleek trance ("Aquadrive"), to hardcore ("Spring Yard"), to symphonic progressive house ("Camargue"). Though the best tracks ("Nightbreed," "Mantra," "Thrust") come with help from the Advent's Cisco Ferreira (maybe this should've been released as a Space Opera LP instead), *4th Sign* is a near-perfect debut. —*John Bush*

**Electronic Highway** / 1995 / R&S ♦♦♦

On *Electronic Highway*, CJ Bolland distances himself from the stark acid-techno and trance of his early career with a set of emotive, symphonic tracks. Though Bolland's rhythms are just as driving, and his use of percussion just as heavy as before, most of the squelchy acid effects have been replaced. On "The Tower of Naphtali," he uses toybox melodies to soften the blow, while a few faraway vintage synth lines spice "Con Spirito" and highlight "Zenith." With help on engineering from David Morley, Bolland also added breakbeats, and the result is the solid early ambient drum'n'bass piece, "Bones." Cisco Ferreira also helps out on two tracks, a remix of "Spoof" and "Drum Tower." —*John Bush*

● **The Analogue Theatre** / Oct. 14, 1996 / Phuture Trax ♦♦♦♦

Bolland's breakout album with a larger crowd continues to display his roots in hard techno while springing a more percussive, wall-of-sound aesthetic closer to Prodigy than Joey Beltram. "The Analogue Theatre," "Counterpoint," and "The Prophet" are up-front trance stormers, and "Electro Power" is an intriguing pastiche of big-beat and acid-rap. Armand Van Helden's mix of the stellar single "Sugar Is Sweeter" adds a bit of polish to the affair, and Bolland's feel for mixing gives the album a good flow. —*John Bush*

## BolzBolz (Andreas Bolz)
*Producer / Neo-Electro, Electro-Techno*

Third Electric's Andreas Bolz doubled up his surname for this solo project, which has grown to three releases of notably high-quality, innovative new-school electro since 1997. Comparatively more uptempo and energetic than his work with Gregor Lutterman as Third Electric, Bolz's solo work under his own name pairs complex, often oddly syncopated rhythms with bold basslines and lively electronics and synth arpeggiation. BolzBolz's debut EP, *32nd Lesson*, appeared on the American label Ersatz Audio, and contained the stripped-down floor-rocker "Music" (previously available only on CD). That track was also the basis for his first EP on Lutterman's Electrocord sub-label, World Electric; "Music Remixes" contained reworkings by Ersatz's Adam Lee Miller (as Plasma Co.) and by BolzBolz himself. A second EP, *Envelope Power*, appeared through World Electric in early 1999, and remains some of the finest new-school German electro ever released, a near-perfect mixture of floor-ready rhythms and head-scratching songwriting. In addition to his BolzBolz and Third Electric work, Bolz also records for Electrocord under the name Funktaxi, with an EP and an LP (*Mild*) to his credit. —*Sean Cooper*

**32nd Lesson [EP]** / Nov. 3, 1997 / Ersatz Audio ♦♦♦♦

Ersatz's Artificial Material's contribution to the *Electrecord 2000* compilation is repaid in kind by Electrecord's BolzBolz (of Third Electric) with this EP of tight, snapping, new wave-leaning electro. "Music" (from Third Electric's uncredited, CD-only full-length) is given its vinyl debut, along with two uptempo tracks, one relying heavily on bassy, repeating synth figures, the other a dirgy, minimal cut with too-excessive vocal samples. —*Sean Cooper*

**Music Remixes [EP]** / 1998 / World Electric ♦♦♦♦

Retakes from BolzBolz and Plasma Co. (Adam Lee Miller of Ersatz Audio) build on the original's stripped down jitter, while a new track, "High Tension Wires" (by Miller together with Bolz and partner Gregor Lutterman as Third Electric), almost steals the show. Hard to find, but worth the trouble. —*Sean Cooper*

● **Envelope Power [EP]** / 1999 / World Electric ♦♦♦♦

A supremely excellent compression of classic electro elements (808 beats, aggressive basslines) and dense, enveloping electronic atmospheres as suitable for home listening as for the DJ set. The title cut builds on the beat from LFO's "Tied Up," murking things up with a dusty bit of reverb and a fierce 303 bassline. The equally great "Manual Control" pairs a popping electronic funk bassline with screwy rhythm patterns and squelchy electronics. Top-notch stuff. —*Sean Cooper*

## Bomb the Bass (Tim Simenon)
b. 1968, Brixton, London, England
*Producer / Electronica, Club/Dance, Acid House, House, Hip-Hop*

Bomb the Bass' Tim Simenon is a sampladelic British hip-hop producer who also co-produced a pair of massive international hits: Neneh Cherry's "Buffalo Stance," and Seal's "Crazy." Born in Brixton of Malaysian and Scottish parentage, Simenon grew interested in dance production after studying studio engineering and DJing at London's Wag Club, a Mecca for fellow breakbeat mavens like S-Express' Mark Moore and Coldcut's Jonathan More and Matt Black. In 1987, Simenon constructed a pastiche of a DJ record titled "Beat Dis" which incorporated samples from Public Enemy to Ennio Morricone to classic television shows *Dragnet* and *The Thunderbirds*. Packaged to resemble a white-label import from America, the track became an underground hit and, after its reissue on Rhythm King, a surprising number two smash on the British charts in early 1988. (Coldcut's "Doctorin' the House" and S-Express' "Theme From S-Express" both followed "Beat Dis" into the Top Ten.)

Later that year, Simenon followed with an LP (*Into the Dragon*) featuring an expanded Bomb the Bass lineup: producer Jonathan Saul Kane (who later recorded as Depth Charge), and vocalists Maureen Walsh and Lauraine Macintosh. Two singles from the album, "Megablast" and an inventive cover of the Burt Bacharach-Dionne Warwick classic "Say a Little Prayer," hit the British Top Ten as well. Also in 1988, Simenon co-produced two tracks for the debut of Neneh Cherry, step-daughter of free jazz trumpeter Don Cherry. Both singles, "Buffalo Stance" and "Manchild," became British Top Ten hits. After completing work on his own studio, he also produced a track for Adamski ("Killer") and mixed a single named "Crazy" for an Adamski protégé, Seal.

With all the outside recording commissions, it took nearly three years for Simenon to ready a follow-up to the first Bomb the Bass LP. *Unknown Territory* finally dropped in 1991, led by another Top Ten single, "Winter in July," and sporting a mid-tempo hip-hop aesthetic that would only earn critical attention several years later after being dubbed trip-hop. He also produced a range of acts, from Eternal to Sinead O'Connor during the early '90s, and more fruits of his collaborative nature arrived in 1995 with the third Bomb the Bass album, *Clear*. The album featured vocal tracks featuring O'Connor, Justin Warfield, Bernard Fowler, Bim Sherman, and Leslie Winer, as well as the instrumental input of Tackhead/On-U Sound compatriots Keith LeBlanc, Doug Wimbish, and Skip McDonald. Simenon again turned to outside work during the late '90s, remixing and producing for David Bowie, Depeche Mode, U2, Gavin Friday, Curve, Booth & The Bad Angel, and Hardfloor. —*John Bush*

**Into the Dragon** / Oct. 1988 / Rhythm King ♦♦♦♦
Though Simenon's breakout hit "Beat Dis" isn't quite as frenetic as contemporary material by Coldcut (or even M/A/R/R/S), the debut Bomb the Bass LP is an intriguing trip through sampledelic hip-hop, electro, acid-house and even dance-pop (as on his other hits, "Don't Make Me Wait" and the Burt Bacharach cover "Say a Little Prayer"). Much of the album mines territory similar to "Beat Dis"—that is, inventive hip-hop tracks like "On the Cut," "Megablast (Hip Hop on Precinct 13)", and "Dynamite Beats" which are somewhat indebted to Mantronix. —*Keith Farley*

**Unknown Territory** / Aug. 1991 / Rhythm King ♦♦♦

● **Clear** / 1995 / 4th & Broadway ♦♦♦♦
Though Bomb the Bass' third album, *Clear*, was originally a scattershot, kinetic dance record, Tim Simenon restructured the record for its American release. The American version of *Clear* demonstrates a distinct trip-hop, techno, jazz, and dub influence, as well as the literary lyical pretentions that were present on the original English release. Simenon created a subdued, multi-layered album, where instruments float in and out of the mix over a deep, laidback groove. All of the rappers on the record are guest stars, including Sinead O'Connor and Justin Warfield. Although their contributions are impressive, the true star of the album is Simenon, who has made an album that proves he isn't stuck in the late-'80s house/techno rut and can compete with '90s artists like Tricky and Portishead. Still, the album highlight comes with a La Funk Mob reworking —*Stephen Thomas Erlewine*

## Bomb20
b. 1979
*Producer / Hardcore Techno*
The Digital Hardcore producer known as Bomb20 impressed the label so much with his criticism of their (comparatively) commercial slant that he gained a record contract of his own. Still just a teenager, he contacted DHR in 1996 to tell them they'd sold out by licensing videos by DHR act Atari Teenage Riot to air on MTV. After sending in a tape of his productions as well, he earned a release on two sublabels, Riot Beats (for "Pigtronics") and Less Than 20 (for *The Choice of the Righteous* EP). Another EP, *Flip Burgers or Die!*, followed in 1998 before his album debut, *Field Manual*. Espousing a violently anti-media, anti-corporate philosophy, he spent six weeks in a German prison during 2000 after being arrested at a demonstration in Berlin. —*John Bush*

● **Field Manual** / Jun. 8, 1998 / DHR ♦♦
Though it's just as extreme a hardcore stance—musically and idealistically—as previous Digital Hardcore material like EC8OR's *All of Us Can Be Rich* and Atari Teenage Riot's *The Future of War*, *Field Manual* sounds less explicit because it's a production act without vocals. Instead of narrative songs like "Deutschland Has Gotta Die," "We Are Pissed," "Start the Riot," or "Delete Yourself," Bomb20 constructs similar productions—dense sonic collage with distorted hardcore beats—and lets vocal samples speak for him. Intriguingly, he bends the will of countless melodramatic movie-trailer voiceovers and various other media samples to make a statement about media itself. Also, in a move straight out of Nation of Ulysses or Underground Resistance, he includes a lengthy essay in the booklet to explain and illumine his views about the increasingly powerful corporate world. Granted, the productions are never as intriguing as the actual views behind them, but give Bomb20 plenty of credit for his principles. —*John Bush*

## Frankie Bones (Frank Mitchell)
*Producer, DJ / Tribal-House, Club/Dance, Techno, House*
Frankie Bones is the most visible DJ and taste-maker of New York's independent techno scene during the '80s and '90s, both through his nation-trotting club appearances and frenetic mix-album schedule (which approaches three per year). After five years of DJ appearances, Bones began producing in 1987, with Tommy Musto as Musto & Bones. Their stellar remixes and tracks for Nu Groove Records made it the home of some of New York's hottest contemporary productions. In 1990, the pair released an album for RCA named *The Future Is Ours*, and the single "All I Want to Do Is Get Away" became a huge hit on dancefloors. Though he separated from Musto soon after their LP, Bones' success gave him entry into the world of international DJing during the early '90s, and his remix work for 808 State and others led to a reputation as one of the preeminent house godfathers. He released almost a dozen CDs during the mid-to-late-'90s, including multiple volumes in the mix-album series *Factory* and *Computer Controlled*, as well as his own production work on the 1998 house chronicle *Technolo-G*. These were followed a year later with a slew of EPs and singles from the New York native. Taking a more commercial path from his independent label Sonic Groove, Bones released the mix CD *You Know My Name* on Moonshine in November of 2000. His brother Adam X is also a high-profile DJ and producer. —*John Bush*

**Houseloop** / Aug. 12, 1996 / Sm:)e ♦♦♦♦

**Factory 101** / Nov. 11, 1997 / X-Sight ♦♦♦

**Technolo-G** / Apr. 7, 1998 / Deep Blue ♦♦♦♦
A megamix of new Bones productions focuses on Brooklyn-style underground techno-funk indebted to electronic dance of all eras: the raw side of early Chicago house ("Jack It Up"), minimalist Detroit ("Just a Little Bit"), rave ("B2B [What U Wanna B]"), and even old-time disco ("Studio 54"). *Technolo-G* is a solid showcase for Bones' tight productions and also gives a good feel for his many DJ slots. —*John Bush*

**Factory 202** / Mar. 23, 1999 / X-Sight ♦♦
The second volume in his series of *Factory* mix albums is chock full of Bones' favorite material—banging techno that just keeps on charging, track after track. Though *Factory 202* does ease listeners in with Dietrich Schoenemann's "Sable Ring" and "Deepest Memory" by Bones' little brother, Adam X, the album hits high-point after high-point through the rest of the set, with tracks by Marco Carola ("Trashed Neurons"), Vector Two ("War Zone 2"), and Bones himself ("Inner Drive"). There may be a few *too many* climaxes for those playing at home, but *Factory 202* is yet another solid document of what it is to see Frankie Bones circa 1999. —*John Bush*

● **Factory 303** / Apr. 18, 2000 / X-Sight ♦♦♦♦
Frankie Bones' third *Factory* collection again focuses on hard, minimal techno, from the martial drums on the opener "Boots on the Run" by Insider to the minimal electro paranoia of "Stalking You" by Detroiter Paris the Black Fu. A DJ who's apparently never learned the meaning of the word stop, Bones hits his peak early on and never really slows down, making for an exhilarating—if potentially exhausting—listen. The buzz saw distortion on "I'm Speaking to You" by Richard Hinge makes for another highlight. —*John Bush*

## Boom Boom Satellites
*Group / Big Beat, Trip-Hop, Club/Dance, Alternative Pop/Rock*
The Tokyo electronic-pop duo Boom Boom Satellites paired singer/guitarist Michiyuki Kawashima and bassist/DJ Masayuki Nakano, fellow university students who first teamed in 1990. Taking their name from a song by Sigue Sigue Sputnik, they earned wide acclaim for their 1995 debut single "Dub Me Crazy," a highlight of noted DJ Fumiya Tanaka's *Abstract Set One* compilation. Signing with the Belgian label R&S, in 1997 Boom Boom Satellites returned with "4 a Moment of Silence," followed later that year by the EP *Joyride*. The full-length *Out Loud* appeared in 1999, followed by the album *Fog Bound* a year later. —*Jason Ankeny*

● **Out Loud** / Feb. 1, 1999 / Epic ♦♦♦♦
It'd be a bit limiting to call Boom Boom Satellites the Japanese version of Prodigy or Chemical Brothers, though the comparison goes a long way to describe the sound of *Out Loud*. "Push Eject" features a breakbeat attack with a set of vocals from Michiyuki Kawashima very reminiscent of Keith Flint (though admittedly he sounds more like Mark E. Smith a couple tracks later). It's clear that this album is much more than just a party record—the vocoder dub of "Limbo" is impeccably programmed, and the live drums by Naoki Hirai add much to "An Owl," with trumpet, sax and flute as well. What sets this album apart from most big-beat casualties is the production—like Si Begg's work as Buckfunk 3000, Boom Boom Satellites embellish their version of rather uncomplicated breakbeat trance with dozens of little sonic touches

that set each track apart. It's not the hackneyed Miles Davis impressions on "Batter the Jam No. 3" that makes this a more important record than Crystal Method, it's just the natural ease of a well-produced album. —*John Bush*

### Boulderdash

*Group / Ambient Techno, Trip-Hop*

Swedish producers Hans Möller and Daniel Skaborn recorded under a variety of names during the '90s, but only gained a modicum of attention worldwide with the 2000 release of their Boulderdash debut, *We Never Went to Koxut Island*. Just part of a thriving Swedish electronic scene that also includes the habitants at Dot Records, the duo began recording early in the decade after assembling their own studio with help from future label-mates Upsalians and Spinform (the latter includes Möller's brother). Aside from the techno project Mnemosyne and experimental drum'n'bass as Juicehead, Möller and Skaborn began producing tracks of complex, ambient techno inspired by early-'90s heroes from British labels Warp, R&S, and Rephlex. Finally, in 2000, the Swedish label Recordings Under Construction released the first Boulderdash album, *We Never Went to Koxut Island*. —*John Bush*

- **We Never Went to Koxut Island** / 2000 / Recordings Under Construction ✦✦✦✦

Though *We Never Went to Koxut Island* is their debut album, prior to its release Boulderdash were recording material for several years. Knowing that, perhaps the complexity on display here shouldn't be quite as startling, but the album is still a left-field gem from a pair of Swedish unknowns. Tortured mid-tempo breakbeats parry with a succession of fragile—but completely developed—melodies and occasional dub effects like delay and echo (note the heavy use of melodica on many tracks). "Window of Opportunity" and "Headless in a Topless Bar" are two highlights. —*John Bush*

### Bowery Electric

f. 1992, New York, NY
*Group / Ambient Pop, Dream Pop, Space Rock, Indie Rock, Trip-Hop*

Manhattan-based drone-rock duo Bowery Electric comprised vocalist/guitarist Lawrence Chandler, a former protege of minimalist composer LaMonte Young, and vocalist/bassist Martha Schwendener. Originally a three-piece rounded out by a series of drummers, Bowery Electric bowed in 1994 with a double 7" on their self-owned Hi-Fidelity Recordings which helped land them on the indie label Kranky, which issued their self-titled debut LP in 1995. With 1996's *Beat*, the duo's swirling, chaotic sound began to incorporate elements of the electronica movement; a subsequent series of 12" remixes by the likes of Disjecta, CHASM, and Immersion further solidified their new affiliation with electronic music, as did 1997's remix collection *Vertigo*. The long-awaited *Lushlife* finally appeared in early 2000. —*Jason Ankeny*

Bowery Electric / Aug. 16, 1995 / Kranky ✦✦✦✦

- **Beat** / Nov. 12, 1996 / Kranky ✦✦✦✦

With *Beat*, Bowery Electric's thick, droning sound begins to move toward electronica, incorporating samplers and sequencers into layers of guitars and bass tones. —*Jason Ankeny*

Vertigo / Aug. 25, 1997 / Beggars Banquet ✦✦✦✦

Consisting of Bowery Electric material remixed by an assortment of artists just across the post-rock/electronica divide from the group, *Vertigo* is a vaguely interesting effort. Remixers including John Roome (Witchman), Jon Tye (Twisted Science), and Colin Newman toughen up the band's textured grooves, resulting in tracks just as abstract as their originals, but given a crisper feel. —*John Bush*

Lushlife / Feb. 22, 2000 / Beggars Banquet ✦✦✦

By now, you pretty much know what to expect from Bowery Electric—great head music filled with dashes of Mo'Wax-informed beats, breathy vocals, and atmospheric flourishes. Those three characteristics are a dime a dozen by now, but somehow BE manages to pull it off without sounding like the umpteenth Portishead knock-off. The duo breathes life into the dead and bloated goat of trip-hop by shedding their own tendency to space out in favor of concentrating more on the pulsing low end. Lawrence Chandler's beats, though highly clichéd at points, land harder than before, and Martha Schwendener's vocals are more prominent. It's their most song-based outing to date, and as a result, it's also their most accessible. At times ("Freedom Fighter,") they even sound assaultive! Yet another Bowery release that feels as comfortable as fresh bedsheets, *Lushlife* lends itself more to head-nodding than nodding off. If it seems too much like a tired, well-trodden road, just pretend the record came out in '95.—*Andy Kellman*

### David Bowie (David Robert Jones)

b. Jan. 8, 1947, Brixton, England
*Vocals, Saxophone, Keyboards, Guitar / Experimental Rock, Blue-Eyed Soul, Proto-Punk, Pop/Rock, Glam Rock, Prog-Rock/Art Rock, Hard Rock*

The David Bowie cliché says he's a musical chameleon, adapting himself according to fashion and trends. While such a criticism is too glib, there's no denying that Bowie demonstrated remarkable skill for perceiving musical trends at his peak in the '70s. After spending several years in the late '60s as a mod and as an all-around music-hall entertainer, Bowie reinvented himself as a hippie singer/songwriter. Prior to his breakthrough in 1972, he recorded a proto-metal record and a pop/rock album, eventually redefining glam-rock with his ambiguously sexy Ziggy Stardust persona. Ziggy made Bowie an international star, yet he wasn't content to continue to churn out glitter-rock. By the mid-'70s, he developed an effete, sophisticated version of Philly soul that he dubbed "plastic soul," which eventually morphed into the eerie avant-pop of 1976's *Station to Station*. Shortly afterward, he relocated to Berlin, where he recorded three experimental electronic albums with Brian Eno. At the dawn of the '80s, Bowie was still at the height of his powers, yet following his blockbuster dance-pop album *Let's Dance* in 1983, he slowly sank into mediocrity before salvaging his career in the early '90s. Out of fashion in the '80s and '90s, it was still clear that Bowie was one of the most influential musicians in rock, for better and for worse. Each of his phases in the '70s sparked a number of subgenres—including punk, new wave, goth-rock, the New Romantics, and electronica. Few rockers ever had such lasting impact.

David Jones began performing when he was 13 years old, learning the saxophone while he was at Bromley Technical High School. Another interesting event happened at the school, when his left pupil became permanently dilated in a schoolyard fight. Following his graduation at 16, he worked as a commercial artist while playing saxophone in a number of mod bands, including the King Bees, the Manish Boys (which also featured Jimmy Page as a session man), Davey Jones, and the Lower Third. All three bands released singles, which were generally ignored, yet he continued performing, changing his name to David Bowie in 1966 after the Monkees' Davy Jones became an international star. Over the course of 1966, he released three mod singles on Pye Records, which were all ignored. The following year, he signed with Deram, releasing the music-hall, Anthony Newley-styled, *David Bowie* that year. Upon completing the record, he spent several weeks in a Scottish Buddhist monastery. Once he left the monastery, he studied with Lindsay Kemp's mime troupe, forming his own mime company, Feathers, in 1969. Feathers was short-lived, and he formed the experimental art group Beckenham Arts Lab in 1969.

Bowie needed to finance the Arts Lab, so he signed with Mercury Records that year and released *Man of Words, Man of Music*, a trippy singer-songwriter album featuring "Space Oddity." The song was released as a single and became a major hit in the UK, convincing Bowie to concentrate on music. Hooking up with his old friend Marc Bolan, he began miming to some of Bolan's T. Rex concerts, eventually touring with Bolan, bassist/producer Tony Visconti, guitarist Mick Ronson, and drummer Cambridge as Hype. The band quickly fell apart, yet Bowie and Ronson remained close, working on the material that formed David's next album, *The Man Who Sold the World*, as well as recruiting Michael "Woody" Woodmansey as their drummer. Produced by Tony Visconti, who also played bass, *The Man Who Sold the World* was a heavy guitar rock album that failed to gain much attention. Bowie followed the album in late 1971 with the pop/rock *Hunky Dory*, an album that featured Ronson and keyboardist Rick Wakeman.

Following the release of *Hunky Dory*, Bowie began to develop his most famous incarnation, Ziggy Stardust—an androgynous, bisexual rock star from another planet. Before he unveiled Ziggy, Bowie claimed in a January 1972 interview with *Melody Maker* that he was gay, helping to stir interest in his forthcoming album. Taking cues from Bolan's stylish glam-rock, Bowie dyed his hair orange and began wearing women's clothing. He began calling himself Ziggy Stardust, and his backing band—Ronson, Woodmansey, and bassist Trevor Bolder—were the Spiders from Mars. *The Rise and Fall of Ziggy Stardust and the Spiders from Mars* was released with much fanfare in late 1972 England. The album and its lavish, theatrical concerts became a sensation throughout England, and it helped him become the only glam-rocker to carve out a niche in America. *Ziggy Stardust* became a word-of-mouth hit in the US, and the rereleased "Space Oddity"—which was now also the title of the rereleased *Man of Words, Man of Music*—reached the American Top 20. Bowie quickly followed *Ziggy* with *Aladdin Sane* later in 1973. Not only did he record a new album that year, but he also produced Lou Reed's *Transformer*, the Stooges' *Raw Power*, and Mott the Hoople's comeback *All the Young Dudes*, for which he also wrote the title track.

Given the amount of work Bowie packed into 1972 and 1973, it wasn't surprising that his relentless schedule began to catch up with him. After recording the all-covers *Pin-Ups* with the Spiders from Mars, he unexpectedly announced the band's breakup, as well as his retirement from live performances, during the group's final show that year. He retreated from the spotlight to work on a musical adaptation of George Orwell's *1984*, but once he was denied the rights to the novel, he transformed the work into *Diamond Dogs*. The album was released to generally poor reviews in 1974, yet it generated the hit single "Rebel Rebel," and he supported the album with an elaborate and expensive American tour. As the tour progressed, Bowie became fascinated with soul music, eventually redesigning the entire show to reflect his new "plastic soul." Hiring guitarist Carlos Alomar as the band's leader, Bowie refashioned his group into a Philly soul band and recostumed himself in sophisticated, stylish fashions. The change took fans by surprise, as did the double album *David Live*, which featured material recorded on the 1974 tour.

*Young Americans*, released in 1975, was the culmination of Bowie's soul obsession, and it became his first major crossover hit, peaking in the American Top Ten and generating his first US No. 1 hit "Fame," a song he co-wrote with John Lennon and Alomar. Bowie relocated to Los Angeles, where he earned his first movie role in Nicolas Roeg's *The Man Who Fell to Earth* (1976). While in L.A., he recorded *Station to Station*, which took the plastic soul of *Young Americans* into darker, avant-garde-tinged directions, yet was also a huge hit, generating the Top Ten single "Golden Years." The album inaugurated Bowie's persona of the elegant "Thin White Duke," and it reflected Bowie's growing cocaine-fueled paranoia. Soon, he decided Los Angeles was too boring and returned to England; shortly after arriving in London, he gave the awaiting crowd a Nazi salute, a signal of his growing, drug-addled detachment from reality. The incident caused enormous controversy, and Bowie left the country to settle in Berlin, where he lived and worked with Brian Eno.

Once in Berlin, Bowie sobered up and began painting, as well as studying art. He also developed a fascination with German electronic music, which Eno helped him fulfill on their first album together, *Low*. Released early in 1977, *Low* was a startling mixture of electronics, pop, and avant-garde technique. While it was greeted with mixed reviews, it proved to be one of the most influential albums of the late '70s, as did its follow-up, *"Heroes."* Not only did Bowie record two solo albums in 1977, he also helmed Iggy Pop's comeback records *The Idiot* and *Lust for Life*, and toured anonymously as Pop's keyboardist. He resumed his acting career in 1977, appearing in *Just A Gigolo* with Marlene Dietrich and Kim Novak, as well as narrating Eugene Ormandy's version of *Peter and the Wolf*. Bowie returned to the stage in 1978, launching an international tour that was captured on the double album *Stage*. During 1979, Bowie and Eno recorded *Lodger* in New York, Switzerland, and Berlin, releasing the album at the end of the year. *Lodger* was supported with several innovative videos, as was 1980's *Scary Monsters*, and these videos—"DJ," "Fashion," "Ashes to Ashes"—became staples on early MTV.

*Scary Monsters* was Bowie's last album for RCA, and it wrapped up his most innovative, productive period. Later in 1980, he performed the title role in the stage production of *The Elephant Man*, including several shows on Broadway. He took an extended break from recording over the next two years, appearing in *Christine F* (1982) and the vampire movie *The Hunger* (1982). He returned to the studio only for his 1981 collaboration with Queen, "Under Pressure," and the theme for Paul Schrader's remake of *Cat People*. In 1983, he signed an expensive contract with EMI Records and released *Let's Dance*. Bowie had recruited Chic guitarist Nile Rodgers to produce the album, giving the record a sleek, funky foundation, and hired the unknown Stevie Ray Vaughan as lead guitarist. *Let's Dance* became his most successful record, thanks to stylish, innovative videos for "Let's Dance" and "China Girl," which turned both songs into Top Ten hits. Bowie supported the record with the sold-out arena tour *Serious Moonlight*.

Greeted with massive success for the first time, Bowie wasn't quite sure how to react, and he eventually decided to replicate *Let's Dance* with 1984's *Tonight*. While the album sold well, and produced the Top Ten hit "Blue Jean," it received poor reviews and was ultimately a commercial disappointment. He stalled in 1985, recording a duet of Martha & the Vandellas' "Dancing in the Street" with Mick Jagger for Live Aid. He also spent more time jet-setting, appearing at celebrity events across the globe, and appeared in several movies—*Into the Night* (1985), *Absolute Beginners* (1986), *Labyrinth* (1986)—that turned out to be bombs. Bowie returned to recording in 1987 with the widely panned *Never Let Me Down*, supporting the album with the *Glass Spider* tour, which also received poor reviews. In 1989, he remastered his RCA catalog with Rykodisc for CD release, kicking off the series with the three-disc box *Sound + Vision*. Bowie supported the discs with an accompanying tour of the same name, claiming that he was retiring all of his older characters from performance following the tour. *Sound + Vision* was successful, and *Ziggy Stardust* re-charted amidst the hoopla.

*Sound + Vision* may have been a success, but Bowie's next project was perhaps his most unsuccessful. Picking up on the abrasive, dissonant rock of Sonic Youth and the Pixies, Bowie formed his own guitar rock combo Tin Machine—with guitarist Reeves Gabrels, bassist Hunt Sales, and his drummer brother Tony, who had previously worked on Iggy Pop's *Lust for Life* with Bowie. Tin Machine released an eponymous album to poor reviews that summer and supported it with a club tour, which was only moderately successful. Despite the poor reviews, Tin Machine released a second album, the appropriately titled *Tin Machine II* (1991), and it was completely ignored.

Bowie returned to a solo career in 1993 with the sophisticated, soulful *Black Tie White Noise;* he recorded the album with Nile Rodgers and his now-permanent collaborator, Reeves Gabrels. The album was released on Savage (a subsidiary of RCA), and received positive reviews, but his new label went bankrupt shortly after its release, and the album disappeared. *Black Tie White Noise* was the first indication that Bowie was trying hard to resuscitate his career, as was the largely instrumental 1994 soundtrack *The Buddha of Suburbia*. In 1995, he reunited with Brian Eno for the wildly hyped, industrial-rock-tinged *Outside*. Several critics hailed the album as a comeback, and Bowie supported it with a co-headlining tour with Nine Inch Nails in order to snag a younger, alternative audience, but his gambit failed—audiences left before Bowie's performance and *Outside* disappeared. He quickly returned to the studio in 1996, recording *Earthling*, an album heavily influenced by techno and drum'n'bass. Upon its early 1997 release, *Earthling* received generally positive reviews, yet the album failed to gain an audience, and many techno purists criticized Bowie for allegedly exploiting their subculture. *hours...* followed in 1999. —*Stephen Thomas Erlewine*

**Station to Station** / 1976 / Rykodisc ◆◆◆◆

Taking the detached plastic soul of *Young Americans* to an elegant, robotic extreme, *Station to Station* is a transitional album that creates its own distinctive style. Abandoning any pretense of being a soulman, yet keeping rhythmic elements of soul, Bowie positions himself as a cold, clinical crooner and explores a variety of styles. Everything from epic ballads and disco to synthesized avant-pop is present on *Station to Station*, but what ties it together is Bowie's cocaine-induced paranoia and detached musical persona. At its heart, *Station to Station* is an avant-garde, art-rock album—most explicitly on "TVC15" and the epic sprawl of the title track, but also on the cool crooning of "Wild Is the Wind," "Word on a Wing," and the disco stylings of "Golden Years." It's not an easy album to warm to, but its epic structure and clinical sound are an impressive, individualistic achievement—as well as a style that proved enormously influential on post-punk. —*Stephen Thomas Erlewine*

☆ **Heroes** / 1977 / Rykodisc ◆◆◆◆◆

Repeating the formula of *Low*'s half-vocal/half-instrumental structure, *Heroes* develops and strengthens the sonic innovations Bowie and Eno explored on their first collaboration. The vocal songs are fuller, boasting harder rhythms and deeper layers of sound. Much of the harder-edged sound of *Heroes* is due to Robert Fripp's guitar, which provides a muscular foundation for the electronics, especially on the relatively conventional rock songs. Similarly, the instrumentals on *Heroes* are more detailed, this time showing a more explicit debt to German synth-pop and European experimental rock 'n' roll. Essentially, the difference between *Low* and *Heroes* lies in the details, but the record is equally challenging and groundbreaking. [The CD reissue includes the previously unreleased instrumental "Abdulmajid" and a remix of "Joe the Lion."] —*Stephen Thomas Erlewine*

★ **Low** / 1977 / Rykodisc ✦✦✦✦✦
Following through with the avant-garde inclinations of *Station to Station*, yet explicitly breaking with Bowie's past, *Low* is a dense, challenging album that confirmed Bowie's place at rock's cutting edge. Driven by dissonant synthesizers and electronics, *Low* is divided between brief, angular songs and atmospheric instrumentals. Throughout the record's first half, the guitars are jagged and synthesizers drone with a menacing robotic pulse, while Bowie's vocals are unnaturally layered and overdubbed. During the instrumental half, the electronics turn cool, which is a relief after the intensity of the preceding avant-pop. Half the credit for *Low*'s success goes to Brian Eno, who explored similar ambient territory on his own releases. Eno functioned as a conduit for Bowie's ideas, and in turn Bowie made the experimentalism of not only Eno, but of the German synth group Kraftwerk and the post-punk group Wire, respectable—if not quite mainstream. Though a handful of the vocal pieces on *Low* are accessible—"Sound and Vision" has a shimmering guitar hook, and "Be My Wife" subverts soul structure in a surprisingly catchy fashion—the record is defiantly experimental and dense with detail, providing a new direction for the avant-garde in rock 'n' roll. —*Stephen Thomas Erlewine*

☆ **Lodger** / 1979 / Rykodisc ✦✦✦✦✦
On the surface, *Lodger* is the most accessible of the three Berlin-era records Bowie made with Brian Eno, simply because there are no instrumentals and there are a handful of concise pop songs. Nevertheless, *Lodger* is still gnarled and twisted avant-pop; what makes it different is how it incorporates such experimental tendencies into genuine songs, something that *Low* and *Heroes* purposely avoided. "D.J.," "Look Back in Anger," and "Boys Keep Swinging" have strong melodic hooks which are subverted and strengthened by the layered, dissonant productions, while the remainder of the record is divided between similarly effective avant-pop and ambient instrumentals. *Lodger* has an edgier, minimalistic bent than its two predecessors, which makes it more accessible for rock fans, as well as giving it a more immediate, emotional impact. It might not stretch the boundaries of rock like *Low* and *Heroes*, but it arguably utilizes those ideas in a more effective fashion. —*Stephen Thomas Erlewine*

☆ **Scary Monsters (And Super Creeps)** / 1980 / Rykodisc ✦✦✦✦✦
Bowie returns to relatively conventional rock 'n' roll with *Scary Monsters*, an album that effectively acts as an encapsulation of all his '70s experiments. Reworking glam rock themes with avant-garde synth flourishes, and reversing the process, Bowie creates dense but accessible music throughout *Scary Monsters*. Though it doesn't have the vision of his other classic records, it wasn't designed to break new ground—it was created as the culmination of Bowie's experimental genre-shifting of the '70s. As a result, *Scary Monsters* is Bowie's last great album. While the music isn't far removed from the post-punk of the early '80s, it does sound fresh, hip, and contemporary, which is something Bowie lost over the course of the '80s. [Rykodisc's 1992 reissue includes re-recorded versions of "Space Oddity" and "Panic in Detroit," the Japanese single "Crystal Japan," and the British single "Alabama Song."] —*Stephen Thomas Erlewine*

**Changesbowie** / Mar. 1990 / Rykodisc ✦✦✦✦
*Changesbowie* is a CD greatest hits collection that revamps the original *Changesonebowie* by adding selections from Bowie's late '70s and early '80s albums. Consequently, it functions as a definitive single-disc introduction to David Bowie, featuring all of his major hits from "Space Oddity," "Changes," "Ziggy Stardust," "Jean Genie," and "Rebel Rebel" to "Heroes," "Ashes to Ashes," "Let's Dance," "Modern Love," and "Blue Jean." One complaint: it wasn't necessary to substitute the "Fame '90" remix for the original to hook completists, since it is inferior and was already issued as a separate single. —*Stephen Thomas Erlewine*

**Singles 1969-1993** / Nov. 16, 1993 / Rykodisc ✦✦✦✦
Taking *Changesbowie* one step further, *Singles 1969-1993* collects all of David Bowie's biggest hits while picking up such overlooked gems as "Drive-In Saturday" and "Loving the Alien." The comprehensiveness and quality of the songs make *Singles* the best Bowie compilation available. Fans will be pleased with the inclusion of the complete lyrics to all of the songs on this two-disc set. —*Stephen Thomas Erlewine*

**Earthling** / Feb. 11, 1997 / Virgin ✦✦✦
Jumping on the post-grunge industrial bandwagon with *Outside* didn't successfully rejuvenate David Bowie's credibility or sales, so he switched his allegiance to techno and jungle for the follow-up, *Earthling*. While jungle is more appropriate than industrial, the resulting music is nearly as awkward. Though he often gets the sound of jungle right, the record frequently sounds as though the beats were simply grafted on top of pre-existing songs. Never are the songs broken open by a new form; instead, they are fairly conventional Bowie songs with fancy production. Fortunately, Bowie sounds rejuvenated by this new form, and songs like "Little Wonder" and "Seven Years in Tibet" are far stronger than the bulk of *Outside*. Still, the record falls short of its goals, and it doesn't offer enough intrigue or innovations to make *Earthling* anything more than an admirable effort. —*Stephen Thomas Erlewine*

**Hours** / Oct. 5, 1999 / Virgin ✦✦
Since David Bowie spent the '90s jumping from style to style—first faux-soul by way of house, then industrial art-rock, and then electronica—it's a shock that *Hours*, his final album of the decade, is a relatively straightforward affair, devoid of any contemporary trends. Not only that, but it feels unlike anything else in his catalog. Bowie's music has always been a product of artifice, intelligence, and synthesis, expanding rock, pop, and soul with ideas and theories borrowed from literature, film, art, and contemporary music. Often, the end result has been art for art's sake, but in the best possible sense—albums that are evocative and unusual, yet visceral and immediate, even when functioning completely at a cerebral level. This was true of commercial moves as well: *Let's Dance* as it was for art-rock just as *Heroes;* both derived from a pop-art idea, but they grew in different directions. Bowie has worked in this fashion since (at least) *The Man Who Sold the World*, but *Hours* is a departure from this method. It is relaxed and natural, as if Bowie, feeling he had nothing left to prove, wrote whatever he wanted. Arriving after two labored albums—where he went out of his way to seem hip—the shift in tone is immediately apparent and quite refreshing, but *Hours'* unique character reveals itself slowly. "Thursday's Child," the album's engaging mid-tempo opener, is a good indication of what lays ahead. It feels like classic Bowie, but it recalls no specific era of his career—a career that is defined by ever-shifting eras. This same sensation follows throughout the album—it all feels familiar, but new. For the first time, Bowie has absorbed all the disparate strands of his music, from *Hunky Dory* through *Earthling*, and has written music from a relatively organic viewpoint. This doesn't mean *Hours* is a work of genius on par with his earlier masterworks; it never attempts to be anything that bold. What it does mean is that it's the first album in a new phase of Bowie's career, one where he has accepted his past and is willing to use it as a foundation for new music. That's the reason why *Hours* feels open, even organic—he's no longer self-conscious, either about living up to his past or creating a new future. It's a welcome change, and it produces some fine music—particularly on the first half of the record, which is filled with such subdued, subtly winning songs as "Thursday's Child," "Something in the Air," "Survive," and "Seven," all of which prominently feature acoustic guitars and reminiscent of *Hunky Dory* tunes. Toward the end of the album, Bowie branches into harder material, with the driving, industrial-based "The Pretty Things Are Going to Hell," and the mildly electronic-flavored "New Angels of Promise." While these aren't quite as successful as the songs on the first half of the album, they share a similar sensibility that elevates them above the also-rans on *Outside* and *Earthling*. And that's what's appealing about *Hours*—it may not be one of Bowie's classics, but it's the work of a masterful musician who has begun to enjoy his craft (again) and isn't afraid to let things develop naturally. —*Stephen Thomas Erlewine*

## The Bowling Green (Micko Westmorland)

*Producer / Drill'N'Bass, Experimental Jungle, Electronica, Jungle/Drum'N'Bass*

Micko Westmorland was one of the only artists associated with the English drill'n'bass scene to rise above the level of fleeting phase. Combining elements of electro, jungle, and downtempo/trip-hop in odd, fidgety, often humorous juxtapositions, Westmorland contributed a track to erstwhile techno/electronica label Rising High's *Further Self-Evident Truths* compilation series before the label folded in 1996. Signing with eclectic label Blue

Planet, the *Mingle* and *Chaise Lounge* EPs appeared that year, followed by an LP, *One Pound Note*, in 1997. Notably, *One Pound Note* was among a string of UK post-techno licensings (also including releases by Squarepusher and Autechre) by Trent Reznor's Nothing label. —*Sean Cooper*

● **Mingle [EP]** / 1996 / Blue Planet ✦✦✦
Micko Westmorland debuted his Bowling Green project on Rising High's *Further Self-Evident Truths Vol. 3* label compilation. Here Westmorland takes his unique blend of weirded out electro-jazz to even more outbound, jungle-inflected heights. While the beats dwell in old-school DMX/Lind territory (read: not much break-sampling), Westmorland's Cubase trickery mashes 'em up large—with a result not far from edgier Atom Heart and Luke "Plug" Vibert. —*Sean Cooper*

**One Pound Note** / Jun. 22, 1998 / Warp/Nothing ✦✦✦

### Boymerang (Graham Sutton)
*Producer / Experimental Jungle, Electronica, Jungle/Drum'N'Bass, Club/Dance*

Boymerang is the drum'n'bass aegis of London-based producer Graham Sutton, better known as one-half of celebrated early-'90s industrial pop group Bark Psychosis. Covering similar territory as dark ambient/electronic dance groups such as Coil and Front 242, Bark Psychosis released only one album and a pair of singles for Virgin before splitting in 1994, due to intense internal conflict. Bark Psychosis' last gig "together" (it was actually only Sutton) took place at the electronic Music Festival in Russia, alongside Seefeel, Autechre, Ultramarine, and Aphex Twin—a lineup that reflected Sutton's new primary musical interest: experimental dance music. Upon his return to the UK, Sutton immersed himself in the drum'n'bass scene, learning the ropes from artists such as Ed Rush, Trace, Fabio, Luke Vibert, Goldie, and Doc Scott before releasing a self-titled EP on 4AD-defect Tony Morley's experimental Leaf label. A mixture of tight jungle programming and frantic, armchair-oriented experimentation, the single accomplished loads for Sutton's rep (to say nothing of Leaf's). Following an additional EP for Leaf and a remix of 2Player's "Extreme Possibilities" for Ninja Tune (next to Vibert in his Wagon Christ guise), Sutton contributed material to a pair of compilations for Jon Tye's Lo Recordings and inked a non-exlusive contract with EMI. Remixes for Collapsed Lung and Sufi followed, as well as an EP for Grooverider's Prototype label, and a track on the Volume compilation, *Breakbeat Science*. His debut full-length *Balance of the Force* appeared on Royal/EMI in May 1997. —*Sean Cooper*

**Still [Single]** / Dec. 23, 1996 / Prototype ✦✦✦
*Still*'s two tracks of relatively straightforward drum'n'bass (particularly by Boymerang standards), lie somewhere between the sparse efficiency of hardstep and the starker, more moody airs of darkside. As with previous material, both tracks show an affectation for hand-crafted breaks and the incorporation of drum machine sounds; elements of electro and techno are obtained here as well. Sutton's skills on bass are put to particularly effective use on the title track. —*Sean Cooper*

**Soul Beat Runna [Single]** / 1997 / Regal ✦✦✦✦
Less bleak and stolid than his Prototype single "Still," or the Reese-laden "Technology" remix, "Soul Beat Runna" places Boymerang on the Leaf tip again, this time with stark, clean machine breaks laid over with a less nasty brand of aqueous atmospheres. Innovative to be sure, but without succumbing to the lingering, post-1996 fever of darkness. —*Sean Cooper*

● **Balance of the Force** / May 12, 1997 / Regal ✦✦✦✦
Graham Sutton let his Boymerang aegis run rampant over the contemporary drum'n'bass map (at time of release, anyway), presenting a cross-section of substyle genre pieces (a diva track, a few techsteppers, a dolphin tune, etc.) as his debut full release. The production is top-notch and a few of the tracks are dynamite, but the album suffers for its lack of focus, sounding like a poorly organized compilation trying to please the public—and succeeding in pleasing no one. As with previous releases and remix work, however, Sutton shines with his techstep abilities. The cachet of tracks utilizing choppy machine-bred breaks and gleaming basslines are the highlights here. —*Sean Cooper*

### The Brand New Heavies
f. 1985, London, England
*Group / Club/Dance, Acid Jazz, Urban, House, Hip-Hop*

Pioneers of the London acid-jazz scene, the Brand New Heavies translated their love of '70s funk grooves into a sophisticated sound that carried the torch for classic soul in an era dominated by hip-hop. Formed in 1985 by drummer/keyboardist Jan Kincaid, guitarist Simon Bartholomew, and bassist/keyboardist Andrew Levy—longtime school friends from the London suburb of Ealing—the Brand New Heavies was originally an instrumental unit inspired by the James Brown and Meters records heard while clubbing the "rare groove" scene in vogue at the time. The trio soon began recording their own music, gaining enormous exposure when their demo tracks were spun at the influential Cat in the Hat Club.

Eventually adding a brass section, the Brand New Heavies built a cult following throughout the London club circuit, surviving the shift which saw the rare groove scene fade in the wake of acid house. After an earlier recording deal with Cooltempo which yielded the single "Got to Give," the Heavies—now including vocalist Jay Ella Ruth—signed with the fledgling indie label Acid Jazz. Recorded on a budget of just £8000, the group's self-titled LP appeared in 1990 to strong critical acclaim, resulting in a licensing deal with the American company Delicious Vinyl. With Ruth out of the band, Delicious Vinyl hand-picked N'dea Davenport as her successor, insisting the Heavies re-record tracks from their debut for their first US effort—also an eponymous release which appeared in 1992.

After scoring at home with "Dream Come True" and "Stay This Way," the single "Never Stop" soon landed on the American R&B charts. The Heavies became the first British group to accomplish such a feat with a debut single (since Soul II Soul several years earlier, at least). A subsequent New York performance augmented by rappers Q-Tip (A Tribe Called Quest) and MC Serch (3rd Bass), inspired the group to begin absorbing hip-hop, and that summer they cut *Heavy Rhyme Experience: Vol 1*—an album including guest appearances by rappers including Main Source, Gang Starr, Grand Puba, and the Pharcyde. 1994's *Brother Sister*, which went platinum in Britain, was Davenport's last recording with the Heavies before beginning a solo career; she was replaced by singer Siedah Garrett in time for 1997's *Shelter*. Two years later the group reappeared with a British best-of album entitled *Trunk Funk: The Best of the Brand New Heavies*; the title was recycled the following year for an American compilation, *Trunk Funk Classics 1991-2000*, which featured a new song recorded with Davenport. —*Jason Ankeny*

● **The Brand New Heavies** / 1991 / Delicious Vinyl ✦✦✦✦
Many of the artists who were part of Britain's soul scene of the late-'80s/early-'90s—including Soul II Soul, Lisa Stansfield, and Caron Wheeler—took a high-tech, neo-soul approach, combining '70s-influenced R&B and disco with elements of hip-hop. The equally impressive Brand New Heavies, however, used technology sparingly, stressed the use of "real instruments," and were unapologetically retro and '70s-sounding. Drawing on such influences as the Average White Band and Tower of Power, the Heavies triumphed by sticking with the classic R&B approach they clearly love the most. Here, the band has a jewel of a singer in N'Dea Davenport, who is characteristically expressive on "Dream Come True" and "Stay This Way." Real horns—not synthesizers made to sound like horns—enrich those gems as well as the sweaty vocal funk of "People Get Ready," "Put the Funk Back in It." and the jazz-influenced instrumental "BNH." While this fine album enjoyed cult hit status, it was sadly ignored by American "urban contemporary" radio. —*Alex Henderson*

**Heavy Rhyme Experience, Vol. 1** / Aug. 3, 1992 / Delicious Vinyl ✦✦✦✦
Between their debut and full-fledged second album, Brand New Heavies released an album of collaborations with some of the brightest stars in hip-hop, such as Gang Starr, Grand Puba, and Main Source. *Heavy Rhyme Experience: Vol. 1* actually works better than their debut, since the rappers bring a gritty street credibility to the group's lush R&B. At its best, the album stands as a splendid fusion of jazz, soul, and hip-hop. —*Stephen Thomas Erlewine*

**Brother Sister** / Mar. 22, 1994 / Delicious Vinyl ✦✦✦
This album finds the BNH heading back to the groove-driven, horn-splashed, hand-clapping funk of their debut album, with N'Dea Davenport stepping back into her role as diva/lead vocalist. Following the string of distinguished rappers who made BNH's sophomore album a brave, if not wholly successful, attempt to infuse rap with the energy of live instruments, Davenport de-

livers the consistency missing from that effort. Repeated listens show this album to be catchier than it initially seems (as long as one avoids "Fake," one of the most irritating songs in a while); when the BNH really lock into a groove, as they do on "Keep Together" (title track), and the instrumental "Snake Hips," they indeed put the funk back in it. —*Peter Stepek*

**Excursions . . . Remixes and Rare Grooves** / 1995 / Delicious Vinyl/Capitol ♦♦

Since the Brand New Heavies were always more club-centric than their contemporaries, it shouldn't come as a surprise that their remix effort, *Excursions: Remixes & Rare Grooves* is entertaining. Nevertheless, it is a bit of a surprise that it's as cohesive as it is, especially considering that it contains a selection of remixes, rare tracks, and new songs. It still pales somewhat to the clearly focused studio efforts, but there are enough gems to make it necessary for hardcore Heavies fans. —*Stephen Thomas Erlewine*

**Shelter** / May 13, 1997 / Delicious Vinyl ♦♦♦

By the time the Brand New Heavies released *Shelter* in 1997, urban R&B was shifting toward the more organic grooves that they helped pioneer in the early '90s. Although the Heavies were into acid-jazz as well, they smoothed over many of the experimental elements of their music in the mid-'90s, leaving behind a seductive, earthy, and jazzy variation of urban soul. This provided the foundation for *Shelter*, their first album featuring Siedah Garrett as lead singer. Garrett's smooth voice helps push the band toward more conventional territory, yet their songwriting is stronger than most of the contemporaries, and their sound is funkier and more convincing. While there are no standout singles on *Shelter*, it's a uniformly engaging listen, illustrating that the Brand New Heavies are one of the great underrated urban R&B bands of the '90s. —*Leo Stanley*

## Breakbeat Era

f. 1998, Bristol, England
*Group / Electronica, Jungle/Drum'N'Bass, Club/Dance*

The Bristol, England-based drum'n'bass project Breakbeat Era was spearheaded by acclaimed producer Roni Size in tandem with DJ Die (also Size's collaborator in Reprazent) and singer Leonie Laws. Their debut LP Ultra-Obscene was released in 1999. —*Jason Ankeny*

● **Ultra-Obscene** / Aug. 30, 1999 / Interscope ♦♦♦♦

Combining the hyperkinetic breakbeats and chilly electronic textures of drum'n'bass with actual song structures and interesting lyrics isn't a new idea anymore—bands like Lamb, Baxter, and Solar Twins have done the same, and Everything But the Girl used drum'n'bass as an escape from their downward spiral into wispy jazz-pop hell. But Breakbeat Era (singer Leonie Laws, DJ Die, and drum'n'bass godfather Roni Size) differs from all of these in that this group comes to rock from drum'n'bass, not the other way around. They also have little time for Baxter's jazz trumpet, the Solar Twins' gauzy pop songs, and EBTG's melodic hooks. Leonie Laws is not a tuneless singer by any means, but her approach is more punk than pop. The instrumental accompaniment is directly borrowed from the "darkcore" subgenre of drum'n'bass, a style typified by minor chords and creepy, robotic basslines. Song titles like "Rancid," "Our Disease," and "Anti-Everything"—all of which sound as though they were nicked from first-wave punk albums—give you an idea of what to expect. Highlights: "Bullitproof," and the brief but super-funky "Max." —*Rick Anderson*

## Danny Breaks (Daniel Whidett)

*Producer / Jungle/Drum'N'Bass, Hardcore Techno, Club/Dance*

Bootstrap producer Danny Breaks is one of few artists from the rave scene's early hardcore days to have successfully followed the style into full-blown jungle, while remaining both innovative and widely respected. Breaks was one of the first big names on former hardcore (and current cornerstone) jungle imprint Suburban Base's roster—recording dancefloor anthems and playlist toppers such as "High Up" (a Top 40 tune), "Peace and Loveism," and "Style Warz" as Sonz of a Loop Da Loop Era. His full-length debut under that name, *Flowers in My Garden* was one of the first long-players in the genre. His roots in hip-hop and turntable tricknology as both a DJ and producer were instrumental in bridging the gaps between post-rave and happy hardcore's scrubbed suburban face and the more streetlevel, working class grit of darkside and hardstep. A suburbanite (residing in Southend), Breaks connected up with Suburban Base in 1991 when he began working at Boogie Times Records (Sub Base is the store's in-house label). "High Up" was the product of Breaks' first attempt at the mixing desk, and his rapid ascent to the recording studio (as well as the popularity of his tunes) persuaded the label to make room on the pressing schedule for all of his projects. Taking a break and working in A&R for Sub Base, Breaks returned in 1995 with his own label, Droppin' Science, releasing periodic volumes of frantic, heavily percussive jungle similar to artists such as Dillinja and Bristol stepper Roni Size. His rep rose, and his label quickly became associated with the front line of nuts'n'bolts hardstep. Droppin' Science's release schedule slowed in 1996 as Breaks played the runaround game with a few major labels (he eventually decided to remain with the underground, signing with Link/Global Communication's Universal Language imprint). Breaks returned to production in early 1997 with "You Ain't Down" (his Universal debut), and the tenth Droppin' Science release, "The Bear/Crime '96." —*Sean Cooper*

**You Ain't Down [Single]** / Sep. 16, 1996 / Universal Language ♦♦♦

This single is a somewhat novel breakbeat tool roughly playable on any speed; tight, oddly treated drums, interspersed with housey filigrees and dirty, artfully clumsy scratching. The emphasis is obviously on drums, and Breaks sporadically skews the ear with odd meters and swing'n'switch beat manipulation. A curiosity well worth investigating. —*Sean Cooper*

● **The Bear/Crime '96 [Single]** / Jan. 20, 1997 / Droppin' Science ♦♦♦♦

Danny Breaks is in top form for his tenth release on his Droppin' Science label. He splits time between dense, snapping techstep breaks on "The Bear" and a funk-soaked, bass-popping snare-feast on "Crime '96." Typical of Breaks' merit as a producer, both tracks are clearly drawn from a range of styles (hardstep, jazzstep, darkside, tech) while at once building and expanding on each with board-work and production trickery recognizably his own (Breaks' drum flanges and snare clusters are signatures). —*Sean Cooper*

**Conscience [Single]** / Jun. 2, 1997 / Droppin' Science ♦♦♦

After Droppin' Science whiz kid Dylan's maniac rewind guarantor, "Virus," Danny Breaks' "Conscience" is, understandably, a bit more conservative—opting for a pair of no-nonsense, well-produced, tech-leaning hardstep tracks over an argument with Dylan's darkcore genius. The subtle, eerie guitar flourishes of "Solar Funk" recalls Photek's "Hidden Camera," while the single's star, "Conscience," is a nasty shake-up of pitched snares, fragmented breaks, and tweaked, bubbling bass squelches. —*Sean Cooper*

## Aril Brikha

b. 1977, Teheran, Iran
*Producer / Minimal Techno, Detroit Techno, Ambient Techno, Techno*

Born in Iran, Aril Brikha is a Swedish producer who records for a Detroit label. Given such far-flung origins, he's naturally able to bring together fans of similarly disparate styles: jazzy house, minimalist Detroit techno, and deeper experimental listening music. Born in Teheran, Brikha moved to Sweden at the age of three. After releasing material on the Swedish labels Plump, Dunkla, and Placktown Sounds, he sent a demo tape to Detroit's Transmat Records (owned by techno legend Derrick May). In mid-1998, Brikha released *The Art of Vengeance* EP on Fragile, a subsidiary of Transmat. The EP gained praise in Detroit circles, and earned Brikha a privileged spot on the rejuvenated Transmat's compilation *Time: Space*. His debut album, 1999's *Deeparture in Time*, was Transmat's first major full-length by a single artist. —*John Bush*

**Art of Vengeance [EP]** / Jun. 15, 1998 / Fragile ♦♦♦

● **Deeparture in Time** / Aug. 10, 1999 / Transmat ♦♦♦♦

There is a lulling calm that makes the techno sounds of Aril Brikha's debut album special. While many artists such as I-F and Luke Slater have released excellent full-length techno albums drawing from the electro sounds of the '80s, Brikha's version of electro doesn't rely on body-rocking beats or nostalgia to be effective. The repetitive drum programming that flows through each of the 11 tracks on *Deeparture in Time* is not innovative, but what makes the album so impressive is Brikha's use of the sounds of the synthesizer to transcend generic electro. Instead of using synthesizer sounds and melodies to complement his beats and rhythms, Brikha's synthesizer exists prominently in each of his tracks, often overshadowing the percussive beats with cosmic sounds. Listening closely, Brikha's formula proves to be rather simple: By using the synthesizer to complicate (and further push) the rhythms of his drum programming, the resultant synergy is more striking than the sum of its two parts. On tracks such as "On and On" and "Setting Sun," Brikha slowly fades in, creating a minimal rhythm from which he builds. Usually two or three minutes in, the track reaches its peak intensity when the multiple elements form a cohesive, yet complex whole. From there the track slowly disassembles until it concludes with a minimal synthesizer or percussive rhythm. These musical puzzles evoke differing moods, depending upon varying degrees of percussion and the tempos. For example, "Groove La Chord" is capable of igniting a dancefloor, while tracks such as "Deeparture in Time" function better as contemplative listening music. —*Jason Stanley Birchmeier*

## Thomas Brinkmann

*Producer / Minimal Techno, Experimental Dub, Experimental Techno*
Alongside Mike Ink, the Basic Channel collective, and Pole, Thomas Brinkmann is one of the leaders in the ongoing German-born study of isolationist dub-inspired techno. Though he's been famed for productions on his own Max, Ernst, and Suppose labels, Brinkmann gained a name in the experimental and techno community for his full-length remixes (or as he terms them, "variations") of material by Richie Hawtin and Mike Ink. The variations were made possible by playback of the original records on a turntable of Brinkmann's own design, which included two tone arms with separate left and right channel outputs.

Brinkmann experimented with carved-groove records since the '80s. He studied art at the Düsseldorf Academy but was reportedly expelled for his philosophies. Influenced by Ryuichi Sakamoto, Steve Reich, Panasonic, and Dan Bell, it was Mike Ink's *Studio 1* singles series that inspired him to begin recording seriously. Brinkmann modified an existing turntable by adding an additional tone arm (one for each output channel, left and right), and slowing down the material to record his own variations. When Ink heard them, he released two EPs of the material on his Profan label (later collected on one CD).

Brinkmann debuted his own productions with the founding of the Ernst label, which released several singles of sharply defined minimalist dub-techno (each using female names for titles) in keeping with the work of Berlin's Basic Channel collective and BC-associate Stefan Betke (aka Pole). Brinkmann also launched two other labels—Max (with male names for titles) and Suppose, which featured full-length releases by Totes Rennen and Weisse Nacht (under the alias "Ester" Brinkmann) Brinkmann's next step involved reworking the dozen 12" singles originally released during 1996 by Plastikman's Richie Hawtin in a series called *Concept*. After traveling from Cologne to Hawtin's base in Canada, Brinkmann thrilled Hawtin with the results. By early 1998, a CD of Brinkmann's *Concept* variations was released on Hawtin's M_nus label. A year later, Brinkmann contributed a volume in the *20' to 2000* series, and inaugurated his own *Ernst* series with "Anna/Beate." —*John Bush*

Studio 1—Variationen / 1997 / Profan ✦✦✦✦
*Studio 1—Variationen* includes 13 tracks of Mike Ink reworkings, sublime electro-dub reminiscent of Panasonic's clips and clicks, as well as the original source recording, Ink's *Studio 1* series. True, the echoed phasing (almost completely separated between left and right channels) can be rather disorienting on first listen—sounding more like the equivalent of a photographic negative than a real picture of a straightahead techno track. The results tend to gel after several listens, as the lag-time of all the repeated effects begins to make some sort of twisted sense. —*John Bush*

• Concept 1 96:VR / 1998 / M_nus ✦✦✦✦
Not quite as jarring on first listen as the *Studio 1* variations, Thomas Brinkmann's second remix album sees him placing tone arms to selected tracks from Richie Hawtin's *Concept* series of singles. The results retain much of Hawtin's originals—the bass drones, muffled explosions, and assorted clicks—but Brinkmann treats them to his trademark phase-and-delay methods. Surface noise revealed by Brinkmann's turntable contributes to the full effect as well. —*John Bush*

Weisse Náchte / Mar. 15, 1999 / Suppose ✦✦✦
Released under his Ester Brinkmann guise, *Weisse Náchte* is an album of avant-electro and downtempo jazz sampling, several tracks of which have recitations by Romanian philosopher E.M. Cioran. There are only a few nods to the acid-dub trademarks of Brinkmann's "Variations" material. —*John Bush*

Ernst 1: Anna/Beate [Single] / 2000 / Ernst ✦✦✦
The first record of this 13-part series—moving all the way through the alphabet—finds the prolific Cologne artist laying down an immensely minimal style of techno characterized by intricate symmetry and light sensation. The rather fascinating array of percussive sounds brought together to form the rhythm tracks of these songs causes the listener to marvel at Brinkmann's mathematical precision. Similarly, a strong sense of ease makes this surprisingly appealing to the ears and not just the senses. Brinkmann doesn't use the harsh style of Roland 909-flavored drum kicks so prevalent in late '90s techno but rather uses feathery beats that sound similar to a group of bouncing rubber balls. Each song also interweaves a certain sound—sometimes a clang, sometimes a bang—that adds a hint of color and personality to these percussive-heavy songs. Don't think of this as ordinary Cologne techno, but rather similar in spirit to Richie Hawtin's *Concept* records. As a singular record exploring a sole idea, this Ernst release should satisfy. Brinkmann's churning out these records may work for DJs, especially with locked grooves and similar motifs, but the more critical home listener may get a bit turned off by the sense of assembly line-like production. —*Jason Birchmeier*

## Broadcast

f. 1995, Birmingham, England
*Group / Ambient Pop, Electronica, Dream Pop, Post-Rock/Experimental, Alternative Pop/Rock*
Space-age pop collagists Broadcast formed in Birmingham, England in 1995. Comprised of vocalist Trish Keenan, guitarist Tim Felton, bassist James Cargill, keyboardist Roj Stevens, and drummer Steve Perkins, the quintet came together from a shared affection for the psychedelic cult band the United States of America—a primary influence on their subsequent work as a group. Debuting in 1996 with the Wurlitzer Jukebox label single "Accidentals," Broadcast immediately won favorable comparisons to Stereolab for their sample-heavy, analogue synth-driven sound; the comparisons continued when they signed to Stereolab's Duophonic Super 45s imprint for their next effort, "Living Room." After the icily atmospheric *Book Lovers* EP, the group moved to Warp Records to release 1997's *Work and Non-Work*, a compilation of their existing singles tracks. The much-anticipated full-length *The Noise Made by People* finally appeared in early 2000, and the *Extended Play Two* EP was issued that fall. —*Jason Ankeny*

• Work & Non-Work / Jun. 9, 1997 / Drag City ✦✦✦✦
Warp's first rock/pop signing since Pulp (yup, Pulp) were Stereolab-soundalikes Broadcast, whose early singles for Wurlitzer Jukebox and the 'Lab's own Duophonic label attracted much attention for their sing-songy fusions of Tortoise-y groovebox meandering and clean-room electronica. *Work and Non Work*, the group's Warp debut, is really nothing more than a compilation of those singles ("Accidentals," "Living Room," and *The Book Lovers EP*, to be exact). As a mini-LP for the new initiate, it serves as a handy one-stop updater, but since most of it appeared elsewhere (within the previous six months) and lacks previously unavailable material, it proves unworthy to fans of any duration. —*Sean Cooper*

The Noise Made By People / Apr. 18, 2000 / Tommy Boy ✦✦✦✦
After being mired in the studio for nearly three years, Broadcast returns with their first proper full-length album *The Noise Made By People*. A collection of more shimmering, weightless pop that is nostalgic for yesterday's visions of the future, it remains on the cutting edge of contemporary music. Where their early singles (collected on 1997's *Work and Non-Work*) painted small, quaint portraits of retro-futurism, *The Noise Made By People* delivers their sound in widescreen, filmic grandeur. Richly layered yet airy pieces (like the album bookends "Long Was the Year" and "Dead the Long Year") seamlessly blend symphonic, electronic, and pop elements into smoky, evocative epics, while synth-based interludes such as "Minus One" and "The Tower of Our Tuning" present Broadcast's more detached, scientific side. Likewise, Trish Keenan's air-conditioned vocals often suggest a robotized Sandie Shaw or Cilla Black, but her humanity peeks out on "Come on Let's Go" and "Papercuts." "Echo's Answer" and "Until Then" are two other highlights of the album—which, despite all of its chilly unearthliness, is a noise made by (very talented) people. —*Heather Phares*

## Susanne Brokesch

**b.** Austria
*Producer / Electronica, Ambient Techno*

Austrian ambient/electronica composer Susanne Brokesch is one of a small-but-growing contingency of female producers releasing innovative experimental music in an unfortunately predominantly male field. Born in Austria and currently residing in Vienna, Brokesch has recorded as Sil, Sil Electronics, and under her own name for such labels as Cheap, Sahko, Tension, and Disko B. She has contributed tracks to a number of Austrian and European experimental music compilations, including *Rancho Relaxo All-Stars* (which also featured Cheap's Patrick Pulsinger and Erdam Tunakan). Although she's never studied music formally, Brokesch's compositions are remarkable for their emphasis on acoustic instrumental sources such as guitars and percussion, which she fuses with electronically generated soundscapes and minimal machine rhythms. Her debut full-length release, *Sharing the Sunhat*, appeared on the typically more dance-oriented Disko B label in 1997, and also showcased her skills as a visual artist (the album's stunning cover and sleeve art are Brokesch's creation). Brokesch also DJs and has supplemented her music career with employment ranging from museum guard to garbage dump attendant. — *Sean Cooper*

- **Sharing the Sunhat** / Apr. 14, 1997 / Disko B ♦♦♦♦

A curious collection of ambient electronics, not least because it appeared on the normally dance-centric Disko B label. Rumored to be the work of the Sil Electronics gang, *Sharing the Sunhat* is closer to the work of Anthony Manning, Panasonic's Mika Vainio, or Australian soundtrack producer Paul Schutze, sporting sprawling environmental soundscapes that are less dark than suggestive, and just a wee bit odd. Switching between angular, furrowed techno, sparse, off-kilter electro, and hissing electronic ambience, *Sunhat* even throws in a shifty lounge-jazz tune, all the while managing an almost narrative coherence that might benefit from filmic accompaniment. Barring that, the album's rich, gorgeous artwork should do fine. — *Sean Cooper*

## Michael Brook

**b.** Toronto, Canada
*Guitar, Bass, Composer, Arranger / Experimental Ambient, Experimental, Techno-Tribal, Electronic, Progressive Bluegrass*

The innovative guitarist and producer Michael Brook was born and raised in Toronto. While studying electronic music and the arts at the University of Toronto, he met trumpeter Jon Hassell, with whom he later toured. Through Hassell, Brook also was introduced to minimalist composer LaMonte Young, under whom he studied Indian music. Working as the house engineer at producer Daniel Lanois' famed Grant Avenue recording studio for a while led to a tenure playing guitar with the Canadian pop band Martha and the Muffins during the late '70s. At the same time, Brook also met Brian Eno, guesting on the 1980 Eno/Hassell collaboration *Possible Musics*. In 1983, he played on Harold Budd's *Magic Realism*.

In 1985 Brook made his solo debut with *Hybrid*, an influential ethno-ambient work recorded with Eno that discovered the middle ground between Western and Indian musical aesthetics and established his unique, heavily-processed "infinite guitar" sound. He spent much of the remaining decade working with Eno, helping create video sculptures and sound installations across the globe. He also became a sought-after producer, helming records for such diverse talents as Roger Eno, Pieter Nooten, Mary Margaret O'Hara, Balloon, and the Pogues. In 1990, Brook returned to world music, producing Youssou N'Dour's acclaimed *Set;* more importantly, he began a continuing collaboration with Pakistani qawaali singer Nusrat Fateh Ali Khan with the seminal *Mustt Mustt*, a fusion of Western ambient and pop sounds with the sacred spiritual music of the East.

After producing *Khaled*, a 1991 project for the Algerian rai vocalist Cheb Khaled, Brook returned to the studio to record his first solo effort in seven years, 1992's stellar *Cobalt Blue*. A rare concert performance given at a party celebrating the album's release was subsequently issued as the limited-edition *Live at the Aquarium*. A pair of projects with the Indian mandolin wizard U. Srinvas, 1994's *Rama Sreemrama*, and the next year's *Dream* followed. In 1996, Brook reunited with Ali Khan for *Night Song*, trailed by work on the score for the Kevin Spacey-directed crime noir *Albino Alligator*. — *Jason Ankeny*

- **Cobalt Blue** / Jul. 1987 / 4AD ♦♦♦♦

Recorded in collaboration with luminaries including Brian Eno and Daniel Lanois, *Cobalt Blue* possesses a depth and complexity which standard ambient recordings lack. Much more than a mere showcase for the technical wizardry of Michael Brook's signature "infinite guitar" sound, the album absorbs a vast range of influences spanning from Middle Eastern rhythms to Spaghetti Western soundtracks, *Cobalt Blue* forges a series of shimmering dreamscapes as provocative as they are evocative. — *Jason Ankeny*

**Live at the Aquarium: London Zoo 21 May 1992** / May 1992 / 4AD ♦♦♦♦

Having an album release party in the London Zoo's Aquarium, where the emphasis would no doubt be on stillness, hush, and the haunting beauty of the deep, suits most 4AD label releases. Given that Brook is known for his mysterious, spare guitar work makes this recording of his solo concert at the aquarium upon the release of *Cobalt Blue* all that more appropriate. Reproducing much of the content of that album (but in a different running order), *Aquarium* consists solely of Brook, his guitar, and preset synth/rhythm patterns. The result is quite fascinating. Whether the listener thinks that the more stripped-down sound of the songs here works better or prefers the generally lusher textures of the studio release, is ultimately be up to individual judgment. Beyond question is the skill Brook uses on his instrument, which thankfully, never transforms into pointless showing off. Those accustomed to his "infinite guitar" sounds (thanks to the likes of U2) might well be surprised at the understated serenity of the performance. Even the most specifically Edge-sounding number, "Ultramarine," sounds more like a calm run-through of one of the Irish musician's pieces instead of a full-on rock-out. The medley of "After Image/Urbana" is an excellent all-around showcase. The first song consists of low E-bow-tinged guitar lines, relaxed and soothing all around, and the second is initially all down to soft strums and a buried rhythm loop. When the song's main melody begins, Brook's performance is at once heartwrenching and soaring, then further supplemented by the increased rhythm punch from his keyboard set-up. If one standout has to be selected, the majestic version of "Lakbossa" is the clear winner. Brook's utterly compelling work is simply jawdropping, tender, and as big as the outdoors all at once. — *Ned Raggett*

**Albino Alligator** / Feb. 11, 1997 / Warner Brothers ♦♦♦

Translating Brook's evocative guitar art into soundtrack music for a Kevin Spacey-directed neo-noir thriller might seem an unusual choice. However, his work here turns into an interesting blend of his own style, smoky late night jazz, and darker, moodier incidental guitar, interspersed with a variety of instrumental touches. One of his sharpest moves lies in the mixing of performers he brings to the effort. Besides stand-up bass and sax, the ney, udu, and srinivas guitar figure into the rotating lineup of instruments he and various collaborators tackle. Brook also plays keyboard on nearly all the tracks, as well as handling a good amount of the bass and drum programming. Given the project's origins, it's striking (if not totally surprising) that most of the pieces hold up as well on their own as do Brook's separate efforts. "Albo Gator" underscores the collaborative nature of the project, with some of Christian Forte's lines from the movie played over the gentle chime of the piece, provided in large part by Jason Lewis' tuned percussion. "Preparation" alone is worth investigating: one of Brook's serene guitar drones and gentle performances, leading into a Morricone-western melody echoing into the distance. Hints of the intense plucking and drive that he brings to many of his pieces bubble under the mix in contrast. "Arrival" starts the album and sets the tone for both film and disc wonderfully—mere hints of Brook's trademark style coming through as a four-performer setup conjures ghosts of legendary past jazz-noir scores. "Miscalculation" is a more upbeat if no less mood-setting effort, Hafez Modirzadeh's short sax tones and Lewis' quick work on tabla and tom-drum setting the tone. A fine, unexpected touch comes with the final track, a cover of the old Harold Arlen number "Ill Wind," with Jimmy Scott and Michael Stipe on vocals, and Flea on bass. — *Ned Raggett*

## Mark Broom

*Producer / Minimal Techno, Tech-House, Club/Dance, Techno*

After a long stint as one of Britain's foremost intelligent techno DJs, Mark Broom began working on production, recording an LP with Black Dog's Ed Handley and Andy Turner as Repeat. He founded several crucial labels—

Pure Plastic, Rewired, Unexplored Beats, 3 Zone, plus Ifach with Peter "Baby" Ford—and began solo recording with a lock on streamlined ambient techno, as well as the more rhythmically dextrous sound of Handley/Turner's later offshoot, Plaid.

Broom began hanging out with the trio Black Dog as early as 1990, DJing at their gigs, and by 1995, he was recording with Ed Handley and Andy Turner as Repeat. The first Repeat release, 1995's *Repeats* LP, made Broom's name as a producer and DJ. He began recording on his own with singles for GPR, Ferox, New Electronica, and Cosmic. His debut album *Angie Is a Shoplifter* appeared in 1996, alongside a wealth of material recorded under a dizzying variety of aliases—Kape I'll Miester, Sympletic, Ted Howler Rhythm Combo, Kruton, and, (again with Handley and Turner) Eco Tourist. Broom also provided remixes for Psychick Warriors Ov Gaia, Ken Ishii, and Nicolette. —*John Bush*

- **Angie Is a Shoplifter** / Oct. 7, 1996 / Pure Plastic ♦♦♦♦

*Angie Is a Shoplifter* is a straightforward look at Broom's roots in moody Detroit techno. Exploring similar ground to mates Black Dog and Stasis, as well as the abstract electro-funk of Plaid, the album includes suitable dancefloor fare such as "The Salsa," alongside tracks designed with the living room in mind. —*John Bush*

## Terry Lee Brown, Jr. (Norman Feller)

b. 1963, Darmstadt, Germany
*Producer / Jazz-House, Tech-House, Club/Dance, House*

One in a growing legion of German producers influenced by the Chicago sound, Terry Lee Brown, Jr. is the working pseudonym of Norman Feller, who produces from his base in a small town south of Frankfurt. Though many Teutons have made their careers on the sound of Detroit-influenced trance, Feller's music reveals no glimpse of its origins. His first productions appeared as Storming Norman on Influence Records, after which he connected with Tom Wax of Phuture Wax Records. Recording for Phuture Wax as Watchman, he cut two of the biggest hard house tracks of 1996, "Watchman's Theme" and "Cut the Midrange." He had already debuted his guise Terry Lee Brown, Jr. (selected simply because it sounded like the name of an American house producer) on Plastic City, and recorded as Twisted Minds, Lectric Cargo, and Wax Scientists. His debut Terry Lee Brown, Jr. album, 1996's *Brother for Real*, was followed by *Chocolate Chords* one year later. Plastic City also released *Selected Remixes* in late 1998, followed two years later with an album of remixes. —*John Bush*

**Brother for Real** / May 6, 1996 / Plastic City ♦♦♦

- **Chocolate Chords** / Oct. 20, 1997 / Plastic City ♦♦♦♦

Not as soulful as many in the Chicago house ranks, but with a warmth and richness which do the title justice, *Chocolate Chords* includes several Terry Lee Brown, Jr. stormers, intricate tech-house tracks which phase in and out—similar to Daft Punk but with more abstraction and less earthiness. Highlights include "The Music," "Chord Progression," and "Here We Go." —*John Bush*

## BT (Brian Transeau)

b. 1973, Washington, D.C.
*Producer / Progressive Trance, Progressive House, Club/Dance, House, Nu Breaks*

His concept of epic house inspired by the classical training received at an early age, Brian Transeau revitalized the British dance community in the mid-'90s and provided a point of entry for later dream-house merchants like Robert Miles, Sash!, and BBE (though Transeau had, for the most part, left the style behind by the time of its pop success during 1997-98). After his debut album appeared in late 1995 (as BT), Transeau hit the dance charts when his remix of Tori Amos' "Blue Skies" became one of the most-played American club tracks the following year. Though he attempted to leave dream-house behind on his second album *ESCM*, Transeau continued to do well with club-goers and critics in Britain as well as America.

Born and raised in Washington, D.C., Brian Transeau played piano from the age of two and began his classical training at thirteen. Even while studying string arrangement and orchestration, Transeau listened to Depeche Mode and Yes. He attended Berklee School of Music in Boston for one year, but dropped out and moved to Los Angeles. He was soon back in Washington, D.C., where he hooked up with longtime friend Ali Shirazinia's new Deep Dish production team. He had already played synthesizer on albums by Salt-N-Pepa and Tyler Collins before debuting on Deep Dish Records with two 1993 singles, "A Moment of Truth" and "Relativity."

The tracks became club hits in Britain, routinely played by super DJs like Sasha and Paul Oakenfold for their epic, symphonic qualities which worked well as a sort of climax at clubs like Cream and Ministry of Sound. Signed to Oakenfold's Perfecto Records, BT continued his success with 1995 singles like "Embracing the Future" and "Loving You More," and did remix work for Mike Oldfield, Seal, and Billie Ray Martin. His debut album *Ima* was a hit with British audiences, though Transeau's name remained largely unheard in his native land.

Transeau's 1996 remix of Tori Amos' "Blue Skies" turned his career when it became a massive club hit in America and Great Britain. By 1997, England received a wave of pop hits in the same line pioneered by Transeau. Dubbed dream-house, artists like Robert Miles and Sash! typified the approach with a wash of new-age or prog-influenced synthesizers, and a chugging beat indebted to trance. Transeau himself attempted to distance himself from the style with his 1998 album follow-up *ESCM*. *Movement in Still Life* followed in mid-2000. —*John Bush*

**Ima** / Nov. 1995 / Perfecto ♦♦♦♦

Arguably BT was in some ways late in the game by the time *Ima* came out—mainly because if there was anything like a "golden age" of uplifting/transcendent/progressive house, it happened in the early '90s rather than the latter half. However, being defiantly out of sync with the times often makes an artistic effort stand out more. While *Ima*'s clean feel, sci-fi/blissed-out song titles (like "Nocturnal Transmission" and "Embracing the Sunshine") and generally happy musings around the beat are miles away from the hip-hop/jungle/big beat styles prevailing elsewhere, it is still a fine if, at times obvious, listen. Certainly anyone interested in trance's aesthetics of beat and build will want to leap over it if they find it. One could slip most of this album on at raves and no one would bat an eye. Samples and sonics indicate an interest in West Coast artists like the Hardkiss collective, but generally BT sounds like he's content in his own world. Sometimes a bit much—the semi-whale sounds on "Embracing the Future (Embracing the Sunshine Mix)" were a cliché long before—but the vibes and other touches on that same track help it and BT out by simply following others' footsteps. The two strongest tracks are unsurprisingly the poppiest, and include vocals. "Loving You More" (included in both a dub version of the original single and a further final instrumental mix) sparkles with energy. The undeniable power of a good (if basic) vocal hook, chopped up and looped in various ways aids as well. More accessible to general listeners is his Cure-tinged collaboration with Tori Amos, "Blue Skies," included in two versions on a bonus disc shipped with initial copies. Said disc also includes a complete remix of *Ima* by Sasha. —*Ned Raggett*

- **ESCM** / Sep. 22, 1997 / Warner Brothers ♦♦♦♦

Continuing pretty thoroughly in *Ima*'s vein, *ESCM* is another collection of ambient-progressive electronic music with as much interest in new age blissouts as dancefloor action. This said, *ESCM* is stronger all around, with a more varied sense of overall rhythm dynamics than the basic build-and-release trance climaxes that were the bread and butter of *Ima*. The opening track "Firewater" illustrates this well with its initial rhythm—a shuddering, slightly distorted tribal drum stomp instead of a straight pulse. Swooping synths and ecstatic vocals mix with deep spoken-word vocals about "fire in the sky"; when the main beats kick in, it is shuffling funk that carries the track to even higher and stronger levels. Concluding with acoustic guitar and rough, soulful vocals, it makes for quite a stunning start, signaling the album's greater ambitions and success at delivering the same. While "Orbitus Teranium" sounds like a tribute to the Orb, the crisp drum machine-generated breakbeat punch of the track is much more BT's affair, spiked with sudden stops, interjections, and laser sounds. As the album continues, hints of polite (if active) drum'n'bass influences and other recent beat touches crop up even as the more familiar techno beats kick in, while quirky, abrupt synth stabs lend a slightly retro air to the proceedings. In this vein, the most retro and successful track is "Lullaby for Gaia," with a high bassline clearly cloning Peter Hook's groundbreaking work for Joy Division and New Order. Jan Johnston's lovely, ethereal vocals, sounding a touch like a very polite Liz Fraser (of the Cocteau Twins) adds the finishing touch to a perfect number. Not everything works, admittedly—"Solar

Plexus," an attempt at semi-industrial rock, has nothing on, say, Prodigy. —*Ned Raggett*

**Movement in Still Life** / Jun. 6, 2000 / Nettwerk ♦♦♦♦
In a turn from his arena-sized, progressive-house origins, Brian Transeau diversifies on his third album. With an inspired cast of co-producers and guest vocalists, *Movement in Still Life* takes on electro-funk and breakbeat techno—with plenty of room for nods to the kind of epic trance that wrote his name on dancefloors all over the world. Three of the biggest names in late-'90s trance (Sasha, Paul Van Dyk, and Hybrid) help out here, and Transeau moves further afield with help from breakbeat maestros Adam Freeland and Kevin Beber on "Hip Hop Phenomenon." Drum'n'bass superstar-in-waiting DJ Rap, and former Opus III vocalist Kirsty Hawkshaw also lend their talents to the album, but the best moments here are pure Transeau. The majestic atmosphere of "Mercury and Solace" and "Godspeed" prove that Transeau can reach as far as he likes for inspiration without sacrificing the sound that made him one of the most noted dance producers in the world. —*John Bush*

## Buckethead

*Guitar / Progressive Metal, Guitar Virtuoso, Funk Metal, Experimental, Heavy Metal, Prog-Rock/Art Rock, Fusion*

Buckethead is one of the most bizarre and enigmatic figures in American underground and experimental music since Parliament-Funkadelic birthed their bevy of cosmic characters in the mid-'70s. An accomplished multi-instrumentalist best known for his virtuosic command of the electric guitar, Buckethead is one of the instrument's most recognizable contemporary innovators. His rapid-fire riffing, near-robotic fretwork, and idiosyncratic lead lines combine elements of Yngwie Malmsteen, Adrian Belew, Slayer's Kerry King, P-Funk's Eddie Hazel, and avant-improv artist John Zorn's Scud-attack sax abuse. His first group, the San Francisco-based metal-funk combine the Deli Creeps, was a regional success, but disbanded before releasing anything. Buckethead's solo career has been more productive, thanks mostly to the motivation of Zorn and Bill Laswell, the latter with whom Buckethead has also recorded and toured (in Praxis). Laswell has also produced a number of Buckethead's solo albums (including *Dreamatorium* and *Day of the Robot*), and has included him on more than a dozen one-off recordings with the likes of Hakim Bey, Bootsy Collins, Anton Fier, Jonas Hellborg, and Bernie Worrell. In addition to releases including 1998's *Colma*, Buckethead also contributed soundtrack material to such films as *Last Action Hero* and *Street Fighter*, returning in 1999 with *Monsters and Robots*. —*Sean Cooper*

**Bucketheadland** / 1992 / Avant ♦♦♦
A two-CD set that probably could have been scaled to one, *Bucketheadland* is a goofy concept album—plotting a bizarre narrative incorporating Japanese robot shows, theme parks, epic battles, Willy Wonka, Buckethead's parents, and lots and lots of toys. Released in Japan on John Zorn's Avant imprint, the album freely mixes arena rock, speed metal, dirty funk, and aimless noodling, and is jam-packed with obscure references that probably make sense only to their author. The second disc is mainly comprised of throwaway techno reworkings of tracks from the first. —*Sean Cooper*

**Giant Robot** / 1994 / Sony Japan ♦♦
A Japan-only rehash of much of the material from *Bucketheadland*, *Giant Robot* is further marred by bad production and the presence of nameless studio musicians backing Buckethead's manic guitar solos, which remain the album's only high point. —*Sean Cooper*

● **Day of the Robot** / Apr. 30, 1996 / Subharmonic ♦♦♦♦
The most consistent and coherent-sounding of Buckethead's releases to date (two qualities usually absent from his earlier works) *Day of the Robot* is most often referred to as his "jungle album" (it features rhythm tracks by UK beat scientist DJ Ninj). The hyperspeed breaks are actually the least interesting aspect of the album, which is notable instead for its steady and inspired chaos-by-design integration of diverse elements (treated guitars, keyboards and pianos, looping bass, etc.)—mainly credited to Laswell's excellent production. —*Sean Cooper*

**Colma** / Mar. 24, 1998 / CyberOctave ♦♦♦
For a guy who takes his sartorial cues from teenage horror flicks (he plays onstage wearing a weird manipulation of a hockey mask), Buckethead sure does make pretty music. It was not always thus—his work with Praxis, for example, has often been somewhat challenging. But on this solo project, on which he plays guitar and bass and is helped out by drummer Brain, the material is surprisingly pleasant, bordering at times on the banal. Titles like "Hills of Eternity" and "Wishing Well" are something of a giveaway—though Brain's beats are fairly funky (and DJ Disc throws in a bit of far-off turntable scratching on a few tracks), these compositions are mostly pretty contemplative, occupying a space just one step away from new age. This isn't necessarily a bad thing, but there are a couple of problems—namely, Buckethead is a lousy bass player. Like many guitarists, he seems to think that playing bass is simply a matter of hitting the root of the chord on the downbeat of the measure. A professional bassist could have contributed enormously to the proceedings (as Bill Laswell does in his guest turn on "Machete"). Another problem is the unimaginative production—which is overly soft and sweet. That said, "Big Sur Moon" is a cool solo guitar piece, and "Machete" really does cook. The rest is merely pleasant. —*Rick Anderson*

**Monsters & Robots** / Apr. 20, 1999 / EMI ♦♦♦♦
Mixing metallic guitar heroics with funk, hip-hop, electronica, and a cinematic soundtrack feel, Buckethead's *Monsters and Robots* is yet another eclectic opus inspired largely by low-budget monster/horror, martial arts, and science fiction movies, especially those of Japan. Like any Buckethead album, the music occasionally meanders, but this outing does improve on its predecessor *Colma* by employing a variety of guest bassists. Primus' Les Claypool (as well as drummer Brain), Bootsy Collins, and Bill Laswell enliven the music's rhythmic underpinnings in ways that Buckethead's own bass playing on *Colma* didn't. Plus, the contributions of guest DJs Phonosycograph Disk, DJ Eddie Def, and Xtrakd are inventive and stimulating, complementing (rather than confusing) the musical mix. It may not be completely consistent, but *Monsters and Robots* offers more than enough musical derangement to satisfy. —*Steve Huey*

## The Bucketheads

f. 1993, New York, NY
*Group / Club/Dance, House*

Kenny "Dope" Gonzalez of Masters at Work formed the studio project known as the Bucketheads to pursue a pumping fusion of his prime influences: disco, house, hip-hop, freestyle, and Latin street music. The sound was exemplified by the Bucketheads' two huge dance hits, 1996's "The Bomb! (These Sounds Fall into My Mind)," and the following year's "Got Myself Together." The quasi-retrospective LP *Dungeon Tapes* was released on Positiva in 1995, followed by the debut album *All in My Mind*. [See Also: Masters at Work, Nuyorican Soul] —*John Bush*

**Got Myself Together [Single]** / 1995 / Henry St./Big Beat ♦♦
Kenny "Dope" Gonzalez quasi-covers the disco classic, using samples of the song title to spark this house jam. He also teams with "Little" Louie Vega for a Masters at Work remix. —*John Bush*

● **All in My Mind** / Aug. 8, 1995 / Henry St./Atlantic ♦♦♦♦
*All in My Mind* explores a great-sounding fusion of disco-funk and house which works well on album tracks like "Jus' Plain Funky," "Sayin' Dope" and "Went," as well as the two breakout singles, "Got Myself Together" and "The Bomb! (These Sounds Fall into My Mind)." —*John Bush*

## Buckfunk 3000 (Si Begg)

*Producer / Experimental Techno, Electronica, Techno*

Recording as Cabbageboy, Si Begg, Bigfoot, and other pseudonyms, Simon Begg produces an energetic, dancefloor-ready fusion of techno and electro as Buckfunk 3000. Signed to Tony Thorpe's Language label, Begg's Buckfunk project produced a trio of singles for Language in 1997 before releasing *First Class Ticket to Telos*, his debut LP, in 1998. While the earlier singles (particularly "PlanetSchockFutureRock") contained a far more pronounced old-school electro flavor, *Telos* is resolutely in the weird techno vein, with straightforward rhythms mixed with off-kilter sounds, and bizarre structural non sequiturs that break up techno's classic conservatism. Begg also owns and operates the Noodles label, co-runs the Mosquito imprint with Cristian Vogel, and has been featured as a remixer for such artists as Sven Vath, Mute, Sluts'n'Strings, and 909. [See Also: Si Begg, Cabbageboy] —*Sean Cooper*

● **First Class Ticket to Telos** / Feb. 23, 1998 / Language ♦♦♦♦
Though listening for signs of "intelligent" life could result in brain damage, *First Class Ticket to Telos* is an irresistible journey through high-intensity

bubblegum trance, reminiscent of how Aphex Twin might soundtrack a video game. There are more ideas in the tracks "Fried Funk & Microchips," "Planet Shock Future Rock," and "Panic Button" than many acts have built entire careers on—and Begg never seems to run out of great effects and tight rhythms. Word to Nintendo: sign this guy up! —*John Bush*

## Harold Budd

b. May 24, 1936, Los Angeles, CA
*Piano, Synthesizer, Producer, Composer, Arranger / Experimental, Avant-Garde, Ambient, Electronic, Neo-Classical*

The American ambient/neoclassical composer most closely allied with the increasingly sympathetic independent-rock underground—through his collaborations with the Cocteau Twins' Robin Guthrie—Harold Budd is one of the few who can very rightly be called an ambient composer. His music, a sparse and tonal wash of keyboard treatments, is inspired by a boyhood spent listening to the buzz of telephone wires near his home in the Mojave Desert town of Victorville, California (though he was born in nearby Los Angeles). Though interested in music from an early age, Budd was 36, married, and had children of his own by the time he graduated from the University of Southern California with a degree in Musical Composition in 1966. He became a respected name in the circle of minimalist and avant-garde composers based in Southern California during the late '60s, premiering his works *The Candy-Apple Revision* and *Unspecified D-Flat Major Chord and Lirio* around the area. In 1970, he began a teaching career at the California Institute of Arts, where he continued to compose, writing *Madrigals of the Rose Angel* in 1972. After leaving the Institute in 1976, Budd gained a recording contract with the Brian Eno-affiliated EG Records, and released his debut album *The Pavilion of Dreams* in 1978. Two years later, he collaborated with Eno on one of the landmark albums of ambient, *Ambient 2: The Plateaux of Mirrors*. After recording two albums for Cantil in 1981 (*The Serpent [In Quicksilver]*) and 1984 (*Abandoned Cities*), Harold Budd again worked with Eno on 1984's *The Pearl*. A contract with Eno's Opal Records resulted in one of Budd's most glorious albums, *The White Arcades*, recorded in Edinburgh with Robin Guthrie of the Cocteau Twins. Budd left Opal after 1991's *By the Dawn's Early Light*, and recorded two albums for Gyroscope: *Music for Three Pianos* (with Ruben Garcia and Daniel Lentz) and the lauded *Through the Hill*, a collaboration with Andy Partridge of XTC. In the mid-'90s, he recorded albums for New Albion and All Saints before signing to Atlantic for the release of *The Room* in mid-2000. —*John Bush*

### The Pavilion of Dreams / 1978 / EG ++++
*Pavilion of Dreams* is a cycle of works composed and recorded by Harold Budd from 1972-1975, each unique in form and inspiration. Strong in electric piano, harp, and voice, this album provides a look at Budd's formative years. —*Backroads Music/Heartbeats*

### Ambient 2: The Plateaux of Mirrors / 1980 / EG ++++
The second album in the *Ambient* series represents the beginning of Eno's fruitful collaboration with pianist Harold Budd; it is also probably Eno's most lyrical work. Subtle and exquisite melodies are played with great sensitivity by Budd while Eno electronically processes the notes of the piano. As is so often the case with Eno's work, the names of the pieces tend to reveal the nature of the music: titles like "First Light," "An Art of Doves," and "Among Fields of Crystal" hint at the pastoral beauty of this sublime and peaceful work. —*Backroads Music/Heartbeats*

### • The Pearl / 1984 / EG ++++
Hearing Budd's piano slowly fade in at the start of "Late October" is one of those perfect moments—it's something very distinctly his own, magnified by Eno's touches and slight echo, it signals the start of a fine album indeed. Acting in some respects as the counterpart to *Ambient 2*, with the same sense of hushed, ethereal beauty the partnership brought forth on that album, *Pearl* is so ridiculously good it instantly shows up much of mainstream new age as the gloopy schlock it often is. Eno is sensed as a performer on the album, if not by his absence then by his very understated presence. The merest hints of synth and whisper play around Budd's performances, ensuring the latter takes center stage. Eno and Daniel Lanois handle production, their teamwork once again overseeing a winner. When bringing themselves closer to the fore, it is still in the subtlest of ways, as with the artificially higher pitched notes from Budd on "Lost in the Humming Air." Part of the distinct charm of the album is the ability of the song titles to perfectly capture the sound of the music—"A Stream With Bright Fish" is almost self-defining. Another key point is Budd's ability to truly capture ambiance in general. "Against the Sky" is a strong example—it can be totally concentrated upon or left to play as atmospherics; it is also at once truly beautiful and a little haunting in an undisturbing manner. Other highlight tracks include the deceptively simple title track, as serene a piece of music as was ever recorded, and the closing "Still Return," bringing *Pearl* to a last peak of beauty. —*Ned Raggett*

### The Serpent (In Quicksilver)/Abandoned Cities / 1984 / Opal ++
Recorded when "ambient" meant Brian Eno rather than enervated techno, the LP and EP collected here were originally released on Budd's own Cantil label in the early '80s. *The Serpent (In Quicksilver)* consists of five solo keyboard works and one very interesting collaboration between Budd and pedal steel player Chas Smith. The latter, titled "Afar," evokes some of the music Brian Eno, Roger Eno, and Daniel Lanois were making at about the same time to accompany an Apollo space mission film. It's echoey and ethereal, and yet the pedal steel sound keeps things tethered to the earth (nothing wrecks the mental image of limitless space quite like the sound of steel guitar). The other pieces are also quite lovely, though not quite as interesting; many sounds are improvised, and are as much about sound treatment as they are about harmonic or melodic development. *Abandoned Cities* is made up of two long pieces for keyboard and electric guitar. In mood, if not sound, they bring to mind Robert Fripp and Brian Eno's *No Pussyfooting* album: the guitar is barely recognizable, and harmonic movement is mostly limited to long suspensions and resolutions. It's a beautiful, dark, shimmery sound though, and will reward your attention or lull you to sleep—whichever you prefer. —*Rick Anderson*

### Lovely Thunder / 1986 / EG ++++
The phrase "Lovely Thunder" suggests a beautiful sound with an undertone of menace. One needs to go no farther than "Gypsy Violin," the last song and centerpiece of the album *Lovely Thunder*, to hear how Harold Budd takes the phrase and forges its musical equivalent. Underneath the plaintive melody of the synthesized violin, and the occasional foghorn-reminiscent bass note, lies a bed of synth chords that are present throughout—sometimes adding notes, sometimes dropping them, sometimes moving a chord up or down a key into dissonance with the rest. The overall result is an undulating base that never quite lets the listener settle onto firm ground, giving the song a distinct edge.

Drones do figure prominently as a musical base for many of the album's other songs, yet the music is generally more akin to the reverberated keyboard treatments Budd utilized to stunning effect on his two collaborations with Brian Eno. Those looking to explore beyond *The Plateau of Mirror* and *The Pearl* would do well to give this album a listen, as they will most likely be challenged and satisfied.

(Cocteau Twins fans will recognize the song "Flowered Knife Shadows" as a slightly edited version of the song "Memory Gongs" from Budd's collaboration with the group on the album *The Moon and the Melodies*.) —*Brian E. Kirby*

### The White Arcades / 1988 / Opal +++
On *The White Arcades*, Budd offers his most varied work yet, due in part to various collaborators such as The Cocteau Twins. For the most part, the music offers a revealing depth and spatial approach, and a readily apparent maturity. There is one track co-composed with Brian Eno called "Totems of the Red-Sleeved Warrior" which soars and drifts from the place explored in *The Pearl*. —*Backroads Music/Heartbeats*

### By the Dawn's Early Light / 1991 / Opal +++
Harold Budd's discs tend to end up in the new age section of record stores, because his music is generally pleasant, quiet, and soothing. But where most new age composers go for the obvious (and sometimes saccharine) melody, Budd veers off into ambiguity; he also lacks the mystical bent that often accompanies the new age style. Instead, his compositional voice is more similar to that of a detached observer—one who creates beauty without getting too involved with it. *By the Dawn's Early Light* finds Budd writing various combinations of viola, guitar, harp, and keyboards. All of the music is lovely, but not all of the compositions sound complete. In several cases, they sound like raw ideas rushed into the studio before their time. Guitarist Bill Nelson

provides much of the interest throughout the album, and the sighing, slithery viola of Mabel Wong lends an occasional turn-of-the-century salon feel to the proceedings. The only really embarrassing moments occur when Budd—whose voice sounds like an unfortunate cross between Garrison Keillor and Kermit the Frog—reads his own poetry. Skip those tracks and you'll be fine. —*Rick Anderson*

## Bugs

f. 1996, San Francisco, CA
*Group / Trip-Hop, Jungle/Drum'N'Bass, Club/Dance, Acid Jazz*

Self-proclaimed "bugs in the system," the duo of Andrew Jervis and Dave "Skyjuice" Biegel came together in 1996 after Jervis spent time as a DJ, and Biegel played bass in hip-hop, reggae, and jazz groups. The music they've made together as Bugs is similarly eclectic, cross-cutting jazz-funk, drum'n'bass, and rare-groove with the overall vibes of acid jazz. Signed to Ubiquity Records, Bugs opened with the 1997 EP *Both Feet in It*, then issued their full-length debut, *Infinite Syndrome*. Biegel also busies himself with two side-projects: his production concern Skyjuice and a breakbeat pop group Puracane—both of which also record for Ubiquity. —*John Bush*

● **Infinite Syndrome** / Nov. 18, 1997 / Ubiquity ♦♦♦

Drum'n'bass artistes everywhere take note: song structures are your friends; the groove never suffers from proximity to a singer; and, lyrics generally impose structure on what can, all too often, otherwise devolve into mere funky longwindedness. Bugs (Andrew Jervis and David Biegel) understand this and as a result, their debut is a rich and spicy stew of thick, dark grooves that throb with contained and organized energy. Various singers lend their talents to the project, including the up-and-coming drum'n'bass chanteuse Terra Deva (who never sounded as sexy on her solo album as she does on the simmering "Broken"), and a woman with the evocative name Storm Large (whose "About You" sounds like something Baxter could have written if English were their first language). The production is virtuosic throughout—note the flanged and delayed percussion on "Let Go" and the tasteful use of jazzy flute on "About You." There's a sly but respectful nod to old-school hip-hop in the power chords and mid-tempo turntablism of "Superscience." Overall, this is one of the most satisfying discs of the year in any genre. —*Rick Anderson*

## LTJ Bukem (Daniel Williamson)

b. 1967, London, England
*Producer, DJ / Electronica, Jungle/Drum'N'Bass, Club/Dance*

Arguably the prime innovator in the development of jungle from its early status as an offshoot of hardcore techno into the respected, stylistic genre it became by the end of the '90s, LTJ Bukem gained fame as an auteur in all fields of the drum'n'bass movement: as a top-flight breakbeat DJ, owner and label-head of the Good Looking/Looking Good stable of labels and, of course, for his recordings—inspired by the lush strings and natural ambience of '70s jazz-fusion masters (like Lonnie Liston Smith and Chick Corea) as well as elegiac Chicago house and moody Detroit techno. Allied with the early-'90s rave and hardcore scene, Bukem began working on production near the end of the '80s. Though his light, airy sound made little sense to his contemporaries, Bukem's style was emulated much more as the jungle scene gained momentum during the mid-'90s. While such producers as Roni Size and Goldie gained the limelight for their solo work, Bukem purposely downplayed his own artistic career in favor of mix albums and label-spanning retrospectives which highlighted dozens of artists from his labels.

Born in London in 1967, Daniel Williamson was adopted and raised in Watford by strict Baptist parents, earning his nickname from the TV series *Hawaii Five-O* ("book 'em, Danno"). He took trumpet lessons as a child, played piano and drums in various school bands, and began listening to a wide range of music—including jazz, fusion, soul, and fusion plus hip-hop and electro. After being expelled from school at the age of 16, Bukem made the natural move to DJ status later in the '80s. Inspired by rare-groove DJs like Tim Westwood and Gilles Peterson, Bukem and several friends set up the Sunshine sound system and played out the latest hip-hop and electro tracks at DJ battles around his Luton base.

When the acid-house explosion hit Britain near the turn of the decade, Bukem gradually stopped going to sound-system battles and began attending the ever-growing raves dotting England's countryside. He began mixing as well, and produced his first track "Logical Progression" in 1990. Bukem soon grew frustrated with a lack of control on his own recordings, however, and in 1991 decided to form his own label, Good Looking Records. Bukem's production style was a continuing anachronism on the rave/breakbeat scene. Early Good Looking tracks like "Demons Theme," "Atlantis," and "Music" provided a soulful, melodic alternative to the prevailing hardcore tracks then in vogue.

By 1994, LTJ Bukem had formed his second label (Looking Good Records) and began the formation of an artist collective—Peshay, Aquarius (aka Photek), PFM, ILS & Solo, Blame, Nookie, Seba & Lo-Tec, Tayla, Funky Technicians—with individuals similarly inclined towards melodicism and epic expanses of sound. In October of that same year, he began the night club Speed at the Mars Bar in order to spread the Good Looking/Looking Good approach to sound. With Bukem and jungle pioneer Fabio spinning breakbeat records while MC Conrad added verbal gymnastics, it soon became one of the most popular clubs in London. Appropriately, Bukem's first full-length release was a mix album, *Mixmag Live!, Vol. 3*, which confirmed his status as one of the top breakbeat DJs in the drum'n'bass scene.

The jungle phenomenon began to crest as a commercial force in 1994, and the appearance of Goldie's *Timeless* one year later signaled the dawn of widespread critical respect for drum'n'bass. Though Bukem signed a major deal as well (through London), he debuted in true label-head fashion, releasing the Good Looking/Looking Good compilation *Logical Progression* instead of a proper solo LP. Bukem did contribute several productions (and mixed tracks for the second disc of the set), but the album definitely portrayed an artist committed to the jungle community more than his own career.

After a subsequent DJ tour of America (his first), Bukem showcased a new direction in late 1996 with *Earth, Vol. 1*. Another compilation (this time spanning his catch-all subsidiary Earth Records), it concentrated on mid-tempo tracks inspired by hip-hop, soul, jazz, and funk—again featuring very few tracks actually by Bukem. The sequel to *Logical Progression* continued the same share-the-wealth strategy—it was helmed and mixed by Good Looking right-hand man Blame. Besides inaugurating yet another mix-album series (*Progression Sessions*) in 1998, Bukem released several additional volumes in both the *Logical Progression* and *Earth* series. *Journey Inwards*, his first full-fledged solo album, followed in the spring of 2000. —*John Bush*

**Mixmag Live!, Vol. 3** / 1995 / Mixmag ♦♦♦♦

Unlike his *Logical Progression* compilation, Bukem's volume in the *Mixmag Live!* series enables him to choose tracks apart from his Good Looking/Looking Good stable, and he ends up using only PFM and his own "Music" single from his roster (though GL/LG artists Funky Technicians do appear, recording for another label). To compensate, Bukem mixes in tracks from the mid-'90s new school, including Source Direct's "Exit 9," and the Photek single "We Can Change the Future" (recorded as Code of Practice). The mixing is a bit more freestyle than on the restricting *Logical Progression*, so enthusiasts who want a true sampling of LTJ Bukem's DJ skills—rather than an overview of his label's output—should spring for this first. —*John Bush*

★ **Logical Progression** / Apr. 1996 / Good Looking ♦♦♦♦♦

The best overview of LTJ Bukem's accomplishments, *Logical Progression* functions three ways: as a Bukem basic-trainer, a retrospective of his Good Looking and Looking Good labels, and as a DJ mix album (though the latter occurs only on disc two). Bukem's most famous recordings ("Demon's Theme," "Music," "Horizons") appear here, as well as the Looking Good anthem "Links" by Chameleon, and contributions from PFM, Peshay, Photek and Funky Technicians. Bukem himself mixes disc two, though the relative constraints inherent in the album's nature make the mixing a bit of a disappointment—at least compared to his volume in the *Mixmag Live!* series. Still, the house influences and steady rhythms make *Logical Progression* perhaps the best introduction to jungle for those not accustomed to hyper-speed breakbeats. —*John Bush*

**Promised Land, Vol. 1** / Aug. 5, 1996 / Mutant Sound ♦♦♦♦

A double-disc collection of LTJ Bukem's mixing talents, *Promised Land, Vol. 1* includes fewer items from his own Looking Good/Good Looking labels, and the lack of intelligent jungle shifts the focus to harder, darker, and earlier tracks than are featured on his *Logical Progression* and *Mixmag* compilations. The mixing is excellent throughout. —*John Bush*

**Earth, Vol. 1** / Nov. 4, 1996 / Good Looking ♦♦♦♦
A compilation of material from an array of Bukem-helmed labels, including flagships Good Looking, Looking Good, Cookin', and Nexus. Accordingly, *Earth, Vol. 1* features a broad range of material. Paul Hunter's Poets of Thought project contributes much of the variety, including two hip-hop tracks and the Latin soul-jazz flavor of "Samba with JC." Other highlights include the debut of Pablo ("Do What You Gotta Do"), Doc Scott's "Tokyo Dawn," and Bukem's "Moodswings." The only drawback is Bukem's sense of conscious artistic vision—each track is described, analyzed, and given purpose, subverting the impact of the album as a whole. —*John Bush*

**Logical Progression, Level 2** / Apr. 28, 1997 / Good Looking ♦♦♦♦
The second volume in Bukem's *Logical Progression* label-overview series is headed by Bukem associate Blame, who contributes several tracks and mixes the second disc (though there is quite a bit of overlap from the first disc). With contributions from Source Direct, PFM, Nookie, and Bukem himself—as well as the vocal skills of MC Conrad and DRS—*Logical Progression* is just as solid as its predecessor, though perhaps less a history lesson than a look at the then-present state of jungle. —*John Bush*

**Earth, Vol. 2** / Sep. 29, 1997 / Good Looking ♦♦♦♦
The *Earth* series features a style of mellow drum'n'bass that samples heavily from the feel and sounds of '70s soul, funk, and jazz music as well as early-'90s instrumental hip-hop. The resulting music is rather dynamic with the freshness of drum'n'bass and nostalgic elements of the past. In addition, the song arrangements do not follow any clear-cut pattern or formula; they always lead the listener down a long, winding path of non-secular aural pleasure. Though the beats of the Good Looking crew aren't nearly as simple or symmetric as hip-hop beats, they flow at a much more sedate pace then the style of drum'n'bass that's most often associated with Bukem and his roster of artists. Artemis' "Silver Down," for example, lays down a jazzy atmosphere of hip-hop beats, layers synth melodies, a shimmering harp, the sounds of rainfall, and even a flute over that. Again, the result seems fresh and modern, yet it's polluted with nostalgic, ghost-like sounds from the past. Bukem's contribution, "Cosmic Interlude," leans heavily toward jazz with an upright bass and looped rhythms of high-hat drum tapping. Much more eloquent than the drum'n'bass-meets-jazz stylings of Roni Size on the *New Forms* album, Bukem's track gleams with beauty, yet it is just one of many quality pieces here. Other exceptional cuts include the sublime texture of Rollercone's "Fictions," the naturalistic sounds of Blu Mar Ten's "Adrift on Deep Water," and the album's intense drum'n'bass climax in DJ Crystil's "Mind Games." Overall, this collection represents the vast possibilities for drum'n'bass as a medium not only for dancing, but also for tranquil contemplation. —*Jason Birchmeier*

**Progression Sessions, Vol. 1** / Jun. 30, 1998 / Good Looking ♦♦♦♦
Quite possibly the smoothest collection of Bukem's trademark drum'n'bass fusion, *Progression Sessions* includes tracks from PHD & Conrad, Seba, Motive One, as well as Bukem himself. —*John Bush*

**Logical Progression, Level 3** / Jun. 30, 1998 / Good Looking ♦♦♦
The third volume in one of Bukem's bewilderingly similar compilation series, *Progression Sessions, Vol. 3* features Bukem mixing in new tracks and classics from Good Looking regulars Blu Mar Ten, Intense, Future Engineers, Voyager, and Big Bud. The sound is smooth drum'n'bass fusion—hardly a new style for Bukem, but undoubtedly fine enough for fans of either the man or the sound. —*Keith Farley*

**Progression Sessions, Vol. 3** / Feb. 1, 1999 / Good Looking ♦♦♦♦
The third volume in one of Bukem's bewilderingly similar compilation series, *Progression Sessions, Vol. 3* features Bukem mixing in new tracks and classics from Good Looking regulars Blu Mar Ten, Intense, Future Engineers, Voyager, and Big Bud. The sound is smooth drum & bass fusion—hardly a new style for Bukem but undoubtedly fine enough for fans of either the man or the sound. —*John Bush*

**Journey Inwards** / Apr. 4, 2000 / Kinetic ♦♦♦♦
Ten years after his mixing career began, and following the release of dozens of compilations focusing on tracks and producers from his Good Looking/Looking Good empire, LTJ Bukem finally released an album of his own. As any listener who's heard any single from any Bukem-headed label will probably be able to guess, his focus here is not quite standard drum'n'bass, but a set of earthy breaks inspired by the smoother end of '70s jazz and fusion. Compared to other jungle pioneers who've recorded expansive double-disc albums (4 Hero, Roni Size, Goldie), Bukem's is most similar in concept and sound to 4 Hero's *Two Pages*, an organic LP with mid-tempo breakbeats and earthy workouts for instrumentalists (not programmers). Even more than 4 Hero, however, Bukem's focus on non-commercial, non-vocal productions is both confident and exemplary. Though it's been easy (and perhaps necessary) to fault Bukem in the past for aping his influences, *Journey Inwards* makes it practically impossible—especially in the context of these productions, so beautiful, detailed, so precisely imagined that they sound as though they've come straight from Heaven's recording studio. From the shimmering waves of his Rhodes keyboard and the undeniably upright bass on the title-track opener (which might be a bit too expansive in its own right), Bukem moves into true drum'n'bass with a sleek, excellent two-stepper called "Watercolours" which features a downplayed, honking sax. He often returns to the Rhodes (it must be his favorite instrument) perhaps a few too many times, but every occurrence is used with the right balance. The breaks programming isn't next-generation, but for each song Bukem finds a pattern that works perfectly with the effects to support it. The second disc is reportedly the downtempo disc, though it's only marginally different from the first. It does indeed concentrate more on influences and genre exercises, from the blaxploitation bliss of "Sunrain" (one of the few vocal tracks on the album) to the soul-jazz strut of "Deserted Vaults." Taken as a whole, *Journey Inwards* is an album of pure brilliance, a work that trumps many of Bukem's past productions and signals, for what may be the first time, that his growing and developing production talents. Truth to tell, there's never been a drum'n'bass double-album that shouldn't have been pared down. With *Journey Inwards*, it's nearly impossible to know what to cut. —*John Bush*

## Burger/Ink

f. 1995, Berlin, Germany
*Drum Programming, Synthesizer / Experimental Techno, Ambient Techno*
Mike Ink, longtime kingpin of Germany's experimental techno scene, formed Burger/Ink with Jörg Burger to release an album for American indie label Matador in 1998. The material was originally recorded in 1996 as part of a two-part EP series for Harvest. [See Also: Mike Ink, Gas, Love Inc.] —*John Bush*

● **Las Vegas** / Sep. 8, 1998 / Matador ♦♦♦♦
Quite distanced from the legion of echo-chamber drumkick records in Mike Ink's catalogue, *Las Vegas* presents a series of languid trance numbers that reprise the deep-sea dub of his Studio 1 recordings—but without the straight-ahead four-four beats. Obviously, Jörg Burger must deserve much of the credit for *Las Vegas*, from highlight tracks "Flesh & Bleed," "Milk & Honey," and "Elvism" to the entire Roxy Music connections inherent in just about every song title on the record. If you buy just one Mike Ink record (alternately: if you can find just one Mike Ink record…), it had better be this one. —*John Bush*

## Buscemi (Dirk Swartenbroeckx)

*Remixing, Producer / Electronica, Trip-Hop*
A smooth mix of earthy breakbeats, classic house, and jazz-funk made Buscemi an interesting addition to the ranks of trip-hop acts. The work of Belgian producer Dirk Swartenbroeckx (who named his project after the American character actor of *Fargo* and *Reservoir Dogs* fame), Buscemi debuted in 1997 with the *Plus Belle Africaine EP* and earned airplay on Kiss FM through Gilles Peterson's radio show. The following year brought the debut album *Mocha Supremo*, and in mid-2000, *Our Girl in Havana*. —*John Bush*

● **Mocha Supreme** / Sep. 22, 1998 / Downsall Plastics ♦♦♦♦
More fast-paced and house-influenced than other European trip-hop acts like Kruder & Dorfmeister, *Mocha Supremo* is an apt title indeed. Tracks like "It Might as Well Be Quiet" and "What the Funk Is Happening?" are slightly chilled versions of the original template for moody house. —*John Bush*

## Byzar

f. 1995, New York, NY
*Group / Illbient, Electronica, Ambient Techno, Ambient Dub*
Connected to the Big Apple illbient crowd along with We, Tipsy, and DJ Spooky, Byzar concentrates on introspective, futuristic dub with heavy bouts

of percussion and overly dark vibes. The group released its debut album *Gaiatronyk Vs. The Cheap Robots* in mid-1997. —*John Bush*

- **Gaiatronyk Vs. The Cheap Robots** / Jun. 30, 1997 / Asphodel ♦♦♦♦
Byzar are, without argument, precisely that on their debut full-length release for Asphodel. Though swiftly pegged as *res logicus* for the DJ Spooky coattail treatment, this roving collective of beat manipulators and signal mutators are operating from far more interesting territory than Spooky's overthought electronic murk. Focusing on off-kilter rhythms and strange and scary monochromatic acoustic and electronic textures, the group's novel sheets of beat-oriented ambient dub-hop recall the more successful moments of Scorn and Techno Animal without falling into the bland repetition and reverb fetishism that tend to mar those groups. A surprisingly mature debut. —*Sean Cooper*

## C+C Music Factory

f. 1990, New York, NY, db. 1994
*Group / Club/Dance, R&B, House, Dance-Pop*

C+C Music Factory wasn't really a group—it's the product of Robert Clivilles and David Cole, two pop-savvy dance producers. In 1990, Clivilles and Cole hired all the singers and created all the tracks for *Gonna Make You Sweat*, C+C Music Factory's first album. While it was prepackaged, it wasn't necessarily faceless; in Freedom Williams, the producers had a solid, if not original or distinctive, rapper. What was really important to the success of the album was how Clivilles and Cole assembled the tracks, blending hip-hop and club sensibilities to mindlessly catchy pop songs. The three hit singles—"Gonna Make You Sweat (Everybody Dance Now)," "Here We Go," "Things That Make You Go Hmmm..."—were very good pop singles, and all of them were massive hits in early 1991.

After their moment in the sun, Williams left for an unsuccessful solo career and Clivilles and Cole released *Greatest Remixes, Vol. 1*, a collection of their work with C+C Music Factory as well as other artists; the album had a hit single with their re-recording of U2's "Pride."

C+C Music Factory released their second album, *Anything Goes!*, in the summer of 1994; it was a moderate hit, spending nine weeks on the charts. Unfortunately, it was the last album the duo ever made—David Cole died of spinal meningitis in early 1995. —*Stephen Thomas Erlewine*

● **Gonna Make You Sweat** / 1990 / Columbia ♦♦♦♦
All their hit hip-hop-pop singles are all here—"Gonna Make You Sweat (Everybody Dance Now)," "Here We Go," and "Things That Make You Go Hmmm..." —*Bil Carpenter*

**Clivilles & Cole's Greatest Remixes, Vol. 1** / 1992 / Columbia ♦♦♦
Featuring new remixes of "Things That Make You Go Hmmm..." and other hits, three new songs, and a cover of U2's "Pride (In the Name of Love)." There's also some material by the Cover Girls and Seduction. —*Bil Carpenter*

**Anything Goes!** / 1994 / Columbia ♦♦♦
C+C Music Factory's first album was an enormous hit, filled with infectious bubblegum dance-pop singles. It was music of the moment, and by the time *Anything Goes* was released, the moment had passed. Clivilles and Cole's production was just as skilled, and several of the hooks on *Anything Goes!* were strong, but the music was too dated to fit into the pop landscape of the mid-'90s. —*Stephen Thomas Erlewine*

**In the Groove** / 1996 / Sony Special Products ♦♦
Anyone looking for the original versions of such C+C Music Factory hits as "Gonna Make You Sweat," "Here We Go" and "Things That Make You Go Hmmm..." will have to stick with the group's debut album, since neither the 1995 compilation *Ultimate* or Sony Music Special Products' budget-priced 1996 sequel, *In the Groove*, fills the bill. *In the Groove* does suffer because of its budget-line origins, since budget-line discs by nature don't contain all the hits, but it's nevertheless discouraging to get just one big hit—the radio mix of "Things That Make You Go Hmmm..."—on the ten-track collection. Sure, having the radio mix of "Pride (In the Name of Love)" is nice, but the rest of the collection contains album cuts of varying interest, especially since they're not as effective when separated from the original albums. As a result, *In the Groove* is a bit muddled, appealing neither to hardcore fans, who already have this material, or to the casual fans who want the hits. Perhaps next time a C+C compilation will be executed properly... —*Stephen Thomas Erlewine*

## Cabaret Voltaire

f. 1974, Sheffield, Yorkshire, England
*Group / Experimental Rock, Post-Punk, Techno, Acid House, Electronic, Industrial*

Though they're one of the most important groups in the history of industrial and electronic music, Cabaret Voltaire are sometimes forgotten in the style's timeline—perhaps because they continued recording long after other luminaries (Throbbing Gristle, Suicide, Chrome) called it quits. Also related to the fact is that CV rarely stayed in one place for long, instead moving quickly from free-form experimentalism through arty white-boy funk and on to house music in the late '80s and electronica the following decade.

When they formed in Sheffield, however, the trio of guitarist Richard H. Kirk, bassist Stephen Mallinder and tape manipulator Chris Watson were closer to performance art than music. Influenced by the Dadaist movement (whence came their name) as well as musical figures Brian Eno and Can, Cabaret Voltaire began recording as early as 1974 but released nothing until their 1978 appearance on Manchester's Factory Records compilation *A Factory Sampler*. Later that year, CV signed to the newly formed Rough Trade label and released the *Extended Play* EP. The record was an insightful, far-seeing release, alternating punk-influenced chargers like "Nag Nag Nag" with more experimental pieces.

The debut Cabaret Voltaire LP *Mix-Up* was just that—an assemblage of driving industrial funk laced with tape loops and sampled effects. The group's intensity helped put them on Britain's independent singles charts (thanks to tracks such as "Silent Command," "Three Mantras" and "Seconds Too Late"), and the release of several live shows proved that Cabaret Voltaire was able to re-create many of their experiments in a concert setting. By the beginning of the '80s, the trio began to diversify by working on film music, collaborative releases, and solo albums—one each for Kirk (*Disposable Half-Truths*) and Mallinder (*Pow-Wow*). The CV album *Red Mecca* showed them working with Arabic elements as well. Watson's departure (for a career in television, and later, the Hafler Trio) provoked Kirk and Mallinder to replace him with Eric Random.

Cabaret Voltaire left Rough Trade in 1983, and inaugurated a new contract with Some Bizzare [sic]/Virgin by shifting their sound, away from raging industro-funk and towards a more danceable form. Keyboard player Dave Ball (Soft Cell) joined the fold, and CV's 1983 LP *The Crackdown* finalized the change. Dividends were quickly paid, as the singles "Sensoria" and "James Brown" (both from *Micro-phonies*) hit the indie charts during 1984. Except for 1985's *The Covenant, The Sword and The Arm of the Lord* (which harked back to the late '70s), Cabaret Voltaire were, with New Order, on their way to a stylish, increasingly commercial hybrid of post-punk, art-funk and the emerging house music scene.

After the simultaneous release of two Kirk solo albums (*Black Jesus Voice* and *Ugly Spirit*) in 1986, the group moved to EMI/Parlophone and worked with Bill Laswell and Adrian Sherwood for their 1987 LP *Code*. The sound of Chicago house had recently blown up in London during 1986-87, and Cabaret Voltaire traveled to the Windy City to record with one of the style's mavericks, Marshall Jefferson. The LP *Groovy, Laidback & Nasty* was the fruit of that intriguing union, and the single "Hypnotised" made the British pop charts, though it also showed CV—for the first time in their 15 years—reacting to the trends instead of creating them.

The group's pioneering work was hardly over, though, as Kirk began working with a new generation of electronic experimentalists based in CV's home of Sheffield. Rob Gretton's Warp Records—which later released work from the cream of Britain's intelligent house/techno crop (Aphex Twin, Black Dog, Autechre)—debuted with *Clonks Coming*, an LP by Kirk's Sweet Exorcist project.

Kirk's increasing devotion to solo work and side projects proved to be the undoing of the group, however, as *Groovy, Laidback & Nasty* was their last album for EMI. During 1993-94, the new-electronica label Instinct released a trio of CV LPs—*Plasticity, International Language, The Conversation*—in the US (licensed from Plastex), after which the band's future appeared cloudy. Kirk continued to record (as Electronic Eye, Sandoz, and himself) while Mallinder moved to Australia, where he has recorded as Sassi & Loco. —*John Bush*

**1974-1976** / 1980 / Industrial ♦♦♦
Ten tracks of Cabaret Voltaire's earliest recordings finds the industrial trio exploring the fringe of experimental music by means of turntable scratching, cut-and-paste techniques (using reel-to-reel tape machines), environmental recordings and even occasional synthesizer textures more akin to Tangerine Dream than Throbbing Gristle, who first released the project on their own label, Industrial Records. The compilation is amazing from a historical standpoint, and surprisingly holds together for more than just historical purposes, even signaling CV's later affinity for electro-pop on the novelty track "Do the Snake." —*John Bush*

**Red Mecca** / 1981 / Mute ♦♦♦♦
Cabaret Voltaire's first consistent record, *Red Mecca* offers a highly stylized revision of Mancini's score for *Touch of Evil* set to a dark, dense electronic landscape. —*Stephen Thomas Erlewine*

★ **2X45** / 1982 / Mute ♦♦♦♦♦
Collecting two separate sessions, one with Watson and one without (the former also with guest drummer Alan Fish of fellow Sheffield experimentalists Hula), *2 x 45* shows the Cabs now well on their way to the perversely upbeat yet ominous funk of their early eighties days. A song like "Breathe Deep" may have things like Kirk's sax and clarinet lines over the stripped-down polyrhythms of Fish and Mallinder, yet the way Mallinder husks the vocals and the claustrophobic feel of the recording don't entirely lend themselves to just going ahead and tearing the roof off the sucker. It's a careful balance the Cabs maintain, but it does work more often than not, while the influence on later industrial-affiliated acts is immediately apparent. Watson's work in the band at this point isn't as noticeable as before, but the drop-in samples on "Yashar" of intense voices asking where all the people on earth are hiding give a sense of where he still turns up. The second session, with a Nort and an Eric Random on drums, guitar, and percussion, is a touch murkier at points but only just. "War of Nerves (T.E.S.)" may start with a tape of a guy talking about tortures involving rats and have Mallinder's distorted, demonic vocals in full effect, but the crisp rhythm punch is still predominant. "Wait and Shuffle" is even, dare it be said, perkier, with a brisk, reggae-touched drum/bass combination and some sprightly keyboards playing around with the sax wails and further found-sound oddities. The lengthy "Get Out of My Face" concludes the session and release on perhaps the quirkiest note yet. Mallinder's cryptic sloganeering peppers things throughout, but it's Kirk's intriguing guitar and the relentless but still somehow fun rhythm push which defines the song best of all. —*Ned Raggett*

**The Crackdown** / 1983 / Some Bizarre ♦♦♦♦
One of Cabaret Voltaire's strongest albums, *The Crackdown* features the band working a number of menacing electronic textures into a basic dance/funk rhythm; the result is one of their most distinctive, challenging records. —*Stephen Thomas Erlewine*

**Micro-phonies** / 1984 / Virgin ♦♦♦♦
Following neatly after *The Crackdown*'s aggressive art-funk-electro combination, *Micro-phonies* shows the duo taking that combination to a stronger level. Having invented the shadowy, murkier side of industrial/noise experimentation, here the Cabs made their equally justified claim at fully kickstarting the beat-heavy crunch such labels as Wax Trax! would pursue shortly thereafter. DAF and the On-U Sound collective deserve as much notice for this, but the Cabs' relatively higher profile in the English/American cultural scene made them the harbingers as much as anyone. Flood's sympathetic co-production with the band is another feather in his cap, and the album sounds just as strong today as upon its release. *Micro-phonies*' most noted tracks are the appropriately funky, horn-heavy "James Brown" and the gripping "Sensoria," which makes for a brilliant album closer, nervous-tension synth signals and a spare but compelling guitar line over another strong beat combination. Subtler moments abound as well, a nice combination of the Cabs' initially understated approach and the greater opportunities available to them in the album's recording. "The Operative" is an unheralded highlight of the release, Mallinder's low-key speak/singing sidling along the crisp but not overpowering rhythm, controlled funk bass and guitar and touches of dub melodica sneaking through the mix. Other hints of the dub influences that the band have always embraced crop up on songs like (unsurprisingly) "Digital Rasta." Throughout the album Mallinder submerges his vocals into the music rather than calling overt attention to them, the reverse of what a lot of later industrial acts would do (often to their detriment). It's a sharp continuation of the Cabs' similar practice from many earlier numbers, here used in a newer musical style. The CD version of *Micro-phonies* includes the fine 12" mixes for "Sensoria" and "Blue Heat," a welcome bonus. —*Ned Raggett*

**The Covenant, the Sword and the Arm of the Lord** / 1985 / Some Bizarre ♦♦♦♦
Named after a radical right-wing American organization—and possibly for that reason simply retitled *The Arm of the Lord* in the States—*Covenant*, self-produced by the group at its longtime studio Western Works, is something of a curious release. While not much like *Code* and the group's absolute nadir, *Groovy, Laidback and Nasty*, *Covenant* still subtly indicates the band's incipient spiral into fairly unremarkable late-eighties mediocrity. Call it a use of already-cliched musical touches copied from others where before Mallinder and Kirk invented sounds everyone else ripped off, but whatever the reason the Cabs here start being less special and more run-of-the-mill. The balance perfected between sheen and punch on *The Crackdown* and *Micro-phonies* is still here, but the stripped-down power of that latter album in particular gets disguised here by intrusive synth-pop and hip-hop elements. Sometimes such new fusions work—"I Want You," with an amusing vocal hook provided from a favorite Cabs vocal source, a TV/radio preacher, has just enough breathy energy and attractiveness to stand out strongly. Many other tracks betray the titular fascination with America, God, and guns the Cabs exorcise here, such as the introductory samples to "Hells Home" and "The Arm of the Lord" itself. Other tracks have definite moments in general, like the quirky combination of percussion on the instrumental break of "Golden Halos." Mallinder gets in some sharp, rumbling bass work at points, and his understated but clear vocal approach still serves him well, while Kirk packs in quite a few fine electronic touches throughout. Still, though, there's just something about this album which feels a bit half-cocked—fans will find something to enjoy, but first-timers should turn elsewhere. —*Ned Raggett*

**8 Crépuscule Tracks** / 1988 / Positive ♦♦♦♦
An expansion of the original *Three Crepuscule Tracks*, *Eight* compiles a variety of slightly random tunes from the group's early eighties days for general consumption. The main cuts are the first, namely the three parts of "Sluggin Fer Jesus." If this cut wasn't the first attempt at what would become one of the most common and ultimately most cliched elements in eighties industrial/EBM—a found-sound tape of an American evangelist over a dance groove—then it was close. Admittedly, at this stage Cabaret Voltaire wasn't dealing in the kinds of massive 'up yours' rhythm assaults later groups like Front 242 would perfect, but the jittery, reggae/dub-touched beats and arrangement on the first part are still fine stuff from the group. The second part starts with just the preacher (or perhaps another one) asking for yet more money, followed by instrumental snippets of the band fading up and then cutting out back into low synth/production murk. The final part, titled "Fools Game," has a heavily tweaked semi-rap and more crazed pastoral ranting floating around a combination of an older, emptier style of Cabaret Voltaire sonics and slight, but only slight, t0uches of the electro-funk then making waves. The remainder of the collection is a bit of a mixed bag, but still has some sharp bits. "Yashar," unexpectedly reappearing here from *2 x 45*, kicks out a stiff beat and jam pretty well, while much of the latter half of the collection explores the balance between shadowy and more 'smooth' beats and production. The unexpected but still successful surprise wrapping *Eight* up is nothing other than a surprisingly faithful if still murky cover of Isaac Hayes' funk classic "Theme from 'Shaft'." Hearing Mallinder go on about the guy who's 'the sex machine to all the chicks' via vocal trickery that makes him sound like he's in a cave is amusing no matter how you slice it. —*Ned Raggett*

**Groovy, Laidback & Nasty** / 1990 / Capitol ♦♦♦
Silent during Britain's acid-house revolution, Cabaret Voltaire returned in 1990 with a clever house crossover album, for which they actually traveled

to Chicago and recorded with house producer Marshall Jefferson in an early British-American meeting of the minds. The result is an album more groovy than nasty, as Mallinder's vocals sound much more pop-oriented than before. Despite possessing a somewhat dated feel even soon after its release, the album showed CV's continued contributions to the growing electronic revolution. —*John Bush*

**The Living Legends** / Jul. 1990 / Mute ♦♦♦♦
If one needs a starting place to discover how an obscure trio of Sheffield sound experimentalists became one of the founders of industrial/EBM music, not to mention a whole range of artists interested in pushing the boundaries of recorded sound, *The Living Legends* is it. Conveniently collecting the series of singles the classic trio line-up released on Rough Trade Records, *Legends* makes for astonishing listening even today, alien now as it was then, and perhaps even more so. Compiled in more or less chronological order with a few exceptions, the tracks range from the quietly mysterious to astonishing, in-your-face sonics. The earliest single, "Do the Mussolini," and its various B-sides initially cast the band as gloomy, dour figures interested in fooling around with tape machines, rhythm boxes and a sense of echo that always made them sound like they were recording in the deep bowels of the earth. The Velvet Underground's "Here She Comes Now" gets an intriguing revamp here, Kirk's guitar buzzing the main riff in the background. After that, things really kick in with the groundbreaking "Nag Nag Nag," brilliantly coproduced by Rough Trade boss Geoff Travis and Red Krayola bandleader Mayo Thompson. Mallinder's abstract aggression as his electronically treated voice roars the title line is breathtaking enough, but the combination of heavily treated guitar and keyboard noise over the basic but effective rhythm pulse adds to the fantastic effect. Many other standouts follow from here, including the lengthy drone/groove of "Walls of Jerico" and the near-clinical push of "Second Too Late," with a gripping duet between a distanced Mallinder vocal and an upfront, vocodered and dead sounding voice. The sense of how the Cabs used everything from the more chaotic end of Krautrock to dub techniques surfaces throughout, capturing the sense of how they at once synthesized past approaches and created new ones. —*Ned Raggett*

**Listen Up with Cabaret Voltaire** / Sep. 1990 / Mute ♦♦♦♦
Given the band's constant outpouring of work in its late '70s/early '80s days via both singles and albums, it's no surprise that enough unreleased or compilation-only material could be brought together to form a two-CD collection. What's a bit more surprising is the quality throughout *Listen Up*, but then again, given the Cabs' abilities in general, it's not too unexpected. The sources for the previously released numbers range from fanzine flexidiscs to John Giorno's *Clean, But It Just Looks Dirty* video compilation, neatly situating the band's wide appeal among any number of undergrounds. The two initial tracks, from a very early Factory Records sampler EP, rank high as masterpieces of ominous threat. "Baader Meinhof" begins with a German speaker, presumably discussing the terrorist group in question, before Mallinder's heavily distorted voice talks over a combination of ambient drift and unnerving noises. "Sex in Secret" introduces a low rhythm box rumble and slightly more clear lyrics, but the heavy echo throughout combined with another combination of gentle and grating sonics marks it once again as Cabaret Voltaire material. Other strong rarities include the lengthy "Loosen the Clamp," with one of the band's most 'industrial' rhythm attacks, and "Trust In the Lord," with one of Mallinder's strongest and clearest vocals over brusque music. When it comes to the numerous unreleased tracks, amid more tentative or less focused material some gems come forth, many showcasing the band's increasing focus on in-your-face electrofunk. "This Is Our Religion" is notable for its Latin/funk rhythm touches, however treated or given a traditional Cabs touch, while "Why" perfectly captures the incipient EBM sound that early Front 242 would use as the basis for their own work. Mallinder's almost passionate vocals are an interesting touch, at least when not fed through the Vocoder. The packaging contains more examples of the band's early cut-up art. —*Ned Raggett*

**Technology: Western Re-Works 1992** / 1992 / Blue Plate ♦♦
Twelve items from the jaggedy universe of Cabaret Voltaire, here given the '90s facelift treatment as they're stripped down for dancefloor functionality. Sometimes it seems *too* smoothed out, though there are times when the original edges will suddenly show through. Nor is it quite as annoying as most of the house mix material making the rounds. —*Steven McDonald*

**International Language** / 1993 / Instinct ♦♦♦♦
*International Language* tones down the few Chicago house elements which had crept into *Plasticity*, replacing them with sublime acid-electro, tribal elements on several tracks and the same emphasis on samples which occasionally distorts the value of the underlying music. Though the melodies and chord progressions sometimes verge on the obvious, *International Language* is a worthy addition to CV's mammoth discography. —*John Bush*

**Plasticity** / Oct. 20, 1993 / Instinct ♦♦♦
Re-emerging with a much more original sound after their 1990 house album, Kirk and Mallinder for the most part rely on abstract electro-inspired ambient techno with extended voice-over samples for *Plasticity*. It certainly wasn't the first time CV had remade themselves without losing elements of their past work (even re-sampling a passage originally recorded over ten years earlier on "Soul Vine [70 Billion People]"). *Plasticity* was an excellent reworking of the house blueprint into the growing fringe of techno not necessarily produced for the dancefloor. The tribal flourishes of "Deep Time" and the obvious signal track "Inside the Electronic Revolution" showcase the duo as continuing visionaries. —*John Bush*

**The Conversation** / 1994 / Instinct ♦♦♦
The most abstract of the three Cabaret Voltaire albums released by Plastex/Instinct, *The Conversation* has the occasional flair of a film soundtrack, especially considering its two-hour sprawl across a double-disc set (the second of which features just one hour-long track). For the most part, however, most tracks just update previous albums *Plasticity* and *International Language*, though several feature darker textures more akin to early-'80s CV output. —*John Bush*

**BBC Recordings 1984-1986** / Jun. 22, 1999 / Pilot ♦♦♦
The results of their trips to Maida Vale during the mid-'80s, *BBC Recordings 1984-1986* includes new versions of the group's industrial-dance scores like "Sensoria" and "I Want You." —*John Bush*

## Cabbageboy (Si Begg)

*Producer / Experimental Techno, Downbeat, Jungle/Drum'N'Bass*

London-based experimentalist Si (Simon) Begg is a member of the notorious Cabbage Head artist collective, formed in 1990 in the midlands town of Leamington Spa, and also including noted dance producers Cristian Vogel and Tim Wright (of Germ). Although, with the exception of a few cassette-only releases as a member of Cabbage Head, he's only been actively releasing music since 1995, Begg's discography (as Cabbageboy, Bigfoot, and Buckfunk 3000, as well as under his own name) has quickly grown to nearly a dozen titles strong, with EPs appearing on such labels as Tresor, Ntone, Eukatech, Language, and Chrome. A restless, often ruthless experimenter with little respect for boundaries, Begg's recorded work (particularly under his Cabbageboy guise) toys incessantly with the conventions of ambient, techno, and drum'n'bass, the results often deviating so sharply from classification that they're simply lost on the listener. His releases (like those of compatriots Vogel, Wright, and Dave Clark) have nonetheless garnered considerable praise from the continental European techno underground, leading to releases on a number of that scene's most popular and respected labels (including Tresor, Mille Plateaux, and MP subsidiary Chrome). Begg's reputation continues to grow at home as well, with a pair of releases on Ninja Tune subsidiary Ntone bringing new, less techno-oriented ears to his awkward, esoteric methods.

Weaned from his teens on a range of progressive music—from prog rock and metal to electro and free jazz—Begg joined Cabbage Head upon being introduced to Cristian Vogel by a mutual friend. After releasing a few cassette projects and hosting a few live events, Vogel and Begg formed the Mosquito label to release dancefloor music with a high quotient of weirdness. Although he released no work of his own through Mosquito, Begg used the time and experience to assemble a studio (now located in Harrow, in northwest London) and focus on A&R and label management. The experience he's since applied to a label of his own, Noodles (launched at the top of 1997). Begg moved to London in the mid-'90s, hooking up with Coldcut's Jonathon Moore and Matt Black through the local music scene. He released his first EP as Cabbageboy, *Sausage Doctor*, on the pair's Ntone label in 1995, following it up with an additional EP, *Planets*, the following year. Begg's connection to Vogel also helped land him a 12" on the somewhat exclusive, extremely selective Tresor label, as well as compilation tracks for Force Inc., K7, Kickin', and Mille Plateaux. Begg's Buckfunk 3000 tracks have also appeared through Moody

Boy Tony Thorpe's Crammed subsidiary Language, with the label issuing his debut album in early 1998. *Genetically Modified* followed a year later. [See also: Si Begg, Buckfunk 3000] *—Sean Cooper*

**Planets [EP]** / Nov. 18, 1996 / Ntone ♦♦♦
Si Begg's second Ntone EP as Cabbageboy is a "dare-you-to-put-your-finger-on-it" sort of affair, with bustling genre references floating in a soup of fuzzy weirdness. The A-side is mostly concerned with electro and jungle, combined in odd, disjointed Cubase jams with a high quotient of funk. The flip is lazy downtempo breakbeat à la Mo'Wax/Wall Of Sound. *—Sean Cooper*

● **Genetically Modified** / Oct. 12, 1999 / Ntone ♦♦♦♦
*Genetically Modified* is Si Begg's third full-length in under two years, though his discography never appears as muddled as it should since each has been recorded under a different alias. Still, the results here are surprisingly similar to his two 1998 LP's, *First Class Ticket to Telos* as Buckfunk 3000 and *Commuter World* as Si Begg. Both were invisible soundtracks whose subjects never quite came into focus—not a big loss considering the incredible productions included. Here it's much the same story, with a concept focusing on genetic engineering. There's an interesting futuristic essay included in the booklet, though apart from the track titles and occasional samples, there's little to give listeners any clue. Begg's immense production talents make this a non-issue, as tracks like "Departure," "Hey Hey We're the Monks," and "Interstellar Love" show off his schizophrenic big-beat/trance fusion. *—John Bush*

## John Cage

b. Sep. 5, 1912, Los Angeles, CA, d. Aug. 12, 1992, New York, NY
Composer / Process-Generated, 20th-century Classical/Modern Composition, Minimalism, Electronic

The most influential and controversial American experimental composer of the 20th century, John Cage was the father of indeterminism, a Zen-inspired aesthetic which expelled all notions of choice from the creative process. Rejecting the most deeply-held compositional principles of the past—logical consequence, vertical sensitivity and tonality among them—Cage created a groundbreaking alternative to the serialist method, deconstructing traditions established hundreds and even thousands of years earlier; the end result was a radical new artistic approach which impacted all of the music composed in its wake, forever altering not only the ways in which sounds are created but also how they're absorbed by audiences. Indeed, it's often been suggested that he did to music what Karl Marx did to government—he leveled it.

Cage was born in Los Angeles on September 5, 1912, the son of an inventor who posited an explanation of the cosmos called the "Electrostatic Field Theory." Later attending Pomona College, he exited prior to graduation to travel across Europe during the early 1930s; upon returning to the US, he studied in New York with Henry Cowell, finally travelling back to the West Coast in 1934 to study under Arnold Schoenberg. Around this time Cage published his earliest compositions, a series of Varèse-inspired works written in a rigorous atonal system of his own device. Relocating to Seattle in 1937 to become a dance accompanist, a year later he founded a percussion ensemble, composing the seminal polyrhythms piece *First Construction (In Metal)* in 1939.

During the late 1930s, Cage also began experimenting with musique concrète, composing the landmark *Imaginary Landscape No. 1*, which employed variable-speed phonographs and frequency tone recordings alongside muted piano and a large Chinese cymbal. He also invented the "prepared piano," in which he placed a variety of household objects between the strings of a grand piano to create sounds suggesting a one-man percussion orchestra. It was at this time that Cage fell under the sway of Eastern philosophies, the influence of Zen Buddhism informing the random compositional techniques of his later work; obsessed with removing forethought and choice from the creative model, he set out to make music in line with the principles of the I Ching, predictable only by its very unpredictability.

Cage's work of the '40s took a variety of shapes: where 1941's *Imaginary Landscape No. 2* was a score for percussion which included a giant metal coil amplified by a phonograph cartridge, 1942's *Williams Mix* was a montage of over 500 pre-recorded sounds, and 1944's *The Perilous Night* was an emotional piece written for a heavily-muted prepared piano. The latter was composed for the Merce Cunningham Dance Company, for which Cage served as musical director from 1943 onward; his collaborations with Cunningham revolutionized modern dance composition and choreography, with the indeterminacy concept extending into these works as well. By the end of the decade Cage's innovations were widely recognized, and in 1949 he was honored with a Guggenheim Fellowship and an award from the National Academy of Arts and Letters.

Cage's most visionary work, however, was still to come: in 1951 he completed *Imaginary Landscape No. 4*, which limited its sound sources to only a dozen radios, with the end result dependent entirely on the broadcast material at the time of performance. That same year he collaborated with a group of performers and engineers to mount the Music on Magnetic Tape project. In 1952, pianist and longtime associate David Tudor premiered Cage's *4'33"*, known colloquially as "Silence;" the composer's most notorious work, it asks the performer to sit at his instrument but play nothing, the environmental sounds instead produced by a typically uncomfortable audience. Concurrently, he delved into theatrical performance (a 1952 performance at Black Mountain College widely regarded as the first "happening") and electronics (*Imaginary Landscape No. 5*, composed for randomly-mixed recordings).

In the wake of 1958's watershed *Concert for Piano and Orchestra*—a virtual catalog of indeterminate notations—Cage continued to immerse himself in electronics as the years went by, most famously in works like 1960's *Cartridge Music*, for which he amplified small household sounds for live performance, as well as 1969's *HPSCHD*, which combined harpsichord, tapes and the like. He also turned to writing, publishing his first book, *Silence*, in 1961, additionally teaching and lecturing across the globe. Elected to the Institute of the American Academy and Institute of Arts and Letters in 1968, he also received an honorary Doctorate of Performing Arts from the California Institutes of the Arts in 1986. Cage died in New York on August 12, 1992. *—Jason Ankeny*

**Aslsp Organ, Vol. 2** / 1991 / Col Legnio ♦♦♦
The title of this suite for piano or organ composed in 1985 refers both to "as slow as possible" and the last paragraph of James Joyce's *Finnegans Wake*—"Soft morning city! Lsp!" There are eight pieces, any one of which must be omitted and any one of which must be repeated. Neither tempo nor dynamics are indicated, only map-like proportions of the notes placement on the page. The music should "sound as it looks." In many works of this period, Cage was relying on the performer's own internal sense of timing rather than employing the extensive clockings of previous works. Each performance is unique, of course, yet the wide range of pitches and aggregate-combinations (with possible registration/timbre changes on an organ) is often evocative without relying on musical "imagery." In the collection *20 Ans de Musique Contemporaine á Metz*, Gerd Zacher, organ. *— "Blue" Gene Tyranny*

**Cheap Imitation** / 1991 / Cramps ♦♦♦
With the composer at the piano. A lovely performance of melodies which are fragments and transformations of melodies for Erik Satie's opera "Socrate" on the death of Socrates. Cage had to produce "cheap imitations" of these melodies for a performance when the rights for the Satie score could not be obtained. *— "Blue" Gene Tyranny*

★ **Singing Through/Vocal Compositions by John Cage** / 1991 / New Albion ♦♦♦♦♦
Beautifully performed pieces from 1942 to 1985 by vocalist Joan LaBarbara with piano and percussion. Contains: A Flower (1950), Mirakus (1984), Eight Whiskus (1984), The Wonderful Widow of 18 Springs (1942) for voice and closed piano, Nowth upon Nacht (1984), Sonnekus (1985), Forever and Sunsmell (1942), Solos for Voice (from the Songbooks)'s 49, 52, 67 (1970), Music for Two (by One) (1984). *— "Blue" Gene Tyranny*

**Diary: How to Improve the World (You Will Only Make Matters Worse)** / 1992 / Wergo ♦♦♦
An eight-CD set of brilliant observations, from the humorous to the speculative to the heart-filling. Cage speaks of lives and notions of the well-known—B. Fuller, Thoreau, the Vietnam War, Meister Eckhart, Schoenberg, being crammed in a subway car and odd confrontations with airplane employees ; of unique and everyday events—unemployment, free worldwide communications, dads and moms, electric clothing, workable anarchy. The typography determines the stereo distribution and level of Cage's voice, the effect of someone talking inside your head, disembodied. (The printed texts additionally used color changes to parallel this effect.) Some of the text, pictures of Cage reading and the clean water supply, and chronologies accompany the discs. *— "Blue" Gene Tyranny*

**Concert for Piano and Orchestra/Atlas Eclipticalis** / 1993 / Wergo ♦♦♦♦
This has got to be one of the finest recordings of Cage's music ever. The careful consideration given to musical and sonic details by the Orchestra of the S.E.M. Ensemble with conductor Petr Kotik, and the wonderful performance of piano soloist Joseph Kubera finally makes understandable in sound Cage's philosophical and poetical insights. In the performance of "Atlas Eclipticalis," for example, we finally hear the ongoing universe of stars, planets, solar winds and asteroids (etc.) much as Cage may have imagined a performance of his work. These musicians play the music with respect, accuracy, and a more-than-ordinary sense of what is beautiful. —*"Blue" Gene Tyranny*

**Fontana Mix and Solo for Voice 2** / 1993 / Hat Hut ♦♦♦
Three parts of the classic tape music piece "Fontana Mix" are superimposed while the "Solo for Voice 2" is performed simultaneously with them. When certain pieces employed the same chance operations or other similar methods in their composition, Cage would often specify in the score that they could be played at the same time. —*"Blue" Gene Tyranny*

**Indeterminancy, New Aspect of Form in Instrumental and Electronic Music** / 1993 / Smithsonian/Folkways ♦♦♦♦
A CD reissue of the legendary early-'60s discs in which Cage relates enlightening and entertaining stories from his life, from ancient texts, from second-hand sources and spontaneous insight, while pieces composed using indeterminant procedures are performed on piano and live electronics by David Tudor. Essential for an understanding of Cage at the root level. (It's OK that the voice is obscured at times.) —*"Blue" Gene Tyranny*

**Music of Changes, Books I-IV** / 1996 / Lovely Music ♦♦♦♦
An exquisitely played and beautiful recording of Cage's masterpiece, one of the most technically difficult pieces in all of piano repertoire. After studying the details of the work with David Tudor, who premiered it, and refining his interpretation in live performance over several years, pianist Joseph Kubera has applied his amazing range of touch and inflection to this accurate and highly musical recording. Because of advanced recording techniques, we are able to hear the fine harmonic and resonant combinations that were scored by Cage, and that form a sort of interior life of the piece. One unique and surprising sound follows the next over wide dynamic (*pppp* to *ffff* applied to each individual event), durational (blazingly fast grace note figures to events or silence held for a page), and pitch ranges (the entire tessitura of the piano is employed). This is one of the first compositions to use organized parameters and chance-operations (using the Chinese *Book of Changes* or *I-Ching*) in its composition. It provides a continually fascinating listening experience. —*"Blue" Gene Tyranny*

**Litany for the Whale** / 1998 / Harmonia Mundi USA ♦♦♦♦
Named after the longest work on the CD, this is an excellent and beautifully performed collection of familiar and rarely given vocal works by John Cage. It is performed by the Theatre of Voices, directed by Paul Hillier, with guest performer/composer Terry Riley. These include: "Litany for the Whale" (for two voices), "Aria No. 2" (for voice and electronics...rolling thunderclouds and other weather and sounds, with vowels and consonants from five languages), "Five" (for five voices...sustained, pure tones...Cage indicates that the notes "should be brushed into being"), "The Wonderful Widow of Eighteen Springs" (the classic song for voice and closed piano, 1942), "Solo for Voice 22 from the Songbooks" (for two voices and electronics...the multiple "meanings" of breath inflections), "Experiences No. 2" (for solo voice, 1948), "36 Mesostics and not re Marcel Duchamp" (two voices and electronics, 1970), "Aria" (for two voices and electronics...a fascinating new realization for two voices...interesting to compare with the classic solo Cathy Berberian realization, 1958), and "The Year Begins to Be Ripe" (from *Songbooks—Solo for Voice 49, Song With Electronics—Relevant: The Year Begins To Be Ripe*, using a text from Henry David Thoreau's journal...for voice and closed piano, 1970). —*"Blue" Gene Tyranny*

## Cajmere (Curtis Alan Jones)

**b.** Apr. 26, 1968, Chicago, IL
*Producer, DJ / Club/Dance, House*

For an international audience reawakening to the influence of Chicago house during the '90s, Curtis A. Jones acted as quite a renaissance leader. Besides donning his straightahead house guise Cajmere and a flamboyant, neon-haired acid-house alter-ego named Green Velvet for several of the most memorable underground house tracks of the decade (including "Preacher Man," "Answering Machine," "Brighter Days," and "Flash"), Jones helmed the two most respected labels in the new school of Chicago house, Cajual and Relief. Though artist-owned labels had become the norm in Detroit, Chicago occurrences were frustratingly rare, despite the fact that the two major house imprints of the '80s, Trax and DJ International, had continually bilked their artists out of money. Cajmere went a long way towards rectifying that situation, releasing records by a diverse cast of producers old and new: DJ Sneak, Glenn Underground, Paul Johnson, Gemini, Tim Harper, and Boo Williams, among others.

The Chicago native began clubbing and buying records while studying at the University of Illinois. He later graduated with a degree in chemical engineering (and even attended several years of grad school at UC-Berkeley), but then returned to his hometown in 1991 with a drive to begin recording and DJing around the area. His first track "Coffee Pot (It's Time for the Percolator)" was released in 1992 as Cajmere on Clubhouse Records. That same year, Cajmere worked on production for "Get With U" by Lidell Townsell, then hooked up with another Chicago vocalist, Dajae. After the pair recorded a breakout single named "Brighter Days," Cajmere decided to form his own Cajual Records to release it. "Brighter Days" ascended to the number two position on the dance charts and became an international smash; it was the perfect remedy to Chicago's quickly deteriorating fortunes, a track which looked back to the '80s boom years but updated the sound with heavier beats, low-end synth and up-to-date programming.

Subsequent Dajae/Cajual collaborations like "U Got Me Up" and "Day by Day" followed, and Cajmere eventually set up his Relief label in 1994. After deciding that the house scene needed a bit more showmanship, he created the alias Green Velvet for live gigs and DJ events. A kind of digital-age Bootsy Collins with impeccable fashion sense, Green Velvet hit the club charts with a trio of anthems from 1995 to 1997: "Flash," "The Stalker," and "Answering Machine." While no full length appeared from either Cajmere or Green Velvet during those years, Cajual/Relief compilations like *The Many Shades of Cajual*, *A Taste of Cajual*, and *Relief: The Future Sound of Chicago* collected all of his best productions. [See also: Green Velvet] —*John Bush*

● **The Many Shades of Cajual** / 1996 / Cajual ♦♦♦♦
Though label-head Cajmere makes only one official appearance ("Horny") on a compilation of his own Chicago label, his production is all over the album. Besides co-writing and producing Dajae tracks like "Day by Day" and "Get Up Off Me," he appears on Derrick Carter's "Dream States" and Terence FM's "Feelin' Kinda High" and (as Green Velvet) remixes one of his own productions. DJ Sneak also makes tight contributions: "Message of Love" and "Sounds From the Pipe." —*John Bush*

**A Taste of Cajual** / Dec. 2, 1997 / Cajual ♦♦♦♦
Cajmere produced four of the tracks on this Cajual compilation, one each as Green Velvet, Chicago Connection and himself, plus Dajae's "Fakes and Phonies." Other stellar new-school Chicago heads appearing are Glenn Underground, Mark Grant, Andre Harris, and Gene Farris. —*John Bush*

## Mira Calix (Chantal Passamonte)

*Producer, DJ / Ambient Techno*

Formerly a career DJ and publicist at Warp Records, Mira Calix was signed to her own Warp recording contract in 1996. Her first single, "Llanga," appeared later that year with an assistance credit from Gescom. The *Pin Skeeling EP* followed in 1998, and her album debut *One on One* in 2000. —*John Bush*

**Pin Skeeling [EP]** / Mar. 9, 1998 / Warp ♦♦♦
Contrary to her DJing or Warp's usual intelli-techno, *Pin Skeeling* is a wash of distorted ambience, with occasional metallic beats providing the only non-textural elements to the songs "Ms. Meteo" and "Sandsings." Mark Clifford's Disjecta earns co-production credits, while Boards of Canada provide a remix of "Sandsing." —*John Bush*

● **One on One** / 2000 / Warp ♦♦♦♦

## Can

**f.** 1968, Cologne, Germany, **db.** 1978
*Group / Kraut-Rock, Experimental, Prog-Rock/Art Rock, Electronic*

Always at least three steps ahead of contemporary popular music, Can was the leading avant-garde rock group of the '70s. From their very beginning, their music didn't conform to any commonly-held notions about rock & roll—not even those of the countercultures. Inspired more by 20th century classical music than Chuck Berry, their closest contemporaries were Frank Zappa or possibly the Velvet Underground. Yet their music was more serious and inaccessible than either of those artists. Instead of recording tight pop songs or satire, Can experimented with noise, synthesizers, nontraditional music, cut-and-paste techniques, and, most importantly, electronic music; each album marked a significant step forward from the previous album, investigating new territories that other rock bands weren't interested in exploring.

Throughout their career, Can's lineup was fluid, featuring several different vocalists over the years; the core band members remained keyboardist Irmin Schmidt, drummer Jaki Leibezeit, guitarist Michael Karoli, and bassist Holger Czukay. During the '70s, they were extremely prolific, recording as many as three albums a year at the height of their career. Apart from a surprise UK Top 30 hit in 1978—"I Want More"—they were never much more than a cult band; even critics had a hard time appreciating their music.

Can debuted in 1969 with the primitive, bracing *Monster Movie*, the only full-length effort to feature American-born vocalist Malcolm Mooney. 1970's *Soundtracks*, a collection of film music, introduced Japanese singer Kenji "Damo" Suzuki, and featured "Mother Sky," one of the group's best-known compositions. With 1971's two-record set *Tago Mago*, Can hit its visionary stride, shedding the constraints of pop forms and structures to explore long improvisations, angular rhythms, and experimental textures.

1972's *Ege Bamayasi* refined the approach, and incorporated an increasingly jazz-like sensibility into the mix; *Future Days*, recorded the following year as Suzuki's swan song, travelled even further afield into minimalist, almost ambient territory. With 1974's *Soon Over Babaluma*, Can returned to more complicated and abrasive ground, introducing dub rhythms as well as Karoli's shrieking violin. 1976's *Unlimited Edition* and 1977's *Saw Delight* proved equally restless, and drew on a wide range of ethnic musics.

When the band split in 1978 following the success of the album *Flow Motion* and the hit "I Want More," they left behind a body of work that has proven surprisingly groundbreaking; echoes of Can's music can be heard in Public Image Limited, the Fall, and Einsturzende Neubauten, among others. As with much aggressive and challenging experimental music, Can's music can be difficult to appreciate, yet their albums offer some of the best experimental rock ever recorded. —*Jason Ankeny*

### Monster Movie / 1969 / Mute ✦✦✦✦
Can's debut is the only full-length, proper release to feature original vocalist Malcolm Mooney, whose free-form ranting is matched by a raw, aggressive dynamic unlike anything else in the group's canon; driving, dissonant songs like the extraordinary "Father Cannot Yell" and "Outside My Door" even owe a rather surprising debt to psychedelia and garage rock. More indicative of things to come is the closer "Yoo Doo Right," a 20-minute epic built on the kinds of hypnotic motifs and minimal rhythms which quickly became Can trademarks. —*Jason Ankeny*

### Soundtracks / 1970 / Mute ✦✦✦
Malcolm Mooney passes the baton to Damo Suzuki for *Soundtracks*, a collection of film music featuring contributions from both vocalists. The dichotomy between the two singers is readily apparent: Suzuki's odd, strangulated vocals fit far more comfortably into the group's increasingly intricate and subtle sound, allowing for greater variation than that allowed by Mooney's stream-of-consciousness discourse. —*Jason Ankeny*

### ☆ Tago Mago / 1971 / Mute ✦✦✦✦✦
With the band in full artistic flower and Suzuki's sometimes moody, sometimes frenetic speak/sing/shrieking in full effect, Can released not merely one of the best Kraut-rock albums of all time, but one of the best albums ever, period. *Tago Mago* is that rarity of the early '70s, a double album without a wasted note, ranging from sweetly gentle float to full-on monster grooves. At least two labels were named after songs from it ("Paperhouse" and "Mushroom"), while the number of bands who have used not only Can, but this album, as a touchstone—especially during the '90s—can't be counted. "Paperhouse" starts things brilliantly, beginning with a low-key chime and beat, before amping up into a rumbling roll in the midsection, then calming down again before one last blast. It almost sounds like a warm-up number for what's to follow. Both "Mushroom," with Liebezeit's intriguingly produced drum line and Suzuki's singing to recommend it, and "Oh Yeah," with Schmidt filling out the quicker pace with nicely spooky keyboards, continue the fine vibe. After that, though, come the huge highlights—three long examples of Can at its absolute best. "Hallelwah"—featuring the Liebezeit/Czukay rhythm section pounding out a monster trance/funk beat; Karoli's and Schmidt's always impressive fills and leads; and Suzuki's slow-building ranting above everything—is 19 minutes of pure genius. The near-rhythmless flow of "Aumgn" is equally mind-blowing, with swaths of sound from all the members floating from speaker to speaker in an ever-evolving wash, leading up to a final jam. "Peking O" continues that same sort of feeling, but with a touch more focus, throwing in everything from Chinese-inspired melodies and jazzy piano breaks to cheap organ rhythm boxes and near babbling from Suzuki along the way. "Bring Me Coffee or Tea" wraps things up as a fine, fun little coda to a landmark record. —*Ned Raggett*

### ☆ Ege Bamyasi / 1972 / Mute ✦✦✦✦✦
The follow-up to *Tago Mago* is only lesser in terms of being shorter; otherwise the Can collective delivers its expected musical recombination act with the usual power and ability. Liebezeit, at once minimalist and utterly funky, provides another base of key beat action for everyone to go off on—from the buried, lengthy solos by Karoli on "Pinch" to the rhythm box/keyboard action on "Spoon." The latter song, which closes the album, is particularly fine, its sound hinting at an influence on everything from early Ultravox songs like "Hiroshima Mon Amour" to the hollower rhythms on many of Gary Numan's first efforts. Liebezeit and Czukay's groove on "One More Night," calling to mind a particularly cool nightclub at the end of the evening, shows that Stereolab didn't just take the brain-melting crunch side of Can as inspiration. The longest track, "Soup," lets the band take off on another one of its trademark lengthy rhythm explorations, though not without some tweaks to the expected sound. About four minutes in, nearly everything drops away, with Schmidt and Liebezeit doing the most prominent work; after that, it shifts into some wonderfully grating and crumbling keyboards combined with Suzuki's strange pronouncements, before ending with a series of random interjections from all the members. Playfulness abounds as much as skill: Slide whistles trade off with Suzuki on "Pinch"; squiggly keyboards end "Vitamin C"; and rollicking guitar highlights "I'm So Green." The underrated and equally intriguing sense of drift that the band brings to its recordings continues as always. "Sing Swan Song" is particularly fine, a gentle float with Schmidt's keyboards and Czukay's bass taking the fore to support Suzuki's sing-song vocal. —*Ned Raggett*

### ★ Future Days / 1973 / Mute ✦✦✦✦✦
Damo Suzuki's final effort is Can's most atmospheric and beautiful record, a spartan collection of lengthy, jazz-like compositions recorded with minimal vocal contributions. Employing keyboard washes to create a breezy, almost oceanic feel (indeed, two of the tracks are titled "Spray" and "Bel Air"), the mix buries Suzuki's voice to elevate drummer Jaki Liebezeit's complex rhythms to the foreground; despite the deceptive tranquility of its surface, *Future Days* is an intense work, bubbling with radical ideas and concepts. —*Jason Ankeny*

### Soon Over Babaluma / 1974 / Mute ✦✦✦
With Suzuki departed, vocal responsibilities were now split between Karoli and Schmidt. Wisely, neither try to clone Mooney or Suzuki, instead aiming for their own low-key way around things. The guitarist half-speaks/half-whispers his lines on the opening groover, "Dizzy Dizzy," while on "Come Sta, La Luna" Schmidt uses a higher pitch that is mostly buried in the background. Czukay sounds like he's throwing in some odd movie samples on that particular track, though perhaps it's just heavy flanging on Schmidt's vocals. Karoli's guitar achieves near-flamenco levels on the song, an attractive development that matches up nicely with the slightly lighter and jazzier rhythms the band comes up with on tracks like "Splash." Also, his violin work—uncredited on earlier releases—is a bit more prominent here. Musically, if things are a touch less intense on *Babaluma*, the sense of a band perfectly living in each other's musical pocket and able to react on a dime hasn't changed at all. "Chain Reaction," the longest track on the album, shows that the combination of lengthy jam and slight relaxation actually can go together rather well. After an initial four minutes of quicker pulsing and rhythm (which sounds partly machine-provided), things downshift into a slower vocal section before firing up again; Karoli's blistering guitar work at this point is striking to behold. "Chain Reaction" bleeds into *Babaluma*'s final song, "Quantum Physics," a more ominous piece with Czukay's bass closer to the fore, shaded by Schmidt's work and sometimes accompanied by Liebezeit. It makes for a nicely mysterious conclusion to the album. —*Ned Raggett*

**Landed** / 1975 / Mute ♦♦

Another erratic waxing features some great guitar and *Babaluma*-style grooves, but is unfocused on the whole. —*Myles Boisen*

**Flow Motion** / 1976 / Mute ♦♦

More pop aspirations and overt use of ethnic textures yield mixed results, as was typical of the band's later years. —*Myles Boisen*

**Can** / 1979 / Mute ♦♦

This one suffers without bassist Holger Czukay, and from overblown pop keyboards. —*Myles Boisen*

**Cannibalism 1** / 1980 / Mute ♦♦♦♦

Given the cohesion of the group's studio albums, Can's songs work surprisingly well in compilation form, as evidenced by *Cannibalism 1*, a collection of tracks taken from the first six years of the group's existence. Covering ground from 1969's *Monster Movie* to 1974's *Soon Over Babaluma* (although nothing from 1973's superb *Future Days* makes the cut), the sampler compiles many of the group's high points (including "Father Cannot Yell," "She Brings the Rain," "Mushroom," and "Soup"), and offers a thorough overview of Can's eclectic musical history to date, even if the abridged versions of cuts like "Mother Sky," "Aumgn," and "Halleluhwah" don't measure up to the full-length renditions featured on the original albums. —*Jason Ankeny*

**Delay ... 1968** / 1981 / Mute ♦♦♦

Although recorded in the late '60s, the material included on *Delay 1968* did not appear commercially until 1981. A collection of cuts featuring early vocalist Malcolm Mooney, these seven songs are among the very first Can ever recorded; while nowhere near as intricate or assured as the group's later work, the visceral energy of tracks like the deranged "Uphill" and "Butterfly" is undeniable. —*Jason Ankeny*

**Cannibalism 3** / 1990 / Mute ♦♦♦

A compilation drawn from the solo releases of various Can members (though it would seem that percussionist Jaki Leibczeit has made his way onto the majority of them) between 1979 and 1991. Curious musical moments keep company with band works, as well as departing for musical territory far divergent from anything known to fans of the band. Fascinating selections that many will find tempting them to acquire full albums. —*Steven McDonald*

**Anthology 1968-1993** / 1995 / Mute ♦♦♦♦

For listeners daunted by the band's long and winding discography, *Anthology 1968-1993* presents short-form highlights like "Spoon," "Future Days," "Moonshake," "She Brings the Rain," and 25 others. Yes, the albums are better places to hear all of these tracks, and there's a typically Cannish disregard for chronology or narrative (i.e., don't hope for liner notes), but this double-disc set is an excellent introduction to the band's 25-year career. —*Keith Farley*

**Sacrilege: The Remixes** / 1997 / Mute ♦♦

Anticipating their detractors with an ironic indictment against purity, Can (yes, the band were consulted) stepped aside while a somewhat ponderous collection of remixers mucked about in their back catalog, *Sacrilege* being the result. Although the album might have been more appropriate a few years earlier (Can sound about as experimental today as your average auto advert) and with a more bizarre slate of remixers (Westbam? *Kris Needs*—), the album is nevertheless an interesting collection of occasionally inspired reinterpretations of classic Can material, with high points hit by Carl Craig's dystopian fog, "Future Days," and Air Liquide's rousing groover "Flow Motion." Of course, Can's own tendency toward self-indulgence means you can hardly fault the worst of these tracks (the Orb's oddly subpar "Halleluwah," U.N.K.L.E.'s forgettable-before-you've-even-finished-with-it stutterer "Vitamin C") for doing the same thing, but that doesn't make them any easier to listen to. —*Sean Cooper*

**Can Box** / May 18, 1999 / Mute ♦♦♦♦

Mute celebrated Can's 30th birthday with the release of the *Can Box*. Formed in Cologne, Germany, in 1968, the feckless sound experimenters went on to reach the lofty cult and seminal status of bands like the Velvet Underground and Mothers of Invention. The three-item box contains a double CD of live music recorded from 1971-1977, a book of history, interviews, reviews, and photos, as well as a video of a 1972 concert and a previously unreleased documentary made in 1988 and 1997. The CD is compiled from cassettes and other non-professional fan recordings with professional sound processing and mastering applied. Four of the pieces are extemporaneous jams that have heretofore not seen the light of day. The tome proves to be of just such rare and personal content. The concert was a free event attended by over 10,000 when Can had placed "Spoon" (available on *Box* album) into the number one chart position. The footage was made with help from Wim Wenders' film editor Peter Przygodda. While this attention brought the group to do a small German tour where each member presented a solo project, there were no plans for a reunion. —*Tom Schulte*

## Benji Candelario

**b.** May 16, 1965, Brooklyn, NY
*Producer, DJ / Garage, Club/Dance, House*

He learned about the spirit of garage and house music first-hand at Larry Levan's Paradise Garage, and Benji Candelario reflected his influences by becoming one of the top New York garage DJs by the '90s. As well as mixing fame, his dozens of remixes and recordings for Cutting, Freeze, Nitegroove, and Kult Records are quite respected in the house community. Candelario listened to soul and funk while growing up in Brooklyn, and gained entry into the '80s underground house scene by hitting clubs like Levan's Paradise Garage and Bond's International with his cousin. It was only a matter of time before he became interested in DJing; after practicing on the decks, he featured at New York hotspots like Redzone, the Building and the Roxy. Candelario began remixing and producing by the late '80s, working with Criminal Element Orchestra and for the label Cutting Records. Recording as Swing 52 with Wayne Rollins, he scored in 1994 with the garage hit "Color of My Skin," while providing remixes for Todd Terry, Ruffneck and Call of the Wild. Candelario recorded several EPs under his own name (including the multi-volume editions *Traxx for the Head* and *Killer Fillers*). His first mixed album, *Havin' It Stateside, Vol. 1*, was released in 1995 on 21st Century Opera Records. —*John Bush*

● **Havin' It Stateside, Vol. 1** / 1995 / 21st Century Opera ♦♦♦♦

Benji Candelario's first mix album has a host of classic Chicago/New York names including Ralphi Rosario, Larry Heard, Maydie Myles, Billie Ray Martin, and Mike Delgado, among others. Throughout, Candelario's mixing skills are excellent but firmly in a garage mold: even though acid jazz hipsters Mondo Grosso are included, it's the King Street Mix of their "Souffles H" that appears here. —*John Bush*

## Cappella

f. 1986, Italy
*Group / Club/Dance, Euro-Pop, House, Dance-Pop*

An Italo-house production team employing up to ten different studios, at least a trio of producers for every production and scores of session workers, Cappella is mostly the creation of producer Gianfranco Bortolotti. Undoubtedly influenced by Motown's assembly-line aesthetic (as well as the '80s British dance team of Stock, Aitken & Waterman), Bortolotti coordinated the work of longtime producers DJ ProfXor, RAF, and DJ Pierre (not the Chicago producer) to create dozens of European club/chart hits under the aliases Cappella, 49ers, Fargetta, RAF, Clubhouse, and East Side Beat. For good or ill, Bortolotti's productions were most responsible for the Italian house phenomenon of the late '80s and early '90s, based on an often-maligned push-button production blueprint which includes only the cheesiest of melodies, samples, piano lines and diva vocals. Each single produced by Bortolotti's Media Productions underwent rigorous testing and remixing for maximum airplay in each country it's released, with only Bortolotti holding the final say on what appears. Throughout the '90s, Cappella was one of the most thoroughly unartistic dance acts—and for the most part, proud of it.

Inspired by the productions of Italo-disco producer and mixer DJ Pierre, Gianfranco Bortolotti began mixing around Italy while at school in the late '70s. The Cappella Project had already debuted as a production team by the end of the decade, though Bortolotti did little more than mix in the music industry until the mid-'80s. In 1987, he produced Cappella's "Bauhaus (Push the Beat)," a club hit throughout Europe and the UK. The following year brought the contintent-wide Top 10 hit "Heylom Halib," which presaged a wave of similar-sounding Italian house tracks during 1989-90. Bortolotti recorded a Cappella album (the cash-in heavy *Heylom Halib*), and scored again with the singles "Be Master in One's Own House" and "House of Energy Revenge." To his credit, he did recruit seminal diva Loleatta Holloway for the single "Take Me Away," less successful than the chart-entries but much better.

After several additional 1992-93 hits ("U Got 2 Know"), Bortolotti decided to make an act of Cappella with the addition of two Brits—Rodney Bishop (formerly with Positive Gang) and Kelly Overett (a vocalist who had worked with SL2). The singles "U Got 2 Let the Music" and "Move on Baby" became Cappella's biggest hits, hitting number one in several countries during 1994. The album *U Got 2 Know* did appreciably well, though Overett left by 1995 (to be replaced by Allison Jordan). Soon however, Cappella appeared to be running on steam. The 1995-96 singles like "Tell Me the Way" and "I Need Your Love" barely made the European charts, and their 1996 album *War in Heaven* fared poorly (though it was released in America). —*John Bush*

**Move on Baby [EP]** / 1994 / London ♦♦
From Italy, Cappella mix above-board house with underground dance on their hit, "Move on Baby," produced by George Maniatis. Several remixes, including one by Armand Van Helden, also appear on this single. —*John Bush*

**Remixes** / 1994 / ZYX ♦♦

• **U Got 2 Know** / 1994 / ZYX ♦♦
Led by continent-wide Hi-NRG hits like "Move on Baby," "U Got 2 Let the Music," and the title track, Cappella's *U Got 2 Know* remains the best place to find the Italian producer's best high-impact, low-intellect dance-pop. —*John Bush*

**Accidentals** / Apr. 11, 1996 / Original Cast Record ♦♦

**War in Heaven** / Apr. 23, 1996 / ZYX ♦♦

**Be My Baby [Single]** / Apr. 21, 1997 / ZYX ♦♦
Cappella's "Be My Baby" is a spy-soundtrack garage barnstormer, and though the vocal is a bit unimpressive, the production more than makes up for it. Included on the 11 remixes for the maxi-single are efforts by R.A.F., DJ ProfXor, DJ Chico Do Forte, and Bismark. —*John Bush*

## Wendy Carlos

b. Nov. 14, 1939, Pawtucket, RI
*Synthesizer / Microtonal, Electronic*

Composer Wendy Carlos spurred electronic music to new commercial heights during the late '60s, popularizing the synthesizer with the enormously successful *Switched-On Bach* album. Born in Pawtucket, Rhode Island on November 14, 1939, Carlos pursued her M.A. in composition under Vladimir Ussachevsky and Otto Luening at Columbia University's famed Columbia-Princeton Electronic Music Center. Following her graduation, she moved to Manhattan, where she found work as a recording engineer. In Manhattan, she met Dr. Robert Moog and, not long afterward, she began playing the Moog synthesizer. Carlos released her first recording, *Switched-On Bach*, in 1968. A showcase for the Moog synthesizer, *Switched-On Bach* interpreted the legendary composer's most renowned fugues and movements via state-of-the-art synth technology; purists were appalled, but the record captured the public's imagination and in time became the first classical album certified platinum by the RIAA. It also earned three Grammy awards. A similar effort, *The Well-Tempered Synthesizer*, followed in 1969. In 1971, Carlos wrote the music for Stanley Kubrick's controversial film *A Clockwork Orange*, introducing the vocoder—an electronic device designed to synthesize the human voice—in her score. After 1976's *Brandenburg Concertos 3-5*, Carlos again worked with Kubrick, providing the score for his 1980 adaptation of Stephen King's *The Shining*. Two years later, she wrote music for the Disney film *Tron*. Subsequent efforts included a spoof of Prokofiev's "Peter and the Wolf" recorded with Weird Al Yankovic and *Switched-On Bach 2000*. —*AMG*

**Switched-On Bach** / 1968 / Columbia ♦♦
The LP that jump-started the entire electronic/classical fusion fad during the late '60s and early '70s, *Switched-On Bach* is a set of rote interpretations performed with Moog synthesizer with little to offer listeners other than those interested in the album for its novelty flavor. —*John Bush*

• **A Clockwork Orange [Original Soundtrack]** / 1972 / East Side Digital ♦♦♦♦
Even before Carlos knew of a film project concerning *A Clockwork Orange*, the composer had begun work on a composition ("Timesteps") based on the book. It's the best piece of music in the score (and one of the most famed in the early history of electronic music), fitting in well next to late-'60s minimalist works by Terry Riley as well as the emerging Tangerine Dream (pre-*Phaedra*). Carlos also pioneered the effect of synthesized vocals (known as a vocoder), and their eerie nature perfectly complemented scenes from the film. Much of the rest of *A Clockwork Orange* is filled with rather cloying synthesizer versions of familiar classical pieces (from Beethoven's Ninth Symphony, Purcell's Music for the Funeral of Queen Mary, Rossini's The Thieving Magpie), similar to Carlos' previous *Switched-On Bach* recordings. Still, it's worthwhile if only for "Timesteps." *A Clockwork Orange* was originally released as a Warner Brothers soundtrack, containing only film cuts (which edited "Timesteps" down from thirteen minutes to only four). Though Carlos released another version with more music, that issue was superseded in 1998 by the release of *A Clockwork Orange: Complete Original Score* by East Side Digital in its comprehensive reissue program. —*John Bush*

**Sonic Seasonings** / 1972 / Columbia ♦♦♦♦
The same year Carlos finalized the score for *A Clockwork Orange*, the composer recorded a double album named *Sonic Seasonings*; it was a complete turn away fom the majestic synthesizer soundscapes and classical inspirations which had marked the movie score. Instead, Carlos recorded large amounts of environmental passages to produce a work which cycled through the four seasons. Beginning with bird calls and a thunderstorm to mark "Spring," Carlos phrases the synthesizers only in terms of the nature sounds heard. They rarely interject themselves, and the result is closer to a nature recording with occasional effects than a synthesizer recording with nature sounds. Of course, there was no precedent for "nature," "environmental" or even "new age" music in 1972—*Sonic Seasonings* was basically the genesis for several entire genres of music two decades later. As part of East Side Digital's Carlos CD reissue campaign, *Sonic Seasonings* was issued as a two-disc set, including the original LP plus a second disc of "natural" recordings, originally begun in 1986 and known as *Land of the Midnight Sun*. —*John Bush*

**Tron [Original Soundtrack]** / 1982 / CBS ♦♦♦♦
Though the film was important mostly for impressionable children, the original soundtrack to Disney's video-game crossover movie *Tron* was a notable landmark in the synthesis of electronic and traditional orchestral music. Given a set of cues from the director, Carlos composed an electronic score for the movie, which was later overlapped with symphonic backgrounds by the London Philharmonic Orchestra and the UCLA Chorus. Despite months of nagging problems in the combination stage, the result is an impressive score that fuses organic and electronic to such a degree that much of the score sounds of a piece. The explicitly electronic portions on tracks like "Tron Scherzo" and "Theme from Tron" are beautifully stilted examples of early '80s sequencer trance with Carlos' soundtrack expertise still in fine form. Though it was available only through its original LP issue and remained out of print throughout the '80s and '90s, rumors surfaced in the late '90s concerning a *Tron* reissue campaign. —*John Bush*

**Digital Moonscapes** / 1984 / Columbia ♦♦
Much was made of this Wendy Carlos outing, featuring the digital synthesizers she helped to design. Unfortunately, the music itself veers uncomfortably between murky electronic experimentalism and weedy pseudo-baroque that does more to irritate than to engage. —*Steven McDonald*

**Tales of Heaven & Hell** / Oct. 13, 1998 / East Side Digital ♦♦♦
"Contains genuinely scary material," reads a sleeve note. "Use caution when listening alone or in the dark." The warning is akin to the kinds of ads they used to run for '50s horror movies, and Wendy Carlos' album of largely instrumental, classically influenced music often recalls the scores of those movies, complete with Latin recitations, creepy sound effects, and whimpering and moaning female voices. But the effect of this "musical drama" is more likely to be mirth than terror, if only because such clichés have been so overdone in soundtrack music. While there are passages of genuine musical interest, the overall conception of Carlos' first album of new material in 12 years is just too silly to take seriously. (Carlos has titled one passage "Clockwork Black," a reference to her score for the film *A Clockwork Orange*.) —*William Ruhlmann*

## Derrick Carter

*Producer, DJ / Jazz-House, Club/Dance, House*
One of the pinnacles of Chicago house music's '90s wave, Derrick Carter began DJing at the age of nine, spinning disco records at family reunions. His debut single "Love Me Right" appeared in 1987, just after he graduated from college. Another single ("Symbols and Instruments," as Mood) appeared in 1989, but the Chicago house scene faded soon after, leaving Carter and other artists with few to play for except themselves. Thanks in part to Cajmere's and Felix Da Housecat's respective labels (Relief, Radikal Fear), Chicago

house made a comeback during the mid-'90s and began to offer impressive newcomers in addition to the old guard. Carter, recording for the Organico label, returned with several singles, and an album as Sound Patrol. In 1995, he began working with a live band as the Sound Patrol Orchestra. Though he hasn't released a production full-length, several mix albums have appeared, including *Cosmic Disco* on MixMag and *Pagan Offering* on Pagan. Carter has also founded two labels (Blue Cucaracha and Classic) and remixed tracks from Chicago's own post-rock heroes Tortoise. —*John Bush*

**The Future Sound of Chicago, Vol. 2** / Jun. 3, 1996 / Ministry of Sound ♦♦♦

- **Cosmic Disco** / May 19, 1997 / DMC ♦♦♦♦
This sublime mix of futuristic tribal house and tech-disco recorded for *Mixmag* features Carter dropping Chicago names like Gene Farris, DJ Sneak, and Green Velvet (plus his own remix of Cajmere's "Only 4 U"). He finds equal time, however, for foreign names like Jedi Knights and Jephte Guillaume. —*John Bush*

**Pagan Offering** / Aug. 31, 1998 / Pagan ♦♦♦
While Carter's *Cosmic Disco* mix mostly concerned Chicago house, *Pagan Offering* shifts the focus overseas to Pagan Records, home of top-flight left-field house by Terry Francis, House of 909, Swayzak, Presence, and Salt City Orchestra. It also includes five unreleased tracks. —*John Bush*

## Kim Cascone

*Producer / Experimental Ambient, Experimental Techno, Dark Ambient, Ambient Techno*

A New York student of electronic music influenced by experimentalists John Cage and Terry Riley, Kim Cascone later moved to San Francisco and founded the Silent label. The label was best known for recordings by Cascone projects PGR, Heavenly Music Corporation, Thessalonians and Spice Barons as well as a 1992 tribute to acid named *Fifty Years of Sunshine* (featuring Nurse with Wound, Psychic TV, Hawkwind, Timothy Leary). After his frenetic release schedule of the early '90s, Cascone took time out to work as a sound engineer for Thomas Dolby's Headspace studios. He returned to active recording with 1999's *Blue Cube*, his first album as Kim Cascone. *Cathode Flower* followed later that same year. [See also: Heavenly Music Corporation, PGR] —*John Bush*

- **blueCube** / 1998 / Rastermusic ♦♦♦♦
Kim Cascone's first release following the dissolution of his popular Heavenly Music Corporation project is also a revisiting of some of the sonic territories of his earlier work as PGR. The album began as a single track to accompany Cascone's contribution to a book of essays about computer music development platform Csound, edited by Richard Boulanger, and expanded into a full-length CD at the behest of Boulanger and others who figured he was onto something. An exploration of themes combining bleeding edge digital technology with rootings about in computer music's prehistory—Cascone used Csound to create acoustical models of early electronic instrument specs—*blueCube* is a musical expostulation on the "alchemical space" specific to composing with machines, and is some of his most enthralling work to date. —*Sean Cooper*

**cathodeFlower** / Nov. 9, 1999 / Ritornell ♦♦♦
This second installment in what Kim Cascone terms the blueCube Triptych is another work of isolationist, experimental ambience inspired by the late-'60s dawn of computer music. Fittingly, Cascone's ode to the era—a time when the Hal 9000 from *2001: A Space Odyssey* epitomized the future-shock wariness that computers would gradually take over their human creators—is a set of dark, paranoid, wind-blown computerscapes, evocative either of deep space or the uninhabited polar regions of Earth. Titles like "vortexShedding (simplex)" and "nullDrift" articulate the feelings conjured by the music, and on the latter, Cascone seems to channel between interstellar radio waves as though he's scanning the heavens for signs of intelligent life. —*John Bush*

## Casino Versus Japan (Erik Kowalski)

*Producer / Electronica, Ambient Techno, Post-Rock/Experimental*
Milwaukee-based producer Erik Kowalski produces tracks of gorgeous listening techno, with baroque, haunting melodies, and distorted trip-hop beats. After over two years of recording on his own, Kowalski released his debut, *Casino Versus Japan*, on Star Star. One year later, *Go Hawaii* followed on Milwaukee's Wobblyhead. Kowalski has also worked with Charles Wyatt as Charles Atlas. —*John Bush*

**Casino Versus Japan** / 1998 / Star ♦♦

- **Go Hawaii** / 1999 / Wobblyhead ♦♦♦♦
Erik Kowalski's second album as Casino Versus Japan is an ambient techno postcard from the nation's sunniest state, though the only obvious references to Hawaii come with the faraway slack-key guitar on the opener "Theme" and the delightful vocal samples of a preschooler on "It's Very Sunny." Elsewhere, *Go Hawaii* is a superb album of chill-out techno-pop—heavy on the spacious synth, minor-key melodies, and crunchy percussion programs. Check "Local Forecast," "Late for School," and "Over Island" for some of the dreamiest techno to come out of the American underground, or "Dielectric Saints" for an atmospheric soundclash between dub and noise-pop. —*John Bush*

## Cassius

f. 1998, Paris, France
*Group / Tech-House, Funky Breaks, Electronica, Neo-Electro, Trip-Hop*
Cassius, a new addition to the top ranks of French electronica circa 1999, actually comprised two of the scene's most experienced producers: Philippe Zdar and Hubert Blanc-Francart (aka Boombass). Besides their productions for Mo'Wax as La Funk Mob, the duo had also manned the boards for several excellent LPs by French rapper MC Solaar. They first met back in the late '80s, working in the same studio (Zdar was an engineer, and Boombass was just learning the trade). Boombass worked with MC Solaar, and combined with Zdar to release two EPs on Mo'Wax as La Funk Mob during 1994. Zdar also teamed with Etienne De Crecy (of Super Discount) to release an LP as Motorbass. Finally, Zdar and Boombass came together in late 1998 as Cassius. Combining the jazzy hip-hop of Boombass with Zdar's phase'n'filter acid-disco, Cassius debuted with the single "Cassius 1999," a club anthem and British Top 20 hit late in 1998. The full-length *1999* appeared early the following year. —*John Bush*

- **1999** / Jan. 25, 1999 / Astralwerks ♦♦♦♦
A sleek and intelligent dance record, Zdar and Boombass' debut is an intriguing update of classic '80s garage and disco in the same fashion that Daft Punk rewired Chicago acid house for 1997's *Homework*. Most of the best tracks here, including "La Mouche" and "Foxxy," weave snippets of diva vocals and flexible basslines into up-front productions with a focus on tight rhythm programming. Unfortunately, too many tracks on *1999* suffer from what can be an unhappy medium—casual pacing for a club tune but rather formulaic production values to make for solid living-room listening. Aside from the single "Cassius 1999," the hip-hop punch of "Mister Eveready" is another highlight. —*John Bush*

## Cerrone (Jean-Marc Cerrone)

b. 1952, Paris, France
*Producer / Club/Dance, Disco, House, Soul*
Jean-Marc Cerrone was one of the most influential disco producers in Europe during the '70s and early '80s, eclipsed only by Giorgio Moroder. Born in Paris in 1952, he studied music as a child and won his first post as the orchestra leader at a Parisian club at the age of 18. After additional work with the French producer Barclay during the early '70s, he released his first solo album, *Love in C-Minor*, in 1976. The title track proved a massive European hit and worked its way into the American Top 40 as well. Although he only placed one more single in the US, Cerrone stayed popular on his native continent over the course of a career spanning a dozen albums. —*John Bush*

- **Love in C Minor** / 1976 / Cotillion ♦♦♦♦
Though it's barely half an hour long, Cerrone's album debut is a masterful sample of mid-tempo disco with an eye towards production prowess instead of chart potential. The full-length includes a 15-minute version of the hit title track, plus a cover of the old Los Bravos hit "Black Is Black." —*John Bush*

**Cerrone 3: Supernature** / 1977 / Gucci ♦♦♦
As its predecessor did, *Supernature* leads off with a lengthy title track that epitomizes chunky producer-driven disco, then explores other avenues with surprisingly leftfield album tracks like the spacy "In the Smoke" and predictably percussion-oriented "Sweet Drums." —*John Bush*

**The Best of Cerrone** / Jan. 9, 1990 / Hot Prod. ♦♦♦♦
Cerrone was a dominant Eurodisco act in the mid-'70s. His music accented both disco's strengths (multi-layered arrangements, a driving, at times almost

overbearing beat, and sophisticated strings) and weaknesses (a stifling lyrical sameness and arrangement/production formula that could quickly grow wearisome). But only Gino Soccio and Georgio Moroder rivaled Cerrone in this style of disco. —*Ron Wynn*

## A Certain Ratio

f. 1977, Sheffield, Yorkshire, England
*Group / Post-Punk, New Wave, Alternative Pop/Rock*

Though formed in Manchester's late-'70s punk scene, A Certain Ratio used an increasing amount of electronics throughout the '80s to become more of a dancefloor-oriented band, much like Factory label-mates New Order. The group (whose name is a pointer to a Brian Eno song) was formed in 1977 by vocalists Simon Topping and Martha Tilson, bassist Jeremy Kerr, guitarist Peter Terrell, and guitarist/trumpeter Martin Moscrop—drummer Donald Johnson later replaced a drum machine. New Order's manager Rob Gretton was impressed by early live shows, and spread the word to Tony Wilson, who signed the group to his fledgling Factory label and became their first manager. In 1979, A Certain Ratio released the cassette-only album *The Graveyard and the Ballroom* (including one side each of studio and live material) and a debut single, "All Night Party."

The punk and industrial grind of ACR's early live shows soon became more danceable and funky—second single "Shack Up" even reached the American R&B Top 50. The proper debut album, *To Each...*, appeared in 1981 and was produced by the band and Martin Hannett. The following two albums, *Sextet* and *I'd Like to See You Again* (both 1982), expanded A Certain Ratio's sound further, encompassing Latin and jazz elements. But Tilson left the band in 1982, and Topping opted out a year later, leaving vocal duties to Kerr and Johnson. Also, Andy Connell joined the group as keyboardist, replacing Peter Terrell.

Frustrated with their lack of commercial success, the group recorded just one more album for Factory, 1986's *Force*, though the company released a singles compilation (*The Old and the New*) around the same time. The next year brought *Live in America* (on the independent label Dojo) and a major-label contract with A&M.

A Certain Ratio fared no better with A&M, however. The full-length *Good Together* was released in 1989 and the mini-LP *MCR* followed one year later, but the band moved to old friend Rob Gretton's label (robs' records) by 1991. *Up in Downsville* appeared in 1992. Creation Records later acquired the rights to ACR's back catalogue and released a remix album with help from Manchester alums Graham Massey, Electronic, the Other Two, and Sub Sub, among others. After a five year hiatus, A Certain Ratio returned in 1997 with *Change the Station*. —*John Bush*

**Graveyard and the Ballroom** / 1979 / Factory ♦♦♦♦

**To Each ...** / 1981 / Factory ♦♦
For A Certain Ratio's debut album, the group dropped much of the bleak dance-punk of early material in place of what sounds like a shallow attempt to seize the baton dropped by gloom giants Joy Division after the death of Ian Curtis. Though Simon Topping's trumpet work occasionally lifts *To Each* over the crop of contemporary synth-popsters, the album is a bit too mired in its own misery to make an impression on listeners. —*Keith Farley*

**Sextet** / Jan. 1982 / Factory ♦♦♦
Released the same year as their debut, *Sextet* upped the energy of A Certain Ratio's dour minimalist dance, with cursory nods to even soul and funk from vocalist Martha Tilson. For the most part, though, the electronics and rhythms are still curiously apart from song structure, making for an oddly distanced record. —*Keith Farley*

● **The Old and the New** / 1985 / Factory ♦♦♦♦
The best place to find out how A Certain Ratio equaled early New Order as far as hypnotic synth-dance was concerned, the compilation *The Old and the New* reaches back into the '70s to cull the best tracks from the group's occasionally entertaining, occasionally disappointing EPs and full-lengths of the era. There are quite a few highlights here, including singles like "Do the Du" and "Shack Up." —*Keith Farley*

**Force** / 1986 / Factory ♦♦
Jettisoning the raw, chilling abandon of their earlier work, *Force* instead layers A Certain Ratio's hybrid of pop, jazz, and funk with shimmering keyboards and guitars. The resulting sound is one that's well-executed and consistent, albeit lacking in potency and spontaneity; the most interesting moments are the most experimental, like the backwards bass on "Bootsy" and the strange drones on "Take Me Down." —*Jason Ankeny*

**Change the Station** / Nov. 25, 1996 / Robs Records ♦♦♦
Arriving six years after *Up in Downsville*, *Change the Station* finds A Certain Ratio in top form, working from a dance-pop foundation and adding flourishes of Manchester funk and ambient house. This time around, vocalists Denise Johnson and Lrona Bailey dominate the proceedings, and their soulful singing gives the songs dimension, helping make *Change the Station* a genuine return to form. —*Stephen Thomas Erlewine*

## Kerri Chandler

b. Sep. 28, 1969, East Orange, NJ
*Producer, DJ / Garage, Club/Dance, House*

One of the best garage producers and remixers during the '90s was Kerri "Kaoz 6:23" Chandler, a native of garage-central New Jersey and a DJ by the time he was nine years old. Influenced by his father (also a mixer in his own time), Chandler also began producing tracks by the time he was 15, with help from fellow Jersey-ites like Tony Humphries, and Michael Watford. His tracks for King St., Strictly Rhythm, Large, Nervous and his own Madhouse Records made him one of the top producers in the garage scene by the early '90s, with a discography including club landmarks like "(You're My) Inspiration," "Hallelujah" and "Stompin' Grounds" as well as more introspective, jazzy works like 1993's *The Atmosphere* EP. Chandler's first LP was 1997's *Kaoz on King St.*, followed a year later by the mix album *Kaoz Theory*. Another mix album, *First Steps*, followed in 2000. Chandler has also recorded under aliases such as K.C.Y.C., Grampa, and Kamar, and worked on remixes for Byron Stingily, Kristine W., Ten City, Robin S., and Martha Wash. —*John Bush*

**Kaoz on King St.** / May 5, 1997 / King St. ♦♦♦♦
*Kaoz on King St.* is a solid full-length spotlighting Kerri Chandler's production mastery. Besides including a few of his classic singles ("Keep Me Inside," "Come Home," "Hallelujah"), the album showcases Chandler's heavy-kick garage beat and high-essence garage-soul. The album features several collaborations as well, including Carole Sylvan and Carolyn Harding (on vocals) plus Hunter Hayes (on saxophone). —*John Bush*

● **Kaoz Theory: The Essential Kerri Chandler** / Sep. 14, 1998 / Harmless ♦♦♦♦

A career-spanning collection from his early releases on Prolific to late-'90s tracks like "See Line Woman" and "Ladbroke Grove," *Kaoz Theory* is a good compilation if not quite essential. There are a few classics ("The Way I Feel," "Glory to God," "Inspiration") and a few rarer productions, plus a solid collaboration track with Joe Claussell titled "Escravos de Jo." —*John Bush*

## Chaos A.D. (Tom Jenkinson)

*Producer / Techno, Acid Techno*

Wishing perhaps to distance himself from the collection of his early recordings released by Rephlex, Tom Jenkinson (aka Squarepusher) issued the material as Chaos A.D. The alias did indeed mark a radically different sound for Jenkinson, mostly hardcore acid techno in the vein of his one-time label-mate Aphex Twin's *Caustic Window* recordings. *Buzz Caner* appeared in 1998. [See also: Squarepusher] —*John Bush*

● **Buzz Caner** / May 25, 1998 / Rephlex ♦♦♦♦
The cover of *Buzz Caner* displays a pile of blank tapes, obviously denoting the mine of unreleased material by Tom Jenkinson. More indebted to acid and trance than the fusion wash displayed by his Warp material, the 12 tracks included are amateurish, occasionally inventive, acid explorations which often sound similar to the rarer items in Aphex Twin's back catalogue. The angry-man vocoder vocals on "Generation Shit" are perhaps the tackiest moment, though the very next track, "Dreaded Pestilence," is inspired and inventive. For the legion of Squarepusher fans who are trainspotters as well, *Buzz Caner* is a must-buy, though the sound is leagues away from most of his recordings. —*John Bush*

## The Chemical Brothers

f. 1989, Manchester, England
*Group / Big Beat, Funky Breaks, Electronica, Trip-Hop, Club/Dance*

The act with the first arena-sized sound in the electronica movement, the Chemical Brothers united such varying influences as Public Enemy, Cabaret Voltaire, and My Bloody Valentine to create a dance-rock-rap fusion which rivalled the best old-school DJs on their own terms—keeping a crowd of people on the floor by working through any number of groove-oriented styles featuring unmissable samples, from familiar guitar riffs to vocal tags to various sound effects. And when the duo (Tom Rowlands and Ed Simons) decided to supplement their DJ careers by turning their bedrooms into recording studios, they pioneered a style of music (later termed big beat) remarkable for its lack of energy-loss from the dancefloor to the radio. Chemical Brothers albums were less collections of songs and more hour-long journeys, chock full of deep bomb-studded beats, percussive breakdowns and effects borrowed from a host of sources. All in all, the duo proved one of the few exceptions to the rule that intelligent dance music could never be bombastic or truly satisfying to the seasoned rock fan; it's hardly surprising that they were one of the few dance acts to enjoy simultaneous success in the British/American mainstream and in critical quarters.

While growing up, both Rowlands and Simons grooved to an eccentric musical diet, ranging from the Smiths and Jesus & Mary Chain to Kraftwerk and Public Enemy. They met while taking the same history course at Manchester University, though neither were native Mancunians—Rowlands enrolled because of the legendary Haçienda nightclub nearby, while Simons acknowledged the city as birthplace to the Smiths and New Order. The pair began sampling Madchester's vibrant nightclub scene together during 1989 and 1990, just at the peak of Britain's fascination with a DJing style named Balearic. Pioneered at the island hotspot of Ibiza during the mid-'80s, Balearic relied on a blend of early house music, Italian disco, rare-groove jazz and funk, Northern soul, hip-hop, and alternative dance. Original Balearic DJs like Trevor Fung, Paul Oakenfold, and Mike Pickering brought the sound back to indie-clubs in London and Manchester, and the style proved very attractive to musical eclectics like Rowlands and Simons.

Though Rowlands was already performing in the alternative-dance group Ariel, the pair began DJing together at the Manchester club Naked Under Leather in 1991. Hardly believing that their weekend project would progress, they took the semi-serious handle Dust Brothers (a tribute to the American production team responsible for one of their favorite albums, the Beastie Boys' *Paul's Boutique*). Despite their doubts, Rowlands and Simons' club night did grow more popular, thanks to the duo's Balearic mix of rare house tracks flavored with hip-hop breakdowns, independent-dance fusions, and ancient second-hand discards. After deciding to try and re-create their unique sound in their tiny bedroom studio, the Dust Brothers emerged with "Song to the Siren," an intriguing example of the new alternative dance scene including sample-victims Meat Beat Manifesto and This Mortal Coil.

After the single was pressed up on a limited release of 500 copies, it began getting attention from Britain's top DJs, initially including an old friend named Justin Robertson but later including Andrew Weatherall and Darren Emerson. Weatherall licensed the single to Junior Boy's Own Records, and after the pair had finished university, they moved back to London to work on another EP (*14th Century Sky*) and a residency at another club. After their third release, "My Mercury Mouth," the duo began to get more high-profile clients for remixing; besides Justin Roberston's Lionrock collective, Primal Scream, Prodigy, and the Charlatans all received treatments.

When lawyers for the original Dust Brothers came calling in 1995, though, Rowlands and Simons were forced to change their name to the Chemical Brothers (the proposed Dust Brothers UK was turned down). Word on the street and nightclub scene was so good that it hardly mattered; their new residency at the Heavenly Sunday Social quickly became one of the hottest clubs in London—documented on the mix disc *Live at the Social, Vol. 1*—and their debut album *Exit Planet Dust* was heavily praised by critics. Another fan of the record, Oasis frontman Noel Gallagher, agreed to lend his vocals to a future single named "Setting Sun," the Chemicals' tribute to one of their own favorites, the Beatles' "Tomorrow Never Knows." The single went to number one in late 1996, and the Chemical Brothers opened up for the giant Oasis concert at Knebworth besides headlining their own shows all over the world. Second album *Dig Your Own Hole* took charge of the top spot on the album charts upon its release in April 1997, and on the wings of America's growing electronica push, the album sailed to number 14 stateside and went gold. The Chemicals released a major-label mix album in 1998, *Brothers Gonna Work It Out*, and followed with their third studio LP, *Surrender*, in 1999. —*John Bush*

☆ **Exit Planet Dust** / Aug. 15, 1995 / Astralwerks ◆◆◆◆◆
The former Dust Brothers make oblique reference to litigation averted on their debut full-length. The Brothers' sound is big on bombast, replete with screeching guitar samples and lots of sirens and screaming divas. A breakthrough album of sorts, *Exit* was, upon its release, one of the few European post-techno albums to make any sort of headway into the stateside market. —*Sean Cooper*

**Loops of Fury [Single]** / 1996 / Astralwerks ◆◆◆◆
*Loops of Fury* is an EP of leftovers released mostly to capitalize on the success of the Brothers' debut. Features a remix by UK techno hero Dave Clarke. —*Sean Cooper*

★ **Dig Your Own Hole** / Apr. 7, 1997 / Astralwerks ◆◆◆◆◆
Taking the swirling eclecticism of their post-techno debut *Exit Planet Dust* to the extreme, the Chemical Brothers blow all stylistic boundaries down with their second album, *Dig Your Own Hole*. Bigger, bolder and more adventurous than *Exit Planet Dust*, *Dig Your Own Hole* opens with the slamming cacophony of "Block Rockin' Beats," and where hip-hop meets hardcore techno, complete with a Schoolly D sample and an elastic bass riff. Everything is going on at once in "Block Rockin' Beats," and it sets the pace for the rest of the record, where songs and styles blur into a continuous kaleidoscope of sound. It rocks hard enough for the pop audience, but it doesn't compromise either the Chemicals' sound or the adventurous, futuristic spirit of electronica—even "Setting Sun," with its sly homages to the Beatles' "Tomorrow Never Knows" and Noel Gallagher's twisting, catchy melody, doesn't sound like retro psychedelia; it sounds vibrant, unexpected, and utterly contemporary. There are no distinctions between different styles, and the Chemicals sound as if they're having fun, building *Dig Your Own Hole* from fragments of the past, distorting the rhythms and samples, and pushing it forward with an intoxicating rush of synthesizers, electronics, and layered drum machines. The Chemical Brothers might not push forward into self-consciously arty territories like some of their electronic peers, but they have more style and focus, constructing a blindingly innovative and relentlessly propulsive album that's an exhilarating listen—one that sounds positively new but utterly inviting at the same time. —*Stephen Thomas Erlewine*

**Chemical Reaction: The Best of British Electronica** / Sep. 30, 1997 / One ◆◆◆
After the Chemical Brothers established themselves as a pop act (at least in England) in 1997, Afrodeisa Records latched upon the ingenious concept of collecting the duo's legendary 12" remixes of other artists on one CD. Due to various licensing problems, Afrodeisa wasn't able to have *Chemical Reaction* feature nothing but Chemical Brothers mixes—six of the 11 tracks are Chemical mixes, the rest being a hodgepodge of original mixes and remixes. Apart from Monkey Mafia's mix of St. Etienne's "Filthy," those five cuts are of negligible worth, but the Chemical cuts are terrific, demonstrating their vast skill as dance producers. The duo completely deconstruct St. Etienne's "Like a Motorway," Leftfield's "Open Up," and Primal Scream's Thin Lizzy tribute "Jailbird," turning them into completely different songs. Essentially, all of the Chemicals' mixes are big beat, but the most remarkable thing is the variety of texture, tones and moods the duo gets out of that style. *Chemical Reaction* might not be the perfect way to become acquainted with these mixes, but for fans who can't find or afford the original singles, it's a worthy addition to their collection. —*Stephen Thomas Erlewine*

**Brothers Gonna Work It Out** / Sep. 22, 1998 / Astralwerks ◆◆◆
To buy time after the success of *Dig Your Own Hole*, the Chemical Brothers released their first DJ mix album, *Brothers Gonna Work It Out*. *Dig Your Own Hole* was one of the handful of electronica albums to find a wide audience in both the UK and the US, largely because of its gigantic, straight-ahead beats. Whether by design or not, it was electronic music that could reach a wide audience because it was about what all rock or pop music is about at its core—rhythm. To their credit, the Chemicals viewed themselves as part of a continuum, not as ambassadors of techno, which is presumably why they used their elevated profile to showcase a style of music unfamiliar to a mass audience with songs unfamiliar to a mass audience. That might lead to the preconception that *Brothers Gonna Work It Out* is a chore or an educational lesson, which couldn't be further from the truth. *Brothers Gonna Work It Out* is a rush, pure and simple. Using their own songs, plus a huge selection of other records and remixes, they've created a relentless, frequently exciting record that pushes forth on the momentum of unpredictable juxtapositions and big, big beats. During the course of the 70-minute disc, the Brothers spin everything—Willie Hutch, Meat Beat Manifesto, Spiritualized, Renegade Soundwave, Manic Street Preachers—which only emphasizes how they've created

their own identity through piecing together remnants of pop and DJ culture, from forgotten favorites to cult classics. Artistically, it doesn't quite match their pair of studio efforts, but it's a nice stopgap for fans awaiting their third full-length album. —*Stephen Thomas Erlewine*

**Surrender** / Jun. 22, 1999 / Astralwerks ♦♦♦♦
By the time of the Chemical Brothers' third album, *Surrender*, the big-beat phenomenon they had done much to engender was more apt to be heard on a soft-drink commercial than the world's hipper dancefloors. And with the growing omnipresence of big-beat's simplistic party vibes threatening to cave in the entire scene, Tom and Ed came to grips with what is—compared to their previous work—a house record. The pounding four-on-the-floor thump of tracks like "Music:Response," "Got Glint," and the duo's take on KLF-style stadium house for the single "Hey Boy Hey Girl" signals that this is a transition record for the Chemical Brothers that could eventually take them back into the straightahead-dance mainstream status enjoyed by acts from Daft Punk to Armand Van Helden.

The irony here is that even considering the changes, *Surrender* still feels very similar to its predecessors. The focus on wave-of-sound production, bucketfuls of old-school vocal samples, and various sirens and beatbox effects sound like they were lifted wholesale from their breakout album, *Dig Your Own Hole*, or their first release, *Exit Planet Dust*. And while a few of the vocal tracks focus on new collaborations, they're along the same lines, making it tough to spot the differences from past albums—the quavering British vocals of Beth Orton have given way to the quavering American vocals of Hope Sandoval, and the Charlatans' Tim Burgess is replaced by New Order's reclusive Bernard Sumner (a sure sign that the Chemicals have moved up a notch on the music-industry food chain). Also, two returning guests (Noel Gallagher and a member of Mercury Rev, Jonathan Donahue) make very similar contributions to the record in the identical places they appeared on *Dig Your Own Hole*. Even besides its simpy title, the Gallagher track "Let Forever Be" is the very same electronica update of the Beatles' "Tomorrow Never Knows" that made their 1996 collaboration single "Setting Sun" a number one hit in Britain. And the Donahue track, "Dream On," is very similar to the indie-psychedelia of "The Private Psychedelic Reel" from *Dig Your Own Hole*. Sure, the Chemical Brothers do this type of music very well; it's just that *Surrender* isn't quite the change of direction they'd been aiming for—it's simply the *same* great album they'd made two years earlier. —*John Bush*

## Neneh Cherry

b. Mar. 10, 1964, Stockholm, Sweden
*Vocals / Pop-Rap, Club/Dance, Urban, Dance-Pop*

The stepdaughter of jazz trailblazer Don Cherry, vocalist Neneh Cherry forged her own groundbreaking blend of pop, dance, and hip-hop which presaged the emergence of both alternative rap and trip-hop. She was born Neneh Mariann Karlssson on March 10, 1964 in Stockholm, Sweden, the daughter of West African percussionist Amadu Jah and artist Moki Cherry. Raised by her mother and her trumpeter stepfather in both Stockholm and New York City, Cherry dropped out of school at age 14, and in 1980 she relocated to London to sing with the punk group the Cherries.

Following brief flings with the Slits and the Nails, she joined the experimental funk outfit Rip Rig + Panic, and appeared on the group's albums *God* (1981), *I Am Cold* (1982), and *Attitude* (1983). When the band broke up, Cherry remained with one of the spin-off groups, Float Up CP, and led them through one album, 1986's *Kill Me in the Morning*. The band proved short-lived, however, and Cherry began rapping in a London club, where she earned the attention of a talent scout who signed her to a solo contract. Her first single, "Stop the War," railed against the invasion of the Falklands Islands.

After attracting some notice singing backup on the The's "Slow Train to Dawn" single, she became romantically and professionally involved with composer and musician Cameron McVey, who, under the alias Booga Bear, wrote much of the material that would comprise Cherry's 1989 debut LP *Raw Like Sushi*. One song McVey did not write was "Buffalo Stance," the album's breakthrough single; originally tossed off as a B-side by the mid-Eighties pop group Morgan McVey, Cherry's cover was an international smash which neatly summarized the album's eclectic fusion of pop smarts and hip-hop energy.

A pair of hits—the eerie "Manchild" and "Kisses on the Wind"—followed,

but shortly after the record's release Cherry was sidelined with Lyme disease, and apart from a cover of Cole Porter's "I've Got You Under My Skin" for the 1990 *Red Hot + Blue* benefit album, she remained silent until 1992's *Homebrew*. A more subdued collection than *Raw Like Sushi*, it featured cameos from Gang Starr and R.E.M.'s Michael Stipe, as well as writing and production assistance from Geoff Barrow, who layered the track "Somedays" with the same distinct trip-hop glaze he later perfected as half of the duo Portishead. While the album was not as commercially successful as its predecessor, Cherry returned to the charts in 1994 dueting with Youssou N'Dour on the global hit "Seven Seconds." After another lengthy layoff spent raising her children, she resurfaced with the atmospheric *Man* in 1996. —*Jason Ankeny*

● **Raw Like Sushi** / May 1989 / Virgin ♦♦♦♦
Those arguing that the most individualistic R&B and dance music of the late '80s and early- to mid-'90s came out of Britain could point to Neneh Cherry's unconventional *Raw Like Sushi* as a shining example. An orthodox and brilliantly daring blend of R&B, rap, pop, and dance music, *Sushi* enjoyed little exposure on America's conservative, urban, contemporary radio formats, but was a definite underground hit. Full of personality, the singer/rapper is as thought-provoking as she is witty and humorous when addressing relationships and taking aim at less-than-kosher behavior of males and females alike. Macho "homeboys" and casanovas take a pounding on "So Here I Come" and the hit "Buffalo Stance," while women who are shallow, cold-hearted or materialistic get lambasted on "Phoney Ladies," "Heart" and "Inna City Mamma." Cherry's idealism comes through loud and clear on "The Next Generation," a plea to take responsibility for one's sexual actions and give children the respect and attention they deserve. —*Alex Henderson*

**Homebrew** / Oct. 27, 1992 / Virgin ♦♦♦♦
Neneh Cherry doesn't get into the studio nearly often enough. Three years passed before the British singer/rapper came out with a second album. Thankfully, she more than lived up to the tremendous promise of *Raw Like Sushi* on the equally magnificent and risk-taking *Homebrew*. Cherry shows no signs of the dreaded sophomore slump—everything on the CD is a gem. She triumphs with a seamless and unorthodox blend of hip-hop, R&B, dance music, and pop, and on "Money Love" and "Trout," the presence of R.E.M.'s Michael Stipe brings rock to the eclectic mix. As humorous as Cherry can be, her reflections on relationships and social issues are often quite pointed. While "Money Love" decries the evils of materialism, the moving "I Ain't Gone Under Yet" describes an inner-city woman's determination not to be brought down by the poverty and drugs that surround her. And "Twisted" is about keeping yourself sane in a world gone insane. Unfortunately, *Homebrew* wasn't the commercial breakthrough Cherry was more than deserving of. —*Alex Henderson*

## Chessie (Stephen Gardner)

f. 1994
*Group / Minimal Techno, Indie Pop, Ambient Pop*

Originally treated as a side project for Lorelei bassist Stephen Gardner, Chessie was his way of experimenting with the guitar while involving his fascination with trains. Gardner started recording in 1994, toying with his six-string and assorted loops to create unique instrumental noise-pop. After Lorelei came to an end in 1996, Gardner had more time to focus on Chessie, and in 1998 Drop Beat Records released his first full-length *Single Series*. Continuing the relationship with Drop Beat, Gardner followed with second album *Meet* in 1999. —*Mike DaRonco*

**Signal Series** / Apr. 13, 1999 / Drop Beat ♦♦

● **Meet** / Nov. 9, 1999 / Drop Beat ♦♦
A collection of lower-than-lo-fi tracks (well, call them sound experiments) recorded between 1993 and 1999, *Meet* begins with a track of over-processed beat-noise that sounds like it was much more fun to record than it is to listen to. The album gradually gives way to a recording of mashed wooden blocks with the attendant heavy distortion, and "Ivy City Interlocking," a track that begins with some soothing ambient textures, abruptly detours into a series of poorly recorded, heavily distorting beats. When Stephen Gardner cleans out the noise, however, he often comes out with some intriguing results, as on the experimental dub of "Brake Test" and "Nowa Huta," which evokes what the Tortoise-Oval soundclash should've *really* sounded like. —*John Bush*

## Chic

**f.** 1977, New York, NY, **db.** 1985
*Group / Disco, Funk*

Chic was the best and most influential disco band of the latter half of the '70s, earning hits with both their own records and the outside productions of co-leaders Nile Rodgers and Bernard Edwards. Beginning their career as the Big Apple Band, the group changed their name to Chic in 1977 after Walter Murphy & the Big Apple Band had a number one hit with "A Fifth of Beethoven." Along with the change in name came a change in music, from fusion to disco. Edwards (bass), Rodgers (guitar), and Tony Thompson (drums) hired Norma Jean Wright and Alfa Anderson to sing, and they recorded a demo of "Dance Dance Dance." Atlantic picked it up in late 1977 after a series of rejections from other record labels; the single sold a million copies in one month, catapulting Chic into the forefront of the disco scene. After Wright left for a solo career, Luci Martin joined the band. Chic's biggest hits—"Le Freak" (No. 1), "I Want Your Love" (No. 7), and "Good Times" (No. 1)—came in 1978-1979, and as disco started to fade, so did the group's popularity. Still, Chic's influence was apparent throughout the '80s; "Good Times" alone spawned Queen's hit "Another One Bites the Dust" (a complete rip-off), and Sugarhill Gang used the record as the foundation for "Rapper's Delight," arguably the first rap single. Nile Rodgers was one of the most successful producers of the early '80s, scoring hits with David Bowie's *Let's Dance*, Madonna's *Like a Virgin*, and Mick Jagger's solo debut, *She's the Boss*. Edwards' solo productions weren't as consistent as Rodgers', but the Power Station's album (which featured Tony Thompson on drums) was a hit. Chic re-formed in 1992, but failed to recapture the fire of its glory days. —*Stephen Thomas Erlewine*

**Chic** / 1977 / Atlantic ✦✦

When Chic's self-titled debut album came out in 1978, many rock critics gave it very negative reviews and failed to see just how rhythmically and harmonically exciting Chic's blend of funk, soul and Euro-disco was. But one critic who often gave Chic favorable coverage was Don Waller, who hit the nail on the head when he exalted the band as "an uptown version of Booker T & the MGs." It was a most insightful analogy—Chic's music was a lot sleeker than Booker T & the MGs' raw, instrumental Memphis soul, but like Booker T, the Niles Rodgers/Bernard Edwards team turned out some of the most infectious and influential R&B party grooves of their era. Although not quite as strong as Chic's next two albums, *C'est Chic* and *Risque*, would be, this highly enjoyable album put the group on the map commercially thanks to the infectious hits "Dance Dance Dance" and "Everybody Dance." Some rock critics saw *Chic* as just another faceless disco production, but in fact, the opposite is true—with this album, Chic fashioned a very distinctive and recognizable sound that proved to be as influential in its era as Booker T & the MGs were in theirs. The sound that Chic established with this album was one that everyone from Queen and ABC, to Sister Sledge, the Sugarhill Gang and Madonna would benefit from. —*Alex Henderson*

**C'est Chic** / 1978 / Atlantic ✦✦

With Chic's second album, *C'est Chic*, all of the pieces in Nile Rodgers and Bernard Edwards' puzzle fell into place perfectly. The group's self-titled debut album had unveiled a winning sound, and on *C'est Chic*, Rodgers/Edwards took it to an even higher level. *C'est Chic* boasted such major hits as "Le Freak" and "I Want Your Love," and the songs that weren't among the hit singles are also superb, including the optimistic "Happy Man," the reflective "At Last I Am Free," the quirky "Funny Bone," and the classy instrumental "Savoir Faire." The infectious opener, "Chic Cheer," quickly caught the attention of New York's emerging hip-hoppers who found its addictive funk groove to be perfect for rapping and mixing. Make no mistake, *C'est Chic* is among Chic's best albums. —*Alex Henderson*

**Risque** / 1979 / Atlantic ✦✦

Chic was very much in its prime when it recorded its third album, *Risque*, which contained hits that ranged from "My Feet Keep Dancing" and "My Forbidden Lover," to the influential "Good Times." That feel-good manifesto is one of the first songs that comes to mind when one thinks of the disco era and the Jimmy Carter years, but Chic's popularity certainly wasn't limited to the disco crowd. The fact that "Good Times" became the foundation for both the Sugarhill Gang's "Rapper's Delight" and Queen's "Another One Bites the Dust" tells you a lot—it underscores the fact that Chic was influencing everyone from early rappers to art rockers. A group that many rock critics were so quick to dismiss was having an impact in many different areas. From hip-hoppers to new wavers in London and Manchester, *Risque* was considered primary listening. And *Risque* is impressive not only because of its uptempo cuts but also because of slow material that includes the lush "A Warm Summer Night" and the dramatic ballad "Will You Cry (When You Hear This Song)." *Risque* is definitely among Chic's essential albums. —*Alex Henderson*

**Real People** / 1980 / Atlantic ✦✦

In the early '80s, Chic's influence on other artists was hard to miss. Change, Fantasy, Luther Vandross, the Talking Heads, Grace Jones and Queen were among the many artists who were incorporating elements of the Chic sound. It was ironic and quite amusing to hear some members of the "Death To Disco!" brigade blaring Queen's "Another One Bites the Dust" on their car stereos during the summer of 1980, for that funk-rock ditty was obviously based on "Good Times." But Chic itself was seeing its popularity start to fade, and fans were realizing that the group had reached its creative peak in the late '70s. Like other albums that Chic recorded in the early '80s, *Real People* is competent but less than essential. Diehard fans will find that while "Rebels Are We," "I Got Protection," and "Chip off the Old Block" are likable and catchy, they aren't in a class with "Good Times" or "Le Freak." This is a decent album, but it's also the work of a group that was past its prime. —*Alex Henderson*

● **Dance Dance Dance: Best of Chic** / Nov. 5, 1991 / Atlantic ✦✦✦✦

You think disco was nothing more than assembly-line funk and freeze-dried beats? Then you need to step into the crisp grooves and walloping boogie found on this stunning collection of Chic's '70s recordings. Such hits as "Good Times," "Dance Dance Dance," and "Le Freak" used the stylistic innovations of James Brown and Sly Stone as a blueprint for a new era of funk. Bernard Edwards' basslines are so provocative they seem to talk, while Nile Rodgers' skeletal guitar runs hark back to Steve Cropper's slashing style. Sure, the songs don't say much. Sure, the dance mixes collected here ramble on after about six minutes. But once you step into these grooves—grooves that influenced an entire generation of artists from David Byrne to Prince—you will realize that these were indeed good times. —*John Floyd*

**Chic-Ism** / Mar. 3, 1992 / Warner Brothers ✦✦

"Doin' That Thing to Me" contains a reference to the mythological wizard Merlin in its lyrics. By some strange twist of nature, mythology was certainly at work when those reviewing *Chic-Ism* on its release in 1992 dismissed it purely because Chic were old hats. In actuality, the worst thing about it is the cover. *Chic-Ism* certainly isn't likely to make album of the century listings, but as Chic albums go, it's fine if a tad '80s, which is to be expected as it was recorded only two years into the '90s. What were critics expecting of Chic—synthesizers à la Kraftwerk? Kicking in with the infectious "Chic Mystique," a little too long at six and a half minutes, it's pretty much business as usual. This leads into "Your Love" and "Jusagroove," both keeping pace before slowing down for "One and Only One." "In It to Win It" is a perfect update of their New York disco-funk style, a recipe that bands like the Brand New Heavies emulated in later years. The last stretch of the album includes "High," a beauty that is close enough a slowed down "Good Times." "MMFTCF (Make My Funk the Chic Funk)," and a better edited reprise of "Mystique" conclude. —*Kelvin Hayes*

## Chicane (Nick Bracegirdle)

*Producer / Progressive -Trance, Progressive-House, Electronica, Trance, Club/Dance, Dance-Pop*

Chicane is the group name for British trance musician and remixer Nick Bracegirdle, who first attracted attention under the name Disco Citizens with the Top 40 UK hit "Right Here Right Now" in 1995. Changing to Chicane, he reached the British Top 20 in late 1996 with "Offshore." He then enlisted Clannad's Maire Brennan for a remake of the Clannad hit "The Theme from Harry's Game" under the title "Saltwater," which reached the UK Top Ten and became an international hit. The first Chicane album, *Far from the Maddening Crowds*, was released in 1997. As a remixer, Bracegirdle transformed Bryan Adams' "Cloud 9" for another major hit in most Western countries. Employing Adams as uncredited vocalist, he then topped the British charts with "Don't Give Up." It was featured on the second Chicane album, *Behind the Sun*, released in Europe in the spring of 2000. This disc reached the Top Ten in Britain and charted across Europe and in the Far East. *Behind the Sun* was released in the US in August 2000. —*William Ruhlmann*

**Chilled** / Aug. 16, 1999 / Edel ✦✦

- **Behind the Sun** / Aug. 8, 2000 / Import ♦♦♦
Nick Bracegirdle, who records under the name Chicane, has a strong pop sense to go with his taste for ambient and trance dance tracks. For one thing, he always employs simple but catchy melodies over his repetitious beats, and for another he cleverly hooks up with some established names looking to extend their appeal into the dance field. "Saltwater," heard here in two different mixes, is a dance treatment of the old Clannad hit "Theme from Harry's Game" (best known in the US for its appearance in a car commercial), complete with Clannad lead singer Maire Brennan. And "Don't Give Up," also heard in two different versions, one of which is a hidden track at the end of the disc, features vocals by Bryan Adams, not that you're likely to recognize him the first time through. When he isn't heating up the dance floor with unlikely guests, Bracegirdle constructs spacy ambient tracks that cool things down, the first of which, "Overture," sounds like something left off a Pink Floyd album from the '70s. Despite international success, the American popularity of this album is likely to be limited to clubs. Not that Americans don't like European dance novelties, but they tend to like them to be more obvious, like Eiffel 65. — *William Ruhlmann*

## Child's View (Nobukazu Takemura)

b. Aug. 26, 1968, Japan
*Producer / Experimental Techno, Ambient Techno*
Child's View was the alias of experimental electronic composer, DJ and producer Nobukazu Takemura, who was born in Japan on August 26, 1968. After beginning his DJing career in high school, he quickly graduated to club appearances throughout Osaka, Kyoto, and Kobe, and in 1987 founded the DJ collective Cool Jazz Productions; a year later, Takemura also joined the Boredoms' Eye Yamatsuka in the influential hip-hop outfit Audio Sports. His initial forays into programming resulted in an appearance on the *Jazz Hip Jap* compilation, and in 1992 Takemura continued expanding his horizons with the formation of the acid jazz group Spiritual Vibes. He released a solo album, also called *Child's View*, in 1994; a remixed edition of the record soon followed, as did remixes for the likes of Tortoise. In 1997, he also collaborated with Japan alumni Richard Barbieri and Steve Jansen on the album *Changing Hands*. The founder of his own label, Idyllic Records International, Takemura adopted the Child's View alias to release the brilliant *Funfair*, issued in the US on Bubble Core Records in early 1999. [See also: Nobukazu Takemura] — *Jason Ankeny*

- **Funfair** / 1999 / Bubble Core ♦♦♦♦
Where so often electronica can be cold and clinical, Nobukazu Takemura crafts richly human soundscapes of remarkable warmth, impressionistic aural collages which achieve a rare balance between man and machine. *Funfair* is arguably his best work to date, infused with a wide-eyed spirit perfectly in keeping with the Child's View alias; the album's center, the 14-minute epic "Pendulum," is a masterpiece of sound and texture, a circus-like loop which incorporates a child's voice to hauntingly ethereal effect. — *Jason Ankeny*

## Children of the Bong

f. 1993
*Group / Ambient Techno, Ambient Dub, Trance*
Daniel Goganian and Rob Henry formed Children of the Bong as a British ambient dub combo, including acoustic guitar and DJ Marin's turntable technology in their live shows. They later decided to go completely electronic, recording several tracks for compilations (*Feed Your Head, Vol. 2, Quadraped Vol. 1*) and — after Planet Dog signed the group — their 1995 debut album. — *John Bush*

- **Sirius Sounds** / Jan. 16, 1996 / MA&M ♦♦
Some albums won't give you life-changing experiences, but they will at least pass the time effectively enough. When it comes to the realm of ambient techno, such an approach is actually more welcome than most. Children of the Bong actually care about beat as well, but though they fool around with dub touches and some often heavy beats, the feeling is more about sweet float à la the lighter side of the Orb. Indeed, that band is the obvious touchstone for what the Children are doing, but lacking the insane, out-of-nowhere touches which transform the Orb into true experimental monsters of odd. The Children would rather live up to their name and just relax a bit, and you can almost smell the burning cannabis as a result. "Underwater Dub," as can be guessed by the name, really hits the stoner flow hard; about the only thing missing is black light and patchouli oil, though admittedly it's not all that distinct a song to begin with. Still, there are enough moments of combined acid squelch and relaxed float that make things worthwhile. "Ionospheric State" is the first song of note, with a melody buried tantalizingly beneath the lead synth crunch and a sharp rhythm roll. Further keyboards in the background accentuate the gentle rise and flow surrounding the main parts of the song. Other tunes of greater note include the nicely energetic "Interface Reality" and the deep bass tug of "Life on Planet Earth," managing to be both a good groove and subtly haunting at the same time. Otherwise, things tend towards the generally pleasant through *Sounds*, as with the nice-but-not-much-to-it "The Veil…" and the tighter dance grooves and vocodered snippets of speaking on "Squigglasonica," which definitely has a fun name to its credit. — *Ned Raggett*

## John Chowning

b. Aug. 22, 1934, Salem, NJ
*Composer / Spectral Music, Electronic*
The father of the digital synthesizer, inventor and composer John Chowning forever altered the face of modern music. Born August 22, 1934 in Salem, New Jersey, he was first exposed to electronic music while studying in Paris, attending live performances by Karlheinz Stockhausen and Pierre Boulez. Upon returning to the US, Chowning arrived at Stanford University in 1962; there a fellow orchestra member passed him a copy of a visionary *Science* magazine piece written by computer music pioneer Max Mathews which confidently predicted that the computer would soon emerge as the ultimate musical instrument. Chowning had never even seen a computer before, but he nevertheless travelled to Mathews' New Jersey offices anyway; he soon returned to Stanford with a box stuffed with computer punch cards, discovering the technology to play them in the university's artificial intelligence department.
Chowning's breakthrough followed in 1967: while experimenting with high-speed vibratos — fluctuations in pitch typically added to electronic sounds to create a heightened realism — he also began toying with a pair of oscillators, modulating one sine wave with the output of the other. What he discovered was a recognizable, richly harmonic tone color at a frequency of around 20Hz, which he was able to manipulate to approximate the sound of clarinets, bassoons and the like. Having hit upon frequency modulation (FM) synthesis, Chowning then spent several years exploring his findings and expanding his sound palette; finally, in 1971 he approached Stanford's Office of Technology Licensing, who in turn sent out feelers to a number of American organ manufacturers. All — Hammond, Wurlitzer, and Lowry among them — rejected the offer; only the Japanese corporation Yamaha understood the possibilities Chowning's discovery offered.
Yamaha, already developing their own digital instruments but enjoying little success, soon acquired a year of exclusive rights to the FM synthesis patent, honing Chowning's ideas and in 1973 building the MAD, the first known all-digital synth ever created. In the meantime, however, Chowning — by definition not an inventor but an electronic music composer and teacher — found himself in hot water with his bosses at Stanford over his meager musical output; he was soon dismissed from the university, and was in Europe when Yamaha came back to license a ten-year deal for the FM rights. The situation proved highly embarrassing for Stanford officials, and they quickly rehired Chowning, offering him the position of Research Associate; he was soon installed as Director of the University's Center for Computer Research and Musical Acoustics, with a professorship to follow in 1979.
The GS-1 digital synth — the first fruits of Chowning's research and Yamaha's development — rolled out of Yamaha's Japanese factories in 1981; although it caused a stir in the marketplace, it was always considered something of a market test. Two years later, Yamaha released the DX-7, a 16-voice polyphonic digital synth with 32 internal memories and a ROM/RAM cartridge slot; overnight, the industry was seemingly turned upside down — the supply simply could not keep up with the demand, and for the next several years Yamaha thoroughly dominated the synth market. The DX-7's success and influence aside, Chowning also left his mark as a composer of computer music; his most notable works included 1971's *Sabelithe*, 1972's *Turenas*, 1977's *Stria* and 1981's *Phone*. — *Jason Ankeny*

- ★ **Phone/Turenas/Stria/Sabelithe** / 1988 / Wergo ♦♦♦♦♦
Lyrical and sophisticated FM synthesis computer music with mysterious and surprising psychoacoustic illusions, like in *Turenas*, the first piece to create

the impression of sound sources moving in a 360-degree space. —*"Blue" Gene Tyranny*

## Chris & Cosey
f. 1981, London, England
*Group / Post-Punk, New Wave, Electronic, Industrial*

After the pioneer industrial rock combo Throbbing Gristle broke up in 1981, Chris Carter and Cosey Fanni Tutti (b. Christine Newby) decided to keep working together. Working under the names Chris and Cosey and CTI (Creative Technology Institute), the duo expanded the dense rhythmic ideas of their former band, adding more accessible synthesized pop elements as their career progressed.

Under the CTI moniker, the duo released their first album, *Heartbeat*, on Rough Trade in 1981; the following year the duo released *Trance*. Rough Trade and Chris and Cosey got in a fight over the retail price of *Trance*, beginning a series of disputes that culminated with the band leaving the label in 1985; they signed with Nettwerk productions in North America and Play It Again Sam in Europe. At the beginning of the '90s, the duo switched to the seminal industrial label Wax Trax! —*Stephen Thomas Erlewine*

**Heartbeat** / 1981 / Wax Trax! ♦♦♦
Chris and Cosey's first album finds the duo still working through the experimental synth-pop of later Throbbing Gristle material. Found sounds and environment-type voices are the only connection to average notions of songwriting, with the machine rhythms and bleak industrial air taking over most of the proceedings. —*Keith Farley*

**Trance** / 1982 / Wax Trax! ♦♦
The connection in the title to medieval chant lends meaning to the differences on Chris and Cosey's second album; here, these dire synth-pop tracks are extended somewhat into unconventional (for rock) territory that explores the modern-day equivalents of non-Western notions of trance music. It is an interesting concept, although the tracks don't always hold up in a purely entertainment sense. —*Keith Farley*

• **Songs of Love and Lust** / 1984 / Wax Trax! ♦♦♦♦
A surprisingly straight-ahead record given the pair's history, *Songs of Love and Lust* is a set of chilling synth-pop tracks with the added emotionless vocals of Cosey herself. They're just as extended as the tracks on *Trance*, though there's a distinct sense that the pair were suffering from a lack of ideas. It's still a solid look at the state of the melancholy synth crowd. —*Keith Farley*

**Exotica** / 1987 / Combat ♦♦
*Exotika* was the duo's first album as part of a North American agreement with Nettwerk Records (also the home of Skinny Puppy) and, while it does represent a leap in technology over their early work, the album still exhibits many of the flaws Chris and Cosey had dealt with since their debut—no focus on songwriting, and too few ideas to make up for that lack. —*Keith Farley*

## Cibo Matto
f. 1994, New York, NY
*Group / Shibuya-Kei, Alternative Dance, Indie Rock, Trip-Hop, Alternative Pop/Rock*

A Japanese-born duo relocated to New York and christened with an Italian band name, Cibo Matto's music mirrored the melting-pot aesthetics of their origins, resulting in a heady brew of funk samples, hip-hop rhythms, tape loops and fractured pop melodies all topped off by surreal narratives sung in a combination of French and broken English. Cibo Matto comprised vocalist Miho Hatori and keyboardist/sampler Yuka Honda, a pair of expatriate Japanese women who arrived in the US independently: Honda, a onetime member of Brooklyn Funk Essentials, settled in New York in 1987, and Hatori, an alum of the Tokyo rap unit Kimidori and a former club DJ, followed six years later. After meeting in 1994, they first teamed in the Boredoms-inspired noise outfit Leitoh Lychee (translated as "frozen lychee nut"); after that band's breakup, the duo formed Cibo Matto, Italian for "food madness" (their love of culinary delights quickly becoming the stuff of legend).

The group soon emerged as a sensation among the Lower Manhattan hipster elite, gaining fame for their incendiary live shows backed by guests including the Lounge Lizards' Dougie Bowne (Honda's ex-husband), Bernie Worrell, Masada's Dave Douglas, and Skeleton Key's Rick Lee. After a pair of acclaimed 1995 independent singles, "Birthday Cake" and "Know Your Chicken," Cibo Matto signed to Warner Bros., surfacing in 1996 with the Mitchell Froom/Tchad Blake-produced *Viva! La Woman*, a delirious, stunningly inventive record celebrating love, food, and love of food. After touring with guest bassist Sean Lennon and Jon Spencer Blues Explosion drummer Russell Simins, the EP *Super Relax* followed in 1997. Lennon, percussionist Duma Love and drummer Timo Ellis were installed as full-time members for the follow-up, 1999's *Stereotype A*. —*Jason Ankeny*

**Cibo Matto [EP]** / 1996 / El Diablo ♦♦♦
This five-track EP assembles the early independent singles which first earned Cibo Matto notice in hipster circles, in some cases offering radically different renditions of material which later resurfaced on the *Viva! La Woman* album. The most startling is "Know Your Chicken," which appears in a wonderfully scuzzy rendition heavily influenced by the Jon Spencer Blues Explosion (whose Russell Simins sits in on drums); the real treat, however, is a wonderfully loopy cover of Soundgarden's "Black Hole Sun," rearranged like a lounge favorite and sung in French. —*Jason Ankeny*

• **Viva! La Woman** / Jan. 16, 1996 / Warner Brothers ♦♦♦♦
Fresh and funky, female and Japanese, the trip-hop/rap duo Cibo Matto have been the recipients of a lot of hype. Fortunately, it's well founded; all trendiness aside, *Viva! La Woman* is an innovative and catchy mix of eclectic samples and stream-of-consciousness lyrics. The likes of Paul Weller, Ennio Morricone, and Duke Ellington combine with observations like "My weight is three hundred pounds...my favorite is beef jerky" (from "Beef Jerky") and "Shut up and eat! You know my love is sweet!" from ("Birthday Cake") in a fun and refreshing way. The tone of the album varies with each song: on tracks like "Sugar Water" and "Artichoke" Cibo Matto plays it spooky and ethereal, while "Birthday Cake" and the single "Know Your Chicken" find them as a couple of cryptic Beastie Girls, tossing off wacky non sequiturs over found soundscapes. Cibo Matto cook up a tasty appetizer of their talent with *Viva! La Woman*. Like their tongue-in-cheek cover of "The Candy Man," Cibo Matto makes everything they bake satisfying and delicious. A diverse and entertaining album, *Viva! La Woman* leaves the listener hungry for more of their crazy food for thought. —*Heather Phares*

**Super Relax [EP]** / Jan. 28, 1997 / Warner Brothers ♦♦♦♦
Granted, the four separate versions of *Viva! La Woman's* sublime "Sugar Water" are unnecessary, but the rest of the material on Cibo Matto's follow-up EP *Super Relax* is superb. No longer relying solely on Yuka Honda's slice-and-dice samples, the duo's sound is considerably more organic this time out; "Spoon" locks into an infectious groove worthy of Luscious Jackson, while the live "BBQ" is breathlessly manic. The highlights, however, are the two covers: the first, a rendition of Antonio Carlos Jobim's "Aguas de Marco" (also found on the benefit LP *Red Hot and Latin*) opens up a vast new global playground of exotic textures and rhythms for the group to romp around in, while their exemplary take on the Stones' "Sing This All Together" proves Honda and vocalist Miho Hatori are equally capable of tackling straightforward rock 'n' roll. —*Jason Ankeny*

**Stereo Type A** / Jun. 8, 1999 / Warner Brothers ♦♦♦
Cibo Matto's eagerly anticipated second album, *Stereo Type A*, reflects growth and change in the band's lineup and sound. Joining the core duo of Yuka Honda and Miho Hatori are new band member Sean Lennon and guests like Arto Lindsay, Caetano Veloso, Sebastian Steinberg of Soul Coughing, and John Medeski and Billy Martin of Medeski, Martin & Wood. The new additions reflect the changing sound of Cibo Matto: relying less on samples and more on their latent funk and jazz elements, *Stereotype A* sounds like summer in New York—eclectic, hot, and funky. Hatori's vocals are her most fluid and assured yet, and Honda's harmonies, particularly on "Moonchild," add a dreamy undercurrent to the sound. Though the hip-hop of "Sci-Fi Wasabi" and filmic quality of "Spoon" (which originally appeared on the *Super Relax* EP) hearken back to old-school Cibo Matto, *Stereotype A's* overall sound is more direct and less fanciful than of their debut album *Viva! La Woman*. Tracks like "Clouds" and "Morning" reflect a nice fusion of the group's old and new sounds, while the brassy "Speechless" and thrash-metal of "Blue Train" round out a delightfully sunny collection from this diverse group. —*Heather Phares*

## Cinematic Orchestra
*Group / Trip-Hop, Jungle/Drum'N'Bass, Club/Dance*

The brilliantly-named Cinematic Orchestra is led by composer/programmer/multi-instrumentalist Jason Swinscoe, who formed his first group, Crabladder, in 1990 as an art student at Cardiff College. Crabladder's fusion of jazz and hardcore punk elements with experimental rhythms inspired Swinscoe to further explore the possibilities of sampling, and by the time of the group's demise in the mid-'90s, he was DJing at various clubs and pirate radio stations in the UK.

The music he recorded on his own at the time melded '60s and '70s jazz, orchestral soundtracks, rhythm loops, and live instrumentation into genre-defying compositions, as reflected on his contribution to Ninja Tune's 1997 *Ninja Cuts 3* collection and his remixes of Ryuichi Sakamoto and Coldcut tracks. The Cinematic Orchestra built on this musical blueprint, letting a group of live musicians improvise over sampled percussion or basslines. The Orchestra included saxophonist/pianist Tom Chant, bassist Phil France, and drummer Daniel Howard, who also recorded the *Channel One Suite* and *Diabolus* EPs for Ninja Tune with Swinscoe. The project's full-length debut *Motion* arrived in 1999 to great acclaim, which culminated in the Cinematic Orchestra's performance at the Directors' Guild Lifetime Achievement Award Ceremony for Stanley Kubrick later that year in London. —*Heather Phares*

● **Motion** / Sep. 14, 1999 / Ninja Tune ♦♦♦♦
Whether to categorize *Motion* as a jazz or electronica album is an intriguing conundrum, because it truly turns out to be a combination of both musical forms, and it is an unequivocally brilliant combination, at that. British arranger/programmer J. Swinscoe—who virtually is the Cinematic Orchestra—gathered samples of drum grooves, basslines, and melodies from various recordings and artists that have inspired and influenced him (spaghetti-western composer Ennio Morricone and Roy Budd's spy film scores, '60s and '70s jazz and soundtrack scores from musicians such as Elvin Jones, Eric Dolphy, Andre Previn, David Rose, and John Morris). He then presented the samples that he had collected to a group of musicians, the core of which consisted of Tom Chant (soprano sax, electric and acoustic piano), Jamie Coleman (trumpet, flugelhorn), Phil France (bass), and T. Daniel Howard (drums), to learn and then improvise. Those tracks, in turn, were sampled and rearranged by Swinscoe on computer to create the tracks that make up this first Cinematic Orchestra album. The album bears all of the atmospheric hallmarks of ambient electronica, as well as Swinscoe's soundtrack inspirations and all the improvisational energy of jazz. Most of the songs are built with wave upon wave of repeated loops and instrumental phrases that work into a groove. Yet it feels at any moment as if the music is about to explode, like a steam whistle boiling to its screaming point. On "One to the Big Sea," for example, the same four-note bassline plays over and over with the same ride cymbal rhythm, but instead of seeming rote or mechanical, the riff just seems to continually bubble up and throb, slowly building anticipation and pressure. When a looped piano riff and horn charts enter the music, the juxtaposition seems almost jarring; yet, as they continue to repeat, in turn, atop the bass and cymbals, you can't help but feel that you're waiting for another dramatic leap, which eventually comes by way of the song's cornerstone: a thrilling drum solo. Each song is just as accomplished in its own way, so expertly arranged by Swinscoe that the impression of both structure and improvisation is created, while never sounding for a moment anything less than organic. The music is constructed piece by piece until it is a seamless whole that lives and breathes on its own merits, much like the soundscapes of DJ Shadow. Regardless of how they were made, though, the songs on *Motion* are by turns eerie, lush, edgy, expansive, gritty, intensely powerful, and gorgeous. Sometimes an album comes along that forces you to reconfigure and reevaluate all of the assumptions you had previously made about music in order to realize how vast and endless the possibilities are; this is one of those albums. —*Stanton Swihart*

## Cirrus

f. 1995, Los Angeles, CA
*Group / Funky Breaks, Trip-Hop, Club/Dance*
Hailed in 1997 as the new Prodigy—mostly by their record label—Cirrus was born in Los Angeles as the project of Aaron Carter and Stephen James Barry. The duo program acid and trance breakbeats for their material, but also added live guitar and bass to appeal to rock crowds at their frantic live shows. After the release of the hotly tipped single "Superstar DJ," Cirrus signed to Moonshine and released *Drop the Break* in April 1997. *Back on a Mission* followed one year later. —*John Bush*

**Drop the Break** / Apr. 15, 1997 / Moonshine Music ♦♦
Not exactly a revolution in the making, *Drop the Break* opts for the familiar tones of house, trip-hop and occasionally breakbeat rave from California's club culture. Several tracks make a break from the norm with actual instruments and polite scratching, but for the most part *Drop the Break* charts a course through the been-there-heard-that forms of electronic dance. —*John Bush*

● **Back on a Mission** / Aug. 25, 1998 / Moonshine Music ♦♦
While electronic music acts such as the Chemical Brothers, Prodigy, and Fatboy Slim propelled their careers with loads of press coverage in the media-savvy UK before bringing their publicity campaigns to the US, Cirrus unfortunately didn't have the same opportunity despite making similar music. Based in Los Angeles, the group merged electronic sounds such as acid and breakbeats with accessible song structures, vocals, and the occasional guitar riff on *Back on a Mission*. The record finds them trying many different styles over the course of ten songs, opening with two guitar riff-driven songs with vocals, followed by an acid-spewing anthem with catchy samples, and then by a rap song. Later songs on *Back on a Mission* don't get quite as ambitious and tend to be suitable acid breakbeat songs with samples. Nothing on this album is as blatantly danceable as the Chemical Brothers' *Exit Planet Dust*, as polluted with catchy hooks as Fatboy Slim's *You've Come a Long Way, Baby*, or as aggressive as Prodigy's *Fat of the Land*. Instead, Cirrus focuses on keeping their beats funky with a broad palette of hi-tech electronic sounds. Unfortunately, the diverse nature of the album prevents it from maintaining a consistent vibe throughout. Listeners may enjoy the rock feel of "Back on a Mission," the acid calamities of "Stop & Panic," or the futuristic Beastie Boys rap of "Abba Zabba," but few will enjoy everything on this album. Had Cirrus stayed true to a concrete dancefloor foundation as Crystal Method did on *Vegas* or stayed true to rock motifs as the Chemical Brothers did on *Surrender*, this album would be a much more enjoyable listen. Instead, it sounds like an indecisive group trying to spread itself thin in hopes of making everyone like something about them; in other words, the group comes off as desperate for appeal. —*Jason Birchmeier*

## Dave Clarke

*Producer, DJ / Electronica, Acid Techno, Hardcore Techno, Club/Dance, Techno*
One of the most respected (and idiosyncratic) techno DJs and producers in the '90s, Dave Clarke began his music career as a hip-hop DJ in the mid-'80s, shifting to acid-house and later rave near the end of the decade. He began recording for Stress (as Pig City) in the early '90s and also appeared on R&S, XL and his own Magnetic North Records. By the mid-'90s, he had gradually shifted away from rave to a brand of straightahead techno with the ferocity of hardcore yet the sublime feelings of classic Detroit techno. A series of three singles named "Red" gained fame during 1995-96 (the last went Top 40 in the UK), as did his ferocious DJ sets.

Clarke's phenomenal album debut *Archive 1* appeared in 1996 on Deconstruction. *Demagnitized*, a compilation of his earlier material on Magnetic North (with additional tracks from Cristian Vogel, DJ Hell and others), was released in 1995. Clarke also mixed two volumes of the crucial electro compilation series *Electro Boogie* for Studio !K7. —*John Bush*

**X-Mix: Electro Boogie** / 1996 / Studio !K7 ♦♦♦♦
Mixed by Dave Clarke, this installment in Studio K-7's *X-Mix* series is the first available on CD as well as VHS; in other words, fans of Clarke can get his mix of electro classics old and new without subjecting themselves to the incredibly cheesy computer-graphics animation for which Studio K-7 is known. Clarke includes Detroit tracks from Model 500, Underground Resistance, and Channel One, as well as Euro-electro from Octagon Man (J Saul Kane) and LFO. Skip the video, but get the CD. —*John Bush*

● **Archive One** / Feb. 5, 1996 / Deconstruction ♦♦♦♦
The hardest, most intense Detroit techno being produced outside of the Motor City appears on *Archive One*, Clarke's first album for Deconstruction and a compilation of sorts from previous singles. Though the downtempo first track and hip-hop flavor of the third start things off on what many of Clarke's fans would consider the wrong foot, the album stomps from the fourth track on—and the inclusion of the A-sides of all three "Red" singles provides the best introduction to Clarke's crucial acid-techno fusion. —*John Bush*

**Electro Boogie, Vol. 2: The Throw Down** / Apr. 13, 1998 / Studio !K7 ♦♦♦♦
Even more stellar as a compilation of crucial electro both past and present, *Electro Boogie, Vol. 2* swaps old-school renegades like Dr. Dre (with the

World Class Wreckin' Cru) and Will Smith (DJ Jazzy Jeff & the Fresh Prince) with underground Detroit acts like Ectomorph, DJ Assault, Aux 88 and Doppleneffekt. The inclusion of 1997's electro anthem "Space Invaders Are Smoking Grass" by I-f only ensures the quality of this compilation, while Clarke's creative mixing and quick cutting from track to track spark the productions to new heights. —*John Bush*

## Clatterbox (David Kempston)

*Producer / Electronica, Neo-Electro*

Although the London-based Clear label kicked off its now celebrated catalog of releases with singles from a range of widely known talent (Reload/Global Communication, Mike Paradinas/µ-Ziq, Acen, and Plaid), they were also quick to cultivate a homegrown stable of lo-fi innovators, including Matthew "Dr. Rockit" Herbert and David "Clatterbox" Kempston. Like Herbert, whose singles and remixes as Wishmountain (for Universal Language) and under his own name (for Phono, Reflective, and SSR, among others) have mined the more pedestrian capacities of the sampler, Clatterbox's sound is reliant on a sort of refined, left-field minimalism. With tracks often composed of only three or four loops judiciously arranged, Kempston's work occasionally suffers for its simplicity. But as with early hip-hop producers such as Man Parrish, the Unknown DJ, and "Pretty" Tony Butler, Kempston's aesthetic forces him to make a little go a long way, often to marvelous effect. It's hip-hop and electro from which Kempston most often draws, of course, but unlike many of the electro nu school, his sound is hardly retro; tracks such as "Matterrox" and "Dunk" may tip their hat here and there with thick, talk box-y bass, handclaps, and rubbery synth work, but his fusion of elements from a range of sources (funk, house, experimental techno, industrial/EBM) with a characteristic humor and knack for extracting musicality from the oddest of sources defies easy dismissal. In addition to his material as Clatterbox proper, Kempston has also released a pair of 12"s on Clear simply titled "Clatterbeats"; stripped-down vignettes intended for DJ use rather than home listening. —*Sean Cooper*

**Clatterbox [Single]** / Dec. 1995 / Clear ♦♦♦
Two slabs of funk-fueled house and electro/hip-hop, stripped-down but dynamic enough to be worth the effort. Kempston's house gear is similar to fellow Clear artist Matthew "Dr. Rockit" Herbert's eponymous work, with a clangy, lo-tech groove supporting sparse melodies and synth bleats. —*Sean Cooper*

• **Eazy Does It** / Apr. 15, 1996 / Clear ♦♦♦♦
Clear makes a full production out of its second Clatterbox release, with both the vinyl and CD versions of *Eazy Does It* sporting a nifty tab-and-slot sleeve. The music rocks similar territory as Clatterbox's self-titled debut EP, although Kempston focuses exclusively on breaks here, a funky fusion of West Coast style hip-hop and early New York and Philly electro predominant. The CD adds the previously vinyl-only debut double 10". —*Sean Cooper*

## Joe Claussell

**b.** 1966, Brooklyn, NY

*Producer, DJ / Jazz-House, Club/Dance, House*

Joe Claussell has long been one of New York City's busiest dance figures, thanks to his work in all areas of the house community: as a highly respected DJ, producer, remixer, label-head (Spiritual Life Music and Ibadan), and record-shop owner (Dance Tracks). Spiritual Life has released tracks from a host of New York nu-house teams including Claussell himself, Mateo & Matos, Blaze, Slam Mode, and frequent production partner Jephte Guillaume. And his Sunday clubnight *Body & Soul* (with fellow residents François Kevorkian and Danny Krivit) recreated the vibes fostered at the birth of modern dance music—David Mancuso's Loft sessions during the early '70s—with a varied mix of vibrant music ranging from Milton Nascimento to Masters at Work to Cesario Evora to Kevin Yost to Fela Kuti. In his productions, he's often mirrored that eclectic mix of styles, dropping in plenty of acoustic instruments and rich percussion patterns.

Like Kevorkian, Claussell is a veteran of the disco era, an enthusiastic participator at DJ sessions from near-legendary figures like Mancuso and Larry Levan. Raised in Brooklyn, he learned musical diversity thanks to the wide-ranging tastes of his seven brothers. He began working at the New York record store Dance Tracks in the late '80s, and after forming a partnership with new owner Stefan Prescott, turned it into one of the leading vinyl sources in the city. Claussell turned to production with a few remixing credits, and in 1996 launched Spiritual Life Music with the single "Stubborn Problems" by Timmy Regisford.

Spiritual Life soon became the home for productions embracing all forms of groove music from the past few decades, as comfortable working through Caribbean folk and salsa rhythms as the expected deep house. (Not surprisingly, the selection at the Dance Tracks store featured the same philosophy at work.) Tight releases by two of New York's best producers (Slam Mode with "Fiat Mistura," and Blaze with "Directions") increased the label's visibility during the mid-'90s, and Claussell moved into production with great singles by Jephte Guillaume ("The Prayer," "Kanpe") during 1997. He also formed a second label, Ibadan, and released his first proper single, the 1997 Brazilian house workout "Escravos de Joe."

The same vibes fostered on Spiritual Life material also found a workout at *Body & Soul*, the Sunday evening club founded by Claussell with François Kevorkian. His first full-length, *Mix the Vibe*, was released on NiteGrooves in 1999, followed later that year by his proper debut, *Language*. A Spiritual Life compilation, *Spiritual Life Music*, is also available. —*John Bush*

• **Mix the Vibe** / Apr. 12, 1999 / NiteGrooves ♦♦♦♦
Though it's difficult to transfer the incredible atmosphere of Claussell's infamous Body & Soul clubnights in New York to a cold slab of plastic, *Mix the Vibe* does an excellent job. Distilling the highlights from two great house labels, NiteGrooves and King Street, Claussell keeps the mood groovy yet intelligent and drops producers such as Masters at Work, Kerri Chandler, Wamdue Kids, and Dimitri From Paris. —*John Bush*

**Body & Soul NYC, Vol. 2** / Jun. 29, 1999 / Wave ♦♦♦
The multifaceted sounds of New York's club scene are compiled on *Body & Soul: NYC, Vol. 2*. The second volume of the series includes Nuyorican Soul's "Black Gold of the Sun," Basement Jaxx's "Samba Magic," Mateo & Matos' "NY Style," Abstract Truth's "(We Had) a Thing," and Cesaria Evora's "Sangue de Beirona." —*Heather Phares*

**Language** / Nov. 29, 1999 / Ibadan ♦♦♦♦
There're two ways to get an understanding of Joe Claussell's music: You can hop on a plane to NYC and head straight to Claussell's world-renowned *Body & Soul*'s Sunday-afternoon tea dance, or you can get his latest disc, *Language*. Going the more practical route, *Language* is a smarter bet. Now, before you start picturing electronic wizardry, laser shows, and hands wavin' in the air, think again folks, 'cause this ain't that kind of party. There's no techno trickery here; no hammering drum machine. Bearing the flowing essence of Afro-house music, jazz, and world beats, *Language* takes you on a chill-out journey of deeply soulful and jazzy ambiance. The conga-rich "Spiritual Insurrection" starts things off, winding through a rhythmic maze of subtle basslines and titillating keyboard arrangements, with the flute taking over the lead on the following track, "Git Wah." On "Kryptic Elements," violin meets flute and conga drum, all caressing each other in a melodious ménage à trois of freeform bliss. Besides one lone vocal track, "Je Ka Jo," the rest of the seven cuts are pure instrumental bliss. Other highlights include "Gbedu 1 Gbedu Resurrection" and the groovy licks of "Mateen's Theme." Executive-produced by Afro-house music legend Jerome Sydenham and Claussell, *Language* is one of several albums over the years that have emerged out of the *Body & Soul* Sunday affair. Claussell's partners François Kevorkian and Danny Krivet both released their own series of albums celebrating Afro-house rhythms, but for the initiated, *Language* speaks volumes. —*Derrick Mathis*

## Kit Clayton

*Producer / Minimal Techno, Experimental Dub, Experimental Techno, Ambient Techno, IDM*

The minimal-to-abstract, somewhat dubby techno of electronic DJ and producer Kit Clayton has appeared on a large number of labels since 1996. Clayton runs several of his own labels, including Cytrax Records and Orthlorng Musorks, but his music—which has garnered praise from such magazines as *The Wire* and *Muzik*—can also be heard on Stefan Betke's Scape label, as well as Mille Plateaux, Organized Noise, Plug Research, Seventh City, Phthalo, and more. Clayton studied at Connecticut's Wesleyan College, learning in the electronic music lab, where he composed interactive pieces. He now works out of his basement studio in San Francisco, not only on music, but on an audio software that helps create systems to generate music with varying randomization—his "day job." He released the EPs *Negative Powers* and *Unreliable Networks* for Cytrax, and debuted on Thomas Brinkmann's Scape label with the praised *Nek Purpalet* EP in mid-1999. Before the end of the year, full-lengths followed on Drop Beat (*Repetition and Nonsense*) and Scape (*Nek Sanalet*). Despite his computer work, Clayton's creations reach beyond "computer music"; for him, computers are just another means of creation to be used along with acoustic, analogue, and digital methods. He has also toured Germany, and created a project to pair visual art with electronic music called "the Mimic and the Model." —*Joslyn Layne*

**Repetition and Nonsense** / Sep. 13, 1999 / Drop Beat ♦♦♦♦
Though Kit Clayton's first album isn't exactly a straightahead techno record, that's the idea that comes to mind when it's compared to his material for Scape (released around the same time). It's not just the focus on four-four beats, either. Most of the effects on *Repetition and Nonsense* are clear, crisp, and high in the mix—miles away from the murky textures of his *Nek Purpalet* EP and *Nek Sanalet* LP. The material here is almost as uniformly excellent as the Scape releases, though its lack of shadow tends to be a drawback. —*John Bush*

● **Nek Sanalet** / Nov. 2, 1999 / Scape ♦♦♦♦
Following on from his *Nek Purpalet* EP earlier in the year, Clayton's first full-length for the Scape label—run by Stefan Betke (aka Pole)—is a masterpiece of experimental dub. Far advanced from the notable progressions made earlier by Berlin's Basic Channel and Chain Reaction crews, *Nek Sanalet* is even a bit more advanced than Betke's own highly regarded work as Pole. The first track, "Nuchu," takes an unintelligible, haunted vocal sample (Aleister Crowley slowed down to the speed of flowing syrup) and rattles it around volleys of cacophonous, echoing percussion and dub effects. The sheer amount of processing done by Clayton's Powerbook must have easily taxed its memory, for absolutely no effects or beats escape the producer's twisted programming sense. True, a bare few of the tracks on *Nek Sanalet*—"Nele" and "Aspoket" come to mind—sound very reminiscent of Clayton's minimal forefathers Basic Channel and Mike Ink, but even these are done amazingly well. For all the techno fans who thought experimental dub was a bit too ingrown and shadowed to make for truly diverting listening, *Nek Sanalet* should mark a surprising change of heart. —*John Bush*

## Clinton

*Group / Electronica, Trip-Hop, Club/Dance, House*
When Cornershop's Ben Ayres and Tjinder Singh took a break from the responsibilities of their main band after the success of *When I Was Born For The Seventh Time*, they formed the political dance duo Clinton. The 1999 single *Buttoned Down Disco* and the 2000 debut album *Disco and the Halfway to Discontent* on Astralwerks introduced this project's more beat and groove-oriented style. —*Heather Phares*

● **Disco and the Halfway to Discontent** / Jan. 25, 2000 / Hut ♦♦♦
As the name Clinton suggests, Ben Ayres and Tjinder Singh's "vacation" from Cornershop delivers a lot of funk mixed with some social commentary. Their debut album, *Disco and the Halfway to Discontent*, explores the politics of dancing—or dance music, at any rate—by applying a stripped-down, lo-fi sensibility to disco's glitter, reggae's groove, and funk's insistent pulse. The opening track, "People Power in the Disco Hour," is one of their best dance manifestos, combining a bare-bones beat with funky bass, wobbly synths, and lyrics like "Disco is the halfway/ To a full discontent/ We're gonna take this movement down to the streets." Though it's starkly rhythmic where Cornershop songs like "Brimful of Asha" are lush and trippy, Singh's appealing vocals and the duo's accessible songwriting provide the link between their two projects. Good moments and ideas abound on *Disco...*, including the sweetly intoned Indian vocals and rousing brass on "Buttoned Down Disco," the rippling electric pianos and snappy drum rolls of "Sing Hosanna," and "Hip Hop Bricks"' low-rider bass, smoky flutes, and processed vocals; however, too many of these good ideas drag on for too long without progressing. "The Hot for May Sound," "Saturday Night and Dancing," "Mr. President," and "Welcome to Tokyo, Otis Clay" all start out with clever melodies and arrangements, and all of them are left underdeveloped. This, added to the album's lo-fi sound quality, sometimes makes *Disco and the Halfway to Discontent* seem like a demo tape for Cornershop's new, dance-inspired direction. With some pruning, this could have been an excellent album, but is merely a fairly enjoyable one instead. Cornershop fans who didn't buy the import of *Disco and the Halfway to Discontent* are rewarded with two bonus tracks: the "Fila Brazilia Disco Frisco Mix" of "Buttoned Down Disco," which keeps the original's sugary vocals and horns and adds sitars and speedy breakbeats to give the song added impact, and "David D. Chambers," a synth and scratching free-for-all set to another stark hip-hop beat. Though this album may please some of Singh and Ayres' fans, it's equally likely to frustrate them as well. —*Heather Phares*

## George Clinton

b. Jul. 22, 1940, Kannapolis, NC
*Producer, Vocals, Keyboards, Synthesizer / Urban, Funk*
The mastermind of the Parliament/Funkadelic collective during the '70s, George Clinton broke up both bands by 1981 and began recording solo albums, occasionally performing live with his former bandmates as the P-Funk All-Stars. Clinton became interested in doo wop while living in New Jersey during the early '50s. He formed the Parliaments in 1955, based out of a barbershop back-room where he straightened hair. The group had a small R&B hit during 1967, but Clinton began to mastermind the Parliaments' activities two years later. Recording both as Parliament and Funkadelic, the group revolutionized R&B during the '70s, twisting soul music into funk by adding influences from several late-'60s acid heroes: Jimi Hendrix, Frank Zappa, and Sly Stone. The Parliament/Funkadelic machine ruled black music during the '70s, capturing over 40 R&B hit singles (including three number ones) and recording three platinum albums.

By 1980, George Clinton began to be weighed down by legal difficulties arising from Polygram's acquisition of Parliament's label, Casablanca. Jettisoning both the Parliament and Funkadelic names (but not the musicians), Clinton signed to Capitol in 1982 both as a solo act and as the P-Funk All-Stars. His first solo album, 1982's *Computer Games*, contained the Top 20 R&B hit "Loopzilla." Several months later, the title track from Clinton's *Atomic Dog* EP hit No. 1 on the R&B charts; it stayed at the top spot for four weeks, but only managed No. 101 on the pop charts. Clinton stayed on Capitol for three more years, releasing three studio albums and frequently charting singles—"Nubian Nut," "Last Dance," "Do Fries Go with That Shake?"—in the R&B Top 30. During much of the three-year period from 1986 to 1989, Clinton became embroiled in legal difficulties (resulting from the myriad royalty problems latent during the '70s recordings of over 40 musicians for four labels under three names). Also problematic during the latter half of the '80s was Clinton's disintegrating reputation as a true forefather of rock; by the end of the decade, however, a generation of rappers reared on P-Funk were beginning to name-check him.

In 1989, Clinton signed a contract with Prince's Paisley Park label and released his fifth solo studio album: *The Cinderella Theory*. After one more LP for Paisley Park (*Hey Man, Smell My Finger*), Clinton signed with Sony 550. His first release, 1996's *T.A.P.O.A.F.O.M.* ("the awesome power of a fully operational mothership"), reunited the funk pioneer with several of his Parliament/Funkadelic comrades from the '70s. Clinton's *Greatest Funkin' Hits* (1996) teamed old P-Funk hits with new-school rappers such as Digital Underground, Ice Cube, and Q-Tip. [See also: Parliament, Funkadelic] —*John Bush*

● **Computer Games** / Nov. 5, 1982 / Capitol ♦♦♦♦
Former Parliament and Funkadelic leader George Clinton made a major comeback under his own name with this album, whose irresistible grooves, vocal choruses, and absurd humor were essentially identical to the music of Funkadelic's salad days. Were you wondering where that "woof-woof" cheer heard on Arsenio Hall and at Black concerts came from? Check out "Atomic Dog." —*William Ruhlmann*

**You Shouldn't-Nuf Bit Fish** / Dec. 1983 / Capitol ♦♦♦
While it kept the funk percolating, George Clinton's follow-up to his post-Parliament-Funkadelic solo debut *Computer Games* didn't boast any tracks as compelling (or as nutty) as "Atomic Dog," though "Nubian Nut" and "Last Dance," which made the R&B Top 40, were fun. Most of the second side was funk without form, a common failing of Clinton's approach. —*William Ruhlmann*

**Some of My Best Jokes Are Friends** / Jul. 1985 / Capitol ♦♦
With technology having taken over R&B in a major way by the mid-'80s, George Clinton made a point of "updating" his P-Funk by being much more

high-tech and using keyboards, drum machines and sequencers extensively. On his third "solo album," *Some of My Best Jokes Are Friends*, Clinton even recruits Britain's very technology-oriented new waver Thomas Dolby to help with the production on a few cuts. *Jokes* is far from his best effort, and sometimes comes across as forced and unnatural. But the CD definitely has its strong points, including the addictive "Bodyguard," the eerie "Bangladesh" and anti-war protest songs "Bullet Proof" and "Thrashin'." With Parliament and Funkadelic, Clinton often had fun making strong social and political statements in a subliminal fashion—this time, however, he's much more direct. Despite its strengths, *Jokes* is an album that only Clinton's most devoted followers should invest in—those exploring his innovations for the first time would do much better to purchase one of his classic Parliament or Funkadelic albums of the '70s (or, for that matter, his first "solo album" *Computer Games*). —*Alex Henderson*

**R&B Skeletons in the Closet** / Apr. 1986 / Capitol ♦♦♦♦
A definite improvement over the uneven *Some of My Best Jokes Are Friends*, the considerably more focused and confident *R&B Skeletons in the Closet* is one of George Clinton's strongest solo efforts. The P-Funkster continues using technology extensively, but this time, his blend of technology and "real instruments" sounds much more natural. Though not quite in a class with Parliament classics like *Mothership Connection* or *Funkentelechy vs. the Placebo Syndrome* or Funkadelic treasures ranging from *Cosmic Slop* to *Uncle Jam Wants You*, *Skeletons* is a superb collection that's well worth acquiring. The CD kicks into high gear with the wildly infectious "Hey Good Lookin'" and maintains that high level of excitement on such driving, sweaty funk treasures as "Do Fries Go with That Shake?," and the appropriately titled "Intense" and the title song. Clinton's eccentricity and outrageous sense of humor serve him well on "Electric Pygmies" and "Mix-Master Suite," an unorthodox, quirky and cinematic ode to hip-hop drawing on everything from jazz to classical music to western movies. Many of Clinton's long-time associates are on hand to help make this album the artistic success it is, including saxman Maceo Parker, trombonist Fred Wesley and the ever-amusing Bootsy Collins. —*Alex Henderson*

**Sample Some of Disc, Sample Some of DAT** / Jan. 1993 / AEM ♦♦♦
Concerned about the huge strides being made in the development of samplers, and the ways in which artists were being sampled by everyone from rappers to plunderphonic collage artists, George Clinton hit on the idea of creating legal, low-cost sample discs based on excerpts from his vast archives. The catch here is that if you use one or more samples from this disc, then you sign over a portion of your royalties to Clinton and company. A good idea, on the surface, but the actual royalty schedule involved was close to heinous, leaving samplers preferring to shell out a hundred dollars or more for license-free discs. This initial disc has some interesting flaws, too, in that the track listing on the inner sleeve has no reference whatsoever to the actual tracks, an error that causes quite a bit of confusion. Finally, the samples (full mixes to solo instrument tracks) represent a more or less ho-hum selection from the vaults. —*Steven McDonald*

**Hey Man, Smell My Finger** / Oct. 1993 / Paisley Park ♦♦♦♦
*Hey Man, Smell My Finger* is everything a great George Clinton album should be—conceptually disjointed, overlong, silly, sloppy, and funky as hell. Thankfully, the music here is his best since *Computer Games*, and the album proves just how responsible he is for much of the music of the '90s, as the irresistible single "Paint the White House Black" illustrates with its numerous cameos. —*Stephen Thomas Erlewine*

**T.A.P.O.A.F.O.M. [The Awesome Power of a Fully Operational Mothership]** / Jun. 1996 / Sony 550 ♦♦
*The Awesome Power of a Fully-Operational Mothership* is the first George Clinton to show signs of a Dr. Dre G-funk influence. Where his previous album, *Hey Man, Smell My Finger*, was pretty much nothing but standard P-Funk, *Awesome Power* slows the beat down just like Dre does on *The Chronic*. The difference is, Dre actually works those grooves into songs where Clinton just lets the funk meander. He doesn't even try to write songs—he operates under the belief that ceaseless jamming and randomly interjected vocals constitutes a good groove. And it does, when given the right source material and musicians. On *Awesome Power*, Clinton has neither. The musicians may have all played with various incarnations of Parliament, but they sound tired and bored on the album—there isn't a single instant when they latch on to a good groove. And what that means is this: On *Awesome Power*, George Clinton sounds more out of touch with contemporary funk and R&B than he ever has. —*Stephen Thomas Erlewine*

**Greatest Hits** / May 9, 2000 / Right Stuff/Capitol ♦♦♦
George Clinton's solo output of the '80s and '90s wasn't as consistent as his work with Parliament/Funkadelic in the 1970s—nonetheless, the P-Funk innovator has had his share of inspired moments as a solo artist, and some of his best solo recordings are united on this collection. Released in 2000, *Greatest Hits* spans 1976-1986 and draws on such solo albums as *Computer Games*, *You Shouldn't-Nuf Bit Fish*, *Some of My Best Jokes Are Friends*, and *R&B Skeletons in the Closet*. The oldest recording is the bonus track, a live Parliament/Funkadelic medley of "Let's Take It to the Stage" and "Do That Stuff" from a 1976 Houston show—most of the selections, however, come from Clinton's Capitol solo albums of 1982-1986. Not surprisingly, the CD opens with "Atomic Dog," Clinton's best known and most essential solo hit. And The Right Stuff's other choices are also wise ones, including "Do Fries Go with That Shake?," "Cool Joe," "Loopzilla," "Hey Good Lookin'," and the quirky rap item "Nubian Nut." *Greatest Hits* isn't the last word on George Clinton's solo career, but if you need a concise introduction to the funkmeister's Capitol efforts of the '80s, it's the logical place to go. —*Alex Henderson*

## Clock DVA

f. 1980, Sheffield, Yorkshire, England
*Group / Post-Punk, Electronic, Industrial, Synth-Pop*
A product of the same mid-'70s Sheffield industrial music community which also gave rise to Throbbing Gristle and Cabaret Voltaire, Clock DVA emerged in 1980 from the ashes of area bands including the Studs, Block Opposite, Veer, and They Must Be Russians, as well as the Future, an early incarnation of the Human League. After a series of shifting lineups, a roster comprised of vocalist Adi Newton, bassist Steven Taylor, guitarist Paul Widger, saxophonist Charlie Collins, and drummer Roger Quail recorded Clock DVA's debut *White Souls in Black Suits*, a cassette-only, improvisational release fusing metallic noise with funk and soul designs which was issued on Throbbing Gristle's Industrial label.

In 1981, the group issued *Thirst*, which abandoned R&B accoutrements in favor of edgy, abrasive electronic noise. Following its release, all of Clock DVA except Newton defected to form Box; after assembling a new lineup of saxophonist Paul Browse, future Siouxsie and the Banshees guitarist John Carruthers, bassist Dean Dennis, and drummer Nick Sanderson, Newton wrangled a major-label deal with Polydor, and Clock DVA soon resurfaced with 1983's *Advantage*, an intense montage of dance beats, piercing feedback and jarring tape manipulations. However, Carruthers and Sanderson both exited following the LP's release; after a brief attempt to forge on as a trio, Clock DVA disbanded in late 1983.

Newton subsequently turned his focus to the Anti Group, an industrial jazz and visual arts project created in tandem with engineer Robert Baker; after a series of singles, he reformed Clock DVA in 1988 with Browse and Dennis, releasing the sample-fueled 1988 EPs *The Hacker* and *The Act*, as well as 1990's full-length *Buried Dreams*, on the Wax Trax! label. By 1991's *Transitional Voices*, Newton's Anti Group partner Baker had replaced Browse; Dennis departed soon after, leaving the remaining duo to record a staggeringly prolific amount of material including 1992's *Man-Amplified*, 1993's *Sign, Black Words on White Paper*, and *Virtual Reality Handbook*, 1994's *150 Erotic Calibrations* and 1995's *Anterior*. —*Jason Ankeny*

**White Souls in Black Suits** / 1980 / Industrial ♦♦♦
A satiric look at British soul through the unblinking eye of the group's slant toward noise and stark drum machines, Clock DVA's debut album radiates a curious energy, a vibe that ironically guarantees more power than their targets ever managed. —*Keith Farley*

**Thirst** / 1981 / Contempo ♦♦♦♦
Their most experimental affair yet, *Thirst* pitched the machine effects to overdrive with a set of obtuse noise-makers from all kinds of unlikely sources. Surprisingly, it's still nominally danceable though the emphasis is solidly on the experimental side of affairs. —*Keith Farley*

● **Advantage** / 1983 / Wax Trax! ♦♦♦♦
The only album released by Clock DVA's second lineup, *Advantage* is near the band's best. Though there aren't many synthesizers, the focus on jarring tape procedures and noise well into the red lines makes for an intense set of songs, enlivened by Adi Newton's evolved vocal style. The atmosphere is

bleak and noir-ish (including a cover of the Velvet Underground's "Black Angels Death Song"), quite similar to early Clock DVA material. —*Keith Farley*

**The Hacker/The Act** / 1988 / Wax Trax! ♦♦♦

## Cluster

f. 1970, Berlin, Germany
*Group / Kraut-Rock, Ambient, Electronic*

The most important and consistently underrated space-rock unit of the '70s, Cluster (originally Kluster) was formed by Dieter Moebius, Hans-Joachim Roedelius and Conrad Schnitzler as an improv group that used everything from synthesizers to alarm clocks and kitchen utensils in their performaces. Continuing on as a duo, Moebius and Roedelius eventually recorded many landmark LPs—separately, as a duo, and with all manner of guest artists from Brian Eno to Conny Plank to Neu!'s Michael Rother—in the field of German space music often termed *kosmische*. Cluster also continued to explore ambient music into the '90s, long after their contemporaries had drifted into tamer new age music or ceased recording altogether.

Cluster originally came out of a Berlin art/music collective named the Zodiak Free Arts Lab, formed by Conrad Schnitzler (one of the leaders of the city's avant-underground), and also including Hans-Joachim Roedelius plus future members of Tangerine Dream, Ash Ra Tempel, and Guru Guru. After Schnitzler and Roedelius met an art student named Dieter Moebius, the threesome formed Kluster in 1970. The group performed around Europe and even in Africa, engaging in wild improv sessions utilizing any instruments they could get their hands on; while touring they met engineer Conny Plank, soon to become a major part of Cluster's recorded output into the late '80s. The first three Kluster LPs, 1970's *Klopfzeichen* and *Zwei Osterei* plus 1971's *Eruption*, consisted of side-long improvisatory jams.

Soon after the release of *Eruption*, Schnitzler left the band for a solo career. Moebius and Roedelius continued on as Cluster and, with the help of Plank, released two eponymous studio albums in 1971 and 1972. An ongoing collaboration with Michael Rother (Neu!) began in 1973, after the duo founded their own private studio out in the German countryside. After inviting Rother down to record, the results were released as the 1974 Cluster LP *Zuckerzeit*, a watershed of electronic pop midway between Cluster, Neu!, and Kraftwerk (the latter just about to explode with their own *Autobahn* LP). That same year, Moebius, Roedelius and Rother formed a Kraut-rock super-group named Harmonia; two excellent albums followed in the next year, *Musik von Harmonia* and *Harmonia De Luxe*, as well as a few sessions with Brian Eno (unreleased until 1997's *Tracks & Traces*).

Eno himself began his own collaboration with Moebius and Roedelius in 1977, when Sky Records released *Cluster & Eno*. The trio also recorded *After the Heat* two years later (technically credited as "Eno Moebius Roedelius"), and after a hiatus of six years resumed the relationship with *Begegnungen* and *Begegnungen II* (both featuring Plank in the lineup as well).

Though Roedelius and Moebius also launched solo careers around this time (1978 and 1983, respectively) they continued to release compelling Cluster material in keeping with *Zuckerzeit*, including *Sowiesoso* in 1976, *Grosses Wasser* three years later and *Curiosum* in 1981.

Besides the Eno collaborations and many other solo works, almost fifteen years passed before the appearance of another Cluster album, 1994's *One Hour*. Moebius and Roedelius continued to work and tour together continually. —*John Bush*

**Klopfzeichen** / 1970 / Hypnotic ♦♦♦
The second offering from Cluster was recorded under the Kluster banner with the original line-up of Conrad Schnitzler, Dieter Moebius, and Hans-Joachim Roedelius. —*Jason Ankeny*

★ **Cluster 71** / 1971 / Philips ♦♦♦♦♦
*Cluster 71* is an excellent balance of the group's early noise period, a growing emphasis on the outer periphery of space music, and a growing minimalist emphasis reminiscent of Steve Reich. The three untitled tracks are exploratory, ever-changing pieces with nominal focuses on guitar distortion and synthesizer wails, though each goes far beyond. *Cluster 71* deserves the many accolades it's been given, and holds up as an early landmark in the history of beatless ambience. —*John Bush*

**Eruption** / 1971 / Marginal Talent ♦♦♦♦
The last album as Kluster, and the last with Conrad Schnitzler a part of the lineup, *Eruption* includes 50 minutes of "Elektronische Musik" recorded live in 1971. Closer to avant-garde and noise than space, it shows the influence of Schnitzler on early Kluster material with forbidding violin lines, heavily distorted organ, and an assortment of tape effects leading the way for several minimalist guitar workouts. Schnitzler himself reissued the album in 1997 through his Plate Lunch label. —*John Bush*

**Zwei Osterie** / 1971 / Schwann ♦♦♦

**Cluster II** / 1972 / Brain ♦♦

**Zuckerzeit** / 1974 / Brain ♦♦♦♦
An unexpected jump from the extended *kosmische* jams of *Cluster 71* into uncharted territory that signaled their direction for years to come, *Zuckerzeit* presented a vision of electronic pop, fusing the duo's haunted melodic sense with crisp, scratchy drum programs that provided a grounded focus to all those synthesizer warbles. Oddly, the ten short tracks have separate composer credits (five each), leading to the assumption that Roedelius handled more evocative synthesizer lines ("Hollywood," "Rosa") while Moebius pushed the group into experimental ground ("Rote Riki," "Caramba"). It's undoubtedly one of the most distinctive records in the Cluster discography, though the simple lack of space rock material makes it a difficult album to recommend from the outset. —*John Bush*

**Sowiesoso** / 1976 / Sky ♦♦♦♦
The evocative toybox melodies (usually the Roedelius compositions) on 1974's *Zuckerzeit* reached their peak with *Sowiesoso*, courtesy of ambling pieces like "Dem Wanderer," the title track and the vaguely Oriental "Halwa." The drum programs are still irresistibly simplistic (not to say simple), but even when *Sowiesoso* stretches out into primarily beatless terrain ("Es War Einmal," "Zum Wohl"), the album retains its power. —*John Bush*

**Cluster & Eno** / 1977 / Skyclad ♦♦♦♦
Brian Eno's first collaboration with Cluster, the best of this album's instrumental pieces are too emotionally rich to waste as mere background music, evoking feelings of hesitancy and regret that rescue the music from mere vapid prettiness. Three tracks in particular indicate things to come. "Wehrmut" is an ethereal synth piece with the pace slowed to a tantalizing crawl. "Steinsame" features a treated guitar playing a slow figure over a dark, almost funereal synth melody. "Schöne Hände" uses watery synth effects to highlight a shivery rhythm pattern. Other pieces dispense with moody atmospherics altogether. Tracks like "Ho Renomo" and "Selange" consist mainly of pounding rhythm patterns lightly embellished by piano or synthesizer, and "Die Bunge" sounds like an electronic goldfinch fluttering around a cartoon horse. While not the unqualified success of their 1978 collaboration *After the Heat*, *Cluster & Eno* remains an important album. Along with Eno's 1978 *Music for Films*, these works helped define the depth and promise of ambient music. —*Michael Waynick*

**After the Heat** / 1979 / Skyclad ♦♦♦
The collaboration follow-up to 1977's *Cluster & Eno* is typically slow-moving and similar to its predecessor, though "Foreign Affairs" and the Eno vocal on "The Belldog" provide more focus. Can's Holger Czukay also guests on several tracks. —*John Bush*

**Grosses Wasser** / 1979 / Skyclad ♦♦♦♦
The best of the proper Cluster LPs recorded between their various Eno collaborations of the late '70s and early '80s, *Grosses Wasser* comprises six tracks of slowly building electronics. While the dark-sounding tracks "Avanti" and "Prothese" sound like a fusion of Tangerine Dream and disco, others including "Isodea" and "Manchmal" recall the early days of *Cluster 71*. —*John Bush*

## Coco Steel & Lovebomb

f. 1992, London, England
*Group / Garage, Club/Dance, House*

Though Coco Steel & Lovebomb grew out of the techno community, the group blends elements of garage, soul and disco with only an ambient techno blueprint. After Coco (aka Chris Mellor) began DJing at the Brighton club Zap, his acid-house sets grew popular in the wake of the late-'80s house explosion. With partner Steel (aka Lene), he formed Coco Steel & Lovebomb, originally growing out of Zap with the single "Feel It" and its follow-ups: "Touch It," "Hold It," "Work It." After taking three years to record their debut album *It!*, the duo released it in 1994. An ambient outing, *New World*, followed in 1997, followed by a remix album two years later. —*John Bush*

● **New World** / Jul. 21, 1997 / Other ♦♦♦
They started out as a pure house outfit, and that's why it's surprising to find

Coco Steel & Lovebomb releasing an ambient album, especially in 1997 when beats reigned supreme. Though some of *New World* uses abstract trip-hop as a base, most of it relies on ambience of the Orb type, exemplified by the album's theme of a trip around the world. It's not that it doesn't work, it just appears that Coco Steel & Lovebomb made a cash-in album years after the fact. —*John Bush*

**It!** / Feb. 16, 1999 / Warp ♦♦

## The Cocteau Twins

f. 1979, Grangemouth, Scotland

*Group / Noise Pop, Ambient-Pop, Dream Pop, Shoegazing, Alternative Pop/Rock*

A group whose distinctly ethereal and gossamer sound virtually defined the enigmatic image of their record label 4AD, the Cocteau Twins were founded in Grangemouth, Scotland in 1979. Taking their name from an obscure song from fellow Scots Simple Minds, the Cocteaus were originally formed by guitarist Robin Guthrie and bassist Will Heggie and later rounded out by Guthrie's girlfriend Elizabeth Fraser, an utterly unique performer whose swooping, operatic vocals relied less on any recognizable language than on the subjective sounds and textures of verbalized emotions.

In 1982, the trio signed to 4AD, the arty British label then best known as the home of the Birthday Party, whose members helped the Cocteaus win a contract. The group debuted with *Garlands*, which offered an embryonic taste of their rapidly-developing, atmospheric sound, crafted around Guthrie's creative use of distorted guitars, tape loops and echo boxes and anchored in Heggie's rhythmic bass as well as an omnipresent Roland 808 drum machine. Shortly after the release of the *Peppermint Pig* EP, Heggie left the group, and Guthrie and Fraser cut 1983's *Head Over Heels* as a duo; nonetheless, the album largely perfected the Cocteaus' gauzy formula, and established the foundation from which the group would continue to work for the duration of its career.

In late 1983, ex-Drowning Craze bassist Simon Raymonde joined the band to record the EP *The Spangle Maker*; as time wore on, Raymonde became an increasingly essential component of the Cocteau Twins, gradually assuming an active role as a writer, arranger, and producer. With their line-up firmly solidified, they issued the 1984 EP *Pearly-Dewdrops' Drop*, followed by the LP *Treasure*, their most mature and consistent work yet. A burst of creativity followed, as the Twins issued three separate EPs—*Aikea-Guinea*, *Tiny Dynamine*, and *Echoes in a Shallow Bay*—in 1985, trailed a year later by the acoustic *Victorialand* album, the *Love's Easy Tears* EP, and *The Moon and the Melodies*, a collaborative effort with minimalist composer Harold Budd.

With 1988's sophisticated *Blue Bell Knoll*, the trio signed an international contract with Capitol Records which greatly elevated their commercial visibility. After 1990's *Heaven or Las Vegas*, the Cocteaus severed their long-standing relationship with 4AD; notably, the album also found Fraser's vocals offering the occasional comprehensible turn of phrase, a trend continued on 1993's *Four-Calendar Cafe*. In 1995, they explored a pair of differing musical approaches on simultaneously-released EPs: while *Twinlights* offered subtle acoustic sounds, *Otherness* tackled ambient grooves, remixed by Seefeel's Mark Clifford. 1996's *Milk and Kisses* LP, on the other hand, marked a return to the band's archetypal style. The Cocteau Twins quietly disbanded while working on an uncompleted follow-up; the posthumous *BBC Sessions* appeared in 1999. —*Jason Ankeny*

**Garlands** / 1982 / 4AD ♦♦

Those hearing *Garlands* for the first time who only know the band's other material will likely be more than a little surprised. Whereas the typical vision of the Twins is of beautiful washes of sounds and exultant vocals from Fraser, on *Garlands* the trio is still only part of the way there. Instead, the best comparison points are to the Cure on *Faith* and *Pornography*, perhaps *Metal Box*-era PiL, a touch of Joy Division here and there—in sum, deep, heavy mood verging on doom and gloom. Bassist Will Heggie, in the only full album he did with the Twins, clearly follows the Peter Hook/Simon Gallup style of low, ominous throb, while Guthrie's guitar work more often than not screeches rather than shimmers. Fraser's singing has a starker edge, unsettling even at its most accessible, sometimes completely disturbing at other times. The strongest track, "Wax and Wane," has the trio creating a powerful but also surprisingly danceable track, the crisp drumbox beat working against Guthrie's compelling atmospherics and Fraser's vocal hook in the chorus. Beyond that and a couple of other moments, though, *Garlands* falters due to something the band generally avoided in the future—overt repetition. Too many of the songs rely on a unified formula that rarely changes; one need only compare to the multiplicity of styles tried on *Head Over Heels* to see the difference. As a debut effort, though, *Garlands* makes its own curious mark, preparing the band for greater heights. Import CD versions contain a complete John Peel session from 1983, with guest vocals from Cindytalk's Gordon Sharpe, which has since been rereleased as part of the *BBC Sessions* package. Two other rarities, "Speak No Evil" and the fine "Perhaps Some Other Aeon," complete the release. —*Ned Raggett*

**Head Over Heels/Sunburst and Snowblind** / 1983 / 4AD/Beggars Banquet ♦♦♦♦

Recorded simply with the duo of Elizabeth Fraser and Robin Guthrie, *Head Over Heels* nevertheless represents a major leap over the Cocteau Twins' earliest work. Fraser's vocals are more assured, and the songs begin to strive as much for substance as atmosphere—"Sugar Hiccup" and "Musette and Drums" mark a move toward more concrete melodies, while "In Our Angelhood" breaks the album's gently hypnotic mood with an agreeably uptempo rhythm. [*Head Over Heels* was reissued on CD with the *Sunburst and Snowblind* EP added as a bonus.] —*Jason Ankeny*

**Tiny Dynamine/Echoes in a Shallow Bay** / 1985 / 4AD/Beggars Banquet ♦♦♦♦

A compilation of two of the trio's EP releases, *Tiny Dynamine/Echoes in a Shallow Bay* is an easy and relatively inexpensive way to sample the Cocteau Twins' non-LP work, although collectors will certainly want the original releases of both, if only for the typically exquisite 4AD label packaging. —*Jason Ankeny*

**Treasure/Aikea-Guinea** / 1985 / Vertigo ♦♦♦♦

A triumph of texture and melody, *Treasure* is the Cocteau Twins' first truly stellar record. The full-length debut of Simon Raymonde, it reveals him to be the final component necessary to make the group's ambitions a reality; songs like "Ivo" and "Pandora (For Cindy)" shimmer with new clarity and focus, while Elizabeth Fraser's vocals grow significantly in resonance and emotional scope, conveying hope, fear, joy, and sorrow in a language more powerful than words. For the CD release of *Treasure*, the *Aikea-Guinea* EP was added as a bonus. —*Jason Ankeny*

**The Moon and the Melodies** / 1986 / 4AD ♦♦

*The Moon and the Melodies* is a collaboration between the Cocteau Twins and keyboardist/composer Harold Budd that fits soundly between the stylistic signatures of the two, both of whom make organic music that relies heavily on electronics. Budd's use of spacious treated piano and keyboard sounds (influenced by a previous collaborator, Brian Eno) combine with the Cocteau Twins' shimmering waves of guitars and Elizabeth Fraser's layered wordless vocals to create what amounts to a soundtrack to a dream about sleeping, with saxophones courtesy of Richard Thomas (of the now defunct Dif Juz) breathing further life into the music. Too bland to be the best introduction to the music of either, but a welcome addition to the collection of fans of both. —*Peter Stepek*

**Pink Opaque** / 1986 / 4AD ♦♦♦♦

After having built up a considerable reputation in the UK and Europe, the Cocteaus first fully reached America via this compilation, cherry-picking some of the group's finest moments for this trans-Atlantic co-release between home label 4AD and then-stateside label Relativity. None of the ten tracks had been released in America before, but whoever assembled the release knew exactly what they were doing in terms of whetting appetites. The only absolute rarity on the disc was "Millimillenary," originally turning up on a compilation tape given away by *New Musical Express*. It's a fine number, recorded soon after Raymonde joined the group—a good mix of the Cocteaus' instrumental lushness and Fraser's vocal acrobatics. The version of *Garlands*' "Wax and Wane" included here is slightly remixed and arguably even better than the original, bringing out everything a little more clearly and powerfully. A sage decision was the inclusion of all three tracks from the *Pearly-Dewdrops' Drops* EP; as flawless as that was, all deserved inclusion, while beginning the compilation with "The Spangle Maker" was also inspired. Other cuts include "Hitherto," "From the Flagstones," "Lorelei," and the then-recent single "Aikea-Guinea." Concluding with the similarly album-ending "Musette and Drums" from *Head Over Heels*, *The Pink Opaque* is a lovely taster for anyone wanting to discover the peerless early years of the Cocteaus. —*Ned Raggett*

**Victorialand** / 1986 / 4AD ✦✦✦

With Raymonde taking a break to work on the second This Mortal Coil album, Fraser and Guthrie made up the Cocteaus for the first full-length follow-up to *Treasure*. Rather than trying for a full-band approach, similar to what was done for *Head Over Heels*, the two instead created a much more simply beautiful effort, with a relaxed air to it. Rhythms are subtler, with bass and drum machine often totally eschewed in favor of Guthrie's delicate guitar filigrees and lush, produced textures. Fraser is, as always, in wonderfully fine voice; her words are quite indecipherable, but the feelings are no less strong for it. "Lazy Calm" starts things perfectly, as deep, heavily-treated guitar strums combine with a heavy flange and guest saxophone from Dif Juz member Richard Thomas. Then the piece builds into a more restrained but still recognizably Cocteau combination of Fraser and Guthrie working in concert. Other songs sparkle with a lovely vivaciousness. Far from being stereotypical arty music to sit around and be gloomy to, two pieces especially shine with a gentle energy: "Fluffy Tufts," with its many-layered ringing strings and Fraser's overdubbed vocals; and the joyful "Little Spacey," with a soft rhythm underlying more sheer electric loveliness. At times, Guthrie strips down nearly completely to acoustic guitar, but by no means totally. He adds heavy reverb and overdubbed lines to create the Cocteaus' wash on such songs as "Throughout the Dark Months of April and May" and "Feet Like Fins," the latter again featuring Thomas, this time on tablas. For all the sweet beauty of *Victorialand*, things end on a quietly dramatic note, but a dramatic one nonetheless. "The Thinner the Air" starts with treated piano and rather spooky guitar leads—the mysterious soloing is especially wonderful—while Fraser then sings with a slightly haunted feeling, concluding with slightly nervous wails. It's an unexpected but effective touch for this fine record. —*Ned Raggett*

● **Blue Bell Knoll** / 1988 / 4AD ✦✦✦✦

The first Cocteaus album to feature a full-band lineup since *Treasure* was also their first full studio record released in America, resulting from the group's stateside deal with Capitol. Much to longtime fans' surprise, the Twins in fact were much more content with Capitol than 4AD, hinting at their eventual full departure from that label. This was all well and good, but the trio's new inspiration didn't fully translate into their work, unfortunately. While *Knoll* has some striking moments that are pure Cocteaus at their best—the opening title track is especially lovely with a keyboard loop leading into Fraser's ever-wonderful vocals, a light rhythm, and a great final Guthrie solo—it's still the band's least noteworthy release since *Garlands*. The feeling throughout is of a group interested in dressing up older approaches that have served them well, but aren't as distinct; the quite-lush arrangements by Guthrie are fine but the songs are a touch more pedestrian. *Knoll* has enough initial steam, however, to ensure that there are reasons to listen, happily. "Athol-Brose" has the inspirational feel that the Twins can easily create. "Carolyn's Fingers," the clear album standout, is perhaps the strongest individual Cocteau song since "Aikea-Guinea," with Fraser singing against herself (one vocal high, another lower) over a rough, hip-hop-inspired rhythm. Guthrie peels off a fantastic main guitar melody, while his solos are peerless; Raymonde, in turn, contributes some supple bass work. After that amazing opening, things slowly but surely slide back a bit; most of the rest of *Knoll* sounds OK enough to listen to, but the heartgripping intensity that defines the Twins at their best isn't present. Pretty moments abound everywhere—the addition of vibes to "Spooning Good Singing Gum" is ear-catching, and the concluding "Ella Megalast Burls Forever" has a sweetly climactic feeling—but *Knoll* could still be greater than it is. —*Ned Raggett*

**Heaven or Las Vegas** / 1990 / 4AD ✦✦✦

Deciding, on the one hand, to scale back the at-times over-pretty sound present on *Blue Bell Knoll* while on the other, to experiment with a new general accessibility—Fraser's vocals in particular are the clearest, most direct they've ever been—the Twins ended up creating their best album since *Treasure*. *Heaven...* is simply fantastic from the start; "Cherry-Coloured Funk" has Guthrie's oft-imitated but never-duplicated processed guitar chimes leading a low-key but forceful rhythm, and Raymonde's grand bass work fleshes it out while Fraser simply captivates, purring with energy and life. Many songs make use of longer openings and closings; rather than crashing fully into a song and then quickly ending, instead the three musicians carefully build up and then ease back. Such cuts are still quite focused, though, almost sounding like they were recorded live instead of being assembled in the studio. Due credit has to be given to the Cocteaus' drum programming; years of working with the machines translated into the detailed work here, right down to the fills. "Fifty-Fifty Clown," starting with an ominous bass throb, turns into a lovely example of Fraser's singing and Guthrie's ability to restrain his playing, filling in space as needed rather than dominating the mix. By no means do the Twins completely turn their back on *Knoll*'s sound; "Iceblink Luck," the lead single, has the same lush feeling but with a newfound energy—the instrumental break is almost a rave-up!—and everything pulses to a fine conclusion. Moments of sheer Cocteaus beauty and power are thick on the ground, including the title track, with its great chorus, and two spotlight Guthrie solos: "Fotzepolitic," a powerful number building to a rushing conclusion, and especially the album-ending "Frou Frou Foxes in Midsummer Fires." Possessed of the same sense of drama and climax of past disc-closers as "Donimo" and "The Thinner the Air," it's a perfect way to end a near-perfect album. —*Ned Raggett*

**Iceblink Luck [EP]** / 1990 / 4AD ✦✦✦

Surprise—you can almost understand what Elisabeth Fraser is singing on this single. The music hovers within intriguing rhythmic structures, Fraser's voice floating sweetly about in the mix. You may not know what "Iceblink Luck" is about, but it sure sounds pretty, as do the two non-LP tracks, "Mizake The Mizan" and "Watchlar." The Twins have always been the alternative answer to new age; this takes them a few steps further. (Available as a 12" vinyl single, and as a compact disc single.) —*Steven McDonald*

**Four-Calendar Cafe** / Sep. 27, 1993 / Capitol ✦✦✦

The Cocteau Twins' first release following their exodus from the 4AD stable, *Four-Calendar Cafe* is also, tellingly, their most earthbound effort; as with *Heaven or Las Vegas*, the emphasis here is on substance as much as style— "Evangeline," "Bluebeard," and "Know Who You Are at Every Age" continue the trio's advance into more accessible melodic and lyrical ground without sacrificing even an ounce of their trademark ethereality. —*Jason Ankeny*

**Milk and Kisses** / Apr. 1996 / Capitol ✦✦

Throughout the '80s, the Cocteau Twins created some of the most beautiful and innovative music of the decade. Liz Fraser's uncanny, gossamer voice and Robin Guthrie's shimmery guitar work both garnered acclaim and inspired bands. *Milk and Kisses* finds the band in a comfortable rut; they've created, and now perfected, a style of music so distinctive that there seems to be little recent creative growth. The result is a beautiful, lush, but somewhat dated and unengaging sounding album that tends to wash over the listener without making any real impact. It is, however, everything that a Cocteau Twins album promises; hypnotic, dreamy, awash in ethereal voices and delicate, liquid guitars. "Tishbite" in particular delivers an accessible dream-pop sound that sounds nice while it's playing but fails to have anything really memorable about it, a problem that plagues most of *Milk and Kisses*. "Half-Gifts," "Rilkean Heart," and "Treasure Hiding" have an airy, otherwordly prettiness to them—but that's about it. Necessary for Cocteau Twins diehards and potentially interesting to those who have never heard the band before, *Milk and Kisses* says nothing, but says it beautifully. —*Heather Phares*

## Coil

f. 1983, London, England

*Group / Experimental, Ambient, Electronic, Industrial*

Initially established in 1983 as a solo outlet for vocalist and percussionist John Balance, the experimental sonic manipulation unit Coil became a full-fledged concern a year later following the arrival of keyboardist/programmer Peter Christopherson, a founder of Psychic TV as well as a member of Throbbing Gristle. After debuting with the 17-minute single "How to Destroy Angels," the duo recruited the aid of Possession's Stephen Thrower, J.G. "Foetus" Thirlwell, and Gavin Friday to record their full-length 1984 bow *Scatology*, an intense, primal work of sculpted industrial noise thematically devoted to the concepts of alchemy and transmutation.

Coil spent the next period of its existence exploring visual media: in late 1984 they recorded a rendition of the Soft Cell smash "Tainted Love," producing a widely banned, hallucinogenic video clip featuring Mark Almond as the Angel of Death; despite considerable controversy at home, the video ultimately found its way to the archives of the Museum of Modern Art. After spending several years working with filmmaker Derek Jarman on the feature *The Angelic Conversation*, Coil issued a remixed edition of their soundtrack; following 1986's *Nightmare Culture*, a collaboration with Boyd Rice produced as split release with Current 93, Christopherson and Balance invited Stephen Thrower to join the group in a full-time capacity. As a trio, they recorded 1986's *Horse Rotorvator,* an LP introducing classical, jazz and Middle Eastern textures into the mix, as well as the EP *The Anal Staircase.*

After 1987's *Unreleased Themes From 'Hellraiser*—a collection of atmospheric Gothic instrumentals commissioned for, but ultimately cut from, the Clive Barker horror film—Coil issued 1988's *Gold Is the Metal With the Broadest Shoulders,* a remixed history of the group's first several years of work. 1990's *Unnatural History,* another career overview, effectively ended the first phase of the band's career; when Coil resurfaced a year later with *Love's Secret Domain,* their music reflected the strong influence of the acid-house culture. Another long layoff brought on by financial difficulties ended in 1995, when the group—now consisting of Christopherson, Balance and Dean McCowall—signed to Nine Inch Nails frontman Trent Reznor's label nothing to release *Backwards.* Additionally, they recorded the LP *Worship the Glitch,* issued under the name ELpH, and in 1996 cut *Black Light District: A Thousand Lights in a Darkened Room,* the first in an ongoing series of "Black Light District" releases. —*Jason Ankeny*

**Scatology** / 1984 / Some Bizarre ✦✦✦

**Horse Rotorvator** / 1987 / K422 ✦✦✦✦
The title *Horse Rotorvator* is explained in the liner notes as a device large enough to 'plough up the waiting world,' created from the bones of the horses of the Four Horsemen of the Apocalypse. The Bay City Rollers this isn't. On the group's second full album, Coil continue the refinement of brute noise and creepily serene arrangements into a truly modern psychedelia, from tribal drumming and death march guitars to disturbing samples and marching band samples and back. Balance shares the same haggard, mystic vocal delivery common to fellow explorers of the edge like David Tibet and Edward Ka-Spel, but he has his own blasted and burnt touch to it all. His lyrical subjects range from emotional extremism of many kinds to blunt, often homoerotic imagery (matched at points in the artwork and packaging) and meditations on death. As a result the cover of Leonard Cohen's "Who by Fire" isn't as surprising as one might think. Past guest Marc Almond appears again on the track with backing vocals, as well as adding them to "Slur," which is composed of an unsettling mix of harmonica, bells, percussion and whatever else can be imagined. Other guests include Almond's then-musical partner Billy McGee, adding a haunting, sometimes grating, string arrangement to "Ostia," which is about the murder of radical Italian filmmaker Pasolini, and Clint Ruin, aka Foetus, adding his typically warped brass touches to "Circles of Mania." Paul Vaughan narrates the lyrics on "The Golden Section," creating a stunning piece that in its combination of demonic imagery and sweeping, cinematic arrangements holds a common ground with In the Nursery. All the guests help contribute to the album's overall effect, but this is Coil's own vision above all else, eschewing easy cliches on all fronts to create unnerving, never easily digested invocations of musical power. —*Ned Raggett*

• **Love's Secret Domain** / 1991 / Wax Trax! ✦✦✦✦
Though Coil's Balance and Christopherson were inspired by the acid-house revolution of the late '80s, their drug-inspired "dance" album isn't quite as indebted to the style as the contemporary work of Psychic TV. The influence comes through mostly in the deranged effects and vaguely surreal air, though several tracks do increase the rhythmic wattage. For the most part, the duo retained the gothic synth-pop of *Horse Rotorvator,* but with a special emphasis on stuttered cut-and-paste sections rather than organic instruments and environmental sublimation. —*John Bush*

**Worship the Glitch** / 1995 / Eskaton ✦✦✦
Recorded with Elph, *Worship the Glitch* is another experimental, uncompromising entry in the Coil disography, perhaps a bit sparer and more minimal. —*John Bush*

**Black Light District: A Thousand Lights in a Darkened Room** / 1997 / Eskaton ✦✦✦
The Coil project Black Light District debuted with an album of broad, minimalistic textures and beatless ambience. Though the vibes are similar to the duo's past work, there are no vocals and few beats; what remains is the restless exploration of sound which Coil have always made a prime concern. —*John Bush*

**Time Machines** / 1998 / Eskaton ✦✦✦✦
Although *Time Machines* wasn't precisely credited to Coil, upon its arrival in early 1998 the CD was the first full-length of new material Balance, Christophersen, et al., released in nearly seven years. An hour-long meditation on drone ostensibly inspired by the psychophenomenological properties of hallucinogenic drugs, *Time Machines* is constructed entirely from cycling, oscillating synth tones, and continues in the vein of shapeless experimentalism established with *Black Light District* and *Worship the Glitch.* Enjoyable, if a mite limited in scope. —*Sean Cooper*

## Coldcut
f. 1986, London, England
*Group / Multimedia, Electronica, Trip-Hop, Club/Dance, Acid House, House, Hip-Hop*

DJs Jonathan More and Matt Black, aka Coldcut, rose to acclaim in the mid-'80s through production and remix work for a number of modern rock, hip-hop, and dance outfits, including Yaz, Lisa Stansfield, Junior Reid, Blondie, Eric B. & Rakim, and Queen Latifah. While that connection has pegged them as a product of the UK acid house and rave scenes, the pair's larger commitment has been to urban breakbeat styles such as hip-hop, ambient dub, and jungle, the three of which have constituted the bulk of their recorded output since their first mid-'80s white-label EP, *Hey Kids, What Time Is It?* Comprising project titles like Hedfunk, Hex, DJ Food, and Coldcut, More and Black have assembled an empire of UK breakbeat and experimental hip-hop through their Ninja Tune/Ntone labels and been a unifying force in underground experimental electronic music through their eclectic radio show, *Solid Steel,* and club and tour dates.

More and Black got their start, not surprisingly, as radio DJs, working at the pirate station Network 21 during the first half of the '80s, and latching onto the snowballing club scene mid- to late-decade. Their claim to early fame, *Hey Kids, What Time Is It?* was modeled on the cut'n'scratch turntable aesthetic of underground deck heroes like Grandmaster Flash and Double D & Steinski. Widely regarded as the UK's first breaks record and an influential force in bringing identity to London's nascent club culture, the record—released as a US import billed to DJ Coldcut to avoid sample litigation—opened as many doors for More and Black as it did for DJs, bringing scads of production and remix work their way. The attention (and sales royalties) also allowed them to launch their Ninja Tune and Ntone labels, which together have been home to some of the most acclaimed and influential artists of London's post-rave underground scene, including DJ Food, Drome, Journeyman, 9 Lazy 9, Up, Bustle & Out, and the Herbaliser.

Although Coldcut was their earliest nom de plume, following a befuddled contract with Arista, the name has languored in legal channels for the past few years. The intervening period found the pair no less active, releasing a flood of material under different names and continuing to work with young groups. 1995 brought the Coldcut name back to More and Black, and the pair celebrated with a mix-CD on the Journeys by DJ label dubbed 70 Minutes of Madness. The release is credited with bringing to wider attention the sort of freestyle mixing the pair have always been known for through their radio show on KISS FM, *Solid Steel,* and their steady club dates, a style that has since taken off through clubs like Blech and the Heavenly Sunday Social. In 1997, Coldcut finally released another full-length, *Let Us Play!* Two years later, the pair followed up with the remix album *Let Us Replay!* —*Sean Cooper*

**Hey Kids, What Time is It? [EP]** / 1987 / White Label ✦✦
With only 500 pressed, Coldcut's "bootie" debut has been known to fetch upwards of a C-note in UK shops. Pretty standard James Brown-and-Jimmy Smith-meet-the-Bomb Squad on frappé, with scratches and left-field references compiled with tight, dizzying precision. —*Sean Cooper*

**What's That Noise?** / Sep. 1989 / Big Life/Tommy Boy ✦✦✦✦
More and Black give breaks the full-length treatment. At times more song-oriented than that implies, the pair move from syrupy house and dancefloor fare to hardcore funk and breakbeat to soupy sonic weirdness. A clear indicator of things to come, the album was reissued stateside by Reprise. —*Sean Cooper*

**Philosophy** / 1994 / Arista ✦✦✦✦
The duo's disastrous major-label debut was worry-free acid jazz made even more palatable by vocalists Ade and China's canned, predictable delivery. The album did produce a minor legend in Mixmaster Morris's remix of "Autumn Leaves," but aside from that it's a dry, muddy beaker with little of interest. —*Sean Cooper*

★ **Journeys by DJ—70 Minutes of Madness** / 1996 / Music Unites/Sony ✦✦✦✦✦
Although this mixed CD is a compilation of material by numerous different

artists (from Harold Budd to Dillinja, Joanna Law to the Jedi Knights), only some of which is the pair's own, it's an ample illustration of the sort of freestyle approach to composition the pair helped popularize. The group jump from style to style at will, drawing out the connections between hip-hop, jungle, techno, electro, ambient, and beyond, with first-rate mixing and turntable work. —*Sean Cooper*

**Coldcut & DJ Food Fight** / Jan. 1997 / Ninja Tune ♦♦♦
The second mix album released by the preeminent DJing team in trip-hop, *Coldcut & DJ Food Fight* is limited by the inclusion of only Ninja Tune artists (including Luke Vibert, Funki Porcini, Up Bustle & Out, DJ Vadim, the Herbaliser and Drome, plus Coldcut and DJ Food themselves). As such, it suffers from a lack of variety, with only several breakbeat tracks to leaven the decidedly trip-hoppish affair. Though Coldcut's mixing and scratching skills are stellar, and the various samples provide sustained interest, the album just doesn't measure up to 1995's classic *Journey by DJ*. While the previous album moved from Boogie Down Productions to Jhelisa Anderson and Mantronix to Photek with grace, the inherent limitations of a Ninja Tunes-only mix LP sinks the whole affair before it begins. (*Coldcut & DJ Food Fight* was released as half of a double-disc compilation called *Cold Krush Cuts*, which also includes DJ Krush's *Back in the Base* mix LP.) —*John Bush*

**Let Us Play!** / Sep. 8, 1997 / Ninja Tune ♦♦♦♦
Decade-long veterans of the electronica scene, label-heads of the respected Ninja Tune Records, owners of their own mix show on Radio 1, and Coldcut still haven't learned to make a good long-player. While Jonathan More and Matt Black were responsible for one of the highlights of electronic music history with their 1996 *Journeys by DJ* compilation, *Let Us Play* shows the duo weighed down by a long cast of collaborators (much as their last proper album, 1989's *What's That Noise?*). While the presence of funk drummer Bernard "Pretty" Purdie, old-school rap impresario Steinski, post-punk and spoken-word firebrand Jello Biafra, tabla specialist Talvin Singh (plus sympathizers like the Herbaliser and Jimpster on production), does provide several highlights—and also testifies to Coldcut's philosophy of throwing hip-hop, electronica, funk and a little bit of a whole lot more into the ring and enjoying the free-for-all—the album moves much slower than Coldcut's mix material (which usually averages two minutes per track, as opposed to six or seven on *Let Us Play!*). Besides the syrupy feel of the LP, the abundance of message tracks ("Noah's Toilet," Biafra's "Every Home a Prison," "Cloned Again") subvert the message of the title, indicative of Coldcut's playful qualities over the years. The lone highlight is the single "More Beats + Pieces," a remake of the 1988 original which was constructed from samples in homage to pioneering hip-hop DJs, who manned two turntables with little opportunity to fall back on samplers and expensive keyboards. —*John Bush*

**Let Us Replay!** / Jan. 26, 1999 / Ninja Tune ♦♦♦
*Let Us Replay!* is a double-disc remix album that also includes a few live tracks from Coldcut's innovative world tour. The reworkings benefit from the recruitment of a variety of wide-ranging but very sympathetic figures including Cornelius, Grandmaster Flash, Shut Up and Dance, Carl Craig, and Mixmaster Morris. The live tracks are a bit less entertaining and are quite similar to their album versions. —*John Bush*

## Ken Collier

*DJ / Techno*
Ken Collier belongs on the same mantel that holds Larry Levan, Frankie Knuckles, David Mancuso, Grooverider, and Kool Herc—esteemed as the true fathers of modern electronic dance music. In the late '70s, Collier was the DJ that inspired Detroit youngsters—and soon to be techno innovators—such as Eddie Fowlkes, Derrick May, and Mike Grant to begin spinning records. After he formed True Disco Productions in 1977, Detroit saw its first serious dance club, *Chessmate*, before becoming the resident at the Motor City's famed *Studio 54 Detroit* in 1979. By the mid-'80s, Collier still reined as the city's most recognized DJ with his appearances at the legendary *Heaven* club, until eventually being eclipsed by his followers, ambitious young DJs such as Jeff Mills and Derrick May. Though he eventually got forgotten in the myths of Detroit—often replaced by the equally influential Electrifying Mojo—he continued spinning in the mid-'90s until he passed away. —*Jason Birchmeier*

## Kimball Collins

b. Orlando, FL
*DJ / Progressive Trance, Club/Dance*
Along with Christopher Lawrence, Kimball Collins is one of the few American trance DJs to rank with British heroes like Paul Oakenfold, Sasha, and John Digweed. Born and raised in Orlando, FL, Collins began DJing in 1987. By the end of the '80s, his clubnights at the Beacham Theater helped jumpstart the dance scene in Orlando, which by the late '90s had become one of America's new rave capitals. He branched out to include DJ gigs all across America, and formed his own PositiVibes Records in 1993. With partner Rich Dekkard, Collins' first single "Hardlife"/"Lushlife" became a double-sided club smash, licensed all over Europe. In 1994, Collins became the first of almost a dozen mixers to helm a volume in the *United DJ's of America* series, and one year later, he released a label mix compilation titled *PositiVibes*. Collins also managed to expand his mixing career into Europe, an area with no shortage of trance DJs eager to take the decks. The Max Music label signed Collins on for a mix-album series in 1999, and released three albums during the next two years—*ICU: Session, Vol. 1, ICU Generation: Trance 2000 Episode 01*, and *Clubnights, Vol. 2: Live at Club Utopia*. —*John Bush*

**Positivibes 1** / 1995 / Stress America ♦♦♦
Kimball Collins mixed this collection of Italian house and disco tracks, including "Nightwalk" by Kama Sutra, "Love Me, Leave Me" by Armante and Virtual Missmo's "Cosmonautica." —*Keith Farley*

● **ICU: Session, Vol. 1** / Jan. 12, 1999 / Max Music ♦♦♦♦
A longtime DJ, Kimball Collins has no fears about playing classic tracks instead of the newest club burners—the self-titled smash by Age of Love is close to ten years old, and Agnelli & Nelson's "El Niño" is no spring chicken either. Other highlights come from Energy 52, Cyrus & the Joker, Billy Hendrix, and "New Life" by Collins himself (with partner Rich Dekkard). —*Keith Farley*

**ICU Generation: Trance 2000 Episode 01** / Nov. 16, 1999 / Max Music ♦♦
Orlando-based DJ Kimball Collins handles the mixing on *ICU Generation: Trance 2000, Episode 01*, a collection of European and American trance singles which lean toward the more upbeat, accessible side of the style. There are shadings of ambient and progressive house as well, and although the compilation doesn't stand head and shoulders above its competition, it's well executed and will appeal to most trance fans. —*Steve Huey*

## Sandra Collins

*Producer, DJ / Progressive Trance, Trance*
Perhaps more than any other genre, electronic dance music spent the 20th century dominated by male DJs and producers, with the occasional vocalist such as Bjork or Tracey Thorn attaining any sort of notoriety. Consider Sandra Collins the first female DJ to reach superstar status in the late '90s electronic dance music explosion. By being one of the first American DJs to champion the traditionally Euro-centric sound of trance, she quickly rose to stardom. Her beginnings on the West Coast at rave parties and at clubs led to her eventual entry into the popular *Tranceport* album series along with a March 2000 cover story for the important New York publication, *Mixer*.

After an early interest in industrial-flavored techno, it wasn't long before Collins was spinning at the West Coast's infamous desert parties in the early '90s. There her musical style become increasingly melodic and ethereal, influenced by the spiritual desert surroundings. By the mid- to late-'90s, she began moving toward the sounds of progressive house and eventually the more epic sounds of trance, much in the style of mid-'90s Sasha and Taylor. By the late '90s, once the elitist class of European trance DJs rose to superstar levels, Collins began moving away from the anthemic sounds that filled the crates of these European DJs and began looking for a more American sound, characterized by West Coast producers such as Deepsky. So on the one hand, she spun trance, a very European sound removed from America, but on the other hand, she favored the handful of American producers in the genre, resulting in a unique sound. This unique sound, coupled with Collins' rarity status as a female, garnered her plenty of attention, catapulting her to notoriety seemingly overnight. Many have criticized the fact that she probably would have never reached such levels of stardom had she been a male—a fact that cannot be argued. Yet despite this criticism, she was awarded the coveted opportunities to first spin at *Woodstock* and then mix the third entry in the extremely popular *Tranceport* series. —*Jason Birchmeier*

● **Tranceport, Vol. 3** / Jun. 6, 2000 / Kinetic ♦♦♦♦
Sandra Collins' set of melancholy yet colorful progressive trance starts slowly and steadily builds towards a fiery, climactic conclusion. The journey seems almost linear as she keeps pushing the mood further and further towards emotional extremity, beginning energetically with the up-tempo sounds of Cass & Slide. These beginning few songs feature small teasing melodies and riffs that allude to what lies ahead but never crosses the line into the realm of hands-in-the-air anthem status. By the sixth song, the music has crept forward to near explosive levels; it is at this moment that Collins drops Chris Zippel's remix of Ultra Violet's "Heaven (Feel and Extremity)." The soft-spoken female vocals of this song soothe the listener and bring a lulling humanity to the set's steaming levels of heat. From this relaxing moment of rest and revelry, the remainder of Collins' set is uphill, first beginning slowly but steadily with the steamy salaciousness of Deep Cover's near-decadent "Deeper Inside" and its downright erotic allusions to euphoric excess. The soft and subtle sounds of the staccato synth melody that introduces L.S.G.'s "I'm Not Existing (O. Lieb Main Mix 2)" soon eclipses the eroticism of "Deeper Inside" and again takes the set to even further heights. The final three songs of this album form a climactic finale characterized by the emotive ups and downs liable to tantalize the listener until the final few explosive peaks of Rank One's "Airwave" conclude Collins' set as well as any song could. The initial journey through Collins' set can be described as nothing less than seductive. Her subtle climb to euphoric excess works brilliantly with its short moment of tranquil foreplay halfway through, showcasing exactly how a DJ constructs a progressive set sure to satisfy the insatiable with its varying degrees of intensity and rich textures. More importantly, Collins never goes overboard on *Tranceport, Vol. 3*, instead choosing to save the climactic anthems only for the final moments of her set rather than take the listener to summits prematurely, a problem plaguing too many trance DJs. —*Jason Birchmeier*

## Colourbox

f. 1981, London, England
*Group / Alternative Dance, Acid House*
One of the legendary 4AD label's earliest and most under-recognized acts, Colourbox was among the first artists outside of the realm of hip-hop to rely heavily on sampling techniques; ultimately, their arty blue-eyed soul—a fusion of far-ranging influences spanning from classic R&B to dub to industrial—reached its commerical and creative apotheosis through their work on M/A/R/R/S' seminal "Pump Up the Volume" project, a reflection of the group's long-standing interest in the burgeoning underground dance music scene of the '80s.

Colourbox was primarily the work of London-based brothers Martyn and Steven Young, who recruited vocalist Debian Curry to sing on their 1982 4AD debut "Breakdown"; Curry was replaced by Lorita Grahame in time for the trio's 1983 re-recording of the same track, this time produced by Mick Glossop. Colourbox's self-titled debut EP—a collection of dub and scratching experiments heralding their first plunge into sampling technology, edited down from three hours of studio sessions—appeared later that same year, with the single "Say You" following in 1984. After another 12", "Punch," the group issued 1985's "The Moon Is Blue," a teaser for their upcoming full-length LP, also a self-titled affair; "Baby I Love You So" and "The Official Colourbox World Cup Theme" both appeared the following year.

In 1987, at the behest of 4AD chief Ivo Watts-Russell, the Young brothers teamed with labelmates AR Kane as M/A/R/R/S to record a single fusing the rhythms and beats from classic soul recordings with state-of-the-art electronics and production. Complete with scratches by champion mixer Chris "C.J." Mackintosh and London DJ Dave Dorrell, "Pump Up the Volume"—a breakthrough effort heralding sampling's gradual absorption from hip-hop into dance music and ultimately the pop mainstream—soon topped the British charts, the first 4AD release to accomplish the feat. Plans for a follow-up never materialized, however; stranger still, despite M/A/R/R/S' success both the Youngs and Colourbox seemed to vanish, with no future recordings forthcoming. —*Jason Ankeny*

● **Colourbox** / 1985 / 4AD ♦♦♦♦
The band's sole full length album was, and is, a lost treasure—though much about its production and general sound firmly places it as a product of the mid-'80s, it was still a stunning debut which covers any number of sounds and styles with aplomb. The result is a unique fusion, where you can't quite guess what will happen from one track to the next, but the sound still resembles the product of one particular vision. The opening songs set the range and ambition of the group straightaway—from the instrumental "Sleepwalker," a truly beautiful piano piece with some extra production touches, the band slams into the sampling/guitar/rock/dance masterpiece "Just Give 'Em Whiskey." Crammed with samples from the likes of Westworld and The Prisoner, it's a total winner of beat, sound, and arrangement. Lorita Grahame makes her first appearance on the next number, the previously released cover of U-Roy's dancehall classic "Say You"—her lovely singing provides the anchor for the album as a whole, matching the multiplicity of Colourbox's approaches with skill. The other cover on the record is often cited as its highlight—a revamping of the Supremes' tremendous "You Keep Me Hanging On," which makes the near contemporaneous take by Kim Wilde seem like the weedy thing it is. There are plenty of other examples of Colourbox reaching for the skies, though: from the mid-century tearjerker gone modern "The Moon is Blue" and the album-closing gentle drama of "Arena" to the aggressive "Manic," which features a snarling guitar solo from William Orbit. There's a slightly curious discrepancy in the album's varying editions—the vinyl version featured an extra record with other tracks and some alternate versions, only half of which ended up on CD. Those included were another take on "Arena" and the amusing samplefest "Edit the Dragon." —*Ned Raggett*

## Common Factor (Nick Calingaert)

*Group / Tech-House, Detroit Techno, Club/Dance, Techno*
Producer Nick Calingaert is the creator of an appealing tech-house fusion that's perfectly in line with his Chicago recording base and Detroit releases. His first Common Factor production, the *1000* EP, appeared on Belgium's SSR in 1996. After being rejected by several British labels, he sent tapes to Detroit's Planet E Recordings. By mid-1998, Planet E head Carl Craig released Calingaert's "In To" single. The *Expanded* EP followed later that year, and in 1999 Planet E issued the debut Common Factor album, *Dreams of Elsewhere*. His follow-up single "Pisces Groove" appeared later in 1999. Calingaert also works with Chris Nazuka as Retroflex (the pair record for Scotland's Soma), and has remixed Chris Simmonds. —*John Bush*

● **Dreams of Elsewhere** / Mar. 23, 1999 / Planet E ♦♦♦
Like many of the other artists on Carl Craig's Detroit-based label, Planet E, Common Factor producer Nick Calingaert bridges the gap between the dance floor and the living room. Beginning with the shimmering synths and calm introspection of "Reflections," the album immerses the listener in its dream world, taking them on an electronic journey into the imaginative and emotional depths of Calingaert's artistic mind. Following this ambient introduction, the music gets much funkier and more uptempo. "Positive Visual" sets the pace of the album with some booming bass in the background and layers of digital melodies working together to form a strong rhythm. What separates this song and a few others on the album from calm techno is the inclusion of sampled vocals. These samples, along with some hints of disco, help "Get Down" and "Horizons" capture the soul and celebratory feel of house music. This blend of techno and house with a relaxed, mellow mood slowly fades after the first three songs. The center of the album—"In To," "The Sky I Stand Under," and "Exploration/ Meaning"—is characterized more by intensity and complexity than funk and soul. The rhythms are more tribal, the sounds are more cosmic, and the album's journey transforms from joyful celebration to nightmarish, hedonistic ecstasy. Near the conclusion of the record, the journey changes once again. "Feel What I Feel," the funkiest and most soulful song on the album, alleviates the intense techno bliss of the preceding songs. After this emotional height, the album concludes with two atmospheric songs of ambient techno. —*Jason Stanley Birchmeier*

**Pisces Groove [Single]** / Aug. 24, 1999 / Planet E ♦♦
On this follow-up to his excellent *Dreams of Elsewhere*, Common Factor producer Nick Calingaert sticks with the upbeat, disco-tinged sound of his early Planet E releases. The A-side, "Pisces Groove," is a straight-ahead techno groover, with some subtly pumping bass, a few programmed percussion loops, and some carefully arranged synthesizer riffs that wiggle and modulate their way through the entire track, sometimes acting as the rhythm, while other times getting dense and consistent enough to act as melodies. On the B-side,

Common Factor again keeps his techno light and smooth, without any compressed banging or pounding. "North Nights" opens with a catchy vocal loop similar in style to the sampled vocals of earlier songs like "Feel What I Feel." The release ends with a fine remix of "Get Down" by Chris Simmonds that doesn't make too many drastic changes to the original. —*Jason Birchmeier*

## Company Flow

f. 1992, Queens, NY
*Group / Underground Rap*

One of the leaders in the return of street-level, non-corporate hip-hop, Company Flow formed in Queens around the trio of rapper/producers El-P and Bigg Jus plus DJ Mr. Len. The trio's dirty, basement-style productions and hard-hitting raps was a welcome addition to the rap scene circa 1997, a time when the Puff Daddy-style of pop/rap ruled the airwaves and charts. Company Flow had debuted more than four years earlier, however, on a 1993 single named "Juvenile Techniques." The trio then formed their own Official Recordings label and released the EP *Funcrusher* one year later. Another single, "8 Steps to Perfection," became an underground hit, and Company Flow teamed up with the independent Rawkus label to release *Funcrusher Plus*, their full-length debut and a compilation-of-sorts mixing old material with new. The instrumentals album *Little Johnny from the Hospitul* followed in 1999. —*John Bush*

- **Funcrusher Plus** / Jul. 28, 1997 / Priority ◆◆◆◆

Harder and more oriented to the underground than Dr. Octagon, Company Flow trump more established artists on their debut album (a collection of singles from 1994-97), released on the independent Rawkus Records. The cover art gives nods to the P-Funk machine as well as A Tribe Called Quest, while rappers Bigg Jus and El-P match the scatological bent of Octagon, but with a style more rooted in '90s rapping and the sing-song delivery of Cypress Hill. The production by El-P and DJ Mr. Len is dark and skeletal, fitting in well with the vocal concerns. —*John Bush*

**Little Johnny from the Hospitul: Breaks & Instrumentals, Vol. 1** / Jun. 15, 1999 / Rawkus ◆◆◆◆

*Little Johnny from the Hospitul* is an instrumental album and a dark affair with slowish textured beats. These aren't your average hip-hop beats, with basic drum loops and DJ scratches thrown in; it's obvious that El-P and DJ Mr. Len spent considerable time constructing the songs. On "Suzy Pulled a Pistol on Henry," the kid from "Bad Touch Example" (on the *Funcrusher Plus* album) gets revenge on the person that molested her. Other standout songs on the album are "Gigapet Ephany," "Wurker Ant Uprise," and the always addicting "Shadows Drown," which features the distant sounds of water to distorted voices to the sounds of electronic locusts. —*Dan Gizzi*

## Conjoint

f. 1996
*Group / Ambient Techno*

The ambient-jazz collective Conjoint included Klaus Berger on vibraphone and Gunter Ruit Kraus on guitar with David Moufang and Jamie Hodge on keyboards, electronics, and programming. Formed in 1996, the group debuted on Moufang's KM20 Recordings with a self-titled 1997 album, and returned in early 2000 with *Earprints*, recorded for Moufang's other label concern, Source. —*John Bush*

- **Conjoint** / Jun. 16, 1997 / KM20 ◆◆◆◆

An interesting electro-jazz summit featuring three "generations" of experimental artists, including David Moufang, vibist Karl Berger (Ornette Coleman, Lee Konitz), new school German avant-garde guitarist Gunter "Ruit" Kraus, and up-and-coming techno experimentalist Jamie Hodge (aka Plus 8's Born Under a Rhyming Planet). Although a superficial listen reveals only the sort of wallpaper-y lounge jazz explored by any number of '70s Blue Note soul-jazz artists (and more recently expanded upon by the likes of Tortoise, Tipsy, the Sea and Cake, etc.), in fact, a subtler mucking about is going on deeper down. Like previous Moufang jazz-related projects, *Conjoint* is a meticulous hybrid of instrumental groove music and minimalist electronica, referencing ambient, electro, and dub through inventive, interwoven dialogues. However (and something of a first where these projects are concerned), samplers are kept largely at bay throughout, relying on an interesting interplay between Berger's omnipresent vibraphone, Kraus' summery guitar work, and Hodge's and Moufang's machines and treatments. Enjoyable and occasionally enthralling. —*Sean Cooper*

**Earprints** / Feb. 8, 2000 / Source ◆◆◆

The sophomore album from Conjoint charts many of the same vibes as 1997's self-titled album for KM20, though that's hardly a drawback. Moufang and Hodge wrap Berger's laidback vibraphone lines and Ruit's sparse guitar pickings—plus a variety of guests on reeds and organ—with a fabric of similarly gentle (but often free-form) atmospherics and electronics. The beats range from crackly trip-hop ("Strange Ideas," "Four Nine") to more precise electro programming ("Walk On!"), even while the surface music remains surprisingly similar. Most of the songs are bookended by short interludes termed "earprints"—unfortunately, the large number of different pieces often gives the experimentation a slight meandering quality. Though it may not survive a full listen, *Earprints* includes a lot of intriguing music. —*John Bush*

## Tony Conrad

b. 1940, Baltimore, MD
*Violin / Experimental Rock, Kraut-Rock, Avant-Garde*

A pioneering force behind the evolution of minimalism, violinist and composer Tony Conrad introduced the idea of "Eternal Music," a droning, mesmerizing performance idiom which employed long durations, amplification and precise pitch to explore new worlds of sound; through both his solo work and through collaborations with artists including LaMonte Young, John Cale and Faust, he forged new creative directions which proved enormously influential on successive generations of artists ranging in background from pop to the avant-garde. Born in Baltimore in 1940, Conrad studied music at Harvard, where he was first exposed to the work of John Cage and David Tudor; among his fellow students were David Behrman, Christian Wolff, and Frederic Rzewski, all of whom later pursued careers in experimental music as well.

After graduating in 1962, Conrad relocated to New York, where he became immersed in the city's burgeoning underground music scene; there he first joined forces with composer and saxophonist LaMonte Young, who at the time was leading an improvisational group including his wife Marian Zazeela on voice-drone, Billy Name (later a staple of Andy Warhol's Factory scene) on guitar, and Angus MacLise on percussion. Conrad approached Young about performing with the group, and by 1963 a new line-up also consisting of Zazeela and the young Welsh musician John Cale began playing about town in an ensemble variously dubbed the Dream Syndicate and the Theater of Eternal Music. Sustaining notes for hours at a time, their improvised dissections of specific harmonic intervals rejected the compositional process, instead elaborating shared performance concepts.

The Dream Syndicate disbanded in 1965, with Conrad, Young and Cale all later staking claim to authoring of the "Eternal Music" aesthetic; Young also held on to the group's live tapes. Still, Conrad and Cale continued collaborating, joining young Pickwick company songwriter Lou Reed and sculptor Walter de Maria in a rock band called the Primitives, on tour in support of their lone single, the Reed-penned "Do the Ostrich." (Conrad also proved a key contributor to early Velvet Underground lore by giving Reed the S&M book from which the band derived its name.) By this time, Conrad had also begun channeling his energies into filmmaking, working as a sound engineer and technical advisor on the experimental features of camp icon Jack Smith, including his 1963 masterpiece *Flaming Creatures*.

In time, Conrad also began directing his own features—among them *The Flicker, Coming Attractions, The Eye of Count Flickenstein* and *Film Feedback*—also composing their respective scores. It was through a German filmmaker travelling in New York City that Conrad first learned of the nascent Kraut-rock scene of the early '70s, and he soon began communicating with the members of Faust. Eventually, he travelled to the group's farm in the northern German community of Wuemme, where a three-day session yielded the 1973 collaboration *Outside the Dream Syndicate*, Conrad's first-ever proper recording. Upon returning to the US, however, he largely abandoned performing to accept a teaching position at the University of Buffalo's Department of Media Study, a job he continued to hold throughout the decades which followed; among his students were the future members of the noise-pop outfit Mercury Rev.

Only in 1993, when Jeff Hunt's Table of the Elements label reissued *Outside the Dream Syndicate*, did Conrad begin considering an active return to performing; he and Faust both soon appeared live at Hunt's first Manganese music festival in Atlanta, and in 1995 Conrad recorded the album *Slapping Pythagoras*, his first new work in over two decades. Next was the single "The

Japanese Room at La Pagode," a collaboration with Gastr del Sol, and in 1996 he issued *Four Violins*, a piece dating back to 1964. A year later, Conrad released *Early Minimalism*, a four-disc collection including not only the aforementioned *Four Violins* but also newly-recorded recreations of vintage Dream Syndicate performances. Collaborations with Jim O'Rourke, the Dead C and Pulp guitarist Mark Webber were all scheduled to follow. —*Jason Ankeny*

**Outside the Dream Syndicate** / 1972 / Caroline ♦♦♦♦
Recorded over a span of three days in 1973, *Outside the Dream Syndicate* was Tony Conrad's first official release; though also credited to the celebrated Kraut-rock band Faust, it's primarily a showcase for Conrad's minimalist drone explorations, an aesthetic fascinatingly at odds with the noisy, fragmented sound of his collaborators. Consisting of three epic tracks, each topping out in excess of 20 minutes, the album is hypnotically contemplative; the music shifts in subtle—almost subliminal—fashion, and the deeper one listens, the more rewarding it becomes. —*Jason Ankeny*

● **Early Minimalism, Vol. 1** / Nov. 18, 1997 / Table of the Elements ♦♦♦♦
The four-disc *Early Minimalism, Vol. 1* is probably the closest modern listeners will come to experiencing the visionary brilliance of the Theatre of Eternal Music at their peak—with an official release of the ensemble's original mid-'60s recordings still nowhere in sight, Tony Conrad has instead assembled a number of latter-day experimentalists (including the always-intriguing Jim O'Rourke) in an attempt to recreate the group's groundbreaking explorations of sound. It's impossible to know to just what extent these new recordings (dating from between 1994 and 1996) have succeeded in recapturing the past, of course, but taken on its own terms this is compelling stuff—minus LaMonte Young's blistering saxophone and Marian Zazeela's vocals, the emphasis is instead on Conrad's violin, which wails with starkly hypnotic power as it weaves through these difficult but rewarding live performances. —*Jason Ankeny*

## Console (Martin Gretschmann)

*Producer / Experimental Techno, Indie Rock*
Console is a side-project for Martin Gretschmann, the lead programmer for the German indie-rockers known as the Notwist. After the second Console album *Rocket in the Pocket* was picked up by a licensing deal through the American mega-indie Matador however, Gretschmann actually earned more attention than his main act. Gretschmann had been recording his own electronic compositions during the recording of the first two Notwist albums, and after the Notwist's 1998 album *Shrink*, he released the first Console LP, *Pan or ama*, on Payola. For his second album, Gretschmann recorded a computer love song titled "14 Zero Zero" that indie tastemakers at Matador got hipped on, and in early 2000, *Rocket in the Pocket* was released through Matador. —*John Bush*

**Pan or Ama** / Jul. 19, 1999 / Payola ♦♦

● **Rocket in the Pocket** / Mar. 21, 2000 / Matador ♦♦♦
From the first track, an inventive neo-electro production with deep, stuttered beats and an inventive use of samples, it's clear that Martin Gretschmann is an excellent producer. On his own side-project holiday away from programming for the indie-electronic pop group the Notwist, Gretschmann displays all of the production talents necessary to succeed in the more intensive arena of listener electronica. Unfortunately, the very next track (it's also the single) is the downright cheesy computer-love cut "14 Zero Zero"—complete with ancient analogue synth, skeletal beats, and all the vocoder vocals anyone can stand in one song. Despite occasional stabs at good production, the song is terribly tacky and comes at least two electro revivals too late to sound like anything but a mistake. (Of course, college-radio programmers everywhere were guaranteed to gush over the single.) Gretschmann moves on to embrace the distorted beats and beatbox flair of top-flight producers like Squarepusher, Si Begg, or Amon Tobin; he shows many great ideas plus the skills to pull them off. It's a shame however, that the worst song here stands to garner him the most attention. —*John Bush*

## Consolidated

f. 1985
*Group / Industrial Dance, Alternative Dance, Club/Dance*
With their confrontational, stridently politically-correct dance music, Consolidated became a small sensation in the early '90s. Not only was the group openly socialist, but the group incorporated all of their messages into their music; their records are unapologetically political and sometimes antagonizingly so. And it was the politics, not their hip-hop/industrial mix, that earned them attention. After a couple of quiet years, Consolidated re-emerged with a new album in the summer of 1994; another long layoff preceded 1998's *Dropped*. —*Stephen Thomas Erlewine*

● **Friendly Fascism** / 1989 / Nettwerk ♦♦♦♦
While Consolidated's political consciousness is commendable, they have apparently spent more time on their lyrics than music. Too frequently, the rhythms are nothing but relentlessly simple, headache-inducing pounding, not subtly textured assaults like Public Enemy. But when their backing tracks do match the fury of their lyrics, the results are quite powerful; too bad that only happens on a third of the album. —*Stephen Thomas Erlewine*

**Play More Music** / 1992 / Nettwerk ♦♦♦
Consolidated play industrial music for those who want more than a night of dancing in blissed-out ecstasy, in a hip-hop style that can appeal to rockers who don't normally like rap/hip-hop. This group presents a serious challenge to those who look the other way hoping that social ills will just disappear on their own. They are, therefore, important. You won't agree with everything you hear on *Play More Music*, but you will be provoked to think about why. —*Roch Parisien*

**Dropped** / Jan. 20, 1998 / Sol 3 ♦♦
The title of *Dropped* is Consolidated's belated reaction to London's termination of their contract with the political dance unit, which likely came about because their sample-heavy, metal-inflected hardcore hip-hop not only wasn't selling by the late '90s, but was also sounding a bit dated. Consolidated responded by carrying on as if nothing has changed—*Dropped* essentially sounds like anything else the band has recorded. That will satisfy some longtime fans, but it also may leave some quite cold. —*Stephen Thomas Erlewine*

## Corduroy

f. 1991, London, England
*Group / Club/Dance, Acid Jazz*
The acid-jazz outfit Corduroy assembled singer/keyboardist Scott Addison, his drummer brother Ben, guitarist Simon Nelson-Smith, and bassist Richard Searle (a former member of '80s one-hit wonders Doctor and the Medics). Formed from the ashes of the short-lived Brit-pop group Boys Wonder, Corduroy played their first gig—a one-off New Year's Eve date—in 1991; the performance proved so successful that its members agreed to continue on full-time, soon signing to the Acid Jazz label and issuing their debut LP, the largely-instrumental *Dad Man Cat*, in 1992. *High Havoc*—the soundtrack to an imaginary film—followed a year later, launching the UK Top Ten hits "Something in My Eye," "The Frighteners," and "London, England." However, in the wake of 1994's *Out of Here* Acid Jazz dropped Corduroy from its roster; after a long hiatus, the group finally landed on the Big Cat label, where they resurfaced in 1997 with *The New You!* —*Jason Ankeny*

**Dad Man Cat** / 1992 / Acid Jazz ♦♦♦
The lounge-kitsch debut from Corduroy spotlights the group's blend of jazz and funk sounds. —*Jason Ankeny*

**Out of Here** / 1994 / Hollywood ♦♦♦

● **The New You!** / Apr. 14, 1997 / Big Cat ♦♦♦♦
Corduroy isn't anything if they're not about style, and *The New You* is their finest creation to date. Working from the same acid-jazz foundation that informed their previous records, the band has added slightly ironic flourishes of lounge music and movie soundtracks while beginning to develop a sophisticated sense of pop craft, largely modeled after Steely Dan. Portions of *The New You* sag under the group's own pretensions, but most of the record is endearingly kitschy, smooth and stylish. —*Stephen Thomas Erlewine*

## Cornelius (Keigo Oyamada)

b. Jan. 27, 1969, Setagaya-ku, Tokyo, Japan
*Producer / Shibuya-Kei, Indie Rock, Alternative Pop/Rock*
Japanese pop-noise savant Cornelius was born Keigo Oyamada, a self-taught guitarist inspired early on by Kiss and Black Sabbath; his musical alias was later chosen as an homage to the film series *Planet of the Apes*. A product of the same Shibuya-kei bubblegum scene that also gave rise to Pizzicato Five, Cornelius debuted in 1993 with the EP *Holydays in the Sun*, the first release from his own Trattoria label; becoming a national teen idol in the wake of

the release of 1994's full-length *The First Question Award*, a year later he issued the album *69/96*, followed in 1996 by the remix LP *96/69*. 1997's *Fantasma* was his creative and commercial breakthrough, a kaleidoscopic, genre-hopping joyride through contemporary musical history which became Cornelius' first American release when it was reissued by Matador a year later. Another pair of remix collections, *CM* and *FM*, followed in 1999. —*Jason Ankeny*

● **Fantasma** / 1997 / Polystar ✦✦✦✦
Cornelius fits right in with the Beastie Boys' Grand Royal aesthetic. He sees no difference between pop and avant-garde, high culture and lowbrow trash—he throws it all together, coming up with completely unexpected combinations. The thrill of hearing hip-hop loops morph into sheets of My Bloody Valentine guitar noise, then into sweet Beach Boys harmonies, is what makes his American debut *Fantasma* such a wonder. It's easy to write Cornelius off as a Japanese Beck, particularly since his pop songcraft is as impressive as the busy, multi-layered production, but it's a little patronizing. Cornelius is operating on his own terms, equally influenced by sunny pop ("Chapter 8— Seashore and Horizon," boasting harmonies by Apples [in Stereo]), garagey hard rock, and kitsch (the cartoonish "Magoo Opening"). He assembles the parts in unpredictable ways—the hard beats of "Mic Check" suddenly give way to floating acoustics; "Chapter 8" literally has a tape recorder stopping and starting the different parts—which is why *Fantasma* is so intoxicating. It is one of those rare records where you can't tell what's going to happen next, and it leaves you hungry for more. —*Stephen Thomas Erlewine*

**CM Cornelius Mix [EP]** / Feb. 2, 1999 / Matador ✦✦✦
Cornelius' *CM* EP applies his whimsical, eclectic sound to songs by artists like Buffalo Daughter, the High Llamas, and Coldcut. The results range from a jazzy electro-pop reworking of Money Mark's "Maybe I'm Dead" to a thrashy, monster-movie version of U.N.K.L.E.'s "Ape Shall Never Kill Ape" to the surfy, cyber-funk breakdown on the remix of Buffalo Daughter's "Great Five Lakes." Fragmented as this may seem, Cornelius' flexible mixing style holds these divergent sounds together. Most of the remixes also use samples from *Fantasma*, providing added sonic cohesion. The analog synth and theremin noisefest on the remix of Coldcut's "Atomic Moog 2000" features snippets of "Star Fruit, Surf Rider"; different samples from that song also pop up on the synthetically pastoral reworking of the Pastels' "Windy Hill," which mixes chirpy electronic noises and breezy synths with the original's sweetly hushed vocals. The electro-tropical makeover of the High Llamas' "Homespin Rerun" and the garage-inflected kraut-rock on the remix of Salon Music's "Galaxie Express" reflect the extremes of Cornelius' sound while presenting different sides of those groups. Though it's not quite as captivating as his own music, *CM* is an interesting and entertaining experiment that will please rabid Cornelius fans. —*Heather Phares*

**FM Fantasma Mix [EP]** / Feb. 2, 1999 / Matador ✦✦✦
Cornelius' *FM* EP lets the artists he remixed on the *CM* EP have a go at reworking songs from his wonderfully inventive *Fantasma* album. In fact, *FM*'s main flaw—if it can be called that—is that the songs that Damon Albarn, the Pastels, U.N.K.L.E., and others try to reshape are so rich and unique in the first place that their remixes generally pale in comparison. Still, Money Mark's sparse, hip-hop transformation of "Mic Check," Buffalo Daughter's laidback version of "New Music Machine," and Coldcut's drum'n'bass remix of "Typewrite Lesson" are original enough to please fans of both Cornelius and the other groups involved. The Pastels' delicate makeover of "Clash" is possibly the EP's best remix, stripping away the song's guitars and drums in favor of fluttering flutes, subtle harmonies, and understated electronic percussion, giving it a very different—yet still recognizable—sound. Likewise, U.N.K.L.E.'s "Free Fall" takes the song in a new but logical direction, mixing narration from *Planet of the Apes* with big beats, sweeping strings, and the original's thrashy guitars. However, while the High Llamas' merry-go-round-meets-jug-band remix of "The Micro Disneycal World Tour" is amusing, it doesn't veer far from Cornelius' version or improve upon it. On the other hand, Albarn's too-clever reworking of "Star Fruits Surf Rider" takes away too much of the original's spacy bossa-nova charm, replacing it with cheesy synths, guttural vocals, and computerized voices. Though it doesn't always show Cornelius or his remixers at their strongest, *FM* is a worthwhile collaboration between some of the most interesting artists of the '90s. —*Heather Phares*

## Cornershop

f. 1992, London, England
*Group / Alternative Dance, Indie Rock, Club/Dance, Alternative Pop/Rock*
Cornershop is a London-based quintet who mix noisy alternative rock sounds with musical influences drawn from lead vocalist/songwriter Tjinder Singh's Punjabi culture. The rest of the band consists of guitarists Ben Ayres and Avtar Singh, sitarist/keyboardist Anthony Saffery, drummer Nick Simms, and percussionist Pete Hall. The group became known in England for its anti-racist politics, an issue at the forefront of Singh's consciousness owing to British maltreatment of Indians in their society. In response to singer Morrissey's experimentation with skinhead imagery, Cornershop burned pictures of him at gigs and at a press conference. Most of the British media dismissed it as a publicity stunt, since the group's musical skills at the time were amateurish at best, if excitingly ragged. A bit more technical polish eventually helped attract the attention of ex-Talking Heads singer David Byrne, who signed the group to his Luaka Bop label in 1995, set up a recording session with poet Allen Ginsberg, and released their acclaimed second album, *Woman's Gotta Have It*. The excellent *When I Was Born for the 7th Time*, highlighted by the hit single "Brimful of Asha" (a tribute to Indian singer Asha Bhosle) followed in 1997. —*Steve Huey*

**Woman's Gotta Have It** / 1995 / Luaka Bop/Warner Bros. ✦✦✦✦
Tjinder Singh's Cornershop has created the perfect hybrid of Western indie-rock and swirling Eastern traditional music: Hindi-pop. It's not like what the Beatles did with sitars nor is it classifiable as world beat: Cornershop is unique. "Jullandar Shere" opens and closes the album on an Eastern note but with a hip-hop twist. It's an adventure in lo-fi noise-pop with the drone of tamboura, native percussion and processed vocal sung in Punjabi providing the rhythm. "Hong Kong Book of Kung Fu" conveys indignation through its angry guitar and spit-sung lyrics. "Call All Destroyer" has Singh leading on funky bass like old-school political-rockers, Gang of Four. The anti-melodies are similar to stock indie-rock, but the sonic dissonance created on dholki, harmonium and flute separates Cornershop from the pack as they reclaim a racial stereotype (that every Asian in Great Britain tends a corner shop)while creating their very own roots music with a message. —*Denise Sullivan*

● **When I Was Born for the 7th Time** / Sep. 8, 1997 / Luaka Bop/Warner Bros. ✦✦✦✦
*When I Was Born for the 7th Time* is a remarkable leap forward for Cornershop, the place where the group blends all of their diverse influences into a seamless whole. Cornershop uses Indian music as a foundation, finding its droning repetition similar to the trancier elements of electronica, the cut-and-paste collages of hip-hop, and the skeletal melodicism of indie-pop. Tying all of these strands together, the band creates a multicultural music that is utterly modern; it is conscious of its heritage, but instead of being enslaved to tradition, it pushes into the future and finds a common ground between different cultures and musics. Like *Woman's Gotta Have It*, large portions of *When I Was Born for the 7th Time* are devoted to hypnotic instrumentals, but the music here is funkier and fully realized. Cornershop hits an appealing compromise between detailed arrangements and lo-fi technology. There may be cheap keyboards and drum machines scattered throughout the album, but they are used as sonic texturing, similar to the turntables, synthesizers, samplers, sitars and guitars that drive the instrumentals punctuating the full-fledged songs. When it chooses, Cornershop can write hooky, immediate pop songs—"Sleep on the Left Side" and "Brimful of Asha" are wonderful pop singles, and "Good to Be on the Road Back Home" is an impressive, country-tinged tale—but what makes *When I Was Born for the 7th Time* such a rich, intoxicating listen is that it balances these melodic tendencies with deceptively complex arrangements, chants, drones, electronic instrumentals, and funky rhythms, resulting in an album that becomes better with each listen. —*Stephen Thomas Erlewine*

## Ferry Corsten

b. Rotterdam, Netherlands
*Remixing, Producer, DJ / Progressive Trance, Trance, Club/Dance*
Otherwise known as System F, Ferry Corsten rose to prominence in the late '90s as one of Europe's top trance DJs, highlighted by an anthem-filled appearance on Ministry of Sound's first *Trance Nation* album. Before attaining such recognition, Corsten began his DJing at the early age of 15, when he would spin at school parties. By his late teens, he was studying to be an electrical engineer, an ambition that was soon eclipsed by his growing interest in

electronic dance music. Soon he was acquiring sound gear to produce his own tracks and started releasing his music under monikers such as Moonman, Pulp Victim, Vera Cocha, Gouryella (with DJ Tiesto), and System F, highlighted by the success of his single "Out of the Blue," which entered the UK's top 20. Yet his most successful work is undoubtably his track "Air," under the guise of Albion, a track that has been championed by many of the world's top DJs (including Paul Oakenfold and John Digweed on their *Global Underground* albums) and has since been re-released in 2000 as *Air 2000* on Platipus with addtional remixes by artists such as Oliver Lieb and Hybrid. Meanwhile, Corsten also won plenty of attention for his high profile remix of Art of Trance's classic "Madagascar." And even though his appearance as the guest DJ on Ministry of Sound's anthem-filled *Trance Nation* debut wasn't the sort of well-composed set one would expect from an experienced DJ such as Corsten, it did help propel his name further into his audience's consciousness. —*Jason Birchmeier*

- **Trance Nation, Vol. 1** / May 17, 1999 / Ministry of Sound ♦♦♦♦
Good luck finding an album that better sums up the enormous hype surrounding trance during the late '90s. On the first *Trance Nation* release, Ferry Corsten (System F, Albion) mixes together a total of 36 of the most popular trance anthems to date, focusing primarily on songs from 1998 but also going back as far as 1992 for the earliest trance anthems: Future Sound of London's "Papua New Guinea," Underworld's "Dark & Long," Age of Love's "Age of Love," BT's "Loving You More," and Robert Miles' "Children." Unfortunately, when a DJ packs 36 of the most massive trance anthems ever on only two CDs without any filler, the mix is going to be rough and unrelenting. Even if Corsten was one of the best DJs in the world, mixing songs such as Energy 52's "Cafe Del Mar (Three 'N' One Mix)" into Paul van Dyk's "For an Angel (PVD E-Werk Club Mix)" isn't going to be easy—climactic tracks such as these need ample foreplay to reach their most promising effects. Without enough lulls, progressive trance such as that featured on this album can begin to sound highly diluted as the listener begins to get increasingly conditioned to giant breakdowns and endless build-ups. Furthermore, due to the progressive nature of these songs and Corsten's decision to cram 18 songs on each disc, one feels cheated by the short track lengths. Finally, for every sublime Robert Miles and Art of Trance song on this CD, there are songs such as the Moonman remix of "The World '99" that are downright gaudy. Yet even when considering these many problems, *Trance Nation* does fare better than many of Ministry of Sound's other compilations that often wander aimlessly from one genre to the next in their mission to capture all the biggest club hits. Furthermore, no album will give naive newcomers a better taste of commercialized progressive trance anthems than this loaded collection. —*Jason Birchmeier*

**Trance Nation, Vol. 2** / Sep. 27, 1999 / Ministry of Sound ♦♦♦

## Cosmic Baby (Harald Bluechel)

b. Feb. 19, 1966, Nuremberg, Germany
*Producer / Ambient Techno, Trance, Club/Dance, Techno*
The techno producer with the most musical training under his belt, Cosmic Baby began his conservatory study at the age of seven, discovered electronic music six years later, and by 1991 he was recording some of the most melodic trance and techno to come from the Continent. Born in Nuremberg in 1966, Harald Bluechel began playing piano at the age of three and was conducted to the Nuremberg Conservatory four years later. After an early affinity for the work of Bela Bartók and Igor Stravinsky, Bluechel began listening to Kraftwerk and Tangerine Dream; he quickly left the conservatory, began picking up electronic equipment and wrote his first synthesizer composition when he was only 14. A move to Berlin to attend that city's University of Arts provided him with a degree in composition as well as sound engineering.

During the late '80s, however, Bluechel encountered the second genre of music which would change his course. Acid-house had become big in Britain, and by 1988 it was being checked in Berlin by early DJs like Westbam and Kid Paul. Bluechel jumped aboard, and after a period during the late '80s composing for radio, he was producing by 1991 with such aliases as Energy 52 (with Kid Paul), Futurhythm and Brainmelter (with DJ Moony Jonzon). His debut album as a solo act, *Transcendental Overdrive* appeared in 1991 on MFS Records and proved an early success story on the German techno scene. Obviously informed by Bluechel's long period in the classical world, the album was melodic trance of the most mature type, while the next year's follow-up *Stellar Supreme* was

another highlight. Bluechel hit the British charts with "Perfect Day" by Visions of Shiva (with Paul Van Dyk), and gained a British/American contract through Logic/Arista for his third album. *Thinking About Myself*, released in 1994, was a more varied album, blending trance workouts like "Cosmic Greets Florida," intriguing classical-techno fusions of material by Debussy and all-over-the-map tracks like "Loops of Infinity." During 1995, he composed music for the film *Futura* and consolidated his position as one of the leading live techno acts with shows all over Europe and America. His fourth album overall, *Fourteen Pieces*, was released in 1996. Three years later the album *Heaven* was released. Bluechel's management concern Cosmic Enterprises is responsible for the label Time Out of Mind. —*John Bush*

**Stellar Supreme** / 1992 / BASE ♦♦

- **Thinking About Myself** / 1994 / Fox ♦♦♦♦
Cosmic Baby's second album is one of the high points of a uniquely Teutonic wish to apply Wagnerian concepts of orchestration and grandeur to techno and trance, in a similar fashion to Sven Väth's *Accident in Paradise*. While Väth is best at constructing beats and rhythms (to the detriment of his bloated quasi-orchestrations), Cosmic Baby proves more than equal to the symphonic task at hand, while his percussion skills rarely arouse any excitement at all. Despite several obvious high points ("Loops of Infinity," "Au Dessous des Nuages," "Cosmic Greets Florida"), the album attempts much but accomplishes little. —*John Bush*

**Fourteen Pieces** / May 27, 1996 / Time Out of Mind ♦♦♦♦

## Couch

f. Munich, Germany
*Group / Indie Rock, Post-Rock/Experimental*
Munich's experimental rock group Couch consists of keyboardist Stefanie Bohm, guitarist Jurgen Soder, bassist Michael Heilrath, and drummer Thomas Geltinger. The group formed in 1993 and found inspiration in classic Kraut-rock groups as well as more current artists such as Slint and Stereolab. Their untitled 1995 debut was a vinyl-only release, but their early works were collected the following year as *Glass Brothers: 1993-1994* on Bulb Records. Their 1997 release, *Etwas Benutzen*, was also their debut for Kitty-Yo, which is also the home of To Rococco Rot, Tarwater, Surrogat, and Laub. Two years later, *Fantasy* arrived and was licensed by Matador Records a year later. —*Heather Phares*

- **Fantasy** / May 4, 1999 / Kitty-Yo ♦♦♦
With *Fantasy*, Couch's third album—and the first re-released by Matador—the Munich quartet makes a quantum leap, blending lush arrangements and direct, memorable melodies into their dynamic instrumentals. Though post-rock fans will hear elements of Stereolab, Neu!, Tortoise, Trans Am, Pell Mell, and the other usual suspects in the album's nine pieces, *Fantasy*'s lively immediacy sets it apart. From the brisk kraut-rock groove of "Ich Bei Davor" to the shimmering, dream pop tinged "Camaro" to the sleek, kinetic "Linie Gegen Strich," Couch delivers an expansive and eclectic sound. "Heimweg 78"'s creative percussion choices and counter-rhythms, "Control"'s bouncy yet graceful melody, and "Gegen Den"'s fluid dynamic shifts define *Fantasy*'s unique but accessible approach, making it perhaps one of the first "post-pop" albums. —*Heather Phares*

## Carl Cox

b. Jul. 29, 1962, Oldham, Manchester, England
*Producer, DJ / Tech-House, Progressive-House, Rave, Club/Dance, Techno, Acid House, House*
A perennial favorite as the best DJ in the world according to fans as well as the major mixing magazines, Carl Cox has been a part of Britain's dance scene from the heady days of disco through to the global clubland of the '90s, with temporary pit-stops covering hip-hop, the rare-groove movement and the immense rave revolution of the late '80s. That large span of time has undoubtedly affected his choice of records, since Cox routinely detours through breakbeat, Italian house and the dance mainstream during his usual sets of hard techno. Perhaps the best testament to his mixing skills is his immense popularity despite his focus on music much more intense than the brand of arena trance spawned by Oakenfold, Sasha, Digweed, and others.

Cox was born in Manchester in 1962, to parents originally from Barbados (they later moved back, after he grew up). Cox began DJing family get-togethers at the age of eight, selecting records from his parents' stack of soul

45s. He was buying his own records soon after, and owned his first pair of turntables at the age of 15. The rest of his teens were spent making spare money at any event he could DJ; though Cox studied electrical engineering in college, he quit after six months and began working various jobs until he could become a full-time DJ.

Cox had followed the musical trends from disco to rare-groove on to hip-hop during the late '70s and early '80s, but the introduction of house into Britain during the middle part of the decade convinced him that he had found his niche. After moving to Brighton in 1986, his reputation bloomed during the acid house explosion of 1988-89; Cox played the opening night at Shoom, one of the defining club nights of Britain's house revolution (as well as other legendary hot-spots like Land of Oz and Spectrum). In front of 15,000 at the 1989 open-air event Sunrise, he unveiled his use of three decks on the mix; that signature technique built him into one of the top DJs of the late '80s and early '90s.

By 1992 Cox had signed an unheard-of long-term production deal with Paul Oakenfold's Perfecto Records and hit number 23 on the British charts with his debut single, "I Want You (Forever)." His second single "Does It Feel Good to You" also reached the Top 40, and he quickly diversified by setting up his own record label (Worldwide Ultimatum) and an international DJ agency (Ultimate). The onset of a more hardcore rave sound (and the fact that he was increasingly becoming pigeon-holed within it) forced Cox to spend several years re-establishing his niche. In a bit of irony, commercial successes like Cox's own steered him away from high-BPM candy-core and towards the still soulful house and techno scene.

Three years after his hit singles, Cox returned with the first volume in what became a genre-defining mix-compilation series, *F.A.C.T.: Future Alliance of Communications and Tecknology*. After the first volume dropped in 1995, surprisingly high sales figures earned a second two years later (released in America as well). One year later, Cox released his first studio full-length with 1996's *At the End of the Cliché*. Mix album *The Sound of Ultimate B.A.S.E.* followed in 1998, with another studio album, *Phuture 2000*, appearing in 1999. One year later, he released the self-explanatory *Mixed Live*, recorded at Chicago's Crobar. —*John Bush*

**F.A.C.T.: Future Alliance of Communication and Tecknology** / Jan. 30, 1995 / React ◆◆◆◆

**At the End of the Cliché** / 1996 / A Worldwide Ultimatum ◆◆◆
Cox's proper studio debut is a soulful, genre-spanning journey through '90s clubland, not unlike his own DJ sets. The *Star Wars* tug of "Tribal Jedi" and the Goa trance of "Phoebus Apollo" provide variety, while "Musky" and "Yum Yum" are minimalist, acid techno barnstormers. Cox only falters when he ventures into the territory of mid-tempo trip-hop; thankfully, it doesn't occur often. —*John Bush*

**Mixmag Live!, Vol. 1** / Jul. 22, 1996 / Mixmag ◆◆◆◆
Carl Cox and Dave Seaman mixed this first volume (cassette only) in *Mixmag*'s series of DJ compilations. *John Bush*

• **F.A.C.T.: Vol. 2: Future Alliance of Community Tecknology** / May 5, 1997 / Moonshine Music ◆◆◆◆◆
Cox's second selection in the *F.A.C.T.* series continued to prove to the world his status as the best DJ. Instead of picking the rarest white-labels as mixers often do, Cox transforms classics of the field like Underworld's "Born Slippy" and Orbital's "Are You There?" so they're just this side of beyond recognition, putting his indelible stamp on anything he touches. The first of the two-disc set comprises the best of hard house, while the second focuses on the downtempo side of techno. —*John Bush*

**Sound of Ultimate B.A.S.E. (Continuous DJ Mix)** / May 19, 1998 / Moonshine Music ◆◆◆◆
The ultimate DJ is back on the music scene; after a departure to circulate the world's club scene and sow his vinyl oats, Carl Cox is back in business. But this time he's brought with him the supremely bassy sounds of his Ultimate B.A.S.E. crew from deep in the heart of England. From the outset, with the floor-cracking jungle bumps of "Bushbaby" by Creative Impulse to DJ Funk's icy cold knocks on "Run," Cox's compilation establishes a presence as unrelenting as its head-throbbing one-two punch of vibes. With a discriminate selection of pure, unadulterated house beats, this compilation can nevertheless make you feel like the picture on the back cover, of Cox standing in front of an over-sized speaker, covering his ears in pain. Keep some aspirin and the power switch handy when planning to listen to this collection of pounding rhythms all the way through. Cox does well to incorporate a variety of house sounds while maintaining a heartfelt, deep, and bass-induced sound, but you would be wise to keep the volume low and not to use headphones. —*Aric Laurence Allen*

**Phuture 2000** / Jun. 15, 1999 / Moonshine Music ◆◆◆◆
Cox makes his bid for the music of the millennium with *Phuture 2000*, his second full production album and the first released in America. As could be expected from one of the world's most traveled DJs, it's an album of diverse styles and tempos, from the percussive energy of the previous year's dance smash "The Latin Theme" to harder techno on "Dr. Funk" and even a nod to the New York super-club on "Tribal Twilo Dance." Whereas many albums beginning with a producer's wish to prove his diversity end up a mixed bag of music that's far too varied to make for a solid listen, Cox knows better than anyone how to pace a set for ultimate entertainment. —*John Bush*

**Mixed Live** / Jul. 25, 2000 / Moonshine Music ◆◆◆◆
The first volume in a special Moonshine series inspired by the hotspot-trotting *Global Underground* mix label and developed by Coxy himself, *Mixed Live* was recorded at "Crobar" in Chicago (and released just two months later). With fully three-quarters of the available channels used to record audience reaction to his set, everybody's favorite DJ mashed it up to his heart's content, and the microphones dutifully recorded every scream from the crowd as he worked through peaks like the tribal funk of Andrew McLoughlin's "Love Story" and Aphrohead's insane party anthem "Cry Baby." A breathtaking balance of hard dancefloor techno and more soulful house (Cox was undoubtedly inspired by playing in the Windy City), *Mixed Live* is perhaps the best mix album Cox has yet recorded. —*John Bush*

## Carl Craig

b. 1969, Detroit, MI
*Producer / Electronica, Detroit Techno, Club/Dance, Techno*

Dancefloor experimentalist and top Detroit techno producer Carl Craig has few equals in terms of the artistry, influence, and diversity of his recordings. Few others have recorded so much quality music in such a variety of styles than Craig, who jammed distorted beat-box samples into lo-fi electro riggings, crafted epic house tracks like his remix of Tori Amos' "God," and recorded the most sublime Detroit techno since godfathers Juan Atkins and Derrick May were at their peak. After an apprenticeship during the late '80s with Derrick May, Craig began releasing his own recordings in 1989, first on May's Transmat imprint and later on his own label, Planet E Communications. During the following decade, Craig spread his work between solo aliases—Paperclip People, Innerzone Orchestra, 69—and his own name. With each new project and each change of musical direction, though, he distinguished himself as one of the few artists to consistently hit the mark with productions whose subtleties in the living room more than matched their infectious energy on the dancefloor.

When he was growing up and attending Detroit's Cooley High, Craig was turned on to a diverse musical diet ranging from Prince to Led Zeppelin to the Smiths. He often practiced on his guitar, but later became interested in club music as well through his cousin, who worked lighting for various parties around the Detroit area. The first wave of Detroit techno had already set sail by the mid-'80s, and Craig began listening to tracks courtesy of Derrick May's radio show on WJLB. He began experimenting with recording techniques using dual-deck cassette players, and later convinced his parents to buy him a synthesizer and sequencer. Craig also studied electronic music, including the work of Morton Subotnick, Wendy Carlos, and Pauline Oliveros. While taking an electronics course, he met a mutual friend of May and passed on a tape including some of his home productions. May loved what he heard and brought him into the studio to re-record one track, "Neurotic Behavior." Completely beatless in its original mix (since Craig didn't own a drum machine), the track was just as sublime and visionary as Juan Atkins' blueprint for cosmic techno-funk, yet called on emotions previously found only on Derrick May's material.

The British fascination with Detroit techno was just beginning to take hold by 1989, and Carl Craig was invited to witness the phenomenon first-hand by touring with May's Rhythim Is Rhythim project (which supported Kevin Saunderson's Inner City on several English dates). The trip became an extended working holiday, as Craig helped out on production for a re-recording of May's classic "Strings of Life" and the new Rhythim Is Rhythim single, "The Beginning." He also found time to record several tracks of his own at R&S Studios in Belgium. On his return to the US, Craig released several R&S tracks on the *Crackdown* EP, recorded as Psyche for May's Transmat Records. Craig then founded Retroactive Records with Damon Booker, and despite working days at a copy shop, continued recording in his parents' basement.

Carl Craig released six singles for Retroactive during 1990-91 (as BFC, Paperclip People and Carl Craig) but the label was dissolved in 1991 due to disputes with Booker. That same year, Craig formed the solo concern Planet E Communications for the release of his new EP *4 Jazz Funk Classics* (recorded as 69). Deliberately lo-fi and gritty with the implementation of funky beatbox samples, tracks like "If Mojo Was AM" presented a new leap forward after the compulsive sheen of Retroactive singles like "Galaxy" and "From Beyond." Besides the distortion of *4 Jazz Funk Classics,* his other Planet E work during 1991 contained off-the-cuff nods to such disparate moods as hip-hop and hardcore techno. The following year's "Bug in the Bassbin" unveiled another Carl Craig alias, Innerzone Orchestra, and added elements of jazz to his beatbox frenzy. In the process, Craig became an uncommon influence on the early progression of the British drum'n'bass movement—DJs and producers often pitched up "Bug in the Bassbin" from 33 to 45-rpm for a do-it-yourself jungle breakbeat.

The release of Paperclip People's "Throw" added disco and funk to Craig's growing list of active inspirations; his natural progression into remixes during 1994 provided the dance world with versions of Maurizio, Inner City, and La Funk Mob tracks plus a stunning reworking of the Tori Amos song "God," that lasted almost ten minutes. Thanks in large part to the Tori Amos remix, Craig soon signed his first contract with major-label exposure, to the Blanco y Negro division of Europe's Mute Records. His first full-length, 1995's *Landcruising,* opened up the Carl Craig sound and gave it an epic feel closer in spirit to his earlier recordings, while the thematic tug of a journey around metro Detroit mirrored Juan Atkins' Model 500 tracks like "Night Drive." *Landcruising* opened up the market for Craig's material and several months later, R&S Records released 69's *Sound of Music,* a compilation of two EPs released the previous year for the Belgian label.

In 1996, the high-profile British house label Ministry of Sound released a new Paperclip People single called "The Floor," composed of hard, clipped techno beats but an elastic bassline and prevalent disco sample that earned it much airplay in house venues. Though he was already one of the most noted names in the world of techno, Craig's reputation began growing in the more general category of mainstream/global dance, and he soon became less tied to the mantle of Detroit techno than many of his contemporaries. Craig helmed one in the series of *DJ Kicks* albums released by Studio !K7 and spent several months based in London. He returned to Detroit later in 1996 to focus on Planet E, which released a Paperclip People album titled *The Secret Tapes of Dr. Eich* (mostly collecting previous singles) and a Psyche/BFC retrospective titled *Elements 1989-1990.* The new year brought the second proper Carl Craig LP, *More Songs About Food & Revolutionary Art.* He spent much of 1998 touring the world as Innerzone Orchestra with a jazzy trio. The project also released an LP, *Programmed,* expanding Craig's full-length output to seven—though only three had appeared under his own name. Two collections appeared during 1999-2000, including the Planet E mix album *House Party 013* and the remix compilation *Designer Music.* [See also: Innerzone Orchestra, Paperclip People, Psyche/BFC, 69] —*John Bush*

**Intergalactic Beats** / 1992 / Planet E ♦♦♦♦

As a various-artists collection of the earliest recordings issued by Carl Craig's excellent Detroit techno label Planet E, in 1991 and 1992, *Intergalactic Beats* possesses undeniable historical significance. Unfortunately, its virtue as a techno monument doesn't make up for its musical weaknesses. Craig composes four of the nine tracks under various aliases: 69, Piece and Shop. Not only are these four tracks the best on the compilation, but they also serve as really the only good reason to spend money on this album. "Ladies & Gentlemen" and "My Machines," the two brilliant 69 tracks taken from 1991's *4 Jazz Funk Classics* EP, start the album off with plenty of style. Various high-tech funk samples are sewn together along some primitive sounding drum programming to form two lengthy disjointed jams. The other Craig tracks, Piece's "Free Your Mind" and Shop's "Nitwit", combine the classic techno sounds of Craig's work as Psyche with the driving electronic funk sound he would go on to produce in the mid-'90s as Paperclip People. Lively and full of energy, these two tracks are more interesting as transitional moments in Craig's artistic evolution than functional as great electronic music. Most of the other tracks on *Intergalactic Beats* aren't really worth spending a lot of time describing. Kenny Larkin's song as Dark Comedy closes the album with some finesse, but relative to his later solo albums such as *Azimuth,* this song pales in comparison. The contributions by Balil and Eevolute stand as average to poor Detroit techno tracks, characterized mostly by their low-budget, primitive sound. Overall, *Intergalactic Beats* will engage listeners interested in the evolution of Detroit techno but will disappoint those searching for quality. Look instead to *Geology,* a compilation released in 1999 examining the finer moments of Planet E's stellar musical past. —*Jason Stanley Birchmeier*

**Landcruising** / 1995 / Blanco Y Negro ♦♦♦♦

A bright, shimmering epic where critics and fans had expected more moody breakbeat electro, the debut Carl Craig LP appeared after years of production work and marked the first of many times when Craig was obviously making his own way, oblivious to what critics might think. Beginning with the sounds of an automobile starting up on "Mind of a Machine" (complete with warning bells and a seatbelt click), Craig introduces us to his man-machine world, where cruising I-96 west of Detroit is a sublime night-time journey, conjuring visions of *Trans-Europe Express* and "Strings of Life" instead of *What's Going On.* The single "Science Fiction," "Technology," the title track and "Einbahn" continue the journey to its close back in the garage. *Landcruising* was a change-up for critics, but as usual, Craig proved up to the expectations. —*John Bush*

**DJ Kicks** / Apr. 8, 1996 / Studio !K7 ♦♦♦

Unlike the typically live (or at least live-sounding) mix albums in the *DJ Kicks* series, Carl Craig did much post-production work on his volume. The result is a collection of complex, reworked techno from Craig's own Planet E label (by Clark, Designer Music and 4th Wave) as well as other crucial techno producers such as Claude Young, Kosmic Messenger, Octagon Man, and Gemini. The addition of a special Carl Craig track—composed entirely with the use of samples from originals included elsewhere on the collection—is a nice touch to what proves to be an admirable collection. —*John Bush*

★ **More Songs About Food and Revolutionary Art** / Mar. 24, 1997 / SSR ♦♦♦♦♦

While Carl Craig's various other musical projects such as Paperclip People, Innerzone Orchestra and 69 may have their niche audience and functional purpose, the music on *More Songs About Food and Revolutionary Art* represents some of the best-crafted, most emotional and beautiful techno ever to come out of Detroit. When Craig relates the music on this album to food and revolutionary art, he isn't joking; the music fuels the mind and soul of the listener with its electronic elegies while pushing the innovative limits of artistic techno beyond simple drum loops and synthesizer melodies. Listeners looking for the dancefloor-inspiring beats of Paperclip People will have their expectations subverted by the rich, subdued emotions of this album. Songs such as "At Les" and "Red Lights" evoke far too many feelings with a far too serious tone for simply dancing. A hazy photo of Craig with his face turned downward as if in prayer, found inside the album liner among other dark graphics, hints at the somber content of the music. The opening track of the album, "Es. 30," diffuses soft synthesizer tones for nearly two minutes before the first foundation-shaking bass beat appears. By this point listeners should begin to feel the elevating effects of Craig's poetic sound. Many selections deserve recognition, beginning with the first real song on the album, "Televised Green Smoke." A carefully assembled grouping of many different rhythm loops, surreal synthesizer notes and thunderous bass beats, this track's foreboding tone only foreshadows what will follow on the album. Nearly every subsequent track heads off on a different musical tangent, some incorporating dissonant piano melodies, looped samples, jazz-like percussion foundations and even smoky female vocals. There are a few moments when the "revolutionary art" goes a bit too far, especially towards the end of the album, in songs such as "Food and Art", but for the most part, as long as one can stomach the occasional experimental excess, this poetic album deserves to be played from start to finish, over and over again. —*Jason Stanley Birchmeier*

**House Party 013: A Planet E Mix** / 1999 / Next Era ♦♦♦♦

*House Party 013* is a collection of Planet E classics dedicated to the people of the Czech Republic and released on the country's Next Era label (the obvious connections between the two heavily industrial regions—Eastern Europe and Detroit—are obvious and unspoken). Just abrasive enough to satisfy fans of harder, Detroit-style techno, but with plenty of dancefloor attitude and house grooves to please clubfans, the collection tracks a few of Craig's Planet E classics ("Galaxy" by BFC, "Floor" and "Steam" by Paperclip People, "Stevie Knows" by Designer Music) plus a bevy of selections from other Planet E artists (Recloose's "Soul Clap 2000," Common Factor's "North Nights," Alton Miller's "Extasol") that prove surprisingly amenable to club consumption when compacted together into a 60-minute mix. —*John Bush*

**Designer Music: The Remixes, Vol. 1** / Jun. 27, 2000 / Planet E ♦♦♦
Carl Craig resurfaces in mid-2000 with *Designer Music, Vol. 1. Designer* is a collection of hand-picked remixes Craig has done over the years, some of which were originally released only on 12" and using the alias "Designer Music," hence, the name of the series. If you are looking for the more popular Tori Amos and Deee-Lite remixes of past, you won't find them on this volume. Rather, *Designer One* is a collection of Carl's more intelligentsia efforts. Starting off the album with remixes of a spacy UFO and a Latin rhythmic Johnny Blas, *Designer* seems to be more of a funky instrumental than something from a techno label. By track four, *Designer Music* breaks out of its shell, when Craig returns to early techno with an incredible remix of Telex' "Moscow Disco." Other mentionables include a unique spin on Inner City's "Good Life" (or "Buena Vida," as called on the album) and Alexander Robotnik's "Problemz." It should be noted that most artists would be torn apart for remixing such classics, but Craig does it proper, with class, and, most importantly, elements of funk and soul. For those fans itching for more of the Paperclip People sound, elements show up on the last two remixes, especially the remix of Ron Trent. With each name that Craig works under, whether it is Innerzone Orchestra, Psyche, or Paperclip People, he displays a different side of his talent and artistic taste. With *Designer Music, Vol. 1*, Craig shows off his ability to break down the essential, recognizable elements of a song and put the pieces back together into a sound that is undeniably his own. —*Diana Potts*

## The Crystal Method
f. 1993, Los Angeles, CA
*Group / Big Beat, Funky Breaks, Electronica, Club/Dance*

L.A.'s Crystal Method have been referred to as America's answer to the Chemical Brothers. A dance-based electronic duo with a definite rock band feel, the comparison would seem appropriate, although it tends to erase what makes the group distinct: a solid base in American hip-hop, rock, soul, and pop. Formed in 1993 by Ken Jordan and Scott Kirkland, Crystal Method is the most recent stop in a string of projects that led them from their native Las Vegas (and some forgettable 4-track stabs at vocal house music), to the early-'90s L.A. rave scene. Drawn in by its youthful idealism, Jordan and Kirkland became absorbed by L.A.'s underground club culture and began knocking out tracks inspired by their experiences. On the strength of one of their demos, Crystal Method signed to Steve Melrose and Justin King's City of Angels imprint in 1994, and their debut single, "Keep Hope Alive," appeared soon after. The title was in reference to L.A.'s waning rave scene (burdened by constant police pressure and a string of random violent incidents) and became something of an anthem due to the endless barrage of remixes and alternate versions that appeared. The pair's demand to be taken seriously as a band (as opposed to the enforced anonymity of most techno acts, and something of a new concept for American dance producers) extended to incessant live performances, and Crystal Method's increasing popularity both in the clubs and among radio jocks led to a deal with Geffen affiliate Outpost Recordings in 1996. The group's debut LP, *Vegas*—an unabashed party record bathed in acid, funk, rock, and big-beat hip-hop—appeared in mid-1997. —*Sean Cooper*

● **Vegas** / Sep. 8, 1997 / Outpost ♦♦♦
Perhaps it's unfair to label Crystal Method as an American Chemical Brothers, since they are contemporaries of, not successors to, the English duo, but the comparison makes sense. Like the Chemicals, Crystal Method is into big beats. There isn't much subtlety to their music, but there doesn't need to be, since their heady fusion of classic, late-'80s hip-hop, rave, techno, and rock is intoxicating on its own. *Vegas*, the duo's debut album, rushes by in a quasi-psychedelic blur, occasionally stopping for ambient detours. There aren't any revelations along the way, but Crystal Method does this crossover techno well, which makes *Vegas* a pleasure. —*Stephen Thomas Erlewine*

## Cubanate
f. 1992, London, England
*Group / Electro-Industrial, Industrial Dance, Industrial*

Marc Heal and Phil Barry, otherwise known as industrial terrorists Cubanate, have explored the hybrid style created by mixing industrial music with the high-speed rhythms of techno. The group formed in London in late 1992 with Heal on vocals and Barry playing guitar, along with keyboard player Graham Rayner and percussionist Steve Etheridge. Cubanate began recording soon after, and played their first live show that same year (with only Heal and Barry). In early 1993, the group signed to Berlin's Dynamica label and released the "Bodyburn" single a few months later. It earned good reviews (Single of the Week according to *Kerrang!*), but Rayner and Etheridge left not long after. Remixer/producer Julian Beeston was added for awhile, but Heal and Barry decided to continue for the time being as a two-piece.

September 1993 brought the duo's debut album *Antimatter*, and the *Metal* EP followed in 1994. Controversy followed Cubanate around the British Isles during a 1994 tour with Carcass, as death threats and near riots caused the *London Evening Standard* to declare that the band had "provoked an outbreak of demented carnage." Late in 1994, Cubanate delivered "Oxyacetylene," the trailer single for second LP *Cyberia*, which appeared in early 1995. Heal and Barry once again enlisted extra members—this time guitarist Shep Ashton and keyboard player Darren Bennett—for a tour with Front Line Assembly, but returned to the duo format for third album *Barbarossa*, released in April 1996. Two years later, *Interference* appeared on TVT. —*John Bush*

**Antimatter** / Jan. 24, 1993 / Dynamica ♦♦
Though no indication appears anywhere on the disc about this, *Antimatter* collects a variety of early singles and tracks from the band rather than being a formal debut album. As such, it promises a lot but doesn't fully deliver. The opening track, "Body Burn," is flat-out amazing, still one of their best tunes and frankly one of the best industrial-dance tunes ever, an energetic blast of sampled beats, thrashed guitar riffs and snarled vocals which distills the spirits of DAF, Nitzer Ebb, and the late '80s Wax Trax! label contingent perfectly. The problem was that it was too perfect, since just about everything else on the disc merely reuses that formula, and what works well once can get more than a little tiring pretty quickly! Whoever put this together seems to acknowledge as much by including two separate remixes of "Body Burn" as well. It doesn't help that Heal's lyrics can verge on the tiresomely obvious for the genre—dominance, revolt, action, some twisted sex to boot? Sure thing! Flecks of the future differences and quirks which would make their future work more distinctive, especially some incorporation of straight-up techno amid the other sonic chaos, crop up at points, but *Antimatter* mostly exists as electronic body music fodder. —*Ned Raggett*

**Cyberia** / 1995 / Dynamica ♦♦♦
A strong but not perfectly successful improvement over *Antimatter* thanks to an increased sonic variety, *Cyberia* deserves more than a little credit for its design sense alone. Located under the clear CD tray in the spine section of every copy, and thus viewed right next to the semi-anguished picture of Heal on the front cover, is a chunk of computer motherboard and transistors, taking the man-machine fetish that electronic music thrives on to new lengths! The music itself? After a quick instrumental bit of vocal ominousness, "Oxyacetylene" rips in, as solid as the earlier "Body Burn" while thankfully not quite sounding exactly like it, as so many of their other early tracks did. Things throughout *Cyberia* generally work a bit better than *Antimatter* due to a stronger sense of different sonic approaches; even the basic but crisp and attention-getting bouncing of small drum tics from speaker to speaker at the start of "Build" makes for a good change. The increasing hardcore techno influence makes for even fiercer sonic underpinnings throughout, while still riffing and shouting with the best of them in industrialville. Small downside: the various remixes included at the end of the disc add little to the originals, and including yet another version of "Body Burn" seems rather pointless —*Ned Raggett*

● **Barbarossa** / 1996 / Dynamica ♦♦♦♦
Finally, Cubanate puts it all together near perfectly, creating 1996's best industrial album by a mile. Relentlessly focusing on creating amazing club-friendly material while trying a number of different approaches throughout, the band sound ready to destroy the world as brutally as possible, while making you dance madly the whole time. Though the opening "Vortech I" sounds like fairly typical Cubanate, the next track, the title song itself, evolves into a

heavy-duty fusion between feedback/industrial beat power and techno speedrush builds and breaks; when Heal suddenly roars "Let's go to work!" during a split-second pause in the music, it all connects. Other numbers like "Exultation" and "Come Alive" aim for similar but thankfully not exact replications of such powerful musical combinations, while songs like "Joy" and "The Musclemen" grapple with unexpected, shuddering percussion patterns for their equally solid effect. Heal's vocals even show hints of subtlety more than once—definitely a new path!—while a number of lyrics sound like he's trying to move beyond the usual dominance/submission/power politics take on things which the genre prefers. The brooding, snaky drive of closing song "Lord of the Flies" showcases the band's abilities well, not least because it's a song which couldn't have been recorded by the band in earlier days—a sure sign of its increasing abilities. —*Ned Raggett*

**Interference** / Apr 14, 1998 / TVT ✦✦✦✦
Cubanate vocalist/songwriter Marc Heal made a conscious effort on *Interference* to improve the intelligence in their lyrics, and he pulls no punches as he talks about real-life situations he was personally involved in. And while the band gained attention and popularity with their industrial-rock earlier albums (1993's *Antimatter*, 1995's *Cyberia*, and 1996's *Barbarossa*), Cubanate have broadened their range a bit, taking more chances with their music, and rhythms in particular. The group can still create a massive wall of electronic sound, as heard on the huge "Isolation," or tunes that hit you directly in the gut (the album opener "IT"). The last song recorded for *Interference*, "IT" became a frustrated rant when Heal couldn't come up with conventional lyrics, all recorded off the top of his head, in one take. And another track, "Voids," was written about the group's last American tour, when Heal began feeling paranoid after combining endless hotel room nights with alcohol. The group has also tried their hand at writing music for video games, the album track "Airport Bar" will appear on the home vid Wing Commander 5—Prophecy. —*Greg Prato*

## Cujo (Amon Tobin)

b. Brazil
*Producer / Jungle/Drum'N'Bass, Club/Dance*
Recording as Cujo for London's Ninebar label, drum'n'bass deviant Amon Tobin fuses hip-hop and jazz compositional ideas with the bustling rhythms of hip-hop and jungle and the bent sonic mayhem of ambient and dub. Unlike rolling junglists such as Alex Reece and Wax Doctor, however, who draw from a softer, "cooler" brand of jazz, Tobin aims to maintain the heat of bop and free, pairing spry, galloping basslines with complex trapset orchestration and shrill, screaming horns. A native of Brazil, Tobin moved to the UK in the mid-'80s, when hip-hop was beginning to take hold and the rhythms of breakbeat electro-funk were replacing reggae and punk as the underground youth music of choice. Currently residing in Brighton, Tobin didn't begin seriously making music until college, but his passion for the sampler, as well as the support and encouragement of no less of breakbeat scientists than Ninebar and Ninja Tune immediately convinced him to forgo a university career to focus on music (he was a few years into a photography degree when he put the whole project on hold). He's since released a trio of EPs (a pair for Ninebar, as well as the *Creatures* EP for Ninja Tune) and as many full-lengths (*Adventures in Foam* as Cujo, plus *Bricolage* and *Permutation* as Amon Tobin). [See also: Amon Tobin] —*Sean Cooper*

● **Adventures in Foam** / Sep. 1996 / Ninebar ✦✦✦
Amon Tobin's impressive full-length debut for the London-based Ninebar label followed a series of head-turning twelves mixing drum'n'bass arrangements with obvious jazz, hip-hop, and Latin and Brazilian influences. Some of those early tracks make it onto *Adventures In Foam*, but the best of the album lay in glimpse-giving moments of genre-mingling such as "The Light" and "Northstar," which spin splintering breaks through shards of '70s fusion and '90s ambient and funk similar in eclecticism to Luke Vibert/Plug, Mung, and the less cheeky side of Squarepusher. The album was reissued by Shadow in 1997 on CD and 2x10". —*Sean Cooper*

## Cul de Sac

f. 1990, Chicago, IL
*Group / Math Rock, Experimental Rock, Post-Rock/Experimental*
Shunning the burgeoning alternative rock movement, Cul de Sac intertwined elements of surf rock, Kraut-rock, Middle Eastern trance and folk music, post-rock psychedelia, and avant-garde to create a unique blend that garnered immediate critical attention. Formed in the early '90s by guitarist Glenn Jones, multi-instrumentalist Robin Amos, formerly of the Girls, and Bullet La Volta drummer Chris Guttmacher, Cul de Sac released their first LP, *Ecim*, on the independent Northeastern label. Bassist and filmmaker Chris Fujiwara played on the release as well and became a permanent member of the band. In addition, steel guitarist and fiddler Ed Yazijian and tape manipulator/collagist Phil Milstein performed on *Ecim*. Dredd Foole guested on vocals, but most of Cul de Sac's material on this and later releases was instrumental. According to Jones, Yazijian left the band because they were "too loud"; he later joined Kustomized.

Early live shows were enhanced by the experimental films of Fujiwara and A.S. Hamrah, adding to the band's eclectic mystique. After a series of singles, a compilation of rehearsal jams was packaged and released as a second LP in 1995 as *I Don't Want to Go to Bed*, an interesting low-fi collection. Cul de Sac collaborated with the legendary John Fahey on 1996's *China Gate*. Three years later the group released the full-length *Crashes to Light, Minutes to Its Fall*. The members of Cul de Sac steadfastly oppose categorization. Their original compositions and recordings have been enhanced by instruments of their own creation, including the Contraption and the Incantor. —*Nick Kemper*

● **Crashes to Light, Minutes to Its Fall** / May 4, 1999 / Thirsty Ear ✦✦✦✦
Cul de Sac has been described as "post-rock," a vague category for bands typically uncategorizable. Cul de Sac weaves instrumental trances around guitarist Glenn Jones' finger picked stylings that recall surf, Middle Eastern, or folk music. He also plays "the Contraption," a Hawaiian lap steel guitar laden with effects pedals and played with kitchen utensils. Synthesist Robin Amos produces distinctive sounds by playing instruments he created himself; his electronic sounds are musical, not a distracting novelty as can sometimes happen in similar situations. Bassist Michael Bloom and drummer Jon Proudman provide a rock-solid yet melodic anchor for the band. All four are virtuoso yet sympathetic musicians—none of them hog the spotlight. *Crashes to Light, Minutes to Its Fall*, the band's fifth album, finds Cul de Sac at its most confident and lyrical. The music is complex and cerebral, yet playful and accessible. This is mind-expanding music of the friendliest sort. Its potential appeal ranges from fans of Pink Floyd or German rock bands of the '70s like Can or Ash Ra Tempel, to surf-rock mavens, or people who say they like the concept of new age music but find the execution dull. "Etaoin Shrdlu," the opening track, ushers in the album gently with percolating electronics and Greek-style fingerpicked electric guitar. Within a few minutes, the listener is catapulted into the stratosphere with a Contraption and electronics duet. From there, the journey is by turns down to earth, as on "A Voice Through a Cloud," and otherworldly, such as "Into the Cone of Cold." "On the Roof of the World" gently touches down with a guitar figure that is alternatively Japanese and Appalachian sounding. Cul de Sac's music is not, as the band name suggests, a street closed at one end; rather, it is a road leading to endless possibilities. —*Jim Powers*

## Current 93

f. 1983, London, England
*Group / Dark Ambient, Experimental, Industrial*
With a glut of industrial-pop hybrids on the market in the '80s and '90s, several bands stayed true to the experimental nature of early industrial music. The Psychic TV axis alone spawned many creative artists, including Current 93's David Tibet, who blends Gothic chanting and haunting atmospherics with industrial noisescapes courtesy of tape loops and synthesizers. Though Tibet doesn't quite have bandmates, he frequently works with a core of collaborators including ex-Psychic TV compatriot John Balance (more famous for his work with Peter Christopherson in Coil); Fritz Haaman, formerly of 23 Skidoo, (like PTV an offshoot of the most influential of the early industrial acts, Throbbing Gristle); Steven Stapleton of Nurse with Wound fame; Rose McDowall of Strawberry Switchblade; and Hilmar Örn Hilmarsson, also a former member of Psychic TV. Steven Stapleton is probably the most frequent member, appearing on virtually all Current 93 releases—a favor which David Tibet returns by working with Stapleton on most projects by Nurse with Wound.

The trio of Tibet, Balance and Haaman debuted in 1983 by recording the single "Lashtah" for Laylah Records. Until the end of the '80s, Tibet—utilizing the various lineups—recorded at a frenetic pace, issuing more than two albums per year for both Laylah and the Maldoror label. By the '90s, Tibet's output and style changed slightly: his productivity slowed somewhat, and the sound grew more subdued, encompassing acoustic folk in its most sinister permutations. —*John Bush*

● **Dogs Blood Rising** / 1984 / Laylah ♦♦♦♦
Having established his art on initial releases, Tibet makes a stunning declaration of purpose on *Dogs Blood Rising*, one of the most frightening, nerve-wracking records ever released. Interspersing quicker tracks and two lengthy evocations of destruction, *Dogs Blood* shows Tibet and his collaborators—including, as always, Stapleton—combining everything from invocations of Yukio Mishima to Christianity in a harrowing blend. Opening track "Christus Christus" sets the tone with its heavily flanged and looped vocals, chanting the title over and over again against a wash of sound, but it's the following track, "Falling Back in Fields of Rape," which truly begins to set this album apart. With guest vocals courtesy of Crass singer Steve Ignorant, who recites lyrics clearly meant to play on both senses of the word 'rape,' everything from recurrent chants of "War!" and other choral moans and varying percussion to heavily treated musical snippets and fragments loops, builds and fades throughout the mix. When a young girl's voice takes over the main lyrics after a snippet of a nursery rhyme is sung, the sheer sense of creepout grows even higher. It's even further intensified as Ignorant's rasping shouts of the main lyric start floating up through the mix like a mantra from hell. "From Broken Cross, Locusts" provides a semi-respite in ways, but only just, chanting from Tibet and others floating low in the mix as a recurrent, strange drum loop sets the overall pace before a sudden, frazzled ending. "Raio No Terrasu (Jesus Wept)" ratchets up everything to the level of apocalypse—the music doesn't pound and explode, but the ever-more pained, wailed voices chanting the title phrase or other similarly disturbed lines, or simply calling and keening unintelligibly, becomes a disturbing, fractured and tape-treated collage of sound. "St. Peters Keys All Bloody" concludes the album on a perversely calm note, with Tibet speaking in a snarl, then softly singing "The Sounds of Silence" and "Scarborough Fair" by Simon and Garfunkel. It's a chilling coda to a striking album. —*Ned Raggett*

**Nature Unveiled** / 1984 / Laylah ♦♦♦♦
Elegant Gregorian chants and cut-and-paste environmental recordings provide a bed for the muddy, disturbing gothic folk on this collection of Tibet's early-'80s recordings. —*John Bush*

## Dan Curtin

b. Youngstown, OH
*Remixing, Producer / Minimal Techno, Tech-House, Detroit Techno, Trance, Club/Dance, Techno*

One of the few American armchair techno producers to directly compete with his British equivalents (As One, Black Dog, B12), Dan Curtin played in a punk band in the early '80s, moved to hip-hop a few years later, and hopped aboard the house/techno explosion by the end of the decade. He began his recording career with 1992's *Tales from the Second Moon EP*, released as Apogee on Peacefrog. Curtin also spent some time a few hours north, working in Detroit with Carl Craig and releasing singles on 33 RPM Records. He really made his name after setting up his own Metamorphic Records in 1992 and releasing the EPs *Planetary* and *Space* (the label was home as well to early recordings by Morgan Geist and Titonton Duvante).

By 1994, Curtin had ranged all over the rapidly expanding electronic dance frontier; besides recording a single for the legendary mainstream house label Strictly Rhythm, he had also released his first album for Peacefrog, one of the leading European imprints for hard, intelligent techno. During the next two years, he released three albums through Peacefrog. Early 1997 brought an association with Japan's Sublime Records, through which Curtin released his fourth LP, *Deception*, plus several EPs during 1997-98. He also recorded with Japan's Tatsuro Hayashi as the Purveyors of Fine Funk, releasing several EPs through Peacefrog. His first album for Elypsia, *Pregenesis*, followed in 1999. —*John Bush*

**The Silicon Dawn** / 1994 / Peacefrog ♦♦♦♦
Tracks like "Parallel," "Devotion," and "A Flash in the Distance" may be difficult to distinguish with contemporary work by British outfits like Black Dog and B12, but *The Silicon Dawn* is an excellent balance of Curtin's stellar 808 drum programs and the ephemeral interstellar strings inspired by prime Detroit material by Derrick May and Carl Craig. —*John Bush*

**Web of Life** / 1995 / Peacefrog ♦♦♦
*Web of Life* compiles much of Curtin's rarer work for his own Metamorphic label, displaying his affinity for blends of jazz and techno-funk. —*John Bush*

**Art and Science** / Oct. 28, 1996 / Peacefrog ♦♦♦

● **Deception** / Mar. 24, 1997 / Sublime ♦♦♦♦
Curtin's first full-length for Sublime shows him in harder territory than previous work, with quite a few techno burners including some acid tweaking reminiscent of Neil Landstrumm. A few tracks include laidback electro-jazz. —*John Bush*

**New World [EP]** / Mar. 30, 1998 / Sublime ♦♦♦
Thankfully over-long at seven tracks, *New World* EP includes several hard-techno workouts with Curtin's usual rhythmic flair, plus a few jazzy tunes with lighter Detroit shadings. —*John Bush*

**Pregenesis** / 1999 / Elypsia ♦♦♦♦
Just as finely programmed and finely produced as his late '90s material for Sublime and Peacefrog, *Pregenesis* shows Curtin coming full circle with productions that highlight his listening debts: from hip-hop to new wave and electro to progressive house. The opener, "Bring It Back," is a fine showcase, weaving Curtin's nods to British ambient techno, rap, and acid-house over the course of its ten minutes. Most of these tracks aren't as hard as his last full-length, 1997's *Deception*, though many of them reflect the same melodic influence that sounds almost Oriental, as if there's a few Yellow Magic Orchestra LPs (or Japanese video games) somewhere in his past. With virtually every track on *Pregenesis*, Curtin makes a peripheral style of music into his own by warping it to his own ends, which are heavy on melancholy melodies and intricate rhythms. The process makes for a diverse, exciting album that never loses its charm. —*John Bush*

## Curve

f. 1991, London, England
*Group / Alternative Dance, Alternative Pop/Rock*

Considering Curve's towering monolith of guitar noise, dance tracks, dark goth, and airy melodies, it's strange that the two core members—guitarist Dean Garcia and vocalist Toni Halliday—met through David Stewart of Eurythmics. Halliday met Stewart while she was a teenager and they remained friends for years; Garcia played on Eurythmics' *Touch* and *Be Yourself Tonight*. The two played together in State of Play, which released one album and two singles in the late '80s to little notice. After the failure of that band, Garcia and Halliday parted ways only to reunite in the beginning of the '90s. Renaming themselves Curve, Halliday and Garcia released three EPs that became independent hits in 1991. Although they were critically acclaimed as well, some members of the UK press attacked Halliday for not being a genuine member of the indie scene. Despite the negative press, their next EP and first album, 1992's *Doppelganger*, hit number one on the UK's indie charts. By the time of the following year's *Cuckoo*, Curve had added two guitarists and a drummer, with Garcia moving to the bass. *Cuckoo* was noisier and more experimental than their previous releases, although it did have a couple of pop songs that were tighter than their usual singles. However, the album didn't make as big a splash in the UK as previous releases; Curve split several months after its release, only to reform in 1997 with the *Chinese Burn* EP. The full-length *Come Clean* followed a year later. —*Stephen Thomas Erlewine*

● **Doppelganger** / Mar. 10, 1992 / Anxious/Charisma ♦♦♦♦
Following a series of single and EP releases that had found chart success in the UK and indie credibility in the States, the British band Curve released their full-length debut *Doppelganger* on Dave Stewart's Anxious label. Led by lead singer Toni Halliday and guitarist Dean Garcia, both of whom had toured with Robert Plant, Curve enlisted production help from Flood for this record. Roaming the same sonic landscape as My Bloody Valentine, *Doppelganger* features the breathy, dreamy vocals of Halliday over top layers of throbbing guitar, dense keyboards, and sledgehammer drumming to create formidable aural textures. At times meandering and unrelenting, tracks like "Already Yours" and "Wish You Dead" are stellar workouts full of rhythm and attitude. The few slower numbers are a nice change of pace with the best results on "Fait Accompli" and the quiet, almost dirge-like "Sandpit," where the less dense instrumentation allows Halliday's vocals to become the focal point. At times menacing and dark and other times more playful, *Doppelganger* is

a bracing listening experience that earned Curve well-deserved attention on both sides of the Atlantic. —*Tom Demalon*

**Pubic Fruit** / 1992 / Anxious/Charisma ✦✦✦
*Pubic Fruit* is not a proper follow-up to Curve's debut full-length, but, instead, it gathers together three of the band's earlier EP releases which had only been released in the UK and adds the previously unavailable 12" version of "Fait Accompli." Despite the album being a compilation of sorts, it holds together quite nicely and provides a good look at the band's work up until their debut release. Much of the material is produced by the band and Steve Osborne and isn't nearly as dense as their debut which benefited from their work with Flood. The non-focus tracks of the EPs are every bit the equal of the songs that eventually found their way onto *Doppelganger* with many of them being true gems. "No Escape From Heaven" features a sultry vocal performance by Toni Halliday over a galloping percussive beat and drive-by bursts of guitar. And "Cherry" is the high-point of this collection. The song starts out quietly with hushed vocals and subtle keyboards before the drums signal a blast of fuzz guitars and everything crashes into a riveting sound collage. —*Tom Demalon*

**Cuckoo** / Sep. 21, 1993 / Anxious/Charisma ✦✦✦✦
Curve's second record finds more mid-tempo songs and a more electronic feel, although producer Flood still manages to bring out the band's dense sonic tendencies. While the music on *Cuckoo* is less aggressive than *Doppelganger*, singer Toni Halliday's lyrics are well defined and still pack a punch. Often playing the woman spurned, but not broken, Halliday takes no quarter. On "Super Blaster" she warns a companion not to start anything that they can't finish and she reads an ex-lover the riot act on "Left of Mother." The music shows more diversity, with a bit of funk injected into the guitars on "Crystal," while "Men Are From Mars, Women Are From Venus" is a hypnotic mid-tempo march. The album closes with the achingly confessional title cut, with Halliday showing a rare sense of vulnerability that is quite effective. Not as immediate as their earlier material and not quite as fulfilling, *Cuckoo* nonetheless will please longtime fans and is a solid introduction for potential converts. —*Tom Demalon*

**Chinese Burn [EP]** / Nov. 4, 1997 / Uptown/Universal ✦✦✦
The *Chinese Burn* EP was the first shot at a comeback by Curve, who spent much of the mid-'90s in limbo. While they were away, Garbage popularized a sound that was remarkably similar to Curve's fusion of drum loops and shoegazing indie-pop. In light of Garbage's success, Curve has decided to delve deeper into dance, as *Chinese Burn* attests. Six of the eight tracks are mixes of the title track, all of which are quite different from each other, but not necessarily compelling. "Chinese Burn" itself is a strong comeback, a tight exciting rush of sound, but the other two tracks are standard-issue Curve. Still, the EP bodes well for the forthcoming full-length comeback. —*Stephen Thomas Erlewine*

**Come Clean** / Mar. 10, 1998 / Uptown/Universal ✦✦✦✦
Just as fans were beginning to wonder if the duo Curve would ever return from their self-imposed exile, they've returned with their best album to date, *Come Clean*. Still combining largely electronic music with alternative hooks and lines, members Toni Halliday and Dean Garcia have returned to a now-popular form of music they helped create years ago. Although the album's two best tracks have previously appeared on their late-1997 EP *Chinese Burn* (the title tracks from both the EP and the full length), there are plenty of other strong tracks in attendance. "Something Familiar" may be the band's most melodically accessible track yet, while the extremely over-driven distortion and abrasive tones of "Dogbone" are just the opposite. Unlike many electronic bands nowadays, the duo makes it clear that they don't just go for musical overkill, as evidenced by the slow electronic groove contained in "Killer Baby," and the mid-paced dance rock of "Cotton Candy." *Come Clean* is the welcome return of a band that deserved attention when they first appeared years ago, and may get it in the electro-friendly late '90s. —*Greg Prato*

## Cut Chemist (Lucas Macfadden)

*Producer, DJ / Turntablism, Underground Rap, Hip-Hop*
As well as being one of the ablest solo turntablists on the globe, Cut Chemist is also a member of two highly rated crews: underground rap kings Jurassic 5 and the Latin-funk band Ozomatli. He came up with the L.A. rap group Unity Committee, and debuted on wax with the B-side of UC's 1993 single "Unified Rebelution." The track, "Lesson 4—The Radio," was a tribute to and continuation of Double D & Steinski's seminal hip-hop collage masterpieces "Lessons 1-3"—and included nods to Indeep, Bob James, Spoonie Gee and Dan Ackroyd.

Soon after the record's release, Unity Committee came together with another group, Rebels of Rhythm, to form Jurassic 5. Cut Chemist kept quite busy with the group, contributing "Lesson 6" to the group's eponymous EP and producing the entire record. He also delved into remixing (DJ Shadow, Liquid Liquid) and outside work (scratching for Less than Jake, appearing with another Los Angeles group, Ozomatli). In mid-1997, Cut Chemist recorded his album debut, *Live at the Future Primitive Sound Session*, with Shorkut of Invisibl Skratch Piklz. His tracks have also appeared on two seminal turntablist compilations, *Return of the DJ, Vol. 1* and *Deep Concentration*. —*John Bush*

● **Live at the Future Primitive Sound Session** / Apr. 7, 1998 / Ubiquity ✦✦✦✦
Working interchangeably, Cut Chemist and Shortkut handled a total of five turntables on this album, recorded live in San Francisco. Unlike the vast majority of turntablist albums, *Live at the Future Primitive Sound Session* ably approximates the incredible excitement of actually *watching* a world-class DJ team in action. Old-school fans will recognize much of the material (from Eric B. & Rakim, Ultramagnetic MC's, Newcleus, Afrika Bambaataa, even a dramatically reworked version of the Beastie Boys' "Egg Man"), but there are quite a few rare grooves in the mix as well—including what could be the first use of Homer & Jethro in a hip-hop context. Continually inventive and entertaining, *Live at the Future Primitive Sound Session* is one of the early turntablist classics. —*John Bush*

## Cybotron

f. 1980, Detroit, MI
*Group / Detroit Techno, Electro, Club/Dance, Techno*
The seminal electro group Cybotron provided the first home for the recordings of techno godfather Juan Atkins. With partner Rick Davis (aka 3070), Atkins recorded several of electro's best moments. The singles "Alleys of Your Mind," "Enter" and "Clear," were dark dystopias of the post-industrial steel city within tight Kraftwerk-inspired funk. Their success prompted Fantasy Records to sign the group, and release 1983's *Enter* LP. Atkins left soon after due to artistic differences (specifically, Davis' defined pop slant), and later defined early Detroit techno with his recordings as Model 500. Davis continued to release albums as Cybotron into the mid-'90s, though the mystical R&B direction of efforts like *Empathy* and *Cyber Ghetto* were quite a turn from the group's beginnings. For fans of electro and techno, Cybotron ended when Juan Atkins left. [See also: Juan Atkins, Model 500, Infiniti] —*John Bush*

★ **Clear** / 1990 / Fantasy ✦✦✦✦✦
The only old-school electro LP with any amount of staying power (thanks in part to its release on Fantasy), this CD release of the Cybotron album previously known as *Enter* includes crucial early singles like "Alleys of Your Mind," "Cosmic Cars" and techno's first defining moment, "Clear." The collision of Atkins' vision for cosmic funk and the arena-rock instincts of Rick Davis result in a surprisingly cohesive album, dated for all the right reasons and quite pop-minded. Ecological and political statements even crop up with the final tracks, "Cosmic Raindance" and "El Salvador." —*John Bush*

**Empathy** / 1993 / Fantasy ✦✦

**Interface: The Roots of Techno** / 1995 / Southbound ✦✦✦✦
*Interface* is basically a reprise of the *Enter/Clear* LP, though it does add to its predecessor's basic lineup with seminal tracks like "Techno City," "Eden," and the House Mix of "Cosmic Cars." It's difficult to recommend however, since the *Clear* LP is so much more widely available. —*John Bush*

## Cylob (Chris Jeffs)

*Producer / Experimental Techno, Electronica, Ambient Techno, IDM*
Another product of Richard "Aphex Twin" James' Rephlex stable, Chris Jeffs' releases as Cylob and Kinesthesia have numbered among the Cornwall-based imprint's most celebrated recent releases. Not nearly as prolific as his friends and sometime-labelmates James and Mike Paradinas (μ-Ziq), Jeffs has nonetheless amassed an impressive catalog of releases in a relatively short period of time. Although he only began experimenting with electronics in 1991, within five years Jeffs released three EPs and three full-lengths—including the cheeky DJ double-pack *Loops and Breaks* (as Cylob) and the sparse ambient of *Empathy Box* (as Kinesthesia)—in addition to remixes for

Aphex Twin, Bochum Welt, and Immersion. Although focusing more recently on a refined brand of ambient breakbeat and techno, Jeffs' stylistic palette includes crunchy, industrial-leaning techno, beatless ambient, and new-school electro-funk. [See also: Kinesthesia] —*Sean Cooper*

● **Cylobian Sunset** / May 27, 1996 / Rephlex ◆◆◆◆
Surprisingly less experimental than either his Kinesthesia twelves or his previous Cylob work (particularly the challenging "Industrial Folk Songs" EP), *Cylobian Sunset* works well as an album, drawing listeners in with evocative melodies and more palatable beats and breaks reminiscent of some of Aphex and µ-Ziq's less caustic Rephlex material. —*Sean Cooper*

**Loops and Breaks** / Jun. 10, 1996 / Rephlex ◆◆
A somewhat humorous double-pack breaks record (e.g., two copies of the same record) modeled on those used by hip-hop and battle DJs for scratching and trick-mixing. The beats are pretty monochromatic (but then, so are most breaks records), leaving the DJ to make something interesting out of Jeffs' skeletal rhythmic sketches. For completists (and, of course, DJs) only. —*Sean Cooper*

**Cylob's Latest Effort [EP]** / 1997 / Rephlex ◆◆◆
Chris Jeffs' first Cylob material since 1996's *Cylobian Sunset* is an abrupt gear-change back into Kinesthesia territory (his other main pseudonym), featuring distortion-heavy electro breaks paired with sometimes-effective, sometimes-not little-kid melodies. Overlong at five tracks (considering how miserably the two shortest fail), but the best of *Latest Effort* is among Jeffs' finest work to date. —*Sean Cooper*

**Previously Unavailable on Compact Disc** / Apr. 13, 1998 / Rephlex ◆◆◆
Including most of the unavailable Chris Jeffs material recorded as Kinesthesia plus Cylob, this collection presents several classic tracks of ambient retro-techno as well as remixes by µ-Ziq, Aphex Twin, and Autechre. —*John Bush*

# D

## D'Influence
f. 1991
*Group / Club/Dance, Acid Jazz, House, Hip-Hop*
The UK acid jazz collective D'Influence comprised vocalist Sarah Anne Webb, guitarist and keyboardist Ed Baden-Powell, keyboardist and multi-instrumentalist Kwame Kwaten and drummer Steve Marston. Debuting in 1992 with *Good 4 We*, the group resurfaced in 1995 with *Prayer 4 Unity;* they also emerged among the leading production teams in contemporary British R&B, helming hits for Mark Morrison and Shola Ama, whose debut LP *Much Love* appeared on D'Influence's own Freakstreet label. Their third album, *London*, followed in 1997. —*Jason Ankeny*

**Prayer 4 Unity** / 1995 / East West ♦♦♦
D-Influence's sophomore album continues the group's trip through funky house rhythms, with Sarah Ann Webb's vocals. Highlights include "Midnite," "Should I" and "Waiting." —*John Bush*

● **London** / May 1997 / Echo ♦♦♦♦
More of a soul band than similar British outfits (Jamiroquai, Brand New Heavies, and Galliano), D'Influence uses their third album to expand the sound into several different directions, including stabs at rapping, gospel, and even salsa. Surprisingly, the genre-crossing works quite well, thanks mostly to the sweet vocals of Sarah Ann Webb. —*John Bush*

## D*Note
f. 1992, London, England
*Group / Ambient Techno, Club/Dance, Acid Jazz, Urban, Hip-Hop*
Primarily the brainchild of musician Matt Winn (nee Wienevski), the British experimental dance act D*Note originally emerged out of London's rare groove scene, with the 1993 debut LP *Babel*—recorded with the assistance of DJ Charlie Lexton and keyboardist Matt Cooper—reflecting a strong acid-jazz background. Hit singles like "Devotion" and "Garden of Earthly Delights," however, recalled house music, while the second D*Note LP, 1995's *Criminal Justice*, plunged into drum'n'bass. In addition to music, Winn also tackled film, rejecting short-form video clips in favor of more ambitious productions like the ten-minute short *Round the Block*. In 1997, he premiered the half-hour featurette *Coming Down*, an acclaimed portrait of the London drug culture. Its soundtrack appeared shortly after the release of the third D*Note album, an eponymous ambient effort issued earlier that same year. —*Jason Ankeny*

**Babel** / Aug. 16, 1993 / TVT ♦♦♦

● **Criminal Justice** / 1995 / TVT ♦♦♦♦
By the time of D*Note's second album, acid jazz had begun to get a bit stale, so Winn & Co. expanded the range of their sound, incorporating a bit of ragga-jungle on the title track (with chatting by MC Navigator), mainstream house on "Garden of Earthly Delights" (with the vocals of Pamela Anderson, sister of Jhelisa), and ambient jazz on "Deep Water." Despite the diversity, D*Note never fails to lose their character through it all, and the acid-jazz fusion comes off remarkably well. —*John Bush*

**D*Note** / Jul. 21, 1997 / VC ♦♦♦
Great moments come few and far between on producer Matt Winn's third D*Note album. Aside from "Waiting Hopefully," whose aggressive vocal from PY (cousin of Carleen Anderson) and piles of breakbeats make it an incredible experience, the jungle-lite rhythms and too-smooth jazzy flourishes make for a less than intriguing album. —*John Bush*

## D'Arcangelo
*Group / Electro-Techno, Ambient Techno, Techno, IDM*
Also behind popular experimental techno group Monomorph (on the Disturbance label), Italian brothers Marco and Fabrizio D'Arcangelo record artful, melodic electro as D'Arcangelo. While the brothers' early discography is populated by nearly a dozen releases of acid and hard techno for such labels as ACV, Out of Orbit, Hot Trax, and Disko B, their more recent work has drawn inspiration from post-techno producers such as Aphex Twin and Autechre, combining intricate rhythmic programming with abstract textures and engaging melodies. The pair's debut EP release entirely in this vein appeared, appropriately enough, through UK-based Rephlex (Richard "Aphex Twin" James' label), and featured a balanced mixture of fast, abrasive rhythms and nostalgia-drenched electronics reminiscent of early Human League, Jean-Michel Jarre, and Depeche Mode. A subsequent release, *Diagrams 10-14*, through Italian electronica label Nature plunged deeper into electro-new wave fusion territory, with a couple tracks almost sounding like Yaz outtakes. Following a split 7" single with Canadian artist Solvent on the latter's Suction label, the brothers released their debut LP on Rephlex. Three years in the making, *Shipwreck* finally appeared in May 1999, and exhibited an evolutionary leap in both production quality and compositional acumen, wedding complex multipart melodies with constantly shifting beats and diverse structures. —*Sean Cooper*

**Diagrams 10-14 [EP]** / 1998 / Nature ♦♦♦
Bouncy, heavy on the melodies and nowhere near as unaccommodating as their earlier releases, D'Arcangelo's debut EP for Nature is some of their most agreeable and engaging work. Of the brothers' many releases, the early new wave influence is strongest here, with bits of the genetic material of Yaz, Depeche Mode and Tangerine Dream in strong evidence. —*Sean Cooper*

● **Shipwreck** / 1999 / Rephlex ♦♦♦♦
Three years in the making and showing it, *Shipwreck* is one of the finest releases from the Rephlex label, and is easily the best D'Arcangelo release to date. Moving from poppy, upbeat electro through dark, splintering mid-tempo experimental tracks and back again, *Shipwreck* leaves behind the simple drum patterns characterizing past efforts, and introduces an atmospheric depth lacking in their comparatively more two-dimensional Rephlex and Nature EPs. Bold and consistently excellent. —*Sean Cooper*

## D'Cruze (Jay D'Cruze)
*Producer / Jungle/Drum'N'Bass, Club/Dance*
Recording for the influential Suburban Base label, breakbeat pioneer Jay D'Cruze produced several excellent early drum'n'bass staples—looking back to the heyday of rave even as they looked ahead to the jungle outbreak of the mid-'90s. After making friends at the Boogie Times shop in Romford, the teenaged D'Cruze debuted in 1993 with "World Within a World," released on the store's emerging imprint Suburban Base. The label soon led the way with the darker sound of hardcore-into-jungle thanks to releases by DJ Hype, Sonz of a Loop Da Loop Era, and Krome & Time. Recording with store-owner Danny Donnelly as Boogie Times Tribe, D'Cruze released two darkcore touchstones: "Real Hardcore" and "The Dark Stranger," the latter anthologized on almost every early jungle compilation worth its salt. Two more classic singles, "Watch Out" and "Lonely," followed before a lengthy absence from the breakbeat scene during its prime crossover years. D'Cruze returned in 1997 with more singles for Suburban Base, DJ Hype's True Playaz, and his own The Bomb label (co-owned with Special K). D'Cruze was one of only three Suburban Base artists to get the full-length treatment, with the 1995 LP *Control*. —*John Bush*

- **Control** / 1995 / Suburban Base ♦♦♦♦

Few jungle producers mashed up drums and vocal samples with the manic intensity of Jay D'Cruze, and the result is this programming-heavy LP, just the second released by Suburban Base in 1995 (after plenty of singles). From the breakdown snare rush and time-stretched chatting that introduces the opener "Come Back," to the metallic mangling of a diva wail and Ginsu-chopped beats on "Ruf Intelligence Revisited," *Control* aptly shows D'Cruze's mastery of the mixing board (uncoincidentally pictured on the front cover). Though he often goes back and forth between house- and ragga-influenced tracks, *Control* is a distinguished early effort at stretching jungle out into the full-length realm. —*John Bush*

**Jungle Innovators, Vol. 1: D'Cruze** / Jul. 16, 1996 / Suburban Base ♦♦♦♦

## DAF

f. 1977, Düsseldorf, Germany, db. 1985
*Group / Post-Punk, Industrial*

Combining elements of industrial, Kraut-rock and post-punk into a minimalist dance sound, Düsseldorf's DAF took their name from the phrase "*Deutsch Amerikanische Freundschaft*," a post-WWII slogan promoting German/American friendship. The group originally consisted of drummer/synth player Robert Gorl, vocalist Gabi Delgado (sometimes Delgado-Lopez), guitarist W. Spelmans, and bassist/keyboardist/saxophonist Chrislo Haas. This lineup recorded the German-only *Ein Produkt der DAF* in 1979 and debuted internationally the next year with *Die Kleinen und die Bosen* ("The Small and the Evil"). Gorl and Delgado moved to London permanently, continuing DAF as a duo, while Haas went on to join Crime and the City Solution. DAF recorded three albums for Virgin during 1981-82 (*Alles Ist Gut, Gold und Liebe, Für Immer*), all sung in German. The pair also found time to appear on the Eurythmics' debut, *In the Garden*. In 1983, the duo disbanded to pursue solo projects. Delgado recorded the solo album *Mistress* that year, and Gorl responded the following year with *Night Full of Tension*, which featured vocals by Annie Lennox. Though DAF re-formed briefly in 1985, the reunion was not recorded. Virgin issued an eponymous British retrospective in 1988. Delgado later began a project named DAF Dos, while Gorl recorded two albums in the late '90s for the techno label Disko B, *Watch the Great Copycat* and *Sex Drops*. —*Steve Huey*

**Ein Produkt der DAF** / 1979 / Warning ♦♦♦

- **Die Kleinen und die Bösen** / 1980 / Mute ♦♦♦♦

After the near-apocalyptic shrieks of *Ein Produkt*, DAF toned down just a touch, but only just, for *Kleinen*. Coming out on Mute as the album did, it helped not merely in establishing the group's cachet, but the label's and, in turn, the whole genre of experimental electronic music in the eighties and beyond. The cover art alone, with the group's name boldly printed white on black in all capitals next to part of a Soviet propaganda poster, practically invented a rapidly overused industrial music design cliché. At the time, though, the group was ironically the most rock they would ever get, with bassist Michael Kemner as well as guitarist Spelmans and electronics performer Haas joining Görl and Delgado. The first half of *Kleinen* was a studio recording with Kraut-rock producing legend Conny Plank, who did his usual fantastic job throughout. The beats are sometimes hollow and always ominous, treated with studio touches to make them even more so, while the squalling, clipped guitar sounds often make nails on chalkboards sound sweet in comparison. Delgado's husky vocals and Görl's spare-but-every-hit-counts drumming on "Osten Währt Am Längsten" are particularly strong, while the electronic rhythms of "Co Co Pino" (Delgado's vocal trills are a scream) and all-out slam of "Nacht Arbeit" can't be resisted. The live side, recorded at London's *Electric Ballroom*, is even more all-out most of the time, starting with the complete noise fest "Gewalt" and then shifting into a series of short, brusque tracks. Delgado pulls off some bloodcurdling screams (and Görl some fairly nutty harmonies as well—check the opening to "Das Ist Liebe") over the din. The musicians themselves sound like they decided to borrow Wire's sense of quick songs while cranking the amps to ten; the resultant combination of feedback crunch and electronic brutality is at times awesome to behold. —*Ned Raggett*

**Alles Ist Gut** / 1981 / Virgin ♦♦♦

Stripped down to the core duo of Görl and Delgado and with Conny Plank again behind the boards with crisp, focused production, with *Alles Ist Gut* ('everything is fine') DAF turned into an honest-to-goodness German hit machine, as detailed in the 1998 Mute reissue's liner notes by Biba Kopf. Even more important and impressive was how they did it—keeping the electronic brutality that characterized them, but stripped down to nothing but Görl's massive drumming, electronic bass and synth tones, and Delgado's deep, commanding singing. The result was and remains massively influential—Nitzer Ebb, to mention one later industrial disciple, would be nothing without this album as a template, while the genre of electronic body music, or EBM, got its undisputed start with the doomladen death disco here. It isn't all just because of machines and politics either. Delgado's lyrical fascination seems to be as much with sex as with power, thus the grunting sounds throughout "Mein Herz Macht Bum" ("my heart goes boom"), to pick one point. Add to that the striking, simple cover design—Delgado on the front, Görl on the back, stripped to the skin and covered in sweat—and maybe Wax Trax! never needed to exist in the first place. "Der Mussolini," DAF's breakthrough hit, still sounds fantastic years later. A perfect case could be made for it as the ultimate industrial music song, with Delgado's at once insistent and sensual singing, lyrics referencing not just Mussolini but any number of fascist figures (as titles of dance crazes, no less!), and Görl's astonishing percussion crunch and bassline. DAF wisely vary things at points, thus the slow, deliberate pulse of "Rote Lippen" and the twinkly keyboard line throughout "Der Räuber Und Der Prinz." With songs like "Als Wär's Das Letzte Mal" and "Alle Gegen Alle" leading the way, though, DAF mainly concentrates on head-on assaults to brilliant effect. —*Ned Raggett*

**Gold und Liebe** / 1981 / Virgin ♦♦

Plank again oversees an album from the duo, while the photo on the cover of Görl and Delgado in what looks like modified bondage gear maintains the sex theme well enough. Put it all together with song titles like "Sex Unter Wasser" ("sex underwater") and "Absolute Körperkontrolle" ("absolute body control") and DAF is tending that much more to the flesh rather than the mind. Things are a just touch less powerful than on *Alles;* opening track "Liebe Auf Den Ersten Blick" has a bass/melody combination that could almost be early Depeche Mode. Most of the time, though, it's only a slight difference by degrees, as pounding monsters like "Ich Will" and the instrumental build of "Absolute Körperkontrolle" demonstrate. Görl's music generally still relies on his forceful percussion and sharp, cutting synth bass in combination, and Plank once again makes it sound fantastic. Additional touches surface throughout, and if *Gold* isn't as immediately varied as *Alles* was, the subtler elements do provide variety. There's almost a lounge feeling to the vibey keyboards on "Sex Unter Wasser," while the rough military drumming on "Muskel" suits the song perfectly. One of the best songs accordingly has one of the best fusions—"Goldenes Spielzeug," with a soft, chime/keyboard melody over a tough bass/drum beat, singing appearing only every so often during its length. Delgado himself, however sex-obsessed he might be this time out, still makes for a strong frontman—certainly, if you don't know German, you can just pretend he's ordering everyone to the dancefloor under pain of death or something similar. *Gold* closes out on a fantastic note with "Verschwende Deine Jugend," a full-on destructive beast in the "Der Mussolini" mode, and "Greif Nach Den Sternen," a steady-paced, almost anthemic number with the trademark DAF blend of brusqueness still intact. —*Ned Raggett*

**Für Immer** / 1982 / Virgin ♦♦

DAF's final album for Virgin, *Für Immer* is another set of spare synth-pop, defiantly non-melodic though not exactly harsh. While Görl's productions usually balance a steady four-four beat with upbeat, repetitive synth progressions and only occasional organic elements, Lopez is all over the place, either sing-speaking in a guttural chant ("A Little Bit of War," "The Gods Are White") or practically crooning like Marc Almond ("In the Jungle of Love," "Fall in Love with Me"). Neither member of DAF contributes much to the album, and except for scattered highlights like "Kebab Dreams," *Für Immer* is a disappointing album. —*John Bush*

**1st Step to Heaven** / 1986 / Ariola ♦♦

## Daft Punk

f. 1992, Paris, France
*Group / Electronica, Club/Dance, House*

In similar company with new-school French progressive dance artists such as Motorbass, Air, Cassius, and Dimitri from Paris, Parisian duo Daft Punk have quickly risen to acclaim by adapting a love for first-wave acid house and techno to their younger roots in pop, indie rock, and hip-hop. The combined talents of DJs Guy-Manuel De Homem-Christo and Thomas Bangalter, the pair's first projects together included Darling, a voiceless indie cover band; their current recording name derives from a review in UK music weekly

*Melody Maker* of a compilation tape Darling were featured on, released by krautrock revivalists Stereolab (their lo-fi DIY cover of a Beach Boys song was derided as "daft punk"). Subsequently ditching the almost inevitable creative cul-de-sac of rock for the more appealing rush of the dancefloor, the pair released their debut single, "The New Wave," in 1993 on the celebrated Soma label. Instantly hailed by the dance music press as the work of a new breed of house innovators, the single was followed by "Da Funk," the band's first true hit (the record has sold 30,000 copies worldwide and seen thorough rinsings by everyone from Kris Needs to the Chemical Brothers).

Although the group had only released a trio of singles ("The New Wave" and "Da Funk," as well as the 1996 limited pressing of "Musique"), in early 1996 Daft Punk was the subject of a minor bidding war. The group eventually signed with Virgin, with their first long-player, *Homework*, appearing early the following year (a brief preview of the album, "Musique," was also featured on the Virgin compilation *Wipeout 2097* next to tracks from Photek, Future Sound of London, the Chemical Brothers, and Source Direct). As with the earlier singles, the group's sound is a brazen, dancefloor-oriented blend of progressive house, funk, electro, and techno, with sprinklings of hip-hop-styled breakbeats and excessive, crowd-firing samples, similar to other anthemic dance-fusion acts such as the Chemical Brothers and Monkey Mafia. In addition to his role in Daft Punk, Thomas Bangalter operates the Roule label and has recorded under his own name (the underground smash "Trax on Da Rocks") as well as Stardust (the huge club/commercial hit "Music Sounds Better with You"). —*Sean Cooper*

★ Homework / Jan. 20, 1997 / Virgin ◆◆◆◆◆
Daft Punk's full-length debut is a funk-house hailstorm, giving real form to a style of straightahead dance music not attempted since the early fusion days of on-the-one funk and dance-party disco. Thick, rumbling bass, vocoders, choppy breaks and beats, and a certain brash naivete permeate the record from start to finish, giving it the edge of an almost certain classic. While a few fall flat, the best tracks make this one essential. —*Sean Cooper*

D.A.F.T.: A Story About Dogs, Androids, Firemen, and Tomatoes [Video] / Mar. 28, 2000 / Virgin ◆◆
*D.A.F.T.: A Story About Dogs, Androids, Firemen, and Tomatoes* features the Parisian electronica duo's videos, along with commentaries, storyboards, and behind-the-scenes footage for each of the clips, remixes, and a live show, "Rollin' & Scratchin' Live in LA." Spike Jonze's popular video for "Da Funk," Michel Gondry's "Around the World," Roman Coppola's "Revolution 909," Seb Janiak's "Burnin'," and the band's self-directed clip for "Fresh" reaffirm the band's musical and visual inventiveness, while the live show features a whopping eight multiple-angle views. The Masters at Work, Ian Pooley, Roger Sanchez, and Armand Van Helden remixes add another layer of depth to this feature-packed DVD, which sets the standard for electronic artists—as well as musicians in general—to present their work in a creative, interactive way. —*Heather Phares*

## Brett Dancer
b. Kalamazoo, MI
*Producer, DJ / House*
After first hearing Chicago house in 1986 and then working alongside Jay Denham and Fanon Flowers while he attended Western Michigan University, Brett Dancer left the Midwest, trading nearby Chicago and Detroit for New York in late 1993. Upon arriving in New York, he built upon the production experience he had attained in Kalamazoo with Denham's Black Nation label, ambitiously starting his own record label, Trackmode. With his own personal label, Dancer began releasing deep house music, heavily influenced by the sounds of both Chicago and Detroit. Furthermore, he also began releasing records on his label by some of these two Midwestern cities most respected artists: Anthony Shakir, Larry Heard, Alton Miller, Boo Williams, Rick Wade, Theo Parrish, among others. In addition to providing an outlet for quality house music, Dancer has also earned substantial respect among the house community for his own productions, many of which are featured on Trackmode along with an excellent contribution to Mike Grant's burgeoning Moods & Grooves label in Detroit. —*Jason Birchmeier*

● The Underground Experience [Single] / 2000 / Trackmode ◆◆◆◆
On the first EP for his Trackmode label, Brett Dancer sets the precedent for the successive releases, showcasing his Chicago-influenced style of deep house. —*Jason Birchmeir*

Black Java Joint [Single] / 2000 / Trackmode ◆◆◆
The *Black Java Joint* EP finds the ever-soulful Brett Dancer further emphasizing his tendency to integrate live musicianship into his tracks, a refreshing tendency that has become a trademark of his style. —*Jason Birchmeier*

## Dandy Jack
b. Santiago, Chile
*Producer / Experimental Techno, Experimental Electro, Electro-Jazz, House*
Dandy Jack is closely associated with Frankfurt-based experimental ambient and techno artists such as Victor Sol, Niko Heyduck, Atom Heart, and Pete Namlook. Originally of Santiago, Chile, Dandy Jack relocated to Frankfurt in the late '80s, where he began releasing solo and collaborative works on Pod, Geometrik, Fax, and, most recently, Atom Heart's Rather Interesting label. His first 12" appeared on Pod under the name Gon, a hard techno single recorded with Atom Heart. His more recent Fax releases—two albums with Victor Sol as X]acks, and the Namlook collaboration *Amp*—have perhaps earned him the widest recognition, but his finest work to date has appeared under his own name on Rather Interesting: the experimental house groover *Dandy Jack and the Cosmic Trousers* and *Dandy Jack and the Plastic Woman*, the latter a mix of fizzy ambient, heavily syncopated electro, and jazzy, experimental electronica. Dandy Jack also performed live as a part of Atom Heart's Lassigue Bendthaus band during their "Render" tour, and has appeared on Rather Interesting's *Real Intelligence* compilation and Geometrik's *Electronic Generators*. —*Sean Cooper*

Amp / 1996 / Fax ◆◆◆◆
Dandy Jack's first collaboration with the gregarious Pete Namlook on the latter's Fax label is a lively foray into experimental beat music, from house and techno to electro and jungle. Although this is Dandy's Fax debut, he doesn't waste any time in setting the tone of this release, which figures closer to his own solo work than to Namlook's. —*Sean Cooper*

Dandy Jack and the Cosmic Trousers / 1996 / Rather Interesting ◆◆◆◆
Flawless progressive techno/house with a strong presence of funk, jazz, and disco. Like most RI gear, Dandy Jack has his tongue in his cheek for much of this, with goofy '60s Latin loungecore rhythms sidling up to solid house grooves and rubbery basslines. —*Sean Cooper*

● Dandy Jack and the Plastic Woman / 1997 / Rather Interesting ◆◆◆◆
Dandy Jack's second full-length for Atom Heart's Rather Interesting label is in full-on AH mode, all bubbling, colliding electro-jazz rhythms and weird, high-wired electronics. Listeners familiar with DJ's earlier work will be surprised to find a pair of (extremely well-done) experimental ambient tracks at the front, but much of *Plastic Woman* is experimental electro/techno in the Atom Heart/Black Dog/Mouse On Mars vein, with enough of a unique take to not sound derivative or dedicational. Excellent. —*Sean Cooper*

## Danmass
f. 1994, London, England
*Group / Big Beat, Club/Dance, Techno*
Formed by London DJs-turned-producers Mr. Dan and Massimo (Bonaddio), Danmass creates tracks of electro-themed old-skool breaks for Dust 2 Dust, the British label they've released material for both separately and as a duo. The pair moved into production in 1995 with the second release on Dust 2 Dust, the "Breakout" single. Later releases from both Mr. Dan and Danmass appeared on the label, and their 1999 debut album *Form Freaks*, became the first single-artist LP released on the label. —*John Bush*

● Form Freaks / May 3, 1999 / Dust 2 Dust ◆◆◆◆
The pairing of a funk musician (Dan) and a techno DJ (Massimo) results in the impressive *Form Freaks*, an electronic mish-mash that moves from rare-groove to big-beat to techno to hip-hop with less static than listeners might expect. The duo's reliance on vintage keyboards and synth give a decidedly retro feel to the proceedings, similar to Air, but with more of a sense of where electronic music's going than where it's been. Twisting from vocal tunes ("Bird," with Harriet Scott) to turntablist hip-hop ("Gotta Learn") to cut-and-paste jazz funk (the club hit "Quake"), Danmass does a little bit of everything, and does it all with a uniform excellence. —*John Bush*

## Dark Comedy (Kenny Larkin)
b. Detroit, MI
*Producer / Detroit Techno, Club/Dance, Techno*
Kenny Larkin's Dark Comedy project debuted in 1996 with the "Plankton" single for his own Art of Dance Records. The following year he released the

Seven Days LP for Belgium's Elypsia Records. [See Also: Kenny Larkin] —*John Bush*

● **Seven Days** / Sep. 16, 1996 / Art of Dance/Elypsia ♦♦♦♦
A bit harder and more isolationist in feel than his regular Kenny Larkin material, Dark Comedy's *Seven Days* deals in clipped beats and high-repetition trance which occasionally sounds more akin to Jeff Mills than Larkin himself. Among many highlights, the best track is the eight-minute minimal epic "Paranoid." —*John Bush*

## Datach'i (Joseph Fraioli)

b. 1977
*Producer / Drill'N'Bass, Experimental Techno, Electronica*
Datach'i's Joseph Fraioli is a manic, sampladelic producer/processor with all the gracelessness (but not artlessness) of experimental-techno producers from Kid606 to Alec Empire. Based in New York, Fraioli released his first work on 1999's *10110101* (Rec+Play). The album earned great reviews in the underground press soon after its release on Caipirinha, and Fraoli followed with his second, *We Are Always Well Thank You*, in 2000. —*John Bush*

● **10110101" (Rec+Play)** / Oct. 19, 1999 / Caipirinha ♦♦♦♦
If you find abstract techno just a little bit too linear, or if you think drum'n'bass would be great if only it were a bit more abrasive, then Datach'i (née Joseph Fraioli) is the guy for you. His debut album opens with what sounds like a breakbeat loop run through a series of flanges and filters, creating a sound so distorted that what were once pitchless beats end up sounding harmonized (harmonized by a coked-up space alien, mind you, but harmonized nonetheless). More surprising is the second track, which can best be described as what *Discreet Music* would have sounded like if Brian Eno suffered from Tourette's Syndrome—it's basically a genuinely beautiful chord progression rendered in cheesy, faux-analog synth tones over a churning, burping drum and bass rhythm track. By track three you're listening to some sort of strange, '50s-era porno recitation and you know that there's no point in thinking about any of this—you're just going to have to turn off your mind and let this guy have his way with it. The two parts of "VCR Powered Carcass" both sound like Skinny Puppy, Ministry, and Roni Size thrown together in a blender; "Leonard Park" is actually kind of funky, which is something of a relief, while "Fried Notes" deconstructs, hilariously, the "Mexican Hat Dance." Listening to some of these tracks on earphones may damage you physically, whereas listening to them on speakers may damage you socially. Proceed with caution. Do proceed, though. —*Rick Anderson*

**We Are Always Well Thank You** / Aug. 22, 2000 / Caipirinha ♦♦♦
More inspired insanity from the King of Intelligent Dance Music (or, as the cognoscenti call it, IDM). Datach'1 works somewhere this side of the abstract groove, revelling in deeply weird (and sometimes downright abrasive) tones and sonorities while almost always leaving a thread of rhymic continuity in the mix. Sometimes, as on the slightly distressing "Free in a Box" and the surprisingly melodic "Merrily We Roll Along", he incorporates breakbeats that are hyperkinetically funky even by jungle standards; on the latter track, a splatter of phase-shifted and distorted sine waves leads into a 168 bpm breakbeat overlaid with a sweet and gently pretty chord progression. On the other hand, "Clown Man" is grooveless without being strictly arrhythmic, and the tweaked, jittery beats on "Memorandum" seem only tangentially related to the moody chords they're up against. That doesn't make those tunes less interesting, just a bit less immediately attractive. But attraction to this sort of music seems to be a matter of genetic predisposition more than anything else—there are some people who simply can't help but be captivated by the deep structural contradictions, the sensuous textures and the astringent tonal qualities of Datach'i's music. There are others for whom it's nothing but supremely irritating noise. Of course, some people feel that way about Bach, too. Their loss. Either way, in the end, this album illustrates how the ideas presented on Datach'i's debut have blossomed into a more realized sound featuring a considerable number of melodic passages in place of the often nursery rhyme-like sounds found on the preceding album. —*Rick Anderson*

## Datacide

b. 1977, Frankfurt, Germany
*Producer / Experimental Ambient, Experimental Techno, Ambient Techno*
Datacide is a side project involving ambient/experimental producers Uwe Schmidt (aka Atom Heart) and Tetsu Inoue. Although their first release on the Frankfurt-based Fax label fit squarely into the analog-heavy ambient and trance styles closely associated with that label, subsequent releases on Schmidt's Rather Interesting label have moved increasingly toward a breezy lounge/electronica fusion, combining elements of kitsch, psychedelia, jazz, and exotica with the pair's quirky rhythms and lush digital ambience. Their third full-length CD under the name, *Flowerhead*, is also the only Rather Interesting title to be licensed for release in the US (it was reissued by Asphodel in 1996).

Schmidt and Inoue began recording together in 1993, after Inoue met Schmidt while vacationing near Frankfurt (where Schmidt lived at the time). They recorded a pair of dance tracks for 12" release on Fax, followed by a full-length which mixed more uptempo trance-oriented techno with beatless ambient and experimental soundscapes. A second Datacide release in a similar, though more ambient vein (and titled, of course, *Datacide II*) appeared the following year before Inoue and Schmidt switched gears for their first Rather Interesting release, *Flowerhead*, an album of laidback ambient-jazz. *Ondas*, released in 1996, upped *Flowerhead*'s weirdness factor significantly, dwelling for most of the album in channel separation experiments which fused the rhythmic abstraction of Atom Heart's recent solo work with the fizzier, more left-field of Inoue's electronic treatments (Inoue's girlfriend, Ingrid, even makes an extended cameo on "mouth trumpet"). —*Sean Cooper*

● **Flowerhead** / 1995 / Asphodel ♦♦♦♦
A mellow, psychedelic jazz/ambient masterpiece, *Flowerhead* leaves most of the dance-music dabblings of Atom Heart and Inoue's earlier releases behind, blending subtle basslines and brushed percussion with shimmering melodies and immersive ambient atmospheres. —*Sean Cooper*

**Ondas** / Nov. 18, 1996 / Rather Interesting ♦♦♦♦
Atom Heart's fourth full-length collaboration with Tetsu Inoue under the Datacide name develops further the "future lounge" concept of the previous, *Flowerhead*, mixing Latin percussion and Baxter-esque string-sweeps with quirky rhythms, jazzy keys-work, and goofy in-joke tangents (Dandy Jack's silly discotheque story; Tetsu's girlfriend Ingrid's mouth-trumpet solo; etc.). The frothy brew is intoxicating, however, and the more organized, "song-y" of the cuts here rate among Atom Heart's finest beatoriented material. —*Sean Cooper*

## Miles Davis

b. May 25, 1926, Alton, IL, d. Sep. 28, 1991, Santa Monica, CA
*Trumpet, Leader, Composer / Jazz-Rock, Modal Music, Hard Bop, Post-Bop, Fusion, Cool, Bop, Jazz-Funk, Hip-Hop*
By the late '60s, Miles Davis had proved himself the major innovator in modern jazz, either spearheading or contributing heavily to most every major movement in jazz since the mid-'40s, from bop to cool to hard bop to modal jazz. With the rise of the new rock consciousness however, and the fragmentation of the jazz scene into mainstream soul-inspired pop or the atonal musings of free jazz, Miles made the most radical change of direction in his career. Beginning with the 1969 landmarks *In a Silent Way* and *Bitches Brew*, and extending to his temporary retirement just seven years later, he stretched out to record almost two dozen studio and live LPs of exploratory music which led the way for jazz to enter the modern age of rock.

Aptly titled fusion or jazz-rock, the new music married the rhythms and amplification techniques of rock 'n' roll with the focus on extemporaneous soloing and group interplay that jazz had made famous. Influenced by the psychedelic inclinations of Jimi Hendrix, Miles Davis confounded fans and purists by masking his trumpet solos with open techniques, wah-wah effects and other means of electrification (he even doubled on organ occasionally). And the trumpeter was just one voice amid the din of a steady backbeat (gained from his favorite soul acts like James Brown and Sly & the Family Stone) and an approach to group soloing which often resulted in hyperkinetic, total improvisation. As his music progressed, Miles shed his jazz sidemen for a band composed largely of African-minded percussionists and rock musicians, a conglomeration of artists better able to engage in the intense, free-form groove music which extended to side-long excursions in the 25- to 30-minute range—usually edited down from jams which originally lasted for hours on end.

That editing process proved very important for ideas about the future direction of music. Instead of the one-take live recordings relied on by jazz artists since the beginning of the century and the simple overdubbing of effects employed by psychedelic rock bands of the time, Miles Davis recorded *everything* his band played during marathon jam sessions, then worked with long-time producer/engineer Teo Macero to sort through material, editing and splicing tapes together for eventual release. The techniques were influenced by *musique concrète* and Stockhausen's ideas about "moment" composition, in which the usual progression of a piece of music is de-stressed in favor of a quasi trance-state style of composition. Though similarly dark in tone and dense in rhythm, his 1969-75 LPs ranged from the distorted acid-blues of *A Tribute to Jack Johnson* to the wild wah-wah funk of *On the Corner*, *Agharta*'s Afro-mystic ambience and *Get Up with It*'s seeming isolationist depression. Many of Miles' more fiery recordings worked a heavy feedback groove picked up in the '80s by industrial-funk groups like Material and, indeed, much of New York's downtown scene. The more muted portions of the fusion years were a heavy influence on the notion of Fourth World and ambient music advanced by Brian Eno and Jon Hassell. In fact, Miles Davis' impact on modern music is so omnipresent as to be often unrecognizable considering the diverse styles and sounds he influenced. —*John Bush*

**This Is Jazz, Vol. 38: Electric** / Dec. 28, 1967-1984 / Sony ♦♦♦
While it's all well and good to have a separate electric music sampler for Miles Davis, this one just won't do. It comes accurately with his very first electric date, featuring Herbie Hancock on Wurlitzer electric piano on "Water in the Pond," and follows the early trail a bit further. But then the CD skips blithely over the three most important electric albums of all, *In a Silent Way*, *Bitches Brew*, and *Jack Johnson*—which is kind of like writing a pocket history of 20th-century Russia and omitting the 1917 Revolution. We land in the '70s with two unrepresentative tracks from *Live-Evil* and *Get Up with It*, a live take of "Spanish Key/The Theme" from the *Fillmore West*, and nothing from the 1972-75 "jungle" band. Davis' "unretirement" in the '80s is dispatched with "Aida," the catchy "U 'n' I" and the essence of his act at the time, "Human Nature." Even the scrambled electric LP from *The Columbia Years* box sums up this era better than this single CD, which though chronologically sequenced, is riddled with too many crucial gaps to be recommended. —*Richard S. Ginell*

**Miles in the Sky** / Jan. 16, 1968-May 17, 1968 / Columbia ♦♦♦♦
The fifth of the six studio albums by the second classic quintet found Davis continuing to move ahead. For the first time, Herbie Hancock is heard a bit on electric piano, guitarist George Benson guests on "Paraphernalia," and the extended performances were just beginning to open themselves to the influences of pop and rock music. This important set of music can be seen as either early fusion, the beginning of the end of the Miles Davis quintet, or both. —*Scott Yanow*

**Filles de Kilimanjaro** / Jun. 19, 1968-Sep. 24, 1968 / Columbia ♦♦♦♦
The sixth and final studio album by Miles Davis' second classic quintet finds the group looking toward early fusion. Herbie Hancock (who doubles on electric piano) and bassist Ron Carter are replaced by Chick Corea and Dave Holland on the two selections from Sept. 24, 1968, although Wayne Shorter and drummer Tony Williams are still key members of Davis' band. The music is less esoteric than his music of a year or two earlier, with funky rhythms and hints at pop and rock music becoming more prevalent although not dominant yet. To many of the jazz purists, this was Miles Davis' final jazz album but to those with open ears toward electronics and danceable rhythms, this set was the predecessor of his next great innovation. —*Scott Yanow*

☆ **In a Silent Way** / Feb. 18, 1969 / Columbia ♦♦♦♦♦
The beginning of fusion (although other groups such as Gary Burton's Quartet with Larry Coryell had hinted strongly at it), this set found Miles Davis for the first time really combining jazz improvising with the rhythms and power of rock. On this LP, Davis jams with an octet (which includes the magical names of tenor-saxophonist Wayne Shorter, keyboardists Herbie Hancock, Chick Corea and Joe Zawinul, guitarist John McLaughlin, bassist Dave Holland, and drummer Tony Williams; all future bandleaders) on two lengthy side-long medleys. Those jazz purists with their minds closed toward electronics of any kind are advised to check out this fairly accessible date before tackling *Bitches Brew*. The strong solos on this early fusion classic might very well win them over. —*Scott Yanow*

★ **Bitches Brew** / Aug. 19, 1969-Aug. 21, 1969 / Columbia ♦♦♦♦♦
No jazz collection is complete without *Bitches Brew*, an influential set that was one of the first successful attempts to form a new music (soon termed fusion) by combining jazz solos with rock rhythms. "Miles Runs the Voodoo Down" is the most memorable of the six lengthy selections, featuring a fascinating ensemble with Davis' trumpet, Wayne Shorter's soprano, Bennie Maupin's bass clarinet, guitarist John McLaughlin, the keyboards of Chick Corea and Larry Young (Joe Zawinul is on some of the other selections), Dave Holland and Harvey Brooks on basses, drummers Jack DeJohnette, Charles Alias, and Lenny White, and percussionist Jim Riley. Not for the close-minded, this music brought many rock listeners into jazz and gave jazz musicians new possibilities to explore. —*Scott Yanow*

**The Complete Bitches Brew Sessions (August 1969-February 1970)** / Aug. 19, 1969-Feb. 6, 1970 / Columbia/Legacy ♦♦♦♦
Columbia's continuing summation of the career of Miles Davis through lavish box-set reissues resumed in 1998 with *The Complete Bitches Brew Sessions*, a four-disc set including all the music from the original 1970 double album *Bitches Brew* plus over two additional hours of music from the six-month period during which the album was recorded. (Some of those tracks were previously released on compilations like *Big Fun* and *Circle in the Round*, but almost one-third of the material lay unissued until this release.) The music is simply fabulous—the simultaneous birth and peak of jazz-rock/fusion, with a host of major players (John McLaughlin, Chick Corea, Joe Zawinul, Wayne Shorter, Jack DeJohnette) and many innovations. There is a bit more evidence of tape hiss than in Columbia's last American remastering of the album, but the revelations of depth and timbre more than make up for it. Though the unreleased selections are distinctly inferior to those released on *Bitches Brew*, "Yaphet," "Corrado" and "Trevere" are intriguing jam sessions that reveal much about the creative process between Davis and producer Teo Macero during recording. Unlike Columbia's previous sets in the series (one treating Davis' period of collaboration with Gil Evans and one featuring the music of his second classic quintet), the *Bitches Brew* sessions lend themselves well to a box set of this type—presenting the music in chronological order does no harm to original LP configurations as it did on previous sets, and the music here is another glowing testament to Miles Davis' importance to the development of jazz in 1969, as in 1949. —*John Bush*

**Big Fun** / Nov. 19, 1969-Jun. 12, 1972 / Columbia ♦♦
This double album features Davis on four side-long jams taken from different sessions during 1969-72. "Great Expectations" features most of the players from *Bitches Brew* along with two sitarists and "Ife" has the trumpeter's 1972 band (with saxophonists Carlos Garnett and Sonny Fortune) but the two best tracks ("Lonely Fire" and "Go Ahead John") are from 1970; the latter features the quintet of Davis, Steve Grossman on soprano, guitarist John McLaughlin, bassist Dave Holland, and drummer Jack Dejohnette. Very interesting if erratic music, it's not essential but fans of Davis' fusion years will enjoy much of it. —*Scott Yanow*

**Live-Evil** / Feb. 6, 1970-Dec. 19, 1970 / Columbia ♦♦♦♦
The first in a continuing series of double-LP extravaganzas released only in Japan in the early '70s, *Live-Evil* mixes four studio tracks from 1970 with four live ones taken from a Washington, D.C. performance in December of that year. Amidst heavy competition, the live tracks—including "What I Say," "Sivad" and "Funky Tonk"—are the highlights, featuring some of Davis' best playing of the decade, plus aggressive work on extended solo spots by John McLaughlin on guitar, Keith Jarrett on keyboards, and Jack DeJohnette on drums. Alternating chaotic deep-groove passages with a few more atmospheric, *Live-Evil* held up for two decades as one of the great import-only Miles Davis albums, until it was reissued in America by Columbia/Legacy in 1997. —*John Bush*

**A Tribute to Jack Johnson** / Apr. 7, 1970 / Columbia ♦♦♦♦
Davis's odd soundtrack for a documentary on the boxer Jack Johnson did not really fit the movie (it was far too modern) but stands alone very well as a strong piece of music. On this straight reissue of the original LP, the two lengthy jams (25-minute-plus versions of "Right Off" and "Yesternow") feature fine playing by a sextet comprised of Davis' trumpet, Steve Grossman's soprano sax, keyboardist Herbie Hancock, guitarist John McLaughlin, electric bassist Michael Henderson, and drummer Billy Cobham. Even listeners who write off the fusion years will find moments of interest on this set. —*Scott Yanow*

**Miles Davis at Fillmore: Live at the Fillmore East** / Jun. 17, 1970-Jun. 20, 1970 / Columbia/Legacy ♦♦♦
The four set-long excursions on this double CD reissue (which for the first time lists the titles of the songs) are full of self-indulgent moments, particularly when Chick Corea and Keith Jarrett almost literally battle each other on their arsenal of electric keyboards but there are also hot solos from Miles Davis and occasionally saxophonist Steve Grossman. This occasionally out-of-control set (which also includes electric bassist Dave Holland, drummer Jack DeJohnette and percussionists Airto) will not win any converts to Davis' fusion years but it does have its humorous (check out the way each night ends with a spaced-out "The Theme") and grooving moments. —*Scott Yanow*

**On the Corner** / Jun. 1, 1972-Jun. 6, 1972 / Columbia ♦♦♦
*On the Corner* is Miles Davis' most controversial album. Jazz purists detest the album, dismissing it out of hand for the very reason that its fans celebrate it—there are no fully-formed songs on the record, just funky rhythmic vamps. Davis assembled a large group of musicians, who aren't credited on the record, and had them play one groove, which demonstrated a heavy debt to Sly Stone. Davis rarely plays trumpet on the record and when he does, it is distorted and processed. Instead, he plays organ, blending into the dense, electric funk. None of the players take extended solos and all of the songs are brief, but improvisation isn't the point of the record. *On the Corner* is about funk and rhythm, not about jazz. With this record, Davis laid the foundation of the genre-blurring hip-hop and acid jazz revolutions in popular music in the '80s and '90s. —*Stephen Thomas Erlewine*

**Get Up with It** / Sep. 6, 1972-Oct. 7, 1974 / Columbia ♦♦♦
This double LP, featuring a variety of Miles Davis' electric ensembles of 1974, has plenty of variety, ranging from a sidelong dirge for Duke Ellington ("He Loved Him Madly") and a dumb but interesting "Red China Blues" to heated jams on "Honky Tonk," "Calypso Frelimo," and "Mtume." Although Davis plays organ rather than trumpet half the time, the dense ensembles and passionate improvisations are creative rather than predictable. —*Scott Yanow*

**Dark Magus** / Mar. 3, 1974 / Tristar ♦♦
The music on this double CD, released domestically for the first time in 1997, was only previously out in Japan and was formerly among the rarest of Miles Davis recordings. Featured is one of the trumpeter's most controversial bands, a noisy ensemble with three guitarists (Reggie Lucas, Pete Cosey, and Dominique Gaumont), electric bassist Michael Henderson, drummer Al Foster, percussionist Mtume, Dave Liebman on tenor, soprano and flute, and guest tenorman Azar Lawrence. The spontaneous music has plenty of repetitive funk sounds from the guitars and bits of aimless rambling, along with some strong moments from Davis and Liebman. If drastically edited, the double CD would have made a killer single disc, for there are some very interesting stretches when magic occurs, but these are often succeeded by over-long vamps. Worth checking out, but not essential. —*Scott Yanow*

**Agharta** / Feb. 1, 1975 / Columbia ♦♦
Recorded the same day as *Pangaea* but not up to its level, this two-LP set features Davis just prior to his six-year retirement. He actually sounds a bit weak on this set (although he takes a rare straightahead solo on "Interlude") but altoist Sonny Fortune has his moments. The dense and rockish ensembles (with the guitars of Pete Cosey and Reggie Lucas) will scare most jazz listeners away. —*Scott Yanow*

**Pangaea** / Feb. 1, 1975 / Columbia ♦♦♦♦
Although Davis' health was shaky at the time of this two-CD set (recorded the same day as the weaker *Agharta*), he has a few strong trumpet solos on these two very lengthy pieces ("Zimbabwe" and "Gondwana"); Davis would drift into retirement for six years shortly after this concert. The music is actually quite rewarding (at least it will be for listeners with open ears) with the dense ensembles and heated solos (Sonny Fortune on soprano, alto and flute and the guitars of Pete Cosey and Reggie Lucas) being quite dangerous, as opposed to the safe fusion of the '90s. *Pangaea* is the finest recording from the least-understood period of Davis's career (1971-75). —*Scott Yanow*

**Panthalassa: The Music of Miles Davis 1969-1974** / Feb. 16, 1998 / Sony ♦♦♦♦
Is it a form of creative blasphemy to alter not only the sequence but the sound of masterworks past? In music, though, the ends quite often justify the means, and grandmaster-mixer Bill Laswell did an undeniably haunting job of reconstructing swatches of Miles Davis' amazing electric music for acid jazz-mutated ears in 1998. Of course, Laswell could claim some license to do so, for the original tracks themselves were subjected to creative editing by Teo Macero. Divided roughly into four sections, *Panthalassa* is a dark, continuous, hour-long, chronological tone poem of remixed electric Davis, from a 15-minute capsule of *In a Silent Way* through 16 minutes from the *On the Corner* sessions and finally nearly half an hour of selections from *Get Up With It*. Offered access to the original multi-track tapes, Laswell sometimes deletes the rhythm sections, brings up hidden instruments, adds Indian and electronic drones from elsewhere on the tapes, constructs moody transitions, and most tantalizingly, unearths passages from the sessions that were being released for the first time. Indeed, the *On the Corner* section yields two new titles to the Davis discography, the highly colored rock/funk "What If" and a sinister march-like "Agharta Prelude Dub." In the end, despite the altered sonic landscape, Laswell accurately evokes in turns the lonely, exquisitely gleaming, nightmarish, despairing moods that Davis was exploring prior to his 1975 retirement, a still much-misunderstood period whose music is far too disturbing and probing to deserve the sellout label. —*Richard S. Ginell*

**Panthalassa: The Remixes** / May 25, 1999 / Sony ♦♦♦
*Panthalassa: The Remixes* is the logical extension of the previous year's *Panthalassa* project, in which long-time aficionado Bill Laswell restructured several Miles Davis recordings in similar fashion to the original production techniques pioneered by Teo Macero on Miles albums *In a Silent Way*, *On the Corner* and *Get Up with It*. Here, several dance producers are brought into the fold, not just to rearrange the material but remix it as well. The versions that work the best are done by producers unafraid to tamper with the tapes: hence, two separate reworkings of "Rated X" (from *Get Up with It*) result in darkside drum'n'bass burners by Doc Scott and Jamie Myerson that find the hyperkinetic energy in the original. The highlight of the entire project is an inexplicably vinyl-only bonus track by DJ Krush, who turns "Black Satin/On the Corner" into a minimalist beat odyssey with several different passages and effective scratching in all the right places. The only real disappointment on *Panthalassa: The Remixes* finds trip-hop deconstructionist DJ Cam creating an uneasy alliance by crudely inserting a loping breakbeat onto Miles' winsome solo from "In a Silent Way." Remix albums are often a mistake for both parties involved, but this one does work on several levels. —*John Bush*

## Roy Davis, Jr.

b. 1970, California
*Producer, DJ / Jazz-House, Garage, Club/Dance, House*
Added on board the Chicago house production team Phuture as a replacement for DJ Pierre, Roy Davis, Jr. later followed his mentor to New York and worked at Strictly Rhythm, recording his own singles for Force Inc., Big Big Trax and Power Music. Originally born in California, Davis moved to Chicago's south side early in his childhood. After being turned on by legendary acid-house pioneers like Phuture and Lil' Louis, he became a DJ and began recording as well with his first single, "20 Below," recorded for the Jack Trax label.

When DJ Pierre began producing for New York-based labels like Jive and Strictly Rhythm during the late '80s, he decided to leave both Chicago and Phuture. Davis spent a year in New York as well, working A&R and production for Strictly Rhythm before moving back to Chicago and stepping into DJ Pierre's place. Davis debuted with 1992-93 Phuture singles like "Rise from Your Grave" and "Inside Out," both of which were recorded for Strictly Rhythm. While Phuture was temporarily on hold in 1994, Davis began concentrating on his own productions again. He released *People from Mars* for Power Music, and recorded singles for Large and Big Big Trax as well. The *Big Big Trax Compilation* was collected in 1996, and *Roy Davis, Jr. & DJ Mix* appeared in 1998. A Phuture reunion (as Phuture 303) resulted in the 1998 album *Alpha & Omega*, after which Davis left the group once again. *Soul Electrica* followed on Peacefrog in 1999. —*John Bush*

• **Secret Mission** / 1995 / Power Music ♦♦♦♦
Over ten tracks, this double-LP set explores dub-house concepts that work equally well in the club and on headphones. —*John Bush*

**Big Big Trax Compilation** / Oct. 14, 1996 / Big Big Trax ♦♦
Davis, Jr.'s mix album for cold front works through deep, tribal, and jazzy house with tracks by Mateo & Matos, Jordan Fields, Kerri Chandler, and Davis himself. —*John Bush*

**Roy Davis, Jr. & DJ Mix** / Mar. 10, 1998 / K-Tel ♦♦♦
**Soul Electrica** / Sep. 6, 1999 / Peacefrog ♦♦♦

## Day One

f. Bristol, England
*Group / Club/Dance, Power Pop, Alternative Pop/Rock, Hip-Hop*

The Bristol-based electronic/rock group Day One consists of vocalist Phelim Byrne and multi-instrumentalist Donni Hardwidge. The duo began collaborating in the mid-'90s, blending the storytelling traditions of hip-hop and British folk along with a slew of musical influences, including jazz and classic rock. Day One's experiments coalesced into a three-song demo, a copy of which made its way to Massive Attack's 3D; soon after, Day One was signed to Melankolic, the pioneering trip-hop group's boutique label. While recording their debut album *Ordinary Man*, the group tried a variety of studios and producers before settling on Mario Caldato Jr., the Beastie Boys' producer of choice. *Ordinary Man* was co-released by Melankolic and Astralwerks in early 2000. —*Heather Phares*

● **Ordinary Man** / Feb. 29, 2000 / Astralwerks ◆◆◆◆

Day One's debut album, *Ordinary Man*, captures the group's unique fusion of folk and hip-hop storytelling traditions and eclectic electronic/acoustic arrangements. The album ranges from blue-eyed hip-hop like "Walk Now, Talk Now" to simple, affecting piano ballads like the title track, but Mario Caldato Jr.'s straightforward production and vocalist Phelim Byrne's appealing, unaffected singing and rapping hold it all together. Shuffling trip-hop beats provide a laidback foundation for most of the songs, but the group adds catchy, humorous lyrics and hooks on "Trying Too Hard" and "I'm Doing Fine," baggy-inspired keyboards on "Bedroom Dancing," and folky guitars on "Autumn Rain," adding to the album's diverse-yet-cohesive appeal. The cheerful, pop-tastic "In Your Life," the yearning, acoustic "Love on the Dole," and the breezy "Waiting for a Break" are among the other highlights of *Ordinary Man*, an impressive debut that places Day One in the ranks of groups like Cornershop and the Beta Band—able to reinvent the pop lexicon but never forgetting to write good songs in the process. —*Heather Phares*

## De La Soul

f. 1987, Amityville, Long Island, NY
*Group / Alternative Rap, Hip-Hop*

At the time of its 1989 release, De La Soul's debut album *3 Feet High and Rising* was hailed as the future of hip-hop. With its colorful, neo-psychedelic collage of samples and styles, and the Long Island trio's low-key, clever rhymes and their goofy humor, the album sounded like nothing else in hip-hop. Where most of their contemporaries drew directly from old school rap, funk, or Public Enemy's dense sonic barrage, De La Soul was gentler and more eclectic, taking in not only funk and soul, but also pop, jazz, reggae, and psychedelia. Though their style earned them critical raves and strong sales initially, De La Soul found it hard to sustain the momentum of their career in the '90s, as their alternative rap was sidetracked by the popularity of the considerably harder-edged gangsta rap.

De La Soul formed while the trio—Posdnous (born Kelvin Mercer, August 17, 1969), Trugoy the Dove (b. David Jude Joliceur, September 21, 1968), Pasemaster Mase (b. Vincent Mason, March 27, 1970)—were attending high school in the late '80s. The stage names of all of the members derived from in-jokes: Posdnous was an inversion of Mercer's DJ name, Sound-Sop; Trugoy was an inversion of Joliceur's favorite food, yogurt. De La Soul's demo tape, "Plug Tunin'," came to the attention of Prince Paul, the leader and producer of the New York rap outfit, Stetsasonic. Prince Paul played the tape to several colleagues and helped the trio land a contract with Tommy Boy Records.

Prince Paul produced De La Soul's debut album, *3 Feet High and Rising*, which was released in the spring of 1989. Several critics and observers labeled the group as a neo-hippie band, because the record praised peace and love, as well as proclaiming that this was the dawning of "the D.A.I.S.Y. age" (Da Inner Sound, Y'all). Though the trio was uncomfortable with the hippie label, there was no denying that the humor and eclecticism presented an alternative to the hardcore rap that dominated hip-hop. De La Soul quickly was perceived as the leader of a contigent of New York-based alternative rappers which also included A Tribe Called Quest, Queen Latifah, the Jungle Brothers, and Monie Love; all of these artists dubbed themselves the Native Tongues Posse.

For a while, it looked as if De La Soul and the Native Tongues Posse would eclipse hardcore hip-hop in terms of popularity. "Me Myself and I" became a Top 40 pop hit in the US (number one R&B), while the album reached No. 24 (No. 1 R&B) and went gold. At the end of the year, *3 Feet High and Rising* topped many best-of-the-year lists, including *The Village Voice*. With all of the acclaim came some unwanted attention, most notably in the form of a lawsuit by the Turtles. De La Soul had sampled the Turtles' "You Showed Me" and layered it with a French lesson on a track on *3 Feet High* called "Transmitting Live from Mars," without getting the permission of the '60s pop group. The Turtles won the case and the decision not only had substantial impact on De La Soul, but on rap in general. Following the suit, all samples had to be legally cleared before an album could be released. Not only did this have the end result of rap reverting back to instrumentation, thereby altering how the artists worked, it also meant that several albums in the pipeline had to be delayed in order for samples to clear. One of those albums was De La Soul's second album, *De La Soul is Dead*.

When *De La Soul Is Dead* was finally released in the spring of 1991, it received decidedly mixed reviews and its darker, more introspective tone didn't attract as big an audience as its lighter predecessor. The album peaked at No. 26 pop on the US charts, No. 24 R&B, and spawned only one minor hit, the No. 22 R&B single "Ring Ring Ring (Ha Ha Hey)." De La Soul worked hard on their third album, finally releasing the record in late 1993. The result, entitled *Buhloone Mindstate*, was harder and funkier than either of its predecessor, yet it didn't succumb to gangsta rap. Though it received strong reviews, the album quickly fell off the charts after peaking at No. 40, and only "Breakadawn" broke the R&B Top 40. The same fate greeted the trio's fourth album, *Stakes Is High*. Released in the summer of 1996, the record was well-reviewed, yet it didn't find a large audience and quickly disappeared from the charts. Four years later, De La Soul initiated what promised to be a three-album series with the release of *Art Official Intelligence: Mosaic Thump*. —*Stephen Thomas Erlewine*

★ **Three Feet High & Rising** / 1989 / Tommy Boy ◆◆◆◆◆

One of rap's most seminal and groundbreaking releases, De La Soul's *Three Feet High and Rising* proved to have as great an influence on alternative rap as Ice-T and N.W.A.'s recordings did on gangster rap. With this innovative and highly experimental debut album, the Long Island visionaries presented a cerebral alternative to hardcore rap's aggression and macho boasting. This softer approach to rap—both musically and lyrically—would have a tremendous influence on A Tribe Called Quest, Digable Planets, the Pharcyde, and other alternative rappers. Drawing on influences ranging from jazz to psychedelic rock and soul to '70s P-funk, De La doesn't hesitate to be abstract and complex. In fact, the album's lyrics aren't always very accessible. Like a lot of jazz, *Three Feet High and Rising* is a challenging CD that reveals more and more of its richness with repeated listening. —*Alex Henderson*

**De La Soul Is Dead** / May 13, 1991 / Tommy Boy ◆◆◆◆

De La Soul throws a curveball at listeners with its second album, *De La Soul Is Dead*, taking a slightly harder and tougher approach, but remaining highly musical, distinctive and recognizable. Though not quite as consistently appealing as the debut, De La Soul is still one of rap's most inviting acts, and remains quite experimental and unpredictable. *De La Soul Is Dead* is less lighthearted than *Three Feet High and Rising*, but offerings like "Oodles of O's" and "Pease Porridge" make it clear that the group can still be enjoyably quirky and eccentric. One song that definitely isn't amusing is "Millie Pulled a Pistol on Santa," an unsettling commentary on child molestation that cuts like a knife without preaching. Like the first album, *De La Soul Is Dead* is a very abstract and cerebral effort that requires several listenings to be fully appreciated. —*Alex Henderson*

**Buhloone Mindstate** / Sep. 21, 1993 / Tommy Boy ◆◆◆◆

Continually trying to live up to the revolution that was their debut, *Buhloone Mindstate* is a return to Daisy Age positive vibes. The beats are big, the samples are fresh, and the melodies are enticing. While the first two albums featured intros and sidelights along the way, *Buhloone Mindstate* has only fifteen tracks (eleven songs). With help from friends Guru, Maceo Parker, and Biz Markie, De La Soul approaches the perfection of *3 Feet High and Rising*, if not the initial effect. —*John Bush*

**Stakes Is High** / Jul. 2, 1996 / Tommy Boy ◆◆◆

Seven years after its debut album, De La Soul was still one of the most unpredictable and risk-taking groups in rap. On the excellent *Stakes Is High*, the Long Island natives continue to thrive on the abstract and the cerebral. Instead of the lightheartedness that characterized *Three Feet High and Rising*, De La favors a harder, tougher approach that's closer to second album *De La Soul Is Dead*. Jazz remains a strong influence for the group, who sample the improvised works of Milt Jackson, Lou Donaldson and Chico Hamilton as well as classic soul by the likes of the Commodores and Sly & the Family

Stone. This eclectic approach certainly didn't hurt the group's popularity in alternative rock and acid jazz circles, but in 1996, rap's hardcore seemed much more interested in gangster rap. —*Alex Henderson*

**Art Official Intelligence: Mosaic Thump** / Aug. 8, 2000 / Tommy Boy ✦✦
De La Soul came storming back after four years of recording inactivity—and practically a decade out of the hip-hop limelight—with a promise to release three full albums in a series they dubbed *Art Official Intelligence*. From the first volume, *Mosaic Thump*, it's clear that despite laudable ambitions, comeback albums should be focused and lean, not as flabby as this one. Unfortunately, the trio of Posdnuos, PA Mase, and Dave (formerly Trugoy the Dove) fall into the same trap they did on 1991's *De La Soul Is Dead;* an inventive, intelligent group attempts to prove themselves flexible enough to survive in a changing music world, and subsequently loses most of their appeal in the process. *Mosaic Thump* begins with "U Can Do (Life)," a surprisingly weak attempt at hip-hop soul. Posdnuos' raps are occasionally thoughtful and clever, but he seems obsessed with being as hardcore as DMX or Jay-Z. Aside from a few solid productions by outsiders (Ad Lib's "My Writes," Jaydee's "Thru Ya City," Rockwilder's "I.C. Y'All." with Busta Rhymes), most of *Mosaic Thump* was produced by De La Soul themselves, and the music is just as limpid and flat as the rapping. —*John Bush*

## Dead Can Dance

f. 1981, Australia
*Group / Spiritual, Dream Pop, Shoegazing, Alternative Pop/Rock, Ethnic Fusion*

Dead Can Dance combines elements of European folk music—particularly music from the Middle Ages and the Renaissance—with ambient pop and world-beat flourishes. Their songs are of lost beauty, regret and sorrow, inspiration and nobility, and of the everlasting human goal of attaining a meaningful existence.

Over the course of their career, Dead Can Dance has featured a multitude of members, but two musicians have remained at the core of the band—guitarist Brendan Perry and vocalist Lisa Gerrard. Perry had previously been the lead vocalist and bassist for the Australian-based punk band the Scavengers, a group who were never able to land a recording contract. In 1979, the band changed their name to the Marching Girls, but they still weren't able to sign a contract. The following year, Perry left the group and began experimenting with electronic music, particularly tape loops and rhythms. In 1981, Perry formed Dead Can Dance with Lisa Gerrard, Paul Erikson, and Simon Monroe. By 1982, Perry and Gerrard decided to relocate to London; Erikson and Monroe decided to stay in Australia.

Within a year, Dead Can Dance had signed a record deal with 4AD. In the spring of 1984, they released their eponymous debut album, comprised of songs the pair had written in the previous four years. By the end of the year, the group had contributed two tracks to *It'll End in Tears*, the first album by This Mortal Coil, and had released an EP called *Garden of the Arcane Delights*. In 1985, Dead Can Dance released their second album, *Spleen and Ideal*. The album helped build their European cult following, peaking at number two on the UK indie charts.

For the next two years, Dead Can Dance were relatively quiet, releasing only two new songs in 1986, both which appeared on the 4AD compilation *Lonely Is an Eyesore*. *Within the Realm of a Dying Sun*, the group's third album, appeared in 1986. In 1988, the band released their fourth album, *The Serpent's Egg* and wrote the score for the Agustin Villarongas film, *El Nino de La Luna*, which also featured Lisa Gerrard in her acting debut.

*Aion*, Dead Can Dance's fifth album, was released in 1990. Also in 1990, the group toured America for the first time, earning rave reviews. The following year, the group was involved in various festivals and theatrical productions. In 1992, the compilation *A Passage in Time* was released on Rykodisc, making it the first American release of Dead Can Dance music. Early in 1993, the group provided the score to *Baraka* and contributed songs to *Sahara Blue*. In the fall of 1993, the group released *Into the Labyrinth*, which became their first proper studio album to receive an American release. *Into the Labyrinth* was a cult success throughout the US and Europe. It was followed by another American and European tour, which was documented on the 1994 album and film, *Toward the Within*. In 1995, Lisa Gerrard released her debut solo album, *The Mirror Pool*. In the summer of 1996, Dead Can Dance released *Spiritchaser* and embarked on an international tour. —*Stephen Thomas Erlewine & Vladimir Bogdanov*

**Dead Can Dance** / 1984 / 4AD ✦✦✦
Early punk backgrounds and the like behind them, Perry and Gerrard created a striking, dour landmark in early-'80s atmospherics on their first, self-titled effort. Bearing much more resemblance to the similarly gripping, dark early work of bands like the Cocteau Twins and the Cure than to the later fusions of music that would come to characterize the duo's sound, *Dead Can Dance* is as goth as it gets in many places. Perry and Gerrard's wonderful vocal work—his rich, warm tones and her unearthly, multi-octave exaltations—are already fairly well established, but serve different purposes here. Thick, shimmering guitar and rumbling bass/drum/drum machine patterns practically scream their sonic connections to the likes of Robin Guthrie and Robert Smith, but they still sound pretty darn good for all that. It's not listed who is handling what instrumentation, but as performers, both are skilled if even then a touch derivative of previous trailblazers. When they stretch that sound to try for a more distinct, unique result, the results are astonishing. Gerrard is the major beneficiary here—"Frontier" explicitly experiments with tribal percussion, resulting in an excellent combination of her singing and the rushed music. Then there's the astonishing "Ocean," where guitar and chiming bells and other rhythmic sounds provide the bed for one of her trademark—and quite, quite lovely—vocal excursions into the realm of glossolalia. Perry in contrast tends to be matched with the more straightforward numbers of digital processing and thick, moody guitar surge; while numbers like "The Trial" and "A Passage in Time" are attractive, they're not Dead Can Dance at its true best. The album does end on a fantastic high note—"Musica Eternal," featuring a slowly increasing in volume combination of hammered dulcimer, low bass tones, and Gerrard's soaring vocals. As an indicator of where the band was going, it's perfect. CD reissues append the *Garden of the Arcane Delights* EP. —*Ned Raggett*

● **A Passage in Time** / Oct. 1991 / Rykodisc ✦✦✦✦
Or more accurately, it was only a matter of time before some sort of introduction to American audiences came about, especially following the band's successful tour of the States, so Rykodisc did the honors with this excellent compilation. It fulfills its brief in spades as a compilation for newcomers and then some—if there's one thing anyone needs to get from the duo, it's unquestionably this. While there's no chronological order to the collection, and the sequencing and arrangement from the original albums are unfortunately if inevitably lost, the choice of songs to feature is completely spot on. The biggest gap is the lack of anything from the self-titled debut and the *Garden of the Arcane Delights* EP, including the track the collection takes its title from. As such songs would jarringly stand out sonically from the rest, though, it's an understandable omission. Nearly every undisputed highlight from the band is included, covering both Perry's and Gerrard's contributions in equal measure. "The Host of Seraphim" here forms the centerpiece of an album rather than the start, while the one-two presentation of "In the Kingdom of the Blind the One-Eyed Are Kings" and "Fortune Presents Gifts Not According to the Book" works wonders here. Two new tracks help to round things out—while both aren't among the most deathless number the band have created, they're still worth the listening to. "Bird" piles on the ambient jungle noises and animals' calls and cries, but is saved from neo-New Age bathos by both its arrangement and the central combination of drumming and Gerrard's singing, here a touch lighter than normal. "Spirit," in contrast, predominantly features electric guitar and strong bass pulse, feeling a bit like a number from the very first album heavily stripped down with a new tension and beauty. Perry's singing suits the performance well, another excellent effort. —*Ned Raggett*

**Into the Labyrinth** / Sep. 14, 1993 / 4AD ✦✦✦
With a regular American deal in place for the first time ever, thanks to 4AD's linkup with the WEA conglomerate, Dead Can Dance made a splash on commercial alternative radio with "The Ubiquitous Mr. Lovegrove," the first single from *Into the Labyrinth*. Raga drones, a strange clattering beat, a haunting wind instrument, orchestral shading and Perry's ever-grand voice make it one of the more unlikely things to be heard on the airwaves in a while. It all begins with yet another jaw-dropper from Gerrard, "Yulunga (Spirit Dance)," with keyboards and her octave-defying voice at such a deep, rich level that it sweeps all before it. Wordless as always but never without emotional heft, the song slowly slides into a slow but heavy percussion piece that sounds a bit like "Bird" from *A Passage in Time*, but with greater impact and memorability. As the album slowly unwinds over an hour's length, the

two again create a series of often astounding numbers that sound like they should be millennia old, mixing and matching styles to create new fusions. Perhaps even more impressive is that everything was performed solely by Perry and Gerrard—no outside guests here, and yet everything is as detailed, lush and multifaceted as many of their past albums. New classics from the band appear almost track for track—Gerrard's a capella work on "The Wind That Shakes the Barley," the gentle beauty of "Ariadne," the rhythmic drive and chants of the title song. The conclusion is a slightly surprising but quite successful cover—"How Fortunate the Man With None," an adaptation of a classic Bertolt Brecht tune about the turn of fortune's wheel. Given a restrained arrangement and Perry's singing, it brings *Labyrinth* to a satisfying end. —*Ned Raggett*

**Towards the Within** / Oct. 25, 1994 / 4AD ♦♦♦♦
A large reason that Dead Can Dance tours and performances were so praised by hardcore fans lay in the band's welcome preference for unknown and otherwise unheard material, rather than simply rehashing expected numbers. Bootlegging of these tracks and performances was understandable and widespread, so involved and passionate was the band's following. 1994 finally brought an official release of this material via the astounding *Toward the Within*, the equal if not superior to the band's studio work. Recorded at a Los Angeles performance from the *Into the Labyrinth* tour, Perry, Gerrard and a five-person band, including Perry's brother Robert, *Toward* shows that the band's magic was clearly not simply something created in studio. Both lead performers are simply in excelsis, their vocal abilities hardly diminished by the rigors of the road—if anything, they sound even more inspired as a result. The range of instruments tackled is testimony to the group's breadth and reach, from the yang ch'in, a Chinese equivalent to hammered dulcimer, to a wide range of drums. As for the songs, only four of the fifteen had been officially released before, including fine takes on "Cantara," "Song of the Sibyl" and "Yulunga (spirit dance)." As for the numerous new delights, Perry has a number of solo or near-solo tracks he performs with acoustic guitar. These include the lovely "American Dreaming" and the mystical set-closing "Don't Fade Away," calling to mind Tim Buckley's sense of scope and vision via Perry's own unique vocal and musical approach. Gerrard's unquestioned highlight is the combination of "Tristan" and "Sanvean," the latter of which is an awesome, widescreen stunner that became an undisputed highlight on her solo debut *The Mirror Pool*. Perhaps the most astonishing numbers are "Rakim," featuring a striking intertwining of Perry and Gerrard's singing, and a version of Sinead O'Connor's "I Am Stretched On Your Grave" that redefines passionate drama. —*Ned Raggett*

**Spiritchaser** / Jun. 25, 1996 / 4AD ♦♦♦♦
What proved to be the final Dead Can Dance album was something of an unusual release—not as different to the rest of the group's work as the first album was, but in areas one can hear the duo wanting to stretch a bit more, however subtly. The tensions that had developed between Perry and Gerrard, personal and otherwise, didn't stop them from creating another fine album, though it has to be said that there's a strong sense the group had at last reached a logical end conclusion. *Spiritchaser* is essentially a 'Dead Can Dance' album as commonly conceived, with all the right elements, instead of the two continuing further explorations to see what else could be done—a summing up rather than a final push forward. Performers from *Toward the Within*, including Ronan O'Snodaigh and Lance Hogan, as well as past album guest Peter Ulrich, appear on some tracks here, most specifically on the opening "Nierika" and "Dedicace Outro." Both are laden with lots of percussion—unsurprising when one realizes that five performers are creating the drumming! Outside of Turkish clarinet by Renaud Pion on the Beatles-sampling "Indus," it's nothing but Perry and Gerrard once again throughout the album, with another combination and arrangement of multiple influences coming to bear. Both Perry and Gerrard are in fine voice throughout, their strong singing still the core centerpiece to their work, but there's almost an air of overfamiliarity to their approaches at this point (perhaps explaining Perry's greater experimentation on his solo debut years later). Interestingly, overtly rock elements like Morricone-styled electric guitar appear at points amid the usual melange of various percussion instruments and arrangements. It works better than might be thought, indicating where things might have gone next for the duo had the two continued on. *Spiritchaser* does at least end on a strong note with the slow, gentle mystery of "Devorzhum," a Gerrard-sung number that makes for a grand conclusion. —*Ned Raggett*

## Mike Dearborn
b. Chicago, IL
*Producer / Club/Dance, Techno, House*
Though he was born on Chicago's south side and grew up listening to house, Mike Dearborn's recordings for Djax-Up-Beats have been embraced more by the worldwide underground techno and tech-house axis. Though he began his production career in the late '80s, Dearborn retired early after being chiseled by a succession of greedy Chicago labels. A deal with the underground Dutch label Djax gave him another shot in 1991. His nine releases for the label—including club classics like "Strictly Underground," "Hardcore Swinger" and "Unpredictable"—made his name around the world as one of the toughest producers around. His full-length debut *Ready for War* dropped in 1999 on the Majesty label. He's also remixed Hardfloor, Joey Beltram and Steve Stoll. —*John Bush*

● **Ready for War** / Mar. 15, 1999 / Majesty ♦♦♦♦
A return for Dearborn from the hard, distorted sounds of his later Djax output, *Ready for War* is nonetheless just as hard a tech-house album as could be expected from the producer of classic Djax releases like "Chaotic State" and "Razorsharp." —*John Bush*

## Sean Deason
b. Detroit, MI
*Producer / Detroit Techno, Club/Dance, Techno*
After a period doing graphic design for hordes of Detroit techno releases, Sean Deason began working on production himself, first for K Hand's Acacia Records, but later for his own Matrix label under aliases such as Project X, Sounds Intangible Nature, Freq and X-313. His production style of driving minimalist funk with sublime, quintessentially Detroit melodies was later tempered by his inspiration from the British drum'n'bass scene, making Deason one of the few Motor City figures to integrate heavy breakbeats into his material.

It was while studying at the Center for Creative Studies that Deason first began working on sleeve-design for records by Juan Atkins, Derrick May, Kenny Larkin and A Guy Called Gerald, including labels like Generator, Acacia and Carl Craig's RetroActive. After being introduced to the basics of sequencing and drum-machine programming by Kenny Larkin and Dan Bell, Deason recorded his first EP, Code 3's "Cyclops," at K Hand's Acacia studios; the record earned airplay on local radio by another friend, Alan Oldham (aka DJ T1000). Deason also worked at Richie Hawtin's studios before forming his own Matrix Records. The label's early releases included singles by the Deason projects Freq and Sounds Intangible Nature as well as the mini-album compilation *Digital Sects* (featuring Larkin, Oldham and Claude Young among others). Signed to Studio !K7, Deason released his first solo album *Razorback* in 1996. One year later, Deason released the Freq LP *Heaven* through Britain's Distance Records. In mid-2000, his new full-length *Allegory & Metaphor* earned comparisons to the likes of Detroit Escalator Company's *Soundtrack 313* for its ability to capture the atmospheric feeling of a city (namely, Detroit) in sound. [See Also: Freq] —*John Bush*

**Razorback** / Oct. 21, 1996 / Studio !K7 ♦♦♦♦
Deason's debut album cycles through Detroit groove-techno with shadings of some intriguing old-school electro. The occasional appearance of drum'n'bass rhythms is more than welcome. —*John Bush*

● **Allegory & Metaphor** / 2000 / Intuit Solar/Matrix ♦♦♦♦
Sean Deason takes Detroit techno into extreme down-tempo territory where emotive subtleties lurk within the tranquil mist of this synth-heavy album. The Detroit artist seems more interested in the bedroom than the dancefloor on *Allegory & Metaphor;* while there are plenty of funky beats on songs such as "Ambience" and "Hip-hoptrak," these rhythms are dramatically eclipsed by the thick layers of serene synth tones that hover throughout the entirety of this record like the mammoth darkness of a bedroom's four corners blanketing the faint light of a flickering candle. For an idea of Deason's gifted ability to transform synth tones into heartfelt poetry, think back to the atmospheric tones of Derrick May's "Icon" or Plastikman's *Consumed* album. The modulating strings of *Allegory & Metaphor* aren't used as background decoration but rather as the most prominent sound on the album. For example, the album's centerpiece, "Zig," carries on for over ten minutes as a synth riff wiggles and worms in a zigzagging manner with heavy layers of phasing un-

til a slow fade into silence. The title track and its album-concluding reprise stand as the album's other noteworthy moments where music surpasses its status as art and enters the domain of sheer beauty. Following the epic nature of "Zig," some may be caught off guard by Deason's lone drum'n'bass track, "Psybadek One," yet for as out of place as one might assume drum'n'bass might sound on a ambient techno album, it surprisingly fits in rather well with the continuity of the album; the song's dense sheets of synth tones and subdued percussion make this possible. In the end, Deason's synth-heavy, bassline-light album challenges Richie Hawtin's synth-light, bassline-heavy *Consumed* album as the best ambient techno album to come from Detroit's long tradition of exceptional techno releases. —*Jason Birchmeier*

## Death in Vegas

**f.** 1994, London, England
*Group / Big Beat, Electronica, Trip-Hop, Club/Dance*
A DJ at the big beat melting-pot The Sunday Social alongside the Chemical Brothers and Jon Carter, Richard Fearless formed a studio project named Death in Vegas to pump out a similar type of audio adrenaline. With the helping hand of Steve Hellier, Fearless spent two years working on material for an LP, then released *Dead Elvis* on Britain's Concrete label in early 1997. After it was licensed for American distribution, the single "Dirt" became a moderate MTV hit later that year. Fearless gained a new production partner (Tim Holmes) as well as a few celebrity guests (Iggy Pop, Bobby Gillespie) for 1999's *The Contino Sessions*. —*John Bush*

**Dead Elvis** / Mar. 17, 1997 / Concrete ♦♦♦
Given Richard Fearless' moonlighting gig as a DJ, *Dead Elvis* is invested with an often overburdened need to push the right buttons, resulting in occasionally formulaic tracks—like the single "Dirt"—which leave little room for surprise. Where Fearless and Hellier opt to explore different waters, dub rhythms and funky acid instead of just sampled guitar riffs, the results are much more impressive. —*John Bush*

• **The Contino Sessions** / Sep. 14, 1999 / Time Bomb ♦♦♦♦
*The Contino Sessions* is a tribute to one of Richard Fearless' heroes, Andy Warhol, as well as the nearing end of the millennium. Fortunately, it's a departure from the big-beat bombast that often threatened to ruin Death in Vegas' first album, *Dead Elvis*. Instead, Fearless has crafted a much more mature record, indebted to the same darkside tendencies that influenced his first but here including music much more suited to the moods and themes. The vocal features for Bobby Gillespie ("Soul Auctioneer") and Iggy Pop ("Aisha") definitely contribute to the proceedings as well. —*Keith Farley*

## Christoph de Babalon

*Producer / Experimental Techno*
Likely due to his lack of bold image, Hamburg-based Christoph de Babalon was somewhat lost in the shuffle of his Digital Hardcore peers, crafting a varying array of largely instrumental tracks that either increase heart rates on the dancefloor or distort the senses in the bedroom. Regardless of his aims, his productions always favored simplicity over complexity and enjoyed a healthy love of doomed cragginess. De Babalon first gained exposure in 1994 for his *I Own Death* EP, which landed in the top ten of BBC DJ John Peel's year-end list. Peel's continued support did nothing to damage de Babalon's "one to watch" status through a clutch of EPs on his own Cross Fade Enter Tainment imprint and Digital Hardcore; his debut LP, *If You're Into it, I'm Out of It* was released in 1997. —*Andy Kellman*

• **If You're Into It, I'm Out of It** / Sep. 8, 1997 / Digital Hardcore ♦♦♦♦
Given the space that a 70-minute double record provides, Christoph de Babalon is given the room he needs to stretch out properly. His EPs are respectable on their own, but his ideas are too numerous and vast to be constricted by EP lengths. The 15 minutes of "Opium" recall Aphex Twin's *Selected Ambient Works, Vol. II*, but stripped of all sense of beauty. Beatless, the track is full of slightly oppressive drones and sampled laughing; the stretched, distorted, and looped cackles surge like waves for an extended length. Much of what follows is nasty drum'n'bass, perhaps qualifying as "junkle". It doesn't quite reach the levels of extremity that the remainder of the DHR roster is prone to. That doesn't mean it's soothing, and one thing the LP has going for it is a resistance to formula and gimmickry. The lone common thread is that everything gets covered in silt. No one can doubt the sense-assaulting capabilities, but they're not achieved by turning every knob to 11.

That also separates the record from the rest of the Digital Hardcore catalog. It might not be as direct, visceral, or punishing, but the soundwaves are just as renegade and commanding of your attention. Most indicative track title: "Nostep." —*Andy Kellman*

## Decoder

**f.** 1995, London, England
*Group / Jungle/Drum'N'Bass, Club/Dance*
Like their more common alias Technical Itch, the work of Darren Beale and Mark Caro as Decoder skirts the leading edge of progressive drum'n'bass, incorporating the moodier elements of jump-up and techstep with a nod toward drum-twisting junglists such as Dom & Roland and the Penny Black label. Although the duo have deepest roots in the late-'80s hardcore breakbeat scene, their material both apart and together has tended toward the darkside, combining dense, unsettling atmospherics with complex, bruising drum patterns and deep subbass groans. In addition to Decoder and Technical Itch (the latter coming from their Bristol-based Tech Itch recording studio), Caro and Beale have also recorded as Kutta (for Rough Tone), T.I.C. (for Back2Basics), and Alpha Proxima (for Au Toi).

The pair's earliest tracks came toward the peak end of the UK hardcore scene; both Beale and Caro were noted DJs, with Beale's recorded work as Orca adding to his notoriety. Introduced by a mutual friend, they released their first record together as Plasmic Life on Bizzy B's Brain Records, and by the early '90s were moving away from the conventions of hardcore, following breakbeat into the less static realms of darkside and hardstep jungle. Still only a part-time collaboration, the pair's partnership deepened after Omni Trio's Rob Haigh heard a Tech Itch track on Kenny Ken's Kiss FM show, leading to their signing with Haigh's home-base Moving Shadow in 1996. The pair produced a number of singles as Technical Itch for the label that same year, with scores of tracks as Decoder and T.I.C. continuing to appear on their own and other labels, marking the pair as one of the more prolific (and increasingly influential) of the new crop. A 1998 Decoder full-length was their first LP out of the gate, though Tech Itch's *Diagnostics* followed one year later on Moving Shadow. —*Sean Cooper*

• **Dissection** / Nov. 2, 1998 / Hardleaders ♦♦♦♦
From the static-garbled vocal sample and sinister piano chords of the opener "Dissected," Decoder revels in the paranoid side of drum'n'bass. As on most solid jungle albums of the late '90s, the rhythms and drum programming don't impress quite as much as the synthetic basslines and effects, but *Dissection* is still worthy of a listen. —*John Bush*

## Deee-Lite

**f.** 1986, New York, NY, **db.** 1996
*Group / Club/Dance, House, Dance-Pop*
With the massive popularity of their hit single "Groove Is in the Heart," Deee-Lite brought the colorful sights and sounds of New York's club culture into the mainstream. Formed in 1986, the trio was led by vocalist Lady Miss Kier (born Kieren Kirby in Youngstown, Ohio) and fleshed out by a pair of DJs, Super DJ Dmitry (a classically-trained guitarist and Russian emigre born Dmitry Brill) and Jungle DJ Towa Towa (born Doug Wa-Chung in Tokyo, Japan).

Fusing house, techno, rap, ambient and funk music with an outrageous visual flair largely influenced by the drag-queen community (Kier's fondness for Fluevog platform shoes helped the '70s fashion revival gather steam), Deee-Lite became hugely popular among New York club denizens, and the trio's own unique cultural make-up earned them a following which ignored racial and sexual boundaries. In 1990, they debuted with the album *World Clique*, a crossover smash thanks to hits like the loping classic "Groove Is in the Heart" (featuring the fluid bass of Bootsy Collins and the saxophone of Maceo Parker) and "Power of Love."

With their 1992 follow-up *Infinity Within*, Deee-Lite's music turned overtly political as songs touched base with hot topics like the environment, safe sex and democracy. Towa Towa left the group soon after; rechristened Towa Tei, he released his solo debut *Future Listening* in 1995. Kier and Dmitry, meanwhile, enlisted DJ Ani for 1994's *Dewdrops in the Garden*, a sensual outing influenced by the growing rave culture. After the release of 1996's remix album *Sampadelic Relics and Dancefloor Oddities*, Deee-Lite disbanded. —*Jason Ankeny*

• **World Clique** / Aug. 1990 / Elektra ♦♦♦♦
Deee-Lite's first and most consistent album, *World Clique* blends DJ Dmitry's

and DJ Towa Tei's groovy, neo-retro house beats with Lady Miss Kier's sultry voice. The result is a nonstop dance album with as much artistic integrity as booty-shakin' power. Even though "Groove Is in the Heart" was the breakout hit from this album, tracks like "Smile On," "What Is Love?," and "World Clique" make this one of the best dance albums of the '90s. —*Heather Phares*

**Infinity Within** / Jun. 23, 1992 / Elektra ♦♦
*Infinity Within* is Deee-Lite's difficult second album. The group's social activism overtakes their instinctive infectiousness, producing well-intentioned but not especially memorable tracks like "I Had a Dream I Was Falling Through a Hole in the Ozone Layer" and "Rubber Lover." —*Heather Phares*

**Dewdrops in the Garden** / Aug. 2, 1994 / Elektra ♦♦♦♦
*Dewdrops in the Garden* sees DJ Towa Tei take a vacation from the band, replaced with DJ On-E—just one of the album's not-so-subtle rave references. The tracks on *Dewdrops in the Garden* are either pseudo-rave instrumentals or witty, funky showcases for Lady Kier's rich vocals. While it's somewhat inconsistent, songs like "Apple Juice Kissin'," "Picnic in the Summertime" and "Call Me" radiate with the group's innate charisma. —*Heather Phares*

**Sampladelic Relics & Dancefloor Oddities** / Oct. 29, 1996 / Elektra ♦♦
*Sampladelic Relics & Dancefloor Oddities* is a collection of remixes of classic Dee-Lite tracks, including "Groove is in the Heart" and "Power of Love." The bulk of the compilation consists of new mixes, and while they do help update Dee-Lite's music for late-'90s dance-clubs, they don't have the visionary power of the original versions—or the remixes from the early '90s, for that matter—making it of interest only to dedicated fans of the group. —*Stephen Thomas Erlewine*

## DeeJay Punk-Roc

b. 1971, Brooklyn, NY
*Producer / Big Beat, Trip-Hop*
DeeJay Punk-Roc was born in Brooklyn, New York back in 1971. The youngest of 6 children, Punk-Roc cut his teeth on the funky sounds of such '70s and '80s stars as Parliament, Barry White, the Isley Brothers, Sugar Hill Gang and Grandmaster Flash; he also began DJing at parties. A troubled teen, he dropped out of high school at 16 years of age, but soon enlisted in the United States Military to put his life back on track. Being stationed in Japan, Germany, and England helped broaden Punk-Roc's mind, and it was after his stint with the military that a friend turned him onto the wonders of writing and recording music. After DJing at a series of parties in a neighborhood school park, he recorded the original track "My Beatbox" for Airdog Recordings (Punk-Roc's UK label). His debut full-length, *ChickenEye*, was released in Britain in mid-1998, and picked up for US distribution through Epic by autumn; it was praised as "the *OK Computer* you can breakdance to" by *Vox* magazine. The mix album *Anarchy in the USA* followed in 1999. —*Greg Prato*

● **ChickenEye** / May 18, 1998 / Independiente ♦♦♦♦
On his debut full-length, *ChickenEye*, DeeJay Punk-Roc introduces his original dance-rich sound. The songs reflect Punk-Roc's specialties—dance/electronic, funk, jazz, and hip-hop, with a production that jumps from retro to current in the blink of an eye. While it was meant to be played on the dancefloor, *ChickenEye* succeeds on the strength of its songwriting; you don't have to be a dance guru to appreciate the irresistible beats and electro-sounds. Featuring Punk-Roc's first-ever single, "My Beatbox," and the other tracks are often just as enjoyable—"Far Out," "No Meaning," and "The World Is My Ashtray" are all tasty dance ditties. By touching upon so many musical styles, DeeJay Punk-Roc turns in an impressive debut. —*Greg Prato*

**Anarchy in the USA** / Jun. 15, 1999 / Moonshine Music ♦♦
Deejay Punk Roc's very own mix album from Moonshine presents a series of big-beat anthems in waiting from Lo-Fidelity Allstars ("Lazer Sheep Dip Funk"), Trinity Hi-Fi ("TV Dinner for One"), Liquitek ("Pheelin' Phased"), Expansion Union ("Worldwide Funk"), and a remix of Roc's own "I Hate Everybody." He only reaches into the back of the crates for one genuine old-school jewel—the 45 King's "1-900 Number"—and the preponderance of big-beat material does weigh the collection down in spots. —*John Bush*

## Deep Dish

f. 1992, Washington, D.C.
*Group / Progressive House, Club/Dance, House*
Initially pigeon-holed as deep-house producers though their blueprint for house music sweeps across trance, techno, and sub-basement dub, the Iranian-American duo known as Deep Dish produced a multitude of club staples during the '90s while harvesting a stellar series of productions for their labels (Deep Dish, Yoshitoshi, Fast Food, and Middle East) by members of the ever-growing Washington, D.C. dance community. While most of Dubfire and Sharam's productions have the epic, grandiose feeling that ties many a house track to its disco forebear, the duo's knack for tight programming and genre-blending have carried them above many of their dance-chart compatriots.

Both Ali "Dubfire" Shirazinia and Sharam Tayebi were born in Iran, though their paths first crossed at a 1991 dance event in Washington, D.C.; both were immersed in the local DJ scene and working part-time at retail jobs they hated. They set up Deep Dish Records in 1992 and debuted with the production "A Feeling" by Moods. In 1993, an old schoolmate of Ali's named Brian Transeau recorded "A Moment of Truth" and "Relativity" for the label; both singles spread the Deep Dish message on dancefloors, and a link with Detroit producer Carl Craig (with whom they swapped mixes) helped the pair's street credibility. By 1994, Dubfire and Sharam were ruling as kings of the D.C. house scene, and had set up the sub-label Yoshitoshi for releases by like-minded compatriots Submarine, Satori, Alcatraz, and Hani. That same year, DJ legend Danny Tenaglia convinced Tribal UK Records to sign Deep Dish for its new Tribal America subsidiary, and the duo hit the dance charts with productions like "High Frequency" and "Casa de X." Deep Dish also made their full-length mix debut in 1995, taking charge of compilations for Tribal America (*Penetrate Deeper*) and Slip'N'Slide (*Undisputed*).

The 1995 single "Hideaway" by De'lacy practically made Deep Dish's career on a commercial and mainstream-dance level; their remix stormed the pop charts and earned them boatloads of additional remix work for Michael Jackson, Tina Turner, Janet Jackson, Pet Shop Boys, Kristine W., Everything But the Girl, the Beloved and the Shamen—Deep Dish even reworked Brian Transeau's collaboration with Tori Amos, "Blue Skies." Dubfire and Sharam added to their mix-album résumé with another Tribal America collection (1996's *In House We Trust*) plus one for Deconstruction (*Cream Separates*) one year later. Just when Deep Dish appeared to be content with releasing a mix album or two each year, the duo released their proper studio debut, *Junk Science*, in 1998. The double-disc mix collection *Yoshiesque* followed a year later and *Renaissance Ibiza* was issued in August 2000. —*John Bush*

**DJs Take Control** / Jun. 3, 1996 / One ♦♦♦

● **Junk Science** / Jul. 6, 1998 / Deconstruction ♦♦♦♦
*Junk Science*, by the Washington, DC duo Deep Dish, was praised by many as one of 1998's best dance albums, and it's easy to understand why. Band members Ali Sirazinia and Sharam Tayebi prove to be masters of the dancefloor, composing tracks that contain many variations in style, as well as unpredictable sonic surprises. Instead of sticking to one dance style as many of today's artists do, Deep Dish incorporate such far-reaching sounds as jazz horns ("Chocolate City [Love Songs])," progressive house ("Sushi"), classic Depeche Mode ("My Only Sin"), and Middle Eastern ("Persepolis"). Also included is a cameo by Everything But the Girl vocalist Tracey Thorn on "The Future of the Future (Stay Gold)" and Deep Dish's 1997 dance smash "Stranded." The band made a conscious effort to move forward musically and look to the future on *Junk Science*, and they've succeeded with a consistent album that's heavy on wonderful sonic experiments. —*Greg Prato*

**Yoshiesque** / Dec. 7, 1999 / Yoshitoshi ♦♦♦♦
Easily as impressive a DJ team as they are at production and remixing, Deep Dish trips through futurist house and R&B with the double-disc mix collection *Yoshiesque*. From the interstellar ambience of the set opener "Dancing in Outer Space" by Atmosfear (remixed by Masters at Work) to deep-groove techno on Ian Pooley's mix of Chaser's "Tall Stories" to the smashing hi-NRG house of their own "Mohammad Is Jesus" to the dizzying trance of S.O.L.'s "Quantensprung" into Underworld's "Jumbo," Deep Dish presents so many attractive angles on electronic dance that boredom—always relevant when listening to a two-and-a-half-hour mix album on headphones or in the car—becomes practically a dead issue. The duo balances faceless-house producers with more rock-friendly groups like Fluke, Lo-Fidelity Allstars, and they even throw in a couple of oldies hits (a Quiver remix of Culture Club's "Do You Really Want to Hurt Me" and the Armand Van Helden remix of War's "Slippin' Into Darkness"). Even while Deep Dish's own production album *Junk Science* occasionally failed to deliver on the promise of perhaps the best track-by-track producers in house music, *Yoshiesque* proves they may be the best mixers as well. —*John Bush*

## Deep Forest

f. 1992, France

*Group / Ambient House, Club/Dance, Ethnic Fusion, Dance-Pop*

Innovatively fusing traditional ethnic musics with state-of-the-art rhythms, the work of Deep Forest was best typified by their 1993 smash "Sweet Lullaby," which brought together the contemporary sounds of ambient techno with the haunting voices of the Pygmies of the central African rain forest. The project was primarily the work of the French keyboardists and programmers Eric Mouquet and Michael Sanchez; after the latter returned from Africa with boxes of records he'd picked up across the continent, he and Mouquet began sampling the native sounds for use with their atmospheric dance tracks, and with the aid of producer Dan Lacksman, their eponymous debut LP appeared in 1993. Propelled by the international hit "Sweet Lullaby," *Deep Forest* was a surprise success; Mouquet and Sanchez soon began work on a follow-up, this time exploring such areas as Mongolia, India and Hungary, recording several tracks with singer Marta Sebestyen. The resulting album, *Boheme*, appeared in 1995; the third Deep Forest record, *Comparsa* followed in 1998, with *Live in Japan* appearing a year later. *—Jason Ankeny*

• **Deep Forest** / May 1993 / Epic ♦♦♦♦

Sampled Baka Pygmy voices flit across a synthesized environment like firefly blips from a video game or disembodied cartoon characters, but the crazy quilt cultural graft is less reminiscent of the giddy but ultimately depressing corporate merger of Bulgarian vocals and disco rhythms on Le Mystère's similarly assembled *From Bulgaria with Love* than it recalls the inestimable charms of Holger Czukay's blend of Arabic vocals and studio-recorded tracks on 1977's "Persian Love." Extraordinary vocals take primacy over workmanlike beats and textures, and the electronics verge toward moodiness instead of force-fitting the buoyancy of the vocals to new age tinkles. But the real genius is a witty manipulation of samples that ranges from the organic to the absurd. *—Bob Tarte*

**Boheme** / 1995 / 550 Music ♦♦♦

Much like Deep Forest's debut album, *Boheme* is a combination of club music and worldbeat. While the album is certainly danceable, it works better as trance-inducing mood music, although it isn't quite as consistent as the debut. *—Stephen Thomas Erlewine*

**Comparsa** / Feb. 17, 1998 / 550 Music ♦♦♦

Deep Forest's third album *Comparsa* continues the world-music potpourri Deep Forest is known for, though there is a pronounced focus on Latin and Caribbean grooves, provided by musicians from Cuba, Belize, Mexico and Madagascar, among other places. Although the nationalities present are truly global, the actual sound of Deep Forest hasn't changed that much, centering mostly on lush new age music with just a bit more of an edge than is usual, plus several tracks with whispered or restrained vocals. For fans of the debut album, *Comparsa* is a noteworthy, though hardly necessary, acquisition. *—John Bush*

## Deep Space Network

f. 1991, Heidelberg, Germany

*Group / Experimental Techno, Electronica, Ambient Techno*

David Moufang, along with figures such as Pete Namlook, Victor Sol, and Uwe Schmidt, is one of the more active members of the German experimental techno scene. His Source label has released single- and LP-length works from Vulva, Deep Space Network, Yoni, View to View, Move D, Reagenz, Spacetime Continuum, and Multiple Void Enjoyment. His own role in some of those projects (View to View, Reagenz, and his main ongoing collaboration with Jonas Grossman, Deep Space Network) has given him a high profile in the global experimental electronic music scene, resulting in his works being reissued by a number of labels, including Instinct and Reflective in the US Although the original releases of many of his recordings can be hard to track down, many of Moufang's and other Source artist's material have been collected on various-artist compilations, including the *Homeworks* and *Headshop* CDs, both released by Source.

Moufang's longest ongoing collaborative association has been with fellow Heidelberg resident Jonas Grossman. Together the pair have released albums as Earth to Infinity and Deep Space Network, as well as in combination with Dutch DJ/musician Dr. Atmo as I.F. on Namlook's Fax label. In 1994, Moufang released a solo CD through Fax, *Solitaire*, and the following year Namlook established the KM20 label as a Fax subsidiary dedicated to DSN and related projects. *Traffic*, the label's first release, was recorded live at the German Love Parade, an annual event somewhat known for spawning loads of live and DJ-set releases (usually of mediocre quality). *Deep Space Network Meets Higher Intelligence Agency* followed in 1997. That same year, Moufang recorded his first album as the head of an atmospheric jazz group named Conjoint. [See Also: Move D] *—Sean Cooper*

• **Big Rooms** / 1993 / Instinct ♦♦♦♦

One of the earlier successful combinations of ambient-leaning soundscapes and vinyl-sourced drum breaks, DSN's first full-length is not as chill as the project's name might suggest. Sill, the beats are atypical and never monotonous, and the tracks mesh instruments, electronics, samples, and rhythms with subtle flair. A nice introduction. *—Sean Cooper*

**Heavy Dose [EP]** / 1993 / Source ♦♦♦♦

Still a bit on the techno tip, with influences straying no farther than what's in the studio. Still, the result is far from monotonous, and a nice sense of dynamics holds throughout. "Number Nine" reappears on the full-length *Big Rooms*. *—Sean Cooper*

**I.F. 1** / 1993 / Fax ♦♦♦♦

A warm, engaging cross-polination of analog electronics with colorful instrumental textures. DSN's reliance on preset Roland drum sounds gets somewhat tedious, but Atmo takes the edge off with sparse, treated percussion samples and lively melodies. *—Sean Cooper*

**Traffic: Live at the Love Parade** / 1996 / KM20 ♦♦♦

Live albums in the world of electronica are notoriously tedious affairs. Nonetheless, *Traffic* is a more-than-worthy follow-up to *Big Rooms*. The pair make up for the limitations of live sequencing and tracking with smart, well thought-out tracks that buoy lightly along on airy electronic beats and sampled stand-up bass licks. A couple tracks lack oomph, but overall the album is surprisingly listenable. Released on Moufang's recently established Fax subsidiary. *—Sean Cooper*

**Deep Space Network Meets Higher Intelligence Agency** / Feb. 24, 1997 / Source ♦♦♦

Deep Space Network's David Moufang and Jonas Grossman team up with Birmingham ambient techno duo Higher Intelligence Agency for a deliriously funky foray into deep space ambient electro. Like HIA's summit with Finnish techno soloist Biosphere (released just prior by Beyond), this album is heavy on the synthetic textures, with bleeps, bloops, and otherwise treated electronics supporting a barrage of abstract, mostly breakbeat machine-born percussion. *—Sean Cooper*

## Deepsky

f. 1992

*Group / Trance, Club/Dance*

The progressive trance duo Deepsky consists of New Mexico natives J. Scotty G and Jason Blum. Their mid-'90s singles for Rampant Records include *Tempest*, which became the theme for MTV's electronica show, "AMP," and "In My Mind," both of which were featured on the label's *Planet Rampant II* singles collection. The duo then moved to Fragrant records, where they collaborated with Shawn Parker as the Dayspring Collective and released the album *Spark*. Deepsky's 1998 single "Stargazer" brought them greater acclaim in the dance world, as did their remixes for artists like Carl Cox and Kaistar. The group relocated to L.A. and, appropriately, switched to the City of Angels label, where they expanded "Stargazer" into an EP. *—Heather Phares*

• **Stargazer [EP]** / Oct. 12, 1999 / City of Angels ♦♦

Though originally released on Fragrant in 1998, "Stargazer" became such an anthem among the trance community that City of Angels—known best for their success with Crystal Method—finally licensed the track and packaged it as a CD-EP with an unnecessary amount of remixes, hoping to reach a crossover crowd of consumers without turntables. The original version of the track attained such popularity for its tremendous build and the resulting explosion. Following a strange lull where the beats drop out, leaving only a strange melody and what sounds like an ultra-synthesized human scream, a fast-moving acid riff drives the song towards its fiery summit, where the galloping bass beats return, inspiring a hands-in-the-air ride through the remainder of the up-tempo track. The countless remixes don't really add anything to the proven effectiveness of the original version and usually just detract from what makes the original version so successful. Thankfully, though, the inclusion of "Cosmic Dancer" does remind listeners that Deepsky isn't merely the one-hit wonder that this EP will have you believe. Still, this release simply takes the proven appeal of the title track too far, resulting in gluttony. —*Jason Birchmeier*

## Definition of Sound
f. 1989, London, England
*Group / Club/Dance, Acid House*

The London-based duo known as Definition of Sound created an appealing and exciting blend of post-acid house hip-hop that merged freestyle, reggae, rap, funk, rock and R&B. One minute the group sounded like Al Green, the next Van Morrison, the next the Ombres. Kevin Clark and Don Weekes met at a mutual friend's house while they were listening to new and rare records and freestyling raps. Weekes, who had recorded with Coldcut's Matt Black and was briefly a member of X Posse, was impressed with Clark's skills and soon the two were working together on material.

The two recorded a demo tape and under the name Top Billin', released two underground hits, "Naturally" and "Straight from the Soul" on the Dance Yard label. The interest generated by the singles led to a deal with Circa Records and a UK following that grew as they opened shows for such visiting acts as KRS-One and Kid-N-Play. The Virgin Records-financed dance label Cardiac signed the group up to a US deal after hearing them at an industry conference.

Their first Cardiac album, *Love and Life: A Journey with the Chameleons* was an adventurous, impressive collection of hip-hop. The first single, "Now Is Tomorrow" was an uptempo jam that featured jangling lead guitar, whooshing flanging effects, soulful vocals by guest singer Elaine Vassell and an inspirational message. It was a hit on dance and rap charts in the middle of 1991. The second single, "Wear Your Love Like Heaven"—a Top Ten UK hit in early 1992, merged streetwise b-boy feel with Donovan's bubble-gum '60s sensibility. The third single, "Moira Jane's Cafe" sounded like it was cut in Memphis with a spoken intro that sounds like Elvis, prominent rock guitar and thick, fatback drums. "Love and Life" was named Rap Album of the Year by Britain's *Record Mirror* and had glowing reviews in *Billboard, Rockpool, The Source* and other stateside publications. Just as it seemed that the Definition of Sound was about to be heard around the world, Cardiac Records folded as a result of EMI's takeover of Virgin.

Their new label, Charisma, took enthusiastic delivery of their sophomore album, *The Lick*, only to be folded in turn into West Coast Virgin a week before it was due to ship. As the corporate dust settled, one of the things buried beneath it was the new Definition of Sound record.

Hard times, no money, no record deal and a yearning to redefine themselves led Definition of Sound into the streets of London to drink in the bittersweet tastes of life, love and despair. After more than a year in which they wrote and recorded nearly thirty new songs, Clark and Weeks signed a deal with Mercury and started making their third album, *Experience*. The clever, finely-crafted songs were exuberant and introspective, from those two self-described "chameleons" of 1991—a little older and a lot wiser. The duo collaborated with famed '80s producer Chris Hughes (Adam & the Ants, Tears for Fears, Robert Plant). The result of that unlikely alliance was, according to *New Musical Express,* "like the delayed hit of a powerful drug"—an indefinable cocktail of '60s pop, psychedelic soul, R&B and various shades of rock, all set in a lush, multi-layered ambient soundscape. —*Ed Hogan*

The Lick / 1992 / Charisma ♦♦

● Experience / Feb. 1996 / Fontana ♦♦♦♦
*Experience* is an inventive, sampladelic album bursting with nods to all sorts of styles from swinging pop to classic soul. Even though the two best tracks ("Boom Boom" and "Pass the Vibes") come first, later songs ("Feels Like Heaven" and "Mama's Not Coming Home") display the Definition duo's continual wish to try out new ideas in sound and expand their repertoire. —*Keith Farley*

## Frank De Groodt
b. 1974, Netherlands
*Producer / Dark Ambient, Ambient Techno*

Frank De Groodt records dark, minimal electro, acid, and techno under the names Sonar Base, the Operator, Urban Electro, and Optic Crux, among others. His records have appeared through such powerhouses of European dance music as Djax-Up-Beats and U-Trax, as well as smaller, more experimental outlets such as Detroit's Monoplaza. Born in 1974 in Holland, De Groodt's electro roots stretch far beyond the style's mid-'90s resurgence; he grew up breakdancing in a working class suburb of Utrecht. De Groodt began making music in the early '90s, and through his Operator and Urban Electro projects (the latter together with Arno Peeters, a.k.a. Spasms) has become one of the style's more respected dancefloor innovators, combining thin, driving beats with sharp synthetic textures and bizarre arrangements. —*Sean Cooper*

● Sonar Bass [Single] / 1997 / U-Trax ♦♦♦♦
Frank De Groodt's double-pack of minimal, mostly breakbeat new-tech was the last release on the noted Utrecht-based experimental dance music label, U-Trax. His only release under the name Sonar Base, it also includes some of his finest work to date, combining clean, delicate drumbox rhythms with glinting synth attacks and dark, sweeping atmospheres. Hard to find but worth tracking down. —*Sean Cooper*

Urban Electro II [Single] / 1997 / DJAX ♦♦♦
Another solid four-tracker of mostly dark, atmospheric electro, though less obviously dancefloor-enslaved than its predecessor. —*Sean Cooper*

Fastgraph [Single] / 1998 / Monoplaza ♦♦♦
Frank De Groodt's brand of austere, electro-based post-techno might seem an odd fit with the Detroit-based Monoplaza label's deliberate quirk. And while this is probably the least "serious" of De Groodt's work, it's equally persistent, all speedy machine breaks and nervous acid squelches. De Groodt's natural lean toward minimalism is also well-placed beside the dry, lo-fi thud of Monoplaza's Le Car and Artificial Material. —*Sean Cooper*

## Vladislav Delay
b. Oulu, Finland
*Producer / Minimal Techno, Experimental Techno, IDM*

A Helsinki producer whose "clicks + cuts" style of ambience makes for easy comparison to countrymates Pan sonic, Vladislav Delay has recorded excellent work for three of Europe's most challenging electronic labels: Chain Reaction, Mille Plateaux, and Thomas Brinkmann's Max.Ernst. He grew up trained in jazz, and still counts Philly Joe Jones—the fiery drummer for the first Miles Davis Quintet—one of his prime influences. Also before entering the world of electronics, Delay took side trips through the music of the globe (Brazilian, Cuban, African). After a few failed experiments with fusing electronics in a band environment, he began producing on his own and grew to love the mid-'90s developments by German labels Chain Reaction, A-Musik, Mille Plateaux, and others. After a series of experimentations during 1996-97 (later released, as by Conoco, on the *Kemikoski* full-length), his first release was *The Kind of Blue* EP, released in 1998 for the Finnish label Huume. During 1999, Delay released singles on Max.Ernst and Chain Reaction, leading to his album debut, *Ele*, on the Australian label Sigma Editions. In early 2000, two more full-lengths followed; first Chain Reaction released *Multila*, then *Entain* appeared on Mille Plateaux. Before the end of the year, Delay had debuted a housier incarnation, Luomo, with the *Vocalcity* LP for Forcetracks. —*John Bush*

Huone/Raamat/Viite [Single] / Jun. 28, 1999 / Chain Reaction ♦♦♦
Vladislav Delay's songs are all about progression, often settling into short lulls of murky clicking and swaying before the sweeping sounds of dub basslines again begin carrying the drifting sounds towards further destinations. The dub bassline-driven A-side of this record, "Huone," seems as if it will never end, continually reshaping itself until its final conclusion. The B-side features two songs, "Raamat" and "Viite," that move away from basslines and rhythm toward a more ambient sound, reminiscent of early Chain Reaction records such as Porter Ricks' "Port of Nuba" and Vainqueur's *Elevation*. The differing styles of sound collage—dub techno and ambient—make this a more varied affair than one will get with most other Delay releases, making it a wonderful place to begin discovering this artist's exciting style. —*Jason Birchmeier*

Multila / Feb. 8, 2000 / Chain Reaction ♦♦♦

● Entain / Mar. 7, 2000 / Mille Plateaux ♦♦♦♦
Vladislav Delay's second full-length release of the year 2000 includes two tracks from 1999's *Ele* EP (on Sigma) plus three new tracks. Throughout, the sound is barely conscious ambience with an unsettling atmosphere and an assortment of click-track detritus that remains compelling 15 minutes and more into tracks like the opener "Kohde" and "Notke." —*John Bush*

## Delerium
f. 1986
*Group / Ambient Pop, Alternative Dance, Alternative Pop/Rock*

One in a multitude of mostly indistinguishable aliases used by Bill Leeb and Rhys Fulber (alongside Frontline Assembly, Intermix, Synaesthesia and Noise Unit) before their breakup in 1996, Delerium was probably the most prolific—though Frontline Assembly was undoubtedly the most well-known. From 1987 to 1997, Delerium recorded over ten albums, mostly for Nettwerk and Dossier. The music encompassed ambient-pop with tribal elements as well, and featured many guest vocalists, including past label-mate Sarah McLachlan, Jacqui Hunt (from Single Gun Theory), Kristy Thirsk (Rose Chronicles) and Lisa Gerrard (Dead Can Dance). —*John Bush*

● **Morpheus** / 1989 / Dossier ♦♦♦♦

One of the first and best Delerium LPs, *Morpheus* leans closer to the pagan death-folk of Current 93 than any of Leeb and Fulber's more industrial recordings. —*John Bush*

**Semantic Spaces** / 1994 / Nettwerk ♦♦♦

After a period focusing on gothic environmental fusion for their Delerium releases, Rhys Fulber and Bill Leeb began recruiting vocalists and moving more toward a Deep Forest style of ethno-dance. —*John Bush*

**Karma** / Apr. 22, 1997 / Nettwerk ♦♦♦♦

Similar to *Semantic Spaces* with its focus on the lighter side of vocal dreampop, *Karma* includes contributions from Sarah McLachlan, Kristy Thirsk, and Jacqui Hunt. —*John Bush*

## Delta 9 (Dave Rodgers)
b. Chicago, IL
*Producer / Hardcore Techno, Industrial*

One of the hardest in the hardcore techno/industrial field, Delta 9 is the alias of Chicago's Dave Rodgers, a man influenced by thrash and industrial as well as dance styles like electro and gabba. Debuting with a series of singles for Drop Bass and Industrial Strength during 1995-96, Rodgers appeared on the *Industrial Fucking Strength* compilation and gained a contract with the increasingly techno-leaning grindcore label Earache. His first album, *Disco Inferno*, was followed later in 1997 by *Alpha Decay*. One year later, he appeared on Vinyl Communications with *VC Mix CD, Vol. 1. Revolution 909* was released in mid-2000. —*John Bush*

**Disco Inferno** / Jan. 28, 1997 / Earache ♦♦

A punishing set of industrial-strength gabba complete with military sound effects, *Disco Inferno* works the same relentless hardcore beats, with variations of the same coming only with the various samples tacked onto them. Remixes of the Delta 9 classics "Son of a Bitch" and "Headstrong" are highlights of the 18-track set. —*John Bush*

● **VC Mix CD, Vol. 1: Unequilibrium** / May 12, 1998 / Vinyl Communications ♦♦

*Unequilibrium* finds Chicago gabba hero Delta 9 mixing tracks from diverse acts (including Kid-606 and Merzbow) who have recorded for the California-based Vinyl Communications. Although the label's status in the indie-noise community makes a gabba collaboration a bit of a head-scratcher, the material is prime gutbucket distortion of all sorts, from guitar feedback to electronics disarray. A few hardcore beats rear their heads, but most of the mix is noise-only. —*John Bush*

## Depeche Mode
f. 1980, Basildon, England
*Group / Alternative Dance, Club/Dance, Post-Punk, Alternative Pop/Rock, Synth-Pop*

Originally a product of Britain's New Romantic movement, Depeche Mode went on to become the quintessential electro-pop band of the '80s; one of the first acts to establish a musical identity based completely around the use of synthesizers, the group began their existence as a bouncy dance-pop outfit but gradually developed a darker, more dramatic sound which ultimately positioned them as one of the most successful alternative bands of their era.

The roots of Depeche Mode (French for "fast fashion") dated to 1976, when Basildon, England-based keyboardists Vince Clarke and Andrew Fletcher first teamed to form the group No Romance in China. The band proved short-lived, and by 1979 Clarke had formed French Look, another duo featuring guitarist/keyboardist Martin Gore; Fletcher soon signed on, and the group rechristened itself Composition of Sound. Initially, Clarke handled vocal chores, but in 1980 singer David Gahan was brought in to complete the lineup; after one final name change to Depeche Mode, the quartet jettisoned all instruments excluding their synthesizers, honing a slick, techno-based sound to showcase Clarke's catchy melodies.

After building a following on the London club scene, Depeche Mode debuted in 1980 with "Photographic," a track included on the *Some Bizzare Album* label compilation. After signing to Mute Records, they issued "Dreaming of Me" in early 1981; while neither the single nor its follow-up "New Life" caused much of a stir, their third effort, "Just Can't Get Enough," became a Top Ten UK hit, and their 1981 debut LP *Speak and Spell* was also a success. Just as Depeche Mode appeared poised for a major commercial breakthrough, however, principal songwriter Clarke abruptly exited to form Yazoo with singer Alison Moyet, leaving the group's future in grave doubt.

As Gore grabbed the band's songwriting reins, the remaining trio recruited keyboardist Alan Wilder to fill the technological void created by Clarke's departure; while 1982's *A Broken Frame* deviated only slightly from Depeche Mode's earlier work, Gore's ominous songs grew more assured and sophisticated by the time of 1983's *Construction Time Again*. *Some Great Reward*, issued the following year, was their artistic and commercial breakthrough, as Gore's dark, kinky preoccupations with spiritual doubt ("Blasphemous Rumours") and psychosexual manipulation ("Master and Servant") came to the fore; the egalitarian single "People Are People" was a major hit on both sides of the Atlantic, and typified the music's turn towards more industrial textures.

1986's atmospheric *Black Celebration* continued the trend towards grim melancholy, and further established the group as a major commercial force. After the superb single "Strangelove," Depeche Mode issued 1987's *Music for the Masses;* a subsequent sold-out tour yielded the 1989 double live set *101*, as well as a concert film directed by the legendary D.A. Pennebaker. Still, despite an enormous fan base, the group was considered very much an underground cult phenomenon prior to the release of 1990's *Violator*, a Top Ten smash which spawned the hits "Enjoy the Silence," "Policy of Truth," and "Personal Jesus."

With the alternative music boom of the early '90s, Depeche Mode emerged as one of the world's most successful acts, and their 1993 LP *Songs of Faith and Devotion* entered the charts in the number one slot. However, at the peak of their success, the group began to unravel; first Wilder exited in 1995, and then Gahan was the subject of a failed suicide attempt. (He later entered a drug rehabilitation clinic to battle an addiction to heroin.) After a four-year layoff, Depeche Mode—continuing on as a trio—released 1997's *Ultra*, which featured the hits "Barrel of a Gun" and "It's No Good." The release of *Singles '86-'98* was celebrated with a major tour. —*Jason Ankeny*

**Speak and Spell** / 1981 / Sire ♦♦♦♦

Though probably nobody fully appreciated it at the time—perhaps least of all the band!—Depeche Mode's debut is at once both a conservative, functional pop record and a groundbreaking release. While various synth pioneers had come before—Gary Numan, early Human League, late '70s Eurodisco and above all Kraftwerk all had clear influence on *Speak and Spell*—Depeche became the undisputed founder of straight-up synthpop with the album's eleven songs, light, hooky and danceable numbers about love, life and clubs. For all the claims about 'dated' '80s sounds from rock purists, it should be noted that the basic guitar/bass/drums line-up of rock is almost twenty-five years older than the catchy keyboard lines and electronic drums making the music here. That such a sound would eventually become ubiquitous during the Reagan years, spawning lots of crud along the way, means the band should no more be held to blame for that than Motown and the Beatles be inspiring lots of bad stuff in the sixties, for instance. Credit for the album's success has to go to main songwriter Vince Clarke, who would extend and arguably perfect the synthpop formula with Yaz and Erasure; the classic early singles "New Life," "Dreaming of Me" and "Just Can't Get Enough," along with numbers ranging from the slyly homoerotic "Pretty Boy" to the moody thumper "Photographic," keep everything moving throughout. Gahan undersings about half the album, and Gore's two numbers lack the distinctiveness of his later work, but *Speak and Spell* remains an undiluted joy. —*Ned Raggett*

### A Broken Frame / 1982 / Sire ♦♦♦

Martin Gore has famously noted that Depeche Mode stopped worrying about its future when the first post-Clarke-departure single, "See You," placed even higher on the English charts than anything else Vince Clarke had done with them. Such confidence carries through all of *Frame*, a notably more ambitious effort than the pure pop/disco of the band's debut. With arranging genius Alan Wilder still one album away from fully joining the band, *Frame* became very much Gore's record, writing all the songs and exploring various styles never again touched upon in later years. "Satellite" and "Monument" take distinct dub/reggae turns, while "Shouldn't Have Done That" delivers its slightly precious message about the dangers of adulthood with a spare arrangement and hollow, weirdly sweet vocals. Much of the album follows in a dark vein, forsaking earlier sprightliness, aside from tracks like "A Photograph of You" and "The Meaning of Love," for more melancholy reflections about love gone wrong as "Leave in Silence" and "My Secret Garden." More complex arrangements and juxtaposed sounds, such as the sparkle of breaking glass in "Leave in Silence," help give this underrated album even more of an intriguing, unexpected edge. Gore's lyrics sometimes veer on the facile, but Gahan's singing comes more clearly to the fore throughout—things aren't all there yet, but they were definitely starting to get close. —*Ned Raggett*

### Construction Time Again / 1983 / Sire ♦♦♦

The full addition of Alan Wilder to Depeche Mode's line-up created a perfect troika that would last another 11 years. The combination of Martin Gore's songwriting, Wilder's arranging, and David Gahan's singing and live star power resulted in an ever more compelling series of albums and singles. *Construction Time Again*, the new line-up's first full effort, is a bit hit and miss nonetheless, but when it does hit, it does so perfectly. From the album's first song, "Love in Itself," something is clearly up; Depeche never sounded quite so thick with its sound before, with synths arranged into a mini-orchestra/horn section and real piano and acoustic guitar spliced in at strategic points. Two tracks later, "Pipeline" offers the first clear hint of an increasing industrial influence (the band members were early fans of Einstürzende Neubauten), with clattering metal samples and oddly chain gang-like lyrics and vocals. The album's clear highlight has to be "Everything Counts," a live staple for years, combining a deceptively simple, ironic lyric about the music business with a purely catchy but unusually arranged blending of more metallic scraping samples and melodica amid even more forceful funk/hip-hop beats. Elsewhere, on "Shame" and "Told You So," Gore's lyrics start taking on more of the obsessive personal relationship studies that would soon dominate his writing. Wilder's own songwriting contributions are fine musically, but lyrically, "preachy" puts it mildly, especially the environment-friendly "The Landscape Is Changing." —*Ned Raggett*

### People Are People / 1984 / Sire ♦♦

The unexpected American success of "People Are People," which remained the band's biggest US hit until the start of the '90s, prompted this Stateside-only compilation, very much a dog's breakfast of new and old songs alike. Earlier album cuts such as "Pipeline" and "Told You So" appear here, but the four new tracks understandably received the biggest attention. The title track itself, though the band members have long since expressed embarrassment over it, is still an engaging, instantly memorable pop hit—if the lyrical sentiments are among Gore's most naively sociopolitical before or since, Gahan delivers them strongly, with Gore providing a fine counterpoint vocal. Musically, the explicit use of sampled metallic crashes and detailed production throughout makes the song one of the strongest incorporations of industrial music techniques in a more listener-friendly manner. Of the three other new tracks, "Get the Balance Right" is the strongest, a wickedly barbed but beautifully sung lyric on political/lifestyle posturing with a killer synthline melody. "Work Hard" veers towards the monotonous, while "Now This is Fun" has a nice moody intro to recommend it. Given that both "People are People" and "Get the Balance Right" ended up on the band's first proper singles compilation, this collection is now rendered one solely for hardcore fans. —*Ned Raggett*

### Some Great Reward / 1984 / Sire ♦♦♦♦

The peak of the band's industrial-gone-mainstream fusion, and still one of the best electronic music albums yet recorded, *Reward* still sounds great, with the band's ever-evolving musical and production skills matching even more ambitious songwriting from Gore. "People Are People" appears here, but finds itself outclassed by some of Depeche's undisputed classics, most especially the moody, beautiful "Somebody," a Gore-sung piano ballad that mixes its wit and emotion skillfully; "Master and Servant," an amped-up, slamming dance track that conflates sexual and economic politics to sharp effect; and the closing "Blasphemous Rumors," a slow-building anthemic number supporting one of Gore's most cynical lyrics, addressing a suicidal teen who finds God only to die soon afterward. Even lesser-known tracks like the low-key pulse of "Lie to Me" and the weirdly dreamy "It Doesn't Matter" showcase an increasingly confident band. Wilder's arrangements veer from big to the stripped, but always with just the right touch—such as the crowd samples bubbling beneath "Somebody" or the call/response a cappella start to "Master and Servant." With *Reward*, Gahan's singing found the metier it was going to stick with for the next ten years and while it's never gone down well with some ears, it still has a compelling edge that suits the material well. —*Ned Raggett*

### Catching Up with Depeche Mode / 1985 / Sire ♦♦♦♦

Like its predecessor, *People Are People*, *Catching Up With Depeche Mode* attempts to fill gaps in the group's extensive discography by compiling singles and album tracks taken from their four previous studio LPs. Dating back to the band's Vince Clarke-penned hits ("Just Can't Get Enough," "Dreaming of Me"), the set culminates with tracks like "Master and Servant" and "Blasphemous Rumours," which bear the full fruit of Martin Gore's dark obsessions. A preview of *Black Celebration* is even offered via "Fly on the Windshield." —*Jason Ankeny*

### Black Celebration / 1986 / Sire ♦♦♦♦

Whether the band felt it was simply the time to move from its most explicit industrial pop fusion days, or whether increased success and concurrently larger venues pushed the music into different avenues, Depeche Mode's fifth studio album saw the group embark on a path that in many ways defined their sound to the present: emotionally extreme lyrics matched with amped-up tunes, as much anthemic rock as they are compelling dance, along with stark, low-key ballads. The slow, sneaky build of the opening title track, with a strange distorted vocal sample provides a curious opening hook, and sets the tone as Gahan sings of making it through "another black day" while powerful drums and echoing metallic pings carry the song. *Black Celebration* is actually heavier on the ballads throughout, many sung by Gore—the most per album he has yet taken lead on—with notable dramatic beauties including "Sometimes," with its surprise gospel choir start and rough piano sonics, and the hyper-nihilistic "World Full of Nothing." The various singles from the album remain definite highlights—such as "A Question of Time," a brawling, aggressive number with a solid Gahan vocal, and the romantic/physical politics of "Stripped," featuring particularly sharp arrangements from Alan Wilder. However, with such comparatively lesser-known (but equally impressive) numbers as the quietly intense romance of "Here Is the House" to boast, *Black Celebration* is solid through and through. —*Ned Raggett*

### Music for the Masses / 1987 / Sire ♦♦♦♦

Initially the title must have sounded like an incredibly pretentious boast, except that Depeche Mode went on a monstrous world tour, scored more hits in America (and elsewhere) than ever before, and picked up a large number of name checks from emerging house and techno artists on top of all that. As for the music the masses got this time around, the opening cut "Never Let Me Down Again" starts things off wonderfully: a compressed guitar riff suddenly slams into a huge-sounding percussion/keyboard/piano combination while anchored to a repeated melodic hook, an ever-building synth/orchestral parts the song's end, and Gahan's vocals (though admittedly, singing one of Gore's more pedestrian lyrics) are of his best. It feels huge throughout, as though recorded at the world's largest arena, instead of in a studio. Other key singles "Strangelove," and the (literally) driving "Behind the Wheel" maintain the same blend of power and song skill, while some of the quieter numbers (as "The Things You Said" and "I Want You Now") show musical and lyrical intimacy could easily co-exist with the big chart-busters. Add to that other winners like "To Have and to Hold," with a Russian radio broadcast start and a dramatic, downward spiral of music accompanied by Gahan's subtly powerful take on a desperate Gore love lyric. The weird, wonderful choral closer "Pimpf," makes Depeche's massive success perfectly clear. —*Ned Raggett*

### 101 / 1989 / Sire ♦♦♦♦

As an event, Depeche Mode's huge (attendance around 80,000) Los Angeles Rose Bowl concert in 1988 remains legendary. No single artist show had sold out the venue since 1980, while the film documentary by Dylan-filmer D.A. Pennebaker clearly demonstrated fans' intense commitment to a near-decade-old band most mainstream critics continued to stupidly portray as a flash in the pan synth-pop effort often still equating quality with having a "real" rock lineup and sound. While they fiddled, the Rose Bowl burned, as *101* demonstrates. For all that Gahan's tour-worn vocals clearly get away from him from time to time (he seems to end every song with the same "Thank you! Thank you very much!" shout), this start to the final encore record of the concert showcases a band perfectly able to carry its music from studio to stage as well as any other combo worth its salt should. Understandably focused on *Music for the Masses* material, the album shows Depeche experimenting with alternate arrangements at various points for live performance. Big numbers like "Never Let Me Down Again," "Stripped," and "Blasphemous Rumors" pack even more of a wallop here. Slower numbers—and more than a couple of ballads—help to vary the hit-packed set, including a fine "Somebody" and "The Things You Said" combination sung by Gore. "Pleasure Little Treasure," while on record an okay B-side, becomes a monster rocker live—the type of unexpected surprise one could expect from a solid band no matter what the music. With a triumphant set of closing numbers, including magnificent takes on "Never Let Me Down Again," "Master and Servant," and the set-ending "Everything Counts," the entire audience sings the chorus well after the song has finally ended. *101* does far better at its task than most might have guessed. —*Ned Raggett*

**Violator** / Feb. 1990 / Sire ♦♦♦♦
In a word, stunning. Perhaps an odd word to use given that *Violator* continued in the general vein of the previous two studio efforts by Depeche: Gore's upfront lyrical emotional extremism and knack for a catchy hook filtered through Wilder's ear for perfect arrangements, ably assisted by top English producer Flood and Gahan's vocal purr. Yet the idea that this record would both dominate worldwide charts (both singles and albums) while song for song being simply the best, most consistent effort yet from the band could only have been a wild fantasy before its release. The opening two singles from the album, however, signaled something was up. "Personal Jesus," at once perversely simplistic, has a stiff, yet arcane funk/hip-hop beat, basic blues guitar chords, and tremendous (thanks to sharp production touches) echoed, snaky vocals. "Enjoy the Silence," a nothing-else-remains-but-us ballad, is pumped up into a huge, dramatic romance/dance number, commanding in its mock orchestral/choir scope, basic as a two-note guitar line anchoring the song. The follow-up single "Policy of Truth" did just fine as well, a low-key Motown funk number for the modern day with a sharp love/hate lyric to boot; even the subtlest of touches like the buried guitar feedback at the end helped add to the overall effect. To top it all off, the album scored on song after song, from the shuffling beat of "Sweetest Perfection" (well sung by Gore) and the ethereal "Waiting for the Night" to the guilt-ridden and loving it "Halo," building into a string-swept pounder. "Clean" wraps up *Violator* on an eerie note, ominous bass notes and odd atmospherics carrying the song. Goth without ever being stupidly hammy, synth without sounding like the clinical stereotype of synth music, rock without ever sounding like a "rock" band, Depeche here reached astounding heights indeed. —*Ned Raggett*

**Songs of Faith & Devotion** / Mar. 23, 1993 / Sire ♦♦♦♦
Between *Violator* and *Songs*, a lot happened: the successes of Jane's Addiction, *Lollapalooza* 1991, and Nirvana rewrote the meaning of "alternative," while another *Lollapalooza* 1991 act, Nine Inch Nails, hit MTV and the airwaves as the most clearly Depeche-influenced new hit band around. In the meantime, Depeche Mode went through some high-profile arguing as Gahan turned into a long-haired, leather-clad rocker, using his own *Lollapalooza* fandom to push for a more guitar-oriented sound. Yet the odd thing about *Songs* is that it sounds pretty much like a Depeche album, only with some new sonic tricks at the hands of Alan Wilder and co-producer Flood. Perhaps even odder is that fact that it works incredibly well all the same. While not as consistent as *Violator*, *Songs* comes packed with strong songs and performances. "I Feel You," opening with a screech of feedback, works its live drums well, but when the heavy synth bass kicks in with wailing backing vocals, even most rockers might find it hard to compete. Gore's lyrical bent, as per the title, ponders relationships through distinctly religious imagery. While the gambit is hardly new, songs like the centerpiece "In Your Room," carefully evolve from a shadowy synth start to a high-volume arena rock throbber; the combination of personal and spiritual love with distinctly erotic overtones, blends perfectly. Outside musicians appear for the first time, including female backing vocals on a couple of tracks, most notably the gospel-flavored "Condemnation" and the uilleann pipes on "Judas," providing a lovely intro to the underrated song (later covered by Tricky). "Rush" is the biggest misstep, a too obvious sign that Nine Inch Nails was a recording-session favorite to unwind to. But with other numbers such as "Walking in My Shoes" and "The Mercy in You" to recommend it, *Songs* continues the Depeche winning streak. —*Ned Raggett*

**Ultra** / Apr. 15, 1997 / Warner Brothers ♦♦♦♦
When news surfaced in 1995 that Alan Wilder had departed Depeche to concentrate on his solo project Recoil, the immediate concern among fans was whether the band would be able to hit past heights again. Though Wilder's profile was always less than Martin Gore's and David Gahan's—and almost even that of Alan Fletcher, whose non-performance live has always been a running joke in the fan community, and who freely admits to generally being around merely to maintain a vibe with his childhood friend Gore—his capability at arranging the songs over the years gave the band its increasingly distinct, unique edge. Combined with Gahan's near suicide and lengthy recovery from drugs, things looked bleak. Happily, *Ultra* turned out a winner. Hooking up with Tim Simenon, longtime UK dance maven and producer of arty fare such as Gavin Friday's *Adam and Eve*, Depeche delivered a strong album as a rejuvenated band. The most immediate change was Gahan's singing. For the first time, he took singing lessons beforehand, and his new control and projection shone, especially on the marvelous "It's No Good," a pulsing, tense yet beautiful song with another deeply romantic Gore lyric. Opener "Barrel of a Gun" continues in the vein of arena-level stompers like "Never Let Me Down Again" and "I Feel You," with huge drum slams and scratching, but *Ultra* mostly covers subtler territory, such as the slightly creepy "Sister of Night" and the gentle "The Love Thieves." Gore sings two winners: the orchestral, slow dance groove "Home" and "The Bottom Line," featuring steel guitar and Can's Jaki Liebezeit on drums, distinctly different territory for Depeche. Closing with "Insight," a quite lovely, building ballad, *Ultra* showed Depeche wasn't ready to quit by any means. —*Ned Raggett*

★ **The Singles 81>85** / 1998 / Mute ♦♦♦♦♦
Replacing the original *Catching Up with Depeche Mode* compilation, *81>85* subtracts two tracks—the lightweight curiosity "Flexible" and "Fly on the Windscreen," which surfaced to better effect on *Black Celebration*—and adds two, the full six-minute remix of "Just Can't Get Enough" and the original version of "Photographic," Depeche's recording debut on a 1980 compilation album. The overall collection remains the same though, namely, a run through the peerless singles that kept the band on the charts in the UK and elsewhere, as well as building up their increasing cult following in America. It's an embarrassment of riches, from such bouncy early hits as "New Life," "Just Can't Enough," and "The Meaning of Love" to the increasingly heavier sound of "Everything Counts," "People Are People," and "Blasphemous Rumors." Nearly all the tracks appear in the original single mixes, some quite different from their album versions, others essentially the same (the one subtle difference in "Somebody" is an echoey percussion pattern buried in the mix, for instance). Two otherwise unavailable singles also appear here: "It's Called a Heart" is pleasant enough, but "Shake the Disease" is great, an obsessive love lyric matched to a wonderful, slow dance melody, and an excellent pairing of Gahan's more aggressive and Gore's gentler vocals. As an introduction to Depeche's brilliant knack for catchy tunes evolving over time into a more challenging (but no less popular) collection of songs, at once defining and expanding the boundaries of synth-pop, look no further. —*Ned Raggett*

**The Singles 86>98** / Oct. 6, 1998 / Reprise ♦♦♦♦
It took Depeche Mode only four years to assemble their first singles compilation, but 12 to release *The Singles 86>98*. Appropriately, the second set was much more ambitious than *The Singles 81>85*, spanning two discs and 20 songs, plus a live version of "Everything Counts." *The Singles 86>98* was an album that many fans, both casual and hardcore, waited patiently for, and for good reason—Depeche Mode was always more effective as a singles band than as album artists. That's not to say that the double-disc compilation is perfect. DM's output fluctuated wildly during those 12 years, as the group hit both career highs and lows. It's possible to hear it all on this set, from "Strangelove" and "Never Let Me Down Again," through "Personal Jesus" and "Enjoy the Silence," to "I Feel You" and "Barrel of a Gun." It's possible that some casual lis-

teners will find that the collection meanders a bit too much for their tastes, but the end result is definitive and, along with *The Singles 81>85*, ranks as Depeche Mode's best, most listenable album. —*Stephen Thomas Erlewine*

## Depth Charge (Jonathon Saul Kane)

*Remixing, Producer / Club/Dance, Techno, Acid House, Hip-Hop*

As Block, Spider, Octagon Man, Grimm Death, and (most often) Depth Charge, DJ/producer Jonathon Saul Kane has been one of the more consistent and innovative forces on the UK dance scene since the late '80s. Recording classic tracks such as "Bounty Killers" and "The Demented Spirit," as well as remixing everyone from Eon, Bomb the Bass, and Sabres of Paradise to Senser, Silver Fox, and S'Express, Kane's work has kept in constant touch with dance music's hip-hop, funk, and electro roots—a fact which places him at the nexus of a number of recent hybrids and resurgent styles. His 1989 Vinyl Solution 12", "Bounty Killers," is roundly considered one of the earliest examples of uptempo trip-hop, mixing chunky sampled breakbeats with brutalizing bass and kitschy kung fu samples (a style which marks his popular Depth Charge work to this day). Additionally, Kane's two labels, D.C. (trip-hop and dub) and Electron Industries (electro and techno), have been responsible for some of the more memorable moments in mid-'90s underground dance music, and have included releases from Damon Baxter (Sem, Deadly Avenger), Ian Loveday (Eon), and Delta, as well as Depth Charge and Octagon Man releases such as "Shaolin Buddha Finger," "10ft. Flowers," "The Legend of the Golden Snake," and *The Exciting World of Octagon Man*. Many of Kane's earlier (1991-1994) Depth Charge releases were compiled on the compilation *Nine Deadly Venoms*, released in 1994. Several singles and EPs followed on DC Recordings during the next few years, but it wasn't until 1999 that Kane returned with another Depth Charge full-length. First, the mix-album *Electro Boogie: Shape Generator* dropped in April 1999, then the production album *Lust* followed in October. *Lust Vol. 2* followed shortly in February of 2000. Kane also helped found Made in Hong Kong, a film festival and video label (through Vinyl Solution) focusing on the promotion and distribution of films in the Hong Kong action cinema genre associated with actors and directors such as Chow Yun Fat, Ringo Lam, Wong Kar-Wai, John Woo, and Jackie Chan. [See Also: Octagon Man] —*Sean Cooper*

**The Legend of the Golden Snake** / 1995 / DC Recordings ♦♦♦
A four-track return to the boards for Jonathon Kane, which finds still more dwelling in the land of kung fu trip-hop. The tracks are actually among his more inventive, however, with minimal dub, dirt-funk, and even flamenco guitar stirring the mix. The EP was also released on CD-single and as a limited-edition 10". —*Sean Cooper*

● **Nine Deadly Venoms** / 1995 / Vinyl Solution ♦♦♦♦
J. Saul Kane's early Depth Charge twelves get the compilation treatment on this full-length debut, which also includes a few new tracks. While the CD sports edits of classic early cuts such as "Bounty Killers" and "Dead By Dawn," the double LP includes the full versions. Although the somewhat formulaic repetition of huge breakbeat/Jackie Chan sample/huge breakbeat can get a bit boring over the distance, the tracks are undeniably catchy, and the energy level (combined probably with a high-volume setting) makes it hardly noticeable. —*Sean Cooper*

**Electro Boogie: Shape Generator** / Apr. 26, 1999 / Studio !K7 ♦♦♦♦
J. Saul Kane's edition in Studio !K7's *Electro Boogie* mix series is an involved, pummeling set of futurist electro, including tracks from Third Electric, Anthony Rother, Echo Park, and Kane's own Octagon Man project with only one throwback: the original Soft Cell version of "Tainted Love." —*John Bush*

**Lust** / Oct. 11, 1999 / DC Recordings ♦♦
Five years from *Nine Deadly Venoms*, Depth Charge returned with an album chock-full of the same uptempo, breakbeat hip-hop he'd pioneered almost a decade before (with plenty of similar kung-fu samples to boot). J. Saul Kane's fusion of hip-hop, techno, and electro was so innovative in the early '90s that it was still popular in dance circles years later, but except for a few intriguing downtempo tracks, it's difficult to hear much on *Lust* that wasn't done years ago on other Depth Charge material. —*John Bush*

## Der Dritte Raum

*Group / Trance, Club/Dance*

The German trance duo Der Dritte Raum ("The Third Rail") paired DJs Andreas Krueger and Ralf Uhrlandt. Signed to Sven Väth's Harthouse label, they debuted in 1995 with the EP *Elektro Disco*, followed soon after by the full-length *Mental Modulator; Wellenbad* followed in 1996, and three years later Der Dritte Raum returned with *Spaceglider*. —*Jason Ankeny*

**Mental Modulator** / Jul. 11, 1995 / Harthouse ♦♦

● **Spaceglider** / Jun. 1, 1999 / Ultra ♦♦♦
Der Dritte Raum's third album ("Raumgleiter" in German), includes twelve aggressive techno-trance epics just one step removed from straightahead trance, the difference being that most trance emphasizes waves of sound while Der Dritte Raum appears to revel in doing more with less. "Infrarot" and "Hale Bopp" are highlights, though many of the tracks sound the same. —*Keith Farley*

## Designer (Casey Rice)

*Producer / Experimental Jungle, Experimental Techno, Indie Rock, Post-Rock/Experimental*

Designer was the drum'n'bass alias of Chicago-based DJ, engineer, and remixer Casey Rice, a longtime Tortoise associate and soundman whose extensive studio credits also include work with Liz Phair, Shrimp Boat, Five Style, and Gastr del Sol. A native of Ohio who relocated to the Windy City during the late '80s, Rice (by day a recording engineer at Brad Wood's Idful Studios) debuted the Designer name in 1996 with the 12" "Vandal"; a remix of the track appeared on the Soul Static Sound label soon after. Subsequent efforts include "Arashi" and "Gebarck Star," the latter released on Stereolab's Duophonic label. Rice additionally teamed with fellow DJ Black Nuclear Power (a.k.a. Trenchmouth's Damon Locks) as Super E.S.P. —*Jason Ankeny*

**This Is It [Single]** / Feb. 12, 1992 / Wads Music ♦♦

● **Vandal [Single]** / Oct. 14, 1996 / Soul Static Sound ♦♦♦
No need to worry about Casey Rice's 12" debut as Designer sounding too much like Tortoise; though he enlists the services of that group's John Herndon and former affiliate Bundy Brown, it's very much Rice's affair. Each of the single's three tracks benefit from subtle flourishes, avoiding the common ills of being too obvious or too clever. Red Red Meat joins Rice on the B-side, and a Larson remix of the A-side nicely hones in on the percussion. What, no diva wails from Liz Phair? —*Andy Kellman*

## Detroit Escalator Co. (Neil Ollivierra)

*Producer / Electronica, Detroit Techno, Club/Dance, Techno, Ambient*

Neil Ollivierra is the Detroit Escalator Co., whose cosmic down-tempo landscapes paint detailed audio pictures of his native Detroit. As the manager of Transmat, Derrick May's label, Ollivierra saw techno evolve from its earliest stages. In 1996 he released *Soundtrack (313)* on Ferox, an album that captures the essence of Detroit through sound bites that Ollivierra collected by riding his bike around the city. His novel *Reality Slap* focused on his early days in the scene and adventures as a label manager. Though demand for the book was high, it was never legally published, as Ollivierra never sought to make money off his efforts. (The only way to get a copy of the thick book was through a photocopy of the original or through a website that Ollivierra maintained and has since taken down.) In 2000, Ollivierra left his position at Transmat to focus on his music and painting. His sophomore album, *Black Buildings*, was issued the same year on Peacefrog records. —*Diana Potts*

● **Soundtrack 313** / Dec. 9, 1996 / Ferox ♦♦♦♦
Under the alias Detroit Escalator Company, Neil Ollivierra makes a strong, soulful debut with *Soundtrack (313)*. In order to really capture the city for the 1996 album, Ollivierra rode his bicycle around Detroit with a DAT player, collecting audio samples. His music is the perfect backdrop for the late nights of empty street calm, when the fog raises from below the streets and traffic lights flash. *Soundtrack (313)* is full of deep, layered emotion and passion—and creates a sound map for the 313 area code city of Detroit. —*Diana Potts*

## Detroit Grand Pubahs

f. Detroit, MI
*Group / Detroit Techno, Electro, Club/Dance, Techno*

The Detroit Grand Pubahs combine silly lyrics and minimal production to create a signature sound. Often labeled a novelty act, the Pubahs are Detroit natives, Dr. Toefinger (Andy Toth) and Paris the Black Fu (Mack Goudy, Jr.). They are mostly associated with their first single, ìSandwichesî, which was carried by both Throw and Jive Electro Records.

Andy Toth, half of the Pubahs, started playing the drums in various bands when he was sixteen and began going to dance parties soon after. Dance music clicked with Toth, and after going to school to be a recording engineer, he took a job at a Detroit recording studio. He worked with many local music acts, including techno pioneer Rob Hood. Toth's production sound can be compared with the minimal, dub nature of Chain Reaction, of whom Toth has been influenced (in addition to the many Detroit techno legends). Vocalist Mack Goudy Jr. (Paris the Black Fu) started DJing around the age of sixteen, inspired by Detroit radio legends the Electrifying Mojo and the Wizard (Jeff Mills). The musical turning point for Mack was at a fashion show where he heard a DJ simultaneously mix two copies of Laid Back's *White Horse*. Mack started buying records through a store he worked at during a brief move to West Virginia. Goudy moved back to Detroit in 1988. His local popularity as a DJ grew steadily thereafter, as a solo act and half of Heckle and Jeckle, with Jon Billebob Williams. With Williams, Paris had an almost regular part in Detroit's "Po' Boy" group of promoters and DJs.

It wasn't until Paris and Toth became co-workers at a restaurant in Royal Oak, Michigan that the two Pubahs met. The two started talking music and soon formed a production partnership. Using Toth's connection at the recording studio he worked at, the Detroit Grand Pubahs were born. The track "Sandwiches" followed soon after, released on Brian Gillespie's label, Throw. The track spread like wild fire through local clubs and gained a lot of local support. The song's playful and pornographic lyrics made it a hit in Detroit, a city that is notorious for often taking an over-serious approach to techno. In addition, the duo's live performance became popular due in part to their off the wall antics, such as wearing wigs, costumes, and Paris stripping down to a thong. Through connections in New York, "Sandwiches" was picked up by Jive Electro—a label associated with such names as Groove Armada. Soon after, "Sandwiches" hit the UK dance charts. In May of 2000, the Detroit Grand Pubahs performed "Sandwiches" and some unreleased tracks to a packed crowd at the first-ever *Detroit Electronic Music Festival*, proving they were more than a one-hit wonder. —*Diana Potts*

- **The Mad Circus [EP]** / 1999 / Throw ✦✦✦✦

An initial listen to "Sandwiches"—the key track—may have you scratching your head at its simplicity. Once you walk away and find that the catchy lyrics and minimal electro beats stick with you, you will understand why this record generated so much hype. In sum, it is very accessible and unbelievably catchy. An anthem if there ever was one, it begins with a simple electro beat that moves at a fairly slow but funky pace. Four bars in, the vocals— courtesy of Paris the Black Fu—begin: "I know you wanna do it/ You know I wanna do it too/ Out here on the dancefloor/ We can make sandwiches/ You can be the bun/ And I can be the burger, girl/ I know you wanna do it/ We can make sandwiches/ So make your thighs like butter, easy to spread/ And we can make sandwiches/ Out here on the dancefloor/ Come on we can do it/ We can make sandwiches." These comedic yet sexually evocative lyrics repeat endlessly for the song's duration as a few other musical elements are added. Its simplicity and repetitive nature make this song inescapable. Also included on *The Mad Circus* are two other pieces: Run/ Stop/ Restore's "Light My Fire (1999 Future Mix)" and Mas 2008's "Anitmaterie Materie." The first is a gimmicky remake of Jim Morrison's classic, done in a comical manner that just doesn't work; the other song by Mas 2008, illustrates the potent style of electro associated with the Twilight 76 parent label. —*Jason Birchmeier*

## Taylor Deupree

*Design / Experimental Ambient, Experimental Techno, Electronica, Ambient Techno, Techno*

Over the years, Taylor Deupree has worked on a considerable amount of projects in music and multi-media. With each musical project he takes on, Taylor shows a different production side of himself, from ambient sounds to hard drum machine driven techno. In the early to late '90s he was part of the acid techno group Prototype 909. This trio's sound can be strongly associated with the early rave style of fast beats and sharp, tweaking, distorted noises. It is through his relationship with Prototype 909 that Taylor would build a strong association with a drum machine, hence the nickname Taylor 808. During Prototype 909's rise to rave popularity, Taylor made time to explore his ambient side. SETI, a project with Savvas Ysatis, and Deupree's solo project, Human Mesh Dance, gave Taylor a chance to explore calmer electronic avenues. Though Taylor has released many works on countless labels, most of his work can be found on Instinct and 12K Records, which is his own label. Taylor Deupree is also very involved in the artistic sub-culture that surrounds electronic music.

Based in Brooklyn, New York, Taylor Deupree's most widely known project is as one third of Prototype 909, a group that also included Dietrich Schoenemann and Jason "BPMF" Szostek. The group was most famous for their live performances and gear, such as rare keyboards, drum machines, and refusal to use a DAT player holding prerecorded music. The band released four full-length albums, *Acid Technology* (Instinct, 1993), *Live 1993-1995* (Instinct, 1995), *Transistor Rhythm* (Instinct, 1995), and *Joined at the Head* (Caipirinha, 1997). Prototype 909 dissolved in the late '90s, but continue to work on projects together and independently.

Taylor Deupree is also half of SETI, a duo named after the research experiment to pick up radio signals from aliens. A relative suggested the name to Taylor for his production alliance with Savvas Ysatis (Omnicron), a long time friend. Both Ysatis and Taylor wanted their music to reflect the mood of the project, which resulted in minimalistic and often experimental sounds and samples. As SETI, Savvas and Taylor put out three full-length releases, *SETI* (Instinct, 1993), *Pharos* (Instinct, 1994), and *Ciphers* (Instinct, 1996). Despite Taylor's worries concerning the use of the name of the highly sensitive experiment, scientists at the SETI Institute actually praised the duo for their work. For *Pharos*, the Institute gave the group sound samples from space and spoken interviews to use on the album. In 1996 Savvas and Taylor formed the label Index, which only released one 12" EP with four tracks from various artists, including Prototype 909's Dietrich Shoenemann. The record is now distributed by Deupree's own label, 12K Records.

In 1993 Deupree started his solo project, Human Mesh Dance. Unlike Prototype 909's knob-tweaking, classic techno sound, Human Mesh Dance would allow Deupree to show his softer, ambient side at the same time that Prototype 909's popularity was rising. His first full-length release as Human Mesh Dance was *Hyaline* (Instinct, 1993). In 1994, he followed with the full-length *Mind Flower*, again on Instict. *Theseceretnumbertwelve* was released in 1997 under much acclaim on 12K Records and marked a new point in Taylor's independence as a solo artist.

Taylor's record label, 12K, is based out of New York and has released a slew of CDs, most in limited editions of 500 or 1000. In 1997, he teamed up with Savvas Ysatis again and released the CD, *Arc vs. Tiny Objects in Space* under the corresponding names. In May of 1998, 12K released the CD, *Alphabet Flasher* by Drum Komputer, which is a name Taylor and former Prototype 909 colleague Schoenemann use when they produce together. That same year Taylor's solo project, *Comma* came out in a limited 500 release, a year later a limited release with Richard Cartier called *Spec* would return Taylor to a paired effort. In April of 2000 the album *.N* was released, and in July Taylor teamed with Tetsu Inoue for *Active/Freeze*. A month later the full-length album, *Polr* was released on Frank Bretschneider's German label, Raster Music.

Besides music, Deupree has had a artistic role in the electronic music culture. Instinct Records gave Taylor an outlet for his work to be noticed, when he took over as their head graphic-design artist. Since his departure from Instinct, he has been highly involved with Caipirinha Productions, the producers of the much acclaimed electronic music documentary, *Modulations*. Taylor Deupree worked on the visually based, futuristic film *Synthetic Pleasures*, where he took charge of the graphic-design work, and contributed to both of the film's soundtracks. —*Diana Potts*

- **.N** / Apr. 11, 2000 / Ritornell/Mille Plateaux ✦✦✦

For *.N*, graphic designer and electronic producer Taylor Deupree focuses on nanotechnology, the science concerned with impossibly miniscule molecules. The field not only converges several different areas of research (chemistry, biotechnology, computer engineering) but is itself a science many experts believe represents a breathtaking venture for scientists and computers in the 21st century. Surprisingly, Deupree manages to bring listeners into the microscopic world of sub-molecular space; his productions are largely free of both bass and rhythm, leaving only brittle, high-frequency sound tools and an abstract production style that sounds just this side of random. The fifth track, "Build," evokes rather well the construction of atoms one molecule at a time, with constant blips of gleaming synth and the occasional burst of faraway computer static. Though Deupree's hardly fettered by any preconceptions of what nanotechnology actually sounds like, these tracks—experimental, freeform, obviously just as focused on the space between sounds as on the sounds themselves—*are* just about what you'd expect to hear while floating from molecule to molecule within individual atoms. And of course nanotechnology is the perfect subject for a producer in league with the heavily computer-processed style dubbed microsound by fellow Ritornell/Mille Plateaux producer Kim Cascone. —*John Bush*

## Terra Deva

*Vocals / Club/Dance*

Influenced by everything from classic soul to jungle, San Francisco singer/songwriter Terra Deva issued her debut LP *Pulled Apart* in 1998. —*Jason Ankeny*

- **Pulled Apart** / Jul. 7, 1998 / OM ♦♦♦♦

What do you get when you put a woman who's a great singer and a good lyricist in the studio with some seriously skilled techno producers? You get great dance music with pretty good words, which is unusual enough to be worth noting. The thing about lyrics is that they tend to want song structure, whereas dance music tends to resist it in favor of extended grooves. So if you think you sense a certain tension between the singing and the grooving here, you're right. The good news is that it's a creative tension, and it results in some very nice pop music. Terra Deva's voice may not be unique, but it sure is lovely, and uniqueness in singers is overrated anyway. "Inside" is slow, smoky, and sexy (even moreso in the goosed-up drum'n'bass remix version that is also provided), and she digs into her Billie Holiday bag on a mambo-ish version of "Speak Low (When You Speak of Love)." "Gratify" is short on melody, but long on expressiveness. The rhythms tend toward a polite drum'n'bass clatter, but there are a few house beats as well, and it's a tribute to the production crew that even the house tracks are interesting and fun to listen to. —*Rick Anderson*

## Richard Devine

*Producer / Electro-Techno, Club/Dance, Techno*

Richard Devine is one of the most talented (if not prolific) of the producers organized around the Miami neo-electro haven of Schematic Records. Based in Atlanta, Devine's productions have the rigid breakbeat swing of prime electro recordings, but also a high degree of DSP (digital signal processing) magic in keeping with Schematic's acknowledged heroes, Autechre. After EPs for a sublabel of Woody McBride's Drop Bass Network and the *Devine* EP on Schematic, the producer began getting a reputation in advanced electronics circles with remixes (of material by Aphex Twin, Chris Deluca, Slicker, and Schematic's own Phoenecia), as well as compilation appearances (*Ischemic Folks* and *Lily of the Valley*, both on Schematic). Turned on to Devine's work by praise from Autechre and his remix of Aphex Twin's "Come to Daddy," Britain's Warp Records hired him in 2000 to record a full-length record. —*John Bush*

- **Polymorphic [EP]** / 1996 / Drop Bass/Six Sixty Six ♦♦♦♦

**Richard Coleman Devine [Single]** / May 4, 1998 / Schematic ♦♦

## Tony De Vit

b. Sep. 12, 1957, Kidderminster, England, d. Jul. 2, 1998, Birmingham, England

*Producer, DJ / Trance, Club/Dance, House*

One of England's most popular DJs before his premature death in 1998, Tony De Vit's brand of sleek, trancey hi-NRG house enlivened Britain's dance scene during the mid-'90s, due to his residencies (at the club Trade and on London's Kiss FM) and his respected labels, Jump Wax and TDV. While working full-time as stock control manager for a thermal-insulation factory beginning in the mid-'70s (and lasting well into the '90s), De Vit began moonlighting as a DJ on the gay club circuit in 1978. He continued to play around the country during the '80s, and in 1992 began a residency at the after-hours club, Trade. There, De Vit's meld of Belgian-hoover trance and nu-style disco became popular with an underground gay audience usually attracted to the more mainstream side of dance.

By the mid-'90s, De Vit had added several DJ awards to his shelf and gained a spot on Kiss FM (after Carl Cox and Judge Jules departed for Radio One). He also began producing, with the singles "Burning Up" and "To the Limit." Both hit the British Top 40 and sparked a heavy remix schedule for De Vit and recording partner Simon Parkes, including East 17, Michelle Gayle, and Louise. During 1996-97, De Vit formed his own labels (Jump Wax and TDV), and released two volumes in the *Global Underground* mix series.

His major-label debut *Trade* documented a night out at his most famed club, and even earned American release through Priority. In 1998, at the peak of his fame, De Vit died of bronchial failure while at a Birmingham hospital. —*John Bush*

**The Remixers: Tony De Vit** / Apr. 29, 1996 / Fantazia ♦♦♦

**Global Underground: Live in Tel Aviv** / Nov. 11, 1996 / Global Underground ♦♦♦

The first installment in Tony De Vit's live DJ-mix series for Global Underground, *Live in Tel Aviv* documents his skill at mixing energetic, uptempo house over the course of two discs. De Vit's excellent taste is on display as well, making it a fine all-around showcase for his talents. —*Steve Huey*

**Live in Tokyo** / 1997 / Global Underground ♦♦♦

Another edition of De Vit's *Live In...* series features the DJ in Japan, mixing tracks from a variety of hardbag labels, including Hooj Choons, Tripoli Trax, as well as his own TDV Records. —*John Bush*

- **Trade** / Apr. 28, 1998 / Priority ♦♦♦♦

The best example of De Vit's high-flying energy trance, *Trade* shows his excellence at DJing and selecting tracks, above and beyond his status as an icon for the dance community. Including De Vit faves like "Cagey Groove" by the KGB, and "Bombay" by Dave Randall, *Trade* has plenty of highlights, best of all being smooth transitions between fast-moving tracks like Brainbashers' "Do It Now" and Da Junkies' "Get Wicked." —*John Bush*

## Devo

f. 1972, Akron, OH

*Group / American Punk, Post-Punk, New Wave, Synth-Pop*

One of new wave's most innovative and (for a time) successful bands, Devo was also perhaps one of its most misunderstood. Formed in Akron, Ohio in 1972 by Kent State art students Jerry Casale and Mark Mothersbaugh, Devo took its name from the concept of "de-evolution"—the idea that instead of evolving, mankind has actually regressed, as evidenced by the dysfunction and herd mentality of American society. Their music echoed this view of society as rigid, repressive, and mechanical, with appropriate touches—jerky, robotic rhythms; an obsession with technology and electronics (the group was among the first non-prog-rock bands to make the synthesizer a core element); often atonal melodies and chord progressions—all of which were filtered through the perspectives of social misfits, outcasts, and flat-out freaks. Devo became a cult sensation, helped in part by their concurrent emphasis on highly stylized visuals, and briefly broke through to the mainstream with the smash single "Whip It," whose accompanying video was made a staple by the fledgling MTV network. Sometimes resembling a less forbidding version of the Residents, Devo's simple, basic electronic pop sound proved very influential, but it was also somewhat limited; and as other bands began expanding on the group's ideas, Devo seemed unable to keep pace. After a series of largely uninteresting albums, the band called it quits early in the '90s, and Casale and Mothersbaugh concentrated on other projects.

Gerald Casale and Mark Mothersbaugh both attended art school at Kent State University at the outset of the '70s. With friend Bob Lewis, who joined an early version of Devo and later became their manager, the theory of de-evolution was developed with the aid of a book entitled *The Beginning Was the End: Knowledge Can Be Eaten*, which held that mankind had evolved from mutant, brain-eating apes currently losing their sanity. The trio adapted the theory to fit their view of American society as a rigid, dichotomized instrument of repression which ensured that its members behaved like clones, marching through life with mechanical, assembly-line precision and no tolerance for ambiguity. The whole concept was treated as an elaborate joke until Casale witnessed the infamous National Guard killings of student protestors at the university; suddenly there seemed to be a legitimate point to be made. The first incarnation of Devo was formed in earnest in 1972, with Casale (bass), Mark Mothersbaugh (vocals), and Mark's brothers Bob (lead guitar), and Jim, who played homemade electronic drums. Jerry's brother Bob joined as an additional guitarist, and Jim left the band to be replaced by Alan Myers. The group honed its sound and approach for several years (a period chronicled on Rykodisc's *Hardcore* compilations of home recordings), releasing a few singles on its own Booji Boy label and inventing more bizarre concepts: Mothersbaugh dressed in a baby-faced mask as Booji (pronounced "boogie") Boy, a symbol of infantile regression; there were recurrent uses of the image of the potato as a lowly vegetable without individuality; the band's costumes presented them as identical clones with processed hair; and all sorts of sonic experiments were performed on records, using real and homemade synthesizers as well as toys, space heaters, toasters, and other objects to create odd textures. Devo's big break came with its score for the short film *The Truth About De-Evolution*, which won a prize at the 1976 Ann Arbor Film Festival. When the film was seen by David Bowie and Iggy Pop, they were impressed enough to secure the group a contract with Warner Brothers. Recorded under the auspices of pioneering producer Brian Eno, *Q: Are We Not Men? A: We Are Devo!* was seen as a call to arms by some, and became an underground hit. Others found Devo's sound, imagery, and material threatening (*Rolling Stone*, for example, called the group fascists). But such criticism missed the point—Devo dramatized conformity, emotional repression, and dehumanization in order to attack them, not to pay tribute to them.

While 1979's *Duty Now for the Future* was another strong effort, the band broke through to the mainstream with 1980's *Freedom of Choice*, which contained the gold-selling single "Whip It" and represented a peak in their sometimes erratic songwriting. The video for "Whip It" became an MTV smash, juxtaposing the band's low-budget futuristic look against a down-home farm setting and hints of S&M. However, Devo's commercial success proved to be short-lived. 1981's *New Traditionalists* was darker and more serious, not what the public wanted from a band widely perceived as a novelty act, and Devo somehow seemed to be running out of new ideas. Problems plagued the band as well: Bob Lewis successfully sued for theft of intellectual property after a tape of Mothersbaugh was found acknowledging Lewis' role in creating de-evolution philosophy, and the sessions for 1982's *Oh, No! It's Devo* were marred by an ill-considered attempt to use poetry written by would-be Reagan assassin John Hinckley as lyrical material.

As the '80s wore on, Devo found itself relegated to cult status and critical indifference, not at all helped by the lower quality of albums like 1984's *Shout* and 1988's *Total Devo*. Alan Myers, sensing a shift toward electronic drums, had departed in 1986, to be replaced by ex-Sparks and Gleaming Spires drummer David Kendrick. Devo recorded (to date) its last album of new material, *Smooth Noodle Maps*, in 1990, after which its members began to concentrate on other projects. Mark Mothersbaugh moved into composing for commercials and soundtracks, writing theme music for MTV's *Liquid Television*, Nickelodeon's *Rugrats*, *Pee-Wee's Playhouse*, and the Jonathan Winters sitcom *Davis Rules*. He also played keyboards with the Rolling Stones, programmed synthesizers for Sheena Easton, and sang backup with Debbie Harry. Buoyed by this success, Mothersbaugh opened a profitable production company called Mutato Muzika. Jerry Casale, meanwhile, who directed most of the band's videos, directed a video clip for the Foo Fighters' "I'll Stick Around." No reunions were expected, but as Devo's legend grew and other bands acknowledged their influence (Nirvana covered "Turnaround," while "Girl U Want" has been recorded by Soundgarden, Superchunk, and even Robert Palmer), their minimalistic electro-pop was finally given new exposure on six dates of the 1996 Lollapalooza tour, to enthusiastic fan response. The following year, Devo released a CD-Rom and again played selected dates on the Lollapalooza tour. —*Steve Huey*

**Q: Are We Not Men? A: We Are Devo!** / Jul. 1978 / Warner Brothers ✦✦✦✦
Devo's debut shows why the band still has a small but rabidly dedicated following well after their artistic peak. Their sound here is mostly guitar-based, with odd melodies and crazily jerky rhythms. With songs about masturbation ("Uncontrollable Urge"), freaks ("Mongoloid"), and technology ("Space Junk"), plus their patented de-evolution philosophy (the anthem "Jocko Homo," about the regression of mankind), and a wickedly deranged deconstruction of "(I Can't Get No) Satisfaction," Devo took punk's anti-mainstream, D.I.Y. spirit and filtered it through the sensibilities of weirdoes, nerds, and outcasts, relentlessly (and bizarrely) satirizing American culture and briefly picking up, attitude-wise, where The Mothers of Invention left off. —*Steve Huey*

**Duty Now for the Future** / Jul. 1979 / Warner Brothers ✦✦✦✦
Most of the aural weirdness on Devo's second album comes from the band's experiments with homemade synthesizer technology. As a result, both the guitars and jerky rhythms play a lesser role in their sound. Although it isn't quite as interesting, it's still appropriately strange, and Devo still doesn't sound quite like anyone else. *Duty* is loosely structured around the theme of everyday corporate drudgery and its effects on individuals. —*Steve Huey*

**Freedom of Choice** / Jul. 1980 / Warner Brothers ✦✦✦✦
*Freedom of Choice*, arguably Devo's strongest musical effort, revolves around relationships, insecurity, and the lack of flexibility in the American psyche. Their arrangements achieve an effective balance between guitars and synths, and the band's highly stylized visual component, this time featuring flower-pot-shaped "energy dome" hats, paid off in the video for "Whip It." The single went gold and helped the album sell over a million copies. Just barely less essential than *Q: Are We Not Men?* —*Steve Huey*

**New Traditionalists** / 1981 / Warner Brothers ✦✦✦
Pegged as a novelty act after the mainstream success of "Whip It" and *Freedom of Choice*, Devo apparently decided to emphasize its underlying ideas about American culture as an antidote. From the opening statement of purpose "Through Being Cool," *New Traditionalists* presents those views in a more straightforward way, with the unfortunate result that Devo is not nearly as absurdly amusing or interesting. The band often comes off as heavy-handed (pointing out on the otherwise terrific "Beautiful World" that the lyrics are intended to be ironic, just in case you didn't get the rather obvious point), as though it wants to make Serious Artistic Statements—but this isn't how Devo's best music works. Furthermore, the band's tendencies toward minimalistic, synth-centered arrangements and melodic deficiencies are much more pronounced here, making the music itself less interesting. *New Traditionalists* does have some very worthwhile moments, but it is disappointing, and it marks the beginning of the band's decline. —*Steve Huey*

**Oh, No! It's Devo** / 1982 / Warner Brothers ✦✦✦
By this point, much of Devo's endearing quirkiness had evaporated. Their sound here was not all that distinguishable from other new wave groups, and apart from a few songs, such as "That's Good" and "Peek-a-Boo," they simply weren't as musically or lyrically interesting as before. Incredibly, it seemed that Devo had not only lost its focus, but was out of ideas as well. Subsequent releases would only confirm this assessment. —*Steve Huey*

**The Greatest Hits** / Dec. 1990 / Warner Brothers ✦✦✦✦
While *Greatest Hits* contains all of the truly necessary items, it also tends to overlook some of the better album tracks from Devo's early period (easily their best work) in favor of a more balanced overview—which means that later albums receive more exposure than they really deserve. The import collection *Hot Potatoes: The Best of Devo* has stronger selections and is the preferred single-disc overview of Devo's career, but if you can't find it and only want one Devo disc, this will do. —*Steve Huey*

**The Greatest Misses** / Dec. 1990 / Warner Brothers ✦✦✦
This compilation, released concurrently with *Greatest Hits*, collects some of the band's stranger experiments, early album tracks, and a few rarities, such as the Booji Boy releases of "Be Stiff" and "Mechanical Man" (both available on the *Hardcore* compilations) and a UK B-side, "Penetration in the Centerfold." It does serve as a good supplement to the *Greatest Hits* collection, even if it is a bit haphazard, but listeners who want more than one Devo disc are advised to go ahead and purchase the first three albums rather than these two compilations—it's a better way to appreciate their achievements, and it's more entertaining. —*Steve Huey*

• **Pioneers Who Got Scalped: The Anthology** / May 9, 2000 / Rhino ✦✦✦✦
Heading into the new millennium, there was no truly definitive Devo compilation on the market, so Rhino attempted to remedy the situation with the double-disc *Pioneers Who Got Scalped: The Anthology*—and did a pretty good job, without quite pulling it off. When faced with a choice, the compilation takes the collector-oriented route by including the rarer version; as a result, buyers get the original Booji Boy-label recordings of "Jocko Homo" and "Mongoloid"; the single remixes of "Snowball," "Baby Doll," and "Disco Dancer"; and the extended dance remixes of "Here to Go" and "Theme From Doctor Detroit." As an added bonus for fans, the beginning and end of each disc features brief sound clips from the group's legendary short films. More problematic though, is the anthology's attempt to present a balanced overview of all phases of Devo's career. While admirable in intent, the fact is that the group's oeuvre grew steadily weaker as time passed, and since disc one runs all the way through their first (and best) four albums, disc two is a pretty bumpy ride. Not that it's worthless—collectors and devoted fans will be thrilled with the inclusion of quite a few songs that had only previously appeared on various movie soundtracks, and it also rescues some worthwhile (if not quite transcendent) singles from obscurity, like the aforementioned "Disco Dancer" and "Post Post-Modern Man." But as a listening experience,

it pales next to the first disc in terms of songwriting, musical invention, and edgy humor. Plus, where the band's early covers reinvented rock standards as comments on alienation and dehumanization, latter-day items like "Bread and Butter" and "Itsy Bitsy Teenie Weenie Yellow Polka Dot Bikini" are strictly novelties and nothing more. The bottom line is, you've got to be a hardcore Devo enthusiast to fully appreciate *Pioneers Who Got Scalped*. If you are, it's a fantastic package; if you want a more basic overview, you're better off with the somewhat disorganized *Greatest Hits* and *Greatest Misses* discs, or the import collection *Hot Potatoes*. It's kind of a shame, though, that in spite of the generally fine job done compiling *Pioneers*, there still isn't a single Devo anthology that distills *all* the best moments from their crucial early years, and throws in just the right (small) number of later singles. —*Steve Huey*

### Dido

*Vocals / Progressive Trance, Club/Dance, Alternative Pop/Rock, Singer/Songwriter*

Electronic pop chanteuse Dido entered London's Guildhall School of Music at age six, and by the time she reached her teens had already mastered piano, violin, and recorder. After touring with a British classical ensemble, she accepted a publishing job, meanwhile singing in a series of local groups before joining the trip-hop outfit Faithless—helmed by her older brother, the noted DJ and producer Rollo—in 1995. As the group's 1996 debut *Reverence* went on to sell some five million copies worldwide, Dido began working on solo material, developing a lushly ethereal sound combining elements of acoustic pop and electronica; signing with Arista, she released her debut LP *No Angel* in mid-1999. —*Jason Ankeny*

• **No Angel** / Jun. 1, 1999 / Arista ♦♦♦
The title notwithstanding, this debut from the former Faithless singer is pretty angelic-sounding stuff. You're bound to think of Sinéad O'Connor, but the comparison is as misleading as it is inevitable. Granted, Dido's ethereal vocals here frequently recall O'Connor; but Dido's music—while inventively augmented with electronics—is generally less adventurous. Ditto *No Angel*'s lyrics, which focus almost exclusively on love, lust, and relationships. That said, the fact remains that this is an auspicious and highly listenable album; atmospheric, seductive, and beautifully produced and sequenced. —*Jeff Burger*

### Dieselboy (Damian Higgins)

b. Steel City, PA
*Producer, DJ / Jungle/Drum'N'Bass, Club/Dance*

The jungle scene has always been centered in Britain, leaving Americans to watch from afar, import the records, and spin occasionally (though rarely very well). Damian Higgins reversed the trends a little bit with his nation-trotting gigs and frequent mix albums released as Dieselboy. Born in Pennsylvania, Higgins began DJing during the early '90s and organized house parties in and around Philadelphia. By 1993, the sound of jungle had begun pumping up America as well as Britain, and Dieselboy made the switch to drum'n'bass. He DJed at jungle events around America, and helmed 1996's Suburban Base jump-up compilation *Drum & Bass Selection USA*. Another Sub Base mix album, *97 Octane*, followed in 1997. Dieselboy's next two albums (*A Soldier's Story, System Upgrade*) appeared on Moonshine, the premiere American mix label. In mid-1999, Higgins began his production career with a single ("Atlantic State") for the respected British concern Technical Itch Recordings, and another single, "Descent," followed later that year for Palm Pictures. Dieselboy's 2000 release *The 6ixth Session* combined a mix disc with a full one of productions. —*John Bush*

**A Soldier's Story** / Jun. 29, 1999 / Moonshine Music ♦♦♦
Alongside DJ Soul Slinger, DJ db and DJ Dara, Dieselboy is one of America's top jungle DJs. The third major mix album he'd released in the past two years, *A Soldier's Story* is his best yet, including tracks from Technical Itch (three total), Jonny L, Danny Breaks, DJ Friction, and Moving Fusion. —*Keith Farley*

• **System Upgrade** / Mar. 18, 2000 / Moonshine Music ♦♦♦♦
For Dieselboy, one of the premiere American drum'n'bass DJs, a system upgrade means getting the latest dubplates on yet another mix album so that it doesn't sound like he's losing touch with the fast-moving, British-based jungle scene. As such, *System Upgrade* includes all-new productions from some familiar labels—Ram, Tech Itch, Moving Shadow, Renegade Hardware—all of which favor the jungle two-step with paranoid bio-tech samples and effects. Admittedly, the once-stale darkstep drum'n'bass sound began getting a bit more interesting after the turn of 2000—thanks in part to excellent producers like Ram Trilogy and Bad Company, both present here. Still, for better or worse, jungle fans are going to get exactly what they're expecting: a dozen or so newish tracks from the top labels in the UK, mixed to perfection. It's the standard drum'n'bass mix album, not so heavy on ideas, but completely up-to-date—that is, until next year's edition appears on the racks. —*John Bush*

### John Digweed

b. 1967, Hastings, England
*Producer, DJ / Progressive Trance, Electronica, Trance, Club/Dance*

Hastings native John Digweed had been DJing for nearly ten years when his DJ remix tape caught the ear of Renaissance promoter Geoff Oakes. He was soon working alongside the likes of another popular Renaissance DJ, Sasha. The new position gave the DJ what he needed for his big breakthrough, and he has continued to prosper since. Soon a Renaissance CD compilation containing some of Sasha and John's best remixes was released. The album was a surprise huge seller, warranting a follow-up, *Renaissance 2*, which soon approached gold status in Europe.

Like Sasha, Digweed isn't limited to remixing other people's records. He promotes shows in Europe under such pseudonyms as Babealicious and Northern Exposure. Sasha and Digweed continued their collaboration with the *Northern Exposure* series, compiling the duo's best remixes for other artists (the second volume was released in 1998 in completely different East and West Coast editions). He scored two Top 30 hits in 1997 with remixes of Chakra's "I Am" and Bedrock's "For What You Dream Of" (featured in the hit movie *Trainspotting*). Digweed also bought a dance club in the south of England in order to perform on a weekly basis. Via the *Global Underground* mix series, he released volumes recorded in Sydney and Hong Kong during 1998, then premiered *Bedrock*—his combination label and production concern—in late 1999. A stateside appearance in the American rave movie *Groove* also increased his stateside visibility. [See Also: Sasha + Digweed] —*Greg Prato*

**Global Underground: Sydney** / Oct. 13, 1998 / Thrive ♦♦♦♦
After collaborating with Sasha on the brilliant *Northern Exposure* series, John Digweed's *Sydney* is a mostly disappointing experience, with the exception of one or two beautiful moments. He has the right idea on this double album by first spinning a dark set of moderately paced deep progressive house with a tribal edge, before moving on to a higher-pitched second set of anthemic trance. Unfortunately, the first set gets boring really quickly, while the second set reaches an immense peak halfway through (which Digweed simply allows to fizzle up through the lackluster finale). When he begins the first set with Fortunato & Montresor's "Imagine," and Liquid Language's "Blu Savannah," Digweed establishes a hypnotic beginning beaming with lush sensuality and warm energy. After the first eight minutes, he lays down one deep tribal house track after another until the bleak lack of color, tone, and variety begins to challenge one's attention span. The final track of the first set, Albion's "Air," concludes the dull set on a very high note with ethereal tones, contrasting the lifelessness of the preceding tracks. Digweed's second set moves at a rapid pace, coming to an intense rushing peak with Deepsky's "Stargazer," and Paul Van Dyk's "Words" halfway through the set. After this heavenly experience, Digweed drops Vintage Millenium's "Propaganda." Other than some novelty vocals—"ecstasy, that's what it's all about"—this track totally kills the momentum established during the preceding tracks. The set sputters towards a dull conclusion that features an unfamiliar version of Crystal Method's "Keep Hope Alive" before finishing off anticlimactically with Ylem's "Out of It." —*Jason Birchmeier*

• **Bedrock** / Nov. 9, 1999 / Ultra ♦♦♦♦
Underground techno originated in the early '80s in cities like Detroit, Toronto, New York City, and London. Prodigy may have been a mainstream success, but DJs/producers like Kevin Saunderson, Stacey Pullen, and Carl Cox have kept it real by remaining exclusively with club gigs and molding most of their adult lives around spinning and scratching across the globe. John Digweed is another techno groundbreaker who has been crafting his DJ skills in the international dance scene since 1989. Aside from being chosen as one of the most prominent DJs by *DJ Magazine* and *Mixmag*, Digweed was

also the first UK DJ to establish his own US residency in the American club market. *Bedrock* is Digweed's double-disc tribute to his decade-old club event, a celebration of superb dance mixing, and innovative artists such as Sandra Collins, Pob & Taylor, Morel, and Tiny Trendies.

Disc one is freshly crisp on tracks like Raff 'n' Freddy's "Listen." BPT's "Moody," which features DJ Danny Morales, broods like a jungle party with sensual vocals, but "Judy" from C12 and Jole is a looping trance tune with electricity so intense, it's almost naughty, yet fascinating. Disc two continues to swirl and sway with bombastic techno grooves on cuts from Escape ("Salina"), and "Over & Out" from Mark Hunt, but Digweed and his musical partner, Nick Muir, appropriately called Bedrock, also contribute the stunning "Heaven Scent." Vivaciously lush with atmospheric ambience and house elements, Digweed is an original. *Bedrock* cuffs the classic and clips the modern; dance music never sounded so enchanting. It's simply about passion, so prepare to be mesmerized by the translucent beauty of John Digweed. —*MacKenzie Wilson*

## Dillinja (Karl Francis)

*Producer, DJ / Electronica, Jungle/Drum'N'Bass, Club/Dance*
One of the more prolific producers in jungle music—with records on over ten labels strong, two of them his own—Dillinja is one of the few drum'n'bass artists who spends more time in the production studio than in clubs. While living in Brixton in the early '90s, he became tipped to jungle by DJ Bryan G, who lived around the corner from him. Fascinated with the sound of drum'n'bass, Dillinja began recording in 1991, releasing tracks on Cybotron, Intelligent IQ, Conqueror, Logic, Lionheart, V, Philly Blunt, and his own Deadly Vinyl label. In 1994, he recorded "The Angels Fell" for Goldie's Metalheadz label and became one of the hottest names in jungle. With his friend Lemon D. (who has also recorded for Metalheadz), Dillinja formed Valve Records, a label that expanded the drum'n'bass aesthetic to include elements of ancient analogue sequences. Though he signed to the major label London for a long-term contract, a planned LP was dropped, and he continued producing multiple singles for the Test label during 1998-99. —*John Bush*

- **The Angels Fell/Ja Know Ya Big [Single]** / 1994 / Metalheadz ♦♦♦♦
While an atmospheric *Blade Runner* sample runs over the top, Dillinja's first single for Metalheadz concentrates on his excellent drum programming, with a stuttered bass kick and waves of renegade snares. —*John Bush*

**Tronic Funk/Thugs [Single]** / Sep. 28, 1998 / Test ♦♦♦

## Dimitri from Paris

*Producer, DJ / Electronica, Alternative Dance, Club/Dance, House*
Compared to his cohorts in the new wave of French dance music, Dimitri from Paris looks much farther afield for his influences. While both Air and Daft Punk make much of their affection for the music of the '70s (prog and disco, respectively), Monsieur Dimitri's inspiration comes from the Continental jet-setting faux-jazz of the '50s and early '60s (exemplified by Dick Hyman, John Barry, and Martin Denny), though the whole is updated by his long years of experience as a house DJ. Based in France, though born in Turkey, Dimitri entered the dance-music community during the mid-'80s by DJing at the French Radio 7. By 1990, his reputation had allowed him to record soundtracks for fashion barons like Chanel, Lagerfeld, and Gaultier. He released two solo EPs during 1993-94, plus the mini-LP *Esquisses*, and contributed to the Yellow Productions compilation *La Yellow 357*. He also remixed hundreds of artists, including Björk, the Brand New Heavies, New Order, James Brown, and Etienne Daho. Dimitri's debut album, *Sacre Bleu*, appeared in late 1996, also on Yellow Productions. Named Album of the Year by *MixMag*, it sold several hundred thousand copies around the world, and finally received an American release in early 1998. The 1997 mix album *Monsieur Dimitri's De-Luxe House of Funk*, however, showed the Frenchman coming back to his house roots. *ICU Session Three* followed in 1999, and the following spring he issued *A Night at the Playboy Mansion*. A second full-length studio effort *Disco Forever* was released in fall 2000. —*John Bush*

- **Sacrebleu** / Jun. 11, 1996 / Yellow Productions ♦♦♦♦
Low on total concept, high on the oh-so-hip cheese factor, French one-man studio whiz Dimitri from Paris dips into the exhausted forum of ironic lounge, spiked with shots of electronic house, with an ambition and enthusiasm found only in a few of his contemporaries (those other French-speaking hipsters, Stereolab, quickly come to mind) on his debut solo album *Sacrebleu*. His winks are a little too self-conscious, and the entire project prattles on a bit too long, but the overall vibe that DJ Dimitri lays down is one of a kinetic French New Wave film scored by a wide-eyed kid—whose hyperactive brain seems to be always working overtime—raised on simultaneous doses of swingin' '60s American junk culture and hip-shakin' Euro-pop. The results resemble something like Esquivel remade, retooled, and reshaped for the '90s dance floor. —*Michael Gallucci*

**Monsieur Dimitri's De-Luxe House of Funk** / Nov. 25, 1997 / Mixmag ♦♦♦♦
A club-centric mix album spanning deep house, Latin, disco, and novelty selections as only Dimitri could choose, *House of Funk* is a tad overladen with his own productions—including his own "Free Ton Style," plus remixes of Brand New Heavies, Björk, and United Future Organization—but there are few quibbles with such a varied, beat-heavy, unmistakably fun mix of tracks. —*John Bush*

**A Night at the Playboy Mansion** / Mar. 28, 2000 / Astralwerks ♦♦♦
On *A Night at the Playboy Mansion*, Dimitri from Paris pulls together some of the best sounds from the past and gives them a fresh twist. The 14-song set includes three freshly remixed songs from the late '70s and the original version of Cerrone's "Give Me Love" from 1977. The entire album has a strong disco feel from beginning to end. The beats thump at a mellow pace with a syncopated sense of funk. This disco sense also comes from the constant appearance of synthesized strings lingering during each song's melodic hook. Most of the 14 songs use vocals to varying effects. For example, the Sunburst Band's "I'll Be There for You (Joey Negro Vocal Mix)" includes a number of vocal tracks acting as background effects, sampled refrains, and peak outbursts. In the end, the heavy use of vocals can wear on the listener, who is more often accustomed to instrumental house tracks rather than an entire set of vocal tracks. Since every song has its own distinct vocal melodies, the set really has no salient peak or rest period. Instead, the entire set comes loaded with vocal hook after vocal hook, and melody after melody until Dimitri from Paris' fiery remix of Ashford and Simpson's "Found a Cure." The set would be more rewarding with a few breathers, but will surely satisfy anyone who appreciates a heavy dose of midtempo disco house loaded with vocals. —*Jason Birchmeier*

## Directions in Music

f. 1995, Chicago, IL
*Group / Experimental Rock, Indie Rock, Post-Rock/Experimental*
The improvisational post-rock trio Directions in Music comprised bassist Bundy K. Brown (an alumnus of Gastr del Sol and Tortoise), drummer Doug Scharin (also of H.I.M., Rex, and June of '44), and guitarist James Warden (a member of 40k). Their self-titled debut album, documenting a three-day session recorded at Chicago's Idful Studios during the spring of 1996, appeared on Thrill Jockey later that year; a single, "Echoes," followed on Soul Static Sound in 1997. —*Jason Ankeny*

- **Directions in Music** / 1996 / Thrill Jockey ♦♦♦♦
*Directions in Music* is the result of a three-day recording session at Chicago's Idful Music. It is a landmark album that represents Bundy K. Brown's commitment to innovation in his post-Tortoise days. For this session, he brings together fellow underground proponents James Warden and Doug Scharin of Rex, Him, and June of 44 fame. The result is an eight-song work of intriguingly radical texture. Taking a standard guitar, bass and drums format and overdubbing, splicing, mixing, and adding various noises, the three create an auditory masterpiece. Both catchy and complex, the album pleases at first listen and astounds thereafter. The dynamics range from the fast-paced euphoria of "4" to the somber "7" (none of the songs are titled.) *Directions in Music* lies somewhere between the erudite Tortoise and a subtle country flavor. The album consistently amazes, and one can only hope that this musical endeavor continues. —*Marc Gilman*

**Echoes [Single]** / 1997 / Soul Static Sound ♦♦♦
Actually billed to Bundy K. Brown's solo Directions aegis, "Echoes" is presumably a mixing-desk/outtakes revisitation of Brown's brilliant 1996 trio outing with Doug Scharin and James Warden, Directions in Music (the pair are propped on the record's inner label). A sort of East Village-via-Kingston soundtrack to some late-afternoon summer daydream, Brown assembles two gorgeous versions of the title track for this brief outing, bringing the fullness of his acumen for arrangement to bare on a marvelously dimensioned assemblage of funky post-rock, soul-jazz, and impressionistic dub with an in-

strumental palette as varied as it is texturally rich and detailed. Released by the eclectic British label Soul Static Sound. —*Sean Cooper*

## Dirty Beatniks

f. 1993, London, England
*Group / Big Beat, Electronica, Trip-Hop, Club/Dance*

A raw, grubby big beat act who filter influences from acid house and old-school rap through breakbeat techno, Dirty Beatniks was formed by friends Neil Higgins and Rory Carille, who met in Dublin during the late-'80s glory days of acid house. After moving to London in 1990, they added bassist/producer Justin Underhill and made their debut remixing for Cujo, Ruby, Akasha, and Marxman. After signing to Wall of Sound, London's favorite beat-specific label, the trio recorded the EP *Bridging the Gap*, then their debut full-length *One One Seven in the Shade* for a 1996 release. After a long break and several personnel changes, Dirty Beatniks returned as (mostly) a duo of Higgins and new member Mau, formerly the vocalist for Earthlings. They released *Feedback* in 2000. —*John Bush*

**One One Seven in the Shade** / Nov. 18, 1996 / Wall of Sound ♦♦

● **Feedback** / Aug. 8, 2000 / Wall of Sound ♦♦♦
Dirty Beatniks return to the music scene after a four-year break with *Feedback*. Most of the original members are gone, except for the founder, Neil Higgins, who has brought aboard Mau Beatnik (former vocalist of Earthlings). Compared to acts such as Propellerheads, the Beatniks serve up a slice of electronic, catchy, eclectic sounds and commentary vocals. —*Diana Potts*

## Disco Inferno

f. 1989, db. 1995
*Group / Ambient Pop, Post-Rock/Experimental, Experimental, Alternative Pop/Rock*

Disco Inferno were formed by teenagers Ian Crause (guitars and vocals), Paul Willmott (bass), Daniel Gish (keyboards), and Rob Whatley (drums) in Essex in 1989. Gish was sacked by autumn of that year and would later join Bark Psychosis; the remaining trio began gigging around London to indifferent pub crowds. The band's early work, summed up on the accurately titled *In Debt*, bears the heavy influence of Joy Division, Wire, and other significant post-punk bands of the late '70s and early '80s. Though derivative and not nearly as experimental and imaginative as the band's later work, the material on *In Debt* successfully pays tribute (and at times rivals) the output of their predecessors. Without knowing it, you might think them to be a Factory band circa 1981—dark, jagged, and haunting.

Crause soon became infatuated with the unique sounds of My Bloody Valentine and the Young Gods, as well as the Bomb Squad's revolutionary production and sampling on Public Enemy's records. A major turning point for Disco Inferno, they began to issue a series of some of the most uncompromising and experimental music of the mid-'90s. The *Summer's Last Sound* EP in 1992 marked this new beginning. Percolating indifference and economic troubles on the part of the band's label, Cheree, came to a head, and Rough Trade came to the rescue and began to issue the band's releases. The new label saved the band's life, as the members believed that they were too challenging for anyone else to understand or care for. The years of 1993 and 1994 turned out to be Disco Inferno's most productive and creative, yielding four EPs and an LP, *DI Go Pop*. Disorienting, confusing, and highly schizophrenic, the challenging releases were in direct contrast to the prevailing Brit-pop scene of the time. They took AR Kane's futurist pop a couple steps further and secured a devout and small following that found solace in their wildly imaginative, peerless nature.

After the *It's a Kid's World* EP, Crause found himself in a creative rut and hadn't the slightest clue as to what their follow-up should entail. Feeling creatively drained from *Go Pop*'s boundary breaking vision and inability to gain sustainable recognition, Crause and company mustered enough creative strength to record *Technicolour*, which didn't find release until '96 and failed to register a blip on the commercial and critical radar. By that time, the group dissolved due to frustration and a seemingly endless, downward financial spiral. The band's last recording session saw posthumous release as a six song EP on the Tugboat label. Crause continued to record under the Floorshow alias, but none of his work surfaced commercially. —*Andy Kellman*

**Summer's Last Sound [EP]** / 1992 / Cheree ♦♦♦♦
The band's last release on the Che label, or more accurately the sublabel Cheree, was the first in five astonishing singles, all containing non-album material, which cemented Disco Inferno's reputation for haunting beauty combined with extreme experimentation. Harnessing the power of sampling and avant-garde production techniques, the band's songs grew ever more ambitious, even as Ian Crause became the best lyricist of the outsider since Morrissey. The title track slowly builds over a weirdly ascending melody line, with the guitar completely transformed into a high, floating edge of sound, while "Love Stepping Out" has only Wilmot's bassline to link it to traditional rock, otherwise indulging in an electronic soundscape, half calmly beautiful, half strangely threatening. Crause delivers his images of decay and, in the latter track, feelings of hatred and loathing for happy couples out parading around with a distanced, lost air, increasing their impact even more. —*Ned Raggett*

● **D.I. Go Pop** / 1994 / Bar/None ♦♦♦♦
Following after three increasingly inventive, truly unique singles ("Summer's Last Sound," "From the Devil to the Deep Blue Sea," "The Last Dance") that demonstrated how thoroughly the band embraced the sampling aesthetic to create a distinct kind of modern art-rock, *Go Pop* embraced the irony of its title with a passion. Pop hooks existed on the record but only in the most spare, hard-to-find forms; otherwise, Disco Inferno was out to create an album to challenge as many listeners as possible without fully embracing a noise approach. In its tension between accessibility and extreme experimentation, *Go Pop* resembles no other album so much as Wire's *154* for the modern day—very English, encompassing a variety of styles and approaches, seemingly totally cryptic yet more touching to the mind, body and soul than anyone might have expected. "In Sharky Water" begins things with water sounds, a basic bass, and a drum slow pulse before turning into an overtly studio-produced thrash combined with shouted lyrics. Every song takes on a different tack, all clearly by the same band while remaining distinctly unique. "New Clothes for the New World" wraps distorted, shuddered vocals around equally strange sounding church bell samples, "Even the Sea Sides Against Us" floats on an acoustic guitar bed endlessly looping around a series of wave sounds and odd keyboard touches, and so forth. It ends with a found-sound tape of a landlady berating the band for playing too loud; it's not the noise but the complexity that leaves your mouth open. Probably one of the only bands truly worthy of the term "post-rock," Disco Inferno is heading in a direction that no previous band has fully embraced. —*Ned Raggett*

**Second Language [EP]** / 1994 / Rough Trade ♦♦♦♦
Following up *D. I. Go Pop* would be a tall order for anyone showing how Disco Inferno kept topping each previous milestone ever more commandingly, but *Second Language* is simply perfect—four songs that never fail to thrill and touch. The title track, according to Crause in contemporaneous interviews, was partially inspired by the Durutti Column and the Chameleons (namely, such bands' majestic guitar beauty and energy). Rather than simply recreate such sound, Disco Inferno hot-wire it, with Crause's guitar/sampler combination running rampant. Harps, spiraling piano loops, Wilmot's clean bass, Whatley's crisp percussion, and more all build through the song until Crause fully cuts loose with a soaring solo that leaves everything the Edge ever tried to do in the dust. "The Atheist's Burden" is relatively more restrained in comparison: low synth pulses start things off, with guitars scraping and surging on the sides rather than up front until the song's final minute—but still with a fine feeling to it. "At the End of the Line" is a cold, clear wonder of a tune, with gorgeous electric guitar raining down from above as bass anchors the rhythm, and Crause's ruminative, stark lyric is delivered with quiet confidence. "A Little Something" is as close as the band ever got to a fun rave-up, and even this was still very much Disco Inferno. Unexpected mixing levels, Crause singing in the same soft, questioning style about being "taught a little song to only sing when things were going horribly wrong," samples everywhere, loveliness, and confusion all at once characterize the song. Arguably the trio's finest moment, and one which humbles most bands' entire careers. —*Ned Raggett*

**In Debt** / Mar. 13, 1995 / Carrot Top ♦♦♦
"In debt" is right—as bandleader Crause freely admitted in interviews in later years, Disco Inferno's beginnings were so clearly inspired by such post-punk luminaries as the Durutti Column, early Wire, and above all else Joy Division, that on first blush it seemed unlikely the band would go further than fine nostalgia. The surprising touch on this compilation of the trio's first single, album, and EP turns out to be how quickly the band started to evolve its own distinct identity. The first two tracks, "Entertainment" and "Arc in

Round," made up the debut single; from the crisp slam of the drums to the intricate, delicate guitar work and non-melodic singing, Disco Inferno's Joy Division fascination hangs so heavy it's almost the work of a tribute band. "Emigre," the original opening track for the first album, is buoyed by a powerful, immediate combination of sparse drumming, digitally echoed riffs and loops, and hints of synth use; the inspirations remain clear, but the song itself is much more their own, brought home with a killer guitar solo and drum break at the end. Similarly fine, soaring numbers such as "Freethought" and more ominous tracks like "Bleed Clean" ("... or does your blood flow in a mess?") mesh with intriguing side efforts like the primarily acoustic "Hope to God." The final four tracks, from the post-album EP, really sees the band take off; "Waking Up" is Disco Inferno's first total masterpiece, opening with an echoed bass note, astoundingly subtle percussion samples, then the deadly calm lyric "A sky without a god is a clear blue sky." "Fallen Down the Wire" rips along to a sudden, unexpected end after an increasingly fierce build-up. All in all, a striking starting point for what was to come next. —*Ned Raggett*

## disJam

f. Hamburg, Germany
*Group / Jazz-House, Club/Dance, Acid Jazz, House*
The Hamburg acid-jazz troupe known as disJam increasingly slanted their instrumental talents toward the electronica and trip-hop crowds. Formed in the early '90s, the band came together around keyboard player Ralf Petter, bassist Sascha Panknin, percussionist Oliver Schumacher, guitarist Volker Kurnoth, and reed player Ole Janssen. The collective soon became popular on the continental acid-jazz scene and recorded their self-titled debut album in 1995 (it also earned American distribution through Instinct's *This Is Acid Jazz* series). Gradually shedding instrumentalists as the focus turned to electronic music and dance-jazz fusion, disJam recorded three albums for Yo Mama, often with help from vocalists (the 1996 album *Phuturing the Poetry of Lemn Sissay* was a collaboration with Sissay, a Manchester poet). In 1998, the band—basically down to a trio of Panknin, Petter, and Schumacher, plus new addition Christoph Kähler on vocals (occasionally) and guitar—signed to Shadow Records and released *Return of the Manchurian*. Once again distributed in America, disJam returned in 2000 with *Hybrid Honey*. —*John Bush*

Disjam / Jul. 11, 1995 / Instinct ♦♦♦

● Hybrid Honey / Feb. 22, 2000 / Shadow ♦♦♦♦
After releasing five albums in just over three years, disJam apparently took a bit more time to record, and the result is easily their best album yet. *Hybrid Honey* is filled with accomplished groove music tied to disco and jazz-funk, with plenty of post-production tactics to add to the keyboards, guitar, bass, and percussion that comprise most tracks. The album is divided in half: the first side is subtitled "Day," the second "Night"; so the more uptempo songs appear early on, while mellow grooves and atmospheric synth take over for the end. *Hybrid Honey* proves not only that disJam have mastery over their instruments, but that they also have dozens of intriguing ideas to drive the musicianship. —*John Bush*

## Disjecta (Mark Clifford)

*Producer / Experimental Techno, Electronica*
Disjecta is the solo side-project of guitarist and electronics composer Mark Clifford, also a member of ambient/post-rock group Seefeel. Unlike Seefeel's warm, serene soundscapes, Clifford's solo work is far less accessible, tying dark, bassy textures to clunky, abrasive beats that recall the more measured moments of labelmates such as RAC and Autechre. Clifford's first work as Disjecta was a pair of singles titled "Looking for Snags," released simultaneously by Warp in early 1996. A full length, *Clean Pit and Lid*, followed soon after. —*Sean Cooper*

● Clean Pit and Lid / 1996 / Warp ♦♦♦
Considerably darker and more rhythmic than his work with Seefeel, Disjecta is Mark Clifford's more techno-derived aegis, combining studio trickery with crisp, chunky beats and basslines that sound closer to the robotic bite of Autechre and RAC. —*Sean Cooper*

## DiY

f. 1989, Nottingham, England
*Group / Rave, Club/Dance, Acid House*
A loose collective of DJs (including DK, Jack, Pezz, Digs & Whoosh, Emma & Pip, DJ Dick, and Pip) who threw massive parties in vacant warehouses and rural areas, Nottingham, England's DiY was begun in 1989 as a response to laws and club procedures that stifled the original ethic of dance culture. As the rave movement grew out of the underground, more people began investigating, and DiY set up its own label for recording projects, called Strictly 4 Groovers. A DiY contract with Warp has also resulted in several singles and an album. —*John Bush*

● 2922 Days / Dec. 15, 1997 / DiY Discs ♦♦♦
DiY's debut album is a set of swirling tribal-house, with a few nods to contemporary "intelligent" styles and trance. For an act not necessarily associated with album productions, it's a pretty solid LP. —*John Bush*

## DJ Assault

*Group / Techno Bass, Electro-Techno, Detroit Techno, Club/Dance, Techno*
DJ Assault has had a large hand in bringing ghetto-tech, aka booty music, from the urban streets of Detroit to the suburban club circuit. The incorporation of electro beats with hardcore, sometimes pornographic lyrics is what makes ghetto-tech highly distinguishable from its other techno cousins. Easily mistaken as a solo act, DJ Assault is actually two men—Craig Adams and Ade' Mainor, aka Mr. De. Together, they run two record labels, Assault Rifle and Electrofunk, which have released Assault's signature tracks, "Crank this Mutha," "Sex on the Beach," and "Ass 'N' Titties."

At the tender age of twelve, Craig Adams began his DJ career spinning at local parties and events in his hometown of Detroit. He took a three-year hiatus to study at the University of Atlanta but soon moved back to Michigan to start producing music in his own studio. Adams finished his studio by adding a local producer, Mr. De. After ill relations with a prior label, the two formed Electrofunk in 1996. Shortly thereafter, they released their first EP, *Terrortech EP*, with the singles "Crank this Mutha" and "Technofreak." The album was a good introduction of the new brand of techno that incorporated heavy bass beats, techno samples, and simple, catchy vocal hooks. During the summer of 1996, Assault released the first *Straight Up Detroit Sh*t (SUDS)* mix CD. Due to the first CD's popularity, Assault released the second volume that September. More popularity would follow the production team with the Ghetto Tech anthems "Ass 'N' Titties" and "Sex on the Beach." After only a year of being in business, Adams and De were able to say that they had sold more records than any other techno artist in the region at that time.

In 1997, due to the amount of production and popularity, Electrofunk split in two—Assault Rifle Records and Electrofunk Records Distribution. This allowed the two to produce and distribute their own material. In April of 1997, *SUDS, Vol. 3* was released along with *Belle Isle Tech*. The latter contained two CDs, one completely rap and the other a compilation of Assault Rifle and Electrofunk releases. The CD offered both sounds of the urban streets to suburban and urban fans. At the end of 1997 DJ Assault released *SUDS, Vol. 4*, which featured 99 tracks and served as an example of the fast style of DJing that developed around ghetto-tech. Unfortunately, Craig and Mainor dissolved their partnership in mid-2000, due to private reasons. Craig immediately started his own label, Jefferson Ave., named for a major street in Detroit that runs from the east to the west side. —*Diana Potts*

● Belle Isle Tech / 1997 / Assault Rifle ♦♦♦
Representing some of the most non-socially redeeming "straight-up ghetto sh*t" to ever come out of Detroit, the sounds of DJ Assault and his partner, Mr. De, are well represented on this release. The first album of this two-record set features the duo's brand of potent gangster rap, which merges the violent egomania of NWA with the pornographic sexism of 2 Live Crew. The second album features a 38-track mix featuring many of the "booty" or "ghettotech" anthems produced by the popular Detroit duo. After experiencing the two very different albums it becomes apparent that Assault and De should stick to producing beats and their booty anthems or else continue to sharpen their rapping skills. Though the ghetto duo do an admirable job of laying rhymes over their hip-hop beats on this, their first attempt at rap, their lack of noteworthy lyrical content becomes stale after the jokes and attitude get old. On the other hand, the accompanying mix CD illustrates exactly why this duo rose to such prominence so quickly. Flying through one pitched-up booty-shakin' track after the next, Assault moves through many of his most revered classics—"Ass 'N' Titties," "Sex on the Beach," "Dick By the Pound"—while also managing to fit in numerous other functional dancefloor tracks. —*Jason Birchmeier*

## DJ Cam (Laurent Daumail)

b. Paris, France

*Producer, DJ / Electronica, Ambient Breakbeat, Club/Dance, Hip-Hop*

Parisian hip-hop devotee Laurent Daumail is one of a few but growing number of French artists updating hip-hop for the chill-out crowd, drawing on the beats'n'samples groundwork of producers such as Rakim, DJ Premier, and Prince Paul and combining it with broad, impressionistic strokes of dub, jazz, and soundtrack-y ambience. Like countrymen the Mighty Bop and La Funk Mob, Cam is stylistically closest to Mo'Wax artists such as DJ Shadow and DJ Krush: minimalist, downbeat instrumental hip-hop built from obscure samples and stomp-box turntable accompaniment, bent and twisted into new, artfully arranged compositions. His debut, 1994's *Underground Vibes*, was released on the tiny French label Street Jazz and was followed by a live recording for the Inflammable imprint (one of only a few "live" recordings in a genre so reliant on the temporal concessions of the recording studio). Dubbed *Underground Live*, the album featured performed extrapolations of many of the tracks from his debut, as well as a few new and improvised tracks. Now nearly impossible to find, those first two albums were reissued in America by Shadow Records, packaged together as the single-CD priced *Mad Blunted Jazz* (particularly useful since acquiring both on import could run more than $50).

Although Cam's music has found little acceptance in his home country, where racial tension has stratified the hip-hop community into rigid definitions of what the music is—and who should be making it (Cam himself is white)—audiences in the UK, Japan, and America have begun picking up on his style. In 1996 Cam was featured on the sprawling Mo'Wax compilation *Headz 2* (among many others) remixed tracks for such artists as Tek 9 and La Funk Mob, and most recently collaborated on live and in-studio projects with Snooze and DJ Krush (he co-wrote a few tracks on the latter's 1997 Mo'Wax release, *Mi Sound*). Cam released *Substances* on Inflammable in 1997. The next year, his major-label debut *The Beat Assassinated* appeared on Columbia Records. In 2000, he released a three-volume series named *The Loa Project*. —*Sean Cooper*

**Underground Vibes** / 1994 / Street Jazz ♦♦♦♦

Cam's debut collection of "abstract hip-hop" finds similar company in artists such as DJ Krush, Howie B., and the Solid Doctor, with pitched down, echo-chamber beats, sparse jazz and funk quotes, and turntable atmospherics combining into a smooth, impressionistic affair. The album was reissued by Shadow records—together with his live Inflammable follow-up, *Underground Live*—as *Mad Blunted Jazz* in 1996. —*Sean Cooper*

**Underground Live** / Jun. 11, 1996 / Inflammable ♦♦♦♦

Live hip-hop albums are hardly common, but then neither is Cam's approach here, seamlessly blending loping, downtempo breaks with thick, dubby basslines, deft, heavily treated scratching, and instrumental samples and vocal drop-ins that make for a solid, tight flow. Cam presents live, tricked-up improvisations of tracks from his debut album, *Underground Vibes*, as well as a few new ones. The album was reissued as disc two of the domestic Shadow label's double Cam release, *Mad Blunted Jazz*. —*Sean Cooper*

• **Mad Blunted Jazz** / Nov. 11, 1996 / Shadow ♦♦♦♦

This handy double-pack combines Cam's first two full-length releases, *Underground Vibes* and *Underground Live*, released on Street Jazz and Inflammable, respectively. Hazy, downtempo instrumental hip-hop with shades of jazz, funk, and soul. —*Sean Cooper*

**Substances** / 1997 / Inflammable ♦♦♦

A far more diverse set of relaxed (and occasionally not so) deviations from clubland, with bits of jungle, electro, and even house creeping into the mix. Cam has broadened the scope of his sound, here; where previous releases tended to focus on sonic depth rather than breadth, atmosphere occupying first chair, *Substances*' sample arrangements are in places almost epic, and the beatwork is far more complex and inventive. —*Sean Cooper*

**The Beat Assassinated** / May 11, 1998 / Columbia ♦♦♦

While *Substances* moved DJ Cam closer to the minimalist beat-camp headed up by DJ Krush, *The Beat Assassinated* is a bit more tied to upfront hip-hop. True, the concrete beats and basement-style productions heard here are far removed from any rap on the charts in America, but the addition of rappers like Channel Live, Silvah Bullet and DJ Djam results in a comfortable balance between underground and mainstream. —*John Bush*

**The French Connection** / 2000 / Shadow ♦♦♦

Borrowing the wider name recognition of mixer DJ Cam, its compadre in the French rap scene, the Parisian avant-hip-hop imprint Artefact Records released this 2000 label retrospective, with tracks from ten different producers. Though none of these artists are well known in the international electronic community, they acquit themselves quite well, each taking the template of downbeat hip-hop and adjusting it thanks to influences from jazz and soundtrack work ("Hide & Seek" by Shinju Gumi, "Spook" by O'Neill), fusion or quiet storm R&B ("Garance" by Art Ensemble, "One of These Days" by Zend Avesta), scratchy, sample-driven American rap (the DJ Cam remix of "More" by Baron Samedi, "Underwater Rhymes" by Doctor L.), and true avant-garde ("Fog Plants" by Naruhisa Matsuoka). DJ Cam's mixing is smooth; it spotlights the diversity of the label, quite underrated considering the quality on display here. —*John Bush*

**The Loa Project, Vol. 2** / Jul. 11, 2000 / Six Degrees ♦♦♦♦

For *The Loa Project, Vol. 2*, DJ Cam expanded his emphasis on cellar-dwelling hip-hop to embrace the legacies of disco and dub, two styles whose roots lie quite close to the beginnings of rap in the early '70s. For "Ganja Man," Cam reprises the bassline from a seminal Augustus Pablo dub version ("King Tubby Meets the Rockers Uptown") to create an intriguing jump-up drum'n'bass track. The French producer also salutes the disco/house axis with several tracks, including the jazzy house jam "Juliet" and the breakbeat filter-disco number "DJ Cam Sound System." Of course, ranging from genre to genre is nothing new for the vast majority of electronic producers, so the risk here becomes losing the distinctive DJ Cam sound to a wash of bland stylistic exercises. Fortunately, his production and beat-mining skills rescue any possible impression of look-what-I-can-do studio theatrics, and Cam also works through plenty of hip-hop territory. The scratchy hardcore musings of "Mental Invasion" are reminiscent of DJ Premier, one of hip-hop's best, and Cam even tips his hat to Timbaland with the hyper-breakbeat R&B of "You Do Something to Me" (featuring China). "Ghetto Love" isn't quite the G-funk jam listeners might expect, instead comprising some quintessentially cinematic dark trip-hop. Despite the diversity, *The Loa Project, Vol. 2* hangs together well since DJ Cam only enlarged his focus to include styles with much kinship to his first love. Note to indie-rock fans: the Frank Black who features on "Candyman" is apparently *not* the former Pixies frontman, though it's unclear from the track and the liner notes just who he is or what he does. —*John Bush*

## DJ Dara

*Producer, DJ / Jungle/Drum'N'Bass, Club/Dance*

Besides the Liquid Sky community, DJ Dara is probably New York's leading exponent of drum'n'bass. He has led several club nights around the city and began recording for Sm:)e Communications with his first album, *Rinsimus Maximus*, released in July 1997. The following year, he returned with the mix album *Full Circle: Drum & Bass DJ Mix*, while both *Renegade Continuum* and *Halfway Home* appeared in 1999. DJ Dara continued his prolific output in early 2000 with *From Here to There*. —*John Bush*

**Rinsimus Maximus** / Jul. 22, 1997 / Sm:)e ♦♦

DJ Dara's first album for Sm:)e Communications is a solid example of bridging jungle and house to good effect, much as Omni Trio's Rob Haigh does on the British side of the Atlantic. The breakbeats are quite steady (he is a DJ, after all) and there's a poppy diva vocal on that all-important second track. The rest of the album focuses on harder material, and though it is quite pleasant, it doesn't seem to have been worked with too much—breakbeat plus bassline thirty seconds later, add effects one minute into the song, and Dara's got himself another track. All this is impressive for an American jungle album but not quite all that compared to most of the British imports. —*John Bush*

• **Full Circle: Drum & Bass DJ Mix** / Aug. 11, 1998 / Moonshine Music ♦♦♦♦

Though his production skills weren't quite up to snuff on 1997's *Rinsimus Maximus*, DJ Dara proves himself an efficient, exciting mixer with the following year's collection *Full Circle*. It's a set of bracing hardstep jungle and tech-step with tracks from Ed Rush & Optical, Matrix, Decoder, DJ SS, Swift, PFM, E-Z Rollers, and DJ Zinc, among others. —*John Bush*

**Halfway Home** / Aug. 24, 1999 / Smile ♦♦♦♦

Dara's second production album is quite a leap from the straight house-influenced breakbeats on 1997's *Rinsimus Maximus*. His recent mix sessions and live dates had included a lot of tough two-step tracks from labels like Renegade Hardware and Technical Itch, so it's no surprise to find that *Halfway Home* has a very similar sound. While a few tracks have piano runs and a sound reminiscent of his earlier material, many of the tracks here ("Heartbeat," "93rd Current") are technological nightmares that rank along the best of Optical and Ed Rush. To say nothing of his mixing skills, Dara's obviously come a long way as a producer and *Halfway Home* is solid proof. —*John Bush*

**From Here to There** / Jan. 25, 2000 / Moonshine Music ♦♦♦
Dara retreats from the darkside a bit on *From Here to There*, opening with a few positive-minded productions including L Double & Serena's "Crazy" and a Klute remix of his own production, "Duplicity." By the fourth track, we're in familiar territory for DJ Dara, with many of the usual suspects: DJ Hype ("The Big 3-Oh"), Decoder ("Hazardous"), Kenny Ken ("Project One"), and John B. ("Prowler," "Progress"). Perhaps sensing that he's in danger of getting a bit stale, Dara takes a more active part in the mix and chooses transitions that don't necessarily flow as smoothly as usual. —*John Bush*

## DJ ESP (Woody McBride)

b. Dec. 6, 1967, Bismarck, ND
*Producer, DJ / Rave, Club/Dance, Acid House*
Mixer, producer, and event-promoter DJ ESP (aka Woody McBride) did much to bring the sound of acid-house and rave to the upper Midwest in the late '80s and early '90s. Born in North Dakota, he moved to Minneapolis in 1988, discovered a burgeoning house scene, and began spinning at clubs and raves around the area. McBride quickly acquired a trademark for his Wall of Bass speaker set-up at DJ gigs and began recording as well with a trio of hard, dark acid EPs from 1993-94 (*Interference, Amplification '94, Bad Acid-No Such Thing*) that inaugurated Milwaukee's Drop Bass Network. He also co-produced tracks with Freddie Fresh (another transplanted Minnesotan) and recorded for Detroiter Alan Oldham's Generator Records, establishing himself along with fellow hard DJ/producers like Adam X, DJ Hyperactive, Damon Wild, and Delta 9. McBride also founded his own label, Communique Records, which released his own tracks plus those by frequent Drop Bass culprits. (An array of Communique sublabels—Head in the Clouds, Country Western, All Ears, MakeOut Music, Sunsuist, Party Rock, Tape—kept him busy as well.) Despite his relentless release schedule, McBride has never attempted a proper full-length. —*John Bush*

• **The Power Hour (Remixes) [Single]** / Nov. 11, 1996 / Virtual ♦♦♦

## DJ Faust

*Producer, DJ / Turntablism, Underground Rap*
DJ Faust is a turntablist with an incredibly dense style of cut-and-paste mixing that leaves little room for pause and entertains shades of original *musique concrèté* producers like Pierre Schaeffer and Pierre Henry. Born in North Carolina but based in Atlanta around the Third World Citizens collective (including DJ Shotgun from Goodie Mob), Faust released his debut *Man or Myth?* in 1998. The *Fathomless* EP followed later that year, trailed in 1999 by *Inward Journeys*. —*John Bush*

• **Man or Myth?** / Jul. 28, 1998 / Bomb Hip Hop ♦♦♦♦
One of the best turntablist debuts on record (or CD for that matter), *Man or Myth?* references dozens of groove classics—from Zapp to Public Enemy to Coldcut to the Steve Miller Band to Mantronix—but cross-cuts through them with such speed and accuracy that Faust remains the focus throughout. While too many turntablists use their albums more for scratching workouts, Faust lets the beats speak for themselves, working in short bursts of scratching only occasionally. Sequenced as one track (although it lists 27 on the back cover), *Man or Myth?* is an essential piece of the instrumental hip-hop puzzle. DJs Shotgun, Craze, and Shortee—from Faust's Third World Citizens collective—feature on a couple of tracks. —*John Bush*

**Inward Journeys** / Aug. 17, 1999 / Bomb Hip Hop ♦♦♦♦
Faust's second album in just over a year is yet another trip through the mind (and turntables) of one of the best DJs out there. It's just as dense as *Man or Myth?* but takes Faust's beatboxing skills even farther along. There's a certain amount of been-there-done-that to the proceedings, but Faust's deft turntable skills rescues any case of the musical blah's. —*Keith Farley*

## DJ Food

*Group / Trip-Hop, Jungle/Drum'N'Bass, Club/Dance*
DJ Food is a collaborative project between Coldcut/Ninja Tune duo Matt Black and Jonathan More, and second-half PC (born Patrick Carpenter) and Strictly (born Kevin Foakes). Although the moniker originally referred only to Black and More's several-volumed series of stripped-down breaks records designed for deck use (i.e. "food" for DJs), club booking demands for the assumedly proper-named DJ Food dictated the pair make an ongoing project of it. Adding PC and Strictly to spice things up (and differentiate DJ Food from Coldcut when they played the same bill), the quartet released a series of 12" singles in various combinations starting in 1994 (including "Freedom"/"Consciousness"), with their proper debut full-length *A Recipe for Disaster* appearing the following year. The quartet also toured Europe, Canada, and America as DJ Food (mainly DJing) and regularly mashed it up side-by-side on Coldcut's weekly KISS FM show *Solid Steel*. PC and Strictly were also hired on by Warp Records to compile and mix a series of Warp releases entitled *Blech* drawing from the influential experimental techno label's back catalog. More and Black continue to split their time between DJ Food and Coldcut, as well as the day-to-day operation of their immensely popular Ninja Tune and Ntone labels. DJ Food's second album, *Kaleidoscope* appeared in April of 2000, to warm reviews. [See Also: Coldcut] —*Sean Cooper*

**Jazz Brakes, Vol. 2** / 1992 / Ninja Tune ♦♦
Available on CD as well as vinyl (though for unknown reasons, since these are mostly tools for DJs), DJ Food's second volume of *Jazz Brakes* includes 23 tracks of two- to three-minute samples and loops, all guaranteed to not upset the mood between tracks in a usual DJ's set. Titles such as "Last Coltrane to Skaville," "Cosmic Jam, Part 1," "Funky Emergency," and "Deadly Serious Bass Party" tell most of the story here. —*John Bush*

• **A Recipe for Disaster** / 1995 / Ninja Tune ♦♦♦♦
Although More and Black's best works are scattered over endless singles, EP, and compilation tracks, *Recipe for Disaster* proves they can pull an album off when they feel like it. Together with a handful of collaborators, the pair split their resources between funky instrumental hip-hop, drum'n'bass, turntable experiments, and armchair trip-hop, providing a good cross-section of the group's various styles. —*Sean Cooper*

**Refried Food, Vols. 1-6** / 1997 / Ninja Tune ♦♦♦♦
The collected output of a number of mix/remix tracks the group released over the course of several months, the *Refried Food* series features some quality reconstructions by Autechre, the Herbaliser, Wagon Christ, Squarepusher, MLO, Journeyman, and others. Released as three double-pack 12"s as well as CD. —*Sean Cooper*

**Kaleidoscope** / Apr. 4, 2000 / Ninja Tune ♦♦♦♦
Apparently comprising recordings from 1996 right up to the year of its release, *Kaleidoscope* continues on from the proper DJ Food debut *A Recipe for Disaster* with a collection of beat-heavy turntablist productions that often hit the high peaks of their close friends Coldcut. Since PC and Strictly Kev *are* DJs first and foremost, *Kaleidoscope* has an atmosphere of cut'n'paste schizophrenia, experimental risk-taking, and rampant comedy reminiscent of their previous mix-album assignments (the Warp compilation *Blech* and Coldcut's *Journeys by DJ*).

As on *A Recipe for Disaster*, however, the production is *much* better than listeners should expect from a pair of turntable-twisters. Jazz is undeniably the backbone of this album, straight from the opener "Full Bleed" where a raw drum kit pounds out stuttered breakbeats with plenty of high-maintenance cymbal work. There are references to all sorts of jazz cats from the cool era, including the fiery Quincy Jones sample that drives "The Riff" and the collaboration with jazz poet Ken Nordine on "The Ageing Young Rebel." The most inventive track is undoubtedly "Break," which turns a spoken-word piece by Lightnin' Rod dealing with billiards (pun definitely intended) into a turntablist high-wire act by repeatedly cutting off the audio between syllables. Even when you've put aside the high-profile musical references and silly sense of humor, though, *Kaleidoscope* remains a great album. Even "Nocturne" and "The Crow," a pair of downtempo tracks with little (on the surface) to recommend them, are still very compelling. With productions these strong, perhaps it's time for PC and Strictly Kev to strip the DJ from their albums just to make sure no one confuses them with part-time producers. —*John Bush*

## DJ Godfather

*Producer, DJ / Electro-Techno, Detroit Techno, Bass Music, Hip-Hop*

DJ Godfather is an influential force in Detroit's vibrant electro underground, which has undergone something of a renaissance in recent years through the work of AUX 88, Brendan "Ectomorph" Gillian, Drexciya, Will Web, and Dopplereffekt. While Detroit's more persistent legacy continues to be techno of the four-to-the-floor variety, artists such as Godfather have mined techno's pre-history—machine-generated breakbeat tracks such as Cybotron's "Clear" and "R-9," Egyptian Lover's "Egypt, Egypt" and "Dance," etc.—fashioning thick, bass-heavy slabs of deep-space and booty-style electro-funk. Although most of Godfather's output to date (released mostly in 12" form on the Detroit-based Twilight 76 label) has been of the old-school/retro ilk, his work with artists such as DJ Dick (as Sector 17) have pushed the style forward as well, bouncing brisk, snapping breaks off rubberband basslines and sheets of warm, slightly foreboding melody. A scratch DJ of renown (and one of only a few to bridge the woefully deep chasm between underground techno and hip-hop), Godfather was featured on the second Bomb Productions turntablist compilation, *Return of the DJ, Vol. 2*. —*Sean Cooper*

**Late Nite [EP]** / 1996 / Twilight 76 ♦♦♦♦
A relatively in-the-pocket fusion of Detroit- and LA-style electro, nonetheless well-conceived and with a good balance of concept and bounce. The A-side features two more or less similar mixes of the title track, with two fast-break electro tracks and a 2-beat floorbanger on the flip. —*Sean Cooper*

**Da Bomb, Vol. 1** / 1998 / Databass ♦
On DJ Godfather's first volume in his *Da Bomb* series, he still seems to be realizing his style and skills, resulting in a somewhat tentative mix. As he would continue do on the improved successive volumes, Godfather focuses primarily on his patented style of booty music: the bass-heavy sounds with a sexually provocative tone created exclusively for the means of dancing—freaky style. Unfortunately, there are some problems with this particular volume. First of all, this volume predates Detroit's ghetto-tech boom, leaving Godfather a little hard up for good booty tracks. Secondly, he tends to force his mixes, making this far from a seamless mix. Similarly, he spends too much time scratching his records rather than mixing them, perhaps impressing a few but frustrating most who could care less about how fast he can scratch. Finally, the tracks tend to be a mix of hip-hop and booty bass music, as if he isn't sure what sort of DJ he wants to be at this point. Thankfully, the successive volumes are drastic improvements. —*Jason Birchmeier*

**Da Bomb, Vol. 2** / 1999 / Databass ♦♦♦
On the second volume in his series of mix CDs, DJ Godfather makes great strides over his mediocre first volume. Essentially, this is practically the same mix—even with the same sort of mini hip-hop set at the end—but this time Godfather mixes are much cleaner, and he has a better arsenal of tracks to choose from. Of the 60 tracks that precede the hip-hop section of the mix, he alternates between Detroit electro such as Drexciya's "Aquatic Beta Particles," bass tracks with catchy vocal chants such as "Get Yo Jit On," and the occasional raunchy booty track such as "Dick 'N' Balls." It's a potent mix that has become his signature style, though it tends to be a bit less pornographic than his succeeding volume. The hip-hop mix that begins with Puff Daddy's "Mo Money, Mo Problems" is the only questionable part of the mix. First of all, the trendiness of hip-hop means that even while the aforementioned Puff Daddy track may have been hot at the time of the mix, it has since become the butt of jokes. Furthermore, when he works tracks such as this into his set, they fit rather well; yet when he goes through an extended series of these records, it sounds too contrived. Finally, the accessible, simple tempo and beats of hip-hop seem far too anti-climatic relative to the craziness of his booty bass and electro tracks. —*Jason Birchmeier*

● **Da Bomb, Vol. 3** / 1999 / Databass ♦♦♦♦
DJ Godfather improves slightly on the third volume of this mix series, to the point of near perfection. Gone are the out of place hip-hop sets that concluded the two preceding volumes, and he manages to present a wider variety of tracks here, with a fun emphasis on booty tracks. The inclusion of tracks by his closest competitor in Detroit's ghetto-tech scene, DJ Assault, only strengthens the mix. Tracks such as "Ass 'N' Titties" and "Shake It Baby," along with a few other Assault classics, fit in perfectly with Godfather's style. Furthermore, Godfather doesn't let his peer steal the show and concludes the set with a great track of his own, "Player Haters in Dis House." The inclusion of Detroit electro classics such as Model 500's "No UFOs"—sounding like it's being spun at 45 rpm rather than 33—only brings more interesting moments to the set. So rather than functioning as strictly a great uptempo dance mix—which it no doubt is—this volume also has more than a few noteworthy moments for trainspotters as well, making it one of the best recorded testaments of Detroit's post-modern style of ghetto-tech DJing. —*Jason Birchmeier*

## DJ Hell (Helmut Josef Geier)

b. 1962, Munich, Germany
*Producer, DJ / Hardcore Techno, Club/Dance, Techno*

DJ Hell (or simply Hell) has balanced Detroit minimalism and Chicago acid house as well as more spacious German trance and hardcore. Beginning his mixing career while still a teenager, Hell moved through punk and new wave to electro, house and hip-hop by the mid-'80s. His DJing gradually led to the start of his production career, and one of his first singles "My Definition of House Music" became a large club hit when reissued by Belgium's R&S Records in 1992. He moved to Berlin to work with Hardwax Records during 1993-94 and also spent time in New York before moving back to his native Munich. Besides releasing his album debut *Geteert und Gefedert* on Disko B in 1994, DJ Hell recorded a volume in the Studio !K7 mix series *X-Mix*. His second full length, *Munich Machine*, also appeared on Disko B—though credited simply to Hell. Besides continuing to DJ around the world, he also ran the International Deejay Gigolos label, which released tracks by Jeff Mills, Christopher Just, and David Carretta, among others. —*John Bush*

**Geteert Und Gefedert** / 1994 / Disko B ♦♦

**X-Mix, Vol. 5: Wildstyle** / 1996 / Studio !K7 ♦♦♦
Yet another volume in Studio !K7's video series matching knowledgeable techno or electro mixes with generally horrid graphics, *Wildstyle* includes great selections from Mike Dearborn, Phortune, and Ron Trent, plus tracks from DJ Hell himself. —*John Bush*

● **Munich Machine** / Nov. 16, 1998 / Disko B ♦♦♦♦
Hell borrowed the title for his second proper album from the Giorgio Moroder supergroup of the '70s, so it's not surprising that *Munich Machine* looks to disco culture for its starting point. But of course, that's only the starting point. *Munich Machine* is a varied collection of acid, techno and house that marries Hell's vision of acid-electro to an assortment of straight-ahead dance tracks and a few truly odd covers—including a stunning remake of the Barry Manilow chestnut "Copacabana" and a reworking of "The Lion Sleeps Tonight" with the lion replaced by a dominatrix. It's not exactly a commercial venture, but *Munich Machine* occasionally possesses the flavor of a retro-disco record like Daft Punk's *Homework*. —*John Bush*

## DJ Hype

*Producer, DJ / Jungle/Drum'N'Bass, Club/Dance*

Although his Ganja Records label and tracks released under his own name and with the Ganja Kru have helped, it's the "DJ" at the front of Hype's name that has proved most important in raising his profile to the level of the Grooveriders, Goldies, and LTJ Bukem's of drum'n'bass. A battle DJ of renown (he represented England in the 1989 DMCs), Hype had a history of electrifying deckwork before moving on from his reggae and hip-hop roots in the late '80s and latching onto house and hardcore. He was an early force on one of London's most influential pirate stations, Fantasy FM, and since then he's consistently topped bills on the international DJ circuit, landing awards for Best Male DJ and Best Radio DJ (in 1994 and 1995, respectively) at the UK's prestigious Hardcore Awards. He's also one of London's popular Kiss FM's biggest attractions and was the force behind Suburban Base's popular multi-volumed mixed compilation series, *Drum and Bass Selection*. A champion of jungle's dancefloor purity, Hype has also rallied consistently against jungle's compartmentalization into artificial "scenes" such as ambient/intelligent and hip-hop/ragga. (Of course, his sets tend to consist almost exclusively of the latter, which somewhat undermines his argument.)

Hype began producing in 1990, engineering and co-producing tracks (including chart-toppers such as "Exorcist" and "The Bee") for hardcore staples Kickin', Strictly Underground, and Sub Base. Although he never lost touch with his breakbeat roots (even going so far as to spin hip-hop instrumentals over house tracks to add a bit of rhythmic flare), it wasn't until he launched his own Ganja label in 1994 (with "Cops") that he began seriously focusing on the post-rave possibilities of sampled breaks. The Ganja label's almost immediate popularity—primarily through floor-fillers such as DJ Krome & Time's "Ganja Man" and DJ Zinc's penultimate 1995 anthem "Super Sharp Shooter"—peaked in late 1995 with *Still Smokin',* a combined-release label compilation between Ganja and cohort Pascal's Frontline imprint, which became one of the highest-selling independent jungle compilations. Re-pressed in 1997, that success also led to a major label deal with MCA's Parousia sublabel and the establishment of True Playaz Music, a Hype-led DJ and production unit also including Zinc, Pascal, and Rude Bwoy Monty. True Playaz, the label, has also come to the fore as one of the more consistent outlets for innovative hardstep, a style that all but disappeared during the jump-up- and techstep-dominated mid-'90s. —*Sean Cooper*

**New Frontiers [EP]** / Aug. 18, 1997 / Parousia ♦♦♦♦
Credited to DJ Hype & the Ganja Kru, *New Frontiers* is a triple-pack EP including six new tracks that range all over breakbeat creation but never fail to recall Hype's roots in the hardcore and ragga-jungle scenes. It's got a couple of steady rollers ("Dense," "No Fear") as well as a jungle two-step ("Plague That Never Ends"), plus nods to old-school rap ("This World"), and even a solid attempt at hardstep soul ("Magic"). It's a clever fusion of old and new, appealing to two generations of Hype/Ganja Kru fans. —*John Bush*

• **True Playaz in the Mix, Vol. 1** / Dec. 15, 1997 / True Play'az ♦♦♦♦
*True Playaz in the Mix, Vol. 1* is an excellent collection of the first eight singles from Hype's True Playaz label, mixed by the man himself and including his own "Peace Love & Unity," as well as excellent jump-up A-sides by Zinc ("Reachout"), Dope Skillz ("No Diggity"), Pascal ("Cool Manouevre"), Swift ("Load"), and Freestyles ("Attack," "Play the Game"). —*John Bush*

## DJ Icey

*Producer, DJ / Big Beat, Funky Breaks, Trip-Hop, Club/Dance*
DJ Icey's breakbeat funk helped jump-start the increasingly fertile dance scene in and around Orlando, Florida during the '90s. Born and raised in the Sunshine State, Icey first got into music via early-'80s synth-pop, industrial, and hip-hop. The boom in club music during the late '80s hooked him as well, and when he began DJing early in the '90s, he usually played out acid-house and funky breaks. He gained a residency at *The Edge,* one of Orlando's seminal clubs, and soon began playing farther afield thanks to the burgeoning US dance underground. (The club later went under, though not before hosting the Chemical Brothers' first American appearance, an invite extended by Icey himself.) When British DJ and longtime A&R kingpin Pete Tong heard an early single produced for Icey's own Zone Records in 1996, he signed the big-beat precursor "Galaxy Breaks" to his ffrr label. Even while spinning in several cities per week, DJ Icey managed to produce a good dozen singles per year for Zone, usually out of his studio in Orlando. His first major mix set, 1997's *The Funky Breaks,* was followed one year later by his full-length production debut *Generate.* Following in the footsteps of notable DJs from Tong to Fatboy Slim, DJ Icey released a volume in the *Essential Mix* series in 2000. —*John Bush*

**The Funky Breaks** / Aug. 11, 1997 / ffrr ♦♦♦
Icey's first major mix album verges from a remix of PM Dawn's "Watcher's Point of View" to Armand Van Helden's reworking of Genaside II's "Narramine" with breakbeat regulars like Headrillaz and Richard F., as well as two tracks ("Grand Canyon Suite" and "Beats-A-Rockin") from Icey himself. —*John Bush*

**Generate** / Jun. 30, 1998 / ffrr ♦♦♦♦
DJ Icey has been a top breakbeat DJ for so long, it's a bit of a surprise that his own full length reveals that he's got some great productions up his sleeve. Though *Generate* includes predictable nods to electro ("Ease the Beat Back Up") and big-beat ("Can't Stop This Track"), each are well done and lead to other interesting tracks, like the straight-ahead acid-techno of "Take the Time" and even beatless leanings on "The Air Is Full of Sound." It's not quite up to the quality of Chemical Brothers/Prodigy territory, but *Generate* is a solid album. —*John Bush*

**Continuous Play** / Mar. 29, 1999 / Zone ♦♦

• **Essential Mix** / Aug. 22, 2000 / Sire ♦♦♦♦
The breaks aren't quite as funky as they used to be, but with his *Essential Mix,* DJ Icey moves the earthy big-beat style forward to embrace futuristic breakbeat trance and electro. Icey also keeps the energy level peaking throughout, even while he ropes in a cast of musically varied producers and remixers, from big-beat rawkers Freestylers to trance maestros Novy Vs. Eniac to Detroit electro mainstay DJ Godfather to symphonic techno forebears Orbital (plus four of his own productions). In an era when the heavily commercial side of progressive trance is usually a DJ's easiest way out, Icey's *Essential Mix* warps the style until it meets his own ends. —*John Bush*

## DJ Keoki (Keoki Franconi)

b. 1968, Panama
*Producer, DJ / Trance, Club/Dance, Techno, House*
Probably the most visible DJ on the mainstream US dance scene, DJ Keoki released a half-dozen mix LPs and, beginning with 1997's *Ego Trip,* his own breakbeat-trance productions as well. Born in Panama but raised in Hawaii, Keoki hit the mainland in the mid-'80s and gained an airline job in New York. While moonlighting at the Danceteria nightclub, he decide to translate his love of music into a DJ career and soon became one of the city's most flamboyant DJs—he dubbed himself "Superstar DJ Keoki" long before he gained *any* fame at all.

After releasing several mixtapes during the early '90s, Keoki gained a licensing deal through Moonshine Music and debuted with a volume in the label's *Journeys by DJ* series in 1994. Several more mix albums followed during the next two years, with Keoki spotlighting his love of deep trance on 1995's *All Mixed Up* and cultivating a sense of humor on the following year's *Disco Death Race 2000.* Though he released his fourth mix LP in 1996 as well, Keoki had already decided to pursue a different path, with the release of his first own-production single, "Caterpillar." The single crested at number three on the dance charts and earned him a spot on that summer's Lollapalooza circuit. After a move from New York to Southern California, Keoki began work on his production debut album and released *Ego-Trip* in July 1997. Always one to stay at least a step ahead of expectations, Keoki returned in 1998 with another mix LP plus an album of *Ego-Trip* remixes (from the Crystal Method, Rabbit in the Moon, Omar Santana, and Cirrus, among others). Djmixed.com followed in 2000. —*John Bush*

**All Mixed Up** / Jul. 4, 1995 / Moonshine ♦♦♦
Keoki's second mix album for Moonshine is yet another set of upfront club-pop tracks, including contributions from Cirrus, Humate, Peter Lazonby, and Union Jack, among others. —*John Bush*

**Disco Death Race 2000** / Mar. 1, 1996 / Moonshine Music ♦♦
The third mix album from Keoki includes such dubious club tracks as Alpha Team's "Go Speed Go," Cranium HF's "Sixteen Bit Suicide" and G-Netic's "Eat Me Raw," as well as other tracks from Anoesis, Skylab 2000, Ispirio Zone, and Interfaco. —*John Bush*

• **The Transatlantic Move** / Oct. 8, 1996 / Moonshine Music ♦♦♦♦
The Transatlantic Move is an annual dance-music festival that usually features most of the most innovative techno artists currently performing. DJ Keoki's *Transatlantic Move* features a selection of highlights from the 1996 festival—including cuts by Richie Hawtin, Kimball Collins, Roger Sanchez, Electric Skychurch, Doc Martin and Josh Wink—as remixed by DJ Keoki himself. The result is frequently intriguing, yet rarely revelatory, meaning that it's an album for Keoki fans, not for the artists that are being remixed. —*Stephen Thomas Erlewine*

**Ego Trip** / Jul. 29, 1997 / Moonshine Music ♦♦♦
Although the production on DJ Keoki's first non-mix album is predictably unsubtle, his mixing skills and feel for how music should flow provides for a more than competent album, especially considering Keoki's low status in the underground. Besides the single "Caterpillar," the Superstar DJ tours through deep house on "Blow" and hits techno on "Wicked." One of the few lapses in judgment is the faux-rap vocal track "Me." —*John Bush*

**Inevitable Alien Nation** / Mar. 24, 1998 / Moonshine Music ♦♦♦
A la Ice-T with *Freedom of Expression,* DJ Keoki puts out a smashing album that pushes the boundaries of dance music and opens with the voice of Jello Biafra and a vision of the penal nation. *Inevitable Alien Nation* is a mix CD of DJ Keoki's "personal favorites." Under his administration, tracks from Coldcut, Junkie XL, Spiritual Being and more work together as a single vision of one killer club experience. Still, different styles rise to the surface and some tracks achieve prominence. The low rub of synth and clattering cowbell on "Useless Man" (Minty) is a smartly arranged intro into a torrent of drum and bass and profanity. The guitar and cymbal intro to "Pleasing the Korean"

(Naked Funk) sets up an energetic arrangement of drum samples and synth beats, smoothly segueing into the "Minty" track. While each track stands alone as powerful techno, it is DJ Keoki's ability continue a groove from one song to another that makes the package greater than the sum of its parts. Also worth noting is the '80s' dance sound of "Dvus" and the fly funk mix in DJ Keoki's treatment of the "Avenging Godfather of Disco." *Inevitable Alien Nation* is a freak-stepping land to escape to, and DJ Keoki is its ambassador. In short, this is what techno should sound like: varied, intelligent, fun, and surprising. —*Thomas Schulte*

**DJmixed.com** / May 9, 2000 / Moonshine Music ✦
No longer dubbed as a "superstar DJ," Keoki seems to have humbled a bit on *DJmixed.com* as he turns in an eclectic though mostly lackluster mix of trance with some other assorted breakbeat sounds. His decision to feature predominantly trance on this particular mix-album comes as no surprise, considering the musical style's alarming popularity in 2000 and Keoki's status as a populist DJ. Thankfully, the album isn't entirely trance and doesn't sound like a Paul Oakenfold or Sasha mix; Keoki instead brings in some strange moments where the music isn't so easily classified. While these moments set the album apart from the generic trance mixes flooding the market in 2000, they also tend to be some of the dullest moments in the mix. By starting the set with DJ Rush's "Grind Me Baby," the listener is instantly left to wonder exactly what sort of precedent Keoki is trying to set for the album, considering this song's cheesy vocal samples. The bad taste in the mouth doesn't stop there, though; the next track, "Big up the Noise," again turns to vocal samples in hopes of generating some sort of pseudo-intensity that the music itself is surely incapable of doing. By the album's halfway point, Keoki has entered the realm of standard trance, eventually concluding a decent run of trance with Liquid Sun's club mix of the *Star Wars* theme. Hardcore fans of the film may cheer or at least grin during this overly extended brand extension, but most will grimace in disgust at Keoki's choice to drop this sheer-novelty moment of formulaic and predictable trance that sums up everything bad about the style. —*Jason Birchmeier*

## DJ Kool (John W. Bowman, Jr.)

b. 1959, Washington, DC
*Producer, DJ / Old School Rap, Go-Go, Club/Dance, Hip-Hop*
A fusion of feel-good go-go music with hip-hop's original block-party aesthetic led DJ Kool to the fore in rap's return to the old school during the late '90s. A veteran of DC's go-go circuit who worked as a warm-up DJ for Rare Essence during the early- to mid-'80s, Kool began recording in 1988 and early on tried to inform the studio art of hip-hop with a live feel in keeping with his experience. His first album *The Music Ain't Loud Enuff* used call and response much like early hip-hop and go-go (and also included the hip-house track "House Your Body," prefaced by a remarkably accurate monologue on the history of house music).

DJ Kool took it to the stage in 1992 with the mini-LP *Twenty Minute Workout*, recorded live in Richmond, Virginia and released on Steve Janis' CLR Records. By the time of 1996's *Let Me Clear My Throat*, mostly recorded live in Philadelphia, the East Coast underground was buzzing about DJ Kool's way with a crowd. American Records won a five-way bidding war and reissued *Let Me Clear My Throat* early the following year; providing remixes of the title track were Funkmaster Flex and DJ Mark the 45 King (whose funky underground hit "The 900 Number" was the basis for the title track in the first place), helping it climb into the Top Five on the rap charts. In mid-2000, he and Fatman Scoop released the remixed Rob Base classic "It Takes Two." —*John Bush*

**The Music Ain't Loud Enuff** / 1990 / Creative Funk ✦✦✦✦
DJ Kool's album debut was an incredibly wide-ranging LP with few similarities to any contemporary hip-hop act, except possibly Mantronix. Including the dancehall ragga track "Raggae Dance," the hip-house track "House Your Body," several crucial sample productions (the title track, "What the Hell You Come in Here For," "How Low Can You Go"), and even the touching R&B production "Pressed Against the Glass," Kool proves himself a master of just about every type of party music then circulating. —*John Bush*

● **Let Me Clear My Throat** / Apr. 1996 / CLR ✦✦✦✦
DJ Kool's *Let Me Clear My Throat* was one of the most invigorating hip-hop records of the mid-'90s, simply because it didn't follow conventional hardcore, alternative, or gangsta rap patterns. Instead, DJ Kool returned to the wild, careening atmosphere of freestyle, old-school hip-hop, anchoring the rhymes with spare scratching and elastic reggae grooves. The result was one hell of a party album, filled with terrific beats and infectious, humorous rhymes. —*Leo Stanley*

## DJ Kool Herc

b. Apr. 16, 195?
*DJ / Old School Rap, Hip-Hop*
DJ Kool Herc is the originator of break-beat deejaying, essentially the essence of hip-hop. By isolating and repeating the "breaks," or most danceable parts, of funk records by Mandrill, James Brown and the Jimmy Castor Bunch, Herc created the prototype for modern day hip-hop. Though others such as Grandmaster Flash perfected and elevated the technique, it was Herc who is credited for its creation.

Beginning his deejaying career in the early '70s at a time when disco was king, Herc immediately distinguished himself by spinning late-'60s funk records by James Brown and Mandrill and isolating their breaks. Among other things, Herc was notorious for throwing all-night parties and invariably present at a Kool Herc party during mid '70s were usually young dancers (called b-boys) who were early incarnations of the breakdancers of the '80s. Another Kool Herc attraction was his mammoth sound-system which was capable of overtaking a party-goer's body, making them literally feel the music.

Herc's career was sidelined, however, when he was stabbed at one of his parties, causing the DJ to curb his activities for several years. Though he was occasionally acknowledged during the '90s, appearing at The Source Awards to talk about hip-hop's early days as well as on the 1994 release *The Godfathers of Threatt* by Public Enemy DJ Terminator X, Herc drifted away from the hip-hop community and ceased to be a key player in the same way he was in the early to mid-'70s. —*Steve Kurutz*

## DJ Krush (Hideaki Ishii)

b. 1962
*Producer, DJ / Electronica, Ambient Breakbeat, Trip-Hop, Club/Dance, Hip-Hop*
Japanese turntablist and producer DJ Krush is one of the few island-nation throw-ups to be embraced by the global hip-hop world. Releasing material through Sony in Japan, Mo'Wax and Virgin in the UK, and Axiom, Shadow, and A&M in America, Krush's heady brand of experimental, (largely) instrumental hip-hop has been praised by everyone from hardcore underground hip-hop 'zines like "The Bomb" to the speckless offices of "Rolling Stone" and "Spin." Beginning as a bedroom DJ in the mid-'80s following the Japanese leg of the Wildstyle tour, Krush moved into mobile DJing, backing up rappers, and eventually solo production. Although his Japan-only debut freely mixed elements of R&B and acid jazz with the beefy breakbeat backbone of mid-tempo hip-hop, Krush's work has since tended more toward the abstract, applying heavy effects and sample manipulation to thick, smart breaks, layered, almost ambient textures, and subtle, inventive scratching. Krush came to larger acclaim in the mid-'90s through his association with the London-based Mo'Wax label, which released his *Strictly Turntablized* in 1994 and *Meiso* in 1996, both reissued stateside by A&M. While *Turntablized* is closer to a collection of DJ tools, *Meiso* is a return of sorts to his earlier work, including rappers such as Guru and CL Smooth on a few tracks and incorporating a wider variety of instrumental sounds and atmospheres. In addition to 1997's *Milight*, Krush also featured on a number of various-artist collections, including Mo'Wax's celebrated *Headz*, as well as *Altered Beats* and *Axiom Dub* (both out on Bill Laswell's Axiom label). *Kakusei* appeared on Mo'Wax/Columbia in 1999, followed by the mix albums *Code 4109* and *Tragicomic* the next year. —*Sean Cooper*

**Strictly Turntablized** / 1994 / Mo'Wax ✦✦✦✦
Basically a DJ tools-type breaks record, *Strictly Turntablized* stands up to repeat listenings thanks to atmospheric production and some interesting needle work. Although horns, piano, and other sampled instruments work their way into the mix, Krush is at his best when he focuses on the beats, evoking mood and emotion through loping percussion and thick bass kicks. —*Sean Cooper*

● **Meiso** / 1996 / Mo'Wax ✦✦✦✦
Krush brings a few rappers back into the fold for his third effort, and the

names are nothing to scoff at: Guru, the Roots, CL Smooth, and Mo'Wax's Deflon Sallahr. The sound is fuller with more studied, focused use of samples, and the scratching and beatwork is top-notch. Guest production work from labelmate DJ Shadow on "Duality" adds tasty spice. The best point of entry into Krush's world. —*Sean Cooper*

**Back in the Base** / Jan. 1997 / Ninja Tune ♦♦
DJ Krush's full-length works have always been a bit hard to swallow given the unyielding predominance of mid-tempo hip-hop, and his contribution to *Cold Krush Cuts*, the double-disc Ninja Tunes mix compilation (one disc of Krush, one of Coldcut), is no different. Restricted to using only Ninja Tune artists (DJ Vadim makes eight appearances!), the material is similar-sounding and repetitious—even more so than DJ Krush's albums. Aside from the chosen records, Krush's mixing skills are okay but overshadowed by Coldcut & DJ Food on the other disc. —*John Bush*

**Milight** / Aug. 18, 1997 / A&M ♦♦♦♦
Not quite as dark as *Strictly Turntablized* or as erratic as *Meiso*, Krush's third album for Mo'Wax is a solid collection of hip-hop instrumentals with vocals on several tracks by Deborah Anderson and the rappers Mos Def and the Japanese Rino (from Lampeye). *Milight* is a casual affair, and by not focusing on the "intelligence" of abstract hip-hop, Krush is able to free his music from the preconceptions which have dogged the genre—and many of the aural-wallpaper LPs which have emerged from it. —*John Bush*

**Ki-Oku** / Jan. 26, 1998 / Instinct ♦♦♦♦
Anyone who remembers trumpeter Toshinori Kondo's work with such thorny avant-gardists as John Zorn, Derek Bailey, and Fred Frith may be a bit taken aback by the extreme accessibility of his collaboration with pioneering turntablist DJ Krush. Much of the music on *Ki-Oku* flirts with smooth-groove jazz—Kondo's muted trumpet line on "Mu-Getsu" sounds an awful lot like something Chris Botti would play, while the duo's instrumental take on the Bob Marley classic "Sun Is Shining" comes off just a little bit muzak-y. On the other hand, "Ki-Gen" and "Ko-Ku" both find Kondo using synthesized treatments in a way that evokes Jon Hassell's work with Brian Eno, while on the latter DJ Krush layers slightly menacing keyboard washes beneath Kondo's unassuming trumpet lines. This is one of those albums that reveals more with repeated listens; if it sounds too easy at first, listen again—there's lots of interesting stuff going on beneath what sometimes sounds like a merely pleasant surface. —*Rick Anderson*

**Kakusei** / Mar. 8, 1999 / Sony International ♦♦♦♦
Despite DJ Krush's many attempts to expand his sound beyond the confines of his own compositional system—bringing in all manner of rappers and acoustical instrumentalists to, perhaps, return the music to the "immediacy of performance"—the question of what makes his music so compelling is easily answered by simply stripping all of that away. And that's precisely what *Kakusei* does. His first "solo" album in two years, and the first not to appear on British label Mo'Wax since his self-titled debut nearly a decade previous, *Kakusei* is without a doubt the best of the best of Krush. Tight, oddly syncopated beats, frayed, sinister samples, and impressionistic turntable work all combined with the perfect balance of movement, dramatic intensity, and straight dopeness. —*Sean Cooper*

**Code 4109** / Apr. 25, 2000 / Tristar ♦♦♦♦
*Code 4109* is the first "proper" mix album from one of trip-hop's reigning DJ masters—his two previous efforts, *Back in the Base* and *Holonic*, were restricted to, respectively, material from the Ninja Tune label and his own work. It's also an excellent compilation, never sacrificing the trademarked earthy grooves on the altar of experimentalism. None of the tracks are obvious inclusions—except for a few of Krush's own productions—and the material that is here has obviously been worked on heavily while on the turntables; Krush transforms, tweak scratches, and attempts all manner of effects on the tracks. From the vicious detuned monster "Back to the Essence" (by Gravity) near the beginning, he spins material from those with similar aesthetics (DJ Cam, the 45 King, Jazzanova) and uses more eccentric inclusions (John Klemmer, Beats International, a Bulgarian choir, Japanese jazz artist Minuro Muraoka) as layering for the stoned beats and haunted basslines on the primary tracks. More so than most of DJ Krush's material, *Code 4109* progresses through different sounds and styles with panache and dexterity. —*John Bush*

## DJ Krust

b. 1968, Bristol, England
*Producer, DJ / Jungle/Drum'N'Bass, Club/Dance*
The co-founder of Bristol's Full Cycle crew (with Roni Size, DJ Die, and Suv), DJ Krust is much noted in the jungle underground for his push-the-envelope productions both alone and in collaboration with Size. Born in Bristol in 1968, Krust was raised on hip-hop and began DJing in the mid-'80s at schools and small clubs around the area. His interests grew to include acid house and rave by the late '80s, and a stint in the group Fresh 4 landed Krust in the middle of the charts, when "Wishing on a Star" made number nine in late 1989. Fresh 4 signed to Virgin but never released another record, so Krust returned to DJing and occasional production work (notably for Smith & Mighty with his brother Flynn, later of Flynn & Flora).

After meeting at the 1990 Glastonbury Festival, DJ Krust and Roni Size soon began to produce tracks together, often in collaboration with DJ Die and Suv. The outfit recorded solo and in tandem for Bryan G and Jumpin' Jack Frost's V Records during the early '90s but then in 1992 formed the Full Cycle label with manager Chris Warton. Along with its sister label Dope Dragon, Full Cycle released several crucial singles and the 1995 label retrospective *Music Box*, through an agreement with Talkin' Loud Records. DJ Krust continued to record for V and Full Cycle and helped out on remixes for Goldie and fellow Bristol crew More Rockers. Size's debut album *New Forms*—with considerable production help from Krust—hit the music world like a bomb in 1997, leading to Krust's own major-label contract the following year (as Krust). His Polygram debut, *True Stories*, was followed in 1999 by *Coded Language*. —*John Bush*

● **Genetic Manipulation [EP]** / Feb. 17, 1997 / Full Cycle ♦♦♦♦
*Genetic Manipulation* is an incredibly varied EP (especially so, considering it's only four tracks deep) that takes Krust from minimal acid textures ("The Last Day") to chunky house chordings ("Brief Encounter"), all filtered through deep, mechanistic drum'n'bass. All in all, it's Krust's best moment yet. —*John Bush*

**Coded Language** / Nov. 1, 1999 / Def Jam ♦♦♦
After many singles and EPs (for Full Cycle and V Recordings) as well as a high-profile gig with Roni Size on the Mercury Award-winning *New Forms* recording, producer Krust goes the way of "intelligent" drum'n'bass (for better and for worse) on his debut album, *Coded Language*. Though both his sense for production and ear for great ideas are still intact, the record suffers from a sense of how self-serious the jungle community has become; the title track features rapper and performance artist Saul Williams solemnly praising the importance of the jungle community, never a good sign for the continuing development of a musical style that's seemed frozen in its tracks since 1996. Krust also enlists a female vocalist named Morgan to contribute vocals on several tracks. He even hired a string quartet for the muted classical flair of "One Moment." *Coded Language* is a very good drum'n'bass album, but it's a shame that Krust didn't focus on his production skills as much as he did on trying to branch out into jungle fusion. —*John Bush*

## DJ Magic Mike (Michael Hampton)

b. 1967, Orlando, FL
*Scratching, Mixing, Producer, DJ / Southern Rap, Bass Music, Hip-Hop*
DJ Magic Mike, the breakthrough bass producer after 2 Live Crew, was the music's most crucial recording artist. An underground label impresario on the order of Master P, Mike's productions were much rougher than the slick Miami bass sound and pursued a gritty old-school vibe—more akin to Ultramagnetic MCs than Luther Campbell—long after most hip-hop producers had gone pop in the late '90s.

The former Michael Hampton began his mixing career before he was even a teenager, spinning at a roller rink and selling mix tapes. By the age of 14, he was hosting a drive-time radio show in his native Orlando. He began concentrating on club work after finishing high school and debuted on wax with 1987's "Boot the Booty" for Vision Records.

One year later, local promoter Tom Reich offered DJ Magic Mike a chance at a half-share in his own Cheetah Records if Mike's releases sold well. His first singles under the agreement, "Magic Mike Cutz the Record" and "Drop the Bass," both became big regional hits, sparking the release of his debut album *DJ Magic Mike and the Royal Posse* in 1989. He took more of a guiding hand over his own instrumental productions for the follow-up, 1990's *Bass Is* the Name of the Game, and the album went gold despite its low vocal content. Mike's breakthrough LP *Ain't No Doubt About It* appeared in 1992, followed by the release of two LPs on the same day in late March; both *BASS: The Final Frontier* and *This Is How It Should Be Done* charted, and the former went gold. Although his recording schedule continued apace during the mid-'90s (and the number of his full-length releases climbed into the double digits), fewer of his LPs charted. Mike picked up the commercial slack with advertising appearances for Coca-Cola and Pioneer and has also worked with Sir Mix-A-Lot, 2 Live Crew, MC Shy D, and Poison Clan. The new millennium saw Mike issue *Magic's Kingdom*, his first album in two years. —*John Bush*

**Bass Is the Name of the Game** / 1988 / Cheetah ♦♦♦♦
Magic Mike's first major LP included at least a half dozen bass classics like "Drop the Bass," "House of Magic," "Feel the Beat" and "Yo." Proof positive of its classic status came in 1998 when it was digitally remastered and reissued by Cheetah. —*John Bush*

**Back to Haunt You!** / 1991 / Cheetah ♦♦♦♦
Recorded as Vicious Base Featuring DJ Magic Mike, *Back to Haunt You!* includes quite a few Magic Mike classics like "It's Automatic," "You Want Bass," and "No Stop to the Madness." —*Keith Farley*

● **The King of the Bass' Greatest Hits, Vol. 1** / 1993 / Cheetah ♦♦♦♦
All of DJ Magic Mike's classic early productions (except for "Magic Mike Cutz the Record") appear on this 1993 Cheetah collection, including "Drop the Bass," "Def and Direct," "Class Is in Session," and "You Want Bass." Mike's scratches and sample work are excellent, though a bit restrained by frequent contributors' raps. There is a bit of overlap with *Foundations of Bass*, but this is the more crucial collection. —*John Bush*

**Foundations of Bass, Vol. 1** / Apr. 29, 1997 / Cheetah ♦♦♦♦
A balanced collection from DJ Magic Mike's entire career pre-1996, *Foundations of Bass* borrows half of its tracks from Mike's first two LPs, focusing more on bass music than the hip-hop slant of the other major Mike collection. —*John Bush*

## DJ Me DJ You

f. 1999, Los Angeles, CA
*Group / Electronica, Indie Rock, Trip-Hop, Club/Dance, Pop/Rock, Alternative Pop/Rock*

Originating in the town nicknamed La La Land, DJ Me DJ You appropriately grab production tools from a catalog of off-beat sources. Comprised of Los Angeles artists Ross Harris and Craig Borell, DJ Me DJ You have produced along side the Dust Brothers, Green Day's Jerry Fin, and Beck. Using samples taken from Indian B-movies and old Italian opera and instructional records, DJ Me DJ You use their cut-and-paste artistic instincts to make music. Other than DJ Me DJ You, Harris and Borell are multimedia artists and half of Sukia, which is signed to the Dust Brothers' label, Ideal, formerly known as Nickel Bag.

Before entering the world as DJ Me DJ You, Craig and Ross also worked with Sasha Fuentes and Grace Monks with the space rock band, Sukia. Sukia served as a perfect production transition to DJ Me DJ You, allowing the two to gain experience in a studio beside production team the Dust Brothers, who have produced for Beastie Boys, Beck, the Rolling Stones, and Marilyn Manson. With Sukia, Craig and Ross also worked under the Dust Brother's label, Ideal, and UK label, Mo'Wax. A good example of Sukia's off center personality is the title of their first album, *Contacto Espacial Con El Tercer Sexo (Space Contact with the Third Sex)* which was inspired by a Mexican comic book about a lesbian vampire and her sidekick, Gary Supermacho.

Craig and Ross broke off of Sukia to perform as DJ Me DJ You and released their first EP in 1999 called *Simplerockmachine*. The EP is eight tracks long and takes samples from hip-hop, Indian film scores and B-movies, that are often found during the duo's hunting trips to thrift stores. Their debut full-length, *Rainbows and Robots*, was released in 2000, again on Emperor Norton Records. Craig and Ross again used the same sample sources used on their previous album, but this time to a more extensive depth. In addition they collaborated with live musicians on drums, sitar, and old keyboards the two collect. Besides producing on their own, DJ Me DJ You have produced music for artists Takako Minekawa, Grand Royal Record's Titans, Beth Orton, Beck, and the Fantastic Plastic Machine.

As individuals, Craig and Ross are involved in the Los Angeles art and music world. Ross compiled the album *The Best of Bruce Haack and Dimension 5* for Emperor Norton, as well as a tribute album to electronic producing pioneer, Haack, benefiting children with autism. He also worked and co-starred in the fictional film *The Recycler* on Propaganda Films. Craig Borell is a graphic designer and does work for the Ideal record label. —*Diana Potts*

● **Rainbows and Robots** / Jan. 25, 2000 / Emperor Norton ♦♦♦♦
With *Rainbows and Robots*, former Sukia members Craig Borrell and Ross Harris (aka DJ Me DJ You) pick up where their old group left off. Comparisons between the two projects may be unfair, but they're also unavoidable. Unfortunately, this album lacks much of the sleazy sense of humor and creativity that made Sukia's *Contacto Especial Con el Tercer Sexo* a kinky, quirky triumph. What's left is a collection of sample-friendly, pseudo-funky analog synth-pop that sounds a bit like backing tracks for the next Beck album. Not that that's a bad thing in and of itself, but it makes Harris and Borrell seem like followers instead of innovators. Though *Rainbows and Robots* is stretched a bit thin at 14 tracks, there are many fun and funky moments on the album. "Earth People," a slinky safari based on samples from a record of the classic children's story The Little Prince; the wittily named space rock epic "Pink Freud"; the loungey, trashy, Sukia-esque "El Pollo Amante"; and the sliced-and-diced robot uprising "Because" are among *Rainbows and Robots*' most distinctive tracks. Though the rest of the album is entertaining, samples from vintage reference and instructional records, synth bleeps and bouncy basslines just don't sound as fresh as they did a few years ago. Here's hoping that DJ Me DJ You's next album pushes the envelope of electronic pop music instead of draining its dregs. —*Heather Phares*

## DJ Pierre (Nathaniel Pierre Jones)

b. Jul. 12, 1965, Harvey, IL
*Producer, DJ / Club/Dance, Acid House, House*

Besides being a crucial DJ and the production wizard partly responsible for the development of Chicago acid-house, DJ Pierre later influenced the sound of New York's more disco-fied house with his tenure as an in-house producer for Strictly Rhythm Records. Born in the Chicago suburbs, Nathaniel Pierre Jones was influenced by the Hot Mix Five, the pioneering DJ team which lit up Chicago's radio airwaves during the early '80s with dance megamixes. Jones later began DJing himself, though he preferred the sound of Italian disco to the blend of soul and American disco that Chicago DJs like Ron Hardy were playing out. When his friend Spanky brought him to the Music Box to hear Ron Hardy in person though, Pierre was convinced—he began spinning records more akin to the burgeoning house sound as well. DJ Pierre began recording on the side with Spanky and another friend named Herb J, working on tracks with an old drum machine and synthesizers.

One of the synthesizers in their studio was the Roland TB-303, a bass-line generator introduced only in the past few years but already a relic littering junk stores at inexpensive prices. After a period of experimentation, the three hit upon an intriguing sound made when the box was pitched much higher than its normal operating frequencies; the squelchy psychedelic sounds enlivened their recordings and more than convinced Ron Hardy to begin playing one track on his reel-to-reel setup at the Music Box. Known at the club as "Ron Hardy's Acid Tracks" and quickly re-recorded for a 1986 release by the three billed as Phuture, "Acid Trax" became one of the biggest house records of the time, the starting point for a whole new style later termed acid house as a tribute. Reportedly, thousands of soundalike records flooded the local market in the next few years, and the originators quickly became forgotten amid the wash of imitators. DJ Pierre kept busy, working on the act Pierre's Phantasy Club with Felix Da Housecat and producing another genuine house classic with "String Free" by Phortune, but he then left Phuture in 1990 with a relocation to New York.

His first single once in Gotham was Photon Inc.'s "Generate Power," a dancefloor barnstormer released on the relatively mainstream dance label Strictly Rhythm. "Generate Power" was the formal debut for Pierre's new production method the Wild Pitch, created with a quickly backspun sample that generated a crispy lightning-strike of sound similar to the acid squelch. Besides featuring on a host of DJ Pierre remixes and productions, it became standard fare for scores of producers during the next few years, just as the sound of the TB-303 had earlier. Pierre continued to remix and produce for Strictly Rhythm and Twisted/MCA, finding additional club hits with "Live & Die" by Audio Clash, another Photon Inc. track named "Love," "Follow Me" by Aly-Us, and "Sound Blaster" by Joint Venture. He also hosted a slew of mix compilations throughout the '90s. —*John Bush*

- **DJ Pierre** / Mar. 16, 1994 / Strictly Rhythm ♦♦♦♦
Strictly Rhythm compiled all of DJ Pierre's best productions for the label during the early '90s, including "Generate Power," "Master Blaster (Turn It Up)," "Live & Die," and "Annihilating Rhythm." It's a crucial collection, mixed by Pierre himself. —*John Bush*

**Mixmag Live!, Vol. 16** / Jul. 22, 1996 / Mixmag Live! ♦♦♦
DJ Pierre's edition in the *Mixmag Live!* series is a half-share with Roger Sanchez. Pierre's side runs the gamut with several of his patented wild-pitch productions, more mainstream vocal house, and the harder side of techno as well. From Felix Da Housecat to Carl Craig, Pierre keeps the mix well in control. —*John Bush*

## DJ Q (Paul Flynn)
b. 1974, Glasgow, Scotland
*Remixing, Producer, DJ / Jazz-House, Tech-House, Club/Dance, House*
Paul Flynn's recordings as DJ Q have an occasional flourish of Detroit techno but mostly rely on tight but vibrant jazzy house. The Glasgow native, who was part of the city's mid-'90s music renaissance (masterminded by Slam and organized through their combined club/label concern, Soma), began DJing early in the '90s as a moonlighting gig from his full-time job, hanging suspended ceilings. Moving to production as well by 1994, Flynn recorded for Dance Mania, Glasgow Underground, and Filter, combining the emotion of Chicago house but with a tighter, more refined aesthetic learned from Detroit producers like Carl Craig. The 1996 single "We Are One" featured Glaswegian poet William Hall intonating over a solid groove-house base, and the track became a hit on the country's more progressive dancefloors. Flynn's debut album as DJ Q, *Face the Music*, appeared in late 1997; *Twenty Four7even* followed in early 2000. —*John Bush*

- **Face the Music** / Oct. 27, 1997 / Filter ♦♦♦♦
DJ Q's *Face the Music* rounds up many of the 12" singles Paul Flynn (aka DJ Q) released between 1995 and 1997, offering proof that he can revive the sound of classic techno and house without making it sound static. His techno is spare and sharp, built from crisp drum loops and jazzy keyboards. It sounds vibrant and alive, occasionally reminiscent of classic techno from the late '80s/early '90s, but it's always danceable and fresh. —*Stephen Thomas Erlewine*

**Twenty Four7even** / Feb. 15, 2000 / Filter ♦♦

## DJ Rap (Charissa Saverio)
b. 1969, Singapore
*Producer, DJ / Jungle/Drum'N'Bass, Club/Dance*
Before emerging from the drum'n'bass underground for a major-label recording contract in 1997, DJ Rap was long one of the best mixers in the business, as well as one of jungle's best (if understated) producers. Born Charissa Saverio in Singapore, she spent her childhood living in various exotic locales around the world (her stepfather was a luxury-hotel manager) before settling in Southampton, England as a teenager. While studying to be a solicitor, Saverio became involved with the British rave scene and soon graduated from clubkid to working as a producer and mixer. Among her first released tracks was 1990's underground breakbeat favorite "The Adored" (as Ambience), recorded with Jeff B. and released on Raw Bass Records. She learned how to mix while promoting a record on the East London pirate station Rave FM, and made her reputation a few years later after standing in for Fabio for a last-minute slot at the Astoria. Rap continued to produce and launched several hardcore/jungle classics of the early '90s, including Engineers Without Fears' "Spiritual Aura," recorded with Aston Harvey (later of the Sol Brothers and Freestylers). DJ Rap formed her own mixing agency, spinning it into the Proper Talent record label as well. Signed to Sony's Higher Ground subsidiary in 1997, she released her first album *Learning Curve* two years later. *Brave New World* followed in mid-2000. The mix album *Brave New World* (a co-headlining gig with Kenny Ken) followed in 2000. —*John Bush*

- **Learning Curve** / May 4, 1999 / Higher Ground/Sony ♦♦♦
For her major-label debut, DJ Rap chose a surprising angle, given her long history as an excellent drum'n'bass DJ and producer. *Learning Curve* is a crossover album so complete there's hardly any traces of drum'n'bass left. Instead, most of the album (especially the radically reconfigured American version) is full-fledged '90s dance-pop, closer to Garbage than Grooverider, with the production gloss and sneering vocals to match. What's even more surprising is that, taken for what it is, *Learning Curve* actually *is* a solid dance-pop album. Rap's vocals are better than expected, the production is inventive and while the songs are still quite far from pop, they're much more than dance fodder. It's a radically different move compared to any other jungle artist's major-label debut, but still, it's surprisingly solid given its emphasis on pop. (The British version includes a few more drum'n'bass tracks, including "Beats Like This," "Audio Technica," and a remix of her classic "Spiritual Aura.") —*John Bush*

## DJ Rolando (Rolando Rocha)
*Producer, DJ / Detroit Techno, Techno*
Though he's one of the later recruits to Detroit's Underground Resistance family, DJ Rolando (aka the Aztec Mystic) became one of the most important figures in the UR organization after two releases: his *Aztec Mystic Mix* compiles all of the label's brightest tracks in a stunning compilation; and his "Jaguar" single is a leftfield dance hit that became a flashpoint for UR's anti-major label stance. Raised in Mexicantown (right next to the Ambassador Bridge on Detroit's southwest side), Rolando grew up mixing the freestyle and hip-hop that was common currency around the area. After he became interested in techno as well and began dropping it into his sets, a friend introduced him to "Mad" Mike Banks, the leader of Underground Resistance and one of the primary figures in Motor City techno.

Rolando soon began DJing around the world as part of the UR organization, and made his production debut on the Underground Resistance tracks "Aztlan" and "Aztec Mystic." He also produced a track ("Mi Raza") for the UR full-length *Interstellar Fugitives*. In early 1999, the B-side of his single "Ascesión/Jaguar" gained airplay in British clubs and on radio, and his *Aztec Mystic Mix* gained even more praise. By the end of the year, "Jaguar" had gained so much attention—much of it in commercial trance circles where UR's pioneering work was barely known—that Sony Germany attempted a tone-for-tone trance remake of the track for potential chart entry and inclusion on DJ albums. Underground Resistance immediately organized an uprising of record-store owners, techno purists, and underground DJs worldwide to protest the recording and boycott its release. Even while *another* megalabel, BMG, considered doing the same thing, Sony backed down and pulled the single. UR responded with *Revenge of the Jaguar: The Mixes*, an EP with remixes by Detroit figures Jeff Mills and Octave One as well as Banks himself. —*John Bush*

★ **The Aztec Mystic Mix** / Jul. 1999 / UR ♦♦♦♦♦
Following up the massive global success of "Jaguar," DJ Rolando, also known as the Aztec Mystic, picks 23 Underground Resistance-related records from his crate for this album, mixing recognized classics, such as the Martian's "Firekeeper," with previously unreleased tracks, like his own "Z Track." Dropping a new track every few minutes, Rolando gives listeners a near assaulting taste of UR's style of Detroit techno—at times unearthly, at other times raw. He opens his mix beautifully with his masterpiece, "Jaguar," which undoubtedly ranks with Rhythim is Rhythim's "Strings of Life" and Model 500's "Ocean to Ocean" as a timeless Detroit techno classic. From there, Rolando focuses primarily on the raw percussive force of various Underground Resistance tracks, occasionally lightening up the mix with the cosmic strings of the Martian every few tracks. When he makes brave transitions from the electronic sci-fi symphonies of the Martian's "Ultraviolet Images" to the raw, sweaty funk of UR's "Soulpower," the tempo changes drastically. A similar change of tempo occurs even more dramatically when he drops "Metamorphasis"—a strange track filled with robotic space probe sounds—for over three minutes before mixing into the fiery, climactic finale of Mad Mike's "Illuminator" and the Suburban Knight's "Midnight Sunshine." This soulful conclusion to the set affirms the fact that Rolando no doubt has a gifted command of the catalog, making this album a wonderful sampler; unfortunately, for as great as this mix truly is, it could benefit from a little more variety. —*Jason Birchmeier*

## DJ Shadow (Josh Davis)
b. 1973, Hayward, CA
*Producer, DJ / Turntablism, Ambient Breakbeat, Trip-Hop, Hip-Hop*
DJ Shadow's Josh Davis is widely credited as a key figure in developing the experimental instrumental hip-hop style associated with the London-based

Mo'Wax label. His early singles for the label, including "In/Flux" and "Lost and Found (S.F.L.)," were all-over-the-map mini-masterpieces combining elements of funk, rock, hip-hop, ambient, jazz, soul, and used-bin incidentalia. Although he'd already done a scattering of original and production work (during 1991-92 for Hollywood Records) by the time Mo'Wax's James Lavelle contacted him about releasing "In/Flux" on the fledgling imprint, it wasn't until his association with Mo'Wax that his sound began to mature and cohere. Mo'Wax released his longest work to date in 1995—the 40-minute single in four movements, "What Does Your Soul Look Like?" which topped the British indie charts—and Davis went on to co-write, remix, and produce tracks for labelmates DJ Krush and Doctor Octagon plus the Mo' trip-hop supergroup U.N.K.L.E.

Josh Davis grew up in Hayward, CA, a predominantly lower-middle class suburb of San Francisco. The odd, White, suburban, hip-hop fan in the hard rock-dominated early '80s, Davis gravitated toward the turntable/mixer setup of the hip-hop DJ over the guitars, bass, and drums of his peers. He worked his way through hip-hop's early years like the heyday of crews like Eric B. & Rakim, Ultramagnetic, and Public Enemy—groups which prominently featured DJs in their ranks. Davis had already been fiddling around with making beats and breaks on a four-track while he was in high school, but it was his move to the northern California cow-town of Davis to attend university that led to the establishment of his own Solesides label as an outlet for his original tracks. Hooking up with Davis' few b-boys (including eventual Solesides artists Blackalicious and Lyrics Born) through the college radio station, Shadow began releasing the *Reconstructed from the Ground Up* mixtapes in 1991 and pressed his 17-minute hip-hop symphony "Entropy" in 1993. His tracks spread widely through the DJ-strong hip-hop underground, eventually catching the attention of Mo'Wax. Shadow's first full-length, *Endtroducing...*, was released in late 1996 to immense critical acclaim in Britain and America. *Preemptive Strike*, a compilation of early singles, followed in early 1998. Later that year, Shadow produced tracks for the debut album by U.N.K.L.E., a long-time Mo'Wax production team that gained superstar guests including Thom Yorke (of Radiohead), Richard Ashcroft (of the Verve), Mike D. (of the Beastie Boys), and others. His next project came in 1999, with the transformation of Solesides into a new label, Quannum Projects. The quasi-compilation *Quannum Spectrum* was released that summer. [See Also: U.N.K.L.E.] —*Sean Cooper*

**Entropy [EP]** / 1993 / Solesides ♦♦♦
Shadow's first full-blown blast of heady, groove-heavy instrumental experiments, released on his own Solesides label, is one continuous track moving from upbeat deck-work and bin-shuddering beats through thick, downtempo head music. The flip is a forgettable vehicle for rapper and labelmate Asia Born (now Lyrics Born). —*Sean Cooper*

**In/Flux [Single]** / Oct. 1993 / Mo'Wax ♦♦♦♦
Although somewhat sloppy, it almost doesn't matter given the scope and originality of the result. Moving from a kinetic, signature Shadow opening through uptempo, funky breakbeats and stoney, textured, downbeat hip-hop, it's easy to see how influential "In/Flux" was on a generation of musicians looking for somewhere to take hip-hop. —*Sean Cooper*

**Lost and Found (S.F.L.) [Single]** / 1994 / Mo'Wax ♦♦♦
A split with DJ Krush, Shadow's side kipes the opening drum break from U2's "Sunday Bloody Sunday," cutting and layering it over chilling guitar and organ samples. The vocal break was lifted, according to Davis, from a late-'60s prison record. —*Sean Cooper*

**What Does Your Soul Look Like? [EP]** / Feb. 1995 / Mo'Wax ♦♦♦♦
"Soul"'s four parts are united in name only, with Shadow moving from solemn breakbeat-noir through alternately light, up-tempo and slower, more questioning moods. Like past releases, his needlework is inspired, with textured, musical scratches that do more than simply accentuate. Shadow's best, most unified work. —*Sean Cooper*

**Hardcore (Instrumental) Hip-Hop [EP]** / Apr. 16, 1996 / Mo'Wax/Excursions ♦♦♦
Shadow on the nepotism tip with his Solesides crew Chief X-Cel and Gift of Gab on the flip. Shadow steals the show with another extended meditation on outbound hip-hop, this time with stronger beatwork than past releases. A throwaway "Scratchapella" and a nice mid-tempo instrumental break run out the side. —*Sean Cooper*

★ **Endtroducing...** / Nov. 19, 1996 / Mo'Wax/ffrr ♦♦♦♦♦
As a suburban California kid, DJ Shadow tended to treat hip-hop as a musical innovation, not as an explicit social protest, which goes a long way toward explaining why his debut album *Endtroducing...* sounded like nothing else at the time of its release. Using hip-hop, not only its rhythms but its cut-and-paste techniques, as a foundation, Shadow created a deep, endlessly intriguing world on *Endtroducing*, one where there are no musical genres, only shifting sonic textures and styles. Shadow created the entire album from samples, almost all pulled from obscure, forgotten vinyl, and the effect is that of a hazy, half-familiar dream—parts of the record sound familiar, yet it's clear that it only suggests music you've heard before, and that the multilayered samples and genres create something new. And that's one of the keys to the success of *Endtroducing*—it's innovative, but it builds on a solid historical foundation, giving it a rich, multifaceted sound. It's not only a major breakthrough for hip-hop and electronica, but for pop music. —*Stephen Thomas Erlewine*

**Camel Bobsled Race (Q-Bert Mega Mix) EP** / 1998 / Mo'Wax ♦♦♦
*Camel Bobsled Race*, Q-Bert's megamix of DJ Shadow music, isn't quite the masterpiece it oculd have been, yet it's hardly a disaster. Recorded live, with both DJs scratching, the mix essentially reconfigures the bulk of *Endtroducing*, adding a couple of singles to the mix. There are layers of new samples and scratches, taken from everything from spoken-word records to jazz. The end result is intriguing and often entertaining, even if it doesn't offer any new revelations. *Camel Bobsled Race* was released as a bonus disc on the US-only singles and B-sides compilation *Preemptive Strike*. —*Stephen Thomas Erlewine*

**Preemptive Strike** / Jan. 13, 1998 / Mo'Wax/ffrr/London ♦♦♦♦
DJ Shadow assembled the singles collection *Preemptive Strike* as a way for American audiences to catch up on his career prior to his debut album, *Endtroducing*. The 11-track album contains three new interludes and three complete singles that he released on Mo'Wax—"In/Flux," "What Does Your Soul Look Like?" and "High Noon"—and a bonus disc, "Camel Bobsled Race," which is a megamix of DJ Shadow material by DJ Q-Bert. Given that *Endtroducing* was a masterpiece of subtly shifting texture, *Preemptive Strike* almost seems purposely incoherent, even though the tracks are sequenced chronologically. The jerky flow can make the album a little difficult to asssimilate on first listen, but it soon begins to make sense, even if it never achieves the graceful flow of the album. Several of the selections on *Preemptive Strike* were available in different forms on *Endtroducing*—parts four and one of "What Does Your Soul Look Like?" are in their original forms here, presented along with one and three, and there's the "extended overhaul" of "Organ Donor." All of these are significantly different than the LP versions, and "What Does Your Soul Look Like?" is necessary in its original, half-hour, four-part incarnation. But the key moments are the seminal "In/Flux," which arguably created trip-hop, and "High Noon," the dynamic, fuzz-drenched single that was his first single release since *Endtroducing*. Those three A-sides are reason enough for any serious fan of the debut to pick up *Preemptive Strike*, but the B-sides and "Camel Bobsled Race" are equally intriguing, making the package a nice summation of DJ Shadow's most important singles through the end of 1997. —*Stephen Thomas Erlewine*

## DJ Sneak

**b.** 1969, Puerto Rico
*Producer, DJ / Club/Dance, House*
One of the second wave of influential Chicago house producers and a member of the vanguard of late-'90s American house producers, DJ Sneak wasn't born in the Windy City but began listening to house soon after his family arrived from Puerto Rico in the early '80s. Because he could speak no English, Sneak gravitated to instrumental music (as well as graffiti art), and became inspired by Chicago legends such as Marshall Jefferson and DJ Pierre. Many of those early innovators had left Chicago for the East Coast by the late '80s, when Sneak was ready to start in the business; by 1992, however, Cajmere had begun a resurgence in the city's classic sound by starting up Cajual Records. Sneak aided in the revolution with a series of singles on Cajual's sister label, the harder-oriented Relief Records. Besides other productions for Strictly Rhythm, Henry St., ZYX, 83 West and Feverpitch (several of which feature Armand Van Helden on co-production, building on the Latin vibes of their heritage), DJ Sneak has also released mix compilations including

1996's *Kinky Trax Collection* and the following year's *Buggin' Da Beats*. —*John Bush*

**Da Pimp Doggy [EP]** / 1995 / Downtown ♦♦♦
From Chicago, DJ Sneak constructed a great disco-inspired party rocker with "All Over My Face." —*John Bush*

**Blue Funk Files** / 1997 / Ultra ♦♦♦♦
Combining the 1996 EP *Blue Funk Files* with the same year's "Hardsteppin' Disko Selection" single (co-produced with Armand Van Helden), the full-length *Blue Funk Files* traces Sneak's Chicago acid minimalism on barnstormers like "Soundz in My Head," "The Grinder," and the A-side of "Hardsteppin' Disko Selection." —*John Bush*

● **Buggin' Da Beats** / May 20, 1997 / Moonshine Music ♦♦♦♦
DJ Sneak compiled this set of future house music, with selections ranging from Kerri Chandler to Global Communication with other tracks by Groove Box, Stephanie Cooke, and Sneak's own "Special K." —*John Bush*

## DJ Soul Slinger (Carlos Slinger)

b. Brazil
*Producer, DJ / Jungle/Drum'N'Bass, Club/Dance*
The leader of New York's breakbeat movement under the banner of Liquid Sky Design (a combination record store, clothing imprint, show promoter, and record label), Carlos Soul Slinger grew up in Brazil but was present in New York during the '70s disco movement and London for both the '80s acid house revolution and the drum'n'bass phenomenon of the '90s. After moving to New York permanently in the early '90s, he introduced jungle DJing stateside and formed the Liquid Sky record store and later, Jungle Sky Records, America's first drum'n'bass label. His debut album *Don't Believe* appeared on Jungle Sky US in late 1997. His mix CD, *United DJs of America, Vol. 14* was released in May of 2000. Several of his tracks have also appeared on the *This Is Jungle Sky* compilation series, and he co-runs two other labels, Tekhed and Home Entertainment. —*John Bush*

**Don't Believe** / Jul. 1, 1997 / Jungle Sky US ♦♦
Like the debut album by DJ Dara, another New York City junglist, *Don't Believe* sounds years out of date compared to similar drum'n'bass work being done in Britain. Disposable breakbeats and simplistic, house-inflected synth lines do little to divert a listener's attention over the course of many overlong tracks. "The Law" is a wondrously executed downbeat excursion, but almost every other track drags on long after it should have ended. —*John Bush*

**Abducted Remixes** / Nov. 25, 1997 / Jungle Sky US ♦♦
A variety of producers and DJs offer remixes of "Abducted," DJ Soul Slinger's successful 1994 collaboration with MC Det. Featured are DJ Ani, T-Power, DJ Wally, WE, the River of Action, DJ Quest and DJ Budda, American Space Travelers, Tube, and Marshall H. —*Steve Huey*

● **United DJs of America, Vol. 14** / May 9, 2000 / DMC America ♦♦♦
Running an incredibly diverse amount of sounds through his twisted head, DJ Soul Slinger, the Jungle legend from Brazil, has produced an album that extends the boundaries of dance music. Featuring the music of Drumsound & Simon Smith, Scitex, Uncle 22, Mike & Ike and the Arsonists, among others, this album fuses together acid house, drum'n'bass, ragga, and the occasional easy listening bit to make something irresistibly funky. —*Stacia Proefrock*

## DJ Spooky (Paul D. Miller)

b. 1970, Washington, D.C.
*Producer, DJ / Illbient, Turntablism, Experimental Techno, Electronica, Post-Rock/Experimental, Trip-Hop*
DJ Spooky (Tha' Subliminal Kid) is the most noted (and notorious) proponent of turntablism, an approach to hip-hop and DJing whose philosophy merges avant-garde theories of *musique concrète* with the increased devotion paid to mixing techniques during the '90s. Though he's overly intellectual at times (to the detriment of his recordings, interviews, and mixing dates), DJ Spooky was a critical figure in spotlighting the DJ as a postmodern poet in his own right. Influenced equally by John Cage and Sun Ra as well as Kool Herc and Grandmaster Flash, few artists did more to mainstream the DJ-as-artist concept than him.

Spooky was born Paul Miller in Washington, D.C. His father was a lawyer and member of the faculty at Howard University, but died when Miller was only three. He inherited his father's record collection which, along with frequent trips around the world (thanks to his mother's international fabric store), opened his eyes to a wide range of music. Growing up in the '80s saw Miller interested in D.C.'s hardcore punk scene and British ska-punk as well as go-go music. While attending college in Maine, Spooky began mixing on his own radio show and attempted to introduce his KRS-One tapes into classroom discussions on deconstruction (an idea made quite conceivable just ten years later). After graduating with degrees in French literature and philosophy, he moved to New York, where he wrote science fiction alongside advertising copy, and pursued visual art as well. He was still into hip-hop, however, and formed the underground Soundlab collective (with We, Byzar, Sub Dub, and others), a scene that later morphed into the illbient movement.

After an assortment of singles and EPs during 1994-95, DJ Spooky gained a record contract from Asphodel in 1996 and released his debut album *Songs of a Dead Dreamer*. The single "Galactic Funk" became a hit on the club scene, leading to recording appearances with Arto Lindsay and remixing spots for Metallica, Sublime, Nick Cave, and Spookey Ruben; Spooky also began writing regular journalist columns, for *The Village Voice* and *Vibe*. As if that didn't keep him busy, he also released the mix album *Necropolis: The Dialogic Project*, recorded a Paul D. Miller solo LP named *Viral Sonata*, and performed in a new digital version of the Iannis Xenakis composition *Kraanerg*. His second proper album, 1998's *Riddim Warfare*, saw DJ Spooky with a cast including disparate indie-world figures from Dr. Octagon to Thurston Moore. He has also mounted visual exhibits at the Whitney Museum in New York, and scored the award-winning 1998 film *Slam*. One year later, he released *File Under Futurism*, a co-production with the Freight Elevator Quartet. —*John Bush*

**Songs of a Dead Dreamer** / Mar. 26, 1996 / Asphodel ♦♦♦♦
The outstanding debut offering from DJ Spooky touches base with everything from trip-hop to ambient to dub to world music and back again. *Songs of a Dead Dreamer*'s one constant is the sound collage aesthetic, which laces the music with the soundtrack of everyday street life—radio static, police sirens, and the like—and informs the album with a distinctly gritty, downtown feel. —*Jason Ankeny*

**Necropolis: The Dialogic Project** / May 21, 1996 / Knitting Factory ♦♦♦
When this album was released in 1995, DJ Spooky (Tha' Subliminal Kid) was not yet the legend of abstract electronica that he would later become. Here he presents an overlong program of remixes by unknown (Byzar, Ben Neill) and relatively famous (Sub Dub, DJ Soul Slinger) electronic dance artists, with some tracks lasting as long as 12 minutes and each featuring a prologue than runs as much as five. The length of these tracks is not a problem in itself, but the random shapelessness of them is. DJ Spooky has an autodidact's love of big words and impatience with coherent syntax ("The anomalies in this mix are coordinate points marking an invisible terrain"), and that combination of intellectual attributes finds direct expression in his music, which is filled with fascinating sounds and textures but is frustratingly bereft of discipline or organization. Hence his remix of Ben Neill's "Grapheme," in which sonic effluvia bob around in a dark sea of noise, and his own "Journey (Paraspace Mix)," a shapeless sound pastiche that mutters and grumbles without ever generating the slightest interest. Those who endure the first half-hour of this 75-minute program will be rewarded by Sub Dub's skanking "Sound-Check" and DJ Soul Slinger's excellent "Abducted (U.F.O. Mix)," but it's hard going until then. There's no excuse for music this potentially interesting to be this boring. —*Rick Anderson*

**Haunted Breaks, Vol. 1 [EP]** / Aug. 18, 1998 / Home Entertainment ♦♦♦
*Haunted Breaks, Vol. 1* is an approximately 40-minute, limited-edition breakbeat EP; it finds Spooky harking back to old-school rave sounds. —*Steve Huey*

● **Riddim Warfare** / Sep. 21, 1998 / Outpost ♦♦♦♦
Though he has his fingers in just about every beat-oriented pot of the late '90s (from hip-hop to trip-hop to drum'n'bass to illbient to turntablism), DJ Spooky managed to control his various inspirations for *Riddim Warfare*, instead of falling prey to the musical-eclecticism-for-its-own-sake concept that often derails similar producers. On the album's half-dozen or so hip-hop tracks, the production is appropriately dense and paranoid for abstract-philosopher rappers like Kool Keith, Sir Menelik, Organized Konfusion, and Killah Priest of Wu-Tang Clan. Elsewhere, Spooky sandwiches the tech-step drum'n'bass stormer "Post-Human Sophistry" right next to a track recorded

live in Brazil with Arto Lindsay (which resembles a fusion of hip-hop with early Weather Report). Only one man could conceive of an album including turntable battles, a workout for Sonic Youth guitarist Thurston Moore, and a spoken-word piece on the same album. Through it all, DJ Spooky makes it work in fine fashion. —*John Bush*

**File Under Futurism** / Sep. 21, 1999 / Caipirinha ♦♦♦♦
DJ Spooky's *File Under Futurism* is the result of a six-month collaboration with the Freight Elevator Quartet, an avant-garde electronic and acoustic group dedicated to pioneering new musical sounds and techniques. *File Under Futurism* features variations on compositions by DJ Spooky that were then reworked and remixed by both Spooky and the Freight Elevator Quartet. Each of the album's pieces reflects society's increasing speed and reliance on technology while exploring different subgenres of electronic music, from the breakbeat-inflected "File Under Futurism (Groove Protocol Mix)" to the minimalist, cello-driven "Downtempo Manifesto," to the heavily-processed digital hardcore of "Experimental Asynchronicity" to the gentler, ambient "Chromatic Aberration." *File Under Futurism* also includes DJ Spooky turntablisms "Interstitial A" and "Interstitial B," as well as Freight Elevator Quartet compositions like "Bring Me My Mental Health" and "The RCA Mark II Synthesizer," which was composed on the first synthesizer ever built. An ambitious and fascinating album, *File Under Futurism* is a rare, successful combination of academics and kinetics. —*Heather Phares*

## DJ T-1000 (Alan D. Oldham)

*Producer, DJ / Detroit Techno, Club/Dance, Techno*
One of Detroit's most talented and venerated techno mixers, DJ T-1000 has been instrumental in the Motor City scene as a label-head and producer as well as DJ. Born Alan Oldham, he spent time as a graphic-design specialist and comics illustrator while studying media at Detroit's Wayne State University. Hired by Derrick May to illustrate the sleeves on a few Transmat releases, Oldham became interested in Detroit's electronic scene, and gradually transformed his Fast Forward radio program on WDET from industrial and fusion into techno. During the show's run, from 1987 to 1992, Oldham introduced thousands of area listeners to Detroit techno via productions from May, Kevin Saunderson, Juan Atkins, Underground Resistance, and Carl Craig—as well as other techno figures like Joey Beltram, Moby, 808 State, and LFO. The show ended in 1992 when an offer to tour with Underground Resistance as the replacement DJ for Jeff Mills proved too difficult to resist. Also in 1992, he formed his own Generator label, the origin of seminal releases by Oldham projects like X-313 ("Interferon," "World Sonik Domination") and TXC-1 as well as tracks by Dave Clarke and Woody McBride. In 1996, Oldham closed Generator and opened a new label, Pure Sonik. He also began DJing around the world, gaining a reputation as one of the best Detroit DJs among considerable competition. The DJ T-1000 mix albums *Supercollider* (a Generator label retrospective) and *Live Sabotage: Live in Belgium* displayed his mixing genius, while his debut production full-length, *Progress*, appeared on Tresor in 1999. Oldham also began recording another album, for Astralwerks. In addition, he has recorded for Djax-Up-Beats, Matrix, and Communique, and done remix work for Terry Lee Brown, Jr. and the Punisher. —*John Bush*

**Supercollider** / Jul. 28, 1997 / Generator ♦♦
● **Progress** / Sep. 28, 1999 / Tresor ♦♦♦
Alan Oldham looks back to the glory days of Detroit techno with a set of hard, dark, occasionally melancholy techno reminiscent of early '90s releases by Underground Resistance and Carl Craig, as well as Oldham himself. The visceral pummeling of "Supernatural (Bangin')" gives way to more atmospheric techno tracks like "Marina" and "Locomia," while Oldham works in trip-hop territory with "Berlin" and "Tonight." —*John Bush*

## DJ Trace (Duncan Hutchinson)

*Producer, DJ / Jungle/Drum'N'Bass, Club/Dance*
DJ Trace was an early member of the tight-knit crew of producers constituting popular techstep drum'n'bass label No U-Turn. Like colleagues Nico and Ed Rush, Trace's first crack at broad exposure came through the *Techsteppin'* compilation, released by the Emotif label and containing a number of tracks licensed from No U-Turn studios. Released in 1995, the compilation helped seed a new direction in drum'n'bass, one characterized by heavy use of electronics, cavernous beats and basslines, and the dystopian histrionics that have since become trademarks of the No U-Turn/Nu Black sound. Trace's 1995 release on Emotif, "The Mutant" (itself a remix of T-Power's "Mutant Jazz"), also spawned a remix of its own, and Ed Rush's "Mutant Revisited" became an influential trial run of tech's by now cliched "hoover" bassline and rolling, relentless breaks. A popular DJ whose schedule busied as No U-Turn's popularity peaked in 1996, Trace moved from the UK to Philadelphia that same year and has participated in a number of US events (including 1997's Big Top tour) both solo and with other members of the No U-Turn crew. —*Sean Cooper*

● **The Return of the Mutant (Mutant Revisited) [Single]** / 1995 / Emotif ♦♦♦♦
The definitive tune of '95 and the ground zero of techstep. The track's relentless breaks and assaultive bassline (courtesy of Ed Rush and an uncredited Dominic Angus) became the blueprint for a hundred knockoff tracks—much of No U-Turn's subsequent catalog was pretty much a footnote to this track—but none could match "Mutant" for style or economy. Essential. —*Sean Cooper*

## DJ Tron

*DJ / Hardcore Techno, Club/Dance*
Having gotten his start in 1991, DJ Tron toured constantly across the United States and Canada for eight years spinning at hardcore parties and distributing mix tapes. Blending his own elements of hardcore punk and twisted techno, Tron dove more into the maniacal side of dance music, which resulted in a part of some controversy and an underground fanbase. His first full-length *Chrome Padded Cell* was released in 1999 and featured a severed hand giving the "sign of Satan"-cuffed fist with the index and pinkie finger sticking out on the cover. —*Mike DaRonco*

● **Chrome Padded Cell** / Apr. 6, 1999 / Highborn ♦♦
Hardcore techno DJ Tron's first full length takes the "hardcore" tag seriously, with many tracks coming off as a sort of techno-punk hybrid. "Dog Will Hunt" appears as an unlisted bonus track. —*Steve Huey*

## DJ Vadim (Vadim Peare)

*Producer, DJ / Electronica, Ambient Breakbeat, Trip-Hop, Hip-Hop*
Hip-hop's influence spread far and wide during the '80s, as witnessed by the growth of the international scene during the following decade. Standing beside brilliant DJs from Japan (Krush) and France (Cam), Russia's DJ Vadim has proved to be the most popular advocate of hip-hop to come out of the former Soviet bloc, triggered mostly by the fact that he moved to Britain early in life. Upon arrival, he set up his own Jazz Fudge Records later that year to issue a demo he called "Derelicts of Conformity" (by Son of Seth). He finally released the recordings early in 1995, as DJ Vadim's *Abstract Hallucinating Gasses* EP.

Britain's top hip-hop and acid jazz DJs began playing the record and, after being scouted by several labels, Vadim signed a contract with Ninja Tune. Several EPs released during 1995-96 showed him to be quite an experimentalist, working heavily with static and noise, never content to let his ideas meander past the two- or three-minute point. His first LP, *U.S.S.R. Repertoire (The Theory of Verticality)*, was released in late 1996. The following year, Vadim began working on acts for Jazz Fudge; he issued the compilation *Sculpture & Broken Sound*, then debuted his own Andre Gurov project with the album *A New Rap Language*. His next project, the highly touted remix album *U.S.S.R. Reconstruction*, appeared in 1998, followed a year later by *U.S.S.R.: Life from the Other Side*. Vadim has also worked as the Bug, with Kevin Martin, Dave Cochran, and Alex Buess. —*John Bush*

**U.S.S.R. Repertoire (The Theory of Verticality)** / Oct. 14, 1996 / Ninja Tune ♦♦♦♦
Of the countless abstract hip-hop LPs released during 1996-97 (with Ninja Tune bearing much of the load), *U.S.S.R. Repertoire* could be one of the best. Vadim's attention to detail when structuring beats, samples and noise is impeccable over the course of the album's 26 tracks. With just the right blend of forbidding atmosphere and subtle funkiness, Vadim created an excellent album his first time out. —*John Bush*

**U.S.S.R. Reconstruction** / Jan. 26, 1998 / Ninja Tune ♦♦♦♦
DJ Vadim selected a baker's dozen of the best producers in the field for work on *U.S.S.R. Reconstruction*. From nu-school electro producers (Reflection, Clatterbox) to more like-minded beat-meisters (DJ Krush, Silent Poets, Kid Koala) and free-form experimenters (Oval, Techno Animal), the album flows

without a hitch through the darkest hip-hop and beat exploration, though the material never becomes as abstract as on Vadim's debut. —*John Bush*

● **U.S.S.R.: Life from the Other Side** / Sep. 14, 1999 / Ninja Tune ◆◆◆◆
DJ Vadim's debut introduced one of the world's best producers in abstract underground rap, a minimalist hip-hopper able to weave a funky break around the slightest piece of noise detritus. After recording a solid remix album (*U.S.S.R. Reconstruction*), Vadim returned in late 1999 with the sophomore-slump-breaking *U.S.S.R.: Life From the Other Side*. Whereas Vadim worked on a miniature scale on his first album, constructing breaks and beats out of abstract noise, here the sound is more upfront and swaggering, much closer to the commercial rap world than before. (Of course, thanks to producers like Timbaland and Swizz Beatz, the commercial rap world had moved much closer to Vadim, as well.) Since he's working with rappers on more than half of the tracks here, Vadim transforms himself from a solo turntablist into a genuine rap trackmaster with catchier riffs and tighter beats than most in Britain's instrumental hip-hop underground. Two tracks, "Viagra" (with El-P from Company Flow) and "English Breakfast" (with Swollen Members), display this excellent fusion by blending the hard-hitting, stutter-stepped style of production perfected by DJ Premier with just a few of the paranoid breaks and hostile atmospheres of Vadim's debut. On a similarly high level as landmarks like Dr. Octagon and Company Flow's *Funcrusher Plus*, *U.S.S.R.: Life From the Other Side* proves Vadim is not only one of the most creative turntablist/producers, but he is also one of the most talented trackmasters in the healthy rap underground. —*John Bush*

## DJ Wally (Keef Destefano)
**b.** New York, NY
*Producer, DJ / Electronica, Ambient Breakbeat, Trip-Hop, Hip-Hop*
A member of New York's Liquid Sky family, DJ Wally began taking trip-hop into new directions with three EPs recorded for his own label, Sams Jointz. The tracks contained an astounding variety of sounds, encompassing ambient, funk, jungle, plus a solid exercise in '70s nostalgia—a reworking of Simon & Garfunkel's classic "Feelin' Groovy." Mo'Wax founder James Lavelle liked what he heard, and licensed one track for his 1996 trip-hop compilation, *Headz II*, a roll call for all the best artists in the new electronica. Early the following year, DJ Wally released his debut album, *Genetic Flaw*, for Liquid Sky's Home Entertainment subsidiary. Paired with DJ Swingsett, Wally released *Dog Leg Left* later that year. *The Stoned Ranger Rides Again* followed in 1999. —*John Bush*

● **Genetic Flaw** / Feb. 25, 1997 / Home Entertainment ◆◆◆◆
Including his classic remake of Simon & Garfunkel's "Feelin' Groovy," *Genetic Flaw* features DJ Wally's explorations through hip-hop, breakbeat, and earthy drum'n'bass. Occasionally, it's too indebted to the illbient scene's abstractions for its own good, but Wally still manages several fine moments. —*John Bush*

**Dog Leg Left** / Aug. 12, 1997 / Ubiquity ◆◆◆
His first album as half of the duo credited as DJ's Wally & Swingsett, *Dog Leg Left* ranges through the blunted drum'n'bass of "Smoking Up the Music" and scratchadelic soul of "Wiggin." For the most part, though, it's acceptable (if a bit bland) downtempo trip-hop, heavy on the vibes but a tad light on the production. —*John Bush*

**The Stoned Ranger Rides Again** / Mar. 30, 1999 / Home Entertainment ◆◆

## DJ Zinc
*Producer, DJ / Jungle/Drum'N'Bass, Club/Dance*
DJ Zinc is probably best known for the virtually undisputed 1995 anthem "Super Sharp Shooter," a fierce, energetic hip-hop/jungle fusion that by year's end had become the very definition of a rinsed-out track. Zinc's career as a DJ and producer, however, stretch quite a ways further back, sketching the steady evolution of hardcore from its house and rave roots through ragga and hip-hop-styled hardstep and beyond. He's worked with a broad range of labels, both respected and virtually unknown (including Back 2 Basics, Congo Natty, Droppin' Science, 2000AD, Brain, and, of course, Ganja), done time on the pirate radio circuit, and DJed as a resident at some of London's most popular underground clubs. Zinc's first production work came in the form of the eight-volume series *Swift and Zinc*, released on Dream Team/Joker Records' Bizzy B's Brain imprint in the early '90s. The collaboration came to an end in 1994 when DJ Swift decided to focus on garage and house (the two still share

studio space). Remarkably, "Super Sharp Shooter" became Zinc's solo debut, and he's since released a number of popular tracks, although none have scaled the heights of his first. He currently records with DJ Hype, Pascal, and Rude Bwoy Monty as part of the Ganja Kru (for MCA sublabel Parousia), as well as for Hype's True Playaz label (as DJ Zinc and Dope Skillz). He continues to DJ on a regular basis. —*Sean Cooper*

● **Super Sharp Shooter [Single]** / 1995 / Ganja ◆◆◆◆
Zinc stuffs gangsta rap, a Public Enemy sample and some incredible beats into the blender on this single, recorded for Ganja. —*John Bush*

## DMX Krew
*Group / Electro-Techno, Club/Dance*
While many acts in the continuing electro-funk revival of the late '90s hid behind aliases and updated the sound considerably, Ed Upton's DMX Krew made few concessions—for better or worse—to music or graphic technology developed later than 1985. Turned on to electro in 1983 after buying a Kraftwerk 7" as a teenager, Upton began recording as DMX Krew in the mid-'90s, with his first album *The Sound of the Street* appearing in 1996 on Rephlex Records. Tracks like "Rock to the Beat," "Move My Body," and "Dance to the Beat" were rough but effective pastiches of spare street-level electro from the glory days, while the high-profile status of Rephlex (the label founded by Aphex Twin) guaranteed Upton a degree of exposure. Rephlex's commitment to electro (as witnessed by its retrospective of electro-bass pioneers Dynamix II) resulted in several additional DMX Krew albums, including 1997's *Ffressshh!* and the following year's *Nu Romantix*. *We Are DMX* followed in 1999. Upton also remixed an electro classic (Herbie Hancock's "Rockit") for Sony, recorded an EP of Kraftwerk covers and released tracks by Bass Junkie, Mandroid, and Biochip C on his own label, Breakin' Records. —*John Bush*

**The Sound of the Street** / Sep. 23, 1996 / Rephlex ◆◆

**Ffressshh!** / Jul. 21, 1997 / Rephlex ◆◆
Updating his criminally retro sound only slightly from the previous year's *Sound of the Street*, Ed DMX still relies on barely thought-out ideas and the novelty effect of vintage electro for *Ffressshh!* It's an interesting album, but one that doesn't quite hold attention for more than a few listens. —*John Bush*

● **Nu Romantix** / Jun. 8, 1998 / Rephlex ◆◆◆
Careful listeners might be able to hear a bit of progression on DMX Krew's third album, though Upton's never far from his vocoder on "Can U Feel the Power?," "End of the Night," and "Mouse" (the latter reminiscent of Newcleus). His disembodied vocals on "You're Not There" are also typically '80s, while a Cylob remix of "I'm All Alone" provides the only link to the last decade of the century. —*John Bush*

## Tod Dockstader
**b.** May 22, 1932, St. Paul, MN
*Composer / Electronic*
Producing a slim but groundbreaking body of work possessed of a truly musical sensibility typically lacking from the tape constructions of his contemporaries, Tod Dockstader was among America's foremost composers of musique concrète, creating electronic soundscapes informed by genuine drama and mystery. Born May 22, 1932 in St. Paul, MN, Dockstader spent his childhood enamoured of radio broadcasts, intrigued not only by the popular programs of the era but also the static and noise separating stations on the dial. In time he turned to producing his own ham radio broadcasts, and while a graduate student at the University of Minnesota he studied film and painting, funding his education by drawing cartoons for local newspapers and magazines.

In 1955 Dockstader relocated to Hollywood, where he was hired as an apprentice film editor at Terrytoons Animation, working alongside future luminaries such as cartoonist Jules Feiffer and director Ralph Bakshi. He soon graduated to writing and storyboarding his own cartoons, earning renown for his "The FreezeYum Story" before relocating to New York in 1958, where he landed a job as an assistant recording engineer at Gotham Recording studios. There Dockstader began collecting interesting sounds, in his off-hours assembling his earliest musique concrète projects. The end result was 1960's *Eight Pieces*, his first major work; shortly thereafter Gotham purchased its first stereo Ampex recorder, allowing Dockstader to revise piece No. 8 for his first stereo project, *Traveling Music*.

On May 20, 1961, New York's WQXR broadcast the world premiere of *Traveling Music* on a program also featuring Edgard Varèse's *Poeme electronique*. That year proved a remarkably productive period in Dockstader's development, as he completed two major works, *Luna Park* and *Apocalypse*. (*Two Fragments from Apocalypse*, also from 1961, consists of a large chunk edited from the latter.) His creations at this time reflect his increasing mastery of the studio and its endless possibilities, making use of techniques including tape-echo antiphony, channel delay, placement and panning. Best labelled as "organized sound," Dockstader's radical construction and manipulation of audio fragments eschew the harmony and rhythm that typically define music, yet their flow, balance and spatial dynamics suggest an artistry far beyond the noisy experiments of his peers.

Revolutionary projects like 1962's *Drone* and 1963's *Water Music* followed, and by the time Dockstader completed his masterpiece, 1964's 46-minute epic *Quatermass*, he had accumulated a sound library of about 300,000 feet of tape equalling 125 hours of source material. A year later, however, his career in musique concrète essentially came to a halt with the test-generator piece *Four Telemetry Tapes*—soon after, Dockstader left his engineering position at Gotham to work as an audio-visual designer at the Air Canada Pavilion at the 1967 Montreal Expo, where he crafted dozens of soundtracks while shooting thousands of slide photographs as well as a film. Concurrently, he also wrote music and book criticism for the *Electronic Music Review* and the *Musical Quarterly*.

Around this same time, the Owl Records label issued three LPs of Dockstader material that were reviewed favorably in a number of national publications, earning him the widest recognition of his career. The exposure, however, proved fruitless—without his Gotham job he was no longer able to access the technology necessary to continue his sound experiments, and without the proper academic background he was denied grants and shut out of electronic music facilities, rejected by the Columbia-Princeton Center among others. The end result was that Dockstader returned full-time to his audio-visual work, in the years to follow writing and producing hundreds of educational filmstrips and videos for schools. His music long out-of-print, his work is finally reissued to great acclaim during the early '80s, becoming a seminal influence on the electronic artists of the following decade. —*Jason Ankeny*

**Quatermass** / 1992 / Starkland ++++

The first of two Dockstader reissues on Starkland, *Quatermass* consists of three compositions, the short works "Water Music" and "Two Moons of Quatermass" plus the 45-minute title work. The first begins predictably with a few water drips but gradually builds to a series of climaxes via sequences of amazing electronic transformations, while the second "Two Moons of Quatermass" consists mostly of veering waves of electronics. The title composition, consisting of five separate pieces, is Dockstader's tour de force. The echoed pounding of the beat in "Tango" reveals Dockstader playing with a variety of shadings and different sounds. Alternately based on composition-based classical as well as pulse music reminiscent of later synthesizer music, *Quatermass* is a warm, passionate tape-music classic that proves Dockstader was the master of American musique concrète and author of quite possibly the most alien recordings ever produced. —*John Bush*

★ **Apocalypse** / 1993 / Starkland +++++

The two stellar reissues of collected Dockstader material on the Starkland label can be separated by their connections to light and darker material. As could be expected, *Apocalypse* concerns the darker edge. Both the 20-minute title track and the included 10-minute "Traveling Music" cultivate a series of chilling atmospheres with few precedents in the academic electronic community. "Traveling Music" does so with a series of clicks and chirps that gradually morph themselves into an undeniable air of menace while "Apocalypse" accomplishes the same with Forbidden Planet effects reminiscent of flying saucers and interstellar explosions plus a series of voice treatments that truly do sound as though they're of alien nature. Also included on the same disc, "Luna Park" turns the laughter of vacationers into chipmunk-frequency effects processed with tremendous amounts of reverb and echo. —*John Bush*

## Dr. Octagon (Keith Thornton)

*Vocals / Underground Rap, Electronica, Trip-Hop, Hip-Hop*

After single-handedly redefining "warped" as the mind and mouth behind the Bronx-based Ultramagnetic MCs, "Kool" Keith Thornton—aka Rhythm X, aka Dr. Octagon, aka Dr. Dooom, aka Mr. Gerbik—headed for the outer reaches of the stratosphere with a variety of solo projects. A one-time psychiatric patient at Bellevue, Keith's lyrical thematics remained as free-flowing here as they ever were with the NY trio, connecting up complex meters with fierce, layers-deep metaphors and veiled criticisms of those who "water down the sound that comes from the ghetto." His own debut single, "Earth People" by Dr. Octagon, was quietly released in late 1995 on the San Francisco-based Bulk Recordings, and the track spread like wildfire through the hip-hop underground, as did the subsequent self-titled full-length released the following year. Featuring internationally renowned DJ Q-Bert (also of the Invisible Skratch Picklz) on turntables, as well as the Automator and DJ Shadow behind the boards, *Dr. Octagon*'s leftfield fusion of sound collage, fierce turntable work, and bizarre, impressionistic rapping found audiences in the most unlikely of places, from hardcore hip-hop heads to jaded rock critics. Although a somewhat sophomoric preoccupation with body parts and scatology tended to dominate the album, Keith's complex weave of associations and shifting references is quite often amazing in its intricacy. The record found its way to the UK-based abstract hip-hop imprint Mo'Wax (for whom Shadow also records) in mid-1996, and was licensed by the label for European release. Mo'Wax also released a DJ-friendly instrumental version of the album titled, appropriately, *The Instrumentalyst: Octagon Beats*. The widespread popularity of the album eventually landed Keith at Geffen splinter DreamWorks in 1997; the label gave *Dr. Octagon* its third release mid-year, adding a number of bonus cuts. In early 1999 however, Keith's alter-ego Dr. Dooom unfortunately "killed off" Dr. Octagon on the opening track of the 1999 album *First Come, First Served* (released on Thornton's own Funky Ass label). Kool Keith signed to Ruffhouse/MCA for his second album under *that* alias, 1999's *Black Elvis/Lost in Space*. —*Sean Cooper*

★ **Dr. Octagon** / May 6, 1996 / DreamWorks +++++

With his 1996 debut release (reissued in 1997 on DreamWorks as *Dr. Octagonecologyst* with a handful of new tracks), Dr. Octagon—a.k.a. Kool Keith—upped the ante and pushed the limits of what was considered hip-hop. Released on the innovative British label Mo'Wax, it caused shockwaves throughout the music community that heard it. Unfortunately, few people actually heard the dizzying and claustrophobic production created by the Automator, the turntable wizardry of DJ Q-Bert, and the insane rhymes of Kool Keith. Without a doubt, this is destined to become not just a hip-hop classic, but a classic album more generally. Released in 1996 during a year that saw an increased amount of sonic experimentation, this release rose to the top for the risks it took. —*Kembrew McLeod*

**The Instrumentalyst: Octagon Beats** / Dec. 9, 1996 / DreamWorks +++

This is essentially the entire *Dr. Octagon* album sans vocals and slightly remixed. If any other artist released an album such as this it would be considered throwaway trash...something for the hardcore fans. But Dr. Octagon's backing tracks are so fresh and original, it's actually nice to just hear the beats minus the rhymes. —*Kembrew McLeod*

## Doctor Rockit (Matthew Herbert)

*Producer / Experimental Techno, Electronica, Neo-Electro, Electro-Techno, House, IDM*

Although his methods may provoke more discussion than his music (at least among chin-stroke types and the British and American dance music presses), Doctor Rockit's Matthew Herbert is an experimentalist of a subtle stripe, combining his love for all styles of dance-based electronic music with a desire to push their modes of expression into new areas. Although Herbert studied music formally, much of his creative impetus has been provided by the compositional potential of digital sampling technology, which he liberally applies to genres such as house, electro, ambient, and techno, fashioning tracks of detail and originality from such mundane objects of everyday life as kitchen flatware, crockery, even his own body. Although the first of his tracks to be released on 12" came out through the Universal Language label associated with Global Communication, the Horn, and Herbert's own Wishmountain project, he's since released a flood of material on the Clear and Phono labels, as Doctor Rockit and Herbert, respectively. With Doctor Rockit, Herbert focuses on old- and new-school electro-funk and housed-up techno, fusing clangy, rattling beats with humorous melodies and leftfield samples and vocal snippets. With his eponymous project, Herbert releases the unlikeliest of experimental house tracks, working within the genre's feel-good, four-on-the-floor arrangements while drastically tweaking its modus operandi. His signature approach has given post-rave house's stale comportment a badly needed shot in the arm, and has (somewhat inexplicably) been widely embraced among mainstream and underground house audiences alike. While continuing to record for both Clear and Phono, Herbert also applied his remixing skills to a number of notable artists, including friend Jonah Sharp of Spacetime Continuum (both on the latter's *Remit Recaps* remix LP and on his Strange Attractor 12" on Phono). After a 1996 full-length on Clear (*The Music of Sound*), Herbert returned to his Doctor Rockit guise in 2000 with *Indoor Fireworks*. [See Also: Herbert, Wishmountain] —*Sean Cooper*

**Ready to Rockit [EP]** / 1995 / Clear ♦♦♦♦
Herbert's debut EP (actually a double-10") on the future-funk Clear label is a weird collection of hitting mid-tempo breakbeat, precious synth-doodle numbers, and lo-fi drum'n'bass, with the clattery beat sampledelia of his Wishmountain and Herbert work in more skeletal form. Some diamonds in the rough, however, include the fizzy electro masterpiece "Worm In My Foot" and the rushed laboratory jungle of "Cameras And Rocks." —*Sean Cooper*

**The Music of Sound** / Nov. 18, 1996 / Clear ♦♦♦♦
Among the most experimental of the neo-electro Clear label's releases, *The Music of Sound* is a trip through the mind of Doctor Rockit's Matt Herbert. His obsession with sounds and sampling technology is still in full force, and several shorter tracks illustrate the experiments—one has a metallic apple being crunched over and over, another dissects the individual words of a mother's question to a child ("Hello baby, want a cookie?"), and yet another reworks the asthmatic blowing of a cool jazz saxophonist. Most of the tracks, however, feature a steady beat at some point and the playful quality throughout makes *The Music of Sound* quite a rewarding journey. —*John Bush*

● **Indoor Fireworks** / 2000 / Lifelike ♦♦♦♦
Another album of amazing tracks that bear the unmistakable prints of Herbert's notoriously grubby sampling fingers, *Indoor Fireworks* ranges from jazz-house to classical to dance-pop to invisible soundtracks to drum'n'bass—all with some semblance of a groove despite the kooky environmental samples. Herbert ranges from the kitchen to the backyard, from his father's automobile to a French café, from an answering-machine message to a trip from his home to his studio. With all this phlegmatic audio detritus, Herbert fashions a series of incredibly funky tracks, like the distorted groove piece "Roman Candle" and the mellow jungle of "Metro." Herbert excels at breezy pop too, with the vocal piece "Summer Love" (vocals by Dani Siciliano) and a self-explanatory track titled "The Whistler." *Indoor Fireworks* also includes what may arguably be a few of the least danceable tracks ever produced by a dance producer: a quintessentially British show-tune named "Hymnformation," a piece named "Music From a Film" performed entirely by the Irish Film Orchestra, and a few tracks scattered throughout that sound surprisingly close to *The Rocky Horror Picture Show* or the Bonzo Dog Band ("This Is the End," "Song with Words"). You often wish Herbert would stick to the dancefloor grooves, considering he's so good at them, but *Indoor Fireworks* is simply too much fun to argue with on anything but a superficial level. —*John Bush*

## Doktor Kosmos (Uje Brandelius)

b. 1971, Stockholm, Sweden
*Keyboards, Engineer, Producer / Electronica, Neo-Electro*
An occasional keyboard player for Swedish kitsch-core unit Komeda, Doktor Kosmos has also recorded albums of deranged yet strangely catchy Casio synth-pop. Born in Stockholm, he explored his fascination with the music of porno-billy by forming the group Handsome Hank and the Hookers at the age of 17. The band later became Doktor Kosmos and the Starlight Orchestra (with him as the lead singer). He recorded one album in Swedish before releasing *Cocktail* on Minty Fresh in 1997. Doktor Kosmos also records occasionally with fellow Swede Magnus ≈ström (aka Friend). —*John Bush*

● **Cocktail** / Sep. 16, 1997 / Minty Fresh ♦♦♦
The childlike yet somewhat obscene wit of Doktor Kosmos knows few bounds, and this delightful album of Casio synth-pop shows his broad range of faux-naive Continental humor, rendered in heavily accented English. For some listeners, the sparse synthesizer rhythms and Tinkertoy melodies will be a bit too much (or little), but *Cocktail* is an enjoyable, eccentric album. —*John Bush*

## Thomas Dolby

b. Oct. 14, 1958, Cairo, Egypt
*Vocals, Keyboards, Guitar, Synthesizer, Producer / New Wave, Synth-Pop*
Though he never had many hits, Thomas Dolby became one of the most recognizable figures of the synth-pop movement of early-'80s new wave. Largely, this was due to his skillful marketing. Dolby promoted himself as a kind of mad scientist, an egghead that had successfully harnassed the power of synthesizers and samplers, using them to make catchy pop and light electro-funk. Before he launched a solo career, Dolby had worked a studio musician, technician, and songwriter; his most notable work as a songwriter was "New Toy," which he wrote for Lene Lovich, and Whodini's "Magic's Wand." In 1981, he launched a solo career, which resulted in a number of minor hits and two big hits—"She Blinded Me with Science" (1982) and "Hyperactive" (1984). Following "Hyperactive," his career faded away, as he began producing more frequently, as well as exploring new synthesizer and computer technology. Dolby continued to record into the '90s, but by that time, he was strictly a cult act.

Dolby's interest in music arose through his interest in computers, electronics and synthesizers. The son of a British archeologist, Thomas Dolby (born Thomas Morgan Robertson, October 14, 1958) originally attended college to study meteorology, but he was soon side-tracked by electronics, specifically musical equipment. He began building his own synthesizers when he was 18 years old. Around the same time, he began to learn how to play guitar and piano, as well as how to program computers. Eventually, his schoolmates gave him the nickname of "Dolby," which was the name for a noise-reduction technology for audiotapes; he would eventually take the nickname as a stage name.

In his late teens, Dolby was hired as a touring sound engineer for a variety of post-punk bands, including the Fall, the Passions, and the Members; on these dates, he would use a PA system he had built himself. In 1979, he formed the arty post-punk band Camera Club with Bruce Wooley, Trevor Horn, Geoff Downes, and Matthew Seligman. Within a year, he had left the group and joined Lene Lovich's backing band. Dolby gave Lovich his song "New Toy," which became a British hit in 1981. That same year, he released his first solo single, "Urges," on the English independent label Armageddon. By the fall, he had signed with Parlophone and released "Europa and the Pirate Twins," which nearly cracked the UK Top 40.

Dolby started playing synthesizer on sessions for other artists in 1982. That year, he appeared on Foreigner's *4*, Def Leppard's *Pyromania*, and Joan Armatrading's *Walk Under Ladders*. Also in 1982, he wrote and produced "Magic's Wand" for Whodini; the single became one of the first million-selling rap singles. Even with all of these achievements, 1982 was most noteworthy for the release of Dolby's first solo album, *The Golden Age of Wireless*, in the summer of 1982; the record reached No. 13 in England, while it was virtually forgotten in America. "Windpower," the first single from the record, became his first Top 40 UK hit in the late summer.

In January of 1983, Dolby released an EP, *Blinded by Science*, which included a catchy number called "She Blinded Me with Science" that featured a cameo vocal appearance by the notorious British eccentric Magnus Pike, who also appeared in the song's promotional video. *Blinded by Science* was a minor hit in England, but the EP and the single became major American hits in 1983, thanks to MTV's heavy airplay of the "She Blinded Me with Science" video. Eventually, the song reached No. 5 on the US charts and it was included on a resequenced and reissued version of *The Golden Age of Wireless*, which peaked at No. 13 in America.

*The Flat Earth*, Dolby's second album, appeared in early 1984 and was supported by the single "Hyperactive." The single became his biggest UK hit, peaking at No. 17. Though *The Flat Earth* reached No. 35 on the US charts, Dolby's momentum was already beginning to slow—none of the singles released from the album cracked the American Top 40. Nevertheless, Dolby was in demand as a collaborator and he worked with Herbie Hancock, Howard Jones, Stevie Wonder, George Clinton, and Dusty Springfield. During 1985, he produced Clinton's *Some of My Best Jokes Are Friends*, Prefab Sprout's *Steve McQueen* (*Two Wheels Good* in the US), and Joni Mitchell's *Dog Eat Dog*, as well as supporting David Bowie at Live Aid. Also in 1985, he began composing film scores, starting with *Fever Pitch*. In 1986, he composed the scores for *Gothic* and *Howard the Duck*, to which he credited himself as Dolby's Cube. That credit led to a lawsuit from the Dolby Labs, who eventually prohibited the musician from using the name "Dolby" in conjunction with any other name than "Thomas."

*Aliens Ate My Buick*, Dolby's long-delayed third album, appeared in 1988 to poor reviews and weak sales, even though the single "Airhead" became a minor British hit. That same year, Dolby married actress Kathleen Beller. For the rest of the late '80s and early '90s, Dolby continued to score films, producing and he began building his own computer equipment. His fourth album, *Astronauts & Heretics*, was released in 1992 on his new label, Giant. Despite the presence of guest stars like Eddie Van Halen, Jerry Garcia, Bob Weir, and Ofra Haza, the album was a flop. The following year, Dolby founded the computer software company Headspace, which released *The Virtual String Quartet* as its first program. For the rest of the '90s, Headspace occupied most of Dolby's time and energy. In 1994, he released *The Gate to the Mind's Eye*, a soundtrack to the videotape *Mind's Eye*. Also that year, Capitol released the greatest hits collection, *Retrospectacle*. — *Stephen Thomas Erlewine*

**The Golden Age of Wireless** / Mar. 1982 / Capitol ♦♦♦♦
This contains Dolby's biggest hit, the humorously quirky "She Blinded Me with Science." Highlights include "Radio Silence," "Europa and the Pirate Twins," "Windpower," "One of Our Submarines," and "Airwaves" — a track that should've been a single. All in all, this is a very solid collection of early-'80s synth-pop. (*The Golden Age of Wireless* originally was released in May 1982 as Harvest/Capitol 12203. In the wake of the success of "She Blinded Me with Science," it was reissued in March 1983 with that track and another added [and two others dropped] as Harvest/Capitol 12271, later reissued on CD as Capitol 46009.) — *Rick Clark*

**Blinded by Science [EP]** / Jan. 1983 / Capitol ♦♦♦
Capitol Records released Thomas Dolby's debut album, *The Golden Age of Wireless*, in May 1982, and it was ignored. But when Dolby came up with a catchy new track called "She Blinded Me With Science," and Capitol borrowed some songs from the LP, added "Science," and released this five-track mini-LP in January 1983. The single (backed by an MTV-friendly video) took off into the Top 10, and in March Capitol issued a revised version of *The Golden Age Of Wireless* with the single added to it, thus making this record redundant. Nevertheless, it encapsulates Dolby synth-pop style particularly well — so well, in fact, that 12 years later, when Capitol came to release the Dolby hits collection *Retrospectacle*, it used four of the five tracks here. — *William Ruhlmann*

**The Flat Earth** / Feb. 1984 / Capitol ♦♦♦♦
A departure from the style of his debut, this moody and atmospheric album adds jazz and Joni Mitchell-esque elements to warm his synth textures. Only "White City" and the single, "Hyperactive!," feature the hard dance beats of his early hits. — *Scott Bultman*

**Aliens Ate My Buick** / Apr. 1988 / EMI/Manhattan ♦♦
Thomas Dolby didn't do his career much good by waiting four years between album releases. Pop music trends shifted away from the quirky synth-pop Dolby had pioneered in 1983-84, and though he employed a heavy funk beat aimed at the discos and even covered a George Clinton song, Dolby seemed less a true dancefloor king than a commentator on the same, especially in such songs as the (non-charting) single "Airhead," "Pop Culture," and "The Ability to Swing." Dolby's flirtation with film had also added an eclecticism to his style that embraced '40s jazz vocalese ("The Key to Her Ferrari") and European balladeering ("Budapest by Blimp"). As ever, Dolby was a man of many ideas, but on *Aliens Ate My Buick* they failed to add up to a coherent statement. — *William Ruhlmann*

**Gate to the Mind's Eye** / Oct. 18, 1994 / Giant ♦♦♦♦
Soundtrack work suits Thomas Dolby, who here turns in a variety of musical settings for a computer animation video that include everything from moody electronic instrumentals and dance tracks to a '30s pop pastiche complete with horn section ("Nuvague"). Five of the nine tracks have vocals, two of which are contributed by Dr. Fiorella Terenzi. Dolby himself sings, raps, and even murmurs Napoleon's words of love to Josephine. As a nonvisual listening experience, it all seems scattered, but *The Gate to the Mind's Eye* demonstrates Dolby's continuing inventiveness. — *William Ruhlmann*

• **The Best of Thomas Dolby: Retrospectacle** / Apr. 4, 1995 / Capitol ♦♦♦♦
After what had seemed like a promising start with "She Blinded Me with Science" in 1983, Thomas Dolby only charted with two other singles in the US (though he had nine chart singles in his native UK, 1981-1992). This 16-track compilation, embracing both his Capitol/EMI and Warner Brothers recordings, demonstrates that Dolby deserved better. His synthesizer-based songs are consistently catchy and clever, and especially notable are early songs like "Urges" and "Leipzig" that have not previously appeared on a US album. "One of Our Submarines," Dolby's cover of Dan Hicks' "I Scare Myself," and "Hyperactive!" all hold up well. Some of the later (non-hit) material from the albums *Aliens Ate My Buick* and *Astronauts & Heretics* is less impressive; a better choice could have been made from those records. But for the most part, this is an efficient collection that justifies its name. — *William Ruhlmann*

## Dom & Roland (Dominic Angus)

*Remixing, Producer / Jungle/Drum'N'Bass, Club/Dance*

Misleadingly plural, Dom & Roland is actually the one-man attack of Dominic Angus, whose slim but steady stream of EPs released through noted drum'n'bass imprints Moving Shadow, Suburban Base, and Doc Scott's 31 Records have represented the harder, darker, more experimental edge of dancefloor-oriented hardstep. Signed by Moving Shadow to a nonexclusive contract in early 1996, Dom's initial singles deviated sharply from the brighter, more melodic thrust of much of the label's back catalog. But Angus' commitment to pushing the hardstep envelope while still pushing bassbins has also meant his tracks have gotten high play among critics as well as DJs, leading to a two-album commitment from the label. A resident of London's Shepherd's Bush, Dom's early connection to the drum'n'bass scene was through friend and early mentor Ed Rush; Dom's launch into production came via Rush collaborator and No U-Turn founder Nick Sykes (aka Nico), to whom Dom payed a nominal fee for studio time and a quick co-write. From there, Dom took classes in studio engineering and production while meeting ends as a restaurant manager. His first proper tracks were released under the name Current Affairs (a collaboration with Brian Ferrier), and his first single under his own name was the grueling "Dynamics/The Planets," released in the early months of 1996. By the end of that year, Angus had racked up four singles and a handful of compilation tracks and remixes (most notably for Flytronix and the Art of Noise's drum'n'bass remix album). Most of his tracks — particularly "The Planets" and both sides of the "Mechanics" twelve — were rinsed so heavily due to the sudden upsurge in darkside hardstep (capped by an uncredited co-write with Ed Rush, Trace, and Nico on one of the year's biggest tunes, "Mad Different Methods"), his profile rose dramatically, leading to remix work for Graham Sutton's Boymerang project and a track on Moving Shadow's 100th 12" release next to Goldie and Rob Playford. The *Industry* album appeared in 1998. — *Sean Cooper*

**Dynamics/The Planets [Single]** / 1996 / Moving Shadow ♦♦♦♦
Dominic Angus' debut solo shot on Moving Shadow shook the jazzstep-dominated British jungle scene to the rafters, updating darkside for the digital age and splintering the loops of the artful rollers into a thousand whizzing, disorienting pieces. The signature Shadow production values are in clear evidence here, but Dom's deft beat treatments are what really edge these two tracks into "classic" territory. — *Sean Cooper*

**Mechanics [Single]** / 1996 / 31 Records ♦♦♦♦
Dom's debut for Doc Scott's 31 label followed the latter's "Shadowboxing" 12", nearly blowing it off decks with a harsh, uncompromising air. The title cut is the ruler here — crackling, near overdriven beats chopped to oblivion under haunting, hissing synth melodies. But both tracks give new meaning to the *dark* side, coming with a sound as dense and artfully composed as it is distinct from the chaotic dirge of much of the techstep crowd. — *Sean Cooper*

• **Industry** / Sep. 28, 1998 / Moving Shadow ♦♦♦♦
Given the number of debut LPs padded out with previous singles, it's a pleasant surprise that each track on Dom & Roland's first full-length is new — though CD-only buyers may be a bit put-off that none of the previous 12"-only burners are present. The sound is pure tech-step, complete with all the menacing undertone and off-kilter effects hitting off the beat that fans would expect (plus a few above-average breakbeats). Two of the most interesting tracks, "Timeframe" and "Anaesthetic," feature Optical co-productions, though the highlight "Elektra" is pure solo Dom. — *John Bush*

## Dopplereffekt

f. Ann Arbor, MI
*Group / Neo-Electro, Electro-Techno, Detroit Techno, Electro, Club/Dance, Techno*

Dopplereffekt are yet another robotic electro act from Detroit to file alongside Drexciya, Ectomorph, and Flexitone. As is par for the course in the Motor City electro scene, identities are unknown, but the emphasis on precise drum programming and effects sounds barely a year or two removed from the classic electric-funk days of 1982. Dopplereffekt debuted in 1995 with a mini-LP for Detroit's Dataphysix label, then released two EPs for the label during 1997—*Infophysix* and *Sterilization*. The countless German references reflect the group's fascination with the classic Kraftwerk sound. After "Sterilization" was included on several mix albums, DJ Hell contacted Dopplereffekt and released the *Gesamtkunstwerk* compilation through his International Deejay Gigolo label in 1999. The alias Japanese Telecom emerged in late 1999 to release the *Rising Sun* mini-LP through the once Ann Arbor-based Intuit-Solar Records. —*John Bush*

● **Gesamtkunstwerk** / Oct. 29, 1999 / International Deejay Gigolos ♦♦♦♦
Including the complete contents of most every Dopplereffekt record released before 2000, *Gesamtkunstwerk* is an excellent display of paranoid, menacing retro-electro straddling the early '80s and the late '90s. As with Kraftwerk classics "Pocket Calculator," "The Robots," and "Home Computer," the social concerns of Dopplereffekt tracks ("Cellular Phone," "Rocket Scientist," "Superior Race," "Speak & Spell") are expressed almost exclusively in the titles, with a minimum of vocal accompaniment. "Sterilization," the act's most famous track thanks to a few compilation appearances, includes just one vocal tag—a robotic "We had to sterilize the population"—but loses none of its post-apocalyptic perfection. Besides the push/pull attraction and repulsion of technology, sex is a big theme ("Plastiphilia," "Pornoactress," "Pornovision") on *Gesamtkunstwerk* as well. At least until their next underground club hit, this collection is all the Dopplereffekt you'll ever need. —*John Bush*

## Download

f. 1995, Vancouver, British Columbia
*Group / Experimental Techno, Industrial*

As industrial and industrial-metal made great inroads on the mainstream charts during the late '90s, many early pioneers continued to record with little fanfare but a large amount of creativity, even if the astounding leaps in technology had largely altered their sound since the heyday of the '80s. Download was originally begun by Skinny Puppy's cEvin Key and Rudolph Dwayne Goettel in 1995 as a side project from their rapidly disintegrating full-time interest. Also a part of Download were Skinny Puppy contributors Anthony Valcic and Ken Marshall, plus Philth and Mark Spybey (from Dead Voices on Air). The debut album *Furnace* was issued on their own SubConscious Records (and distributed by Cleopatra) in late 1995; several months earlier, however, Goettel had died from a heroin overdose.

Skinny Puppy disbanded in 1996 after the release of its final album (*The Process*), and Download continued with two EPs early in the year. The first, (*Microscopic*) included remixed tracks from *Furnace*, while the second (*Sidewinder*) was the group's first release for Nettwerk Records (though not for Key, who had released many on Nettwerk through Skinny Puppy). Their second album *The Eyes of Stanley Pain* followed in mid-1996, and began to show the effect of the electronic dance music which Skinny Puppy had influenced a full decade before. The film soundtrack *Charlie's Family* appeared on Metropolis Records in 1997, followed by Download's third proper album (*III*) in October 1997. *Effector* was released three years later. —*John Bush*

**Sidewinder [EP]** / Apr. 30, 1996 / Nettwerk ♦♦♦♦
Companion to Download's second album, *The Eyes of Stanley Pain*, *Sidewinder* is its namesake—a collection of remixes and new material which may not have fit onto the album for various reasons, but still very worthy in their own right. This means that some tracks on this EP, namely "Shemaesin" and "Im5," make for even more challenging listening than anything on the album itself since they can wander off and do their own thing, discarding traditional musical structures and forms to replace them with Download's experimentations with harsh, sculpted electro sounds and complex arrangements. It would really be these tracks which give *Sidewinder* its appeal to existing fans, alongside the elegant remix of "Attallal" (from Download's first album release, *Furnace*) by haujobb. The remixes from *The Eyes of Stanley Pain* ("Sidewinder," "Glassblower," and "Base Metal") may serve to hook new listeners, however, since these mixes are still close to the originals and are fairly representative of the album's sound overall. —*Theo Kavadias*

**The Eyes of Stanley Pain** / May 28, 1996 / Nettwerk ♦♦♦♦
Released prior to the split between cEvin Key (of Skinny Puppy fame) and Mark Spybey (from Zoviet France and Dead Voices On Air) due to artistic differences, *The Eyes of Stanley Pain* is perhaps more accessible than their previous releases. Although Key's Skinny Puppy roots permeate the sound, *The Eyes of Stanley Pain* (along with the simultaneously released remixes, *Sidewinder*) marks a remarkable progression from them, making it perhaps the most cohesive Download material at the time of its release. Some of the material moves from something remarkably more coherent compared to earlier releases, featuring danceable tracks such as "Possession" and "Outafter," without sacrificing the intense electronic experimental sound usually associated with the band. Other tracks provide the surreal contrast of soft melody and the methodically haphazard use of sharp sound ("Base Metal"), while yet others provide an unexpected mix of both (such as "Collision"). As for musical structures and ideas as to what music should actually sound like, Download continues to throw it all out and invent their own as they go. Added to all this is the haunting presence of guest vocalist Genesis P. Orridge, hailing from one of the earliest industrial acts, Throbbing Gristle, and more recently, Psychic TV. This range and diversity of elements creates a depth not present on earlier releases. At once accessible and musically very challenging, *The Eyes of Stanley Pain* has definitely become one of the benchmarks of the industrial style, and is probably the first album any listener, new or old, should investigate when exploring Download's experimentation with electro sound. —*Theo Kavadias*

● **III** / Oct. 21, 1997 / Nettwerk ♦♦♦♦
Download's second album for Nettwerk, *Download III*, finds cEvin Key toning down his industrial roots in favor of longer stretches of experimental electronica. That's not to say that he has completely abandoned industrial—after all, this is one the founding fathers of the genre—but there's simply more texture and interesting detours than before, making it of interest to listeners who usually find industrial noisy and impenetrable. —*Stephen Thomas Erlewine*

## Dreadzone

f. 1994, London, England
*Group / Ambient Dub, Trance, Club/Dance, Techno*

The British dance group Dreadzone rose from the remnants of the short-lived Screaming Target, itself an outgrowth of Big Audio Dynamite. Screaming Target comprised Don Letts, Greg Roberts, and Leo Williams, in collaboration with producer and remixer Tim Bran; when Letts exited, Bran signed on with the team of Roberts and Williams, and the trio rechristened themselves Dreadzone. A dub band relying heavily on sampling and other elements of electronica, they debuted in 1993 with the LP *360∞*. Two years later, *Second Light* featured guest appearances from Mad Professor and Leftfield's Earl 16; "Little Britain," the trio's breakthrough UK hit, followed in 1996, with the LP *Biological Radio* appearing the next year. —*Jason Ankeny*

● **360∞** / 1993 / Creation/TriStar ♦♦♦♦
This duo uses rhythms based on reggae and some trance-techno; that's not incredibly new, but Dreadzone manage to create a fresh sound. Most tracks are uptempo, and some sped-up dub livens the mix to produce a solid, but not head-spinning, album. —*John Bush*

**Second Light** / 1995 / Virgin ♦♦♦
The collective formed from Big Audio Dynamite weave Celtic influences into their heavy dub sound. —*John Bush*

## The Dream Team

f. 1994, London, England
*Group / Jungle/Drum'N'Bass, Club/Dance*

The Dream Team (aka the Dynamic Duo) are a steadily rising duo whose releases on their own Joker imprint have made it one of the most popular underground labels for straightahead, no-bones jump up-style drum'n'bass. Going by the names Bizzy B. and Pugwash, the pair began working together in 1994 after releasing a smattering of solo tracks (Bizzy on his Brain imprint, Pugwash as Double Dipped on I.D.), hooking up through the network of producers and DJs which constitutes the London underground breakbeat scene. Locking up drum'n'bass in its literal form, the pair's Joker work expands upon the rhythmic focus of jump-up mainstays such as Shy FX and DJ Hype, releasing floor-filling party tracks with a fresh, complex rhythmic edge. Although two of the group's biggest tunes—"Stamina" and "Raw Dogs"—were released on hardcore mainstay Suburban Base shortly after the pair began working together, Joker has been the focus of their activities since its inception in 1995, peaking at the start of 1997 with a full-length release, *The Drum'n'bass World Series*, a collection of new tracks and exclusive mixes from Decoder, Rude Bwoy Monty, and Trend. That year also saw the release of album, *Trilogy*, on Sega/Suburban Base Records. In addition to running Joker and releasing and remixing tracks, Bizzy and Pugwash both DJ, (Pug had a regular slot on the noted Kool FM), the increasing exposure taking them well beyond the London underground pirate scene and into party slots in Europe and the States. —*Sean Cooper*

**The Dream Team** / Jan. 14, 1997 / B-Mas ♦♦♦♦

- **The Drum'n'bass World Series** / Feb. 10, 1997 / Joker ♦♦♦♦
*The Drum'n'bass World Series* was released at the beginning of 1997 to coincide with the Joker label's two year anniversary and is its 25th release. An old-school jump-up fiend's delight, the album is a club-bound collection of romping steppers in the Hype/Coolhand Flex vein. All of the tracks included on the vinyl version are exclusives—either new tracks or new mixes of existing tracks (including reworkings by Decoder, Trend, and Rude Bwoy Monty)—with the CD adding a few bonus cuts from the Joker archive. —*Sean Cooper*

## Dreamfish
f. 1993
*Group / Ambient*

Although Dreamfish's discography includes only two titles, the group is deeply linked to the resurgence of post-rave ambient music and the birth of one of the genre's most important and prolific labels, Fax. The combined project of Fax label impresario Pete Namlook and new-ambient guru Mixmaster Morris (who also records under the name Irresistible Force), Dreamfish's first and most significant CD was released in 1993. *Dreamfish* was among the first entirely beatless releases to appear on Fax (which prior to its reincarnation as an ambient label was known for releasing melodic hard trance), and joined the Orb's *U.F. Orb*, the KLFs *Chill Out*, and Irresistible Force's *Flying High* in announcing an important new strain of environmental electronic music. (It remains among Fax's finest moments.) Taking its name from a tropical fish known and consumed for its psychedelic properties, the album's four tracks are probably among the closest approximations of that experience you're likely to find. Buoyed along by warm, lush waves of analog synth and spare bits of percussion (high-hats, subtle, bell-like clave figures), tracks such as "School of Fish" and "Fishology" became immediate chill room staples. Namlook and Morris finally revisited the Dreamfish project in 1996, although for a number of reasons (not all of them entirely their fault; ambient as a whole sounded nowhere near as fresh as it had several years earlier) the somewhat ill-conceived *Dreamfish 2* failed to scale the heights—or is that depths—occupied by its predecessor. The original *Dreamfish* was reissued by the Rising High label shortly after its first appearance, and the CD remains in print via Fax's Ambient World sublabel. —*Sean Cooper*

- **Dreamfish** / 1993 / Fax ♦♦♦♦
The first release in Fax's PW series—and one of only a handful of Fax albums also released on vinyl—Pete Namlook and Mixmaster Morris's first collaboration remains among the very finest moments in the Fax label's vast catalog. Where the long-running association of ambient music with outer space was willingly courted by groups such as the Orb and even Morris's own Irresistible Force, *Dreamfish* headed instead for aquatic depths, and tracks such as "Fishology" and "School of Fish" are a pure immersion experience—the kind of music for which you'll willingly court cliché by listening to it entirely in the dark, and possibly under chemical influence. An essential, enduring classic of new-school ambient. —*Sean Cooper*

**Dreamfish 2** / 1996 / Fax ♦♦
A disappointing follow-up to the classic first *Dreamfish*, this sequel is a merely adequate collection of deep, echoey, ultimately quite disposable ambient. The 24-minute "Submerge" is the only standout track, with the other 30-plus minutes suffering from a surfeit of reverb and a dearth of worthwhile ideas. —*Sean Cooper*

## Mike Dred
*Producer / Experimental Techno, Techno, IDM*

Mike Dred (aka Chimera, Judge Dred, and the Kosmik Kommando) makes acid-tinged experimental techno geared both for the dancefloor and for home listening. A member of the UK's extended West Country experimental techno family (which also includes Reload, the Aphex Twin, and Matt Herbert), Dred drew early inspiration from European synth-pop groups like Kraftwerk and the Human League, as well as the American electro scene spreading like wildfire in the mid-'80s London underground. Although he's recorded for a variety of different labels, including R&S, R&S offshoot Diatomyc (which he helps run), and his own Machine Codes label, the bulk of his material has appeared on Richard James' Rephlex imprint, mostly under the Kosmik Kommando and Chimera names. Reportedly hooking up with the label after meeting some friends of James' on a train en route to a rave in Cologne, Dred's penchant for harsh, relentlessly experimental acid and techno fit neatly into the Rephlex vision, and Dred's first *Kosmik Kommando* EP was among the first 12"s the label released. Dred's Rephlex discography has since grown to include two full-length albums (one each under the KK and Chimera names) and five EPs, with releases on Diatomyc and Machine Codes numbering close behind. His first proper album, *Virtual Farmer*, appeared in late 1998. [See Also: Kosmik Kommando] —*Sean Cooper*

**Machine Codes: 93-97 (First Compilation)** / Aug. 19, 1997 / Machine Codes ♦♦♦

- **Virtual Farmer** / Oct. 19, 1998 / Warp ♦♦♦♦
Credited to Mike Dred and Peter Green, *Virtual Farmer* unites the computer-age acid-funk of Dred's fellow Rephlex acts Bochum Welt and Cylob with an attention to the swirling noise loops and assorted static reminiscent of contemporary material by Autechre. Indeed, Dred even takes it a bit farther on tracks like "Cornucopian 105" and "Nautilus 110." —*Keith Farley*

## The Dreem Teem
f. 1994, London, England
*Group / Speed Garage, Garage, Club/Dance, House*

Different from the rap group and the drum'n'bass unit with a similar name, the Dreem Teem are (with Tuff Jam) the kings of speed garage, the manic dance style which brought crowds of club kids back to house music from jungle in the late '90s, in large part because speed garage producers hijacked many techniques from drum'n'bass, including rewinds, vocals on the ragga tip, DJs adept at scratching, and even the occasional breakbeat lifted from jungle. The Dreem Teem is a trio of DJs and occasional producers, all of whom entered London's club scene during the glory days of acid house in 1988-89: Timmi Magic (born London; August 23, 1968), Mikee B (born Kingston, Jamaica; December 10, 1967), and DJ Spoony (born London; June 27, 1970). They worked separately during the early to mid-'90s, but later met up at the Arches, where DJ Spoony's residency anticipated the development of speed garage in Britain. After getting together as a DJ team (with Timmi focusing on the mixing while Spoony scratched and Mikee worked as the selector), the Dreem Teem released a 1997 mix set on the 4 Liberty label, *The London Dreem Teem in Session*. —*John Bush*

- **The London Dreem Teem in Session** / Jul. 21, 1997 / 4 Liberty ♦♦♦♦
Released around the same time as another crucial speed garage compilation, Tuff Jam's *Underground Frequencies, Vol. 1*, the Dreem Teem's *In Session* is a perfect complement, focusing on tracks more tied to the underground like DJ Disciple, R.I.P., and the Dreem Teem's own Timmi Magic. —*John Bush*

## Drexciya
f. 1993, Detroit, MI
*Group / Neo-Electro, Electro-Techno, Detroit Techno, Club/Dance*

Although they released only five EPs in their first ten years recording together, controversial Detroit techno duo Drexciya became one of the most celebrated and influential names in American experimental techno. One of the few groups using techno as a political tool in effecting criticism of racial inequity and inner-city recovery, Drexciya have brought a wider social and aesthetic agenda to a style in which allegiance to the beat is typically the only prerequisite. Closely associated with the "Mad" Mike Banks label group Underground Resistance and operating in the classically covert tradition of "faceless" techno (the pair's identities remain a mystery), the group's reputation at the bleeding edge of Detroit-school experimentation is pretty much universal, with everyone from Jeff Mills to Mike Paradinas getting in namechecks. Despite their steadfastly underground attitude, Drex's records have found release through such internationally renowned labels as Warp and Rephlex. Offering an often relentless fusion of early electro and techno with elements of acid and industrial music, Drexciya's fast-beat backbone and tough-as-nails rhythmic bite are among the most austere and uncompromised in contemporary techno. Reportedly, the group record their material live, which gives much of their music (particularly their Shockwave and Underground Resistance releases) a vital, immediate feel. Much of their UR output was collected on 1997's *The Quest*, and a full-length (*Neptune's Lair*) followed on Tresor in 1999. —*Sean Cooper*

**Deep Sea Dweller [Single]** / 1994 / Shockwave ♦♦
Drexciya's debut four-tracker on Shockwave was the blast that led to the group's involvement with Underground Resistance, and "Deep Sea Dweller's" mix of burning acid and funky-fueled, mid-tempo electro gives a good indication of why. A bit more derivative than the Drexciya to come, but a tight, surprisingly resilient EP nonetheless. —*Sean Cooper*

**Drexciya, Vol. 1: Aquatic Invasion [EP]** / Feb. 1994 / UR ♦♦♦♦
A storming techno/electro-funk three-tracker, decidedly lo-fi but with enough guts and attitude to make it both listenable and danceable. Shades of acid and industrial combine with burly 808 breaks on two of the tracks, while the third is a Kraftwerkean two-beat workout with an almost Euro-pop feel. —*Sean Cooper*

**Drexciya, Vol. 2: Bubble Metropolis [EP]** / Apr. 1994 / UR ♦♦♦
Drexciya's second mission for Underground Resistance is a largely breakbeat, almost frighteningly self-assured six-track EP. The group play the poles of optimism and dystopian hopelessness expertly, switching between Chicago-styled arm-wavers and focused Motor City calls to arms with ease. Techno in the truest sense. —*Sean Cooper*

**Drexciya, Vol. 4: The Unknown Aquazone [EP]** / Aug. 1994 / Shockwave ♦♦
The fourth installment is a double-EP, and at 12 tracks is loosely categorizable as the pair's first album. —*Sean Cooper*

**Drexciya, Vol. 5: The Journey Home [EP]** / Oct. 1995 / Warp ♦♦
Despite their ideological pretensions, the Drex duo opt for a twelver on the comparatively establishmentarian Warp label, riding the crest of the mid-1995 electro revival buoyed by Elecktroids, the Jedi Knights, and Mike "Jake Slazenger" Paradinas. Unfortunately, the goods got lost somewhere in transport, as *Journey* is a quick, disappointing stab at mid-fi electronic breakbeat miles in depth and quality from their Shockwave and UR material. —*Sean Cooper*

● **The Quest** / Jul. 7, 1997 / Submerge ♦♦♦♦
Drexciya's inspired blend of subaquatic techno-funk has been influential far beyond the group's level of recognition. Formerly restricted to periodically repressed and unfortunately not well-distributed 12" releases, the group's fusion of old-school electro and techno-pop rhythms with screaming acid lines and alternately dark and uplifting melodic textures should finally find a wider audience thanks to this CD compilation. Collecting no less than 28 tracks across two CDs (a nine-track double-pack was also issued), *The Quest* is the definitive Drexciya and one of the most amazing documents of Detroit post-techno yet released. —*Sean Cooper*

**Neptune's Lair** / Oct. 26, 1999 / Tresor ♦♦♦♦
Though a quick glance at the track titles—"Organic Hydropoly Spores," "Polymono Plexusgel," "Triangular Hydrogen Strain," "Oxyplasmic Gyration Beam"—lends the impression that this is yet another Drexciyan work wherein the music, though stellar enough, isn't quite as important as the subaquatic science-fiction themes, *Neptune's Lair* proves as solid a piece of musicianship as the act has ever recorded. The album mostly disdains the frog-like neo-retro vocal samples that often shifted emphasis away from the music on the *Drexciya* EPs, and simply pushes through with a set of mid-tempo, paranoid electro gems. The production is still reminiscent of the classic electro era, but never feels as tied to the vintage synth as before. Admittedly, there's a bit much to digest on the 20 tracks, but *Neptune's Lair* is yet another bright spot in the Detroit electro-techno revival. —*John Bush*

## Drome (Bernd Friedmann)

*Producer / Ambient Breakbeat, Ambient Dub, Trip-Hop*
Drome is the earlier, more techno- and dub-infused pseudonym of Nonplace Urban Field/Some More Crime member Bernd Friedmann. With his first singles and a full-length appearing on the Toxiktrakks label and more recent material released through Wigwam and Ninja Tune, Friedmann's signature restlessness with respect to convention is clearly nascent in his Drome work, most obviously in his knack for odd combinations. Although Friedmann's releases as Drome have thinned in recent years, the name is widely regarded in association with the development of downtempo breakbeat and trip-hop, with a sample-heavy ambient- and dub-influenced take on hip-hop-styled beats and a clear, atmospheric nod to home listening over the dancefloor. A native of Berlin, Friedmann's commitment to accelerated mutation also earned him a spot on the Ntone sampler, *Earthrise* (a two-disc set released by the American Instinct label in 1995), as well as a touring partner in Uwe Schmidt, aka Atom Heart, who accompanied Friedmann on a series of live dates in Australia and Japan toward the end of 1996. Friedmann's Nonplace Urban Field material has occupied the bulk of his time of late, with releases such as *Raum Fur Notizen* and *Golden Star*, as well as remixes for Unitone Hi-Fi, Bowery Electric, and Hab taking Drome's genre-obliterating aesthetic deeper still into the forests of abstraction. [See Also: Nonplace Urban Field] —*Sean Cooper*

**Dromed** / 1991 / Silent ♦♦
A bizarre fusion of psychedelic ambient and industrial leaning, EBM-esque techno. Hopelessly dated by now (Friedmann himself quickly moved on to more *de jour* fusions of ambient, hip-hop, dub, and jungle), the album is at least interesting for its vision and lack of compromise. —*Sean Cooper*

● **The Final Corporate Colonization of the Unconscious** / 1995 / Ntone ♦♦♦♦
An underrecognized classic of downtempo/experimental ambient dub-hop, with melodic depth and accomplished production often lacking in more popular benefactors of the sound. Drome's sound here is quite a distance in refinement from the earlier Toxiktrakks material, but as with earlier releases, *Colonization* is ripe with tweaked, perverse arrangements, combining musique concrète, dub reggae, hip-hop, jazz, house, and even hardcore breakbeat techno in ways that somehow make perfect sense. —*Sean Cooper*

## The Drum Club

f. 1991, London, England
*Group / Progressive House, Club/Dance, House*
Disenfranchised and frustrated with Britain's early-'90s rave scene, former club promoters and DJs Charlie Hall and Lol Hammond formed the Drum Club as a combination production/remix act. Inspired by groups like Spiral Tribe, DiY, and Tonka on the emerging free-festival circuit, the duo toured with Orbital on the MIDI Circus during 1993, and their debut album *Everything Is Now* appeared soon after, on Big Life Records (also the home of the Orb). After remixing Hardkiss, Psychick Warriors Ov Gaia, and System 7 among others, the pair was soon tagged as one of the hottest remixing teams in Britain. Their follow-up *Drums Are Dangerous* was a breakthrough of sorts, earning an American release through Instinct in 1994. Instinct also documented Hall and Hammond's crucial concert appearances on 1995's *Live in Iceland*. Later that year, however, Hammond formed the breakbeat act Slab! with Nina Walsh. —*John Bush*

**Everything Is Now** / 1993 / Big Life ♦♦♦♦
For their album debut, Hammond and Hall drafted studio regulars Steve Hillage, Emma Anderson (of Lush), and Kate Holmes from Frazier Chorus to add a touch more musicianship to their progressive trance. The LP's live feel is enhanced by Drum Club's ease in a concert setting, and though most of the tracks trace the same club-grooves as could be expected, several tracks expand on dance parameters. —*John Bush*

● **Drums Are Dangerous** / 1994 / Instinct ♦♦♦♦
Another attempt to expand the sound of the dancefloor into the living room—despite the track title "Rock 'N' Roll Is Dead"—includes more song-oriented tracks, with vocal contributions from Saffron (later of Republica), Kirsty Hawkshaw, and KLF-regular Maxine Harvey. *Drums Are Dangerous* is quite a success, much more mature in sound than the debut, though just as consistently danceable. —*John Bush*

**Live in Iceland** / 1995 / Instinct ♦♦♦
In the liner notes, the Drum Club thank "All those who have the courage and conviction to take their music out of the studio and leave the DAT machines at home." This good live set shows Hammond and Hall weaving trance and ambient tracks together, with guest Anabel Simmons on the didgeridoo. —*John Bush*

## Drum Island

f. 1996, Norway
*Group / Ambient Dub, Trip-Hop*

The Norwegian ambient dub trio Drum Island comprised ex-Ismistik member Ole J. Mjos, Apollo Records co-founder Torbjorn Brundtland, and promoter-turned-DJ Rune Lindbek. Under the name Those Norwegians, the group issued a series of 12" singles on the UK label Paper Recordings before evolving into Drum Island, issuing their brilliant self-titled debut LP on Apollo in late 1997. —*Jason Ankeny*

- **Drum Island** / 1998 / R&S ++++

Rarely are groups so perfectly named as Drum Island; the moniker is utterly evocative of their sound, a heady blend of isolationist dub textures and tropical rhythms lapped by cool waves of cocktail jazz. Dreaming of a sun-drenched Caribbean paradise from a snowbound Scandinavian perspective, this remarkable debut LP is both sultry and alien, its cinematic samba and conga grooves tempered by ambient elements all cold to the touch; floating not in water or in space but in the area between, *Drum Island* is a world unto itself, and a trip well worth taking. —*Jason Ankeny*

## Dub Pistols

f. 1996, London, England
*Group / Big Beat, Trip-Hop, Club/Dance*

The continuing ascendancy of big-beat techno with punk-rock attitude continued unabated with the Dub Pistols, a lager-swilling quintet headed by ex-club promoter Barry Ashworth and featuring guitarist John King, bassist Jason O'Bryan, programmer Bill Borez, and turntablist Malcolm Wax. Ashworth, who had been turned on to the vibes of Ibizan house in the mid-'80s, began promoting clubs in Britain later in the decade. He went overground by 1989 with Deja Vu, a much-loved club night for Madchester bands like Happy Mondays and the Stone Roses. After a bust-up with police during another of his events, 1991's *Eat the Worm*, Ashworth and several friends decided to form the band Deja Vu, a London-centric band with Madchester influences. After signing with Cowboy and releasing a couple of singles, the group released one album (*Gangsters, Tarts & Wannabes*) but broke up by 1996.

Inspired by the Chemical Brothers and Jon Carter's *Heavenly Social* club night, Ashworth began DJing himself. He was recruited to remix "Blow the Whole Joint Up" by Carter's Monkey Mafia, and got his new group Dub Pistols signed to Concrete Records as a consequence. The band debuted in late 1996 with the singles "There's Gonna Be a Riot" and "Best Got Better." By the time of their 1998 debut album *Point Blank*, big-beat appeared to have run its course. Dub Pistols remained an infectious live draw, however, startling audiences in Britain and around the world. —*John Bush*

- **Point Blank** / Oct. 5, 1998 / A&M +++

After recording nothing but EPs, the Dub Pistols delivered their first full-length album with *Point Blank*, one of late 1998's more noteworthy examples of electronica. The thing that makes the Pistols' electronica/big beat more substantial than similar efforts is their broad-minded outlook and willingness to incorporate a variety of influences. While a lot of late-'90s electronica could wear thin quickly (especially outside of a club setting), the less predictable Pistols manage to hold one's attention for a longer period and usually avoid becoming boring or one-dimensional. *Point Blank* kicks into high gear with the infectious, Public Enemy-influenced rap/dance number "Unique Freak" before drawing on everything from acid house and techno ("Blaze the Room") to ska ("Cyclone") and dubwise reggae ("Ghetto"). To be sure, this is club music first and foremost, but even those who could have cared less about going to a rave could sit down and admire the Pistols' efforts to avoid electronica's limitations. They don't avoid them altogether—toward the end of the CD, the tracks start to sound mechanical and impersonal. But part of the time, *Point Blank* provides a memorable and risk-taking visit to clubland. —*Alex Henderson*

## Dub Syndicate

f. 1980, London, England
*Group / Ambient Dub, Club/Dance, Dub*

Drummer Style Scott joined Adrian Sherwood's influential On-U Sound dub label in the late '70s and played on Sherwood's influential releases as the New Age Steppers (with vocalist Bim Sherman, horn player Deadly Headley, melodica player Dr. Pablo, and a large guest lineup). Scott later formed his own band, Dub Syndicate, which soon became—with the possible exception of African Headcharge—On-U Sound's most popular act. Though not a group per se, Style Scott and producer Sherwood explore reggae, dub, and dancehall by collaborating with some of reggae and dub's greatest talents, including Lee "Scratch" Perry, Skip McDonald, U-Roy and, in a bit of posthumous sampling of an old friend, Prince Far I (on 1990's *Stoned Immaculate*).

Debut album *Pounding System* (1982) and the following year's *One Way System* were both reissued in America by ROIR. A project with Dr. Pablo titled *North of the River Thames* didn't earn a domestic release, but 1985's *Tunes from the Missing Channel* was licensed to EMI. An import-ony project with Lee "Scratch" Perry called *Time Boom 'De Devil Dead* followed in 1986, but 1990's *Strike the Balance* appeared on the Island subsidiary Mango. On-U Sound, in conjunction with the American label Restless, began an ambitious reissue effort with three volumes of the *Classic Selection* series (similar to African Headcharge's *Great Vintage* series) but continued to make new Dub Syndicate projects such as *From the Secret Laboratory* and *Stoned Immaculate* available only on import. Restless, though, did eventually give *Stoned Immaculate* and 1994's *Echomania* domestic releases. In 1996, Dub Syndicate released both an album of new material (*Ital Breakfast*), and the remix album *Research & Development*, with reworkings of tracks from the entire Dub Syndicate catalogue by Zion Train, Soundclash, Iration Steppas, and the Rootsman. Four years later, the performance album *Live at the Maritime Hall* was released. —*John Bush*

- **Classic Selection, Vol. 1** / 1989 / On-U Sound ++++

Dub Syndicate is a reggae collective with a constantly shifting lineup that revolves around the rhythmic nucleus of drummer Lincoln Valentine "Style" Scott and bassist Errol "Flabba" Holt (who are perhaps better known as the rhythm section for Roots Radics). Other members regularly featured include On U Sound mainstays Skip McDonald (guitar) and Carlton "Bubblers" Ogilvie. Equally important to the band's sound, however, is the production style of On-U label chief Adrian Sherwood, whose signature sound brings together a bass-heavy roots sound with such decidedly avant-garde twists as found sounds and spoken-word vocal samples. *Classic Selection Vol. 1* compiles several previously released singles and album tracks along with 11 previously unavailable recordings, and features vocals from Bim Sherman, the bizarre poet Andy Fairley, and numerous other unidentifiable sources (one track uses a repeated sample of someone saying "Good things are happening with intercommunications, baby"). As is usually the case with Dub Syndicate albums, Sherwood's production prowess is a central figure in the sound. All tracks were recorded between 1984 and 1988, and all are excellent. —*Rick Anderson*

**Strike the Balance** / 1990 / On-U Sound +++

*Strike the Balance* features vocal contributions from mainstay Bim Sherman and a guest appearance by Shara Nelson on a cover of Serge Gainsbourg's "Je t'aime." —*Steve Huey*

**Classic Selection, Vol. 2** / 1991 / On-U Sound ++++

Like its predecessor, this is a generous collection of new and old tracks from the UK's premier roots reggae band. As usual, the focus is on instrumental groove music, though voices are punched in regularly. This collection features more creepy poetry from Andy Fairley ("Your head will become a crazy bulbous punchbag of sound, lead-weight, and fearsome") and more of Bim Sherman's light, gauzy crooning, along with the requisite bizarre vocal samples. "Style" Scott and "Flabba" Holt keep things tight and heavy on drums and bass, respectively, but Adrian Sherwood's production takes center stage, as the bass shakes the walls and other instruments fly around the room crazily. This is ominous, exhilarating, frightening music that shows how interesting and creative it's possible to get while remaining within the confines of a genre as stylistically defined as reggae. —*Rick Anderson*

**Echomania** / 1994 / Restless ++++

This disc finds Dub Syndicate back to full strength. Thanks to an all-too-brief distribution arrangement with Restless Records in the US, this is one On-U title that should be relatively easy to find in the States, and it will make a fine introduction for newcomers to the band's strange but wonderful art. Drummer "Style" Scott and bassist "Flabba" Holt keep everyone together with monstrous reggae riddims, while Adrian Sherwood tears things up around them from his perch at the mixing board. Lee "Scratch" Perry makes a couple of hilarious cameo appearances, in one case sentencing all "heads of government" to "poverty and famine and hardship and bad luck." When guitarist Skip McDonald sings, you can hear echoes of his past work with Tackhead and intimations of what will come with Strange Parcels. Everywhere the rhythms are airtight and relentlessly propulsive. One song manages to quote successfully the American gospel standard "Walking in Jerusalem Just Like John." A rare and wonderful recording. —*Rick Anderson*

**Stoned Immaculate** / Oct. 11, 1994 / Restless ♦♦♦♦
Though this outing suffers from the absence of regular bassist Flabba Holt (instead, all basslines are played by keyboardist Noel Brownie, and keyboard bass just doesn't cut it for roots reggae), it still provides significant amounts of pleasure both traditional (Prince Far I's stentorian pronouncements, "Style" Scott's martial drumbeats) and experimental (Adrian Sherwood's typically over-the-top production). The found vocal snippets are sometimes more anonymous (that could be anyone saying "Watch, operatah—jus' lick back de riddim fi I, seen—") and sometimes more specific (that has to be Jim Morrison intoning "Out here we're stoned...immaculate"). The rhythms themselves sometimes sound a bit generic, but not objectionably so. All in all, a slightly more restrained but still rewarding album from this consistently fine band. —*Rick Anderson*

**Research and Development** / Nov. 12, 1996 / On U Sounds ♦♦♦
For fans of Britain's notorious On-U Sound label, the prospect of a Dub Syndicate remix album is cause for drooling anticipation. Although Dub Syndicate's lineup varies, its core membership is the same as that of Roots Radics, the most important reggae studio band since the Revolutionaries. The big difference between the two groups is producer Adrian Sherwood, whose over-the-top dubwise production makes On-U recordings instantly identifiable.

So if *Research and Development* disappoints, it may be due to overinflated expectations. As it turns out, the remixes of such classic Dub Syndicate fare as "2003 Struggle" and "Dubaddisaba" (by D.J. Scruff and Soundclash, respectively) do rock hard—it's just that they don't rock that much harder than the original versions. "Jamaican Jig," remixed by Abashanti, actually rocks softer. On the other hand, Tribal Drift does a bang-up job on "Hey Ho," letting it coast along on a slightly beefed-up beat for a couple of minutes, then slingshotting it off into jungle territory. And Rootsman gets well dread on a slow, thunderous remix of "Ravi Shankar." So while it's not all it could have been, *Research and Development* isn't exactly a waste of money, either. —*Rick Anderson*

**Mellow & Colly** / Aug. 17, 1998 / Lion & Roots ♦♦♦♦
*Mellow & Colly* is essentially a collaboration between Style Scott and Scientist; it's only half of the project, as Adrian Sherwood mixed his own version and released it as *Fear of a Green Planet*. In addition to drummer Scott, featured musicians include guitarist/sitarist Nicky Skopelitis and tabla player Bill Buchan. —*Steve Huey*

## Dubstar

f. 1994, Newcastle, England
*Group / Alternative Dance, Club/Dance, Dance-Pop*
The British dance-pop outfit Dubstar formed in Newcastle, England in 1994. Comprised of vocalist Sarah Blackwood, keyboardist/programmer Steve Hiller, and guitarist Chris Milkie, the trio soon recorded a demo containing a cover of Billy Bragg's "St. Swithin's Day," quickly earning a contract with the Food label. After their first single, "Stars," reached the UK Top 40 in the summer of 1995, Dubstar issued their acclaimed debut LP, *Disgraceful*. In the early weeks of 1996, "Not So Manic Now" became the group's breakthrough hit; their sophomore effort *Goodbye* appeared the following year. —*Jason Ankeny*

**Disgraceful** / Oct. 1995 / Food ♦♦♦♦
Somewhat of a triumph, especially for a British band of the '90s with no hint of Beatles influence or tortured vocals. Instead we are treated to a smorgasbord of nifty melodies, some very good lyrics, and Sarah Blackwood's lovely vocals. For the most part, the sound (led by Stephen Hague's glossy production) is layered synths, sometimes Erasuresque (as on "Anywhere"), with programmed beats, and here or there, the odd jangly guitar à la the Sundays ("St. Swithins Day," written by Billy Bragg). The singles "Stars" and "Not So Manic Now" are sumptuous, and even when the guitar delves into grungy terrain on the title track, reminiscent of *Garlands*-period Cocteau Twins, they still pull it off. Only on "Not Once, Not Ever" and "The Day I See You Again do they come slightly unstuck—not much to complain about on a debut. —*Kelvin Hayes*

● **Goodbye** / Sep. 16, 1997 / PolyGram ♦♦♦♦
Dubstar sounds like the name of a reggae act, but in fact, *Goodbye* offers very lush, atmospheric, and British-sounding synth-pop and dance-pop that inspired quite a few comparisons to St. Etienne, as well as the Pet Shop Boys and New Order. The Newcastle, England trio had become popular in the UK in 1995, and it was in 1997 that this CD introduced Dubstar to American shores. While St. Etienne is the most obvious influence on melancholy songs like "Can't Tell Me," "Stars," and "No More Talk," it's important to stress that Dubstar projects an attractive and recognizable personality of its own. Sarah Greenwood's waif-like vocals are as icy cool as the high-tech production, but as aloof as she can be, Greenwood allows a lot of vulnerability to come through on this striking, melodically rich effort. —*Alex Henderson*

## Dubtribe Sound System

f. 1991, San Francisco, CA
*Group / Club/Dance, House*
Two disenfranchised Gen-Xers known as Sunshine and Moonbeam Jones record as Dubtribe Sound System, blending the peace-and-love vibe of the '60s with non-MIDI tribal-house music on close to a dozen cross-country American trips. Since they don't use computers during their live performances, the duo improvise vocals, drum programming, and keyboard work. Originally formed as Dubtribe, the pair signed to the Organico label and released several singles in late 1993, followed by the album *Sound System*. The live *Selene Songs* followed in 1995. After changing their name to Dubtribe Sound System, they released *Bryant Street* in 1999 on Organico. —*John Bush*

**Selene Songs** / 1995 / Organico ♦♦♦
Recorded at various live dates, *Selene Songs* presents the San Francisco dubsters at their most ambient, with few beats to disturb the feeling. —*John Bush*

● **Bryant Street** / Feb. 23, 1999 / Jive ♦♦♦♦
Dubtribe's third album, *Bryant Street*, recalls '70s deep funk and soul, though with an assortment of distinctly '90s updates, including acid breakbeats and tribal house. Although there are plenty of melodies floating through the LP, the dub influences inherent in the duo's name come through on several tracks, including "Samba Dub," "Wednesday Night," and "Loneliness in Dub." —*John Bush*

## Curd Duca

*Artwork, Producer / Ambient Techno, Trip-Hop*
The productions of electronic mood-music figure Curd Duca look back to the late-'60s dawn of popular synthesizer music, the age of Wendy Carlos' classical-synth fusions and studio producers who experimented with computer music by yoking it to pop pieces. Duca's been in the music business since the early '80s, originally playing keyboards for the German groups Auch Wenn Es Seltsam Klingen Mag and 8 Oder 9—the latter released a half-dozen LPs during the '80s. In 1992, he recorded his solo debut, *Easy Listening*, the first in what became a five-volume series on Normal Records that took up most of the subsequent four years. Moving to the solid experimental/techno label Mille Plateaux in 1997, Duca released *Switched-On Wagner*, a series of synthesizer translations of works originally by the German romantic giant Richard Wagner. The following year, he inagurated yet another series, *Elevator*, each volume of which included dozens of short tracks in a muzaky mode. —*John Bush*

**Elevator** / Mar. 16, 1998 / Mille Plateaux ♦♦♦

**The Best of Curd Duca** / Mar. 24, 1998 / Asphodel ♦♦♦♦

**Elevator 2** / Apr. 20, 1999 / Mille Plateaux ♦♦

● **Elevator 3** / May 30, 2000 / Mille Plateaux ♦♦♦♦
Self-described as "digitalanalog mood music," Curd Duca's *Elevator 3* album jams together 48 short pieces of sound montage, using digital processing to splice together and manipulate warm acoustic sounds. Five of the songs employ the soothing vocals of Carin Feldschmid, bringing these otherwise entirely abstract pieces closer to our schema of a traditional song; the humanity of her voice elevates these songs to the status of being the most memorable moments on the album. Yet even these few songs with vocals tend to pass by unconsciously as Duca quickly transitions from one song to the next so smoothly that only the most attentive listeners will notice. And keep in mind that Duca doesn't expect the listener to be attentive; he doesn't call it mood music for nothing. The music tends to flow in a stream of consciousness-like manner, from one brief moment of acoustic sound to the next. There are few salient moments and virtually no dominant rhythms, only subtly pulsing beats, fading samples, and breaths of quiet noise. This lack of salient attributes

combines with the short track length and seamless transitioning to create the essence of poetic mood music that never gets tedious or monotonous; it isn't funky, melodic, or very beautiful, but it is rather calming. —*Jason Birchmeier*

## The Durutti Column

f. 1978, Manchester, England
*Group / Alternative Dance, Post-Punk, Alternative Pop/Rock*

The Durutti Column was primarily the vehicle of Vini Reilly, a guitarist born in Manchester, England in 1953. As a child, Reilly first took up the piano, drawing inspiration from greats like Art Tatum and Fats Waller, before learning to play guitar at the age of ten. Despite an early affection for folk and jazz, Reilly ultimately became swept up by the punk movement, and in 1977 he joined the group Ed Banger and the Nosebleeds.

In 1978, Factory Records founder Tony Wilson invited Reilly to join a group dubbed the Durutti Column, the name inspired by the Spanish Civil War anarchist Buenaventura Durruti and a Situationists Internationale comic strip of the '60s. Along with Reilly, the nascent band included guitarist Dave Rowbotham, drummer Chris Joyce, vocalist Phil Rainford, and bassist Tony Bowers; following a handful of performances, Rainford was fired, and after recording a pair of tracks for the EP *A Factory Sampler*, Rowbotham, Joyce, and Bowers broke off to form the Moth Men, leaving the Durutti Column the sole province of Vini Reilly.

Recorded with the aid of a few session musicians and released in a sandpaper sleeve, the debut *The Return of the Durutti Column*, a collection of atmospheric instrumentals, appeared in 1980. With 1981's pastoral *LC*, recorded with drummer Bruce Mitchell (who remained a frequent collaborator), Reilly attempted vocals on a few tracks, and continued expanding his palette with a pair of explorations of chamber music, 1982's *Another Setting* and 1984's *Without Mercy*. Electronic rhythms, meanwhile, emerged as the pivotal element of 1985's *Say What You Mean, Mean What You Say*.

After 1985's live effort *Domo Arigato*, *Circuses and Bread* marked a return to the densely-constructed guitar textures of previous works, while 1987's eclectic *The Guitar and Other Machines* ranked among the Durutti Column's most ambitious works to date. In 1988, Reilly backed Morrissey (also an alumnus of the Nosebleeds) on his solo debut *Viva Hate* before returning the Durutti Column to release a 1989 LP titled *Vini Reilly*, another diverse affair which incorporated vocal samples from Otis Redding, Annie Lennox, Tracy Chapman, and opera star Joan Sutherland.

1990's aggressive *Obey the Time* preceded 1991's *Lips That Would Kiss Form Prayers to Broken Stone*, a collection of singles, rarities, and unreleased material. After a long layoff, the Durutti Column returned in 1995 with *Sex and Death*, followed a year later by *Fidelity*, which fused dance beats with Reilly's guitar lines. *Night in New York* arrived in 1999. Among Durutti alumni, Chris Joyce and Tony Bowers achieved the greatest success as members of Simply Red; tragically, founding guitarist Dave Rowbotham was slain by an axe murderer in 1991, inspiring the Happy Mondays song "Cowboy Dave." —*Jason Ankeny*

**The Return of Durutti Column** / 1979 / Factory ♦♦♦♦
*The Return of the Durutti Column*'s record jacket—a cardboard sleeve designed to wreak havoc on all the albums alongside it in the bin—is its only nod to punk abrasiveness; otherwise, Vini Reilly's debut seems to have been created in a vacuum, its shimmering, evocative guitar instrumentals owing nothing to the era which spawned it. Inventively produced by Martin Hannett, the disc immediately sets forth Reilly's trademark guitar sound, a singular hybrid of electric and acoustic textures; songs like the opening "Sketch for Summer" possess a remarkable lightness of tone and spirit, with a surefooted sense of environmental beauty. —*Jason Ankeny*

**LC** / 1981 / Factory ♦♦♦♦

**Without Mercy** / 1984 / Factory ♦♦♦
Named in honor of Keats' *La Belle Dame Sans Merci*, the two-part *Without Mercy* ranks among the Durutti Column's most beautiful and ambitious works, a hauntingly minimal record not dissimilar from chamber music. Employing strings and horns in addition to the more standard guitar, piano, and electronic percussion, the piece achieves a mournful poignancy as emotionally satisfying as anything in Vini Reilly's catalog. —*Jason Ankeny*

**Guitar & Other Machines** / 1988 / Venture ♦♦♦
As the title indicates, *The Guitar and Other Machines* represents the Durutti Column's increasing expansion into electronics, a move heralding an even greater sonic scope than per usual. Paradoxically, however, the album is one of Vini Reilly's most emotionally resonant, employing a number of guest vocalists which lend a much-needed human dimension to the ambitious soundscapes; Reilly himself even steps behind the microphone for the ghostly "Don't Think You're Funny." —*Jason Ankeny*

● **Vini Reilly** / 1989 / Factory ♦♦♦♦
Produced by Stephen Street, *Vini Reilly* is the Durutti Column's finest hour, a stunningly prismatic album that captures the group at its most deeply wrought and eerily beautiful. The opener, "Love No More," sets the record's tone, cutting and pasting vocal samples into a heartbreakingly wordless reverie backed by one of Reilly's most intricate compositions; samples abound throughout the record, always employed with rare skill and grace, and the songs channel a vast reservoir of influences from funk to opera to evoke a singularly spectral atmosphere. —*Jason Ankeny*

## The Dust Brothers

f. 1983, Los Angeles, CA
*Group / Alternative Dance, Club/Dance, Hip-Hop*

The Dust Brothers were among the preeminent producers of the '90s, helming records for everyone from Beck to Hanson while influencing countless others with their signature cut-and-paste marriage of hip-hop and rock. Not to be confused with the British production duo the Chemical Brothers, who began their career under the same name before receiving a cease-and-desist order, the Los Angeles-based Dust Brothers were Mike Simpson and John King, who met in 1983 while working at the Pomona College radio station. They originally teamed to DJ at parties, and by the end of the decade scored a production deal with the Delicious Vinyl label. In 1989, they scored chart success producing debuts from rappers Tone-Loc (the monster hit "Wild Thing") and Young M.C., but their most distinctive early work was on the Beastie Boys' groundbreaking *Paul's Boutique*, widely acclaimed among the most innovative and influential albums of the period for its pioneering use of digital sampling. In the years to follow, the Dust Brothers emerged among the most sought-after remixers and producers in the industry, working on projects for everyone from White Zombie to Technotronic to Shonen Knife; they also founded their own label, Nickel Bag (later changed to Ideal), and in 1996 helmed Beck's extraordinary *Odelay*. Branching out even further, in 1997 they produced Hanson's chart-topping "MMMBop," as well as a handful of tracks from the Rolling Stones' *Bridges to Babylon* LP. Their first full-length solo record was the score for the 1999 film *Fight Club*. —*Jason Ankeny*

● **Fight Club [Original Soundtrack]** / Jul. 27, 1999 / Restless ♦♦♦♦
The score to David Fincher's controversial, subversive film *Fight Club* was composed and performed by the Dust Brothers, whose production and remixing work with artists like the Beastie Boys, Beck, and the Chemical Brothers helped shape the sound of the '90s. Their music for *Fight Club* reflects their own hip-hop and dance roots, as well as the film's edgy, underground tone in its blend of trip-hop, drum'n'bass, and electro elements. —*Heather Phares*

## Titonton Duvante

b. Jul. 2, 1973, Columbus, OH
*Producer / Club/Dance, Techno*

Long a regarded techno producer through his associations with Dan Curtin and Morgan Geist, Titonton Duvante began coming into his own during 1998-99 with the single "Endorphin" and his first full-length, *Voyeurism*, both superb fusions of electro, synthesized jazz, and highly melodic techno. From Columbus, Ohio, Duvante was classically trained but also listened to Detroit techno and later, drum'n'bass. He debuted on record with the "Embryonic" single for Dan Curtin's Cleveland-based Metamorphic label, and also contributed to the "Titonton & Morgan" single co-released by Geist's Environ label and Phono UK. Duvante also formed part of the ele_mental collective and the 21/22 Corporation label, which released material from Charles Noel (as Monochrome) and Todd Sines (as Cron) plus the respected *Trace Elements* compilation series. He also recorded for Multiplex, SSR, and his own Residual label, recruiting John Tejada, Boo Williams, and Todd Sines to record for it as well. His debut full-length *Voyeurism* appeared on the StarBaBy label in 1999. Duvante is also an excellent DJ (with a series of *Double Edged* mixtapes), known to dip into drum'n'bass as well as classic techno and electro. —*John Bush*

**Extrapolation (Remixes) [Single]** / Nov. 2, 1998 / Metamorphic ♦♦♦
The "Extrapolation" remix disc includes three tracks: one by Dego (of 4 Hero)

that pits hard techno against tech-step drum'n'bass with intriguing results. The other two are electro and techno workouts by Metamorphic label-head Dan Curtin. —*John Bush*

- **Voyeurism** / Mar. 14, 1999 / Starbaby ◆◆◆◆
Using nothing more than his 808 and 303 boxes to work with on most tracks, Titonton's first LP showcases his flair for haunted acid melodies and crisp rhythm productions, in keeping with the work of occasional co-producer Morgan Geist. *Voyeurism* is a different work than Geist's superb album *The Driving Memoirs*, but equally excellent for fans of exquisitely produced mood-techno. —*John Bush*

## The Dylan Group

f. 1996, New York, NY
*Group / Indie Rock, Post-Rock/Experimental, Club/Dance*
Ambient duo the Dylan Group teamed Dylan Cristy (a noted jungle DJ as well as co-founder of the New York-based Bubble Core label) and Adam Pierce (also known for his work as the anagrammatic Mice Parade). Set apart from their contemporaries by their use of live instruments—primarily vibraphone and drums—the Dylan Group appeared on a handful of compilations, as well as a split release with H.I.M., before issuing their full-length debut *It's All About (rimshots and faulty wiring)* in 1998. *Re-Interpreted*, a collection of remixes by the likes of Bundy K. Brown and Nobukazu Takemura, followed later that year, and in 1999 the Dylan Group (now a four-piece additionally featuring Scott McGovern and Tyler Pistilli) resurfaced with *More Adventures in Lying Down*. *Ur-Klang Search* appeared a year later. —*Jason Ankeny*

**It's All About (rimshots & faulty wiring)** / Feb. 24, 1998 / Bubble Core ◆◆◆

**Re-Interpreted** / Apr. 28, 1998 / Bubble Core ◆◆
The remix album *Re-Interpreted* includes solid reworkings of Dylan Group favorites by colleagues H.I.M. and Nobukazu Takemura (aka Child's View) plus We, D, Squelch, and Number One Dog. —*Keith Farley*

- **More Adventures in Lying Down** / Mar. 23, 1999 / Bubble Core ◆◆◆
The Dylan Group's first album after becoming a true band marks their midway point between an early focus on live music and the growing programmability of their peers in the post-rock community. The band makes a powerful statement by leading off with "Stay (And We'll Make Such Sweet Music)," an Astrud Gilberto chestnut that benefits from the interplay of vibes and drums. "Spaghetti" includes an acoustic version of what would be jungle breakbeats, "The Pipes" is a tape experiment involving a series of clattering noises and *More Adventures in Lying Down* even includes a live track recorded at *the Knitting Factory*. It's an interesting fusion of live and pre-programmed music. —*Keith Farley*

## Dynamix II

f. 1985, Miami, FL
*Group / Bass Music, Electro, Club/Dance*
Miami's David Noller and Scott Weiser, aka Dynamix II, are among a very few of the first wave of American electro and bass music artists to have successfully translated their old-school credentials into new-school relevance. The producers behind classic roof-raisers "Bass Generator," "Ignition," and "Just Give the DJ a Break," Noller and Weiser carved out a signature niche in early electro with a kitchen-sink-style megamix approach, amplifying electro's energy level, deepening the low-end, and playing up its robotic themes with ample vocoded vocals and squirty electronics. The group formed in 1985 after Noller, a local DJ who had recently started making tracks, met Weiser and the two began building a studio together. Noller was signed to Bass Station records at the time, and Dynamix appeared through a handful of other Miami labels before the pair set up their eponymous imprint in 1988. Although mostly of only local interest beginning in the late '80s, when electro died out in favor of rap, the group got a big boost nearly a decade later, when UK-based label Rephlex—owned by Richard James, aka Aphex Twin—reissued *Electro Megamix: 1985-Present*, an all-in-one-place collection of their biggest tunes from over the years, and originally released on the Joey Boy label in 1997. A stream of new material has appeared since then, including "We Are Your Future" and "The Plastic Men," both through Joey Boy. A collaboration with British producer Ian Loveday, aka Eon, also appeared through Wax Trax!/TVT in 1999. Additionally, Dynamix II have remixed fellow Florida group Rabbit in the Moon and Expansion Union. Most of their LPs and singles from throughout the years remained in print. —*Sean Cooper*

**Dynamix II: The Album** / 1990 / Dynamix ◆◆◆
**Bass Planet** / Nov. 16, 1993 / Dynamix II ◆◆

- **Electro Bass Megamix: 1985 to Present** / Nov. 11, 1997 / Joey Boy ◆◆◆◆
An excellent Dynamix II collection and a great pointer to how exciting electro really can be, *Electro Bass Megamix* runs through every feted Dynamix II single in the mix format they were created to serve. It just wouldn't be a proper compilation without "Just Give the DJ a Break," "Feel the Bass," and "Bass Generator," though the album hits other high points with "Hypnotic 808" and "DJ's Go Berzerk." The collection was reissued in 1998 by Rephlex with the title *Electro Megamix*. —*John Bush*

# E

### E-Dancer (Kevin Saunderson)
b. Detroit, MI
*Producer / Detroit Techno, Club/Dance, Techno*
Just one of the myriad aliases Kevin Saunderson used to release singles on his own KMS label during the late '80s and early '90s, E-Dancer was also the pseudonym under which Saunderson released one of his first actual solo LPs, 1998's *Heavenly*. [See Also: Kevin Saunderson, Inner City] —*John Bush*

- **Heavenly** / Jul. 28, 1998 / Planet E ♦♦♦♦
Detroit techno pioneer Kevin Saunderson's E-Dancer album, *Heavenly*, functions nearly as well as his *Faces & Phases* collection as an excellent introduction to his hard-hitting, pumping techno. Whereas *Faces & Phases* may sound a bit primitive with its mediocre sound quality, *Heavenly* sounds fresh and timeless. Classics such as "Velocity Funk," "The Human Bond," and "Feel the Mood" have a high-tech, polished shine, while some of Saunderson's other early classics, such as "Pump the Move," get fresh remixes. In addition to these classics, there are a few songs not found on *Faces & Phases*, including an excellent remix of "World of Deep" by Carl Craig and a remix of "Heavenly" by Juan Atkins. When these more cosmic practitioners of down-tempo techno re-engineer Saunderson's pumping rhythms, the results are quite interesting. Craig smooths out the pounding "World of Deep" by toning down the punishing bass beats and sensually moving the song's synthesized tones into the foreground. Atkins also tones down the abusive percussion of Saunderson's original mix of "Heavenly" and reorganizes the song's structure into a much less coherent flow, focusing more on the complex nature of spirituality rather than the euphoric side. A few of the remaining tracks, such as "Banjo" and "Oombah," don't have the same intensity or luster as the aforementioned tracks. They could have used some remixing or perhaps have been eliminated. They aren't terrible by any means, but when compared to some of Saunderson's best work, they make for an uneven album. Yet even though *Heavenly* may not be comprised of brilliant techno from start to finish, its highlights overshadow nearly anything found on the crude though thoroughly comprehensive *Faces & Phases* collection. —*Jason Stanley Birchmeier*

### Eat Static
f. 1989, Frome, England
*Group / Electronica, Ambient Dub, Trance*
A techno-based, UFO-obsessed side project of Ozric Tentacles' Merv Pepler (keyboards, drum patterns, samplers) and Joie Hinton (keyboards, samplers) along with synth player Steve Everitt, Eat Static formed in Frome, England in 1989. After making their initial appearances performing before and after Ozric shows, Eat Static issued their first few singles on their own Alien label before signing to Planet Dog, debuting with the album *Abduction* in 1993. The follow-up, 1994's *Implant*, proved so successful that Peplar and Hinton exited Ozric permanently; the *Epsylon* EP appeared the next year, with the *Bony Incus* EP surfacing in 1996. A year later the album, *Science of the Gods* was released on Mammoth Records. —*Jason Ankeny*

**Implant** / 1994 / Planet Dog ♦♦
This offshoot of Ozric Tentacles uses alien sound effects and a heavy bass with some synth work. Very danceable, but the samples can wear thin. —*John Bush*

**Epsylon** / 1995 / Planet Dog/Mammoth ♦♦
Although trance and techno are the main elements here, the group also uses Eastern samples on *Epsylon*. This US version of the album includes three bonus tracks, including a great mix of "Gulf Breeze." —*John Bush*

**Abduction** / Sep. 12, 1995 / Mammoth ♦♦♦

- **Science of the Gods** / Oct. 21, 1997 / Mammoth ♦♦♦♦
Two years on from their third album *Abduction*, Eat Static's *Science of the Gods* shows a marked improvement over the duo's previous output. Adding a few impressive breakbeats tied to both jungle and hip-hop, but never sacrificing their allegiance to psychedelic and alien-obsessed techno/trance, *Science of the Gods* hits several highpoints, including "Interceptor," "Contact…," and "Bodystealers." —*John Bush*

### EC8OR
f. 1993, Berlin, Germany
*Group / Gabba, Electronica, Hardcore Techno*
Cologne-bred, Berlin-based Patric C. (aka EC8OR) is one of the most prolific of the younger generation of "digital hardcore" artists combining hardcore breakbeat and gabber techno with elements of punk rock, speed metal, and experimental noise. Recording and performing under a half dozen pseudonyms (including Eradicator, E-De Cologne, Irish Coffee, and Test-Tube Boy), Patric C.'s EC8OR work is usually in collaboration with teen punk vocalist Gina D'Orio (formerly of the Lemonbabies and Throw That Beat), and through their association with Alec Empire's Digital Hardcore Recordings label, they've managed to become one the most popular and well-known artists on the German hardcore scene. Using only an Amiga 500 (a cheap, somewhat obsolete desktop computer with built-in sequencing and sampling capabilities), Patric began recording in 1991 after quitting school to immerse himself in the emerging rave scene. Releasing tracks literally out of his travel bag, Patric's first twelves of relatively straightforward techno appeared through Cologne's noted Structure label group (which included imprint's such as DJ Ungle Fever, Mono Tone, and Profan along with artists such as Mike Ink, Air Liquide, and Biochip C.). Patric's love of hip-hop, punk, and death metal didn't show through in the music until he began making breakbeat gabber, however—a style which linked him with hardcore acid and techno labels such as Shockwave, Fischkopf (through which he released his debut LP, *Agit-Prop*), and, eventually, DHR. The group's association with the latter label has probably been the most crucial; in addition to a number of singles and the self-titled EC8OR full-length (released in late 1995), DHR's distribution deal with American label Grand Royal translated into a far larger audience for their music, with *World Beaters* following in 1998. Two years later EC8OR released the full-length *The One and Only High and Low*. —*Sean Cooper*

**EC8OR** / 1995 / DHR ♦♦

- **All of Us Can Be Rich** / Aug. 12, 1997 / Grand Royal ♦♦♦
Take lots of distorted vocals, drum machine beats, Slayer-esque guitars and redundant samples, and smudge this all together to get a very cliché '90s industrial band; add to the fact that their material sounds as if it was recorded in their mom's basement and you've got EC8OR. Having listened to one too many Ministry records in high school, the duo of Patric Catani and Gina V. D'orio took all their frustrations (assuming from not fitting in with the popular crowd) by screaming songs like "We Are Pissed" along with sloppy industrial rhythms that flow as smoothly as Homer Simpson with his shoelaces tied together. They at least get an "A" for effort in trying to take themselves way too seriously. —*Mike DaRonco*

**World Beaters** / Aug. 25, 1998 / DHR ♦♦
It's difficult to imagine EC8OR upping the ante for their second wide-release album, but *World Beaters* does it with higher BPMs, more distortion, and even fewer intelligible lyrics than the duo's previous album. It also lacks the mindless revolutionary hilarity of prime 1996-era singles like "Cocaine Ducks" and "Spex Is a Fat Bitch," but "Until Everything Explodes" and "The Shit You Dig" come very close. —*John Bush*

**The One and Only High and Low** / Sep. 19, 2000 / Digital Hardcore ♦♦
Unfazed by any musical or technological fads within the world of electronic dance since their last release, 1998's *World Beaters*, the D.I.Y. duo EC8OR doesn't change much for their fifth album overall. Patric Catani's production is (as usual) a no-attention-span, post-rave spin on the ragged metal-riff samples of classic Def Jam productions by Rick Rubin in the late '80s, complete with all manner of light-speed thrash breakbeats and continual changes of tempo. Though the sound won't surprise any listeners even vaguely familiar with the Digital Hardcore aesthetic, *World Beaters* shows EC8OR growing even more intriguing than DHR's flagship, Atari Teenage Riot. Catani and Gina D'Orio avoid the played-out digital-hardcore blues by leavening their occasionally stand-offish attitude with tongue-in-cheek numbers like "Gimmy Nyquil All Night Long" and "Zero Heroes." —*John Bush*

## The Ecstasy of Saint Theresa

f. 1993, Czechoslovakia
*Group / Ambient*
The Czechoslovakian ambient group the Ecstasy of St. Theresa comprised vocalist/keyboardist Irna Libowitz, sound designers Jan Muchow and Petr Wegner, bassist Jan Gregar, guitarist John Moore, multi-instrumentalist Misa Klimkova, keyboardist Colin Stuart, flautist Vladimira Jestrabova and percussionist Katie Hecker. Debuting in 1993 with the EP *…fluidtrance centauri…*, they returned the following year with the Guy Fixsen-produced full-length *Free-D (Original Soundtrack)*; a remix EP, *Astrala Vista*, was the only Ecstasy of St. Theresa release in the months and years to follow, although the group continued performing live. —*Jason Ankeny*

• **Free-D (Original Soundtrack)** / 1994 / Free ♦♦♦♦
*Free-D (Original Soundtrack)* exists in a kind of musical limbo—while it possesses elements of everything from ambient techno to dream pop to new age, it refuses to adhere to any strict sonic definition for too long. For one, the reliance on live instruments like cellos and flutes lends the Ecstasy of Saint Theresa's soundscapes a distinctly human pulse, but at the same time the music is clearly electronic in structure and design, textured by droning keyboard washes and synthetic rhythms. Moreover, while the record's soft contours and muted hues evoke the aesthetics of ambient, it simply refuses to fade into the backdrop—the formlessness of the songs ensures that they're in seemingly constant flux, a shape-shifting fusion of spectral vocals, enigmatic samples, and abstract beats. Ultimately, it's *Free-D*'s refusal to accept easy categorization that makes it so compelling—it's a singular experience in deep listening. —*Jason Ankeny*

**Astrala Vista [EP]** / 1994 / Free ♦♦
The *Astrala Vista* EP features five remixes of work by the semi-ambient Czech group Ecstasy of St. Theresa, including turns by Disco Inferno, Twin Freaks, Bandulu, and the group itself—the music falls solidly within the style of pleasingly bleepy electronics but also has a sense of movement and dynamics that's typically hard to find in remix releases. —*Nitsuh Abebe*

## Ectomorph

f. 1994, Detroit, MI
*Group / Neo-Electro, Electro-Techno, Detroit Techno, Club/Dance*
Though they're unknown to all but a select few in the American and European underground, Detroit electro duo Ectomorph are on the leading edge of a new wave of American dance music artists reconnecting techno to its roots in Motor City funk and soul via electro. Like early Detroit artists such as Juan Atkins and Carl Craig who sought to explore the fusion of man and machine in a wholly electronic musical form, Ectomorph dwell on the pros and cons of the machine aesthetic. But where many of those artists eventually left the rigid funk of the beatbox break behind for the steady pulse of a disco or house beat (electro all but disappeared in the mid- to late-'80s, following the birth and ascendance of full-blown techno), Ectomorph, as well as likeminded artists such as Drexciya, Flexitone, Dopplereffekt, and DJ Godfather continue to draw from the legacy of figures such as James Brown, Funkadelic, the Bar-Kays, and the Meters. Although their music bears little resemblance to the free-wheeling acoustical jams of many of those groups, Ectomorph's affection for swung, meter-stepping rhythms and disorienting blasts of analog fuzz trace out a direct, recognizable connection.

Formed by bedroom arms Brendan "BMG" Gillen and Gerald (as the former member of Detroit new wave group the Batteries likes to be known) in 1994, Ectomorph have released twelves and a handful of compilation tracks for labels such as Sabotage, Serotonin, Astralwerks, and Submerge. Their influence and reputation have more than exceeded their comparatively limited output, with DJs regularly citing them as favorites and European electro revivalists routinely biting their style. Ectomorph's first release, the *Subsonic Vibrations* EP, was released in 1994 (the record also included a pair of looped-rhythm lock-grooves; a signature of the group); the four-track "Stark" EP followed the following year, with tracks on Astralwerks' *Detroit: Beyond the Third Wave* and Sabotage's *Electro Juice* exposing the group to a much wider audience. Additionally, Gillen and Gerald have recorded for Carl Craig's Planet E label under the name Flexitone, releasing a pair of singles and a track on the label compilation *Elements of and Experiments with Sound*. Gerald also records as one-half of Detroit electro group Drexciya, with Gillen's solo work appearing most often through Audiohypnose. Gerald left the duo in 1996, and was replaced by Erika Sherman. In 2000, DJ Godfather and Carlos Souffront started accompanying the group, taking over DJ Rotator's original slot. [See Also: Flexitone] —*Sean Cooper*

• **Stark [EP]** / 1995 / Interdimensional Transmissions ♦♦♦♦
Ectomorph go lock-groove crazy with their second self-released 12", coming up with no less than 10 locking figures before even bothering to lay down a single track. The EP's three other long-players are somewhat typical minimalist Detroit electro, with a perhaps more playful presence on the low-end and a goofy, two-beat throw-back tacked on at the end. —*Sean Cooper*

**Subsonic Vibrations [Single]** / 1995 / Interdimensional Transmissions ♦♦♦
Four tracks (plus two lock grooves) of bleached out, deep-space electro. Hints of Drexciya can be found in the ranting, caustic bleeps of "Skin," but Ectomorph's comparatively more subdued minimalism is the leading impress here. —*Sean Cooper*

**Abstraction [EP]** / May 12, 1997 / Interdimensional Transmissions ♦♦
Ectomorph's third blast from the electro dimension is probably their lowest-fi, most minimal to date. Although much of the bleepwork of the previous releases has been stripped out to focus on the rhythmic dynamic between drums and bass, sparse, squelchy accents appear here and there. These are definitely *beat* tracks, however, with clattering, reverbed 909 patterns played off against wobbly, surging basslines and on-the-one kicks worthy of James Brown's tricked-out mini. —*Sean Cooper*

**Destroy Your Powercenters [EP]** / Aug. 2, 1999 / Interdimensional Transmissions ♦♦♦♦
Ectomorph's fourth release for the label is a daring step in the effort to push the limits of vinyl as a format. The a-side contains two mixes of "Subversion" set up as a double groove—where each mix starts at the outer edge of the record on its own groove. In effect, the listener/dj is forced to closely examine the piece of art—er—vinyl to discover what is hidden and discern which cut pleases more or has a preferred function. The track itself exploits a highly processed vocal utterance for syncopation against Ectomorph's unmistakable rhythmic didacticism to reach the moody space also explored in the first three releases. "(We Have Come To) Destroy Your Power Centers (Beats)" is a bonus rhythm piece with a unique and schizophrenic approach to programming—while the B-side opener "Only in Shadows" is an even further fracture from the groove set by ectomorph's prior releases—it's got a four-to-the-floor kick!—This rhythmic assumption submits to the warmth of a bassline that evokes Fingers under a spooky high line. "Slither" brings back good ole' "funky electro beat" for another cut of dark psychedelia. "Destroy Your Power Centers" stands on its own as a vinyl oddity while it describes the evolution of Ectomorph seen in the context of their discography. —*Carlos Julio Souffront*

**Breakthrough/Magnetic (Dub Version) [Single]** / 2000 / i.t. ♦♦♦♦
"Breakthrough" b/w "Magnetic (Dub Version)" trades in Interdimensional Transmissions lingering penchant for the vinyl gymnastics of lock and concentric grooves and inside-out tracking for a more conventional functionality—the DJ tool. As for the music—its approach follows the formatting's cue (or is it the other way around?)—it's a dance record. It's not that the first four Ectomorph releases weren't danceable, but with "Breakthrough," Ectomorph utters its most succinct and reverent statement in the dialogue of the electro-dance tradition. "Magnetic (Dub Version)" functions in its own right; the slinky monotone groove adds mood and rhythmic didacticism to whatever party it's invited to. Perhaps the most dramatic evolution of Ectomorph's sound, this record will endure. —*Carlos Souffront*

## Todd Edwards
b. 1973
*Producer, DJ / Jazz-House, Speed Garage, Garage, Club/Dance, House*

Though he gets less credit from stateside DJs and producers (at least compared to labelmates like Armand Van Helden), Todd Edwards created an innovative blend of rhythmic, cut-and-paste vocal samples, rubbery basslines, and slapping percussion that helped propel Britain's Sunday club scene into the genuine cultural phenomenon of speed garage. Based in New Jersey, Edwards began producing for Nervous, the New York house label, during the early '90s. His 1993 "Guide My Soul" single, recorded as the Messenger, established a prototype for garage music that retained the soul and grit but avoided the overly polished airs much of the music had acquired. One year later, "The Praise" (as the Sample Choir) continued Edwards' irresistible, unique production style — which often utilizes dozens of different samples, many of them himself — and he also worked with two "real" vocalists, Kim English ("Tomorrow") and Veda Simpson ("Oohhh Baby").

In 1994, Edwards recorded several tracks for an upcoming New Jersey jazz-house label, i! Records. One year later, his second proper release on the label, "Saved My Life," became a big club hit and earned license in Britain through Pete Tong's ffrr Records. He provided remixes for several dance hits, by Robin S., Wildchild, Indo, St. Germain, the Beloved, and label-mate Kevin Yost. In 1999, Nervous collected his productions on a CD collection, and i! Records released *Prima Edizione*, a quasi-compilation including four new tracks. Edwards also released an EP with Tuff Jam, and completed a co-production for inclusion on Daft Punk's sophomore album. —*John Bush*

**Prima Edizione** / Jan. 18, 1999 / i! Records ♦♦♦♦
Released on the mostly downtempo label i! Records, *Prima Edizione* doesn't so much present a new side of Todd Edwards as it tweaks the soulful, jazzier side of his previous productions. Mostly comprised of tracks from i! releases past, the album also includes four new tracks featuring the (now) veteran producer's take on the omnipresent filtered-disco style and ambient house (a beatless version of his single classic "Fly Away"). Edwards' dancefloor productions usually reward close listening, so it's no surprise that this collection of home-oriented electronics hits the same peaks as his singles. —*John Bush*

● **Todd Edwards' Nervous Tracks** / Oct. 19, 1999 / Nervous ♦♦♦♦
*Todd Edwards' Nervous Tracks* collects eleven tracks from the label's most distinctive producer, offering plenty of evidence (as if any were necessary) how Edwards forged the style that launched Britain's garage and 2-step scene. On highlights like "Guide My Soul," "The Praise," and "So Real," Edwards dices not just the words from split-second vocal tags, but bare syllables, then pours them into a fast-forward mix of pointed beats and cymbal-heavy percussion. The effect is invigorating and contagious, so it's no surprise that when upcoming British garage producers like MJ Cole and Tuff Jam began looking for role models, they emulated Edwards. Even the vocal productions, "Oohhh Baby" by Veda Simpson, and "Tomorrow" by Kim English, are excellent. —*John Bush*

## The Egyptian Lover (Greg Broussard)
*Producer / West Coast Rap, Old School Rap, Electro, Club/Dance, Urban*

One of the most innovative producers of the old-school/electro era, Egyptian Lover's Greg Broussard recorded a parade of singles during the '80s that proved influential for decades. Influenced himself by Kraftwerk/hip-hop soundclashes like Afrika Bambaataa's "Planet Rock" and Man Parrish's "Hip-Hop Be Bop (Don't Stop)," as well as the extroverted black-lover soul of Prince and Zapp, Broussard began recording from his Los Angeles base in 1983. One year later, he emerged with the breakdancing anthem "Egypt, Egypt," released on the Freak Beat label. Similar to excellent tracks being produced all over America — from Detroit (Cybotron) to New York (Mantronix) — "Egypt, Egypt" and successors "What Is a DJ If He Can't Scratch," "And My Beat Goes Boom," and "Computer Love (Sweet Dreams)" spent much time in DJ crates during the '80s and '90s. Broussard also released several LPs during the mid-'80s, including 1984's *On the Nile* (practically a greatest-hits compilation), 1986's *One Track Mind*, and 1988's *Filthy*; the first two appeared on his own Egyptian Empire label. After several years away from music, he returned in 1994 with *Back From the Tomb* and the following year's *Pyramix*. —*John Bush*

● **On the Nile** / 1984 / Egyptian Empire ♦♦♦♦
Based around a conceptual and thematic slant, Egyptian Lover's debut album includes all his best-known early hits — "Egypt, Egypt," "What Is a D.J. If He Can't Scratch," "Computer Love (Sweet Dreams)," "Girls," and "My House (On the Nile)." —*Ron Wynn*

**One Track Mind** / 1986 / Egyptian Empire ♦♦
**King of Ecstasy: The Best of Egyptian Lover** / Dec. 1, 1995 / DMSR ♦♦♦♦
This Egyptian Lover hits collection includes extended mixes of a few tracks from his mid-'80s heyday ("Lover," "Egypt, Egypt") but hardly qualifies as a definitive collection of Broussard's best. —*Ron Wynn*

## 808 State
f. 1988, Manchester, England
*Group / Club/Dance, Acid House, House*

A pioneer of the acid house sound, 808 State formed in Manchester, England in 1988 when Martin Price, the owner of the city's legendary record store Eastern Bloc and the founder of the independent label Creed, first joined forces with local musician and producer Graham Massey. After teaming with collaborator Gerald Simpson, 808 State recorded its debut EP *Newbuild* in 1988, and also began remixing tracks for groups like the Inspiral Carpets. After Simpson exited to form his solo project A Guy Called Gerald, Price and Massey enlisted DJs Andrew Barker and Darren Partington (known together as the Spinmasters) for the recording of 1989's *Quadrastate* EP, which earned the group a huge club hit with the track "Pacific." After signing with ZTT, they released the album *808:90*, which was embraced by the burgeoning rave culture. 808 State's next single, "The Only Rhyme That Bites," recorded with hip-hopper MC Tunes, marked a dramatic shift into hardcore rap, but was another huge hit. A series of diverse singles followed, culminating in the 1991 album *Ex: El*, which featured guest vocals from New Order's Bernard Sumner and Bjork; the same year, 808 State also wrote, produced and performed the music for the MC Tunes LP *The North at Its Heights*. In 1992, Price left to work as a solo producer, later forming his own label, Sun Text. The remaining trio continued on in 1993 with *Gorgeous*, and handled remix work for the likes of David Bowie, Soundgarden and Bomb the Bass before returning with the experimental *Don Solaris* in 1996. The *808:88-98* compilation followed two years later. —*Jason Ankeny*

**Newbuild** / 1988 / Creed State ♦♦♦♦
The group's 1988 debut — the only material recorded with A Guy Called Gerald — is straightahead acid-house, minus the genre experimentations that characterize later albums such as *808:90*. Nevertheless, the mid-'90s generation of techno progressives (including Aphex Twin) saluted this album's raw edge as a major influence. In 1999, Aphex Twin reissued *Newbuild* on his Rephlex label. —*John Bush*

**90** / 1989 / ZTT ♦♦♦♦
808 State's debut album release on ZTT Records wasn't the first major UK house/techno release, but arguably, it was the most important at the time, gaining a reputation over the years as a true classic in the field of electronic music. While not remarkably different from its many American precursors, *90* not only established that Britain could do things just as well as the States, it also helped to fully lay the groundwork for the '90s electronic revolution that continues to play out in the UK. Arguably, 808 at this point weren't always pushing edges: "Magical Dream" and "Ancodia" have a decided gentility to their grooves. That said, "Cobra Bora" has an aggro edge, mixing gentler impulses with something more clipped and rough, not to mention a wickedly clever sample of the a cappella opening to Van McCoy's "The Hustle," clearly pointing the way to the monstrous groove of *Cubik* in a year's time. "Pacific 202, '90s classic number, fuses the two strains perfectly, with its soft synth and sax combination riding an insistent bass groove that's just a little bit more forceful than might be expected. The concluding tracks, such as "808080808," are closer to being in-your-face danceable, though with interesting tweaks along the way, such as "Donkey Doctor"'s echoed vocal sample and sudden mid-song break to a softer groove. —*Ned Raggett*

**Quadrastate [EP]** / 1989 / Creed ♦♦♦
Spinmakers Partington and Barker joined 808 State for a classic example of lush, beautiful house, which laid the groundwork for some synth-heavy ambient house. The single "Pacific State" became the group's biggest hit to date. —*John Bush*

● **Utd. State 90** / Jun. 1990 / Tommy Boy ♦♦♦♦
The canard regarding American releases of British records, from the Beatles on down, has been that the stateside company screws up, rearranges, or dras-

tically pares down the original release. Quite happily for all concerned, American label Tommy Boy got its version of the 90 album almost exactly right. While the track order was drastically changed (and the 60-second concluding track, "The Fat Shadow," removed), there was no real disruption of flow, and seven bonus tracks were added to create a full CD's worth of early 808 in one easy package—a perfect gift for American fans. The new tracks come from a variety of sources, most being earlier (or later) singles or remixes done exclusively for this release. Of these, "Cubik" is the clear standout—three-and-a-half minutes of utterly compelling techno force, led off by what would shortly become one of the most commonly imitated and ripped-off electronic basslines ever. "Kinky National," while derived from the *Quadrastate* EP's "State Ritual," appears here with an almost industrial feel to it, armed with an ominous bass riff and a stiffer, complex percussion pattern. "Revenge of the Girlie Men" is another reworking of a decent *Quadrastate* track, "Disco State," minus samples from the band IOU. "State to State," the final *Quadrastate* recycle, remains more or less in its original form. Two fine, new remixes of "Pacific 202"—numbered "212" and "718"—appear at the end of the disc, while "Boneyween" appears to be the one wholly new track, a fast-paced house thump driven by some great squiggly keyboard melodies. The end result remains the best way to listen to early 808 State, and is a near-perfect demonstration of the band's work. —*Ned Raggett*

**Ex:El** / May 9, 1991 / Tommy Boy ♦♦♦♦
Starting with the sparkling "San Francisco," which begins with a chiming keyboard introduction before turning into a relentless pounder of a track overlaid with a constantly changing series of melodies, *Ex:El* captures 808 State at their absolute best. None of their subsequent albums quite matched *Ex:El*'s perfect blend of art, mass appeal, and Zeitgeist (one of the most commonly used vocal samples in techno, *Willy Wonka*'s "We are the music makers," made its first major appearance here, on "Nephatiti"). A major change here from past releases is the increasing variety and power of the State's percussion: beats are heavier and more staggered, embracing earlier flirtations with hip-hop and industrial music with even greater success, as heard on heavy-duty groovers like "Leo, Leo." A sign of how influential *Ex:El* ended up being can be seen in how one of the commonest clichés of UK techno albums—the guest appearance of a noted indie/alternative rocker on a track or two—got its start from the cameo vocals here. Fellow Mancunian dance pioneer Bernard Sumner of New Order sings one of his patented gentle ruminations over "Spanish Heart," a nice piano-led number with a solid backbeat. Meanwhile, even more notably, the Sugarcubes' Björk lends her swooping singing to the lower-key but still active "Qmart" and the dramatic, flamenco-tinged "Ooops," establishing a partnership with the State's Graham Massey that would result in his working on many of her solo projects, including *Army of Me*. Add to all this two of the best techno singles from the early '90s—"In Yer Face," a subtly politicized anti-American slammer, and the almighty "Cubik" (in America replaced by an astonishing remix of the same song, the original having appeared on *Utd. State 90*)—and *Ex:El* stands out all the more strongly. A true masterpiece. —*Ned Raggett*

**Gorgeous** / Jan. 19, 1993 / Tommy Boy ♦♦♦
*Gorgeous* is 808 State's most vocal-oriented effort, and features a number of fairly anonymous and forgettable guest singers. The record is most successful when it sticks to the group's trademark atmospheric dance instrumentals, although even those are fairly run-of-the-mill. —*Jason Ankeny*

**Don Solaris** / Jun. 17, 1996 / ZTT ♦♦♦♦
Although Bristol's first breakthrough acid-house band hadn't disappeared entirely from the production scene, their sporadic recordings following '93's *Gorgeous* were limited either to Japanese-only pressings or to members of their fan club, State to State. *Don Solaris*, the group's first widely available album in more than four years, is thus something of a return for the group. And somewhat surprisingly, it's accomplished stuff, successfully avoiding the twin slumps of blandness and derivativeness that so often attends the post-hiatus of once innovative groups. The album roams freely from anthemic acid-house to trip-hop to jungle to dense, warping electro, with studio chops that raise well-written songs to a higher level of listenability. Although vocal contributions from the likes of M. Doughty of Soul Coughing, Louise Rhodes of Lamb, and James Dean Bradfield of the Manic Street Preachers occasionally prove intrusive, the group deftly integrate pop song structure with a focused experimentalism. —*Sean Cooper*

**808:88-98** / Jun. 2, 1998 / ZTT/Universal ♦♦♦♦
*808:88-98* is a terrific compilation that contains many of the highlights of the groundbreaking house group's first ten years. Their biggest club hits are here, along with a handful of new mixes of such songs as "Pacific" and "Cubik," plus a new song, "Crash." It's a comprehensive, entertaining retrospective that not only works as a good introduction, but also provides an excellent summation of their achievements. —*Stephen Thomas Erlewine*

## Einstürzende Neubauten

f. Apr. 1, 1980, Berlin, Germany
*Group / Experimental Rock, Post-Punk, Industrial*
Along with Cabaret Voltaire and Throbbing Gristle, Germany's Einstürzende Neubauten ("collapsing new buildings") helped pioneer industrial music with an avant-garde mix of white-noise guitar drones, vocals verging on unlistenable at times, and a clanging, rhythmic din produced by a percussion section consisting of construction materials, hand and power tools, and various metal objects. Neubauten was founded by vocalist/guitarist Blixa Bargeld and percussionist and American expatriate N.U. Unruh in Berlin as a performance art collective; their early activities included a seemingly inexplicable half-naked appearance on the Berlin Autobahn, where the duo spent some time beating on the sides of a hole in an overpass. The group's early lineup also included percussionists Beate Bartel and Gudrun Gut, plus contributor and sound engineer Alexander Van Borsig; their earliest recordings are mostly unstructured, free-form noise issued on various cassettes and singles, including their first single, "Fuer den Untergang," 1981 EP *Schwarz*, and 1982 album *Kollaps*. Some of these recordings are compiled on the *80-83 Strategies Against Architecture* collection, with live shows on the cassette-only *2 X 4*. Bartel and Gut were replaced by ex-Abwarts member F.M. Einheit (who served as Neubauten's chief machinery operator) in 1983, when guitarist and electronics expert Alexander Hacke and Abwarts bassist Marc Chung also joined. A tour of England opening for the Birthday Party resulted in a contract with Some Bizarre Records, which released the slightly more structured *Portrait of Patient O.T.*, as well as consternation from club owners and journalists over Neubauten's stage demolitions and frequent ensuing violence.

When Nick Cave left the Birthday Party and formed his backing band the Bad Seeds, Bargeld became the guitarist and toured and recorded with Cave over most of the decade. He remained with Neubauten, however, which released *1/2 Mensch* in 1986, showcasing its wider range of expression. The group disbanded briefly but soon re-formed, and have released albums off and on since then for Elektra, signing to Trent Reznor's Nothing label for 1998's *Ende Neu*. While Bargeld remains a Bad Seed, Van Borsig and Hacke contributed to the remainder of the Birthday Party's recordings as Crime and the City Solution. In May of 2000 Einstürzende Neubauten released the full-length *Silence Is Sexy* on Mute Records. Elektra reissued both *Strategies Against Architecture* compilations on CD, while most of the group's '80s albums remain available on the independent Thirsty Ear label. —*Steve Huey*

● **Strategies Against Architecture '80-'83** / 1984 / Positive ♦♦♦♦
A double-disc collection spanning 1980 to 1983, *Strategies Against Architecture* works surprisingly well considering Einstürzende Neubauten's resistance to solid retrospectives. Compiling tracks from their 1982 debut *Kollaps* plus much live work and a few unreleased cuts, tracks like "Stahlversion," "Schmerzen Mören," and "Zum Tier Machen" illustrate the group's experimental aesthetic with what is a surprisingly listenable flair. —*John Bush*

**Half Mensch** / 1985 / Some Bizarre ♦♦♦♦
Though it's a bit less intentionally noisy than previous Neubaten material, *Half Mensch* is, in a way, the group's masterpiece. The inspired use of such "traditional" instruments as a grand piano alongside the band's characteristic blazing percussion make for a record similar more to their compositional influences like Stockhausen than their nearest contemporaries, like Throbbing Gristle or Cabaret Voltaire. The record that showed Einstürzende Neubaten could rise above the concept of noise for its own sake to reach another level of noise-oriented post-punk music, *Half Mensch* is an excellent feat of industrial music. —*John Bush*

**Haus der Luege** / 1989 / Rough Trade ♦♦
Like its predecessor *Fuenf auf der Nach Oben Offenen Richterskala, Haus der Luege* ("House of Lies") represents a detour from the trademark Neubauten noise into low-key, subtle textures. While the group hasn't forgone found industrial sounds, they've instead integrated them more thoroughly into the songs; while the volume is restrained, the music is still taut, relying on the unpredictability of the new approach for its intensity. —*Jason Ankeny*

**Tabula Rasa** / Feb. 16, 1993 / Elektra ♦♦♦♦
A surprisingly restrained Neubauten outing, *Tabula Rasa* favors mood and atmosphere over noise and fury. —*Jason Ankeny*

**Ende Neu** / Jul. 23, 1996 / Mute ♦♦♦
On their 1996 release *Ende Neu* (ending-new), the quintessential scientists of the post-avant-garde abstain from focusing on listener disintegration tactics as they did on prior albums, but opt instead to hone their craftsmanship in new compositional areas. Some followers of their earlier material might object to the obvious and comparatively conventional song structure and style that is displayed on *Ende Neu*, picking up a power tool to highlight a piece rather than centering the entire work around it, or leaving a stage before setting it ablaze—but the destruction has already been performed, and now they are erecting the brave new anti-building of musical art. Exploring intricate processions of time and toying with melodious harmonies, Blixa Bargeld and Co. seem to have matured gracefully. The opening cut, "Was Ist Ist," is a furious, fast-paced slander on the constant wanting of mankind while simultaneously serving as a tongue-in-cheek remark on how absolute, scientific power overrules impossibility. From there, *Ende Neu* continues to musically rewrite the band's style, using familiar topics such as ethereal chaos ("Die Explosion Im Festspielhaus"), cosmic complacency ("The Garden"), revolt ("Installation No.1"), and even a Kafka-esque piece, "Der Schacht Von Babel." This is the first release since the departure of founding band member Mark Chung, and it is obvious that the remaining members have taken the time to contribute to the void left by his departure. *Ende Neu* delivers a precision-fed matrix of audio-encrypted knowledge in a manner not like the chaotic Neubauten of the early '80s, but more strategic, and more mature. —*Greg Matherly*

**Ende Neu Remixes** / Sep. 8, 1997 / Mute ♦♦
The legion of differently minded artists that have been inspired by Einstürzende Neubauten makes for an intriguing remix album, based on the group's 1996 record, *Ende Neu*. Spanning Jon Spencer, Pan sonic, Barry Adamson, Techno Animal, Thomas Fehlmann, Panacea, Kreidler, and Alec Empire, this cast of remixers show themselves to be perhaps a bit too reverent to original material, though Panacea deconstructs the title track in a blaze of post-industrial hardcore. —*John Bush*

**Silence Is Sexy** / May 23, 2000 / Mute ♦♦♦♦
Odds are *no one* banked on Einstürzende Neubauten lasting 20 years—not even Blixa Bargeld's gran. What were the odds of such a destructive band surviving that long? Did the Stooges ever stand a chance of writing a song called "1989"? Not likely. How about the Sex Pistols making album ten, let alone five? Not a chance. More importantly, who would have thought that the milestone year would see the release of one of Neubauten's best albums? After all, they appeared to be treading water after 1996's *Ende Neu*; die-hard fans were waning in number, a result of the group's apparent death march toward more awkwardly contemporary material. Though *Silence Is Sexy* might retain some of the band's recent song-based developments (unsavory to some), its closest touchstone is 1987's *Richterskala*. They might not be as unsettling as they were in their early days, but they still know how to mess things up.

"Sabrina" is one of the tracks that brings to mind their excellent album from 1987. Swaying strings and plaintive percussive taps frame Bargeld's whispers as he waxes like a bawdier Bryan Ferry: "It's not the red of the dying sun/The morning sheets' surprising stain/It's not the red of which we bleed." The boys take a couple smoke breaks during the following title track. Bargeld's drags are higher in the mix than Alexander Hacke's bassline. The closing chorus is provided by a crowd at a Mexican concert. The next three tracks are spit out so quickly that they nearly trip over each other in succession.

Bargeld puts his science/philosophy/Mr. Wizard cap on a couple times, most unfortunately when he gives his view on the perception of beauty on "Beauty." Without the verbal subject matter, the title is still fitting; Hacke, Bargeld, and Rudi Moser cook up a beautiful atmospheric track that isn't nearly as enjoyable due to Bargeld's spiel.

As with *Richterskala*, restraint is a key element. Bargeld doesn't *really* let his vocal chords rip until the 12th track, "Redukt," and their trademark clangorous overload isn't struck upon very often. Those who reveled in Neubauten's undead bass sound will find the record goes down a treat, too. At nearly 70 minutes, it's a bit sprawling, but it allows the gang to represent every element that has made them vital and influential to experimental music throughout the last two decades. Irregardless of your pickiness with Neubauten's material—what you like/hate about them—anyone could piece together 40 minutes of the record for an ace -Cliff's Notes version. It's going to be difficult for Neubauten to top this monster. (Early editions came with a second disc, consisting solely of the 19-minute long "Pelikanol." A scraping, hypnotic track, Bargeld uses his voice as a drone instrument to great effect.) —*Andy Kellman*

## Elecktroids

f. 1995
*Group / Neo-Electro, Electro*

A one-off, Warp-released side-project that nobody seems willing to go on record about, mysterious electro outfit Elecktroids have been rumored to be the work of everyone from Detroit underground legends Drexciya to Mark Bell of Manchester bleep popularizers LFO. Whatever the case, Elecktroids are a well-produced, if vaguely tongue-in-cheek, outfit combining elements of contemporary "listening techno" with early Detroit electro influences and obviously Kraftwerk-derived themes of technological aggrandizement. The group released the *Kilohertz* EP in 1995, at the crest of a putative "electro revival" launched by UK label Clear; *Elektroworld*, the group's only full-length to date, followed shortly after. Despite apparently came-and-went release status, Elecktroids have enjoyed a somewhat enduring popularity, making it onto two different Warp "best of" compilations as well as contributing two tracks to popular electro mix session *X-Mix: Electro Boogie*, put together by techno producer/DJ Dave Clarke and released by the K7 label in 1997. —*Sean Cooper*

● **Elektroworld** / 1995 / Warp ♦♦♦♦
An enduring throw-up of the 1995 electro revival launched by labels such as Clear, Pharma, and Rephlex, *Elektroworld* is a slickly produced, if mostly in-the-pocket collection of Kraftwerk-inspired electro. Although a retro vibe predominates, included among *Elektroworld*'s more obviously cheek-tonguing cuts are "Floatation" and "Perpetual Motion," which rate among the best from new-styled electro artists such as Drexciya and Plaid. —*Sean Cooper*

## Electric Company

f. 1995, Los Angeles, CA
*Group / Noise Pop, Ambient Pop, Dream Pop, Indie Rock, Shoegazing, Experimental, Alternative Pop/Rock*

The recordings of Electric Company are the end result of indie-rock figurehead Brad Laner's relentless experimentation within a range of post-punk styles, from avant-garde rock to thrash to alternative pop to electronica. His work as Electric Company is nominally based within electronica, though it's more of a studio hybrid embracing guitar-rawk, drum'n'bass and noise. A long-time fan of experimental/improv artists from Beefheart to Throbbing Gristle to the Residents, Laner founded his first band Debt of Nature at the age of 14. The group recorded several tracks for New Alliance in 1982 and opened for Sonic Youth and the Swans in 1986 before Laner founded another group, Steaming Coils, which released three albums of their own. He also played with seminal Los Angeles trance-rockers Savage Republic before forming his most famous group, Medicine, in 1991.

The first American band signed to Britain's super-indie Creation Records, Medicine earned praise from alternative critics for their extreme interpretation of My Bloody Valentine's noise-pop revolution. The group's first album *Shot Forth Self Living* was issued on Creation scant months after their formation, and distributed in the States via Def American. Two albums followed before Medicine broke up in 1995, the year of Laner's solo debut as Electric Company, *A Pert Cyclic Omen*. Though Laner's other major post-Medicine project Amnesia recorded albums in 1997 and 1998, he returned with two more Electric Company records, *Studio City* for Island and *Omakase* for Vinyl Communications. In addition, Laner has collaborated with members of sympathetic groups Mercury Rev and the Vas Deferens Organization, and recorded as part of the neo-prog band Lusk. —*John Bush*

**A Pert Cyclic Omen** / Aug. 8, 1995 / Warner Brothers ♦♦♦♦
Brad Laner was certainly a busy guy in the mid-nineties—there was Medicine, his primary project, but he also had his hand in a vast number of side-projects. Electric Company is, of course, one of these, and it falls on the more abstract end of Laner's work—*A Pert Cyclic Omen* lays out atmospheric loops and noisy drones that simply drift peacefully on to their conclusions. This could be rightly viewed as a slightly monochromatic proposition (and the fact that each song's title is an anagram of "Electric Company" only

heightens the lack of distinction between them), but Laner does lend some variety to his selections—"P.A. Intercom Cycle" has a stormy ambience, "Polymeric Accent" lays out a steady and very noticeable loop, "A Pert Cyclic Omen" has a vaguely tribal feel, and "Electro Amp Cycle" turns into something like a deconstructed samba. The album may not appeal to fans of Laner's more pop-oriented projects, but it's an appealing and surprisingly listenable endeavor nonetheless. —*Nitsuh Abebe*

**Electric Company Plays Amnesia** / 1997 / Supreme/Island ♦♦♦♦
Released only as a limited-edition extra disc with the first run of Amnesia's *Cherry Flavor Night Time*, this is, indeed, simply Laner remixing his band, but doing so in such a radical fashion that it's far more appropriate to term it an Electric Company release in full. Taking each track from the original album in order and revamping it completely, *Plays* succeeds so well that it makes one hope that other artists would engage in similar moves. The original songs, with their dreamy post-shoegaze crunch, turn into aggressive, abstract compositions in Laner's hands, as the opening number "Suzurro" makes clear. Drum loops are started, stopped, reintroduced, distorted, and cut short, as are guitar blasts, bass rumbles, and all sorts of hard-to-determine sounds. Tempos constantly shift, while anything close to hummable rapidly gets chucked. The similarities *A Pert Cyclic Omen* had to Main's frosty sense of creeping doom are retained here, but the other line of descent would have to be the Bomb Squad at their most "out-there" (the massive hip-hop beats plus the "everything on top of everything else" approach never fails in the right hands). Where things remain somewhat straightforward, as in the charging pulse and rumble of "Stay Away," these adaptations are still millions of miles away from the originals. Among the strongest numbers are "The Unlikely Faucet," where a barely there rhythm and static-laden crackling combines with a series of extreme feedback shimmers, and "External," where various ominous background drones mix with sudden interjections of audio vérité noise (barking dogs, airplane engines, etc.). Ending with an unlisted bonus track of a woman talking about her discovery of a hermaphrodite infant while babysitting—accompanied by yet another strange rhythm and more cut-up vocal samples—*Plays* is challenging and fascinating listening. —*Ned Raggett*

● **Studio City** / Mar. 10, 1998 / PolyGram Island ♦♦♦♦
Make no mistake—*Studio City* is an apt title for Brad Laner's second album of rhythm-and-noise experimentation as Electric Company. After a period ensconced in his own little electro laboratory, Laner returns with a set of tracks poised to turn the relatively harmless (by 1999) jungle breakbeat on its head. Measuring once and triggering twice for his collection of rhythm samples, Laner concocts a set of off-kilter rhythms for each track that never quite settles into a predictable rhythm. The deep bass and queasy effects of "Throb Ear" or the percussion detritus of "Darken an' Glubbering" prove Laner's much more concerned with musical experimentation than consistent music. Virtually all of the tracks are solo creations, though the keyboards of Ken Gibson do appear on three tracks. —*John Bush*

**Omakase** / Apr. 13, 1999 / Vinyl Communications ♦♦♦♦
After getting major-label commitments out of the way with 1998's *Studio City*, Brad Laner returned one year later with an album for Vinyl Communications, Southern California's premiere home for avant-garde electronics (courtesy of recordings by Lesser and Kid-606). Of course, his last record was hardly crossover material, and *Omakase* sows much of the same ground. There's a bit less focus on the beat here, and a few tracks reminiscent of electronica heroes like Mouse on Mars. Also, at least according to the song titles (including "A Cereal Syria," "Minidisco," and "Randy Alien"), Laner appears to have bitten by Vinyl Comm's humor bug. —*John Bush*

## Electric Skychurch

f. 1993, Los Angeles, CA
*Group / Electronica, Ambient Techno*
Los Angeles-based ambient techno mystics Electric Skychurch comprised composer and producer James Lumb, vocalist Roxanne Morganstern, and percussionist Alex Spurkel. Formed in 1993, the trio began attracting notice through their performances on the L.A. underground dance scene, often appearing at the Full Moon Gathering raves. The first Electric Skychurch single, "Creation," appeared in early 1994, followed a year later by the LP *Knowoneness*, a record notable for its use of live instruments—strings, didgeridoos, pianos, bongos—in tandem with antique analog synths. The atmospheric *Together* EP followed in 1996. —*Jason Ankeny*

● **Knowoneness** / Jul. 18, 1995 / Moonshine ♦♦
An album uniting organic, analog, and digital elements into a collection of visionary soundscapes, *Knowoneness* sweeps from ethno-ambience to sequencer trance to deep ambient dub. The trippy (some would say dippy) vocals on tracks like "Radiate" veer close to relegating *Knowoneness* into overly mystical Deep Forest/Enigma territory. —*John Bush*

## The Electrifying Mojo

b. Little Rock, AR
*DJ / Detroit Techno, Club/Dance*
The sparks that fired the great conflagration of techno in Detroit were in no small part provided by the Electrifying Mojo, a late-'70s and early-'80s DJ who made it his occupation to "save Detroit and the world from the musical blahs." Born and raised in Little Rock, Arkansas, he joined the Air Force and began to DJ at his base in the Philippines. When he returned to the US, Mojo worked a few years in radio before deciding to enter law school at the University of Michigan. He worked as a college DJ, amazing audiences with an incredibly broad range of genres and artists. After college, he moved to Detroit and began to apply the same techniques to his off-hours shift on a local radio station, encompassing the Clash, Prince, the B-52s, Madonna, Kraftwerk, and Depeche Mode. Techno pioneers Juan Atkins and Derrick May (among many others) listened and were introduced to a broad range of music, from punk to electronic pop. The pair began working for Mojo, producing lengthy mixes that then appeared on the show. While both Atkins and May moved on to record during the late '80s, the Electrifying Mojo continued to DJ, occasionally shuffling between different radio stations. —*John Bush*

## Electronic

f. 1989, Manchester, England
*Group / Indie Pop, Chamber Pop, Dream Pop, Alternative Dance, Indie Rock, Brit-pop, Alternative Pop/Rock*
One of the first supergroups from post-punk Great Britain, Electronic is the on-off project formed by New Order's Bernard Sumner and Johnny Marr, former guitarist of the Smiths. The duo released "Getting Away with It" in December 1989, with both Sumner and Neil Tennant of the Pet Shop Boys on vocals. The single just missed the Top Ten in England, but was the end of Electronic for over two years; Sumner and Tennant returned to their respective groups while Marr played on albums by The The and Billy Bragg.

Electronic's sophomore single "Get the Message" finally appeared in April 1991, and an eponymous debut album followed in June. The non-album single "Disappointed" was released just over a year later. Sumner then returned to New Order to record their sixth album *Republic*, while Marr returned to his sideman role with The The and the Pretenders. The duo reunited to record again—this time with help from former Kraftwerk member Karl Bartos—and released *Raise the Pressure* in July 1996. Newly signed to the Koch label, Electronic issued their third full-length *Twisted Tenderness* four years later. —*John Bush*

● **Electronic** / May 28, 1991 / Warner Brothers ♦♦♦♦
Electronic's debut album fuses Marr's impeccable riff-oriented songwriting, Sumner's yearning vocals, and mid-tempo post-acid-house beats not quite as hard-hitting as New Order's recent *Technique* LP. The singles "Getting Away With It" (with the Pet Shop Boys' Chris Lowe and Neil Tennant), "Feel Every Beat," and "Get the Message" are solid pop songs just as sublimely infectious as the best of New Order. The only misstep is "Feel Every Beat," a lightweight rap featuring none other than Sumner on vocals. —*John Bush*

**Raise the Pressure** / Jul. 9, 1996 / Warner Brothers ♦♦♦
Electronic began as a side project for New Order's Bernard Sumner and the Smiths' Johnny Marr, dabbling in the sort of '80s synth-pop pioneered by the former's band. *Raise the Pressure* is not so firmly planted in that genre—there's still a good deal of retro electronica, but Marr brings in more guitar work, making the album more of a straight-ahead pop affair. Some of the songs are Brit-pop at its finest ("Forbidden City," "For You"), and others hint at New Order's *oeuvre* ("Dark Angel")—some engage in a more danceable pop style reminiscent of the Pet Shop Boys. Solid writing and a few new tricks keep it from becoming an exercise in mid-'80s English nostalgia. —*Nitsuh Abebe*

### Electronic Eye (Richard H. Kirk)

*Producer / Ambient Techno, Ambient Dub*

Former Cabaret Voltaire member Richard H. Kirk is widely regarded as contemporary techno's busiest man, a distinction he's picked up through a release schedule that keeps discographers sweating and diehard fans near bankruptcy. No doubt, that work ethic developed during Kirk's time with CV, who, in their nearly 20 years together, released as many albums and even more EPs. Kirk's not far behind as a solo artist, splitting just over half that total between his three ongoing projects—Sandoz, Electronic Eye, and works released under his own name—as well as collaborations with British DJ Parrot (as Sweet Exorcist) and heaps of singles and EPs. While the Sheffield-based Cabaret Voltaire began as an electronics-and-tape-loops outfit with obvious ties to other English post-industrial experimentalists like Throbbing Gristle, Einsturzende Neubauten, and Chrome, the group eventually penetrated a pop-group context while retaining the edge of dystopia and isolation at the core of their earlier work. Kirk's solo work has evolved along similar lines, although he works more toward integrating technology with more humanitarian concerns. His stylistic palette—mostly house, early techno, and ambient—and the inclusion of tracks on compilations released by the Warp label have pegged Kirk as an evangelist of "intelligent techno," but his solo work actually comes off closer to sample-heavy ambient house and techno. His affection for African and tribal percussion and thematics connect his various works in obvious ways, and many of his albums have been reissued domestically. [See Also: Richard H. Kirk, Sandoz] —*Sean Cooper*

- **The Idea of Justice** / 1995 / Beyond ✦✦✦✦
Still more funky, sampledelic ethno-techno from Kirk, with Parliament-style guitars sitting next to South American hand drums and electronic beats. —*Sean Cooper*

### Elektric Music

f. 1992, Düsseldorf, Germany

*Group / Club/Dance, Alternative Pop/Rock, Dance-Pop*

Though Kraftwerk released little during the '90s, one of its former members, Karl Bartos, produced some very Kraftwerk-esque synth-pop during the decade as Elektric Music. He wasn't an original member of the pioneering German electronic group (Florian Schneider and Ralf Hütter were the core duo), but Bartos played on Kraftwerk records from 1975's *Radio-Activity* until 1986's *Electric Cafe*. He left soon after, and though Kraftwerk produced no more music during the late '80s or '90s, Bartos formed his own project named Elektric Music, debuting with the 1992 single "Crosstalk." One year later, first album *Esperanto* included work by OMD's Andy McCluskey. Bartos collaborated with Bernard Sumner and Johnny Marr in the super-group Electronic during 1996-97, then released his next album *Electric Music*, a much more pop-oriented project than expected. —*John Bush*

- **Esperanto** / Jun. 7, 1994 / Atlantic ✦✦✦
The Kraftwerk comparisons would be unmissable even without the obvious connections, though *Esperanto* updates the sound with deeper grooves and a little bit of techno-funk. The lyrical concerns for guest Andy McCluskey are also taken straight from Kraftwerk 101—witness song titles like "TV," "Crosstalk," and "Kissing the Machine" (the latter a musical ringer for prime *Pacific Age*-era OMD). —*John Bush*

- **Electric Music** / Aug. 25, 1998 / East West ✦✦✦
Quite similar to the second album released by the Sumner/Marr project Electronic, Bartos' own second album jettisons much of the electronic influences in favor of breezy guitar-pop indebted to New Order and Pet Shop Boys. Though the opener "Young Urban Professional" has much of the Kraftwerk sound (complete with vocoder), succeeding tracks rely on straightahead alternative pop. The results are surprisingly solid, especially for fans of New Order following Bartos after his work in Electronic. He even contributes his own vocals (with the same impassive emotion of Sumner himself) to tracks like "Sunshine" and "Call on Me." —*John Bush*

### Elementz of Noise

f. 1995, London, England

*Group / Jungle/Drum'N'Bass, Club/Dance*

One of the more dynamic duos in jungle's techstep movement, Alan Clark and Justin Maughan recorded a non-stop barrage of singles for labels such as S.O.U.R., Emotif, Smokers Inc., Mind Switch, and Elements of Sound. Clark, who had begun working as a soul/funk DJ in the early '80s, moved on to production in Britain's heavy rave scene by the end of the decade. He recorded with several bands including the hardcore techno act PSI Division, and became friends with Justin Maughan, another member of PSI Division with whom he worked at the record store Bass Generator.

After parting ways with the group, the duo began recording and DJing together. After meeting with Dave Stone, co-owner of S.O.U.R. Records (Sound of the Underground), Elementz of Noise was born. From the S.O.U.R. sub-label Emotif came singles like "Astral," "Neon," "Sights and Sounds," and "Psyche," plus tracks for seminal S.O.U.R./Emotif compilations *Tech Steppin'* and *Shapeshifter: A Jazzstep Injection*. —*John Bush*

**Chillin' on Tha Funk [Single]** / Oct. 7, 1996 / S.O.U.R. ✦✦

**Mephisto/Torch [Single]** / Jul. 21, 1997 / Smokers Inc. ✦✦✦✦

- **The Remixes: Neon/D4 Toxic Waste [Single]** / Nov. 23, 1998 / Emotif ✦✦✦✦
Two sides of tearing tech-step, *The Remixes* features a Ray Keith remix of "Neon" while the flip has an Elementz of Noise remix of Keith's "D4 Toxic Waste." —*Keith Farley*

### Paul Elstak

*Producer / Gabba, Hardcore Techno, Club/Dance*

Paul Elstak was the crown prince of Dutch gabba, the variant of hardcore techno that consistently sought the darkest, fastest electronic dance music possible in a post-apocalyptic nihilistic frenzy. Though the Rotterdam producer was later reviled by many of his hardcore brethren because of his surprising chart leanings, his 1992 single "Where the Fuck Is Amsterdam?" by Euromasters practically created the gabba style. Later singles like "Rotterdam" and "The Nightmare Continues" were also popular on the emerging scene but by 1995, Elstak had pulled back from the dark side. Instead, he followed a more light-hearted hi-NRG style—prepared with help from the Dutch production crew the Klubbheads—that resulted in a series of Top Ten Dutch pop hits including "Life Is Like a Dance," "Luv U More" (a cover of the Sunscreem hit), "Don't Leave Me Alone," and "Rave On." His first full-length *May the Forze Be with You* appeared in 1996. —*John Bush*

- **May the Forze Be with You** / Nov. 25, 1996 / Bluemusic ✦✦
Elstak's 1996 LP makes no mention of his dark past, focusing instead on "happy" hits like "Life Is Like a Dance," "Don't Leave Me Alone," and "Luv U More." The album even comes in separate versions for fans of pop or hardcore, but neither approach the menace of his pre-1995 work—which is best found on period compilations. —*John Bush*

### Emergency Broadcast Network

f. 1990

*Group / Experimental Techno, Electronica*

More of a multi-media organization than a band, Emergency Broadcast Network construct video pastiches much as techno artists use samplers to create audio effects. Josh Pearson (Public Relations Programmer) and Gardner Post (Systems Manager) met at the Rhode Island School of Design in the early '80s and began to experiment with video samples, adding DJ Ron O'Donnell in 1990. Packing a Chevy truck with all their gear, the trio followed the 1991 Lollapalooza tour around America, broadcasting soundtracked videos to somewhat confused concertgoers. The band's first release, in the form of a video (*Commercial Entertainment Product*) and an audio CD (*Behavior Modification*), appeared in 1992 on TVT. EBN gained a huge audience later that year when U2 used one song as an opening for their Zoo TV tour. In 1995, the trio released their second album, but also spent time producing videos for the likes of Coldcut and other electronica favorites. —*John Bush*

- **Telecommunication Breakdown** / 1995 / TVT ✦✦✦
Audio terrorists Emergency Broadcast Network make much better video directors than producers; on their debut, an assortment of sub-minute-long tracks (most chock full of nonstop political and social commentary) conspire to create a difficult listen. The single "Electronic Behavior Control System" is a highlight, and there are several other fine moments, but they're often difficult to find. —*John Bush*

## Alec Empire

b. May 2, 1972, Berlin, Germany
*Producer / Experimental Techno, Electronica, Ambient Techno, Hardcore Techno, IDM*

The founder of Berlin's Digital Hardcore Recordings, Alec Empire created some of the most musically diverse works of the '90s, recording both as himself and with the trio Atari Teenage Riot. Empire was often identified with (and pigeon-holed for) his ATR productions—lo-fi breakbeats played at the speed of thrash which simultaneously embraced the energy of punk, the uncompromising ferocity of industrial music, and the futurism of techno. On his solo albums, however, Empire ranged through isolationist ambient, electro, breakbeat, hard techno, even twisted lounge music. As such, he gained fans in several fields while recording for the German experimental/electronic label Mille Plateaux. Still, his first American exposure came when the Beastie Boys' Grand Royal Records signed Atari Teenage Riot in 1996.

Born on May 2, 1972, in West Berlin, Alec Empire was early influenced by rap and the breakdancing scene. Later he began listening to early punk, and played in several bands during the late '80s. By the turn of the decade, Empire became fascinated by the sound of acid and techno, though he detested the drug culture inherent to raves. He began recording EPs for Force Inc—as well as its subsidiary Mille Plateaux—and formed Atari Teenage Riot in 1992, with Carl Crack and Hanin Elias. A slightly more rock-oriented project, ATR nevertheless focused on the extreme: their political themes and screamed vocals were inspired by punk, but the music concentrated on acid synth and distorted breakbeats. After an Atari Teenage Riot deal with British Phonogram collapsed, Empire used the cash in hand from the Phonogram contract to found Digital Hardcore Recordings in 1994, releasing EPs that year by himself as well as EC8OR, DJ Bleed, and Sonic Subjunkies.

In 1995, Mille Plateaux released three Alec Empire albums: the compilation *Limited Editions 90-94*, his proper debut album *Generation Star Wars*, and *Low on Ice (The Iceland Sesssions)*. That same year, Atari Teenage Riot recorded *1995*, the first album to be released on Digital Hardcore. After two 1996 LPs, *Hypermodern Jazz 2000.5* and *Les Etoiles de Filles Mortes*, Empire issued his first album for Digital Hardcore, *The Destroyer*. Soon after, the DHR collective—including ATR and EC8OR—toured the States at the invitation of Grand Royal Records, the label operated by the Beastie Boys. Grand Royal began releasing 7" singles by Empire, ATR, and EC8OR at the end of 1996. Early the following year, many of Empire's albums were given US releases by his self-formed Geist Records, and Atari Teenage Riot released its American debut *Burn Berlin Burn*. [See Also: Atari Teenage Riot] —*John Bush*

**Low on Ice (The Iceland Sesssions)** / Mar. 1995 / Mille Plateaux ✦✦✦✦
One of Alec Empire's few consistent LPs, *Low on Ice (The Iceland Sessions)* presents a series of polar soundscapes, isolationist in form and quite dubby in execution. Even though the beats often grow caustic, the vibes are chilled and quite similar to much ambient music. —*John Bush*

**Generation Star Wars** / Jun. 1995 / Mille Plateaux ✦✦✦
The first Alec Empire album to alternate the hardest hardcore breakbeats with more free-form ambient and environmental passages, *Generation Star Wars* is a brutal but often engaging listen, sampling drug talk and, bizarrely, Marv Albert's broadcast of a New York Knicks game for several minutes. Moving from extreme to extreme doesn't make for a nicely flowing album, but *Generation Star Wars* often packs a punch. —*John Bush*

**Limited Editions 1990-1994** / Sep. 1995 / Mille Plateaux ✦✦✦
Presenting selected tracks of Empire's earliest recordings, *Limited Editions* includes British white-labels and recordings from the French TNI label, as well as early-'90s singles for Force Inc, like the 1992 EP *SuEcide 1-3*. Most tracks lie much closer to early hardcore techno than his later solo output, though his work with Atari Teenage Riot is forecasted on several tracks. —*John Bush*

● **The Destroyer** / 1996 / Digital Hardcore ✦✦✦✦
The first Alec Empire album actually released on Digital Hardcore, *The Destroyer* is a festival of hardcore breakbeats in line with most of *Generation Star Wars* and his productions for Atari Teenage Riot. —*John Bush*

**Hypermodern Jazz 2000.5** / 1996 / Mille Plateaux ✦✦✦✦
For *Hypermodern Jazz 2000.5*, Empire varied the beats but rarely invoked the extreme tempo changes which characterized other material. The result is an interesting fusion of techno and jazz, often touching on electro, downtempo breakbeat and acid. "God Told Me How to Kiss" and "Unknown Stepdancer" are two highlights. —*John Bush*

**Les...toiles des Filles Mortes** / Dec. 2, 1996 / Mille Plateaux ✦✦✦
Empire's second album of 1996, *Les...toiles de Filles Mortes* is a collection of completely beatless tonal soundscapes with minimal changes. It's a difficult album, more similar to tectonic plate shifts than the earthquake shuddering of his industrial breakbeat work. On the whole, though the music isn't representative, it succeeds better than his other, more scattered, solo recordings. —*John Bush*

**The Geist of Alec Empire** / Oct. 20, 1997 / Geist ✦✦✦✦
A three-disc set collecting material from the five LPs recorded for Mille Plateaux between 1990 and 1996, *The Geist of Alec Empire* is an efficient distillation of the tremendously varied work Empire has done; from the faux easy-listening *Hypermodern Jazz 2000.5* and the disturbed glacial fluctuations of *Low on Ice*, to the distorto-breakbeats on *The Destroyer* and *Generation Star Wars*. All in all, it's a fabulous collection that works much better than Empire's often schizophrenic solo albums. —*John Bush*

**The Curse of the Golden Vampire** / Jun. 15, 1998 / Digital Hardcore ✦✦
Though both acts have little trouble producing excellent work on their own, the collaboration between Empire and Techno Animal comes off as a distinct disappointment. *The Curse of the Golden Vampire* takes each act's trademark—industrial breakbeats and darkside dub soundscapes, respectively—and merely blends them together, resulting in a project which sounds as though separate studios were used for recording. Fans of either Empire or Techno Animal will obviously enjoy the sound, but few promises are actually delivered. —*John Bush*

## Empirion

f. 1993, Essex, England
*Group / Club/Dance, Techno*

Debuting with the acid-trance rocker "Narcotic Influence," which was voted one of the 100 greatest dance singles of all time by no lesser an authority than *Mixmag*, Empirion formed in 1993 at an Essex club featuring resident DJ Jamie Smart. Smart, who had spent time bumming around with the Prodigy's Liam Howlett (the two both worked at a car wash), met up with reformed industrialist Bob Glennie, and rock 'n' roller Oz, and the trio soon formed Wanted Records, recording "Narcotic Influence" in just two days. Unlike the Prodigy, however, Smart, Glennie and Oz all take an equal part in recording and running the label. Later singles "Quark" and "Ciao" furthered the band's reputation as forward-thinking dance hooligans, and Smart's DJ sets at Prodigy shows also increased their fame until Beggars Banquet signed the trio to a major-label contract. The debut album *Advanced Technology* was released in early 1997. —*John Bush*

● **Advanced Technology** / Apr. 8, 1997 / Beggars Banquet ✦✦✦✦
A surprisingly straight-ahead debut for such a hyped group in the midst of genre-bending from every side, *Advanced Technology* includes nods to previous Empirion material like "Narcotic Influence" and "Quark," as well as the more mellow sounds for the final track, the epic "New Religion." —*John Bush*

## Endemic Void (Danny Koffey)

*Producer / Jungle/Drum'N'Bass, Club/Dance*

Easy-chair jungle outfit Endemic Void have carried out one of the more successful fusions of jazz, dub, and spacy ambient atmospherics in a drum'n'bass context. The one-man project of dance music producer Danny Koffey (previously known for his work with more straightforward acid house and techno outfits Slipstream and Strictly Rockers), Endemic Void began as a side-project deviation from the rigid demands of those groups, although the project's popularity quickly transformed it to full-time status. Signing with ex-Moody Boyz Tony Thorpe's Language label in 1995, Endemic Void released a 12" and the debut *Equations* LP in 1996, which earned instant praise as some of the most listenable examples of drum'n'bass to still maintain a hard, innovative edge. Remixes for artists such as Meat Beat Manifesto and the Swedish Dot label's Quant followed, with Reinforced's Shogun and No-U-Turn's Nico Sykes in turn trying their hands at EV originals. EV tracks have also been featured on popular compilations such as *Breakbeat Science*. —*Sean Cooper*

● **Equations** / Nov. 4, 1996 / Language ✦✦✦✦
The spate of electronic jazz-fusion records of the early '70s provided well-known jungle producers from LTJ Bukem to Photek to Kid Loops with acres

of material from which to sample and crib their own atmospheres. Quite possibly the best of these "fusion fusions," *Equations* by Endemic Void wasn't given half the hype it deserved. Danny Koffey's Rhodes keys are tender and fragile in all the right places on the intros to "Lion Stone" and "Inner Daze," though they inevitably give way to a set of beefed-up basslines and stellar breaks programming practically unequalled in the field of living-room jungle. It's difficult to quibble with *Equations* at all, but if there's any problem here it's that all of the material is angled at the exact same spot in the hearts of fusion lovers—if that's your cup of tea, though, the album will sound irresistible throughout. —*John Bush*

## Enigma

f. 1990, Ibiza, Spain
*Group / Club/Dance, Ethnic Fusion*

With their 1991 hit "Sadeness," Enigma brought the new age fascination with Gregorian chants and old-world culture to the clubs; the resulting single was both unique and irresistible. The rest of the album followed that pattern successfully, although without quite matching the stunning success of the hit single. On their second album, 1994's *Cross of Changes*, some of the old-world elements remained, but the new age angle came to the forefront in a set of slick, radio-friendly dance-pop. *Enigma 3: Le Roi Est Mort, Vive Le Roi* followed in 1996. A side project, Trance Atlantic Airwaves, issued *The Energy of Sound* in 1998. The fourth Enigma record, *The Screen Behind the Mirror*, followed in early 2000. —*Stephen Thomas Erlewine*

- **MCMXC A.D.** / 1990 / Charisma ✦✦✦✦
Driven by the Gregorian chants of the hit single "Sadeness Part I," Enigma's debut album is an interesting fusion of new age sensibilities and dancefloor rhythms. —*Stephen Thomas Erlewine*

**The Cross of Changes** / Feb. 8, 1994 / Charisma ✦✦✦
*The Cross of Changes* casts a wider net than Enigma's debut, mysterious and pulsating, drawing on everything from Arabic signatures ("The Eyes of Truth") to native American chanting ("Silent Warrior"). Sultry, sensuous, and ethereal, live and sampled female vocals—both spoken and harmonic—make up Cretu's layered choir. Subtle trance and dance, washes of atmosphere, new age mysticism, and synthesized dramatics. —*Roch Parisien*

**Le Roi Est Mort, Vive Le Roi** / Nov. 26, 1996 / Virgin ✦✦✦
Enigma burst on the scene in the early '90s with a pretty nifty schtick: dance beats and lush chord washes underpinning such exotica as muttered French sex talk and Gregorian chant, all unified by a bizarre theme somehow related to the Marquis de Sade. The concept was never as original as some people thought (Mark Stewart's &Maffia had set plainchant to electrofunk as far back as 1984), but it worked nicely, and "Sadeness" (har har) was an international dance-club hit. Two albums later, Michael Cretu (the individual who records under the Enigma moniker) doesn't seem to have done much to expand upon his original ideas. The monks are still there, floating in a murky club mix, though this time they're joined by a cool Mongolian ensemble as well. Cretu is singing more, which is unfortunate since his voice is mediocre and his lyrics silly, but the occasional high point does emerge, such as the darkly lovely "The Child in Us." Most of the album, however, is twaddle. Song titles like "Morphing Thru Time," "Beyond the Invisible," and (I kid you not) "Odyssey of the Mind" will give you a good idea of what to expect—lots of atmosphere, lots of reverb, lots of sternly intoned lyrics about, er ... something or other. What's missing is musical interest. Overall, the cool packaging is the only thing noteworthy about this disappointing effort. —*Rick Anderson*

**The Screen Behind the Mirror** / Jan. 18, 2000 / Virgin ✦✦
Enigma's fourth album *The Screen Behind the Mirror* continues Michael Cretu's explorations into ambient new age, Gregorian chant, world music, and dance rhythms. Cretu's vocals play a more prominent role than on earlier Enigma albums, which, unfortunately, often detracts from the songs' other diverse elements—which include church bells, Middle Eastern and European choirs, sensuous female vocals, and a wide array of ethnic percussion and instruments. The album's pieces are mixed together continuously and are united thematically by samples and reinterpretations of Orff's "O Fortuna" and other material from *Carmina Burana*, giving songs like "Endless Quest," "The Gate," and "Smell of Desire" a flowing, cohesive feel. Though it doesn't reveal significant growth or change in Enigma's work, *The Screen Behind the Mirror* will please fans of the group's other atmospheric works. —*Heather Phares*

## Brian Eno (Brian St. Baptiste de la Salle Eno)

b. May 15, 1948, Woodbridge, Suffolk, England
*Vocals, Keyboards, Synthesizer, Producer, Composer, Arranger / Experimental, Glam Rock, Prog-Rock/Art Rock, Ambient, Electronic*

Ambient pioneer, glam-rocker, hit producer, multimedia artist, technological innovator, worldbeat proponent and self-described non-musician—over the course of his long, prolific and immensely influential career, Brian Eno was all of these things and much, much more. Determining his creative pathways with the aid of a deck of instructional, tarot-like cards called Oblique Strategies, Eno championed theory over practice, serendipity over forethought, and texture over craft; in the process, he forever altered the ways in which music is approached, composed, performed, and perceived, and everything from punk to techno to new age bears his unmistakable influence.

Brian Peter George St. John le Baptiste de la Salle Eno was born in Woodbridge, England on May 15, 1948. Raised in rural Suffolk, an area neighboring a US Air Force base, as a child he grew enamored of the "Martian music" of doo-wop and early rock 'n' roll broadcast on American Armed Forces radio; a subsequent tenure at art school introduced him to the work of contemporary composers John Tilbury and Cornelius Cardew, as well as minimalists John Cage, LaMonte Young, and Terry Riley. Instructed in the principles of conceptual painting and sound sculpture, Eno began experimenting with tape recorders, which he dubbed his first musical instrument, finding great inspiration in Steve Reich's tape orchestration "It's Gonna Rain."

After joining the avant-garde performance art troupe Merchant Taylor's Simultaneous Cabinet, as well as assuming vocal and "signals generator" duties with the improvisational rock unit Maxwell Demon, Eno joined Cardew's Scratch Orchestra in 1969, later enlisting as a clarinettist with the Portsmouth Sinfonia. In 1971 he rose to prominence as a member of the seminal glam band Roxy Music, playing the synthesizer and electronically treating the band's sound. A flamboyant enigma decked out in garish makeup, pastel feather boas and velvet corsets, his presence threatened the focal dominance of frontman Bryan Ferry, and relations between the two men became strained; finally, after just two LPs—1972's self-titled debut and 1973's brilliant *For Your Pleasure*—Eno exited Roxy's ranks to embark on a series of ambitious side projects.

The first, 1973's *No Pussyfooting*, was recorded with Robert Fripp; for the sessions Eno began developing a tape-delay system, dubbed "Frippertronics," which treated Fripp's guitar with looped delays in order to ultimately employ studio technology as a means of musical composition, thereby setting the stage for the later dominance of sampling in hip-hop and electronica. Eno soon turned to his first solo project, the frenzied and wildly experimental *Here Come the Warm Jets*, which reached the UK Top 30. During a brief tenure fronting the Winkies, he mounted a series of British live performances despite ill health; less than a week into the tour, Eno's lung collapsed, and he spent the early part of 1974 hospitalized.

Upon recovering, he traveled to San Francisco, where he stumbled upon the set of postcards depicting a Chinese revolutionary opera, which inspired 1974's *Taking Tiger Mountain (By Strategy)*, another sprawling, free-form collection of abstract pop. A 1975 car accident which left Eno bedridden for several months resulted in perhaps his most significant innovation, the creation of ambient music: unable to move to turn up his stereo to hear above the din of a rainstorm, he realized that music could assume the same properties as light or color, and blend thoroughly into its given atmosphere without upsetting the environmental balance. Heralded by the release of 1975's minimalist *Another Green World*, Eno plunged completely into ambient with his next instrumental effort, *Discreet Music*, the first chapter in a ten-volume series of experimental works issued on his own Obscure label.

After returning to pop structures for 1977's *Before and After Science*, Eno continued his ambient experimentation with *Music for Films*, a collection of fragmentary pieces created as soundtracks for imaginary motion pictures. Concurrently, he became a much-sought-after collaborator and producer, teaming with the German group Cluster as well as David Bowie, with whom he worked on the landmark trilogy *Low*, *"Heroes,"* and *Lodger*. Additionally, Eno produced the seminal No Wave compilation *No New York* and in 1978 began a long, fruitful union with Talking Heads, his involvement expanding over the course of the albums *More Songs About Buildings and Food* and 1979's *Fear of Music* to the point that by the time of 1980's world music-inspired *Remain in Light*, Eno and frontman David Byrne shared co-writing credits on all but one track. Friction with Byrne's bandmates hastened Eno's departure from the group's sphere, but in 1981 he and Byrne reunited for *My Life in the Bush of Ghosts*, a landmark effort which fused electronic music with a pioneering use of Third World percussion.

In the interim, Eno continued to perfect the concept of ambient sound with 1979's *Music for Airports*, a record designed to calm air passengers against fears of flying and the threat of crashes. In 1980, he embarked on collaborations with minimalist composer Harold Budd (*The Plateau of Mirror*) and avant-trumpeter Jon Hassell (*Possible Musics*) as well as Acadian producer Daniel Lanois, with whom Eno would emerge as one of the most commercially successful production teams of the '80s, helming a series of records for the Irish band U2 (most notably *The Joshua Tree* and *Achtung Baby*) which positioned the group as one of the world's most respected and popular acts. Amidst this flurry of activity, Eno remained dedicated to his solo work, moving from the earthbound ambience of 1982's *On Land* on to other worlds for 1983's *Apollo Atmospheres and Soundtracks*, a collection of space-themed work created in tandem with Lanois and Eno's brother Roger. In 1985, Eno resurfaced with *Thursday Afternoon*, the soundtrack to a VHS cassette of "video paintings" by artist Christine Alicino.

After Eno produced John Cale's 1989 solo effort *Words for the Dying*, the duo collaborated on 1990's *Wrong Way Up*, the first record in many years to feature Eno vocals. Two years later he returned with the solo projects *The Shutov Assembly* and *Nerve Net*, followed in 1993 by *Neroli; Glitterbug*, a 1994 soundtrack to a posthumously-released film by Derek Jarman, was subsequently reworked by Jah Wobble and issued in 1995 as *Spinner*. In addition to his musical endeavors, Eno also frequently ventured into other realms of media, beginning in 1980 with the vertical-format video *Mistaken Memories of Medieval Manhattan*; along with designing a 1989 art installation to help inaugurate a Shinto shrine in Japan and 1995's *Self-Storage*, a multimedia work created with Laurie Anderson, he also published a diary, 1996's *A Year with Swollen Appendices*, and formulated *Generative Music I*, a series of audio screen-savers for home computer software. In August of 1999, *Sonora Portraits*, a collection of Eno's previous ambient tracks and a 93-page companion booklet was published. —*Jason Ankeny*

**(No Pussyfooting)** / Nov. 1973 / EG ♦♦♦♦
At the same time Brian Eno was working on *Here Come the Warm Jets*, he was flexing his experimental muscle with this album of tape delay manipulation recorded with Robert Fripp. In a system later to be dubbed Frippertronics, Eno and Fripp set up two reel-to-reel tape decks that would allow audio elements to be added to a continuing tape loop, building up a dense layer of sound that slowly decayed as it turned around and around the deck's playback head. Fripp later soloed on top of this. *No Pussyfooting* represents the duo's initial experiments with this system, a side each. "Heavenly Music Corporation" demonstrates the beauty of the setup, with several guitar and synth elements building on top of each other, the music slowly evolving, and Fripp ending the piece with low dive-bombing feedback that swoops over the soundscape, bringing the piece to its conclusion. "Swastika Girls," on the other hand, shows how the system can be abused. With too many disconnected sounds sharing the space, some discordant, some melodic, the resulting work lacks form and structure. Eno and Fripp later refined the system on *Evening Star* and Eno's solo album *Discreet Music*. Fripp would take the system and base whole albums and live appearances around it (particularly *Let the Power Fall*). But it was here on *No Pussyfooting* where it all started. —*Ted Mills*

★ **Here Come the Warm Jets** / Jan. 1974 / EG ♦♦♦♦
Eno's solo debut, *Here Come the Warm Jets*, is a spirited, experimental collection of unabashed pop songs on which Eno mostly reprises his Roxy Music role as "sound manipulator," taking the lead vocals but leaving much of the instrumental work to various studio cohorts (including ex-Roxy mates Phil Manzanera and Andy Mackay, plus Robert Fripp and others). Eno's compositions are quirky, whimsical and catchy, his lyrics bizarre and often free-associative, with a decidedly dark bent in their humor ("Baby's On Fire," "Dead Finks Don't Talk"). Yet the album wouldn't sound nearly as manic as it does without Eno's wildly unpredictable sound processing; he coaxes otherworldly noises and textures from the treated guitars and keyboards, layering them in complex arrangements or bouncing them off one another in a weird cacophony. Avant-garde yet very accessible, *Here Come the Warm Jets* still sounds exciting, forward-looking and densely detailed, revealing more intricacies with every play. —*Steve Huey*

**Taking Tiger Mountain (By Strategy)** / Nov. 1974 / EG ♦♦♦♦
Continuing the twisted pop explorations of *Here Come the Warm Jets*, Eno's sophomore album, *Taking Tiger Mountain (By Strategy)*, is more subdued and cerebral, and a bit darker when he does cut loose, but it's no less thrilling once the music reveals itself. It's a loose concept album—often inscrutable, but still playful—about espionage, the Chinese Communist revolution, and dream associations, with the more stream-of-consciousness lyrics beginning to resemble the sorts of random connections made in dream states. Eno's richly layered arrangements juxtapose very different treated sounds, yet they blend and flow together perfectly, hinting at the directions his work would soon take with the seamless sound paintings of *Another Green World*. Although not quite as enthusiastic as *Here Come the Warm Jets*, *Taking Tiger Mountain* is made accessible through Eno's mastery of pop song structure, a form he would soon transcend and largely discard. —*Steve Huey*

☆ **Another Green World** / Nov. 1975 / EG ♦♦♦♦♦
A universally acknowledged masterpiece, *Another Green World* represents a departure from song structure and toward a more ethereal, minimalistic approach to sound. Despite the stripped-down arrangements, the album's sumptuous tone quality reflects Eno's growing virtuosity at handling the recording studio as an instrument in itself (a la Brian Wilson). There are a few pop songs scattered here and there ("St. Elmo's Fire," "I'll Come Running," "Golden Hours"), but most of the album consists of deliberately paced instrumentals which, while often closer to ambient music than pop, are both melodic and rhythmic; many, like "Sky Saw," "In Dark Trees," and "Little Fishes," are highly imagistic, like paintings done in sound which actually resemble their titles. Lyrics are infrequent, but when they do pop up, they follow the free-associative style of albums past; this time, though, the humor seems less bizarre than gently whimsical and addled, fitting perfectly into the dreamlike mood of the rest of the album. Most of *Another Green World* is like experiencing a soothing, dream-filled slumber while awake, and even if some of the pieces have dark or threatening qualities, the moments of unease are temporary, like a passing nightmare whose feeling lingers briefly upon waking but whose content is forgotten. Unlike some of his later, full-fledged ambient work, Eno's gift for melodicism and tight focus here keep the entirety of the album in the forefront of the listener's consciousness, making it the perfect introduction to his achievements even for those who find ambient music difficult to enjoy. —*Steve Huey*

**Discreet Music** / Dec. 1975 / EG ♦♦♦♦
Taking a cue from Satie's idea of "musique d'ameublement" (furniture music), music that just exists like furnishings in an apartment, played so as not to draw attention to itself (not really Muzak, a company which seeks to produce a more intentional work-product effect), Eno created several albums of what he termed "ambient music" which combined a softer style of pattern music (influenced by Bryars, Nyman, Harold Budd) with environmental noises. *Discreet Music* is probably the best of these, using an Oliveros-style "tape delay arrangement to slowly change patterns of repeating sounds. —*"Blue" Gene Tyranny*

**Evening Star** / 1976 / EG ♦♦♦♦
Robert Fripp's second team-up with Brian Eno was a less harsh, more varied affair, closer to Eno's then-developing idea of ambient music than what had come before in *No Pussyfooting*. The method used, once again, was the endless decaying tape loop system of Frippertronics but refined with pieces such as "Wind on Water" fading up into an already complex bed of layered synths and treated guitar over which Fripp plays long, languid solos. "Evening Star" is meditative and calm with gentle scales rocking to and fro while Fripp solos on top. "Wind on Wind" is Eno solo, an excerpt from the soon to be released *Discreet Music* album. The nearly 30-minute ending piece, "An Index of Metals," keeps *Evening Star* from being a purely background listen as the loops this time contain a series of guitar distortions layered to the nth degree, Frippertronics as pure dissonance. As a culmination of Fripp and Eno's experiments, *Evening Star* shows how far they could go. —*Ted Mills*

☆ **Before and After Science** / May 1978 / EG ♦♦♦♦♦
*Before and After Science* is really a study of "studio composition" whereby recordings are created by deconstruction and elimination: tracks are recorded and assembled in layers, then selectively subtracted one after another, resulting in a composition and sound quite unlike that at the beginning of the process. Despite the album's pop format (mostly three and four-minute songs), the sound achieved is unique and strays far from the mainstream. Eno also exper-

iments with his lyrics, choosing a sound-over-sense approach. When mixed with the music, these lyrics create a new sense or meaning, or the feeling of meaning, a concept inspired by abstract sound poet Kurt Schwitters and employed on many recordings by Eno. (This concept is epitomized on the track "Kurt's Rejoinder," on which we actually hear samples from Schwitters' "Ursonate.") *Before and After Science* opens with two bouncy, upbeat cuts—"No One Receiving," featuring the offbeat rhythm machine of Percy Jones and Phil Collins (Eno regulars during this period), and "Backwater." Jones' analog delay bass dominates on the following "Kurt's Rejoinder," and he and Collins return on the mysterious instrumental "Energy Fools the Magician." Robert Fripp solos over Phil Manzanera's rhythm on the rocking "King's Lead Hat," the Talking Heads being the subject of the lyrics (Eno had just begun to produce their albums at this time). The last five tracks on the CD (the entire second side of the album format) display a serenity unlike anything in the pop music field. These compositions take on an occasional pastoral quality, pensive and atmospheric. Cluster join Eno on the mood-evoking "By This River," but the album's apex is the final cut, "Spider and I". With its misty emotional intensity, the song seems at once sad yet hopeful, evoking images vague yet precise. The music on *Before and After Science* at times resembles *Another Green World* ("No One Receiving") and *Here Come the Warm Jets* ("King's Lead Hat") and ranks alongside both as the most essential Eno material. —*David Ross Smith*

### Music for Films / Oct. 1978 / EG ♦♦♦
Recorded intermittently between 1975 and 1978, *Music for Films* compiles moody, instrumental electronic pieces intended as soundtrack material for imaginary motion pictures; the songs are brief and fragmentary, ranging from the haunting "Sparrowfall" to the luminous, densely layered "Quartz." —*Jason Ankeny*

### ★ Ambient 1: Music for Airports / Mar. 1979 / EG ♦♦♦♦♦
Four subtle, slowly evolving pieces grace Eno's first conscious effort at creating ambient music. The composer was in part striving to create music that approximated the effect of visual art. Like a fine painting, these evolving soundscapes don't require constant involvement on the part of the listener. They can hang in the background and add to the atmosphere of the room, yet the music also rewards close attention with a sonic richness absent in standard types of background or easy-listening music. —*Linda Kohanov*

### Fourth World, Vol. 1: Possible Musics / 1980 / EG ♦♦♦
*Fourth World Vol. 1: Possible Musics* is a collaboration between the trumpeter Jon Hassell (who gets top billing) and synthesizer player Brian Eno. The "fourth world" seems to be located somewhere in the Sudan, if the album's cover picture is any indication. (That's in the middle of Africa, just south of Egypt, for you geography neophytes.) And the music consists of Hassell's haunting trumpet sounds, coupled with Eno's atmospheric synthesizer sounds and "treatments," playing over a variety of percussion instruments. Typical of both musicians, the music is slow and trance-like, and typical of Middle Eastern music, it has an odd, often wailing tonality that is, however, more otherworldly than, um, fourth-worldly. —*William Ruhlmann*

### ☆ My Life in the Bush of Ghosts / Feb. 1981 / Sire ♦♦♦♦♦
A pioneering work for countless styles connected to electronics, ambience and third-world music, *My Life in the Bush of Ghosts* expands on the fourth-world concepts of Hassell/Eno work with a whirlwind 45-minutes of world-beat/funk-rock (with the combined talents of several percussionists and bassists including Bill Laswell, Tim Wright, David van Tieghem, and Talking Heads' Chris Frantz) that's also heavy on the samples—from radio talk-show hosts, Lebanese mountain singers, preachers, exorcism ceremonies, Muslim chanting, and Egyptian pop, among others. It's also light years away from the respectful, preservationist angles of previous generations' field recorders and folksong gatherers. The songs on *My Life in the Bush of Ghosts* present myriad elements from around the world in the same jumbled stew, without regard for race, creed, or color. As such, it's a tremendously prescient record for the future development of music during the '80s and '90s. —*John Bush*

### Ambient 4: On Land / Apr. 1982 / EG ♦♦♦♦
Eno's most masterful ambient effort to date was created as a musical antidote to the confusion of life in New York City. An earthy sense of repose underlies intricate sonic essays. —*Linda Kohanov*

### Music for Films 2 / 1983 / EG ♦♦♦
Like its predecessor, *Music for Films, Vol. 2* collects more of Eno's scores for nonexistent motion pictures. —*Jason Ankeny*

### Apollo: Atmospheres & Soundtracks / 1983 / EG ♦♦♦♦
An exquisite experiment, *Apollo* takes Eno's spacescapes from albums like *Another Green World* and arranges them with some heavenly pedal steel guitar by Daniel Lanois. The recording engulfs the listener and captures the feel of space travel, weightlessness, and other sensations vividly. It's also perhaps Eno's warmest record ever. In the end, it comes off sounding not unlike a Grateful Dead experiment, with Lanois' lazy pedal steel sounding quite similar to Jerry Garcia's playing on David Crosby's "Laughing." An excellent nighttime vehicle. —*Matthew Greenwald*

### Begegnungen / 1984 / Gyroscope ♦♦♦♦
A prime compilation from the Eno/Cluster family, *Begegnungen* features previously released solo, duo, and trio recordings circa 1976-1984. These include pieces from various configurations of Eno, Moebius, Roedelius, Plank, and percussionist Mani Neumeier. The compositions are strong and inventive, and the music, an eclectic mix of progressive Kraut-rock and artistic, ambient electronica, is the best of its genre. All the material is synth-based and mostly upbeat, even bubbly at times, as in the jumpy "Nervos" (from Moebius' *Tonspuren*) and the quirky, rhythmic "Pitch Control" (from the exquisite *Zero Set*), which features electronic horse whinnies.

"Johanneslust" and "The Belldog" are highlights. From Roedelius' *Durch die Wuste*, the vibrant, reflective "Johanneslust" stands out with its acoustic guitar-like synthesizers and ambient landscape; and "The Belldog" (*After the Heat*), the only vocal track on the album, benefits from industrial overtones, musically and lyrically. Based in a warm, synthetic rhythm, "The Belldog" features beautifully mood evoking Eno vocals. And the song takes on an air of importance and sophistication with its epic quality. Honorable mention goes to Moebius' and Plank's "Two Oldtimers," a bright, almost playful composition from *Rastakraut Pasta*.

The album's cover photograph by Michael Weisser is one of several photos he created for Sky Records, including *Begegnungen II* and *Old Land*. *Begegnungen II* is an excellent follow-up, released the same year as the first. It contains different songs from *Begegnungen* but draws from most of the same album sources. And *Old Land*, strictly an Eno/Cluster compilation, contains all of the Eno/Cluster tracks found on the *Begegnungen* pair, plus more. —*David Ross Smith*

### Thursday Afternoon / 1985 / EG ♦♦♦
Eno's creative endeavors have recently shifted to sound-and-light installations, involving unconventional use of video monitors. This CD-only 1985 album was conceived as the soundtrack to one of his experimental videos, which, believe it or not, can be viewed properly only with the TV on its side. This uninterrupted 61-minute piece is probably the first recording created specifically to take advantage of the length of the CD format. Muted piano notes hang suspended in the air, while a soft monochordal synthesizer ambience slowly and subtly unfolds. Perhaps more than any other of his works, *Thursday Afternoon* epitomizes what Eno calls his "holographic" compositional style, where any brief section of the music is truly representative of the whole. The mood here is spacious and distinctly contemplative. —*Backroads Music/Heartbeats*

### Begegnungen II / 1985 / Gyroscope ♦♦♦
More offerings from Eno, Moebius, Roedelius, Plank, and Neumeier, *Begegnungen II* is the equivalent of its predecessor. The tracks on the compilation (recorded in 1976-1983) are an appealing mix of artsy electronic ambiance and progressive Kraut-rock. Eno's mechanical "Broken Head" stands out as the only vocal track—a dark, almost oppressive industrial tune not unlike early Gary Numan, but warmer. "Speed Display," originally recorded for Moebius, Plank, and Neumeier's *Zero Set*, is a fantastic showcase for Mani Neumeier's speed and endurance as a percussionist. He generates an incredible rhythmic groove, supplemented by sparkling synthesizer flourishes. Roedelius shines with two contributions to the set. His atmospheric "Mr. Livingstone," an Asian-influenced synth piece with complementary percussion, is pleasantly reminiscent of the opening to "The Colony of Slippermen" from Genesis' *Lamb Lies Down on Broadway*. Along similar lines, the warm colors of "Langer Atem" may have been inspired by Eno's more melodic ambient work, perhaps *Music for Films*. Elsewhere on the record, Moebius and Plank's "Conditionierer" scores as upbeat, quirky synth-rock. The well-crafted recordings on the *Begegnungen* albums are easily some of the most interesting compositions by all involved; the albums therefore serve as excellent introductions to the musicians' work. —*David Ross Smith*

**Wrong Way Up** / Oct. 1990 / Opal ♦♦♦♦
Both Eno and Cale have always flirted with conventional pop music throughout their careers, while reserving the right to go off on less accessible experiments, which means they've always held out the promise that they would make something as attractive as this synthesizer-dominated collection, on which Eno comes as close to the mainstream as he has since *Another Green World*, and Cale is as catchy as he's been since *Honi Soit*. The result is one of the best albums either one has ever made. —*William Ruhlmann*

**Nerve Net** / Sep. 1992 / Opal ♦♦
For the record, this was not Brian Eno's first attempt at rock 'n' roll. Not counting his time with Roxy Music (hardly rock 'n' roll, let's face it), he also made several solo albums in the '70s that were clearly intended as approaches to pop music—they were sideways approaches, of course, shaped by the intellectual distance he has always kept between himself and the music that arises from the forces that he puts into motion, and they were far from unqualified successes. Nor is this his first attempt at getting funky; that was *My Life in the Bush of Ghosts*, a deeply weird (but kind of fun) collaboration with head Talking Head David Byrne. But this is his most rocking solo album in years, and also his funkiest. That's not to say it's either funky or rock 'n' roll, but it does manage to be lots of fun in a slightly inhuman, claustrophobically funky sort of way. The list of participants includes several of the usual suspects (Robert Fripp, Robert Quine, Roger Eno), as well as a few surprises (Benmont Tench, John Paul Jones) and a raft of unknowns. The sound, which doesn't vary much from track to track, is compressed and dense, with lots of heavily treated and synthesized percussion. On "What Actually Happened," for example, drummer Richard Bailey plays a distinctly organic funk part through what sounds like a battery of effects, while a bassist and guitarist do indistinguishable things and Eno messes around with everything and throws in samples. "Juju Space Jazz" features both Quine and Fripp (the latter credited with "early '50s club guitar") as well as Eno playing such instruments as "African organ" and "tenor fax" (har har). Bailey is back funking things up on "Distributed Being," on which Fripp also plays a rather retiring solo. Overall, this album is quite fun but nothing to get too awfully excited about. —*Rick Anderson*

**The Shutov Assembly** / Oct. 1992 / Opal ♦♦♦
If *The Shutov Assembly* is reminiscent of Brian Eno's earlier "ambient" music projects dating back to *Discreet Music* (1975), it shouldn't be surprising. Recorded between 1985 and 1990, the atmospheric, slow-moving sound patterns are more, the artist contends, like paintings than music. *The Shutov Assembly*, dedicated to Russian painter Sergei Shutov, is, like the similar works in his catalog (he cites *Music for Films, On Land, Music for Airports, Thursday Afternoon*, and *Nerve Net*, as well as *Discreet Music*), as much a concept as a record. —*William Ruhlmann*

**Neroli** / Aug. 3, 1993 / Caroline ♦♦
Named after an oil derived from orange blossoms intended as an aid for clear thoughts, *Neroli* is subtitled "Thinking Music Part IV"; an hour-long electronic piece, it represents Eno at his most ambient, with no rhythmic pulse and only scattered hints of melody. —*Jason Ankeny*

**Eno Box II: Vocals** / Nov. 16, 1993 / Virgin ♦♦♦♦
The first of two retrospective box sets devoted to the groundbreaking work of Brian Eno, *Eno Box II* concentrates on his pop and vocal material, including some selections from the unreleased *My Squelchy Life*. Although his music still makes the most sense in the context of his albums, *Eno Box II* is solid crash-course introduction to his work, which remains as revolutionary today as it was when it was released. —*Stephen Thomas Erlewine*

**Headcandy** / 1994 / Ion ♦♦
*Headcandy* brings us back full circle to the trippy light shows of the psychedelic '60s. Featuring a 30-minute dose of pleasing ambient/techno instrumentation (accessible via audio CD player or CD-ROM) courtesy of Brian Eno, the visual effects are multiplied throughout a darkened room by the refractive glasses included with the disc, similar to those cheapie cardboard 3-D movie throw-aways. Unless you must own everything that the prolific Mr. Eno has ever recorded, *Headcandy* makes an interesting one-time curiosity piece only, about as enduring as black light art. However, this might be practical software for those kind of parties where everyone is equipped with the requisite eyewear and fueled with mind-altering substances. —*Roch Parisien*

**Eno Box I: Instrumentals** / Mar. 22, 1994 / Virgin ♦♦♦♦
This is one of the nicest box sets released in a while, from the outer box to the design of the accompanying booklet. The selection of tracks covers everything from Eno's earliest instrumental explorations through to an assortment of collaborations with artists such as David Bowie and Jon Hassell. This is a great set for owners of CD changers—the structure of these three discs allows a continuous performance in which the music develops over a period of almost four hours. Despite the ambient nature of some of the material, it's never boring. An excellent job. —*Steven McDonald*

**The Drop** / Jul. 7, 1997 / Thirsty Ear ♦♦
*The Drop* finds Brian Eno replicating the floating, trancy sound of *Neroli*, creating a shimmering collection of ambient music. Although *The Drop* illustrates that ambient doesn't all sound the same—it can be soothing and scary, sometimes both at once—the album doesn't particularly hold the listener's interest, as the shifting electronic soundscapes never reveal any substantial compositions. It's intriguing for a while, but by the time the 74 minutes of *The Drop* have finished, the album has made little lasting impression. —*Stephen Thomas Erewine*

## Eon (Ian Loveday)
*Producer / Trance, Club/Dance, Techno, Acid House*
Mostly the work of Ian Loveday, Eon was an early hit on the acid-house club scene with sountrack-sampling trance hits like "Spice," "Basket Case," and "Light Colour Sound." Loveday was an electronics fan from early on, beginning his recording career during the mid-'80s with a simple setup including only a drum machine and keyboard. His first proper Eon single, 1988's "Light Colour Sound," was pushed along by a close friend, Colin Faver, who played the track during his sets for the noted pirate station Kiss FM. Two singles from 1992, "Basket Case" and "Spice" (the latter sampled *Dune*), became proper club hits in America as well as Britain, and debut album *Void Dweller* was an early full-length success for the dance world.

Several tracks on the album had benefitted from collaborations, with Depth Charge's J Saul Kane and Peter "Baby" Ford (Loveday returned the favor with production for a track on Ford's *Bford9*). He also provided remixes for Bizarre Inc's *Energique* album, then branched out even farther with singles for Ford's Trelik Records (recorded as Minimal Man) and Kane's Electron Industries label. No LPs were forthcoming, but Loveday continued to record increasingly minimal, trance-inspired tracks. —*John Bush*

● **Void Dweller** / Sep. 8, 1992 / Columbia ♦♦♦
The sampladelic acid-house LP *Void Dweller* includes the two crucial Eon singles "Spice" and "Basket Case" as well as a few solid album tracks like "Fear: The Mind Killer" and "Final Warning." —*Keith Farley*

## Erasure
f. 1985, London, England
*Group / Alternative Dance, Club/Dance, Alternative Pop/Rock, House, Dance-Pop*
Following the disbandment of the short-lived synth-pop group Yazoo, former Depeche Mode member Vince Clarke formed Erasure in 1985 with singer Andy Bell. Like Yaz and Depeche Mode, Erasure was a synth-based group, but they had stronger dance inclinations, as well as a sharper, more accessible sense of pop songcraft, than either of Clarke's previous bands. Furthermore, Erasure had the flamboyantly eccentric Andy Bell—one of the first openly gay performers in pop music—as its focal point. Bell's keening, high voice and exaggerated sense of theatricality became the band's defining image. In their native Britain, Erasure was successful from their inception. After a few years, the duo achieved commercial success in America with 1988's "Chains of Love," but they remained, in essence, a cult band on both sides of the Atlantic, cultivating a dedicated fan base over the course of their career.

Before forming Erasure, Clarke was one of the founding members of the groundbreaking synth-pop outfit, Depeche Mode. He left after recording only one album with the group, choosing to form Yaz with Alison Moyet instead. After Yaz released two albums, Moyet left to pursue a solo career. Clarke participated in a short-lived alliance with vocalist Feargal Sharkey and producer Eric Radcliffe, called the Assembly, in 1984. Following a single with vocalist Paul Quinn, he decided to form Erasure. Clarke placed an advertisement for vocalists within a British music newspaper and received over 40 demo tapes, from which Andy Bell was selected as his partner.

Released in 1986, Erasure's first album, *Wonderland*, received poor reviews and weak sales upon its release. The duo quickly followed the album with "Sometimes," a preview from their forthcoming second album. "Sometimes" reached number two on the UK charts, beginning a string of successful singles that would run into the '90s. *The Circus,* the group's second album, was released in the spring of 1987 and peaked at number six on the UK charts. *The Innocents,* Erasure's third album, became their first number one album in Britain upon its release in 1988. The album featured the group's first American hit, "Chains of Love," which reached number 12 in the US; its follow-up, "A Little Respect," peaked at number 14 in America. At the end of 1988, Erasure released the *Crackers International* EP, which reached number two in Britain.

Erasure's fourth album, *Wild!,* appeared in 1989 and like its predecessor, it reached number one in the UK, as did its successor, 1991's *Chorus.* Erasure released the *Abba-Esque* EP, a tribute to the Swedish pop group ABBA, in 1992, it became their first number one single in the UK. Later that year, Erasure released a compilation of their British singles, *Pop! The First 20 Hits.* Two years later, the duo released its fifth album, *I Say I Say I Say,* which featured the hit single, "Always," their first American hit since 1988. Erasure's eponymous sixth album was released in the fall of 1995. It was followed in the spring of 1997 by *Cowboy. Loveboat* surfaced three years later. —*Stephen Thomas Erlewine*

**Wonderland** / May 1986 / Sire ♦♦♦♦
The duo's full debut was a sparkling collection of synth-pop tunes that made up in enthusiasm and immediate catchiness what it lacked in overall variety or any sense of artistic progression from Clarke's past. Though production, one of Flood's earliest high-profile efforts, is detailed and often lush, anyone who had followed Clarke's career wouldn't be surprised by anything on *Wonderland.* Soaring melody lines, hints of melancholia, dancefloor-oriented beats, it's all there. Bell's vocals merely tie the connections to the past further, his at times too shrill for comfort falsetto inevitably echoing Yaz' Alison Moyet as well as one-time Assembly vocalist Feargal Sharkey. Allowing for all these inevitable reminders, though, still means *Wonderland* is well worth a listen. The key reason is the smash UK single "Oh l'Amour," which rapidly became a staple for American modern rock stations as well. A lovely a cappella opening and instantly catchy hook, not to mention sprightly performances from Clarke and Bell both (the latter wisely undersings rather than pushing the flamboyance, letting loose more on the chorus), ensured its classic status. The two other singles, "Who Needs Love like That" and "Heavenly Action," aren't quite as strong but work in the general formula quite well regardless. Other album cuts are a touch more scattered in quality; nothing is awful, but there are some definite highlights. The slightly slower "Cry So Easy" has a great chorus, giving Bell a chance to show his chops, while "March on Down the Line" moves with a fine positive energy, an anthem without calling attention to itself as such. "Say What" is an interesting mostly instrumental, aside from a gang shout or two of the title, letting Clarke's compositional abilities come to the fore on their own. CD versions include remixes of "Who Needs Love like That" and "Oh l'Amour," the second being quite fine. —*Ned Raggett*

**The Circus** / Mar. 1987 / Sire ♦♦♦
Having gotten familiar with each other and the public on *Wonderland,* Clarke and Bell aim their sights higher with its follow-up, sometimes stumbling but otherwise making a more distinct all-around album while losing none of the key pop smarts that ensured the band's success. Flood once again mans the production boards, helping bring out Clarke's greater number of individual touches and approaches to great effect. It can be the queasy synth whoosh on "Don't Dance," the chunky pseudo-guitar blasts on lead track and single "It Doesn't Have to Be," or the funhouse keyboards on the title song, a cautionary environmental tale, all testaments to Clarke's ever-strengthening pushback of synth-pop's presumed sound and cliches. Bell in turn is finding more to do with his voice, his breathy crooning more seductive and affecting, while his high-volume calls to musical arms generally avoid hyper-ear-piercing levels in favor of general appeal. Exceptions do crop up, admittedly "Sexuality," which has a slightly clumsy chorus to begin with, and Bell's histrionics don't help it. But when the two members are on, they're on in a big way, and the two major hit singles from *The Circus* are prime examples of Erasure in excelsis. "Victim of Love" has Bell showing off some great soul chops right from the start over an inspiring, charging melody, while "Sometimes" contains a strong dance beat and Clarke's synth/acoustic guitar mix underscoring Bell's call for love. Elsewhere, the band's social conscience makes itself known without sounding obvious, especially on "Hideaway." Detailing the coming-out of a young man to his family and his resultant need to leave home, it makes its point with drama but not histrionics, Bell's multi-tracked chorus at once uplifting and empathetic. The CD version includes remixes of "Sometimes" and "It Doesn't Have to Be," along with a soft take by Clarke on Edvard Grieg's classical standby "In the Hall of the Mountain King." —*Ned Raggett*

**The Innocents** / Apr. 1988 / Sire ♦♦♦♦
Having built up a strong fan base and back catalogue in just a couple of years, Erasure turned into a full-blown pop phenomenon thanks to *The Innocents,* winning the British equivalent of the Grammy for album of the year and spawning a big American hit single, "Chains of Love." Accompanied by a video from Throbbing Gristle/Coil mastermind Peter Christopherson, the sassy, upbeat number, with fine backing vocals in part from early Soul II Soul singer Caron Wheeler, was a great calling card for the album as a whole. Stephen Hague took over as producer from Flood, perhaps smoothing out some points for a more general mainstream appeal but otherwise letting the strengths of the songs speak for themselves. It begins with another single and stone-cold classic, "A Little Respect," with a charging beat/acoustic guitar/synth arrangement and a flat-out fantastic performance from Bell, especially on the ascending chorus. Guest performances help flesh out a number of songs quite well. Wheeler and others reappear on "Yahoo!," a gospel-touched (musically and lyrically) number, while noted session performers the Kick Horns add just that to the "please come back" punch of "Heart of Stone." On their own, though, the duo continues in the same general vein of earlier releases while the Erasure formula of dance/synth/soul was now clearly established through and through; thankfully the combination of slight variety and overall performance prevents the album from dragging. *The Innocents'* ballads are perhaps a touch prettier than the lyrics would make them out to be, but if the sheen of songs like "Hallowed Ground" cuts away from the sometimes blunt images of poverty and hopelessness Bell calls up, the music still has a solid power. The CD version adds a fine original, "When I Needed You," and a fun cover of the Phil Spector/Ike and Tina Turner classic "River Deep, Mountain High." —*Ned Raggett*

**Crackers International [EP]** / Sep. 1988 / Sire ♦♦♦
This six-track EP helped bridge the gap between the April 1988 release of *The Innocents* and the October 1989 release of *Wild!* "Stop!" and "Knocking on Your Door" (both heard in original and 12" remix versions). They were typical hi-NRG Erasure tracks, with driving dance beats and forceful tenor vocals by Andy Bell, but they did not embrace the broader pop audience the group had reached with the 1988 singles "Chains of Love" and "A Little Respect." "She Won't Be Home" was a Christmas song, reflecting the seasonal release of the EP in November 1988 in the UK. —*William Ruhlmann*

**Wild!** / Oct. 1989 / Sire ♦♦
In the UK, *Wild!,* Erasure's fourth album, topped the charts, just as its predecessor, *The Innocents,* had done, spinning off four hit singles in the process. But in America, where *The Innocents* had been Erasure's commercial breakthrough, it was a different story. Maybe it was the leadoff single, "Drama!," a hardcore dance track with ponderous lyrics about "the infinite complexities of love," but *Wild!* saw Erasure falling back on its disco audience rather than continuing to expand into the mainstream. The group tried different sounds, beginning with a piano instrumental and including the Spanish-flavored "La Gloria," but much of the material was just more of the synthesized dance tracks familiar from previous records. Despite their continuing appeal at home, Erasure seemed to be stagnating creatively. —*William Ruhlmann*

**Chorus** / Oct. 1991 / Sire ♦♦
*Chorus,* Erasure's fifth album, was a look back at its earliest synth-pop style, after the relatively eclectic approach taken on its predecessor, *Wild!* Vince Clarke's instrumental tracks employed familiar electronic keyboard sounds, rather like the synth-dance music of the early '80s that he pioneered with Depeche Mode and Yaz. That was good enough to give Erasure its third straight UK #1 and four more hit singles, but in the US, where the title track just stumbled into the lower reaches of the singles charts, the group had fallen back on a dance-oriented cult following, its music sounding dangerously old-fashioned. —*William Ruhlmann*

● **Erasure Pop!: The First 20 Hits** / Nov. 24, 1992 / Sire ♦♦♦♦
*Pop!: The First 20 Hits* is exactly what it claims to be—a collection of Erasure's

biggest singles, which makes it the best place to get acquainted with this synth-pop band. — *Stephen Thomas Erlewine*

**Erasure** / Oct. 24, 1995 / Elektra ♦♦♦
It's been a long way from the bouncy dance hits of Erasure's early days to this thoughtful, expansive collection whose eponymous title suggests a new beginning. The 11 tracks run 71½ minutes, leaving room for extended instrumental passages. (The lack of breaks between the songs contributes to the sense of a single long musical piece.) But it isn't so much the length as the slower tempos and reflective lyrics, which often conflate romance with religion, that make *Erasure* the group's most ponderous album. "Fingers & Thumbs (Cold Summer's Day)" is the obvious uptempo dancefloor hit, but that's an atypical track on an album that finds Andy Bell singing about fear and grace and sanctuary. Maybe AIDS is the subtextual subject in all this, or maybe Bell and Clarke are just getting philosophical after seven albums. Whatever the reasons, they are becoming the Pink Floyd of the synth-pop set. — *William Ruhlmann*

**Cowboy** / Apr. 22, 1997 / Warner Brothers ♦♦
For *Cowboy*, Erasure hooked up with Depeche Mode producer Gareth Jones, and the record appropriately has some light trip-hop and ambient flourishes. Nevertheless, Erasure can't change their modus operandi no matter how hard they try, and the result is a new sound that never sounds new. Furthermore, Andy Bell and Vince Clarke have hit a songwriting rut, and all of the songs blend together, with very few individual tunes standing out, suggesting that the group is beginning to run out of ideas. — *Stephen Thomas Erlewine*

## ESG

f. 1978, South Bronx, New York
*Group / Old School Rap, Electro, Club/Dance*

An art-funk ensemble from the South Bronx, ESG was formed by sisters Renee, Valerie, and Marie Scroggins, all of whom handle vocals and percussion, and friend Leroy Glover (bass). ESG's music is centered around the sisters' complex polyrhythms, with atmosphere supplied by bass and pop-flavored guitar. During their first incarnation, the group signed with 99 Records and issued a debut self-titled EP in 1981 that featured three live and three studio songs, the latter produced by the legendary Martin Hannett (Joy Division, etc.). 1982's *ESG Says Dance to the Beat of the Moody* EP continued in a similar vein, as did their first full-length album, 1983's *Come Away with ESG*. ESG disbanded shortly thereafter, but unexpectedly re-formed in the early '90s, heralding their comeback with a self-titled 1991 compilation of previously released material. The group's work had become popular among hip-hop artists searching for samples, with such acts as TLC, the Wu-Tang Clan, the Beastie Boys, Big Daddy Kane, and indie rockers Unrest all making use of ESG beats; the group addressed this issue on the 1992 12" EP *Sample Credits Don't Pay Our Bills*. *ESG Live!* appeared in 1995, featuring both old and new material. The group continued to record during the late '90s, and even added Scroggins daughters Chistelle and Nicole. The major retrospective *A South Bronx Story* appeared on Universal Sound in 2000. — *Steve Huey*

**Come Away with ESG** / 1983 / 99 ♦♦

★ **A South Bronx Story** / 2000 / Universal Sound ♦♦♦♦♦
To grasp the widespread appeal of ESG, first consider that they played the opening night of *the Hacienda* and the closing night of *the Paradise Garage*. *The Hacienda* was based in Manchester, England, a venue run by Factory, the label whose flagship acts included the dark funk of A Certain Ratio and the increasingly dancefloor-oriented New Order. The late Larry Levan had ESG close out *the Paradise Garage*, the infamous and eclectic dance club located in New York. But most crucial to the realization of ESG's legacy is documented in the samples found on scads upon scads of hip-hop tracks. The four Scroggins sisters (and a friend on percussion, Tito Libran) didn't have a concept in mind when they made their pioneering music. Their sparse sound was more a result of doing what they could with what they had. The sisters' mom bought them their instruments, and they later gathered up numerous cheap percussion devices to add accent. Major kudos to Universal Sound for compiling ESG's best works for *A South Bronx Story*. Until 2000, the group's scant material had been nearly impossible to find. The most legendary inclusion is the Martin Hannett-produced 7" EP that was originally released on Factory (later released as a 12" by US no wave indie 99 with live tracks backing it). This release featured their trademark track "Moody," which ended up

being listed as a Top 50 classic by nearly all of New York's dance clubs; it was also immortalized on a volume of Tommy Boy's excellent *Perfect Beats* series, lodged between Liquid Liquid and Strafe. Though not their best moment, it summed up their sound quite well: dynamic, near-dub bass, random (not ramshackle) percussion that complemented the song, and sparsely chanted/sung vocals. Like the remainder of their recorded output, it featured the three "R"s: rhythm, rhythm, and more rhythm. Also on the debut EP was their most sampled "UFO"; the nauseous siren trills at the beginning found sped-up use in at least half a dozen rap tracks in the late '80s and early '90s. Big Daddy Kane and LL Cool J used it, and the Bomb Squad slyly swiped it for Public Enemy's "Night of the Living Baseheads."

Also compiled on the disc are selections from their follow-up EP and LP from the early '80s, as well as their "comeback" record from 1991. Arguably their best moment was "Dance." With its jumpy Motown rhythm, post-punk bass, and narrative/old school vocals, it sounds like a wild mix of the Supremes and *Metal Box*-era Public Image Limited. Deborah's bass, though not as musicianly, captures the spirit of PiL's Jah Wobble copping Motown session bassist James Jamerson.

As a whole, their output was energetic and extremely fun. The LP from 1991 wasn't as revolutionary as their earlier work, but it wasn't without its moments. Instead of sounding more James Brown-driven on the early records, the later LP sounds more Meters-derived in spots. "Erase You" features some streetwise lines: "Erase you/Just like a drawing/Erase you/Flush you like my toilet/Erase you/Show you I'm a woman."

Definitely a treasure to be sought out, *A South Bronx Story* is essential for any hip-hop head, post-punk connoisseur, dance fanatic, or Luscious Jackson fan. That's an amazing accomplishment: to cross that many boundaries with such limited resources. — *Andy Kellman*

## Esion

f. 1995
*Group / Indie Pop, Electronica, Techno*

A one-man industrial-dance outfit based in Ann Arbor, Michigan, Esion was formed by singer/songwriter and Eastern Michigan University School of Music graduate Don Kline. Although classically trained, Kline's songwriting displays more modern influences, mixing elements of industrial, pop, funk, techno, hip-hop, jazz, and rock 'n' roll. After a brief stint in early 1995 as the singer for local jazz group the Jazz Cabinet, Kline began experimenting more with electronic music and began recording and performing as Esion. After debuting with an EP, he released his first full-length album, *Lickity Split*, in 1996. One year later, *En Route* appeared on Kline's own Xenograph Music label. Kline also licensed songs to MTV for use on their *Making the Video* television series. — *AMG*

● **En Route** / 1998 / Xenograph Music ♦♦♦
Kline's second full album as Esion is a deft, accomplished work of singer/songwriter electronica, reminiscent of synth-pop and European industrial, but also focused on innovating the form itself. Kline ranges much farther than most in search of new musical fusions, moving from the dreamy 303 ambience of "Xero-G" to electronic samba on "13 Machine," to the breakbeat-techno pastiche "Unoquattro" (the latter is an instrumental). On many tracks, there's a sense of minor-chord melancholy that contributes to the mood and makes the album a cohesive whole. It's a solid album, balancing the playful experimentation of Kline's productions, a voice capable of many subtleties, and an arranging sense that ties the two together with no visible seams. — *John Bush*

## Euphonic

*Group / Jungle/Drum'N'Bass, Club/Dance, Techno*

Euphonic are a drum'n'bass duo consisting of Rob Henry and "DJ Nick" Trimm; Henry had been in Children of the Bong, while Trimm was previously a graffiti artist. After remixing such artists as Pig, Ultrafunkula, and Armand Van Helden, Euphonic issued their debut LP, *S/T*, on the Different Drummer label in 1998. — *Steve Huey*

● **Euphonic** / Mar. 10, 1998 / Different Drummer ♦♦♦♦
Euphonic's self-titled debut EP features guest appearances by a number of Brooklyn underground dance music figures, including Dr. Israel, Soothsayer, Trumystic Sound System, and vocalists Hedlam and Jennifer Achono. — *Steve Huey*

## Eurythmics

f. 1980, London, England, db. 1990
*Group / Pop/Rock, New Wave, Synth-Pop*

Eurythmics were one of the most successful duos to emerge in the early '80s. Where most of their British synth-pop contemporaries disappeared from the charts as soon as new wave faded away in 1984, Eurythmics continued to have hits until the end of the decade, making vocalist Annie Lennox a star in her own right, as well as establishing instrumentalist Dave Stewart as a successful, savvy producer and songwriter. Originally, the duo channelled the eerily detached sound of electronic synthesizer music into pop songs driven by robotic beats. By the mid-'80s, singles like "Sweet Dreams (Are Made of This)" and "Here Comes the Rain Again" had made the group into international stars and the group had begun to experiment with their sound, delving into soul and R&B. As the decade wore on, the duo's popularity eroded somewhat — by the late '80s, they were having trouble cracking the Top 40 in America, although they stayed successful in the UK. During the early '90s, Eurythmics took an extended hiatus, as both Lennox and Stewart pursued solo careers.

The origins of Eurythmics lay in the Tourists, a British post-punk band of the late '70s formed by Lennox and Stewart. The pair met in London while she was studying at the Royal Academy of Music. Stewart had recently broken up his folk-rock group Longdancer and was writing songs with guitarist Pete Coombes. Immediately after meeting, Stewart and Lennox became lovers and musical partners, forming a group called Catch with Coombes, which quickly evolved into the Tourists in 1979. Though the band only was together for two years, the Tourists released three albums — *The Tourists, Reality Effect*, and *Luminous Basement* — which all were moderate hits in England; two of their singles, "I Only Want to Be with You" and "So Good to Be Back Home Again," became Top Ten hits.

During 1980, Lennox and Stewart's romantic relationship dissolved and, along with it, so did the Tourists. Though they were no longer lovers, Lennox and Stewart decided to continue performing together under the name Eurythmics and headed to Germany to record their debut album. Featuring support from various members of Can, and Blondie's drummer Clem Burke, among others, the duo's debut *In the Garden* was released in 1981 to positive reviews, but weak sales. Following the failure of *In the Garden*, Stewart set up a home studio and Eurythmics recorded a second album, *Sweet Dreams (Are Made of This)*, which was released in 1983.

"Love Is a Stranger" was the first British single pulled from the album and it became a minor hit in the fall of 1982, a few months before the LP appeared. The title track was released as a single in the spring, and it rocketed to number two on the UK charts; shortly afterward, it climbed to number one on the American charts. "Sweet Dreams (Are Made of This)" was helped enormously by its stylish, androgynous video, which received heavy airplay from MTV, who had only recently become a major influence within the music industry. After "Sweet Dreams," Eurythmics re-released "Love Is a Stranger." It reached the UK Top Ten (number 23 US), beginning a string of hit singles that ran for a year. *Touch*, the duo's third album, was released toward the end of 1983 and it continued their success throughout 1984, spawning the hits "Who's That Girl?" (number 3, UK; number 21, US), "Right By Your Side" (number 10, UK; number 29, US), and "Here Comes the Rain Again" (number 8, UK; number 4 US). During the course of 1984, Annie Lennox's theatrical gender-bending was becoming increasingly notorious, which helped their record sales. At the end of the year, they released the soundtrack for the film adaption of *1984*, which received poor reviews and sales, despite the Top 10 UK placing of its single, "Sexcrime (Nineteen Eighty-Four)."

Released in the spring of 1985, Eurythmics' fourth album, *Be Yourself Tonight* boasted a tougher, R&B-influenced sound and featured a duet with Aretha Franklin, "Sisters Are Doin' It for Themselves." The duet became one of three hit singles from the album, in addition to "Would I Lie to You?" (number 17, UK; number 5, US), and "There Must Be an Angel (Playing with My Heart)" (number 1, UK; number 22, US). *Revenge*, released the following year, followed the R&B and soul inclinations of *Be Yourself Tonight* to a harder-rocking conclusion. Though the album peaked at number 12 in the US and spawned the number 14 hit "Missionary Man," its sales were noticeably weaker than its predecessor. In the UK, the group was slightly more popular — "Thorn In My Side" reached the Top Ten — but it was evident that the group was past the point of their peak popularity.

As appropriate for a group passing their commercial pinnacle, Eurythmics began branching out into other areas. During 1985 and 1986, Dave Stewart produced a number of superstars, including Bob Dylan, Daryl Hall, Tom Petty, and Mick Jagger. Annie Lennox began a short-lived acting career, appearing in *Revolution*. Eurythmics reconvened in 1987 to release *Savage*, which was greeted with mixed reviews and weak sales. That same year, Stewart married Siobhan Fahey, a former member of Bananarama that had also appeared in the "Love Is a Stranger" video; she would later be a member of Shakespeare's Sister, which was prodcued by Stewart. In 1988, Lennox had a hit duet with Al Green with "Put a Little Love in Your Heart," taken from the *Scrooged* soundtrack. The following year, Eurythmics released *We Too Are One*, which sold well in Britain, reaching number one, but poorly in America, despite "Don't Ask Me Why" becoming their first Top 40 hit since "Missionary Man." Furthermore, the reviews were decidedly mixed on the album.

Eurythmics quietly went on hiatus of 1990, releasing *Greatest Hits* the following year. Lennox began a solo career in 1992, releasing *Diva*, an album that would eventually sell over two million copies. Stewart continued producing records and writing film soundtracks, as well as forming a band called Spiritual Cowboys. In 1995, he officially launched a solo career with the release of *Greetings from the Gutter*. Lennox and Stewart reformed Eurythmics in 1999, releasing *Peace*, their first new studio album in a decade. — *Stephen Thomas Erlewine*

**In the Garden** / 1981 / RCA ✦✦✦

Eurythmics' debut album, *In the Garden*, is the missing link between the work of the Tourists, who included both Dave Stewart and Annie Lennox, and 1983's commercial breakthrough, *Sweet Dreams (Are Made of This)*. Co-produced by Kraftwerk producer Conny Plank at his studio in Cologne, Germany, it has some of the distant, mechanistic feel of the European electronic music movement, but less of the pop sensibility of later Eurythmics. The chief difference is in Lennox's singing; even when the musical bed is appealing, Lennox floats ethereally over it, and the listener doesn't focus on her. As a result, *In the Garden* wasn't much of a success, though when Eurythmics streamlined their sound and emphasized Lennox's dominating voice on subsequent releases, they found mass popularity. — *William Ruhlmann*

**Sweet Dreams (Are Made of This)** / Jan. 1983 / RCA ✦✦✦✦

Much commotion was caused by the MTV video clip for the hit title track from their breakthrough second album, which played up vocalist Annie Lennox's androgynous image. — *Donna DiChario*

**Touch** / Nov. 1983 / RCA ✦✦✦✦

The follow-up to the success of *Sweet Dreams* showed a more confident Lennox and Stewart, ready to expand their stylistic range. It contains the Top 40 hits "Here Comes the Rain Again," "Who's That Girl," and "Right by Your Side." — *Scott Bultman*

**Touch Dance** / May 1984 / RCA ✦✦

*Touch Dance* is a remix album that takes four of the album tracks from *Touch* and extends and reconfigures them. "The First Cut," "Cool Blue," and "Paint a Rumour" are presented in vocal and instrumental versions, mixed either by Francois Kevorkian or John "Jellybean" Benitez. "Regrets" is presented only in a vocal version mixed by Kevorkian. The result will be of interest to DJs and to those curious about the various ways that a song can be reconstituted, but not to general listeners, since the remixes do not noticeably improve upon the originals. — *William Ruhlmann*

**1984 (For the Love of Big Brother)** / Nov. 1984 / RCA ✦✦

While it is not billed as an Original Motion Picture Soundtrack, this album does contain, as a jacket note indicates, "music derived from Eurythmics" original score of the motion picture *1984*, and it was treated as a side project for marketing purposes, not as Eurythmics' full-fledged fourth new studio album. Fair enough. Much of the album is instrumental, and the closest thing to a pop song, "Sexcrime (Nineteen Eighty-Four)" (which was a Top Ten hit in the UK), like the other vocal numbers, relates to the movie's future fiction theme. As such, the album is substandard if judged as an independent Eurythmics album, adequate if judged as a soundtrack. — *William Ruhlmann*

**Revenge** / Jul. 1986 / RCA ✦✦✦

On their fifth album, Eurythmics moved away from the austere synth-pop of their previous work and toward more of a neo-'60s pop/rock stance. "Missionary Man" (which went Top 40 as a single in the US and charted in the UK) featured a prominent harmonica solo, while "Thorn in My Side" had a chiming guitar riff reminiscent of The Searchers and a fat sax solo. Of course, the primary element in the group's sound remained Annie Lennox's distinctive alto voice, which was still impressive even if the material was slightly less so. *Revenge* was a successful album, reaching the Top Ten in the UK and going gold in the US, but it was a disappointment compared to their last three albums. And creatively, it was a step down as well—there was nothing here that they hadn't done a little better before. —*William Ruhlmann*

**Savage** / Nov. 1987 / RCA ♦♦
If *Revenge*, Eurythmics' fifth album, marked a slight fall-off in the group's commercial and artistic accomplishments, *Savage*, their sixth collection, confirmed that decline. In the US, the album failed to generate a substantial hit single and sold poorly compared to previous efforts. In the more faithful UK, the album hit the Top Ten and spun off four chart singles, but none that matched earlier hits. Musically, Eurythmics, for the most part, abandoned the more conventional pop/rock they recently had been pursuing, returning to the synthesized dance music and arch tone of their early hit "Sweet Dreams (Are Made of This)." But they still seemed less inspired than before. —*William Ruhlmann*

**We Too Are One** / Sep. 1989 / Arista ♦♦♦
Switching to Arista Records in the US, Eurythmics made their last album together with *We Too Are One*, and they went out in style. Calling upon a broad pop range, their seventh album was their best since *Be Yourself Tonight* in 1985. The sound was varied, the melodies were strong, and the lyrics were unusually well crafted. In retrospect, the album can be seen as a dry run for Annie Lennox's debut solo album, *Diva* (1992); songs like "Don't Ask Me Why" (which grazed the US Top 40) serve as precursors to the dramatic ballads to come. There is, however, an air of romantic resignation throughout *We Too Are One*, appropriate to its valedictory nature. The disc spawned four chart singles in the UK and returned Eurythmics to number one in the album charts, but it did not substantially improve Eurythmics' reduced commercial standing in the US, confirming that it was time for Lennox and Dave Stewart to pursue other opportunities. —*William Ruhlmann*

● **Greatest Hits** / May 1991 / Arista ♦♦♦♦
It may have taken them a little while to get going, but when the Eurythmics hit their stride with their second album *Sweet Dreams (Are Made of This)*, they began a hit streak that defined them as one of the most commercially successful and musically satisfying new wave bands of the '80s. For six years, the group was reliable, turning out at least one great single on each album, none of which sounded identical. Yet all were recognizable as the work of Dave Stewart and Annie Lennox. *Greatest Hits* summarizes those glorious years and while it misses a couple of hits—a bad thing when the sublime "Right By Your Side" is concerned, but not when "Sexcrime (Nineteen Eighty-Four)" is—it remains an excellent collection. It might not follow a strict chronological order, but it flows nicely, revealing that the band that produced such chilly synth-pop classics as "Sweet Dreams," "Here Comes the Rain Again," "Love Is a Stranger," and "Who's that Girl?" were capable of delivering equally captivating light pop and ballads ("There Must Be an Angel [Playing with My Heart]," "Don't Ask Me Why," "Thorn in My Side"), ersatz soul ("Sisters Are Doin' It for Themselves") and hard-driving rock 'n' roll ("Missionary Man," "I Need a Man"). Few of their contemporaries were capable of such range, and *Greatest Hits* proves that the best of the Eurythmics' work were undeniable pop classics. —*Stephen Thomas Erlewine*

**Peace** / Oct. 19, 1999 / Arista ♦♦♦
Nearly a decade after Eurythmics went on an unannounced, virtually unnoticed hiatus in 1990, Annie Lennox and Dave Stewart returned with the heavily publicized *Peace*. During their time off, neither member was exceptionally busy. Lennox had a huge hit with her 1992 solo debut, *Diva*, but its 1995 successor, the all-covers *Medusa*, failed to maintain her momentum. Still, *Medusa* fared better than Stewart's three solo albums of the '90s, none of which generated much chart action or critical notice. Curiously, both Lennox and Stewart were silent after 1995, which means that reuniting really wasn't a sacrifice, since their solo careers had stalled. In fact, it was a wise idea to reteam, both commercially and artistically, since their best and most popular music was made together. While it's no great surprise they reunited, it is odd that *Peace* so strongly resembles *Diva*. True, Eurythmics were moving toward the melodramatic grandeur of *Diva* on their final '80s album, *We Too Are One*, yet they still had an innate sense of quirkiness and a desire to take risks. In 1999, they're more about craft, which only emphasizes the maturity of the music. That's not entirely a bad thing, even if it means that *Peace* needs a couple of spins before the songs begin to register. Lennox and Stewart know how to write gently insinuating melodies and how to richly layer their tracks with small sonic details, weaving lush tapestries of sound. It's an alluring sound, and *Peace* keeps its mood throughout. Even when they attempt to revisit their Stonesy tendencies, as on "Power to the Meek" and "I Want It All," the songs play as sleekly and smoothly as the ballads that dominate the record. In one sense, that's good, because it means that *Peace* keeps a consistent tone from front to back, but it also means that most of the songs blend together. There are no standout singles here—they're all part of a piece, for better or worse—and that's the hardest thing to accept about the record. Eurythmics were one of the best singles bands of the '80s, turning out at least one terrific single with each record. It's hard not to miss that gift on *Peace*—for all its virtues, it doesn't have any grabbers or growers. Even so, *Peace* is a successful debut for Eurythmics, Mach 2. It's classy adult-pop, delivered with style and grace. If fans of the duo's groundbreaking new wave don't warm to it, that's fine—it wasn't made for them in the first place. —*Stephen Thomas Erlewine*

## Everything But the Girl

f. 1982, Hull, England
Group / *Alternative Dance, Club/Dance, Pop/Rock, Alternative Pop/Rock*
Originating at the turn of the '80s as a leader of the lite-jazz movement, Everything But the Girl became an unlikely success story more than a decade later, emerging at the vanguard of the fusion between pop and electronica. Founded in 1982 by Hull University students Tracey Thorn and Ben Watt, the duo took their name from a sign placed in the window of a local furniture shop, which claimed "for your bedroom needs, we sell everything but the girl." At the time of their formation, both vocalist Thorn and songwriter/multi-instrumentalist Watt were already signed independently to the Cherry Red label; Thorn was a member of the sublime Marine Girls, while Watt had issued several solo singles and also collaborated with Robert Wyatt.

Everything But the Girl debuted in 1982 with a samba interpretation of Cole Porter's "Night and Day"; the single was a success on the UK independent charts, but the duo nonetheless went on hiatus as Thorn recorded a solo EP, *A Distant Shore*, while Watt checked in with the full-length *North Marine Drive* in 1983. EBTG soon reunited to record a cover of the Jam's "English Rose" for an "NME" sampler; the track so impressed former Jam frontman Paul Weller that he invited the duo to contribute to the 1984 LP *Cafe Bleu*, the debut from his new project, the Style Council.

Everything But the Girl's own beguiling 1984 debut *Eden* followed on the heels of the single "Each and Every One," a UK Top 40 hit. The jazz-pop confections of the group's early work gave way to shimmering jangle-rock by the time of 1985's *Love Not Money*, while a subtle country influence crept into the mix for 1986's lush, orchestral *Baby, the Stars Shine Bright*. The beautifully spare *Idlewild* followed in 1988, spawning the single "I Don't Want to Talk About It," a poignant cover of a song by the late Crazy Horse guitarist Danny Whitten, which became EBTG's biggest hit to date, landing at the number three spot on the British charts.

Watt and Thorn travelled to Los Angeles to record 1990's slick, commercial *The Language of Life*, produced by Tommy LiPuma and featuring a guest appearance by jazz great Stan Getz. After a return to pop textures with 1991's *Worldwide*, Everything But the Girl mounted a series of club performances which resulted in 1992's *Acoustic*, a spartan set of covers (including Elvis Costello's "Alison," Bruce Springsteen's "Tougher Than the Rest," and Mickey and Sylvia's "Love Is Strange") which presaged the coming ascendancy of the "Unplugged" concept. In the wake of the record's release, Watt fell prey to Churg-Strauss Syndrome, a rare auto-immune system disease which brought him to the brink of death; after a year in recovery, he wrote several new songs which the duo recorded for inclusion on *Home Movies*, a 1993 hits collection.

In 1994, EBTG collaborated with dub-trance innovators Massive Attack on their LP *Protection;* Thorn's vocal turn highlighted the hit title track, and the cinematic Massive Attack sound clearly informed Everything But the Girl's own 1994 effort *Amplified Heart*, another strong and eclectic outing featuring an appearance by guitar great Richard Thompson. In 1995 the soulful single "Missing" was innovatively remixed by Todd Terry, and after first becoming a club sensation, the track blossomed as a major international hit, reaching the number two position on the US pop charts. More importantly, Terry's remix, combined with the lessons of the Massive Attack sessions, launched the duo into an entirely new—and equally satisfying—musical direction: with 1996's brilliant *Walking Wounded*, Everything But the Girl dove headfirst into electronica, crafting sophisticated, assured excursions into trip-hop and drum'n'bass. In 1999, the duo reappeared with *Temperamental*. —*Jason Ankeny*

**The Best of Everything But the Girl** / 1996 / Blanco Y Negro ♦♦♦♦
*The Best of Everything But the Girl* is divided between selections from their early records and remixes of '90s hits, such as "Missing." Consequently, the album draws a slightly misleading portrait of their career, yet it still functions as an excellent introduction to the band, since it features many of their best songs, including "Apron Strings." —*Stephen Thomas Erlewine*

★ **Walking Wounded** / May 21, 1996 / Atlantic ♦♦♦♦♦
With *Walking Wounded*, Everything But the Girl put an acceptable face on trip-hop, jungle and techno, opening up the world of experimental dance music to a new audience. At its core, Everything But the Girl is a pop group, which means they automatically abandon the free-form song structures that characterize most of trip-hop and techno. In a sense, that dilutes the impact of the music, but the duo found a way around that by seamlessly incorporating the rhythms into carefully crafted songs. They work the same ground as Massive Attack, but their songwriting is more accessible and less adventerous than the groundbreaking Bristol group. Furthermore, Everything But the Girl never approach the tarnished glamour of Portishead, the kineticism of Bjork, or the brilliantly evocative soundscapes of Tricky. Essentially, the beats are used as window-dressing—the group's music hasn't changed that much. —*Stephen Thomas Erlewine*

**Everything But the Girl Vs. Drum & Bass** / Oct. 22, 1996 / Atlantic ♦♦♦♦
The *Everything...Drum & Bass* EP is comprised of remixes of several tracks from Everything But the Girl's first full-fledged dance album, *Walking Wounded*. Most of the EP consists of fine remixes of the album's title track, but the best cut is a version of "Single" remixed by Photek. —*Stephen Thomas Erlewine*

**Temperamental** / Sep. 28, 1999 / Atlantic ♦♦♦♦
Everything but the Girl's resurrection as a sophisticated electronica outfit may have been unpredictable, but it certainly revitalized the duo's music. Prior to 1996's *Walking Wounded*, the duo had taken their charming, jazzy acoustic pop as far as it could go. Adding electronica, primarily drum'n'bass and trip-hop, to the equation broke their potential wide open, as the captivating, seductive *Walking Wounded* proved. It was such a drastic, fulfilling departure that it did raise the question of where they go from here; its 1999 sequel, *Temperamental*, answers that by offering more of the same, except just a little different. *Temperamental* tempers the lightly skittering drum'n'bass and eliminates trip-hop, yet retains the same feel as *Walking Wounded*. House music—everything from classic '80s house to contemporary house—serves as the musical foundation, which actually opens the doors for slight jazzy inflections, along with long, hypnotizing instrumental passages (most notably on "Compression"). Weirdly, it also serves as a good setting for a batch of songs that are essentially in the singer/songwriter vein. In fact, there aren't as many clear pop hooks here as there were on *Walking*. "Five Fathoms," "Tempermental," and a couple of other tracks work as singles, but the album is more of a meditative, reflective piece, like a singer/songwriter album—except it's dressed in sultry, evocative electronic dance music. That means, of course, that *Temperamental* isn't all that different than its predecessor, but its blend of house, electronica, pop, jazz, and folk is equally satisfying as that landmark album. —*Stephen Thomas Erlewine*

## Experimental Audio Research

f. 1993
*Group / Experimental Ambient, Ambient Techno, Space Rock, Indie Rock, Post-Rock/Experimental, Experimental*

Experimental Audio Research—EAR for short—was a loosely affiliated assembly of performers primarily spearheaded by Spectrum frontman Sonic Boom; from time to time, the group also included, among others, My Bloody Valentine's Kevin Shields, God's Kevin Martin and AMM's Eddie Prevost. As a revolving exercise in guitar-based noise, each EAR release radically differed from the ones preceding it, spanning the divide between weightless ambience and dense sheets of feedback; the project was introduced via 1994's *Mesmerised*, and was followed a few months later by the *Pocket Symphony*, released solely on 5" vinyl. (As befitting Sonic Boom's own affection for record collecting, the releases that followed in 1995—*Hydroponic* and an untitled effort—appeared only as a 10" and 8" picture-disc recording, respectively.) Although released in 1996, the *Beyond the Pale* LP was originally intended as the first Experimental Audio Research release, and was actually recorded in 1992; *Phenomena 256* followed that August. Next up was 1997's *The Köner Experiment*, a nod to minimalist Thomas Köner, who also appeared on the disc; *Millennium Music* followed in 1998, with subsequent releases including *Data Rape*. —*Jason Ankeny*

**Mesmerized** / Jun. 15, 1994 / Sympathy for the Record Industry ♦♦♦
Produced by Sonic Boom, *Mesmerized* sounds much like an extended Spacemen 3 intro with spacier effects. Surprisingly, the band's avant-garde racket is calm and relaxing when not at loud volumes. —*John Bush*

**The Köner Experiment** / Mar. 31, 1997 / Space Age ♦♦
If you're home really late at night and you randomly spin the radio dial to see what you pick up, you just might end up falling asleep to burbling, phased-out static. To distinguish such an act from listening to *The Köner Experiment* might be harder than you think. Here, the Experimental Audio Research collective restrain their avant-garde indie noise-rock to come up with ten untitled tracks that try to explore the seedlings of collaborator Thomas Köner's more minimalist philosophies. Fortunately, such pretension doesn't necessarily make for a stillborn experience. When these pieces sound like an insomniac's heartbeat, pulsing along to an unsettling world of twilight paranoia, the effect is deeply disturbing. There's a mechanist's glare to a number of these tracks. An exhausted lucidity probably points to one of the most potent and coherent constructions of all the EAR releases so far. You just have to ignore those times when the album subjugates itself with pointless irregularity and you'll be happier not knowing when the band shoegazes off into that middle-distance. —*Dean Carlson*

● **Millennium Music** / Jan. 20, 1998 / Atavistic ♦♦♦♦
Experimental Audio Research—comprised this time of Sonic Boom & Pete Bassman of Spectrum, Eddie Prevost of A.M.M., and Tom Prentice of God—follow the minimalist *The Köner Experiment* with *Millennium Music*, arguably their most dense and complex work to date. Armed with an arsenal of vintage synthesizers, voltage-controlled electronics and theremins—as well as both acoustic and electric guitars—EAR sets out to make a sweeping millennial statement, the music attempting to evoke both the prehistoric era and the digital age and seemingly everything in between; given its grandiose designs, *Millennium Music* is often surprisingly successful, a challenging but ultimately rewarding work executed with the same dedication to innovation which has thus far marked all of the releases in the EAR oeuvre. —*Jason Ankeny*

## E-Z Rollers

f. 1995, Norfolk, England
*Group / Jungle/Drum'N'Bass, Club/Dance*

The duo of Jay Hurren and Alex Banks defined the easy-rolling two-step of Moving Shadow Records during the late '90s with their recordings as E-Z Rollers, after developing hardcore breakbeats earlier in the decade as JMJ & Richie and Hyper On Experience. Both were originally involved in the mid-'80s rare-groove and hip-hop scene around their native East Anglia, promoting shows and DJing as well. They moved into house as well after the rave explosion, and while Banks increasingly concentrated on production work in his home studio during the early '90s, Hurren continued to mix at events, usually billed as JMJ.

The duo began recording (separately at first) after meeting emerging jungle don LTJ Bukem—Banks with Hyper On Experience and Hurren with JMJ & Richie (as well as the solo project Parallel World). Hurren and Banks' various singles for Rob Playford's Moving Shadow and Bukem's Good Looking—"Montana" and "Universal Horn" as JMJ & Richie, "Thunder Grip" and "Lords of the Null Lines" as Hyper-On Experience, "Second Encounta" and "The Rhodes Tune" as Flytronix—helped write the template for smooth drum'n'bass with plenty of jazz texture but swift rhythms to keep the vibes moving in clubs.

After meeting up with vocalist Kelly Richards at one of their gigs, Hurren and Banks decided to form E-Z Rollers around the threesome. Their debut album *Weekend World* appeared in mid-1996, followed by several additional singles for Moving Shadow and the full-length follow-up *Weekend World*. Hurren and Banks have also worked on production for Foul Play and Peshay. —*John Bush*

**Dimensions of Sound** / Jul. 15, 1996 / Moving Shadow ♦♦♦♦
*Dimensions of Sound* proves an apt title for E-Z Rollers' debut album; the trio

sample frosty ambience for "The Morning After," and provide a trip to Bollywood on "Passage to India," and make several other stops on their way through the world of slightly chilled drum'n'bass. Photek contributes a remix of "Rolled into One." —*John Bush*

**Retro/Subtropic [Single]** / Mar. 10, 1997 / Moving Shadow ♦♦♦
E-Z Rollers returned to Moving Shadow in early 1997 after the success of their first album with a 12" of smooth jazzy tech-step and, on the flip, more ambient textures. —*John Bush*

● **Weekend World** / May 11, 1998 / Moving Shadow ♦♦♦♦
E-Z Rollers' sophomore album explores territory much closer to the jazzy coffee-table side of drum'n'bass than the group's previous output. The beats are mostly simple two-steps, though the background effects and basslines are quite strong, whether on vocal tracks like "Tough at the Top" or rougher tracks like the tech-step roller "Soundclash." The final result is a good blend of jungle's lighter sound with the occasional darker texture. —*John Bush*

# F

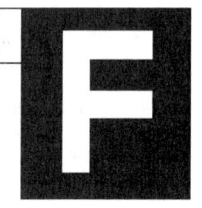

### Adam F (Adam Fenton)
b. 1972, Liverpool, England
*Producer / Electronica, Jungle/Drum'N'Bass, Club/Dance*

Adam F is a drum'n'bass outsider who's nonetheless managed to turn his musical ear into a successful string of tracks colliding jungle's mellower rhythms with jazz, soul, funk, and dreamy ambience. Born Adam Fenton in Liverpool in 1972, he's the son of '70s glam rocker Shane Fenton, aka Alvin Stardust; his uncle recorded under the name Rory Storm in Rory Storm and the Hurricanes (Ringo Starr held their drum chair prior to joining the Beatles). Adam F led a musical childhood which centered around his father's sizable record collection, mainly '70s soul-jazz and funk fusioners such as Stevie Wonder, Marvin Gaye, and Earth, Wind, & Fire. His most high-profile gig before he discovered dance music came at the age of 17, when he toured America as the keyboardist for a reformed Moody Blues. Adam's first jungle tracks—"Lighter Style" and "Criminal Activity"—were cut'n'paste crowd pleasers composed by literally picking up the latest club hits and approximating their styles. He's since moved on to a more individual approach (represented on more recent tracks such as "Metropolis" and "F-Jam"), signing with Perfecto in 1995 to further pursue a more conventionally instrumented hybrid of jazz- and funk-fueled drum'n'bass (his first single for the label featured Van Morrison's guitarist and Sade's flautist). —*Sean Cooper*

● Colours / Nov. 10, 1997 / Astralwerks ♦♦♦♦
Adam F's debut album *Colours* runs the gamut of drum'n'bass styles, from the propulsive dance floor to sophisticated adult contemporary crossover. He flourishes between those two extremes, when he concentrates on either '70s funk workouts or cinematic soundscapes. If Adam F had concentrated on those two styles, *Colours* would have been a thoroughly impressive debut. Since it's weighed down by lesser material that was intended to showcase his diversity, the album is merely promising, which isn't bad at all, especially since the best moments are addictive in their own way. —*Stephen Thomas Erlewine*

### Fabio (Fitzroy Heslop)
b. Sep. 27, 1965, London, England
*Producer, DJ / Jungle/Drum'N'Bass, Club/Dance*

Fabio is the pioneering breakbeat DJ who, along with Grooverider, brought drum'n'bass into the British club scene. A DJ since the early '80s rare-groove and hip-hop periods, he was born in London and grew up in Brixton. Though he went to college for awhile and worked as an insurance agent, his burgeoning mixing career soon took center stage. A soul fan and early friend of fellow DJs Colin Dale and Tim Westwood, Fabio first made his name on the pirate station Phase 1 and got hooked on house music by 1986.

With Grooverider, Fabio hosted several popular after-hours house events during the late '80s. During the early '90s, he formed two of the seminal club-nights for drum'n'bass, *Rage* and *Speed*. At the former, he and Grooverider provided the early darkside to hardcore techno while the latter saw Fabio and LTJ Bukem charting the course of an increasingly experimental-minded scene. Though he concentrated on mixing while Grooverider added production credits to his résumé, Fabio and his Creative Source label proved crucial to the early development of producers like Alex Reece, Wax Doctor, and Hidden Agenda. He was also slotted to mix the second volume in the mix-album series *Promised Land*. —*John Bush*

● Promised Land, Vol. 2 / May 20, 1997 / Paradigm ♦♦♦♦
LTJ Bukem passed the baton to his jungle forefather Fabio for the second volume in the *Promised Land* series. Fabio responded with an epic two-disc collection that ranges from the polished end of drum'n'bass (Funky Technicians, Voyager, Fokus, Adam F) to harder material from DJ Trace, Big Bud, and Code Blue. —*Keith Farley*

### Faithless
f. 1995, London, England
*Group / Progressive Trance, Progressive House, Club/Dance, House, Dance-Pop*

A prime house-pop group and consistent club act, Faithless is at its core a duo of producers Rollo and Sister Bliss. Before the group officially came together in 1995, Rollo had produced a previous club hit ("Don't You Want Me" as Felix in 1992), plus an album for Kristine W. and remixes for the Pet Shop Boys, Björk, and Simply Red. Sister Bliss, a piano and violin prodigy from the age of five, converted to acid house in 1987, and quickly became one of the UK's best house DJs, also recording several singles as herself. Though the two had begun producing together as early as 1993, Faithless became a stable quartet two years later with the addition of vocalists Jamie Catto (previously in the Big Truth Band) and Maxi Jazz (from the Soul Food Cafe Band). The group attained worldwide status the following year with the singles "Salva Mea" (one of the biggest dance hits of the year), "Insomnia," and "Reverence." The debut Faithless album, also titled *Reverence*, appeared in late 1996 on Rollo's Cheeky Records, and was picked up for distribution by Arista the next year. *Sunday 8pm* followed in 1998, and was reissued in 1999 with a collection of remixes titled *Saturday 3am*. —*John Bush*

● Reverence / Nov. 11, 1996 / Arista ♦♦♦♦
The debut Faithless album includes all of the group's early hits ("Salva Mea," "Insomnia," "Reverence") sung by regular vocalist Maxi Jazz, as well as guests Pauline Taylor and Dido. —*John Bush*

Sunday 8pm / Sep. 21, 1998 / Arista ♦♦
The second album from UK electronic dance collective Faithless has neither the rampant grooves nor the arrogant idealism to qualify it as anything more than a random, standard dancefloor record with redundant beats and hoary ideas. Clearly, though, more was intended; the theme running throughout *Sunday 8pm* is one that celebrates club life with an almost religious enthusiasm. The dreamy soundscapes here alternate between elegantly spiritual (and very new age) drifts and dull, tuneless forays into spacy nowhereland—and the occasional misguided R&B trips lack soul (not all that surprising, considering the coldness of this band's electronica). The one keeper is "God Is a DJ," eight minutes of club worship that repeats the refrain "This is my church" so relentlessly that you begin to wonder if the Faithless altar includes a turntable and synthesizer along with the usual celebratory offerings. —*Michael Gallucci*

### Michael Fakesch
*Producer / Electronica, Electro-Techno*

Munich-based producer Michael Fakesch's work is more widely known via Funkstorung, the name he records under with partner Chris De Luca. Funkstorung have released almost a dozen records in just three years together, mostly through the obscure Acid Planet imprint and, more recently, their own label Musik Aus Strom. Funkstorung's records typically deploy a dark, rough, hard-edged electro aesthetic vaguely reminiscent of a slightly less obsessive Autechre. Fakesch's solo work, however, while retaining the gritty production values, pursues a bleaker, far more introverted tack, with a studied focus on melody and slower, more plodding rhythms. Fakesch followed a not uncommon progression from late '80s hip-hop (Public Enemy, Paris) and old-school electro (Grandmaster Flash, Man Parrish)—he was a semi-professional breakdancer—to the techno explosion that took hold in Germany in the early '90s. His solo output to date consists of the two-part *Demon* EP (1997) and the 1999 full-length *Marion*. —*Sean Cooper*

**Demon 1 [EP]** / 1997 / Musik Aus Strom ♦♦♦♦
Four artfully lo-fi tracks are either melancholic ambient electro or kinetic breaks, depending on the speed they're played (the record doesn't indicate which). Similar to Autechre and less hackneyed Mike "μμ-Ziq" Paradinas, Fakesch applies meticulously textured layers of distortion to his rhythms while immersing subtle, haunting melodies in liberal baths of reverb. Also accompanied by the equally impressive "Demon 2," "Demon 1" includes a remix by Skam/Planet Mu artist Boards of Canada. —*Sean Cooper*

• **Demon 2 [EP]** / 1997 / Musik Aus Strom ♦♦♦♦
The second of a two-part series, "Demon 2" is Fakesch's best solo work to date, arriving at the prefect balance of chaos and quietude. Five tracks blend textured, sputtering beats with aching melodies and warping digital effects, resulting in some of the more affecting music to be released by the Munich-based Musik Aus Strom label (also home to Fakesch's other main project, Funkstorung). Includes a remix by Dylan Nathan, aka Jega, of Skam/Planet Mu. —*Sean Cooper*

**Marion** / Dec. 14, 1999 / Musik Aus Strom ♦♦♦
Funkstorung's Michael Fakesch blends old and new material on his debut full-length, *Marion*, which features four tracks taken from Fakesch's *Demon* EPs and six newly recorded pieces. Overall, it continues his move toward refining and expanding upon his increasing Autechre influence, although there's a less robotic, mechanized feel to Fakesch's work. —*Steve Huey*

## Fantastic Plastic Machine (Tomoyuki Tanaka)

b. Kyoto, Japan
*Producer / Shibuya-Kei, Club/Dance, Alternative Pop/Rock, Dance-Pop*
The most producer-driven act in the Japanese pop movement known as Shibuya-kei, Fantastic Plastic Machine was formed by Tomoyuki Tanaka. Though he has the basic stylistic tastes requisite of the Shibuya-kei artist (namely lounge music, bossa nova, French pop, and soft rock), Tanaka has more of a club mentality, driven by his long experience as a DJ. Born in Kyoto, he entered the music business in the late '80s as a bassist for a ten-piece trad-rock band known as Margarine Strikes Back. Absorbed into dance music and the acid-house movement near the turn of the decade, he formed a DJ team called Sound Impossible and began spinning a mix of French and Brazilian pop, soundtrack music, and exotica. At one Sound Impossible show, longtime Deee-Lite turntablist Towa Tei convinced Tomoyuki Tanaka to begin recording again, and Fantastic Plastic Machine was born. Tanaka contributed tracks to two compilations (*Sushi 3003, Fish Smell Like Cat*) and remixed Combustible Edison before signing to Pizzicato Five's Readymade Records. His self titled debut album was released in 1998, and distributed in America by Emperor Norton. *Luxury* followed one year later. —*John Bush*

• **Fantastic Plastic Machine** / May 26, 1998 / Emperor Norton ♦♦♦♦
Like similar releases from artists including the brilliant Cornelius and Pizzicato Five, Fantastic Plastic Machine's self-titled debut is a wild, breakneck ride through the history of pop music, slicing and dicing elements of house music, bossa nova, drum'n'bass, and hip-hop, all filtered through a distinctly Japanese worldview. —*Jason Ankeny*

**Luxury** / Apr. 6, 1999 / Emperor Norton ♦♦♦
*Luxury* is a bit more dance-oriented than its predecessor, as Fantastic Plastic Machine downplays the kitsch factor in favor of contemporary electronic sounds and beats. However, there are still plenty of lounge, bossa nova and classic pop influences. —*Steve Huey*

**M** / Jun. 29, 1999 / Emperor Norton ♦♦♦
The final volume from a trilogy of remix albums, *M* features remixers from North and South America giving different spins to Fantastic Plastic Machine's futuristic lounge. Artists like Swamp, Los Amigos Invisibles, the Angel, and Hive rework songs like "You Must Learn All Night Long," "Disco for Jackie," "Honolulu Calcutta," and "The Girl Next Green Door." —*Heather Phares*

## Mark Farina

*DJ / Funky Breaks, Trip-Hop, Club/Dance*
Making a name for himself mainly as a DJ, Mark Farina has had a large hand in the building of San Francisco's house music scene. Originally from Chicago, Farina is in the same generation of Chicago house music legends Derrick Carter and Cajmere. Mostly associated with the *Mushroom Jazz* series of releases, Farina is known for his down-tempo, but dance floor friendly style of mixing jazz, house and hip-hop.

Mark Farina started DJing at the age of fifteen in his home town of Chicago. The city's large hand in the creation of house music had a strong influence on Farina and acted as a large source of inspiration for his DJing. In college, at Northwestern University's radio station WNUR, Farina and his airwaves partner Derrick Carter produced a Friday night radio show for two years. During this time Farina released *Mood* as part of the trio, Symbols and Instruments. British Magazine *The Face* rated *Mood* above artists such as New Order and Deee-Lite in their 1989 year-end music poll.

Shortly after his time at Northwestern University, Farina relocated to San Francisco. Using his musical influences, Farina made a mixtape of downtempo house tunes called *Mushroom Jazz*. Soon after, the album's title spawned a type of sound and grew popular due in part to Farina's weekly residency at a club local club called *Jazid Up*. The local notoriety eventually resulted in a CD of the same name on Om Records in October of 1996 and led to a global tour, which Mark headlined. In 1996 Farina also produced another continuous-mix CD, *Seasons One*, on Domestic Records. The second installation in the series, *Mushroom Jazz, Vol. 2*, was released in 1998, once again resulting in another promotional tour led by the now seasoned DJ. Farina released two more mix CDs in 1998, *United DJs of America, Vol. 9* (Moonshine) and *Imperial Dub, Vol. 1* (Studio !K7). After a string of mix CDs, Farina released an original work in 1998, "Midnight Calling." The track went virtually unnoticed due to the fact that Farina's mix CDs and DJing appearances were receiving most of the promotional attention. In 1999 the first in a series of CDs by Om Records, meant to highlight San Francisco DJs, debuted with Mark Farina. The CD showcased Farina's style of mixing jazzy downtempo and disco vocal oriented tracks. The CD was also released as a triple vinyl pack containing, in their entirety, all the songs Farina used for the CD. —*Diana Potts*

• **Mushroom Jazz** / Oct. 22, 1996 / OM ♦♦♦
Farina's hypnotic dance-floor jazz creates a trippy background mix and an enjoyable look at some promising new artists for those willing to listen. That being said, it's not a seamless mix, containing some jarring transitions. Tracks that don't fade into the background are the international hit single by Blue Boy, "Remember Me," and Mr. Electric Triangle's "Bossa Nova." As much as he forges a unique, mellow sound, he is inescapably influenced by DJs like Gilles Peterson. —*Ryan Randall Goble*

**Mushroom Jazz, Vol. 2** / Oct. 20, 1998 / OM ♦♦♦
DJ Mark Farina handles the mixing on *Mushroom Jazz, Vol. 2*, a collection of mellow acid-jazz tracks by various artists that actually holds together quite well. Farina's added samples help give a sense of unity to the whole album, and his house influences add a bit of variety. —*Steve Huey*

## Farley & Heller

f. 1991, London, England
*Group / Progressive Trance, Club/Dance, House*
Although prominent house DJs and producers individually, London-based remixers Terry Farley and Pete Heller enjoyed their greatest notoriety working as a duo. They first surfaced in the early '90s as part of Andrew Weatherall's Boys Own collective, making their debut with a hugely popular remix of the Farm's "Groovy Train"; hits for Espiritu ("Francisca"), Sunscreem ("Perfect Motion"), K Klass ("Don't Stop"), and Secret Life ("As Always") followed. Farley and Heller also earned wide renown when their mix of M People's "Open Your Heart" topped *Billboard's* club charts in 1995. A year later they reunited to assemble a two-disc entry into the *Journeys by DJs* beatmix series, with their own "Ultra Flava" 12" appearing at much the same time. In addition to working under the own names, Farley and Heller additionally recorded as Roach Motel, an outlet for their more underground projects; they also joined producer Gary Wilkinson in the lush garage techno trio Fire Island, as well as teaming with Weatherall and Hugo Nicholson in Bocca Juniors. Their other pop remix projects include work with New Order ("Regret"), Michael Jackson ("Blood on the Dancefloor"), his sister Janet ("When I Think of You"), Kylie Minogue ("Where Has the Love Gone?"), U2 ("Salome"), and Pet Shop Boys ("Go West"). —*Jason Ankeny*

• **Journeys by DJ, Vols. 1-2** / Oct. 28, 1996 / Music Unites ♦♦♦♦
An excellent trip through the main avenues and backroads of house music from the beginning of the '90s, Farley & Heller's double-disc *Journeys by DJ* extravaganza features nods to plenty of American heroes like Armand Van

Helden ("Psychic Bounty Killer"), Masters at Work ("Mack Daddy Shoot"), Funky Green Dogs ("The Way"), Benji Candelario ("Central Park"), and George Morel ("Morel's Groove"), as well as fellow British house/garage producers Black Science Orchestra ("Save Us"), St. Germain ("Alabama Blues"), and CJ Bolland ("Sugar Is Sweeter"). For fans of mainstream club music, there are few better ways to groove than this two-hour-plus set. —*Keith Farley*

## Farley Jackmaster Funk (Farley Keith Williams)

**b.** Jan. 25, 1962, Chicago, IL
*Producer, DJ / Club/Dance, Acid House, House*

When a new style of music first cracks the pop charts, the hit is usually a deliberate crossover by an artist having little to do with the music's original pioneers. The first house single to reach the charts, however, was recorded by seminal Chicago DJ and producer, Farley Jackmaster Funk. His cover of Isaac Hayes' "Love Can't Turn Around" made the Top Ten in mid-1986—ironically, not in his home country but in the UK—at the same time that he was one of the biggest names in Chicago house. Born in 1962, Farley began DJing while still a teenager. He first made his name in 1981, broadcasting on Chicago's WBMX-FM with Ralphi "The Razz" Rosario, Kenny "Jammin" Jason, Mickey "Mixin" Oliver, and Scott "Smokin" Seals as the Hot Mix 5—the legendary DJ team which broke house music for a wider Chicago audience. Farley also appeared at the legendary Warehouse Club (mixing alongside Frankie Knuckles), and then began a residency at the Playground (later the Candy Store) which set in stone his reputation as one of the city's top DJs.

Known as Farley Keith or Farley Funkin' Keith up to that point, he began recording in 1984 with the single "Jack the Bass," which inaugurated the highly popular jacking craze in Chicago house. After two more singles ("Funkin' with Drums Again," "Give Yourself to Me") for Trax Records, he rechristened himself Farley Jackmaster Funk and released "Love Can't Turn Around," with vocals by Darryl Pandy (often mistaken for Farley on the accompanying video). The single hit the number nine spot on the British pop charts and stunned hundreds of Chicagoans, who had no idea their records were becoming popular across the ocean.

"Love Can't Turn Around" wasn't followed by any other big international hits—"As Always" made a brief UK entry in 1989, while "It's You" was a local club draw—and by the late '80s, he had lost his DJ residency as well. Fortunately, Farley made a smooth transition to an even more lucrative sport—the global DJ circuit, where the prospect of hearing an American original brought thousands of club-goers. Never one of the most prolific recording artists in a style of music known for single-a-month release schedules, Farley moved into hip-hop in the early '90s, but returned to house by the mid-'90s with a new protege vocalist, Melanie. He also recorded new material with two other house legends (Adonis and Chip E) as Black Balls, and also released a volume in the mix series *House Music Movement*. —*John Bush*

● **House Music Movement** / Sep. 15, 1998 / Mastertone ♦♦♦♦
Farley Jackmaster Funk's edition in the *House Music Movement* series features a host of his own remixes and remixes—old and new—including "Love Can't Turn Around," "Child of God," "No Competition," "Lift Him Up," "He's My Best Friend," and "Before It's Too Late" as well as tracks from Roger Sanchez, Erick Morillo, Mousse T. and others. A bonus disc includes an intriguing interview with the man himself. —*John Bush*

## Farmers Manual

**f.** 1995, Vienna, Austria
*Group / Experimental Techno, Experimental Electro, Electronica*

Austrian electronic experimentalists Farmer Manual comprise a casual collective of musicians, DJs, computer geeks, and net freaks who count music as only one of a number of ongoing projects. The group's identity is as mysterious as the periodic transmissions from their Vienna studios (which began appearing in 1996), but their releases have managed to capture an international audience for their strident bird-flip to dance-based electronic music convention. Released by labels such as Mego, Ash, and Ash sublabel Tray, titles such as "FM," "fsck," and *No Backup* (a CD+ title and Mego's first full-length production) have pushed the envelope of musical intelligibility well off the map, spraying burbling, obverse rhythmic structures with blasts of noise and distortion, closely paralleling the approach of Panasonic or more recent Autechre. The group's full-length debut, *No Backup*, is a collection of drawn-out discombobulations of standard rhythmic and melodic structures, while the 12" only "FM" (meant as the vinyl alternative to the CD, but featuring none of the same tracks) contains more than a dozen brief sketches of minimal electro, many ending in lock-grooves (the tracks' bare repetition tend to beg the question of why they bothered with anything beyond a lock in the first place, but...). The group have also dabbled in drum'n'bass-style rhythmic programming (most prominently on their Tray 12" "fsck") and have conducted a number of live Internet broadcasts via their handsome website at http://www.farmersmanual.co.at). —*Sean Cooper*

● **No Backup** / May 7, 1996 / Mego ♦♦♦♦
Impeccable, meticulously destructured electronic tangents are constructed from a minimum of constituent elements (a couple of drum machines, a synthesizer—maybe—and any number of sound modification devices). Like many on the Vienna scene, Farmers Manual use cheap technology to maximum effect, and prefer mucking about with assumptions about the "proper" rendering of beat-oriented (and sometimes beatless) electronic music designed for a post-dancefloor audience. Both fascinating and musically enjoyable, *No Backup* is among Mego's finest releases to date. —*Sean Cooper*

**fsck** / Aug. 19, 1997 / Ash International ♦♦♦♦
More abstract genre abuse from the Vienna collective, this time spreading a multitude of ambient, electro, and drum'n'bass reductions across 99 tracks geared toward those of deficited attention span. The easy comparison would probably run something like a cross between Panasonic, Merzbow, and Photek, but Farmers Manual bring a humor and lackadaisical production *vivance* to the proceedings that make their strange, somewhat abrasive musical oddities as enjoyable to hear as they are fascinating to stretch out in. —*Sean Cooper*

**Explorers_We** / May 18, 1998 / OR ♦♦♦
If exploiting the microscopic compositional possibilities enabled by digital recording and editing technologies can be considered a distinct new genre, then *Explorers_We* is its first masterpiece. At first blush formless and chaotic, the CD's hour-plus collage of vocal bits, sound bytes, and fractured song fragments begins gradually to cohere into something remarkable and seductive. Farmers Manual write songs like frozen juice containers—concentrated, and requiring a bit of elbow work. But once the right ratio of ideation and assent has been found, *Explorers_We* is a true delight. —*Sean Cooper*

## Gene Farris

*Producer, DJ / Club/Dance, House*

Though Gene Farris is one in the new school of Chicago DJ/producers, his sound looks back to disco and funk even more than the requisite house sound of the Windy City. He recorded singles for Cajmere's Cajual/Relief and European labels Force Inc. and Soma before his debut album *Fruity Green* appeared in 1997 on Force Inc. After one more album for the label (1998's *Planet House*), he moved to Soma for *This Is My Religion* in 2000. —*John Bush*

**Fruity Green** / Jan. 6, 1997 / Force Inc ♦♦
**Planet House** / Feb. 2, 1998 / Force Inc ♦♦♦
Gene Farris' *Planet House* is a collection of dance tracks drawing equally from disco and house music; it sounds as good at home as it does in the clubs. —*Steve Huey*

● **This Is My Religion** / Jul. 25, 2000 / Soma ♦♦♦♦
Farris' second album cycles through many of the Chicago producer's musical interests, from jazzy house (complete with trumpet samples) on "The Grail," contemplative tech-house on "Origins," and on several tracks ("Confession," "The Gospel," "The Big Doobie," "Let Yourself Go"), extroverted filter-disco club stompers. These are all done well, but they can't hold a candle to the irresistible, tragically brief interludes "This Is My Religion" (the intro) and "Smoke Session Pause" (halfway through the album), a pair of excellent down-tempo sample tracks. Another highlight is "I Wanna Love You," complete with smoking synth-groove and a bridge worthy of a classic Donna Summer track. Everything Farris does he does quite well, and though he's never pioneering a new sound on *This Is My Religion*, his devotion and worship are evident. —*John Bush*

## Fatboy Slim (Norman Cook)

**b.** Jul. 13, 1963, Bromley, England
*Producer, DJ / Big Beat, Funky Breaks, Trip-Hop, Club/Dance*

Norman "Jacker-Of-All-Genres" Cook, in addition to his former occupations as bassist for the Housemartins and one third of acid-house hitmakers Pizzaman, is also the man behind one of the most popular of the new flock of English "brit hop" producers, Fatboy Slim. Releasing his Fatboy material through club staple Skint, Cook's raucous blend of house, acid, funk, hip-hop, electro, and techno has added to his already formidable reputation as one of the foremost all-around producers on the UK club scene. Born in Bromley on July 13, 1963, Cook joined the Hull-based pop group the Housemartins in 1986, replacing founding member Ted Key. After the group split the following year, Cook became involved with the burgeoning acid-house scene, pairing with producers Tim Jeffery and JC Reid toward the end of the decade to form Pizzaman. The trio nailed three Top 40 hits together ("Trippin' on Sunshine," "Sex on the Streets," and "Happiness") before Cook splintered off to record with similarly-styled outfits Freakpower and Beats International in the early '90s. He's shut most of his other production activities down in recent years to focus on his latest incarnation, Fatboy Slim, which to date includes a trio of singles and the full-length *Better Living Through Chemistry*. Cook was also called in to add his remixing skills to Jean-Jacques Perrey's proto-electronica classic "Eva," released as a 12" and CD single in 1997. In addition to his FBS work, Cook also recorded the *Skip to My Loops* sample CD, a popular studio tool sporting a melange of sample-ready drum loops, analog squelches, and assorted noises. In early 1998, his remix of Cornershop's "Brimful of Asha" spent several weeks at number one in the British charts. Fatboy Slim's eagerly anticipated second LP *You've Come a Long Way, Baby* followed later that year. The album went platinum in the US and spawned two international hits, "The Rockafeller Skank" and "Praise You," which also boasted a Spike Jonze-directed video that earned three MTV Video Music Awards as well as two Grammy nominations. "The Rockafeller Skank," "Praise You," and other songs from *You've Come a Long Way, Baby* ended up on countless soundtracks and commercials, cementing Fatboy Slim's unique position as a critically acclaimed and immensely popular act. Cook also recorded several mix albums, including the first disc of the Radio 1 compilation *Essential Selection, Vol. 1* and his own *On the Floor at the Boutique*. The latter was released domestically in the US in early 2000 to help fans withstand the wait for his third album, *Halfway Between the Gutter and the Stars*, which arrived that fall. [See Also: Beats International] —*Sean Cooper*

**Better Living Through Chemistry** / 1996 / Astralwerks ◆◆◆◆
Fatboy Slim is one of DJ Norman Cook's many aliases, and has proven to be his most popular and successful yet. Although he consistently racks up dance hits in his native England (each under a different surname), he didn't achieve global success until the re-release of *Better Living Through Chemistry* in '97. On the insistence of his friends the Chemical Brothers, Cook released the track "Going Out of My Head" as the album's first single. Due to its popular video and instantly catchy sample from the Who classic "I Can't Explain," Cook earned his first US hit. Another unlikely sample used to great effect was featured in the track "Michael Jackson," which used a snippet of Negativland's "Negativland." "The Weekend Starts Here" is similar to the Beastie Boys' funk instrumentals, featuring distant organ and lazy harmonica blowing (which sounds an awful lot like the harmonica phrase at the beginning of Black Sabbath's "The Wizard"). Recommended to those who can't get enough of today's popular technoid-sampled-alternative-dance style. —*Greg Prato*

**On the Floor at the Boutique** / Aug. 25, 1998 / Skint ◆◆◆◆
The hook here isn't so much the big-beat compilation itself as it is the DJ who mixed the program—none other than the funk soul brother himself, Fatboy Slim. Better known to those over 30 as Norman Cook, bass player for the Housemartins and later the brains behind the charming reggae-funk outfit Beats International, he's now the king of big beat, a club music subgenre dedicated to phat, stoopid beats and pure dancefloor fun. *On the Floor at the Boutique* was recorded live as Fatboy mixed it at Brighton, England's *Big Beat Boutique*, and it's guaranteed to ruin the carpet at any party. There are contributions from artists as established as Fred Wesley (with his Horny Horns, not the Famous Flames) and the Jungle Brothers, and as obscure as DJ Tonka (whose "Phun-Ky" is an album highlight) and Bassbin Twins. It should come as no surprise that Fatboy Slim himself delivers some of the best moments on the program, including the deeply weird "Michael Jackson" and his irresistible Top 40 hit "Rockafeller Skank." Outstanding. —*Rick Anderson*

● **You've Come a Long Way, Baby** / Oct. 12, 1998 / Astralwerks ◆◆◆◆
Fatboy Slim's debut album *Better Living Through Chemistry* was one of the surprises of the big-beat revolution of 1996—an eclectic blowout, all tracked to thunderous loops and masterminded by Norman Cook, a former member of the British pop band the Housemartins. It might not have been as startlingly fresh as the Chemical Brothers, but the hard-hitting beats and catchiness, not to mention consistency, of *Better Living* was a shock, and it raised expectations for Fatboy Slim's second album, *You've Come a Long Way, Baby*. And that record itself was something of a surprise, since it not only exceeded the expectations set by the debut, but came damn close to being the definitive big-beat album, rivaling the Chemicals' second record, *Dig Your Own Hole*. The difference is, Cook is a record geek with extensive knowledge and eclectic tastes. His juxtapositions—the album swings from hip-hop to reggae to jangle-pop, and then all combines into one sound—are wildly original, even if the music itself doesn't break through the confines of big beat. Then again, when a record is this forceful and catchy, it doesn't need to break new stylstic ground—the pleasure is in hearing a master work. And there's no question that Cook is a master of sorts—*You've Come a Long Way, Baby* is a seamless record, filled with great imagination, unexpected twists and turns, huge hooks and great beats. It's the kind of record that gives big beat a good name. —*Stephen Thomas Erlewine*

**Signature Series, Vol. 1: Greatest Remixes** / Feb. 15, 2000 / Intersound ◆◆◆◆
*Signature Series, Vol. 1: Greatest Remixes* is a ten-track collection of Norman Cook postproductions, though the claim in the title is doubtful, considering Cornershop's "Brimful of Asha" and the Beastie Boys' "Body Movin'" are nowhere to be found. Still, the ones that *are* here are excellent. Cook's production skills are impeccable, and his knack for both a cleverly tweaked, oddball old-school sample and an irresistible groove are displayed to even better effect than on his original albums. Most of the inclusions here originally came from the dance community—the licensing fees are always cheaper—and though it's more of a budget-label cash-in than anything else, it turns out well. Highlights include remixes of Stretch'n'Vern's "Get Up! Go Insane!," Christopher Just's "I'm a Disco Dancer (And a Sweet Romancer)," Wildchild's "Renegade Master" (originally by the late Roger McKenzie, a friend of Cook's), and the surprisingly mid-tempo "E.V.A." by tape-music pioneer Jean-Jacques Perrey. Over the course of ten tracks, Cook's tricks of the trade pop up just a bit too often to make for a solid listen, but fans and collectors alike will enjoy *Signature Series, Vol. 1: Greatest Remixes*. —*John Bush*

**Halfway Between the Gutter and the Stars** / Nov. 7, 2000 / Astralwerks ◆◆◆◆
The cover of Norman Cook's breakout Fatboy Slim album, *You've Come a Long Way, Baby*, was a good clue to the contents, picturing as it did thousands of LPs straining the racks in Cook's record room—undoubtedly just a small portion of his massive collection of sampling material. Inside, Cook unfolded a party record for the ages, long on fun (though understandably short on staying power), chock full of samples pillaged from all manner of obscure soul shouters and old-school rap crews, triggered and tweaked *ad nauseam*. With his third LP, *Halfway Between the Gutter and the Stars*, Cook pulls away slightly from the notoriously fickle pop charts and crossover kids courted on his last record. Instead, he makes a conscious attempt to inject some real hedonism back into the world of dance—he *is* a DJ, after all—and sure enough, the cover matches those aims: it's a long shot on a beach (Ibiza or some other far-flung shore), with the sun shining out of someone's behind. The intro even pokes gentle fun at the loved-up R&B tradition with an extended sample from some bygone soul artist waxing overly poetic about his girlfriend. From there, Cook tears into an acid-techno rampage named "Star 69," a track that takes few prisoners and sounds closer to Plastikman than Propellerheads, though it does include the Fatboy Slim trademark—a rather blue vocal sample repeated continually for nigh on a minute (funnily enough, the track was entirely removed from the clean version of the album).

Despite the torrid pace set early on, there's still quite a bit of the used-bin scavenger left in Cook; the most patented big-beat anthems here, "Ya Mama" and "Mad Flava," include all the expected displays of crowd-moving hip-hop calls, unhinged beatbox funk, continual drum breakdowns, and plenty of rawk riffs. The first single "Sunset (Bird of Prey)" is another potential crossover move, featuring what is easily the album's most recognizable sample source—Jim Morrison from the Doors. Borrowing from Morrison's posthumous LP of poetry *An American Prayer*, the "collaboration" works better than could be expected, with Morrison's pseudo-mystical, surreal vocal— "Bird of prey, flying high/In the summer sky, gently passing by"—floating over some comparatively atmospheric breakbeat funk by the Fatboy.

Sniffy electronica purism aside though, Cook remains, if not the best overall producer in the dance world, certainly in its top rank, with an excellent ear for infectious hooks, tight beats, and irresistible grooves. On advice from friends the Chemical Brothers, Cook recruited collaborators for the first time—nu-soul diva Macy Gray, funk legend Bootsy Collins, fellow superstar DJ/producer Roger Sanchez—and the two tracks with Gray, "Love Life" and "Demons," are arguably the highlights of the entire album. In a similar fashion to David Holmes, Cook's ample production talents are served best with a vocalist lending focus, and "Love Life" is a seven-minute ride veering from dirty, warped funk to noise-heavy hip-hop breakdowns while Gray scats, growls, and purrs with clearly audible glee. After Bootsy's joint (the surprisingly bland "Weapon of Choice") and a hackneyed social-message track ("Drop the Hate"), Gray returns to save the album with another unbelievable performance on the half-resigned, half-hopeful gospel soul of "Demons." The closer, "Song for Shelter," is a masterful stroke of sun-splashed house recorded with help from Roger Sanchez and an ecstatic serenade to the dance music experience by Roland Clark (interpolated from his single "I Get Deep"). In all, *Halfway Between the Gutter and the Stars* is possibly Norman Cook's best possible statement after being—nearly simultaneously—picked up by a multitude of notoriously fickle pop consumers and thrown away by his previously rock-solid dance fan base. The hooks are unmissable and there's plenty of big-beat techno from a master of the form, but there's also a good amount of mature material that would undeniably appeal to many listeners in the dance world if they ever condescended to give it an objective listen. —*John Bush*

## Fauna Flash

f. Munich, Germany
*Group / Trip-Hop, Jungle/Drum'N'Bass, Club/Dance*

Fauna Flash is a German duo who have brought jungle to a country that is infamous for its love of hard, classic techno beats. Christian Prommer and Roland Appel make up the duo who have been admired by such jungle hierarchy as Metalheadz posse members Grooverider and Fabio. The two broke away from traditional German techno in 1992 when the band experienced duo started playing live drums at raves in German clubs. In 1994 they stepped into the studio to gain experience and a year later released their first tracks for Compost Records. The popularity and positive endorsement from DJs such as Peshay, Kemistry & Storm, and Giles Peterson landed the two 12" exclusive release on Peshay's label, Elementz. Their track &At the Movies was also put on the popular jungle compilation *Promise Land 3*. Besides their various 12 releases, Prommer and Appel work with fellow Compost artist Rainer Trüby as the Rainer Trüby Trio. Though they produce jungle, Roland and Appel take influence from jazz and '80s fusion. —*Diana Potts*

● **Aquarius** / Jan. 12, 1998 / Compost ♦♦

Munich jungle outfit Fauna Flash sounded a bit out of the loop, so to speak, on their debut album *Aquarius*. Unlike the producers in Britain's large and diverse jungle community, Germany doesn't have much of a drum'n'bass scene to call on for support, so Fauna Flash end up recycling ideas from established UK acts like Roni Size or L.T.J. Bukem. The results are sometimes pleasant, but rarely compelling. —*John Bush*

## Faust

f. 1971, Wumme, Germany
*Group / Kraut Rock, Experimental, Prog-Rock/Art Rock*

"There is no group more mythical than Faust," wrote Julian Cope in his book *Kraut-rocksampler*, which detailed the pivotal influence the German band exerted over the development of ambient and industrial textures. Producer/overseer Uwe Nettelbeck, a onetime music journalist, formed Faust in Wumme, Germany in 1971 with founding members Hans Joachim Irmler, Jean Herve Peron, Werner "Zappi" Diermaier, Rudolf Sosna, Gunther Wustoff, and Arnulf Meifert. Upon receiving advance money from their label, Nettelbeck converted an old schoolhouse into a recording studio, where the group spent the first several months of its existence in almost total isolation, honing their unique, cacophonic sound with the aid of occasional guests like minimalist composer Tony Conrad and members of Slapp Happy.

Issued on clear vinyl in a transparent sleeve, Faust's eponymously-titled debut LP surfaced in 1971; although sales were notoriously bad, the album—a noisy sound collage of cut-and-paste musical fragments—did earn the group a solid cult following. Another lavishly-packaged work, *Faust So Far*, followed in 1972, and earned the group a contract with Virgin, who issued 1973's *The Faust Tapes*—a fan-assembled collection of home recordings—for about the price of a single, a marketing ploy which earned considerable media interest. After *Outside Dream Syndicate*, a collaboration with Tony Conrad, the band released 1973's *Faust IV*, a commercial failure which resulted in the loss of their contract with Virgin, who refused to release the planned *Faust 5*.

When Nettelbeck turned his focus away from the group, Faust disbanded in 1975, and the members scattered throught Germany; however, after more than a decade of playing together in various incarnations, Faust officially reunited around the nucleus of Irmler, Peron, and Dermaier for a handful of European performances at the outset of the '90s. In 1993, they made their first-ever US live appearance backing Conrad, followed by a series of other stateside performances; after several live releases, a pair of new studio albums, *Rien* and *You Know FaUSt*, followed in 1996. *Ravvivando* appeared three years later. —*Jason Ankeny*

**Faust** / 1971 / Recommended ♦♦♦♦

The impact of Faust cannot be overstated; their debut album was truly a revolutionary step forward in the progress of "rock music." It was pressed on clear vinyl, packaged in a clear sleeve, with a clear plastic lyric insert. The black X-ray of a fist on the cover graphically illustrates the hard core music contained in the grooves, an amalgamation of electronics, rock, tape edits, acoustic guitars, musique concrète, and industrial angst. The level of imagination is staggering, the concept is totally unique, and it's fun to listen to as well. —*Archie Patterson*

**Faust So Far** / 1972 / Recommended ♦♦♦♦

Faust's second album moves closer to actual song structure than their debut, but it still remains experimental. Songs progress and evolve instead of abruptly stopping or cutting into other tracks. The opening song "It's a Rainy Day, Sunshine Girl" begins as a repetitive 4/4 beat played on toms and piano with the title sung over the top. But for seven minutes the song adds instruments, including a lush analog synth line, and ends in a memorable sax riff. Faust's lyrical side appears on the acoustic "Picnic on a Frozen River" and "On the Way to Adamäe," whereas its abrasive side pops up on "Me Lack Space." "So Far," a jam shared by guitar, horns, and tweedy keyboard, rolls along with a funky hypnotic beat and wailing processed synths. And on "No Harm," the crazed delivery of such lines as "Daddy, take the banana, tomorrow Sunday" makes one want to believe something profound is going down. In terms of scope and the wealth of ideas, this is probably the most balanced of their first four albums. —*Ted Mills*

**Faust IV** / 1973 / Virgin ♦♦♦♦

*Faust IV* is an album of intriguing vacillations between chugging, motorische Kraut-rock (occasionally bordering on jazz-rock) and a series of effervescent, alluring folk-pop songs such as "Sad Skinhead" and "Jennifer." The group gets the balance just right by inserting jagged guitar chords and hints of experimentalism into the pop songs, and by never letting the instrumental tracks range too far into avant-garde territory. It's easily Faust's most listenable album, though hardly a commercial move. —*John Bush*

**The Faust Tapes** / 1973 / Cuneiform ♦♦♦♦

This was the release that "broke" Faust to a British audience, mostly because of a marketing gimmick whereby the then-infant Virgin label sold it in shops for half a pound. Still, it's no mean feat to sell 50,000 copies of rock this avant-garde, no matter what the cost. A continuous 43-minute piece with about 26 discrete passages (which makes it hell to zero in on a specific bit on CD), it roams from crash'n'mash drums and fierce art-rock jamming to rather pretty, if inscrutable, bits of folk-rock and spoken word, with odd shards of melody sticking out like glass in a tire. There are rough reference points to Zappa in the torrid editing and British Canterbury bands in the goofier, more rock-driven parts, but this is even less immediately accessible, taking a few plays to get a grip on, though most pop-oriented listeners won't get that far. —*Richie Unterberger*

**Munich and Elsewhere** / 1986 / Recommended ♦♦♦

Leftovers from the early part of the '70s that are consistent enough with the Faust anything-goes vibe to be considered worthy of investigation by anyone who values their proper albums as well. There's no consistent focus, which in turn is entirely consistent with the nature of a band so enigmatic. It's been reissued in its entirety on the *Seventy One Minutes Of* CD, which adds a substantial amount of additional rare material, and is thus the recommended alternative to hunting down the original release. —*Richie Unterberger*

- **71 Minutes of Faust** / 1996 / Recommended ✦✦✦✦
Basically an expanded version of *Munich and Elsewhere* (which was itself a compilation of unreleased material), with the addition of the unreleased LP *Faust Party Three* (parts of which had previously appeared only as limited edition EPs and singles), as well as two previously unreleased tracks. Parts wed brutal drum patterns to insistently repetitive guitar riffing; there are prog-rock keyboard passages that slightly recall Soft Machine. "Don't Take Roots" sounds like an unintentional satire of the cheap California psychedelia that you might hear on a late-'60s youth culture exploitation flick. Sometimes it even sounds like a parody of early King Crimson-type pomp rock. It would be nice to have some liner notes explaining exactly what comes from where, but basically what you need to know is that it was all recorded in Germany from 1971 to 1975, and is on par with the quality of the albums they actually released during that time. —*Richie Unterberger*

**You Know FaUSt** / Feb. 25, 1997 / Recommended ✦✦✦
Faust's comeback album *You Know FaUSt* is a surprisingly vital return, finding the group at the wild, recklessly experimental peak of *The Faust Tapes* and *Faust IV*. Largely shedding the blistering *musique concrète* of their reunion concerts, the band concentrates on creating mainly instrumental soundscapes of synthesizers, organs, horns, droning guitars, and pulsating rhythms. While the sound isn't as revolutionary as it once was, it is undeniably more accomplished—and frequently just as exciting—as their earlier recordings. —*Stephen Thomas Erlewine*

**Faust Wakes Nosferatu** / Mar. 3, 1998 / Klangbad ✦✦✦
*Faust Wakes Nosferatu* was composed as a sort of companion piece to the classic vampire film *Nosferatu*, and Faust's music runs the gamut from delicate, ambient minimalism to cacophonous rock passages. —*Steve Huey*

**Ravvivando** / May 11, 1999 / EFA ✦✦✦✦
With touring and recording becoming something of a regular occurrence in the '90s, Faust was actually resembling a proper band. Although the group had been somewhat active since its semi-retirement in the mid-'70s, this album represented something of a mini-comback on the heels of a concurrent international tour for these Kraut-rock legends as founding members Zappi Diermaier and Hans-Joachim Irmler carried the torch. *Ravvivando* is full with some of the best Velvet Underground minimalist-noise-rush this side of My Bloody Valentine, even if you miss the complete audio-visual aspect of their insane pyrotechnic shows (see *The Faust Concerts*). Interestingly, there are brief parodies/tributes to their fellow Germans Amon Düül ("Take Care"), Cluster ("Ein Neurer Tag") and Neu! "T-Electronique"—perhaps not surprising from a band that once self-consciously called a song "Kraut-rock." With the amusing carnival-like "Dr' Hansl," the monster-movie blues of "Livin' Toyko," the eerie, chanted "Apokalpyse" and the anthemic, spiritual "Du Weibt Schon," this represents something of a new twist in their career. It has more to do with the collage quality of *Rien* (1995) than the wonderfully goofy *IV* or their early tape experiments. An intriguing phase for an always unpredictable group. —*Jason Gross*

## Felix Da Housecat (Felix Stallings, Jr.)

b. 1972, Chicago, IL
Producer, DJ / Club/Dance, Acid House, House

Second-wave Chicago house impresario Felix Da Housecat entered the elite via his recordings as himself, Thee Maddkatt Courtship, Aphrohead, Sharkimaxx) as well as his ownership of Radikal Fear Records, one of the premiere Chicago labels of the '90s. An introduction to Chicago legend DJ Pierre during the mid-'80s gave the 15-year-old Felix Stallings, Jr. the kickstart he wanted, and with some help from Pierre, he produced his first single "Phantasy Girl" in 1987.

His parents discouraged his growing club lifestyle, however, and after high-school graduation Stallings left the scene entirely to attend Alabama State College. Over the course of a few years, he lost all interest in house music, though his girlfriend got him back into it. After calling DJ Pierre (who had moved to New York's Strictly Rhythm label), Felix began mixing and producing again. By 1992, he had a hit with the single "Thee Dawn" on Guerilla Records. His popularity soared in Europe, and the following year's "By Dawn's Early Light" and "Thee Industry Made Me Do It" cemented his reputation.

Not long after Stallings formed Radikal Fear Records, the label became one of the top house imprints in the world, thanks to releases from Mike Dunn, DJ Sneak, and Armando as well as Felix himself. During 1995, he released his debut full-length *Alone in the Dark* (as Thee Maddkatt Courtship) on Deep Distraxion. Hot on its heels came the label collection *Radikal Fear: The Chicago All Stars* and a Housecat DJ album titled *Clashbackk Compilation Mix*. Another production LP, *Metropolis Present Day—Thee Album*, followed in 1998. One year later, Stallings appeared extra busy; in addition to his first album as Aphrohead, he also released another Maddkatt Courtship LP, the highly praised *I Know Elektrikboy*. Felix Da Housecat has also remixed Diana Ross, Kylie Minogue, Black Science Orchestra, and X-Press 2. [See Also: Maddkatt Courtship] —*John Bush*

**Transmissions, Vol. 2** / 1997 / Virgin Music Canada ✦✦✦
Felix Da Housecat's volume in the *Transmissions* series features a surprising amount of techno—with tracks by Ian Pooley, Speedy J, Joey Beltram, and Plastikman—as well as house masters like Phuture and Felix's own Aphrohead project. —*John Bush*

- **Clashbackk Compilation Mix** / Nov. 4, 1997 / K-Tel ✦✦✦✦
Released by Cold Front, the dance division of none other than K-Tel Records, Felix Da Housecat's *Clashbackk Compilation Mix* is an excellent mix of hard-edged house including a few of his production aliases—Aphrohead ("Blindmanwilly," "While They Watch"), Maddkatt Chronicles ("Vengeance of a Madman," "Mommy Why?"), and Felix Da Housecat himself ("Zeka's Solar Device"). Though there aren't any other big-name producers (L.A. Williams and Spanky are the biggest), Felix sets an intense groove from the opening seconds and rarely lets go. —*John Bush*

**Metropolis Present Day—Thee Album** / 1998 / Radikal Fear ✦✦✦✦
*Metropolis Present Day* is an intriguing LP, including past singles like "Footsteps of Rage!" and "Metropolis" as well as interesting stylistic excursions such as "Marine Mood." Robert Hood provides a remix of "Footsteps," among other highlights including "Somekinda Special" and "B 4 Wuz Then." —*John Bush*

## Fennesz (Christian Fennesz)

Guitar, Producer / Experimental Techno, Experimental Electro, Electronica, Ambient Techno

Vienna-based guitarist Christian Fennesz is one of the city's many artists associated with the noted Mego label, which releases mostly freeform ambient and experimental electronica. Similar in some respects to the work of Seefeel or Experimental Audio Research, Fennesz's six-string soundscapes are both darker than the former and more complex and intricate than the latter, combining dense, multilayered sheets of treated guitar and synth with thin, odd-metered electronic percussion and engaging sampler work. A former member of Austrian underground experimental rock group Maische, Fennesz has also collaborated with Mego artist Peter "Pita" Rehberg on his *Seven Tons for Free* CD, as well as performed ensemble pieces for conceptual and multimedia art installation. His first solo work for Mego, the *Instrument* EP, was released in 1996, and featured 4 tracks of stunning, uncompromised ambient and electro-acoustic, combining elements of experimental electro/techno with heavily treated guitar and electronics. *Hotel Paral.lel* followed in 1997, and three years later Fennesz returned with *Plus Forty Seven Degrees 56' 37" Minus Sixteen Degrees 51' 08"* and *Music for an Isolation Tank*. —*Sean Cooper*

**Instrument [EP]** / 1997 / Mego ✦✦✦✦
Four tracks ranging from deep, melodic ambient bliss to shuffling, rhythmically randomized experimental electronica. Given the EP's title, the fractured, out-of-register-whammy-bar/bridge shot gracing the cover, and an obvious nod to six-string obscurantists such as My Bloody Valentine and Seefeel on a pair of the tracks, it's safe to say much of the music originated with the relatively traditionalist (from the standpoint of electronica, anyway) medium of the guitar. The results, however, are anything but predictable, with uniformly inventive deployments of the instrument's combinatorial possibilities (effects boxes, looping figures, sequenced sound collage) filling the EP's 20-plus minutes. —*Sean Cooper*

- **Hotel Paral.lel** / 1997 / Mego ✦✦✦✦
As bizarre as it was, Christian Fennesz's previous release for Mego—the "Instrument" EP—is made positively accessible by this, his full-length debut. Skipping across droning, machinic ambient, minimal experimental techno, and abstract beat-oriented electronica, the album draws copiously from compositional styles the artist clearly (and thankfully) has nothing but a passing interest in. Points of reference might include, by turns, Main, Porter Ricks, Nonplace Urban Field, and Throbbing Gristle, but like other Mego artists

such as General Magic and Farmers Manual, Fennesz manages to sustain a consistent assault on stylistic convention while remaining at the same time positively listenable and anything but pretentious. Although the guitar seems less present than on "Instrument," its appearance on "Blok M" and "Fa," among others, makes for some singularly beautiful moments. The album's standout closer, "Aus," is a stunning example of post-genre complexity made more notable by how strangely catchy it is. —*Sean Cooper*

### Il Libro Mio [EP] / 1998 / Tanzhotel ♦♦♦
This special 3" CD release features Fennesz's composition for an Austrian ballet company celebrating the work of 15th century Italian painter Jacopo Carrucci, also known as Pontormo. It's hard to imagine what sort of dancing might be accompanied by Fennesz's fractured computerscapes, but these 20 minutes of stuttering electronics, digital fuzz, and dam-bursting sample collage are a welcome addition to Fennesz's too-brief discography. Much less structured and accommodating than his previous works, but enjoyable nonetheless. —*Sean Cooper*

### Fennesz Plays [Single] / Feb. 2, 1999 / Mego/Moikai ♦♦
Much ballyhoo was made of this two-track 7" featuring Fennesz's "covers" of the Rolling Stones and Brian Wilson. In spite of enthusiastic testimony to the contrary, "Paint It Black" and "Don't Talk (Put Your Head on My Shoulder)" don't bear even the remotest resemblance to the originals. The reissue of the record's less than ten minutes of abstract guitar textures by the American label Moikai says more for Moikai label chief Jim O'Rourke's penchant for pop subversion than for the intrinsic quality of the music, which though interesting enough, simply doesn't approach Fennesz's other releases. For completists only. —*Sean Cooper*

## FFWD
f. 1993, London, England
*Group / Ambient Techno*

FFWD stands for Thomas Fehlmann (Sun Electric), Robert Fripp, Kris Weston, and Dr. Alex Paterson (the latter two of the Orb), and as that lineup suggests, was probably ambient's first supergroup. Although a one-off project with no certain plans of reconvening, the album resulting from the few days in the studio spent recording it is a landmark of experimental ambient and surprisingly unlike the various projects its contributors are known for. Closest in feel perhaps to some of the Orb's more recent releases (*Pomme Fritz* and *Orbus Terrarum*), *FFWD* deviates strongly in its sparseness and subtlety. Fripp's guitar is heavily atmospheric and subjected to the sort of heaping effects processing Fehlmann and Weston are known for; Paterson reportedly recorded hours of the virtuoso just noodling around on his six-string and assembled the bits into usable passages only after the fact. Thanks to inspired arrangements and an emphasis on texture, *FFWD* is also one of only a few albums to successfully figure the guitar in a central position without sounding off-balance or obligatory.

In addition to his early experiments with Brian Eno on such albums as *No Pussyfooting* and *Evening Star*, Fripp has also worked on other occasions with new ambient luminaries such as Future Sound of London and has released a pair of *Soundscapes* performances recorded during a solo tour. Weston (aka Thrash) left the Orb in 1995 to pursue a solo project, and Fehlmann's Sun Electric has released several full-lengths and a handful of EPs. —*Sean Cooper*

● **FFWD** / 1994 / Inter-Modo & Discipline ♦♦♦
A fast-forward of sorts for new-school ambient, which had begun to stagnate by the time Fripp & Co. organized this summit. Horse hooves, wind-up toys, a clock being smashed, mutilated tablas, even the light shuffle of a book's pages being turned all figure somewhere in the mix. Superlative song-ordering and attention to mood and flow make complete listening a must. Exemplary and essential. —*Sean Cooper*

## Fifty Foot Hose
f. 1967, db. 1970
*Group / Psychedelic*

Fifty Foot Hose was one of the most unusual '60s San Francisco psychedelic bands, in part because they weren't really that psychedelic. Like a few other acts of the time (most notably the United States of America), they were trying to fuse the contemporary sounds of rock with electronic instruments and avant-garde compositional ideas. Only one album resulted from the ambitious enterprise, and that record (*Cauldron*, 1968) still remains unknown to all but hardcore collectors. Although an erratic work, it was intriguing for its mix of jazzy psychedelic rock tunes with electronic sound effects that anticipated future models of synthesizers, but sounded fiercer and more primitive.

Fifty Foot Hose was founded by bassist Cork Marcheschi, who had previously been in a conventional rock/R&B band, the Ethix. Under Marcheschi's prodding, in 1967 the Ethix released one wildly atonal single, "Bad Trip," whose violent musique concrète foreshadowed the avant-garde postures of his subsequent group. (In fact, "Bad Trip" was *more* avant-garde than anything Fifty Foot Hose would record. Apparently it was played once on a local underground radio station, and then never again.) Interested in the ideas of experimental composers like Edgar Varése, John Cage, Terry Riley, and George Antheil, Marcheschi constructed his own electronic instrument from a combination of elements like theremins, fuzzboxes, a cardboard tube, and a speaker from a World War II aircraft bomber.

Fifty Foot Hose was filled out by guitarist David Blossom and his vocalist wife Nancy, who brought both psychedelic and jazz influences to the band, and a couple of musicians who had played with Marcheschi in other acts. A home demo successfully demonstrated their fusion of electronic effects and songs that were loosely in tune with the San Francisco psychedelic vibe. It led to a deal with Limelight, a subsidiary of Mercury that focused more upon experimental music than conventional rock and pop outings.

*Cauldron* was perhaps more interesting for its experimental textures than the sometimes routine compositions—eerie electronic swoops and jolts swam through the background and foreground of the tracks, enhanced by techniques like putting instruments through an FM transmitter. The jazzier and spookier tunes worked better than the bluesier hard rock items, yet it was an admirably risk-taking effort. But, ultimately, a pretty uncommercial one—although they got some live work in San Francisco, the album was heard by few at its time of release. Fifty Foot Hose was finished, ironically, by the temptations of a much more commercial project when the musical *Hair* came to San Francisco, most of the members joined the production to satisfy their need for more reliable income. Interest in the group resurfaced in the '90s, as they became recognized as precursors to the electronic rock sounds of groups like Throbbing Gristle. Marcheschi is now a respected sculptor, specializing in public work using neon, plastic, and kinetic characteristics. —*Richie Unterberger*

### Cauldron / 1968 / Limelight ♦♦♦
The Fifty Foot Hose's only album features a variety of musical styles, from swirling, trippy ballads to heavier, new wave-like rock songs. There is also a spacey version of "God Bless the Child" for good measure. The record features stereo panning and many other effects done more smoothly than on other records of the era. The CD reissue contains three bonus tracks, two songs from their demo, and a 1966 pre-Hose dada-esque noise freak-out by Cork and two friends. —*Jim Powers*

● **Cauldron Plus** / 1996 / Big Beat ♦♦♦♦
A CD reissue of their rare 1968 LP, with the addition of seven interesting bonus tracks. *Cauldron* itself is erratic but fascinating. When married to routine blues-rock, the electronic squiggles seem to be covering up the inadequacy of the basic material, and the occasional bleats of pure electronic passages will bore rock-oriented listeners. Yet when combined with lilting-but-disquieting jazz-psychedelic compositions, like the title track and "If Not This Time," it's genuinely original, similar in feel to the oscillation-toned rock of the United States of America (though the USA's one-shot album was more consistent and smoothly produced). The bonus tracks include the four-song home demo that got them their Limelight contract (two of the cuts would be re-recorded on the LP); except for the rambling and indulgent "Desire," these are up to par with what came out officially. Topping things off are both sides of the "Bad Trip" single by Cork Marcheschi's previous group, the Ethix; the willfully inaccessible blasts of noise-rock are among the most uncommercial and downright difficult relics of the psychedelic era that ever made it onto vinyl. —*Richie Unterberger*

## Fila Brazillia
f. 1991, Hull, England
*Group / Electronica, Ambient Techno, Trip-Hop*

Hull-based duo Fila Brazillia are the most popular and acclaimed of the noted Pork Recordings stable. Formed in 1991 by producers Steve Cobby and Dave McSherry, Fila followed Cobby's association with Ashley & Jackson, a moderately successful pop/dance group signed to Big Life! which went belly up as the label began demanding more and more pop and less dance. Returning to his native Hull from Manchester, Cobby met DJ/dabbler Dave Pork, and the two forged a creative alliance which continues to this day. Hooking up with McSherry to form Fila, the group's first 12", "The Mermaid," was released that same year on Pork's fledgling imprint (formed, actually, specifically for the occasion), gaining instant acclaim among DJs and headphonauts alike for its innovative fusion of funk, dub, house, hip-hop, and acid jazz. The group followed their debut single with a string of full-length releases (*Old Codes, New Chaos, Maim That Tune,* and *Black Market Gardening* among them) which were instrumental in building Pork's reputation as one of the most consistent and respected of England's vast ocean of underground breakbeat/trip-hop labels. More recent releases have integrated elements of pop and drum'n'bass on a number of tracks. Fila's rep has also translated into a number of acclaimed remixes, including Lamb's "Cotton Wool," the Orb's "Toxygene," and DJ Food's "Freedom" (over a dozen of which were featured on the two-disc collection *Brazilification*.) In addition to Fila, Cobby is also an active member of other Pork stable acts such as Solid Doctor (his solo guise) and Heights of Abraham, both of which have released a number of full-length recordings. —*Sean Cooper*

**Old Codes, New Chaos** / 1994 / Pork ◆◆

**Maim That Tune** / 1995 / Pork ◆◆◆
Experimental technoheads Fila Brazillia really mix it up on *Maim That Tune,* constructing various takes on techno, including elements of spaghetti Western, hip-hop, house, and African music. —*John Bush*

**Mess** / Apr. 29, 1996 / Pork ◆◆◆

**Black Market Gardening** / Nov. 11, 1996 / Pork ◆◆◆◆

**Luck Be a Weirdo Tonight** / Jun. 23, 1997 / Pork ◆◆◆◆
Even more experimentally hyper than on previous LPs, Fila Brazillia cross-fertilize styles with abandon on *Luck Be a Weirdo Tonight,* resulting in such genre-bending as prog-blaxploitation and space-disco, as well as more straightahead fusions like lounge-disco. —*John Bush*

**Power Clown** / Aug. 31, 1998 / Pork ◆◆◆◆
The eclecticism and the organic warmth of Fila Brazillia's electronica continue to amaze on *Power Clown,* one of their finest efforts to date. Laidback jazz-funk grooves straight out of the '70s are the foundation of the record, but hints of Stevie Wonder-esque soul, hip-hop, bossa nova, ambient, spacey techno, house, minimalist electro, big-beat, and trip-hop all pop up here and there, as do touches of ethnic percussion, acoustic guitar, saxophone solos, new age-y synth flourishes, and the occasional odd vocal sample or sound effect. What really pushes *Power Clown* over the top, though, is that the group maintains their focus throughout, never meandering and changing things up often enough to keep the grooves from becoming repetitive. One of the finest and most overlooked electronic-dance releases of 1998. —*Steve Huey*

● **Brazilification** / Jun. 6, 2000 / Kudos ◆◆◆◆
Just like Kruder & Dorfmeister's excellent *K&D Sessions,* Fila Brazillia's *Brazilification* is a continuous-mix set of down-tempo remixes spanning two discs, and it's just as stellar a compilation of material, too. Though Fila Brazillia doesn't quite have the reputation on the decks, like K&D they'd been not only one of the busiest remixing teams during the late '90s but also one of the best. Freed from the "serious" art of long-form recordings and given a focus by the originals (many of which are pop songs by alternative bands), Cobby and McSherry sound even better here than on their albums (where frequent genre excursions and long jams occasionally make for rather bland trip-hop). As you'd expect from the cover photo, which shows the anoraked pair larking about on a hillside, the duo knows how to have fun as well; they toy with their vocoders to give a hilarious canary-in-a-ring-modulator effect to the vocals of Moloko's Roisin Murphy on their remix of "Lotus Eaters." Though many of the best remixes come on the first disc (Radiohead's "Climbing up the Walls," U.N.K.L.E.'s "Berry Meditation," the Orb's "Toxygene"), one of Brazillia's best moments on wax—the alternately blissful and drum-heavy rework of Lamb's "Cottonwool"—finally appears late on the second disc. For those too busy to track down remixes, *Brazilification* is not only a perfect complement to the Pork Recordings pair but a worthy introduction. —*John Bush*

## Final (Justin Broadrick)

*Producer / Dark Ambient*
Final is the only solo alias among Justin Broadrick's many ongoing projects, which include Godflesh, Ice, Techno Animal, and Painkiller. Specializing in malevolent space music of the kind also practiced by Bill Laswell projects on Axiom Dub and Subharmonic, Final began in 1993 with the release of *One* on Subharmonic. The inevitable *2* followed three years later, while *The First Millionth of a Second* appeared on Manifold in 1997. Broadrick has also contributed remixes to material by David Kristian. —*John Bush*

**One** / 1993 / Subharmonic ◆◆◆

**The First Millionth of a Second** / Aug. 7, 1997 / Manifold ◆◆◆◆
The seven tracks on *The First Millionth of a Second* work through incredibly textural, wall-of-noise ambience, though several tracks have uncanny melodic lines ("Quark," "Critical Thresholds") running through them. —*Keith Farley*

● **Solaris** / Sep. 29, 1998 / Alley Sweeper ◆◆◆◆
The results of sessions from summer 1995 recorded by Broadrick live to two-track, the *Solaris* EP includes three tracks of expansive ambient noise created mostly by guitar distortion and other effects detritus. *Solaris* was filled out for a 1998 CD reissue with the addition of a fourth track, the 30-minute "Dying Star." —*Keith Farley*

## Fingers Inc.

**f.** 1985, Chicago, IL, **db.** 1988
*Group / Club/Dance, Acid House, House*
The top early Chicago house group and the first outlet for the production genius of Larry Heard, Fingers Inc. was formed in 1985 by Heard with vocalists Robert Owens and Ron Wilson. Though the group often took a sideline to Heard's solo jaunts as Mr. Fingers, at their best they rivalled Ten City with expressive club gems like "You're Mine," "It's Over," and "A Love of My Own." The group also spawned the first (and some say best) house LP, 1988's *Another Side.* That album was basically the end of Fingers Inc., though; Heard produced singles by Owens and Wilson, but then moved on to a solo career by the end of the decade. [See Also: Larry Heard, Mr. Fingers] —*John Bush*

● **Another Side** / 1988 / Indigo Music/Jack Trax ◆◆◆◆
The only LP from Fingers Inc. was the first full-length in the genre and an unabashed house classic. Obviously, it's chocked with uptempo singles perfectly primed for the dancefloor ("Bye Bye," "Music Take Me Up," "Distant Planet"), and vocalist Robert Owens' gospel flavor and strong voice is a special treat. What makes *Another Side* more than just a statistic, however, is Heard's surprising adeptness at sustaining interest over the course of a full album. His flare for melancholy had been previously hinted at only by the Detroit techno producers, and it resulted in the rare mainstream house LP that succeeded on several levels. —*John Bush*

## Carl Finlow

*Producer / Electro, Techno*
Voice Stealer is one of many bylines used by eclectic dance music producer Carl A. Finlow, whose slick, sophisticated fusions of a range of dance music styles have appeared variously on the Soma, 20:20 Vision, Subvert, Klang, Phono, and SSR labels. Following on the heals of bold, bouncy hybrids of electro and new wave such as Le Car's "Automatic" and I-F's "Space Invaders Are Smoking Grass," Finlow's 1998 debut as Voice Stealer, *The All-Electric House,* was one of the more interesting, well-crafted album-length amalgams of those styles to appear. Fusing new wave's and electro's two strongest attributes—cool, detached melodic and vocal accompaniment and thin, rubbery drumbox funk—*The All-Electric House* escaped cliche partially by the novelty of its combination, and partially because Finlow was the one doing the combining. Although much of his work to date has clustered around standard, breakbeat, and progressive house—he helped form the popular underground label 20:20 Vision, has released records through 20:20 as Random Factor and Urban Farmers, and is the imprint's in-house producer—the fastest growing segment of Finlow's solo discography is in the vein of his Voice Stealer material, and includes collaborative releases with Ralph Lawson (the "Droid Funk" EP) and Daz Quayle (under the name Scarletron, primarily for Electron Industries), as well as the four-track *Il.ek.tro* EP, released

under his own name by Klang Elektronik in mid-1998. One year later, *Il.ek.tro 2* followed. [See Also: Voice Stealer] —*Sean Cooper*

● **Il.ek.tro [EP]** / 1998 / Klang Electronik ✦✦✦✦
Almost a concentrated reduction of Carl Finlow's album-length electro update *The All-Electric House* (released under the name Voice Stealer), "Il.ek.tro" contains some of Finlow's finest work to date. Forward-looking cuts such as "Carbon Academy" and "Threads Part Two" tread heavily syncopated territory, while the show-stealing "Tune In (To the System)" combines austere, slightly silly vocals with solid mid-tempo breaks and velvety synth slides. Excellent. —*Sean Cooper*

**Electrocide [EP]** / 1998 / SCSI ✦✦✦
Released under the name Silicon Scally on Daz "Scarletron" Quayle's SCSI label, the *Electrocide* LP is Finlow's stab at a dance record. It's adequate, but still a far cry from his best work as Voice Stealer, Random Factor, and Il.ek.tro —*Sean Cooper*

**Too Fast into the Future [EP]** / 1998 / 20:20 Vision ✦✦✦✦
*Future* is most similar to Finlow's Voice Stealer project, although heavier new wave and techno-pop influences make for softer edges and a more developed, "songier" feel. Though unlikely, it's not exactly implausible to imagine tracks like "Broken Mirror" and "When Daylight Fades" gaining radio play. Some of Finlow's best work to date. —*Sean Cooper*

**Il.ek.tro 2 [EP]** / 1999 / Klang ✦✦✦
Faster in tempo and more consistently oriented toward the dance floor than its predecessor, Finlow and Daz Quayle's second *Il.ek.tro* EP is another solid release both for the increasingly popular German label Klang and for the increasingly prolific Finlow and Quayle. These four tracks are a little denser and more repetitive than past releases by either artist might have predicted, but interesting hand-made sounds and odd rhythms make for a solid EP. —*Sean Cooper*

## The Fireman

f. 1993, London, England
*Group / Ambient House, Club/Dance*
What would seem to be one of the oddest examples of electronica crossover was the Fireman, an ambient project concerning producer and occasional Orb-collaborator Youth plus the dean of British rock, Sir Paul McCartney. In truth however, McCartney had been involved in London's electronic and avant/garde music scene during the mid-'60s—he even prepared the tape loops and effects for the Beatles' famed "Tomorrow Never Knows," probably the most famous use of *musique concrète* in history.

The Fireman collaboration began in 1993, just at the height of the boom in downtempo house, when a mostly featureless red LP named *Strawberries Oceans Ships Forest* appeared on the shelves of record stores. A bout of rumor-mongering reminiscent of the 1977 Beatles-are-Klaatu scam quickly gave way to the fact that McCartney had indeed been a part of the project. The album was licensed to America (through Capitol) as well, though it received little press. Though the album smacked of a one-off, the Fireman returned in 1998 with a second album, *Rushes*. —*John Bush*

**Strawberries Oceans Ships Forest** / Feb. 14, 1994 / Capitol ✦✦✦✦
Almost as surprising as the fact that Paul McCartney and Youth were participating in an ambient house project was the fact that the Fireman's debut LP succeeds on most accounts. Though it's difficult to judge the level of McCartney's input, most tracks are quite melodic and samples or effects often give the feel of a regular framework. Overall, it may be just a bit too tame for fans of Youth or the Orb, but it will please more than a few Beatles fans. —*John Bush*

● **Rushes** / Oct. 20, 1998 / Capitol ✦✦✦✦
Following the path of ambient techno into more freeform territory, Youth and McCartney deliver a second album that trades the mid-tempo beats for slow-moving workouts heavy on the electronics, though a few guitars do see their way into the mix. —*Keith Farley*

## Cevin Fisher

b. Oct. 26, 1963, East Orange, NJ
*Producer / Garage, Club/Dance, House*
One of the breakout house producers of the late '90s, though he'd been working for a decade before, Cevin Fisher is responsible for a growing number of club favorites including "Freaks Come Out," "(You Got Me) Burnin' Up," "Music Saved My Life," and "House Music." Fisher began DJing while in his teens, first in his father's New Jersey bar and at various college gigs, but later in a spot at the mecca for garage music, Club Zanzibar. From there, he moved to New York in the late '80s and began working on production with employees like Motown and Arthur Baker's Shakedown Studios. Convinced by Danny Tenaglia to begin recording on his own, he debuted with several anthemic tunes like "House Is a Feeling" (as Sunday School) and "Hands on Love," songs that carried on the vibes of early house pioneers Tony Humphries and Larry Heard. Early singles "The Way We Used To" and "Shine the Light" earned international clubplay, though it was 1998's "The Freaks Come Out" that pushed him into the mainstream house stratosphere. Released on at least five different labels, the single made Fisher's reputation as a suave producer, with preeminent vocals on his cuts. Two compilations appeared in 1999, the mixed *Dangerous Disco* and the Nervous compilation *Cevin Fisher's Nervous Tracks*. One year later, *Underground 2000* appeared on Razor & Tie. Fisher has also remixed Quincy Jones, Chaka Khan, Robert Miles, and Kevin Aviance. —*John Bush*

**Dangerous Disco/My First CD** / Mar. 15, 1999 / United DJs ✦✦✦✦
This 13-track mix album features Fisher on the decks and includes plenty of his best remixes—"Women Beat Their Men" by Submission, "The Break 98" by Arthur Baker—plus his own classic cuts "Freaks Come Out" and "House Music." —*Keith Farley*

**Cevin Fisher's Nervous Tracks** / Nov. 2, 1999 / Nervous ✦✦✦
*Cevin Fisher's Nervous Tracks* contains eight cuts associated with Fisher, including two each from Potion, Reverend, and House Under Moon, plus one apiece from All Purpose and People Underground. Though the tracks are challenging and interesting enough, most of Fisher's big club hits appeared on other labels. —*Stephen Thomas Erlewine*

● **Underground 2000** / Mar. 7, 2000 / Razor & Tie ✦✦✦✦
Including eight tracks of his productions for New York's Maxi Records (plus four remixes), *Underground 2000* includes plenty of Fisher classics—garage standards like "(You Got Me) Burnin' Up" and "The Way We Used To," as well as the rough Latin grooves of "Music Saved My Life" and "Mas Groove"—compiled in a quasi-mix format. Few to none of the best garage producers can make records as strong from a futuristic production sense as they are on the raw soul feeling that's inherent in great dance music; this collection is all the proof listeners need that Cevin Fisher hits those highs on a consistent basis. —*John Bush*

## Flanger

*Group / Trip-Hop*
Atom Heart's and Bernd Friedmann's Flanger project is produced by the combination of traditional jazz elements with experimental filtering and editing techniques. For the 1999 album *Templates*, Flanger used drums, bass, piano, and vibraphone, then put the product through their own editing process with the end product of unrecognizable instruments. The June 1999 release was hosted by the well-respected Ninja Tune Records, home of artists including Kid Koala, DJ Food, and Funki Porcini. *Midnight Sound* followed in fall 2000. —*Diana Potts*

● **Templates** / Feb. 8, 1999 / Ntone ✦✦✦✦
Flanger's *Templates* collects the two EPs of the same name into one album of avant-garde electronic music that balances techno and jazz elements in a minimalist, experimental approach. Though the ideas are progressive, tracks like "Full on Scientist" and "Studio Tan" are witty, organic workouts that are as friendly as they are challenging. —*Heather Phares*

## Flexitone

f. 1995, Detroit, MI
*Group / Electro-Techno, Detroit Techno, Club/Dance*
Flexitone is yet another bubble-up from the identity-shy Detroit underground. Combining the funky electro experiments of Underground Resistance and deep sea dwellers Drexciya with the stark, bleached-out minimalism of Synapse and Ectomorph, Flexitone number among a new breed of Detroit artists re-engaging techno's pre-history in the electronic breakbeat. In fact, the project is yet another pseudonym of electro/techno duo Ectomorph, the more common disguise of Brendan "BMG" Gillen and Gerald (also of Drexciya). The pair have released only a handful of tracks as Flexitone (through Carl Craig's Planet E imprint), but they've numbered among some of the most focused, evolved dance-based experimental electronic music to emerge from the American underground since Cybotron and Model 500. Flexitone's debut, "The Pulse of Evolution," appeared on the Planet E label compilation *Elements*

of and Experiments with Sound, and an alternate mix of that track kicked off the group's first EP/picture disc for Planet E, "Rotoreliefs" (with disc art a reproduction of Marcel Duchamp's painting of the same name). The group's follow-up, "Nausicaa," appeared the following year, and continued in the same vein of atmospheric, downtempo electro as "Rotoreliefs," this time with a more complex melodic presence. Although Flexitone's tracks are unlikely to show up in the sets of any dancefloor DJs, they occupy similar territory with artists such as Autechre, Disjecta, Cylob, Bochum Welt, and Panasonic, rounding out the slight-but-growing American arm of dance-based experimental electronic listening music. [See Also: Ectomorph] —*Sean Cooper*

● **Electricity/Nausicaa [Single]** / Dec. 9, 1996 / Planet E ♦♦♦♦
Three tracks of delicate, minimalist downtempo electro in the Autechre, Ectomorph, Bochum Welt vein. Flexitone's beatwork remains inspired and ever-shifting, but the most striking aspect of *Nausicaa*'s title track is its melodicism, with oblique, contrapuntal themes twisting and fusing like mutating strands of DNA. A Himadri remix of "Nausicaa" also appears. —*Sean Cooper*

## A Flock of Seagulls

f. 1980, Liverpool, England
*Group / New Romantic, New Wave, Synth-Pop*

As well-known for their bizarrely teased haircuts as their hit single "I Ran (So Far Away)," A Flock of Seagulls was one of the infamous one-hit wonders of the new wave era. Growing out of the synth-heavy and ruthlessly stylish new romantic movement, A Flock of Seagulls was a little too robotic and arrived a little too late to be true new romantics, but their sleek dance-pop was forever indebted to the short-lived movement. The group benefitted considerably from MTV's heavy rotation of the "I Ran" video in the summer of 1982, but they were unable to capitalize on its sudden success and disappeared nearly as quickly as they rocketed up the charts.

Hairdresser Mike Score (lead vocals, keyboards) formed A Flock of Seagulls with his brother Ali (drums) and fellow hairdresser Frank Maudsley (bass) in 1980, adding guitarist Paul Reynolds several months later. The group released its debut EP on Cocteau Records early in 1981, and while the record failed to chart, its lead track "Telecommunication" became an underground hit in Eurodisco and new wave clubs. The band signed a major-label contract with Jive by the end of the year, and their eponymous debut album appeared in the spring of 1982. "I Ran (So Far Away)" was released as the first single from the album, and MTV quickly picked up on its icily attractive video, which featured long shots of Mike Score and his distinctive, cascading hair. The single climbed into the American Top 10, taking the album along with it. In the UK, "I Ran" didn't make the Top 40, but "Wishing (If I Had a Photograph of You)" reached number ten later that year; in America, that single became a Top 40 hit in 1983, after "Space Age Love Song" peaked at number 30. "Wishing" was taken from the group's second album, *Listen* (1983), which was moderately successful.

However, the band's fortunes crashed shortly after the release of *Listen*, as 1984's *The Story of a Young Heart*, failed to produce any hit singles. Reynolds left after the album and was replaced by Gary Steadnim; the band also added keyboardist Chris Chryssaphis. The new lineup was showcased on 1986's *Dream Come True*, which failed to chart. Shortly after its release, the band broke up. Mike Score assembled a new lineup of A Flock of Seagulls in 1989, releasing the single "Magic" and touring the USA. The band failed to make any impact and most of the band left by the end of the year. The band continues to tour worldwide, although with major changes to its members, and in 1995 released a new album: *The Light at the End of the World*. —*Stephen Thomas Erlewine*

**A Flock of Seagulls** / 1982 / Jive ♦♦♦
The Liverpool quintet A Flock of Seagulls first gained attention in the dance clubs with "Telecommunication," included on this debut release. The band benefited from heavy play on MTV and quickly became known for its outrageous fashion and lead singer Mike Score's waterfall-like haircut. However, its self-titled debut is an enjoyable romp that was set apart from other synth-heavy acts of the time by Paul Reynolds' unique guitar style. The kinetic "I Ran (So Far Away)" became a video staple and a Top Ten radio hit. "A Space Age Love Song," with its synthesizer washes and echo-laden guitar also managed to score at radio. The rest of the album consists of hyperactive melodies, synthesizer noodlings, and electronic drumming. The lyrics are forgettable. In fact, they rarely expand on the song titles, but it's all great fun and a wonderful collection of New Wave ear candy. —*Tom Demalon*

**Listen** / 1983 / Jive ♦♦
Following their gold-selling Top Ten debut, A Flock of Seagulls returned in 1983 with *Listen*. Mike Howlett again handled the production chores, but the band errantly chose to pursue even more reliance on electronics, which gives *Listen* a bit of a sterile feel. Nonetheless, there are still several tracks here that are as strong as their debut, even if, as a whole, the album isn't as consistent.

*Listen* spawned only one hit, but it's a gem; the multi-layered, hypnotic "Wishing (If I Had a Photograph of You)." Other standouts include the eerie, moody "Nightmares," with its sparse guitar and synthesizer squawks and a surprisingly effective ballad "Transfer Affection." Ultimately, the band loses the plot on the second half, when they seem to forget melodies and focus on hardware. Although, the Bill Nelson-produced "(It's Not Me) Talking" is a bracing, breakneck tempo return to their interest in aliens, *Listen* is most likely to be enjoyed most by fans of the band only. —*Tom Demalon*

**The Story of a Young Heart** / Aug. 1984 / Jive/Arista ♦♦♦
Faced with declining sales and a sound that was already becoming considered passe, A Flock Of Seagulls retooled a bit for its third album *The Story Of A Young Heart*. Steve Lovell stepped into the producer's role and the band eased up on its heavily synthesized approach for more of a Euro-pop feel to no avail. The less-cluttered, more-polished sound of album is undermined by the limited vocal ability of singer Mike Score. His monotonal delivery fails to imbue the songs with any warmth. "The More You Live, The More You Love" is as good as anything they've done and gave the band one final chart hit stalling at number 54. Otherwise, the best stuff is near the end and sounds most reminiscent of their debut. "Over My Head" and "Heart Of Steel" bound along but sound thin. However, they almost recapture their hyperkinetic glory with "Remember David." *The Story Of A Young Heart* is the sound of a band slowly losing momentum. —*Tom Demalon*

● **The Best of A Flock of Seagulls** / 1987 / Jive ♦♦♦♦
Every good song A Flock of Seagulls ever recorded is available on this fine collection, including the new wave classic "I Ran (So Far Away)" plus "Wishing (If I Had a Photograph of You)" and others. —*Stephen Thomas Erlewine*

## Fluke

f. 1989, London, England
*Group / Electronica, Club/Dance, Techno, House*

A three-piece combo who managed to make inspired music during the '90s while blazing a path through most of the popular electronic styles of the decade, Fluke was formed by occasional vocalist Jon Fugler, Mike Tournier, and Mike Bryant in 1989 after the three had spent several years living in the same combination house and recording studio. At first an eclectic, widely inspired house-pop act, the three later moved into trip-hop (and the British charts) during the mid-'90s before another leap into big-beat video-game soundtracks by the end of the decade.

Bitten by the acid-house bug in 1988, Fugler, Tournier, and Bryant began recording with two singles informed by more-than-competent guitar work, soaring techno-funk and plenty of pop inspiration as well. "Thumper" and "Joni" (the latter sampling Joni Mitchell's "Big Yellow Taxi") brought Fluke much attention in the growing electronic sphere, and they signed a one-off album deal with indie-rock kingpins Creation for their debut full-length, 1991's *Techno Rose of Blighty*. After completing another record deal with Virgin that same year, Fluke released a live album *Out (in essence)* and their sophomore masterpiece *Six Wheels on My Wagon*, an album of poppy, occasionally dreamy ambient-trance which included several previously released singles. By 1995, Fluke had even hit the British charts (with the singles "Bullet" and "Tosh") and their third LP *OTO* marked a bit of a departure for the trio, a downbeat, jazzy path just beginning to be name-checked as trip-hop. Hitting the charts in an even bigger way during their 1997 return, the trio released "Atom Bomb," a high-energy number recorded for the Virgin video-game soundtrack *Wipeout 2097*. The single and video also introduced fourth member Arial Tetsuo, an anime race-car driver come to life as concert figurehead Rachel Stewart. *Risotto*, Fluke's fourth LP, fit in nicely with the growing fanaticism surrounding big-beat techno, though the trio held on to their trance and trip-hop inclinations as well. —*John Bush*

**Techno Rose of Blighty** / 1991 / Creation ♦♦♦♦

**Six Wheels on My Wagon** / 1993 / EMI ♦♦♦♦
With a delightful, trance-pop record that resulted in chart entries for singles like "Groovy Feeling" and the ironic "Electric Guitar," Fluke's stature does not suffer

for their perceived descent from the heights of intelligent electronic dance into the less rarefied air of popular music. There are still plenty of moments for production-oriented bliss on "Spacey (Catch 22 Dub)" and "Eko." —*Keith Farley*
OTO / 1995 / Circa ♦♦♦

● Risotto / Sep. 23, 1997 / Astralwerks ♦♦♦♦
Fluke's fourth album altogether finds remixed tracks from 1995's *OTO* alongside a few new titles. The polished techno-funk of previous records, which sometimes grew a bit tired, is nicely expanded on with big-beat numbers like the video-game soundtrack "Atom Bomb" plus moderate breakbeats on several tracks, and "Goodnight Lover," which drifts into soundtrack ambience. —*John Bush*

## Flying Saucer Attack

f. 1993, Bristol, England
*Group / Ambient Pop, Experimental Rock, Dream Pop, Space Rock, Indie Rock, Post-Rock/Experimental*
Formed in Bristol, England in 1993, the elusive avant-noise project Flying Saucer Attack primarily comprised the duo of singers/guitarists David Pearce and Rachel Brook, refugees from the group Lynda's Strange Vacation who formed FSA as an outlet for their interest in home-recording experimentation. Drawing influence from Kraut-rock, folk, and dream-pop, they bowed with the single "Soaring High," followed by an eponymously-titled 1993 debut LP which buried the group's narcoleptic vocals and amorphous songs under dense, organic sheets of feedback.

After 1994's *Distance*, a collection of atmospheric singles and unreleased material, FSA emerged in 1995 with *Further*, a remarkably evocative work which transported the group's hypnotic guitar wash into a uniquely pastoral setting. *Chorus*, another singles compilation, followed later in the year, and with it came a declaration of the end of the group's initial phase, setting the stage for Flying Saucer Attack's continued evolution as one of the decade's most innovative and ambitious groups. 1997's *New Lands* was the first fruit of this new FSA, now a Pearce solo project exploring the possibilities of sampling; Brook, meanwhile, focused on her side group Movietone, a similarly blissed-out excursion into sound. FSA followed up *New Lands* three years later with *Mirror*. —*Jason Ankeny*

Distance / 1994 / VHF ♦♦♦
*Distance* is a compilation of early singles and unreleased tracks from Flying Saucer Attack's short career. Only half of the album's eight tracks could be considered songs; the rest are looped feedback workouts that sound eerily ambient. Even the four "songs" are distorted beyond belief, producing a caterwaul reminiscent of My Bloody Valentine's prime work. —*John Bush*

Flying Saucer Attack / 1994 / VHF ♦♦♦♦

● Further / Apr. 17, 1995 / Drag City ♦♦♦♦
*Further* perfects the "rural psychedelia" concept explored on earlier Flying Saucer Attack recordings—a ghostly, rainswept album, its acoustic textures and muted hues evoke a far more organic atmosphere than the duo's previous work, conjuring a gorgeously pastoral soundscape cloaked in shadows and fog. Although FSA's signature feedback still sparks and crackles underneath the album's surface, highlights like "In the Light of Time" and "Come and Close My Eyes" suggest a new intimacy and warmth—woven around David Pearce's deep, somnambulent vocals. The songs' stark acoustic settings possess a spectral beauty which previous singles only hinted at, capturing an otherworldly blissfulness as intoxicating as it is elusive. —*Jason Ankeny*

Mirror / Jan. 18, 2000 / Drag City ♦♦♦
The sweeping billows of sound that begin "Space (1999)," the opening track of *Mirror*, Flying Saucer Attack's first album of the 21st century, set the tone for this ride on the clouds. The blurring of lines between noises and notes, of sounds and music, give this album a soothing and ambient feel. Atmospheric guitars layer the background, simple basslines provide the anchor, and sound effects take the sound further into space. Dave Pearce's gentle vocals keep the album a mellow affair throughout, except for the out-of-place "Chemicals," which unfortunately breaks the mood with its quasi-industrial feel. Some of the songs do seem to wander aimlessly, however, and *Mirror* occasionally gets tangled in its own loose web. Overall, these surges of sound are best enjoyed in the late evening or early morning hours, depending on your intention. Both results are great. Either you will enter one of your most relaxed states of sleep or will awaken as if by a wave of feathers. —*Jason Kane*

## Foetus (J.G. Thirlwell)

b. Melbourne, Australia
*Producer / Experimental Rock, Post-Punk, Industrial*
Despite the constant shifts in name (from Scraping Foetus Off the Wheel to Foetus Uber Frisco to Foetus All Nude Revue) and the less frequent variations in aesthetics (all focused around the same unforgiving sonic attack), the music manufactured under the prolific Foetus umbrella was solely the product of one J.G. (Jim) Thirlwell. A native of Melbourne, Australia, Thirlwell relocated to London in 1978, where he conceived the basic Foetus concept—impenetrable panoramas of extremist noise built on tape loops and syncopated rhythms—as an alternative to the constraints of rock music.

Finding no takers for his work, Thirlwell created his own label, Self Immolation, to issue his debut single "OKFM," which appeared under the first of the innumerable variants of the Foetus name, Foetus Under Glass. As You've Got Foetus on Your Breath, he released his full-length debut, *Deaf*, later that year. Thirlwell spent the next several years exploring his brand of industrial sounds as a solo artist, issuing a steady stream of LPs, EPs, singles, and compilations before adopting another alias, Clint Ruin, and teaming with ex-Swan Roli Mosimann in 1986 to record the album *Dirtdish* as the duo Wiseblood.

After 1988's *Thaw* (recorded as Foetus Interruptus), Thirlwell formed Foetus Corruptus with other members of the Swans, Hugo Largo and Unsane; both the 1989 "official bootleg" *Rife* and 1990's more above-board *Male*—credited to Foetus in Excelsis Corruptus Deluxe—documented the group's live set. Out of the experience grew Steroid Maximus, a group employing much of the same personnel which produced instrumental music for the scores of imaginary films on 1991's *Quilombo* and 1992's *Gondwanaland*. With 1995's *Gash*, Thirlwell entered the ranks of the major labels thanks to a deal with Sony; the LP, as well as the subsequent EP releases *Null* and *Void*, earned the rare distinction of appearing under the simple name Foetus. —*Jason Ankeny*

Hole / 1984 / Thirsty Ear ♦♦♦
Belying the fact that J.G. Thirlwell was long pigeon-holed as an industrial artist, *Hole* veers from downtown blues to surf-raunch to paranoid industrial dance and back with few pauses. Listeners expecting to catch their breath at some point may be a bit startled, since *Hole* never lets up and resists easy classification. Highlights include "Clothes Hoist" and "I'll Meet You in Poland, Baby." —*Keith Farley*

● Nail / 1985 / Thirsty Ear ♦♦♦♦
*Nail* is possibly the best Foetus album; it apparently hopes to piss off all potential listeners by working through as many warped sounds and styles as possible. Though Thirlwell's sense of humor is sometimes hard to take (check the faux-cinematic "Theme from Pigdom Come" and "Overture to Pigdom Come"), the sheer range of this music is hard to believe. —*Keith Farley*

Bedrock [EP] / 1987 / Self Immolation-Some Bizzare-Relativi ♦♦♦
A five-track EP including a few versions of the bluesy title track, *Bedrock* also includes the Foetus ode to musique concrète via a pair of crushing tracks that reveal Thirlwell's nearly successful assault on music. —*Keith Farley*

Rife / 1988 / Invisible ♦♦
Recorded on the supporting European tour for *Thaw* in 1988, *Rife* is an authorized bootleg finding Jim Thirlwell backed by a band tagged Foetus Corruptus, which also includes Algis Kizys, Norman Westberg, Ted Parsons, and Raymond Watts. *Rife* was reissued in the US in 1998. —*Steve Huey*

## A Forest Mighty Black (Bernd Kunz)

b. Freiburg, Germany
*Producer / Electronica, Trip-Hop*
A Forest Mighty Black is one of the few outposts for jazzy downtempo in Germany. Fronted by producer Bernd Kunz, the outfit debuted with "Candyfloss" and "Fresh in My Mind," two of the first three singles appearing on Munich's respected Compost label (also the home of recordings by Fauna Flash, Funkstörung, Beanfield, and Turntable Terranova). A Forest Mighty Black gained positive praise for their refreshing blend of Brazilian and fusion influences with trip-hop, and appeared on several compilations from the Acid Jazz label. First album *Mellowdramatic* was released in 1997, followed one year later by *Mellowdramatic Remixed*. A Forest Mighty Black have also provided remixes of their own for United Future Organization, another electronic act notably influenced by the music of Brazil. —*John Bush*

- **Mellowdramatic** / Dec. 8, 1997 / Compost ♦♦♦♦
Nominally based around a series of hard bop and film-music samples amplified with crunchy beats, *Mellowdramatic* is an exceptional record of downtempo grooves and late-night Rhodes keyboards. Producer Bernd Kunz has an excellent sense of atmosphere concerning what a laidback trip-hop album should be, illustrated by tracks like "Minigame," "Everything," and "Duo Trippin'." —*Keith Farley*

## Fortran 5
f. 1989, London, England
*Group / Ambient Techno, Alternative Dance, Club/Dance*
Recruiting a bevy of oddball-celebrity sidemen and guest vocalists—sampled or otherwise—somewhat blurred the backbone of the group, but David Barker and Simon Leonard recorded several albums of inspired ambient techno as Fortran 5. Indebted to such culprits of British whimsy as Syd Barrett and Monty Python, the duo usually recorded with samplers blazing, the unholy result of which included bizarre pop collisions like Donna Summer and the Pretenders or the Champs' "Tequila" and thrash-metal. With roots in the Mute Records artists I Start Counting, the pair debuted with 1990's "Crazy Earth," a dreamy acid-house track counting Barrett among its sample victims. Several singles followed during 1990-91, including "Heart on the Line" with (live) vocals by Miranda Sex Garden.

The debut Fortran 5 LP was *Blues*, released in 1991; it included contributions from Can's Holger Hiller, Orb's Kris Weston (aka Thrash) and noted DJ Colin Faver. The weirdest collaboration, however, was a cover of Syd Barrett's "Bike," with vocals obtained by posthumously sampling various lines from legendary comedian and *Carry On* film star, Sid James—the group was perhaps saved from a court case since producer on the session was Sid James' son Steve. Following the LP were several high-profile singles, including "Look to the Future" (with live vocals by Sly Stone alumnus Larry Graham) and "Persian Blues" (with Neil Arthur of Blancmange).

The sampling shenanigans continued on Fortran 5's second full-length, *Bad Head Park*. The "Sid Sings Syd" theme was resurrected, with celebrated British actor Derek Nimmo unwittingly lending his vocals to a cover of Derek & the Dominos' "Layla," while Barker and Leonard also called upon John Barry and media coverage of the Gulf War to enhance their compositions. The duo featured no collaborators and few samples on their third, the 1995 concept album *Avocado Suite*. Fortran 5 also remixed Erasure, Inspiral Carpets, Miranda Sex Garden, and Laibach. —*John Bush*

**Blues** / Oct. 1991 / Elektra ♦♦
It's not quite as outrageous as it was (hopefully) meant to be, but *Blues* is a solid collection of early-'90s ambient techno that earns extra points for the covers of "Heart on the Line" and "Bike." —*Keith Farley*

- **Bad Head Park** / Jun. 1993 / Mute ♦♦♦
Just a tad more focused on the music than the shenanigans for their second album, Fortran 5 turn in a solid set of ambient techno and listening music headed by tracks like "Persian Blues" and "Time to Dream." —*Keith Farley*

**Avocado Suite** / May 1995 / Mute ♦♦
*Avocado Suite* is a sample-laden album of Fortran 5's playful techno and trance jams. —*John Bush*

## Foul Play
f. 1991
*Group / Jungle/Drum'N'Bass, Club/Dance*
One of the most important collectives in breakbeat dance's shift from hardcore to jungle during the early '90s, Foul Play was responsible for seminal drum'n'bass tracks like "Open Your Mind," "Being with You," and their remix of Omni Trio's "Renegade Snares" (all recorded for Moving Shadow Records). The trio of Steve Bradshaw, John Morrow, and Steve Gurley began releasing material in the early '90s, on their own Imprint label as well as Section 5 and Oblivion. From 1992 to 1994, Foul Play recorded a raft of classic tracks for Moving Shadow. Though Gurley left in 1994 to join Rogue Unit, the remaining duo kept working on producing and released only the second artist full-length on Moving Shadow, 1995's *Suspected*. Foul Play also founded another label, Panik Records, though Bradshaw's tragic death in 1998 left the group's future cloudy. Morrow returned the following year with a new project, Foul Play Productions, organized with producer Neil Shepherd. —*John Bush*

- **Suspected** / 1995 / Moving Shadow ♦♦♦♦
The album debut for the British duo includes new versions of past singles "Open Your Mind," "Music Is the Key," and "Total Control" (the latter an Origin Unknown remix) alongside original productions on "Artificial Intelligence" and "Ignorance." The drum programming is stunning, a peak easily the best achieved on any drum'n'bass LP before or since. With an impressive roster of remix/engineering helpers (Omni Trio, Hopa & Bones, Rob Playford) and a varied repertoire encompassing soul, funk, and trip-hop in addition to hardcore breakbeats, *Suspected* is one of the best early full-lengths produced by the jungle scene. —*John Bush*

## 4E (Can Oral)
*Producer / Electro-Techno, Electro, Club/Dance, Techno*
An original Structure label-group artist with dozens of releases on Koln-based imprints such as DJ Ungle Fever, XXC3, Eat Raw, and Pharma, NYC-based experimental electro producer Can Oral is the man behind an array of pseudonyms. Recording most often as 4E and Khan, Oral's discography is also littered with such monikers as Bizz O.D., Gizz T.V., El Turco Loco, and Fuzz DJ. One of only a handful of European producers to move to the US in order to jumpstart the dozing underground, Oral includes NY's Temple Records (the store he opened under Manhattan's Liquid Sky Clothing), as well as record labels Temple and Liquid Sky among his ongoing commitments. The brother of Air Liquide's Can Oral, Can was (along with artists such as Mike Ink, J. Berger, and Biochip C's Martin Damm) an active contributor to early Structure labels such as Blue and DJ Ungle Fever, the center of the German acid/techno explosion during the '90s heyday of experimental acid and techno. Can began recording as 4E after moving to New York (the name was the address of his first flat, which doubled as his studio), and has since released a number of EPs and full-lengths as both 4E and Khan, most notably on Force Inc./Mille Plateaux and his own fast-expanding Liquid Sky, Home Entertainment, and Temple labels. Stylistically, Oral treads closest to experimental hip-hop and electro, fusing gritty 303 chirps and smooth electronic atmospheres with kicking, mid-tempo breaks constructed from familiar drum sounds and patterns. His 1996 debut for Liquid Sky sister label Home Entertainment, *Blue Note* is ambient electro in the vein of B12, Jonah Sharp, and Autechre/Gescom, with none of the more caustic resonances that defined his earlier, more dancefloor-friendly work in evidence. Oral operates and plays at the weekly club, Killer, and has worked on material with noted experimental/ambient composer Tetsu Inoue. [See Also: Khan] —*Sean Cooper*

**4E** / 1996 / Pharma ♦♦♦
Typical Pharma-style mid-tempo hip-hop/electro—dirty, lo-fi, and almost live-sounding. —*Sean Cooper*

**Next [Single]** / 1997 / Sockett ♦♦
This four-tracker is 4E's first release for an American label other than his own, in this case for Freddy Fresh's Minneapolis-based Sockett imprint. Although previous Sockett releases have tended toward a more club friendly brand of housey techno, 4E's twelve is a pretty solid slab of minimal, experimental electro. One ("Gentle Killer") is on the melodic, downtempo tip and the remaining three similar in quirk and percussive bounce to previous releases for Blue, Force Inc., and his own Home Entertainment label. —*Sean Cooper*

- **4E4ME4YOU** / Apr. 27, 1998 / Mille Plateaux ♦♦♦♦
The beats on *4E4ME4YOU* are even slower than Khan's normally languid tempos, but he fills the numerous gaps with a variety of gutter-level effects and distortion. Khan also introduces his partner DJ Snax, for help on a couple of tracks. —*Keith Farley*

## 4 Hero
f. 1989, Dollis Hill, London,
*Group / Jungle/Drum'N'Bass, Club/Dance*
Consistently on the front lines of the drum'n'bass battleground, the duo of Dego (McFarlane) and Mark Mac (Mark Clair) nevertheless failed to receive the exposure of luminaries like Goldie and Roni Size, mostly because they didn't release much 4 Hero material during jungle's crucial crossover years, from 1994 through 1997. Despite beginnings in London's hip-hop underground during the mid-'80s, the duo moved into the hardcore/rave scene later in the decade and recorded classics like "Mr. Kirk's Nightmare" and "Journey from the Light" for one of the scene's best labels, their own Re-

inforced Records. The tracks were among the first to chart the darkside of the rave scene and presage the more sinister tendencies of drum'n'bass. Quite ironic then, that while the jungle scene caught up with (and grew increasingly obsessed by) 4 Hero's innovations during the late '90s, the duo had already moved on to a more polished, fusion-inspired sound with their major-label breakout, 1998's *Two Pages*.

In the beginning, the name 4 Hero did actually mark the presence of a quartet. Mark Mac and Dego first hooked up with Iain Bardouille and Gus Lawrence in 1986, through their mutual adoration for hip-hop and involvement in the Strong Island FM pirate radio station, which operated out of London's Camden area. By 1989, Mark Mac and Dego were recording percussive breakbeat experiments and becoming increasingly involved with the rave and hardcore breakbeat scene, while Bardouille and Lawrence gradually moved into management of the quartet's newly formed Reinforced Records. The label debuted with the *Rising Sun* EP by Mark and Dego, credited to 4 Hero. The second EP, *Combat Dance*, became a big seller in the dance community, though a shady distributor reneged on payment of the profits. The pair criss-crossed the country during the late '80s and early '90s, DJing and playing at raves while they struggled to earn enough money for Reinforced to stay afloat. After approaching the group at one show, Goldie began working as an A&R man and engineer for the label. He soon became a familiar face at Reinforced headquarters, and learned much about production techniques from Dego and Mark Mac.

Though it was still in the rave scene, 4 Hero's subsequent recordings also revealed a growing interest in the flip side of rave's increasingly elegiac feeling. The single "Mr. Kirk's Nightmare" included samples of a policeman telling a suburban father that his son has died of an overdose, and the statement of intent in the titles "Journey from the Light" and "Cookin' Up Ya Brain" was self-evident. 4 Hero's 1991 LP debut *In Rough Territory* also sketched a sinister path through the breakbeat scene, leagues ahead of other producers and on the cutting edge of a style that wouldn't peak for well over five years later.

Instead of continuing down the darkside breakbeat path however, 4 Hero began to diversify. Dego introduced his Tek 9 side-project, which united his love of hip-hop, jazz fusion, and occasional breakbeats, while Mark Mac debuted the straightahead hard techno of Nu Era. Two compilation albums were the next LP releases for Reinforced—*Calling for Reinforcements* and *Definition of Hardcore*—with obvious contributors 4 Hero and Tek 9 alongside newer projects like Goldie's Rufige Cru and Mark Mac's Manix. Three years after its debut LP, 4 Hero released another album, *Parallel Universe*. The smooth sound reflected more of a debt to old-school Detroit techno and Chicago house, much farther away from the hardcore of *In Rough Territory*. As jungle began to explode as a commercial force in 1994, 4 Hero were often name-checked as godfathers of the movement. (Great Britain's BBC-TV even borrowed the title of a Tek 9 track for its jungle documentary, *A London Sumtin'*.)

The duo was relatively silent during 1995, though Reinforced continued its release schedule with a debut full-length from Nookie (*The Sound of Music*), another compilation (*Jungle Book*) and several singles from Doc Scott. One year later, Mark Mac released a Nu Era full-length (*Beyond Gravity*) and Dego put out the first Tek 9 LP, *It's Not What You Think It Is!!?!* As well, Dego and Mark Mac added yet one more alias to their stable during 1996, with a self-titled album recorded as Jacob's Optical Stairway. Released on R&S Records, the LP became the duo's most polished effort extant, with high-pitched synth and spacey fusion breakbeats, in addition to help from technocrat Juan Atkins and dance superstar Josh Wink. Three years after their last proper full-length, Dego and Mark Mac signed to the British nu-groove label Talkin' Loud and released their third album *Two Pages*, tied to earthier forms of jazz-fusion than their Jacob's Optical Stairway material. [See Also: Jacob's Optical Stairway] —*John Bush*

**In Rough Territory** / 1991 / Reinforced Rivet ♦♦♦

After only a few releases on their Reinforced imprint, Dego and Mark Mac released their debut 4 Hero album, an LP that pre-existed the UK hardcore movement's transformation into jungle. As such, *In Rough Territory* is just that: a raw album which fuses energetic rave atmospheres with the emerging complexities of breakbeat drum'n'bass; track titles like "No Sleep Raver," "Can't Strain My Brain," and "May the Wicked Perish in the Fire of Hell" say much about the mood of the album. With its repeated vocal sample serving as the lead-up to the actual nightmare, the early 4 Hero trademark "Mr. Kirk's Nightmare" is by far the best track here. Although most rave/hardcore acts disappeared overnight, 4 Hero began working its sound into what emerged as drum'n'bass. —*John Bush*

★ **Parallel Universe** / 1995 / Reinforced ♦♦♦♦♦

A vast improvement over their 1991 debut, *Parallel Universe* was the album that showed what jungle was capable of in the full-length medium. While the UK charts were caught up in ragga-jungle mania, Dego and Mark Mac wedded their unsurpassed, futuristic breakbeats-immaculate (check "No Imitation" for proof) with inspiration including keyboard stringwork from Chicago house, a few sci-fi themes from the Detroit auteurs, and the glossy experimentalism of early-'70s jazz fusion. Along with LTJ Bukem's Good Looking crew, 4 Hero and the sound of *Parallel Universe* pre-figured electronica's obsession with "intelligent" jungle during 1995-96. The duo dip into R&B/house territory with a few diva vocals, which somewhat subverts the innovative feel of a drum'n'bass classic. Thankfully, the out-of-print album was reissued by Crammed Discs in 1998. —*John Bush*

**Two Pages** / Jul. 13, 1998 / PolyGram ♦♦♦♦

It's nearly impossible to listen to 4 Hero's *Two Pages* without thinking about the incredible success enjoyed by the jungle movement (and Roni Size's *New Forms* LP in particular) during the three-year gap which separated Dego and Mark Mac's second album from their third. With LTJ Bukem, the duo was one of the first jungle acts to desert hardcore for the astral drift of jazz-fusion atmospheres, and *Two Pages* is about as fusion-soaked as it gets. The first of the two discs includes the more downtempo R&B, almost orchestral side of 4 Hero, quite indebted to jazz luminaries like Pharoah Sanders, Lonnie Liston Smith, and Roy Ayers. Many of the instruments are live contributions, while vocalists as wide-ranging as poet Ursula Rucker and Digable Planets rapper Butterfly make appearances. The second disc is the dancefloor (read: tighter) half of the album, skirting through dense soundscapes of paranoid breakbeats. As could be expected, more than two hours of music is way too much for listeners to work their way through, and a heavy editing job would have made this a stellar album instead of the flawed and somewhat bloated album it turned out to be. For drum'n'bass fans, the real highlights come with second-disc tracks like "We Who Are Not as Others" and "In the Shadows"—as it is, they're so terrific as to nearly justify purchase by themselves. (The American version of *Two Pages* edited the album down to fit on a single disc, and added several tracks not available on the British two-CD version.) —*John Bush*

**Two Pages Reinterpretations** / Apr. 20, 1999 / PolyGram International ♦♦♦

Unlike many acts, Dego and Mark Mac had nothing to prove with their remix album, so *Two Pages Reinterpretations* spotlights a few of 4 Hero's up-and-coming favorites in the dance community instead of getting in bigger or more critically respected names to draw in neophytes. Many of the renditions are downtempo or jazzy house, with cuts by Jazzanova, Ron Trent, Shawn J. Period and Sonar Circle proving that 4 Hero's interests lie far afield from drum'n'bass. It's still a bit of an irony that the biggest name here—house legends Masters at Work—contributes the best remix: a smooth garage rendition of "Starchasers." —*John Bush*

## Four Tet (Kieran Hebden)

*Producer / Experimental Techno, Post-Rock/Experimental, Trip-Hop*

Spawned from the urge to do something apart from his post-rock band, Fridge, Kieran Hebden started recording electronic music under the name Four Tet. His full-length 1999 release, *Misnomer* was put out on the UK's, Output Recordings. *Misnomer* was a follow up to his first full length, *Dialogue* and many prior 12" releases, including one done with dub pioneer, Pole. With the Four Tet project, Hebden strives to use a balance of organic and programmed sounds.

Kieran Hebden gained music experience as part of the high school band Fridge, composed of bandmembers Sam Jeffers and Adem Ilham. The band has released several CDs, including a box set, to a rather loyal fan base. When the members of Fridge went off to college, it gave Hebden some time to play with music ideas he hadn't had time for while concentrating on the band. Hebden credits hip-hop, which was far from what Fridge was doing, as an inspiration to play with samples and different kinds of rhythmic beats. Hebden mostly admired the producer Dark Child ("The Boy is Mine" by Brandy and Monica and Whitney Houston's "It's Not Right, But It's Okay") as well as Takemura and Timbaland, who use such unique instruments as the thumb piano. Eager to experiment, Hebden bought a computer and began collecting drum and sound samples. Though his tracks sound contrary, Hebden produces all the Four Tet tracks in his flat using only his computer to loop, slice and paste downloaded samples and rhythms. His first full length was *Dialogue*, which was noticed by dub pioneer, Pole (Stefan Betke). The two eventually collaborated for the 12", *Four Tet vs. Pole*, which includes an original song by each and then a remix of the track done by the opposing artist. Shortly after, on the tail end of 1998, Four Tet released the full length *Misnomer*. At around the same time of the release of *Misnomer*, Fridge was signed to a major label, Go-Beat, which is owned by Polydor Records. This allowed Hebden and the rest of his band mates to quit their day jobs and fully concentrate on Fridge and their other music projects. —*Diana Potts*

**ThirtySixTwentyFive [Single]** / Aug. 10, 1998 / Output ♦♦♦♦
The *ThirtySixTwentyFive* single, which actually lasts around 35 minutes, is Four Tet's most ambitious project so far. Four Tet is comprised of Fridge member Kieran Hebden, who often uses spare Fridge material to incorporate into his DJ mixes. The vinyl edition of the single is pressed as a double album, but the second side of each album is blank, thus, allowing DJs to mix the two together simultaneously. The music is more haunting and abstract than the other Four Tet releases. Whereas the full length "Dialogue" and the other singles have a consistent, catchy sound, "ThirtySix" explores straight-ahead beats, voice overs, background noise (the sound of an ambulance siren creeps in and out all through the album), and sampling. There is an initial theme repeated throughout, but by the end of the song it has morphed into something completely different. Perhaps the best way to describe "ThirtySix" is not as dance oriented as other Four Tet material; it's more experimental without being completely abstract. Hebden is able to incorporate a variety of sounds within one 35-minute piece without bombarding the listener with too many noises. This might not be the best introduction to Four Tet, but rather an extension and experimentation with previous themes. —*Marc Gilman*

● **Dialogue** / Feb. 15, 1999 / Output ♦♦♦♦
Some people might think it's easy to explain Four Tet: "It's electronica." It might be easiest to wince at these people and concede, "Yes, well sort of." Four Tet, the one-man DJ project of Fridge's Kieran Hebden, doesn't fit so easily into any one category. True, there are beats, samples, and other aspects of turntablism to his music, but there are also live instruments and very real sounding drum tracks—"organic electronic" might be one way to describe it. *Dialogue* is Four Tet's first proper album (a slew of remixes and 12"s have come before and after). Sometimes the record is jazzy: heavy acoustic bass and scattered drums, but alternately, tabla and sitar are the key focus of the final track. It seems that Hebden is quite happy in any musical setting he creates. None of the album sounds contrived, and there's an underlying earnestness that provides real credibility. Some of the record sounds, at times, like the more sampled passages of Fridge, but not as austere. If you're feeling fed up with stale, predictable electronica, or feeling ready to brave the shores of the electro-isle, this is an excellent album. —*Marc Gilman*

## Eddie "Flashin'" Fowlkes

**b.** 1962, Detroit, MI
*Producer, DJ / Detroit Techno, Club/Dance, Techno*
Though he was present at the birth of Detroit techno, Eddie "Flashin'" Fowlkes was often overlooked in favor of the more press-hyped "Belleville Three" (Juan Atkins, Derrick May, Kevin Saunderson). Still, Fowlkes' template of futuristic techno blended with elements of mellow deep-house and a touch of Motown soul was name-checked with surprising frequency by British and German producers aware of the debt they owed to Detroit's first guard. The style, dubbed "Black Technosoul" by Fowlkes himself, was illustrated in hilarious fashion on the cover of an LP as some kind of interplanetary switched-at-birth scenario.

A big fan of Motown and soul while growing up, Fowlkes began mixing while still in high school and made the move to become a full-time DJ after a stint in business college. He often DJed at the fabled Detroit club Music Institute and first recorded in 1986 with the "Goodbye Kiss" single for Juan Atkins' Metroplex Records. Fowlkes also recorded for KMS, 430 West (the seminal single "Inequality"), and Play It Again Sam during the late '80s and early '90s, and released his debut full-length, the hard and soul LP *Serious Techno, Vol. 1* in 1991.

After several Detroit producers experienced tremendous success abroad, Fowlkes gained an album contract with Germany's Tresor Records and recorded in Berlin with the in-house production team 3MB (aka Moritz Von Oswald and Thomas Fehlmann), resulting in 1993's *The Birth of Technosoul*. Another LP from the sessions (*Deep Detroit Techno Soul, Vol. 1*) emerged that same year, and Fowlkes began recording for other European labels like Infonet, Back to Basics, and Peacefrog as well. His third album for Tresor, *Black Technosoul*, followed in 1996. —*John Bush*

**Deep Detroit Techno Soul, Vol. 1** / Aug. 15, 1993 / Pow Wow ♦♦♦

● **The Birth of Techno Soul** / Oct. 15, 1993 / Pow Wow ♦♦♦♦
The result of Fowlkes' trip to Berlin is a solid collection of early-'90s groove techno that forms the basis of his man-machine philosophy, with titles like "Computee," "My Soul," and "Move Me." In truth, several tracks were recorded in Detroit, but most feature the studio talents of Thomas Fehlmann and Moritz Von Oswald (aka Maurizio). —*John Bush*

**Black Technosoul** / Jun. 3, 1996 / Tresor ♦♦
*Black Technosoul* illustrates exactly how Eddie Flashin' Fowlkes takes the machine-like sounds of classic Detroit techno and re-organizes this aesthetic to ultimately function similar to the classic Chicago house records by Marshall Jefferson and Larry Heard that had been so influential to Fowlkes. So when he refers to these songs as "black technosoul," Fowlkes actually presents an excellent summary of these sounds: derived from two predominantly black music cultures—Detroit and Chicago—with the techno sounds of Detroit and the sweaty, body jacking soul of classic Chicago house. Rarely has this merger of these two neighboring Midwestern cities' styles been this aggressively merged—not even Kevin Saunderson, Green Velvet, Theo Parrish, Gemini, or Carl Craig were able to keep their music this well balanced—so it is rather exciting to hear Detroit techno with such straight-up party attitude and Chicago house with such a mechanical feel; unfortunately though, the music seems a bit too compromised to be considered classic. By trying to bring two different styles together, certain elements must be discarded—namely techno's mysticism and house's organicism, in this case—leaving these songs with a glossy facade but an arguably hollow sense of substance. —*Jason Birchmeier*

## John Foxx (Dennis Leigh)

**b.** Chorley, Lancashire, England
*Vocals, Guitar / Post-Punk, Prog-Rock/Art Rock, Ambient, Synth-Pop*
John Foxx was born in Chorley, Lancashire in the north of England. A child intellectual, reading the manifesto's of *the Futurists* at age 9, a career in the arts beckoned as Foxx enrolled at the Royal College of Art in London before forming the band Ultravox. After 3 albums, including one produced by the now legendary Brian Eno, Foxx left in '79.

His first solo disc, *Metamatic*, was issued in 1980 through his own label metal beat, with Virgin handling distribution. With the exception of some bass, the sound was completely synthetic. It became his biggest selling album, featuring the single "Underpass."

A livelier album, *The Garden*, followed a year later, named after the studio where it was recorded and which Foxx would frequent for the next few years. The opening "Europe After the Rain" is perhaps his finest moment. *The Garden* also included a version of the "Lord's Prayer (Pater Noster)" sung in Italian to a disco beat! Initial copies came with a booklet entitled "Church," complete with Foxx's photomontage images, poems, and lyrics.

1983's *The Golden Section* was one of the few Foxx releases produced by an outsider, Zeuss B. Held. As with *The Garden* it peaked slightly lower down at 27. If that was a shame, it was nothing compared to the shock of his fourth and final album for some time, *In Mysterious Ways*, charting at number 85 on its release in 1985. Two singles featured; both failed to chart despite the usually stunning Foxx illustrations on the sleeve, especially on "Stars on Fire."

After this John Foxx vanished, his name bearing "whatever happened to..." conversations. On the sleeve notes for 1992's compilation *Assembly*, Foxx hinted he was totally disinterested in the mid-'80s music scene. He spent his time lecturing (helping shoot the video to techno band LFO's debut namesake single), illustrating book covers, and collaborating with Bomb the Bass mainman Tim Simenon on the short-lived project *Nation 12*.

In 1997 Foxx re-appeared almost as mysteriously as he had disappeared with two new albums: *Cathedral Oceans* and *Shifting City* (with Louis Gordon). The former was primarily ambient in nature and namechecked musician Harold Budd who, during an interview, cited Foxx "a fantastic artist." —*Kelvin Hayes*

● **Metamatic** / 1980 / Virgin ♦♦♦♦
Foxx's solo debut after leaving Ultravox!, *Metamatic* achieves the same emotional transcendence as his previous group's early highlight *Systems of Ro-*

mance, despite a new reliance not just on synthesizers but on a musical framework dependent on them. On *Metamatic*, Foxx cultivates a curious air of disinterest that never seems truly bored, but is much more extreme than even his unarguably distant vocal style for Ultravox!. It holds up as one of the peaks of the early '80s fascination with emotionless, Kraftwerk-inspired synth-pop. —*John Bush*

**The Garden** / 1981 / Metal Beat/Virgin ♦♦♦
As could be gleaned from the title, John Foxx's second album isn't nearly the stark synthesizer record of his debut. In fact, there are a few organic instruments in the mix and a relaxed musical tone that matches Foxx's ruminations on religion and mysticism. Though fans expecting another *Metamatic* may have been disappointed, Foxx proved with *The Garden* that he was an artist and not merely a musician. —*John Bush*

**John Foxx** / 1981 / Virgin ♦♦♦♦

**The Golden Section** / 1983 / Virgin ♦♦♦♦
Another radically different record to file next to his first two, the third solo album by John Foxx focused on fusing the experimental fringe of synth-pop with a melodic preoccupation that almost put him into crossover territory. Capped by the superb single "Endlessly," *The Golden Section* again distanced Foxx from the glut of synth bands on the market. —*John Bush*

**Cathedral Oceans** / Oct. 7, 1997 / Resurgent ♦♦♦
The first CD release of John Foxx's ever-evolving *Cathedral Oceans* piece, usually married in performance to a series of visual projections. The music is built around layers of delay and echo effects. —*Steve Huey*

## Laila France

*Producer / Electronica, Alternative Pop/Rock*
Electronica ingenue Laila France was first hired by avant-popster Momus after she answered a newspaper ad asking for a singer reminiscent of Italian soft-porn films. With the production expertise of Momus, she released her 1997 debut album *Orgonon* for Bungalow Records and provided vocals for the self-titled album by the Japanese pop group Fantastic Plastic Machine. —*John Bush*

● **Orgonon** / Nov. 17, 1997 / Bungalow ♦♦♦
She sounds just as amateurish as Momus obviously wanted her to be, but Laila France's debut album is enlivened by stellar poptronica production by Momus—with a bit of help from Robin Rimbaud (aka Scanner) and Douglas Benford (aka Si-Cut.db). Tracks like "Japanese Especially," "The Pink Song," and "Trance Cocktail Airlines" have the classic air of Brigitte Bardot-type sex-kitten glamor, though the lyrics occasionally go just a bit too far ("The Sensations of Orgasm," "First Love Blood") down those roads (probably also intentional on Momus' part.) —*John Bush*

## Terry Francis

b. Jul. 28, 1966, Epsom, England
*Producer, DJ / Tech-House, Club/Dance, House*
His sleek fusion of techno and house made him a top British DJ, but Terry Francis has also helmed a series of solid productions, both as Housey Doingz (with Nathan Coles) and under his own name. Based in Croydon, Francis worked at the Swag record store and began DJing an irresistible blend of electro-techno and earthy house during the early '90s. His Wiggle clubnight gained fans around the country, and was eventually spun into a label as well. With Wiggle compatriot Coles, he recorded one of the label's early club hits, Housey Doingz's *Piano EP*. The like-minded househeads at Pagan Records (founded by House of 909) offered him a full-length deal, which brought Housey Doingz's *Loving It* album in mid-1997. Francis also recorded singles for Checkpoint and Surreal, and debuted an ongoing mix series *Architecture* in early 1998. The album also earned release in America, courtesy of Ark 21. By the end of the year, the second volume of *Architecture* appeared on Pagan. —*John Bush*

● **Architecture** / Feb. 16, 1998 / Ark 21 ♦♦♦
*Terry Francis Presents Architecture* finds the DJ mixing together a number of house tracks from different artists, tying them together with his signature tech-house style. The music has a warm, melodic vibe that makes it interesting listening for people who don't want to dance. Four of the cuts on the album are new, exclusive tracks from Francis, and the record also includes the Francois Kevorkian mix of Ame Strong's "Tous Est Blue." —*Leo Stanley*

**Architecture, Vol. 2** / Nov. 9, 1998 / Pagan ♦♦♦♦

## Christopher Franke

b. Apr. 6, 1953, Berlin, Germany
*Keyboards, Synthesizer, Producer / Minimalism, Progressive Electronic, Adult Alternative*
A longtime member of the pioneering German electronic unit Tangerine Dream, keyboardist/composer Christopher Franke was born in Berlin on April 6, 1953, subsequently studying classical music and composition at the Berlin Conservatory. While playing in the jazz-rock group Agitation Free, he and his mentor, Swiss avant-garde composer Thomas Kessler, set up a sound studio and began teaching courses in improvisation, laying the groundwork for what would become the Berlin School of Electronic Music. Through the school, Franke met Edgar Froese and Peter Baumann, joining them in Tangerine Dream in 1970; he remained with the group for nearly two decades, during that time greatly expanding the parameters of electronic music through his contributions to landmark records including *Zeit*, *Atem*, and *Phaedra*, as well as influential film soundtracks like *Sorcerer*, *Risky Business*, and *Legend*. One of the first musicians to explore the full creative scope of the synthesizer, Franke proved particularly innovative in employing sequencers as percussion instruments, forging the dense, throbbing sound which became Tangerine Dream's trademark during the mid-to-late '70s. He left the group in 1988 to mount a solo career, settling in Los Angeles two years later to pursue film work; in 1991, in addition to forming the Berlin Symphonic Film Orchestra (BSFO), Franke issued his debut solo album *Pacific Coast Highway*. In 1993 he founded his own label, Sonic Images, subsequently releasing several collections of his music for the syndicated sci-fi series *Babylon 5*, as well as his continuing solo recordings. Three years later Franke released *Perry Rhodan Pax Terra* which was followed in 1989 by *Epic*. —*Jason Ankeny*

● **Pacific Coast Highway** / 1991 / Private Music ♦♦♦♦
Franke's first solo album is surprisingly melodic, highly accessible, and immaculately produced. As the title suggests, this music would make the perfect soundtrack for a drive up the California coast. The innovative sequencer work of his Tangerine Dream years has given way on this album to more predictable pop electronic orchestrations that would easily fit into new adult-contemporary radio formats. —*Linda Kohanov*

**New Music for Films, Vol. 1** / 1993 / Varèse Sarabande ♦♦♦
A nicely balanced collection of cues from three different motion pictures (*Eye of the Storm*, *McBain*, and *She Woke Up*) performed by Franke and his Berlin Symphonic Film Orchestra (best known now for their work on *Babylon 5*). This is excellent music for creative thinking and creative dreaming, and even for getting the blood stirred up a bit. Just don't expect to do anything particularly meditational! —*Steven McDonald*

**Babylon 5 [Original Soundtrack]** / May 18, 1995 / Sonic Images ♦♦♦
The first soundtrack to the science-fiction television series *Babylon 5* features selections from several original shows, plus a few pieces inspired by the show. For fans of the program or Christopher Franke's sweeping new age music, this is an excellent collection, featuring some of his very best and most evocative compositions. —*Rodney Batdorf*

**Klemania** / May 23, 1995 / Sonic Images ♦♦
*Klemania* is Christopher Franke's tribute to the electronic music festival of the same name. Appropriately, it's an enchanting collection of ambient music with a strong worldbeat undercurrent, and it's quite an intriguing journey. —*Rodney Batdorf*

**Celestine Prophecy** / 1996 / Priority ♦♦♦
Christopher Franke's adaptation of James Redfield's best-selling book *The Celestine Prophecy* is layered with worldbeat flourishes, drawing from all manners of Eastern and ancient musics. Franke layers rhythms and sonic textures, from African percussion to sampled pianos and high falsetto vocals. By and large, the soundscapes are evocative, even if they aren't necessarily evocative of the book itself. Nevertheless, *The Celestine Prophecy* is yet another impressive work from one of the most gifted and adventurous new age composers of the '80s and '90s. —*Rodney Batdorf*

**Pacific Blue [Original Soundtrack]** / Aug. 5, 1997 / Sonic Images ♦♦
The soundtrack to *Pacific Blue* is comprised entirely of music written and performed by Christopher Franke, who attempts to approximate the show's extreme Southern California mentality by layering the album with heavy rock, surf tunes, and soothing instrumentals. For anyone who's a fan of the show, the results are familiar and entertaining, but for listeners unfamiliar

with *Pacific Blue*, the soundtrack will be sporadically entertaining. Nevertheless, Franke's instrumental facility and his capablity to emulate a number of styles makes the record an impressive effort. —*Stephen Thomas Erlewine*

**Transformation of Mind** / Nov. 4, 1997 / Earth Tone ♦♦♦♦
*Transformation of Mind* is an ambitious project, merging Christopher Franke's evocative, hypnotic contemporary instrumentals with Deepak Chopra reading from his 1991 book, "Unconditional Life." The recording is complemented by a multi-media section on its disc, one that features photography from Bruce Heinemann. For listeners not in tune with new age philosophy, *Transformation of Mind* can seem indulgent, but it's a remarkably well-executed project from all standpoints, from Franke's music and Chopra's prose and poetry, down to Heinemann's nature photographs. It's one of the true original works in the new age field during the late '90s. —*Rodney Batdorf*

## Frankie Goes to Hollywood
f. 1980, Liverpool, England, db. 1987
*Group / Club/Dance, New Wave, Dance-Pop*

On the back of an enormous publicity campaign, Frankie Goes to Hollywood dominated British music in 1984. Frankie's dance-pop borrowed heavily from the then-current hi-NRG movement, adding a slick pop sensibility and production. What really distinguished the group was not their music, but their marketing campaign. With a series of slogans, T-shirts, and homoerotic videos, the band caused enormous controversy in England and managed to create some sensations in the United States. However, the Frankie sensation was finished as soon as it was started; by the release of their second album *Liverpool* in 1986, the group's audience had virtually disappeared.

Based in Liverpool, Frankie Goes to Hollywood formed in 1980, comprising ex-Big in Japan vocalist Holly Johnson, vocalist Paul Rutherford, guitarist Nasher Nash, bassist Mark O'Toole, and drummer Peter Gill. Originally, the group was called Hollycaust, but they changed their name to Frankie Goes to Hollywood—taken from an old headline about Frank Sinatra's acting career—by the end of the year. The band didn't make anything of note until 1982, when they appeared on the British television program "The Tube" with a rough version of the video for "Relax." The appearance attracted attention from several record labels as well as record producer Trevor Horn. Horn contacted the band and signed them to his label, ZTT. Late in 1983, Frankie's first single, the Horn-produced "Relax"/"Ferry Cross the Mersey," was released. A driving dance number, "Relax" featured sexually suggestive lyrics that would soon lead to great controversy.

Around the time of the release of "Relax," Frankie's promotional director Paul Morley, a former music journalist, orchestrated a massive, intricate marketing campaign that soon paid off in spades. Morley designed T-shirts that read "Relax" and "Frankie Says…," which eventually appeared across the country. The group began playing up their stylish, campy homosexual imagery, especially in the first video for "Relax." The video was banned by British TV and a new version was shot. Similarly, Radio 1 banned the single and the rest of the BBC radio and television networks quickly banned the record as well. Consequently, "Relax" shot to No. 1 in January of 1984 and soon sold over a million copies. Frankie's second single, the political "Two Tribes," was released in June of 1984. The single, which was also produced by Trevor Horn, entered the charts at No. 1; it went gold in seven days. "Two Tribes" stayed at No. 1 for nine weeks and eventually sold over a million copies. While it was on the top of the charts, "Relax" went back up the charts, peaking at No. 2.

Frankie-mania had taken England by storm, yet it took a while to catch on in America. "Relax" peaked at No. 67 in the spring of 1984, while "Two Tribes" just missed the Top 40 in the fall. *Welcome to the Pleasuredome*, the band's Trevor Horn-produced debut double album, entered the UK charts at No. 1, and their third single, the ballad "The Power of Love," also reached No. 1. *Welcome to the Pleasuredome* reached No. 33 in early 1985 in the US, prompting the re-release of "Relax"; this time around, it made it into the American Top Ten.

"Rage Hard," the first single from their second album, peaked at No. 4 in the UK during the summer of 1986. It was followed by the release of *Liverpool*, which reached No. 5 on the British charts. Frankie Goes to Hollywood began their final tour in early 1987; by April, the band had broken up. Holly Johnson went on to pursue a solo career, which began in earnest in 1989, after a long legal battle with ZTT. Paul Rutherford also began a solo career, yet neither his nor Johnson's were particularly successful. Johnson was diagnosed with AIDS in the early '90s and subsequently retired from music. —*Stephen Thomas Erlewine*

**Welcome to the Pleasuredome** / 1984 / ZTT/Island ♦♦♦♦
Upbeat British dance music with melodramatic vocals and lyrics that are sexually and politically provocative. The sound of Frankie Goes to Hollywood swept Britain in the years 1983-1985. Here is the wide-screen debut double album, containing the hits "Relax," "Two Tribes," "The Power of Love," and the title track. —*William Ruhlmann*

● **Bang! The Greatest Hits** / Mar. 22, 1994 / ZTT/Island ♦♦♦♦
Frankie Goes to Hollywood hyped their debut album *Welcome to the Pleasuredome* so much that when their second record, *Liverpool*, failed to live up to expectations, their career was effectively over. That didn't stop them from releasing greatest-hits albums, however, nor did it stop the inevitable wave of '80s nostalgia that surged forth in the '90s. To cash in on whatever meager Frankie nostalgia that may have existed, *Bang! Greatest Hits by Frankie Goes to Hollywood* appeared in 1994 and was reissued in 1998, when the rights shifted to Universal Records. *Bang!* is as good a compilation of Frankie's material as could be assembled, featuring no less than eight songs from *Pleasuredome* (including, of course, "Relax," "Two Tribes," "The World is My Oyster" and "Bang") and five songs from *Liverpool*. There were a couple of good songs stranded on the second album ("Ferry Cross the Mersey," "Rage Hard") and certain casual fans may enjoy having those singles on the same disc with the hits, but the fact remains that Frankie can only truly be understood (and, to a certain extent, truly enjoyed) on *Pleasuredome*. That debut stood on its own, sounding unlike any other record of its time, and it contained all of the big hits in the first place. Consequently, many casual listeners will be satisfied with simply acquiring that record, even if the album versions were slightly different than the singles. If they feel otherwise, *Bang!* will serve as the definitive singles collection, satisfying both the hardcore and casual fan. —*Stephen Thomas Erlewine*

## Freaky Chakra (Daum Bentley)
*Remixing, Producer / Electronica, Ambient Techno, Club/Dance*

An excellent addition to the West Coast's psychedelic groove movement alongside Tranquility Bass, Single Cell Orchestra, and Spacetime Continuum, Daum Bentley's Freaky Chakra project combined funk, earthy techno, and elements of classic industrial music for his debut LP, 1995's *Lowdown Motivator*. A fan of hip-hop and industrial until the nascent rave scene hit San Francisco in the late '80s, Bentley began recording in the early '90s and appeared live in early incarnations of Miguel Fierro's Single Cell Orchestra. Introduced to Tranquility Bass' Mike Kandel through Fierro, Bentley passed him a demo tape and released the debut Freaky Chakra single "Halucifuge" on Kandel's Exist Dance Records.

One year later Bentley was signed to the surging independent Astralwerks, which released his first album *Lowdown Motivator* in 1995. Comprising a range of material recorded as early as 1990, the LP earned glowing praise from critics, as did the stormy battle-clash *Freaky Chakra Vs. Single Cell Orchestra*. Bentley resurfaced in 1997 with the EP *Year 2000*, and his second proper full-length *Blacklight Fantasy* was released one year later —*John Bush*

**Lowdown Motivator** / 1995 / Astralwerks ♦♦♦♦
*Lowdown Motivator* occasionally moves closer to the rich, diverse ecotapestry of Future Sound of London's *Lifeforms* than the work of Bentley's compatriots around San Francisco. Despite the ambient leanings, earthy beats are never far behind on the album, and Bentley has good instincts when it comes to constructing and mixing rhythms around his effects. —*John Bush*

**Budded on Earth to Bloom in Heaven [EP]** / Nov. 1995 / Astralwerks ♦♦♦
This extended-length six-cut EP includes vocals by Curve's Toni Halliday and a remix by Single Cell Orchestra. Even discounting the additional help, *Budded on Earth…* covers a lot of territory, remaining danceable and engaging throughout. —*John Bush*

**Freaky Chakra Vs. Single Cell Orchestra** / Sep. 9, 1996 / Astralwerks ♦♦♦♦
● **Blacklight Fantasy** / Apr. 21, 1998 / Caroline/Astralwerks ♦♦♦♦
The debut should have been difficult to top, but *Blacklight Fantasy* has no problem accomplishing the mission. An updated blend of slightly psychedelic effects and deep-beat electro grooves propels songs like "Downspace," "Year 2000," and the title track. —*John Bush*

## Freeform (Simon Pyke)

*Producer / Experimental Jungle, Experimental Techno, Experimental Electro, Electronica, Ambient Techno, IDM*

London's Simon Pyke releases angular, almost algorithmic experimental electro under the name Freeform. Expanding on the rhythmic and percussive elements of a style first seriously pursued by artists such as Coil, Autechre, and RAC, Pyke's Freeform material is at times even more lab-coat than the above, playing dense, sparking rhythmic figures off one another in complex, shifting patterns that manage to suggest ambient, experimental electro, techno, dub, and industrial all at once. After releasing an album on Ambient Soho house label Worm Interface and a stunning EP on Skam (co-owned by Autechre and fast becoming one of future electronica's most popular scouting-grounds), Pyke was snapped up by Sheffield's Warp label in 1995. His Warp debut, a double 12"/CD-EP entitled *Prowl*, was a mixture of the dirty experimental fracture of his previous Skam work and the more hi-res, circuitous electro-lounge of Warp and Clear artists such as Plaid, Gregory Fleckner Quintet, and Dr. Rockit. Although he never followed up with a full-length for the label, Pyke contributed a new track to a promo-only cassette compilation given out by Warp during a European label tour, as well as to the 1996 Worm Interface compilation, *Frequencies*. After his second album for WI, 1997's *Heterarchy*, he released three albums in three years for three labels: Headphone (*Pattern Tub*), Sprawl (*Me Shape*), and Sub Rosa (*Green Park*). —*Sean Cooper*

**Elastic Speakers** / 1995 / Worm Interface ♦♦♦
Simon Pyke uses clever synth patterns and eclectic techno rhythms on this refreshing album. —*John Bush*

● **Prowl [EP]** / 1996 / Warp ♦♦♦♦
Freeform's Simon Pyke zeroes in on one or two of the themes of his earlier work—mostly electro and ambient—for his Warp debut. A double-pack EP with just four tracks in tow, the release isn't nearly as varied as his previous material, but benefits greatly from a sense of focus. "Lebanon" and "Brieflei" are the high-points here, with shifting melodies and odd time signatures helping reinvent electro for the martini-swilling armchair set. —*Sean Cooper*

**Free [EP]** / Jul. 8, 1996 / Skam ♦♦♦♦
Simon Pyke's *Free* EP was the first non-Autechre-related Skam release, and proved there was more to the label than the mask-donning tactics of one of electronica's most respected names. Cutting across electro, dub, ambient, and experimental noise, *Free* was a restless, difficult affair that, though flawed and at times overly repetitive, suggested enough new vistas to be worthy of credit. Sheffield's Warp imprint apparently agreed—the five-tracker was enough to land Pyke a contract with the label in 1995, just as it was released. —*Sean Cooper*

**Glob [EP]** / 1997 / Musik Aus Strom ♦♦♦
"Glob" is Freeform's Simon Pyke's first proper release for the Musik Aus Strom label, whose releases by Funkstorung, Michael Fakesch, and Andre Estermann have stumbled over similar territory as Freeform releases on Skam and Worm Interface. Lodged between the more textured ambience of his recent *Heterarchy* and the goofball clown-funk of EPs such as "Prowl" (on Warp) and "Palavalamp" (on Worm Interface), "Glob"'s tracks play like grade school science projects; fascinating little machines that bob and twitch and squirm and pop without going much of anywhere, but keep you in a state of rapt attention nonetheless. —*Sean Cooper*

**Heterarchy** / 1997 / Worm Interface ♦♦♦♦
Although his earlier releases for Worm Interface, Warp, and Skam were notable for their blunt abuse of rhythmic convention, Simon Pyke's second full-length for WI (his first being *Elastic Speakers*) is a minimal question mark of apparently beatless (thought not lacking in percussion) ambient/electronica. Constraining himself to only three or four textural flavors through the course of 12 tracks, Pyke constructs a fascinating series of sonic vignettes (many under three or four minutes), each like a little sonic puzzle the logic of which is slowly revealed through repeat listenings. Quite a bit different, then, from the audacity of his previous work, but fantastic nonetheless. —*Sean Cooper*

**Pattern Tub** / 1998 / Headphone ♦♦♦♦
While the overwhelming majority of Freeform's released work has involved a certain thumbing of nose and extending of tongue, Simon Pyke's first release for Bobby Bird's (ex-Higher Intelligence Agency's) Headphone label is surprisingly serious. More subdued than past releases such as *Elastic Speakers* and *Prowl*, *Pattern Tub* is similarly intricate, trading brashness for subtlety, but maintaining the level of compositional complexity that carried his previous albums. While the closing track—15 minutes of mostly untreated traffic sounds gathered via Pyke's bedroom window —is an unfortunate cap to an otherwise excellent album, "Poundland" and "Monza Lecta" (the latter a duet with Bit-Tonic's Iris Garrelfs) are some of Pyke's most original songs to date. —*Sean Cooper*

## Adam Freeland

b. Aug. 7, 1973, Welwyn Garden City, England
*Producer, DJ / Tech-House, Club/Dance, Techno, Nu Breaks*

Adam Freeland is the DJ, label-head, and producer most often hailed for the fusion of breakbeat and techno (sometimes branded nu-skool breaks) on righteous mix albums like 1996's *Coastal Breaks* and 2000's *Tectonics*. Based in Brighton, Freeland began DJing in 1991, originally mixing deep house and later drum'n'bass. After becoming an in-demand DJ around Britain and to a lesser degree in Europe for his mixing skills and innovative sound, Freeland released his first mix album, *Coastal Breaks*, in 1996. He began producing around the same time, teaming with Kevin Beber as Tsunami One and hitting it big in underground circles with the single "No. 43 With Steamed Rice Please" on Fuel. The second volume in the *Coastal Breaks* series followed in 1998, and he formed his own label, Marine Parade (named after a seaside road in Brighton). In 1999, another Tsunami One production—"Hip Hop Phenomenon," recorded with American trance producer BT—became a hit. Earning scads of best-new-DJ reviews from magazines as well as no less an authority than Carl Cox, Freeland returned to the mix-album realm in 2000 with *Tectonics*, licensed to American audiences through Ultra Records. An avid fan of surfing and snowboarding, Freeland has DJed at numerous snowboarding events as well as clubs worldwide. His remixing credits include the Orb, Headrillaz, Orbital, Deejay Punk Roc, and Dylan Rhymes. —*John Bush*

**Coastal Breaks, Vol. 1** / Nov. 11, 1996 / Distinctive ♦♦♦♦

**Coastal Breaks, Vol. 2** / Jul. 21, 1998 / Xtreme Entertainment ♦♦♦

● **Tectonics** / May 2, 2000 / Ultra ♦♦♦♦
Just as the disparate styles in electronic dance began drifting, like continents, so far apart it seemed unlikely they'd ever be within hailing distance of each other again, one of Britain's brightest young DJs brought them all back into the fold. On *Tectonics*, Adam Freeland compiled a selection of tracks that hark to techno as much as trance, house as much as breakbeat, and made a fresh form out of the strengths of many different styles. Freeland simultaneously assimilates the mid-tempo breakbeats and analog paranoia of drum'n'bass, the streamlined flair and elegance of progressive trance, and the edge and hardness of techno, with delicious, refreshing results. Many of the tracks are associated with Britain's growing tech-house movement, with Freeland compatriots like Layo & Bushwacka, Kevin Beber, and ILS making appearances. (Freeland himself comprises half of Tsunami One, whose "Hip Hop Phenomenon" collaboration with BT is included here). Just as the dozens of dance styles out there began getting codified (and stale), Freeland took the best parts of each and produced one of the year's brightest mix albums. —*John Bush*

## Freestyle (Tony Butler)

*Producer / Electro-Techno, Electro, Techno, Hip-Hop*

One of the most prolific and influential of the '80s electro artists, Miami-based producer Tony Butler recorded a string of popular club tracks on Power/Jam Packed and his own Music Specialist label in the mid-'80s, helping build the electro legacy that would give birth to Miami-style bass music and freestyle (named after Butler's primary pseudonym). As well, he influenced '90s post-techno artists such as Autechre and Biochip C. Butler's earlier tracks under his own name, and they are all electro classics, with singles such as "Fix It in the Mix," "Jam the Box," and "Get Some" exploring a thinner, more stripped-down sound similar to Man Parrish and Cybotron. Butler's tracks with Freestyle are perhaps the more well known, and include such club staples as "It's Automatic," "Don't Stop the Rock," and "The Party Has Begun." His more commercial, pop-oriented writing and production work with Trinere, Debbie Deb, and Shannon, however, remain his claim to fame. Butler continues to live and record in Miami. —*Sean Cooper*

● **Freestyle** / Jul. 5, 1990 / Pandisc ♦♦♦♦
One of the few (occasionally) available Freestyle collections from Pandisc,

this self-titled disc includes just eight tracks, though it has most of the best: "Don't Stop the Rock," "It's Automatic," "The Party's Just Begun," and "Come to My House," plus a wild "Freestyle Mega Mix." —*John Bush*

**Don't Stop the Rock** / Jul. 22, 1997 / Hot Productions ♦♦♦♦

## Freestylers

f. 1996, London, England
*Group / Big Beat, Funky Breaks, Electronica, Trip-Hop*

More old-school hip-hop, electro and ragga than big-beat techno (though they're often pigeon-holed that way), the Freestylers were formed by the trio of Matt Cantor, Aston Harvey and Andrew Galea. All three were British b-boys back in the day, and were heavily involved in Britain's dance scene by the late '80s, both as DJs and producers—Cantor recording as Cut'n'Paste, 2 Fat Buddhas, and Freska All Stars, among others, Harvey as Blapps! Posse (author of the 1990 breakbeat classic "Don't Hold Back"). Harvey had also worked with Rebel MC and Definition of Sound, but after meeting Galea, the pair began recording together as Sol Brothers and soon brought Cantor into the fold as well.

Taking the name Freestylers from their first sample (Freestyle's "Don't Stop the Rock"), the trio released their first single, "Drop the Boom (AK-48)" and formed their own Scratch City Records to release it. The track was a prime slice of vocoderized electro, and became an underground club classic as far afield as bass-driven Miami. The *Freestyle EP* followed late in 1996, and Freestylers also released singles on Freskanova (home of Cantor's many solo projects). The group even managed a chart hit (and *Top of the Pops* appearance) with 1998's "B-Boy Stance," a collaboration with vocalist Tenor Fly. A spate of remixing followed, for Audioweb, Afrika Bambaataa and the Jungle Brothers (the latter a pair of the Freestylers' prime influences). The trio also helmed the big-beat compilation *FSUK 2* and contributed a Radio One Essential Mix (where Beenie Man, Public Enemy, the Fall and Whodini all rubbed elbows). Live appearances at Glastonbury and around the European festival circuit met with much praise, and the Freestylers finally released their debut album *We Rock Hard* in 1999. —*John Bush*

• **We Rock Hard** / Jul. 14, 1998 / Freskanova ♦♦♦♦
Though it's more of a run through their back-catalogue than a proper debut, *We Rock Hard* comes through on the title's claim, with little of the push-button, big-dumb-techno aspects of most big-beat acts. Focusing on electro, ragga, breakbeat, and a closing jungle workout ("Warning") with chatting by MC Navigator, the Freestylers up the ante for Britain's old-school big-beat merchants. —*John Bush*

## Freq (Sean Deason)

*Producer / Detroit Techno, Club/Dance, Techno*

A more varied project for Sean Deason than his standard work as himself or Sounds Intangible Nature, Freq debuted with singles for Deason's own Matrix label before hitching up with Britain's Distance Records. The full-length *Heaven* appeared on Distance in mid-1997. [See Also: Sean Deason] —*John Bush*

• **Heaven** / Jun. 16, 1997 / Distance ♦♦♦♦
Sean Deason's first full-length as Freq came just one year after his proper debut, *Razorback*, and it shows him branching out into a wide array of styles inspired by, but nowhere near derivative of, his Detroit home. Appearing much more comfortable working under an alias, Deason goes through hard and dark techno on "Xirtam 2," but moves into positively lush territory with "Dreamtime." He's also one of the few Detroit producers to verge into drum'n'bass territory, and on "Fury," he shows he's one of the best American producers in the mostly British medium. The genre experimentations on *Heaven* work because the music itself is just as solid on its own merits. —*John Bush*

## Freddy Fresh (Frederick Schmidt)

b. New York, NY
*Producer, DJ / Electronica, Electro-Techno, Trip-Hop, Club/Dance, Techno, House, Hip-Hop*

Freddy Fresh is among the most active and prolific American underground dance music artists, having released more than a hundred records on a dozen different labels in less than half a decade. Born and bred in New York, Fresh's name is more often associated with the Minneapolis scene, to which he relo-cated in the late '80s after kick-starting a passion for hip-hop and house music production. Fresh formed his longest-running record label—Analog Recordings—in Minneapolis, and his label empire has since grown to include a host of sublabels (first Butterbeat and EMF, and now Socket and Boriqua), as well as Analog's UK arm. In addition to a growing stateside audience, Fresh is also one of the few contemporary non-Detroit techno/electro musicians to have a strong European following, and his records for Experimental, Harthouse, and Martin "Biochip C" Damm's Anodyne label have strengthened his international presence. Although Freddy's release history has included tracks in just about every style from hip-hop and house to techno and trance, his roots and most consistently pursued affectation lay in electro; his records thrive on buzzing modular analog noises and resolutely dirty production techniques, resulting in a distinct, instantly recognizable brand of funky, minimal, somewhat experimental dance music.

Although Fresh grew up a gothic rock/new wave junkie, a trip to the "boogie down" Bronx with his girlfriend (now his wife) in 1984 introduced him to the thriving NYC hip-hop scene. Instantly smitten, Fresh began collecting DJ tapes (Shep Pettibone, Jeff Mills, Frankie Bones, anything he could get his hands on) and, of course, records—everything from Jonzun Crew and Newcleus to Liquid Liquid and Cerrone, Bill Withers and Cat Stevens—and his collection has since grown to over 10,000 strong (making his side-gigs as a DJ a bit easier). Fresh's first work behind the boards came via Bronx legends Boogie Down Productions, with Fred remixing a track for a B-side release (although good luck finding it, and Fred recommends you don't try!). From there, Freddy began piecing tougher a studio, collecting many of the ancient analog synths that give his records their distinct, almost studio-jam feel (he mixes all his tracks live). In 1992, after releasing debut singles on Nu Groove and Silvo Tancredis' Experimental imprint, Fresh established his first label, Analog, to release his own tracks. The label and its offshoots have since attracted such weighty names as Thomas Heckman, Tim Taylor, Cari Lekebusch, DJ Slip, the Bassbin Twins, and Biochip C. In 1995, Fresh inked a contract with noted German techno label Harthouse, and his second full-length, *Accidentally Classic*, was released by the label's UK arm in late 1996, with a Harthouse US reissue following close behind. His third album, *The Last True Family Man*, followed on Harthouse Eye Q. Additionally, Fresh has released records through Wisconsin-based acid stronghold Drop Bass Network, Labworks, and noted German electro label Electrecord. —*Sean Cooper*

**Analog Space Funk** / Oct. 7, 1996 / Analog ♦♦♦

• **Accidentally Classic** / Jan. 28, 1997 / Harthouse ♦♦♦♦
Although most of Freddy Fresh's Harthouse gear has sat on the housey techno side of the fence, *Accidentally Classic* is dominated by thin, 808 breaks and atmospheric melodies that give it a certain old-school Sheffield feel. Fresh roped in buddy/D-Jaxx producer Tim Taylor for mixdown, and the album is noticeably more polished than the usual lo-fi Fresh gear. Surprising. —*Sean Cooper*

**The Last True Family Man** / Feb. 22, 1999 / Eye Q ♦♦♦♦
Freddy Fresh's killer fusion of electro and breakbeat funk dovetailed nicely with the big-beat fad of 1998-99, giving his third album *The Last True Family Man* a perfect springboard. The album lives up to the hype as well, with plenty of irresistible big-beat party tunes like "Badder Badder Schwing" (a Fatboy Slim collaboration) and "It's About the Groove." The title, a pointer to his domestic bliss, spotlights the differences between Fresh and most big-beat producers; there are quite a few laidback tracks and interludes, much more inventive than run-of-the-mill sample madness but lacking much of their frenzy as well. —*John Bush*

## Fretless AZM (Max Brennan)

b. Isle of Wight, England
*Producer / Jazz-House, Electronica, Ambient Techno, Trip-Hop*

One of the more organic (sounding) producers in the field of electronic music, multi-instrumentalist Max Brennan works from his base on the Isle of Wight, a relatively isolated outpost in the middle of the English Channel. The solitude must undoubtedly accelerate his recording schedule, since during 1996-97 Brennan released a total of seven LPs under his three main aliases: the quasi solo acts Fretless AZM, Universal Being, and Maxwell House (many of whose releases also feature the work of Brennan compatriots Paul Butler and Rupert Brown). The blueprint of all three projects are much akin, a locked-groove variation on deep jazz-funk, minus its earthy qualities and more indebted to the cosmic reckonings of Sly and George Clinton electro-funk with slapped bass and rhythm schemes borrowed from worldbeat.

A painter/decorator and veteran of several live funk bands before he emerged as a producer in 1995 with the Fretless AZM project, Brennan recorded several EPs plus the debut Fretless AZM album *From Marz with Love* during 1996. He had already debuted the spacier, more downtempo Universal Being project with two LPs recorded that same year for Holistic (*Holistic Rhythms* and *Jupiter*). Before the end of the year, Brennan had released *another* album by *another* project, the self-titled debut for Maxwell House on Peacefrog Records. The year 1997 brought two more Fretless AZM LPs, *Astral Cinema* and *Distant Earth*, as well as the second Maxwell House album. In 1998, he unveiled a new pseudonym for Holistic—his own. Max Brennan's *Alien to Whom?* was released in June 1998, just two months after the fourth Fretless AZM full-length in total, *Oceans of Light*. Brennan also released EPs for Beau Monde as O.H. Krilll and for Phono as Cide. *Millennium Butterflies*, again credited to Fretless AZM, followed in early 2000. —*John Bush*

**Star Seed Signals [EP]** / 1995 / Holistic ♦♦♦
Fretless AZM move from fusion workouts to deep house with enviable ease on this single for the Holistic label. —*John Bush*

**From Marz with Love** / Aug. 12, 1996 / Holistic ♦♦

• **Astral Cinema** / May 27, 1997 / Holistic ♦♦♦♦
Max Brennan's fusion of the organic and the electronic is so well-blended that it's virtually impossible to tell which parts of *Astral Cinema* were jammed live and which were programmed in the studio. Though continual bass-centric grooves and track structures have a similar feel over the course of an LP, just about every track offers a unique perspective on futuristic jazz-funk. —*John Bush*

**Distant Earth** / Jun. 16, 1997 / Holistic ♦♦

**Oceans of Light** / Apr. 20, 1998 / Holistic ♦♦♦
Brennan appeared to be growing as a musician as his Fretless AZM project continued. Fourth album *Oceans of Light* revealed glimpses of improvisation among its deep grooves and the occasional excursion into beatless electronics. Though most tracks require a few listenings to fully reveal themselves, it's a well-planned journey. —*John Bush*

## Freur

f. 1981, Cardiff, Wales
*Group / Pop/Rock, New Wave, Synth-Pop*
Freur was an arty synth-pop band from Cardiff, Wales, notable for two reasons: first, vocalist Karl Hyde and keyboardist/programmer Rick Smith went on to form the seminal electronica group Underworld; secondly and far less importantly, the group initially used an unpronounceable glyph as its name over a decade before the concept occurred to Prince. The idea was for the quintet to keep itself as remote and distant as possible, both as an artistic statement and publicity gimmick, and it did help in the latter department early on. In addition to Hyde and Smith, who formed the group in 1981, Freur included ex-Fabulous Poodles drummer Bryn Burrows, Alfie Thomas, and John Warwicker. A record deal was inked in 1983, and a demo version of their debut album's title track, "Doot Doot," became a minor hit in Britain and a smash success in Europe. However, the album was unable to support the single's success with any consistency, and the title of 1985's *Get Us Out of Here* proved prophetic, as the band split up. Smith and Hyde later formed an early version of Underworld with two other Freur alumni in 1988, but the latter pair was long gone by the time Underworld achieved its most influential incarnation. —*Steve Huey*

• **Doot-Doot** / 1983 / Oglio ♦♦♦
Freur's debut album was an ambitious but uneven experiment in early techno, a set of synthesized beats and keyboard riffs. Occasionally, as on the title track, there was enough quirky humor and hooks to make it an enjoyable exercise in dance-floor grooves, but the record just as often meandered around in an attempt to find the appropriate sonic textures. Since Freur eventually evolved into Underworld, *Doot-Doot* is an interesting piece of history, but judged as music, it pretty much stands as a fitfully entertaining artifact of its time. [Oglio's reissue contains a handful of singles and 12" mixes as bonus tracks.] —*Stephen Thomas Erlewine*

**Get Us Out of Here** / 1985 / CBS ♦♦

## Fridge

f. 1995, Putney, England
*Group / Electronica, Ambient Techno, Indie Rock, Post-Rock/Experimental*
The British post-rock trio Fridge comprised guitarist Kieran Hebden, bassist Adem Ilhan, and drummer Sam Jeffers, longtime friends from the Putney area who began playing music together while attending school. A chance record shop encounter with another friend helped put the group in contact with Output label chief Trevor "The Underdog" Jackson, who signed them the next day; the first Fridge record, the single "Lojen," was released in early 1997, with all three members still in their teens. The full-length *Ceefax* followed a few months later, but it was their final release of 1997, the epic *Anglepoised* EP, which won the group their first significant radio airplay and critical raves; the equally brilliant *Lign*—a tandem 7" and 12" release with no overlapping tracks—appeared during the early weeks of 1998. The second Fridge LP, *Semaphore*, arrived that March, and was followed by *Orko*, another 7" and 12" doublepack; the EP was their last new material for Output, with the trio signing to Go Beat! soon after. A two-disc collection of their Output singles, *Sevens and Twelves*, was issued in late 1998, with a full album, *EPH*, following the next year. In addition to his work in Fridge, Hebden also recorded material under the names Four Tet and Joshua Falken. —*Jason Ankeny*

**Ceefax** / Mar. 10, 1997 / Output ♦♦♦

**Semaphore** / Mar. 16, 1998 / Output ♦♦♦♦
Fridge's second studio album is simultaneously sprawling and streamlined, a dense, wildly eclectic work which, while epic in scope, is rendered with exacting precision and minimalist grace. Darker and more enigmatic than the trio's previous outings, *Semaphore* possesses a sensual allure that the studied musings of their post-rock peers otherwise lack—"A Slow," as lugubrious and muted as its title suggests, is also insinuatingly lovely, while the liquid basslines, squawking saxophones, and the whispered spoken-word samples of "Lo Fat Diet" evoke a sinister dreaminess. "Lign," which clocks in at just 18 seconds, is in its way the quintessential Fridge moment—beautiful, hypnotic, but always just out of reach. —*Jason Ankeny*

• **Seven's and Twelve's** / Oct. 19, 1998 / Output ♦♦♦♦
Assembling all of Fridge's single and EP sides from their 1997 debut *Lojen* through to 1998's *Orko*, the two-disc *Seven's and Twelve's* highlights the trio's stunning diversity as well as their impressive mastery of sound and structure. Given the relatively brief time frame during which all of the material originally appeared, the only thing more remarkable than Fridge's prolificness is its sheer consistency—much of *Seven's and Twelve's* is brilliant, the product of a group which emerged with its all-encompassing sonic vison fully-formed. From the seductive, slo-mo bloom of the epic "Anglepoised" to the squiggly electronics of "For Force" to the airy dub of "Asthma," each cut evokes its own distinct textures and atmospherics, linked together by a warmth and accessibility rare for music so fiercely intelligent. —*Jason Ankeny*

**EPH** / Jun. 14, 1999 / Go! Beat ♦♦♦♦
Fridge always presents some interesting music on its records; the only problem is that they tend to be a bit inconsistent. From the brilliant early LP *Semaphore* to much more obscure projects like *Indisguise*, a joint venture with D, the band is constantly pushing the limits of electro-instrumental music. *EPH* continues this trend but, in the end, is less fascinating than previous releases. There are certainly highlights, and the album grows more interesting with repeated listens, but it still comes up a bit short. The album's bookends, "Ark" and "Aphelion," are quite good, as are the shorter "Meum" and "Tuum." Unfortunately, the rest of the album is weighed down by all-too-similar songs. Clearly the band spent a great deal of time on the details—overdubbed second drum tracks and creepy background sounds pervade the album—but, ultimately, all this hard work pays few dividends. Although *EPH* is an interesting album in its own right, it just doesn't stand up to the band's other releases. —*Marc Gilman*

## Friend (Magnus Åström)

*Producer / Electronica, Neo-Electro*
The excitable new-school electro drum'n'bass of Friend formed part of the highly respected Swedish label Dot, which broke out of the gate in early 1997 with four impeccable EPs—one each by Hab, Tupilaq, Quant, and Friend. Both "Chromosome for Sale" and the later "Sauna Sessions" were pieces of

electro-jungle fusion tuned with an unusually fine hand, and on Friend's double-pack *Single of the Week* EP, he received help from friend Doktor Kosmos (of Komeda) for a surprisingly straightahead quasi-pop song. Friend's debut album *Hot Rod* appeared on Dot in September 1997. —*John Bush*

### Single of the Week [EP] / Sep. 1997 / Minty Fresh ♦♦♦♦
Friend's second EP for Sweden's Dot Records, produced in conjunction with Komeda keyboard player Doktor Kosmos, features remixes from the best of London's Clear label: Metamatics, Clatterbox, and Daniel Ibbotson. The double 12" was reissued on CD by the American Minty Fresh. —*John Bush*

### ● Hot Rod / Sep. 26, 1997 / Dot ♦♦♦♦
Not quite as essential as hab's *maPOd*, its predecessor on Dot Records, *Hot Rod* practices a similar jag of ultra-clean electro effects and skittery drum'n'bass across tracks like "Kites (Are Nice)," "Eklekto" and "Fetma." —*John Bush*

## Robert Fripp
b. May 16, 1946, Dorset, England
*Keyboards, Guitar, Producer / Experimental, Prog-Rock/Art Rock*
Throughout his career, guitarist Robert Fripp has continually pushed the boundaries of pop music, as well as pursuing many avant-garde and experimental musical ideas. Fripp began playing professionally with the League of Gentlemen in the mid-'60s, providing instrumental support to many American singers that were touring England. During this time he began Giles Giles and Fripp with Pete and Mike Giles. The trio only released one album, 1968's *The Cheerful Insanity of Giles Giles and Fripp*, yet the group soon evolved into King Crimson.

Following the release of their 1969 debut album *In the Court of the Crimson King*, King Crimson became one of the most respected progressive rock acts of its era. From 1969 to 1974, Fripp was the one mainstay in the group, leading it through its various musical incarnations.

During this time, he pursued several side projects away from King Crimson. Fripp recorded two albums with Brian Eno—*No Pussyfooting* (1972) and *Evening Star* (1974). Both of the albums featured the musicians experimenting with avant-garde techniques, including Fripp's "Frippertronics." "Frippertronics" featured layers of guitars and tape loops, producing a harmonically-rich, humming sound; it became a familiar sound on his records. Fripp also produced a handful of albums, mainly records by experimental jazz outfits.

In 1974, Fripp disbanded King Crimson and retired from music. Three years later, he returned to the business, playing on David Bowie's *"Heroes."* Soon afterward, he produced and played on Peter Gabriel's second self-titled album, as well Daryl Hall's *Sacred Songs*. Fripp released his first solo album, *Exposure*, in 1979. *God Save the Queen/Under Heavy Manner* appeared the following year, and in 1981, he assembled a new lineup of King Crimson. While that band recorded and performed, he also led a new band which borrowed its name from his first group, the League of Gentlemen. After releasing three albums, the new version of King Crimson broke up in 1984; the League of Gentlemen split soon afterward.

Fripp released *God Save the King* in 1985 and began teaching guitar, dubbing his students and school the League of Crafty Guitarists; he released an album recorded with his Crafty Guitarists in 1986, the same year he released the first of two collaborations with his wife, Toyah Wilcox. Fripp re-formed the '80s lineup of King Crimson in late 1994, releasing *Thrak* in 1995. He returned to recording solo in 1997, releasing *That Which Passes*. —*Stephen Thomas Erlewine*

### (No Pussyfooting) / Nov. 1973 / EG ♦♦♦♦
At the same time Brian Eno was working on *Here Come the Warm Jets*, he was flexing his experimental muscle with this album of tape delay manipulation recorded with Robert Fripp. In a system later to be dubbed Frippertronics, Eno and Fripp set up two reel-to-reel tape decks that would allow audio elements to be added to a continuing tape loop, building up a dense layer of sound that slowly decayed as it turned around and around the deck's playback head. Fripp later soloed on top of this. *No Pussyfooting* represents the duo's initial experiments with this system, a side each. "Heavenly Music Corporation" demonstrates the beauty of the setup, with several guitar and synth elements building on top of each other, the music slowly evolving, and Fripp ending the piece with low dive-bombing feedback that swoops over the soundscape, bringing the piece to its conclusion. "Swastika Girls," on the other hand, shows how the system can be abused. With too many disconnected sounds sharing the space, some discordant, some melodic, the resulting work lacks form and structure. Eno and Fripp later refined the system on *Evening Star* and Eno's solo album *Discreet Music*. Fripp would take the system and base whole albums and live appearances around it (particularly *Let the Power Fall*). But it was here on *No Pussyfooting* where it all started. —*Ted Mills*

### Evening Star / 1976 / EG ♦♦♦♦
Robert Fripp's second team-up with Brian Eno was a less harsh, more varied affair, closer to Eno's then-developing idea of ambient music than what had come before in *No Pussyfooting*. The method used, once again, was the endless decaying tape loop system of Frippertronics but refined with pieces such as "Wind on Water" fading up into an already complex bed of layered synths and treated guitar over which Fripp plays long, languid solos. "Evening Star" is meditative and calm with gentle scales rocking to and fro while Fripp solos on top. "Wind on Wind" is Eno solo, an excerpt from the soon-to-be-released *Discreet Music* album. The nearly 30-minute ending piece, "An Index of Metals," keeps *Evening Star* from being a purely background listen as the loops this time contain a series of guitar distortions layered to the nth degree, Frippertronics as pure dissonance. As a culmination of Fripp and Eno's experiments, *Evening Star* shows how far they could go. —*Ted Mills*

### ● Exposure / 1979 / EG ♦♦♦♦
Conceived as the third part of an MOR trilogy that included Peter Gabriel's second album and Daryl Hall's *Sacred Songs*, *Exposure* is concerned with a marketplace that Fripp saw as hostile to experimentation and hungry for product. Strangely, then, *Exposure* is one of his most varied and successful rock albums, offering a broad selection of styles. "Water Music I and II" is pure Frippertronics; "Disengage" and "I May Not Have Had Enough of Me but I've Had Enough of You" are angular, jagged rock like he would make with the reformed King Crimson; "North Star" is a soulful ballad led by Daryl Hall on vocals, and a less bombastic version of "Here Comes the Flood" with Peter Gabriel singing, making for a melancholic ending. Peter Hammill, Terre Roche, and Narada Michael Walden also add vocals to a pleasant experiment in pop, Fripp style. —*Ted Mills*

### Let the Power Fall / 1981 / EG ♦♦♦
*Let the Power Fall (An Album of Frippertronics)*—"Frippertronics" is the name Robert Fripp gives to his instrumental pieces constructed with an electric guitar and a tape recorder. It is characterized by long-lined instrumental passages with sustained notes that reverberate in interesting repetitions and variations. —*William Ruhlmann*

### I Advance Masked / 1982 / A&M ♦♦♦
Many a guitar fan would have predicted that a summit between legendary guitarists Andy Summers (the Police) and Robert Fripp (King Crimson) would result in a guitar solofest. But the music on their first collaboration together, *I Advance Masked*, stresses guitar textures and moods over indulgent soloing. Although the recording sessions weren't entirely enjoyable for Summers (who was experiencing marital problems at the time), some very beautiful music can be found on the resulting album. The music for the track "Girl on a Swing" does an excellent job of conveying the song's title in one's mind, and the duo's guitars weave wonderful polyrhythmic guitar lines throughout "China—Yellow Leader." "The Truth of Skies" is an atmospheric piece, created by a wash of keyboard sounds and guitar dissonance, while "New Marimba" would have sounded right at home on an early-'80s King Crimson album. *I Advance Masked* has a dreamlike quality to it, and is definitely not typical rock music. It's highly recommended to fans of these two great and original guitarists. —*Greg Prato*

### God Save the King / 1985 / EG ♦♦♦♦
When King Crimson was on hiatus from the mid-'70s to the early '80s, guitarist Robert Fripp took a three-year break from the music industry. When he decided to return to music, he formed a new band, the League of Gentlemen. Breaking away from Crimson's trademark progressive sound, Fripp enlisted the help of Sara Lee on bass, and Johnny Toobad on drums (later replaced by Kevin Wilkinson). The trio released a total of two albums, 1980's *Under Heavy Manners/God Save the King* and 1981's *The League of Gentlemen*. The 1985 release *God Save the King* was a revised compilation of both releases, with additional parts added by Fripp. David Byrne lends his unmistakable vocal stylings to the track "Under Heavy Manners," while the trio

shine on the album's remaining tracks, all instrumentals. "Inductive Resonance" contains some classic '60s keyboard sounds, while "Heptaparaparshinokh" shows off Fripp's playing at its quirkiest. The opening title track is lengthy (over 13 minutes long), but keeps your attention with Fripp's guitar constantly weaving solos over a funky, repetitive bassline supplied by Lee. A great album, which shows what a shame it is that the League of Gentlemen didn't remain together for a few more albums. —*Greg Prato*

**Network** / 1985 / EG ♦♦♦♦
This is a 20-minute compilation EP consisting of three tracks from Fripp's *Exposure* album and featuring such sidemen as Phil Collins, Brian Eno, Daryl Hall, and Peter Gabriel, and two tracks from the League of Gentlemen album *God Save The King*. As such, it touches upon both Fripp's more pop-oriented work and his more experimental work, making for a good introduction to him. —*William Ruhlmann*

**1999 Soundscapes: Live in Argentina** / 1994 / Discipline ♦♦♦
The five selections that make up Robert Fripp's *1999* album were selected from 12 different live, improvised performances recorded in Buenos Aires, Argentina in 1994. And although some King Crimson fans will be confused by Fripp's musical departure, he's said that his soundscape material is his most immediate and personal work, since the improvised performances can change from night to night, depending on the circumstances. Also, it is pretty fascinating just how many different tones, colors, and textures Fripp creates with just a guitar, guitar synthesizer, and effects pedals (it sounds almost like a full electronic orchestra at times). Fripp also chose not to edit or cut any of the songs on *1999* (except for one), so the songs sound exactly the way they did when Fripp first improvised them in front of an Argentinean audience back in '94. If you want to check out Fripp's Frippertronics technique, which he talks about often in interviews (Fripp describes the technique as being based on "delay, repetition, and hazard"), *1999* is an adequate introduction. —*Greg Prato*

**Radiophonics: 1995 Soundscapes, Vol. 1** / 1995 / Discipline ♦♦♦
On his first volume in the Soundscapes series, Robert Fripp shuns his rock side and chooses to explore experimental, new age-like sounds instead. The selections on *Radiophonics* were culled from a seven-night stand of concerts that Fripp played in Buenos Aires, Argentina from April 3 to April 9, 1995; in the liner notes, Fripp himself admits trying to test the audience's patience, generosity of spirit, and listening capabilities. With that said, you should expect that this isn't your typical record—it's almost as if Fripp is a painter, splashing his canvas with all different kinds of colors and textures. The album transmits many different feelings, from haunting and eerie (the track "Atmosphere") to comforting and relaxing ("II Elegy—For Mothers and Children"). This is not a typical guitar hero solo album; in fact, the guitar doesn't even sound like a guitar at any point on the record. But if you're in search of a sedate recording that will clear your mind, Robert Fripp's *Radiophonics, 1995 Soundscapes Vol. 1* will do the trick. —*Greg Prato*

**A Blessing of Tears: 1995 Soundscapes, Vol. 2** / 1995 / Discpline ♦♦♦♦
When Robert Fripp's mother passed away in 1993, he chose the new age sounds of his soundscape series to serve as a tribute to her. The liner notes in the CD booklet contain a beautifully written eulogy (by Fripp himself) about the interesting life of his mother Edie. Fripp does an excellent job of conveying his grief in the eight selections that comprise *A Blessing of Tears*, while his sorrow is evident in some of the tracks' titles—"The Cathedral of Tears," "A Blessing of Tears," etc. All of the tracks were recorded live during a week-long US West Coast tour, and it differs from the preceding Soundscapes release, *Radiophonics*, because its sole purpose is obviously not to test his audience's "listening capabilities." Fripp has once again successfully put his most personal and heartfelt feelings into his music, the proof being heard throughout the beautiful *A Blessing of Tears, 1995 Soundscapes Vol. 2*. —*Greg Prato*

**That Which Passes: 1995 Soundscapes, Vol. 3** / 1996 / Discipline ♦♦♦
Unlike the two previous volumes of Robert Fripp's soundscapes series, the third release, *That Which Passes*, is not a completely improvised affair. These tracks have been edited from the original live recordings (recorded at two venues in '95—the Goethe Institute of Buenos Aires and the Washington Square Church). On the preceding *Vol. 2*, Fripp issued a collection of instrumentals directly influenced by the death of his mother, and while Fripp does admit that the loss of his mother still affected the music's outcome a bit, *That Which Passes* is influenced by the general theme of "reflections on mortality and dying," and is not a carbon copy of its predecessor. The music still has a relaxing, somber quality to it, and does a good job of taking the listener on a textured musical journey throughout its duration. Fans of soothing new age and ambient instrumentals will surely enjoy Robert Fripp's *That Which Passes*. —*Greg Prato*

**The Gates of Paradise** / Apr. 28, 1998 / Discipline ♦♦♦♦
Fripp continues his soundscape series with this typically evocative piece. As with his other work of this period, the theme touches on devotional and spiritual matters, with Fripp painting challenging and solitary impressions with "Frippertronic" brushstrokes. The new age set will most likely balk at his more dissonant passages, but King Crimson fans and those with a taste for the unusual will delight in his ascetic excess. —*Tim Sheridan*

## Edgar Froese

b. Jun. 6, 1944
*Mellotron, Keyboards, Guitar, Bass, Synthesizer, Producer, Leader, Composer, Arranger / Ambient, Progressive Electronic, Adult Alternative, Electronic*

The only continuing member of the pioneering synthesizer group Tangerine Dream, Edgar Froese also proved to be one of the most ambitious in releasing solo albums alongside the voluminous output of the band. Considered a master of the Mellotron, the early keyboard device (made famous by the Moody Blues) that produced its sound through key-activated tape loops of actual recordings of orchestras, choirs, and other acoustic sounds. Though it still drew from TD's trademark sequencer sound, Froese's solo recordings have a more direct and personal quality, and often feature his penchant for rock-style guitar work.

Even while Tangerine Dream was releasing career classics *Phaedra* and *Rubycon* during 1974-75, Froese began his solo career with the two records *Aqua* and *Epsilon in Malaysian Pale*, quite similar in style to contemporary work by Tangerine Dream. During the rest of the '70s, Froese released four more solo albums during TD's breaks, followed in 1983 by *Pinnacles*. By that point, Froese was the undisputed leader of Tangerine Dream and could release material which would have appeared as solo work during the previous decade. The 1995 Virgin collection *Beyond the Storm* summed up his solo career. —*Linda Kohanov*

**Aqua** / 1974 / Blue Plate ♦♦♦♦
The solo debut from the leader of Tangerine Dream is a set of four synthesizer pieces, free-form and pastoral. The lengthy title track is quite naturalistic, organized around a series of synth bubbles and water sounds, while "NGC 891" reflects Froese's interest in space-rock. —*John Bush*

● **Epsilon in Malaysian Pale** / 1975 / Blue Plate ♦♦♦♦
As lush and entrancing as listeners are led to believe from the exotic foliage on the cover, *Epsilon in Malaysian Pale* is the Froese solo record closest in sound to Tangerine Dream. The light sequencer trance and waves of statuesque synthesizer effects on "Maroubra Bay" are quite similar to TD's work on *Rubycon* (released that same year), and it's just as beautiful and hypnotic. The title track however, is an atmospheric flute piece that forsakes the sequencer for most of its length. —*John Bush*

**Macula Transfer** / 1976 / Brain ♦
An album of guitar and synthesizer soundscapes, *Macula Transfer* was composed by Tangerine Dream founder Edgar Froese in 1975 and 1976 during the different airline flights that give the tracks their titles. Though the LP does make good traveling or background music, most of it is emotionally ambiguous, without enough detail or variety to reward active listening. An exception is the standout track "Quantas 611," a slow, moody synth piece that would sound at home on Brian Eno's *Music for Films* or Aphex Twin's *Selected Ambient Works, Vol. 2*. "OS 452," with its driving rhythm guitar over synth washes, sets the pace for the rest of the LP. "AF 765" adds organ and solo guitar to the mix, with a quickening pace at the end that prefigures techno tracks like Moby's "Thousand." "PA 701" features more complex rhythms, with chorus effects reminiscent of those used by Popol Vuh. —*Michael Waynick*

**Beyond the Storm** / 1995 / Virgin ♦♦♦♦
The prog-rock pioneer released this solid two-disc set in 1995, chronicling his entire solo career. —*John Bush*

## From Within

*Group / Ambient Techno*

From Within is an unlikely ambient techno collaboration between Canadian acid techno legend Richie Hawtin and prolific ambient composer Pete Namlook, whose collaborative partners also include such artists as Klaus Schulz, Mixmaster Morris, Tetsu Inoue, Bill Laswell, and Burhan Ocal, among a dozen others. From Within combines Namlook's signature sweeping synths with Hawtin's sharp beats, producing a sound not dissimilar from Higher Intelligence Agency and the more beat-oriented side of Global Communication. The pair have produced three From Within CDs to date, with all three originally appearing on Namlook's limited-quantity Fax label. The CDs were reissued via Fax sublabel World in 1996, and Hawtin re-released them once again on his Plus 8 label in late 2000. —*Sean Cooper*

- From Within 1 / 1994 / Fax ♦♦♦♦
- From Within 2 / 1995 / Fax ♦♦♦

## Front Line Assembly

f. 1986, Vancouver, British

*Group / Electro-Industrial, Industrial Dance, Industrial*

Front Line Assembly was the best-known of the various electronic music projects undertaken by the prolific Vancouver-based duo of Bill Leeb (vocals, synthesizers) and Rhys Fulber (synthesizers and samplers). After working in the mid-'80s under the pseudonym Wilhelm Schroeder with Skinny Puppy, the Austrian-born Leeb formed the industrial/techno-based Front Line Assembly in 1986 with Fulber—who initially joined on as a studio assistant—and synth-player Michael Balch. After a handful of compilation appearances and cassette-only releases, Front Line Assembly issued its first three full-length efforts— *The Initial Command*, *State of Mind* and *Corrosion*—on a monthly basis between December 1987 and February 1988. Later in 1988, *Corrosion* was reissued, along with a subsequent mini-album titled *Disorder*, and a number of exclusive bonus tracks, as *Convergence*.

In 1989, the group returned with the album *Gashed Senses & Crossfire*, which contained the dance-flavored singles "Digital Tension Dementia" and "No Limit." A European tour in support of the record yielded a live album—titled, simply, *Live*—that was released and deleted on the same day in a limited edition of 4,000 pressings. After Balch departed Front Line Assembly in 1990, Fulber stepped in as a full partner; the streamlined duo soon released the electro-styled album *Caustic Grip*, while 1992's *Tactical Neural Implant* found the group's music moving in a more hard-edged disco direction. By 1994, the sound evolved yet again, with the album *Millennium* displaying a newfound reliance on guitars; both the title track and "This Faith" scored as club hits. Fulber departed the lineup by 1997, while his replacement Chris Peterson debuted with 1998's *Monument*. *Implode* appeared one year later. —*Jason Ankeny*

**State of Mind** / 1988 / Cleopatra ♦♦♦

The second full-length record from Front Line Assembly, *State of Mind* was also the second of three albums the group released on a month-by-month basis between December 1987 and February 1988. Recorded with the group's original line-up of Bill Leeb and Michael Balch, the album finds Front Line in an experimental dance music mode typical of its early work. —*Jason Ankeny*

**Millennium** / 1994 / Roadrunner ♦♦♦

Rhys Fulber and Bill Leeb returned in late 1994 after a two-year silence (as FLA, at least) with *Millennium*, a heavy album that combines their usual aggressive industrial electronics with a lot of guitars and some hip-hop rhythms. It's an admirable stab at bending genres, but the album doesn't flow from start to finish as great ones do. —*John Bush*

**Remix War** / Jun. 1996 / Cleopatra ♦♦♦

*Remix War* features a number of Front Line Assembly songs as remixed by Die Krupps and a selection of Die Krupps selections remixed by Front Line Assembly—hence, the "remix war" that the title refers to. It's a fun exercise for fans of either band, but if you aren't familiar with either group, it's a little uneventful. —*Stephen Thomas Erlewine*

- **Reclamation** / Oct. 7, 1997 / Roadrunner ♦♦♦♦

The influential industrial/electronic band Front Line Assembly was far ahead of its time. Although later technoid groups would achieve far more popularity (Nine Inch Nials, Prodigy), most of today's electro sounds were first laid down by Front Line Assembly. Formed in Vancouver, Canada back in 1986, FLA was one of the first groups (along with Skinny Puppy and Ministry) to fuse dance music with elements of both rock and alternative. Shouted vocals, repetitive synthesizers, and drum machines, eerie sound effects, and darkly futuristic lyrics were all present in the mix. *Reclamation* is essentially a best-of compilation covering 1989–1993, but also includes remixes and hard-to-find B-sides, making it the perfect introduction to the band and an indispensable addition to longtime fans' collections. Included are all of the group's underground hits—"Digital Tension Dementia" (in a new Contagion Mix form), "Provision," and "No Limit." FLA's best-known single, "Mindphaser," was a big club hit in '92, and it's easy to understand why—contagious dance beats and affected vocals with a monstrous Euro-accent spell success in the techno genre. The group has been quiet of late; Rhys Fulber is the only FLA member remaining active (producing tracks for the electronic-heavy metal band Fear Factory). And although the group never truly broke through in America like they did in Europe, it seems like FLA's music would be better appreciated in this heavily computerized day and age. —*Greg Prato*

**Flavour of the Weak** / Jan. 13, 1998 / Metropolis ♦♦

With Rhys Fulber gone, Bill Leeb turns out a Front Line Assembly album with the assistance of Chris Peterson. *Flavour of the Weak* finds the duo fusing their trademark sound with various popular dance sounds of the late '90s, especially drum'n'bass and electronica. —*Steve Huey*

**Cryogenic Studios** / Aug. 11, 1998 / Cleopatra ♦♦

*Cryogenic Studios* compiles tracks not only from Frontline Assembly, but from Bill Leeb's major side projects—Delerium, Synaesthesia, Pro>Tech, and Equinox—as well, making it a handy introduction to the range of his talents, even if it isn't his most consistent release. —*Steve Huey*

**Re-Wind** / Aug. 18, 1998 / Metropolis ♦♦♦

*Re-Wind* is a two-disc set of remixed material originally featured on the *Flavour of the Weak* album; the more aggressive first disc belongs entirely to Bill Leeb, while the second features contributions from Front 242, Collide, Tim Schuldt, Kalte Farben, Eat Static, Cydonia, and Fini Tribe. —*Steve Huey*

**Monument** / Sep. 22, 1998 / Roadrunner ♦♦♦

Similar to the 1997 release *Reclamation*, *Monument* is essentially a best-of compilation, with several previously unavailable remixes included. With selections taken solely from their 1989-1993 period (what many fans feel was their peak), all of the tracks on *Monument* have been edited together by band producer/co-collaborator Greg Reely. Proving to be a worthy companion to *Reclamation*, the album shows once and for all why many put Front Line Assembly in the same class as other influential electro bands from the same era (Ministry, NIN, Meat Beat Manifesto, etc.). The same harsh vocals and repetitive electronic percussion that Front Line Assembly used extensively in the early '90s have been inherited by such present-day bands as Fear Factory and Stabbing Westward—"Big Money (remix)," "Mental Distortion," "Virus (Cauterized Mix)," and "Laughing Pain" are all prime examples. Containing over 73 minutes of music, *Monument* is another fine compilation of Front Line Assembly. —*Greg Prato*

**Implode** / Apr. 27, 1999 / Metropolis ♦♦♦♦

While 1994's *Millennium* showed what raging guitars and a metal slant could do to Front Line Assembly's heavy industrial sound, *Implode* adds an advanced concentration of electronics and drum'n'bass rhythms. Songs like "Retribution" and the single "Prophecy" are just as dark and storming as previous FLA material but with a crucial update to the production. —*Keith Farley*

## Full Moon Scientist

f. 1994, London, England

*Group / Electronica, Club/Dance, Techno*

Recording for progressive house imprint Hard Hands and later the more sympathetic electro-eccentrics at Botchit & Scarper, Full Moon Scientist was formed by Walsh and Rowlands for a genuine brand of experimentalism within the confines of electronica. After recording several EPs for Hard Hands during 1995, including the shroom-nightmare EPs *Shrub-A-Dub* and *Mondaymorningdread*, the duo released their debut album, *The Men in White Coats*, also on Hard Hands. Silent for the most part during 1996, Full Moon Scientist returned the following year on Botchit & Scarper, also the home of new-school crusties like the Knights of the Occasional Table, Freq Nasty and Purple Kola. First, the "Doc Hope" single appeared in September 1997, followed by *Do We Look Like Comedians?* one month later. —*John Bush*

**The Shrub-A-Dub [EP]** / 1995 / Hard Hands ♦♦
This EP of remixes from *The Men in White Coats* album includes a dub remix from Vinyl Blair and an ambient workout courtesy of Tony Thorpe. —*John Bush*

• **Do We Look Like Comedians?** / Oct. 6, 1997 / Botchit & Scarper ♦♦♦
Although occasionally too humorous and referential for its own good, Full Moon Scientist cross-pollinates house, trip-hop and trance to good effect on their sophomore effort, recorded for Botchit & Scarper. —*John Bush*

## Fun-Da-Mental

f. 1991, London, England
*Group / British Rap, Club/Dance, Hip-Hop*
In 1991, Aki Qureshi ("Propa-Gandhi") saw a need in his homeland of Great Britain for a music group devoted to publicizing the social injustice directed at members of its Asian and Afro-Caribbean communities, and the collective Fun-Da-Mental was born. Qureshi built a following by releasing singles on his own independent label, Nation Records, and integrating multimedia spectacles into the group's concerts. Dave "Impi-D" Watts joined the group in 1993, and together, the two formed the musical core of Fun-Da-Mental, writing most of the worldbeat-influenced music, integrating tapes of recorded speeches into the songs and taking their turns rapping. Their 1994 debut, *Seize the Time*, features eight lyricists and five rappers altogether; *Erotic Terrorism* followed in 1998. —*Steve Huey*

• **Seize the Time** / 1995 / Mammoth/Atlantic ♦♦♦♦
Aimed at an Asian audience, Fun-Da-Mental mixes politics and music in a true "in-your-face" way. Musically, they are likely to sample radical politicians and any sounds that catch their ear. A double CD, its track listing omits their "Countryman" single. Their material addresses issues pertinent to the Asian experience. "Countryman" itself is highly hypnotic, lyrically sharp, and a revealing exploration of host nation attitudes. —*Ken Hunt*

**Erotic Terrorism** / May 5, 1998 / Beggars Banquet ♦♦♦♦
Fun-Da-Mental's fourth full-length keeps the group at the front of the "Asian Underground" movement, melding electronic club rhythms with elements of Indian and Pakistani music; like Cornershop and Asian Dub Foundation, their material reflects the multicultural experience with insight and honesty, and *Erotic Terrorism* is a record as eye-opening as it is danceable. —*Jason Ankeny*

## Trevor Fung

b. Jul. 29, 1961, Hammersmith, London, England
*DJ / Club/Dance, Acid House, House*
Trevor Fung began DJing with Paul Oakenfold in a club on the Spanish Mediterranean island Ibiza in 1987, gradually making it a cosmopolitan hotspot for Fung's "Balearic" style of mixing pop and indie-rock with house. Other DJs such as Danny Rampling, Nicky Holloway, and Johnny Walker later came to check it out and brought the emerging style back to the London clubs, which were into hip-hop and not much else. Rampling and Holloway soon set up their own house nights and Oakenfold followed also, pushing house to the forefront of British club life in the late '80s while Fung took charge of the Ibiza crowd and journeyed to London for huge one-off events. He continued to DJ well into the '90s, at locations all over the world. —*John Bush*

• **Classic House** / Aug. 4, 1998 / DCI ♦♦♦♦
More than most other DJs, Trevor Fung knows what classic house should be all about, and he proves it with this mix album, sourcing acid-house and techno back to Chicago and Detroit with plenty of focus on old-guard classics by Mr. Fingers, Marshall Jefferson, Reese & Santonio (aka Kevin Saunderson), Ralphi Rosario, Frankie Knuckles, Armando, and many more. *Classic House* is more than just a history lesson; it's an exciting, double-disc trip through some of the best electronic dance music ever recorded. —*John Bush*

## Funk D'Void (Lars Sandberg)

b. Mar. 10, 1971, Glasgow, Scotland
*Remixing, Producer / Jazz-House, Tech-House, Club/Dance, Techno*
On the techno side of tech-house, Lars Sandberg's streamlined recordings as Funk D'Void enlivened the fertile Glasgow techno scene during the mid-'90s courtesy of Soma Recordings, the label owned by local scene-heads Slam. He began DJing hip-hop and house around Glasgow in the mid-'80s and later began recording as well, sparked by a drive to hear his own tracks on the dance floor. Sandberg named his production alias in tribute to George Clinton, whose P-Funk concert machine often featured a mythical Scrooge character named Sir Nose d'Void of Funk who was inevitably forced to give it up by the end of the show. After hooking up with Soma for the 1995 single "Jack Me Off," tracks like "Soul Man" and "Bad Coffee" began hitting the clubs as well. Sandberg released the debut Funk D'Void album *Technoir* on Soma in 1997. Also, his Chaser project (with Nigel Hayes) made waves of its own with the album *Game On*, also on Soma. Another Sandberg alias, United States of Sound, recorded two singles for the Bomber label. The second Funk D'Void full-length, *Imitate*, appeared in late 2000. —*John Bush*

• **Technoir** / Jun. 23, 1997 / Soma ♦♦♦♦
Featuring several club classics previously released on Soma as well as the more recent single "Lucky Strike," *Technoir* does a good job of juggling old and new, though Sandberg proves better at producing dance material than his downtempo tracks. —*John Bush*

## La Funk Mob

f. 1991, Paris, France
*Group / Electronica, Trip-Hop, Club/Dance, Hip-Hop*
Although MC Solaar was the only French rapper of note during the '90s, several hip-hop production crews made inroads in the quintessentially American style, including DJ Cam, the Mighty Bop, and La Funk Mob. The latter team, formed by Boom Bass and Philippe Zdar in the early '90s (though Boom Bass had worked with Solaar on his first two solo albums, weaving samples from Black Sheep to Serge Gainsbourg), debuted with a track on the 1993 compilation album *Jimmy Jay Présente "Les Cool Sessions"* and signed to Britain's seminal Mo'Wax for two 1994 EPs, *Tribulations Extra Sensorielles* and *Casse les Frontieres, Fou les Têtes en L'air* ("Breaking Boundaries, Messing Up Heads"). Little was heard from the duo during 1997-1998; two side-projects (Motorbass and L'homme Qui Valait 3 Milliard) saw European releases, and Boom Bass again provided production work for MC Solaar on his third album, *Paradisiaque*. The duo resurfaced as Cassius in 1999 for the purpose of French progressive house. —*John Bush*

**Breaking Boundaries, Messing Up Heads [EP]** / Apr. 1994 / Mo'Wax ♦♦♦♦
A double 10" set, La Funk Mob's second release for Mo'Wax includes a "Techno Disc" (with a great Carl Craig remix) and a "Hip-Hop Disc." —*John Bush*

• **Tribulations Extra Sensorielles [EP]** / Aug. 1994 / Mo'Wax ♦♦♦♦
An extended EP of clean trip-hop and electro minimalism, *Tribulations Extra Sensorielles* is a Mo'Wax highlight, sparked by "Ravers Suck Our Sound." —*John Bush*

## Funkadelic

f. 1968, Detroit, MI, db. 1981
*Group / Psychedelic, R&B, Funk*
Though they often took a back chair to their sister group Parliament, Funkadelic furthered the notions of black rock begun by Jimi Hendrix and Sly Stone, blending elements of '60s psychedelia and blues plus the deep groove of soul and funk. The band pursued album statements of social/political commentary while Parliament stayed in the funk singles format. But Funkadelic, nevertheless, paralleled the more commercial artist's success, especially in the late '70s when the interplay between bands moved the Funkadelic sound closer to a unified P-Funk style.

In the grand soul tradition of a backing band playing support before the star takes the stage, Funkadelic began by supporting George Clinton's doo wop group, the Parliaments. By mid-1967, Clinton's backing band included his old friend Billy "Bass" Nelson (b. January 28, 1951, Plainfield, NJ) and guitarist Eddie Hazel (b. April 10, 1950, Brooklyn, NY). After several temporary replacements on drums and keyboards, the addition of rhythm guitarist Lucius "Tawl" Ross (b. October 5, 1948, Wagram, NC) and drummer Ramon "Tiki" Fulwood (b. May 23, 1944, Philadelphia, PA) completed the lineup.

The Parliaments recorded several hits during 1967, but trouble with the Revilot label backed Clinton into a corner. He hit upon the idea of deserting the Parliaments' name and instead recording their backing group, with the added vocal "contributions" of the former Parliaments—same band, different name. Billy Nelson suggested the title Funkadelic, to reflect the members' increased inspiration from LSD and psychedelic culture. Released in 1970, Funkadelic's self-titled debut album listed only producer Clinton and the five members of Funkadelic—Hazel, Nelson, Fulwood, and Ross, plus organist Mickey

Atkins—but it also included all the former Parliaments. Keyboard player Bernie Worrell also appeared on the album uncredited, even though his picture was included on the inner sleeve with the rest of the band.

Worrell (b. April 19, 1944, Long Beach, NJ) was finally credited on the second Funkadelic album (1970's *Free Your Mind... And Your Ass Will Follow*). He and Clinton had known each other since the early '60s, and Worrell soon became the most crucial cog in the P-Funk machine, working on arrangements and production for most later Parliament/Funkadelic releases. His strict upbringing and classical training (at the New England Conservatory and Juilliard), as well as the boom in synthesizer technology during the early '70s, gave him the tools to create the horn arrangements and jazz fusion-inspired synth runs that later trademarked the P-Funk sound. Just after the release of their third album, *Maggot Brain*, P-Funk added yet another big contributor, Bootsy Collins. The throbbing bassline of Collins (b. October 26, 1951, Cincinnati, OH) had previously been featured in James Brown's backing band, the J.B.'s (along with his brother, guitarist Catfish Collins). Bootsy and Catfish were playing in a Detroit band in 1972 when George Clinton saw and hired them.

The Clinton/Worrell/Collins lineup premiered on 1972's *America Eats Its Young*, but soon after its release, several original members left the camp. Eddie Hazel spent a year in jail after a combination drug possession/assault conviction, and both Tawl Ross and Billy Nelson left as well. Funkadelic hired teenaged guitar sensation Michael Hampton as a replacement, but both Hazel and Nelson would return for several later P-Funk releases.

Funkadelic moved to Warner Bros. in 1975 and delivered its major-label debut, *Hardcore Jollies*, one year later to lackluster sales and reviews. In 1977, Funkadelic recorded what became its masterpiece (and arguably the best P-Funk release ever), 1978's *One Nation Under a Groove*. During the most successful year in Parliament/Funkadelic history, Parliament hit the charts first with "Flash Light," P-Funk's first R&B number one. "Aqua Boogie" would hit number one as well late in the year, but Funkadelic's title track to *One Nation Under a Groove* spent six weeks at the top spot on the R&B charts during the summer. The album, which reflected a growing consistency in styles between Parliament and Funkadelic, became the first Funkadelic LP to reach platinum (the same year that Parliament's *Funkentelechy Vs. the Placebo Syndrome* did the same).

At just the point that Funkadelic appeared to be at the top of its powers, though, the band began to unravel. Several members formed a new Funkadelic, then began recording during 1981. Clinton eventually jettisoned both the Parliament and Funkadelic names (but not the musicians), and began his solo career with 1982's *Computer Games*. [See Also: Parliament, George Clinton] —*John Bush*

**Free Your Mind... And Your Ass Will Follow** / 1970 / Westbound ◆◆◆
Not quite as promising as its title and classic cover would indicate, *Free Your Mind and Your Ass Will Follow* is full of faux religious rambling and spacey studio overdubs and effects, yet still manages to pull it off in the endearing Clinton style of blending soul, heavy metal, gospel, and bad sci-fi movies, coming up with gems such as "Friday Night, August the Fourteenth" and "Funky Dollar Bill." —*Julian Katz*

**Funkadelic** / 1970 / Westbound ◆◆◆
The music is serious but George Clinton is as tongue-in-cheek as ever. The album opens up with his voice, proposing "If you will suck my soul, I will lick your funky emotions," and proceeds in and out of that vein for forty minutes. This album is raw and pure funk, with often twangy guitars and deep, low yet prominent basslines. It takes the quirky, basic groove of the Meters and renders it heavy and grungy, while maintaining the straight-faced humor that Clinton has made famous. —*Julian Katz*

**Maggot Brain** / 1971 / Westbound ◆◆◆◆
Perhaps the best early Funkadelic album, *Maggot Brain* showed guitarist Eddie Hazel's increased contribution to the band on the ten-minute title track, which epitomizes the P-Funk machine by working a Hendrix-fronting-the-Family Stone vibe. The album also increased the group's commercial status (with the 27 R&B single & "I Wanna Know If It's Good for You"), but its abstract thematical content discouraged less adventurous listeners. One exception was "You and Your Folks, Me and My Folks," which spoke of the beauty of an interracial romance. "Can You Get to That," the third single culled from the album, proved that Funkadelic remembered the sweet soul music on which most of its members had been reared. —*John Bush*

**America Eats Its Young** / 1972 / Westbound ◆◆◆
An ambitious double-LP, *America Eats Its Young* featured Funkadelic's first attempt at overt political criticism—the cover made the title explicit by depicting the Statue of Liberty gorging on infants. Besides the political commentary and the ecology bender of "If You Don't Like the Effects, Don't Produce the Cause," the band still manages to groove on several tracks, such as "Loose Booty" and "Biological Speculation." A bit bloated and definitely worthy of an editing job, *America Eats Its Young* still comes packed with great songs. —*John Bush*

**Cosmic Slop** / 1973 / Westbound ◆◆◆◆
Funkadelic's fifth LP backs away from the political commentary of *America Eats Its Young*, making it more of an inheritor to the unrestrained funk of *Maggot Brain* than anything else. Instead, the band is ready to get on the good foot, with classic tracks like "No Compute" and the title track, another long instrumental jam in the same league as the *Maggot Brain*'s title song. —*John Bush*

**Standing on the Verge of Getting It On** / 1974 / Westbound ◆◆◆
Funkadelic returned to the charts with *Standing on the Verge of Getting It On*; both the title track and "Red Hot Mama" fared well with R&B listeners, and the band's sixth album proved to be the smoothest, most flowing album the band had produced up to that point. Unlike previous albums, which used the Parliaments' doo wop past occasionally, *Standing on the Verge of Getting It On* is consistently based in rock. Though highlights are not especially frequent, the album was a solid stab at creating the kind of brilliance later found on *One Nation Under a Groove*. —*John Bush*

**Hardcore Jollies** / 1976 / Warner Brothers ◆◆◆◆
In 1976, George Clinton enjoyed much greater commercial success than before and became more than a cult figure—only he didn't do it with Funkadelic. Parliament's 1976 albums *Mothership Connection* and *The Clones of Dr. Funkenstein* were what made him one of the most successful artists in soul and funk. Of course, Parliament and Funkadelic were essentially the same band, but while Parliament had an immediacy that appealed to singles-minded Black radio, Funkadelic remained basically album-oriented. Although more direct and less self-indulgent than early Funkadelic dates like *Maggot Brain* and *America Eats Its Young*, *Hardcore Jollies* was far from an album of hit singles. But it was definitely an album of irresistible funk grooves, and no Clinton devotee should be deprived of the joys of "Comin' Round the Mountain," the eerie "You Scared the Lovin' Out of Me," or an inspired remake of "Cosmic Slop." The guitar-crunching title song demonstrates how hard Clinton could rock, but in those days, album-rock radio wouldn't touch Funkadelic no matter how much heavy guitar some of its songs employed. —*Alex Henderson*

**Tales of Kidd Funkadelic** / 1976 / Westbound ◆◆◆
Some leftover jams, songs, and funk pieces from the Funkadelic era. George Clinton was in the midst of moving Funkadelic to another label, and the Westbound folk released a bunch of vault material to get another Funkadelic album on the market. There were still some fine cuts, but the random element prevented it from being a great album because it lacked the thematic organization and vision Clinton provided for the concept LPs. —*Ron Wynn*

★ **One Nation Under a Groove** / 1978 / Warner Brothers ◆◆◆◆◆
Early on *One Nation Under a Groove* George Clinton asks the rhetorical question "Who Says a Funk Band Can't Play Rock?" Only a fool needs to ask for the answer, since the answer is the album itself. *One Nation Under a Groove* is the most fully-realized slice of P-Funk. Parliament put out albums as funky as this, but they got bogged down in their concepts, while Funkadelic always traded too heavily in psychedelic cliches and art-rock trappings to really let loose. But that's not the case with *One Nation*. On this record, the concept is underplayed, letting the funk come to the forefront. Some died-in-the-wool Funkadelic fans might lament the lack of electric guitar freak-outs, but no matter—this is music of a supreme vision. Besides, the guitars are there, pushing along the funk in an effortless fashion, which helps draw attention to the vocals, which are alternately sexy and downright hilarious. Don't think of *One Nation Under a Groove* as a collection of songs. Think of it as one sustained funk symphony, and you'll be on the right track. Clinton never got this consistently funky again. —*Leo Stanley*

**Uncle Jam Wants You** / 1979 / Warner Brothers ◆◆◆◆
Fueled by the wildly addictive single "(Not Just) Knee Deep," *Uncle Jam*

*Wants You* became one of Funkadelic's best-known albums. Nonetheless, this isn't all that commercial an effort. Like its predecessor, *One Nation Under a Groove*, *Uncle Jam* sold respectably thanks to a major hit, but only contained one truly visible single. For George Clinton, Funkadelic still functioned as Parliament's more esoteric, less radio-friendly alter ego. Pearls like "Foot Soldiers" (which incorporates bits of the World War I anthem "When Johnny Comes Marching Home," among other things), the goofy "Field Maneuvers," and the cute ballad "Holly Wants to Go to California" aren't the stuff that radio hits are made of, although the shadowy "Freak of the Week" could have been a major hit with the right promotion and exposure. Consistently entertaining, this is among the many Funkadelic albums that are truly essential. —*Alex Henderson*

**The Electric Spanking of War Babies** / 1981 / Warner Brothers ✦✦✦✦
With George Clinton, a humorous phrase could be nothing more than playful tomfoolery, or it could be a double-entendre with a deep political meaning. The phrase "electric spanking of war babies" falls into the latter category—it referred to what the funk innovator saw as the US government using the media to promote imperialistic wars. To Clinton, the American media functioned as a propaganda machine during wartime. But whether or not one cares to examine its hidden political messages, *Electric Spanking* is an above-average party album. *Spanking* falls short of the excellence of *One Nation Under a Groove* and *Uncle Jam Wants You* and didn't boast a major hit single, but amusing funk smokers like "Electro-Cuties" and "Funk Gets Stronger" aren't anything to sneeze at; nor is the reggae-influenced "Shockwaves." *Spanking* turned out to be the last album Clinton would produce under the name Funkadelic—when he hit the charts again in 1983, Mr. P-Funk was billing himself as a "solo artist." —*Alex Henderson*

**Music for Your Mother** / Mar. 31, 1993 / Westbound ✦✦✦✦
This two-disc set collects all the great Funkadelic singles and B-sides and presents them in remastered glory. The list includes such gems as "Funky Dollar Bill," "Cosmic Slop," "Let's Take It to the Stage," and "I'll Bet You." Unfortunately, some of Funkadelic's finest efforts were album-length and/or suite pieces, so some brilliant material not issued on singles was omitted. But it's as comprehensive a collection as possible under the circumstances (lacking the later material owned by Priority), and Rob Bowman's notes are extensive and nicely done. —*Ron Wynn*

### Funki Porcini (James Bradell)
*Producer / Electronica, Ambient Breakbeat, Ambient Techno, Trip-Hop*
Funki Porcini is artist and DJ James Bradell, whose swirling mixtures of downtempo breaks, smooth ambiance, and disjointed drum'n'bass helped put the Coldcut-owned, South London-based Ninja Tune label on the map. The first single from his 1995 Ninja debut, *Hed Phone Sex*, "Long Road" (with a B-side, "Poseathon," littered with Bongwater samples) was featured on a number of compilations cashing in on the fashionability of "trip-hop," but Porcini's brand of laidback, atmospheric breakbeat is less gimmicky than that connection suggests. His follow-up to *Hed Phone Sex*, *Love, Pussycats, and Carwrecks*, is filled with jittery, jazz-laden drum'n'bass with a good dose of usually quite twisted humor. Bradell played North America with the Coldcut conglomerate DJ Food as part of the 1996 Unexploded Bomb tour, and has grown increasingly in-demand as a remixer, disorganizing tracks by everyone from Journeyman to the Mike Flowers Pops. His third album in total, *Ultimately Empty Million Pounds*, launched in 1999 and was soon followed by an EP, *Zombie*. —*Sean Cooper*

**Hed Phone Sex** / Nov. 14, 1995 / Shadow Records ✦✦✦✦
At times overly smooth and straying a bit too close to mindless acid jazz, Bradell's solo debut nonetheless carries promising weight, with detailed ambient and dub textures filling out opium-inspired slow-breaks and begging deep, reclined (and, as the title implies, singular) listening. The domestic Shadow reissue adds a second CD of remixes and bonus tracks. —*Sean Cooper*

**Love, Pussycats, and Carwrecks** / Jun. 17, 1996 / Ninja Tune ✦✦✦
Porcini bags the doped-up, downbeat vibe of his first LP, *Hed Phone Sex*, bouncing breaks off of breaks in seemingly random combination. A wonderfully disorienting cluster of new directions. —*Sean Cooper*

• **The Ultimately Empty Million Pounds** / Mar. 29, 1999 / Ninja Tune ✦✦✦✦
Funki Porcini's first album since the boom in spy-soul breakbeat made famous by Fatboy Slim has quite a bit of material in similar territory, easily forgivable considering he'd been working the same line for five years. *The Ultimately Empty Million Pounds* has a few moments of aimless drifting, but it's also liberally sprinkled with entertaining samples, killer beats, and great ideas, especially on appropriately titled tracks like "Rockit Soul," "Theme from Sugar Daddy," and "Reboot." —*John Bush*

### Funkmaster Flex (Aston Taylor)
b. Aug. 5, 19??, New York, NY [The Bronx]
*DJ / Old School Rap, Club/Dance, Hip-Hop*
Funkmaster Flex was long among the top DJs on the New York hip-hop scene, parlaying his success on radio into a career as a prominent producer and remixer. Born Aston Taylor in the Bronx, his father was also a DJ, playing house parties and dancehalls in his native Jamaica. Also influenced by pioneering jocks including Red Alert, Flex bought his first set of turntables at the age of 16, eventually becoming an assistant to another of his DJ heroes, KISS-FM's Chuck Chillout; when Chillout was unable to make it to the studio once in 1987, Flex covered for him on the air, soon earning a regular broadcast slot. Chillout later moved to WBLS, taking Flex with him as a DJ; the latter soon became a favorite at Manhattan clubs and industry parties, ultimately attracting the attention of programming chiefs at Hot 97 WQHT. There he emerged as one of the most prominent hip-hop DJs in New York, soon making his remixing debut with "Dope on Plastic;" "Six Million Ways to Die," and "C'mon Baby" followed, and in late 1995 Funkmaster Flex issued the acclaimed LP *The Mix Tape, Vol. 1: 60 Minutes of Funk*. A second volume appeared in 1997, with a third following a year later. In 1999, Flex returned with *The Tunnel*. —*Jason Ankeny*

• **The Mix Tape, Vol. 1: 60 Minutes of Funk** / Nov. 21, 1995 / RCA/Loud ✦✦✦✦
Funkmaster Flex's *The Mix Tape—Volume 1* recalls hip-hop's past while pointing toward its future. Featuring a wide array of hip-hop styles graced by amazing freestyle raps by some of the '90s top MCs, the album sounds like a mix tape compiled from the radio and 7" singles—there's simply nothing but first-rate music, with no filler whatsoever. Although there are elements of old school rap as well as modern funk, the daring production and stunning rhymes make *The Mix Tape* a rarity of mid-'90s hip-hop—it's a record that sounds like none of its competition. It announces itself as an instant classic. —*Stephen Thomas Erlewine*

**The Mix Tape, Vol. 2: 60 Minutes of Funk** / Feb. 11, 1997 / RCA ✦✦✦✦
*The Mix Tape, Vol. 2: 60 Minutes of Funk* is every bit as engaging as its predecessor, capturing Funkmaster Flex as he spins through a stack of modern and classic hip-hop and R&B, with various guest rappers freestyling while he does so. The energy is equal to *Vol. 1*, and while some listeners might find the relentless but seamless mixing to be a little amelodic and irritating, any true hip-hop fan will consider the album a treasure. —*Leo Stanley*

**The Mix Tape, Vol. 3: 60 Minutes of Funk, The Final Chapter** / Aug. 11, 1998 / RCA ✦✦✦✦
The third (and final, according to the album's subtitle) chapter of New York DJ Funkmaster Flex's mix albums is the best of the bunch, a gritty combination of old- (A Tribe Called Quest, House of Pain, Naughty By Nature) and new- (Missy Elliott, Wu-Tang Clan, Busta Rhymes) school rappers. Flex's deft skill at remixing some familiar tunes—he often takes a minute or two of a cut and works brand new beats, as well as some exclusive freestyling courtesy of top-name artists themselves, into the grooves—makes *The Mix Tape* more than just a lazy compilation of radio hits. Still, when you get down to it, it really doesn't amount to much more than 75 minutes (despite the title's claim of only 60) of a guy spinning some of his favorite records, albeit with style. —*Michael Gallucci*

**The Tunnel** / Dec. 7, 1999 / Def Jam ✦✦✦✦
It takes a pretty connected man to assemble the most star-studded rap album ever released. *The Tunnel* features all of the biggest and best MCs in hip-hop—DMX, Jay-Z, Nas, Method Man, Eminem, LL Cool J, Snoop Dogg, Capone-N-Noreaga, Mary J. Blige, Redman & Erick Sermon, Raekwon—freestyling over tracks, most of them produced by Rockwilder or Funkmaster Flex himself. The affair is somewhat similar to his popular mixtape series, which alternated hip-hop classics with guest appearances from MCs inserted between standard productions. The mere presence of all these incredible rappers is more than enough to push *The Tunnel* over the top, and the addition of a live freestyle between 2Pac and the Notorious B.I.G. recorded in 1993

makes it worthwhile for that track alone. Among many highlights, "True" with Method Man, "For My Thugs" with Jay-Z, "We in Here" with the Ruff Ryders, and "Ill Bomb" with LL Cool J are the best here. —*Keith Farley*

## Funkstörung
f. 1994, Munich, Germany
*Group / Experimental Techno, Electro-Techno, Ambient Techno, IDM*

Munich's Funkstörung have been described as the German Autechre, a description which probably has less to do with their sound than the interest the group has attracted to their Musik Aus Strom label. Similar to Autechre's Skam label, Musik Aus Strom (German, roughly, for "synthesizer music") has become one of the more collectible, obsessed-over underground electronica labels, coveted as much for the Skam-esque enigma about them as the increasing exchange between the two labels' rosters (a connection the two sealed in 1997 with the release of the limited edition *Mask* series, a collaboration between the labels and their respective artists).

Composed of Michael Fakesch and Chris De Luca (both barely into their 20s), Funkstörung's more recent excursions into dark, muddy, lo-fi electro and instrumental hip-hop were preceded by a number of relatively straight-ahead techno records on Bunker sublabel Acid Planet beginning in 1994. The duo were contacted soon after by none other than Aphex Twin's Rephlex label about releasing some material, but stalled plans and unanswered phone calls led the pair to forego the label-shopping route early on, and most of their most significant material to date (with the exception of a few compilation tracks and a single for Compost) has appeared through MAS. Although the Bunker singles far outnumber their later self-released material, MAS twelves such as "Zeit," "Breakart," and "Artificial Garbage" compose the group's more sophisticated, mature sound.

The hotly pursued *Mask* series has also done much for the group's visibility; limited to between 100 and 500 copies per release (in successively increasing quantities), *Mask* releases to date have included tracks from Funkstörung and Skam's Jega, Bola, and Boards of Canada. In 1999, Studio !K7 released the remix collection *Additional Productions*, and Funkstörung returned one year later with their full-length debut, *Appetite for Disctruction*. —*Sean Cooper*

**Funkenstort [Single]** / Apr. 28, 1997 / Compost ♦♦
Funkstörung's first release through the relatively high-profile German trip-hop and electronica label Compost presents the same brand of lo-fi, electronics-propelled beat music they've released through their Musik Aus Strom and Mask labels. Elements of hip-hop and drum'n'bass predominate to a greater extent than with previous 12"s, although the tracks seem more sketches than full-blown songs. Good for what it is but by no means great. —*Sean Cooper*

**Post Art [Single]** / May 11, 1998 / Chocolate Industries ♦♦
**Additional Productions** / May 4, 1999 / Studio !K7 ♦♦♦♦
This eight-track remix compilation features indie techno heroes Funkstörung reworking tracks by an array of artists from Björk to Wu-Tang Clan to Finitribe to East Flatbush Project to Various Artists and Visit Venus. The duo's trademarked style (trademarked by Autechre, that is) is in full effect and though remix compilations usually aren't a good source for original productions, *Additional Productions* fills the bill quite nicely. —*John Bush*

● **Appetite for Disctruction** / Apr. 25, 2000 / Studio !K7 ♦♦♦♦
*Appetite for Disctruction* is nothing short of a post-modern masterpiece. Post-modernism may have become passé, killed by its own irony and countless moronic interpretations, but understand it or not, care for it or not, there is little doubt that post-modernism and its deconstruction of culture have dominated intellectual thought post-Vietnam and into the new millennium. Post-modernism may be played out, but there is always room for one more statement of the times and of the future, especially if it as brilliant as *Appetite for Disctruction*. The album is electronica with a statement, a deconstruction of the musical trends of our times. Funkstörung presents a complete concept. From the art direction of the jewel case to the irony of the liner notes to the mundane song titles to the name of the album itself, *Appetite for Disctruction* is a cohesive vision: the smashing of previous musical boundaries and the unity of these genres into something completely new.

Funkstörung creates an aural world of maddeningly complex soundscapes. *Appetite for Disctruction* takes the listener on a such a lush mental trip that it is difficult to wrap your mind around it as a whole. Moving seamlessly from trip-hop to soul music to head-nodding dance beats to the bleeps of sci-fi imagery to straight-up hip-hop to general cacophony, *Appetite for Disctruction* is an experiment in sound. This isn't mass-market, pop-friendly, Fatboy Slim electronica. It is the exploration of the genre and all of its influences from new wave to hip-hop to R&B to computer programming. Along with Kraftwerk's pioneering work and Underworld's artistry, Funkstörung's *Appetite for Disctruction* is an essential piece of electronica for the collector's vaults. —*Brian Musich*

## Funky Derrick (Mederic Nebinger)
*Producer / Electronica, Club/Dance, House*

The alias of Frenchman Mederic Nebinger, Funky Derrick specializes in disco-sampled retrodelia with nods to commercial house. As a child, Nebinger played piano and listened to disco as well as Tangerine Dream. He studied law and worked in advertising, though after an introduction to the music of DJ Pierre, he bought a sampler and began producing. He recorded sporadically during the '90s, including singles for the French labels Rave Age and Deja Vous, before being signed to Twisted/MCA under his Funky Derrick guise. Debut album *Boogie Dawn* appeared in 1999. —*John Bush*

● **Boogie Dawn** / Sep. 22, 1998 / MCA ♦♦♦
Though it's more adept at building grooves from the sample up than on any new sounds, Funky Derrick's *Boogie Dawn* is an interesting record, hardly serious but all the more fun for it. Singles like "Keep It Up" and "Bang Liberation" weave the usual vocal snippets around elastic basslines and mainstream house effects. Overall, it's a great record for disco and electronica fans looking for music that straddles the divide between uptempo music for home as well as the club. —*John Bush*

## Funky Green Dogs
f. 1994, Miami, FL
*Group / Progressive House, Club/Dance, House*

Murk boys Oscar Gaetan and Ralph Falcon were hyped more on respect than sales figures before they broke out of the American dance mainstream with two of the biggest hits of 1996-97, "Fired Up!" and "The Way" by Funky Green Dogs. Gaetan and Falcon had been producing for their own Murk Recordings since the early '90s, and had earned club-play with hits by Liberty City ("Some Lovin'," "If You Love Someone") and remixes of Madonna, Pet Shop Boys, the Beloved and RuPaul, among others. After recording a Liberty City LP beginning in 1995, the pair turned around and released it as Funky Green Dogs, an alias which had graced only one of their previous recordings. The trailer single "Fired Up!" became a big hit on dancefloors (and charts) with remixes by Danny Tenaglia. After the album *Get Fired Up* appeared in late 1996, second single "The Way" hit number one on the dance charts. The duo added new vocalist Tamara, a native of the Bahamas, for their second album, *Star*. [See Also: Murk] —*John Bush*

● **Get Fired Up** / Oct. 22, 1996 / MCA ♦♦♦♦
The debut Funky Green Dogs album is the best place to get extended versions of the duo's two big hits "The Way" and "Fired Up!," though that's hardly the only good thing about *Get Fired Up*. The singles are placed first and second in the album configuration, leaving Gaetan and Falcon plenty of room to stretch out. Though "Some Kind of Love," "Until the Day" and "Why?" have the same basic blueprint as "The Way," they are all quality productions easily in the same league as FGD's more famous tracks. —*John Bush*

**Star** / Feb. 23, 1999 / MCA ♦♦♦♦
Though they've added a new singer and moved a bit farther toward actual songwriting, the Murk boys prove they still know their way around some crucial tribal-house grooves. The vocalist Tamara adds more emotional flair to Funky Green Dogs than past records, and the single "Body" is more than just an interesting club tune. —*John Bush*

## F.U.S.E. (Richie Hawtin)
*Producer / Ambient Techno, Club/Dance, Techno*

A Richie Hawtin pseudonym which predated even the more famed Plastikman, F.U.S.E. debuted in 1991 with the fourth single on Hawtin's +8 Records, "Approach & Identify." Given wider issue later that year on the +8 compilation *From Our Minds to Yours*, F.U.S.E. released several more singles during 1992, then the album *Dimension Intrusion* in 1993. Released on Warp Records (Britain's premiere label for the new listening techno), the LP gained

Hawtin many converts, especially when it was released in America as well, by TVT Records. While Hawtin increasingly concentrated on his Plastikman project, new F.U.S.E. releases became more and more rare. [See Also: Richie Hawtin, Plastikman] —*John Bush*

● **Dimension Intrusion** / Sep. 14, 1993 / TVT ♦♦♦♦

*Dimension Intrusion* alternates minimalist stompers like "F.U." and "Train-Trac" with more melodic, contemplative material. The latter made Hawtin a perfect match for the other producers in Warp's *Artificial Intelligence* series (B12, Black Dog, Polygon Window). Despite his direct Detroit inspirations—exemplified on the requisite automobile track "Nitedrive"—Hawtin encounters familiar territory on *Dimension Intrusion*'s more downtempo tracks: "A New Day," the title track and "Into the Space." —*John Bush*

## Futique

f. 1995, New York, NY

*Group / Electronica, Ambient Breakbeat, Ambient Techno, Trip-Hop*

Yet another pseudonym for the work of Taylor Deupree (aka Taylor 808) and Savvas Ysatis (aka Omicron)—that is, besides S.E.T.I. and Arc—Futique make the alias rather necessary, since the duo's material is surprisingly different from their usual glut of sparse ambience. Hip-hop beatboxes and Crooklyn dub make appearances alongside the jazzy rhythms on Futique's debut, *Luv Luv* (recorded, as always, for the Instinct label). *Mr. So & So* followed in 1996, and *Go Low* appeared three years later. —*John Bush*

**Luv Luv** / Aug. 6, 1996 / Instinct ♦♦

**Paging Mr. So & So** / Aug. 19, 1997 / Instinct ♦♦♦♦

The second Futique album expands on the Crooklyn dub inspirations of the duo's debut, in a fashion similar to bands like We, Tipsy, and DJ Spooky. The beats are a bit more prominent, and the jazz influence is underplayed somewhat. "Sister Freak" and "Rawhide" provide several highlights. —*John Bush*

● **Go Low** / Dec. 1, 1999 / Shadow ♦♦♦♦

Futique's third album *Go Low* serves up more fun, stylish electro-jazz with equal doses of cheese and atmosphere. Highlights include the sly, funky "Lionel Shuffle," the stark, pseudo-Asian melody of "Perpetual Spirit" and "Sugar in the Raw," with its overlapping, syncopated beats and minimalistic horns and organs. "C-Nut" and "Bubble Trouble" also reveal how Futique's sparse but effective arrangements belie the musical skill behind the kitsch. —*Heather Phares*

## Future Forces, Inc.

f. 1995, Vauxhall, London,

*Group / Jungle/Drum'N'Bass, Club/Dance*

Although Future Forces appeared on the drum'n'bass scene a bit later than most producers, they and the label group they help run (which includes Trouble on Vinyl, Renegade, and Renegade Hardware) have risen to fast prominence through their style of deep, futuristic hardstep. The Vauxhall-based duo of Darren Bridge and Jason Maldini, Future Forces formed in 1995 when Bridge and Maldini were introduced by a mutual friend. Holing up in Maldini's modest studio, the two began putting together simple jump-up cuts and releasing them through Trouble on Vinyl. Working their sound into a harder, more aggressive style (combined with the growing influence of techstep), more recent FF releases (such as "Dead by Dawn" and "Constant") have reflected a more mature approach to production and arrangement, with hard-as-nails breaks combining with more subtle melodic and atmospheric elements. The group recently began DJing as well (primarily as a dub plate-driven promotional device for their various artist and label projects), and the pair are involved individually in a number of solo projects; Bridge as D-Bridge and Monochrome, and Maldini as Subphonics. Future Forces were also featured on the Renegade Hardware compilation *The Way-Out Chapter*. —*Sean Cooper*

● **Dead by Dawn [Single]** / Nov. 25, 1996 / Renegade Hardware ♦♦♦♦

**Symetrix/Cold Fusion Renegade [Single]** / Mar. 10, 1997 / Renegade Hardware ♦♦♦♦

## Future Loop Foundation (Mark Barrott)

b. 1971, Sheffield, Yorkshire, England

*Producer / Ambient Techno, Jungle/Drum'N'Bass*

An ambient-inspired jungle producer more intent on recording solid full-lengths than jump-up singles, Mark Barrott recorded for Planet Dog Records, known more for its crusty psychedelic trance than breakbeat futurism. Barrott, born in Sheffield, played piano as a child and became intrigued with synthesizers. He had a rudimentary home-studio setup by the early '90s, after acid-house, ambient, and the first wave of jungle had made successive waves in England. Barrott began recording downtempo drum'n'bass in 1995, and signed to Planet Dog in the hopes that he'd have more of a chance to release full-lengths. The following year brought his first, *Time & Bass*, and the LP was licensed to America as well.

Later in 1996, Barrott composed music for VH1's Worldwide Fashion Awards. He also assembled a Future Loop Foundation live show, which played at Talvin Singh's Anokha club and toured with Planet Dog's package Megadog. He also recorded the first session for Radio One's *One in the Jungle* show, and released his second LP *Conditions for Living* in 1998. With a new addition to the fold, none other than Planet Dog-head Michael Dog, Barrott returned in 2000 with *Phunk Roc*. —*John Bush*

● **Time and Bass** / Jul. 29, 1996 / Mammoth ♦♦♦♦

The debut LP by Future Loop Foundation, though understandably more focused on the easychair than the dancefloor, manages to stir the blood more than most ambient-jungle producers out there, content to drip a Lonnie Liston Smith sample and some bird calls over their breakbeat collection. Barrott's drum programming is better than most of his competition (check "Carla's Dream"). Aside from the percussion, *Time and Bass* ranges far and wide—from the electronic pulse of "I Want to Believe," to diva-oriented mainstream jungle ("Kinetic Pioneers," "Spirit Catcher"), to the Photek/Bukem-style of drum'n'bass naturalism on "Discovery" and "Shake the Ghost." Indeed, *Time and Bass* makes for an excellent after-hours album. —*Keith Farley*

**Conditions for Living** / Nov. 9, 1998 / Planet Dance ♦♦♦

**Phunk Roc** / May 16, 2000 / Global Fusion ♦♦

By the year 2000, with drum'n'bass on the wane for several years, breakbeat producers were forced to tighten their belts and really give listeners something new to break away from the crowd. Unfortunately, *Phunk Roc*, the third album released by Future Loop Foundation, doesn't really separate itself at all. Barrott and Michael Dog constructed a tight, streamlined album—halfway between jazzy drum'n'bass, jump-up, and the more psychedelic leanings of previous Planet Dog material—but there's little to grasp on to and few ideas that haven't been heard on countless jungle albums previously. Give them credit for tailoring the entire album as a continuous work (and for mixing things up with the languorous down-tempo track "Coming Down"), but for the most part *Phunk Roc* just cruises on by without making much of a statement. —*John Bush*

## Future Pilot A.K.A. (Sushil K. Dade)

*Producer / Experimental Techno, Electronica*

Formerly the bassist for a host of Scottish indie-pop bands (including Soup Dragons, Telstar Ponies, and BMX Bandits), Glasgow's Sushil K. Dade debuted his own project, Future Pilot A.K.A., with several collaborational EPs with guests ranging from Two Lone Swordsmen to rock producer legend Kim Fowley to the Fall's Brix Smith to Scottish jazzman Bill Wells to the Pastels. His full-length debut, *Vs. A Galaxy of Sound*, was a double-disc compilation culled from the EPs. —*John Bush*

● **Future Pilot A.K.A. Vs. A Galaxy of Sound** / Mar. 23, 1999 / Beggars Banquet ♦♦♦♦

Not quite a remix collection, not quite a collaborational album and not quite a proper album, it's difficult to place *A Galaxy of Sound* other than to just proclaim it an experimental record that charts Sushil K. Dade's fascination with music ranging from techno to dub to ethno-ambient to bhangra to indie-rock. Over the course of 20 tracks, Dade invited a series of wide-ranging musical figures—including techno experimentalists Two Lone Swordsmen, jazz multi-instrumentalist Bill Wells, former Fall personage Brix Smith, fellow Indians Cornershop, '60s rock auteur Kim Fowley, Suicide's Alan Vega and cuddle-popsters the Pastels—to contribute to a record that easily earns its title. —*John Bush*

## Future Sound of London

f. 1989, London, England

*Group / Electronica, Ambient Techno, Trip-Hop, Club/Dance, Techno*

First recognized as the dance duo behind such club hits as "Stakker" (as Humanoid) and "Papua New Guinea," Future Sound of London have since become one of the most acclaimed and respected international experimental ambient groups, incorporating elements of techno, classical, jazz, hip-hop, electro, industrial, and dub into expansive, sample-heavy tracks, often exquisitely produced and usually without easy precursor. Notoriously enigmatic and often disdainful of the press, the group's Garry Cobain and Brian Dougans have worked their future-is-now aesthetic into a variety of different fields, including film and video, 2- and 3-D computer graphics and animation, the Internet, radio broadcast, and, of course, recorded music. Although they usually disdain their earlier work as play-for-pay clubfare not representative of their contemporary musical vision, many of the thematic concerns of their earlier 12"s and their first, heavily dance-oriented LP, *Accelerator*, have followed them into their more recent work. Usually filed under "ambient," that work is often much more than that, drawing from the history of experimental electronic music with a relentlessness that has helped to push the calmer elements of that genre's reputation into decidedly more difficult directions. The pair has also grown in repute as remixers, obliterating tracks by Curve, Jon Anderson, David Sylvian & Robert Fripp, and Apollo 440 and rebuilding pieces of almost majestic complexity with the remnants. The duo's later works, *Lifeforms*, *ISDN*, *Dead Cities*, and the *My Kingdom* EP among them, are important stopping points on the road of rabid hybridization characteristic of post-rave European experimental electronica (ambient, jungle, trip-hop, ambient dub, etc.), and the pair's somewhat punk rock attitude despite their success has done much to underscore the scene's underground roots. [See Also: Amorphous Androgynous] —*Sean Cooper*

**Accelerator** / 1991 / Cleopatra ◆◆◆◆
Still quite rooted in a dance music aesthetic, *Accelerator* shows shades of things to come in its dense, effusive orchestration and experimental beats. A satisfying first effort. —*Sean Cooper*

**The Far-Out Son of Lung and the Ramblings of a Madman [EP]** / 1994 / Virgin ◆◆◆
Originally released on white-label, this four-track collection of highlights from the group's ISDN concerts hit like a genrecidal bomb, working jazz, hip-hop, funk, and ambient simultaneously, and forcing eventual release of the full-length collection, *ISDN*. —*Sean Cooper*

**Lifeforms (Remixes) [Single]** / 1994 / Astralwerks ◆◆◆
This quick-but-quality EP showcases FSOL-as-remixers, vigorously working over the title track of their recent album with a variety of different results—beatless ambient to pounding techno—all of it top-notch. Cocteau Twin Liz Fraser's trippy, expansive vocals contribute much. —*Sean Cooper*

★ **Lifeforms** / May 27, 1994 / Astralwerks ◆◆◆◆◆
A groundbreaking double-CD collection of shimmering, detailed ambient techno, self-indulgent at times, but breathtakingly so. Dougans and Cobain approach sound like sculpture here, fashioning commonplace sounds like birds' wings, waves, and dopplering machinery into impressive, multilayered, three-dimensional objects, at once digital and oddly human. —*Sean Cooper*

**ISDN** / Oct. 1994 / Astralwerks ◆◆◆◆
A masterful, nearly seamless fusion of ambient, trip-hop, soul-jazz, electro, industrial-leaning techno, and styles yet unclassified, reportedly recorded live for ISDN uplink to various radio stations around the world (hence the name). The Astralwerks reissue plays havoc with the track listing, subtracting three cuts, substituting a pair from the *Farout* EP, and adding a new track, "Kai," but the decision to issue a double-vinyl version was a good one. —*Sean Cooper*

**My Kingdom [Single]** / Oct. 14, 1996 / Astralwerks/Virgin ◆◆◆◆
Feeling the waters in early '96 with a typically anonymous 12" entitled "We Have Explosive," FSOL mark their follow-up this time, both lexically and stylistically, by returning to the dense forest of sonic abstraction characteristic of their earlier work. Unlike "Explosive"'s abrasive amyl-house vibe, "Kingdom" brings together the lush ambiance of *Lifeforms* with the focused, somewhat dark edge of *ISDN*, moving through five mixes (four on the vinyl version), all of them otherwise unavailable, of the track derived from their *Dead Cities* album. Downtempo, drum'n'bass-esque fast-breaks, and foggy ambient electro all find play here. A welcome return to form. —*Sean Cooper*

**Dead Cities** / Oct. 29, 1996 / Astralwerks/Virgin ◆◆◆◆
FSOL's penchant for sustained thematics registers here in an extended narrative of decay, with *Blade Runner*-esque themes (and even a *Blade Runner* sample!) running through over an hour of stunning aural collage. As usual, the music is impossible to pin down, moving from beatless ambient through downbeat breaks, fast jungly rhythms, and dense, noisy passages reminiscent of *ISDN*'s more formless segments. Perhaps not as experimental as previous efforts, *Dead Cities* is also more mature, relying more on smart arrangements than production gimmickry. A limited pressing of the CD also included a nearly 200-page book of stories, graphics, and video stills. —*Sean Cooper*

**We Have Explosive [Single]** / Apr. 1, 1997 / Astralwerks/Virgin ◆◆◆
The poppy standout from FSOL's *Dead Cities* LP gets the usual extended remix treatment on this nine-part opus single. Originally released under the name Semtex months in advance of *Dead Cities*, "We Have Explosive" gets a re-release here, with a pair of remixes each by Leon Mar/Oil (aka Arcon 2) and Curtis Mantronik (half of the original electro duo Mantronix), as well as a number of takes by the group themselves (the vinyl version contains the original, Mar and Mantronik mixes, and the CD's epic "Pt. 5"). Like past remix singles, this one's all over the map, the original sound files recombined in a range of stylistic deployments, from jungle-y breakbeat to downtempo and old-school hip-hop/electro. Good, but not great. —*Sean Cooper*

## Fuxa

f. 1995, Detroit, MI
*Group / Space Rock, Indie Rock, Post-Rock/Experimental*
Detroit-based experimental rock duo Fuxa focused on a lo-fi, electronics-heavy blend of droning, treated guitars, vintage synths (most often the Hammond B-3), and sparse percussion in the vein of Loop, Spacemen 3/Spiritualized, and Amp. Comprised of Randall Nieman and Ryan Anderson, the group formed in 1995 after Nieman left Dearborn-based space-rock group Windy & Carl to purse other projects. He hooked up with Anderson, who'd recently severed his ties with another local group, Asha Vida, and a common interest in arcane instruments and electronics led the pair to each form a label—Nieman with Mind Expansion and Anderson with Astro Lanes—to put out collaborative material. What followed was a veritable flood of releases, not only on Mind Expansion and Astro Lanes, but labels such as Burnt Hair, Alley Sweeper, Che, and Darla, most of them meticulously conceived with an eye toward collectibility (hand-cut and numbered sleeves, colored vinyl, strategic split recordings, etc.). The result was Fuxa's quick ascension to cult status, buoyed by split recordings with artists such as Orange Cake Mix, Flowchart, Bright, and Stereolab. The group were also featured on Virgin UK's mammoth post-rock companion *Monsters, Robots, and Bugmen* in 1996 and conducted a brief UK tour as Stereolab's support that same year. The group released several full-lengths (including *Three Field Rotation*, which collects their first three singles and adds two new tracks). Though they were reportedly sitting on enough material for about a dozen more, the group disbanded before the end of the decade. —*Sean Cooper*

**3 Field Rotation** / 1995 / An I/Mind Expansion ◆◆◆
*3 Field Rotation* compiles Fuxa's 7" singles that were released in 1994 and 1995 on small labels. This traces the group's development into a knob-twiddling ambient space-rock outfit with interesting ideas. While the album is interesting, the time limits of the 7" makes it more difficult for these songs to freely stretch out and unfold the way they should. In many cases these "songs" seem to end before they begin, but there are still some outstanding compositions that make this collection worthwhile. —*Kembrew McLeod*

● **Very Well Organized** / Nov. 11, 1996 / Mind Expansion ◆◆◆◆
Fuxa's first proper full-length (*Three Field Rotation* was basically just a compilation of EP tracks), *Very Well Organized* is an ocean apart from their debut. Gone are the fuzzy amateurishness and the deliberate obstinance of "First Abductions" and "100 White Envelopes," replaced by a subtler, more committed exploration of vintage analog's capacity for warmth. The group have been quoted as wanting to produce happy music in the face of the American indie underground's premium on po-faced white-boy depression, and *Organized* is their strongest bid for that to date. The Hammond is at the center of many of the tracks here, the result being a kind of ambient church music as goofy and unpretentious as it is challenging and hypnotic. —*Sean Cooper*

## FX Randomiz

*Producer / Experimental Techno, Electronica, Post-Rock/Experimental*
Cologne, Germany's enigmatic A-Musik label has produced some of the most fascinatingly complex reshufflings of experimental ambient and post-techno. And while his name typically only makes it onto his own releases, Felix "F.X." Randomiz has been involved in one way or another with most of them. A con-

tributor to the electronica etchings of such artists as Pluramon, Holosud, Schlammpeitziger, and, most notably, Mouse on Mars (on the group's popular *Autoditacker* LP and together with MOM's Jan St. Werner as Slow), F.X. Randomiz blends elements of each of those projects into a highly synthetic, vertical melange as solid as it is precarious. His cheerful, wobbly, sampler-abusing electronica is probably most in the vein of glitch-miners like General Magic, Mouse on Mars, and even some Atom Heart, but the sheer density of his tracks can make them all the more demanding on the listener. Randomiz finally broke out of contributor mode in 1996, contributing the standout version on Schlammpeitziger's "Freundlichbaracudaremix" 10", released that year by A-Musik in extremely limited quantities. His debut LP, *Goflex*, appeared on A-Musik in 1998. Similar in its chimey imprecision to many of the artists that in 1997–98 help put Cologne on the experimental post-techno map, the album's crammed, lo-fi flutter seemed even more avoidant than most. —*Sean Cooper*

● **Goflex** / Oct. 13, 1997 / A-Musik ♦♦♦♦

*Goflex* is Randomiz's first long-form (well, actually not that long) release for A-Music, following his wonderfully kludgey recast of labelmate Schlammpeitziger on the latter's "Freundlichbarracudaremix" 10". Unlike that track, however, *Goflex* is extremely dense; Randomiz here approaches songwriting in a vertical rather than horizontal or linear fashion, piling dizzying, disorienting sequences of melodic decay atop one another and giving only the slightest of rhythmic clues as to where the music's center might be. The result makes for fascinating—though occasionally tedious and exhausting—listening; the best of it places Randomiz next to fellow Cologneers Marcus Schmickler and Mouse On Mars as among the most interesting of the city's current bumper-crop of musical innovators. —*Sean Cooper*

# G

## G Flame & Mister G (Colin McBean)
*Producer / House*

As G Flame and Mr. G, Colin McBean moved away from the hard techno he had produced with Cisco Ferreira as the English duo known as the Advent. After spending the mid to late '90s as a highly regarded duo, McBean began concentrating on a techno-influenced style of house music that retained the Advent's knack for producing elaborate and highly textured tracks for the dance floor but that integrated the sense of soul and groove that commonly gets associated with house. Besides releasing EPs on Metal Box and Phoenix G, McBean also released G Flame and Mr. G material on Mike Grant's Detroit-based Moods & Grooves label. —*Jason Birchmeier*

- **Give 'N' Take [EP]** / 2000 / Moods & Grooves ♦♦♦
The hard tech-flavored house of G Flame & Mr. G may sound a bit out of place on the otherwise deep house-orientated Moods & Grooves label from Detroit, but there is little denying its worth as a peak-hour DJ record, capable of sending most any crowd into a frenzy. There are primarily two songs here—"Swing Crewz II" and "Pulsez"—along with a dub version of the former; both songs follow a similar template of stomping up-tempo percussion and phasing high-end synth riffs. While the low-end rhythms remain constant, the high-end synths phase through muted phases before then prominently rising to the foreground, creating a frenzied moment of peak intensity. As a less punishing and more house-orientated continuation of the Purpose Maker school of repetitive percussive maelstroms colored with the occasional catchy sound, *Give 'N' Take* functions excellently as the sort of driving record that can take a crowd to a new level. —*Jason Birchmeier*

## Gabrielle
*Vocals / Club/Dance, Dance-Pop*

British house/R&B vocalist Gabrielle was a nightclub singer when she wrote "Dreams"; after she recorded it in 1993, the single set a record for highest chart entry by a debut act when it hit No. 2 in England. A week later, "Dreams" was the No. 1 single in the land, and Gabrielle picked up a Brit Award for Best Newcomer. Her debut album *Find Your Way* sold over a million copies worldwide, and paved the way for her sophomore self-titled album, released in 1996 and produced by the Boilerhouse Boys. In 2000, Gabrielle followed up with her third album, *Rise*. —*John Bush*

- **Gabrielle** / 1996 / Go! ♦♦♦♦
Gabrielle's eponymous second album isn't all that dissimilar from her debut *Find Your Way*. It's still the same mix of appealingly lightweight pop, urban soul and Eurotrash disco that made the debut a success, and it still has the same ratio of winners to clunkers. So, there's not much different at all, but that's not bad, because the singles, including "Give Me a Little More Time," are fine pop concoctions that make *Gabrielle* a frothy, guilty pleasure. —*Stephen Thomas Erlewine*

## Galliano
f. 1988, London, England
*Group / Club/Dance, Acid Jazz*

The first act signed to the groundbreaking acid-jazz label Talkin' Loud, Galliano formed in 1988 around acid house DJ Rob Gallagher but later turned to laidback and jazzy soul with heavy emphasis on live presentation and environmental issues. A loose collective during its first years, the group comprised Gallagher with raps and turntables, vocalist Valerie Étienne (aka Auntie Val), guitarist Mark Vandergucht, bass player Ernie McKone, drummer Crispin Taylor, keyboard player Mick Talbot (formerly with the Style Council), and contributors Brother Spry, Daddy Smith, and, occasionally, Roy Ayers. Galliano's first release was the 1989 single "Frederick Lies Still," a tender play on the *Superfly* anthem "Freddie's Dead" by Curtis Mayfield. The band's debut full-length, *In Pursuit of the 13th Note*, followed two years later on Talkin' Loud. After 1992's *A Joyful Noise Unto the Creator*, Galliano received an American contract and released *What Colour Our Flag* as a basic trainer (the album compiled the best tracks from the first two LPs). *The Plot Thickens*, issued in 1995, was the group's proper US debut. A year later, Galliano returned with *4 (Four)*. —*John Bush*

**A Joyful Noise Unto the Creator** / 1993 / Talkin' Loud ♦♦♦♦

**What Colour Our Flag** / 1994 / Talkin' Loud/Mercury ♦♦♦
These tracks were originally recorded during 1991 and 1992 in London when the group called itself the Galliano Project. They blended strident protest poetry and commentary with Afro-Latin and African rhythms, hard bop, jazz-rock, funk, and pop arrangements. The results were spectacularly uneven; some selections had riveting lyrics and exciting performances, while others were musically dreary, with rambling verse or unimpressive vocals. But the 14 songs presented here are noteworthy even when they fail, for they're a product of musicians and performers trying something inspiring and frustrating, risky and calculated. Their efforts deserve careful scrutiny, even if they don't always merit praise. —*Ron Wynn*

- **The Plot Thickens** / 1995 / Talkin' Loud/Phonogram ♦♦♦♦
Though the grooves are just as tight five years on from the debut Galliano album, *The Plot Thickens* features the group's expanded eco-political focus on "Twyford Down" and "Long Time Gone." Elsewhere, "Blood Lines" and "Rise and Fall" chart sing-along acid-jazz. —*Keith Farley*

**Live at the Liquid Rooms** / 1997 / Talkin' Loud ♦♦♦♦
Recorded live in Tokyo in 1996, *Live at the Liquid Rooms* improves on Galliano's studio albums by offering funkier rhythms and jazzier musical interludes, thereby proving that they are stronger and more talented than the average acid-jazz collective. —*Stephen Thomas Erlewine*

## Ganger
f. 1995, Scotland, db. 1999
*Group / Experimental Dub, Experimental Rock, Indie Rock, Post-Rock/Experimental*

The Scottish post-rock quartet Ganger formed in 1995, its original members—bassists Stuart Henderson and Graham Gavin, drummer James Young and guitarist Lucy McKenzie—coming together out of a shared affection for the classic Kraut-rock sound. Debuting with the EP *Half Nelson*, 20-minute impromptu jams like "Jellyneck" characterized the group's early approach, but as their music grew more disciplined and eclectic the line-up began to crumble, with McKenzie the first to exit to pursue a career in the visual arts. After Gavin quit in 1997, Henderson and Young recruited ex-Fukiyama bassist Natasha Noramly and guitarist Craig B., with the revitalized Ganger resurfacing in early 1998 with the EP *With Tongues Twisting Words;* the full-length *Hammock Style* followed later that year, but the band had broken up by 1999. —*Jason Ankeny*

- **Hammock Style** / 1998 / Domino ♦♦♦♦
The lingering usage of the term "postrock" has seemingly outdated itself, and indeed if a new label for non-mainstream or indie bands had to be created it would be "post-postrock." The label has become a nasty one, avoided by anyone wishing to preserve their artistic independence. The Scottish band Ganger, is one such band. It's not surprising that Ganger is a product of Scotland, notorious for musical innovators including the likes of Belle & Sebastian, Mogwai and many others. *Hammock Style* is their first full length effort,

and at present, the album is solely distributed by Britain's Domino label, leaving American consumers to pay a slightly higher fee, albeit for some excellent music. In Ganger, one hears many influences—the droning melodies of Tortoise, hushed vocals à la Kim Gordon and complex Slint-esque arrangements. But the reason for this album's success is Ganger's synthesis of these sounds into one unique voice. The album's beauty is carefully mediated by close attention to detail and enthusiastic spontaneity. The shortcomings of the term "postrock" are apparent after one listen to this album, and it is impossible to characterize this band as anything other than good; musical genres need not apply. The album starts strong with the trio of "Cats, Dogs and Babies Jaws," "Upye," and "Capo (South of Caspian)." These songs provide a catchy and bold beginning to the album, drenched in energetic melody and thumping rhythm. One feels, as sung by bassist Natasha Noramly, "lost in the city of sound." Lost in a good sense though, where over-preoccupation with direction is unproductive, and complete immersion in the moment is necessary. Ganger runs the gamut of noise, lilting melody and rock-stomp on *Hammock Style* and it makes for a great album. The songs on this album are a bit shorter, but better crafted than Ganger's three previous single releases. *Hammock Style* is a welcome respite for anyone fed up with the jargon and labeling of modern music. Put simply, this album is good. —*Marc G. Gilman*

**Canopy EP** / Jan. 12, 1999 / Merge ✦✦✦✦
The music of Glasgow, Scotland's Ganger was criminally under-heard across the Atlantic in the band's brief lifetime. Indeed, *Canopy*, an EP pressed for the band's maiden US tour with Mogwai in the fall of 1999, wound up as its final release. Ganger's brilliant blend of rhythm, texture, and bass-driven warmth had just begun to hit its stride on 1998's magnificent *Hammock Style*, and this EP shows a clear pattern of growth from that release. In particular, the vocals that graced nearly half of the tracks on *Hammock Style* have been cast aside, allowing the music to tug on the heartstrings in way most instrumentals never do. "State Conversation" initially recalls the crystalline beauty of the instrumentals on Bundy K. Brown's *Directions in Music* album, before an abrupt rhythm change generates a spell of head-nodding bliss. Elsewhere, Ganger demonstrates the art of restraint on the title track and "Standing on the Shoulders of Giants," which kicks around in the same major key for over six minutes. A darker vibe emerges on the Sonic Youth-ish "Now We Have You," while the 42-second "Hai!" revels in a jubilant, major-key riff. One will never know how great this band could have become.—*Jonathan Cohen*

## Garbage

f. 1993, New York, NY
*Group / Alternative Dance, Alternative Pop/Rock*
Garbage built on the sonic landscapes of My Bloody Valentine, Curve, and Sonic Youth, adding a distinct sense of accessible pop songcraft. Garbage was the brainchild of producers Butch Vig, Duke Erikson, and Steve Marker. Initially, Garbage was an informal jam session between the three producers held in Marker's basement, but they eventually recruited vocalist Shirley Manson, who had previously sung with Angelfish and Goodbye Mr. MacKenzie.

Vig is a native of Viroqua, Wisconsin, who learned to play piano as a child and drums as a teenager. He attended the University of Wisconsin briefly before pursuing a career in music instead. The first band he joined after leaving college was Spooner, who he played drums with. Also in Spooner was Erikson, who sang and played guitar with the band. Marker was a native of New York who moved to Wisconsin to attend college. He became a fan of Spooner and began recording their songs. Vig left Spooner shortly afterwards, but he kept in touch with the band. After a few years, Spooner became Firetown and Vig played drums in the new outfit.

Firetown broke up in the late '80s, without achieving much success. Prior to the formation of Firetown, Vig and Marker bought an eight-track cassette recorder together and set up a makeshift studio in a local warehouse. This studio was dubbed Smart Studios and Vig recorded numerous local punk and alternative bands at the warehouse. By the late '80s, Smart had become one of the hippest recording studios in America. Many records released on Touch & Go, Sub Pop, and Twin/Tone, among other indie labels, were made at Smart. Vig and Smart broke into the big time in 1991, after he produced Nirvana's *Nevermind*. *Nevermind* elevated Butch Vig to the status of a superstar producer and for the next two years, he produced numerous American alternative superstars, including Sonic Youth, Smashing Pumpkins, and L7.

Shortly after Vig became a star, he and Marker began playing together, eventually asking Erikson to join them. Hence, Garbage was officially formed in 1993, after Erikson joined the duo. After a year of playing, they hired Shirley Manson after seeing Angelfish on MTV. Manson began her musical career at an early age, joining Goodbye Mr. MacKenzie as a teenager; she played keyboards and sang backing vocals in the band. For the next few years, she toured with the band before leaving to form Angelfish, whom she led through an eponymous 1994 album.

Garbage recorded their debut album in late 1994 and early 1995. Their eponymous first album appeared in the fall of 1995 on Almo Sounds. After receiving support from radio and MTV, the album began to climb the charts toward the end of 1995, when the second single, "Queer," received heavy airplay. By the summer of 1996, *Garbage* had gone gold in the United States, and shortly afterward it achieved platinum status, as "Only Happy When It Rains" and "Stupid Girl" became radio hits.

After a brief break, Garbage began work on their second album in the summer of 1997. The record, entitled *Version 2.0*, was released in May the following year, preceded by the single "Push It." —*Stephen Thomas Erlewine*

● **Garbage** / Aug. 15, 1995 / Almo Sounds/Geffen ✦✦✦✦
Garbage's self-titled debut has all the trappings of alternative rock—off-kilter arrangements, occasional bursts of noise, a female singer with a thin, airy voice—but it comes off as pop, thanks to the glossy production courtesy of drummer Butch Vig. Not only is the sound of the record slick and professional, but all the songs are well-crafted pop songs. Unfortunately, only a handful of the songs are memorable, but those that are—"Vow" and "Queer," in particular—are small, trashy alternative pop gems. —*Stephen Thomas Erlewine*

**Version 2.0** / May 12, 1998 / Almo Sounds ✦✦✦
Neither a flat-out retread nor a full-fledged progression, *Version 2.0* is almost too accurate a title for Garbage's second album. Everything that made *Garbage* a success is here—Shirley Manson's seductive strength, strong pop sensibility, a production that falls halfway between alternative rock and techno—presented in a slightly newer form. *Version 2.0* may be gilded with fresh drum loops and shiny, computerized production, but it lacks the thrilling immediacy of the debut. It isn't that Garbage's sound is no longer appealing—it's that high-tech production has a tendency to make the songs sound the same. That was a problem with the debut as well, but it's discouraging to find that those flaws are repeated, not solved. Still, when Garbage pulls it all together, the results are irresistible, and there are just enough moments on the album—including "Special," "Push It," "Temptation Waits" and "I Think I'm Paranoid"—to make it a successful follow-up, even if it isn't a brave step forward. —*Stephen Thomas Erlewine*

## Laurent Garnier

b. Feb. 1, 1966, Boulogne Sur Seine, France
*Producer, DJ / Club/Dance, Techno, Acid House, House*
A former staffer at the embassy in London, Frenchman Laurent Garnier began DJing in Manchester during the late '80s and became by the following decade one of the best all-around DJs in the world, able to span classic deep house and Detroit techno, the harder side of acid/trance and surprisingly jazzy tracks as well. He added production work to his schedule in the early '90s, and recorded several brilliant LPs with a similar penchant for diversity.

One of the first Europeans to begin mixing American house music in Britain, Garnier was one of the prime cogs in the late-'80s Madchester scene. His DJing at Manchester's legendary Haçienda club provided a major inspiration for the Stone Roses and Happy Mondays to begin adding house rhythms to rock music. Garnier shifted his attention back to France in the early '90s, running the Wake Up club in Paris for three years and gradually moving into recording as well. For the FNAC label, Garnier released "French Connection" and the *Bout de Souffle* EP; after the label went under, though, he formed the F Communications label with Eric Morand (a friend who had also worked for FNAC). He had amassed quite a discography by the mid-'90s, but his first LP *Shot in the Dark* wasn't launched until 1995. His second, *30*, appeared in 1997, followed by the retrospective *Early Works*. After trotting the globe with multiple DJ appearances during the late '90s, Garnier returned to the production realm with *Unreasonable Behaviour*, released in early 2000. —*John Bush*

**Mixmag Live!, Vol. 19** / 1995 / Mixmag ✦✦✦
Laurent Garnier mixed this nineteenth volume in *Mixmag*'s series of DJ compilations. —*John Bush*

**RawWorks** / 1996 / Never ♦♦♦♦
*RawWorks* works as a quasi-best-of compilation and an American introduction to Garnier, including three tracks from his *Shot in the Dark* album, most of the *Club Traxx* EP, plus remixes of Jazz Juice and Alaska (aka Wax Doctor and Alex Reece) and the unreleased track "Orgasm." —*John Bush*

**Laboratoire Mix** / Oct. 21, 1996 / React ♦♦♦♦
Garnier was a DJ before he was producer, and his long experience in the booth informs the *Laboratoire Mix*. Moving from classic Chicago house both past ("Jungle Wonz") and present (Green Velvet's "Help Me") into hard trance and acid with tracks from Neil Landstrumm and Robert Armani, Garnier even drops his own track "The Force" in the middle of a spin through Detroit (Kosmic Messenger, K Hand, Aux 88, Juan Atkins). Superb selection, great flow and a wide range of material make the two-disc set one of the best DJ mixes around. —*John Bush*

• **30** / Mar. 31, 1997 / Never ♦♦♦♦
*30* is a seemingly effortless blend of classic Chicago jacking house with minimalistic acid funk and the occasional detour into trip-hop and ambient house. Enhanced by Garnier's long-time DJ work, the superb mix and feel for what should come next inform production skills to an incredible degree. The single "Crispy Bacon" is one of the seminal moments in the history of acid, while "Sweet Mellow D" and the mid-tempo "ForMax" provide other highlights. The superb jacking theme "The Hoe" and "Flashback" (dedicated to the recently deceased Armando) are two of the more overtly Chicago-inspired tracks, but *30* is a stunning album throughout. —*John Bush*

**Early Works [2-CD]** / Apr. 28, 1998 / Arcade ♦♦♦♦
Compiled nearly a decade after their initial creation, the nine songs from 1992-93 captured on *Early Works* illustrate Garnier's one-time infatuation with dark acid techno epics. None of the songs conclude before the five-minute mark, as the renowned French producer weaves warped 303 acid lines across the busy landscape of his relaxed tempo soundscapes. The resulting effect can be downright creepy bliss, such as during the opening moments of "Water Planet," or nightmarishly alarming at other times when he sacrifices any hint of colorful melody for bleak techno motifs. Of these nine songs, the listener will most likely fall under the hypnotizing spell of "Acid Eiffel." This 13-minute song builds slowly from one faint track of modulating sound to another, resulting in a giant, pulsing acid techno anthem in the ranks of Plastikman's best. Garnier may have grown out of his acid techno phase, but the previously hard-to-find songs on *Early Works* show just how masterful the French artist had become at constructing this picturesque style of tranquil electronic music. —*Jason Birchmeier*

**Unreasonable Behaviour** / Mar. 28, 2000 / Import ♦♦♦♦
More complex and idiosyncratic than his previous full-length works (and much less danceable as a consequence), *Unreasonable Behaviour* focuses on mid-tempo jams in the verge between evocative techno, electro-jazz, and even melancholy synth-pop. If 1997's *30* was his Chicago album, this one is definitely the Detroit installment, from the Motor City shoutouts at the end of the excellent "Communications From the Lab" to the future-imperfect electro track "Greed (Part 1+2)." Still, most of these tracks come closer to updated jazz-fusion than techno, with highlights like "City Sphere," "The Sound of the Big Babou," and "Forgotten Thoughts" driven by fuzzy, distorted melodies with dreamy synthesizer lines over the top and an emphasis on live (-sounding) drumming. He'd surely think twice before plugging any of these tracks into one of his DJ sets, but *Unreasonable Behaviour* is a solid fusion of jazz and techno. —*John Bush*

## Gas (Wolfgang Voigt)

b. Cologne, Germany
*Drum Programming, Synthesizer, Producer / Experimental Techno, Ambient Techno*

Besides the wealth of chiselled echo-techno he's recorded as Mike Ink, M:I:5, Love Inc. and Studio One, Berlin producer Wolfgang Voigt released several albums of more expansive music as Gas. Voigt debuted the project with the *Modern* EP on his own Profan Records in 1995, then released *Gas* two years later on Mille Plateaux. In contrast to his previous work's stark austerity, the *Gas* LP presented tracks of murky ambience with even murkier percussion. *Zauberberg* followed in 1998, and two years later Voigt returned with *Pop*. [See Also: Burger/Ink, Mike Ink, Love Inc.] —*John Bush*

**Gas** / Feb. 11, 1997 / Mille Plateaux ♦♦♦♦
**Zauberberg** / Feb. 9, 1998 / Mille Plateaux ♦♦♦♦
The second of Wolfgang Voigt's Gas albums, *Zauberberg* employs an assortment of beautiful strings shimmering above pools of eerie electronic ambience. Whereas the succeeding Gas albums tend to present slightly different moods for each song, *Zauberberg* sticks to one main tone throughout its duration. The homogeneous nature of the album accentuates its mood, pulling the listener deeper and deeper into its foreboding world of synthesized melancholy. Some songs on the album diverge slightly, adding other elements such as a distant, thumping bassline and a constant rain shower of crackling noises that make the CD version of this album sound like a dusty vinyl record. But for the most part, Voigt sticks to a consistent approach from song to song. The Brian Eno-like ambience lingering in the background of every song sets a haunting foundation, reflected analogously with the red-tinted forest depicted on the album's cover. This analogy towards surreal darkness is no joke; these songs could well function as the soundtrack to a haunted house. In terms of melody, Voigt constructs these songs with loops, creating hints of melody as certain string sounds appear every 20 seconds or so. These hints of melody are really the only salient element in these songs beside the dense ambience brooding at the foundation of these songs. When describing the components of *Zauberberg* with words, the music may seem homogeneous and lackluster, yet these often negative characteristics end up being positive qualities on this album. Similar to Eno's *Music for Airports*, Voigt has mastered the fine line between boredom and beauty. On the surface, nothing seems to happen, but the astute listener will notice the rich textures and powerful moods, which tend to be consistent from one song to the next. —*Jason Birchmeier*

**Königsforst** / Mar. 29, 1999 / Mille Plateaux ♦♦♦
When music seems as abstract and as disconnected from identifiable semantics as the sparse dronings epics of Gas's *Königsforst*, visual cues such as the cover art can assume enormous importance. In the case of this particular album, the cover art and inside jacket contain text-free images of a lightly wooded forest submerged in hazy orange tones. This surreal image oddly correlates quite effectively with the haunting sounds of the music found within the album's eerie packaging. With *Königsforst*, the infamous man of many masks, Wolfgang Voigt, leads the listener down a hallucinogenic path into a haunted aural forest of blurry sounds swirling slowly like leaves swaying in the wind or ghosts hovering in the far distance. The gothic tone of this music's droning horn-like string sounds operates on one's unconscious. The sounds are heard yet are extremely intangible and difficult to pinpoint. One cannot name a particular sound with the exception of the occasional deeply buried dub bassline. The altered sounds drone on and on in loops of mesmerizing circles, capable of putting even the most high-strung individual into catatonia. At the end of the journey through *Königsforst*, one feels as though a dream has just concluded. The listener is left with no salient memories of the music—no melodies, riffs, rhythms, identifiable sounds, or vocal hooks—yet a sense of abduction remains, a feeling that one has just been carried away into a phantom-like realm of gaseous invisible creatures only to be abruptly brought back a jarring sense of reality. —*Jason Birchmeier*

• **Pop** / Mar. 28, 2000 / Mille Plateaux ♦♦♦♦
Of the many remarkable ambient albums released by the Frankfurt, Germany-based label Mille Plateaux, the works of Gas always seems to stand out above the rest. With *Pop*, the man behind the Gas moniker, Wolfgang Voigt, brings some light to the haunting haziness of his previous album, *Königsforst*. Rather than reveling entirely in the dark passageways of eerie droning strings, Voigt integrates terrestrial sounds such as trickling streams of water and wind to his surreal soundscapes on the beginning half of the album. Yet even though the prolific German artist attempts to bring a sense of humanity to his austere music, *Pop* still immerses the listener into a alien domain of unearthly sound more dynamic that his previous musical journeys. The epic songs loop endlessly in hypnotizing repetition as tiny alterations in the resonance and tone function as a means of increasingly disorienting the listener. The farther one ventures into this album, the farther one ventures away from the secular world of human voices, passing cars, and chirping birds. In the word of Gas, one loses touch with humanity as droning strings of various feels swirl endlessly in orbiting intervals of rising and fading salience. The secular traces of water and wind that open *Pop* fade quickly, pulling the listener further and further away from any sense of reality. By the thumping

conclusion of the album, even the tranquil sense of hallucination becomes eclipsed by the album's intense peak, where the music speeds up until listeners feel as though they are either unwillingly falling down a drain into the farthest depths of the album or frantically racing to an eventual escape from Voigt's all-encompassing world of Gas. —*Jason Birchmeier*

## Gastr del Sol

f. 1991, Louisville, KY

*Group / Math Rock, Experimental Rock, Indie Rock, Post-Rock/Experimental*

Gastr del Sol was the most prominent vehicle of indie-rock stalwart David Grubbs, a former member of Squirrel Bait, Slint and Bastro. With Gastr del Sol, the Louisville, Kentucky-born vocalist/guitarist/pianist's evolution from conventional rock music into more intricate and sophisticated tone patterns became complete; debuting with the 1993 EP *The Serpentine Similar*, the group—a shifting aggregate of talents which initially inclued bassist Bundy K. Brown and drummer John McEntire—began exploring their new approach, taking off from often improvisational performances to embark on highly idiosyncratic sonic adventures. With the single "20 Songs Less," guitarist, composer, and tape manipulator Jim O'Rourke signed on, and following the departure of Brown, and with the decreased involvement of McEntire, Gastr del Sol became a kind of catch-all tag for Grubbs and O'Rourke's many eclectic projects; the acoustic *Crookt, Crackt or Fly* followed in 1994, as did the EP *Mirror Repair*. With 1995's *The Harp Factory on Lake Street*, Grubbs and O'Rourke composed a single 17-minute orchestral piece, while with 1996's *Upgrade and Afterlife* they returned to more more traditional dynamics to create their most beautiful and intriguing work to date. O'Rourke left Gastr del Sol in 1997, shortly after completing work on *Camoufleur*, which was released in January 1998. —*Jason Ankeny*

**Crookt, Crackt, or Fly** / 1994 / Drag City ✦✦✦✦

With the enigmatic *Crookt, Crackt, or Fly*, Gastr del Sol's focus shifted to the dual guitars of David Grubbs and Jim O'Rourke, translating into a strange but frequently sublime acoustic recording shaded by vague hints of tape manipulations and only the occasional touch of percussion. It's music of extremes—the songs are either very brief or very long, the lyrics are often inscrutable, and the music is wildly unpredictable, rejecting standard tonalities and compositional structures in favor of an elusive, baffling but nevertheless intoxicating otherness. —*Jason Ankeny*

**Mirror Repair [EP]** / Jan. 1, 1995 / Drag City ✦✦✦

Like its predecessor, *Crookt, Crackt or Fly*, the *Mirror Repair* EP finds Gastr del Sol spinning a series of elliptical, unpredictable compositions, some with cryptic lyrics. The centerpiece is undoubtedly the near-nine-minute "Eight Corners," which is built around a gentle piano figure that is interrupted at times by chaotic blurts from horns and tape effects, while adding barely audible sonic coloring at others. "Dictionary of Handwriting" is a more driving piece with an abrupt ending, utilizing electric guitar arpeggios and even some percussion. The songs' overall unpredictability is again striking, but perhaps even more notable is the sonic detail Grubbs and O'Rourke achieve using mostly minimal instrumentation. Accessible it isn't, but concentrated listening will bring ample rewards. —*Steve Huey*

**Serpentine Similar** / Aug. 1, 1995 / Teenbeat ✦✦✦✦

**The Harp Factory on Lake Street** / Aug. 1, 1995 / Table of the Elements ✦✦✦

*The Harp Factory on Lake Street* is an intentional departure from Gastr del Sol's main line of work—aside from the formality of a name change, it could almost be considered a one-off side project. The record consists of one 17-minute orchestral composition, recruiting various Chicago musicians (Jeb Bishop, John McEntire, Bob Weston) to create a decidedly abstract and ambient work from largely traditional instruments. The result is sparse and unstructured, and times, and adopts a wall-of-sound approach at others; some of David Grubbs' melodic piano work emerges at points as well. *The Harp Factory on Lake Street* may not be of much interest to those who enjoy the pop aspects of Gastr del Sol's other work, but it fits well with the more experimental work of Chicago's "post-rock" and avant-jazz musicians. —*Nitsuh Abebe*

• **Camoufleur** / Jan. 20, 1998 / Drag City ✦✦✦✦

Jim O'Rourke's last album with Gastr del Sol is a subdued, meditative affair, bringing together elements of folk, jazz, film music and the avant-garde. "The Seasons Reverse" opens the album with a deceptive, gentle melody and strummed, hushed guitars. Its sound and leisurely pace set the tone, but not the style, for the rest of the album. Each track is intricate and layered, but the music isn't overly complex. Instead, *Camoufleur* is quiet and minimal, requiring attentive listening. Only "The Seasons Reverse" and the closer "Bauchredner," with its unexpected, catchy horn-driven coda, are straightforward. The remainder of the album demands concentration. Given some time, the album opens up, revealing layers of modest beauty. It's a nice way for O'Rourke to leave the fold, and it certainly suggests that David Grubbs is far from finished musically, whether he chooses to continue with Gastr del Sol or not. —*Stephen Thomas Erlewine*

## Gearwhore (Brian Natonski)

*Producer / Electronica, Ambient Techno*

Gearwhore is the alter ego of DJ and recording engineer Brian Natonski, who took the name from his obsession with top-quality recording equipment. Natonski began his career as an engineer at Chicago Trax Studio, later moving to Orange County and founding his own label, Fatal Data, with his partner Shaheen. Natonski issued singles under the Gearwhore alias, among others, and produced Skylab 2000's "Auburn." In 1997, Gearwhore signed with the Astralwerks label, issuing *The Passion* EP that year as a precursor to his full-length debut, 1998's *Drive*. —*Steve Huey*

• **Drive** / Jul. 28, 1998 / Astralwerks ✦✦

Brian Natonski (aka Gearwhore) whips up electronica that's cold and danceable. As with most techno-throb of this sort (save work by the Chemical Brothers or Tranquility Bass), there isn't much melody here to speak of. It's all breakbeats and the occasional power chord. But if that's just what you're looking for, go no further than the onion-peel rhythm layers of "Accelerator" or the creatively percussive sampling on "11:11." —*Tim Sheridan*

## Morgan Geist

b. New Jersey

*Producer / Detroit Techno, Club/Dance, Techno, IDM*

A New Jersey boy initially inspired by Great Britain's take on the sound of Detroit, Morgan Geist eventually tracked the roots of techno back to Motor City innovators like Derrick May. Unlike many influenced by tracks like "Strings of Life" and "Nude Photo," Geist placed equal weight on the emotional power of Detroit techno as well as tight programming and combustive percussion. When he began listening to music, however, it was the sound of early-'80s synth-pop heroes like Devo, Severed Heads and Depeche Mode. The early British techno of 808 State and Black Dog were his point of entry into instrumental dance music, and he soon began collecting masses of synth gear while studying at Oberlin College. After he passed a demo tape on to Dan Curtin, the producer signed Geist up for singles on his Metamorphic Records. Geist later formed his own Environ label, releasing excellent statements of purpose which showed his affinity for the more emotional, midtempo strains of house music as well as the spartan ethic of Detroit techno. In 1997, he hooked up with London's neo-electro label Clear and released *The Driving Memoirs*. The following year saw the issue of *Environ: Into a Separate Space*, a collection of work for his own label. —*John Bush*

• **The Driving Memoirs** / Nov. 24, 1997 / Clear ✦✦✦✦

Dedicated to the memory of his sister (who died in a car accident), Morgan Geist designed *The Driving Memoirs* as an auditory account of a long road trip, placing it in similar company with Detroit landmarks by Carl Craig (*Landcruising*) and Model 500 ("Night Drive: Time, Space, Transmat"). In a bit less than an hour, Geist cruises through ten tracks of exquisite, finely tuned techno with an eye to the percussion-programming finesse of Black Dog (circa *Bytes*) and the reflective, haunting electro-jazz of early As One. But *The Driving Memoirs* does much more than cycle through its influences; taken in whole, it's a state-of-the-art techno masterpiece that's more than worthy of its predecessors and arguably the best release to come from the highly respected Clear label. —*John Bush*

**Morgan Geist Presents Environ: Into a Separate Space** / Feb. 2, 1998 / Phono ✦✦✦✦

A retrospective covering the first three records released on Geist's Environ label, *Into a Separate Space* includes one track from the first issue (*Premise* EP) plus all six tracks from the *Remnants* EP and the *Titonton & Morgan* EP (recorded with Titonton Duvante). Though the tempos are a bit quicker than Geist's full-length debut, these tracks have a similar emphasis on moody strings and crisp, beatbox percussion, especially compared to his later recordings for Clear and Multiplex. Also included are two exclusive tracks, though both are brief atmospheric pieces. —*John Bush*

## Gemini (Spencer Kincy)

*Producer / Club/Dance, Acid House, House*

One of the most forward-looking producers in the continuing Chicago renaissance of the '90s, Gemini recorded for nu-house labels like Cajual and Relief in 1993 but later issued singles and LPs for such wide-ranging imprints as Disko B, Peacefrog, Distance, Makeout Music, NRK and later, his own co-founded Guidance Records. He began recording early in the decade, and gained fame for the minimalist flavor of Cajual twelves like "Tangled Thoughts" and "Duality." Gemini debuted his album work in late 1997 with two almost concurrent LPs, *In and Out of the Fog and Lights* and *Imagine-A-Nation*. His third full-length *In Neutral* was released before the end of the year, showing him to be anything but that. —*John Bush*

**A Moment of Insanity [EP]** / 1995 / Planet E ♦♦

This four-song EP finds courageous Chicago house producer Gemini (Spencer Kincy) recording for Carl Craig's Detroit techno label Planet E. All four of these tracks retain a repetitive rhythmic minimalism that may be a bit dull for those interested in just listening instead of dancing or DJing. This, of course, isn't to say that these tracks are inferior by any means. In fact, the looped rhythms of *A Moment of Insanity*—with their thumping 4/4 bass drums, interstellar synths, and occasional deviations from the repeating loop—make it hard to just sit there and listen. Similar to Craig's Paperclip People recordings, this is excellent dance music that breaks away from the formulaic norms of Chicago house without suffering in terms of quality. One can only wish that there were more deviations from the looped rhythms. The tracks are funky, cosmic, and sensual, but also a tad boring for listeners relaxing in their living rooms. —*Jason Stanley Birchmeier*

● **Imagine-A-Nation** / Sep. 1, 1997 / Relief ♦♦♦♦

The most wide-ranging of Gemini's trio of 1997 LPs, *Imagine-A-Nation* progresses through the expected acid minimalism but also detours through Native American percussion and intriguing brass on "Native to America" and sly funk/disco basslines on "Falling Leaves" and "Don't Look Back." —*John Bush*

**In and Out of Fog and Lights** / Sep. 8, 1997 / Peacefrog ♦♦♦

Gemini's second 1997 album finds the Chicago house producer concentrating on relentlessly minimalist grooves and percussion, with only the barest of melodies working for each track. Definitely designed as a collection for the dancefloor more than the living-room, the album works nevertheless with a raft of entertaining songs including "Deep Shade" and the vocal track "Prelargonium." —*John Bush*

**In Neutral** / Dec. 1, 1997 / Distance ♦♦

The odd man out of Gemini's first three LPs, *In Neutral* is more roughly an experimental album, with acid tweaks and wiggly basslines providing a few focus points for the far-out tracks. —*John Bush*

## Genaside II

f. 1989, Brixton, London, England

*Group / Jungle/Drum'N'Bass, Club/Dance, Techno, Acid House, Hip-Hop*

Creators of a seminal moment for drum'n'bass back in 1991, Genaside II returned more than five years later with their debut full-length, a piece of high-powered, breakbeat futurism influenced by Manga animé. Basically a duo of Chilly Phatz and Koa Bonez (aka Kaos De Keeler) with engineer Charlie Meats, the crew was raised on the hard-life streets of Brixton and inspired by urban raggamuffins like Rebel MC and Ray Keith.

Debuting in 1989 with the cut-and-paste ragga-terrorism of "Fire When Ready," Phatz and Bonez followed with the 1991 single "Narramine." Intersplicing the sweet soulful vocals of Sharon Williams with blistering breakbeat ragga, the single became a major mover on the hardcore techno scene. Along with "Mr. Kirk" by 4Hero, Genaside II defined the growing move towards darkness in hardcore, years before drum'n'bass emerged overground. Despite additional singles like "Hellraiser" (recorded with Ray Keith and featuring a beat later borrowed by Prodigy for "Firestarter"), personal problems kept the duo out of commission for several years.

By 1995, Phatz and Bonez had sorted things out and even signed to the major-label-connected Internal. After a live date with the New Power Generation, mutual friends introduced the duo to the Wu-Tang Clan while in America. As a result, Genaside II's 1996 debut album *New Life 4 the Hunted* featured Wu-associate Cappadonna as well as Eek-A-Mouse and Rose Windross. *Ad Finite* followed in 1999. —*John Bush*

**New Life 4 the Hunted** / 1996 / Internal/London ♦♦♦

After almost a decade, Genaside II's debut LP shows the duo allied to contemporary acts (like Headrillaz) sitting on the divergence which separated breakbeat techno from full-fledged drum'n'bass. Obviously a pair of mature producers, Phatz and Bonez recruited vocalists Rose Windross (from Soul II Soul) for some classic house flavor, Eek-A-Mouse and Killermen Archer for ragga attitude, and Wu-Tang's Cappadonna for an interesting hip-hop/breakbeat collaboration. Though the album also includes a version of their 1991 classic "Narramine," it strays surprisingly close to a bland listen, with few full-fledged ideas holding together the many vocal tracks. —*John Bush*

● **Ad Finite** / Sep. 21, 1999 / Never ♦♦♦♦

Genaside II released their second full-length, *Ad Finite*, with an American distribution contract in hand, thanks to the patronage of Tricky (who was undoubtedly inspired by the group's acid-breakbeat terrorism from way back). The album improves on 1996's somewhat stillborn *New Life 4 the Hunted*, with better production and more of a focus on the music itself — the first album carried the art of vocal collaborations a bit too far. The pair obviously didn't spend much of their time trawling for beats; even middling old-school fans will recognize just about every break used on *Ad Finite*, along with the sirens and effects from many a classic hip-hop record. It should be obvious, though, that what really counts is not the beats themselves, but what you do with them. Genaside II are among the best dance producers at layering their productions with interesting effects, and every break on *Ad Finite* you've heard before is used differently than you've ever heard it. The single "Mr. Maniac" and "50,000 Whats?" are invigorating darkside productions. The social critique inherent on Genaside II's earlier material is still being caned, from the opener — a British female paraphrases Gil Scott-Heron's "The Revolution Will Not Be Televised" for London circa 1999 — to tracks like "Casualties of War," "Paranoid Thugism," and "Streets of San Fran Brixton." Still more tied to the aesthetic of 1989 than 1999 (that's a good thing), Genaside II make big beat serve their own ends, and the result is a raging political record miles away from the mindless dance of Fatboy Slim. —*John Bush*

## General Magic

f. 1994, Vienna, Austria

*Group / Experimental Techno, Experimental Electro, Electronica*

"Accidental electronica" duo General Magic is perhaps the strangest, least stylistically constrained project on the Austrian Mego label's roster. Formed by label bosses Ramon Bauer and Andi Pieper around the same time they established Mego (GM's collaboration with Peter Pita Bauer, *Fridge Trax*, was the first Mego release), GM released a pair of twelves on Mego, as well as a mini-LP (*Live and Final Fridge*) on Source before releasing the full-length CD *Frantz* in 1997. (The album was recorded in both Austria and Germany, where Bauer maintains the label's Berlin studio, and contains source material sampled from the rail line connecting the two cities.) Like Panasonic and Autechre, General Magic limit their tonal color palette to only a few categories of sound (drum machine, EQ, distortion, reverb) but manage to construct tracks of exquisite detail and, somehow, variety, with influences (where they are even recognizable) including dub, funk, techno, ambient/electro-acoustic, and hip-hop. As with those other groups, the key to General Magic's success is Bauer and Pieper's accomplished production, with even the dirtiest, most artifact-laden of sounds displaying a polished sheen that makes GM's music often more fascinating then affecting (although a few of the group's songs are actually quite moving). —*Sean Cooper*

**Fridge Trax [EP]** / 1995 / Mego ♦♦♦

The concept: throw a bunch of contact mics into a dozen or so different refrigerators in various states of disrepair, shut the door, record the ensuing racket, and fashion an EP of music with those sounds as the only raw material. As limited in scope as such a project might sound, *Fridge Trax* is a fascinating listen. The range of sounds Pita and General Magic (Peter Rehberg, and Ramon Bauer and Andi Pieper, respectively, all of the Vinnese Mego label) are able to extract from such seemingly unmusical sources is nothing short of phenomenal, from blunt, funky breakbeats and warbling basslines to weird, shivery drones and echoing atmospherics. —*Sean Cooper*

**Live & Final Fridge** / 1996 / Source ♦♦♦

As if a four-track EP weren't enough, Peter Rehberg (Pita) and Ramon Bauer and Andi Piper (General Magic) return to the icebox graveyard to assemble an entire album of tracks sourced from ailing refrigerators. Even better produced and with an overall tighter, more composed feel than the similarly conceived Mego 12", "Fridge Trax," *Live & Final Fridge* is somehow an improvement over its short-form predecessor (a potentially silly assessment until one actually *hears* it). Again, the sounds are lively and amazing in their diversity, with skittery beats, zinging electronics, and any number of bizarre noises forcing you to pay that much more attention to the sounds of your own fridge each time you open the door. —*Sean Cooper*

**Faßt** / 1997 / Touch ♦♦♦♦
As the liner notes recall, this collaboration between Ramon Bauer (one half of General Magic) and Peter Rehberg (all of Pita) was sourced from "broken DAT tapes, personal mistakes and total machine failure." The statement's similarity to post-techno experimenters Oval is confirmed by the odd scratched-disc textures, bursts of electricity and static. Nevertheless, the album is a bit more rugged than Oval's slightly chilled response to technology-gone-wrong, and is more listenable as a result. —*John Bush*

● **Frantz!** / Apr. 1997 / Mego ♦♦♦♦
Although the electronica feeding frenzy was building to a frothing head when it appeared, General Magic's full-length debut, *Frantz*, contained the real soul and sense of the term; electronic music inspired by dance musics such as hip-hop, techno, and electro (as well as non-dance or sub-dance musics such as ambient and electroacoustic), but totally and completely uninterested in dance music per se. *Frantz* is 14 tracks of uninterrupted brilliance; a minimal, focused assault on convention carried out with low-key noise, distortion, a decent dose of funk, and enough humor to keep perspective. In terms of pushing electronica into still less derivative territories (no minor-key pad refrains here, kids), *Frantz* is one of the most important, accomplished albums released in years. —*Sean Cooper*

## The Gentle People

f. 1995, Los Angeles, CA
*Group / Electronica, Lounge, Ambient Techno*
Tri-continental ambient lounge group the Gentle People are a bizarre amalgam of influences and affinities, combining the esoteric club culture of the '90s with the cocktails-and-tiki-trinkets kitsch of the '50s, hitting just about every opportunity for nostalgic, cheesball second-hand embarrassment in between. Signed in the UK to Richard "Aphex Twin" James' Rephlex imprint since 1995, the group's relaxed brand of sugar-coated, vocal-based easy listening is a far cry from the typically abrasive lo-fi machine music of that label. With members originating in America, the UK, and Australia (the band is based in Los Angeles, the four-piece (including cartoonish "members" Dougie Dimensional, Laurie LeMans, Valentine Carnelian, and Honeymink) have nonetheless attracted a committed international following, with releases appearing in both the UK and Japan and material showing up increasingly on American compilations of loungecore and exotica (a marketing trend which hit its peak in 1995-96). In addition to a number of national and international tours and festival engagements, the group have also remixed tracks for the likes of Pizzicato 5, as well as having their bubbly fare popped, smeared, and otherwise disheveled by the likes of Luke Vibert, Aphex Twin, DJ Wally, and many others. Following the 1997 album *Soundtracks for Living*, the Gentle People returned two years later with *Simply Faboo*. —*Sean Cooper*

**Journey** / 1996 / Rephlex ♦♦

● **Soundtracks for Living** / Jan. 6, 1997 / Rephlex ♦♦♦
The cover art for the Gentle People's 1997 Rephlex full-length—the band in full space race/cocktail-chic regalia standing before a bubblegum-pink background, their name gloriously rendered in plump, soap-bubble lettering—is perhaps the best indication of what to expect here. The group's bluntly non-threatening concoction of sugar-drenched cheese—all fluffy exotica, 101 Strings-style muzak, and wispy, wordless backing vocals—is tough to get through even two tracks of without either an exceedingly strong will or a good stiff drink. —*Sean Cooper*

**Simply Faboo** / Sep. 14, 1999 / Rephlex ♦♦♦
The Gentle People's *Simply Faboo* delivers more swinging, exotica/electronica grooviness, and adds a slight edge to their frothy sound. Songs like "Stepford Zombie," "Shopping World," and "Hungover" reveal the flip side of the candy-colored world that "Magic Kingdom," "Gentle People Are Love" and "Parfum" depict. —*Heather Phares*

## Gerd (Gert-Jan Bijl)

*Producer / Jazz-House, Ambient Techno, Club/Dance, Techno*
Gerd is the nom de plume of Gert-Jan Bijl, better-known as one-half of Rotterdam techno duo Sensurreal. Although most of Bijl's creative time is spent with his partner Dirk-Jan Hanegraaf working on Sensurreal-related projects (the group have released material on Prime, Beam Me Up!, and Op-Art), the presence of the group's studio in his living room has meant Bijl's downtime woodshedding has led to an increasing stock of solo material. Portions of that material began appearing in 1994, with singles for Jochem "Speedy J" Paap's now-defunct Beam Me Up! label, more recently, Bijl had two singles come out the same day on two of the UK's most esteemed dance labels, Pork and Universal Language. Bijl's solo material is, not surprisingly, quite close to the dreamy, melodic breakbeat techno of his Sensurreal work, though perhaps with a deeper engagement of funk and downtempo hip-hop (particularly on his self-titled Pork single). A full-length for Universal Language, *This Touch Is Greater Than Moods*, was released in 1997. —*Sean Cooper*

**Vulcan Princess** / Feb. 10, 1997 / Universal Language ♦♦♦
Gert-Jan Bijl's debut solo shot for Link/Reload's Universal Language imprint is well nigh indistinguishable from Sensurreal, save perhaps for the emphasis on syncopation and a more overwhelmingly funk-fueled backing break. The same lush melodies obtain, however, along with the deep, bassy foundation of the group's early Prime and Malego singles. —*Sean Cooper*

● **This Touch Is Greater Than Moods** / May 26, 1997 / Universal Language ♦♦♦♦
Sensurreal's Gert-Jan Bijl picked the formula for his latest round of Gerd work with his earlier Universal Language singles and here doesn't alter it an iota, with *Touch* an amazingly lush and atmospheric, ultimately quite harmless collection of coffee-table techno. Mostly breakbeat and with a high index of jazz and funk chops circulating in the mix (rubbery basslines, minor-key synth glissandos, etc.), the album is extremely well done (if a little boring). Appropriately released on Reload/Global Communications' Universal Language imprint, the album sounds much like the tracks appearing under those names a few years prior, underscoring as well how little new ground is being covered here. —*Sean Cooper*

## Germ

f. 1992, Birmingham, England
*Group / Experimental Techno, Ambient Techno*
British techno outfit Germ are one of the most influential, under-recognized forces of innovation in the European experimental electronic music scene. Formative figures on the early UK techno map, Germ (along with the General Production Recordings label, through which they've released the entirety of their catalog) were defining the vocabulary of "composerly" dance-based electronic listening music long before labels such as Warp, Rephlex, and Rising High (labels which have since received a good deal of the credit for inventing same) existed. Adapting many of dance music's formal characteristics to decidedly non-dancefloor ends, Germ combine the tropes of techno, house, and electro with a conceptual base deriving from contemporary classical, electroacoustic, industrial, and experimental jazz. Although the band is most closely associated with Birmingham's Tim Wright, Germ is actually a group effort, including contributions from trombonist Hilary Jeffrey, double-bassist Matt Miles, and producer Jon Dalby (who has also recorded a number of EPs for GPR under his own name). Germ have released a pair of full-length albums and several singles to date, consistently pushing techno's synthetic, highly deterministic structures into new areas of complexity and chance, drawing most often from jazz and industrial/musique-concrete. Inspired by other dance deviants such as the Black Dog, BEAST (an artist collective in Wright's native Birmingham, which Wright credits with sparking an interest in electronics-based composition early on), and the On-U Sound stable, Germ's focus on texture, chance, and movement within the context of dance music's reliance on minimal, repetitive rhythmic figures also allies them with 20th-century composers such as Steve Reich and Philip Glass. —*Sean Cooper*

**Gone** / 1994 / GPR ♦♦♦

● **Parrot** / 1995 / GPR ♦♦♦♦
N.J. Bullen (ex-Scorn) appears on two tracks, "Owt" and "Asp." —*Sean Cooper*

## Gescom

**f. 1995, Sheffield, Yorkshire,**
*Group / Experimental Techno, Neo-Electro, Electro-Techno, Club/Dance, Techno, IDM*

Shrouded in conjecture and just a wee bit of good fun, Gescom is the more dancefloor-friendly identity of Sean Booth and Rob Brown, aka Autechre. The bulk of the pair's Gescom material (save for an EP a piece on "future funk" label Clear and David Moufang's Source label, as well as a mail-order-only 12" offered to members of the group's fanclub) has been issued through the Manchester-based experimental techno label Skam, owned and operated by occasional collaborator Andy Maddocks. Focusing on the more uptempo tendencies of Autechre paired with a harder, rougher, more driving rhythmic edge, Gescom material remains committed to the more adventurous side of electro/techno even as it gives DJs a bit more backbeat to work with. The group hit a bit of notoriety (apart, of course, from the thick-and-thin dedication of Ae trainspotters) when a track ("Mag") from their second Skam twelve was included on South London breakbeat virtuosos Coldcut's celebrated *Journeys by DJ* mix session. The first Gescom full-length, *MiniDisc*, appeared in 1998. [See Also: Autechre] —*Sean Cooper*

### Gescom 1/Gescom 2 [EP] / 1995 / Skam ♦♦♦
This two part double-pack released seperately (then reissued together) is the most dance-y of Booth and Brown's catalog. Although the crunchy beats of Autechre's hardest material are in evidence, Gescom distinguishes itself with faster, more abrasive rhythms, more sampledelic arrangments, and even a bit of humor. —*Sean Cooper*

### Gescom EP [#1] / 1995 / Skam ♦♦♦
Although Gescom/Autechre's debut for their own Skam label was in reality preceded by a promo-only 12" entitled "Lego Feet," this relatively more obtainable four-tracker will have to suffice as a first shot. Somewhat lo-fi but nonetheless quite listenable ambient/industrial electro, thinner and somewhat soupier than their Autechre work, but noticeably related in sound and concept. —*Sean Cooper*

### Gescom EP [#2] / 1995 / Skam ♦♦
Gescom is Autechre's more dancefloor-friendly aegis, and the third release on their Skam label back that claim up amply. A shade too loopy for casual listening, DJs snapped this up for their thick, shuttering breaks and minimal architecture. —*Sean Cooper*

### ● The Sound of Machines Our Parents Used [EP] / 1995 / Clear ♦♦♦♦
A hair closer to their Autechre material but still goofy enough to be a Clear release. Reportedly the group released it as a joke, but the result is anything but laughable. Accomplished, if not essential, stuff. —*Sean Cooper*

### Gescom EP [#3] / Jun. 24, 1996 / Skam ♦♦♦
Released in a clear bubble-pack sleeve, Gescom's third Skam installment is basically one four-part track. Slicing up treated vocal samples with odd-metered beats and bass rhythms, "Key Nell" occasionally strays into quasi-Rephlex industrial territory, and is probably the group's least-accessible material to date. —*Sean Cooper*

### Mini Disc / Jul. 27, 1998 / Touch ♦♦♦♦
A change-up from the beat-orientation of most Gescom material, the world's first MD-only release is a 45-track, hour-long collection of assorted ambient noise and other detritus, most of which sounds as though it came straight from Autechre's samplers with no editing to speak of. Designed to be played on a random setting (MD technology allows skips throughout a disc with no lag time), the album works quite well considering its avowed purpose. Since Gescom and Autechre have always phrased their electronics experimentation with plenty of beats though, it's difficult to take *Mini Disc* as anything more than a cast-off. —*John Bush*

## Ghost

**f. 1988, Tokyo, Japan**
*Group / Neo-Psychedelia, Indie Rock, Alternative Pop/Rock*

A collective of psychedelic-minded Japanese musicians headed by guitarist Masaki Batoh, Ghost records commune-minded free-range psychedelia with equal debts to the Can/Amon Düül axis of Kraut-rock, as well as West Coast psych units like Blue Cheer and Jefferson Airplane. Batoh grew up in Kyoto, where he attended a private school well-geared to spark his interest in rock music, from Dylan and Pink Floyd to the Velvet Underground. Later, he formed Ghost with a large and varying lineup, centered around contributors such as Michio Kurihara, Kazuo Ogino and Taishi Takizawa. According to reports, the group lived a nomadic existence, drifting from ruins of ancient temples to disused subway stations around the Tokyo area.

The band began releasing their work with the albums *Ghost* and *Second Time Around*, each appearing during 1991-92. The American independent Drag City licensed each of the albums for distribution, and L.A.'s The Now Sound picked up two of Batoh's solo albums, *A Ghost from the Darkened Sea* and *Kikaokubeshi* (released together as well under the title *Collected Works*). Two more Ghost titles, *Tune In, Turn On, Free Tibet* and *Snuffbox Immanence*, were released simultaneously in 1999. A year later, the group teamed with kindred spirits Damon and Naomi for *Damon and Naomi with Ghost*. —*John Bush*

### Ghost / 1991 / Drag City ♦♦♦
Give points to Ghost for defying expectations right from the start of its first album, at least if one is coming in merely expecting a drifty, new age type of experience. "Sun is Tangging" may start off fairly quietly, but then it explodes in a noise fest and then returns to a calmer acoustic serenity throughout. With that as a fine surprise starting point, Batoh and company enter fully into their fascinating acid-folk-jam world with a strong number of songs. The group and its many guests—no less than eleven—explore everything from droning mysticism that sounds like it was recorded in mist-shrouded jungle temples to heavy duty percussion-led songs that will make any Amon Düül fan smile in happiness. Given this wide range, Batoh's particular vision feels not merely like a tribute to his musical forebears but a striking new synthesis, while his main collaborators at this point match his dreams well. Mu Krishna, the chief percussion player, does a particularly fine job on his own or with various guests throughout, also contributing 'whisper,' as the credits name it. One moment where Batoh gets to step fully to the fore is the lovely "I've Been Flying," where his soft acoustic playing and understated but still strong singing floats above a lovely electric guitar solo from then guest performer Kurihara. The immediately following "Ballad of Summer Rounder" is just as grand, Batoh's tender, evocative singing and playing accompanied about four minutes in by Takizawa's flute and guest drummer Shigeru Konno's steady, restrained percussion. It eventually ends in a classic jam, Takizawa switching to sax and going off over the head-nodding beat as Batoh seems almost to be speaking in tongues or mantras. "Rakshu" wraps up this quite fine debut with an intoxicating, hushed blend of percussion—gongs, bells, blocks—and Batoh's prayerful singing. —*Ned Raggett*

### ● Second Time Around / 1992 / Drag City ♦♦♦♦
Ghost's second album, following one year on from the self-titled debut, saw a slight shift in the line-up, with Krishna out on percussion, replaced by Iwao Yamazaki. Guest performer Kazuo Ogino also became permanent, introduced from the start with his Celtic harp on the opening "People Get Freedom," while multi-instrumentalist Takizawa and bassist/singer Kohji Nishino continued from before. Batoh as always remained the center around which all revolved, with even more eerily beautiful and powerful music than before. All members were credited with a large number of percussion instruments, from bell tree and Tibetan bells to 'some nameless bells and stones,' further intensifying the aura of ancient and mysterious rites that hangs through Ghost's music. The blend of influences both Western and Eastern results in a series of fine syntheses, perhaps even stronger than on *Ghost*. "Higher Power," with oboe and finger cymbals among much more, and "First Drop of the Sea," which could almost be a calmer Scott Walker number from the late '60s at points, both capture this sense of broad listening to grand effect. Batoh can be straightforward as he chooses, thus the title track, for one example. He almost sounds a bit like Bowie in lighter cabaret mode (an approach he generally maintains throughout the record) even while the acid folk atmosphere gently kicks along, sometimes with quiet drama in the arrangements. When the band fully kicks in, as on the rolling "Forthcoming from the Inside," everything achieves powerful heights as a result. His lyrics throughout are often quite striking—his images of ceremonies, seeking the spiritual amid the mundane and more often make a lot more sense than the fuzzier hoo-hah coming from his West Coast psych/Kraut-rock forebears. This is especially striking in the case of the former, given that English isn't his first language. —*Ned Raggett*

### Lama Rabi Rabi / Nov. 19, 1996 / Drag City ♦♦
The incipient fascination with and appreciation of Tibetan culture by Batoh started to fully emerge with this album, in both title, design (the title is shown on the cover art in the style of the Tibetan alphabet, while art from that cul-

ture appears on the back) and similar other signifiers. Not that *Lama Rabi Rabi* is strictly about that country or its situation—Ghost would wait some years more for its specific effort on that front—but it does showcase the sense of depth Batoh brings to his art, evident throughout this strong album. The lengthy, fascinating "Mastillah" starts *Lama* on a striking high, with a series of percussive instruments meshed with acoustic drones and low, wordless mantras, leading to a steady rhythm pace from Yamazaki through a shimmering combination of the above, mixed with flute and stringed instruments. The immediately following "Rabirabi" makes this sense of religious celebration even stronger, with Batoh's slightly distorted vocals carrying through a rhythm-driven number, at once rock (thanks especially to the bass) and not, punctuated further by a chorus chanting the title. From there on in the majority of *Lama* addresses the heavier jam side of the band, where acoustic instruments easily have the force of their electric counterparts and often predominate. The banjo/flute/booming drum combination of "Mex Square Blue" and the more conventionally psych-fried "Bad Bone" are two fine examples. The more stripped-down, hushed folk side of Ghost emerges as well. "Into the Alley" is stunningly lovely, Batoh and his acoustic guitar accompanied by a variety of subtle background shadings from other instruments, while the brief "My Hump is a Shell" combines piano, guitar and what sounds like a musical saw to rich effect. Most striking of all would be "Agate Scape," an eleven-minute piece with both quiet beauty and echo-laden instrumental builds. —*Ned Raggett*

**Snuffbox Immanence** / Apr. 20, 1999 / Drag City ♦♦♦♦
With a slightly reshuffled line-up—Ogino now clearly became Batoh's chief collaborator, while new percussionist Setsuko Furuya accompanied the returning Kurihara, cellist Hiromichi Sakamoto and two brass players—Ghost on *Snuffbox* created another striking, beautiful album. With its senses of fusions now firmly grasped, able to slide from trumpet and flute-accompanied folk on the opening "Regenesis" to the initially acoustic then ragingly electric "Sad Shakers," Ghost achieved levels of inspiration that easily equaled many of Batoh's original role models. One of those early sources gets saluted in a sharp way—the Rolling Stones' "Live With Me" gets a piano/vibe-heavy remake here, with Furuya getting to showcase his abilities in particular. Another neopsych masterpiece is the title track—Batoh's truly cool, spaced-out lyric gets backed perfectly by Ogino's harpsichord, his own acoustic and crunching electric guitar work, and plenty of production effects and tweaking for effect. The at-times underrated sense of playfulness which crops up in Ghost's work gets some airing here. "Soma" ends by shifting from a gentler flow to a quicker ending led by Batoh's banjo, while "Fukeiga" has similar fun with the vibes and Batoh's electric soloing offset against his clear acoustic work. Still, though, it's the sense of spiritual power and mantra-based music and performance that comes through the strongest on *Snuffbox*, a mostly calm and understated affair for its length. The fine instrumental "Daggma," with Ogino and Furuya's combination of keyboard and percussion instruments backed by Sakamoto's cello, is at once melancholic and uplifting. Batoh also clearly feels thoroughly comfortable with switching between his native tongue and English, splitting the amount sung in each language down the middle. "Hanmiyau" closes *Snuffbox* with a flourish, piano, guitar reverb and more, Batoh's serene lyrics echoing up from the depths. —*Ned Raggett*

**Tune In, Turn On, Free Tibet** / Apr. 20, 1999 / Drag City ♦♦♦♦
Conceived as a companion release to *Snuffbox*—the two albums were released within a few weeks of each other and share some art—*Free Tibet* is definitely much more the socially forceful flip side to that lovely album. The same core five-person line-up records here, but as photos and an impassioned essay from the liaison office of the Dalai Lama demonstrate, the goal is what's stated right in the title. Given Batoh's open inspiration, spiritually and musically, from that region, recording what amounts to both a celebration and call to action makes perfect sense. Certainly Ghost aren't interested in simply recording a tribute to Tibetan music—while the opening track "We Insist" starts with various Tibetan wind instruments, the focus is on Batoh, who speaks rather than sings, his words distorted heavily, the effect almost that of a government official dictating one's fate. The same sense of beautiful serenity that so often pervades Ghost's work is more than clear here—all it takes is a listen to the grand "Way of Shelkar" to show that, its blend of Batoh, guitars, keyboards and other instruments achieving a wondrous calm. Other songs like "Lhasa Lhasa" and "Change the World" deliver the key message with the same sweet grace. The album climaxes with the mind-blowing title track, the longest from

the group has ever done at over half an hour long. Whether it was carefully planned or a jam session, it's a stunner, ranging from acoustic gentility to percussion craziness to nuclear-strength electric roars, sometimes switching from one section to another on a dime. There's one interesting link to *Snuffbox* in terms of music—as on that album, Ghost here salute a musical forebear, in this case Tom Rapp. His Pearls Before Swine track "Images of April" gets a stripped-down, softly whispered cover here, both a worthy tribute to the original and a showcase for Batoh's own considerable work. —*Ned Raggett*

## Walter Gibbons

**d.** 1994
*Mixing, Producer, DJ / Disco, House*
One of the dance figures whose influence and exposure far exceed his actual name-recognition association, Walter Gibbons pioneered the concept of the remix and 12" single in America. Influenced by Jamaican dub producers, Gibbons began altering tracks for his DJ sets in the early '70s, then took his innovations to the studio and recorded the first commercially available remix singles. He started his career as a DJ, and became one of the most popular mixers in New York by the early '70s. Gibbons began working for Salsoul Records in 1976, and recorded his first remix singles that year, Double Exposure's "Ten Percent" and the Salsoul Orchestra's "Nice 'N' Nasty." Utterly transformed with the addition of echo/reverb effects borrowed from dub and drum breaks, the singles influenced dozens of producers (and DJs).

As well, the tracks' influence hardly ended away from the dancefloor. Released on the 12" vinyl format at a cheap price, they became incredibly popular and soon spurred other labels (including the majors) to begin releasing their own 12" remix singles as well. Gibbons also worked on tracks for West End and Gold Mind during the late '70s, but was inactive for several years. He returned in 1984 with his most seminal record yet, a classic on New York's growing garage scene known as "Set It Off." Gibbons' original soon became the "Roxanne, Roxanne" of the garage community, swamped by dozens of remakes and answer tracks, including versions by C. Sharp, Maquerade, Number 1 and Strafe (the latter is undoubtedly the most-heard and definitive). He also remixed a 1986 Arthur Russell single for Sleeping Bag, Indian Ocean's "Tree House/School Bell," but later left the recording industry altogether. He died in 1994. —*John Bush*

## Clifford Gilberto Rhythm Combination

**f.** 1997
*Group / Drill'N'Bass, Electronica, Jungle/Drum'N'Bass*
Another fusion-soaked drill'n'bass production unit along the lines of Squarepusher and Animals on Wheels, the Clifford Gilberto Rhythm Combination debuted on the 1998 Ninja Tune *Funkungfusion* compilation, then released their debut album *I Was Young and I Needed the Money* later that year. The group also remixed Ninja Tune label-heads Coldcut. —*John Bush*

● **I Was Young and I Needed the Money** / Oct. 5, 1998 / Ninja Tune ♦♦♦
At its best, this album sounds like Stevie Wonder possessed and traveling at light speed; at its worst, it sounds like a battlefield of sonic carnage. "Deliver the Weird" is sure to go down as a classic drill'n'bass cut with its nuclear keyboard and bass work; this is where Gilberto is at his most potent. "Giant Jumps" makes playful allusions to Coltrane's *Giant Steps*. "Ms. Looney's Last Embrace" showcases his ability to integrate a wide variety of sources to his sound and keeps you laughing with him, not at him. Unfortunately, this album never comes into focus because Gilberto deals with his influences in separate parts as opposed to a whole. —*Ryan Randall Goble*

## Philip Glass

**b.** Jan. 31, 1937, Baltimore, MD
*Keyboards, Conductor, Composer / Original Score, 20th Century Classical/Modern Composition, Avant-Garde, Minimalism, Ethnic Fusion*
Philip Glass was unquestionably among the most innovative and influential composers of the 20th century; postmodern music's most celebrated and high-profile proponent, his myriad orchestral works, operas, film scores and dance pieces proved essential to the development of ambient and new age sounds, and his fusions of Western and world music were among the earliest and most successful global experiments of their kind. Born in Baltimore, Maryland on January 31, 1937, Glass took up the flute at the age of eight; at just 15, he was accepted to the University of Chicago, ostensibly majoring in

philosophy but spending most of his waking hours on the piano. After graduation he spent four years at Juilliard, followed in 1963 by a two-year period in Paris under the tutelage of the legendary Nadia Boulanger. Glass' admitted artistic breakthrough came while working with Ravi Shankar on transcribing Indian music; the experience inspired him to begin structuring music by rhythmic phrases instead of by notation, forcing him to reject the 12-tone idiom of purist classical composition as well as traditonal elements including harmony, melody and tempo.

Glass' growing fascination with non-Western musics inspired him to hitchhike across North Africa and India, finally returning to New York in 1967. There he began to develop his distinctively minimalist compositional style: his music consisting of hypnotically repetitious circular rhythms; while quickly staking out territory in the blooming downtown art community, Glass' work met with great resistance from the classical establishment, and to survive he was forced to work as a plumber and later as a cab driver. In the early '70s he formed the Philip Glass Ensemble, a seven-piece group composed of woodwinds, a variety of keyboards, and amplified voices; their music found its initial home in art galleries but later moved into underground rock clubs, including the famed Max's Kansas City. After initially refusing to publish his music, Glass formed his own imprint, Chatham Square Productions, in 1971; a year later, he self-released his first recording, *Music with Changing Parts*. Subsequent efforts like 1973's *Music in Similar Motion/Music in Fifths* earned significant notoriety overseas, and in 1974 he signed to Virgin UK.

Glass rose to international fame with his 1976 "portrait opera" *Einstein on the Beach*, a collaboration with scenarist Robert Wilson. An early masterpiece close to five hours in length, it toured Europe and was performed at the Metropolitan Opera House; while it marked Glass' return to classical Western harmonic elements, its dramatic rhythmic and melodic shifts remained the work's most startling feature. At much the same time, he was attracting significant attention from mainstream audiences as a result of the album *North Star*, a collection of shorter pieces which he performed in rock venues and even at Carnegie Hall. In the years to follow, Glass focused primarily on theatrical projects, and in 1980 he presented *Satyagraha*, an operatic portrayal of the life of Gandhi complete with a Sanskrit libretto inspired by the Bhagavad Gita. Similar in theme and scope was 1984's *Akhnaten*, which examined the myth of the Egyptian pharoah. In 1983, Glass made the first of many forays into film composition with the score to the Godfrey Reggio cult hit *Koyaanisqatsi;* a sequel, *Powaqqatsi*, followed five years later.

While remaining best known for his theatrical productions, Glass also enjoyed a successful career as a recording artist. In 1981, he signed an exclusive composer's contract with the CBS Masterworks label, the first such contract offered to an artist since Aaron Copland; a year later, he issued *Glassworks*, a highly successful instrumental collection of orchestral and ensemble performances. In 1983, he released *The Photographer*, including a track with lyrics by David Byrne; that same year, Glass teamed with former Doors keyboardist Ray Manzarek for *Carmina Burana*. 1986's *Songs of Liquid Days*, meanwhile, featured lyrics from luminaries including Paul Simon, Laurie Anderson and Suzanne Vega, and became Glass' best-selling effort to date. By this time he was far and away the avant-garde's best-known composer, thanks also to his music for the 1984 Olympic Games and works like *The Juniper Tree*, an opera based on a fairy tale by the Brothers Grimm; in 1992, Glass was even commissioned to write "The Voyage" for the Met in honor of the 500th anniversary of Christopher Columbus' arrival in the Americas—clear confirmation of his acceptance by the classical establishment. In 1997, he scored the Martin Scorsese masterpiece *Kundun; Dracula*, a collaboration with the Kronos Quartet, followed two years later. —*Jason Ankeny*

**Einstein on the Beach** / 1979 / Atlantic ++++
This opera, composed in 1975 and premiered in 1976, is scored for four principal actors, 12 singers doubling as dancers and actors, a solo violinist, and an amplified ensemble of keyboards, winds and voices. It is imbued with the postmodern spirit both in its non-linear, poetic, mystic narrative and the floating, eternal world created by the shifting, mathemetically precise patterns of Glass' modal music. There are three primary visual sets linked to three musical themes that recur within the work: trains (recalling the metaphors Einstein used to illustrate the theory of relativity, and with which he played as a child), a trial setting (modern life and modern science examined), and a spaceship (a metaphor for transcendence, and/or an escape from nuclear disaster). Also Einstein himself appears midway between the orchestra and the stage as a violinist (his hobby) and observer/witness. There are also additional spoken texts written by Christopher Knowles, Samuel M. Johnson, and Lucinda Childs, which appear in various arrangements for single and multiple voices. This work locates itself as a midpoint between the composer's early-'70s work linking rhythmic and harmonic structures and his later series of operas and vocal works and film scores employing expanded narrative and/or timbral experiments. —*"Blue" Gene Tyranny*

**Koyaanisqatsi** / 1982 / Antilles ++++
Parodied more than once, derided, blessed, hailed as a wonder, and decried as a travesty, this (abbreviated) soundtrack is capable of generating fascination and annoyance, often simultaneously. The truth is that this isn't merely minimalism—it's expressive minimalism, with some impressive nuances. Given the space to breathe, the music here is breathtaking, and becomes even more so when properly linked, in its full form, with the film's visuals. The later *Powaqqatsi* did not live up to the first film in either a visual or musical respect. —*Steven McDonald*

**Songs from Liquid Days** / 1986 / CBS ++++
*Songs from Liquid Days* became Philip Glass' most popular and successful recording. The title holds the clue to the music's accessibility: these are songs, providing a more familiar and comfortable format for appreciating the world of minimalism than Glass' operas or instrumental pieces. Working with such lyrical collaborators as David Byrne and Suzanne Vega, he created art music which sounds radio-friendly. There is also great variety displayed on this album. While the musical backing is unmistakably Philip Glass, the arrangements and vocal treatments range from the coolly subdued chamber music of "Freezing," featuring the Kronos Quartet and Linda Ronstadt, to the appropriately electrifying and almost New Wave-ish "Lightning." The album's highlight, however, is the opener, a ten-minute opus called "Changing Opinion." With unusually oblique lyrics courtesy of Paul Simon, it condenses the odd excitement and drama of a minimalist opera into a single creative burst of melody, rhythm and momentum. The minimalist composers originally wanted to reconnect Western art music with a broad popular audience. On that basis, *Songs from Liquid Days* may be their single greatest achievement. —*Freddy Stidean*

**A Thin Blue Line** / 1989 / Atlantic ++++
The soundtrack to Errol Morris' documentary *The Thin Blue Line* emphasizes story over music; the interviews which make up the majority of the film—a crusading effort which led to the the release of its subject, Randall Adams, from a Texas prison—are presented on record as they were on screen, with Glass' chamber orchestra music hovering in the background. The result is a soundtrack which comes remarkably close to capturing the power of its source film; even without the moving images, this is a chilling document. —*Jason Ankeny*

★ **Music in 12 Parts** / 1990 / Venture +++++
Philip Glass is renowned for his style of pattern music, presented in its most developed form in this early work, still one of his best. Glass developed a method of writing that simultaneously retained the sense of the timeless "present" while bringing new thoughts about melody and harmony in a non-virtuosic sense. On *Music in 12 Parts* (as well as his opera *Akhnaten*), these ideas are very elegant and profound, while at times Glass verges on the direct appeal of a movie-music sensibility as in *1000 Airplanes on the Roof*. For having this range, he remains a very controversial composer. —*"Blue" Gene Tyranny*

**Glassworks** / 1993 / Columbia ++
With a richer sound and variation of timbres than in the usual Glass keyboard renditions, Donald Joyce plays, with great attention and feeling, various solo works by Glass on a large church organ. Appealing. —*"Blue" Gene Tyranny*

**Music with Changing Parts** / 1994 / Elektra/Nonesuch ++
A re-issue of the 1971 recording. Glass at his most fundamental and best. —*"Blue" Gene Tyranny*

**Heroes Symphony** / Mar. 1997 / Point Music ++
Like *Low* before it, *Heroes* was one of David Bowie's most experimental and avant-garde records, so it made sense that Philip Glass would follow the *Low Symphony* with the *"Heroes" Symphony*, adapting Bowie and Brian Eno's

original, minimalistic synthesized sketches for full orchestra. Surprisingly, Glass' arrangements and orchestrations—including charting the title track for a big band—are less adventurous than the original recordings, which actually robs the music of its impact. However, the new arrangements emphasize the icy allure of the original compositions, and the shimmering, glassy textures sound coldly beautiful. Nevertheless, the *"Heroes" Symphony* doesn't quite hold together as an actual symphony, but it remains an intriguing listen, even if it is a disarmingly unchallenging one. —*Stephen Thomas Erlewine*

**Kundun** / Nov. 25, 1997 / Elektra/Asylum ♦♦♦♦
Philip Glass' soundtrack to Martin Scorsese's Dalai Lama epic *Kundun* captures the grace, beauty, joy and melancholy within the film. Glass uses familiar minimalist structures, but works with traditional Tibetan instrumentation and monks, giving the music an alluringly otherworldly feel. It's an entirely original, evocative score, and one of Glass' high-water marks in the field. —*Stephen Thomas Erlewine*

## Global Communication

f. 1991, Cornwall, England
*Group / Jazz-House, Ambient House, Electronica, Ambient Techno, Jungle/Drum'N'Bass, Club/Dance, House*

No other electronic dance act made so many recordings in such a wide range of styles (and with such impressive results) as the duo of Mark Pritchard and Tom Middleton. After coming together in 1991, the pair began recording music whose range spanned all of electronic dance music, though many were recorded under aliases—industrial techno as Reload, electro-funk as Jedi Knights, progressive house as Link, jungle as the Chameleon and most famously, ambient and house as Global Communication. Their 1994 LP *76:14*, recorded as Global Communication, was a notable high-point of the early-'90s ambient house movement.

The partnership began in 1991, when Pritchard and Middleton formed Evolution Records (named after a Carl Craig track) to release their own dancefloor-oriented house and techno. (Middleton had previously recorded with Aphex Twin while Pritchard had been half of the duo Shaft, responsible for the British Top Ten rave hit "Roobarb & Custard"). The first three releases on Evolution were EPs recorded as Reload by Pritchard/Middleton in 1992-93—*The Reload, The Autoreload*, and *The Biosphere*. The records were excellent Detroit-inspired tracks, brooding and eerie but nonetheless highly danceable. Reload first gained fame on the Infonet label (the brief dance subsidiary launched by Creation Records) with an EP and the 1994 full-length *A Collection of Short Stories*. Global Communication, which matched the unsettling ambience of Reload but with a focus on warmer rhythms, debuted on Evolution 004, otherwise known as *The Keongaku* EP. Though GC's full-length debut *Pentamerous Metamorphosis* followed soon after, it wasn't quite a proper album per se; it was in fact an extended remix of Chapterhouse's *Blood Music* LP.

With the ambient house boom in full force by 1994, Pritchard and Middleton's downtempo project became more important than Reload. They signed to Dedicated and released *76:14* in mid-1994. The album later gained an American release, and made many critic's best-of lists that year. Global Communication released *Remotion* in late 1995, though this album consisted of remixes also, including material from the out-of-print *Pentamerous Metamorphosis* LP along with reworkings of material by Jon Anderson, Nav Katze and Warp 69.

Never a team to rest on their laurels, Pritchard and Middleton added another side project to their résumé in late 1994 when Jedi Knights released the debut single for nu-school electro label Clear Records. Though a full-length was more than a year in coming—*New School Science* appeared in March 1996—the debut 12" sparked an electro revival in England, and anticipated later Clear moonlightings by µ-Ziq (as Tusken Raiders), Matt Herbert (as Doctor Rockit) and Autechre (as Gescom). Jedi Knights also appeared on the May 1995 label retrospective *The Theory of Evolution* along with other Evolution projects such as Reload, Link/e621 and non-Pritchard/Middleton artists such as Jak & Stepper (aka Dave Kempston and Stevie Horn) and Matt Herbert's Wish Mountain project.

Evolution was soon replaced by Pritchard and Middleton's new label venture: Universal Language Productions, the home of new releases by Gerd, Max 404, Danny Breaks and Droppin' Science, among others. The duo also debuted yet another project in early 1996—the Chameleon had first appeared in 1994 remixing Link's "Archetype Arcadian," and as jungle began to grow in popularity during 1995-96, LTJ Bukem signed the Chameleon to his Good Looking stabel for the single "Links." It appeared in January 1996, and was compiled later that year on Bukem's *Logical Progression* compilation.

Perhaps fearful of spreading themselves too thin, Pritchard and Middleton cut back on their side-project work by early 1997; though no LPs were forthcoming, the pair did issue two new Global Communication singles ("The Way/The Deep," "The Groove") signalling a new direction toward the lush sounds of dancefloor-friendly deep house and funk. Middleton also stepped out on his own with *A Jedi's Night Out*, an entry in "Mixmag"'s series of DJ albums. By the end of the decade, both were working on solo projects (Middleton's Cosmos project produced a big Ibizan club hit during 2000 with "Summer in Space"), though they promised they'd work together again. [See Also: Jedi Knights, Reload] —*John Bush*

**Pentamerous Metamorphosis** / Dec. 1993 / Dedicated ♦♦♦♦
Ostensibly a remix of an entire Chapterhouse album though few traces of the original remain, *Blood Music: Pentamerous Metamorphosis* appeared one year before the first proper Global Communication album and included early versions of songs from that LP. Much more minimalistic and slow-moving than its follower, the album includes a few moments as crucial as *76:14* but for the most part emerges as a bit still-born compared to the high peaks to which Pritchard and Middleton would later ascend. —*John Bush*

★ **76:14** / Jun. 1994 / Dedicated ♦♦♦♦♦
Tempering the industrial tilt of their previous Reload material with slower, more graceful rhythms and an ear for melody unmatched by any in the downtempo crowd, Mark Pritchard and Tom Middleton produced the single best work in the ambient house canon. The tick-tock beats and tidal flair of "14:31" are proof of the duo's superb balance of beauty with a haunting quality more in line with Vangelis than Larry Heard (though both producers were heavy influences on the album). On several tracks the darkside appears to take over—the pinging ambience of "9:39"—but for most of *76:14* the melodies and slow-moving rhythms chart a course toward the upbeat and positive. —*John Bush*

**Maiden Voyage [Single]** / Oct. 1994 / Dedicated ♦♦♦
Available as two separately released singles, *"Maiden Voyage"* includes a Spiritualized remix and the eco-ambience of "Funk in the Fridge." —*John Bush*

**A Theory of Evolution** / Apr. 1995 / Wax Trax! ♦♦♦♦
*A Theory of Evolution* is a compilation of releases on Evolution Records (consisting mostly of Global Communication aliases Reload, Link, Chameleon and Jedi Knights). Tracks from the first three *Evolution* EPs by Reload are intriguing listens for the acid- and Detroit roots-techno originally favored by Pritchard and Middleton, though later stylistic change-ups make appearances as well, like "Pubic Funk" by Jedi Knights. —*John Bush*

**Remotion** / Feb. 20, 1996 / Hit It! Recordings ♦♦♦
An album compiling most of GC's post-production work, *Remotion* includes remixes of material by Jon Anderson, the Grid, Nav Katze, Reload, Warp 69, and Chapterhouse. —*John Bush*

**The Way/The Deep [Single]** / Nov. 25, 1996 / Dedicated ♦♦♦♦
Global Communication's initial foray into straight-ahead house music is surprisingly successful, comprising two tracks of progressive house with enough twists and spins to keep headphone boffins interested. Available as a separately released double pack, the single features a Secret Ingredients remix. —*John Bush*

## Global Goon (Johnny Hawk)

b. 1967, Liverpool, England
*Producer / Electronica, Ambient Techno, IDM*

According to his press bio, Global Goon's Johnny Hawk is a former shepherd from Liverpool who earned a recording contract after moving to London and rooming with Richard D. James (aka Aphex Twin) for a time. Hawk had worked in the capital for a multimedia company while making music on the side; after moving into a shared house with James, he released his first album *Goon* on Rephlex in 1996. Rumors that Goon actually *was* Aphex Twin persisted even after the release of *Cradle of History* two years later. —*John Bush*

● **Goon** / Dec. 2, 1996 / Rephlex ♦♦♦♦
*Goon* does sound remarkably similar to Aphex Twin material: some verita-

bly cheesy synth-work over a simple, infectious melody, an occasional vocal reminiscent of the trippy leanings of the Incredible String Band, and overreaching everything, an aburdist sense of humor. Though the vocal track becomes a bit tedious, the instrumental offerings are more than up to snuff actually, including several songs akin to Aphex's *Selected Ambient Works* or work by Cylob ("The Owl, Pussycat," "Clapping Song") and a few that detour the ambient vibe into intriguing hip-hop territory, such as "Metal Buffalo." With music this enjoyable, it doesn't really matter who is doing the recording —*John Bush*

**Cradle of History** / Apr. 6, 1998 / Rephlex ♦♦♦

## Globo

*Group / Trip-Hop, Club/Dance*
The sampladelic trip-hop act Globo released their debut album *This Time It's Globo...* on Hydrogen Dukebox in May 2000, though not before a questionable sample on their single "13" attracted a lawsuit and delayed its release. —*John Bush*

● **This Time It's Globo...** / May 23, 2000 / Hydrogen Dukebox ♦♦
*This Time It's Globo...* is an ambitious work of cross-genre pollinization, though it recycles a few too many clichéd sounds for its own good. The opener "Onward" begins as a big-beat track but gradually turns to an odd pastiche of easy listening and techno before attempting to summon the acid-house glory of Primal Scream circa *Screamadelica*. The track sums up Globo's hodgepodge of techno, dub, trip-hop, and acid-house; it's a sound that hits all the right notes but never really accomplishes much in the way of new ideas or sounds. The eccentric vocal samples on "Globo Conspiracy" and "Autosleeper" make for a bit of diverting listening, but too often Globo simply goes through the motions instead of making solid dance music. —*John Bush*

## Godflesh

f. 1988, Birmingham, England
*Group / Industrial Metal, Heavy Metal, Grindcore*
Godflesh was formed in 1988 by ex-Napalm Death guitarist and Head of David drummer Justin Broadrick and bassist G.C. Green. The band's sound has been tagged as grindcore, with its heavy, ultra-detuned guitars and bass and plodding tempos. Industrial and experimental influences are also easy to spot in the drum machine and various noises, effects, and tape loops; depending on the album, the group's sound may run either way. Godflesh chiefly makes mood music, and the mood is one of intense, depressed rage. The group's discography is rather tangled, with various singles and EPs out in addition to albums like 1992's *Pure*, 1996's *Songs of Love and Hate* and 1999's *Us and Them*. Broadrick has drawn praise from the musical community for his unique guitar playing and musical style and has been hailed as a major innovator. He is also a member of Final and Techno Animal. —*Steve Huey*

● **Pure** / 1992 / Earache ♦♦♦♦
On *Pure*, trudging hip-hop beats combine with ghastly undead-android distorted vocals and bludgeoning, bone-crunching guitars to produce the musical equivalent of a steamroller. Grim, brutal and merciless, Godflesh's uncompromising blend of industrial dub and grindcrusher guitars could flatten even the most optimistic spirit in a matter of seconds. The closer "Pure II" turns the tables however, with almost 25 minutes of isolationist dub-noise. —*David Kent-Abbott*

**Merciless** / 1994 / Earache ♦♦♦
A highly layered and textured EP with an abundance of sounds, effects, and tape manipulation, there's even a simple melody on "Flowers." This ranks among their better work and holds attention more consistently than some of the group's full-length albums. —*Steve Huey*

**Selfless** / 1994 / Earache ♦♦♦
*Selfless* is more subdued and moody, managing to be both dark and strangely soothing at the same time; Justin Broadrick even comes close to singing on occasion. The CD is over 78 minutes long, so the band inevitably falls into repetition and meanders in spots. Fans of their heavier work may be disappointed, but most of *Selfless* works well as angry, depressed mood music. —*Steve Huey*

**Love and Hate in Dub** / Jun. 24, 1997 / Earache ♦♦♦♦
Justin Broadrick's electronic and acoustic proclivities intersected once before, on the 1991 remix EP *Slavestate*. Where those mixes were wrought with an almost industrial-techno stiffness, *Love and Hate In Dub* (which sources Godflesh's 1996 trio release, *Songs of Love and Hate*) reflects Broadrick's more recent occupations: heavy ambient dub and nasty, paint-peeling drum'n'bass. The result is a more lithe, slithery redivision of Godflesh's metallic murk, some tracks echoing with deep, bassy drones, others pummeling away with odd rhythmic timbres and quasi-jungular patterns. —*Sean Cooper*

## Godspeed You Black Emperor!

f. 1994, Montreal, Quebec,
*Group / Experimental Rock, Space Rock, Indie Rock, Orchestral*
The instrumental, multi-media Montreal group Godspeed You Black Emperor! creates extended, repetition-oriented chamber rock. The minimal and patient builds-to-crescendo of the group's compositions result in a meditative and hypnotic listen that becomes almost narrative when combined with found sound splices, and the films of their visual collaborators. GYBE! formed in 1994, and that year self-released a limited-run (33 copies) cassette entitled, *All Lights Fucked on the Hairy Amp Drooling*. The band's next recording, *F#A#(Infinity)*, was initially a limited run release of 550 LPs on the Canadian label Constellation, but was picked up by Kranky and released onto CD as well. Early 1999 brought the EP *Slow Riot for New Zero Kanada* (released by both labels) and increased recognition for a band intent on retaining anonymity. Nevertheless, interest in GYBE! only continued to grow among new music fans with much positive attention from *The Wire* magazine, the band's participation in the John Peel-produced Peel Session for the London BBC, and the group's consistently impressive live shows, including their performance at Quebec's 1999 new music festival, *FIMAV* and the tour with Labradford later that year. GYBE! performances generally include at least nine or more musicians and a projectionist. The instrumentation consists of three guitars, two basses, French horn, violin, viola, cello and percussion. 2000 brought about the release of *Lift Your Skinny Fists Like Antennas to Heaven*, pushing their diverse orchestral rock sound even further into the universe. —*Joslyn Layne*

**F#A#(Infinity)** / 1996 / Kranky ♦♦♦♦
"We are trapped in the belly of this horrible machine, and the machine is bleeding to death." Few albums begin with such promise and foreboding, but this first full-length from Canadian genius collective Godspeed You Black Emperor! succeeds in the first few moments. *F#A#(Infinity)* contains three compositions that run the gamut from grotesque to sublime. The term "composition" seems an appropriate one to use as this band does not write songs. Each piece is at least fourteen minutes in length, consisting of three to four sections. The band, a nine member unit consisting of guitar, drums, bass, strings, keyboard, marimbas and woodwinds, intersperses voice-over narrative with sprawling instrumental melodies. The arrangements move slowly, building from hushed silence to cathartic crescendo and back again. The narratives that accompany the music meditate on the corruption of the American government and the seeming emptiness of the postmodern era. At times, it seems that the music might offer hope, but alternatively, the haunting melodies can serve to emphasize the confusion encountered in these stories. As "Dead Flag Blues," the album's first track, unfolds, the speaker's voice is undercut by a poignant string melody and the piece builds to a beautiful peak. "Dead Flag Blues" is a four part arrangement in an apparently symphonic pattern. A theme is stated, followed by a quiet interlude out of which the tension builds to disaster/epiphany and finally a quiet reprise of the initial melody is given. The albums second piece, "East Hastings," follows a similar pattern producing brilliant results. "Providence" is the album's final piece, a bit longer than the others, but lacking the consistency and unity of its counterparts. The music on this album is unique and powerful. One would be hard-pressed to find any imitators of this revolutionary musical form created by GYBE! Its origins are as much avant-classical as they are rock 'n' roll, and the band has a achieved a true synthesis of the two forms, expanding them to new boundaries. This music is inherently inexplicable, and this is its beauty. —*Marc G. Gilman*

**Slow Riot for New Zero Kanada [EP]** / Mar. 16, 1999 / Constellation ♦♦♦♦
A low hum is the first thing heard. It's nearly an inaudible sound, like the opening of Beethoven's Ninth Symphony. Soon other instruments join and overlap: strings, guitar, and glockenspiel. For a while, the listener hovers in a mist feeling the musical waves ebb and flow, warning of impending danger.

In these moments, uncertainty breeds and devours the weak, swallowing them whole. This is probably Mile End, the location alluded to in the liner notes of the Canadian ensemble Godspeed You Black Emperor!'s *Slow Riot for New Zero Kanada*. Mile End is described in detail, and the influence of this locale on the recording of the *Slow Riot* must have been immense. In fact, the best way to describe this album is as a direct result of Mile End's setting: the abandoned buildings, haunting forest, burned out railroad cars, and empty train tracks. All of these physical images pervade the tone of this album: they are its sadness, beauty, and anger. The darkness is there too. Once immersed in Mile End, it's near impossible to find your way out. The darkness limits your freedom, and at the same time hides you from the rest of the world. You are alone and it is both frightening and liberating. As for the music, there's really not much to say. If this description of Mile End appeals to you or intrigues you then it will be a worthwhile listen. "Moya," the album's first piece, is a lot like weathering a torrential downpour: torn between moments of uncertainty a final deluge occurs absorbing everything in its path. The second piece, "BBF3," is a history lesson set to music, a story of dysfunctional government, militias, and human rights. This one album spans the emotions of terror and delight in 30 minutes. The same feelings of fear and triumph found in Beethoven can be found here, and there is perhaps no better endorsement for such music. —*Marc Gilman*

- **Lift Your Skinny Fists Like Antennas to Heaven** / Sep. 12, 2000 / Kranky ♦♦♦♦

*Lift Your Skinny Fists Like Antennas to Heaven*, the much-anticipated follow-up to Godspeed You Black Emperor's *Slow Riot*, is a double-disc achievement of four works (each with multiple parts): "Storm," "Static," "Sleep," and "Antennas to Heaven." It is a windfall for any fan of ambient pop, orchestral rock, space rock, or simply lush string arrangements who understands how powerful love, melancholy, and frustration can be. The main complaint voiced by critics of Godspeed's music is that their works just repeat the same pattern: start out sparse and slow, build-build-build, crescendo. While there are certainly crescendos, there is no such predictable pattern repeated among the works on *Lift Your Skinny Fists Like Antennas to Heaven*—it's loaded with dynamics, unexpected sections, strong emotions and beauty.

The album opener, "Storm," is a leap for GYBE! that, alone, makes this release worth getting. It's a rapturous work that rises with a potent melancholy, driven by heartrending emotions. "Storm" vents a powerful frustration (each listener can insert their own reasons why) with majestic screams of strings, guitars, and layers, resulting in a climactic and passionate soaring. It eventually winds down into an exhausted aftermath of piano, underlying drones, and frustrated rants. The second piece, "Static," is a wandering, isolationist piece of bleak expanses shaded with darker emotions, but the remaining two works raise the album back up to the impressive standard set by the opening cut, though with less furor and even more loveliness. "Sleep" opens with an elderly gentleman reminiscing about Coney Island, and his frank and amusing narration briefly recalls the recordings of David Greenberger and scenes from the documentary *Vernon, FL*. This narration is followed by a slow and melodic piece featuring a pseudo-theremin effect amidst all of the other instrumentation. "Antennas to Heaven" opens with someone playing acoustic guitar, singing "What'll We Do with the Baby-O," soon washed over with sound, which then gives way to a brief chorus of glockenspiels, and on.

During most of *Lift Your Skinny Fists Like Antennas to Heaven*, musical and emotional opposites alternate as regularly, and naturally, as breathing: delicate string work and rock-out guitar and drums, spoken word and walls of sound, gracious and possessed, tip-toes and cliff-diving, dark hallways and blinding sunshine. —*Joslyn Layne*

## Goldfrapp

*Producer, Vocals / Electronica, Alternative Pop/Rock*
Bath, England's singer/composer/keyboardist Allison Goldfrapp began exploring music as a part of her studies as a Fine Art Painting major at Middlesex University, mixing sound, visuals, and performances in her installation pieces. While she was still in college, she appeared on her friend Tricky's 1995 debut *Maxinquaye*, which led to appearances on albums from other cutting-edge electronic artists, including Orbital's *Snivilisation* and Add N to (X)'s *Avant Hard*. By the late '90s, Goldfrapp began honing her own compositions; one of her friends passed some of her demos on to composer Will Gregory. Finding much in common in their musical tastes and approaches, the duo took Allison's surname as the name for their collaboration. After signing to Mute in 1999, Goldfrapp delivered their debut album, *Felt Mountain*, in fall 2000. —*Heather Phares*

- **Felt Mountain** / Sep. 19, 2000 / Mute ♦♦♦♦

Though her collaborations with Tricky, Orbital, and Add N To X focused on the sheer beauty and power of her singing, on her debut album *Felt Mountain* Allison Goldfrapp also explores more straightforward styles. Together with composer/multi-instrumentalist Will Gregory, Goldfrapp wraps her unearthly voice around songs that borrow from '60s pop, cabaret, folk, and electronica without sounding derivative or unfocused. From the sci-fi/spy film hybrids "Human" and "Lovely Head" to the title track's icy purity, the duo strikes a wide variety of poses, giving *Felt Mountain* a stylized, theatrical feel that never veers into campiness. Though longtime fans of Goldfrapp's voice may wish for more, the exuberant, intoxicating side of her sound, lovelorn ballads like "Pilots," "Deer Stop," and "Horse's Tears" prove that she is equally able at carrying—and writing—more traditional tunes. A strange and beautiful mix of the romantic, eerie, and world-weary, *Felt Mountain* is one of 2000's most impressive debuts. —*Heather Phares*

## Goldie (Clifford Price)

b. 1966, Walsall, England
*Producer, DJ / Electronica, Jungle/Drum'N'Bass, Club/Dance*
The first superstar produced by the breakbeat jungle movement, Goldie popularized drum'n'bass as a form of musical expression just as relevant for living-room contemplation as techno had become by the early '90s. Though he hardly developed the style, and his later reliance on engineers like Rob Playford and Optical to capture his sound puts into question his true musical importance, Goldie became one of the first personalities in British dance music, his gold teeth and b-boy attitude placing him leagues away from the faceless bedroom boffins which had become the norm in intelligent dance music. For the first time, England had a beat-maestro and tough-guy head that could match the scores of larger-than-life hip-hop stars America had produced, and the high profile of drum'n'bass as the first indigenously British dance music made Goldie a figure of prime importance. After spending several years working on his production skills at Reinforced Records (the home of 4 Hero), he founded Metalheadz Records, which released seminal dark-yet-intelligent singles by Source Direct, Photek, J. Majik, Optical, Lemon D, Wax Doctor and Peshay, among others. In 1995, Goldie released *Timeless*, one of jungle's first and best full-length works of art. The album put him squarely at the top of the drum'n'bass heap—at least in the minds of critics and mainstream listeners—though his follow-up *SaturnzReturn* displayed an ambitious, personal side of Goldie hardly in keeping with jungle's producer mentality.

A native of Walsall, England, Goldie was born to a Scottish-Jamaican couple and put up for adoption (for this reason, he refuses to reveal his true name). He bounced around child-care homes and several sets of foster parents during his childhood years, and became fascinated with the rise of hip-hop, break-dancing and graffiti art. By 1986, he was involved with break-dancing crews around his home of Wolverhampton; after making several trips to London for all-day break-dancing events (and to see hip-hop pioneer Afrika Bambaataa), Goldie appeared in the English documentary on graffiti art called *Bombing*. He also spent time in New York and Miami (working in a market stall selling customized gold teeth), but returned to England by 1988.

For a time, Goldie worked at the Try 1 shop in Walsall (also selling gold teeth), then moved to London. He began hanging out with two fellow heads from the British hip-hop scene, Nellee Hooper and 3-D (later of Massive Attack), and by 1991 he'd been introduced to the breakbeat culture that birthed jungle; at the seminal club-night Rage, DJs Grooverider and Fabio pitched ancient breakbeats up to 45-rpm, blending their creations with the popular rave music of the time. Goldie was hooked on the sound of raw breakbeat techno, and he gradually switched his allegiance to jungle from the British hip-hop scene that later generated trip-hop.

Through his girlfriend DJ Kemistry (later to make her name with the mixing duo Kemistry & Storm), Goldie hooked up with Dego and Mark Mac, two of the most influential figures in the emerging drum'n'bass scene. The duo's Reinforced Records and recordings as 4 Hero were fostering an increasingly artistic attitude to the music, and Goldie learned much about breakbeat production and engineering at their studios. He recorded his first single as Ajax Project, then debuted on Reinforced as Metalheadz with two 1992 singles, "Killermuffin" and "Menace." The 1993 single "Terminator" broke him within the jungle scene—besides pioneering the crucial jungle concept of time-stretching (basically extending a sample without altering its pitch) the single evinced the growing separation between the uplifting rave scene and its emerging dark side, reliant on breakbeats and restless vibes.

The name was later taken for his influential Metalheadz Records, which released material from a legion of crucial jungle artists—Photek, Doc Scott, Dillinja, Source Direct, Peshay, J Majik, Alex Reece, Lemon D. and Optical among others. Later singles such as "Angel" and remixes for 4 Hero's Reinforced label spread Goldie's fame, and in 1995 he signed a contract with London Records. His first major-label single was "Timeless," and his debut album of the same name followed in August 1995. He gained additional fame in early 1996, when an American tour supporting Björk sparked a relationship between the two and led to a brief engagement period before they called off a wedding. Goldie resurfaced in 1998 with a high-profile follow-up—*SaturnzReturn*, an epic two-disc set including one track, "Mother," which broke the sixty-minute barrier itself. The album tanked with critics and fans, leading to a return to the underground later that year with the *Ring of Saturn* EP. Goldie also mixed a two-disc volume in the *INCredible* series of mix albums compiled by Ovum. —*John Bush*

**Inner City Life (Remix) [Single]** / 1995 / Metalheadz ✦✦
Jungle's first superstar gets help from 4 Hero and Doc Scott, while Goldie remixes one himself on this 1995 single. —*John Bush*

★ **Timeless** / Aug. 1995 / ffrr ✦✦✦✦✦
Respected by the underground for his production skills and lauded by the press for his star potential, Goldie's album debut proved he was no fluke on either count. But from the first few minutes of *Timeless*, new listeners might wonder what's so different about jungle and its first superstar. The sweeping synths and lilting female vocals that form the intro to the title-track opener could be taken from any above-average house anthem. All questions are answered, however, once the beat kicks in. Manic, echoey percussion rolls around and through the song while a muscular dub bassline pounds additional sonic territory. The beat fades in and out, appearing and re-appearing with all the stealth of a charging rhino. The seven other tracks are just as uncompromising, even adopting a hip-hop beat for the R&B flavor of "State of Mind." Though jungle might be jarring for first-time listeners unused to midtempo melodies functioning as a bed for hyperspeed beats, *Timeless* makes it a much smoother ride. —*John Bush*

**SaturnzReturn** / Jan. 27, 1998 / ffrr ✦✦
Goldie's debut album *Timeless* established him as the king of jungle. Spanning two discs and boasting the epic, 20-plus minute "Timeless," *Timeless* was filled with ambition and invention, and it bristled with the thrill of the new—it sounded as if the music was being invented as you heard it. The debut was so astonishing that it, in many ways, painted Goldie into a corner for his follow-up, *SaturnzReturn*. Goldie not only had to equal its consistency, but he had to offer fresh dimensions to the now-familiar drum'n'bass rhythms. Superficially, *SaturnzReturn* at least delivers in terms of scale and ambition. Running a little over two and a half hours and including a mini-symphony as its first track, the double-disc set is bursting with promise. Unfortunately, it fails to reach the dizzying heights of its predecessor, and its very ambitions feel like burdens. "Mother," the amorphous hour-long pseudo-symphony that comprises the first disc, collapses before the drums are even heard. After 20 minutes of atmosphere, a surge of intriguing rhythms wash up, only to fade away after another 20 minutes to reveal a simplistic, simple-minded symphonic theme that is never developed. If the second disc had been a masterpiece, it would have been easy to forgive the excesses of "Mother," but it suffers from a near-crippling schizophrenia. Divided between harrowing, dark aural journeys and slick, club-ready R&B, the disc never develops a consistent mood and often is sunk by overlong, misguided tracks. With its waves of processed Noel Gallagher guitars and garbled Goldie vocals, "Temper Temper" never quite hits as hard as it should, and it never has the impact of the gutsy KRS-One collaboration, "Digital." Those two vocal tracks are hardly the closest Goldie comes to accessiblity—"Believe" and "I'll Be There for You" have slick soul textures, with layered keyboards, wah guitars and wailing divas. These soul excursions last too long, and are intercut with dark jungle explorations that have scary rhythmic structures, but no sense of purpose. There are some very provocative textures scattered throughout these ten tracks, and Goldie's skill for hyperactive drum programming can be astonishing, but that astonishment fades quickly since the music never goes anywhere—it just meanders forever, as the drums slowly lose their power and turn into a tinny din of noise. As a result, Goldie sounds confused, as if he wants to push forward but doesn't know how. With some serious editing, *SaturnzReturn* would have been a powerful record, but as it stands, its bloated running time and pretentious, formless songs only obscure Goldie's considerable talent. —*Stephen Thomas Erlewine*

**Ring of Saturn [EP]** / Dec. 8, 1998 / London ✦✦✦✦
After the negative response to his two-disc sophomore album *SaturnzReturn*, Goldie's next major release was (thankfully) an EP, albeit a ten-track, 60-minute EP. Fortunately, *Ring of Saturn* returns the producer to exactly what made his reputation: the tightest breakbeats and most original effects around. *Ring of Saturn* begins with a VIP remix of "Mother"—a track whose album version was over an hour long—that drastically improves the original simply by trimming the endless wash of swirling orchestration that began and closed the track in its original incarnation. Signs of Goldie's particular affinity for excess (read: super-slick jazz-fusion) are still noticeable; the emphasis single is a cover of Bobby Caldwell's quiet-storm chestnut "What You Won't Do for Love" with longtime Goldie collaborator Diane Charlemagne on vocals. The other unreleased tracks however, are leaner and much more tied to underground jungle than anything on *SaturnzReturn*, and it's a much better release. Rounding out the EP are remixes—by Optical and Grooverider—of the Noel Gallagher collaboration "Temper Temper," and both are excellent examples of twisted industrial tech-step. —*John Bush*

**INCredible Sound of Drum'n'Bass** / May 3, 1999 / Incredible ✦✦✦
He's known more for his production expertise and musical vision than his skills behind the turntables, but Goldie has been a DJ almost as long as he's been a producer. And despite the fact that it's not his specialty, *INCredible Sound of Drum'n'Bass* is a solid album. Though his mixing isn't up there with the best (Grooverider, Fabio, Bukem), Goldie's track selection is excellent. Almost half of the tracks either originally appeared on Goldie's Metalheadz label or were produced by close compatriots. The nepotism is hardly a problem, however, since Metalheadz released a raft of crucial singles—"Pulp Fiction" by Alex Reece, "The Angels Fell" by Dillinja, "To Shape the Future" by Optical, "The Warning" by Grooverider's Codename John project, "Here Come the Drumz" by Doc Scott, "Your Sound" by J. Majik—that can only help any collection they're on. The second disc also includes two of Goldie's earliest productions, "Manslaughter" and "Terminator." Goldie usually plays out most of the songs before moving on to the next, but drops in plenty of twists to keep listeners into it. True, a better mix album by a less popular name would never sell in the numbers this one has, but Goldie proves with *INCredible Sounds of Drum'n'Bass* that his status as jungle superstar number one is untouched. —*John Bush*

## Gong
f. 1968
*Group / Freakbeat, Canterbury Scene, British Psychedelia, Space Rock, Experimental, Psychedelic, Prog-Rock/Art Rock, Avant-Garde, Electronic*
Gong slowly came together in the late '60s when Australian guitarist Daevid Allen (ex-Soft Machine) began making music with his wife, singer Gilli Smyth, along with a shifting line-up of supporting musicians. Albums from this period include *Magick Brother, Mystic Sister* (1969) and the impromptu jam session *Bananamoon* (1971) featuring Robert Wyatt from the Soft Machine, Gary Wright from Spooky Tooth, and Maggie Bell. A steady line-up featuring Frenchman Didier Malherbe (sax & reeds), Christian Tritsch (bass), and Pip Pyle (drums) along with Allen (glissando guitar, vocals) and Gilli Smyth (space whisper vocals) was officially named Gong and released *Camembert Electrique* in late 1971, as well as providing the soundtrack to the film *Continental Circus* and music for the album *Obsolete* by French poet Dashiel Hedayat.

*Camembert Electrique* contained the first signs of the band's mythology of the peaceful Planet Gong populated by Radio Gnomes, Pothead Pixies, and Octave Doctors. These characters along with Zero the Hero are the focus of Gong's next three albums, the *Radio Gnome Invisible Trilogy*, consisting of *Flying Teapot* (1973), *Angel's Egg* (1974), and *You* (1975). On these albums, protagonist Zero the Hero is a space traveler from Earth who gets lost and finds the Planet Gong, is taught the ways of that world by the gnomes, pixies, and Octave Doctors and is sent back to Earth to spread the word about this mystical planet. The band themselves adopted nicknames—Allen was Bert Camembert or the Dingo Virgin, Smyth was Shakti Yoni, Malherbe was Bloomdido Bad de Grasse, Tritsch was the Submarine Captain and Pyle the Heap. Over the course of the trilogy, Tritsch and Pyle left and were replaced by Mike Howlett (bass) and Pierre Moerlen (drums). New members Steve Hillage (guitar) and Tim Blake (synthesizers) joined.

After *You*, Allen, Hillage, and Smyth left the group due to creative differences as well as fatigue. Guitarist Allen Holdsworth joined and the band drifted into virtuosic if unimaginative jazz fusion. Hillage and Allen each released several solo albums and Smyth formed Mothergong. Nevertheless the trilogy line-up has reunited for a few one-off concerts including a 1977 French concert documented on the excellent *Gong est Mort, Vive Gong* album. Allen also reunited with Malherbe and Pyle as well as other musicians he had collaborated with over the years for 1992's *Shapeshifter* album. Hillage also worked as the ambient techno alias System 7. A number of Gong-related bands have existed over the years, including Mothergong, Gongzilla, Pierre Moerlin's Gong, NY Gong, Planet Gong and Gongmaison. —*Jim Powers*

**Magick Brother** / 1970 / Affinity ♦♦
In 1970, the world got its first taste of the original pothead pixie, Daevid Allen's Gong, as *Magick Brother* was released in France on the BYG label. Allen's wife, Gilli Smyth, penned all the tunes on the album, and Allen's now-classic "Ph.P." drawing style graces the inside of the gatefold. Leaning a little toward the pop end of the spectrum, *Magick Brother* is a fairly light album, devoid of the blatant psychedelic/hippie qualities which shine through so brilliantly on the later *Camembert Electrique*. Smyth's "space whispering" makes its debut on the opening track, though the album is not as spacy as it is ethereal. "Gong Song" is a highlight, with lyrics describing a pothead pixie who came down from the planet Gong to sing his green song...the roots of the Gong myth. Allen's guitar sound is a bit flat and hollow throughout the project, dynamics taking a back seat in most of these recordings. He relies on distortion and various guitar augmentations, but this all works quite well in the context of the collective sound. Much of the vocal harmonizing on the album is typical of many '60s pop troupes and sounds fairly dated today. Didier Malherbe's sax and flute playing spices up this mostly pop-oriented prog-rock outing, helping to make this a cut above the radio norm. Although this is an interesting release, especially for its status as the first Gong project, it is not typical Gong and is not recommended as a starting point for sampling the band's recordings. —*David Ross Smith*

**Camembert Electrique** / 1971 / Charly ♦♦♦♦
This is a classic, the epitome of the band's early Daevid Allen phase with Ph.P.'s (pothead pixies) in full, blazing glory. In its infancy, Gong was a unique prog rock band that branched out in all directions at once while most other prog bands chose simply one path or another. *Camembert Electrique* is a testament to that. The band's eclectic "electric cheese" rock is a mixture of psychedelic rock, spacey atmospherics and lyrics, and doses of jazz often presented with a pop sensibility, yet always intense. From the first cut on *Camembert* we're transported to planet Gong via the voice of a "radio gnome" who drops in intermittently to remind us we're not in Kansas anymore. Daevid Allen leads the band through several compositions musically (not lyrically) reminiscent of, and possibly influenced by, early King Crimson—a hard, raw-edged sound propelled by a strong guitar-sax-percussion combo. Drummer Pip Pyle played on only a few Gong sessions; he is a major figure here, as is saxophonist Didier Malherbe. Both are up front on the wailing progressive rocker "You Can't Kill Me," which also features guitarist Allen in top form. Allen's declarative "I've Bin Stone Before," the first part of an inventive three-song medley, is of particular interest; introductory church organ and avante-garde sax make this another unique Gong experience. But the real gem on *Camembert* is "Tropical Fish: Selene." This jazzy composition is the most involving and intricate piece on the recording. The band moves tightly through several progressive movements and Gilli Smyth scores with her trademark "space whispering." *Camembert Electrique* remains undated after almost thirty years and hovers "strong and steamin'" over most of the Gong catalogue. —*David Ross Smith*

**Continental Circus** / 1971 / Philips ♦♦♦
Gong performed the soundtrack for *Continental Circus*, Jerome Laper- rousaz's film about the 1970 Grands Prix 500cc. Laperrousaz also collaborated with Gilli Smyth on the compositions, which are tighter and more intricate than the band's previous release, *Magick Brother*. This is possibly the smallest number of musicians involved on any Gong project, and it shows in the sound of the music—straightforward progressive rock with no surprises. Keys and synth are kept to a minimum as the band plunges forth with the standard guitar, bass and drums. Malherbe's playing (sax/flute) has not yet moved to the forefront, and the band decided to drop the psychedelic angle for this outing. Much of the music is strictly guitar-driven, with the final instrumental cut resembling early King Crimson, as is the case on several cuts from the following, far superior release, *Camembert Electrique*. [There is a bootleg version of *Continental Circus* in existence with twice as many tracks.] —*David Ross Smith*

**The Radio Gnome Invisible, Pt. 1: Flying Teapot** / 1973 / Charly ♦♦♦
You know you're in for a treat when the personnel section on an album reads as follows: Dingo Virgin (Daevid Allen), Hi T. Moonweed (Tim Blake), the Good Witch Yoni (Gilli Smyth), Bloomdido Bad de Grass (Didier Malherbe), the Submarine Captain (Christian Tritsch), Venus de Luxe (Francis Linon), Lawrence the Alien (Laurie Allen), Francis Bacon (Francis Moze), Rachid Whoarewe (Rachid Houari), and Steve Hillside (Steve Hillage). Produced by Georgio Gomelski (Giorgio Gomelsky), notable for his work with the Yardbirds, Brian Auger, and Magma, this relatively early Gong project is a great representation of the Allen-era Gong. Though not as intricate as its follow-up companion piece, *Angel's Egg*, *The Flying Teapot* is more of a true prog/space-rock outing, where hippy-trippy lyrics and space whispering abound, as evidenced in the opening track, "Radio Gnome Invisible."

The following cut, "Flying Teapot," is the sprawling highlight of the album. At times reminiscent of some early Weather Report jams, though not as jazzy, the tune features prominent bass, standout percussion/drums, and space whispering courtesy of Smyth. Improvisational groaning and percussion bring this jam to a close. "Pothead Pixies" is a fun pop (pot?) tune which probably received very little, if any, airplay due to the lyrics, followed by Blake's brief synth interlude, "The Octave Doctors and the Crystal Machine." "Zero the Hero and the Witch's Spell," another lengthy composition, features Malherbe's sax playing, which, at this early point in the Gong evolution, is credited for most of the jazz sounds heard in the music (remember, Pierre Moerlen has yet to join the band). This cut becomes quite heavy near its end before making a clever transition into the final cut, "Witch's Song/I Am Your Pussy." Here we hear Smyth's strange, sexually explicit lyrics, which she embellishes with ethereal voicings and cackling. This, combined with a jazzy sax from Malherbe and some very groovy musical lines near the closing, make for another fun tune. —*David Ross Smith*

**Expresso** / 1976 / Virgin ♦♦♦♦
A studio album of excellent instrumental jazz-rock from percussionist Pierre Moerlen's band, featuring guitarist Allan Holdsworth's fluid guitar. —*Michael G. Nastos*

**Gazeuse!** / 1976 / Virgin ♦♦♦
*Gazeuse!* was the first in a successful line of strictly jazz-rock sessions for percussionist Pierre Moerlen and company—compositions that stressed jazz more than rock and which generally strayed away from lyrical content. This 1976 recording, also released under the title *Expresso*, was the band's first completely instrumental album, a companion piece to the later, somewhat warmer *Expresso 2* which is quite similar in sound and structure. To say *Gazeuse!* is percussive is an understatement. Drummer Moerlen is accompanied by brother Benoit and Mirielle Bauer on vibraphones with Mino Cinelu playing other assorted percussion. "Percolations" is a showcase for this foursome: Part one, a display of beautiful vibes and xylophones; Part two, a technically superb drum solo. Pierre's playing is fierce in this second part, exhibited by some truly volatile drumming near the close. Allan Holdsworth is the sole guitarist on the album and contributes two of his own compositions. His "Night Illusion" is a standout and reminiscent of Bill Bruford's *Feels Good to Me* on which Holdsworth collaborated around the same time. Longtime Gong member Didier Malherbe adds spice to the proceedings with jazzy flute on "Shadows Of" and prominent sax on the slightly funky "Esnuria." —*David Ross Smith*

**Shamal** / 1976 / Virgin ♦♦♦
Between Daevid Allen's departure from the band and Pierre Moerlen's "official" takeover of the band, there is *Shamal*. This transitional album contains

none of the Allen-inspired psychedelia, but also very little of Moerlen's jazz influence. *Shamal* is, for the most part, a progressive rock album, half vocal, half instrumental. Its most accessible tune, the opening "Wingful of Eyes," had the potential for airplay if only it hadn't been so lengthy. Penned by Mike Howlett, his not-so-great-but-appealing vocal style and lyrics will grow on you, given the opportunity. "Bambooji," mostly instrumental, opens with Didier Malherbe's flute, which at times gives this tune an Asian sound. Percussion and flute dominate and yield a Scottish feeling as well. "Mandrake" is the soft, laidback piece on the album, followed by the closing title cut, a slight foreshadowing of the sound Pierre Moerlen and company assumed on the next several albums. Moerlen, an outstanding, classically trained drummer/percussionist, along with Jorge Pinchevsky on violin, color this piece with a Mahavishnu Orchestra hue, although it's still distinctly Gong. —*David Ross Smith*

**Gong Est Morte, Vive Gong** / 1977 / Tapioca ♦♦♦
Recorded live at the Hippodrome in Paris. Wildly eclectic, with Daevid Allen. —*Michael G. Nastos*

● **Live Etc.** / 1977 / Virgin ♦♦♦♦
The essential *Live Etc.* sports incredible live versions of material from four Gong albums (*Camembert Electrique, Flying Teapot, Angel's Egg, You*) and one studio track which had been recorded in 1974 as an attempt at a single. The live material, recorded 1973-75, consists of performances from several different incarnations of the band, making this an excellent starting point for anyone interested in sampling Gong. Abundant and overflowing with infusions of space, prog, and jazz, this melting pot of a band stands alone in its eclectic delivery of the goods. Highlights include Moerlen's percussion solo on "Flying Teapot," and Malherbe's sax solo on "Zero the Hero...," and Hillage's guitar work on the spacy "Radio Gnome Invisible." "Where Have All the Flowers Gone" is Gong's attempt at a single; while somewhat mainstream, even this piece pushes the envelope for the airwaves. "6/8 Tune" is a superb jazzy instrumental, a kind of foreshadowing to the CD's final four tracks, which are for the most part instrumental and very progressive. The tracks blend together to form the climax and highlight of this great live album, and exhibit the jazziness that would become an integral sound in the band's future releases. Recorded after Allen's departure, this is the personnel that would go on to record *Shamal*, though no tracks from that album show up here. *Live Etc.* originally ended with the tune "Ooby-Scooby Doomsday" (another attempt at a pop hit), but at 79 minutes, the CD format could not hold it, and it has been tacked on to the end of the *Angel's Egg* compact disc release. —*David Ross Smith*

**Expresso 2** / 1978 / Virgin ♦♦♦
As interesting and fun as the Daevid Allen-period was, the name Gong became more meaningful in the context of the music as percussionist Pierre Moerlen assumed the role of bandleader. An emphasis on percussives of all sorts became clear on *Gazeuse*, the band's first completely instrumental album, and the music became much jazzier, though never considered jazz.

*Expresso 2* finds Pierre Moerlen's Gong at their peak. Like their previous studio release, *Gazeuse*, the album is instrumental, the music is very polished, the sound very clean. Vibes and xylophone dominate on this album, somewhat reminiscent of the sound Zappa achieved through Ruth Underwood on *One Size Fits All* just three years earlier. The first two tracks, "Heavy Tune" and "Golden Dilemma," are the highlights here, partially due to the fact that the rest of the cuts all blend together and sound quite similar. The listener is pleasantly assaulted with a barrage of vibes, yet what a unique sound it is when heard on a rock-oriented album. Guitar combos rarely get much better than on "Heavy Tune," as Mick Taylor rips out leads over Allan Holdsworth's grinding rhythm guitar. The collective guitar sound achieved is one of restrained power; however, the piece can comparatively be considered a rocker. Gong shifts to a different gear with the following track, "Golden Dilemma," a faster-paced, jazzy piece with incredible solos from guitarist Bon Lozaga. Formerly of Curved Air, Darryl Way's violin is a highlight on "Sleepy" and "Boring" (neither of which apply). "Sleepy," awhich combines Way's violin with Holdsworth's guitar leads, prefigures the sound of the first UK album (Holdsworth went on to form UK with violinist Eddie Jobson). A very short album, *Expresso 2* is possibly the strongest of the post-Allen Gong, and an essential album. —*David Ross Smith*

**Time Is the Key** / 1979 / Arista ♦♦♦
The instrumental *Time is the Key* ushers Moerlen's Gong into the new age. A lighter version of their previous release, *Downwind*, the band plays mostly progressive rock-based compositions with a drastically different personnel. Peter Lemer's keys, coupled with the sound of vibes and electravibe in particular, give the music a generic, new age sound at times. Hanny Rowe is a prominent figure on most of the cuts, his playing being one of the most memorable aspects of this album. Gong never had such a strong bassist—their music never stressed it—but Rowe is up front here, displaying leadership capabilities by occasionally carrying the music. This is most evident on the carnival-like "Supermarket" and "An American in England".

As on *Downwind*, the jazz element is minimal, showing up only in "Arabesque Intro & Arabesque," the most impressive material on the disc. Here, Allan Holdsworth (who appears on only three cuts) plays lead over Bon Lozaga's rhythm, and Moerlen's heavyweight percussion and tympani take the prize. Other percussive highlights include the opener, "Ard Na Greine" (vibes and tympani), and the guitar-rocking "Bender." —*David Ross Smith*

**25th Birthday Party** / Oct. 10, 1995 / Griffin Music ♦♦♦♦
On October 8 and 9, 1994, Gong celebrated its 25th anniversary with a massive festival at The Forum in London. In addition to Gong, sets were played over the two days by Kevin Ayers, Tim Blake, "Shapeshifter" Gong, Here & Now, Fluvius, Shortwave, Planet Gong, Kangaroo Moon, and the Invisible Opera Company of Tibet. This classic Gong lineup, which hadn't played together since 1977, consisted of Daevid, Gilli, Didier, Tim Blake, Mike Howlett, Pip Pyle, Steffi Sharpstrings, and Shyamal Maitra; no particular era of Gong is most represented here, but rather a mix of personalities from throughout the band's history. Judging by this two-CD set commemorating the event, it was an amazingly energetic two days, as the Gong repertoire was infused with new life, sounding fresh and current, with new variations and tunes inserted throughout. As a psychedelic and alternative rock institution, Gong proves here that it still has the vitality and ability to entertain a new generation of fans. —*Jim Powers*

## Robert Gordon

b. Sheffield, Yorkshire, England
*Producer / Ambient Techno, Club/Dance, Techno*
Robert Gordon's influence on the sound and direction of UK techno and electronica is hardly suggested by his discography, which includes only a handful of EPs and a single full-length. Among the first to combine the techno sound of Detroit with more pronounced electro, new wave, and techno-pop influences, Gordon releases under such names as XON, Unique 3, Sector, and (the most recognizable of the bunch) Forgemasters are generally considered the ground zero of the UK bleep and intelligent techno styles now associated with artists such as Richard Kirk and LFO. A native of Sheffield, Gordon was the founder of Warp Records, through which he released his debut (along with Shaun Maher and Winston Hazel) as Forgemasters, "Track with No Name," in 1992. He was a contributor to Unique 3's now-legendary "The Theme" (although he was not credited), and Gordon-related releases have appeared on such labels as FON, Network, and David Moufang's Source imprint. Source released his only solo full-length to date, *Projects*, in 1996, and a full-length collaboration with Pete Namlook, *Ozoona*, also appeared on the latter's Fax label that same year. The bulk of Gordon's most recognizable work, however, has been for other artists, and his production discography includes Pop Will Eat Itself, Cabaret Voltaire, DJ Mink, Yazz, the Human League, and Stacey Q, among many others. —*Sean Cooper*

**Ozoona** / 1996 / Fax ♦♦♦
A somewhat disappointing summit between Gordon and Fax magnate Pete Namlook made more bearable by the knowledge that it was recorded more than two years previous to its release. The style is somewhat middle-of-the-road ambient techno *a la* early Higher Intelligence Agency or a less complex Stefan Robbers, with the album's production quality its strongest suit. —*Sean Cooper*

● **Projects** / 1996 / Source ♦♦♦♦
Something of a Source Records retrospective for Gordon, collecting several 12" tracks and one-off collaborations with the likes of Richie Hawtin and Source's David Moufang. The sound is a little dated, perhaps (many of the tracks were either released years earlier or have been sitting around for as long), but the tracks are all exceedingly well-written, and the fact that few have made music of this sort (bleepy, gimmick-free minimal

techno with a high index of rubbery funk) makes them more than novel. —*Sean Cooper*

## Manuel Göttsching
b. Sep. 9, 1952, Berlin, Germany
*Keyboards, Guitar, Synthesizer / Kraut Rock, Ambient*
Both as a founding member of the Kraut-rock group Ash Ra Tempel and through his later solo work, Manuel Göttsching was among the true innovators of the musical aesthetic later dubbed electronica, with his 1984 release *E2-E4* remaining a seminal building block in the subsequent development of styles ranging from techno to house to contemporary ambient music. Born in 1952 and raised in West Berlin, Göttsching gave up his classical music training at the age of 14 to begin performing with a variety of local groups, eventually turning to electronics and improvisational techniques. In 1970 he formed Ash Ra Tempel with ex-Tangerine Dream drummer Klaus Schulze and schoolmate Hartmut Enke; the group was quickly signed by the Berlin-based OHR label, issuing their self-titled debut LP the following year.

As electronics began making a bigger and bigger impact on the German music scene, Ash Ra Tempel emerged at the vanguard of the new technology, acquiring new equipment with seemingly each passing performance; after 1982's *Schwingungen*, the group even played live in Switzerland with Dr. Timothy Leary, a collaboration which yielded 1973's *Seven Up*. By the following year both Schulze and Enke had left the group, however, with Göttsching forging ahead as a solo artist now working simply as Ashra; around this same time he issued *Inventions for Electric Guitar*, a groundbreaking soundscape which greatly furthered his experiments with electronics. Subsequent releases including 1977's *New Age of Earth* continued his guitar manipulations; during the middle of the decade, he also played in the group the Cosmic Jokers.

Göttsching and Schulze reteamed in late 1981 for an improvisational tour; at the end of their run they agreed to soon hook up again to appear in Hamburg. The day before he left Göttsching sat down in his studio to create a piece of music to listen to on the airplane; the end result was a 58-minute experimental piece dubbed *E2-E4*, a collage of treated guitar lines, icily atmospheric synths and cutting-edge beats. Never intending for the track to see the light of day, he did not issue it until 1984, the first of his albums to appear under his own name. *E2-E4* soon became a major favorite on the underground club circuit, where it was regularly spun in sets featuring New Order and other key innovators of the moment despite its creator's admission that it was never created with dance audiences in mind.

In 1989 Göttsching was contacted by a group of Italian DJs wishing to release a remix of *E2-E4*; he agreed, even travelling to Italy to play guitar on the track. Retitled due to licensing restrictions, it appeared as an eponymous release credited to Sueño Latino, going on to become a worldwide club smash which eventually topped the UK dance charts. Ironically, it sold more copies than all of Göttsching's previous recordings combined. That same year, he also resurrected the Ashra name to release the LP *Walkin' the Desert*, his first collection of new music in some time. In the years to follow, Göttsching continued working on new Ashra material, also taking on a variety of outside projects like composing music for fashion shows. *E2-E4* also remained an electronica touchstone, sampled by artists including Junior Vasquez and Carl Craig. [See Also: Ash Ra Tempel] —*Jason Ankeny*

★ **E2-E4** / 1984 / Racket ◆◆◆◆◆
*E2-E4*, one of the few records Göttsching released under his own name, has earned its place as one of the most important, influential electronic records ever released. It's also the earliest album to set the tone for electronic dance music; simply put, it just sounds like the mainstream house produced during the next two decades. Similar to previous Ashra albums like *New Age of Earth* and *Blackouts*, it does so with a short list of instruments—just the nominal drum machine and a pulsing guitar line in the background plus some light synthesizer work. What sets it apart from music that came before is a steadfast refusal to follow the popular notions of development in melody and harmony. Instead, *E2-E4* continues working through similar territory for close to an hour with an application to trance-state electronics missing from most of the music that preceded it. Though the various components repeat themselves incessantly, it's how they interact and build that determines the sound—and that's the essence of most electronic dance music, that complex interplay between several repetitive elements. —*John Bush*

## Gramm (Jan Jelinek)
*Producer / Experimental Dub, Experimental Techno, Ambient Techno*
Jan Jelinek's productions as Gramm and Farben are some of the warmest examples in what is usually a very cold style of electronics, the heavily experimental German dub scene. Based in Berlin, Jelinek debuted with three Farben singles released on Klang Electronik during 1998-99. After signing to David Moufang's Source Records, he recorded his first LP (*Personal Rock*) as Gramm. —*John Bush*

● **Personal Rock** / Jan. 11, 2000 / Source ◆◆◆◆
Though many producers have pushed forward the clicks-and-cuts style of experimental ambience developed by German experimentalists Oval (among others), few have been able to match their knack for making abstract cuts into pieces of undeniable beauty. Jan Jelinek's first LP as Gramm is one of the precious few, and it's obvious from the opener "Legends/Nugroove," a track that drifts along with droning, melancholy synth accompanying the various extreme-frequency percussion detritus in the track. While the beats are slightly more straight-ahead on "Type Zwei" (another highlight), the atmospherics are similarly down-tempo, nocturnal, and even dizzying at times. Though they're stated simply and rarely vary from track to track, the synths are also extremely effective at creating a reflective mood. For all the abstract chill-out fans who need a bit more to dwell on than four-four or breakbeats, *Personal Rock* offers almost as much experimentation as beauty. —*John Bush*

## Grandmaster Flash (Joseph Saddler)
b. Jan. 1, 1958, Barbados, West Indies
*Producer, Leader, Arranger, DJ / Old School Rap, Electro, Club/Dance, Hip-Hop*
DJ Grandmaster Flash and his group the Furious Five were hip-hop's greatest innovators, transcending the genre's party-music origins to explore the full scope of its lyrical and sonic horizons. Flash was born Joseph Saddler in Barbados on January 1, 1958; he began spinning records as teen growing up in the Bronx, performing live at area dances and block parties. By age 19, while attending technical school courses in electronics during the day, he was also spinning on the local disco circuit; over time, he developed a series of groundbreaking techniques including "cutting" (moving between tracks exactly on the beat), "back-spinning" (manually turning records to repeat brief snippets of sound) and "phasing" (manipulating turntable speeds)—in short, creating the basic vocabulary which DJs continue to follow even today.

Flash did not begin collaborating with rappers until around 1977, first teaming with the legendary Kurtis Blow. He then began working with the Furious Five—rappers Melle Mel (Melvin Glover), Cowboy (Keith Wiggins), Kid Creole (Nathaniel Glover), Mr. Ness (Eddie Morris) and Rahiem (Guy Williams); the group quickly became legendary throughout New York City, attracting notice not only for Flash's unrivalled skills as a DJ but also for the Five's masterful rapping, most notable for their signature trading and blending of lyrics. Despite their local popularity, they did not record until after the Sugarhill Gang's smash "Rapper's Delight" proved the existence of a market for hip-hop releases; Flash and the Five's debut, "Superrappin'," followed on the Enjoy label in 1979, and a year later they signed with the famed Sugar Hill Records.

Grandmaster Flash and the Furious Five's Sugar Hill debut, 1980's "Freedom," reached the Top 20 on national R&B charts on its way to selling over 50,000 copies; its follow-up, "Birthday Party," was also a hit. 1981's "The Adventures of Grandmaster Flash on the Wheels of Steel" was the group's first truly landmark recording, introducing Flash's "cutting" techniques to create a stunning sound collage from snippets of songs by Chic, Blondie and Queen. Flash and the Five's next effort, 1982's "The Message," was even more revelatory—for the first time, hip-hop became a vehicle not merely for bragging and boasting but for trenchant social commentary, with Melle Mel delivering a blistering rap detailing the grim realities of life in the ghetto. The record was a major critical hit, and it was an enormous step in solidifying rap as an important and enduring form of musical expression.

Following 1983's anti-cocaine polemic "White Lines," relations between Flash and Melle Mel turned ugly, and the rapper soon left the group, forming a new unit also dubbed the Furious Five. After a series of Grandmaster Flash solo albums including 1985's *They Said It Couldn't Be Done*, 1986's *The Source* and 1987's *Ba-Dop-Boom-Bang*, he reformed the original Furious

Five line-up for a charity concert at Madison Square Garden; soon after, the reconstituted group recorded a new LP, 1988's *On the Strength*, which earned a lukewarm reception from fans and critics alike. Another reunion followed in 1994, when Flash and the Five joined a rap package tour also including Kurtis Blow and Run-D.M.C. A year later, Flash and Melle Mel also appeared on Duran Duran's cover of "White Lines." —*Jason Ankeny*

#### The Message / 1982 / Sugar Hill ♦♦♦♦
Grandmaster Flash & The Furious Five merged the Afrocentric consciousness expressed by such early rappers as Gil Scott-Heron and The Last Poets with b-boy production to create "The Message," an all-time rap anthem. It was the focal point of this LP, which also included "It's Nasty" and "Scorpio," two other strong cuts that might have been winners on their own. Unfortunately, rather than a starting point, this album proved to be their ultimate peak. —*Ron Wynn*

#### The Source / 1986 / Elektra ♦♦♦
Grandmaster Flash's follow-up to *The Message* was his first minus The Furious Five. Things weren't the same from a compositional or performance standpoint, as his raps seemed weaker and his rhymes almost devoid of crispness, humor or insight. Only "Ms. Thang" and "Street Scene" offered any hint of the incisiveness or vision depicted in "The Message." —*Ron Wynn*

#### Da Bop Boom Bang / 1987 / Elektra ♦♦
The fire was gone and the imagination and flair diminished on this 1987 album. Grandmaster Flash sounded too tired on such cuts as "Big Black Caddy," "Get Yours," and "U Know What Time It Is" to recapture the spirit and bristling intensity that made "The Message" an anthem. He was sadly more effective doing nonsense like "Them Jeans." —*Ron Wynn*

#### On the Strength / 1988 / Elektra ♦
Grandmaster Flash & The Furious Five tried to regroup on this 1988 release, but old school hip-hop had been lapped by the charge of the new school. There was little interest or response to such cuts as "Tear The Roof Off" and "Boy Is Dope," while "Fly Girl" and "Magic Carpet Ride" sounded dated and weary. —*Ron Wynn*

#### Greatest Hits / 1989 / Sugar Hill ♦♦♦♦
Flash was the DJ and the Furious Five were the best multiple rappers around, moving from the music's low-rent dance origins (it was Flash who began cutting in repeated portions of other records) and party spirit to the "message" approach that took over in the mid '80s, prefigured in "The Message." Much of what came later started here. —*William Ruhlmann*

#### ♠ Message from Beat Street: The Best of Grandmaster Flash / Apr. 19, 1994 / Rhino ♦♦♦♦♦
Grandmaster Flash was one of the most important, groundbreaking rap artists of the early '80s, and all of his most important records—with and without Melle Mel and the Furious Five—are collected on this essential 11-track disc, which includes the classic tracks "The Message" and "White Lines (Don't Don't Do It)." —*Stephen Thomas Erlewine*

#### Adventures of Grandmaster Flash: More of the Best / Jul. 1996 / Rhino ♦♦♦♦
Although many of Grandmaster Flash's best, biggest, and most groundbreaking work was compiled on *Message from Beat Street: The Best Of*, *The Adventures of Grandmaster Flash: More of the Best* is necessary for any comprehensive rap collection. The rest of Grandmaster Flash's most important singles, many of which have not appeared on compact disc before, are coralled onto this single-disc. On the whole, the album concentrates on the group's latter-day efforts for Elektra Records, but the cream of the album is the handful of singles for Sugarhill, including the pioneering "The Adventures of Grandmaster Flash on the Wheels of Steel," which presents the group at its freshest and most innovative. Some of the Elektra recordings are a little rote and by-the-book, but the Sugarhill songs help make this an essential purchase. —*Stephen Thomas Erlewine*

#### Adventures on the Wheels of Steel / 1999 / Sugarhill/Sequel ♦♦♦♦
For old-school fanatics who need still more Sugar Hill material, even after Rhino's massive five-disc set *The Sugar Hill Records Story*, Sequel packaged a three-disc box of material recorded by Grandmaster Flash and the Furious Five (plus a few cuts headed by Grandmaster Melle Mel). *Adventures on the Wheels of Steel* spans all the way from their earliest, pre-Sugar Hill recordings (the great singles "Super Rappin' No. 1" and "Flash to the Beat") to the mid-'80s material recorded after Grandmaster Flash split from Sugar Hill (both he and Melle Mel headed collectives composed of former members of the Furious Five). Of course, anyone even vaguely interested in this set is already going to own quite a few of these tracks, from the big Furious Five hits "The Message" and "White Lines" to much-anthologized classics like "Birthday Party," "New York New York," "The Showdown," "Scorpio," and "Message II (Survival)." Where this collection really begins to excel, and attract collectors, is the large number of rarities included. Sure, most old-school fans have "The Adventures of Grandmaster Flash on the Wheels of Steel," but how many have even heard Melle Mel's 1984 update "The New Adventures of Melle Mel"? And the Furious Five were well-known for their social critiques, but after Grandmaster Flash left the fold the group continued to record solid message tracks like "Jesse" (for Jesse Jackson's 1984 presidential campaign), the con-man game "Hustlers Convention," and "Vice." Truth to tell, there are only a pair of unreleased tracks on *Adventures on the Wheels of Steel*, but at least half of these 34 tracks have never been seen on compact disc. —*John Bush*

## Mike Grant

*Producer, DJ / Techno, House*

At the end of the '90s, Mike Grant re-emerged as one of the leading figures in Detroit's growing house scene after spending the majority of the decade and late '80s pursuing other ambitions. When Grant's fresh Moods & Grooves label began raising more than a few eyebrows with its catalog of releases by many of Detroit's best house producers—as well as many other soulful non-Detroit artists such as G Flame & Mr. G and Brian Harden—few knew that he has been a key figure in the Motor City's early to mid-'80s electronic dance scene as a talented DJ. His musical career began at an early age, influenced by Detroit's fledging music scene and his uncle, the general manager at a local R&B/dance radio station, WKWM. By 1980, the young Grant had joined a DJ collective known as Men of Music while become close friends with schoolmate Blake Baxter. Grant and Baxter began swapping DJ tactics and mix tapes, with Grant eventually joining Baxter's DJ group, the Beat Sound Company. A few years later, in 1983, Grant was scoring club residencies in Detroit alongside legends such as Ken Collier and also managed to make appearances on *The Scene*, a video dance show on WGPR alongside other local superstars such as Jeff Mills. During this mid-'80s era, Grant's reputation as one of the city's top DJs led to eventual friendships and partnerships with many of that eras other top DJs, most notably future techno legends Eddie Fowlkes, Derrick May, and Juan Atkins. During the summer of 1985, he became a member of Detroit's first radio mix show, *Street Beat*, where alongside his other talented peers, the foundation for what would later become early Detroit techno was ultimately formed.

Yet while Atkins, May, Mills, and Kevin Saunderson began creating the first techno records in the mid to late '80s—and becoming global legends in the process—Grant stayed true to his decision to join the military. During this time, he continued to DJ on the military base and in Seattle, where he practically introduced the sounds of Detroit techno to the unsuspecting West Coast. Following his time in the military, Grant then studied telecommunications in Chicago and began his career in this same field, while occasionally returning to his hometown for the occasional performance. In the late '90s, he planned his return, beginning with a recording as Black Noise on Metroplex Records, titled "Nature of the Beast." This dark, monstrous techno record renewed interest, cumulating with its inclusion on mix CDs such as Juan Atkins' *Wax Trax! Mastermix* and DJ T-1000's *Live Sabotage*. But it wasn't techno that Grant would soon find recognition with but rather the soulful grooves of house music. Instead of just DJing and producing tracks, he went to the lengths of starting his own label, Moods & Grooves, and began releasing the work of his peers—such as Alton Miller and Brett Dancer—as well as his own music. By mid-2000, the label had received substantial acclaim—including a high-profile appearance by Grant at the landmark *Detroit Electronic Music Festival*—and plans were underway to start additional labels focusing on techno and urban sounds. —*Jason Birchmeier*

#### ● It's a Detroit Thing... [EP] / May 17, 1999 / Moods & Grooves ♦♦♦♦
As his debut on his own Moods & Grooves label, Mike Grant's *It's a Detroit Thing...* offers two lengthy sides of soulful music, each with an accompanying piece of music. The A-side features "Hypnotize," a tech-

feeling track with the funky dancefloor percussion of deep house that features a truly haunting vocal sample ("music in my dreams"). An accompanying reprise beginning with a short a cappella segment only adds to this song's allure. The B-side features "Sunlight," a serene synth-heavy track with an extending synth intro titled "Rest in Peace, My Brother" that seamlessly leads into "Sunlight." These two main tracks showcase a wonderful combination of tech-flavored synths and deep house rhythms, while also keeping creative DJs in mind with the accompanying reprise and intro. —*Jason Birchmeier*

## Chris Gray

b. Nov. 13, 1970, Greenwood, MS
*Producer / Jazz-House, Club/Dance, House*
The productions of deep house expert and Chicago historian-of-sorts Chris Gray tug at the same compelling heartstrings as classic producers like Larry Heard and Marshall Jefferson. Inspired by Heard as well as Blaze, Ron Trent and the Wamdue Project, Gray grew up in Mississippi completely unaware of developments in the Windy City. After his cousin passed him an early house mix tape in 1987, he began listening to the music intently. Three years later, he had formed the Deephouse Projekt, an information-gathering source about the genesis of house music in Chicago. Gray graduated from Mississippi State University in 1992, and moved to Chicago to begin working on production. His first two EPs, *The Moonchildren* and *Very Moody*, were statements of purpose reflecting a deep appreciation for Heard classics like "Can You Feel It" and "Mystery of Love." Both appeared on Britain's Freetown/Subwoofer Records, and Gray's 1997 debut LP *A Deeper Level of Understanding* was also given a British release via Music Is...Records. He recorded for American labels like DC 10, providing remixes for Kevin Elliott, Greg Cash and Larry Heard himself (on *Dance 2000, Part 3*). Gray's sophomore album *Fish & Luvconfushun* was released in mid-1998. One year later, *Emotional Distortion* appeared on Deep 4 Life. —*John Bush*

**A Deeper Level of Understanding** / May 19, 1997 / Music Is... ♦♦♦♦

**Fish & Luvconfushun** / Jun. 29, 1998 / Kickin'/Fragmented ♦♦♦♦
A mild, jazzy trip through deep house with plenty of sweeping science-fiction synth along for the ride, Chris Gray's *Fish & Luvconfushun* includes several highlights—"All the Love," "Who 2 Luv" and the title track. —*John Bush*

● **Emotional Distortion** / May 31, 1999 / Deep 4 Life ♦♦♦♦
One of the best of Chicago's throwback house producers, Chris Gray pushes it to another level with his third full-length *Emotional Distortion*. The title is perfect for Gray's heart-breaking style of production—heavy on the minor-chord synthesizer fills long a trademark of Chicago's best producers. Though the 14 tracks never range too far outside the boundaries of jazz-house, highlights such as "Undoubted Luv," "As the Sun Sets," and the title track make for pure musical bliss. —*John Bush*

## Green Velvet (Curtis Alan Jones)

b. Apr. 26, 1968, Chicago, IL
*Producer, DJ / Progressive Trance, Tech-House, Progressive House, Club/Dance, House*
Green Velvet, initially created by house don Cajmere (aka Curtis Jones) as an outlet for his non-vocal productions and frequent DJing gigs, grew to become even more popular than the man himself, thanks to club singles like "Preacher Man," "Answering Machine" and "The Stalker." Each were infectious, undeniably fun records with simple vocal taglines and a wonderful sense of humor. Jones, who had nurtured the Chicago house renaissance of the '90s with his Cajual Records, gained immense success in 1993 with the Cajmere single "Brighter Days" (vocals by Dajae). Later that year, he formed the sub-label Relief mostly for instrumental tracks by himself and others.

Besides releases from DJ Sneak, Gemini and Paul Johnson, Green Velvet figured on many of the early Relief singles, including its first, "Preacher Man" as well as "Flash" (also released on the British Open label), "The Stalker" and 1997's hilarious "Answering Machine." Jones began to do supplement his Green Velvet DJing schedule with quasi-live gigs as well, and released his first LP in 1999. His self-titled release on F-111 one year later compiled a dozen of his earlier club hits. [See Also: Cajmere] —*John Bush*

**Answering Machine [Single]** / Sep. 29, 1997 / Cajual ♦♦♦♦

**Preacher Man [Single]** / Jun. 15, 1998 / Musicman ♦♦♦

**Constant Chaos** / Feb. 22, 1999 / Musicman ♦♦♦♦
The first Green Velvet full-length takes a musical bed formed from Kraftwerk and Gary Numan, electro-funk, and Chicago's mechanistic jacking house craze to frame Cajmere's fascinating vocal concerns—which range from emotionless intonations to much more emotive yelling. The bizarre song material balances tech-apocalypse ("Save the World," "Technology's Out of Control") and paranoid musings on all manner of occurrences related to alien encounters ("Abduction") and love life ("Thoughts," "Strange"). Though none of the previous Green Velvet club favorites are reprised for his album, Cajmere has created a raft of future classics, all along the same lines. —*John Bush*

● **Green Velvet** / Apr. 4, 2000 / Warner Brothers ♦♦♦♦
If you happen to be a house fan who's attempted in vain to turn someone on to the form with failing results, a couple spins of *Green Velvet* just might do the trick. This 2000 release through Warner dance subsidiary F-111 ties up some of his more accessible tracks throughout the previous years, and due to its wide-open distribution channels, it's the easiest work of the man to find. To the average electronica fan—the one who's been limited to the likes of big beat and trip-hop, at least—the most distinctive aspect of Green Velvet's tracks would be his monologues and skit-type "episodes." His production skills have always been highly regarded, but it's the always *hilarious* goings-on through the likes of "Flash," "Answering Machine," "Water Molecule," and "Abduction" that might reel in the house-phobes. Repeated listening will likely make the listener appreciate the actual musicality within. House might not typically feature instantly grabby hooks like Fatboy Slim and the Chemical Brothers, or the torpid headphone symphonies of Tricky and Portishead, but there's plenty of house that can thrill without benefit of the dancefloor.

"Flash" (from 1995) takes the parents of ravers on a guided tour through "Club Bad," wherein Velvet points out the various deviant things that the kids get up to without supervision. "This is not the thing to do!" "Answering Machine" outlines a *really* bad week for the producer. From Monday through the weekend, he gets a daily phone message—each of them a bummer. A girlfriend informs him that the baby isn't his, so the engagement ring won't be necessary; his landlord informs him of impending eviction ("The naked girl that was running down the hall last week didn't help."); his psychic friend directs him to *never* leave the apartment; a girlfriend-stealing mate phones to let him know that the party he threw at the producer's apartment was the bomb. "The Stalker" sounds like part two of Kevin Saunderson's obsessive Reese track "Just Another Chance." Where Saunderson merely seemed like an in-heat, deep-breathing lover bent on infatuation, the predator in "The Stalker" has lost it, sounding completely demented and detached from reality.

Musically, the tracks are just as satisfying, if not more so. Though his production frequently gains positive comparisons to the mid-to-late '80s mind-emptying/machinist jack tracks, Green Velvet also dips into the electronic side of late '70s/early '80s post-punk and early Prince. The driving, perverse nature of "Red Light" fits comfortably between the Normal's "Warm Leatherette" and Soft Cell's "Sex Dwarf," and musically sits in the company of Suicide's second album. The programmed percussion on "Thoughts" is straight out of *Purple Rain*-era Prince, and "Destination Unknown"'s opening throbs are an update on the ones heard on "Dirty Mind." These highlights hardly scratch the surface—the compilation is an endless barrage of bright spots, surely enough to entertain and convert house-phobes and definitely a concise way to please the already informed. Most definitely the renaissance Superman of the house scene, Green Velvet is deserving of any Chemicals worshipper or Moby-phile. Don't let the yellow feather Mohawk intimidate you. —*Andy Kellman*

## Jeff Greinke

*Percussion, Producer / Dark Ambient, Electro-Acoustic, Ambient*
Electro-acoustic composer Jeff Greinke is, like similar-sounding artists Robert Rich and Vidna Obmana, one of the younger contemporary principals of space music, approaching production and composition with an architect's feel for context, depth, and movement. Like many of his contemporaries (particularly in North America), Greinke was producing introspective, experimental electronic music many years prior to its recent popularization in ambient and isolationist electronica, releasing much of his

most significant work either on cassette or through tiny independent labels with limited distribution. Currently based in Seattle, Greinke studied meteorology at Penn State and began producing and performing electronic music in 1980. Working at first in an academic setting with extensive gear at his disposal, Greinke opted instead to assemble his own, comparatively spartan studio. Influenced by the soundscape experiments of composers such as Brian Eno and David Moss (particularly the latter's *Terrains*), Greinke began integrating thin, sweeping electronics with heavily treated samples and sound effects, percussion, and extensive use of digital and analog effects, giving his music a spatial depth which many have compared favorably with Eno's *On Land*. More recently, Greinke has incorporated an increasingly prominent rhythmic focus, filling in the more static approach of his early recordings with heavier instrumentation and percussion. As a solo artist, Greinke has recorded a number of albums for Multimood, Silent, and his own label, Intrepid, which he formed with artist/sculptor/producer and frequent collaborator Rob Angus in 1982. He has contributed tracks to numerous dark/industrial ambient and experimental/electro-acoustic compilations, alongside artists such as Rich, Obmana, DJ Spooky, Biosphere, Kathleen Amacher, Alan Lamb, and Michael Stearns. Additionally, Greinke is a founding member of the 4th world ethno-ambient/jazz quartet Land, who have recorded a number of albums for the Australian Extreme label. Also a visual artist of some note, Greinke has exhibited his photography (which also graces many of his album covers) and composed soundtracks for film and video. —*Sean Cooper*

● **Cities in Fog** / 1985 / Projekt: Archive ♦♦♦♦
This double-disc reissue by Projekt includes Greinke's debut album from 1985 (originally released on his own Intrepid label) along with the newly recorded *Cities of Fog 2*. Though the original lacks the accomplished sound-layering techniques of Greinke's later work, it possesses an uncanny flair for mood, texture and depth of recording. The new material is in much the same dark ambient vein, thogh "Melt" features some dustbin percussion lines. —*Jason Ankeny*

**Changing Skies** / 1990 / ♦♦♦
Utilizing his uncanny skills for sculpting sound, Jeff Greinke creates strange new worlds of raging alien beauty where he submerges his listeners into atmospheres that throb with exotic rhythms and shimmer and flow like mercury. Mysterious, sensual, etheric, melancholy and sometimes foreboding, *Changing Skies* is sure to please those who appreciate and enjoy the likes of Harold Budd, Brian Eno, Mychael Danna and Steve Roach. —*Backroads Music/Heartbeats*

**Lost Terrain** / 1992 / Silent ♦♦♦
This 1992 entry from Jeff Greinke is strongly suggestive of some of the works of Harold Budd and the cooler ambient pieces of Brian Eno. The often opaque shades of "Changing Skies," his previous release, give way here to culturally flavored hues that drift through dreamlike states with similar theme variations. A journey into night, *Lost Terrain* has the feeling of exploring forgotten landscapes of both inner and outer worlds. The first cut, "Terrain of Memory," will strike a sympathetic chord with those who like Budd's *The White Arcades* in its cool, dark ambience. "The Cry," with its Indonesian-influenced percussion, sharpens the senses, like walking into the pitch-black entrance of a strange forest at dusk. Fans of Eno's *Ambient 4: On Land* will like "The Moor" in all of its deep-space/alien grandeur. "River of Wood" couches the listener in an almost psychedelic sea of bamboo percussion and voice, while "Falling Away" touches with gentle strokes of synthesized moonlight, lulling us into the twilight of consciousness. This is truly an album for intrepid masters of introspection. —*Heartbeats*

**In Another Place** / 1993 / Linden Music ♦♦♦♦
This release marked a major step forward in the ongoing evolution of Jeff Greinke's electronic music. Where there was once a predominance of smoky haze there is a delicate luminosity and playfulness, with a new feeling of freshness and vitality that never surfaced on his previous releases. Even when he applies his characteristic treated piano and synthesizer to the gothic romanticism of the title cut, his hands convey a greater level of confident sensitivity and technical precision. Along with these stylistic changes one can detect more "heart" in Greinke's performance. There is less of the "alien" and more of the "human" to connect with this time around. —*Backroads Music/Heartbeats*

## The Grid

f. 1988, London, England
*Group / Electronica, Club/Dance, Techno, Acid House*
The Grid formed in the late '80s when Richard Norris—who collaborated with Psychic TV on the group's acid-house album *Jack the Tab*—hooked up with ex-Soft Cell member Dave Ball. The duo recorded the single "Floatation" in 1990 with vocalist Sacha; the debut album *Electric Head* appeared the same year, fusing the best of late-'80s house and techno into a poppy yet danceable mix. Follow-up *4,5,6* (1992) included contributions from Sun Ra and Robert Fripp, among others. Ball & Norris rode the crest of their British hit single "Swamp Thing" for the 1994 album *Evolver*, their slickest and most focused yet. *Music for Dancing* followed one year later. —*John Bush*

**Electric Head** / 1990 / East West ♦♦
Powered by "Floatation," the debut album assembles the Grid's house/techno inspirations with a pop blueprint for success. —*John Bush*

● **4,5,6** / 1994 / Deconstruction ♦♦♦♦
Much work as remixers provoked Norris & Ball to look for co-conspirators on their second album; consequently they reeled in vocalists like Yello's Dieter Meier and Faust's Dagmar Krause—along with helpers Robert Fripp and Phil Manzanera. The result has an even broader range than the debut, but still holds together beautifully. —*John Bush*

**Evolver** / 1995 / Deconstruction ♦♦
The huge success of "Swamp Thing" proved that the Grid had arrived, and *Evolver* is the result: a confident, focused album that encompasses the duo's influences but nevertheless stakes out new ground. —*John Bush*

**Music for Dancing** / Oct. 1995 / Deconstruction ♦♦♦

## Groove Armada

f. London, England
*Group / Electronica, Ambient Techno*
London's dance duo Groove Armada consists of Tom Findlay and Andy Cato. The group formed in the mid-'90s after being introduced by Cato's girlfriend and soon started their own club, also named Groove Armada (after a '70s discotheque), which featured their spinning. By 1997 they released a handful of singles, including "4 Tune Cookie" and "At the River;" their debut album *Northern Star* followed the next year. 1999 saw the release of *Vertigo*, which made the top 20 of the British charts and silver status the UK. The album's singles achieved similar heights, including "I See You Baby," which was remixed by Fatboy Slim. The group followed this success with a stint as Elton John's opening band and the US release of *Vertigo* in early 2000. An album of remixes followed shortly after, featuring post-productions by DJ Icey and Tim "Love" Lee —*Heather Phares*

**Northern Star** / Mar. 9, 1998 / Tummy Touch ♦♦♦
This is what happens when you let George Clinton fans start experimenting with ambient house. True—unlike what their name probably implies, Groove Armada stumble off much more into funk's flamboyant territory than groove's hypnotic subtlety, which actually isn't so bad. Because here in the band's debut album, *Northern Star*, such genre tweaking works nearly every time. You get the primal rhythms of "Entrance to Zanzibar" or the Air-like French house of "Dirty Listening," and it sounds soothing as well as unique. It's as if Ninja Tune's mischievous ambient artists (Funki Porcini, The Irresistible Force, etc.) were reinforced by small spikes of traditional melodies instead of just "quirky" samples. The album does tend to shilly-shally by repeating such tricks (the less said about "M2 Many," the better)—possibly because the straight-ahead spectral ambience or hands-in-the-air booty shaking haven't bitten the band just yet. Even worse, why Groove Armada's majestic "At the River" is strangely absent from the album is anybody's guess (thankfully, this oversight was rectified later in the band's *Vertigo*), which means that as a statement, *Northern Star* might overall leave one with a plain aftertaste, but the smart laidback funk of the album will surely have most curious palettes satisfied. —*Dean Carlson*

● **Vertigo** / May 24, 1999 / Pepper ♦♦♦♦
Groove Armada's second album finds the pair expanding on the sonic range of 1998's *Northern Star*, spreading out to Franco-electronic pop ("Dusk, You and Me"), big-beat techno ("If Everybody Looked the Same"), and laidback funk grooves (the masterpiece titled "At the River"). Though it often seems

they're throwing change-ups more to show listeners what they can do, *Vertigo* achieves the effortless grace of a varied repertoire. —*John Bush*

**Back to Mine** / Apr. 4, 2000 / Ultra ♦♦
It must be slightly frustrating to be Groove Armada. With the Fatboy Slim remix of "I See You Baby" slowly becoming Groove Armada's unrepresentative single that everybody seems to know, this personal installment into the *Back to Mine* mix series is where the heart of the band beats the most. No, this mix album is not a quick-draw of all sorts of proto-stupid, club-friendly gunplay to make people shake that ass. Instead it's an opportunity to help once again show people that the band is more about putting their firearms on the nightstand, resting one's behind on a comfy couch, and putting on some slow, amorous grooves. For starters, choosing songs like their great rhythmic romantic take on A Tribe Called Quest's "Description of a Fool" or the effective beats of Tony D can do nothing but help. Really, how many other bands would later holster Al Green right next to Roots Manuva? About midway through, though, it does delve into some seriously trite slap-jazz. These excursions (think BBG and Sir Raymond Mang) show just how dangerous it can be for musicians in the trip-hop realm to veer perilously close to Kenny G instead of Tricky. Regardless, *Back to Mine* is generally a mix that traces around an interesting idea: maybe the more trip-hop stylings of musicians have more in common with, say, Barry White than Brian Eno? That might not be so wrong. Because if the mainstream world considers Groove Armada to be the type of musicians to get to watch somebody wobble their buttocks, their actual mentality is more about the music to play after you get that person to go home with you. It wouldn't be so bad if more pacifists like Groove Armada were sheriffs from time to time. —*Dean Carlson*

## Groove Theory
f. 1991, New York, NY
*Group / Club/Dance, Urban, House, Soul, Hip-Hop*
Groove Theory is a duo consisting of former songwriter and session vocalist Amel Larrieux, a New York native, and former Mantronix rapper Bryce Wilson. When they met in 1991 through a mutual friend, both were dissatisfied with their musical careers: Larrieux's voice wasn't capable of the Whitney Houston/Mariah Carey vocal gymnastics expected of black female vocalists, and Wilson wanted a chance to put his unused production talents to work. The two each recognized in the other a chance to express themselves musically in ways they had been looking for, and Groove Theory was born. The group's music is calmer than most hip-hop, concerning itself with romance and sensuality. Their self-titled debut album appeared in 1995. —*Steve Huey*

● **Groove Theory** / Nov. 1995 / Epic ♦♦♦
Vocalist Amel Larrieux (Groove Connection) and producer Bryce Wilson (of Mantronix) teamed up as Groove Theory for an album of cool, laid-back soul/house, rooted in R&B and hip-hop. From the delicious trip-pop singles "Baby Luv" and "Tell Me" to more expansive material on "Good 2 Me" and "You're Not the 1" there's a lot to be excited about on this album, not least of which is Larrieux's seductive vocals. —*John Bush*

## Grooverider (Roger Bingham)
b. Apr. 16, 1967, Dulwich, London, England
*Producer, DJ / Jungle/Drum'N'Bass, Club/Dance*
Hardcore/drum'n'bass DJ and producer Grooverider has over the years become almost synonymous with the London drum'n'bass scene. A DJ for over a decade spinning everything from soul-jazz and acid-house to hip-hop and hardcore breakbeat, "Grooverider the Hardcore Provider," as he's come to be known, has followed the evolution of drum'n'bass up from its earliest roots in breakbeat techno and happy hardcore on through to contemporary styles such as ambient and techstep. A residing DJ at some of London's biggest-name clubs (including Rage and his own long-running, highly lauded Metalheadz night at Blue Note), Grooverider's influence, not only on the sound but also the politics and ideology of jungle, is probably rivaled only by Goldie's (and then with not nearly the flamboyance). A DJ since his early teens, Rider (born Roger Bingham) spun everything from acid jazz and deep house with the South London Sound System and pirate station FAZE FM before landing a residency with Rage, an institution of early-'90s hardcore thrown under the umbrella of London's biggest weekly, Heaven. Fired from an apprenticeship in accounting when he couldn't make it jibe with nights out spinning 'til 4 a.m., Grooverider went full-time with DJing when he was hired on at Rage, and began producing music shortly after.

Rider recorded his first tracks (as Codename John) for his newly launched Prototype label in late 1993, at the height of the reign of ragga and jump-up. Fusing breakbeat with elements of rave, acid, and techno, Grooverider's approach on tracks such as "Dreams of Heaven" and "Deep Inside" pushed for a crossover of jungle's most important historical constituents—hardstep, darkside, and the music's hardcore past—an approach soon popularized by so-called "techstep" artists such as Origin Unknown, Ed Rush, and Boymerang. In time, Prototype would become synonymous with futuristic dancefloor drum'n'bass that nonetheless refuses the conservatism most often associated with the dancefloor. Early releases on the label include Ed Rush's "Kilimanjaro," "Threshold" by Dillinja's Cybotron project, and Boymerang's massive "Still" (tracks from these releases all appear on Prototype's first full-length release, *The Prototype Years*). Grooverider signed a non-exclusive recording deal with Sony subsidiary Higher Ground in 1996—*The Prototype Years* was the first fruit of that, followed in 1998 by his proper solo debut *Mysteries of Funk*. Prototype remains active as well. —*Sean Cooper*

**Grooverider's Hardstep Selection, Vol. 2** / 1995 / Kickin ♦♦♦
This Grooverider-mixed collection of ragga and darkstep drum'n'bass includes tracks by Tom & Jerry, Dillinja, and J Majik. —*Keith Farley*

**Grooverider Presents: The Prototype Years** / 1997 / Higher Ground/Proto ♦♦♦♦
A definitive compilation of solid, consistently quality dancefloor tracks from the Rider's own Prototype imprint. Featuring a score of classic cuts from Boymerang, Lemon D, Ed Rush, and John B., as well as new material from Rush and Fierce, Optical, Matrix, Dillinja's Cybotron project, and Groove himself (as Codename John), *The Prototype Years* is a high-water mark of progressive, dancefloor-oriented drum'n'bass, with tight, chrome-dipped production and superior, innovative arrangements obtaining across the board. Although the artists' predilection for the dark side may at first appear simply *du temps* (the album was, after all, released in early 1997, during the height of techstep's reign in the clubs), each track maintains a notable degree of focus and integrity, drawing enough from each of the corners of the breakbeat world to remain just this side of trendiness. The CD version adds bonus tracks from the Prototype catalog, as well as a second disc mixed by Groove himself, also featuring the previously unavailable Dom & Roland remix of Boymerang's "Still." Nothing short of essential. —*Sean Cooper*

● **Mysteries of Funk** / Sep. 28, 1998 / Higher Ground ♦♦♦♦
After ten years of being the best drum'n'bass mixer around as well as running his own stellar label, jungle godfather Grooverider finally released an album of his own, and it's worthy of the hype. While the beats on *Mysteries of Funk* are reminiscent of tracks recorded for his Prototype label by Matrix Fierce and Optical (the latter did much engineering work on the album), Grooverider has made them his own with atmospheres dedicated to the science-fiction end of jazz and fusion. "Rainbows of Colour" and "Imagination" are expansive four-minute diva tracks, and while there is an excellent darker track ("Where's Jack the Ripper"), *Mysteries of Funk* succeeds most when Groove is wrapping his drum'n'bass two-step around a distinctly mainstream attention to house and fusion ambience. It's wholly an artist record (whereas *The Prototype Years* was a tracks collection), but *Mysteries of Funk* succeeds on all its points. —*John Bush*

## Scott Grooves (Patrick Scott)
*Producer / Jazz-House, Tech-House, Club/Dance, Techno, House*
Yet another young name to add to the roster of soulful Detroit techno proteges who work in elements of house, Scott Grooves played keyboards for Kevin Saunderson's Inner City before working on production under his own name, with singles and an LP for Soma Records. While Grooves was growing up, his jazz-musician father influenced him to begin playing drums, keyboards and guitar. Though he continued to stress his musicianship, Grooves' time with Inner City and working in Record Time—Detroit's prime shop for techno—inspired him towards techno instead of jazz. After Scotland's Soma Records released his debut single "A New Day" in 1997, the following year brought a full-length, *Pieces of a Dream*. —*John Bush*

● **Pieces of a Dream** / 1998 / Soma ♦♦♦♦
Scott Grooves' long affinity for jazz comes through loud and clear on his debut album for Soma. Featuring an update of Wes Montgomery's "Bumpin'" on

Sunset" (here titled "Bumpin' on the Underground") and a soaring version of Lonnie Liston Smith's classic "Expansions" (recorded with Roy Ayers on vibes), *Pieces of a Dream* incorporates soul, disco, funk and house into a primal brew of jazz-fusion. "The Mothership Re-Connection" incorporates a live Parliament gig—with the permission of George Clinton himself, and recorded at his own Detroit Disc Studios—while the single "A New Day" translates an epic piano riff into a European dancefloor hit. All told, *Pieces of a Dream* is a soulful epic, just as noteworthy coming from Detroit as anywhere else. —*John Bush*

## Jephté Guillaume

b. Haiti
*Bass, Producer / Jazz-House, Club/Dance, House*

The burgeoning organic direction of deep house during the late '90s—which gathered influences from disco to jazz-funk to Brazilian jazz—was pushed along by Jephté Guillaume, not just a producer and vocalist but an in-demand bassist around New York's hip-hop and acid jazz scene since the early '90s. Born in Haiti, Guillaume moved to New York as a child, fleeing the Duvalier regime along with his family. Once settled, he began playing at an early age, learning bass while his brother Donald worked on drums. By the beginning of the '90s, the two began recording with the Haitian-music group Rara Machine. Guillaume also played with the world collective Vodu 155, and with the post-bop acid jazz group Abstract Truth.

Amidst much work in group situations, Jephté Guillaume also began recording on his own and released his debut single, "One Respect," in 1994 for the house label Metropolitan. By 1997, "The Prayer" (his first single for Joe Claussell's *Spiritual Life Music*) became a massive underground house hit, driven by deep Latin vibes, acoustic guitar, and Guillaume's own vocals. Hot on its heels came a series of similar recordings ("Kanpé," "Lakou-A," and "Ibo Lele") for Spiritual Life, each balancing Guillaume's knowledge of Caribbean grooves with the increasingly organic feel of New York house (thanks in part to Claussell's popular club-night, *Body & Soul*). His album debut *Voyage of Dreams* appeared on Chrysalis in 1998. Most of Guillaume's Spiritual Life work was collected on the compilation, *Spiritual Life Music*. —*John Bush*

- **Voyage of Dreams** / Sep. 28, 1998 / Chrysalis ++++

## Gus Gus

f. 1995, Reykjavik, Iceland
*Group / Electronica, Alternative Dance, Indie Rock, Trip-Hop*

Being a quirky co-ed nine-piece from Reykjavik, Iceland, Gus Gus was almost bound to inspire comparisons to the Sugarcubes, though the onset of ten years caused the group to inherit the influences of electronic fuzz and trip-hop rhythms rather than the bout of post-punk lunacy which inspired the Sugarcubes during the late '80s. Begun as a cinema concern in early 1995 by filmmakers Stefán Árni and Siggi Kjartansson, the group was gradually expanded to include musicians such as DJ Herb Legowitz and programmer Biggi Thórarinsson as well as singer/songwriters Daníel Ágúst, Hafdís Huld and Magnús Jónsson (former actors all), a cinematographer (Steph) and a producer (Baldur Stefánsson). The band's decidedly indie sensibilities led to their signing by 4AD after a four-part series of dance mix EPs during 1996. Among a handful of groups in the late '90s with access to both close-knit dance circles as well as the notoriously uptight indie community, the group gained support from LFO (with Mark Bell's remix of "Believe"), and one of London's most celebrated DJ stores, Fat Cat Records, while playing their first date in England. Given a combined US/UK release due to 4AD's agreement with Warner Bros., their debut album *Polydistortion* hit the stores in April 1997. *This is Normal* followed in 1999, and one year later the anthology release *Gus Gus Vs. T-World* appeared. —*John Bush*

- **Polydistortion** / Apr. 8, 1997 / 4AD/Warner Brothers ++++

Taking dashes of the quirky pop on which their countrymen the Sugarcubes relied, Gus Gus nevertheless use more of a songwriter's approach to electronica and trip-hop on their debut album; though the rhythms and effects are delightfully abstract, most songs have a surprisingly tight lyrical structure holding them together. Because they are a nine-piece outfit, Gus Gus has almost as many songwriting combinations as there are tracks on the album, which proves to make *Polydistortion* a varied and wide-ranging album. Initial copies of the US album contained a second disc featuring four extra tracks, including the LFO remix of "Believe." —*John Bush*

**This Is Normal** / Apr. 27, 1999 / Warner Brothers ++++

Gus Gus' second album, *This Is Normal*, heralds their discovery that they are first and foremost a pop band. While the spacious, sophisticated electronica they developed on their debut (*Polydistortion*) is still evident, *This Is Normal*'s smooth, streamlined finish has more than a nodding acquaintance with dance-pop. Though *Normal* is certainly less weird than its predecessor, it remains floating outside of the mainstream, but swims a little closer to it. Looking to explore individual normality within the album's 11 tracks, Gus Gus' multiple singers and songwriters expound on sex, fame, youth and love. "Ladyshave" features sly vocals from Daniel Agust and a slightly kinky premise, while Hafdis Huld's breathy soprano elevates "Teenage Sensation," "Superhuman" and "Blue Mug" to an icy, remote beauty. As with *Polydistortion*, Gus Gus continues to be more convincing on their albums' quiet, introspective moments. The mannered chamber pop of "Bambi" and the pretty atmospherics of "Dominique" are among the highlights of *This Is Normal*, while dance-oriented songs like "Very Important People," "Starlovers" and "Love Vs. Hate" probably sound less flat and distant in one of the group's amazing multimedia concerts. The innovative beats and arrangements on Gus Gus' debut are missed here, but *This Is Normal* is still a fine blend of accessibility and invention. —*Heather Phares*

**Gus Gus Vs. T-World** / Apr. 18, 2000 / 4AD/beggar's banquet +++

Though this album is credited to the kings of Icelandic techno known as Gus Gus, it actually consists of tracks recorded in the mid-'90s by a duo consisting of Gus Gus charter members Herb Legowitz and Biggi Veira, who were known at that time as T-World. Although everything here is beat-driven and deeply informed by the Detroit techno and deep house traditions, the seven tracks on this disc are ultimately better suited to the chill-out room than the dance floor; the grooves on compositions like "Anthem" and "Earl Grey" are solid, yet the musical textures are consistently soft and warm rather than driving. "Purple," with its stuttering breakbeat and ethereal female vocal sample, comes closest to being a party anthem, while everything else moves in something approaching dreamtime. There's nothing especially innovative in this music, yet it seems to get more interesting the more you listen to it. —*Rick Anderson*

## A Guy Called Gerald (Gerald Simpson)

f. Feb. 16, 1967
*Producer, DJ / Jungle/Drum'N'Bass, Club/Dance, Acid House, House*

Mancunian house and techno innovator Gerald Simpson is the odd post-rave musician who's been able to find a successful voice in a wide variety of different styles. Starting with Chicago house and moving through Detroit techno, acid house, electro, hardcore techno, and currently drum'n'bass, Gerald's been an influential contributor to most of recent dance music's most important stopping points. Although his highest-profile moment came in the form of the late-'80s ubiquitous club hit "Voodoo Ray," Gerald's been widely recognized as an important force in the nascent London hardcore and jungle scenes, influencing key figures like Goldie, Dego, and Dillinja, and keeping the style moving forward beyond the more confrontational concerns of its early years.

Simpson's first recorded work was in collaboration with fellow Manchester group 808 State, whose early combinations of electro and hip-hop beats with elements of anthemic house and techno and slick production created some of UK acid house's earliest club staples. Simpson appeared on 808's debut, *Newbuild*, and co-wrote one of the group's biggest hits—"Pacific State"—although he was not credited (he got his jabs in later with a single titled "Specific Hate"). Leaving the group in the late '80s to pursue a solo career, Gerald's first blast was also his biggest—"Voodoo Ray"—which solidified his reputation in the clubs and landed him a major-label recording contract. After a string of moderately successful releases for Sony, Gerald was released from the label when they refused to release his album *High Life Low Profile*. Disappearing from the music scene for a few years, Gerald resurfaced with *28 Gun Bad Boy*, released on his own Juice Box label. The album was a mutational cobblestone on the way to full-blown drum'n'bass and continues to be namechecked to this day. Gerald released *Black Secret Technology* in 1995, and focused on his DJing schedule and occasional singles releases during the rest of the decade. Finally, in 2000, he released *Essence* on Studio !K7. —*Sean Cooper*

**Automanikk** / 1989 / Columbia ++++

A Guy Called Gerald's first solo album, recorded for the major label CBS/Columbia, is a journey through sampladelic acid-house with a few haunted melodies gained from his exposure to Detroit techno, notably on "Subscape" and "Eyes of Sorrow." The Motor City's own Derrick May and Carl Craig provide remixing on "FX (Mayday Upgrade)," while elsewhere Kraftwerk inspriations show up on "Automanikk" and he delivers a remixed version of "Voodoo Ray" named "Voodoo Ray Americas." *Automanikk* was an excellent exception to the many acid-house cash-ins littering the landscape around the turn of the decade. —*John Bush*

**28 Gun Bad Boy** / 1992 / Juicebox ✦✦
A bleak collection of post-rave hardcore with a minimalism and rhythmic focus clearly influential on current-day jungle. —*Sean Cooper*

★ **Black Secret Technology** / 1995 / Juicebox ✦✦✦✦✦
The first full-length release in a style that, like its close relatives hip-hop and techno, began as a 12" genre. The album laid much important groundwork for experimental junglists like Photek, Subtropic, and Goldie, with the styles more common rhythmic brashness informed by a bit of perspicacity, making for a measured, eminently listenable collection. —*Sean Cooper*

# H

## Bruce Haack
b. May 4, 1931
*Synthesizer, Producer / Obscuro, Computer Music, Educational, Space Age Pop, Electronic*

Bruce Haack was one of the most musically and lyrically inventive children's songwriters of the '60s and '70s. Despite—or perhaps because of—his intended audience, his music was unusually expressive, combining homemade analog synths, classical, country, pop and rock elements and surreal, idealistic lyrics. Haack's innovations and desire to teach still sound fresh, making his music a favorite with fans of analog synths and esoteric recordings. Contemporaries like Raymond Scott and followers like Luke Vibert and Add N to (X) championed his unique musical vision, which embraced concepts like "Powerlove" and turned household appliances into synthesizers and modulators.

This musical vision appeared at age 4, when Haack started picking out melodies on his family's piano, and expanded; by age 12, he gave piano lessons and played in country & western bands as a teen. His upbringing in the isolated mining town of Rocky Mountain House in Alberta, Canada gave Haack plenty of time to develop his musical gifts.

Seeking formal training to hone his ability, Haack applied to the University of Alberta's music program. Though that school rejected him because of his poor notation skills, at Edmonton University he wrote and recorded music for campus theater productions, hosted a radio show, and played in a band. He received a degree in psychology from the university; this influence was felt later on in songs that dealt with body language and the computer-like ways children absorb information.

On the merits of one of his theatrical scores, New York City's Juilliard School offered Haack the opportunity to study with composer Vincent Persichetti; thanks to a scholarship from the Canadian government, he headed to New York upon graduating from Edmonton in 1954. At Juilliard, Haack met a like-minded student, Ted "Praxiteles" Pandel, with whom he developed a lifelong friendship. However, his studies proved less sympathetic, and he dropped out of Juilliard just eight months later, rejecting the school's restrictive approach.

Throughout the rest of his career, Haack rejected restrictions of any kind, often writing several different kinds of music at one time. He spent the rest of the '50s scoring dance and theater productions, as well as writing pop songs for record labels like Dot and Coral. Haack's early scores, like 1955's *Les Etapes*, suggested the futuristic themes and experimental techniques Haack developed in his later works. Originally commissioned for a Belgian ballet, *Les Etapes* mixed tape samples, electronics, soprano and violin; the following year, he finished a musique concrète piece called *Lullaby for a Cat*.

As the '60s began, the public's interest in electronic music and synthesizers increased, and so did Haack's notoriety. Along with songwriting and scoring, Haack appeared on TV shows like *I've Got a Secret* and *The Tonight Show with Johnny Carson*, usually with Pandel in tow. The duo often played the Dermatron, a touch and heat-sensitive synthesizer, on the foreheads of guests; 1966's appearance on *I've Got a Secret* featured them playing 12 "chromatically pitched" young women.

Meanwhile, Haack wrote serious compositions as well, such as 1962's *Mass for Solo Piano*, which Pandel performed at Carnegie Hall, and a song for Rocky Mountain House's 50th anniversary. One of his most futuristic pieces, 1963's *Garden of Delights*, mixed Gregorian chants and electronic music and was one of Haack's favorites. Unfortunately, this work was never broadcast or released in its complete form.

Haack found another outlet for his creativity as an accompanist for children's dance teacher Esther Nelson. Perhaps inspired by his own lonely childhood, he and Nelson collaborated on educational, open-minded children's music. With Pandel, they started their own record label, Dimension 5, on which they released 1962's *Dance, Sing & Listen*. Two other records followed in the series, 1963's *Dance, Sing & Listen Again* and 1965's *Dance, Sing & Listen Again & Again*. Though the series included activity and story songs similar other children's records at the time, the music moves freely between country, medieval, classical and pop and mixes instruments like piano, synthesizers and banjo, and the lyrics deal with music history or provide instructions like "When the music stops, be the sound you hear," resulting in an often surreal collage of sounds and ideas.

The otherworldly quality of Haack's music was emphasized by the instruments and recording techniques he developed with the *Dance, Sing & Listen* series. Though he had little formal training in electronics, he made synthesizers and modulators out of any gadgets and surplus parts he could find, including guitar effects pedals and battery-operated transistor radios. Eschewing diagrams and plans, Haack improvised, creating instruments capable of 12-voice polyphony and random composition. Using these modular synthesizer systems, he then recorded with two two-track reel-to-reel decks, adding a moody tape echo to his already distinctive pieces.

As the '60s progressed and the musical climate became more receptive to his kind of whimsical innovation, Haack's friend, collaborator and business manager Chris Kachulis found mainstream applications for his musical wizardry. This included scoring commercials for clients like Parker Brothers' Games, Goodyear Tires, Kraft Cheese and Lincoln Life Insurance; in the process, Haack won two awards for his work. He also continued to promote electronic music on television, demonstrating how synthesizers work on *The Mr. Rogers Show* in 1968, and also released *The Way Out Record For Children* later that year.

Haack's records were about to get even more way-out, however: Kachulis did another important favor for his friend by introducing Haack to psychedelic rock. Acid rock's expansive nature was a perfect match for Haack's style, and in 1969 he released his first rock-influenced work, *The Electric Lucifer*. A concept album about the earth being caught in the middle of a war between heaven and hell, *The Electric Lucifer* features a heavy, driving sound complete with Moogs, Kachulis' singing, and Haack's homegrown electronics and unique lyrics, which deal with "Powerlove"—a force so strong and good that it will not only save mankind but Lucifer himself. Kachulis helped out once more by bringing Haack and *Lucifer* to the attention of Columbia Records, who released it as Haack's major-label debut.

As the '70s started, Haack's musical horizons continued expanding. After the release of *The Electric Lucifer*, he struck up a friendship with fellow composer and electronic music pioneer Raymond Scott. They collaborated and experimented with two of Scott's new instruments, the Clavivox and Electronium. Unfortunately, nothing remains of their collaboration, and though Scott gave Haack a Clavivox, he didn't record with it on his own. However, he did continue on *Lucifer's* rock-influenced musical with 1971's *Together*, an electronic pop album that marked his return to Dimension 5. Perhaps in an attempt to differentiate this work from his children's music, he released it under the name Jackpine Savage, the only time he used this pseudonym.

Haack continued making children's albums as well, including 1972's *Dance to the Music*, 1973's *Captain Entropy*, and 1974's *This Old Man*, which featured sci-fi versions of nursery rhymes and traditional songs. After relocating to Westchester, PA to spend more time with Pandel, Haack focused on children's music almost exclusively, writing music for Scholastic Magazine Records like "The Witches Vacation" and "Clifford the Small Red Puppy." He also released *Funky Doodle* and *Ebenezer Electric* (an electronic version of

Charles Dickens' *A Christmas Carol*) in 1976, but by the late '70s, his prolific output slowed; two works, 1978's *Haackula* and the following year's *Electric Lucifer Book II*, were never released.

However, *Haackula* seems to have inspired Haack's final landmark work, 1981's *Bite;* the albums share several song titles and a dark lyrical tone different from Haack's usually idealistic style. Though *Bite* is harsher than his other works, it features his innovative, educational touch: a thorough primer on electronics and synthesizers makes up a large portion of the liner notes, and Haack adds a new collaborator for this album, 13-year-old vocalist Ed Harvey.

Haack's failing health slowed Dimension 5's musical output in the early '80s, but Nelson and Pandel kept the label alive by publishing songbooks like *Fun to Sing* and *The World's Best Funny Songs*, and re-released selected older albums as cassettes, which are still available today. Haack died in 1988 from heart failure, but his label and commitment to making creative children's music survives. And while Dimension 5's later musical releases — mostly singalong albums featuring Nelson — may lack the iconoclastic spark of the early records, Nelson and Pandel's continued work reveals the depth of their friendship with Haack, a distinctive and pioneering electronic musician. —*Heather Phares*

### Dance Sing and Listen Again / 1964 / ♦♦♦

1962's *Dance, Sing & Listen* marks Bruce Haack's debut as a children's composer. The first part of the *Dance, Sing & Listen* series, the album includes medieval, country, classical and pop styles in its embrace, interpreting the songs with a mix of electronic and acoustic instruments. From the boogie-woogie of "Introduction" to the electronic-classical hybrid of "Medieval Dances," Haack's wide-ranging musical vision has free reign on *Dance, Sing & Listen*. "Sunflowers" is an activity song in which children imagine they are sunflowers, from seed to bloom; behind Esther Nelson's instructions, Haack provides fizzy, bubbling keyboard effects, a vaguely African guitar line and bongos as accompaniment. In other hands this might be a simple activity song; with Nelson and Haack's creative approach, it borders on sci-fi spoken word.

Similarly, tracks like "Eine Kleine Gebouncemusik" feature discussions between Nelson, Haack and the children they recorded the album with, resulting in a parallel-dimension version of *Kids Say the Darnedest Things*. The sprightly, keyboard-based "Gebouncemusik" is a quintessential Haack work, referencing Mozart's "Eine Kleine Nachtmusik" as well as Hindemith's concept of "gebrauchmusik," or "utility music," which can have a specific musical purpose or be played by anyone. Only Haack, however, could come up with such a unique array of elements and blend them into something even more distinctive. —*Heather Phares*

### The Way-Out Album for Children / 1968 / ♦♦♦♦

After a three-year drought of Dimension 5 releases, Bruce Haack, Esther Nelson and Ted Pandel returned in 1968 with *The Way Out Record for Children*. This album found the trio edging toward the acid rock-influenced direction they explored on later releases like *Electric Lucifer*, but also included activity and story songs like the ones on the *Dance, Sing and Listen* series.

As with those records, *The Way Out Record for Children* features an "Introduction" to the Dimension 5 gang, and movement songs like "Medieval Dancing." "School for Robots," an ear-body coordination game, features robotic vocals created by Haack speaking in a monotone and tapping his Adam's apple; this low-budget innovation is just another manifestation of his practical but innovative approach. The song also reflects Haack's silly sense of humor in puns like "Greetings, fellow robots. I hope oil goes well with you... Here is your robot music. Do not rust until you can dance to it." Electronic experimentation is apparent on the instrumental "Rubberbands," which mixes a bouncy, almost random synth melody with the elastic "boing" of a Jew's harp. *The Way Out Record* also features artwork by Haack's friend and manager Chris Kachulis, who contributes vocals on a few songs as well. —*Heather Phares*

### The Electronic Record for Children / 1969 / ♦♦♦

Like *The Way Out Record for Children*, 1969's *The Electronic Record for Children* adds more freaked-out fun to the basic menu of electronic-based story and activity songs shared by all the Dimension 5 releases. This time, Bruce Haack and Esther Nelson pretend they are on a spaceship orbiting the earth, and this theme plays out in their between-song banter as well as on songs like "Mara's Moon" and "Clapping with Katy," where the duo calls a friend on earth to play a clapping game with her. "Sing" and "Upside Down" are sweet slices of electronic pop, while "Saint Basil" includes a trip to the planet of the singing mice and a choir of Greek children, and the sound-effect laden instrumental "Listen" reflects the wilder side of Haack's imagination. As always, *The Electronic Record for Children* showcases the sparkling creativity, humor, and wonder of Haack and company. —*Heather Phares*

### The Electric Lucifer / 1970 / CBS ♦♦♦♦

After hearing late '60s rock 'n' roll from his friend Chris Kachulis, Bruce Haack added acid rock to his already diverse sonic palette. The result was 1970's *Electric Lucifer*, a psychedelic, anti-war song cycle about the battle between heaven and hell. The underlying concept of this concept album is "Powerlove," a divine force that not only unites humanity but forgives Lucifer his transgressions as well. But though this album extolls the healing powers of peace and love, *Electric Lucifer* uses often menacing music and lyrics to get its point across. "War" depicts the battle royale between good and evil with a martial beat and salvos from dueling synthesizers; a child's voice murmurs "I don't want to play anymore," and a funereal synth melody replaces the electronic battle march. Haack's marriage of rock rhythms and unique electronics creates a sound unlike either his previous work or the era's psychedelic rock, but songs like "Incantation" and "Word Game," with their percolating beats, buzzing synths, and vocoders, are much trippier than most acid rock. The strangely forlorn "Song of the Death Machine" sounds a bit like a short-circuiting HAL singing "My Darling Clementine," while "Word Game" features cool, dark electro-rock and brain-teasing lyrics like "Ray of sun/Reason/Knowledge/No legends." Kachulis sings on both of these tracks, and his deadpan vocals complement the weirdness going on around him nicely. His involvement with *Electric Lucifer* also includes aiding the album's release on Columbia Records; though it was Haack's only major label release, *Electric Lucifer* remains musically innovative and subversive. —*Heather Phares*

### Dance to the Music / 1972 / ♦♦♦♦

The 1972 album *Dance to the Music* is one of the best expressions of Dimension 5's aesthetic, mixing Bruce Haack and Esther Nelson's inspired outlook and folk, pop, and classical elements and filtering them through homespun electronics. Activity songs like "When the Music's Over" and "Squarefinger" update musical chairs and square dancing with the Dimension 5 approach, which means doing a square dance with your fingers and receiving instructions like "when the music's over, be the sound you hear."

Hints of bluegrass and country can be heard in *Dance to the Music*, particularly on "EIO (New MacDonalds Have a Form)," an update of "Old MacDonald Had a Farm" that celebrates the body and its parts, explaining, "Your form results mostly from the way your genetic program programs you," and "Liza Jane," which features electronic banjos and a shuffling tempo. The album also features some of Dimension 5's most psychedelic moments, including "Surprise," a sound collage piece that ranges from music-hall pop to "America the Beautiful," and "Soul Transportation," which is one of the simplest, yet most creative explanations of meditation ever recorded. Haack and Nelson intone directions like, "You just sort of relax and let your head go where it wants to" and "Now make sure there is nothing like furniture near you so you don't *really* trip." The duo guides the listener through a group meditation experience, noting, "At this point some children feel that they are all one child, made of many children," and the hovering space-synth background music shifts to very trippy, Indian-based electronic music. The subtle layers of humor, education, musical skill, and electronic whimsy present in all of Dimension 5's albums are especially evident on *Dance to the Music*, making it one of Haack's finest works. —*Heather Phares*

### ● Hush Little Robot / Oct. 6, 1998 / QDK Media ♦♦♦♦

1998's *Hush Little Robot* is the most comprehensive and easily available release of Bruce Haack's pioneering electronic music. This German collection culls its tracklisting from his middle works, emphasizing 1969's rock concept album *The Electric Lucifer* and the 1974 children's album *This Old Man*. The result is a mix of robotic nursery rhymes and dark, psychedelic electronic rock, the two extremes of Haack's repertoire. *Hush Little Robot*'s lighthearted tracks, like "School for Robots," "This Old Man," and "Thank You" feature banjos and Haack's vocal impersonations of a computer and an old man, along with plenty of random bleeps and bloops from his homemade synths. The best of the children's songs jam their lyrics full of educational information, as well as silly puns and voices: "Bods" features a sparkly keyboard line and lyrics about how body language conveys more than words—pretty far-out stuff for 1974. The eastern-tinged "Shine On" is a mantra explaining the properties of light, and "Elizabeth Foster Goose" explores the history of nursery rhymes in Haack's uncommon style. Haack's experimental side also shines on *Hush Little Robot*. "Rubberbands," from 1968's *The Way Out Album for Children*, is not only one of the earliest pieces on the album, but also one of its most adventurous, featuring echo-drenched synths interrupted by boinging noises and squeaks that sound like a robot with some loose gears. And *Electric Lucifer's* spooky, acid-tinged numbers like "Incantation" and "Word Game" feature rolling bass, droning keyboards, and electronic percussion for a very different—but not unrecognizable—take on psychedelic rock. "Word Game" in particular is a high point in Haack's career, containing both the wide-ranging sonics and cryptic lyrics that are its trademarks. Atop fuzz bass and phased keyboards, vocalist Chris Kachulis intones "Universe: one poem. Love: E-V-O-L. Evolve. Revolve: To love again." *Hush Little Robot* completes the Haack experience with two college radio interviews he did around the release of *Electric Lucifer*. Though his music ably speaks for itself, hearing the soft-spoken Haack explain his synthesizers and the peaceful, futuristic themes of his music adds an extra dimension of understanding. A tantalizing glimpse at Haack's prolific body of work, *Hush Little Robot* is a must for fans of vintage synths and esoteric recordings.—*Heather Phares*

## hab (Hans Carlsson)

b. Sweden
*Producer / Electronica, Neo-Electro*

Brooklyn-based artist Hans Carlsson makes intricate melodic electro with vague echoes of hip-hop and drum'n'bass under the name hab. A native of Sweden, Carlsson's earliest musical involvement was with a number of punk and alternative rock bands (he plays guitar and sings), among them a four-piece called Mouth that made it as far as a major-label contract (on Warner subsidiaries Telegram and Reprise in Sweden and America, respectively) before dissolving in 1994 under the weight of an archetypally "corporate rock" experience. Carlsson spent subsequent years traveling from Sweden to Holland to Paris, and finally to the Hasidic neighborhood of Williamsburg in Brooklyn (site of a sort of late-'90s New York bohemian renaissance), where he's recorded most of his material. The first of that material began appearing through Sweden's Dot label after a demo of Carlsson's work was upped by then-Dot artist Krister Linder (of Tupilaq); Linder's and Carlsson's debut EPs for the label were among its first releases and helped garner Dot the attention that transformed the label into something of an overnight sensation. Carlsson followed that 12" up with a full-length in September of 1997; titled *maPOd*, the album is a stunning collection of both rhythmically stunning and melodically engaging post-techno, interweaving thin, intricately syncopated percussion with thematic figures that are given far more focus and development than is typical of even the most armchair-oriented of electronica. —*Sean Cooper*

### Hab [EP] / 1997 / Dot ♦♦♦♦

Hab is a newcomer to the Swedish Dot label, which arrived on the scene nearly fully formed (and with a rep to match!) in early 1997, simultaneously releasing four singles of crafted, high-quality experimental electronica. A rare American presence in a decidedly European artform, hab (a native of New York) also represents one of the strongest Stateside contributions to date, as evidenced by this debut EP of sharp, scientific ambient electro. Like most of the rest of Dot's catalog, *Hab* features a pair of original tracks and a pair of remixes on the flip (by Nonplace Urban Field and Paul Frankland, aka Journeyman). All four tracks are solid, solid stuff, the hab tracks sounding a bit like a more melodic Autechre and the NUF and Journeyman mixes courting the outer edges of, respectively, frantic electro/jungle and breakbeat-driven ambient dub. —*Sean Cooper*

### ● maPOd / Oct. 20, 1997 / Dot ♦♦♦♦

Brooklyn-via-Gothenberg, Sweden artist hab's *maPOd* was the first full-length to appear through the Swedish Dot label, and among the first and most significant releases of new-school electronica to (sort of) originate on American shores. Similar in some respects (though at the same time quite singular and original) to the emotive, deeply melodic machine music of Warp artists such as Autechre and the Black Dog, hab's lilting, slightly melancholy, downbeat melodic electro lies somewhere between those two artists, fusing a charming, engagingly *human* compositional sensibility with the oddest of sounds and shifting, curiously syncopated rhythms. *maPOd* is easily on par with the best of hab's international contemporaries, and equally essential.—*Sean Cooper*

## Hafler Trio

f. 1980, Sheffield, England
*Group / Experimental Rock, Ambient*

Prolific and enigmatic, the Hafler Trio masterminded some of the most challenging and innovative sonic experiments of their time—defining music as simply organized sound, their unique synthesis of electronics, samples and tape loops probed the psychoacoustic power of noise, exploring not only its sensory effects but its physical ramifications as well. Formed in Sheffield, England in 1980 by Cabaret Voltaire alum Chris Watson and Andrew McKenzie, the Hafler Trio was never a three-piece in any actual sense—in fact, the third member originally credited to the line-up, one Dr. Edward Moolenbeek, was (according to an interview with McKenzie in the March/April 1991 issue of *Option* magazine) reportedly an expert in psychoacoustic research who edited the journal *Science Review* during the 1930s.

Much of the Hafler Trio's mystique stems from the deliberate misinformation the group consistently set forth—although their records regularly came packaged with deluxe graphs, diagrams, and essays detailing the purported effects of sound on the listener, the scientific authenticity of their "findings" is debatable; for example, their 1984 debut, *Bang! An Open Letter*, claims to be based on the studies of an acoustic researcher named Robert Spridgeon, complete with bibliography. Spridgeon later proved to be a complete fabrication, however, and over the course of subsequent efforts including 1985's *Alternation, Perception and Resistance—A Comprehension Exercise* EP, 1986's *Three Ways of Saying Two—The Netherlands Lectures* and *Dislocation*, the Hafler Trio continued baffling audiences with a deluge of propaganda, clouding perceptions to increase the visceral impact of their music.

By 1987's double-LP *A Thirsty Fish*, Watson had exited H30, leaving McKenzie the sole constant member; its follow-up, *intoutof*, heralded a new approach, rejecting the cut-and-paste noise and abrasive drones of earlier releases in favor of a more hypnotically ethereal sound. 1991's *Kill the King* announced the beginning of a trilogy which continued on with *Mastery of Money* and *How to Reform Mankind;* acclaimed in many quarters as the Hafler Trio's finest work, these three records diametrically oppose the soothing, placating effects of most ambient musics—*Mastery of Money*, with its extensive use of low-frequency tones, is a particularly unnerving and discomforting experience. Subsequent releases include 1992's *Fuck* and 1994's *One Dozen Economical Stories*, a collaboration with filmmaker Peter Greenaway. In 1996, the Hafler Trio also mounted *Who Sees Goes On*, a series of thematically-linked limited-edition releases. —*Jason Ankeny*

### ● Kill the King / 1991 / Silent ♦♦♦♦

The first major album after Watson left, *Kill the King* was recorded for Kim Cascone's Silent Records, a home for isolationist ambience throughout the world. With the help of Adi Newton and John Duncan among others, Andrew McKenzie constructed over an hour of fathomless space music, reliant on field recordings as well as various electronics and similar in fact to Cascone's work as PGR. The beginning of a new period for Hafler Trio, and an excellent christening. —*John Bush*

### Mastery of Money / 1992 / Touch ♦♦♦

### How to Reform Mankind / 1993 / Touch ♦♦♦♦

### One Dozen Economical Stories / Oct. 10, 1994 / Sub Rosa ♦♦♦♦

### Bang! An Open Letter/Walk Gently Through the Gates of Joy / 1995 / Grey Area/Mute ♦♦♦♦

As the Hafler Trio's experimental sound is far from everyone's cup of tea, the two-fer release *Bang! An Open Letter/Walk Gently Through the Gates of Joy* is a smart way for budget-minded consumers to pick up a large chunk of the group's music without a great deal of risk. The first, Hafler Trio's debut album, is stil one of their best efforts, and the second includes several previously unreleased tracks as well as the 1985 EP *Alternation, Perception and Resistance*. It's easily the best document of Hafler Trio's abrasive post-punk period still available. —*Jason Ankeny*

## Hal Featuring Gillian Anderson

f. 1996
*Group / Electronica, Club/Dance*

The British ambient techno collective Hal made headlines in 1997 when they teamed with "X-Files" star Gillian Anderson to record the single "Extremis." The project originated with the BBC documentary series "Future Fantastic," hosted by Anderson and featuring theme music by Hal (Raheen, Savage, and Px, respectively). In time, the actress became so enamoured of the group's music that she agreed to collaborate with them on a one-off single, lending vocals and starring in the video for the track "Extremis." The song also appeared on *Future—A Journey Through the Electronic Underground*, a collection of techno, ambient, and drum'n'bass tracks hand-picked by Anderson herself. —*Jason Ankeny*

● **Extremis [Single]** / May 12, 1997 / Virgin ♦♦
The only release by Hal was the single "Extremis," an ambient-trance number whose only claim to fame is the mystical, sung-spoken vocals by Gillian Anderson. It's basically a toss-away, essential for *X-Files* fans but hardly worth a passing glance for any music fans. —*John Bush*

## Herbie Hancock

b. Apr. 12, 1940, Chicago, IL
*Piano (Electric), Keyboards, Piano, Synthesizer, Leader, Composer / Electro, Modal Music, Hard Bop, Post-Bop, Fusion, Jazz-Funk, R&B, Funk*

Throughout his career, Herbie Hancock was one of the most restless artists on the musical scene, continually shuttling between pop music, club grooves and more traditional jazz recordings. It's a testament to his ability that he continually succeeded—in a commercial *and* artistic sense—whether he was playing hard bop during the '60s, Afro-centric space jazz in the early '70s, liquid synthesizer funk and disco-pop just a few years later, and in the '80s, the first mainstream recordings to acknowledge hip-hop and techno as musical forces. Though his first LPs as a leader were straightahead acoustic hard bop, Hancock was influenced by his mentor Miles Davis to begin using electric piano later in the decade; his was a vital contribution to the original jazz-rock/fusion masterpiece, Miles' *In a Silent Way*.

After leaving Blue Note to sign a contract with Warner Brothers, Hancock recorded an elegant funk album named *Fat Albert Rotunda* and in 1969 formed a sextet that evolved into one of the most exciting, forward-looking jazz-rock groups of the era. Now deeply immersed in electronics, Hancock added the multiple ARP synthesizers of Dr. Patrick Gleeson to his Echoplexed, fuzz-wah-pedaled electric piano and clavinet; the recordings became spacier and more complex rhythmically and structurally, creating their own corner in the avant-garde. By 1970, all of the musicians used both English and African names (Herbie's was Mwandishi). Forced to land the mothership when it failed to pay the bills, Hancock moved on to the next step—a terrific funk group whose first album, *Head Hunters*, with its Sly Stone-influenced hit single "Chameleon," became the biggest-selling jazz LP up to that time. Now handling all of the synthesizers himself, Hancock's heavily rhythmic comping often became part of the rhythm section, leavened by interludes of the old urbane harmonies. Hancock recorded several electric albums of mostly superior quality in the '70s, followed by a turn into disco around decade's end. In the meantime, however, Hancock refused to abandon acoustic jazz. A reunion of the trend-setting 1965 Miles Davis Quintet (Hancock, Ron Carter, Tony Williams, Wayne Shorter, with Freddie Hubbard sitting in for Miles) at New York's 1976 Newport Jazz Festival led to several tours and recording dates as V.S.O.P. during the following 15 years.

Hancock continued his chameleon ways in the '80s, first and foremost with 1983's *Future Shock*. Produced by Bill Laswell and featuring Grand Mixer D.ST on turntables, the single "Rockit" became an MTV hit and one of the most prominent tracks in the electro wave. Much of *Future Shock* was on a similar plane to Michael Jackson's pop giant *Thriller* of the year before, but Hancock's vocoderized vocals and programmed percussion became big influences on techno and dance. During the '80s, Hancock often traveled back and forth between what jazz purists termed "pop" albums (1984's *Sound-System*, 1988's *Perfect Machine*) and more jazz-centric projects, like playing with the brothers Marsalis and George Benson. He once more delved into hip-hop with 1995's *Dis Is Da Drum*, but also recorded straigtahead efforts like the following year's *The New Standard*. —*Richard S. Ginell & John Bush*

☆ **Mwandishi: The Complete Warner Bros. Recordings** / Oct. 3, 1969-Feb. 17, 1972 / Warner Archives ♦♦♦♦
This two-CD set reissues the complete contents of three LPs: *Fat Albert Rotunda*, *Mwandishi*, and *Crossings*. The earliest session (extensions of generally memorable funk themes used in a Bill Cosby cartoon) features the keyboardist in a sextet on most selections with tenor-saxophonist Joe Henderson, trumpeter Johnny Coles, and trombonist Garnett Brown; two songs use a 15-piece group. However the bulk of this set showcases Hancock's regular sextet of the era (which was comprised of trumpeter Eddie Henderson, Benny Maupin on bass clarinet, alto flute and soprano, trombonist Julian Priester, bassist Buster Williams, and drummer Billy Hart); the later session also adds Patrick Gleeson's moog synthesizer. *Mwandishi* and *Crossings* are explorative and loosely funky avant-garde, yet influenced by rock and funk. The results are often quite fascinating, but this group (which only recorded one further album for Columbia) was a commercial flop, which Hancock would eventually break up in favor of the Headhunters. —*Scott Yanow*

**Fat Albert Rotunda** / Oct. 3, 1969+Dec. 8, 1969 / Warner Bros. ♦♦♦♦
Centered around some soundtrack music that Hancock wrote for Bill Cosby's *Fat Albert* cartoon show, this was Herbie's first full-fledged venture into jazz-funk—and his last until *Head Hunters*—making it a prophetic release. At the same time, it was far different in sound from his later funk ventures, concentrating on a romping, late-'60s-vintage, R&B-oriented sound with frequent horn riffs and great rhythmic comping and complex solos from Hancock's Fender-Rhodes electric piano. The syllables of the titles alone—"Wiggle Waggle," "Fat Mama," "Oh! Oh! Here He Comes"—have a rhythm and feeling that tell you exactly how this music saunters and swaggers along—just like the jolly cartoon character. But there is more to this record than fatback funk. There is the haunting, harmonically sophisticated "Tell Me a Bedtime Story" (which ought to become a jazz standard), and the similarly relaxed "Jessica." The sextet on hand is a star-studded bunch, with Joe Henderson in funky and free moods on tenor sax, Johnny Coles on trumpet, Garnett Brown on trombone, Buster Williams on bass, and Tootie Heath on drums. Only Williams would remain in the electric Hancock Sextet to come. Also trumpeter Joe Newman, saxophonist Joe Farrell, guitarist Eric Gale, and drummer Bernard Purdie make guest appearances on two tracks. An engaging, friendly record, it is now available on CD as part of *Mwandishi: The Complete Warner Bros. Recordings*. —*Richard S. Ginell*

**Mwandishi** / Dec. 31, 1970 / Warner Bros. ♦♦♦♦♦
With the formation of his great electric sextet, Herbie Hancock's music took off into outer and inner space, starting with this landmark album (available on CD in the *Mwandishi* double set) recorded in a single session on New Year's Eve. Ever the gadgeteer, Herbie plays with electronic effects devices—reverb units, stereo tremelo, and Echoplex—which all lead his music into spacier, open-ended directions very much influenced by Miles Davis' electric experiments, rendering it from post-bop conventions. There are just three tracks: the insistent 15/4-meter Afro-electric-funk workout "Ostinato (Suite For Angela)," the inquisitive "You'll Know When You Get There" with its ethereal Hancock voicings, and trombonist Julian Priester's "Silent Way"-influenced "Wandering Spirit Song" which eventually dips into tumultuous freeform. Eddie Henderson emerges as a major trumpet soloist here, probing, jabbing, soliloquizing; Bennie Maupin comes over from Lee Morgan's group to add his ominous bass clarinet and thoughtful alto flute; and Buster Williams' bass and Billy Hart's flexible drums propel the rhythm section. Santana's Jose "Chepito" Areas and Leon "Ndugu" Chancler also add funky percussive reinforcement to "Ostinato," along with guitarist Ron Montrose. The group's collective empathy is remarkable, and Hancock had only begun to probe the outer limits with this extraordinary music. —*Richard S. Ginell*

**Crossings** / Dec. 1971 / Warner Bros. ♦♦♦♦
With the frenzied knocking of what sounds like a clock shop gone berserk, *Crossings* takes the Herbie Hancock Sextet even further into the electric avant-garde, creating its own idiom. Now, however, the sextet has become a septet with the addition of Dr. Patrick Gleeson on Moog synthesizer, whose electronic decorations, pitchless and not, give the band an even spacier edge. Again, there are only three tracks—the centerpiece being Hancock's multifaceted, open-structured suite in five parts called "Sleeping Giant." Nearly 25 minutes long yet amazingly cohesive, "Sleeping Giant" gathers a lot of its strength from a series of funky grooves—the most potent of which explodes at the tail end of Part Two—and Hancock's on-edge Fender Rhodes electric piano solos anticipate his funk adventures later in the '70s. Bennie Maupin's "Quasar" pushes the session into extraterrestrial territory, dominated by Gleeson's wild Moog effects and trumpeter Eddie Henderson's patented fluttering air trumpet. Even stranger is Maupin's "Water Torture," which saunters along freely with splashes of color from Hancock's spooky Mellotron and fuzz-wah-pedaled Fender Rhodes piano, Gleeson's electronics, and a quintet of voices. Still a challenging sonic experience, this music (which can be heard

on Warner's *Mwandishi* two-CD set) has yet to find its audience, though the electronica-minded youth ought to find it dazzling. —*Richard S. Ginell*

**Sextant** / 1972 / Columbia ♦♦
Herbie Hancock's first recording for the Columbia label, *Sextant* is a transitional album, closer to the electronic experimentation of *Crossings* and *Mwandishi* than to the funk that was to follow beginning with his next release, *Headhunters*. Still, glimpses of the future can be heard on "Hidden Shadows," propelled by Buster Williams' funky bass riff doubled by bass clarinetist Benny Maupin. The sideclong "Hornets" sounds like it was lifted off of Miles Davis' *Live-Evil*. This was the final recording by the Herbie Hancock Sextet, and provides an interesting look at an artist on the move. —*Jim Newsom*

★ **Head Hunters** / 1973 / Columbia ♦♦♦♦♦
*Head Hunters* was a pivotal point in Herbie Hancock's career, bringing him into the vanguard of jazz fusion. Hancock had pushed avant-garde boundaries on his own albums and with Miles Davis, but he had never devoted himself to the groove as he did on *Head Hunters*. Drawing heavily from Sly Stone, Curtis Mayfield and James Brown, Hancock devloped deeply funky, even gritty, rhythms over which he soloed on electric synthesizers, bringing the instrument to the forefront in jazz. It had all of the sensibilities of jazz, particularly in the way it wound off into long improvisations, but its rhythms were firmly planted in funk, soul and R&B, giving it a mass appeal that made it the biggest-selling jazz album of all time (a record which was later broken). Jazz purists, of course, decried the experiments at the time, but *Head Hunters* still sounds fresh and vital two decades after its initial release, and its genre-bending proved vastly influential on not only jazz, but funk, soul and hip-hop. —*Stephen Thomas Erlewine*

**Death Wish** / 1974 / One Way ♦♦
Herbie Hancock extends the reach of his *Head Hunters*-vintage electric music into the soundtrack field, with some switchbacks to earlier styles and old-fashioned movie suspense music thrown into the eclectic mix. Jerry Peters provides the requisite orchestral backgrounds, and the wah-wah guitar licks give some indication as to where Herbie's funk music would be going in the future. The main title music is the best track—tense, streaked with Hancock's echo-delayed electric piano and understated orchestrations. A good deal of the record, alas, is filled by listless film cues that are meaningless without the action in front of you. Still, the results are, in general, more intriguing than usual for the film genre. —*Richard S. Ginell*

**Dedication** / Jul. 29, 1974 / CBS/Sony ♦♦♦
This is a unique experiment in the Hancock discography, recorded in Tokyo in just one day during a tour of Japan. Side one contains two introspective, complex solo acoustic piano tracks: "Maiden Voyage" and "Dolphin Dance," which are notable since they date from a period when Hancock was supposedly totally immersed in electronics. Side two has two even more unusual things—"Nobu," a one-man show recorded in real time with the sample-and-hold feature of an ARP 2600 synthesizer providing a rhythm section for Hancock's electric keyboards, followed by "Cantaloupe Island," with a pre-recorded synth bassline. Side two is a fascinating look-back at the charms and stringent limitations of mid-'70s analog keyboards, as well as a challenge to Hancock's on-the-wing inventiveness—and despite some inevitable stiffness in the rhythm, he comes through with some colorful work. This would be the first of several Japan-only Hancock albums from the '70s, an indication that Japanese jazz fans were (and perhaps still are) far more open-minded and free-spending than their American counterparts. —*Richard S. Ginell*

**Thrust** / Aug. 26, 1974 / Columbia ♦♦♦
The follow-up to the breakthrough Headhunters album was virtually as good as its wildly successful predecessor: an earthy, funky, yet often harmonically and rhythmically sophisticated tour de force. There is only one change in the Headhunters lineup—swapping drummer Harvey Mason for Mike Clark—and the switch results in grooves that are even more complex. Hancock continues to reach into the rapidly changing high-tech world for new sounds, most notably the metallic sheen of the then-new ARP string synthesizer which was already becoming a staple item on pop and jazz-rock records. Again, there are only four long tracks, three of which ("Palm Grease," "Actual Proof," "Spank-A-Lee") concentrate on the funk, with plenty of Hancock's wah-wah clavinet, synthesizer textures and effects, and electric piano ruminations that still venture beyond the outer limits of post-bop. The change-of-pace is one of Hancock's loveliest electric pieces, "Butterfly," a match for any tune he's written before or since, with shimmering synth textures and Bennie Maupin soaring on soprano (Hancock would re-record it 20 years later on *Dis Is Da Drum*, but this is the one to hear). This supertight jazz-funk quintet album still sounds invigorating a quarter of a century later. —*Richard S. Ginell*

**Man-Child** / Jan. 1976 / Columbia ♦♦♦
Perhaps the funkiest album of Herbie Hancock's early- to mid-'70s jazz/funk/fusion era, *Man-Child* starts off with the unforgettable "Hang Up Your Hang Ups," and the beat just keeps coming until the album's end. "Sun Touch" and "Bubbles" are slower, but funky nonetheless. Hancock is the star on his arsenal of keyboards, but guitarist Wah Wah Watson's presence is what puts a new sheen on this recording, distinguishing it from its predecessors, *Headhunters* and *Thrust*. Others among the all-star cast of soloists and accompanists include Wayne Shorter on soprano sax, Stevie Wonder on chromatic harmonica, and longtime Hancock cohort Bennie Maupin on an arsenal of woodwinds. —*Jim Newsom*

**Direct Step** / Oct. 17, 1978-Oct. 18, 1978 / Columbia ♦♦♦♦
For the rabid audiophiles in Japan, Herbie Hancock went to Tokyo to record a direct-to-disc LP that later became one of the world's earliest CD releases. Due perhaps to the arduous one-take-only nature of the direct-to-disc process, Hancock takes the rare step of using a second keyboardist, Webster Lewis, to handle the multiple electronic textures; the rest of the cast is a quorum of Headhunters (Bennie Maupin, reeds; Paul Jackson, bass; Bill Summers, percussion), plus guitarist Ray Obiedo and drummer Alphonse Mouzon. Understandably, the music sometimes sounds a bit inhibited and structured but there are some refreshingly jarring rhythmic disruptions in "Butterfly." "Shiftless Shuffle" eventually develops a fine roadhouse groove, and the extended "I Thought It Was You" cuts the original version on *Sunlight*. The excellent LP sound is superior to that of the CD—especially the rock-solid bass and drums. —*Richard S. Ginell*

**Feets, Don't Fail Me Now** / 1979 / Columbia ♦
Herbie Hancock's electric records up until this point were marked by intelligence and adventure, even at their most earthy. But no, this one doesn't have an ounce of either. Herbie falls hook, line, and sinker for the disco fad and submerges his personality underneath the plastic vocals and the idiot four-on-the-floor disco beat. Hancock's own gauzy vocals through a Sennheiser vocoder are embarrassing, and even his synthesizer work sounds coarse and gimmicky. This time, even the purists were right; this is of no interest to jazz listeners and it isn't even good disco. —*Richard S. Ginell*

**Magic Windows** / 1981 / Columbia ♦♦
This is an improvement over Hancock's disco-era productions since at least it is grounded in Herbie's own '70s funk outings ("Chameleon," etc.) instead of generic dance music. Technically, this is an R&B album—not disco—with funkier, more flexible rhythm sections, more intriguing electronic instrumental decorations by Hancock, and some first-class instrumental contributions by the Brothers Johnson, the Escovedo family and Michael Brecker. Herbie even gives himself solo breaks on "Magic Number" and "Satisfied with Love" that redeem both tracks and there is a spooky foretaste of techno-pop on "The Twilight Clone." True, this album is still dominated by the R&B vocals of Sylvester, Gavin Christopher, and Vicki Randle but Hancock's own sonic signatures make this record listenable. —*Richard S. Ginell*

**Future Shock** / 1983 / Columbia ♦♦♦♦
Herbie Hancock completely overhauled his sound and conquered MTV with his most radical step forward since the Sextet days. He brought in Bill Laswell of Material as producer, along with Grand Mixer D.ST playing scratch turntables—and the immediate result was "Rockit," which makes quite a post-industrial metallic racket. Frankly, the whole record is an enigma; for all of its dehumanized, mechanized textures and rigid rhythms, it has a vitality and sense of humor that make it difficult to turn off. Moreover Herbie can't help but inject a subversive funk element when he comps along to the techno-beat—and yes, some real, honest-to-goodness jazz licks on a grand piano show up in the middle of "Auto Drive." —*Richard S. Ginell*

**Sound-System** / 1984 / Columbia ♦♦♦
In the grand tradition of sequels, *Sound-System* picks up from where *Future Shock* left off—if anything, even louder and more bleakly industrial than be-

fore (indeed, "Hardrock" is "Rockit" Mk II with a heavier rock edge). Yet Hancock's experiments with techno-pop were leading him in the general direction of Africa, explicitly so with the addition of the Gambian multi-instrumentalist Foday Musa Suso on half of the tracks. "Junku," written for the 1984 Olympic Games with Suso's electrified kora in the lead, is the transition track that stands halfway between "Rockit" and Hancock's mid-'80s Afro-jazz fusions. Also "Karabali" features an old cohort, the squealing Wayne Shorter on soprano sax. Despite succumbing a bit to the overwhelming demand for more "Rockits," Hancock's electric music still retained its adventurous edge. *—Richard S. Ginell*

**Perfect Machine** / Oct. 1988 / Columbia ♦♦♦
Set upon recapturing the pop ground he had invaded with *Future Shock*, Hancock relies upon many of the former's ingredients for yet another go-'round on *Perfect Machine*. High-tech producer Bill Laswell is back, so is scratchmaster D.ST—and armed with a warehouse of mostly digital keyboards, Hancock adds the distinctive bass of Bootsy Collins and the Ohio Players' vocalist Sugarfoot, who always sounds as if he had just swallowed something. The music is mostly thumping, funk-drenched techno-pop which still has some verve, particularly the designated single "Vibe Alive" and the "Maiden Voyage" interlude as heard through an electronic fun-house mirror. But this is not really an advance over Hancock's early-'80s pop projects. This would be Hancock's last album for at least seven years as he concentrated upon film projects and reunions with Miles Davis alumni (there was also an aborted deal with the Qwest label). As such, *Perfect Machine* is an appropriate end to this chapter in his career. *—Richard S. Ginell*

**Return of the Headhunters!** / 1998 / Verve ♦♦♦
After a two-decade-long hiatus, Herbie Hancock's Headhunters returned to action in 1998 with their funk groove pretty much intact, allowing for some technological and stylistic updating. The core of the band—the too-long-neglected Bennie Maupin (saxes, bass clarinet), Paul Jackson (bass), Bill Summers (percussion), and the group's second drummer, Mike Clark—still has the complex funk telepathic interplay down pat, though occasionally the rhythms are simplified for contemporary audiences. Hancock himself only appears on four tracks, where he tries to comp and stomp out on latter-day digital instruments (alas, he doesn't quite generate the same superfunky feeling that he once could on analog clavinets, Fender-Rhodes pianos, and ARP synths). Billy Childs fills the keyboard chair in more genteel fashion on the other six tracks, with occasional help from Patrice Rushen, Mark Goodman, and Darrell Smith. The main hangup here is that the revived Headhunters didn't come up with much memorable material, the strongest tracks being the back-to-1974 retro workout "Funk Hunter," the rhythmically tricky "Kwanzaa," and "Watch Your Back," which features the obligatory rap honoring elder statesmen of music (strange how reverential the nominally rebellious younger set often can be). *—Richard S. Ginell*

## K Hand (Kelli Hand)

*Producer, DJ / Detroit Techno, Club/Dance, Techno, House*
One of the best Detroit DJs during the late '80s, Kelli Hand set up her own Acacia Records in 1988 and later began producing albums in earnest during the mid-'90s, recording precise acid stormers as well as a growing number of tracks more on the verge of jazzy progressive house. She had spent time clubbing in New York (mostly at Larry Levan's *Paradise Garage*) before she began buying house records in the mid-'80s. Hand later became a DJ, mixing sets around the Motor City with an equal weight on house as well as techno.

After K Hand founded Acacia Records, she began releasing tight Detroit classics like "Think About It," "Everybody," "Flash Back," and "Mystery." By 1994, Hand was being name-checked by an international audience, and the release of her breakout single "Global Warning" on Warp that same year cemented her status as one of the top Detroit producers—not just one of the top female producers. High-profile compilation appearances on *Trance Europe Express, Vol. 2* and *Detroit: Beyond the Third Wave* extended her fame.

K Hand entered the album ranks in 1996 with *On a Journey*, the first non-DJ release for Belgium's Studio !K7. Six months later, *Ready for Darkness* followed on Distance Records, and two months after her sophomore LP, the third was in the can as well. *Soul*, recorded for Germany's Ausfahrt, combined progressive house flavors with a distinctly jazzy sound showing Hand's continued risk-taking stance regarding her Detroit roots. Her second Studio !K7 album, *Art of Music*, appeared in 1998 and her debut for Ausfahrt (*Fan-*

*tasy*) followed one year later. Hand has also provided house remixes for Carl Craig's Paperclip People and Argonic. *—John Bush*

**On a Journey** / Oct. 21, 1996 / Studio !K7 ♦♦♦
K Hand's debut album recycles several singles from her own Acacia Records, mini-masterpieces of distorted Detroit techno with disco loops and phased acid effects, but also an emphasis on delicate strings reminiscent of Derrick May. *—John Bush*

● **Acacia Classics, Vol. 1** / 1997 / Acacia ♦♦♦♦
Though it's listed as a various-artists compilation, all 13 tracks on *Acacia Classics, Vol. 1* are K Hand productions, and the album includes every classic track she produced for her own label. From early productions like "Flash Back" and "Think About It" (the latter with credits from Mad Mike and Jeff Mills) to "Ready for the Darkness" and "Street Knowledge," Hand proves herself a capable producer. The album is dedicated to two of her DJ heroes, Detroit's Ken Collier and New York's Larry Levan. *—Keith Farley*

**Ready for Darkness** / Mar. 31, 1997 / Distance ♦♦♦♦
The follow-up to the sprawling *On a Journey* distills the essence of hard Detroit techno into a tight minimalist groove. Though the beats seldom stray from a standard four-four kick, "Horizon," "Cycle," and the title track all feature Hand's cleverly distorted loops. *—John Bush*

**Soul** / May 26, 1997 / Ausfahrt ♦♦♦
A natural given the title, *Soul* is the most laidback album of K Hand's entire career. Swapping jazzy lines and vocal samples for the acid phasing of her earlier material, Hand works in moody breakbeats and basslines to give her tracks a strong emotional tug. Much closer to progressive house than anything out of the techno camp, *Soul* is another impressive addition to the diverse K Hand discography. *—John Bush*

**The Art of Music** / May 12, 1998 / Studio !K7 ♦♦♦♦
*The Art of Music* is a return of sorts for K Hand, back to her minimalist Detroit roots after the jazz excursions on *Soul*, though occasional flourishes do much to unite the styles. Hand's third album in just over a year sees debts to electro and techno blossom into a fully formed style, reminiscent of the explorations of mood techno with Juan Atkins' Model 500 material, especially on tracks like "Census" and "Eternal." *—John Bush*

**Fantasy** / Jan. 26, 1999 / Ausfahrt ♦♦♦

## Beaumont Hannant

b. York, England
*Producer / Ambient Techno, Techno, IDM*
A wildly eclectic producer who released four LPs during 1993-94 but then all but retired his solo work for a place in the trip-hop duo Outcast, Beaumont Hannant began DJing in 1986 after attending several hip-hop mixing competitions. During the late '80s he was heavily into electro, techno, and hip-hop as well as indie-rock (he even managed fellow natives of York Shed Seven for a while). Hannant began working on production in 1993 with the EP *Tastes and Textures, Vol. 1* for GPR Records. One track, "Awakening the Soul," appeared on the *Positiva Ambient Collection*, and Hannant released his debut album, *Basic Data Manipulation (Tastes and Textures, Vol. 2)* that same year. In 1994, Hannant recorded an unbelievable three full-lengths (*Texturology, Bitter Sweet, Sculptured*) for GPR, each possessing a breath-taking variety of styles.

By 1995, however, Hannant had begun to diversify his talents, providing remixes for Autechre, Björk and Ned's Atomic Dustbin, producing indie-folkie Lida Husik and beginning the group Outcast with his engineer Richard Brown. The duo signed to One Little Indian and released their debut album *Out of Tune* in 1996. Hannant appeared to have returned to his solo guise as well at the end of the year with the release of a GPR double-pack EP titled *Notions of Tonality*. *—John Bush*

● **Sculptured** / 1995 / General Productions ♦♦♦
Beginning with the pseudo electro-folk of "Ormeau" (with vocals by Lida Husik) and continuing through aggro-techno "Toxicity" (rap by Paul Edmeade), *Sculptured* broadened the spectrum of electronic listening music. The sheer variety of music makes it a difficult listen, but the tracks do work very well on their own. Unsurprisingly, Hannant thanks over 200 artists in the liner notes, from LFO to Mahler to the Kinks to Shed Seven. *—John Bush*

**Notions of Tonality, Vol. 1 [Single]** / Dec. 2, 1996 / GPR ♦♦

## Happy Mondays

f. 1985, Manchester, England, db. 1992
*Group / Madchester, Alternative Dance, Club/Dance, Alternative Pop/Rock, House*

Along with the Stone Roses, the Happy Mondays were the leaders of the late '80s/early '90s dance club-influenced Manchester scene, experiencing a brief moment in the spotlight before collapsing in 1992. While the Stone Roses were based in '60s pop, adding only a slight hint of dance music, the Happy Mondays immersed themselves in the club and rave culture, eventually becoming the most recognizable band of that drug-fueled scene. The Mondays' music relied heavily on the sound and rhythm of house music, spiked with '70s soul licks, and swirling '60s psychedelia. It was bright, colorful music that had fractured melodies that never quite gelled into cohesive songs.

Unwittingly or not, the Happy Mondays personified the ugly side of rave culture. They were thugs, pure and simply—they brought out the latent violence that lay beneath the surface of any drug culture, even one as seemingly beatific as England's late '80s/early '90s rave scene. Under the leadership of vocalist Shaun Ryder, the group sounded and acted like thugs, especially in comparison with their peace-loving peers, the Stone Roses. Ryder's lyrics were twisted and surrealistic, loaded with bizarre pop culture references, drug slang, and menacing sexuality. Appropriately, their music was as convoluted. The Happy Mondays were one of the first rock bands to integrate hip-hop techniques into their music. They didn't sample, but they borrowed melodies and lyrics and, in the process, committed rock blasphemy. For a band that celebrated their vulgarity and excessiveness, the Happy Mondays appropriately came undone by their addictions, but they left behind a surprisingly influential legacy, apparent in everyone from dance bands like the Chemical Brothers to rock 'n' rollers like Oasis.

With their second album, 1988's *Bummed*, the Happy Mondays became British superstars, particularly lead singer Shaun Ryder. *Pills 'n' Thrills & Bellyaches*, released in 1990, marked the height of the band's popularity, creativity, and influence; although the record made the Top 100 albums chart in America, it didn't establish them as stars in the US.

After that, the fall was quick. By the time they released their last studio album, *Yes, Please*, Manchester had disappeared from public consciousness; it sold respectably, but the group didn't have the commercial impact that they had just two years before. Besides the lack of public interest, Shaun Ryder had become addicted to heroin, tearing the band apart in the process. At a high-level record contract meeting, Ryder walked out for some "Kentucky Fried Chicken," which was the band's slang for heroin. Ryder never returned and the group quickly fell apart.

Shaun Ryder and the Mondays' full-time dancer Bez re-emerged in the mid-'90s with Black Grape. The band released their critically acclaimed debut, *It's Great When You're Straight...Yeah!*, late in the summer of 1995. Black Grape's sound pursued the same direction as the Mondays, only with a harder, grittier edge to their sound and lyrics. *—Stephen Thomas Erlewine*

**Squirrell & G Man Twenty-Four Hour Party People Plastic Face Carnt Smile** / Apr. 1987 / Factory ♦♦
Produced by John Cale, Happy Mondays' debut album is a haphazard affair that concentrates on bare-boned funk exercises, only occasionally landing on the colorful, swirlingly eclectic mixture of funk, hip-hop, and pop that would become the band's signature sound. *—Stephen Thomas Erlewine*

**Bummed** / Nov. 1988 / Elektra ♦♦♦♦
The Happy Mondays first essayed their fusion of dance-club beats, hip-hop, funk and rock 'n' roll on *Bummed*. A considerable improvement from the unfocused *Squirrel and G-Man*, *Bummed* is slightly inconsistent, but the group's sound is beginning to gel. In particular, Shaun Ryder's incoherent bluster of non sequiturs, surreal imagery and verbal threats is coming into its own, and it adds a sense of menace to dark grooves like "Lazy Itis," "Mad Cyril," and "Wrote for Luck." The latter was remixed by Vince Clarke after the album's release, and the new version, which was included on later pressings, was the hardest dance the group had yet attempted, suggesting the direction they would follow on their next album. *—Stephen Thomas Erlewine*

★ **Pills 'n' Thrills & Bellyaches** / Apr. 1990 / Elektra ♦♦♦♦♦
A swirling, neo-psychedelic kaleidoscope of hallucinogenic drugs, trippy beats, borrowed hooks, and veiled threats, *Pills 'n' Thrills & Bellyaches* is the Happy Mondays' masterpiece and the peak of the entire Madchester craze.

Where the Stone Roses were pop classicists, the Happy Mondays pushed pop into the Ecstasy age. The Mondays' cut-and-paste rhythms and melodies are clearly influenced by hip-hop and electronic dance music, and their songs have the same sort of twisted internal logic, subverting conventional pop song structures while reinterpreting oldies, occasionally stealing entire songs and claiming them as their own (John Kongos' "He's Gonna Step On You Again" is transformed into "Step On," LaBelle's "Lady Marmalade" provides the basis for "Kinky Afro"). Most of the musical collage is the creation of producers Paul Oakenfold and Steve Osborne, but the vision of *Pills 'n' Thrills & Bellyaches* belongs to Shaun Ryder, who reveals himself as a surreally gifted lyricist. Lifting melodies at will, Ryder paints a bizarre vision of modern urban life, fueled by sex, drugs, violence, and dead-end jobs—and instead of lamenting the state of affairs, he celebrates them in his hoarse, arhythmic, tuneless holler. His thuggishly surreal sense of humor and appropriation of hooks became enormously influential on British rock 'n' roll in the '90s, particularly on Oasis' sense of style. *—Stephen Thomas Erlewine*

**Yes, Please** / Sep. 22, 1992 / Elektra ♦♦
By the time of 1992's *Yes, Please*, The Happy Mondays had succumbed to the excessive lifestyle they had so enthusiastically promoted. Lead singer Shaun Ryder, who had always acted as both the mouthpiece and musical visionary for the band, sounds as if he couldn't be bothered and the music reflects his disinterest. In the hands of Chris Frantz and Tina Weymouth (Talking Heads, Tom Tom Club), the group's music loses much of its distinctive, thuggish edginess, as well as its reliance on current dance trends, becoming faceless, undistinguished dance-pop sludge. *Yes, Please* was not a particularly good way to say goodbye. *—Stephen Thomas Erlewine*

**Double Easy: The US Singles** / Sep. 14, 1993 / Elektra ♦♦♦
The Happy Mondays' drug-soaked vision worked best on individual songs, so the concept of a singles collection seems ideal. However, the band's two groundbreaking and popular albums—*Bummed* and *Pills 'n' Thrills & Bellyaches*—have distinct musical visions, and work better as records than *Double Easy*, which fails to be a captivating listen, even though it includes nearly every one of their finest songs. *—Stephen Thomas Erlewine*

**Loads (& Loads More)** / Oct. 30, 1995 / London ♦♦♦♦
With the exception of *Pills 'n' Thrills & Bellyaches*, the Happy Mondays had difficulty expanding their ideas into full albums, which makes the singles compilation *Loads* all the more useful. It contains all of the band's hit singles—"Step On," "Kinky Afro," "Hallelujah," "Lazyitis," "W.F.L.," "Tokoloshe Man," "Loose Fit," "Bob's Yer Uncle," "24 Hour Party People," "Mad Cyril"—plus several important album tracks, making it an excellent distillation of the band's career; as an album, only *Pills 'n' Thrills* provides better listening, and *Loads* is arguably just as good as an introduction, especially for casual fans. The first 10,000 copies of *Loads* included an extra disc, *Loads More*, a compilation of remixes making their debut appearance on CD, including Bernard Sumner's "Freaky Dancing," Mike Pickering's "Delightful," Martin Hannett's "Lazyitis," and Vince Clarke's "W.F.L."; all of the remaining mixes are by Paul Oakenfold. Since the remixes date from the height of Happy Mondays' career, they provide useful insight on the band's talents as a dance group. *—Stephen Thomas Erlewine*

## Brian Harden

b. Chicago, IL
*Producer / Club/Dance, House*

Nurtured on the jazz sounds of artists such as Miles Davis and Herbie Hancock, as well as the burgeoning mid-'80s house scene in his hometown of Chicago, Brian Harden was well primed for a career as a musician. Despite his lack of formal musicianship, he began producing jazz-influenced house in the early '90s for recognized Chicago labels such as Dancemania and Relief. By the end of the decade, his music received substantial praise after he released a series of EPs titled *The Nubirth Project* on Mike Grant's Detroit-based house label, Moods & Grooves. *—Jason Birchmeier*

● **The NuBirth Project, Vol. 1 EP** / Oct. 11, 1999 / Moods & Grooves ♦♦
Brian Harden's Moods & Grooves debut finds him again accentuating his pumping rhythms with a welcome sense of musicianship. On all three tracks, he integrates live keys into his arrangements, bringing both a sense of color and spontaneity to the mostly syncopated percussion. Furthermore, "Palladium" features some excellent synth work, while a horn loop drives "The Horn." The way Harden uses bridges and other short intermissions to break up

the often repetitive nature of house also makes these songs sound less like studio creations and more like an actual live band. This organic feel makes Harden's work here perfect to integrate into a set featuring many of his Detroit deep house peers: Theo Parrish, Rick Wade, Kenny Dixon Jr., Rick Wilhite, Alton Miller, and former Detroit area producer Brett Dancer. —*Jason Birchmeier*

## Hardfloor

f. 1991, Berlin, Germany
*Group / Electronica, Trance, Club/Dance, Acid House*
One of the most popular and well-known German techno artists, Hardfloor is comprised of Oliver Bondzio and Ramon Zenker. Forming in 1991 as the German acid and techno scenes were just beginning to solidify around artists such as Sven Vath, Pete Namlook, David Moufang, and DJ Criss, Bondzio and Zenker came together at the behest of a mutual friend. The former already an established DJ and the latter a successful studio producer, Hardfloor released the 11-minute "Acperience" single soon after deciding to inject a bit of bombast into the German scene. Utilizing since-standard compositional tools like long, melody-driven buildups and elaborate percussion breaks, the track became an instant dance floor anthem and made Hardfloor a sought-after name for remix and production work. Although the pair recorded briefly for the Eye Q label, most of the group's work has come out through Sven Vath's influential Harthouse imprint, including a number of full-length releases and a consistent schedule of 12"s and EPs. Although the pair have since evolved from the more simplistic floor-movers of their earlier work, incorporating elements of hip-hop, electro, breakbeat techno, and post-acid house styles like trip-hop and intelligent dance, the group remains committed to the smoldering edge of acid, with 909 and 303 sounds comprising the lion's share of their recognizable sound. Hardfloor remix credits include Mike Oldfield, the Shamen, and Mory Kante, and both Bondzio and Zenker also release their own and others' material through their respective Jakpot and No Respect labels. The duo adopted the alias DaDamnPhreakNoizPhunk for the 1999 acid-breakbeat adventure, *Electric Crate Digger*. —*Sean Cooper*

**Funalogue [EP]** / 1994 / Harthouse ♦♦♦♦
Over-the-top hardcore acid-techno, thick and imposing. —*Sean Cooper*

**Tb Resuscitation** / 1994 / Planet Earth ♦♦♦

**DaDamPhreakNoizPhunk [EP]** / 1995 / Harthouse ♦♦♦
*DaDamPhreakNoizPhunk* is a six-track EP of freestyle hip-hop beats wedded to Hardfloor's patented acid-trance, with surprisingly positive results. —*John Bush*

**Respect** / 1995 / Harthouse ♦♦♦
Hardfloor reach out to the Chicago, Detroit, New York, Belgium, and UK innovators on their second full-length effort, a credit-where-credit-is-due type outing not nearly as water-treading as much of their earlier '90s material was. Confident if slightly redundant. —*Sean Cooper*

**Strikeout [Single]** / 1996 / Harthouse ♦♦♦
On first listen, Bondzio and Zenker appear to have left their acid and trance roots behind, trading stomping beats and squidgy 303 lines for funky hip-hop and electro breaks. But the sound is still signature Hardfloor, and as trendy as doing a breakbeat record was upon its release, *Strikeout* is still an extremely well-done record, and a tribute to the group's diversity. —*Sean Cooper*

● **The Best of Hardfloor** / Sep. 8, 1997 / Eye Q ♦♦♦♦
Six years after their debut release, Hardfloor compiled 19 tracks consisting of their best moments, including obvious classics like "Acperience" and "Into the Nature," as well as "Once Again Back," "Dubdope," and "Mahogany Roots." The second disc alternates Hardfloor remixes of New Order, Depeche Mode and Robert Armani with reworkings of original Hardfloor material by Surgeon and Dave Angel, among others. —*John Bush*

**All Targets Down** / Nov. 16, 1998 / Harthouse ♦♦♦

**Electric Crate Digger** / Apr. 6, 1999 / Studio !K7 ♦♦♦
*Electric Crate Digger* is the full-length continuation of a two-part EP series begun in 1995 and subtitled "Hardfloor Presents DaDamPhreakNoizPhunk." Given that fact, it's much easier to see the album in light of Hardfloor's developing interest in breakbeats than as the big-beat crossover record it certainly sounds like. Still, Bondzio and Zenker are much better producing full-on trance than these rather lame sample pastiches. —*John Bush*

## Hardkiss

f. 1991, San Francisco, CA
*Group / Trance, Club/Dance, Techno*
Scott, Gavin, and Robbie, the Hardkiss brothers, ruled the underground San Francisco club scene during the '90s with a mixture of acid, trance, and breakbeat techno. World-class DJs all, the brothers also run their own Hardkiss label, releasing material as themselves plus myriad other artists, including Rabbit in the Moon and Scott's God Within project. It was Scott and Gavin who formed the group in the early '90s after experiencing Britain's 1989 Summer of Love firsthand while studying in Europe. Returning to the States, the two began promoting and organizing massive raves on the East Coast, but later moved out to San Francisco to share the vibe with the West as well. Hooking up with old friend Robbie and christening themselves Hardkiss, the trio began recording material for their eponymous label. Though few releases appeared on anything other than vinyl, the label compilation *Delusions of Grandeur* serves as a good primer to the Hardkiss sound. Scott, Robbie, and Gavin have each released compilations detailing their mixing skills as well. —*John Bush*

● **Delusions of Grandeur** / Oct. 31, 1994 / Hardkiss ♦♦♦♦
The debut Hardkiss album is truly a communal affair, with associates like the Drum Club, Rabbit in the Moon and Jon Drukman providing mixes and production. A variety of past and present Hardkiss label material is represented, including "Out of Body Experience," "Phoenix," "Pacific Coast Highway," and "Drums Are Dangerous." —*John Bush*

## Hardknox

f. 1996
*Group / Big Beat, Trip-Hop, Club/Dance*
The British big-beat duo Hardknox formed in 1996 when DJs Steve P. (a.k.a. Skycutter and Immortal Minds) and Lindy Layton (formerly of Beats International) joined forces. They released their debut single "Coz I Can" that year on the Skint Label, also the home of Fatboy Slim; *NME* gave it Single of the Week honors, which they also bestowed on the group's second effort, the *Psychopath* EP. The duo's hard-hitting, dancefloor-friendly style made them in-demand remixers, tweaking songs from diverse acts like Orgy, the Crystal Method, and Faith No More. 1998 found Hardknox appearing on compilations like *The Big Beat Conspiracy, Vol. 1* and *Monster Breaks: A Collection of Big Beat Finery*. The following year the duo appeared at Woodstock '99 and released their full-length debut, *Come in Hard*. —*Heather Phares*

● **Hardknox** / Sep. 28, 1999 / Jive ♦♦
Hardknox's self-titled full-length debut features more of the aggressive big-beat that their singles on Skint and appearances on compilations introduced. The album also features guest vocal appearances by Schooly D, and tracks like "Come In Hard" set the tone for their somewhat repetitive, but not totally unenjoyable dance music. —*Heather Phares*

## James Hardway (David Harrow)

b. London, England
*Producer / Electronica, Jungle/Drum'N'Bass, Club/Dance*
Drum'n'bass fusionary James Hardway works most often with cool jazz textures, though he is largely immune to the purist poses of many jungle producers. Known before the mid-'90s under his birth name David Harrow (and reportedly related to Al Capone), Hardway has worked with an impressive cast of British producers, from Genesis P-Orridge to Adrian Sherwood and Jah Wobble to Andrew Weatherall. During the early '80s, Hardway lived in Germany and acted in films before getting into the Berlin music scene. He recorded an album in 1983 (as David Harrow), and worked with European electro-pop star Anne Clark on several albums. Hardway also appeared with Jah Wobble on the continent, but relocated to London by 1986, where he was swept up by the acid-house phenomenon.

Hardway divided his time during the late '80s and early '90s between dub units (Adrian Sherwood's On-U Sound System, Lee Perry) and the burgeoning electronic community, working as a producer with Psychic TV and many others. After ranging into jungle/drum'n'bass during 1995, he debuted his James Hardway guise with an impressive 1996 LP, *Deeper, Wider, Smoother, Shit*. The album was all the more noteworthy considering he played all live instruments (except for flute) and covered programming as well. Hardway displayed a talent for writing songs also, with a credit for Billie Ray Martin's 1996 club hit "Your Loving Arms." After the release of his second, 1997's *Welcome to the*

*Neon Lounge*, Hardway earned an American contract through Shadow. The label collected tracks from his two albums to date for the 1998 compilation *Easy Is a Four Letter Word*. After the practically obligatory remix collection *Reshuffle and Spin Again*, Hardway returned with his third proper album, *A Positive Sweat*. Hardway's recordings as Technova have also appeared on Andrew Weatherall's Emissions Audio Output Records. —*John Bush*

**Deeper, Wider, Smoother, Shit** / Jul. 15, 1996 / Recordings of Substance ++++
Though many tracks rely on only slim percussion lines and the occasional atmospheric trumpet sample or live flute solo by Clive Bell, James Hardway's take on moody breakbeat of the jazz-hipster variety is a diverting one. It is Hardway's clever programming and innate sense for when a break becomes a bit too stale which enlivens *Deeper, Wider, Smoother, Shit* and makes it an intriguing LP. —*John Bush*

**Welcome to the Neon Lounge** / Nov. 18, 1997 / Recordings of Substance +++
Similar to Amon Tobin's increased use of samples from the bop and swing eras, James Hardway looked a bit farther back than the '60s and '70s when picking samples for use on his second LP. The result is another album of intelligent, moving drum'n'bass, although the differences between this and Hardway's debut are negligible. —*John Bush*

• **Easy Is a Four Letter Word** / Aug. 18, 1998 / Shadow ++++
An American collection balancing the best tracks from his first two albums, *Easy Is a Four Letter Word* proves that, fused with the right jungle beats, easy-listening lounge jazz can be very challenging listening. Portions of the record feature saxophone, flute, and double bass parts that were recorded live. —*Steve Huey*

**A Positive Sweat** / 1999 / Recordings of Substance +++
For *A Positive Sweat*, Hardway again moved closer toward emphasizing live instrumentation and vocal tracks over just programming. Much of the album was actually recorded in the studio during loose jam sessions, with Hardway only going over the tapes afterwards to insert additional breakbeats. The results are well-produced but overly smooth in spots, more akin to '90s mainstream soul than most drum'n'bass. While Amanda Ghost contributes most of the vocals, Hardway himself steps out for "Go On." —*John Bush*

**Reshuffle and Spin Again** / Apr. 27, 1999 / Recordings of Substance ++
Hardway's remix collection tends toward the dark side of drum'n'bass, with reworkings by T-Power (the highlight by far), Icarus, Nucleus & Paradox, and Resonator. —*John Bush*

## Ron Hardy

d. 1991
*Producer, DJ / Acid House, House*
Ron Hardy is the only man who can test Frankie Knuckles' status as the godfather of Chicago house music. Though he never recorded under his own name and left little evidence of his life, Hardy was the major name in Chicago dance music from the late '70s to the mid-'80s. By 1974, he had already effected a continuous music mix—with reel-to-reel machines plus a dual-turntable setup—at the club Den One. Several years later, Hardy played with Knuckles at a club called the Warehouse and though he spent several years in Los Angeles, he later returned to Chicago to open his own club, the Music Box. While Knuckles was translating disco and the emerging house music to a straight southside audience at the Power Plant, Hardy's 72-hour mix sessions and flamboyant party lifestyle fit in well with the uptown, mostly gay audience at the Music Box. A roll-call of major Chicago producers—including Marshall Jefferson, Larry Heard, Adonis, Phuture's DJ Pierre, and Chip E—all debuted their compositions by pressing up acetates or reel-to-reel copies for Hardy to play during the mid-'80s. Lingering problems with heroin addiction forced him to leave the Music Box around 1986 and though he continued to DJ around the area, Hardy wasn't around when Chicago became house music's mecca later in the decade. He died in 1991. —*John Bush*

## Harmonia

f. 1973, Forst, Germany, db. 1976
*Group / Kraut Rock, Experimental*
Though Harmonia began as a sideline excursion for Hans-Joachim Roedelius and Dieter Moebius of Cluster and Michael Rother of Neu!, the group became one of the most legendary in the entire Kraut-rock/*kosmische* scene with the release of several mid-'70s LPs.

After two studio albums recorded as Cluster, Roedelius and Moebius moved out to the German countryside to build their own studio in the village of Forst. After several disappointments in his attempt to expand Neu! into a live unit, Rother retreated to Cluster's studio for a series of relaxed, improvisational jam sessions that wedded Cluster's exploratory space music with the chugging rhythms and guitar sense of Rother. The debut Harmonia LP, *Musik von Harmonia*, appeared in 1974 (with an accomplished live track, recorded in Amsterdam). Though Rother also continued with Neu! to create another Kraut-rock classic, *Neu! '75*, Harmonia remained his focus for another LP, 1975's *Harmonia de Luxe*. Brian Eno had proclaimed Harmonia "the world's most important rock group," and he eventually joined the proceedings for several 1976 sessions—the legendary results of which lay unreleased for over twenty years, until Rykodisc acquiesced with the release of *Tracks & Traces*. Though Cluster and Eno continued their collaboration during the late '70s, Rother began a solo career with 1978's *Sternthaler*. —*John Bush*

• **Musik von Harmonia** / 1974 / Brain ++++
From the opener "Watussi," *Musik von Harmonia* sounds radically different from much of the German electronic music before it, a clever fusion of Cluster-style space with up-front drum machines that suggests a more atmospheric version of Kraftwerk. Much of the album continued in the vein of previous Cluster material (including the live track "Sehr Kosmisch"), but for the most part this was a new direction for German music, and an excellent one. —*John Bush*

**Harmonia de Luxe** / 1975 / Brain ++++

**Tracks & Traces** / Nov. 4, 1997 / Rykodisc ++++
The great lost album of the space-rock movement until a late-'90s resurrection by Rykodisc, *Tracks & Traces* (released as Harmonia 76) includes nine tracks of languid, spaced-out brilliance. Though a few tracks have vocals from Eno, most of the material here is prime synthesized bliss (e-guitar, e-bass and drum machine notwithstanding), from the building organ-like chords of the 15-minute "Sometimes in Autumn" to what sounds like a fusion of *kosmische* and blaxploitation funk on the opener, "Vamos Companeros." Perhaps not as consistently excellent as the first Harmonia LP, but definitely worthy of reissue. —*John Bush*

## Mick Harris

*Keyboards, Drums, Producer, Programming / Dark Ambient, Ambient Dub, Industrial*
Closely allied with post-industrial dub terrorists such as Bill Laswell, Techno Animal, James Plotkin, Robert Musso, and Anton Fier, Birmingham-based artist Mick Harris is something of a study in extremes. A drummer with noted death metal outfit Napalm Death through the group's late-'80s/early-'90s heyday, Harris began experimenting with monochrome ambient and dub styles toward the tail end of his association with that group. Releasing material through Earache as Scorn (his ambient dub aegis) and through Sentrax as Lull, in addition to other sporadic projects, his genre-spanning activities have done much to jar the minds, expectations, and record collections of audiences previously kept aggressively opposed. To the present, Scorn and Lull, along with John Zorn's experimental jazz-dubcore outfit Painkiller have remained Harris' primary ongoing projects, although one-off collaborations with the likes of James Plotkin, Nicholas Bullen, Bill Laswell, and Martyn Bates are common. Harris formed Scorn in 1991 in collaboration with bassist Nick Bullen, incorporating elements of ambient, industrial, dub, rock, and hip-hop. The group (though pared back to just Harris following *Evanescence*) have released a number of increasingly well-received full-length recordings, including the remix LP *Ellipsis*, which features outbound reworkings by the likes of Coil, Autechre, Laswell, and Germ. Harris' solo work as Lull focuses on darker, more "isolationist" ambient soundscapes, some of which have been reissued domestically by Laswell's now-defunct Subharmonic imprint. [See Also: Lull, Scorn] —*Sean Cooper*

**Somnific Flux** / 1995 / Subharmonic ++
On the two tracks which comprise *Somnific Flux*, Harris and Laswell combine to create sinister percussion-filled dronescapes. —*John Bush*

**Overload Lady** / Apr. 28, 1997 / Sub Rosa +++
Billed as a drum'n'bass album, *Overload Lady* fits the bill only on the tech-

nical scale. As with many albums from the noise/illbient/industrial community which take on a style rooted in clubs, the tools are present, but the total effect is more than lacking. The drum programming isn't inferior to contemporary production, but the music has a lack of focus and direction which subvert any positives the album might contain. —*John Bush*

● **Murder Ballads: Complete Collection** / Oct. 20, 1998 / Invisible ◆◆◆◆
*Murder Ballads* is a three-CD set reissuing the trilogy of *Drift*, *Passages*, and *Incest Songs* previously put out by Harris (Scorn) and Martyn Bates (Eyeless in Gaza). The three albums naturally belong together for their highly stylized content. Each one is a set of original compositions inspired by, and closely following, the patterns of the West European/American folk murder ballad. While gory stories on the TV news may seem to indicate a dark curiosity pandering to contemporary man, Harris and Bates' work reminds us that such stories have always found an audience and gained life in frequent retelling. Mick Harris provides the forlorn, desolate soundscapes that have caused this music to be termed isolationist, or even post-isolationist. These attenuated pieces average about 20 minutes each. Over this cold, abandoned, synthesizer soundscape Bates intones a morbid, chilling, blue-eyed soul of syllables stretched out a gallow's length. The combination of this sanguine poetry and chilling ambient darkwave is intensely fascinating to the point of being disturbing. Harris and Bates deserve high praise for so totally incorporating this blood-drenched footnote on music history as to create such a worthy body of work to add to and continue the murderous game. The set, in an understated gold and black package, includes fittingly antique artwork and complete lyrics. —*Thomas Schulte*

## Paul Haslinger

*Keyboards, Guitar, Synthesizer, AMG Contributor, Composer / Experimental, Ambient, World Fusion*

Trained at the Academy of Music in Vienna, Austria, Paul Haslinger graduated straight into active work in the European music business, first recording with Hypersax, culminating in his joining Tangerine Dream in time for the recording of *Underwater Sunlight*. Haslinger brought a certain amount of structure to the band's compositions, resulting in some of the more improvisational elements being jettisoned; the change in direction shaped the progress of the group into the '90s.

Haslinger remained with Tangerine Dream until the end of 1990, pursuing graduate studies in music between recording dates and live tours, appearing on more than fourteen albums, regular and soundtrack, before his departure (a fifteenth album, the soundtrack to *The Park Is Mine*, appeared in 1992).

In 1991, he began a collaboration with Lightwave, a French experimental group. He relocated to Los Angeles at the same time, eventually creating a studio that he dubbed "The Assembly Room." His pace of work has never slackened—two albums with Lightwave, the release of *Future Primitive* (under his surname only), and the release of *World Without Rules* are the tip of the iceberg. Haslinger has provided music for everything from interactive CD-ROMs to convention openings. He has also developed his own unique musical processes to help drive his creativity and to lead him interesting musical directions, with the Coma Virus album *Hidden* displaying some of the results of these "Assembly strategies." —*Steven McDonald*

**World Without Rules** / 1996 / RGB ◆◆◆

● **Score** / Jan. 26, 1999 / RGB ◆◆◆◆
Haslinger's second album for RGB Records is another world-fusion effort, albeit with a cinematic scope and more of an emphasis on chunky grooves. A few tracks, including the highlight "When Worlds Collide," are virtually pop songs, while much of the album explores contemporary instrumental music and reveals influences from trip-hop and dance music. Though Haslinger's production work is edgy and skillful throughout, the Eastern chanting and vocals on many tracks may bother fans of traditional dance music. —*John Bush*

## Jon Hassell

b. Mar. 22, 1937, Memphis, TN

*Trumpet, Leader, Composer / Experimental, Fusion, Avant-Garde, Techno-Tribal, Minimalism, Ambient, Ethnic Fusion*

Trumpeter Jon Hassell was the originator and unrivalled master of the musical aesthetic he dubbed Fourth World—in his own words, "a unified primitive/futuristic sound combining features of world ethnic styles with advanced electronic techniques." Born March 22, 1937 in Memphis, TN, he attended Rochester, NY's Eastman School of Music and Washington, DC's Catholic University before studying in Europe under the legendary Karlheinz Stockhausen. After subsequent collaborations with minimalist pioneers La Monte Young and Terry Riley, Hassell mounted a number of solo pieces known collectively as the Landmusic Series; the most famous of these so-called "sound monuments" was 1969's *Solid State*, an electronic project which evoked the gradual erosion of sand dune formations via a tuned mass of vibrations.

Beginning in 1972, Hassell studied classical Indian music under the tutelage of Pandit Pran Nath, modifying Nath's vocal techniques to the trumpet to develop the Fourth World concept, which he introduced with 1978's *Vernal Equinox*. The jazz-inspired *Earthquake Island* appeared a year later, and in 1980 Hassell issued *Possible Musics/Fourth World Vol. 1*, a collaboration with Brian Eno. (A sequel, *Dream Theory in Malaya/Fourth World Vol. 2*, was quick in forthcoming.) Through Eno, he also began working with a series of experimental pop acts, appearing on records by Talking Heads, David Sylvian and Peter Gabriel; in 1982, Hassell additionally scored Magazzini Criminali's Venice production of *Sulla Strada*, earning an Ubu award for Best Music for a Theatrical Work.

Following 1983's *Aka-Dabari-Java/Magic Realism* (co-produced by Daniel Lanois), Hassell did not resurface on record until 1986's *Power Spot;* in the interim, he composed *Pano de Costa*, a string quartet piece recorded by the Kronos Quartet for their *White Man Sleeps* LP. *The Surgeon of the Nightsky Restores Dead Things by the Power of Sound* followed in 1987, and that same year Hassell collaborated with the Burkina Faso percussion ensemble Farafina, a union which spawned 1989's *Flash of the Spirit*. The hip-hop-inspired *City: Works of Fiction* appeared in 1990, and four years later he launched *Dressing for Pleasure;* subsequent projects include *Lurch*, an experimental dance piece choreographed by Gideon Obarzanek, and 1999's *Fascinoma*, on which Hassell collaborated with Ry Cooder and Jacky Terrasson. *Hollow Bamboo* was issued a year later. —*Jason Ankeny*

**Earthquake Island** / 1979 / Tomato ◆◆◆
"Miles Davis meets the Bermuda Triangle" on Hassell's first album with Miroslav Vitous, Nana, Dom Um Romao, and Badal Roy. Stunning music and cover art. —*Michael G. Nastos*

★ **Fourth World, Vol. 1: Possible Musics** / 1980 / EG ◆◆◆◆◆
*Fourth World Vol. 1: Possible Musics* is a collaboration between the trumpeter Jon Hassell (who gets top billing) and synthesizer player Brian Eno. The "fourth world" seems to be located somewhere in the Sudan, if the album's cover picture is any indication. (That's in the middle of Africa, just south of Egypt, for you geography neophytes.) The music consists of Hassell's haunting trumpet sounds, coupled with Eno's atmospheric synthsizer sounds and "treatments," playing over a variety of percussion instruments. Typical of both musicians, the music is slow and trance-like, and typical of Middle Eastern music, it has an odd, often wailing tonality that is, however, more otherworldly than, um, fourth-worldly. —*William Ruhlmann*

**Fourth World, Vol. 2: Dream Theory in Malaya** / 1981 / EG ◆◆◆
An academic feel proceeds from the subject matter, a meditation on the inspirational seed of artistic composition. It takes its lead from the dreamtelling of Malaysian aborigines, the Senoi, whose environment, beliefs, and music shape Hassell's approach. —*Bob Tarte*

**Flash of the Spirit** / 1988 / Intuition ◆◆
Taking a vacation from abstraction, Hassell kicks out a near set of dance tunes with Burkino Faso musicians, Farafina. So great is his exhilaration, he even gives us peeks at the natural timbre of his trumpet. It was produced by Hassell, Daniel Lanois, and Brian Eno. —*Bob Tarte*

## HAT

f. 1994

*Group / Experimental Techno, Electronica, Electro-Jazz, Ambient Techno*

Acronymic globetrotter trio HAT are the combined efforts of, in order, Japan's Haruomi Hosono, Germany's Uwe Schmidt (a.k.a. Atom Heart), and New York's Tetsu Inoue. The group's on-again/off-again collaborations have to date produced two CD-only releases, each bringing together elements of ambient, techno, electro, jazz, pop, lounge, and exotica. Occasionally demanding and always entertaining, both albums number among all three artists' finest recent releases, each successfully fusing Hosono's mastery of offbeat pop with Schmidt's bizarre rhythmic frameworks and Inoue's elegant, alluring digital acousmatics. The group's self-titled debut was released on Schmidt's Rather

Interesting label in 1995. A visionary and effortless electronic fusion with a heavily improvisational feel, the CD was reissued by Hosono's Tokyo-based Daisyworld imprint in 1996, and the success of the disc in Japan led to a follow-up, *DSP Holiday*, recorded and released in 1998. *DSP Holiday* showed a deeper concern for accessibility—probably driven as much by the popularity of the first disc in Japan as by each artists' growing interest in porting abstract digital sound experiments into a pop framework—although that's hardly a criticism; the disc is at least its predecessor's equal. —*Sean Cooper*

● **DSP Holiday** / 1998 / Daisyworld ♦♦♦♦
HAT's second disc of aisle-spanning electronica is a more laid-back affair. Released this time on Hosono's Daisyworld label, *DSP Holiday* is all afizz with sampled percussion, bossa nova rhythms, and references to Japanese pop and eazy-breezy jazz. All cue to Daisyworld's installed base of plastic-dipped lounge-a-holics, of course, but *DSP Holiday* is an incredibly weird and wonderful recording all the same. Schmidt's penchant for knowing when to pull the rhythmic rug completely out from underneath a song plays a crucial role in keeping the kitsch at bay, but the album as a whole proves yet another object lesson in the value of summing up parts. —*Sean Cooper*

## haujobb

f. 1993, Germany
*Group / Electro-Industrial, Industrial Dance, Industrial*
Their style a synthesis of industrial electronics and dance music, haujobb formed in Germany in 1993 around the trio of Dejan Samardzic, Daniel Meier, with B. Junemann. After the release of a cassette-only album named *Drift Wheeler*, haujobb signed to Off Beat Records and in 1993 released a proper debut, *Homes and Gardens*. The trio toured Germany and issued the album in the States, but said farewell to Junemann in 1995, just after the release of *Freeze Frame Reality*. A split release with :wumpscut: titled *The Remix Wars, Strike 1* appeared one year later, and Haujobb also contributed remixes to Front Line Assembly and Download; cEvin Key returned the favor on the *Frames* remix EP. Their third album, *Solutions for a Small Planet*, appeared in 1996, followed by the two-disc *Matrix*, which included remixes as well as individual samples so bedroom boffins could remake tracks from *Solutions for a Small Planet* themselves. Haujobb returned two years later with *Ninetynine*; an accompanying remix collection followed in 1999. —*John Bush*

**Freeze Frame Reality** / 1995 / Off Beat ♦♦♦
German industrial band haujobb use a Skinny Puppy influence as a springboard to fresh ideas, combining an increased use of electronics and a touch of ambient dub. —*John Bush*

**Frames [EP]** / 1995 / Off Beat ♦♦♦♦
*Frames*, released late in 1995, is haujobb's addition to the trend of industrial bands to release albums featuring remixes of their own songs by their contemporaries. In this case, haujobb are in good company, since *Frames* features not only their new reinterpretations of their material but have alongside them artists such as Forma Tadre, Mentallo & the Fixer, and cEvin Key from Download. Almost all the material on *Frames* was featured in its original form on their previous album, *Freeze Frame Reality* (though the US Pendragon release also has the original material from their first single, "Eye Over You," as bonus tracks). On the whole, the remixes featured on this EP are more forceful and sometimes more aggressive than the elaborate electronic soundscapes featured on earlier haujobb releases, but this is not to say that existing fans of this outfit will be disappointed—the complexity is still there, but has been mediated into stronger beats and heavier sounds with very different feels and textures to the originals. They often very closely reflect the music of the guest remixer, especially in cEvin Key's case, which is probably the best outcome for any good remix release. The one track which bears exception to all of this is the "A4—Main Title," which has haujobb delving into their string arrangements again, though in this case the strings are not attached to any industrial number they've performed. This track was rumored to be a composition for introductory credits of the movie *Alien 4* and shows that haujobb's talents are not confined to the electro-industrial sound. After all this experimentation with a number of artists, *Frames* ends with the feel of a collection of interesting sketches rather than a polished album release, yet it is as successful a venture musically as any other album released by this band, especially for existing fans. —*Theo Kavadias*

● **Solutions for a Small Planet** / Oct. 29, 1996 / Metropolis ♦♦♦♦
As haujobb's third major album release, *Solutions for a Small Planet* marks a departure from their previous definitive style. The intricate electronic soundscapes and detailed attention to samples and voices are all still present, but a new progressive techno feel permeates this release. Some elements of this album seem reminiscent of the remixing they have done between this album and the second for electro-industrial bands such as Front Line Assembly, Download, and Wumpscut. Within this new style, haujobb have again shown that their complex intensity functions for both their danceable upbeat tracks (such as "Rising Sun" and "Deviation") and the slower attention-to-sounds tracks in the vein of "Nature's Interface." Throughout all these changes, however, haujobb have retained both their intricacy and clinical approach to sound that they defined for themselves with their previous release, *Freeze Frame Reality*. —*Theo Kavadias*

**Ninetynine** / May 4, 1999 / Metropolis ♦♦♦♦
With *Ninetynine*, haujobb begins to open up its sound to the influence of more experimental electronica, helped no doubt by frontman Daniel Meyer's dabblings with a variety of other groups and remix projects. The sound of the record is minimalistic, sometimes featuring female vocalists, and more ethereal than past Haujobb releases, continuing the progression hinted at by *Matrix*. —*Steve Huey*

**Ninetynine Remixes** / Nov. 23, 1999 / Metropolis ♦♦♦♦
haujobb's *Ninetynine Remixes* features nine reconfigurations of tracks from the group's *Ninetynine* album, casting them in a more ambient and minimalistic light. Tracks like haujobb's own remix of "Pulsar" and "Overflow (Red Sparrow Mix)" emphasize the percussive aspects of their music as well as their flair for creating cold, spare, yet somehow moving synth melodies. "Overpulse (Combination by Photic Sonar)" fuses together "Pulsar" and "Overflow" with darkly beautiful results. "Overflow (Infam Remix)" and "Overflow (For a Space Remix)" reveal different aspects of the original's ethereal-dance vibe and Vanessa Briggs' vocals, while "Cutedge (60:60 Architect Remix)" and "Ninetynine (S'Apexed)" take haujobb's stark but atmospheric style to new heights. —*Heather Phares*

## Richie Hawtin

b. Jun. 4, 1970, Danbury, England
*Producer, DJ / Minimal Techno, Electronica, Acid Techno, Club/Dance, Techno*
Although of English and Canadian origins, Plastikman's Richie Hawtin is closely connected with the current Detroit techno scene associated with figures such as Kenny Larkin, Stacey Pullen, Eddie Fowlkes, and Derrick May. His Plus 8 label—co-owned and operated with John Acquaviva—is one of the most influential experimental dance music imprints, and Hawtin's own tracks recorded as Plastikman and F.U.S.E. are highly regarded as faithful, intelligent, forward-stepping updates of the Detroit sound. A DJ of renown and growing in repute as a remixer, Hawtin's visibility as one of experimental dance music's more important and innovative figures has been on the rise since the release of his debut Plastikman album, *Sheet One*.

Born in the English burgh of Danbury in 1970, Hawtin's parents moved to Canada when he was nine. An early interest in electronic-based pop and dance music turned serious when Hawtin discovered the tracks being pumped out of his neighbor-across-the-river Detroit. Beginning as a DJ in 1987, Hawtin quickly became involved in composition through his direct involvement in Detroit's tight-knit community of musicians and producers. Combining early influences from European synth-pop groups like Kraftwerk and New Order with the stripped-down techno-futurism of Detroit innovators such as Juan Atkins and Derrick May, Hawtin's tracks are as steeped in Motor City tradition as they deviate from it in terms of texture and rhythmic complexity. Although 12"s through Plus 8 and the European NovaMute label have all been pretty dancefloor-oriented, Hawtin's attention to techno-based listening music has been just as focused through his full-length albums. [See Also: F.U.S.E., Plastikman] —*Sean Cooper*

**Concept 1 96: CD** / Oct. 19, 1998 / M_nus ♦♦♦
Over the course of a year Richie Hawtin released a 12-volume set of records—one every month—known as the *Concept* series. *Concept 1 96: CD* collects 15 of the compositions from these now hard-to-find records. Unlike the material Hawtin releases as Plastikman and F.U.S.E., this album focuses entirely on the cognitive, rather than the physical or sensory side, of electronic dance music. Each of these tracks arranges and manipulates electronically produced sounds as an abstract expressionist painter would treat a canvas.

Through the use of deep bass frequencies, his sounds sometimes seem to come to life, becoming tangible as they rattle the interior of one's home or creep down one's spine. As artistic expression, this collection bursts at the seams with interesting ideas and some truly creative sounds, but is probably too devoid of melody and rhythm for fans of Hawtin's 303-based work. —*Jason Birchmeier*

★ **Decks, EFX & 909** / Nov. 2, 1999 / Nova Mute ♦♦♦♦♦
The next step after his *Mixmag* live album from 1995 and the increasing minimalism of his subsequent Plastikman material (the *Consumed* LP), *Decks, EFX & 909* presents Richie Hawtin displaying not only his talents as a mixer but also as a producer. An extension of his live sets (though not entirely recorded live), the album was produced using turntables, an effects processor and Roland pedal, plus a TR-909 drum machine for added beats, and employs a degree of improvisation rarely seen on mix albums. Cycling through 38 tracks in just over an hour, Hawtin ranges through driving, minimalist techno with inclusions from Richard Harvey, Jeff Mills, Surgeon, Pacou, Heiko Laux, Vladislav Delay, Maurizio, Rhythm & Sound, Marco Carola, and a few of his own tracks. The result of Hawtin's obvious labor of love is a mix album that manages to be simultaneously intense and moody, pummeling yet restrained. The beats are clipped and precise, rarely deviating from a 120 BPM pace. Though fans might resent the fact that it wasn't recorded live, *Decks, EFX & 909* simply couldn't have been done well in a live setting—at times, Hawtin has four records spinning at once, and the layers of sound he adds to the show makes this album the highly effective statement on techno that it is. Another devastating release from North America's most effective dancefloor experimentalist. —*John Bush*

## Headrillaz

f. 1994, London, England
*Group / Big Beat, Funky Breaks, Club/Dance*
South London big beat trio Headrillaz produce caustic, bombastic uptempo trip-hop in the Chemical Brothers/Monkey Mafia mold, fusing rock-based samples and attitude with elements of house, techno, and club-bound hip-hop. Formed in 1995 as an offshoot of Ninja Tune acid-jazz/trip-hop group Slowly, Headrillaz is the brother/stepbrother team of Casper, Saul, and Darius Kedros, all of whom have been producing music in one form or another since their early teens. The name Headrillaz first surfaced as a remix credit on one of a string of experimental Brit-hop twelves following Slowly's demise (the Kedros brothers released a number of singles as Tranquil Elephantizer and Trunk), and continued as a proper project after London producer Howie "B" Bernstein saw the group dirty up a DATs'n'tables performance in a club. Bernstein insisted on releasing their 1996 debut 12", "Weird Planet," on his own Pussyfoot label, and the group followed up with two more twelves—"Screaming Heads" and "Spacefuck"—before releasing the full-length *Coldharbour Rocks* in 1997. A singles compilation mostly, *Coldharbour* collected the best of the group's Pussyfoot output to date and added a few unreleased cuts. The trio's live performances also escalated to the band level, with a full touring ensemble landing gigs at major UK festivals such as Tribal Gathering and Glastonbury. —*Sean Cooper*

● **Coldharbour Rocks** / Jun. 30, 1997 / Pussyfoot/V2 ♦♦♦♦
The debut album by Headrillaz includes a collection of their early singles like "Spacefunk," "Hot 'N' Bovvud," and "Screaming Headz") mines similar ground to the Chemical Brothers, specifically uptempo big-beat techno with enough vocal samples and siren calls to interest those not used to electronic music with little or no traditional structure. In general, *Coldharbour Rocks* has fewer ideas than contemporary work by the more popular Chemical Brothers; though it is enjoyable enough in its own right, many artists have done better. —*John Bush*

## Larry Heard

b. May 31, 1960, Chicago, IL
*Keyboards, Producer / Jazz-House, Club/Dance, Acid House, House*
He never sold as many records as some of the other Chicago house producers, but Larry Heard is arguably the best to come out of the scene, providing the crucial marriage between the warmth and communal feeling of disco and the energy and futurism of house music. His classic mid-'80s singles on Trax Records—as Larry Heard and Mr. Fingers, as well as Fingers Inc. with the addition of vocalists Ron Wilson and Robert Owens—set the template for every house-influenced producer to come later, and scores of dance artists have name-checked him as providing the best moments in house music's history. Unlike many of his Chicago house contemporaries, Heard's discography is quite large, with several albums released under each of his three major pseudonyms plus several albums during the '90s recorded as Larry Heard.

Born on Chicago's South Side in 1960, Heard began buying records at an early age and was influenced by his parents' jazz and gospel collection. Though he practiced on guitar and bass as a youth, he joined a friend's band playing drums after bluffing his way through an audition at the age of 17. Heard began practicing with fervor and became quite good, though he took a civil-service job as well to pay the bills. While playing with a variety of local bands during the late '70s and early '80s (including one with future house star Adonis on bass), Heard was introduced to many different types of synthesizers, and he gradually became more interested in playing keyboards than drums. Heard finally opted out of the band setup in 1984, bought a synthesizer/drum machine combo and began producing music. After a few days with the gear, he had recorded three tracks later recognized as serious pinnacles of Chicago house, among them "Mystery of Love," "Washing Machine," and "Can You Feel It." His lack of connections in the club scene made it difficult to get the tracks listened to, though Heard finally debuted on wax with a 1985 single for DJ International named "Donnie." Instead of being credited to Larry Heard however, the single appeared as the It, and was co-written by street poet Harry Dennis. Later, on one of his infrequent trips into the club/party scene, Heard met up with Robert Owens. Owens was then working as a DJ though he was (more importantly) an incredibly talented gospel-styled vocalist. Heard and Owens decided to form Fingers Inc., with the addition of Ron Wilson.

The nascent Chicago house scene was just about to explode with recording activity, and Heard released nearly a dozen singles during 1986-87, for both Trax and DJ International. Fingers Inc. contributed Chicago classics like "Mystery of Love," "You're Mine," "Distant Planet," and "Bring Down the Walls" while Mr. Fingers dropped quite possibly the most sublime house single ever released, "Can You Feel It." (Though by no means a hard and fast rule, Fingers Inc. releases were usually vocal tracks, while Heard used the tag Mr. Fingers as his solo outlet.)

By the end of the '80s, Heard's name was being dropped by many in the new wave of British producers influenced by American house music. He continued recording in earnest, and released one of the first house full-lengths with the 1988 Fingers Inc. LP *Another Side* for Jack Trax Records. The following year, Jack Trax released Heard's original 1984 instrumental demos as the Mr. Fingers album *Amnesia*, even though he had never given consent to the album's issue. Despite its barely legal status, the LP showcased the first flowering of Heard's genius with several impeccable tracks. His large production role on the 1989 debut album by Lil' Louis (of "French Kiss" fame) was noticed by the major labels and by the beginning of the '90s, Heard was being offered contracts by several labels. He recorded additional material with Harry Dennis, though Dennis' continuing drug problems gave Heard a desire to strike out on his own.

After finally signing to MCA as a solo act in 1991, Heard issued his first major-label album one year later. Mr. Fingers' *Introduction* charted an intriguing balance between floor-filling garage house and several tracks of polished jazz-fusion; Heard's undying influence among DJs and producers alike made the album quite an international success. Though it graced the American dance charts as well, MCA attempted to interfere with the production of its follow-up *Back to Love*, and later refused to release the album at all. It finally appeared in 1995 on Black Market Records, the label formed by Heard's friend and former manager Ren Galston.

By the time *Back to Love* was released however, Heard had already recorded and released another album, his first as simply Larry Heard. The album *Sceneries Not Songs, Vol. 1* (and its follow-up) both expanded on Heard's commitment to inner space rather than the dancefloor. He returned to a style more tied to traditional house with 1996's *Alien* and the following year's *Dance 2000*. In late 1997, Heard suddenly declared that he had quit recording to take a computer-programming job in Memphis. Despite his apparent retirement from music, two more albums of new tracks filtered out in 1998. Yet another, *Genesis*, followed in 1999. [See also: Fingers Inc., Mr. Fingers]—*John Bush*

**Sceneries Not Songs, Vol. 1** / 1994 / Black Market ♦♦♦♦
The jazzier tracks from Larry Heard's only album for MCA coalesced in 1995 on the first of his *Sceneries Not Songs* full-lengths. Heard extends the fusion

as well, covering the prevailing ambient house boom (of which he was a prime influence). —*John Bush*

★ **Classic Fingers** / 1995 / Black Market ✦✦✦✦✦

Spotlighting Larry Heard's seminal production work during the '80s and '90s, *Classic Fingers* includes obvious Mr. Fingers/Fingers Inc. milestones like "Mystery of Love," "Distant Planet," and "Amnesia," plus quite a few obscure productions like "Shine" by Kriss Coleman, "Play It Loud" by House Factors, "Blast Off" by Gherkin Jerks, and the It's "Gallimauffry Gallery." Though it's quite an obscure compilation (available in 1- and 2-CD incarnations), *Classic Fingers* is the best way to get the most material by Larry Heard. —*John Bush*

**Sceneries Not Songs, Vol. Tu** / 1995 / MIA ✦✦✦

First gaining fame in the early '80s as Mr. Fingers, Chicago-based house music pioneer/MIDI programmer Larry Heard helped pave the way for what now some call ambient house, while others label it acid jazz. His major label debut on MCA, *Introduction*, enjoyed success on both the dancefloor and smooth jazz radio in the States and overseas.

On *Sceneries Not Songs, Vol. Tu*, Heard continued the winning formula. The opener, "Crystal Fantasy," inspires good feelings with an airy mix, soaring strings, and solid handclaps. The misty "Romantic Sway" is in the mode of Paul Hardcastle's Jazzmasters with light rhythm box, soft, slow synth swells, and vibraphonic lead lines.

There are a number of melodic dance workouts here. "Carla Dance" has tasty percussion and jazzy acoustic and electric piano solos. Despite its name, "Techno-Centric" isn't hyper-kinetic but rather sparse and mid-tempo with jazzy, upper-register piano and unassuming synth textures. "Night Images" is good mood music for a lovely conversation. "Ice Castles" has stomp funky bass and xylophone solos. "Nature's Bliss" has an openness that's built around gentle conga, shaker, and tambourine that leaves plenty of space for comping piano and clear synth flute lines. The oh-too-short mid-tempo "Precious Tears" has an otherworldy synth lead, slapped congas, and harmonica riffs. Though his vocals are missed, Larry Heard paints deft, aural "sceneries" on *Sceneries Not Songs, Vol. Tu*. —*Ed Hogan*

**Alien** / Apr. 8, 1996 / Black Market ✦✦✦✦

Larry Heard's productions always hinted at deepest outer space, but *Alien* was his first actual science-fiction record. It's almost as polished as the most mainstream dance production, but just as sublime as any Detroit producer. Heard's house roots often show themselves, while the chords and shimmering production make this an album almost on par with Heard's mid-'80s peak. —*John Bush*

**Dance 2000** / Nov. 10, 1997 / Distance ✦✦✦✦

Even though it wasn't the last album of new Larry Heard material, *Dance 2000* would have been a quality departure for the most respected Chicago house producer. The LP is stocked with deep grooves and Heard's seminal synthesizer textures on tracks like "Dancefloor Seduction" and "Hydrogenation." Stylistically, it's very similar to his earliest recordings, no mean feat at that. —*John Bush*

**Dance 2000, Part 2** / Aug. 3, 1998 / Distance ✦✦✦

**Parrains de la House** / Nov. 24, 1998 / Mirakkle ✦✦✦✦

## Heaven 17

f. Oct. 1980, London, England
*Group / New Romantic, New Wave, Synth-Pop*

Taking their name from the Anthony Burgess novel *A Clockwork Orange*, the UK techno-pop trio Heaven 17 grew out of the experimental dance project the British Electric Foundation, itself an offshoot of the electro-pop outfit Human League. The core of Heaven 17 was comprised of Martyn Ware and Ian Craig Marsh, a pair of onetime computer operators who first teamed in 1977 as the Dead Daughters, a duo which integrated synthesizer patterns with a heavy reliance on tape loops. Soon, Ware and Marsh were joined by Philip Oakey and Adi Newton and changed their name to the Human League, where they remained before exiting together in 1980.

As a means of establishing the synthesizer as an expressive, human instrument, Marsh and Ware formed the British Electric Foundation, a production project which employed a variety of musicians and singers including Tina Turner, Sandie Shaw and Gary Glitter. The B.E.F.'s debut, 1980's *Music of Quality and Distinction, Vol. 1*, also included vocalist Glenn Gregory, a former photographer whom Ware and Marsh met at a Sheffield drama center; in 1981, the duo enlisted Gregory for Heaven 17, the first and most successful B.E.F. alter ego, and debuted with the single "(We Don't Need This) Fascist Groove Thang," a minor hit banned by the BBC over its title. An album, *Penthouse and Pavement*, followed the same year.

By the release of 1983's *The Luxury Gap*, the B.E.F. had fallen by the wayside, and Heaven 17 had become Ware and Marsh's primary focus; the LP proved highly successful, spawning the hit singles "Temptation," "Come Live with Me," "Crushed by the Wheels of Industry," and "Let Me Go." The follow-up, *How Men Are*, was another British hit, but the group receded from view after its release; when they returned in 1986 with the album *Pleasure One*, it was with a number of guest musicians and vocalists.

After the commerical failure of 1988's *Teddy Bear, Duke & Psycho*, Heaven 17 officially disbanded; Ware focused on production chores, and worked on Terence Trent D'Arby's debut *Introducing the Hardline According to Terence Trent D'Arby*. In 1990, he and Marsh resurrected the B.E.F. aegis, releasing *Music of Quality and Distinction, Vol. 2* the following year. In 1996, a reformed Heaven 17 returned with *Bigger than America*. —*Jason Ankeny*

**Penthouse and Pavement** / 1981 / Virgin ✦✦✦✦

● **The Best of Heaven 17: Higher & Higher** / Aug. 24, 1993 / Virgin ✦✦✦✦

*The Best of Heaven 17: Higher & Higher* is an extensive, 17-track collection that contains all of the group's best moments, including "Temptation" and "(We Don't Need This) Fascist Groove Thang," plus several album tracks, lesser-known singles, and remixes of their two greatest hits. It's too much music for casual fans, especially since the sequencing is slightly illogical, and it's not comprehensive enough for dedicated collectors, but *Higher & Higher* remains an adequate overview of the synth-pop band's career. —*Stephen Thomas Erlewine*

**Bigger than America** / 1996 / WEA ✦✦

By 1988's *The Luxury Gap* album, Heaven 17 seemed to have taken a holiday, and their only further releases by the early '90s were two *Greatest Hits* albums (one in Europe and one in America). Martyn Ware spent his time producing other acts like Erasure and their *I Say I Say I Say* album. But in 1998, ten years after Heaven 17's last "studio" album, Marsh, Ware, and Gregory came back larger than life with *Bigger Than America*. The album contains a collage of sounds ranging from their early Human League days to the latest cutting-edge '90s electronica. Unlike so many other synth-pop acts, Heaven 17 doesn't rely on the barrage of beats and orchestra hits to conceal poor lyrical content. Glenn Gregory is a sensational vocalist and together with Marsh and Ware has written intelligent lyrics that take center stage in the songs. "Do I Believe" and "Maybe Forever" are the best examples with their percussionless, minimalistic instrumentation taking a back seat to Gregory's voice. These songs have a simple, vintage feel, like Yaz's "Ode to Boy" using only a few synth sounds to carry them through. Heaven 17 fans will recognize their trademark sound on *Bigger Than America*. Traces of their classic songs like "Temptation," "Let Me Go" and "Come Live with Me" prevail on the new album. In fact, many of the sounds even seem to go back as far as the Human League's "Circus of Death" and "Being Boiled." This does not mean the album is retro; it just draws some of the elements from their history. The single "Designing Heaven" is as contemporary as anything Erasure, the Pet Shop Boys, or the Human League have done recently. Another carry-over is the underlying theme of technology in many of their lyrics that mirror older songs like "Crushed by the Wheels of Industry."

The album contains two bonus remixes of the single, "Designing Heaven," one of which was remixed by veteran producer Giorgio Moroder and another with Gregory singing in German. The first of the two mixes relies on drum and bass, while the second is more of a remake with only lyrical changes. As a whole, the album is well-constructed synth-pop. Heaven 17 has made a great comeback with *Bigger Than America*. If you like Heaven 17 or early Human League, you will love this album. —*Paul Fucito*

**Retox/Detox (Remixed)** / Sep. 8, 1998 / Eagle ✦

In what seems to be an attempt to remain hip and important, Heaven 17 came up with this mess. It seemed like a good idea: '90s DJs (such as Freddie Fresh, Molella, Adrian Sherwood, and more) remixing some of Heaven 17's best-known hits, plus two new recordings of older hits ("Fascist Groove Thang" and "Let Me Go"), but in reality, the result is a big disappointment. This is a real shame, especially since they chose this as the follow-up to their wonderful reunion CD *Bigger Than America*. And Heaven 17 have only themselves to blame, as they assembled this project and were responsible for the whole thing. The real problem with this dance-oriented CD is that the mixes are not very good, and they do nothing to enhance the original songs. In fact, these new mixes take away everything that was good about Heaven 17. Gone are the addictive pop melodies, and in their place are these overlong, drawn-out, boring mixes. Also, the repetition of songs is a big problem. Is there any real need for three mixes of "Geisha Boys and Temple Girls"? It's a second-rate Heaven 17 song at best, and as six-minute dance mixes, it becomes quite unbearable. In fact, there is a total of 13 songs spread over two CDs, with all but four songs remixed twice. This is truly sad, given the wealth of material spread over the six studio releases by Heaven 17. All but one (Giorgio Moroder's remix of 1996's "Designing Heaven") are new mixes, and fans would be better off searching out the original 12" singles for truly creative sounds. It is hard to say for whom this package was designed, as the average dance listener will probably find this whole thing somewhat sloppy and not too danceable, and Heaven 17 fans will be running for the original versions as soon as the CD begins. Fans of this band, and of the '80s sound, would be better served by searching out the 1993 best-of, *Higher and Higher*, and leaving this mess alone. —*Aaron Badgley*

## Heavenly Music Corporation (Kim Cascone)

*Producer / Electronica, Ambient Techno*

American composer and sound designer Kim Cascone may be more recognizable in his former role as head of Silent Records, the label he founded in the mid-'80s, but his recordings as Spice Barons, Thessalonians, PGR, and, most often, Heavenly Music Corporation or his own name, have been equally visible. A soundtrack composer through the early '80s before striking out on his own, Cascone studied electronic music arrangement and composition formally at the Berklee College of Music in the early '70s before studying with Dana McCurdy at Manhattan's New School in 1976. Subsequently working as assistant musical supervisor under director David Lynch on both *Twin Peaks* and *Wild at Heart*, Cascone left Hollywood for San Francisco in the mid-'80s to pursue solo composition, forming Silent Records in 1986 after self-releasing his first PGR album, *Silence*. Though far more abrasive and conflicted than much of his later work, PGR's use of texture and compositional chance is a constant through the whole of Cascone's oevre. A number of PGR titles followed—both on Silent and the RRRecords, Noctovision, and Permis de Construire labels—and Cascone has since gone on to record primarily as Heavenly Music Corporation, releasing the bulk of his work through Silent. Deriving the name from the seminal recording by Brian Eno and Robert Fripp on their 1973 collaboration *No Pussyfooting*, HMC's focus, with some exception, has been on beatless ambient, beginning in 1993 with *In a Garden of Eden* (composed just prior to the birth of Cascone's son, Cage), and working through a series of releases in the mid-'90s. Working toward increasingly abstract aural sculptures, HMC's dabbling with the club culture most new ambient composers look to for inspiration has stretched no further than the spares rhythms that pervade *Consciousness III* and some of *Lunar Phase*, with the lion's share of his material drawing from early electronic and musique concrète composers such as Morton Subotnick, John Cage, and Luciano Berio. Cascone left Silent in 1996 to pursue design and composition at Headspace, a multimedia company started by Thomas Dolby. [See Also: Kim Cascone, PGR] —*Sean Cooper*

**In a Garden of Eden** / 1993 / Silent ♦♦

The liner notes of the seven-track *In a Garden of Eden* release make a number of vaguely flaky claims; it was created for use in a "technomystical chill room" in Goa, India, uses a process of "sublingual hypgnosis" to induce a "theta state" in the listener's brain and actually warns against driving an automobile or operating heavy machinery while listening to it. The record is the sort of thing one would expect after reading this; a completely ambient collection of synth washes and burbles of the mellowest variety, occasionally verging on new-age territory and always retaining a soothing appeal. How much of this is due to "sublingual hypgnosis" is anyone's guess, but the album serves as well as any other release of this sort—it's not an artistic or musical entry into the ambient world, but simply a collection of soothing tones to space out to. —*Nitsuh Abebe*

**Consciousness 3** / 1994 / Silent ♦♦♦

The second Heavenly Music Corporation outing is a more upbeat affair, combining Cascone's textural flare with elements of house and techno. Apparently inspired by the movie *Logan's Run*, the album is the most accessible of the HMC catalog, and also the least impressive, relying too often on canned beats and uninteresting melodies. —*Sean Cooper*

**Lunar Phase** / 1995 / Silent ♦♦♦♦

The most ambitious of Cascone's HMC albums, *Lunar Phase* is also the most successful, fusing thick, echoing textures with shimmering melodic lines and subtle, largely beatless rhythms. Composed in part for broadcast on the Japanese ambient satellite/radio station St. Giga, the album is a solid, consistently high-quality work. —*Sean Cooper*

● **Anechoic** / Feb. 1996 / Silent ♦♦♦♦

Highly derivative of its predecessor, *Lunar Phase*, *Anechoic* is still an impressive collection of new ambient. Deep tones and sparse melodies combine with artful, slowly evolving structures, this time almost devoid of percussion. —*Sean Cooper*

## Christoph Heemann

b. 1965

*Producer / Experimental Rock, Experimental Techno, Ambient Techno*

Christoph Heeman's recordings with H.N.A.S. and as a solo act reflect his inheritance of a number of rich European legacies: Kraut-rock, the industrial cut-ups of Nurse with Wound and Cabaret Voltaire, and the idea of the invisible soundtrack which has intrigued many independent-minded producers from Brian Eno to Paul Schütze. In 1983, the teenaged Heemann formed H.N.A.S. (*hirsche nicht aus sofa*, roughly translated as Moose Without a Sofa) with Achim Flaan (aka Achim P. Li Khan).

Amidst a parade of obscure cassette-only releases on their own Dom Records, the duo's first major album, 1985's *Abwassermusik* reflected an interest in collages of samples, tape loops and found sounds, often repeated *ad infinitum*. For 1986's *Melchior*, an expanded H.N.A.S. lineup worked with the very sympathetic Steven Stapleton (of Nurse with Wound) and issued the album on Stapleton's United Dairies labels. The group released two more LPs during 1986-87, *Im Schatten Der Möhre* and *Küttel im Frost* (both on Dom).

Meanwhile, Christoph Heemann had begun working farther afield, with an assortment of figures in the noise underground. He recorded a remix-by-mail project with Merzbow (*Sleeper Awake on the Edge of the Abyss*), appeared with Chicago guitarist Jim O'Rourke's Illusion of Safety, recorded with H.N.A.S.'s own Andrea Martin, and released work as Mimir with Legendary Pink Dots mainman Edward Ka-Spel. Heemann's first solo work, the 1992 EP *Über Den Umgang Mit Umgebung und Andere Versuche* (released on Robot Records), effectively ended H.N.A.S. as a recording entity (though Achim P. Li Khan continued with the Damenbart and Brigitte projects).

Christoph Heemann's first album work, *Invisible Barrier*, appeared on the Australian Extreme Records in 1993. Inspired by filmmakers Alain Resnais and Louis Malle, he recorded *Aftersolstice* one year later, for the Barooni label. Following his third solo album, 1997's *Days of the Eclipse*, Heemann again branched out to work on other projects, among them another Mimir release, several dates with Illusion of Safety, and a role in the recording of the Current 93 album *In a Foreign Land, In a Foreign Town* with David Tibet and Steven Stapleton. —*John Bush*

**Invisible Barrier** / 1993 / Extreme ♦♦♦

An invisible soundtrack in Heemann's continuing series, *Invisible Barrier* alternates environmental recordings with other unidentified forms of slightly unsettled ambience. The result is barely conscious, definitely needing some sort of visual counterpart to balance the sound. —*John Bush*

**Aftersolstice** / 1994 / Barooni ♦♦♦

The second solo project from Heeman (formerly of H.N.A.S.) is an album of alternately orchestral and machine-driven ambience, with various found sounds and samples livening the mix. —*John Bush*

● **Days of the Eclipse** / 1997 / Barooni ♦♦♦♦

The follow-up to *Invisible Barrier*, this time dedicated to Russian director Andrei Tarkovsky, progresses through similar found-sound ambience and environmental recordings as well as passages with more conscious orchestration. —*John Bush*

## Heldon

f. 1974, db. 1978

*Group / Experimental, Prog-Rock/Art Rock, Electronic*

Led by guitarist Richard Pinhas, the French group Heldon released seven groundbreaking albums, melding electronic and rock forms, from 1974 to 1978. Pinhas also recorded six albums under his own name. Pinhas was heavily influenced by Robert Fripp; this shows in his guitar playing, and in the titles of several of his compositions. While early LPs sometimes evoked the sound of Fripp & Eno, Heldon evolved in its own direction. The release of *Heldon IV: Agneta Nilsson* saw the group heading toward a more intense, menacing sound. *Heldon V: Un Reve Sans Consequence Speciale* was the first to feature the "classic" lineup of Pinhas, drummer Francois Auger and keyboard player Patrick Gauthier. These three would be the key personnel on Heldon's last four albums. The entire Pinhas/Heldon catalog was reissued on CD by Cuneiform, several featuring bonus live tracks. —*Jim Dorsch*

### Heldon II: Allez Teia / 1975 / Cuneiform ♦♦♦

Inexplicably, Pinhas repudiated this reissue in a 1992 interview, along with its sequel, *It's Always Rock and Roll*, as recordings that "did not stand time." Heldon was not yet a proper band at this stage, and had only Georges Grunblatt assisting Pinhas on Mellotron, guitars, and ARP synthesizers. Perhaps Pinhas is embarrassed, in retrospect, at the recording's general lack of originality. Overt homage is paid to influences, with a song titled "In the Wake of King Fripp" (named after King Crimson's second release, *In the Wake of Poseidon*). Another piece on the CD is dedicated to "Fripp and Eno." The relationship with Fripp and Eno's two collaborations, *No Pussyfooting* and *Evening Star*, is indeed pronounced on several tracks, but since this was a sound that neither Eno nor Fripp stuck with for very long, further elaborations of it are always welcome. One curious aspect of this recording (and perhaps another source of discomfort for Pinhas in retrospect) is that a visual attempt has been made to affiliate Pinhas and/or his music with angry young student radicals (the cover has a photo of a club-wielding policeman chasing a young protestor), but the music itself is not in the least bit angry or violent. Pinhas even plays acoustic guitar on several tracks, and adds a Mellotron string section on several others, creating a sound which is almost incipient New Age. However, several other pieces such as "Fluence," with its minor keys and abstract, watery drones, and the following piece, "St. Mikael Samstag Am Abends," have more substantial elements of darkness or mystery. There are worse things than an album which sounds in part like Fripp and Eno circa *Evening Star*, and Pinhas's retrospective judgment of this recording is much too harsh. —*William Tilland*

### Interface / 1976 / Cuneiform ♦♦♦♦

Heldon's real excellence as a band is dramatically demonstrated with this fine recording. A dashing young left-wing intellectual, Pinhas was something of a cult figure in his native France, or at least had the potential to be one, but he wisely rejected the role of rock 'n' roll guitar hero with backing band, in favor of something much more interesting and radical. Patrick Gauthier on Moogs and Francois Auger on percussion had played with Pinhas on and off for the previous several years, and at this point they had developed into a solid sympathetic unit with a strongly rhythmic orientation. The intricate interlocking rhythms, created by percussion and several synthesizers, have a proto-techno quality at times, and suggest both the German group Can and, on at least one piece, early Ash Ra Tempel. Some of the Grateful Dead's long, free-form jams might also serve as a touchstone, and tracks like "Bal-a-fou" even begin with loose, vaguely psychedelic fragments which gradually coalesce into a very trippy and propulsive collective improvisation. On several pieces, Pinhas's Fripp-inspired guitar lines provide still another layer of intensity. The tour de force is the long title piece which ends the CD. At close to 20 minutes, it builds slowly, gradually adding layers of rhythmic complexity with drums, synthesized percussion, sequencers and Pinhas's electric guitar, which doesn't even show up until nine minutes into the piece. —*William Tilland*

### Stand By / 1979 / Egg ♦♦♦♦

This was Heldon's last studio release, although the reissued *Rhizosphere* CD includes a 1982 Heldon concert recording with slightly different personnel. *Stand By* features the classic trio lineup of the brilliant Francois Auger on percussion, Patrick Gauthier on keyboards and Pinhas on guitars, keyboards and electronics, with some additional assistance from Didier Batard on bass, Didier Badez on sequencers and Klaus Blasquiz doing voices. The two long pieces on the CD are an interesting contrast. The title piece starts with some nasty distorted fuzz guitar from Pinhas over ponderous, menacing bass and drums. King Crimson at its most aggressive could be considered a model, but this track is also very close to the so-called "zheul" sound of Magma, another French prog-rock band of the period, which shared Pinhas' interest in science fiction motifs, among other things. Later in the piece, the band switches gears somewhat with a slightly quicker tempo, but then after a minutes settles back into a grinding, heavy metal sound. After a short and much jauntier electronic interlude comes the second long piece, "Bolero," which uses the well-known Spanish rhythm in an opening section, but then moves into a long space jam which is anchored by a strong sequencer pulse. The result is some very effective "kosmiche" space music, much in the vein of early Klaus Schulze. From a later vantage point, the musical style here is quite familiar, but what makes Heldon's piece a superior thing of its kind is Auger's imaginative percussion, Pinhas's loose, soaring guitar improvisation on top of the precise electronics, and the general interplay among musicians and between acoustic, electric and electronic instruments. Not cookie-cutter stuff by any means, this piece gives the German audionauts such as Schulze and Tangerine Dream some worthy competition. —*William Tilland*

### Heldon V: Un Reve Sans Consequence Speciale / 1981 / Inner City ♦♦♦♦

This is one of Heldon's most impressive recordings. It offers the continuity of a group sound throughout, with Pinhas' keyboards and guitars supported by Francois Auger playing drums and percussion on most tracks, and additional assistance from Patrick Gauthier on Moog synthesizers and either Didier Batard or Janick Top on bass. Stylistically, it's a great leap forward from previous Heldon releases, and much closer to the fusion jazz of, say, Mahavishnu Orchestra, than to conventional psychedelic or prog-rock. The five pieces (one in both a live and a studio version) have no real melodies or themes; rather, they use simple patterns and chord sequences as guidelines, and let the musicians improvise around them. The opening "Marie Virginie C." almost sounds like late Coltrane free jazz, or perhaps like Hendrix at his most frenzied, with guitars and synthesizers howling, and Auger thrashing wildly in the background. Speaking of Auger, he has to be one of the great rock drummers of the era—not just in France but in all of Europe. He's fast, ferocious and very funky. The second piece on the CD, the very African-sounding "Elephanta," is a showcase for his percussive talents, and through the miracle of overdubbing, he sounds like an entire ethnic percussion orchestra. Another long piece, "Toward the Red Line," has a hard-edged techno quality (in 1976!), thanks to Auger's motoric drumming and the swirling rhythmic pulse of electronic sequencers. For all the fuss made about the experimental nature of early Tangerine Dream, it is doubtful that they ever did anything more radical than this. Gauthier is also a key member of this group, laying down ostinato patterns on mini-Moog and Moog bass which substantially thicken the group sound and allow Pinhas to soar over the top with electric guitar and his own keyboards. Neither Pinhas or Gauthier is the least bit shy about coaxing some ungodly howls, moans and growls out of his electronics, and their consistent willingness (even eagerness) to get down and dirty gives the music its backbone. This is a very powerful and confident recording, and many years later it remains one of the most successful examples even of electronic instruments used in an experimental rock context. —*William Tilland*

### • Electronique Guerilla/It's Always Rock and Roll / 1993 / Cuneiform ♦♦♦♦

Between 1974 and 1982, Frenchman Richard Pinhas recorded at least twelve LPs either under the Heldon name or his own, alternating between guitars and keyboards himself and accompanied by a variety of associates on guitars, drums and analog synthesizers. This double CD reissue includes Heldon's very first release, *Electronique Guerrila*, and their third, *It's Always Rock and Roll* (itself a double LP originally). These releases are sometimes referred to as *Heldon I* and *Heldon III* (*Heldon II*, otherwise known as *Allez Teia*, was recorded earlier in 1975). In spite of the rather aggressive album titles, these early recordings are mellow to the point of ambient, and inscrutably (or perversely), there's very little music in the entire program which would be considered rock 'n' roll by any stretch of the imagination. (Very unobtrusive drums appear only on several of the later tracks on the *Rock and Roll* reissue.) Most musical biographies of Heldon/Pinhas speak of the Eno/Fripp influence, and indeed, Pinhas encouraged the connection in early interviews by referring to the two English musicians in terms bordering on hero worship. But Pinhas is too modest. Much of the better-known electronic trance music that Pinhas and Heldon seem to be imitating, e.g., early Tangerine Dream, Soft Machine, Fripp and Eno, etc., actually comes after these early Heldon recordings—or is occurring at roughly the same time. Aside from Fripp/Eno's *No Pussyfooting*, only the first edition of Fripp's King Crimson band could be considered as an obvious influence, but Pinhas doesn't use vocalists, and seldom demonstrates any delusions of prog-rock grandeur on these releases. If Pinhas is paying homage to Fripp on these recordings, then he is also extending Fripp as well, with the wailing sustain of Pinhas' heavily processed guitar gliding over the top of a number of looped and sequenced synthesizer patterns to good effect. By later standards, the electronic equipment used by Heldon is almost laughably antique, and the concepts may also seem simple and predictable to a more sophisticated audience. Nonetheless, there is a purity and conviction to this music, and a dark, slightly sinister element perhaps best exemplified in the long "Dr. Bloodmoney," a title inspired by the great sci-fi writer Philip K. Dick. Like Dick, Pinhas has a talent for messing with your head, and combines overlapping patterns in such a way that time itself sometimes seems suspended. —*William Tilland*

## Robert Henke

*Producer / Experimental Techno, Ambient Techno*

Producer Robert Henke is better known as one-half of Monolake, the popular minimal techno group associated with Berlin's Chain Reaction label. While that project has brought Henke more notoriety, his most evolved and studied work to date has appeared eponymously, on his own Imbalance Computer Music label. Forsaking, for the most part, the rhythmic pulse of Monolake, solo releases such as *Piercing Music* and *Floating.Point* have focused on the expressive capacity of wholly digitally produced sonic environments, combining crashing waves of FM synthesis with slight clicks, buzzes, drones, and thin, computer-bred noise. Closely related to the comparatively more esoteric works of academic composers such as Francois Bayle, John Chowning, and Bernard Parmegiani (who number among his primary influences), Henke's solo work combines aesthetic aspects of electro-acoustic and acousmatic musics with the less aggravated atmospheres of ambient and experimental post-techno, including him among such company as Terre Thaemlitz, Kim Cascone, and Oval. —*Sean Cooper*

**Piercing Music** / 1995 / Imbalance Computer Music ♦♦♦

● **Floating.Point** / Aug. 4, 1997 / Imbalance Computer Music ♦♦♦♦
Where with his Monolake material Henke is apt to abuse the organic right out of his real-life recordings, his solo work often follows the opposite path, constructing the sounds of such apparently natural phenomena as insects, birds, and crashing waves from the raw material of dimensionless digital noise. This is a subtext of *Floating.Point* (the title refers to the iterative slippage inherent in digital signal processing), which—concept or no—is also some of the current scene's most satisfying digital ambient. —*Sean Cooper*

## Pierre Henry

b. Dec. 9, 1927, Paris, France
*Synthesizer, Composer / Musique Concrète, Electronic*

The celebrated French composer Pierre Henry was among the pivotal forces behind the development of musique concrète, becoming the first formally educated musician to devote his energies to the electronic medium. Born in Paris on December 9, 1927, he began training at the Paris Conservatoire at the age of ten, studying piano under Nadia Boulanger and percussion under Felix Passerone while also attending the classes of Olivier Messiaen. Still, Henry had little regard for traditional musical instruments, preferring instead to privately experiment with nonmusical sound sources; over time, he grew fascinated with the notion of incorporating noise into the compositional process, and perhaps unsurprisingly first attracted notice in performing circles for his prowess as a percussionist.

In 1949, Henry joined the staff of the RTF electronic studio, founded by Pierre Schaeffer five years earlier; he soon immersed himself completely in electronic music, heading the Groupe de Research de Musique Concrète throughout the greater part of the '50s. Henry soon began compiling a "sound herbal," a catalog of any sound potentially useful from a musical standpoint—everything from animal cries to editing techniques to speed variations, all of which he deemed superior to conventional instrumentation. It inspired 1950's *Symphonie pour un homme seul*, a 12-movement work cowritten by Henry and Schaeffer employing the sounds of the human body; solo pieces including 1951's *Le microphone bien tempere* (the first attempt at notated musique concrète), *Musique sans titre* and *Concerto des ambiguites* (which combined live piano with its own recorded distorted sounds) all broke new ground as well.

In 1952, Henry produced the first musique concrète ever commissioned for commercial films when he scored Jean Grémillon's *Astrologie;* a year later, at the Donaueschingen Festival, he premiered *Orpheé 53*, the first musique concrète piece composed for the stage. Henry also frequently collaborated with choreographer Maurice Béjart, a pairing which yielded 1955's *Arcane*, 1956's *Haut-voltage*, 1962's *Le Voyage*, 1963's *La Reine*, 1967's *Messe pour le temps présent* and 1971's *Nijinsky, clown de Dieu*—in all, he scored more than 30 films and stage productions during his long career. In 1958, Henry left the RTF, and in 1960 he teamed with Jean Baronnet to found the Apsone-Cabasse Studio, the first private electronic music workshop in France; concurrent was his realization that for musique concrète to evolve, it would need to begin incorporating the electronic aesthetics pioneered in other areas of the world.

Towards that end, in 1959 Henry composed both *Coexistence* and *Investigations,* trailed a year later by *La noire a soixante*, which fused musique concrète with pure electronics. Throughout the decade to follow, his music adopted increasingly spiritual and meditative qualities; 1968's *La Messe de Liverpool*, in fact, was commissioned for the consecration of that city's Cathedral of Christ the King. Spoken Biblical text was also prominent in *L'apocalypse de Jean*, which was debuted in Paris on October 30, 1968 at a 24-hour celebration of Henry's music. A year later, he premiered *Ceremony*, which included music by the pop band Spooky Tooth. By the '70s, his primary interest was large-scale works complete with elaborate lighting effects, among them *Mise en musique de corticolart* and *Kyldersttück*.

During the mid-'70s, Henry's project frequently paid homage to his own inspirations—1975's *Futuriste* celebrated the Italian futurist Luigi Russolo and his 1913 work *The Art of Noises*, while 1979's *La Dixieme Symphonie* served as a follow-up to Beethoven's nine symphonies. Continuing to work regularly throughout the years that followed in a vast range of musical contexts—he even collaborated with the American alternative rock trio Violent Femmes—in 1997 Henry completed *Interieur/Exterieur*, a work commissioned by Radio France which he declared the culmination of his life's work. His influence on contemporary music was underlined by the concurrent release of the LP *Metamorphosé*, which featured remixes of his work by the likes of Coldcut, DJ Vadim, William Orbit, Fatboy Slim and Funki Porcini. —*Jason Ankeny*

**Variations Pour une Porte et un Soupir** / 1965 / Limelight ♦♦♦♦

● **Messe Pour Le Temps Présent** / 1967 / Philips ♦♦♦♦
Though it's perhaps Henry's best-known work, *Messe Pour Le Temps Présent* isn't the best display of the powers of musique concrète. Similar to the glut of crossover moog-rock albums around the same time, Henry's occasional bursts of searing computer static are accompanied by a faux '60s go-go beat. It's an intriguing release, but works better for novelty fans and beginners who would rather have a gradual immersion into musique concrète. It earns its stars however, for its reissue on a French CD that also inludes several of Henry's other compositions, including "Variations Pour une Porte et un Soupir." —*John Bush*

**Ceremony** / 1969 / Island ♦♦

**Metamorphosé: Messe Pour Le Temps Présent** / Aug. 18, 1997 / ffrr ♦♦♦♦
One of the originators of *musique concrète* gets his material remixed by some late-'90s inheritors of his experimentation. Among the cast are contributions from Coldcut, DJ Vadim, William Orbit, Fatboy Slim, and Funki Porcini, all of whom rework Henry compositions into what is an obviously more danceable context. Despite Henry's many statements about the new electronica as little more than a new generation of pop music, the collisions work surprisingly well (though far more for fans of the remixers than of Henry's work). —*John Bush*

## Scott Henry

*DJ / Progressive House, Trance, Club/Dance, House*

Though one may not instantly assume the Washington DC area a breeding ground for talented DJs and renowned clubs, but, in fact, Scott Henry has made the area his stomping ground, with both his highly populated DJ performances and his legendary clubs. Like many other electronic dance music artists from the DC area—Deep Dish, John Selway, BT, Charles Feelgood—Henry first became infatuated by the many early rave events occurring on the East Coast. Yet, even before these experiences, he had been already spinning records since being a freshman at Towson State College near Baltimore, Maryland in 1985. In 1990, he had moved on to techno and house, ultimately forming a weekly event called Orbit with Feelgood, which lasted until 1992. Next came Fever, a still-running weekly party in Baltimore featuring world class DJing talent. Henry didn't stop there, though, also starting the more ambitious Friday night event known as Buzz in DC. This gigantic event draws clientele from up and down the East Coast with some of the best DJ lineups imaginable. Of course, all the while, Henry has been improving his DJing skills, often known to drift from breaks to funky techno and from progressive house to the occasional dose of trance, as captured on his Ultra Records debut mix, *Buzz: The Sounds of the Nation's Capitol*. —*Jason Birchmeier*

● **Buzz: The Sounds of the Nation's Capital** / Aug. 22, 2000 / Ultra ♦♦♦
For his first widely distributed mix album, longtime Washington DC icon Scott Henry lays down a trendy set of pumping progressive house tracks that often creeps close into trance territory. The inclusion of so many updated dance classics—Green Velvet's "Flash," Lil Louis' "French Kiss," Hashim's "Al-Naafiysh"—and such a heavy proportion of Timo Mass remixes—four of the 15 tracks—are what makes this album so trendy; it's hard to think that such an emphasis on of-the-moment anthems will endure over time. Still, if one looks past Henry's populist stance, this set really gets off to a wonderful beginning: a three-track run of Green Velvet's "Flash (Timo Maas' Dirty Dub)," Josh Wink featuring Lil Louis' "How's Your Evening So Far," and Oliver Lieb's "Metro (US Mix)." Following this run of peak-hour intensity, the album dies down a bit, gaining steam again at the conclusion when Henry drops KilaHurtz's "West on 27th (A Tribe Called KHz Mix)," a mammoth progressive house track, followed by yet another Maas remix. If only Henry could maintain the energy that the album's start emanates this would be an amazing mix; unfortunately he can't. Furthermore, the fact that he relies so much on updated versions of already-proven classics—"Flash" and "French Kiss"—also cheapens the thrill a bit. Yet, in the end, newcomers that may not be familiar with these tracks should be blown away, and one can't help but feel that Henry is catering to a more populist crowd here. —*Jason Birchmeier*

## The Herbaliser

f. 1992, London, England
*Group / Electronica, Ambient Breakbeat, Ambient Techno, Trip-Hop, Hip-Hop*

The Herbaliser are one of the more purely hip-hop-oriented acts on Ninja Tune's roster of sample-based pocket-funk. Combining deft, mid-tempo beats, well-chosen jazz and funk figures, sparse scratching, and even the odd rap, Herbaliser bridge the gap between dusty B-side instrumental hip-hop and London's new school of psychotropic beat scientists. Formed by Ollie Teeba and Jake Wherry in the early '90s, Herbaliser, unlike many of London's abstract beat scene's acid house-steeped big-name artists, trace their roots to American jazz and funk (Roy Ayers, Johnny Pate, Ramsey Lewis), as well as old-school hip-hop (particularly of the New York variety—DST, Sugarhill, Jungle Brothers). A bass player in acid jazz/funk group the Propheteers, Wherry met local DJ Teeba in South London, where they both currently live. The pair assembled a few tracks in Wherry's tiny studio, which they subsequently passed to Ninja Tune bosses Matt Black and Jonathan More (aka Coldcut) in a club. The group were signed to the label shortly after.

Herbaliser released a few warmly received EPs on Ninja Tune in 1994 and 1995 (the hard-to-find *Real Killer* is the best of these) before dropping their debut LP, *Remedies*, which brought both the group and the then up-and-coming Ninja label much attention. While that album capitalized more directly on London's burgeoning underground breakbeat scene, freely mixing styles into a funky, sample-heavy amalgam closer to beat-heavy acid jazz, subsequent singles ("Flawed Hip-Hop," "New & Improved") subtracted the schmaltzier bits from the mix, focusing in and expanding upon the group's hip-hop foundation. *Blow Your Headphones*, their second LP, presented a solid hour-plus of the same, simultaneously taking aim at UK "trip-hop"'s tendency toward gimmick and noodle over depth and kick. *Very Mercenary* followed in 1999.

Recent remixes by the group have included DJ Food, Raw Stylus, and label foremen Coldcut's "Atomic Moog," the last of which went to number one on the UK singles chart. A touring act as well, Herbaliser assemble a full-blown band for live performances, with Wherry's bass and Teeba's turntable tricks supported by a three-piece horn section and live drums and percussion. Wherry has also released solo material through the Parisian Big Cheese label (under the name the Meateaters) and continues to work with the Propheteers. —*Sean Cooper*

**Remedies** / 1995 / Ninja Tune ♦♦♦
Herbaliser's DJ-friendly jazz/funk/hip-hop fusion is well stated on this debut. Although later releases trim back the album's occasional excess of instrumental samples, a few standout tracks and solid production throughout makes *Remedies* a pleasing, if limited, listen. —*Sean Cooper*

● **Blow Your Headphones** / Mar. 11, 1997 / Ninja Tune ♦♦♦♦
Herbaliser is the most hip-hop of the Ninja Tune lot, and previous releases (such as *Remedies* and the *New and Improved* EP) have illustrated a knack for filling out the jazz and funk roots of hip-hop while remaining both deep and kicking. *Blow Your Headphones* ups the ante considerably, with a non-stop soul-drop that pushes the beats even further forward and thins the extraneous samples and genre-references. The result is less differentiable from straight-ahead hip-hop (save for the fact the album's mostly instrumental), but is also less derivative of acid and soul jazz, a connection that tended to mar their previous work. —*Sean Cooper*

**Very Mercenary** / Apr. 20, 1999 / Ninja Tune ♦♦♦♦
A bit more Carnaby Street than South Bronx (compared to 1997's *Blow Your Headphones*), the Herbaliser's third album works in '60s spy-funk territory to a degree unseen in the group's discography. Though the emphasis on uptempo trip-hop with an old-school edge is carried throughout, *Very Mercenary* also hits instrumental tracks like "Missing Suitcase" and "Goldrush" that include a full band. A bit less necessary than their previous, but a solid record indeed. —*Keith Farley*

## Herbert (Matthew Herbert)

*Producer / Jazz-House, Tech-House, Experimental Techno, Electro-Techno, Club/Dance, House*

Although his methods may provoke more discussion than his music (at least among chin-stroke types and the British and American dance music presses), Matthew Herbert is an experimentalist of a subtle stripe, combining his love for all styles of dance-based electronic music with a desire to push their modes of expression into new areas. Although Herbert studied music formally, much of his creative impetus has been provided by the compositional potential of digital sampling technology, which he liberally applies to genres such as house, electro, ambient, and techno, fashioning tracks of detail and originality from such mundane objects of everyday life as kitchen flatware, crockery, even his own body. Although the first of his tracks to be released on 12" came out through the Universal Language associated with Global Communication, the Horn, and Herbert's own Wishmountain project, he's since released a flood of material on the Clear and Phono labels, as Doctor Rockit and Herbert, respectively. With Doctor Rockit, Herbert focuses on old- and new-school electro-funk and housed-up techno, fusing clangy, rattling beats with humorous melodies and left-field samples and vocal snippets. With his eponymous project, Herbert releases the unlikeliest of experimental house tracks, working within the genre's feel-good, four-on-the-floor arrangements while drastically tweaking its modus operandi. His signature approach has given post-rave house's stale comportment a badly needed shot in the arm, and has (somewhat inexplicably) been widely embraced among mainstream and underground house audiences alike. While continuing to record for both Clear and Phono (almost a full dozen of his tracks appeared on Phono's two-disc compilation *The End of the Beginning*), Herbert also applied his remixing skills to a number of notable artists, including friend Jonah Sharp of Spacetime Continuum, Harold Budd, Atom Heart, Moloko, Motorbass, Super Furry Animals, DJ Food, Hardfloor, and Presence, among others. Vocalist Dani Siciliano joined Herbert for the 1998 LP *Around the House*. His first mix album, *Let's All Make Mistakes*, appeared on Tresor in 2000. [See Also: Doctor Rockit, Wishmountain] —*Sean Cooper*

**100 Lbs.** / 1996 / Phono ♦♦♦♦
The best tracks from his first three limited-edition Phono twelves and some new goodies fill out a solid stack of future-house grooves. The tongue is definitely in the cheek on many of these tracks, but so are the heart and soul where they should be, with Herbert's power at evoking the best aspects of all-night sweaty warehouse parties in top form. The triple-pack vinyl version sports a slightly different track listing. —*Sean Cooper*

**Parts 1, 2 & 3** / Apr. 29, 1996 / DC Recordings/Electron ♦♦♦
Few producers can work their way around vicious club grooves even while they're prominently sampling *Beavis & Butthead*, but Herbert makes it work, managing to effortlessly balance both sides of the intelligent/dance coin. It's

more a collection of singles than a proper album (and there's some overlap from *100 Lbs.*), but *Parts 1, 2 & 3* is a brash, irresistible set. —*John Bush*

- **Around the House** / Jul. 27, 1998 / Phonography ◆◆◆◆

With the addition of vocalist Dani Siciliano on several tracks, *Around the House* is much more suited to straight-ahead dance music than Herbert's previous work. The deep liquid basslines and staccato kitchen-sink percussion (reminiscent of a more skeletal Chic) are working in support of something—namely, Siciliano's languorous vocals—and Herbert proves quite adept at backing a singer. —*John Bush*

**Let's All Make Mistakes** / 2000 / Tresor ◆◆◆◆

Though genius sampler/producer Matthew Herbert is less known for his mixing skills, his first DJ album succeeds on the same terms as his production work by toying with the formula of techno and concocting some seriously entertaining dance music. From the beginning, Herbert flaunts his lack of experience by skewering the more perfectionist aspects of dance DJs, talking to himself during the intro: "Now, I must remember/I'm a human, I'm allowed to make mistakes." As for the musical portion of *Let's All Make Mistakes*, Herbert finds a range of producers in touch with his vision of skittery, frenetic, vaguely organic electro and acid house, calling on producers like Si Begg, Mr. Oizo, Isolée, and Nightmares on Wax who share his half-serious outlook on serious dance. Herbert also allies himself with sound architects farther afield, but still with common links to both the minimalist bent and fascination with the music of sound. Detroiters Plastikman, Theo Parrish, and DBX, plus Chicago freakazoid Green Velvet, all show up with hard, trance-state techno that works well in context. Of course, what's a producer's mix album without plenty of his own tracks? Herbert obliges with five of his own productions (scattered across three aliases) plus his remix of Moloko's "Sing It Back." Relentless, addictive, and deliciously fun, *Let's All Make Mistakes* is a mix-album classic from a man with no business making mix albums. —*John Bush*

## Hexstatic

f. 1990, London, England
*Group / Funky Breaks, Trip-Hop, Club/Dance*

Though they're best known in the music world as the award-winning visual arm of audio cut'n'paste experts Coldcut, Hexstatic (previously Hex) have broken down the barriers between music, multimedia, and computers ever since they created the first computer-generated pop video ("Coldcut's Christmas Break") in 1990. Graphic-design artists Robert Pepperell and Miles Visman formed Hex along with Coldcut's Matt Black and Jonathan More. While working on videos for artists including Kevin Saunderson, Queen Latifah, and Spiritualized, Hex programmed a video game (*High Banana*) in 1991 and inaugurated a series of multimedia CD-ROMs just one year later with Global Chaos CDTV, which united music, graphics, and video games into one product. A series of successors (Escape, Global Chaos, Digital Love) preceded the release of 1994's *AntiStatic*, another CD-ROM simultaneously released on CD and vinyl by Coldcut's NTone Records.

Throughout the '90s, Hex accompanied Black and More's live performances with visuals, and Pepperell also developed the CD-ROM portion of Coldcut's 1997 LP *Let Us Play* plus the software used during the world tour. Though Pepperell and Visman later left Hex, fresh blood came in the form of Stuart Warren Hill and Robin Brunson. Their first work for Coldcut, the "Timber" video, won awards for its innovative use of repetitive video clips synced to the music. In 2000, they released *Rewind*, their own album for NTone. Obviously a digital-edge release, the two-disc set combined CD-ROM and DVD capabilities to a fully synchronized music/video release. —*John Bush*

- **Rewind** / Aug. 22, 2000 / NTone ◆◆◆◆

Multimedia experts Hexstatic undoubtedly have a special interest in communication, so it's no surprise the duo uses its first LP (recorded for their pals at Ninja Tune) to poke fun at the continually confusing digital age. After an intro wherein celebrity announcer Don Pardo reassures audiences that technical difficulties are being attended to for nigh on a full minute, the group launches into "Communication Break-Down," with scattered samples—modem-connect noise, wrong numbers, answering machine messages, and various interference—serving as a bed for Coldcut-style turntablist trip-hop. On the next track, "Deadly Media," a parade of random Japanese vocal snippets gradually organize themselves around rigid 808 breakbeats for a fascinating, hilarious track. Like their award-winning "Timber" video for Coldcut,

which chopped and spliced visuals in a similar manner that turntablism does to music, *Rewind* makes complete sense; on these tracks, the percussion lines and beats aren't the only elements serving the rhythm. Though the production is solid, many of the other tracks here use some overly familiar blueprints—especially for Ninja Tune artists—from kung-fu samples (on a track actually *named* "Ninja Tune,") to video game electro ("Vector,") and even the age-old favorite: porn-film samples ("The Horn"). Good music abounds, but Hexstatic proves much more pioneering in the visual realm than the musical. (One place they *really* shine is on the second multimedia disc, which offers an excellent video for each track and a style of choosing videos that will warm the hearts of *Battletech* fans.) —*John Bush*

## Higher Intelligence Agency

f. 1992, Birmingham, England
*Group / Ambient Techno, Ambient Dub*

The Birmingham-based Higher Intelligence Agency is composed of DJ/musician Bobby Bird and occasional collaborator Dave Wheels. Musically, they pitch their creative tent somewhere between the ambient and experimental techno camps, with breakbeat, electro-style rhythms and a song-oriented melodic and harmonic base informing the bulk of their most recent work. The group formed in 1992 as a live experiment performing at Bird's Oscillate parties (which played early host to such acts as Autechre, Orbital, Mixmaster Morris, and Scanner), and has since grown into a full-on creative force, releasing a pair of albums and as many EPs. Although perhaps not as prodigious as many of their peers, HIA's focus is on quality rather than quantity, and their released material is uniformly well-produced and meticulously crafted. In addition to constant touring and the ongoing Oscillate schedule, HIA have also performed commissioned work for museums and festivals. While still bent on working together, Bird has largely taken over HIA's reigns while Wheels pursues a solo project, and has completed remixes for Freeform and Obconic. Collaborations in 1996 with Frankfurt's Deep Space Network and Geir Jenssen of Biosphere also produced an album apiece, the former (*Deep Space Network Meets Higher Intelligence Agency*) on DSN's Source label and the latter (*Polar Sequences*) on Beyond. Another collaborational series, *S.H.A.D.O.* with Pete Namlook, began in 1997 and resumed two years later. —*Sean Cooper*

**Colourform** / 1993 / Waveform ◆◆◆

Ambient-techno with emphasis on the techno. A nice, consistent album but lacking the humanness of later efforts. —*Sean Cooper*

**Reform [EP]** / 1994 / Beyond ◆◆◆

An EP of *Colourform* material refashioned by Autechre, Mixmaster Morris, A Positive Life, and Pentatonik. The Autechre and Pentatonik versions are the scorchers here, although all four tracks are of high quality. —*Sean Cooper*

- **Freefloater** / 1995 / Beyond ◆◆◆◆

One of the finest examples of ambient electro released to date, *Freefloater* manages to be at once complex and accessible, laying melodic hooks over funky, often syncopated rhythm patterns and austere bass figures. Warm and detailed, it's easily HIA's best work.—*Sean Cooper*

**Polar Sequences** / 1996 / Beyond ◆◆◆◆

A collaboration between Biosphere's Geir Jenssen and Bobby Bird of Higher Intelligence Agency, commissioned by the Norwegian government for live performance at the 1995 Polar Music Festival. Suitably frosty melodies and glacial textures provide the framework for compositions utilizing the natural environment of the Arctic Circle for inspiration and source material (snow falling, ice cracking and splitting, the clang of cable car mountain lifts, etc.), to often remarkable effect. Sparse beats occasionally bubble up, but the focus is definitely on the icy edge of Arctic life. —*Sean Cooper*

**Nothing** / 1997 / Headphone ◆◆◆◆

The first release on Higher Intelligence Agency's Bobby Bird's Headphone imprint (a sublabel of Frankfurt ambient powerhouse Fax) is System Error's *Nothing* (featuring Bird with somebody named Brian Duffy, whom we can only assume isn't the identically named American astronaut). The album charts a similar and wonderfully diverse path through the sort of spacy deep ambient-electro as other of Bird's recent releases (*Deep Space Network Meets HIA*, *S.H.A.D.O.*) and is, of course, exceedingly listenable, utilitzing an interesting array of odd-shaped beats and handcrafted sounds and atmospheres. About two-fifths beatless, *Nothing* is some of Bird's most focused, consistent work to date. —*Sean Cooper*

## Steve Hillage

b. Aug. 2, 1951, England
*Vocals, Guitar, Synthesizer, Producer / Space Rock, Prog-Rock/Art Rock, Avant-Garde*

A guitarist who first found fame in the progressive-rock era only to later resurface as an ambient techno cult hero, Steve Hillage was born August 2, 1951. In 1967 he co-founded the group Uriel with bassist Mont Campbell, organist Dave Stewart and drummer Clive Brooks; the unit subsequently continued on as the trio Egg upon Hillage's 1968 departure for university. He did not return to music for another three years, reuniting with Stewart in 1971 in Khan, which recorded the 1972 prog-rock effort *Space Shanty* before soon splitting.

After touring in support of Kevin Ayers, Hillage joined Gong, winning acclaim for his echo- and delay-heavy brand of guitar work over the course of the group's 1972-1975 "Radio Gnome Invisible" trilogy (consisting of the LPs *Flying Teapot, Angel's Egg,* and *You*). In 1975 Hillage went solo with the album *Fish Rising,* the first fruits of a longstanding writing partnership with keyboardist Miquette Giraudy. He next travelled to New York to cut 1976's *L,* produced by Todd Rundgren and featuring guest appearances from Utopia as well as jazz great Don Cherry.

At the peak of the punk era, Hillage's work was by no means fashionable, but he pressed on regardless; in 1977 he issued *Motivation Radio,* an album recorded with Malcolm Cecil (the creator of an influential early electronic project, the studio-synthesizer T.O.N.T.O.). 1978's *Green,* 1979's *Rainbow Dome Musick* (an early ambient outing) and *Open,* and 1983's separately released *For to Next/And Not Or* followed, but as interest in his music continued to dwindle, Hillage turned to production, helming records for the likes of Robyn Hitchcock and Simple Minds.

By the close of the '80s, Hillage had largely disappeared from music; however, in 1989 he was visiting the ambient room of a local club when, much to his surprise, his own *Rainbow Dome Musick* began to play. He introduced himself to the DJ, one Alex Paterson, and soon Hillage was working with Paterson's seminal group the Orb; out of their collaboration grew a new Hillage-Giraudy project, System 7, a dance collective also comprised of club luminaries including Paterson and fellow DJ Paul Oakenfold.

After debuting with an eponymously titled 1991 LP, System 7 plunged completely into blissed-out ambient sound on 1993's *777,* which reached the Top 40 on the UK album charts. 1994's *Point 3* appeared in two different versions: the first, *The Fire Album,* offered heavy beats and rhythms, while *The Water Album* featured drumless mixes of the same music. With 1996's *Power of Seven,* System 7 turned to Detroit techno, recruiting the services of mixers Carl Craig and Derrick May. —*Jason Ankeny*

*L* / 1976 / Blue Plate ♦♦♦♦
Heavy glissando guitar jazz-rock with Don Cherry. Essential statement. —*Michael G. Nastos*

*Green* / 1978 / Blue Plate ♦♦♦
On Steve Hillage's 1978 release, *Green,* the underground prog-rock fan favorite issues more of his trademark thinking-man's music. Fans of mid- to late-'70s Pink Floyd will want to check this album out, since it possesses many of the same musical qualities, due to the fact that it was produced by Floyd drummer Nick Mason along with Hillage. Although not as consistent as some of his other albums, it certainly has its moments. Hillage's recurring sci-fi influence is still felt in his music, especially on such tracks as "Sea Nature," "UFO Over Paris," and "Unidentified (Flying Being)." Hillage uses the same band that appeared on his *Motivation Radio* album, which helps make Hillage's twisted songs even better (like his other albums, the musicianship is top-notch). Besides comparisons to Floyd, the album's music is also similar to David Bowie's late-'70s experimental electronic phase (check out the track "Crystal City," with vocals almost identical to Bowie). Hillage fans will definitely not be disappointed with *Green.* —*Greg Prato*

● *Rainbow Dome Music* / 1979 / Blue Plate ♦♦♦♦
An album of two extended pieces, *Rainbow Dome Music* is a must-buy for new-age rock fans. —*Michael G. Nastos*

## H.I.M. (Doug Scharin)

*Producer / Experimental Dub, Post-Rock/Experimental, Experimental*
The experimental dub alias of indie staple Doug Scharin (a former member of Codeine who later drummed in June of 44 and Rex while also collaborating on Bundy K. Brown's Directions in Music), H.I.M. debuted in 1995 with the 12-minute "Chemical Mix," a track on the *Crooklyn Dub Consortium: Certified Dope, Vol. 1* compilation. A full-length, *Egg,* followed on the Southern label in early 1996, trailed later that year by the 12" *Chill and Peel.* In 1997, H.I.M. returned with *Interpretive Belief System,* as well as a self-titled split release with the ambient duo the Dylan Group. *Sworn Eyes* followed in 1999. —*Jason Ankeny*

H.I.M./The Dylan Group / May 5, 1997 / Bubble Core ♦♦♦

● Interpretive Belief System / Aug. 5, 1997 / WordSound ♦♦♦♦
*Interpretive Belief System* is an extraordinary confluence of scattershot percussion, hip-hop attitude and dub vibes from the starter "Port of Entry" to the excellent closer "Second Chance." —*Keith Farley*

*Sworn Eyes* / 1999 / Perishable ♦♦♦
Jazz-oriented experimental music from the Chicago post-rock crowd, with HIM constant Doug Scharin aided by guitarist Jeff Parker (from Tortoise and Isotope) and other musicians associated with outfits such as Rex and Chicago Underground Duo. The drowsy, but not quite narcotic, dreamscapes of these instrumentals owe much to Jon Hassell (particularly in the woozy and wobbly effects/treatments) and the early electric fusion of Miles Davis. Unlike its forebears, HIM uses '90s loops and edits, as well as dub and hip-hop rhythms (as on "Trace Elements"). As with much of Hassell's work, the atmosphere is somewhat akin to traveling through an electric underwater jungle. —*Richie Unterberger*

## Dr. Samuel J. Hoffman

b. Jul. 23, 1903, Manhattan, New York City, NY, d. Dec. 6, 1967
*Theremin / Television Music, Film Music, Space Age Pop, Experimental, Electronic*

Dr. Samuel J. Hoffman was among the driving forces behind the rise of the theremin, helping popularize the bewitching electronic instrument on stage, on record and—perhaps most importantly—in film. Hoffman was born in Manhattan on July 23, 1903, where (according to Charlie Lester's comprehensive theremin website at http://www.137.com/theremins/) he originally studied violin under Ovide Musin. Despite his musical prowess, he later attended med school, earning a degree in podiatry; concurrently, he played in the bands of Meyer Davis and Jolly Coburn, adopting the stage name Hal Hope. Hoffman acquired his theremin sometime during the mid-'30s, forming an electronic trio that caused a sensation on the New York City club circuit. Upon relocating to Los Angeles during the early '40s, he continued performing live, this time attracting the attention of Hollywood; when the famed composer Miklos Rozsa needed a theremin for his score to the 1945 Alfred Hitchcock classic *Spellbound,* he contacted Hoffman, and the subsequent success of the film made him and the theremin a hot property throughout the movie business. Hoffman went on to lend his talents to other films, including *The Lost Weekend, The Day the Earth Stood Still, The Delicate Delinquent,* and *The 5,000 Fingers of Dr. T;* he also recorded a series of LPs, among them 1947's *Music Out of the Moon,* 1948's *Perfumes Set to Music,* and 1949's *Music for Peace of Mind.* Countless television contributions additionally followed prior to his death on December 6, 1967. —*Jason Ankeny*

● Music Out of the Moon/Perfumes Set to Music/Music for Peace of Mind / 1999 / Basta ♦♦♦♦

## David Holmes

b. Feb. 14, 1969, Belfast, Northern Ireland
*Producer, DJ / Funky Breaks, Electronica, Club/Dance, Techno*

David Holmes is the among the best in a growing cadre of invisible-soundtrack producers inspired by the audio verité of classic film composers—Lalo Schifrin, John Barry, Ennio Morricone—as well as the usual stable of dancefloor innovators and a large cast of jazz/soul pioneers to boot. Similar to the work of Howie B., Barry Adamson, and Portishead's Geoff Barrow, Holmes' productions are appropriately spacious and theatrical, though usually focused on future club consumption as well. His first album, hotly tipped in England, rose the stakes significantly for his second. *Let's Get Killed* hardly disappointed, gaining critical and artistic success given the constraints of instrumental dance music. The increased exposure even helped him hire in on Hollywood's bankroll to provide the score for the 1998 feature film *Out of Sight.*

Born in Belfast the youngest of ten children, David Holmes listened to punk rock as a child and began DJing at the age of 15—his sets at pubs and clubs around the city during the next few years embraced a range of grooves including soul-jazz, Mod-rock, Northern soul and disco. Holmes also worked as an underground concert promoter and wrote a fanzine as well, though he was still just a teenager when the house and techno boom hit Britain in the late '80s. Soon he was integrating the new dance music into his mixing, and his club night Sugar Sweet became the first venue for serious dance music in Northern Ireland. Back-and-forth contact between England and Northern Ireland brought Holmes into contact with leading DJs Andrew Weatherall, Darren Emerson and Ashley Beedle. After familiarizing himself with the studio, he began recording with Beedle (later of Black Science Orchestra) to produce the single "DeNiro" (as Disco Evangelists), a sizeable dancefloor hit in 1992. The following year, his Scubadevils project (a collaboration with Dub Federation) appeared on the first volume of the seminal compilation series *Trance Europe Express*.

That first taste of success brought David Holmes much remixing work during 1993-94, for Weatherall's Sabres of Paradise, St. Etienne, Therapy?, Fortran 5, Sandals, and Justin Warfield, among others. He later signed to Go! Discs and in 1995 released his debut album *This Film's Crap, Let's Slash the Seats*. Besides the cinema-terrorist persona evoked in the title, the album featured other ties to the cinema: the single "No Mans Land" had been written in response to the controversial Guildford 4 film *In the Name of the Father*. Television director Lynda La Plante ended up using many of the tracks from the album for her series "Supply & Demand", and one track was used in the Sean Penn/Michael Douglas film *The Game*. Holmes' first proper soundtrack, the Marc Evans film *Resurrection Game*, appeared in 1997. The experience inspired Holmes to travel to New York and gather a wealth of urban-jungle environment recordings, compiled and mixed into his second proper album, *Let's Get Killed*. He followed with the remix collection *Stop Arresting Artists*, and in 1998 scored the A-list Hollywood feature *Out of Sight* with a prescient set of groove-funk. (The attention also earned him a place in *Entertainment Weekly*'s list of the Top 100 Creative People in Entertainment.) His single "My Mate Paul" even featured as the theme music to the Sony Playstation game Psybadek. *Essential Mix 98/01* followed later that year, and in 1999 *This Film's Crap, Let's Slash the Seats* was reissued with a bonus disc of rarities and unreleased tracks. Holmes issued his third studio effort *Bow Down to the Exit Sign* in September 2000. —*John Bush*

**This Film's Crap, Let's Slash the Seats** / 1995 / Go! Discs ◆◆◆◆
Holmes' debut sets out his bent for film music from the get-go with the single "No Man's Land," a kettle full of madness brewed with sampled church bells and door-slams framed by a lock-step military beat. The ballad "Gone" has a similar feel for the cinematic, though plenty of other tracks kick as hard as anything else in the clubs, particularly the acid stormer "Slash the Seats." An American reissued added a bonus disc with remixes and several tracks featuring vocals by Sarah Cracknell of St. Etienne. —*John Bush*

**Let's Get Killed** / Oct. 7, 1997 / A&M ◆◆◆◆
On David Holmes' second album, the first to be released in America, he explores with even greater depth his fascination with original soundtrack material. Recording snippets of conversation on the streets of New York with his DAT recorder, Holmes returned to England and weaved the vocal samples around his amorphous embrace of several electronic styles, including big-beat techno of the type favored by the Chemical Brothers, intelligent drum'n'bass (as on the title track) and the gentler soundtrack-feel of ambient house. The effect created *is* like that of a soundtrack and even though *Let's Get Killed* isn't attached to a film, it flows with energy and grace. —*John Bush*

**Stop Arresting Artists** / May 1998 / Go! Beat ◆◆◆◆
*Stop Arresting Artists* is a feature-length remix of David Holmes' acclaimed second album, *Let's Get Killed*. Holmes farmed the record out to a diverse array of remixers, including Andrew Weatherall and the Stereo MC's, keeping a piece of it for himself. These are hardly rote, by-the-books remixes—these reveal new unexpected levels to each track without stripping away the original identity. *Stop Arresting Artists* still has that disoriented urban vibe that made *Let's Get Killed* such a unique experience; it's just seen from a different angle. —*Stephen Thomas Erlewine*

**Essential Mix 98/01** / Nov. 2, 1998 / ffrr ◆◆◆◆
Holmes' *Essential Selection* guest slot from BBC Radio One is a double-disc set with room for plenty of soul chestnuts (Marlena Shaw, James Brown, the Googie Rene Combo, Rare Earth), several tracks so square they're hip (Percy Faith, Don Sebesky, Brigitte Bardot, Ananda Shankar), plus a few "standard" choices including tracks by Plaid, Skylab, Jurassic 5 and Holmes himself. The mixing is masterful and the track selection is inspired. —*John Bush*

● **Bow Down to the Exit Sign** / Sep. 12, 2000 / Polygram International ◆◆◆◆
A vast improvement over the intriguing but rarely focused *Let's Get Killed*, David Holmes' third solo album benefits from his growing status as a producer to watch—and specifically, from his ability to snag the talents of big-name vocalists. As on his soundtrack for the feature film *Out of Sight*, Holmes excels when he's providing a propulsive yet not overly self-conscious background for the prime focus, whether it's an action scene in a film or a song-oriented framework on an album. Recruiting the top rank of like-minded bluesy vocalists from the alternative world—Bobby Gillespie (from Primal Scream), Jon Spencer (from the Blues Explosion), Martina Topley Bird (a Tricky collaborator), and an excellent newcomer, Carl Hancock Rux—Holmes plays on all the same heavy dub/soul/funk trademarks as on *Let's Get Killed*, but constructs excellent productions with a tight, live, organic sound. Though Gillespie's "Sick City" is yet another Stonesy, tossed-off performance, the production on the track makes it a stomper of raging rocktronica. Elsewhere, on tracks like "Incite a Riot" and "69 Police," Holmes calls up dub ghosts from original Jamaican keyboard extraordinaire Jackie Mittoo to scruffy indie rock inheritors like Dub Narcotic. While his previous work came off as soundtrack material in desperate search of a film to accompany it, *Bow Down to the Exit Sign* is very much a fully formed record. —*John Bush*

## Holosud

f. 1996, Cologne, Germany
*Group / Experimental Techno, Experimental Electro, Electronica, Post-Rock/ Experimental*

Holosud is the combined talents of Joe Zimmerman and Felix Randomiz, both in-house artists of Koln's noteworthy A-Musik label. Randomiz records for A-Musik as F.X. Randomiz, and Zimmerman as Schlammpeitziger; together as Holosud they record heavily sequenced music exploring by turns the darker and more comic corners of current electronica. Holosud's self-titled-debut EP appeared in 1996, and helped make a name for A-Musik as a source of innovative experimental electronic music only vaguely connected to even the most bizzarre tangents of post-techno. The group's debut LP, *Fijnewas Afpompen*, appeared in 1998, and built upon its predecessor by adding goofy melodic elements reminiscent of Randomiz's solo work. —*Sean Cooper*

● **Holosud [EP]** / 1997 / A-Musik ◆◆◆◆
Four tracks of sampler resuscitation clearly inspired by, but still quite a distance from, the experimental dance music of fellow Kolners Mouse on Mars, Mike Ink and so forth. Quite a bit darker and more complex than most other A-Musik fare, *Holosud* is nonetheless among the young label's most impressive releases to date. —*Sean Cooper*

**Fijnewas Afpompen** / 1998 / A-Musik ◆◆◆
One of the best releases to come from the A-Musik label, *Fijnewas Afpompen* is also the most reminiscent of Cologne heroes Mouse on Mars. Over a series of plodding electro stomps, innumerable waves of clicks, clacks and explosions surf high in the mix. The highlights "Alaune" and "Kettsmarock" are busier still than Mouse on Mars' famously cluttered productions. That noted German sense of humor is on display for "Saftsocke im Zimmergarten," the illogical but hilarious fusion of Cologne-style eclectronics with hillbilly twang. —*John Bush*

## Hood

f. 1991, Leeds, England
*Group / Indie Rock, Post-Rock/Experimental*

The Leeds, England-based lo-fi bliss-popsters Hood comprised Andrew Johnson, Chris Adams, Richard Adams, John Evans, Craig Tattersall, and Nicola Hodgkinson. The group debuted in 1992 with the 7" "Sirens"; after 1993's "Opening into Enclosure," a year later they issued *Cabled Linear Traction*, which collected their two earlier singles. Absent throughout 1995, the next year Hood returned with a barrage of new material—after three singles ("Lee Faust Million Piece Orchestra," "A Harbour of Thoughts," and "I've Forgotten How to Live," all of them issued on different labels), the group also released the full-length *Silent '88*. *Secrets Now Known to Others*, a ten-track EP of material recorded for but not included on *Silent '88*, appeared in 1997, as did the album *Structured Disasters*. Though it wasn't released in America, *The Cycle of Days and Seasons* followed on Domino in 1999. —*Jason Ankeny*

**Cabled Linear Traction** / 1994 / Slumberland ♦♦♦
Hood's debut album balances artfully tuneless indie-pop reminiscent of Pavement with several tracks of more abstract instrumental passages. —*Keith Farley*

● **Silent '88** / 1996 / Slumberland ♦♦♦♦
Though it's a bit similar to their debut, *Silent '88* shows that Hood's rustic dream-pop smarts have intensified even while their adventures into noisier territory have taken them farther afield. Nothing describes their visions of post-rock better than song titles like "Smash Your Head on the Cubist Jazz," "The Hidden Ambience of a Lost Art," and "Delusions of Worthlessness." —*Keith Farley*

**Rustic Houses Forlorn Valleys** / Apr. 14, 1998 / Domino ♦♦♦

## Robert Hood

*DJ, Producer / Minimal Techno, Detroit Techno, Club/Dance, Techno*
Robert "Noise" Hood makes minimal Detroit techno with an emphasis on soul and experimentation over flash and popularity. Recording for Metroplex, as well as the Austrian Cheap label and Jeff Mills' Axis label, Hood also owns and operates the M-Plant imprint, through which he's released the bulk of his solo material. Hood was a founding member, along with Jeff Mills and Mike Banks, of the Underground Resistance label, whose influential releases throughout the early- and mid-'90s helped change the face of modern Detroit techno and sparked a creative renaissance. Infusing elements of acid and industrial into a potent blend of Chicago house and Detroit techno, UR's aesthetic project and militant business philosophy were (and remain) singular commitments in underground techno. Hood left Detroit (and UR) with Jeff Mills in 1992, setting up shop in New York and recording a series of 12" EPs with Mills. Through the mid-'90s, Hood has focused on his solo work, setting up M-Plant in 1994 and releasing singles such as "Internal Empire," "Music Data," and "Moveable Parts." Although his desire to remain underground has been replaced by an urge to reach a wider audience, Hood remains fiercely critical of artistic and economic movements destructive to inner-city communities and has combined his musical enterprises with outreach and social activist ends. In 1994, Berlin's techno-centric Tresor label released his debut full-length, *Internal Empire*, and Cheap released *Nighttime World* the following year. During the rest of the decade, Hood focused on DJ dates as well as a string of singles for M-Plant. Finally, in 2000, the second volume in the *Nighttime World* series appeared on M-Plant. [See Also: The Vision] —*Sean Cooper*

**Internal Empire** / 1994 / Tresor ♦♦♦♦
Hood's solo debut defines his minimalist manifesto, with a conventional four-tour beat underpinning series of skeletal machine effects. Except for a few synthesizer backings on one track, all of the music on *Internal Empire* serves the rhythm tracks, from the trancestate pulses on "Minus" and "Parade" to the title track's percussion breakdowns. Thankfully reissued on Tresor in 1998. —*John Bush*

● **Nighttime World, Vol. 1** / 1995 / Cheap ♦♦♦♦
Compared to the minimalist lock-step of *Internal Empire*, Hood's second album *Nighttime World* is practically a soul album—even the cover looks more like *What's Going On* than *X-101*. On the first track, "Behind This Door," he conjures a few string flourishes and a surprisingly chunky bassline to evoke the nightlife, while the title track, "Electric Nigger," and "The Color of Skin" all trade in Hood-style minimalism for a bit more focus on fleshed-out productions, including even acoustic pianos. Of course, there's still a trademark glazed-eye trance workout ("Untitled"). Unlike *Internal Empire*, this one functions as more than just a collection of great tracks. And it's great to see Hood's growth as a producer not posing a threat to his sound. *Nighttime World* is still one of the most inventive full-lengths to come out of Detroit. —*John Bush*

**Moveable Parts, Chapter 2 [Single]** / Feb. 10, 1997 / M-Plant ♦♦♦♦
Hood's control of minimal Detroit trance continued on this 1997 twelve. "The Grey Area" gets the nod as best track. —*John Bush*

**Nighttime World, Vol. 2** / 2000 / M-Plant ♦♦
Perhaps wisely, for his second volume in the *Nighttime World* series, Rob Hood moved away from the increasingly popular minimalist sound he'd pioneered. Instead of the skeletal, loop-based Detroit trance of *Internal Empire* and the first *Nighttime World* (plus his recent singles-based work), Hood layers multiple synth lines: all with heavily evocative, organic-sounding presets that haven't been heard in this fashion for many years, especially in the future-sensitive Motor City. He also acknowledges the influence of hip-hop; "The Key to Midnight," "Untitled," and "Silent Hill" sound halfway between Wu-Tang Clan and a down-tempo Ken Ishii. These surprisingly slick, hardly danceable originals are so emotive they sound odd when placed in proximity to Hood's usual spare, minimalist productions (a few of these do appear, most notably "Teflon" and "Darkroom"). Even with a few beautiful, spiritual down-tempo tracks like "Peace (Closing Theme)," *Nighttime World, Vol. 2* is a very difficult listen, especially for fans of the sound Hood made famous.—*John Bush*

## Hooverphonic

f. 1995, Brussels, Belgium
*Group / Ambient Pop, Adult Alternative Pop/Rock, Alternative Pop/Rock*
The Belgian ambient pop band Hooverphonic featured vocalist Liesje Sadonius, guitarist/programmer Alex Callier, keyboardist Frank Duchêne, and guitarist Raymond Geerts. Known simply as Hoover across Europe, the group made their initial splash contributing the song "2Wicky" to the soundtrack of the 1996 Bernardo Bertolucci film *Stealing Beauty*, followed a year later by the full-length *New Stereophonic Sound Spectacular*. Sadonius left Hooverphonic a short time later, and was replaced by vocalist Geike Arnaert in time to record 1998's *Blue Wonder Power Milk*. *The Magnificent Tree* followed two years later. —*Jason Ankeny*

● **Blue Wonder Power Milk** / Aug. 11, 1998 / Epic ♦♦♦
Hooverphonic's fusion of indie pop, art-rock, techno, ambient and electronica is a hit-or-miss proposition. It's either breathtaking in its cool, shimmering electronics, or it falls flat, sounding beautiful but signifying nothing. On their debut, their moments of brilliance outweighed the lesser tracks, but they just break even on their follow-up, *Blue Wonder Power Milk*. Certainly, the tracks that do work are even more spectacular than anything on their debut, creating an unusual, futuristic, jazzy variation on techno that has a strong melodic undercurrent. When it falls flat, it's only because it meanders without melodies or structure to provide a through line. Still, Hooverphonic's occasional mastery of sonic texture makes *Blue Wonder Power Milk* worth repeated listens. —*Stephen Thomas Erlewine*

## Haruomi Hosono

b. 1947, Tokyo, Japan
*Keyboards, Bass, Producer / Ambient Techno, Club/Dance, Techno, Worldbeat, Ambient, Electronic*
Haruomi Hosono, overshadowed by his Yellow Magic Orchestra bandmate Ryuichi Sakamoto, has still forged a unique path through ambient music, building on the advances made by the soundscapes of Brian Eno during the '70s, though he recorded his first album before Eno had even joined Roxy Music. Born in Tokyo in 1947, Hosono studied sociology at Rikkyo University, forming several bands while still in school. His first solo album, *April Fool*, was released in 1969.

Throughout the early and mid-'70s, he played the part of studio musician and bassist, and formed two fusion projects, Happy Band and Tin Pan Alley. Later in the '70s, he began recording tape and synthesizer experiments which culminated in the album *Cochin Moon*, released on the Japanese King Records. By 1978, his group Harry Hosono & the Yellow Magic Band had sprung into Yellow Magic Orchestra, with Ryuichi Sakamoto and Yukihiro Takahashi. Coming just a few years after electro futurists Kraftwerk and Tangerine Dream, YMO pursued a similar trail, later incorporating synth-pop and new wave as well and becoming Japan's most successful band during the '80s—even though they had broken up by 1984.

Even while Yellow Magic Orchestra was still around, Hosono had been busy with other projects. With three labels to his credit (YEN, Non-Standard and Monad Music) and releases on those labels under guises such as S-F-X, Mercuric Dance and—most prolifically—F.O.E. (Friends of the Earth), Haruomi Hosono stayed active into the late '80s. He composed scores for the films *Paradise View* and *The Tales of Genji*, but became disgusted with the industry and withdrew from music altogether by the turn of the decade. The pioneers of ambient house began to namecheck Yellow Magic Orchestra in the early '90s—even producing a YMO remix album called *High Tech/No Crime* featuring the Orb plus many others—and Hosono returned with 1992's *Medicine Compilation from the Quiet Lodge*. Albums for Creation and Polygram followed during the mid-'90s. —*John Bush*

**Medicine Compilation from the Quiet Lodge** / 1992 / Tristar ♦♦♦♦

Mental Sports Mixes / 1994 / Creation ♦♦♦

• N.D.E. / Jul. 15, 1995 / PolyGram ♦♦♦♦
Produced by Bill Laswell, *N.D.E.* is an album of driving instrumental electronics, a few of which chart a downtempo, dubby affair probably influenced by Laswell himself. The focus is mostly on techno-pop that smacks of Hosono's prime work, away from YMO as well as in it. —*Keith Farley*

## House of 909

f. 1995, Bournemouth, England
*Group / Tech-House, Club/Dance, House*

Along with Basement Jaxx, House of 909 is one of the few British production teams able to rival their American counterparts in the creation of mainstream deep house. Anchored by the trio of Nigel Casey, Trevor Loveys, and Affie Yussuf, the collective also includes the production talents of Jamie Cox and Martin Howes. Centered around Casey's House of 909 imprint, productions by Voices from Beyond, Future Soul Orchestra, and Shakedown became proper club hits in Britain during the mid-'90s. The collective's beginnings also lie with Casey, a pioneering house DJ on Britain's South Coast during the late '80s and '90s. He originally formed 909 Perversions Records after meeting Affie Yussuf, who had recorded for Force Inc and founded his own Ferox label.

After producers Trevor Loveys and Jamie Cox joined the fold, House of 909 Records was born. The label debuted in 1996 with EPs from Future Soul Orchestra and Voices from Beyond, deep tracks which looked back to classic American productions by Larry Heard and Deep Dish but with a distinctly British flair. The group then hit paydirt when Pagan Records licensed House of 909's *Deep Distraction EP*. The mix collection *Soul Rebels* followed in 1997, and the team came together for their first new album, *The Children We Were*, in 1998. —*John Bush*

Soul Rebels / Aug. 26, 1997 / Pagan ♦♦♦♦
Trevor Loveys' House of 909 project have been one of the champions of British deep house. This first full-length is a quasi-compilation, including tracks from the early EPs *Future Soul Orchestra* and *Voices from Beyond* as well as much new material. Highlights such as "Movin On" and "Distant Cry" echo their Chicago predecessors well, while the low production values prove quite a boon in a style of music jam-packed with productions polished to perfection but devoid of any soul. —*John Bush*

• The Children We Were / Sep. 21, 1998 / Pagan ♦♦♦♦
The proper album debut by House of 909, is an excellent British house record—a bit more evocative than it is danceable. Still, the atmospherics on tracks like the title track and "So Much Love 4 You" give way to groovy house vocals. Occasionally, the trio lean just a bit too close to their roots in the classic Chicago house of Larry Heard and others, but that never dampens the excellent productions on *The Children We Were*. —*John Bush*

## Housey Doingz

f. 1995, Croydon, England
*Group / Club/Dance, House*

An irresistible fusion of house music's progressive end with a tighter feel tied to techno, Housey Doingz is based around the Croydon club-night Wiggle and led by resident DJs Terry Francis and Nathan Coles. The crew hit the map with British club-goers during 1996, thanks to the infectious singles "Piano" and "Doing It," the latter released on the Pagan label run by compatriots at House of 909. One year later, Housey Doingz earned a full-length with the release of *Doing It (Livin' It, Lovin' It, Largin' It)*. —*John Bush*

• Doing It (Livin' It, Lovin' It, Largin' It) / Jul. 1, 1997 / Ark 21 ♦♦♦♦
Just when house seemed to be old hat in the wake of intelligent dance music, jungle, and speed garage, Housey Doingz made it a force for quality music with this collection, mixed by the Doingz' own Terry Francis and culled from their labels, Wiggle and Eye 4 Sound. The sound is pure house, with little concession to other styles, but still succeeds with the little touches that most house production ignores. *Doing It* is one of the most consistently invigorating house collections of the late '90s. —*John Bush*

## Hrvátski (Keith Fullerton Whitman)

*Producer / Experimental Jungle, Jungle/Drum'N'Bass*

Hrvátski is the recording alias of schizoid drum'n'bass producer Keith Fullerton Whitman, whose Reckankreuzungsklankewerkzeuge (RKK) label has offered some of the most prosaic experimental-electronic recordings of the late '90s, in league with electro-noise from labels like V/Vm and Diskono. A Berklee College of Music dropout in 1995 and a former metal columnist for *Guitar Player*, Whitman recorded dozens of tracks during the late '90s but released very few of them, even after forming RKK and releasing the *Attention: Cats* compilation in 1998. Finally, RKK compiled various Hrvátski recordings for the full-length release *Oiseaux 96-98* in 1999. Hrvátski also works for Forced Exposure, the noted record store based in Boston. —*John Bush*

• Oiseaux 96-98 / 1999 / Reckankreuzungsklankewerkzeuge ♦♦♦♦
Approaching two full decades into its lifespan, the classic "Amen" break—culled from the Winston Brothers' "Amen" single—had driven hundreds of hip-hop and jungle recordings. Still, it'd probably never been cut and chopped or sliced and diced quite like it was on this compilation of late-'90s recordings from the hard drive of Keith Whitman. The opener, "Routine Exercise," belies its title with a flurry of processed beats that never quite lose the rhythm, while "Atelier" gets trigger-happy on the sample with multiple breaks going off at different times. Apart from the focus on percussion programming, there's really not much else going on except for a few melodies and atmospheres (courtesy of jazz or cinema samples). But given the raft of other breakbeat-happy drill'n'bass records in the racks, it's a bit of a surprise that Hrvátski keeps the proceedings surprisingly funky—he's liable to shift directions at any moment, but never loses his feel for the beat in hand. All in all, *Oiseaux 1996-1998* is a good record to hunt down for those who've worn out their copies of Plug's *Drum'n'bass for Papa*. —*John Bush*

## Keith Hudson

b. 1946, Kingston, Jamaica, d. 1984
*Drums, Producer / Dub*

Ominously known as "The Dark Prince of Reggae," Keith Hudson was born into a musical family in Kingston, Jamaica in 1946. His musical education began as Hudson worked as a sort of roadie for Skatalite and Jamaican trombone king Don Drummond. By age 21, Hudson, who had been trained as a dentist, sunk his earnings into his own record label, Inbidimts, and had a hit with Ken Boothe's recording of "Old Fashioned Way." Not long after this chart success, the suddenly hot Hudson was producing some of the biggest names (and soon-to-be biggest names) in reggae—John Holt, Delroy Wilson, Alton Ellis, and the great toasters U-Roy and Dennis Alcapone, all of whom benefited from what would be Hudson's trademark production style: groove-centered, bass/drum-dominated, lean and mean stripped-down riddims. By the mid-'70s, Hudson began releasing more solo work, hitting paydirt from the start with his 1974 debut, *Entering the Dragon* and his intense second record, *Flesh of My Skin*, an ominous, dark record that earned Hudson his title as reggae's "Dark Prince." In 1976, Hudson relocated to New York City and worked pretty much nonstop, producing as well as recording solo records up until 1982. He succumbed to lung cancer in 1984, at age 38, robbing reggae of one its greatest, most adventurous, and unheralded producers and performers. —*John Dougan*

Entering the Dragon / 1974 / Atra import ♦♦♦♦
Hudson's debut shows off his songwriting ability and, perhaps most important, his production skills. As is the case with much of Hudson's solo work, it's primal stuff—that is, minimalism rules the day, and there is not too much in the way of fancy mixing effects and aural wizardry. But Hudson, who by the time of this recording had produced some big names in Jamaican music, learned his lessons well, and his time as a producer/student pays off in this remarkably assured and confident debut. —*John Dougan*

• Pick a Dub / 1974 / Blood & Fire ♦♦♦♦
In his excellent book *England's Dreaming*, Jon Savage refers to *Pick a Dub* as "the greatest dub album ever, twelve cuts, all fantastic." I heartily concur with Savage's assessment, with the lone caveat being that I think there are some Lee Perry and King Tubby sides that might be as good. That caveat notwithstanding, *Pick a Dub* is sensational, arguably the crowning achievement of Hudson's career. In fact, coming as early as it did in the development of dub (it was originally released in 1974), it is seminal work, a landmark in progressive remixing on a par with early King Tubby, Augustus Pablo, and Rupie Edwards. What makes this record so scintillating is the intensity of the bass and drums, and Hudson's relatively naked production. There are not a lot of goofy sound effects and studio screwing-around, just buckets of blood and sweat all rolled into a seductive slab of percussive heaviness that will rattle every filling in your head. Once a forgotten obscurity, *Pick a Dub* was

rescued by the folks at Blood and Fire, who re-released it in 1994. Go buy it today. —*John Dougan*

**Brand** / 1979 / Pressure Sounds ♦♦♦♦
Another amazing chunk of dub, *Brand* is the dub version of Hudson's *Rasta Communication*. And if you think *Pick a Dub* was tough to find, *Brand* was assumed to have fallen into a crack in the universe. Only available at outrageous collector's prices, *Brand* was finally rescued by producer and dub mastermind Adrian Sherwood for his label Pressure Sounds. Exhilarating and powerful, *Brand* proves that *Pick a Dub* was no fluke and that Hudson was simultaneously writing and rewriting the book of dub. Rhythmically dense and intense (thanks to bassist Ranchie and drummer Sly Dunbar), *Brand* is sinewy instead of slick, powerfully direct instead of playfully obscure. If you're hep to Hudson's vibe after listening to *Pick a Dub*, then you won't be able to live another day without *Brand*. —*John Dougan*

**Flesh of My Skin** / 1988 / Atra ♦♦♦♦
The record that "demonized" Keith Hudson, a doom-and-gloom bass-heavy retreat into the dark recesses of one's psyche. Loaded with intense, at times violent, imagery, this is an intense record with oppression and racism as its main subject matter. Interestingly, according to reggae scribe Steve Barker, the original master tapes have disappeared. As a result, the album only exists in a remixed version, not by Hudson but by his engineer Sid Bucknor, and was re-released in 1988. Still, I haven't heard any complaints about Bucknor's remix; after all, he was the engineer on the original session. —*John Dougan*

**Studio Kinda Cloudy** / 1988 / Trojan ♦♦♦♦
An excellent, borderline indispensable collection of Hudson's best production work featuring songs by Alton Ellis, Dennis Alcapone, John Holt, and Delory Wilson. Although it's easy to focus on Keith Hudson the solo performer, his talents in the studio behind a mixing board were as good as any of the big-name producers in Jamaica. What is even more amazing is how young Hudson was (early 20s) when he worked on much of this material. An important piece of reggae history. —*John Dougan*

## Human League

f. 1977, Sheffield, Yorkshire,
*Group / New Romantic, Club/Dance, New Wave, Synth-Pop, Dance-Pop*
Synth-pop's first international superstars, the Human League was among the earliest and most innovative bands to break into the pop mainstream on a wave of synthesizers and electronic rhythms, their marriage of infectious melodies and state-of-the-art technology proving enormously influential on countless acts following in their wake. The group was formed in Sheffield, England in 1977 by synth players Martyn Ware and Ian Marsh, who'd previously teamed as the duo Dead Daughters; following a brief tenure as the Future, they rechristened themselves the Human League after enlisting vocalist Philip Oakey. The trio soon recorded a demo, and played their first live dates; they soon tapped Adrian Wright as their "Director of Visuals," and his slide shows quickly became a key component of their performances.

Signing with the indie label Fast, in 1978 the Human League issued their first single, "Being Boiled"; a minor underground hit, it was followed by a tour in support of Siouxsie and the Banshees. After a 1979 EP, *The Dignity of Labour Parts 1-4*, the group released their first full-length effort, *Reproduction*, a dark, dense work influenced largely by Kraftwerk. *Travelogue* followed the next year, and reached the UK Top 20; still, internal tensions forced Ware and Marsh to quit the group in late 1980, at which time they formed the British Electronic Foundation. Their departure forced Wright to begin learning to play the synthesizer; at the same time, Oakey recruited bassist Ian Burden as well as a pair of schoolgirls, Susanne Sulley and Joanne Catherall, to handle additional vocal duties.

The first single from the revamped Human League, 1981's "Boys and Girls," reached the British Top 50; recorded with producer Martin Rushent, the follow-up "Sound of the Crowd" fell just shy of the Top Ten. Their next single, "Love Action," reached number three, and after adding ex-Rezillo Jo Callis the League issued "Open Your Heart," another hit. Still, their true breakthrough was the classic single "Don't You Want Me," from the album *Dare!*, both topped their respective charts in England, and went on to become major hits in the US as well. A tour of the States followed, but new music was extremely slow in forthcoming; after a remix disc, *Love and Dancing*, the Human League finally issued 1983's *Fascination!* EP, scoring a pair of hits with "Mirror Man" and "(Keep Feeling) Fascination."

The much-anticipated full-length *Hysteria* finally surfaced in mid-1984, heralding a more forceful sound than earlier Human League releases; the record failed to match the massive success of *Dare!*, however, with the single "The Lebanon" earning insignificant airplay. The group soon went on indefinite hiatus, and Oakey recorded a 1985 solo LP with famed producer Giorgio Moroder titled simply *Philip Oakey and Giorgio Moroder*. To the surprise of many, the Human League resurfaced in 1986 with *Crash*, produced by the duo of Jimmy Jam and Terry Lewis; the plaintive lead single "Human" soon topped the US charts, but the group failed to capitalize on its comeback success, disappearing from the charts for the remainder of the decade.

When the Human League finally returned in 1990 with *Romantic*, their chart momentum had again dissipated, and the single "Heart Like a Wheel" barely managed to rise into the Top 40. The record was the band's last with longtime label Virgin; now a trio consting of Oakey, Sulley and Catherall, they ultimately signed with the East/West label, teaming with producer Ian Stanley for 1995's *Octopus*. The album went largely unnoticed both at home and overseas, with the single "Stay with Me Tonight" issued solely in the UK. New material is reportedly forthcoming. —*Jason Ankeny*

**Reproduction** / 1979 / Virgin ♦♦♦
Pop fans a bit put off by Human League's dispassionate vocals on their breakout hit "Don't You Want Me" would have been shocked by the degree of emotionlessness heard two years earlier on the band's 1979 album debut. The trio of Marsh, Ware and Oakey all handled vocals and synthesizers to create a set of grim, rigid tracks that revealed a greater lack of humanity than even Kraftwerk. It's a surprise that Human League hit the British charts at all (the single "Empire State Human"), since this could well be the most detached synth-pop record ever released. —*John Bush*

**Travelogue** / 1980 / Virgin ♦♦
The Human League's second album, *Travelogue*, was its first to be released in the US (Not that you would have noticed at the time, given the limited distribution; the album subsequently was picked up for reissue by Virgin/Atlantic in 1988). It was also the last to feature the nearly original lineup of Martyn Ware, Ian Marsh, Philip Oakey, and Adrian Wright. Already, the band's synthesizer textures and Oakey's mannered voice were starting to lean in a pop direction, but much of this album retained the austere tone of earlier synthesizer groups such as Kraftwerk and Tangerine Dream. The conflicting musical directions led to a split in the band after this album, with Ware and Marsh forming Heaven 17 and Oakey and Wright reorganizing a new version of the Human League. Ironically, both ventures were more pop-oriented than before. —*William Ruhlmann*

★ **Dare** / 1981 / A&M ♦♦♦♦♦
Martin Rushent's fresh, clean production keeps the synthesized music from being too cluttered, while Philip Oakey's voice is used for its self-consciously melodramatic effect and contrasted with the untrained singing of Joanne Catherall and Susanne Sulley. The hits are "Don't You Want Me" and (in England) "The Sound of the Crowd," "Love Action (I Believe in Love)," and "Open Your Heart," but the album also works as a consistent piece. —*William Ruhlmann*

**Love and Dancing** / 1982 / A&M ♦♦
Credited to "The League Unlimited Orchestra" in homage to Barry White's Love Unlimited Orchestra, *Love and Dancing* carried a sleeve note that read, "This album contains instrumental versions of previously released songs by the Human League specially remixed and produced by Martin Rushent." (Actually, one song was new, and there are a few vocal choruses.) The songs had been released previously on *Dare* so if you always thought "Don't You Want Me" was a great track with obnoxious vocals, this is the album for you. —*William Ruhlmann*

**Fascination!** / 1983 / A&M ♦♦♦
Instead of following *Dare*, its internationally successful third album, with another full-length effort, the Human League re-emerged with this under-27-minute, six-track EP, which consists of the one new track on its *Love and Dancing* remix album, plus the A- and B-sides of its post-*Dare* singles "(Keep Feeling) Fascination" (in two versions) and "Mirror Man." Both those songs were hits in the pop-synthesizer style of *Dare*, but the group's failure to produce a new album after 19 months was an indication of the instability it would suffer for the rest of its career. —*William Ruhlmann*

**Hysteria** / 1984 / Virgin ♦♦
The Human League's two-and-a-half-year effort to come up with a follow-up

to *Dare* resulted in *Hysteria*, which tinkered with the hit formula, demoting producer Martin Rushent to computer programmer on only a few cuts. It was probably a mistake to release the politically oriented "The Lebanon" as the first single, especially in the US, where the country is called merely "Lebanon" and where the band was known primarily for the romantic "Don't You Want Me." That song wasn't typical of the album, which featured a remake of the earlier hit ("Don't You Know I Want You"), but was mostly filled with nondescript synthesizer dance tracks that barely deserved to be called songs. *Hysteria* was the Human League's opportunity to consilidate their worldwide success with *Dare;* instead, they slumped slightly at home and put their career in jeopardy in America. — *William Ruhlmann*

### Greatest Hits / 1988 / A&M ++++
*Greatest Hits* reminds that popular tracks like "Don't You Want Me" successfully bridged the gap between dance, pop, and rock audiences. With "Being Boiled," the 16-strong collection even offers a token sample of the League's earliest, more experimental machine music approach—although their atmospherically funereal cover of the Righteous Brothers' "You've Lost That Loving Feeling" should also have made the cut. Includes the rather engaging new recording "Stay with Me Tonight" from the currently active version of Phil Oakey and friends. — *Roch Parisien*

### The Very Best of the Human League / Jul. 14, 1998 / Ark 21 ++++
In the summer of 1998, the Human League set out on tour with the reunited Culture Club, both bands hoping to capitalize on the New Wave nostalgia that was slowly sweeping the country. The tour naturally provided an ideal opportunity for a new hits collection, *The Very Best of the Human League*. Essentially, it's a slightly reworked version of *Greatest Hits*, sharing all the obvious tracks ("Don't You Want Me," "Love Action (I Believe in Love)," "Mirror Man," "Fascination (Keep Feeling)," "Human," "Being Boiled," "The Lebanon"), and subsituting earlier cuts like "The Sound of the Crowd" and "Open Your Heart" for middle-of-the-road '90s singles "Tell Me When," "Stay with Me Tonight," "Heart Like a Wheel" and "One Man in My Heart." Clearly, this collection is for fans who prefer *Crash* to *Dare*, and they'll likely be satisfied, since it's fairly consistent. That said, *Dare* fans should note that this album features a genuine rarity in "Together in Electric Dreams," Philip Oakey's collaboration with Giorgio Moroder for the 1984 film *Electric Dreams*. It doesn't pop up all that often on either Human League releases or various-artists collections, which means this is all the more valuable for collectors, who may also enjoy the "Audio Liner Notes" which feature the group retelling their history. The Snap remix of "Don't You Want Me," however, will be of little interest to either camp. — *Stephen Thomas Erlewine*

## Human Mesh Dance (Taylor Deupree)
*Producer / Electronica, Ambient Techno*

Similar to his work with Savvas Ysatis as SETI, Taylor Deupree's Human Mesh Dance project explores an isolationist headspace comprised of psychedelic soundscapes with minimal beatwork and carefully hoarded samples. The debut *Hyaline* was released in 1994 on Instinct Records, the label which issues many of Deupree's various aliases (and also employs him as graphic designer). One year later, second album *Mindflower* appeared, followed in 1997 by *The Secret Number Twelve*. — *John Bush*

### • Hyaline / 1994 / Instinct ++++
The Human Mesh Dance debut full-length is a well-crafted piece of organic ambience, heavy on the organics on tracks like "Smooth Sea, Clear Sky," "Sunflower," and "Signs of Life." — *John Bush*

### Mindflower / 1995 / Instinct +++
A bit darker than the debut, *Mindflower* looks midway between sky and space for inspiration on "Satellites (Ring the Sky)," "Birth of a Perfect Planet," and "Deep Phase." — *John Bush*

## Tony Humphries
b. Nov. 3, 1957, Brooklyn, NY
*Producer, DJ / Garage, Club/Dance, House*

One of the few DJs whose career at the hub of dance music (New York) spanned the '70s, '80s, and '90s, Tony Humphries is one of the most important names in the evolution of house. His status is especially vaunted, considering his role in the development of garage music (also known as the Jersey Sound, in honor of Humphries' work at Newark's Club Zanzibar). Though Larry Levan is considered the seminal garage DJ (his Paradise Garage club gave its name to the style), Humphries nurtured the style throughout the '80s and '90s and was potentially Levan's equal at inspiring audiences to higher and higher flights of dancefloor bliss.

Born in Brooklyn in 1957, he began collecting records at the age of ten and joined a DJ club while at college in Manhattan. Humphries had never considered a career in music, but when his job in the editorial department of New York's *Daily News* was temporarily halted due to a strike early in the '80s, he never looked back. Humphries began working at a record store and spent his extra time spinning at New York's 98.7 KISS-FM in 1981. One year later, he debuted with a residency at the Club Zanzibar in nearby Newark, New Jersey.

Though Larry Levan's DJing at the Paradise Garage gave a name to the soulful New York variant of early house music later termed garage, Humphries was just as instrumental in bringing the sound to a wide audience. Every major East Coast producer coming up in the late '80s and early '90s name-checked him with vigor, and his DJing was also influential on many second-wave British acts. The UK connection came in handy by the turn of the decade—Humphries became one of several American DJs to make a name (and quite a large paycheck) on British shores. Several years later, the London super-club Ministry of Sound tapped Humphries for an exclusive deal to DJ and produce for its club/label combo, and Humphries also worked on remixing for Chaka Khan, Deee-Lite, the Sugarcubes, and Janet Jackson, among others. Besides mix albums for Strictly Rhythm and Tribal UK, Humphries has recorded several of his own productions as the Tony Humphries Project. — *John Bush*

### Tony Humphries Strictly Rhythm Mix / 1993 / Strictly Rhythm +++

### This Is the Sound of Tribal UK, Vol. 2 / Feb. 1996 / I.R.S. ++++
Tony Humphries mixed this 1995 double-album compilation of classic and exclusive Tribal UK material, including tracks from Junior Vasquez, Deep Dish, Fallout Shelter, Absolute US, Liberty City, and Salt City Orchestra, among others. — *John Bush*

### • Take Home the Club / Mar. 25, 1997 / Bassline ++++
A club compilation that features the requisite dancing female and barely even lists Humphries' name on the cover, *Take Home the Club* is still one of the best documents of the garage king's impeccable talent for mixing and selecting records. The way the vocal tag on the opener (Colonel Abrams' "I'm Not Gonna Let") slides into the next track, the track shout-outs to Humphries favorites like Connie Harvey and Jocelyn Brown, the emphasis on solid, hook-filled tracks—all of these make this such an exuberant, joy-filled occasion that listeners actually get a sense of the immense energy and vibes fostered in classic clubs like Humphries' own *Zanzibar*. Simply put, it's one of the most important, enjoyable mix albums ever released. — *John Bush*

## Steve "Silk" Hurley
b. Nov. 9, 1962, Chicago, IL
*Producer, DJ / Club/Dance, Urban, House*

One of the most important producers for the early popularity of Chicago house, Steve "Silk" Hurley precipitated the founding of a major early house label (DJ International), recorded house music's first number one single and was the first to branch out to encompass pop and hip-hop within the house framework. Born on the south side of Chicago, Hurley began listening to contemporary R&B/funk of bands like Parliament/Funkadelic, the Gap Band, and the Ohio Players. Influenced to become a DJ by the disco hot mixes he heard on local radio, Hurley manufactured his own mixing setup out of spare parts after a trip to Radio Shack. He studied engineering at the University of Illinois (and later at junior college), but dropped out by 1981 to concentrate on music full-time.

As a crucial early DJ, Hurley's name was made in 1983 at a club called the Candy Store. With his friend and roommate Farley Keith, he promoted house music parties and also mixed on local Chicago radio station WBMX-FM. After Jamie Principle's rough bedroom demos became huge crowd favorites wherever he DJed, Hurley began buying synthesizer and recording gear; he emerged with several rough beat tracks, then recruited Keith Nunnally to add vocals and named the project JM Silk. His single "Shadows of Your Love" was the first release on DJ International (the label had been financed by Hurley and owner Rocky Jones). The B-side "Music Is the Key" quickly made the single a double-sided Chicago hit and set the Hurley sound blueprint: a cavalcade of stuttering beats balancing an insistent melodic quality which mirrored Nunnally's soulful vocals. The addition of a rap—the first on a house record—only added to the epic quality of the single.

In 1986, Farley Keith had stunned the Chicago community when he hit the British Top Ten with "Love Can't Turn Around," recorded as Farley Jackmaster Funk. Hurley, however, claimed the track was a blatant theft of one of his own productions—the two stopped speaking to each other—and got his revenge by trumping Farley's success with his next production, "Jack Your Body." Borrowing the bassline from the club classic "Let No Man Put Asunder" by First Choice and adding the sampled stutter technique from "Music Is the Key" (though here on the vocals instead of percussion), the single hit number one in Britain in early 1987 and proved the most successful of the dozens of tie-in singles which swept Chicago house during the jacking craze of 1987.

Like Frankie Knuckles, Marshall Jefferson, and several other Chicago producers, Hurley spent more of the late '80s and early '90s working on production and remixing than actual recording; he provided club treatments for the likes of Michael Jackson, Madonna, Janet Jackson, CeCe Peniston, Inner City, New Order, Black Box, and En Vogue, winning Remixer of the Year honors at the 1991 British Dance Awards. After forming his own Silk Productions company, Hurley gradually branched into hip-hop and R&B production as well. —*John Bush*

- **Work It Out** / 1989 / Atlantic ✦✦✦

## Hybrid

*Group / Progressive Trance, Club/Dance*

Hybrid is a trio of remixers based in the Welsh city of Swansea: Mike Truman, Chris Healings, and Lee Mullin. Meeting while going to clubs in the early '90s, the three made their own remixes of recordings, eventually earning assignments from record companies to pursue their hobby professionally. Finally, they were signed to Distinct'ive Records and embarked on making an ambitious first album, *Wide Angle*, in Moscow, using such talents as singer Julee Cruise and the 90-piece Russian Federal Orchestra. "Finished Symphony," which reached the UK singles charts in July 1999, featured the orchestra. It was followed into the charts in September by "If I Survive," featuring Cruise on vocals, and by *Wide Angle* itself. Picked up for release in the US by Kinetic (distributed by Reprise, a division of major label Warner Records), *Wide Angle* was reconfigured for its American appearance in September 2000. The group then served as the opening act on Moby's US tour that same fall. —*William Ruhlmann*

- **Wide Angle** / Sep. 19, 2000 / Kinetic ✦✦✦✦

Though the late '90s witnessed the advent of dozens of progressive trance DJs and producers, few attempted to record a production LP. They preferred instead to release scads of mix albums, most of which purported to take listeners on a journey but did little more than offer frequent breakdowns and same-sounding tracks. Finally, the British team Hybrid delivered the goods with their full-length debut *Wide Angle*. Befitting the cinematic nod in the title, Hybrid often bedrocks their productions with film-music flourishes indebted both to traditional orchestration and the rock-based John Barry school of soundtracking; even when they're spinning through futuristic, warped trance with a roster of cutting-edge effects to impress even the most callused *Global Underground* fan, there's an undeniably cinematic grandeur to these productions. Hybrid utilizes slow-moving strings and gradually building chords, straight out of Gorecki's "Symphony No. 3," but surprisingly effective in this context. They also do well with collaborations, recruiting Julee Cruise for three beautiful tracks, the album highlights "I Know," "If I Survive," and "Dreaming Your Dreams." In similar fashion to the way Orbital—another team with a good grasp of symphonic techno—warped acid house and techno so they'd make as much sense on headphones as on the dancefloor, Hybrid bends the template of progressive trance to fit on the full-length realm, and with equally impressive results. (The American version of *Wide Angle* differs from the British one issued a year earlier in that two tracks featuring Cruise, "High Life" and "Fatal Beating," are missing, and three tracks, "Kill City [Edit]," "Kid 2000 [Edit]," and a second version of "Altitude," have been added. The tracks also seem to have been mixed and edited differently.) —*John Bush*

# I

## I:Cube
*Producer / Tech-House, Trip-Hop, Club/Dance, Hip-Hop*

French techno/house producer I:Cube (aka Nicholas), along with such artists as Air, Motorbass, and Daft Punk, was one of the most hyped underground acts on Paris' resurging dance scene during 1996-97 (with the difference that, instead of the industry, it was those artists doing the hyping). Similar in some respects to his colleagues, I:Cube's near-comprehensive fusion of the range of minimal electronic dance musics—a molten concoction of funk, soul, electro, trance, Chicago house, and Detroit techno—first surfaced through the "Disco Cubism" single (on popular Parisian DJ Gilb-R's Versatile label) in 1996. Made all the more amazing by the discovery that it was the work of a teenage schoolboy, the single's popularity was upped considerably by the full-length debut, *Picnic Attack,* which appeared the following year. Informed by a heavy dose of driving, minimal, trance-oriented techno, the album helped distinguish I:Cube's style from that of his more press-hounded countrymates (and attracted a fair amount of hounding on its own). A surprising and consistently inventive release, the album (along with Daft Punk's *Homework* and the Sourcelab label compilations) gave considerable weight to the notion that Paris' dance underground is among the least stylistically segregated around, producing innovative, compositionally accomplished music both clear in focus and broad in scope. *Adore* followed in 2000. —*Sean Cooper*

● **Picnic Attack** / Jun. 2, 1997 / Versatile ✦✦✦
One of the more interesting, inventive releases among the new crop of Parisian house/techno talent, I:Cube's full-length debut for Versatile covers similar territory to other recent debuts from Motorbass and Daft Punk. I:Cube ups the trance quotient, however, making for a driving brand of funky, soulful techno with both depth and velocity. Cleaner, tighter production also adds to the album's appeal. —*Sean Cooper*

## I-F
f. 1993, Den Haag, The Netherlands
*Producer, DJ / Neo-Electro, Electro-Techno, Electro, Techno*

Dutch outfit I-F produces thin, minimal electro and techno punctuated by somewhat obvious but inventively reconstituted influences tracing to late '70s and early '80s American and Italian disco and British new wave and technopop. Heavily melodic and often incorporating thick, dense basslines that bounce along with a force equal to or exceeding that of the beat, I-F tracks such as "Superman," "Quest," "Playstation No. 1," and the massive club hit "Space Invaders are Smoking Grass" helped reinitiate the use of bizarre, synthetic-sounding lyrics, pushing beyond the odd sampled vocal of most dance music and into full-on verse-chorus-verse arrangements that recall the heyday of British new romantic groups such as Visage, the Normal, and Fad Gadget.

Based out of the Dutch urban center of Den Haag, I-F is largely the work of one producer—known as Ferenc—although the close-knit qualities of the Den Haag underground and a preponderance of like-sounding artists (including Unit Moebius, Electronome, Funkstorung, and a dozen others) on I-F-associated labels such as Viewlexx, Acid Planet, and Murdercapital makes uncredited collaborations a distinct likelihood. Focusing first on hard-hitting acid and techno, Ferenc released a number of limited-run EPs through those labels (as both Beverly Hills 808303 and I-F) before hooking up with higher-profile German label Disko B in 1996. I-F's Disko B releases marked a shift in style; the two-part *Portrait of a Dead Girl* series began playing up the electro and new wave influences, incorporating rhythmic syncopation, vocals, and strong, simple melodies. I-F's debut LP, *Fucking Consumer,* was released by Disko B in the summer of 1998, and remains one of the most memorable new-school electro albums to date. I-F's by-far most widely known track, however—"Space Invaders Are Smoking Grass"—appeared in the interim, debuting on the Detroit-based Interdimensional Transmission label, which kicked off its four-part EP series *From Beyond* with the cut. Also compiled onto *Fucking Consumer,* "Space Invaders" became one of 1997's biggest anthems, receiving track-of-the-year kudos from no less a bassbin-hugging tastemaker than *Jockey Slut* magazine, spawning an IT remix 12", and flooding the label's Ann Arbor, MI offices with licensing requests.

I-F material continued to appear at a higher-than-average clip throughout 1998, including a collaborative 12" for the Austrian Sabotage label (under the name Lonny and Melvin) and a second full-length LP/CD, *The Man from P.A.C.K.* In addition to his production work, Ferenc continues to operate Hotmix Electro-nix, a mail-order business often referred to as the Dutch Submerge, originally formed in 1990 and now an important European distribution hub for underground experimental dance music. —*Sean Cooper*

**Portrait of a Dead Girl, Vol. 1 [Single]** / Aug. 5, 1996 / Disko B ✦✦✦
The first of a two-part 12" series for Disko B, featuring material previously available only via the artist's limited-run Viewlexx label. A four-tracker of decidedly unconventional electro and techno, *Dead Girl*'s two standouts are "I do Because I Couldn't Care Less"—a ruthless, dissonant electro stormer satirizing techno's devolution into pop mediocrity (the track's title is a nose-thumb at Aphex Twin's 1995 album *I Care Because You Do*)—and the chafing doomsday electro-pop of "Superman." —*Sean Cooper*

**Portrait of a Dead Girl, Vol. 2 [Single]** / 1997 / Disko B ✦✦✦✦
("Space Invaders Are Smoking Grass Remix") The massive crossover success of I-F's contribution to Interdimensional Transmission's four-part "From Beyond" series prompted this savvy remix 12". The A-side features an extended recast pairing a bright, snapping two-beat with the original's unmistakable thin 808 beats and perhaps the most impossibly great bassline in dance music history. On the flip are the track's original version and "Secret Desire," a preview from I-F's forthcoming IT full-length, *The Man from P.A.C.K.* —*Sean Cooper*

**Space Invaders Are Smoking Grass/Secret Desire [Single]** / Mar. 2, 1998 / Interdimensional Transmission ✦✦✦✦
*Space Invaders Are Smoking Grass* was I-F's first full release for IT, offering extended access to the timeless electro anthem originally released on the first installment of the label's record series *From Beyond.* Surely the song to forever change the label's and artist's profiles, "Space Invaders" evokes traditions in Italian disco and new wave in addition to electro with its irresistible melody, galloping disco bassline, and textured, primitive vocoded rap over-top. The track is a sharp departure from I-F's previous work in its more overt reference to "retro" influences. On this release, the original track is coupled with I-F's own "Extended Dance Remix" as it were as well as a teaser of an instrumental version of "Secret Desire"—a song included on I-F's subsequent full length for IT, *The Man from P.A.C.K.* —*Carlos Julio Souffront*

● **Fucking Consumer** / May 4, 1998 / Disko B ✦✦✦✦
*Fucking Consumer* is one of the most solid and well-formed examples of literally new-school electro. Combining the thin, angular beats of '80s breakdance music with melodic, vocal, and rhythmic elements culled from new wave and techno-pop, tracks such as "Disko Slique," "Theme from Sunwheel Beach Bar," and the inimitable "Space Invaders Are Smoking Grass" count among some of the boldest, most distinctive experimental electronic dance music of the post-rave era. Fairly monochromatic and formed mostly of alternately combined drum patterns and melodic and rhythmic textures, the tracks are also quite composed, making of them a clear, if somewhat bizarre, sibling of pop—simple and repetitive, yet engaging and vastly entertaining. The CD version adds a number of hard-to-find cuts from early I-F releases,

including the standout "Cry" and the morose-but-silly closer, "End Theme," which features a cameo by vocalist Gitane Demone of legendary goth-rock band Christian Death. —*Sean Cooper*

**The Man from P.A.C.K.** / 1999 / Interdimensional Transmissions ++++
I-F's second album in as many years and the first full-length artist's release on the Interdimensional Transmissions label, *The Man from P.A.C.K.* is substantially more stripped down than much of I-F's other recent work. Still, the bouncy basslines are there, though somewhat subdued, and the thin electronics that back gated, snapping snares are unmistakable. The album takes a few additional listens to appreciate properly, but it's the equal of the comparatively more gripping *Fucking Consumer* once inside. "Secret Desire," "The Getaway Scene," and "Midnight Connection to Mars" are particularly impressive. The CD version features a number of non-LP bonus cuts. —*Sean Cooper*

**The Theme from P.A.C.K. [Single]** / May 3, 1999 / Interdimensional Transmission +++
This 12" contains two mixes of a track also included on the I-F full-length release *The Man from P.A.C.K.* Side A is an extended 12" version offering a longer introductory rhythm workout with I-F's always impeccable programming—complete with the P.A.C.K. signature snare-as-punishment. The B-side contains a Parallax Corporation remix chronicling I-F's departure from the "P.A.C.K. sound" into a fresh style of analog disco with an emphasis on simple melodies, galloping basslines, and sophisticated dance arrangements. —*Carlos Souffront*

**Mixed Up in the Hague, Vol. 1** / 2000 / Panama ++++
I-F's *Mixed Up in the Hague* is an excellent dance-history lesson focusing on the electro-disco that's been such an influence on his productions. Wisely avoiding most of the endlessly compiled electro classics ("Planet Rock," "Rockit," "Clear") that tend to bore advanced listeners, I-F instead looks back to the motorized sequencer disco of the late '70s and early '80s with a parade of excellent obscurities. (Featuring track titles but no list of performers is undoubtedly not an oversight but a challenge to potential trainspotters out there.) The more familiar tracks include "Manmade" by Man Parrish, "The Chase" by Giorgio Moroder, a remix (cover?) of Kraftwerk's "Tour de France," "Space Is the Place" by Newcleus, "Problemes d'Amour" by Alexander Robotnick, and "Dirty Talk" by Klein + MBO. The mix is raw and hands-on too, with almost two dozen tracks squeezed into an hour of mixing. —*John Bush*

## Daniel Ibbotson

*Remixing, Producer / Jazz-House, Tech-House, Neo-Electro, Club/Dance*
Balancing his affinity for new-school deep house beats with an early fixation for jazzy textures, indie-rock, and Warp's bleep techno, Daniel Ibbotson is a producer-by-accident, a home-production aficionado who put together a demo tape during 1995 while studying at the Glasgow School of Arts for his photography degree. After sending it to the electro label Clear Records (whose buzzed-about résumé included incarnations of µ-Ziq, Black Dog, and Global Communication), the label released some of the material as the *Souped-Up EP* in August 1996. More than enough material was left for an entire album, released in 1998 for the Clear spin-off Reel Discs. Ibbotson also remixed Friend & Doktor Kosmos, and appeared on the Compost collection *Future Sound of Jazz, Vol. 3;* he returned in 1999 with *Frequency and Phase.* —*John Bush*

● **New Stories** / Oct. 27, 1997 / Reel Discs ++++
An album of diverse moods and tempos, *New Stories* inflects house with jazz-funk and mild electro along the lines of Ian O'Brien or Matthew Herbert, though with less humor and diva orientation than the latter. Highlights include the smooth-flowing opener "Jazz by Design," the title track, and "Skyscraper Trees." —*John Bush*

**Stream Lines** / Dec. 7, 1998 / Glasgow Underground ++
While Ibbotson's take on textured jazz-house is pleasing enough, *Stream Lines* is definitely an album of diminishing returns. It's very similar to his first album, with only the occasional disco sample to invigorate a few tracks. —*John Bush*

**Frequency and Phase** / Dec. 14, 1999 / Glasgow Underground +++
*Frequency and Phase* is Daniel Ibbotson's third album in just over two years, and from the first few tracks, it shows. The early '80s R&B raunch of the opener, "Coming to Get You," goes on a bit too long, and the follow-up "Island Song" never gets going at all. Still, he ups the ante from his last full-length, *Stream Lines,* matching his house inspiration (the crisp percussion and loose-booty basslines) with synth-horns, bongos, and electric piano that sound more like '80s porn soundtracks than electronic listening music. It's occasionally closer to electronica muzak than futuristic dance, but *Frequency and Phase* is a good groove throughout. —*John Bush*

## Ice

f. 1992
*Group / Underground Rap, Ambient Dub, Hip-Hop*
The darker visions of industrial-strength trip-hop plus death-metal raging equals the intense dub-hop of Ice. A side-project-of-sorts formed around Godflesh's Justin K. Broadrick and God's Kevin Martin (the same lineup comprising Techno Animal), Ice formed in the early '90s with additional bandmembers Dave Cochrane and Alex Buess. The quartet released *Under the Skin,* their debut LP, in 1993. Broadrick and Martin both kept quite busy with other work—for Techno Animal, Final, Godflesh, God, and others—and released only the 1995 remix EP *Quarantine.* Finally, in 1998, Ice returned with their second album *Bad Blood* and new drummer Lou Ciccotelli, plus collaborators like Sebastian Laws and Scott Harding of New Kingdom, Blixa Bargeld, DJ Vadim and El-P from Company Flow. —*John Bush*

**Under the Skin** / 1993 / Pathological ++

● **Bad Blood** / Oct. 20, 1998 / Morpheus ++++
*Bad Blood* is a collision of gut-bucket beats, basement production, and what occasionally sounds like a grindcore vocalist trying to rap. Those vocal collaborations come from Sebastian Laws (also of New Kingdom), Blixa Bargeld, and WordSound label favorite Sensational. Aside from Broadrick and Martin, New Kingdom's Scott Harding and DJ Vadim also work on production, resulting in a dense, broiling sludge of industrial-dub (not half bad at that). —*John Bush*

## Icons

f. 1994
*Group / Jungle/Drum'N'Bass, Club/Dance*
Blame and Justice, two of the foremost names in intelligent jungle production (along with their longtime compatriot LTJ Bukem), began working together in the early '90s. After recording singles for Moving Shadow, the duo formed their own Modern Urban Jazz label, and in 1996 issued the debut Icons album, *Emotions with Intellect.* —*John Bush*

● **Emotions with Intellect** / Oct. 14, 1996 / React America ++++
Blame and Justice's polished, jazzy drum'n'bass productions walk the line between Goldie's house-oriented jungle and the organic futurist fusion of LTJ Bukem. On *Emotions with Intellect,* the duo let their synthesizers do the mood enhancement while a crucial set of breaks provides reserves of intellect. It's undoubtedly an emotional album, and intelligent at that, though its slightly overhyped status can make it hard to cope with. —*John Bush*

## Idjut Boys

f. London, England
*Group / Garage, Club/Dance, House*
Dan Tyler and Conrad McDonnell, aka Idjut Boys, are an English duo whose music formula includes combining a sense of humor with music. With tracks entitled "Frogs Arrrse" and "Life: The Shoeing You Deserve," it's clear that Tyler and McDonnell keep the pressure and often seriousness of the hectic music industry in perspective.

Tyler and McDonnell met in the late '80s in Cambridge while Conrad was working as a lifeguard and McDonnell was studying at university. Both men met at Brighton's "Tonka" night events, where they discovered a shared passion for similar music. Soon after, both moved to London and established the U-Star parties. In addition to lending their own talents, Tyler and McDonnell hosted New York DJs Hector Romero and Ted Patterson. The Idjut's combination of classic house and a touch of techno soon caught on, and landed the duo gigs DJing all over the world. After the release of their fourth 12", in 1994, McDonnell and Tyler established U-Star Records. Their release "Not Reggae" was admired by such production legends as Francois Kevorkian. The Idjut Boys have produced and remixed the likes of Lighthouse Family, Sound 5, and Dimitri from Paris. After releasing a slew of 12"s, in February of 2000 the Idjuts released the mix CD *Saturday Nite Live* on Nuphonic Records. The CD featured a techno and house mix of Idjut Boys favorites including Francois K.'s mix of Femi Kuti, Shoki Shoki, Sweat Shop, and Aril Brikha. —*Diana Potts*

Life: The Shoeing You Deserve / Mar. 29, 1999 / Glasgow Underground ++++
Just as silly and self-unserious as listeners could expect from the title, *Life: The Shoeing You Deserve* features the Idjut Boys & Quakerman making disco music with punk attitudes, a work ethic that results in unpolished nonproductions quite far removed from the wave of progressive trance consistently caned by Britain's laziest DJs. —*John Bush*

• Saturday Nite Live / Mar. 28, 2000 / Nuphonic ++++
By their name alone, Idjut Boys sound as if they should be a cheeseball techno act, but Dan Taylor and Conrad McDonnell are quite the contrary on their first mix CD, *Saturday Nite Live*. Though all the tracks sound to be vintage *Paradise Garage* finds, they are all relatively new releases. *Saturday Nite Live* is a nonstop flow of funk-influenced garage-style house music. The track selection, including Isolee, Aril Brikha, and a Francois K. remix of Femi Kuti, have just the right amount of variety to keep the energy flowing. What would normally be an odd mix from Brikha's pure synthesizer sound to the deep house sound of Victor Davies' vocal "Run Away Train" works beautifully with Idjuts behind the wheel. Where most would fumble, *Saturday Nite Live* makes a master puzzle out of odd, classic, and soulful pieces. —*Diana Potts*

## Brandi Ifgray

*Piano, Producer / Electronica, Ambient Techno, Trip-Hop, Club/Dance*
During the '80s, Brandi Ifgray led the group Shadowplay, which alternated the sound of smoky jazz with alternative punk energy. By the '90s, Ifgray was working in electronica, and his debut album *Le Mutant* was produced by Finnish lounge impresario Jimi Tenor. The album appeared on Finland's Sahko Records in 1997, and was licensed to American audiences through EFA. —*John Bush*

• Le Mutant / Apr. 28, 1997 / Sahko +++
Ifgray is a friend of the Finnish funk lizard Jimi Tenor, and covers much of the same territory with an interesting take on vocal-oriented electronic music. There's little doubt that *Le Mutant* could come from the polar north, and though it's inspired by Tenor as well as Björk, the album covers a wide range of styles over the course of 60-odd minutes. —*John Bush*

Stargaze / Mar. 29, 1999 / Sahko +++
Again employing Jimi Tenor in the producer's chair, Brandi Ifgray utilizes more live instrumentation on *Stargaze*, which lends the jazzy elements of his electronica something of a fusion flavor; a choir even pops up in places. —*Steve Huey*

## Ryoji Ikeda

*Producer / Experimental Techno, Minimalism, Electronic*
Japanese minimalist electronic composer Ryoji Ikeda is a leading figure among the new crop of computer-based musicians exploring the aesthetic possibilities opened up by digital production technologies. Released through his own CCI Recordings, the UK-based Touch label, and Staalplaat, among others, Ikeda's music engages the digital recording and production process directly, playing up subtle glitches and interruptions typically edited out of that process and combining them with profoundly complex and disjointed collages of samples, pure-tone electronics, and heavily treated digital noise. More recent releases have added elements of the experimental post-techno subgenre-scape to Ikeda's hard-disk stew, with bits of jungle, dub, and minimal techno cropping up between the crackles and whines. Vaguely related— at least in spirit— to American minimalists and computer composers such as LaMonte Young, Steve Reich, Terre Thaemlitz, and John Bischoff, Ikeda's work is also in close harmony with German and Austrian post-techno artists such as Farmers Manual and Rehberg/Bauer, with whom he has collaborated live. Mostly unknown in Japan, his work as a solo artist and in collaboration with Japanese audio/video troupe Dumb Type has gained him a wider audience in the US and Europe. —*Sean Cooper*

+/- / 1997 / Touch ++

• 0°C / 1998 / Touch ++++
A dizzying, physically exhausting tour de force of rootless sonic meltdown, with acoustic samples, electronic beats, tone-based electronics, and all manner of clicks, clacks, static, and noise running through a digital blender and regurgitated in blasts alternately impenetrable and just barely there. Dense, difficult, and enjoyably enlightening all at once. —*Sean Cooper*

Time/Space / 1998 / Staalplaat ++++
Forty minutes of music spread across two 3" CDs, each mapped to the themes indicated in the title. "Time" is a collage of jet engines, morse code patterns, and almost painfully high frequencies, while "Space" is reminiscent of Ikeda's +/-: pure, static sine waves combined slowly and to odd effect. In other words, a great introduction to the major themes of Ikeda's released work to date, and all told, some of his finest. —*Sean Cooper*

20' to 2000 / 1999 / Noton ++
Ikeda's contribution to German label Noton's 12-volume *20' to 2000* series is mostly what you'd expect, although the combination of digital static and cycling pure tones is somehow less interesting than usual. For series completists only. —*Sean Cooper*

## In the Nursery

f. 1981, Sheffield, Yorkshire,
*Group / Experimental Rock, Film Music, Post-Punk*
Formed in Sheffield, England by brothers Klive and Nigel Humberstone in 1981, In the Nursery explored a strange fusion of industrialized military rhythms and classical and film soundtrack music. Devoted more to the former in their early years, the band debuted in 1983 with the mini-album *When Cherished Dreams Come True*, also contributing to several compilations over the next two years. After the 1985 *Temper* EP, the group's initial lineup had evaporated, leaving only the Humberstone brothers to record their first full-length effort, 1986's *Twins*, which began to explore classical influences in greater depth. Percussionist Q and French bilingual vocalist Dolores Marguerite C were added for 1987's *Stormhorse*, which was intended to resemble the soundtrack to an imaginary film. 1988's *Koda* continued in this vein; in 1989, Wax Trax! released a compilation of the band's early work entitled *Counterpoint*. In 1990, In the Nursery altered its approach somewhat for the more graceful, refined *L'Esprit*, on which C's vocals played a prominent role for the first time. *Sense* (1991) and *Duality* (1992) were the group's most film soundtrack-like albums yet, and that direction finally culminated in an official soundtrack, 1993's *An Ambush of Ghosts*. The 1994 concept album *Anatomy of a Poet* followed, along with several collaborative projects under the alias Les Jumeaux. *Scatter*, an extensive retrospective, was released on the band's own ITN Corporation label in 1995; meanwhile, the track "White Robe" was licensed by Warner Bros. for *Interview with the Vampire*, and the single "Hallucinations?" appeared in several different films. From 1996-97, the group's soundtrack work has expanded, with contributions to the television series *La Femme Nikita* and a new score for the silent film *The Cabinet of Dr. Caligari*; there have also been several more releases under the Les Jumeaux moniker. —*Steve Huey*

Prelude (1983-1985) / 1985 / ITN Corporation ++
Formative is indeed the word here, as the sheer symphonic sweep of ITN in future years here is all but absent. Instead, this collection of the early EP *When Cherished Dreams Come True* and various singles tracks showcases a band much more in line with dank, hardscrabble post-punk than with orchestral power. Many of the tracks sound fairly anonymous in comparison to later works, but strong examples of the brothers' ability with a dramatic song crop up more than once, as with the compelling "Mystery," which builds to a frenzied climax while retaining the same quietly forceful singing tone throughout. Unusual arrangements also appear from time to time, as with the heavily produced guitar line on "A to I," which initially sounds like a keyboard melody more than anything else, and "Lost Prayer" and "And Your Eyes," both of which mostly eschew guitars for a synth-heavy approach (the latter is especially compelling, very much a taste of where ITN would go next). The brothers' singing ability varies from cleaner if at-times strained vocals to much more darkly ominous efforts that, combined with the definite post-Joy Division feel of much of the music, especially with the strong Peter Hook-style basslines, calls to mind such similarly energetic gloomsters as And Also the Trees or Crispy Ambulance. Ant Bennet's live drumming does the trick fairly well, on tracks like "Witness (to a Scream)" and "Sentient" already showing shades of the militaristic percussion which would become central to future ITN releases, and the Humberstones' work on guitar and bass is more than serviceable, adding touches like saxophone and bells from time to time to introduce some welcome, unexpected variety amidst the sometimes-overwhelming gloom. Still, while hardly a problem to listen to, *Prelude* very much has the feel of a work in progress—an interesting snapshot of a band's early days, but not much more. —*Ned Raggett*

**Twins** / 1986 / ITN Corporation ♦♦♦♦
Assisted at points by Elaine McLeod on female vocals and Gus Ferguson on cello in place of the departed Bennet, the Humberstones take a notable step forward from rock aesthetics to a much more elaborate, involved kind of music—the opening track alone, "Timbre," with a muffled but relentless pulse and a slightly distorted sample of Bulgarian choir singing, makes for an intriguing start. The use of electronic drums throughout gives *Twins* a very stiff feel at times, but otherwise the musical combinations on display are supple, almost fluid. The title track's mix of male and female singers, vocal samples, heavily produced guitar, and a variety of keyboard melodies and shadings along with the percussion is much more its own beast than earlier tracks, a general mix that continues more or less throughout the record with odd little diversions, as with the almost jazzy "Joaquin." A number of the songs veer towards the outright industrial at times. "Intertwine" slams into gear with a pounding beat sample, while "Workcorps" almost has an all-too-appropriate title in this regard—but notably ITN are not so much interested in death-disco as sheer mood and power, more Test Dept. and Einsturzende Neubaten than Ministry. Some of the tracks exhibit an increasing reach in artistic inspiration—"Profile 63" revolves around a series of John Kennedy speech snippets, while the sweetly haunting "Judgment of Paris" refers to Greek mythology. With the *Temper* EP added as a bonus on the ITN corporation rerelease, including the excellent "Breach Birth" (graced with some of the most strange, abstract vocals ever laid down on tape) and "Arm Me Audacity" demonstrating the abilities of ITN at their aggressive, very consciously arty best, *Twins* remains an underrated, fascinating album. —*Ned Raggett*

**Koda** / 1988 / Wax Trax! ♦♦♦♦
While in many ways a logical continuation of the aesthetic demonstrated on *Stormhorse*—predominantly instrumental compositions, utilizing synthesizers to create mock-orchestral pieces—*Köda* suffers a touch in comparison. For whatever reason, many of the string samples sound just a little too shrill and, especially from the vantage of time, simply cheesy, a little too obvious. Unavoidable perhaps, but the bombastic surge of the opening track "Rites," for one, is undercut when you can just sense that the sometimes hypertrebly melodies are direct from the keyboard. This aside, however, *Köda* is a fine record nonetheless, not as much of a distinct progression from the previous album but possessed of numerous subtle touches throughout, as with the woodwind shadings on the gentle "Te Deum." Overall, the emphasis is on the big and at-times overwhelming, notably on the pounding "Scherzo," with even fragmentary pieces suggesting movements in a Wagnerian epic production. The haunting, complex "Ascent" is the centerpiece of the record, majestic in its scope and wonderfully arranged. Q's snare drumming once again adds a distinct, powerful flair to the proceedings, while Dolores Marguerite provides dramatic narration more than once, mostly in French. Gary Talpas' explanatory liner notes read practically like those of a normal classical release; if the intent is ironic, it's awfully hard to tell. On its own, though, *Köda* is more than fine as a collection of striking mood pieces, regardless of any intent as a uniform creation. The ITN Corporation reissue adds two key single tracks from the same time, the rushing "Compulsion" and the magnificent "Libertaire," as beautiful and powerful a summation of the ITN sound as any, with sweeping horns, strings, and organ counterbalanced against delicate, gentle passages. —*Ned Raggett*

**L'Esprit** / 1990 / Wax Trax! ♦♦♦♦
The Humberstone brothers' first out-and-out masterpiece, *L'Esprit* remains as compelling and lovely an album as it did upon initial release. Taking their love of the dramatic, romantic, and theatrical to even greater heights, their musical complexity was never so involved before, their sense of creating soul-tugging beauty never so fully realized. Right from the opener—"To the Faithful," featuring a now-rare but all the more effective for it vocal from the Humberstones over a forceful but never strident string line accentuated by horns and Q's excellent drumming—*L'Esprit* truly is a soundtrack to an non-existent film. The potential to dream up any number of climactic scenes or meaningful visual passages to such solid pieces as the choral-accompanied "Azure Wings" or the storm-cloud-laden "Retaliation," with its rolling beginning and stately pace, reveals itself time and again. Wisely, ITN step back from creating solely epic pieces here, allowing for the slightly jazz/French pop feel of "Sesudient," with appropriate vocals from Dolores Marguerite, as well as other slight changes from the norm. The big change here, though, is an increasing allowance for the subtlest of touches to help drive many of the pieces, as with a series of harp flourishes on "Soeurette," as well as simply toning things down in general. Far from weakening the effect of the music, it makes *L'Esprit* that much more enjoyable by means of variety. One piece always seems to especially stand out per album; here "Scenes of Childhood" is the clear winner, with a low pulse heralding a simply beautiful string line that gently develops throughout the song. The extra tracks on the ITN Corporation rerelease are not bad at all, but do not add much to what is already a magnificent effort on its own. —*Ned Raggett*

**Duality** / Aug. 18, 1992 / Third Mind ♦♦♦♦
Perhaps ITN's most carefully composed and performed release up to this point, *Duality* builds on the various strengths of earlier works—the basic performance style established on *Stormhorse*, the sweep and range of *L'Esprit* and the increasing subtlety provided by both that and *Sense* resulting in an album that is not simply pleasant but truly inspiring and evocative. "Belle Epoque" begins *Duality* with a mix of piano, strings, horns, chorus effects, and Q's snare drumming, here a little more restrained and all the more effective for it, that is instantly memorable. Very much in line with the filmic nature of earlier releases, it practically begs to be the musical backdrop of some lush romantic drama. The hints of dancefloor-based experimentation crop up again as well, with "Always" providing a particularly sharp example, as shuddering bass and a low-key funk beat underpin a dramatic narrative piece and another lovely orchestral arrangement, while "Pulse" lives up to its title, having just that lurking at the base of the piece. String arrangements here often take on quite a rhythmic approach as well, continuing in the line of experimental percussion touches from before. More so than most of their releases, *Duality* also contains a lot of poetry and recitation with the various songs. Unlike, say, the somewhat overripe efforts of the Moody Blues in past years, ITN's selections and performances match together perfectly; whoever the uncredited male narrator is on "Corruption," he brings a commanding voice to some quite Romantic with a capital R lyrics in concert with Dolores Marguerite as a strong, exquisite musical piece unfolds and builds behind them. In all, another fine album indeed from the brothers Humberstone. —*Ned Raggett*

**Anatomy of a Poet** / 1994 / EFA ♦♦♦♦
The portentous opening track "Bombed" makes for a fine start here, combining as it does the established ITN sound and approach—Dolores Marguerite's sung/spoken lyrics, exquisite synth strings and so forth with newer elements such as Jill Crowther's oboe and a very arty but effective exploration of dance bass and beats. What makes *Anatomy* stand out even more, however, is hinted at in the album's title—this collection very much explores poetry on a number of levels, taking the increasing narrative approach from *Duality* to newer heights. English author Colin Wilson is the featured spoken-word performer throughout; his low but clear voice meshes well with the dramatic flow of the music, as on the title track, which features Wilson interpreting a poem by Victorian writer Ernest Dowson over an inspired, complex arrangement. Other poets quoted include Yeats, Wilde (Wilson's recital of whom over a lovely piano-based arrangement also featuring Crowther is a definite album highlight) and the lesser known James Elory Flecker, while other musical guests include Lemon Kittens/Shock Headed Peters veteran Karl Blake taking lead vocals on a moody version (featuring guitar!) of Scott Walker's "The Seventh Seal." Q continues his fine work on snare drum, as always, while electronic percussion takes the definite fore on such techno-based tracks as "In Perpetuum," featuring another of the brothers' now quite rare turns on vocals along with Dolores Marguerite, and a dramatically reworked version of the *Ambush* track "Hallucinations?," both combining the orchestral drama of ITN with the dancefloor better than anyone might have guessed (the ITN Corporation reissue of the album adds two further remixes of "Hallucinations?" as well). Proudly, self-consciously reaching for the artistic and unafraid to show it, *Anatomy* is yet another milestone in the Humberstones' continuing career. —*Ned Raggett*

**Stormhorse** / 1994 / Import ♦♦♦
Right from the opening notes, as synth-strings swirl to begin "Tempest," the Humberstones serve note that they have made their next step forward with their music, and a striking step it is. Though soon outstripped by following releases in artistic terms, in many ways *Stormhorse* remains the crucial album of ITN's early years, for a variety of reasons. First and foremost, the band's musical approach—electronic orchestration, supplemented by a further variety of keyboards and piano—has remained essentially unchanged

from this album forward, becoming even more involved and subtle with the years and the increasing pace of technology, but still quite powerful and beautiful in its initial stages here. Second, two sidemembers who have remained with the band in one fashion or another since, first appeared on this album—female vocalist Dolores Marguerite C, possessed of a quietly powerful soprano voice, and Q, who exclusively plays military snare drums for the band, and does so excellently, with precise, careful fills and extended drum rolls building to climactic moments. Finally, the oft-commented sense of ITN's music as cinematic truly begins here; while hard to capture in words, the symphonic/industrial feeling of *Stormhorse* lends itself to being envisioned as backing music for a dramatic epic. Certainly it's no accident that the credits refer to the album as being the "original soundtrack to the [nonexistent] film." While few tracks stand out on their own, as a whole *Stormhorse* sets and maintains its lush, portentous mood throughout. It's all the more fascinating to realize that the Humberstones have no formal classical training; the opportunities created by technological advances to create whole worlds of sound have been enthusiastically pursued by the band from the start, and especially from this album on. —*Ned Raggett*

● **Scatter** / 1995 / ITN Corporation ♦♦♦♦
*Scatter* is that rare beast among career-spanning compilations, a collection that both serves as an excellent introduction to the band's oeuvre as well as packed with enough fine obscurities and new treats to make it equally essential for longtime fans. Following no particular chronological course, *Scatter* runs from the first releases up to the then most-recent, sometimes in unexpected ways. "Mystery," from the debut EP release of ITN's post-punk guitar days, receives a radical sonic update and remix as "Mystere" to match more current ITN sounds, and does so with power and drama both. Other new remixes include an even lovelier version of *Duality*'s "Belle Epoque," "Twins," and *Sense*'s "Sixth Sense," while the rarities include "Epitaph," "Seraphic," and a remix of "Workcorps," all from long deleted compilations and all quite good indeed. An unissued track from the *Anatomy* sessions appears as well—"The Painter," featuring another fine Colin Wilson narration of a poem, in this case Yeats' "Under Ben Bulben," over exquisite musical backing. The hands-down winner of all the new and rare songs, however, is their remix of the Sabres of Paradise's "Haunted Dancehall," an absolutely stunning reworking of the already grand techno cult classic into a lush, chilling anthem. The selection of older tracks can't be faulted at all; while not every peak could be included, such key ITN tracks as "To the Faithful," "The Pearl," and "Miracle of the Rose II" showcase the band at their neo-classical best, while even earlier tracks as "Huntdown" give a fine reminder of the band's rougher origins. Add to that a jam-packed booklet with testimonials from numerous musicians and writers, plus a variety of rare photos and artwork, and there's no doubt: *Scatter* is a must have on all fronts, no exceptions. —*Ned Raggett*

**Feathercut** / Jun. 28, 1996 / ITN Corporation ♦♦♦♦
Officially released under the band's Les Jumeaux (French for "the twins," unsurprisingly!) identity, *Feathercut* came about as a chance for the Humberstones to explore more dance-oriented sides of their music which they felt were distinct from work done as ITN. As perhaps an emphasis of this, neither Dolores Marguerite nor Q appear anywhere on the album, though sometime collaborator Dee de Rocha does contribute lyrics and singing. The opening title track, a fine ambient-inflected piece, gives a good indication of the album as a whole, while the mix of string synth and piano has the ITN feel to it. Overall things are gentler, with the dance touches that might be buried a bit in the mix on an official ITN release—electronic drum pulses, keyboard synths, and clearly synth (as opposed to synth as orchestral piece) parts—given a greater prominence. One or two tracks aside, *Feathercut*'s feel is a relaxing mood rather than the high drama of ITN's regular releases; it makes for a solid contrast as a result. One of the more interesting influences that crops up throughout is dub; while the production touches are light, it can still definitely be heard on such songs as "Carroussella," "Miracle Road," and "Late Poem." Perhaps unsurprisingly as a result, de Rocha's singing on the first two tracks slightly echoes the work of similarly dub-influenced groups as Massive Attack. The experimentation with rhythm ITN regularly explore logically surfaces here as well; "Cyflo" is a good example, with a variety of sounds providing extra percussion over a bass sequencer loop. While not as strong as the best of ITN's albums, *Feathercut* still has a lot going for it as a pleasant listening experiences, and more importantly, can stand alone rather than simply being heard as a side project. —*Ned Raggett*

**Asphalt** / Jan. 13, 1998 / EFA ♦♦♦♦
Beginning with a series of light drones and construction sounds before settling into a muffled pulse beat with gentle synths, the beginning of the second of ITN's commissioned silent film soundtracks provides an almost ambient industrial note to the movie, a melodramatic though obscure German mystery from the late '20s noted for its sets and cinematography. When "Sobriety I" begins, though, with its haunting piano melody and melancholy arrangement, we are clearly back in the realm of ITN drama, more gentle than on many of their albums, but nonetheless wonderful to hear as always from the band. As with the soundtrack to *Caligari*, *Asphalt* is composed and played solely by the Humberstones (while a couple of tracks certainly sound like oboist Crowther is playing on them, no specific credits for other players are present in the liner notes). Similarly to *Caligari* as well, mood setting rather than specific songs is the major goal, complementing the film source rather than overwhelming it. However, *Asphalt* feels just that bit more standalone than the *Caligari* soundtrack, a little more strong on its own qualities. The contrast between piano and other arrangements is used excellently on a number of pieces, such as "Precious," which also works in a shuffling trip-hop beat to boot. Similar contrasts appear between full-string arrangements and distorted, bubbling percussion on "Metropole," while other tracks, like the appropriately ominous "Underworld," combine rather than contrast elements for uniform effect. Overall an air of mysterious decadence carries through the album, something at once beautiful and disturbing—the gentle, music box tones of "Opulence" especially stand out in this regard—making *Asphalt* a most intriguing listen, regardless of your knowledge of the film in question. —*Ned Raggett*

**The Man with a Movie Camera** / Apr. 20, 1999 / EFA ♦♦♦♦
Third in the series of commissioned silent film soundtracks by the band, the original movie is a late-'20s Soviet avant-garde documentary, regarded by some critics to be as radical and innovative as Buñuel's *Un Chien Andalou* in terms of film technique. ITN for the first time use one of their regular side players on an entry in this series—flautist Lindemann—who adds subtly but strongly to the instrumental mix throughout (his low bass flute tones on "Camera Lucida" are a good instance of how he incorporates himself into the work). Again, as with the other soundtracks, the individual pieces serve to construct an overall mood rather than fully standing out on their own. The feeling of this soundtrack compared to the previous ones is how light and open it can feel at times; there is a gentle but strong exultance present which perhaps matches the positive hopes of the new world meant to be constructed in the USSR, which the film no doubt captures. "City Awakening," for instance, feels like exactly that, almost like a sunrise captured in music (and accentuated by a striking rhythm loop that sounds like softly ringing metal throughout the track), while "Accelerated Life" builds up in subtly dramatic fashion, a grand arrangement getting grander and more life-affirming as it goes. Percussion and rhythm throughout mostly come via pulsing but gentle sequencer loops as opposed to the more upfront samples on their other work, in its own way underscoring the confident futurism of the film (though notably, the rhythm on "Parallax," the majestic standout piece on the album, comes mostly from cymbals!). Once more, ITN demonstrates its almost empathetic ability to create striking music for the film medium. —*Ned Raggett*

## Incognito

f. 1981, London, England
*Group / Club/Dance, Acid Jazz, Funk, House*
An acid jazz project with surprisingly deep roots in the '70s jazz/funk/fusion world, Incognito was originally formed by Jean-Paul Maunick (aka Bluey) and Paul "Tubbs" Williams. Both were leaders of the late-'70s disco-funk group Light of the World, who scored several moderate British hits including a cover of "I Shot the Sheriff." Just after the release of Light of the World's third LP (*Check Us Out*), Maunick and Williams shifted the lineup slightly and renamed the conglomeration Incognito.

Incognito debuted with the single "Parisienne Girl" and released the 1981 LP *Jazz Funk*, but were inactive during the rest of the '80s. Maunick continued to write material for his group, even while working with Maxi Priest and others. (Williams later moved to Finland.) By the beginning of the '90s, DJ legend and early Incognito fan Gilles Peterson had founded the Talkin' Loud label, and he made Incognito one of his first signings. The 1991 single "Always There" (with vocals by Jocelyn Brown) became a Top Ten hit as part of Britain's booming acid jazz scene, prompting the release of Incognito's second album overall, *Inside Life*. It was largely a studio affair, with Maunick and engineer Simon Catsworth directing a large cast with many of the best musicians in Britain's fertile groove community.

With 1992's *Tribes Vibes & Scribes*, Maunick added a more established vocalist, the American Maysa Leak. A cover of Stevie Wonder's "Don't You Worry 'bout a Thing" became another Incognito hit, and the album ascended Britain's pop charts even as it rose on America's contemporary jazz charts. Third album *Positivity* became the group's biggest album success, with much attention across Europe as well as Britain. Leak unsuccessfully attempted a solo career with Blue Note, leading to the temporary vocal replacement Pamela Anderson (not the *Baywatch* pin-up) on 1995's *100 Degrees and Rising*. Leak returned, though, appearing on the following year's *Beneath the Surface*. Incognito later expanded its discography with 1996's *Remixed*, 1998's *Tokyo Live*, and 1999's *No Time Like the Future*. —*John Bush*

**Inside Life** / 1991 / Verve/Forecast ♦♦♦♦

● **Tribes, Vibes and Scribes** / 1992 / Verve ♦♦♦♦
This England-based dance and funk but mostly jazz band brings nothing but energy to this project. The production is sleek, and the arrangements are precise. Maysa Leakey reaches her higher notes without abandoning the fullness of her unwavering lower range. Half of the songs on this album utilize her vocals, while the others are instrumentals. The instrumental tracks feature bebop-influenced solos, in particularly "L'Arc En Ciel De Miles," which is an admirable tribute to the late famous jazz trumpeter. However, each song's solo is just as riveting as the next. The one constant on this album is the steady strum of bassist Randy Hope-Taylor. Contrary to the group's name, their music is anything but incognito—it's excellent and as conspicuous as ever. —*Craig Lytle*

**Positivity** / 1994 / Talkin' Loud ♦♦♦
This is an excellent collection of jazz and fusion numbers featuring the wholesome, peerless vocals of Maysa Leak and group newcomer Mark Anthoni. With gritty, urban rhythms and painstaking arrangements, Leak's radiant vocals ring with invitation. The lyrical content is upright and substantive. All the songs have an aggressive backbeat regardless of their tempo, providing an unobstructed platform for these artistic musicians to express their chic brand of music. Group leader Jean-Paul "Bluey" Munick's vision of intertwining various genres of music (bebop, soul, classical, dance, etc.) into one incomparable sound is exemplary. —*Craig Lytle*

**100 Degrees and Rising** / Jun. 6, 1995 / Talkin' Loud ♦♦♦
On *100 Degrees and Rising*, the pioneering acid house outfit Incognito turn in another first-rate record, featuring their trademark mixture of jazz, soul, and funk. There's not much to distinguish *100 Degrees* from their previous handful of records, but the band is smooth, accomplished and deep, finding new variations on their trademark sound. —*Stephen Thomas Erlewine*

**Remixed** / Jul. 15, 1996 / PolyGram ♦♦
*Incognito Remixed* features a number of the group's tracks for Talkin' Loud/Verve remixed by stars like Pete Rock and Roger Sanchez. Some of these 12 songs have previously been released, but the bulk of the disc have never been easily available—most are promotional-only remixes. Frequently these versions, including a steaming "Always Threre," actually improve on the original take, offering deeper, more textured grooves. In fact, it is arguably the finest, most consistent Incognito album available. —*Leo Stanley*

**Beneath the Surface** / Oct. 21, 1996 / PolyGram ♦♦♦
*Beneath the Surface* finds original lead singer Maysa Leak returning to the Incognito fold. Coincidentally or not, the record finds the group moving deeply into smooth, laidback, jazzy soul. It's a seductive sound and the group executes it well, even though there ironically isn't that much substance beneath the surface. —*Leo Stanley*

## Indian Ropeman (Sanj Sen)

*Producer / Funk, Hip-Hop*

Brighton native Sanj Sen, known as Indian Ropeman, took his stage name from a '60s tune by Julie Driscoll. Ropeman has toured often, performing at clubs and festivals, appearing with British hip-hop groups as well as indie-rock bands. His sound has been described as a heady mixture of Indian-influenced breakbeat, sitar funk, hip-hop, and dance. Ropeman, with his expertise with synths, sequencers, and samplers, has released a number of singles under the Skint Records label, such as "Dog in the Piano," "66 Meters," and "Sunshine of Your Love." At times he also uses the backup of a scratch DJ, a drummer, and a guitarist. In 1999, Ropeman released his debut album, *Elephant Sound*. The bass-heavy LP showcases tracks like "Dominant Tonic," "Stand Clear," and "Your Own Enemy." —*Charlotte Dillon*

● **Elephant Sound** / May 24, 1999 / Elephant Music ♦♦
The moonlit Eastern dance rhythms and oasis-fresh sitar funk that the Ropeman ladles out from his debut album present grooves most dancefloor mix-crafters hear only in their sweetest dreams. *Elephant Sound* graciously presents 11 sweeping instrumentals that escalate with a kind of New Age space-movie buildup. "Mission To The Moog" is a postmodern hip-hop floor trembler, which features bitchin' samples from Mission Control and Neil Armstrong on his Apollo 11 journey à la the old Nels Peterson All-Star sample orgies. More journeys into the unknown include the obscure but ultimately mesmerizing "Dog In The Piano," with silly lyrics and more than a little Tipper Gore-infuriating morphology. Other choice moments include the sparkly "Chairman Of The Board" and the brittler, poppier "Your Own Enemy," which brings new techno oomph to a genre that has threatened to flatten out and die of late. Released as a single, "66 Metres" features the freakish banshee vocals of Shahin Badar, last heard on "Smack My Bitch Up." Brighton-based production swami Sanj Sen is the button-man behind all this unchecked fun, managing to make a record that combines the most agreeable moments of Prodigy and Fatboy Slim in a single sleeve to be proud of.—*Becky Byrkit*

## Indio

*Group / Detroit Techno, Ambient Techno, Club/Dance, Techno*

Lansing techno veteran John Beltran formed Indio with fellow producers Sam McQueen and Seth Taylor. Recording for Derrick May's pioneering Transmat label, Indio released their self-titled debut in late 1999. [See Also: John Beltran] —*John Bush*

● **Indio** / Dec. 7, 1999 / Transmat ♦♦♦♦
Consisting of techno veteran John Beltran, Seth Taylor, and Sam McQueen, Indio's debut focuses on an ambient techno sound designed to invoke emotions and feelings within the relaxed mind of the listener. Unlike techno aimed to incite frenzied dancing with relentless bass beats and percussion, as in the case of Jeff Mills or Adam Beyer, Indio's techno utilizes hypnotic synthesizer tones and melodies with little, if any, pounding bass. While each of the nine tracks retains unique elements differentiating themselves from the others, all share some formal tendencies. First of all, a sense of rhythm arises from subdued drum loops that tend to focus on complex timing and arrangement. This lingering percussive background is then submerged in a dense flow of rich saturated synthesizer tones, notes, and melodies. These synthesized sounds characterize the individual songs with a sense of contemplative emotion and feelings of smooth sensuality. Melodies intermingle with ambient walls of tone while ghostly sounds howl like undecipherable cries from another world. This album deserves to be played from start to finish, since there are no weak tracks worth skipping. Each reinterprets similar emotions, which usually tend to be melancholy and contemplative. The final track on the album, "Snowdrifts"—also found on the excellent Transmat compilation *Time: Space*—stands out as the album's pinnacle. Eliminating the percussive rhythmic backbone found in the preceding eight tracks, "Snowdrifts" leaves the listener alone in a cold shower of swirling synthesizer tones until the stormy ambience finally fades to a lonely moment of silence. —*Jason Stanley Birchmeier*

## The Infesticons

*Group / Underground Rap, Trip-Hop, Club/Dance*

Underground-rap impresario Mike Ladd has recorded several LPs of sewer-level hip-hop, both under his own name and as the Infesticons. A big funk fan as a kid, he played drums in a punk band while living around New York during the early '80s and got into hip-hop in 1985. After years of freestyle rhyming (closer to urban poetry than straight-out rapping) and producing, Ladd released his first solo album *Easy Listening for Armageddon* in 1997 for Scratchie/Mercury. One year later, the "Blah Blah" single followed on Big Dada, and in 2000 his second LP *Welcome to the Afterfuture* appeared on his own Like Madd Music. Later that year, Ladd signed his new alias the Infesticons to Big Dada/Ninja Tune and released *Gun Hill Road*. Ladd also released a single for the Beastie Boys' Grand Royal label, in their *Blow Up Factor* series. —*John Bush*

● **Gun Hill Road** / May 30, 2000 / Big Dada ♦
The cream of the underground hip-hop crop—a gaggle of lost gangstas and

a Beastie Boy collaborator—comprise the wild and should-be-wonderful mob collectively know as the Infesticons, spearheaded by the inimitable Mike Ladd. It should be wonderful but it isn't: *Gun Hill Road* suffers mightily from blurred vision, splintered beats, tuneless loops, too much noise, and a low rap standard. The sound is pure N.Y.C. underground and stellar moments abound, but the overall impact is scattershot. A stunning wealth and breadth of talent, anti-playa attitude, and derangement are on display here, but the feeling is showy and spotty. Highlights have to be Saul Williams' reassuringly nutcase "Monkey Theme," Rob Smith's waveless proto-rap "Chase Theme," and Dana & Majesticon 69's transsexual/freak/funk show "Shampoo Theme." There are some reverential moments to funkadelia and many of Smith and Majesticon's movements are often sheer labyrinths of voicescapes in the most ambitious of the rap traditions. This record might suit the connoisseur bent on impressing his or her guests with sheer weirdness and rudeness, but it ultimately does the genre—and the venerable musicians—no favors as a showpiece of innovative modern music. —*Becky Byrkit*

## Infiniti (Juan Atkins)

*Producer / Detroit Techno, Club/Dance, Techno*

A reservoir for Juan Atkins' more sublime, home-listening recordings than his dancefloor project Model 500, Infiniti released EPs for Atkins' own Metroplex as well as Tresor, and Tresor issued a compilation of his Infiniti releases in 1996. The first proper Infiniti album appeared towards the end of 1998; *Never Tempt Me* followed a year later. [See Also: Juan Atkins, Cybotron, Model 500] —*John Bush*

- **The Infiniti Collection** / May 27, 1996 / Tresor ++++

Home to several of Atkins' most beautiful productions of the '90s, *The Infiniti Collection* wisely collects recordings from a variety of labels, including Tresor itself, Peacefrog, New Electronica, Radikal, and Atkins' own Metroplex. Though most of the tracks are straightahead techno, Atkins informs each with his crucial sense of sublimity and vision, from the bubbly melodicism of "Sunshine" to the glowing ten-minute high of "Think Quick" (mixed by Maurizio). —*John Bush*

**Skynet** / Sep. 29, 1998 / Tresor ++++

Only the second solo full-length of Atkins' long career (after Model 500's *Deep Space*), *Skynet* strengthens the links between the godfather and his many acolytes in England and Germany. While his '80s work influenced Brit acts like the Black Dog and B12, here Atkins sounds influenced by that sound in turn and relies on a production style much more subtle than on his very R&B-ish Model 500 material. It's akin to the divide on his '80s tracks between the evocative mood music of "Night Drive (Time Space Transmat)" and the full-throttle machine techno of "No UFOs." (The American version adds two bonus tracks.) —*John Bush*

## Information Society

f. 1985, Minneapolis, MN
*Group / Club/Dance, Dance-Pop*

An agreeable dance outfit with ties to industrial music, techno, and funk plus an equally appreciable pop sense, Information Society hit the danceclubs and later the charts with their infectious breakout single, 1988's "What's on Your Mind (Pure Energy)." The group, a quartet formed in Minneapolis by James Cassidy, Paul Robb, Kurt Harland (aka Kurt Valaquen), and Amanda Kramer, signed to Tommy Boy Records a few years later and recorded a self-titled debut album. The single "What's on Your Mind (Pure Energy)," propelled by a Leonard Nimoy sample and Valaquen's smooth, assured vocals, became a club hit and eventually landed at number three in the pop charts. Later that year, "Walking Away" hit the Top Ten as well, and the album reached gold-certified status. Kramer left soon after, however, to record with the Golden Palominos, 10,000 Maniacs, and also on her own. Information Society's sophomore album, similar to not-so-famous follow-ups by dance-popsters EMF and Jesus Jones, was more than competent but mostly ignored by critics who had pegged them as one-hit wonders. Several singles managed shallow chart exposure, but after the third album (1994's *Peace & Love, Inc.*), both Robb and Cassidy exited. Harland continued on, releasing the industrial-tinged *Don't Be Afraid* for Cleopatra Records in 1997. —*John Bush*

- **Information Society** / 1988 / Tommy Boy ++++

An infectious update of the classic synth-pop most famous earlier in the decade, Information Society's self-titled debut sounds most similar to British groups like ABC and Pet Shop Boys, though hits like "What's on Your Mind," "Walking Away," and the cover of "Lay All Your Love on Me" manage to inject the affair with elements of industrial dance and hip-hop. All in all, it's a much better album than expected from the group many dismissed as mere one-hit wonders. —*John Bush*

**Hack** / 1990 / Tommy Boy ++

The Minneapolis-based synth-pop group Information Society scored in 1988 with the Top Ten hits "What's On Your Mind (Pure Energy)" and "Walking Away," both from the band's platinum-selling self-titled debut album. The band released the more experimental *Hack* in 1990; although it contains a few tunes that are just as good as those on the debut, the album is marred considerably by repetition and excess. "Think," the first single, became a minor hit single in 1990, with good reason; the tune could have fit in quite well with the insanely catchy dance-pop of the debut. Unfortunately, there are only a handful of tracks on *Hack* that show off Information Society's strengths. The band's best songs from the debut ("What's On Your Mind," for example) mixed Latin rhythms with somewhat dark synth-pop and vocalist Kurt Harland's snide delivery, which is reminiscent of the Thompson Twins' Tom Bailey. On *Hack*, too many of the tunes drag (like the unbearable "Fire Tonight") and sound alike ("Now That I Have You" is a virtual rewrite of "Think"), and the overuse of sound effects and production gimmicks suggests Information Society was attempting a more aggressive (or perhaps obnoxious) sound. Instead, this approach adds unnecessary weight to the material, and the pop sensibility that made the debut album so successful has all but disappeared. This album is also cluttered with annoying, pretentious between-song sound collages that serve no purpose other than to test the skip mechanism on CD players. If Information Society had spent a little more time coming up with actual songs instead of worthless filler, and if the band had focused more on hooks instead of production, *Hack* may have kept them from becoming a flash in the pan. The handful of good songs here prove the band could have maintained its success, but it was not to be. It tanked, not even going gold and failing to yield even one major hit. Information Society released *Peace and Love, Inc.* in 1992, which failed to re-establish the band as hitmakers. —*William Cooper*

**Insoc Recombinant** / Apr. 6, 1999 / Cleopatra ++

This double CD contains one CD of sounds and one of video. The sounds are Information Society pieces remixed by artists like Spahn Ranch, Leæther Strip, Electric Hellfire Club, THC, David J of Love and Rockets, and others. More interesting and powerful are the five videos on the second CD. These are un-remixed, original InSoc videos. Included are .avi files for "What's on Your Mind," "Peace and Love," "Walking Away," "Think," and "Going, Going Gone." —*Tom Schulte*

## Mike Ink (Wolfgang Voigt)

b. Cologne, Germany
*Producer / Minimal Techno, Experimental Dub, Experimental Techno, Techno*

Mike Ink is one of Europe's leading producers of minimalist pure house and techno, released primarily under his own name and as Love Inc., M:I:5, and Gas. After kick-starting the German acid scene during 1991-92 and releasing some of the style's more popular tracks, Ink reoriented his focus on the essentials of a distinctively German brand of minimalist techno, launching the Profan and Studio 1 labels, all widely hailed in the techno underground as among the finest sources of purist European dance music. His analytical, almost religious affection for the four-on-the-floor beat (and not much else!) definitely places him against the dominant trends of the hyper-hybridized post-rave dance music environment into which he's released the bulk of his material, but also gained his work acclaim alongside that of labels such as Concept and Basic Channel.

A native of Cologne, Germany, Ink, together with artists such as Biochip C., J. Burger, and Air Liquide, was a founding member of the Structure label group, which included the Blue, Monotone, and DJ Ungle Fever labels, largely responsible for the early '90s German acid house revival. Unlike his early colleagues, however, Ink has resisted the urge to diversify, sticking to his puritanical aesthetic through a series of EPs and album-length releases for Force Inc., Extreme, Trans Atlantic, Burger Industries, and his own Profan and Studio 1 labels. Breaking his various stylistic pursuits into definite chunks, Ink reserves the Love Inc. name for his more commercial house tunes, while

M:I:5 and his own name usually grace his techno releases, and Gas is reserved for his beatless experimentations. Ink's *Respect*, released on Force Inc. in 1994, is a good introduction, and remained among his most acclaimed work. Ink material has trickled out from a variety of sources since, including a 1996 single for Warp, a Love Inc. LP for Force Inc., several Gas full-lengths through Mille Plateaux, and, his American debut in 1998, the J. Burger collaboration *Las Vegas* (released as Burger/Ink). He also collected his Studio 1 and M:I:5 material for two separate 1997 CD compilations. [See Also: Burger/Ink, Gas, Love Inc.] —*Sean Cooper*

**R.E.S.P.E.C.T.** / 1994 / Force Inc ♦♦♦
The first American release of Mike Ink material came on this mini-album released on Sm:)e Recordings. The double 10" includes several tracks of Ink's early techno-funk minimalism, with remixes from Luke Slater's Planetary Assault Systems, Air Liquide's Jammin' Unit and Dr. Walker. —*Keith Farley*

**Polka Trax [EP]** / Oct. 28, 1996 / Warp ♦♦♦
A mini-album/maxi-single for Sheffield's Warp label, collecting the original and remixes of Ink's previous single "Paroles" (including reworking by Autechre and Tpower) and four versions of the title track, "Polka Trax." The oddball humor of Ink's Love Inc. project is equally in place here, although musically he probes the edges of jazzy breakbeat techno. —*Sean Cooper*

**Studio 1** / Apr. 7, 1997 / Studio 1 ♦♦♦♦
The *Studio 1* CD compiles tracks and edits plus some new material from Mike Ink's series of ten 12"-only singles released on his label. The name of the game throughout focuses on straightahead, minimalist house grooves with little ornamentation other than Ink's focus on dubwise effects. Neophytes may wonder what the fuss is, though repeated listenings bear a few more insights into Ink's inner-space concepts. —*John Bush*

● **Maßstab 1:5** / Jan. 12, 1998 / Profan ♦♦♦♦
Actually an Ink side project released as M:I:5, *Maßstab 1:5* presents 11 tracks of repetitive, minimalist dub-dance. Most work through distinctive three-note bass rhythms dropping in and out of the mix, a languid beat-per-second tempo and sets of off-kilter, backtracked effects designed to hit simultaneously in left and right channels only once every five occurrences (hence the title). Potentially bland or hypnotic, depending on the point of view, these tracks revealed Ink as a master of post-rave beat experimentation. —*John Bush*

## Inner City

f. 1988, Detroit, MI
*Group / Club/Dance, House, Dance-Pop*

The group that took Detroit techno to the masses via the British charts and the world's dancefloors, Inner City was no crossover act—rather, an intense collaboration between a noted Chicago house vocalist and one of the most influential Detroit producers of the '80s. Both Paris Grey and Kevin Saunderson were well-known for their contributions to the club music of their respective communities well before their 1989 debut album. Saunderson did more to advance techno than anyone except Juan Atkins and Derrick May, through his releases as Tronik House, Reese, E-Dancer, and Essaray; Grey recorded several house classics, including "Don't Make Me Jack." Between the two (and later addition Ann Saunderson, Kevin's wife), Inner City topped dance charts in America and Britain 11 times, hit Britain's Top 40 eight times and sold over six million records.

The group was formed in 1987 when Saunderson, still in college and recording out of his basement studio, produced a track he felt needed lyrics. After Chicago vocalist Paris Grey (b. Shanna Jackson) was recommended by Chicago producer Terry Baldwin, the two collaborated on the single "Big Fun." It was finally released late in 1988 on the Virgin compilation *Techno: The New Dance Sound of Detroit*, and hit the British charts in a surprising crossover success. Signed to Virgin soon after, Saunderson and Grey hit again later that same year with the Top Ten single "Good Life." Their debut album *Paradise* (*Big Fun* on its American issue) reached the UK Top 20, though it largely failed to cross over on the American pop charts. *Paradise Remixed* followed in 1990 and later singles "Ain't Nobody Better," "Watcha Gonna Do with My Lovin'," and "That Man (He's Mine)" lit up dancefloors around the world, spreading the word about techno to thousands of mainstream clubbers familiar only with house music. Inner City's second album *Fire* did less well than the first, in part because Virgin had pressured the group into an American version of Soul II Soul. After the popular single "Back Together Again" and third album *Praise*, the group went on a hiatus, as Saunderson returned to his more experimental roots with work as the Reese Project. Inner City returned to the charts with 1994's "Do Ya" and "Share My Life," and continued to be a vital recording concern well into the late '90s. [See Also: Kevin Saunderson, E-Dancer] —*John Bush*

★ **Big Fun** / 1989 / Virgin ♦♦♦♦♦
In the '80s and '90s, a lot of dance music has spotlighted female singers with thin, weak voices who seem on the verge of death. But house music has often been a home to expressive, big-voiced divas who can truly wail—a fine example being Paris Gray of the duo Inner City. Along with producer/composer Kevin Saunderson, Gray was responsible for some of the most rewarding dance music of the late '80s and early '90s. *Big Fun*, Inner City's debut album, is full of house songs that enjoyed extensive dance club exposure, including "Good Life," "Do You Love What You Feel," "Ain't Nobody Better," and the title song. While Saunderson's production is decidedly high-tech, Gray's warm, passionate singing is mindful of dance music's heritage and underscores its soul and gospel roots in a delightful way. Unfortunately, Inner City never crossed over to the R&B or pop markets as Virgin Records hoped—an irony considering that *Big Fun* is so much more individualistic and soulful than most of the generic efforts which dominated Black radio in 1989. —*Alex Henderson*

**Fire** / 1990 / Virgin ♦♦♦
Inner City escaped the dreaded sophomore curse with its consistently enriching second album, *Fire*, which provides such inspired, gospel-influenced house music treasures as "My Heart's Not Here with You," "Lovelight," "What Does It Take," and "That Man (He's All Mine)." Like its predecessor, *Big Fun*, *Fire* shows Paris Gray to be a singer of depth and substance, and Kevin Saunderson to be an inventive, distinctive producer. Inner City's vision remained positive, and "Hallelujah" and "Unity" are fine examples of the uplifting "love/peace/togetherness" theme that's common in house music. Though Saunderson liked to call Inner City's music "techno-house," both *Big Fun* and *Fire* are very melodic and accessible albums lacking the type of abrasiveness associated with techno. Once again, Inner City fared well in club and dance-music circles, but unfortunately, enjoyed little exposure in the R&B and pop markets. —*Alex Henderson*

**Praise** / 1992 / Virgin ♦♦♦

## Innerzone Orchestra

f. 1992, Detroit, MI
*Group / Jazz-House, Detroit Techno, Club/Dance*

The preserve for jazz-oriented recordings by Detroit techno auteur Carl Craig, Innerzone Orchestra first came together in the early '90s to record one of the most respected singles of Craig's career, "Bug in the Bassbin," for his own Planet E Recordings. With Craig on programming and a group including percussionist Francisco Mora Catlett (a former pupil of Max Roach and member of Sun Ra's Arkestra, plus a leader on his own for Capitol), keyboard player Craig Taborn (a member of the James Carter Quartet as well as a sideman with the Art Ensemble of Chicago and Dave Holland), and Rodney Whitaker on upright bass, the band played only scattered dates during the mid-'90s while Craig recorded under his own name. Innerzone Orchestra finally hit the studio in 1999, recording their full-length debut *Programmed* for Astralwerks. Live dates including New York's Central Park SummerStage followed later that year. Craig also set up a new jazz subsidiary of Planet E named Community Projects, with Catlett contributing the first release, his own *World Trade Music* LP. [See Also: Carl Craig, Paperclip People, Psyche/BFC, 69] —*John Bush*

**Bug in the Bassbin [Single]** / 1992 / Planet E ♦♦♦♦
Originally released as half of a double pack along with Planet E's first compilation *Intergalactic Beats*, the *Bug in the Bass Bin* 12" is easily one of techno's most important releases because in sounding so different from anything else "techno" it helped to push out the boundaries of what techno could be. Apparently if you heard it in 1992 and played it at 45 rpm, then you heard a very early drum'n'bass record. However, listening to the track at the arguably correct speed of 33 rpm is no less inspiring. Produced by Carl Craig, "Bug in the Bass Bin" is an alien funk gem with a unique two-bar loop of a couple of different sampled breakbeats, a deep bassline, and a high line directly referencing the disco classic "Let No Man Put Asunder." Though the two B-sides "Nitwit" and "Surreal" are usually criminally under-hyped, they are just as timeless and bizarre as the flip side. "Nitwit" is a soaring dance track

that incorporates a couple of Craig's trademarks of breakbeats and a highly textured synth riff into some of the conventions of Detroit techno rhythm programming. "Surreal" closes out this indispensable landmark record and is probably Craig's most aptly titled track. The high synth line pitch bends in such a bizarre timbre and close repetition to be instantly hypnotic, while the orchestral stabs and funky breakbeat-down commands the dance. This 12" is one of the rarest things in techno—a flawless record of uncompromising creativity. —*Carlos Souffront*

● **Programmed** / 1999 / Astralwerks ♦♦♦♦
Legions of dance producers have used jazz as a crutch, sampling crackly old Blue Note LPs to get just the right vibes for their productions (or occasionally even recruiting actual musicians to appear on tracks), but then paying little attention to how—or, a more important concern, if—those elements work within their own creations. Leave it to Carl Craig, the most artistic, uncompromising techno producer around, to produce an album on par with the best recent work in either field. The beats are more upfront than on Craig's last solo record (*More Songs About Food and Revolutionary Art*), but this album has a very similar concept; it's a work of electronic music in the abstract that rejects the accepted standards of any style of music, whether it's techno, electronica, jazzy house, or recent fusion. As can be guessed from the title, *Programmed* is not an acoustic, band recording—although several tracks feature the full Innerzone Orchestra (no more than four pieces), most are just as programmed as Craig's previous work. Still, percussionist Francisco Mora Catlett and keyboard player Craig Taborn do have a large presence on the album, from the sublime electro-jazz on "Basic Math" and "At Les" (a new version of the Carl Craig standard) to the gorgeous comping of Taborn over thick, frenetic acid lines on "Eruption."

*Programmed* is undoubtedly Craig's show though, and more than anything else highlights his range of production talents. When he sets his sights on hip-hop for "The Beginning of the End" (with vocals by Lacksi-daisy-cal), Craig produces a startling track with impossibly deep, crisp beats that immediately separate the song from anything ever produced by rap juggernauts from Dr. Dre to Timbaland. The title track takes a hip-hop beat standard and turns it over and into itself, continually phased out of control over a set of oddly structured synth-stabs. Craig also gives nods to invisible soundtracks on "Manufactured Memories" and "Architecture" (the latter recorded with Richie Hawtin), reflecting the influence of Vangelis' 1982 soundtrack to *Blade Runner*. And on "People Make the World Go Round," he constructs a few well-placed strings as a folk-slanted framework for the soulful vocal. If *Programmed* can be faulted at all, it's for the sense that Craig is doing *too* much here, tackling too many different styles of music; the fact is, that feeling exists for only a short time until the album's many facets come together with a surprising grace. —*John Bush*

## Tetsu Inoue
b. Tokyo, Japan
*Producer / Experimental Ambient, Electronica, Ambient Techno, Ambient*
A native of Tokyo, Japan, Tetsu Inoue is an ambient composer whose solo and collaborative works with the likes of Pete Namlook, Jonah Sharp, and Atom Heart are important documents of new school ambient and experimental electronic. Inoue began playing music in high school, starting on guitar in pop/rock cover bands. He began experimenting with synthesizers and early monophonic sequencers, inspired by the fusion of pop, psychedelic rock, and experimental electronic pioneered by groups like Pink Floyd, Tomita, and particularly Yellow Magic Orchestra, and by the mid-'80s was scoring for ballet and small dance groups. Tetsu Inoue moved to New York around 1986, securing an apartment before heading for an extended stay in San Francisco, where he played guitar in karaoke bands and began working with SF-based composer Naut Humon. He returned to New York soon after, continuing to amass demo material, and headed for Germany in the late '80s, where he met Uwe Schmidt (Atom Heart) and Pete Namlook. Although ostensibly on vacation, Inoue recorded his first work for release while in Frankfurt (*Station Rose*, a collaboration with Schmidt, on Cyclotron) and, upon his return to New York, began working with Namlook on a number of different projects. Although dabbling in dance music styles such as techno and trance during this period, he was moving increasingly toward strictly ambient composition, and Namlook's noted Fax label would release several of his albums through the early to mid-'90s. Most of his best solo and collaborative works appear there, including *2350 Broadway* and *Shades of Orion* with Namlook, *Electro Harmonix* with Jonah Sharp, and *Ambiant Otaku*, *Organic Cloud*, and *Slow and Low* as a solo artist. His mature aesthetic centers around a fusion of, by turns, haunting and contemplative soundscapes layered with heavily treated samples and field source materials, and occasional, usually sparse percussion. It's most elegantly stated on such works as *MU* (with Atom Heart as Masters of Psychedelic Ambiance) and *World Receiver*. —*Sean Cooper*

**2350 Broadway** / 1993 / Fax ♦♦♦♦
A seminal, almost fabled release spanning two CDs and recorded in real time (no pre- or post-production and no overdubs). Remarkably engaging for its simplicity, the set was subsequently reissued by popular demand and spawned a pair (and counting) of follow-ups in the series. —*Sean Cooper*

**Ambiant Otaku** / 1994 / Fax ♦♦♦♦
Tetsu Inoue's first solo work on Fax and a highly sought-after collectible. Some of the tracks bear a passing resemblance to Brian Eno's early generative experiments (*Discreet Music, Evening Star*) but Inoue's take is decidedly contemporary, with pillowy, mellifluous synth passages occasionally accented by subtle beats and lilting melodies. —*Sean Cooper*

**Shades of Orion** / 1994 / Fax ♦♦♦♦
Tetsu Inoue's second full-length collaboration with Pete Namlook splits evenly between beatless and beat-oriented ambient, with spacey, immersive textures and subtle arrangments. High production values and the wealth of creative territory covered make for one of the finest early Fax releases. —*Sean Cooper*

**Organic Cloud** / 1995 / Fax ♦♦♦♦
More austere than *Ambiant Otaku*, it's also less varied, although the album ranks among his finest works. Sprawling but focused soundscapes with breathy atmospherics and subtle, complex rhythms. —*Sean Cooper*

**Slow and Low** / 1995 / Fax ♦♦♦
Tetsu Inoue's experimental tendencies take full reign on his third Fax solo work. Heavily hacked samples and field recodings abound, and though not as immediately engaging as his early work, repays close attention with a depth of shape and color. —*Sean Cooper*

● **World Receiver** / Jun. 11, 1996 / Instinct ♦♦♦♦
An engulfing combination of *Slow and Low*'s brazen experimentalism, and *Otaku* and *Cloud*'s concentrated ambiance and subtle melodiousness. Ostensibly a concept album integrating field recordings gathered from his travels around the world, the album is much more integrated and involved than much of his early solo work. His best work to date. —*Sean Cooper*

**Time 2** / Dec. 2, 1996 / Fax ♦♦♦
Although it's always hard to tell who's leading and who's following in a Namlook production, it's safe to say this latest collaboration between Namlook and NY producer Tetsu Inoue has benefited from both musicians' recent excursions to the more beat-oriented side of the tracks (Namlook with *Ozoona* and *Amp*, Inoue with *Hat, Ondas*, and *Instant Replay*). Most of *Time2* is dominated by skittery jungle-esque rhythms reminiscent of Atom Heart (particularly on the Namlook/Atom Heart Fax release *Jet Chamber 2*), although Inoue's signature hand-picked synth patches are in equal evidence. —*Sean Cooper*

**Psycho-Acoustic** / May 19, 1998 / Tzadik ♦♦♦♦
*Psycho-Acoustic* is a strange release for Tetsu, for more reasons than one. First, much of his discography to date has appeared on ambient, techno, and post-techno labels such as Fax, Pod, and Rather Interesting; Tzadik is an experimental music label formed by jazz iconclast John Zorn in 1995, releasing mostly jazz-freak, art-punk, noise, and contemporary compositional and computer music from artists such as David Shea, James Tenney, Masada, Ruins, Anthony Coleman, Derek Bailey, and David Slusser. Allegiances aside, however, *Psycho-Acoustic* also contains by far some of the strangest music of Tetsu's career. Ditching the warm, continuous tones and atmospheres of favorites such as *Organic Cloud* and *World Receiver*, *Psycho-Acoustic* is 40 dense, demanding minutes of experimental desktop abuse, all bleeps, bloops, hard edits, and short blasts of chrome-clean digital noise. Still, as disjointed and plastic as many of the pieces seem, echoes of Tetsu's previous concerns remain (particularly those of more outward-leaning discs such as *Slow and Low*); the texture-heavy "Modu Lotion" and the quirky but wonderfully engaging duet with New York drum machine composer Ikue Morie, "Tom & Tone," stand out in this respect. —*Sean Cooper*

**Waterloo Terminal—Architettura Series 2** / Oct. 20, 1998 / Caipirinha ♦♦♦♦

The second release in Caipirinha's Architettura series, *Waterloo Terminal* was inspired by Nicholas Grimshaw's steel and glass structure, which lay on the UK end of the massive underwater Chunnel. More than merely providing the aesthetic impetus for the music, Grimshaw's Terminal provided the raw material; Tetsu scanned schematics of the building into his computer and used a software program to "convert" the picture files into sounds, with which he then composed. Tetsu's second album of mostly computer-generated music, *Terminal* is also more approachable than the previous *Psycho-Acoustic*, revealing a fascinating depth of detail the further into the recording the listener is willing to go. It's still many orders of abstraction beyond even the least rooted of his popular Fax releases, but the points of continuity are many, and *Terminal* more than proves Tetsu's caliber in a medium (computer music) he's only just begun to explore. —*Sean Cooper*

## Insides

f. 1992
*Group / Dream Pop*

Ambient pop duo Insides teamed singer/bassist Kirsty Yates and guitarist/programmer J. Serge Tardo, who previously joined forces under the name Earwig. Signing to 4AD's Guernica imprint, the duo debuted in 1993 with the disquieting *Euphoria;* a year later, label chief Ivo Watts-Russell issued *Clear Skin* (consisting of a single 38-minute ambient piece) without Insides' permission, and the group parted ways with the company soon after. Landing on the Third Stone label, in 1997 they contributed a track to the *A Taste of Third Stone Records Vol. 2* sampler, next resurfacing in mid-2000 with the full-length *Sweet Tip.* —*Jason Ankeny*

● **Euphoria** / 1993 / 4AD ♦♦♦♦

Insides' elusive and icy electronic pop explores the darkest, seamiest corners of love and sex—their songs capture the emptiness and hostility that surface when the afterglow fades, ugly scenes punctuated by eruptions of violence, waves of self-loathing, and caresses that are cold to the touch. Singer/bassist Kirsty Yates' vocals are eerily dispassionate, detailing her sordid tales of physical intimacy and emotional distance with alarming candor—songs like "Darling Effect," "Skin Divers," and "Skykicking" are brutally revealing, giving voice to thoughts and feelings perhaps better left unspoken. The bitter irony of the album's title aside, *Euphoria* is harrowing and deeply disturbing, yet strangely beautiful—as unforgiving as it is unforgettable. —*Jason Ankeny*

**Clear Skin** / 1994 / Guernica ♦♦♦♦

The lushly packaged *Clear Skin* consists of a single 38-minute instrumental piece which doesn't move forward so much as it expands—built around an endlessly repeating programmed rhythm (Eastern in both its influence and texture), the music seems to be running to stand still, gradually absorbing additional layers of sound while remaining firmly rooted in its most basic ideas. Despite its ambient origins, *Clear Skin* does everything but fade into the backdrop of its environment—depending on the listener's mood, it's either hypnotic or torturous, beautiful in its stark simplicity or unnerving in its excessive self-indulgence; either way, it's another fascinating statement from a group for whom provocation is much more than a marketing conceit. —*Jason Ankeny*

## Invisibl Skratch Piklz

f. 1995, San Francisco, CA
*Group / Turntablism, Underground Rap*

The Invisibl Skratch Piklz are a rotating crew of hip-hop DJs whose tactile acrobatics are more accurately served by the term "turntablist" (coined by Piklz founder DJ Q-Bert). Currently a quintet (although their lineup shifts constantly), the group's core consists of Q-Bert (Rich Quitevis), "Mixmaster Mike" Schwartz, and Shortkut (J. Cruz), with newcomers D-Styles and Yoga Frog replacing founding member DJ Disk (Lou Quintanilla) in 1996. Individually and as a group, the Piklz's reputation in the hip-hop underground is undisputed, and journos get a kick out of describing how they were asked by the world's most prestigious international DJ association (DMC) to stop competing since they were discouraging other DJs from even bothering to enter. But it's the leaps the group have made since they retired from competition that have proved most impressive, dragging turntable tricknology into new and wholly autonomous territories of musicianship currently being developed by a new generation of bedroom virtuosi, with turntable groups such as the X-Men, the Beat Junkies, and the Skratch Piklz at the forefront.

Although the members have known each other and practiced and played together for years (most notably under the names FM20, Dirt Style Productions, and the Turntable Dragons), the Invisibl Skratch Piklz officially formed in 1995. Citing the underground vitality of turntablism and its distance from the comparatively stale commercial rap scene, the Piklz's stated intent was to focus on the art of DJing (defined by skills such as cutting, scratching, and beat juggling) in order to develop and expand its musical potential. Beginning with a five-part series of mixtapes called the *Shiggar Fraggar Show* (recorded for Oakland-based hip-hop writer/promoter Billy Jam's pirate radio show, *Hip-Hop Slam*), the group quickly evolved from a hybrid of more traditional cutting, scratching, and trick DJing into an autonomous "turntable orchestra," scratching out by hand (on as many as 5 turntables at once) a unified montage of beats (i.e., manually scratched kick, snare, hi-hat, etc.), basslines (i.e., continuous bass tones manipulated by hand and with the turntable's speed and pitch controls), wah-wah pedal effects, and extremely intricate and controlled scratch textures. The first fully formed examples of this emerging aesthetic, "Invasion of the Octopus People," appeared on the underground turntablist compendium, *Return of the DJ*, and was later included on Bill Laswell's similarly styled *Altered Beats* (released on Axiom in 1996). Additional international tours, guest appearances, videotapes, and compilation tracks have brought these innovations to a wider audience, often to people previously unaware of the music's potential and sophistication.

Although an awareness of the mechanics of scratching is helpful in understanding the group's innovations, the music's logic (as well as its stylistic moorings, from hip-hop to jazz and beyond) is pretty self-evident, a fact which led to a recording deal with the Asphodel label in 1997. Their first release, *The Invisibl Skratch Piklz Vs. Da Klamz Uv Deth*, is a 12"/CD+ best-of, compiling bits of the group's various routines from the past few years. A dozen or so other mixtape snapshots of the members' ever-evolving sound also exist, as well as a handful of breaks records (among them *Battle Breaks, Booger Breaks, Toasted Marshmallow Feet Breaks,* and *Eardrum Medicine*) which are also standards of the scene, continually selling out pressing after pressing within weeks. Additionally, Q-Bert contributed turntable work on Kool Keith's immensely popular *Dr. Octagon* LP, and members of the Piklz have also appeared on recordings by Saafir, Ras Kass, MCM and the Monster, and Praxis. —*Sean Cooper*

● **Invisibl Skratch Piklz Vs. Da Klamz Uv Deth [EP]** / Jul. 28, 1997 / Asphodel ♦♦♦

The ISP's debut vinyl release under their own name is a long-form EP collaging together bits and pieces of their live routines from over the previous year or so. Pared back to the trio of QBert, Shortkut, and Mixmaster Mike, the 12" features the group's trademark abstract turntable deviations, wrapping thinly sliced references from soul, rock, jazz, funk, and old-school hip-hop (Doug E. Fresh, Too hort, Soulsonic Force, Cybotron) around hand-scratched beats, basslines, and constantly shifting rhythmic textures. Not as minimal and controlled as similar passages from the group's earlier cassette-only releases and compilation tracks (and therefore suffering a little from sloppiness), but also a bit more fun. Blast 1's gorgeous cover art is also worth noting. —*Sean Cooper*

**The Shiggar Fraggar Show, Vol. 1** / Aug. 1998 / Old School Slam ♦♦♦

Not exactly the Piklz's proper long-form debut, *The Shiggar Fraggar Show, Vol. 1* is a live album including segments from a Bay Area pirate-radio show done with ISP members Mixmaster Mike, Q-Bert, Shortkut, Apollo, and DJ Disk. It's just a bit slow out of the gate and doesn't move with the same grace as other fine turntablist moments (like Cut Chemist and Shortkut's *Live at the Future Primitive Sound Session*), but the volatile scratchwork and entertaining samples keep things interesting. Once the tempo picks up, the album steams ahead with bucketfuls of old-school flavor. —*John Bush*

## IO (Patrick Pulsinger)

*Producer / Experimental Techno, Electronica, Techno*

Austrian techno experimentalist Patrick Pulsinger is one of a very few Vienna-bred electronic musicians to reach acclaim in the wider dance music world. Although Pulsinger has recorded in just about every vein of electronic dance music—from house and techno to minimal electro and warped downbeat—his take on each is usually one of pushing established boundaries in unexpected directions, leading to a cult-like status among DJs (and often exceeding the amount of play his records actually receive). Perhaps best known for the unlikely acid jazz hit "City Lights," a collaboration with countrymate Dorfmeister (of the production team Kruder & Dorfmeister), the bulk of Pulsinger's recorded work (including the *Porno* full-length for Disko B and a series of EPs and an album as IO) hasn't been nearly so straight-ahead. Released mostly on his own Cheap label, that work has drawn from Detroit techno and Chicago house, funk, jazz, soul, and disco, and hip-hop and electro-funk, with Pulsinger warping the years and spaces separating these elements until they seem to congeal into a logical whole. Like many of his peers, Pulsinger doesn't stick with any one brand-name too long, and his discography is rittled with aliases, including Sluts'N'Strings, Restaurant Tracks, and Showroom Recording Series. Although the Cheap label's early discography (singles like "Summerbreeze" and the Robert Hood full-length *Nighttime World, Vol. 1*) were geared more toward a club atmosphere, that direction is being increasingly abandoned in recent releases such as "Showroom Recording Series, Vol. 2" and "Mean Clown Welcome," which display instead a brand of cheeky bedroom electronica similar to labels such as Clear and Evolution. [See Also: Private Lightning 6, Patrick Pulsinger] —*Sean Cooper*

**Claire [Single]** / 1995 / Cheap ♦♦♦
A double-pack of off-leaning minimal breakbeat and techno gear, with acoustical samples blended cleanly with fizzing electronics. The best of this EP later went on to form the core of IO's Mo'Wax/Excursions EP, also featuring remix work by Mark Broom and Andrea Parker. —*Sean Cooper*

● **Attack, Sustain, Decay, Release** / 1996 / Cheap ♦♦♦♦
One of the Cheap label's only CD releases (the other being Robert Hood's "Nighttime World"), *ASDR* is a compilation of earlier IO material released through Cheap. The curious title derives from a common filter device used in analog sound synthesis. —*Sean Cooper*

## Irresistible Force (Morris Gould)

*Producer, DJ / Ambient House, Electronica, Ambient Breakbeat, Ambient Techno, IDM*

DJ, musician, journalist, and self-described "international cheerleader of ambient," Mixmaster Morris has been one of the most visible—and most active—proponents of new ambient and electronic music. As renowned for his inventive, wide-casting DJ sets as for his original works under the Irresistible Force name, Morris's influence on the direction of post-rave electronica has been enormous. From his relentless tour schedule, weekly playlists, and monthly release reviews, to his extensive website chronicling the evolution of ambient and experimental electronic music, Morris has helped bring a whole range of otherwise obscure artists (from Terre Thaemlitz to Photek; Ken Ishii to Robert Rich) to a wider audience. And while his holographic suits, Zippy connections, and soundbite approach to musical evangelism might seem a bit ridiculous, his commitment to the music and the quality of his ongoing contribution is undeniable.

English-born Morris Gould got his start as a DJ in the early '80s—not in warehouse party chill rooms, but in dive-bar punk clubs spinning experimental rock, jazz, electronic, and other assorted weirdness in between bands. Eventually taking his deck proficiency and rapidly expanding record collection to pirate station Network 21 (where he worked with Jonathan More and Matt Black of Coldcut), Morris earned his nickname from his eclectic radio shows, during which he might pair Terry Riley with Tibetan monks or Captain Beefheart with Amazonian field recordings. After finishing college in the mid-'80s, Morris worked in computer systems administration before forming Irresistible Force with friend Des de Moor in 1987. The pair played clubs and toured with Meat Beat Manifesto, eventually releasing a single before Morris dissolved the partnership in 1989. Retaining the name, Morris delved deeper into the growing UK rave scene, touring with the Shamen in 1989, playing side gigs and parties, and organizing London's first ambient club events, Telepathic Fish.

Although Morris had experimented with real-time tape loops and low-rent electronics since the mid-'80s, it wasn't until the early '90s that he began to seriously pursue recording. He released his first full-length work, *Flying High*, on the Rising High label, and recorded a celebrated collaboration with Frankfurt ambient composer Pete Namlook, *Dreamfish*. Both albums landed Morris at the forefront of the new ambient movement—a position he graciously accepted—and a string of remix work for the likes of Coldcut, the Shamen, Barbarella, Rising High Collective, and Higher Intelligence Agency followed. Growing problems with his label, however, would plague Morris into the recording of his second album, with was delayed for two years. Following the release of *Global Chillage* in 1995, Morris dissolved his relationship with Rising High and began recording for old friends Coldcut on their Ninja Tune label. The 1998 full-length *It's Tomorrow Already* was the first under the new deal. —*Sean Cooper*

★ **Flying High** / 1993 / Instinct ♦♦♦♦♦
Along with the Orb's *Adventures Beyond the Ultraworld* and the KLF's *Chill Out*, one of the first and finest of the new ambient crop. Morris' mix of electronic and organic textures and epic song lengths helped set the standard (and was responsible for not a few clichés). All but one track, tellingly, features the word "high" in the title; the one that doesn't is called "Symphony in E." Essential. —*Sean Cooper*

**The Underground [EP]** / 1993 / Instinct ♦♦
An unfortunate collection of throwaway dance tracks hurried through RH's release process at the height of Morris' acclaim. —*Sean Cooper*

**Global Chillage** / 1995 / Astralwerks ♦♦♦♦
Not as groundbreaking and perhaps not as satisfying as *Flying High*, Morris' follow-up is a nonetheless well-crafted, if occasionally nostalgic second effort. A focus on rhythm and a much more synthetic feel dominate, with a playful, grounded approach taking the place of the debut's more airborne thematics. —*Sean Cooper*

**It's Tomorrow Already** / Sep. 21, 1998 / Ninja Tune ♦♦♦♦
Morris let nearly 1,000 tomorrows pass between his second and third albums, but it was apparently time well spent. While the period separating *Global Chillage* from *It's Tomorrow Already* was one of the most explosive in post-rave electronica, Morris didn't let the rootless eclecticism he's long championed in his DJ sets follow him into the recording studio. *Tomorrow* is remarkably consistent and suffers little from the overzealousness that tends to plague music that knows too much about itself. Many of the tracks display the same fusion of warm synths, pattery rhythms, and drug-aligned voice-overs that fill *Chillage* and the still-classic *Flying High*, but the loose organicism of Ninja-styled downtempo (as on "Nepalese Bliss" and the title cut) makes a nice addition to the mix. —*Sean Cooper*

## ISAN

f. 1991, Reading, England
*Group / Electronica, Ambient Techno, Post-Rock/Experimental*

Robin Saville and Antony Ryan's releases as ISAN are characterized by simple rhythms, pop-inflected song structures, and strong, committedly analog melodies. Originally from Reading, England, the duo emerged from the electronica underground in the mid-'90s, at a time when groups like Autechre and Aphex Twin were bringing increasing levels of abstraction and disjunction to electronic post-techno. Dodging that approach, ISAN joined artists such as Solvent, B. Fleischmann, Sweden's Pluxus, and Kraut-rock-electronica fusionists To Rococo Rot in making their music warm, inviting, and accessible. Like many of those artists, ISAN (perhaps inadvertently) draw on the '70s and '80s electronic experiments of Hans-Joachim Roedelius, Jean-Michel Jarre, early new wave, and *Another Green World*-era Brian Eno. Releases on indie-hybrid labels like Static Caravan, Liquefaction Empire, and Foundary— among them several limited and hard-to-find 7"s—earned ISAN a crossover audience from the start. The group's profile got a boost in 1999 when they were signed to electronica powerhouse Warp Records; their first release for the label was a remix of Seefeel's "When Face Was Face," included on Warp's 10th anniversary release *Remixes*. —*Sean Cooper*

● **Beautronics** / 1998 / Tugboat ♦♦♦♦
Robin Saville and Anthony Ryan began experimenting together in 1991, releasing a string of singles on UK indie labels such as Wurlitzer Jukebox and Bad Jazz, but by the time of this debut album, the duo maintained their musical relationship long-distance—from separate English towns. Such distance served as little roadblock, however, because ISAN is at least partly about self-confessed technical ineptitude. The duo utilize cheap analog equipment as a purposeful restriction on themselves, with the goal of creating modern music that belies its source, and this debut certainly achieves that goal. *Beautronics* is like a splatter painting of mechanized sounds in which beauty and electronics are inseparable components of the music; in fact, where there is congruence of the two, there are songs. The nature of the music is for the most part ambient, full of simple, wobbly analog synth squiggles and even simpler drumbeats, but the

music itself is far from unsophisticated or slight. Although Saville and Ryan would likely cringe at such a notion, their music is sneakily intelligent, full of tonal color and textural skill masked by the apparent sparseness of the songs. Color is, in fact, a large thematic thread on the album; one song, the chirping "Paintchart," crystallizes this theme perfectly. Some of ISAN's songs could easily accompany a children's TV or puppet show (though it would admittedly have to be a rather warped one), as there is something naïve and wistful about them. Between the songs there are also short sound sketches with titles such as "Tint2-Rosy Apples" and "Tint5-Glittery Disco Blue" that further extend the painterly approach of ISAN, adding both coloring and depth to the album. At times, the music suggests the bumping-together of metals, the eerie whirring of computer control panels, and the apocalyptic screech of sirens, all of which accentuate the fact that we humans have already become at least half-machine ourselves, at least in spirit. But it is also done in such a manner as to throw suspicion on the whole process, to weaken the seriousness and claustrophobia brought to millennial electronic music trends. Like Autechre, ISAN doesn't make anything easy for the listener. The music is stripped bare, and left to its own devices, to do its own work. All the hard, carved-out edges remain. There is no slickness, no overcomplication. And that, ironically, makes *Beautronics* even more of a complex achievement. —*Stanton Swihart*

**Digitalis** / 1999 / Liquefaction ✦✦✦
*Digitalis* definitely lives up to its name. The two-piece UK ensemble ISAN provides a heavy layer of synth-ridden instrumentals with a backing array of drum machines. No heavy guitars, no angst-filled industrial metal, no campy sci-fi movie samples, this is just smooth, minimal pop that leans heavily towards the digital aspect of soothing new wave. —*Mike DaRonco*

**Salamander** / 1999 / Morr Music ✦✦
One has to appreciate anybody who tries to toss a little good humor into the po-faced playground of electronic instrumentalists. Which is why it was easy to smile at the soundtrack-to-an-imaginary-children's-show template of ISAN's early work. The trouble with *Salamander* is that one wishes the band would finally change the channel every once in awhile. This effort does feel different than past works, but in a bad way. Instead of floating along a wash of melodic assurance in works like *Beautronics* or *Digitalis*, this album constantly feels distracted. The flow is stop-start and haggard, as if ISAN is so bent on infusing humor into the electronic scene that they are unintentionally decreasing their attention span with every release. "Braille Foundry," for example, closes off the album with repetitive (yet touching) circles of tunefulness, and "Effokl" is Vangelis' *Blade Runner* score if it got distracted from the monotone adults and just started to play paddle-ball. Even these very defective highlights, though, only heighten the failed roundabouts of the other songs surrounding them. So it's possible *Salamander* will be a signal to the band that merely going against the tide of a genre can only go so far. Fans can only hope that ISAN will soon find that remote control and once again prove their unpretentious talents are just aching for new—and interesting—experiments in sound. —*Dean Carlson*

## Ken Ishii

b. 1970, Tokyo, Japan
*Producer, DJ / Detroit Techno, Club/Dance, Techno*
Japanese techno artist Ken Ishii is among the most innovative, experimental composers in contemporary techno. Although working in and drawing from a decidedly dancefloor-oriented, Detroit-derived framework, Ishii's exploration of avant-garde compositional techniques like chromaticism and the prominent influence of digital synthesis figures him as strongly deviant from Motor City aesthetic tradition. A Tokyo native, Ishii's work is most resonant in feel perhaps to the work of Derrick May, though the influence of more artful electronic experimentalists like Yellow Magic Orchestra and Haruomi Hosono also figure prominently. Although Ishii has only been releasing music since the early '90s—recording under his own name for the R&S label, as well as Rising Sun (for ESP), Utu (Plus 8), Flare (Sublime), and Yoga (ESP)—his 1993 and 1994 R&S works, as well as his Sublime CD *Reference to Difference* are all benchmarks of techno futurism. Incorporating elements of British bleep and breakbeat techno, as well as elements of the 20th century avant-garde, Ishii's finest work expands on techno's rigid rhythmic structure, wedging in elements of chaos and disruption. Like the Black Dog, B12, and other armchair experimentalists, Ishii's music is often praised by DJs who nonetheless refuse to give his often challenging records much play. Although until only recently unknown in Japan and just a step above obscure on the global techno scene, Ishii's 1995 release *Jelly Tones* opened his work out onto a larger audience, prompting a world tour and growing repute as compsoser and DJ. In addition to a continuous performance and DJing schedule, Ishii also remixed tracks for Keiichi Suzuki, Tokyo Skaparadise Orchestra, Cova, and Masatoshi Nagase. *Sleeping Madness*, his first album for R&S in four years, dropped in 1999. —*Sean Cooper*

● **Innerelements** / 1994 / R&S/Sony ✦✦✦✦
Collects the best material from his earlier "Deep Sleep," "Pneuma," and "Tangled Notes" releases for R&S/Apollo and adds three new tracks. Reissued by Sony, the album is an excellent, relatively easy-to-find introduction to Ishii's oevre. —*Sean Cooper*

**Tangled Notes [Single]** / 1994 / R&S ✦✦✦✦
A relentless, cacophonous collection of outbound experimental techno, with a clanging, bleeting harmonic wallop edged on by disjointed rhythms and complex arrangements. A masterpiece of future-form techno and criminally underacknowledged. —*Sean Cooper*

**Jelly Tones** / 1995 / R&S ✦✦✦
Accompanied by a full-length video by noted Japanese animator Morimoto (*Akira*) and a *Jelly Tones* CD-ROM, Ishii's 1995 album was a self-professed stab at taking techno-derived music to a mass audience. The result is a pop-oriented techno album that, while nowhere near as satisfying as his previous work, is an important step toward removing Ishii's music from the ghetto of dancefloor ambivalence. A pair of 12"s from the album includes remixes by Wagon Christ, Luke Slater, Dave Angel, Ian Pooley, and Frank De Wolf. —*Sean Cooper*

**Extra [Single]** / 1995 / R&S ✦✦✦✦
The video-game techno wizard from Japan gets some of the best remixers of the year, in the form of Dave Angel and the two Lukes, Vibert and Slater. —*John Bush*

**X-Mix: Fast Forward & Rewind** / May 1997 / Studio !K7 ✦✦✦
Ishii blends quite a few disparate elements into his volume of the *X-Mix* series, from Renegade Soundwave to Basement Jaxx to Coldcut and Jedi Knights. —*John Bush*

**Sleeping Madness** / Nov. 1, 1999 / R&S ✦✦✦✦
Ishii's first album for R&S in four years shows what he's been up to in the last half of the '90s: tracking further developments in experimental dub (thanks to the Germans) and techno-jazz (thanks to the Brits and Americans). And though the references to varying forms of listening techno crop up quite a bit, most of these productions aren't chained to the chill-out couch by any means. They're just as sleek and fast-moving as Ishii's classic productions, and reliant on the same bubbling groove. So it's the best of both worlds: a new sound, but one with Ishii's feel for traditional techno. —*John Bush*

## Isotope 217

f. 1996, Chicago, IL
*Group / Experimental Rock, Indie Rock, Post-Rock/Experimental*
The Chicago-based jazz-funk fusion ensemble Isotope 217 featured guitarist Jeff Parker along with percussionists John Herndon and Dan Bitney, all three better known for their work in Tortoise; the roster on the group's 1997 Thrill Jockey label debut, *The Unstable Molecule*, also includes trumpeter Rob Mazurek, bassist Matt Lux, and trombonist Sara P. Smith. *Utonian_Automatic* followed in 1999, along with a split collaboration with Commander Mindfuck and Designer. A year later, *Who Stole the I Walkman?* was released. —*Jason Ankeny*

● **The Unstable Molecule** / Nov. 4, 1997 / Thrill Jockey ✦✦✦✦
Isotope 217, one of Rob Mazurek's numerous Chicago jazz side projects, finds itself in a precarious position somewhere between post-rock and jazz. Isotope grew out of weekly jam sessions around the Chicago area, and are put on record for the first time. Recruiting members of Tortoise (Dan Bitney, John Herndon, and Jeff Parker) for this effort, there is a pronounced lo-fi vibe, which is counteracted by Mazurek's jazz ambition. The end result is an album that is neither straightahead jazz or space-rock, but a quirky, funk-flavored, astute musical venture. Tracks like "Kryptonite Smokes the Red Line" and "La Jetee" explore mellow spaces and employ the uses of varied instrumentation including cello and other strings. "Audio Boxing" and "Beneath the Undertow" rely on catchy horn arrangements and precise construction, while providing a counterpoint to the subdued nature of the other tracks. *The Un-*

*stable Molecule* will satisfy anyone who has a taste for out-of-the-ordinary jazz, and an inclination toward funk would not hurt either. It provides a consistent listen, but must be understood as a bridge between two genres. It is a serious effort to assimilate a post-rock sound with contemporary jazz, and it succeeds well. —*Marc Gilman*

**Utonian_Automatic** / Aug. 10, 1999 / Thrill Jockey ♦♦♦♦
Isotope 217's second album, *Utonian Automatic*, contains more angular, extended fusion experiments like the jagged, noisy opener "Luh" and the quietly skewed "Rest for the Wicked." The group's percussive elements come to the fore on "Looking after Life on Mars," while "New Beyond"'s moody, murky keyboards settle the song into an uneasy lull. Over the course of *Utonian Automatic*'s seven tracks, Isotope 217 expand their experimental style, making it even more diverse and challenging. —*Heather Phares*

**Who Stole the I Walkman?** / Aug. 8, 2000 / Thrill Jockey ♦♦
Ever consider that there might a few too many bands inspired by Tortoise? Isotope 217 is here to make sure you do, with every electronic shimmy up their post-rock, jazz-funk pole. At least it's easy to applaud the effort. In the same year America celebrated the likes of a Debbie Gibson silicon-enhanced replica or literally any number of jock rockers, there's something to be said for trying to update the self-important club of jazz in a restorative context. It just too often sounds like the band members are playing in different studios. The awful "Moot Ang" tries to locate that thin line between impromptu Arkestra-like passion and childish interpretations of a PBS jazz special. Somewhere else the brief "Kidtronix" manages to show an immense wealth of ridiculousness even as it implodes on its own instruments in less than two minutes. If the band stopped trying to be sophisticated and just became sophisticated, they would cope better. As in "Meta Bass" or "Space Kirkits," for instance, the mixture of ambient dub pneumatics and obscure melody is enchanting. The album especially shines when it takes a turn into some new French house *cul-de-sac* of Carter Burwell's *Being John Malkovich* score. For the most part, though, this third album sags on its dependence on the "jazz intelligent" ideal. Too much, too late. Either way, *Who Stole the I Walkman?* is an album that often changes about 43 times in the span of a minute, but you'd usually be too lost in a numb daze to notice. —*Dean Carlson*

# J

## Jacob's Optical Stairway
f. 1995, London, England
*Group / Jungle/Drum'N'Bass, Club/Dance*
Jacob's Optical Stairway is, if possible, an even more streamlined and lush drum'n'bass project for Mark Mac and Dego than their usual 4 Hero guise. During 1995, JOS recorded a 12" and a self-titled debut LP for Belgium's R&S Records, with help from contributors including Juan Atkins and Josh Wink. [See Also: 4 Hero] —*John Bush*

- **Jacob's Optical Stairway** / 1995 / R&S ♦♦♦♦
Carrying the science-fiction theme of 4 Hero's *Parallel Universe* over to their Jacob's Optical Stairway side-project, Dego and Mark Mac crafted an album of understated breakbeats with high strings and synthwork, in addition to vocals by an R&B-inspired diva (Samantha Powell). The duo also enlisted Detroit hero Juan Atkins and new electronica stalwart Josh Wink to work on two tracks: "The Fusion Formula" and "The Naphosisous Wars," respectively. —*John Bush*

## Jam & Spoon
f. 1991, Frankfurt, Germany
*Group / Electronica, Trance, Club/Dance, Techno*
Heralded among the pioneers of trance, the Frankfurt, Germany-based duo of producer Jam El Mar and Mark Spoon (aka Markus Loeffel) made an enormous impact in 1992 with their groundbreaking remix of the self-titled single by Age of Love. After the first Jam and Spoon EP, *Tales from a Danceographic Ocean*—which contained their influential hit "Stella"—the duo unleashed a barrage of remixed material for Moby ("Go"), Frankie Goes to Hollywood ("Relax"), Deep Forest and others, all to massive club play; the single "Right in the Night (Fall in Love with Music)" followed in 1993, the first of several of the duo's recordings to feature the American-born vocalist Playka. That same year, Jam and Spoon issued their full-length debut LP, the two-volume *Tripomatic Fairytales 2001 and 2002*, which saw a move away from the pile-driving beats of earlier efforts towards a more commercial sound. In 1996, the duo returned with *Disco 2001*, an album recorded under the alias Tokyo Ghetto Pussy. Though the next Jam and Spoon LP (1997's *Kaleidoscope*) didn't cause much of a splash, a remix of "Stella" became a worldwide club hit in 1999. —*Jason Ankeny*

- **Tripomatic Fairytales 2001** / Apr. 1993 / Epic ♦♦♦♦
The first of Jam & Spoon's separately released but thematically linked *Tripomatic Fairytales* focuses on uptempo eco-techno and trance, as on the highlights "Heart of Africa," "Neurotrance Adventure," "Stella," and "Odyssey to Anyoona." Most of the 14 tracks here float along without nearly as many ideas as they should have, but they compile a frequently entertaining set. —*Keith Farley*

**Tripomatic Fairytales 2002** / Jun. 1993 / Epic ♦♦♦

**Kaleidoscope** / Jul. 28, 1997 / Sony ♦♦♦
Though *Kaleidoscope* may not be as impressive as earlier material by the duo, it represents another step forward for progressive trance. From straight-ahead tracks like "Garden of Eden" and the single "Don't Call It Love" (with vocals by Plavka) to more tongue-in-cheek material—"So Called Techno Track" and the Miles-tribute "Mark Runs the Voodoo Down"—Jam & Spoon keep on keeping on with determination and class. —*Keith Farley*

## James Bong
f. 1993, Copenhagen, Denmark
*Group / Experimental Techno, Electronica, Ambient Techno*
Morten Remmer and Thomas Knak from James Bong are sound-sample experimentalists akin to Matthew Herbert's Doctor Rockit project, able to marry dubby mid-tempo grooves to what is often a literally kitchen-sink style of production. The Danish duo began producing in the early '90s as part of a tangled collective comprising such solo and group projects as Future 3, How Do I, Dub Tractor, Opiate, and Jet (some of which included Remmer's brother Anders and the keyboard talents of Jesper Skaaning). James Bong signed up to Britain's 2 Kool Recordings and released a few 1995-96 EPs, including "General Weirdness" and "Mr. Kiss Kiss Bong Bong." While Future 3 released its debut album in 1995, JB followed one year later with *C'est Trés Bong*. The duo have also appeared on April Records' compilation series *Boredom Is Deep and Mysterious*, and remixed countrymen Deepfried Toguma. —*John Bush*

- **C'est Trés Bong** / Sep. 23, 1996 / 2 Kool ♦♦
Their style is most often too introspective for their own good (especially when stretched out to LP length), and James Bong's album debut lacks energy. True, there are a few deep grooves to tighten up those mid-tempo skeletal effects, but they're far too infrequent to save the album. —*John Bush*

## Mike James
*Producer, DJ / Techno*
While Derrick May went on to become an undeniable legend in the history of electronic dance music for his innovations as a techno artist and DJ, Mike James received little to no recognition for his contributions to May's timeless anthem, "Strings of Life." Of course, before the duo even produced the track, May had a reputation as a talented producer and reportedly handled the bulk of the production for "Strings of Life," though the occasional May critic does often raise the issue of James' contribution. —*Jason Birchmeier*

## Jamiroquai
f. 1992, London, England
*Group / Adult Alternative Pop/Rock, Trip-Hop, Club/Dance, Acid Jazz, Alternative Pop/Rock, Urban, Dance-Pop*
An intriguing development in the '90s British clubscene, Jamiroquai came together in 1992 with a blend of house rhythms and the influence of '70s soul, personified by vocalist Jason Kay, an occasional dead-ringer for Stevie Wonder. Also including drummer Derrick McKenzie, keyboard player Toby Smith, bassist Stuart Zender, and vibes player Wallis Buchanan, the group debuted in October 1992 with the single "When You Gonna Learn?" on Acid Jazz Records. Signed to Sony soon after, Jamiroquai released its debut album *Emergency on Planet Earth* in 1993. The album exploded in the UK, hitting number one on the album charts and going platinum. *The Return of the Space Cowboy* followed the first album into platinum territory upon its release in 1995, and though *Travelling Without Moving* had a slower start upon its release in 1996, it became the first Jamiroquai album to make moves across the Atlantic. The album hit gold, and earned the group several MTV Video Music Awards. *Synkronized* followed in 1999. —*John Bush*

**Emergency on Planet Earth** / Aug. 10, 1993 / Columbia ♦♦♦♦
Jamiroquai made a large initial splash in 1993 with *Emergency on Planet Earth*, a psychedelic melange of tight, funky rhythms, acid rock intimations, and '70s soul melodies. Frontman Jay Kay introduces himself with an environmentally oriented manifesto inside the sleeve, and his lyrics smack of idealist "save the planet" revolution. But this revolution would be held on the dancefloor, if the band's impressive rhythm section had anything to say about it. Horns, string arrangements, and a didgeridoo provide full texture on most of the album's tunes, and the socially aware party vibe raged into the UK's number one album slot. For a debut, *Emergency* shows quite a range of diversity, from the uptempo jazzy instrumental "Music of the

Mind" to the stop-start funk of "Whatever It Is, I Just Can't Stop." —*Troy Carpenter*

● **Return of the Space Cowboy** / 1995 / Columbia ◆◆◆◆
Jason Kay's dead-on Stevie Wonder impersonation drives the acid jazz and funky R&B of Jamiroquai. He takes on social issues such as homelessness and Native Americans' rights. A good album, but constant tempo changes keep the groove from flowing. —*John Bush*

**Travelling Without Moving** / Sep. 9, 1996 / Epic Sony ◆◆◆◆
*Travelling Without Moving* deepens the acid jazz and '70s soul fusions of *Return of the Space Cowboy*, yet it doesn't have the uniform consistency of its predecessor. Nevertheless, Jamiroquai's fusions sound more fully realized with each outing, which makes its patchy songwriting forgivable. —*Stephen Thomas Erlewine*

**Synkronized** / Jun. 8, 1999 / Sony ◆◆◆◆
Three years after their breakout *Travelling Without Moving*, Jamiroquai returned with another album that charts Jay Kay's continuing fascination with club-bound music of the '70s—from disco to jazz-funk to rare-groove to later Motown—but also shows signs of maturity. Produced by Kay with Al Stone, who also collaborated on *Travelling Without Moving*, the album includes several tracks (like the single "Canned Heat") that work infectious acid-jazz grooves, and Kay's hipster vocals give out feel-good vibes through a set of ambiguously good-time lyrics. Though other tracks show a bit of an electronica update to the affairs, each still spotlights how strong and tight the band is. It may not be a leap ahead in sound, but *Synkronized* is another solid Jamiroquai record. —*John Bush*

## Jammin' Unit (Cem Oral)
*Producer / Electronica, Ambient Dub, Techno, Acid House, IDM*

Cem "Jammin' Unit" Oral is better known as one half of German acid/techno group Air Liquide, but has released more material as a solo artist. Recording (as with his partner Ingmar "Walker" Koch) under a seemingly endless array of pseudonyms—including Cube 40, Zulutronic, Bionic Skank, G104, and Ultrahigh—Oral was one of the most prolific artists on the early German acid scene and helped organize Cologne's influential Structure label group (which included the Blue, Structure, and DJ Ungle Fever imprints). His more recent work has appeared through Sm:)e, Pharma, Force Inc., and once-popular UK techno imprint Rising High, which released his debut full-length as Jammin' Unit (*Jammin' Unit Discovers Chemical Dub*) in 1995. An active producer and engineer since 1991, Oral produced mainstream house and techno for some of German's most commercial labels before following his distortion-ridden muse in more experimental directions. His nickname, Jammin' Unit, derives in part from the German pronunciation of Cem ("jam"). [See Also: Zulutronic] —*Sean Cooper*

**Jammin' Unit Discovers Chemical Dub** / 1995 / Rising High ◆◆
Jammin' Unit (from Air Liquide) explores the world of dub-electronica on this Rising High release. —*John Bush*

● **Deaf, Dub, & Blind** / Mar. 24, 1997 / Instinct ◆◆◆◆
Air Liquide's Cem Oral (aka Jammin' Unit) has pursued the integration of dub with electronic dance styles such as acid and techno since his earliest releases on Structure, Force Inc., and Rising High. *Deaf, Dub, & Blind*, his debut full-length for Blue Planet (reissued in 1997 by Instinct) is one of his biggest successes. Although archetypal dub elements, such as loping basslines and tons of reverb, are present, so too are more subtle engagements of the style in meter, phrasing, and instrumentation (muted rhythm guitars and chiming percussion pop up in the unlikeliest of places). —*Sean Cooper*

**Are You Prepared?** / Dec. 7, 1998 / Pharma ◆◆◆

## Japan
f. 1974, London, England, **db.** 1982
*Group / New Romantic, New Wave, Prog-Rock/Art-Rock*

Japan's evolution from rather humble glam-rock beginnings into stylish synth-pop (and beyond) made the British group one of the more intriguing and successful artists of their era. Formed in London in 1974, Japan began its existence as a quintet comprised of singer/songwriter David Sylvian, bassist Mick Karn, keyboardist Richard Barbieri, drummer (and Sylvian's brother) Steve Jansen, and guitarist Rob Dean. In their primary incarnation, the group emulated the sound and image of glam rockers like David Bowie and the New York Dolls; Sylvian's over-the-top vocals, much in the vein of Bryan Ferry, also earned Japan frequent (if derisive) comparisons to Roxy Music.

After winning a label-sponsored talent contest, they were signed to Germany's Ariola-Hansa Records in 1977 and debuted a year later with a pair of LPs, *Adolescent Sex* and *Obscure Alternatives*, which received little notice at home or in the US but did find favor among Japanese audiences. With 1979's *Quiet Life*, Japan made a tremendous leap into more sophisticated stylistic and subtle territory; a subsequent hit single covering Smokey Robinson's "I Second That Emotion" further underscored the newfound soulfulness of their music.

1980's *Gentlemen Take Polaroids* continued to broaden Japan's scope, incorporating a variety of exotic influences into their increasingly atmospheric sound. With 1981's *Tin Drum* (recorded minus Dean), the band peaked: tapping sources as diverse as funk and Middle Eastern rhythms, the album moved beyond pop confines into experimental tones and textures, and scored a UK smash with the single "Ghosts."

However, *Tin Drum* also proved to be Japan's swan song: long-simmering differences among the band members came to a head when Karn's girlfriend moved in with Sylvian, and the group disbanded in 1982. The individual members quickly forged ahead with their projects: Sylvian began a successful solo career and also entered into a series of collaborations with performers like Ryuichi Sakamoto, Holger Czukay, and Robert Fripp, while Karn issued a 1982 solo LP, *Titles*, before founding the short-lived duo Dali's Car with Bauhaus' Peter Murphy. In 1986, meanwhile, Jansen and Barbieri issued *Worlds in a Small Room* under their own names before recording together as the Dolphin Brothers.

In 1987, Karn released *Dreams of Reason Produce Monsters*, a solo LP which featured contributions from Sylvian and Jansen, spurring rumors of a reunion which came to fruition in 1989 when the four principal members reteamed under the name Rain Tree Crow. By the time an eponymously-titled album appeared in 1991, however, relations had again dissolved in acrimony, and the musicians went their separate ways; while Sylvian continued working independently, as the decade wore on Karn, Jansen, and Barbieri occasionally reunited in various projects while also maintaining solo careers. —*Jason Ankeny*

● **Quiet Life** / 1979 / Fame ◆◆◆◆
*Quiet Life* is the album that transformed Japan from past-tense glam rockers into futuristic synth-popsters, though they'd been leaning in that direction for awhile. It's also a solid proto-romantic synthesizer record, enhanced by Karn's superb fretless-bass work and Sylvian's smooth, sneering vocals spread over pop hits like the title track and "Fall in Love with Me." —*Keith Farley*

**Gentlemen Take Polaroids** / 1980 / Blue Plate ◆◆◆◆
The group's debut for Virgin, *Gentlemen Take Polaroids* is a bit slicker on the synthesizer side but less satisfying as an album; it sounds slightly more dated than other entries in the Japan discography. Still, it includes the hit title track, a few other solid tracks, and two pastoral synthesizer exercises named "The Art of Swimming" and "Taking Islands in Africa" (the latter recorded with Yellow Magic Orchestra's Ryuichi Sakamoto). —*Keith Farley*

**Tin Drum** / 1981 / Blue Plate ◆◆◆◆
On *Tin Drum*, Japan finally dropped their Bowie/Roxy fixations and began making their own music. The heavy Oriental influence, centered ironically more on China than Japan itself, is apparent from the cover shot (featuring a poster with the beatific face of Mao smiling down) to songtitles like "Cantonese Boy" and "Visions of China" (the latter a medium-sized hit in Britain). Yet even beneath the surface, *Tin Drum* is a record indebted to Asian music. The synthesizer textures and percussion on the opener "Talking Drum" point to the Orient, and Sylvian uses his voice less like a rock star and more like another instrument in the mix, even on the Top Five hit "Ghosts." Karn's fretless bass, Barbieri's keyboards, Sylvian's voice—each sounds out similar ground and balances the others so perfectly that they frequently sound like one instrument. —*Keith Farley*

**Gentlemen Take Polaroids/Tin Drum/Oil on Canvas** / Oct. 4, 1994 / Caroline ◆◆◆◆
Caroline combined Japan's three early-'80s albums for Blue Plate—*Gentlemen Take Polaroids*, *Tin Drum*, *Oil on Canvas*—in one slip-cased box set in 1994. For any fan who had yet to replace their vinyl with CDs, this is an ideal purchase, but collectors who already own the discs may want to think about

this set twice, since it contains no bonus tracks or new packaging. —*Stephen Thomas Erlewine*

## Jean Michel Jarre

b. Aug. 24, 1948, Lyon, France
*Vocals, Keyboards, Synthesizer, Producer, Leader, Composer, Arranger / Multimedia, Club/Dance, Progressive Electronic, Adult Alternative, Electronic*
Celebrated as the European electronic music community's premier ambassador, composer Jean-Michel Jarre elevated the synthesizer to new peaks of popularity during the '70s, in the process emerging as an international superstar renowned for his dazzling concert spectacles. The son of the famed film composer Maurice Jarre, he was born August 24, 1948, in Lyon, France, and began studying piano at the age of five. Abandoning classical music as a youth, Jarre became enamoured of jazz before forming a rock band called Mystere IV; in 1968, he became a pupil of the musique concrète pioneer Pierre Schaeffer, joining the Groupe de Recherches Musicales. His early experiments in electro-acoustic music yielded the 1971 single "La Cage"; the full-length *Deserted Palace* followed a year later.

Jarre's early works were largely unsuccessful, and give little indication of the work to follow; as he struggled to find his own voice, he wrote for a variety of singers including Francoise Hardy, and also composed for films. Seeking to push electronic music away from its minimalist foundations as well as the formal abstractions of its most experimental practitioners, he slowly developed the orchestrated melodicism of his 1977 breakthrough effort *Oxygène*, an enormous commercial hit which reached the number two spot on the UK pop charts. The follow-up, 1978's *Equinoxe*, was also a smash, and a year later Jarre held the first in a series of massive open-air concerts at the Place de la Concorde in Paris, the estimated one million spectators on hand earning him a place in the Guinness Book of World Records.

Only in the wake of 1981's *Les Chants Magnétiques* ("Magnetics Fields") did Jarre mount a proper tour, traveling to China with a staggering amount of stage equipment in tow; the five performances, performed backed by some 35 traditional instrumentalists, later generated the LP *Concerts in China*. 1983's *Music for Supermarkets* instantly became one of the most collectible albums in history—recorded for an art exhibit, only one copy was ever pressed, selling at a charity auction for close to $10,000. The master was then incinerated, guaranteeing the record's rarity. Jarre's next proper release was 1984's *Zoolook*, which failed to connect with audiences with the same success as its predecessors; a two-year hiatus followed before he resurfaced on April 5, 1986, with an extravagant live performance in Houston celebrating NASA's silver anniversary; in addition to the over one million in attendance, it was also broadcast on global television.

*Rendez-Vous* appeared a few weeks later, and after another highly visual live date in Lyon, Jarre assembled the best material from the two events as the 1987 concert LP *Cities in Concert—Houston/Lyon*. *Revolutions*, featuring the legendary Shadows guitarist Hank B. Marvin, followed in 1988, and a year later a third concert LP, dubbed simply *Jarre Live*, hit stores. After 1990's *En Attendant Cousteau* ("Waiting for Cousteau"), Jarre mounted his biggest live experience yet, with an attendance of over two and a half million fans converging on Paris to see him perform in honor of Bastille Day. The decade to follow proved surprisingly quiet, however, and apart from the occasional live appearance Jarre was largely removed from the limelight; finally, in 1997 he issued *Oxygène 7-13*, updating his concepts for a new musical era. —*Jason Ankeny*

★ **Oxygène** / 1977 / Dreyfus ♦♦♦♦♦
This album conveys the excitement and freshness you'd expect from a talented young man embarking on a career in what was still a relatively unknown and unjaded electronic music scene. Sometimes innocent and introspective, other times ambitious and even a little spooky, this is a must for anyone interested in electronic music. —*Linda Kohanov*

**Equinoxe** / 1978 / Dreyfus ♦♦♦
Progressive, multilayered electronic music, it features glistening sequencer patterns, flowing melodies, and futuristic special effects that sound like you're blasting off into outer space. After all these years, most of it holds up. —*Linda Kohanov*

**Les Chants Magnétiques** / 1981 / Dreyfus ♦♦♦♦
*Les Chants Magnétiques* was the third of Jarre's albums in a row to update Tangerine Dream's atmosperic sequencer trance for a synth-pop and mainstream crossover audience. The side-long "Les Chants Magnétiques Part 1" is the capstone of the album, while parts two through five move through driving electronic pop and several passages more indebted to Jarre's past in the *musique concrète* scene. It's often just as melodic and inventive as *Oxygène*, though not as consistently creative. —*John Bush*

**Zoolook** / 1984 / Dreyfus ♦♦♦♦
On the first departure of his career since 1977's *Oxygène*, Jean-Michel Jarre combined an actual band and processed vocal samples—recorded in 25 different languages—with his rich, melodic synthesizer pop. The rhythm is often propelled by guttural vocal snippets, as on "Ethnicolor" and "Zoolookologie." That's not half as disconcerting for those used to his previous work as the album's art-funk backing: Adrian Belew on guitar, Marcus Miller on bass, and Yogi Horton on drums, plus Laurie Anderson on one track. Though *Zoolook* is interesting throughout, the tracks with Jarre alone are often the best, reprising the classic *Oxygène* sound. —*John Bush*

**Rendez-Vous** / 1986 / Dreyfus ♦♦♦
Just after his live performance in Houston to celebrate NASA's anniversary, Jean-Michel Jarre released *Rendez-Vous*, an appropriately cosmic-sounding album of glittering synth-pop. It consists of the same music heard at the Houston concert and shows Jarre moving closer to conventional rock territory, though still with his distinct blueprint. The final track, "Last Rendez-Vous: Ron's Piece," was composed by Jarre for astronaut Ron McNair and was intended to be the first musical piece played and recorded in space. McNair's historic duty was cut short, however, by the Challenger shuttle disaster of January 1986. —*John Bush*

**Waiting for Cousteau** / 1990 / Polygram ♦♦♦♦
*Waiting for Cousteau* was another in a long line of concept albums by Jean-Michel Jarre, this one based, as the title would suggest, on the life and work of French oceanographer and film-maker Jacques Cousteau.

As he has always done, Jarre used his music to conjure up perfect images of his subject matter. The three part "Calypso" series is no exception, and it is easy to imagine tropical islands in warm Caribbean seas. Complete with steel drums, the "Calypso" series is as good as anything Jarre had produced since at least *Zoolook*, if not *Oxygène*.

*Waiting for Cousteau*, however, is a different matter. Comprising nearly 47 minutes of ambient electronica, the track is simply tedious. It is worth noting that on cassette versions of *Waiting for Cousteau* the title track was reduced by almost half its length, making it much more palatable. —*Jonathan Lewis*

**Images: The Best of Jean Michel Jarre** / 1991 / Dreyfus ♦♦♦♦
*Images* is a solid overview of Jean-Michel Jarre's recordings for Epic, containing the majority of his best-known material and most accessible work. It may not be of interest to collectors and longtime fans, since it doesn't contain anything unexpected, yet it's an excellent introduction for the curious. —*Stephen Thomas Erlewine*

**Chronologie** / 1993 / Disques Dreyfus ♦♦♦
For fans of Jean-Michel Jarre, *Chronologie* contains more of Jarre's proven ability to blend familiar sounds in the New Music tradition into unusual, inventive compositions. The uninitiated will find *Chronologie*'s blend of 19th Century classical musical themes with pop, rave, and rap sounds downright danceable. Many of the pieces begin with a classical sound—in one song it's deeply resonating pipe organ—and almost invariably pick up the tempo quickly and slide right into a Gloria Estefan beat. —*MusD*

**Oxygène 7-13** / May 20, 1997 / Sony ♦♦♦
*Oxygène 7-13* continues where Jean-Michel Jarre left off 20 years before, that is, the last track ("Part 6") of 1977's *Oxygène*. Much had changed in the interim, for both Jarre and synthesizer technology. The result is a set of uptempo, highly melodic electronic trance reminiscent of Steve Hillage's work of the time, as well as German trance producers like Sven Väth. Though it will sound best to those already familiar with his music, Jarre's influence was considerable, and he continued to prove it in the late '90s. —*John Bush*

## Jaz Klash

f. 1995
*Group / Jungle/Drum'N'Bass, Club/Dance*
The Cup of Tea breakbeat act Jaz Klash is a collaboration between the Bristol trip-hop duo More Rockers and American hip-hop producer the Angel. Born in Brooklyn, the Angel was living in Los Angeles by the early '90s, when she began working for Delicious Vinyl. She worked on remixing for the Phar-

cyde, Brand New Heavies, Spearhead, and Donald Byrd, also composing music for soundtracks (*Gridlock'd*, *Playing God*). After More Rockers' Rob Smith and Peter D remixed her track "Step into the Light" in 1995, the trio got together at the suggestion of More Rockers' managaer Simon Goffe. The one-off meeting produced material for the 1997 full-length *Thru the Haze*, recorded with keyboard help from Jacky Terrasson and Brian Auger. The Angel later returned stateside to work on her own projects, Supa Crucial and 60 Channels. —*John Bush*

● **Thru the Haze** / Jun. 2, 1997 / Cup of Tea ◆◆◆◆
Perhaps the best thing out of Bristol drum'n'bass since *New Forms*, the debut album from the collaborative trio Jaz Klash is a set of jungle jazz with a definite edge to it, courtesy of live instrumentation by noted jazz keyboardists Jacky Terrasson and Brian Auger. The drum programming by More Rockers and the Angel is superb and distinctive, while even the Angel's own vocals on two tracks come off quite well. *Thru the Haze* also includes two remixes by Roni Size associates Die and Suv, plus an Angel remix of the title track. —*John Bush*

## Philip Jeck

*Turntables, Producer / Experimental Ambient, Ambient Techno*
In similar territory to Christian Marclay and David Shea, Philip Jeck is an avant-garde turntablist, plunderphonic sample terrorist, and performance artist whose most famous installation, Vinyl Requiem, included no less than 180 turntables. After studying the visual arts at Dartington College in Devon, Jeck began a performance career that found him at art galleries as well as warehouse parties, where he emulated the turntable tricks of American hip-hop DJs like Grandmaster Flash. It was during a five-year collaboration with contemporary dancer Laurie Booth though, that Jeck developed a more personal and experimental style of music-making allied with Canadian John Oswald's style of plunderphonics sampling. Jeck's 1993 Vinyl Requim installation with Lol Sargent utilized 180 turntables as well as 12 slide projectors and two film projectors and won a Performance Award from *Time Out* magazine. The following year, he appeared on the Blast First! compilation *Deconstruct* alongside Christian Marclay, John Oswald, Bruce Gilbert Stock, and Hausen & Walkman and in 1995, Jeck released his debut album *Loopholes* for Touch. *Surf* followed four years later. —*John Bush*

**Loopholes** / 1995 / Touch ◆◆◆
Philip Jeck rejects the digital future for some vintage analogue textures on *Loopholes*, and easy rhythms blend the disparate parts into a pleasant whole. —*John Bush*

● **Surf** / Jan. 25, 1999 / Touch ◆◆◆◆
Philip Jeck's second album, *Surf*, continues his fascination with analog sounds and recording techniques; samples and loops are taken mostly from vintage vinyl, while Jeck's rhythms keep the sonic textures from floating away. —*Steve Huey*

## Jedi Knights

f. 1995
*Group / Neo-Electro, Electro-Techno, Club/Dance*
One of the more endearing pseudonyms of Global Communication's Tom Middleton and Mark Pritchard, Jedi Knights spearheaded Britain's electro revival of 1994-95 with the single "May the Funk Be with You." Resembling nothing so much as a fusion of electro-funk with the cantina band from *Star Wars*, Jedi Knights also released a rare GC-related full-length, 1995's *New School Science*. The duo continued to use Jedi Knights, for big-beat frenzy on singles like "Big Knockers" and "Catch the Break." [See Also: Global Communication, Reload] —*John Bush*

**May the Funk Be with You [Single]** / Jan. 1995 / Clear ◆◆◆
This single, part of a series of electro side-projects on Clear (also including μ-Ziq as Tusken Raiders, Autechre as Gescom, and members of Black Dog as Plaid), features Global Communication as Jedi Knights. In true electro-funk fashion, the 12" has a great vocoder bit. —*John Bush*

● **New School Science** / Apr. 8, 1996 / Universal Language ◆◆◆◆
A fusion of '80s electro and its requisite *Star Wars* fixation with the hilarious concept feel of a Parliament-Funkadelic LP, *New School Science* sees the Jedi Knights on a continuing mission to "restore the funk across the universe." Included are slightly altered versions of tracks from their Clear single ("May the Funk Be with You," "Noddy Holder") and new tracks which make up for a slight lack of ideas with non-stop fun. "Dances of the Naughty Knights" works around a sample from *Monty Python and the Holy Grail* ("We are the knights who say ni!") and the occasional vocoder bits are spot-on. There are also two links to Jedi Knights' more celebrated incarnation: a house-centric Masters at Work tribute and the atmospheric ambience of the final track. —*John Bush*

## Marshall Jefferson

**b.** Sep. 19, 1959, Chicago, IL
*Producer, DJ / Club/Dance, Acid House, House*
One of the original innovators in Chicago house, Marshall Jefferson had a hand in several of the music's most influential early tracks. As a solo act, he recorded 1986's "Move Your Body"—sub-titled and unanimously acclaimed "The House Music Anthem." Jefferson also helped record Phuture's "Acid Tracks," the first and best acid house single. Later, amidst a wave of acid-inspired records, he grew tired of the sound and moved into a more spiritual form of music later termed deep house; along with Larry Heard, he became one of its best producers.

Jefferson was born in Chicago in 1959, the son of a police officer and a school teacher. Heavily into hard rock like Black Sabbath and Deep Purple during the '70s, he attended university to study accounting, but left after three years to take a job in the post office. By 1983, friends began taking him to Chicago's Music Box club; after being exposed to Ron Hardy's influential mixing style, Jefferson soon realized that house music had a real feeling to it, unlike the commercial disco sound he was accustomed to hearing on the radio. House artists like Jesse Saunders and Jamie Principle had begun releasing records by that time, and Jefferson felt the need to begin recording as well. He bought a synthesizer/sequencer combo and passed several of his newly recorded tapes on to Ron Hardy. The legendary DJ liked what he heard and began dropping the tracks into his set.

During the two-year period from 1985 to 1986, Marshall Jefferson released half-a-dozen of the biggest club hits in Chicago. His first release, "Go Wild Rhythm Trax," appeared on Virgo Records in 1985. Later that year he produced his friend Sleazy D's "I've Lost Control," and the track became a big club hit. "Move Your Body," another recording first introduced by Hardy, was given a full release on Trax Records in 1986; the single immediately dropped a bomb on Chicago crowds, who soon began acknowledging the track as house music's defining moment.

Less than one year after "Move Your Body" however, Chicago was forced to react to another important milestone, the onset of acid house. The trio known as Phuture (DJ Pierre, Spanky, and Herb J) had recently recorded some material using the acid squelch of Roland's TB-303 synthesizer, and with Marshall Jefferson's help, they entered the studio to record a full version. Phuture emerged from the studio with "Acid Trax," one of the most influential songs in the history of house. Several months after its release, it had spawned literally *hundreds* of imitators and answer versions; soon the Chicago house scene had become swamped with tracks soaked in the squelchy reverbs of the TB-303.

Given the lack of variety in the scene, Jefferson quickly tired of acid house. Instead of continuing with acid, he recorded an atmospheric slice of house inspired by the original vibe he had experienced at the Music Box back in the early '80s. The track, "Open Your Eyes," took its place alongside contemporary productions by Larry Heard, signalled a new feeling in house music, named deep house for its level of emotion and organic beauty.

Unlike many Chicago house producers, Jefferson managed to make a good living during the late '80s and early '90s, when house music went global almost overnight and the bottom dropped out of Chicago's fraternal club scene. Several Marshall Jefferson productions not recorded under his own name, such as Hercules' "Lost in the Groove," Jungle Wonz's "The Jungle," and Kevin Irvine's "Ride the Rhythm" all became sizeable club hits. Also, he masterminded the career of the pre-eminent house vocal group Ten City from 1988 through 1992, and began DJing around Europe after being offered several high-profile spots in 1989. Jefferson spent much of the '90s remixing and DJing, but did record under his own name for the 1997 album *Day of the Onion*. —*John Bush*

**Day of the Onion** / Feb. 4, 1997 / KTM ◆◆◆◆
Similar to the work of Larry Heard, the other chief producer of deep Chicago house during the late '80s, Marshall Jefferson's first actual solo album (after a decade-long production career) is a contemplative affair. Though the beats

are by no means downtempo, the polished synthesizer textures add an occasionally melancholy air to the proceedings. —*John Bush*

★ **Past Classics** / Feb. 2, 1998 / Fierce ✦✦✦✦✦

Though many of Marshall Jefferson's classic productions are on compilations, *Past Classics* is the best place to find many Jefferson tracks in one place. Ten tracks are included, from the obvious—"Move Your Body (The House Music Anthem)" and Jungle Wonz's "The Jungle"—to less-noted material like "Time Marches On." —*John Bush*

## Jega (Dylan Nathan)

*Producer / Experimental Electro, Electronica, Jungle/Drum'N'Bass, IDM*

Mancunian Dylan Nathan is one of a new generation of artists to begin producing electronic music inspired by UK artists such as Orbital and Aphex Twin, but without having much interest in or contact with the UK acid house explosion from which those artists originally issued. Recording under the name Jega for a growing number of labels, Nathan's well-composed hybrids of new wave, electro, ambient, and, more recently, drum'n'bass are widely lauded in the international experimental electronic underground; his releases for noted Manchester-based, Autechre-affiliated label Skam are among the label's best. Nathan got his start after close friend Mike Paradinas (aka μ-Ziq, who also owns the Planet Mu label) urged him to get a few pieces of gear and begin making tracks. The results of that initial push were released by Skam in 1996 as the *Jega EP*, which was followed in mid-1997 by an additional self-titled 12" (sometimes referred to as the *Card Hore EP*). Nathan has also released tracks through Skam/Musik Aus Strom co-project, Mask, and provided a remix for MAS co-owner Michael Fakesch's *Demon 2 EP*. The full-length release *Spectrum* appeared on Paradinas' Planet Mu in 1998, followed by an American contract with Matador. Two years later, Nathan returned with *Geometry*. —*Sean Cooper*

**Jega EP [#1]** / Jul. 15, 1996 / Skam ✦✦✦✦

Dylan Nathan's first release for hometown experimental label Skam is almost a mini-album in length, and features seven tracks of surprisingly original dark, melodic electro and heavily syncopated breakbeat. Nathan's tracks are starkly minimal, but also quite effective, pairing simple minor-key melodies with crisp, snapping machine rhythms and sparse electronic atmospheres, recalling at once Man Parrish, early Berlin, and Mike "μ-Ziq" Paradinas. —*Sean Cooper*

**Jega EP [#2]** / Aug. 11, 1997 / Skam ✦✦✦

At six tracks long, Jega's second EP for Skam is just a track shy of his debut, though not as essential. The first track grafts Luke Vibert's beatbox vocal cut-up from his "Extreme Possibilities" remix onto a supercharged drum'n'bass framework, but doesn't take it anywhere particularly interesting. In fact, the drum'n'bass-oriented tracks are the least worthy here, primarily since jungle's rate of evolution is too rapid for d'n'b dabblers whose tracks end up sounding instantly dated. A pair of ambient-electro corkers ("Oak Hanger," "Stainless Steel Drum"), however, as well as two short-ish downbeat/electronica sketches, make this one worth tracking down. —*Sean Cooper*

**Spectrum** / Jul. 6, 1998 / Matador ✦✦✦

Dylan Nathan's assortment of fragile melodies and schizophrenic percussion programming puts him right in line with the early output of Rephlex acts like Aphex Twin and μ-Ziq. *Spectrum* wears that influence on its sleeve, for better and worse. The result is an album of delightfully inventive, perhaps overly humorous "listening techno" that comes complete with two drill'n'bass corkers ("NIA" and "Manic Minor"), as many dark drum'n'bass tunes ("Intron.ix" and "Pitbull"), plus distinctively μ-Ziq melodies for the backgrounds of most other songs. Still, Nathan proves his programming skills are on a par with Paradinas or James on several tracks, including the time-stretched pins-and-needles of "Musical Chairz" and the jazzy "Red Mullet." —*John Bush*

● **Geometry** / Oct. 17, 2000 / Matador ✦✦✦✦

With *Geometry*, Dylan Nathan pulls back slightly from the drill'n'bass bent of his first LP (*Spectrum*) to embrace the vintage synth-electronics and labor-intensive programming of his early Skam material. The opener "Alternating Bit" is a dark track that layers deep sub-bass and increasingly warped drum programs over waves of symphonic-synth straight out of Wendy Carlos' classic *Tron* soundtrack. Elsewhere, Nathan proves his immense skills not only at inventing melodies but also submerging said melodics within an array of kitchen-sink effects and next-level programming. The highlight is "Recursion," a start-stop sequencer track with razor-wire percussion programs, slow-moving paranoid-synth, and a multitude of effects that sound alarmingly similar to early-'80s flight-simulator games. Nathan reprises the classic haunted-electro sound of Skam with "Doric" and the title track. —*John Bush*

## Jellybean (John Benitez)

b. 1959, New York City, NY [South Bronx]
*Producer / Club/Dance, House, Dance-Pop*

One of the finest remixers and producers during the post-disco days of the '80s, Jellybean worked with many pop stars during the decade. Born in the South Bronx in 1959, John Benitez was collecting records from an early age; after he attended a nearby disco club called the Sanctuary in the mid-'70s, he became immersed in the growing disco scene and soon became one its best DJs as well as an early producer with his own reel-to-reel machine. After appearances at the clubs Experiment 4 and Xenon, Benitez moved on to such prestigious showplaces as Studio 54 and the Electric Circus. With the dawn of the '80s (and the death of disco), he continued DJing with a residency at Manhattan's Fun House (beginning in 1981), and also hosted a dance show on New York's WKTU.

Jellybean's burgeoning production and remix career went into full gear during 1981-82; he reworked seminal tracks from Rockers Revenge, the Jimmy Spicer Bunch, and Afrika Bambaataa, then watched as two of his remixes from 1983's *Flashdance* soundtrack ("Flashdance" and "Maniac") became sizeable hits. Madonna, an early club regular who admired Benitez for his DJing as well as his production skills, drafted him to write and produce a track for her debut album later in 1983. Their collaboration "Holiday" became her first hit, and Madonna returned the favor by co-writing another Top 20 hit for Jellybean, "Sidewalk Talk" from his 1984 EP *Wotupski*. His 1987 debut album *Just Visiting This Planet* featured Jellybean in his usual production role though his name appeared on the sleeve; despite the mainly unknown guest vocalists, the single "Who Found Who" with Elisa Fiorillo became another Top 20 hit. His second album, 1988's *Jellybean Rocks the House*, was a much tighter affair though it featured no hits.

Though his solo career took precedence, Jellybean spent more time during the late '80s working on remixes and productions for other pop stars, including Sting, Whitney Houston, Eurythmics, Debbie Harry, Sheena Easton, Book of Love, and Debbie Gibson. Though he released his third album in 1991 (*Spillin' the Beans*), Benitez kept to a low profile for the most part during the '90s, doing consistent remix and production work. In 1995, he founded H.O.L.A. Recordings (Home of Latino Artists) for Latin-dance releases. —*John Bush*

**Wotupski [EP]** / 1984 / EMI America ✦✦✦

Remix/production great Jellybean Benitez signed a separate artist deal with Liberty Records in the mid-'80s, and his first release was an EP that had some nice dance-pop cuts, including "Sidewalk Talk," a song written by Madonna. Outstanding sound and interesting arrangements. —*Ron Wynn*

**Just Visiting This Planet** / 1987 / Chrysalis ✦✦

Jellybean Benitez is one of the greatest producers and mixers in recent dance music history, but it's hard to call most of his releases as a matter "albums." They're impressively produced and arranged sequences, with faceless vocals running in and out of some superbly constructed arrangements. There's much on this album that's really ear-catching, but its lyric and performance content doesn't match its technical brilliance. —*Ron Wynn*

● **Jellybean Rocks the House** / 1988 / Chrysalis ✦✦✦✦

Jellybean Benitez made serious impact as a performer as well as a producer and remixer with this late '80s album, one of two he did with Chrysalis. He landed two chart hits and extensive urban-contemporary radio airplay, plus serious club and dance attention. As always, the production, arrangements, and studio work were brilliant, more than enough to mask frequently routine vocals. —*Ron Wynn*

**Spillin' the Beans** / 1991 / Atlantic ✦✦

After recording a few albums for Chrysalis, Jellybean Benitez moved to Atlantic with the generally disappointing *Spillin' the Beans*. A producer, writer, and mixer as talented as Jellybean should be recording excellent albums, but instead, much of this dance-pop/R&B collection (which often wastes the talents of female vocalists like Niki Harris, DeAnna Eve, and Cindy Valentine) is surprisingly mediocre. The album does contain a few impressive cuts, including the amusing "Love Is a Contact Sport," the infectious deep house number "What's It Gonna Be" (an appropriate vehicle for Harris), and the Caribbean-flavored "Secret Weapon" (available only as a bonus track on the CD version). But for every worthwhile offering, there are three unimpressive ones. Jellybean is capable of much more. —*Alex Henderson*

**Jellybean's House Party** / Apr. 4, 2000 / Jellybean ♦♦♦

## Jessamine

f. 1992, Galion, OH, **db.** 1999
*Group / Space Rock, Indie Rock, Post-Rock/Experimental*

Drone-rockers Jessamine formed in the college town of Galion, OH before relocating to Seattle, where they earned notice for "Your Head Is So Small...," a 1994 single on the Sub Pop label. After signing to Kranky, Jessamine—vocalist/guitarist Rex Ritter, bassist/vocalist Dawn Smithson, keyboardist Andy Brown, and drummer Michael Faeth—issued their self-titled debut in 1995; their follow-up, *The Long Arm of Coincidence*, was released a year later. *A Pox on You*, a collaboration with Spectrum, followed, as did the singles collection *Another Fictionalized History*; their third studio LP, *Don't Stay Too Long*, appeared in 1998. Just after the release of *Living Sound*, an archival live outing recorded with Experimental Audio Research ringleader Sonic Boom, Jessamine disbanded. —*Jason Ankeny*

● **Jessamine** / May 26, 1995 / Kranky ♦♦♦♦

Over a series of tuneless vocals and duets, Jessamine's debut album presents some of the most intriguing noise-pop since My Bloody Valentine and Medicine were in their heyday. From the textural noise of the opener, it might be assumed that the group pursues distortion for its own sake, though later vocal tracks "Secret," "Royal Jelly Eye Cream," and "Inevitably" each include delicious pieces of guitar distortion that accent the fragile melodies exceptionally well. Slipping between abstract noise akin to label-mates Labradford and bass-driven pop songs may not be for everyone, but Jessamine does it better than most. —*Keith Farley*

**Long Arm of Coincidence** / Sep. 2, 1996 / Kranky ♦♦♦♦

The band's sophomore album stretches out their heavy dream-pop inspirations to accept accomplished, noisy dream-pop on "Step Down" and "Say What You Can." Though Dawn Smithson has at best a tenuous hold on her vocals, the hazy productions and accompanying rhythm section do much to lift these songs above expectations. —*Keith Farley*

**Another Fictionalized History** / Sep. 16, 1997 / Histrionic ♦♦♦♦

**Living Sound** / Dec. 7, 1999 / Histrionic ♦♦♦

Recorded live in Seattle in 1996, *Living Sound* features the four-piece fleshed out with help from EAR's Sonic Boom. The group plays together well, though fans of both Jessamine and Sonic Boom/EAR will know exactly what to expect. Over a shuffling rhythm that drops in and out of the mix, Andy Brown (Micromoog, Farfisa), Rex Ritter (guitar, effects), and Sonic Boom (theremin, EMS) provide waves of atmospheric improvisation. There aren't any moments of pure bliss, but the focus on ambient noise rarely grows boring. —*John Bush*

## Jeswa (Josh Kay)

*Producer / Electro-Techno*

Better-known for his work with partner Romulo Del Castillo under the names Soul Oddity and Phoenecia, Miami-based Josh Kay released the *Skone* EP on Schematic in 1997. —*Sean Cooper*

● **Skone [EP]** / Jul. 28, 1997 / Schematic ♦♦♦♦

Although Schematic's first two releases were found by many to compare a little too favorably to UK IDM-founts like Autechre and the Black Dog, Jeswa's debut for the label remains on the respectable end of influence, integrating the odd rhythms and quirky percussion of those groups with a greasy, head-bucking funk decidedly American in origin. A four-tracker laboring for the most part in mid- to downtempo electro territory, Jeswa also draws liberally from early bleep techno and the cinematic cartoon electronica of Mouse on Mars and Atom Heart. —*Sean Cooper*

## Jhelisa (Jhelisa Anderson)

*Vocals / Trip-Hop, Club/Dance, Acid Jazz, House, Soul*

Best-known as the vocalist for the Shamen on several hits from their 1993 album *Boss Drum*, Jhelisa Anderson gained a solo contract in 1994 from Dorado Records after storming the charts on such Shamen singles as "LSI (Love Sex Intelligence)." Though much of her previous work had portrayed her as a diva, she cooled things down beginning with her first solo album, 1995's *Galactica Rush*, a mellow LP with shadings of soul and jazz mixed in with electronic flourishes. Two years later, Jhelisa put out her second, *Language Electric*. She has had several remixes of her songs issued and also released an acoustic EP. —*John Bush*

**Galactica Rush** / Jan. 31, 1995 / Planet Earth ♦♦

● **Language Electric** / Mar. 10, 1997 / Dorado ♦♦♦

Jhelisa's second album for Dorado finds her delving into darker territory, both musically and lyrically—with themes ranging from child abuse to prearranged marriage. Her own arrangements and music-writing enhance the personality of *Language Electric*, and the mood is understated, though the range of sounds—from loose funk and ambient-soul to occasional techno—sounds more reminiscent of her work with the Shamen. Fellow Dorado act Outside (Matt Cooper) sits in on piano. —*John Bush*

## Jimpster (Jamie O'Dell)

*Producer / Funky Breaks, Electronica, Jungle/Drum'N'Bass*

Ambient-jazz, jungle producer Jamie O'Dell was near the top of the hype list for 1997, his Jimpster project upped by the likes of Mixmaster Morris and Coldcut. However, as jungle's avant-garde veered into techstep territory and "ambient" and "jazz" switched from drum'n'bass adjectives to unsavory invectives, Jimpster's appeal switched from the dancefloor to the armchair, gaining popularity instead (like Squarepusher and Cujo's Amon Tobin) among electronica audiences. His string of EPs, released through the Manchester-based Freerange label, found a welcome audience in those repelled by techstep's murky, bleating hoovers but craving something a little more sophisticated than the rolling, housey breaks and pad washes characteristic of most dancefloor-ambient and jazz-drum'n'bass. His debut full-length, *Martian Arts*, was a compilation of those Freerange singles, and was released by the New York-based Instinct label in mid-1997.

Like Squarepusher and Cujo, O'Dell takes his jazz influence in not always obvious directions, with results often pleasantly recalling '70s fusion acts such as Weather Report, Herbie Hancock, and *Bitches Brew*-era Miles Davis without stooping to excessive sampling (O'Dell draws from live session tapes recorded in his studio). A student of jazz and contemporary composition when he began cutting records, O'Dell is also one of many musicians in his family; his mother is a jazz singer on the London circuit and his father is the drummer for jazz-funk fusion combo Shakatak. Jimpster is also a popular live act, with bassist Cheyne Towers and sax/flute blower Roger Wickham backing up O'Dell's samplers and Atari. The proper debut Jimpster LP *Messages from the Hub* was released on Kudos in 1999 and the eclectic compilation *Scrambled* was issued a year later. —*Sean Cooper*

● **Martian Arts** / Jun. 10, 1997 / Instinct ♦♦♦♦

A handy compilation of Jimpster's various and hard-to-find twelves for the Freerange label, indeed ranging free, from mutant jazz-jungle to swirly downtempo breaks. Some of the tracks veer dangerously close to quiet storm territory, but the arrangements are uniformly accomplished and the production top-notch. A number of the tracks feature bass and flute accompaniment by Cheyne Towers and Roger Wickham. —*Sean Cooper*

**Messages from the Hub** / Apr. 12, 1999 / Kudos ♦♦

After his debut album, Jimpster makes a bid for being a serious artist that, for the most part, falls flat. The energy and flair of his first EPs are gone, replaced with quiet introspection worthy of Air or quiet-storm junglism (Endemic Void minus the breaks). A few tracks, including "Static Dynamic" and "Shivering Sands," benefit from his introspective touches, but listening to an entire album of fusion wash can be a trial unless you're a big fan of the Rippingtons. —*John Bush*

## Jive Bunny and the Mastermixers

f. 1988, London, England
*Group / Club/Dance, Acid House, Dance-Pop*

Jive Bunny and the Mastermixers anticipated the megamix boom of the mid- to-late '90s, assembling a seemingly endless series of dancefloor-friendly medleys of pop oldies. The brainchild of British producers John Pickles and Ian Morgan, Jive Bunny came out of nowhere in 1989 to top the UK charts with their debut single "Swing the Mood"; when the follow-ups, "That's What I Like" and "Let's Party," both reached number one as well, the duo became only the third act in history (behind Gerry & the Pacemakers and Frankie Goes to Hollywood) to score chart-topping singles with each of their first three releases. *Jive Bunny—The Album* appeared in 1989 as well; subsequent singles including "That Sounds Good" and "Can Can You Party" reached the British Top Ten, but the group's stay in the limelight was brief and 1990's *It's Party Time* failed to repeat the commercial impact of its predecessor. Still, new Jive Bunny collections continued appearing throughout the decade, among them *Havin' a Party, Beach Party, Jive Bunny Christmas*, and *Biggest Party on the Planet*. —*Jason Ankeny*

**Jive Bunny: The Album** / 1989 / Atco ✦

● **The Best of Jive Bunny** / Oct. 24, 1994 / Music Club ✦✦
True, there are only 12 tracks on this Jive Bunny collection, but that could be more than enough for any novelty fan hungry for the extreme commercial end of dance-pop rip-offs. The album includes the two big hits "Swing the Mood" and "That's What I Like" plus various genre exercises like "Rock 'n' Roll Party Mix" and "Roaring Twenties." —*Keith Farley*

**Can Can You Party** / Aug. 28, 1996 / Stardust ✦✦
Another half-hearted release in the Jive Bunny series includes medleys and mega-mixes of songs like "Surfin' USA," "Money Mony," "Wooly Bully," "The Locomotion," "At the Hop," "Great Balls of Fire," "Runaway," "Sweet Little Sixteen," "Johnny B. Goode," and "Bye Bye Blackbird." —*Jason Ankeny*

## Joi
f. 1992, London, England
*Group / Electronica*

1999 seemed to be the year that Joi, the group featuring Asian/Anglo DJ/vocalist brother Haroon and Farook Shamsher, had envisioned for nearly a decade. After years of building a following in London clubs, the self-described "original Asian backbeat fusionists" had successfully toured North America and had released a groundbreaking album, *One and One Is One*, on the Astralwerks subsidiary of Peter Gabriel's Real World label. Combining Asian chants, India-influenced melodies, westernized dance music, and hip-hop, the Shamsher brothers had been embraced by the popular music world. The headliners of the "Freshworld" Free Music Festival in London, Joi received a BBC Asian Music award in 1999. While VH-1 claimed that Joi "mesh the fabrics of underground dance, Indian percussion, trance-inducing chants, and a rhythm far more futurist than old-school funk," MTV said, "They've concocted a batch of four-on-the-floor dance numbers that incorporate relentlessly upbeat and free-spirited sound." Just as the momentum of the band's rise peaked, Haroon Shamsher was forced to shut down operations when his brother fell victim to a heart attack and died on July 8, 1999. After a four month period of mourning, Shamsher pulled together a new line-up for the group and began to pick up the pieces, touring as the opening act for the British tour by Eurythmics. Natives of Bengal, India, the Shamsher brothers first attracted attention in the early '90s as member of the Joi Bengal Sound System. Their debut single, "Desert Storm," was released in 1993. Masters of the new studio technology, they often appeared at DAT/DJ session in London clubs where they artistically mixed DATS with vinyl and on-line sampling and live percussion by Bongo Paul. —*Craig Harris*

● **One and One Is One** / Feb. 23, 1999 / Astralwerks ✦✦✦
Given the high quality of the dance music coming out of London's Asian Underground movement these days—Talvin Singh's *O.K.* and the Asian Dub Foundation's *Rafi's Revenge* were two of 1999's best albums—you'd expect better than this from Joi, a duo consisting of brothers Farook Shamsher and Harron Shamsher, who proved their mettle with an excellent remix on the Nusrat Fateh Ali Khan tribute album *Star Rise*. But on their debut full-length they tend to lose focus and go a bit soft. Despite the complex and beautiful percussion textures on "Everybody Say Yeah" and singer Susheela Raman's inspired performance on "Asian Vibes" (not to mention a great drum'n'bass mix on "ESY-SHJ" courtesy of Spring Heel Jack), the album never feels like it gets all the way off the ground. "Heartbeat," with its mediocre house groove, is a bust from the first measure, and although "India" starts off promisingly with a bracing bhangra rhythm, it eventually trails off into a boring 4/4 rock beat and little else. Make no mistake—nothing on this album is less than pleasant, but too, not much of it is more than just pleasant. —*Rick Anderson*

## Grace Jones
b. May 19, 1952, Kingston, Jamaica
*Vocals / Club/Dance, Disco, Dance-Pop*

Entertainer and model Grace Jones has a European flair but a hard, stilted singing style. Jones is on the cutting edge of reggae-style dance music, although commercial success evades her. Jones renewed her career in the '90s, though she's done more acting than singing since releasing *Bulletproof Heart* in 1989 for Capitol. She had a featured role in the Eddie Murphy film *Boomerang* in 1992; *Private Life: The Compass Point Sessions*, a retrospective of her work for Island, followed in 1998. —*Bil Carpenter*

**Muse** / 1979 / Island ✦✦✦
A fine dance and club album, *Grace Jones* was still essentially a disco act when she recorded this album at the end of the '70s. The campy tendencies and flat vocals were subordinated to the array of cross-rhythms, textures, and production devices buttressing the tracks. Jones did some outstanding numbers during this era, but seldom utilized her voice beyond either a decorative or supporting role. She wasn't (and still isn't) a soulful or great singer, but future albums would demonstrate that she could do more things than mouth lines and insert herself into rhythm tracks. —*Ron Wynn*

**Warm Leatherette** / 1980 / Island ✦✦✦✦
Grace Jones teamed with the great reggae production duo of Sly Dunbar and Robbie Shakespeare on this 1980 album, and made the transition from straight dance and club act into quasi-pop star with reggae and urban contemporary leaning. The single "Private Number" was one of her best, and the overall album had more energy and production gloss than previous LPs that had been aimed completely at the club market. It helped that Jones seemed enthused about the session and really put herself into the songs. —*Ron Wynn*

● **Nightclubbing** / 1981 / Island ✦✦✦✦
Actress, model, and disco/reggae sensation Grace Jones enjoyed her greatest pop success with this album. Sly Dunbar and Robbie Shakespeare's production gave Jones a thin reggae veneer, while also providing her with a sensational hit in "Pull Up To The Bumper." The song's suggestive lyrics and quasi-reggae feel helped make it a club smash and Top Ten R&B hit. Jones alternated between being coy and aggressive on this record, which was one of the last hurrahs for Sly And Robbie's "taxi" beat pop-reggae sound. —*Ron Wynn*

**Living My Life** / 1982 / Island ✦✦✦
Grace Jones essentially retired from music after this album and became a film actress for three years. The album followed her definitive *Nightclubbing* and was a commercial disappointment, although it had some nice material and excellent production and arrangements. But she often sounded distant and detached, and not even the great support could totally overcome Jones' less than enthusiastic performances. —*Ron Wynn*

**Slave to the Rhythm** / 1985 / ZTT/Island ✦✦✦✦
An audio biography of Grace Jones, produced by Trevor Horn, it's a sonic treat along the lines of Yes' *90125* or Frankie Goes to Hollywood's first album (both produced by Horn). The music ranges from slick R&B runaway grooves to striking audio montages, interrupted occasionally by conversation about Jones's life. Serious ear candy. —*Scott Bultman*

## Howard Jones (John Howard Jones)
b. Feb. 23, 1955, Southampton, Hants, England
*Vocals, Keyboards / Pop/Rock, New Wave, Synth-Pop*

Howard Jones was one of the defining figures of mid-'80s synth-pop. Jones' music merged the technology-intensive sound of new wave with the cheery optimism of hippies and late-'60s pop. Jones racked up a string of hits in the mid- and late '80s before he retreated into being a cult figure in the '90s.

A native of Southampton, England, Jones learned how to play piano at the age of seven. By the time he was a teenager, his family had relocated to Canada, which is where he joined his first band, a progressive-rock group called Warrior. Eventually, Jones moved back to England, where he played in a number of different groups. In the mid-'70s, he enrolled in the Royal Northern College of Music. After he dropped out of college, he played with a variety of local Southampton jazz and funk bands. Eventually, Jones began performing as a solo artist. At these solo shows, Jones performed only with synthesizers and drum machines. For these one-man concerts, Jones had a mime called

Jed Hoile perform. After a few years of solo performing, Jones attracted the attention of John Peel, who offered the keyboardist a BBC session. Soon, Jones was opening for new wave synth-pop acts across England. By 1983, he had signed with WEA in England and Europe; in America, he signed to Elektra.

Howard Jones released his first single, "New Song," in England in the fall of 1983 and it became a big hit, peaking at number three. His second single, "What Is Love," was released a few months later and it reached number two. *Human's Lib*, Jones' debut album, was released in the spring of 1984 and quickly rose to number one in England. Thanks to repeated exposure on MTV, the album became a moderate hit in the US. Later in 1984, "New Song" and "What Is Love" became American Top 40 hits, while "Pearl in the Shell" became his third British Top Ten single.

In 1985, Jones phased Hoile out of his live show, formed a touring band, and released his second album, *Dream into Action*. The record became his most successful album, reaching number ten and going platinum in the US and spawning the hit singles "Things Can Only Get Better," "Like to Get to Know You Well," "Life in One Day," and "Look Mama." In the spring of 1986, he released *Action Replay*, an EP of remixes that featured a new version of "No One Is to Blame" from *Dream into Action*. "No One Is to Blame" became Jones' biggest US hit, peaking at number four. The relatively weaker chart placement of number 16 in the UK was indicative of his future in England—his next single, "You Know I Love You...Don't You?," taken from his third album *One to One*, became his last British Top 40 hit.

Jones released his fourth album, *Cross That Line*, in the spring of 1989. The first single from the album, "Everlasting Love," became a number one adult contemporary hit in America, reaching number 13 pop. However, the album stalled at number 65. Jones returned three years later with *In the Running*, a set that saw him abandoning synthesizers for piano. The album didn't make the charts. Following the release of *The Best of Howard Jones* in 1993, Elektra dropped him. Instead of seeking a new record contract with another major label, Jones hit the road in 1994, performing acoustic shows. At the 1994 shows, he sold *Working in the Backroom*—an album he recorded at his home studio and released on his own label, Dtox Records—at his concerts. For the next two years, Jones continually toured America and Europe. In 1996, he released *Live Acoustic America* on PLM Records; *People* followed two years later. —*Stephen Thomas Erlewine*

**Human's Lib** / 1984 / Elektra ◆◆◆◆
His debut album is almost entirely performed on synthesizers. The material on *Human's Lib*, like all of the following albums, is very inconsistent; Jones either writes hits or flops, with very little in between. Contains two of Jones' best songs, "New Song" and "What Is Love?" —*Iotis Erlewine*

**Dream into Action** / 1985 / Elektra ◆◆◆◆
This album shows the synthesizer pop idol at the height of his creativity—*Dream Into Action* is definitely the most interesting of Jones' albums. It contains some of his best songs—"Things Can Only Get Better," "Life in One Day," and "No One Is to Blame." The CD includes two bonus tracks, "Bounce Right Back" and "Like to Get to Know You Well," both of which are worthwhile additions. —*Iotis Erlewine*

**Action Replay** / 1986 / Elektra ◆◆
This is a six-track mini-album that includes an updated version of "No One Is to Blame" featuring Phil Collins on percussion. This album really isn't worth buying, especially if you have the other Jones albums. —*Iotis Erlewine*

**One to One** / 1986 / Elektra ◆◆
This is Jones' most musically mature and toned-down album. The synthesizers are less overbearing than on the previous albums, yet the songs are mediocre. *One to One* reached number ten in the UK, but did not fare as well in the US, peaking at number 56. This album features the revamped "No One Is to Blame," which is inferior to the original version. —*Iotis Erlewine*

**Cross That Line** / 1989 / Elektra ◆◆
After a three-year wait, this album was a bit of a disappointment. Musically, it is his best yet, but it lacked a certain energy that the others had. The songs seemed to replace vivacity with length. The album didn't do very well on the charts; the number 13 single (US), "Everlasting Love," was the biggest hit. Ironically, the best song on this album, "Out of Thin Air," does not use a single synthesizer but instead is a solo piano piece performed by Jones himself. After all those years of electronic music, a song featuring a real instrument is a welcome relief. —*Iotis Erlewine*

● **The Best of Howard Jones** / Jun. 29, 1993 / Elektra ◆◆◆◆
*The Best of Howard Jones* successfully distills all the hits and highlights from his albums onto one disc. It could be all the Howard Jones you'll ever need. —*AMG*

## The Jonzun Crew

f. 1981, Boston, MA
*Group / Electro, Club/Dance*
Michael and Soni Johnson, who were born in Florida, formed the Jonzun Crew in Boston with Steve Thorpe and Gordy Worthy. Mixing electro-funk with comic/novelty lyrics, the foursome recorded sizable hits in 1982 and 1983 with "Pack Jam (Look out for the OVC)" and "Space Cowboy." Michael Johnson left the group in 1986 for a solo career, but didn't do much beyond one A&M release. He had more impact as the person who discovered New Edition and as the writer/producer of their hit "Candy Girl." —*Ron Wynn*

● **Lost in Space** / Nov. 1983 / Tommy Boy ◆◆◆
Michael and Soni Johnson enjoyed a little notoriety on the club and urban contemporary circuit with this early-'80s album that was kind of a mild elaboration on the George Clinton/Parliament/Funkadelic space traveler theme. The Jonzun Crew wasn't as musically or lyrically compelling as Clinton, although the single "Space Cowboy" was a Top 20 R&B hit, and "Electro Boogie Encounter" had its moments. But this was more silly/novelty material than inspired or satirical vision, and ultimately couldn't establish the band as a serious act. —*Ron Wynn*

**Cosmic Love** / 1991 / Critique ◆◆
The Jonzun Crew couldn't duplicate the mild success they enjoyed in the mid-'80s with their mix of offbeat humor, electronic backbeats, and quasi-mystical/space analogies. This album lacked the charm, unpredictable air, and otherworldly aura of its predecessor and never generated much action or attention. It was well produced but otherwise forgettable. —*Ron Wynn*

## Journeyman (Paul Frankland)

*Producer / Electronica, Ambient Techno, Trip-Hop*
UK producer Paul Frankland is best known for his recordings as Woob for the popular Nottingham-based ambient dub label Em:t Recordings. Frankland is also signed to Ninja Tune subsidiary Ntone as Journeyman, a project that has produced a pair of full-length recordings to date. *Mama 6*, the first of those, was among Ntone's first releases; available only on CD, it featured a heady blend of alternately house-y and downtempo beats, lush electronics, and quixotic samples, and it quickly went out of print. 1997's *National Hijinx* benefitted from Ninja Tune's growing prosperity by receiving a much larger pressing and availability on both vinyl and CD. The album also swapped out the rhythmic lope of the debut on several tracks for a quasi-junglist sensibility, although even the uptempo cuts manage to remain just as calm and reposed. [See Also: Woob] —*Sean Cooper*

**Mama 6** / 1996 / Ntone ◆◆◆

● **National Hijinx** / Aug. 26, 1997 / Ntone ◆◆◆◆
Journeyman is Paul Frankland of Woob's more full-bodied project. Maintaining the spare, amplified downbeat textures of the latter, Frankland with Journeyman focuses his attention on the cavernous spaces between Woob's echoing beats and mesmerizing rhythms, adding greater movement and a gorgeous depth of detail. As with much material by Woob, Journeyman's *National Hijinx* is replete with movie references which match the music's cinematic wanderings stroke for stroke. A few of the tracks toy with drum'n'bass figures, but always in ways that suggest a more purposive engagement; Frankland hasn't "gone jungle" as so many have (a good half of the album is beatless ambient, as well). This is polished, complex stuff, and a fascinating listen on the scale of FSOL or Ntone labelmates Neotropic. —*Sean Cooper*

## The Jungle Brothers

f. 1986, New York, NY
*Arranger / Jazz-Rap, Alternative Rap, Club/Dance, Hip-Hop*
Although they predated the jazz-rap innovations of De La Soul, A Tribe Called Quest, and Digable Planets, the Jungle Brothers were never able to score with either rap fans or mainstream audiences, perhaps due to their embrace of a range of styles—including house music, Afrocentric philosophy, a James Brown fixation, and of course, the use of jazz samples—each of which has been the sole basis for the start-up of a rap act. Signed to a major label for 1989's

*Done by the Forces of Nature*, the JB's failed to connect on that album—hailed by some as an ignored classic—or the follow-up, *J Beez Wit the Remedy*.

Mike Gee (b. Michael Small; Harlem, NY), DJ Sammy B (b. Sammy Burwell; Harlem, NY), and Baby Bam (b. Nathaniel Hall; Brooklyn, NY) came together as the Jungle Brothers in the mid-'80s and began their recording career at the dance label Idler's. The result of the sessions, *Straight Out the Jungle*, was released in early 1988. The album's Afrocentric slant gained the Jungle Brothers entry into the Native Tongue Posse, a loose collective formed by hip-hop legend Afrikaa Bambaataa including Queen Latifah (and, later, De La Soul and A Tribe Called Quest). The album's most far-out cut was "I'll House You," a collaboration with house producer Todd Terry and an early experiment in what later became known as hip-house.

Though *Straight Out the Jungle* had not sold in large quantities, Warner Bros. signed the trio in 1989 and released a second album, *Done by the Forces of Nature*, that same year. Though it was issued around the time of De La Soul's groundbreaking *3 Feet High and Rising* LP and gained just as many positive reviews, the album was overlooked by most listeners. The Jungle Brothers' chances of mainstream acceptance weren't helped at all by a four-year absence after the release of *Done by the Forces of Nature*, inspired mostly by Warner Bros. marketing strategies. Finally, in the summer of 1993, *J Beez Wit the Remedy* appeared, complete with a sizeable push from Warner Bros.; unfortunately, the large amount of promotion failed to carry the album. Obviously not learning from their earlier mistakes, Warner Bros. also delayed the release of the group's fourth album, *Raw Deluxe*, until mid-1997. *V.I.P.* followed in early 2000. —*John Bush*

- **Straight Out the Jungle** / 1988 / Warlock ♦♦♦♦
The trio's debut is powered by muscular funk riffs underpinned by an Afrocentric sensibility and a sharp sense of humor. —*John Floyd*

**Done by the Forces of Nature** / Nov. 1989 / Warner Brothers ♦♦♦♦
By injecting some vocal delicacy and some clever samples into their moderately militant message, they made a second album that elaborates on their own winning formula. —*John Floyd*

**J Beez Wit the Remedy** / Jun. 22, 1993 / Warner Brothers ♦♦♦
Nearly four years after *Done By the Forces of Nature*, the Jungle Brothers return with a hazy, funky album, filled with their brand of literate hip-hop. Although they've made some stylistic progressions since the last record, it wasn't enough to be a completely groundbreaking release, nor was it commericial enough to break them out of their critically acclaimed/cult status. Instead, it was another solid, inventive album that didn't receive the attention it deserved. —*Stephen Thomas Erlewine*

**Raw Deluxe** / Jun. 3, 1997 / Gee Street ♦♦♦
The Jungle Brothers' career was plagued with delays and setbacks, which resulted in each of their albums being released several years after they were officially due. Their fourth effort, *Raw Deluxe*, is no different. The Jungle Brothers remain one of hip-hop's most inventive crews, crafting remarkably sophisticated, jazzy beats and rhyming with skill and intellegence, but they sound more as if they were aligned with late-'80s trends, not the styles of the late '90s. This isn't a bad thing, since they are musically and lyrically gifted, but it also makes *Raw Deluxe* sound more like an artifact than a blazing comeback. —*Stephen Thomas Erlewine*

**Jungle Brothers: Remixes** / Oct. 27, 1998 / Gee Street ♦♦♦

**V.I.P.** / Jan. 4, 2000 / Polygram International ♦♦♦♦
Even though the JB's originated the highly influential Native Tongues clique (De La Soul, A Tribe Called Quest), their ten-year run of musical mischief has been anything but native. Spearheaded by the acid beats of the Propellerheads' Alex Gifford, their latest foray, *V.I.P.*, is yet another experimental set, one that highlights the exquisite chemistry of group members Baby Bam and Mike G. While the JB's don't fit the traditional hip-hop image, that's part of their appeal, as their innocent, party-oriented raps hold one purpose—to get your back up off the wall. —*Matt Conaway*

## Junior Varsity km

f. 1997, Texas

*Group / Experimental Jungle, Indie Pop, Experimental Rock, Ambient Techno, Space Rock*

Not to be confused with the similarly-named Houston indie-pop band, drum'n'bliss project Junior Varsity km was the guise of San Francisco-based electronic artist Kenric McDowell. Releasing his debut EP *Style for Life* on local Darla Records in 1997, he returned the following year with both *You're Fabulous* and *Taking Care of You*, the latter a contribution to the label's ongoing "Bliss Out" series. The two-volume *Teledesic Disco* set followed in 1999. —*Jason Ankeny*

- **Teledesic Disco, Vol. 1** / Jul. 13, 1999 / Darla ♦♦♦

**Teledesic Disco, Vol. 2** / Jul. 13, 1999 / Darla ♦♦

## Junkie XL (Tom Holkenberg)

b. Netherlands

*Producer / Big Beat, Electronica, Club/Dance, Techno*

The big-beat electronica project Junkie XL was largely the work of Amsterdam-based remixer Tom Holkenberg, previously known for his work with acts like Nerve and Fear Factory. Beginning his career at the age of 14, Holkenberg initially played in area funk and reggae units, later switching to alternative rock; while working in a music store, he first began experimenting with synthesizers and technology, and in 1996 won the Grand Prix of the Netherlands as best house music producer. After completing Junkie XL's 1997 debut LP *Saturday Teenage Kick*, a blend of electronica and rock, he enlisted rapper Rude Boy (an alumnus of Urban Dance Squad), DJ Frankie D, drummer Baz Mattie, and guitarist Renee van der Zee to transform his one-man studio project into a working band. —*Jason Ankeny*

- **Saturday Teenage Kick** / Dec. 8, 1997 / Roadrunner ♦♦♦
Junkie XL's debut is often more interesting in theory than in execution; as an attempt to combine rock and electronica on an equal basis, *Saturday Teenage Kick* is an admirable effort, but too often the ideas simply don't jell. Lacking the dense, complex production of acts like the Chemical Brothers or Prodigy, the album never achieves the visceral power it's seeking—it's too dance-oriented for rock listeners, and vice versa. —*Jason Ankeny*

## Juno Reactor

f. 1991

*Group / Goa Trance, Trance, Club/Dance, Techno*

Best-known for injecting former porn star Traci Lords with some hi-NRG trance on her 1995 solo album, Ben Watkins and co. have pursued a fusion of Goa trance and techno on their own recordings as Juno Reactor. Watkins, who has produced Alison Moyet and worked with Youth (in both the Empty Quarter and Brilliant), formed his own band in the late '80s, the Flowerpot Men (not to be confused with the '60s band of the same name). Not long after, Watkins retreated to travel around the world with a portable DAT recorder, using the results to soundtrack a traveling art exhbition. After meeting up with Stefan Holweck, an old comrade from Brilliant, the duo formed Juno Reactor with Mike Maguire and occasional contributors Johan Bley and Jens Waldenback.

Juno Reactor hit big on the dancefloor with a 1993 single, "High Energy Protons," and signed to Mute Records. Later that year, the group released its debut album, *Transmissions*, and toured as the Orb's support slot for chillout-room duty; a deal with Orb's Inter Modo label resulted in 1994's *Luciano*. The hype increased a year later as Traci Lords recruited the group to produce her debut album, *1000 Fires*. Signed to Wax Trax! a year later (but on Blue Room Released in Europe), Juno Reactor returned with their third album, *Beyond the Infinite*, in 1996. *Bible of Dreams* followed in 1997 and *Shango* in fall 2000. Watkins' side-projects include Psychoslaphead and Electrotete. —*John Bush*

**Transmissions** / 1993 / NovaMute ♦♦
*Transmissions* leads off with Juno Reactor's biggest club hit to date, "High Energy Protons," a curious track that translates three-chord heavy metal through some 303 acid with a few suitably trippy vocals. The rest of the album has more of the same, alternately spacey or psychedelic. It's occasionally reminiscent of the Orb's ambient dub, especially on the astronaut-sampling "Luna-Tic." —*John Bush*

**Beyond the Infinite** / Mar. 12, 1996 / Wax Trax! ♦♦
Whether you believed Goa trance was the LSD-inspired wave of the future or just another bastardization of third-world culture, Juno Reactor has been plunging forward as if they don't care how close the genre could come to disaster. This might be a good time for the band to get a devil's advocate implanted inside their heads. *Beyond the Infinite* offers more of the east meets west dance sentiments thrown together in a surprisingly tiresome manner

and its overall feeling of flipped-out exclusivity damages any of the band's mighty aspirations. "Silver" can have all the sitar friendliness to satisfy those prone to psychedelics, "Magnetic" nods along to the twirling excesses of an outdated pre-jungle beat, yet these efforts make the sober listener simply feel left out of a loop. It doesn't make things easier that the band has yet to choose which path to take. In "Samurai," for example (the track used in promoting Arnold Schwarzenegger's *Eraser*), there is more of a Photek-like, oriental focus on techno-trance operations than ever before. Which is an interesting new attempt; even though it feels stilted, confused, and just an excuse to steal the keyboards from the Cure's "A Forest." With its mystified sense of native adoration and tiring execution, *Beyond the Infinite* is an album signifying a band at a crossroads. They've now exposed about five musical directions to take, and it might take less (or more) drugs to show which path is the correct one. —*Dean Carlson*

- **Bible of Dreams** / 1997 / TVT ♦♦♦
All too often, techno recordings that sounded exciting in the clubs of the late '80s and early to late '90s didn't hold up well at home, where their limitations became quite obvious. *Bible of Dreams*, on the other hand, is interesting both on and off the dance floor. Instead of simply concerning itself with the number of beats per minute it can provide, Juno Reactor delivers trance to sit down and listen to. The mostly instrumental material (though with scattered soundbites and samples) is varied, and the group fuses trance with everything from Middle Eastern music ("God Is God") to heavy metal ("Swamp Thing"). —*Alex Henderson*

## Jurassic 5

f. 1993, Los Angeles, CA
*Group / Turntablism, Underground Rap, Hip-Hop*
Though there's actually six of them, Jurassic 5 got everything else right on their self-titled debut EP. Part of the new rap underground of the late '90s (along with Company Flow, Mos Def, Doctor Octagon, and Sir Menelik), the sextet—the MCs Marc 7even, Chali 2na, Zaakir, and Akil and producers Cut Chemist and DJ Nu-Mark—came together in 1993 at the Los Angeles cafe/venue named the Good Life. The six members were part of two different crews, Rebels of Rhythm and Unity Committee; after collaborating on a track, they combined into Jurassic 5 and debuted in 1995 with the "Unified Rebellion" single for TVT Records. At the tail end of 1997, the *Jurassic 5 EP* appeared and was hailed by critics as one of the freshest debuts of the year (if not the decade). Both Cut Chemist and Chali 2na are also part of the Latin-hop collective Ozomatli, while Chemist himself has recorded several mix-tapes plus the wide-issue album *Future Primitive Soundsession* (with Shortkut from Invisibl Skratch Piklz). The year 2000 found the group on tour with Fiona Apple and on the Warped Festival, just in time for the release of *Quality Control* that summer. —*John Bush*

**Jurassic 5 [EP]** / Oct. 13, 1997 / Rumble/Pickininny ♦♦♦♦
Clocking in at just about one-third the running time of your average rap album circa 1997, Jurassic 5's debut was the most refreshing hip-hop release of the year, and not just because it abandoned the epic-length concepts of the rap mainstream. With old-school vibes to spare, excellent rhythmical raps, and the production genius of Cut Chemist and DJ Nu-Mark, *EP* finally delivered on all the diverse talents promised by the growing hip-hop underground. "Jayou" is a flute-loop classic, and "Concrete Schoolyard" has that nostalgic "can it all be so simple" vibe so rarely heard from hip-hop. —*John Bush*

- **Quality Control** / Jun. 6, 2000 / Interscope ♦♦♦♦
In June 2000, almost seven years after their formation, underground rap's most lauded crew finally hit with a full-length. Great expectations aside, *Quality Control* hits all of the same highs as Jurassic 5's excellent EP of three years earlier, stretching out their resume to nearly an hour with a few turntablist jaunts from resident beat-jugglers DJ Nu-Mark and Cut Chemist. The formula is very similar to the EP, with the group usually going through a couple of lines of five-man harmonics before splitting off for tongue-twister solos from Zaakir, Chali 2na, Akil, or Mark 7even. As expected, there are plenty of nods to old-school rap, from "LAUSD," with its brief tribute to hip-hop classic "The Bridge" by MC Shan, to "Monkey Bars," where the group claim inspiration—yet just a bit of distance—from their heroes ("Now you know us but it's not the Cold Crush, four MC's so it ain't the Furious / Not the Force MCs the three from Treacherous, it's a blast from the past from the moment we bust"). Though critics and uptight rap purists might fault them for not pushing the

progression angle enough, Jurassic 5's rhymes are so devastating and the productions (by Nu-Mark and Cut Chemist) are so unstoppable that it hardly even matters whether the group is really old-school or not. —*John Bush*

### Juryman (Ian Simmonds)

*Producer / Ambient Breakbeat, Ambient Techno, Trip-Hop, Jungle/Drum'N'Bass*
Juryman is the trip-hop side project of Ian Simmonds, who has released material on Ninja Tune's Ntone offshoot, SSR, and his own ATL imprint. Formerly of pop house group the Sandals (who had a huge hit in the early '90s with "Feet"), Simmonds went solo after problems with the group's label forced them to break up (his label, ATL—All That's Left—is an ironic tribute to that sobering experience). Although his solo releases began appearing around the time of post-Mo'Wax bandwagon-jumping, Simmonds' tracks have a studied complexity that distinguish them from the breakbeat wallpaper of the spliff-soaked downbeat set. He released his first two 12"s, "Juryman 1" and "Juryman 2," on ATL before heading to Ninja Tune's experimental Ntone arm for "Juryman 3." His fourth single (care to guess its title?) appeared on Crammed subsidiary SSR in 1997, and included more full-blown drum'n'bass rhythmic elements. The full-length *Mail Order Justice* followed later that year, recorded with recording partner Luke Gordon (aka Spacer), the in-house engineer at Howie B.'s Pussyfoot studio. Simmonds' second full-length *Last States of Nature* appeared under his own name on Studio !K7. —*Sean Cooper*

- **Mail Order Justice** / Oct. 14, 1997 / SSR ♦♦♦♦
*Mail Order Justice* is an album of close fusion breaks, usually clocking in at a mid-tempo pace but often relieved by a few drum'n'bass breakdowns. It's obvious that Simmonds and Gordon are excellent programmers and old studio hands, following up the beats closely with deep bass licks and atmospheric effects. Simmonds' own understated, half-spoken vocals don't exactly improve tracks like "Prophet & the Fool," but the production more than makes up for any lack of vocal prowess. Guests include Dagmar Krause and, on the title track, rapper Simon Anniky. —*John Bush*

### Justice (Tony Bowes)

b. 1972, Luton, Bedfordshire, England
*Producer / Jungle/Drum'N'Bass, Club/Dance*
One of the more connected jungle producers, and a respected name in the field of Bukem-style polished drum'n'bass, Justice (Tony Bowes) co-owns the Modern Urban Jazz label and records as Icons with Blame. His own productions—as Justice, Justice & Tertius, and Glider State—have appeared on Basement, Creative Wax, Echo Drop, and Recordings of Substance.

Raised in Luton, Justice began producing at the age of 17 with newfound friend Conrad Shafie (aka Blame). The two met while studying media at college in Dunstable, and went into the studio in 1991 to try their hand at producing hip-hop tracks. Instead, they emerged with "Death Row," one of the earliest examples of hardcore breakbeat. While the rave scene progressed into self-parodic fluff, Blame and Justice continued producing, both together and on their own. Pushed into new directions by the early influence of LTJ Bukem's "Music," the duo formed Modern Urban Jazz Records. Justice compiled and mixed a Modern Urban Jazz compilation, and united with Blame as Icons for the stellar 1996 LP *Emotions with Intellect*. His debut album as a solo act, *Viewpoints*, was released in 1998. *Hears to the Future* followed two years later. —*John Bush*

**Justice Presents Modern Urban Jazz, Vol. 1** / Oct. 6, 1997 / Creative Wax ♦♦♦♦
After working as Icons with Blame, Justice compiled a selection of mostly unreleased jungle tracks which, despite the title, doesn't rely on the type of mellow, jazzy drum'n'bass that tends to drag over the course of most mix LPs. With occasional partner DJ Pulse in tow, Justice cycles through tracks by Louis Coltrane, Endemic Void, Seeka, and Krash. —*John Bush*

- **Viewpoints** / Jul. 13, 1998 / Recordings of Substance ♦♦♦♦
Though the lighter, jazzier side of jungle has been Tony Justice's usual haunt, his debut production album includes nods to Detroit techno, electro, and hip-hop as well as the more downtempo side of breakbeat. Despite working through a variety of styles, Justice remains steady on the controls, and since each track bears his unmistakable hand, *Viewpoints* maintains its flow with incredible ease. On an album consisting mostly of highlights, the moody

chords on "Gemini Reprise," and the infectious two-step rhythm slaps on "More Air," and the vacuum-style hip-hop of the criminally short "Intention" make for brilliant listening. —*John Bush*

**Mixed Substances** / Mar. 1, 1999 / Recordings of Substance ♦♦♦
Fans of electronica in general and drum'n'bass in particular will get a huge kick out of this strange little mid-priced gem of an album, assuming that they can find it (it purports to be a "very limited edition"). It consists of tracks taken from various releases on the Recordings of Substance label, mixed live by Justice at a Brixton club called *The Junction* in December 1998, and released here as an uninterrupted dance mix. The tracks vary in mood from James Hardway's jazzy "Illustrated Man" to Magnetic's chilly, computer-based "Bull Roaring" and the darker "Moon Palace" by Icarus. No track on this compilation is less than very good, and it would make an excellent introduction to the state of the art of British drum'n'bass for anyone who's curious. Those who are already hip to the genre will enjoy it just as much. —*Rick Anderson*

# K

## K-Alexi (K-Alexi Shelby)
*Producer, DJ / Club/Dance, Acid House, House*

K-Alexi Shelby recorded for prime Chicago house labels Trax and DJ International, Derrick May's seminal techno label Transmat, and later, European labels ACV and Djax-Up-Beats. He is responsible for several early acid-house classics ("All for Lee-Sah," "Essence of a Dream," "It's Me") and produced one of the rare house full-lengths, *Don't Cha Want It*— He began DJing in the early '80s, and as part of the Risque Rhythm Team (later Risque II and Risque III), Shelby recorded "The Jacking Zone," "Essence of a Dream," and "More than Just a Dance," all 1986-87 classics on the emerging house scene. For Trax, he also produced "Hot Swing" and the album *Trick Tracks* as K. Kool.

After connecting with Detroit's Derrick May (who was a regular in Chicago), K-Alexi recorded "All for Lee-Sah" on May's Transmat Records, and also worked with later Chicago mainstays like Fast Eddie and Mike Dunn. Shelby also released one of the few LPs on DJ International, 1991's *Don't Cha Want It*—, and made the switchover to his growing European fanbase during the early '90s with singles for Djax-Up-Beats, ACV, and others. Though he recorded more rarely during the '90s, K-Alexi released two full-lengths, *Flawless Victory* in 1996 and *Brings You Absolute Power* one year later. —*John Bush*

**Don't Cha Want It**— / 1991 / DJ International ♦♦

**Flawless Victory** / 1996 / ACV ♦♦♦

● **Brings You Absolute Power** / Oct. 27, 1997 / Nepenta ♦♦♦♦

K-Alexi's 1997 LP for Nepenta showed why he's one of the best of the original Chicago DJs and producers still working. Besides knowing how to move a crowd while on the decks, he's also a master at producing tracks of his own, and this tightly crafted album of breakbeat acid house displayed one of the old guard still producing with flair. The drum programs, turntable spinbacks, and crowd-raising samples on "Dance with Me," "Do You Want More?," and "You Get Down" bring back memories of classic Chicago nightspots. K-Alexi gets into afterhours material also, with a few downtempo jazzy tracks ("Effects of My High," "To Love a Spy") as well as breakbeat techno ("Bass & Drum Superbrew"). —*John Bush*

## K-klass
*f. 1988, Wrexham, Wales*
*Group / Progressive House, Club/Dance, House*

One of the more omnipresent remixing teams on the British house scene of the '90s, K-klass emerged in the late '80s, founded by Andy Williams and Carl Thomas after the demise of their previous band Interstate (who had played with 808 State on the early house scene). The Welsh duo added Paul Roberts and Russ Morgan, and began recording with 1990's *Wildlife* EP. Late the following year, K-klass' single "Rhythm Is a Mystery" reached the Top Five and they began their continual residence in the club charts with later singles "Don't Stop," "Let Me Show You," and "What You're Missing," from their debut album, 1993's *Universal*.

By the mid-'90s, K-klass had begun to move away from the original blueprint of British house and towards a more mainstream, song-oriented approach—though one which embraced trance, nu-disco, and even ambient house. K-klass remixes of Whitney Houston, Blondie, Frankie Knuckles, M People, Lulu, Bizarre Inc., and Bobby Brown became sizeable dancefloor hits. The 1996 K-klass LP *Remix and Additional Production* displayed their allegiance to post-production, perhaps to the detriment of their own recording career. —*John Bush*

● **Remix and Additional Production** / Apr. 15, 1996 / Deconstruction ♦♦♦

By 1996, K-klass were much more popular for their remixes (especially in America) than their own productions, so it's fitting that they released *Remix and Additional Production* instead of a production album. Besides straying a bit too far toward the mainstream side of the club charts, it's a fine collection of tracks never previously available in any kind of wide-issue release. —*John Bush*

**K2** / Oct. 12, 1998 / Parlophone ♦♦

## François K (François Kevorkian)
*b. Jan. 10, 1954, Rodez, France*
*Producer, DJ / Club/Dance, Disco, House*

Only Frankie Knuckles can lay claim to straddling a longer span of time in the thick of dance music than François Kevorkian. And though his name is no more than vaguely familiar to many dance fans, Kevorkian's influence is immense. Beginning with his production work for the crucial disco label Prelude during the late '70s and extending through an immense quantity of remixes and productions for legions of pop bands during the following decade, few producers did more to mechanize and refine the disco template into music clearly recognizable as house. After moving from his native France to New York City in the mid-'70s, Kevorkian learned the art of mixing from the era's most influential DJs (Walter Gibbons, Jellybean, Larry Levan). He began producing early reel-to-reel cut-ups, patterned on dub techniques, which pushed bouts of much-needed experimentalism into disco. He then brought the dance treatment to scores of alternative bands and pop stars who needed it during the '80s and '90s. Unfortunately, Kevorkian never spent as much time on his own productions, releasing very few singles though he helmed his own imprint, Wave Records.

Born in Rodez, France, in the mid-'50s, Kevorkian grew up in the suburbs of Paris, playing drums in several bands while studying biochemical engineering and pharmacy in college. After deciding to chuck in his studies, he moved to New York and began playing with any pick-up bands he could find. His first important work in the club-scene came when Kevorkian took a part-time gig at the club Galaxy 21 providing live fill-in drums for the DJ, Walter Gibbons. Though the club later closed, Kevorkian moved on to another named Experiment Four and became friends with its resident, Jellybean Benitez.

Kevorkian soon began producing his own tracks after he learned that Benitez owned a four-track reel-to-reel machine. Hoping to warp tracks for maximum dancefloor consumption, Kevorkian recorded dub-inspired cut-and-paste megamixes with splice and edit techniques, even adding special effects gained from movies and other sources. (One of his first productions, a version of "Happy Song and Dance" by Rare Earth, was a New York club staple for years afterward.) In mid-1977, he started DJing at a club known as New York, New York—the premiere disco spot after Studio 54. While working there, Kevorkian met DJ legend Larry Levan and the two became fast friends. After Kevorkian was tapped for an A&R position at the disco label Prelude, he began working at the label's studios with Levan, creating mixes for the West End and Salsoul imprints as well as Prelude. Kevorkian's mix for Musique's 1978 single "Push Push (In the Bush)" went gold—despite an obvious lack of chart action—and his productions for another Prelude act, D-Train, resulted in additional club hits like "You're the One for Me," "Music," and "Keep On."

A talent for studio mixing and his requisite dancefloor credentials made François Kevorkian one of the most in-demand producers during the '80s. An increased momentum during the decade for general dance music pushed labels to request special nightclub versions of pop songs for the dance crowd, and Kevorkian obliged hundreds of times, for such groups as Yaz, the Smiths,

Depeche Mode, Diana Ross, Adam Ant, U2, Kraftwerk, Matthew Sweet, the Pet Shop Boys, Thomas Dolby, Ashford & Simpson, and Erasure, among many others. In 1987, he founded Axis Studios as well, which provided a home for recording by Madonna, C+C Music Factory, Mariah Carey, and Deee-Lite.

Given his busy studio schedule, it's no wonder Kevorkian neglected his DJing during most of the '80s. He returned to form in 1990, and traveled to Japan with Larry Levan for several high-profile gigs. Kevorkian became a label-owner as well in the '90s; his Wave imprint provided a home for several of his own productions, including 1997's pioneering *FK-EP*. The best document of his DJing skills, *Essential Mix*, appeared in 2000. —*John Bush*

**FK-EP** / 1995 / Wave ♦♦♦

**FK-EP and Beyond** / Apr. 2, 1996 / Wave ♦♦♦♦
An expanded repackaging of the previous year's *FK-EP*, this nine-track collection includes the full four tracks from the seminal original release, plus remixes of each by fellow New York heroes the likes of Danny Tenaglia and Todd Terry, Angel Moraes, and Matthias Heilbronn & Mike Delgado. Kevorkian's prescient originals blend mid-tempo house-era percussion and basslines with sequencer-trance effects and moody synthwork, walking a fine line between house, garage, trance, and down-tempo with elan. It's a sublime sound using production methods that would only grow ubiquitous years later in the progressive trance scene. —*John Bush*

**Hypnodelic [Single]** / Aug. 11, 1997 / Wave ♦♦♦♦
A precious four-track EP among the first Kevorkian productions actually released under his own name, *Hypnodelic* uses house music only as a starting point for Kevorkian's explorations into jazz, funk, and soul plus several ambient grooves. —*John Bush*

● **Essential Mix** / May 2, 2000 / Polygram International ♦♦♦♦
*Essential Mix*, François Kevorkian's two-disc meditation on the New York City dance scene over the preceding quarter-century, is appropriately expansive and all-embracing. The evident pan-global vibes and emphasis on funk and fusion will strike a chord for those who've been exposed to his sets at *Body & Soul*, the seminal NYC nightclub organized by himself, Joe Claussell, and Danny Krivit. As such, we hear tribal-funk tracks from Kyoto Jazz Massive ("Nacer do Sol"), Bob Holroyd ("African Drug"), Jephte Guillaume ("La-Kou-A"), Jazzanova ("Caravelle"), Billy Cobham ("Storm"), and Akwaaba ("Just Pillau"), as well as the funk side of the breakbeat spectrum with James Brown ("There Was a Time"), Tower of Power ("Squib Cakoo"), Earth, Wind & Fire ("In the Stone"), D Train ("Keep On"), and George Benson ("Song for My Brother"). Sprinkled among these are more eclectic dancefloor favorites—left field dance tracks ("Home Computer" by Kraftwerk, "Throw" by Carl Craig's Paperclip People project), two tracks by NYC hip-hop legends (A Tribe Called Quest, De La Soul), and a trio of Chicago house nuggets (Adonis' "No Way Back," Lil Louis' "Jazzmen," Virgo's "Free Yourself"). These aren't necessarily the best dance tracks to make it big in New York between the mid-'70s and the end of the century, but Kevorkian's steady hand and supreme knowledge makes it one of the best dance compendiums ever assembled. —*John Bush*

### Kandis (Jens Massel)
*Producer / Minimal Techno, Experimental Dub, Experimental Electro, Electro-Techno*
Kandis was the project name under which the first two releases on the Cologne-based Karaoke Kalk label appeared. A pseudonym of KK co-owner Jens Massel, Kandis' drowsy ambient electronica is similar to that of the more abstract of Mouse on Mars or the more minimal of Simon "Freeform" Pyke or the Austrian Mego label. Although Kandis is not the only artist associated with Karaoke Kalk, Massel's *Senter* and *Vol Wok* EPs are the most distinctive of the lot, and, though pressed in extremely limited quantities, are more than worth the effort in tracking down. —*Sean Cooper*

**Senter [EP]** / Jul. 28, 1997 / Karaoke Kalk ♦♦♦
Karaoke Kalk's reputation for innovative environmental electronica has been growing steadily since the release of this, its first 12" EP. A three-tracker ranging from the minimal throb of Panasonic to breezy melodic electro with a burp-and-wheeze factor approaching that of Mouse on Mars. —*Sean Cooper*

● **Val Wok [EP]** / Jul. 28, 1997 / Karaoke Kalk ♦♦♦♦
The second release from the Karaoke Kalk label is a five-track slab of acceptably ponderous electronica in the vein of Cologne-based artists such as FX Randomiz, Markus Schmickler, and 8m2 Stereo. Also vaguely similar to some of Mouse On Mars' rhythmic abstractions circa *Iaora Tahiti* (though minus the excessive sampling), *Val Wok* is an exceptional collection of tracks clearly inspired by dance music structures without coming anywhere near the dancefloor. Recommended particularly to fans of minimal beat-abusers such as Freeform and Farmers Manual. —*Sean Cooper*

### Ray Keith
b. Aug. 19, 1967, Colchester, England
*Producer, DJ / Jungle/Drum'N'Bass, Club/Dance*
From rare-groove to acid house to hardcore to jungle, Ray Keith remained one of the most steady DJs on England's breakbeat scene during the '80s and '90s. After a remix of Orbital's "Chime," he moved into production with apparent ease and became a respected drum'n'bass label-head as well. Born in Colchester, Keith began DJing by the early '80s and followed English beatfreaks through soul, hip-hop, and rare-groove until the acid-house and hardcore explosion of the late '80s and early '90s. By the middle of the '90s, he had become one of the most inspired drum'n'bass DJs and remixers. His own productions, including the jump-up anthem "Terrorist," began taking center stage by the mid-'90s and Keith formed three separate labels—Penny Black, Dread, and UFO—in 1996. He has worked in close association with Gavin Cheung (aka Nookie) and also works at one of the premiere dance shops in Britain, Black Market Records. Keith released the Penny Black collection *Breakage, Vol. 1* in 1997, followed by a solo debut of sorts, 1999's *UFO Presents Contact*. —*John Bush*

● **Penny Black Presents Breakage, Vol. 1** / Aug. 1997 / Penny Black ♦♦♦♦
Presenting the best from Ray Keith's Penny Black records, *Breakage* is a barrage of terrifying techstep from one of the form's true originators including tracks from several Keith aliases like Twisted Anger as well as selections from his engineer partner, Nookie. —*John Bush*

**Contact** / Feb. 15, 1999 / UFO ♦♦♦
The double-disc set *Contact* presents the first fruits of Keith's UFO Records label, home to his more experimental (read: album-oriented) productions. Fortunately, the left-field productions don't suffer on the dancefloor at all, with hardcore dark-menace productions "There's Something Out There" and "Da Funk Fang" alongside old-school burners like "Class of 89" and "303 Mayhem." —*John Bush*

### DJ John Kelley
b. Japan
*DJ / Progressive Trance, Funky Breaks, Electronica, Rave, Club/Dance*
An acid-funk DJ who helped push the popular West Coast sound of breakbeat trance by rinsing it all over the nation, DJ John Kelley is best known for his sets at *Full Moon Gatherings*. The influential series of raves held in the deserts outside Los Angeles during the mid-'90s created an emergent sound, led by breakout producers like Crystal Method, Überzone, Bassbin Twins, and Electric Skychurch. Born on a US Air Force base in Japan, Kelley grew up in Southern California and began going to raves outside the city during the mid-'90s. He also became interested in the turntable arts, and after *Full Moon Gatherings* promoter/spinner DJ Daniel heard one of Kelley's mixtapes, he began playing at the raves as well. In 1996, Kelley released a mix album—explicitly patterned after his rave sets—with the descriptive title *Funkydesertbreaks*. The compilation became an underground hit, sparked an American tour where Kelley spotlighted the style, and prompted a sequel one year later. In 1998, he released *Knee Deep*, a mix album more aligned with global trends in trance and techno. The 1999 collection *Highdesertsoundsystem* was a slight return to the *Funkydesertbreaks* sound; a second volume appeared a year later. —*John Bush*

● **Funkydesertbreaks** / Aug. 6, 1996 / Moonshine Music ♦♦♦♦
An album of typically American funky breakbeats and psychedelic trance from the cream of the crop, including Uberzone, the Crystal Method, Electric Skychurch, Omar Santana, and Psychedelic Research Lab. John Kelley's mixing is more than proficient, but the generally unexciting flavor and lack of subtlety in the material drags the compilation down a bit. —*Keith Farley*

**Funkydesertbreaks, Vol. 2** / Jun. 24, 1997 / Moonshine Music ♦♦♦

**Highdesertsoundsystem** / Jul. 27, 1999 / Moonshine Music ♦♦♦♦
Several years after his breakthrough with the *Funkydesertbreaks* series, John

Kelley returns to his roots in tribal-house and funky techno with spotlight tracks from Jan Driver ("Drive By"), Mac Zimms ("Silicon Valley"), DJ Dan ("That Zipper Track"), and Dave Randall ("Bombay"). —*Keith Farley*

**Highdesertsoundsystem, Vol. 2** / Jun. 27, 2000 / Moonshine ♦♦♦♦
With the second volume in his *Highdesertsoundsystem* series, John Kelley moves away from the breaks sound of his *Funkydesertbreaks* albums and the hard house sound of his first volume in this series in favor of a more trance-influenced sound, instantly evident just by the track selection. Tracks such as Trancesetters' "Roaches," Killahurtz's "West on 27th," and two Timo Maas productions—"Riding on a Storm" and "Eclipse"—aren't exactly underground tracks, having appeared on more than a few mixes. Sure, these are great tracks. No one can blame Kelley for having bad taste, but these aforementioned tracks, in particular, make him seem like a generic *Global Underground*-wannabe DJ; thankfully though, Kelley compensates by including tracks by Joel Mull ("Mole"), G Flame ("How Knows"), and Ben Simms ("Work It") that bring a more raw, non-accessible edge to his mix. This refreshing blend of powerful Hooj Choon-orientated trance stompers and harder material by big name techno producers makes an interesting mix that rarely occurs. Furthermore, the way Kelley mixes from the trance into the techno and back showcases his courage and skill as a DJ. Yet even though this is a rather impressive mix, one cannot help but wonder about his inconsistencies as a DJ. He began with a hard acid breaks-style mix (*Funkydesertbreaks*) then moved on to a hard, almost-tribal house sound (*Highdesertsoundsystem*), and now he embraces the trance that has always been foreshadowed in his mixes and hard techno, a truly rare combination. Perhaps this inconsistency can be seen as evolution or a daring edge of experimentation rather than an attempt to latch onto trends; either way, it results in a good mix, which, in the end, is all that really matters. —*Jason Birchmeier*

## Khan (Can Oral)

**b.** Jun. 7, 1965
*Producer / Experimental Techno, Electro-Techno, IDM*
An original Structure label-group artist with dozens of releases on Cologne-based imprints such as DJ Ungle Fever, XXC3, Eat Raw, and Pharma, NYC-based experimental electro producer Can Oral is the man behind an array of pseudonyms. Recording most often as 4E and Khan, Oral's discography is also littered with such monikers as Bizz O.D., Gizz T.V., El Turco Loco, and Fuzz DJ. One of only a handful of European producers to move to the US in order to jumpstart the dozing underground, Oral includes NY's Temple Records (the store he opened under Manhattan's Liquid Sky Clothing), as well as record labels Temple and Liquid Sky among his ongoing commitments. The brother of Air Liquide's Cem Oral, Can was (along with artists such as Mike Ink, J. Burger, and Biochip C's Martin Damm) an active contributor to early Structure labels such as Blue and DJ Ungle Fever, the center of the German acid/techno explosion during the '90s heyday of experimental acid and techno. Can began recording as 4E after moving to New York (the name was the address of his first flat, which doubled as his studio), and has since released a number of EPs and full-lengths as both 4E and Khan, most notably on Force Inc./Mille Plateaux and his own fast-expanding Liquid Sky, Home Entertainment, and Temple labels. Stylistically, Oral treads closest to experimental hip-hop and electro, fusing gritty 303 chirps and smooth electronic atmospheres with kicking, mid-tempo breaks constructed from familiar drum sounds and patterns. His 1996 debut for Liquid Sky sister label Home Entertainment, *Blue Note*, is ambient electro in the vein of B12, Jonah Sharp, and Autechre/Gescom, with none of the more caustic resonances that defined his earlier, more dancefloor-friendly work in evidence. Oral also operated and played at the weekly club, Killer, and worked on material with noted experimental/ambient composer Tetsu Inoue. Released in 1997, *Silent Movie, Silver Screen* was his first album for noted New York label Caipirinha. Two years later though, he signed a contract with the indie-rock imprint Matador and released *1-900-Get-Khan*. *Passport* followed in early 2000. [See Also: 4E] —*Sean Cooper*

**Blue Note** / Jun. 4, 1996 / Home Entertainment ♦♦♦♦
Khan-man Can Oral's debut for his second stateside label venture, Home Entertainment, is smooth, mid- to downtempo ambient electro with an instrumental hip-hop feel. While the rhythmic patterns generally stay on the safe side of conservative, Oral's knack for mood and shifting harmonic passages make for an extremely listenable full-length release. —*Sean Cooper*

**Silent Movie, Silver Screen** / Oct. 7, 1997 / Caipirinha ♦♦♦
Khan's first explicitly soundtrack-oriented venture was this 1997 album for Caipirinha, dedicated to a range of obtuse films and people including *The Cabinet of Dr. Caligari*, Leni Riefenstahl, Baron Munchausen, Carmen Miranda, and Kenneth Anger. The music is prime distorted electro-techno as few other than Khan do it. —*Keith Farley*

**1-900-Get-Khan** / May 4, 1999 / Matador ♦♦♦♦
*1-900-Get-Khan* is more than just a collection of songs charting the harsher side of downtempo breakbeat and minimalist techno. Similar to David Holmes' *Let's Get Killed*, Khan's first album for the American super-indie Matador is the soundtrack to a European's attraction for the seamier side of New York. While the cover is set up with ads for a personal section, the title itself is also a functioning 1-900 number, available for $2.99 per minute. The songs inside are well-produced, though a few too many imply the illicitness with simple add-ons like a descending bassline or vibraphone twinkles. Still, "Jet Lounge Blues," "Nowhere," and "Body Dump" showcase the effect of Khan's thematic scope—the latter track even features Julee Cruise intoning lines like "carpet fibers don't lie." An extension of his 1997 recording *Silent Movie, Silver Screen*, *1-900-Get-Khan* is an excellent invisible soundtrack. —*John Bush*

● **Passport** / Jan. 25, 2000 / Matador ♦♦♦♦
An excellent package for the American market, *Passport* catches vinyl tracks and unreleased material (circa 1993 through 1998) from no less than nine of Can Oral's varied aliases, many including long-time cohorts like brother Cem Oral and Ingmar Koch (aka Dr. Walker). Though compilations that collect material from a variety of sources (or pseudonyms) often sound a bit disjointed, each of the beefy electro-techno tracks on *Passport* work well together. Fittingly, there are more tracks from the popular 4E and Khan than from any other alias, though two of the best tracks ("G.E.N.A.T.T.A.C.K.Z.," "Time Square-No Time") come from the Khan & Walker alias Global Electronic Network. —*John Bush*

## Praga Khan (Maurice Engelen)

*Producer / Rave, Club/Dance, Acid House*
Belgian studio wizard Praga Khan produced several of the rave world's biggest hits, under his own name as well as in conjunction with band projects (Lords of Acid, Digital Orgasm, Channel X) masterminded by the MNO production team composed of Khan, producer Oliver Adams, and vocalist Jade 4U. Born Maurice Engelen, Khan worked as a DJ in Belgium's growing acid/trance/newbeat scene of the late '80s and held court at Brussels' seminal Happy House club. He began recording as well in 1988 with a project named Shakti, a fusion of house and Indian music featuring the vocals of Nikkie Van Lierop (aka Jade 4U). The pair recorded two dozen singles from 1988 to 1991, under aliases including Praga Khan, Lords of Acid, Jade 4U, Major Problem, and Dirty Harry.

After meeting producer Oliver Adams in 1991, Khan and Jade 4U formed a production collective known as MNO—short for Maurice/Nikki/Oliver—and recorded a series of Brit-pop hits that year. Aimed between the uplifting spirit of house music and the growing darkside of rave and trance excess, the singles "Running Out of Time" and "Startouchers" (as Digital Orgasm), "Groove to Move" (as Channel X), and "Injected with a Poison" and "Rave Alert" (as Praga Khan Featuring Jade 4U) all made the British charts during 1991-92. Despite its controversial drug connotations, "Injected with a Poison" reached the number 16 spot (and hit number one in Japan). The trio's Lords of Acid project began conquering dancefloors as well, with the 1991 single "Take Control" and the *Lust* LP one year later.

While Lords of Acid gradually turned into an industrial dance group (with plenty of guitars and cartoonish sexual songwriting), the MNO team continued to diversify, beginning in 1992 with a major-label US album contract for Lords of Acid and Digital Orgasm (DO)—both courtesy of Rick Rubin's American Recordings. While the resulting LPs (*DO It* and Lords of Acid's *Voodoo-U*) weren't quite the commercial juggernaut Rubin hoped for, both increased the visibility of Belgian trance (and European dance music as a whole) in America, especially with alternative and college-radio audiences. Lords of Acid even undertook a stateside tour and attempted to cross over with the popular industrial crowds. The Japanese label Avex contracted Channel X to release an album; the title track of 1994's *Take It to the Top* became their second number one single in Japan.

During a small lull in the recordings of the several MNO-based acts, Khan released a full-length, *Conquers Your Love,* under his own name. He also scored music for several feature films, including *Basic Instinct, Sliver, Strange Days,* and *Virtuosity.* He also did remix work for Alice in Chains, White Zombie, and Jean-Michel Jarre. Lords of Acid returned in 1997 with *Our Little Secret,* and Khan released his second "solo" album *Pragamatic* in 1998. Additional solo albums appeared in 1999 (*Twentyfirstcenturyskin*) and 2000 (*Mutant Funk*). —*John Bush*

**Conquers Your Love** / Oct. 29, 1996 / Never ♦♦

● **Pragamatic** / Jun. 2, 1998 / Antler-Subway ♦♦♦
Praga Khan's second album of pounding high-energy Euro-trance is also reminiscent of more recent developments in German industrial dance and electronic body music (which he undoubtedly influenced himself). Along with a reworking of Khan's rave classic "Injected with a Poison," *Pragamatic* includes a few solid vocal tracks—"Luv U Still," "Remove the Armour," and "I Want You." —*Keith Farley*

## Kid Koala (Eric San)

b. 1975, Vancouver, British Columbia, Canada
*Producer, DJ / Turntablism, Underground Rap, Electronica, Club/Dance, Hip-Hop*

Chinese-Canadian turntablist Kid Koala was born Eric San in Vancouver, British Columbia in 1975. Classically trained on the piano, San instead put his fingers to work on a pair of Technics 1200s starting in the late '80s. He was a college pub DJ and bedroom turntable manipulator for nearly a decade before landing a recording deal with UK experimental hip-hop duo Coldcut's Ninja Tune imprint in 1997. San's eclectic approach to sound collage is actually closer to the latter's far-flung beat experiments than the old-school New York and L.A. references which most often form the canon of the scratch DJ's art. It's also a circle-closer of sorts: San's nascent mixing aesthetic was influenced early on by classic Coldcut records such as "(Hey Kids) What Time Is It?" and their "7 Minutes of Madness" massacre of Eric B. & Rakim's "Paid in Full." In fact, the coincidence of Koala signing to his heroes' label (despite the fact that it's based thousands of miles away and home mostly to instrumental trip-hop and computer-funk producers) was less a coincidence than it would at first appear; San managed to arrange an "inadvertent" car ride with the group when their label's Stealth tour passed through Montreal in 1996, making sure his mix tape, "Scratchappyland," was in the car stereo well beforehand. Excerpts from that tape doubled as Kid Koala's identically titled solo debut when Ninja Tune, duly impressed, released it as a 10" in July of 1997. Koala also appeared on the second volume of the Bomb's *Return of the DJ* compilation, his track "Static's Waltz" another excerpt from his mix tape. Subsequent Ninja Tune releases included Kid Koala remixes of DJ Food's "Scratch Yer Head" and (fittingly) Coldcut's classic "Beats and Pieces," plus the 2000 full-length *Carpal Tunnel Syndrome.* —*Sean Cooper*

● **Scratchappyland [Single]** / 1997 / Ninja Tune ♦♦♦♦
Eric "Kid Koala" San's Ninja Tune debut was an identically named segment from his "Scratchappyland" mixtape. Located somewhere between the goofier moments of turntable groups such as the Invisible Skratch Piklz and the Beat Junkies and the schizophrenic sound collage of Coldcut and Steinski, the record is littered with obscure references culled from children's records and dust-caked dime-store novelties. Extremely rare but worth tracking down. —*Sean Cooper*

**Carpal Tunnel Syndrome** / Feb. 22, 2000 / Ninja Tune ♦♦♦
*Carpal Tunnel Syndrome* is Kid Koala's first commercially available album. He put out the now legendary mix tape *Scratchcratchratchatch,* which once he signed to Ninja Tune was trimmed down and turned into *Scratchappyland,* a promo record that Ninja Tune sent out to publicize their new DJ prodigy. *Carpal Tunnel Syndrome* uses hundreds of sounds; Kid Koala samples anything from the movie *Revenge of the Nerds* to Winnie the Pooh. Although this album could have been longer (it's only 37 minutes), it still has many songs that are worth hearing, such as "Music for Morning People," "Barhopper 2," and "Roboshuffle." —*Dan Gizzi*

## Kid Loco (Jean-Yves Prieur)

*Producer / Ambient Pop, Alternative Dance, Trip-Hop, Club/Dance*

An easy-listening trip-hopster similar in style and intent to his countrymen Air and Dimitri from Paris, Kid Loco has an even stronger following in the long tradition of French pop characterized by Serge Gainsbourg. Otherwise known as Jean-Yves Prieur, he began playing the guitar at the age of 13 and played in several French punk groups during the early '80s. He moved on to production as well by the end of the decade, and moved on to reggae and hip-hop with a band named Mega Reefer Scratch. By 1996, Prieur had built his own studio, christened himself Kid Loco, and released the *Blues Project EP* for Yellow Productions. The full-length *A Grand Love Story* appeared one year later, earning praise from many in the indie-rock and electronica community. A remix album was released in 1998. Prieur also accompanied St. Etienne's Sarah Cracknell for a rendition of "The Man I Love" from the Gershwin tribute *Red Hot + Rhapsody,* and has remixed Stereolab, Pulp, Mogwai, the High Llamas, Dimitri from Paris, and Talvin Singh. The reconfigured *Prelude to a Grand Love Story* appeared in 1999 as Loco's US full-length debut, and the remix album *Jesus Life for Children Under 12 Inches* followed later that same year. —*John Bush*

● **A Grand Love Story** / Nov. 25, 1997 / Yellow Productions ♦♦♦♦
*A Grand Love Story* is an irresistible romp through the light-hearted, pastoral side of trip-hop by way of orchestral-pop paragons like Bacharach, Gainsbourg, and Love. Songs like the single "Relaxin' with Cherry" and "She's My Lover" are beautiful pop songs, constructed mostly from sampled material with a few live guitar and basslines plus vocals by Prieur and the Pastels' Katrina Mitchell. If the '70s fixations of Air were shifted back a decade, the results would be quite close to *A Grand Love Story.* —*John Bush*

**Prelude to a Grand Love Story** / Jun. 15, 1999 / Atlantic ♦♦♦
France's Kid Loco presents a special stateside release, 1999's *Prelude to a Grand Love Story,* which reconfigures songs from his first album, *A Grand Love Story.* Loco's multifaceted electronic music embraces everything from abstract techno to trip-hop, giving it a romantic spin. *Prelude* features the single "She's My Lover" in its original version, as well as remixes by Tommy Hools and St. Etienne, and includes mixes of "Love Me Sweet" by Jim O'Rourke and "Relaxin' with Cherry" by Dimitri from Paris. —*Heather Phares*

**Jesus Life for Children Under 12 Inches** / Sep. 21, 1999 / WEA International ♦♦♦♦
An excellent set compiling Kid Loco's outside productions for like minds (Saint Etienne, Pulp, High Llamas) and less so (Pastels, Talvin Singh, Mogwai, Kat Onoma), the *Jesus Life for Children Under 12 Inches* remix album presents Loco-ized versions some justifiably excellent tracks, made even more solid by the producer's knack for balancing old and new influences, and retaining the spirit of the original even while he pulls out his production bag of tricks. (The American version trades the Saint Etienne and High Llamas remixes for ones by Gak Sato and Badmarsh + Shri.) —*Keith Farley*

**DJ Kicks** / Oct. 19, 1999 / Studio !K7 ♦♦
In the late '90s, it may be seen as obsolete to try and release a compilation that is neither 1) trance nor 2) trance. Yes, while the popular dance world was spinning on its own narrow axis, there were still musicians like Kid Loco bucking the trends and releasing chill-out albums like this: his own clandestinely mischievous installment in the *DJ Kicks* series. The problem is that despite such a non-conformist stance, there's something wrong in its unpleasant mesh of moods. This means that while including songs such as the easy-breathing trip-hop of Jazzanova's "Introspection" or the cycling mantra of Underworld's "Blueski" make for an interesting mix, the fact that they are so close next to so many songs centered around childish jabs (a pornosampling track by Common Ground, the cartoon-squealing track by Tom Tyler, etc.), the tones tend to cancel each other out. Loco seems lost in deciding whether to make a straight-forward, jazz-centric, chill-out album or a slightly nutty experiment. If he went confidently into one direction, the results would have been much better. Because, again, for every magnetic track like Boards of Canada's "Happy Cycling," there is a silly track like a remix of Deep Season's "Jesus Christ Almighty" right next door. In other words, right when the mood is being set, the listener is covertly being taken into another. Which isn't such a bad plan. It's just poorly done since these exact shifts seem sadly slipshod instead of effective. This methodology of going for the chill-out and simultaneously trying to tickle your ribs just grates after awhile. So in the end, Loco's mixing skill and urge to fiddle with chill-out templates are laudable. However, the entire compilation still feels defective, and an opening sample probably best explains the reason why: a man asks, "Don't you know I'm loco?" While the answer might be, "yes," it might also be, "not loco enough." —*Dean Carlson*

## Kid Loops (Jamie Lexton)

*Producer / Jungle/Drum'N'Bass, Club/Dance*

Combining his love for science fiction, old-school hip-hop, and the lush side of Detroit techno and jazz fusion, Jamie Lexton's productions as Kid Loops skirt the edge where raw breakbeat chemistry becomes bland coffee-table fare (a place once inhabited by several fusion legends as well). A native of North London, Lexton listened to Public Enemy, Stetsasonic, and Mantronix as a child, and began working in the studio with help from his brother Charlie, who co-owns the Filter label and records as Cool Breeze. His studio prowess and wide-eyed youth gained him the name Kid Loops, and he recorded his first single "Alien Resident" for Filter in 1995. Lexton again worked with his brother on *Kid Loops Vs. Cool Breeze*, an LP released as Special Projects in late 1996. Singles followed for All Good Vinyl and Filter once again, before Lexton's proper debut album, *Time Quake*, was released in mid-1997. —*John Bush*

**Kid Loops Vs. Cool Breeze [Single]** / Nov. 25, 1996 / Filter ♦♦

● **Time Quake** / Jul. 1997 / Ultra ♦♦♦
Jamie Lexton's debut album as Kid Loops walks that uncomfortable line between intelligent drum'n'bass and coffee-table fare that sounds pleasant enough to passing listeners but doesn't really push the envelope. Besides the vocoderized vocals on his Eric B. & Rakim homage "The Microphone Fiend" and some tweaked scratching on "Wicked Loops," *Time Quake* is an album of fits and starts, solid but lacking real innovation. —*John Bush*

## Kid 606 (Michael Trost Depedro)

b. Jul. 27, 1979, Caracas, Venezuela

*Producer / Experimental Techno, Post-Rock/Experimental, Hardcore Techno, IDM*

Inspired by hardcore techno, indie-punk, noise-rock, and a liberal dose of heavy metal, the recordings of Kid 606 are a highlight of the growing American indie-electronica scene. His lack of seriousness regarding "intelligent techno" (conspicuous in his attitude as well as his recordings) and fondness for breakbeat thrash places him in line with Digital Hardcore advocates Atari Teenage Riot and electronics deconstructivists such as Add N (To X). A native of Venezuela, the Kid moved to San Diego early in life. After becoming interested in samplers, he began recording and released some material with Spacewurm and Ariel, two acts associated with the Southern California label Vinyl Communications. After the demise of both, Kid 606 debuted on his own with a full-length for VC, 1998's *Don't Sweat the Technics*. A split-compact-disc with Lesser gained release later that year, as well as the VC EPs *Unamerican Activity* and *Dubplatestyle*. In mid-2000, Kid 606 released *Down with the Scene*, his first album for the experimental Ipecac label associated with Faith No More's Mike Patton. He also works in the side-project DISC with Lesser and Matmos. *P.S. I Love You* was also released in mid-2000.—*John Bush*

**Don't Sweat the Technics** / May 26, 1998 / Vinyl Communications ♦♦
Long on ideas but just a bit short on coherence or development, the Kid's proper album debut cycles through sample- and static-heavy hardcore gabba/techno. Though humor is a big part of *Don't Sweat the Technics* (check the interlude "She's Defective"), Kid 606 is a much better producer than he'd like you to believe, from the stomping percussive title track to inclusions like "Silver Egg" and "You Mean This Much Right Now." —*John Bush*

**Unamerican Activity [EP]** / Aug. 11, 1998 / Vinyl Communications ♦♦
He had released two practically LP-length works in less than a year (including the LSR/Kid 606 split) before *Unamerican Activities* came out, but this style of drum'n'bass industrial thrash must be quite easy to produce. As examples of the style go, it's just as good (or bad) as any of his others. —*John Bush*

● **Down with the Scene** / Jun. 20, 2000 / Ipecac Recordings ♦♦♦
Fortunately, Kid 606's first album for the (comparatively) high-profile Ipecac Recordings proves just as uncompromising, schizophrenic, and hilarious as his previous recordings, ridden with blasts of skull-cracking static, breakbeat noise, and tortured found-sound vocal samples—all digitally processed to within an inch of their lives. From the R&B-goes-hardcore "Secrets 4 Sale" (with vocals by label associate Mike Patton) to song titles like the IDM-baiting "Luke Vibert Can Kiss My Indie-Punk Whiteboy Ass," "It'll Take Millions in Plastic Surgery to Make Me Black," "GQ on the EQ," "Two Fingers in the Air Anarchy Style," and "My Kitten," Kid 606 injects a much-needed sense of humor into the experimental/hardcore scene. That may not be enough to warrant any more than two or three listens, but there's at least a 50-50 balance between senseless distortion and well-programmed tracks with a semblance of a groove. —*John Bush*

**P.S. I Love You** / Oct. 17, 2000 / Mille Plateaux ♦♦♦
*P.S. I Love You* moves far away from the manic break beats and blatant noise barrages of Kid 606's *Down with the Scene*, instead embracing the clicks + cuts sound of Mille Plateaux circa 2000. It's a refreshing change. Though there's little denying the fact that *Down with the Scene's* no-holds-barred attitude towards abrasive sound assembly wowed masses of people, it now sounds quite juvenile when held up against the elegant, mannered sounds of *P.S. I Love You*. As mentioned, the maelstrom breakbeat avalanches of Kid 606's previous work are notably absent here, as is his blatant punk attitude. Without these rude sounds, the music relies on lush ambient waves of sound, characterized primarily by their twitching textures and their subtle glitches. The question does arise as to exactly how derived this music is, especially given the sudden surge in this glitch/clicks + cuts sound's popularity in addition to Kid 606's notorious image as a sly figure. Yet even if Kid 606 is merely raping earnest artists such as Vladislav Delay and Sutekh of their textures—a highly suggestive assumption—one cannot deny the appeal of his album; like other artists such as Moby, sometimes it is best to separate the artist from his work in order to best appreciate the music as just music. On Kid 606's past albums, stripping away his persona also meant stripping away much of the music's appeal, while here the opposite is true—no audience baiting, just amazing music. —*Jason Birchmeier*

## Kid Spatula (Michael Paradinas)

*Producer / Experimental Techno, Ambient Techno, Techno, IDM*

The Mike Paradinas alias Kid Spatula debuted in 1995 with *Spatula Freak*, his first album for an American label, Kim Cascone's Reflective. Five years later, Paradinas returned to the pseudonym for *Full Sunken Breaks* on his own Planet µ label. [See Also: Jake Slazenger, µ-Ziq] —*John Bush*

● **Spatula Freak** / Nov. 7, 1995 / Reflective ♦♦♦♦
Pushing the envelope of the electronic music genre, Michael Paradinas stalks adventurous sounds and unusual musical directions. Another alias for the man known also known as µ-Ziq, Kid Spatula follows the blueprint of his *In Pine Effect* album, mixing distinctive drum tracks (in beat and timbre) with orchestral synth, odd piano tinkling, and a wide array of ambient samples. Not as musically dense as *In Pine Effect*, these arrangements are more sparse, but no less fertile. "Trunk" is an emotive piece driven by big bass thuds overlaid with a repitive synth figure and embellished with xylophone, horn, and cello; "Chisholm" follows a light piano riff until ambushed by complex, cymbal-heavy percussion for a crackling, crunchy rhythm; while the in-your-face factory-inflected "Metal Thing 1" has more corners and sharp edges than a cubist painting. Paradinas' rich and intricate work continues to represent him as not only a prolific talent, but a prodigious one. —*Chris Parker*

**Full Sunken Breaks** / 2000 / Planet µ ♦♦♦
More than four years after the first Kid Spatula album, Mike Paradinas revisited the alias with *Full Sunken Breaks*, a treasure chest of what sounds like outtakes from the 1999 µ-Ziq LP *Royal Astronomy*, plus a few tracks that didn't quite suit the flavor of his other full-lengths. Perhaps it's just overappreciation of the quality of material Paradinas relegates to his indie-label side projects, but several tracks here sound much better than those included on µ-Ziq LPs. For the most part, they're a world away from the brittle, metallic experimentation of 1995's *Spatula Freak* and much closer to the processed breakbeat freakery of µ-Ziq material ever since 1997's *Urmur Bile Trax*. Definitely more than just a collection of throwaway tracks designed for collectors only, *Full Sunken Breaks* hits almost as many highs as Paradinas' µ-Ziq full-lengths. —*John Bush*

## Kinesthesia (Chris Jeffs)

*Producer / Experimental Techno, Ambient Techno, IDM*

Another product of Richard "Aphex Twin" James' Rephlex stable, Chris Jeffs' releases as Cylob and Kinesthesia have numbered among the Cornwall-based imprint's most celebrated recent releases. Not nearly as prolific as his friends and sometime-labelmates James and Mike Paradinas (µ-Ziq), Jeffs has nonetheless amassed an impressive catalog of releases in a relatively short period of time. Although he only began experimenting with electronics in

1991, within five years Jeffs released three EPs and three full-lengths—including the cheeky DJ double-pack *Loops and Breaks* (as Cylob) and the sparse ambient of *Empathy Box* (as Kinesthesia)—in addition to remixes for Aphex Twin, Bochum Welt, and Immersion. Although focusing more recently on a refined brand of ambient breakbeat and techno, Jeffs' stylistic palette includes crunchy, industrial-leaning techno, beatless ambient, and new-school electro-funk. [See Also: Cylob] —*Sean Cooper*

**Kinesthesia, Vol. 1 [EP]** / Oct. 1993 / Rephlex ♦♦♦

**Kinesthesia, Vol. 2 [EP]** / Jan. 1994 / Rephlex ♦♦

● **Empathy Box** / Aug. 1994 / Rephlex ♦♦♦♦
Released as a bare white vinyl LP and similarly styled CD at the height of electronica's Return to the Beat, Jeffs' third Kinesthesia volume is a defiantly spare, (mostly) beatless affair, with dark textures and spare, elongated melodies taking Jeffs' normally quite oppositional style in new directions. A bit more work getting into but ultimately worth it. —*Sean Cooper*

## King Britt & Sylk 130
f. Philadelphia, PA
*Producer, DJ / Jazz-House, Electronica, Club/Dance, House*

Growing up in southwest Philadelphia, house DJ/producer King Britt was raised in a household filled with music, from James Brown to Duke Ellington. He began buying records at the age of seven, and gradually amassed a collection of over 10,000 singles. Britt saw the beginnings of the local rap scene evolve with Schooly D., Three Times Dope, Steady B., DJ Cash Money, and DJ Jazzy Jeff & the Fresh Prince. His tastes also expanded to include Depeche Mode, Roxy Music, Kraftwerk, Front 242, and the Smiths. While attending Temple University, he began producing his own tracks and also met Ishmael Butler (aka Butterfly), who introduced Britt to his jazz-rap group Digable Planets. Acquiring the nickname Silkworm, he toured with the group for more than two years. Through a mutual friend, he also met Josh Wink, and the duo soon began tooling around in their respective bedroom/MIDI recording studios. The result was a worldwide dance hit, 1993's "Tribal Confusion" by E-Culture. Britt and Wink formed their own label, Ovum Recordings, and worked on production as well as remixing, for artists including Tori Amos, Donna Lewis, Solsonics, and Mary Wilson.

King Britt first hatched the idea for a solo album while touring with Digable Planets. A soundtrack fan without the money to make a feature film, he decided to record the music for a fake movie, enlisting hometown talent—dubbed the Sylk 130 collective—including legendary bassist Jamaaladeen Tacuma, drummer Darryl Burgee, keyboardist James Poiser, vocalist Alison Crockette, poet Ursula Rucker, rapper Tony "Capital A" Green, and guitarist Monnette Sudler. *When the Funk Hits the Fan* was released on Ovum/Sony in 1998, and followed by *The Remixes* one year later. —*Ed Hogan*

● **When the Funk Hits the Fan** / Jan. 27, 1998 / Sony ♦♦♦♦
DJ King Britt and his Sylk 130 collective debut with the impressive *When the Funk Hits the Fan*, a seamlessly retro concept album exploring a day in the life of a teenage DJ spinning records circa 1977. A celebration of the soul, funk, and jazz which inspired Britt himself, the album is a pastiche of songs and skits, perfectly evoking the spirit of the late '70s while firmly entrenched in contemporary sounds as well; it's this same timeless quality which makes cuts like "Last Night a DJ Saved My Life," "Gettin' into It," and "The Reason" so effective. —*Jason Ankeny*

**When the Funk Hits the Fan: The Remixes [EP]** / Mar. 30, 1999 / Sony ♦♦
These remixes cover material from the brief history of this eclectic dance outfit led by King Britt. Laying out equal parts soul, funk, hip-hop, and disco, the disc is a phat little party in one slim package. —*Tim Sheridan*

## King Tubby (Osbourne Ruddock)
b. 1941, Kingston, Jamaica, d. Feb. 1989, St. Andrews, Jamaica
*Producer / Dub*

Dub music had to come from somewhere, and the consensus is that it came from the mind and four-track mixing board of Osbourne Ruddock, known far and wide as King Tubby. Born in Kingston, Jamaica in 1941, Tubby began his career in the mid-'50s repairing radios and DJ sound systems. Near the end of the decade, Tubby went to work cutting and mixing records for Jamaican impresario and Treasure Isle label honcho Duke Reid, recording hit singles by popular singers such as the Melodians and Phyllis Dillon. It was while working with Reid that Tubby began what seemed to be a deceptively simple bit of experimentation: he would remix songs starting by dropping the vocal track, boosting parts of the instrumental track (e.g., suddenly there would be nothing but bass or rhythm guitar), and add subtle effects like echo or delay to the instruments he had isolated. The immediate impact of this process of dub mixes was that songs became hits twice. Tubby was remixing recognizable tracks like the Melodians' "You Don't Care," and played for the crowds who gathered to dance to the mobile sound systems, the effect was mesmerizing. Reggae historian Steve Barrow, writing about the crowd reaction to Tubby's first public airing of his dub mixes, notes "the crowd did a quick double take and then went wild, pushing down the fence until it was flattened and then rushed in, knocking the speaker boxes flying." Tubby had clearly stumbled on to something very powerful with dub.

Soon Tubby, relying on extremely primitive four-track recording and mixing equipment, was the mixer in demand for most of Jamaica's big-name producers such as Reid, Vivian Jackson (aka Yabby You), and Winston "Niney" Holness. However, his most prodigious period of creativity was during the mid-'70s, when Tubby worked with Bunny Lee. Lee relied on Tubby's brilliance for mixing dub tracks of Lee's studio band the Aggrovators. Virtually every record released on Lee's labels (Jackpot, Justice, and Attack) featured a dub mix done by or supervised by Tubby (the mixers he supervised were none other than Prince Jammy and Philip Smart, aka "Prince" Philip). This prolific output and the success of many of the records had cemented Tubby's reputation as the King of Dub. Tubby eventually opened his own studio and continued to engineer and produce records for Lee, and was also a crucial part of a series of roots-heavy releases on Carlton Patterson's Black and White label.

By the start of the '80s, Tubby was on top of his game, running his studio, training a new generation of mixers, picking and choosing artists he wanted to work with, and in general becoming comfortable with being a reggae icon. This ended abruptly and brutally in February 1989, when Tubby was shot and killed during a robbery outside of his home in St. Andrew, Jamaica. Violence has claimed many great reggae musicians and producers, and the loss of King Tubby was especially significant due to his groundbreaking technique and his role as a teacher who passed the word and science of dub down to succeeding generations who took Tubby's trip even farther out than he had. —*John Dougan*

★ **King Tubby Special 1973-1976** / 1989 / Trojan ♦♦♦♦♦
This two-disc set brings together some of the finest dub mixes ever produced by the legendary King Tubby. The first disc compiles 13 tracks played by the Observer Allstars and originally produced by Winston "Niney" Holness; the second consists of 17 cuts by the Aggrovators (produced by Bunny Lee) and includes the collection's title track, a deejay talkover featuring the great U Roy. King Tubby's approach to dub was always distinctive; his mixes are distinguished by a touch that is sweet-sounding and endlessly creative, balancing innovation with respect for the original even during the most drastic deconstruction of a song. And unlike some other dub producers, Tubby generally left swatches of the vocal line in place, dropping it in and out of the mix and applying dirty analog echo, sometimes subtly changing the lyrical focus. This collection's unusually helpful liner notes will help interested listeners find original versions of many of the tracks. A truly essential dub collection. —*Rick Anderson*

**If Deejay Was Your Trade** / 1994 / Blood & Fire ♦♦♦♦
Another in a seemingly endless series of excellent reissue by the Blood and Fire label. This features some superb Tubby mixes from 1975-79. Fat bass and drums create a Spectorish wall of sound that envelops the other players, as Tubby's savvy behind a mixing board is frequently awesome. Not much overlap with the two-LP set *King Tubby's Special*, it deserves a place in your CD bin if you've caught the dense Tubby vibe and are hungry for more. —*John Dougan*

**Dub Gone 2 Crazy** / Jul. 22, 1996 / Blood & Fire ♦♦♦♦
An excellent second collection of dub mixed by Tubby and Lloyd "Prince Jammy" James. Many of the tracks were taken from recordings by Johnnie Clarke, and feature Tubby and Jammy cutting loose with their trademark echo explosions, combined with machine gun fire, outer space blips and boinks, all rolled together with the sinewy rock steady beat provided by the Aggrovators. Although the remixes of the Clarke tracks are stellar, it's the dub version of the Jah Stitch and Dr. Alimantado track "The Barber Feel It" (here called "The Poor Barber") that gets my blood pumping. A little wilder than the first Blood and Fire collection of Tubby dub, this is the first time these tracks (all of which were released as singles) have been anthologized in this manner. A real treat. —*John Dougan*

**Dangerous Dub** / Nov. 12, 1996 / Greensleeves ++++
A collaboration between dub mixmaster/studio whiz King Tubby and dancehall tough Jah Screw, *Dangerous Dub* is a 13-track collection of some of the heaviest roots dub around. The two spent nights mixing tracks in King Tubby's studio located in the perilous, crime-rife ghetto of west Kingston—hence the name *Dangerous Dub*. Pounding, mind-blowing basslines and supple guitar tracks are provided by studio mainstays Flabba Holt and Bingy Bunny, both of whom appear on countless reggae and dub recordings. They provide a nice balance to the rat-a-tat ratcheting sounds King Tubby is famous for. The best cut by far is "Hungry Belly Dub," a remake of the classic reggae standard "Bandulo." Along with "London Bridge Special," *Dangerous Dub* is a great introduction to dub at its finest. —*Matthew Hilburn*

## Richard H. Kirk

b. Sheffield, Yorkshire, England
*Keyboards, Guitar, Producer / Experimental Techno, Electronica, Ambient Techno*

Former Cabaret Voltaire member Richard H. Kirk is widely regarded as contemporary techno's busiest man, a distinction he's picked up through a release schedule that keeps discographers sweating and diehard fans near bankruptcy. No doubt, that work ethic developed during Kirk's time with CV, who, in their nearly 20 years together, released as many albums and even more EPs. Kirk's not far behind as a solo artist, splitting just over half that total between his three ongoing projects—Sandoz, Electronic Eye, and works released under his own name—as well as collaborations with British DJ Parrot (as Sweet Exorcist) and heaps of singles and EPs. While the Sheffield-based Cabaret Voltaire began as an electronics-and-tape-loops outfit with obvious ties to other English post-industrial experimentalists like Throbbing Gristle, Einsturzende Neubauten, and Chrome, the group eventually penetrated a pop-group context while retaining the edge of dystopia and isolation at the core of their earlier work. Kirk's solo work has evolved along similar lines, although he works more toward integrating technology with more humanitarian concerns. His stylistic palette—mostly house, early techno, and ambient—and the inclusion of tracks on compilations released by the Warp label have pegged Kirk as an evangelist of "intelligent techno," but his solo work actually comes off closer to sample-heavy ambient house and techno. His affection for African and tribal percussion and thematics connect his various works in obvious ways, and many of his albums have been reissued domestically. [See Also: Electronic Eye, Sandoz] —*Sean Cooper*

**Virtual State** / 1993 / Wax Trax! ++++
Kirk's debut solo Warp album is an opus of sorts, with melodic passages and themes reappearing throughout. Obscure indigenous samples combine with standard and breakbeat techno and ambient textures, vocal, chanted, and spoken word snippets, and accomplished rhythmic programming. Reissued by Wax Trax!/TVT in 1994. —*Sean Cooper*

● **The Number of Magic** / 1995 / Wax Trax! ++++
Similar to his first for Warp, Kirk uses an incredibly wide variety of sources for this album of gorgeous ambient ethno-funk, including electro, bleep, techno and Eastern melodies. In fact, on one track, "Monochrome Dream," Kirk combines jazz, dub, spacey-ambient, and Latin rhythms, all at the same time (!). "Lost Souls on Funk" and "So Digital" are excellent as well, slightly more downtempo than the latest Cabaret Voltaire material and deftly produced like few others could do. Despite the disparity of genres, *The Number of Magic* holds together perfectly. —*John Bush*

**Alphaphone, Vol. 1: Step, Write, Run** / Nov. 25, 1996 / Alphaphone ++++
*Step, Write, Run* collects most of the material released in the first year of operation of Kirk's previously vinyl-only, dance-oriented Alphaphone label, including tracks from Cold Warrior, Yellow Square, Papadoctrine, and International Organization (Kirk pseudos one and all). The two-CD set is a nice blend of straight-up Kirk/Sandoz/Electronic Eye-styled techno and more meandering mid-tempo breakbeat fare. —*Sean Cooper*

## Klein & M.B.O.

f. 1980
*Group / Club/Dance, Disco*

Italian post-disco stalwarts Klein & MBO were formed around the nucleus of Tomas Ramirez Carrasco and M. Boncaldo. During the mid-'80s, singles like "Dirty Talk," "Wonderful," and "The MBO Theme" became big hits in both the emerging New York garage scene and Chicago's house community. Little else is known about the duo, though their singles remained DJ favorites well into the next decade. —*John Bush*

● **Dirty Talk [Single]** / 1981 / ++++

**The MBO Theme [Single]** / 1981 / +++

## The KLF

f. 1987, Liverpool, England, db. May 1992
*Group / Ambient House, Rave, Club/Dance, Newbeat, Acid House, House*

More than any pop band in history, the KLF ripped off the music industry for a bucketful of loot and got away with it—as illustrated in their own guidebook to creating number one singles, *The Manual*. Bill Drummond and Jimi Cauty applied the tactics of punk shock-terrorism to late-'80s acid house and became one of Britain's best-selling artists (recording also as the JAMS and the Timelords) just before their retirement in 1992. The duo then deleted their entire back catalogue—a potential loss in the millions of pounds—and declared they wouldn't release another record until peace was declared throughout the world.

The son of a Scottish preacher, Bill Drummond (b. William Butterworth; April 29, 1953; South Africa) ran away from home to become a fisherman before enrolling in a Liverpool art school in the late '70s. He became involved in Liverpool's punk scene, and in 1977 formed the short-lived punk band Big in Japan with Holly Johnson (later of Frankie Goes to Hollywood) and Ian Broudie (the Lightning Seeds). A year later, Drummond co-founded the Zoo label (with Dave Balfe), serving as manager and producer for the Teardrop Explodes and Echo & the Bunnymen through the early '80s. After both bands left Zoo for the majors, Drummond followed by joining WEA as an A&R man; there, he signed Strawberry Switchblade, Zodiac Mindwarp, the Proclaimers, and Brilliant. He quit the business in 1986, though, and released the solo album *The Man* one year later for Creation Records. The album was a satiric goodbye to music, voicing Drummond's hope that he would never be involved in the industry again.

With his retirement only six months old, Drummond decided to make a hip-hop record. He called an old friend, Brilliant's Jimi Cauty (b. 1954), to help with production and technology. A week later, the duo—christened the Justified Ancients of Mu Mu, or the JAMS for short—recorded the sample-heavy pastiche "All You Need Is Love." The single, released that May, was followed a month later by the JAMS' debut album *1987 (What the Fuck Is Going On?)*, which continued the sonic piracy with long passages lifted from the Beatles, Led Zeppelin, and ABBA. As a matter of course, ABBA objected to the sampling, and in September the Copyright Protection Society demanded that all copies be recalled and destroyed. Instead, Drummond and Cauty traveled to Sweden, hoping that a personal meeting with ABBA would resolve the situation. Locked out of the group's Stockholm studio, the pair decided to return to England, stopping only to burn 500 copies of *1987* in a Swedish field. (The incident was photographed and serves as the cover for the best-of album *History of the JAMS*.) Cauty and Drummond kept the album in the spotlight though, by advertizing in *The Face* magazine five remaining copies for sale at the price of £1000 each. They eventually sold three, gave one away, and kept the last. In October 1987, the JAMS released an edited version of the album called *1987 (The JAMS 45 Edits)*, with specific instructions on how to recreate the original *1987* at home.

A second album, *Who Killed the JAMS?*, appeared early in 1988, but it was superseded by the May release of "Doctorin' the Tardis" (recorded as the Timelords). Incorporating samples from Gary Glitter, Sweet and the theme to *Dr. Who*, the single hit number one in the British charts and eventually became one of the most popular sports anthems of all time. Within six months, "Doctorin' the Tardis" was collected on two JAMS compilations, the American *History of the JAMS a.k.a. The Timelords* and the British double-LP *Circa 1987: Shag Times*. Six months later, Cauty and Drummond compiled their knowledge of popular success and the music industry, publishing *The Manual* with a statement of purpose included in the subtitle: "How to have a number one the easy way—The Justified Ancients of Mu Mu reveal their zenarchistic method used in making the unthinkable happen."

Cauty and Drummond's second novelty single, "Kylie Said to Jason" (credited to the KLF, or Kopyright Liberation Front), proved a flop in July 1989, so the pair changed directions later that year. Jettisoning the beats of their previous work but retaining the samples and effects, the duo played a major part in the development of the '90s boom in ambient music. Cauty and Drummond recorded the classic *Chill Out* album in late 1989, mixing source material from two DAT machines onto a cassette recorder during a live session. Concurrent to the *Chill Out* project, Cauty had actually formed another ambient house forerunner, the Orb, with Dr. Alex Paterson. The duo recorded "A Huge Ever Growing Pulsating Brain That Rules from the Centre of the Ultraworld" in addition to material for an album, but split early in 1990—with Paterson taking the name for his future recordings. Cauty then deleted Paterson's contributions. rerecorded large portions and released the results credited only as *Space*.

Obviously, the KLF's ambient recordings weren't going to top the charts, so later in 1990 Cauty and Drummond moved back to acid house and earned the greatest success of their career. The single "What Time Is Love?"—the first volume in what became known as the Stadium House Trilogy—hit number five on the UK singles charts in August 1990. "3 A.M. Eternal" took over the number one spot in January 1991, and *The White Room* LP topped the album charts upon its release in March. The final single in the trilogy, "Last Train to Trancentral," also made Top Ten. The KLF's success carried into Europe during 1991, and even the Americans caught on by September, pushing "3 A.M. Eternal" to number five and *The White Room* into the Top 40 album charts. The US-only "America: What Time Is Love?" reached number 57 in November 1991, and early in 1992 "Justified and Ancient"—the surprising pairing of the KLF with country queen Tammy Wynette—almost reached the American Top Ten. Cauty and Drummond, the best-selling singles act in the world during 1991, were on the verge of becoming superstars.

The duo had other plans in mind, though. Voted Best British Group by BPI and the Brit Awards, the KLF were scheduled to perform at a London awards ceremony on February 13, 1992. Cauty and Drummond did show up, but horrified the formal audience with a hardcore thrash version of "3 A.M. Eternal" (performed with the justifiably named Extreme Noise Terror) that also included Drummond spraying the crowd with blanks from an automatic rifle and the post-performance announcement, "The KLF have left the music industry." Topping their already extreme actions, Cauty and Drummond delivered the carcass of a dead sheep—plus eight gallons of blood—to the lobby of the hotel after-party. The industry and press reaction was overwhemingly negative, but Cauty and Drummond had already made their mint. Promising that no more releases were forthcoming until peace reigned around the world, they officially retired from music on May 5, 1992—the date commemorated the 15th anniversary of Drummond's emergence in the music industry, with Big in Japan. To convince the public that it wasn't simply a scam to sell more records, Drummond and Cauty deleted the entire back catalogue of KLF Communications.

Though the KLF did return one year later, it was not to release music but to provide a commentary on the art world. First, a series of newspaper adverts commanded the world to "Abandon All Art Now." Cauty and Drummond—thinly veiled as the K-Foundation—then announced that they would be awarding a prize of £40,000 to the worst work of art that year. Winner Rachel Whiteread (who had also won England's Turner Prize) refused the award, prompting a ceremony in which the K-Foundation vowed to burn the prize money. Whiteread accepted the award just seconds before the bills were torched, and donated the money to charity.

In August 1994, the artists formerly known as KLF managed to outdo themselves yet again. After physically nailing £1,000,000 to a board—an act which necessitated the largest cash withdrawal in UK history—Cauty and Drummond showed the money around England as a work of art entitled "Nailed to the Wall." Then, on the island of Jura, in the presence of one journalist and one cameraman, they burned the entire sum as yet another bizarre commentary on the art world.

Cauty and Drummond's first recording in almost three years appeared later that year. Though peace didn't rule the world in late 1994, the K-Foundation honored the historic peace accord between Yitzhak Rabin and Yasser Arafat by releasing—only in Israel—an ultra-limited-edition single, a novelty cover song entitled "K Sera Sera," recorded with the Red Army Choir. Drummond and Cauty also recorded a track as the One World Orchestra for the *HELP* charity album in 1995. In late 1997, the KLF finally re-emerged (as 2K) and released the single "\*(\*)\*k the Milennium" on Mute. —*John Bush*

**1987 (What the Fuck Is Going On?)** / May 1987 / Atlantic ♦♦
Sample-heavy to the point where the presence of original material becomes questionable, *1987* is a hilarious record filled with the KLF's comments on music terrorism and their own unique take on the Run-D.M.C. type of old-school rapping. Tracks like "Don't Take Five Take What You Want," "Hey Hey We Are Not the Monkees," and the rather more obviously criminal "All You Need Is Love" only confirms the eternal existence of this LP within bootleg collections (though several tracks did appear in different versions on *The History of the JAMs a.k.a. The Timelords*). —*John Bush*

**The History of the JAMs a.k.a. The Timelords** / 1988 / TVT ♦♦♦♦
Interesting more for its sample-and-scatter philosophy than the thick Scottish brogue with which Drummond tries to emulate Run-D.M.C., *The History of the JAMs a.k.a. The Timelords* takes no prisoners—Dave Brubeck's familiar saxophone riff from "Take Five" is looped onto the James Brown-style jam "Don't Take Five (Take What You Want)," Whitney Houston "guests" on the hilarious "Whitney Joins the JAMs" (a dry run for the later, actually *live*, appearance of Tammy Wynette), and assorted other stars of the past also make appearances (including the Beatles, MC5, Jimi Hendrix, and Petula Clark). Aside from the novelty tracks—which wear as thin as their production values quite soon—this is the only available KLF full-length containing "Doctorin' the Tardis," perhaps the most popular sports anthem ever recorded. —*John Bush*

★ **Chill Out** / Jan. 1990 / Wax Trax! ♦♦♦♦♦
One of the initial works in the ambient house canon, *Chill Out* is the practically beatless soundtrack to a late-night journey along the Gulf Coast, and the track titles tell much of the story: "Six Hours to Louisiana, Black Coffee Going Cold," "3AM Somewhere Out of Beaumont," "Elvis on the Radio, Steel Guitar in My Soul." Recorded live by Drummond and Cauty (with much unintended help from sample victims Elvis Presley, Fleetwood Mac, and the throat singers of Tüva), *Chill Out* consists largely of fragmented, heavily reverbed steel guitar, environmental sounds (birds, trains), occasional synth, and an angelic vocal chorus repeating the KLF's own "Justified and Ancient" theme. Throughout, Drummond and Cauty display an instinctive talent for wallpaper music that's truly diverting, making *Chill Out* one of the essential ambient albums. —*John Bush*

☆ **The White Room** / Mar. 1991 / Arista ♦♦♦♦♦
After the incredible success of their "Doctorin' the Tardis" single in 1988 (better known as that theme from *Dr. Who*), Drummond and Cauty had plenty of money to hire talented musicians (instead of merely sampling them, as on their early recordings). *The White Room* is the result, an album bursting with hit singles that nevertheless flows as well as any concept album. Often overlooked as a classic from the acid house era (mostly because of the KLF's retirement one year later), *The White Room* represents the commercial and artistic peak of late-'80s acid house. —*John Bush*

## Klute (Tom Withers)

*Producer / Jungle/Drum'N'Bass, Club/Dance*
Experimental jungle producer Tom Withers is one of the more pigeonhole-proof of the London drum'n'bass set. Releasing tracks primarily as Klute and Override, his talent for composing the most relentlessly exploratory of tracks within the language of dancefloor drum'n'bass (as opposed to artful noodlers such as Plug, Mung, and Squarepusher) has played a role in pushing jungle beyond the more loopy confines of its "ambient" and "jazzy jungle" offshoots. While somewhat classifiable as an ambient junglist himself, Withers' tracks flit about with such pace and contradiction as to distance his work from the more manageable output of artists such as Alex Reece and LTJ Bukem. A guitarist in the semi-legendary British punk band the Stupids before finding the next level of extreme in the exploding hardcore (as in, hardcore techno) underground, Withers released a few spotty white-labels of straightahead dancefloor fare in the early '90s before settling into experimental breakbeat by 1993.

Withers' path through the labyrinth of underground labels—from Certificate 18, Deep Red, and Octopus to Crammed subsidiaries Selector and Language—brings his two most distinctive characteristics into focus; complicated, disjointed rhythms and tense, often melancholy melodic themes. While darkness constitutes an important component of many of his tracks (particularly his Certificate 18 and Octopus singles), it's often paired with a lighter, more dynamic thrust that gives his tunes an almost epic feel. Withers' Selector releases as Phume (together with Dave Campbell, ex-Hi-Ryze) are lighter still, with elements of techno and house combining with jungle's brisker BPMs. In addition to his regular schedule of twelves, Withers' production resume includes remix work for Sumosonic and Octopus labelmates Stranger (aka Inky Blacknuss), as well as releases as Tongue, Tom Tom, and Dr. No. *Casual Bodies*, released in 1998, was his first full-length. [See Also: Override] —*Sean Cooper*

- **Casual Bodies** / Nov. 16, 1998 / Certificate 18 ♦♦♦♦
A solid collection of what made Klute a special act within the drum'n'bass community, *Casual Bodies* includes plenty of nods to old-school techno (as on Withers' previous singles) plus dubbed-out material on "Arrival" and live drumming by the man himself on "Blood Rich." —*Keith Farley*

## Frankie Knuckles (Frank Warren Knuckles, Jr.)

b. Jan. 18, 1955, New York City, NY [South Bronx]
*Producer, DJ / Club/Dance, Acid House, Urban, House*

The man many call the godfather of house, Frankie Knuckles began DJing in New York in the early '70s while still a teenager, years before the disco boom which proved to be the first flowering of modern dance music. Ten years later he was in Chicago, putting together megamixes of old disco hits with new drum-machine percussion for an appreciative audience at crucial clubs like the Music Box and the Warehouse. Another decade on from those first formative steps for house music, Knuckles was back in his New York home, working as a producer and remixer for the biggest pop stars in the business. His career spans more time than any dance producer and without him, the landscape would be immeasurably different.

Born in the Bronx in 1955, Knuckles listened to a lot of jazz as a child, thanks to his sister's record collection. He studied commercial art and costume design before taking his first job as a DJ in 1971. Several years later, he hooked up with childhood friend Larry Levan and the two began working at Nicky Siano's New York club, the Gallery. Levan later moved to the Continental Baths, and Knuckles worked at another club for several months before rejoining Levan. Again, Levan left—this time to set up his own club, the Soho Place—and Knuckles continued on until the Continental Baths was closed. A group of entrepreneurs initially approached Levan about becoming the DJ at a club they were starting in Chicago; instead of abandoning the interest in his own club, he declined but suggested his friend Frankie Knuckles.

Knuckles moved to Chicago in 1977 and began DJing at the Warehouse, spinning Salsoul and Philadelphia Int'l records in front of a crowd unused to the New York DJing style, which included beat-mixing and the addition of percussion fills (from a separate turntable) to spruce up the sound of traditional soul. In 1983, Knuckles opened his own club, the Power Plant. While Ron Hardy was entrancing a largely gay, uptown crowd at the Music Box, Knuckles introduced the sound to many of the Southside producers who made waves during the '80s: Marshall Jefferson, Larry Heard, Adonis, Steve "Silk" Hurley, and at least half a dozen others.

After more than 15 years spinning vinyl, Frankie Knuckles began recording as well, debuting with several singles released on the seminal Trax Records. Such efforts as "Your Love," "Baby Wants to Ride," "You Got the Love," and "Angel" (most credited to Knuckles though vocalist Jamie Principle undoubtedly exercised some influence) were among the best tracks released in the Chicago house explosion of the mid-'80s. Knuckles also recorded for Danica ("Let the Music Use You") and worked with younger producers like Marshall Jefferson as well as future Fingers, Inc. vocalist Robert Owens. Just as Chicago house began spreading worldwide during 1986-87 though, Knuckles returned to New York. He formed Def Mix Productions with David Morales (one of the other major names in house music) and began working on house treatments for the biggest pop stars of the '80s and '90s, including Michael Jackson, Diana Ross, Chaka Khan, Inner City, and En Vogue.

Despite the popularity of house in the international arena, the godfather of the music waited several years before the major labels came calling for something other than a remix. Finally, Virgin signed him to an artist contract in 1991 and released his debut album *Beyond the Mix*. The singles "The Whistle Song," "Rainfalls," and "Workout" moved up the dance charts, though the album failed to connect with pop or R&B fans. Knuckles continued to produce singles and remix tracks, while his second album *Welcome to the Real World* was released in 1995. —*John Bush*

**Beyond the Mix** / 1991 / Virgin ♦♦♦
Any serious fan of house music knows the name Frankie Knuckles. Like Marshall Jefferson, he commands the type of respect in the genre that Grandmaster Flash enjoyed in hip-hop. When Knuckles signed with Virgin, the enthusiasm was high among house aficionados; but in fact, his Virgin debut, *Beyond the Mix*, isn't the all-out dancefloor extravaganza many were predicting it would be. The CD definitely has its strong points—including Lisa Michaels' seductive vocals on "Sacrifice" and the haunting "Rain Fall" and Shelton Becton's gutsy performances on "It's Hard Sometime" and the gospel-influenced "Soon I Will Be Done." At its best, *Beyond the Mix* is far superior to most of the songs heard on urban contemporary radio in 1991. But "Godfather" and "Party in My House" are routine hip-house numbers that are virtually indistinguishable from countless other fusions of rap and house recorded in the early '90s. —*Alex Henderson*

**Welcome to the Real World** / 1995 / Virgin ♦♦♦
As on his major-label debut, producer Frankie Knuckles uses many different dance concepts to vary the attack on his second album for Virgin, including the singles "Whadda U Want (From Me)" and the number one dance hit "Too Many Fish." —*John Bush*

★ **Best of Frankie Knuckles** / 1999 / Mirakkle ♦♦♦♦♦
The best (and only) collection of Knuckles' diverse production hits during the '80s, *Best of Frankie Knuckles* includes "Your Love," "Baby Wants to Ride," "Let the Music Use You," "You've Got the Love," and "Waiting on My Angel," among others. —*John Bush*

## Gottfried Michael Koenig

b. 1926, Magdeburg, Germany
*Composer / Musique Concrète, Atonal, Electronic*

Composing and generating sound via computer technology as early as the mid-'60s, Gottfried Michael Koenig was a pivotal force in cementing the emerging relationship between music and electronics. Born in Magdeburg, Germany, in 1926, Koenig studied composition at the Detmold School of Music before relocating to Bonn, where he pursued his interest in computer engineering. Between 1954 and 1964, he worked alongside Karlheinz Stockhausen at the electronic music studios of the Westdeutscher Rundfunk (WDR) in Cologne, collaborating with other aspiring composers including György Ligeti and Mauricio Kagel; in 1956, Koenig completed his first major electronic piece, *Klangfiguren II*, followed a year later by *Essay*.

During the early '60s, Koenig began writing a program—named simply Project 1, or PR1—designed to compose and generate music via the computer; when in 1964 he accepted the position of creative director with the Institute for Sonology in Utrecht, Holland, he took the software with him, putting on the finishing touches three years later. While at Utrecht, Koenig also began experimenting with the Variable Function Generator, a machine developed by physics student Stan Templaars able to generate sound using roughly the same technology as an analog sequencer. Hitting upon the idea of treating the VFG as an oscillator, between 1967 and 1969 Koenig used the machine to compose a series of groundbreaking pieces known collectively as the *Funktionen*.

In 1968, Koenig also began work on a second program, PR2; its complicated design made it difficult to use, however, and so PR1 remained his primary outlet for computerized composition. He continued tinkering with PR1 for years to follow, in 1978 introducing VOSIM oscillators to the project to create an extended program christened PRIX; a series of subsequent additions resulted in another upgrade, PRIXM, and the completion of 1979's *Output*. When the Institute of Sonology was relocated to the Hague in 1986, Koenig retired from his post to focus full-time on computerized composition as well as developing new musical programs; in 1991, he also published the first in a series of theoretical writings titled *Aesthetic Practice*. —*Jason Ankeny*

- **Langfiguren II (Soundfigures) (1955-56)/ Essay (1957-58)/Terminus 1 (1962)** / 1990 / BVHaast ♦♦♦♦
This collection of material by electronic pioneer Gottfried Michael Koenig includes three classic pieces, *Langfiguren II*, *Essay*, and *Terminus*. It's classic pointillistic electronic music. —*"Blue" Gene Tyranny*

## Komputer

f. 1995, London, England
*Group / Neo-Electro, Electro*

If you didn't figure it out from the name, the first notes of Komputer's debut album should point the way toward the group's obvious fixation with German electro-pop godfathers Kraftwerk. The British trio—Simon Leonard (lyrics, keyboards), David Baker (vocals, keyboards), and Jane Brereton (drums)—copied the trademark analog synth, computerized vocals, and mid-tempo rhythms of Kraftwerk, thereby functioning more as a tribute band than an actual force. Their album *The World of Tomorrow* was released in October 1997 by Mute. —*John Bush*

- **The World of Tomorrow** / Oct. 1997 / Mute ♦♦♦♦
Consciously retro in an electro-pop kind of way, *The World of Tomorrow* succeeds because the group doesn't try to sidestep their obvious debt to Kraftwerk. The analog synthesizers, vocoderized singing, and lockstep beats all point to the godfathers of techno, and Komputer does a good job of it. They even manage to push the envelope a bit farther, with commentary—albeit superficial—on tracks like "Bill Gates" and "More Automation." As a tribute LP, *The World of Tomorrow* is excellent. —*John Bush*

## Thomas Köner

*Producer / Ambient*

One of the few musicians with ties to the unrelated but somewhat connected fields of contemporary avant-garde, techno, and indie-rock, Thomas Köner has released albums of sparse ambience for the Barooni label, recorded similarly skeletal and lo-fi techno (with Andy Mellwig) as Porter Ricks, and appeared on albums by Bill Laswell's Divination as well as Sonic Boom's EAR collective. A native of the Netherlands, Köner began recording with 1991's *Nunatak Gongamur*, the first in a series of LPs for the Dutch Barooni label. The next two, *Teimo* and *Permafrost*, were later collected onto one disc by Mille Plateaux, and followed by *Aubrite* in 1996. That same year, Köner appeared on *Distill*, an album by the Bill Laswell-based ambient dub project Divination—which called a roll of experimentalist composers, including Paul Schütze, Pete Namlook, Anton Fier, Haroumi Hosono, Mick Harris, and Tetsu Inoue. Also lending his name—literally—to an EAR (Experimental Audio Research) album titled *The Köner Experiment*, he produced the work with rhythm and programming help from Andy Mellwig. Mellwig and Köner had already recorded several EPs of shadowed techno as Porter Ricks (later collected on the Chain Reaction quasi-compilation *Biokinetics*). The Köner solo effort *Kaamos* followed in 1998. —*John Bush*

- **Teimo/Permafrost** / Feb. 10, 1997 / Mille Plateaux ♦♦♦♦
As Thomas Köner's experimental minimalism is certainly not everyone's cup of tea, the *Teimo/Permafrost* two-fer is a relatively easy way for the curious to get a solid idea of just what his music is all about. —*Jason Ankeny*

**Kaamos** / Apr. 20, 1998 / Mille Plateaux ♦♦♦
Thomas Köner's first album for Mille Plateaux continues the abstract tones and sublime white-noise of earlier LPs, though occasional crackles and low-end bass gives some element of focus to the proceedings. —*John Bush*

## Kooky Scientist (Fred Gianelli)

*Producer / Minimal Techno, Club/Dance, Techno, Acid House*

An experimental producer based in Boston, Fred Gianelli recorded with Psychic TV's acid-house incarnation in the mid- to late '80s, but then went on to a series of diverse recordings for several labels. A veteran of music since the late '70s, Gianelli worked with Genesis P. Orridge and the Psychic TV crew for several years, appearing on 1990's *Towards the Infinite Beat*, later gaining a deal through Wax Trax! for a 1992 LP, *Fred*. After forming his own Telepathic Recordings label for left-field experimentation with an arsenal of manufactured and altered electronics, Gianelli submerged for several years until recording the atmospheric *Telepathic Romance* LP for the similarly styled Finnish Sähkö label. Perhaps needing to flex his dancefloor muscles once again, Gianelli signed with Richie Hawtin's Plus-8 imprint as Kooky Scientist, and released the acid-oriented *Unpopular Science* in early 1997. —*John Bush*

- **Unpopular Science** / Apr. 15, 1997 / Never ♦♦♦♦
An entertaining look into the bizarre soundlab of the Kooky Scientist, *Unpopular Science* features test-tube rhythms boiling and frothing while Gianelli explores the far reaches on "Old Vs. Heav" and "Cash Flow." There are several fairly straightahead tracks (which work just as well), but most of the album focuses on intriguingly weirded-out techno. —*John Bush*

## The Kosmik Kommando

*Producer / Experimental Techno, Acid Techno, IDM*

Mike Dred (aka Chimera, Judge Dred, and the Kosmik Kommando) makes acid-tinged experimental techno geared both for the dancefloor and for home listening. A member of the UK's extended North Country experimental techno family (which also includes Reload, the Aphex Twin, and Matt Herbert), Dred drew early inspiration from European synth-pop groups like Kraftwerk and the Human League, as well as the American electro scene spreading like wildfire in the mid-'80s London underground. Although he's recorded for a variety of different labels, including R&S, R&S offshoot Diatomyc (which he helps run), and his own Machine Codes label, the bulk of his material has appeared on Richard James' Rephlex imprint, mostly under the Kosmik Kommando and Chimera names. Reportedly hooking up with the label after meeting some friends of James' on a train en route to a rave in Cologne, Dred's penchant for harsh, relentlessly experimental acid and techno fit neatly into the Rephlex vision, and Dred's first *Kosmik Kommando* EP was among the first 12"s the label released. Dred's Rephlex discography has since grown to include two full-length albums (one each under the KK and Chimera names) and five EPs, with releases on Diatomyc and Machine Codes numbering close behind. [See Also: Mike Dred] —*Sean Cooper*

**Kosmik Kommando [EP]** / 1993 / Rephlex ♦♦♦

- **Freaquenseize** / 1994 / Rephlex ♦♦♦♦
Mike Dred's only full-length for Rephlex as the Kosmik Kommando consists of bracing acid-techno heavy on the experimentation and accountably low on any type of funk. Highlights include "Lost Horizon," "The Futurist," and "Quondam," the latter available only on the CD version (which includes several extra tracks). —*Keith Farley*

## Koxbox

f. 1992, Copenhagen, Denmark

*Group / Progressive Trance, Goa Trance, Trance, Club/Dance*

Formed in Copenhagen early in the '90s, Koxbox made some of the first moves toward the psychedelic trance sound that became a standard later in the decade. The duo was formed by Frank E (aka Frank Madsen) and Peter Candy, who first met back in 1980 while playing in rock bands around Copenhagen. They became friends, and presented their own show on Danish radio, moving into techno by the end of the '80s. The first Koxbox productions appeared on WTP Records, which got them signed to the leading European trance label, Harthouse. Their debut album, 1995's *Forever After*, was recorded with the help of third member Ian Ion, a studio engineer and producer. As trance exploded during the '90s, Koxbox recorded for two of the best labels on the scene, Blue Room Released ("Stratosfear") and T.I.P. ("Reoscillated"). The second Koxbox album, *Dragon Tales*, appeared on Blue Room Released in 1997. Unfortunately, Frank E and Peter Candy's working relationship soured by 1999 and Koxbox appeared to call it quits. —*John Bush*

- **Forever After** / Aug. 25, 1995 / Harthouse ♦♦♦♦
The debut album from Koxbox presents the trio working through psychedelic trance before the style had any rules. The pulsing rhythms and digitally precise acid lines are stiff, but the range of ideas on tracks like "Space Interface" and "Point of No Return" belie the formality. *Forever After* is not only an excellent artifact of the early-'90s trance scene; it's a landmark for much of the trance music that came afterwards. —*John Bush*

**Dragon Tales** / 1997 / Blue Room Released ♦♦♦

## Kraftwerk

f. 1970, Düsseldorf, Germany

*Group / Kraut-Rock, Club/Dance, Electronic*

During the mid-'70s, Germany's Kraftwerk established the sonic blueprint followed by an extraordinary number of artists in the decades to come. From the British new romantic movement to hip-hop to techno, the group's self-described "robot pop"—hypnotically minimal, obliquely rhythmic music performed solely via electronic means—resonates in virtually every new development to impact the contemporary pop scene of the late 20th century, and as pioneers of the electronic music form, their enduring influence cannot be overstated. Kraftwerk emerged from the same German experimental music community of the late '60s which also spawned Can and Tangerine Dream; primary members Florian Schneider and Ralf Hütter first met as classical music students at the Dusseldorf Conservatory, originally teaming in the group Organisation and issuing a 1970 album, *Tone Float*. Schneider and Hütter soon disbanded Organisation, rechristening themselves Kraftwerk (German for "power station"), beginning work on their own studio (later dubbed Kling Klang), and immersing their music in the fledgling world of minimalist electronics. Their 1971 debut, titled simply *Kraftwerk 1*, offered a hint of their unique aesthetic in its earliest form, already implementing innovations including Schneider's attempts at designing homemade rhythm machines.

A series of lineup shifts followed, and at one point Hütter even left the group; however, by the release of 1972's *Kraftwerk 2*, he and Schneider were again working in tandem. Recorded without a live drummer, the album's rhythms relied solely on a drum machine, creating a distinctly robotic feel without precedent—the concept of purely technological music was, at the time, utterly alien to most musicians, as well as listeners. A series of well-received live performances followed before Kraftwerk began work on their breakthrough third LP, 1973's *Ralf and Florian*. Honing their many ambitions down to a few simple yet extraordinarily innovative concepts, their music began growing more and more revelatory—even their clean-cut, scientific image was in direct opposition to the dominant pop fashions of the time. Kraftwerk's first album to be issued in the US, 1974's *Autobahn* was an international smash; an edited single version of the epic title track was a major hit at home and abroad, and in America the previously unknown group reached the upper rungs of the pop albums chart. Performed in large part on a Moog synthesizer, *Autobahn* crystallized the distinctive Kraftwerk sound while making the group's first clear overtures towards conventional pop structure and melody, establishing a permanent foothold for electronic music within the mainstream.

Kraftwerk resurfaced in 1975 with *Radio-Activity*, a concept album exploring the theme of radio communication; indicative of the group's new global popularity, it was released in both German and English-language editions, the latter appearing early the following year. Train travel emerged as the subject of 1977's *Trans-Europe Express*, which marked an increased movement towards seeming musical mechaninization; the line became even further blurred with the follow-up, 1978's aptly titled *The Man Machine*, a work almost completely bereft of human touches. By this time, the members of Kraftwerk even publicly portrayed themselves as automatons, an image solidified by tracks like "We Are the Robots." Having reached the peak of their influence, however, the group disappeared from view, the first of many extended absences to follow; they did not return to action prior to 1981's *Computer World*, a meditation on the new global dominance of technology—a society their music long ago predicted and predated. After topping the British charts with the single "Computer Love," Kraftwerk again vanished, enjoying a five-year layoff culminating in the release of 1986's *Electric Cafe*. By now, however, pop music was dominated by synthesizers and drum machines, and the group's stature flagged; but for a 1991 best-of collection titled *The Mix*, they remained silent in the years to follow, finally releasing a new single, "Expo 2000," in late 1999. —*Jason Ankeny*

### Kraftwerk 1 / 1971 / Philips ♦♦♦♦
Leaving the free-form improvisation of their earlier group Organisation behind them, Ralf Hütter and Florian Schneider moved into the realm of disciplined electronic rhythms with *Kraftwerk 1*, and the rest was history: while not an artistic triumph comparable to the group's best work, their debut is nonetheless hypnotic and innovative, at times close in spirit to the work of Steve Reich or Terry Riley in its minimalist construction. —*Jason Ankeny*

### Kraftwerk 2 / 1972 / Philips ♦♦♦
For their second Kraftwerk album, Ralf Hütter and Florian Schneider took the *sturm und drang* of the industrial revolution and implanted it into a musical core that consisted of electronic soundscapes and metronomic rhythmic pulsations, especially on the 17-minute opener "Klingklang." The future sound of industrial music was fashioned on this album and its predecessor. —*Archie Patterson*

### Ralf and Florian / 1973 / Warner Brothers ♦♦
An extension of their improvisational live performances, Kraftwerk's third LP curbs their obsessive minimalism to achieve a more complete sound; a softer, smoother record largely dominated by electric piano and textured electronic percussion, it marks the duo's first true overtures toward melody and, by extension, dance music, setting the stage for the breakthroughs of *Autobahn* the following year. —*Jason Ankeny*

### ★ Autobahn / 1974 / Warner Brothers ♦♦♦♦♦
Although Kraftwerk's first three albums were groundbreaking in their own right, *Autobahn* is where the group's hypnotic electro-pulse genuinely came into its own. The main difference between *Autobahn* and its predecessors is how it develops an insistent, propulsive pulse which makes the repeated rhythms and riffs of the shimmering electronic keyboards and trance-like guitars all the more hypnotizing. The 22-minute title track, in a severely edited form, became an international hit single and remains the peak of the band's achievements—it encapsulates the band and why they are important within one track—but the rest of the album provides soundscapes equally as intriguing. Within *Autobahn*, the roots of electro-funk, ambient and synth-pop are all evident—it's a pioneering album, even if its electronic trances might not capture the attention of all listeners. —*Stephen Thomas Erlewine*

### Radio-Activity / 1975 / Capitol ♦♦♦
A concept album exploring themes of broadcast communications, *Radio-Activity* marked Kraftwerk's return to more obtuse territory, extensively utilizing static, oscillators, and even Cage-like moments of silence to approximate the sense of radio transmission; a pivotal record in the group's continuing development, the title track—the first they ever recorded in English—is their most fully realized electro-pop effort to date, while "The Voice of Energy" precipitates the robot voice so crucial to their subsequent work. —*Jason Ankeny*

### ☆ Trans-Europe Express / 1977 / Capitol ♦♦♦♦♦
Although *Autobahn* was a left-field masterpiece, *Trans-Europe Express* is often cited as perhaps the archetypal (and most accessible) Kraftwerk album. Melodic themes are repeated often and occasionally interwoven over deliberate, chugging beats, sometimes with manipulated vocals; the effect is mechanical yet hypnotic. Thematically, the record feels like parts of two different concept albums: one a meditation on the disparities between reality and image ("Hall of Mirrors" and "Showroom Dummies" share recurring images of glass, reflection, illusion, and confused identities, as well as whimsical melodies), and the other the glorification of Europe. There is an impressive composition paying homage to "Franz Schubert," but the real meat of this approach is contained in the opening love letter, "Europe Endless," and the epic title track which shares themes and lyrics with the following track, "Metal on Metal." The song "Trans-Europe Express" is similar in concept to "Autobahn," as it mimics the swaying motion and insistent drive of a cross-continent train trip. What ultimately holds the album together, though, is the music, which is more consistently memorable even than that on *Autobahn*. Overall, *Trans-Europe Express* offers the best blend of minimalism, mechanized rhythms, and crafted, catchy melodies in the group's catalog; henceforth, their music would take on more danceable qualities only hinted at here (although the title cut provided the basis for Afrika Bambaataa's enormously important dancefloor smash "Planet Rock"). —*Steve Huey*

### The Man Machine / 1978 / Capitol ♦♦♦♦
*The Man Machine* is closer to the sound and style that would define early new wave electro-pop—less minimalistic in its arrangements and more complex and danceable in its underlying rhythms. Like its predecessor, *Trans-Europe Express*, there is the feel of a divided concept album, with some songs devoted to science fiction-esque links between humans and technology, often with electronically processed vocals ("The Robots," "Spacelab," and the title track); others take the glamour of urbanization as their subject ("Neon Lights" and "Metropolis"). Plus, there's "The Model," a character sketch which falls under the latter category but takes a more cynical view of the title character's glamorous lifestyle. More pop-oriented than any of their previous work, the sound of *The Man Machine*—in particular among Kraftwerk's oeuvre—had a tremendous impact on the cold, robotic synth-pop of artists like Gary Numan, as well as Britain's later new romantic movement. —*Steve Huey*

### ☆ Computer World / 1981 / Warner Brothers ♦♦♦♦♦
The first of Kraftwerk's many extended periods of silence was broken with the release of *Computer World*, a record exploring the ramifications of living in a society dominated by technology. A tightly honed, starkly minimalist effort, its implementation of recent technological advances yields a brighter and sharper sound than ever before; the single "Pocket Calculator" typifies the group at their most playful, while "Home Computer" eerily presages the emergence of techno and house music later in the decade. —*Jason Ankeny*

### Electric Cafe / 1986 / Elektra ♦♦♦
Five long years after *Computer World*, Kraftwerk finally resurfaced with another LP, *Electric Cafe;* the rest of the pop music industry having finally caught up with the group's vision, they no longer seem so innovative and inspired—indeed, the record's brief running time (under 36 minutes) seems indicative of

a lack of ideas and new directions, with the spartan opening tracks "Technopop" and "Musique Non-Stop" virtually interchangeable and the remaining cuts surprisingly mainstream in both form and content. —*Jason Ankeny*

**The Mix** / Jun. 11, 1991 / Elektra ✦✦✦
By the early '90s, it was quite apparent just how far-reaching Kraftwerk's influence had been. From techno to hip-hop to industrial music to house, numerous others were undeniably indebted to the group. Dance clubs had long been a key part of Kraftwerk's following, and the dance market was the obvious target of *The Mix*—a collection of highly enjoyable, often clever remixes. While novices would do better to start out with *Trans Europe Express* or *The Man Machine*, hardcore Kraftwerk followers shouldn't pass up these remixes of such classics as "Trans Europe Express," "The Robots," "Autobahn," and "Radioactivity." One could nitpick about the absence of "Neon Lights" and "Europe Endless," but the bottom line is that this CD was a welcome addition to the Kraftwerk catalogue. —*Alex Henderson*

**Expo 2000 [Single]** / Dec. 28, 1999 / EMI ✦✦
Kraftwerk's first new song after a nearly 20-year break, this song was commissioned for *Expo 2000* in Hanover, Germany. In fact, they received such a lucrative commission for it that German taxpayers complained about their paycheck.

The song is audibly Kraftwerk; the simple melodies and drumbeats are there. However, instead of sounding innovative, it has started to sound a bit dated. It is still good, but one would think that a group inventive enough to write "Trans Europe Express" in 1977 could do better in 2000. —*Joshua Landau*

## Kreidler

f. 1994, Düsseldorf, Germany
*Group / Electronica, Ambient Techno, Experimental*
Kreidler is a Düsseldorf-based side-project of Stefan Schneider, bassist with Cologne neo-Kraut-rock group To Rococo Rot. Kreidler is similar to that group in its attempts to combine catchy, acoustic-based compositions (e.g., guitar, bass, drums) with bizarre electronic tangents, a tact that allies them with such American post-rock outfits as Tortoise and Trans Am. However, Kreidler's approach is both more filled out than the former and less derivative than the latter, and is probably closer to countrymen Can or Faust than any of the more contemporary rock-based extrapolators. The group records for Kiff SM and produced their first album, *Weekender*, in 1996. The remix EP *Resport* featured work from Jim O'Rourke and Ln, among others. Their second album *Appearance and the Park* earned a record deal with Mute. —*Sean Cooper*

**Weekender** / Nov. 18, 1996 / PIAS ✦✦✦
**Resport [EP]** / Jun. 30, 1997 / Stewardess ✦✦✦
● **Appearance and the Park** / May 25, 1998 / Mute ✦✦✦✦
It's a bit difficult to get electronics and more standard instruments to sound good together, and it seems as though Kreidler was experimenting more than playing on their first album. The concept works much better on *Appearance and the Park*, and sounds similar to American post-rock units like Rome or Trans Am, though with fewer influences from rock. —*John Bush*

## David Kristian

*Producer / Minimal Techno, Experimental Techno, Electronica, Ambient*
Based in Montreal, David Kristian has looked far back into electronic music's past to unite his vision of soundtrack music and experimental electronics. Inspired by the first completely electronic film score, 1956's *Forbidden Planet* by Louis and Bebe Barron, Kristian recorded a 1997 album (*Cricklewood*) as a tribute to the radical sound experiments that the Barrons used to record it. Kristian's recording career began in the early '80s while working at a cable-television station in New Brunswick. Deciding to produce his own scores to science-fiction/animation shorts aired on the station, he composed soundtracks consisting of tape loops and analogue experiments tied to the heyday of science fiction in the '50s.

Though Kristian continued to record during the '80s, it wasn't until 1994 that his first album *Synaesthesia* earned a release, on Discreet/Indiscreet. The straightahead flavor of the album's rhythms belied Kristian's focus on experimental productions. Two EPs, *Clubfoot* and *Ectopic Beat*, charted a newfound fascination with drum'n'bass and earned him fans within the techno community. Kristian responded with a change-up, the relatively beatless *Cricklewood* album released on Alien8. He has also recorded with Toronto's Gregory De Rocher (aka Lowfish), and released the remix work *Woodworking*. —*John Bush*

● **Cricklewood** / 1997 / Alien8 ✦✦
David Kristian's first release for the Canadian Alien8 label, more closely associated with avant-noise terrorists such as Aube and Merzbow, is likely to attract an entirely new audience to the label. For a moment, anyway; probably just long enough for them to skip through the first three or four tracks of *Cricklewood* before passing it over to their "trade" pile. Ostensibly Kristian's tribute to the soundtrack of famous B-horror flick *Forbidden Planet*, *Cricklewood* is all echoey test tones and modulating drones, and not a whole lot else. Fans of schizo-ambient/noise crossover acts such as Merzbow, Lustmord, and Fushitsusha may find Kristian's abstract, buzzing analog extremism of passing interest, but those who picked up *Cricklewood* on the strength of the sort of jittery experimental electronica featured on compilations by Lo Recordings and Worm Interface, as well as on his Drop Beat EP, *Ectopic Beat*, should probably stear clear. —*Sean Cooper*

## Kruder & Dorfmeister

f. 1993, Vienna, Austria
*Group / Electronica, Trip-Hop*
The trip-hop production duo of Peter Kruder and Richard Dorfmeister has gained more fame for its stellar remixes and DJ sets than as producers of its own work. By engineering reworkings of tracks by a cast of artists ranging from William Orbit and Bomb the Bass to Bone Thugs-N-Harmony and United Future Organization, the Austrian duo became one of the most respected names in the dancefloor community.

Kruder & Dorfmeister's standing increased with the issue of two acclaimed 1996 DJ albums: *Conversions* for Spray/BMG and *DJ Kicks* for Belgium's Studio !K7. After forming their own G-Stone Records, the pair found a distribution deal with Quango and released the *G-Stoned* EP in mid-1996. Though they remained busy with remix work and DJ gigs during 1997, it wasn't until late 1998 that another release appeared, *The Kruder & Dorfmeister Sessions*. Dorfmeister also appears in the side-project Tosca with Rupert Huber, while Kruder released an album on G-Stoned in 1999 as Peace Orchestra. [See Also: Tosca, Peace Orchestra] —*John Bush*

**Conversions: A K&D Selection** / Feb. 1996 / Shadow ✦✦✦
Kruder & Dorfmeister's *Conversions: A K&D Selection* is the pair's first full-length DJ album, establishing their mastery of downtempo trip-hop mixes while sprinkling some organic, grooving drum'n'bass and techno in for good measure. —*Steve Huey*

**DJ Kicks** / Apr. 1996 / Studio !K7 ✦✦✦✦
Though it's a close race, the duo make for better DJs than producers, as witnessed by their volume in the *DJ Kicks* series. Beginning with downbeat trip-hop including Herbaliser, Statik Sound System, and Thievery Corporation, Kruder & Dorfmeister flow through jazzy drum'n'bass (with Aquasky and JMJ & Flytronix) and techno (with Hardfloor and Showroom Recordings). K&D sound much more relaxed and involved than on their own *G-Stoned* EP. —*John Bush*

**G-Stoned [EP]** / Aug. 1996 / Quango ✦✦✦✦
*G-Stoned* is a four-track EP packed with some of the rawest, most intense trip-hop ever recorded. The melange of syrupy beats and languid samples display Kruder & Dorfmeister with an impeccable grasp of constructing sounds, though the tracks seem to wander a bit before reaching their conclusion. —*John Bush*

★ **The K&D Sessions** / Oct. 13, 1998 / Studio !K7 ✦✦✦✦✦
While Kruder & Dorfmeister remained unwilling to release a "proper" album even several years after their breakout, *The K&D Sessions* is proof positive they're still doing what they do best—making the most blissfully blunted music the world has ever heard. The two-disc set is first and foremost a K&D mix album, to add to the two they'd already released. It's also a remix collection, though; each of the 21 tracks are reworkings (by Kruder, Dorfmeister, or both) for artists including Roni Size, Lamb, David Holmes, Bomb the Bass, Depeche Mode, Bone Thugs-N-Harmony, Sofa Surfers, and Count Basic. As could be expected, *The K&D Sessions* is earthy, downtempo and acid-based, even moreso than previous mix albums by the pair. The pinging vocal

samples that echo through the duo's remix of "Bug Powder Dust" by Bomb the Bass prove amply that Kruder & Dorfmeister have a better handle on 21st-century dub techniques than any other producers out there, and the impossibly deep beats on almost every track simply couldn't have been recorded by any other act. Yes, it's a bit of a shame that the pair still hadn't released an album of own-productions, but with (re)mix albums this stunning and accomplished, Kruder & Dorfmeister hardly needed one to gain respect. —*John Bush*

## Eric Kupper
*Keyboards, Producer, DJ / Club/Dance, House*

A keyboard player for several post-punk bands before hitting the house remix-session circuit in the '80s, Eric "K-Scope" Kupper made his dance debut providing keys for top remixers like David Morales, Arthur Baker, and Frankie Knuckles, who recorded Kupper's "The Whistle Song" for his 1990 album *Beyond the Mix*. Kupper later made the move to production himself, working on tracks with PM Dawn, Connie Harvey, and RuPaul as well as remixes for Kate Bush, Army of Lovers, and 808 State. He debuted his own project, K-Scope, on two 1995 EPs for Tribal America, then released his debut album *From the Deep* later that year. *Instant Music* followed in 1998. —*John Bush*

**The K-Scope Project [EP]** / 1995 / Tribal America ✦✦
Kupper stakes an R&B-inflected house style on his debut single, recorded for Tribal America. —*John Bush*

● **Instant Music** / Aug. 25, 1998 / MCA ✦✦
The second album by Eric Kupper & K-Scope got a wider release (through Tribal/MCA) than its predecessor. While "Latin Blues, Part 1" and "The Run" lean toward '70s jazz-funk with Kupper's keys over a bed of not-quite-ready-for-the-mainstream house, a few others venture into rather free-form territory. —*Keith Farley*

# L

## Jonny L (Jonny Listners)
*Producer / Rave, Jungle/Drum'N'Bass, Club/Dance*

After blowing up in the early-'90s hardcore techno scene and spending several years out of the spotlight, Jonny L's status as a rave castoff underwent heavy modification when his drum'n'bass deviations became quite respected in the dance community. He's one of the few dark-side jungle producers with a distinctive style, his productions enervating the favored two-step clichés with retrofitted 303-style acid effects that are the audio equivalent of hi-res computer monitors. A constant on Britain's XL Recordings—along with Prodigy—since 1992, Jonny L debuted with straightahead rave staples like "Love You So," "Ooh I Like It" (a number 73 hit in Britain) and "Make Me Work." By the mid-'90s, he turned to more expansive releases like "2 of Us" and the *Tychonic Cycle* EP, reminiscent of intelligent jungle LTJ Bukem style. The 1997 "Piper" single and *Sawtooth* LP were glowing returns to his hardcore breakbeat origins and highlights of the year in the drum'n'bass arena (foreshadowing the dark, intelligent scene termed neuro-funk). *Magnetic* followed one year later. —*John Bush*

**Sawtooth** / Nov. 17, 1997 / XL Recordings ♦♦♦♦
*Sawtooth* was a long time in coming but definitely worth the wait. Besides the 1997 club anthem "Piper," the album includes several jump-up basement anthems like "S4" and others, continuing Jonny L's status as one of the pre-eminent jungle producers. —*John Bush*

● **Magnetic** / Nov. 2, 1998 / XL Recordings ♦♦♦♦
Just one year on from his last LP, Jonny L returned with the next step. Though it doesn't have the completely unrestrained malevolence of *Sawtooth*, *Magnetic* betters its predecessor as a showcase for Jonny L's excellent and tremendously inventive production feel. He works the classic Zeppelin levee break into "Hard Clip (Interlude)" and offers at least six tracks of pure brilliance (including each of the first three). The album's several collaboration tracks (vocalist Lady Kier (Deee Lite) and British rapper Silvah Bullet) are rather hit and miss, but they're the only failings on a brilliant album. —*John Bush*

## L.A. Style
f. 1991, db. 1995
*Group / Rave, Club/Dance*

L.A. Style made chart history in 1992 when their single "James Brown Is Dead" became the first rave track to appear in *Billboard*'s weekly pop rankings. Primarily the work of producers Denzil Slemming, Maxx Mondino, and Fonny DeWulf, L.A. Style debuted with the "James Brown" single, far and away their biggest hit. A self-titled LP followed in 1993, but by the time the group resurfaced a year later with the single "Raving on L.A. Style," their 15 minutes of fame had elapsed. —*Jason Ankeny*

● **L.A. Style** / 1993 / Arista ♦
L.A. Style's only album includes the obligatory singles "James Brown Is Dead" and "Raving on L.A. Style," but the album tracks suffer from one-note ideas and little flair for execution. —*Keith Farley*

## Labradford
f. 1992, Richmond, VA
*Group / Experimental Rock, Indie-Rock, Post-Rock/Experimental*

Consisting of bassist Robert Donne, guitarist/vocalist Mark Nelson, and Carter Brown on keyboards, Labradford are an experimental ambient/post-rock group from Richmond, Virginia. Incorporating electronics as well as non-traditional arrangements and production techniques, the group's sound-track-y, effects-heavy sonic landscapes operate in a vein closely allied with groups such as Experimental Audio Research, Flying Saucer Attack, and Gastr del Sol, and have earned the group high praise among a diverse variety of different audiences. The trio have released material through American indies Merge and Kranky, as well as the Kiwi rock label Flying Nun and Stereolab's Duophonic imprint. Though occasionally incorporating vocal and rhythmic elements, the group relies most often on the drone aesthetic, mixing looping guitar effects and long keyboard passages with snippets of barely-audible vocals and assorted found objects on records like 1994's *Prazision*, 1995's *Stable Reference*, 1996's self-titled effort and 1997's *Mi Media Naranja*. 1999 brought the release of a new album, *E Luxo So*. —*Sean Cooper*

**Prazision** / 1994 / Kranky ♦♦♦♦
As the premiere release on Kranky, which would become one of the '90s most notable US indie labels for its series of adventurous releases, *Prazision* already holds a certain place in the history books. Regardless of who put it out, however, this excellent debut would command attention for introducing Labradford and its marvelous drone/ambient sound to the world. Inspired by such cult-level titans of '80s drone as Spacemen 3 and Loop [whose ex-members almost immediately championed the band after *Prazision*'s appearance], the then duo's ability to create seemingly stark [but quite layered and complex the more you listened to it], echoed modern psychedelic masterpieces made itself apparent from the beginning. Notably, the band eschewed conventional percussion of any sort, relying on singer/guitarist Nelson's simple but effective guitar parts—usually consisting of a series of a few notes, repeated in sequence and given reverb—to carry the rhythm, while keyboards and organs explored all varieties of ambient and melodic approaches. Nelson's lyric delivery serves him best when simply reciting rather than singing, as on the beautifully chilling "Sliding Glass," and though the overall effect of his quiet, half-whispered vocals is very Spacemen 3-derivative, it certainly doesn't hurt the album any. The trump card here is "Gratitude," a keyboard-led piece which is in fact Labradford's own series of thank-yous to friends, family and labels for their support, delivered using a Vocoder. At once amusing and quite cool to listen to, it's a nicely unexpected touch on a solid first record. —*Ned Raggett*

**A Stable Reference** / 1995 / Kranky ♦♦♦♦
Having established their sound, Labradford took the admirable step on its sophomore release with extending it to further levels rather than simply refining what was already there, as well as adding bass player Robert Donne to the line-up. Whether various live appearances with Main in fact had an impact, Labradford here resembles that extremely avant-garde group in creating honest-to-goodness "post-rock" as originally defined by critic Simon Reynolds—music reliant on rock instruments but avoiding bluesy riffs and pop hooks in favor of sheer light and shade, very much at home in the studio. The biggest change on *Reference* has remained a near-constant ever since, namely the removal of lyrics and vocal parts from almost all tracks, outside of some extremely understated and intentionally buried in the mix bits scattered through the record. Other long-running motifs started to appear as well—astoundingly obscure cover art, short and/or nonsensical terms for song titles, such as "SEDR 77," and even more attention on mix complexity, with subtle yet important sonic elements and samples scattered through the songs. The middle track of the release remains the most noteworthy—"Eero," a long, doomy song consisting almost entirely of guitar reverb—without guitar—and dark keyboard drones echoing into the far distance. Songs like "Mas" and "Balanced on Its Own Flame" retain the greatest similarity to *Prazision* due to the echoed, deliberate guitar playing and general pace, yet in the end *Reference* already points to the increasingly more challenging albums in Labradford's near future. —*Ned Raggett*

**Labradford** / 1996 / Kranky ♦♦♦♦
On the band's self-titled third effort, rhythm in a traditional sense appears for

the first time, with drum machines and other percussion patterns often mixed low but still notable. "Phantom Channel Crossing" starts the album on a wonderful note, with a clunky, machine-like sample carrying the track, before sliding into the equally fine "Midrange," combining many familiar elements from past efforts—whispered vocals, deliberate guitar pluckings, organ drones and otherwise, string accompaniment—into a drifting, mesmerizing whole. While not as notably a different step forward as *Reference*, Labradford here works its changes on a more low-key basis; the feeling is of refinement rather than sudden changes. It's also the band's shortest album yet—barely 40 minutes long—but with only seven songs to share that time, the general feeling of relaxation mixed with understated tenseness remains as prominent as ever. Many of the most effective touches of the album don't call attention to themselves, but weave into the song to create the overall effect, such as the metronome pulse and intentionally discordant strings on "Scenic Recovery." Just when you think you have the band pegged, they tweak the recipe in new and surprising ways—the hallmark of the band's overall career. —*Ned Raggett*

● **Mi Media Naranja** / 1997 / Blast First! ♦♦♦♦
For all of the group's first three albums each being intriguing, engaging listens, there was no hint that *Media* would be as flat out amazing as it was. Yet it was, and remains Labradford's best album yet, an accomplished meshing of all the various elements to their sound over previous releases into one near-perfect sonic document. Making a specific benefit out of turning the minimal into something maximal always was the band's major ability, but it gets showcased here to a new, breathtaking extent. "S" sets the scene just right, with Mark Nelson's trademark deliberate echoed guitar plucking and all manner of ambient keyboard touches joined by gentle strings and, most notably of all, a crisp, dub-inflected rhythm, spare but forceful. Add to this an overlay near the start of the song of a high frequency pitch—not annoying, but noticeable—and the end impression is of a band in full command of how to create detailed but not overly busy songs, compelling in their understated beauty. The album is packed with such high points and subtle sonic touches—the sample of a child and slight bossa-nova rhythm on "WR," the loops of running liquid and distant engines behind twinkly keyboard sounds—and then all that behind the usual guitar/organ interplay—on "I," along with cryptic found-sound man-on-the-street statements dropped in at various points to boot. Quietly fascinating and endlessly listenable, *Media* turns what had been a very good band indeed into a masterful one. —*Ned Raggett*

**E Luxo So** / May 10, 1999 / Kranky ♦♦♦♦
The underrated but present Labradford sense of humor turns up here in an amusing way—namely, the six song titles for the band's fifth record, which when read in order are in fact the album credits: recording studio, side players and so forth. Besides being entertainingly wry, this emphasizes even more than the one and two letter songtitles from *Media* that Labradford are much more about musical than any lyrical intent—something always apparent, but even more so here, on the band's first full instrumental release. Compared with the low-key complexity of *Media*, *Luxo* is far more minimal and a bit less gripping as a result, though not by much. The keyboard-provided rhythm on "with John Morand and assisted by Brian Hoffa" helps make it one of the quirkiest songs yet Labradford have done, while having piano instead of organ playing against the guitar makes it even more distinct. "Dulcimers played by Peter Neff. Strings played" actually verges on being modern classical, consisting almost solely of piano and a string quartet, with the exception of a sudden interruption of what sounds like a door opening and closing and various gears turning. "and Jonathan Morken. Photo provided by" has more of the in-depth sound layering expected of Labradford, with what sounds like a series of record pops helping to provide some of the rhythm beneath a piano/organ/guitar combination, but generally this is a more spacious sounding effort from the band, and not a bad one at all. —*Ned Raggett*

## Laika
f. 1993, London, England
*Group / Ambient-Pop, Dream-Pop, Indie-Rock, Post-Rock/Experimental*
Like their namesake—the dog rocketed into orbit by the Soviets and renowned as the first living creature to exit the earth's atmosphere—Laika travelled the spaceways, forging a distinct and wildly experimental fusion of hip-hop, jazz, electronica, dub, and Kraut-rock without earthly precedent. A kind of Too Pure label all-star team comprised of former Moonshake vocalist/programmer Margaret Fiedler and bassist John Frenett, onetime PJ Harvey drummer Rob Ellis and noted producer Guy Fixsen, as well as ex-God percussionist Lou Ciccotelli and saxophonist/flautist Louise Elliott, Laika formed in London during the autumn of 1993; their debut EP, *Antenna*, appeared the following summer. *Silver Apples of the Moon*, the group's acclaimed full-length debut, followed in late 1994; after a hiatus and the departure of Frenett, Laika resurfaced with *Sounds of the Satellites* in early 1997, garnering even greater critical praise. *Good Looking Blues* appeared in 2000. —*Jason Ankeny*

**Silver Apples of the Moon** / 1995 / Too Pure ♦♦♦♦
A visionary debut, *Silver Apples of the Moon* channels the full scope of modern music: hip-hop, dub, jungle, acid-jazz, electronica—you name it, it's here. Contradictions and ironies fuel the record: a feather-light surface sheen masks a dark, complex rhythmic undertow, while Margaret Fiedler's gentle, whispery vocals act as camouflage for the perversity and malice at the heart of highlights like "Marimba Song," "44 Robbers," and "Honey in Heat." —*Jason Ankeny*

● **Sounds of the Satellites** / Feb. 24, 1997 / Too Pure ♦♦♦♦
During the three long years which passed between the release of *Silver Apples of the Moon* and its follow-up, *Sounds of the Satellites*, the dub, trip-hop, and drum'n'bass sounds which made Laika so distinctive and original the first time out became commonplace; never given their proper due as pioneers of electronica anyway, their prospects for creating music of similar depth and invention appeared to grow dimmer and dimmer as time went on. Miraculously, *Sounds of the Satellites* is even better than its predecessor, a simultaneous expansion of the band's sonic palette and a brilliant refinement of their past innovations. The pivotal difference between Laika and other similarly inclined artists is their unparalleled sense of atmosphere: far removed from the pummeling insistence of groups like Prodigy or the Chemical Brothers, Laika also avoids the cinematic film-noir ambience of Portishead in favor of a subdued, dreamlike labyrinth of sound—the album is, by turns, claustrophobic ("Breather"), sexy ("Almost Sleeping"), and menacing ("Shut Off/Curl Up"). Rarely is electronic music so suggestive, so fluid, or so human; *Sounds of the Satellites* exists in its own orbit, so far ahead of its contemporaries as to be off of the map. —*Jason Ankeny*

**Good Looking Blues** / Apr. 18, 2000 / Too Pure ♦♦♦♦
For a band that named itself after the first dog in outer space—and previous albums called *Sounds of the Satellites* and *Silver Apples of the Moon*—you'd think Laika would make spacey ambient music with a focus on quirky beats. And they do, sometimes. The emphasis, though, of *Good Looking Blues*, the London quartet's third album, is to give equal attention to Margaret Fiedler's smooth, somewhat gothic- and soul-influenced vocals and the band's mixture of rock, slow electronic, and sit-on-your-couch dance music. Fiedler, who went to grade school with Liz Phair in Winnetka, Illinois and later played in a Smiths-sounding college band with Moby, speak-sings dark fictional stories about life's basic themes: love, sex, death, and work. But it's not quite that simple. For instance, on one of the album's standouts, "Black Cat Bone," she tells a story of a woman who kills her evil husband with voodoo: "Rocks for my pillow and sand for my bed/For better or worse, I left him for dead." Laika's talent is crafting a particular mood. This mood, however, is difficult to explain. With songs about nights of apologies on "Moccasin," a lover man leaving on "T Street," and working for the man until death do you part on "Widow's Weed," you can't deny that Laika is dealing with themes of depression and wallowing in sadness. And even though you wouldn't call the sound upbeat, it is indeed mesmerizing, tranquil, and head-bobbing. —*Amy Schroeder*

## Lamb
f. 1994, Manchester, England
*Group / Electronica, Jungle/Drum'N'Bass, Club/Dance*
Mancunian downtempo/drum'n'bass duo Lamb were one of the first groups to add a lyrics-based vocalist to steadfastly jungle-based productions. Unlike other vocal-based groups (such as Everything But the Girl and the Sneaker Pimps) who've dabbled in rolling breaks as a quiet accompaniment to a clearly dominant vocal lead, Lamb dwell in brash musical contrasts and, occasionally, contradictions that make their songs as musically complex and exploratory as they are vocally catchy. Formed in 1994 by producer Andrew Barlow and vocalist Louise Rhodes (the former an in-house engineer for So What management, the latter a daughter of folk-singer parents and a bud-

ding songstress), Lamb nailed a contract with Mercury subsidiary Fontana almost straight out of the gate.

The group's calling card, the "Cotton Wool" single, already showed fieldleaders such as Gerald Simpson and Fila Brazillia were on their side (each contributed a remix). But if anything it was the untouched title track that illustrated Lamb's commitment to keeping the music interesting (the track rows along on a thick double-bass sample and absolutely brutalizing drum sequences) while filling it out with a big dose of tunefulness. An additional single ("Gold") followed, with Lamb's self-titled debut released in the Fall of 1996 to widespread acclaim. Like the previous singles, much of *Lamb* explores song-oriented deployments of jungle, but the album also adds elements of downtempo and ambient-ish electro-jazz as well, making for one of the most diverse, stylistically mature debuts in recent memory. Most recently, Rhodes lent her vocals to Sheffield legends 808 State's *Don Solaris* LP (on the track "Azura"), and the success of Lamb's debut also brought a fair amount of remix work their way. The pair also added touring to their repertoire (*Lamb*'s release was followed by a European tour with labelmates Galliano), combining their electronics-heavy productions with live instrumentalists. Second album, *Fear of Fours*, appeared in 1999. —*Sean Cooper*

**Cotton Wool [Single]** / 1996 / Fontana ♦♦♦♦
This one exploded out of Lamb's Manchester studios and onto just about every DJ deck in town. Three-quarters of Lamb's debut single is dominated by remixes—and able ones at that, from the likes of Fila Brazillia and A Guy Called Gerald—but all sound utterly tame next to the original, with full-auto drum breaks exploding around Louise Rhodes' wrenching, seductive torch. Amazing. —*Sean Cooper*

★ **Lamb** / May 13, 1997 / Fontana ♦♦♦♦♦
Using the post-modern torch music of Portishead as a foundation, Lamb spins out into new sonic territories on its eponymous debut album. The group sports a heavier techno influence, incorporating the buzzing rhythms of drum'n'bass into their music in particular, yet they cut their modernistic electronic influences with a dark sense of melodicism. Most of the album is devoted to jazzy songs that are broken apart by Andrew Barlow's synthesizers and sampler, and are anchored by Louise Rhodes' seductive vocals, which prevent the electronics from becoming cold. It's sophisticated urban music, one that's miles away from the avant-garde sensibilities of Tricky and the haunted romanticism of Portishead, or even the pop leanings of Sneaker Pimps and the soul-inflected grooves of Morcheeba. Instead, Lamb is classy, detached and cool—a more club-oriented and less melodic variation of *Everything But the Girl's Walking Wounded*. Although *Lamb* may run a little long, it's one of the more hypnotic by-products of trip-hop yet released. —*Stephen Thomas Erlewine*

**Fear of Fours** / May 17, 1999 / Fontana ♦♦♦♦
While their debut was practically a revolution in the development of a satisfactory fusion of singer/songwriter vocals and drum'n'bass, Lamb's second album sets the bar much higher. As on the band's debut, Andy Barlow proves he's one of the most capable and inventive producers in the electronic community. He also still sounds inspired by the fiery side of bop as well as more muted chamber music, from the dexterous synthetic bass and intricate drum programs on "Little Things" to the restrained beats and orchestral tug of "All in Your Hands" and "Bonfire." Similar to the rather deflated return of Portishead in 1997, though, *Fear of Fours* suffers from Louise Rhodes' tendencies to play up her voice as a torch diva, overemoting and often coming off as girlish or whiny on many tracks. Thank goodness, then, for lengthy instrumentals like "Ear Parcel," which begins with the pastoral sounds of twinkling bells and croaking frogs but later whips up a few frenzied breakbeats as a bed for a sampled trumpet solo. —*John Bush*

## Neil Landstrumm

*Producer, DJ / Experimental Techno, Club/Dance, Techno*
Based in Edinburgh, Scotland, Neil Landstrumm has played upon the verge of experimental techno music, a form no less innovative though its steady beat has been perceived as having little room for intelligent musicians. Influenced by the Sheffield school of industrial bleep techno pioneered by LFO, Landstrumm is also respectful of colleague Cristian Vogel, who more than shares his tendencies toward the obtuse. Landstrumm began producing in the early '90s within a variety of groups, but began solo production in 1993. He met Vogel one year later while DJing at Edinburgh's Sativa club, and released a single for Vogel's Mosquito label; the duo also combined for several EPs recorded as Blue Arsed Fly. Landstrumm began recording for Peacefrog Records through Vogel's connection to Luke Slater, and released his first album *Brown for August* on Peacefrog in 1995. Increasingly splitting production chores with occasional partner Tobias Schmidt—who records on his own as well—he released his second LP, *Understanding Disinformation*, in 1996 for Berlin's sympathetic Tresor label. Landstrumm's formation of the Scandinavia label that year took up much of his time, with the release of solid singles by Adam X, Stephen Brown, and others; nevertheless, in 1997 he managed to issue another full-length, *Bedrooms & Cities*. *Pro Audio* followed a year later. —*John Bush*

**Understanding Disinformation** / Jul. 29, 1996 / Tresor/Logic ♦♦♦♦

● **Bedrooms & Cities** / Oct. 6, 1997 / Tresor ♦♦♦♦
Neil Landstrumm's second home, the US, gets name-checked all over *Bedrooms & Cities*. Besides the obvious—track titles like "Miami Vice," "Minneapolis Bass Treatment," and "Tension in New York"—there's the music itself, still linked to his early Sheffield/Warp influences but also reliant on specifically American innovations such as funk and bass-driven dance. Through it all is Landstrumm's trademarked preference of twiddling with wild-pitched acid and distortion instead of choosing the usual path. —*John Bush*

**Pro Audio** / Sep. 22, 1998 / Tresor ♦♦♦
Recorded in Brooklyn, *Pro Audio* takes Landstrumm once more into his old stomping grounds; that is, stomping techno with an assortment of lurching, careening acid lines to unsettle those four-four beats and trad drum machines. The formula is in just a little danger of growing stale, leading to a bit of difficulty in differentiating between tracks from this album and ones from Landstrumm's earlier work (though the title "Down on the A" reveals its New York origins). Spotlight tracks "Vectrex" and "Gigolos Trapped in Retro Hell," tap into some great experimental grooves. —*John Bush*

## Ulf Langheinrich

*Producer, Composer / Experimental Techno, Ambient Techno*
As one-half of Viennese multimedia performance group Granular-Synthesis, Ulf Langheinrich explores the interface of time, vision, technology, and subjectivity, bringing these components into uneasy proximity in order to foreground relationships of codetermination. A featured artist at world renowned exhibitions and festivals such as Japan's *Nagoya Biennale* and Austria's *Ars Electronica*, Granular-Synthesis (which includes Langheinrich and co-producer Kurt Hentschlager) were introduced to American audiences in 1996 via the New York-based Asphodel label's *Recombinant* tour, during which the group presented its audiovisual work-in-progress, "Motion Control"—an arresting, multi-panel projection of the face of Japanese performance artist Akemi Takeya digitally manipulated and reorganized to suggest a sort of hyperkinetic stasis. Asphodel sublabel Sombient subsequently released a solo work by Langheinrich; titled *Degrees of Amnesia*, the 72-minute CD presents 13 wonderfully varied digital ambient landscapes utilizing, among other software-based production techniques, granular synthesis—a method of digital sound design whereby sounds are reduced to their smallest possible quanta, or "grains," and organized and manipulated to achieve otherwise unattainable levels of sonic depth and detail. —*Sean Cooper*

● **Degrees of Amnesia** / Jan. 20, 1998 / Asphodel ♦♦♦♦
Ulf Langheinrich's first solo full-length for an American label, *Degrees of Amnesia* is comparable to the intricate digital abuses of electronic minimalists such as Mika Vainio and Porter Ricks. However, unlike much of those artists' work, Langheinrich seems intent upon bridging the atomization of sound (via digital sound production technologies such as granular synthesis) with an enduring musicality. Langheinrich joins in this fashion academic computer musicians espousing a sort of "chaos music," but who nonetheless remain often woefully off-target in terms of aesthetics. On the contrary, assembling rich, oddly affecting landscapes of engulfing ambience and dense, digital noise, *Degrees of Amnesia* is a fascinating, immensely rewarding disc. —*Sean Cooper*

## Kenny Larkin

b. Detroit, MI
*Producer / Detroit Techno, Club/Dance, Techno*
Third Wave techno artist Kenny Larkin is the member of a new school of Detroit-based musicians taking the city's famous brand of hard-edged musical futurism into new and innovative areas. Although he missed out on the style's

formative years in the mid- to late '80s due to a stint in the military, Larkin, a Detroit native, was brought up to speed upon his return by the likes of Juan Atkins and Derrick May, the latter of whose weekly radio shows inspired Larkin to pursue music production. Heavily rooted in house, Larkin quickly incorporated techno's formal characteristics into a brazen-yet-refined style that places his music somewhere in between Detroit and Chicago, combining house's more swinging rhythmic vibe and soft edge with techno's muscular backbeat and experimental zeal. He released a pair of 12"s—"We Shall Overcome" and "Integration"—on the Richie Hawtin/John Acquaviva label Plus 8 in the early '90s before moving on to release material through Buzz, Warp, and R&S. Massively influential on British and German, as well as American strains of techno, his tracks have appeared on a number of notable compilations documenting new-school Detroit talent. His exposure abroad has also translated, as with a number of Detroit originals such as Jeff Mills and Carl Craig, into a level of European success far surpassing that at home. [See Also: Dark Comedy] —*Sean Cooper*

- **Azimuth** / 1994 / Warp ♦♦♦♦
Larkin's work has evidenced a sharp turn away from the dancefloor, incorporating compositional elements of ambient and armchair techno, while remaining true at least in spirit to his roots. *Azimuth* is a pretty successful example of this trend, although the combination works best on tracks such as "Funk in Space" where rhythmic play is given fuller reign. —*Sean Cooper*

**Metaphor** / 1995 / R&S ♦♦♦♦
Larkin's second full-length arguably betters his debut, charting much of the distinctive geography found on *Azimuth*. The highlights here, including the title track plus "Nocturnal" and "Loop 1," use the same whirling space-funk and haunted-synth techno from *Azimuth*, with a better attention to his 808 programming. What lifts *Metaphor* above its predecessor comes with its detours, into beatless territory with "Java" and the dense looped techno reminiscent of his Dark Comedy alias on "Catatonic (First State)." —*John Bush*

## Bill Laswell

b. Feb. 12, 1955, Salem, IL
*Bass, Producer, Arranger / Electronica, Dark Ambient, Club/Dance, Experimental, Dub, M-Base, Prog-Rock/Art-Rock, Fusion, Avant-Garde, Ambient, Modern Creative*

A longtime linchpin of the New York City underground music scene, Bill Laswell was among the most prolific artists in contemporary music; as a performer, producer, and label chief, his imprint is on literally hundreds of albums, the majority of them characterized by a signature sound fusing the energy of punk with the bone-rattling rhythms of funk. Born on February 12, 1955, in Salem, Illinois, he initially played guitar, but soon switched to bass; raised primarily in the Detroit area, he honed his skills in local funk outfits before relocating to New York in 1978. There Laswell formed Material, an outlet for his experimental approach towards sounds ranging from jazz to hip-hop to worldbeat; originally the backup unit for Daevid Allen, the group soon began working on its own, issuing its debut EP *Temporary Music* in 1979.

In addition to fronting Material, Laswell also mounted a solo career, issuing *Baselines* in 1982 on Celluloid, a label he partly owned and operated. Appearances on key recordings from the likes of David Byrne, John Zorn, Fred Frith, and the Golden Palominos served as a virtual nexus of the downtown NYC community, and in 1983 he broke into the mainstream with his production work on Herbie Hancock's smash "Rockit," which he also co-wrote; the follow-up LP, *Sound-System*, won him a Grammy. Throughout the mid-'80s Laswell was everywhere, playing bass on LPs from artists including Mick Jagger, Peter Gabriel, Yoko Ono, and Laurie Anderson; he also joined the avant group Curlew, and produced a number of African acts.

In 1986, Laswell joined guitarist Sonny Sharrock, drummer Ronald Shannon Jackson, and saxophonist Peter Brotzmann in the group Last Exit; a second solo LP, *Hear No Evil*, appeared two years later, and after a long hiatus he also resurrected Material in 1989 with *Seven Souls*. Another project, the hip-hop-flavored Praxis, was resumed after close to a decade of inactivity with 1992's *Transmutation (Mutatis Mutandis)*. In 1990, Laswell formed another label, Axiom, to explore his interest in the new sounds of ambient and techno; where in the past his work rarely appeared solely under his own name, by the middle of the decade he was issuing several solo records annually in a wide range of styles from dub to jazz. He also remained among the most prolific producers in the business, collaborating with the likes of Dub Syndicate, Pete Namlook, Buckethead, and DJ Spooky. —*Jason Ankeny*

**Baselines** / Mar. 1982 / Rough Trade ♦♦♦
Even though Bill Laswell was already immersed in numerous projects since the end of the '70s, including leading his loose ensemble Material, he didn't release a solo record until 1984, and *Baselines* was quite a strange album. On the one hand, there's "Upright Man," one of the most infectious grooves Laswell has ever conceived, boasting ace bass playing and a weird taped sermon as sort-of lead vocals. Then there's "Work Song," which is funky and catchy and features Phillip Wilson's somewhat off-beat drumming (pun intended). The other tracks are more experimental, weird, and don't catch on as well—although they all reward repeated listening, for at first the listener might get lost between Ronald Shannon Jackson's irate drumming, Michael Beinhorn's acid-drenched synths and snippets of tapes and shortwave, the stuttering horns of George Lewis and Ralph Carney, the undescribable contributions of Fred Frith, and the vocalisms and percussion (rhythmic and non-rhythmic) David Moss provides. It's an interesting record, but it's not essential listening, and beginners or fans of Laswell's less avant-garde music won't get much out of this. If the somewhat comparable *Memory Serves* by Material left you craving more, you might want to give this album a try. —*Chris Genzel*

- **Hear No Evil** / 1988 / Venture ♦♦♦♦
A wonderful producer and bassist whose albums are more rock and instrumental pop than jazz. —*Ron Wynn*

**Axiom Ambient: Lost in the Translation** / 1994 / Axiom ♦♦♦♦
Bassist/producer Bill Laswell has long been one of the most important figures in New York's downtown scene, a frequent collaborator with artists as diverse as Fred Frith, the Master Musicians of Joujouka, PIL, the Golden Palominos, Jonas Hellborg, and many, many more. As prime mover in the constantly shifting musical collective known as Material, he has produced and played on some of the best experimental rock albums of the '80s and '90s, including 1994's stellar *Hallucination Engine* (Axiom 314-518 351-2), and lately his work has been more and more informed by a strange sort of cybermysticism, a mood which has found its perfect manifestation in "Axiom Ambient: Lost in the Translation." This two-disc set includes remixes of tracks previously performed by Material as well as several new compositions, most of them clocking in at well over ten minutes. Laswell's sound is warmer than that of many of his electronic compatriots and actually includes sounds found in nature, and even if there isn't much to hold your attention, you can fall asleep and have groovy dreams. —*Rick Anderson*

**Psychonavigation** / 1994 / Subharmonic ♦♦♦
The brainchild of ambient music deans Laswell and Pete Namlook, *Psychonavigation* is explained most succinctly by its title. Beautiful synth and looped vocal samples are layered over chill-out percussion and ambling rhythms. There is some diversity: The second track deserts the positive vibe and introduces disturbing vocals. —*John Bush*

**Silent Recoil** / 1995 / Low ♦♦
For the launch of yet another label, Bill Laswell produced an album with only three tracks of ambient-dub. The lilting atmospherics somehow work when attached to an immense bassline. —*John Bush*

**Subsonic, Vol. 2: Bass Terror** / 1995 / Sub Rosa ♦♦
Instead of a collaboration between Laswell and the ex-member of Scorn, *Subsonic 2* includes a lengthy track from each: Laswell's contribution explores dark percussive ambience, while Bullen uses a dub groove to flavor his ambience. —*John Bush*

**Web** / 1995 / Subharmonic ♦♦♦
Some of the most abrasive, industrial leaning ambient of either of these composers' careers. Chains rattle, voices whisper menacingly, and dark, dissonant textures and deep bass drones collide on a trio of extended tracks united by the questionably thematic topic of digital communications technology. Difficult but rewarding. —*Sean Cooper*

**Equations of Eternity** / 1996 / WordSound ♦♦
A collaboration between Bill Laswell, Scorn's Mick Harris, and the Italian Eraldo Bernocchi, *Equations of Eternity* is a much more exciting prospect than much of Laswell's earlier material on Axiom Records. The combination of slowly progressing bass and abrasive drum programming—each done with ponderous care—puts the album over the top, and though it's difficult

to pinpoint each member's contributions, it hardly matters on an album this enjoyable. —*John Bush*

**Sacred System, Chapter One: Book of Entrance** / 1996 / ROIR ✦✦✦
Fans of Bill Laswell will salivate at the prospect of an all-reggae outing from the master producer and bass god. And at first listen, he bears out most expectations: the grooves are heavy, intelligent, and well-constructed. But as the disc wears on, it also becomes increasingly clear that he made one serious mistake in making this album: he played and produced everything himself, and the resulting sound is kind of sterile. Blame it in part on the crispy-clean digital keyboard sound that varies not at all from track to track, but part of the problem lies in the fact that all of the musical ideas clearly come from one person. Laswell's a genius, but so is Prince; that doesn't mean that there shouldn't be someone there helping him sort the brilliant ideas from the mediocre ones, not to mention contributing a few different musical gestures just to keep things interesting. That said, this is a gorgeous piece of well-textured reggae background music. But if you want more than that, check out the followup (*Sacred System: Chapter Two*). —*Rick Anderson*

**Sacred System, Chapter Two** / 1997 / ROIR ✦✦
On *Sacred System: Chapter Two*, bassist and producer extraordinaire Bill Laswell makes good on the partly unfulfilled promise of 1996's *Sacred System Chapter One: Book of Entrance*. The difference, in this case, is a small ensemble of guest musicians who include Material guitarist Nicky Skopelitis, a tabla virtuoso named Bill Buchen, and jazz cornettist Graham Haynes (son of legendary bop drummer Roy Haynes). Whereas *Chapter One* was a rather arid solo project, *Chapter Two* comes completely to life with the various contributions of its ensemble players: Skopelitis mostly lays back and contributes lovely textures, while Haynes defines cavernous aural spaces with his echoey, jazzy horn lines, and Buchen delivers almost impossibly intricate percussion figures. Laswell himself seems more energized, as well, and his basslines sound deeper, heavier, happier. This is a deeply satisfying compilation of groove music from one of groove's greatest living exponents. —*Rick Anderson*

**Equations of Eternity, Vol. 2: Veve** / Aug. 4, 1998 / WordSound ✦✦✦
*Equations of Eternity 2: Veve* (voodoo) was recorded in three separate countries; Mick Harris laid down the beats in England, Bill Laswell added bass in the US, and producer Eraldo Bernocchi put the finishing touches on the tapes in Italy. It all makes for jarringly powerful rhythms and an eerie, sparse atmosphere. —*Steve Huey*

**Jazzonia** / Aug. 25, 1998 / Douglas ✦✦✦✦
The concept which Bill Laswell and Alan Douglas conceived for this CD has been tackled by various musicians with varying results, taking the jazz tradition of the past and updating them for the present, with hip-hop beats and the like. This mixture has often enough resulted in lukewarm acid jazz or, worse yet, cynical cash-ins, although gems can be found. Thanks to Laswell's unique vision, however, the music on this disc is nothing short of amazing. The renditions of vocalese jazz standards (including "Moody's Mood for Love," Stan Getz's "Little Boy Don't Get Scared," and Duke Ellington's "Cottontail") are built around a vocal duo from Brooklyn: Asante and Laswell himself. He doesn't just play his dubby bass, but also programmed the hip-hop beats and contributed sounds in general (some of which were taken from his earlier releases: compare "Blue" to "33" from *Valis II*). That's not all, however; apart from the soulful vocals of Asante, singers include Dana Bryant (whose voice is incredibly sexy), Alicia Renee, and even rap pioneer Grandmaster Melle Mel. Amina Claudine Myers, who plays some funky organ and electric piano on various tracks, also sings on one track. Adding to the hip-hop element are turntablists Roc Raida and DXT; Laswell himself also does some scratching. The jazz element is brought in by saxophonist Byard Lancaster and cornetist Graham Haynes (both restrained and intense at once) and the subdued, bluesy guitar work of Brandon Ross and Nicky Skopelitis. Finally, Karl Berger is an important voice on most of the tracks; he not only arranged and conducted the Material Strings (sounding romantic but cliché-free), but also plays vibes and keyboards. Two tracks deserve special mention: "Blue" (a Joni Mitchell cover) is the only instrumental track, apart from the one-minute and 47-second "Fade" at the end of the disc—and it's pure melancholy, thanks to Berger's textures and Haynes' echoey cornet. The other one is "Cottontail," which Laswell treated with a drum'n'bass loop and some priceless "walking dub bass." Bootsy Collins has a short cameo on this track. The biggest plus of this album is that it's never afraid of being sentimental, with its full strings and lush arrangements, but at the same time it's completely free of cheese and

clichés. Laswell has indeed blended various styles into a fresh and original sound which sounds traditional and new at once. Who says that staying in the tradition has to imply sounding like a xerox of it? —*Chris Genzel*

**Broken Vessels** / 1999 / Velvel ✦✦✦✦
The length of time between the initial appearance of Todd Fields' movie about out-of-control paramedics and the release of this album of music "from and inspired by" the film would indicate a rather typical Laswellian post-production condition. In other words, rather than release an album that compiles cues and themes from the motion picture score, Laswell has instead reconstructed the work to provide more structural cohesiveness indicated by the way the tracks segue from one to the next, and the structural cohesiveness of several of them, indicating that short cues have been repeated, combined, and modified to create a song-like structure.

Otherwise, the album provides a condensed trip through many of Laswell's touchstones—ambient drones, modified world music elements, cracking funk, ear-bleed level rock, explosively percussive rhythm structures, and so on. Nicky Skopelitis provides terrific support via some blazing guitar work, while Lance Carter's drumming seems (in terms of Laswell's production methods) less significant by far. *Broken Vessels* is not one of Laswell's milestones, by any means, but it is an engaging and propulsive recording. —*Steven E. McDonald*

**Invisible Design** / Mar. 23, 1999 / Tzadik ✦✦✦✦
Though Bill Laswell is no stranger to his inner creative genius, there is something about the complete free reign that the Tzadik label routinely gives its artists that seems to bring out their best work. So it is not surprising that *Invisible Design*, his first Tzadik album, hums with energy and the poetic grace of a well-executed thought. The overwhelming element throughout is a kind of meditative flow—with synth elements and lingering bass notes floating in and out like breath. The percussive element of some of his other albums is not to be found here—this is a work of pure contemplation. Deeply spiritual, the album also creates a landscape of chill and emptiness. It is nearly never dark, but sometimes gives the impression of light viewed from a place of shadow. A few pieces show contrast—"Black Aether" alternates the atmospheric elements with swaths of grind and buzz, and "Oceans of Borrowed Money" trades the slow, lingering bass of many of the other tracks for something more uptempo and funky. The result is active, but never frenetic or tense. *Invisible Design* may echo elements of Laswell's other ambient projects, but this is a unique project and nowhere yet has he produced a record that is so consistently good from start to finish. —*Stacia Proefrock*

**Imaginary Cuba** / Sep. 14, 1999 / RCA ✦✦✦✦
Bassist and producer Bill Laswell has dabbled in several varieties of African music over the long and circuitous course of his career, with uneven results. But Latin America is a region he's left largely alone, until now. *Imaginary Cuba* finds him taking an approach somewhat similar to the one he employed on his *Off World One* project—building on a foundation of field recordings, he constructs complex and often dub-inflected sound collages that sound like no one but Laswell while still maintaining respect for the music's origins. Laswell's distinctive bass style—heavy, yet almost singingly melodic—and his penchant for dubwise echo and fade techniques are what make this music recognizably his, but the raw materials that form its basis come from Cuban artists like Tata Guines, Frank Emilio, and the Septeto Nacional. Massed, trance-inducing drums, music-hall piano, call-and-response vocals and various unidentified stringed instruments are all part of the mix, and the rhythmic stew that Laswell cooks up using all of these ingredients is rich, thick, and spicy. Highly recommended. —*Rick Anderson*

**Emerald Aether: Shape Shifting/Reconstructions Of Irish Music** / Mar. 14, 2000 / Shanachie ✦✦
This project had such potential. Celtic music lends itself very nicely to being mixed with modern dance beats, and no one makes such cultural fusions work better than Bill Laswell—witness in particular his very fine *Imaginary Cuba* album and countless other bubbly multicultural musical stews. On *Emerald Aether*, the idea was to take tracks from Shanachie's enviably deep Celtic catalog (including performances by singer Karan Casey, flutist Matt Molloy, piper Jerry O'Sullivan, and the band Solas) and place them like green jewels in Laswell's trademark space-funk settings. And in several cases, it works really well—"The Stride Set," a set of reels by Solas, is nicely energized by Laswell's breakbeats, and the echoey ambience he applies to O'Sullivan's "Wind Chimes and Nursery Rhymes" works very well, too. But too many of

these tracks are ruined by Laswell's ignorance (or, it seems more likely, simple disregard) of modal harmony in general and the key centers of the individual songs in particular. His settings of Karan Casey's performances add chord washes that bear no apparent harmonic relationship to the keys Casey is singing in, which means that her singing clashes unpleasantly with the music that is supposed to be supporting her. The same thing happens rhythmically with the dubwise drum'n'bass setting that Laswell builds for Matt Molloy's rendition of "The Hare in the Heather" — there's no reason why the beats couldn't have meshed with Molloy's played rhythms, and the final product would have much more compelling if they had. Despite some inspired moments, this album is a real disappointment overall. —*Rick Anderson*

**Dub Chamber 3** / Apr. 25, 2000 / Roir ♦♦♦♦
There's no doubting Bill Laswell's sincere love of dub (the reggae subgenre that anticipated remix culture by about 20 years). As one of the finest and most tasteful bass players on the planet, Laswell's grounding in reggae is evident in every note he plays, and his mystical, experimental production style has always been heavily influenced by such dubmasters as King Tubby, Scientist, and Lee "Scratch" Perry. But for all of the experimentalism (and sometimes downright abrasiveness) of many of his projects, he has been fairly criticized in the past for getting mushy when he gets into an explicitly dubwise context. Most notoriously, he managed to squander a great opportunity when he turned an entire album's worth of classic Bob Marley material into soupy multi-culti muzak. But the third volume in his *Sacred System* trilogy (called, confusingly, *Dub Chamber 3*) is more muscular than some of his other dubwise excursions, and although there's not much here to challenge the mind, the dreamy flavor of this music is consistently fortified by sturdy beats and Laswell's inimitably tasty basslines. The album consists of four long tracks; on all of them, he's joined by guitarist Nicky Skopelitis, and two of them also feature the playing of Norwegian trumpeter Nils Petter Molvaer, whose treated trumpet gives everything a beautiful, eerie sheen. Other guests include bassist Jah Wobble, percussionist Karsh Kale, and pianist Craig Taborn. Recommended. —*Rick Anderson*

## LaTour

f. 1990, Chicago, IL
*Group / Club/Dance, Acid House, Dance-Pop*
LaTour was the alias of Chicago-based house producer William LaTour, who in 1991 scored a major club crossover smash with the novelty hit "People Are Still Having Sex," featured on his self-titled debut LP. Subsequent attempts to repeat this early success — like the follow-up "Allen's Got a New Hi-Fi" — failed, however, and 1993's *Home on the Range* appeared to little notice, with LaTour dropping entirely out of sight soon after. —*Jason Ankeny*

● **LaTour** / 1991 / SMASH ♦♦
The rule on LaTour's debut is sampladelic acid house, a bit more inventive than most, but still a bit too sex-obsessed to qualify for further interest. —*John Bush*

**Home on the Range** / 1993 / SMASH ♦♦

## Laub

f. Berlin, Germany
*Group / Experimental Techno, Ambient Techno*
An experimental indie-electronics act based in Berlin, Laub was formed in the mid-'90s by programmers Antye Greie-Fuchs and Von Jotka. The pair debuted in 1997 with the *Kopflastig* LP, released on Kitty-Yo — home to companion acts like Tarwater and Gonzalez, and also the site of Greie-Fuchs' dayjob. After adding percussionist Sebastian Vogel, Laub returned in 1999 with *Unter Anderen Bedingungen Als Liebe* and an accompanying remix album, *Intuition*. —*John Bush*

**Kopflastig** / 1997 / Kitty Yo ♦♦♦

**Unter Anderen Bedingungen Als Liebe** / May 4, 1999 / Kitty-Yo ♦♦♦

● **Intuition (Remixes)** / Oct. 26, 1999 / Kitty-Yo ♦♦♦♦
A collection of remixes featuring source material from *Unter Anderen Bedingungen Als Liebe, Intuition* features genre exercises and interpretations from various Laub well-wishers (Gonzales, Blond, Schneider TM, Pole, Rechenzentrum) plus a few of the more beat-oriented experimentalists in the electronic scene (Coldcut, Clifford Gilberto Rhythm Combination, Richard Thomas). Gonzales' deep and dark "Wake up Remix" is one of the highlights, as is Schneider TM's gloriously lo-fi "Urlaub Widergefühlich Remix." —*John Bush*

## Christopher Lawrence

*DJ / Progressive Trance, Trance, Club/Dance*
Christopher Lawrence is a sleek trance DJ who's risen to the top of the field — in America, at least — and helmed several mix albums as well as produced his own work and remixed others. Before he'd been DJing for more than a few years, Lawrence released the 1997 mix album *Rise* on the Fragrant label. One year later, he signed a production contract with the respected Scottish label Hook Recordings, and watched as "Navigator" and "Shredder" became proper British club hits, extending his name and resume across the globe. During 1999, he released two more mix albums, *Temptation* (for City of Angels) and the label retrospective *Hook Recordings*. Signed to the American mix label Moonshine Music, Lawrence delivered his fourth collection *Trilogy, Part One: Empire* in 2000. —*John Bush*

**Temptation** / Feb. 23, 1999 / City of Angels ♦♦♦
*Temptation* is a DJ album spotlighting Christopher Lawrence's mixing talents, as well as featuring a version of his "Shredder" single. —*Steve Huey*

● **Hook Recordings** / Apr. 27, 1999 / Egil Music ♦♦♦♦
When the Scottish trance label Hook decided to release a retrospective, who better to spin the mix than "America's top trance DJ" Christopher Lawrence, the producer of two Hook singles himself. The result, *Hook Recordings*, is Lawrence's best mix album, perhaps because it's as much a labor of love than a day at the office. Obviously, the tracks must be given some credit; although they're statuesque and self-important as only trance can be, they're also much harder and more minimal than the norm, sticking to the point with no reliance on over-the-top effects or continuous breakdowns. Highlights come from X-Cabs (own remixes of "Prophase" and "Neuro"), DeNiro ("Evolver"), and Dawntreader ("Dominion"), while Lawrence's pair of inclusions also do well. Lawrence strips these tracks down to the bone so much so that a few techno fans may even find themselves crossing the fence to give this one a try. —*John Bush*

**Trilogy, Part One: Empire** / Feb. 22, 2000 / Moonshine Music ♦♦
*Trilogy, Part One: Empire* is an 11-track set of sleek club trance that strays only occasionally from the hypnotic, vaguely eerie template of 120-bpm acid trance. Lawrence does gradually move into anthem territory with extroverted, individual selections — Baby Doc's "Hard Work," his own "Renegade," and the nu-house of "Twin Town" by Ian Wilkie Vs. Timo Maas — but far too much of the mix blends together into background music: perfect for a coffeehouse or smart bar (and not too bad on the dancefloor either), but not the most diverting listen. —*John Bush*

## Layo & Bushwacka

*Group / Tech-House, Club/Dance, Techno, Nu Breaks*
The duo of Layo Paskin and Matthew "Bushwacka" B. are better known as co-owner and resident DJ, respectively, at the End, the tech-house club founded by the Shamen's Mr. C. Matthew B. had recorded singles for Sound as a Pound and Plank before he was signed up to DJ at *the End*. The club soon became one of the best in England, and spurred a record label as well for related productions. Several singles and the first album by Layo & Bushwacka appeared on End Recordings, as did several singles produced by Paskin and Mr. C as the Usual Suspects. —*John Bush*

● **Low Life** / Oct. 25, 1999 / End Recordings ♦♦♦♦
Despite several respected singles and remixes, Layo Paskin and Matthew "Bushwacka" B. were still better known as DJs than producers before 1999. All that changed with *Low Life*, however. The duo's first production LP is a varied album that flirts with Miami bass, electro, funk, Italian house, Latin percussion, and breakbeat techno (often in the same song), while still rarely deserting their pioneering tech-house foundation. Much more streamlined and dance-friendly than competitive acts like Leftfield or the Chemical Brothers, *Low Life* succeeds at nearly everything it attempts — a surprise given the amount of cross-genre pollination going on here. —*John Bush*

## Le Car

f. 1995, Detroit, MI, db. 1998
*Group / Neo-Electro, Electro-Techno, Detroit Techno, Club/Dance*
Detroit duo Le Car make quirky, lo-fi listening techno reminiscent of Kraftwerk and Gary Numan, as well as more recent upgrade artists such as Elecktroids, Dopplereffekt, and Ectomorph. Consisting of Adam Miller and Ian Clark, most of Le Car's material to date (including the *Autofuel* and *Au-*

*tograph* EPs) has appeared on Miller's Ersatz Audio and Monoplaza imprints, established by Miller and partner/producer Robert Saltz in 1995 with the idea to pair dancefloor tracks with more experimental B-sides. Although EA's first few releases stuck to that program, more recent singles have shifted almost exclusively toward left field. Le Car were featured on the *Electro Juice* and *Five* compilations released by Austrian electronica label Sabotage alongside remarkably similar-sounding artists such as Patrick Pulsinger, Def Con, and the Private Lightning Six. In addition to the Le Car singles, Ersatz Audio has released tracks by Miller and Clark solo projects (Artificial Material and Lesseninglesson, respectively), as well as the 1996 compilation EP *Omniolio* and the major retrospective *Auto-Biography*. —*Sean Cooper*

### Autofuel [EP] / 1996 / Monoplaza ♦♦

Four tracks and two vignettes released on newly established Erstaz Audio sublabel Monoplaza. While standard-fare floorbang is hinted at with two of the tracks, this is weird, weird stuff, pitching its tent on grins'n'winks-filled territory similar in some respects to Dopplereffekt and Bochum Welt, but with a rhythmic complexity reminiscent of Atom Heart or some Patrick Pulsinger. —*Sean Cooper*

### Autograph [EP] / 1997 / Monoplaza ♦♦♦

Le Car's second 12" bares much resemblance to the first; beats made of cheap plastic, cheeky, humorous electronic noises put to use where melodies and basslines might normally be, etc. However, unlike "Auto Fuel," few of the tracks here move beyond 4-track sketches, although some interesting ideas are presented. —*Sean Cooper*

### Automatic [EP] / Oct. 27, 1997 / Sabotage ♦♦♦♦

*Automatic* is a mini-LP of sorts, and Le Car's first official release on the Austrian Sabotage label, whose own predilections toward good-natured cheek-tonguing makes Le Car's brand of lo-fi new wave/electro a logical fit. *Automatic* is essentially five tracks and three short vignettes, the former amounting to some of the group's most melodically and rhythmically integrated work to date. Foregrounding the inclination toward late-'70s/early-'80s weirdo technopop far more implicit in earlier recordings, Le Car manage whole songs—and good ones, too—where past releases settled for sketches. —*Sean Cooper*

### ● Auto-Biography / Aug. 31, 2000 / Ersatz Audio ♦♦♦♦

Die-hard fans of the electro-pop Detroit duo Le Car will foam over this collection, and those not familiar will be properly introduced with *Auto-Biography*. Jack Pulvine (of now defunct Monoplaza Records) and Adam Lee Miller (half of Adult and the Ersatz Audio label) released five 12"s (including their remix album) as Le Car to date. *Auto-Biography* is a perfect journal of Le Car's take on the relationship between man and music machine. Surprisingly, the CD is the first full-length from the duet and features tracks from the out of print *Automatic* mini-LP on Craft Records, a division of the Vienna based Sabotage Communications. Some never released tracks and edits in addition to a remix by G.D.Luxxe rounds out the CD nicely. To the new listener, Le Car functions as a surface audio reminder of the electronic poppy background music used in breakdancing films from the '80s. With a closer listen, Pulvine and Miller's music becomes simplistic and complicated and the devoted relationship with their music and gear is heard. Though this music is clearly and intentionally mechanical, the human presence cannot be denied. While striving to fill dance floors is the goal for many electronic acts and essential to the industry balance, so are the acts that redefine and push boundaries by more simplistic and quieter means. Le Car's mechanical sound is evened out with a subtle and lurking presence of humor. The CD's hidden track is a perfect example, but divulging the reason would be similar to giving away the surprise ending to an incredible film. *Auto-Biography* embodies precise, simplistic, and creative production, while keeping it comprehensible and simultaneously challenging. —*Diana Potts*

## Tim "Love" Lee

b. Jan. 19, 1970, Cambridge, England
*Producer / Trip-Hop, Club/Dance*

A trip-hop producer who also appears influenced by the smarmier side of Italian soft-porn soundtracks and the singles-bar scene, Tim "Love" Lee formed his own Peace Feast and Tummy Touch labels in 1996 to release tracks by Groove Armada, Waxploitation, and his own name. Singles like "Again Son," "Ruffbut," and "Nu Pholk Sound" treated trip-hop with an earthy edge. "Badder Bongo" was the trailer for his first LP, *Confessions of a Selector*, which was released in Britain in 1998. An American release through Silent followed later that year, with *Call Me "Lone" Lee* appearing in the spring of 2000. —*John Bush*

### ● Confessions of a Selector / 1997 / Silent ♦♦♦♦

Breezy jazz-funk, a little bit of disco, and porn soundtracks inform Tim "Love" Lee's debut, all produced with a variety of late-'70s and early-'80s B-movie soundtrack staples like cheap synthesizers, sarod, bongos, vocoder, and vibes. The only concessions to the '90s are the beats—edgy, well-programmed, and just enough of a presence to lift *Confessions of a Selector* above the many stale trip-hop and nu-disco albums released around the same time. —*John Bush*

### Tim "Love" Lee's XXX-Mas Selection [EP] / Dec. 7, 1998 / Tummy Touch ♦♦♦

### Call Me "Lone" Lee / Apr. 25, 2000 / Tummy Touch ♦♦

A qualified disappointment after a remarkable debut, *Call Me "Lone" Lee* offers little more than a few sleazy-listening tracks whose links to the '70s are just a bit too direct to qualify as anything more than camp or nostalgia. Partially compiled from previous singles releases, "Bed Sheet Shuffle," "One Night Samba," and the two-part "Triple X Togetherness" prove far more intriguing track titles than actual productions. One exception: the narcoleptic country haze of "Go Down Dixie." —*John Bush*

## Leftfield

f. 1991, London, England
*Group / Progressive House, Electronica, Club/Dance, House*

The production team which brought house music back from the brink of commercial mediocrity, Leftfield made it safe for artistic producers to begin working in a new vein termed progressive house. Paul Daley (a former member of A Man Called Adam and the Brand New Heavies) and programmer Neil Barnes combined the classic soul of early Chicago and New York house with the growing *Artificial Intelligence* school of album-oriented techno to create classic, intelligent dance music. When legal hassles over ownership of the Leftfield name prevented the pair from recording their own music after the release of their debut "Not Forgotten," they turned to remixing, establishing their early reputation for reworking tracks by artists ranging from Stereo MC's and David Bowie to Yothu Yindhi and Renegade Soundwave. Finally, with their courtroom battles successfully behind them, they formed their own Hard Hands label in late 1992 and issued the single "Release the Pressure," featuring reggae vocalist Earl Sixteen; "Song of Life" followed, and in 1993 Leftfield scored their first major hit with "Open Up," recorded with John Lydon. Their debut LP *Leftism* was released in 1995; the long awaited *Rhythm and Stealth* followed four years later. —*Jason Ankeny*

### ★ Leftism / 1995 / Hard Hands/Columbia ♦♦♦♦♦

*Leftism* spans most of Daley and Barnes' singles output from 1992 to 1995 (excepting only "Not Forgotten") and adds several new tracks. Far from being just a stale progressive house LP, it spans a wide range of influences (tribal, dub, trance) and includes a good mixture of vocal tracks (with Toni Halliday, John Lydon, and Earl Sixteen) and instrumental workouts. —*John Bush*

### Rhythm and Stealth / Aug. 31, 1999 / Columbia ♦♦♦♦

Perhaps wishing to move from progressive-house flagwavers to trip-hop super-producers on a par with Massive Attack, Leftfield returned after almost five years of silence with a set of blunted trip-hop jams, stoned to say the least—though glimmers of their house background do show through. Aside from a few uptempo stormers ("Double Flash," "Swords") reminiscent of a slightly less frenetic Jeff Mills, house fans looking for anthems worthy of "Not Forgotten" might be disappointed. The grooves on *Rhythm and Stealth* are a bit too languid and the productions a bit too intricate for dancefloor consumption. The one track that may make fans yearn for the heady days of 1993, "El Cid," begins with the ephemeral synth for which Leftfield has been known, but soon moves into breakbeat territory. Hip-hop pioneer Afrika Bambaataa makes an appearance on the excellent "Afrika Shox," taking the mic on a brutal electro throwdown. As *Rhythm and Stealth* shows time and time again, it's definitely not 1993 anymore, and Leftfield has moved on with a grace and mastery of production seldom seen in the dance world. —*John Bush*

## Legendary Pink Dots

f. 1980, London, England
*Group / Experimental Rock, Post-Punk, Industrial*

Formed in London in 1980, Legendary Pink Dots moved to Amsterdam in the middle of the decade. Members throughout the band's career have been

Edward Ka-Spel (vocals, keyboards) and Phil Knight (keyboards), also known as the Silver Man, with a shifting supporting cast over the years. The Dots' music is by turns melodic pop and exotic psychedelia, with classical influences, sampling, and relentlessly dark, violent, apocalyptic lyrics. After several releases for Mirrodot and Inphaze during the early '80s, the group signed to Play It Again Sam distribution for 1985's *The Lovers*, and released much of their best material (1990's *Crushed Velvet Apocalypse*, 1991's *The Maria Dimension*) on the label. Even as Legendary Pink Dots neared their two-decade anniversary, the group continued to tour Europe and America quite consistently, appreciated by several generations of dark industrial/goth audiences (and documented by the 2000 live album *Farewell, Milky Way*). —*Steve Huey*

**Chemical Playschool 10** / 1981 / Mirrodot ♦♦♦
Recorded between 1990 and 1995, *Chemical Playschool* is a double-disc set that includes five tracks included with limited editions of *The Maria Dimension*. Though it sounds good, the total package is less accessible than most of the Dots' admittedly obtuse recordings of psychedelic electronica. —*John Bush*

● **Under Triple Moons** / Apr. 29, 1997 / ROIR ♦♦♦♦
*Under Triple Moons* is a compilation of electro-experimentalists the Legendary Pink Dots' early material. All of the tracks were previously very hard to find, since they were only issued on cassettes non-commercially (for fans only), and were personally compiled by the band's singer and leader, Edward Ka-Spel. Ka-Spel's name may be familiar to Skinny Puppy fans, since he's collaborated with them often, but *Under Triple Moons* sounds nothing like Skinny Puppy's volatile music. What you'll find here are icy cold synthesizers merged with hard to decipher lyrics sung in a heavy European accent ("Amphitheatre," "Frosty," "Splash," etc.). Although it doesn't rank with the Pink Dots' best work, it's still recommended to hardcore fans of the band. —*Greg Prato*

**Nemesis Online** / Dec. 8, 1998 / Soleilmoon ♦♦♦
This impressive, moody release from the nearly 20-year-old group Legendary Pink Dots starts assertively. "Dissonance" earns its title from an over-modulated crunch of a rhythm married to a reverberated Western acoustic guitar rhythm. Over this, vocalist Edward Ka-Spel (now the Prophet Qa'Se-pel) intones a surreal tale of incarceration for the criminal that does not harmonize with society. The harsh crunch continues on into an instrumental track, "Jasz," and its glimpses of shards broken from the sounds of piano and saxophone. Before pivoting into mostly more ambient and reflective pieces Legendary Pink Dots is known for, you are treated to the strongest track of this collection. "As Long As It's Purple and Green" is a telling and lucid exploration of a psychotic's inner workings more recited (with a snarl) than sung over a breakbeat and loops similar to those in "Jasz." Again, the self-defined individual finds himself instantly cast out and confined from society at large. The ending is, of course, dissonant. Thus passing the storm, nine selections of Legendary meditation mixed with some upbeat numbers like more breakbeat and horn in "Zoo" and the heavy metal guitar in "Is It Something I Said?" follow. Of these, "Ghost" begins in the tranquility of an electric piano melody to breed the sanguine looped chant "blood on the door/blood on the stairs…" "A Sunset for a Swan" is perhaps the most quirky, sounding as it does like a New Orleans street band singing Syd Barrett poetry with electronica/carnival production. —*Tom Schulte*

## Legion of Green Men

f. 1994, Burlington, Ontario,
*Group / Ambient Techno, Club/Dance, Techno*
Alexander Addicus and Rupert J. Lloyd have applied their warped visions of ambient breakbeat, dub, and trip-hop to sampling experimentation under such messed-up aliases as Zeuxis & the Painted Grapes, Empirical Sleeping Consort, Alkahest and, most often, Legion of Green Men. Based in the relatively quiet metropolis of Burlington, Ontario, the duo formed their own Post Contemporary label in the early '90s and organized around a production team named Incarnate. Two 1994 releases as Legion of Green Men, the single "Midnight Genius" and debut LP *Spatial Specific*, earned Addicus and Lloyd a bit of credibility around the country and gave them a record-distribution deal through fellow Canadian Richie Hawtin's Plus 8 label. Virgin Canada picked up the baton too, giving the album worldwide release. The duo had already moved on however, with the debut of dub alias Zeuxis & the Painted Grapes for a 1995 LP titled *Mystic Songs from the Sanitorium*, released through Post Contemporary. They also recorded EPs as Incarnate and Alkahest before dropping their long-awaited sophomore album as Legion of Green Men, 1999's *Floating in Shallow Water*. —*John Bush*

● **Spatial Specific** / 1994 / Virgin Music Canada ♦♦♦
*Spatial Specific* is an imaginative but occasionally frustrating debut album from the Ontario duo. From the first two tracks (both of which feature a repetitious vocal sample repeated *ad infinitum* with a couple of effects to change the sound), it's clear that sonic experimentation is the name of the game here, a fact which doesn't always make for enjoyable listening. To the credit of the Green Men, they do pull off several effective fusions of gadgetry and grooves on tracks like "Extended Shadows" and "Veneration of the Goddess," it's just that they're a rather rare occurrence. —*John Bush*

**Floating in Shallow Water** / 1999 / Post Contemporary ♦♦♦

## Leila

b. Iran
*Keyboards, Producer / Electronica, Indie Rock*
Moving from a supporting keyboard role with Björk and Galliano to put out her own record on Aphex Twin's Rephlex Records, Leila is the rare female electronica songwriter that doesn't sing, choosing instead for her album *Like Weather* to use vocals from friends and even her own sister. Born in Iran, she spent part of her childhood there but was forced to flee to London with her family. She became interested in DJing as well as keyboards, and left college to play with Björk on her first album, 1994's *Debut*. Leila graduated to sound engineer for the second Björk LP, and began setting up her own home studio. Signed to Rephlex Records for a solo album, she released the single "Don't Fall Asleep" in 1997 and *Like Weather* the following year. *Love Story* appeared in 1999. —*John Bush*

● **Like Weather** / Mar. 30, 1998 / Rephlex ♦♦♦♦
Even compared to the dozens of edgy electronica songwriters appearing in the wake of Björk, *Like Weather* is quite a shot out of left field. Though many songs' anti-production values mark them as bedroom records in the vein of Rephlex geeks like Cylob or Bochum Welt, many of the vocal songs are downtempo symphonies worthy of Massive Attack. With a bit of studio tweaking reminiscent of Aphex Twin himself, the single "Don't Fall Asleep" has an assortment of unnatural frequencies, from the pitched-down, practically tune-less vocals to scattered dub explosions and pointed beats. The overall tone, though tremendously eclectic, is of an experimentalism far in advance of other electronic singer/songwriter acts out there. —*John Bush*

## Robert Leiner

b. Aug. 1, 1966, Boras, Sweden
*Producer / Ambient Techno, Trance, Club/Dance, Techno, Acid House*
Unlike the majority of electronic artists, who can flip-flop between hardcore tracks and more downbeat material but rarely excel at both, Robert Leiner recorded excellent uptempo acid tracks as Source and (later) the Source Experience, meanwhile releasing under his own name one of the best ambient techno albums of the '90s, *Visions of the Past*. Born in Sweden in 1966, Leiner began DJing at the tender age of 15 and set up his own studio just a few years later. After recording tracks for several different labels in his homeland, he moved to Ghent, Belgium, and began working for R&S Records as a technical consultant and sometime artist.

Leiner's first release on R&S, an ultra-rare 12" recorded in 1992, was followed by his appearance on *In Order to Dance, Vol. 4* as Neuromancer. The following year, he issued his debut LP as Source, *Organized Noise*. After releasing a masterpiece of pure acid techno in keeping with contemporary work by the Aphex Twin and others, Leiner threw a curveball: *Visions of the Past*, released as himself. The LP alternated between passages of ambient warmth echoing the Orb with more disturbing elements which signalled a turn in the flavor of electronica. Other than a single for the album though, it was the last work Leiner released as himself. Instead he began recording as the Source Experience in 1994, issuing *Different Journeys* on R&S and undertaking a grand DJ tour of Europe during 1995. Two additional 12"s appeared during the year (*Synaesthesia* and *Zyklus*) but Leiner kept much closer to the underground than during his early career. [See Also: Source] —*John Bush*

● **Visions of the Past** / Feb. 1994 / Apollo/R&S ♦♦♦♦
Arguably the most underrated electronic album of 1994, *Visions of the Past* alternates between songs of uptempo trance beauty and slower ambient cuts

so sinister that the flesh crawls. The best example of the former is "Aqua Viva," a 12-minute dolphin epic with dolphin sounds; of the eerie tracks, "Northern Dark," "Dream or Reality," and the title track are the most paranoid. —*John Bush*

## Cari Lekebusch

b. 1972
*Producer / Minimal Techno, Club/Dance, Techno*

Though his productions haven't been major innovators on the techno scene, Cari Lekebusch has consistently recorded dozens of singles under pseudonyms like Mr. James Barth, Braincell, and Vector, as well as his own name. Raised in Stockholm, Lekebusch began collecting records from an early age, and taped his own musical experiments. He began DJing professionally and organized parties around the area during the late '80s.

Several years later, Lekebusch began producing records part-time as well, after assembling his gear to found Hybrid Studios. He recorded for labels like Planet Rhythm, Loop, Plumphouse, R&S, ffrr, Svek, Proper NYC, Drumcode and Harthouse, later forming his own labels—Hybrid Productions, Audio Pollution, Trainspotters Nightmare—with Planet Rhythm owner Glen Wilson. Hybrid expanded by the late '90s to become a design company also, and Lekebusch released his first LP in 1996—*Man of Many Theories* as Braincell. Another full-length, Mr. James Barth's *Stealin' Music*, was released in 1998, and Lekebusch finally released an LP under his own name early the following year. He has also remixed for Claude Young, Steve Stoll, Surgeon, and Adam Beyer, among others. —*John Bush*

● **Det Jag Vet** / Mar. 8, 1999 / Hybrid ✦✦✦✦

*Det Jag Vet* collects over 25 tracks by one of the most prolific techno producers out there, including remixes and unreleased cuts in addition to Lekebusch's best-known tracks. It's set up like a DJ set, with just two or three minutes devoted to each hard, funky track before it moves to the next track. —*Keith Farley*

## Lemon D (Kevin King)

b. 1974
*Producer, DJ / Jungle/Drum'N'Bass, Club/Dance*

Lemon D is the most often used recording name of South London jungle producer Kevin King. The man behind the Planet Earth label as well as a number of 12"s for Metalheadz, Prototype, V Recordings, and Epic, King's reputation as a strong, economical producer of dancefloor drum'n'bass has risen steadily since his work began appearing in the early '90s. His soulful tracks maintain a distinct jazz feel without resorting to excessive sampling, and while his drum programming lay on the more pedestrian side of jungle's manic polyrhythms, his production skills make them more than listenable. King's career got a boost in 1993 when he hooked up with the Metalheadz stable, leading to engineering work with J. Majik and Dillinja and, eventually, a few releases of his own on the influential label. His curious pseudonym is an oblique reference to his label's (Lemon D/Le Monde, French for "the world"), and has graced remix productions for Art of Noise. In 1997, King inked a long-term contract with Belgian techno label R&S and co-founded the Valve label with Dillinja, to release the pair's harder, more relentless material. —*Sean Cooper*

**Jah Love [Single]** / 1995 / Conqueror ✦✦

"Jah Love" injects some jazz and funk into the mix, while the able bassline propels everything along at a danceable clip on this Conqueror release. —*John Bush*

● **Urban Style Music [Single]** / 1995 / Metalheadz ✦✦✦✦

"Urban Style Music" blends his brand of jungle with laidback hip-hop, West Coast style. —*John Bush*

**Going Gets Tuff [Single]** / Nov. 25, 1996 / Prototype ✦✦✦

Probably the least innovative of Prototype's brief catalog, "Going Gets Tuff" is nonetheless likable stuff. A bit darker, perhaps, than past 12"s, Lemon D's knack (similar to Bristoleans DJ Krust and Roni Size) for squeezing a mature soulfulness out of a bare minimum of elements is in top shape here. —*Sean Cooper*

## Les Rythmes Digitales (Stuart Price)

b. 1978, Paris, France
*Producer / Big Beat, Electronica, Trip-Hop*

More akin to French nu-disco compatriots like Daft Punk than his Wall of Sound label-mates, Jacques Lu Cont's Les Rythmes Digitales project bridges the gap between the quintessentially early-'80s phenomenon of synth-pop and more contemporary styles like acid house and trip-hop. Lu Cont is actually of British origin, however; he was born Stuart Price to a Reading couple vacationing in Paris. Both were classical pianists, but Stuart was turned on to the twin towers of electro—Kraftwerk and Afrika Bambaataa—at an early age. He also became interested in noted French proto-electronica figures like Pierre Henry and Jean-Jacques Perrey, and began experimenting with synthesizers as a teenager. Mark Jones from Britain's Wall of Sound Recordings gained a demo-tape from a third party, invited Price to begin recording for the label, and even concocted his Gallic alias (years before Daft Punk and Air made French citizenship a hot property).

The first Les Rythmes Digitales single was 1996's electro-shocked "Kontakte," followed closely by the debut album *Liberation*. Price looked to another of his influences for his second Wall of Sound single; "Jacques Your Body (Make Me Sweat)" was a streamlined acid-disco epic, the title a clever pun on Chicago house kingpin Steve "Silk" Hurley's hit from ten years earlier. Price began a DJ residency spinning '80s hits, and even provided a few remixes, for decade classics like Heaven 17's "(We Don't Need This) Fascist Groove Thang" and Robert Palmer's "Addicted to Love" as well as label-mates Dirty Beatniks. Les Rythmes Digitales became a noted live act as well, playing 1998's Reading Festival (a hometown gig for Price) and headlining a Wall of Sound label tour through Britain and Europe. A new single, "(Hey You) What's That Sound?," anticipated his second album, and featured none other than Boy George in its accompanying video. —*John Bush*

**Liberation** / Jul. 8, 1996 / Wall of Sound ✦✦✦

● **Darkdancer** / May 24, 1999 / Wall of Sound ✦✦✦✦

While his debut LP ran with the Wall of Sound crowd to the detriment of some interesting ideas, Jacques Lu Cont came into his own with the second Les Rythmes Digitales album. Consider *Darkdancer* Lu Cont's senior thesis in the major course of study: "History of Dance Music: The Early to Mid-'80s." And give him straight A's because he's obviously done his homework and actually studied the texts, without resorting to rote memorization and subsequent regurgitation come test time. Every club-oriented stylistic speed-bump of the decade is right here, including the era of female dance-pop before Madonna (yes, it did exist) with "Take a Little Time," an earnest little electro-groover that earns Lu Cont bonus points for utilizing the crucial '80s diva Shannon. "Hypnotise" is a nice little electro-paranoia track to fit in with Bambaataa's "Planet Rock," and "Brothers" takes on streamlined dance intellectualism à la New Order (with a straining pseudo-bassline to match). The house era is probably best represented, with nods to Chicago jacking house—complete with stuttered vocal tags—on the standouts "Jacques Your Body (Make Me Sweat)" and "Music Makes You Lose Control." Even when he strays into territory last inhabited by Level 42, as on "Sometimes" (with Nik Kershaw on vocals), a great song and a great production rescues Lu Cont from anything potentially cringe-worthy. That's the secret of *Darkdancer*; well-written songs, excellent production skills, and a sense of fun that takes no prisoners make originality seem like an academician's game. —*John Bush*

## Lesser

f. 1995, San Diego, CA
*Producer / Experimental Techno, Jungle/Drum'N'Bass*

J Lesser is an indie sampler terrorist stranded halfway between the heavily fraternal scenes organized around conventional drum'n'bass and unconventional noise. His formative career includes time spent playing with a Metallica cover band in San Diego, and with figures who later formed the indie bands Crash Worship and A Minor Forest. Lesser contributed the debut release for the San Diego indie-electronica label Vinyl Communications with 1996's *Excommunicate the Cult of the Live Band*. *Gigolo Cop*, and *Welcome to the American Experience* followed in one-year intervals, while a split-compact-disc with Kid-606 was released in 1998. Besides appearing with Matmos and Kid-606 as DISC, Lesser has also recorded as $157 and Backfire. —*John Bush*

**Excommunicate the Cult of the Live Band** / Oct. 8, 1996 / Vinyl Communications ✦✦

**Welcome to the American Experience** / Jan. 13, 1998 / Vinyl Communications ✦✦✦

Lesser explores the noisiest, most assaultive regions of indie-jungle on his album, *Welcome to the American Experience*. —*Jason Ankeny*

- **Split Compact Disc** / Jun. 9, 1998 / Vinyl Communications ◆◆◆◆
  *Split Compact Disc* includes six tracks by Lesser and ten by Kid-606 and makes for the best album released by either producer. Lesser's half is a barrage of electronica noise overload occasionally reminiscent of an indie-powered Mouse on Mars and perfect for listeners with no attention span. Kid's portion focuses on mangled breakbeat assaults and lo-fi sampler experimentation. —*John Bush*

## Larry Levan (Lawrence Philpot)

b. Jul. 18, 1954, Brooklyn, NY, d. Nov. 8, 1992, New York, NY
*Producer, DJ / Garage, Club/Dance, Disco, House*

Neglected by many because of his early death and lack of recording, Larry Levan is one of the seminal names in dance music, a legendary influence during the '70s and '80s. Influenced by David Mancuso's seminal Loft parties, which presaged disco by more than five years, Levan took his cue and transferred those communal vibes to clubland with one of the most famed nightspots ever, the Paradise Garage. For more than ten years, Levan's garage style was a wildly eclectic mix including any tracks (or parts of tracks) that would make people dance, including Motown and Philly soul, Afro-Cuban and Italian disco to new wave, punk, and classic hard rock. He influenced hordes of hardcore club-goers and a wave of DJs ranging from Tony Humphries to Paul Oakenfold. More than anyone, Levan set the tone for New York disco in the '70s and garage/house music during the '80s. By the '90s, mainstream New York dance swung to a diverse cast of dance artists, who had in common the one thing that united the records on Levan's decks: they were all soulful.

Levan began his first DJ residency while still a teenager, at a New York club called the Gallery in 1971. Both there and at his next club, the Continental Baths, Levan worked with (and profoundly influenced) the future godfather of house, Frankie Knuckles. After setting up the Soho Place midway through the decade, Levan joined the Paradise Garage in 1977 and began changing the face of dance music. Unlike other disco clubs around the city—including the notoriously hip, but musically flat Studio 54—the Paradise Garage featured a nightclub built on music, with attendees who were preferential about the music they danced to, not who they were seen by. Levan and engineer Richard Long supervised construction of what has been called the best sound system ever produced, and spent hours before opening each night to make sure that acoustics, speaker placement and atmosphere were perfect. To give club-goers the ultimate dance experience, Levan used an assortment of subtle tricks; during the night, he would even upgrade the quality of his musical selections and turntable needles until music, mixer and dancers hit their peak simultaneously. (The Paradise Garage's sound system was so good in fact that it was later bought by the London super-club Ministry of Sound, carefully disassembled, shipped overseas, and installed in a new space.)

By the beginning of the '80s, disco's flame had been extinguished by a glut of sub-par recordings and rabid anti-disco movements. Levan continued playing to an increasingly underground (though still ecstatic) audience. He also began working on studio production as well, recording remixes and special dance versions of pop songs for labels like Salsoul, Prelude, and West End as well as the occasional major label. Though many of his 12" productions were obscurities of the highest order (except in the crates of privileged DJs), tracks by the Peech Boys, Jimmy Castor Bunch, First Choice, Loleatta Holloway, and Skyy became certifiable dance classics. By the mid-'80s, the sound of New York/Chicago house music had begun to infiltrate England.

In an ironic twist, however, the man who did much to pave the way for dance music wasn't around during its rebirth. By September 1987, the Paradise Garage had closed its doors. Though Levan appeared on several remixes and productions during the late '80s and early '90s, he spent only a fraction of his time in the studio compared to during his heyday. Levan returned to the DJing booth on a 1992 trip to Japan with François Kevorkian, though he died as a result of AIDS complications later in the year. —*John Bush*

**Paradise Garage** / Dec. 5, 1995 / Salsoul ◆◆◆◆
*Paradise Garage* includes seven actual Levan post-productions from the vaults of Salsoul Records—previously released as the LP *Larry Levan's Greatest Hits, Vol. 2*. Each runs over six minutes, and the selections ("I Got My Mind Made Up" by Instant Funk, "Double Cross" by First Choice, and an epic 13-minute mix of "Make It Last Forever" by Inner Life Feat. Jocelyn Brown) include ones many clubbers would expect to hear on an average night at the Paradise Garage. It's a great look at one of the seminal names in dance music history, and one of the only albums of its type available. —*John Bush*

★ **Live at the Paradise Garage** / Sep. 5, 2000 / Strut ◆◆◆◆◆
Larry Levan is one of the few legendary figures in contemporary dance music, a DJ and remixer whose reliance on audiophile-level sound, in both the clubs he played and the records he selected, set a standard that, according to many witnesses, has never been equaled. In the years after his death in 1992, dance fans were forced to content themselves with his remix work, which admittedly, made for some great post-productions. Despite the lack of material, his legend has persisted primarily as a DJ, and primarily for his residency at one of the most revered clubs in the history of dance, the Paradise Garage. And in late 2000, more than 20 years after it was recorded, a relic from another era appeared on the British rare groove label Strut Records. High expectations notwithstanding, Levan comes through with a stunning, invigorating 80-minute set of disco movers and sweet Philly soul, the performances almost as uplifting and the bass almost as chunky as they must've sounded at the original SoHo nightspot. Though it's virtually untouched by Levan's notorious genre-bending (the Clash's "Should I Stay or Should I Go" was a Garage favorite), *Live at the Paradise Garage* is one of the best, and best-sounding, documents of the disco era ever produced. And it's a rare latter-day disco fan who will have heard many of these tracks before; though many of the artists are familiar (the Supremes, Cher, Shalamar, the Chi-Lites, Ashford & Simpson), Levan selected songs with great productions or the right tone to reflect his moods. Though the spotlight is clearly on Levan's mixing, a few highlights do appear, including "Angel in My Pocket" by Change, "By the Way You Dance (I Never Knew It Was You)" by Bunny Sigler, and "Get on the Funk Train" by Giorgio Moroder's Munich Machine. Clearly a labor of love (as well as an invaluable musical and historical document) from the people at Strut, *Live at the Paradise Garage* includes a complete history of both the club and Levan himself, as well as dozens of photos and reminiscences from inheritors like François Kevorkian, Danny Tenaglia, Joe Claussell, and Danny Krivit included in its 36-page book. —*John Bush*

## LFO

f. 1988, Sheffield, Yorkshire,
*Group / Club/Dance, Techno, House, IDM*

The Sheffield techno duo of Mark Bell and Gez Varley have a reputation that, at first glance, might seem to exceed them. Having released only two records and not many more singles in their eight years together, the pair's apparently meager contribution would hardly seem to bear out the claim that they've been one of British techno's most important, agenda-setting groups. Nonetheless, early singles such as "We Are Back," "Freeze," and "Love Is the Message" from their debut *Frequencies*, as well as "Tied Up" from the more recent *Advance*, have indelibly marked British techno with Detroit's progressiveness, electro's funk, and an unflinching, uniquely British experimentalism. Taking their name from the foundational component of the synthesizers—the low frequency oscillator (kind of like calling a rock group Power Chord)—the pair were approached by the London-based Warp label in the late '80s, after tapes the pair had put together on some junky, second-hand equipment caught the ears and dancefloors of local clubs and DJs. Both Bell and Varley admit to roots in the early- and mid-'80s hip-hop and electro invasions as well as the more obvious British acid house explosion, and their affectation for thick electronic breaks, vocoder samples, and sparse, modal melodies derive largely from that source. (LFO are also one of only a few—with 808 State and Coldcut—to find domestic reissue through the New York-based hip-hop label Tommy Boy, making obvious a connection between British experimental techno and American hip-hop and electro-funk that hasn't until only very recently been followed up on.) Releasing their bass-heavy debut in 1991 to universal acclaim, the pair were silent for the next five years, with rumors of a follow-up surfacing from time to time failing to produce anything. Reportedly working with early Depeche Mode member Alan Wilder and Karl Bartos of Kraftwerk (none of that material's ever seen light), LFO finally resurfaced in 1995 with the ironically titled "Tied Up," followed several months later by *Advance*. The group also remixed tracks for Björk and the Sabres of Paradise, but broke up soon after. Varley went on to a solo career, while Bell worked on tracks for Björk's *Homogenic* LP. —*Sean Cooper*

★ **Frequencies** / Oct. 1, 1991 / Tommy Boy ♦♦♦♦♦
Definitive collection of the new style electro-techno, with composition and dynamics taking equal play with groove and DJ-friendliness. Reissued by Tommy Boy in the US, the hip-hop connection was apparent in the few breakbeat tracks, but for the most part the record leans more toward acid house and techno for its cues. Recommended. —*Sean Cooper*

**Advance** / 1996 / Warp ♦♦♦♦
Nearly legendary as the album-that-almost-never-happened, *Advance* was a full five years in the making, with hardly a peep of new material in between. The result isn't as essential as their debut, but growth and maturity are evident, particularly in the focus and depth of composition. The material flows nicely, with the heavier, more body-oriented material broken up by contemplative, atmospheric ambient interludes. —*Sean Cooper*

## Like a Tim (Tim van Leijden)

*Producer / Electronica, Electro-Techno, Club/Dance, IDM*
Like a Tim is Netherlands-based electronica deviant Tim van Leijden, whose idiot-(s)avant-garde abusements of hip-hop and techno have appeared mostly on the D-Jax label. One for the "Yeah, I buy his records...Sorted!...Play them out? Are you joking?" file, Leijden's surprisingly listenable beat-hiccups are similar in some respects to artists such as Atom Heart and Patrick Pulsinger, but with a typically stronger, more minimal hip-hop foundation (Mantronix, Schooly D) which those artists often trade out. Following a high-profile remix session for countrymate Speedy J's major label debut ("Ni Go Snix," released by Mute in early 1997), Leijden was roped in by Cornwall-based acid/electronica label Rephlex to give a few tracks the Like a Tim makeover. Leijden is also a gifted graffiti artist (his visual style equally as idiosyncratic as his musical), and his illustrations grace the labels and sleeves of most of his releases; he returned in 2000 with *Red and Blue Boxing*. —*Sean Cooper*

**Remixes [EP]** / 1997 / Rephlex ♦♦♦
"Like A" Tim Leijden attacks a few recent treats from the Rephlex catalog, including tracks from Bochum Welt's "Feelings On a Screen," DMX Krew's "Can't Hide Your Love," and Cylob's "Diof '97." However, where one might normally expect Leijden's mixes to be led even further astray by the already off source material (c.f. his warped remix of Speedy J's equally warped "Ni Go Snix"), the effect is more one of cross-cancellation, with suprisingly conventional recapitulations of mid-'80s lo-fi electro holding most of the tracks together. Not bad, particularly, just not... *weird* enough. —*Sean Cooper*

● **Yeah Right** / May 11, 1998 / Geist ♦♦♦
Tim's first proper album, recorded for Alec Empire's Geist label, is a collection of no-frills Casio synth-pop injected with plenty of no-attention-span hip-hop attitude. It takes remarkable patience to sit through an entire album with titles like "Booming Is Business" and "I Got a Blaster, Now All I Need Is a Ghetto" telling the story, but Tim's infectious cover of "Legs"—yes, the ZZ Top chestnut—just might raise a few smiles. —*John Bush*

## Lil' Louis (Louis Sims)

b. Chicago, IL
*Producer, DJ / Club/Dance, Acid House, House, Dance-Pop*
One of the most popular Chicago house producers during the late '80s thanks to his massive club hit "French Kiss," Lil' Louis was also the only Chicago producer to successfully deal with the major labels; he released two albums for Epic, and only left the label at his own instigation. Born in Chicago, Louis was the son of blues drummer Robert "Bobby" Sims, who recorded for Chess and played with B.B. King. He grew up with nine siblings and played both drums and bass as a child, then began DJing in the mid-'70s (he earned his nickname after appearances at the club River's Edge while still in middle school). By the end of the decade he had his own club, the Future, where he began working on his editing techniques, thanks to a cassette deck and later a reel-to-reel recorder.

By the '80s, Lil' Louis was hosting the biggest house parties in Chicago, and he began recording his productions around that time as well. His first single "How I Feel" appeared on his own label, and he began collaborating with Marshall Jefferson on several tracks—"Seven Ways to Jack" by Hercules, Byron Stingily's "I Can't Stay Awake." In 1987, his new single "French Kiss" became a local hit, then a platinum-selling international classic after being licensed to CBS and ffrr. The success triggered a major-label contract through Epic, and the release of his debut album *From the Mind of Lil' Louis* in 1989. Charting a course across jazz-fusion and R&B as well as house, the LP was one of the best produced by any of the Chicago figures, and included session contributions from Larry Heard, Die Warzau, and his own father on drums. From the album, the moody single "I Called U" became another club hit. His follow-up LP, the more stylistically unified *Journey with the Lonely*, didn't fare as well and Lil' Louis retired from recording for over four years, preferring instead to set up his own studio in New York and work on production with Babyface and Me'Shell NdegeOcello. He returned by collaborating with "Little" Louie Vega of Masters at Work and also worked on production for Black Magic. —*John Bush*

● **From the Mind of Lil' Louis** / 1989 / Epic ♦♦♦♦
One of the better LPs from the Chicago house scene, *From the Mind of Lil' Louis* makes the obvious inclusion of several past hits like "French Kiss" and "I Called U." Pushing the album into another sphere however, are the great collaborations which occur. Larry Heard's input on tracks like "Blackout," "Tuch Me," and "6 A.M." is stellar, and uptown Wax Trax! industrialists Die Warzau even appear on production and mixing. Despite several tracks which fail to reprise the sexy soul of "French Kiss," Lil' Louis' debut album is a triumph. —*John Bush*

**Journey with the Lonely** / Apr. 1992 / Epic ♦♦♦
Unlike the collaboration-heavy first Lil' Louis LP, *Journey with the Lonely* is an introspective affair with fewer helpers. Tracks like "Club Lonely," "Dancing in My Sleep," and the closer "Jazzmen" veer quite far away from "French Kiss" with regards to their mood and intention, even though the chords and beatwork may be similar. —*John Bush*

## Lilith

f. 1991, Chicago, IL
*Group / Experimental Techno, Dark Ambient, Ambient Techno, Experimental, Ambient, Industrial*
The combined efforts of producer Scott Gibbons and vocal contributor Rachel Wilson, Lilith is an experimental electronic/dark ambient group with feet planted with equal force in industrial and "power electronics." Unlike artists normally associated with the latter two genres, however, Lilith's music is conceived from the standpoint of simplicity and resourcefulness, with Gibbons' artful approach to the musical potential of mundane objects and only very minimal production trickery substituted for industrial/noise music's curt, often messy impudence. A graduate of the University of Chicago Master's program in the Philosophy of Religion, Gibbons' undergraduate and graduate careers were split between books and unhindered improvisational outings, first with the Chicago ensemble New Elementals, then solo as Nipple Runs and Laughingwind. The Elementals was as renowned for their live performances (which often included elaborate costumes, theater, and pyrotechnics), and Gibbons has retained his taste for extreme performance both as a solo artist and with Lilith.

Gibbons released several self-produced tapes—both with the Elementals, as well as under his solo guises—before forming Lilith in 1991 with vocalist Rachel Wilson, with whom he'd worked sporadically in the past. Like earlier material, Gibbons' Lilith tapes were dominated by an unsettling mixture of sparse, treated instruments and percussion, but with increasing truck given to a heavily conceptual approach to found sound and everyday objects (rocks on *Stone*, voice and breath on *Redwing*). Unlike many sound hackers, however, Gibbons prefers real-time manipulation, with single-track studio improvisations limiting generational sound experiments to arrangement and composition (although he does use computers, primarily for real-time processing). Gibbons' Lilith material finally began finding a larger audience in 1992, with his first official release, *Stone*, issued by the Belgian experimental label Sub Rosa, and he's since been featured on compilation releases side by side with such artists as Locust and David Toop. Gibbons' ongoing interest in the extremes of spirituality and sexuality also continue to inform his music, with themes deriving from Theosophy, Crowleyan numerology, and sexual deviance cropping up both in song-titles and conceptual motifs. —*Sean Cooper*

**Stone** / 1992 / Sub Rosa ♦♦♦♦

**Orgazio** / 1994 / Sub Rosa ♦♦♦

**Redwing** / 1994 / Sub Rosa ♦♦♦

● **Field Notes** / Feb. 9, 1999 / World Domination ♦♦♦♦
The first Lilith album for World Domination is nominally constructed from field recordings, though as could be expected from past recordings, the re-

sults reveal little about the sound sources. What does appear on the album is deep sub-bass with an assortment of porous-sounding clicks and clacks, progressing into a miniature symphony of isolationist ambience. As with the best work by single-sample-only artists like Aube, the results are impressive—not only in consideration of their sources, but from a pure-sonic viewpoint as well. —*John Bush*

## Alison Limerick

*Vocals / Alternative Dance, Club/Dance*

Singer Alison Limerick began her music career during the mid-'80s — after attending the London School of Contemporary Dance, lending backing vocals to high-profile recordings like the Style Council's 1985 LP *Our Favourite Shop*. A year later 4AD label chief Ivo Watts-Russell tapped her to appear on *Filigree and Shadow*, the second album from his all-star This Mortal Coil project; Limerick also appeared on the follow-up, 1991's *Blood*. Work with Peter Murphy (1992's *Holy Smoke*) followed before Limerick finally made her solo debut in 1994, teaming with renowned dance producers David Morales and Frankie Knuckles for hits including "Where Love Lives" and the UK Top 20 smash "Make It on My Own"; the full-length *With a Twist* appeared the same year. The 1996 remix collection *Club Classics* followed, and a year later Limerick returned with "Put Your Faith in Me." —*Jason Ankeny*

**With a Twist** / Apr. 4, 1994 / Arista ♦♦♦

- **Club Classics** / 1996 / Arista ♦♦♦
They may not be the original versions that clubbers and radio fans will recognize, but the mixes on *Club Classics* make for a good overview of Limerick's singles-heavy career. The nine-track album includes extended remixes of her big hits, "Where Love Lives" and "Make It on My Own," plus a Kenlou (aka Masters at Work) mix of "Getting It Right" and a Romanthony remix of "Where Love Lives." —*John Bush*

## Lionrock (Justin Robertson)

*Producer / Big Beat, Funky Breaks, Electronica, Club/Dance, House*

Producer Justin Robertson began recording as Lionrock in 1991 after plotting a successful career as a DJ and remixer. Aloof from the limelight and popular almost despite himself, Robertson took an almost laughably conventional route to a level of success reached by probably less then one percent of dance music producers. A native of Manchester, Robertson earned a degree in philosophy before taking a job as (what else) a record clerk in the Eastern Bloc record shop, where he began collecting the funkier side of progressive house and DJing on a regular basis. After remixing a track for Mad Jack on in-house label Creed (his mix of "Feel the Hit" became something of a underground smash), Robertson was subsequently flagged down by the likes of the Shamen, Candyflip, the Sugarcubes, and Erasure to lend his evolving signature to their material. As his style matured, he became associated with the burgeoning Balaeric scene (a hodge-podge subcategory of house encompassing a range of influences, from rock and R&B to disco and garage). Robertson released his solo debut, "Roots and Culture"/"Lionrock," on his own Most Excellent label in 1992. After peaking a few brows and spawning another round of remix work, Robertson was courted by pop/dance label Deconstruction, with whom he signed in 1993.

Robertson released an additional EP, *Packet of Peace*, on Deconstruction in April of 1993 before settling in to record his full-length debut. Released late the following year, *An Instinct for Detection* was an ambitious effort to say the least, featuring scads of instrumentation resolutely un-traditional by UK dance music standards, mixed and matched with dirty house breaks and aggressive but accessible arrangements. Although the record was met warmly, its subtle abuse of pop (in the Beach Boys, not Mariah Carey sense) was lost on many, and it remains something of a cult favorite. Robertson embarked on an elaborate tour following the album's release, and the presence of guitars, percussion, and drum kit on the stage of a Lionrock show became standard from word go. In 1996, the popular mix-CD series *Journeys by DJ* contracted a mixed set from Robertson, resulting in a massive two-disc set spanning the range not only of Lionrock's influences, but of the last two decades of electronic dance music as a whole. Robertson continues to be a popular remixer, and Lionrock releases (including 1995's *An Instinct for Detection* and 1998's *City Delirious*) appear on a sporadic basis. —*Sean Cooper*

**An Instinct for Detection** / 1995 / Deconstruction ♦♦♦♦
Justin Robertson's Lionrock blends club music, hip-hop (with Manchester rapper MC Buzz B), and elements of dub on this 1995 debut album. —*John Bush*

- **City Delirious** / Mar. 16, 1998 / Time Bomb ♦♦♦♦
The second album from Justin Robertson's crew of British DJ renegades (this time with some live guitars and an MC tossed into the frantic mix) covers a lot of electronica ground on its 14 songs, sticking pretty close to classic surging house through the stretch. And while quite a bit of it is incidental — the vocals are simply layered atop the wildly stammering instrumental tracks, just as sampled dialogue was randomly piled onto *An Instinct for Detection* — the best cuts on *City Delirious* (particularly the block-party electro-ska of "Rude Boy Rock") find as much inspiration on the sweaty dancefloor as they do in the gimmick-strewn studio in which the album was made. Lionrock's big beat is also more accessible this time around, trading in some of the more obscure musical references of the past for actual, timely tuned rhythms. —*Michael Gallucci*

## Liquid Liquid

f. 1980, New York, NY
*Group / Electro, Post-Punk*

The minimalistic funk grooves of New York's Liquid Liquid consisted almost entirely of percussion grooves with a smattering of bass, plus congas, marimba, and the occasional vocal thrown in. The quartet consisted of Scott Hartley (drums, percussion, talking drum), Richard McGuire (bass, percussion, piano, guitar), Salvatore Principato (percussion, vocals), and Dennis Young (percussion, marimba, roto-toms). The band released three EPs during its existence — 1981's *Liquid Liquid* and *Successive Reflexes*, and 1983's *Optimo*. The latter contained the track "Cavern," which became the basis for Grandmaster Flash's "White Lines (Don't Do It)." In 1997, Grand Royal Records released a collection of those three EPs, plus a 1982 performance, *Live from Berkley Square*. —*Steve Huey*

- **Liquid Liquid** / Aug. 11, 1997 / Grand Royal ♦♦♦♦
The angular, bass-propelled funk grooves of Liquid Liquid laid the groundwork for post-rock bands like Tortoise and Ui more than a decade before the fact — stripped of all excess and artifice, their hypnotically dub-like sound offered a starkly minimalist counterpoint to the prevailingly lush production of the concurrent disco movement, in the process impacting the development of everything from hip-hop to drum'n'bass. This superbly packaged 18-track retrospective collects the sum of Liquid Liquid's official output, recorded between 1981 and 1983, and all things considered, it's remarkable just how prescient and modern the group's music really was. Although only the standout, "Cavern" (the basis for the Grandmaster Flash rap classic "White Lines"), is even remotely familiar in any strict sense, the remaining material, with its thickly fluid basslines and circular rhythms, will undoubtedly strike a chord of recognition in anyone versed in the sonic motifs of post-rock and electronica. Ui's Sasha Frere-Jones is thanked on the sleeve, but in truth he's the one owing the debt — for all intents and purposes, post-rock (and a whole lot more) starts here. —*Jason Ankeny*

## Lithops (Jan St. Werner)

*Producer / Experimental Techno, Electro-Techno*

Lithops is the solo guise of Jan Werner, known to most as half of popular Cologne/Düsseldorf-based duo Mouse on Mars. Also a member of abstract ambient outfit Microstoria, Werner tends toward middle ground with his Lithops material, fusing the smooth digital weirdness of Microstoria with the smudgy, off-kilter beats and warm, imperfect textures of more recent Mouse on Mars releases such as *Instrumentals* and *Glam*. Lithops tracks rub the outer edges of inferential electronics, and often sound as though they began their lives as happy little studio accidents, all fumbly, peripatetic rhythms emerging from a haze of muffled bass and overdriving synth textures. Although Werner's first Lithops tracks trace only to 1995, a flood of material has quickly appeared, beginning with the two-track "Wackler/Khan" 12", issued by tiny Cologne-based imprint Eat Raw, and shifting into high-gear with a pair of full-lengths released in 1998. Werner and MoM partner Andi Toma's vinyl-only Sonig label issued the first of those — the drab, gauzy *Uni Umit* — in early 1998, while the Eat Raw's LP *Didot* followed only months later. Although it didn't receive quite the initial distribution push of Sonig's first release — MoM's excellent *Instrumentals* LP, reissued stateside by Thrill Jockey — *Uni Umit* is equally as splendid, wrapping thick, organic textures around sparse rhythms, bizarre electronics, and thick, strapping, resonant bass. (The album got a Stateside CD reissue in 1998, via Jim O'Rourke's Moikai label.) *Didot*, for its part, was slightly better-produced and rhythmically further flung than its predecessor, but both satisfy to a more or less equal degree. An additional 1998 release came in the form of the "Turbino" 7", released by the otherwise unrelated Static Caravan label. —*Sean Cooper*

**Tubino [Single]** / 1998 / Static Caravan ♦♦♦
This quick and dirty two-track 7" is half Mouse on Mars-ish electro-dub, half bruised, undulating freeform ambient. But while both "See Through" and "Filterbend" rate among Lithops' best material to date, the obscurity of the label means that unless you already own it, you're not likely to find it. Worth searching for, however. —*Sean Cooper*

● **Uni Umit** / Feb. 2, 1998 / Sonig ♦♦♦♦
The second release on Mouse on Mars' in-house imprint, Sonig, Jan Werner's *Uni Umit* is a delightful collection of smudgy, impressionistic electronica similar in feel to the less structured of MoM's material, as well as to other Cologne-based artists such as Kandis/Senking and F.X. Randomiz. Featuring only a handful of casual, willfully underproduced cuts incoporating elements (vague, abstracted ones) of ambient, electro, house, and even musique concrète, *Uni Umit* is brief but satisfying, revealing layer upon layer of obscure detail with each listen. —*Sean Cooper*

**Didot** / May 4, 1998 / Eat Raw ♦♦♦♦
Released just months after his full-length debut, *Didot* is Jan Werner's second album of mirthful, crayon-drawn electronica under his solo Lithops guise. With slightly cleaner production and a more varied stylistic palette than its predecessor (*Uni Umit*, released on his and Mouse On Mars partner Andi Toma's Sonig label), *Didot* skips through jittery house and electro, dense post-rock, and moist, foggy beatless ambient, subsuming each bizarre twist under the same generally unifying theme of weird samples and fractal electronics. Structure and thematic development are given clearer focus on *Didot*, making it the more accessible of the two LPs (not that that word might otherwise be appropriately applied to either). —*Sean Cooper*

## Live Human

f. 1996, San Francisco, CA
*Group / Turntablism, Underground Rap, Hip-Hop*
San Francisco's experimental turntablist trio Live Human formed in 1996, when turntablist DJ Quest (a.k.a. Carlos Aguilar), drummer/percussionist Albert Mathias and bassist Andrew Kushin united their diverse musical experiences to create spontaneous, constantly mutating instrumental hip-hop. Among their other credits, Aguilar worked with DJ Shadow on tracks for Quannum and Handsome Boy Modeling School, helped found the DJ crew Space Travelers and collaborated on 1992's *Hamster Breaks*, one of the first breakbeat records tailored to the needs of scratch DJs; multi-percussionist Mathias maintains a solo recording career and tours and performs at universities and dance festivals as a teacher, composer and accompanist; and Kushin performs in Closer To Carbon, an experimental string ensemble, and co-founded the label Out Of Round Records. Kushin and Mathias also performed together in the similarly progressive collective Contraband and Thread, saxophonist Charles Sharp's free-jazz trio. Live Human debuted their hybrid of sampling and live improvisation 1997's *Live Human Featuring DJ Quest*, which was released by Cosmic Records in a limited-edition vinyl pressing of 1000 copies. Later that year, London's Fat Cat label licensed four of the album's songs for release in Europe and the UK as the EP *Live Human: Improvisessions*. Fat Cat also released 1999's *Orange Bush Monkey Flower* single, which preceded Live Human's second full-length *Monostereosis: The New Victrola Method*. The album was re-released in the US by Hip-Hop Slam in early 2000, just a few months before the group made their Matador debut with *Elefish Jellyphant*. —*Heather Phares*

● **Monostereosis: The New Victrola Method** / May 24, 1999 / Fat Cat/Hip Hop Slam ♦♦♦♦
The three-man turntablist rhythm section Live Human debuted with *Monostereosis*, an LP originally recorded for Britain's Fatcat Records but later reissued on the American Hip Hop Slam label. With drummer Albert Mathias and Andrew Kushin laying down bedrock rhythms, DJ Quest gets plenty of space to stretch out on his turntables. As you'd expect from a live crew, the emphasis here isn't so much an old-school rap redux as it is an attempt to exploit the infinitely expressive turntable as a true instrument. Even while he's scratching and sampling to his heart's delight, Quest ranges quite far for his samples, from the squawking horn-section blasts on the opener "Onetwothree" to a sitar and jaw harp "Grasshopper." The intense old-school funk of "Orangebush-monkeyflower" leads right into reverb territory with "Percodan," while "The E Pod" is an excellent skate-anthem-in-waiting. A record posed somewhere between Booker T. & the MG's and Invisibl Skratch Piklz, *Monostereosis* is one of the freshest turntablist items down the pipe in several years. —*John Bush*

**Elefish Jellyphant** / Jul. 11, 2000 / Matador ♦♦♦♦

## Lo Fidelity Allstars

f. 1996, London, England
*Group / Big Beat, Funky Breaks, Electronica, Trip-Hop*
A six-piece big-beat band with more of a rock 'n' roll slant than the other acts on the big-beat boutique Skint Records, Lo Fidelity Allstars marry rumbling dub basslines with breakdown-organ riffs borrowed from soul tunes and a care-free attitude reminiscent of the Madchester glory days of Happy Mondays and Stone Roses. The group was originally formed in mid-1996 by a turntable wizard known as the Albino Priest, a Leeds native who worked at the Tower Records in London's Piccadilly Circus, and vocalist Wrekked Train. The duo gradually added members during the year, all of whom took absurd nicknames—keyboard player Sheriff Jon Stone, bassist A One Man Crowd Called Gentile, engineer the Many Tentacles, and a drummer named the Slammer.

Lo Fidelity Allstars began recording and sent a demo tape to Skint label-boss Damian Harris; after Harris saw them play live, he signed them. The group's first three singles for Skint were "Kool Roc Bass," "Disco Machine Gun," and "Vision Incision," all of which appeared during 1997 (just at the peak of big-beat frenzy in England thanks to recent releases by Fatboy Slim and Bentley Rhythm Ace). The Lo Fi debut album *How to Operate with a Blown Mind* followed in 1998. By the end of the year, Wrekked Train had left the band because of artistic differences; Albino Priest became the band's nominal frontman in time for 1999's *How to Operate with a Blown Mind*. The band followed up in 2000 with the mix album *On the Floor at the Boutique*. —*John Bush*

● **How to Operate with a Blown Mind** / May 25, 1998 / Sony ♦♦♦♦
With an effortless grace unmatched by even their Skint label-mates, Lo-Fidelity Allstars segue between acid-house, hip-hop, punk, soul and disco on their debut album. Previous high-energy singles like "Vision Incision" and "Kool Roc Bass" are included, along with new tracks like the surprising hi-NRG/electro fusion on "Lazer Sheep Dip Funk" and early-'80s funk reminiscent of Prince or Jamiroquai on "Battle Flag" (with Pigeonhed). On occasion however, the Allstars' attempt at a varied sound backfires; "I Used to Fall in Love" and "Vision Incision" are harshly distorted urban ballads with sub-Liam Gallagher whining in place of vocals. —*John Bush*

**On the Floor at the Boutique** / Feb. 8, 2000 / Sony ♦♦♦♦
The official compilation from the mecca of breakbeat techno, Brighton's *Big Beat Boutique*, *On the Floor at the Boutique* includes no less than 21 tracks and must qualify as one of the most diverse mix albums ever released. Mixers (and Skint Recordings heroes) the Lo-Fidelity Allstars grab tracks from an assortment of producers, from Blackstreet to Les Rythmes Digitales, Trouble Funk to Armand Van Helden, Boogie Down Productions to '60s soulstress Felice Taylor. Even more surprising is the natural feel of the proceedings: none of the selections sound forced, making *On the Floor at the Boutique* an excellent collection. —*John Bush*

## Locust (Mark Van Hoen)

b. London, England
*Producer / Experimental Techno, Electronica, Ambient Techno, Club/Dance, IDM*
Locust's Mark Van Hoen occupies the shadier, more melancholic side of contemporary ambient, assembling records of unmistakable beauty out of shards of dark, somewhat foreboding textures and arrangements. A London native active in the film and commercial music business before concentrating full-time on recording for release, Van Hoen has produced a string of highly thought-of releases for the R&S subsidiary Apollo in a relatively short period of time. He's quoted Steve Reich, David Sylvian, Kraftwerk, and Brian Eno as early influences, but more recently has been attempting to pursue paths of creative conception opened up by John Coltrane and Karlheinz Stockhausen. Although earlier releases focused on sprawling, mostly beatless experimental soundscapes, his more recent work has incorporated elements of breakbeat styles such as trip-hop and jungle—mostly in terms of produc-

tion techniques, as opposed to aesthetic qualities, and with decidedly Locust flair. *Truth Is Born of Arguments* was the first release of this sort, and included heavy, distorted percussion and complex, looping polyrhythms similar to (although much more sluggish than) those found in drum'n'bass.

Not always the ambient misanthrope, Van Hoen splits his creative activity between Locust and a number of ongoing collaborative ventures, among them Autocreation (techno) and Involution (post-techno experimental electronic), the latter with Seefeel frontman Daren Seymour. Van Hoen's also completed a number of remixes for Seefeel and As One, among others, and has recently incorporated elements of multimedia and performance art into his live appearances. Van Hoen also released the occasional recording under his given name, including 1996's *Last Flowers from the Darkness* and 1999's *Playing with Time*. —*Sean Cooper*

**In Remembrance of Times Past** / 1994 / Apollo ♦♦♦
Collects demos, four-track experiments, and otherwise unreleased material recorded during the mid- to late '80s. —*Sean Cooper*

**Truth Is Born of Arguments** / 1995 / Apollo ♦♦♦♦
A collection of austere, somewhat paranoid beat-oriented experimental ambient, similar in feel and tone to his earlier material, though with decidedly deviant stylistic features. Song titles include gems like "I Feel Cold Inside Because of the Things You Say," "I Believe in a Love I May Never Know," and "Inside I Am Crying." —*Sean Cooper*

● **Morning Light** / Jun. 23, 1997 / Apollo ♦♦♦♦
The Locust vocal album *Morning Light* includes nine gorgeous pop songs sprinkled with four short tracks of electronic atmosphere. Van Hoen is at his best here, creating pleasantly distorted, effervescent electro-pop productions for vocalists including Holli Ashton, Wendy Roberts, and Craig Bethell. Moving from folk-pop to orchestral electro to hi-NRG trance (occasionally in the same song), Van Hoen frames his singers with sympathetic productions. It's a wonder that his productions cover so much territory and still make for *any* kind of pop songs, much less supremely effective ones, but *Morning Light* works throughout. —*John Bush*

## Loop Guru

f. 1992, London, England
*Group / Electronica, Ambient Techno, Ambient Dub, Trance*

A global fusion duo which deftly combined old-world music and sound with new-world attitude and technology, Loop Guru primarily comprised bassist/guitarist Salman Gita (born Sam Dodson) and programmer Jamuud (a.k.a. Dave Muddyman), both longtime staples of the London club scene. After meeting in 1980 at the introduction of future Trans Global Underground member Alex Kasiek, the two men frequently found themselves performing on the same bill, discovering a mutual dissatisfaction with the restraints of rock music while forging a common bond from their shared interest in tape loops and worldbeat rhythms. Gita and Jamuud soon began experimenting with a mixing desk, which they plugged into a series of tape recorders, DAT machines, VCRs, and so forth; after playing a number of instruments as simultaneous accompaniment, they ultimately created sound collages from what resulted, incorporating samplers and computers into the mix as technology progressed.

Under the name Loop Guru, they debuted in 1992 with "Mrabet"—a nod to the Moroccan writer and Paul Bowles confidante—which took "Single of the Week" honors in the *NME* (an award also handed to the follow-up, "Paradigm Shuffle"). With Iranian-born vocalist Sussan Deyhim, they next issued the *Sussan-tics* EP, a multiple-remix project, followed in 1994 by their full-length debut *Duniya*. In 1995 Loop Guru signed to the North-South label, entering into a unique agreement to release both a "pop record" and a more experimental work on an annual basis. The first fruits of the deal arrived in the form of *Amrita*, a more conventional effort, and *The Third Chamber*, an hour-long ambient "single"; in 1996, they issued the third volume in their *Catalogue of Desires* ambient series (the first two were available only at concerts), along with *Moksha*, a collection of sessions from the John Peel show. *Loop Bites Dog* followed in 1997. In 1999, the complete *Catalogue of Desires* was reworked and remixed into a single-disc release, *The Fountains of Paradise*. —*Jason Ankeny*

● **The Third Chamber** / 1995 / North South ♦♦♦♦
Much like Transglobal Underground (who they're often identified with), Loop Guru incorporate Eastern rhythms and instruments into electronic-based dance-friendly music. *The Third Chamber*, however, lies closer to the source (and farther away from dance music) than Transglobal Underground. —*John Bush*

**Amrita... All These & the Japanese Soup Warriors** / Oct. 1995 / Pinnacle ♦♦♦
Loop Guru's sophomore album grounds the team's ethereal melodies, chants, vocals, and effects with a heavy dub/house beat. —*John Bush*

**Duniya** / Nov. 1995 / Waveform ♦♦♦

**Catalogue of Desires, Vol. 3: The Clear White Variation** / Apr. 8, 1996 / Guru ♦♦
*Catalogue of Desires, Vol. 3* (the first two volumes were sold only at Loop Guru concerts) constitutes some of the group's most ambient-oriented work. Cleopatra reissued this album in 1999, three years after its original release. —*Steve Huey*

**Loop Bites Dog** / Sep. 29, 1997 / World Domination ♦♦
It's a rare Loop Guru album that sounds much different from its predecessor, and *Loop Bites Dog* hardly varies the formula, with ambient-breakbeat productions, worldbeat-inflected female vocals and the vaguely symphonic feel of a grandiose concept album taken far more seriously than it should be. —*John Bush*

**The Fountains of Paradise** / Jun. 15, 1999 / Cleopatra ♦♦♦
Through the '90s, Loop Guru recorded three installments in a series of ambient projects they called *Catalogue of Desires*. The first two were cassettes sold only at the group's concerts, while the third volume was officially released in 1996. *Fountains of Desire* plucks portions of the material from the initial two volumes, remixing and reworking it into an updated single-disc collection that in places actually improves on the originals, even if there are still some dull, overly repetitive passages that don't quite achieve the desired hypnotic effect. However, there are some interesting worldbeat-flavored touches sprinkled throughout that help make up for it, at least for more dedicated fans. —*Steve Huey*

## Looper

f. 1998
*Group / Indie Pop*

Looper was the electronic-inspired side project of Belle and Sebastian bassist Stuart David; after debuting in mid-1998 with the Sub Pop single "Impossible Things," the full-length *Up a Tree* followed in March of 1999. Upon completing work on Belle and Sebastian's *Fold Your Hands Child, You Walk Like a Peasant* album, David left the group to focus on Looper full-time, touring with the Flaming Lips prior to releasing *The Geometrid* in the spring of 2000. —*Jason Ankeny*

**Up a Tree** / Mar. 9, 1999 / Sub Pop ♦♦
Although Looper is a Belle and Sebastian side project, fans of the Scottish group's lush, wispy pop confections looking for similar sounds here will be sorely disappointed—on his own, Stuart David rejects the ornate strings and horns of B&S in favor of electronic textures and trip-hop beats, and while there's a definite pop dimension to *Up a Tree*, it's secondary at best. The album is cut from the same cloth as David's "Spaceboy Dream" from B&S' *The Boy with the Arab Strap*, the lone bit of filler on an otherwise extraordinary record; his fascination with electronica reaches a much greater potential here, but there's still no shaking the feeling that *Up a Tree* was released thanks solely to its pedigree, and without regard to its actual merit. —*Jason Ankeny*

● **The Geometrid** / May 9, 2000 / Sub Pop ♦♦♦
Looper returns with *The Geometrid*, another collection of Stuart David's home-spun electronic pop. As befitting the fact that Looper is now David's main project, the album has a more polished feel than its predecessor *Up a Tree*, as well as more of an electronica vibe, particularly on the dancefloor send-up "Mondo '77" and the bleep-tastic "Modem Song." But David's sweet pop sensibilities reign supreme on most of the album's songs, especially "On the Flipside," "Money Hair," and "These Things." Sometimes Looper's singalong antics wear thin, as on the overly long "Uncle Ray" and "Bug Rain," but curious Belle & Sebastian devotees and *Up a Tree* fans will find more than a few things to like about *The Geometrid*'s unaffected, unpretentious style. —*Heather Phares*

## Lords of Acid

f. 1988, Brussels, Belgium
*Group / Alternative Dance, Club/Dance, Newbeat, Acid House, House*

Lords of Acid's exaggeratedly sexual acid house dance music gained a cult following with their 1991 album, *Lust*. Previously, the band had released three singles that laid the groundwork for the dense, throbbing *Lust* and its club hits, "Rough Sex" and "I Must Increase My Bust." Between their debut and their second album, 1994's *Voodoo-U*, the group added industrial elements to their sound and became a more straightforward, band-oriented group. At the time of their second album, Lords of Acid was led by Lady Galore (born Ruth Mcardle; vocals) and featured bassist Lord T. Byron (born Frank Vloeberghs), keyboard player Shai De La Luna, and drummer McGuinnes (born Kurt Liekens). Subsequent efforts include 1997's *Our Little Secret* and 1999's *Expand Your Head*. —*Stephen Thomas Erlewine*

● **Lust** / Oct. 25, 1991 / Antler-Subway/Caroline ♦♦♦♦
Lords of Acid's debut album is the best representation of their dirty, sex-crazed acid-house dance music, featuring the club classics "I Sit on Acid" and "I Must Increase My Bust." —*David Jehnzen*

**Voodoo-U** / 1994 / Warner Brothers ♦♦
Previously an acid-house group, Lords Of Acid use more industrial sounds, along with some reggae and ska, on *Voodoo-U*. Songs such as "The Crab Louse" and "Drink My Honey" aren't recommended for queasy stomachs. —*John Bush*

**Our Little Secret** / Jul. 22, 1997 / Never ♦♦♦
*Our Little Secret* isn't remarkably different from Lords of Acid's previous album, *Voodoo-U*—it's still the same mix of throbbing dance-club beats, industrial noise, metallic guitars and sexual kitsch as before. In many ways, *Our Little Secret* actually improves on *Voodoo-U*, offering sharper productions, funnier songs and catchier hooks, even if the group's ability to outrage is beginning to wane. —*Stephen Thomas Erlewine*

**Expand Your Head** / Jul. 27, 1999 / Never ♦♦
Driven by the club anthem "Am I Sexy?," Lords of Acid again works the porn-dance angle they'd been pursuing ever since early-'90s singles like "Rough Sex" and "I Must Increase My Bust," though their S&M themes and unsubtle topics had put the troupe right into the mainstream, along with the late-'90s ascendance of Marilyn Manson and others. Still, it's a one-trick pony that doesn't hold listeners interest over the long haul of an LP, despite credible production by Praga Khan. —*Keith Farley*

## Love Inc.

f. 1991, Berlin, Germany
*Group / Club/Dance, Techno, House*
Mike Ink is one of Europe's leading producers of minimalist pure house and techno, released primarily under his own name and as Love Inc, M:I:5, and Gas. After kick-starting the German acid scene 1991-92 and releasing some of the style's more popular tracks, Ink reoriented his focus on the essentials of a distinctively German brand of minimalist techno, launching the Profan and Studio 1 labels, all widely hailed in the techno underground as among the finest sources of purist Euopean dance music. His analytical, almost religious affection for the four-on-the-floor beat (and not much else!) definitely places him against the dominant trends of the hyper-hybridized post-rave dance music environment into which he's released the bulk of his material, but also gained his work acclaim alongside that of labels such as Concept and Basic Channel.

A native of Cologne, Germany, Ink, together with artists such as Biochip C., J. Burger, and Air Liquide, was a founding member of the Structure label group, which included the Blue, Monotone, and DJ Ungle Fever labels, largely responsible for the early '90s German acid house revival. Unlike his early colleagues, Ink has resisted the urge to diversify, sticking to his puritanical aesthetic through a series of EPs and album-length releases for Force Inc, Extreme, Trans Atlantic, Burger Industries, and his own Profan and Studio 1 labels. Breaking his various stylistic pursuits into definite chunks, Ink reserves the Love Inc. name for his more commercial house tunes, while M:I:5 and his own name usually grace his techno releases (Gas is reserved for the odd experimental track). [See Also: Burger/Ink, Gas, Mike Ink] —*Sean Cooper*

● **Life's a Gas** / Sep. 30, 1996 / Force Inc ♦♦♦♦
The first album release for any Mike Ink pseudonym, *Life's a Gas* is a set of electro-jazz soundscapes also indebted—surprisingly—to pop music, with the inclusion of a vocal track. Also included is a version of the Ink track "R.E.S.P.E.C.T." —*Keith Farley*

## Low Res (Danny Zelonky)

b. Milwaukee, WI
*Producer / Experimental Techno, Techno*
Danny Zelonky's Low Res project is just one of the diverse cast of artists assembled around the Plug Research label, the West Coast's home for experimental techno. Born in Milwaukee, Zelonky studied musique concrète at a local conservatory and began recording in 1994. Changes in locale from New York to Tokyo to North Hollywood brought Zelonky into contact with a range of artists and music, resulting in the release of his 1996 single "Amuck" on Tokyo's Sublime label plus Detroit's Metroplex (the imprint run by techno godfather Juan Atkins). In 1996, the Low Res track "Multiratio" appeared on *Plug Research & Development*, a compilation released by the Los Angeles-area label gradually gaining a worldwide name for stateside experimental techno. His debut album *Approximate Love Boat* appeared on Plug Research as well, towards the end of 1998. Around the same time, Zelonky recorded material for the long-awaited second LP by Juan Atkins' Model 500 project (1999's *Mind and Body*), and also released an LP on Mille Plateaux as Crank. —*John Bush*

● **Approximate Love Boat** / Nov. 2, 1998 / Plug Research ♦♦♦♦
*Approximate Love Boat* is a concept LP, concerning a group of aliens forced to reconstruct Earth music after a computer error destroys the results of their field trip away from their solar system. The music journeys far beyond trite space clichés to territory closer to the waves-of-static and industrial beatmash of far-flung material by Autechre or Pan sonic. —*John Bush*

## Lowfish (Greg de Rocher)

b. Toronto, Canada
*Producer / Electronica, Electro-Techno, Ambient Techno*
Toronto-based producer Gregory DeRocher records energetic lo-fi experimental electro as Lowfish. Released mostly on his and partner Jason "Solvent" Amm's own Suction label, DeRocher's music combines the stripped-down approach of early new wave and industrial acts such as Human League and Skinny Puppy with the melodic edginess of *Selected Ambient Works 1*-era Aphex Twin. DeRocher's first tracks were recorded and released on cassette under the name Pest(e) before Suction was established in 1997. Following two split EPs, one with Amm and one with Montreal's David Kristian, Lowfish's *Fear Not the Snow and Other Lo-Fiiing Objects* appeared on Suction in early 1999. A bursting collection of short, noisy, spontaneous electronica pairing raw drum machine rhythms with up-front, alternately aggressive and plaintive electronics, the CD drew widespread acclaim. DeRocher has remixed work for David Kristian and Kid606, among others, and released material through labels such as Lo Recordings, Switch, City Center Offices, and Alien8. —*Sean Cooper*

**Suction 001 [EP]** / 1997 / Suction ♦♦♦
A generous debut from Canadian electronica label Suction, featuring six tracks (three apiece) from label proprietors Greg de Rocher (as Lowfish) and Jason Amm (as Solvent). Rushing to the Rephlex analogy might at first seem appropriate, but melodic and textural elements tracing to industrial/ebm and new wave raise the obscure-concept level a bit higher than much of the acid/electro/ambient crunch appearing on Aphex' label. Closer to the Skam/Mask/V/VM brand of dark, atmospheric ambient electro, with touches of drum'n'bass on two of the three Lowfish tracks. —*Sean Cooper*

**Suction 002 [EP]** / 1997 / Suction ♦♦♦♦
Toronto's lowfish (Greg De Rocher) and Montreal's David Kristian pair up for the second all-Canadian release on the former's Suction label. The artists split two tracks apiece over the two sides, moving through minimalist distortion science; manic, squelchy electro; dizzying, multi-layered breaks; and a sort of sci-fi electronica recalling the B-movie ambience of Robert Wise and Roger Corman. —*Sean Cooper*

● **Fear Not the Snow and Other Lo-Fiing Objects** / 1999 / Suction ♦♦♦♦
Self-described as "robot music from Canada," Lowfish's debut CD is reminiscent of early Aphex Twin cross-bred with the raw electro of I-f and the brash analog bounce of Visage or the Normal. Inspirational and pure. —*Sean Cooper*

## Alvin Lucier

b. 1931, Nashua, NH
*Liner Notes, Composer / 20th Century Classical/Modern Composition, Minimalism, Electronic*
A trailblazing force in psycho-acoustic music, avant-garde composer and performer Alvin Lucier was born in Nashua, NH, in 1931; educated at Yale and Brandeis, he also spent two years in Rome on a Fulbright Scholarship before returning to Brandeis in 1962 to teach and conduct the university's chamber chorus. His breakthrough composition, *Music for Solo Performer (1964-65)*

for *Enormously Amplified Brain Waves and Percussion*, was the first work to feature sounds generated by brain waves in live performance; biological stimuli played an increasing role in Lucier's subsequent work as well, most notably through his notation of performers' physical movements. Acoustical phenomena, meanwhile, was the subject of 1970's landmark *I Am Sitting in a Room*, in which several sentences of recorded speech were simultaneously played back into a room and re-recorded there dozens of times over, the space gradually filtering the speech into pure sound. 1980's *Music on a Long Thin Wire* was a further extension of Lucier's fascination with the physics of sound—a conceptual piece featuring a taut 50-foot wire passed through the poles of a large magnet and driven by an oscillator, the amplified vibrations yielded beautifully ethereal results. A professor at Wesleyan University from 1970 onward, Lucier's later works additionally included a number of sound installations as well as works for solo instruments, chamber ensembles, and orchestra. —*Jason Ankeny*

**Music for Solo Performer (1964-65) for Enormously Amplified Brain Waves and Percussion** / 1982 / Lovely Music ♦♦♦♦
The first musical work to use brain waves to generate sound. World instruments, as well as a cardboard box and a trash can are vibrated by loudspeakers placed near and under them, as bursts and trains of the amplified alpha waves disturb the cones of the speakers. —*"Blue" Gene Tyranny*

• **I Am Sitting in a Room** / 1990 / Lovely Music ♦♦♦♦
A new music classic. 32 repetitions of a simple line of text over 40 minutes, constantly broadcast and re-recorded in a room until the nodal tones of the room and the voices undergo a magical transformation of a sense of person and place into a sense of universal presence. Lucier is the dean of psycho-acoustic music. —*"Blue" Gene Tyranny*

**Crossings** / 1991 / Lovely Music ♦♦♦♦
Pure, profound, and classic. Complex ideas realized simply. This CD includes the pieces "In Memoriam Jon Higgins" (1984) / "Septet for Three Winds, Four Strings and Pure Wave Oscillator" (1985) / "Crossings" (1982) for small orchestra with slow-sweep pure wave oscillator. —*"Blue" Gene Tyranny*

**In Memoriam Jon Higgins (1984) / Septet for Three Winds, Four Strings** / 1991 / Lovely Music ♦♦♦♦
In "Crossings" for a small orchestra of 16 players equally divided on either side of the stage, a slow-sweep pure-wave oscillator slowly ascends throughout the entire seven-octave range of the orchestra. During this ascent, the instrumentalists, cued by video monitors, catch onto and hold a particular pitch—before, during, and after that same pitch is played from the oscillator. As the pitches slowly move toward each other, you can hear the beat of the frequencies slow down until reaching a steady pitch with no beating. Then the beating speeds up again as the oscillator moves away from the instrument's pitch. "The resultant patterns of deceleration-stasis-acceleration form the basic gestures of the work" (Lucier). For all their seeming simplicity, Lucier's works provide a deep listening experience of great dignity and elegance. —*"Blue" Gene Tyranny*

**Music on a Long Thin Wire** / 1992 / Lovely Music ♦♦
Recording of an installation made on May 10, 1979 in the Rotunda of the US Customs House, Bowling Green, New York City. The wire was extended 80 feet through the oval of the Rotunda and was driven by one pure wave oscillator. The wire played itself: all changes in volume, timbre, harmonic structure, rhythmic and cyclic patterning, and other sonic phenomena. —*"Blue" Gene Tyranny*

**Panorama** / 1996 / Lovely Music ♦♦
Four innovative and intriguing works based on the poetry of physical phenomena. "Wind Shadows" (1994) for two pure wave oscillators and trombonist, in which diverse tuning modulations (three cycles above and three cycles below given pitches) produce spinning wave illusions. In "Music for Piano with One or More Snare Drums" (1990) overlapping patterns of piano tones cause snare drums to resonate defining a geography of the performance space. In "Music for Piano with Amplified Sonorous Vessels" (1990) the interior resonances of small vessels, such as wine glasses, sea shells, clay pots, bamboo cups etc., placed near the piano are amplified over loudspeakers, their sound in turn creating interference patterns. "Panorama" (1993) employed a photograph of the Swiss and Austrian Alps as a score for a trombonist who would "draw" the mountains by sliding tones, punctuated at peaks by a pianist's single tones and intervals. —*"Blue" Gene Tyranny*

## Lull (Mick Harris)

*Producer / Experimental Ambient, Experimental Techno, Dark Ambient, Ambient Dub, Ambient*

Closely allied with post-industrial dub terrorists such as Bill Laswell, Techno Animal, James Plotkin, Robert Musso, and Anton Fier, Birmingham-based artist Mick Harris is something of a study in extremes. A drummer with noted death metal outfit Napalm Death through the group's late-'80s/early-'90s heyday, Harris began experimenting with monochrome ambient and dub styles toward the tail end of his association with that group. Releasing material through Earache as Scorn (his ambient dub aegis) and through Sentrax as Lull, in addition to other sporadic projects, his genre-spanning activities have done much to jar the minds, expectations, and record collections of audiences previously kept aggressively opposed. To the present, Scorn and Lull, along with John Zorn's experimental jazz-dubcore outfit Painkiller have remained Harris' primary ongoing projects, although one-off collaborations with the likes of James Plotkin, Nicholas Bullen, Bill Laswell, and Martyn Bates are common. Harris formed Scorn in 1991 in collaboration with bassist Nick Bullen, incorporating elements of ambient, industrial, dub, rock, and hip-hop. The group (though pared back to just Harris following *Evanescence*) have released a number of increasingly well-received full-length recordings, including the remix LP *Ellipsis*, which features outbound reworkings by the likes of Coil, Autechre, Laswell, and Germ. Harris' solo work as Lull focuses on darker, more "isolationist" ambient soundscapes, some of which have been reissued domestically by Laswell's now-defunct Subharmonic imprint; a move to Relapse yielded 1996's *Continue* and 1998's *Moments*. [See Also: Mick Harris, Scorn] —*Sean Cooper*

**Cold Summer** / 1994 / Sentrax ♦♦♦
Desperate, beatless, oddly beautiful soundscapes, similar in tone to Harris' work as Scorn, though without many of the more rhythmic, structured elements. Reissued in 1995 on Bill Laswell's Subharmonic label. —*Sean Cooper*

**Continue** / Sep. 24, 1996 / Relapse ♦♦♦

• **Moments** / Jun. 23, 1998 / Relapse ♦♦♦♦
Reportedly inspired by Mick Harris' deep affection for the soundtrack to the classic David Lynch film *Eraserhead*, Lull's fifth full-length effort is utterly hypnotic stuff. Digitally edited from 33 separate sections to form one continuous soundscape pattern, its ebb and flow makes for transfixing listening. —*Jason Ankeny*

## Lustmord (Brian Williams)

b. Wales

*Producer / Experimental Ambient, Dark Ambient, Ambient, Industrial*

While his days are spent working on sound design for Hollywood scores by Graeme Revell, sound designer Brian Williams records experimental ambience and dark space music as Lustmord. His recordings have been embraced by a variety of ambient fans, ranging from the '70s traditionalists at the Hearts of Space label to the ambient techno experimentalists at Plug Research. Born and raised in Wales, Williams first performed as Lustmord in 1980 as a series of unannounced "support slots" at larger gigs, with Williams simply leaping onstage and performing until security became aware of the situation. Though understandably brief, the rock terrorism gained Williams contact with like minds in the proto-industrial scene including SPK and Throbbing Gristle. He soon began appearing with SPK on tour and in the studio, and in 1982 released a self-titled Lustmord LP, including work by Coil's John Balance and Nocturnal Emissions' Nigel Ayers. His second album *Paradise Disowned* (released by SPK's Side Effects label in 1984), featured recordings made in a variety of subterranean locales including the crypt at Chartres Cathedral, Dunster Abattoir in Bangor, Wales, and on the oceanfloor. By that time, Williams had also taken over the running of Side Effects.

Though he released no additional Lustmord material during the rest of the '80s, Williams did record (and do sound research) for albums by Current 93, Nurse with Wound, SPK, Chris & Cosey, and SPK member Graeme Revell's solo project *The Insect Musicians*. Lustmord returned in 1990 and released a pair of albums for Side Effects, *The Monstrous Soul* in 1992 and *Place Where the Black Stars Hang* in 1994. Williams moved to California in the mid-'90s after being recruited by Graeme Revell to work on his sound library for the scores of feature films including *Mighty Morphin Power Rangers*, *Street Fighter*, *Teenage Mutant Ninja Turtles*, *The Crow*, and *Spawn*, among others.

Another Williams collaboration, this with space-music pioneer Robert Rich, debuted with the 1995 release of Rich's *Stalker* album, recorded for Hearts of Space. One year later, Williams responded to requests from the ambient techno DJ community for Lustmord material on vinyl by releasing a single for Plug Research. The recording inspired his next project, a collaborative live album named *Lustmord Vs. Metal Beast* that skirted the edges of dark-ambient techno. He also has several ongoing projects including Arecibo, Isolrubin BK, and Terror Against Terror. —*John Bush*

**Lustmord** / 1983 / Sterile ♦♦

**Heresy** / 1990 / Soleilmoon ♦♦♦
Sound-sourced from an assortment of deep-acoustic spots including sewers and subterranean caves, *Heresy* is a suitably dark hour-long trip through ambient-noise. —*Keith Farley*

● **The Place Where the Black Stars Hang** / 1994 / Soleilmoon ♦♦♦♦
*The Place Where the Black Stars Hang* is an album of a single track (it actually includes five indexed songs), progressing from unerringly spacious, dark tones to Gothic vocal atmospheres and more ambient ones that recall heartbeats. It's an excellent, vacuous record. —*Keith Farley*

**Lustmord Vs. Metal Beast** / 1997 / Soleilmoon/Side Effects ♦♦♦♦
Despite the occasional references to previous Lustmord material, *Vs. Metal Beast* is easily the most distinctive album of Brian Williams' career. Recorded in June 1997 for broadcast over Orange County's KUCI-FM, the album presents Williams in collaboration with Shad T. Scott (aka Metal Beast), labelhead of Isophlux Records. While several tracks retain the spacious noise for which Williams is known, many of them, such as "Open Towers Emerge" and "Heart of a Dog," display fusions of dark ambience with the rhythmic chaos of Isophlux acts like Scott himself and Lexaunculpt. The balance between old-guard ambient and new-style techno makes for a great listen. Though long-time Lustmord fans may have trouble getting into it, *Lustmord Vs. Metal Beast* is a solid collaboration. —*Keith Farley*

## M People

f. 1990, Manchester, England
*Group / Club/Dance, House, Dance-Pop*

The visionary behind the hit-making British house team M People is Mike Pickering (b. March 1958; Manchester), a respected DJ who played in Quando Quango, booked several early shows by the Smiths, and signed Happy Mondays and James to Factory Records while working A&R during the mid-'80s. Pickering later moved from Factory to the dance label Deconstruction, where he signed acts in addition to recording material with his own band, T-Coy. He formed M People in 1990 with Heather Small (b. Jan. 20, 1965; London) and former Orange Juice member Paul Heard (b. Oct. 5, 1960; London).

The group signed to DeConstruction in 1991, and released the single "Colour My Life" that May. Second single "How Can I Love You More," propelled by Small's deep soul vocals, became a UK hit and spawned the 1992 album *Northern Soul*. Later that year M People issued the remix work *Northern Soul Extended*, and then began a blockbuster 1993 with "Movin' on Up." The album *Elegant Slumming* was also a hit, earning the group a BRIT award as Best UK Dance Act. The following year, *Bizarre Fruit* continued M People's success, and was followed in 1997 by *Fresco*. During the next two years, a pair of collections appeared: *Classic M People* and *Testify*. —*John Bush*

● **Elegant Slumming** / 1994 / Epic ♦♦♦♦
Including no less than five British Top Ten singles and several other chart entries stretching back to 1992, *Elegant Slumming* is easily M People's best album. From the driving British house of "One Night in Heaven" and the nu-disco slant of "Moving on Up" to more downtempo soul on "Colour My Life," vocalist Heather Small is confident and aggressive while the production by Mike Pickering and Paul Heard backs her up with an exquisite touch. —*Keith Farley*

**Bizarre Fruit** / 1995 / Epic ♦♦♦♦
The Manchester, England-based trio M People scored in 1994 with a series of British Top Ten hits from its debut album *Elegant Slumming;* both "Moving on Up" and "One Night in Heaven" became US dance club smashes, thanks to an endearing mixture of house and R&B and Heather Small's startling vocal presence. Fortunately, M People did not suffer the dreaded sophomore slump; the 1995 release *Bizarre Fruit* continues in much the same vein as its predecessor.

*Bizarre Fruit* is chock full of funky house grooves, and Small's deep, soulful vocals add just the right touch to the mix, making M People considerably warmer than most contemporary dance acts. The "Moving on Up" soundalike "Open Your Heart" was a major club success in its own right. In addition to the obvious dance appeal, "Open Your Heart," like most of M People's music, has a touch of '70s R&B in the mix. The album's opener "Sight for Sore Eyes" has a grandiose gospel-influenced intro before kicking into the funky groove and a melody similar to Technotronic's "Pump Up the Jam." The jazzy "Search for the Hero" and the retro-soul tune "Precious Pearl" are also highlights.

M People, unlike many mid-'90s dance music acts like C+C Music Factory and the Real McCoy, deserves kudos for releasing an album just as entertaining and consistent as its debut. *Bizarre Fruit* is a worthy follow-up to *Elegant Slumming* and should please those who enjoy a little soul when hitting the dancefloor. —*William Cooper*

**Northern Soul** / Oct. 1995 / Deconstruction ♦♦♦

**Fresco** / 1997 / Deconstruction ♦♦
M People spent a considerable amount of time on *Fresco,* the group's fourth album, crafting a record that would break them out of the Euro-pop straitjacket and establish them as an international dance-pop act. In other words, *Fresco* is less a club album than it is a radio record, filled with carefully-constructed songs with strong rhythms, sturdy hooks, and pop-soul melodies. Too bad that much of the record simply isn't as memorable. Sure, there are several potential singles with naggingly catchy melodies and the entire production is appealingly glossy and accessible, but the songs simply aren't there and neither is the charming, unashamed brashness of their early work. A few songs—the garage techno of "Angel St.," the catchy house of "Fantasy Island" and the sweeping orchestrated pop of "Just for You"—make the album worthwhile, but on the whole *Fresco* is a distressing step backward for a group that had yet to make a false move. —*Stephen Thomas Erlewine*

**Testify** / May 25, 1999 / Sony ♦♦
Using their *Classic M People* compilation as a springboard, the trio released another collection in 1999, though *Testify* is nowhere near as essential. The new compilation includes the three new songs originally from the greatest-hits package (one of which is the title track), and a few of the group's best album tracks from past years; it is rounded out by new remixes of classic hits "Moving on Up," "Colour My Life," and "How Can I Love You More?" It's a curious collection, unessential for beginners and rather frustrating for collectors. —*John Bush*

## Timo Maas

*Producer, DJ / Progressive Trance, Electronica, Trance, Club/Dance*

Düsseldorf's Timo Maas is mostly associated with his involvement in Germany's trance scene as a DJ and producer. Often misspelled by Americans as Timo Mass, the man who portrays an evil persona gained a large global following at the height of the global trance music scene, which had a large push from DJs such as Paul Van Dyk and Sandra Collins in the mid- to late '90s.

Maas' first exposure to music came via listening to the radio when he was young. He bought his first record when he was nine and his first pair of turntables when he was 17. His earlier gigs were around Germany playing mostly Top 40 records at bars, sneaking in the occasional techno record. In 1982 he played his first real official set in the basement of a friend's house at a party and was booked a lengthy six years later for his first official all-techno gig. He was introduced to the rave scene in 1992, in its early German days, through a booking at an Easter rave. Following were a long string of big rave events and local exposure. The production bug first bit Maas in the early '80s when he was listening to James Brown clips, but his first record, "The Final XS," was not released until 1995. Called cheesy by Maas himself, the record did not do very well in most markets. Shortly after, he teamed with producer Gary D and the two released the more successful "Die Herdplatte" record. Gary D also landed Maas a residency at one of Hamburg, Germany's larger known clubs, Tunnel, from 1994 to 1996. However, the relationship did not last long due to a personal dispute.

Maas bounced back shortly after through connections in London with Leon Alexander and Stephan Sutterthwaite. The two Englishmen connected the German producer with the Bristol-based progressive house club Lakota. In addition, Alexander and Sutterthwaite had a hand with Hope Recordings, which Maas would come to release many singles through and be largely involved with, in addition to Hope Management. He has recorded and remixed albums under a series of monikers, including Orinoko for Sony, Germany. He also records with manager and mate Leon Alexander under Mad Dogs and Englishmen. In 2000, Timo Maas took a residency at New York City mega-club Twilo with colleagues Deep Dish of the label Yoshitoshi. In October of 2000 he released the full-length album *Music for the Maases* on Hope Recordings through Kinetic. —*Diana Potts*

- **Music for the Maases** / Oct. 3, 2000 / Kinetic ♦♦
Timo Maas smacks down a double whammy in more ways than one with the double mix CD *Music for the Maases*. Not only are there two CDs, but all the tracks used for the mixes are either original productions or remixes by Maas under his own name or his many aliases. Unless you are a huge Timo Maas fan, it will probably be more Maas than you can handle. The mix fluxes from tech house to the deeper realms of trance, for which the Frankfurt native is most associated with. Respected by such big names as Paul Oakenfold and Pete Tong, Maas adds another notch to his long resume with the 2000 release of *Music for the Maases*. —*Diana Potts*

## C.J. Mackintosh (Christopher John Mackintosh)

b. Dec. 29, 1962, Paris, France
*Keyboards, Producer, DJ / Club/Dance, House, Hip-Hop*

C.J. Mackintosh has long been one of the most high-profile DJs on the British clubscene, from an early career as one of Europe's best hip-hop mixers and a mainstream introduction via the one-shot wonder "Pump Up the Volume" (by M/A/R/R/S) through to his residency spinning house/garage sets at the London super-club Ministry of Sound. Born in Paris though he grew up in London, Mackintosh was introduced to DJing by his brother (both had been buying records from an early age). The pair set up their own sound-system (as a part-time gig from running a car-parts export firm) and began throwing parties with the booming sound of rare-groove and early Sugar Hill hip-hop. Mackintosh's first residency, at a joint named the Flim Flam Club, helped him secure duties creating megamixes at Serious Records. In 1987, Mackintosh won the English wing of the prestigious DMC World Mixing Championships and joined the Nasty Rox, Inc. production team formed by another noted British DJ, Dave Dorrell. (Mackintosh replaced Nellee Hooper, later of Massive Attack and Soul II Soul.)

That same year, Ivo Watts-Russell, the head of the respected independent rock label 4AD, assembled a studio group (including members of 4AD acts Colourbox and AR Kane) to create a hip-hop/acid house crossover track. Looking to hire the top DJs available for scratching duties, Watts-Russell made the natural choice of champion mixer Mackintosh and the Nasty Rox, Inc. team. The resulting single, titled "Pump Up the Volume" and shipped out as by the group M/A/R/R/S, became a club sensation; it the Top 10 in Britain in 1987 and ascended to the Top 20 in America one year later.

Though M/A/R/R/S never released another record, Mackintosh's reputation allowed him a quick transition into the world of remixes; with Dorrell, he worked on productions for C&C Music Factory, Barbara Tucker, Coldcut, Inner City, and Public Image Limited. His early hip-hop influences allowed him success with more mid-tempo R&B jams as well, on remixes for Whitney Houston, Janet Jackson, Sounds of Blackness, Sly & Robbie, De La Soul, Guru's Jazzmatazz, and D-Mob.

When Mackintosh began mixing at the Ministry of Sound, probably the best-known nightclub in Britain, the selections were all house and garage. He released several mix albums, either alone or allied with other top DJ talents (such as Farley & Heller and Todd Terry) and his Love Happy project hit the charts with the 1995 anthem "Message of Love." A highly publicized feud with Ministry of Sound caused Mackintosh to abruptly resign his residency in 1996, though he continued to DJ around the world. —*John Bush*

**Mixmag Live!, Vol. 3** / Jan. 1996 / Moonshine ♦♦♦
Mackintosh shared this third volume in the *Mixmag Live!* series with Sasha. —*John Bush*

- **Colours: The Full Spectrum** / Oct. 27, 1997 / ♦♦♦♦
A double-pack including mix work by Mackintosh plus Farley & Heller, *Colours: The Full Spectrum* is a solid, somewhat exciting collection of chart-bound trance and house, enlivened solely by Mackintosh's mixing skills. —*Keith Farley*

## Mad Professor (Neal Fraser)

b. Guyana
*Vocals, Drums, Percussion, Producer, Arranger / Dub*

A mastery of electronic gadgetry has been expressed through the imaginative recordings produced by Mad Professor (Neil Fraser). Working from his own studios, Mad Professor has overseen more than one hundred albums including groundbreaking remixes for Massive Attack, Sade and Pato Banton. A native of Guyana, Mad Professor earned his professional name for his childhood fascination for electronics. At the age of nine or ten, he built a radio from scratch. Moving to London, at the age of thirteen, Mad Professor continued to experiment with electronics. Although he bought a semi-professional reel to reel tape recorder in 1975, he was unable to record in sync. This prompted him to purchase more and more equipment. By the following year, he had begun experimenting with dubbing. Over the years, Mad Professor's studio, which he named "Ariwa", after the Nigerian word for sound, has continued to evolve. Opened in a south London house in 1979, it moved to a much larger space in the Peckham ghetto the following year. During the four years that the studio remained at the site, Mad Professor found that the seemingly unsafe location cost him much of his clientele. After a brief return to the original house, the studio relocated to its present site in Whitehorse Lane. —*Craig Harris*

**Feast of Yellow Dub** / 1984 / RAS ♦♦♦
It's fashionable to slag British producer Mad Professor these days. And it's true that his sound, a digitally clean yet sonically adventurous combination of Lee Perry-style quirkiness and rootswise rhythm, is distinctive enough and his output prolific enough that he does open himself up to charges of repetition. It might be fair to call him the Vivaldi of reggae: he borrows from himself shamelessly, and you can generally identify a Mad Professor production within about four bars. But really, that's not necessarily a bad thing. And when you team him up with a personality as strong as that of Yellowman—Jamaica's famous Afro-albino toaster—the results can be outstanding, as they are here. Actually, Yellowman's contributions are pretty passive; this is a collection of Yellowman singles in dub versions by the Professor, and Yellowman's voice only pops into the mix occasionally. Even then, it's often digitally manipulated past recognizability; fans who pay close attention may recognize "A Dose of Diseases" as the dub version of "AIDS" and "Some Wild Western Peppers" as the dub of "Wild Wild West." Roots Radics provide the instrumental raw material for this crazy dub concoction, and as usual their performances are impeccable. —*Rick Anderson*

**Who Knows the Secret of the Master Tape—** / 1987 / RAS ♦♦♦♦
More creative instrumentation and plenty of dub madness make this album a unique offering in a sometimes overdone field. —*Myles Boisen*

**Hijacked to Jamaica: Dub Me Crazy Pt. II** / 1991 / RAS ♦♦♦
Part II of the *Dub Me Crazy* series was actually done in Jamaica, rather than in The Professor's England home. —*Myles Boisen*

**It's a Mad, Mad, Mad Professor** / 1994 / Ariwa ♦♦♦♦
Mad Professor is a British reggae producer whose incredibly prolific output rivals that of Jamaica's legendary sound factories of the late '60s and early '70s in both quantity and quality. His particular genius is an ability to produce music that is completely modern in sound and technique but that nevertheless draws heavily on the "roots and culture" tradition of golden-era Jamaican reggae. His collaborations with Pato Banton, Macka B, and the legendary Lee Perry (whose influence is felt heavily in Mad Professor's work) have brought him fame in the broader reggae community, while the *Dub Me Crazy* series on his Ariwa label (distributed by RAS in the US) has earned him the adoration of dub fans around the world. This sampler is the place for a neophyte to begin. It includes rarities and tracks from his earlier albums, all "Recorded in Dubarama." That means that instruments and voices fly in and out of the mix, echoing crazily and careening off into the darkness only to return when you least expect them. Mad Professor doesn't do the introspective, mystical dub of so many of his predecessors—there's always an intense energy and a mischievous sense of humor at work, even on his more political material. —*Rick Anderson*

**Beyond the Realms of Dub: Dub Me Crazy—The Second Chapter** / Sep. 3, 1996 / Ariwa ♦♦♦
On this, the second installment in the *Dub Me Crazy* series, the Mad Professor opens simply by saying "Tune into dub me crazy part two" just before plunging headlong into ten tracks of space-age dub that are sure to twist your brain up nice and tight. After all, that's the goal here, right? At times, some of the tracks sound a bit too much like a '70s video game with low batteries and seem too crammed with extraneous electronic noises. Sometimes it works, like on "Elastic Plastic," and at other times it doesn't, like on "Africa 1983 Dub." Indeed, on tracks like the steel drum-laced "English Connection," simpler is better. Despite the few weak tracks, true Mad Professor fans will find satisfaction in his characteristic deep-space piano chords that seem to re-

verberate forever, basslines that will nail you to a wall, and just the right amount of quirkiness thrown in for good measure. —*Matthew Hilburn*

● **Ras Portraits** / Jul. 8, 1997 / Ras ✦✦✦✦

Ras designed *Ras Portraits* as a concise introduction to a particular artist's recordings for the label. Since the information behind Ras releases is always shady, it's difficult to discern the origin of tracks on *Ras Portraits*, but the disc is one of the better collections of Mad Professor material that Ras has released, and listeners curious about his albums for the label should start here. It should not, however, be seen as a definitive introduction to his music in general. Among the featured tracks on the Professor's *Ras Portrait* are "Dub Science," "Beyond the Realms of Dub," "Zion," "Holokoko Dub," "Sistren Version," "Buccaneer's Cove," "Hi-Jacked to Jamaica," "Fire on Mt. Sinai," "Black Skin, White Minds," "Anti-Racist Broadcast," and "Harder Than Babylon."
—*Stephen Thomas Erlewine*

**Dubtronic** / Aug. 24, 1998 / Ariwa ✦✦

This is a disappointingly pedestrian outing from Mad Professor, a genius producer whose solo work has been maddeningly uneven in the '90s. Although he practically holds the patent for the UK lovers rock sound and has done fine work with such artists as Lee "Scratch" Perry, Kofi, and Sandra Cross, he hasn't been able to translate his production prowess into consistently interesting solo projects. *Dubtronic* is a collection of instrumentals featuring the fine Robotiks band and cameo appearances by Perry and several others, and the most interesting thing about the album is the degree to which it downplays explicit reggae rhythms in favor of slick and mild-mannered funk. "Boombox Dub" and "Boombox Version II" relieve the tedium somewhat with a deep, slow groove and interesting sound effects, but "Drum & Bass in the Asylum" is a thoroughly boring piece of generic jungle, and "Bedroom Sensation" is an equally tiresome attempt at instrumental lovers rock. It all adds up to a sort of easy-listening version of modern reggae. —*Rick Anderson*

**Fire in Dub** / Nov. 10, 1998 / Ariwa ✦✦✦✦

Okay, pay close attention: *Fire in Dub* is the dub version of Lee Perry's *Dub Fire* (ARICD 134), which is not itself a dub album and which was released in the US at the same time as this one. It's important that you not get confused, because *Dub Fire* is a relatively crummy disc, while this one is really very good. The difference? Perry's increasingly dissolute vocals are left out for the most part, which leaves nothing but the rock-solid backing tracks of the Robotiks band for Mad Professor to play with. The Professor has made some pretty boring music on his own over the last ten years, and this album makes it clear what's been missing: live musicians. Give him flesh and blood to work with, and he can wreak serious havoc: note the demented rhythmic brilliance of "Can't Control the African" (based on "Place Called Africa") and "Don't Try to Capsize I" (based on "Rock My Boat"). It's amazing how much fun Lee Perry can be when you only hear his voice occasionally. —*Rick Anderson*

## Thee Maddkatt Courtship (Felix Stallings, Jr.)

*Producer / Club/Dance, House*

One of the more consistent pseudonyms Chicago producer Felix Da Housecat used for EPs and singles during much of the '90s, Thee Maddkatt Courtship also served as the base for many of his studio full-lengths, including 1995's *Alone in the Dark* and 1999's *I Know Elecktrikboy*. [See Also: Felix Da Housecat] —*John Bush*

● **I Know Electrikboy** / Oct. 4, 1999 / ffrr ✦✦✦✦

*I Know Electrikboy* is a loose concept album from the mind of Felix Da Housecat, a work that functions more as a love song to house music and to the dance scene in general. The concept presents a futuristic world in need of a musical savior due to an invasion of consumer-minded, imperialist Earthlings bent on taking over music as they know it. The hero, Electrikboy, uses his numerous aliases, connection to the underground, and, above all, the power of music to stifle any attempts at detection. Thematically, *I Know Electrikboy* balances two kinds of songs: those dealing with the communal power of dance scenes ("My Life Muzik," "Zone 2 Nite," "My Fellow Boppers") and more than a few laments about the passing—or worse, the gradual commercialization—of those same scenes ("Where Is Your Past?," "Electrikboy," "Cosmic Pop"). The allegories to the increasingly mainstream dance industry and to Felix himself are obvious, so it's probably a good thing that he doesn't attempt to stretch the concept too far. The focus on *I Know Electrikboy* is squarely on the music, and as such, there are a few of the best productions of his career here (granted, some were gathered from previous singles). As befits an album concerning the dance scene, most of these productions are aligned with several historical periods in electronic dance music—mid-tempo disco-funk inspired by Giorgio Moroder, raw early '80s R&B, Chicago house (obviously), and just a little bit of acid. Many of the tracks have vocals (either by Tyrone Palmer, Harrison Crump, or Felix himself) and Felix perfectly balances a free-form style of soulful songwriting with a stricter production sense that still wouldn't suffer on the dancefloor. Throughout, he skates a very thin line separating the direct and the implied, vocal and instrumental. It's an intriguing statement about music for those looking to find it, but *I Know Electrikboy* is above all an excellent musical statement in its own right. —*John Bush*

## Madonna (Madonna Louise Veronica Ciccone)

b. Aug. 16, 1958, Rochester, MI

*Vocals, Producer / Club/Dance, Pop/Rock, Adult Contemporary, Dance-Pop*

After a star reaches a certain point, it's easy to forget what they became famous for and concentrate solely on their persona. Madonna is such a star. Madonna rocketed to stardom so quickly in 1984 that it obscured most of her musical virtues. Appreciating her music became even more difficult as the decade wore on, as discussing her lifestyle became more common than discussing her music. However, one of Madonna's greatest achievements is how she manipulated the media and the public with her music, her videos, her publicity, and her sexuality. Arguably, Madonna was the first female pop star to have complete control of her music and image.

Madonna moved from her native Michigan to New York in 1977, with dreams of becoming a ballet dancer. She studied with choreographer Alvin Ailey and modeled. In 1979, she became part of the Patrick Hernandez Revue, a disco outfit who had the hit "Born to Be Alive." She traveled to Paris with Hernandez; it was there that she met Dan Gilroy, who would soon become her boyfriend. Upon returning to New York, the pair formed the Breakfast Club, a pop/dance group. Madonna originally played drums for the band, but she soon became the lead singer. In 1980, she left the band and formed Emmy with her former boyfriend, drummer Stephen Bray. Soon, Bray and Madonna broke off from the group and began working on some dance/disco-oriented tracks. A demo tape of these tracks worked its way to Mark Kamins, a New York-based DJ/producer. Kamins directed the tape to Sire Records, who signed the singer during 1982.

Kamins produced Madonna's first single, "Everybody," which became a club and dance hit at the end of 1982; her second single, 1983's "Physical Attraction," was another club hit. In June of 1983, she had her third club hit with the bubbly "Holiday," which was written by Jellybean Benitez. Madonna's self-titled debut album was released in September of 1983; "Holiday" became her first Top 40 hit the following month. "Borderline" became her first Top Ten hit in March of 1984, beginning a remarkable string of 17 consecutive Top Ten hits. While "Lucky Star" was climbing to No. 4, Madonna began working on her first starring role in a feature film, Susan Seidelman's *Desperately Seeking Susan*.

Madonna's second album, the Niles Rodgers-produced *Like a Virgin*, was released at the end of 1984. The title track hit No. 1 in December, staying at the top of the charts for six weeks; it was the start of a whirlwind year for the singer. During 1985, Madonna became an international celebrity, selling millions of records on the strength of her stylish, sexy videos and forceful personality. After "Material Girl" became a No. 2 hit in March, Madonna began her first tour, supported by the Beastie Boys. "Crazy for You" became her second No. 1 single in May. *Desperately Seeking Susan* was released in July, becoming a box office hit; it also prompted a planned video release of *A Certain Sacrifice*, a low-budget erotic drama she filmed in 1979. *A Certain Sacrifice* wasn't the only embarrassing skeleton in the closet dragged into the light during the summer of 1985—both *Playboy* and *Penthouse* published nude photos of Madonna that she posed for in 1977. Nevertheless, her popularity continued unabated, with thousands of teenage girls adopting her sexy appearance, being dubbed "Madonna Wannabes." In August, she married actor Sean Penn; the couple had a rocky marriage that ended in 1989.

Madonna began collaborating with Patrick Leonard at the beginning of 1986; Leonard would co-write most of her biggest hits in the '80s, including "Live to Tell," which hit No. 1 in June of 1986. A more ambitious and accomplished record than her two previous albums, *True Blue* was released the following month, to both massive commercial success (it was a No. 1 in both the US and the UK, selling over five million copies in America alone) and critical acclaim. "Papa Don't Preach" became her fourth No. 1 hit in the US While her musical career was thriving, her film career took a savage hit with the November release of *Shanghai Surprise*. Starring Madonna and Sean Penn, the comedy received terrible reviews, which translated into disastrous box office returns.

At the beginning of 1987, she had her fifth No. 1 single with "Open Your Heart," the third number one from *True Blue* alone. The title cut from the soundtrack of her third feature film, *Who's That Girl?*, was another chart-topping hit, although the film itself was another box office bomb. 1988 was a relatively quiet year for Madonna, as she spent the first half of the year acting in David Mamet's *Speed the Plow* on Broadway. In the meantime, she released the remix album *You Can Dance*. After withdrawing the divorce papers she filed at the beginning of 1988, she divorced Penn at the beginning of 1989.

*Like a Prayer*, released in the spring of 1989, was her most ambitious and far-reaching album, incorporating elements of pop, rock and dance. It was another No. 1 hit and launched the No. 1 title track and "Express Yourself," "Cherish," and "Keep It Together," three more Top Ten hits. In April 1990, she began her massive *Blonde Ambition* tour, which ran throughout the entire year. "Vogue" became a No. 1 hit in May, setting the stage for her co-starring role in Warren Beatty's *Dick Tracy;* it was her most successful film appearance since *Desperately Seeking Susan*. Madonna released a greatest hits album, *The Immaculate Collection*, at the end of the year. It featured two new songs, including the No. 1 single "Justify My Love," which sparked another controversy with its sexy video; the second new song, "Rescue Me," became the highest-debuting single by a female artist in US chart history, entering the charts at No. 15. *Truth or Dare*, a documentary of the *Blonde Ambition* tour, was released to positive reviews and strong ticket sales during the spring of 1991.

Madonna returned to the charts in the summer of 1992 with the number one "This Used to Be My Playground," a single featured in the film *A League of Their Own*, which featured the singer in a small part. Later that year, Madonna released *Sex*, an expensive, steel-bound soft-core pornographic book that featured hundreds of erotic photographs of herself, several models, and other celebrities — including Isabella Rossellini, Big Daddy Kane, Naomi Campbell, and Vanilla Ice — as well as selected prose. *Sex* received scathing reviews and enormous negative publicity, yet that didn't stop the accompanying album, *Erotica*, from selling over two million copies. *Bedtime Stories*, released two years later, was a more subdued affair than *Erotica*. Initially, it didn't chart as impressively, prompting some critics to label her a has-been, yet the album spawned her biggest hit, "Take a Bow," which spent seven weeks at No. 1. It also featured the Bjork-penned "Bedtime Stories," which became her first single not to make the Top 40; its follow-up, "Human Nature," also failed to crack the Top 40. Nevertheless, *Bedtime Stories*, marked her seventh album to go multi-platinum.

Beginning in 1995, Madonna began one of her most subtle image makeovers as she lobbied for the title role in the film adaptation of Andrew Lloyd Webber's *Evita*. Backing away from the overt sexuality of *Erotica* and *Bedtime Stories*, Madonna recast herself as an upscale sophisticate, and the compilation *Something to Remember* fit into the plan nicely. Released in the fall of 1995, around the same time she won the coveted role of Evita Peron, the album was comprised entirely of ballads, designed to appeal to the mature audience that would also be the target of *Evita*. As the filming completed, Madonna announced she was pregnant and her daughter, Lourdes, was born late in 1996, just as *Evita* was scheduled for release. The movie was greeted with generally positive reviews and Madonna began a campaign for an Oscar nomination that resulted in her winning the Golden Globe for Best Actress (Musical or Comedy), but not the coveted Academy Award nomination. The soundtrack for *Evita*, however, was a modest hit, with a dance remix of "Don't Cry for Me Argentina" and the newly-written "You Must Love Me" both becoming hits.

During 1997, she worked with producer William Orbit on her first album of new material since 1994's *Bedtime Stories*. The resulting record, *Ray of Light*, was heavily influenced by electronica, techno, and trip-hop, thereby updating her classic dance-pop sound for the late '90s. *Ray of Light* received uniformly excellent reviews upon its March 1998 release and debuted at number two on the charts. Within a month, the record was shaping up to be her biggest album since *Like a Prayer*. Two years later she returned with *Music*, which reunited her with Orbit and also featured production work from Mark "Spike" Stent and Mirwais, a French electro-pop producer/musician in the vein of Daft Punk and Air. —*Stephen Thomas Erlewine*

### Madonna / 1983 / Sire ++++
Madonna's self-titled debut was one of the strongest dance records of the early '80s, featuring a state-of-the-art production and a handful of great songs. Although her voice was still quite thin at this point, Madonna projected a powerful charisma, bringing slight material like "Everybody," "Physical Attraction," and "Burning Up" to life. However, it was on well-constructed pop songs like "Borderline," "Lucky Star," and "Holiday" that the record became truly impressive, as the material matched Madonna's performance. All three of the songs became hits and wrote the blueprint for dance-pop divas that dominated much of the remaining decade. —*Stephen Thomas Erlewine*

### Like a Prayer / 1989 / Sire ++++
Out of all of Madonna's albums, *Like a Prayer* is her most explicit attempt at a major artistic statement. Even though it is apparent that she is trying to make a "serious" album, the kaleidoscopic variety of pop styles on *Like a Prayer* is quite dazzling. Ranging from the deep funk of "Express Yourself" and "Keep It Together," to the haunting "Oh Father" and "Like a Prayer," Madonna displays a commanding sense of songcraft, making this her best and most consistent album. —*Stephen Thomas Erlewine*

### ● The Immaculate Collection / 1990 / Sire ++++
On the surface, the single-disc hits compilation *The Immaculate Collection* appears to be a definitive retrospective of Madonna's heyday in the '80s. After all, it features 17 of Madonna's greatest hits, from "Holiday" and "Like a Virgin" to "Like a Prayer" and "Vogue." However, looks can be deceiving. It's true that *The Immaculate Collection* contains the bulk of Madonna's hits, but there are several big hits that aren't present, including "Angel," "Dress You Up," "True Blue," "Who's That Girl," and "Causing a Commotion." The songs that are included are frequently altered. Everything on the collection is remastered in Q-sound, which gives an exaggerated sense of stereo separation that often distorts the original intent of the recordings. Furthermore, several songs are faster than their original versions and some are faded out earlier than either their single or album versions, while others are segued together. In other words, while all the hits are present, they're simply not in their correct versions. Nevertheless, *The Immaculate Collection* remains a necessary purchase, because it captures everything Madonna is about and it proves that she was one of the finest singles artists of the '80s. Until the original single versions are compiled on another album, *The Immaculate Collection* is the closest thing to a definitive retrospective. —*Stephen Thomas Erlewine*

### Erotica / Oct. 20, 1992 / Maverick +++
While it didn't set the charts on fire like her previous albums, the ambitious *Erotica* contains some of Madonna's best and most accomplished music (including the hit singles "Deeper and Deeper" and "Rain"), even if it runs a bit long. —*Stephen Thomas Erlewine*

### Bedtime Stories / Oct. 25, 1994 / Maverick ++++
Perhaps Madonna correctly guessed that the public overdosed on the raw carnality of her book *Sex*. Perhaps she wanted to offer a more optimistic take on sex than the distant *Erotica*. Either way, *Bedtime Stories* is a warm album, with deep, gently pulsating grooves; the album's title isn't totally tongue-in-cheek. The best songs on the album ("Secret," "Inside of Me," "Sanctuary," "Bedtime Story," "Take a Bow") slowly work their melodies into the subconscious as the bass pulses. In that sense, it does offer an antidote to *Erotica*, which was filled with deep but cold grooves. The entire production of *Bedtime Stories* suggests that she wants listeners to acknowledge that her music isn't one-dimensional. She has succeeded with that goal, since *Bedtime Stories* offers her most humane and open music; it's even seductive. —*Stephen Thomas Erlewine*

### Ray of Light / Mar. 3, 1998 / Warner Brothers ++++
*Ray of Light* is the first self-conscious album in Madonna's catalog, the first time that she genuinely seems worried about keeping up with the times. In some ways, she had good reason to worry. At the time she released *Ray of Light*, she hadn't released an album of new material in four years; during that time, she revamped her image, scoring her first successful movie role in *Evita* and becoming a mother. All of these superficially indicated that she was out of touch with contemporary dance culture, but Madonna decided to hit back at those suspicions hard, enlisting respected techno producer William Orbit to helm *Ray of Light*. Unlike other veteran artists who tried to come to terms

with "electronica" (U2, Robbie Robertson), Madonna was always a dance artist, so it's no real shock to hear her sing over breakbeats, pulsating electronics, and blunted trip-hop beats. What is a shock is that it works. Part of the reason behind the album's success is that Madonna and Orbit haven't gone for full-out techno. They've reigned in the beats, tamed electronica's eccentricities, and retained her flair for pop melodies, creating the first mainstream pop album that comes to terms with techno. Sonically, it's the most adventurous record she has made, but it's far from inaccessible, since many of the songs have strong melodic hooks, whether it's the swirling title track, the meditative opener "Substitute for Love" or the ballad "Frozen." However, there's a certain distance to the music. Madonna had singing lessons for *Evita*, and the lessons stuck—her performance on *Ray of Light* is her most mannered, technically precise singing on record. Combined with the stylish, detached electronic music and self-consciously mature lyrics, the singing helps make *Ray of Light* the most mature and restrained album in Madonna's catalog. And while that's an easy achievement to admire, it's not necessarily an easy one to love. —*Stephen Thomas Erlewine*

**Music** / Sep. 19, 2000 / Warner Brothers ♦♦♦♦
Despite all the pre-release hype surrounding 1998's *Ray of Light*, Madonna's embrace of electronica was hardly a startling development, considering that she had been on the cutting edge of dance since she became a superstar; she always knew what was new and hip. Still, the positive reviews *Ray of Light* garnered were a new development, since it was the first time that Madonna was universally treated like a serious artist—all because of a production by William Orbit and an album that was self-consciously somber, even when it let loose. Given the positive reception from critics and audiences alike, it's little wonder that she decided to up the ambition and electronica quotient on her next album, 2000's *Music*. Filled with vocoders, stylish neo-electro beats, dalliances with trip-hop, and, occasionally, eerie synthesized atmospherics, *Music* blows by in a kaleidoscopic rush of color, technique, style, and substance.

It's an album with so many layers and tricks that it's easily as self-aware and earnest as *Ray of Light*, where her studiousness complimented a record heavy on spirituality and reflection. Here, she mines that territory occasionally, especially as the record winds toward its conclusion, but overall she applies her new tricks toward celebrations of the music itself. That's not only true of the full-throttle dance numbers—the Mirwais showcases "Music" and "Impressive Instant," the William Orbit collaborations "Runaway Lover" and the trippy "Beautiful Stranger" rewrite, "Amazing"—but also for ballads like "I Deserve It" and "Nobody's Perfect," where the sentiments are couched in electronic effects and lolling, rolling beats. Ultimately, that results in the least introspective or revealing record Madonna has made since *Like a Prayer*, yet that doesn't mean she doesn't invest herself in the record.

Working with a handful of producers—mainly Mirwais, who co-helmed six of the ten tracks, but also Orbit, Guy Sigsworth, and Mark "Spike" Stent in various collaborations—she has created an album that is her most explicitly musical and restlessly creative since, well, *Like a Prayer*. She may have sacrificed some cohesion for that willful creativity—*Music* never achieves the tonal unity of her three main '90s albums—but it's hard to begrudge her that, since it's such an appealing, addictive record. Perhaps it could have been sequenced a bit better, so the songs flow together seamlessly, yet that's easy to forgive since so much the album works exceptionally well. If, apart from the haunting closer "Gone," the Orbit collaborations fail to equal *Ray of Light* or "Beautiful Stranger," they're still sleekly admirable, and they're offset by the terrific Sigsworth/Stent mid-tempo cut "What It Feels Like for a Girl" and Madonna's thriving partnership with Mirwais. This team forms the heart of the record, and they're responsible for such stunners as the intricate, sensual, folk-psych "Don't Tell Me," the eerily seductive "Paradise (Not for Me)," and the thumping title track, which sounds funkier, denser, sexier with each spin. Whenever she works with Mirwais, *Music* truly comes alive with the spark and style Madonna intended, yet enough of the rest of the album succeeds to make it another latter-day artistic triumph for Madonna. —*Stephen Thomas Erlewine*

## Main

f. 1991, Croydon, England
*Group / Experimental Ambient, Experimental Rock, Dark Ambient, Post-Rock/Experimental, Experimental*

Upon the 1991 dissolution of the British trance-rock quartet Loop, bassist Neil McKay and John Wills formed the Hair and Skin Trading Company, leaving guitarists Robert Hampson and Scott Dawson to found the highly-experimental Main, a project combining the aesthetics of ambient music with layered tapestries of droning electric guitar textures and dark, ominous soundscapes. Main's debut EP releases, 1991's *Hydra* and 1992's *Calm*—later collected as the *Hydra-Calm* LP—were their most aggressive, as well as the closest to conventional rock idioms; beginning with 1992's stellar *Dry Stone Feed*, the duo began exploring ambient sounds, gradually eliminating all traces of percussion and rhythm from their work.

With 1993's *Firmament* and the triple-LP set *Motion Pool*, Main began pushing into "drumless space," a realm of cold, alien sound with little resemblance to conventional musical structure; 1994's *Firmament II* severed all remaining ties to tradition, focusing instead on two epic, abstract environmental pieces with no earthly precedent or connection. After 1995's *Ligature*, a collection of early material remixed by the likes of Paul Schütze, Jim O'Rourke, and Paul Kendall, Main mounted *Hz*; their most ambitious project yet, it compiled a series of six monthly EPs pushing harmonic drones, industrial intensity and atmospheric minimalism to their furthest extremes. Upon completing the third installment in the *Firmament* series, Dawson left the duo in late 1996, and Hampson continued Main primarily as a solo project, soon returning with *Firmament IV*. —*Jason Ankeny*

● **Dry Stone Feed [Single]** / 1992 / Beggars Banquet ♦♦♦♦
The bridge between Robert Hampson and Scott Dawson's previous work in Loop and the drumless space aesthetic perfected on subsequent Main projects including the *Firmament* and *Hz* series, *Dry Stone Feed* is arguably the pivotal release in the duo's catalog, a mesmerizing work essential to understanding their past as well as their future. Opening with the grinding "Cypher," each successive track systematically strips away another element of conventional musical design, gradually obliterating cherished notions of structure, shape, and form to arrive at "Pulled from the Water," an epic environmental noise collage which itself gives way to the title track, a pulsating, buzzing alien abstract. Disturbing, gripping, and ferociously brilliant. —*Jason Ankeny*

**Firmament** / 1994 / Beggars Banquet ♦♦♦♦
With the first record in the ongoing *Firmament* series, Main severs its remaining ties to musical tradition, slipping out of the nooses of melody and rhythm to plunge fully into a brave new world of sound. Capturing an otherworldly environment which is by turns mysterious, disorienting, and sinister, *Firmament* is shorn completely of the patterns and motifs which typify standard ambient music—these four tracks (titled simply with Roman numerals) are instead like field recordings captured on an alien landscape, devoid of even the vaguest hint of human consciousness. —*Jason Ankeny*

**Motion Pool** / Apr. 1994 / Beggars Banquet ♦♦♦♦
Starting out with "VII," a continuation in both sound and song-title sequence of the absolute minimalism of the first *Firmament* release, *Motion Pool* for the most part focuses on the abstract ominousness of the band's earlier work, dealing in, as the slogan for the album puts it, "...drumless space." Such space is not devoid of rhythm, though, and the established pattern of clipped, looped bass and guitar pieces combined with various production and studio touches, with Robert Hampson's vocals snaking out of the ambient fog, reestablishes itself on such tracks as "Crater Scar" and "Reformation." "Spectra Decay" sounds a little more normal in context, centering on an open-ended repeating riff, though everything around it remains as cryptic and moody as it has ever been. Towards the end, things return to the nearly evanescent beginning, as such songs as "Heat Realm" and, unsurprisingly, "VIII" often times sound barely there, low pulses of bass, minimal reverb echoes, and the subtlest of background hums and hisses filling the tracks. "Heat Realm" itself practically disappears towards its end, resulting in having to crank the volume to hear the actually quite lovely sonic touches in the final minutes. It may sound unlistenable, but the tracks have their own quiet, compelling nature to them, not ambient enough to simply ignore but not hooky enough to hum. Given how future releases would aim even further down this particular route, *Motion Pool* remains a key release for the band, a last stop with their initial [and even then quite obscure] style before almost completely embracing the outer reaches of what makes a song a song. —*Ned Raggett*

**Firmament II** / Nov. 1994 / Beggars Banquet ♦♦♦♦
Taking and running with its predilection for utterly avant-garde approaches to rock, as well as lengthy, open-ended compositions, Main continues the series of *Firmament* release with its most compelling release to that time.

Though only consisting of two nearly half-hour long tracks, "IX" and "X," continuing that particular series of numbered songs, both succeed as fascinating examples of guitar reinvention, constantly shifting and changing as they go. "IX" starts with strange, echoing rhythms (apparently solely guitar created, as seems to always be the case with the band) before turning into a series of up and down notes and further odd pulses. After a sudden silence, a newer series of feedback shimmers starts, then turns into a moody wash with odd scribbling noises around the edges. Strange squeals herald a rumbling background of distortion and looped feedback scratches that builds into a lengthy drone, fading into hissing, guitar ringing, and almost liquid noises before ending the track. "X" takes a similarly winding path, starting quietly then turning into more ominous background rumbles and loops and seemingly disconnected, free-floating sounds of feedback and riff chunks. This slowly changes into a more upfront sequence of layered noise, from the gentle to the not-so-much, before quieting and turning into a more soothing hum of reverb and a slow, mantralike loop of noise, with odd stabs of trebly feedback lurking deep in the mix, all of which changes in various low-key ways before concluding. Striking and at times quite, quite beautiful in an alien way, *Firmament II* is Main at its challenging best. —*Ned Raggett*

**Ligature (Remixes) [EP]** / 1995 / Beggars Banquet ◆◆◆◆
Where most remix collections transform an artist's original recordings into something dislocated and alien, in the case of Main—for whom dislocation and alienation are aesthetics unto themselves—the exact opposite is true; *Ligature* restores the human element to the duo's work, and although it would be misleading to suggest that the disc's eight tracks (five reworked by Main themselves and the others reimagined by Paul Kendall, Paul Schütze, and Jim O'Rourke, respectively) are easy to swallow, their relative warmth and physicality lend an accessibility to the proceeedings which other releases lack. —*Jason Ankeny*

**Hydra-Calm** / Aug. 22, 1995 / Atlantic ◆◆◆◆
Collecting the content of two vinyl EPs and adding a lengthy bonus track, "Thirst," named after Main's studio, *Hydra-Calm* provides a good launching point for Robert Hampson's further explorations of the outer musical void. Unsurprisingly, many of the tracks sound a lot like later-period Loop, though with an even more minimal, stripped down vibe. Emphasis throughout is on rhythm and repetition, which would become an even stronger trademark of Main's than Loop's, with any change in the songs occurring at the most subtle levels. "Flametracer" starts things off in fairly familiar territory, with its heavy guitar crunches and Robert Hampson's echoed, murky vocals, but the mechanistic sheen lent to the track separates it from the likes of Loop stompers such as "Straight to Your Heart." After that, things get more abstract as they go, from "Time Over (Dub)"'s glazed guitar lines and the two-note riff turning into open-ended feedback of "Suspension" to the quite unsettling, bass-heavy "Feed the Collapse." "Thirst" itself pointed the way forward more than initially realized, being nothing but twenty minutes of near silence broken by feedback whines and scrapes. Numerous comparisons were made upon release to sources of inspiration in Kraut-rock; certainly the X-ray cover shot and translucent packaging clearly references Faust's similarly-constructed debut, while the emphasis on minimal machine-produced rhythms calls to mind both Can and Neu!. This said, Main manage the unique trick of referencing musical ancestors without exactly sounding like them, exploring areas of the same abstract, consciously and proudly experimental music in its own method rather than retracing steps. A difficult but intriguing start. —*Ned Raggett*

**Hz** / May 21, 1996 / Beggars Banquet ◆◆◆◆
Originally issued in 1995 as a series of six monthly EPs, the resulting two-disc compilation *Hz* is Main's masterpiece, an exploration of pure cosmic sound so deep and so vast that it seems to echo into infinity. Even in comparison to the soundscapes of the *Firmament* series, the noises and textures of *Hz*'s six suites are stunningly evocative—dedicating "Corona" to David Lynch's longtime sound editor Alan Splet and "Kaon" to Sun Ra sideman John Gilmore, Main conjures the otherworldly spirits of both, assembling bleakly hypnotic, unsettlingly vivid documents of what the liner notes ominously dub "stellar evolution." It's music which seems to exist in a void, and its buzzing, rumbling and droning textures capture and twist the imagination in ways conventional music never could. —*Jason Ankeny*

**Deliquescence** / 1997 / Beggars Banquet ◆◆◆◆
That such a studio-bound act as Main could perform live may seem something hard to believe—though the bandmembers never actively call attention to it, listening to the many albums and singles over the years shows clearly that they thrive on arranging and playing sounds, loops, and backgrounds just so, investing seemingly improvised or simple tracks with an incredible degree of complexity. Wisely on the one hand, challengingly on the other, Main approached the live performance here, recorded for a French music festival, predominantly as an opportunity to play wholly new material perhaps indeed truly improvised this time, though one can never be sure. The band are known to use premade CDs and a variety of players to generate sounds on stage, so what in fact might sound like sudden uses of the guitar may indeed simply be prerecorded instances of just that used in a new context—a not unexpected approach, perhaps. "Particle Suspension" and "Phase Space" manage the neat trick of living up to their titles; everything sounds like it's floating randomly in the air, and silence rather than sound characterizes both pieces. While rhythms of feedback and random noise, not to mention the ever trusty dub bass underpinning, propel both songs along, both tracks sound intentionally fragmentary, even incomplete by Main's own standards. "Outer Corona" revisits the flanged and fuzzed riff from the *Corona* EP on *Hz*, but after that it returns to the new and even more obscure, finally ending with "Valency," simply fading out and away at the end. What audience there is can barely be heard, if at all; it could almost be a rehearsal or experiment by the band—and maybe it was, ultimately—but the results are, as to be expected with Main, uniquely compelling. —*Ned Raggett*

**Firmament III & IV** / Sep. 8, 1998 / Beggars Banquet ◆◆◆
Continuing the *Firmament* series where it left off with *II*, *III* features the band once again pushing even their own far-reaching extremes; if not as flat-out amazing as the previous entry, *III* still shows that Main's ability to create unexpected arrangements out of the most unlikely of source materials, and then to create an atmosphere of unrelenting uneasiness verging into unspoken anger, is second to none. Consisting of five tracks, two featuring fellow avant-garde artist Paul Schütze on "elution samples," though nothing is immediately different on said tracks than might otherwise be expected; all vocals and anything resembling an immediate hook is unsurprisingly absent. The first track begins with crackling static, guitar noises bubbling up from under, and so forth, but the second number, "XII," has a much more compelling feel to it with a central bell-like rhythm—as always with Main, whether or not it really is a bell can't be determined, but it holds the track while all kinds of low key, barely there sonic activity kicks around deep in the mix, ending on what sounds like a series of subharmonic touches. "XIII" and "XIV," the tracks featuring Schütze, have more sudden cuts between activity and silence, but otherwise develop the general mood of seeming ambiance over busy but buried arrangements. "XV" closes things on a weirdly beautiful note, thanks to a choral effect at points, but with more than enough screeching, muffled rhythms and other elements to remind you that, yep, Main it is, operating on its own rules and eternally proud of that. And who can argue with such great results? —*Ned Raggett*

## J Majik (Jamie Spratling)

b. 1978
*Producer, DJ / Electronica, Jungle/Drum'N'Bass, Club/Dance*
Though he's one of the youngest members of the Metalheadz stable, Jamie Spratling debuted back in 1992 with tracks recorded for the Planet Earth label. Similar to the other Metalheadz, Majik's 12"s are dark affairs, with some of the best drum'n'basslines around, though he leavens the brew with jazzy flourishes, like the Spanish guitar prevalent on the flip side of his first single for Metalheadz, "Your Sound." Living in Northwood, England, he began DJing in the early '90s—while in his early teens—and recorded "6 Million Ways to Die" in 1992 as DJ Dextrous. Two more singles followed for Planet Earth before the *real* DJ Dextrous became known to him, after which he turned to the alias J. Majik for his 1994 debut on Metalheadz, "Your Sound." The track was an undeniable classic, and later showed up on the *Platinum Breakz* compilation. Besides later singles for Metalheadz such as "Jim Kutta" and "Arabian Knights," Majik records for Mo'Wax as well as his own Infra Red label, which released his debut LP, *Slow Motion*, in mid-1997. —*John Bush*

● **Slow Motion** / Aug. 25, 1997 / Infra Red ◆◆◆◆
J. Majik's uncanny ability to grab elements of recognizable jungle styles and drag them kicking and screaming into new, undefined areas appears in droves on this debut full-length. Although, like his more recent Infra-Red releases, much of *Slow Motion* dabbles in the shadowy dungeons of tech-step,

the effect is more the cyborgian dystopia of *Blade Runner* or William Gibson than the dopey dirge-and-bass normally found dwelling in darkness. About half the material here is previously unavailable, making *Slow Motion* a nice catch-up course as well as being a vehicle for Majik's emerging, mature sound. Additionally, the latter third of the album features the dreamy downtempo material Majik released on the Mo'Wax label under the name Innervisions. —*Sean Cooper*

## A Man Called Adam

f. 1987, London, England
*Group / Jazz-House, Club/Dance, Acid Jazz, House*

From acid-jazz collective to mellow Ibizan house masterminds, A Man Called Adam have pursued much the same fusion of gentle jazz/house rhythms with classic pop songwriting despite the progression of stylistic identifiers used to describe their sound. Comprised of Sally Rodgers and Steve Jones, the group has not only courted the middle-aged coffee-table crowd with a sophisticated sense of pop songcraft, but also kept a close connection to the dance community, courtesy of their ownership of Other Records, a jazz-house label with releases from Coco Steel & Lovebomb, Rosie Gaines, and Maria Naylor. A Man Called Adam's ethereal female vocals and inspirations from jazz as well as house make for easy comparisons with Everything But the Girl, though Rodgers and Jones gradually became more pop-slanted during the '90s, as EBTG leaned closer and closer to the dancefloor.

A Man Called Adam was originally founded as a jazz band, led by Sally Rodgers, Steve Jones, and Paul Daley (later to form Leftfield). Signed to the pioneering Acid Jazz Records enabled the group to find more gigs, and debut with a pair of singles. These early recordings, "A.P.B." and "Earthly Powers," reflected more recent influences—namely the acid-house explosion which had rocked British clubs and charts during the late '80s. Winnowed down to a threesome of Rodgers/Jones/Daley, A Man Called Adam signed to Big Life in 1990 and just missed the British Top 40 that year with "Barefoot in the Head." After Daley left the fold, Rodgers and Jones followed with their first LP, *The Apple*. Unhappy with their treatment by Big Life (a sentiment echoed by the Orb at the same time), Rodgers and Jones decided to form their own label, Other Records, with design artist and longtime friend Steve "Jaffa" Gribbin.

Perhaps due to their new interests in label management, Rodgers and Jones didn't release much A Man Called Adam material during the mid-'90s. (They did have some input on the *Fear of Flying* LP released by Other act Sensory Productions, and released singles on Other as Beachflea). By the end of the decade, the brand of uptempo yet slightly melancholy jazz-house pioneered by the duo became incredibly popular as a soundtrack for British club-kids vacationing in the dancefloor paradise known as *Ibiza*. The singles "Easter Song," "Estelle," and "All My Favourite People (Stay with Me)" became *Ibiza* anthems, and A Man Called Adam made appearances on many club compilations. The pair's second album, *Duende*, finally appeared in 1998. —*John Bush*

**The Apple** / 1991 / ♦♦♦

● **Duende** / Jun. 29, 1998 / Other ♦♦♦♦
Seven years can be a lifetime in the dance world, and the differences between A Man Called Adam's debut and their sophomore album *Duende* prove the fact. While the anthems, "Easter Song" and "All My Favourite People (Stay with Me)," are the quickest point of entry for casual listeners, most every track on the album is a laidback treasure and a potential Balearic classic. —*John Bush*

## Jake Mandell

*Producer / Experimental Techno, Electro-Techno, Techno, IDM*

One of listening techno's brightest young producers thanks to acclaimed albums for Worm Interface and Force Inc, Jake Mandell began working in electronics while at high school in Boston. He studied classical piano and jazz as well, but ended up a biochemistry major in college. Surprisingly, biochem—and his specialty, enzyme structures—turned out to be a suitable course of study preliminary to an electronics career, for Mandell soon began shaping his productions after the complex computer software used in the modeling of proteins. After a single recorded for his own Primedeep label, his first proper release was 1997's *Midwest* EP, the title a reference to his new home in Minneapolis. Early in 1999, Mandell's full-length debut *Parallel Processes* gained praise in experimental-electronics circles (and comparisons to programming heroes like Autechre) for its balance of intricate effects programming and deep grooves. Releases followed for Pitchcadet, Carpark, and Kodama (the latter a full LP) before his second major album, the increasingly minimalist work *Quondam Current*, appeared on Force Inc in 2000. —*John Bush*

**Parallel Processes** / Mar. 23, 1999 / Worm Interface ♦♦♦♦
About what you'd expect from a biochem major, *Parallel Processes* proves one of the densest, most elaborately imagined works of the listening-techno brigade. Borrowing the restless air of drum'n'bass programming, but substituting his own labyrinthine effects processors instead, Mandell occasionally bests the heavily respected Autechre at weaving the most complex balance of rhythm and noise ever heard in the techno realm. As such, it's a bit of a surprise that tracks like "Gamtev" and "Untitled 44" have melodies at all, but here too Mandell does it extremely well. One of the brightest debuts in the advent of late-'90s complextronics. —*John Bush*

● **Quondam Current** / Feb. 1, 2000 / Force Inc ♦♦♦♦
After one album recorded for the indie-experimental label Worm Interface, Jake Mandell moved to Germany's Force Inc and delivered an album much closer to the latter label's penchant for driving, minimalist techno that's just a bit heavier on the beat than the effects. Contrary to much of his prior output, most of these tracks would easily make it on the dancefloor; the highlights ("Emulsified Ossature," "Jabot," the Basic Channel-inspired "Red Auscultation") feature pounding grooves and harsh breakbeats learned from the drum'n'bass crowd. Still, *Quondam Current* is a cauldron of experimental textures, a work that features all manner of electronically enhanced clicks, pops, and scratches layered five or six at a time. —*John Bush*

## Manna

f. 1991, Sheffield, Yorkshire,
*Group / Electronica, Ambient Techno*

While many a Sheffield native occupies an important place in the history of European experimental techno—the city produced Robert Gordon, LFO, Richard H. Kirk, and 808 State, among others—none have mixed professional extremes more than producers Jonathan Quarmby and Kevin Bacon. Known in the world of ambient and experimental techno as Manna, Quarmby and Bacon are perhaps better known in the land of AOR, where their CV includes labels such as Elektra, Polydor, Wau! Mr. Modo, BMG, and Island, and artists such as Robert Palmer, Finley Quaye, Audioweb, Longpigs, and the Gyres. Although work released under Manna's own name includes only two full-lengths and several singles (all through Belgium-based R&S offshoot, Apollo), the group's role in filling in the gaps in interest between the dancefloor and the home listening audience has been important as well.

Formed in 1991, Manna released their debut single—"R-Earth"—that same year on Wau! Mr. Modo (home, at the time, of the Orb). A bit of an underground hit, the track was licensed by R&S sublabel, Apollo, which signed the group in 1993. Manna's self-titled debut followed in 1995, and displayed the more upbeat, funk-fueled brand of ambient techno the label had begun to be known for (through Apollo artists such as Tournesol and Sun Electric). The group's sound is a clean, warm mix of analog synths and sampled and carefully treated percussion, combined with 808 and 909 drum sounds (usually altered or muted in the mix) and more standard acoustical instruments (guitar, bass, traps). The group also shies away from multitracking, preferring to mix elements live in the studio (the fold-out on their Apollo debut depicts the scattershod arrangement of their Sheffield studio). Manna continued to record between other, more mainstream production work, and their Apollo follow-up *5:1* appeared in 1998. —*Sean Cooper*

● **Manna** / 1995 / Apollo ♦♦♦♦
Manna's debut for Apollo followed only a single, "R-Earth" (released on Wau! Mr. Modo and included on the vinyl version of *Manna*). Although producers Jonathan Quarmby and Kevin Bacon's tertiary relationship to the experimental electronic scene is revealed in the naiveté of some of the arrangements, they more than make up for it in the production, which is nothing short of shimmering. And while many of the tracks fall into a somewhat static mold of ambient techno explored years earlier by artists such as Speedy J and Biosphere, the group's knack for hand-painted sounds and deep atmospherics makes for an extremely listenable update. —*Sean Cooper*

**Our Earth [Single]** / 1995 / Apollo ♦♦
Manna's debut track for Mr. Modo, reworked here and paired with the album track "From Heaven." A bit heavier than most of the Sheffield duo's Apollo longplayer (and those who bought the vinyl won't need this; "Our Earth" appeared

there, though not on the CD), the track is a dub-heavy fusion of ambient atmospherics, slow-break science, and noisy, dissonant textures. —*Sean Cooper*
5:1 / Mar. 16, 1998 / Apollo ♦♦♦

## Anthony Manning

*Producer / Experimental Techno, Electronica, Ambient Techno, Electro-Acoustic*

English experimental electronic composer Anthony Manning maintains something of an odd connection to the stylistic involutions of his contemporaries. Although he uses the tools of the techno trade, dabbles in some of dance music's less obvious rhythmic structures, is signed to a techno label (Irdial), and appeals most often to admirers of dance-based experimental electronica, his music is closer in its concerns to academic and minimalist composers such as Steve Reich, LaMonte Young, and Morton Feldman. Manning's compositions for synthesizer and drum machine are generally written on graphic scores, with the final shape of his pieces—while still a combination of planning and the accidents of timbre and shape resulting from the nature of programmable instruments—determined, in certain respects, before a single note is played. His 1994 Irdial debut, *Islets in Pink Polypropylene*, was composed for a single instrument—the Roland R8 drum machine—and his subsequent full-length, 1996's *Chromium Nebulae*, was a similarly austere smudge of off-kilter analog experimentation, with Manning's focus on hand-made sounds and interacting textures more often than not surprassing any overtly "musical" intent. Manning's work has also been featured on the Ash International compilation *A Fault in the Nothing*, and his third album for Irdial, *Concision*, was released in early 1998. —*Sean Cooper*

**Islets of Pink Polypropylene** / 1995 / Irdial ♦♦
A bubbling rhythm and synth-driven bleep electronica fuel this LP-only release from the innovative Irdial label. —*John Bush*

● **Chromium Nebulae** / May 27, 1996 / Irdial ♦♦♦♦
A dark, brooding meditation on electro-symphonic minimalism, Manning's *Chromium Nebulae* is his most accomplished, satisfying work to date. Manning's aversion to presets translates his music into a collection of alien, sometimes threateningly synthetic soundscapes, giving the listener little footing in the predictable, but also offering much to those willing to abandon prejudice. *Chromium Nebulae*, along with the entire Irdial back catalog, was reissued in 1997. —*Sean Cooper*

**Concision** / Jan. 20, 1998 / Irdial ♦♦♦
Manning's third Irdial album shows he hasn't stopped expanding his methods. Although he's still pursuing the kind of fusion of post-classical and ambient/experimental electronica evident in his previous work, *Concision* finds him adding rhythmic elements more immediately recognizable to the post-techno lot—machine-bound breaks set in a downbeat electro lope. Where these appear (on only a handful of cuts, actually), they are less the bleating pulse of a dance track than the sketching of a framework (an unfortunately underdeveloped one) for the interlocking explorations of melody and timbral nuance that organized his previous recordings. Recurring themes seem to tie much of *Concision* into a solid, coherent package, while the tracks switch restlessly between austere solo piano, haunting drones, and stolid, fuzzy, *Blade Runner*-esque atmospheres. A nice listen now and again. —*Sean Cooper*

## Kurtis Mantronik (Kurtis El Khaleel)

b. Sep. 4, 1965, Jamaica
*Producer / Big Beat, Electronica, Hip-Hop*

One of the most influential hip-hop producers of the '80s, Kurtis Mantronik returned in the mid-'90s with a solo career that showed him fitting in well with the legion of big-beat artists he had inspired. As the nominal leader of Mantronix, he produced a good half-dozen early rap classics, including "Basslines," "Ladies," and "King of the Beats." By the late '80s however, Mantronik had moved into R&B and house; after Mantronix disintegrated in 1991, he spent several years working on production, then left music altogether. He returned in the mid-'90s with the mini-LP *Burn the Elastic* and his first full-length, *I Sing the Body Electro*. Praise for the album spurred him to re-form Mantronix and begin recording a new LP. —*John Bush*

● **I Sing the Body Electro** / Sep. 1, 1998 / Oxygen Music Works ♦♦♦♦
*I Sing the Body Electro* is that rare exception to the rule that influential artists should never attempt a ten-years-later comeback trying the same style their current inheritors have made commercial. Mantronik's production methods are completely up to date (and then some), resulting in an album that perfectly balances old-school sampladelic hip-hop with the breakbeat-energized dance music of the late '90s. "King of the Beatbox V 3.0," "Bass Machine Re-Tuned," and "On the Beatbox" are stunning returns to the glory days of Mantronix, while vocal tracks like "Mad," "Push Yer Hands Up," "One Time, Feel Fine" show that Mantronik's trackmaster skills could easily light up the world of mainstream rap, just as they did almost 15 years earlier. —*John Bush*

## Mantronix

f. 1984, New York, NY, db. 1991
*Group / Old School Rap, Electro, Club/Dance, House, Hip-Hop*

Over and above their standing as one of the best and most innovative groups from hip-hop's golden age, Mantronix provided rap music with its first man-machine, Kurtis Mantronik. A turntable master who incorporated synthesizers and samplers into the rhythmic mix instead of succumbing to the popular use of samples simply as pop hooks, Mantronix exploited technology with a quintessentially old-school attitude which had little use for instruction manuals and accepted use. After the hip-hop world began to catch up with Mantronik's developments, he moved from hardcore rap to skirt the leading edge of club music, from electro to ragga, techno, and house. And though he never found a rapper worthy of his immense production talents, Mantronik inspired dozens of DJs and beatmeisters around the world during the next decade—in hip-hop, mainstream dance music, and the new electronica—even while his records were practically impossible to find (many snapped up, no doubt, by those same aspiring DJs).

Mantronik was born Kurtis Khaleel in Jamaica, though his family soon moved to Canada and ended up in New York by the late '70s. Mantronik soon began DJing around the city, and was working behind the decks at Manhattan's Downtown Records when he met MC Tee (born Touré Embden). After the duo had assembled a demo tape, they gave it to William Socolov, president of Sleeping Bag Records. He signed Mantronix soon after hearing it, and released their debut single "Fresh Is the Word." The track lit up New York's streets and clubs during 1985, and brought the full-length *Mantronix: The Album* early the following year. Two new singles, "Ladies" and "Basslines" became big street hits as well, and even crossed over to join the first wave of hip-hop chartmakers in Britain.

By that time, Mantronix had also begun working on A&R at Sleeping Bag, where he signed EPMD, produced KRS-One's first credit ("Success Is the Word" by 12.41) and helmed other intense tracks by Tricky Tee, Just-Ice, and T La Rock. The second Mantronix LP, *Music Madness*, continued to keep the duo fresh in the clubs. The increasing popularity of hip-hop gave Mantronix a chance at a major-label contract, and by 1987 the duo had signed with Capitol. *In Full Effect* emerged the following year, and portrayed Mantronix jettisoning many of his more hardcore inclinations in favor of a fusion of dance and R&B, an early precursor to hip-house. The production excursion "Do You Like...Mantronik?" proved that Mantronik's ear for clever beats remained, however. And Mantronix's success in England prompted several of the first sampladelic hits, like "Pump Up the Volume" by M/A/R/R/S and "Theme from S'Express" by S'Express.

Soon after *In Full Effect*, MC Tee left to join the Air Force. Mantronik replaced him with Bryce Luvah (the cousin of LL Cool J) and DJ Dee (Mantronik's own cousin). With 1990's *This Should Move Ya*, Mantronix made the move from hip-hop into more straightahead house. With vocalist Wondress in tow, a pair of Mantronix singles stormed the British Top 20, including the Top Five "Got to Have Your Love." He still used the rappers, but continued to work in dance with 1991's *The Incredible Sound Machine*. As a group entity, Mantronix disappeared at that point. Mantronik began producing other acts—mostly female vocalists or freestyle acts—and later exited music altogether. He returned in the mid-'90s as a breakbeat elder statesman, recording as Kurtis Mantronik and providing remixes for EPMD, Future Sound of London, and Doctor Octagon. A Mantronix respective and several album reissues began filtering out in 1999, and Mantronik began recording a new group album later that year. —*John Bush*

**Mantronix: The Album** / 1985 / Sleeping Bag ♦♦♦♦
Mantronix's finest album remains this intriguing debut, when Mantronik and rapper MC Tee scored with what was then an imaginative and unusual mix of dance and hip-hop production styles and sensibility with soul and R&B vo-

cals. They weren't house, or rap, or urban contemporary, but a wonderful hybrid of all these and more, including touches of dancehall reggae and even pop and funk. The album had two fine singles in "Bassline" and "Ladies" and made Mantronix a hot property. —*Ron Wynn*

**In Full Effect** / 1988 / Capitol ♦♦♦
The Capitol debut for Mantronix, and the final album featuring rapper MC Tee. This album skirted the lower regions of the pop charts and had a less abrasive, smoother sound, although the patented dance/hip-hop/urban contemporary fusion hadn't been affected. But overall, it wasn't quite as risky or spirited as their Sleeping Bag records, despite Mantronik's continuing production excellence. —*Ron Wynn*

**This Should Move Ya** / 1990 / Capitol ♦♦♦
Mantronix switched labels in the late '80s, moving from the independent Sleeping Bag to the major label Capitol. This was their second Capitol album, and it worked out fine. Although the lineup had now changed, with Bryce Luvah and D.J.D. on board rather than MC Tee, the group had another strong single in "Got To Have Your Love," and Capitol was providing Curtis "Mantronik" Kahleel with a bigger push and sharper production and sound. But the underground spirit that permeated Mantronix's Sleeping Bag albums was missing, as was the quirky air that marked their past singles. —*Ron Wynn*

**The Incredible Sound Machine** / Mar. 18, 1991 / Capitol ♦♦
Mantronix's high-tech and futuristic approach fared better in clubs and dance music circles than among b-boys and hip-hoppers, but make no mistake: the New York group created some of the most memorable rap of the mid-'80s. Unfortunately, things began unraveling for Mantronix artistically when it left the small (and now defunct) Sleeping Bag Records for Capitol. A pedestrian effort that surprisingly, favors R&B, new jack swing, and house music over rap, *The Incredible Sound Machine* contains nothing that's even a fraction as imaginative as Mantronix's Sleeping Bag recordings. Rapper MC Tee is gone, and leader/producer Kurtis "Mantronik" Khaleel is joined by singer Jade Trini, among others. Trini's singing isn't bad—it's the material that's so forgettable and generic. —*Alex Henderson*

**Bass Machine Re-Tuned** / 1997 / Oxygen Music Works ♦♦♦
One-half of innovative hip-hop/electro duo Mantronix (namely, Kurtis "Mantronik" Khaleel) back behind the "Bass Machine" for this '90s-style update. The three-track single includes remixes of the electro classic by Riz Maslen (of Neotropic) and Florida-based producer Omar Santana, whose mid-'80s electro and funky breaks-based tracks were as influential as Mantronix's own. Great stuff. —*Sean Cooper*

★ **The Best of Mantronix 1985-1999** / Mar. 15, 1999 / Virgin ♦♦♦♦♦
A solid Mantronix compilation (though UK only) for all those unable to find the out-of-print originals, *The Best of 1985-1999* includes undeniable hip-hop classics like "Bassline," "Ladies," and "King of the Beats" as well as a new single, "Push Yer Hands Up" (which had first appeared on Mantronix's 1998 solo album). —*John Bush*

## Christian Marclay

*Turntables, Producer / Turntablism, Experimental*

Christian Marclay was the first non-rap DJ to make an artform out of the turntable, treating the instrument as a means to rip songs apart, not bridge them together. A longtime associate of Downtown improv figures John Zorn, Elliott Sharp, and Butch Morris as well as Kronos Quartet. After a period studying at the Massachusetts College of Art, Marclay was inspired artistically by Joseph Beuys and musically by Cage and the Fluxus group. He noted the experimental applications made possible by using the turntable in ways hardly recommended by owners manuals, and began performing as early as 1979. Marclay's methods included standard scratching, playback on damaged turntables, the actual destruction (and reassembly) of vinyl to record the results, and creating musical juxtapositions by mixing together a variety of radically different artists. His 1985 installation *Footsteps* included a gallery floor lined with thousands of records for people to walk over (the results were packaged and sold). His 1988 LP *More Encores* featured tributes to a variety of musical figures, including "John Cage" (recorded by gluing together pieces of several records to create one) and "Louis Armstrong" (using a hand-cranked gramophone to alter the pitch). Though he recorded much more sparingly in the '90s, Marclay continued to appear on Zorn projects including several editions of his *Filmworks* series. The Atavistic label has released the retrospective *Records 1981-1989. Moving Parts* was released in mid-2000. —*John Bush*

**More Encores: Christian Marclay Plays the Music Of . . .** / 1988 / ReR ♦♦♦♦

**Black Stucco/In "Imaginary Landscapes"** / 1989 / Elektra/Nonesuch ♦♦♦♦

Marclay plays turntables—using the clicks of vinyl discs, by scratching, back-and-forth manual rotation, mixing, varispeed etc.—using recordings as artifacts of society. He has also created art objects with the same records—"Footsteps" is a one-sided record containing the sounds of footsteps. 3500 copies were spread on the floor of the Shedhalle galleries in Zurich and people were invited to walk on them over the course of 6 weeks, and 1000 of the records with dirt and scratches were made available by Gelbe Musik. He has also made a "record without grooves" with a gold label housed in a black velour cover with golden writing, signed, and numbered. —*"Blue" Gene Tyranny*

● **Records 1981-1989** / Jun. 10, 1997 / Atavistic ♦♦♦♦
*Records 1981-1989* is a fascinating collection of Marclay's work during the '80s, the results of hours of home recordings—using up to eight turntables and various other instruments of his own making—plus many live performances (one track comes from a nationally televised appearance on the David Sanborn/Hal Willner program *Night Music*). Marclay did much more than just scratching and sampling for these tracks—"One Thousand Cycles" uses an increasing variety of repeated samples and clicks to create a complex rhythm of its own, while "Pandora's Box" varies the speed on its array of plunderphonics. (Though the latter sounds like an easy contemporary of late-'90s major-label turntablist LPs, it was originally released on a 1984 avant-indie compilation from Sweden that also featured Sonic Youth and Live Skull.) —*John Bush*

## Marley Marl (Marlon Williams)

b. Sep. 30, 1962, Queens, NY
*Producer, DJ / Old School Rap, Hip-Hop*

One of old-school rap's first (and finest) super-producers, Marley Marl organized under his Cold Chillin' Records banner an incredible roster of crucial rappers—including his cousin MC Shan, Big Daddy Kane, Biz Markie, Roxanne Shante, Kool G Rap, and Master Ace. His pioneering use of sampling techniques (best heard on 1986's "The Bridge" by MC Shan) was credited with increasing rap's accessibility. Besides his countless outside productions, Marl also recorded two rather inconsistent albums of his own, with backing tracks serving as vehicles for displaying a vast array of guest performers. Marl continued producing into the late '90s (including high-profile LPs by Capone-N-Noreaga, Rakim, and Fat Joe) and also hosted a weekly rap radio show in New York. —*Steve Huey*

**In Control, Vol. 1** / 1988 / Cold Chillin' ♦♦♦♦
*In Control, Vol. 1* is a greatest-hits package (of a sort) featuring singles Marley Marl produced for his stable of artists on the Cold Chillin' label. Mostly though, the album serves to show exactly how important Marley Marl was to the advancement of hip-hop. Before him, hip-hop relied mostly on primitive, artificial sounding 808 drum machine beats. Marley Marl transformed the genre completely with his stock of drum loops, most lifted from James Brown records. His crisp beats enlivened hip-hop and set the tone for the sample madness that would eventually consume producers. *In Control, Vol. 1* includes some of the best moments from the producer's hip-hop revolution. Rap heavyweights Biz Markie and Heavy D. try their hand at a Barry Manilow impression on their transformation of "We Write the Songs." Master Ace and Action attempt some hip-hop upliftment on "Keep Your Eyes on the Prize," and Master Ace, Craig G., Kool G. Rap, and Big Daddy Kane, join forces for one of the best posse cuts in hip-hop history, "The Symphony." While some of these rappers, most notably Heavy D. and Big Daddy Kane, would go on to further success, none ever would sound this tight again. Marley Marl's groundbreaking production and the strength of the various MCs showcased on *In Control, Vol. 1* make the album a must for anyone even remotely interested in hip-hop's history. —*Christopher Witt*

**In Control, Vol. 2** / 1991 / Cold Chillin' ♦♦♦
By the time of the release of Marley Marl's *In Control, Vol. 2*, three years after the release of Vol. 1, hip-hop had changed paths. In 1988 Marley Marl's repertoire of drum loops and James Brown samples were revolutionary, but

in 1991 they were anything but fresh. Even worse Big Daddy Kane, Biz Markie, and most of the other artists who made *In Control, Vol. 1* such a success had parted ways with Marley Marl. On *In Control, Vol. 2*, the producer relies on a new set of artists. Unknowns such as MC Amazing, MC Cash, and Kevy Kev try their best, but they can't summon the energy of Marley's original roster. A couple of unfortunate R&B songs and an excursion into reggae do nothing to lift the album. —*Christopher Witt*

● **House of Hits** / Jun. 11, 1995 / Cold Chillin' ✦✦✦✦
A 15-track collection of Marley Marl's best productions, *House of Hits* features every one of the super-producer's absolute best joints. The track listing—including "The Bridge" by MC Shan (a rare six-minute-plus extended mix), "Eric B. for President" by Eric B. & Rakim, "Make the Music with Your Mouth Biz" by Biz Markie, "Raw" by Big Daddy Kane, "Roxanne's Revenge" by Roxanne Shanté—works double-duty as an old-school-classics compilation, irrespective of production credits. Listening to *House of Hits*, it becomes clear that Marl's Cold Chillin' Records was a stable of hip-hop standards unmatched by any label save Def Jam and Sugarhill. —*Keith Farley*

## M/A/R/R/S
f. 1987, London, England, db. 1988
*Group / Club/Dance, Acid House, Dance-Pop*
M/A/R/R/S' lone single "Pump Up the Volume" remains a watershed in the history of sampling, heralding its gradual absorption from hip-hop into dance music and ultimately the pop mainstream. The 1987 record was the brainchild of 4AD chief Ivo Watts-Russell, who assembled M/A/R/R/S' line-up from the ranks of label acts Colourbox and AR Kane; the concept behind the single was to fuse the rhythms and beats from classic soul recordings with state-of-the-art electronics and production, complete with scratches by champion mixer Chris "C.J." Mackintosh and London DJ Dave Dorrell. Originally mailed in an anonymous white label to a group of 500 influential DJs, "Pump Up the Volume" derived its title from the Eric B. & Rakim rap snippet that was the disc's most obvious sample; it appeared commercially six weeks later, debuting in the Top 40 of the UK charts and eventually reaching Number One, where for untold listeners it served as an introduction to the nascent underground dance scene. "Pump Up the Volume" was also a hit overseas, but plans for a follow-up never materialized as M/A/R/R/S quickly disintegrated in the wake of financial squabbling, becoming a one-hit wonder of rare influence. —*Jason Ankeny*

● **Pump Up the Volume [Single]** / 1987 / Atlantic ✦✦✦✦
Though label affiliates pressed for more, the only release by M/A/R/R/S was this 1987 single, an early hip-hop/dance crossover hit that doesn't seem as surprising in hindsight but still hasn't lost its edge. Four mixes of the title track are included, plus a bonus AR Kane B-side, "Anitina." —*John Bush*

## Billie Ray Martin
b. Berlin, Germany
*Vocals / Club/Dance, Dance-Pop*
Techno diva Billie Ray Martin was born in Berlin and raised in London; initially influenced by jazz and cabaret, during the mid-'80s she led a Motown-inspired soul band dubbed Billie and the Deep, gaining her first exposure on the Berlin club circuit. After moving back to England in 1987, she formed the dance-pop group Electribe 101, scoring a series of club hits including "Talking with Myself." Eventually going solo, Martin debuted in 1996 with *Deadline for My Memories;* the first single, "Your Loving Arms," not only reached the UK Top Ten but also topped the American club charts, while its follow-up "Running Around Town" fell just shy of the US Top Ten. Martin resurfaced in 1999 with the *Crimes & Punishment* EP. —*Jason Ankeny*

● **Deadline for My Memories** / Jun. 25, 1996 / Magnet ✦✦✦
Brian "BT" Transeau provided a bare-bones production for Martin's debut album, though the singles "Your Loving Arms" and "Running Around Town" are magical electro-pop tracks. —*John Bush*

## Doc Martin
*Producer, DJ / Club/Dance, Techno, House*
Long one of the most innovative and influential DJs on the West Coast club circuit, Doc Martin began spinning house records in San Francisco in 1986, quickly winning a cult following among warehouse party denizens for his eclectic tastes and skill at mixing the crowd with the music. After several years of masterminding epic eight-hour sets at clubs including Flammable Liquid and Sunday Love, Martin relocated to Los Angeles, where he soon took up residency at the Metropolis. By the mid-'90s, he was also the first West Coast DJ to hold a number of residencies in New York, appearing at clubs including the Roxy, Twilo, and the Tunnel; also a favorite among London crowds, he regularly spun sets at venues including Cream, Back to Basics, and Lakota. In 1996 Martin contributed the fifth volume in the *United DJ's of America* compilation, followed later that year by *Unlock Your Mind*. A series of 1997 EPs preceded the release of *The House Music Movement* a year later. —*Jason Ankeny*

**United DJ's of America, Vol. 5: West Coast** / Feb. 20, 1996 / DMC ✦✦✦
Doc Martin's most easily available mix album, *United DJ's of America* includes tracks by Doctor Dub, Terence FM, the Absolute, and Sweet Drop, among others. —*John Bush*

● **Unlock Your Mind** / Sep. 3, 1996 / Moonshine Music ✦✦✦✦
Despite his name-DJ status, Doc Martin selects quite a mix of more underground dance names, including I:Cube and Jedi Knights as well as DJ Sneak and Terry Lee Brown, Jr. —*John Bush*

## Massive Attack
f. 1987, Bristol, England
*Group / Electronica, Alternative Dance, Trip-Hop, Club/Dance, Alternative Pop/Rock*
The pioneering force behind the rise of trip-hop, Massive Attack was among the most innovative and influential groups of their generation; their hypnotic sound—a darkly sensual and cinematic fusion of hip-hop rhythms, soulful melodies, dub grooves, and choice samples—set the pace for much of the dance music to emerge throughout the '90s, paving the way for such acclaimed artists as Portishead, Sneaker Pimps, Beth Orton, and Tricky, himself a Massive Attack alumnus. Their history dates back to 1983 and the formation of the Wild Bunch, one of the earliest and most successful sound system/DJ collectives to arrive on the UK music scene; renowned for their seamless integration of a wide range of musical styles from punk to reggae to R&B, the group's parties quickly became can't-miss events for the Bristol club crowd, and at the peak of their popularity they drew crowds so enormous that the local live music scene essentially ground to a halt.

When the Wild Bunch folded during the mid-'80s, two of its members—"Mushroom" Vowles and "Daddy G" Marshall—teamed with local grafitti artist 3D (born Robert Del Naja) to form Massive Attack in 1987; another Wild Bunch alum, Nellee Hooper, split his time between the new group and his other project, Soul II Soul. The group's first single, "Daydreaming," appeared in 1990; it featured the sultry vocals of singer Shara Nelson and raps by Tricky, another onetime Wild Bunch collaborator. The classic "Unfinished Sympathy" followed, as did another compelling effort, "Safe from Harm." Finally, in 1991 Massive Attack issued their debut LP, *Blue Lines;* while by no means a huge commercial success, the record was met with major critical praise, and was dubbed an instant classic in many quarters. Nelson, featured on many of the album's most memorable tracks, exited for a solo career soon after, and the group then confusingly changed their name to simply "Massive" to avoid any implication of approval for the UN's policy towards Iraq; in the wake of the disastrous US tour that followed, many were quick to write the band off right then and there.

After a three-year layoff, Massive Attack—their full name now properly reinstated—resurfaced with *Protection;* again working with Hooper and Tricky, they also brought into the fold vocalist Nicolette, as well as Everything But the Girl's Tracey Thorn. Three singles—"Karmacoma," "Sly," and the title track—were released from the LP, which was also remixed in its entirety by the Mad Professor and issued as *No Protection*. A lengthy tour followed, and over the next several years, Massive Attack's solo work was primarily confined to remixes for artists including Garbage; they also worked with Madonna on a track for a Marvin Gaye tribute album. Finally, to promote their appearance at the annual Glastonbury music festival, the group issued a new EP, *Risingson*, during the summer of 1997. The third full-length Massive Attack effort, *Mezzanine*, appeared in mid-1998; in addition to reggae singer Horace Andy, making his third consecutive LP appearance with the group, vocal chores were handled by the Cocteau Twins' Elizabeth Fraser and newcomer Sara Jay. —*Jason Ankeny*

★ **Blue Lines** / Aug. 6, 1991 / Virgin ✦✦✦✦✦
At the time of its 1991 release, *Blue Lines* was a startlingly fresh album. Before Massive Attack, few dance collectives attempted to fuse hip-hop rhythms

with hypnotic, trance-like pop melodies and soul instrumentation. All of the album has a dark, muted quality, making the tracks blend together seamlessly. While that might mean the songs are indistinguishable from each other, Massive Attack offers enough subtle variations in the rhythms and arrangements to keep the record a mesmerizing listen. —*Stephen Thomas Erlewine*

**Protection** / 1994 / Virgin ♦♦♦♦
While it wasn't as fresh and innovative as *Blue Lines*, Massive Attack's second album, *Protection*, was a fine album that refined the group's atmospheric fusion of soul, pop and hip-hop, yet it offered no new musical ideas. —*Stephen Thomas Erlewine*

**No Protection: Massive Attack Vs. Mad Professor** / 1995 / Circa ♦♦♦♦
*Protection* was widely considered a disappointing follow-up to Massive Attack's groundbreaking debut, *Blue Lines*. Where their debut bent all of the conventional hip-hop, dub reggae, and soul rules, *Protection* essentially delivered more of the same. Perhaps that's the reason why Mad Professor's remix of the album, *No Protection*, was welcomed with open arms by both Massive Attack fans and critics. Mad Professor has returned the group to their experimental, cut-and-paste dub reggae and hip-hop roots. He has gutted the songs—twisting and reassembling the vocal tracks, giving the songs deeper, fuller grooves and an eerily seductive atmosphere. In other words, he has made *Protection* into a more daring and fulfilling album with his remixes. —*Stephen Thomas Erlewine*

☆ **Mezzanine** / Apr. 27, 1998 / Virgin ♦♦♦♦♦
Between the 1994 release of *Protection* and its follow-up, 1998's *Mezzanine*, trip-hop had worked its way into the mainstream. Massive Attack, however, remained something of a cult institution—they had some chart success, yet they stayed the province of hip clubgoers and musicians, many of whom appropriated the band's innovations on hit records of their own. As they labored over their third album, Massive Attack's music grew progressively bleak, even as they worked to add live instrumentation to their sound. Consequently, *Mezzanine* feels alive with paranoia, vital in its own dread. Musically, it isn't a great step forward—it's a development of *Blue Lines* and *Protection*, not a departure—but the focused darkness makes it feel more coherent than their previous records, even if it doesn't sound as fresh as *Blue Lines*. In fact, on a casual listen the album may seem a little like a retread, since there aren't really any new sounds, but the key to the album is in the subtle textures—how the murmuring "Risingson" becomes chilling, how Elizabeth Fraser's vocals on "Teardrop" offer no comfort. Ultimately, *Mezzanine* is a carefully crafted and intensely personal record that is the group's most challenging and arguably rewarding effort to date. —*Stephen Thomas Erlewine*

## Masters at Work
f. 1990, New York, NY
*Group / Garage, Club/Dance, House*

The duo of "Little" Louie Vega and Kenny "Dope" Gonzalez are the preeminent production/remix team in house music, their nom de plume Masters at Work standing behind dozens of the biggest club hits and remixes of their time. Effectively soundtracking the freewheeling American nightclub scene of the '90s, Vega and Gonzalez blended their love of the disparate music coming from New York's underground clubs during the 1980s—disco, the freewheeling garage scene, emerging house and hip-hop styles, Latin freestyle—to enormously influence the mainstream dance sound as it coalesced during the following decade. Besides their productions, remixes, and appearances as Masters at Work, Vega and/or Gonzalez are also involved in a good dozen other projects (including Nuyorican Soul, KenLou, the Bucketheads, and the Untouchables), many of which appear on the duo's own MAW Records label.

Both Vega and Gonzalez were born to parents living in New York (the Bronx and Brooklyn, respectively), though of Puerto Rican heritage. Consequently, both were early influenced by the Big Apple's fertile salsa scene during the '70s. (Vega's uncle is the renowned salsa vocalist Hector Lavoe, and his father played saxophone in Latin groups for over 30 years, while Gonzalez' father Hector Torres is also a salsa expert.) During the early '80s, both were noted DJs around New York, though Vega immersed himself in house and freestyle while Gonzalez entered the rap scene. (The separate interests came in handy later, as dance fan Vega concentrated on songwriting and groove-making while hip-hop head Gonzalez programmed beats and samples.) The pair were also working separately as producers, and Vega had already made a name for himself working on dozens of freestyle tracks and remixes by Nice & Smooth, Information Society, and India. Gonzalez, working as a mobile DJ with a team calling themselves the Masters at Work, founded his own Dope Wax Records and worked on production for all of the major New York dance labels: Strictly Rhythm, Nervous, Cutting, and Big Beat. In 1987, he loaned out the name Masters at Work to Todd Terry for the 1987 single "Alright Alright" (a huge club hit), then Terry returned the favor one year later by introducing him to Vega.

After comparing notes, the pair decided that combining their wide range of influences could be an interesting experiment. They released their first Masters at Work single, the appropriately titled "Blood Vibes," on Cutting Records. Since Vega still had remixing contracts from his solo days, the pair decided to apply the MAW treatment first to Debbie Gibson's "One Step Ahead." The dance community was reasonably shocked to hear a disposable pop artist given a respectable, even exciting, dance sound.

House production teams rarely released albums of their own productions under their own name, but a Masters at Work LP appeared in 1993, on Cutting Records. The album mixed older singles with newer productions, and featured guest slots for vocalists like Jocelyn Brown and India (the latter of whom is also Vega's wife) plus producers like Todd Terry and Maurice Joshua. The reputation of Vega and Gonzalez grew soon and they received pleas from most of the major labels to contribute remixes, adding to their resume Michael Jackson, Donna Summer, Madonna, St. Etienne, George Benson, Brand New Heavies, Lisa Stansfield, Deee-Lite, Everything But the Girl, Chic, Soul II Soul, Neneh Cherry, Ce Ce Peniston, and dozens more.

Though Masters at Work were still a relatively underground phenomenon in 1993, the success of singles like "The Nervous Track" (as the Latin-vibed Nuyorican Soul), "Love and Happiness" (as River Ocean), "I Can't Get No Sleep," and "When You Touch Me"—each with vocals by Vega's wife, India—caused their associated label Strictly Rhythm to give them their own MAW Records subsidiary. The discofied Gonzalez side-project known as the Bucketheads reigned the dance charts during 1995-96 with two number one singles, "The Bomb (These Sounds Fall into My Mind)" and "Got Myself Together."

In early 1997, the MAW duo issued the most high-profile release of their career (at least in terms of the music establishment), a self-titled full-length as Nuyorican Soul. Recorded with input from a host of jazz and Latin pastmasters (George Benson, Roy Ayers, Tito Puente, Charlie Sepulveda, Dave Valentin), the album spawned several club hits, including "Runaway" and "It's Alright, I Feel It." The following year, Masters at Work compiled some of their best productions for *Masterworks: Essential KenLou House Mixes* and *MAW Records: The Compilation, Vol. 1*. Two years later, BBE trumped both with the release of the four-disc box *Tenth Anniversary Collection, Pt. 1 (1990-1995)*. [See Also: The Bucketheads, Nuyorican Soul] —*John Bush*

**The Album** / 1993 / Cutting ♦♦♦
The debut full-length by Masters at Work begins with several tracks of midtempo ragga hip-hop ("Give It to Me" with Screechie Dan, "The Buddah Chant") and ends with a few tracks of premiere vocal house—"Can't Stop the Rhythm" (with Jocelyn Brown) and "I Can't Get No Sleep" (with India). Although it'd be easy to say that beathead Gonzalez and the more house-minded Vega each masterminded one side of the album separately, it's more of a collaborative effort than it appears. The link point comes with several short breakbeat sample tracks, like the highlight "Get Up" (though it's just over two minutes) and "Blood Vibes." Though it's not as convincing as many of MAW's singles, *The Album* is a solid summation of what made Masters at Work the best American house unit during the '80s and '90s. —*John Bush*

**Mixmag Live!, Vol. 10** / 1995 / Mixmag ♦♦♦♦
Dave Seaman and Masters at Work mixed this tenth volume (cassette only) in *Mixmag*'s series of DJ compilations. —*John Bush*

**Sessions, Vol. 5** / 1995 / Ministry of Sound ♦♦♦
The undisputed kings of New York house in the '90s, "Little" Louie Vega and Kenny "Dope" Gonzalez serve up a great double-disc mix of the '90s' top house hits on *Sessions, Vol. 5*. Featured tracks include Hardrive's "Deep Inside," "Can't Wait to Get No Sleep 95" and "Moonshine"; "Come and Be Gone" by The Bucketheads; Lou 2's "Freaky," and "Stay Together" by Barbara Tucker (all Masters at Work productions). Contributions from artists unconnected with Vega and Gonzalez include Kim English's "I Know a Place," Jasper Street

Company's "A Feeling," David Morales's "Philadelphia," Donna Blackely's "Gotta New Love," "There Will Come a Day" by Absolute, "Keep On" by M&S, and Rochelle Fleming's "Suffer." —*John Bush*

**Masterworks: Essential KenLou House Mixes** / Jan. 20, 1998 / Harmless
◆◆◆◆

Covering the history of house according to Masters at Work, *Masterworks* is the place for all of MAW's best club remixes, from the early reworking of St. Etienne's "Only Love Can Break Your Heart" to diva workouts like Kathy Brown's "Can't Play Around," Neneh Cherry's "Buddy X," and Barbara Tucker's "Beautiful People." Gonzalez and Vega's decision to turn the retrospective into a mix album was a good one, providing an hour of non-stop MAW productions. —*John Bush*

★ **MAW Records: The Compilation, Vol. 1** / Feb. 3, 1998 / Strictly Rhythm
◆◆◆◆◆

A more diverse collection than *Masterworks* (though both include MAW-related hits "Moonshine" and "The Bounce"), *MAW Records: The Compilation, Vol. 1* collects essential tracks from the two-year history of Vega and Gonzalez' own label. It alternates genre workouts like the Latin-tinged "MAW War" and "India con Lavoe" with more mainstream dancefloor fillers such as Ruffneck's "Everybody Be Somebody" and KenLou's "What a Sensation." The highlight for both production *and* delivery, however, comes with the 12-minute remix of "To Be in Love," an M.F.S.B. cover with MAW's effortless, chunky disco production flowing seamlessly under a definitive, outboard, near-scatting vocal by India and live add-ons by keyboard player Albert "Sterling" Menendez and bassist Gene Perez. An excellent blend of straight-ahead house, disco flashbacks, mid-tempo tracks, and Latin excursions, *The Compilation, Vol. 1* provides the best introduction to the stunning, diverse resumé of Masters at Work. —*John Bush*

**The Tenth Anniversary Collection, Pt. 1 (1990-1995)** / May 23, 2000 / Import ◆◆◆◆

Masters at Work's *Tenth Anniversary Collection* is a prescient, inestimably valuable four-disc compilation of MAW tracks covering the first five years of what may be the greatest partnership in house music. As surprising as it is to see a single-artist house box set, perhaps the label of release (BBE) makes it a bit more fathomable, considering MAW's Kenny Dope has mixed volumes in two different BBE series (*Hip Hop Spectrum* and *Strange Games and Funky Things*). Still, BBE spared no expense with this box, licensing tracks from many different labels—always a problem considering the large number of outside productions MAW takes on—and fashioning a lavish box with stellar liner notes to complete the set. Thanks also in part to "Little" Louie Vega and Kenny "Dope" themselves, *The Tenth Anniversary Collection* is also compiled excellently. Since separate discs cover vocal productions, dubs or remixes, beat workouts, and club tracks, fans of Masters at Work for different reasons can focus on facets of their production genius, whether it's a tight club track or a glorious vocal production. Rare and influential MAW tracks ("Blood Vibes," "Justa 'Lil' Dope," "The Bounce," "Our Mute Horn") share space with elegant, evocative vocal productions (Marc Anthony's "Ride on the Rhythm," Martha Wash's "Carry On," Barbara Tucker's "I Get Lifted"), while the duo's best remixes (for Tito Puente, Lisa Stansfield, Simply Red, Ce Ce Peniston, and Alison Limerick) show their diversity. Of course, four discs may be too much for any but devoted fans, but there's so much great house music packed into this set, it's definitely worth taking a chance for anyone interested in the history of dance music. —*John Bush*

## Mateo & Matos

f. 1989, New York, NY
*Group / Jazz-House, Tech-House, Club/Dance, House*

One of the most gifted and focused production teams in the New York house underground, John "Roc" Mateo and Eddie "E-Z" Matos were both educated in the warm vibe of disco first-hand by listening to classic DJs on New York radio during the late '70s, among them Shep Pettibone, Tony Humphries, and Jonathan Fearing. That original link from disco informed their own productions for Henry Street, NiteGrooves, Nervous, and a host of other labels during the '90s.

The pair first met in 1985 and became DJ partners soon after. Later that year, they were introduced to "Little" Louie Vega (several years before he joined Kenny "Dope" Gonzalez to become Masters at Work) and learned much from Vega about recording-studio protocol, including production and engineering. Mateo & Matos earned their first high-profile DJ gig at Hector Cruz's mobile House Nation club and spent much of the rest of the '80s DJing in a variety of locales. By 1989, the duo began using what they'd learned from "Little" Louie Vega in their own productions. After recording half-a-dozen singles for their own Final Cut Records, Mateo & Matos' reputation began to spread and they recorded for Oxygen Music Works, Henry Street, Nervous, NiteGrooves, and Spiritual Life during the mid-'90s. Their debut production album, *New York Rhythms*, appeared on Scotland's Glasgow Underground label in 1997. One year later, the second volume appeared. In 1999, *The Many Shades of Mateo & Matos* earned domestic distribution through Glasgow Underground. —*John Bush*

● **New York Rhythms** / Oct. 27, 1997 / Glasgow Underground ◆◆◆◆

The equivalent of sublime Detroit techno for the more mainstream New York house crowd, *New York Rhythms* is an hour-long set with none of the floor-filling tricks of the trade used by many commercial-oriented producers and DJs. Instead, Mateo & Matos succeed simply by working though various deep house grooves, always imbued with soul and a surprising degree of majesty. Highlights include the Latin-tinged standout "Summer Groove." —*John Bush*

**New York Rhythms, Vol. 2** / Sep. 28, 1998 / Glasgow Underground ◆◆

**The Many Shades of Mateo & Matos** / Nov. 1, 1999 / Glasgow Underground ◆◆◆

Mateo & Matos expand their production focus on *The Many Shades...*, inserting a couple of short breakbeat tracks and spoken-word interludes into the usual brace of disco cut-ups and mellow house productions. It's an intriguing diversion, but the straight-ahead house tracks here—"Got a Message" is the best—far outshine any of the stylistic detours. —*John Bush*

## Material

f. 1979, New York, NY
*Group / Experimental Rock, Post-Punk, Prog-Rock/Art Rock, Avant-Garde, Ambient, Funk*

One of the most high-profile projects of the endlessly prolific bassist and producer Bill Laswell, Material pioneered a groundbreaking fusion of jazz, funk, and punk which also incorporated elements of hip-hop and world music well before either's entrance into the mass cultural consciousness. Formed in 1979, the first Material line-up consisted of Laswell, multi-instrumentalist Michael Beinhorn, and drummer Fred Maher, all three staples of the downtown New York City underground music scene. The group, plus Kramer and a few others backed Gong's Daevid Allen during his NY visit, resulting in the album *About Time*, by New York Gong. After Material's debut LP under their own name, *Temporary Music*, the group's ranks swelled to include figures ranging from Sonny Sharrock to Henry Threadgill to Fred Frith, additions which yielded 1981's superb *Memory Serves*. A guest list running the gamut from Nile Rodgers to a then-unknown Whitney Houston distinguished the avant-funk of 1982's *One Down*, the final Material LP before a nearly decade-long hiatus; Laswell finally reassembled the troops in 1989 to record the atmospheric *Seven Souls*, which spotlighted the spoken-word performances of the legendary William S. Burroughs. 1991's *The Third Power* brought the group back to its soulful roots, with guests including Herbie Hancock, Sly & Robbie, Maceo Parker, and the Jungle Brothers; after 1994's *Hallucination Engine*, another four-year hiatus preceded the release of the remix collection *The Road to the Western Lands. Intonarumori* followed in 1999. —*Jason Ankeny*

● **Memory Serves** / 1981 / Restless ◆◆◆◆

Material was a prolific band in the early '80s, and if you had to pick just one of the many EPs and LPs that came out around this time, this is the one to take. First of all, just check out the personnel—it's a who's who of the downtown avant-party set: Bill Laswell and Michael Beinhorn, of course, aided and abetted by the likes of Fred Frith, Sonny Sharrock, Henry Kaiser (and those are just the guitarists), violinist Billy Bang, drummer Anton Fier, and too many more to mention. The sound is consistently challenging yet just as consistently rewarding; Laswell's bass is front-and-center most of the time, churning out funky and angular lines that provide a solid foundation for more outré sounds like Frith's prepared guitar and George Lewis's splayed trombone on "Memory Serves" and the scratchy violin and edgy seven-beat melody of "Metal Test." "Conform to the Rhythm" indulges Beinhorn's singing at its tuneless, Orwellian worst, but there's far more to recommend than to criticize on this album. Strongly recommended. —*Rick Anderson*

**Temporary Music 1 [EP]** / 1981 / Red Music ♦♦
**Temporary Music 2** / May 1981 / Restless ♦♦♦

Okay, ready? Here goes: tracks one through four are the contents of *Temporary Music 1*, the first EP by Material, which then consisted of bassist Bill Laswell, keyboardist Michael Beinhorn, and a few of their downtown friends. Tracks five and six are both sides to an early single. Tracks seven through ten were originally released as *Temporary Music 2*, and tracks 11 and 12 were originally part of an EP entitled *American Songs*—the rest of the EP consisted of the two sides of that early single mentioned above. And in case you're not confused enough, this CD duplicates an early and now quite rare vinyl LP called *Red Tracks*, except for a different song order and the addition of two extra cuts. The music? For the most part, it's not quite as interesting as the disc's colophonic history. Lots of plodding, samey rhythms and dreary, glowering songs with titles like "Slow Murder" and "On Sadism." There are enough exceptions to make the album recommendable, though, including the confrontational "Discourse" and the skronky "Dark Things," which features a flanged percussion sound that was unusual for the period. A worthy effort from a band that would later do much better. —*Rick Anderson*

**One Down** / 1982 / Restless ♦♦♦

*One Down* marked a distinct shift in sound for Material, the avant-garde downtown pickup group organized around bassist Bill Laswell and keyboardist Michael Beinhorn. The edgy experimentalism that characterized earlier efforts like *Temporary Music* and *Memory Serves* is downplayed here in favor of funk and disco tunes delivered with a minimum of weirdness. Sure, it sounds dated but that doesn't make it less attractive. Laswell is a master of funk bass, and with guests like drummer Yogi Horton, guitarist Nile Rodgers, and singers Nona Hendryx and Whitney Houston (just before she became a superstar on her own), he didn't really have much chance to go wrong. Highlights include "Take a Chance" and the strutting "I'm the One;" if you want something a little more challenging, check out Archie Shepp's squalling sax solo on the Houston vehicle "Memories." This is straightahead turn-of-the-80s funk at its old-fashioned best from the folks you'd have least suspected of harboring such sympathies. —*Rick Anderson*

**Seven Souls** / 1989 / Virgin ♦♦♦♦

This release of *Seven Souls* should not be confused with the original issue, which came out on the Virgin label in 1989 and is now out of print. The Triloka reissue improves on the original by adding four remixed versions to the regular album tracks (placing them, strangely, at the head of the program instead of at the end) and by printing the William Burroughs texts which function as the album's focal point. Those texts are fascinating and disturbing: on the title track, Burroughs explains ancient Egyptian beliefs about the gradual process of death underneath. On "Soul Killer," he speculates on whether the soul can survive nuclear assult, while the band attempts, apparently, to simulate nuclear devastation musically (the result is much more musically interesting in its remixed version). "The Western Lands" is the album's masterpiece, a travel guide for the soul with an eerily funky accompaniment of melodic eight-string bass and one-drop drumming. The remix is even better. In its original version, this was only a pretty good Material album; in this reissue, it's among the band's best. —*Rick Anderson*

**The Third Power** / 1991 / Axiom ♦♦♦

Material has never really been a band—it's basically a constantly shifting constellation of musicians whose center of gravity is producer and bassist Bill Laswell and keyboardist Michael Beinhorn. Certain musicians are frequently included (in the old days, Fred Frith and Anton Fier; these days, Nicky Skopelitis and Sly Dunbar), but each album usually features a drastically different lineup from the last, and often a new stylistic approach as well. *The Third Power* is Material's foray into reggae/hip-hop fusion. Beinhorn is conspicuously absent on this album (and has remained so since, rendering Material's name basically synonymous with Laswell's), and Laswell abdicates the bass chair to Robbie Shakespeare; all the drums are played by his cohort Sly Dunbar. Sidemen include Bootsy Collins, Olu Dara, Herbie Hancock, and James Brown's old horn section. Vocals are provided by members of the Jungle Brothers, the Last Poets, Shabba Ranks, and others. That kind of diversity would lead to anarchy on any other record, but Laswell has been chaos into revelation for years. Sly and Robbie keep everything pumping nicely, the rappers keep it interesting, and Nicky Skopelitis' off-kilter guitar keeps reminding you that this really is a Material album. The mood is surprisingly constant, maybe a little too much so; Shabba's raggamuffin chanting on "Reality" isn't treated much differently from the Bob Marley cover that closes the album. But it's a nice mood. Pity the whole thing clocks in at just over half an hour. —*Rick Anderson*

**Hallucination Engine** / 1993 / Axiom ♦♦♦

By the mid-'90s, Material was simply another word for Bill Laswell, so as Laswell's fascination with ambient mysticism grew, so did Material's tendencies in that direction. After 1991's dark and reggae-inflected *The Third Power, Hallucination Engine*'s long, spacy jams aren't exactly a dramatic departure, but the combination of Wayne Shorter and various North African elements is certainly interesting. In fact, the array of guest musicians is more diverse than ever: Trilok Gurtu, Jonas Hellborg, Zakir Hussain, Bootsy Collins—the list goes on and on and even includes William Burroughs (who intones a hilarious list of "Words of Advice" over a churning mid-tempo funk groove). In his ambient mode, Laswell has been accused of turning too little music into too much track length, and there's some justice to those criticisms; here, "Black Light" and the unbelievably well-named "Eternal Drift" both plod along for far too long with far too little development. But that William Burroughs track kicks in just as you're about to fall asleep, and it's followed immediately by a very funky and very jazzy remix of "Cucumber Slumber." "The Hidden Garden/Naima" proposes an interesting juxtaposition of Arabic pop song and modal jazz, with dramatic and beautiful results, while "Shadows of Paradise" brings the album to a close with a gentle whimper, not a bang. —*Rick Anderson*

**The Road to the Western Lands** / Mar. 10, 1998 / Triloka ♦♦♦

This generous remix album delivers five versions of "The Western Land" and two of the title tracks from Material's *Seven Souls* album, which was originally released on the Virgin label in 1989 and was reissued by Triloka in 1997. (Tracks one and seven are duplicated on the full album.) All of the remixes are radical departures from the album tracks on which they're based, and you might never guess that all the "Western Land" mixes are based on the same original version if it wasn't for the wisps of William Burroughs' laconic spoken-word vocals fluttering in and out of all of them. There are lots of big names here, including Talvin Singh (who weighs in with an attractively funky, if unexciting, selection), DJ Olive, and DJ Soul Slinger (who gets more radical with the source material, messes around more with Burroughs' voice and creates extremely intricate rhythms, to compelling effect). Spring Heel Jack take a sort of ambient approach, with frankly boring results. But Bill Laswell's ten-minute excursion on "Seven Souls" is a revelation. Recommended with minor reservations. —*Rick Anderson*

**Intonarumori** / Sep. 28, 1999 / Palm ♦♦♦♦

Things sure have changed since Material (then a trio consisting of bassist/producer Bill Laswell, drummer Fred Maher, and keyboardist Michael Beinhorn) released its first EP of mildly abrasive experimental art-funk in 1979. These days Beinhorn and Maher are out of the picture, and Material is just a name that Laswell gives once and a while to one of his many collaborative projects. This time out, Material is Laswell and a motley crew of rappers and DJs. The disc package is emblazoned with the defiant slogan "Rapping is still an art," which tends to raise one's expectations somewhat. Those expectations are more or less borne out, too. As is his wont, Laswell provides instrumental settings that are dark, rhyhmically complex and bone-shakingly bass-heavy; on top of his foundational beats there are expert turntable manipulation from the likes of DXT (known to old school aficionados as Grandmaster D.ST) and phonosycographDISK, rapping by Ramm Ell Zee, Scotty Hard, Killah Priest, Flavor Flav, and others, and even a cameo appearance by wispy-voiced art-pop singer Lori Carson (whose "All That Future," a collaboration with funky keyboard legend Bernie Worrell, turns out to be one of the album's highlights). Flavor Flav is his typical off-the-wall self on "Burnin,'" while Killah Priest gets arryhmically serious on the six-minute recitation "Temple of the Mental." Alicia Blue provides the aptly titled "Flow," and Kool Keith weighs in with "Conspiracies," a lyrical theme that keeps returning throughout the album. The only weak point on the album comes, unfortunately, at the very end, with Ramm Ell Zee's obnoxious and stupid "Hisstory." Highly recommended overall. —*Rick Anderson*

## Max Mathews

*Programming / Computer Music, Electronic*

The father of computer music, pioneering researcher Max Mathews programmed the first-ever computer-generated sounds, setting into motion a technological and creative revolution which continues to this day. A telecommunications engineer and amateur violinist working in Bell Telephone Laboratories' acoustic and behavioral reseach department during the mid-'50s, Mathews was originally assigned to explore the digital transmission and recording of speech patterns, a process he realized could be easily adapted to the composition and playback of music as well. In 1957, he created the first music-synthesizing program, MUSIC 1, effectively transforming the computer into a new kind of instrument, one theoretically capable of generating any sound transmitted through a loudspeaker.

The development of the MUSIC II program — run on an IBM 704 and written in assembler code — quickly followed, and in 1959 Mathews developed MUSIC III, designed for a new wave of IBM transistorized 7094 machines which were much faster and easier to use than their antecedents. Where these first three experimental programs were all written in assemble language, MUSIC 4, developed by Mathews in conjuction with fellow Bell researcher Joan Miller, was the first widespread computer sound synthesis program to be written in Fortran. The rapid evolution of his work inspired Mathews to publish a visionary 1963 *Science* magazine piece confidently predicting that the computer would soon emerge as the ultimate musical instrument: "There are no theoretical limits," he wrote, "to the performance of the computer as a source of musical sounds."

Work on MUSIC V, running on IBM 360 machines, was completed in 1968, improving upon its predecessor by including re-entrant instruments (i.e. an instrument being reactivated in a piece in which it's already active), allowing sounds to be called upon as many times as necessary. Two years later, Mathews pioneered GROOVE (Generated Real-time Output Operations on Voltage-controlled Equipment) — the first fully-developed hybrid music synthesis system, it allowed the composer/conductor to manipulate sound in real time. Developed on a Honeywell DDP-224 computer with a simple cathode ray tube display, disk, and tape storage devices, GROOVE produced sound via an interface for analogue devices and two 12-bit digital-to-analog convertors, its input devices consisting of a 24-note keyboard, four rotary knobs, and a rotary joystick.

Mathews next teamed with inventor Robert Boie to develop the Radio Baton, a hyperinstrument allowing the user to conduct a computer orchestra with a simple wave of the wand over an electromagnetic field. In 1987, he left the research and develop field to accept a position as professor of music in the Center for Computer Research in Music and Acoustics at Stanford University in California; in later years he also regularly toured the lecture circuit, typically demonstrating the Radio Baton in action. Mathews also pioneered another computer music program called Conductor; another interactive real-time graphic multimedia program was dubbed "MAX" in his honor. Remaining active in computer-generated music into the '90s, Mathews predicted that by 2010, "almost all music will be made electronically, by digital circuits." — *Jason Ankeny*

## Matmos

f. 1995, San Francisco, CA
*Group / Experimental Techno, Electronica, Ambient Techno*
Matmos were one of the more unlikely left-field experimental electronic acts to appear when their self-titled debut was quietly released on their own Vague Terrain label at the beginning of 1997. Based in San Francisco and completely out of the largely UK-dominated electronica loop, the duo (Andrew Daniel and Martin Schmidt) stood little chance of being heard among the din of marketing budgets and entrenched proppers of popular mainstays such as Warp, Rephlex, and Astralwerks and encroaching big-name acts such as the Chemical Brothers and Prodigy. Closer in spirit to the American indie underground (a notion buoyed by a flood of early press in fixtures such as *Alternative Press*, *Magnet*, and *Option*), the group were also embraced by hardcores of the Autechre/Aphex/μ-Ziq ilk, leading to a feature in highbrow UK AG stalwart *The Wire* and interest from a number of notable European labels.

Although only the pair's first release, *Matmos*' microscopic abuse of sourcings as varied as electric guitars, freshly cut hair, the amplified neural activity of crayfish, and the human voice (there are a few synthesizers and drum machines in there as well) was instantly distinguishing, conveying an experimental ardor several flow diagrams removed from the more dance-entrenched UK electronica scene. While with *Matmos* that experimentalism is elevated to method, in fact both Schmidt's and Daniel's musical pasts are littered with strange associations, the most bizarre of which is probably King G and the J Krew, a "white funk/rap" outfit which also included Jason Noble (currently of indie salon/string quartet group Rachel's). Schmidt was a founding member of avant-garde electronic group X/I and worked with San Francisco-based experimental music collective IAO Core alongside current members of groups such as Amber Asylum and Tipsy. Matmos began as a long-distance tape exchange project while Daniel was living in London (he's originally from Kentucky), with the pair settling in the San Francisco Bay Area (where Daniel is pursuing a Ph.D.) in the mid-'90s. Schmidt, a visual artist, also comanages the San Francisco Art Institute's New Genres department. — *Sean Cooper*

● **Matmos** / 1997 / Vague Terrain ◆◆◆
*Matmos* is an extended meditation on the musical potential of weird noises. Integrating a range of distinctly non-musical sound sources (hair, breath, crustacean brain activity, etc.) into familiar contemporary forms such as electro, jungle, techno, and dubby downtempo breakbeat, the result is a perversion of both esoteric noise music and the (comparatively) more accessible electronica of artists such as Autechre, Locust, and μ-Ziq, which it most closely (but still only vaguely) resembles. Terrifically strange. — *Sean Cooper*

**Quasi-Objects** / Jun. 16, 1998 / Vague Terrain ◆◆◆
The duo's second full-length release on their own Vague Terrain imprint is both an improvement and a disappointment. On the plus side, the material is oceans better production-wise, more thoughtfully arranged, and more fully developed. However, Matmos tend to let the schtick of let's-make-tracks-entirely-out-of-weird-noises get the better of their aesthetic judgement, and too much of *Quasi-Objects* ends up being little more than flat-falling justification for whoopie cushion samples, stretched banjos, and chopped-up voice. Still, more than a few tracks — "Cloth Mother/Wire Mother" and "Always Three Words" among them — are both sonically perplexing *and* engaging. — *Sean Cooper*

## Matrix (Jamie Quinn)

*Remixing, Producer / Jungle/Drum'N'Bass, Club/Dance*
Jamie Quinn is the owner of Metro Records and a frequent recording partner of his brother Matt (aka Optical). The duo debuted on the first two Metro releases, Matrix's "Double Vision" and Optical's "Shining," and also worked together on singles for Positiva and Metalheadz. Solo Matrix tracks have appeared on Ruff Element, New Identity, and Prototype as well. Quinn was the natural choice to mix the *Metro Level 01* collection in 1999, and he released an album debut (*Sleepwalk*) the following year. — *John Bush*

**The Message '96 [Single]** / Oct. 14, 1996 / New Identity ◆◆
**Double Vision [Single]** / Sep. 15, 1997 / Metro ◆◆
**Mute 98/Convoy [Single]** / Apr. 6, 1998 / Prototype ◆◆
**Metro Level 01** / Aug. 9, 1999 / Metro ◆◆◆
● **Sleepwalk** / 2000 / Metro ◆◆◆
The sound surely won't surprise fans who know to expect down-and-dirty two-step drum'n'bass from either of the Quinn brothers, but Matrix's debut full-length is a surprisingly tight record, including a raft of great new productions like "Asylum," "Gap the Mind," "Apache," and the down-tempo piece "Angel." — *John Bush*

## Maurizio (Moritz Von Oswald)

*Producer / Minimal Techno, Experimental Dub, Experimental Techno, Electronica, Ambient Techno, Ambient Dub*
Maurizio is the operating name of Moritz Von Oswald, the Berlin-based musician and entrepreneur who owns a half-share in Basic Channel Records and co-produced the label's various releases, a wildly influential series of fuzzy EPs with purposefully low production values recorded under the aliases Cyrus, Quadrant, Phylyps, and Radiance. Von Oswald reserved his solo work for the Basic Channel sub-label M, which issued a half-dozen Maurizio EPs during the mid-'90s. Understandably, the Maurizio sound is quite similar to Basic Channel's, though Von Oswald is often more taken with pounding dub basslines and a somewhat cleaner production style, which gives his EPs a better chance on dancefloors.

Von Oswald was originally a Berlin-area percussionist who worked on LPs by the Associates and Holger Hiller during the late '80s, and also played in one of the last incarnations of Palais Schaumburg. By the end of the decade he'd made the leap from drummer to producer, working with fellow Palais

Schaumburg member Thomas Fehlmann as 3MB, the in-house production team at Berlin's Tresor Records. While involved with Tresor, he recorded with Detroit techno pioneer Juan Atkins and remodeled one of Atkins' Infiniti tracks, "Think Quick," into one of the most sublime techno productions ever released. It was an intriguing Berlin-Detroit collaboration which signalled the continuing close link between the two cities. (In 1995, Von Oswald again worked with Atkins for the debut Model 500 album, *Sonic Sunset*.)

While still working at Tresor in 1993, Von Oswald had formed Basic Channel Records with partner Mark Ernestus. The immediately recognizable BC sound, a ruddy take on Detroit techno with minimal changes and maximum echo-chamber droning capacity, asserted itself with nine vinyl-only EPs during the next few years, recorded as various aliases including Cyrus, Quadrant, Phylyps, and Radiance, though all were presumably Von Oswald and Ernestus. In the meantime, the Maurizio project had begun recording in 1993, with the first release on M Records, the *Ploy* EP. After being remixed by the Orb, it was reissued by the British WAU! Mr. Modo and even appeared on the second *Excursions in Ambience* compilation. M Records next released an EP by Vainqueur, then concentrated on Maurizio yet again with five EPs during the next three years.

Besides M and Basic Channel, Von Oswald had also founded sub-labels Rhythm & Sound, Burial Mix, and Imbalance, though he later turned over management of the latter to Robert Henke (of the duo Monolake). Except for Maurizio's "Ploy," none of the Basic Channel/Maurizio material had appeared on cassette or CD, thanks to the duo's polemical stance about vinyl. Finally in 1995, a Basic Channel sampler was released, though most of the tracks were viciously edited to fit more than three or four tracks onto a seventy-minute CD. Maurizio released a similar compilation by 1997, followed by Basic Channel compatriots Porter Ricks, Vainqueur, and Monolake. —*John Bush*

**Ploy [EP]** / 1992 / M ✦✦✦
Beginning with "Ploy (Strategic Mix)," Maurizio lays down a punishing foundation of straightahead, syncopated rhythm, which is driven primarily by a pounding bass beat and a rattling layer of high-hat percussion. An alien-sounding riff then appears and continues to loop throughout the song. The second track, "Eleye," isn't nearly as harsh or extreme, featuring an ambient buzz lingering in the background and strange wind-like swooping sounds. Underground Resistance highlight the AA-side of the record with their rendition of "Ploy"; lasting for several minutes, the UR version has little in common with the original, but it stands as the stronger version of the two with its slower pace and more relaxed feel. —*Jason Birchmeier*

**Domina [EP]** / 1994 / M ✦✦✦✦
For the third M record, Maurizio again collaborates with another artist to present two quite different versions of one song. Originally penned by Maurizio, "Domina" was also remixed by Detroit artist Carl Craig for this record and stands as one of the best songs ever written by either of these artists. Maurizio's version of "Domina" foreshadows the sound pursued for the remainder of the M series. The deeper, bass-driven rhythms thump along in a seemingly syncopated fashion for the majority of the piece's duration. The beats are of the lowest frequencies and are more felt than heard, needing a subwoofer to reproduce their deep sound. Just as Underground Resistance offered a mellower and more sensual version of Maurizio's original mix on *Ploy*, Carl Craig's version of *Domina* takes away all the pounding extremity of Maurizio's version and replaces it with drifting layers of gentle synthesizer tones and a vocal sample. —*Jason Birchmeier*

**M 4 [EP]** / 1995 / M ✦✦✦✦
Beginning with *M 4*, Maurizio began to release records with similar characteristics, perfecting his signature style in the process. As he had done exceptionally on the previous M record, *Domina*, Maurizio began stripping away many of the more excessive elements of his techno, such as synthesizers and harsh percussion, in favor of a more minimal style. On the two untitled sides of *M 4*, the songs thump along gracefully with deep, dub-style bass beats and little else besides a few simple, little, looped riffs that phase and modulate subtly throughout the song. There are few salient characteristics, such as melodies, breakdowns, or vocals, leaving only a deep, thumping rhythm and some juxtaposing high-pitched sounds sprinkled on top. The repetitive nature also makes the record even more hypnotic by seeming almost monotonous to casual listeners, but it is found to be loaded with small fluctuations upon closer listening. —*Jason Birchmeier*

**M 4.5 [EP]** / 1995 / M ✦✦✦✦
Maurizio's *M 4.5* functions as a continuation of the sounds originally released on the preceding record in the M catalog, *M 4*. *M 4.5* rearranges the deep, bass-driven rhythms and strips away many of the foregrounded riffs, leaving only a simple high-hat percussion rhythm and a muted riff that fades in and out of the song endlessly. There are few changes at all throughout the 12-plus minutes of *M 4.5*; the song sounds almost like a locked groove. The repetitive nature of its endless loops gives *M 4.5* a powerful, hypnotic quality that is capable of either mesmerizing listeners on the dance floor or putting them to sleep. The flip side, less than a minute long, strips away the bass beats, leaving only the phasing, high-pitched sounds. —*Jason Birchmeier*

**M 6 [EP]** / 1996 / M ✦✦✦✦
For *M 6*, Maurizio again returns to the deep, bass-driven style of minimal techno that makes up the later half of the M series. Again, thumping sub-frequency basslines capable of shaking walls pound for the duration of these epic songs, while subtle riffs and sparse high-hat percussion offset the monotone bassline. The riffs on *M 6* still phase and modulate somewhat sporadically, as they have on previous M records. In fact, they sound almost aquatic on *M 6*, giving the two versions of the record a nautical feel. —*Jason Birchmeier*

**M 7 [EP]** / 1997 / M ✦✦
The sounds of *M 7* prove a fitting conclusion to the popular series of records by Maurizio, as each release has become increasingly minimal. On *M 7*, Maurizio takes this application of minimalism about as far as it can possibly go. Every one of the few sounds used for this record sounds muted, faded, and decayed. The bass-driven rhythm of each version thumps hard and deep, but each is also more felt than heard due to the sub-frequency levels. The endlessly looping monotone rhythms are complemented with a juxtaposing high-hat percussive rhythm that taps gently in step with the bassline flowing deeply underneath it. Once again, Maurizio employs a subtle riff that phases and modulates as if it was being transmitted from a distant source; it seems echoed, muted, and weak. As distant and decayed as the sounds are, though, there is a surreal beauty that remains. —*Jason Birchmeier*

● **Maurizio** / Jul. 14, 1997 / Basic Channel ✦✦✦✦
Concentrating on volumes four through seven in the M Records series, *Maurizio* collects edits of seven tracks, adding one original 12" mix and one unreleased mix. Each of the nine tracks layer heavy dub effects and synthwork over mid-tempo house rhythms with plenty of echo and reverb. Besides its necessity for collectors due to the unreleased track, the disc is also the best place to start for those unable or unwilling to use a turntable. Given the fact that the originals are so long and basically unchanging, the edits occasionally work better than the originals, although they aren't the versions that a vinyl-phile like Maurizio necessarily wanted listeners to hear. —*John Bush*

## Mause

f. 1996, Vienna, Austria
*Group / Electronica, Techno*

Gerhard Potuznik and Tex Rabinowitz combine '70s-style vocal techno-pop arrangements with grubby electronica and indie-rock under the name Mause. Reportedly the duo's attempt to fuse an admiration for such far-reaching influences as Depeche Mode, the Melvins, and early-'80s American breakdance music, Mause are almost as bizarre in delivery as in description. Short for "Die Mause" (the mice), Mause formed in Vienna in 1996, and released their first material through Falsch, an Internet-based sublabel of Mego (for whom Potuznik has also recorded under his own name). The group released its proper debut, *Teen Riot Gunther-Strackture*, shortly after. A more than album-length dismantling of stylistic barriers, *Teen Riot* moves at an almost schizophrenic clip through new wave, techno, electro-jazz, trip-hop, indie, and pop, combining the representative features of each into a dense, often comical amalgam. Mego co-released Mause's second album, *Made in Japan*, in 1998 with Morbid Records. The group perform live regularly, and Potuznik and Rabinowitz also record under the name Gerhard Deluxe for the Cheap and Craft labels. —*Sean Cooper*

● **Teen Riot Gunther-Strackture** / 1997 / Morbid ✦✦✦
A quirky, humorous collection of genre abuse combining elements of electro, techno, synth-pop, indie-rock, and other assorted weirdness, Mause's debut LP is an extremely entertaining (if somewhat novel) collection of vaguely experimental electronic pop. Fun but somewhat thin. —*Sean Cooper*

**Made in Japan** / 1998 / Morbid/Mego ✦✦

## Richard Maxfield

**b.** Feb. 27, 1927, Seattle, WA, **d.** 1969
*Composer / Atonal, Electronic*

Groundbreaking electronic composer Richard Maxfield was born in Seattle on February 2, 1927. According to the biographical entry located at /www.virtulink.com/mela/main.htm, as a child he studied piano, and later played clarinet in the Seattle All Youth Orchestra, even writing a symphony while still in high school. After a stint in the Navy, Maxfield spent a year at Stanford University, transferring to the University of California in 1947 to study under composer Roger Sessions. Upon graduating in 1951 he was awarded the Hertz Prize before travelling to Europe and befriending the likes of Pierre Boulez and Karlheinz Stockhausen; during a subsequent trip abroad, he also met Christian Wolff, John Cage, and David Tudor. After spending 1958 in New York studying under Cage at the New School, the following year Maxfield assumed Cage's teaching duties, tapping LaMonte Young as his assistant; instructing his students in the art of creating music from exclusively electronic sources, he is widely believed to be the first true teacher of electronic music in America.

Also in 1959, Maxfield completed his first major electronic piece, "Sine Music (A Swarm of Butterflies Encountered Over the Ocean);" over the next five years, he wrapped up no less than two dozen new works, primarily created via a cut-and-paste method assembled from randomly-chosen pieces of tape containing pre-recorded and manipulated sound sources spliced together with blank passages of assorted duration. Maxfield then continued adding and dropping passages from each piece, often creating what he dubbed inter-masters—i.e., multiple tape reels played simultaneously to generate a new master recording. His home studio arsenal at this time essentially consisted of a pair of tape recorders, several sine-square wave generators, microphones, a homemade mixer and turntable, assorted filters, switches, amplifiers and speakers, and finally a reverberation machine dubbed a "Dynamic Spacexpander." Maxfield was likely the first American to generate electronic music by means of building his own equipment, and may also have been the first outside of European circles to compose pure electronic music removed from the principles of musique concrète.

Maxfield's visibility in the New York art underground was raised considerably by his standing as a member of the Fluxus movement, with performances at various downtown performances spaces, including appearances at the famous loft concert series mounted by LaMonte Young at Yoko Ono's loft during 1960 and 1961. He also tenured as a recording engineer at Westminster Records, and additionally served as Musical Director of the James Waring Dance Company. In 1966 Maxfield left New York for California, teaching at San Francisco State College for two years. There he released his best-known work, a recording titled simply *Electronic Music;* originally issued in 1967 on the Advance label, it featured both tape constructions and ensemble performance pieces, including collaborations with David Tudor and others. In 1968, Maxfield relocated to Los Angeles; tragically, he committed suicide the following year at the age of 42. —*Jason Ankeny*

● Night Music in "New Sounds in Electronic Music" / Odyssey ♦♦♦♦
Exquisite pre-synthesizer electronic music made—like his pieces "Sine Music" (1959) and "Trinity Piece" (1960)—with only the supersonic bias signal of a tape recorder and a supersonic sawtooth waveform from an oscilloscope producing audio range difference tone "ghosts." Identical in feeling to a response to the sound of birds and insects on a summer night in a city park. —*"Blue" Gene Tyranny*

## Derrick May

**b.** Apr. 6, 1963, Detroit, MI
*Producer, DJ / Detroit Techno, Club/Dance, Techno*

Of the Belleville Three, the cadre of early Detroit producers who tested the limits of spirit within electronic dance music and changed the integrity of the form forever, Derrick May's reputation as an originator remained intact despite more than a decade of recording inactivity. While Juan Atkins is rightly looked at as the godfather of techno, with a recording career beginning in the electro scene of the early '80s and encompassing some of the most inspired tracks in the history of dance music, and Kevin Saunderson is the Detroit producer with the biggest mainstream success through his work with vocalist Paris Grey as Inner City, May's position as an auteur eroded slightly during the '90s due to a largely inexplicable lack of activity. As far as influence counts as part of the equation, however, May recorded the techno tracks which top dance producers point to as the most original and influential. The classic Derrick May sound is a clever balance between streamlined percussion-heavy cascades of sound with string samples and a warmth gained from time spent in Chicago, enraptured by the grooves of essential DJs like Ron Hardy and Frankie Knuckles. May's Transmat Records label was the home of his best material, cuts like "Nude Photo," "Strings of Life," "Kaos," and "It Is What It Is," most produced from 1987 to 1989 as Rhythim Is Rhythim. And though his release schedule all but halted during the '90s, he continued DJing around the world and honed Transmat into one of the most respected techno labels in the world.

Derrick May was born in Detroit in 1963, a single child raised largely by his mother. At the age of 13, he began attending school in the suburb of Belleville; there he met Juan Atkins and the two began trading mix-tapes, Atkins providing May's entry into the world of Parliament, Kraftwerk, and Gary Numan. When his mother moved to Chicago, May stayed in Detroit with another friend, Kevin Saunderson, to finish school. By 1981, Atkins had taught May and Saunderson the essence of DJing as well, and the trio formed Deep Space Soundworks, a collective existing to present their favorite music at parties and clubs. May and Atkins also began working with a local DJ named the Electrifyin' Mojo—the man who first introduced Atkins to Kraftwerk and early synth-pop—by creating elaborate megamixes for use on Mojo's radio show.

After high-school graduation May attended university on a football scholarship. He soon tired of the academic life though, and returned to Detroit, where he worked in an arcade. During his frequent trips to Chicago to visit his mother, he had gotten hooked up with Chicago's familial house scene, then in its infancy. May was fascinated by the warmth and community feeling engendered at spots like the Power Plant and the Music Box, where DJs Frankie Knuckles and Ron Hardy used elaborate turntable set-ups and reel-to-reel machines to create mastermixes which re-invoked the spirit of disco even while pushing music forward. May brought Saunderson to the clubs several times as well, and stayed in Chicago for up to a year. When he again returned to Detroit, the need for a club to call his own caused May and the Deep Space family to found the Music Institute. It soon became the hub of Detroit's ever-growing underground musical family, a place where May, Atkins, and Saunderson DJed along with cohorts Eddie "Flashin" Fowlkes and Blake Baxter. The club invigorated a badly fractured sense of community for many residents, and changed the lives of second-wave technocrats like Carl Craig, Stacey Pullen, Kenny Larkin, and Richie Hawtin.

Though May owned a Roland TR-909 synthesizer, he had done little actual recording by the early '80s. When Juan Atkins hit the big time in 1981 with the local success of his group Cybotron, it influenced May to begin recording seriously. He debuted on wax with "Let's Go" (the third release on Atkins' Metroplex Records) and then founded his own Transmat label, a Metroplex subsidiary named after Atkins' track "Night Drive (Time, Space, Transmat)." May introduced Rhythim Is Rhythim, his most important guise, with the Transmat single "Nude Photo." The producer soon followed up with more future classics of the genre: "Freestyle," "Strings of Life," "It Is What It Is," and "Kaos."

Of those first singles, "Strings of Life" hit Britain in an especially big way during the country's 1987-88 house explosion, and May became one of the first American techno artists to tour England. He was also recruited heavily as a remixer, for pop bands—eager to gain credit in clubland—as well as straight dance acts. A series of setbacks around the turn of the decade appeared to sour May's fortunes, though. The fertile British rave scene, which had grown in strength from 1986 to 1990, was overwhelmed by music growing ever more frenetic in order to compete with increasing drug intake. Quite soon, most of the successes in British dance music were native hardcore or rave-pop groups (Altern-8, Sunscreem, Prodigy) while much of clubland forgot its American inspirations in favor of chart-bound novelty tracks.

In 1991, May looked ready to return in a big way; at one point, he considered forming a Kraftwerk-styled techno super-group named Intelex with Atkins and Saunderson. Though negotiations to sign with Trevor Horn's ZTT Records looked promising, the deal eventually fell through, and May later declined several invitations by major labels. In fact, he quit making music for the most part by late 1991 (despite consistent rumors to the contrary), though he did work with ambient pioneer Steve Hillage on tracks for the debut album of Hillage's System 7 project. May continued to DJ around the world, and maintained his standing in the eyes of many top-flight producers. His Transmat label continued to find a home for many of the finest techno singles ever compiled, including tracks by Stacey Pullen's Silent Phase, Juan Atkins' Model 500, Joey Beltram, K-Alexi, Carl Craig's Psyche, and Kenny Larkin's Dark Comedy. Finally, in 1995, Sony Japan compiled his most innovative tracks onto the single-disc retrospective *Innovator,* and May contributed a song to the soundtrack for Sony's video game *Ghost in the Shell.* [See Also: Rhythim Is Rhythim] —*John Bush*

**Mayday Mix** / Jul. 28, 1997 / Open ♦♦♦♦
May's contribution to the *Mix-Up* series (which also included sets by Kevin Saunderson, Jeff Mills, and Ken Ishii) isn't quite as frenetic as Mills' own, but he packs quite a few records into his set and plays around with just about every one, including May regulars like Lil' Louis' "French Kiss," Phuture's "Spank Spank," and "Dance" by Pal Joey. Since May was much more of a DJ than a producer during the '90s, *Mayday Mix* is quite an important document of his intense sessions. —*John Bush*

★ **Innovator** / Oct. 28, 1997 / Transmat ♦♦♦♦♦
This double album compiles the majority of Derrick May's key recordings from the late '80s as Rhythim Is Rhythim. The album's deceptive track listing has a total of 27 tracks on the album, but listeners should keep in mind that 11 of those 27 last less than two minutes; despite this disappointment, though, the many full-length versions still make this collection a necessity. These classic tracks from the early days of Detroit techno retain a rich aura of emotion and mystique rarely found in the often formulaic genre. Produced with synthesizers and primitive drum machines, each of the tracks on *Innovator* consists of the same sounds: looped synthesizer melodies floating in the foreground above a complex array of programmed percussion rhythms. What may surprise techno listeners most, though, is the minimal use of monotonous, hard-hitting bass beats—a tendency found in the majority of techno and house music. May's strength lies in his use of melody and rhythm to complement the spiritual and cosmic motifs surrounding his music without having to rely on mindless 4/4 beats. Included on *Innovator* are two versions of May's best-known techno anthem, "Strings of Life." In addition, some of the stronger tracks previously released on May's Transmat label are here, including "It Is What It Is," "Nude Photo," and "The Beginning." There are also May's collaborations with Carl Craig—"Kao-tic Harmony" and "Drama"—as well as his excellent collaboration with D-Wynn, "R-Theme." Interestingly, the many short interludes hint at many other beautiful tracks waiting to be released. —*Jason Birchmeier*

## MC 900 Ft. Jesus (Mark Griffin)

b. Dallas, TX
*Producer / Industrial Dance, Alternative Dance*
Taking the name MC 900 Ft. Jesus from an Oral Roberts' sermon, the Dallas native, Mark Griffin, began recording in the late '80s. MC 900 Ft. Jesus' first records were bracing fusions of hip-hop, industrial, and spoken word, with hints of jazz. He became a favorite on college radio with his 1990 debut *Hell with the Lid Off* and 1991's *Welcome to My Dream,* yet he never established much more than a cult following. Laying low for a couple years, MC 900 Ft. Jesus returned with his most popular record to date in 1994, *One Step Ahead of the Spider.* Featuring the hit single "If I Only Had a Brain," the record was calmer than his earlier work, incorporating more elements of jazz and funk; it was a hit on both alternative radio and MTV. —*Stephen Thomas Erlewine*

**Hell with the Lid Off** / 1990 / Nettwerk ♦♦♦♦
This is eccentric rap and hip-hop from whiteboy MC 900 Ft Jesus (Mark Griffin) and DJ Zero, a Texan who supplies some fierce cuts on the turntable. One of the few Caucasian rap artists that stays true to the traditions of rap, *Hell with the Lid Off* features "I'm Going Straight to Heaven," "Truth Is out of Style," and "Spaceman." —*John Book*

**Welcome to My Dream** / 1991 / Nettwerk ♦♦♦
Mark Griffin continues his weird ways and records an album that is more personal and political than the debut. Although not credited, DJ Zero is still part of the group. —*John Book*

● **One Step Ahead of the Spider** / Jun. 28, 1994 / American ♦♦♦♦
MC 900 Ft. Jesus reached his artistic maturity with *One Step Ahead of the Spider,* a dense set of jazzy hip-hop highlighted by the single "If I Only Had a Brain." —*Stephen Thomas Erlewine*

## Meat Beat Manifesto

f. 1987, London, England
*Group / Electronica, Ambient Techno, Acid House, Industrial*
Beginning in 1987 as an experimental/industrial duo inspired by the cut-and-paste attitudes of hip-hop and dub, Meat Beat Manifesto increasingly became a vehicle for its frontman Jack Dangers to explore the emerging electronics of techno, trip-hop, and jungle. Though the group was initially pegged as an industrial act (simply appearing on Wax Trax! Records was enough to do the trick), their approach to studio recordings influenced many in the new-electronica community during the '90s, even while Dangers remained a superb producer working in much the same way.

Born John Corrigan in 1967 in Swindon, England, Dangers played with Jonny Stephens in the pop band Perennial Divide in the mid-'80s. The two formed Meat Beat Manifesto in 1987 initially as a side-project, and released the singles "I Got the Fear" and "Strap Down" that year. The dense, danceable material surprised many critics used to the duo's previous work, and the singles received good reviews.

Dangers and Stephens left Perennial Divide by 1988 and recorded an album that same year—using a touring group of up to 13 members for occasional live shows. The tapes were damaged in a fire, so the two recorded *Storm the Studio* a year later. Just as dense and sample-heavy as the first singles, *Storm the Studio* included four songs but added three remixes of each—no need to explain the title—encompassing high-energy dub, hip-hop, and noise-rock. With an American deal through Wax Trax!, Meat Beat Manifesto became known in the US as an industrial band, though Dangers and Stephens felt themselves pigeonholed.

The duo moved to the US soon after, and formed a rough political collective with the members of Consolidated and the Disposable Heroes of Hiphoprisy. (Jack Dangers and Consolidated's Mark Pistel co-produced early Disposable Heroes material.) Meat Beat Manifesto, meanwhile, continued their audio terrorism on *99%,* a 1990 album that added some jazzy rhythms to the collage of noise. That same year, Wax Trax! recycled the remaining tapes from the aborted first album and released them as *Armed Audio Warfare.*

When Dangers and Stephens signed away from Wax Trax! to the major label Elektra in 1992, the duo finally shook the industrial tag that had stuck with them before. Instead, the media christened the follow-up *Satyricon* a techno album, due to both the duo's tour of the US with Orbital and Ultramarine, and the album's groove-heavy update of old synth groups such as Depeche Mode. Dangers' early material began to be name-checked as at least a partial motivation for the drum'n'bass movement—due to the studio mechanics inherent in the music. The 1996 double-album *Subliminal Sandwich* increased Dangers' devotion to the experimental side of electronica. *Actual Sounds and Voices* followed in 1998. —*John Bush*

**Armed Audio Warfare** / Apr. 1989 / Wax Trax! ♦♦♦
This 1989 album, compiled from B-sides and early singles, is dominated by distorted mechanics and feedback. —*John Bush*

**Storm the Studio** / Aug. 1989 / Wax Trax! ♦♦♦
This four-track mini-album contains hip-hop and dub-inflected remixes of three early singles plus the new track "Re-Animator." —*John Bush*

**Satyricon** / 1992 / Elektra ♦♦♦♦
The first outright dance record from Jack Dangers, *Satyricon* forsakes most of the noise for deep hip-hop/techno grooves and a quasi-rap vocal style. —*John Bush*

**Version Galore** / 1995 / Play It Again ♦♦
Uptempo yet chunky dub versions of several singles appear on this 1991 album, including two mixes from Andrew Weatherall (Sabres of Paradise). —*John Bush*

**Subliminal Sandwich** / 1996 / Play It Again Sam ♦♦♦♦
Sounding like virtually none of his contemporaries (except perhaps Future Sound of London), Jack Dangers puts industrial textures to work as a mask for intense vocal samples and breakbeat rhythms plus the occasional organic instrument like guitar and even clarinet. Though *Subliminal Sandwich* sprawls a bit over the course of its two discs (much like FSOL's *Lifeforms*), it only rarely fails to excite. —*John Bush*

● **Actual Sounds and Voices** / Aug. 28, 1998 / Nothing ♦♦♦♦
Coming back strong on their eighth release overall, Meat Beat Manisfesto (led by mastermind Jack Dangers) issued one of their finest albums yet, *Ac-*

tual *Sounds and Voices*. Instead of using samples of already-recorded drum parts like they've done in the past, Dangers pieced together a studio group, which included saxophonist Bennie Maupin and synth programmer Pat Gleeson, both members of Herbie Hancock's '70s band Headhunters. A massive amount of jamming ensued, freeform style. Dangers went back to the tapes afterwards, and picked out his favorite parts, which later turned into the compositions that make up the album. Standouts include "Everything's Under Control," "Oblivion/Humans," and "Acid Again," to name a few. With such popular electronic artists of today constantly using samples of past MBM tracks (including Prodigy, Chemical Brothers, Fat Boy Slim, and others), the band couldn't have picked a better time to re-emerge. —*Greg Prato*

## Meco (Meco Monardo)

b. Nov. 29, 1939, Johnsonburg, PA
*Producer / Disco*

Producer and studio musician Meco marked a confluence of the two dominant pop-culture preoccupations of the late '70s, shooting to fame on the heels of a chart-topping disco rendition of the theme to *Star Wars*. Born Meco Monardo in Johnsonburg, PA, in 1939, he took up the trombone at the age of nine, and later earned a scholarship to the Eastman School of Music in Rochester, NY. There Meco formed a jazz trio with fellow students Chuck Mangione and Ron Carter, later enlisting with the West Point Army Band. From 1965 to 1974, Meco worked as a studio player, and also landed a number of arranging gigs, most notably on Tommy James' "Crystal Blue Persuasion." He additionally arranged and performed the music on a series of television commercials.

Meco's breakthrough arrived in 1974 when he co-produced the Gloria Gaynor smash "Never Can Say Goodbye," followed by the Carol Douglas masterpiece "Doctor's Orders." In 1977, Meco saw the George Lucas film *Star Wars* on the day of its release and quickly became obsessed, seeing the picture numerous times; while admiring producer John Williams' score, he felt the music lacked commercial possibilites, and soon contacted Casablanca Records chief Neil Bogart about the possibility of a disco version. Working with veteran Broadway arranger Harold Wheeler, Meco recorded *Star Wars and Other Galactic Funk*; soon the first single, "Star Wars Theme/Cantina Band," rose to number one. Although he recorded similar music inspired by films including *The Wizard of Oz* and *Close Encounters of the Third Kind*, Meco remained most closely associated with *Star Wars*, even recording a highly successful Christmas album based on the movie; he retired from music in 1985, later working as a commodities broker in Florida. —*Jason Ankeny*

● **The Best of Meco** / Feb. 4, 1997 / Polygram ◆◆◆◆
*The Best of Meco* is an exhaustive and carefully assembled collection of the producer/keyboardist's disco-fied renditions of popular movie themes; opening with his biggest hit, "Star Wars Theme/Cantina Band," the disc also includes singular performances of the "Theme from Close Encounters," "Themes From The Wizard of Oz," and "Love Theme from Superman (Can You Read My Mind?)" plus most of his breakout recording *Star Wars and Other Galactic Funk*. While certainly a one-of-a-kind document of the cultural forces at work during the late '70s, at over 74 minutes in length, it's nevertheless guaranteed to tax the endurance of all but the most devoted fans. —*Jason Ankeny*

## Mekon (John Gosling)

*Producer / Big Beat, Electronica, Trip-Hop, Club/Dance*

John Gosling's work for Wall of Sound Records as Mekon has anticipated a barrage of stylistic changes during the mid-'90s, from trip-hop to big-beat techno and the general influence of American hip-hop in electronic culture. Debuting in 1994 with "Phatty's Lunchbox" (just the second release on Wall of Sound), Gosling pioneered the blueprint for the dance music popularized years later by Prodigy and Chemical Brothers: breakbeat trip-hop invested with a lot of energy and old-school attitude. Future singles blazed new trails as well, through contributions from "Mad" Frankie Fraser (on the gangsta-oriented "Revenge of the Mekon") and Schoolly D (for "Skool's Out"). Gosling released his first Mekon album, *Welcome to Tackletown*, in June 1997 and has remixed Wall of Sound labelmate Agent Provocateur. —*John Bush*

● **Welcome to Tackletown** / Nov. 18, 1996 / Wall of Sound ◆◆◆◆
Providing the darker side to big-beat extravaganzas by the Chemical Brothers and others, *Welcome to Tackletown* looks back to the old school of hip-hop for most of the way, on previous singles like "Phatty's Lunchbox" and "Revenge of the Mekon" plus new tracks like "Skool's Out" and the title cut. —*John Bush*

## Chris Meloche

*Producer / Experimental Techno, Ambient Techno, Electro-Acoustic*

Canadian composer Chris Meloche has been writing music for electro-acoustic and multimedia performance since the early '80s, releasing only a portion of that work on small-run cassettes and, more recently, experimental ambient labels. Although his formal training has been limited, Meloche has pursued independent study of Stockhausen, Reich, Cage, Riley, and Subotnick, as well as Throbbing Gristle, Can, Brian Eno, and Tangerine Dream. His compositions tend toward the more textural, experimental side of ambient electronics, incorporating elements of the lived environment in sprawling compositions often several hours in length. In 1982, Meloche formed M104 with Werner Albert, the pair performing live and composing for silent film accompaniment. More recently, Meloche has focused on his solo work through commissioned works supported by the Canada Council and the Ontario Arts Council, with works for radio performance and broadcast comprising the bulk of his activities. Often exceeding several hours in length, some of those works have begun to appear (albeit in condensed form) on CD, most notably through the Frankfurt-based Fax label (*Recurring Dreams of the Urban Myth* and *Wireless*) and Silent Records (*Distant Rituals*). Meloche is also a founding member of the Canadian Electroacoustic Community and the World Forum for Acoustic Ecology, and hosts the weekly electronic music show *Wired for Sound* from his home in Ontario. —*Sean Cooper*

**Recurring Dreams of the Urban Myth** / 1994 / Fax ◆◆◆
A condensed version of a six-hour composition premeried in Canada in May of 1994, Meloche's debut for the Fax label incorporates elements of city ambiance (buses, crowd noise, radio signals, etc.) and electronic feedback in organic, cyclical arrangments. Somewhat laborious over the course of its 72 minutes (let alone six hours!), *Urban Myth*, much as its source material, works best as aural wallpaper; a suggestive, subconscious soundtrack to other activities. —*Sean Cooper*

● **Wireless** / 1995 / Fax ◆◆◆◆
Like its predecessor in 1994's *Recurring Dreams of the Urban Myth*, *Wireless* draws from the urban environment in assembling dense, disorganized soundscapes of subtle beauty. Unfolding slowly over the course of an hour, *Wireless*, as its name suggests, utilizes radio waves in combination with treated elecronics, with results closer in feel to electro-acoustic experimentalists such as Carl Stone and Morton Subotnick than the warm, often more active ambient the Fax label is known for. —*Sean Cooper*

## Mephisto Odyssey

f. 1993, San Francisco, CA
*Group / Trance, Club/Dance, Techno, House*

The acid-trance project Mephisto Odyssey was formed in late 1993 by Bay Area DJ Mikael Johnston, Barrie Eves, and Orpheos Dejournette. The trio began recording dancefloor favorites such as "Dream of the Black Dahlia," "The Motive," "Get Down," and "Catching the Skinny," and released their debut album (named after their latest single) on the City of Angels label. After being hired to remix Jane's Addiction's "So What!," they were signed to Warner Bros. Records. Josh Camacho, a DJ, then joined the group. An EP, *The Lift*, was released in the spring of 2000, followed in August by Mephisto Odyssey's major-label debut, *The Deep Red Connection*. —*John Bush*

● **The Deep Red Connection** / Aug. 8, 2000 / Warner Brothers ◆◆
Production units like Mephisto Odyssey get a lot of work as remixers but come up against a challenge when they try to make their own records because what they do, constructing interesting rhythm tracks out of drums, percussion, and synthesizer patterns, seems like only part of what it takes to make music. Since they are not much interested in melody, lyrics, and singing, they tend to import those elements. That's the case here, with raps, toasting, and vocals by guest performers added to eight of the 13 tracks. While the guests add variety, providing the excuse, for example, to slow down the pace to a reggae dub style in "Soundman Connection," featuring Mad Lion, for the most part the vocals seem like vestigial elements, especially because Mephisto Odyssey is such an inventive musical collective. The most interesting and compelling tracks are instrumentals like "Sexy Dancer" and the aptly named "Red Drums" that expose the group's ability to assemble inven-

tive rhythm patterns. Unlike many of their peers, they do not feel required to stuff the sound picture, and they are, in fact, at their best when they deconstruct the overall sound into its elements without ever losing the beat. The only vocal track that matches the background is "Wish," featuring Paula Frazer, who adds a wistful touch to Mephisto Odyssey's music. Next time, maybe they should dispense with the guest stars. —*William Ruhlmann*

## Merzbow (Masami Akita)

*Guitar, Effects, Producer / Noise, Dark Ambient, Experimental*

Merzbow is the alias of Masami Akita, one of the world's most prolific practitioners of eardrum-assaulting Japanese noise. Starting in 1981, Merzbow issued literally dozens of releases on a monthly basis; however, his first official US collection, *Venereology*, did not come out until 1994. His second stateside release, the psychedelia-tinged *Pulse Demon*, appeared in 1996; like its predecessor, the record was mastered at abnormally high audio levels to further amplify the extreme nature of Merzbow's work. —*Jason Ankeny*

**America Salutes Merzbow** / Apr. 5, 1996 / Vinyl Communications ♦♦♦

**Age of 369/Chant 2** / May 7, 1996 / Extreme ♦♦♦♦

**Pulse Demon** / May 28, 1996 / Release ♦♦

Merzbow's second American release offers more of the deafening white noise that is his trademark, mastered for maximum loudness. Not for the faint of heart, but ideally suited for the hard of hearing. —*Jason Ankeny*

● **Scumtron: A Tribute to Merzbow** / Jun. 16, 1997 / Mute ♦♦♦♦

Standing next to two deafening Merzbow originals ("Eat Beat Eat 1," "Eat Beat 2"), remixers Autechre, Jim O'Rourke, Panasonic, and Russell Haswell can't help but come off a bit muted. The best contribution is Bernhard Günter's atmospheric mix, which comes off as a photographic negative of the usual Merzbow material. —*John Bush*

**1930** / May 19, 1998 / Tzadik ♦♦♦♦

There's a wider variety of unexpected sounds than those normally heard in a Merzbow listening session in this sonic inundation. Unguessed-at dimensions are accessed through *1930* via sensory overload of oscillations, infinitely layered static, frequencies from pitch to buzz—an explosion could get lost in this, and many do. It is the sounds of tuning in the radio, only to catch the low end frequencies of an earthquake. Music has long explored—and exploited—its ties to emotions; the genre of noise, it seems, has moved on to exploring sound's physical effects. Merzbow, the leader of Japanese noise, has learned how to use sound to operate on your brain; he utilizes indiscernible frequencies to poke pinholes in your eardrums and bleed out your preconceived notions of sound, music, and how they can affect you. This listening experience is not simply a result of sheer volume (Merzbow is generally listened to *very* loudly): even while turned down low, the sounds all combine into an irresistible force that messes with your physical being. It will scramble your brain, until consciousness barely registers anything but sound. [Note: This is, however, a somewhat temporary effect.] —*Joslyn Layne*

## Metamatics

f. 1996, London, England

*Group / Jazz-House, Neo-Electro, Club/Dance, Techno, IDM*

One of the best new artists to come out of the high-profile Clear Records camp, Metamatics was formed by Lee Norris and Dominic Kennedy. Similar to the fragile melodies of µ-Ziq but with an emphasis on spare downtempo breakbeats and crispy percussion, Norris and Kennedy debuted on Clear with four EPs during early 1997. Their debut album *A Metamatics Production* appeared in April of that year. After Kennedy's departure, *Neo Ouija* followed in 1998, on the Japanese P-Vine label. Metamatics resurfaced two years later with *Spook Tinsel Shoal* and *Project Unison* (the latter a collaboration with Clatterbox). —*John Bush*

● **A Metamatics Production** / Apr. 7, 1997 / Clear ♦♦♦♦

Covering the four Metamatics EPs released on Clear during early 1997, *A Metamatics Production* charts the duo's course across abstract drum'n'bass and polar electro soundscapes. Equally comfortable working with breaks as with a four-four beat, Metamatics' sublime Detroit shadings and crisp percussion makes Kirk Degiorgio's As One project its closest precursor. The sublime electro update "Dope for the Robot" is the highlight. —*John Bush*

**Neo Ouija** / 1998 / P-Vine ♦♦♦♦

Another LP of exquisitely produced new-school electro, *Neo Ouija* balances floating synth effects with detailed percussion work on the high end and fluid bass on the low. Though the atmospherics occasionally let the album down, the highlights here—including "Escher Escalator," the title track, and the highly melodic "Vanishing Point"—are stellar examples of the Clear label sound at its peak. [One year after its Japanese release, *Neo Ouija* also appeared on Britain's Hydrogen Dukebox.] —*John Bush*

**Spook Tinsel Shoal** / Jun. 13, 2000 / Hydrogen Dukebox ♦♦♦

## Mice Parade (Adam Pierce)

*Producer / Indie Rock, Post-Rock/Experimental*

The experimental electronica/post-rock of New York's Mice Parade, a.k.a. Adam Pierce, blends live instrumentation, layers of overdubs, and intricate percussion into a distinctive, playful sound. Mice Parade's 1998 debut single *My Funny Friend Scott* introduced Pierce's genre-bending style, which he expanded on with that year's full-length debut *The True Meaning of Boodleybaye*. With 1999's *Ramda*, Pierce upped the ante once more by recording the tracks and mixing the album in one take, lending it an improvised feel. 2000 saw the release of *Collaborations*, which featured contributors like Curtis Harvey, Jim O'Rourke, Doug Scharin, Aki Tsuyoko and Nobukazu Takemura. —*Heather Phares*

● **The True Meaning of Boodleybaye** / Jul. 25, 2000 / Bubble Core ♦♦♦♦

The one-man-band project of Adam Pierce, Mice Parade's *The True Meaning of Boodleybaye* is a winsome piece of jagged D.I.Y. indie pop. Though the heavy drum kit and overall recording approaches the lowest of the lo-fi, Pierce floats a series of precious melodies over the top on tracks like "A Dance by Any Other Name" and "My Workday in May." The impression is oddly similar to what an emo band might sound like if they tried to do their own version of electronica: halfway between Add N to (X) and Sunny Day Real Estate. —*John Bush*

## The Micronauts

f. 1994, Paris, France

*Group / Electronica, Acid Techno, Club/Dance, Techno*

Parisian electro duo the Micronauts teamed Christophe Monier (who previously recorded under his own name as well as the alias Discotique) and Canadian-born George Issakidis, who migrated to France in 1990. The two met while working on the fanzine *Eden*, and in 1995 released the Micronauts 12" "The Jazz"; the record was championed in the press by the Chemical Brothers, and in turn Monier and Issakidis remixed the Chemicals' hit "Block Rockin' Beats." Subsequent Micronauts releases including 1996's "Get Funky Get Down" followed before the duo signed to Astralwerks to make their American debut with 1999's "The Jag" and the following year's *Bleep to Bleep*. —*Jason Ankeny*

**Jag [Single]** / May 25, 1999 / Astralwerks ♦♦♦

After signing to Virgin's Astralwerks/Science electronica division, the Micronauts generated high expectations and substantial hype with their song, "The Jag." As an edited three and a half-minute song, "The Jag (Radio Edit)," functioned as a nice example of the murky area where electronica becomes pop music and vice versa. The song uses some strong vocal hooks—"Ohh, baby, what you done to me/you make me feel so good inside/everything's gonna be/close to you/you make me feel so alive"—some tame electro funk, some disco strings samples, and some samples of women moaning in moments of celebration. In other words, the ingredients are firmly positioned for a wonderful pop song trading guitars and drums for electronica's most proven formal motifs. Of course, three and a half-minutes is a pretty short time for any strong musical ideas to evolve beyond simple presentation. Thankfully, the Micronauts also offer an 11-minute version of the song that takes these same musical ideas and stretches them to the breaking point by adding much more funk and beats without diffusing the song's melodic core centered on the vocal hooks. This full-length version makes one tremendously eager for more. It's no wonder Astralwerks and Science were so adamant about getting this song heard, even if they had to press a CD just to get this song into the hands of the public. This French duo may have gotten initial attention due to the unprecedented success of fellow French artists Daft Punk and Air, but "The Jag" proves that there is substantial evidence for the excitement. —*Jason Birchmeier*

● **Bleep to Bleep** / Mar. 29, 2000 / Science/Virgin ♦♦♦♦

The title of the Micronauts' (mini-)LP debut is just as good as any, considering all but one of the songs feature "bleep" in the title, and there's a four-part series entitled "Baby Wants to Bleep." It's also completely in keeping with the duo's aesthetic, which injects a sense of humor and off-hand charm into the often sterile and increasingly academic field of acid techno. They function as a near-perfect incarnation of classic acid acts like Altern-8 or the KLF, both of whom produced great music but also recognized and exploited, for comic effect, Britain's acid revolution during the early '90s. With all the mayhem and track-to-track flow of the best hip-hop DJs (even though they're performing on 303s and 909s instead of turntables), the Micronauts tear their way through squelchy acid hysteria and continually test the upper limits of the frequency range. Though most of the humor is inherent in the track titles, the music is so kinetic that it's easy to envision Monier and Issakidis smirking behind their boxes even as they were programming the album. Except for the heavily processed freeform-electronics piece ("Bleeper 0+2") that cuts the album in two, *Bleep to Bleep* offers plenty of tweaked acid patterns and quite a few trips through heavy reverb. —*John Bush*

## Microstoria
f. 1994, Düsseldorf, Germany
*Group / Experimental Techno, Electronica, Ambient Techno, Post-Rock/ Experimental, IDM*
Microstoria is a side project of Oval's Markus Popp and Jan St. Werner of Mouse on Mars. Combining Oval's fetish for CD scarification with MoM's odd instrumentation and breezy, subtly inchoate arrangements, the pair's combined efforts come off much as one might expect. The group debuted with a pair of albums on the German Mille Plateaux label falling somewhere between the more engaging techno-exotica of St. Werner's main focus and the sometimes gruelling abstraction of Popp's. Both releases were reissued by Stateside post-rock imprint Thrill Jockey (Tortoise, Rome, Trans Am), which also released the remix effort *Reprovisers* in 1997. —*Sean Cooper*

**Init Ding** / 1995 / Mille Plateaux ✦✦✦
Markus Popp (Oval) and Jan St. Werner (Mouse on Mars) combined as Microstoria in 1995 for an album of left-field electronic experimentation. —*John Bush*

**_snd** / Jun. 3, 1996 / Mille Plateaux ✦✦✦
Less chattery and abstract than previous work, with technique and acoustics given equal play. Popp and St. Werner seem odd bedfellows at first, but the subtle parallels in compositional concern become clearer as the album rolls on. Difficult listening, perhaps, but worth it. —*Sean Cooper*

● **Reprovisers** / Apr. 21, 1997 / Mille Plateaux ✦✦✦✦
Although Microstoria began as something of a low-budget distraction, the Oval/Mouse on Mars side project has steadily become one of the Mille Plateaux label's highest profile groups (thanks also in part to American indie label Thrill Jockey's committed reissue program). *Reprovisers* suggests as much by gathering together an impressive range of remix talent to attack tracks from the group's two LPs. The results are, as expected, fascinating, ranging from the humorous, structured abstractions of Ui and Stereolab to the refractive minimalism of Jim O'Rourke and Mouse on Mars, to the stuttery, disjointed spasms of Christophe Charles. —*Sean Cooper*

## Midfield General (Damian Harris)
*Producer / Big Beat, Funky Breaks, Trip-Hop, Club/Dance*
Not just another big-beat act invading the LP realm a couple of years too late, Midfield General is the recording alias of Skint label-boss Damian Harris. A prime architect of the sound of big beat, Harris grew up listening first to punk, then hip-hop, and finally acid house; after moving to Brighton to study art, he began DJing and promoting clubs around the city. In 1994, his music knowledge landed him a job at Loaded Records, where former Housemartin Norman Cook—a friend of Harris' since his days working at the Rounder store in Brighton—recorded as Pizzaman.

Harris and Cook's mutual vision brought about Cook's first single as Fatboy Slim, "Santa Cruz." After releases by Arthur and Hip Optimist (aka Andy Barlow, later of Lamb), Harris debuted his Midfield General project in 1994 with "Worlds/Bung." Almost overnight, the label became famous around Great Britain as ground zero for the full-on collision between acid-house mayhem, old-school-rap attitude, and hook-heavy sampladelic trip-hop later dubbed big beat—after the Skint club night *Big Beat Boutique*, held at Brighton's Concorde. Releases by Req, Bentley Rhythm Ace, Hardknox, and Lo Fidelity Allstars cemented the catalog, and after Fatboy Slim's second album *You've Come a Long Way Baby* became an international phenomenon, Harris inaugurated a global deal with Sony. Taking most of a year off from the office to concentrate on recording, he finally released his debut album *Generalisation* in 2000. Harris also mixed the third volume in Skint's *On the Floor at the Boutique* series. —*John Bush*

● **Generalisation** / Jul. 10, 2000 / Skint ✦✦✦✦
It's not easy being part of the big-beat elite. By the time 2000 runs around, you're ignored by the electronic aristocracy, shunned like an illegitimate son at a Thanksgiving dinner party, and expected to sound exactly like Fatboy Slim. Yet under his *nom de plume* of Midfield General, Skint label owner and musician Damian Harris takes the "who gives a toss" approach to create a moody, antsy collection of breaks, beats, and a steadfast refusal to die. Luckily, music loves an iconoclast. One of the first warning signs of a quality comeback in the world of big beat was most assuredly Harris' own *On the Floor at the Boutique, Vol. 3* mix album because much like that mix, *Generalisation* retains the unpretentious breakbeats and infectious eclecticism that made big beat such a good idea in the first place. Over here, for example, "General of the Midfield" combines a swishing house beat with pogo-ing bass licks. Or even close by, "Stigs in Love" goes from high keyboard notes and then slowly mutates into a jungle-influenced monster. Both songs certainly show how so much other dance music is tragically conservative. However, not all is as effective. One aspect of the album that one has to quickly become acclimated to is its odd shift of moods. From the fantastic thumps of the old favorite "Devil in Sports Casual" to the cartoonish electro-pulses of "Ricky 39" to the odd fatherly addendum of "Birthday," the album feels uncertain what mood to keep bouncing off of within its own time constraints. As if to prove the point, "Reach Out"—the song a scant three tracks in—is *Generalisation*'s summit. It should remind listeners of the inventive nostalgia of songs like Fatboy Slim's "Praise You" or Groove Armada's "At the River," yet it wisely avoids the former's idiosyncratic nature and the latter's melodrama. Linda Lewis' vocals keep cycling to new heights as Harris keeps the song's expressive musical character building until everything has an emotive sheen. Which all helps make *Generalisation* a follow-up uppercut to Harris' *On the Floor at the Boutique* comeback punch. A dignified (albeit erratic) album that renews big beat's varied personality as well as its emotional potential. —*Dean Carlson*

## Boris Midney
b. Russia
*Engineer, Producer, Arranger / Progressive Trance, Club/Dance, Disco*
Pioneering dance music producer/arranger Boris Midney was among the principal architects of the Eurodisco sound—one of the first to exploit the full potential of 48-track recording, his trademark blend of strings, horn, and percussion created a sound as deep and lush as any heard during the disco era. Born in Russia, Midney was a classically-trained composer who started out writing film scores; turning to disco, however, he discovered his true calling, and working under a number of guises including Caress, Beautiful Bend, the USA/European Connection, Masquerade, Double Discovery, Companion and Festival, he produced an enormously prolific body of work from his New York City studio ERAS. Relatively quiet during the '80s and early '90s, Midney resurfaced in 1999 with the techno-influenced *Trancesetter*. —*Jason Ankeny*

● **Boris Midney Anthology** / Apr. 13, 1999 / OZ ✦✦✦✦

**Trancetter** / Sep. 7, 1999 / Max Music ✦✦✦
A long-time engineer for disco labels including Prelude and T.K., Midney updated his sound considerably for *Trancetter*, a set of progressive trance anthems aligned to superstar DJs like Paul Oakenfold and Sasha. Of course, Midney's wealth of experience in dance music is bound to pay off with a set of dividends much different than any current faves, and *Trancetter* does include some interesting fusions of old-school disco and new-style trance. —*Keith Farley*

## The Mighty Bop (Christophe Le Friant)
*Producer, DJ / Club/Dance, Acid Jazz, Urban*
The man behind such productions as the Mighty Bop (downtempo hip-hop), Bob Sinclar (house), and Réminiscence Quartet (acid jazz), is Chris the French Kiss (aka Christophe Le Friant), a Parisian DJ and head of the crucial French label Yellow Productions as well as a producer. Le Friant began DJing in 1987 while still a teenager, and formed Yellow Productions in 1993 with Alain Ho,

Several of the first releases on Yellow were by Le Friant: the Mighty Bop's "Messe Pour le Temps Present," Réminiscence Quartet's "Roda Mundo," and his first LP, the French hip-hop summit *The Mighty Bop Meet DJ Cam et La Funk Mob*. Alongside releases from a parade of excellent French sources, including DJ companions Dimitri from Paris and Kid Loco, Yellow also hosted two more Mighty Bop LPs during 1996-97, *La Vague Sensorielles* and *Autres Voix, Autres Blues*.

Eager to inject some fun into the burgeoning French house underground, Le Friant borrowed the name Bob Sinclar (from a character in the well-known French film *Le Magnifique*) and in 1997 produced his first Sinclar EP, *A Space Funk Project*. Soon enough, he had an entire Bob Sinclar LP ready to go, and *Paradise* appeared on Yellow just in time for summer 1998. One of the album's tracks, "Gym Tonic," began getting some clubplay in France thanks to its bouncy house vibe and incessant singalong chorus (lifted from a Jane Fonda workout record). A huge anthem during the summer season in Ibiza, "Gym Tonic" looked ready to explode on the charts until Fonda sought legal action for the illegal sample. Perhaps wary of overly burdensome commercial success, the song's coproducer—Daft Punk's Thomas Bangalter, who'd just recorded his own breezy house delight, Stardust's "Music Sounds Better With You"—refused to have even a remixed version released as a single. Nevertheless, assorted bootlegs cropped up and by October a mysterious artist named Spacedust—probably just a major-label-fronted cash-in attempt—hit the top of the charts in Britain with an almost identical remix of the Sinclar-Bangalter original, entitled "Gym and Tonic." (Another crass Spacedust move, covering Bangalter's solo hit with the slimly disguised title "Music Feels Good With You," dropped like a rock.)

With all the offending samples removed, Sinclar's *Paradise* LP was re-released worldwide in 1999. He also worked on remixes, providing tracks by Bangalter himself, Ian Pooley, Second Crusade, and the Yellow project Tom & Joyce with additional production. Le Friant returned to the Mighty Bop alias in 2000 with the retrospective mix collection *Spin My Hits*. [See Also: Bob Sinclar] —*John Bush*

**Meet DJ Cam Et La Funk Mob** / 1995 / Yellow Productions ♦♦♦

• **Spin My Hits** / 2000 / Yellow Productions ♦♦♦♦
Downtempo hip-hop at its most nocturnal and statuesque, Mighty Bop's influences come from a variety of sources. Start with rap's golden age (for the beats), early New York and Chicago house (for the atmospheric synth), and a liberal dose of jazz and R&B (for the instrumentation and overall vibes). The French turntablist covers Bricusse/Newley's "Feeling Good," and even titles one of his tracks "Moody's Mood" (though resemblances to the James Moody standard are slight). Elsewhere, "Freestyle Liguistique" is a solid minor-key hip-hop track with rapping by EJM, and the album hits another downtempo high with "Sea, Sex & Fleurs," a sultry beat piece featuring vocals by Louise Vertigo. Overall, *Spin My Hits* is a delightful mix trip through the Mighty Bop back catalog. —*John Bush*

## Robert Miles (Roberto Concina)
b. Nov. 3, 1969, Switzerland
*Producer, DJ / Progressive House, Trance, Club/Dance, House*
Italian dream-house DJ Robert Miles rose from relative obscurity to score one of the biggest and most unlikely hits of 1996 with his monster single "Children." Born Roberto Concina in 1969 to a military family stationed in Switzerland, he did not return to Italian soil until the age of five, settling in the town of Fagagna. Raised primarily on the classic American soul sound of the '70s, Miles began studying piano as a teen, and at 13 began DJing local house parties. By the late '80s he was regularly spinning hardcore trance sets at Venice area clubs under the name Robert Milani, eventually adopting the name Miles as symbolic of the musical journey awaiting him; in time he assembled a basic studio system comprising a sampler, mixer, keyboard, and 32-track digital board, accepting production work with the Italian label Metromaxx.

"Children" was inspired by a collection of photos taken by Miles' father while stationed in war-torn Yugoslavia; the DJ was equally disturbed by the growing number of deaths plaguing the Italian rave community, and he soon began work on "Children," a simple, piano-driven instrumental anthem produced at a cost of only £150. Originally issued in 1994, the single slowly emerged as an international blockbuster, topping charts in Germany, France, Holland, and Belgium on its way to becoming the biggest European single of 1996; it also fell just shy of reaching the Top 20 on the American pop charts.

After its follow-up, "Fable," Miles issued his debut LP *Dreamland*, with its remix companion *Dreamland II* appearing a short time later. He resurfaced in 1997 with *23 AM*. —*Jason Ankeny*

• **Dreamland** / Jul. 1996 / Arista ♦♦♦♦
Robert Miles' debut album *Dreamland* is a hypnotic tapestry of synthesizers and guitars that encaptures the listener in a mesmerizing web of melodic new age music. Occasionally, his music is so light is disappears into the air, but most of *Dreamland* is magical. —*Sara Sytsma*

**23 AM** / Nov. 24, 1997 / Arista ♦♦♦
Inspired by everything he saw and absorbed on the supporting tour for *Dreamland*, *23 AM* is Robert Miles' atmospheric plea for uniting together saving the earth from the excesses of man. At its core, it's an ambient album, filled with spacy, synthetic textures, repetitive keyboard lines, and sound effects. Miles uses ambient as a foundation, and he often spins off into dance-club tracks where divas (either Kathy Sledge, Nancy Danino, or Barbara Prunas) sing his humanistic lyrics. There are interesting ideas throughout *23 AM*, but they're not always executed well—often, the ambient interludes are meandering and the vocal tracks are colorless—but there are enough interesting moments to make the album of interest to any fan of *Dreamland*. —*Stephen Thomas Erlewine*

## Alton Miller
b. May 18, 1966, Detroit, MI
*Producer, DJ / House*
Of the many figures central to Detroit's thriving electronic dance music scene that began in the mid-'80s and has carried on to the present, some figures such as Alton Miller have played important roles but never managed to attain the mythical status that has been granted to many of the city's more legendary figures. Growing up in the '70s, Miller soaked up the musical environment surrounding him in the Motor City, taking a particular interest in the sounds of Motown, Philadelphia, Parliament-Funkadelic, and Santana. It was during the early '80s once the dance music-crazed Miller become friends with a young Derrick May that he decided to start spinning records, citing Chicago DJs such as Ron Hardy and Frankie Knuckles as prime influences. By the latter part of this same decade, Miller joined forces with George Baker and Chez Damier to start *the Music Institute*, a short-lived but legendary Detroit club that has since become near-mythical, thanks to the pioneering techno efforts of figures such as May. Following the demise of *the Music Institute*, Miller took an interest in Conga drumming in addition to DJing, which led to a period between 1989 and 1991 where he toured world with his music. He then joined forces once again with May, first as an employee of the artist's Transmat record label, then as Aphrodisiac, the title under which he would begin releasing his music. Besides his EP on the Transmat-affiliated label, Fragile, he also released his music on Kevin Saunderson's KMS label and a series of EPs on the Serious Grooves label. By the mid- to late '90s, he increased his presence in the Detroit area through a number of DJ performances and continued to release his music on renowned labels such as Carl Craig's Planet E, Mike Grant's Moods & Grooves, and Distance. —*Jason Birchmeier*

• **Song of the Drum [EP]** / Mar. 1, 1999 / Moods & Grooves ♦♦♦♦
This EP's title is suiting; Alton Miller's percussive work on these three songs truly stands out in the often formulaic realm of house, where a pumping 4/4 808 beat seems the norm. Instead, Miller brings his background as a percussionist to the forefront of these tracks, where the intricate layers of modest percussion and accentuating basslines make these songs wonderful for a dancefloor. Furthermore, he also manages to bring some nice synths into the mix, along with some vocals on the EP's standout track, "Africa '99." Rarely does house sound so organic—the antithesis of the glossy house anthems heard in all the mega-clubs. —*Jason Birchmeier*

## Jeff Mills
b. Jun. 18, 1963, Detroit, MI
*Producer, DJ / Minimal Techno, Detroit Techno, Trance, Club/Dance, Techno*
Jeff Mills, along with Robert Hood, Carl Craig, and Joey Beltram, is one of the biggest American names in techno. Championed for his music's relentless pursuit of hardness and his stripped-down, almost industrial DJ sets, Mills is the latest in a long line of Detroit-bred talent to take on an international reputation. A founding member of noted Motor City institution Underground

Resistance, Mills helped build the artist roster and label ideology (as well as much of its back catalog) with partners "Mad" Mike Banks and Robert "Noise" Hood before moving to New York in 1992 to pursue more vigorously his solo and DJ career (with a resident spot at the legendary Limelight and a recording contract with the noted German label Tresor). (Although rumors of bad blood between the early UR crew have been denied by all involved, Mills' decision to split was apparently total, with Banks all but repudiating his involvement with Mills and Mills distancing himself from the continuing political militancy of Banks and the UR organization.) Mills' UR-related releases (including "The Punisher," and "Seawolf") are stripped-down and erratic, fusing elements of hardcore acid and industrial techno to the sparse Detroit aesthetic. Not surprisingly, his post-UR sound hasn't eased a bit, although UR's penchant for the four-track sound has been replaced by higher quality production.

Prior to his involvement in UR, Mills was a DJ at Detroit public radio station WDET (he was also studying architecture at the time), spinning everything from Meat Beat Manifesto and Nine Inch Nails to Chicago house and underground Detroit techno. He began producing in the mid-'80s, working with Tony Srock on the project the Final Cut. Mills met Banks through a local garage group Members of the House, who Banks was working with in the late '80s. Mills remixed a track on a Members 12", and his and Banks' shared love for Chicago soul and the harder edge of Detroit techno blossomed into Underground Resistance as a combined business and creative enterprise. The pair, along with Robert Hood, recorded several EPs and singles together, including tracks such as "Waveform," and "Sonic," before Mills defected to New York in 1992 to pursue a residency at the Limelight club and a solo career recording for Tresor and his own label, Axis. Mills' discography includes two full-length volumes of *Waveform Transmissions* for Tresor, a live album and rarities collection for the British label React, and the first album in a new contract with Sony Japan, as well as a handful of 12" EPs on Axis and several collaborations with Robert Hood on his M-Plant label. In 2000 Mills took more memorable action by scoring a new soundtrack for Fritz Lang's 1926 masterpiece *Metropolis*. —*Sean Cooper*

**Waveform Transmission, Vol. 1** / 1992 / Tresor ◆◆◆
Jeff Mills' earliest solo work is captured here on *Waveform Transmission, Vol. 1*, an album that redefined notions of the adjectives "hard" and "banging" within the techno community circa 1993. Upon an initial listen, one may be instantly overwhelmed by the intensity of Mills' barrage of pounding 909 kick drums and other sub-frequency rhythms, along with the breakneck pace at which he loops these rhythms. To top off the dense sub-rhythms and the nauseating intensity of these songs, he also adds some screeching hi-frequency riffs for an additional element of sonic assault. The album's highlight comes on "Changes of Life," the one song to stray from the fairly generic template that Mills had created for himself on this particular release. This cut may instantly sound like a reinterpretation of Derrick May's "Strings of Life" with its use of traditional piano sounds. Rather than use the piano as a tool for generating melody as May had done on his legendary track, however, Mills uses it as a tool for generating rhythm. The piano notes bang just as hard as his punishing 909 kick drums, thereby using a traditionally harmonious instrument for ferocity. Though the songs on *Waveform Transmission, Vol. 1* advance his ideas about techno to harsher and more complicated areas of construction, relative to his later work on Axis, they also sometimes use brutality as a substitute for quality. He doesn't get any harder than he does on this album, but even though his later work finds the fine balance between harsh industrial pounding and surreal tonal quality, one can't help but see how influential this particular album at its introduction was to the entire school of producers interested in the harsher extremes of the techno spectrum. —*Jason Birchmeier*

**Atlantis** / 1993 / Pow Wow ◆◆
Never short on ideas, Jeff Mills conceptualized a full-length techno album investigating the myth of Atlantis as a follow-up to his preceding concept album, *X-102 Explores the Rings of Saturn*. The 16 song titles on *Atlantis* are the only linguistic devices used by Mills—with the exception of two enclosed maps of the mythical city in the CD jacket—to tell his tale, forcing the listener to connect short titles such as "The Gardens" and "Eruption" with the abstract sounds of his techno. Relative to any other non-lyrical forms of music, Mills actually succeeds in his aim to inject a sense of color and story into his music by incorporating a diverse palette of alien sounds and varying moods. The songs on *Atlantis* aren't intended to function as dance music but rather as individual pieces of an engaging whole like chapters in a novel. Unfortunately, though Mills succeeds to a certain extent with his intentions of instilling a sense of story into his music, the music itself isn't that engaging. The strange, alien sounds he uses to characterize the underlying percussive foundation of his songs can't be described as beautiful or melodic, and the songs themselves aren't repetitious enough to function as groove-orientated dance music. So while Mills' ambition and imagination are unparalleled within the world of electronic music and deserve ample recognition, *Atlantis* never reaches its full potential, sounding far too purposefully abstract and a bit too contrived for casual listening; one can appreciate Mills' grand intentions for the record, but it just doesn't compare to his later output on Axis. —*Jason Birchmeier*

**Mecca [EP]** / 1993 / Axis ◆◆◆◆
For the fourth release on his Axis label, Jeff Mills flavored his then-unique style of techno a bit with ideology. Etched into the inner groove of *Mecca*'s A-side is the statement "Balance is the essential component," and a yin-yang symbol is etched into the B-side. Mills carries this rather simple ideology into his music, crafting a light and surreal A-side—featuring "Inner-self" and "Yantra"—with little to no pounding or banging basslines. Then on the B-side, he lays down three tracks of rather hard-hitting aggressive techno with plenty of banging and pounding. "Step to Enchantment (Stringent)" especially stands as one of Mills' most DJ-friendly compositions, with its inescapable 909 drum kicks, rustling high-hat percussion, and the simple yet so catchy riff that has become a trademark similar to "The Bells." In terms of Mills' early Axis records, there are few that compare to *Mecca* in terms of both quality and utility; it has both atmospheric compositions and pumping dancefloor tracks, making it a useful record for any techno DJ creative enough to manipulate the juxtaposition. —*Jason Birchmeier*

**Growth [EP]** / 1994 / Axis ◆◆◆
Moving further away from the banging percussive techno mayhem of his *Waveform Transmission* albums on Tresor, *Growth* finds Jeff Mills producing a less dance-friendly style of techno that's more focused on exploring surreal melodies than laying down the usual dose of syncopated rhythms. These untitled compositions fluctuate between moments of collective serenity characterized by soft synth tones before often getting interrupted by alien melodies and the occasional series of percussive beats—a near perfect balance between the many oft-polarized aspects of techno. Furthermore, Mills accentuates this difficult brand of techno with the underlying ideology of "growth" and a well-constructed locked groove in the middle of side B that creates it's own endless track, characterized by a laser sound firing once every rotation. —*Jason Birchmeier*

**Waveform Transmission, Vol. 3** / 1994 / Tresor ◆◆
A collection of Jeff Mills' mid-'90s minimal techno, more oriented towards DJs and dancefloors than home listening pleasure, this album features some excellent tracks that share similar formal tendencies. The somewhat apparent template practiced by Mills on this album makes it difficult to differentiate between the individual tracks since they all hit hard, move fast, and feel scrambled. They each lumber along with so much eardrum-shattering power that it seems as if the music extends its strength outwards from the speakers in a malicious attempt to overload the senses of the listener. It's almost impossible to avoid the symmetrically positioned, numbing 909 bass beats as they push the strange, alien melodies of songs such as "DNA" far into the background. These characteristically idiosyncratic tracks bear the stamp of Mills' trademark style, which would soon evolve to more poetic extremes on his own Axis and Purpose Maker labels. Placed within the context of a DJ's eclectic set, these repetitious tracks sound amazing, but aren't quite as effective as individual songs since they tend to get a bit monotonous. He had discovered a formula for an aggressive, minimal style of techno that would soon be emulated by legions of Northern European techno producers. —*Jason Birchmeier*

**Humana [EP]** / 1995 / Axis ◆◆◆◆
The four tracks on *Humana* have little in common with the heavily rhythmic style of inescapable tribal techno so often associated with Jeff Mills. Here, Mills decreases the intensity of his techno by first cutting out any pounding or banging percussion, using heavily diluted bass beats in their place. Next, the pace of the tracks is considerably decreased, giving them a sedate feel. Finally, Mills incorporates a broad palette of hi-frequency sounds similar to those used on *Growth*. Here though, the sounds are much more pleasing to

the ear, and they're arranged with more variety and less looped cycles. *Humana* doesn't have any song titles nor any melodic hooks that will stick with the listener after the record stops spinning. In lieu of these, he focuses on tone and motif through use of the album's soft, tranquil sound palette and its allusions towards the innate beauty of humanity. —*Jason Birchmeier*

**The Dancer [EP]** / 1996 / Purpose Maker ♦♦♦
The four songs on this first release in the Purpose Maker series share similar qualities, characterized most notably by repetitive grooves that loop for long periods of time. The "locked" sound of these sounds—909 bass kicks, high-hat percussion rhythms, some odd yet subtle samples—aid the DJ's ability to mix records at a quick rate and also make it easy for people to feel the rhythm, resulting in dancing. This first release contains four equally stunning songs that execute this simple formula for great dancefloor techno with genius accuracy and functions also as an omen for the other amazing Purpose Maker records to come. —*Jason Birchmeier*

★ **Live at the Liquid Room, Tokyo** / May 20, 1996 / React ♦♦♦♦♦
For years this legendary mix CD remained the primary illustration of how Jeff Mills almost single-handedly redefined the art of techno DJing. A former hip-hop DJ in Detroit, Mills' DJing technique focuses heavily on crosscutting, backspins, sudden stops, and a constant focus on continually mixing in sounds from a new record, all at a breakneck pace liable to induce a heart attack. The constantly forward-moving continuity of Mills' September 28, 1995, three-hour performance at the Liquid Room in Tokyo never gets boring or even reaches a lull. Even if a given listener dislikes a particular record that Mills happens to spin, it only takes anywhere from 30 seconds to two minutes for him to mix in a new track. While Mills' technical skills are worthy of recognition, the primary reason this album has attained such high stature arises from the countless hard techno classics littered throughout this 67-minute album. He drops 17 of his own tracks, including masterpieces such as "Casa," "The Bells," and "Step to Enchantment" while also including tracks by Richie Hawtin, Joey Beltram, Surgeon, and Advent; he even devotes over three minutes to Rhythim Is Rhythim's late-'80s Detroit techno anthem "Strings of Life." Though most DJs modestly avoid populating their sets with their own tracks, Mills' releases are of such high quality that this attribute ends up being a strength; this all-around excellent album establishes a benchmark for all techno DJs. —*Jason Birchmeier*

**The Other Day [EP]** / Aug. 12, 1996 / Axis ♦♦
Here Mills presents some different styles in the short context of this 12" record: two upbeat tracks with a cheery vibe, two contemplative small chunks of bleak ambience, and a final pumping track that assaults the listener with a barrage of high-frequency sounds and occasional spurts of showering white noise. The up-tempo songs will appeal to the DJ-types looking for some energetic techno to rock with, while the two short ambient tracks should appeal to about anyone with their stark darkness, which will work wonders as a quick lull in a DJ's set or as music to zone out to. The eclectic nature of the record doesn't allow for a greater overall motif, as found in *Humana*, but the diverse range of music does make it an engaging record well worth investigating for anyone who appreciates Mills' knack for prolific creativity. —*Jason Birchmeier*

**Kat Moda [EP]** / Nov. 18, 1996 / Purpose Maker ♦♦♦♦
If one Jeff Mills record more than any other became a staple of mid- to late-'90s techno, it would probably have to be *Kat Moda*. It became almost a given that any techno DJ owned at least one copy of this record, primarily for "The Bells." This song has everything a DJ can want in a quality techno record for the dancefloor: a catchy piano melody perfect for humming or whistling to, a quick and slamming bass kick compressed beyond belief, some showering high-hats, a suspense generating synth riff, and a refreshing sense of minimalism. The other three tracks on this record remain consistent to "The Bells," with "Kat Race" doing little but replacing the piano melody with a subtler riff. The key to these songs is the locked-in-place percussive loops that Mills lays down as the foundation for his tracks; seldom does the rhythm alter itself, never changing tempo and rarely changing its composition. —*Jason Birchmeier*

**Very [EP]** / Nov. 18, 1996 / Axis ♦♦
On his *Very* EP, Jeff Mills presents four untitled songs with different tempos but similar auras. Two of the songs ride pounding basslines and bring in a few high-frequency riffs to further the rhythm. Mills also makes sure to keep tweaking these two pumping tracks, fading out the bassline for lulling moments and also bringing the riffs in and out of the mix. The two other songs on this record feature pounding basslines for their foundation and rather rich oceans of eerie, echoed synth. Each of these two songs also makes excellent use of high-hat percussion to bring a sense of rhythm to the tracks and add some subtle melodies for a sense of beauty. The perfect balance between energy and ambience on *Very* works well, while similar dark, echoed sounds and the occasional appearance of females speaking in a foreign tongue establish the consistent motif that shadows over the entire record. —*Jason Birchmeier*

**The Other Day** / May 19, 1997 / React ♦♦♦
A rarities compilation of Jeff Mills' work for his own Axis Records, *The Other Day* isn't the best place to begin if you're interested in Mills' brand of hardcore Detroit techno. In fact, much of the material here isn't at all hardcore; instead, Mills concentrates on half-thought ideas and tracks without much percussion at all. It's an interesting look at the process of composition, but isn't really intended for newfound fans. —*John Bush*

**Steampit [EP]** / Nov. 24, 1997 / Purpose Maker ♦♦♦
Like a massive stampede of rabid horses storming through a gigantic echoing cavern, the four galloping tracks on the *Steampit* EP reinforce the popularly held notion that Jeff Mills' Purpose Maker records evoke a certain animalistic aura. Each of the four tracks has its personal nuances that color the song and give it character, but an emphasis on a pumping-fist-in-the-air style of pounding rhythm densely constructed out of many different percussive sounds remains constant to all four. One may get caught in these hypnotizing rhythms and may miss the intricate changes in the songs, where one rhythmic loop slowly eclipses another in these compressed arrangements. Yet for as fascinating as it is to listen as Mills stitches together one stomping rhythm on top of another, losing oneself in the mesmerizing whole tends to be the most rewarding approach to these songs. —*Jason Birchmeier*

**Purpose Maker Compilation** / Jun. 1998 / Purpose Maker/Watts ♦♦♦
The 14 tracks on this compilation come from Mills' various Purpose Maker EPs, which tend to feature his more dance floor-oriented style of hard-hitting, rhythmic techno, flavored with a hint of tribal motifs. Nowhere near as formulaic and predictable as his mediocre *Waveform Transmission, Vol. 3* nor as wildly unpredictable and diverse as his *The Other Day* album, the tracks comprising *Purpose Maker Compilation* fit a certain template, but incorporate enough different sounds and arrangements to make each track freshly unique. Tracks such as "Reverting" and "Fly Guy" feature strange rolling basslines capable of infiltrating one's nervous system, while others such as "Paradise" and "The Bells" inject a mood of ecstatic dance floor mayhem into the more serious tone of the album. On this album, Mills finds the perfect combination of creativity and utility that is as brilliant as it is danceable, without ever getting boring or monotonous. However, these pieces could use a bit more variety in terms of tempo, sound, or structure. —*Jason Birchmeier*

**From the 21st** / Jan. 30, 1999 / Sony Japan ♦♦♦
*From the 21st* finds Jeff Mills focusing on an experimental style oriented towards listening rather than DJing or dancing. Many of Mills' albums from the '90s, such as *Purpose Maker Compilation* and *Live at the Liquid Room*, found the ever-inventive artist focusing on aggressive, high-energy, uptempo techno primarily characterized by pounding percussion. On this album, though, he heads more in the direction of the material found on *The Other Day*, the diverse collection selectively picked from his Axis record label. There are a few tracks, such as "B2F-7" and "31J56-4," that feature underlying bass beats conducive to dancing, but, overall, listeners won't find much rhythm on this album. For the most part he abandons the punishing low-frequency percussion of his previous albums for a more contemplative style that appeals to the cognitive processes of listening rather than affective responses. This album furthers many of the more experimental ideas originally proposed on his mid-'90s Axis EPs. On one hand, none of these tracks follow any familiar template or use familiar sounds like the acid lines of the Roland 303, instead sounding alien and original. Yet from the opposing perspective, the tracks can get dull unless one is in the mood for an adventure into Mills' theories about the farthest limits of what music could possibly evolve into, foreshadowing the style he would eventually feature on his Tomorrow label. —*Jason Birchmeier*

**Preview [EP]** / Sep. 6, 1999 / Axis ♦
*Preview* marks the first release from Jeff Mills' third record label, Tomorrow, which functions as a outpost for the sounds of the future, similar to how his

Axis label showcases experimentation and Purpose Maker showcases DJ tracks. Upon first listen, *Preview* sounds fascinating. The music side includes three short pieces of calm techno that place their focus more on texture and mood than rhythm or energy. The flip side of the record includes a long spoken word piece titled "Glen21" that features a conversation about the future, where an interviewer asks daring questions about how time will change the world and what the music of the future will sound like. Overall, *Preview* will definitely intrigue the listener on the first two or three listens, but once the surprises wear off and once the ideas get old this is a record that will start to collect some dust. —*Jason Birchmeier*

## Russell Mills
*Producer / Ambient Techno*

Multi-media artist Russell Mills first earned notice in music circles for his cover designs for acts including Brian Eno, David Sylvian, Harold Budd, Nusrat Fateh Ali Khan, Robert Fripp, and Nine Inch Nails; in between exhibiting his paintings, assemblages, and collages throughout the globe, he also collaborated with Eno on the book *More Dark than Shark* and with Sylvian on the audio/video installation *Ember Glance: The Permanence of Memory*. Mills' first foray into music came in 1982, when he worked with ex-Wire members Bruce Gilbert and Graham Lewis (then recording as Dome) on the ambient album *Mzui/Waterloo Gallery*. In 1996, Mills issued his debut ambient recording *Strange Familiar*, which featured the infinite guitar of co-writer Michael Brook; the all-star *Pearl & Umbra* followed in early 2000, with Mills having adopted Undark as the name of his shifting backing group. —*Jason Ankeny*

• **Strange Familiar** / 1996 / Em:t ♦♦♦♦
In 1996, art-design maestro Russell Mills assembled the tremendously impressive Undark collective—both Brian and Roger Eno, David Sylvian, Bill Laswell, the Edge, Kevin Shields, Robin Guthrie, Hywel Davies, etc.—for an LP of guitar-damaged beatscapes and textured invisible-soundtracks. *Strange Familiar* is an astonishing work, ebbing and flowing better than any other album in recent memory. Mills and his crew don't always wait for the next track marker to introduce a new theme, resulting in a work that pays huge dividends over the course of a full listen. (For example, Michael Brook's infinite guitar ceases long before the end of his showcase track "Stone's Egg," leaving Mills more than ten minutes to deconstruct a groove that begins with a cavernous bassline and warped percussion but ends up with little more than a few solitary bells.) This fusion of electronic and organic, future and past, begs for a new term to describe it; perhaps the time has come for the next step on from Hassell/Eno's *Fourth World* of the '80s, a Fifth World of ethno-electronic sound. This is definitely an album of such excellence to be able to trumpet a new revolution in sound. —*John Bush*

**Pearl & Umbra** / Jan. 1, 2000 / Instinct ♦♦♦♦
Russell Mills' *Pearl & Umbra* fuses world music, electronic, and rock influences into intense, predominantly instrumental songs like the droning, percussive "Swallow Crystals," the tribal, passionate "Canyon: Split Asunder," and the jazzy, brass-driven "All Wise Fly (Pneuma)." The album also features contributions from like-minded musicians such as Bill Laswell, Harold Budd, Roger Eno, Paul Schutze, Robin Guthrie, and Brian Eno. David Sylvian's world-weary vocals add to the delicate unease of "Rooms of Sixteen Shimmers," while Susan Deyhim's warm, passionate vocals add another layer of mystery to "Heaven Dips," and Clodagh Simond's brogue adds a Celtic tinge to the cover of Syd Barrett's "Golden Hair." "Causes, Causes, Causes" and "Cage of Air" pit winding, wailing guitars against pummeling polyrhythms and pulsing basslines. Every bit as intricate and engaging as *Undark*, *Pearl & Umbra* adds warmth and resonance to Mills' musical chiaroscuro. —*Heather Phares*

## Takako Minekawa
*Vocals, Producer / Shibuya-Kei, Alternative Pop/Rock*

Singer/songwriter Takako Minekawa stands apart from many of the other female recording artists from Japan. Instead of creating faceless, saccharine pop, Minekawa crafts her unique brand of pop from her personal obsessions—cats, keyboards, French pop—and her sweet, girlish voice.

A child movie and TV star in Japan, Minekawa was always interested in music and formed her first group *Lolita* with some college friends. This morphed into *Fancy Face Groovy Name* in 1990, which also included Kahimi Karie. After playing in a number of groups, Minekawa was ready to strike out on her own. She released her solo debut *Chat Chat* in 1994, which she followed up with 1995's *A LittleTouch of Baroque In Winter* and 1996's *Roomic Cube* (released the following year in the US).

With each album, Minekawa's writing and arrangements showed a more refined mix of innocence and complexity. However, her ideas were still fresh and playful, as the 1998 remix EP *Recubed*—which featured *Roomic Cube* songs remixed by friends like Sukia, the Pulsars, and Buffalo Daughter—showed. *Cloudy Cloud Calculator*, Minekawa's most independent statement yet, was released at the end of 1998; it was followed by 1999's *Fun 9* and 2000's *Maxion EP*. —*Heather Phares*

**Chat Chat** / 1995 / Polystar ♦♦♦
With her little-girl voice, a penchant for toy instruments, and a list of credits that thanks Raggedy Ann alongside Black Sabbath, Takako Minekawa shows all signs of a terminal case of the cutes on her debut recording, *Chat Chat*. That's not to say that cute can't be fun. Minekawa's cover versions—including Eddie Cochran's "Summertime Blues," the Beatles' "Drive My Car," and songs by Victoria Williams and country crooner Tom T. Hall—are always interesting. Meanwhile, her original compositions lean toward the wistful. While the arrangements here are decidedly more conventional (and guitar-oriented) than the albums that follow, 1995's *Chat Chat* provides the first encounter with a distinctive pop voice. —*Michael Jourdan*

• **Roomic Cube** / Feb. 18, 1997 / What Are Records? ♦♦♦♦
Based on the concept of a "room" being Takako Minekawa's favorite place for creating music, *Roomic Cube* finds a place for everything. Co-written and produced with her friends in Buffalo Daughter, the album stretches her sound: while her more usual style of minimal, poignant songwriting shows up on tracks like "Sleep Song" and "Never/More," the tracks Buffalo Daughter collaborated on reflect the group's affection for busy arrangements and sound effects. This gives *Roomic Cube* a somewhat schizophrenic feel, but appealingly so. "Klaxon!," "Wooooog!," and "1.666666" in particular hint at Buffalo Daughter's penchant for noisy funk and rock. "T.T.T. (Turntable Tennis)" is a happy medium of the artists' styles, featuring hints of guitars, witty samples, and sound effects on top of a ping-pong table rhythm. Though the album tends to run hot and cold, it ends up being the right sonic temperature. —*Heather Phares*

**Recubed [EP]** / Aug. 21, 1998 / Emperor Norton ♦♦
1998's *Recubed* EP features six songs from Takako Minekawa's *Roomic Cube* album, remixed by friends like Land of the Loops, the Pulsars, Trans Am, and Buffalo Daughter. Each track on the EP reflects elements of both Minekawa and the remixing artist, and they're all a pretty good fit. Trans Am's remix of "T.T.T. (Turntable Tennis)" adds a computery menace to the track, while the Pulsars' take on "Fantastic Cat" enhances the song's innate new-wave sheen. Since Buffalo Daughter collaborated with Minekawa on most of *Roomic Cube's* songs, their remix of "Klaxon!" sounds only a little different than the original, but DJ Me/DJ You of Sukia brings that group's trademark collage style to "1.666666," cutting and pasting at will. An interesting collaboration of like-minded musicians and friends. —*Heather Phares*

**Cloudy Cloud Calculator** / Oct. 13, 1998 / Emperor Norton ♦♦♦♦
Takako Minekawa's fourth album, *Cloudy Cloud Calculator*, is one of her finest and most unique moments. Where Buffalo Daughter's collaboration on Minekawa's previous album, *Roomic Cube*, sometimes overshadowed her basically minimalist style, *Cloudy Cloud Calculator* gives Minekawa's songs room to breathe. "Milk Rock" makes the most out of a vibe bassline, breakbeats and her breathy vocals, and "Phonobaloon Song"'s deceptively simple vocals and keyboard arrangement covers a spectrum of emotions. Minekawa's sense of humor makes its presence felt on most of the songs, especially "Cat House," which features sampled kitties meowing to a bouncy synth beat. "Black Forest" and "International Velvet" create a lush, filmic mood, while "Cloud Chips," "Kraftpark," and "Kangaroo Pocket Calculator" suggest a slightly playful, somewhat ominous futuristic world. Minekawa saves one of the best tracks for last, a remake of Joe Meek and the Tornadoes classic "Telstar," redone with a Martin Denny-like arrangement and exotica beat. *Cloudy Cloud Calculator*'s highly inventive, restrained pop shows that Minekawa has hit her stride as a songwriter and arranger. —*Heather Phares*

**Ximer [EP]** / Jun. 22, 1999 / Emperor Norton ♦♦♦
*Ximer* is an eight-song EP featuring remixes and alternate takes of songs

from Takako Minekawa's album *Cloudy Cloud Calculator*. Guest remixers like Cornelius, Kid Loco, and Oval take on "Milk Rock," "Black Forest," and "International Velvet," respectively. An acoustic version of "Cloud Cuckoo Land" rounds out the collection. —*Heather Phares*

**Fun 9** / Jul. 6, 1999 / Emperor Norton ♦♦♦♦

Takako Minekawa's third full-length US release *Fun 9* delivers more of her inventive electronic pop, and includes collaborations with co-producers Cornelius and DJ Me/DJ You, the side-project of Sukia's Craig Borrell and Ross Harris. Not surprisingly, this means that while *Fun 9* retains Minekawa's playful musical vision—evident in songs like "Shh Song," "Spin Spider Spin," and "Fancy Work Funk"—it also presents her ideas in a more eclectic and polished style. From the breathy, overlapping vocals and synth blips of the album opener "Gently Waves," to "Tiger"'s bouncy, lunar funk and "Plash"'s breakbeat bossa nova, Minekawa fashions a wide array of lush, lighthearted songs into an album that is as self-assured as it is fun. —*Heather Phares*

## Attilio Mineo

b. Aug. 28, 1918, Brooklyn, NY
*Producer / Exotica, Electronic*

Space-age pop composer and arranger Attilio Mineo was born in Brooklyn, NY, on August 28, 1918; after graduating high school he played piano in a series of big bands, subsequently leading his own orchestra on and off for close to three decades. Regularly writing songs with wife Toni, Mineo often accepted commissioned projects to fund his more personal work, and in 1962 he agreed to record musical accompaniment for a Seattle World's Fair attraction dubbed the Bubbelator, a transparent and spherical elevator housing up to 150 passengers. Sold alongside the Bubbelator, Mineo's resulting LP, *Man in Space with Sounds*, combined electronic melodies, alien sound effects and spoken-word introductions, quickly selling out its limited pressing and becoming a sought-after collectors item among exotica aficionados prior to its 1998 reissue on Subliminal Sounds. —*Jason Ankeny*

● **Man in Space with Sounds** / 1962 / Subliminal Sounds ♦♦♦

## Ming + FS

f. 1996, Brooklyn, NY
*Group / Illbient*

New York City drum'n'bass duo Ming + FS pioneered their own self-described "junkyard" sound, deftly mixing-and-matching elements of old-skool hip-hop, jungle, electro, turntablism, and live instrumentation. Ming + FS met in 1996 while the former was spinning trip-hop sides at a house party, and after teaming weeks later to collaborate on a series of breakbeat tracks, they signed to the Brooklyn Music Limited under the name Leadfoot. In 1997, the duo also opened their own recording studio, Madhattan, as well as a label of the same name; remixing material for everyone from DJ Spooky to the Notorious B.I.G., Ming + FS also earned notoriety for a series of EPs including *NY's Lucky Charm* and *Junkyard Drum'n'Bass I*. Their entry to the *This Is Jungle Sky* mix series preceded the 1999 release of their full-fledged debut LP *Hell's Kitchen*. —*Jason Ankeny*

● **Hell's Kitchen** / Aug. 24, 1999 / OM ♦♦♦♦

Though listeners might guess (correctly) that Ming + FS belong to New York's illbient scene from the cover and album title, the production duo come off in a similar manner to Japanese producers like Fantastic Plastic Machine and Pizzicato Five. While FS takes on the turntables for most tracks (in addition to occasional keyboards), Ming plays guitar and Moog. The pair's productions are tight, very tied to breakbeat jungle but with plenty of old-school hip-hop flavor. Ming + FS scatter guest rappers throughout the album with care, using BLESTeNATION for the jump-up jungle of "Unison" and an appropriately darkside dub slant to the streets-is-watching track "CLS" featuring Mack & Youngblood. Ming + FS have dozens of good ideas on *Hell's Kitchen*, and they never repeat themselves on this excellent debut. —*John Bush*

## Ministry

f. 1981, Chicago, IL
*Group / Industrial Dance, Industrial Metal, Heavy Metal, Alternative Pop/Rock, Industrial*

Until Nine Inch Nails crossed over to the mainstream, Ministry did more than any other band to popularize industrial dance music, injecting large doses of punky, over-the-top aggression and roaring heavy metal guitar riffs that helped their music find favor with metal and alternative audiences outside of industrial's cult fan base. That's not to say Ministry had a commercial or generally accessible sound: they were unremittingly intense, abrasive, pounding, and repetitive, and not always guitar-oriented (samples, synthesizers, and tape effects were a primary focus just as often as guitars and distorted vocals). However, both live and in the studio, they achieved a huge, crushing sound that put most of their contemporaries in aggressive musical genres to shame; plus, founder and frontman Al Jourgensen gave the group a greater aura of style and theater than other industrial bands, who seemed rather faceless when compared with Jourgensen's leather-clad cowboy/biker look and the edgy shock tactics of such videos as "N.W.O." and "Just One Fix." After 1992's *Psalm 69*, which represented the peak of their popularity, Ministry's recorded output dwindled, partially because of myriad side projects and partially due to heroin abuse within the band, but continued to resurface through the rest of the decade.

Ministry was formed in 1981 by Alain Jourgensen (b. Oct. 8, 1958, Havana, Cuba); he had moved to the US with his mother while very young and lived in a succession of cities, eventually working as a radio DJ and joining a new wave band called Special Affect (fronted by future My Life With the Thrill Kill Kult leader Frankie Nardiello, aka Groovie Mann). Featuring drummer Stephen George, Ministry debuted with the Wax Trax! single "Cold Life," which—typical of their early output—was more in the synth-pop/dance style of new wavers like the Human League or Thompson Twins. The album *With Sympathy* appeared on the major label Arista in 1983 and followed a similar musical direction, one that Jourgensen was dissatisfied with; he returned to Wax Trax! and recorded several singles while rethinking the band's style and forming his notorious side project the Revolting Cocks.

In 1985, with Jourgensen the only official member of Ministry, the Adrian Sherwood-produced *Twitch* was released by Sire Records; while not as aggressive as the group's later, more popular material, it found Jourgensen taking definite steps in that direction. Following a 1987 single with Skinny Puppy's Kevin Ogilvie (aka Nivek Ogre) as PTP, Jourgensen once again revamped Ministry, with former Blackouts bassist Paul Barker officially joining the lineup to complement Jourgensen's rediscovery of the guitar; fellow ex-Blackouts William Rieflin (drums) and Mike Scaccia (guitar), as well as vocalist Chris Connelly, were heavily showcased as collaborators for the first of several times on 1988's *The Land of Rape and Honey*. With Jourgensen and Barker credited as Hypo Luxa and Hermes Pan, respectively, this album proved to be Ministry's stylistic breakthrough, a taut, explosive fusion of heavy metal, industrial dance beats and samples, and punk aggression. 1989's *The Mind Is a Terrible Thing to Taste* built on its predecessor's artistic success, and *In Case You Didn't Feel Like Showing Up (Live)* was recorded on its supporting tour, introducing other frequent Ministry contributors like drummer Martin Atkins (later of Pigface) and guitarist William Tucker (as well as featuring a guest shot from Jello Biafra). Jourgensen next embarked on a flurry of side projects, including the aforementioned Revolting Cocks (with Barker, Barker's brother Roland, Front 242 members Luc Van Acker and Richard 23, and many more), 1000 Homo DJs (with Biafra, Rieflin, and Trent Reznor), Acid Horse, Pailhead (with Ian MacKaye), and Lard (again with Biafra, Paul Barker, Rieflin, and drummer Jeff Ward).

In late 1991, Ministry issued the single "Jesus Built My Hotrod," a driving rocker featuring manic nonsense vocals by co-writer Gibby Haynes of the Butthole Surfers; its exposure on MTV helped build anticipation for the following year's full-length *Psalm 69* (subtitled *The Way to Succeed and the Way to Suck Eggs*, although the only title that appears on the album consists of a few Greek letters and symbols). The record reached the Top 30 and went platinum, producing two further MTV hits with "N.W.O." and "Just One Fix," and Ministry consolidated its following with a spot on the inaugural Lollapalooza tour that summer (joined by new guitarist Louis Svitek). However, drug and legal problems sidelined the band in the wake of its newfound popularity, resulting in the clouded *Filth Pig* being released in 1995, too late to capitalize on their prior success. More problems with drugs and arrests followed, and Jourgensen returned to some of his side projects, recording a new album with Lard, among others. In 1999, the new single "Bad Blood" was featured prominently in the sci-fi special-effects blockbuster film *The Matrix*, setting the stage for the release of *Dark Side of the Spoon* (the title a reference to the band's heroin problems) later that summer. Guitarist William Tucker committed suicide in May 1999. —*Steve Huey*

**With Sympathy** / 1983 / Arista ♦♦

**Everyday Is Halloween** / 1984 / Wax Trax! ♦♦
More technical music and industrial metal from Ministry, they were still considered a bit danceable then. The album has influenced many industrial bands of today. —*John Book*

**Twelve Inch Singles (1981-1984)** / 1985 / Wax Trax! ♦♦♦
Included are all of their best-known hits and great songs before they got signed by a major label (Sire). Early techno-industrial music from the early '80s. —*John Book*

**Twitch** / 1986 / Sire ♦♦♦
The name Ministry brings to mind images of big dumb guitars and arena rock sensibility. But before they created their influential third album *The Land of Rape and Honey*, there was *Twitch*. And this album probably owes more to Front 242 than anything. The only thing remotely resembling their later music is the use of psychotic sampling that Al Jourgensen and Paul Barker will always be known for. A good example being "Like You" the first track on album. Other differences include Patty Jourgensen singing on the song "The Angel" and Al Jourgensen actually trying to sound unaggravated at times. It's interesting though repetitive at times ("Crash and Burn"), and if you care to listen to Mr. Jourgensen's rants, he really does have something to say. "Isle of Man" tells the story of the arrival of Columbus and how the persecution of the Indians will be revisited on the offenders in time. Make no mistake: this sounds nothing like any of Ministry's other albums, listeners may hear how they became what they did. —*Alan Esher*

● **The Land of Rape and Honey** / 1988 / Sire ♦♦♦♦
*The Land of Rape and Honey* represented Ministry's stylistic breakthrough, combining assaultive percussion, samples, synths, and (sometimes) crunching guitars with distorted, barking vocals. For all the emphasis on the group's metal/industrial fusion, it's really only the first three (and best) tracks on *Rape and Honey*—"Stigmata," "The Missing," and "Deity"—that employ guitars extensively. The remainder of the album merely suggests heavy metal aggression through its electronic and sampled elements; it is far more industrial in feel, even though it's just as dark. Ministry was the industrial band that, more than any other, appealed to metal fans, and it was *The Land of Rape and Honey* that began to lay claim to that status. —*Steve Huey*

**Mind Is a Terrible Thing to Taste** / Nov. 1989 / Sire ♦♦♦♦
In what many consider to be Ministry's peak, the band creates another wonderful album to follow *The Land of Rape and Honey*. Fusing thrash guitars with excellent synth and percussion work, Ministry lay the foundation for even more followers of the band's music. But what makes the album even more commendable is the unique flair and the avoidance of cliché elements that have brought down the guitar-heavy industrial-rock genre. Purists might argue that Ministry has given up these roots; but it's plain to see that the roots remain, and are only revamped by the necessary progression of a band that has been around for so many years. The sound is Ministry's, most definitely. —*Marc van der Pol*

**Psalm 69: The Way to Succeed & The Way to Suck Eggs** / Jul. 14, 1992 / Sire ♦♦♦♦
Although this is Ministry's most accessible album, it is not a sellout. Al Jourgensen and company never let the intensity up, with the machine-like grind of the rhythm section constantly driving the same sixteenth-note rhythms again and again. "Just One Fix" is the best track on a remarkable, intense album, which also includes the single "Jesus Built My Hotrod." —*Stephen Thomas Erlewine*

**Filth Pig** / 1995 / Sire ♦♦
Distracted by drugs, arrests, and replacing nearly the entire lineup of Ministry, Al Jourgenson took nearly four years to complete *Filth Pig*. Instead of being a carefully constructed masterpiece, the record is a monotonous attack of relentless guitar noise. And although Jourgenson does keep his promise of reducing the number of samplers and synthesizers used on the album, the new approach sounds like a retreat into heavy metal, not a brave step forward. Slowing the songs down slightly and turning up the guitars results in a muddled quagmire. Without the blitzkrieg barrage of samples and clean metallic attack, Ministry sounds strangely castrated, and it doesn't help that Jourgenson's songs are neither catchy nor powerful. *Psalm 69* may have been too concise for longtime Ministry fans, but at least it packed a punch. On the surface, *Filth Pig* is noisier, but it has no power. —*Stephen Thomas Erlewine*

**Dark Side of the Spoon** / Jun. 8, 1999 / Warner Brothers ♦♦
Having struggled back to their feet after another round of arrests and drug problems (not to mention the suicide of guitarist William Tucker), Ministry ambitiously attempts to broaden their signature sound with *Dark Side of the Spoon*. While it is a better record than the monotonous din that was *Filth Pig*, that's largely because of a few strong moments propping up a number of surprisingly bland attempts at aggression. Tunefulness was never Ministry's strong point, and several songs are built on rudimentary vocal melodies rather than jackhammer riffs and samples (although "Whip and Chain" isn't bad). While it's admirable that the group is trying new things this far into its career, it never settles on a definite approach, thus sounding a little directionless. Besides, not everything they're trying is new; a few parts are reminiscent of the more synth-oriented days prior to *The Land of Rape and Honey*, while some of the dark humor that used to fill Revolting Cocks albums pops up here and there ("Nursing Home," for example). The problem with the latter is that in the past, when Ministry displayed a sense of humor, it was performed as though they might snap at any second; here, it sounds a little dopey—not that that's necessarily bad, it just seems ineffectual next to, say, the gonzo gibberish of "Jesus Built My Hotrod." It would be a mistake to say that the album is a complete failure; "Supermanic Soul" and "Bad Blood" integrate some of the noisiness of *Filth Pig* with sound effects and classic Ministry riffs, while the otherwise dull "Eureka Pile" successfully works in some Eastern-tinged female vocals. But it does become apparent—especially over the second half of the album—that the band simply doesn't sound as fearsome as they once did, and so, overall, *Dark Side of the Spoon* can't be considered the successful expansion of their sound that would bode well for the future. —*Steve Huey*

## Mirwais (Mirwais Ahmadzai)

b. 1961, Switzerland
*Producer / Trip-Hop, Club/Dance, House*
Though he is known as one of the leading lights in France's dance music scene, producer/composer/multi-instrumentalist Mirwais Ahmadzai was born in Switzerland to Italian and Afghani parents. After moving to Paris at age six, he immersed himself in music, learning the guitar before he hit his teens. A few years later, he started the electronic/punk/disco hybrid Taxi Girl, who released the 1981 album *Seppuku*. The group disbanded after eight years of playing together; Mirwais then formed the folk-pop outfit Juliette et les Independants with his girlfriend. A decade later, he returned to electronic music after hearing drum'n'bass for the first time. His single "Disco Science" became a hit on the French club circuit and attracted Madonna's attention; she was so impressed with it that she invited Mirwais to produce the bulk of her 2000 album *Music*. His own solo debut album *Production*, which took the stripped-down, playful electro sound of fellow Frenchmen Daft Punk to a poppier level, arrived in the US shortly before *Music* was released. —*Heather Phares*

● **Production** / Aug. 8, 2000 / Sony International ♦♦♦♦
On his aptly named debut album *Production*, hot French producer Mirwais marries the stylish playfulness of contemporaries like Air and Daft Punk with an even more direct pop sensibility. Not only does this explain why he was the ideal choice to produce the bulk of Madonna's *Music*—in fact, that album's best track, the brittle ballad "Paradise (Not for Me)," is included here—but it also results in a collection of songs that are as clever and intelligently crafted as they are danceable. Though most of Mirwais' stylistic touches (stark, sculpted electro beats, running basslines, and vocoders galore) aren't really new, the freshness and innocence he brings to them are—this is a man who named his label Naive, after all. *Production*'s electro-pop works equally well taken as a whole or song by song: from the slinky-yet-funny album opener "Disco Science," which appropriates the irresistibly catchy foghorn vocals from the Breeders' "Cannonball" and puts them in an entirely different context, to the dreamy, brooding house of "Never Young Again," Mirwais invigorates these vintage elements with the energy of someone hearing and playing them for the first time. Despite its name, *Production* has much more than pristine sonics in its favor. —*Heather Phares*

## Mr. C (Richard West)

b. Jan. 2, 1964, London, England
*Producer, DJ / Tech-House, Club/Dance, Techno, Nu Breaks*
His rapping for the Shamen made him one of the most ubiquitous MCs in Britain during the early '90s, but by the end of the decade Mr. C became one

of the most respected DJs around the world. Born Richard West in London, he emerged as a leading DJ and label head (of Plink Plonk) by the late-'80s house explosion in Britain. Introduced to the Shamen's Colin Angus at one of the seminal *Spiral Tribe* events of the era, Mr. C was invited to join the group after the death of bandmember Will Sin in 1990.

One year later, his deft Cockney rap, added to a remix of 1989's "Move Any Mountain," helped the single storm the Top Five in England. During 1992, the Shamen returned to the Top Five four times, led by Mr. C on the number one lads-on-E anthem "Ebeneezer Goode" as well as "LSI" and "Boss Drum." As the Shamen slipped from the charts during the mid-'90s, Mr. C returned to the dance underground and his first love, DJing. His first mix albums, 1996 volumes in the *X-Mix* and *Mixmag Live!* series, made clear his focus on American techno from Detroit to New York. By 1997, his Sub-terrain residency at the club he co-owns, *The End*, made it one of the hottest spots in England, with a hard but danceable tech-house fusion. Mr. C also inaugurated a new label, End Recordings, and produced three singles during 1998-99. In 2000, the tech-house mix set *Subterrain 100% Unreleased* appeared on Engine. —*John Bush*

X-Mix, Vol. 6: The Electronic Storm / Apr. 22, 1996 / Studio !K7 ♦♦♦

• Mr. C Presents Subterrain 100% Unreleased / Jun. 20, 2000 / Engine ♦♦♦♦

One of the most under-rated DJs in Britain, Mr. C changed the rules for your average mix album circa 2000 with *Subterrain 100% Unreleased*. Based on the award-winning club night he hosts at The End in London, the disc is based (as the title attests) on tracks recorded especially for the album. Thanks to the dozens of exciting DJ/producers that have appeared at the club, Mr. C was able to recruit a stellar list of producers, including Stacey Pullen, Derrick Carter, Dave Angel, Layo & Bushwacka, Gene Farris, Charles Webster, Terry Francis, and Cari Lekebusch. Punters searching for a bucketful of trance anthems or radio hits will undoubtedly be disappointed, though listeners who look a bit deeper will find 16 tracks of deep, soulful techno, mixed intelligently and with care by one of the music's best DJs. Two of the highlights come from the man himself, "Electroniche" and a remix of Mr. James Barth's "For the Lords." *Subterrain 100% Unreleased* definitely isn't the album for listeners who like their anthems huge and their breakdowns unmissable, but it is one of the best techno compilations of the year. —*John Bush*

## Mr. Fingers (Larry Heard)

*Producer / Club/Dance, Acid House, House*

While Larry Heard produced dozens of classic Chicago vocal tracks with the trio Fingers Inc., he reserved Mr. Fingers as a pseudonym for his solo career. During the mid-to-late-'80s, Heard alternated Mr. Fingers EPs—over-stocked with classics like "Mystery of Love," "Can You Feel It?," and "Washing Machine"—with the more commercially substantial recordings of Fingers Inc. By 1988 however, the group had split; after working on production with Kym Mazelle, Lil Louis, and Ricky Dillard among others, Heard signed to MCA and debuted with 1991's *Introduction*. He returned in 1994 with *Back to Love*, then appeared to retire Mr. Fingers in favor of recordings simply as Larry Heard. [See Also: Larry Heard, Fingers Inc.] —*John Bush*

Amnesia / 1989 / Jack Trax ♦♦♦♦

The first Mr. Fingers LP out of the gates, though of dubious origins, is a classic compilation of the earliest, and most inspired, recordings by Larry Heard. Liberally sprinkled with seminal tracks like "Can You Feel It?," "Washing Machine," "Slam Dance," and "Bye Bye," *Amnesia* became virtually impossible to find several years after its release and remains one of the most sought-after documents of Chicago house. Though perhaps not worth the high price from collectors, it remains a brilliant Larry Heard collection. —*John Bush*

• Introduction / 1992 / MCA ♦♦♦♦

Heard's solo debut (of a sort) blends essential club tracks like "Closer," "On My Way," and "What About This Love" with material more in keeping with his producer mentality and rock background. Selections like "On a Corner Called Jazz," "Waves Against the Shore," and "We Can Work It Out" provide Heard with a chance to stretch out into intriguing jazzy house. The differences between individual tracks are somewhat slight, and most of the album clocks in at an easy-going mid-tempo gait. While it's a bit over-polished, and there are a few too many vocal tracks (delivered in essentially the same style), *Introduction* is a fine album. —*John Bush*

Back to Love / Aug. 1994 / Black Market International ♦♦♦

The belated follow-up, originally scheduled for release on MCA, continues Heard's fascination with a blend of jazz-house fusions and tracks closer to the classic Chicago house that was then almost a decade old. —*John Bush*

## Mr. Oizo (Quentin Dupieux)

*Producer / Club/Dance, Techno*

Though it's a sure bet he'll linger in the minds of most only for his omnipresent Levi's advert and 1999 European chart-topper "Flat Beat," music-video director Quentin Dupieux turned in some excellent electronic productions as Mr. Oizo. Far from the madding crowds of ad-oriented hipster trance or jungle, "Flat Beat" was a mid-tempo techno production with heavily distorted effects and a playful nature that fit perfectly with the visual focus, a sock puppet. While still a teenager, Dupieux began directing short films for French television, and turned in no less than eight works between 1994 and 1998. His associations with the music world began in 1997, when leading French dance citizen Laurent Garnier serendipitously bought a car from Dupieux's father. Dupieux directed the video for Garnier's "Flashback" single, as well as the long-form video *Nightmare Sandwiches* starring and featuring music by Garnier. That year, he also moved into music production, with his debut single *"1"* appearing on Garnier's F Communications label. After the video he (naturally) directed for second single "M-Seq" landed on an adagency desk, he was tapped to direct the commercial that launched Levi's vaunted non-denim line of trousers. The eccentric advert—featuring a puppet named Flat Eric maniacally bobbing his head to the music in the passenger seat of a Chevelle while a nonplussed human driver concentrated on the road—soon became famous across Europe, and the single (also on F Communications) hit number one all across the continent. (It eventually sold over two million copies.) The obligatory full-length *Analog Worms Attack* followed in October, and earned American distribution early the following year. Dupieux also directed the video for "Party People" by Alex Gopher. —*John Bush*

• Analog Worms Attack / Feb. 22, 2000 / Mute ♦♦♦♦

The album debut for Quentin Dupieux may not have received worldwide distribution had it not been for its most publicized track, the notorious Levi's advert and crossover hit named "Flat Beat." But it's doubtful Dupieux will turn into a one-hit wonder—and if he does, there's always his directing career—since *Analog Worms Attack* is an inventive album that somehow marries the experimental side of techno (Cristian Vogel, Laurent Garnier) with the outrageous flair of novelty tracks usually seen on, well, television commercials. Even including "Flat Beat" (which was wisely added only as a bonus track), the highlights are "Monophonic Shit" and "No Day Massacre," two tracks that blend surprisingly deep grooves and oddball effects. It's not so much a sense of humor that Dupieux displays here; it's closer to the playful side of quasi-pop electronica fashioned by Mouse on Mars and Like a Tim. Fans of the trademarked "Flat Beat" sound will find much to love as well ("Smoking Tape" and "Flat 55" are most similar to the hit), making *Analog Worms Attack* a left-field treat for both pop-culture seekers and genuine music fans. —*John Bush*

## Mr. Scruff (Andrew Carthy)

b. Feb. 10, 1972, Macclesfield, Cheshire, England
*Producer, DJ / Electronica, Ambient Techno, Trip-Hop*

Mr. Scruff's breakbeat noodlings have been some of the more playful and summery of the British trip-hop lot, with ultra-clean production and an economic approach to sampling distinguishing his music from spliff-tokers and bombasts alike. The authorial nickname of Manchester native Andy Carthy (his neatly trimmed beard being the source), Mr. Scruff attracted the buzz of DJs and critics alike with the 1995 Rob's Records release, "Sea Mammal" (a semi-veiled tribute to Boogie Down Productions' seminal "My Philosophy"), which combined the dime-store aesthetic of a Luke Vibert or Howie B. with more tempered, straightahead rhythms and subtle funk, soul, and electro references. The appearance soon after of the *Frolic EP* on Rob's subsidiary Pleasure—which took the breezier, tea-room quotidian feel of his debut a few Sunday afternoon steps further—turned buzz to blare for Carthy, with remix offers from the likes of DJ Food and Lamb flowing in. 1997 brought an EP ("Large Pies") for noted Bristol label Cup of Tea, as well as Scruff's eponymous debut full-length. *Keep It Unreal*, his debut for Ninja Tune, followed in

1999. A rabid record collector, Scruff's frequent DJ sets include everything from '60s and '70s soul-jazz and funk, scratchy old reggae and dub 45s, classic hip-hop, schmaltzy vocal pop, and new-school electronica. —*Sean Cooper*

**Frolic EP (Part 2) [EP]** / 1995 / Pleasure ♦♦♦
A solid remix EP featuring tracks from Scruff's first two EPs taken 'round the back for a good seeing-to by the little-known Programmers Revenge (on the stunning jeep-rocker "Chicken in a Box") and Votel ("Sea Mammal"). Styles range from the dancefloor-ready to headphone-bound production subtleties, each track revealing its own charms. —*Sean Cooper*

**Mr. Scruff** / May 12, 1997 / Pleasure ♦♦♦
Mr. Scruff's debut album has many of the same problems of those in the abstract trip-hop camp (too abstract, not enough energy), but the sheer range of Scruff's sample-spotting and genre obliteration overwhelms any boredom inherent in his style of straightahead trip-hop. —*John Bush*

• **Keep It Unreal** / Jun. 1, 1999 / Ninja Tune ♦♦♦♦
Thanks to imaginative programming on tracks like the single "Honeydew," *Keep It Unreal* is yet another accomplished work by breakbeat maestro Mr. Scruff. The vibes definitely triumph over any progression on these tracks, but the album's diverse moods and tempos work magic. The galloping gait and what sounds like a Louis Jordan sample power "Get a Move On" while the next track "Midnight Feast" has the late-night feel of a Portishead single. The single "Honeydew" has a rich, soulful vocal that lifts the song into Soul II Soul territory while the cagey, metallic drum programs sound straight off a driving new wave single. "Cheeky" is a deep-groove house number with bright piano lines and an echoed diva vocal. Several tracks are reminiscent of Amon Tobin's swing-era plunderphonics, but most everything here is original, well-done, and prime Mr. Scruff. —*John Bush*

## Mix Master Mike (Michael Schwartz)

b. 1970
*DJ / Turntablism, Underground Rap, Hip-Hop*
Mix Master Mike (b. Michael Schwartz in 1970) first attracted attention as a member of the Invisibl Skratch Piklz, one of the most acclaimed DJ collectives of their era—three-time winners of the annual world scratching competition, they were eventually barred from entering as a result of a lack of any solid competition. Debuting in 1996 with *Michristmasterpiece Muziks Worst Nightmare*, Mike's skills eventually brought him to the attention of the Beastie Boys, who recruited him to serve as the DJ on their 1998 LP *Hello Nasty* and on tour; his second solo record, *Anti-Theft Device*, appeared that same summer. —*Jason Anhony*

• **Anti-Theft Device** / Jul. 21, 1998 / Asphodel ♦♦♦♦
Mix Master Mike's prowess on the turntables is breathtaking—he scratches with uncanny skill, his abilities equal parts scientific precision and reckless innovation. *Anti-Theft Device* is even stronger than his debut *Michristmasterpiece Muziks Worst Nightmare*; his sampling sources are more clever and more obscure, all seamlessly integrated into a crazed tapestry of beats and sounds. —*Jason Ankeny*

## MK (Marc Kinchen)

*Producer / Garage, Club/Dance, House, Dance-Pop*
Marc Kinchen is one of the most idiosyncratic house producers of the '90s, tempering his feel for soulful New York-styled garage with the energy of hard techno, learned from time spent working in Detroit at Kevin Saunderson's KMS Studios. And though he's one of the few top-flight producers that doesn't work as a DJ, Kinchen's productions rarely reveal that lack of experience. His debut recording, First Bass' "Separate Minds," was released on the KMS compilation *Techno 1*. Kinchen also recorded several singles as MK before he moved to Brooklyn in 1991, formed his own Area 10 Records and released the single "Burning."

It became a moderate club hit, and led to remixing for the Shamen, Tom Tom Club, the B-52's, Bobby Brown, and D-Influence. Soon, Kinchen was one of the hottest producers in mainstream house, and in late 1992 he signed to Charisma for an album deal. Kinchen's full-length debut was 1993's *Surrender*, credited to MK Featuring Alana (aka Alana Simon) and featuring the singles "Always" and "Love Changes," which became deep house club hits worldwide. Kinchen continued to remix (for Pet Shop Boys and Opus III, among others) and recorded both as himself and 4th Measure Men. —*John Bush*

• **Surrender** / Sep. 21, 1993 / Virgin America ♦♦♦
*Surrender* is a solid production house album, with Marc Kinchen at the helm for irresistible tracks like "Always" and "Love Changes," plus vocalist Alana doing her best Donna Summer impersonation. Kinchen's production expertise saves many of the album tracks from being the mere throwaways that clutter most mainstream house albums, but *Surrender* is still an album most notable for its singles. —*John Bush*

## MLO

f. 1995, London, England
*Group / Electronica, Ambient Techno, Trance, Club/Dance*
Englishman Jonathon Tye and Australian Peter Smith met in London, where they formed the ambient techno outfit MLO in the mid-'90s. After recording two EPs during 1996 (*Two Voyages* and *Garden*), the duo released their debut full-length *Plastic Apple* later that year. After its release, the group appeared to stall as Tye spent much time working with his solo project Twisted Science and on the roster for his Lo Recordings imprint. —*John Bush*

• **Plastic Apple** / Oct. 7, 1996 / SU ♦♦♦♦
One of the overly neglected but generally solid full-lengths from the ambient house generation, *Plastic Apple* reveals influences from a range of sources. From the hip-hop lilt of the opener "DJ Food's Sonic Soup" to the tongue-in-cheek naturalism of the closer "Birds 'N' Flutes 'N' Shit," Tye and Smith reveal their sense of humor over a set of slightly chilled, completely inventive electronics. —*Keith Farley*

## Moby (Richard Melville Hall)

b. Sep. 11, 1965, Darien, CT
*Vocals, Mixing, Producer, DJ / Electronica, Ambient Techno, Trance, Club/Dance, Techno, Pop/Rock, Alternative Pop/Rock, House*
Moby was one of the most controversial figures in techno music, alternately praised for bringing a face to the notoriously anonymous electronic genre, as well as being scorned by hordes of techno artists and fans for diluting and trivializing the form. In either case, Moby was one of the most important dance music figures of the early '90s, helping bring the music to a mainstream audience both in England and in America. Moby fused rapid disco beats with heavy distorted guitars, punk rhythms, and detailed productions that drew equally from pop, dance, and movie soundtracks. Not only did his music differ from both the cool surface textures of ambient music and the hedonistic world of house music, but so did his lifestyle—Moby was infamous for his devout, radical Christian beliefs, as well as his environmental and vegan activism. "Go" became a British Top Ten hit in 1991, establishing him as one of the premier techno producers. By the time he came to the attention of American record critics with 1995's *Everything Is Wrong*, his following from the early '90s had begun to erode, particularly in Britain. Nevertheless, he remained one of the most recognizable figures within techno, even after he abandoned the music for guitar-rock with 1996's *Animal Rights*.

Born Richard Melville Hall, Moby received his nickname as a child; it derives from the fact that Herman Melville, the author of *Moby Dick*, is his great-great granduncle. Moby was born and raised in Darien, Connecticut, where he played in a hardcore punk band called the Vatican Commandos as a teenager. Later, he briefly sang with Flipper, while their singer was serving time in jail. He briefly attended college, before he moved to New York City, where he began DJing in dance clubs. During the late '80s and 1990, he released a number of singles and EPs for the independent label Instinct. In 1991, he set the theme from David Lynch's television series *Twin Peaks* to an insistent, house-derived rhythm and titled the result "Go." The single became a surprise British hit single, climbing into the Top Ten. Following its success, Moby was invited to remix a number of mainstream and underground acts, including Michael Jackson, Pet Shop Boys, Brian Eno, Depeche Mode, Erasure, the B-52's, and Orbital.

Moby continued performing at dances and raves throughout 1991 and 1992, culminating in a set at 1992's *Mixmag* awards where he broke his keyboards at the end of his concert. *Moby*, his first full-length album, appeared in 1992. In 1993, he released the double A-side single "I Feel It" / "Thousand," which became a moderate UK hit. According to the *Guinness Book of Records*, "Thousand" is the fastest single ever, appropriately clocking in at 1000 beats a minutes. That same year, Moby signed a record contract with Mute and his first release was *Ambient*, which compiled unissued material recorded between 1988 and 1991. Later that year, *The Story So Far*, a collection of singles released on Instinct, appeared. In 1994, the single "Hymn"—one of the first fusions of gospel, techno and ambient music—was released.

In 1994, Moby signed a major-label contract with Elektra Records in the US. *Everything Is Wrong*, his first album released under the deal, appeared in the spring of 1995 to uniformly excellent reviews, especially in the American press, who had previously ignored him. Despite the promotional push behind the album and his popular sets at the 1995 Lollapalooza, the album wasn't a commercial success. The following year, Moby suddenly abandoned techno to record heavy guitar rock for *Animal Rights*, which received mixed reviews. A partial return to electronica, 1997's *I Like to Score*, was followed by 1999's *Play*. Surpassing everyone's expectations, the album became a platinum hit and reached number one in the UK, while *Play*'s tracks were licensed by dozens of advertisers and compilers. —*Stephen Thomas Erlewine*

★ **Moby** / 1992 / Instinct ♦♦♦♦♦
After recording a string of dance classics culminating with the pop hit "Go," Moby released his full-length debut balancing those songs with a few decidedly inventive album tracks. Moby's melodic sense developed much quicker than other early techno producers; despite the criticisms leveled at his later direction (or lack thereof), his first album is a masterpiece of challenging, unrepetitive, beautifully programmed rave-techno. Though the familiar tracks "Drop a Beat," "Next Is the E," and "Go" are the highlights here, the final two tracks, "Slight Return" and "Stream," are fine examples of early chill-out techno. —*John Bush*

**Early Underground** / Apr. 28, 1993 / Instinct ♦♦♦♦
A fifteen-track compilation of Moby's early career, collected from seven releases, this album fails to show the diversity that makes his self-titled LP such a joy. The tracks here are acceptable early rave-techno, but they won't appeal to those who think repetition is a sign of artistic deficiency. Most of the vocal samples are typical fare for the early '90s, but "Go (Original)" is more than worthy. —*John Bush*

**Ambient** / Aug. 17, 1993 / Instinct ♦♦♦
Hoping to cash in on the ambient house craze in 1993, Instinct Records released a collection of Moby's softer tracks (which, to his credit, had been recorded long before). Tracks like "My Beautiful Blue Sky," "Piano and Strings," and "Myopia" showcase his talent for majestic orchestral sounds and melodic synth layered over slower beats and percussion. —*John Bush*

**Everything Is Wrong** / Mar. 14, 1995 / Elektra ♦♦♦♦
For his first major-label album, Moby pulled out all the stops, trying to fit as many different styles as possible into 50 minutes. From fast breakbeats to pseudo-industrial trash, ambient trance to dance-pop, Moby tries it all. It's not quite a statement of genius—for all the bluster, there really isn't that much difference between his songs, which are nearly all standard three-chord progressions; it's all in the production. What ties everything together is Moby's understanding of the beat. The pulse holds steady throughout the record, making it sound like a very good night at a club. —*Stephen Thomas Erlewine*

**Animal Rights** / Feb. 11, 1996 / Elektra ♦♦
Just as the rock mainstream was turning its attentions toward techno, Moby abandoned electronic music to refashion himself as an alternative rocker—sort of like a cross between Nine Inch Nails and Smashing Pumpkins—for *Animal Rights*. Moby attempted rock on *Everything Is Wrong*, but on *Animal Rights*, his thin, pseudo-industrial guitar riffs dominate the proceedings, with his ambient soundscapes being pushed to the back of the record. Though Moby could be commended for having the courage to diversify, he simply isn't very good at alternative rock—his voice is thin and undistinguished, his rhythms are too tight, his guitars sound anemic and he can't write a hook. In fact, he even buries the hook in his ill-conceived cover of Mission of Burma's post-punk classic "That's When I Reach for My Revolver." Consequently, *Animal Rights* ranks as one of the classic failed albums, right alongside Sinead O'Connor's big-band *Am I Not Your Girl*. (The American edition of *Animal Rights* contained five bonus tracks not available on the original British version, which was released in the fall of 1996.) —*Stephen Thomas Erlewine*

**Rare: Collected B-sides** / Aug. 1996 / Instinct ♦♦♦
*Rare: Collected B-sides* isn't just for the die-hard Moby fan. Compiling a number of B-sides and non-LP singles on a single disc, *Rare* features a few run-of-the-mill remixes, but usually these alternate versions offer a significantly new spin on the songs. More importantly, tracks like the notorious "Thousand"—which zips by at the impossibly fast speed of a thousand beats per minute—are included, making it a necessary listen for any dedicated fan of Moby. —*Stephen Thomas Erlewine*

**I Like to Score** / Aug. 26, 1997 / Elektra/Asylum ♦♦♦
Considering that Moby's music is most effective in small doses, perhaps it shouldn't be a surprise that the compilation *I Like to Score* is a strong record. However, it does come as a surprise, since Moby's music usually sounds too insular for the kind of shifting, provocative atmospherics needed for effective film music. Here, on this collection of cinematic instrumental work, Moby demonstrates that he can capture the mood and feeling of a film while retaining his musical identity. Nothing here is particularly complex, and not all of it works—his reworking of John Barry's "James Bond Theme" sounds like a major studio's idea of what the kids are listening to these days—but by and large, *I Like to Score* is every bit as effective as Moby's official releases. —*Stephen Thomas Erlewine*

**Play** / Jun. 1, 1999 / V2 ♦♦♦♦
Following a notorious flirtation with alternative rock, Moby returned to the electronic dance mainstream on the 1997 album *I Like to Score*. With 1999's *Play*, he made yet another leap back toward the electronica base that had passed him by during the mid-'90s. The first two tracks, "Honey" and "Find My Baby," weave short blues or gospel vocal samples around rather disinterested breakbeat techno. This version of blues-meets-electronica is undoubtedly intriguing to the all-important NPR crowd, but it is more than just a bit gimmicky to any techno fans who know their Carl Craig from Carl Cox. Fortunately, Moby redeems himself in a big way over the rest of the album with a spate of tracks that return him to the evocative, melancholy techno that's been a specialty since his early days. The tinkly piano line and warped string samples on "Porcelain" frame a meaningful, devastatingly understated vocal from the man himself, while "South Side" is just another pop song by someone who shouldn't be singing—that is, until the transcendent chorus redeems everything. Surprisingly, many of Moby's vocal tracks are highlights; he has an unerring sense of how to frame his fragile vocals with sympathetic productions. Occasionally, the similarities to contemporary dance superstars like Fatboy Slim and the Chemical Brothers are just a bit too close for comfort, as on the stale big-beat anthem "Bodyrock." Still, Moby shows himself back in the groove after a long hiatus, balancing his sublime early sound with the breakbeat techno evolution of the '90s. —*John Bush*

**Songs 1993-1998** / Jul. 11, 2000 / Elektra/Asylum ♦♦♦
When *Play* became a breakout hit in 1999, Elektra readied a basic trainer for listeners new to Moby's practically trademarked style of down-tempo house baroque. Ranging from the *Move EP*, his major-label debut, to the soundtrack-inspired *I Like to Score*, *Songs 1993-1998* trawls the back catalog to pluck tracks on the same atmospheric level as *Play* classics like "Porcelain" or "South Side." Many of these tracks—especially ones from *Everything Is Wrong* and *Animal Rights*—sound much better in this format, divorced from the rock flame-outs that often surrounded them on the original albums. And though the version of his classic "Go" is actually a re-recording from 1998, it's a solid update that retains much of the original but never sounds like a pointless remake. *Songs 1993-1998* also spotlights Moby's continuing excellence in a number of genres, including a few of his Hi-NRG house singles from the mid-'90s ("Feeling So Real," "Move"), as well as his frequently beautiful ambient excursions ("God Moving Over the Face of the Waters," "The Rain Falls and the Sky Shudders"). It's a shame that the compilation completely skips his seminal early productions ("Drop a Beat," "Next Is the E") and a few rarities would've been nice for collectors, but *Songs 1993-1998* will satisfy fans of *Play* waiting for a new album. —*John Bush*

## Mocean Worker (Adam Dorn)

*Producer / Electronica, Jungle/Drum'N'Bass, Club/Dance*

The ranks of jazzy drum'n'bass swelled to a maneagable degree with the debut of Mocean Worker, the recording alias of jazz producer Adam Dorn. Dorn's father Joel was one of the stalwart producers at Atlantic Records during the '60s and '70s, helming sessions by Coltrane and Mingus as well as pop records like Roberta Flack's "Killing Me Softly," Bette Midler's debut album and the Allman Brothers' *Idlewild South*. Adam, a bass player and vocalist, studied at Berklee College of Music and worked extensively in the music industry as well, with artists ranging from David Sanborn to Hal Willner to Chaka Khan. Father and son have also produced archival reissues released by their own 32 Records (the catalogue also proved helpful when Dorn began sampling sources like Mahalia Jackson and Slim & Slam's Slam Stewart).

The Mocean Worker project came about almost by accident, the results of a series of half-serious recording sessions. After realizing the quality of the music he'd created, Dorn released his first Mocean Worker album *Home Movies from the Brain Forest* in 1998 on the punk label Conscience. Dorn moved to the Island subsidiary Palm Pictures for his second, *Mixed Emotional Features* in 1999. *Aural & Hearty* was issued the following year. —*John Bush*

● **Home Movies from the Brain Forest** / Apr. 7, 1998 / Conscience ++++
Jazzy drum'n'bass is hardly the full story on Mocean Worker's debut album. From the darkside noir of "American Tabloid" (a James Ellroy tribute) to the excellent roots/standards homage on the evocative "Summertime/Sometimes I Feel Like a Motherless Child," Dorn pulls off a minor masterpiece of the field. And the drum programming—usually an after-thought with album-oriented junglists—shines throughout, including on the highlights "What's Wrong" and "Overtime." —*John Bush*

**Mixed Emotional Features** / Feb. 23, 1999 / Island ++++
Mocean Worker is otherwise known as Adam Dorn, and when he's not indulging his beat-freak proclivities on his own, he helps his father Joel run the 32 Jazz reissue label. Among other things, this means that he doesn't have much trouble clearing samples, and he uses that enhanced level of access in a number of highly creative ways on this album. The most impressive of these is on the cleverly titled "Counts, Dukes, and Strays," an acid jazz tour de force constructed entirely out of samples from compositions by Count Basie, Duke Ellington, and Billy Strayhorn. But he knows other secret handshakes, as well: "Times of Danger" is a pitch-perfect homage to TV spy-show soundtracks, and "Detonator" is an equally fine addition to the dark drum'n'bass tradition. He's swinging without a net on "Mycroft," which combines Sherlock Holmes dialogue with Hawaiian steel guitar, and he manages to pull it off. Almost every track has moments like these. This is an album that bears up under repeated listenings, which is not always the case with electronic dance music. —*Rick Anderson*

**Aural & Hearty** / Sep. 26, 2000 / Palm ++
After proving himself one of the more adept drum'n'bass producers on his first two sets, Adam Dorn branched out his Mocean Worker project considerably for his third LP, *Aural & Hearty*. The results aren't completely disastrous—Dorn's production talents are as tight as usual—but the parade of genre workouts on this album makes it all a bit tiring (though it must've been a fun one to record). After a short intro, *Aural & Hearty* begins with a beyond played-out big beat redux named "Hey Baby" (guess what the predominant vocal sample turns out to be), and the track is only partially redeemed by Dorn's production finesse and the guest scratching of Roc Raida (from the X-Ecutioners). The song with the highest expectations coming in, a Bono collaboration titled "Air Suspension," also turns out a distinct disappointment; Dorn frames Bono's tossed-off vocal with little more than a few bland acid-techno riffs and a vocal tag lifted straight from a Timbaland record. The rest of the genre is *Aural & Hearty* soundchecks—easy-tempo groove on "Tres Tres Chic," Brazilian samba on the scratchy cut "Velvet Black Sky," filtered disco on "Astroglide," beatbox techno on "Step"—are pleasant enough, but quite clichéd coming on the heels of Dorn's inventive mastery of dark drum'n'bass and trip-hop on his previous material. "Intothinair" is one of the bare few highlights, a stab at paranoid tech-house with a devastating analog bassline and shimmering synth (Dorn apparently loved the bassline effect, considering he used it in two other tracks on the album). —*John Bush*

## Model 500 (Juan Atkins)
b. Detroit, MI
*Producer / Detroit Techno, Club/Dance, Techno, House*
The source for most of Juan Atkins' prime material, Model 500 was the Detroit godfather's guise for over a decade. Beginning with the 1985 classic "No UFO's" and extending to the release of his first proper LP (1995's *Deep Space*), the alias made Atkins' reputation with ten singles for his own Metroplex Records and several others for the Belgian R&S label. The same year *Deep Space* dropped, R&S also released a compilation including the best of Model 500's Metroplex material. [See Also: Juan Atkins, Cybotron, Infiniti] —*John Bush*

★ **Classics** / 1995 / R&S +++++
*Classics* makes it all clear—here are the roots of later developments such as techno-funk, acid-house, rave and trance, most released years before the forms became popular. Spanning the years 1985 to 1990 (in roughly chronological order), tracks like "No UFOs," "Sound of Stereo," "Night Drive," and "The Chase" form one of the most consistent, forward-looking discographies of the decade, alternately noisy and sublime. —*John Bush*

**Deep Space** / May 1995 / R&S +++
The first proper Model 500 full-length combines Juan Atkins' two favorite conceptual themes. Delineated by the spacy track titles and highways (M69, M24) for track numbers, *Deep Space* focuses on science fiction and automobile journeys through the course of its mostly instrumental tracks. —*John Bush*

**Mind and Body** / Mar. 8, 1999 / R&S ++++
Atkins' second full-length of Model 500 material spews out all the styles that Atkins had been influenced by over the past few years, including such far-ranging sounds as commercial R&B, drum & bass, British techno, and trip-hop. Though it's interesting to see Atkins' take on such a wide variety of music, it makes for a schizophrenic album, enjoyable in fits and starts but hardly a classic worthy of the master himself. —*John Bush*

## The Modernist (Jörg Burger)
*Drum Programming, Synthesizer / Minimal Techno, Experimental Dub, Experimental Techno, Techno*
Under the monikers Burger Industries, the Bionaut, and the Modernist, Cologne, Germany's Jörg Burger has proven himself one of the city's most prominent and influential techno producers and composers. Burger's collaborations with fellow Cologne native Wolfgang Voigt (a.k.a. Mike Ink) shaped their individual careers as well. Initially inspired by the pop scene in London, where both Burger and Voigt resided in the early '80s, the pair became acid techno converts when they returned to Germany.

By 1988, they were recording electronic music influenced by both pop and acid techno, though Voigt's music had a minimal, rhythmic bent while Burger's was warmer and more melodic. Two of Burger's early tracks appeared on the 1989 compilation *Teutonic Beats*, which was produced by Thomas Fehlmann. Two years later, Burger and Voigt formed their first label, Trance Atlantic, on which Burger released *Burger Industries: Vol. 1*. In 1993, after a move to Frankfurt to work with Air Liquide's Jammin' Unit and Dr. Walker and the creation of two other labels, Structure (which released Burger's first Bionaut album, 1992's *Everybody's Kissing Everyone*) and Blue, Voigt and Burger put their collaboration on a temporary hiatus. Burger returned to Cologne and, along with recording artists like Cristian Vogel and Thomas Heckmann, he put his creative energies into Bionaut and one-off single projects, a new label, Eat Raw, a dance magazine called *House Attack*, and a record store, Delirium.

He also contributed to the relaunch of the EMI Harvest label, which released Bionaut's 1995 longplayer *Lush Life Electronica* as well as the 1996 Burger/Ink album *Las Vegas* and the Modernist's debut, 1997's *Opportunity Knox*, which were both received warmly by publications like *Spex*, *Muzik*, *Jockey Slut*, and *Mixmag*. Around this time Burger also founded Granit, a graphics and illustration studio responsible for the artwork on all of his projects' covers.

By 1999, Burger moved from EMI/Harvest to Sony, where he created the Popular Organisation, which featured a triumverate of labels: the dancefloor-oriented Popular Tools, the experimentally-based Popular Sound and Popular Music, which released electronically-inclined pop. Popular Tools released the Modernist's second album *Explosion* in Europe in late 1999; the album was released in the US by Matador Records—who also released the domestic version of *Las Vegas*—in early 2000 with new artwork and extra tracks. [See Also: Burger/Ink] —*Heather Phares*

**Opportunity Knox** / Nov. 10, 1997 / Harvest ++

● **Explosion** / Apr. 18, 2000 / Matador ++++
Burger's second album as the Modernist explores the growing compatibility between '90s house and the experimental slant of German minimalists spearheaded by Mike Ink (Burger's sometime recording partner). Though the lock-step four-four beats, whipcrack cymbal work, and echoed, dubby effects heard on most of these tracks are reminiscent of Ink's Studio 1 material, Burger adds a good deal of atmosphere to his productions. Whether it's the contemplative guitar on "Manson Soup," the quasi-vibes lines on "Inspiratio," or the comparatively dense layers of audio bliss on "Eurojah (Immigrant Dub)," Burger allows his tracks a bit more room than most self-conscious ex-

perimentalists would, and they blossom in the fresh air. Though the cumulative effect of *Explosion* is still rather samey, Burger's talents make him one of the most underrated German electronic producers of his day. [The American release via Matador added three tracks to the European issue, including the Popular Tools singles "Mrs. New Deal" and "Architainment, Pt. 1."] —*John Bush*

## Moebius

*Synthesizer, Producer / Kraut Rock, Ambient, Electronic*

From his early work with the pioneering Kraut-rock band Cluster to his later solo recordings, Dieter Moebius remained one of the most innovative and prolific voices in contemporary electronic music, anticipating movements from ambient to techno years before the fact. By day a student at Berlin's Akademie Grafik, Moebius was moonlighting as a cook at an area restaurant when in 1969 he was befriended by Conrad Schnitzler, a key figure in local avant-garde circles, and invited to join Kluster, a band Schnitzler was forming with fellow underground artist Hans Joachim Roedelius. The trio released their debut LP *Klopfzeichen* in 1970; in the wake of their third album, 1971's *Kluster und Eruption*, Schnitzler exited to pursue a solo career, and Moebius and Roedelius continued on as a duo, modifying the name to Cluster.

Working with famed producer Conrad Plank, Cluster began to move increasingly towards more structured soundscapes—with 1974's *Zuckerzeit*, they even pursued an electronic pop sound similar in spirit to Kraftwerk. Moebius and Roedelius also teamed with Neu!'s Michael Rother in Harmonia, releasing a pair of much-acclaimed mid-'70s LPs which caught the attention of Brian Eno, who in response collaborated with the trio on a legendary session (released much later as *Harmonia 76*) heralding a turn towards ambient textures (and influencing the sound of the 1976 Cluster album *Sowiesoso*). Roedelius and Moebius subsequently worked with Eno on 1977's *Cluster and Eno* and 1979's *After the Heat* as well; in the wake of 1981's *Curiosum*, however, they dissolved Cluster, with both pursuing solo endeavors.

Moebius' first subsequent effort was 1981's *Material*, a second collaboration with Plank (his proper solo debut, *Rastakraut Pasta*, had appeared two years earlier); together, they produced some of the most experimental recordings of their respective careers, creating harsh mutant soundscapes which over time gave way to the proto-ambient textures of 1986's *En Route*, their final work before Plank's untimely death. Concurrently Moebius also teamed with Gerd Beerbohm for 1982's *Strange Music* and 1983's *Double Cut*, both explorations of pure noise; meanwhile, with the solo album *Tonspuren* (also from 1983), Moebius clearly anticipated the emergence of techno. Apart from teaming with Karl Renzeinhuasen in the duo Ersatz, during the early '90s he also reunited with Roedelius to revive Cluster. —*Jason Ankeny*

• **Tonspuren** / 1983 / Gyroscope ♦♦♦♦

The first true Moebius solo album, *Tonspuren*, collects ten short electronic pop songs that coast along on lo-fi rhythms and an assortment of creaking, chirping, and wheezing synthesizer lines. Although most feature rather simple melodies, Moebius stretches out a bit on "Contramio" and "Furbo." —*Keith Farley*

**Double Cut** / 1984 / Skyclad ♦♦♦♦

The second of two collaborations involving Moebius and Gerd Beerbohm, *Double Cut* sounds miles away from the relatively harmless electronic/pop experiments of solo work by Moebius or Cluster. Consisting of only four extended tracks, the album expresses the dark side of electronics courtesy of the repetitive trance-state on "Hydrogen" and "Minimotion." *Double Cut* is much closer to electronic inheritors in the experimental and techno fields than Moebius' usual new age pursuits. —*Keith Farley*

**Zero Set** / 1984 / Skyclad ♦♦♦♦

Recorded at Conrad Plank's studio in 1982, *Zero Set* is a highly percussive affair with Mani Neumeier. The album is saturated in drum and synth rhythms and polyrhythms, resulting in compositions that are energetic and infectious. The opener, "Speed Display," is the granddaddy of them all. This superb, driving piece of synth-Kraut-rock showcases Neumeier's percussive "speed display," so to speak. The following cut, "Load," seems almost borne of the first, with an obscure synthesized vocal, steady percussion flourishes, synth spritzes, and industrial overtones. "Recall" is reminiscent of early Can and features a Sudanese vocal, and the closing track, "Search Zero," is representative of the entire project: a quirky, percussive, progressive synth-rock composition. *Zero Set* is impressive; to date, it's possibly the most interesting

project on which the three musicians have worked. Two of the tracks, "Speed Display" and the textured, bubbly "Pitch Control," also appear on Sky Records' excellent *Begegnungen* compilations. —*David Ross Smith*

**Rastakraut Pasta/Material** / 1996 / Gyroscope ♦♦♦♦

This two-fer combines a pair of albums recorded by Moebius & Plank: 1979's *Rastakraut Pasta* and 1981's *Material*. On the former, languid drum machines frame several interesting exercises in alien pop, from the vocoder experimentation on "News" and "Missi Cacadou" to the title track's hilarious fusion of reggae and kraut-rock. (Can's Holger Czukay appears on bass for three tracks.) Though *Material* begins with a straightahead synth-rocker (including prominent guitar and a quicker pace), it's a more unusual album than its predecessor. The tracks "Infiltration" and "Tollkühn" trade in the drum machines for sets of far-flung synthesizer passages. In all, two solid albums of electronic-minded Kraut-rock. —*John Bush*

**Ludwig's Law** / Dec. 1, 1998 / Drag City ♦♦

*Ludwig's Law* includes the previously unheard results of a 1983 session involving long-time collaborators Moebius and Conny Plank plus Mayo Thompson, the frontman of notorious American underground rockers Red Krayola. The results are actually quite close to a fusion of two styles: the ambling electronic pop of Moebius/Cluster and the more percussive experimentalism of Red Krayola. Most tracks have odd half-sung, half-spoken voicings probably best left off the tapes. It's an interesting match-up, if not quite a meeting of the minds. —*Keith Farley*

## Mogwai

f. 1996, Glasgow, Scotland

*Group / Experimental Rock, Space Rock, Indie Rock, Post-Rock/Experimental*

The cosmic post-rock band Mogwai was formed in Glasgow, Scotland, in 1996 by guitarist/vocalist Stuart Braithwaite, guitarist Dominic Aitchison, and drummer Martin Bulloch, longtime friends with the goal of creating "serious guitar music." Towards that end they added another guitarist, John Cummings, before debuting in March 1996 with the single "Tuner," a rarity in the Mogwai discography for its prominent vocals; the follow-up, a split single with Dweeb titled "Angels vs. Aliens," landed in the Top Ten on the British indie charts. Following appearances on a series of compilations, Mogwai returned later in the year with the 7" "Summer"; after another early 1997 single, "New Paths to Helicon," the group issued *Ten Rapid*, a collection of their earliest material. Around the time of recording the superb 1997 EP *4 Satin*, former Teenage Fanclub and Telstar Ponies member Brendan O'Hare joined the lineup in time to record their debut studio LP *Mogwai Young Team*, exiting a short time later to return to his primary projects Macrocosmica and Fiend 1. Again a quartet, Mogwai next issued 1998's *Kicking a Dead Pig*, a two-disc remix collection; the *No Education No Future (Fuck the Curfew)* EP appeared a few months later. In 1999, they released *Come on Die Young*. —*Jason Ankeny*

**Ten Rapid** / Aug. 12, 1997 / Jetset ♦♦♦♦

*Ten Rapid* compiles the bulk of the singles Mogwai released between 1995 and 1997, but the tone of the music is so consistent, it could have all come from the same session. Like a post-rock band, Mogwai is about subtle, shifting sonics and repetition, but they are hardly as precious or cerebral as any post-rock group. Each of their songs sounds as if it goes around in a circle, surrounding itself in interlocking, mathematical patterns. While there are waves of feedback washing over the album, the music itself sounds like it's in the distance. Their habit of burying vocals (which aren't featured that often in the first place) also keeps Mogwai from reach, and nothing on *Ten Rapid* is immediately engaging, even though it is intriguing. With repeated listens, the album reveals its hidden layers, and the music becomes hypnotic in its gradual, deliberate pace and interwoven guitars. —*Stephen Thomas Erlewine*

• **Young Team** / Oct. 21, 1997 / Jetset ♦♦♦♦

*Young Team*, Mogwai's first full-length album fulfills the promise of their early singles and EPs, offering an complex, intertwining set of crawling instrumentals, shimmering soundscapes, and shards of noise. Picking up where *Ten Rapid* left off, Mogwai uses the sheer length of an album to their advantage, recording a series of songs that meld together—it's easy to forget where one song begins and the other ends. The record itself takes its time to begin, as the sound of chiming processed guitars and murmured sampled vocals floats to the surface. Throughout the album, the sound of the band keeps shifting, and it's not just through explosions of noise—Mogwai isn't merely jamming, they have a planned vision, subtly texturing their music with small, telling details.

When the epic "Mogwai Fears Satan" draws the album to a close, it becomes clear that the band has expanded the horizons of post-rock, creating a record of sonic invention and emotional force that sounds unlike anything their guitar-based contemporaries have created. —*Stephen Thomas Erlewine*

**Come on Die Young** / Apr. 6, 1999 / Chemikal Underground/Matador ✦✦
"Too much, too soon" is a tattered rock 'n' roll cliche, but it continues to tell the tale of many young bands, such as Glasgow's acclaimed post-rock collective, Mogwai. Usually, the phrase is hauled out to describe an intoxicated downward spiral by bands that had too much success all at once, but that's not the case here. Mogwai suffered too much praise—too many accolades from critics, too much reverence from underground hipsters. The damned thing is, the singles compilation *Ten Rapid* and the debut *Young Team* were records that deserved all the acclaim they earned, but a funny thing happened while Mogwai was recording their much-anticipated second album, ironically titled *Come On Die Young*—the band went stale. *Young Team* was teeming with unexpected ideas, sounds and structures; *Come On Die Young* is a lethargic trawl through post-Slint and Sonic Youth territory. Where their free-form noise improvisations were utterly enthralling on their earlier records, the ebb and flow is entirely too familiar throughout *Come On Die Young,* largely because they follow the same pattern on each song. And each cut blends into the next, creating the impression of one endless track that teeters between deliberately dreamy crawls and random bursts of noise. Granted, that was the blueprint for *Young Team,* but there is little dynamicism anywhere on *Come On Die Young.* Mogwai repeat the same riffs with the same inflection, never pushing themselves toward new sonic territory, yet never hitting a mesmerizing trance. It feels like a degraded photocopy of their earlier records—it's possible to discern the initial spark that made them fascinating, but this current incarnation is too smudged and muddy to hold attention on its own terms. Perhaps *Come On Die Young* wouldn't have seemed as disappointing if it hadn't arrived on the wave of hype and expectation, but the truth is, it pales in comparison to their own work, plus the work of such peers as Aerial M. Actually, there's another cliche that applies to *Come On Die Young*—"the sophomore slump." Fortunately, Mogwai's previous work indicates they're savvy enough to make sure this record is just a slump, not a premature death. —*Stephen Thomas Erlewine*

## Moloko

f. 1993, Sheffield, Yorkshire,
*Group / Electronica, Trip-Hop, Club/Dance, House*

The Sheffield-based dance-pop duo Moloko is the end result of Irish-born singer Roisin Murphy's attempt to pick up mixer/producer Mark Brydon at a 1994 party with the come-on, "Do you like my tight sweater? See how it fits my body." Brydon saw musical potential in her attitude, and the two formed a creative and romantic partnership.

Murphy, who never sang outside of the shower before, was a newcomer to the music business. However, Brydon had many years of experience with UK house music acts House Arrest and Cloud 9, helped found Sheffield's Fon studios, and remixed artists like Eric B & Rakim and Psychic TV. Soon after forming Moloko, they released their debut single, "Where Is the What If the What Is in the Why?," and signed to Echo Records.

The band's full-length debut, inevitably named *Do You Like My Tight Sweater?,* came out in 1995 and was an equal mix of Murphy's slinky attitude and Brydon's musical prowess. The album combined dance, funk, and trip-hop elements in an approach similar to Portishead or Massive Attack but with a sense of humor and sass unique to Moloko. Though the album's US release occurred nearly a year later, the single "Fun for Me" was featured prominently on the *Batman & Robin* soundtrack and received some radio airplay.

Moloko toured with kindred musical spirits such as Pulp, built a home studio, and recorded the follow-up to *Do You Like My Tight Sweater?,* titled *I Am Not a Doctor.* Released in 1998 (and late 1999 in the US), the album continued in Moloko's witty, funky tradition. The group's third album, *Things to Make and Do,* was issued in the UK in the spring of 2000. —*Heather Phares*

● **Do You Like My Tight Sweater?** / Nov. 1995 / Echo ✦✦✦✦
The aptly named *Do You Like My Tight Sweater?* slinks and bounces on a funky backbone of fat basslines and innovative beats that support singer Roisin Murphy's sly, theatrical vocals and lyrics. Part catwoman, part roid, her singing ranges from a knowing purr to an androgynous growl and creates characters like party weirdos, dominatrixes, killer bunnies, and ghosts.

As dramatic as her vocals are, however, Murphy is an anti-diva; her musical surroundings equal her singing in importance. The other half of *Do You Like My Tight Sweater?*'s individuality comes from Mark Brydon's arrangements, which combine fluid tempos, sudden breakbeats, witty sound effects, and unearthly keyboards in sci-fi grooves that appeal to the brain and body.

Standout tracks like "Fun For Me," "I Can't Help Myself," "Lotus Eaters," and "Party Weirdo" mix sensuality, technology, funk, and electronica in a unique and stylish blend. While some of the sillier songs like "On My Horsey" and "Dirty Monkey" disrupt the flow of *Do You Like My Tight Sweater?,* the danceable creativity of Moloko's debut overrides its quirks. —*Heather Phares*

**I Am Not a Doctor** / Aug. 24, 1998 / Mushroom ✦✦✦✦
*I Am Not a Doctor* could have been called "Moloko 2.0." A better integration of tech appeal and sex appeal than the group's debut *Do You Like My Tight Sweater?,* Moloko's singing, writing, and musical reach are all upgraded on *I Am Not a Doctor.* The result is a more entertaining and less self-conscious album.

Songs like "The Flipside," "Blink," and "Pretty Bridges" offer a stylized, pop take on jungle, while the ballads "Downsized," "Caught in a Whisper," and "Should've Been Could've Been" mix pathos with the band's dry wit. The deadpan new wave of "Sorry," the cyberfunky "The Id," and the techno torch-song "Sing It Back" show off Moloko's expanded range.

Musically and vocally, Roisin Murphy and Mark Brydon blend their talents more smoothly on *I Am Not a Doctor.* Murphy's voice melds with the horns, strings, and keyboards backing her, while real and electronic drums punctuate each song expressively. A balance of contradictions, Moloko keeps inventiveness and listenability high on their second album. —*Heather Phares*

## Money Mark (Mark Ramos Nishita)

b. Detroit, MI
*Keyboards, Producer / Indie Pop, Electronica, Indie Rock, Trip-Hop, Soul-Jazz*
Money Mark is the alias of Mark Ramos Nishita, a keyboardist whose funky, retro-flavored riffs earned him the unofficial title of the fourth Beastie Boy. Born in Detroit to a Japanese-Hawaiian father and a Chicano mother, Nishita moved to the West Coast when he was six; some years later, he hooked up with the Dust Brothers production team, and began overdubbing keyboards for the Delicious Vinyl label. While working as a handyman, Nishita accepted a job repairing the Beastie Boys' Silverlake, CA home; soon, he became a pivotal member of the group's Grand Royal Posse, and performed on both 1992's *Check Your Head* and 1994's *Ill Communication.*

Recorded at his home studio, Money Mark's solo debut *Mark's Keyboard Repair*—a loose, infectious collection of fuzzy organ noodlings performed on vintage equipment—appeared in 1995 as a set of three 10" records issued on the Los Angeles-based label Love Kit. Although the small pressing sold out almost instantly, the first record in the series found its way to Britain and the offices of Mo'Wax founder James Lavelle, who quickly flew to L.A. to meet with Nishita; a deal was struck, and *Mark's Keyboard Repair* was reissued in late 1995. *Push the Button* followed in 1998. —*Jason Ankeny*

● **Mark's Keyboard Repair** / 1995 / Mo'Wax ✦✦✦✦
Money Mark was the keyboardist on the Beastie Boys' *Check Your Head* and *Ill Communication.* Both albums demonstrated his influence, with his thick, funky organ appearing all over the place. On his own, Money Mark creates music that is quite similar to the instrumental tracks on the two Beastie albums, but his music is grittier and jazzier. *Mark's Keyboard Repair* sounds like a lo-fi, indie rock variation of '60s soul-jazz, particularly the records of Jimmy Smith and John Patton. Mark's attention span is extremely short—some of the songs don't last a minute—but the songs keep the same laidback groove flowing throughout the album. *Mark's Keyboard Repair* features a full 30 songs on its American release—the original English version clocked in with 20—but it is rarely boring. Only the groove is important on the album, and Money Mark never lets it stop. —*Stephen Thomas Erlewine*

**Push the Button** / May 4, 1998 / A&M ✦✦✦✦
Lacking the kaleidoscopic ambience of *Mark's Keyboard Repair,* Money Mark's second album, *Push the Button,* is a more cohesive affair than its predecessor. That doesn't mean it sticks to one style, either. Mark tries his hand at jazz, soul, funk, pop, and even ballads over the course of *Push the Button,* but where the sheer brevity of the numerous songs on *Keyboard Repair* made it seem like a colorful sketchbook, the songs here form a greater work. Not only has he taken the time to connect the songs, he also has decided to sing, adding further depth and color to his funky palette. While his vocals are a little flat,

they fit the laidback vibe of the record, and on occasion, they really connect. Propelled by a relaxed shuffle and jazzy organ, "Hand In Your Head" is a gem of a summer single, and "Rock in the Rain" and "Maybe I'm Dead" aren't far behind, either. It may be removed from the lo-fi soul-jazz miniatures of *Keyboard Repair*, but *Push the Button* has a real soulful charm of its own—one that's equally seductive. —*Stephen Thomas Erlewine*

## Monk & Canatella

f. 1994, Bristol, England
*Group / Ambient Techno, Trip-Hop*
Bedsit trip-hop duo Monk & Canatella were formed by Simon Russell and Jim Johnston after each had long been involved in the Bristol community (scene-leaders Portishead even dedicated a song to them). They debuted on Cup of Tea Records with 1995's *Fly Fishing* EP, which gathered good reviews from the British music weeklies and radio DJs. The EP and its follow-up "I Can Water My Plants" were early investigations into the more domestic, indie-rock side of trip-hop. After getting an American release via *Cup of Tea: A Compilation* on Quango, Monk & Canatella released their debut album, *Care in the Community*. —*John Bush*

● **Care in the Community** / Apr. 21, 1997 / Cup of Tea ♦♦♦
On their debut album, Monk & Canatella's limp-wristed take on bedsit trip-hop makes Portishead sound like N.W.A. Besides the evidence inherent in track titles such as "I Can Water My Plants" (not to mention the muso poetry therein) and "Fish," the shambling beats and occasional surprise tell the listener that this is dance music overly inspired by alternative rock of the '80s. —*John Bush*

## Monkey Mafia

f. 1995, London, England
*Group / Big Beat, Funky Breaks, Electronica, Club/Dance, House*
Monkey Mafia's brand of big-beat "Brit-hop-amyl-house" is similar in respects to that of the Chemical Brothers, Fatboy Slim, and artists associated with the Skint and Wall of Sound labels. The production arm of Essex-born DJ Jon Carter's many club-related activities, the project began in 1995, following a string of tracks for Wall of Sound under the name Artery and coinciding with his residency at Heavenly's influential anything-goes weekly, the Sunday Social. Carter's musical past actually reaches quite a bit farther back than London's post-acid house big-beat scene; he was the member of a number of pub-rock and psychedelic cover bands while studying philosophy in Southampton. As such, his influences run a far wider berth than usual suspects such as Kraftwerk, Public Enemy, and Double D & Steinski, including obscure old-school hip-hop and electro, '60s rock and soul, and his longest-running obsessions, dancehall and reggae.

Carter moved to London around 1993, learning engineering and production working in the studios of (oddly) hardcore and jungle labels such as Trouble on Vinyl and No U-Turn. He passed a demo of ragga-tinged mid-tempo breakbeat tracks he assembled in his spare time to Wall of Sound's Mark Jones, who released a few of them before losing Carter to de-Construction in 1995. Carter's debut for the label, "Blow the Whole Joint Up," appeared that same year. An instant hit among the capital's flourishing acid-hop scene, the track earned Carter remix work for Prodigy and Saint Etienne, as well as a steady stream of DJ gigs (the latter of which tended to limit his release schedule). A pair of EPs managed to trickle out however, including 1996's "Work Mi Body" and 1997's "Lion in the Hall." The long-awaited full-length *Shoot the Boss* appeared in late 1998. —*Sean Cooper*

● **Shoot the Boss** / May 4, 1998 / Heavenly ♦♦♦♦
British DJ/keyboardist Jon Carter is the mastermind behind Monkey Mafia, who finally issued their debut full-length *Shoot the Boss* in 1998 (after several EPs and singles such as "Work Mi Body," and *15 Steps EP*, etc.). By remixing tracks for such popular alternative rock artists as Kula Shaker, Supergrass, and Prodigy (Carter has toured with the latter), Carter made quite a name for himself. *Shoot the Boss* shows that although Carter is interested in electronic dance, he wants to also keep a "human" element to his music. By including an MC named Dougie, turntable master First Rate, bassist Dan, and drummer Tom, Monkey Mafia contains the best of both worlds. The music is a combination of reggae, hip-hop, dance, electronic, and alternative— "Make Jah Music," "Blow the Whole Joint Up," and "Lion In the Hall" contain each of these musical elements. —*Greg Prato*

## Mono

f. 1996, London, England
*Group / Electronica, Alternative Dance, Adult Alternative Pop/Rock, Trip-Hop, Club/Dance*
Influenced by cool jazz, '60s pop, and classic film-soundtracks, the trip-hop duo Mono formed around vocalist Siobhan De Maré and producer Martin Virgo, a one-time member of Nellee Hooper's production team which worked on Massive Attack's seminal "Unfinished Sympathy" as well as Björk's *Debut*. After Virgo hooked up with De Maré in mid-1996, the pair recorded the *Life in Mono* EP and signed to Mercury by the end of the year. After working on their debut album *Formica Blues*, Mono gained a comparatively high profile through an appearance on the soundtrack to the American film *Great Expectations*. *Formica Blues* was released in America in February 1998, six months after its British appearance. —*John Bush*

● **Formica Blues** / Sep. 1997 / PolyGram ♦♦♦♦
Equal parts trip-hop and lounge, pop and film music, Mono's *Formica Blues* is a startling, fresh debut album. Producer/songwriter Martin Virgo used to work with Nellee Hooper, one of the key dance producers of the early '90s, and he has taken Hooper's knack for making underground beats and ideas accessible. Virgo's songs blend the sleekness of '60s easy listening with strong melodies and fresh trip-hop beats—often, the music sounds like the middle ground between St. Etienne's cheery retro dance-pop and Everything But the Girl's club-conscious *Walking Wounded*. *Formica Blues* would be enjoyable simply on sonic terms, since the stylish production is endlessly alluring, but Virgo's songs give the music depth and vocalist Siobhan De Mare's breathy croon adds a human edge, resulting in a thoroughly enchanting debut. —*Stephen Thomas Erlewine*

## Mono Junk (Kimmo Rapatti)

*Producer / Acid Techno, Club/Dance, Techno*
Years before loop-based experimental techno became a stock-in-trade for scores of producers around the world, Finnish producer Kim Rapatti was recording minimal productions for more than a dozen labels worldwide. Based in Turku, he began releasing material on his own Dum Trax label in 1990, utilizing multiple aliases including Mono Junk, Detroit Diesel, Mars 31, Coopers, Unik, Melody Boy 2000, and occasionally his own name. A 1995 Dum Trax compilation was followed by his first full-length, *Gloom*. By the mid-'90s, Rapatti's rigid, isolationist sound became much-hyped in the techno world and he recorded for top labels including Plug Research, Sähkö, 12K, Neuton, Interdimensional Transmissions, Trope, and i220. —*John Bush*

**Dum Trax** / 1995 / Dum ♦♦
Ostensibly a label compilation spotlighting Finn Kim Rapatti's Dum Records, *Dum Trax* turns out to be virtually a Rapatti solo album. Besides tracks from his most famous guise Mono Junk, such Rapatti aliases as Mars 31, Melody Boy 2000, and Detroit Diesel are featured on *Dum Trax*. The productions are mid-tempo Detroit acid fusions, leaning quite close to Aphex Twin's earlier *SAW* material, but with a bit less nuance. Most of the tracks are taken from 1993-94 Dum singles, though several are exclusives. —*John Bush*

● **Gloom** / 1995 / Dum ♦♦♦
Listeners clued in by the title may not be surprised by the stark, ambient tilt to classic acid house accomplished by Kim Rapatti on his Mono Junk project. True to the Rapatti aesthetic, the 303/909 combination and a few old-school tools (sinewave generators, etc.) are responsible for a large majority of the total sound heard on *Gloom*, though as usual, he makes the limitations work for him instead of against. The epic "Enter" is a deep 303 reverb nightmare similar to contemporary Plastikman, while "Sonorous" is more melancholy than haunting, courtesy of a relaxed beat and some surprisingly tinkly, bell-like melodies. Though a few tracks never really break out of their atmospheric/experimental mold, *Gloom* is an often fascinating listen, caught in the verge between academic '70s electronics and bare '90s acid techno. —*John Bush*

## Monolake

f. 1995, Berlin, Germany
*Group / Minimal Techno, Experimental Dub, Experimental Techno, Electronica, Ambient Techno, IDM*
Monolake is among the most acclaimed artists associated with the Berlin-based Basic Channel/Chain Reaction label group, run by Moritz "Maurizio"

von Oswald and home to such champions of minimalist austerity as Vainqueur, Substance, and (initially) Porter Ricks. Consisting of Robert Henke and Gerhard Behles, the group have recorded just under a dozen singles for the Chain Reaction and Din labels, as well as a full-length CD, *HongKong*, released by CR in 1997. Monolake's music sits at the intersection between abstract computer music and the more dance-derived techno redux of their CR labelmates. Behles studied formally at Utrecht's Institute of Sonology (a noted fount of electronic experimentation formed in the late '60s by Stan Tempelaars and Gottfried Michael Koenig). Behles and Henke met at Berlin's Technical University, where Behles taught and Henke was studying sound engineering for film. Monolake formed somewhat by accident, when a first round of collaborative improvising in the studio led to a handful of tracks from which their first single, "Cyan," was soon pressed. A number of follow-up releases appeared in 1995 and 1996, with the best of these eventually joining new material on the 1997 CD release, *HongKong*, an important release both for Chain Reaction (it's widely considered the label's finest) and Monolake (whose previously vinyl-only 12"s reached a somewhat small, specialist audience). The full-length *Interstate* followed in 1999, along with the EP *Gobi: The Desert*.

In addition to his work with Behles, Henke is a mastering engineer for Maurizio's Dubplates & Mastering (the D&M inscription can be found on the run-out groove of many a European techno release), and also operates the Imbalance Computer Music label, home to the more experimental reaches of Chain Reaction and Basic Channel artists such as Andi Mellweg (of Porter Ricks), Wieland Samolak, and Henke himself. —*Sean Cooper*

● **HongKong** / Dec. 15, 1997 / Chain Reaction ♦♦♦♦
*HongKong* compiles some of Monolake's most beautiful works that had previously been released on vinyl exclusively. There may not be any purer examples of this German duo's sound than the opening track of the album, "Cyan." Integrating strange, animalistic noises from a distant invisible jungle with a cushioned, thumping bassline, delicately tapping percussion, and occasional high-frequency synthesized notes, Monolake's tone blends dubbed organic serenity with computerized harmony. With most of the tracks lasting upwards of ten minutes, this compilation may be too excessively odd for some, while also being one of the most tranquil forms of electronic music for others. The album ends with two tracks from Monolake's release on the Din label and the previously unreleased "Mass Transit Railway." Not nearly as epic or as cinematic as the other numbers, these final three still incorporate strange samples, such as waves crashing on the side of a boat and a montage of Asian voices. These peculiarities only figure into the first minute or so of each respective track before Monolake moves toward the disoriented style of minimal, monotone techno of the Basic Channel label. As a sampler of Monolake's early releases, *Hong Kong* functions effectively, featuring a range of differing sounds that comprise a music quite unlike any that's been produced outside of Germany. —*Jason Birchmeier*

**Interstate** / Mar. 23, 1999 / Monolake/Imbalance ♦♦♦♦
A worthy follow-up to one of the best full-lengths of Berlin's experimental camp, *Interstate* continues in the pulse vein but breaks up all hints of the flowing trance-states on *HongKong* by attaching waves of distortion apparently grabbed from Autobahn source recordings. It's a more up-front record than its predecessor, while the emphasis on solid programming and unheard sounds keeps it in the same category: excellent. —*Keith Farley*

**Gobi: The Desert [EP]** / Aug. 23, 1999 / Chain Reaction ♦♦♦♦
Monolake releases such as *Hong Kong* and *Interstate* draw directly on the lived environment, fusing wispy minimal techno with field recordings of waves, insects, and bustling streets until the latter begin losing all reference to origin, even to reality. The group's *Gobi EP* takes the opposite tack, conjuring earthy hums, chilling night winds, chirping microscopic fauna, and distant, bassy rumbles from the thin air of the digital recording studio. If this is just the ambient M.O. ported to the desktop, so be it; the results are far more stunning and transporting than any mere replicant methodology could possibly achieve. Entirely beatless, and therefore quite unlike the group's previous releases, it's also some of their strongest work to date. —*Sean Cooper*

## Moody Boyz (Tony Thorpe)
*Producer / Techno, Acid House, House*
Moody Boyz was one of the more adventurous names in UK house and techno during and immediately following the height of the London acid house movement. The nom de plume of producer Tony Thorpe (both solo and with occasional collaborators), Moody Boyz produced some of the first English acid records and is widely credited with helping inspire both jungle and "intelligent techno" artists by combining elements of dub, hip-hop, electro, and traditional African musics within a dancefloor-friendly techno framework. Releasing a number of 12"s on XL and William Orbit's Guerrilla label, Moody Boyz titles including "Funky Zulu" and "Destination Africa" are now considered classics, while the remix version of *Product of the Environment* (cleverly dubbed *Recycled*) is one of the earliest examples of the now-common techno remix album. Thorpe also helped bring artists such as In Sync and Digidub to prominence by featuring them as remixers. In addition to his own work, Thorpe also reworked tracks for System 7 and was the in-house remixer for acid-house charlatans the KLF at the height of their popularity, adding credibility and grit to chart-busting hits such as "3 A.M. Eternal," "What Time Is Love?," and "Last Train to Transcentral."

Thorpe curtailed his Moody Boyz activities in 1994, following the appearance of the *Recycled* double EP. He joined the SSR/Crammed label in 1995 (*Product of the Environment* was also reissued by Crammed) as an A&R rep, heading up the experimental dance end of the imprint at the helm of the Language sublabel, home to such artists as Endemic Void, Tao, Phosphorous, and Si Begg's Buckfunk 3000 project. —*Sean Cooper*

**Destination Africa [Single]** / 1994 / Crammed ♦♦♦
Two more mixes of the track from the *Product of the Environment* LP, one each treading tribal drum'n'bass and uptempo trip-hoppy/breaks territory. Good but hardly essential. —*Sean Cooper*

● **Product of the Environment** / 1994 / Guerilla ♦♦♦♦
A visionary collection of subtly innovative techno and tribal house, with heaps of African and Caribbean influences fitted neatly into tracks fusing odd time signatures, shifting rhythms, and lush atmospheres. Although Thorpe's earlier twelves probably resulted in more dance-floor play, this is a record to be proud of. —*Sean Cooper*

**Recycled for the Environment** / Dec. 15, 1994 / SSR ♦♦♦♦
Billed as an EP, this is basically a full-length collection of remixed versions of tracks from the Moody Boyz' *Product of the Environment* LP. The 2x12" features mostly lesser-known remixers (at the time, anyway) such as Insync, The Arc, and Digidub, as well as Andrew Weatherall together with Dave Hedger under their Lords of Afford moniker. Styles range from lush tribal techno to murky ambient and spacy electro, each offering an inspired extrapolation of Thorpe's originals. —*Sean Cooper*

## Moodymann (Kenny Dixon, Jr.)
*Producer, DJ / Tech-House, Detroit Techno, Club/Dance*
Kenny Dixon, Jr.'s outspoken views on the state of black techno and his aversion to publicity put him in a league occupied by few Detroit producers other than Underground Resistance supremo "Mad" Mike Banks, though his tech-house productions as Moodymann are soulful in a league few could expect. Dixon began producing early in the '90s, and inaugurated his own KDJ Records in 1994 with the *Moody Trax* EP. Following singles like "The Day We Lost the Soul" and "I Can't Kick This Feelin When It Hits" proved one of the best fusers of short, soulful disco samples to the harder minimalist Detroit techno. Further singles for After Midnight, Music Is…, and Carl Craig's Planet E Records (including the brilliant *Dem Young Sconies* EP) solidified Dixon's place in Detroit techno, though his stance on promotion remained firm. Much of his KDJ output appeared on 1997's *A Silent Introduction*, while the following year's *Mahogany Brown* brought much new material. *Forevernevermore*, released in 2000, collected more of his KDJ material and added several new tracks as well. —*John Bush*

★ **A Silent Introduction** / Oct. 20, 1997 / Planet E ♦♦♦♦♦
The ultra-smooth house music of Kenny Dixon Jr.'s Moodymann project doesn't follow any formula and can vary heavily from one track to the next. On any given track there can be horns, guitar licks, vocals, handclaps, gentle percussion and even crowd applause. What Dixon seems to have done is to sample some of the most genuine moments of '70s funk and disco records and then assemble these parts into a whole that doesn't fit into any stylistic trend or time frame. By making his house sound a bit rough, heavily sedated and well-aged, Dixon adds new flavor to a genre lacking creativity in the late '90s. Each of the ten tracks on *Silent Introduction* possesses its own unique beautiful characteristics, but it is the epic tracks that truly demand countless listens. The first of these epic classics follows the opening track and begins

with Dixon's spoken words drifting over a modulating siren of ambience. When Dixon finally concludes his ode to "the real niggaz from Detroit who struggle everyday, just to live, eat, and breathe," the first thumping bass beats of "I Can't Kick This Feeling When It Hits" begin unleashing the very feeling the song speaks of. Throughout the upbeat dancefloor scorcher, the sample of a female voice singing the song's hook is repeated endlessly until it begins to act as one of the minimally looped percussion rhythms of the track. The most intense song on the album, "Music People," picks up the mostly downtempo pace of the album at its halfway point. A dense layer of funky samples and basslines, the track peaks when a male vocalist sings, "Welcome to our world of merry music," brilliantly followed by a slick horn bridge. Immediately following Dixon's outro speech at the conclusion of "Music People" come the opening notes of "Sunday Morning." Even though this track doesn't technically become dancey until about five minutes in, when the bass drum starts kicking, there are some interesting female diva humming vocals, chirping birds, human chatter, and some traditional jazz instrumentation. —*Jason Stanley Birchmeier*

**Misled [EP]** / 1998 / KDJ ♦♦♦♦
Of Kenny Dixon, Jr.'s many Moodymann records, the *Misled* record in particular stands out as an example of how he subtly brings in a sense of quiet yet hard-hitting ideology. The record's label sets up a comparison of the suburban and inner-city life, aiming derogatory comments towards suburban youths as posers: "The City: a place where most suburban kids think they're from/Detroit: A place where neggahs roam, neggahs like me/don't be misled!" The epic title track opens with a sample from Curtis Mayfield's "Freddie's Dead"; from there the sounds of inner-city life—sirens, car horns, cars driving by, and various hustle and bustle—fade and a synth melody kicks off two sides of thick funk, accentuated throughout by an excellent use of vocal samples. The undeniable funky old-school feel of this record makes it one of his best. —*Jason Birchmeier*

**Mahogany Brown** / Apr. 20, 1998 / Peacefrog ♦♦♦♦
The proper debut album for Moodymann, *Mahogany Brown* alternates mellowed-out disco dubs like "Brown Mahogany" and "Stoneodenjoye" with more aggressive tech-house tracks like "Me and My People's Eyes." Though it would be nearly impossible to top *A Silent Introduction*, the singles compilation released one year before, Kenny Dixon, Jr. does a tremendous job skirting the slender divide between sublime Detroit techno and more soul-inflected house like the work of Terrence Parker. —*John Bush*

**Forevernevermore [Single]** / Aug. 10, 1998 / KDJ ♦♦♦
Complain all you want about this release by Kenny Dixon, Jr. as Moodymann being only one-sided. It may not be big on quantity, but it compensates in terms of quality. The ten-minute track moves rather quickly with an uptempo underlying rhythm composed of several percussive sounds that integrate a funky guitar riff into its loop. Every 30 seconds or so, the music comes to a halt, sounding as if someone has stopped the record with their hand. At other moments within the song, the sound of human voices in a bar or restaurant appear momentarily before drifting away. At another moment about three and a half minutes in, the song reaches a calm lull before rearranging itself. The rhythm gets reconstructed with a bongo sound while the guitar gets replaced by a piano. This second phase of the song has a faster pace and a stronger sense of rhythm, perfect for increasing the energy on a dancefloor. —*Jason Birchmeier*

**Shades of Jae (Parts 1 & 2) [Single]** / May 31, 1999 / KDJ ♦♦♦♦
Some of Kenny Dixon, Jr.'s Moodymann records serve as wonderful records for home listening while others function better as records for the dancefloor. Of Dixon's many wonderful records—and there are many—*Shades of Jae* is arguably his quintessential dancefloor record. Released in 1999 and still heard to this day by a wide-ranging roster of house DJs in and outside of the Detroit area, *Shades of Jae* had to have been written with a DJ in mind. First of all, there are two versions of the song that work well when mixed together (assuming that a DJ has two copies). Secondly, the song has to be one of the most funky records ever written, with the syncopated collage of quiet jingling, subtle handclaps, keyboard melodies, and soul-drenched vocal samples. Finally, Dixon makes this song funky *without* using a bassline, which is almost unheard of, especially for a house anthem. The second, shorter version doesn't mess around with the anticipatory foreplay of the first, instead delivering the kick drum beats for the duration of the song. —*Jason Birchmeier*

## Moonshake

**f.** 1991, London, England, **db.** 1997
*Group / Indie Pop, Ambient Pop, Dream Pop, Indie Rock, Alternative Pop/Rock*

Experimental pop outfit Moonshake was led by Dave Callahan, the onetime frontman of the C-86 group the Wolfhounds; after several years away from the music scene, he resurfaced in early 1991, placing an ad in *Melody Maker* calling for bandmates. Among those who responded were vocalist Margaret Fiedler, bassist John Frenett, and drummer Michael Rother, and within just four days of their formation, Moonshake—so named after a track on Can's *Future Days* LP—entered the studio to record their debut EP *First* for Creation Records. After jumping to the Too Pure label, the group resurfaced later in 1992 with the *Secondhand Clothes* EP, followed shortly by the *Beautiful Pigeon;* the full-length *Eva Luna*—a brilliant collision of breakbeats and guitar noise drawing influence from disparate sources ranging from dub to krautrock to hip-hop—brought their prolific year to a close. After the 1993 EP *Big Good Angel* EP, Fiedler—who shared vocal and songwriting duties with Callahan—and Frenett quit to form Laika; adding new bassist Matt Brewer and saxophonist Raymond M. Dickaty, Moonshake recorded 1995's *The Sound Your Eyes Can Follow*, a radical departure from previous efforts which almost completely eliminated guitars in favor of a vast palette of samples. After 1996's *Dirty & Divine*, Callahan relocated from London to New York, a move which hastened Moonshake's mid-1997 break-up. —*Jason Ankeny*

● **Eva Luna** / 1992 / Matador/Atlantic ♦♦♦♦
The only full-length album recorded by Moonshake's original lineup, *Eva Luna* is bursting with ideas and tension; dissonant instrumental lines careen off of both noisy samples and spacey dream pop textures, resting on a bed of hypnotic dub bass grooves and deliberate, deeply funky percussion. Just as exciting as the seemingly alien soundscapes is the precarious coalition between singers and songwriters Dave Callahan and Margaret Fiedler, who weave their divergent songwriting and performance approaches into something of a double-sided personality. Callahan delivers his tales of despairing cynicism and rage over modern urban life with theatrical growls and nasal wails, while Fiedler's hushed murmurs and understated purr belie the aggression lurking under her songs' often nightmarish psycho-sexual dramas. Above all, *Eva Luna*'s sound collages are dark and edgy, regardless of whether their overall tone is mellow or furious; the album's dense layers of sonic detail and the ebb and flow between Callahan and Fiedler's contrasting songwriting styles make it a richly inventive, endlessly fascinating listen—and unfortunately the only full-length album of its kind in the group's oeuvre. Matador's American reissue appends the three tracks from the "Secondhand Clothes" single. —*Steve Huey*

**The Sound Your Eyes Can Follow** / 1995 / Too Pure/American ♦♦♦

**Dirty & Divine** / May 21, 1996 / C/Z ♦♦♦♦
*Dirty and Divine* shows Moonshake painting their soundscapes with an intriguing sonic palette. As might be expected for a band named after a Can song, they draw from that band's hypnotic, minimalist grooves, but also incorporate bits of jazz, hip-hop, and dub, as well as the contemporary influence of Stereolab, even if they aren't as melodic as that band. —*Steve Huey*

## David Morales

**b.** Aug. 21, 1961, Brooklyn, NY
*Remixing, Producer, DJ / Club/Dance, House*

Known (and often derided) for his occupation as remixer to the stars during the '90s, David Morales was one of the pioneers of house music in New York, an original head from the '70s who weathered the change-over from disco to house and teamed up with Frankie Knuckles to form the leading early remix team, Def Mix. During the '90s the dance mainstream became aligned to many of his stylistic trademarks—vocal breaks, uptempo piano riffs, plenty of strings—resulting in clichés attributed to both of them. Also, Morales hasn't been involved in own-name record production as much as his few peers (Knuckles, Junior Vasquez, Todd Terry), but Morales found a dancefloor hit with the 1994 single "In De Ghetto."

His beginnings were certainly not so refined; born in Brooklyn to Puerto Rican immigrants, Morales lived his early life in quite a rough section of the Brooklyn projects and was once shot while growing up. He dropped out of high school after ninth grade, and worked as a cook while supplementing his meager living with a job as a DJ (he had been collecting records since the age of 14). Turned on to disco at crucial clubs like the Loft and the Paradise Garage, Morales was soon working at the Garage as well after hooking up with For the Record, an early DJ management firm. His reputation spread during the late '70s and early '80s until he had DJed at every major club in the New York area. One of the first underground house hits in the New York area, "Do It Properly" (by 2 Puerto Ricans, a Black Man, and a Dominican) was a production helmed by Morales, with Chep Nunez, Robert Clivilles, and David Cole. Moving on to remix and production work during the '80s, he hooked up with another major house legend, Frankie Knuckles (through For the Record) to form the Def Mix Productions crew, and his Red Zone remixes became known as important sign-posts in the developing progressive house movement.

Increasingly though, as dance music began appealing to a wider clientele, Morales' mixes attuned themselves more to the mainstream of dance and his material often garnered airplay on daytime radio as well as in nightclubs. After making his name in the pop charts with an early Def Mix for Seal, he began working with a role call of the era's major pop stars: Mariah Carey, Madonna, Michael Jackson, U2, Janet Jackson, Tina Turner, and Björk, among them. A major-label contract with Mercury resulted in the 1994 single "In De Ghetto," a reasonable club hit, and Morales' debut album, *The Program*. He's also a top-flight DJ, known for pushing a sound much harder than that found on his own remixes. —*John Bush*

**The Program** / Jul. 20, 1993 / PolyGram ◆◆◆
The debut David Morales album is quite a community affair, considering the producer recruited names like legendary reggae sidemen like Sly & Robbie and Collin York plus dance supremos Peter Daou and Eric Kupper. Despite a too-many-cooks air hanging over the proceedings, the title track and "In Da Ghetto" are infectious singles. —*John Bush*

● **United DJ's of America, Vol. 4** / Jul. 18, 1995 / DMC ◆◆◆◆
A two-disc set with David Morales on the first and his remix partner Frankie Knuckles on the second, *United DJ's of America, Vol. 4* showcases great sets by both DJs. Morales selects tracks from Lee Genesis, Disco Elements, Maydie Myles, and DJ Dexter, while Knuckles goes for more of a soul/garage vibe with Kerri Chandler, Romanthony, Kathy Sledge, and Barbara Tucker, as well as Way Out West and Deep Dish. —*John Bush*

**Ministry of Sound Presents: The Sessions, Vol. 7** / Feb. 17, 1997 / Ministry of Sound ◆◆◆

## Morcheeba

f. 1995, London, England
Group / Electronica, Trip-Hop, Club/Dance, Alternative Pop/Rock, Urban
The most groove-oriented act in the mid-'90s female-fronted electronica crowd, Morcheeba rely on the sweet, fluid vocals of Sky Edwards and a laid-back mix of fusion, funk, and blues produced by brothers Paul and Ross Godfrey, on beats/scratches and guitar/keyboards respectively. The trio was formed in 1995 when the Godfreys decided to go out on their own after co-producing six tracks for David Byrne's album *Feelings*. They submitted several tapes of their instrumental demos to labels around London, but received little interest in return. After hooking up with vocalist Edwards at a party, however, their music began to gel and Morcheeba signed to the China label. After the release of two EPs (*Trigger Hippie* and *Music That We Hear*), the trio issued their debut album, *Who Can You Trust?* It appeared on the American Discovery label in late 1996, and Morcheeba toured the US with Live and Fiona Apple the following year. *Big Calm* followed in 1998 and *Fragments of Freedom* was released two years later. —*John Bush*

**Who Can You Trust?** / Sep. 24, 1996 / Discovery ◆◆◆◆
Slower, smoother, and more soulful than Portishead and less pop-oriented than the Sneaker Pimps, Morcheeba has an alluringly dark sound that nevertheless remains accessible. As their debut *Who Can You Trust?* illustrates, the trio has a keen sense of how to make a pop melody seem dangerous and foreign by having it crawl out of the murk of creeping beats and ominous samples. Although the group lacks the visionary spark of Tricky and Portishead, and their songs aren't as bracing as the Sneaker Pimps, Morcheeba has a distinctive, idiosyncratic sound that makes *Who Can You Trust?* entrancing. Although the latter half of the album tends to sound a little samey, without many beats or hooks to distinguish each song, the album remains a hauntingly atmospheric—and quite terrific—debut. —*Stephen Thomas Erlewine*

● **Big Calm** / Mar. 16, 1998 / Sire ◆◆◆◆
Realizing that trip-hop was a dead end, at least as far as hipness goes, Morcheeba expanded their sonic palette on their second album, *Big Calm*. Trip-hop and dance rhythms remain, but the trio has spent more time writing songs, crafting an album where pop, lounge, film soundtracks, reggae, jazz, and electronica all peacefully coexist. Consequently, *Big Calm* is a stylistic tour de force, evidence that Morcheeba has turned into a mature, sophisticated group with impeccable taste. Occasionally, the album can sound a little distant, as if the fusions and productions were more important than the actual songs, but the trio is so musically adept, and Sky Edwards' voice is so enchanting, that *Big Calm* become irresistible in its own way. —*Stephen Thomas Erlewine*

**Who Can You Trust?/Beats & B-Sides** / Dec. 1, 1998 / Sire ◆◆◆
The limited-edition *Who Can You Trust?/Beats & B-Sides* appends an eight-cut bonus disc to Morcheeba's engagingly atmospheric 1996 debut; while the added material is far from revelatory, fans of the group will want the extras anyway, primarily for the intriguing remixes of songs including "Killer Hippie," "Tape Loop," and "Shoulder Holster." —*Jason Ankeny*

**Fragments of Freedom** / Aug. 1, 2000 / Sire ◆◆
Even though Morcheeba was one of the later, straggling entries in the trip-hop phenomenon, their previous albums succeed because of the interplay between Sky Edwards' sweetly sensual, airy voice and the band's correspondingly mellow grooves. Unfortunately, their third album *Fragments of Freedom* scraps most of their signature sound for half-baked experiments in R&B, acid jazz, and hip-hop. Though it's certainly understandable that the group would want to move away from the dead-and-buried trip-hop sound that defined them originally, it seems that Morcheeba are just using bands like Brand New Heavies and M People as sonic templates instead of Tricky and Portishead. The bland, overly slick production softens any impact that soulless soul songs such as "Rome Wasn't Built in a Day" and "Love Is Rare" might have had, and while Edwards may be blessed with a *soulful* voice, she's unconvincing belting out pseudo-sultry lyrics like "Is that a rocket in your pocket?" The group's misguided forays into hip-hop are even worse; Mr. Complex's guest rap on "Love Sweet Love" sounds like it was surgically grafted from another track entirely, and while Bahamadia's appearance on "Good Girl Down"'s celebration of sisterhood makes more sense, it still sounds out of place with Edwards' essentially refined, delicate style. Not every song on *Fragments of Freedom* is ill-conceived, however; the opening track, "World Looking In," ranks among their finest, and the steel drum instrumental "A Well Deserved Break" is pretty and refreshing. Despite its annoying, overpowering synth bass, "Shallow End" boasts a lilting, seductive melody that showcases Edwards' voice instead of fighting against it, and the title track is a pleasant enough piece of trip-hop pastiche. But for the most part, *Fragments of Freedom*'s contrived attempts to bring the funk to Morcheeba's sound are as fake and painful as a forced smile. —*Heather Phares*

## David Morley

Producer / Electro-Techno, Ambient Techno, Electro, Techno, Ambient
Although producer David Morley has been involved in a range of recording projects, encompassing trance and techno as well as the more ambient and "intelligent" offshoots thereof, his work has been marked by a consistent experimentalism, earning him a reputation as a compositional innovator among producers, DJs, and home listeners the world over. Born and raised in England, Morley's name is most often associated with the Belgian techno scene, primarily due to early R&S releases as Spectrum, TZ4, and under his own name which helped to solidify the label's nascent sound. Spectrum's "Brazil," recorded with R&S owner Renaat Vandepapeliere, was a visionary fusion of dancefloor techno/trance and ambient/experimental strains that helped earn R&S its association as an important force at the fore of European dance music. Morley, together with Outlander's Marcos Salon, was also behind the fourth release (known as TZ4) in R&S' *Test Zone* series, an important signpost in R&S' early development. In 1994, Morley released his first two EPs under his own name—*Evolution* (the first release on R&S sublabel Apollo) and *Shuttle* (on R&S-proper)—both exploratory ambient/electro classics that sit neatly next to the works of such artists as Biosphere, Aphex Twin, and Higher Intelligence Agency as early examples of ambient/intelligence techno. More recently, Morley has released increasingly dark and tex-

tural works, both solo and in combination with former Inky Blacknuss collaborator/current Mo'Wax signee Andrea Parker. In addition to the pair's Infonet EP *Angular Art* (1995), Morley and Parker recorded the *Too Good to Be Strange* EP (Apollo, 1995) under the name Two Sandwiches Short of a Lunchbox, as well as contributed tracks to R&S ambient sublabel Apollo's second label comp *The Divine Compilation*. Morley's debut full-length, *Tilted*, appeared on Apollo in 1998. —*Sean Cooper*

**Shuttle [EP]** / 1994 / R&S ♦♦♦

Morley steps up to R&S proper for his second EP, although his brand of thumpy ambient techno hasn't become any more (or less) danceable. Five tracks here, with a reworking of the celebrated "Evolution," as well as some striking melodic and textural work filling out another solid release. —*Sean Cooper*

**Angular Art [Single]** / 1995 / Infonet ♦♦♦♦

Yet another David Morley/Andrea Parker's one-off (see also Two Sandwiches Short of a Lunchbox), this time for the Infonet label. "Angular Art" is a far cry indeed from the English techno imprint's usual floor-stomp fare, wedding deep, ominous piano lines with blunt, monochromatic electro beats (ala Parker's "Melodious Thunk"). Some of both Parker and Morley's finest (if somewhat simplistic) work to date. —*Sean Cooper*

● **Stardancer [EP]** / 1996 / Apollo ♦♦♦♦

Four tracks of ambient-leaning experimental music, two beat-oriented, which consistently beguile even the formalist's attempts at classification. Morley's rep for almost unerring innovation finds verification in the classic but nonetheless wholly original waves of deep, lush analog synth passages, wed on one of each of the sides' two tracks to a warped, pulsing, almost implicit beat. Essential. —*Sean Cooper*

**Tilt [Single]** / Sep. 1, 1997 / R&S ♦♦♦

Breaking a year-plus silence during which Morley's Apollo full-length, *Aquarium*, grabbed the title for Most Distended Release Delay in the label's history, *Tilt* was likely released as an attention-span saver, designed to cool the fidgets of Morley die-not-that-hards. Ponderous, then, it appeared on R&S, but it's at least a 50-50 split between Morley's older, danceable stuff and a more engrossing brand of downbeat ambient/electro-dub approached with 1996's *Stardancer* EP. Not Morley's best, neither is *Tilt* his worst. —*Sean Cooper*

**Tilted** / Jan. 19, 1998 / Apollo ♦♦♦♦

## Giorgio Moroder

b. Apr. 26, 1940, Ortisei, Italy
*Synthesizer, Producer, Composer / Pop/Rock, Disco, Dance-Pop*

One of the principal architects of the disco sound, producer and composer Giorgio Moroder was born in Ortisei, Italy, on April 26, 1940. Upon relocating to Munich, Germany, he established his own studio, Musicland, and recorded his debut single "Looky, Looky" in 1969; his first LP, *Son of My Father*, was released in early 1972. Around that time Moroder was introduced to fellow aspiring musician Pete Bellotte, with whom he formed a production partnership; in collaboration with singer Donna Summer, the duo was to become one of the most powerful forces in '70s-era dance music, their success beginning with the release of 1974's *Lady of the Night*. Summer's *Love to Love You Baby* followed in 1975; the title track, clocking in at close to 17 minutes in length, was an international smash, its shimmering sound and sensual attitude much copied in the years to follow.

At their mid-'70s peak, Moroder, Bellotte, and Summer were extraordinarily prolific, releasing new albums about once every six months. Concept records like 1976's *A Love Trilogy* and *Four Seasons of Love* culminated with the release of 1977's *I Remember Yesterday*, a trip through time which climaxed with the smash "I Feel Love." With its galloping bassline and futuristic, computerized sheen, the single was among the watershed hits of the disco era, and helped propel Summer to new prominence as the reigning diva of the dancefloor.

In 1978, Moroder made his initial foray into film music, winning an Academy Award for his score to Alan Parker's *Midnight Express*. Summer's double LP *Bad Girls* followed in 1979, becoming a massive hit and spawning such chart-topping singles as "Hot Stuff" and the title cut. After one final studio LP, 1980's *The Wanderer*, the Moroder/Bellotte/Summer team disbanded, and the disco era began drawing to a close.

In the early '80s, Moroder focused primarily on films; after producing the soundtracks for pictures including *American Gigolo* and *Cat People*, he turned to 1983's *Flashdance*, earning his second Oscar for the hit "Flashdance...What a Feeling," performed by Irene Cara. In 1984, Moroder courted controversy from film purists for his contemporary electro-pop score to the restored release of Fritz Lang's silent-era masterpiece *Metropolis*. After contributing to the soundtrack of the 1986 hit *Top Gun*, he turned increasingly away from dance music to focus on rock, producing the album *Flaunt It*, the debut from the heavily hyped British flash-in-the-pan Sigue Sigue Sputnik. In the years to follow, Moroder kept a low profile on the pop charts, although he remained a fixture on film soundtracks. In the '90s, he also turned to remixing, debuting with a reworking of Eurythmics' "Sweet Dreams (Are Made of This)" and going on to tackle material from Heaven 17 and others. —*Jason Ankeny*

**Knights in White Satin** / 1976 / Oasis ♦♦

★ **From Here to Eternity** / 1977 / Casablanca ♦♦♦♦♦

*From Here to Eternity* is Moroder's quasi-instrumental masterpiece, a continuous mix of banging Eurodisco complete with vocoder effects and this statement on the back cover—"Only electronic keyboards were used on this recording." The metallic beats, high-energy impact, and futuristic effects prove that Moroder was ahead of his time like few artists of the '70s (Kraftwerk included), and the free-form songwriting on tracks like "Lost Angeles," "First Hand Experience in Second Hand Love," and the title track are priceless. The 1985 quasi-compilation *From Here to Eternity...And Back* included most of the original album plus new tracks and a remix of the single "Chase." —*John Bush*

**Midnight Express** / 1978 / Atlantic ♦♦♦♦

Though there are a few queasy pop/vocal tracks, Moroder's soundtrack to *Midnight Express* earns points for an array of exploratory synthesizer pieces (including "Wheel" and "Cacaphoney") as well as its opener, "Chase." One of Moroder's biggest hits, the track bounces back and forth between melodic disco and hypnotic sequencer trance just one step removed from the likes of Tangerine Dream. —*John Bush*

**16 Early Hits** / 1991 / BMG ♦♦♦

With an assortment of early tracks recorded between 1966 and 1972, *16 Early Hits* focuses on novelty songs, straightahead rock 'n' roll, and several examples of late-'60s electronic bubblegum. It's a bit of a surprise to find Moroder's distinctive songwriting sense and flair for using odd instruments (and production techniques) in place this early, it's only recommended for *fanatical* Moroder fans or those who don't mind incredibly Beatle-esque pop music. —*John Bush*

## Mother Mallard's Portable Masterpiece Co.

f. 1969, Ithaca, NY
*Group / Electronic*

The world's first synthesizer ensemble was formed by David Borden in 1969, initially as a live band to perform their own versions of classics from the classical/minimalist repertoire of Terry Riley, Steve Reich, Robert Ashley, and Philip Glass. Borden had been working as composer-in-residence for the Ithaca, New York school district when he became aware of developments in synthesizer technology by Bob Moog. After being invited to Moog's nearby company, Borden became one of the first to test-drive the revolutionary Moog synthesizer. (His ignorance of module synthesizers helped along many design changes that made Moogs much more user-friendly than their predecessors.) Intrigued with the idea of live synthesizer performance in a band setting, Borden joined with Steve Drews and (later) Linda Fisher. After several performances associated with Cornell University (where Borden also worked) as well as a few in-store demonstrations for Moog, Mother Mallard began recording in 1970. They continued to perform in various live settings, but wasn't able to release material until 1973, when Judy Borsher agreed to found Earthquack Records to release material by the group (she also replaced Fisher). The group's self-titled debut album appeared that year, followed by *Like a Duck to Water* in 1976. Though Mother Mallard gradually disintegrated as a recording concern, Borden continued to record as a solo artist; in the early '90s, Mother Mallard reunited to perform several live shows and returned again later in the decade. In 1999, Cuneiform released the retrospective *1970-1973*. —*John Bush*

**Mother Mallard's Portable Masterpiece Co.** / 1973 / Earthquack ♦♦♦♦

**Like a Duck to Water** / 1976 / Earthquack ♦♦♦

• **1970-1973** / Jan. 18, 1999 / Cuneiform ♦♦♦♦
This reissue of the earliest work by Mother Mallard's Portable Masterpiece Co. includes all of their first album, plus almost 20 minutes of previously unreleased material. The group wore their minimalist influences quite well, resulting in tracks which take the cycling repetitions of work by Steve Reich into new territory altogether, as on the 12-minute "Music." Most of the music here is a bit beyond minimalism; in fact, it's much closer to exploratory protospace music or new age on the highlights "Ceres Motion" and "Cloudscape for Peggy," the latter of which was composed around the time acts like Tangerine Dream and Cluster were just getting started. —*John Bush*

## Motorbass

f. 1994, Paris, France
*Group / Electronica, Club/Dance, House*

Philippe Zdar and Etienne De Crecy are the names behind Parisian disco house duo Motorbass, whose romping '70s updates released on the Cassius and Source labels have been instrumental in reviving the Parisian underground dance music scene and bringing to it international attention. Although, like similar hype targets Daft Punk, Motorbass have scarcely more than a few singles and an album to their name, their mature, confident fusion of hip-hop and funk with the party vibe of disco and the driving soul of house has made their name almost synonymous with innovative club music. Formed by Zdar and Crecy in 1994, the group's first releases, "Motorbass" and "Transfunk," followed their work behind the boards on noted French artist MC Solaar's first two albums. Zdar grew up in the south of France (his primary musical focus growing up was as the drummer in a speed metal band), and moved to Paris after discovering jazz in his late teens. Immersing himself in music production, Zdar met Crecy early on and the pair's gradual exposure to Paris' acid-house underground added Chicago and New York influences such as Marshall Jefferson and Giorgio Moroder to the mix. *Pansoul*, the group's 1996 debut, was praised upon its release as an almost instant classic, and played a catalytic role in bringing attention to the Paris underground in 1996—attention which has since brought groups such as Dimitri, Daft Punk, and Air (whose self-titled EP on Source was reissued by trip-hop stronghold Mo'Wax that same year) to wider recognition. In addition to Motorbass, Philippe Zdar is also the main force behind Mo'Wax dance-funk group La Funk Mob, who've released a pair of singles and a mini-album through the label. —*Sean Cooper*

• **Pansoul** / Jul. 1, 1996 / Cassius ♦♦♦♦
The only album released by Motorbass is a solid LP of retro-disco with minimal grooves and no more than a short vocal sample or two to drive most tracks. This sort of thing was much easier to take before Daft Punk upped the ante with *Homework*, but the attention to detail on tracks like "Ezio" and "Fabulous" make it a solid album. —*Keith Farley*

## Mouse on Mars

f. 1993, Düsseldorf, Germany
*Group / Experimental Ambient, Experimental Techno, Electronica, Electro-Techno, Ambient Techno, Post-Rock/Experimental, IDM*

German post-techno duo Mouse on Mars are among a growing number of electronic music groups dabbling in complex, heavily hybridized forms that include everything from ambient, techno, and dub to rock, jazz, and jungle. The combined efforts of Andi Toma and Jan St. Werner (of Cologne and Düsseldorf, respectively), MoM formed in 1993, reportedly after Werner and Toma met at a death metal concert. Working from Werner's studio, the pair fused an admiration for the early experiments of Kraut-rock outfits like Can, Neu!, Kluster, and Kraftwerk into an off-beat update including influences from the burgeoning German techno and ambient scenes. A demo of material found its way to London-based guitar-ambient group Seefeel, who passed it on to the offices of their label, Too Pure. MOM's first single, "Frosch," was released by the label soon after, and was also included on the debut album, *Vulvaland*. Immediately hailed for its beguiling, inventive edge that seemed to resist all efforts at easy "schublade" (an even less flattering approximation of the English "pigeonhole"), *Vulvaland* was reissued in 1995 by (oddly) Rick Rubin's American Recordings label, who also released their follow-up, *Iaora Tahiti*, soon after. More upbeat and varied than their debut, the album made some inroads into the American marketplace, but the group's somewhat challenging complexity and steadfast refusal to pander make widespread popularity unlikely. They returned in 1997 with three different releases—the EP *Cache Coeur Naif*, the LP *Autoditacker*, and the vinyl-only *Instrumentals*. Another vinyl-only release (*Glam*) appeared in 1998, and was followed a year later by the "official" follow-up to *Autoditacker*, *Niun Niggung*. Although remixes are rare, the group have been appearing with increasing frequency on compilations of experimental electronic music, including Volume's popular *Trance Europe Express* series. They were also prominently featured on a pair of tribute albums—*Folds and Rhizomes* and *In Memoriam*—dedicated to French poststructuralist philosopher Gilles Deleuze. Werner also records as half of the duo Microstoria (with Oval's Markus Popp) and solo as Lithops. —*Sean Cooper*

**Vulvaland** / 1994 / Too Pure/American ♦♦♦♦
A wibbly, barely digital match of ambient texturology with experimental strains of techno, dub, and krautrock. While the flip relies too heavily on four-on-the-floor ambient house clichés, the A-side is a prize, cultivating a weird, electronics-based avant-pop vibe as successful as it is unique. —*Sean Cooper*

★ **Iaora Tahiti** / Oct. 3, 1995 / Too Pure/American ♦♦♦♦♦
More upbeat and with far greater detail than the debut, *Iaora Tahiti* proves Werner and Toma haven't stood still. The pair's fondness for all things lo-fi follows them here, but just as evident is a depth and punch lacking in their earlier material. Jungle-style programming pops up on the first single, "Bib," as well as elements of dub, funk, industrial, film soundtracks, and musique concrète. Their finest work to date. —*Sean Cooper*

**Cache Coeur Naif [EP]** / 1997 / Too Pure ♦♦♦♦
In 1997, while American bands were struggling to incorporate the trendy gadgetry of electronica into their acts and major labels were running around trying to sign Their Own Private Chemical Brothers, many of the European scene's more stalwart experimentalists (Aphex Twin, Warp Records, Mark Van Hoen, Witchman) were drawing on the catchiness of the pop tradition by adding vocalists, quoting '70s soul and jazz in their music, and/or (in Warp's case) signing jazz-funk (Jimi Tenor, Red Snapper) and rock (Broadcast) acts to their rosters. Mouse On Mars make their bid on the former with "Cache Coeur Naif," a 4-track EP (and the group's first release under their own name in more than 2 years) featuring Stereolab vocalists Mary Hansen and Laetitia Sadier. While only one of the songs features vocals in anything like a "pop" sense (verse-chorus-etc.), each incorporates at least a Hansen whisper or a Sadier purr (en Francaise, natch) wrapped around gloriously off-kilter, bleached-out dub-electro rhythms and the usual, Mars-bound assortment of wheezy bleeps, whirrs, and crackles. An excellent return. —*Sean Cooper*

☆ **Autoditacker** / Aug. 18, 1997 / Thrill Jockey ♦♦♦♦♦
*Autoditacker* finds Mouse on Mars continuing to grow and improve, adding textures and detail to their dense, electronic soundscapes without compromising their sound. They still are indebted to Kraut-rock and dub, but they continue to add new sounds and styles to their music, including long ambient stretches and flirtations with drum'n'bass. There are no silent moments on *Autoditacker*—every inch of the tape is filled with rhythms, keyboards, and electronic squiggles. Each listen reveals new layers of the group's intricate arrangements, and the shifting instrumentation and themes recall the best adventurous jazz in terms of unpredictability. It's another stunning record in a distinguished, inventive catalog. —*Stephen Thomas Erlewine*

**Instrumentals** / Oct. 13, 1997 / Sonig ♦♦♦♦
While previous releases such as *Vulvaland* and *Iaora Tahiti* had more or less of their share of remarkable moments, *Instrumentals* is the closest thing yet to the sort of album the best of those moments suggested Mouse On Mars was capable of. Unlike the jittery pop electronica of MoM's only months-previously issued *Autoditacker*, *Instrumentals* (released on their newly launched Sonig label) profiles the group's more relaxed, experimental side, working tracks up out of a mush of warm, sputtery electronics and vaguely bouncing rhythms. The album is only about 70 percent new material (it includes MoM's contributions to two Sub Rosa compilations dedicated to the work of philosopher Gilles Deleuze), but the placement of the two recycled tracks in the context of an album of which the rest matches them in both quality and atmosphere makes *Instrumentals* undoubtedly MoM's most enjoyable and consistent effort. Vinyl only, but worth buying a turntable for. —*Sean Cooper*

**Glam** / Jul. 20, 1998 / Sonig ♦♦♦♦
This LP of warm, grubby electronica was originally recorded as the soundtrack to an American film staring Tony "Who's the Boss?" Danza, and finally saw general (if somewhat limited) release in 1998, after it became clear the film

would never be completed. Despite the passage of time, however (most of these tracks date from '93 and '94), *Glam* contains some of Toma and Werner's most compelling material to date, and listens like a sort of combined laboratory/proving ground for the dauby, impressionistic abstraction later pursued on the 1997 MoM LP *Instrumentals* and by Werner side project Lithops. The least "genrefied" of MoM's already exceptionally itinerant discography, *Glam* is also wonderfully diverse, mixing tracks containing clamorous, sometimes goofy rhythms with introspective cuts consisting of little more than patterned clicks and raspy, absorbing organ drones. —*Sean Cooper*

**Niun Niggung** / 1999 / Domino ♦♦♦♦
From the first few seconds of Mouse on Mars' sixth full-length, it appeared that Germany's most inventive duo had deserted the bubble'n'squeak electronica they'd trademarked and instead gone the way of instrument-driven post-rockers like Tortoise or Kreidler. There's a chamber quartet in attendance, and a hushed air that sounds almost mature. After a minute of suspense though, things go all wibbly and electronic fans will find themselves back in the happy preserves of prime Mouse on Mars. The duo's vision of techno on *Niun Niggung* is impeccably perfectionist but texturally messy and surprisingly organic: it's electronic dance as produced by robotic hillpeople. The highlight is "Super Sonig Fadeout," a propulsive track that begins with several moments of metallic distortion. Slowly, ingeniously, the noise organizes itself into a loping, incredibly funky beat that drives the rest of the track. The music on *Niun Niggung* far too much fun to provoke the question of whether Toma and St. Werner have progressed or not (which is always a matter for serious analysis in electronic circles), but the album does occasionally sound more like an attempt to duplicate the Mouse on Mars formula than the real thing. [The British and German release of *Niun Niggung* included a radically different configuration from the American release.] —*John Bush*

## Move D (David Moufang)

f. 1993
*Group / Ambient Techno, Club/Dance, Techno*
In addition to his solo recordings for Source, Fax, and Compost, Move D's David Moufang has also partnered with Jonas Grossman (as Deep Space Network) and Jonah Sharp (as Reagenz) to produce many of the best explorations of leftfield techno and trip-hop recorded during the '90s. In 1992, he founded Source Records (based in Heidelberg, Germany) with Grossman, and the pair released their first material together that same year, as Earth to Infinity. One year later, Moufang and Grossman released their first Deep Space Network LP, *Big Rooms*, and the album received American distribution through Instinct. Moufang branched out in a big way during 1994-95: he released the solo album *Solitaire* on Fax, the Move D debut *Kunststoff* on Source, and collaborated with Spacetime Continuum's Jonah Sharp as Reagenz for a self-titled album on Reflective.

Moufang's often confusing timeline continued in 1996 with another Move D release (*Exploring the Psychedelic Landscape*) and two more DSN works, *Deep Space Network Meets Higher Intelligence Agency* and *Traffic: Live at the Love Parade*. In 1997, he inaugurated yet another project, an ambient-jazz unit known as Conjoint. [See Also: Deep Space Network] —*John Bush*

● **Solitaire** / 1994 / Fax ♦♦♦
Moufang's first solo project for Fax is a pretty minimal affair, similar to the *I.F.* series but without quite the breadth of sounds. Moufang restricts himself to an 808 and maybe two or three synths for the entirety of the disc, which shifts track to track between moody, soundtrackish ambient and more upbeat techno- and electro-derived listening music. —*Sean Cooper*

**Kunststoff** / 1994 / Source ♦♦♦
Offbeat experimental techno not dissimilar from his Reagenz and Earth to Infinity projects. —*Sean Cooper*

## µ-Ziq (Michael Paradinas)

b. 1971, Wimbledon, London, England
*Remixing, Producer / Experimental Techno, Electronica, Ambient Techno, Jungle/Drum'N'Bass, Techno, IDM*
One of the premiere names in the field of electronic home-listening music, Mike Paradinas' recordings retained the abrasive flavor of early techno pioneers and explored the periphery of experimental electronica even while coddling to his unusual ear for melody, the occasional piece of vintage synthesizer and distorted beat-box rhythms. While his side-projects—including Diesel M, Jake Slazenger, Gary Moscheles, Kid Spatula, and Tusken Raiders—have often emphasized (or satired) his debts to jazz, funk, and electro, Paradinas reserved his most original and exciting work for major album releases as µ-Ziq. Early µ-Ziq LPs were based around the most ear-splitting buzz-saw percussion ever heard (in a musical environment or otherwise), with fast-moving though deceptively fragile synthesizer melodies running over the top. As Paradinas began weaving his various influences into a convincing whole, his work became more fully developed (though possibly not as exciting), a fluid blend of breakbeat hip-hop and drum'n'bass with industrial effects and the same brittle melodies from his earlier work.

Born in Wimbledon (though he grew up in several other spots around London), Paradinas began playing keyboards during the early '80s and listened to new wave bands like Human League and New Order. He joined a few bands in the mid-'80s, then spent eight years on keyboards for the group Blue Innocence. During that time, however, Paradinas had been recording on his own as well with synthesizers and a four-track recorder. When Blue Innocence disintegrated in 1992, he and bass player Francis Naughton bought sequencing software and re-recorded some of Paradinas' old material. After the material was played for Mark Pritchard and Tom Middleton—the duo behind Global Communication and Reload as well as heads of Evolution Records—they wanted to release it; recording commitments later forced Pritchard and Middleton to withdraw their agreement, though by that time Richard D. James (aka Aphex Twin) had also heard the tracks and agreed to release a double-album for his label, Rephlex Records.

The debut album for µ-Ziq (paraphrased from the side of a blank tape and pronounced "mew-zeek") was 1993's *Tango N' Vectif*. The LP set the template for most of Paradinas' later work, with at times shattering metal-cage percussion underpinning a collection of rather melodies. The Rephlex label was just beginning to flourish, with added journalistic attention paid to Aphex Twin's recent *Selected Ambient Works 85-92*, and though James began to feature less in label-doings than co-founder Grant Wilson Claridge, later Rephlex work by Cylob, Luke Vibert (aka Wagon Christ), Seefeel, and Squarepusher made it among the cream of electronic home-listening labels.

When Naughton began taking college more seriously (something Paradinas had attempted briefly, from 1990 through 1992), he officially bowed out of µ-Ziq. Second album *Bluff Limbo* was scheduled to be released in mid-1994, though only 1000 copies made it out of the gate. (It was officially issued by Rephlex in 1996 after Paradinas served papers on the label.) Paradinas' first major-label release came later in 1994, after he undertook a remix project for Virgin Records. The EP *µ-Ziq Vs. The Auteurs* was one of the most high-profile examples of the remix-by-obliteration movement, a burgeoning hobby for many electronica producers in which a pop-song reworking would bear no resemblance to—or trace of—the original.

Though the EP was hardly a prime mover in the sales category, Virgin signed Paradinas to a hefty contract and gave him his own Planet µ sub-label to release his own work as well as develop similar-minded artists. Written into his own contract was a provision for unlimited recording under different names, and during 1995 Paradinas definitely took it to task: he unveiled three aliases and released as many albums in less than a year's time. The nu-skool electro label Clear released his debut single as Tusken Raiders early in the year; it mined the fascination with *Star Wars* and electro music shared by producers like Global Communication, Aphex Twin, and James Lavelle, head of Mo'Wax Records. Clear also released the first Paradinas alias full-length, Jake Slazenger's *MakesARacket*, later in 1995. Although they were still audible, the LP downplayed his electro influences in favor of some rather cheesy synthesizer figures and a previously unheard debt to jazz-funk.

The distortion re-appeared on Paradinas' second LP of the year, *Spatula Freak* by Kid Spatula. The first American-only release of a Paradinas album (it appeared on Jonah Sharp's San Franciso-based Reflective Records), its sound had the metallic feel of the first two µ-Ziq LPs but with a less-dense production job. Just one month after *Spatula Freak*, Paradinas released his first proper µ-Ziq LP for a major label, *In Pine Effect*. The album included tracks recorded from 1993 to 1995, and though it was quite a varied album, the distance appeared to give it quite a disjointed feel.

Paradinas spent 1996 releasing a second Jake Slazenger album (*Das Ist Ein Groovy Beat Ja?* for Warp) and his first as Gary Moscheles (*Shaped to Make Your Life Easier* for Belgium's SSR/Crammed Discs). Both LPs journeyed further down the queasy-listening route of the first Slazenger record, with departures into '80s-style party funk and surprisingly straightahead soul jazz. He also owned a half-share in the Rephlex-released *Expert Knob Twiddlers* (credited as Mike & Rich), the fruit of Paradinas' 1994 recordings with the Aphex Twin.

Paradinas entered 1997 ready to undertake the most ambitious style makeover in his career; the fusion of his home-listening techno with the hypertensive rhythms of street-level drum'n'bass. One year earlier, Aphex Twin had released a single of schizophrenic jungle noodlings ("Hangable Auto Bulb"), and Tom Jenkinson's Squarepusher project had provided the first convincing headphone drum'n'bass act. Paradinas waded into the pool with *Urmur Bile Trax, Vols. 1&2*, a double-EP also released as one full-length compact disc. Though the change-over wasn't completely convincing, the next μ-Ziq full-length more than made up for expectations. *Lunatic Harness* presented a complete synthesis of the many elements in Paradinas' career, from synth-jazz-funk and beat-box electro through to ambient techno and jungle. Though still unable to break through to a mainstream which had recently accepted Prodigy and the Chemical Brothers into the fold, Paradinas and μ-Ziq were introduced to many rock fans after he toured America as the support act for techno chanteuse Björk. [See Also: Kid Spatula, Jake Slazenger] —*John Bush*

☆ **Tango N' Vectif** / Nov. 1993 / Rephlex ♦♦♦♦♦
This album immediately paired the young bedroom rat as a contemporary of Richard "Aphex Twin" James, on whose label it appeared. The offbeat envelope-pushing themes and occasionally heavily distorted percussion sees the comparison through, but that's where the similarity ends. His only full-length work with former bandmate Francis Naughton. —*Sean Cooper*

**Bluff Limbo** / May 1994 / Rephlex ♦♦♦♦
Historically interesting from the standpoint of his later work—shades of Jake Slazenger and Kid Spatula can be heard here—*Bluff Limbo* is nonetheless overly repetitive, relying heavily on the distortion-pedal aesthetic by now a cliche of Rephlex artists (Aphex Twin, Cylob, and Kinesthesia). The album was originally issued promo-only in 1994 (and then with different track listings across formats!) and finally saw proper release in mid-1996. —*Sean Cooper*

**μ-Ziq Vs. The Auteurs [EP]** / Oct. 1994 / Hut/Astralwerks ♦♦♦
An album of remixes of material by solemn British pop group the Auteurs, from their 1993 album *Now I'm a Cowboy*. Unlike remix projects which pair track with doting (or at least neutral-to-positive) fan, this one is notable for Paradinas' well-publicized disdain for the music. He shows as much on the thorough hatchet job to which he submits four of the album's tracks. —*Sean Cooper*

**In Pine Effect** / Oct. 31, 1995 / Astralwerks ♦♦♦♦
His most stylistically developed album under the μ-Ziq name to date. Although Paradinas is big on insisting his music isn't for dancing, most of the tracks here feature a familiar dancefloor pulse, with alternately arresting and sidesplitting melodies floating above signature percussion and some interesting brass work. "Phiesope" even samples Kristen Hersh! —*Sean Cooper*

**Urmur Bile Trax, Vols. 1 & 2** / Feb. 4, 1997 / Astralwerks/Planet μ ♦♦♦
μ-Ziq's Mike Paradinas dives head-first into breakbeat madness with this double-EP/LP of experimental jungle. Released as two different 12"s of roughly the same length (the CD merely collects both), *Urmur Bile Trax* is similar to the recent fast-break experiments of artists such as Luke "Plug" Vibert and Richard "Aphex Twin" James, opting for highly disjointed, complex drum programming and odd, multilayered noise collage instead of consistent groove or dancefloor friendliness. —*Sean Cooper*

★ **Lunatic Harness** / Jun. 30, 1997 / Astralwerks ♦♦♦♦♦
Mike Paradinas' first success story from the frontlines of ambient/electro/drum'n'bass experimentation comes via his second attempt, *Lunatic Harness*. Following the brief but for the most part uninteresting toybox chop-up of 1996's *Urmur Bile Trax*, the album escapes the mire of noncommittal cheekiness (an affectation that also damaged some of his Jake Slazenger work) by returning to early releases such as *Tango 'N Vectif* and *Bluff Limbo* for inspiration, fusing pretty, affecting melodies and dynamic ambient atmospheres with beats that manage a tight balance between structured groove and complete chaos. —*Sean Cooper*

**Royal Astronomy** / Jul. 27, 1999 / Astralwerks ♦♦♦♦
After the drum'n'bass updates on his previous full-length, *Royal Astronomy* in large part returns Mike Paradinas to the green pastures of his youth—electroslanted melodic techno and post-rave ambience with an eye on classics of his early career like *Tango 'N Vectif*. From the cinematic opener "Scaling" and the simple melodies of the single "The Fear" (with vocals by a Japanese-born, British-based author named Kazumi), Paradinas keeps it simple throughout. Indeed, the pendulum bass and synth-strings on "Gruber's Mandolin" could have been taken stock-and-barrel from either of his first two Rephlex albums. Still, there are breakbeats all over this record—and on two of the best tracks, the gorgeous production titled "Carpet Muncher" and "Autumn Acid," a song slightly reminiscent of Aphex Twin's "Windowlicker." There's also plenty of hip-hop attitude on other tracks, from the Gang Starr sample on "The Motorbike Track" to the turntable spinbacks on "The Hwicci Song." For the most part, it's obvious that Paradinas' sampler has moved on and gained for it. —*John Bush*

## Joel Mull

**b.** 1975, Stockholm, Sweden
*Drum Programming, Synthesizer, Producer, DJ / Minimal Techno, Club/Dance, Techno*
Along with his other Swedish peers such as Adam Beyer and Oliver Ho, Joel Mull has been reshaping the sound of techno during the '90s at a young age, emerging as one of the genre's most promising future producers. His musical career began at an early age, six, when he received his first synthesizer, eventually playing for numerous bands during his teens as both a drummer and a keyboard player. In 1991, he attended his first electronic dance music party, heard techno, and began making it his life. By 1993 he bought a sampler, a pair of Technics turntables, and a mixer; he was then a full-fledged techno artist. By the end of the decade, he had recorded for esteemed Swedish labels such as Beyer's Code Red and Christian Smith's Tronic, while also holding down some residencies at Swedish clubs such as Turbulence and also appearing at Berlin's Love Parade with his brand of pummeling techno. —*Jason Birchmeier*

● **Safety Session [EP]** / Jul. 28, 1997 / Code Red ♦♦♦
This EP showcases exactly why Joel Mull has risen to the top of the Swedish camp of techno producers pushing techno towards more percussive heights. —*Jason Birchmeier*

## Murk

**f.** 1991, Miami, FL
*Group / Progressive House, Club/Dance, House*
The toast of the American house underground during the '90s, Cuban American producers Oscar Gaetan and Ralph Falcon stand behind several of the decade's best house tracks, dark numbers whose soulful vocal lines and high charting position bely an acid-tinged ruggedness at odds with the candyfloss arrangements of many dance hits. Most were recorded for their Murk Recordings label—later licensed through MCA/Tribal America—under a variety of aliases and projects including Liberty City, Funky Green Dogs, Deep South, and Coral Way Chief. Gaetan and Falcon grew up together in Miami, and though Falcon spent four of his teenage years at a Georgia military school, both discovered and began enjoying house music independently. The duo gradually entered the Miami dance scene, influenced by early domestic producers Farley Jackmaster Funk and Todd Terry as well as later British comers including A Guy Called Gerald.

After producing a single called "Tricky Jazz" for the local DSR Records, Gaetan and Falcon followed with Mission Control's "Outta Limits," which appeared on an Atlantic compilation in 1992. By that time the pair had already set up Murk Recordings and released singles as Intruder and Interceptor. Their next production was Liberty City's "Some Lovin'," a sublime piece of hypnotic mellowed-out trance recorded with singer Bebe Dozier, a family friend. The single broke them to an international audience, and the Murk boys were soon being called on to DJ around the world.

In 1993, MCA's division of Tribal America responded to the fame, licensing the Murk catalogue in total and issuing *Murk: The Singles Collection*. That same year, another Liberty City single, "If You Really Love Someone," became another club hit. The duo remixed Madonna, Pet Shop Boys, the Beloved, and RuPaul. During 1994, both Gaetan and Falcon concentrated on label ventures of their own (Gee Man Soul and Miami Soul Records, respectively) but then came together to record a Liberty City LP. When the album came out in 1996, however, it was under yet another alias from their early Murk days, Funky Green Dogs. *Get Fired Up* became a crossover hit, thanks to the number one dance single "Fired Up!" and another club hit, "The Way." In 1999, the pair released a volume in the mix series *United DJ's of America*. [See Also: Funky Green Dogs] —*John Bush*

- **Murk: The Singles Collection** / Nov. 16, 1993 / IRS ♦♦♦♦
This early compilation includes Murk tracks by Intruder, Interceptor, Liberty City, and the Funky Green Dogs from Outer Space. The Liberty City track "Some Lovin'" is one of the highlights. —*John Bush*

**Essential Murk & Funky Green Dog Mixes** / May 26, 1998 / Harmless ♦♦♦

A stellar compilation of remixes by various solo and group Falcon/Gaetan aliases, including several for themselves as well as outside productions like Donna Summer, Olive, JayDee, Tin Tin Out, and Boris Dlugosch, among others. —*Keith Farley*

**United DJ's of America: Murk Starring in Miami Vice** / Jul. 27, 1999 / DMC America ♦♦♦

The duo of Oscar Gaetan and Ralph Falcon united for this volume in the *United DJ's of America* series, set in Miami and starring not only the Murk boys but also many of the stars from their production roster, including Funky Green Dogs and Fire Island. The mix is intense and well-ordered, definitely a highlight for mainstream-dance fans from a series of mix albums that have rarely failed to please. —*Keith Farley*

## Muslimgauze (Bryn Jones)

b. 1961, Manchester, England, d. Jan. 14, 1999
*Producer / Experimental Ambient, Experimental Techno, World Fusion*

Bryn Jones was not a practicing Muslim and never went to the Middle East. His recordings as Muslimgauze, however, qualified him as one of the Western artists most explicitly slanted in his favor of the Palestinian liberation movement. Since the Manchester-native's works were instrumental, most of the political statement was inherent in the packaging: Witness titles such as *Fatah Guerrilla, Return of Black September, Hebron Massacre, Vote Hezbollah, United States of Islam*, and *The Rape of Palestine*. Jones could have been a potentially controversial figure if his releases were available in anything except severely limited editions—usually less than one thousand copies of each. Despite their lack of prominence, Jones' blend of found-sound Middle Eastern atmospheres with heavily phased drones and colliding rhythm programs were among the most startling and unique in the noise underground.

Formed in 1982 to protest the Israeli invasion of Lebanon, Muslimgauze's first release was the *Hammer & Sickle* EP, which appeared in 1983 as a response to the Soviet invasion of Afghanistan. During the '80s, Jones averaged almost two Muslimgauze albums per year, plus additional EPs and limited releases (of 500 copies each). With 1990's *Intifaxa* he earned his first release on Extreme Records, an American label with releases by Robert Rich and Paul Schütze. Five albums followed for Extreme in the next four years, while a half-dozen were released on the Dutch Staalplaat, distributed in the States as well through Soleilmoon. As the decade progressed, Muslimgauze's output became even more concentrated—five albums in 1994, six a year later, and an unbelievable eight LPs in 1996. The experimental/noise underground increased in visibility during the late '90s, with Muslimgauze productions gradually encompassing heavier beats and a style close in execution to post-industrial beat-heads Techno Animal, Download, and Scorn. The Muslimgauze project ended tragically in 1999 when Jones died suddenly of a rare blood disease. A number of posthumous releases including *Lo-Fi India Abuse* (partially a collaboration with dub collective Systemwide) and the nine-disc *Box of Silk and Dogs* soon followed. —*John Bush*

**Abu Nidal** / Sep. 1987 / Limited Editions ♦♦♦♦
Dedicated to the PLO and named after one of the most notorious (or alternately most heroic) Palestinian fighters of the time, *Abu Nidal* is one of the better Muslimgauze releases, creating rich, deep music from the basic sources of Arabic and other Muslim backgrounds. The title track immediately commands attention here; while Muslimgauze always had a knack for instant, spot-on atmospherics, "Abu Nidal" stands out as one of the best examples of his talent. Its drifting, sensuous wind sounds and synths create a lovely drone web behind the relentless but not overpowering live percussion drive, all of which is occasionally accentuated by a counterpoint rhythm of bells or other drums. "Green is the Color of the Prophet" takes a slightly gentler approach to the same basic form, but one that's just as striking; it's an ominous dance hinting at something not quite right, while still alive with the joy of performance. "Fatwa" is perhaps the most immediately Western of the tunes, if only because of its more straightforward drum machine punch and pound, almost more akin to contemporaneous Wax Trax! releases, though entirely lacking in guitars. With the sidelong "Gulf War" as the remaining song on the album, *Abu Nidal* is both a fine piece of music and a masterful piece of political agitprop. —*Ned Raggett*

**Iran** / 1989 / Staalplaat ♦
An important release, and not just musically—this turned out to be the first album by Muslimgauze for Staalplaat, the Dutch-based label that, with its sister company Soleilmoon in the United States, proved to be Bryn Jones' staunchest supporter, releasing the lion's share of his massive discography over the course of the '90s and beyond. Only three songs long, *Iran* still deserves attention if only for the killer opening track alone, an extended remix of "Lion of Kandahar." It's a slamming song with a pulsating beat that alternately takes over then subsides back into the mix, as other drums and percussion play around it. Bells, drones, and synth strings flesh out the overall piece, at times doing a radical revamp of the core beat as well. As an example of Muslimgauze's radical fusion of styles, it's near perfect. "Qom" has its points, with a strange, echoing clatter providing the main rhythm among many as the song slowly but surely builds. It still falls a touch flat, however, against the brilliant opening track. "Intifadah" brings it all to a fine conclusion; cymbal clashes herald yet more throbbing beats, occasionally dropping many of the rhythm tracks in various combinations. Some nicely unexpected shifts in tempo are provided, as string and sitar noises, among others, slide out of the speakers. —*Ned Raggett*

**Coup D'etat/Abu Nidal** / 1992 / Soleilmoon ♦♦♦♦
The re-release of these two recordings, which had been long out of print at the time, brought some changes to what had been done before. The first side of *Abu*, the lengthy "Gulfwar," was left off entirely, while *Coup*'s "Una Voca" was removed in favor of three other songs: "Tabula Rasa II" and "Tonton Macoutes II," sequels of sorts to the originals from *Coup*, and "Jarnail Singh," an otherwise unavailable song which, for the most part, gently lopes along to a nicely ambient background, right down to bird calls and other noises from nature. There's an odd little vocal/noise loop of a false ending to keep the listener a bit on edge, though! Meanwhile, the packaging was revamped to include a variety of new images from around the Muslim world. —*Ned Raggett*

**Betrayal** / 1993 / Staalplaat ♦♦
The first Muslimgauze release after the initial peace agreement between Israel and the PLO in late 1993, *Betrayal* has a memorable cover featuring the handshake between Yitzhak Rabin and Yasser Arafat, with its title boldly, simply printed on it. The album dedication itself is "to a united Arab response," so expecting the album, recorded mere days after the handshake, to be a new explosion of musical anger would be the logical conclusion. As it happens, though, *Betrayal* isn't that far removed from *Veiled Sisters;* while not as minimalist, if not repetitive, as that particular release, *Betrayal* relies on the same basic tools of gentle, steady electronic percussion and low-level bass and keyboard shadings. The most immediate changes lie with the various vocal samples on some of the tracks; while not immediately intelligible per se, you get scraps and hints from them, expressing a range of negative emotions regarding the initial peace pact. At the same time, often a subtle but nonetheless effective sense of omen and dire warning lurks throughout the music; the use of bass tones in particular doesn't seem that far removed from what Massive Attack eventually came up with years later on *Mezzanine*. Also, as with *Veiled Sisters*, even the most low-key of changes has a large effect in context, such as the metallic clattering added to the electronic pulsing on the second "Nabius." Overall, the feeling is meditative; this is the kind of music you could put on for a quiet moment, but it's not exactly easy listening in any sense of the word. —*Ned Raggett*

**Citadel** / 1994 / Extreme ♦♦♦
A mixed bag on this effort, *Citadel* was released a couple of years after Muslimgauze stopped recording for Extreme Records; therefore it was possibly compiled from outtakes or other random sources as a result. A number of songs feel more like random noodles than necessarily completed songs; while this has often been a complaint about Muslimgauze's work, it isn't quite as bad here as it is elsewhere, and even the more generic numbers usually have a little something going for them, like the soft wind instrument sounds on "Dharam Hinduja" or the near dubwise production (and, rather surprisingly, dry English spoken vocals at the end!) on "Masawi Wife &

Child." The title track has some strong percussion to its credit, up very high in the mix, with a synth-plucked string loop providing the main melody. "Beit Nuba" and "Ferdowsi" stand out as being two of the most ambient tracks in the Muslimgauze catalog; the beat is present in both, but it's heavily mixed down. "Opel" has much more of a rough electronic/industrial feeling to it than many of the Muslimgauze tracks from around the same time, which is an interesting and unexpected touch for the album; while "Shouf Balek" is equally heavy on the electronics, the effect is much more tinny and chintzy. Rather surprisingly, "Infidel" was chosen as a single from the album; given that it doesn't stand out all that much from any other average Muslimgauze track, its selection seems based on whim more than anything else. —*Ned Raggett*

### Al-Zulfiquar Shaheed / 1994 / T.4 ♦♦♦

Unexpectedly released by Muslimgauze on French label T4 after almost exclusively working with Soleilmoon and Staalplaat for some time, *Shaheed* is no idle one-off. It contains some impressive work even by the band's standards. Consisting of only four tracks, *Shaheed* showcases Bryn Jones' ability to create lengthy, detailed compositions. Continuing the tradition of impressive album openers, "Sadhu" is a 22-minute monster which takes the basics from many Muslimgauze songs—Arabic percussion, droning keyboards, and heavily echoed, dub-styled production—and stretches them even further. The obsessive focus on rhythm at the heart of Jones' work really comes out here, especially over a series of build-ups and sudden halts within the song as it progresses. "Shaheed" mixes hard-to-interpret vocal samples from what sound like a variety of Arabic speakers with a clipped, sharp rhythm push. "Mosaic Palestine" could well be what its title says it is, given all the various samples at play in it, though no exact source is noted for any of them; the core musical track is an attractive, minimal arrangement of stringed instruments and various beats and bells. "Ayodhya Skin and Stone" closes things with a near half-hour effort, often using the shimmering synth string/light percussion combination familiar from releases like *Veiled Sisters*. Here, however, the drumming is live rather than machine-generated, and its intensity changes, rises, and falls throughout the song. Adding more heavily echoed samples and removing or altering the organ tones from time to time results in an often disturbing, murky composition which, while still recognizably Muslimgauze, has its own unique appeal to it. —*Ned Raggett*

### Blue Mosque / 1994 / Staalplaat ♦♦

While "Muzzel of Deceit" isn't as strong an introduction to this double-disc effort as earlier tracks were for their respective albums, it's still a fair effort. It shows Muslimgauze continuing the work begun on *Zealot*, where dub-wise production techniques blend with drones and at times slamming beats,—"Freedom Fighter" being a great example of this (why Muslimgauze hasn't been more readily sampled by other artists remains a mystery)—to create a very modern form out of traditional types of music. "Bir Zeit" stands out here, due to its aggressive electronic feel and distorted rhythm track elements (intentional here as compared to *Zealot*); though the track is mixed relatively low, it sets up an excellent air of looming menace thanks to the strange whispering throughout the track. "Futile Arad Search" is another fine piece; it relies on a strange percussion loop that seems constructed from anything but regular percussion instruments which are set against a slightly more conventional rhythm that surfaces from the wash of sound in the mix. Particularly striking is one part where little but a soft drum machine beat and the sudden shudder of a tambourine come to the fore. Other songs worthy of attention include "Fadhan," with its wheezing electronics layered below a traditional drum performance, the jaunty swing of "Bandit Queen," with its quirky keyboard hook, and the slow, compelling crawl of "Pakistani Nuclear Box." Longer tunes like "Rattan Kiss" sometimes succeed, and sometimes don't; occasionally rising from the music's foreground is the unfortunate slide from entrancing minimalism to relative boredom which can afflict Muslimgauze releases. While not quite up to the same level as *Zealot*, *Blue Mosque* is still another fine Muslimgauze release. —*Ned Raggett*

### Hebron Massacre / 1994 / Soleilmoon ♦♦♦

Written and recorded in a one-day session shortly after the titular event—the February 24, 1994, murders of a number of Palestinians by a crazed Jewish settler at Hebron's Cave of the Patriarchs—the one-track *Hebron Massacre* remains one of the bitterest and most straightforward indictments of Israel ever recorded by Muslimgauze. Given that Bryn Jones' entire musical career concerned such indignation in one way or another, that's saying something, but here his cause isn't limited to the blunt design of the release, featuring news clippings about the tragedy. Mixing a number of samples from interviews in response to the killings, the song has a shrill edge to it, thanks to the chillingly sharp main keyboard synth line set against soft but persistent percussion beats, with a low bass rumble further propelling the track. Simple in comparison to his other works, it still retains a sharp musical and lyrical power with enough alien beauty to make it worth repeated listens. —*Ned Raggett*

### Gun Aramaic / 1995 / Soleilmoon ♦♦♦♦

"Saladin Mercy" begins *Gun* on a familiar touch, perhaps almost too familiar; while a certain consistency to Muslimgauze's work is no surprise, Bryn Jones generally varies things from album to album just enough to create distinct, different listening experiences for each release. Still, "Saladin" feels like something which easily could have been on his previous Soleilmoon/Staalplaat release *Maroon*, with its blend of the drones from earlier pieces and the more recent tweaking and heavy variety in the rhythms throughout the song. The following track, the first "8 am, Tel Aviv, Islamic Jihad," sets things more to rights, with a combination of sharp pulses, echoing roars, and what sounds like a domestic squabble between a couple caught on tape—a characteristically strange combination which again works out quite nicely in the end. A little more than most Muslimgauze releases, *Gun* is very environmental in terms of its composition; the reliance on conversational snippets throughout almost turns the album into a soundtrack for a non-existent film. As is often the case for Muslimgauze, the most fascinating elements of *Gun* often are the simplest, such as the persistent, slow-rising beat in the first "Opiate and Mullah," or the shift from near silence to an elegant, slightly creepy keyboard arrangement about thirteen minutes into "Oil Prophets (pt. 1, 2, 3)." *Gun* wraps things up on a very moody note with the dark rumblings concluding "Oil Prophets (pt. 4, 5)" and the quite brief but deep, moody drones of the second "Opiate and Mullah," making for a slightly unexpected end to a fair album. —*Ned Raggett*

### Maroon / 1995 / Staalplaat ♦♦♦♦

Noteworthy for its attractive paperboard, intense blue ink packaging alone, *Maroon* isn't just all looks; the first piece, the brief "Intro," is a mini-masterpiece of echoed singing and punchy digital beats, at once an expected track from Muslimgauze and something just a little bit different. While not completely a distinct change from the past or an undisputed high point of his career, *Maroon* does have Bryn Jones again doing what he loves to do and, for the most part, doing it very well indeed, with little changes thrown in along the way. The first "Thimble Cups of Urdu" demonstrates this nicely; while initially reminiscent of such zoneouts as *Veiled Sisters*, the intricate layering of many different percussion lines, rising and falling within the mix, along with buried bass and eerily soft keyboards, quickly establishes it as being a much more complex beast. The first "Harem of Dogs," meanwhile, is a flat-out winner, beginning with a sudden, high-volume shimmer of synth strings leading into the main piece; it's very upfront, in comparison to many similar pieces which take a more relaxed approach, and it really conveys the flavor of actually being in the middle of something, thanks in part to the many conversational snippets shot through the mix and left relatively free of production touches. The second "Harem" has a similar feel but its own distinct part, when nothing but a reverse cymbal loop obsessively plays on before the strings slide back in one last time. The remaining tracks on the album aren't quite as distinct as these numbers in particular, but together they all result in another generally fine Muslimgauze release. —*Ned Raggett*

### Azzazin / 1996 / Staalplaat ♦♦♦♦

Shorter than many of Muslimgauze's '90s albums—13 untitled songs over 45 minutes—*Azzazzin*, originally released as part of the limited-edition subscription series, feels more like a collection of random experiments than a cohesive piece of work per se. If not something that would intrigue the casual listener, the hardcore fan will likely find something of interest on the various tracks here. Starting with an extremely minimal opening number—it's no surprise Finnish experimental duo Pan Sonic are Muslimgauze fans, based on this track—*Azzazzin* has a much more electronic feeling than most of Bryn Jones' other albums, eschewing the traditional elements used elsewhere for a rough, quietly aggressive and disturbing feel. Comparisons with Aphex Twin aren't too far off the mark here, but this is still clearly a Muslimgauze release than any sort of ripoff. The fourth track, with its unpredictable keyboard snarls over a low, quiet pulse, and the sixth and seventh songs, with distorted, high-pitched noise tones mixed with a soft series of bass notes and a slight spoken-word interjection from time to time, are some of the strong points from this intriguing release. Beats are used in an extremely limited way throughout *Azzazzin*, with rhythm, always a key component of Jones' work, more suggested at points by the nature of the keyboard lines than anything else. Closing with an equally minimal track, *Azzazzin* won't be everyone's cup of tea, but adventuresome listeners will find themselves rewarded. —*Ned Raggett*

**Deceiver** / 1996 / Staalplaat ♦♦♦
Starting off with the quite lengthy first title track, which begins as a heavy-stomp monster that either is sampling a John Bonham drum part or is doing its best to sound like it is, then alternates between quieter and louder passages, *Deceiver* is another excellent entry in the limited-edition release series begun by *Izlamaphobia*. Like that other double-disc release, which showcased Bryn Jones moving into newer, less familiar sonic realms with his work, *Deceiver* has Muslimgauze *working in extremis* on a variety of fronts, if not quite as much (though pretty darned close nonetheless) as the earlier effort. One thing that definitely does carry over from *Izlamaphobia* is Jones' love for crunching drum and percussion sounds used in immediate, in-your-face approaches. Standouts in this vein, to name just two out of many, include "A Parsee View," one of the sharpest and most danceable things Muslimgauze released, with a massive beat and tight groove accompanied by what sounds like heavily-amplified clapping, and the very untypical "Herod-1," anchored around a pumped-up series of bass synth lines and a swirling, wordless female vocal sample. "Herod-2" takes the bass and gets even crazier with it, with backwards percussion and many strange twists and turns. The full blend of punch and experimentalism which characterized *Izlamaphobia* does crop up at points here as well, as with "Morsel of Sand," with several interlocked percussion lines, some quite clear and some heavily treated, accompanied only by a flute, and the body-rocking first "Jagdish Masjid of Light," which even has some wah-wah guitar snuck into the funk. The second "Jagdish" is no slouch either, with distortion and sonic overload worthy of Autechre to boot on top of everything else. —*Ned Raggett*

**Fatah Guerrilla** / 1996 / Staalplaat ♦♦♦♦
Muslimgauze expands into ever-more lengthy projects with this three-disc release, each disc being at least an hour long and separately titled. On *Fatah*, Bryn Jones manages a neat encapsulation of the various styles and phases of Muslimgauze, intentionally or not, over the course of the entire work. The first disc, *Muhammadunize*, has what could be called a classic feel to it, with a very familiar blend of drones, string instruments, and synths, and varying percussion/breakbeat patterns, in turn mixed with a number of hard-to-catch vocal samples. It's a formula used many times in the past by Jones, yet somehow he still manages to keep things just fresh enough, investing songs like the first and second "Khalifate" and especially both slamming versions of "Imad Akel" with enough unexpected touches. He incorporates the basic power of his work in the tracks as well, with both beauty and a nervy, hard-to-define tension as the songs progress. *Tajik and Persian Blind*, the second disc, generally fits in the vein of *Izlamaphobia* or *Deceiver*—the title track from the latter briefly resurfaces as "Deceive for Yourself"—with the combination of massive beats (e.g., "Shisla Nain Royal Bidjar") and aggro-arty, Aphex Twin-styled production ("Dizurt"); the one-ringer "Negev Gulag," recorded three years previously, is thrown in as well. As might be guessed from its title, the final disc, *Chechnya Over Dub*, plays up the dub aesthetics which are always lurking at the heart of Muslimgauze's work—though generally in more abstract and indirect senses than might be expected—while also mixing and matching all of the previously mentioned strands, from the bass-heavy rumble of "Resume and Shaduf" to the utterly minimal ambience of "Sari of Acidic Colours." The whole release is a bit much to take all in a row, but the set is, nonetheless, another good effort from Jones. —*Ned Raggett*

• **Zouriff Moussa** / 1997 / Staalplaat ♦♦♦♦
Instead of the drones and mostly beatless atmospheres of many previous Muslimgauze recordings, *Zouriff Moussa* presents quite a danceable switch for Bryn Jones. Dedicated to a Palestinian martyr, the album sounds like a cleaner version of Techno Animal, with Eastern influences instead of dub. "Turkquoize Label" and "Brazil Marijuana" are surprisingly infectious, with distorted breakbeats and the patented Muslimgauze phased-channel drone. There are 24 tracks spread across more than an hour, so there isn't a large amount of time for each track, though several are presented in suites, like "Anti Arab America." For messed-up beat fans who are able to find it, *Zouriff Moussa* is close to a crucial purchase. —*John Bush*

**Mort Aux Vaches** / Aug. 4, 1998 / Staalplaat ♦♦
One of the few live Muslimgauze recordings, *Mort Aux Vaches* finds Bryn Jones at the *VPRO* studios with some pre-recorded material and samples, plus a band of local musicians and guests including "percussionists" Ryan Moore and Werner Durand. Consisting of one long track, the music begins with atmospheric effects with an Arabian air, then picks up with distorted live drums, forbidding vocal samples, and effects from Jones plus several solos on flute and theremin. The balance between live interaction and programming makes for a great recording. —*John Bush*

**Hussein Mahmood Jeeb Tehar Gass** / Nov. 23, 1999 / Soleil Moon ♦♦♦♦
The way the fine track "Bilechik Mule" begins *Hussein*, a listener would be forgiven for thinking that it sounds like anything but Muslimgauze; while rhythm, as always, is still central, the clattering mechanical beat is quite unlike the vast majority of his recordings, and the high-pitched sound loop added to it is equally unexpected. As a way to confound expectations—and in and of itself—the song is a good start to one of Muslimgauze's most direct records, which was also Bryn Jones' last major release before his untimely death in early 1999. While none of his passion has subsided, *Hussein* does come across as being lighter in tone, even jaunty at points compared to many past releases, as the galloping title track ably demonstrates. Add to that the quirky keyboards on "Nazareth Arab" and you have a downright amusing start to *Hussein*. In turn, tougher tracks, such as the semi-jungle "Sarin Odour," aren't as fierce in comparison to other raging numbers of the past, but they still have a solid energy to them, while moodier songs like "Turkish Purdah" and the very dub (right down to the melodica) "Istanbul" also keep the groove going. Intentional static is introduced on various tracks as well, which is not something that Jones has been well known for in the past. The static provides an even rougher edge to songs like the electrodub "Uzi Mahmood 7." Given the breadth of his work up until his passing, it would be hard to say that *Hussein* would be the signpost to even more changes and developments in style, but it does definitely demonstrate that Jones went out on top, as challenging and listenable as ever. —*Ned Raggett*

**Muslimgauze Remixes, Vol. 2** / Dec. 7, 1999 / Soleil Moon ♦♦♦
What's the essential difference between a Muslimgauze remix of Muslimgauze material and just a new Muslimgauze recording? That's a fair question, and it's one that Jones himself compounds by not identifying the source material for this remix collection. (Not only does he not share any information about the original tracks remixed here, he also, in typically perverse fashion, doesn't even bother to list the names of the tracks on the package. You'll have to put it in the CD player in order to determine that it consists of ten individual tracks.) But if it's impossible to analyze these remixes in relationship to their source material, it's still possible to evaluate their independent musical quality, which is startlingly consistent and high. The North African scales and percussion textures that you'd expect from Muslimgauze are as apparent as ever, but there are also strong reggae and dub accents, particularly on the first, fourth, and fifth (with its Augustus Pablo-ish melodica part) cuts. There's not a ton of melodic interest here, but the rhythms and instrumental textures are consistently complex and attractive enough to maintain interest. Highly recommended. —*Rick Anderson*

## My Bloody Valentine

f. 1984, Dublin, Ireland
*Group / Dream Pop, Shoegazing, Alternative Pop/Rock*
Like the Velvet Underground, Sonic Youth, and the Jesus & Mary Chain before them, My Bloody Valentine redefined what noise meant within the context of pop songwriting. Led by guitarist Kevin Shields, the group released several EPs in the mid-'80s before recording the era-defining *Isn't Anything* in 1988, a record that merged lilting, ethereal melodies of the Cocteau Twins with crushingly loud, shimmering distortion. Though My Bloody Valentine rejected rock 'n' roll conventions, it didn't subscribe to the precious tendencies of anti-rock art-pop bands. Instead, it rode crashing waves of white noise to unpredictable conclusions, particularly since their noise wasn't paralyzing like the typical avant-garde noise-rock band: It was translucent, glimmering, and beautiful. Shields was a perfectionist, especially when it came to recording, as much of My Bloody Valentine's sound was conceived within the stu-

dio itself. Nevertheless, the band was known as a formidable live act, even though they rarely moved, or even looked at the audience, while they were on stage. Their notorious lack of movement was branded "shoegazing" by the British music press, and soon there were legions of other shoegazers—Ride, Lush, the Boo Radleys, Chapterhouse, Slowdive—that, along with the rolling dance-influenced Madchester scene, dominated British indie-rock of the late '80s and early '90s. As shoegazing reached its peak in 1991, My Bloody Valentine released *Loveless,* which broke new sonic ground and was hailed as a masterpiece. Though the band was poised for a popular breakthrough, they disappeared into the studio and didn't emerge over the next five years, leaving behind a legacy that proved profoundly influential in the direction of '90s alternative rock.

Born in Queens, New York, Kevin Shields' family moved to Dubin, Ireland, when he was six years old. In his teens, he became obsessed with pop music, eventually playing in Complex with his childhood friend Colm O'Ciosoig. In 1984, Shields and O'Ciosoig formed My Bloody Valentine with vocalist Dave Conway and keyboardist Tina, taking their name from a slasher horror film. The group relocated to Berlin, where they released the Birthday Party-influenced EP *This Is Your Bloody Valentine* on the Tycoon label in 1985 to little notice. The following year, the band moved to London, where they added bassist Debbie Googe. By the summer, they had signed to Fever and had released the EP *Geek!,* which again was ignored. Later that year, the group moved to Kaledoscope Sound, releasing *The New Record By My Bloody Valentine* EP, which illustrated a Jesus & Mary Chain influence. The following year, the band moved to the Primitives' Lazy Records, releasing *Sunny Sundae Smile* early in the year. That EP was the first My Bloody Valentine record to mesh airy melodies with grinding guitars, but the two EPs that followed in 1987—*Strawberry Wine* and *Ecstasy*—were more focused and acclaimed. Conway left the band by the end of the year and was replaced by vocalist/guitarist Bilinda Butcher, whose breathy vocals fit the group's evolving sound more appropriately.

My Bloody Valentine's new sound coalesced with the group's first full-fledged album, 1988's *Isn't Anything.* Released on Creation Records, *Isn't Anything* was greeted with enthusiastic reviews in the UK music press and the band's following increased dramatically by the end of the year; in fact, their reputation had become large enough to attract the attention of Sire/Warner Bros. in the US, who became the group's American label. Two other EPs, *Feed Me With Your Kiss* and *You Made Me Realise,* were also quite popular, and by the beginning of 1989, bands that based their sound on My Bloody Valentine's droning swirl began to appear. The group retreated to the studio in 1989 to record their followup, which meant that only one EP, *Glider,* was released during that year. By the spring of 1990, it was becoming clear that the followup to *Isn't Anything* wouldn't be appearing anytime soon, and reports about Shields' growing perfectionism began to circulate in the UK weekly music press. Soon, it became apparent that the band's lengthy recording sessions were crippling Creation Records, but the group's audience was still passionate, despite the inactivity: The *Tremelo* EP was released at the end of 1990 to considerable acclaim, and managed to climb into the UK Top 40.

When My Bloody Valentine's second album, *Loveless,* finally appeared in late 1991, it was greeted with uniformly excellent reviews and it became a hit within the UK, reaching number 24 on the charts. In America, the group made significant inroads, particularly by supporting Dinosaur Jr. Despite the band's acclaim and growing audience, *Loveless* didn't sell in numbers to recoup its reported $500,000 recording cost and Creation dropped the band from their label; Creation wouldn't fully recover until 1994, when they signed Oasis. My Bloody Valentine signed with Island and entered the studio at the end of 1992 to record a new album. In 1993, the group contributed a James Bond cover to a charity compilation.

And then... nothing happened.

Shields built a home studio with his Island advance and reportedly completed two separate albums, but scrapped them both. Often, the studio ran into technological problems. Between 1993 and 1997, both Googe and O'Ciosoig left the band, leaving only Shields and Butcher; after driving a cab for about a year, Googe formed Snowpony in 1996. There were signs that My Bloody Valentine were emerging from hiding in 1996, when the group contributed to the Wire tribute album *Whore* and Shields played on Experimental Audio Research's *Beyond the Pale.* Still, no new My Bloody Valentine material appeared. —*Stephen Thomas Erlewine*

**This Is Your Bloody Valentine** / 1985 / Tycoon ✦
My Bloody Valentine's debut album *This Is Your Bloody Valentine* is an unfocused and derivative collection of post-punk goth-rock that offers no indication of the revolutionary guitar sound the group would later create. —*Stephen Thomas Erlewine*

**Isn't Anything** / 1988 / Creation/Sire ✦✦✦✦
The first of My Bloody Valentine's two landmark albums, *Isn't Anything* combines delicate, brittle melodies and big guitars. "Lose My Breath" and "No More Sorry" highlight Belinda Butcher's understated but charismatic voice, while guitars take the spotlight on "Cupid Come." Songs like "Sue Is Fine" and the seminal "Feed Me with Your Kiss" point toward the band's future sound of fuzzed-out, multi-tracked guitars and blissful male-female vocal harmonies. An underrated and surprisingly accessible album. —*Heather Phares*

**Ecstasy & Wine** / 1989 / Lazy ✦✦
*Ecstasy & Wine* combines the 1987 EPs *Strawberry Wine* and *Ecstasy* on one compact disc. *Strawberry Wine* finds the band moving closer to their lush, shimmering neo-psychedelia, while *Ecstasy* finds the group incorporating dissonance and layers of feedback into sounds established on *Strawberry Wine,* thereby offering a rough blueprint for *Isn't Anything.* —*Stephen Thomas Erlewine*

**Glider [EP]** / 1989 / Sire ✦✦✦
The *Glider* EP finds My Bloody Valentine exploring the different harmonics in their dissonances and distortion, creating floating layers of sound that are hypnotic in their ebb and flow. The first song, "Soon," is one of the group's greatest sound paintings, filled with evocative textures and eerie, disembodied rhythms, while the title track is nearly as fascinating, making *Glider* an essential addition to a My Bloody Valentine library. —*Stephen Thomas Erlewine*

★ **Loveless** / Nov. 5, 1991 / Sire ✦✦✦✦✦
One of the best and most influential albums in '90s alternative rock, *Loveless* puts the band's innovative sonic style over lyrical substance. And the sonic styles of *Loveless* change constantly: Drums bludgeon the listener's ears and fade into nothingness; guitars whine like chainsaws and hum like cellos. The intricate mix of feedback—guitar washes and dreamy harmonies on songs like "Til Here Knows When" and "Blown a Wish"—is awe-inspiring; though it takes My Bloody Valentine many years of work to complete their albums, it's easy to understand why when the results are this breathtaking. —*Heather Phares*

## My Life with the Thrill Kill Kult

f. 1986, Chicago, IL
*Group / Alternative Dance, Alternative Pop/Rock, Industrial, House*
Most house-based dance music is either completely devoid of content or has a fairly serious political consciousness. Not so with My Life with the Thrill Kill Kult. With its schlocky mix of samples, synths, beats, Satan, and sex, the group is a hyped-up, stylized psychdelic/Industrial dance troupe that revels in bad taste of all kinds. And the sheer tastlessness of their records gained a large cult following in the early '90s, culminating in their 1991 *Sexplosion* album and its single, "Sex on Wheels." Though albums like *13 Above the Night, Blue Buddha,* and *A Crime for All Seasons* didn't achieve the same prominence as *Sexplosion,* the group cranked out its sleazy sounds for the better part of the '90s. —*Stephen Thomas Erlewine*

**Confessions of a Knife** / 1990 / Wax Trax! ✦✦✦✦

**Kooler Than Jesus** / 1990 / Wax Trax! ✦✦✦

● **Sexplosion!** / 1991 / Interscope ✦✦✦✦
Though My Life with the Thrill Kill Kult has fared well among supporters of underground industrial and gothic music, the fairly accessible *Sexplosion!* consists of, for the most part, what is essentially melodic, high-energy Eurodance music—but with quite a difference. Loaded with soundbites and references to S&M, bondage, and sexual misadventures, *Sexplosion!* is deliberately outrageous and over-the-top. With song titles like "Leathersex," "The International Sin Set," and "Sex on Wheels," it's clear that the Thrill Kill Kult loves shock value. But this highly cinematic and often amusing CD is so tongue-in-cheek and self-consciously erotic that it's hard to regard the unique, distinctive Thrill Kill Kult as genuinely subversive. Rather, *Sexplosion!*'s main aim is to have fun and entertain—and on that level, it's quite sucessful. —*Alex Henderson*

**Crime for All Seasons** / Jun. 10, 1997 / Red Ant ♦♦♦

By the time My Life With the Thrill Kill Kult released *Crime for All Seasons* in 1997, they had spent too much time away from the spotlight and their audience, and the industrial/rave audience had declined sharply. So, the album was generally ignored, but this doesn't necessarily mean that the album was terrible. In fact, it isn't that much weaker than their other albums, which were similarly inconsistent, and it offers enough fine moments to keep fans happy, even though it does raise questions of whether the group has run out of ideas. —*Stephen Thomas Erlewine*

**Dirty Little Secrets** / Oct. 26, 1999 / Rykodisc ♦♦

*Dirty Little Secrets* is a compilation of 18 remixes of Thrill Kill Kult material, with eight having been previously unreleased. Some add new elements to the tracks, while others pretty much retain the original feel with one or two different sounds in the mix. It doesn't feature an all-star lineup of big-name remixers, as some of these projects do; it's simply a variety of recastings of songs from throughout the band's career, and in that regard, it's a fun listen, even if a few tend to drag on rather longer than they should. —*Steve Huey*

## Jamie Myerson

b. 1975, New Jersey

*Producer / Jungle/Drum'N'Bass, Club/Dance*

One of the few American producers fluent in drum'n'bass during the early '90s, Jamie Myerson explored the more melodic (if not muzaky) side of jungle and trance, in league with fellow new-age breakbeat producers like Adam F. and E-Z Rollers as well as straightahead dream-house merchants Sash! and Robert Miles. Myerson recorded for 4 Hero's Reinforced Records from 1993 to 1995 before signing with an American, Josh Wink's Ovum Recordings, for a Columbia-distributed major-label contract. Growing up in southern New Jersey, Myerson listened to alternative rock and played drums in several bands, but also built up his budding bedroom studio with synthesizer gear. During 1991, he began tuning in to a local college radio station to hear the new sounds of breakbeat and techno from England, primarily early hardcore labels like Moving Shadow and Reinforced.

Still just a teenager, he began producing tracks in that mold. When he learned that Dego—co-owner of Reinforced and a member of the seminal drum'n'bass team 4 Hero—was in nearby Philadelphia as part of a DJ tour, Myerson traveled to the event and passed him a demo tape. Dego encouraged him to continue recording and, in 1994, released his first single "Find Yourself" (as JLM Productions) on the Reinforced EP *Enforcers, Vols. 6 & 7* in 1994. At that point, Myerson was the only American producer recording for a strictly jungle label in England. Myerson produced three additional singles for Reinforced (and one for Belgium's Crammed Discs) before releasing his first domestic single on Sm:)e Recordings in 1996. Soon after, he signed to Josh Wink's Ovum Recordings, distributed through Columbia. Myerson's debut album, *The Listen Project*, was released in April 1998. His sophomore effort *Sky City: Lift Me Up* was issued two years later. —*John Bush*

● **The Listen Project** / Apr. 7, 1998 / Ovum/Columbia ♦♦

Although Jamie Myerson's intial singles were quite good, the success of *Listen*, his full-length debut, still comes as something as a surprise. In essence, he's an American counterpart to Roni Size, finding a middle ground between layered, polished club music and progressive, rhythmically intricate jungle. Apart from Carol Tripp's appearance on "Rescue Me," there aren't many vocals on the album, but that doesn't mean it's inaccessible—the layers of intertwining beats and keyboards are more mesmerizing on their own, creating a provocative, fascinating debut. —*Stephen Thomas Erlewine*

## Mysteryman (D. Pier)

*Producer / Electronica, Electro-Techno, Ambient Techno, Electro*

While its birthplace may have been Stateside, much of the most interesting and innovative dancefloor electro to appear since the early '90s has come from Europe, and specifically Germany. Not surprising, given Kraftwerk's influence on American artists such as Juan Atkins and Afrika Bambaataa, but since techno is almost the national pastime and breakbeats are mostly left to the English, the quality of the material is remarkable. One of the more notable recent sources of German electro has been the Overexposed label, a sublabel of hardcore techno imprint Overdrive. Although Overexposed appeared at first a dabblers' sublabel for Overdrive artists, it quickly took on an identity of its own, thanks largely to the work of D. Pier, aka Mysteryman, whose releases have dominated the label's release schedule to date. Showing a strong rooting in Detroit and L.A. styles (particularly Drexciya, Model 500, and Egyptian Lover), Pier's interest in updating the sound for contemporary sensibilities is obvious in his fusion of classic beat patterns with inventive syncopation and a sharp digital edge (particularly on his "Life in a Tube" 12"). Pier's tracks are also mainlined by a spry, sometimes subtle experimentalism rare in producers aiming their jams at the dance floor. —*Sean Cooper*

● **Mysteryman, Vol. 2** / Dec. 2, 1996 / Overexposed ♦♦♦♦

While clearly a nod to Detroit masters such as "Mad" Mike Banks and Drexciya, "Mysteryman 2" is electro-funk with a bit of hormone circulating in its blood. A five-track double-EP and D. Pier's second for Overexposed, "Mysteryman 2" is the label's strongest to date, with tight, uptempo electro beats and deep, full basslines hinting slightly toward a Miami sound. Pretty much club tracks, then, but brisk, smart composition and the odd lyric make it work at home, too. —*Sean Cooper*

**Life in a Tube [Single]** / 1997 / Overexposed ♦♦♦♦

Another killer jammy from the mysterious D. Pier. Again on Overdrive's electro imprint, Overexposed, these are space-race booty breaks from the year 2010, all deep, thunderous kicks and twittering, angular hi-hats, cowbells, and claves. Reminiscent of LFO's "Tied Up" or an Autechre-via-Miami redux, the flip side's "The Cold Fog" and "Contact" are all you need, with the title track a competent but somehow less inspired uptempo roller. —*Sean Cooper*

# N

### Naked Music NYC
*Group / Urban, R&B, House*
A revolving collection of artists led by songwriter Jay Denes, Naked Music NYC aligned itself with the so-called "New Soul" scene which also included Erykah Badu, Maxwell, and D'Angelo. Their debut LP, *What's on Your Mind?*, appeared in mid-1998. —*Jason Ankeny*

- **What's on Your Mind?** / Jun. 23, 1998 / OM Records ✦✦✦
Naked Music NYC looks to the heyday of '70s-era soul for inspiration on *What's on Your Mind?* While the group assimilates their influences well, they don't really bring anything new to the sound. As a break from the monotony of contemporary R&B aesthetics the album is entirely welcome, but taken solely on its own terms it doesn't leave much of a lasting impression. —*Jason Ankeny*

### Pete Namlook (Peter Kuhlmann)
*Producer / Ambient-House, Ambient, Electronic*
If most artists in contemporary electronica are like islands unto themselves, turning out tracks in relative anonymity, Pete "Namlook" Kuhlmann is a whole continent. A dizzyingly prolific composer who's steadily built up an entire industry around his Frankfurt-based Fax label, Namlook's name is inextricably linked with the post-rave resurgence of ambient music, and many of his solo and collaborative recordings with the likes of Mixmaster Morris, Tetsu Inoue, Klaus Schulze, Bill Laswell, Richie Hawtin, Geir Jenssen, Dr. Atmo, Burhan Ocal, Atom Heart, Jonah Sharp, Charles Uzzell-Edwards, and David Moufang, among many others, number among the most lauded and influential in new ambient. Although Namlook got his start releasing quasi-new age (as Romantic Warrior) and hard trance (as Sequential, 4Voice, Escape, Deltraxx, and a host of others), he and his label have become synonymous with new ambient since Fax began exclusively releasing the style shortly after the label formed in 1992. Fax helped give shape to ambient's new school by allowing the artists to freely experiment while making a living from their music. (Fax's label structure confers the majority of its profits to its artists.) Countless Fax releases, particularly those dating from 1993 and 1994, are considered classics of contemporary electronic ambient, and while the label has suffered a certain degree of repetition in recent years, Fax remains one of the most important and influential German electronic music labels. Namlook has been criticized for adopting a quality-over-quantity approach—his label's release schedule was up to a CD per week for more than a year, and currently produces 24 per year, many of them Namlook's own—but he's succeeded in attracting a devoted, ravenous following that allows him and his label to continue releasing new music. Fax has released more than 250 full-length CDs, dozens of 12"s, and several compilations—including the sprawling 4-CD *Ambient Cookbook*, which remains the best introduction to the label—and has expanded to included four Fax-related labels and two subsidiary labels (Rather Interesting and Headphone, run by Atom Heart and Higher Intelligence Agency's Bobby Bird, respectively). Fax releases have been licensed for reissue by R&S, Music Man, Rising High, Instinct, and Injection. With distributors on three continents and a small universe of Web sites devoted to reviewing, trading, and collecting Fax titles, the label and its proprietor have long since passed the stage of phenomenon and crossed over to institution.

Musically, Namlook draws most recognizably on the synthscapes of artists such as Klaus Schulze and Hans Jochim Roedelius, combing the droning electronics of those artists with, depending on the project or collaborator, ethnic instrumentation (tabla, tambouri, oud), environmental samples (rain, voices, arriving and departing trains, wildlife), sweeping electronic treatments (the bubbly undercurrents of *Dreamfish* or the drifting synthetic landscapes of *2350 Broadway*), and minimal acoustic and electronic rhythms (jungle, electro, techno, and trance). His collaborations tend to outdo his solo recordings, although a few of his solo works are among Fax's finest. Though hard to find, the two volumes of *The Definitive Ambient Collection* offer a good introduction to Namlook's early work. Subsequent compilations of more recent material have appeared at somewhat regular intervals; due to the wide variety of styles pursued by various projects, compilations may be the best place to start. —*Sean Cooper*

**The Definitive Ambient Collection** / 1992 / Rising High ✦✦✦✦
Including almost a full dozen snippets of what are usually hour-long works by Namlook and co., *The Definitive Ambient Collection* includes a variety of early Fax highlights from the albums *Air 1, 4Voice*, and others. Though edits of longer works rarely work well in these circumstances, *The Definitive Ambient Collection* works better than most, mostly because it's presented as a mix album. It's a good place to start, but listeners will find it increasingly unnecessary after hearing the sources of these tracks. —*Keith Farley*

**The Fires of Ork** / 1993 / Fax ✦✦✦
A less-than-characteristically beat-oriented collaboration with Namlook and Biosphere's Geir Jenssen on the former's noted Fax label. It's a nonetheless stellar four track CD, with lush, well-composed material split evenly between uptempo feet movers and sprawling, stirring ambient. Reissued by Apollo with different artwork. —*Sean Cooper*

**2350 Broadway** / 1993 / Fax ✦✦✦✦
A seminal, almost fabled release spanning two CDs and recorded by Namlook and Tetsu Inoue in real time (no pre- or post-production and no overdubs). Remarkably engaging for its simplicity, the set was subsequently reissued by popular demand and spawned a pair (and counting) of follow-ups in the series. —*Sean Cooper*

**The Definitive Ambient Collection, Vol. 2** / 1994 / Rising High ✦✦✦
The second volume of collected Namlook material on Fax balances interstellar excursions like "Trip to Mars" and "Trip to Polaris" with the ambient figure's eco-ambient works, including "Duane Sky." —*Keith Farley*

**The Dark Side of the Moog** / Oct. 10, 1994 / Fax/PK ✦✦✦✦
The noteworthy first meeting of '70s space hero Klaus Schülze and his '90s inheritor Pete Namlook, *The Dark Side of the Moog* is an hour-long journey into vintage space territory, quite similar to Schülze classics *Timewind* or *Moondawn*, perhaps because he was using analogue synthesizers for the first time in many years. —*Keith Farley*

- **Air 1+2** / Oct. 25, 1994 / Instinct ✦✦✦✦
An American release combining Namlook's first two *Air* albums on a two-disc set, *Air 1+2* forms one of the most evocative displays of ambient music ever recorded, and is arguably Namlook's solo masterpiece. *Air 1* is a set of gusty ambience with the appropriately titled tracks "Wind" and "Breeze," plus a series of impressionistic female French vocal samples placed over lazy, brooding space music. The second disc consists of 11 tracks that work through ethno-ambience with added effects from a didgeridoo and a rain stick. Namlook seems to have disregarded Eno's definition of ambient as aural wallpaper, since the two hours of music here include some of the most addictive, compulsively listenable instrumental electronics ever recorded. —*Keith Farley*

**Silence 1+2** / 1995 / Instinct ✦✦✦✦
The second pairing of Fax imports for a double-disc domestic issue, *Silence 1+2* spotlights Namlook's first two collaborations with Fax regular Dr. Atmo. Mostly beatless, the music is a bit more brooding and sinister than most Fax

material, even with the bird calls and nature sounds on the 20-minute highlight "Garden of Dreams." —*Keith Farley*

**The Dark Side of the Moog 2** / Apr. 2, 1995 / Fax/PK ♦♦♦♦
The second in the series of Namlook/Schulze collaborations, *The Dark Side of the Moog 2* consists of the hour-long track "A Saucerful of Ambience" (the entire series includes Pink Floyd references). As on the first, the music is beatless space music (minus the tremendous feelings of depth on most of Schulze's works), though artificial effects similar to bird calls and faraway bells punctuate the mix continually. —*John Bush*

**Jet Chamber 3** / 1997 / Fax ♦♦♦♦
Fax's eventual plunge into breakbeat madness comes, not surprisingly, via Atom Heart's Uwe Schmidt, who here twists the aesthetic of the sampled break into its most musical form. As with past *Jet Chamber* releases, Fax honcho Pete Namlook is along for the ride, but his input seems limited to some rather ponderous bass, guitar, and synth accompaniments that pair awkwardly with Schmidt's dense, vibrating beats. —*Sean Cooper*

**Psychonavigation 3** / 1997 / Fax ♦♦♦♦
Since the *Psychonavigation* series seems to be reserved for Namlook and Bill Laswell's more deep-space-oriented collaborations (and often with a somewhat gloomy tone), it's not surprising that this third in the series is a shadowy, somewhat Geiger-esque affair. While a funk-fueled breakbeat track (the only obvious instance of bass guitar during the course of the hour) makes an appearance toward the end of the recording, much of the material is concerned with shifting, overlapping tones and frequencies which combine, harmonize and reverbate. Sparse vocal samples accentuate Namlook's extended Synthi and Trautonium passages, with Laswell's deep, monochromatic bass textures providing an ample anchor point. —*Sean Cooper*

**The Dark Side of the Moog 6** / 1997 / Fax +49-69/450464 ♦♦♦♦
Of all the collaborations that Pete Namlook has made since founding his Fax label in the early '90s, it is arguable that his pairings with Klaus Schulze have been the most consistently fascinating. Namlook and Schulze are probably well aware of their unique musical chemistry, as this was their sixth release in only three years (they have since slowed down to about one a year since then). What makes the partnership work so well, if at times unevenly, is the fact that both men are able to fuse their distinct musical voices into a seamless whole. Like its predecessors, "VI" is a single song broken into six sections. After the moody first section of barely intelligible voices, the disc launches itself into a space rock/techno maelstrom that barely slows in tempo for the rest of its hour-plus length. Poking through this unceasing mix of sequencer runs, pings, and thumps are fluid guitar leads, keyboard melodies, and seemingly random vocal samples. The album reaches its climax with "Part V", a 24-minute piece that rises and ebbs upon a constant rhythm to present a trance-inducing effect that makes the song pass by much quicker than its length would suggest. Bill Laswell once again makes a guest appearance, although it isn't clear exactly what his contribution is precisely, and the typically sparse liner notes are of no help in that regard. Although it is tempting to state that Namlook and Schulze simply overwhelmed Laswell's work, it is much more likely that the three have achieved such synchronicity in terms of their musical ideals that their individual voices have merged into a singular, cohesive sound. Listening to this collaboration certainly bears that theory out. —*Brian Kirby*

## Natural Calamity

f. 1991, Tokyo, Japan
*Group / Shibuya-Kei, Alternative Pop/Rock*
The Shibuya-kei trio known as Natural Calamity is a bit of an anachronism compared to others in the rich Japanese pop scene characterized by Cornelius and Pizzicato Five. The earthy trip-hop blues produced by Shunji Mori and Kuni Sugimoto, plus American Stephanie Heasley's countrified vocals come in marked contrast to Tokyo's many French/Brazilian/exotica aficionados. Mori and Sugimoto met in the early '90s, and produced their first album *Dawn in the Valley* for File Records, owned by Toshio Nakanishi of Love T.K.O. *Let It Come Down* and *Sundance* followed, as well as the collaboration LP *Group of Gods*, recorded with Nakanishi and Masayaki Kudo (who form half of the trip-hop quartet Skylab). While Sugimoto was spending some time in London, he met Stephanie Heasley, who was working at the Tower Records store in Piccadilly Circus. After recording in London and Spain as a trio, Natural Calamity signed to the Idyllic/Toy's Factory label and released *Andulucian Moon*. Hyped in the Japanese press, the group earned American distribution through the Dust Brothers' Nickelbag label for their second LP, 1998's *Peach Head*. The inevitable remix album followed, with contributions by Stock, Hausen & Walkman, the Dust Brothers, Buffalo Daughter and Kool Keith. —*John Bush*

● **Peach Head** / Aug. 11, 1998 / Nickelbag ♦♦♦♦
If the musical environment of *Peach Head* is lazy, the music itself is not. Instead, Natural Calamity creates textured songs that build on themselves, creating lovely, fragile drones, sometimes with a distinctly folksy psychedelic or space-rock flavor, sometimes entirely pop, but always stretched and elongated. But the music never even begins to drag. Each song is like an unraveling, and it is not uncommon for a song to sound as if it is just kicking into gear at the three-minute mark. Their songwriting is accomplished, assured, and varied, while the duo stretch their instruments to the limit, seemingly playing them as if they are completely different instruments, and they frequently sound as if they are melting right in their players' hands. "Dark Water & Stars" has a Caribbean feel with Shunji Mori's reverbed tremolo guitars sounding something like steel drums being played under water, creating a queasy but mellow feel, at least until the electronic, space-age alien sounds appropriate the song. Never has pedal steel guitar sounded as futuristic as it does on "Tomorrow," a beautiful, sleepy song. "So Good" combines the best of the pop and psychedelic-folk sides of Natural Calamity. The vocal melody can only be called pop, but stretched over slowly finger-picked guitar and completely relaxed drumming, the song becomes expansive and open. The Dust Brothers remix of "As You Know" is an example of Natural Calamity as a progressive pop band, as the song incorporates unusually crisp and steady drumming and little snatches of scratching. An upbeat bassline by Kuni Sugimoto guides the melody, and Mori's guitars are not to be found throughout. This in contrast to the original version of the song, which takes the exact same melody but softens all the elements, adding Mori's liquid-toned playing, bouncy organ, and water effects with squealing electronic doodles. Stephanie Heasley's vocals barely peek through the futuristic haze. She deserves special mention here. Her voice is supple and malleable, and her melodies swim along with the flow of the music rather than cutting through and disrupting it. When she needs to be quiet, she is, but Heasley also helps keep the music from collapsing in on itself when it slows to a walk, and makes the somewhat more upbeat songs, such as "And That's Saying a Lot," sound sexy and just slightly risque. When Heasley sings "I'm a woman of very few words/And that's saying a lot," she is so suggestive that it is almost too much to bear. But that phrase could just as easily describe Natural Calamity as a band. They prefer to let their music do most of the talking for them. *Peach Head* is perfect chill-out mood music. —*Stanton Swihart*

## Negativland

f. 1979, Berkeley, CA
*Group / Sound Collage, Post-Punk, Experimental*
A Firesign Theatre for the post-punk era, Negativland was a conceptual group specializing in multimedia manipulation, pop prankishness and cultural terrorism. Initially comprised of Mark Hosler, Richard Lyons, and David Wills, Negativland formed in Berkeley, California in 1979. Initially, projects like their 1980 eponymous debut and 1981's *Points* consisted of tape loops and cut-and-paste audio montages, but by 1982, when they began hosting their own radio show, *Over the Edge*, the trio had begun incorporating music, sampling, skits and phone-ins into the mix.

With the addition of master tape-manipulator Dan Joyce, Negativland's self-described "cultural jamming" grew more complex and intricate, and in 1985 they issued *Over the Edge Volume 1: JamCon '84*, a remarkably dense sonic pastiche of looped noise, media pranks, original music and general mayhem taken from their radio program. Their assault on the media stepped up with the release of 1987's *Escape from Noise*, which featured the track "Christianity Is Stupid;" after reading about a Minnesota teen who murdered his parents with an axe, Negativland issued a mock press statement falsely claiming that "Christianity Is Stupid" influenced the boy's lethal behavior. A media furor ensued, and the group became the center of considerable controversy, never once cracking a smile. The prank later became fodder for 1989's *Helter Stupid*, which detailed the origins and aftermath of the stunt while simultaneously exploring the ready manipulation of the press.

After three more 1990 cassettes taken directly from *Over the Edge*, Negativland issued 1991's *U2* EP, its most ambitious statement yet. Packaged to look like a U2 single titled "Negativland," the record featured a cover of the Irish mega-band's hit "I Still Haven't Found What I'm Looking For," played on kazoos and synthesizers; added to the mix was a bootleg tape of a studio rant by deejay Casey Kasem, who seethes "That's the letter U and the number 2...These guys are from England and who gives a shit?" The joke turned sour, however, when U2's label, Island, and the band's publishers brought suit against Negativland and their label, SST; ultimately, *U2* was recalled and destroyed, its copyrights reassigned, and damages recovered.

Bloodied but unbowed, Negativland soldiered on, dedicating 1992's *Guns* to "the members of our favorite Irish rock band, their record label and their attorneys." (U2 themselves, it should be noted, later incorporated many of Negativland's notions of media manipulation and cultural appropriation into their blockbuster *Zoo TV* tour.) Following the lawsuit, the group's focus remained centered on issues of free speech, corporate greed, and intellectual properties; they published two books, 1992's *The Letter U and the Numeral 2* and 1995's *Fair Use*, and starred in a documentary, *Sonic Outlaws*. Their subsequent audio releases consisted primarily of material from *Over the Edge; Dispepsi*, their first full-length collection of new material since 1993's *Free*, appeared in 1997. *The ABC's of Anarchy*, a split EP with Chumbawamba, followed two years later. —*Jason Ankeny*

### Negativland / 1980 / Seeland ♦♦
Right from the outset, Negativland were provocateurs, throwing antagonistic soundbites over top of a jumble of jagged sound collage, melodic acoustic guitar, and the sound of power tools. The debut, which features 20 tracks identified only by their number, is far less cohesive than the works that made them a thorn in the side of record companies, but there are still quite a few moments of inspiration to be found here. Some are plain-out musique concrète, but others fuse noise with conventional song structure...sort of like the Beach Boys making guest appearances on a Throbbing Gristle session. Each album is handmade, with whatever wallpaper samples happen to be kicking around, decorated by incongruous little snapshots from a previous age. —*Sean Carruthers*

### Escape from Noise / 1987 / SST ♦♦♦♦
While the sound collage of Negativland's first three studio albums pointed in the band's ultimate direction, they were really rough sketches compared to *Escape From Noise*. *Escape* is a full-on audio assault, more musical than ever, but with tight and well-constructed sound sections thrown in. Instead of simply a collection of sounds and snippets, however, each cut on *Escape From Noise* picks a target and takes aim. "Quiet Please" takes on market research in the world of radio. "Michael Jackson" is a laundry list of pop stars being charged with creating commercial pop. "Sycamore" turns happy, shiny, new preplanned communities into something far more sinister. Although some other tracks ("Yellow, Black and Rectangular," "Car Bomb") don't really take on particular targets, they're fun nonetheless. Probably the most accomplished piece is the strangely creepy "Time Zones," which talks about how many time zones there are in the Soviet Union (there are 11, by the way, and it's not even funny). Although it wasn't apparent at the time, the centerpiece of the album would be "Christianity Is Stupid," a prime example of how sound bites can be rearranged to say whatever you want them to say. (The full sound bites appear on the album *Helter Stupid*, the first half of which was inspired by a media frenzy after the band suggested that a murder may be attributable to "Christianity Is Stupid," as an excuse to get out of having to tour in the wake of this album, which turned out to be a much bigger success than anyone expected.) Scattered throughout the album are unexpected guest appearances from some of the biggest names in underground music, including Jello Biafra on "toilet flushing," the Residents on "hoots and clanging," and the Grateful Dead's Jerry Garcia and Mickey Hart on mouth sounds and "processed animals." In addition to better-constructed material, the production quality on *Escape From Noise* is also top-notch, making it a joy to listen to. Although future works would prove more controversial, this is probably Negativland's masterwork. —*Sean Carruthers*

### ● Helter Stupid / 1989 / SST ♦♦♦♦
After the relative success of 1987's *Escape From Noise* album, studio project Negativland found itself in the strange position of being expected to go on a money-losing tour. To get out of the tour, the band cooked up a phony press release linking their song "Christianity Is Stupid" to a multiple murder, claiming that federal officials had told the band not to leave town. This prank quickly spiraled out of control, with many media sources taking their news from each other instead of reality. This media circus became the basis for the first half of the album *Helter Stupid*, which deconstructs the media, the controversy, and sensationalism. Although the root of all of this material is perhaps ethically questionable, "Helter Stupid" is a brilliant lampoon of the media and makes the listener question just what is being fed to them as "information." Filling out the album is a series of "Perfect Cut" tracks, which meld together tons of singles from the '70s and then get Negativland audio blender treatment. Although the songs have their moments, they're not really enough to sustain half an album, especially after such a good start. —*Sean Carruthers*

### Fair Use: The Story of the Letter U and the Numeral 2 / Feb. 17, 1995 / Seeland ♦♦♦♦
Using *The Letter U and the Numeral 2* as its foundation, *Fair Use* uses the same documents and material but goes further in depth, adding far more material. It raises a number of issues that one would expect to be raised by the poster boys of copyright infringement: What is public domain? What qualifies as parody? What, ultimately, constitutes "fair use" under the copyright laws? Although the subject matter and the reams of documents are really a bit weighty for those only casually interested in the subject, those who care will find it a substantial and interesting read. —*Sean Carruthers*

### Over the Edge, Vol. 1Ω: Starting Line / Jul. 7, 1995 / Seeland ♦♦♦
This typically provocative Negativland release is assembled from the group's long-lived radio show, and consists primarily of looped noise, media pranks, and fleeting moments of original music. —*Jason Ankeny*

### Dispepsi / Jul. 29, 1997 / Seeland ♦♦♦
Targeting a monolithic soft drink company—namely, Pepsi—is a tricky thing, even for anarchic sonic terrorists like Negativland. After all, they got burned once before, when they did the Casey Kasem/U2 parody, "U2," a song that resulted in lawsuits that nearly gutted their career. This time around, however, the targets were receptive—Pepsi allowed Negativland to put them through their standard sonic cuisenart, probably thinking that it functioned as an album-length advertisement. And, weirdly enough, it does. By the late '90s, corporations had co-opted enough "alternative" techniques in their advertising to make this aural collage sound as if it was styled for modern rock radio commercials. Still, there are some pleasures on *Dispepsi*, particularly how Negativland has restyled their signature sound to have easy, lightweight accessiblity, but the album remains a mixed blessing. —*Stephen Thomas Erlewine*

## Ben Neill

**b.** North Carolina
*Keyboards, Trumpet, Producer / Electronica, Jungle/Drum'N'Bass, Ambient*
Trumpeter Ben Neill successfully bridged the gap between ambient music and the avant-garde, further blurring aesthetic boundaries with the development of his mutantrumpet, a revolutionary electro-acoustic hybrid of conventional trumpet and synthesized sound. A native of North Carolina and a product of classical training, Neill relocated to New York City during the mid-'80s, immersing himself in the downtown experimental music scene; increasingly fascinated with minimalism, he studied under the legendary La Monte Young, and with the aid of the synthesizer pioneer Robert Moog designed the first mutantrumpet, an instrument fit with three bells, six valves, a trombone slide, and an analog processing system whch allowed him to create any number of open, muted, and electronic sounds.

In 1984, Neill completed *Orbs*, his first major composition for mutantrumpet, percussion, and audio/visual projections; pieces including 1985's *Mainspring*, 1987's *Money Talk* and 1988's *Abblasen House* followed prior to his breakthrough work *ITSOFOMO (In the Shadow of Forward Motion)*, a 1989 collaboration with visual artist David Wojnarowicz. A year later Neill travelled to Amsterdam's Steim Studios to develop a new, MIDI-capable mutantrumpet; the upgrade resulted in the addition of a number of switches, knobs, and pressure-sensitive pads allowing the player to trigger and modify a variety of sounds and sequences, as well as lights and projections, all in real time. *After Haydn*, a collaboration with electronic composer Nicolas Collins, followed in 1991.

Neill then began a six-year stint as curator of the downtown NYC performance space The Kitchen, a position which served as his gateway into the burgeoning electronic music scene. Presenting performances by everyone from John Cage to Jim O'Rourke to Future Sound of London, he began increasingly absorbing electronic influences into his work and was particularly fascinated by the local "illbient" movement; originally created as an installation/performance piece, Neill's 1995 album *Green Machine* instead evolved into a full-blown dance music project, complete with 12" remixes from the likes of Single Cell Orchestra and DJ Spooky. The latter resurfaced on 1996's *Triptycal*, and Neill also spent the better part of 1997 appearing with Spooky and video sampling innovator's Gardner Post "Sci-Fi Lounge" tour. *Goldbug* followed a year later. —*Jason Ankeny*

**Mainspring** / 1992 / Ear-Rational ♦♦♦♦
In addition to pieces featuring Neill's invention the mutatrumpet, a combination of three trumpets plus slide, which makes rapid change between a variety of sonorities possible, an electronic processing system by Robert Moog, and a computer program by David Behrman have both been designed to work with the mutatrumpet. This CD exemplifies the idea of "unified multisidedness" in its sounds and compositional style. For example, in "Mainspring" (1985) after a fanfare type intro, into a riff-steady march tune over a half-stepping accompaniment with steel guitar country music slides and, later, a solo for the bridge that is really delightful and peculiar. "Dis-solution 2" (1986) is for mutatrumpet, percussion, and pitch-sensing electronics (David Behrman) providing a lovely treble shadow, and "No More People" (1988) with text by Stevie Smith for soprano and band is a classic aria over constantly intense telegraphic figures. Wow.... —*"Blue" Gene Tyranny*

**678 Streams** / 1994 / New Tone ♦♦♦♦
Both the pitch and rhythmic elements for this piece written in 1993 are based on the frequency ratio 6:7:8 and their overtones. Each of the three bells of the composer's originally designed mutantrumpet instrument supplies one of the three sets of harmonics. Sounds from this instrument interactively trigger materials stored in the computer—drum and other percussion sounds, sweeping arpeggios of drone chords (whose cross-rhythms constantly recombine), small trilling figurations, and echoes of Neill's live playing. The hypnotizing effect is like a set with Miles Davis, Terry Riley, and David Behrman on the same bandstand, plus Neill's unique musical sensibilities toward the vast worlds of cross-cultural modal music that are a touchstone of postmodern pattern (so-called "minimal") music. —*"Blue" Gene Tyranny*

**Green Machine** / Sep. 5, 1995 / Astralwerks ♦♦♦♦

**Triptycal** / Sep. 9, 1996 / PolyGram ♦♦♦
Although it retains traces of the illbient influences which textured the previous *Green Machine*, DJ Spooky even makes a cameo appearance. *Triptycal* pushes Ben Neill closer to more straightforward ambient territory, largely favoring atmosphere over groove. As his mastery of the mutantrumpet grows, Neill's playing becomes more and more evocative—the album's dreamscapes move easily from minimalist rhythms to dense drum'n'bass beats, complete with a sensual warmth which belies the record's intellectual rigors. —*Jason Ankeny*

● **Goldbug** / Jun. 16, 1998 / Antilles/I.L.S. ♦♦♦♦
For a trumpet player, Neill proves himself a masterful drum'n'bass merchant and an excellent keyboardist to boot on his 1998 album *Goldbug*. From the opening track "Tunnel Vision," Neill's blend of breakbeats and occasional mutantrumpet solos sounds better than many producers in the drum'n'bass community. There are some notable guests (including DJ Spooky and Page Hamilton), but they appear on few tracks and never take the focus away from Neill's excellent album. —*Keith Farley*

## Neotropic (Riz Maslen)

*Remixing, Producer / Experimental Techno, Electronica, Ambient-Breakbeat, Ambient Techno, Trip-Hop*

One of the most prominent of a growing population of women composers working in post-techno experimental electronics, Riz Maslen's work as Neotropic and Small Fish with Spine combines ambient, dub, and electro with shards of house, hip-hop, and drum'n'bass. Although she's released nowhere near the amount of material as labelmates such as Coldcut and London Funk Allstars, consistency and a stylistic listlessness have proven key in elevating her to near peer status. Signing with the NTone and R&S labels in the mid-'90s (as Neotropic and Small Fish with Spine, respectively) with only a compilation track and a four-track EP to her name, Maslen has wasted no time filling her vida with some of the finest recent examples of downbeat breakbeat and experimental ambient-dub.

Ironically, Maslen's career in the upper reaches of the European experimental dance establishment didn't begin until she moved to New York, where she released the *Stickleback* EP through Apple-housed dance label Oxygen Music Works. After a pair of tracks on a compilation for Ninja Tune offshoot NTone, Maslen headed back to London in 1995 to release the *Tumble Weed* EP and, the following year, a single ("Laundrophone") and album (*15 Levels of Magnification*) for the label. Belgium-based R&S' release of her self-titled *Small Fish with Spine* EP followed soon after. Maslen has also risen to acclaim through her association with the Future Sound of London, with whom she appeared on UK music show *Top of the Pops*, as well as collaborated with on a number of their recordings. Her second for Ninja Tune was 1999's *Mr. Brubaker's Strawberry Alarm Clock*. [See Also: Small Fish with Spine] —*Sean Cooper*

● **15 Levels of Magnification** / 1995 / NTone ♦♦♦♦
The theme here is paranoia, the title deriving from the zooming capabilities of government surveillance cameras. Like earlier Neotropic work, styles mix pretty freely, though with a more integrated, atmospheric bent permeating elements of electro, hip-hop, dub, and drum'n'bass. —*Sean Cooper*

**Tumble Weed [EP]** / 1995 / NTone ♦♦♦
Riz Maslen's debut Neotropic release fits snugly into the NTone catalog, with dubby beats and odd electronics dominating. Although Maslen skips from style to style on tracks such as "From Small Acorns" and "Here I Am," the overall effect is quite similar to Future Sound Of London (with whom Maslen has worked on occasion), with lush synth washes accenting lazy, weirded out beats and off-kilter samples. —*Sean Cooper*

**15 Levels of Magnification (Remixes) [Single]** / Sep. 23, 1996 / NTone ♦♦♦
While Riz Maslen's soupy, downtempo ambient breakbeat might seem the last candidate for the Leon Mar (aka darkcore junglist Arcon 2) remix treatment, Mar's recent release on Future Sound Of London in-house label EbV (as Oil) and Maslen's own past work with the group clarifies things a little. Mar's remix is the pick of the litter, here, a stomping techstep number with a bassline to make Maslen proud. The rest varies from uptempo trip-hop to warped electronic weirdness from DJ Food and Maslen herself (the CD-version adds several more). —*Sean Cooper*

**Mr. Brubaker's Strawberry Alarm Clock** / Oct. 19, 1998 / NTone ♦♦♦
Over three years removed from her Neotropic debut, Riz Maslen returns to beat territory with another collection of sampladelic, slightly atmospheric, breakbeat techno. True to the title, there are a few psychedelic/garage flourishes, more reminiscent of the '60s than the '90s. The wheezing electro drive to "Under Violent Objects" underlines a series of paranoid strings while "Improved Industrial Dwellings" and "Vacetious Blooms" prove Maslen's way with beats and effects hasn't suffered from the absence. The album's not quite as compulsively listenable as *15 Levels of Magnification*, but given the uncompromising excellence of her debut, that's hardly a drawback. —*Keith Farley*

## Neu!

f. 1971, Düsseldorf, Germany, db. 1975
*Group / Obscuro, Proto-Punk, Kraut-Rock, Art-Rock/Progressive-Rock, Electronic*

While little-known and relatively unheralded during their brief existence, the Kraut-rock duo Neu! cast a large shadow over later generations of musicians, and served as a major influence on artists as diverse as David Bowie, Sonic Youth, Pere Ubu, Julian Cope, and Stereolab.

Neu! formed in Düsseldorf, Germany in 1971 after multi-instrumentalists Michael Rother and Klaus Dinger both split from Kraftwerk. Recorded in the space of four days with Can producer Conrad Plank, the duo's self-titled debut appeared early in 1972, and quickly established their affection for minimalist melodies and lock-groove rhythms. While virtually ignored throughout the rest of the world, the album sold extremely well in West Germany, resulting in a tour with support from Guru Guru's Uli Trepte and Eberhard Krahnemann.

Rother and Dinger returned to the studio in 1973 for *Neu! 2*, where a shortfall of cash allowed the duo to complete only two songs, "Super" and "Neueschnee," which they subsequently remixed at varying and disorienting speeds in order to flesh out a full-length album. After the record's release, Rother joined Dieter Moebius and Joachim Roedelius of Cluster to form Harmonia, but Neu! officially reunited in 1975 to record *Neu! 75*. After its release, they again disbanded; Rother continued on as a solo performer, while Dinger and drummer Hans Lampe formed La Dusseldorf. In the mid-'80s, Rother and Dinger reformed yet again, although the recording sessions, titled *Neu! 4*, did not officially surface until 1996. —*Jason Ankeny*

● **Neu!** / 1972 / Billingsgate ✦✦✦✦
Neu!'s visionary debut is an intensely visceral record which reinvents rock in its own visage: a shifting soundscape of drones, feedback, proto-ambient textures, processed effects, and industrial rhythms hung upon minimalist melodies, the album has few precedents, and the fingerprints of its influence are still smeared across experimental music decades later. —*Jason Ankeny*

**Neu! 2** / 1973 / United Artists ✦✦✦✦
A perverse effort, *Neu! 2* mocks the very concept of recorded music: after a lack of cash forced the group to curtail their studio sessions after finishing only a handful of songs, they simply remixed the singles "Super" and "Neueschnee" at various speeds—complete with scratches and pops—to ensure enough material for a full-length LP. Other tracks consist simply of music being played back in the studio, ending when the needle is pulled off the turntable; another concludes with the sound of a cassette being eaten by a tape machine. Confrontational, subversive and brilliant. —*Jason Ankeny*

**Neu! 75** / 1975 / United Artists ✦✦✦
A work of polar extremes, *Neu! 75* is essentially a group record in name only; anticipating the duo's imminent breakup, the album splits evenly between the diametrically opposed work of Klaus Dinger and Michael Rother, resulting in a jarring juxtaposition of Rother's ambient minimalism and Dinger's proto-punk abrasion. —*Jason Ankeny*

**Neu! 4** / 1996 / Captain Trip ✦✦
Recorded sometime in the mid-'80s but not released until over a decade later, *Neu! 4* picks up where the duo left off in 1975, exploring the extremes of both white noise and ambient beauty. Like *Neu! 2*, the album fills out with remixes of the basic tracks, but where the earlier effort simply varied playback speeds, the material on *Neu! 4* undergoes radical, even alien transformations. Much of the record predates '90s electronic music with remarkable foresight: "Fly Dutch II" is a spacy techno loop which stakes out territory later claimed by Mouse on Mars, "Danzing" is a brutal electro experiment, and "86 Commercial Trash" is constructed around samples from German television advertisements. —*Jason Ankeny*

## Neuropolitique (Matthew Cogger)

b. London, England
*Producer / Electronica, Club/Dance, Techno, Acid House*

Neuropolitique is Matt Cogger, a London-based producer whose influential records on the ART, Peacefrog, and New Electronica labels were some of the first examples of UK-bred techno exploring a distinctly Detroit aesthetic. A mixture of steady, pulsing rhythms and melodic and harmonic phrasing with a slight experimental edge, Cogger has made no secret of the influence artists such as Juan Atkins and Derrick May have had over his music. But he has also managed to sidestep the relentless accusations of plagiarism which have plagued UK colleagues such as Kirk Digiorgio and B12. Raised in a London suburb where his exposure to electronic music began early on (he bought Mike Oldfield's *Tubular Bells* at the age of seven), Cogger nonetheless received no formal training, his complex arrangements a function of his engineering experience and a commitment to mastering his gear. To date, that commitment has sealed a pair of full-lengths for New Electronica and a current contract with noted experimental imprint Irdial.

Cogger's first exposure to dance music was (not uncommonly) electro and early hip-hop, which he helped promote as a member of a sound system which also included Lee Purkis (aka Insync of 10th Planet). As hip-hop became more commercial, Cogger became increasingly interested in the emerging acid house movement, picking up the legendary *House Sound of Chicago* compilation in 1986 and immersing himself in the club scene. Drawn to the bizarre experiments of early Detroit techno, Cogger met up with Derrick May at a party in 1989 and made offhanded plans to visit the producer at his Detroit home. Two months later, Cogger was knocking on May's door, having left London to dry out from acid house's drug-addled "summer of love" and learn something about this music he couldn't leave alone. Cogger began working at May's studio, engineering a number of popular records, and soon cutting tracks with Marty Bonds, including "Mind You Don't Trip." His first solo work was the "Artemis" single, later released on Kirk Degiorgio's Applied Rhythmic Technology (A.R.T.) label (Cogger met Degiorgio at May's studio when Degiorgio was over from London on a record-buying trip). A.R.T.'s assocation with the New Electronica label led to Cogger releasing a number of influential tracks and a trio of full-lengths on the label as Neuropolitique (derived from a book by Timothy Leary). —*Sean Cooper*

**Are You Now or Have You Ever Been....** / 1995 / New Electronica ✦✦✦
Matt Cogger's 1995 long player is agreeable but not exactly challenging percussion-heavy techno. —*John Bush*

● **Beyond the Pinch** / 1997 / New Electronica ✦✦✦
*Beyond the Pinch* is a ponderous collection of whitecoat techno and hardcore-leaning rave-esque breakbeat. Matt Cogger's long proven his affection for a leisurely stroll down the road less traveled, and in that respect, *Beyond the Pinch* is signature Neuropolitique, from its (literally) cheeky cover to the swirling masses of artfully dirtied electronics clogging up well-composed electro, techno, and hardcore-leaning breakbeat circa 1991. Not a particularly standout album in any other respect than its steadfast refusal of popular trends (what, no jungle?), but then that applies to most of Cogger's work. Good not great. —*Sean Cooper*

## Jason Nevins

b. 1970, New York, NY
*Producer, DJ / Club/Dance, Hip-Hop*

Cut-and-paste mixmaster Jason Nevins was born in New York City in 1970; he began DJing while working at his college radio station at Arizona State University, and upon returning to the East Coast began creating his first remixes. After producing a handful of compilation tracks, he issued his self-titled debut EP in 1994, followed in 1995 by the full-length *Green*. Remixes for Janet Jackson and Lil Kim followed before Nevins rocketed to international fame in 1997 with his mix of the Run-D.M.C. classic "It's Like That," which topped pop charts across Europe on its way to selling over three million copies. Much of Nevins' subsequent work also reflected his love for '80s hits, with reworkings of Run-D.M.C.'s "It's Tricky" and Rob Base's "It Takes Two" as well as Falco's "Der Kommissar" and Toni Basil's "Mickey" appearing soon after. —*Jason Ankeny*

● **It's Like That [Single]** / Sep. 1, 1997 / Sm:)e ✦✦
Somewhere between commercial crossover and downright exploitation, Nevins' big-beat dance remix of "It's Like That" soared to the number one spot on charts all over Europe, though with little fanfare in his home country. In his hands, "It's Like That" became a pumping breakbeat burner that didn't sound half-bad on the dancefloor but quickly lost its steam on car radios or home systems. It stands as a '90s curiosity, and not much else. —*Keith Farley*

**It Takes Two [Single]** / Feb. 9, 1998 / Sm:)e ✦

**It's Tricky [Single]** / Mar. 23, 1998 / Epidrome ✦

## New Order

f. 1980, Manchester, England
*Group / Alternative Dance, Club/Dance, Post-Punk, New Wave, Alternative Pop/Rock, Synth-Pop, House, Dance-Pop*

Rising from the ashes of the legendary British post-punk unit Joy Division, the enigmatic New Order triumphed over tragedy to emerge as one of the most influential and acclaimed bands of the '80s; embracing the electronic textures and disco rhythms of the underground club culture many years in advance of their contemporaries, the group's pioneering fusion of new wave aesthetics and dance music successfully bridged the gap between the two worlds, creating a distinctively thoughtful and oblique brand of synth-pop appealing equally to the mind, body, and soul. New Order's origins officially date back to mid-1976, when guitarist Bernard Sumner (formerly Albrecht) and bassist Peter Hook—inspired by a recent Sex Pistols performance—announced their intentions to form a band of their own. Recruiting singer Ian Curtis and drummer Stephen Morris, they eventually settled on the name Joy Division, and in 1979 issued their landmark debut LP, *Unknown Pleasures*.

After completing sessions for Joy Division's sophomore effort, *Closer*, Curtis hanged himself on May 18, 1980; devastated, the remaining trio immediately disbanded, only to re-form a few months later as New Order with the addition of keyboardist Gillian Gilbert. With Sumner assuming vocal duties, the new group debuted in March 1981 with the single "Ceremony," a darkly melodic effort originally composed for use by Joy Division. The LP *Movement* followed a few months later, and when it too mined territory similar to New Order's previous incarnation, many observers were quick to dismiss the band for reliving former glories. However, with their next single, "Everything's Gone Green," the quartet first began adorning their sound with synthesizers and sequencers, inspired by the music of Kraftwerk as well as the electro beats coming up from the New York underground; 1982's "Temptation" continued the trend, and like its predecessor was a major favorite among clubgoers.

After a year-long hiatus, New Order resurfaced in 1983 with their breakthrough hit "Blue Monday;" packaged in a provocative sleeve designed to recall a computer disk, with virtually no information about the band itself — a hallmark of their mysterious, distant image — it perfectly married Sumner's plaintive yet cold vocals and abstract lyrics with cutting edge drum machine rhythms ideal for club consumption. "Blue Monday" went on to become the best-selling 12" release of all time, moving over three million copies worldwide. After releasing their brilliant 1983 sophomore album *Power, Corruption and Lies*, New Order teamed with the then-unknown producer Arthur Baker to record "Confusion," another state-of-the-art dance classic which even scraped into the American R&B charts. The group's success soon won them a Stateside contract with Quincy Jones' Qwest label; however, apart from a pair of singles, "Thieves Like Us" and "Murder," they remained out of the spotlight throughout 1984.

Heralded by the superb single "The Perfect Kiss," New Order resurfaced in 1985 with *Low-Life*, their most fully realized effort to date; breaking with longstanding tradition, it actually included photos of the individual members, suggesting an increasing proximity with their growing audience. *Brotherhood* followed in 1986, with the single "Bizarre Love Triangle" making significant inroads among mainstream pop audiences. A year later the group issued *Substance*, a much-needed collection of singles and remixes; it was New Order's American breakthrough, cracking the Top 40 on the strength of the newly recorded single "True Faith," which itself reached number 32 on the US pop charts. The remixed "Blue Monday 1988" followed, and in 1989 — inspired by the Ecstasy-fueled house music which their work had clearly predated and influenced — New Order issued *Technique;* their most club-focused outing to date, it launched the hits "Fine Time" and "Round and Round."

After recording the 1990 British World Cup Soccer anthem "World in Motion," New Order went on an extended hiatus to pursue solo projects; Hook formed the band Revenge, longtime companions Morris and Gilbert recorded a series of television themes as the Other Two, and, most notably, Sumner teamed with ex-Smiths guitarist Johnny Marr and Pet Shop Boys frontman Neil Tennant in Electronic, which scored a Top 40 hit with the single "Getting Away With It." Finally, New Order reconvened in 1993; *Republic* was their biggest hit to date, falling just shy of the US Top Ten despite charges from longtime fans that the band had lost its edge. A major tour followed, although rumors of escalating creative conflicts plagued the group; refusing to either confirm or deny word of a breakup, New Order simply spent the mid-'90s in a state of limbo, with Sumner eventually recording a long-awaited second Electronic LP and Hook mounting another new project, Monaco. "Brutal," the first new effort from New Order in a number of years, was featured on the soundtrack of the 2000 film *The Beach*. —*Jason Ankeny*

### Movement / 1981 / Factory ♦♦♦
New Order's debut album *Movement* bridges the gap between the synthesizer-heavy music the group would later develop and Joy Division's languid, morbid drone. *Movement* pointed the way toward New Order's future by featuring more synthesizers than any of Joy Division's records, as well as more accessible hooks and melodies. —*Stephen Thomas Erlewine*

### Power, Corruption and Lies / 1983 / Qwest ♦♦♦♦
New Order's second album was their giant step out of the looming shadow of Joy Division, clearly establishing their own unique and innovative musical identity. Seamlessly incorporating Gillian Gilbert's lush synth patterns into the mix, *Power, Corruption and Lies* springs from the propulsive, almost liquid bass of Peter Hook and the increasingly strong compositional skills of Bernard Sumner to firmly install the group as a cutting-edge electronic dance unit, one with unsurpassed reserves of humanity and depth — tracks like "Age of Consent" and the shimmering "Your Silent Face" speak to the mind and the body in equal measure. The US release also appended their breakthrough club hit "Blue Monday," a masterpiece of the genre. —*Jason Ankeny*

### Low-Life / 1985 / Qwest ♦♦♦♦
New Order's evolution from from post-punk survivors to state-of-the-art electronic unit became complete with the superb *Low-Life*, the first of their albums to receive a proper American release. Tracks like "Sub-Culture" and "The Perfect Kiss" represent dance-pop at its very finest — propulsive, smart and edgy, they combine lush synth patterns and programmed beats with a level of emotional investment seemingly at odds with its environs, creating a tension which keeps the music fresh and involving where other club hits from the era now seem dated and vacuous. In spite of their new technological mastery, the group remains as eccentric and unpredictable as ever — "Elegia" is a delicate instrumental piece, while the opening "Love Vigilantes" is quite nearly a folk song, complete with a squawking harmonica intro, and is utterly unlike anything else in the New Order catalog; still, it succeeds brilliantly, the work of a band at the very top of its game. —*Jason Ankeny*

### Brotherhood / 1986 / Qwest ♦♦♦♦
One of the least-synthesized albums in New Order's discography, *Brotherhood* offers the simultaneous peak of the group's hook-filled songwriting (not just on the single "Bizarre Love Triangle") and Peter Hook's trademark basswork, which takes a plaintive, upper-register lead on highlights like "Weirdo" and "Broken Promise." As usual, the lines dividing organic and electronic are quite fuzzy, resulting in stark drum-machine lines for the tender ballad "All Day Long." Sumner's fondness for bizarre, enigmatic lyrics continues apace with songs like the closer ("Every second counts, when I am with you/I think you are a pig, you should be in a zoo"). —*John Bush*

### Substance / 1987 / Qwest ♦♦♦♦
*Substance* is a double-disc set collecting New Order's singles, including several songs that were never available on the group's albums, at least in these versions. While there are a couple of re-recordings of earlier singles, most of *Substance* consists of 12" single mixes designed for dance club play. Arguably, these 12" mixes represent New Order's most groundbreaking and successful work, since they expanded the notion of what a rock 'n' roll band, particularly an indie-rock band, could do. *Substance* collects the best of their remixes and in the process it showcases not only the group's musical innovations, but also their songwriting prowess — "Temptation," "Blue Monday," "Bizarre Love Triangle," and "True Faith" are some of the finest pop songs of the '80s. Although it is a double-disc set, *Substance* isn't overly long. Instead it offers a perfect introduction to New Order, while providing collectors with an invaluable collection of singles. —*Stephen Thomas Erlewine*

### ☆ Technique / 1989 / Qwest ♦♦♦♦♦
The first post-acid house masterpiece of British pop, *Technique* presents New Order doing what they'd done best for close to a decade — writing brilliant left-field pop songs and consistently blurring the line between electronic dance and alternative pop. From the driving singles "Fine Time," "Run" and "Round & Round," it would appear that *Technique* was the band's most dance-slanted record yet, though rockier album tracks like "Love Less" and "All the Way" reveal the band having it both ways. "Mr. Disco" proves that the group's baffling sense of humor is still intact. —*John Bush*

### Republic / May 11, 1993 / Qwest ♦♦♦♦
Pulling back slightly from the raw, dance-oriented *Technique*, New Order took a break for four years and then crafted another slice of prime guitar-pop. In keeping with previous work, *Republic* simply borrows elements of contemporary innovations in club music to frame a set of effortlessly enjoyably alternative pop songs. As on *Technique*, the singles ("World," "Spooky") are the most danceable on the record, while lyrical concerns are among the most direct of the group's career, including "Ruined in a Day" and "Times Change," sure signs of the demise of Factory Records. —*John Bush*

### The Rest of New Order / 1995 / London ♦♦♦

### ★ The Best of New Order / Mar. 14, 1995 / Qwest ♦♦♦♦♦
Instead of presenting New Order as a progressive dance band as *Substance* did, *The Best of New Order* showcases New Order the pop band, condensing most of their hit singles onto one disc. A couple of remixes are thrown in (Shep Pettibone takes over "Blue Monday"), and several classics, including "Temptation" and "Ceremony" are missing, but it is still a concise explanation of why the group was one of the most important dance groups of the '80s. —*Stephen Thomas Erlewine*

### Video 586 [Single] / Sep. 22, 1997 / Kudos ♦♦♦♦
A single 20-minute track recorded in the early '80s but never available in anything like its full form, *Video 586* is a pure synthesizer track except for Peter Hook's rumbling low-end. Reminiscent of an extended mid-tempo dub of the

early single "Everything's Gone Green," the track plods occasionally but is remarkable purely for its view of New Order as a synthesizer band in the midst of the crossover-heavy synth-pop crowd of the early '80s. —*John Bush*

## Kenneth Newby

*Sampling, Producer / Experimental Ambient, Electro-Acoustic, Ambient*
Electro-acoustic composer Kenneth Newby has released a number of "deep listening" recordings on the Hearts of Space, Extreme, Fathom, and City of Tribes labels, both solo and as a member of Trance Mission and Lights in a Fat City. A student of Western and nonWestern musical traditions alike, Newby has studied Balinese and Javanese music and dance firsthand and is a noted scholar of computer music (many of his pieces involve algorithm-based compositional techniques). Like Jon Hassell, Steve Roach, and Pauline Oliveros, among others, Newby's music is a studied integration of ancient and traditional acoustic elements with meticulous and controlled electronic sound generation and manipulation devices, bringing together such influences as Western classical, ambient, and gamelan with sophisticated technology and a contemporary feel.

Born in the UK, Newby moved from his second home, Canada, to the San Francisco Bay Area in the late '80s, where, among other things, he worked with pre-*Wired* newtech mag *Mondo 2000* as a writer and editor. He began working with local artists such as Stephen Kent and Beth Custer (with whom he would eventually form Trance Mission), and hooked up with the then-San Francisco-based Hearts of Space label, which released his solo debut, *Ecology of Souls*, in 1992. His longest group projects to date are Lights in a Fat City and Trance Mission, both of which involve more pronounced rhythmic and harmonic elements than his solo work (Newby plays a range of string and percussion instruments). His collaboration with Stephen Kent and Steve Roach, *Halcyon Days*, was released in 1996, and is probably his most well-known release. City of Tribes released his second solo album, *Sirens*, in 1997; an expansive landscape of dreamy tribal ambient, it's among his finest work to date. —*Sean Cooper*

**Ecology of Souls** / 1994 / Hearts of Space ♦♦♦♦
Complex, textured layers of sound weave and unfurl on this newly remastered version of Kenneth Newby's 1993 solo release. Responsible for the primal soundings of Lights in a Fat City and the world beat experience of Trance Mission, composer and multi-instrumentalist Newby envisions and sculpts atmospheric frameworks. Percussion, acoustic instruments, didgeridoo, vocal chants, and natural sound environments are fused with the suling gambuh, a meter-long bamboo flute that is tremendously flexible in terms of range of technique, to create an effective and provocative tool communicating a variety of emotions. —*MusD*

• **Sirens** / Apr. 29, 1997 / City of Tribes ♦♦♦♦
Newby's solo return after a four-year absence, *Sirens* is an immersive collection of ambient and environment electro-acoustic music with strong though restrained Middle Eastern and Southeast Asian influences. Newby intertwines a number of wordless vocal sources with drones, sparse percussion, and contributions on harp, rebab, bull fiddle, and didgeridoo from an assembly of guest artists. A strong, consistent album. —*Sean Cooper*

## Newcleus

f. 1979, Brooklyn, NY
*Group / Old School Rap, Electro*
Although they recorded only two albums, Newcleus contributed one true electro classic in "Jam on Revenge (The Wikki-Wikki Song)," which has been immortalized on hundreds of hip-hop mix tapes and often included in even techno DJ's sets. The origins of Newcleus lay in a 1977 Brooklyn DJ collective known as Jam-On Productions, including Ben "Cozmo D" Cenac, his cousin Monique Angevin and her brother Pete (all teenagers and still in high school). Many members—MCs as well as DJs—came and went as the group played block parties all over the borough, and by 1979, the group centered around Cenac, his future wife Yvette "Lady E" Cook, Monique Angevin, and *her* future husband, Bob "Chilly B" Crafton. (The foursome named their group Newcleus as a result of the coming together of their families.)

By this time, Cenac had begun to accumulate a collection of electronic recording equipment, and the quartet recorded a demo tape of material. With several minutes left at the end of the tape, Newcleus recorded a favorite from their block parties, with each member's vocals sped up to resemble the Chipmunks. The track, "Jam-On's Revenge," impressed producer Joe Webb more than the other Newcleus material, and it became the group's first single, released in 1983 on Mayhew Records. A huge street success, the track became known unofficially as "the Wikki-Wikki song" (after the refrain); when it was re-released later that year on Sunnyview Records, it had become "Jam on Revenge (The Wikki-Wikki Song)."

The single hit Top 40 on the R&B charts in 1983, and its follow-up "Jam on It" did well on even the pop charts. "Computer Age (Push the Button)" was a more mature single, with accomplished rapping and better synthesizer effects, and it also hit the R&B Top 40. The first Newcleus LP, *Jam on Revenge*, was a bit of a disappointment, and their second album, *Space Is the Place*, did even more poorly upon release in 1984. Without a single as noteworthy as "Jam on Revenge" or "Computer Age," and with the advent of Run-D.M.C.'s organic, rock-influenced approach to rap music, Newcleus faded quickly. Though the Cenacs and the Craftons continued to record sporadically until 1989, they didn't hit the R&B charts after 1986. —*John Bush*

**Jam on Revenge** / 1984 / Sunnyview ♦♦

• **Jam on This!: The Best of Newcleus** / Jul. 22, 1997 / Rhino ♦♦♦
Newcleus deserve mention in any history of electro/hip-hop of the early '80s because of two certifiable classics: "Jam on Revenge (The Wikki-Wikki Song)" and "Computer Age (Push the Button)." Two tracks hardly fill a major compilation album, and at first glance, the group wouldn't appear to deserve their own best-of set; however, the compilers at Rhino did a good job of selecting tracks from the group's two albums, 1984's *Jam on Revenge* and the following year's *Space Is the Place* (a reference to jazz mystic Sun Ra). Other than the obvious hits, great album tracks include "Auto-Man," "I Wanna Be a B-Boy" and "Let's Jam." —*John Bush*

## Nico (Nick Sykes)

*Producer, DJ / Jungle/Drum'N'Bass, Club/Dance*
Artist/producer Nico is the production mind behind No U-Turn (NUT) Records and NUT sublabel Nu Black, whose releases by Ed Rush, DJ Trace, Spidernet, and under Nico's own name have been closely associated with the steady darkening of jump-up and techstep-style jungle. Although in particular Ed Rush has recently found wider exposure through his association with Emotif, Grooverider's Prototype imprint, and progressive mainstay Metalheadz, both Nico and NUT (as well as sublabels Saigon and Nu Black) have benefited from the rise in popularity. Although tracks out under his own name are few (he prefers to work in combination), his work behind the boards engineering such anthems as "Bloodclot Artattack," "Guncheck," and "Mothership," as well as several of the tracks on Emotif's lauded *Techsteppin'* compilation (so many, in fact, that it listens almost like a NUT best-of!) set him among the most important and influential jungle producers of the mid-'90s.

Prior to his work in the jungle scene, Nico worked in more middle-of-the-road engineering and production; he didn't hear jungle until Ed Rush—who lived just down the block—showed up at his studio with a few records. At first turned off by the brashness of the sound, Nico roped in Rush after an adjustment period and began producing tracks out of his apartment studio. After a string of largely forgettable releases, the pair issued their first record on Nico's newly formed NUT label. Entitled "Bloodclot Artattack," the track's taut, aggressive drums and monster basslines found a small but committed audience among those tiring of jungle's jazzier, more atmospheric turn (c/o of Bukem, Alex Reece, Spring Heel Jack, et al.). Following a string of moderately received twelves by Rush, Spidernet (Pete Parsons of DeeJay and Lucky Spin), and DJ Trace, as well as the release of *Techsteppin'* on Emotif, Nico formed the Nu Black label as an experiment. The label issues no dubplates or white labels—signatures of the high turnover scene—and its releases are shipped in plain black sleeves with just a small sticker indicating the artist and release number. The first three releases on the label—"Mothership," "Input," and "Amtrak"—shipped more copies than any previous NUT release, and are widely credited with jungle's return to the darkside. —*Sean Cooper*

**Mothership [Single]** / 1995 / No U-Turn ♦♦♦

• **Input [Single]** / 1996 / Nu Black ♦♦♦♦
Nu Black's second and perhaps most celebrated release, "Input" is a split with 19-year-old DJ Fierce, a Nu Black office lackey to whom Nico promised a shot behind the boards. Two tracks of eerie, atmospheric darkness, here, with thick, echoing breaks spinning through half the side before a pair of basslines to wake the dead show up. Storming. —*Sean Cooper*

## Nicolette (Nicolette Okoh)

b. 1964, Glasgow, Scotland
*Vocals / Ambient Techno, Trip-Hop*

From rare-groove to rave to trip-hop and soul, Nicolette was one of the most eccentric dance vocalists of the '90s, working with everyone from the one-shot rave act L.A. Style to electro futurists like Plaid. Born in Scotland though she was raised in Nigeria, France, and Switzerland, Nicolette debuted with the single "Wicked Mathematics" after being one of the first signings by the eponymous label run by Shut Up and Dance. Her debut album, 1992's *Now Is Early* showed her to be an uncommonly mature talent who wrote her own songs (some engaged in political commentary) and featured a warm, crystalline voice. Besides various vocal gigs (including Massive Attack's *Protection*), Nicolette rarely recorded during the next four years. Finally in 1996, she was signed to Gilles Peterson's Talkin' Loud Records. Her second album, *Let No-One Live Rent Free in Your Head*, appeared that same year. Nicolette also contributed an edition in Studio !K7's *DJ Kicks* series. —*John Bush*

**Now Is Early** / 1992 / Studio !K7 ♦♦♦♦
Nicolette's first album, with the Shut Up and Dance production team, charts an intriguing course between her soulful, house-influenced vocal work and the more hardcore production sound. —*John Bush*

● **Let No One Live Rent Free in Your Head** / 1996 / Talkin' Loud ♦♦♦♦
Quite similar to Björk as one of the most eccentric female vocalists in electronic music, Nicolette also knows how to pick producers who get the best out of her songs. She selected Plaid to mix it up on her political-minded single "No Government," while elsewhere the singer works with Alec Empire, 4Hero, and Felix (Roni Size and Dillinja help out with remixes). *Let No One Live Rent Free in Your Head* is one of the most glowing moments of mid-'90s vocal electronica. —*John Bush*

## Nightmares on Wax

f. 1988, Yorkshire, England
*Group / Electronica, Trip-Hop, Club/Dance, Techno, IDM*

The combined project of George Evelyn and Kevin Harper, Nightmares on Wax were one of the brightest spots on the post-rave British techno map of the early '90s. Although since pared back to just Evelyn and a handful of contributors, N.O.W.'s debut album, *A Word of Science*, was, along with early tracks by LFO, Tuff Little Unit, and Tricky Disco, a crucial bridge between the competing influences of New York house and electro, Detroit techno and soul, London rave and acid, and the burgeoning eclecticism of the years to come. Forming in the late '80s in West Yorkshire as an extension of Evelyn and Co.'s b-boy crew the Soul City Rockers, N.O.W.'s first singles, "Dextrous" and "Aftermath," were both highly regarded, and the latter shot into the pop singles Top 40. The subsequent album laid a good deal of the groundwork for the downtempo experimental hip-hop/electro-funk worked over by Mike Paradinas, Luke Vibert, Spacer, and others, and earned the group a secure spot among techno's select crew of next-step innovators. The group nonetheless disbanded following *Science*'s release, with Harper leaving to pursue a DJ career and Evelyn turning out a smattering of house tracks on Warp's Nucleus subsidiary before settling into bedroom woodshed mode. Following a four-year hiatus, Evelyn resurfaced with a track on the Mo'Wax *Headz* compilation and, soon after, *Smoker's Delight*, basically an instrumental hip-hop album with a distinctively British eclecticism. Still involved with the same sorts of genre-spanning sampler-and-sequencer experiments, *Smoker's Delight* is also less obvious, suited more to repeat listenings than previous material. The same was also true for 1999's *Carboot Soul*, Evelyn's first album as part of a deal with American indie label Matador for domestic distribution. In 2000, N.O.W. produced the first new material by De La Soul in several years, included on an EP (*The Sound of N.O.W.*) featuring the rap pioneers. Later that year, Studio !K7 issued the mix album, *DJ Kicks*. —*Sean Cooper*

**A Word of Science** / 1991 / Warp ♦♦♦♦
One of the first album-length statements of British techno and a crucial map for post-rave experimental beat music. —*Sean Cooper*

**Smoker's Delight** / 1995 / Warp ♦♦♦♦
Evelyn's solo step is a whole delightfully unreducible to its parts, which, as with earlier releases, is largely electro, hip-hop, and soul, with bits of Latin percussion and downtempo funk thrown in. The album spawned a pair of somewhat forgettable remix EPs, and was reissued by TVT immediately upon release. —*Sean Cooper*

● **Carboot Soul** / Apr. 12, 1999 / Matador ♦♦♦♦
Four years on from *Smoker's Delight* and, fortunately, little has changed for Evelyn's Nightmares on Wax project. While he could've easily been forgiven for following the nu-beat crowd and inserting a few prescient big beats into the blunted trip-hop formula, it's all clear from the opener "Les Nuits" (a N.O.W. theme of sorts, repeated from *Smoker's Delight*) that we have on hand a return to form, not a turn away from the trip-hop style that took such a beating during the late '90s. The lazy-day soul samples driving tracks like "Morse" and "Finer" are perfect examples that instrumental hip-hop doesn't have to resort to the usual producer's bag of tricks to make for music leagues beyond the average. There's also a focus here lacking from previous material; fewer interludes make for a more concentrated listening experience. All in all, *Carboot Soul* is one of the best arguments yet for the continuing development of trip-hop beyond mere coffee-table fare. —*John Bush*

**DJ Kicks** / Sep. 26, 2000 / Studio !K7 ♦♦♦♦
George Evelyn, one of the best production ears in trip-hop, came a bit late to the mix-album field (his volume in the series had actually been planned since 1995), but definitely came correct anyway. *DJ Kicks* spins through a raft of nu-school hip-hop (Aim, Blackalicious, Freddy Fresh, Syrup, Type), classic old-school producers from A Tribe Called Quest ("Award Tour") to Kenny Dope ("Get on Down," "Superkat"), and tosses in a few of his own N.O.W. tracks to boot. Just as supremely chilled as the best Nightmares on Wax material. —*John Bush*

## Nine Inch Nails

f. 1989, Cleveland, OH
*Group / Industrial Metal, Club/Dance, Heavy Metal, Alternative Pop/Rock, Industrial*

Nine Inch Nails, the one-man band of Trent Reznor, brought industrial music to the masses with 1989's *Pretty Hate Machine*. With its electronic rush, incessant beats, and distorted guitars, the album appeared to be like much industrial music on the surface, yet Reznor wrote pop songs, not the soundtrack to a personal horror movie. NIN's scarred, harsh soundscapes were bleak enough, yet Reznor's lyrics raise the despair and self-loathing to new heights; at times, his relentless darkness can veer dangerously close to self-parody.

*Pretty Hate Machine* wasn't a hit when it was released; it charted in 1990 and stayed on the charts for years afterward. By the time Reznor assembled a band for the first Lollapalooza tour in 1991, the group had a sizable following that only grew with NIN's ferocious performances on the tour. Legal troubles with his record company delayed the release of a second album; in 1992, he released a stop-gap EP, *Broken*, that was harder and more abrasive than the debut, yet still conformed to conventional song structures; it debuted in the *Billboard* Top Ten. With their second full-length album, Reznor showed his true roots—'70s progressive rock. *The Downward Spiral* was promoted as a concept album, a cohesive piece of work; it also featured ex-King Crimson guitarist Adrian Belew. Still, NIN is able to straddle two seemingly opposing genres easily, gaining alternative and mainstream hard rock fans alike; whether he likes it or not, Trent Reznor is the man that made industrial palatable for pop fans, and audiences eagerly anticipated his third album, 1999's *The Fragile*. In fall 2000, the remix album *Things Falling Apart* was released. The album featured previously unavailable material and several remixes, as well as showcasing work by Adrian Sherwood, Dave Ogilvie, Charlie Clouser, and more. —*Stephen Thomas Erlewine*

★ **Pretty Hate Machine** / Nov. 1989 / TVT ♦♦♦♦♦
The reason *Pretty Hate Machine* gained a huge cult following is that Trent Reznor didn't make an industrial album in the strict sense of the term; his songs are pop songs played in an industrial style. Meanwhile, he constructs a towering monument of angst and hatred in his lyrics, perfect for legions of alienated adolescents. As Reznor says, "I'd rather die than give you control," and he proves it throughout *Pretty Hate Machine*. Full of hooks, beats, and abrasive noise, *Pretty Hate Machine* gave a generation of adolescents a martyr as well as a great way to vent anger. —*Stephen Thomas Erlewine*

**Broken [EP]** / Sep. 22, 1992 / Interscope ♦♦♦♦
After the unexpected success of *Pretty Hate Machine*, Trent Reznor found himself unable to enjoy it. Instead, he became embroiled in an ugly lawsuit with his record company, which prevented him from releasing any new ma-

terial for three years. Although *Broken* is only an EP, the wait was more than worth it. Those who fell in love with the pseudo-industrial *Pretty Hate Machine* will likely be alienated by the raging, angry assault of *Broken*. Instead of blaming everyone else for his troubles, Reznor turns his anger inward. "Wish" and "Happiness in Slavery" are busier, angrier, and noisier than anything on *Pretty;* the songs still have hooks, but the hooks are the noise. The anger on *Broken* is real, not feigned; for those who can stomach undiluted rage, *Broken* is a masterpiece. —*Stephen Thomas Erlewine*

**Fixed [EP]** / Nov. 1992 / Interscope ♦♦♦
Even more than *Broken*, the limited-edition *Fixed* EP sounds like an attempt by Reznor to whittle down the size of his audience. The remixes on *Fixed* totally distort all of the original meanings and intents of the original versions on *Broken;* it's the closest Reznor has come to pure industrial music. While the remixes completely rearrange the songs, *Fixed* is additional proof that NIN is not a flash in the pan. A bold artistic move, and not for the faint of heart. —*Stephen Thomas Erlewine*

**The Downward Spiral** / Mar. 8, 1994 / Interscope ♦♦♦♦
Although Trent Reznor designed *The Downward Spiral* as a concept album about despair and anger, these are familiar themes for Nine Inch Nails; it's up to the music to carry the album. And it does carry the album, featuring harder guitars and more brutal beats. However, the songwriting has slipped and the aggression sounds forced. —*Stephen Thomas Erlewine*

**Further Down the Spiral [EP]** / May 30, 1995 / Island ♦♦
While it's marketed as an EP, *Further Down the Spiral* is essentially the single for "Hurt," which is included here in its live version, the same version that's used in the video. However, what makes the disc worth investigating is the remixes. Like *Fixed* before it, *Further Down the Spiral* deconstructs and reassembles the tracks from the platinum *The Downward Spiral*, reconfiguring the music in ways that are frequently more interesting and challenging than the original versions. —*Stephen Thomas Erlewine*

**The Fragile** / Sep. 21, 1999 / Interscope ♦♦♦
Never mind that it took Trent Reznor a long, long time to deliver Nine Inch Nails' second album; the anticipation that greeted *The Downward Spiral* was nothing compared to what awaited its sequel, *The Fragile*. Like *Spiral*, *The Fragile* appeared five years after its predecessor, but the wait seemed longer. After all, between 1989's *Pretty Hate Machine* and *Spiral*, Reznor released numerous stop-gap EPs, remixes, and even toured, slowly building the ravenous following that devoured the second album. *Spiral* not only satiated those fans, but it made Reznor into a superstar and a critic's darling, and neither camp could wait to see where he was going to go next. Once he retreated to his New Orleans studio in 1996, there was little clue to what direction that may be. Word of some collaborators drifted out of the ether—Alan Moulder returned as co-producer, engineer, and mixer; Adrian Belew contributed some guitar; Dr. Dre did some mixing—which only increased expectations that the sequel would top its predecessor. All of those names, plus concept album guru Bob Ezrin (who "provided final continuity and flow"), are credited on *The Fragile*, but everybody's contribution is filtered through Reznor, who has the only discernable signature on the album. That's no great shock, since NIN has always been Reznor's vehicle, but what is shocking is how *The Fragile* feels like no great leap forward, musically or lyrically. As the first five songs unwind, all of Nine Inch Nails' trademarks—gargantuan, processed distorted guitars, ominous electro rhythms, near-ambient keyboards, Reznor's shredded vocals and tortured words—are unveiled, all sounding pretty much how they did on *Spiral*. Upon closer inspection, there are some new frills, particularly in the quiet sections, yet these aren't apparent without some digging. And what's on the surface isn't necessarily inviting, either. There is nothing as rhythmic or catchy as "Closer," nothing as jarring as the piano chorus of "March of the Pigs," no ballad as naked as "Hurt." Ultimately, there are no great singles, which is remarkable for a 23-track double-disc album. That's not to say that Reznor doesn't try for something immediate and visceral: He pulls out all the stops on "We're in This Together" and winds up sounding like Filter. Indeed, every time he stretches for a hate anthem, he misses the mark; he either recycles old ideas or sounds restrained. Fortunately, *The Fragile* begins to live up to its title once the first side is over. Subsequently, there are detours into empty, noisy bluster (some of which, like the Marilyn Manson dis "Starfuckers, Inc.," work quite well) but they're surrounded by long, evocative instrumental sections that highlight Reznor's true gifts. He may not always write memorable songs, but he knows how to arrange and how to create interesting sonic juxtapositions. For instance, with its unsettling martial rhythms and Germanic synthesized brass, "Pilgrimage" is scarier than any of his pummeling testosterone fests. Throughout its long running time, *The Fragile* is compelling when it's vulnerable, when Reznor steps away from his trademark rage in favor of crafting delicate, alternately haunting and pretty soundscapes. These are quite captivating on their own, yet they cast a dark shadow upon the industrial bluster, which sounds canned, even self-parodic, in comparison. Since they provide a change of pace, these flirtations with self-parody fit nicely into the flow of the album, which never feels indulgent, even though it runs over 100 minutes. Still, *The Fragile* feels like a let down in many ways. There's no denying that it's often gripping, offering odd and interesting variations on NIN themes, but that's the problem—they're just variations, not progressions. Considering that it arrives five years after *Spiral*, that is a disappointment; half a decade is plenty of time to redefine an artist's signature sound, as NIN proved with their first two albums. That's not to say that it's impossible to tell where the time went—Reznor's music is immaculately crafted and arranged, with every note and nuance gliding into the next, and that alone takes time—but he and Moulder spent more time constructing surfaces than songs. Those surfaces can be enticing but since it's just surface, *The Fragile* winds up being vaguely unsatisfying, even with all of its virtues. —*Stephen Thomas Erlewine*

## Nitzer Ebb

f. 1982, Chelmsford, Essex,
*Group / Industrial Dance, Post-Punk, Industrial*
Before the majority of industrial acts added guitars and became the heavy metal of the '90s, Nitzer Ebb produced hard-hitting electronic music with the Teutonic bent and abrasive edge of early industrial music, plus the vocal chanting and beat-heavy flavor of the late-'80s alternative and Balearic dance scene. Formed in Chelmsford, Essex in 1982 by vocalist Douglas McCarthy, drummer Bon Harris, and keyboard player David Gooday, the group began experimenting with synthesizers and drum pads, fusing their affinity for dark goth and punk rock with the emerging technology. After several popular shows around London during 1984, PWL producer Phil Harding began working with Nitzer Ebb and recorded their first single, "Isn't It Funny How Your Body Works," which appeared on the band's Power of Voice Communications label in 1985. Three more singles followed during 1985-86 before Nitzer Ebb signed to Mute in late 1986; the first Mute recordings were the singles "Murderous" and "Let Your Body Learn" in early 1987, just before the release of their debut album, *That Total Age*. After the single "Join in the Chant" was remixed by producer Flood (Nick Cave, Erasure), it became one of the crucial tracks in the growing alternative/Balearic dance scene, played out alongside Chicago house, Detroit techno, and Northern soul.

After the release of *That Total Age*, Nitzer Ebb toured Europe with Depeche Mode, and the pop sensibilities appeared to inspire them. By the time of their second album, *Belief*, Gooday had disappeared (to be replaced by Julian Beeston) and Flood had taken over the producer's role from Harding, nudging Nitzer Ebb closer to the dancefloor and shearing away the militaristic bent of much of their earlier recordings. Singles like "Hearts and Minds," "Shame" and "Lightning Man" were loaded with the cold aggression of earlier recordings, working well on dancefloors as well as college radio stations; the 1990 single "Fun to Be Had" even reached number two on the dance charts. The following year's *Ebbhead* further consolidated their position with alternative audiences, with at least two well-known singles, "I Give to You" and "Godhead." As a whole, though, the album showed Nitzer Ebb a bit confused as to where industrial music was going. Nitzer Ebb virtually disappeared from active music-making for the next four years, finally reappearing in 1995 with their fifth album, *Big Hit*. —*John Bush*

● **That Total Age** / Nov. 5, 1987 / Geffen ♦♦♦♦
A towering album of harsh, minimalistic synthesizers, rhythms, and samples, *That Total Age* established Nitzer Ebb as one of the most distinctive alternative dance-rock combos of the late '80s. —*Stephen Thomas Erlewine*

**Belief** / Jan. 9, 1989 / Geffen ♦♦♦♦
*Belief* is essentially the same record as *That Total Age*, but Nitzer Ebb's sonic assault remains just as impressive on their second album. —*Stephen Thomas Erlewine*

**Showtime** / Feb. 26, 1990 / Geffen ♦♦♦♦
Not quite as hard-hitting a record as *Belief* but just as cold and minimalistic,

*Showtime* was the best-flowing Nitzer Ebb album in their discography. Each of the previous LPs contained better individual singles, but only *Showtime* worked from start to finish and still featured two amazing singles, "Lightning Man" and "Fun to Be Had". —*John Bush*

**Ebbhead** / Sep. 30, 1991 / Geffen ♦♦♦
An ambitious though slightly flawed expansion of the trademark Nitzer Ebb sound, *Ebbhead* featured what had become an album standard: two impeccable singles, "I Give to You" and "Family Man," and a subdued, slightly drawn-out sound on several other tracks which slowed everything down. The singles alone almost make it a worthwhile purchase, but *Ebbhead* drags a bit too much. —*John Bush*

**Big Hit** / Mar. 27, 1995 / Geffen ♦♦
*Ebbhead* captured Nitzer Ebb at their peak, but its delayed followup, *Big Hit*, is a disappointment, finding the group at a loss for ideas. Even the addition of a new member, Jason Payne, cannot spark Douglas McCarthy and Bon Harris to new levels. Part of the problem is that Nitzer Ebb decided to rely on more traditional rock instruments—loud guitars, bass, and drums—abandoning their electronic and industrial elements to a certain degree. The result is a muddled, uneven collection that fails to move the group forward. —*Stephen Thomas Erlewine*

## Nonplace Urban Field (Berndt Friedmann)

*Producer / Experimental Techno, Electronica, Ambient Techno, Ambient Dub*
NUF is the experimental solo alter ego of Drome collaborator Berndt Friedmann, whose collaborative works under that name have been influential reference points on the map of post-rave ambient dub and trip-hop. Where Drome's more organic approach to sampledelic breakbeat ambient and digital dub has placed the group next to artists such as Coldcut and Deep Space Network, however, NUF is closer to the outskirts of genre hybridity occupied by the Orb, Transcend, James Bong, and Uwe Schmidt, bringing house, techno, ambient, dub, jazz, and genres unnamed into close proximity. Although NUF's first full-length work leaned more toward wholesale genre integration, subsequent releases (particularly the "mini-album" *Raum Fur Notizen*) tended increasingly toward abstraction, constructing complicated, often humorous amalgams of dub, jungle, electro, jazz, and Latin. Based in Cologne, Friedmann's NUF material has also been released on the industrial techno label Toxxikk Trakks and on Incoming!'s digidub compilation series, *Serenity Dub*. In 2000, Friedmann released *Burnt Friedmann Con Ritmo* through Stefan Betke's Scape label. [See Also: Drome] —*Sean Cooper*

**Nuf Said** / 1995 / Incoming! ♦♦♦
Berndt Friedmann's debut full-length by his NUF project is dence ambient-dub-house with sprinklings of breakbeat and jazz. The overwhelming dancefloor orientation of much of the material can make extended listening somewhat taxing, but the production is tops and Friedmann's knack for unlikely combinations is impressive. —*Sean Cooper*

**Mini Album/Raum Fur Notizen** / Sep. 23, 1996 / Incoming! ♦♦♦♦
With *Notizen*, Friedmann ditches the dancefloor pastiche and heads for bleached-out jungle territory, colliding beatbox patterns and effects loops to dazzling effect. Similar to the polyrhythmic experiments of Atom Heart and Elfish Echo, though with more of a dub foundation. —*Sean Cooper*

● **Golden Star** / Jun. 9, 1997 / Incoming! ♦♦♦♦
A jam-packed hybrid of new tracks and remixes from his previous three albums, *Golden Star* is also the most satisfying, consistently engaging NUF release to date. In addition to a handful of new tracks which follow up on Friedmann's previous mini-album's (*Raum Fur Notizen*) warped, idiosyncratic charm, *Golden Star* features such artists as Scanner, Pink Elln, Solid Doctor's Steve Cobby, Porter Ricks, Pluramon, 8m2 Stereo, and O. Braun, pulling, twisting, clipping, weaving, and otherwise abusing NUF's source tapes. Drawn through as many individual styles as Friedmann is apt to combine in a single track (experimental ambient, house, minimal techno, funky electro-jazz, downtempo, and rapid-fire drum'n'bass), the album is uniformly intriguing, each artist taking full inspiration from Friedmann's stylistic restlessness. —*Sean Cooper*

**Burnt Friedmann Con Ritmo** / Aug. 1, 2000 / Scape ♦♦♦
A frequently intriguing recording to file alongside those of Señor Coconut Y Su Conjunto, *Burnt Friedmann Con Ritmo* is a much more consciously straight-faced fusion of electronics with Latin and jazz. These eight tracks feature skittery comping on keyboards with angular vibes and an assortment of percussion improv—at times only slightly aligned with Latin rhythms. Fronting the most likely nonexistent disposable rhythm section, Friedmann recruited sidemen including Cologne's Josef Suchy for guitar on five tracks and South American transplant Atom Heart (aka Señor Coconut himself) for Moog on one track. Thanks largely to Suchy's minor-key musings, "Destination Unknown" is a highlight, as is Atom Heart's feature on the 12-minute "Das Wesen Aus Der Milchstrasse." —*John Bush*

## Nookie (Gavin Cheung)

*Producer / Jungle/Drum'N'Bass, Club/Dance*
Besides working on engineering for material by Ray Keith, Gavin Cheung has recorded myriad drum'n'bass highlights as Nookie and Cloud 9, releasing his material on some of the most respected labels on the hardcore/jungle scene—Moving Shadow, Reinforced, Penny Black and Labello Blanco as well as his own, Daddy Armshouse. An early fan of hip-hop and electro, Cheung was a member of a breakdance crew that also recorded several sessions during the mid-'80s. After studying for several years, he began working in a record store around the time of the acid-house explosion of the late '80s. Debuting on wax with a ragga/hip-hop remix of Ninjaman's "Zig It Up" in 1989, Cheung was a proper player in Britain's growing hardcore techno scene of the early '90s. Cheung recorded for Moving Shadow as Cloud 9, and recorded several of the nascent jungle community's most infectious tracks, including the much-anthologized "You Got Me Burnin" and "Mr. Logic." His Nookie alias received much attention too, as Cheung released one of the earliest jungle LPs, 1995's *The Sound of Music* (for 4 Hero's Reinforced Records). Besides working on tracks with Ray Keith and helping out Moving Shadow label-mate Rob Haigh's Omni Trio project (for the LP *Music for the Next Millennium*), he remixed Tek 9 and Goldie, and also collaborated with Chicago house pioneer Larry Heard for the 1997 single "Mystical People," released on Labello Blanco. —*John Bush*

● **The Sound of Music** / July 4, 1995 / Selector ♦♦♦♦
Released just after *Parallel Universe* by 4 Hero, Nookie's debut full-length is another high-point for drum'n'bass, with previous burning singles "Only You" and "Give a Little Love" alongside a Foul Play remix of the title track and Cheung's own remix (as Cloud 9) of "Drummer of Doom." —*Keith Farley*

**Mystical People [Single]** / Jan. 20, 1997 / Labello Blanco ♦♦♦

## The Normal

f. 1978
*Group / New Wave, Synth-Pop*
A short-lived outfit whose existence is conveniently documented by a lone 1978 single, the Normal was an alias for Daniel Miller, owner of Mute Records. Through the likes of Cabaret Voltaire and Depeche Mode, Miller's label was responsible for opening thousands of minds to the possibilities of electronic music. Despite the Normal's low profile and minimal output, their "T.V.O.D."/"Warm Leatherette" single added its own significant contribution to the then-new electronic pop playing field. The B-side, written in tribute to J.G. Ballard's auto-wreck fetish novel *Crash*, carried relentless pulsing, clinical snapping, and detached vocal chants; it's since become a classic in the realm, having been covered by the likes of Grace Jones and Chicks on Speed. As the Normal, Miller also contributed to an experimental live EP with Robert Rental entitled *Live at West Runton Pavilion;* Miller briefly dedicated himself to synth-pop covers of classic rock songs as the Silicon Teens as well. —*Andy Kellman*

● **T.V.O.D./Warm Leatherette [Single]** / 1978 / Mute ♦♦♦♦
A pivotal, early release of electronic new wave, this single oddly gained more notoriety for its B-side, "Warm Leatherette." Amidst jolting zaps, pops, and blipping skips, Daniel Miller robotically intones about the pleasures of car crash as foreplay: "A tear of petrol is in your eye/The hand brake penetrates your thigh/Quick—let's make love/Before you die." The track sounds like a darkly cartoonish version of a malfunctioning dot matrix printer: clinically pristine, minimal, and sinister. A brief flash that caused countless ripples, it sounds just as fresh two decades after its creation. [The single was later reissued on CD.] —*Andy Kellman*

## the notwist

f. 1989, Weilheim, Germany
*Group / Indie Rock, Alternative Pop/Rock*
Formed near Munich as a hardcore punk band, the notwist gradually began to embrace a fusion of classic '80s indie-pop songwriting and scruffy electronic

backings indebted to Oval and Autechre. The quartet is comprised of brothers Markus and Micha Acher (on vocals/guitar and bass, respectively) plus programmer/keyboard player Martin Gretschmann and drummer Martin Messerschmidt. Their self-titled 1989 debut and 1992's *Nook* were rough-and-tumble punk LPs. Third album *12* marked the group's first flirtation with electronics, though the chord structures and vocals of Markus Acher marked the nowtist more as an alternative band. The band then gained an American distribution deal with Zero Hour, and after *12* was reissued, fourth album *Shrink* appeared in 1998. Gretschmann has also recorded on his own as Console. —*John Bush*

**12** / 1995 / Zero Hour ✦✦✦

German post-rockers the notwist take an unconventional approach to making dance-pop on *12*. Though the occasional use of grinding analogue synthesizers makes for a style far from the mainstream, the linear thrust of rock is apparent throughout the album. The result is music harking back to alternative-pop icons like Dinosaur Jr. and Sonic Youth, as well as experimental-techno producers Oval and Autechre. A limited-edition American release includes a bonus disc of remixes. —*John Bush*

● **Shrink** / Sep. 8, 1998 / Zero Hour ✦✦✦✦

The group's second album has tighter pop songs (though the chords are still a bit derivative of Dino Jr.) and an edgier production sense reminiscent of Pan sonic and other electronic experimenters underlying on tracks like "Day 7," "Another Planet" and "Chemicals." The fusion of bubbly electronics and ragged guitar-pop works better than expected, lifting *Shrink* above a raft of other post-rock acts. —*John Bush*

## Null (Kazuyuki K. Null)

*Guitar, Producer / Experimental Ambient, Experimental Rock, Noise-Rock, Space-Rock, Industrial*

Aside from the extremity of his work with Japanese grind/death/noise rockers Zeni Geva, K.K. Null reserved his solo projects for music just as intense but with more diversity. That range is simply astonishing considering that virtually all of his recordings consist of a patch cord or two (plus occasional treated vocals) fed in to Null's assortment of guitar and effects pedals. Null creates intense wall-of-noise machine music as well as droning isolationist material, which provides a surprsisingly effective update of Southeast Asia's atonal gong music. Besides a number of one-man albums for such labels as Table of the Elements, Manifold, Charnel House, Alleysweeper, and his own Nux Organization label, he has also recorded with sympathizers such as Masami Akita (aka Merzbow), James Plotkin, Jim O'Rourke, and Fred Frith—plus as a member of the side-project groups Yona-Kit, Absolut Null Punkt, and YBO2. —*John Bush*

● **Sonicfuck USA.** / 1990 / Nux Organization ✦✦✦✦

K.K. Null's first solo album was a 1990 live concert recorded in America (roughly half in San Jose and half in San Francisco). The title is quite apt, considering Null's assault on the senses via guitar and voice; both are treated beyond all recognition, resulting in caterwauls of metallic noise-skronk that approach the sound of a poorly recorded chainsaw. Making the most extreme passages of Sonic Youth appear comparable to a Peter Frampton solo is hard work indeed, but Null fits the bill with ease. —*John Bush*

**Aurora** / 1994 / Caroline ✦✦✦✦

Null and James Plotkin, two grindcore extremists of past days, collaborate on *Aurora* to create dark ambient music. Despite being recorded on a primitive four-track, this is an intensely textured and brooding release. "Dead Moon Ritual" brings the listener to an eerie, yet tranquil void, only for that tranquillity to be disrupted by sparsely placed echoing bells. "Sawtooth Swirl," on the other hand, is a superb psychedelic experience, bringing to mind James' band OLD during the *Musical Dimensions of Sleastak* years. Compared to Plotkin's other contemporary efforts, this is definitely among his best work. —*Marc van der Pol*

**Ultimate Material II** / 1995 / Fourth Dimension/Dirter ✦✦✦

This 1995 double-LP set expands Null's horizons with adventures into comparatively new age territory, though exploratory and anachronistic enough to be considered avant-garde. —*John Bush*

**Ultimate Material III** / 1995 / Manifold ✦✦✦

Another collection of out-of-this-world noise performed without samplers or synthesizers, *Ultimate Material III* consists of two half-hour workouts for K.K. Null with only guitar, percussion, and voice. The first track is a bracing motorized wail while the second begins with a muted version of the first, only to explode into similar noise and effects. —*John Bush*

**Absolute Heaven** / Aug. 1, 1995 / Nux Organization ✦✦✦

*Absolute Heaven* contains three pieces, the capstone of which is the 36-minute second track, recorded in 1991. Amidst a background of jangling gong-like sounds (as usual, guitar and connected effects pedals are the only instruments used) is a scathing chainsaw tear of guitar feedback and distortion, gradually faded out to reveal occasional smoke-belch eruptions and more droning gongs. —*John Bush*

**New Kind of Water** / 1996 / Charnel House ✦✦✦✦

Including Null with special guest Jim O'Rourke, *New Kind of Water* is a series of improvised guitar duets, two of which were recorded live at Chicago's Lounge Axe. It's yet another album in Null's catalogue of guitar tracks that appear to be anything but, this one reminiscent of Southeast Asian gongs and droning organs; the live tracks though, are less processed, hence closer to normal electric guitar. The music is among Null's most atmospheric and beautiful, only occasionally droning or repetitious. —*John Bush*

**Terminal Beach** / Dec. 30, 1996 / Manifold ✦✦✦✦

Inspired by a J.G. Ballard story, *Terminal Beach* consists solely of K.K. Null's guitar/vocal loops, treatments,. and live playing, all multitracked. It's an impressive achievement that moves from the abstract sound sculptures of "Voice of Eternity" to pummeling machine-trance on the 17-minute "War Dance." Though the range can be astonishing and difficult to cope with, *Terminal Beach* is a revelatory listen. —*John Bush*

## Gary Numan (Gary Anthony James Webb)

b. Mar. 8, 1958, Hammersmith, London, England
*Vocals, Keyboards, Synthesizer / New Romantic, New Wave, Electronic, Synth-Pop*

Gary Numan managed to incorporate the electronic innovations of Kraftwerk, Brian Eno, and David Bowie into pop music, creating some of the first synth-pop hits of the new wave era. Numan originally performed under the name Tubeway Army, which had a chart-topping British single with "Are 'Friends' Electric?" The first record he released under his own name, 1979's *The Pleasure Principle,* featured the international hit "Cars;" the single hit No. 1 in the UK and reached the US Top Ten. Throughout the early '80s, Numan was one of the most popular artists in the UK, amassing several Top Ten hits and two No. 1 albums. Around 1983, his career began to slip, as each record became indistinguishable from the other. Even as he fell out of the Top Ten, Numan held on to his diehard fans. He continued to record into the '90s, releasing *Fury* in 1998 and *Dramatis Project* in mid-2000. —*Stephen Thomas Erlewine*

**Tubeway Army** / Nov. 1978 / Beggars Banquet ✦✦✦✦

The classic, long-out-of-print self-titled debut by Gary Numan's Tubeway Army has finally been reissued by Beggars Banquet, who have done a masterful job remastering the tracks and adding a live set from 1978 as a bonus. In the past, many have felt that Numan's debut disc didn't measure up to his later triumphs (1979's *Replicas,* 1980's *Telekon,* etc.), but listening to it today, you discover that it's the most underrated of all his early albums. Numan & the Tubeway Army were one of the first new wave/punk bands (along with Kraftwerk and Devo) to successfully fuse robotic synthesizers with rock 'n' roll. Gary Numan's guitar riffing is more prominent here than on any other of his albums, which gives the tunes a splendid *Ziggy Stardust* feel at times. Kicking things off with several strong compositions—"Listen to the Sirens," "The Life Machine," and "Friends"—the album sags momentarily in the middle ("My Love Is Liquid"), but soon returns to its high standards with "Are You Real?" and "Jo the Waiter." The reissue of *Tubeway Army* wraps up with the 13-track *Living Ornaments '78: Live at the Roxy* set, which was previously released only as a bootleg. Although lo-fi, it's an audience recording containing songs that didn't make it to the debut. [Note: In addition to bonus tracks, all of the Gary Numan/Begggars Banquet re-releases contain classic photographs and informative liner notes by Numan biographer Steve Malins.] —*Greg Prato*

**Replicas** / 1979 / Atco ✦✦✦✦

By the release of their second album, *Replicas,* Gary Numan was the undisputed focal point and leader of icy electro-punkers Tubeway Army. And the move proved to be massively successful back home in the UK, where both the album and the single "Are 'Friends' Electric?" topped the charts. The band had made a conscious effort to streamline the sound heard on their 1978 self-titled debut—the distorted guitar riffs were played on Moog synthesizers instead, and Numan had perfected his faux-space-age persona. And the paranoia that is very evident in the lyrics and vocals on Numan's next release, *The Pleasure Principle*, can be detected on *Replicas*. Another near-perfect album by the band, highlights are many—"Me! I Disconnect From You," "The Machman," "You Are In My Vision," and one of the most underrated new wave/synth-driven compositions of the whole era, the chilling ballad "Down In the Park." And out of all the Gary Numan/Beggars Banquet reissues, *Replicas* contains the strongest bonus tracks, such as never-heard outtakes from the recording sessions, including "The Crazies," "Only a Downstat," and the B-side to the original "Are 'Friends' Electric?" single, "We Are So Fragile." [Note: In addition to bonus tracks, all of the Gary Numan/Begggars Banquet re-releases contain classic photographs and informative liner notes by Numan biographer Steve Malins.] —*Greg Prato*

**The Pleasure Principle** / Sep. 1979 / Arista ◆◆◆◆
The most popular of all the Gary Numan albums is undeniably 1979's *The Pleasure Principle*. The reasons are simple—there is not a single weak moment on the disc, it contains his sole US (No. 1 worldwide) hit, "Cars," and new drummer Cedric Sharpley adds a whole new dimension with his powerful percussion work. *The Pleasure Principle* is also one of the first Gary Numan albums to feature true ensemble playing, especially heard within the airtight, killer groove of "Metal" (one of Numan's all-time best tracks). Starting things off with the atmospheric instrumental "Airlane," the quality of the songs get stronger and stronger as the album progresses—"Films," "M.E.," "Observer," "Conversation," the aforementioned "Cars," and the UK Top Ten hit "Complex" all show Numan in top form. The 1998 reissue contains three unreleased instrumentals (one the B-side to the "Cars" single, "Asylum"), as well as four live tracks. If you had to own just one Gary Numan album, *The Pleasure Principle* would be it. [Note: In addition to bonus tracks, all of the Gary Numan/Begggars Banquet re-releases contain classic photographs and informative liner notes by Numan biographer Steve Malins.] —*Greg Prato*

**Telekon** / 1980 / Arista ◆◆◆◆
Gary Numan's follow-up to the flawless *The Pleasure Principle* was 1980's *Telekon*. Although it was another mega-hit back home in England (his third consecutive No. 1 album), Numan could not follow up his massive new wave hit "Cars" in the US, where he was unjustly slapped with the one-hit wonder tag. *Telekon* would also turn out to be the last true classic Numan album, as monetary problems and an unfocused attempt to try different musical forms (as well as a short-lived retirement) would steer him away from his original vision. Although *Telekon* was indeed a strong album, it could have been even stronger if it included the UK Top Ten singles "I Die: You Die" and "We Are Glass" (both were recorded during the *Telekon* sessions). Numan experimented with funk for the first time in his career ("Remind Me to Smile"), but there were still plenty of chilling synth excursions to keep the Numan faithful satisfied—"This Wreckage," "The Aircrash Bureau," "I'm An Agent," and "I Dream of Wires" are all choice cuts. The 1998 Beggars Banquet re-release eventually did include both the UK singles, as well as several other rarities, including a bare "piano version" of "Down In the Park." [Note: In addition to bonus tracks, all of the Gary Numan/Begggars Banquet re-releases contain classic photographs and informative liner notes by Numan biographer Steve Malins.] —*Greg Prato*

**I, Assassin** / 1982 / Atco ◆◆◆◆
Although it showcases his trademark sound to a fine effect, the repetitive, formulaic songwriting of *I, Assassin* suggests that Gary Numan had hit a brick wall with his robotic, synthesized pop. —*Stephen Thomas Erlewine*

**Warriors** / 1983 / Beggars Banquet ◆◆
Former Be-Bop Deluxe leader Bill Nelson was brought in to produce this album and provide some soaring lead guitar work, but the collaboration with Numan was beset by difficulties involving Numan's ego and approach to recording. While Nelson's production is evident on many tracks and his guitar is heard in several places, much of this is business as usual (a B-side, "Poetry and Power," features more Nelson and has gone on to a great deal of popularity, especially with the Gravity Kills cover on *Random*). The science fiction influences here are Robert A. Heinlein's *The Moon Is a Harsh Mistress* and Harlan Ellison's "'Repent, Harlequin!' Cried the Tick-Tock Man." While there is some evidence of confusion as to his direction, the music and songwriting has more energy than anything on the predecessor, *I, Assassin*, with some genuinely engaging moments along the way. —*Steven McDonald*

**Berserker** / 1984 / Numa ◆◆◆
Originally released in 1984 on his own Numa label, *Berserker* is one of the most synthesizer-heavy albums from Numan's mid-'80s period, with tracks like "My Dying Machine," the title track and "A Child with the Ghost," written in tribute to longtime friend and bass player Paul Gardiner. —*John Bush*

**Metal Rhythm** / 1988 / Illegal ◆◆◆
Numan's career had stalled somehow during the first run of his own record label, leading him to sign a deal with IRS for several albums—a deal that would lead to frustrations galore for Numan, who found himself suddenly constrained by a record company's idea of what Gary Numan should be. This did not affect Numan immediately, mind you—*Metal Rhythm* is an energetic return to form, with some great moments in songs such as "New Anger" and "America." The basic theme of the album is the rebirth of a pop star … alas, it would be downhill for a while after this. IRS took cuts from this and several prior albums and cobbled together the patchwork of *New Anger*, and the slide began in earnest. —*Steven McDonald*

**Machine + Soul** / 1992 / Numa ◆◆
Lightning must have struck Numan for this album—he either wanted to be Janet Jackson or Prince, or both. The backing vocalists wail on, the music thumps along in a zombielike attempt at funk, and the whole works staggers grimly along like a bad attempt at white-boy soul. It's not all bad—just terribly painful. —*Steven McDonald*

**Archive, Vol. 1** / Oct. 22, 1996 / Rialto ◆◆◆
Rialto's *Archive, Vol. 1* is a 16-track collection that balances live versions of greatest hits and latter-day studio recordings from Gary Numan. Certainly, this is the kind of record that will irritate casual fans, who will want the original hit versions of "Are 'Friends' Electric?" and "Cars," and the recordings are specialized or interesting enough for collectors, so it falls into a weird limbo that pleases neither extreme. —*Stephen Thomas Erlewine*

**The Best of Gary Numan: 1984-1992** / 1997 / Emporio ◆◆◆
Gary Numan had stopped having hits several years before 1984, which is where *The Best of: 1984-1992* chooses to begin. During the late '80s, Numan began to concentrate more on sonic textures, creating glassy, shimmering soundscapes with his synthesizers and abandoning the robotic funk that made "Cars" and "Are 'Friends' Electric?" into hits. While the latter is included in a stilted live version, none of his best moments are featured on this collection. Nevertheless, it does feature the cream of a highly uneven era, and that alone makes it a worthwhile addition to his catalog. For many casual fans, *The Best of: 1984-1992* will be all they need from Numan's latter-day recordings, if they need it at all. —*Stephen Thomas Erlewine*

● **Premier Hits** / Mar. 25, 1997 / Beggars Banquet ◆◆◆◆
In the US, Gary Numan is remembered as a one-hit-wonder, while back home in his native England, he continued to crank out hit after hit and became a superstar in the process. His icy space-age persona and sound may be forever associated with early 80's British new wave (Flock of Seagulls, early-Duran Duran, etc.), but he was the originator, and today seems pretty darned original. Numan was a scholar of the David Bowie *Ziggy Stardust*-era, who used Bowie's space alien approach as a starting point. While retaining his futuristic lyrics, Gary stripped *Ziggy*'s sound free of the distorted guitar riffing and posturing, and replaced it with clinical synthesizers and a standoffish stage persona. His music also gives off a paranoid vibe at times, as evidenced on the hits "I Die: You Die" and "Are 'Friends' Electric?" But Numan's songs can also sedate you ("Down In the Park"), while other times sneak up on you (the unexpected punk rocker "Bombers"). And of course there's his sole US hit, "Cars," which sounds like a not-so-distant ancestor to fellow futuristic weirdos Devo. —*Greg Prato*

**Exile** / Feb. 10, 1998 / Cleopatra ◆◆◆
Instead of returning to his groundbreaking, retro (by today's standards) synth work of the early '80s, Gary Numan tackles twitching electro-rock reminiscent of Nine Inch Nails on 1998's *Exile*. A comeback album of sorts, *Exile* does the job of proving that Numan still has what it takes to remain relevant in the '90s alternative scene, but it's not exactly the magnificent return to form that Numan fanatics were expecting prior to its release. Since he is an originator (listen to 1979's *Replicas* and 1980's *The Pleasure Principle* for the proof), it's hard to accept that *Exile* is so familiar-sounding to his technoid contemporaries of the '90s. Still, it seems like ages since Numan has sounded so committed on record, as heard on the single "Dominion Day," plus the tracks "Dead Heaven"

and "Dark." Also included on the US CD version as a bonus track is a recent live reading of his 1979 classic "Down in the Park," which showed that Numan can still nail his signature sound. *Exile* confirms that the great Gary Numan is close to being back on the right musical track. —*Greg Prato*

**Remodulate: The Numa Chronicles** / Aug. 4, 1998 / Cleopatra ♦♦♦♦
*Remodulate: The Numa Chronicles* is a two-CD retrospective covering Gary Numan's output for his own Numa label from 1984-1995; however, fans looking for a concise overview of that period should be warned that the second CD consists of live material from throughout Numan's career. Also, some fans will appreciate the fact that some singles on the first disc are included in their extended versions, while others might find that they detract from the overall playability. [Note: the vinyl release of *Remodulate* contains two bonus tracks.] —*Steve Huey*

## Nurse with Wound

f. 1978, London, England
*Group / Experimental Rock, Dark Ambient, Experimental, Industrial*
A loose experimental project formed in 1978 by Steven Stapleton, Nurse with Wound has explored abstract music—influenced by Kraut-rock, freewheeling jazz improvisation and Throbbing Gristle but including a heavy debt to French surrealists Dali and Lautréamont—with an overpowering release schedule of limited-edition albums and EPs. Stapleton worked with an ever-changing list of collaborators during the early years of Nurse with Wound, though Current 93's David Tibet has been the only frequent recording companion during the '80s and '90s. Nurse with Wound's first three albums (*Chance Meeting on a Dissecting Table of a Sewing Machine and an Umbrella, To the Quiet Man from a Tiny Girl* and *Merzbild Schwet*) reflect a naked, minimalist slant with long periods of quiet suddenly interrupted by guitar chords inspired by the avant-garde wing of psychedelia/jazz-rock, chains, music boxes, and found-sound recordings. By the early '80s, Stapleton had begun to incorporate noisy, abrasive rhythms that put him more in line with contemporary EBM masters like Skinny Puppy and SPK. Though Stapleton continued his surrealist slant, he often moved back to more empty recordings. These works—beginning with *Soliloquy for Lilith* in 1988—came to light in the context of the growing ambient/electronic movement, however, putting Nurse with Wound squarely in line with music trends for the first time. Stapleton recorded two split-singles with Stereolab during 1995, and continued his hectic, uncompromised release schedule from his base in Southern Ireland. —*John Bush*

• **Chance Meeting on a Dissecting Table of a Sewing Machine and an Umbrella** / 1979 / United Dairies ♦♦♦♦
The debut Nurse with Wound album lies halfway between the more tuneless explorations of Kraut-rock and the new industrialism practiced by Throbbing Gristle and Cabaret Voltaire. Across three lengthy tracks, obtuse guitar freakouts are used to frame distorted synthesizers and mostly rhythm-less drum machines. Though it frequently defies easy analysis, *Chance Meeting* is one of the more glowing examples of uncompromising industrial-noise of the '70s. —*John Bush*

**Homotopy to Marie** / 1982 / United Dairies ♦♦♦♦
**Soliloquy for Lilith** / 1988 / Idle Hole ♦♦♦
**A Sucked Orange** / 1989 / United Dairies ♦♦♦♦
The peak of Stapleton's intense art-of-sampling period, *A Sucked Orange* includes 20 tracks, most consisting of just one repetitive sample gradually reworked over the course of several minutes. Though it's not the most exciting Nurse with Wound release, Stapleton conjures extensive trance-states by relying on just one sound, and that's quite fascinating by itself. —*John Bush*

## Nuyorican Soul

f. 1996, New York, NY
*Group / Latin-Dance, Club/Dance, House*
Better known as the dance production team Masters at Work, Kenny "Dope" Gonzalez and Lil' Louis Vega became Nuyorican Soul for an EP in 1996 and an eponymous full-length one year later. Much like Guru's jazz-rap fusion project *Jazzmatazz*, *Nuyorican Soul* united jazz legends with newer talents in a celebration of jazz, R&B, and dance, with most tracks including Latin styles befitting the heritage of Gonzalez and Vega. [See Also: The Bucketheads, Masters at Work] —*John Bush*

• **Nuyorican Soul** / Mar. 11, 1997 / Giant Step/Blue Thumb ♦♦♦♦
All-star albums are usually dodgy affairs, but the over-arching talents—and more importantly, production experience—of Masters at Work's Kenny Dope and Lil' Louie Vega keep *Nuyorican Soul* from being overburdened with cooks. Roy Ayers, George Benson, and Jazzy Jeff contribute prominently to four tracks, and vocalists Jocelyn Brown and India (Louie's wife) are heard as well, but over half of the album is comprised of instrumental tracks—several which include Tito Puente on vibes and timbales, flutist Dave Valentin, trumpeter Charlie Sepulveda, organist/arranger Hilton Ruiz, and trombonist Steve Turre. In keeping with Masters at Work's heritage, most of the album is Latin in feel and jazzy in composition, but with ever-present synths and piano runs that belie their heavy dance heritage. If *Nuyorican Soul* is one of the best all-star dance albums to date, it is for lack of competition. —*John Bush*

## Michael Nyman

b. Mar. 23, 1944, London, England
*Piano, Composer / Original Score, Avant-Garde, Minimalism*
Celebrated for his modular, repetitive style, minimalist composer Michael Nyman was among experimental music's most high-profile proponents, best known in connection with his film scores for director Peter Greenaway. He studied at the Royal Academy of Music and King's College, London under communist composer Alan Bush and Thurston Dart, a musicologist specializing in the English Baroque. Under Dart's tutelage, Nyman was introduced to 16th- and 17th-century English rounds and canons, their repetitive, contrapuntal lines highly influencing his own later work; Dart also encouraged him to travel to Romania in the interest of seeking out the country's native folk music traditions. Upon graduating during the mid-'60s, Nyman found himself disconnected from both the pop music of the times and the school of modern composition heralded by Stockhausen; as a result, from 1964 to 1976, he worked not as a composer but as a music critic, writing for publications including *The Listener, New Statesman,* and *The Spectator*. In a review of British composer Cornelius Cardew, he first introduced the word "minimalism" as a means of musical description.

During this same period, Nyman did continue performing, appearing with artists ranging from the Scratch Orchestra and Portsmouth Sinfonia to Steve Reich and the Flying Lizards. In 1974, he wrote the influential book *Experimental Music—Cage and Beyond*, an exploration of the influence of John Cage on a generation of composers and performers. Perhaps its most profound impact was on Nyman himself, who through writing the book seemed to discover his own muse; in 1976 he accepted an invitation from Harrison Birtwistle, Director of Music at the National Theatre, to arrange a number of 18th-century Venetian popular songs for a production of Goldoni's *Il Campiello*. Nyman's arrangements consisted of medieval instruments—rebecs, sackbuts and shawms, bass drums, soprano saxophones, and the like—designed for maximum loudness to produce a distinctive instrumental color; when the production ended, he began composing original music merely to keep the same group of musicians together. Originally an acoustic unit, when rechristened the Michael Nyman Band in the early '80s, amplification became essential to their aesthetic.

Nyman's first major success came in 1982 with the score to the Greenaway film *The Draughtsman's Contract;* his subsequent collaborations with Greenaway on pictures including 1988's *Drowning By Numbers,* 1989's *The Cook, the Thief, His Wife and Her Lover* and 1991's *Prospero's Books* remain among his most high-profile works, their notoriety coming at the risk of overshadowing his forays into opera, chamber music, vocal music, and dance scores. The signatures of Nyman's work include not only his use of propulsive repetition, but also a palette of idiosyncratic instrumental touches—thumping keyboards, "rude" bass clarinets and baritone saxophones, and extreme high and low octave doublings. Mozart was a central influence in much of his work, including 1976's *In Re Don Giovanni* and 1983's *I'll Stake My Cremona to a Jew's Trump;* Schumann, meanwhile, was the major inspiration behind the acclaimed 1986 chamber opera *The Man Who Mistook His Wife for a Hat,* while Bartok shades 1988's *String Quartet No. 2,* commissioned for the Indian dancer and choreographer Shobana Jeyasingh.

In 1990, Nyman composed *Six Celan Songs,* a work based on the poems of Paul Celan, for the German cabaret singer Ute Lemper, with whom he first worked on the score for *Prospero's Books.* His most emotional compositions to date, they served as the clear impetus for his score to Jane Campion's 1992 film *The Piano*, easily Nyman's best-known work; like so many of his compositions, he obsessively reworked the music to *The Piano* time and time again, the haunting melodies reappearing arranged for standard piano concerto, for two pianos, for chamber ensemble, for soprano saxophone and strings (*Lost and Found*) and for soprano and string quartet (*The Piano Sings*). While 1992's *The Upside-Down Violin* reflected Nyman's continuing fascination with traditional ethnic musics, 1993's *MGV*, or *Musique a Grande Vitesse*, returned to the propulsive sounds of the Michael Nyman Band. Other major works include 1992's *Time Will Pronounce*, 1993's *Yamamoto Perpetuo* (a composition for unaccompanied violin written for Alexander Balanescu), 1994's solo harpsichord work *Tango for Tim*, and 1995's *String Quartet No. 4*. Among Nyman's film scores: 1995's *Carrington* and 1997's *Gattaca*. —*Jason Ankeny*

- **Waltz** / 1982 / New Tone ♦♦♦♦

Composed in 1982, this piece for band of multiple saxes, brass, clarinets, two violins, and piano, is built on an interior conflict—a simple, rather maudlin waltz pattern is confronted by a wildly squawking and squealing gaggle that "attempt to destroy it. Officium before its time." (Nyman) The effect is engagingly surreal and drolly humorous and definitely not your usual three-four stomp. —*"Blue" Gene Tyranny*

**A Zed and Two Noughts** / 1990 / Virgin ♦♦♦

Score for the film by Peter Greenway. Nyman's filmscores make effective use of baroque harmonies (Pergolesi, Vivaldi, Purcell...often in traditional "chain of suspensions" technique) and Phil Glass-like harmonies (Wagnerian thirds mixed with modal scales) combined with obsessive patterns in the British "minimalist" style to make a sound of his own. Excellent production by composer David Cunningham. —*"Blue" Gene Tyranny*

**The Piano Concerto** / 1994 / Pauline Oliveros ♦♦♦

Notwithstanding the rather droll British joke of the title, and barely skirting a style of Romantic period kitsch, this piece still features surprising harmonic changes and lovely melodies à la Nyman, and retains the post-modern "edge" of his earlier film music. The concerto is of course based on Nyman's music for Jane Compton's award-winning movie *The Piano*. —*"Blue" Gene Tyranny*

**Gattaca [Original Soundtrack]** / Oct. 21, 1997 / Virgin ♦♦♦

Michael Nyman's soundtrack to the paranoid futuristic thriller *Gattaca* is appropriately haunting and challenging, filled with chilly, evocative soundscapes. —*Rodney Batdorf*

# O

## O Yuki Conjugate
f. 1982, Nottingham, England
*Group / Experimental Ambient, Ambient*

The British experimental ambient unit O Yuki Conjugate was formed in Nottingham in 1982 by multi-instrumentalists Andrew Hulme and Roger Horberry; inspired by the atmospheric guitar instrumentals of the Durutti Column, they began experimenting with keyboards and tape loops, adding percussion to the mix before debuting with the soundscapes of 1984's *Scene in Mirage*. A three-year gap preceded the release of the follow-up, *Into the Dark Water*, the first of many extended absences from the contemporary music scene; only in 1991 did O Yuki Conjugate again resurface, issuing *Peyote* on the Projekt label. *Undercurrents (In Dark Water)*, which assembled both older material and latter-day recordings, appeared a year later. After 1994's superb *Equator*, the group released *Sunchemical*, a collection of remixes. Hulme and Horberry additionally collaborated on dance music under the name Symetrics, with the former also heading the groups A Small Good Thing and Sons of Silence as well as recording *Fell* with Paul Schütze. —*Jason Ankeny*

● **Peyote** / 1991 / Projekt ♦♦♦♦
O Yuki Conjugate's dark tribal ambience features aggressive rhythms and invigorating textures, moody yet melodic, with menacing undercurrents. Trance-like and inviting nonetheless, O Yuki Conjugate inhabit some netherworld between ethnic, ambient, improvised and experimental sounds. Built largely on ghostly layers of percussion, this intriguing release suggests ceremonies of ancient worship, or other tribal rites. For the hearty and courageous listener, *Peyote* is a musical trip well worth taking. —*Backroads Music/Heartbeats*

**Undercurrents (In Dark Water)** / 1992 / Staalplaat ♦♦♦♦
*Undercurrents* is warmer yet far more ghostly than *Peyote*. There is a drifting, dreamlike quality of slow motion balanced by the vibrations of exotic tribal percussion. The hauntingly melancholy and erotic vocals of Maddy Alty spin around your emotional body like the silken strands of a gossamer web. Delicate yet sparse intonations of the flutes conjure up images and feelings related to water. Their soft mercurial phrasings appear and then disappear like an underground river snaking its way through a labyrinth of caves. —*Backroads Music/Heartbeats*

**Equator** / 1995 / Staalplaat ♦♦♦♦

## Paul Oakenfold
b. Aug. 30, 1963, London, England
*Producer, DJ / Progressive Trance, Goa-Trance, Trance, Club/Dance, Acid House, House*

Paul Oakenfold is the DJ, remixer, and producer who did more than anyone else to break house music in Britain during the late '80s. During 1987-88, Oakenfold hosted a series of crucial club nights which introduced thousands of Brits to house music. Just a few years later, he helped push the new dance crossover into the charts by master-minding hit productions by Happy Mondays (among others) and forming one of the most successful dance labels of the '90s, Perfecto Records. Even well over a decade after his emergence, Oakenfold remained, quite simply, dance music's most popular DJ.

Born in London in 1963, Oakenfold began mixing at the age of 16, and hooked up with friend Trevor Fung to play soul and rare-groove at a basement bar in Covent Garden. He also spent some time in New York during the late '70s, working for Arista Records and soaking up the disco scene through Larry Levan's genre-spanning sets at the Paradise Garage. Back in England by the early '80s, Oakenfold worked as a club promoter and British agent for the Beastie Boys and Run-D.M.C. He continued DJing as well, and eventually ended up at the Project in 1985-86, one of the first venues for house music in England. With Fung and another friend named Ian St. Paul, Oakenfold was introduced to the exploding club-scene on the vacation island of Ibiza (near the coast of Spain) during 1987 and imported the crucial mix of house, soul, Italian disco and alternative music later dubbed the Balearic style.

During 1988-89, house music and the Balearic style gestated at several Oakenfold-run club nights (Future at the Sound Shaft, then Spectrum and Land of Oz at Heaven) before emerging above terra firma as a distinctly British entity. Oakenfold and Steve Osborne had been working with new dance converts Happy Mondays, and their production for the 1989 Happy Mondays' single "(W.F.L.) Wrote for Luck" was voted Dance Record of the Year by the *NME*. The duo's production for the Happy Mondays' break-out full-length *Pills 'n' Thrills 'n' Bellyaches* placed them squarely in the vaunted territory of other new dance producers like Andrew Weatherall (who achieved similar success with Primal Scream's *Screamadelica* from the same year). Soon, major labels were lining up to have Oakenfold and Osborne remix their biggest pop stars including U2, Simply Red, New Order, the Cure, Massive Attack, M People, Arrested Development, the Shamen, the Stone Roses, and even Snoop Doggy Dogg (some as Perfecto, the combination remix service and RCA-connected record label founded by the pair in 1990). The Oakenfold/Osborne team were nominated by BPI as Best Producers from 1990 to 1993.

By the mid-'90s, dance music had reached the mainstream of British radio and culture, with Paul Oakenfold at the front of a new wave of globe-trotting DJs; he toured with U2 and supported live gigs by INXS, the Orb, Simply Red, Boy George, and Primal Scream. On Britain's ever-growing club circuit, he inaugurated the London super-club Ministry of Sound early in the '90s and became a resident at Britain's other super-club, Liverpool's Cream, instead of taking big money for independent gigs. He also cut down his remix schedule to less than five per year, concentrating instead on the release of half-a-dozen mix albums, including several volumes in the *Journeys by Stadium DJ* series. Oakenfold left Cream in 1999, after which Virgin commemorated the occasion with the release of *Resident: Two Years of Oakenfold at Cream*. *Perfecto Presents Another World* arrived the following year. —*John Bush*

**Journeys by Stadium DJ** / 1994 / Planet Earth ♦♦♦
A more pop-oriented collection than Oakenfold's later mix discs, *Journeys by Stadium DJ* includes several vocal tracks but showcases Oakenfold's seamless mixing ability to good effect. Making appearances are tracks by the Shamen, Spooky, Leftfield, and Oakenfold's own Perfecto remix of U2's "Lemon." —*John Bush*

● **Global Underground: Oslo** / Jun. 9, 1997 / Boxed ♦♦♦♦
A double-disc set recorded live in Norway, *Global Underground* sees Oakenfold joining clubbers on a varied trip through breakbeat, progressive-house, and trance, mixed to perfection and with little doubt of who the world's best DJ is. The track listing includes productions by LTJ Bukem, Omni Trio, Taucher, Astral Projection, and Cruzeman, plus Oakenfold's own production on the breakout hit "You're Not Alone" by Olive. —*John Bush*

**Tranceport** / Nov. 3, 1998 / Kinetic ♦♦
Superstar DJ Paul Oakenfold's (he was the opening act on U2's Zoo TV tour) first overground album of remixes and recycled beats is a highly thematic sampler platter featuring 11 underground dance/electronica artists made even more cult-worthy by Oakenfold's occasionally dashing facelifts. But *Tranceport* is no mere mix tape of the Oakenfold '98 Experience. Taking tracks by such artists as the Dream Traveler, Gus Gus, and Agnelli + Nelson, Oakenfold slips new tricks and grooves into the work, in essence cre-

ating brand new multi-BPM beasts in the process. The atmospheric techno offshoot trance often can be a smothering listen, drifting miles above the ozone with little or no purpose (or end in sight); here, Oakenfold makes it inviting—a beautifully textured music that reveals a little something more about itself with each listen. A major achievement of the genre. —*Michael Gallucci*

### Global Underground: New York / Jan. 19, 1999 / Thrive ♦♦
On the *New York* album, Paul Oakenfold often disregards continuity and seamless mixing to even further degrees than on other albums such as *Tranceport*. Even though it's overly apparent when Oakenfold drops a new track, he at least focuses his efforts on a beautiful track selection for this set, which is mostly trance and features a surprisingly large percentage of vocal tracks, such as Jamie Myerson's "Rescue Me." Separating these songs are progressive pieces that build to intense sensory heights before swooping into deep synth-saturated ambience. Appearing near the end of the second set, CM's "Dream Universe" follows this progressive template perfectly, as it slowly drops into a symphonic ocean of synthesized waves for nearly three minutes before flying angelically towards heavenly peaks of rhythmic aural sensation towards the end of the track. However, Oakenfold's inability to sustain continuity leaves the album feeling fragmented. For example, the second set begins wonderfully with hints of drum'n'bass in Ambrosia's "Inside Your Arms" then reaches a sudden lull with the sublime opening notes of Talisman & Hudson's ethereal masterpiece, "Leave Planet Earth." Just when it seems as though the set is going to begin building, it comes to almost a complete halt yet again, as Oakenfold fades in Junk Project's "Composure," and then finally shifts gears with Albino's "Air." Similarly, the first set is a mixed affair highlighted by a few moments of genius, such as the climax of Greece 2000's "3 Drives on Vinyl" and the bliss of Life on Mars' "Life in Mind" [Note: both the UK and US versions of this album have the same songs.] —*Jason Birchmeier*

### Resident: Two Years of Oakenfold at Cream / Mar. 15, 1999 / Virgin ♦♦♦
*Resident* serves as a retrospective album featuring many of the trance anthems Oakenfold made famous during his two-year residency at the British club *Cream*. Featuring recorded crowd reactions, this double album often feels as if one is actually listening to Oakenfold perform one of his many legendary sets at the club. The crowd reactions provide the sort of communal feel one gets a club but usually doesn't hear on other DJ mix albums, such as those on the Global Underground label. Many of the 24 trance and progressive-house tracks featured on *Resident* are remarkable works, such as Tilt and Paul Van Dyk's "Rendezvous" and Matt Darey's mix of Agnelli + Nelson's "El Nino." Unfortunately, many of these same tracks can be found on Oakenfold's other albums from the late '90s. Even so, *Resident* diffuses the compressed intensity of *Tranceport* and brings continuity to the jagged flow of *Global Underground: New York*. The first set focuses more on progressive house tracks with vocals, while the second set features many of the best hands-in-the-air anthems of this particular era. —*Jason Birchmeier*

### Perfecto Presents Another World / Sep. 19, 2000 / Sire ♦♦
Perhaps realizing that the market for progressive trance mix albums was fast approaching saturation amidst a raft of inferior products, Paul Oakenfold displayed a touch more variety with his 2000 edition, *Perfecto Presents Another World*. Scattered all over this collection are the usual trance producers (Timo Maas, Salt Tank, Tone Depth, LSG) and signings to his Perfecto label one would expect, but Oakenfold also incorporates snippets from more atmospheric sources, including Dead Can Dance and Vangelis' soundtrack classic, *Blade Runner*. And he even tapped Perfecto stalwart Quivver to apply the trance treatment to Led Zeppelin's "Baby I'm Gonna Leave You," a process that doesn't transform the song as much as it applies a sleek backing to a few of Robert Plant's bluesier vocal lines. Except for these stylistic detours (two tracks from *Blade Runner*, with one each from Dead Can Dance and the group's vocalist Lisa Gerrard), *Another World* is the same old trance album. There are a few intriguing anthems that manage to wear out their welcome over the course of seven minutes and up, plenty of breakdowns to maintain attention on the dancefloor, and an overall pleasant sound that simply floats by without making much of a positive impact. Oakenfold is probably treading dangerous ground here, considering that nods to traditional non-dance artists fly right over the heads of his core audience, even while they seem like calculated gestures to those who recognize the references. —*John Bush*

## Vidna Obmana (Dirk Serries)
b. Antwerp, Belgium
*Producer / Experimental Ambient, Electro-Acoustic, Ambient*

Belgian producer Dirk Serries, aka Vidna Obmana, is a prolific composer of deep ambient and electro-acoustic music, utilizing slow, shifting electronic figures and sparse environmental recordings to construct long, minimalist, often extremely personal textural works. Taking his nom de plume from the Yugoslavian for "optical illusion" (a concept which carries much weight in his composing, as well), Serries has released material through a wide range of different labels, including Projekt, Amplexus, Extreme, Hic Sunt Leones, Syrenia, ND, and Multimood. Serries began recording experimental noise musics in the late '80s, working solo and in combination with artists such as PBK, exploring the more abrasive side of electronic composition. Beginning with the release in 1990 of *Shadowing in Sorrow*, however, (the first part of what would come to be known as Vidna's ambient *Trilogy*) Serries began moving toward an almost isolationist ambient aesthetic, exploring themes of calm, solitude, grief, and introspection in long, moving pieces which tended to chart similar ground as American space music artists such as Robert Rich, Michael Stearns, and Steve Roach (Serries has since collaborated with both Rich and Roach). The first two movements of *The Trilogy—Sorrow*, as well as its follow-up *Passage in Beauty*—were self-released by Serries in 1990 and 1991, with the third volume, *Ending Mirag*, appearing the following year on the American ND label. The album was praised as some of the finest post-classical experimental electronic music of its time, and the Stateside connection finally opened his music up to an American audience, leading also to his association with Sam Rosenthal's Projekt label (the entire *Trilogy* was finally reissued by Projekt sister label Relic as a boxed set in 1996, with several new Vidna releases also appearing in the interim).

Although his textural recordings form the core of his output to date, Serries' more recent solo and collaborative works (such as *The Transcending Quest*, *Echoing Delight*, and *The Spiritual Bonding*) have also found him pushing the minimalism of his earlier works into the Fourth World territories of artists such as Jorge Reyes, Michael Stearns, and Jon Hassell, setting lush, dreamy soundscapes in a larger, more engaging rhythmic framework (usually with contributions from percussionists Djen Ajakan Shean and Steve Roach). Still, many compilations and retrospectives of his earlier or unreleased work have appeared in recent times so as to confuse somewhat the trajectory of his development, which at any rate seems to trade more or less equally between the freeform conceptual landscapes of his earlier Projekt, Relic, and ND works and the more structured interactivity of the Extreme and Amplexus releases. Collaborations have also increasingly occupied Serries' time, with full-length works with Steve Roach (*Well of Souls*, *The Spiritual Bonding*), Robert Rich (*The Spiritual Bonding*), Asmus Tietchens (a self-titled collaboration for Syrenia), Sam Rosenthal (*Terrace Of Memories*), and Djen Ajakan Shean (*Parallel Flaming*) appearing all within the space of only a few years. Both *Landscape in Obscurity* and *The Shape of Solitude* followed in 1999, and in the spring of 2000 Obmana returned with *Echo Passage* and *Surreal Sanctuary*. —*Sean Cooper*

### Music for Exhibiting Water with Contents: Soundtrack for the Aquarium / 1993 / Hybrids ♦♦♦
A collection of music composed to accompany the opening of the Antwerp Zoo aquarium, incorporating sound design of seemingly aqueous intent, as well as layered, looping samples of underwater life (dolphins, whales, etc.). —*Sean Cooper*

### Memories Compiled / 1994 / Relic ♦♦♦♦
A two-CD set collecting many early, previously unreleased looped pattern experiments from 1988-89. Also featuring contributions from early collaborator PBK, the set covers similar, thought not quite as successful ground as textural works such as *Trilogy* and *River Of Appearance*. Probably more interesting as a single disc, over the course of two the lack of variation becomes somewhat tedious. —*Sean Cooper*

### The Spiritual Bonding / 1994 / Extreme ♦♦♦
Produced by Steve Roach with guest appearances by Robert Rich, Alio Die, and Djen Ajakan Shean. —*Sean Cooper*

### Still Fragments / 1994 / ND ♦♦♦
Vidna Obmana's second release for the ND label features fragments from live performances in Hamburg, Germany and Antwerp, Belgium. —*Sean Cooper*

**The Transcending Quest [Single]** / 1995 / Amplexus ♦♦♦♦
Vidna's debut for Stefano Gentile's limited run 3" Amplexus label is a delightful fusion of his textural and composerly sides, with high-res environmental recordings (wind, bells, crickets) accenting deep drones and slow, resonant percussion. The disc in its totality was also included on Projekt's Amplexus compilation, *Collected Works*. —*Sean Cooper*

**Well of Souls** / 1995 / Projekt ♦♦♦
A two-CD collaboration with Steve Roach. —*Sean Cooper*

**River of Appearance** / 1996 / Projekt ♦♦♦♦
The first solo Vidna Obmana work in three years is a surprising return to textural composition, particularly since intervening collaborations with Djen and Steve Roach have revealed the more restless side of Serries' compositional persona. Still, an overarching focus on melody and dynamics distinguishes *Appearance* from earlier program works such as the *Trilogy*, combining mood with movement in far more obviously "musical" ways. —*Sean Cooper*

● **The Trilogy** / 1996 / Relic ♦♦♦♦
A rare treat much-anticipated by out-of-the-loop Obmana fans, *The Trilogy* collects a trio of full-length recordings self-released by Vidna's Dirk Serries and through tiny American experimental electronic label ND, featuring hands down the composer's finest, most accomplished textural works to date. While three discs might seem excessive for a compositional style relying heavily on looping and repetition, the pieces never seem indulgent or overlong (indeed, they occasionally seem almost too short), with each disc sketching out an emotional space all its own. The first and last word in Vidna-style ambient. —*Sean Cooper*

**Crossing the Trail** / Apr. 7, 1998 / Projekt ♦♦♦♦
Belgian composer Dirk Serries, aka Vidna Obmana, has crafted a well-polished, smooth stone that glistens in the river of Sound. His minimalist, trancewalk, dreamtime whispers on *Crossing the Trail* rate right up there with Steve Roach, Robert Rich, and Nik Tyndall, to mention just a few. In fact, Roach guests on this release having collaborated with Vidna Obmana in past creations. Seamless, drifting, boundless, lilting, waves and rivulets of sound wash over you in the 69-plus minutes, that pass by in a timeless void. Seven journeys await you, each pouring into the next, "Encountering Terrain" to "Trail Dwelling" and into "Forest Arrow." I hear a percussive, gently driven trilogy, flowing from the headwaters of imagination to the broad expanses of vision. "Mission Ground" glides you out onto a still lake of mists and ominous foreboding. "The Esoteric Source" is passage inside a great Temple, the Hall of Records, spanning this tributary of Time we know as Life. Vidna Obmana opens the ineffable gates of lucid dreaming with this piece. "The Giant Traveller" speaks to me of secrets now learned, we walk now in wisdom, unafraid of the darkness and the pace is our own. "This Splendid Place" is the dimension of all our aspirations, now complete. Pain is past. Sorrow is unknown. Quicksilver, ebony dark seas caress the shores of the Overworld. Here is the land of the undiscovered way, the paths few trod, the pass through the snow-covered mountains on the edge of Being. Vidna Obmana guides the soul in *Crossing the Trail*. Vidna Obmana has learned his lessons well and offers a gift of thanks. —*John W. Patterson*

## Ian O'Brien
*Producer / Jazz-House, Tech-House, Club/Dance, Techno*
Ian O'Brien's tech-house-jazz fusion put him on the map in 1996 as one of the most talented young dance producers, thanks to genre-bending singles for Ferox like "Intelligent Desert" and "Monkey Jazz." After his full-length *Desert Scores* dropped in February 1997, O'Brien began concentrating on more soulful, nu-disco output like a remix of Lisa Stansfield's "The Line" and his single for 4th Wave, "It's an Everyday World." His second LP, *Gigantic Days*, followed in 1999. —*John Bush*

● **Desert Scores** / Feb. 17, 1997 / Ferox ♦♦♦♦
Ian O'Brien's first LP alternates an extremely danceable form of tech-house (on tracks like "Mad Mike Disease") with more listener-oriented jazzy downtempo ("Dark Eye Tango," for one). Taken as a whole, *Desert Scores* is an impressive LP charting a type of interbreeding which puts O'Brien in league with As One's Kirk DeGiorgio and Daniel Ibbotson as the most balanced electronic/jazz fusion producers Britain offered during the late '90s. —*John Bush*

**Gigantic Days** / Apr. 26, 1999 / Peacefrog ♦♦♦
Doing for '80s electro-jazz what As One's *Planetary Folklore* did for more Afro-centric '70s fusion, Ian O'Brien's second album of techno/jazz fusion is another success, exploring the best of both worlds with an attention to production detail and beats often lacking in the electronic realm. Though a few tracks also lean uncomfortably close to the jazz-wank-lite heard on much of *Planetary Folklore*, O'Brien mixes up the productions slightly, from the funky keys on "Where Does the Past End and the Present Begin?" to the sublime atmospheres on the 12-minute closer "The Question of Value." —*John Bush*

## Octagon Man (Jonathon Saul Kane)
*Producer / Electronica, Techno*
As Block, Spider, Octagon Man, Grimm Death, and (most often) Depth Charge, DJ/producer Jonathon Saul Kane has been one of the more consistent and innovative forces on the UK dance scene since the late '80s. Recording classic tracks such as "Bounty Killers" and "The Demented Spirit," as well as remixing everyone from Eon, Bomb the Bass, and Sabres of Paradise to Senser, Silver Fox, and S'Express, Kane's work has kept in constant touch with dance music's hip-hop, funk, and electro roots, a fact which places him at the nexus of a number of recent hybrids and resurgent styles. His 1989 Vinyl Solution 12", "Bounty Killers," is roundly considered one of the earliest examples of uptempo trip-hop, mixing chunky sampled breakbeats with brutalizing bass and kitschy kung fu samples (a style which marks his popular Depth Charge work to this day). Additionally, Kane's two labels, D.C. (trip-hop and dub) and Electron Industries (electro and techno), have been responsible for some of the more memorable moments in mid-'90s underground dance music, and have included releases from Damon Baxter (Sem, Deadly Avenger), Ian Loveday (Eon), and Delta, as well as Depth Charge and Octagon Man releases such as "Shaolin Buddha Finger," "10ft. Flowers," "The Legend of the Golden Snake," and *The Exciting World of Octagon Man*. Many of Kane's earlier (1991-94) Depth Charge releases were compiled on the double LP *Nine Deadly Venoms*, released in 1994. Kane also helped found Made in Hong Kong, a film festival and video label (through Vinyl Solution) focusing on the promotion and distribution of films in the Hong Kong action cinema genre associated with actors and directors such as Chow Yun Fat, Ringo Lam, Wong Kar-Wai, John Woo, and Jackie Chan. [See Also: Depth Charge] —*Sean Cooper*

● **The Demented Spirit [EP]** / 1990 / Vinyl Solution ♦♦♦♦
Listening back, it's hard to believe *The Demented Spirit* was recorded in 1990, a year when acid house was the law of the land and electro was what your boring older brother was still listening to. As uncool as it was then, these tracks sound fresh and remarkably innovative with a bit of distance on them, pairing emerging desktop tech with ominous synth patches and complex and ultimately quite funky beatwork. —*Sean Cooper*

**The Exciting World of Octagon Man** / 1995 / Electron Industries ♦♦♦
J. Saul Kane's debut long-player under his electro-infused Octagon Man guise was hotly anticipated a full five years after the release of the now-legendary "Demented Spirit" single, and it does not disappoint. Like the angular rhythms and sparse, metallic thunk of that early single, *The Exciting World* is the sound of machine sex through the thin walls of an hourly-rated motel, all dampened clicks and grinding clatter. —*Sean Cooper*

**10 Ft. Flowers [EP]** / 1997 / Electron Industries ♦♦
A double 10" of sadly uninspired, dirt-caked electro. While the lo-fi production of previous Octagon Man releases seemed to add a layer of textured rust to electro's machinery aesthetic, these tracks just sound badly done, and rushed to boot; ponderously average minimal loops that for all intents may as well be locked grooves. —*Sean Cooper*

## Octave One
f. 1989, Detroit, MI
*Group / Techno-Bass, Detroit Techno, Club/Dance, Techno*
One of the more anachronistic teams in the Detroit techno underground, Octave One's rough-and-tumble production values gel with most Motor City crews but for Lawrence Burden and his two brothers, the focus is completely on music with little political or social aesthetics behind their tracks. Burden originally began DJing in 1987 in a collective named VLE Nu AGE, then recorded a single in 1989 with the help of brothers Lynell and Lenny plus Anthony Shakir, Jay Denham, and Juan Atkins. Originally released on Derrick May's Transmat Records, "I Believe" made waves after being compiled onto the British Detroit compilation *Techno! The New Dance Sound of Detroit*, helping the Burdens form Direct Beat/430 West Records (originally located

at 430 West 8 Mile Road in Detroit). The labels became favored names for hard-hitting electro-bass tracks from Aux 88, Alien FM and Underground Resistance mainman Mad Mike Banks. Besides later Octave One output like "The X Files," the *Foundation* EP and the *Cymbolic* mini-LP, 430 West released several volumes in the bass compilation *Detroit: Techno City* and Direct Beat obliged with the compilation *Techno Bass: The Mission*. In late 1997, Octave One released their debut album, *The Living Key (To Images from Above)*. The following year brought *The Collective*, a look at the group's back catalogue. Releases from other Octave One incarnations have also appeared, including Never on Sunday, Random Noise Generation (RNG), and Metro D. —*John Bush*

**The Living Key (To Images from Above)** / Oct. 13, 1997 / 430 West ✦✦✦✦
Of the many acts in Detroit's techno underground, Octave One are perhaps the most difficult to place. The trio's productions are filled with warm chunky grooves, though their occasionally minimalist style is too raw to invite comparisons to techno-soul mavericks like Terrence Parker or Kenny Dixon, Jr. Consisting of tracks from two separately released EPs, *The Living Key (To Images from Above)* solidly balances the hard and the soul on tracks like "Covenant" and "Emissary." —*John Bush*

● **The Collective** / Sep. 1, 1998 / 430 West ✦✦✦✦
The Octave One retrospective includes all of their best work for 430 West as well as their 1990 debut, "I Believe." Later tracks like "Empower," "DayStar Rising" and "The Symbiont" are perfect examples of some of the smoothest, most inventive techno-funk to come out of Detroit. —*John Bush*

## The Odd Toot (Simon Smith)

*Producer / Drill'N'Bass, Jungle/Drum'N'Bass, Club/Dance*
Simon Smith is an inventive Scottish producer who's been (understandably) pigeon-holed into the drill'n'bass scene for his idiosyncratic use of samples and notable lack of attention span when it comes to packing his tracks full of ideas and sound. Reportedly classically trained, Smith began releasing his productions in 1997, after an association with James Hardway helped earn release for the Odd Toot's *Hot Rock Tee* EP on Hardway's Recordings of Substance. The *Bampot* album followed later that summer, and Smith moved to the related Hydrogen Dukebox label for 2000's *Mental Money*. —*John Bush*

**Bampot** / Jul. 14, 1997 / Recordings of Substance ✦✦
Like Tom Jenkinson's Squarepusher project, the Odd Toot's Simon Smith produces freakout drum'n'bass but diverges from the usual jazz fusion noodling to encompass ragga and dancehall inspirations as well. Reportedly, the odd title is Scottish slang for "silly bastard," and it's as good a pointer to Smith's production style as any. —*John Bush*

● **Mental Money** / Apr. 25, 2000 / Hydrogen Dukebox ✦✦✦
Much more controlled than the sample chaos spread all over the first Odd Toot record, *Mental Money* is an excellently recorded album of trip-hop and jungle indebted to the tongue-in-cheek lewd fantasies of Aphex Twin. Inventive drum manipulation makes "Moo Says" a highlight, and "Shoddy Rudder" includes brass and saxes, plus the High Llamas' Sean O'Hagan on guitar. —*John Bush*

## Mike Oldfield

b. May 15, 1953, Reading, Berkshire, England
*Keyboards, Percussion, Guitar, Bass / Progressive-Rock/Art-Rock, Progressive-Electronic*
Composer Mike Oldfield rose to fame on the success of *Tubular Bells*, an eerie, album-length conceptual piece employed to stunning effect in the film *The Exorcist*. Oldfield began his professional career at the age of 14, forming a folk duo with his sister Sally; a year later, the siblings issued their debut LP, *Sallyangie*. By the age of 16, he was playing bass with Soft Machine founder Kevin Ayers' group the Whole World alongside experimental classical arranger David Bedford and avant-jazz saxophonist Lol Coxhill; within months, Oldfield was tapped to become the band's lead guitarist prior to recording the 1971 LP *Shooting at the Moon*.

*Tubular Bells*, originally dubbed *Opus 1*, grew out of studio time gifted by Richard Branson, who at the time was running a mail-order record retail service. After its completion, Oldfield shopped the record to a series of labels, only to meet with rejection; frustrated, Branson decided to found his own label, and in 1973 *Tubular Bells* became the inaugural release of Virgin Records. An atmospheric, intricate composition which fused rock and folk motifs with the structures of minimalist composition, the 49-minute instumental piece (performed on close to 30 different instruments, virtually all of them played by Oldfield himself) spent months in the Number One spot on the UK charts, and eventually sold over 16 million copies globally. In addition to almost singlehandedly establishing Virgin as one of the most important labels in the record industry, *Tubular Bells* also created a market for what would later be dubbed New Age music, and won a Grammy for Best Instrumental Composition in 1974.

The follow-up, 1974's *Hergest Ridge* (named after Oldfield's retreat in a remote area of Herefordshire) also proved phenomenally successful, and dislodged *Tubular Bells* at the top of the British chart. With 1975's *Ommadawn*, he explored ambient textures and world music; however, the emergence of punk left Oldfield baffled, and he retreated from sight for three years following the LP's release. He resurfaced with 1978's *Incantations*, which featured the single "Guilty," a nod to the disco movement; *Platinum*, issued a year later, kept its eye on the clubs, and featured a dance version of the Philip Glass composition "North Star." With 1980's *QE 2*, Oldfield moved completely away from his epic-length pieces and travelled into pop territory, a shift typified by the album's cover of ABBA's "Arrival." He continued in a pop vein for much of the '80s, as albums like 1983's *Crises*, 1984's *Discovery* and 1987's *Islands* encroached further and further upon mainstream accessibility. In 1992, Oldfield teamed with producer Trevor Horn for *Tubular Bells II*, which returned him to the top of the UK charts. *The Sound of Distant Earth* appeared two years later, followed by a third *Tubular Bells* update in 1998. —*Jason Ankeny*

● **Tubular Bells** / 1973 / Virgin ✦✦✦✦
The then-newly-formed Virgin Records allowed Oldfield a year to complete this 49-minute conceptual effort, which required him to record eighty tracks of himself playing 28 different instruments. *Tubular Bells* achieved Top Ten chart success in the US when it was used in the soundtrack for the film *The Exorcist*, selling over 10 million copies. —*Scott Bultman*

**Tubular Bells II** / 1992 / Warner Brothers ✦✦✦
Like it's predecessor, the composer plays virtually all the instruments, including guitars, mandolin, banjo, piano, organ, synthesizers, percussion, and—of course—tubular bells. *II* opens with quiet TB passages that echo the original and use it as a launch pad without merely reproducing what has come before. The 70-minute composition flows nicely from ambient movements to those featuring Oldfield's fluid electric guitar work. Twenty years later, this reprise risked being over-pretentious; instead, Oldfield incorporates passages that are downright playful and irreverent. —*Roch Parisien*

**The Elements: The Best of Mike Oldfield 1973-1991** / Nov. 16, 1993 / Virgin America ✦✦✦✦
A very succinct walk through Mike Oldfield's first two decades of music-making, *Elements* includes edits of extended Oldfield perennials like *Tubular Bells*, *Ommadawn*, and *Amarok*, plus glimpses of his surprisingly keen pop wit by way of hits like "Family Man" and "Moonlight Shadow." Much of the material is uncommonly folksy ("In Dulci Jubilo," for instance), but the album provides the best perspective on Oldfield's varied career. —*John Bush*

**XXV: The Essential** / Nov. 17, 1997 / WEA ✦✦✦✦
*XXV: The Essential* is a good overview of highlights from Mike Oldfield's Virgin and Warner recordings. Some of the tracks are included in their original form, while others—including, inexplicably, *Tubular Bells III*—are present in edited or remixed versions. It's not a bad sampler, but it's frustrating since it doesn't present the original recorded versions of each song. Nevertheless, it is an adequate summary of Oldfield's '90s recordings. —*Stephen Thomas Erlewine*

**Tubular Bells III** / Sep. 22, 1998 / Warner ✦✦✦
*Tubular Bells III* is a record quite similar to his second update of the original classic, recorded just six years previous. The production methods are a bit more polished and the tone is more serious, but the music remains dreamy, somewhat over-evocative new-age-with-a-beat music, quite similar to Enigma—thanks to the Eastern textures of vocalist Amar on three tracks. There are a few occasional moments of levity, however, including the raging guitar stormer "Outcast," and a remake of Oldfield's early-'80s hit "Man in the Rain." —*John Bush*

## Olive

f. 1994, London, England

*Group / Electronica, Downbeat, Ambient Dub, Adult Alternative Pop/Rock, Trip-Hop, Club/Dance*

The epitomy of the quieter, coffee-table side of singer/songwriter electronica and trip-hop, Olive was formed by producers Tim Kellett and Robin Taylor-Firth (former members of, respectively, Simply Red and Nightmares on Wax) with vocalist Ruth-Ann Boyle. Kellett connected with Boyle while playing keyboards for a live incarnation of the Durutti Column (he manipulated her tape-looped vocals while on stage), and asked her to join him in a new recording project. With Kellett writing lyrics and the addition of Taylor-Firth, the trio recorded three songs and found plenty of labels ready to bid for their services. RCA Records won out and released "You're Not Alone" in 1995. Though it took almost a year to catch on with British audiences, the single eventually hit number one and sold half a million copies. America proved passingly fond of the track as well, making a home near the Top 40 for it. Their second album *Trickle* arrived in 2000 on Maverick Records. —*John Bush*

**Extra Virgin** / 1996 / RCA ♦♦♦

A year after its initial release, Olive's debut album, *Extra Virgin*, finally produced a number one British hit with "You're Not Alone," a low-key lite-trip-hop number with a graceful melody. It's a strong single, and there are similarly strong moments on *Extra Virgin*, yet Olive don't stand out from the post-Portishead pack. Like Everything But the Girl, they are essentially a folky, pop-oriented group that uses the stoned rhythms of trip-hop as hip window-dressing. Since that rhythm is appealing on its own terms, it doesn't matter that Olive uses it as ornamentation, especially since they use it well. What is a problem is their lack of consistent songwriting. Only a few songs match the singles "You're Not Alone" and "Miracle" in terms of memorable, melodic construction, and the weaker tracks tend to float by on their admittedly entrancing production. And that leaves *Extra Virgin* an intriguing debut, but not necessarily one that promises great things from Olive. —*Stephen Thomas Erlewine*

● **Trickle** / 2000 / Maverick ♦♦♦♦

Where most trip-hop artists downplay melody as a matter of principle, Olive (keyboardist/trumpeter/producer Tim Kellett and vocalist Ruth-Ann) embraces it almost defiantly, maintaining the rhythmic interest of electronica and the generally dark undercurrents of trip-hop while simultaneously delivering tunes that are swooningly lovely without ever sounding quite commercial. The lead track on the band's Maverick debut is perhaps its best: "Love Affair" glides on an updraft of sampled strings and a subtly jungle-flavored breakbeat, while the sung melody (especially in the chorus, where the chord progression takes an unusual and delightful turn) climbs from peak to emotional peak. The rest of the program is almost as good, from the slow and funky "Trickle" and a tweaked and bleepy version of the 10cc classic "I'm Not in Love" to a slightly Latin-tinged kiss-off song titled "Creature of Comfort." (Several minutes after the end of the album's last track is a hidden song called "Take My Hand.") Highly recommended. —*Rick Anderson*

## Pauline Oliveros

b. May 20, 1932, Houston, TX

*Accordion, Composer / 20th-Century Classical/Modern Composition, Minimalism, Electronic*

Avant-garde composer Pauline Oliveros pioneered the concept of Deep Listening, an aesthetic based upon principles of improvisation, electronic music, ritual, teaching and meditation designed to inspire both trained and untrained performers to practice the art of listening and responding to environmental conditions in solo and ensemble situations. Oliveros received her first musical instruction from her mother and grandmother—equally inspired by the sounds of nature, she committed to pursuing a career in music early in life, studying composition at San Francisco State College during the early '50s and playing french horn in an improvisational group which also included pianist Terry Riley. Later recognized primarily for her prowess on the accordion, during the mid-'60s she served as the first director of the Tape Music Center at Mills College, followed by a 14-year teaching stint at the University of California at San Diego which concluded upon her relocation to Kingston, New York in 1981. In the intervening years Oliveros established herself among the most original thinkers in contemporary music, known initially for the "Sonic Meditations," her earliest attempts at absorbing environmental sounds into the musical process. The same concept was at the heart of the Deep Listening series, a collection of 30 pieces composed between 1971 and 1990. During the mid-'80s, she also established the Pauline Oliveros Foundation, which spread the Deep Listening gospel through recordings, lectures, and retreats. —*Jason Ankeny*

**Lullaby for Daisy Pauline/In "Sleepers"** / 1985 / Finnadar ♦♦♦

In the collection *Sleepers*, written in 1979 for her new niece and namesake, this is an example of Oliveros' work written in graphs with verbal instructions that call for the meditative and "deep listening" involvement of groups of performers and often of the audience members as performers themselves. "Hum the sound of pleasure as if you were serenading your best loved infant... play with the MMM sound by adding vowels and dipthongs between the M's using any repetitions or prolongations... stay open to your own sensations and imagine gradually expanding your awareness to sensing your surroundings..." It goes without saying that realizations of this piece are often beautiful. Much of Oliveros' work continues to explore the meditative solo state (especially her compelling spontaneous accordion playing, with and without electronics) and highly imaginative and perceptive musical instruction scores (*Crow Two, El Relicario de los Animales, The Wheel of Life, Sonic Meditations*, etc.) that create situations to increase the possibilities of group interaction(s) and intuition. —*"Blue" Gene Tyranny*

● **The Roots of the Moment** / 1988 / Hat Art ♦♦♦♦

Oliveros with accordion in just intonation within an interactive electronic environment created by Peter Ward. An amazing hour-long live creation (improvisation)... images of valleys, other universes, whatever comes to mind... an exercise in true "deep listening"as she refers to the concerts her foundation presents in upstate New York. —*"Blue" Gene Tyranny*

**Deep Listening** / 1989 / New Albion ♦♦♦♦

On this project, released by the progressive San Francisco label New Albion, accordionist Pauline Oliveros has teamed up with trombonist Stuart Dempster and vocalist Panaiotis to produce a remarkable album of atmospheric space music. The recording took place inside a huge cistern at an army fort, an acoustic space characterized by tremendous reverberation. The unlikely instruments—primarily accordion, trombone, didjeridoo, and voice—produce sustained tones that are subtly modulated by the extraordinary acoustics, making it often seem as if there were more instruments present, or as if this music has been electronically processed—neither of which is the case. All the music was improvised on site, with the musicians banging on metal pipes and found objects on the final track. The effect is remarkable, immersing the listener in a hypnotic field of shifting resonance, in a truly profound experience of deep listening. —*Backroads Music/Heartbeats*

**Crone** / 1992 / Lovely Music ♦♦♦

Oliveros on accordion with electronics creating various illusionary movements in space. Beautiful. —*"Blue" Gene Tyranny*

**St. George and the Dragon/In Memoriam Mr. Whitney** / 1996 / Mode ♦♦♦♦

**Alien Bog (1967)/Beautiful Soop (1966)** / 1997 / Pogus ♦♦♦♦

Two fabulous early electronic works both employing the legendary Buchla Box 100 analog synthesizer and realized at the Tape Music Center at Mills College (now called the Center for Contemporary Music). *Alien Bog* evokes a place deep in the natural world far from humankind's civilizations—low gentle thumps at ground level, high cycling bird-like sounds, sustained cricket calls, quick side-to-side flights of unknown critters, and low calls of immense animals in the distance, all cycle contrapuntally to create a peaceful yet bizarre environment. The charming *Beautiful Soop* for reciting voices and electronics incorporates poetic fantasy texts from classic literature: *The Jabberwocky*, excerpts from *Alice in Wonderland*, and so on. The voices take on a fantastical aspect when processed through tape-delays (echoes and accumulative modulations), and the voices also are continually mixed with surrealistic and often humorous electronic sounds. After 27 minutes the fantasy build-up reaches an engrossing (and to some listeners, ironic) plateau, and the narrative voice fades, stuck in the repeating groove of a vinyl record. An unpretentious, enjoyable, yet pioneering work. —*"Blue" Gene Tyranny*

**Duo for Accordion and Bandoneon with Possible Mynah Bird Obbligato (See-saw)** / 1998 / Musicworks ♦♦♦♦

In the collection *Musicworks #70* with Pauline Oliveros on accordion, David Tudor on bandoneon, and Ahmed the Mynah bird, this piece is an absolute delight with punctuated accordion, bandoneon sounds, hissings, and a kind of bird barking and squeaking. Another wonderful experiment in interspecies communication. —*"Blue" Gene Tyranny*

## Omni Trio (Rob Haigh)

*Producer / Jungle/Drum'N'Bass, Club/Dance*

Actually the single force of one Rob Haigh, Omni Trio's sunny brand of intricate, orchestrated drum'n'bass has been growing in acclaim since the onset of ambient or intelligent jungle in the mid-'90s brought names such as L.T.J Bukem, Spring Heel Jack, and TPower to the fore. Into his 30s, Haigh already had a decade on most of those names, a fact communicated in the often more eclectic influence behind his tunes—from Carl Craig and Mantronix to Miles Davis and Can. An acolyte of London's mid-'80s experimental industrial/avant-garde scene, Haigh's first Omni Trio releases—a series of 12"s issued in distinctive, color-coded sleeves—started to appear in the early '90s. Following on the heels of early hardcore and darkside techno, Haigh's tunes were among the first composed outside of jungle's immediate dancefloor loop, and were early examples of the music's potential to draw on a wide range of sources (ambient, house, jazz, soul) for influence. His first full-length album, *Volume 1: The Deepest Cut*, was released on Moving Shadow in 1995 and combined many of those early 12" tracks—"Mystic Stepper," "Renegade Snares"—with some stunning production and remix work by Foul Play (on "Snares"), among others. His proper debut, *Haunted Science*, was released by Moving Shadow in 1996; *Skeleton Keys* followed in 1997. In addition to his increasingly successful career as a recording artist and remixer, Haigh also owns and operates a record shop in Hertford. —*Sean Cooper*

**Volume 1: The Deepest Cut** / 1995 / Moving Shadow ♦♦♦♦
A cross-cutting collection of the finest moments of Haigh's early singles, reworked for re-release and supported by three new tracks. A perfect combination of soulful melody and tearing drum'n'bass percussion. The CD includes two bonus tracks. —*Sean Cooper*

• **Music for the Next Millennium** / Aug. 1995 / Sm:)e ♦♦♦♦
Including classics like "Renegade Snares," "Living for the Future," "Rollin' Heights," and "Thru the Vibe," *Music for the Next Millennium* is a crosscutting collection of the finest moments of Haigh's early singles, reworked for release on a full-length and supported by three new tracks (plus an additional two on CD). A perfect combination of soulful melody and tearing drum'n'bass percussion. Released in Britain as *The Deepest Cut.* —*Sean Cooper*

**Haunted Science** / Aug. 12, 1996 / Moving Shadow ♦♦♦♦
Omni Trio's Rob Haigh knows how to create a relentless drum'n'bass rhythm track, and he knows how to change the mood of a song by subtly shifting rhythmic textures. *Haunted Science* has a few weak spots where Haigh simply meanders without stumbling onto anything interesting, but at its best, the album showcases the power of jungle. —*Stephen Thomas Erlewine*

**Skeleton Keys** / Sep. 29, 1997 / Moving Shadow ♦♦♦
*Skeleton Keys* doesn't vary much from the polished, house-inspired drum'n'bass Rob Haigh has been engineering since the early '90s. Though his third proper album as Omni Trio features only one diva vocal (on "Red Rain"), all elements of the earlier albums are still in place—vaguely familiar breaks, gradually tweaked and twisted beyond recognition, with infectious synthwork and an overall spartan production that leaves the listener craving just a bit more. All this familiarity is by no means bad, however, and the presence of a downtempo groove on the title track puts it all into focus. —*John Bush*

## One Dove

f. 1991, Manchester, England
*Group / Electronica, Alternative Dance, Club/Dance, Techno*

One Dove's 1993 debut album, *Morning Dove White*, featured production by techno mastermind Andrew Weatherall. Under his direction, the band became one of the hippest names in techno and alternative circles in late 1993. Though they broke up before recording a follow-up, vocalist Dot Allison returned in 1998 with a solo career. —*Stephen Thomas Erlewine*

• **Morning Dove White** / Oct. 19, 1993 / ffrr ♦♦♦♦
A nearly perfect mixture of techno and pop, *Morning Dove White* succeeds because the hooks and melodies are given priority along with the rhythm tracks. Vocal parts float in and out of the mix, wrapping themselves around melodic, muscular guitar and keyboards; the hypnotic single, "White Love," sets the direction for the album. —*Stephen Thomas Erlewine*

## Optical (Matt Quinn)

*Producer / Jungle/Drum'N'Bass, Club/Dance*

Matt Quinn's recordings as Optical skirt the atmospheric side of neuro-funk drum'n'bass, with the paranoid musings of a handful of industrial-strength British producers like Ed Rush, Source Direct, and Quinn's brother Jamie, who records as Matrix. Jamie and Matt began releasing singles on their own Metro Records from a West London base, with Matrix's "Double Vision" alongside Optical's "Shining" as the label's opening shots. Optical recorded for a half-dozen other imprints as well, including Goldie's Metalheadz and Grooverider's Prototype. The producer's two contributions to those labels (respectively, "To Shape the Future" and "Grey Odyssey") raised his profile considerably after gaining re-release on CD compilations—Goldie's *Platinum Breakz II* and Grooverider's *The Prototype Years*. He had already earned a reputation as one of the most hotly tipped producers of 1997 when another classic single for Prototype, "Moving 808s," hit big late that year.

By 1998, Quinn had been tapped to contribute his engineering expertise to two of the most hyped jungle LPs of the year—Goldie's *SaturnzReturn* (replacing Rob Playford) and Grooverider's *Mysteries of Funk*. He also earned co-production credits on Dom & Roland's *Industry*, and continued to release single after single of intense, *Predator*-styled drum'n'bass. After forming his own label, Virus, with No-U-Turn Records don Ed Rush, he was co-billed with Rush on a five-LP set titled *Wormhole*, the first full-length to actually carry Optical's name. —*John Bush*

**To Shape the Future [Single]** / Apr. 28, 1997 / Metalheadz ♦♦♦♦
Optical's first single for Metalheadz alternates a rumbling, synth-tech effects line with some intriguing breakbeat percussion slap. —*Keith Farley*

• **Moving 808s [Single]** / Nov. 17, 1997 / Prototype ♦♦♦♦
One of the best drum'n'bass singles of the year, "Moving 808s" was recorded for Grooverider's Prototype Records, and is also available on *The Prototype Years* compilation. —*Keith Farley*

## 'O'Rang

f. 1993, London, England
*Group / Trip-Hop*

Bassist Paul Webb and drummer Lee Harris were bandmates for a decade in the influential British band Talk Talk. A year after the band's final release—1992's critically acclaimed *Laughing Stock*—Harris and Webb built a studio which they dubbed The Slug. Once the studio was up and running, the duo allowed all sorts of musicians to come in and improvise with them, using the resulting music as source material with which to create the music heard on 'O'Rang's albums. The band's recorded debut was the EP, *Spoor* (1994), followed by two full lengths, *Herd of Instinct* (1995), and *Fields & Waves* (1996). The recordings were originally released on Echo Records, and later picked up and reissued (except for the EP) in 1997 by Chicago's Hit It! Recordings, followed a year later by the new *Remixes*. 'O'Rang features Webb and Harris on a variety of instruments, incorporating dub rhythms, various percussion, and thickly layered atmospherics to create a rock music that has been highly praised by UK publications such as *The Wire*, *The Times* of London, and *Melody Maker*. —*Joslyn Layne*

• **Herd of Instinct** / 1995 / Echo ♦♦♦♦
*Herd of Instinct* is a few trancy steps away from *Fields & Waves*, the collection of precise and lovely soundscapes that followed it. On *Herd of Instinct*, Paul Webb and Lee Harris take their usual spacy vocals, dubby bass, and exotic percussion into less melodically structured areas, beating, droning, and washing along without the attentive sense of composition that would mark later releases. —*Nitsuh Abebe*

**Fields & Waves** / 1996 / Echo ♦♦♦♦
The second album from Talk Talk rhythm section Lee Harris and Paul Webb is a seducing mixture of hypnotic techno rhythms, pan-ethnic sounds, and ear-grabbing samples. Most of the listener's time is spent enjoying an instrumental experience. There is no singer, per se, but vocals and speech are incorporating as more winning sounds in this successful mix. Only on the unfortunately modern rock leaning "Seizure" and "Moratorium" is this formula tampered with. The more I listen to his CD, though, the more these "tracts" strike me as just a nervous twitch on the face of an otherwise easy to like personality. I am focusing on my dislike for Webb's singing there because 'O'Rang is the most engrossing when disembodies. When I am floating on an

organic mesh of samples and sonic structure, I want the paradise for myself. Enjoying a wilderness landscape, I no more want a reminded of the civilization left behind that I want a reminder of the culture left behind when I am taking in the 'O'Rang sunset soundscape. A direct connection to an outer headspace is made by the pictures that accompany each track and offer Global Positioning taken from satellite. Intelligent, melodic electronica that is visually suggestive. *—Thomas Schulte*

## The Orb

f. 1989, London, England
*Group / Ambient House, Electronica, Ambient Techno, Ambient Dub, Club/Dance*

The Orb virtually invented the electronic genre known as ambient house, resurrecting slower, more soulful rhythms and providing a soundtrack for early-morning ravers once the clubs closed their doors. The group popularized the genre as well, by appearing on the British chart show *Top of the Pops* and hitting number one in the UK with the 1992 album *U.F.Orb*. Frontman Dr. Alex Paterson's formula was quite simple: he slowed down the rhythms of classic Chicago house and added synth-work and effects inspired by '70s ambient pioneers Brian Eno and Tangerine Dream. To make the whole a bit more listenable—as opposed to danceable—obscure vocal samples were looped, usually providing a theme for tracks which lacked singing.

Paterson had worked as a roadie for Killing Joke during the '80s, and began to be influenced by the explosion of Chicago house music in England during the mid-to-late-'80s. He joined the A&R department of EG Records—the home of Brian Eno himself—and first recorded as the Orb with Jimi Cauty (who had played in the Killing Joke side-project Brilliant and later gained fame as one-half of the KLF). The duo's first release as the Orb, a failed acid-house anthem named "Tripping on Sunshine," appeared on the 1988 compilation album *Eternity Project One*. In May 1989, the Orb released the *Kiss* EP, a four-tracker dedicated to—and heavily sampled from—New York's KISS-FM. Paterson had begun to DJ in London around this time, and Paul Oakenfold recruited him to man Land of Oz, the chill-out room at his club Heaven.

Paterson's ambient sets incorporated a wide array of samples and sound effects, ranging from BBC nature recordings to NASA space broadcasts and special effects. With those samples mixed underneath the music of ambient pioneers such as Eno and Steve Hillage, his sets became popular alternatives for dancefloor victims and worn-out club kids. Hillage happened to be in the room one night when Paterson sampled his *Rainbow Dome Musick* album. The two became friends and later recorded together, Hillage contributing guitar to the Orb's "Blue Room" single and Paterson working on the debut album by Hillage's System 7 project (or 777, as it is known in the States due to copyright problems with Macintosh).

The Orb's first actual foray into ambient house appeared in October 1989 on Paterson's WAU!/Mr. Modo label. The 22-minute single "A Huge Ever Growing Pulsating Brain That Rules from the Centre of the Ultraworld," which sampled ocean noises and Minnie Riperton's "Loving You," actually hit the UK charts that year. The single became popular with indie-kids as well as club DJs, and earned Paterson and Cauty the chance to re-record the song in December 1989 for a John Peel session. (That version was released two years later, alongside their second session, on the Orb's *Peel Sessions* album.)

In early 1990, Dave Stewart asked Paterson and Cauty to remix his single "Lilly Was Here"; the track hit the UK's Top 20, and the Orb's remix work soon became just as popular as their original material. Erasure, Depeche Mode, Yello, Primal Scream, and more than 20 other bands eventually received the remix treatment before Paterson began to cut back his remixing work in 1992. (One of the only outside remixes of Orb material occurred around this time when breakbeat pioneers Coldcut remixed the *Kiss* EP for a US-only single.)

Alex Paterson and Jimi Cauty had been recording an album during the turn of 1989-90, but the two split in April 1990—a result of Paterson's fear that the Orb had become known more as a KLF side-project than an original act. Cauty stripped Paterson's contribution to the recordings and released the eponymous album—credited simply as Space—later that year. (Cauty released another ambient album that year: *Chill Out*, this time with his KLF partner Bill Drummond.)

In the meantime, Alex Paterson had been working with Youth (from Killing Joke) on the new track "Little Fluffy Clouds," with a melody incorporated from composer Steve Reich. The single appeared in November 1990, sparking the wrath of the sampled Rickie Lee Jones, whose dialogue with Levar Burton—from the PBS-TV children's program *Reading Rainbow*—was sampled for the chorus and title of the track; Big Life later settled out of court for an undisclosed sum. Though the single failed to place in the charts, its laidback vibe made it a big hit on the dancefloor.

Youth's other commitments made it unable for him to become a permanent member of the Orb, so Paterson decided to recruit Kris Weston (nicknamed Thrash for his punk/metal roots), a young studio engineer who worked on "Little Fluffy Clouds" and had recently left his previous band, Fortran 5. The Orb performed live for the first time just after the pairing, early in 1991 at London's Town & Country 2 with Steve Hillage on guitar. The group's live dates soon became their forte, breaking down the boundaries which had previously separated electronic music from rock. An Orb show encompassed the best elements of performance hall and club, with colorful light shows and visuals, and a relaxed, positive groove rarely found in electronic circles.

All this was fine and good, but the Orb had not yet released an album, the vehicle which virtually all modern musicians use to make artistic statements. Finally, in April 1991, *The Orb's Adventures Beyond the Ultraworld* was released in England to considerable critical acclaim. Its popularity extended to the general public as well, pushing the double-album into Great Britain's Top 30 LP charts.

By mid-1991, the Orb had signed a deal to release *Ultraworld* in the States, but were forced to edit the album down to one disc. (The full double-disc version was later released in the US by Island.) Paterson and Thrash toured Europe during 1991, and compiled the Orb's first two *Peel Sessions* in November 1991. One month later, the duo released *The Aubrey Mixes* as a Christmas special. The album, a remix compilation with reworkings by Steve Hillage, Youth, and Jimi Cauty, was deleted on the day of its release, but still managed to place in the UK Top 50.

In June 1992, the new single "Blue Room" hit the British Top Ten. The longest single in chart history at just under 40 minutes, it earned the Orb a spot on *Top of the Pops*, where they ruminated over a chess game and waved at the camera while a three-minute edit of the single played in the background. Released in July, the album *U.F.Orb* concentrated not on space, but the beings that inhabit it. (The actual 'Blue Room' is an installation where the US government allegedly keeps the relics of a 1947 saucer crash outside Roswell, NM.) It hit number one on the British album charts, and also did well with critics, who praised it and the duo's sold-out tour of England.

The non-album single "Assassin"—originally slated to feature vocals from Primal Scream's Bobby Gillespie—followed in October, and it reached No. 12 on the British charts. The US release of *U.F.Orb* appeared two months later, with initial copies including a second disc with the full version of "Blue Room" plus mixes of "Assassin." A limited LP release of *U.F.Orb* in England included a live recording of the Orb's appearance at London's Brixton Academy in 1991. (The date was later released on video with an added CD soundtrack as *Adventures Beyond the Ultraworld: Patterns and Textures*.)

Though the Orb had released several hours of recordings and many remixes during its first three years of existence, the beginning of 1993 prompted a dry spell of over a year and a half. The problem wasn't a lack of material; Paterson and Thrash continued to record, but Big Life Records had begun a controversial campaign to reissue several early singles. The Orb threatened to release no new material until the label promised to cease and desist, and negotiations stalled while the duo looked to opt out of their contract. In the meantime, Big Life spent 1993-94 reissuing five CD singles and two other 12" releases, including "Little Fluffy Clouds" (which hit the British Top Ten), "Huge Ever Growing Pulsating Brain" and "Perpetual Dawn" (the second single from *Ultraworld*).

Paterson finally signed an international deal with Island in 1993 and released the stop-gap *Live 93* later that year. The double-disc set—which hit No. 23 in the album charts—included highlights from Orb appearances in Europe and Japan, and featured another clever dig at Pink Floyd: the cover has a large stuffed sheep suspended over a power station, alá the Floyd's *Animals* cover.

The Orb's first studio release for Island appeared in June 1994. *Pomme Fritz* (a "little album") was quite a departure from ambient house, the field that had since caught up with Paterson's revolution of the late '80s. The album has a schizophrenic quality that portrays the group caught between two worlds: the pastoral ambience of the first two albums, and the harsher, almost industrial, rhythms which the Orb were pushing forward. *Pomme Fritz* made No. 6 on the British charts, but critics hated it, charging that Paterson had finally disappeared up his own arse. They even compared him to Pink Floyd's own Syd Barrett, who masterminded the psychedelic classic *Piper at the Gates of Dawn*, but later slipped out of the band as the world's first—and most popular—acid casualty.

*Pomme Fritz* was also a watershed in that the role of Kris Weston had diminished highly. Credited on *Pomme Fritz* only as an engineer, Weston did appear with Paterson on the August 1994 side-project FFWD, the collaboration between Robert Fripp, Orb members Paterson and Weston, and Orb contributor Thomas Fehlmann (hence the name: Fripp, Fehlmann, Weston, and Doctor). By early 1995, Weston finally left the Orb to devote time to his own projects, though no material has since surfaced. Before the duo separated, however, they teamed for the Orb's most famous live appearance: on a rave bill at *Woodstock 2* with Orbital, the Aphex Twin, and Deee-Lite.

Taking up the slack from Weston's departure was Thomas Fehlmann. The Orb had previously remixed a single from his Sun Electric project, and most of *Pomme Fritz* was recorded at his Berlin studios. Finally, almost three years after *U.F.Orb*, the new and improved group released the Orb's third studio LP, *Orbus Terrarum*. With a concept and a sound rooted firmly on terra firma, the album's dense rhythms and return to natural samples heralded a turn away from the cosmic fascination within ambient house—which had been nurtured in large part by *Ultraworld* and *U.F.Orb*. During 1995, Paterson and Fehlmann mounted an ambitious world tour. After the release of a double-disc remix compilation, the Orb returned to the great beyond with the spacey sounds of 1997's *Orblivion*. The retrospective *U.F.Off* followed in 1998, and though Paterson and Co. finished their fifth studio effort *Cydonia* soon after, Island delayed its release until the new millennium. —*John Bush*

★ **The Orb's Adventures Beyond the Ultraworld** / Aug. 1991 / Big Life ◆◆◆◆◆

Much like the early Orb-related project recorded as Space, *Adventures Beyond the Ultraworld* simulates a journey through the outer realms—progressing from the soaring ambient-pop of "Little Fluffy Clouds" and the stoned "Back Side of the Moon" (a veiled Pink Floyd reference) to "Into the Fourth Dimension" and ending (after more than two hours) with the glorious live mix of "A Huge Ever Growing Pulsating Brain." A varied cast of samples (*Flash Gordon*, space broadcasts, foreign-language whispers) and warm synthesizer tones provide a convincing bed for the mid-tempo house beats and occasionally dub-inflected ambience. With a clever balance of BBC Radiophonics Workshop soundtracks, '70s ambient meister-works by Eno, Hillage, and Floyd plus the steady influence of Larry Heard's sublime Chicago house, *Adventures Beyond the Ultraworld* is the album that defined the ambient house movement. —*John Bush*

**Aubrey Mixes: The Ultraworld Excursions** / Jan. 10, 1992 / Caroline ◆◆◆◆

Including reworkings of *Ultraworld* material by Pal Joey, Kris Needs, Readymade, and Youth, among others, *Aubrey Mixes* is an interesting though hardly essential album. —*John Bush*

☆ **U.F.Orb** / Mar. 1992 / Big Life ◆◆◆◆◆

The commercial and artistic peak of the ambient house movement, *U.F.Orb* strides past the debut with more periods of free-form ambience and less reliance on a standard four-four beat. From the opener "O.O.B.E." through the bass-heavy gait of "Blue Room" and "Towers of Dub," the flow is more natural and ranges farther than most would have expected. The bevy of contributors (including Steve Hillage, Jah Wobble, Youth, Thomas Fehlmann, and Slam) never threaten to overload the proceedings, though the minimalist sampling of *Ultraworld* is replaced by a production focus much more dense and busy, especially on the rain-forest-on-Saturn ethno-ambience of "Close Encounters." Elsewhere, Paterson maintains his fascination with the earthy dub basslines of Mad Professor and Lee Perry even while he's indulging in flights of fancy indebted to Sun Ra. —*John Bush*

**Live 93** / Nov. 22, 1993 / Island ◆◆◆◆

Although the thought of an Orb live album may raise some eyebrows, the resulting double-CD set is amazing, a complete representation of the group in concert and living proof that techno is indeed a live, as well as recorded, art form. Besides, the consistent Pink Floyd jokes on the record (as well as the brilliant cover art) are hilarious. —*Stephen Thomas Erlewine*

**Pomme Fritz [EP]** / Jun. 13, 1994 / Island Red ◆◆◆

The first hint that the Orb might have taken their work a bit too far, *Pomme Fritz* is a "little album" (only 40 minutes) which swaps the interterrestrial-journey concept with some sort of psychedelic culinary preoccupation on tracks like "More Gills Less Fishcakes" and "We're Pastie to Be Grill You." Those two were the Orb's most experimental to date—garbled vocal samples further twisted into unintelligibility, wheezing synthesizer lines about to break down, and few remnants of the beats from *U.F.Orb*. The other six tracks are closer to straight-ahead ambient techno, though with a rhythmic dexterity far beyond their contemporaries. The beautiful ambient grooves of "Alles Ist Schoen" make it the highlight. —*John Bush*

**Orbus Terrarum** / Apr. 4, 1995 / Island ◆◆◆◆

The perfect response to a music-scene swamped by what Paterson himself called "lame ambient noodling for seventy minutes," *Orbus Terrarum* brings the mothership back to earth for a collision with some surprisingly harsh percussion and noisy synth. The melodies and dub lines of previous Orb recordings are still in the mix, and the esoteric bent of *Pomme Fritz* is muted somewhat. *Orbus Terrarum* is definitely not the place to start, but it's still a worthy successor to *U.F.Orb*. The final track "Slug Dub" is an ambient epic with vocal samples taken from a children's story. —*John Bush*

**Auntie Aubrey's Excursions Beyond the Call of Duty** / Jul. 15, 1996 / Deviant ◆◆◆◆

A double-disc compilation of over two and a half hours of remixes, *Excursions* includes Orb reworkings of well-known bands (Primal Scream, Erasure, Depeche Mode, Killing Joke) and more obscure acts (Keiichi Suzuki, Love Kittens). Several mixes sound a bit dated and the scattershot quality of the set can distract listeners, but the inclusion of several epiphanous moments (Material's "Praying Mantra," Primal Scream's "Higher than the Sun," and Sun Electric's "O'Locco") makes the album worthwhile for fans. Included is a thick book including colorful discographies and an interesting essay. —*John Bush*

**Orbscure Trax: The Rare Excursions** / 1997 / Island ◆◆◆

*Orbscure Trax* was a digipak promo CD given away with purchased copies of the Orb's 1997 CD, *Orblivion*, primarily to boost sales during the group's spring '97 tour. Hardly a throw-away gimmick, however, the 70-minute-plus disc contains some extremely high-quality material, beginning with the Ganja Kru's hardstep take on *Orblivion*'s first single, "Toxygene," and moving through unreleased mixes such as "Molten Love (Berlin Session Film Mix)" and "Bedouin," as well as rare versions of perennial faves such as "Little Fluffy Clouds," "Oxbow Lakes," and "Plateau." —*Sean Cooper*

**Orblivion** / Feb. 24, 1997 / Island ◆◆◆◆

If the Orb's 1995 release *Orbvs Terrarvm* was an extended meditation on the earthbound, the band's follow-up in *Orblivion* rises from the muck of primordial ectoplasm for a guided tour of late-20th-century Western culture's more paranoid face. From the Cold War (the album kicks off with Kennedy's intoning of the immortal invective "Are you now, or have you ever been..."), to the pre-millenial ranting of David Thewlis' warped, apocalyptic monologue from Mike Leigh's *Naked* ("The bar code! The ubiquitous bar code!"), *Orblivion* does for post-industrial-turn-of-the-century mania what earlier albums such as *The Orb's Adventures Beyond the Ultraworld* and *U.F.Orb* did for aliens and flying saucers. Like the previous record—an effusive mix of sprawling environmental textures, clanging, treated percussion, and humorous, trainspotterly samples—*Orblivion* brings with it another adjustment in mood, combining elements of downbeat, electro, and drum'n'bass with dense, soupy amalgams of treated electronics and shimmering rhythms. *Orblivion* also evidences a renewed interest in the more immediately engaging, upbeat pop of "Perpetual Dawn"- and "Little Fluffy Clouds"-era Orb, with a deeper, more embellished sound marked, in all likelihood, by the first fulltime contributions from former engineer Andy Hughes (who replaced Kris Weston after the latter's departure in 1994). Dub is still the organizing principle of the Orb's music, however, and whatever one's opinion of the actual album (reactions are likely to range from "genius" to "aimless") the production is undeniably amazing. —*Sean Cooper*

**U.F.Off: The Best of Orb** / Oct. 5, 1998 / PolyGram ◆◆◆◆

A brief, twelve-track trip through the Orb' singles archive, *U.F.Off* includes mixes of just about every single from "A Huge Evergrowing Pulsating Brain" through "Toxygene" (though not in strictly chronological order). Singles compilations for electronic artists hardly ever fit the bill for long-time listeners or neophytes, yet this one is put together well and remains a solid addition to any collection. The double-disc version inludes additional remixes plus a few unreleased tracks ("Mickey Mars," "Pi"). —*Keith Farley*

## William Orbit (William Wainwright)

*Keyboards, Remixing, Producer / Electronica, Ambient Techno, Trance, Electronic*

Ambient pioneer, studio master, and omnipresent dance remixer William Orbit began his musical career in the new wave band Torch Song. Even while the group recorded several albums for IRS, Orbit remained in the studio to learn the ropes and began producing and remixing for artists including Sting, Madonna, Prince, the Human League, Erasure, and Belinda Carlisle. Orbit concurrently recorded his own material, and released his first solo album *Orbit* in 1987. That same year, he inaugurated the ambient project Strange Cargo, which released follow-up albums in 1990 and 1993. Also during the late '80s, Orbit latched onto the acid-house explosion in England and founded one of the scene's most notable labels, Guerilla Records. Orbit's own Bassomatic recorded for Guerilla alongside British progressive acts Spooky and React 2 Rhythm plus excellent Chicago producers Felix Da Housecat and DJ Pierre. Through Virgin, Bassomatic also released an album, *Set the Controls for the Heart of the Bass*.

Though his release schedule slowed slightly during the '90s, William Orbit continued producing and remixing at a furious pace. He also founded a new label, N-Gram Recordings, and prepared to release the classical-crossover work *Pieces in a Modern Style* as the Electric Chamber. The album, which featured electronic interpretations of classical pieces, drew angry protests from composers Arvo Pärt and Henryk Górecki, and they helped block the album's release. In 1998, after 15 years of behind-the-scenes post-production, Orbit's name hit the mainstream thanks to his helming the Madonna comeback album *Ray of Light* (Orbit not only produced the entire LP, but co-wrote many of the tracks). The album won Grammy awards for Best Pop Album and Best Dance Recording, and its success led to a host of remixing and production work, including Blur's 1999 album *13*. In 2000, Orbit finally released *Pieces in a Modern Style*, and the album became an unexpected hit thanks to Ferry Corsten's trance remix of Samuel Barber's "Adagio for Strings." —*John Bush*

### Strange Cargo / 1988 / IRS ✦✦✦

Recorded between 1984 and 1987, Orbit's first *Strange Cargo* release is a dynamic album of quirky mood music, with the producer exploiting the full range of his synthesizer presets and evoking a quintessentially '80s style of Fourth World digitalia. Though it's all well produced, most of these tracks are suited more for use as musical beds on the Discovery Channel, and "Via Caliente" and "Riding to Rio" may be too bright and happy for fans of his later work. Still, "Silent Signals," "The Secret Garden," and "Scorpions" are contemplative ambience in league with early Tangerine Dream. —*John Bush*

### Strange Cargo 2 / 1991 / Capitol ✦✦✦✦

*Strange Cargo 2* finds Orbit moving (slowly) away from the synth-horn solos and overall sound of new age/contemporary instrumental. Though there's a few more electronics on this record, he still seems uncommonly fixated with textural touches like Spanish guitar, and the effect is still much more Windham Hill than Warp. Still, the Indian fusion pieces "777" and "The Thief & the Spirit" are highlights, with a series of masked vocal samples creating eerie moods. —*John Bush*

### • Strange Cargo 3 / 1994 / IRS ✦✦✦✦

The last and best of the *Strange Cargo* albums, *3* matches elegant sequencer trance and understated organic instruments (piano, guitar) with ethnic-fusion and soft house rhythms. It's the only *Strange Cargo* record with vocals, with Beth Orton making an early appearance (more earth mother than neo-folky) on the beautiful ambient-trance single "Water From a Vine Leaf." "Into the Paradise" and "The Story of Light" are variations on the same form (and produced almost as well), while Orbit borrows on hip-hop and dub for "Time to Get Wize," with the toasting of Divine Bashim. While still tied to the '80s *Fourth World* aesthetic of its predecessors, on *Strange Cargo 3* Orbit begins to move toward a more completely electronic form of music in keeping with the productions of his Guerilla label. —*John Bush*

### The Best of Strange Cargo / Feb. 20, 1996 / IRS ✦✦✦✦

Compiling tracks from his three *Strange Cargo* albums (with recordings dating from 1984 to 1994), William Orbit displays a range of recording styles, drifting from the ambient-pop of "Water from a Vine Leaf" with Beth Orton to recordings more obsessed with trance and world rhythms. —*John Bush*

### Pieces in a Modern Style / Feb. 22, 2000 / Warner Brothers ✦✦✦

After years of making his own esoteric ambient albums and paying for them by doing dance remixes for pop acts, William Orbit hit the big time in 1998 by co-writing and producing Madonna's *Ray of Light* album. With his own debut solo album on Madonna's label, he returned to his esoteric pursuits, programming a variety of calm classical pieces into his computer and rearranging them to one extent or another. Samuel Barber's "Adagio for Strings" came off relatively unscathed, but by the time he got to "Ogives Number 1" by Erik Satie, Orbit was mixing in the sounds of a helicopter, as if he were Francis Ford Coppola doing sound design work on *Apocalypse Now* with the Doors' "The End." Handel's "Largo from Xerxes" remained recognizable, but Beethoven's "Triple Concerto" was largely transformed. No matter whose music he was reformulating, however, Orbit worked gently, creating an album that, if it technically belonged beside Wendy Carlos' *Switched-On Bach*, was actually more reminiscent of Brian Eno's *Discreet Music*. It may seem surprising, then, to note that "Adagio for Strings" landed on the US and UK dance charts, but that was only in Ferry Corsten's remix (actually, an entirely different version, full of the usual thundering percussion), which was included along with an ATB version on a separate CD with the album. Though Orbit was already at work on the new Madonna album at the time that *Pieces in a Modern Style* was released, from the sound of it you'd have thought he was really angling to get film scoring jobs. —*William Ruhlmann*

## Orbital

f. 1987, Sevenoaks, Kent, England
*Group / Electronica, Ambient Techno, Club/Dance, Techno*

Orbital became one of the biggest names in techno during the mid-'90s by solving the irreconcilable differences previously inherent in the genre: to stay true to the dance underground and, at the same time, force entry into the rock arena, where an album functions as an artistic statement—not a collection of singles—and a band's prowess is demonstrated by the actual performance of live music. Though Phil and Paul Hartnoll first charted with a single, the 1990 British Top 20 hit "Chime," the duo later became known for critically praised albums. The LPs sold well with rock fans as well as electronic listeners, thanks to Orbital's busy tour schedule, which included headlining positions at such varied spots as the *Glastonbury Festival, the Royal Albert Hall and Tribal Gathering*.

The brothers Hartnoll—Phil (b. Jan. 9, 1964) and Paul (b. May 19, 1968)—grew up in Dartford, Kent, listening to early-'80s punk and electro. During the mid-'80s, Phil worked as a bricklayer while Paul played with a local band called Noddy & the Satellites. They began recording together in 1987 with a four-track, keyboards and a drum machine, and sent their first composition "Chime" (recorded and mastered onto a cassette tape for a total production cost of £2.50) into Jazzy M's pioneering house mix show *Jackin' Zone*. By 1989, "Chime" was released as a single, the first on Jazzy M's label, Oh-Zone Records. The following year, ffrr Records re-released the single and signed a contract with the duo—christened Orbital in honor of the M25, the circular London expressway which speeded thousands of club-kids to the hinterlands for raves during the blissed-out Summer of Love. "Chime" hit No. 17 on the British charts in March 1990, and led to an appearance on the TV chart show *Top of the Pops*, where the Hartnolls stared at the audience from behind their synth banks. "Omen" barely missed the Top 40 in September, but "Satan" made No. 31 early in 1991, with a sample lifted from the Butthole Surfers.

Orbital's untitled first LP, released in September 1991, consisted of all new material—that is, if live versions of "Chime" and the fourth single "Midnight" are considered new works. Unlike the Hartnolls' later albums, though, the debut was more of a collection of songs than a true full-length work, its cut-and-paste attitude typical of many techno LPs of the time. During 1992, Orbital continued their chart success with two EPs. The *Mutations* remix work—with contributions from Meat Beat Manifesto, Moby and Joey Beltram—hit No. 24 in February. Orbital returned Meat Beat's favor later that year by remixing "Edge of No Control," and later reworked songs by Queen Latifah, the Shamen, and EMF as well. The second EP, *Radiccio*, reached the Top 40 in September. It marked the Hartnolls' debut for Internal Records in England, though ffrr retained control of the duo's American contract, beginning with a US release of the debut album in 1992.

The duo entered 1993 ready to free techno from its club restraints, beginning in June with a second LP. Also untitled, but nicknamed the "brown" album as an alternative to the "green" debut, it unified the disjointed feel of its predecessor and hit No. 28 on the British charts. The Hartnolls continued the electronic revolution that fall during their first American tour. Phil and Paul had first played live at a pub in Kent in 1989—before the release of "Chime"—and had continued to make concert performance a cornerstone of their appeal during 1991-93, though the US had remained unaware of the fact. On a tour with Moby and the Aphex Twin, Orbital proved to Americans that techno shows could actually be diverting for the undrugged multitudes. With no reliance on DATs (the savior of most live techno acts), Phil and Paul allowed an element of improvisation to the previously sterile field, making their live shows actually sound live. The concerts were just as entertaining to watch as well, with the Hartnolls' constant presence behind the banks—a pair of flashlights attached to each head, bobbing in time to the music—underscoring the impressive light shows and visuals. The early 1994 release of the *Peel Session* EP, recorded live at the BBC's Maida Vale studios, cemented onto wax what concert-goers already knew. That summer proved to be the pinnacle of Orbital's performance ascent; an appearance at *Woodstock 2* and a headlining spot at the *Glastonbury Festival* (both to rave reviews) confirmed the duo's status as one of the premier live acts in the field of popular music, period.

The US-only *Diversions* EP—released in March 1994 as a supplement to the second LP—selected tracks from both the *Peel Session* and the album's single "Lush." Following in August 1994, *Snivilisation* became Orbital's first named LP. The duo had not left political/social comment completely behind on the previous album—"Halcyon + On + On" was in fact a response to the drug used for seven years by the Hartnolls' own mother—but *Snivilisation* pushed Orbital into the much more active world of political protest. It focused on the Criminal Justice Bill of 1994, which gave police greater legal action both to break up raves and prosecute the promoters and participants. The wide variety of styles signalled that this was Orbital's most accomplished work. *Snivilisation* also became the duo's biggest hit, reaching No. 4 in Great Britain's album charts.

During 1995, the brothers concerned themselves with touring and headlining the *Glastonbury Festival* in addition to the dance extravaganza *Tribal Gathering*. In May 1996, Orbital set out on quite a different tour altogether; the duo played untraditional, seated venues—including the prestigious Royal Albert Hall—and appeared on stage earlier in the night, much like typical rock bands. Two months later, Phil and Paul released "The Box," a 28-minute single of orchestral proportions. It screamed of prog-rock excess—especially the inclusion of synth harpsichords—and appeared to be the first misstep in a very studied career. The resulting *In Sides*, however, became their most acclaimed album, with many excellent reviews in publications that had never covered electronic music. It was over three years before the release of Orbital's next album, 1999's *Middle of Nowhere*. —*John Bush*

**Orbital** / Oct. 1991 / ffrr ♦♦♦♦

The US version of Orbital's debut album serves as a good primer to the group's early history, including standard versions of the early singles "Chime," "Omen," "Satan" and "Midnight," in addition to two B-sides which showed Phil and Paul's first stab at varying their Kraftwerk-inspired sound. "Belfast" (from the "Satan" single) is a warm, mid-tempo synth track inspired by Depeche Mode; "Choice," at the other extreme, is an aggro-house piece with vocal samples (i.e. "Wake Up!") that recall socially conscious punks like Crass. —*John Bush*

**Diversions [EP]** / 1992 / ffrr ♦♦♦

★ **Orbital 2** / 1992 / ffrr ♦♦♦♦♦

Opening with a looped *Star Trek* sample, Orbital's second album progresses through eight tracks of warm, unrepetitive techno in what sounds more like a DJ mix album than an LP, with no bows to mainstream sensibilities. Here, the duo's acknowledged inspiration from Kraftwerk, present before but always in the background, came to the fore. The brilliant manner in which the Hartnolls weave several synth lines, samples, sung vocals, and percussion—mathematically precise but still beautifully orchestrated—updated Kraftwerk's mastery of minimalist electronic music. One of the highlight of the '90s techno movement, the 'brown' album is still Orbital's most exciting work. —*John Bush*

**Snivilisation** / Aug. 23, 1994 / ffrr ♦♦♦♦

The political commentary inherent in 1994's *Snivilisation* extended even to the Top 30 single "Are We Here?," whose Criminal Justice Bill Mix voiced Phil and Paul's concern over what the bill might lead to—silence. Musically, the album delivers on the diverse promises of early B-sides "Choice" and "Belfast," with more harbingers to their thrash background—especially on "Quality Seconds"—and the addition of a third member, vocalist Alison Goldfrapp, on two songs. The shuffling, quasi-Eastern jungle rhythms of "Are We Here?," a beautiful piano run to begin "Kein Trink Wasser" and the glorious ambient climax "Attached" also reflect the fact that *Snivilisation* is Orbital's most varied LP. —*John Bush*

☆ **In Sides** / Mar. 1996 / ffrr/London ♦♦♦♦♦

*In Sides* isn't Orbital's best album, or the most accomplished, but it is the most definitive. It pulses with the energy of the debut, the lush flow of the second, and the conceptual theme of *Snivilisation*. The focus this time, though, is ecology. "The Girl with the Sun in Her Head" was recorded on a Greenpeace bus using only solar power, and "Dwr Budr" (Welsh for 'dirty water') also criticizes the misuse of natural resources. Phil and Paul's respect for the jungle/drum'n'bass movement showed in the moderate breakbeat rhythms on several tracks. —*John Bush*

**Middle of Nowhere** / Apr. 5, 1999 / PolyGram International ♦♦♦♦

Electronica routinely covers more ground, more quickly, than any style of music on the planet; the hottest new sound in January is old hat by March and downright foolish to even mention in June. Orbital, however, is the great constant in the world of techno. The brothers Hartnoll manage to turn in excellent albums, every few years, that occasionally reference the latest sound but rarely vary from the chord-heavy melodics of their debut single, "Chime." Though it took a bit longer to release, *Middle of Nowhere* is another typically excellent Orbital album. Experiments with breakbeats and other styles of music made interesting mixers of their previous two albums, *Snivilisation* and *In Sides*, and this fifth album includes nods to big-beat techno ("I Don't Know You People") and soundtrack composers. The latter is hardly a surprise, considering the Hartnolls' sideline gig as score composers (*Event Horizon*, *The Saint*). The opener, "Way Out," adds trumpet solos and a symphonic grandeur—reminiscent of John Barry's scores for the James Bond films—to the quintessential Orbital sound. Even considering the lack of real progression in sound, *Middle of Nowhere* reflects the pair once again making all the right moves and not slowing down a bit. —*John Bush*

## Orchestral Manoeuvres in the Dark

f. 1978, Liverpool, England

*Group / Alternative Dance, New Romantic, Post-Punk, New Wave, Synth-Pop*
Featuring the core members Paul Humphreys and Andy McCluskey, the Liverpudlian synth-pop group Orchestral Manoeuvers in the Dark (OMD) formed in the late '70s. Humphreys and McCluskey began performing together in school, playing in the bands VCL XI, Hitlerz Underpantz, and the Id. After the Id split in 1978, McCluskey was with Dalek I Love You for a brief time. Once he left Dalek, he joined with Humphreys and Paul Collister to form OMD. The group released their first single "Electricity" on Factory Records; the record led to a contract with the Virgin's subsidiary DinDisc. Using their record advance, McCluskey and Humphreys built a studio, which allowed them to replace their 4-track recorded with drummer Malcolm Holmes (formerly of the Id) and Dave Hughes (formerly of Dalek I Love You).

In 1980, the group released their self-titled debut album. *Organisation* appeared the same year, which featured the UK Top Ten single "Enola Gay."; Hughes was replaced by Martin Cooper after its release. The band's next few albums—*Architecture and Morality* (1981), *Dazzle Ships* (1983), *Junk Culture* (1984)—found the band experimenting with their sound, resulting in several UK hit singles. Recorded with two new members, Graham and Neil Weir, *Crush*, their most pop-oriented album, found more success in America than in Britain, as the single "So in Love" hit No. 26 on the charts. "If You Leave," taken from the *Pretty in Pink*, soundtrack was their biggest American hit, climbing to No. 4 in 1986. *The Pacific Age* was released the same year, yet America was the only country where it was popular. Shortly after its release, the Weir brothers left the band, followed by Holmes, Cooper, and Humphreys. McCluskey continued with the band, releasing *Sugar Tax* in 1991; in the meantime, Humphreys formed the Listening Pool.

After *Sugar Tax* failed to gain an audience, OMD returned with *Liberator* in 1993, which also was ignored. It was followed three years later with *Universal*. *The OMD Remixes* appeared in 1998. —*Stephen Thomas Erlewine*

**Orchestral Manoeuvres in the Dark** / 1980 / Virgin ♦♦♦♦

A very quirky, nervous album of clockwork synth-pop that avoided the lockstep imposed by primitive technology, mainly by dint of Andy McCluskey's twitchy, frantic bass and vocals and a quirky tape machine. Includes the re-recorded version of "Electricity" (their first single) as well as "Red Frame, White Light" and "Messages," two cuts that seem to promote muscle spasms as dance methodology. — *Steven McDonald*

**Organisation** / Nov. 1980 / Virgin ♦♦♦
OMD's second album *Organisation* finds the group adding an actual drummer, which has the effect of deepening the band's dark, swirling synth-pop. While *Organisation* isn't as thoroughly impressive or unexpected as the debut, its best songs, most notably the single "Enola Gay," demonstrate that the band's craft is improving. — *Stephen Thomas Erlewine*

**Architecture & Morality** / Nov. 1981 / Virgin ♦♦♦♦
With their third album *Architecture & Morality*, OMD attempt to make their synth-pop sound organic, and the result is an uneven but fascinating collection of somber dance-pop highlighted by the eerie hit singles "Joan of Arc" and "Souvenir." — *Stephen Thomas Erlewine*

**Dazzle Ships** / 1983 / Virgin ♦♦♦
With *Dazzle Ships*, OMD push their sonic boundaries to the extreme, incorporating found sounds, studio effects and altered tapes in attempt to create a concept album about the history of technology. Despite their efforts, the end result isn't very captivating since the group concentrated on texture, not songs, but some of those sounds are well worth investigating. — *Stephen Thomas Erlewine*

**Junk Culture** / 1984 / A&M ♦♦♦♦
*Junk Culture* finds OMD reintegrating crisp pop melodies into their sound while moving far away from pop song stucture. Instead, the group explores modern dance rhythms and production styles—there are more complex rhythm tracks on *Junk Culture* than any of their other albums, and "Tesla Girls" even incorporates hip-hop scratching. It's an fascinating, frequently captivating listen, and represents a significant comeback for the duo. — *Stephen Thomas Erlewine*

**Crush** / 1985 / A&M ♦♦♦♦
Following through on the pop inclinations of *Junk Culture*, OMD recorded a full-fledged mainstream pop album with *Crush*. Considerably calmer and more accessible than their previous records, the album may be less adventurous than their earlier work, but the breezy melodic charm of dance-pop singles like "So in Love" make *Crush* a thoroughly winning album. — *Stephen Thomas Erlewine*

**The Pacific Age** / 1986 / A&M ♦♦
OMD flirted with the mainstream on *Crush*, so some fans might find *The Pacific Age* a welcome return to esoteric, cryptic music. However, the album is loaded down with pompous, unrealized concepts and weak melodies, making it one of the most tedious and trying albums in their catalog. — *Stephen Thomas Erlewine*

• **The Best of O.M.D.** / 1988 / A&M ♦♦♦♦
*The Best of OMD* is a 16-track collection that features all of the group's hit singles, from "Enola Gay," "Souvenir" and "Joan of Arc" to "Tesla Girls," "So in Love" and "If You Leave," adding 12" mixes of "We Love You" and "La Femme Accident" for good measure. It's a thorough and entertaining retrospective, and it's all that most casual fans will need. — *Stephen Thomas Erlewine*

**Sugar Tax** / Jun. 11, 1991 / Virgin ♦♦♦
*Sugar Tax* is the first album OMD recorded without Paul Humphreys, and while the record is less adventurous than most of the group's previous albums, that's not necessarily due to his absence. Instead, OMD began a slow decline into light soul-inflected synth-pop in the late '80s, and *Sugar Tax*, while thoroughly competent, is nothing more than predictably refined and pleasant dance-pop. — *Stephen Thomas Erlewine*

**Liberator** / Jun. 29, 1993 / Virgin ♦♦
OMD have rarely been as dance-oriented as they are on *Liberator*, a collection of retro-disco and contemporary '90s club cuts. While it is far from the experimental and edgy synth-pop that earned the group rave reviews in the early '80s, it is an enjoyable, lightweight collection of appealing dance-pop. — *Stephen Thomas Erlewine*

**Universal** / 1996 / Virgin ♦♦
*Universal* is a rote collection of synth-pop and dance-pop from OMD, demonstrating only a fraction of the sophisticated craft that made its predecessor *Liberator* enjoyable, and none of the adventurous spirit of their '80s records. — *Stephen Thomas Erlewine*

**The OMD Singles** / Nov. 17, 1998 / Virgin ♦♦
Looking back on 20 years of creative growth since the electro-pop band's inception, *The OMD Singles* is logically and chronologically arranged. The earliest recordings, 1980's "Electricity" and "Messages" prove electric messages were being channeled from such German pioneers as Kraftwerk and Neu. These English boys were enamored of melody, though, and it was not long before such dulcet, song-like structure became self evident, as in 1984's "Tesla Girls." From then on, it is a steady climb in coherence, with synth rhythms downplayed in order to bring the melodic theme to the front. The pinnacle of this progression is OMD's memorable "So In Love" (1985) and "If You Leave" (from 1986's *Pretty in Pink*). The album closes with their last hit, 1996's glam influenced autobiography "Walking on the Milky Way." Last original member, Andy McCluskey, has blessed this greatest hits package as the final swan song for the long-lived group. Originating in post-punk synth experimentation and closing in dated, but still strong, pop productions, *The OMD Singles* is an excellent timeline of the band whose sound covered in a single career that same territory explored by the Human League, Erasure, Yaz, New Order, and beyond. — *Thomas Schulte*

**The Peel Sessions: 1979-1983** / Apr. 24, 2000 / Virgin ♦♦♦♦
Yet another release from the John Peel/BBC archives, and in this case it is a clear winner. OMD was one of the most original and unique sounding bands of the '80s, and they were also one of the most beguiling. To the average listener, they were a synth-pop group chock full of hits. Yet there was another side to this band, and it is that side that is displayed on this release. The music here, recorded live in the studio for the BBC, has the trademark melodic hooks, but it also features some of their more creative sounds. Even well-known songs such as "Enola Gay" take on a new life here. Rougher, rawer, and much more experimental. Fans also have the opportunity to hear some tracks from their very much underrated *Dazzle Ships* performed "live." Those particular tracks are downright eerie, especially "ABC Auto-Industry." But brilliant nonetheless. The CD is well recorded, and the playing is tight and exciting. To round off the CD, there is a bonus track of the original 7" version of "Electricity" (released on the Factory label). This alone is worth the price of the CD. Andy McCluskey and Paul Humphreys have never sounded so good and so alive and energetic on any of the studio releases. Highly recommended. — *Aaron Bagdley*

## Origin Unknown

f. 1990, London, England
Group / Jungle/Drum'N'Bass, Club/Dance

East London jungle imprint Ram Recordings (along with labels such as Droppin' Science, Flex, Infa-Red, and No U-Turn) is closely associated with a new wave of drum'n'bass innovators, twisting darkside and hardstep into future-fueled, increasingly entropic configurations that draw as often from the dry, brittle technologism of techno and electro as from jungle's more uppity roots in hip-hop and ragga. Entirely owned and operated by partners Andy C. and Ant Miles, Ram's back-catalog is near-filled with Ant- and Andy-related projects such as Concept 2, Desired State, and perhaps their most well-known and best-respected pseudonym, Origin Unknown. Formed in Essex in 1990, Ram was a product of the area's vibrant pirate radio underground; the label shares roots with hardcore staple Suburban Base (and Sub-Base's storefront, Boogie Times), producers Dillinja, Cool Hand Flex, and DJ Hype, and pirate frequencies such as Centreforce and Sunrise. Andy and Ant's working relationship (the pair set up a studio and began recording together in 1990) grew out of a shared dissatisfaction with more mainstream dance music production and an increasing fascination with exploding breakbeat culture, which by 1992 had grown to critical mass in London's East End.

The pair's early releases include remix and engineering work for Suburban Bass and an assortment of artists, but Ram was already in the works by the time they were seriously laying down tracks, and by the release of their fourth 12"—"The Touch"/"Valley of the Shadows"—Ram's trademark of dark, pointed, brazenly technological hardstep was picking up speed in the clubs. That single's B-side, in fact, was one of the earliest blasts from darkside's more bleepy cousin, techstep (popularized by Ed Rush, Trace, Doc Scott, etc). Rather than following tech's leaders through the murk of fear and isolation, however, Andy and Ant have turned instead to a process of refinishing; an approach similar to techno, with the focus on the details and subtlety and finesse substituted for the brash beats'n'bass attack of techstep's front guard. The breaks still shred through the fabric of their tracks, but rolling beats in the Ram sense never equal soft and sweet, and a nervous, adamant jitter of electronics is usually in tow.

The pair took the formula to new heights in late 1996, coming up with arguably one of the biggest tunes of the year with the Origin Unknown remix of Busta Rhymes' "Whoo-Ha." And while Ram and sister label Liftin' Spirits (home primarily to Miles-related projects) have remained for the most part 12" driven, the pair joined ranks with labels such as Metalheadz, Infa-Red, and Reinforced by releasing *The Speed of Sound* in early 1997, a full-length collection of new cuts and exclusive mixes from the entire Ram family (which also includes Shimon and Stakka & K-Tee, among others). The following year, Andy C, Miles, and Shimon released three lauded singles (as Ram Trilogy) and followed with the full-length *Molten Beats* in 1999. In addition to their work together with Ram and Liftin' Spirits, Ant and Andy continue a long reign as in-demand remixers, as well as DJing (Andy) and working on solo material (Miles records as Higher Sense for Moving Shadow). [See Also: Ram Trilogy] —*Sean Cooper*

● **The Speed of Sound** / 1996 / RAM ◆◆◆◆
Though *The Speed of Sound* is more a Ram Recordings compilation than an Origin Unknown full-length, it's near essential for fans wishing to save $50 by skipping the many vinyl-only singles. Including paranoid classics like "Valley of the Shadows" as well as more straight-ahead club burners like "Roll On," *The Speed of Sound* is an excellent document of jungle's continuing development during the late '90s. —*Keith Farley*

**Valley of the Shadows [Single]** / Jul. 1, 1996 / RAM ◆◆◆◆

## Jim O'Rourke
b. 1969, Chicago, IL
*Multi Instruments, Guitar, Producer, Composer / Experimental Rock, Indie Rock, Post-Rock/Experimental*

American post-classical composer Jim O'Rourke has been a key component in the increasing overlap of the American and European experimental music avant-garde, working in everything from jazz and rock to ambient and electro-acoustic and building many a bridge in between. A Chicago native, his work has found equal truck with experimental jazz and noise fanatics, chill room denizens, and bedroom experimentalists, and has had the resultant effect of cross-polinating many otherwise isolated compositional communities. Dealing most often with prepared guitar in improvisational group settings, O'Rourke has also released a fair bit of material as a soloist, although more often in the electro-acoustic/musique concrète vein. He's collaborated with such contemporary improv heroes as Derek Bailey, Henry Kaiser, Eddie Prevost, and Keith Rowe (of English improv group AMM), KK Null, David Jackman (Organum), and early Kraut-rock experimentalists Faust. O'Rourke is also engaged in an ongoing exploration of experimental rock as a member of Gastr Del Sol, who've released albums through the Teen Beat and Table of the Elements labels.

Beginning with guitar at the age of six, it wasn't until his collegiate career at DePaul University that O'Rourke's interest in the less obvious possibilities of the instrument led him through the early catalogs of the post-classical and electro-acoustic traditions. While at DePaul, O'Rourke completed much of the work that would constitute his first few releases. He also had the opportunity to meet up with noted improvisational guitarist Derek Bailey, whose invitation to O'Rourke to play at the British improv festival Company Week led to further collaborative projects with Bailey, Henry Kaiser, Eddie Prevost, and David Jackman. O'Rourke began working with Dan Burke's Illusion of Safety project in the early '90s, releasing three albums through Staalplaat and Tesco before moving on to form experimental "rock" group Gastr Del Sol with David Grubbs. Although focusing more on collaboration after a string of solo releases in the early '90s, O'Rourke has shifted back to solo work of late, releasing *Terminal Pharmacy* through John Zorn's Tzadik label and completing commissioned pieces for the Kronos Quartet and the Rova Saxophone Quartet. In 1995, O'Rourke was invited by German experimental electronic label Mille Plateaux (Oval, Steel, Microstoria) to conduct an extended remix of their entire back catalog. He also produced and co-wrote a good portion of innovative German outfit Faust's Table of the Elements release, *Rien*. Subsequent releases include 1997's acclaimed *Bad Timing* and its equally brilliant follow-up, 1999's *Eureka*. —*Sean Cooper*

**Rules of Reduction [EP]** / 1993 / Metamkine ◆◆◆◆
A 17-minute *musique concrète* work from O'Rourke, who has also worked with Illusion of Safety. Strange, dense, dreamlike music segments mix with more ethereal music and sounds of traffic, car horns, children playing, and speeches. —*William I. Lengeman III*

**Terminal Pharmacy** / 1995 / Tzadik ◆◆◆
With *Terminal Pharmacy*, Jim O'Rourke creates a soundscape so calm and minimal that some people, lacking patience for the seeming formlessness, could do entirely without it, while others will find themselves repeatedly putting it in their CD player at home, work, or wherever they need warmth dispersed throughout the air. Seeping steadily from the edge of silence comes crackles, thin fuzz, and extended string tones. Less narrative than what "electro-acoustic" usually refers to, "Cede" hums at the back of your mind. Given almost a minute of silence in between, the second piece then begins; sounding like a very quiet improvisation, the instruments whisper bowed rounds, a conversation in tininess that grows bolder at moments. —*Joslyn Layne*

**Bad Timing** / Aug. 25, 1997 / Drag City ◆◆◆◆
With *Bad Timing*, O'Rourke attempts a return to the organic atmosphere of acoustic guitar from his explorations in electronica. The album consists of four songs clocking in at roughly ten minutes each, and is characterized by O'Rourke's ambient acoustic exploration. Three of the tracks enlist various instruments from cello to trumpet and even drums. The songs are highly textured and require patience, as they slowly evolve from abstract riffs into clear melodies. The album encompasses a rich dynamic range despite the seeming limitations that acoustic guitar could impose. There is a fair amount of splicing and mixing, which attests to the fact that O'Rourke has not completely dispensed with his passion for electronic music, but these interludes often provide a unique perspective. The highlight of the album is the final track, "Happy Trails," which begins with distorted acoustic noise, followed by an upbeat country rhythm provided by Tortoise's John McEntire. In sum, *Bad Timing* is a consistent effort and well worth a listen, especially during the mellow early morning hours. —*Marc Gilman*

● **Eureka** / Feb. 16, 1999 / Drag City ◆◆◆◆
It's a good bet to expect the unexpected with Jim O'Rourke—no matter which hat he's wearing (solo artist, bandmate, producer, remixer, etc.), each of the endlessly prolific projects that bears his name takes on a shape and identity all its own while retaining the originality and ingenuity that have become the hallmarks of his singular body of work. *Eureka* is perhaps his most stunning and surprising detour yet, a full-blown excursion into lush, melodic pop; granted, there's something inherently perverse about the very notion of O'Rourke and Chicago underground cronies like trombonist Jeb Bishop and cornetist Rob Mazurek tackling such classicist stuff, but instead the album is short on irony and long on affection—in fact, its most subversive dimension is its very real mainstream appeal. What's most fascinating about *Eureka* is that its big, bright pop is actually the perfect showcase for O'Rourke's mastery of sound—highlights like the epic opener "Women of the World" and a joyously schmaltzy cover of the Bacharach/David chestnut "Something Big" are crafted with remarkable care and depth, the former in particular building and blooming in truly majestic fashion. On a conceptual level, of course, it's easy to view *Eureka* as another in a long line of deconstructionist experiments, a reading more overtly avant songs like "Movie on the Way Down" and "Through the Night Softly" certainly bears out; on a deeper level, however, it's a true labor of love, and its sheer exuberance and creativity go further in re-shaping the pop aesthetic than any pure intellectual exercise ever could. —*Jason Ankeny*

**Halfway to a Threeway [EP]** / Jan. 20, 2000 / Drag City ◆◆◆◆
Jim O'Rourke returns to the melodic pop of *Eureka* on his EP *Halfway to a Threeway*. The music is almost as warm and cuddly as the stuffed frog and bear on the cover, but the lyrics are a bit strange—a little demonic, even. Nonetheless, it's hard to find an album this consistent and compulsively listenable. The first track, "Fuzzy Sun," is triumphant, setting the stage for the instrumental "Not Sport, Martial Art." "Not Sport" swings, builds to a crescendo, and then something curious happens: Right before the song darts back into the groove, there's an audible exhale, perhaps from O'Rourke himself. It's this subtle buildup and release of tension—a bated breath released at the precise moment—that sells the album. It's perfect. The final song, and title track, "Halfway to a Threeway," finds a female-obsessed O'Rourke singing about a love who's plagued by "epilectpic fits" and other weird problems. The song is basically a solo acoustic arrangement, and kind of Nick Drake-ish in it's beauty, so the subject matter comes as a bit of a surprise. If you liked *Eureka*, buy this album. It is, as O'Rourke mumbles at one point during the title track, "sweet but short." —*Marc Gilman*

## Beth Orton

b. Dec. 1970, Norwich, England
*Songwriter, Vocals, Guitar / Alternative Folk, Adult Alternative Pop/Rock, Trip-Hop, Folk-Rock*

Singer/songwriter Beth Orton combined the passionate beauty of the acoustic folk tradition with the electronic beats of trip-hop to create a fresh, distinct fusion of roots and rhythm. Orton debuted as one half of the duo Spill, a one-off project with William Orbit which released a cover of John Martyn's "Don't Wanna Know About Evil." She continued working with Orbit on his 1993 LP *Strange Cargo 3*, co-writing and singing the track "Water from a Vine Leaf" before appearing with the group Red Snapper on their first singles "Snapper" and "In Deep." In 1995 Orton teamed with the Chemical Brothers for "Alive: Alone," the ultimate track on their *Exit Planet Dust* LP. After assembling a backing band comprised of double bassist Ali Friend, guitarist Ted Barnes, keyboardist Lee Spencer, and drummer Wildcat Will, she finally issued her 1996 debut EP *She Cries Your Name;* her stunning full-length bow *Trailer Park*, produced in part by Andrew Weatherall, followed later in the year. In 1997, Orton released the superb *Best Bit* EP, a move towards a more organic, soulful sound highlighted by a pair of duets with folk-jazz legend Terry Callier; the full-length *Central Reservation* followed in 1999. *—Jason Ankeny*

**Trailer Park** / 1996 / Heavenly ♦♦♦♦

A folkie for the electronica age, Beth Orton brilliantly bridges the gap between acoustic songcraft and digital dance beats with her extraordinary debut album *Trailer Park*. Fusing the plaintive emotional power of the singer-songwriter tradition with the distanced cool of trip-hop rhythms, Orton creates a fresh, distinct and surprisingly organic sound without obvious precedent; blessed with a warm, ethereal voice capable of adapting comfortably to spartan folk ("Whenever," a touching cover of the Spector/Greenwich/Barry-penned "I Wish I Never Saw the Sunshine") buoyant pop ("Live As We Dream," "How Far") and spacy, densely-layered electronica ("Tangent," "Touch Me With Your Love"), she shifts gears with remarkable ease, the depth and clarity of her unique perspective connecting even the most disparate tracks together into a unified whole. Simply put, *Trailer Park* is one of the most promising and innovative debuts of its era. *—Jason Ankeny*

**Best Bit [EP]** / 1997 / Heavenly ♦♦♦♦

*Best Bit* is a masterpiece in miniature, a four-track EP of stunning vision and depth; Orton's first substantial release since her groundbreaking debut album *Trailer Park*, it moves away from the electronic textures of her previous work to forge a more organic compound of folk, dance-pop, and jazz. The title track, with its loose, swinging trip-hop rhythms and treated background vocals, is closest in spirit to the album, but by the second cut, the evocative "Skimming Stone," Orton is in uncharted territory, juxtaposing moody piano-jazz with spaced-out guitar textures. The revelation of *Best Bit*, however, is the record's second half, a pair of breathtaking duets with singer Terry Callier: the first, a cover of Fred Neil's "Dolphins," represents folk-jazz fusion at its finest and most eccentric, with Orton's ethereal presence matching perfectly with Callier's warm, soulful croon. No less wonderful or touching is the closing "Lean on Me," a Callier original featuring Orton's most impassioned vocal turn to date—proof positive that under her remote electronic rhythms there beats a fragile human heart. *—Jason Ankeny*

• **Central Reservation** / Mar. 9, 1999 / Arista ♦♦♦♦

On her stunning sophomore album *Central Reservation*, Beth Orton slips free of the electronic textures that colored her acclaimed 1996 debut *Trailer Park*, stripping her music down to its raw essentials to produce a work of stark simplicity and rare poignancy. With the exception of a pair of Ben Watt-produced tracks ("Stars All Seem to Weep" and a remix of the title cut), *Central Reservation* rejects synthetic sounds and beats altogether in favor of an organic atmosphere somewhere between folk, jazz and the blues; the focal point is instead Orton's evocatively soulful voice, which invests songs like "Sweetest Decline" and "Feel to Believe" with remarkable warmth and honesty. It's a risky move creatively as well as commercially—after all, the club culture was the first to champion Orton's talents—but it pays off handsomely; for all its brilliance, elements of *Trailer Park* already feel dated, but the new material possesses a timelessness that recalls the best of Nick Drake or Sandy Denny, with a haunting beauty to match. And while much has been made of the melancholy that pervades her music, ultimately *Central Reservation* is first and foremost a record about hope and survival; its emotional centerpiece, the seven-minute "Pass in Time" (a spine-tingling duet with legendary folk-jazz mystic Terry Callier), grapples with the death of Orton's mother, but its underlying message of healing and perseverance is powerfully life-affirming—her music hasn't merely discovered the light at the end of the tunnel, it's now bathing in it. *—Jason Ankeny*

## O.S.T. (Chris Douglass)

b. Edinburgh, Scotland
*Producer / Electronica, Ambient Techno*

O.S.T. (Original Soundtrack, as well as a few other, less printable pseudos) is the one-man ambient/experimental electro project of DJ/producer Chris Douglass. A native of Edinburgh, Douglass left Scotland at the age of ten for San Francisco, where he's lived ever since. Raised on a heaping diet of John Coltrane and Max Roach (his mother is a jazz fanatic), he added early-'80s breakdance music to his list of influences when artists such as Egyptian Lover and Uncle Jamm's Army began defining the sound of California hip-hop and electro (Douglass himself spent his share of time perfecting backspins on squares of discarded cardboard and linoleum). Combining the above two styles with the more melancholic elements of British and European rock and Euro-pop groups such as the Smiths, Kraftwerk, and Morton Subotnick, Douglass began producing music in 1993, and released his first 12" on Detroit's Switch label (an arresting three-tracker of bizarre rhythmic noise experiments) the following year.

Although he originally planned on relocating to techno's birthplace, Douglass moved back to San Francisco shortly after the Switch 12" was released and began working on an album for Jonah Sharp's Reflective label. The album never appeared, and that and a handful more of gone-nowhere EP and LP release plans with labels such as Skam and Plug Research have resulted in as many as 500 tracks and four complete albums lying dormant in Douglass' DAT cachet. O.S.T. material finally began appearing with more frequency starting in 1996, beginning with his remix of Spacetime Continuum's "Simm City" on the latter's *Remit Recaps* CD alongside the likes of Carl Craig, Autechre, and Higher Intelligence Agency. Subsequent twelves for Qliphothic and noted London label Worm Interface, as well as twelves for compilations on XLR8R and Plug Research (both under the name Rook Vallade), appeared in 1996 and 1997. Douglass also performs live periodically, appearing on bills in America and the UK next to such names as Spacetime Continuum, Derrick May, Eric Hill, and post-rockers Trans Am. *—Sean Cooper*

• **Aspire [Single]** / 1997 / Qliphothic ♦♦♦

O.S.T.'s first proper 12" following his Switch debut and an almost depressing number of fallen-through release plans reveals an even darker fusion of moody ambient and electro than previous. The beat patterns have been stepped up here, with syncopation tossing about in a soup of austere electronics and hissing atmospheres. O.S.T.'s already lo-fi aesthetic dips a little too deep into the murk at times, with the beats often muffled by the density of the mix, but fans of the Skam and V/VM labels should find this quality four-tracker a welcome addition. *—Sean Cooper*

## Otaku

f. 1998, San Francisco, CA
*Group / Ambient Dub, Trip-Hop*

The dub/trip-hop production team Otaku came together in San Francisco in 1998, originally to soundtrack an art exhibition comprising alien artifacts. Brothers Colonel 32 and NaN had already been recording for several years, however, utilizing the reams of samples collected on their hard drives as well as their growing mixing skills. Influenced by earthy beat-oriented scenes from hip-hop, dub, the Orb, and Brooklyn's illbient scene, the pair recorded *Bitwise Operators* and released it on the Malvado label in mid-2000. They also composed the title track for an internet-only sci-fi series named *Pix and Rez*. *—John Bush*

• **Bitwise Operators** / Jul. 4, 2000 / Malvado ♦♦♦

A bit of an anachronism in the San Francisco electronics scene, Otaku creates dark trip-hop with deep beats, often mashing up rhythms mid-track like the best turntablists. Occasionally reminiscent of big beat techno at a slightly slower tempo, *Bitwise Operators* features fragile, cinematic melodies. The two-part "Dub Bass" summons the spirit of the Orb with several minutes of gently wandering ambient dub, complete with heavy basslines, reverbed effects, and plenty of nonsensical vocal samples (lifted from a few too-obvious sources like *The Simpsons* and *Happy Gilmore*). —*John Bush*

## Oval
f. 1993
*Group / Minimal Techno, Experimental Techno, Electronica, Ambient Techno, Post-Rock/Experimental, Electronic, IDM*

Although Oval are perhaps more well-known for how they make their music than for the music they actually make, the German experimental electronic trio have provided an intriguing update of some elements of avant-garde composition in combination with techniques of digital sound design, resulting in some of the most original, if somewhat challenging electronic music of the contemporary scene. Originally composed of Markus Popp, Sebastian Oschatz, and Frank Metzger, Oval gradually became the work of just Popp, with Metzger providing most of the visual and design work. The bulk of Popp's work, released through the Force Inc.-related Mille Plateaux label, incorporates elements of what could be described as "prepared compact disc"—manually marred and scarified CDs played and sampled for the resultant, somewhat randomly patterned rhythmic clicking. Layered together with subtle, sparse melodies and quirky electronics, the results are often as oddly musical as they are just plain odd. Popp brought this approach to bare on the first full-length Oval releases—*Wohnton, Systemische* and *94 Diskont*—as well as a number of compilation tracks. Although a rung below marginal in their home country and even more obscure in the States, Oval's remixes of Chicago post-rock group Tortoise brought them in contact with American audiences; both *Systemische* and *94 Diskont*, as well as Markus Popp's work as Microstoria (with Mouse on Mars' Jan St. Werner) were reissued domestically by Thrill Jockey in 1996. One year later, the *Dok* LP featured Oval's collaboration with Christophe Charles. After 1999's *Szenario* EP, Popp and co. returned in 2000 with *Ovalprocess*. —*Sean Cooper*

**Wohnton** / 1993 / Thrill Jockey ♦♦♦
Even on their debut album back in 1993, Oval were heavy into CD-skip experimentation, though the big surprise on this skeleton-in-the-closet is the surprising number of vocal tracks. The resulting collision between experimental techno and pop actually works quite well, and several songs here (notably "Allesin Gedanken" and "Hallodrauflen") work better with vocals than they would've as simple tracks. The production is years ahead of its time as well, pointing the way toward futurist techno at the same time many electronic groups were attempting to sound like the Orb. —*John Bush*

**Systemische** / 1994 / Mille Plateaux ♦♦
Slightly overbearing over the course of its 11 tracks, the best of *Systemische* is truly remarkable in its unlikely musicality. The group is at its best when the clickety-clackety rhythms are backgrounded to concentrate on melodic and thematic development. —*Sean Cooper*

★ **94 Diskont** / 1995 / Mille Plateaux ♦♦♦♦♦
Oval's second proper collection of digitally damaged electronica adds a far wider range of sound and texture to the blender than the previous *Systemische*. The vinyl Mille Plateaux version included a bonus 12" of remixes by Scanner, Mouse on Mars, and Jim O'Rourke. —*Sean Cooper*

**Dok** / Jan. 20, 1998 / Thrill Jockey ♦♦♦♦
Recorded in collaboration with Tokyo-based artist Christophe Charles, *Dok* continues Oval's manipulation of digital technology with typically innovative results. Beginning with Charles' field recordings of various ringing bells assembled from around the world, these static peals mutate into fluid, linear songs, complete with rhythm indices and bass tones; through extensive processing, beautifully organic music is somehow created, and like previous Oval releases, *Dok* forces listeners to reassess everything they believe to be true about the nature of sonic shape and form. —*Jason Ankeny*

**Szenariodisk** / Jun. 22, 1999 / Thrill Jockey ♦♦
Like many other electronic projects, Oval is difficult to describe. Markus Popp has had a hand in loads of interesting projects, from the minimalist/experimental Microstoria to the Jim O'Rourke and David Grubbs combo Gastr del Sol. On *Szenariodisk*, Popp puts his many hats to work in creating a cerebral, complex result. One hears echoes of the click-oriented compositions of Nobukazu Takemura combined with electronic-sounding feedback, vaguely vocal-sounding samples, and a plain old synthesizer. The music is extremely contemplative; it's too detailed to be background sound and requires focused attention to be fully appreciated. The track listing is a bit misleading, as it seems that five of the songs are comprised of two tracks each and the final track consists of only one section. It is nearly impossible to discern any type of link between the two-part tracks. Most tracks have clicking in the background; this is especially true of "Episonik," the first track, as well as "Kardio V." The clicks provide a vague sense of rhythm in an otherwise timeless space. The second half of "Episonik" is essentially washed-out electronic distortion punctuated by bells that ring every five seconds or so. Perhaps the best piece on the album is "Par," which has an identifiable melody poised far behind waves of synthesized noise. This sheds some light on what might be an essential element of Popp's aesthetic: taking what could be an easily hummable melody and rearranging it to be barely recognizable. Nonetheless, Popp loses none of the melodic beauty behind his songs; rather, he constructs something equally as beautiful. [*Szenariodisk* compiles tracks from the two Oval EPs *Szenario* and *Aero Deko*.] —*Marc Gilman*

**Ovalprocess** / Jun. 20, 2000 / Thrill Jockey ♦♦♦♦
By the time of *Ovalprocess*, Oval's fifth full album, the clicks-and-cuts style of experimental ambience Markus Popp and company helped develop nearly a decade before was being championed all over the world, from Tokyo (Nobukazu Takemura) to Berlin (Pole) to Sheffield (SND) to San Francisco (Kit Clayton). All of which makes it a bit of a surprise that *Process* remains a distinctive work. The scratchy bass hum and high-pitched, atonal effects heard on most every track are very nearly Oval trademarks, and despite the focus on experimentation, *Ovalprocess* retains yet another hallmark of the group's productions: it's a remarkably beautiful album. Granted, this won't quite signify to listeners unfamiliar with the genre, but when the album climaxes (on the ninth untitled track) with a droning organ melody heard faintly above a cacophony of glitch static, electronics fans might just find themselves wiping their eyes from the wonder of it all. Even among considerable competition, Oval remains the very best at making beautiful music out of civilization's sonic detritus. —*John Bush*

## Override (Tom Withers)
*Producer / Jungle/Drum'N'Bass, Club/Dance*

Experimental jungle producer Tom Withers is one of the more pigeonhole-proof of the London drum'n'bass set. Releasing tracks primarily as Klute and Override, his talent for composing the most relentlessly exploratory of tracks within the language of dancefloor drum'n'bass (as opposed to artful noodlers such as Plug, Mung, and Squarepusher) has played a role in pushing jungle beyond the more loopy confines of its "ambient" and "jazzy jungle" offshoots. While somewhat classifiable as an ambient junglist himself, Withers' tracks flit about with such pace and contradiction as to distance his work from the more manageable output of artists such as Alex Reece and LTJ Bukem. A guitarist in the semi-legendary British punk band the Stupids before finding the next level of extreme in the exploding hardcore (as in, hardcore techno) underground, Withers released a few spotty white-labels of straight-ahead dancefloor fare in the early '90s before settling into experimental breakbeat by 1993.

Withers' path through the labyrinth of underground labels—from Certificate 18, Deep Red, and Octopus to Crammed subsidiaries Selector and Language—brings his two most distinctive characteristics into focus; complicated, disjointed rhythms and tense, often melancholy melodic themes. While darkness constitutes an important component of many of his tracks (particularly his Certificate 18 and Octopus singles), it's often paired with a lighter, more dynamic thrust that gives his tunes an almost epic feel. Withers' Selector releases as Phume (together with Dave Campbell, ex-Hi-Ryze) are lighter still, with elements of techno and house combining with jungle's brisker BPMs. In addition to his regular schedule of twelves, Withers' production resume includes remix work for Sumosonic and Octopus labelmates Stranger (aka Inky Blacknuss), as well as releases as Tongue, Tom Tom, and Dr. No. [See Also: Klute] —*Sean Cooper*

● **Future Paranoia [Single]** / 1995 / Octopus ♦♦♦♦
Withers' debut three-tracker under his Override moniker is lush-yet-chilly abstract drum'n'bass, with rinsed breaks given fresh treatment through odd rhythmic arrangements and complex syncopation. Withers manages to be

both dark and optimistic at the same time, edging minor-key synth melodies over cascading strings and bar-to-bar rhythmic variations. Recommended. —*Sean Cooper*

**Consume and Destroy [EP]** / Dec. 2, 1996 / Octopus ♦♦♦♦
Tom Withers' most complex and intricate beat manipulation to date appears on his *Consume and Destroy* EP, released by Octopus toward the end of 1996 at the height of the resurgence of darkside. "Destroy" echoes a fascination for this style with its moody patches and killing, warped basslines, but Withers' knack for lilting melodies and delicate rhythmic themes puts this twelve in a class by itself. The CD version (Octopus' first EP-length CD release) adds tracks from previous Override single, "Future Paranoia," as well as an otherwise unavailable track. —*Sean Cooper*

# P

## Jochem Paap
*Producer / Ambient House, Ambient*

Jochem Paap is the birth name of the Dutch former DJ wizard and current production king Speedy J. Except for scattered contributions to various-artists compilations, Paap kept his real name out of the recording sphere until 1999, when Pete Namlook's Fax Recordings released two discs of ambient material recorded during the past couple of years. [See Also: Speedy J] —*John Bush*

● **Vrs-Mbnt-Pcs 9598 1** / 1999 / Fax ♦♦♦♦
From the mind behind Speedy J, *Vrs-Mbnt-Pcs* is a seven-track collection of beautiful, chiming ambience with nothing more than an occasional bass tone for harmony and faraway synthesizer to accompany the slowly building melancholia. Most tracks are quite similar to each other, though the comparatively brief "Flm" (just like in the title, fill in the missing vowel) is rather more cinematic, reminiscent of Aphex Twin's *Selected Ambient Works II*. Though Paap's best known for his experimental techno productions, he displays considerable talents here, creating space music tracks that stand alongside masters like Tangerine Dream and Klaus Schulze. —*John Bush*

**Vrs-Mbnt-Pcs 9598 2** / 1999 / Fax ♦♦♦

## Augustus Pablo (Horace Swaby)
b. 1954, St. Andrews, Jamaica, d. May 18, 1999
*Melodica, Keyboards, Piano, Synthesizer, Organ, Producer / Dub*

The name never gained the international recognition of Bob Marley's, but Augustus Pablo is one of reggae's legitimate legends, a pioneer who flipped the genre completely upside down. Along with producer King Tubby, Pablo almost singlehandedly invented dub, wherein reggae's fat bass and popping drums are twisted and contorted until they crack like bullwhips and rumble like syncopated earthquakes. This is instrumental music: voices will emerge from the supple rhythms only to trickle into an echo-shrouded void, forsaking their contribution to the bedrock grooves. And Pablo's haunting splashes of melodica (which at times conjure images of Ennio Morricone's Sergio Leone soundtracks) gave his music a sound that is immediately identifiable and as singular as anything Marley managed. Born Horace Swaby, as a youngster he hung around Kingston's jostling recording studios, watching the masters. There he met the original Augustus Pablo—the Upsetters keyboardist Glen Adams—who invented the name and played the melodica, the odd instrument that gave reggae its "Far East" sound. Adams moved to the States in 1971 and left the concept to Swaby, who began recording in 1972. As Augustus Pablo, he released a string of brilliant singles over the next five years on his Rockers label. The best of those singles are collected on *Original Rockers*, and his best early album is *King Tubby Meets Rockers Uptown* (1976). He continued working for decades, occasionally striking a balance between the technical wizardry of his Tubby years and the slick production style of modern reggae. Though Pablo's later work only occasionally matched the breathtaking innovation of his prime material 1981's *East of the River Nile* equaled his early triumphs—the results weren't always great but they were always interesting. He died of a nerve disorder on May 18, 1999 at the age of 46. —*John Floyd & Roger Steffens*

**King Tubbys Meets Rockers Uptown** / 1976 / Shanachie ♦♦♦♦
A compilation of the best King Tubby/Augustus Pablo collaborational sides available, *King Tubbys Meets Rockers Uptown* was released in 1976 to capitalize on the popularity of the title track, one of the seminal dub sides of all time. (It was so popular that Island flipped the original, "Baby I Love You So" by Jacob Miller, onto the B-side of the single for the first time.) The other 11 tracks are all variations on the same superb form, super tuff rhythms and echoplexed melodica lines, with the rock-solid contributions of bassist Robbie Shakespeare and members of Bob Marley's band. —*John Bush*

**East of the River Nile** / 1977 / Shanachie ♦♦♦♦
The best of the pure instrumental albums in Pablo's catalog, *East of the River Nile* finds the melodica master stretching out on various keyboards and strings as well on earthy, meditative tracks like "Chant to King Selassie I," "Jah Light" and "Natural Way." Though this is explicitly a nondub occasion, "Natural Way" does get its own version with "Nature Dub." —*John Bush*

**Original Rockers** / 1979 / Shanachie ♦♦♦
*Original Rockers* is a solid introduction to Pablo's haunting melodica playing, and includes brief flashes of his dub inspiration on "Tubby's Dub Song" and "Rockers Dub." As usual, the lineup is superb—Robbie Shakespeare, Aston and Carlton Barrett, Earl Chinna Smith, and Bobby Ellis, among others. Though much of the album is instrumental, Dillinger guests on "Brace a Boy." —*John Bush*

**Rockers Meet King Tubby Inna Fire House** / 1981 / Shanachie ♦♦
Another early gem, *Rockers Meet King Tubby Inna Fire House* shows the influence of dub pioneer King Tubby plus Prince Jammy. —*Myles Boisen*

**Rockers International Showcase** / 1991 / Rykodisc ♦♦
While many of Augustus Pablo's albums are entirely instrumental, *Rockers International Showcase* finds him working with various singers as well as dubwise and dancehall toasters (the reggae equivalent of rappers). Toasters, in fact, have been embracing Pablo's tracks for decades. The more memorable singing on this diverse CD is provided by Yami Bolo on the angry "Poor Man Cry," Icho Candy on the sobering "Pray" and Junior Delgado on "Money" (which has an ambience recalling early to mid-'70s soul). Less distinguished is Bunnie Brissett's appearance on the run-of-the-mill lover's-rock number "Begging For My Love." Not outstanding but generally enjoyable, *Rockers International Showcase* is a project Pablo's more devoted followers will want. —*Alex Henderson*

★ **Classic Rockers** / 1995 / Island ♦♦♦♦♦
This generous collection of classic, rare, and previously unissued tracks is part of an outstanding reissue series from Island Jamaica (Island Records' reggae-specific imprint). The Augustus Pablo album may be the best of the bunch. It opens with the classic Jacob Miller song "Baby I Love You So," and is immediately followed by the dub version of that track ("King Tubby Meets the Rockers Uptown"), which may well be the single best dub cut ever recorded. Instrumentals and vocal tracks by Pablo-produced artists follow, including a couple of previously hard-to-find Delroy Wilson tracks with their dub versions, and two classic performances by Junior Delgado and the late Hugh Mundell. Run, don't walk, to your nearest music store to get this one. —*Rick Anderson*

**Presents DJ's from the '70s & '80s** / Sep. 23, 1997 / Big Cat ♦♦♦
Not a compilation as much as an update of Augustus Pablo's classic productions from the '70s and '80s, the album works much better than most packages of re-recorded hits, since Pablo still manages to inject the spirit of creativity into each track. —*John Bush*

## Pacou (Lars Lewandowski)
b. 1972, Berlin, Germany
*Producer / Minimal Techno, Club/Dance, Techno*

A banging techno producer and DJ based in Berlin, Pacou translated his influences from raw, early dance pioneers like Underground Resistance and Todd Terry into productions of no-nonsense techno on a par with minimalists like Jeff Mills and Surgeon. Born Lars Lewandowski in Berlin in 1972, Pacou listened to synth-pop before getting into the first wave of acid-house and techno, courtesy of the German capital's fertile dance community. He began producing in 1993, and turned his occasional DJ spots at the legendary *Tresor* club into a residency by 1995. A steady stream of dubplates—often dropped in his own sets—announced the arrival of Pacou's first release, the 1996 EP *Reel Techno* on Tresor, followed by his album debut *Symbolic Language*. For his second, *No Computer Involved*, Pacou stretched out with a set of radically different productions, each utilizing a different studio setup. After setting up his own label, LL Records, for releases by an array of producers (including the pseudonym Agent Cooper), Pacou returned in 2000 with *State of Mind*. —*John Bush*

● **Symbolic Language** / Jul. 21, 1997 / Tresor ◆◆◆◆
*Symbolic Language* displays the influence of the techno and house music Pacou was inspired by, especially Todd Terry and Underground Resistance. —*Steve Huey*

**No Computer Involved** / Aug. 10, 1998 / Tresor ◆◆
True to its title, Pacou's second full-length LP, *No Computer Involved*, was conceived, played, and recorded without the use of computers. —*Steve Huey*

**State of Mind** / Feb. 15, 2000 / Tresor ◆◆◆
Long on the pummeling beats and hypnotizing effects but just a bit short on actual ideas, *State of Mind* doesn't quite work in the confines of full-length headphone music. Pacou's production and drum programming is precise (especially on highlights like "Think Twice" and "Format 2"), but these tracks work best in a DJ set, not in a living room. —*John Bush*

## Palm Skin Productions (Simon Richmond)

*Producer / Electronica, Trip-Hop, Club/Dance, Acid Jazz*
Palm Skin Productions specialize in darkside dub excursions, heavy on the downtempo breakbeats, jazzy flourishes, and gut-bucket percussion. It's all the work of one Simon Richmond, though occasional collaborator Chris Bowden often appears on saxophone. Richmond first worked as a percussionist for the Talkin' Loud label's in-house session team K Collective, working on tracks by Jhelisa, Neneh Cherry, and D*Note. He began recording as Palm Skin Productions in 1994, and appeared on the 4th & Broadway compilation series *Rebirth of Cool* with the track "Spock with a Beard." Richmond followed with two 1996 singles for Mo'Wax Records, "Like Brothers" and "The Beast," then moved to Hut for his debut album *Remilixir*. He has also remixed Galliano, Global Communication, United Future Organization, D*Note, and the Jon Spencer Blues Explosion. —*John Bush*

● **Remilixir** / Sep. 1996 / Hut ◆◆◆◆
*Remilixir* shows Simon Richmond undoubtedly invigorated by the experience he gained from his work at Talkin' Loud Records; it's easily one of the best-produced trip-hop albums to date, with Richmond showing off a range of influences including jazz fusion, funk, spaghetti western soundtracks, '70s space music, Afro-Cuban percussion styles, and even a touch of classical music on the closer "Beethoven Street." Three tracks midway through the album form a beautiful miniature suite. An early acid jazz percussion vibe forms the accompaniment to the jazz riffs on "Osaka" (with Chris Bowden on saxophone and Neil Yates on trumpet) which segues right into the restrained acid effects and subtle big-beat posturing of "Trouble Rides a Fast Horse," which jumps in turn to the exquisite Tangerine Dream sequencer trance of "Flipper." The single "Condition Red" is the highlight of the album however, topping Tricky at his own game of trip-hop darkness. *Remilixir* rarely fails to entice. —*John Bush*

## Pan American (Mark Nelson)

*Producer / Experimental Rock, Space Rock, Indie-Rock, Electronic*
A more beat-oriented solo project for guitarist/vocalist Mark Nelson of Labradford, Pan American debuted with a self-titled album on Kranky in 1998. Nelson recorded a track for the British experimentalist-electronic label Fat Cat's *Split* series, and also played live with pedal-steel genius B.J. Cole. His second Pan American LP, *360 Business/360 Bypass*, appeared in early 2000 with collaborations from Chicago trumpeter Rob Mazurek and the members of Low. —*John Bush*

**Pan American** / Mar. 23, 1998 / Kranky ◆◆◆◆
Mark Nelson of Labradford fame has gone solo under the name Pan American. Splinters of whispers, chilly organs, faint hints of guitars, space-dub bass, and ratcheting electronic pings and blips recall early Aphex Twin, but the spacewalking sound is warmer, richer, and more bewitching. Unlike Labradford, which at times can be a bit arch, Nelson brings things down to the point at which the music is an enveloping primordial ooze which lulls and pacifies. That's not to say it's boring—far from it. In fact, Nelson's adeptly structured sonic landscapes are lush, dense, and intricate. Many of the tracks play on a similar theme, which makes them flow into one another with a calming seamlessness. In a further effort at sublime tranquillity, "Lake Supplies" utilizes a soothingly hypnotic hammer dulcimer for an additional mystic quality. *Pan American* is not something to put on when in search of a pick-me-up, but it makes for some of the best unwinding music around. —*Matthew Hilburn*

● **360 Business/360 Bypass** / Jan. 31, 2000 / Kranky ◆◆◆◆
Mark Nelson's second album as Pan American has a similar sound to his debut, and a similar charm as well. Recorded with Casey Rice, *360 Business/360 Bypass* is a work of atmospheric, melancholy dub minimalism whose closest stylistic companions are experimental-techno producers (Pole, Basic Channel, Senking), though with analogue elements instead of digital. Thanks to his large body of work with Labradford, Nelson knows how to structure long freeform tracks for maximum effect, and the result is a collection of tracks that are uniformly beautiful despite (or possibly because of) their sparse feel. True, "Code" would have been much more beautiful without the added vocals of Mimi Sparhawk and Al Sparhawk from Low, and Rob Mazurek's trumpet doesn't contribute to "Double Rail" as much as it takes away from it, but *360 Business/360 Bypass* is nevertheless an excellent piece of ambient minimalism. —*John Bush*

## Panacea (Matthias Mootz)

b. Summerhausen, Germany
*Producer / Industrial Dance, Electronica, Jungle/Drum'N'Bass, Club/Dance*
Panacea's Mathias Mootz is one of the first German drum'n'bass producers to make a significant dent among the somewhat insular London jungle crowd, creating a bridge of sorts between the UK jungle scene and its Berlin-based antagonist in the "digital hardcore" of Alec Empire, Shizuo, Atari Teenage Riot, etc. Although Mootz's work is reported to be only marginally accepted in his home country (and despite high praise by Empire), the brutalizing, overdriving, near industrial breakbeats and buzzing, hoover-esque basslines of tracks such as "Stormbringer" and "Torture" share much with Berlin hardcore artists. Mootz's most obvious influence is the first he's apt to namecheck—Ed Rush. But the appearance of unlikely samples (Autechre, My Bloody Valentine) and IDM-ish electro-breaks on his less rinsed tracks make him not nearly the one trick pony he at first appears. Hailing from the countryside town of Summerhausen, Mootz's musical roots lie in the early hardcore breakbeat of industrial dance artists such as Front 242, early Prodigy, and Nitzer Ebb. One of the first new artists to record for Force Inc.'s experimental beat music offshoot Chrome, Mootz released no less than three singles his first three weeks out of the gate. He immediately captured the attention of the ever-darkening drum'n'bass scene by taking the harsh, dusty darkcore of Rush, Trace, Dom & Roland, and Elementz of Noise a step forward, fusing dozens of sharp, redlining breaks and swampy bass rolls (often two or three at once) with dense, gaseous electronics, vocoder samples, and doom-bleating synths into a malicious, chaotic soup. Following "Stormbringer," "Tron," and "Day After," Chrome issued the LP *Low-Profile Darkness*, with the vinyl a sort of extended double 12" and the CD adding tracks from the earlier twelves. Additionally, Mootz remixed a track by related-labelmate Mike Ink (his Panacea took the odd man out in a double-pack of minimal house and techno takes on Ink's "Respect"). *Twisted Designz* followed in 1998 with an American release to boot, while Mootz also issued an EP and full-length under his hardcore acid alias, Bad Street Boy. The third Panacea LP, released in 1999, was a collaboration with Japanese vocalist Hanayo. One year later, he released a volume in Caipirinha's *Architettura* series focused on the city of Brazilia. —*Sean Cooper*

**Species [EP]** / 1997 / Gyration ◆◆◆◆
Panacea's first release away from the Chrome label is also probably his strongest to date. Although not as immediately impressive as, say, "Torture" or "Stormbringer," "Species" relies less on gimmick to make its point, focusing on smart, syncopated drum cut-ups and subtle production manipulation over blind distortion and endless hoover blasts. Mootz seems to have taken to heart complaints that his tracks are too dense to sound like anything other than noise and murk over a PA, turning the chaos down a few notches and putting a bit of time and energy into production quality. Released by up and coming German drum'n'bass label Gyration. —*Sean Cooper*

**Stormbringer [Single]** / Feb. 10, 1997 / Chrome ♦♦♦♦
Mathias Mootz's Panacea calling card is this two tracker of fierce, unrelenting darkcore jungle, vaguely echoing the No U-Turn lot and experimental jungle deviants such as Slack Dog and Shizuo, but upping the dirge factor and adding about a bazillion overlapping samples to the din. "Stormbringer" shuffles through more than a half dozen breaks (including the metallic snap of Autechre's "Second Bad Vilbel"), while the flip's "Jacob's Ladder" is a hissing mess of crushing drums and dirt-caked distortion. *—Sean Cooper*

**Low Profile Darkness** / Feb. 17, 1997 / Chrome ♦♦♦♦
Panacea managed a 12" a week for Force Inc. subsidiary Chrome before coming out with his debut full-length less than two months after his first material appeared. Like the widely hailed singles, *Low Profile Darkness* lives up to the hype and then some, throwing wide-spinning curves with dark electro tracks like "Low-Tek Intro" and "Am I Losing U," as well as the to-be-expected range of darker-than-thou fraying, distorto techstep. Despite it's somewhat headbangerly appeal, *Darkness* manages to remain interesting throughout. The CD version also includes a few holdovers from the earlier EPs, as well as two previously unavailable non-LP tracks. *—Sean Cooper*

● **Twisted Designz** / Apr. 20, 1998 / Chrome ♦♦♦♦
*Twisted Designz* brings even more relentless darkness from Panacea, and a return-to-the-source affinity for the industrial music of the late '80s. Less tied to the military two-step than before, Mootz calls into battle an assortment of wild-pitched acid-synth and several diabolical horror samples to create one of the most evil-sounding releases in the drum'n'bass movement. *—John Bush*

**Hanayo in Panacea** / Oct. 13, 1998 / Chrome ♦♦♦
Panacea's trademark Germanic drum'n'bass lockstep meets its vocal equivalent on this collaboration with the Japanese tortured vocalist Hanayo. The highlights here, including "Ich Steh an Deiner Krippen Hier" and "Hallo Hitler" (the latter originally compiled on *Electric Ladyland 5*), have all the distorted breaks and Front 242 leanings that Panacea fans expect while Hanayo attempts to win over converts to her style of little-girl-lost screaming and screeching. It's not only a good pairing, it's an intriguing direction for Panacea (and the course of vocal-electronica as a whole). Mootz would have faced a diminishing-returns backlash against his style of up-front EBM drum'n'bass had there not been some sort of difference to these proceedings. *—John Bush*

**Brasilia Architettura** / Mar. 21, 2000 / Caipirinha ♦♦
Pay close attention now: *Brasilia* is the fourth installment in the Caipirinha label's *Architettura* series, an ongoing film and CD project that is meant to document a synergistic relationship between architecture and electronic music. Brasilia itself is a city in Brazil designed by famous architect Oscar Niemeyer; he zoned the city and designed all of its buildings, but apparently neglected to include things like sidewalks, resulting in what has been referred to as a "bizarrely futuristic ghost town" in which beautiful curvilinear buildings house thoroughly isolated human beings. Panacea is the name of a German techstep artist who has written a program of 20 impressionistic pieces of abstract techno music designed to invoke the feelings of spiritual void and modernistic bleakness inspired by the city of Brasilia. And sure enough, he succeeds on this consistently interesting but rarely very enjoyable disc, which sounds a bit like R2D2 on acid. Many tracks are rhythmic, but there aren't very many grooves—breakbeats try repeatedly to elbow through the punishing waves of gray and white noise on "No Verve-2," though "Onerous (My Slickness)" features a consistent pulse from what sounds like a deeply damaged drum machine. In between these two tracks is "Void of Safety," the one which comes closest of any on this album to providing any moments of actual beauty. The whole thing is worth hearing, but it's rather hard to imagine anyone replaying it frequently for pleasure. However, to be sure, pleasure doesn't seem to be what Panacea is trying to get at here. *—Rick Anderson*

## Pan sonic

f. 1992, Turku, Finland
*Group / Minimal Techno, Experimental Techno, Electronica, Ambient Techno, IDM*

Finnish minimalist techno group Pan sonic are among the most active and well-known artists from that country's tiny experimental techno underground, and the first to reach acclaim at an international level. Pursuing the jagged edges of minimal techno and hardcore, the group has earned an enduring association with industrial and noise music through their incorporation of antiseptic production techniques and power-tool electronics, landing them in 1995 on the English Mute label's experimental subsidiary Blast First! (most of their catalog to date has since appeared there). The affinity lay more at the surface, however, as Pan sonic are better understood as a collision between Jeff Mills and Mike Ink—dance-based electronic music with a maximum of impact, realized through a minimum of extraneous detail. Known for junking together studio equipment from spare parts and ancient analog debris, Pan sonic's search for the untried in techno is their compositional M.O., placing them closer to the music's Detroit roots than is often understood.

Formed in Turku in the early '90s, Pan sonic began as the duo of Mika Vainio and Ilpo Väisänen. As with most Finnish techno groups, Pan sonic's earliest beginnings lay with the Sahko/Puu imprint, the focus of the Northern European techno scene and home to such artists as Kirlian, Philus, ÿ (Vainio's solo guise), Mono Junk, and Jimi Tenor. Pan sonic released its self-titled debut single through Sahko in 1994 before being joined by third member Sami Salo and landing a contract with Blast First! the following year. The group's first BF! release, *Vakio*, was a full-length CD/triple-10" boxed set featuring the same brand of furtive, passively aggressive techno, though with a fuller, more thought-out sound. Soon after *Vakio*'s release in 1995, Salo left the group (apparently to join the Army), and Pan sonic's subsequent releases—the *Osasto EP* and the group's 1997 sophomore long-player, *Kulma*—noted his absence by their comparatively harder, less subtle tone.

Pan sonic added live performance to their regular repertoire in 1996, playing a number of gigs throughout Europe and Japan, as well as touring with the gothic rock group the Swans. Vainio moved to London in 1997, where, in addition to his continuing commitment to Pan sonic, he continues to record as ÿ (his third full-length under that name, *Olento*, was issued on Sahko just prior to *Kulma*'s release). He has also released work on Sahko, Puu, and Cheap as Tekonivel, Orchestra Guacamole (with Jaakko Salovaara), and Kosmos (with Jimi Tenor), as well as remixed tracks for Björk and Tactile. Pan sonic have also been featured on several compilation albums, including *A Fault in the Nothing* (Touch, 1996) and *Funktion 1: Finnish Techno Collection* (Function, 1996). By 1998, an inevitable confrontation with the Japanese manufacturing giant also known as Pan sonic had resulted in a name-change of sorts, to Pan sonic. The missing letter re-surfaced the following year, as the title of the duo's third album. Vainio and Väisänen also recorded the *Endless* LP (as VVV) with the addition of Suicide vocalist Alan Vega. *—Sean Cooper*

**Vakio** / 1995 / Blast First! ♦♦♦♦
The then trio's debut album shows Pan sonic already well on its particular voyage into capturing the spirit of total innovation via strictly electronic means. The high-pitched opening tone of "Alku" mutates into a rapid pulse of sound before "Radiokemia" introduces what for many is the sound of the band, with minimal, cutting electronic percussion accompanied by bursts of static. The variations and changes Pan sonic can create with such a seemingly simple formula are nearly endless, as "Radiokemia," with its drop-outs and astonishingly subtle builds, and the rest of *Vakio* proceeds to demonstrate. The depth and power of the group's rhythm punch is astonishing, shown throughout the album. Even when the drum notes or hits are slightly buried via production or echo, as on the slow whine of "Tela," their power can't be resisted, technology taken to a higher degree. The general alternation between one-note pieces and more complex, beat-heavy numbers continues throughout *Vakio*, though some tracks blend the two sides. "Graf" is a fine example, its main line underscored by what could almost be called a chugging train sound. Hints of more traditional approaches to techno surface from time to time, thus the varying percussion lines on "Vaihe," which sound as much like an intro to a separate song than a tune in and of itself, or the solid groove of "Hapatus." The trio certainly doesn't shy away from flat-out noise either—"Hetken" begins with a sustained tone before erupting into a soundfest then just as suddenly shifting back to another tone. "CSG-Sonic" and "Sahkotin" close out *Vakio* well. The first repeats the opening gambit of "Alku" with a different core sound, while the second builds into probably the album's strongest, most commanding dance effort without losing the edge that makes Pan sonic so distinct. *—Ned Raggett*

**Kulma** / Jan. 27, 1997 / Blast First! ♦♦♦

● **Endless** / Jul. 21, 1998 / Mute ♦♦♦♦
Unlike many creative collaborations of its kind, *Endless* actually works—the

noisy, minimalist techno ethic of Pan sonic members Mika Vainio and Ilpo Väisänen fits the aggressive vocals of Alan Vega like a glove, pushing both camps in new musical directions without sacrificing their own pre-established identities. —*Jason Ankeny*

**A** / Feb. 22, 1999 / Mute ♦♦♦
Similar to contemporary albums released by Autechre and Aphex Twin, Pan sonic went even farther down the road of abstract electronics with their third proper album *A*, though it was a much shorter journey for the likes of Vainio and Väisänen than most others. The result is an album of unrestrained noise and texture with few concessions to rhythm. —*John Bush*

## Paperclip People (Carl Craig)

b. Detroit, MI
*Producer / Electronica, Detroit Techno, Club/Dance, Techno, House*
Though it's basically just another incarnation of Carl Craig's innovative career, Paperclip People is his most dancefloor-slanted project, resulting in productions quite distinct from the albums he released as himself. Recording several singles during 1996 for Britain's Open Records (run by the super-club Ministry of Sound), Paperclip People's unique fusion of tweaked acid-dub and house raised consciousness about Craig on mainstream dancefloors. Late in 1996, he collected Paperclip People singles with additional new material for *The Secret Tapes of Dr. Eich*. In late 1998, the single "4 My Peepz" was released on Planet E. [See Also: Carl Craig, Innerzone Orchestra, Psyche/BFC, 69] —*John Bush*

**Remake (Uno)/Remake (Duo) [Single]** / 1994 / Planet E ♦♦♦
This 12" is not only Carl Craig's homage to the seminal proto-techno anthem *E2-E4* by Kraut hero Manuel Göttsching but is also the earliest re-emergence of Craig's Paperclip People moniker on the Planet E label. Though this record, like much of Craig's music, is a reverent nod to the songs that inspire him, it doesn't stand out on its own as well as many of his other sample-based tracks. He temporarily lost his knack for making the old samples sound new again; instead, this one sounds more like its two primary elements pasted together unimaginatively. Göttsching's soaring melody of heart-aching beauty is almost perverted (in the bad way) by Craig's signature drums. If it weren't for Basic Channel's and Derrick May's gorgeous renditions of *E2-E4*, one might have to say that perfect records ought not to be remixed. But in avoiding such a gross overstatement, it is more fair to say that Craig simply fell off on this one. —*Carlos Souffront*

**The Floor [EP]** / Jun. 17, 1996 / Open ♦♦♦
*Floor* is Carl Craig's long-awaited follow-up to the wildly successful *Throw* by his disco-revamped-as-techno-house project Paperclip People. It is fair to say that this record's downfall is its transparent effort to simply re-employ *Throw*'s fail-safe formula of an extended monolithic groove that straddles the line between house and techno. While Craig's sample-based dance music usually looks back to disco's legacy while taking a step forward, "Floor" looks back to *Throw*'s legacy and stagnates. The one element that distinguishes "Floor" is its haunting atmosphere; it is easily one of Craig's most spooky dance tracks. The B-side tracks "Floor(Drums)" and "Oscillator" confirm this sense of artistic stagnation because while "Oscillator" is an incredible song, it's one that Carl Craig had already released years before on Retroactive. *Floor* isn't a bad 12", but it's not as artistically progressive as Carl Craig can be. —*Carlos Souffront*

**Throw [Single]** / Aug. 12, 1996 / Open ♦♦♦♦
*Throw* was originally released as the "throwaway" B-side for the first 12" on the UK label Open. But after putting a world of both techno and house headz into a frenzy, Carl Craig then re-released it were it belonged, on the A-side of a Planet E 12". "Throw" is the perfect testament to how the best dance records are usually the simplest. There's something about this basic half-bar looped bassline, sampled from the breakdown of another one of Craig's favorite disco records, that makes for an utterly infectious dance epic. The track's finishing touch is that bit of signature Craig quirkiness, which in this case is a silly falsetto solo in the song's extended breakdown. This record has an interesting irony to it because while "Throw" was named literally and indeed as a throwaway B-side to Craig's remake of Manuel Gottsching's *E2-E4*, "Remake" ended up being the true throwaway. For the B-side of the Planet E release, Craig's remake was substituted by Basic Channel's reshape of the same seminal German proto-techno record. "'Remake' Basic Reshape" is a stunning masterpiece where Basic Channel, in their impeccable tastefulness, styl-

izes the key elements of *E2-E4* to maintain their unmistakable sound. Surely one of this label's finest releases, in addition to being the only Planet E record issued on several different colors of vinyl, *Throw* is no throwaway. —*Carlos Souffront*

★ **The Secret Tapes of Dr. Eich** / Dec. 2, 1996 / Open ♦♦♦♦♦
Representing the dance-music side of multi-talented Detroit electronic musician Carl Craig, the bizarre electronic funk of Paperclip People has more in common with the Chicago house sounds of artists such as Green Velvet than Detroit techno pioneers Derrick May or Juan Atkins. Before listeners are even able to get the album in the stereo, the weird motifs form preconceptions. The Paperclip People are something of a Kraftwerk parody: Eich on electronics, Me on tapes, Son on subliminal vocals, and Sche on samples. Craig's live Paperclip People performances incorporate these postmodern elements as he performs in a white lab coat, usually alongside three mannequins.

*The Secret Tapes of Dr. Eich* compiles the Paperclip People EPs from the early '90s. Included on the compilation are classics such as "The Climax," "Throw," and "Floor." While much of Craig's other output focuses on a contemplative style of smooth Detroit techno as equally suited to meditating as dancing, his party-oriented Paperclip People material is not only lighthearted and fun, but its bass beats rumble at a fairly consistent 4/4 rhythm. The spiritual melodies populating Craig's *More Songs About Food and Revolutionary Art* album or the artistic experimentation of his Innerzone Orchestra album *Programmed* are almost nowhere to be found. The album has a nostalgic feel, sounding like an alien hybrid of Chicago house and disco with a bit of Detroit's creativity. Tracks such as "My Neighborhood" thump with plenty of bass while cymbals occasionally crash, P-Funk-style basslines intermingle, and the classic synthesized strings of disco float above. Other tracks such as "Paperclip Man" and "Oscillator" pick up the pace, raging with dancefloor intensity as Craig adds a funky arrangement of oddly synthesized sounds to the bumping bass and electronic handclaps. The dancefloor functionality and crazed party attitude of this album are its strengths, but make it too intense for times when the listener just wants to relax. —*Jason Stanley Birchmeier*

**4 My Peepz [EP]** / Nov. 24, 1998 / Planet E ♦♦♦♦
A fabulous return for Craig's Paperclip People project, *4 My Peepz* includes both sides of the previous 12"—"4 My Peepz (Shot)" and "4 My Peepz (Stabbed)"—plus two new tracks and a remix of "The Climax." The A-side is a brooding piece of lockstep techno-funk with minimal changes, a killer bridge, and Craig intoning the title just twice during the 11-minute track. —*John Bush*

## Anthony Pappa

*DJ / Progressive Trance, Trance, Club/Dance, House*
Though Anthony Pappa had already made the rounds at many of England's top clubs such as *Renaissance*, *Cream*, *Bedrock*, and *Ministry of Sound*, it wasn't until he was awarded the first volume in Global Underground's ambitious *Nu Breed* series that many really gave him a close look. He won Australia's DMC DJ championship at the tender age of 15—there has always been something special about Pappa. Since those late teen years DJing in Australia, he has left for the electronic music Utopia of England, where he had hopes of becoming one of the world's top DJs. By his early 20s, he was acknowledged as a gifted DJ and was spinning around the world but never reached the elite heights of true superstar status alongside the world's Sashas and Paul Van Dyks. With his own albums in both *Renaissance* and *Global Underground*'s popular series of mix CDs, he has come one step closer to attaining his ambition of becoming one of the world's top DJs. —*Jason Birchmeier*

● **Global Underground: NuBreed** / Mar. 7, 2000 / Boxed ♦♦
While the concepts underlying the inaugural release of Global Underground's *NuBreed* series are both intriguing and refreshing, Anthony Pappa's mix unfortunately doesn't quite reach the preconceived expectations most loyal Global Underground listeners have. A few songs into the first set, these exceptions seem to be fulfilled as the Melbourne DJ drops some driving, straightahead progressive house tracks that forcefully move the momentum forward and start the first set off on a high note. Unfortunately, this sense of excitement soon fades as Pappa never really moves away from this style of music. He maintains the same tempo, aura, and style of tracks throughout the first set, which ultimately reaches a depressing anticlimax during the ex-

tended lull of Humate's "Welcome to the Future" remix (an otherwise wonderful song that would fit better in the middle of the set as a momentary valley perfect to build upon). Pappa's second set heads into trance territory, favoring the epic style of trance with its steady linear rhythms, slow shifts in momentum, and a lingering sense of heavenly aura evoked through distant synths. But again, Pappa never fleshes out his set, dropping one similar track after another. Eventually, he moves his set into a breaks-influenced flavor of trance during the fluctuating nine-minute ride through Hi-Fi Bugs' "Lydian & the Dinosaur," yet for as wonderfully majestic as this song may be, it still isn't the hands-in-the-air anthem one wants at the end of a DJ set. —*Jason Birchmeier*

## Andrea Parker

**b.** Apr. 2, 1972
*Producer, DJ / Electronica, Electro-Techno, Trip-Hop*
A classically trained cellist and former session vocalist, Andrea Parker's brilliant darkside electro-techno productions for Mo'Wax, R&S, and Sabrettes displayed an artist with impeccable programming skills but also an increasing desire to integrate her own training into the mix. She began recording on her own in the early '90s, and became a DJ by 1993. One year later, she began collaborating with David Morley, first for Infonet Records on the *Angular Art* EP, then for R&S on the *Too Good to Be Strange* EP (the former appeared under Morley's name, the latter as Two Sandwiches Short of a Lunchbox). Morley contributed engineering to Parker's 1996 solo debut for Mo'Wax, the 40-minute EP *Melodious Thunk*. Her second EP for Mo'Wax, *Rocking Chair*, featured London's Royal Philharmonic Orchestra alongside sampled beats and effects. She also remixed Depeche Mode, Lamb, the Orb, Ryuichi Sakamoto and Steve Reich before beginning work on her actual debut full-length, *Kiss My ARP*. In the meantime, she contributed a volume in Studio !K7's *DJ Kicks* series in 1998. —*John Bush*

**Ballbreaker/Some Other Level [Single]** / Jul. 13, 1998 / Mo'Wax ♦♦♦
After the somewhat overwrought orchestral single "Rocking Chair," this two-track 10" is very much a return to form for Parker, who on "Ballbreaker" and "Some Other Level" teams back up with longtime collaborator David Morley to record some of her best work to date. Marrying the stark minimalism of her Mo'Wax debut *Melodious Thunk* with the haunted melodies of her work with Morley as Two Sandwiches Short of a Lunchbox and as Angular Art, these tracks strike a perfect balance between electro's spare, chromium funk and dark ambient's isolationist atmospheres. —*Sean Cooper*

**DJ Kicks** / Oct. 13, 1998 / Studio !K7 ♦♦♦
Andrea Parker's contribution to Studio !K7's long-running mix series *DJ Kicks* is, expectedly, heavy on electro past and present. The set's timing aside, it's market-driven; electro's periodic "revivals" are almost as predictable as the scores of second-rate tracks full of preset 808 beats and overzealous vocoders that inevitably follow. K7 at least had the sense to call in someone with the knowledge and skill to put an interesting set together. Parker's *DJ Kicks* also does double duty as a peek behind the curtain of her own fascinating, still-developing sound. The mixing is adequate, but Parker's set is ultimately about track selection, and most of what's offered here is excellent, including classics like 69's "Desire," Model 500's "Night Drive," Man Parrish's "Hip Hop Be Bop (Don't Stop)," and C.O.D.'s "In the Bottle," as well as relative newcomers like Drexciya, Dopplereffekt, Voigt Kampff, and Gescom (a.k.a. Autechre). —*Sean Cooper*

• **Kiss My ARP** / Feb. 23, 1999 / Mo'Wax ♦♦♦♦
The debut from acclaimed DJ and slightly less acclaimed electronica artist Andrea Parker is a winning mix of the electronic and the organic, a rather dark but never depressing examination of the psyche that relies equally on vintage synthesizers (hence the album title), cutting-edge beatcraft, and real orchestral string arrangements. And she sings pretty well, too. The album opens with the downbeat and contemplative "The Unknown," on which a minor chord progression and how-low-can-you-go bassline are leavened by big synth washes and a soaring chorus. "In Two Minds" is a fairly abstract synth piece with pizzicato violins and a chirping analog noise that Allen Ravenstine would kill for. "Sneeze" charmingly samples the sound of Parker sneezing into a surprisingly funky four-bar rhythm loop and also uses analog synthesizer to approximate the sound of water-pot percussion. "Return of the Rocking Chair," however, is a ponderous and annoying waste of time, but everything else on this album is well worth listening to. —*Rick Anderson*

## Terrence Parker

*Producer, DJ / Detroit Techno, Club/Dance, House*
One of the prime producers of soulful house music with an edge (granted he's from Detroit), Terrence Parker started out a hip-hop DJ but later blended a wealth of influences (from techno, soul, disco, jazz and even downtempo) to give his recordings a unique flavor midway between hands-in-the-air house and the more sublime sound of Detroit techno. Among his dozens of aliases, the two most vaunted are Seven Grand Housing Authority and his own name, for which he's released several LPs for Studio !K7.

When Parker began DJing in the early '80s, he mixed early Whodini and Run-D.M.C., though after hearing the work of Chicago's Jesse Saunders, he began integrating house and techno into his sets as well. Parker made the move to production in 1988 after borrowing a friend's keyboard. During the late '80s and early '90s he recorded as Madd Phlavor, the Minimum Wage Brothers, the Lost Articles, Plastic Soul Junkies, Disco Revisited, and Disciples of the Jovan Blade.

When his tracks "The Question" and "Love's Got Me Higher"—both by Seven Grand Housing Authority—became club hits in Europe during 1993-94, Parker made the move to a full-length with 1996's *Tragedies of a Plastic Soul Junkie*, recorded for Studio !K7 under his own name. Seven Grand Housing Authority released its debut LP, *No Weapons Formed Against Me Shall Prosper*, the following year and Parker returned with his second solo jaunt, *Detroit After Dark*. Parker also saluted his hip-hop past by organizing the Studio !K7 compilation series *3 Minute Blunts*, which featured Detroit artists trying their hand at hip-hop production. He's also managed three labels, Primary, Intangible, and Makin' Madd Music. In 1998, Parker released a pair of limited-edition discs of demos through Intangible, and he issued several volumes of his own mix sets through his own company. —*John Bush*

• **Tragedies of a Plastic Soul Junkie** / Oct. 28, 1996 / Studio !K7 ♦♦♦♦
Terrence Parker's debut album is an intriguing collection of tracks with many of the trademarks of house (piano lines, strings), though his ear for samples and wiggly basslines—both equally infectious—easily bring him into techno's territory. Besides uptempo selections like "Pure Disco" and "Piano Circus," Parker mixes the album up with the earthy grooves of the downtempo-jazz song "A Track for O.J. Simpson (The Acquittal)" and the vaguely hip-hop "Plastic Soul Junkie." —*John Bush*

**Detroit After Dark** / Oct. 20, 1997 / Studio !K7 ♦♦♦♦
On his second album for Studio !K7, Terrence Parker hones the deep house grooves of 1996's *Tragedies of a Plastic Soul Junkie* and injects a distinctly "Detroit" sense of afterhours soul. The result is an album by turns danceable as well as downtempo, rather than a party record for excessively mechanical techno-heads. —*John Bush*

## Parliament

**f.** 1970, Detroit, MI, **db.** 1980
*Group / R&B, Funk*
Inspired by Motown's assembly line of sound, George Clinton gradually assembled a collective of over 50 musicians and recorded the ensemble during the '70s both as Parliament and Funkadelic. While Funkadelic pursued band-format psychedelic rock, Parliament engaged in a funk free-for-all, blending influences from the godfathers (James Brown and Sly Stone) with freaky costumes and themes inspired by '60s acid culture and science fiction. From its 1970 inception until Clinton's dissolving of Parliament in 1980, the band hit the R&B Top Ten several times but truly excelled in two other areas: large-selling, effective album statements and the most dazzling, extravagant live show in the business. In an era when Philly soul continued the slick sounds of establishment-approved R&B, Parliament scared off more white listeners than it courted. The Clinton congregation also proved a heavy influence on the first wave of electronic dance, techno pioneers like the Motor City's own Juan Atkins, Derrick May, and Carl Craig, as well as house legends Larry Heard and Frankie Knuckles.

The P-Funk aggregation actually dates back to 1955, when George Clinton (b. July 22, 1941, Kannapolis, NC) formed a New Jersey doo wop group named the Parliaments. Based out of a barbershop back room where Clinton straightened hair, the Parliaments released only two singles during the next ten years, but frequent trips to Detroit during the mid-'60s—where Clinton began working as a songwriter and producer—eventually paid off their investment. After their 1967 hit "(I Wanna) Testify," the Parliaments ran into trouble with their label and refused to record any new material. Instead of waiting for a settlement, Clinton decided to record the same band under a new name: Funkadelic. Founded in 1968, the group began life as a smoke screen, claiming as its only members the Parliaments' backing band, but in truth including Clinton and the entire Parliaments lineup. Even though he regained the rights to the Parliaments name in 1970 and recorded the first Parliament LP (*Osmium*) that same year, Clinton decided to focus on the firing-on-all-cylinders Funkadelic and the group released their self-titled debut in 1970 as well.

Though keyboard player Bernie Worrell (b. April 19, 1944, Long Beach, NJ) had played on the original *Funkadelic* album, his first credit with the conglomeration appeared on Funkadelic's second album, 1970's *Free Your Mind...And Your Ass Will Follow*. Clinton and Worrell had known each other since the New Jersey barbershop days, and Worrell soon became the most crucial cog in the P-Funk machine, working on arrangements and production for virtually all later Parliament/Funkadelic releases. His strict upbringing and classical training (at the New England Conservatory and Juilliard), as well as the boom in synthesizer technology during the early '70s, gave him the tools to create the synth runs and horn arrangements that later trademarked the P-Funk sound. Two years after the addition of Worrell, P-Funk added its second most famed contributor, Bootsy Collins. The muscular, throbbing bassline of Collins (b. Oct. 26, 1951, Cincinnati, OH) had already been featured in James Brown's backing band (the J.B.'s) along with his brother, guitarist Catfish Collins, and Clinton hired them soon after seeing them playing in a Detroit band.

After recording five Funkadelic LPs between 1970 and 1974, the collective pulled up stakes and began recording as Parliament. After signing with Casablanca in 1974, Parliament hit with "Up for the Down Stroke" (No. 10 R&B, No. 63 pop), which appeared in mid-1974 and reflected a more mainstream approach than Funkadelic, with funky horn arrangements reminiscent of James Brown and a live feel that recalled Kool & the Gang. It became the biggest hit yet for the Parliament/Funkadelic congregation. The third Parliament LP, *Mothership Connection*, was arguably the peak of Parliament's power, sparked by three hit singles: "P. Funk (Wants to Get Funked Up)," "Tear the Roof Off the Sucker (Give Up the Funk)," and "Star Child." In addition to Bootsy Collins, the album featured two other James Brown refugees: horn legends Maceo Parker and Fred Wesley.

Several internal squabbles during 1977 apparently didn't phase Clinton at all; the following year proved to be the most successful in Parliament's history. In January, "Flash Light"—from the Parliament album *Funkentelechy Vs. the Placebo Syndrome*—became the collective's first number one hit. Early in 1979, Parliament hit number one yet again with "Aqua Boogie" from its eighth album, *Motor-Booty Affair*. Parliament's ninth album, *Gloryhallastoopid (Or Pin the Tale on the Funky)*, was released later in 1979 and showed a bit of a slip in the previously unstoppable Clinton machine. Despite a few hits during 1980, Clinton began to be weighed down that year by legal difficulties arising from Polygram's acquisition of Parliament's label, Casablanca. Jettisoning both the Parliament and Funkadelic names (but not the musicians), Clinton began his solo career in 1982 and continued to tour and record during the '80s as the P-Funk All Stars. [See Also: Funkadelic, George Clinton] —*John Bush*

**Up for the Down Stroke** / 1974 / Casablanca ✦✦✦✦
The first album by Clinton's revamped Parliament remains a perfect introduction, although its best songs are on their *Greatest Hits*. —*John Floyd*

**Chocolate City** / 1975 / Casablanca ✦✦✦
The title track was a masterpiece, one of George Clinton's satirical triumphs. Whether you think it was a political work or not, everything clicked—the production, comic lead vocals, lyrics, and arrangements. The remainder of the album wasn't quite that strong, but was still excellent. It mixed every Clinton element: chaotic jamming, quirky outlook, hilarious vocals, and that sense of the casually absurd that Clinton championed. —*Ron Wynn*

**Clones of Dr. Funkenstein** / 1976 / Casablanca ✦✦✦✦
George Clinton had his otherworldly, controlled, chaotic vision well in gear for this album. He milked the Frankenstein notion, creating a mad scientist and sonically documenting his warped funk notions. Clinton got instrumental assistance from a crack corps that included keyboardist Bernie Worrell, saxophonist Maceo Parker and trombonist Fred Wesley, plus numerous vocalists, guitarists, and instrumentalists. The album went gold, although it wasn't as inspired or successful as *Mothership Connection*. But such songs as "Dr. Funkenstein," "I've Been Watching You (Move Your Sexy Body)," and "Everything Is On The One" were quintessential Parliament jams. —*Ron Wynn*

**Mothership Connection** / 1976 / Casablanca ✦✦✦✦
This was *the* Parliament masterpiece. It mixed creative and clever satirical takeoffs on James Brown, Sly Stone, and classic black radio with the kind of loose, inventive improvising seldom heard in R&B or soul circles. The narratives were swift and humorous and the music crackling, fast-moving, and progressive. The title cut, "Tear The Roof Off The Sucker (Give Up The Funk)," and others marked the beginning of Clinton and Parliament/Funkadelic's evolution into national celebrities. —*Ron Wynn*

**Gloryhallastoopid** / 1979 / Casablanca ✦✦✦
Although at the time this album was viewed as a disaster, there has been some critical reassessment in past years. It was certainly not as inspired, brilliantly executed, or memorable as any one of many '70s Parliament or Funkadelic gems, but it did have its own humorous/bizarre outlook. Clinton was being torn in many directions and plagued by money problems, so he didn't give it the attention it probably needed. Still, it deserves a revisit by Clinton fans who tossed it aside in disgust the first time around. —*Ron Wynn*

● **The Best of Parliament: Give Up the Funk** / Jun. 6, 1995 / Mercury Funk Essentials ✦✦✦✦
To some, boiling Parliament's legacy down to a single-disc collection is the equivalent of heresy, since most fans treat each album as an individual work of art. Still, there is no denying that Parliament was an untouchable singles act, recording some of the greatest soul/funk singles of the '70s. For those listeners that just want an introduction, or only need the hits, *The Best of Parliament: Give Up the Funk* is the ideal choice. A more complete and logical collection than the previous *Greatest Hits (The Bomb)*, *The Best of Parliament* supplies all of the great group's greatest hits, from "Up for the Down Stroke" and "Tear the Roof off the Sucker" to "Flash Light" and "Aqua Boogie." For those that can only handle the funk in moderation, there is no better collection. —*Leo Stanley*

## Man Parrish

*Producer / Electro, Club/Dance, Hip-Hop*
Although he produced only a handful of tracks of renown and disappeared into obscurity almost as quickly as he had emerged from it, Manny Parrish is nonetheless one of the most important and influential figures in American electronic dance music. Helping to lay the foundation of electro, hip-hop, freestyle, and techno, as well as the dozens of subgenres to splinter off from those, Parrish introduced the aesthetic of European electronic pop to the American club scene by combining the plugged-in disco-funk of Giorgio Moroder and the man-machine music of Kraftwerk with the beefed-up rhythms and cut'n'mix approach of nascent hip-hop. As a result, tracks like "Hip-Hop Be Bop (Don't Stop)" and "Boogie Down Bronx" were period-defining works that provided the basic genetic material for everyone from Run-D.M.C. and the Beastie Boys to Autechre and Andrea Parker—and they remain undisputed classics of early hip-hop and electro to this day. A native New Yorker, Parrish was a member of the extended family of glam-chasers and freakazoids that converged nightly on Andy Warhol's Studio 54 club. His nickname, Man, first appeared in Warhol's *Interview* magazine, and his early live shows at Bronx hip-hop clubs were spectacles of lights, glitter, and pyrotechnics that drew as much from the Warhol mystique as from the Cold Crush Brothers.

Influenced by the electronic experiments of Klaus Nomi and Brian Eno as well as by Kraftwerk, Parrish together with "Cool" Raul Rodriguez recorded their best-known work in a tiny studio sometimes shared with Afrika Baambaata, whose own sessions with Arthur Baker and John Robie produced a number of classics equal to Parrish's own, including "Wildstyle," "Looking for the Perfect Beat," and the infamous "Planet Rock." What distinguished "Hip-Hop Be Bop," however, was its lack of vocals and the extremely wide spectrum of popularity it gained in the club scene, from ghetto breakdance halls to uptown clubs like Danceteria and the Funhouse. After he discovered a pirated copy of his music being played by a local DJ, Parrish found his way to the offices of the Importe label (a subsidiary of popular dance imprint Sugarscoop), with whom he inked his first deal. He released his self-titled LP shortly after, and the album went on to sell over 2 million copies worldwide. Following a period of burn-out, Parrish recorded and remixed tracks for Michael

Jackson, Boy George, Gloria Gaynor, and Hi-NRG group Man2Man, among others, and served as road manager for the Village People. While Parrish's subsequent material has achieved nowhere near the success or creative pitch of his earlier work, he continues to record from his Brooklyn studio and is a frequent DJ at New York SM clubs. His second LP, *Dreamtime*, appeared on Strictly Rhythm in 1997. —*Sean Cooper*

**Man Parrish** / 1982 / Polydor ✦✦✦✦

While most of Man Parrish's first LP hasn't stood up very well, it's almost impossible to hear "Hip-Hop Be Bop (Don't Stop)" too many times, and "Man Made" is a lost classic nearly the equal of Parrish's best-known work. Parrish's disco roots are apparent in the tracks "Street Clap" and "Heatstroke," the latter of which first appeared on the soundtrack to a porno movie. —*Sean Cooper*

• **The Best of Man Parrish: Heatstroke** / Dec. 24, 1996 / Hot Productions ✦✦✦✦

*The Best of Man Parrish: Heatstroke* is a stellar 14-track collection that contains all of the production legend's big hits and cult favorites, including "Hip Hop Be Bop (Don't Stop)," "Six Simple Synthesizers," "Techno Trax," "Hip Hop Rebop," "Pray," "Brown Sugar," "Hey There Homeboys," "Who Me," and "Boogie Down Bronx." —*Stephen Thomas Erlewine*

**Dreamtime** / Jul. 14, 1998 / Hot Productions ✦✦✦

## Theo Parrish

*Producer / Tech-House, Detroit Techno, Techno*

With a style similar to Moodymann's take on Detroit tech-house as a melange of distorted disco-funk and boogie, Theo Parrish originally grew up in Chicago but moved to the Motor City by the time of his late-1996 *Baby Steps* EP on Elevate Records, a subsidiary of 7th City. From the EP, his Chicago tribute "Lake Shore Drive" later appeared on the Kenny Dixon/Moodymann release "Inspirations of a Small Black Church," and Parrish also worked on tracks by Rick Wilhite, Dewayne Davis, and Pandemonium. He continued through 1997 with singles for his own Sound Signature label plus Music 15 and Filth. In late 1998, Peacefrog released two Theo Parrish LPs, both of which were issued on CD as *First Floor*. Also a stellar DJ, Parrish is renowned around Detroit for his sets of downtempo jazz-funk and disco. —*John Bush*

• **First Floor, Parts 1&2** / Nov. 2, 1998 / Peacefrog ✦✦✦✦

*First Floor* includes the complete contents of the two EPs Parrish recorded for Peacefrog during 1998. After an excessively spare opener, the collection moves into a succession of excellent tracks ("Sweet Sticky," "Paradise Architects," "Electric AlleyCat," "JB's Edit") driven by distorted, scratchy, trance-like sample snippets borrowed from disco and jazz-funk. (The back cover even shows Parrish soaking in a bath of records with Ron Carter and Isaac Hayes LPs visible.) Parrish's ingenious use of drum programming and effects add-ons tie each track together just the way a great DJ should. It's the next best thing to seeing him spin. —*John Bush*

**Sound Signature Sounds** / 2000 / Sound Signature ✦✦✦

## Marco Passarani

b. Rome, Italy

*Producer / Experimental Techno, Club/Dance, Techno*

Italian electronica producer Marco Passarani has been referred to as Rome's answer to the Aphex Twin. Although his idiosyncratic fusion of ambient, electro, and techno places a premium on distortion boxes and simple but affecting three-part melodies, releases such as "2099" and "It Will Be What It Was" (both appearing under the name Passarani 2099 on his own Nature imprint) are equally, if not more, indebted to Kraftwerk and Bochum Welt—in other words, Euro and new wave influences not as pronounced in Richard James' work. A DJ since he discovered hip-hop and electro in his early teens, Passarani began producing in the classic Chicago tradition, playing machine beats and electronics over minimal dance records in order to spruce them up and bring them closer to the music he was hearing in his head. Reacting against the commercial side of the Italian scene, which during the early '90s was dominated by throwaway house and techno, Passarani and partners Andrea Benedetti and Sandro Nasonte founded a string of labels (including Sysmo, Mystic, and the most recent, Nature Recordings) committed to the experimental extremes of dance culture's ever-increasing polysemy. This commitment to fostering dance music's lunatic fringe—as well as Passarani's on-going affection for plainly weird UK- and Detroit-based groups such as Aphex, Ectomorph, Drexciya, Cylob/Kinaesthesia, and Dopplereffekt—led to the interlocking of Rome's electronica underground with artists and labels such as Underground Resistance, Direct Beat, Cheap, Reference, Acid Planet, Fax, Warp, and Rephlex. Passarani also helped establish the Remix distribution company in 1990, which has since grown into the largest Italian dance music importer. In addition to his Nature releases, which tend toward the more abstract and composely, Passarani has released straightforward dance music as well through Alan Oldham's Generator label. —*Sean Cooper*

• **Passarani 2099 [EP]** / 1995 / Nature ✦✦✦✦

**It Will Be What it Was [EP]** / 1996 / Nature ✦✦✦

## Peace Orchestra

*Group / Electronica, Trip-Hop, Club/Dance*

With the Kruder & Dorfmeister collective apparently unwilling to produce a studio album as a duo, Peter Kruder debuted his Peace Orchestra alias in 1999 for a self-titled album of blissfully stoned beats and a cinematic/orchestral flair. [See Also: Kruder & Dorfmeister, Tosca] —*John Bush*

• **Peace Orchestra** / Aug. 24, 1999 / G-Stone ✦✦✦✦

*Peace Orchestra*, the debut album by Kruder & Dorfmeister's Peter Kruder, suffers little for its lack of both producers. The kind of trance-state trip-hop that sounds freshly minted by God himself, these nine tracks belie the notion that trip-hop is a style scavenger, content to paste sampled jazz-funk over a few hip-hop breaks. *Peace Orchestra* is so lovingly crafted, so finely detailed that comparisons with the glut of trip-hop sinking the market seems almost laughable (yes, it's that good). A languid clarinet line does a slow waltz with K&D's oft-used shuffle-beat on the highlight "Meister Petz," while "Double Drums" works a mutated tech-synth line with strong breakbeats. Kruder's musical sense comes from a variety of musical capitals, including Rio de Janeiro (the fine, delicate swing), New York (the jazz chords and shadings), East L.A. (Latin percussion), and London (acid house). Only Kruder (or perhaps Dorfmeister) could distill so many elements into one cohesive album without risk of blandness or musical fragmentation. —*John Bush*

## Peanut Butter Wolf (Chris Manak)

b. San Mateo, CA

*Producer, DJ / Turntablism, Underground Rap, Electronica, Hip-Hop*

Among the true talents in the late-'90s new skool of old-school hip-hop, Peanut Butter Wolf began DJing as a teenager and became quite an entrepreneur at his San Jose, CA high school, selling mix tapes of his turntable work. He debuted on wax in 1989 with "You Can't Swing This" on All Good Vinyl, recorded with a smooth MC named Lyrical Prophecy. By the end of the year, PBW began working with MC Charizma, and the two gelled quickly, perfecting their skills at block parties and shows with the likes of the Pharcyde, House of Pain, and Nas. Just after the duo gained a record deal with Hollywood Basic in 1992, Charizma was shot and killed.

Unsure of where to turn without the talents of his MC, Peanut Butter Wolf began issuing strictly instrumental work, including his first release, *Peanut Butter Breaks* on Heyday Records. Tracks followed for the Bomb label (on the excellent *Return of the DJ* compilation) as well as OM Records. Though the MC had ruled the world of hip-hop since the mid-'80s, selected DJ crews began to get exposure in the dance underground by the late '90s, including DJ Shadow, the Invisbl Skratch Piklz, and the X Men (whose name was later changed to the X-Ecutioners, for copyright reasons). Peanut Butter Wolf joined the elite as well, recording for dance labels 2 Kool (the *Lunar Props* EP) and Ninja Tune (remixing the Herbaliser) as well as contributing production work for fellow old-schooler Kool Keith. With the foundation of his Stone's Throw label, PBW began developing tracks recorded earlier with MC Charizma and released work by another Bay Area crew, Fanatik. —*John Bush*

**Phanatik Beats** / Sep. 30, 1996 / Stone's Throw ✦✦✦✦

**Super Duck Breaks** / Nov. 18, 1996 / Stone's Throw ✦✦✦

• **My Vinyl Weighs a Ton** / Jan. 18, 1999 / Copasetik Recordings ✦✦✦✦

After more than a decade in the rap industry, this release marks the prolific producer/DJ's first solo album. Based in the influential Bay Area hip-hop scene, his work with Kool Keith and Rasco elevated his status as a producer. Even Cypress Hill and alt-rockers Garbage have sampled his work (without credit). With the album's title serving as an ode to Public Enemy and an understated description of his record collection, *My Vinyl Weighs a Ton* offers production styles from the block rocking "Definition of Ill", featuring Planet Asia, to the hypnotic sampling of "Run the Line" with baritone lyricist Rasco. And while many hip-hop tracks are known for having multiple MCs share mic time, Peanut Butter Wolf serves up an all-DJ cut with 11 of the world's most talented wax spinners (Cut Chemist, A-Trak, Rob Swift, etc.) rotating in a vinyl challenge. *My Vinyl Weighs a Ton* is undeniably a landmark album, offering one of the genre's most varied, humorous and progressive collections. —*Craig Robert Smith*

## The Peech Boys
f. 1980, New York, NY, db. 1984
*Group / Garage, Club/Dance, Dance-Pop*
Alternately known as the New York Citi Peech Boys or N.Y.C. Peech Boys, this underground funk-rock unit recorded one of the early hits in the New York house/garage scene with 1981's "Don't Make Me Wait." Despite recording for West End and Island in the early '80s, the Peech Boys never made it out of the gate commercially despite cutting some intriguing songs. Formed by vocalists Bernard Fowler, Robert Kasper, Michael de Benedictus, Darryl Short, and Steven Brown, the group came together under the wing of seminal DJ Larry Levan at the Paradise Garage. After much club success with "Don't Make Me Wait," the Peech Boys recorded an LP for Island in 1983 but split not long after. Fowler continued to work as a background vocalist and arranger on tracks for the Rolling Stones, Herbie Hancock, Gil Scott-Heron, Sly & Robbie, Yoko Ono, and Philip Glass, among others. —*Ron Wynn*

• *Life Is Something Special* / 1983 / Island ♦♦♦

## Daniel Pemberton
*Producer / Ambient, Electronic*
Influenced by statuesque electronic artists the likes of Jean-Michel Jarre, Tomita, and Vangelis, ambient composer Daniel Pemberton began collecting keyboard gear from an early age and wrote a tips column for a video-game magazine to earn enough money for increasingly high-end equipment. He also began recording his own compositions, and passed a tape on to Mixmaster Morris at one of his gigs. When word (as well as additional tapes) continued to spread, Pemberton recorded his debut album *Bedroom*, which gained release in late 1994 for Pete Namlook's highly collectible Fax Records. The Mixmaster Morris connection also led to work for Coldcut's Ninja Tune label, including a DJ Vadim remix released on the latter's *U.S.S.R. Reconstruction* LP. —*John Bush*

• *Bedroom* / Nov. 21, 1994 / Fax Sub-Label ♦♦♦♦
*Bedroom* filters the ambient and space inspirations of most Fax material through Pemberton's own influences on the composer side of new age and electronics. The result is an evocative album ranging from atmospheric nature pieces ("Antarctica," "Lost Caves") to more upfront productions ("Phoenix," "Submerge," "Novelty Track"). Though the mood is sublime throughout, frequent listens reveal the depth behind Pemberton's production prowess. —*John Bush*

## Perrey-Kingsley
f. 1965, db. 1967
*Group / Obscuro, Space Age Pop, Electronic*
In the mid-'60s, Frenchman Jean-Jacques Perrey—an electronic musician who had helped popularize the Ondioline, a keyboard which produced sounds similar to the violin and the flute—teamed up with American composer and arranger Gershon Kingsley for a couple of albums of then-futuristic electronic pop. Using tape recorders, scissors, and splicing tape they recorded variations on pop motifs that, while kitschy from a latter-day perspective, represented the state-of-the-art in electronic sounds at the time. Two LPs, *The In Sound from Way Out!* and *Kaleidoscopic Vibrations*, were released by Vanguard in the late '60s. Perrey also recorded several albums of Moog music as a solo artist, and came back into vogue in the '90s with a feature in the book *Incredibly Strange Music*. Everyone from Stereolab and µ-Ziq to the Beastie Boys to hip-hop super-producer Timbaland featured ideas borrowed from Perrey-Kingsley prominently on tracks of their own, while Perrey began recording again, both on his own and with fellow Frenchmen Air. —*Richie Unterberger*

*The In Sound from Way Out!* / 1966 / Vanguard ♦♦
From a technical standpoint, this early attempt to bring electronic music to the masses is commendable. The result of (according to the liner notes) 275 hours of work and several miles of tape, these electronically modified sounds were combined with electronic sounds from oscillators, tone generators, and feedback loops to create something resembling pop melodies. Live musicians then embellished these materials with both electronic and natural instruments. The problem is, the end product (certainly after 30 years have removed the novelty value of electronic tones) is cheesy enough to skirt the boundaries of kitsch, with a boxy, mechanical texture and a music-box-run-amok feel that makes it sound like a direct ancestor of Hot Butter's 1972 hit instrumental "Popcorn." There is a goofy charm to the mischievous placement of burps, gurgles, animal noises, and naive outer space-tinged themes. But with material that would be far more at home on the soundtrack of a children's TV cartoon than a work of contemporary composition, this album is more of a curiosity than anything else. —*Richie Unterberger*

*Kaleidoscopic Vibrations* / 1967 / Vanguard ♦♦

• *The Essential Perrey & Kingsley* / 1988 / Vanguard ♦♦♦♦
*The Essential Perrey & Kingsley* brings together each track from the two LPs Perrey-Kingsley recorded for Vanguard, *The In Sound from Way Out!* and *Kaleidoscopic Vibrations*. As such, it's an obvious first purchase, though the liner notes are scant. —*John Bush*

## Jean-Jacques Perrey
b. Jan. 20, 1929
*Producer / Musique Concrète, Space Age Pop, Electronic*
Recording both as a solo artist and in collaboration with Gershon Kingsley, Jean-Jacques Perrey helped popularize electronic music with a series of albums in the '60s that used Moog synthesizers, the ondioline, and magnetic tape. His work was never intended to be part of the avant-garde, as Perrey himself cheerfully declared in his liner notes. His goal was to popularize electronic music by deploying it in happy, simple tunes and arrangements. That's why his music falls far closer to easy listening/space age pop than any sort of cutting edge—and that is also why his music sounds more cheesily nostalgic than futuristic these days.

In the early '50s, Perrey became fascinated by the ondioline, a keyboard instrument that anticipated the synthesizer with its emulation of other instruments. He dropped out of medical school to become a sales representative for the ondioline, and by the early '60s he'd moved to the US to work in television, radio, and the recording studio. His '60s albums for Vanguard, both as a solo act and half of Perrey-Kingsley, were his most widely circulated, giving Perrey a chance to demonstrate his arsenal of electronic instruments, treatments, and tape manipulations. The actual results were bouncy and childish, perhaps betraying more of Perrey's considerable background in radio/TV jingles than may have been intended. Treated more as novelties than innovations, they came back into vogue when Perrey was profiled in RE/SEARCH's *Incredibly Strange Music* book in the '90s. Perrey returned to France in 1970, where he continued to work in radio, TV, soundtracks, and other musical projects. By the '90s he had begun recording again, first in a collaboration with French electronica duo Air, then with an album of his own, *Eclektronics*. —*Richie Unterberger*

• *The Amazing New Electronic Pop Sound of Jean Jacques Perrey* / 1968 / Vanguard ♦♦♦♦
"What I have tried to do," wrote Perrey in the liner notes to this album, "is to bring the electronic sonorities to popular music." This he accomplished via the ondioline, Moog, magnetic tapes, electronic instruments, and other gizmos. He also wrote or co-wrote most of the material on this disc, which sounds like nothing so much as late-'60s instrumental "mood" music albums as refracted through a slightly more ambitious, electronic lens. It's really not something you can put on again and again, but it's kind of fun nonetheless. The arrangements have a kind of desperately trendy go-go-type charm, borrowing occasionally from familiar folk and pop melodies like "Frere Jacques" and "Georgy Girl." —*Richie Unterberger*

*Moog Indigo* / 1970 / Vanguard ♦♦♦
In comparison to his 1968 album *The Amazing New Electronic Pop Sound*, Perrey's 1970 effort concentrated, as the title indicates, more heavily on the Moog synthesizer. Other than that, it's more of the same late-'60s background pop mood music through a primitive electronic filter. The melodies and arrangements are colored a wee bit more by vague heavy rock and soul influences, which are most evident in the first track, "Soul City." But it's still

wholeheartedly cheerful, nonthreatening stuff, as you might guess from titles like "Country Rock Polka" and "Flight of the Bumblebee," not to mention the cover of "Hello Dolly." "Passport to the Future" is an ironic title in light of the track's liberal lifts from the Tornados' classic instrumental, "Telstar," which had been recorded almost a decade earlier. —*Richie Unterberger*

Eclektronics / Jun. 15, 1998 / Basenotic ♦♦♦♦

## Lee "Scratch" Perry

b. 1936, St. Mary's, Jamaica
*Vocals, Percussion, Producer, Leader, Composer / Political Reggae, Roots Reggae, Jungle/Drum'N'Bass, Dub, Rocksteady*

Some call him a genius, others claim he's certifiably insane, a madman. Truth is, he's both, but more importantly, Lee Perry is a towering figure in reggae—a producer, mixologist, and songwriter that, along with King Tubby, helped shape the sound of dub, and made reggae music such a powerful part of the pop music world. Along with producing some of the most influential acts (Bob Marley and the Wailers and the Congos to name but two) in reggae history, Perry's approach to production and dub mixing was breathtakingly innovative and audacious—no one else sounds like him—and while many claim that King Tubby invented dub, there are just as many who would argue (myself included) that no one experimented with it or took it further than Lee Perry.

Born in the rural Jamaican village of St. Mary's in 1936, Perry began his surrealistic musical odyssey in the late '50s working with ska man Prince Buster selling records for Clement "Coxsone" Dodd's Downbeat Sound System. Called "Little" Perry because of his diminutive stature (Perry stands four foot eleven inches), he was soon producing and recording for Dodd at the center of the Jamaican music industry Studio One. After a falling out with Dodd (throughout his career Perry has a tendency to burn his bridges after he stops working with someone), Perry went to work at Wirl Records with Joe Gibbs. Perry and Gibbs never really saw eye to eye on anything and in 1968 Perry left to form his own label, called Upsetter. Not surprisingly, Perry's first release on Upsetter was a single entitled "People Funny Boy," which was a direct attack upon Gibbs. What is important about the record is that, along with selling extremely well in Jamaica, it was the first Jamaican pop record to use the loping, lazy, bass-driven beat that would soon become identified as the reggae "riddim" and signal the shift from the hyperkinetically upbeat ska to the pulsing, throbbing languor of "roots" reggae.

From this point through the '70s, Perry released an astonishing amount of work under his name and numerous, extremely creative, pseudonyms: Jah Lion, Pipecock Jakxon, Super Ape, the Upsetter, and his most famous nom-de-plume, Scratch. Many of the singles released during this period were significant Jamaican (and UK) hits, instrumental tracks like "The Return of Django," "Clint Eastwood," and "The Vampire," which cemented Perry's growing reputation as a major force in reggae music. Becoming more and more outrageous in his pronouncements and personal appearance (when it comes to clothing, only Sun Ra can hold a candle to Perry's thrift-store outfits), Perry and his remarkable house band, also named the Upsetters, worked with just about every performer in Jamaica. It was in the early '70s after hearing some of King Tubby's early dub experiments that Perry became interested in this form of aural manipulation. He quickly released a mind-boggling number of dub releases and eventually, in a fit of creative independence, opened his own studio, Black Ark.

It was at Black Ark that Perry recorded and produced some of the early, seminal Bob Marley tracks. Using the Upsetters rhythm section of bassist Aston "Familyman" Barrett and his drummer brother Carlton Barrett, Perry guided the Wailers through some of their finest moments, recording such powerful songs as "Duppy Conqueror" and "Small Axe." The good times, however, were not long, especially after Perry, unbeknownst to Marley and company, sold the tapes to Trojan Records and pocketed the cash. Island Records head Chris Blackwell quickly moved in and signed the Wailers to an exclusive contract, leaving Perry with virtually nothing. Perry accused Blackwell (a white Englishman) of cultural imperialism and Marley of being an accomplice. To this day, Perry refers to Blackwell as a vampire, and accuses Marley of having curried favor with politicians in order to make a fast buck. These setbacks did not stem the tide of Perry releases, be they of new material or one of a seemingly endless collection of anthologies. Perry was also expanding his range of influence, working with the Clash, who were huge Perry fans, having covered the Perry-produced version of Junior Murvin's classic "Police and Thieves." Perry was brought in to produce some tracks for the Clash, but the results were remixed more to the band's liking. All this hard work was wreaking havoc with Perry's already fragile mental state, leading to a breakdown. The stories of his mental instability were exacerbated by tales of massive substance abuse (despite his public stance against all drugs except sacramental ganja) which reportedly included regular ingestion of cocaine and LSD; one potentially apocryphal story even had Perry drinking bottles of tape head-cleaning fluid. But these stories, as with much surrounding Perry, blur fact and fiction. One story that was true was that Black Ark, and everything in it, burned to the ground. Perry claims bad wiring as the culprit, but the more familiar and commonly accepted story is that Perry burned the studio down in a fit of acid-inspired madness, convinced that Satan had made Black Ark his home. Whatever the case, the site of Perry's greatest moments as a producer had been reduced to (and remains) a pile of rubble and ash. Soon after the fire that consumed Black Ark, Perry, increasingly fed up with the music business in Jamaica (which by all accounts is corruption personified), decided to leave.

Despite the considerable lows in his career, today Perry remains busy and, so it seems, reasonably happy. Although he's less in demand as a producer, his solo work remains very strong, and his continuing influence can be felt in the contemporary dub music of the Mad Professor (another former Perry protege that Perry now treats with disdain), and some post-rave electronica music. Even the Beastie Boys gave Perry his props in a rhyme on their release *Ill Communication*, and later added him to the bill of performers at a concert for Tibetan freedom. The man called Scratch lives in Switzerland and continues to cook up a psychedelic brew of music that, along with being ahead of its time, will warp your head, in a good way, assuming that you're up to the challenge. In 1997, Island (the label started by the vampire Chris Blackwell) released *Arkology*, a three-disc compilation of Perry recordings.

A word or two about Perry's discography: it's massive, unwieldy, and although there are plenty of great records, there's almost as much crap. The lack of quality control has little to do with Perry, but rather with sleazebags trying to rip off his legacy. After King Tubby's murder in 1989, his studio was looted, and many of Perry's tapes were stolen. Some of these recordings have shown up on poorly mastered, and expensive, anthologies. Releases on Trojan, Rounder's reggae subsidiary label Heartbeat, and Island (and its subsidiary label Mango) are generally excellent and are the best place to start building your Perry collection. Smaller labels like Seven Leaves and the French-based Lagoon Records (which seems like a semilegit bootleg label) are hit-and-miss propositions, and those inclined to check out recordings on these labels are encouraged to proceed with caution. Avoid releases on the Rohit label, if only for their lousy production and tacky, grade-Z packaging. Also, as with King Tubby recordings, purchasing a Perry release means you might be buying a record he produced, but not necessarily performs on. That said, happy hunting and listening. —*John Dougan*

**Super Ape** / 1976 / Mango ♦♦♦♦
As it says on the cover, "Dub it up, blacker than dread," and that bit of rastaspeak accurately describes the vibe of the great record. The Upsetters are in reeling and rollicking good form, and Perry's mastery of the mixing board is made manifest on tracks like "Zion's Blood" and "Dread Lion." The accent is bass heavy, which in reggae is no surprise, but here Boris Gardener's bass is so propulsive and commanding, and Perry mixes it so far upfront, that it will shake your foundations. This is one of the few early Perry releases where his personality is less dominant than that of the band, but it only takes a few spins for Scratch's blood and fire to become evident. —*John Dougan*

**Dub Messenger** / 1980 / Tassa ♦♦
An artist as willfully bizarre (and as prolific) as Lee "Scratch" Perry is bound to make a few missteps, and this is one of them. Although the insert gives performance credit to the Upsetters, there isn't a single analog instrument to be heard on this album, leading to the strong suspicion that all the music was produced on a keyboard by Perry and/or producer Lloyd "Bullwackies" Barnes. The sound is sterile and flat, and though the album is partially redeemed by Perry's typically off-kilter rantings on such subjects as international finance, nursery rhyme characters and the nature of the cosmos, there is none of the sonic adventurousness that marks the best of his work. We've come to expect almost anything from Scratch, but blandness comes as an unpleasant surprise. —*Rick Anderson*

**History, Mystery and Prophesy** / 1984 / Mango ✦✦
Perry's weakest Island/Mango release. All the rough edges are gone, and Perry's berserk charm is in short supply. Still, because it's Perry, there are tracks to recommend ("Heads of Government" being the most notable), but there are plenty better Perry records to be had. —*John Dougan*

★ **Reggae Greats** / 1984 / Mango ✦✦✦✦✦
Almost the same track listing as 1979's *Scratch on the Wire*, but far less expensive and easier to find. My caveat with Mango's *Reggae Greats* series is they don't offer a lot of liner information and use unimaginative graphics. But you will get "Police and Thieves," and no reggae collection is complete without it. —*John Dougan*

**Time Boom X De Devil Dead** / 1987 / On-U Sound ✦✦
For those familiar with the work of British dubmeister and producer extraordinaire Adrian Sherwood, the thought of he and Scratch working together sets off fits of near-Pavlovian salivating. This collaboration is excellent, and Perry and Sherwood (both of whom traffic in an idiosyncratic sound and approach to production) sound perfectly suited as collaborators. What helps considerably is the effectiveness of Sherwood's band the Dub Syndicate, who rock a little harder than the Upsetters and create edgier, more brittle soundscapes for Perry to romp through and Sherwood to produce (although it should be noted that Perry had a hand in the production too). Perry's toasting and singing are not as manic as on *Battle of Armagideon*, but he delivers the goods on tracks like "S.D.I." and "Allergic to Lies." Out of print on vinyl, this is a Perry recording deserving of a CD reissue if it hasn't been already. —*John Dougan*

**Chicken Scratch** / 1989 / Heartbeat ✦✦
Of all the reissues of Perry's early career, this is the most illuminating, because it captures the youthful Lee Perry (in his early 20s) singing ska music. Backed by the phenomenal Skatalites, featuring trombonist Don Drummond, saxophonists Tommy McCook and Roland Alphonso, and keyboardist Jackie Mittoo, Perry belts out such Studio One ska/pop classics like "Please Don't Go," "Man to Man" (which features backing vocals by the very youthful trio of Bob Marley, Bunny Wailer, and Peter Tosh), and "Solid as a Rock." The songs skitter along, filled to the brim with exuberance, and the Skatalites (as usual) are a joy to hear, banging out double-time rhythms with reckless abandon. Adding to the fun are female backing vocalists the Soulettes and the Dynamites, the former featuring Bob Marley's wife Rita. This is rarely heard Perry music, and considering how far from this music he is today, it's almost hard to imagine him recording it. If you are building a Lee Perry library, absolutely, positively make this one of your purchases. —*John Dougan*

**Mystic Warrior** / 1989 / RAS ✦
Perry's collaboration with fellow oddball Neal "The Mad Professor" Fraser yielded this good, but nonessential release. This version, as opposed to the dub version, adds Fraser's techno magic to the proceedings, lending a more contemporary feel, but Perry's ranting is even more unfocused and lunatic than usual and never really gets anything going verbally. Recommended to those whose love for Perry has turned into something resembling an addiction. —*John Dougan*

**Build the Ark** / 1990 / Trojan ✦✦✦
The last of Trojan's three-record (two-CD) collections of Perry's crucial Black Ark production work of the '70s. And, as was the case with the previous collections (*The Upsetter Box* and *Open the Gate*), there's absolutely no good reason not to own this collection too. If you're thinking that three double-CD sets of Lee Perry is starting to sound like overkill, look at it this way—that's like saying you've breathed enough air, and now you don't need any more. As with recordings of Sun Ra, there's always a reason (like amazing music, for a start) to add more Lee Perry to your collection. And with this release you will be able to get you hands on Junior Murvin's amazing "Cross Over" (nearly as good as "Police and Thieves"), Winston Heywood's "Long, Long Time," and Eric Donaldson's "Freedom Street." This is the sound of Black Ark at its most exciting and prolific, and remains a testament to Perry's genius as a producer, mixer and arranger. A heavy groove indeed. —*John Dougan*

**From the Secret Laboratory** / 1990 / Mango ✦✦
The second collaboration between Perry and his acolyte Adrian Sherwood, and, as was their first meeting (*Time Boom X De Devil Dead*), it's a perfect mixture of Perry's manic toasting and singing and the sinuous beat supplied by the Sherwood-led Dub Syndicate and the Roots Radics band. Money and attacks on capitalism (specifically the World Bank) fuel Perry's ire on this disc, but just when the going gets heavy, Scratch pulls out a tribute to cartoon detective Inspector Gadget, as well as a great cover of Leroy Sibbles' "Party Time." As with their earlier release, Perry and Sherwood work well together, perhaps due to Sherwood's fondness for psychedelicizing his dub mixes and Perry's preference for flat-out weirdness. In any event, this collaboration between pupil and teacher is one of the better releases of Perry's recent vintage. —*John Dougan*

**Black Ark in Dub** / Oct. 4, 1993 / Lagoon ✦✦✦✦
A fine collection of early Perry dub packaged in what seems to be a semilegit, bootleg way. This label is tied in (I think) with the French label Lagoon, which has released the Perry-produced Bob Marley session (two CDs, both of them essential). This is a good selection; Perry remixes are typically audacious and crazy, but there's little enclosed information telling you when the tracks were cut. Lack of information is an ongoing problem with Perry releases, since his entire output defies any kind of authoritative historical treatment. Still, this is worthy of your time, even if it doesn't provide the big buzz of some of Perry's other, more far-out experiments. —*John Dougan*

**Experryments at the Grassroots of Dub** / 1995 / RAS ✦✦✦
Lee "Scratch" Perry is the undeniable mastermind behind some of reggae's greatest moments. These days, however, it's hard to say whether he is still the genius he once was or whether he has assumed the role of reggae's clown prince. *Experryments at the Grassroots of Dub* shows a bit of both sides. Each track begins with a short, spoken-word journey into Perry's warped mind, but most of the music is top-notch, if slightly over-synthed. Perry's cast includes the Mad Professor, who now tours with him, on drums and William the Conqueror on bass and keyboards. "Sky High Dub," a reworking of Bob Marley's "Natty Dread Rides Again," reaches into the stratosphere and "Dub Wise Experryments," with its underlying flute loops shows Perry at his "experrymental" best. "Pooping Dub Song," however, should have been flushed, as it simply doesn't fit with the rest of the album. In the words of Perry, this album is, for the most part, "Soopboib." —*Matthew Hilburn*

**Super Ape Inna Jungle** / 1995 / RAS ✦✦
The first thing you should know is that this is *not* a jungle version of Lee Perry & the Upsetters' *Super Ape* album. Instead, it's a collaboration between Perry and the production team of Douggie Digital and Juggler, who basically provide beds of bass-heavy jungle as musical settings for scraps of Perry's vocals. The profit margin on a project like this has got to be pretty high, but that doesn't mean there's anything wrong with the music. On "Nasty Spell," the jumpy breakbeats, synthesized chords, and sonar blips roil and surge beneath Perry's barely intelligible utterances. He makes himself clearer on the equally propulsive "Why Complaining?" (though, as usual, he's not saying much that will make sense to the earthbound mind). The last two tracks on the disc are both relatively straightforward dub mixes by Mad Professor. These would've been more effective breaking the tension at intervals during the program, but, hey, that's why CD players are programmable. —*Rick Anderson*

**Voodooism** / 1996 / Pressure Sounds ✦✦✦✦
Not a collaboration in the truest sense of the word, this collection of Black Ark sides from the mid-'70s represents some of Perry's best work, and thanks to Adrian Sherwood's Pressure Sounds label, all of the fire and madness of these sides, long assumed lost, can be enjoyed. The tracks here are Perry at his most playful, with lots of bass-heavy vibe colliding with goofy sound effects and clattering percussion. But for those hungry for the deep, dark mix that Perry was cooking up at Black Ark circa 1974-1979, you can't do any better than this. Of course, Sherwood would be the one to get it all on one disc, but if he hadn't, it probably would never have been done. And a cursory spin will make you shout thanks. —*John Dougan*

**Arkology** / 1997 / Island Jamaica ✦✦✦✦
Purportedly the definitive Lee Perry compilation, the three-CD set *Arkology* is loaded with good intentions and is carefully constructed, but with a back catalogue like Perry's, where it's nearly impossible to find out what's what, definitive in this case is a dream. Still, the compilers have done a fine job of providing an overview of Perry's career that makes sense musically, historically, and culturally. For those who want to jump headlong into Perry's world (assuming of course that you don't mind parting with the $40 it'll cost you to do so), then this is the way to go; otherwise I'd recommend taking the money

and buying two to three individual releases. *Arkology*'s foundation is the 1979 anthology *Scratch on the Wire;* the compilers took those tracks and added a significant number of remixes and a few previously unreleased dub tracks to give it some weight. And that is perhaps the set's biggest drawback—it doesn't cover quite enough of Perry's career. Remixes are nice, but a representative sampling of the early, mid- and late periods at Black Ark would have been better, as well as a few of the early-'60s ska tracks that didn't make it onto Heartbeat's excellent *Chicken Scratch* compilation. There are also some irritating audio considerations here. I love compact disc technology, but sometimes reggae reissues lose that warm, extremely loud bass sound that is crucial to the riddims. That's not always the case on this release, but there are some moments when you wish there was just a little more blood coming from the speakers. So, all that said, is *Arkology* worth it? Absolutely. I would recommend it with this lone caveat: Don't think that this large purchase will give you all the crucial Lee Perry recordings. It provides a good overview and is an excellent introduction, but consider it the start, rather than the completion, of your journey with Scratch and the Upsetters. —*John Dougan*

**Technomajikal** / Jun. 3, 1997 / ROIR ♦♦
Lee "Scratch" Perry's 1997 release, *Technomajikal*, is a collaboration with Dieter Meier of Yello. It can be described as electronic reggae, but the music's organic sound and feeling has certainly not diminished. The story behind how this unlikely collaboration came to pass is interesting. Perry had been living in Switzerland, and since Meier lives there as well, he tracked Perry down and talked about laying down some tracks in his Zurich recording studio. Perry accepted the invite, and soon was singing and rapping over acoustic tracks laid down by Meier, which were later replaced by a more electro accompaniment. Perry refused to record his vocals the accustomed way, as he sang into a microphone while sitting outside the studio with a pair of headphones on. The finished album easily appeals to both dance enthusiasts and fans of reggae/dub, with several tracks featured as official versions, then repeated as either remixed radio versions or instrumentals (such as "UFO Attack," "Maxi Merlin," and "X-Perry-Ment"). —*Greg Prato*

**Dub Fire** / 1998 / Ariwa ♦♦
Some things never change. For instance, Lee "Scratch" Perry is still one of the funniest characters in the world of reggae music. Other things do change: for instance, these days he sings even worse than he did in the '70s. (The liner notes refer to his "uncanny vocal resemblance to Bob Marley," but only the congenitally uncritical and the slightly deaf will agree with that assessment.) Those vocal limitations are especially obvious in light of his material, which includes several old Marley tunes ("Soul Rebel," "Rock My Boat") and one associated with the great Junior Byles ("Place Called Africa," here presented as "Africa Place"). Mad Professor's canny production and the cool, assured backing of the Robotiks band save this album from the scrap heap, but barely. Lyrical nadir: the unbelievably puerile "Doctor Dick." —*Rick Anderson*

## Persona (Eric Cook)

*Producer / Experimental Techno*
Drummer-turned-producer Eric Cook worked with noise-rockers Gravitar and blues-rockers Bantam Rooster before turning to electronic music in the late '90s. Based in Dearborn, Michigan, Cook began playing in 1985, and spent time in several local bands before joining Gravitar in 1992. He appeared on several of the band's albums, including the celebrated debut *Gravitaativaravitar,* before joining Bantam Rooster in 1994. Cook began spending more time on his electronic solo recordings (a hobby since 1991) after breaking his ankle in early 1998. By the end of the year, he'd completed his first full album, *Maximal*. It earned release on California's Vinyl Communications the following year. —*John Bush*

• **Maximal** / Jun. 29, 1999 / Vinyl Communications ♦♦♦
Like other releases on Vinyl Communications by Kid606 and Lesser, hardcore techno designed for the living room doesn't seem like such a bizarre prospect after listening to Eric Cook's debut as Persona. The drummer for noise-rockers Gravitar emphasizes a diverse sonic palate, definitely in keeping with his former band. On tracks like the opener "Release the Dogs," "Dingspumm," and "Counting Time in Flu Season," Cook constructs dense walls of distorted metallic percussion, then breaks them all down with legions of effects-processing tools; in fact, he rarely even pauses between tracks. At times, it all gets a bit overwhelming—there must be enough ideas here to pad out five albums. Fortunately, he takes a few sidetrips: into paranoid breakbeat (albeit, *distorted* breakbeat) on "Thumper," and with the live-sounding drums "Waiting for Matika." Vinyl Communications also tacked on five remixes, by Kid606, Lesser, Marumari, Totemplow, and Cook's fellow suburban Detroiter Warn Defever (from His Name Is Alive). —*John Bush*

## Peshay (Paul Pesce)

*Producer, DJ / Electronica, Jungle/Drum'N'Bass, Club/Dance*
An early protegé to Goldie while the two worked on production at 4 Hero's Reinforced Records during the early '90s, Peshay's style of jungle/drum'n'bass, influenced both by house and the more polished forms of jazz fusion, allies itself both with Goldie and 4 Hero. A breakbeat DJ from early in his career, Peshay debuted on wax with Reinforced in 1993, recording the *Protegé* EP before joining Goldie's Metalheadz stable and releasing its second single, "Psychosis." He also recorded several twelves with LTJ Bukem's Good Looking Records, including "The Piano Tune" and "19.5." Though hampered by a serious illness which sidelined him during jungle's breakout year of 1995, Peshay returned in 1996, remixing singles from Goldie's *Timeless* ("Inner City Life" and "Angel") and contributing tracks to the Mo'Wax compilation *Headz II*. Signed up to Mo'Wax, Peshay released the "Miles from Home" single in mid-1998 and worked on material with Photek's Rupert Parkes. The label's practical dissolution by the following year led to delays for the expected full-length, though by July 1999 Peshay's debut album—also called *Miles from Home*—appeared on the Island Blue label. Following *de rigeur* for top-flight jungle producers, he also formed his own label, Elementz Records, which released twelves from Decoder and Technical Itch. —*John Bush*

**The Piano Tune/The Vocal Tune [Single]** / 1995 / Good Looking ♦♦♦

**Jah VIP Rollers (Mix) [Single]** / 1996 / Metalheadz ♦♦♦♦

**Miles from Home [Single]** / Apr. 27, 1998 / Mo'Wax ♦♦♦♦
Peshay's first single for Mo'Wax is an epic journey through the interstellar realms of drum'n'bass, courtesy of space-age effects and a legion of solid breaks programming. The flip side includes an Underdog remix. —*Keith Farley*

• **Miles from Home** / Jul. 19, 1999 / Island Blue ♦♦♦
Long delayed because of release problems with Mo'Wax, Peshay's debut funnels his jazz influences—not just the slick end of '70s fusion and disco, but the hard boppin' '60s as well—into a solid album of breakbeat dance. The jazz'n'breaks angle is done better than most, thanks to input from two of the jungle scene's prime engineer/producers, Decoder and (on two tracks) Photek. The title track is an obvious highlight (it actually appeared on Mo'Wax as a single more than a year earlier), and the live bass and piano on "Live at 2:37" are a welcome attempt to continue integrating jazz improv with drum'n'bass. The rap track "End of Story" also works very well, with vocals by J-Live and beautiful Fender Rhodes playing by Illinton. For most of the album though, the results argue well on paper but end up a bit dry and overly respectful in the final analysis. *Miles from Home* has a few notable highs, but seems too polished and labored over to work as a truly great album. It's difficult to dispel the impression that it suffered from the extra studio time. —*John Bush*

## Pet Shop Boys

f. Aug. 1981, London, England
*Group / Alternative Dance, Club/Dance, Pop/Rock, House, Dance-Pop*
Postmodern ironists cloaked behind a veil of buoyantly melodic and lushly romantic synth-pop confections, the Pet Shop Boys' cheeky, smart, and utterly danceable music established them among the most commercially and critically successful groups of their era. Always remaining one step ahead of their contemporaries, the British duo navigated the constantly shifting landscape of modern dance-pop with rare grace and intelligence, moving easily from disco to house to techno with their own distinctive image remaining completely intact. Satiric and irreverent—yet somehow strangely affecting—the Pet Shop Boys transcended the seeming disposability of their craft, offering wry and thoughtful cultural commentary communicated by the Morse code of *au courant* synth washes and drum-machine rhythms.

Pet Shop Boys formed in London in August 1981 when vocalist Neil Tennant (a former editor at Marvel Comics who later gained some notoriety as a journalist for *Smash Hits* magazine) first met keyboardist Chris Lowe (a onetime architecture student) at an electronics shop. Discovering a shared passion for dance music and synthesizers, they immediately decided to start a band. Dubbing themselves the Pet Shop Boys in honor of friends who worked in such an establishment—while also obliquely nodding to the sort of names prevalent among the New York City hip-hop culture of the early '80s—the duo's career first took flight in 1983, when Tennant met producer Bobby "O" Orlando while on a writing assigment. Orlando produced their first single, 1984's "West End Girls." The song was a minor hit in the US but went nowhere in Britain, and its follow-up, "One More Chance," was also unsuccessful.

Upon signing to EMI, the Pet Shop Boys issued 1985's biting "Opportunities (Let's Make Lots of Money)"; when it too failed to attract attention, the duo's future appeared grim, but they then released an evocative new Stephen Hague production of "West End Girls," which became an international chart-topper. Its massive success propelled the Pet Shop Boys' 1986 debut LP *Please* into the Top Ten, and when "Opportunities" was subsequently reissued, it too became a hit. *Disco*, a collection of dance remixes, was quickly rushed into stores, and in 1987 the duo resurfaced with the superb *Actually* which launched three more Top Ten smashes—"It's a Sin," a lovely cover of the perennial "Always on My Mind," and "What Have I Done to Deserve This?," a duet between Tennant and the great Dusty Springfield. A documentary film titled *It Couldn't Happen Here* was released the following year.

Also in 1988, Pet Shop Boys issued their third studio LP, the eclectic *Introspective*. The single "Domino Dancing" was their final Top 40 hit in the US The following year, the duo collaborated with a variety of performers, most notably Liza Minnelli, for whom they produced the 1989 LP *Results*. They also produced material for Springfield, and Tennant joined New Order frontman Bernard Sumner and ex-Smiths guitarist Johnny Marr in the group Electronic, scoring a hit with the single "Getting Away With It." The Pet Shop Boys reconvened in 1990 for the muted, downcast *Behaviour*, produced by Harold Faltermeyer. 1991 saw the release of their hit medley of U2's "Where the Streets Have No Name" and Frankie Valli's "Can't Take My Eyes Off You," and was followed in 1993 by *Very*, lauded among the duo's finest efforts to date. After a three-year absence, the Pet Shop Boys resurfaced with *Bilingual*, a fluid expansion into Latin rhythms. *Nightlife* followed in 1999. —*Jason Ankeny*

**Please** / 1986 / EMI America ♦♦♦
A collection of immaculately-crafted and seamlessly-produced synthesized dance-pop, The Pet Shop Boys' debut album *Please* sketches out the basic elements of the duo's sound. At first listen, most of the songs come off as mere excuses for the dance floor, driven by cold, melodic keyboard riffs and pulsing drum machines. However, the songcraft that the beats support is surprisingly strong, featuring catchy melodies that appear slight because of Neil Tennant's thin voice. Tennant's lyrics were still in their formative stages, with half of the record failing to transcend the formulaic constraints of dance-pop. The songs that do break free—the crass "Opportunities (Let's Make Lots of Money)," and the lulling "Suburbia," and the hypnotic "West End Girls"—are not only classic dance singles, they're classic pop singles. —*Stephen Thomas Erlewine*

**Disco** / Oct. 1986 / EMI America ♦♦
Released at the height of dance-pop in 1986, The Pet Shop Boys' remix album *Disco* defiantly asserted the roots of the current trend with the title. And with its long remixes, *Disco* is designed to be pumped at a dance floor. As casual listening, it gets a bit tedious, but even at these extended lengths, the melodic craft of The Pet Shop Boys' material shines through. —*Stephen Thomas Erlewine*

**Actually** / Jun. 1987 / EMI America ♦♦♦♦
With their second album *Actually*, The Pet Shop Boys perfected their melodic, detached dance-pop. Where most of *Please* was dominated by the beats, the rhythms on *Actually* are part of a series of intricate arrangements that create a glamorous but disposable backdrop for Neil Tennant's tales of isolation, boredom, money, and loneliness. Not only are the arrangements more accomplished, but the songs themselves are more striking, incorporating a strong sense of melody, as evidenced by "What Have I Done To Deserve This?," a duet with Dusty Springfield. Tennant's lyrics are clever and direct, chronicling the lifes and times of urban, lonely, and bored yuppies of the late '80s. And the fact that dance-pop is considered a disposable medium by most mainstream critics and listeners only increases the reserved emotional undercurrent of *Actually*, as well as its irony. —*Stephen Thomas Erlewine*

**Introspective** / Apr. 1988 / EMI America ♦♦♦
Featuring a mere six tracks, most of them well over six minutes in length, *Introspective* was a move back to the clubs for The Pet Shop Boys. Over the course of the album, they incorporated various dance techniques that were currently in vogue, including Latin rhythms and house textures. The title isn't entirely an arch joke, however. Like *Actually*, *Introspective* was an exploration of distant, disaffected yuppies, which naturally resulted in a good deal of self-analyzation. Melodically, the essential song structures were as strong and multi-layered as the previous album, yet that was hard to hear beneath the varying rhythmic textures that composed the bulk of each track. Nevertheless, the mixes are more compelling than the remixes on *Disco* and the songs include several of their best numbers, including "Left to My Own Devices" and "Domino Dancing," as well as the reconstruction of "Always On My Mind" and a cover of Blaze's club classic "It's Alright." —*Stephen Thomas Erlewine*

**Behavior** / Oct. 1990 / EMI America ♦♦♦♦
*Behavior* was a retreat from the deep dance textures of *Introspective*, as it picked up on the carefully-constructed pop of *Actually*. In fact, *Behavior* functions as The Pet Shop Boys' bid for mainstream credibility, as much of the album relies more on pop-craft than rhythmic variations. Although its a subtle maneuver, it would have been rather disastrous if the results weren't so captivating. Tennant takes this approach seriously, singing the lyrics instead of speaking them. That doesn't necessarily give the album added emotional baggage—all of the distance and detachment in the duo's music is not a hinderance, it's part of the concept—but it does result in an ambitious and breathtaking pop album, which manages to include everything from the spiteful "How Can You Expect To Be Taken Seriously?" to the wistful "Being Boring." —*Stephen Thomas Erlewine*

★ **Discography: The Complete Singles Collection** / Nov. 5, 1991 / EMI America ♦♦♦♦♦
Most of The Pet Shop Boys' albums are well-crafted and thoroughly intriguing in their own right, but dance-pop is a medium that is driven by hit singles. *Discography* collects all the duo's numerous hit singles, including a handful of nonalbums tracks, in their original 7" single mix, which occasionally varies from the album version, particularly in the case of the *Introspective* material. Presented chronologically, the singles not only demonstrate the band's increasing musical sophistication, they illustrate what fine songwriters Tennant and Lowe are. These 19 songs form one of the most consistent and innovative bodies of work of its era. Some of the production techniques have dated slightly, but the music has remained impressive. —*Stephen Thomas Erlewine*

**Very** / Oct. 5, 1993 / ERG ♦♦♦♦
Because they work in a field that isn't usually taken seriously, The Pet Shop Boys are often ignored in the rock world. But make no mistake—they are one of the most talented pop outfits working today, witty and melodic with a fine sense of flair. *Very* is one of their very best records, expertly weaving between the tongue-in-cheek humor of "I Wouldn't Normally Do This Kind of Thing," the quietly shocking "Can You Forgive Her?," and the bizarrely moving cover of The Village People's "Go West." Alternately happy and melancholy, *Very* is The Pet Shop Boys at their finest. —*Stephen Thomas Erlewine*

**Bilingual** / Sep. 1996 / Atlantic ♦♦♦
As a title, *Bilingual* is a double-edged sword. Disregard it's sexual connotations and concentrate on its musical implications—*Bilingual* is a rich, diverse album that delves deeply into Latin rhythms. It's not a crass, simplistic fusion, where the polyphonic rhythms are simply grafted over synthesizers and a disco pulse. Instead, *Bilingual* is an enormously subtle album, with shifting rhythms and graceful, understated melodies. The music isn't the only thing subtle about the album—Neil Tennant's voice and lyrics are nuanced, suggesting more than they actually say. Furthermore, *Bilingual* consists of the most optimistic, happy set of songs the Pet Shop Boys have ever recorded. Whether it's the smooth disco of "Before" or the insistent rhythms of "Se a Vida e," *Bilingual* is filled with joyous, if subdued, sounds. If anything, it's further proof that even if the Pet Shop Boys aren't gracing the top of the charts as frequently as they did during the late '80s, they are crafting albums that are more adventurous and successful than they did when they were one of the top acts in pop music. —*Stephen Thomas Erlewine*

**Nightlife** / Nov. 2, 1999 / Sire ♦♦♦
*Nightlife* is a loose concept album—more of a song cycle, really—about nightlife, naturally. There's not really a specific story, it's more of a collection of moods and themes, from love to loneliness. In that sense, it's not that dif-

ferent from most Pet Shop Boys albums, and, musically, the album is very much of a piece with such latter-day efforts as *Very* and *Bilingual*, which is to say that it relies more on craft than on innovation. Depending on your point of view, this may not be such a bad thing, since the Pet Shop Boys are the masters of subtle craft and masterful understatement. Such skills serve them well when they're essentially following familiar musical territory, which they are on *Nightlife*. At its core, the record is very much like *Very*—a clever, skillful updating of classic disco, highlighted by small contemporary dance flourishes, and infused with a true sense of wit, sophistication, and intelligence. The Pet Shop Boys do this music better than anyone else ever has, and they're at the top of their form here, but it's hard to get beyond the initial impression that they've done this before. Each individual song works beautifully, from the wistfully dejected "I Don't Know What You Want But I Can't Give It Any More" to the exhilarating Village People homage "New York City Boy." But as a whole, *Nightlife* seems less than the sum of its parts, largely due to the familiarity of the music. Repeated listens help erase that impression, since increased exposure to these songs makes them feel like a large part of the group's catalog, but *Nightlife* remains an album that's largely impressive because of its craft and not its inspiration, which ultimately makes it feel like a second-tier album in the groups' catalog. —*Stephen Thomas Erlewine*

## Gilles Peterson

*DJ / Northern Soul, Trip-Hop, Jungle/Drum'N'Bass, Acid Jazz, Funk, Hip-Hop*
Gilles Peterson may be the British equivalent to Motown's Berry Gordy in that these two men were responsible for sounds that changed the face of music history. Raised in South London by French/Swiss parents, Peterson grew up speaking French at home and English everywhere else. At 18, Peterson began DJing around London, ultimately spinning at the now-famous Dingwalls club in Camden. His sets covered the spectrum of urban music, from jazz to funk to soul and back to hip-hop. Out of this Peterson co-founded the Acid Jazz label with some colleagues. The name itself was a joke between northern soul fan Eddie Piller and Peterson, but it soon became the catch phrase for the smooth, hip-hoppin', funk-influenced jazz that spread around the globe as both a sound and fashion. Acid Jazz became home to such artists as Brand New Heavies, Jamiroquai, Mother Earth, and Courtney Pine. At the same time Peterson created compilations not only for his own label, but for Blue Note and Prestige. Peterson's work re-opened the jazz floodgates that seemed lodged shut for so long. While many jazz purists rejected the acid jazz movement, it rekindled an interest in jazz as a whole, keeping it alive in the 25-and-under demographic. Artists like Pharoah Sanders and Roy Ayers came back from obscurity and into the mainstream, largely because of Peterson's work. Peterson expanded his vision by creating the Talking Loud label, which came to include some of England's most innovative drum'n'bass artists like 4-Hero and Roni Size. Teaming up with one-time Talking Loud A&R man and DJ Norman Jay, Peterson's critically acclaimed *Journey by DJs: Desert Island Mix* captured the pair's love and understanding of music history. Two years later, Peterson followed up with a volume in the *INCredible Sound* series of mix albums. He continued to connect artists like Sun Ra to Roni Size to Gang Starr and back to Miles Davis with ease on his internationally syndicated radio shows On Jazz and Kiss FM. —*Ryan Randall Goble*

**JDJ Presents: Desert Island Mix** / Sep. 22, 1997 / JDJ ♦♦♦♦
Some mixes create a mood; the best ones force the listener to pack up their mind and take a journey. Two of the most cultivated ears in all of England, Peterson and Norman Jay, each perform one mind-numbing set on this two-disc masterpiece. Blending the finest rare-groove, hip-hop, Northern soul, jungle, jazz, and every shade in between, these sets ebb and flow with passion. Jay's mix has more of a house flavor, in contrast to Peterson's jazzier explorations. Subtle sounds demarcate every twist and turn of this piece; listen for interesting sprinkles of Herbie Hancock, Average White Band and Sun Ra tastefully flavoring some of their songs. Look out for Jay's wild remix of the Hall and Oates hit "Maneater," the two funky versions of "A Love Supreme," and the ultra-rare track "What's Wrong with Groovin'" by Letta Mbulu on Peterson's mix. For anyone who's never heard these men spin live—this is as close to their musical heaven as you'll get. —*Ryan Randall Goble*

• **INCredible Sound of Gilles Peterson** / Oct. 25, 1999 / Incredible ♦♦♦♦
The Gilles Peterson entry in the *INCredible Sound* series of various artists compilations allows at-home listeners to experience what a set of the DJ's musical choices might be like at one of his club appearances. His approach is amazingly eclectic, managing to include everything from a cover of introspective folky Nick Drake's "River Man" to Minnie Riperton's "Les Fleur" and Pharoah Sanders' "Rejoice." Just looking at the list of selections, you wouldn't think they could work together as a coherent collection, much less get and keep a dancefloor moving. But the key is sequencing: Peterson has a wonderful sense of how one track can flow into another, moving the musical mood 180 degrees without disturbing the listener or abruptly changing the beat. Alterations of the pace are always gradual enough to sustain continuity, yet over the course of the album the music changes styles frequently, incorporating a witty rap on "Your Revolution," Sarah Jones' sexual-denial take-off on Gil Scott-Heron's "The Revolution Will Not Be Televised" that might have been entitled, "Your Revolution Will Not Happen Between These Thighs," before concluding with a flurry of tracks featuring Latin percussion. Peterson is a musical generalist with a much broader sense of what dance music can be than most DJs, especially those in the US, and the result can be heard on this consistently engaging compilation. (*INCredible Sounds of Gilles Peterson* was initially released in the UK in 1999; it was picked up for US release by Epic Records on August 15, 2000.) —*William Ruhlmann*

## PFM

f. 1993
*Group / Electronica, Jungle/Drum'N'Bass, Club/Dance*
Not to be confused with the '70s Italian prog-rock group of the same name, PFM were the source of some of the most popular ambient/intelligent jungle tunes—including "One and Only" and "For All of Us"—during the style's 1995-96 heyday. Pairing hard, rolling amen breaks with warm, fizzing analog melodies and lysergic atmospherics, PFM's best material sits next to early Photek, Peshay, Source Direct, and LTJ Bukem tracks such as "Dolphin Tune," "Stone Killer," and "Music" as spearheading a more listener-friendly style of drum'n'bass, one which has since attracted the widest audience of jungle's many offshoots. The duo of Mike Bolton and Jamie Saker, PFM (longform: Progressive Future Music) were among the earliest artists associated with LTJ Bukem's Good Looking/Looking Good labels, releasing such early tracks such as "Wash Over Me" and "The Western Tune" to great acclaim and helping to solidify the now-prevailing label's characteristic sound. The duo released a few more singles in 1996 before dissolving their relationship with Good Looking in 1997. —*Sean Cooper*

**The Western Tune/Hypnotising [Single]** / 1994 / Good Looking ♦♦♦
• **For All of Us/The Mystics [Single]** / Jun. 3, 1996 / Good Looking ♦♦♦
One of the first of Good Looking's CD-single releases pairing two artists' singles on one disc, PFM's "For All of Us" appears here with Peshay's "The Mystics," with both mining a similar sound: hard, splintering amen breaks and lilting, almost melodramatic analog melodies. Not either artist's best work, but extremely light on the ears nonetheless. —*Sean Cooper*

## PGR (Kim Cascone)

*Producer / Experimental Ambient, Dark Ambient, Ambient Techno*
American composer and sound designer Kim Cascone may be more recognizable in his former role as head of Silent Records, the label he founded in the mid-'80s, but his recordings during the early '90s as PGR, Spice Barons, and Thessalonians plus during the mid-'90s as Heavenly Music Corporation, were equally as visible. A soundtrack composer through the early '80s before striking out on his own, Cascone studied electronic music arrangement and composition formally at the Berklee College of Music in the early '70s before studying in with Dana McCurdy at Manhattan's New School in 1976. Subsequently working as assistant musical supervisor under director David Lynch on both *Twin Peaks* and *Wild at Heart*, Cascone left Hollywood for San Francisco in the mid-'80s to pursue solo composition, forming Silent Records in 1986 after self-releasing his first PGR album, *Silence*. Though far more abrasive and conflicted than much of his later work, PGR's use of texture and compositional chance is a constant through the whole of Cascone's oevre. A number of PGR titles followed, including 1992's *Chemical Bride* and 1995's *The Morning Book of Serpents*, though Cascone later went on to record primarily as Heavenly Music Corporation, releasing the bulk of his work through Silent. Cascone finally left the label in 1996 to pursue design and composition at Headspace, a multimedia company started by Thomas Dolby. Three years later, he reappeared on the recording scene with *Blue Cube*, an album released as himself. [See Also: Kim Cascone, Heavenly Music Corporation] —*Sean Cooper*

**The Chemical Bride** / 1992 / Silent ♦♦♦
Cascone's first major release as PGR includes eight tracks of viscous audio concrete, ranging from the sinister drones of "Headful of Blue Sun" to the slightly less sinister gaseous ambience of "Oceanic & Atmospheric." —*John Bush*

● **The Morning Book of Serpents** / 1995 / Silent ♦♦♦♦
*The Morning Book of Serpents* consists of rare and previously unreleased odds and ends from Kim Cascone's sparse catalog of recordings. While he coyly avoids specifying the instruments he uses, everything sounds like it is done on either guitar or synthesizer, and most of the pieces in this collection function less as music than as sound sculpture—this stuff isn't about melody and harmony, but rather about sound. "Euphoria, Order and Chaos," which dates from the early '80s, sounds like unaccompanied prepared guitar and frankly could have been lifted directly from one of the Fred Frith/Henry Kaiser albums on the Metalanguage label, or from Frith's long-gone and sorely missed *Live in Japan* box set of the same period. That's a high compliment, by the way. The noises Cascone coaxes from his guitar sound like they were produced by contemplative but articulate alien life forms. "Microbes" is three minutes too long at 7:21, whereas "Eight Corners of the Horizon" packs a lot of interest into one minute. "Floods and Chairs" is perhaps the most moving work in this collection: It manages to be atmospheric without being spacy—the dripping water and dark, foreboding chord progression give a tensely urban feel to the piece. Though clearly not for everyone, this really is a remarkable album. —*Rick Anderson*

**A Hole of Unknown Depth** / Feb. 6, 1996 / Silent ♦♦♦♦

## Phats & Small

*Group / Club/Dance, House*
The production team of Phats and Small found much of their success in lending a hand to the European rebirth of disco and progressive house. Brighton, UK, natives Russell Small and Jason Phats gained popularity with the dance singles "Turn Around" and "Feel Good."

Russell began his DJing career at thirteen when he started his own mobile DJ business, being escorted by his father to weddings and parties. Small acknowledges the business did not last because of his dislike of slow ballads and his inability to stop swearing over the mic. Odds against him, Small turned his focus to DJing and house music. How exactly Russell and Jason met, depends on who you ask, though the two have jokingly said they met on a Brighton dancefloor and instantly knew it was a production match made in heaven. The disco driven 1999 release "Turn Around" reached number two in the national charts and was followed closely with the similar "Feel Good." In September of that same year they did several remixes of Earth Wind and Fire's "September" and released it under the title "September '99." Phats and Small are often grouped with other commercial dance artist and long time friend, Fatboy Slim (Norman Cook), as they are both from Brighton and have brought a lot of attention to the English suburb. Phats and Small have brought large numbers to the town with their monthly club night, Mutant Disco, at Brighton's Zap Club. In 1999, Phats and Small released their first full length, *Now Phats What I Small Music*, with the help of singer Big Ben, whose voice is featured on both "Turn Around" and "Feel Good." —*Diana Potts*

● **Now Phats What I Small Music** / Nov. 15, 1999 / Multiply ♦♦
The duo of Jason Phats and Russell Small were responsible for two of clubland's biggest singles in 1999, "Turn Around" and "Feel Good." Their debut album, despite the cheeky title, presents only variations on a form of the filtered disco-cheese present on the singles. As infectious as they are on the radio or dancefloor, Phats & Small's productions just don't work very well for home listening, especially when the same ideas are repeated throughout an album. Still, this may be the best place to get both singles. —*John Bush*

## Phoenecia

f. 1994, Miami, FL
*Group / Electronica, Neo-Electro, Electro-Techno, IDM*
Unlikely heirs to the legacy of Miami hip-hop represented by Maggotron, 2 Live Crew, Tony Butler, and MC A.D.E., beat decomposers Phoenecia combine bass music's boom with the glitchy, angular, digitally processed postelectro of Autechre, RAC, and other artists associated with the British Warp label. Originally releasing music as Soul Oddity, producers Romulo Del Castillo and Joshua Kay formed Phoenecia in 1997, when their sound took a more minimalist turn, focusing on complex percussive figures and fractured rhythms. Preceded by a pair of releases as Jeswa (Kay) and Metic (Del Castillo) for the Miami-based Schematic imprint, Phoenecia's first track appeared on Detroit label Interdimensional Transmissions' *From Beyond* compilation series. "Roba" recalled their Soul Oddity work while stripping out the melody and a good deal of clutter, leaving only the buckingest of robotic beatbox fragments and a squirting, jittering bassline. The *Randa Roomet* EP, their debut proper, appeared through Warp shortly after, and featured four tracks in a more expanded, vaguely dancefloor-ready style. A handful of remix and compilation tracks later appeared through Chocolate Industries, Nature, Alien8, and Schematic, which the pair took over operation of in 1997. [See Also: Soul Oddity] —*Sean Cooper*

● **Randa Roomet [EP]** / Dec. 15, 1997 / Warp ♦♦♦
The first proper release by Soul Oddity side project Phoenecia. The group's debut track, "Roba" (for the "From Beyond" series, on the Interdimensional Transmissions label) introduced a style of sparse, abstract, lo-fi electro similar to tracks the pair have released separately as Jeswa and Metic, among others. "Randa Roomet" is comparatively more straightforward, although the Escher-like layers of clicky percussion and frantic, ricocheting rhythms are still oceans from what you're likely to encounter dancefloors filling up to. Nonetheless, "Thong," the third of this four-track double-pack, is arguably one of the most advanced and accomplished breakdance tunes released since the late '80s. —*Sean Cooper*

**OddJobs [EP]** / Aug. 9, 1999 / Schematic ♦♦
The seven-track *OddJobs* remix EP features two versions from the Phoenecia alias Soul Oddity, as well as one each from a few friends (Richard Devine, Push Button Objects, Takeshi Muto) and compatriots from Detroit (Ectomorph) and England (Autechre). Except for the warped bass shots of PBO's production and the stuttered experimental techno of Richard Devine's, the first Soul Oddity remix is best, with an acid-era siren paving the way for some heavily processed neo-electro. —*John Bush*

## Photek (Rupert Parkes)

b. 1971, Ipswich, England
*Producer / Electronica, Jungle/Drum'N'Bass, Club/Dance*
Though Goldie became the first superstar of jungle, the recordings of Rupert Parkes—as Code of Practice, Aquarius, Studio Pressure, the Truper, and Sentinel, but most famously as Photek—made him an easy pick for the style's most artistic and intelligent producer. Working his way through street-level hardstep (on early productions for Certificate 18 and Street Beats) and airy, sub-aquatic "dolphin" tunes for LTJ Bukem's Good Looking label, Parkes finally arrived at a sound that pushed the bounds of drum'n'bass from the dancefloor into the realm of breakbeat headspace. Unlike most jungle producers, Parkes has never DJed and rarely goes to clubs. His incredibly intricate rhythm programming—often requiring weeks of computer preparation—and the unmissable aura of paranoid menace on recordings such as "The Hidden Camera" and "UFO" exerted quite an influence on the return of dark-style drum'n'bass during the late '90s.

As a teenager, Parkes listened to electro, techno, and hip-hop as well as the more free-form side of jazz and fusion. Thanks to a sampler bought with a £2000 loan from the Trust of the Prince of Wales, he began producing tracks and first appeared on Paul Solomon's Certificate 18 Records with singles as Studio Pressure. He also recorded for Basement (as Sentinel) and Street Beats (the Truper) before initiating a series of 12" singles for his own Photek Records, which gave him credentials and led to releases on Goldie's Metalheadz label and LTJ Bukem's Good Looking, as well as a remix for the Therapy? single "Loose."

After Parkes had released more than 80 tracks of drum'n'bass on half a dozen labels, he was approached by Virgin and signed to a five-album deal with the label's Science imprint (provided he was allowed to continue recording for other independent labels as well). Parkes' first release on Science was *The Hidden Camera* EP, which appeared in May 1996. The second Science single "Ni-Ten-Ichi-Ryu" displayed an increasing interest in applying the lessons of martial arts to his programming (the title is Japanese for "two swords, one technique"). Virgin compiled the latter two releases on 1997's *Risc Vs. Reward*, then released the debut Photek album *Modus Operandi* in September 1997. Much-hyped though little-praised, the album was followed by 1998's *Form & Function*, a compilation including several original Photek Records tracks plus remixes and new tracks. During the next two years, Parkes focused on his new Photek Productions label, and finally released a second LP, *Solaris*, in 2000. —*John Bush*

**The Hidden Camera [EP]** / Jun. 11, 1996 / Science ◆◆◆◆
Photek's first release for the Virgin subsidiary is a nicely packaged double-pack of tight, impeccably produced experimental drum'n'bass not too dissimilar from the material released through his own label. The opener, "KJZ," is the EP's finest track, shuffling along on a fluid layer of crash and ride cymbals and a finely detailed, rubbery acoustic bassline. A pair of mixes of the title track bridge the gap between the two twelves, and the remaining track is a brief throwaway that could've used a bit more development. —*Sean Cooper*

**Risc Vs. Reward** / Jul. 22, 1997 / Astralwerks ◆◆◆◆
Not quite the proper full-length fans had been waiting for, *Risc Vs. Reward* collects the six tracks from his first EP and single for Science ("The Hidden Camera" and "Ni-Ten-Ichi-Ryu") including two mixes of "The Hidden Camera" itself, the slow-motion drum'n'bass arts of the opener "KJZ," and the two sides of his second, "Ni-Ten-Ichi-Ryu" and "The Fifth Column." —*John Bush*

**Modus Operandi** / Sep. 9, 1997 / Astralwerks ◆◆◆◆
After releasing more than one hundred tracks on singles, scattered over half a dozen labels and as many pseudonyms, Rupert Parkes finally issued his first long-player in late 1997, and it seems the lack of time restraints got the better of him. Parkes is near idolized in the jungle underground for his obsession with detail when patterning his breaks, but his take on paranoid drum'n'bass wears out its welcome less than halfway through the album. While electronic artists usually mix up styles on full-lengths to make the lack of song structure less of a liability for home listeners, Parkes seems resistant to diversity (three small exceptions are the Detroit-inspired "Aleph 1" and two downtempo tracks, "124" and the title song). Much of this criticism is the kind leveled at a stellar artist who could (or should) have brought excellent work onto a higher plane altogether, but the fact remains that *Modus Operandi* is a difficult listen, even for fans. —*John Bush*

● **Form & Function** / Sep. 14, 1998 / Astralwerks ◆◆◆◆
The Photek Records label, home to six singles between '95 and 1996, included several of the most stunning drum'n'bass productions ever heard. "Rings Around Saturn," "UFO," "The Seven Samurai," and "The Physical" each take their place as the tracks that made a name for Rupert Parkes in the jungle community. One year after the release of his debut LP, Science/Astralwerks used the collection *Form & Function* to compile those singles for all the fans who'd missed out on all that vinyl-only material. The problem is, *Form & Function* includes only *four* originals from Rupert Parkes' pre-LP 12" output (two are unlisted), substituting instead remixes of several tracks plus two new productions. Sympathetic producers Digital, Peshay, Doc Scott, and J Majik take the scissors to Photek classics "The Lightening," "Rings Around Saturn," "The Water Margin," and "UFO," while Photek remixes his own "The Seven Samurai" and "Resolution." Though there are several excellent productions here, it's all a bit troubling since jungle producers rarely look back to rewrite history. The new tracks, "Knitevision" and "Santiago" almost rescue the proceedings with excellent turns; the former works wonders around an understated bassline and martial-arts programming while the latter features off-kilter snares and offsetting synth. Still, what could have been an essential look at what is arguably the best back catalog in drum'n'bass is transformed into a disappointing remix collection. It's especially a shame, considering the first six singles (A-sides and B-sides) would have fit perfectly onto a 75-minute disc. —*John Bush*

**Solaris** / Sep. 19, 2000 / Astralwerks ◆◆◆◆
Finally released from the artistic pressure and unrelenting hype surrounding his full-length debut (1997's *Modus Operandi*), Photek producer Rupert Parkes moved on to embrace Chicago acid house and minimal techno with his sophomore *Solaris*. Whereas *Modus Operandi* portrayed an artist trapped within the style he'd pioneered (paranoid drum'n'bass), *Solaris* sounds more like an album Parkes actually *wanted* to make (instead of the one his fans expected). Indebted to hard-edged Chicago acid track producers like Adonis and Armando, Parkes constructed brittle, distorted drum-machine breaks (instead of the usual endlessly tweaked skittery breakbeats) and matched them with claustrophobic analog effects, most of which hark back at least a decade or so. Parkes also made the acid house connections direct by enlisting help for two vocal tracks from Chicago institution Robert Owens (Fingers Inc.).

The first Owens track, "Mine to Give," attacks with suprisingly unwavering beats and a rumbling bassline straight out of the Windy City sound of the late '80s. The other Owens contribution, a smooth production named "Can't Come Down," is more reminiscent of Parkes' productions for LTJ Bukem's Good Looking Records (like the atmospheric jungle classic "Pharaoh"). In fact, only one track here ("Infinity") flirts with the drum'n'bass darkside fans and critics had pigeonholed Photek in, though there's an undeniable air of paranoia and menace throughout the album. Near the end, Parkes even salutes the growing legion of experimental-techno producers with a trio of excellent minimalist down-tempo tracks: an ambient isolationist track named "Aura" and two brittle trip-hop productions, "Halogen" and "Almost Blue Heaven" (the latter with vocals from Simone Simone). For better (and occasionally for worse), *Solaris* is just as dense and intensive a package as Photek's previous work. Still, the range of styles points to a more ambitious future. —*John Bush*

## Phuture

f. 1985, Chicago, IL
*Group / Club/Dance, Acid House, House*
Phuture only released a handful of tracks (plus an album a full decade after their debut), but have remained a legendary act in the development of Chicago house for their stomping 1987 single "Acid Trax," the track that began and defined the acid house sound. The group was formed by DJ Pierre, synthesizer fan Spanky, and Herb J in 1985 as a recording entity to produce records for Pierre to mix into his sets at several crucial Chicago clubs. After being turned on to the high-pitched squelch of the Roland TB-303 synthesizer (marketed as a bassline machine for solo guitarists), the trio emerged from the studio with a track they called "In Your Mind." Ron Hardy previewed the song at his legendary club the Music Box—where it became known as "Ron Hardy's Acid Track"—and Phuture re-made the cut with production by Marshall Jefferson. Released on Trax Records in 1987, the single created a dividing point between the Chicago sound before and after it, with hundreds of "Acid Trax" imitations flooding the local market. After it caught on in Britain as well, the single soundtracked the wave of club madness which coalesced in the rave movement by the end of the decade.

Despite recording one single with immense influence on dancefloors around the world, Phuture etched a rocky path during the rest of the '80s. Herb J left after their follow-up single "We Are Phuture," and was replaced by an up-and-coming producer, Roy Davis, Jr. DJ Pierre left several singles later, and was himself replaced by Damon Neloms (aka Professor Trax). The lineup of Spanky, Davis, Jr., and Neloms recorded 1992's "Inside Out" but then the group lay dormant for several years. In 1996, Phuture returned as Phuture 303 (with the addition of L.A. Williams) and released the album *Alpha & Omega* one year later. —*John Bush*

● **Acid Trax [Single]** / 1987 / Trax ◆◆◆◆
Sweeping in on a wave of stark drum programs and atmospherics that sound closer to tape hiss than anything intentional, the 11-minute megalith-on-wax of "Acid Trax" is an incredibly raw cut—witness the plodding four-four beats and lack of a bridge. Still, the superb acid squelch, ripe for the picking by DJs across the world, continued to impress long after the first hundred or so "covers" and answer records flooded the dance racks. —*John Bush*

**We Are Phuture [Single]** / 1988 / Trax ◆◆◆◆

**Rise from Your Grave [Single]** / 1991 / Strictly Rhythm Gold ◆◆◆◆

## Piano Magic

*Group / Ambient Pop, Dream Pop, Indie-Rock*
The experimental pop melancholia of Piano Magic was primarily the work of founder Glen Johnson—the group's sole constant member. He maintained a strict revolving-door roster policy, ensuring that no two recordings or live shows ever featured the same lineup. On the strength of their first demo tape, Piano Magic was signed to the Ché label, issuing their debut single "Wrong French" in 1996 and earning "Single of the Week" honors from *Melody Maker* in the process. "Wintersport" appeared the following year, and the group's third single, the Wurlitzer Jukebox label release "For Engineers," sold out its original pressing within a week. Piano Music's first full-length effort, *Popular Mechanics*, closed out a prolific 1997, with the next year offering split releases with Icebreaker, Matmos, and tourmates Low in addition to *A Trick of the Sea*, their contrbution to Darla Records' ongoing *"Bliss Out"* ambient series. The album *Low Birth Weight*, the group's first release for new label

Rocket Girl, was released in mid-1999, soon followed by the singles "Amongst the Books, An Angel" and "There's No Need for Us to Be Alone." —*Jason Ankeny*

● **A Trick of the Sea: Bliss Out, Vol. 13** / Jul. 13, 1999 / Darla ♦♦♦♦
Darla's monthly *Bliss Out* series continues with Piano Magic's nautically obsessed excursion into strikingly broody waters. Featuring two somnolent 20-minute ambient halves, most of the attention should actually be directed toward the title track. As it drifts through about three or four main phases— melodic mantras, underwater pulses, beat-less cries—its core, grieving vocals by Lucy Gulland punch with the affecting force of a sonic boom. For that reason alone, *Trick of the Sea: Bliss Out, Vol. 13* is surely a quiet masterstroke. A drowned grandeur that is difficult to resist, it seduces you like a mermaid taking you down to the bottom of the ocean to open your lungs to the sea. —*Dean Carlson*

**Low Birth Weight** / Jun. 13, 2000 / Rocket Girl ♦♦♦

## Pink Floyd

f. 1965, London, England
*Group / Multimedia, British Psychedelia, Album Rock, Psychedelic, British Invasion, Prog-Rock/Art Rock*

Pink Floyd are the premier space-rock band. Since the mid-'60s, their music has relentlessly tinkered with electronics and all manner of special effects to push pop formats to their outer limits. At the same time they have wrestled with lyrical themes and concepts of such massive scale that their music has taken on almost classical, operatic quality, in both sound and words. Despite their astral image, the group was brought down to earth in the '80s by decidedly mundane power struggles over leadership and, ultimately, ownership of the band's very name. Since that time, they've been little more than a dinosaur act, capable of filling stadiums and topping the charts, but offering little more than a spectacular recreation of their most successful formulas. Their latter-day staleness cannot disguise the fact that, for the first decade or so of their existence, they were one of the most innovative groups around, in concert and (especially) in the studio.

While Pink Floyd are mostly known for their grandiose concept albums of the '70s, they started as a very different sort of psychedelic band. Soon after they first began playing together in the mid-'60s, they fell firmly under the leadership of lead guitarist Syd Barrett, the gifted genius who would write and sing most of their early material. The Cambridge native shared the stage with Roger Waters (bass), Rick Wright (keyboards), and Nick Mason (drums). The name Pink Floyd, seemingly so far-out, was actually derived from the first names of two ancient bluesmen (Pink Anderson and Floyd Council). And at first, Pink Floyd was much more conventional than the act into which they would evolve, concentrating on the rock and R&B material that was so common to the repertoires of mid-'60s British bands.

Pink Floyd quickly began to experiment, however, stretching out songs with wild instrumental freak-out passages incorporating feedback, electronic screeches, and unusual, eerie sounds created by loud amplification, reverb, and such tricks as sliding ball bearings up and down guitar strings. In 1966, they began to pick up a following in the London underground; onstage, they began to incorporate light shows to add to the psychedelic effect. Most importantly, Syd Barrett began to compose pop-psychedelic gems that combined unusual psychedelic arrangements (particularly in the haunting guitar and celestial organ licks) with catchy melodies and incisive lyrics that viewed the world with a sense of poetic, childlike wonder.

The group landed a recording contract with EMI in early 1967 and made the Top 20 with a brilliant debut single, "Arnold Layne," a sympathetic, comic vignette about a transvestite. The follow-up, the kaleidoscopic "See Emily Play," made the Top Ten. The debut album, *The Piper at the Gates of Dawn*, also released in 1967 and may have been the greatest British psychedelic album other than *Sgt. Pepper's*. Dominated almost wholly by Barrett's songs, the album was a charming funhouse of driving, mysterious rockers ("Lucifer Sam"), odd character sketches ("The Gnome"), childhood flashbacks ("Bike," "Matilda Mother"), and freakier pieces with lengthy instrumental passages ("Astronomy Domine," "Interstellar Overdrive," "Pow R Toch") that mapped out their fascination with space travel. The record was not only like no other at the time; it was like no other that Pink Floyd would make, colored as it was by a vision that was far more humorous, pop-friendly, and light-hearted than those of their subsequent epics.

The reason Pink Floyd never made a similar album was that *Piper* was the only one to be recorded under Barrett's leadership. Around mid-1967, the prodigy began showing increasingly alarming signs of mental instability. Syd would go catatonic onstage, playing music that had little to do with the material, or not playing at all. An American tour had to be cut short when he was barely able to function at all, let alone play the pop star game. Dependent upon Barrett for most of their vision and material, the rest of the group was nevertheless finding him impossible to work with, live or in the studio.

Around the beginning of 1968, guitarist Dave Gilmour, a friend of the band who was also from Cambridge, was brought in as a fifth member. The idea was that Gilmour would enable the Floyd to continue as a live outfit; Barrett would still be able to write and contribute to the records. That didn't work either, and within a few months Barrett was out of the group. Pink Floyd's management, looking at the wreckage of a band that was now without its lead guitarist, lead singer, and primary songwriter, decided to abandon the group and manage Syd as a solo act.

Such calamities would have proven insurmountable for 99 out of 100 bands in similar predicaments. Incredibly, Pink Floyd would regroup and not only maintain their popularity, but eventually become even more successful. It was early in the game yet. The first album had made the British Top Ten, but the group were still virtually unknown in America, where the loss of Syd Barrett meant nothing to the media. Gilmour was an excellent guitarist, and the band proved capable of writing enough original material to generate further ambitious albums, Waters eventually emerging as the dominant composer. The 1968 follow-up to *Piper at the Gates of Dawn*, *A Saucerful of Secrets*, made the British Top Ten, using Barrett's vision as an obvious blueprint, but taking a more formal, somber, and quasi-classical tone, especially in the long instrumental parts. Barrett, for his part, would go on to make a couple of interesting solo records before his mental problems instigated a retreat into oblivion.

Over the next four years, Pink Floyd would continue to polish their brand of experimental rock, which married psychedelia with ever-grander arrangements on a Wagnerian operatic scale. Hidden underneath the pulsing, reverberant organs and guitars and insistently restated themes were subtle blues and pop influences that kept the material accessible to a wide audience. Abandoning the singles market, they concentrated on album-length works, and built a huge following in the progressive rock underground with constant touring in both Europe and North America. While LPs like *Ummagumma* (divided into live recordings and experimental outings by each member of the band), *Atom Heart Mother* (a collaboration with composer Ron Geesin), and *More...* (a film soundtrack) were erratic but each contained some extremely effective music.

By the early '70s Syd Barrett was a fading or nonexistent memory for most of Pink Floyd's fans, although the group, one could argue, never did match the brilliance of that somewhat anomalous 1967 debut. *Meddle* (1971) sharpened the band's sprawling epics into something more accessible, and polished the science-fiction ambience that the group had been exploring ever since 1968. Nothing, however, prepared Pink Floyd or their audience for the massive mainstream success of their 1973 album, *Dark Side of the Moon*, which made their brand of cosmic rock even more approachable with state-of-the-art production, more focused songwriting, an army of well-time stereophonic sound effects, and touches of saxophone and soulful female backup vocals.

*Dark Side of the Moon* finally broke Pink Floyd as superstars in the United States, where it made No. 1. More astonishingly, it made them one of the biggest-selling acts of all time. *Dark Side of the Moon* spent an incomprensible 741 weeks on the *Billboard* album chart. Additionally, the primarily instrumental textures of the songs helped make *Dark Side of the Moon* easily translatable on an international level, and the record became (and still is) one of the most popular rock albums worldwide.

It was also an extremely hard act to follow, although the follow-up, *Wish You Were Here* (1975), also made No. 1, highlighted by a tribute of sorts to the long-departed Barrett, "Shine on You Crazy Diamond." *Dark Side of the Moon* had been dominated by lyrical themes of insecurity, fear, and the cold sterility of modern life. *Wish You Were Here* and *Animals* (1977) developed these morose themes even more explicitly. By this time Waters was taking a firm hand over Pink Floyd's lyrical and musical vision, which was consolidated by *The Wall* (1979).

The bleak, overambitious double concept album concerned itself with the material and emotional walls modern humans build around themselves for survival. *The Wall* was a huge success even by Pink Floyd's standards, in part because the music was losing some of its heavy-duty electronic textures in favor of more approachable pop elements. Although Pink Floyd had rarely even released singles since the late '60s, one of the tracks, "Another Brick in the Wall," became a transatlantic No. 1. The band had been launching increasingly elaborate stage shows throughout the '70s, but the touring production of *The Wall*, featuring a construction of an actual wall during the band's performance, was the most excessive yet.

In the '80s, the group began to unravel. Each of the four had done some side and solo projects in the past, more troublingly, Waters was asserting control of the band's musical and lyrical identity. That wouldn't have been such a problem had *The Final Cut* (1983) been such an unimpressive effort, with little of the electronic innovation so typical of their previous work. Shortly afterward, the band split up—for a while. In 1986, Waters sued Gilmour and Mason to dissolve the group's partnership (Wright had lost full membership status entirely). Waters lost, leaving a Roger-less Pink Floyd to get a Top Five album with *Momentary Lapse of Reason* in 1987. In an irony that was nothing less than cosmic, about 20 years after Pink Floyd shed its original leader to resume its career with great commercial success, they would do the same again to his successor. Waters released ambitious solo albums to nothing more than moderate sales and attention, while he watched his former colleagues (with Wright back in tow) rescale the charts.

Pink Floyd still has a huge fan base, but there's little that's noteworthy about their post-Waters output. They know their formula, they can execute it on a grand scale, and they can count on millions of customers—many of them unborn when *Dark Side of the Moon* came out, and unaware that Syd Barrett was ever a member—to buy their records and see their sporadic tours. *The Division Bell*, their first studio album in seven years, topped the charts in 1994 without making any impact on the current rock scene, except in a marketing sense. Ditto for the live *Pulse* album, recorded during a typically elaborate staged 1994 tour, which included a concert version of *The Dark Side of the Moon* in its entirety. Waters' solo career sputtered along, highlighted by a solo recreation of *The Wall*, performed at the site of the former Berlin Wall in 1990, and released as an album. It was reported in the summer of 1996 that Syd Barrett was lying ill in a Cambridge hospital, unable or unwilling to regulate his diabetic condition. —*Richie Unterberger*

**The Piper at the Gates of Dawn** / Aug. 5, 1967 / Capitol ◆◆◆◆
The title of Pink Floyd's debut album is taken from a chapter in Syd Barrett's favorite children's book, *The Wind in the Willows*, and the lyrical imagery of *The Piper at the Gates of Dawn* is indeed full of colorful, childlike, distinctly British whimsy, albeit filtered through the perceptive lens of LSD. Barrett's catchy, melodic acid-pop songs are balanced with longer, more experimental pieces showcasing the group's instrumental freakouts, often using themes of space travel as metaphors for hallucinogenic experiences—"Astronomy Domine" is a poppier number in this vein, but tracks like "Interstellar Overdrive" are some of the earliest forays into what has been tagged space-rock. But even though Barrett's lyrics and melodies are mostly playful and humorous, the band's music doesn't always bear out those sentiments—in addition to Rick Wright's eerie organ work, dissonance, chromaticism, weird noises, and vocal sound effects are all employed at various instances, giving the impression of chaos and confusion lurking beneath the bright surface. *The Piper at the Gates of Dawn* successfully captures both sides of psychedelic experimentation—the pleasures of expanding one's mind and perception, and an underlying threat of mental disorder and even lunacy. This duality makes *Piper* all the more compelling in light of Barrett's subsequent breakdown, and ranks it as one of the best psychedelic albums of all time. —*Steve Huey*

**A Saucerful of Secrets** / Jun. 29, 1968 / Capitol ◆◆◆
A transitional album on which the band moved from Barrett's relatively concise and vivid songs to spacy, ethereal material with lengthy instrumental passages. Barrett's influence is still felt (he actually did manage to contribute one track, the jovial "Jugband Blues"), and much of the material retains a gentle, fairy-tale ambience. "Remember a Day" and "See Saw" are highlights and on "Set The Controls for the Heart of the Sun," "Let There Be More Light," and the lengthy instrumental title track, the band begins to map out the dark and repetitive pulses that would characterize their next few records. —*Richie Unterberger*

**Ummagumma** / Nov. 1969 / Capitol ◆◆◆
For many years, this double LP/CD was one of the most popular albums in Pink Floyd's pre-*Dark Side of the Moon* output, containing a live disc and a studio disc all for the price of one (in the LP version). The live set, recorded at Mothers, Birmingham, and The Manchester College of Commerce in June 1969, is limited to four numbers, all drawn from the group's first two LPs or their then recent singles. (One would love to know if there was more music played at those shows, and if it was taped, and if the tapes survived.) Featuring the band's second line-up (i.e. no Syd Barrett), the set shows off a very potent group, their sound held together on stage by Nick Mason's assertive drumming and Roger Waters' powerful bass work, which keeps the proceedings moving no matter how spaced out the music gets. They also sound like they've got the amplifiers to make their music count, which is more than the early band had. "Astronomy Domine," "Careful With That Axe Eugene," "Set The Controls For The Heart of the Sun," and "A Saucerful of Secrets" are all superior here to their studio originals, done longer, louder, and harder, with a real edge to the playing that was mostly only suggested in the originals. Even "Astronomy Domine," a product of Syd Barrett's tenure with the original group, is sharper here. David Gilmour's crunchy guitar keeping it a good axe-man's showcase even in the absence of the author, while "A Saucerful of Secrets" from the album of that name is played and sung with a slashing attack throughout its 13 minute length. The studio disc was more experimental, each member getting a certain amount of space on the record to make their own music—Richard Wright's "Sysyphus" was a pure keyboard work, featuring various synthesizers, organs, and pianos. David Gilmour's "The Narrow Way" was a three-part instrumental for acoustic and electric guitars and electronic keyboards and Nick Mason's "The Grand Vizier's Garden Party" made use of a vast range of acoustic and electric percussion devices. Roger Waters' "Grantchester Meadows," a lyrical folk-like number unlike almost anything else the group ever did, was the only part of the studio set that found a lasting place in the group's repertoire, featured on their 1971 tour and in the concert special from the Fillmore West. In 1994 the album was remastered and reissued in a green slipcase, in a version a lot louder and sharper (and cheaper) than the original CD release. The reissue also comes with a poster and recreates the album's original interior and restores the original front cover (the owners of the copyright in the soundtrack to *Gigi*, the album cover which could be seen in the original *Ummagumma* LP cover, had the image on the album jacket airbrushed out after the first pressing—it's back here). —*Bruce Eder*

**Meddle** / Oct. 30, 1971 / Capitol ◆◆◆◆
With *Meddle*, Pink Floyd instrumentally arrived at an airy ensemble sound, which would eventually find full flower on their 1973 classic *The Dark Side of the Moon*. This approach is particularly evident on "Echoes," a periodically languorous jam that takes up one half of the album. Nevertheless, there are enough sonic concepts and pleasant melodies at work on this album to make it worthwhile to the Floyd fan looking to dig deeper than *The Dark Side of the Moon* or *The Wall*. —*Rick Clark*

**Obscured by Clouds** / Jun. 1972 / Capitol ◆◆
Like *More*, *Obscured By Clouds* was a soundtrack album Pink Floyd threw together quickly for a film by Barbet Schroeder. Songs like "Free Four" show Roger Waters developing the songwriting skills that would catapult Pink Floyd to mass stardom with its next new release, *Dark Side of the Moon*. —*William Ruhlmann*

★ **Dark Side of the Moon** / Mar. 24, 1973 / Capitol ◆◆◆◆◆
By condensing the sonic explorations of *Meddle* to actual songs and adding a lush, immaculate production to their trippiest instrumental sections, Pink Floyd inadvertently designed their commercial breakthrough with *Dark Side of the Moon*. The primary revelation of *Dark Side of the Moon* is what a little focus did for the band. Roger Waters wrote a series of songs about mundane, everyday details which aren't that impressive by themselves, but when given the sonic backdrop of Floyd's slow, atmospheric soundscapes and carefully placed sound effects, they achieve an emotional resonance. But what gives the album true power is the subtly textured music, which evolves from ponderous, neo-psychedelic art-rock to jazz fusion and blues-rock before turning back to psychedelia. It's dense with detail, but leisurely paced, creating its own dark, haunting world. Pink Floyd may have better albums than *Dark Side of the Moon*, but no other record defines them quite as well as this one. —*Stephen Thomas Erlewine*

**Wish You Were Here** / Sep. 12, 1975 / Columbia ◆◆◆◆
Pink Floyd followed the commercial breakthrough of *Dark Side of the Moon* with *Wish You Were Here*, a loose concept album about and dedicated to their founding member Syd Barrett. The record unfolds gradually, as the jazzy tex-

tures of "Shine On You Crazy Diamond" reveal its melodic motif, and in its leisurely pace, the album shows itself to be a warmer record than its predecessor. Musically, it's arguably even more impressive, showcasing the group's interplay and David Gilmour's solos in particular. And while it's short on actual songs, the long, winding soundscapes are constantly enthralling. —*Stephen Thomas Erlewine*

**Animals** / Oct. 2, 1977 / Columbia ✦✦✦
Consisting of heavily reworked songs that had long been a part of Pink Floyd's live repertoire and were now given an Orwellian overview, *Animals* found Pink Floyd acting as the mouthpiece for Roger Waters' increasingly vitriolic takes on modern life. The result was one of its less successful later efforts. —*William Ruhlmann*

**The Wall** / Nov. 30, 1979 / Columbia ✦✦✦✦
Roger Waters constructed *The Wall*, a narcissistic, double-album rock opera about an emotionally crippled rock star who spits on an audience member daring to cheer during an acoustic song. Given its origins, it's little wonder that *The Wall* paints such an unsympathetic portrait of the rock star, cleverly named "Pink," who blames everyone—particularly women—for his neuroses. Such lyrical and thematic shortcomings may have been forgivable if the album had a killer batch of songs, but Waters took his operatic inclinations to heart, constructing the album as a series of fragments that are held together by larger numbers like "Comfortably Numb" and "Hey You." Generally, the fully developed songs are among the finest of Pink Floyd's later work, but *The Wall* is primarily a triumph of production—its seamless surface, blending melodic fragments and sound effects, makes the musical shortcomings and questionable lyrics easy to ignore. But if *The Wall* is examined in depth, it falls apart, since it doesn't offer enough great songs to support its ambition, and its self-serving message and shiny production seem like relics of the late-'70s Me Generation. —*Stephen Thomas Erlewine*

## Pizzicato Five

f. 1984, Tokyo, Japan
*Group / Shibuya-Kei, Indie Pop, Alternative Dance, Club/Dance, Alternative Pop/Rock, Dance-Pop*

Godfathers of the Shibuya-kei scene, Tokyo kitsch-pop deconstructionists Pizzicato Five originally began taking shape as far back as 1979, when university students Yasuharu Konishi and Keitaro Takanami first met at a local music society meeting. Agreeing to form a band, they soon recruited fellow society member Ryo Kamamiya; their search for a suitable vocalist proved frustrating, however, and only in late 1984 did they settle on singer Mamiko Sasaki. The first Pizzicato Five single, "Audrey Hepburn Complex," followed a year later, and in 1986 the group issued their debut LP, *Pizzicato Five in Action*. A slew of subsequent records established them among the most popular acts in Japan, in spite of a series of line-up fluctuations which saw both Kamamiya and Sasaki exit in 1988, replaced soon after by vocalist Takao Tajima (who in turn quit the following year). Beginning with the 1990 single "Lovers Rock," Maki Nomiya was the new P5 vocalist. Their popularity at home continued to soar, and in 1994 the American indie label Matador agreed to issue the compilation EP *Five by Five*. Takanami quit shortly after its release, however, reducing the group to a duo. After a pair of other US compilations, *Made in USA* and *The Sound of Music by Pizzicato Five*, in 1997 they issued *Happy End of the World*, the first of their LPs to enjoy simultaneous Japanses and American release. *The International Playboy and Playgirl Record* followed two years later, and the group's last proper album of the millennium, *Pizzicato Five (tm)*, appeared in November 1999. —*Jason Ankeny*

**Couples** / 1987 / CBS/Sony ✦✦
With *Couples*, their first full-length album, Pizzicato Five still struggled to find their identity. As would be their norm, the cover art is quite stylish: a blurry color close-up of a bathroom cup, a tube of toothpaste, and two toothbrushes. This unfocused romanticism is pleasant enough, but the vocals by Mamiko Sasaki and Ryo Kamomiya lack emotion and fail to click with the lush, Burt Bacharach-esque arrangements, making most of them that much sleepier. A few uptempo tracks stand out—"What Now Our Love," "Odd Couple" (which naturally quotes the sitcom theme)—but this effort still falls short of establishing the P5 personality. —*Pat Padua*

**Belissima!** / 1988 / CBS/Sony ✦✦✦
A slogan announces: "People, Let's get stoned with Pizzicato Five!" This is no call to hippie arms but to a stoned soul picnic. After a few false starts, Pizzicato Five changed their lineup, and a more powerful singer makes all the difference on *Belissima!* The album introduces Tajima Takao, "Genius," who makes like a Japanese soul crooner. Where P5's previous singers were stilted, Tajima Takao floats over these Sound of Philadelphia grooves, finally giving P5 the push they needed. Ersatz soul, perhaps, but confident ersatz soul. Their sound is filled out with organ, harmonica, sax, congas, the kind of soul-jazz instrumentation Tajima Takao took with him when he left P5 to form Original Love. But in the second half of the album, his vocals revert to the sleepy woodenness of his predecessors. Ironic, since part of *Couples* would help form the backing track for a song that would help introduce his successor Maki Nomiya, "Baby love child." Still, an auspicious debut, and Pizzicato Five would get even better. —*Pat Padua*

● **Made in USA** / 1994 / Matador ✦✦✦✦
Although it's not billed as such, the group's stateside debut is actually a compilation of tracks from their 15 or so albums. You need a taste for irreverent sampling and ironic deconstruction of lightweight pop idioms to dig this. But within that narrow field, Pizzicato Five are as good as it gets. They devise fare that's both funky and funny, made more human than most such projects by Maki Nomiya's fetching vocals. —*Richie Unterberger*

**Romantique 96** / Sep. 30, 1995 / Triad/Columbia ✦✦✦✦
If *Overdose* was Konishi's tribute to New York, or the New York of his mind, *Romantique 96* is his version of France, a France of the '60s (of course), of Michel Legrand, Serge Gainsbourg, Jean-Luc Godard, and *Last Year in Marienbad*. The music on the album may detour from that path (the rap on "Icecream Meltin' Mellow" or the bizarre Plastics cover "Good") but a majority of the tracks are some of the lushest orchestrations since *Couples*. Singer Maki Nomiya makes good as a chanteuse on "The Awakening," "Triste," and the *trés romantique* "Tokyo, Mon Amour." There's also a touch of melancholia in the lyrics and the melodies are more pronounced here than on other recent albums. The album's other notable track is "Flying High," which marks the major label debut of Fantastic Plastic Machine, who, according to Konishi, rented the track space out like one would rent a room in an apartment. —*Ted Mills*

**The Sound of Music by Pizzicato Five** / Oct. 31, 1995 / Atlantic ✦✦✦✦
The second of Matador's compilations of Pizzicato Five's Japanese releases, with an emphasis on *Bossanova 2001* and *Overdose*. There are a few rarities scattered throughout: "Fortune Cookie," an obscure B-side, and "No. 5," from Readymade Recordings in 1991. The St. Etienne remix of "Peace Music," nine minutes of loops and distortion, unbalances this collection, but most of the selection is cohesive enough to listen to all the way through. —*Ted Mills*

**Happy End of the World** / Sep. 9, 1997 / Capitol ✦✦✦✦
*Happy End of the World* is the first album of entirely new material that Pizzicato Five released in the United States, but it doesn't necessarily represent a great leap forward for the dance-lounge duo. Pizzicato Five continued to blend light '60s pop, '70s disco, and '80s dance with an ironic flair on *Happy End of the World*, but the energy level is turned down a bit. It's a surprisingly laidback album, but that's not necessarily a bad thing—the lush arrangements have an engaging, low-key charm, and the beats are nice and subtle. *Happy End of the World* runs a little too long, and no song stands out as a single, but it's an engaging record that suggests there may be more to the Pizzicato Five than kitsch. —*Stephen Thomas Erlewine*

**Pizzicatomania** / Jun. 30, 1998 / Teichiku/Non Standard ✦✦
*Pizzicatomania!* collects minor remixes of material from Pizzicato Five's first two EPs, *The Audrey Hepburn Complex* and *Pizzicato V in Action*, plus a few more tracks from that era. This set bids farewell to what is actually the group's least golden era, and does little to rescue the slight, uninspired production and singing. "From Party to Party" finds some of the spark that would make their later, eclectic dance-pop so memorable—namely, an infectious beat that resembles at once sleighbells and crickets—but Mamiko Sasaki is too limited a singer to make this rise above the merely cute. Still, they are cute, if not yet transcendently so. —*Pat Padua*

**Playboy & Playgirl** / Aug. 25, 1998 / Matador ✦✦✦
*Playboy and Playgirl* begins with the kind of collage-heavy imagined soundtrack that marked *Happy End of the World*. With that out of the way, they get back to the inspired, eclectic popcraft that is their strength. Hookier and more danceable than their previous album, this is a welcome return to songwriting for the dynamic duo. Think Burt Bacharach without the self-pity, with a

smidgen of Motown and Stax. Keyboard timbres run the gamut of the Pizzicato imagination from faux-harpsichord to spacy funk. Singer Nomiya Maki puts her unpretentious stamp over everything from *Sgt. Pepper's* pomp to '60s R&B horns to symphonic dancefloor beats to introspective pastorals. While P5 may be in with the lounge crowd, they never feel superior to their cheesy predecessors. Avoiding the sometimes smug, reactionary irony of the new exotica, Yasuharu Konishi's diverse influences are held together by his all-embracing slice of the pop spectrum. A joyous record. [Note: *Playboy & Playgirl* was released in Japan in 1998 under the title *The International Playboy & Playgirl Record*. Matador's 1999 American release cuts the third track, "International Pizzicato Five Mansion," and substitutes "La Règle du Jeu" later in the album's running order.] —*Pat Padua*

**Pizzicato Five (tm)** / Nov. 20, 1999 / Columbia ♦♦♦♦
The last Pizzicato Five release of the decade, this 12-track CD is tainted with a little melancholic *fin de siècle*, especially in tracks such as "20th Century Girl" and "Goodbye Baby and Amen," the latter a duet with once-Pizzicato Five lead vocalist Takao Tajima. But other than that, this is typical late-period Yasuharu Konishi, a breathless collage of distorted organ, speed lounge, dense rhythmic pile-ups, even Faust-like metal ("Loudland!"). Only "Wild Strawberries," with its riff stolen from Francoise Hardy, is reminiscent of their sound at the start of the '90s. Nods to the past: Konishi indulges his own fanboy wishes by working with '60s Japanese idol singer Mieko Hirota, letting her sing "Perfect World" in a Spencer Davis Group-type arrangement; Konishi polishes off a song from 1987's *Couples*, "Serial Stories," for Nomiya Maki. An improvement over their previous album. —*Ted Mills*

**Remixes 2000** / May 2, 2000 / Sony International ♦♦♦♦
Tracks from *Pizzicato Five (tm)* and the *Darlin' of Discotheque* EP get the remix treatment from a group of recent Japanese DJs and musicians, a majority of them from Konishi's label. Mansfield's remix of "One Two Three Four Five Six Seven Eight Nine Ten Barbie Dolls" adds some super kitsch swing to the proceedings, while Cubismo Grafico turns "Tout Tout Pour Ma Cherie" into a pop-metal song circa 1979. Konishi adds his own mix, a "Groove Room Suite" that combines "Love Again" with a Mieko Hirota-sung "Darlin' of Discotheque." All the artists seem to be on the same wavelength as the group, resulting in a consistently listenable experience. —*Ted Mills*

## Plaid

f. 1991, London, England
Group / *Electronica, Neo-Electro, Electro-Techno, Ambient Techno, Club/Dance, IDM*

Although Plaid pre-existed the association, the duo's Ed Handley and Andy Turner spent most of their early recording years with third-wheel Ken Downie as the dancefloor-confounding Black Dog Productions. Meshing well with Downie's vision of heavily hybridized post-techno and obscurantist thematics, the pair brought several nascent Plaid tracks to the Black Dog table on the group's debut, *Bytes*, a collection of tracks recorded by various iterations of the three members. The group recorded several albums and EPs throughout the early and mid-'90s, helping to forge a style of dance music one step removed from the 12" considerations of the average faceless techno act. Handley and Turner (whose mutual love for early hip-hop contributed to BDP's more bawdy, street-level grit) split from Downie in 1995, and since then have rechanneled their efforts full-time into their first project, releasing an EP on the neo-electro Clear label before signing to Warp. The pair also recorded an album with European techno figure Mark Broom under the pseudonym Repeat, two tracks of which also made it onto the *South of Market* EP, released on Jonah Sharp's similarly located Reflective imprint. Most of Plaid's material has been issued in the US through Nothing, including the full-length albums *Not for Threes* (1998) and *Rest Proof Clockwork* (1999). In 2000, the pair released *Trainer*, a retrospective including much of their early EP work. —*Sean Cooper*

**Mbuki Mvuki** / 1991 / Black Dog Productions ♦♦♦
Plaid's obviously dancefloor-flavored grooves are heavy on the polyrhythms (their debut is often considered an important stepping stone in the evolution of drum'n'bass). Bantu, according to the group, for "dance so hard you take your clothes off," the album is a Black Dog-esque fusion of many styles, including elements of ambient and Latin jazz. One for the trainspotters until its reissue in 2000 as part of the double-disc *Trainer*. —*Sean Cooper*

**Mind Over Rhythm Meets Plaid on the Planet Luv [EP]** / 1995 / Rumble ♦♦♦
A double-10" of anonymous dancefloor fodder barely recognizable as Plaid (and who the heck are Mind Over Rhythm, anyway?). Half the tracks are billed to Plaid, with the rest either MOR or co-composed tunes. Not worth the effort of tracking down. —*Sean Cooper*

**Android [EP]** / Mar. 1995 / Clear ♦♦♦♦
One of the brighter spots in the Clear catalog is Plaid's collection of heavily percussive neo-electro and drum'n'bass. Released just after the "official" breakup of Black Dog Productions (Ken Downie continues to record under the BDP name), the EP differs from the quirkier Black Dog material in its denser, more cohesive structure and DJ-friendliness. —*Sean Cooper*

**Undoneson [Single]** / Sep. 8, 1997 / Warp ♦♦♦
Plaid's first single for Warp and their first EP-length (though only barely) release of new material under their own name in more than five years. Those pining for the rhythmic complexity of Plaid's work with Ken Downie as Black Dog Productions or of the reissue tracks on the 1995 Clear EP may be disappointed by two-thirds of this one. "Headspin" and the title track, though nicely enough arranged, stick pretty close to loop-and-lock drum programming. Plaid shines, however, in the least likely of places, with melodic and timbral cross-stitching at points stepping into the circle of greatness occupied by BDP's *Spanners* and *Temple of Transparent Balls*. A pleasant (if flawed) return. —*Sean Cooper*

**Not for Threes** / Oct. 13, 1998 / Nothing ♦♦♦♦
Plaid's second full-length release, *Not for Threes*, is separated from its predecessor by one of the most celebrated side trips in electronic listening music's brief but broad history. As members of Black Dog, Ed Handley and Andy Turner (together with Ken Downie) helped set the standard for experimental techno, bringing a daring range of influences together in a space consistently characterized by quality and innovation. As such, great things were expected of *Threes*, and with a couple exceptions, the pair deliver. Although treading far closer than any Black Dog material ever did to the sort of pop electronica of Plaid's interim work with Bjork (who appears here on the gorgeous "Lilith"), *Threes* is ambitious on different terms, moving from the abused and distorted breaks of "Extork" and "Prague Radio" to a balanced radio-friendliness that never sacrifices ingenuity for ease. A handful of tracks feature vocals throughout, and while the results had the predictable effect of irritating BD purists, they actually work remarkably well (partly because the tracks contain absolutely no trace of compositional compromise). A few of the tracks ("Headspin," "Abla Eedio," the too-brief "Seph") sit easily beside the very best Black Dog. —*Sean Cooper*

**Peel Sessions [EP]** / Apr. 20, 1999 / Nothing ♦♦♦

**Rest Proof Clockwork** / Jun. 21, 1999 / Warp ♦♦♦♦
On the surface, Plaid's second full-length charts similar territory as their debut, with the same intriguing mix of old-school flow and electronic programming clout, plus an odd tendency to play with certain synth presets — steel drums, for instance — that would make most electronica technicians cringe. True, there's a bit more hip-hop flavor on this one, like the faux turntablism on the excellent tracks "Shackbu" and "Little People." And the novelty angle Plaid have occasionally nodded to in the past is out on two tracks especially: the vocoderized bossa-nova number "New Bass Hippo" and "Dang Spot," the kind of popcorn electronica that harks back to Perrey & Kingsley. When it comes down to it, the technical differences between *Rest Proof Clockwork* and Plaid's debut *Not for Threes* are minimal. Still, there's a certain soul to this album that displays the maturing ex-breakdancers progressing even after more than ten years of recording. In fact, two of the most beautiful tracks of Plaid's long career are right here. The first is "Buddy," a yearning downtempo track with echoing effects; the second is "Dead Sea," a beatless piece of glorious synth-strings which evoke past civilization just as achingly as "The Crete That Crete Made" (from *Temple of Transparent Balls*, the 1993 album by Handley and Turner's former concern, the Black Dog). So, in sum, *Rest Proof Clockwork* is yet another production masterpiece to file on the shelf with the rest of Plaid's work. The element that puts them far, far ahead of every other beatminer out there is a growing sense of spirit that lets the machines do the singing. —*John Bush*

★ **Trainer** / 2000 / Warp ♦♦♦♦
After negotiations broke down between former Black Doggers Ken Downie,

Ed Handley, and Andy Turner, what was projected to be a three-disc set with nearly all the existing Black Dog Productions rarities became instead a two-disc set of Handley/Turner productions recorded during the first half of the '90s. *Trainer* is still a near-essential document of early British techno, including a raft of rarely heard classics like "Scoobs in Columbia," "Norte Route," and "Angry Dolphin," plus the entirety of their ultra-rare *Mbuki Mvuki* mini-LP. The Handley/Turner production aesthetic balanced sublime, Detroit-inspired synth with hyper-kinetic drum programs and breakbeat madness years before England's love affair with jungle. Grabbing tracks from far-flung but like-minded labels like ART, Planet E, A13, and Clear, *Trainer* includes over two hours of warped acid house from a B-boy perspective—it's hardly a coincidence that Black Dog Productions shared initials with South Bronx's finest. —*John Bush*

## Planet Patrol

f. 1982, New York, NY, **db.** 1984
*Group / Electro, Urban, Funk, Dance-Pop*
Produced and organized by early hip-hop impresarios Arthur Baker and John Robie, Planet Patrol walked an intriguing line between electro and the classic Motown sound. The quintet of vocalists (led by Herb Jackson) only produced one album, but it is one of the few classic LPs of the electro era. —*John Bush*

• **Planet Patrol** / Dec. 1983 / Twenty One ♦♦♦♦
This early-'80s collection of Arthur Baker and Afrika Bambaataa's groundbreaking hip-hop creations has some Todd Rundgren and Gary Glitter covers thrown in for spice. Electro-funk at its best. —*John Floyd*

## Planetary Assault Systems (Luke Slater)

*Producer / Club/Dance, Techno*
Even while productions under his own name have explored electro and listening techno, Luke Slater's Planetary Assault Systems guise remained the home for his productions closest to the percussive, banging techno he produced during the early '90s. The alias began quite early too, with a series of four *Planetary Funk* EPs recorded for Peacefrog during 1992-94 (collected on 1995's *Archives*). His first full-length under the guise, *Electric Funk Machine*, appeared in 1997 and was followed one year later by *The Drone Sector*. [See Also: Luke Slater] —*John Bush*

**Archives** / Feb. 5, 1995 / Peacefrog ♦♦♦♦
*Archives* features nine tracks from Slater's *Planetary Funk* EP series, including a raft of sleek hard techno classics ("Booster," "In From the Night," "Starway Ritual") as well as (slightly) more atmospheric cuts ("Twighlight," "Flightdrop"). —*John Bush*

**Electric Funk Machine** / Feb. 3, 1997 / Peacefrog ♦♦♦♦

• **The Drone Sector** / Nov. 9, 1998 / Peacefrog ♦♦♦♦
Slater's second full album as Planetary Assault Systems is bookended by five tracks of trademarked tough-as-nails phased techno, akin to his early work. The three downtempo productions in between ("You Thought It," "Jay Track One," and the beatless "Long Lost") lift *The Drone Sector* to a higher plane altogether, showing Slater with a knack for atmospherics that's just as impressive as the energy of his straight-ahead tracks. —*John Bush*

## Plastikman (Richard Hawtin)

b. Jun. 4, 1970, Danbury, England
*Producer, DJ / Minimal Techno, Experimental Techno, Electronica, Ambient Techno, Acid Techno, Club/Dance, Techno, Ambient*
His style formed by a fusion of the barest acid-house and straitjacket-tight Detroit techno, Richie Hawtin became one of the most influential artists in the world of techno during the '90s, even while sticking to out-of-date synth dinosaurs like the Roland TB-303 and TR-808. Hawtin combined lean percussion and equally spare acid lines into haunting techno anthems which kicked with more than enough power for the dancefloor while diverting headphone listeners as well. While even his early recordings were quite minimalistic, he streamlined the sound increasingly over the course of his recording career. From the early '90s to the end of the decade, Hawtin's material moved from the verge of the techno mainstream into a yawing abyss of dubbed-out echo-chamber isolationism, often jettisoning any semblance of a bassline or steady beat. Hawtin released material on his own +8 Records under several aliases—some in tandem with co-founder John Acquaviva—and made the label one of the best styled in Detroit techno of the '90s. He earned his pedigrees from worldwide fans of techno for his best-known releases, as Plastikman (for NovaMute) and F.U.S.E. (for Warp/TVT).

While original Detroit technocrats like Juan Atkins and Derrick May were changing the face of electronic music in the mid-'80s, Richie Hawtin was growing up across the river in Windsor, Ontario. A British native, born in 1970, he moved to Canada with his family at the age of nine. Introduced to '70s electronic/minimalist pioneers Kraftwerk and Tangerine Dream by his father (who was a robotics engineer for General Motors), Hawtin began DJing at the age of 17—as DJ Richie Rich—and soon landed gigs at Detroit hotspots like the Shelter and the famed Music Institute, home to all-night club sessions led by May and Kevin Saunderson. Though many of Motown's innovators were skeptical of the skinny white Canadian, Richie Hawtin's formation of +8 Records helped deflect much of the criticism.

Hawtin and +8's co-founder, John Acquaviva, began working together in 1989, originally to make a Derrick May megamix for use on the radio. They later emerged from Acquaviva's studio with several original recordings. The duo issued one single, "Elements of Tone" as the first release on +8 Records (credited to States of Mind), and sat back while many in the techno world puzzled over who was responsible. The label's later releases—by Kenny Larkin, Jochem Paap (aka Speedy J) and Mark Gage (aka Vapourspace) in addition to various Hawtin/Acquaviva projects—made the label famous for laboratory-precise techno based on slowly evolving and shifting acid lines. The aggressive sound matched the work of the label/artist collective Underground Resistance as the best techno to come out of Detroit in the early '90s, thanks to a slow-down in the work of past masters Atkins, May, and Saunderson. Demand grew at the same time for Hawtin's excellent acid-inspired DJing.

The Plastikman project debuted in 1993 with two releases for +8—the seminal "Spastik" single and an album, *Sheet One*. Hawtin's first wide release, however, came with the alter-ego F.U.S.E. (short for Further Underground Subsonic Experiments). A more varied and melodic project than Plastikman (but not by much), F.U.S.E. released the album *Dimension Intrusion* for the British Warp Records in late 1993. As part of the label's *Artificial Intelligence* series, *Dimension Intrusion* was also licensed to Wax Trax!/TVT for release in America. (Hawtin joined such ambient techno heroes as the Aphex Twin, Black Dog, Autechre, and B12, all receiving their wide-issue debuts.) Later, NovaMute signed an agreement with +8 and another Hawtin-founded label, Probe; *Sheet One* was reissued in 1994, followed by the second Plastikman LP, *Musik*. Much more restrained than *Sheet One*, the album fit in well with the growing ambient techno movement. All told, Hawtin was responsible for the release of three albums and a good sized EP in the span of just one year.

That impressive schedule was shattered in 1995, when Hawtin was entangled in difficulties resulting from a sudden crackdown on his usual procedure of crossing the American border to perform. Refused entrance for more than a year, he lost his inspirational grounding with the Detroit scene and found it difficult to continue recording for his third Plastikman album, *Klinik*. While he waited for re-entry, Hawtin spent time setting up the sublabel Definitive, and continued to DJ around the world. Though he recorded scattered singles for +8 and related imprints, his only full-length release that year was an excellent entry in the *Mixmag Live!* series, taken from a DJ set recorded at the Building in Windsor. By the time he was able to return to America, he had changed his musical direction and eventually abandoned the *Klinik* album.

Hawtin returned in 1996 to his release schedule; during each month of the year, he issued a completely unadorned single recorded as Concept 1 (some were later collected on *Concept 1 96:CD*, mixed by Hawtin). Desperately minimal works, even compared to his earlier material, the singles showed Hawtin's reaction to the new-school of barely there techno coming from German labels like Basic Channel, Chain Reaction, Profan, and Studio 1—all of them originally influenced in no small way by Plastikman recordings. Finally, in early 1998, he released his third Plastikman LP, *Consumed*, which proved to be just as brutally shadowed as the Concept 1 material. The continued experimentalist direction showed Hawtin coming full circle, back to his position on the leading edge of intelligent techno. Many of the unreleased *Klinik* recordings surfaced in late 1998 on the compilation *Artifakts [BC]*. [See Also: F.U.S.E., Richie Hawtin] —*John Bush*

**Sheet One** / 1993 / Nova Mute ◆◆◆◆
One of the first records to turn the 303 acid box upside down from glorious high to isolationist low, Plastikman's first album focuses on laser-precise minimalist rhythms to drive a series of echo-box acid lines that gradually acquire power over the course of the album's lengthy album tracks like the ten-minute "Drp," "Glob," and "Plasticine." —*John Bush*

★ **Musik** / Nov. 8, 1994 / Plus 8 ◆◆◆◆◆
Richie Hawtin didn't just produce full-length albums; his albums were conceptual pieces that flowed from one track to the next with smooth continuity—from a strange audio experiment in sparse, symmetrically designed drum programming to epic electronic trips fueled by swarms of tapping percussion and haunting, lifelike acid sounds. Similar to other Plastikman albums such as *Consumed*, the beginning and end of *Musik* are simply amazing in the epic scope of their cinematic exercises in computerized funk, while the middle of the album consists of short, strange experiments in mood, tone, and shape. The first two tracks, "Konception" and "Plastique," take up nearly 20 minutes of the album with their relentless, percussive electro rhythms and shrieking, alien-sounding electronic melodies. From there things get a bit slow-paced and at times dull, as Hawtin drops musical ideas rather than progressive songs. But just when things get a bit too experimental for pleasure, Hawtin concludes the album with two of the mind-encompassing sort of tracks that have propelled the name Plastikman beyond connotations of an avant-garde composer to the stature of artistic genius. Not only can he impress you with his theories, but he can also sweep your feelings away on his epic audio excursions into inhuman sensory overload. —*Jason Birchmeier*

**MixMag Live!, Vol. 20: Plastikman** / 1995 / Mixmag ◆◆◆◆
Though recorded in the studio rather than at an actual live performance, *Mixmag Live!* comes close to being the equivalent of a shortened version of Hawtin's all-night performances. Consisting of 22 tracks—including a few signature tracks—*Mixmag Live!* clocks in at nearly an hour, as Hawtin gives each track only a short moment before adding the next, often overlapping multiple tracks. At times the results are mind-blowing, as only the most knowledgeable listener can distinguish one from another, when multiple tracks are layered, or when the next track enters. The abundance of thumping bass beats and body-moving rhythm will surely please listeners who view techno as a means to dancing, but it may be a little too sensory-overloading for listeners accustomed to the calming sounds of other Plastikman albums, such as *Consumed* or *Musik*. The highlight of the album comes about a third of the way through, when Hawtin drops a montage of percussive symmetry with the trilogy of 909-driven tracks from the early '90s, "Spastik," "Spaz," and "Helikopter." —*Jason Birchmeier*

**Consumed** / May 18, 1998 / Nova Mute ◆◆◆◆
After achieving global fame in the techno world with his previous albums, intense live performances, and legendary Detroit parties, Richie Hawtin's first full-length Plastikman release in years shocked many listeners with its move toward the depths of minimal ambience. In form and structure the music on *Consumed* doesn't deviate much from Hawtin's previous Plastikman album, *Musik*. What differs are the sounds and technique applied to these forms and structures. Nearly every sound on *Consumed* registers in the lowest bass frequencies, except for the barely audible synths hovering, shadowlike, far behind the wall-shaking basslines. The album retains the ability to submerge listeners with its continuity, motifs, and overall tone but never claims to be dance music. One track slowly merges with the next while the emotional tone instilled by Hawtin never wavers from consuming, contemplative alienation. The beginning two tracks ("Contained" and "Consume") and the concluding two ("Inside" and "Consumed") demand notice with their epic scope and emotional radiation. Sandwiched between these heavy tracks rest some shorter variations of the deep, minimal bass executions of German artists such as Maurizio and the Chain Reaction camp. Some were upset by the sedate feel of this album, but most acknowledged its status as a highly personal album evoking an impressive aura of poetic realization. —*Jason Birchmeier*

**Concept 1 96:CD** / Jun. 30, 1998 / M_nus ◆◆◆◆
Over the course of a year, Richie Hawtin released a 12-volume set of records—one every month—known as the *Concept* series. *Concept 1 96: CD* collects 15 of the compositions from these now hard-to-find records. Unlike the material Hawtin releases as Plastikman and FUSE, this album focuses entirely on the cognitive rather than the physical or sensory side of electronic dance music. Each of these tracks arrange and manipulate electronically produced sounds as an abstract expressionist painter would treat a canvas. Through the use of deep bass frequencies, Hawtin's sounds sometimes come to life, becoming tangible as they rattle the interior of one's home or creep down one's spine. Among other strange characteristics, the tracks aren't named but rather numbered. Outside of their running time and shape, differentiating the 15 tracks becomes a bit difficult, since many of the songs share the same sonic attributes, and also because there are multiple tracks named "Four," "Five," "Eight," "Eleven," and "Twelve." Rather than speaking individually about the separate tracks, it's better to think of them as separate components, in a whole, that is the audio equivalent of a sensory-altering installation art exhibit. As artistic expression, this collection bursts from the seams with interesting ideas, but may be too devoid of melody and rhythm for many. —*Jason Birchmeier*

**Artifakts [bc]** / Nov. 2, 1998 / NovaMute ◆◆◆◆
A consuming inhuman atmosphere of computerized drum convulsions and eerie, yet relaxing, synthesized strings establish the foundation to *Artifakts (bc)*—the leftover remnants of an abandoned Plastikman album known as *Klinik*. Each song becomes more and more complicated before slowly subtracting each layer of complication, then drifting into the next song's construction. Outside of the smooth continuity of the opening three down-tempo tracks—that foreshadow the ambient sound Hawtin would move to on *Consumed*—the remainder of the album consists of quite different tracks. "Hypokondriak" and "Skizofrenik" expand the use of excessive percussion of his classic track "Spastik," and then later on the *Sickness* EP. Unfortunately, these two songs aren't very listenable, and some may even find them unbearable. Two other tracks, "Rekall" and "Are Friends Electrik?," deserve recognition as quite possibly the two best on the album. Though *Artifakts (bc)* doesn't possess the continuity or consistent motifs of other Plastikman albums such as *Consumed* or *Sheet One*, the songs themselves are of high quality and worth experiencing. —*Jason Birchmeier*

## Rob Playford

b. Hertfordshire, England
*Producer, DJ / Jungle/Drum'N'Bass*

Rob Playford has been referred to as "the busiest man in jungle," and has probably had his hands in more aspects of the business, art, and culture of hardcore and drum'n'bass than any other single person. A DJ, recording artist (2Bad Mice, Kaotic Chemistry, Metalheads), label owner (Moving Shadow), and ultra-visible dance music proponent, Playford, like Goldie, Grooverider, and DJ Hype, has been a staple on the hardcore scene since it traded its helium-shrill vocal samples and rave whistles for chopped-up breaks and thunderous basslines in the early part of the '90s. An important catalyst of jungle's post-rave growth spurt, Playford's 2Bad Mice project helped push breakbeat beyond its rave trappings, and, with Moving Shadow as his engine, has played a crucial role in supporting jungle's growth as an autonomous art form.

A native of Hertfordshire (just north of London), Playford DJed house and techno through the late-'80s height of the acid house movement, following the music into its harder element at decade's turn. He self-released his own track, "Orbital Madness," and became a touch point for young artists and bedroom producers seeking advice on how to break into the scene. Rather than continuing to funnel talent to other labels, however, Playford formed Moving Shadow in 1990 (assisted by a "how-to" book on running a small business), both to release his own material and those of up-and-coming hardcore artists such as Blame, Mixrace, Flytronix, Danny Breaks (as Hyper On Experience), and Earth Leakage Trip. Initially selling records out of the trunk of his car, the steady growth of the hardcore and jungle scenes, as well as the consistent quality of the music finding its way to Moving Shadow, meant the label quickly became a full-time commitment.

Moving Shadow's early catalog was dominated by Playford-related projects, including 2Bad Mice, the influential trio Playford formed in 1991 with Sean O'Keefe and Simon Colebrooke. They released a number of club hits through the early '90s (including "Waremouse"), and are widely credited with releasing the first serious glimpse of drum'n'bass in 1992's massive "Bombscare." One of Moving Shadow's first chart successes, "Bombscare" charted in both the UK (No. 43) and the US (No. 23) and has sold through a number of pressings, reissues, and remixes. Playford's other main musical venture—Metalheads (the artist, not the label), together with Goldie—have released a number of singles, including the massive hit "Inner City Life," arguably one of the most crucial moments in jungle's crossover to widespread acceptance. The pair also worked together on Moving Shadow's much-hyped 100th release, titled simply "The Shadow" and billed to Playford, Goldie, and Dominic Angus (of MS's Dom & Roland). The Metalheads tag has also been attached to a number of remixes, including post-Happy Mondays group Black Grape and the soundtrack for *Mission: Impossible*. Playford also engineered on Goldie's full-length debut, *Timeless*.

Moving Shadow's incessant drum'n'bass PR extended in the mid-'90s to a series of regional compilations (including *Storm from the East* and *Transcentral Connection*), and the label has increasingly pushed the full-length format, with albums by Omni Trio, Foul Play, and E-Z Rollers all appearing. The label's stable has also grown to one of the most solid and acclaimed on the current scene, with new-crop artists such as Ed Rush, Dom & Roland, and Technical Itch all signing on. A reissue label, Re-Animate, was established in 1996, and MS's publishing arm has handled licensing for such popular UK TV shows as *Eastenders* and *Father Ted*. In addition to the success of his label and recording projects, Playford was also the recipient of a special award for outstanding industry contributions at the 1996 UK hardcore awards. —*Sean Cooper*

● **The Shadow [EP]** / 1997 / Moving Shadow ◆◆◆
The much to-do'd 100th 12" release on Playford's Moving Shadow label was this collaboration with Goldie and Dominic Angus. Accompanied by two other remix twelves (featuring Dom & Roland and Underworld), "The Shadow" is competent, though by no stretch monumental stuff, and a couple notches below the stew one might expect from these chefs' combined kitchens. —*Sean Cooper*

**Shadow (Remix)** / Aug. 11, 1997 / Moving Shadow ◆◆

## Plug (Luke Vibert)

*Producer / Drill'N'Bass, Experimental Jungle, Electronica, Jungle/Drum'N'Bass, Club/Dance*

Luke Vibert, who had previously provided the links between trip-hop and the intelligent/ambient wing with material recorded as Wagon Christ, did the same to jungle/drum'n'bass with his releases as Plug. During 1995-96, long before notable gear-heads began experimenting with breakbeats, Vibert released three EPs of rangy, schizoid drill'n'bass for the British label Rising High. Later in 1996, the Plug LP *Drum'n'bass for Papa* appeared on Blue Planet. One year later, Nothing/Interscope—the label headed by Nine Inch Nails' Trent Reznor—gave it an American release and Vibert remixed a NIN single as well. Perhaps fearing a potential breakthrough in the States, Vibert returned to the Wagon Christ alias in 1998 [See Also: Wagon Christ, Luke Vibert] —*John Bush*

**Plug 1 [Single]** / 1995 / Rising High ◆◆
Released at the height of Wagon Christ-mania (such as it was), Plug's identity remained a mystery until sweating trainspotters with the Next Big Thing on their minds forced the issue. Four tracks of goofed-out cut'n'slash drum'n'bass, with the emphasis on reworked jazz clichés and over-the-top rhythmic manipulation. —*Sean Cooper*

**Plug 2 [Single]** / 1995 / Rising High ◆◆
More of the same in this series, with the drum patterns even more complex and the ersatz-jazz-tweak aesthetic best exemplified (in word and deed) by the b-side's three mixes of "Cheesy." The approach begins to wear on repeat listenings, although the effects-driven percussion arrangements never cease to force a smile. —*Sean Cooper*

**Plug 3 [Single]** / 1996 / Rising High ◆◆
Kettle drums and West Coast g-funk number among Vibert's passions on his third Plug outing. A hairless jazz-derived than some of his earlier material and probably meant equally for DJs as for armchair junglists. The beat chopping is more restrained, with more than a passing glance given to development and flow. —*Sean Cooper*

**Plug 1 & 2 [EP]** / Jul. 15, 1996 / Plug ◆◆◆
This reissue inexplicably lops off a pair of tracks, but the double-pack format makes for handy storage (and a lower price!) for these crucial, sought-after tracks. —*Sean Cooper*

**Drum'n'bass for Papa** / Jul. 29, 1996 / Blue Planet ◆◆◆◆
Vibert tones down the dime-store jazz cheese for his first Plug long-player, opting for a subtler, far more enjoyable brand of weirdness. Although not as immediately satisfying as his earlier Plug work, Vibert's attention to detail and skill for tying together loose ends—from tablas and sitars to chimey children's-book melodies and sprangy timestretched beats—is expert. It's still drum'n'bass, but, like the best of his earlier twelves, it's also much more than that. —*Sean Cooper*

★ **Drum'n'bass for Papa/Plug 1, 2 & 3** / Sep. 9, 1997 / Nothing/Interscope ◆◆◆◆◆
The double-disc Americanized version of *Drum'n'bass for Papa* resequenced and remixed the original album and added an entire hour's worth of Plug rarities for the second disc. The extra inclusions are virtually each track from the first three Plug singles (recorded before the album and originally released on Rising High). The material from the EPs is quite similar to and definitely up to the level of the LP's quality, perhaps concentrating more on Vibert's experimental streak and his roots in hip-hop. There are a few more old-school vocal samples, downtempo breakdowns in the middle of tracks, and even more of a focus on production than on the original *Drum'n'bass for Papa*. For American listeners, the two-disc set is a no-brainer and overseas buyers might even consider ordering the import. —*John Bush*

## Pluramon

f. 1995, Cologne, Germany
*Group / Experimental Dub, Experimental Techno, Experimental Electro, Ambient Techno, Post-Rock/Experimental*

"Post-rock" as a fusion of the instrumentation and song structures of rock 'n' roll with those of a range of more commercially marginal styles such as dub, ambient, techno, and Kraut-rock has been asserted primarily to be an American phenomenon, an assertion usually supported by reference to groups such as Tortoise, Labradford, Jessamine, Rome, and others associated with Chicago's Kranky and Thrill Jockey labels. But while many of those groups have been instrumental in propogating the style to a wider audience, English and European artists such as Stereolab, Broadcast, Circle, and Kreidler have seen to some of the post-rock picture's more innovative brushstrokes. Marcus Schmickler's Pluramon project is best heard in this context. A sort of collaborative orchestra assembled from bits and bobs of freeform acoustic/analog and hard disk sessions, Schmickler's group has achieved some of the more remarkable hybrids of standard guitar/drums/bass, abstract electronics, and nontraditional instruments. Where dub tends to surface as the organizing principle of much American post-rock, Pluramon's music seems informed by far broader timbral and organizational perspectives.

Based in Cologne, Pluramon was formed by Schmickler in 1995. Although the focus of the project was in counterpoint to the heavily sample-based post-techno of his then-recent solo work *Onea Gako*, the desire to fuse acoustics and electronics in contexts geared toward the exploration of new musical forms stretched back to his work in the early '90s with two groups, Pol and Kontakte (whose releases appeared on French label Odd Size). Both groups were heavy on guitars, acoustic drums, and wind instruments and paired live, sometimes improvisational sessions with subsequent treatments and electronic overdubs. Pol and Kontakte also provided some of the contributors that would be absorbed by Pluramon, including Georg Odijk (founder of the A-Musik label and record shop) and Frank Dommert (another A-Musik local and a schoolmate of Schmickler's).

Pluramon's first release, the full-length *Pickup Canyon*, was released in 1995 by Mille Plateaux, sublabel of German techno juggernaut Force Inc. A heady, filmic fusion of electronic atmospheres, disembodied guitar, and sparse, wafting percussion, *Canyon* was widely lauded as one of the most original rearticulations of the '70s German Kraut-rock movement associated with Can, Neu, Amon Düül, and others. (That the record also included a brief appearance by former Can drummer Jaki Liebezeit brought the point home with a certain force.) But the group's strongest statement of solidarity with the Kraut-rock tradition was made with its follow-up album, finally released in 1998, again by Mille Plateaux. *Render Bandits* was a much more full-blown fusion of Canesque musical structures and bizarre sonic interventions tracing to sources both acoustic (including instruments such as glockenspiel, picadongs, and nickel strings) and electronic (broad use of effects and digital sound processing, echoing Schmickler's intervening solo work, *Wabi Sabi*, released by A-Musik in 1997). Two years later, in mid-September, *Bit Sand Riders* was released on Mille Plateaux [See Also: Marcus Schmickler] —*Sean Cooper*

**Pickup Canyon** / Jul. 1, 1996 / Mille Plateaux ◆◆◆
A vague, sparse, sketchbook study of structured electro-acoustics featuring

ambling guitar arrangements, nonspecific electronic textures, and, on at least one track, the calming pulse of former Can drummer Jaki Liebezeit. An interesting collection of songs clearly informed by standard rock structures, but still sounding (thankfully) nothing like rock. —*Sean Cooper*

• **Render Bandits** / Jun. 8, 1998 / Mille Plateaux ♦♦♦♦
Like its predecessor, *Pickup Canyon*, Pluramon's second effort seems quite focused on getting only just close enough to any one genre to suggest an affiliation before quickly retreating into a haze of other stimuli. *Render Bandits* turns that haze into a dust storm at points, with a sometimes daunting buzz of electronics and blasted acoustic treatments nearly (that is to say, not quite) obliterating the music's sturdy rhythmic foundation. A much fuller-bodied recording is the result, with tracks such as "Tel Bell," "Syth," and "Hintergrund" matching the very best of far more widely lauded post-rockers such as Tortoise. —*Sean Cooper*

## Pole (Stefan Betke)

*Producer / Experimental Ambient, Experimental Dub, Experimental Techno, Electronica, Ambient Techno, Techno, IDM*

Although you won't find his name in their catalog, Stefan Betke has been closely associated with the Berlin-based Basic Channel label and BC artists such as Maurizio, Monolake, and Vainqueur. Like those artists' bassy, dub-laden reductions of techno and house, Betke's work (appearing so far on the Kiff SM and Din labels under the name Pole) has been all about doing more with less. Snaps, clicks, crackles, and smudgy bass atmospheres occupy the whole of Pole 12"s such as "Tanzen" and "Raum Eins/Raum Zwei," as well as Betke's aptly titled series of CD releases issued by Kiff and distributed to American audiences by Matador. Where most Basic Channel releases cling fearlessly to the throbbing momentum of 4/4 minimalism, Betke draws complex, intricate rhythms from the crisp analog haze, layering rich, ghosted melodies over multitracked tape hiss and a barrage of syncopated skips and stutters. Betke's tracks thus share more with off-kilter Colognese such as Oval, Mouse on Mars, and Kandis than with his implied colleagues at Basic Channel studios. Still, his music retains the stark emptiness of Berlin post-techno, though it's far more interesting (and far less dance-friendly) than the comparison might suggest. Betke's nom de plum derives, as usual, from a sound-processing device, the Waldorf 4 Pole-Filter, from which issue the strained creaks and crackles that identify his music. —*Sean Cooper*

### Raum Eins/Raum Zwei [Single] / May 4, 1998 / Din ♦♦♦
Basically two versions of the same track, Betke's debut 12" is a strong, simple statement of the Pole aesthetic. Forging an uncanny alliance between gorgeous ambient, minimal techno, and abstract electronic dub, these tracks move—through swift, progressive stages—into a kind of bubbly, immersive stasis. —*Sean Cooper*

• **1** / Jul. 27, 1998 / Kiff SM ♦♦♦♦
Stefan Betke's nine variations on damaged dub minimalism recall the best of Basic Channel techno while steering well clear of the monotony factor. As with Pole's first singles, these tracks materialize out of a haze of stuttering fuzz, bouncing thin shimmers of echoing synth off of ambiguous rhythms and taught, bulging bass. Those who have followed Betke's Kiff career up the ranks to CD status will be disappointed to see the full contents of his previous 12" "Tanzen" included here, but it's at least nice to have it all in one place. An excellent debut. —*Sean Cooper*

**Tanzen [Single]** / Oct. 1998 / Kiff SM ♦♦♦♦
Stefan Betke's second 12" is a gloriously engaging transliteration of German analog techno-minimalism, trading the rhythmic drone of his Basic Channel brethren for weird downtempo rhythms comprised of clicks, taps, and thuds several levels of abstraction beyond the most mechanical drum machine beat. Isolationist electronic dub, icy and beautiful. —*Sean Cooper*

**2** / Feb. 1, 1999 / Matador ♦♦♦♦
Following Matador's compilation of Pole's earliest material released in the US as *1*, the New York label released a second album of the Berlin artist's material as *2*. The six-song record fits somewhere between the structural exercises of *1* and the ambient minimalism of *3*, released a year later in summer 2000. By the time Matador released *2*, a substantial amount of hype surrounded Pole producer Stefan Betke's music. His relationship to the Chain Reaction camp in Berlin was cited numerous times along with his dub influences. These exciting comparisons to Basic Channel and Lee "Scratch" Perry gave journalists plenty to write about. But underlying this hype, Pole proceeded to undeniably progress artistically on *2*. The album retains *1*'s interest in musical ideas and structural possibilities, but it moves beyond mere theory to create six songs that affect the listener emotionally as well as cerebrally. The six songs of *2* put a greater emphasis on the underlying bassline, flirting with the listener's preconceived notions of rhythm and how it should operate. Besides the hints of funk that differentiate *2* from its predecessor, the album also tends to more evenly distribute the ideas of *1* into every song rather than just one or two songs. What results is a more cohesive sound from the opening moments of "Fahren" to the closing moments of "Weit." This consistency signals the evolution of a signature style for Betke that makes comparisons to artists such as Maurizio less valid. With *2*, the artist has differentiated himself away from his influences. Furthermore, *2* isn't nearly as abstract or minimal as *3*, making it a better starting point for first-time Pole listeners still accustomed to looping basslines and accessible rhythms. —*Jason Birchmeier*

**3** / Jun. 20, 2000 / Matador ♦♦♦♦
On Pole's third full-length collection, producer Stefan Betke's dub moves further towards ambient minimalism. The structure and rhythm on his previous album, *2*, disintegrate on *3* into songs full of space occupied by reverb, where the listener's mind subjectively inserts unconscious assumptions about what sounds belong in these gaps. Betke's minimalist approach subtracts many of electronic music's institutionalized motifs such as percussion, synth melodies, and thumping 4/4 rhythms. Without this extra baggage, pulsing dub basslines drive the songs while distorted remnants of synth notes, and Betke's infamous crackles bring life to the low-end. A casual listen won't unearth the beauty of the eight songs on *3;* one needs to play these songs on a powerful sound system at loud volumes to discover the many sublime nuances lurking beneath the surface of this music. The pulsing basslines flow from the speakers with trickling delight, creeping into one's bones as the frequencies vibrate the listener's spine and most other tangible objects within a close radius of the subwoofer. In addition to these rich low-end sounds, one truly doesn't hear the subtle pops and snaps at a modest volume. Once the music truly consumes one's ears, these muted and near-silent sounds become increasingly salient, serving as a sort of spontaneously conceived, free-form machine poetry. Some songs such as "Karussell" include bouncy basslines evoking a sense of rhythm, but even the most rhythmic moments of this album probably won't incite any dancing. The songs of *3* are strictly cerebral catalysts, altering the mood of a context with their gloomy aura of disorientated sounds. *1* and *2* functioned similarly, but those albums devoted more attention to structure and rhythm. The heightened abstraction of *3* with its intended minimalist aesthetic takes a more liberal approach to dub techno, reaching even harder for an unparalleled touch of the sublime. —*Jason Birchmeier*

## Polygon Window (Richard D. James)

*Producer / Ambient Techno, Techno, IDM*

Richard James' recorded his first album for Warp as part of the label's *Artificial Intelligence* series. Polygon Window's *Surfing on Sine Waves* was released in late 1992, and earned James' first American release the following year via Warp's package deal with TVT Records. [See Also: Aphex Twin] —*John Bush*

★ **Surfing on Sine Waves** / Nov. 1992 / Warp ♦♦♦♦♦
Call it ironic that the Aphex Twin's first US album release was under a pseudonym, but given the many names Mr. James has used over the course of his career, perhaps it's just as well. Regardless of name or intent, on *Surfing* he serves up a great collection of abstract electronic/dance madness, caught somewhere between the driftiness of his more ambient works at the time and the rave-minded nuttiness of "Digeridoo." The opening track, "Polygon Window," plants its feet firmly in both camps, with a brisk series of beats playing against the slightly dark, slightly quirky keyboard sounds with which the Twin first made his name. It's a good harbinger for the rest of *Surfing*, which satisfies, if not always astonishes, like Aphex does at his best. "Quoth," the single from the album, is a great dancefloor pounder. Though not as exultant and slowly building as "Digeridoo," it does makes its point with bluntness and power, consisting nearly solely of drums and percussion samples. "Quino Phec" is the album-ending counterpart; it's a mostly calm composition with only slight drums low in a mix that floats along inoffensively enough. The trademark wiggy humor of the Twin crops up at points as well, with the distorted video game robot voice on "UT1–Dot" intoning something about "electronic techno music" being one of the more noticeable examples. *Surf-*

ing is more a diversion in the end than anything else, not quite Aphex-by-numbers but not one of his great leaps forward either. Newcomers would do better with the *Classics* and *Selected Ambient Works 85-92* compilations first, when it comes to recordings from this time period. —*Ned Raggett*

## Ian Pooley

b. 1975, Mainz, Germany
*Producer, DJ / Minimal Techno, Tech-House, Club/Dance, Techno*
Over the course of his more than twenty singles for Force Inc, the prime German label for forward-looking techno, Ian Pooley has been inspired by the minimalist sound of Detroit as well as deep house. Born in Mainz, Germany, Pooley began collecting records and DJing at the age of 12 and became firmly entrenched in the classic Detroit sound of Derrick May and Juan Atkins while still a teenager. Along with his long-time friend DJ Tonka, Pooley began recording as T'N'I with the *Low Mass* EP, just the second release on Force Inc. The label was just beginning to gain a reputation as one of the premiere Continental venues for futuristic techno, with releases by Love Inc., Alec Empire, and Biochip C. DJ Tonka and Pooley recorded an EP with Alec Empire, plus several additional singles as Space Cube, but then separated.

Beginning as a solo act in 1994, Pooley continued to record for Force Inc.; his reputation soon grew with EP releases like *Twin Gods* and *The Celtic Cross* as well as the singles "Rollerskate Disco" and "The Chord Memory." He hooked up with John Acquaviva's Definitive label, and also released his debut album *The Times* for Force Inc. During 1996-97, Pooley provided remixes for Deee-Lite, Yello, the Cardigans, Dave Angel, Green Velvet, Love Inc., and Ken Ishii. His second album *Meridian* was released on Sony/V2 in 1998. Pooley has also appeared on over a dozen compilations for Force Inc. and Mille Plateaux, including *In Memoriam Gilles Deleuze* and the first two volumes of the *Electric Ladyland* series. In 2000, he returned with the full-length *Since Then*, an album with a more Brazillian flavor than previous Pooley works. —*John Bush*

**The Times** / Apr. 8, 1996 / Force Inc ♦♦♦♦

• **Meridian** / Jun. 22, 1998 / V2 ♦♦♦♦
While the majority of *Meridian* walks the consistently blurry line between deep house and Detroit techno, the album moves farther afield with the earthy breakbeat track "What's Your Number?," and disco-funk on "Followed," and even quasi-post-rock for "Disco Love." Of the more straight-ahead tracks, "Cold Wait" and the serene beauty of "Flatlet" make for two highlights. —*John Bush*

**Since Then** / 2000 / V2 ♦♦♦
Surely not the first Northern European to lose his head after escaping to sunnier climes, Ian Pooley intended his second album for V2 as an audio travelog (to accompany the pictorial one included in the booklet) of his visits, spanning Brazil to Barcelona and Malta to Montreal. As such, most of these tracks are warm disco-tech movers, reminiscent of Latin '70s dance-fusion (Azymuth, Salsoul Orchestra) and perfect for Ibizan beach parties. Some of the tracks are filtered very similar to the wave of Stardust inheritors, though Pooley's deft touch on the programming immediately rescues these tracks from being mere imitators. Two familiar-sounding tracks, "Coracao Tambor" and "900 Degrees," feature Rosanna and Zélia. Though the music's undoubtedly not quite as exciting as the geography it was inspired by, *Since Then* is a breath of fresh air on a stifling summer day. —*John Bush*

## Pop Will Eat Itself

f. 1986, Stourbridge, England, db. 1996
*Group / Alternative Dance, Alternative Pop/Rock*
Taking their name from an *NME* feature on the group Jamie Wednesday (later known as Carter the Unstoppable Sex Machine), the archetypal grebo band Pop Will Eat Itself formed in Stourbridge, England in 1986. Comprised of vocalist/guitarist Clive Mansell, keyboardist Adam Mole, drummer Graham Crabb and bassist Richard Marsh, PWEI began their existence as a Buzzcocks-influenced indie guitar band, and issued their self-produced debut EP *The Poppies Say Grrr* in 1986.

While recording their follow-up *Poppiecock*, PWEI became immersed in sampling, drawing material from sources ranging from James Brown to Iggy Pop; soon Crabb emerged from behind his drum kit to join Mansell as co-frontman, and a drum machine was installed in his place. Honing a fusion of rock, pop, and rap which they dubbed "grebo," the Poppies kickstarted a small revolution. By the release of their 1987 full-length debut *Box Frenzy* and the hit "There Is No Love Between Us Anymore," grebo—the name quickly given the entire subculture of similarly grimy and raunchy bands—was all the rage in the British music press.

The influence of hip-hop was even more pronounced on singles like "Def. Con. One." and "Can U Dig It?," both included on Pop Will Eat Itself's 1989 masterpiece *This Is the Day... This Is the Hour... This Is This!*, their debut for RCA. "Touched by the Hand of Cicciolina," an ode to the Italian porn-actress-turned-politician, was another hit, while 1991's *Cure for Sanity* marked an increasing interest in dance music. By 1992's *The Looks or the Lifestyle*, PWEI even added a live drummer, Fuzz (born Robert Townshend), to expand their ever-mutating sound.

In early 1993, the Poppies issued their biggest UK hit, "Get the Girl, Kill the Baddies"; ironically, later that same year the group was dropped by RCA. After signing to Infectious in Britain, they were picked up in the US by Nothing, a label owned by longtime fan Trent Reznor. Sporting a harder-edged, funk-metal sound, PWEI resurfaced in 1994 with *Dos Dedos Mis Amigos*. Prior to the release of a 1995 remix record, *Two Fingers, My Friends*, Crabb exited the group to focus on his side project, Golden Claw Musics. March later gained fame in the big-beat act Bentley Rhythm Ace. —*Jason Ankeny*

• **This Is the Day... This Is the Hour... This Is This!** / 1989 / RCA ♦♦♦♦
The sampling chaos that runs through Pop Will Eat Itself's breakout album includes nods to hip-hop, acid-house, heavy metal, synth-pop, soul—basically anything the Poppies could get their grebo little samplers on. The results, though dated, are consistent fun for listeners who can stand the old-school British rhymes on hits like "Can U Dig It" and "Def.Con.One." The last half of the album provides opportunity to stretch out, as "Shortwave Transmission on Up to the Minuteman" and "Satellite Ecstatica" illustrate. —*Keith Farley*

**Dos Dedos Mis Amigos** / 1994 / Interscope ♦♦♦
Pop Will Eat Itself goes industrial. Well, not really, but the shift to Trent Reznor's Nothing label shows in the music. The guitars are harder-edged, and the drumbeats are less dancy and more driving. Despite all that, the album maintains the Poppies' unique sense of humor. Songs range from the dark club favorite "Ich Bin Ein Auslander" to the entertaining denunciation of the Royal Family on "Familus Horribilus." This album, although not all that representative of the rest of their discography, is certainly worth finding for any fan of the band. —*Joshua Landau*

**Two Fingers, My Friends** / Mar. 6, 1995 / Infectious ♦♦♦♦
The remix album accompanying Pop Will Eat Itself's final album, *Dos Dedos Mis Amigos*, includes a range of solid remixers including the Orb, Renegade Soundwave, Fun-Da-Mental, Foetus, Transglobal Underground, and Apollo 440. —*John Bush*

**Wise Up Suckers** / 1996 / Camden ♦♦♦
A sort of best-of album, RCA released this disc after Pop Will Eat Itself broke from the label. Due to their rights to the back-catalog, this disc was produced with no input from the band. Although a good introduction to their pre-*Dos Dedos Mis Amigos* work, fans would serve themselves and the band better by acquiring *This Is the Day, This Is the Hour, This Is This!*, and *Dos Dedos Mis Amigos*. —*Joshua Landau*

## Popol Vuh

f. 1969, Munich, Germany
*Group / Kraut-rock, Ethnic Fusion, Progressive Electronic, Neo-Classical*
Of the many now-legendary artists to emerge from the Kraut-rock movement, few anticipated the rise of modern electronic music with the same prescience as Popol Vuh—the first German band to employ a Moog synthesizer, their work not only anticipated the emergence of ambient, but also proved pioneering in its absorption of worldbeat textures. At much the same time Popol Vuh was formed in Munich in 1969, another group of Norwegian descent, adopted the same name, an endless source of confusion in the years to follow. Both were inspired by the holy book of Guatemala's Quiche Indians and according to Mayan researchers the title roughly translates as "meeting place." Keyboardist Florian Fricke was deeply immersed in Mayan myth at the time he formed the group with synth player Frank Fiedler and percussionist Holger Trulzsch, and his interests were reflected in the spiritual themes of their 1970 debut, *Affenstunde*.

The follow-up two years later, *In den Gärten Pharaos*, was Popol Vuh's creative breakthrough, an intensely meditative work fusing ambient textures with organic percussion. In its wake, however, Fricke converted to Christianity, a move which sparked a rejection of electronics in favor of traditional ethnic instrumentation including guitars, oboe and tamboura; he then tapped Japanese soprano Djong Yun to lend vocals to 1972's lovely *Hosianna Mantra*. Fricke next teamed with onetime Amon Düül II drummer Daniel Fichelscher for the next Popol Vuh LP, *Seligpreisung*. Its follow-up, 1975's *Einjager und Siebenjager*, remains widely considered among the group's most stunning efforts. That same year, they began a lengthy creative partnership with the celebrated filmmaker Werner Herzog which yielded soundtracks for features including *Aguirre, Wrath of God, Fitzcarraldo* and *Nosferatu*.

Throughout the latter half of the '70s, Popol Vuh's fascination with global sounds and instruments continued, with the prominence of sitars, tablas, and tamboura percussion on LPs like 1977's *Herz aus Glas* and 1979's *Die Nacht der Seele: Tantric Songs* earning their latter-day sound descriptions like "raga rock." In 1978, Fricke founded the Working Group for Creative Singing and also became a member of the Breathing Therapy Society, traveling the world to lecture on both subjects; ultimately, his outside passions began to overshadow his work in Popol Vuh, and as the '80s dawned the group began losing steam, calling it quits after 1983's excellent *Agape Agape*. After reuniting two years later for *Spirit of Peace*, Fricke again reassembled Popol Vuh for the 1997 LP *Shepherd's Symphony*. —*Jason Ankeny*

**In the Gardens of Pharao/Aguirre** / 1983 / Celestial Harmonies ♦♦♦
This reissue includes the complete contents of two Popol Vuh classics, 1971's *In den Gärten Pharaos* and 1974's *Aguirre*. *In den Gärten Pharaos* ("In the Gardens of Pharao") was the first true work of "sacred music" by Florian Fricke. Consisting of two extended works (the second of which was recorded live), his mixture of electronics and church organ with assorted winds and percussives conjures up visions of deep, mystical emotion, marking the dawn of new age music, and still today is a wonder to behold. Though *Aguirre* jettisoned the electronics in favor of piano and electric guitar, its six lengthy pieces are nevertheless quite atmospheric and meditative. —*Archie Patterson*

• **Tantric Songs/Hosianna Mantra** / 1991 / Celestial Harmonies ♦♦♦♦
A meditational feast halfway between religious/classical trance music and Germanic space music of the time, this reissue of 1972's *Hosianna Mantra* and 1979's *Die Nact der Seele–Tantric Songs* on Celestial Harmonies includes some of the most beautiful music Popol Vuh ever recorded. Though the electronics had been forsaken, the music is still quite evocative— "Mantra of the Touching of the Earth" and "Angel of the Air" (both from *Tantric Songs*) present slow-moving piano passages, punctuated by sitar and tambura. *Hosianna Mantra* includes much beautiful work by Fricke on piano and harpsichord, Conny Veit on electric guitar, and Djong Yun reciting Biblical passages on "Kyrie," "Blessing," and the title track. Most of the best new age music was recorded before the term was even coined, and these two albums easily hit that mark. —*Jenna Woolford*

## Porcupine Tree

f. 1991
Group / Experimental Rock, Post-Rock/Experimental, Experimental, Prog-Rock/Art Rock

A member of No Man, Steven Wilson has been recording experimental prog-rock as Porcupine Tree since the mid-'80s. His first wide release, *On the Sunday of Life*, appeared in 1991 on Delerium Records. *Up the Downstair* (Delerium), *The Sky Moves Sideways* (C&S; 1995), *Signify* (1997, Delerium) and *Coma Divine* (1999, Delerium) are also available, as are two limited-edition collections of outtakes, *Yellow Hedgerow Dreamscape* and *Staircase Infinities*. Wilson's live band includes keyboardist Richard Barbieri (Japan), bass player Colin Edwin, and percussionist Charles Maitland. *Lightbulb Sun* followed in 2000. —*John Bush*

• **The Sky Moves Sideways** / Oct. 1995 / C&S ♦♦♦♦
*The Sky Moves Sideways* is among Porcupine Tree's most ambitious works, containing a two-part, 35-minute title track as a centerpiece. Although there are a few dull moments on the piece, it's by and large an impressive piece of neo-prog-rock that grounds the flightier aspects of the album and makes *The Sky Moves Sideways* one of their better records. —*Stephen Thomas Erlewine*

**Staircase Infinities** / Jan. 1996 / Blueprig ♦♦♦
A collection of several outtakes recorded around the same time as Porcupine Tree's 1993 debut, *Staircase Infinities* offers music ranging from Syd Barrett-esque folk to ambient space-rock, prog-rock, and psychedelic guitar jamming. Some material was previously released on 10" vinyl only. —*Steve Huey*

**Signify** / 1997 / Delerium Delec ♦♦♦
With *Signify*, Porcupine Tree moves toward ambient and electronica without abandoning their neo-prog roots. Occasionally, the group sounds as if they're trying too hard, pushing chilly ambient electronics into their music without questioning whether they need to be there or not, but most of the album works, creating a hypnotic blend of prog-rock structure and ambient texture. —*Stephen Thomas Erlewine*

**Voyage 34: The Complete Trip** / Jun. 6, 2000 / Delerium ♦♦
*Voyage 34*, originally a two-volume EP series from 1992-1993, was expanded into "The Complete Trip" after Steven Wilson remixed and added production for its eventual re-release seven years later. Documenting the ill effects of an acid trip by a frequent user (the first 33 were fine), the four-phase work begins with a straight-laced narrator explaining the events leading up to the trip, with straight-ahead (though slightly exploratory) guitar work by Wilson over a mid-tempo drum section. Thankfully, the album gradually moves into more ambient climes, with trippy vocal samples framing the mood throughout the final phases. Including a thick booklet with most of the narration repeated alongside surreal artwork, *Voyage 34: The Complete Trip* is a bit self-serious and pseudo-mystical even without the music to add to it, an intriguing experiment but hardly a work to stand on its own. —*John Bush*

## Porter Ricks

f. 1994, Berlin, Germany
Group / Minimal Techno, Experimental Dub, Experimental Techno, Electronica, Detroit Techno, Ambient Techno

Named for a character on the '60s TV show *Flipper*, Porter Ricks specializes in subaquatic dub techno, providing the closest touchstone to the static hum and fuzzy beatwork of their quasi label-mates Basic Channel. A collaboration between ambient maestro Thomas Köner and beatmeister Andy Mellwig, the duo debuted with three 12"s on the Basic Channel sublabel Chain Reaction during 1995-96. Filtering out any of the harder effects from Detroit techno and Plastikman material with what sounded like an affinity for undersea SONAR frequencies and wind-tunnel ambience, the singles became quite popular with the growing experimental techno scene of the mid-'90s (and even influenced Plastikman in return). By the time of the 1996 CD collection *BioKinetics* on Chain Reaction, Porter Ricks had moved on to Force Inc with the double-pack *Redundance* EP, plus the singles "Spoil" and "Exposed." The duo also recorded a single for Barooni before collecting their Force Inc material onto a self-titled 1997 CD. Two years later, the Techno Animal collaboration *Symbiotics* appeared. Köner also has a long-running solo career, with a half-dozen albums recorded for Barooni. —*John Bush*

**Port of Nuba [EP]** / 1995 / Chain Reaction ♦♦♦♦
On the *Port of Nuba* record, the Porter Ricks duo explores two variations of a disjointed composite of rhythms. The A-side introduces listeners to the physical sounds of "Port of Nuba," with its overlapping collection of galloping basslines and rhythm tracks. The B-side leaves those physical sounds and explores the more surreal, aquatic sounds of "Nautical Nuba." Both of these tracks last around nine minutes and don't deviate much from their arrangement, except for slow modulations and a continuous emphasis on phasing the tracks. Essentially, "Port of Nuba" and "Nautical Nuba" are the same song, with the latter being simply a much more altered take on the former, alluding to its nautical nature. Strangely enough, the surreal B-side, "Nautical Nuba," stands out as the stronger version; its heavy use of filtering and phasing eases the nauseatingly tangible presence of the A-side's somewhat punishing nature. —*Jason Birchmeier*

**Nautical Dub [EP]** / Jan. 1996 / Chain Reaction ♦♦♦
Over the course of their previous two releases on Chain Reaction, Porter Ricks had slowly moved away from the traditional style of techno associated with the Detroit techno popularized by labels such as Underground Resistance. Instead, they look to Berlin for influence on this record, particularly to the work of Basic Channel. On this record's two tracks—"Nautical Dub" and "Port Gentil"—the pummeling Roland 909 bass kicks of Jeff Mills have been replaced by the intangible dub basslines of Maurizio, creating an almost invisible sense of underlying rhythm. The many assembled sounds and rhythms swirl, eclipse, accentuate, and enhance one another like one large pulsing montage of propulsive ambience. —*Jason Birchmeier*

★ **BioKinetics** / Sep. 16, 1996 / Chain Reaction ♦♦♦♦♦

Porter Ricks' *BioKinetics* album is one of the most important releases in the Chain Reaction label's deep catalog, collecting tracks from their three early releases as well as some previously unreleased material. Moving away from techno's traditional connotations of being a style composed of syncopated, pounding Roland 909 kick drums layered with simple synthesizer melodies, string arrangements, or 303 acid riffs, Porter Ricks incorporates heavily altered percussive sounds or dub basslines in their place. Furthermore, the tracks aren't entirely syncopated, with various rhythms sometimes slowly drifting in and out of sequence, causing the tracks to sound more natural or live rather than computerized. Most importantly though, the work compiled on *BioKinetics* wouldn't function well as the type of techno a DJ would spin at a club since listeners would have an awfully difficult time dancing to it. Songs such as "Port of Nuba" and "BioKinetics 1" don't have consistent rhythms, instead sounding rather disjointed and scrambled; unfortunately, these are the weakest moments on this album. Rather it is tracks such as "Nautical Dub," "BioKinetics 2," "Port of Gentil," and "Nautical Zone" that make this such a noteworthy album. These songs don't even worry about incorporating percussion; instead, they focus on a montage of various rhythms registering at a variety of frequencies to create a piece of music whose rhythmic elements cover all ends of the sonic spectrum, from rumbling sub-frequencies to subtle rhythms that emanate from the tweeters of listeners' speakers. The tendency of this album's tracks to fit either one template or another makes this an inconsistent album, but the few magnificent tracks are ultimately worthy of investigation. —*Jason Birchmeier*

**Porter Ricks** / Dec. 15, 1997 / Mille Plateaux ♦♦♦♦

The second Porter Ricks album, compiled from singles released after the duo left the Basic Channel fold, represents quite a change from their previous output. Unlike the sound of *BioKinetics*, Porter Ricks circa 1997 had virtually abandoned the scratchy, lo-fi take on ambient dub and techno championed by most Basic Channel groups. Instead, the album has a clean sound which enables the listener to hear the impeccable production which must have been included on previous releases but was simply unhearable. Whether listeners like their Porter Ricks with surface noise or not, the basic blueprint has remained the same—impeccable. —*John Bush*

**Symbiotics** / Nov. 2, 1999 / X ♦♦♦♦

On *Symbiotics*, two of the best production teams in the field of experimental techno—PR and Techno Animal—hook up for a dream gig that surpasses expectations, even for the notoriously critical electronic underground. It all begins with the opener, "Polytoxic 1," an impossibly dense, claustrophobic production that shudders along on a mid-tempo beat and an ominous bassline pushed far past the redline. Though nothing else on the album equals "Polytoxic 1," there's a lot of great material here, including "Phosphoric" and "Hydrozoid", both excellent productions. At times, however, it's difficult to tell how much interplay actually went on between the two duos—on a few tracks, Porter Ricks' click-track ambience is simply layered over Techno Animal's thudding beats and echoey percussion. Still, even if they just e-mailed the audio files back and forth, *Symbiotics* is a dazzling album. —*John Bush*

## Portishead

f. 1991, Bristol, England
*Group / Electronica, Adult Alternative Pop/Rock, Trip-Hop, Alternative Pop/Rock*

Portishead may not have invented trip-hop, but they were among the first to popularize it, particularly in America. Taking their cue from the slow, elastic beats that dominated Massive Attack's *Blue Lines* and adding elements of cool jazz, acid house, and soundtrack music, Portishead created an atmospheric, alluringly dark sound. The group wasn't as avant-garde as Tricky, nor as tied to dance traditions as Massive Attack; Instead, the band wrote evocative psuedo-cabaret pop songs that subverted their conventional structures with experimental productions and rhythms of trip-hop. As a result, Portishead appealed to a broad audience—not just electronic dance and alternative rock fans, but thirtysomethings who found techno, trip-hop, and dance as exotic as worldbeat. Before Portishead released their debut album *Dummy* in 1994, trip-hop's broad appeal wasn't apparent, but the record became an unexpected success in Britain, topping most year-end critics polls and earning the prestigious Mercury Music Prize. In America, it also became an underground hit, selling over 150,000 copies before the group toured the US. Following the success of *Dummy*, legions of imitators appeared over the next two years, but Portishead remained quiet, as they worked on their second album.

Named after the West Coast shipping town where Geoff Barrow grew up, Portishead formed in Bristol, England in 1991. Prior to the group's formation, Barrow had worked as a tape operator at the Coach House studio, where he met Massive Attack. Through that group, he began working with Tricky, producing the rapper's track for the *Sickle Cell* charity album. Barrow also wrote songs for Neneh Cherry's *Homebrew*, though only "Somedays" appeared on the record. Around the time of Portishead's formation, he had begun to earn a reputation as a remix producer, working on tracks by Primal Scream, Paul Weller, Gabrielle, and Depeche Mode. Barrow met Beth Gibbons, who had been singing in pubs, in 1991 on a job scheme. Over the next few years, the pair began writing music, often with jazz guitarist Adrian Utley who had previously played with both Big John Patton and the Jazz Messengers.

Before releasing a recording, Portishead completed the short film *To Kill a Dead Man*, an homage to '60s spy movies. Barrow and Gibbons acted in the noirish film and provided the soundtrack, which earned the attention of Go! Records. By the fall, Portishead had signed with Go! and their debut album, *Dummy*, was released shortly afterward. *Dummy* was recorded with engineer Dave MacDonald, who played drums and drum machines, and guitarist Utley, who rounded out Portishead's lineup.

Both Barrow and Gibbons were media-shy—the vocalist refused to participate in any interviews—which meant that the album received little attention outside of the weekly UK music press, which praised the album and its two singles, "Numb" and "Sour Times," heavily. Soon, Go! and Portishead had developed a clever marketing strategy based on the group's atmospheric videos that began to attract attention. *Melody Maker*, *Mixmag*, and *The Face* named *Dummy* as 1994's album of the year, and early in 1995, "Glory Box" debuted at No. 13 without any radio play. Around the same time, "Sour Times" entered regular rotation on MTV in America. Within a few weeks, *Dummy* and "Sour Times" were alternative rock hits in the US. Back in the UK, the album had crossed over into the mainstream, becoming a fixture in the British Top 40. In July, the record won the Mercury Music Prize for Album of the Year, beating highly-touted competition from Blur, Suede, Oasis, and Pulp.

Following the Mercury Music Prize award, Barrow retreated to Coach House to begin work on Portishead's second album. The self-titled record finally appeared in September 1997. The live *PNYC* followed late the next year. —*Stephen Thomas Erlewine*

★ **Dummy** / Oct. 1994 / PolyGram ♦♦♦♦♦

Portishead's album debut is a brilliant, surprisingly natural synthesis of claustrophobic spy soundtracks, dark breakbeats inspired by frontman Geoff Barrow's love of hip-hop, and a vocalist (Beth Gibbons) in the classic confessional singer/songwriter mold. Beginning with the otherworldly theremin and martial beats of "Mysterons," *Dummy* hits an early high with "Sour Times," a post-modern torch song driven by a Lalo Schifrin sample. The chilling atmospheres conjured by Adrian Utley's excellent guitar work and Barrow's turntables and keyboards prove the perfect foil for Gibbons, who balances sultriness and melancholia in equal measure. Occasionally reminiscent of a torchier version of Sade, Gibbons provides a clear focus for these songs, with Barrow and company behind her laying down one of the best full-length productions ever heard in the dance world. Where previous acts like Massive Attack had attracted dance heads in the main, Portishead crossed over to an American, alternative audience, connecting with the legion of angst-ridden indie fans as well. Better than any album before it, *Dummy* merged the pinpoint-precise productions of the dance world with pop hallmarks like great songwriting and excellent vocal performances. —*John Bush*

**Portishead** / Sep. 30, 1997 / Go! Beat/London ♦♦♦♦

Portishead's debut album *Dummy* popularized trip-hop, making its slow, narcotic rhythms, hypnotic samples, and film-noir production commonplace among sophisticated, self-consciously "mature" pop fans. The group recoiled from such widespread acclaim and influence, taking three years to deliver their eponymous second album. On the surface, *Portishead* isn't all that dissimilar from *Dummy*, but its haunting, foreboding sonic textures makes it clear that the group isn't interested in the crossover success of such fellow travellers as Sneaker Pimps. Upon repeated plays, the subtle differences between the two albums become clear. Geoff Barrow and Adrian Utley recorded original music that they later sampled for the backing tracks on the album, giving the record a hazy, dreamlike quality that shares many of the same signatures of *Dummy*, but is darker and more adventurous. Beth Gibbons has taken the opportunity to play up her tortured diva role to the hilt, emoting wildly over the tracks. Her voice is electronically phased on most of the tracks, adding layers to the claustrophobic menace of the music. The sonics on *Portishead* would make it an impressive follow-up, but what seals its success is the remarkable songwriting. Throughout the album, the group crafts impeccable modern-day torch songs, from the frightening, repetitive "Cowboys" to the horn-punctuated "All Mine," which justify the detailed, engrossing production. The end result is an album that reveals more with each listen and becomes more captivating and haunting each time it's played. —*Stephen Thomas Erlewine*

PNYC / Nov. 10, 1998 / PolyGram ♦♦♦
By the end of the decade, artists realized that CD and CD-R bootlegs of live performances were in high demand, which meant that they could profit by officially releasing certain "special" live performances. Portishead's one-night stand at New York City's Roseland Ballroom, released as *PNYC*, certainly qualifies as one of those "special" occasions. Performing with a 35-piece orchestra, Portishead runs through selections from their two albums, favoring their second slightly. On the surface, it doesn't seem like the orchestra would add much to the performances, especially since the arrangements remain similar, but their presence makes the music tense, dramatic, and breathtaking. This is especially true of the material from *Portishead*. On album, several of these songs sounded a little flat, but here, they soar right alongside such staples as "Mysterons," "Sour Times," and "Glory Box." That alone doesn't necessarily make *PNYC* revelatory—instead, it deepens a listener's understanding of the artist, much like the Tindersticks' *The Bloomsbury Theatre, 12.3.95*. Which means, of course, that it's much more compelling and essential than the average live album. —*Stephen Thomas Erlewine*

## Potuznik (Gerhard Potuznik)

*Producer / Neo-Electro, Electro-Techno*

Austrian producer Gerhard Potuznik is one of the most accomplished and prolific producers associated with Vienna's Cheap, Morbid, and Sabotage family. An on-again/off-again member of electro/techno/experimental pop groups Private Lightning Six and Mause, he's spent much of his career releasing music as Potuznik and Gerhard Deluxxe. His first EP, "Up North They Are Free," appeared on Cheap in 1996, and contained mostly weird techno and breakbeat fusions accentuated by bits of disco, funk, and acid. Starting with the "Deluxe" EP in 1997, however, Potuznik's weirdness factor got a big boost. Combining odd instrumental and acousmatic samples in a framework of mid-tempo electro and '80s revivalist techno-pop, "Deluxe" was leaps and bounds beyond both his previous material and much of the dirgy downtempo that Vienna was becoming known for at the time of its release. "Spiral Architect" appeared on Sabotage sublabel Craft in 1998, and mined jungle's fashionable rhythms, though with decidedly experimental aplomb. His debut LP under his own name, *Amore Motore (Autobahn)*, appeared on Mego that same year. A stripped-down vamp on one of Kraftwerk's most famous songs, the album was a largely negligible collection of simple drumbox rhythms with pop overtones. Following a handful of compilation tracks, Potuznik's finest work to date, *Concorde*, appeared on Cheap in early 1999. An expanded edition of *Concorde* earned American distribution by the end of the year. —*Sean Cooper*

Amore Motore (Autobahn) / Aug. 4, 1998 / Mego ♦♦♦
- Concorde / 1999 / Cheap ♦♦♦♦
A collaboration with Mego's Ramon Bauer (aka General Magic), *Concorde* is an ambitious hybrid of electro, pop, disco, hip-hop, funk, ambient, noise, and computer glitch music with few immediate precursors. —*Sean Cooper*

## Presence (Charles Webster)

*Producer / Club/Dance, House*

Tasteful nu-groove and trip-hop soul producer Charles Webster emigrated from Britain to the United States after working with American techno mavericks including Juan Atkins and Derrick May. The producer, engineer, and recording artist has worked with R&S and Hardkiss, but gained fame with his Love from San Francisco label. Webster's acid-inspired productions as Presence ("My Baby," "A Better Day," "Sense of Danger") became deep house standards, though much more respected in Britain than America. A Love from San Francisco compilation was released in 1995, though Presence's debut full-length didn't appear until 1999. —*John Bush*

- All Systems Gone / Feb. 22, 1999 / Pagan ♦♦♦
The brainchild of Englishman Charles Webster, the architect of Love from San Francisco, Presence is more of a soul collective than a traditional recording project. Similarities to such projects as Style Council and Innocence are inevitable, but Presence is a wholly unique and fresh undertaking. Combining classic soul songwriting with some futuristic dance/house grooves, *All Systems Gone* is also buttressed by several fabulous vocal performances, most notably ex-Massive Attack's Shara Nelson, who's reading of "Sense of Danger" is truly magnificent. Probably the first classic record of the 21st century. —*Matthew Greenwald*

## Pressure Drop

f. 1990, London, England
*Group / Electronica, Ambient Techno, Club/Dance*

The UK dub dance duo Pressure Drop comprised DJ/producer partners Justin Langlands and Dave Henley, both of whom first surfaced during the mid-'80s spinning records at London clubs and warehouse parties. Forming Pressure Drop in 1990, their early singles reflected the eclecticism of their DJing work, drawing on influences including funk, northern soul, ska, acid house, and hip-hop. Upon completion of their 1992 debut LP *Upset*, their label Big World folded. The German company IDE bought their contract, and as a result only about two thousand copies of the record were actually released in their native Britain. After 1993's dark *Front Row* met a similar fate, Pressure Drop issued little further material for several years, finally arranging for their *Change the Silence* EP to appear on Leftfield's Hard Hands label in 1995; the full-length *Elusive* followed in 1997. —*Jason Ankeny*

Tearing the Silence / 1995 / Hard Hands ♦♦♦
- Elusive / Oct. 1997 / Hard Hands ♦♦♦♦
Similar to Massive Attack, Pressure Drop uses filtered symphonic strings, acoustic guitar passages and slow beats to produce their introspective dub symphonies. There are points on the album when they do it even better than their contemporaries. —*John Bush*

## Pressure Funk

*Group / Club/Dance, Techno*

Two years on from the first single delivered by Slam's Stuart MacMillan and Orde Meikle under their alias Pressure Funk, the full-length *Twisted Funk* appeared on Soma in early 1999. [See Also: Slam] —*John Bush*

- Twisted Funk / Mar. 29, 1999 / Soma ♦♦♦♦
Slam's Stuart McMillan and Orde Meikle know better than to let up just because they've released a full-length under an alias, and the first Pressure Funk LP proves to be just as pummeling a ride through techno and funk as their Slam material—heavy on the subtleties but with plenty of big sounds to entertain dancefloor residents. Though previous singles such as the title track and "Raw Spirit" get the best play, the album works from beginning to end (a pleasant surprise given its hour-plus length). —*John Bush*

## Pressure of Speech

f. 1993, London, England
*Group / Electronica, Club/Dance, Techno*

Mickey Mann is best known for his production and engineering work for one of the rave movement's first and biggest pop throw-ups, the Shamen. Originally a psychiatric nurse who worked in the same hospital with the Shamen's Colin Angus and Will Sin, and actually introduced the two), he formed his own group, Pressure of Speech, in 1993 along with partners DJ Stika (a DJ with London's Spiral Tribe) and Luke Losey (a lighting engineer for the KLF, the Orb, and Curve, among others). The name derives from a psychological affliction characterized by manic and extreme ranting, an apt if hyperbolic description of PoS' penchant for musical information overload. The group was signed by another of Mann's long-standing affiliations, Orbital's Internal label (Mann is Orbital's live sound engineer and co-produced their *Brown Al-*

bum), after being featured on Planet Dog's notable *Feed Your Head* compilation. PoS combine the rhythmic elements of Detroit and UK techno with evocative, sometimes gloomy atmospherics, and, like Orbital, have been known to pepper their otherwise dancefloor/chill room-straddling tracks with overt political and social commentary (as evidenced by album and track titles such as *Art of the State* and "Assume Nothing"). The group was given their first serious Stateside exposure via Hypnotic Records, who licensed several of the group's tracks, as well as remixes by the likes of Higher Intelligence Agency and Vapourspace, for compiling onto the US-only EP *Phase 1*. —*Sean Cooper*

- **Phase 1 [EP]** / Aug. 26, 1997 / Cleopatra ♦♦♦
*Phase 1* is a stateside calling card of sorts for UK techno trio Pressure of Speech, whose previous activities include engineering duties for the Shamen and Orbital and live events with the Orb and Irresistible Force. A remix EP featuring such artists as Higher Intelligence Agency, Vapour Space, Orbital, and Scanner, *Phase 1* ranges from banging techno to more experimental ambient and electro-funk, and is both a nice introduction to and departure from this lesser-known group's dense, unusual sound. —*Sean Cooper*

**50 Years of Peaces** / Aug. 25, 1998 / Cleopatra ♦♦♦
*50 Years of Peaces* alternates a few tracks approaching hardcore techno and trance (quite close to the Hypnotic label's major backer, Cleopatra) with more free-form recordings, like the tribal/environmental atmospherics of "Chelyabinsk" and "Dum Dum." —*John Bush*

## Pretty Tony (Tony Butler)

b. Miami, FL
*Producer / Electro, Club/Dance, Techno*
One of the most prolific and influential of the '80s electro artists, Miami-based producer Tony Butler recorded a string of popular club tracks on Power/Jam Packed and his own Music Specialist label in the mid-'80s, helping build the electro legacy that would give birth to Miami-style bass music and freestyle (named after Butler's primary pseudonym), as well as influence '90s post-techno artists such as Autechre and Biochip C. Butler's earlier tracks under his own name are all electro classics, with singles such as "Fix It in the Mix," "Jam the Box," and "Get Some" exploring a thinner, more stripped-down sound similar to Man Parrish and Cybotron. Butler's tracks with Freestyle are perhaps the more well known, and include such club staples as "It's Automatic," "Don't Stop the Rock," and "The Party Has Begun." His more commercial, pop-oriented writing and production work with Trinere, Debbie Deb, and Shannon, however, remain his claim to fame. Butler continues to live and record in Miami. —*Sean Cooper*

**Fix It in the Mix [Single]** / 1984 / Music Specialist ♦♦♦
A party tune from top to bottom, "Fix It in the Mix" also ably illustrates Butler's status as one of the more dynamic producers on the early electro scene, with frequent breaks and dynamic rhythmic programming drawing the blueprint for so-called "intelligent dance music" a decade in advance. —*Sean Cooper*

- **Get Some [Single]** / 1985 / Music Specialist ♦♦♦♦
Carried along by a clanging, almost industrial backing rhythm and sparse, kicking electro beat, "Get Some" was years ahead of its time in terms of pushing the compositional envelope of dance music. The flip contains a more dub-influenced version of the title track, with echoing beats and the odd vocoder snippet the only remaining elements. —*Sean Cooper*

## Darren Price

b. 1970, Woking, London, England
*Producer, DJ / Electronica, Club/Dance, Techno*
Allied with respected British techno producer/DJs like Luke Slater and Dave Angel, Darren Price recorded for Junior Boy's Own and toured the world as Underworld's offical DJ but later made waves of his own with some of the most pure, undistilled techno being made in Britain. Born in Woking, Price was turned on to electro and hip-hop during the early '80s and began practicing the fine art of mixing with an ancient turntable set-up. The acid-house explosion of the late '80s captivated Price in a similar fashion, and after hanging out at the seminal club-night Shoom, he hooked up with resident DJ Andrew Weatherall and began working at Weatherall's Junior Boy's Own Records.

Price soon made the leap to production as well, and recorded for JBO with Gary Lindop and Eric Chiverton as Centuras. Despite splitting with the duo later on, Price continued recording and issued hot tracks for NovaMute during 1995-96. Fellow Junior Boy's Own act Underworld recruited Price as the resident DJ on their world tour during 1996, and one year later Price released his debut album *Under the Flightpath* (the title a reference to the location of his studio, near Heathrow). —*John Bush*

- **Under the Flightpath** / Jun. 10, 1997 / Mute ♦♦♦♦
One of the few British producers who can pull off an album of pure techno, Price looks to his influences (from early electro through Underground Resistance) to provide the template for exploration on tracks like "Counterpoint," "Airspace," and "Things Change." Only occasionally does he turn to a richer production style, for moody tracks such as "Blueprint." —*John Bush*

## Primal Scream

f. 1984, Glasgow, Scotland
*Group / C-86, Electronica, Alternative Dance, Club/Dance, Acid House, Alternative Pop/Rock, Rock 'n' Roll, House*
Primal Scream's career could in many ways be read as a microcosm of British indie rock in the '80s and '90s. Bobby Gillespie formed the band in the mid-'80s while drumming for goth-tinged noise-rockers the Jesus & Mary Chain, who were the exact opposite of Primal Scream—the latter specialized in infectious, jangly pop on its early records. After a brief detour to punky hard rock, the group reinvented themselves as a dance band in the early '90s, following through on the pop and acid-house fusions of the Stone Roses and Happy Mondays. With the assistance of producers Andrew Weatherall and Hugo Nicholson, Primal Scream created the ultimate indie-pop and dance fusion album, *Screamadelica*, in 1991. *Screamadelica* broke down boundaries and changed the face of British pop music in the '90s, helping to make dance and techno acceptable to the rock mainstream. Instead of following through on the promise of the album, Primal Scream retreated to Stonesy boogie for their 1994 follow-up *Give Out But Don't Give Up*. When that record was greeted with indifference, they returned to dance-rock fusions with 1997's *Vanishing Point*, which re-established the group as a major force in British rock.

Bobby Gillespie (vocals) formed Primal Scream in 1984, while still drumming for the Jesus and Mary Chain. On its initial releases, Primal Scream was a group of '60s revivalists, crafting hooky, guitar-driven pop songs. The band signed to Creation Records in 1985, and over the next year, they released a pair of singles. However, Primal Scream didn't really take off until the middle of 1986, when Gillespie left the Mary Chain and guitarists Andrew Innes and Robert Young joined the band. "Velocity Girl," a rush of jangly guitars, was a B-side that wound up on *NME*'s C86 cassette compilation, a collection of underground pop groups that defined the UK's mid-'80s indie-pop scene. The band's debut, *Sonic Flower Groove*, fit into the C86 sound. After the band rejected the initial version recorded with Stephen Street, they re-recorded the album with Mayo Thompson, and the record was finally released in 1987 on the Creation subsidiary, Elevation. The album was well received in the British indie community, as was its 1989 follow-up *Primal Scream*, which demonstrated hard rock influences from the Rolling Stones and New York Dolls to the Stooges and MC5.

As the '80s drew to a close, Britain's underground music scene became dominated by the burgeoning acid-house scene. Primal Scream became fascinated with the new dance music, and they asked a friend, a DJ named Andrew Weatherall, to remix a track from *Primal Scream*, "I'm Losing More Than I'll Ever Have." Weatherall completely reworked the song, adding a heavy bass groove echoing dub reggae, deleting most of the original instrumentation (even the layers of guitars), and interjecting layers of samples, including lines of Peter Fonda's dialogue from *The Wild Angels*. The new mix was retitled "Loaded," and it became a sensation, bringing rock 'n' roll to the dance floor and dance to rock 'n' rollers. "Come Together," the first single from their forthcoming third album, was in much the same vein, and was similarly praised.

For their third album *Screamadelica*, Primal Scream not only worked with Andrew Weatherall and Hugo Nicholson, the pair who essentially designed the sound of the album, but also with the Orb and former Stones producer Jimmy Miller. The resulting album was a kaleidoscopic, neo-psychedelic fusion of dance, dub, techno, acid house, pop, and rock, and it was greeted with rapturous reviews in the UK. Released in the spring of 1991, *Screamadelica* also marked an important moment in British pop in the '90s, helping to bring techno and house into the mainstream. The album was a massive success, winning the first Mercury Music Prize in 1992.

In the wake of the groundbreaking *Screamadelica*, most observers wondered what Primal Scream would do next, yet few would have predicted their retreat to '70s hard rock for *Give Out But Don't Give Up*. Released in 1994, the album was eagerly awaited, but its Stonesy hard rock was not well received, and it was a relative commercial failure. More importantly, it hurt the group's reputation as innovators, a situation they reacted to with the title track to the hit 1996 film, *Trainspotting*. Primal Scream's contribution to the soundtrack was a return to the dance stylings of *Screamadelica*, only darker. The band continued to work on their next album, entitled *Vanishing Point*, over the course of 1996, finally releasing it to enthusiastic reviews in the summer of 1997. *XTRMNTR* followed in the spring of 2000. —*Stephen Thomas Erlewine*

★ **Screamadelica** / Oct. 8, 1991 / Sire ♦♦♦♦♦
*Screamadelica* is an impressive, innovative album that seamlessly combines classic rock with the throbbing beat of the dance club. While it doesn't contain any concise pop songs besides "Movin' On Up," the album is remarkably consistent and proved that it was possible to inject some true grit into the highly stylized world of techno, house, and rave. —*Stephen Thomas Erlewine*

**Vanishing Point** / Jul. 7, 1997 / Reprise ♦♦♦♦
Primal Scream found themselves in danger of losing their hip audience in the wake of their misconceived trad-rock record, *Give Out But Don't Give Up*. As a reaction, they returned to the genre-bending, electronic dance-rock of the seminal *Screamadelica* for *Give Out*'s follow-up, *Vanishing Point*. Instead of recycling the dazzlingly bright neo-psychedelia of *Screamadelica*, Primal Scream reaches deep into cavernous dub and '60s pop. *Vanishing Point* is a dark, trippy album, filled with mind-bending rhythms and cinematic flourishes. The addition of former Stone Roses bassist Mani to the Scream gives their music an organically funky foundation that has been lacking. Over those rhythms are samples, reverbed guitars, and synthesizers that echo spy movies, Southern soul, and the Stones. Above anything else, *Vanishing Point* is about sound and groove. Words remain a weak point for Bobby Gillespie, who only manages cohesive lyrics on the swirling "Burning Wheel" and "Star," but that is a secondary concern, since Primal Scream is at its best when working the rhythms. Songs like "Kowaliski" and, in particular, the extended instrumentals of "Get Duffy" and "Trainspotting" illustrate that the group is still capable of creating exotic, thoroughly entrancing sounds, which is what makes *Vanishing Point* a remarkable comeback. —*Stephen Thomas Erlewine*

**Echo Dek** / Oct. 27, 1997 / Creation ♦♦♦♦
Released a mere three months after *Vanishing Point*, *Echo Dek* finds Primal Scream turning over the master tapes for the record to Adrian Sherwood, who remixes eight of the songs ("Stuka" is done twice) and takes them farther out into left-field territory. *Vanishing Point* was already quite adventurous, sinking deep into dub and ambient cocktail territory, but Sherwood confirms the experimental bent of the record with *Echo Dek*. Only a few songs are twisted beyond recognition, the rest simply follow the original versions to their logical conclusion, offering elastic grooves, disembodied vocals and bottomless bass. Most remix albums are only of interest to hardcore fans, but Sherwood's clever, dynamic work makes *Echo Dek* of interest to anyone curious about contemporary dance. —*Stephen Thomas Erlewine*

**XTRMNTR** / May 2, 2000 / Astralwerks ♦♦♦♦
Whenever indie music seems lost in its own self-righteous, unchallenging, inoffensive fundament, Primal Scream rides in to try and save it all. So just as *Screamadelica* tried to encapsulate the importance of ecstasy culture, or *Vanishing Point* tried to exorcise their own insanity, *XTRMNTR* is a nasty, fierce realization of an entire world that has also lost the plot. The album starts with a gloriously vindictive sample of a kid commanding "Kill All Hippies," and this roughly states the album's modus operandi. There are songs shouting with furious, feedback-splayed anger ("Blood Money," "Exterminator"), songs of club-based revolt (both house-influenced versions of "Swastika Eyes"), and songs of utterly manic desperation ("Accelerator"). The album only lurches when lead singer Bobby Gillespie's weedy vocals can't keep up with the black noise of the music. "Insect Royalty" meanders and mumbles with a blank approach. "Pills" is a half-realized hip-hop song, with Gillespie diminishing its power on every verse (it only saves itself when it caps the song off with the album's central theme: "Sick fuck fuck sick fuck fuck sick fuck..."). Thankfully, Scream's highs, such as the gentleness of "Keep Your Dreams" (sounding like the third sibling to 1991's "I'm Coming Down" or 1997's "Star"), as well as the inversely monstrous and apocalyptic "MBV Arkestra (If They Move, Kill 'Em)," shower down with purely visceral poise. The album is not the flawless statement against complacency the band seemed to strive for, but it succeeds at tearing heads off, shooting fascists, and quickly asking questions later with unbelievable fury. For these reasons alone, it easily serves as one of the band's highest marks. These aren't the aggro-simpleton maneuvers of bands like Rage Against the Machine or Korn; the implosive production and sheer political belief prove that ingenuity must come hand in hand with "statement" if an idea is to come across effectively. *XTRMNTR* is simply a protest—sonically as well as lyrically—and maybe this would be a fine time to once again rally behind something worthwhile. —*Dean Carlson*

## Prince (Prince Rogers Nelson)

**b.** Jun. 7, 1958, Minneapolis, MN
*Vocals, Keyboards, Drums, Guitar, Bass / Neo-Psychedelia, Club/Dance, Pop/Rock, Urban, Rock 'n' Roll, Funk, Dance-Pop, Soul*

Few artists have created a body of work as rich and varied as Prince. During the '80s, he emerged as one of the most singular talents of the rock 'n' roll era, capable of seamlessly tying together pop, funk, folk, and rock. Not only did he release a series of groundbreaking albums, he toured frequently, produced albums, and wrote songs for many other artists, and recorded hundreds of songs that still lie unreleased in his vaults. With each album he has released, Prince has shown remarkable stylistic growth and musical diversity, constantly experimenting with different sounds, textures, and genres. Occasionally, his music can be maddeningly inconsistent because of this eclecticism, but his experiments frequently succeed. No other contemporary artist can blend so many diverse styles into a cohesive whole.

Prince's first two albums were solid, if unremarkable, late '70s funk-pop. With 1980's *Dirty Mind*, he recorded his first masterpiece, a one-man *tour de force* of sex and music; it was hard funk, catchy Beatlesque melodies, sweet soul ballads, and rocking guitar-pop, all at once. The follow-up, *Controversy*, was more of the same, but *1999* was brilliant. The album was a monster hit, selling over three million copies, but it was nothing compared to 1984's *Purple Rain*.

*Purple Rain* made Prince a superstar; it eventually sold over ten million copies in the US and spent twenty-four weeks at No. 1. Partially recorded with his touring band The Revolution, the record featured the most pop-oriented music he has ever made. Instead of continuing in this accessible direction, he veered off into the bizarre psycho-psychedelia of *Around the World in a Day* (1985), which nevertheless sold over two million copies. In 1986, he released the even stranger *Parade*, which was in its own way was as ambitious and intricate as any art-rock of the '60s; however, no art-rock was ever grounded with a hit as brilliant as the spare funk of "Kiss."

By 1987, Prince's ambitions were growing by leaps and bounds, resulting in the sprawling masterpiece *Sign O' the Times*. Prince was set to release the hard funk of *The Black Album* by the end of the year, yet he withdrew it just before its release, deciding it was too dark and immoral. Instead, he released the confused *Lovesexy* in 1988, which was a commercial disaster. With the soundtrack to 1989's *Batman* he returned to the top of the charts, even if the album was essentially a recap of everything he had done before. The following year he released *Graffiti Bridge*, the sequel to *Purple Rain*, which turned out to be a considerable commercial disappointment.

In 1991, Prince formed The New Power Generation, the most versatile and talented band he has ever assembled. With their first album, *Diamonds and Pearls*, Prince reasserted his mastery of contemporary R&B; it was his biggest hit since 1985. The following year, he released his twelfth album, which was titled with a cryptic symbol; in 1993, Prince legally changed his name to the symbol. In 1994, after becoming embroiled in contract disagreements with Warner Brothers, he independently released the single "The Most Beautiful Girl in the World," which became his biggest hit in years. Later that summer, Warner released the somewhat half-hearted *Come* under the name of Prince; the record was a moderate success, going gold.

In November 1994, as part of a contractual obligation, Prince agreed to the official release of *The Black Album*. In early 1995, he immersed himself in another legal battle with Warner, proclaiming himself a slave as the company refused to release his new record, *The Gold Experience*. By the end of the summer, a compromise was reached, and the album was released in the fall. In the summer of 1996, Prince released *Chaos & Disorder*, his last album of original material for Warner Brothers. Setting up his own label, NPG, he resurfaced later that same year with the three-disc *Emancipation*, which was designed as a magnum opus that would spin off singles for several years and be supported with several tours. However, even his devoted cult following needed considerable time to digest such an enormous compilation of songs; once it was clear that *Emancipation* wasn't the commercial blockbuster he hoped it would be, Prince assembled a long-awaited collection of outtakes and unreleased material called *Crystal Ball* in 1998. With *Crystal Ball*, Prince discovered that it's much more difficult to get records to an audience than it seems; some fans who pre-ordered their copies through Prince's website (from which a bonus fifth disc was included) didn't receive them until months after the set began appearing in stores. To top off this flood of material, Prince released a new one-man album, *New Power Soul*, three months after *Crystal Ball*; even though it was his most straightforward album since *Diamonds and Pearls*, it didn't do well on the charts, partially because many listeners didn't realize it had been released.

A year later, with "1999" predictably an end-of-the-milennium anthem, Prince issued the remix collection *1999 (The New Master)*. A collection of Warner Bros.-era leftovers, *Vault: Old Friends 4 Sale*, followed that summer, and in the fall Prince returned to Arista with the all-star *Rave Un2 the Joy Fantastic*. —*Stephen Thomas Erlewine*

**For You** / 1978 / Warner Brothers ♦♦
On his debut album *For You*, Prince shows exceptional skill for arranging and performing mainstream urban R&B and funk, but his songwriting remains conventional. Only on the mildly racy "Soft and Wet" does he demonstrate a personal touch, but the song is still more of a promise than a fulfillment. While *For You* isn't a bad record, it is merely a pleasant one, and it offers very little indication of his staggering talents. —*Stephen Thomas Erlewine*

**Prince** / 1979 / Warner Brothers ♦♦♦
Expanding the urban R&B and funk approach of his debut, *Prince* is a considerably more accomplished record than his first effort, featuring the first signs of his adventurous, sexy signature sound. Although the album is still rather uneven, a handful of songs rank as classics. "I Wanna Be Your Lover" is excellent lite-funk and "Why You Wanna Treat Me So Bad?" is a wonderful soulful plea, but "I Feel for You," a sexy slice of urban R&B with a strong pop melody, is the true masterpiece of *Prince*, indicating the major breakthroughs of his next album, *Dirty Mind*. —*Stephen Thomas Erlewine*

☆ **Dirty Mind** / 1980 / Warner Brothers ♦♦♦♦♦
Neither *For You* or *Prince* was adequate preparation for the full-blown masterpiece of Prince's third album, *Dirty Mind*. Recorded in his home studio, with Prince playing nearly every instrument, *Dirty Mind* is a stunning, audacious amalgam of funk, new wave pop, urban R&B, and pop, fueled by grinningly salacious sex and the desire to shock. Where other pop musicians suggested sex in lewd double entendres, Prince left nothing to hide—before its release, no other rock or funk record was ever quite as explicit as *Dirty Mind*, with its gleeful tales of oral sex, threesomes, and even incest. Certainly, it opened the doors for countless sexually explicit albums, but to reduce its impact to mere profanity is too reductive—the music of *Dirty Mind* is as shocking as its graphic language, bending styles, and breaking rules with little regard for fixed genres. Basing the album on a harder, rock-oriented beat than before, Prince tries everything—there's pure new wave pop ("When You Were Mine"), soulful crooning ("Gotta Broken Heart Again"), robotic funk ("Dirty Mind"), rock 'n' roll ("Sister"), sultry funk ("Head," "Do It All Night") and relentless dance jams ("Uptown," "Partyup"), all in the space of half an hour. It's a breathtaking, visionary album, and its fusion of synthesizers, rock rhythms, and funk set the style for much of the urban soul and funk of the early '80s. —*Stephen Thomas Erlewine*

**Controversy** / 1981 / Warner Brothers ♦♦♦♦
*Controversy* continues in the same vein of new wave-tinged funk on *Dirty Mind*, emphasizing Prince's fascination with synthesizers and synthesizing disparate pop music genres. It is also more ambitious than its predecessor, attempting to tackle social protest ("Controversy," "Ronnie, Talk to Russia," "Annie Christian") along with sex songs ("Jack U Off," "Sexuality"), and it tries hard to bring funk to a rock audience and vice versa. Even with all of Prince's ambitions, the music on *Controversy* doesn't represent a significant breakthrough from *Dirty Mind*, and it is often considerably less catchy and memorable. Nevertheless, Prince's talents as a musician make the record enjoyable, even if it isn't as compelling as most of his catalog. —*Stephen Thomas Erlewine*

★ **1999** / 1982 / Warner Brothers ♦♦♦♦♦
With *Dirty Mind*, Prince had established a wild fusion of funk, rock, new wave, and soul that signalled he was an original, maverick talent but it failed to win him a large audience. After delivering the soundalike album *Controversy*, Prince revamped his sound and delivered the double album *1999*. Where his earlier albums had been a fusion of organic and electronic sounds, *1999* was constructed almost entirely on synthesizers by Prince himself. Naturally, the effect was slightly more mechanical and robotic than his previous work and strongly recalled the electro-funk experiments of several underground funk and hip-hop artists at the time. Prince had also constructed an album dominated by computer-funk, but he didn't simply rely on the extended instrumental grooves to carry the album—he didn't have to when his songwriting was improving by leaps and bounds. The first side of the record contained all of the hit singles and, unsurprisingly, they were the ones that contained the least amount of electronics. "1999" parties to the apocalypse with a P-Funk groove much tighter than anything George Clinton ever did, "Little Red Corvette" is pure pop and "Delirious" takes rockabilly riffs into the computer age. After that opening salvo, all the rules go out the window—"Let's Pretend We're Married" is a salacious extended lust letter, "Free" is a elegaic anthem, "All the Critics Love U in New York" is a vicious attack at hipsters and "Lady Cab Driver," with its notorious bridge, is the culmination of all of his sexual fantasies. Sure, Prince stretches out a bit too much over the course of *1999* but the result is a stunning display of raw talent, not wallowing indulgence. —*Stephen Thomas Erlewine*

**Purple Rain** / 1984 / Warner Brothers ♦♦♦♦
Prince designed *Purple Rain* as the project that would make him a superstar, and, surprisingly, that is exactly what happened. Simultaneously more focused and ambitious than any of his previous records, *Purple Rain* finds Prince consolidating his funk and R&B roots while moving boldly into pop, rock, and heavy metal with nine superbly crafted songs. Even its best-known songs don't tread conventional territory: the bass-less "When Doves Cry" is an eerie, spare neo-psychedelic masterpiece; "Let's Go Crazy" is a furious blend of metallic guitars, Stonesy riffs and a hard funk backbeat; the anthemic title track is a majestic ballad filled with brilliant guitar flourishes. Although Prince's songwriting is at a peak, the presence of the Revolution pulls the music into sharper focus, giving it a tougher, more aggressive edge. And, with the guidance of Wendy and Lisa, Prince pushed heavily into psychedelia, adding swirling strings to the dreamy "Take Me With U" and the hard rock of "Baby I'm a Star." Even with all of his new, but uncompromising forays into pop, Prince hasn't abandoned funk, and the robotic jam of "Computer Blue" and the menacing grind of "Darling Nikki" are among his finest songs. Taken together, all of the stylistic experiments add up to a stunning statement of purpose that remains one of the most exciting rock 'n' roll albums ever recorded. —*Stephen Thomas Erlewine*

**Around the World in a Day** / 1985 / Paisley Park ♦♦♦
*Purple Rain* made Prince sound like he could do anything, but it still didn't prepare even his most fervent fans for the insular psychedelia of *Around the World In a Day*. Prince had made his interior world sound fascinating and utopian on *Purple Rain*, but *Around the World In a Day* is filled with cryptic religious imagery, bizarre mysticism, and confounding metaphors, which were drenched in heavily processed guitars, shimmering keyboards, grandiose strings and layers of vocals. As an album, the record is a bit impenetrable, requiring great demands of the listener, but individual songs do shine through—"Raspberry Beret" is a brilliant piece of neo-psychedelia with an indelible chorus, "Pop Life" is a snide swipe at stardom that emphasizes Prince's outsider status, "Condition of the Heart" is a fine ballad, "America" is a good funk jam, "Paisley Park" is heavy and slightly frightening guitar psychedelia, while the title track is a sunny, kaleidoscopic pastiche of *Magical Mystery Tour*. The problem is, only a handful of the songs have much substance outside of their detailed production and intoxicating performances, and the album has a creepy sense of paranoia that is eventually its undoing. —*Stephen Thomas Erlewine*

### Parade (Music from the Motion Picture "Under the Cherry Moon") / 1985 / Paisley Park ♦♦♦♦

Undaunted by the criticism *Around the World in a Day* received, Prince continued to pursue his psychedelic inclinations on *Parade*, which also functioned as the soundtrack to his second film, *Under the Cherry Moon*. Originally conceived as a double album, *Parade* has the sprawling feel of a double record, even if it clocks in at around 45 minutes. Prince and the Revolution shift musical moods and textures from song to song—witness how the fluttering psychedelia of "Christopher Tracy's Parade" gives way to the spare, jazzy funk of "New Position," which morphs into the druggy "I Wonder U"—and they're determined not to play it safe, even on the hard funk of "Girls and Boys" and "Mountains," as well as the stunning "Kiss," which hits hard with just a dry guitar, keyboard, drum machine, and layered vocals. All of the group's musical adventures, even the cabaret-pop of "Venus De Milo" and "Do U Lie?," do nothing to undercut the melodicism of the record, and the amount of ground they cover in 12 songs is truly remarkable. Even with all of its attributes, *Parade* is a little off-balance, stopping too quickly to give the haunting closer "Sometimes It Snows in April" the resonance it needs. For some tastes, it may also be a bit too lyrically cryptic, but Prince's weird religious and sexual metaphors are developing into a motif that actually gives the album weight. If it had been expanded to a double album, *Parade* would have equaled the subsequent *Sign O' the Times*, but as it stands, it's an astonishingly rewarding near-miss. —*Stephen Thomas Erlewine*

### The Black Album / 1987 / Warner Brothers ♦♦♦

Apart from the Beach Boys' *Smile*, few unreleased albums cultivated the myth of Prince's *The Black Album*. Originally scheduled for release in November of 1987—when it would have followed the double-album *Sign O' the Times* by just a matter of months—Prince pulled the album just weeks before its release. Several thousand copies, mostly on vinyl, had already been pressed and were immediately destroyed; rumors persisted for years that a handful of compact discs were also manufactured. Almost immediately, a legend grew around the album, that Prince refused to release it because he believed it was too bleak and that Warner Brothers didn't want to promote the album because of its explicit lyrical content. Bootleg copies of the album spread as quickly as the rumors, and by the end of 1988, it was arguably the most bootlegged album in history. In the fall of 1994—when Prince's commercial standing was in decline and after most diehard fans had obtained a copy of the record—*The Black Album* was suddenly released officially as a limited edition, most likely as a way for Prince to free himself from his record contract. And at that time, the general public learned what Prince fans had known for many years—*The Black Album* was fun, but not much more. With *The Black Album*, Prince recorded an album that was intended to silence all the critics that claimed he abandoned his funk and R&B roots. Every song on the brief eight-song collection is pure funk or R&B, from the slamming opener "Le Grind" to the smooth urban ballad "When 2 R In Love" (which happened to appear on *Lovesexy*, the album Prince released instead of *The Black Album*). Some of the tracks genre exercises are and nothing more. Occasionally, such as the lame attack on hardcore rappers "Dead On It," the music is flat-out embarassing, but the best moments of *The Black Album* is when Prince's indulges in his joyously perverse humor. On "Bob George," possibly the strangest song he ever recorded, Prince alters the tape so his voice sounds like a menacing baritone drawl and he growls threats to his lover, who just had an affair with Prince—or, as Bob George calls him, "that skinny motherfucker with a high voice." "Cindy C" is a lascivious declaration of lust for supermodel Cindy Crawford, during which Prince claims he'll "pay the usual fee" to sleep with her. And "Superfunkyfragicalisexy" and "2 Nigs United 4 West Compton" burn with the best James Brown, George Clinton, and Sly Stone tracks. So, *The Black Album* might have salvaged his R&B reputation if it was released in 1987. Instead it became a legendary record that doesn't quite deserve its widespread reputation. It's a nice little gem that is primarily of interest to dedicated fans, but it doesn't quite hold the attention of casual fans. —*Stephen Thomas Erlewine*

### Sign O' the Times / 1987 / Paisley Park ♦♦♦♦

Sprawling, eclectic and messy, Prince's second double-album, *Sign O' the Times*, falls into the tradition of great chaotic double albums like *The Beatles*, *Exile On Main St.*, and *London Calling* that are great because of their overreaching, seemingly haphazard scope. In short, it's the album where Prince shows nearly all of his cards, from bare-bones electro-funk and smooth soul to pseudo-psychedelic pop and crunching hard rock. In between, he touches on gospel, blues, and folk, among many other stylistic flourishes. Originally intended as a triple-album set called *The Crystal Ball*, *Sign O' the Times* was the first album Prince recorded without the Revolution since 1982's *1999* (the band does appear on the in-concert raveup, "It's Gonna Be A Beautiful Night") and the effect on him is liberating—he is free to dive into all the styles he merely hinted at on *Around the World In A Day* and *Parade*. The music sounds open and, usually, inviting, even though many of these songs are the most cryptic, insular songs he's ever written. Most of these songs are leftovers from the aborted Camille project, an alter-ego Prince created that was personified with the use of sped-up tapes. Camille is the voice that sings "If I Was You're Girlfriend," the most disarming and bleak psycho-sexual song Prince ever wrote, as well as the equally chilling "Strange Relationship." The fraying relationships are weighted by the a social chaos Prince hints at throughout the album with his apocalyptic imagery of drugs, bombs, empty sex, abandoned babies and mothers, and AIDS. But he also balances the despair with hope, whether it's God ("The Cross"), love ("Adore," "Forever In My Life"), or just having a good time ("Play in the Sunshine," "It's Gonna Be A Beautiful Night"). In it's own roundabout way, *Sign O' the Times* is the sound of the late '80s—it's the sound of the good times collapsing and the natural reaction to retreat to your own world, so you can just dance all those problems away. It's an endlessly fascinating and provocative listen. The album was a hit, but not at the magnitude of his previous records. Nevertheless, *Sign O' the Times* was one of the last times an artist this diverse, perverse. and bloody eccentric could top the charts. —*Stephen Thomas Erlewine*

### Lovesexy / Feb. 1988 / Paisley Park ♦♦♦

It's nearly impossible to judge *Lovesexy* as anything but a hastily assembled substitute for the withdrawn *Black Album*, which does the record a disservice. An exactingly sequenced song cycle—the compact disc didn't have index markings to separate the individual tracks—*Lovesexy* is quite a different record than not only *The Black Album*, but anything else Prince had recorded. Where *Dirty Mind* was single-minded in its lust, *Lovesexy* connects the carnal with spiritual, and the calmness of the music reflects this outlook. Even when the record dips into hard funk, such as on the title track or the single "Alphabet Street," there's a relaxed, casual quality to the music that is shocking after the dense paranoia of *Parade*, *Sign O' the Times* and *The Black Album*. Prince intends to enter a new phase of maturity with such considered music and ambitious lyrical themes, but neither his music nor his lyrics are consistently well-stated over the course of the album. A handful of tracks are worthwhile—the sappy ballad "When 2 R In Love," the moving "I Wish U Heaven," the weird psychedelia of "Anna Stesia" and "Glam Slam," as well as the wonderful "Alphabet Street"—but it is his weakest album since *Controversy*. —*Stephen Thomas Erlewine*

### The Hits 1 / Sep. 14, 1993 / Paisley Park ♦♦♦♦

The primary fault with Prince's two-part *Hits* collection is that both volumes are missing some important singles and are sequenced incoherently, thereby failing to give an accurate impression of his astonishing musical growth. However, they do contain enough necessary items to illustrate why he was one of the most influential and gifted musicians of the '80s, as well as providing a reasonable introduction and compilation for casual fans. *Hits 1* contains a good cross-section of his biggest hits—"When Doves Cry" (presented in an edited version), "When You Were Mine," "Let's Go Crazy," "1999," "Sign O' the Times," "Alphabet Street," "Diamonds and Pearls," "7"—plus new items like a "Pink Cashmere" and "Nothing Compares 2 U" (a Prince song that Sinead O'Connor took to No. 1) which are nearly as good as the familiar tracks. However, it provides an incomplete portrait, making *Hits 2* a necessary purchase. —*Stephen Thomas Erlewine*

### The Hits 2 / Sep. 14, 1993 / Paisley Park ♦♦♦♦

Like *Hits 1*, *Hits 2* presents an illogically sequenced cross-section of some of Prince's biggest hits and most notorious songs, including "Dirty Mind," "I Wanna Be Your Lover," "Head," "Delirious," "Little Red Corvette," "I Would Die 4 U," "Raspberry Beret," "Kiss," "U Got the Look," "Cream," and "Purple Rain." Two new tracks, "Peach" and "The Pope," are included among the 18 cuts and while they don't match the rest of the songs (or the new cuts on *Hits 1*), they are nevertheless enjoyable. On the whole, *Hits 2* is a slightly stronger collection than its predecessor, but it still gives a rather incomplete portrait—if you buy *Hits 2*, you need to buy *Hits 1*. —*Stephen Thomas Erlewine*

## Prince Paul (Paul Huston)

b. Apr. 2, 1967
*Producer / Underground Rap, Alternative Rap, Hip-Hop*

Beginning his career as a DJ for Stetsasonic, rapper and producer Prince Paul has lent his skills to albums by Boogie Down Productions, Gravediggaz, MC Lyte, Big Daddy Kane, and 3rd Bass, among others. Paul's big break came when he produced De La Soul's *3 Feet High and Rising* album. Shattering the acknowledged rules of hip-hop production, he sampled not only funk, but all types of music to create fresh and original backing tracks. By throwing in comedy sketches as well, Prince Paul and De La Soul completely ushered in a new era for hip-hop. In 1994, Paul returned to rapping, joing RZA and Stetsasonic member Fruitkwan in Gravediggaz, a side-project that debuted with *6 Feet Deep*. He also began working with the new elite in underground rap, recruiting the Automator, New Kingdom's Scott Harding, and Spectre for his debut solo album, 1997's *Psychoanalysis: What Is It? A Prince Among Thieves* followed in 1999, and later that year Paul formed Handsome Boy Modeling School with the Automator to release the album *So...How's Your Girl?*. —*Steve Kurutz*

**Psychoanalysis: What Is It?** / Oct. 21, 1997 / Tommy Boy ♦♦♦
From George Clinton and De La Soul to Ornette Coleman and Frank Zappa, a lot of great artists haven't hesitated to be self-indulgent. It's a question of *how* self-indulgent an artist chooses to be, and on *Psychoanalysis (What Is It?)*, Prince Paul is much too self-indulgent for his own good. Known for his membership in the group Stetsasonic and for producing De La Soul, Queen Latifah and others, Paul has an impressive resume. But this unfocused, incoherent CD wasn't his finest hour. Though it contains a few worthwhile rap tunes (including "Psycho Linguistics" and "J.O.B.—Das What Dey Is"), *Psychoanalysis* isn't a rap album so much as a collection of soundbites, samples, and dialogue played over tracks. Overall, the album is pointless and serves no purpose other than Paul's desire to amuse and entertain himself. Paul may have gotten a few laughs out of it, but listeners will be left out in the cold and find themselves asking if there is a point to all this. —*Alex Henderson*

● **A Prince Among Thieves** / Feb. 23, 1999 / Tommy Boy ♦♦♦♦
Known to his mother as Paul Huston, Prince Paul's diverse resume includes membership in the influential jazzy outfit Stetsasonic, and the morosely creative Gravediggaz. He's also produced for De La Soul, George Clinton, and the Beastie Boys. Perhaps best known for his humor and unpredictability, Prince Paul surprises again with what may be the first true rap musical, *A Prince Among Thieves*. The storyline, told through songs and interludes produced by Prince Paul, involves an aspiring rapper (Tariq), on the verge of a major record deal. Without the necessary funds for a quality demo tape, he begins a hustling journey through New York. Standout verses come courtesy of Kool Keith as a weapons dealer ("Crazy Lou's Hideout"), Chris Rock as a junkie ("My First Day") and Everlast as an overzealous policeman ("The Men in Blue"). Seamlessly combined skits and album tracks make this a hip-hop opera worth seeing at the Met. —*Craig Robert Smith*

## Jamie Principle (Byron Walton)

b. Jul. 5, 196?, Chicago, IL
*Vocals, Producer / Club/Dance, Acid House, House*

Scattered among the classic productions of the mid-'80s Chicago house scene are those of Jamie Principle, the first to record song-based house music and the closest to a songwriter in the entire community. Principle never received his proper respect, since many of his best singles were only released years after their (usually ecstatic) introduction on the Chicago club-scene. Also, the balance of input between Principle and producer Frankie Knuckles has never been defined, resulting in singles credited to "Frankie Knuckles Presents," "A Frankie Knuckles Production," or occasionally just "Frankie Knuckles" instead of what should perhaps have been acknowledged as Principle co-productions.

He was born Byron Walton on Chicago's south side, and early on differed from the majority of future house producers by gaining inspiration from a novel group of artists: David Bowie, Depeche Mode, Prince, and Human League instead of the almost requisite mixture of Parliament/Funkadelic and obscure disco. He played drums and clarinet as part of a band while attending church, and by 1980 had decided to try making music on his own. With a synthesizer and his own live drum accompaniment, Principle began writing songs and later bought a four-track recorder to set them down on tape. A mutual friend, José Gomez, introduced his recordings to the don of Chicago DJs, Frankie Knuckles, and Knuckles began dropping Principle songs—still on reel-to-reel tape—into his sets at the Warehouse.

One of the tracks, "Your Love," became a huge hit at the clubs and on the Hot Mix 5's radio show. Finally, in 1985, two years after house music had debuted on wax, "Your Love" was released on Trax Records. Another previously unreleased gem, "Waiting on My Angel," was released on Person Records one year later. According to reliable rumor, Knuckles attempted to sell an unreleased Principle single to both of the two major Chicago house music labels, Trax *and* DJ International, at the same time and without his permission; soon, Principle had distanced himself from the producer, and released the dis record "Knucklehead" in response.

The B-side of "Your Love" on its Trax issue was "Baby Wants to Ride," a piece of X-rated funk which made clear Jamie Principle's allegiance to Prince. The ffrr label licensed the single in 1988 and it became a major international club hit. Principle hit the Americans with two singles for Atlantic ("Cold World" and "Date with the Rain," produced with Steve "Silk" Hurley) but then signed to the Smash subsidiary of PolyGram. The singles from his 1991 album *Midnite Hour* did moderately well in clubs but Principle's increasingly pop-slanted productions alienated club-goers and simultaneously failed to cross over into pop markets. He continued producing and appeared on Jesse Saunders' *Chicago Reunion* album in 1993. —*John Bush*

● **Midnite Hour** / 1991 / Smash ♦♦♦
The house/R&B crossover that never happened, *Midnite Hour* features several sexy funk tracks that put the Prince back into Principle—"You're All I've Waited 4," "Hot Body," and the title track—but instead of hitting the dancefloors, Smash pointed the album straight at the radio stations and failed miserably. It's obviously still worth hearing, since Principle was one of house music's best songwriters, but the nonhouse efforts sound dated and somewhat embarassing. —*John Bush*

## Private Lightning 6

f. 1995, Vienna, Austria
*Group / Electronica, Electro-Techno*

PL6 is the tongue-in-cheek, legends-in-their-own-minds supergroup led by Austrian DJs/producers Patrick Pulsinger and Erdam Tunakan. Joined variously from track to track by fellow Viennese electro-jazz obscurantists Gerhard Potuznik, F. Sokol, and Def Con, among others, the group has released an album and a handful of compilation tracks through such labels as Sabotage and Morbid, including the full-length two LP/CD *They Came Down*. Like more recent Pulsinger incarnations such as Sluts'N'Strings & 909 and Showroom Recordings, PL6 move freely between funky downtempo jazz-hop and exploratory, heavily syncopated electro. [See Also: IO, Patrick Pulsinger, Sluts'N'Strings. —*Sean Cooper*

● **They Came Down** / 1996 / Morbid ♦♦♦
PL6's long awaited full-length debut does not disappoint, coming with a diverse array of electronic strangeness drawing from electro, hip-hop, jazz, and techno. Although a couple tracks never really make it past drawing-board status, enough of this album strikes the right balance of groove and self-indulgent sampler abuse to make it worth recommending. —*Sean Cooper*

## Prodigy

f. 1990, Braintree, Essex, England
*Group / Big Beat, Electronica, Rave, Club/Dance, Techno*

Prodigy navigated the high-wire balancing artistic merit and mainstream visibility with more flair than any electronica act of the '90s. Ably defeating the image-unconscious attitude of most electronic artists in favor of a focus on nominal frontman Keith Flint, the group crossed over to the mainstream of pop music with an incendiary live experience that approximated the original atmosphere of the British rave scene even while leaning uncomfortably close to arena-rock showmanship and punk theatrics. True, Flint's spiky hairstyle and numerous piercings often made for better advertising, but it was producer Liam Howlett whose studio wizardry launched Prodigy to the top of the charts, spinning a web of hard-hitting breakbeat techno with king-sized hooks and unmissable samples. Despite electronic music's diversity and quick progression during the '90s—from rave/hardcore to ambient/downtempo and back again, thanks to the breakbeat/drum'n'bass movement—Howlett modified Prodigy's sound only sparingly, swapping the rave-whistle effects and ragga samples for metal chords and chanted vocals proved the only major difference in the band's evolution from their 1991 debut to their worldwide breakthrough with third album, *The Fat of the Land*. Even before the band took its place as the premiere dance act for the alternative masses, Prodigy had proved a consistent entry in the British charts, with over a dozen consecutive singles in the Top 20.

Howlett, the prodigy behind the group's name, was trained on the piano while growing up in Braintree, Essex. He began listening to hip-hop in the mid-'80s and later DJed with the British rap act Cut to Kill before moving on to acid house later in the decade. The fledgling hardcore breakbeat sound was perfect for an old hip-hop fan fluent in uptempo dance music, and Howlett began producing tracks in his bedroom studio during 1988. His first release, the EP *What Evil Lurks*, became a major mover on the fledgling rave scene in 1990. After Howlett met up with Keith Flint and Leeroy Thornhill (both Essex natives as well) in the growing British rave scene, the trio formed Prodigy later that year. Howlett's recordings gained the trio a contract with XL Records, which re-released *What Evil Lurks* in February 1991.

Six months later, Howlett issued his second single "Charly," built around a sample from a children's public-service announcement. It hit No. 1 on the British dance charts, then crossed over to the pop charts, stalling only at No. 3. (It wasn't long before a copycat craze saw the launch of rave takeoffs on *Speed Racer*, *The Magic Roundabout*, and *Sesame Street*) Two additional Prodigy singles, "Everybody in the Place" and "Fire/Jericho," charted in the UK during late 1991 and early 1992.

Prodigy showed they were no one-anthem wonders in late 1992, with the release of *Prodigy Experience*, one of the first LPs by a rave act. Mixing chunky breakbeats with vocal samples from dub legend Lee "Scratch" Perry and the Crazy World of Arthur Brown, it hit the Top Ten and easily went gold. During 1993, Howlett added a ragga/hip-hop MC named Maxim Reality (Keeti Palmer) and occupied himself with remix work for Front 242, Jesus Jones, and Art of Noise. He also released the white-label single "Earthbound" to fool image-conscious DJs who had written off Prodigy as hopelessly commercial. Late 1993 brought the commercial release of "Earthbound" (as the group's seventh consecutive Top 20 singles entry, "One Love").

After several months of working on tracks, Howlett issued the next Prodigy single, "No Good (Start the Dance)." Despite the fact that the single's hook was a sped-up diva-vocal tag (an early rave staple), the following album *Music for the Jilted Generation* provided a transition for the group, from piano-pieces and rave-signal tracks to more guitar-integrated singles like "Voodoo People." The album also continued Prodigy's allegiance to breakbeat drum'n'bass; though the style had only recently become commercially viable (after a long gestation period in the dance underground), Howlett had been incorporating it from the beginning of his career. *Music for the Jilted Generation* entered the British charts at No. 1 and went gold in its first week of release. The album was also nominated for a Mercury Music Prize, as one of the best albums of the year.

Prodigy spent much of 1994 and 1995 touring around the world, and made a splashy appearance at the 1995 Glastonbury Festival, proving that electronica could make it in a live venue. The group had already made a transition from the club-rave circuit to more traditional rock venues, and the Glastonbury show set in stone the fact that they were no longer just a dance group. Flint's newly emerged persona — the consummate in-your-face punk showman and master of ceremonies for the digital-age crowd — provided a point of reference for rock critics uncomfortable covering Howlett (whom they saw as a glorified keyboard player).

Prodigy's incessant road schedule left little time to record, but Howlett managed to bring out the next new Prodigy single in March 1996. "Firestarter" entered the British charts at No. 1, though the video was almost banned due to complaints about arson fixation; many *Top of the Pops* viewers complained that Keith Flint had scared their children. An unmissable guitar hook and Flint's catcall vocal antics — his first on record — made it a quick worldwide hit and though "Firestarter" wasn't a major success in the US, its high-profile spot in MTV's *Buzz Bin* introduced Prodigy to many Americans and helped fuel the major-label push for electronica during the following year (though Prodigy did reject collaborative offers from David Bowie, U2, and Madonna). In the middle of the electronica buzz, Prodigy dropped their third album, *The Fat of the Land*. Despite rather obvious attempts to court mainstream rock fans (including several guest-vocalist spots and an L7 cover), the LP entered both British and American charts at No. 1, shifting several million units worldwide. The next Prodigy full-length was 1999's *The Dirtchamber Sessions*, a mix album helmed by Howlett. —*John Bush*

★ **Experience** / Oct. 20, 1992 / Elektra ♦♦♦♦♦

One of the few noncompilation rave albums of any worth, *Experience* balances a supply of top-this siren whistles and chipmunk divas with Howlett's surprising flair at constructing track after track of intense breakbeat techno. Almost every song sounds like a potential chart-topper (circa 1992, of course) while the true singles "Your Love," "Charly," "Music Reach 1/2/3/4," and "Out of Space" add that extra bit of energy to the fray. More than just a relic of the rave experience, *Experience* shows Prodigy near the peak of their game from the get-go. —*John Bush*

☆ **Music for the Jilted Generation** / Feb. 28, 1995 / Mute ♦♦♦♦♦

Prodigy's response to the sweeping legislation and crackdown on raves contained in 1994's Criminal Justice Bill is an effective statement of intent. Pure sonic terrorism, *Music for the Jilted Generation* employs the same rave energy that charged their debut *Experience* up the charts in Britain, but yokes it to a cause other than massive drug intake. Compared to their previous work, the sound is grubbier and less reliant on samples; the effect moved Prodigy away from the American-influenced rave and acid house of the past and toward a uniquely British vision of breakbeat techno that was increasingly allied to the limey invention, drum'n'bass. As on *Experience*, there are so many great songs here that first-time listeners would be forgiven for thinking of a greatest-hits compilation instead of a proper studio album. After a short intro, the shattering of panes of glass on "Break & Enter" catapults the album ahead with a propulsive flair. Each of the four singles — "Voodoo People," "Poison," "No Good (Start the Dance)," and "One Love" — are excellent, though album tracks like "Speedway" and "Their Law" (with help from Pop Will Eat Itself) don't slip up either. If *Experience* seemed like an excellent fluke, *Music for the Jilted Generation* was the album that announced Prodigy was on the charts to stay. —*John Bush*

**The Fat of the Land** / July 1, 1997 / XL Mute/Maverick/Warner Bros. ♦♦♦♦

Few albums were as eagerly anticipated as *The Fat of the Land*, Prodigy's long-awaited follow-up to *Music for the Jilted Generation*. By the time of its release, the group had two No. 1 British singles with "Firestarter" and "Breathe," and had begun to make inroads in America. *The Fat of the Land* was touted as the album that would bring electronica/techno to a wide American audience; in Britain, the group already had a staggeringly large following that was breathlessly awaiting the album. Liam Howlett toiled on the record for well over a year, which meant that many observers were expecting the album to be an unqualified masterpiece. *The Fat of the Land* falls short of masterpiece status, but that isn't because it doesn't deliver. Instead, it delivers exactly what anyone would expect: intense hip-hop-derived rhythms, imaginatively reconstructed samples and meaningless shouted lyrics from Keith Flint and Maxim. Half of the album does sound quite similar to "Firestarter," especially when Flint is singing; his hyperactive antics play better live than on record. Still, Howlett is an inventive producer, and he can make empty songs like "Smack My Bitch Up" and "Serial Thrilla" kick with a visceral power, but he is at his best on the funky hip-hop of "Diesel Power" (which is driven by an excellent Kool Keith rap) and "Funky Shit," as well as the mind-bending neo-psychedelia of "Narayan" (featuring guest vocals by Crispian Mills of Kula Shaker) and the blood-curdling cover of L7's "Fuel My Fire," which features vocals by Republica's Saffron. All those guest vocalists mean something — Howlett is at his best when he's writing for himself or others, not his group's own vocalists. But this is a minor point, because *The Fat of the Land*, even at its most predictable, is invigorating. "Firestarter" and all of its rewrites capture the fire of Prodigy at its peak, and the remaining songs have imagination that give the album weight. *The Fat of the Land* doesn't have quite enough depth or variety to qualify as a flat-out masterpiece, but what it does have to offer is damn good. —*Stephen Thomas Erlewine*

**The Dirtchamber Sessions, Vol. 1** / Apr. 6, 1999 / Beggars XL ♦♦♦♦

As though he wasn't the feature player on each of the three Prodigy albums preceding it, *The Dirtchamber Sessions* presents Liam Howlett in a solo setting. But here, instead of showing off his production wizardry, his long history as a DJ and mixing abilities are on display. They're proved more than up to the task, as Howlett plays mix n'match with over 50 records from his hip-hop and funk past. While the Chemical Brothers' mix album (released the year before) showcased the duo digging deep in their record crates for a set of soul chestnuts and rare finds, Howlett's selection and feel for the flow of a mix is superior. Including tracks by the JB's, Herbie Hancock, the 45 King, L.L. Cool J, the Sex Pistols, and Jane's Addiction, Howlett chooses grooves familiar to all and improvises around them (as any old-school DJ would think obvious) instead of mixing between two tracks like few have ever heard. The result is an enlightening, practically flawless mix album. —*John Bush*

## Propaganda
f. 1983, Düsseldorf, Germany
*Group / Club/Dance, New Wave, Synth-Pop*

Synth-pop band Propaganda was formed in Germany by vocalist Claudia Brücken and drummer Michael Mertens plus keyboard players Susanne Freytag and Ralf Dorper. The quartet moved to England in 1983 and signed to ZTT Records, also the home of Frankie Goes to Hollywood and Art of Noise. Propaganda's first single, "Dr. Mabuse," reached the British Top 30 in early 1984, but the band's second release was more than a year in coming. Finally, in May 1985, "Duel" trumped the debut single by hitting No. 21.

Propaganda's first album *A Secret Wish* appeared one month later, and the resulting tour necessitated the addition of bassist Derek Forbes and drummer Brian McGee—both formerly with Simple Minds. After the release of the remix album *Wishful Thinking* later that year, Dorper became the first original member to leave the band, and Propaganda splintered soon after, due to a prolonged legal battle to leave ZTT. The group finally re-emerged in 1988 with Mertens, Forbes, McGee, and American vocalist Betsi Miller. The quartet signed with Virgin, and released *1234* in 1990. The single "Heaven Give Me Words" broke the British Top 40 in 1990, and "Only One Word" placed modestly later that year.

Meanwhile, Claudia Brücken—who had stayed with ZTT in large part because of her marriage to label-owner Paul Morley—formed Act with Thomas Leer. The duo charted "Snobbery and Decay" in mid-1987 and released their only album, *Laughter, Tears, and Rage* in 1988. Brücken became a solo act by the turn of the decade, and charted only one single, "Absolut (E)," from her 1991 album *Love, And a Million Other Things*. Though neither the band nor Brücken had recorded recently, rumours flew during the mid-'90s that a Propaganda reunion was in the works. —*John Bush*

• **A Secret Wish** / 1985 / Island ++++
With guests including David Sylvian, Heaven 17's Glenn Gregory, and Steve Howe, *A Secret Wish* is synth-rock with an eye toward orchestrated pop as well as a bit of sampler experimentation in the grand ZTT tradition of Art of Noise. There's a distinct lack of songwriting on the album, and though the synth-grooves are tight enough to keep it flowing for most of its length, *A Secret Wish* occasionally falls flat from its own weight. —*Keith Farley*

**Wishful Thinking** / 1985 / ZTT/Island +++
In the '80s, remix records were usually either solipsistic synth noodling with very little appeal for the average listener or, worse still, crass commercial attempts to eek a few additional dollars from die hard fans. Propaganda was apparently prepared to answer accusations of that sort. The record jacket for *Wishful Thinking*, their 1985 collection of remixed "disturbdances" of songs from their debut, *A Secret Wish*, defends the remix concept with a quotation from Goethe: "and refashioning the fashioned/ lest it stiffen into iron/ is a work of endless vital activity." Somehow *Wishful Thinking* seems deserving of Goethe's defense. These remixes are vital and original creations in their own right. At times they even seem to surpass the quality of the original poppier versions. The driving dance beats, mesmerizing gothic chords, and swirling ambient guitars create a melancholic ethos of considerable artistic merit. Perhaps the key is the reduction in emphasis on the sometimes grating sing/shout vocals by Claudia Brucken and Susan Freytag. And though some mixes do begin to get dull when they are reduced to thumping bass and grinding drums, the vast majority of this project is more dynamic than that. —*Evan Cater*

**1234** / 1990 / Charisma +++
*1234* was not only Propaganda's first album for Charisma—it was also the first album the group had recorded since its legal battle with ZTT and the first since its personnel changes of 1988. Keyboardist Michael Mertens (Propaganda's only remaining original member) and Simple Minds graduates Derek Forbes (bass) and Brian McGee (drums) were still on board, although singer Claudia Brucken had been replaced by Betsi Miller, an American vocalist who fit in nicely. While *1234* isn't Propaganda's best album and falls short of essential, it's generally decent. "Heaven Give Me Words," "Only One Word," and "Wound in My Heart" are examples of Propaganda doing what it did well: lush, atmospheric synth-pop. Attractive melodies were Propaganda's forté, and the group's post-Brucken lineup provided its share. *1234* is the work of a group that was past its prime, but still had some things to say musically. —*Alex Henderson*

## Propellerheads
f. 1996, Bath, England
*Group / Big Beat, Funky Breaks, Electronica, Trip-Hop, Club/Dance*

Proponents of the much-maligned big-beat style of dance music (i.e. the Chemical Brothers), the Propellerheads—keyboardist/bassist/DJ Alex Gifford and drummer/DJ Will White—sprang out of Bath, England in 1996 to achieve almost overnight success in the UK with their brand of unabashed party techno, which combines strains of hip-hop, acid house, jazz-funk, and spy-film soundtracks. Gifford began his career as a studio musician, playing keyboards for Van Morrison and saxophone for the Stranglers, among others, before joining dance collective the Grid. After a stint on the staff of Peter Gabriel's Real World Studios, where he helped write and produce the well-received *Arcane* compilation, Gifford decided to start recording his own music, and sought out local drummer White. In 1996, the duo released its first EP, *Dive*, on Wall of Sound; almost immediately, the title track was licensed by Adidas for use in a television commercial. The follow-up, *Take California*, appeared later that year, and the title track became a significant underground big-beat success. The 1997 *Spybreak!* EP was another hit, demonstrating the duo's love for spy-film soundtracks; later in the year, the group hit the British Top Five with a remake of the Bond theme "On Her Majesty's Secret Service," recorded for the compilation *Shaken and Stirred: The David Arnold 007 Project*. Remixes for acts like Luscious Jackson, Soul Coughing, and 808 State followed, and Propellerheads signed to DreamWorks. The band made its US debut in 1997 with a self-titled CD5, which contained the new single "Bang On!," as well as several old and new tracks. In early 1998, the Propellerheads released their full-length debut, *Decksanddrumsandrockandroll*, to generally positive reviews. —*Steve Huey*

• **Decksanddrumsandrockandroll** / Jan. 26, 1998 / Wall of Sound ++++
Really, the title says it all—*Decksanddrumsandrockandroll* is about as close to rock 'n' roll as big-beat techno is going to get. Taking their cue from the Chemical Brothers, the Bath-based duo Propellerheads offer a set of pummeling, ultra-loud beats that may dabble in funk, house, hip-hop, soul and rap, but which all come out sounding as aggressive as rock. Not that there's anything wrong with that—at its best, big beat is as invigorating as any other music—but Propellerheads don't have the finesse, innovation or style of the Chemical Brothers, the leading propenents of big beat. When they shake the beat up, whether on the wah-wah drenched "Velvet Pants" or the pair of John Barry/James Bond tributes (a reworking of their cover of "On Her Majesty's Secret Service" and "History Repeating"), it sounds like a tactical move, since they know they can't spend the entire album on thundering dance cuts like "Bang On!" and "Take California." That said, *Decksanddrumsandrockandroll* remains a strong big-beat album, even if it ultimately doesn't reveal anything new, because the duo knows how to craft a hard-hitting, infectious rhythm track. And while that doesn't make them the next Chemical Brothers, it does make them the best in this style since the Chemicals. —*Stephen Thomas Erlewine*

## Prototype 909
f. 1993, New York, NY
*Group / Electronica, Club/Dance, Techno*

More than just a history experiment, Prototype 909 focuses on making forward-looking techno using mostly early-'80s synthesizers, like the Roland TB-303 and TR-808. Disdaining most MIDI setups, Taylor Deupree (aka Taylor 808), Dietrich Schoenemann, and Jason Szostek usually opt to compose their music on the fly, both at live appearances and on recorded works. The trio debuted in 1993 with *Acid Technology* for Instinct, while *Transistor Rhythm* and *Joined at the Head* followed at two-year intervals. The relaxed schedule is due in part to the fact that Prototype 909 is more of a side project than a regular band; Deupree also works as Human Mesh Dance and with the groups S.E.T.I. and Futique, while Schoenemann has X-Out and Szostek appears with BPMF and Decameron. Both Schoenemann and Szostek also record for Disko B as Rancho Relaxo. —*John Bush*

**Acid Technology** / 1993 / Sonic ♦♦♦
Prototype 909's early document of the acid-house revival, *Acid Technology* balances the minimalism of Plastikman with the spacier projects of the New York Instinct scene (including Taylor 808's own Human Mesh Dance and Futique projects). The result is an album just as hard-hitting as much other acid-techno, but informed by the ambience of Taylor's other recordings. —*John Bush*

**Transistor Rhythm** / 1995 / Sonic ♦♦♦

**Live '93-'95** / Aug. 29, 1995 / Instinct ♦♦

● **Joined at the Head** / Sep. 2, 1997 / Caipirinha ♦♦♦♦
*Joined at the Head* ably defeats the old adage that humor doesn't belong in techno, with ten tracks of driving acid-techno enlivened by the occasional odd bit of comedy—either actual or implied—from the cover shot (a computer-morphed photo of the threesome actually "joined at the head") to the quirky acid lines of "Housebroken" and the mere titles "Theme to Ravewatch" and "The Kids Don't Care." The music is up to the test too, hardly out of place on the country's harder dance floors as well as a few living rooms. —*John Bush*

## Psyche/BFC (Carl Craig)

*Producer / Detroit Techno, Club/Dance, Techno*
The reservoir for Carl Craig's earliest, most seminal sides, Psyche and BFC recorded several singles for Transmat, Fragile, and Craig's own Retroactive during 1989 and 1990. Long pointed to as the birth of the second wave in Detroit techno, the tracks were collected for release on Craig's Planet E Records in 1996. [See Also: Carl Craig, Innerzone Orchestra, Paperclip People, 69] —*John Bush*

★ **Elements 1989-1990** / 1996 / Planet E ♦♦♦♦♦
*Elements 1989-1990* compiles much of Carl Craig's earliest output before he started his own private Detroit techno label, Planet E, and began to achieve increasing levels of popularity with side projects such as Innerzone Orchestra and Paperclip People. While nowhere near as brilliant as Craig's other techno album from the '90s, *More Songs About Food and Revolutionary Art*, this compilation demonstrates rather effectively just exactly why Detroit pioneers such as Derrick May and Mike Banks took Craig under their wings. Formally, Craig shadows all 12 of the recordings on this compilation with drifting layers of synthesizer tones, which linger in the distance throughout each of the tracks, evoking mysterious inhuman moods. While Craig's ambient synthesizer provides the emotional character, his primitive sampler and drum machine produce fuzzy percussive rhythms propelled with distorted bass beats. The haunting synthesizer melody of tracks such as "It's a Shame"—a Derrick May anthem at the legendary Musical Institute—radiate like beaming glimpses into non-secular heavens. Similarly, the terribly distorted vocals on "Chicken Noodle Soup" and "Crackdown" may be the effect of low-budget recording, but they add ghostly feelings of ancient dreams lingering somewhere deep in the decayed remnants of Detroit. Even though fuzzy static sound of *Elements 1989-1990* doesn't compare to the striking clarity of Craig's later work, its cobwebs and dusty decay provide it with tones of antiquity. Like long-forgotten childhood memories, the re-release of these now impossible-to-find early Detroit techno recordings is reason to celebrate. At times rough around the edges and perhaps a bit too simple in relation to Craig's later work, their efficient simplicity functions as the bridge between May's pioneering work as Rhythim Is Rhythim and Craig's more evolved output on *More Songs About Food and Revolutionary Art*. Within these songs lies an element of naiveté and a strong sense of ambition that will never be duplicated by Craig again, no matter how grand his ideas or genius his craft. —*Jason Stanley Birchmeier*

## Psychic TV

f. 1979, London, England
*Group / Experimental Rock, Experimental, Acid House, Alternative Pop/Rock, Industrial*
After Genesis P-Orridge dissolved the seminal industrial-rock outfit Throbbing Gristle, he and Gristle cohorts Peter Christopherson and Cosey Fanni Tutti, plus Geoff Rushton, formed Psychic TV in 1979 as a means of continuing their confrontational, shock-oriented approach to music and their multimedia live performances. Psychic TV draws much of its inspiration from the literary underground, including situationist philosophy, William Burroughs (a professed fan), the Marquis de Sade, and Philip K. Dick. The group also claims to be the mouthpiece for its own quasi-religious group, the Temple Ov Psychick Youth. P-Orridge has been branded a dangerous deviant in several publications, and police raided his home in 1992, seizing videos, books, and magazines following a television show concerning child abuse in which a Psychic TV performance art video was shown out of context.

As for the music itself, Psychic TV's earlier years continued in the experimental vein of Throbbing Gristle's work, encompassing melodic pop, barely listenable white noise, gentle ballads, industrial found-sound collages, spoken-word pieces, and experiments with ethnic instruments and world music, all tied together by a dadaist sensibility. *Force the Hand of Chance*, the group's first album, was released in 1982; during the '80s, Psychic TV's prodigious output totaled over 20 albums. Much of this stemmed from a publicity stunt beginning in 1986 for which the group attempted to release one live album, each from a different nation, on the 23rd of each month for 23 months. Even though the group didn't quite achieve its goal, the fourteen albums Psychic TV released in eighteen months was enough to get the group into the *Guinness Book of World Records*. Christopherson and Rushton both left the group rather early on to form Coil, and Psychic TV has since become an open-ended collective with contributors such as Alex Fergusson, formerly of Alternative TV. Psychic TV scored a minor UK pop hit in 1986 with "Godstar," a tribute to Rolling Stones guitarist Brian Jones, and 1988 saw the group's first album release in America with *Allegory and Self*.

Beginning in 1988, P-Orridge became a pioneer on the British club and rave scene. Records from the Chicago house scene by Frankie Knuckles and Farley Jackmaster Funk made their way to London, and when P-Orridge noticed the word "acid" on one of them, he dubbed the British psychedelic variation "acid house" and began recording and experimenting with the style on *Jack the Tab: Acid Tablets, Vol. 1* and *Towards Thee Infinite Beat*. P-Orridge has since released albums under the name Psychic TV as well as using a variety of aliases to produce "compilation" albums actually featuring all his own music. Several Psychic TV collections, as well as new material, have continued to appear in the '90s; the best of the retrospectives are the two singles compilations *Hex Sex* and *Godstar*, and the 1999 overview *Best Ov: Time's Up*. —*Steve Huey*

**Force the Hand of Chance** / 1982 / Some Bizarre ♦♦♦
The debut Psychic TV album has all of the hallmarks of the group's radical inspirations: light '60s pop on "Just Drifting (For Caresse)" and "Stolen Kisses," more orchestrated instrumental work for the later "Caresse," and several free-form passages with bizarre spoken-word material from Genesis himself. *Force the Hand of Chance* also features the input of Peter "Sleazy" Christopherson, just before he founded Coil with John Balance. —*John Bush*

**Dreams Less Sweet** / 1983 / Thirsty Ear ♦♦♦
Their second album, released in 1983, *Dreams Less Sweet* fluctuates between industrial pieces and heavily orchestrated pop, employing exotic instruments like the Tibetan thighbone in additon to a number of found sounds. —*Jason Ankeny*

● **Allegory and Self** / 1988 / Revolver ♦♦♦♦
Beginning with "Godstar," Psychic TV's tribute to Brian Jones complete with Stonesy guitar licks, *Allegory and Self* balances surprisingly straight-ahead alternative pop with more experimental tracks using tape cut-ups or extended synthesizer freeforms. P-Orridge makes for quite an ambitious frontman, crooning like Love and Rockets' Daniel Ash on "We Kiss" and producing a series of guttural roars for "Southern Comfort." "She Was Surprised" even bears the first fruits of Psychic TV's fixation with sampladelic acid house. It may not be a characteristic Psychic TV (if such an animal exists), but *Allegory and Self* may well be the best introduction for beginners. —*John Bush*

**Jack the Tab: Acid Tablets, Vol. 1** / 1988 / Castalia ♦♦♦

**Kondole** / 1989 / Temple ♦♦♦♦

**Towards Thee Infinite Beat** / Apr. 1990 / Wax Trax! ♦♦♦♦
Although it tends toward unvarying sampladelic acid house, *Towards Thee Infinite Beat* is a good place to start for Psychic TV's dance phase. —*John Dougan*

**Beyond Thee Infinite Beat** / Aug. 1990 / Wax Trax! ♦♦♦
This *Infinite Beat* remix album includes reworkings of tracks by a host of PTV associates, including Dave Ball, Andy Falconer, Jack the Tab, and Evil Eddie. Although most of the tracks have the blander qualities of much acid

house, Falconer's mix of "Bliss" and DJ Sugar Jay's mix of "Horror House" are a bit together than most. —*John Bush*

**Presents Ultrahouse: The Twelve Inch Mixes** / 1992 / Wax Trax! ♦♦

**Hex Sex: The Singles, Pt. 1** / 1994 / Cleopatra ♦♦♦♦
The pop end of Psychic TV gets the full treatment with this singles collection, released on the Cleopatra label, including faithful covers of '60s standards like the Beach Boys' "Good Vibrations" and Serge Gainsbourg' "Je T'aime Non Plus," culture-icon tributes "Roman P." and "Godstar" plus later singles like "Hex Sex" and "Love War Riot." Though Genesis P-Orridge's vocals are occasionally tuneless, *Hex Sex* is a good summation of one of the more bizarre "pop" bands of the '80s. —*John Bush*

**Godstar: The Singles, Pt. 2** / 1995 / Cleopatra ♦♦

**Cold Blue Torch** / Apr. 1996 / Cleopatra ♦♦
On *Cold Blue Torch*, members of Skinny Puppy, Prong, Pigface, and Spahn Ranch remix material from the preceding Psychic TV album *Trip Reset*. —*Jason Ankeny*

**The Origin of the Species** / Mar. 24, 1998 / Invisible ♦♦♦♦
Five years of Psychic TV (1987-1992) are examined in this two-CD sampler packaged in Psychic TV's trademark exploitation of the power of the vulgar image. This is the first of a three-part series chronicling the group. Ten of the 21 tracks are previously unreleased. "Infinite Beat" and succeeding tracks identify Psychic TV as primogenitors of electronica, creative sampling and the club mix while flirting with psychological principles of mind control. Such is the typical combination of outre and superficially commercial material that is the Psychic TV fare and guaranteed to maintain their cult following. It is certainly no understatement to say that without this group's envelope-pushing fusion of machines and rock instrumentation you could never have gotten to the now thoroughly explored realms of acid house and techno. A 30-page, full-color booklet details each track with text from the mind of founding member, Genesis P-Orridge (also of preindustrial noise experimenters Throbbing Gristle). Allowing full immersion of this suggestive, cryptic, neo-psychedelic beat music is truly a mind altering experience. A couple hours after partaking of these doses, one can be assured that Psychic TV aspired, and often succeed at, employing guitars, drums, keyboards and sequenced sounds toward recreating an expansive, hallucinogenic, paradigm challenging drug experience…that you can dance to. —*Thomas Schulte*

**Best Ov: Time's Up** / Jun. 29, 1999 / Cleopatra ♦♦♦♦
While it isn't quite a definitive overview, *Best Ov: Time's Up* is easily the best single-disc introduction to Psychic TV, featuring such crucial singles as "Godstar" (in both 7" and 1994 versions), "Roman P.," "United '94," and more. Some of the single mixes present are very difficult to locate elsewhere, making this package enticing for devoted fans as well. —*Steve Huey*

**Origin of the Species, Vol. 2** / Aug. 31, 1999 / Invisible ♦♦♦
The two-disc *Origin of the Species, Vol. 2* rescues a sizable number of Psychic TV house tracks from out-of-print obscurity. The first disc is drawn from the albums *Jack the Tab: Acid Tablets, Vol. 1* (1988) and *Tekno Acid Beat* (1989), while the second disc features the *Ultradrug* material issued in 1995. The *Jack the Tab* cuts are the most interesting, having been issued as a fake various-artists compilation and actually featuring Psychic TV working with former Soft Cell keyboardist Dave Ball and writer Richard Norris. Since the tracks here aren't culled from as wide a variety of sources as the first volume of *Origin of the Species*, it isn't quite as consistent a listen, but it does capture the group at their acid-house peak, and all of this material has been very difficult to find for a long time. —*Steve Huey*

## Psychick Warriors Ov Gaia

f. 1989, The Netherlands
*Group / Dark Ambient, Ambient Techno, Techno*

Just as light-hearted ambient house began to hit the mainstream in the early '90s, Psychick Warriors Ov Gaia foreshadowed a move to sinister downtempo music, more influenced by Coil and Psychic TV than the Orb. The Dutch group's shadowy nature and lack of connection to the close-knit dance community mystified some (their live shows were often performed behind large screens), but the band's sound—organic tribal-trance with an understated use of samples—became quite influential, as many groups mirrored the move to darker rhythms later in the decade.

The lineup for Psychick Warriors Ov Gaia—Reinier Brekelmans, Bobby Reiner, and Robert Heynen with soundman/producer Tim Freeman—originally played in an industrial band called the Infants in 1985. Later in the '80s, the group appeared as Sluagh Ghairm ("spirits cry"), but by the end of the decade they had become known as Psychick Warriors Ov Gaia—the name signifying membership in the Temple Ov Psychick Youth, the occult collective founded by Psychic TV's Genesis P. Orridge (though Psychick Warriors weren't connected musically to Psychic TV). In 1990, the band released their debut single "Exit 23," a minimalistic trance epic with a haunting vocal sample from Timothy Leary ("return, to the source"). As with all their future work, it appeared on Belgium's Kk Records. The second single "Maenad" was an upbeat tribal house mover, also focused squarely on the dance floor.

The 1992 debut album *Ov Biospheres and Sacred Grooves* showed that Psychick Warriors could stride the fence between floor-filling organic trance and dark ambience quite well. On tracks such as "Obsidian" and the Drum Club remix of "Exit 23" (added to the American Restless release), the chilling ambient groove easily overpowered any textured beats.

After a single release for "Obsidian" and the Heynen/Freeman side-project called Disciples Ov Gaia (on which they remix "The Key," from *Ov Biospheres and Sacred Grooves*), Heynen left to form Exquisite Corpse, a group that focused on the minimal tribal rhythms evident on "Maenad." Three very different projects occupied Psychick Warriors during 1993-94. The first was *Psychick Rhythms, Vol. 1*, a six-track EP of beats that—the package warned—was designed "for mixing, for breaks, for possession, for collectors." The second was a session for John Peel's BBC radio show, quite an honor for a continental electronic band. The three-tracker featured two titles remixed from *Psychick Rhythms* and the exquisite ambience of "Dust," a track that had first appeared on the *Trance Europe Express, Vol. 1* compilation. The "Out Now" single appeared in Spring 1994, consisting of the ambient title track, a remix of "Dust," and two songs in more of a house vein.

By 1995, the Psychick Warriors' lineup consisted of Brekelmans and Freeman, plus new members Joris Hilckmann and Reinoud Van Den Broek. The "Kraak" single and a new LP, *Record of Breaks*, returned to the tribal rhythms of the first album, but still represented a textured ambient sound unlike any other band of the moment. Though *Record of Breaks* never received a full American release, the American double-disc compilation *History of Psychick Phenomenon* included most of the album, along with the entire "Obsidian" CD-5 and selections from the singles for "Exit 23," "Maenad," and "Kraak." —*John Bush*

● **Ov Biospheres & Sacred Grooves** / 1992 / KK ♦♦♦♦
This seamless album, propelled by "Obsidian" and "Exit 23," is perhaps the eeriest work to come out of the ambient house genre. The sounds are organic in form, intoxicatingly repetitive, and miles away from the positive melodies of The Orb or others. PWOG excel in long, steadily evolving pieces, and it's well documented on *Sacred Grooves*. —*John Bush*

**Record of Breaks** / 1995 / Kk ♦♦♦♦
Psychick Warriors' second album locks into an even harder dark trance groove than the debut, using textured sounds and heavy, even beats to pound listeners into submission. —*John Bush*

**A History of Psychick Phenomenon** / Sep. 17, 1996 / Never ♦♦♦♦
*History of Psychick Phenomenon* is a somewhat mysterious two-disc American collection which includes some material from *Record of Breaks* plus various singles tracks from "Exit 23," "Kraak," and "Obsidian." —*John Bush*

## The Psychonauts

*Group / Trip-Hop, Club/Dance*

Functioning as the house DJs for Mo'Wax Records, the Psychonauts recorded the 1998 mix album flashback *Time Machine*. One year later, the duo made their production debut with the single "Hot Blood/Invading Space." —*John Bush*

● **Time Machine: A Mo'Wax Retrospective Mix** / Oct. 12, 1998 / Mo'Wax ♦♦♦♦
On *Time Machine*, the Psychonauts spin through a dense turntablist mix of Mo'Wax favorites, close to 50 tracks in no less than half an hour. Obviously, label stalwarts (DJ Shadow, DJ Krush, U.N.K.L.E., Dr. Octagon) get much of the table time here, though the Psychonauts' obvious familiarity with the catalog enables them to dredge a few obscure classics as well: La Funk Mob's "Motor Bass Gets Phunked Up," Andrea Parker's "Melodious Thunk," Luke Vibert's "Welcome," and the Psychonauts' own remix of Liquid Liquid's "Scraper." A near-crucial document for Mo'Wax collectors, *Time Machine*

would undoubtedly get the nod for wider audiences too if only it still appeared in record stores. —*John Bush*

## Public Enemy

f. 1982, Long Island, NY
*Group / Hardcore Rap, East Coast Rap, Hip-Hop*

Public Enemy rewrote the rules of hip-hop, becoming the most influential and controversial rap group of the late '80s and, for many, the definitive rap group of all time. Building from Run-D.M.C.'s street-oriented beats and Boogie Down Productions' proto-gangsta rhyming, Public Enemy pioneered a variation of hardcore rap that was musically and politically revolutionary. With his powerful, authoritative baritone, lead rapper Chuck D rhymed about all kinds of social problems, particularly those plaguing the Black community, often condoning revolutionary tactics and social activism. In the process, he directed hip-hop towards an explicitly self-aware, pro-Black consciousness that became the culture's signature throughout the next decade. Musically, Public Enemy was just as revolutionary, as their production team the Bomb Squad, created dense soundscapes that relied on avant-garde cut-and-paste techniques, unrecognizable samples, piercing sirens, relentless beats, and deep funk. It was chaotic and invigorating music, made all the more intoxicating by Chuck D's forceful vocals and the absurdist raps of his comic foil Flavor Flav. With his comic sunglasses and an oversized clock hanging from his neck, Flav became the group's visual focal point, but he never obscured the music. While rap and rock critics embraced the group's late '80s and early '90s records, Public Enemy frequently ran into controversy with their militant stance and lyrics, especially after their 1988 album *It Takes a Nation of Millions to Hold Us Back* made them into celebrities. After all the controversy settled in the early '90s and once the group entered hiatus, it became clear that Public Enemy was the most influential and radical band of its time.

Chuck D (b. Carlton Ridenhour, August 1, 1960) formed Public Enemy in 1982, as he was studying graphic design at Adelphi University on Long Island. He had been DJing at the student radio station WBAU, where he met Hank Shocklee and Bill Stephney. All three shared a love of hip-hop and politics, which made them close friends. Shocklee had been assembling hip-hop demo tapes, and Ridenhour rapped over one song, "Public Enemy No. 1" around the same time he began appearing on Stephney's radio show under the Chuckie D pseudonym. Def Jam cofounder and producer Rick Rubin heard a tape of "Public Enemy No. 1" and he immediately courted Ridenhour in hopes of signing him to his fledgling label. Chuck D initially was reluctant, but he eventually developed a concept for a literally revolutionary hip-hop group—one that would be driven by sonically extreme productions and socially revolutionary politics. Enlisting Shocklee as his chief producer and Stephney as a publicist, Chuck D formed a crew with DJ Terminator X (b. Norman Lee Rogers, August 25, 1966), and fellow Nation of Islam member Professor Griff (b. Richard Griff) as the choreographer of the group's backup dancers, the Security of the First World, who performed homages to old Stax and Motown dancers with their martial moves and fake Uzis. He also asked his old friend William Drayton (b. March 16, 1959) to join as a fellow rapper. Drayton developed an alter-ego called Flavor Flav, who functioned as a court jester to Chuck D's booming voice and angry rhymes in Public Enemy.

Public Enemy's debut album, *Yo! Bum Rush the Show*, was released on Def Jam Records in 1987. Its spare beats and powerful rhetoric were acclaimed by hip-hop critics and aficionados, but the record was ignored by the rock and R&B mainstream. However, their second album *It Takes a Nation of Millions to Hold Us Back* was impossible to ignore. Under Shocklee's direction, PE's production team, the Bomb Squad, developed a dense, chaotic mix that relied as much on found sounds and avant-garde noise as it did on old-school funk. Similarly, Chuck D's rhetoric gained focus and Flavor Flav's raps were wilder and funnier. *A Nation of Millions* was hailed as revolutionary by both rap and rock critics, and it was—hip-hop had suddenly became a force for social change. As Public Enemy's profile was raised, they opened themselves up to controversy. In a notorious statement, Chuck D claimed that rap was "the Black CNN," relating what was happening in the inner city in a way that mainstream media could not project. Public Enemy's lyrics were naturally dissected in the wake of such a statement, and many critics were uncomfortable with the positive endorsement of Black Muslim leader Louis Farrakhan on "Bring the Noise." "Fight the Power," Public Enemy's theme for Spike Lee's controversial 1989 film *Do the Right Thing*, also caused an uproar for its attacks on Elvis Presley and John Wayne, but that was considerably overshadowed by an interview Professor Griff gave the *Washington Times* that summer. Griff had previously said anti-Semitic remarks on stage but his quotation that Jews were responsible for "the majority of the wickedness that goes on across the globe" were greeted with shock and outrage, especially by White critics who previously embraced the group. Faced with a major crisis, Chuck D faltered. First he fired Griff, then brought him back, then broke up the group entirely. Griff gave one more interview where he attacked Chuck D and PE, which led to his permanent departure from the group.

Public Enemy spent the remained of 1989 preparing their third album, releasing "Welcome to the Terrordome" as its first single in early 1990. Again, the hit single caused controversy as its lyrics "still they got me like Jesus" were labeled anti-Semitic by some quarters. Despite all the controversy, *Fear of a Black Planet* was released to enthusiastic reviews in the spring of 1990, and it shot into the pop Top 10 as the singles "911 Is a Joke," "Brothers Gonna Work It Out," and "Can't Do Nuttin' for Ya Man" became Top 40 R&B hits. For their next album, 1991's *Apocalypse 91...The Enemy Strikes Black*, the group re-recorded "Bring the Noize" with thrash metal band Anthrax, the first sign that the group was trying to consolidate its white audience. *Apocalypse 91* was greeted with overwhelmingly positive reviews upon its fall release, and it debuted at No. 4 on the pop charts, but the band began to lose momentum in 1992 as they toured with the second leg of U2's Zoo TV tour and Flavor Flav was repeatedly in trouble with the law. In the fall of 1992, they released the remix collection *Greatest Misses* as an attempt to keep their name viable, but it was greeted to nasty reviews.

Public Enemy was on hiatus during 1993, as Flav attempted to wean himself off drugs, returning in the summer of 1994 with *Muse Sick-N-Hour Mess Age*. Prior to its release, it was subjected to exceedingly negative reviews in *Rolling Stone* and *The Source*, which affected the perception of the album considerably. *Muse Sick* debuted at No. 14, but it quickly fell off the charts as it failed to generate any singles. Chuck D retired Public Enemy from touring in 1995 as he severed ties with Def Jam, developed his own record label and publishing company, and attempted to re-think Public Enemy. In 1996, he released his first debut album, *The Autobiography of Mista Chuck*. As it was released in the fall, he announced that he planned to record a new Public Enemy album the following year.

Before that record was made, Chuck D published an autobiography in the fall of 1997. During 1997, Chuck D reassembled the original Bomb Squad and began work on three albums. In the spring of 1998, Public Enemy kicked off their major comeback with their soundtrack to Spike Lee's *He Got Game*, which was played more like a proper album than a soundtrack. Upon its April 1998 release, the record received the strongest reviews of any Public Enemy album since *Apocalypse '91: The Enemy Strikes Black*. After Def Jam refused to help Chuck D's attempts to bring PE's music straight to the masses via the internet, he signed the group to the web-savvy independent Atomic Pop. Before the retail release of Public Enemy's seventh LP, *There's a Poison Goin' On...*, the label made MP3 files of the album available on the internet. It finally appeared in stores in July 1999. —*Stephen Thomas Erlewine*

**Yo! Bum Rush the Show** / 1987 / Def Jam ✦✦✦✦

When their debut was released in 1987, very few rap groups even approached Public Enemy's musical or political stance. Listening to the first album now, it's surprising how few of the songs are actually political—the sheer force of the sound fools the listener into thinking Chuck D is saying more than he actually is. Still, "Megablast," "Public Enemy No. 1," and "Miuzi Weighs a Ton" carry a small amount of political rhetoric. Much sparer than later releases, the album is carried over the top by Chuck D's bulldozer roar. —*Stephen Thomas Erlewine*

★ **It Takes a Nation of Millions to Hold Us Back** / 1988 / Def Jam ✦✦✦✦✦

Arguably the best hip-hop album ever made, *It Takes a Nation of Millions to Hold Us Back* was a huge leap forward not only for Public Enemy, but for all of hip-hop. PE's signature sound—a barrage of found sounds, densely woven samples, and noisy tape loops—was evident for the first time, courtesy of The Bomb Squad. Chuck D's lyrics, full of revolutionary rhetoric yet managing to avoid being hysterical, matched the aural onslaught. The group's political stance would be meaningless if the music didn't put it over the top throughout, and that does happen on "Black Steel in the Hour of Chaos," "Night of the Living Baseheads," "Rebel Without a Pause," "Don't Believe the Hype," and "Bring the Noise," in particular. There isn't a weak moment on the album. A landmark recording. —*Stephen Thomas Erlewine*

☆ **Fear of a Black Planet** / 1990 / Def Jam ✦✦✦✦✦
Public Enemy's artistic and commercial winning streak continued with its third album, *Fear of a Black Planet*. While other East Coast rappers were content to boast about their prowess on the microphone, Public Enemy always had a lot to say. Though a few stinkers are included—the worst offender being the homophobic "Meet the G That Killed Me"—they are by far outnumbered by the gems. From "Burn Hollywood Burn" (a brutally honest attack on racism in the film industry) to the optimistic "Brothers Gonna Work It Out," the politically charged rappers have no problem maintaining the level of excellence they reached on *It Takes a Nation of Millions to Hold Us Back*. A gut-level attack on incompetence in the 911 system, "911 Is a Joke" illustrates just how on-target PE could be—in fact, it should be stressed that the song precedes by several years the incident in which 911 operators in Philadelphia came under attack for doing nothing to help a youth who was being beaten to death. And once again, PE's producers, the Bomb Squad, provide a collage of samples that is as imaginative as it is bombastic. —*Alex Henderson*

**Apocalypse 91... The Enemy Strikes Black** / Oct. 1, 1991 / Def Jam ✦✦✦✦
Although it falls short of the excellence of *Fear of a Black Planet* and *It Takes a Nation of Millions to Hold Us Back*, PE's fourth album proved that the Long Islanders could still be extremely stimulating—both lyrically and musically. This time, the obvious winners include "Shut Em Down" (a commentary on liquor stores profiting from human suffering in the Black commmunity) and "By the Time I Get to Arizona" (an angry reflection on that state's refusal to celebrate Martin Luther King's birthday in the early '90s) and an invigorating rap/metal remake of "Bring the Noize" featuring thrash headbangers Anthrax. Although produced by the Imperial Grand Ministers of Funk instead of the Bomb Squad, the album boasts exactly the type of production one associates with PE—abrasive, hard, and dissonant. Unfortunately, PE's popularity would decline considerably after the album—and considerably less talented N.W.A. clones would be selling a lot more albums. —*Alex Henderson*

**Muse Sick-N-Hour Mess Age** / Aug. 23, 1994 / Def Jam ✦✦
Public Enemy took a full three years between *Apocalypse 91* and *Muse Sick-N-Hour Mess-Age*. During that time, numerous hip-hop styles had come and gone, making Public Enemy seem hopelessly outdated by the time they actually released their fifth record. With the exception of the *Greatest Misses* compilation, *Muse Sick* didn't fare as well on the charts as the group's three previous albums, nor was it well-received critically, receiving the poorest reviews of any of the group's efforts. And, again discounting *Greatest Misses*, *Muse Sick* is PE's weakest album. Conceptually, it's all over the place, as Chuck D strikes out at a number of his usual targets but without the focused, intelligent rage of *Nation of Millions* or *Fear of A Black Planet*. Similarly, the music careens out of control, as they try to incorporate recent hip-hop innovations to their signature sound. Nothing on the record sounds forced, but the album does sound directionless, which tends to cancel out the number of solid tracks on the album. Public Enemy doesn't necessarily seem outdated or musically bankrupt on *Muse Sick-N-Hour Mess-Age*—they just appear unsure of themselves. —*Stephen Thomas Erlewine*

**He Got Game** / Apr. 21, 1998 / Def Jam ✦✦✦
Four years is a long time in hip-hop, but it seems that Public Enemy has been away even longer. Delivered at the height of the popularity of blunted, ignorant G-funk, *Muse Sick-N-Hour Mess Age* went ignored upon its release in 1994, and PE faded from view shortly afterward. Which means that when *He Got Game*—nominally a soundtrack to Spike Lee's basketball drama, but in reality more of an individual album—was released in the spring of 1998, it seemed like Public Enemy hadn't been active since 1991's *Apocalypse 91*. Seven years out of the spotlight both hurt and helped PE. With Chuck D pushing 40, there's no question that they're a veteran act, but the late '90s are friendlier to their noisy, claustrophobic hip-hop than the mid-'90s, largely because hip-hop terrorists like the Wu-Tang Clan, Jeru the Damaja, and DJ Shadow were bringing the music back to its roots. PE follows in their path, stripping away the sonic blitzkrieg that was the Bomb Squad's trademark and leaving behind skeletal rhythm tracks, simple loops, and basslines—in other words, this is hardcore. Taking on the Wu at their own game—and, if you think about it, Puff Daddy as well, since the simple, repetitive loop of Buffalo Springfield's "For What It's Worth" on the title track is nothing more than a brazenly successful one-upmanship of Puff's shameless thievery—doesn't hurt the group's credibility, since they do it *well*. Listen to the circular, menacing synth lines of the opening "Resurrection" or the scratching strings on "Unstoppable," and it's clear that Public Enemy can compete with the most innovative artists in the younger generation, while "Is Your God a Dog" and "Politics of the Sneaker Pimps" prove that they can draw their own rules. That said, *He Got Game* simply lacks the excitement and thrill of prime period PE—Chuck D, Terminator X, and the Bomb Squad are now seasoned, experienced craftsmen, and it shows, for both and better and worse. They can craft a solid comeback like *He Got Game*, but no matter how enjoyable and even thought-provoking the album is, that doesn't mean it's where you'll turn when you want to hear Public Enemy. —*Stephen Thomas Erlewine*

**There's a Poison Goin' On...** / Jul. 20, 1999 / Atomic Pop ✦✦✦
Opening with a sonic collage straight out of *Fear of a Black Planet* and rushing into the extraordinary "Do You Wanna Go Our Way—?—," *There's a Poison Goin' On...* comes out of the gates sounding like classic Public Enemy, which is exactly what Public Enemy intended. It's what they needed to sound like, after all. Their slight sonic change-up on *He Got Game* didn't result in a hit, but the problem wasn't with that record, it was with its proposed follow-ups (including remixes), which Chuck D wanted to bring directly to the public through the internet. Def Jam wouldn't hear of it, and the label and PE soon sank into a bitter feud that ultimately resulted in the band signing with web-friendly label Atomic Pop, who initially released *Poison* as downloadable MP3s before pressing compact discs. In a way, the feud was a good thing for PE, since it brought them media attention, which is a rare thing for a veteran hip-hop band, even one as universally acclaimed as Public Enemy. Such increased exposure also brought a minor controversy over "Swindlers Lust," which was perceived as anti-Semitic by some critics, but this outrage was isolated, never spilling over into the mainstream because Public Enemy was now at the margins of hip-hop. They were no longer considered cutting-edge among certain quarters, and younger kids never picked up their records, so the only place for this controversy to reside was among the rock critics and aging fans who remembered when *It Takes a Nation of Millions* changed the world ten years prior to the release of *Poison*. The natural by-product of this is that they're the only ones that paid attention to the album. Chuck D is smart, though, and he must have known that this would have been the case when he was recording the album, since it consciously copies PE's past and never really breaks from that blueprint. In some respects, that's a disappointment, since *He Got Game* showed that PE could subtly incorporate modern hip-hop and do it better than some modern acts, but *There's a Poison Goin' On* is nevertheless a strong album, even if it is doggedly classicist. It's also dogmatic, with Chuck D preaching to the converted about the evils of the record industry and conformity in hip-hop, which does become a little trying by the end of the record, but it won't matter because he delivers lyrically and PE delivers musically. It does so in a manner that's entirely familiar to fans of Public Enemy, but that's not really a problem, since it offers a solid continuation of *Apocalypse 91*. It may not be a hit, but it's not dated, and ultimately, it's their most satisfying record in several years—which is a subtle difference that only the converted will notice. —*Stephen Thomas Erlewine*

## Public Image Ltd.

f. 1978, London, England
*Group / Post-Punk, Experimental, Alternative Pop/Rock, Alternative Dance*
Public Image Ltd. (PiL) originally was a quartet led by singer John Lydon (formerly Johnny Rotten, b. Jan 31, 1956) and guitarist Keith Levene, who had been a member of the Clash in one of its early lineups. The band was filled out by bassist Jah Wobble (John Wordle) and drummer Jim Walker. It was formed in the wake of the 1978 breakup of Lydon's former group, the Sex Pistols. For the most part, it devoted itself to droning, slow-tempo, bass-heavy noise rock, overlaid by Lydon's distinctive, vituperative rant.

The group's debut single, "Public Image," was more of an uptempo pop/rock song, however, and it hit the UK Top Ten upon its release in October 1978. The group itself debuted on Christmas Day, shortly after the release of its first album, *Public Image*. Neither the single nor the album was released in the US.

*Metal Box*, the band's second UK album, came in the form of three 12" 45 RPM discs in a film cannister. It was released in the US in 1980 as the double album *Second Edition*. (By this time, PiL was a trio consisting of Lydon, Levene, and Wobble.) The third album, not released in the US, was the live *Paris in the Spring* (1980). Lydon and Levene, plus hired musicians, made up the group by the time of *The Flowers of Romance* (1981), the much-acclaimed fourth album, which reached No. 11 in the UK.

In 1983, PiL scored its biggest UK hit, when "This Is Not a Love Song" reached No. 5. By this time, however, Levene had left, and the name from here on would be, more than anything else, a vehicle for John Lydon (though with a comparatively steady lineup). A second live album, *Live in Tokyo*, appeared in England in 1983.

The following year saw the release of *This Is What You Want... This Is What You Get*, only PiL's third album to be released in the US, though it now had six albums out. It marked the start of Lydon's move toward a more accessible dance-rock style, a direction that would be pursued further in *Album* (1986) (also called *Cassette* or *Compact Disc*, depending on the format), notably on the hit "Rise," as well as on *Happy?* (1987) and *9* (1989) In 1990, PiL released the compilation album *The Greatest Hits, So Far*, and in 1991 came the new album, *That What Is Not*. After completing his memoirs in late 1993, Lydon decided to put an end to PiL and pursue a solo career. —*William Ruhlmann*

★ **Metal Box** / Jul. 1980 / Warner Brothers ♦♦♦♦♦
From presentation to sound to ideology, PiL was determined to remain as far away from traditional rock trappings as possible. Seeing themselves as more of a "collective" than a band, the group managed to keep the word "boundaries" out of their vocabulary for at least the first four years of their existence. Their first three records are hallmarks of uncompromising, challenging post-punk, hardly sounding like anything of the past, present, or future. Sure, there were touchstones that got their imaginations running—the bizarreness of Captain Beefheart, the open and rhythmic spaces of Can, and the dense heaviness of Lee Perry's productions fueled their creative fires—but what they achieved with *Metal Box* was a completely unique hour of avant garde noise. Or anti-rock, as they called it.

Originally packaged in a film canister as a trio of 12" records played at 45 RPMs, the bass and treble are pegged at 11 throughout, with nary a tinge of mid-range to be found. It's all scrapes and throbs (dubscrapes?), not to mention John Lydon's caterwauling about such subjects as his dying mother, resentment and murder—certainly not a record to get the party hopping. Guitarist Keith Levene splatters silvery, violent, percussive shards of metallic scrapes onto the canvas, much like a restrained Jackson Pollack. Jah Wobble and Martin Atkins lay down a molasses-thick rhythmic foundation throughout that's just as funky as Can's Czukay/Leibezeit and Chic's Edwards/Thompson. No, really—much of the record flat-out *grooves*.

*Metal Box* might not be recognized as a groundbreaking record with the same reverence as *Never Mind the Bollocks*, and you certainly can't trace numerous waves of bands who wouldn't have existed without it like the Sex Pistols record, but it's tones have sent miasmic reverberations through a much broader scope of artists and genres. Like a virus.

[*Metal Box* was issued in the States in 1980 with different artwork and cheaper packaging under the title *Second Edition;* the track sequence differs as well. The UK reissue of *Metal Box* on CD boasts better sound quality than the *Second Edition* CD.] —*Andy Kellman*

**The Flowers of Romance** / 1981 / Warner Brothers ♦♦♦♦
As opposed to the axis of throbbing bass and guitar slashings of *Metal Box*, *The Flowers of Romance* is centralized on razor-sharp drums and typically haranguing vocals. No dubwise grooves here—bassist Jah Wobble was kicked out prior to the recording for ripping off PiL backing tracks for his solo material. And growing more disenchanted with the guitar, Keith Levene's infatuation with synthesizers was reaching a boiling point. His scythe-like guitar is truly brought out for only one song. Stark and minimal are taken to daring lengths, so it's no surprise that Virgin initially balked at issuing the heavily percussive record.

"Four Enclosed Walls" opens with something of a mechanical death rattle and John Lydon's quavering warble, framed by backwards piano and Martin Atkins' spartan, dry-as-a-bone drumming. His rapier-like drums seem to serve a similar purpose to Levene's guitar on *Metal Box*. An unsteady drum pattern and fragile, wind chime-like guitar from Levene shape "Track 8," a bleak look at sexual relationships. Lydon adds color with pleasant imagery of Butterball turkeys and elephant graves. "Under the House" and "Francis Massacre" are the most violent tracks due to Atkins' machine gun firing and Levene's chilling atmospherics. Lydon lashes out at zealous fans on the only bottom-heavy tune, "Banging the Door": "The walls are so thin/ The neighbors listen in/ Keep the noise down."

Perhaps the band's most challenging work (in the avant garde sense), it's just as "love it or hate it" as *Metal Box;* it'll either go down a treat or like a five pound block of liverwurst. [The UK version adds three bonus tracks: an instrumental version of "The Flowers of Romance," "Another," (essentially "Graveyard" with vocals) and "Home Is Where the Heart Is." The latter two can be found on *Plastic Box*.] —*Andy Kellman*

**Happy?** / 1987 / Virgin ♦♦♦♦
Continuing with the deceptively pop-oriented studio sheen of *Album, Happy?* is a set of outwardly friendly material, which reveals its fractured melodies and concepts upon closer inspection. Song for song, *Happy?* isn't quite as strong as *Album*, but it continues its predecessor's sound to a fine effect. —*Stephen Thomas Erlewine*

**9** / 1989 / Virgin ♦♦♦
Not only does *9* expand on the pop leanings of the two previous PiL albums, it adds elements of dance music and funk. At first, the record might seem a bit too slick, but it reveals more subtexts with each listen, although the music isn't quite as involving as the songs on *Album* and *Happy?*. —*Stephen Thomas Erlewine*

**The Greatests Hits, So Far** / 1990 / Virgin ♦♦♦♦
*The Greatest Hits, So Far* is a solid, but not quite satisfying 14-track overview of Public Image Ltd.'s career from 1978 to 1990. Starting with their debut single, "Public Image," the collection moves through the group's early, experimental period to their dance-rock sound of the mid- to late '80s. While there's no faulting the material, the band's move toward the mainstream means that the disc isn't quite cohesive and also produces a sharp dividing line around its halfway point—the first half sounds fresher and more eclectic, while the second is more accessible yet not quite as distinctive. There are great songs to be found in both areas, but those more enamored of the group's early material might find that period underrepresented. However, it is a good way to get most of the best material from PiL's more uneven albums, as well as an excellent (if incomplete) introduction to Lydon's post-Pistols work. —*Steve Huey*

## Pulse

*Group / Minimal Techno, Club/Dance, Techno, Acid House*
Germans Tommi Eckhart and Klaus Loschner (aka DJ Good Groove) met in 1992, and formed Pulse to create minimal, driving techno. The two first appeared remixing on the Disko B label, remixing Caesar's "Don't You Do It." Pulse signed to Harthouse and in early 1993, released "Outlaw Parts I and II." Eckhart and Loschner's debut album, *Surface Tensions*, appeared in 1994. Eckhart is also part of the trance group Perry & Rhodan, while Loschner, as DJ Good Groove, has recorded two volumes of *Drummatic Tales.* —*John Bush*

● **Surface Tensions** / 1995 / Harthouse ♦♦
Pulse's first album works gradually shifting trance tones into minimalist rhythms occupied only by extreme frequencies—either the most twee treble or hardly audible sub-bass. Infrequent use of vocals gives *Surface Tensions* a distant, spacey sound. —*John Bush*

## Patrick Pulsinger

*Producer / Experimental Techno, Ambient Techno, Techno*
Austrian techno experimentalist Patrick Pulsinger is one of a very few Vienna-bred electronic musicians to reach acclaim in the wider dance music world. Although Pulsinger has recorded in just about every vein of electronic dance music—from house and techno to minimal electro and warped downbeat—his take on each is usually one of pushing established boundaries in unexpected directions, leading to a cult-like status among DJs (and often exceeding the amount of play his records actually receive). Perhaps best known for the unlikely acid jazz hit "City Lights," a collaboration with countrymate Dorfmeister (of the production team Kruder & Dorfmeister), the bulk of Pulsinger's recorded work (including the *Porno* full-length for Disko B and a series of EPs and an album as IO) hasn't been nearly so straight-ahead. Released mostly on his own Cheap label, that work has drawn from Detroit techno and Chicago house, funk, jazz, soul, and disco, and hip-hop and electro-funk, with Pulsinger warping the years and spaces separating these elements until they seem to congeal into a logical whole. Like many of his peers, Pulsinger doesn't stick with any one brand-name too long, and his discography is rittled with aliases, including Sluts'N'Strings, Restaurant Tracks, and

Showroom Recording Series. Although the Cheap label's early discography (singles like "Summerbreeze" and the Robert Hood full-length *Nighttime World, Vol. 1*) were geared more toward a club atmosphere, that direction was increasingly abandoned in releases such as "Showroom Recording Series Vol. 2" and "Mean Clown Welcome," which display instead a brand of cheeky bedroom electronica similar to labels such as Clear and Evolution. [See Also: IO, Private Lightning 6] —*Sean Cooper*

**Carrera** / 1997 / Cheap ♦♦♦

More madcap, funk-fueled breakbeat weirdness from Cheap's Patrick Pulsinger and Erdam Tunakan. Like previous Sluts material, *Carrera* steers clear of the freakbeat electro territory explored by the pair's *Showroom Recordings Series* and remixes for Lamb and A Forest Mighty Black, settling instead into spacy electronic trip-hop with heaps of funk and jazz references. Although *Carrera* would have made a solid 12", the presence of a few weak tracks and a pair of ponderous disco numbers reduce the album's overall effectiveness. —*Sean Cooper*

● **Porno** / Jan. 20, 1998 / Disko B ♦♦♦♦

This Pulsinger invisible soundtrack is an eight-track set of surprisingly straight-ahead electro and techno, with little of the jazzier material heard on *Carrera*. Tracks like "Risk," "A Piece of Me," and "Treated" are laboratory-precise speciments, including only the occasional echoed-dub effects. —*John Bush*

## Push Button Objects (Edgar Farinas)

*Producer / Electronica, Ambient Techno, Trip-Hop, Club/Dance, Techno, IDM*

Edgar Farinas is the Miami-bred producer behind Push Button Objects, whose artful fusions of hip-hop, electro, and jungle have appeared through the American Schematic and Chocolate Industries labels, and through the UK-based imprint Skam. While hip-hop remains the core element of the PBO sound, Farinas combines the raw beats with treated electronics, bizarre samples, and rhythmic deviations mostly foreign to hip-hop's mid- to downtempo lope. His debut EP appeared through the Schematic label, now owned and operated by Josh Kay and Rom Castillo of Phoenecia and Soul Oddity, and remains his best work. Much ballyhooing attended his first Skam EP, due to the label's connection with electronica auteurs Autechre, but that EP is easily his least interesting work to date. —*Sean Cooper*

● **Push Button Objects [EP]** / Jul. 21, 1997 / Schematic ♦♦♦♦

Credited to one Edgar Farinas, PBO's debut four-tracker of slow-oozing acid hip-hop is similar in parts to German Structure-based groups such as Air Liquide, Red Light District, 4E, and (earlier, slower) Biochip C. Forsaking the thin-drum approach of previous Schematic releases, Farinas' big beats, gurgling basslines, and loop-slice changeups make for easily the most distinctive Schematic release to date. —*Sean Cooper*

**Return Home [Single]** / May 11, 1998 / Chocolate Industries ♦♦♦

It's not quite the revolution in sound of the previous Schematic single, but this single for Chocolate Industries features all the revolving electro patterns and toybox melodies electro-techno fans could want, as well as a Gescom remix of "Non-Existent." —*John Bush*

**Push Button Objects [Single]** / 1999 / Skam ♦♦

The wildstyle cover is probably the best thing about this mostly drab and uninspired collection of featureless downtempo. For completists only. —*Sean Cooper*

# Q

## Q-Burns Abstract Message (Michael Donaldson)
*Remixing, Producer / Club/Dance, Techno*

Q-Burns Abstract Message is the alter ego of Orlando, Florida DJ/producer/remixer Michael Donaldson. A member of the city's Eighth Dimension collective, Donaldson's eclecticism has graced several compilations, EP, and single releases for various labels, and remixes for artists including Faith No More and Us3. After nabbing the opening slot on the Chemical Brothers' US tour, Donaldson was signed to the Astralwerks label in 1997. His debut single, "Touchin' on Something," was released late in the year, and the singles collection *Oeuvre* followed in 1998. —*Steve Huey*

**Oeuvre** / May 19, 1998 / Astralwerks ♦♦♦♦

An excellent introduction to the Q-Burns aesthetic, *Oeuvre* assembles eight tracks previously available only as singles and compilation tracks—among them "Toast," "141 Revenge Street," and "Flava Lamp"—as well as the outtakes "Bugeyed Sunglasses" and "Puff the Magic." Most intriguing is the all-new "Touchin' on Something," intended as an appetizer for the upcoming full-length *Feng Shui*. —*Jason Ankeny*

● **Feng Shui** / Sep. 22, 1998 / Astralwerks ♦♦♦♦

The proper debut by Donaldson's Q-Burns Abstract Message project is a bright spot for leftfield American electronica, easily comparable to more celebrated British producers from Orbital to the Chemical Brothers. *Feng Shui* is a bit more melodic and also more tied to Florida's breakbeat rave scene, but Donaldson ranges far and wide for his musical ideas, with nods to Latin, psychedelia, R&B, and even Kraut-rock (the results of which include an unlikely Faust cover—"Jennifer" from *Faust IV*—that manages reverence for the original as well as a pioneering spirit of its own). Though worldwide listeners often look to Britain for full-length electronica odysseys, *Feng Shui* proves they're found all over. —*John Bush*

## Finley Quaye
*Vocals, Producer / Electronica, Adult Alternative Pop/Rock, Trip-Hop*

Purportedly the uncle of Tricky and the brother of prominent guitar sideman Caleb Quaye, Finley Quaye could definitely have relied on nepotism to get himself a recording contract. Fortunately, his sweet voice and feel for a soul groove were the leading indicators in his signing to the Haiku label. After collaborating with A Guy Called Gerald and becoming friends with Iggy Pop, Quaye recorded his debut album, *Maverick A Strike*, and released it in 1997. He then began recording vocals for Tricky's third album. —*John Bush*

● **Maverick A Strike** / Oct. 1997 / 550 Music ♦♦♦

A fusion of his own light reggae singing, urban-contemporary production qualities, and mid-tempo trip-hop rambling, Finley Quaye's debut album is an enjoyable effort. Particularly impressive is the range of Quaye's voice, from a distinctive high tenor to barely audible whispering. In fact, the only problem with *Maverick A Strike* is the singer's lack of emotion; even while his voice stretches out on the highlight, "I Need a Lover," it doesn't appear as though he cares much about the song. —*John Bush*

# R

## Rabbit in the Moon
f. 1993, Orlando, FL
*Group / Funky Breaks, Trance, Club/Dance*

Somewhere between performance art and dancefloor trance, Rabbit in the Moon was formed in Orlando, Florida by the duo of Steve McClure and David Christophere. Similar in style to Keith Flint's status as nominal frontman for Prodigy, McClure provides most of the visual entertainment during the act's frenetic live show—his costumes more in keeping with a horror film than a rave—while Christophere takes care of all the programming. The duo recorded several singles for Hallucination before debuting on Hardkiss Records with the 1994 single "Phases of an Out of Body Experience." Christophere provided remixes for an assortment of artists, including Goldie, Orbital, Sarah McLachlan, White Zombie, Cosmic Baby and Garbage—many collected on *Rabbit in the Moon Remixes, Vol. 1*. Rabbit in the Moon also collaborated with Humate on a pair of singles for Superstition, and in 1999 issued the full-length *Floorid.a*, as well as a sequel to their first remix collection, aptly titled *Remixes, Vol. 2*. — *John Bush*

- **Rabbit in the Moon Remixes, Vol. 1** / Jun. 23, 1998 / Hallucination ♦♦♦♦
A remix collection that also functions as a continuous-mix album, this nine-tracker includes Rabbit in the Moon's most famed remixes, Goldie's "Inner City Life" and Orbital's "Are We Here," as well as others by artists ranging from Sarah McLachlan to Astral Pilot to White Zombie. —*John Bush*

**Rabbit in the Moon Remixes, Vol. 2** / Oct. 26, 1999 / Hallucination ♦♦♦
The second volume in Rabbit in the Moon's growing remix series (still without a proper full-length to show for their career) selects reworkings for artists including Smashing Pumpkins ("The End Is the Beginning Is the End"), Garbage ("Milk"), Love and Rockets, and the Stone Roses, among others. —*Keith Farley*

## Radiohead
f. 1989, Oxford, England
*Group / Brit-pop, Alternative Pop/Rock*

Radiohead was one of the few alternative bands of the early '90s to draw heavily from the grandiose arena-rock that characterized U2's early albums. But the band internalized that epic sweep, turning it inside out to tell tortured, twisted tales of angst and alienation. Vocalist Thom Yorke's pained lyrics were brought to life by the group's three-guitar attack, which relied on texture—borrowing as much from My Bloody Valentine and Pink Floyd as R.E.M. and the Pixies—instead of virtuosity. It took Radiohead a while to formulate their signature sound. Their 1993 debut, *Pablo Honey*, only suggested their potential, and one of its songs, "Creep," became an unexpected international hit, its angst-ridden lyrics making it an alternative rock anthem. Many observers pigeonholed Radiohead as a one-hit wonder, but the group's second album, *The Bends*, was released to terrific reviews in the band's native Britain in early 1995, and the group steadily promoted the album over the next year. It eventually won widespread acclaim from fellow musicians and critics, as well as strong sales, establishing the group as something more than a one-hit wonder.

Thom Yorke (vocals, guitar), Ed O'Brien (guitar, vocals), Jonny Greenwood (guitar), Colin Greenwood (bass) and Phil Selway (drums) formed Radiohead as students at Oxford University in 1988. Initially called On a Friday, the band began pursuing a musical career in earnest in the early '90s, releasing the *Drill* EP in 1992. Shortly afterward, the group signed to EMI/Capitol and released the single "Creep," a fusion of R.E.M. and Nirvana highlighted by a noisy burst of feedback prior to the chorus. "Creep" was a moderate hit, and their next two singles, "Anyone Can Play Guitar" and "Pop is Dead," built a small following, even as the British music press ignored the group. *Pablo Honey*, Radiohead's debut album, was released to mixed reviews in the spring of 1993. As the band launched a European supporting tour, "Creep" became a sudden smash hit in America, earning heavy airplay on modern rock radio and MTV. On the back of the single's success, Radiohead toured the US extensively, opening for Belly and Tears for Fears. All the exposure helped *Pablo Honey* go gold, and "Creep" was re-released in the UK at the end of 1993. This time, the single became a Top Ten hit, and the band spent the following summer touring the world.

Although "Creep" made Radiohead a success, it also led many observers to peg the band as one-hit wonders. Conscious of such thinking, the group entered the studio with producer John Leckie to record their second album, *The Bends*. Upon its spring 1995 release, *The Bends* was greeted with overwhelmingly enthusiastic reviews, all of which praised the group's deeper, more mature sound. However, positive reviews didn't sell albums, as Radiohead struggled to be heard during the UK's summer of Brit-pop and as American radio programmers and MTV ignored the record. The band continued to tour as the opening act on R.E.M.'s prestigious *Monster* tour. By the end of the year, *The Bends* began to catch on, thanks not only to the band's constant touring, but also to the stark, startling video for "Just." The album made many year-end Best of the Year lists in the UK, and early in 1996 the record re-entered the British Top Ten and climbed to gold status in the US During the first half of 1996, Radiohead continued to tour before re-entering the studio that fall to record their third album, *OK Computer*, which was released in the summer of 1997. Three years after their critically-acclaimed, media-praised third album, Radiohead maintained their perfectionist nature on their eclectic fourth album *Kid A*, released in October 2000. Yorke said he was mentally distraught after the massive success of *OK Computer*, and the mounting emotion captured on *Kid A* reflects such open-ended catharsis.—*Stephen Thomas Erlewine*

**The Bends** / Apr. 4, 1995 / Capitol ♦♦♦♦
*Pablo Honey* in no way was adequate preparation for its epic, sprawling follow-up, *The Bends*. Building from the sweeping, three-guitar attack that punctuated the best moments of *Pablo Honey*, Radiohead create a grand and forceful sound that nevertheless resonates with anguish and despair—it's cerebral anthemic rock. Occasionally, the album displays its influences, whether it's U2, Pink Floyd, R.E.M., or the Pixies, but Radiohead turn clichés inside out, making each song sound bracingly fresh. Thom Yorke's tortured lyrics give the album a melancholy undercurrent, as does the surging, textured music. But what makes *The Bends* so remarkable is that it marries such ambitious, and often challenging, instrumental soundscapes to songs that are at their cores hauntingly melodic and accessible. It makes the record compelling upon first listen, but it reveals new details with each listen, and soon it becomes apparent that with *The Bends*, Radiohead have reinvented anthemic rock. —*Stephen Thomas Erlewine*

★ **OK Computer** / Jul. 1, 1997 / Capitol ♦♦♦♦♦
Using the textured soundscapes of *The Bends* as a launching pad, Radiohead delivered another startlingly accomplished set of modern guitar rock with *OK Computer*. The anthemic guitar heroics present on *Pablo Honey* and even *The Bends* are nowhere to be heard here. Radiohead have stripped away many of the obvious elements of guitar rock, creating music that is subtle and textured, yet still has the feeling of rock 'n' roll. Even at its most adventurous—such as the complex, multi-segmented "Paranoid Android"—the band is tight, melodic and muscular, and Thom Yorke's voice effortlessly shifts from a sweet falsetto to vicious snarls. It's a thoroughly astonishing demonstration of musical virtuosity, and becomes even more impressive with repeated listens, which reveal subtleties like electronica rhythms, eerie keyboards, odd time signatures and syncopated rhythms. Yet all of this would simply be showmanship if the songs weren't strong in themselves, and *OK Computer*

is filled with moody masterpieces, from the shimmering "Subterranean Homesick Alien" and the sighing "Karma Police" to the gothic crawl of "Exit Music (For a Film)". *OK Computer* is the album that establishes Radiohead as one of the most inventive and rewarding guitar-rock bands of the '90s. —*Stephen Thomas Erlewine*

**Kid A** / Oct. 3, 2000 / Capitol ◆◆◆◆

The overwhelming critical success of *OK Computer* hardly made the task ahead for Radiohead any easier. For fans that waited for the group's next move with baited breath, Radiohead was expected to deliver nothing short of the greatest album of all time, or at least a *Sgt. Pepper's* for the new millennium. The creative breakthrough arrived when the band embraced electronica—a move that was nearly a cliché by the end of the '90s, since everyone from U2 to Ricki Lee Jones dabbled in trip-hop or electro. The difference is, not only did Radiohead flirt with the genre on *OK Computer*, but their quietest moments always shared a similar chilly feel as electronica. That's why the wholehearted electronic conversion on *Kid A* fits, but it also helps that Radiohead doesn't take the easy route and simply add some club beats or sonic collage techniques. Instead, they strove to bring themselves in line with the "intelligent dance music" of Autechre and Aphex Twin, where the skittering electronic beats never are infectious and the sonic surfaces are stylishly dark and unsettling. To their immense credit, Radiohead doesn't sound like carpetbaggers, because they share the same post-post-modern vantage point as their inspirations. As a result, *Kid A* is easily the most successful electronica album from a rock band—so much so that it doesn't sound like the work of a rock band, even if it does sound like Radiohead. Still, it never is as visionary or stunning as *OK Computer*, and it doesn't really repay the intensive time it demands in order for it to sink in. This is still, quiet music that drifts by on not just the first listen, but on the first several listens. Hearing the aural seams on the songs can be distracting, but the real problem of *Kid A* is that it's a challenge to the group's audience that doesn't always live up to its end of the bargain. Of course, any experiment that yields mixed results still yields results, and there are some moments here that positively shimmer with genius: the hypnotic way "Everything in Its Right Place" unfolds, how the disquieting title track trumps many electronica acts at their own game, the gentle despair of "How to Disappear Completely," how Radiohead spins their trademark sound on "Optimistic," and especially the clustered paranoia of "The National Anthem," the hardest-rocking thing here and the one song that surpasses expectations raised by *OK Computer*. Given the stasis of Radiohead's peers, these moments are enough to make *Kid A* a qualified success and one of 2000's necessary listens, even if it doesn't match its predecessor. —*Stephen Thomas Erlewine*

## Rae & Christian

f. 1995

*Group / Electronica, Trip-Hop, Club/Dance, House*

Rae & Christian emerged in the late '90s as a successor to the many stellar British production teams of the '90s, updating the rich urban grooves of Soul II Soul and Massive Attack with a bit more emphasis on classic hip-hop. The duo of Mark Rae and Steve Christian, often helped out by vocalist Veba, began recording together in 1995. Grand Central Records released several of their collaborative singles—as well as a few solo singles by Rae—beginning in 1996. The duo's debut album, *Northern Sulphuric Soul*, was released in late 1998. —*John Bush*

● **Northern Sulphuric Soul** / Oct. 5, 1998 / Grand Central ◆◆◆◆

*Northern Sulphuric Soul* features the duo navigating the slender divide between jazzy hip-hop, mid-tempo nu-soul, and mainstream house. Nine of the thirteen tracks feature guest vocalists, from Texas and Veba (the latter a Rae & Christian regular) to the Jungle Brothers, Jeru the Damaja, and JVC Force. Surprisingly, R&C are equally masterful on the dance tracks and the hip-hop cuts; though most of the songs aren't exactly barn-burners, it's obvious that every aspect of these productions have been labored over. Dance listeners can always count on deep basslines, but hardly ones that are as intricate as they are on *Northern Sulphuric Soul*. —*John Bush*

**Mixer Presents Rae & Christian** / May 23, 2000 / DMC ◆◆◆

DJ's Mark Rae and Steve Christian mixed this collection featuring some of the strongest club music on both sides of the Atlantic. One of the best tracks is their own "Play On," which features the work of the Jungle Brothers. Other highlights come from Face & Feline, DJ Spinna, Riton, and Tuff Crew. —*Stacia Proefrock*

## Dave Ralph

*DJ / Progressive Trance, Progressive House, Trance*

A true DJ veteran, Dave Ralph first started DJing back in 1977 and has since climbed to the elite position of being one of the world's most recognized DJs, holding residencies in both America and Europe as well as spinning at festivals as large as *Woodstock* and *Love Parade*. But back when Ralph first began spinning records, he didn't necessarily have high aspirations of being an innovative DJ, instead focusing on pleasing his given audience with the sounds they wanted to hear. When he heard Larry Heard's legendary "Washing Machine" back in the mid-'80s, Ralph heard his calling, making the long commute regularly to London to pick up the latest vinyl. Since then, he has slowly built his reputation, holding residencies at esteemed clubs such as *Cream* and *Shelley's*, and eventually hooked up with Paul Oakenfold's Perfecto label. After serving as Oakenfold's opening DJ on the 1996 Perfecto tour, it has been nothing but glory for Ralph, as he has gone on to become a world-renowned champion of the evolving trance sound, being awarded the closing slot at *Woodstock* and as the featured DJ in Kinetic's second volume in their popular *Tranceport* series. By the end of 2000, he had relocated to the sunny beaches of Florida to reside, holding residencies at some of the US's top clubs such as Washington D.C.'s *Buzz*, and Detroit's *Motor*, in addition to releasing *Love Parade: Berlin* in late 2000, furthering his status as one of the most embraced trance DJs in the US —*Jason Birchmeier*

● **Tranceport, Vol. 2** / Nov. 2, 1999 / Kinetic ◆◆◆

Following on from the first volume in the series (mixed by Paul Oakenfold), Dave Ralph's *Tranceport II* works through two discs of progressive trance. Ralph is a bit more inspired by the breakbeat end of trance than Oakenfold (who has a tendency for Eurodance), and the collection benefits from it. His song selection and musical sense also trump Oakenfold's, and *Tranceport II* includes some excellent tracks, starting with the opener, "Rabbitweed," by fellow trance DJ Sasha. Ralph balances tracks by what are fast becoming the usual trance producers (Art of Trance, X-Cabs, Jam & Spoon) for this sort of collection with comparatively left-field figures like Luke Slater, Oliver Lieb, and Resistance D. Though he puts his imprint on the collection, any DJ mix album that averages over eight minutes per track (as this one does) reveals a distinct lack of energy and enthusiasm—like the glut of albums by superstar DJs, *Tranceport II* is more of a collection of tracks (albeit well-selected tracks) than a mix album. Perfect for your hipper shoe stores, but maybe not the best diversion of listeners' time. —*John Bush*

**Love Parade: Berlin** / Oct. 3, 2000 / Kinetic ◆◆

Dave Ralph's album-length ode to Berlin's fabled *Love Parade* finds him trading in the expansive sounds found on his *Tranceport II* album for this straight-ahead set of up-tempo progressive house. While most of the 12 tracks feature some sort of momentary lull, for the most part, these songs keep their BPMs rather high and focus on energy rather than melody or epic moods. It's a rather unfortunate decision. Ralph's move from England to Miami, Florida may perhaps explain his new sound—supposedly representative of what he spun at 2000's *Love Parade*—yet no matter the motive, the set could really use a little variety in terms of mood or tempo. Songs such as Tatoine's "Music" or Timo Maas' update of Green Velvet's "Flash" surely fit a certain mood and tempo; no one's arguing that. The only moments when this mood or tempo change throughout the course of the mix come during each track's momentary melodic lull and during the final track of the set, Torsten Stenzel's take on Moby's "Porcelain." To be honest, it's an embarrassing way to end the set; there are many better remixes of this stunning track, and this one is by far one of the worst. For as dull as this album will seem to seasoned fans of trance-related music, it should appeal to new-comers with its easily digestible consistency—there are few surprises here and even fewer risks. And perhaps this was exactly the underlying mission that Ralph and, more likely, Kinetic was aiming for: commercial accessibility. —*Jason Birchmeier*

## Ram Trilogy

f. 1998

*Group / Jungle/Drum'N'Bass, Club/Dance*

Already responsible for a raft of drum'n'bass classics recorded throughout the '90s, Ram Recordings' bosses Andy C and Ant Miles—formerly known as Origin Unknown—united with fellow Ram producer Shimon to form Ram Trilogy. Fittingly, the three debuted with a trio of epic singles during the last half of 1998, the industrial-strength anthems "No Reality/Scanners," followed by "Mind Overload/Intercity" and "Chase Scene/Terminal 1." All three singles took as their template the darkstep style becoming increasingly ubiquitous throughout the jungle scene (a sound pioneered by Origin Unknown themselves), but advanced the cause considerably with a legion of future-shock beats and effects. A year later, the notoriously media-shy team emerged from the underground with the first full-length ever released on Ram Recordings, *Molten Beats*. [See Also: Origin Unknown] —*John Bush*

**Part 1: No Reality/Scanners [Single]** / Aug. 24, 1998 / Ram ♦♦♦♦

**Part 2: Mind Overload/Intercity [Single]** / Oct. 5, 1998 / Ram ♦♦

**Part 3: Chase Scene/Terminal 1 [Single]** / Dec. 14, 1998 / Ram ♦♦♦

● **Molten Beats** / Nov. 8, 1999 / Ram ♦♦♦♦
Ram Trilogy's full debut was undeniably built with the same blueprint used by most dark drum'n'bass producers, but for once the neuro-funk sound gets challenged a bit. The trio take plenty of care with their production, moving the sound away from brittle metallics to embrace a variety of sounds. The drum programming is an advance as well; though the difference isn't astounding, it's clear they've constructed their beats from the ground up, and the overall result is an album that clearly separates Ram Trilogy from the ranks of sound-alike jungle. —*John Bush*

## Danny Rampling

b. Jul. 15, 1961, Streatham, London, England
*DJ / Trance, Club/Dance, Acid House, House*
Danny Rampling has been one of the most famous DJs on the British house scene since its beginnings. After being exposed to the original Balearic vibes on Ibiza, Rampling returned to London, founded several seminal club nights and DJed on pirate radio until the music he helped push went mainstream and landed him a spot on Radio 1. Born in Streatham, London, he began DJing while still a teenager, and became enmeshed in the capital's fertile soul/rare-groove scene during the '80s. On a 1987 visit to the Spanish vacation island of Ibiza, however, Rampling was first introduced to the crucial blend of soul, Italian disco, American house/garage and alternative dance termed Balearic.

Rampling, with friends Paul Oakenfold, Nicky Holloway and Johnny Walker, eventually returned to Britain and spread the news about Ibiza through club nights, pirate radio, and the growing community of warehouse parties later to morph into the rave scene. Rampling's Shoom was perhaps *the* most important club night for early house music; though only a few hundred clubbers were exposed to the new sound at Shoom, it proved the vital spark for later clubs and raves which numbered thousands of entries. Though the club was gone by 1989, Rampling had already begun playing in Europe and in 1990 founded another classic club night, Pure. His sound progressed from acid house to harder trance during the '90s, and he joined the BBC's Radio 1 in 1996 with a popular show, *The Love Groove Dance Party*. (He's also released several double-disc mix sets based on the show.)

Rampling released mix albums for Metropole, Mixmag, and Dragonfly, and began recording for Deconstruction with his Millionaire Hippies project. Always known as one of the hardest clubbers on the scene, Rampling suffered a breakdown from exhaustion during 1997, then was dropped by Deconstruction after not producing another Millionaire Hippies record. Signed to Distance Records, he returned in 1998 with new productions and another mix album, *Club Nation*, recorded for Virgin. —*John Bush*

**Mixmag Live!, Vol. 4** / 1995 / Mixmag ♦♦♦♦
Graeme Park and Danny Rampling mixed this fourth volume in *Mixmag*'s series of DJ compilations. —*John Bush*

● **The Love Groove Dance Party, Vols. 1 & 2** / 1996 / Metropole ♦♦♦♦
A double-disc set, the first two volumes in Rampling's *Love Groove Dance Party* series are an epic journey through house and trance featuring tracks by Urban Blues Project, Patrick Prins, Indica, Mory Kante, Roger Sanchez and Chez. —*John Bush*

## The Real McCoy

f. 1993, Berlin, Germany
*Group / Club/Dance, Euro-Dance, Hi-NRG, House*
A trio of Olaf Jeglitza, Patricia Petersen and Vanessa Mason, the Real McCoy formed in Berlin in 1993 and soon became popular throughout Europe with the chart-topping hit "Another Night." In late 1994, the single hit number three on the American charts, as did the following year's "Run Away." Their debut album *Another Night* went double-platinum by late 1995, and *One More Time* followed in 1997. —*John Bush*

● **Another Night** / 1994 / Arista ♦♦♦♦
The Real McCoy's debut album is the one with most of their hits, including "Run Away," "Come and Get Your Love," "Another Night" and "Automatic Lover," most of which were produced by Shep Pettibone. It's obviously an album balancing hit singles with identical-sounding filler, but since most of the group's biggest successes are included, it's a handy hits package. —*John Bush*

**Real McCoy** / 1995 / Arista/Hansa ♦♦♦♦

**On the Move** / Jun. 6, 1995 / ZYX ♦♦

**One More Time** / Mar. 25, 1997 / Arista ♦♦
Disappointing sophomore effort from German dance trio. The Real McCoy scored in late 1993 and 1994 with the dreamy club smashes "Another Night" and "Runaway," and solid tunes such as "Automatic Lover" and "Come and Get Your Love" also became minor dancefloor sensations. 1997's *One More Time*, however, barely registers; only the title track, a catchy, lightweight piece of pop fluff, makes any kind of impression. Most of *One More Time* is empty filler, and a couple of moments are unbearable: the silly "I Wanna Come (With You)" teases with the provocative title but fails to deliver, and the absurd Euro-pop remake of Shania Twain's "If You're Not in It for Love (I'm Outta Here)" is awful, but it isn't even bad enough to be fun. And the forced sexiness of Olaf Jeglitza's deep, half-whispered, melodramatic vocal style can really wear thin over the course of an entire album. European dance acts rarely have a long shelf life, and this album proves the Real McCoy is no exception. Stick with the debut. —*William Cooper*

**Remix Album** / Aug. 11, 1998 / BMG International ♦♦

## Rebel MC (Michael West)

b. 1965, London, England
*Vocals, Producer / Jungle/Drum'N'Bass, Club/Dance*
The '80s popster turned proto-jungle revolutionary was born Michael West in 1965 in London. He formed Double Trouble in the early '80s with Michael Menson and Leigh Guest, releasing the ska-pop hit "Street Tuff." Rebel MC later gained fame in England as a pop/rapper, but by 1991 he had released *Black Meaning Good*, an album that presaged jungle with hardcore techno married to dub basslines and ragga toasters such as Barrington Levy and P.P. Arnold. His 1992 singles "Rich Ah Getting Richer" and "Humanity" also showed the new direction. "Code Red"—released as Conquering Lion—became an outright jungle smash in 1994, bringing the jungle movement to the British masses. —*John Bush*

● **Rebel Music** / 1990 / Desire ♦♦♦

## Rechenzentrum

f. Berlin, Germany
*Group / Minimal Techno, Experimental Techno*
The minimal electronics duo Rechenzentrum formed in Berlin around producer Marc Weiser and design artist Lillevaen. Weiser, a DJ and vocalist as well, organized *the Berlin club night Maria Am Ostbahnhof* and the festival *Club Transmediale*. Lillevaen worked with artists including Christine Hill and Blixa Bargeld before coming together with Weiser as the visual half of Rechenzentrum. The duo remixed Tarwater, Laub, and Elektronauten then released their self-titled debut on Kitty-Yo in 2000. Weiser has also recorded as Le Hammond Inferno for Bungalow. —*John Bush*

● **Rechenzentrum** / May 30, 2000 / Kitty-Yo ♦♦♦
Though the drum programs and effects are clinical and precise in the hallowed tradition of minimal techno, Rechenzentrum's self-titled debut remains a very warm and engaging record. Similar to electronic recidivists from Stereolab to Appliance to Fridge, Marc Weiser makes sure there's plenty of personality to his productions, and it's clear from the opener "Absent Minded," in which the skeletal beats don't quite overwhelm the gentle synthesizer atmospheres and barely there whisperings from a female vocal. And though the three-part "Da Hilsbach Triptychon" is heavily processed in the modern *musique concrète* aesthetic, the programming is downright funky and playful. Many of the tracks are variations (albeit heavily tweaked variations) on a steady four-four beat, but there are many great ideas on this collection. By doing to minimal techno what Mouse on Mars do to its experimental cousin, Rechenzentrum fashioned an engaging, entertaining first album. —*John Bush*

## Recloose (Matt Chicoine)

*Group / Detroit Techno, Club/Dance, Techno*

Recording as Recloose, Matt Chicoine is the Detroit producer whose notable EPs for Carl Craig's Planet E label explore upbeat, sample-based trip-hop instead of the synth-based techno often heard in the Motor City. Unsure of his career direction after graduating with a degree in English from the University of Michigan in nearby Ann Arbor, Chicoine—previously a resident mixer known as DJ Bubblicious—began exploring electronic recording as well. According to Detroit legend, while working in a take-out joint, he slipped one of his tapes into an order from techno don Carl Craig, and Craig signed him to Planet E. His first EP, 1998's *So This Is the Dining Room*, earned great reviews around Detroit. In 1999, just after recording the *Spelunking* EP, Chicoine helped fill out Craig's Innerzone Orchestra for live performances around the globe. Though his releases had been primarily home-listening experiences, he also DJed and performed at several far-flung spots. In anticipation of a Recloose full-length, he released the "Can't Take It" single in early 2000. —*John Bush*

**So This Is the Dining Room [EP]** / Mar. 17, 1998 / Planet E ✦✦✦✦

On Recloose's debut EP, he ambitiously integrates several different styles of music into a synergy of scrambled sampled percussion, jazzy horns, and a taste for free-form structuring. Though short—with only three extended songs and two short songs—*So This Is the Dining Room* is a brave record full of ambition and grand ideas that isn't quite as effective in practice as in theory, but a noteworthy record nonetheless. As a whole, it aims to break down stylistic barriers with its heavy use of percussive samples (rather than drum machines) and its tendency to blend many different sounds into a jazz-like structure. At times the funk and melody aren't quite enough to propel the music to levels of brilliance. As funky and melodic as "MYM230 (R.I.P.)" may be, it doesn't compensate for the sloppy electronic jazz of "Dislocate." Chicoine would neatly remedy this problem on his next release, the much more realized *Spelunking*. —*Jason Birchmeier*

● **Spelunking [EP]** / Sep. 14, 1999 / Planet E ✦✦✦✦

On his second EP for Planet E, Detroit artist Matt Chicoine makes impressive strides, surpassing his previous release not only in terms of quality but also consistency. Whereas *So This Is the Dining Room* was daring, yet at times overambitious in its eclectic execution, Chicoine seems to have found a style that he feels comfortable with, focusing his efforts on laying down energetic funk. The tracks here move along at a steady pace that doesn't quite reach peak dancefloor velocity but comes pretty close. Chicoine's ingredients on this record tend to be dub-style basslines that thump more than kick, organic high-frequency percussion sounds, and the occasional soulful vocal snippet (whenever he wants to bring a sense of humanity to a given song). The sedate "Insomnia in Dub" proves to be the most magical cut on the record. While the other numbers may emanate energy, this tranquil track, with its smooth, deep bassline and horn sample, evokes visions of a faintly lit room diffused with smoke and incense. The vocal snippets, piano melodies, and guitar notes that occasionally appear during the song elevate the mood tremendously with their human emotion, proving that Detroit may indeed continue to be the breeding ground for innovative electronic music that still manages to retain a sense of soul. —*Jason Birchmeier*

## Red Snapper

f. 1994, London, England
*Group / Electronica, Trip-Hop, Acid Jazz*

Notable for their pioneering synthesis of acoustic instruments and electronic textures, the British acid jazz trio Red Snapper comprised guitarist David Ayers, double bassist Ali Friend and drummer Richard Thair. Formed in 1993, the group's debut EP *The Snapper* appeared the following spring; after two more EPs, *Swank* and *Hot Flush*, Red Snapper signed to the acclaimed Warp Records label, where their early singles were later compiled as *Reeled and Skinned*. The full-length *Prince Blimey* was released in 1996, followed two years later by their American debut *Making Bones*. In 2000, the English trio released *Our Aim Is to Satisfy Red Snapper*. —*Jason Ankeny*

**Reeled and Skinned** / 1995 / Warp ✦✦✦

The first Red Snapper full-length is an EP collection including three tracks each from *Snapper*, *Swank* and *Hot Flush* originally released on the Flaw Recordings label. Though the tracks are a bit skeletal, collaborations with Sabres of Paradise ("Hot Flush") and Beth Orton ("Snapper," "In Deep") come off quite well. —*Keith Farley*

**Prince Blimey** / Sep. 9, 1996 / Warp ✦✦✦✦

The Snapper finally leave the trip-hop pretensions behind and churn out a wild and wonderful collection of future-retro ambient/jazz/funk/drum'n'bass. Though the performances are capable enough, what really makes this record smoke is the slightly, well, warped production, as if the whole thing were recorded in a subterranean boho bar south of the equator. Occasionally fumbling onto an unfortunate (fl)acid jazz vibe, *Prince Blimey*'s occasional botches are few enough to make this record more than worth it. —*Sean Cooper*

● **Making Bones** / Sep. 28, 1998 / Warp ✦✦✦✦

A full decade of acid jazz never produced a more stunning fusion of electronic music with live instrumentation than *Making Bones*. Poised halfway between Sly & Robbie and Roni Size, Red Snapper's first album for a worldwide audience surfs a wave of breakbeat funk that includes nods to dub, punk, soul, drum'n'bass and hip-hop. The rock-steady rhythm section of Richard Thair (drums) and Ali Friend (bass) holds the groove better than any sampler, tying together radically different material like classic British soul on "Image of You," metallic drum'n'bass on "The Sleepless" (with excellent rapping by MC Det) and the fusion update "Bogeyman" (with trumpeter Byron Wallen). It's obvious the Snapper have mastered all aspects of '90s electronic dance, and *Making Bones* is proof positive. —*John Bush*

**Our Aim Is to Satisfy Red Snapper** / Oct. 17, 2000 / Matador ✦✦✦✦

Nearly as astonishing as 1998's excellent *Making Bones*, Red Snapper's third full album again finds the instrumental trio comping over a wealth of great musical ideas wedded to dub, soul-jazz, big-beat, disco, even hard rock. "Shellback" features a pounding Zeppelin breakbeat from drummer Richard Thair and a processional bassline of Ali Friend setting up vocalist Karime Kendra, who floats serenely over the entire production. Kendra resurfaces elsewhere, showing an enviable range by transforming herself into an extroverted diva for the breakbeat disco track "The Rough and the Quick." "The Rake" is a torrid beatbox-funk number with a nasally vocal effect straight out of P-Funk, while "Bussing," "Belladonna," and "They're Hanging Me Tonight" are atmospheric groove cuts with more allegiance to a classic jazz unit like Weather Report than any trip-hop act out there. Red Snapper never appear to run out of ideas or energy, and excellent production and recording unite the disparate styles into a jewel of an album. —*John Bush*

## Alex Reece

*Producer, DJ / Jungle/Drum'N'Bass, Club/Dance*

Though he's most interested in acid house and early Detroit techno, Alex Reece came to prominence in the mid-'90s as a jungle star. His interest in techno began in the late '80s, when acid house was popular. Reece gradually earned enough money to buy turntables and a decent vinyl collection. He then began DJing and worked for Basement Records in 1992, engineering for Wax Doctor. Quitting his job to concentrate on making his own music, Reece first tried his hand at house (recording with brother Oscar as Exodus), but found it too formulaic. He realized that there was much more to explore in jungle/drum'n'bass, so he began to experiment.

His initial releases appeared on the Sinister, Creative Wax and Moving Shadow labels, but Reece made his name with Goldie's Metalheadz Records. Singles like "Basic Principles" and "Pulp Fiction"—with its trademark lurching bassline—became jungle standards, showcasing his minimalist style, a sound partly inspired by his fixation with acid house. In fact, the case might be made that Reece's music isn't jungle at all, since most of his beats are quite steady. It is only the occasional percussion break and off-beat rimshots that spin his work into jungle territory.

No matter if he's a junglist or a house maven, Reece cemented his reputation quite well with additional recordings as Jazz Juice (for Precious Materials), Lunar Funk (for Mo'Wax) and the Original Playboy (for R&S). In early 1996, he landed a major-label deal when Island recruited him for their Quango subsidiary. His debut album *So Far* was released in September 1996. While the album was received well in most circles, the jungle underground—led by Goldie—had practically disowned Reece by that time, disgusted with his "commercial" leanings. —*John Bush*

**Pulp Fiction/Chill Pill [Single]** / 1995 / Metalheadz ✦✦✦✦

- **So Far** / Aug. 5, 1996 / Quango/Island ♦♦♦
Call the album "jungle for the dance masses." *So Far* comes from noted junglist Alex Reece, but newcomers to breakbeats will have no trouble tapping their feet or keeping in rhythm to any of the songs here. Reece's massive "Pulp Fiction" single appears here as "Pulp Friction," and though the bassline is majestic, the beats are what matter in jungle; Reece just doesn't have what it takes to put him into Goldie/Photek territory. Goldie's *Timeless* is probably the closest touchstone to *So Far*, since both albums lean very close to house music—female diva vocals, skittery piano and synth lines, etc. But in the end, Goldie spins heads while Alex Reece simply makes them bob. —*John Bush*

**Al's Records Series, Vol. 1** / Apr. 14, 1997 / Al's ♦♦
Though it was released as a various-artists compilation, this 12-track collection of material from Reece's own label includes ten of his own productions, mostly house-derived drum'n'bass minimalism. —*Keith Farley*

## Reel 2 Real

f. 1993, New York, NY
*Group / Club/Dance, House*
The producer of one of the biggest dance hits of the '90s, "I Like to Move It"—plus a half-dozen other Top 20 hits in Great Britain—Reel 2 Real is masterminded by Erick Morillo, a New York DJ who sought to combine the energy of Latin-house music with reggae rhythms and textures. Morillo, who is of Columbian and Dominican heritage, began DJing in his early teens and studied production at New York's Center of Media Arts. After working on remixes for several reggae singles, he teamed up with a toaster, the General, for "Muevelo," a platinum-selling single popular in Latin communities. Another big mover on the dancefloors, "The New Anthem/Funk Buddha," brought him the attention of the Strictly Rhythm label. Signed to the label and introduced to the Trinidad-born vocalist Mad Stuntman (aka Mark Quashie), Morillo formed Reel 2 Real and released the group's first single, "I Like to Move It," in 1993.

By the following year, the single had exploded on the world's dancefloors, spawning the *Move It!* album. The LP did well on the charts, and produced four British hit singles. Morillo continued to DJ and released the mix compilation *Live & More* in early 1996. Before the end of the year, Reel 2 Real had released its second album, *Are You Ready for Some More?*, with vocal contributions from Michael Watford, Barbara Tucker and Althea McQueen, among others. Morillo gained a higher profile that year after providing DJ duties for MTV's *Singled Out*. He also hooked up with Latin American heart-throbs Proyecto Uno for the Cuban barnstormer, "Mueve la Cadera." —*John Bush*

**Move It!** / 1995 / Positiva ♦♦

- **Are You Ready for Some More?** / Sep. 17, 1996 / Strictly Rhythm ♦♦♦
Reel 2 Real's sophomore album is a bit less focused on hit singles, especially so considering it doesn't contain the megahit "I Like to Move It." Though there are plenty of charting singles included—the title track "Mueve la Cadera (Move Your Body)," "Jazz It Up,"—Morillo attempts to diversify, including another update of the Gamble-Huff chestnut "Now That We Found Love" and the ballad "Love Hurts." He's only occasionally successful, though, making one wish he'd stick to hit singles. —*John Bush*

## Reflection

f. 1995, Tokyo, Japan
*Group / Electronica, Electro-Techno, Ambient Techno, IDM*
The first Japanese signings to London's notorious Clear Records, Reflection seem to have more on their minds than simply updating '80s electro with the tweak of '90s technology. A production trio of Ichiro (programming) and Kenji Taniguchi (programming, occasional guitar) with supervisor Nobukazi Takemura, Reflection deals in intelligent electro, working in flourishes of everything from bossa nova spice to acid squelching—basically any style of exotica within reach of the last forty years. The group's first release for Clear was mid-1997's *Transparent* EP, after which came their debut album, *The Errornormous World*. Hot on its heels appeared a remix album, *The Morerroronus World*, with contributions from 4 Hero, As One, Plaid, Morgan Geist and Hidden Agenda. —*John Bush*

- **The Errornormous World** / Jul. 7, 1997 / Clear ♦♦♦♦
Attacking dance music with the usual flair of Japanese producers possessing a wealth of instruments and effects at their beck and call, Reflection blend new-school electro (like almost any artist on the Clear label) with touches of jazz, hip-hop, bossa nova, and even church organs in the most absurd places on their debut album. —*John Bush*

**The Morerroronus World** / Nov. 10, 1997 / Clear ♦♦♦
Reflection's remix album featured reworkings by mostly sympathetic artists from the vein of jazzy/electro/techno fold, including Clear labelmates past and present like Plaid, Morgan Geist and As One plus producers farther afield such as Hidden Agenda and the Freestyle Man. —*John Bush*

## Steve Reich

b. Oct. 3, 1936, New York, NY
*Composer / Tape Music, 20th Century Classical/Modern Composition, Avant-Garde, Minimalism*
Following in the footsteps of La Monte Young and Terry Riley, composer Steve Reich is widely considered the third major pioneer of minimalism; credited as the innovator behind phasing—a process whereby two tape loops lined up in unison gradually move out of phase with each other, ultimately coming back into sync—his early experiments in tape manipulation also anticipated the emergence of hip-hop sampling by well over a decade. Reich was born October 3, 1936 in New York City, and later studied philosophy at Cornell University; while at the Juilliard School of Music, he turned to composition, finally landing at Mills College in Oakland, California under the tuteleage of avant-garde composers Luciano Berio and Darius Milhaud. During his collegiate years, Reich supported himself by drumming professionally; however, when his academic career drew to a close in 1963, he turned to driving a cab.

Around that same time, Reich completed his first major compositions, *Pitch Charts* and the experimental film score *Plastic Haircut*. 1964's *Music for Three or More Pianos* was his first work to make use of tape loops, followed a year later by the landmark *It's Gonna Rain*, a phased piece constructed out of a 13-second sample of a sermon by the minister Brother Walter. Reich again applied his phasing manipulations to the recorded voice on 1966's *Come Out*, but with 1967's *Piano Phase* and *Violin Phase* he began employing the process on acoustic instruments. Subsequent works continued expanding the parameters of the phasing concept—while the above-mentioned *Violin Phase* could be played with one violin and electronic tape or with four violins, 1971's extended *Drumming* (inspired by a journey to Ghana) was scored for four pairs of bongos, three marimbas, three glockenspiels, and voice.

Reich's subsequent work veered from quintessential minimalism (1972's self-explanatory *Clapping Music*) to orchestral compositions (1976's *Music for Eighteen Musicians*, again everything its title promises), with the latter aesthetic becoming his primary focus in later years. Rarely recorded throughout his first decades as an artist, during the '80s Reich's major works finally began appearing on album, among them 1988's brilliant *Different Trains*, a Holocaust-inspired piece created for live string quartet, pre-recorded string quartet and sampled voices. (On LP it was paired with *Electric Counterpoint*, a composition for jazz guitarist Pat Metheny which was later sampled by the UK ambient duo the Orb on their hit "Little Fluffy Clouds.") Reich's Jewish heritage continued playing a central role in his later work as well—1994's multi-media piece *The Cave* retold the story of the prophet Abraham. As Reich's trailblazing work came into fashion with the wave of late-'90s electronica, the remix album *Reich Remixed* appeared in 1999. —*Jason Ankeny*

★ **Music for 18 Musicians** / 1978 / ECM ♦♦♦♦♦
Nonesuch's 1998 issue of *Music for 18 Musicians* was originally released as part of the ten-disc box set *Works*. It's a new digital recording of Reich's most famous piece, and it's the only single-disc release of the piece. It's a fine, nearly definitive, recording of one of the most influential contemporary classical compositions of the late 20th century. —*Leo Stanley*

**Music for a Large Ensemble** / Feb. 1980-Mar. 1980 / Ecm ♦♦♦
*Music for a Large Ensemble, Violin Phase* features Reich's "phase music" techniques. —*Michael P. Dawson*

**Early Works** / 1987 / Elektra/Nonesuch ♦♦♦♦
These historical recordings were difficult to find (usually on out-of-print compilations) for a long time so it's gratifying to have them readily available in one place. The two important tape pieces here from the mid-sixties, "Come Out" and "It's Gonna Rain", have their sound sources originating in police brutality and apocalyptic evangelism. Reich takes his sources and turns them into two short tape loops repeated rapidly as they gradually go out of synch with each other—what's revealed are the intricacies of the human voice. "Come Out" takes the voice fragment and turns it into a hall-of-mirror set of

voices over shuffling beat and wah-wah that are actually a by-product of subtleties of the voice and almost unrecognizable as the original vocal sample. It becomes a scary psychedelic funk piece that Funkadelic or Can would have been proud of. "It's Gonna Rain" is similarly looped and phased as the preacher's admonition is transformed, moving in and out of synch as the piece progresses with the second part of the piece especially full of fierce, terrifying swirls of noise. After taking musique concrète to another level, Reich decided to try to make similar strides with instrumental music. The two other pieces here, "Piano Phase" and "Clapping Music", represent this new direction in his work. Re-recorded here in 1986 and 1987, their intricate, layered patterns should be familiar to fans of another one of Reich's masterpieces, "Music for 18 Musicians". *Early Works* is a must-have introduction for anyone interested in the roots of minimalist music. —*Jason Gross*

**Different Trains/Electric Counterpoint** / 1989 / Elektra/Nonesuch ♦♦♦♦
In an acoustic equivalent to interactive electronics, Reich creates a rhythmic tape of train whistles of the 1930s and '40s and of speakers recalling train rides of the past in the USA. and in Nazi-occupied lands . The natural pitch inflections of the voices are then transferred to pitches for the instruments. A rich emotional experience akin to his earlier pieces "It's Gonna Rain" (1965) and the shocking "Come Out" (1966) (both on Elektra / Nonesuch 79169-2) …a more interesting use of the rather mechanistic edge of his pattern music. —*"Blue" Gene Tyranny*

**The Cave** / Oct. 24, 1995 / Nonesuch ♦♦♦♦
*The Cave* is a December 1994 piece featuring the Steve Reich Ensemble (conducted by Paul Hillier) in collaboration with video/text writer Beryl Korot. The story concerns the only place in the world where both Jews and Muslims are allowed to worship, a mosque in Hebron supposed to be the Cave of the Patriarchs where Abraham and many of his descendants were buried. Reich's ensemble includes four vocalists, four percussionists, three vocalists and a five-piece string section. The work begins with regimented percussion and follows through short spoken-word parts and longer sung passages. In several of the spoken-word parts, the harmonics are echoed in the string section (one of Reich's most recognizable and appealing devices), and although the content may be uninteresting to those not familiar with the ongoing Israeli-Arab differences, *The Cave* is a fascinating piece. —*John Bush*

**Works: 1965-1995** / 1997 / Elektra/Nonesuch ♦♦♦♦
Of the composers generally referred to as "minimalist" (a label almost universally rejected by those to whom it is applied), three have had a substantial and direct impact on modern music both popular and classical since the '60s: Philip Glass, Steve Reich and, to a somewhat lesser degree, John Adams. (Other important early minimalists, including La Monte Young and Terry Riley, have impinged on the general popular consciousness mostly by virtue of their formative influence on the Glass/Reich/Adams triumverate.) Of the big three, Reich has made the most consistently interesting music in both harmonic and rhythmic terms. Glass has had the greater commercial success and Adams has worked in larger forms with more prestigious orchestras, but Reich has been most consistently successful in setting repetitious, slow-changing patterns into complex, genuinely interesting and musically compelling structures. As he has repeatedly and adamantly stated, his is not "trance" music—he expects the listener to pay close attention, and his music amply rewards those who do.

This monumental ten-CD retrospective collects the original recordings of almost all of Reich's published music. ("New York Counterpoint," "Eight Lines," "Four Organs" and "Music for 18 Musicians" are newly recorded for this collection.) It documents his progression from early tape pieces, deceptively simple compositions which foreshadowed his later work with phase shifting and canonic structures, to the recent choral/orchestral works that demonstrate once and for all that Reich's music is far from "minimal" in any meaningful sense of the term. All of the most famous works are included, notably "Music for 18 Musicians," "The Desert Music" and "Different Trains," which many consider to be his masterpiece, but there are some curious exclusions—his groundbreaking "Violin Phase" is missing, for example, not to mention the charming "Music for Pieces of Wood" ("Clapping Music," from the same period, is included) and his gorgeous composition for flutist Ransom Wilson, "Vermont Counterpoint." But this box set is still an essential purchase for anyone with a serious interest in modern art music. The packaging is beautiful, and the accompanying booklet includes full track and personnel listings, a chronology of Reich's career, appreciative notes from fellow musicians and an excellent new interview by Jonathan Cott. —*Rick Anderson*

**Reich Remixed** / Mar. 29, 1999 / Nonesuch ♦♦♦
Since he's one of the most influential classical composers for later electronica producers, it's only natural that Steve Reich should get his own remix collection, to file alongside Pierre Henry and others. This ten-track collection includes some of the most respected new producers in the field—from beat veterans Coldcut, Howie B and Kurtis Mantronik to relative newcomers Andrea Parker and Nobukazu Takemura (aka Child's View)—dissecting the gorgeous sounds of Reich classics like "Music for 18 Musicians" and "Come Out" for a younger audience. And though it's difficult to think of Reich's usual followers appreciating these remixes for what they are, the cast is one of the best for a remix album in recent memory. Coldcut's version of "Music for 18 Musicians" is quite faithful, retaining the luxuriant waves of sound that make the original one of the best-sounding pieces of music ever recorded. Kurtis Mantronik, one of the best hip-hop producers of all time, puts his legendary drum programming abilities to the test by taking on "Drumming," Reich's study of African percussion. Two of the tracks, by Tranquility Bass and DJ Spooky, are megamixes that use material from several different Reich compositions. There have been far too many subpar remix albums in the late '90s devoted to bands who don't deserve them, but *Reich Remixed* is both a worthy cause and an excellent production. —*John Bush*

## Reload
f. 1991, Cornwall, England
*Group / Ambient Techno*
The first incarnation of producers Mark Pritchard and Tom Middleton, Reload graced the first three releases for the duo's own Evolution Records. *The Reload, The Autoreload* and *The Biosphere* (each released in 1991) matched the moodier side of Detroit techno with acid-house and sweeping synthesizer lines borrowed from soundtrack music. A brief contract with Infonet Records resulted in two additional EPs and the 1993 full-length *A Collection of Short Stories,* though Pritchard and Middleton virtually retired the Reload name by 1994, when their first LP as Global Communication was released. Reload remixes of Slowdive, Aphex Twin and Nav Katze have also appeared. [See Also: Global Communication, Jedi Knights] —*John Bush*

● **A Collection of Short Stories** / 1993 / Infonet ♦♦♦♦
A stunning first full-length for the Pritchard/Middleton duo, *A Collection of Short Stories* charted the dark side of the ambient techno coin long before many had been turned on to the music at all. Alternating the automated-machinery chug of tracks like "Teq" and "Ahn" with more sweeping (but similarly dark) moods on "Peschi," "Rota Link" and "1642 Try 621," the album provides the soundtrack to a night in a possessed auto factory; hissing steam and banging metallic percussion punctuate the moods effectively, while an included book of short stories gives the music a focus if desired. Even the lighter, dreamier side which would later appear on Global Communication releases is given airtime on the ethereal "Le Soleil Et La Mer." Unjustly slept on when first released by Infonet, *A Collection of Short Stories* was reissued in America in 1997. —*John Bush*

**Auto Reload EP, Vol. 2 [EP]** / 1994 / Infonet ♦♦♦
The *Auto Reload EP* includes remixes by Black Dog and Reload-offshoot Global Communication, LP versions of "Le Soleil Et La Mer" and "The Biosphere," and a new track called "Phase 4." —*John Bush*

## Renegade Soundwave
f. 1986, London, England
*Group / Alternative Dance, Club/Dance, Industrial*
Formed in London during the late '80s, Renegade Soundwave applied the punk and industrial ethic to both dub and dancefloor electronica, in good company with fellow sound terrorists throughout the decade, from Cabaret Voltaire to Skinny Puppy and Meat Beat Manifesto. The trio of Gary Asquith, Danny Briottet and Carl Bonnie debuted on Rhythm King with the 1987 single "Kray Twins," and moved to Mute one year later for an EP, *Biting My Nails.* Though Renegade Soundwave spent two years recording material for an album, the release of *Soundclash* and *In Dub* within six months vindicated them somewhat. The group's only hit, "Probably a Robbery" (from *Soundclash*), made the British Top 40 early in 1990, but Bonnie left later that year for a solo career. Asquith and Briottet spent several years in isolation before emerging in 1994 with the "Renegade Soundwave" single and the album *How You Doin?* After playing their first live date in history during late 1994,

the duo released *Brixton* and *The Next Chapter of Dub* the following year. The compilation *RSW 87-95* emerged in 1996. — *John Bush*

**Soundclash** / 1989 / Mute ♦♦♦

Recycling American hip-hop and British dub to form their own unique sound aesthetic, Renegade Soundwave cover a lot of territory on their debut album. Though the rapping is subpar, productions like the opener "Blue Eyed Boy" (featuring the same sample later used by Public Enemy for "By the Time I Get to Arizona") and their cover of the old English Beat classic "Can't Get Used to Losing You" reveal a solid focus on the audio terrorism possible from sampling. *Soundclash* also includes Renegade Soundwave's charting single "Probably a Robbery" and the title track from their previous EP *Biting My Nails*. — *John Bush*

● **In Dub** / 1990 / Elektra ♦♦♦♦

*In Dub* is a double album featuring versions of several previous tracks plus much new material recorded with the assistance of Flood and Holger Hiller. Selections like "Thunder," "Transition," and "Deadly" are skeletal echo-chamber rhythm tracks devoid of much melody or effects, though "Holgertron" does sample the *Dr. Who* theme with panache. — *John Bush*

**How You Doin—** / 1994 / Mute/Elektra ♦♦♦

Briotett and Asquith recorded their first album as a duo with 1994's *How You Doin?* Tracks like "Funky Dropout," "Last Freedom Fighter" and "Renegade Soundwave" do a good job at fusing industrial music and dance with James Brown's funky-drummer aesthetic. — *John Bush*

**RSW 87-95** / Jul. 29, 1996 / Mute ♦♦♦♦

Renegade Soundwave's *RSW 87-95* collects the bulk of the dance trio's singles of the late '80s and early '90s, featuring a selection of remixes and album tracks to round out the retrospective. It's an excellent introduction to a frequently intriguing dance outfit. — *Stephen Thomas Erlewine*

## Repeat

f. 1994, London, England
*Group / Experimental Techno, Club/Dance, Techno*

An only periodically revisited side project of producers Mark Broom and Ed Handley and Andy Turner of Plaid, Repeat have nonetheless issued a relative wealth of material in their short existence. Beginning with their 1996 A13 debut, *Repeats*, the group also released a selection from that album on Jonah Sharp's Reflective label as the *South of Market* EP. A four-track EP, *Canada*, followed in 1997 on Broom's Unexplored Beats label (named for his London studios, where all Repeat material thus far has been conceived). The group have also contributed tracks to various compilations, including A13's celebrated *Experimenta*, also featuring material by the Black Dog, Thomas P. Heckmann, and a solo Broom. Musically, Repeat is closer to Plaid's funky brand of listening techno than Broom's more straight-ahead, booming fare, with *Canada* containing the chunkiest of the group's tracks. Heavily syncopated and with an emphasis on movement and development, the group incorporate rhythms less traveled, shifting percussion elements in ways that confound expectation, similar in respects to Plaid's work with Ken Downie as the Black Dog (particularly on the latter's *Bytes*). — *Sean Cooper*

**Repeats** / 1996 / A13 ♦♦♦

The trio of Mark Broom and Plaid's Ed Handley and Andy Turner knocked out this quick nine-track full-length of jerky listening techno for their A13 debut. Although it's clear the group spent about a weekend putting the material together, enough is stuffed between the jarring electronics and angular, odd-metered rhythms to make for a solid, repeatable listen. Fans especially of mid-period Atom Heart, B12, and early Black Dog should apply. — *Sean Cooper*

**South of Market [EP]** / 1996 / Reflective ♦♦♦

Released on Jonah Sharp's similarly located San Francisco-based Reflective imprint, *South of Market* takes two of *Repeats*' finest tracks—"End Up" and "Fish Stew"—and adds a third Sharp/Turner/Handley collaboration, "Soon," recorded during the SF leg of a Plaid tour. Oddly, it's the new track that stands out, suggesting the propriety of further Sharp/Plaid collabs which have, to date, yet to materialize. — *Sean Cooper*

● **Canada [EP]** / 1997 / Unexplored Beats ♦♦♦♦

A four-track of meandering, downtempo experimental electro released on Broom's own Unexplored Beats label. Although "Canada" is probably the least innovative of UXB's brief-but-classic cachet of releases, the tracks are enjoyable enough slices of minimal, funky electro/techno, focusing as elsewhere on subtle (if somewhat monotonous) perambulations of rhythm. "Canada" also marks an improvement in production over earlier works, with dense percussion and a sharpness of detail. — *Sean Cooper*

## Republica

f. 1995, London, England
*Group / Electronica, Alternative Dance, Club/Dance, Alternative Pop/Rock*

As Brit-pop remained popular in England during the mid-'90s, Republica hit the charts with a sound closer in feel to '80s indie-dance groups such as the Pet Shop Boys and New Order. Vocalist Saffron was born in Nigeria, and began singing with club-staples N-Joi and the Shamen, as well as Jah Wobble. By 1995, she had met keyboard players Tim Dorney (previously with Flowered Up) and Andy Todd (who has produced Barbra Streisand and Bjork, among others). They began writing songs, and after recruiting guitarist Johnny Male and drummer Dave Barborossa, Republica debuted with the single "Out of the Darkness." UK indie-dance label Deconstruction signed the group and released its self-titled debut. From the album, "Ready to Go" became a hit both in England and in the States, where it stormed the alternative Top Ten during late 1996. The follow-up, 1998's *Speed Ballads*, only gained British distribution. — *John Bush*

● **Republica** / Jul. 29, 1996 / RCA ♦♦♦♦

Republica essentially sounds like they're stuck in 1990, when house and rave were just beginning to make their presence felt in dance-pop—which, to more critical ears, will mean they sound dated during the mid-'90s, when jungle, drums'n'bass, ambient and all other forms of techno are finally edging their way into the mainstream. And that argument would be relevant if Republica were attempting to work in that genre, but as their eponymous debut indicates, they have no interest in hardcore techno—they just want to dance. Working with strong, accessible hi-nrg beats and catchy choruses, the trio has a bright, energetic sound that is quite infectious when tied with the right melodies, such as on the hit singles "Ready to Go" and "Drop Dead Gorgeous." If they had more than one sound, however, *Republica* would be even more entertaining, but as it stands, the record is a stretch of pleasantly numbing dance-pop punctuated by two terrific singles. — *Stephen Thomas Erlewine*

**Speed Ballads** / Nov. 1998 / Deconstruction ♦♦♦

While it was released only in the UK, Republica's sophomore release *Speed Ballads* exhibits some remarkable growth. Detractors always felt that the band was the commercialization of other similar groups such as Garbage, yet Republica's music has a definite pop leaning that sets them apart from some of their contemporaries. Since Republica is more or less a studio creation—more about "production" than being a band, really—it's not surprising that the project employed a team of all-star producers including Alan Winstanley and the Lightning Seeds' Ian Broudie. What resulted was a cycle of ten tracks in an album far more diverse than their debut. While the disco-metal that ruled their first record has been pushed to the back of the mix here—only some of the songs actually have the same pounding rhythms on the debut—the songwriting has come exceptionally far. It's especially noticeable on the excellent single "Try Anything," a moving power-ballad that's also awash in beats. Other highlights include the hard-driving "From Rush Hour With Love" and the spacey "Fading of the Man." — *Jason Damas*

## Req

*Producer / Funky Breaks, Electronica, Ambient Breakbeat, Trip-Hop*

Brighton graffiti artist/producer Req in some respects embodies the cliches of British underground club music; no formal musical training whatsoever; a youth spent tagging, DJing, and breakdancing in the wake of the first wave of hip-hop culture to hit the UK; a knack for pushing received artistic sensibilities to their breaking point and coming up with exciting new directions in the offing. Req's music, however, is hardly clichéd, combining a warped, abstract approach to sampled breaks with a knack for extracting a haunting moodiness out of even the most minimal of electronic and sampledelic soundscapes. One of the UK's most respected graffiti artists, Req began writing in 1984, after the Beat Street tour hyped his senses to the basic tenets of hip-hop. Although he only began making music by the time he was into his late 20s, Req's years spent bedroom DJing refined his instinct for effective compostition, a skill which tends to compensate for his music's somewhat limited sonic palette. Req's debut for esoteric beathead imprint Skint (home also to Fatboy Slim and Bentley Rhythm Ace) was his *Garden* EP, four tracks of breathy downtempo hip-hop similar to the breakbeat abstractions of DJ

Krush and DJ Cam. With stated influences spanning from early Detroit techno and old school hip-hop, to the Black Dog, Req's tracks are more stylistically rooted in the Mo'Wax/Cup of Tea camp, stripping hip-hop of its extraneous elements and focusing on the bass, the beats, and the atmosphere around them. *Req: One*, his debut Skint full-length (with wraparound cover displaying a mural of his artwork), was released in 1997, and was praised highly by everyone from Coldcut to *The Wire*. —*Sean Cooper*

**Req: One** / Mar. 3, 1997 / Skint ♦♦♦
Req takes the opportunity of the longform format to spread his sound out a bit, resulting in an alternating collection of rooted, downtempo beat music and floaty, meandering ambience. Req's stated intention with *Req: One* was for the music to "hint at a direction" without ever actually settling down into one, an interesting approach one would expect to prompt self-righteous cries of "MUSO!" but for the fact that Req's inspired amateurism is too honest and freeflowing to warrant it. Overall, pretty samey-sounding, but a good listen. —*Sean Cooper*

● **Frequency Jams** / Feb. 16, 1998 / Skint ♦♦♦♦
Like its predecessor, the undersung *One*, Req's *Frequency Jams* is a blurry, choppy assemblage of fractured rhythms and lo-fi Tascam experimentalism. And as with his debut, Req more than makes up in concept what he lacks in craft, dragging a for-all-intents *purist's* hip-hop into some of the most interesting, inventive corners of instrumental beats. Highlights include the heavy-on-the-attack old school rhythms of "I (Linn Mix)" and Req's haunting, fuzzy, lonesome tribute to the African finger piano, "Mbira." —*Sean Cooper*

## Resistance D

f. 1994
*Group / Trance, Club/Dance, Techno*
The trance outfit Resistance D was formed by the duo of Pascal F.E.O.S. and Maik Maurice. After the pair released *The Human EP* for Planet Earth in 1994, *The Best of Resistance D* followed in 1995 on Harthouse/Eye Q Records. Although they remixed Jean-Michel Jarre's "Oxygène" in 1997, Resistance D recorded little during the late '90s. As a solo act however, Pascal F.E.O.S. continued recording for Planet Vision and Ongaku, and dovetailed nicely into the progressive trance movement of the late '90s. —*John Bush*

● **The Best of Resistance D** / 1995 / Harthouse/Eye Q ♦♦♦♦
Like many acts on the Harthouse label, Resistance D pursue a driving, minimalist trance with waves of acid-synth. Though somewhat derivative, *The Best of Resistance D* is a fine effort. —*John Bush*

## Rhythim Is Rhythim (Derrick May)

*Producer / Detroit Techno, Club/Dance, Techno*
As the name under which Derrick May produced his many prototypical techno classics in the late '80s, Rhythim Is Rhythim remains one of the most esteemed guises in techno's short history. Though the handful of Rhythim Is Rhythim classics are primarily the product of May's forward-looking sense of musical creativity, it is important to remember that there were occasional contributors. Most significantly, some of Carl Craig's earliest production work appears on the Rhythim Is Rhythim tracks "Drama," "Kao-tic Harmony," and the 1989 version of "Strings of Life." In addition, Thomas Barnett and Mike James contributed to "Nude Photo" and "Strings of Life," respectively, while D-Wynn collaborated with May for the Rhythim Is Rhythim spin-off R-Thyme ("R-Theme" and "Illusion"). Yet for the most part, it was entirely May's gifted vision as an innovator that led to one Rhythim Is Rhythim classic after another. Beginning with "Nude Photo" as the first release on his Transmat label, May produced nothing but classics in his short life as a producer from 1986 to 1991. During this period, "Nude Photo" and the piano-driven "Strings of Life," in particular, became anthems in England's exploding late '80s rave scene. Other less anthemic songs such as "Beyond the Dance (Cult Mix)," "It Is What It Is," and "Icon (Montage Mix)" were championed for their mystical sound, consisting simply of synthesizer melodies and light percussive rhythms. In 1998, May compiled the majority of his Rhythim Is Rhythim songs on the *Innovator* double album; unfortunately, many previously unreleased tracks appear in abbreviated form. [See Also: Derrick May] —*Jason Birchmeier*

**Icon/Kao-tic Harmony [Single]** / 1988 / Transmat ♦♦♦
The two tracks May left as his swan song function—"Icon" and "Kao-tic Harmony"—stand as a testament to his startling growth over the course of only a few years as a composer. "Icon" opens with a ridiculously fast-paced foundation of percussive rhythms; lacking a thumping 4/4 bass beat, the rhythm's complexity feels overwhelming for a moment until an elegiac synthesizer melody slowly fades over the top of the speedy percussion at a pace more suited for lullabies than dancing. Though these two elements contrast with one another, it is exactly this contrast that makes this track so touching and seductive. While one element of the song evokes adrenaline and energy, the other soothes the listener with its soft blanket of synthesized teardrops. The B-side of *Icon* is a collaboration between the teacher, May, and his protégé, Carl Craig—"Kao-tic Harmony"—which maintains the aura of melancholy emitted during "Icon," taking the cosmic sounds of May's otherworldly synthesizers to an extreme unlike anything in May's catalog. Rich in reverb and echo, synthesizer melodies open the track free of any percussion. After what seems like an improvised synthesizer solo, a fast-paced percussive rhythm enters, again free of any thumping bass beats to hold the track together. —*Jason Birchmeier*

● **Beyond the Dance [EP]** / 1989 / Transmat ♦♦♦♦
For this record, Derrick May took an otherwise excellent song from his *It Is What It Is* record, "Beyond the Dance," and gave it an epic remix, completely restructured the song, first by greatly expanding its scope to epic status, then rearranging the rhythms. For the first several minutes of "Beyond the Dance (Cult Mix)," May has submersed the rearranged high-hat percussive rhythms from the original in layers of his sensual synthesizer. One of the synthesizer layers lingers in the background, casting a shadow of melodic beauty; the other layer is the chorus of string stabs that were the highlight in "Beyond the Dance" 's original mix. "Beyond the Dance (Bizzaro Mix)" from the B-side is much shorter and sounds remarkably like the first version, while "Sinister (Trolley Mix)" functions well as yet another wonderful extension of the Rhythim Is Rhythim sound. —*Jason Birchmeier*

**It Is What It Is/Beyond the Dance [Single]** / 1989 / Transmat Classics ♦♦♦♦
Though "Strings of Life" may be the song forever associated with Derrick May's groundbreaking style of sensual techno in the late '80s, the title track to the sixth release by Transmat may be his quintessential song in terms of style. A fairly simple song, "It Is What It Is" perfectly summed up the brand of techno May found success with as Rhythim Is Rhythim. There are two other songs on this release that sound similar to "It Is What It Is," but aren't quite as melodic: "Feel Surreal" and the original version of "Beyond the Dance." Both lay down complex percussive rhythms composed of different tones and timbres. "Beyond the Dance" uses the same sort of orchestral stabs that elevated "Strings of Life" to such surreal heights. Anthemic, colorful, and celebratory, these stabs make the song; without them, it would be nothing but a bland drum-machine exercise. "Feel Surreal" also has some melodic moments, courtesy of May's deft synthesizer work. —*Jason Birchmeier*

## Robert Rich

b. California
*Percussion, Guitar, Flute, Synthesizer, Producer, Leader, Composer, Arranger / Microtonal, Experimental Ambient, Space, Techno-Tribal, Electro-Acoustic, Ambient, Ethnic Fusion, Progressive Electronic*
Although his music is often consigned to the new age bins of record stores and the bulk of his work has been released on labels more closely associated with that classification, Robert Rich's solo and collaborative recordings have proven extremely influential on a range of new school ambient and experimental artists. Although barely into his 30s, Rich's association with earlier space-music pioneers such as Steve Roach, Kevin Braheny, and Michael Stearns also makes him one of the few of that generation to have interfaced creatively with the new wave of experimental electronic composers.

A California native, Rich began experimenting with electronics in the late '70s before attending Stanford University, where he completed a degree in psychology. While at Stanford, Rich's involvement in the university's prestigious Center for Computer Research in Music and Acoustics expanded his interest in electronic composition, as well as bringing him in contact with a wide range of non-traditional, non-Western musical ideas. Rich's performance of several all-night "sleep concerts" during this period also helped solidify an aesthetic focus on psychoacoustics, perceptible in early recordings such as *Geometry* and *Trances/Drones*.

Rich's more mature works such as *Rainforest* and *Propagation* have sought to combine that interest with more recognizable electro-acoustical elements (Rich plays a wide range of instruments, from synths and effects racks to hand drums and flute), but the influence of digital sound manipulation has also moved increasingly to the fore. Inspired by the more textural works of artists like SPK and Throbbing Gristle, Rich's interest in the edgier side of electronic composition has also earned him a reputation among fans of gothic, industrial, and dark ambient, made most obvious by his collaboration in 1995 with Brian Williams of Lustmord. In addition to his more ambient-leaning works, Rich also plays in the experimental pop band Amoeba. He is also a scholar of Just Intonation, writing regularly on the topic and co-authoring the software program JICalc. He released *Inner Landscapes* in 1999, and *Humidity: Three Concerts* a year later. —*Sean Cooper*

**Rainforest** / 1989 / Hearts of Space ✦✦✦
1989's *Rainforest* combines Robert Rich's fine compositional ability and just intonation approach and a spectrum of ethnic influences into a musical evocation of the rainforest. Synthesizers, African thumb pianos, marimbas, gamelans and bamboo flute join in polyrhythmic, textural pieces like "Mbira" and "Drumsong." Rich's compositional skill gives "The Forest Dreams of Bach" transcultural appeal, mixing counterpoint and a Bach-like progression with a gamelan processional rhythm. Part of the proceeds from *Rainforest* support the Rainforest Action Network, a non-profit organization dedicated to saving the world's rainforests. —*Heather Phares*

**Strata** / 1990 / Fathom ✦✦✦✦
This highly regarded collaboration between Rich and Steve Roach uses layers of the earth as a metaphor for exploring layers of the psyche. With a wide variety of acoustic and electronic instruments, the two create surreal landscapes of throbbing world music rhythms, broad synthesizer washes, and ethereal sounds. —*Linda Kohanov*

**Propagation** / 1994 / Fathom ✦✦
The most "musical" (in the traditional sense) of Rich's solo works, *Propagation* takes to its logical conclusion a compositional goal Rich often refers to as "glurp," or something like digital/organic synthesis. Oddly, "glurpy" is exactly what much of the album is best described as. And a bit too glurpy in points, with unlikely art pour l'art electro-acoustical pairings often taking precedent over Rich's more evocative side. —*Sean Cooper*

**Yearning** / 1995 / Fathom ✦✦
A collaboration with sarod player Lisa Markow focusing on the theme of the Indian alap. Essentially an album-length expansion of the pair's work together on *Propagation*. Though somewhat precious, *Yearning* is also quite often breathtakingly beautiful, with Rich's subtle textures and melodies complementing Markow's accomplished improvisations. —*Sean Cooper*

★ **Stalker** / Nov. 1995 / Fathom ✦✦✦✦✦
A stunning masterpiece of evocative, slightly ominous environmental ambient inspired by the Andrei Tarkovsky film of the same name. Not nearly as composed as much of Rich's previous work, *Stalker* is also far more powerful, with deep, subterranean soundscapes taking the place of melodic and harmonic movement. —*Sean Cooper*

**A Troubled Resting Place** / 1996 / Fathom ✦✦✦
A collection of hard-to-find solo outings previously released on small-run labels such as Amplexus and Side Effects, *A Troubled Resting Place* showcases some of the finest examples of Rich's open-ended, penetrating approach to music. A slightly restive, alien feel permeates the album's tracks, thanks to Rich's use of just intonation in his compositions and the mix of flutes, steel guitar, incidental noise and synths in his arrangements on tracks like "Bioelectric Plasma." Reminiscent of *Stalker*, the calm austerity of *A Troubled Resting Place* explores Rich's use of music as a possibility, not as an end in itself. —*Heather Phares*

**Trances/Drones** / May 7, 1996 / Extreme ✦✦✦✦
During the period 1979-1984, Robert Rich was busy with psychology studies, Sleep Concerts and developing his musical style via a series of different experiments, ranging from solo work to performances that buried the audience in layers of sound from all directions. The music on *Trances/Drones* is drawn from that period, including all of the *Trances* and *Drones* material, plus the title track from *Sunyata*, Rich's first release, and the previously unreleased "Resonance." The music here is wonderfully relaxing (more so with the *Trances* material than with *Drones*) and perpetually fascinating. There's a lot more going on in most of the material here than would be expected at first blush—layer after layer of swirling textures and tones—and you'll find that interrupting one of these pieces is generally a shock: Rich has a talent for finding the internal rhythms of the body, which means you should allow the music to let you go gently (which, in the end, it does). —*Steven McDonald*

**Fissures** / 1997 / Fathom ✦✦✦✦
*Fissures* brings together two influential innovators of dark ambient-leaning electro-acoustic composition. Specifically, the album combines Rich's knack for integrating a range of acoustic instruments (dulcimer, PVC flutes, steel guitar) into alien, otherworldly atmospheres with Alio Die's talent for depths-plumbing, remarkably spatial arrangements which are as uncannily musical as they are subtle and mesmerizing. While the album echoes moments of both artists' previous work (Rich's collaboration with Brian Williams, *Stalker*, as well as Alio Die's 1995 Amplexus release, *Suspended Feathers*), *Fissures* manages a singular, wholly organic fusion of the two. —*Sean Cooper*

**Numena/Geometry** / 1997 / Fathom ✦✦✦
This Fathom reissue of two early Rich releases makes a handy companion to the composer's more fully formed recent work (particularly the dark ambient albums *A Troubled Resting Place* and *Stalker*). Although the albums are very different from one another, their respective foci—*Numena*'s psycho-acoustical organicism, *Geometry*'s sense of melodic symmetry and balance—combine as the two guiding principles of most of Rich's composing throughout his career. As a whole, *Geometry* has aged the least gracefully of the two, inflected as it is with a by now new age-y melodicism that detracts from the less specific groping of the album's lush textural support. *Numena*, however, sounds as focused and exploratory as it did when it was recorded; remarkable, since over a decade has passed. —*Sean Cooper*

**Seven Veils** / Aug. 18, 1998 / Hearts of Space ✦✦✦✦
Robert Rich is a master alchemist at weaving exotic ethnic sounds onto an ambient electronic background tapestry. On *Seven Veils*, Rich takes from the Middle East desert tones that speak of slender minarets, ancient landscapes, and the wealth of forgotten nations buried in the fertile crescent. Adding to the richness of this offering, these melodies are not as often sampled as they are played on live instrumentation. Indeed, the instruments of diverse cultures are brought to bear on incarnating these pseudo-Arabic stylings. Guitar, played hauntingly and sparsely, as a flavoring instrument, is prominent. Rich himself plays the lap steel guitar throughout the album, and avant-garde journeyman experimental guitarist David Torn is present on two tracks. The melody is actually most often rising from Rich's bamboo and PVC flutes. Their warm resonance and the human sound of respiring they bring goes far to make this a warm and intimate recording. Subtle but diverse percussion is enhanced with rubber band marimba and dulcimer in setting a foundation for these tracks. The highlight is a 15-minute piece, "The Book of Ecstasy." Over three "chapters," the listener is taken from a lonely percussion introduction sparkling with ghost-like effected treble sounds of guitar and electronics to Torn's sonorous guitar solo. Finally, the listener goes alight in "A Veiled Oasis" where the flute and cello (courtesy of Hans Christian of Amoeba) mark the boundaries of a cool, moonlit island in a harsh sea of sand. This Muslim psychedelia is a must for every shrinking world audiophile. —*Tom Schulte*

## Terry Riley

b. Jun. 24, 1935, Colfax, CA
*Keyboards, Piano, Composer / Tape Music, 20th Century Classical/Modern Composition, Minimalism, Ambient, World Fusion*

Minimalist pioneer Terry Riley was among the most revolutionary composers of the postwar era; famed for his introduction of repetition into Western music motifs, he also masterminded early experiments in tape loops and delay systems which left an indelible mark on the experimental music produced in his wake. Riley was born June 24, 1935 in Colfax, California, and began performing professionally as a solo pianist during the '50s; by the middle of the decade he was studying composition in San Francisco and Berkeley, where among his classmates was fellow minimalist innovator La Monte Young. Influenced by John Coltrane and John Cage, he began exploring open improvisation and avant-garde music, and in 1960 composed *Mescalin Mix*, a musique concrète piece composed for the Ann Halprin Dance Company consisting of tape loops of assorted found sounds.

By the early '60s, Riley was regularly holding solo harmonium performances beginning at 10:00 pm and continuing until sunrise, an obvious precursor of the all-night underground raves to follow decades later. After graduating Berkeley in 1961, his next major work was 1963's *Music for the Gift*, composed for a play written by Ken Dewey; among the first pieces ever generated by a tape delay/feedback system, it employed two tape recorders—a setup Riley dubbed the "Time Lag Accumulator"—playing a loop of Chet Baker's rendition of Miles Davis' "So What." The loop effect sparked Riley's interest in repetition as a means of musical expression, and in 1964 he completed his most famous work, the minimalist breakthrough *In C;* a piece constructed from 53 separate patterns, it was a landmark composition which provided the conception for a new musical form assembled from interlocking repetitive figures.

In time, Riley also learned to play saxophone, introducing the instrument into his so-called all-night flights; these epic improvisational performances became the basis for his most successful recordings, 1968's *Poppy Nogood and the Phantom Band* and the following year's *A Rainbow in Curved Air*, the music's cyclical patterns and etheral atmospherics predating the rise of the ambient concept by several years. In 1970, Riley made the first of many trips to India to study under vocal master Pandit Pran Nath, with whom he frequently performed in the years to come; another collaborator was John Cale, a pairing which resulted in the 1971 LP *Church of Anthrax*, arguably Riley's most widely-known recording outside of experimental music circles. Throughout the '70s, he also taught composition and North Indian Raga at Mills College in Oakland, California.

A pair of early '70s live performances—one in L.A., the other in Paris—resulted in the 1972 album *Persian Surgery Dervishes*, a work of meditative machine music clearly prescient of the trance sound to follow. Around the same time, while on staff at Mills, he befriended David Harrington, violinist of the Kronos Quartet; their camaraderie yielded a total of nine string quartets, the keyboard quintet *Crows Rosary* and *The Sands*, a concerto for string quartet and orchestra commissioned by *the Salzberg Festival* in 1991. Another Riley/Kronos collaboration, 1989's *Salome Dances for Peace*, was even nominated for a Grammy. Recording less and frequently as the years passed, Riley agreed to stage a performance celebrating the silver anniversary of *In C* which was then released in 1990. —*Jason Ankeny*

**Rainbow in Curved Air** / 1967 / Columbia ✦✦✦✦

**Poppy Nogood and the Phantom Band All Night Flight, Vol. 1** / 1968 / Cortical Foundation ✦✦✦✦

*Poppy Nogood and the Phantom Band* is scored for organ, saxophone, and the echo-inducing time-lag accumulator (aka the Phantom Band). The piece's first incarnation was as a six-hour all-night concert during 1968, and later as the back of a CD reissue of the previous year's *Rainbow in Curved Air*. Finally, a 40-minute edit of the concert was released in 1997; it shows Riley's growing Eastern influence and droning minimalism, quieting only for the last five minutes. —*John Bush*

**In C** / 1989 / Celestial Harmonies ✦✦✦✦

Performed by the Shanghai Film Orchestra, conducted by Wang Yongji. Truly celestial and a different feeling than American / European performances of this famous piece. This CD also contains David Mingyue Lang's gorgeous *Music of a Thousand Springs* and his *Zen (Ch'an) of Water*. Highly recommended. —*"Blue" Gene Tyranny*

★ **Rainbow in Curved Air/Poppy Nogood and the Phantom Band** / 1990 / CBS ✦✦✦✦✦

A CD re-issue of the classic 1969 recording. After several graph compositions and early pattern-pieces with jazz ensembles in the late 50's and early 60's (see "Concert for Two Pianists and Tape Recorders" and "Ear Piece" in La Monte Young's book—"An Anthology"), Riley invented a whole new music which has since gone under many names (minimal music—a category often applied to sustained pieces as well—pattern music, phase music, etc.) which is set forth in its purest form in the famous "In C" (1964) (for saxophone and ensemble, CBS MK 7178). "Rainbow in Curved Air" demonstrates both the straightforward pattern technique, but also has Riley improvising with the patterns, making gorgeous timbre changes on the synthesizers and organs, and presenting contrasting sections that has become the basic structuring of his current works ("Candenza on the Night Plain" and other pieces, Kronos Quartet, Gramavision R22Z-79444, 2 CDs; "Salome Dances for Peace" (1989), Kronos Quartet, Elektra/Nonesuch 79217-2, 2 CDs; and the recently premiered and as-yet-unrecorded "The Jade Palace" (1991), commissioned and played by The St. Louis Symphony. Scored for large orchestra with extra percussion and electronics, some of this work's 7 movements are: "Star Night," "Blue Lotus," "The Earth Below," and "Island of the Rhumba King.") —*"Blue" Gene Tyranny*

**Cactus Rosary (A Semi-Secular Song for Bruce Conner)** / 1993 / Artifact Music ✦✦✦

As the pun on "semi-circular" in the title implies, this music emphasizes the side-to-side as well as foreground-to-background musical dimensions—for example, gradual tuning changes generate beats that move tones in the space, a shaker sweeps from left-to-right, and repeated words of the text (e.g., "I was born, born, born, born... in India, India, India, India") gradually disappear into deep silence. A mesmerizing and original piece. —*"Blue" Gene Tyranny*

**Persian Surgery Dervishes** / 1993 / Newtone ✦✦✦

A welcome re-issue on two CDs of Riley's '70s masterpiece. Exquisite playing and a phenomenal experience of constantly evolving creation. —*"Blue" Gene Tyranny*

**Terry Riley: Zeitgeist-Intuitive Leaps** / 1994 / Work Music London ✦✦✦

This CD by the group Zeitgeist contains two works by Riley which he personally supervised and created in close cooperation with the group. These performances are perhaps the best ones recorded of Riley's music played by others. *The Room of Remembrance* (1987) is built around five melodic phrases, each of which serves as a "door"...when the musicians go out they are in the realm of improvisation and must construct ways to re-enter the room. The internal story of the piece is built around the image of a "medicine man," having expired in the wintry north of future America, being carried slowly up an icy incline as "snow clams" chant the Om Mane Padme Hum. A beautiful hymn in steady jazz-voiced chords opens the first section, and is interrupted at times by jolly phrases that recall gamelan music; snowflake patterns and windy tremolos are added, making the aural landscape wintry. Rushing patterns follow. The piece concludes with a subdued but fuller textured repeat of the initial hymn in steady chords. *Salome's Excellent Extension* (1989) is in four sections for quartet (piano, marimba, sax, vibraphone/steel drum) and part a series of works with a similar title: the string quartets called *Salome Dances For Peace*. This work offers a unique combination of the rich harmonic and gestural field of American West Coast jazz with Riley's pattern and Indian music sensibilities, with occasionally themes of a 1920s French "Les Six" turn. —*"Blue" Gene Tyranny*

**Reed Streams** / Apr. 20, 1999 / Cortical Foundation ✦✦✦✦

Terry Riley's debut work, 1966's *Reed Streams*, has been unavailable for over 30 years. 1999's reissue on the Cortical Foundation label features Riley's groundbreaking keyboard trance pieces, remastered from the original tapes, in all their droning, psychedelic glory. Along with "Untitled Organ (1964-66)" and "Dorian Reeds (1966)," the reissue includes a psychedelic big-band version of "In C—Mantra," the classic minimalist favorite. —*Heather Phares*

## Rinôçerôse

f. 1995, Montpellier, France
*Group / Electronica, Trip-Hop, Club/Dance*

The self-proclaimed house-with-guitars unit known as Rinôçerôse formed in 1995 around the French duo of Jean-Philippe Freu and Patou Carrie, from the ashes of two indie bands. Recording for the Spanish label Elefant, the pair released an eponymous debut soon after coming together (recorded with help from programmer Johnny Palumbo), then assembled a seven-piece band to tour the country. Soon, the French major label PIAS signed the duo and released the EP *Le Mobilier* in 1998. A support gig for Underworld in Paris cemented the group's rather tenuous credentials in the dance world, and Rinôçerôse released their album debut *Installation Sonore* on V2 in mid-1999. —*John Bush*

● **Installation Sonore** / Sep. 6, 1999 / V2 ✦✦✦

Culling inspirations from only the most stylish late-'90s dance acts (Daft Punk, Basement Jaxx, Underworld), Rinôçerôse focuses in on lush, filtered disco (with the requisite clipped beats and streamlined sound) as a pad for frontmen Freu and Carrie to layer their accomplished guitar work. While the guitar lines occasionally sound gimmicky or muzaky—closer to Steely Dan than Underworld—the duo often succeed in transcending the boundaries of house-with-guitars. Though the opener "La Guitaristic House Organisation" begins with a few clichés, the interstellar-overdrive effects near the end of the track rescue it from oblivion. And on several other tracks, added flute and Latin percussion make for some solid pan-global vibes. For all the lap steel, talkbox, bottleneck, wah-wah, fuzz guitar, whammy bars, e-bow, and Spanish guitar in evidence, the programming work of Johnny Palumbo bears much of the burden. Thankfully, he's at least slightly ahead of the curve—though it's easy to see the concept dating quickly and poorly. —*John Bush*

## Steve Roach

b. 1955, California

*Didjeridu, Percussion, Flute, Synthesizer, Producer / Spiritual, Space, Techno-Tribal, Ambient, Ethnic Fusion, Progressive Electronic, Electronic*

A longstanding leader in contemporary electronic music, composer and multi-instrumentalist Steve Roach drew on the beauty and power of the earth's landscapes to create lush, meditative soundscapes influential on the emergence of ambient and trance. A onetime professional motorbike racer born in California in 1955, Roach—inspired by the music of Tangerine Dream, Klaus Schulze, and Vangelis—taught himself to play synthesizer at the age of 20; debuting in 1982 with the album *Now*, his early work was quite reminiscent of his inspirations, but with 1984's *Structures from Silence* his music began taking enormous strides, the album's expansive and mysterious atmosphere inspired directly by the natural beauty of the southwestern US Subsequent works including 1986's three-volume *Quiet Music* series honed Roach's approach, his dense, swirling textures and hypnotic rhythms akin to environmental sound sculptures.

In 1988, inspired by the Peter Weir film *The Last Wave*, Roach journeyed to the Australian outback, with field recordings of aboriginal life inspiring his acknowledged masterpiece, the double-album *Dreamtime Return*. A year later, he teamed with percussionist Michael Shrieve and guitarist David Torn for *The Leaving Time*, an experiment in ambient jazz. After relocating to the desert outskirts of Tuscon, Arizona, Roach established his own recording studio, Timeroom, and in the years to follow grew increasingly prolific, creating both as a solo artist and in tandem with acts including Robert Rich, Michael Stearns, Jorge Reyes and Kevin Braheny—in all, close to two dozen major works in the '90s alone, all of them located at different points on the space-time continuum separating modern technology and primitive music. —*Jason Ankeny*

**Traveler** / 1983 / Fortuna ♦♦
This earlier release displays Roach's command of the electronic pop sound. Not all of this album stands up to critical listening, but the good cuts are great, and the influence of Schulze and Jarre is unmistakeable. —*Backroads Music/Heartbeats*

**Structures from Silence** / 1984 / Fortuna ♦♦♦♦
This influential album of extended works marked the emergence of his serene, yet haunting synthesizer breaths. —*Linda Kohanov*

**Dreamtime Return** / 1988 / Fortuna ♦♦♦♦
Roach's sojourn into the mythological mind of the Australian aborigines demonstrates that electronic music's greatest potential may lie in bringing our most elusive dreams and ancient memories into focus through potent, highly imaginative soundscapes. Altered chords that breathe ever so slowly, floating textures, digitally sampled aboriginal instruments, primitive trance rhythms, and arresting abstract sounds lead you through an unfolding maze of sonic dimensions that depict a sense of mystery and confrontation with the unknown. The double CD has 38 minutes of music not in the cassette version. —*Linda Kohanov*

**Western Spaces** / 1990 / Chameleon ♦♦♦
This reissue of Roach and Kevin Braheny's first evocation of the American Southwest features several selections not included on the original 1987 version. This album is a classic in the progressive electronic and ambient genres. —*Linda Kohanov*

**Now/Traveler** / 1992 / Fortuna ♦♦♦♦
This CD reissue features music from Roach's first two albums, originally recorded in 1982 and 1983. Both are excellent examples of his early, high-energy, sequencer-based style, with some hints at his developing ambient and tribal leanings. —*Linda Kohanov*

**World's Edge** / 1992 / Fortuna ♦♦♦♦
I can quickly summarize *World's Edge* in saying this a wonderfully executed blending of all those things that worked so well in *Structures from Silence* and *Dreamtime Return* Disc One incorporates a healthy dose of the Aboriginal percussives into Roach's trademark swelling drone-breathing synths. A perfect balance of tension-release, anticipation-relaxation, and trancezone/world-stopping is woven in a fine tapestry of ethereal soundworlds. Ten tracks ranging from 3:05 to 10:25 offer some of Roach's best works for the blank-stare, alpha-waved, drool-inducing moments. Disc Two offers essentially another hour of one nonstop Roachscape, transporting you even further through massive gong calls, synthvoice wordless chants, Tibetan ruins among Cydonian foothills, crumbling on the dust storm-eroded face of Mars, now welcome your naked soul. I hear Roach's *The Magnificent Void* here too. This is Roach as best as I can describe for you. As I do for only a select handful of artists—I highly recommend you ambient-heads and electronic tunes-devotees make sure this is in your collection. —*John Patterson*

● **Suspended Memories, Forgotten Gods** / 1993 / Hearts of Space ♦♦♦♦
In *Forgotten Gods*, Roach, Reyes, and Saiz explore an added dimension in space music. They have incorporated various drums and percussion instruments—prehistoric flutes, clay pots, bones, rainsticks, chanting—which lend their music a uniquely dreamlike, shamanic ritual sound. The three shared Roach's desert home for a week, where they connected with each other intuitively through their shared medium of music. The result is this improvised feast of sound where the lines between the ancestral and the futuristic melt away into the immediacy of now. —*MusD*

**Kiva** / Oct. 3, 1995 / Fathom ♦♦♦♦
Ron Sunsinger, a Native American tribal artist and musician, joins two space music pioneers on *Kiva*, an atmospheric recreation of sacred tribal ceremonies representing the directions of the Four Winds. For the Southwest tribes, a *kiva* is a circular subterranean structure used for ceremony and ritual; other tribes may use a canopy of trees, the circular space of a Sun Dance, or a cavern. For this recording, Ron Sunsinger obtained, with permission, field recordings of traditional ceremonies. The musicians then brought the *kiva* space into their music studio. Each wind direction is preceded by an atmospheric passage of chanting, nature sounds, and rattles. "East Kiva: Calling in the Midnight Water" features chanting with the rattles and rapid drumbeats of a peyote ceremony. The space music continues the ceremony to an expanded heartbeat, with horns signaling breakthroughs of thunder strikes. A more celestial space is heralded by organ tones and crickets. Hearing the overlapping layers of sound and the progression allows the listener's mind to travel, while still being connected to the ceremonial music and rhythms. Ghostly voices usher in the passage to "South Kiva: Mother Ayahuasca." Here, breathy whistles and a hypnotic twang of a stringed instrument begin a trance that takes off on one of the most dramatic space blastoffs on record. It climaxes through shouts and ceremonial purging, a sacred song, and whistling; the organ/chanting drone background is very trippy with its sonic infinity pattern of organ tones, chanting, jungle birds, and distorted drumming. "West Kiva: Sacrifice, Prayer and Visions" includes the powerful pow-wow drumming, singing, and stomped bells of the Native American Sundance. The space music collides sounds and rhythms—a dizzying and hallucinatory clash of reality and illusion. The music then "passes out" and takes the listener on a voyage through a sonic tunnel where all time is suspended. The final "North Kiva: Trust and Remember," recorded in a cavern, thunders with resonant drums and the growls of the didgeridoo. This recording is an excellent introduction to space music and the shamanic experience. You'll find it's not a free ride. —*Carol Wright*

**Halcyon Days** / 1996 / Fathom ♦♦♦♦
The liner notes explain that the ancient Greeks believed that somewhere in the world, the gods calmed the storms of winter for two weeks so the descendants of Alcyon, the once human kingfisher, could lay their eggs on still waters. *Halcyon Days*, the album, is an interpretation—a mixture of space music and ethnic instruments—of this mythical event, and not quite as "quiet" as I would imagine these days to be. At any rate, they are not the quiet you'd find on an angel cloud, but the sultry peacefulness (the sound of the saxophone helps here) you'd find at the edge of a swamp. One thing for sure: the storms may stop, but life doesn't. Joining forces on this odyssey are space music maestro Steve Roach, Stephen Kent (didgeridoo, drums and percussion, cello-sintir, and ocarinas), and Kenneth Newby (various "sound shape-shifting" and exotic instruments). The Halcyon world comes to life as rhythms burble on world percussion instruments, didgeridoo drones swirl like mosquitoes or croak like frogs. Space music effects slither like snakes, create eerie mists, buzz in flight, or plummet in delirium. The music is very cohesive and atmospheric; if removed from the context of the legend, most cuts on *Halcyon Days* are suitable for trance-dance; "Calyx Revelation" is suitable only for trance, period. Very trippy. —*Carol Wright*

**Cavern of Sirens** / Jun. 10, 1997 / Projekt ♦♦♦
This is head music in the extreme: Roach's spacy synth atmospheres are offset by Obmana's croaking chant for a dreary, trippy aural experience. The extended

pieces never really get anywhere, but that's not the point, is it? Suffice to say, this stuff is best enjoyed in altered states of consciousness. — *Tim Sheridan*

**On This Planet** / Sep. 16, 1997 / Fathom ♦♦♦♦
The cover of this recording offers two of the many faces of this planet. One is a craggy, misty place of eerie cold, the other a wind-worn ancient desertscape. Both extremes are intense, lonely and extremely inviting in their inhospitableness. It is like being drawn toward the knife. This challenging "dark ambient" composer asks you to experience his compositions loud. This is no unobtrusive sonic background, but a sound atlas to the nether regions. The creations are wrought with didgeridoo, clay pots, varied percussion including synthesizers, conversation and electronic respirations. This is a condensation of material developed for and by his '97 tour. I know I rue the day I passed up the opportunity to witness that! — *Thomas Schulte*

**Dust to Dust** / Apr. 7, 1998 / Projekt ♦♦♦
Open, dusty spaces are familiar images in the musical world of Steve Roach, but he gives his favorite subject an entirely new twist on this 1998 collaboration with Roger King. Harking to the ghosts of the Old West, this variation comes courtesy of the harmonica, an instrument new to Roach recordings. It is brought to the fore here, underpinned by King on various guitars and Roach's ever-present electronics. The duo drenches their instruments in a healthy dosage of reverb, occasionally letting phrases drift off entirely. This technique imbues the music with the impression of viewing yellowed photographs of frontiersmen in a long-forgotten family album. A suite of songs beginning with "A Bigger Sky" and concluding with "First Sunrise" delve into a deeper space that fans will recognize, dissolving all ties with the physical realm by utilizing whispered voices and gradually inserting Roach's trademark rhythmic sequences. But it is the traditional instruments that truly stand out on this album, allowing the listener to imagine a time and place now relegated to myth. Roach once again proves himself a restless experimenter who consistently chooses talented collaborators that will enable him to expand both his own musical vision, and that of his listeners. — *Brian E. Kirby*

● **Dreaming... Now, Then: A Retrospective 1982-1997** / Mar. 9, 1999 / Celestial Harmonies ♦♦♦♦
A prescient collection of tracks ranging from 1982's *Now* to 1994's *Artifacts* (with two unreleased tracks from 1997 rounding out the later material), *Dreaming... Now, Then* is easily the best collection of Steve Roach material available, displaying the excellence of early recordings from his debut albums, compiling almost 20 minutes of music from his landmark *Dreamtime Return* and catching the best tracks from his more expansive albums. For listeners who prefer his early material however, the CD reissue *Now/Traveler* may be a better choice. — *John Bush*

**Light Fantastic** / Sep. 21, 1999 / Fathom ♦♦♦♦
Roach's second album of 1999 is, like the first, a collaboration with Vir Unis, though the material departs Roach's usual field of geographical inspiration for the realm of visible light. The six lengthy tracks coast over waves of ambient bliss with a series of skittery percussion lines that manage to draw on the physics of light refraction quite well. Another featured player, Vidna Obmana, brings his mastery of ambient noise to the mix, though the credits are a bit difficult to cipher (Obmana: "fujara sample food performance"). With his tamboura, Stefin Gordon fills in the Eastern slant to "The Reflecting Chamber." In total, *Light Fantastic* is a very digital work, continually plumbing the depths of crisp sound and gong-like reverberations. As usual with material by Roach, mere descriptions fail to conjure the acres of beautiful, expansive sound produced. The analogy of light that inspired the work is perhaps the best description of all. — *John Bush*

## Alexander Robotnick (Maurizio Dami)

b. 1950
*Producer / Synth-Pop, Disco*
The alias of jazz keyboard player and vocalist Maurizio Dami, Alexander Robotnick existed for several years during the mid-'80s as an Italian synth-pop/disco crossover for the Italian label Materiali Sonori. Robotnick enjoyed a healthy fan base far beyond Europe, however, as thousands of import copies of the single "Problèmes d'Amour" ended up influencing many later house and techno pioneers in Chicago and Detroit.

Dami, who began his musical career during the early '80s with visions of being an electronic cabaret singer, bought two Roland synthesizers (the seminal TR-808 and TB-303) to begin recording. Convinced by Materiali Sonori's Giampiero Bigazzi to move into the still fertile Italian disco scene to score a quick hit, Dami recorded "Problèmes d'Amour" and released the single on the Materiali Sonori subsidiary Fuzz Dance in 1983. It became quite an import hit in America's underground club scene, and sparked the mini-LP *Ce N'est Qu'un Début* that same year. Additional singles like "Computer Sourire" and "C'est La Vie" appeared on Fuzz Dance during the mid-'80s, but Dami had already moved on by then, later recording under his own name and as GMM, then playing with the ethno-ambient band Masala in the '90s. — *John Bush*

● **Problèmes d'Amour [Single]** / 1983 / Fuzz Dance ♦♦♦♦
**Ce N'est Qu'un Début [EP]** / 1984 / Materiali Sonori ♦♦♦

## R.O.C.

f. London, England
*Group / Electronica, Trip-Hop*
Although formed in London in 1983, the electronic trio R.O.C. went largely unknown for over a decade as writer/programmer Patrick Nicholson (who formed the group alongside guitarist Fred Browning) focused on his work as tour promoter for British acts performing in Eastern Europe. Only with the 1993 arrival of Colorado-born vocalist Karen Sheridan did R.O.C. (once believed to be an acronym for Reincarnation of Christ) truly begin to take shape, issuing a series of five independent singles which led to their signing with the Setanta label. After releasing their debut LP in early 1996, R.O.C. moved to Virgin which reissued the album later that year. — *Jason Ankeny*

● **R.O.C.** / May 21, 1996 / Bar/None ♦♦♦
ROC's debut album is a swirling journey through the deepest depths of post-Tricky trip-hop, as well as much more atmospheric material (with no less depressing subject matter). Though vocalist Karen Sheridan sweeps in on the opener "Desert Wind" with a narcoleptic haze of slide guitar and heavenly organ chords, tracks like "Excise" and a twisted cover of "Plastic Jesus" (from *Cool Hand Luke*) chart the dark side of trip-hop. — *John Bush*

## Rocker's Hifi

f. 1991, Birmingham, England
*Group / Illbient, Electronica, Ambient Dub, Trip-Hop, Club/Dance*
Recycling the dub aesthetic of the '70s and applying it to '90s trip-hop and electronica, Rocker's Hifi formed in 1991 when DJ Dick (aka Richard Whittingham), a reformed punk, rare-groove and acid-house mixer, met up with rock 'n' roller Glyn Bush. At first known as Original Rockers (a salute to an Augustus Pablo LP), the duo borrowed a friend's mixer and began cutting it up on their debut single "Breathless," recorded for the pair's Cake label. After renaming the imprint Different Drummer and themselves Rocker's Hifi — in deference to Pablo's request — DJ Dick and Bush added a rapper named MC Farda P. and released "Push Push." By the time of their debut album *Rockers to Rockers* (more a collection of singles than a full-length work), the group began moving heavily into ambient dub and what later became known as trip-hop. A licensing deal with Island and positive reviews from critics gained them notice, and a well-received tour of the UK and US proved that the studio boffins could rock the joint as well. After the release of a dub remix album, *Music Is Immortal*, Rocker's Hifi came back with their second full-length, *Mish Mash*. — *John Bush*

**Rockers to Rockers** / 1995 / Gee Street ♦♦♦
In 1995, Richard Whittingham and Glyn Bush finally received a domestic release for their 1993 debut album. *Rockers to Rockers* explores trance rhythms with equal parts dub, hip-hop and ragga thrown into the mix. Highlights include "D.T.I. (Don't Stop the Music)" and "Push Push." — *John Bush*

● **Mish Mash** / Mar. 25, 1997 / Warner Brothers ♦♦♦♦
Another interesting fusion of dub and trip-hop with more straight-ahead techno and trance qualities, *Mish Mash* sees the duo maturing in style and technique. Standout tracks include the Bacharach-David sampling "Uneasy Skanking" and the final track, a Clash reworking named "Queen of the Ghetto." — *John Bush*

**Overproof** / Oct. 19, 1998 / Different Drummer ♦♦♦

## Roedelius (Hans Joachim Roedelius)

*Synthesizer, Producer / Space Rock, Kraut Rock, Ambient, Neo-Classical*
From his early work with the pioneering Kraut-rock band Cluster to his later, more ambient solo recordings, Hans Joachim Roedelius remained one of the most innovative and prolific voices in contemporary electronic music. Born in Berlin in 1934, he drifted through a series of odd jobs before turning to

music, later collaborating with conceptual artist Conrad Schnitzler in a series of experimental bands including Plus/Minus, Noises and the Human Being. In 1968, Roedelius and Schnitzler were among the co-founders of the Zodiak Free Arts Lab, a group of avant-garde artists from a variety of creative disciplines which quickly became one of the driving forces of the Berlin underground scene; with Dieter Moebius, they formed Kluster in 1969, performing extended improvisational live dates throughout West Germany.

Cluster released their debut LP *Klopfzeichen* in 1970; in the wake of their third album, 1971's *Kluster und Eruption*, Schnitzler exited to pursue a solo career, and Roedelius and Moebius continued on as Cluster. Working with famed producer Conrad Plank, the duo began to move increasingly towards more structured soundscapes—with 1974's *Zuckerzeit*, they even pursued an electronic pop sound similar in spirit to Kraftwerk. Roedelius and Moebius also teamed with Neu!'s Michael Rother in Harmonia, releasing a pair of mid-'70s LPs which caught the attention of Brian Eno, who in response collaborated with the trio on a legendary session (released much later as *Harmonia 76*) heralding a turn towards ambient textures (and influencing the sound of the 1976 Cluster album *Sowiesoso*). Roedelius and Moebius subsequently worked with Eno on 1977's *Cluster and Eno* and 1979's *After the Heat* as well.

In the interim, Roedelius made his solo debut with 1978's *Durch die Wüste*; after Cluster went on hiatus in the wake of 1981's *Curiosum*, he plunged fully into solo work, regularly releasing several new LPs each year. Although most of these projects pursued ambient paths—the multi-chapter *Selbstportrait* series, 1981's *Lustwandel*, 1987's *Momenti Felici* and 1992's *Friendly Game* all being good examples—others like 1982's *Offene Türen* and 1992's *Sinfonia Contempora I* explored more dissonant electronic soundscapes. Additionally, Roedelius worked in a series of mediums including theatre, dance and film, collaborating with everyone from Holger Czukay to Peter Baumann; in 1990, he and Moebius also reunited for *Apropos Cluster*, and the duo continued working together throughout the decade to follow. —*Jason Ankeny*

● **Durch die Wüste** / 1978 / Skyclad ✦✦✦✦
The debut Roedelius album is an excellent showcase of the producer's talents in producing exquisite instrumental music for reflection. Though these tracks often stray from beatless space music (the opener "Am Rockzipfel" flits back and forth between electronic hard rock and space), the musical structures employed certainly suggest ambience, from the classical melodies of the title track to the gaseous atmosphere of "Glaubersalz." —*Keith Farley*

**Lustwandel** / 1981 / Sy ✦✦✦✦
Meditative and quite reminiscent of contemporary new age music, *Lustwandel* features Roedelius on a series of quiet piano solos, backed by atmospheric synthesizers that occasionally take what sound like classical backing. —*John Bush*

**Wenn der Südwind Weht** / 1981 / Skyclad ✦✦✦✦
The fact that *Wenn der Südwind Weht* possesses a similar cover photo (a pair of feet dangling over the edge of a pond) to the first Roedelius album is a good pointer to the album's similar sound. The ten tracks here are playful synthesizer exercises, many with Roedelius' patented high-pitched melodies, reminiscent of a theremin. "Auf Leisen Sohlen" and the title track are highlights. —*John Bush*

**Offene Türen** / 1982 / Skyclad ✦✦✦✦

**Auf Leisen Sohlen** / 1994 / Transmitter ✦✦✦

## Romanthony (Anthony Moore)
*Producer / Garage, Club/Dance, Acid House, House*
Romanthony is a new-school acid garage producer who routinely summons both the raw soul and the raw sound of originals from the glory days of acid house and garage during the late '80s. Though he's much more an underground name in his native America than Europe (where he has released several full LPs and collections), two Romanthony co-productions (and a vocal) for the second album released by fans Daft Punk helped lift his status in the mainstream dance scene. Born Anthony Moore, he began producing in the garage mecca of New Jersey, specializing in high-energy, low-fidelity productions during an era in which dance productions became ever more mainstreamed. Released on his own Black Male label—he also owns Orange and World—club assaults like "Floorpiece" and "Let Me Show You Love" presented an aggressive, extroverted dancefloor persona, straight out of Prince's playbook and akin to Chicago's Green Velvet.

Despite local popularity for his tracks and mixes, Romanthony was nowhere near a worldwide name until the mid-'90s, when Britain's Azuli Records released a full-length collection of Black Male productions titled *Romanworld*. His trademarked throwback acid house became a hot sound by the end of the decade, and the growing house mecca of Scotland became an early convert, with a raft of singles on Glasgow Underground. His first proper album, *Instinctual*, was a collaboration with Glasgow Undeground's DJ Predator. *Live in the Mix* followed on Distance in 1999, and another retrospective (*R.Hide in Plain Site*) appeared on Glasgow Underground in 2000. —*John Bush*

**Bring U Up** / 1995 / Black Male ✦✦

**Romanworld** / Mar. 17, 1997 / Azuli ✦✦✦✦

**Instinctual** / Mar. 1, 1999 / Glasgow Underground ✦✦✦
A garage and disco throwback record with plenty of "hands in the air" samples but not a lot of emotion, *Instinctual* is a bit of a disappointment compared to Romanthony's previous work. —*John Bush*

● **Live in the Mix** / Jun. 14, 1999 / Distance ✦✦✦✦
An irresistible ride through hard house that brings back the spirit of pummeling DJ sessions on New York's Kiss-FM, *Live in the Mix* is a hard-hitting compilation of tracks from the three major labels helmed by Romanthony (Orange, World, Black Male), including five numbers from the man himself. Romanthony obviously knows these tracks well, from female-vocal productions for Nyree ("Dance With Me," "Good Times," "I Like It") to hip-house breakdowns from MC Gift ("Beatrock") to his own tracks. It's on his own tracks, particularly the back-to-back anthems "Floorpiece" and "Under/Main" where *Live in the Mix* peaks. Proof positive why he's Daft Punk's favorite DJ. —*John Bush*

## Rome
f. 1993, Chicago, IL
*Group / Experimental Dub, Ambient Dub, Post-Rock/Experimental*
Thrill Jockey instrumental duo Rome are, like many of the acts on the Chicago-based independent label, generally grouped in as loose adherents of "post-rock," a period-genre arising in the mid-'90s to refer to rock-based bands utilizing the instruments and structures of the music in a non-traditionalist or otherwise heavily mutated fashion. Unlike other Thrill Jocky artists such as Tortoise and Trans-Am, however, Rome draw less obviously from the past, using instruments closely associated with dub (melodica, studio effects), ambient (synthesizers, found sounds), industrial (machine beats, abrasive sounds), and space music (soundtrack-y atmospherics), but fashioning from them a sound which lay clearly beyond the boundaries of each. Perhaps best described as simply *experimental*, Rome formed in the early '90s as the trio of Rik Shaw (bass), Le Deuce (electronics), and Elliot Dick (drums). Based in Chicago, their Thrill Jockey debut was a soupy collage of echoing drums, looping electronics, and deep, droning bass, with an overwhelmingly live feel (the band later divulged that much of the album was the product of studio jamming and leave-the-tape-running styled improvisation). Benefiting from an early association with labelmates Tortoise as representing a new direction for American rock, Rome toured the US and UK with the group (even before the album had been released), also appearing on the German Mille Plateaux label's tribute compilation to French philosopher Gilles Deleuze, *In Memoriam*. Although drummer Elliot Dick left the group soon after the first album was released, Shaw and Deuce wasted no time with new material, releasing the "Beware Soul Snatchers" single within weeks of its appearance. An even denser slab of inboard studio trickery, "Soul Snatchers" was the clearest example to date of the group's evolving sound, though further recordings failed to materialize. —*Sean Cooper*

● **Rome** / 1996 / Thrill Jockey ✦✦✦✦
Rome's dreamy, disorienting debut is a warped, slow-motion paste-up job, featuring elements of dub, ambient, and foamy electronics against a solid, time-shifting backbone of live drums and loping bass. The most dub-like of the "post-rock" lot, Rome are also the least-derivative, running their influences through enough compositional randomizers to come up with something both immediately compelling and enduringly satisfying. —*Sean Cooper*

## Ronnie & Clyde
f. 1995, London, England
*Group / Illbient, Electronica, Trip-Hop, Club/Dance*
Breakbeat trainspotters and reflexive sample merchants John Ross and Rob Fitzpatrick formed Ronnie & Clyde. After about a year of recording, the duo be-

gan putting in over-time with their sampler and dealt the results to Swim Recordings. Though the label was more noted for post-acid theorists than rudeboy inheritors, label-head Colin Newman liked what he heard and issued Ronnie & Clyde's first single "The Last Hand" in 1996. After appearing on the Leaf compilation *Invisible Soundtracks*, Ross and Fitzpatrick released another single in 1997, then their debut album *In Glorious Black and Blue*. —*John Bush*

- **In Glorious Black and Blue** / Oct. 7, 1997 / World Domination ♦♦♦♦
Though it's completely instrumental, Ronnie & Clyde's debut album proves darkly melodic. Besides well-thought-out breakbeats and noir-ish effects that completely suit the title, occasional downtempo passages give *In Glorious Black and Blue* a calming, hypnotic flair. —*John Bush*

## Ralphi Rosario

*Producer, DJ / Club/Dance, Acid House, House*

He became a famed mainstream/house producer and remixer by the '90s, but Ralphi Rosario will forever be known as the author of house's most infectious hit, "You Used to Hold Me," as well as his status as a member of the illustrious Hot Mix 5 radio team that consistently lit up Chicago's WBMX during the '80s with the best house tracks of the day. The Hot Mix 5 also had a record label, which released "You Used to Hold Me" as well as crucial Rosario followups like "Pieces" and "I Want Your Love." He hit the dance charts consistently during the late '80s and '90s for labels including NiteGrooves, Henry St. and Jus' Trax. A 1994 re-release of "You Used to Hold Me" brought dozens of remixes, including Masters at Work, Danny Tenaglia, Hula & K. Fingers, DJ Hyperactive and Maurice Joshua. Rosario has himself remixed and produced for Pet Shop Boys, Gloria Estefan, Deee-Lite and Debbie Gibson. —*John Bush*

**Gotta New Love** / Apr. 16, 1995 / Underground ♦♦♦

- **Parrains de la House** / Nov. 24, 1998 / Mirakkle ♦♦♦♦
The first hits collection for Ralphi Rosario presents a host of tracks often compiled on best-of-house sets but never available together. Besides his careermaker "U Used to Hold Me," *Parrains de la House* includes later Rosario classics like "I Want You," "Una Cosa de Amor" and "In the Night." —*John Bush*

## Roupe (Rupert Brewer)

*b. London, England*
*Producer / Electronica, Ambient Techno, Jungle/Drum'N'Bass*

Roupe is Rupert Brewer, a London-based producer whose fusions of techno, jazz, funk, electro, ambient, and electronic experimentation have earned him comparisons to such innovators of "intelligent techno" as the Black Dog, Tony Thorpe, Richard H. Kirk, and Beaumont Hannant. Brewer released two full-lengths—one, *Strom*, on GPR sublabel Neuron Musique; the other, the essential *Entelechy*, on Resource—before signing with Swedish upstart label Dot in 1997. A Roupe remix was featured on the self-titled debut EP by Dot artist Quant, and Brewer's first single for the label, "Transport Solutions," appeared in December. —*Sean Cooper*

- **Entelechy** / Feb. 24, 1997 / Resource ♦♦♦♦
Although *Strom*, his full-length debut (on short-lived GPR sublabel Input Neuron Musique) was a more derivative affair, Rupert Brewer's second outing is a mini-masterpiece of listener-oriented post-techno. Like the Black Dog, to which the best of *Entelechy* favorably compares, Roupe approaches dancefloor-friendly rhythms with an artful complexity, composing rich, multi-dimensional songs—instead of static, utilitarian trax—with constantly shifting rhythms and textures. —*Sean Cooper*

**Transport Solutions [EP]** / Dec. 15, 1997 / Dot ♦♦♦
Roupe's first Dot EP is funkier and a bit more playful than his previous work, pairing skipping, mid-tempo breakbeats with sassy basslines and sweet, delicate melodies. The second track, "Herbie Strides Again," is built around a VSOP-era Herbie Hancock sample and is, accordingly, among Roupe's jazziest tracks. Like other Dot releases, "Transport Solutions" sports two originals and two remixes—one from fellow Dotian Friend, the other from the London-based Clear label's Metamatics. A solid if somewhat unimaginative release. —*Sean Cooper*

## Rozalla

*b. Zimbabwe*
*Vocals / Rave, Club/Dance, Acid House, House*

A native of Zimbabwe, Rozalla first gained success in the early '90s as a vocalist for the Band of Gypsies production team. The single "Everybody's Free" became a big hit in 1993, leading to her nickname "Queen of Rave." She released an album soon after and remained a familiar name on European and American dance charts during the '90s, though 1995's *Look No Further* featured more R&B and soul elements than previous productions. —*John Bush*

**Everybody's Free** / 1992 / Epic ♦♦

- **Look No Further** / 1995 / Epic ♦♦
Though the bouncy basslines mark Rozalla's second album as dance-pop, the production—by Frankie Knuckles, Joey Negro and Jellybean (among others)—includes nods to soul, techno, hip-hop and house. —*John Bush*

## Ruby

*f. 1994, Seattle, WA*
*Group / Trip-Hop, Club/Dance, Alternative Pop/Rock*

Ruby was the alias of singer Lesley Rankine, previously the frontwoman of Scottish noise-provocateurs Silverfish. After leaving the group in the wake of their 1993 LP *Fuckin' Drivin' or What*, Rankine relocated from London to Seattle to collaborate with producer Mark Walk, with whom she'd previously worked on material for the industrial collective Pigface. Dubbing the project Ruby—a name shared by both of their maternal grandmothers—Rankine and Walk created a sonic backdrop closer to electronica than the abrasive rock of the singer's past work, with the acclaimed LP *Salt Peter* appearing in 1995. The remix EP *Stroking the Full Length* followed a year later. —*Jason Ankeny*

- **Salt Peter** / Nov. 1995 / Creation ♦♦♦♦
Formerly of the aggressive feminist punk outfit Silverfish, Leslie Rankine renamed herself Ruby in 1995 and changed her musical tactics. Instead of hard-edged post-punk, Ruby's music is a dark, eerie fusion of trip-hop and industrial, with quietly menacing beats and droning synths. Although it could be said that she was simply trend-hopping with *Salt Peter*, Ruby's music is substantially better than Silverfish—it's more provocative, as well as better written. Not all of the album works, but *Salt Peter* remains a promising debut. —*Stephen Thomas Erlewine*

**Stroking the Full Length [EP]** / Oct. 29, 1996 / Sony ♦♦♦♦

## Ed Rush (Ben Settle)

*Producer, DJ / Jungle/Drum'N'Bass, Club/Dance*

Jungle producer Ed Rush's name has become almost synonymous with the word "dark." With a steady string of 12" releases dragging drum'n'bass to hell and back, forcing taught, kettle-sized snare snaps through ringing rides and thunderous, superdense basslines, Rush, together with oft collaborator Nico Sykes, has been almost singularly responsible for jungle's eventual (re)turn to the darkside. Recording most often for Nico-related labels No U-Turn and Nu Black, Rush has also more recently begun to cast his net farther out, bringing his brooding, dank-heavy brand of nightmare drum'n'bass to such labels as Prototype and Metalheadz. First introduced to jungle through late-period hardcore (tracks such as 2 Bad Mice's "Bombscare" and Doc Scott's "Here Come the Drums"), Rush began producing after hooking Nico (a for-hire producer who lived on Rush's block) on the sound. The pair released a few forgettable tracks before buckling down and working on putting together a new sound. Nico formed No U-Turn in 1993 as a vehicle for that sound, and the pair's first proper Ed Rush twelve, "Bloodclot Artattack," was released that same year.

Although he'd already been making tracks for a couple years, Rush's reputation began to grow in the wake of the 1996 backlash against the smooth, rolling atmospherics of ambient and heavily jazz-oriented jungle (Bukem, Alex Reece, Wax Doctor, PFM, etc.). With several tracks on the genre-coining compilation *Techsteppin'* (released by Emotif), and with darkness once again coming to the forefront among the DJs, Rush tracks such as "Guncheck," "Bloodclot Artattack," "Subway" (recorded with Dom of Dom & Roland), and "Check Me Out" began showing up in more and more (and more and more influential) DJ sets. Releases on Speed/Blue Note DJ Grooverider's Prototype label ("Kilimanjaro"), as well as twelves for Metalheadz ("Skylab") and Nico's No U-Turn offshoot, Nu Black ("Mad Different Methods," "Amtrak") further cemented Rush's rep at the forefront of a new style. Although he remains a free agent, demand for Rush tracks (as well as remixes) means he's been playing the field, releasing increasing quantities of material on a number of labels, both large and small. And while the over-the-top rumble of darkside techstep is bound to wane in popularity, Rush's most recent work has proven he's not reliant on the novelty of that sound. —*Sean Cooper*

**Mad Different Methods [Single]** / Jun. 17, 1996 / Nu Black ♦♦♦♦
The perfect blend of jump-up energy and darkside horrorcore atmospherics. The A-side's title track is on a more restrained hip-hop edge, with the flip given the overdrive treatment, all scissor hi-hats, noisy blasts, and polyrhythmic madness. As bold and efficient a statement of the Ed Rush/Nico sound as exists. —*Sean Cooper*

**Skylab/Density/The Raven [Single]** / Oct. 14, 1996 / Metalheadz ♦♦♦
Far more restrained than his No U-Turn and Nu Black tracks, "Skylab" (Rush's debut for Goldie's Metalheadz label) is nonetheless a solid, satisfying release. The title cut is the keeper here, with a long ambient-ish intro preceding some tight, tech-leaning hardstep. —*Sean Cooper*

• **Torque** / Mar. 10, 1997 / No U-Turn ♦♦♦♦
Released at the height of the label's popularity, No U-Turn's artist compilation *Torque* is a pummeling, rock-solid introduction to the force that brought darkcore jungle to a new level of menace in 1996. Home to Ed Rush, Nico, DJ Trace, and newcomer Fierce, No U-Turn's (as well as NUT sublabel Nu Black's) steady output—all muddy, hissing electronics; unruly, superdense, overlapping basslines; and splintering, driving breaks—arguably dominated the jungle scene in the latter half of 1996, spawning hordes of imitators. The album features several new tracks as well as a few classics from the catalog, with the CD-version adding a bevy of additional tracks as well as bonus disc of NUT material mixed live by Ed Rush (including the previously unreleased Boymerang remix of Rush & Nico's "Technology"). —*Sean Cooper*

**Wormhole** / Nov. 16, 1998 / Virus ♦♦♦♦
Another two-disc collection including an album of regular tracks plus a bonus mix of tracks from the first, *Wormhole* finds the two most hyped producers in the drum'n'bass community, Optical and Ed Rush, together on an album of new tracks. Though it's a little thin on the drum programming side, highlights like "Mystery Machine," "Compound," "Slip Thru" and "Millennium" display a progress of sorts on the effects route, the air of paranoid menace even more pronounced than on the previous Ed Rush full-length update, 1997's *Torque*. —*John Bush*

## Arthur Russell

b. 1951, Iowa, d. Apr. 4, 1992
*Cello, Producer, Composer / Minimalism, Classical, Disco, Hip-Hop*

Arthur Russell was a formally trained cellist and composer with a background in Indian classical music, and a resume highlighted by collaborations with Allen Ginsberg and Philip Glass. His involvement in Manhattan's downtown performance scene of the '70s resulted in a long running association with the Kitchen. The same Arthur Russell was also a quirky songwriter, a producer of one shot disco singles, a founding partner of seminal hip-hop/dance label Sleeping Bag, and a principle designer of the dubby, underground club sound that bridges the gap between the disco era and the first stirrings of house and garage music. Yet, despite a career that seemed contradictory on the surface, he produced a body of work notable for its focus, integrity, and singularity.

Russell and his cello moved from Iowa to San Francisco in the early '70s, where he studied at a school founded by Hindustani (North Indian) music master Ali Akbar Khan. It was during this West Coast period that he began his association with Ginsberg by providing musical accompaniment for many of the poet's performances. Russell moved to New York in the mid '70s, where he collaborated in the Flying Hearts, a rock project that involved the likes of David Byrne, Rhys Chatham and Peter Gordon. In 1979, Russell produced "Kiss Me Again," the first disco single for Sire records, and made his reputation as a dance music producer with Loose Joint's "Is It All Over My Face" for West End. The club mix of this single was one of the earliest efforts by Paradise Garage DJ Larry Levan, and qualifies without doubt as a prototype of what came to be known as the Garage sound. In 1982, under the name Dinosaur L, Russell released *24-24 Music* on his own Sleeping Bag label. The 12" single from this album, a Francois Kevorkian remix of "Go Bang," epitomized the loose, jazzy, somewhat minimalist underground sound that would inform Chicago house. Though the record was not a huge dancefloor smash, it was an influential turntable hit, finding its way into many radio mixes and supplying the identifying sample for Todd Terry's "Bango."

In 1983, Russell released a portion of a larger instrumental composition as the *Tower of Meaning* LP, as well as another Loose Joints single. His 1986 *World of Echo* was a one man show of quietist original songs in a solo cello and vocal format that seemed designed to be overheard. *World of Echo* embodies the link between the two sides of Russell's output. The unusually percussive cello accompaniment evident on the album versions of "Wax the Van," "Let's Go Swimming" and "Treehouse" could be preliminary sketches for the keyboard and drum versions of those tunes that appeared on Russell produced 12" singles. Though *World of Echo* received a favorable critical reception in the UK music press, Russell remained relatively obscure throughout his life, which was ended by AIDS in 1992. In 1994, a retrospective of previously unissued material was released as *Another Thought*. —*Richard Pierson*

• **Tower of Meaning** / 1983 / Chatham Square ♦♦♦♦
Julius Eastman conducting an almost medievally pure music in which tone combinations of two or three notes tuned to modal/raga scales are played by various instrumental groups. There is a love of listening to the pure combinations per se, as they are delivered at a regular, moderate pace...then, unpredictibly, rich or dissonant chords will be held that open your mind's ear, and take your breath away....The sudden ceasing of the music at certain points also has a similar effect. —*"Blue" Gene Tyranny*

**World of Echo** / 1986 / Upside ♦♦♦
An incredible assemblage of solo versions of this influential and unique downtown musician. Contains the songs and instrumentals written from 1980-1986: "Soon-To-Be Innocent Fun/Let's See," "Tower of Meaning / Rabbit's Ear/Home Away from Home," "Tone Bone Kone," "Answers Me," "Being It," "Place I Know/ Kid Like You," "She's the Star/ITake This Time," "Treehouse," "See-Through," "Hiding Your Present from You," "Wax the Van," "All-Boy All-Girl," "Lucky Cloud," and "Let's Go Swimming." Subtle, transcendental with gentle rock beats and new music influences in patternings and textures. —*"Blue" Gene Tyranny*

**Another Thought** / 1994 / Point ♦♦♦♦
Though it consists of material that is leagues away from his classical or dance productions, Arthur Russell's posthumous collection *Another Thought* is an excellent set of home recordings compiled by friends. The songs are brittle folk-pop numbers straight out of left field, often augmented only by Russell himself on cello. It's simply another radical look at one of experimental music's most varied talents. —*Keith Farley*

## S

### S'Express (Mark Moore)
*Producer / Club/Dance, Acid House, House, Dance-Pop*
Performing under the name S'Express, young British DJ Mark Moore scored a number one hit in his homeland in 1988 with "Theme from S'Express," a record that helped pave the way for the subsequent hegemony of the sampladelic acid-house sound on the pop charts. Moore released an album, *Original Soundtrack*, in 1989, strongly influenced by '70s disco. He followed one year later with *Intercourse*. —*Steve Huey*

- **Original Soundtrack** / May 24, 1989 / Capitol ♦♦♦

**Intercourse** / May 1990 / Rhythm King ♦♦
All too often, dance music has emphasized beats and tracks at the expense of vocal personality. But there's no shortage of expressive singing on S'express's *Intercourse*, one of the more noteworthy dance albums of 1991. The duo consists of keyboardist Mark Moore and vocalist Sonique, whose passionate, brassy wailing is an obvious asset on exuberant numbers like "Twinkle (Step Into My Mind)," "Nothing to Lose" and "Find 'Em, Fool 'Em, Forget 'Em." For all its high-tech, European-sounding slickness, *Intercourse* sounds like the result of genuine artistic inspiration, not the product of a musical assembly line or a marketing meeting. In the US, the CD didn't do much in the pop or R&B markets, but in dance clubs, S'express was well received. —*Alex Henderson*

### Cheb i Sabbah
**b.** Algeria
*Producer, DJ / Electronica, Club/Dance, Ethnic Fusion*
Algerian-born, San Francisco-based DJ Cheb i Sabbah's greatest musical affinity lies with London's fusion-minded Asian Underground movement, typified by the likes of bhangra-influenced electronic musicians like Talvin Singh and Asian Dub Foundation. However, Sabbah draws to a large extent on more traditional Indian music, basing his compositions on the structures and trance-like, meditative qualities of classical ragas. His early projects included poet Ira Cohen's *The Majoon Traveler* (1994), on which he remixed music by Don Cherry, Ornette Coleman, and various world musicians; his collaboration with Timothy Leary, "Why Are You Here?," appeared on Scorn's 1995 album *Ancient Lights and the Blackcore*, and he contributed to various compilations, including the Psychic TV remix project *Cold Blue Torch* and the Bill Laswell-headed *Chakra: The Seven Centers*. Sabbah's acclaimed full-length debut album, *Shri Durga*, was released in 1999; it was followed the next year by *Maha Maya: Shri Durga Remixed*, a more freewheeling set which featured similarly minded guest remixers like Transglobal Underground, Bally Sagoo, and the State of Bengal, among many others. —*Steve Huey*

- **Shri Durga** / Apr. 27, 1999 / Six Degrees ♦♦♦♦

Most Asian-European dance fusion of the '90s has come from London's Asian Underground scene, and has drawn primarily on bhangra sources for its Asian content. DJ Cheb i Sabbah's project, on the other hand, is based on classical traditions, specifically the Hindustani music of northern India; perhaps not surprisingly, the music is accordingly less dancehall-oriented, though DJ Cheb (with the help of bassist Bill Laswell and drummer Kevin Carnes, among others) does indeed lay on the funky beats in most cases. But all of the compositions are based on traditional ragas, and the beats often come after prolonged and contemplative preludes, during which the raga is stated in its traditional vocal or traditional setting. On "Ganga Dev," for example, the singer starts off accompanied only by a drone, and is then joined by tabla and sitar after a couple of minutes, and only then do Laswell's bass and Carnes' drums come in to funk things up. Most tracks follow this pattern, and the overall effect is more soothing than booty-moving. If you want to party, pick up *Maha Maya*, the companion album to this one which features many of the same compositions in clubbier mixes. This one's for the chill-out room. Both are highly recommended. —*Rick Anderson*

**Maha Maya: Shri Durga Remixed** / Feb. 22, 2000 / Six Degrees ♦♦♦♦
The Algerian-born DJ Cheb i Sabbah released *Shri Durga* in 1999, setting something of a new standard in South Asian dance music. Where Asian Underground upstarts and worldbeat fusioneers tend to throw equal parts bhangra, drum'n'bass, rock, reggae, and funk into the mix, Cheb i Sabbah took recordings of classical Indian performers and gave them restrained (but sometimes tastefully funky) modern treatments. *Maha Maya*, on the other hand, throws such caution to the wind, and with very pleasing results. It's kind of like a DJ festschrift: Cheb i Sabbah has fans in high places, and several of them contributed funked-up remixes of tracks from *Shri Durga* to make this album. Thus we have State of Bengal's junglist approach to "Shri Durga," Bally Sagoo's Detroit techno take on "Kese Kese," and TJ Rehmi's bhangra-fied "Durga Puja." Best of all may be Fun Da Mental's slowly churning, alternate remix of "Shri Durga." The program is bracketed by two of Cheb i Sabbah's own remixes. Fans of modern club music and the Asian Underground scene should consider this an essential purchase, along with the original album. —*Rick Anderson*

### The Sabres of Paradise
**f.** 1992, London, England, **db.** 1995
*Group / Electronica, Ambient-Techno, Club/Dance, Techno, IDM*
Andrew Weatherall's Sabres of Paradise were one of the UK's most celebrated experimental techno groups. A combined effort of Weatherall and collaborators Jagz Kooner and Gary Burns, the group released a flood of singles and EPs, many of which were collected on compilations released by Warp and Weatherall's other main focus: the Sabrettes label, with releases from Plod and Slab, among others. Born in Windsor, Berkshire, Weatherall considers himself a DJ first, and his exhausting schedule of deckwork has been arguably as influential as his records, inspiring scores of other DJs and anticipating trends in trance-techno, inelegant dance, and even trip-hop. Still, tracks such as "Smokebelch," "Theme," "Wilmott," and the expansive *Haunted Dancehall* did much in helping to push the post-techno envelope beyond the often staid conventions of the dance floor. Weatherall also gained visibility through remix and production work, working with Primal Scream and Scottish ambient-pop group One Dove, and reworking tracks for James, the Orb, Bjork, Therapy?, Happy Mondays, Future Sound of London, Bomb the Bass, Skylab, and Moody Boyz. His mixing skills can be sampled firsthand via the three-CD collection *Cut the Crap*, released by Six by 6 Records.

After dissolving his Sabres of Paradise project and label, Weatherall set up the tripartite Emissions label group and launched his latest, perhaps most prodigious musical venture, Two Lone Swordsmen. A collaboration with Emissions engineer Keith Tenniswood, 2LS was formed in early 1996. The group speaks the same language of warped, downtempo grooves as much previous Sabres work (particularly "Smokebelch" and "Wilmott"), but opts instead for a syntax of minimal electronics and taut, brittle electro-funk for structure and guidance. The group's first full-length release, 1996's *The Fifth Mission*, was a whopping double-CD/triple-LP, both preceded and followed by additional EPs of new material ("Tenth Mission" and "Third Mission"). A few months later, the group issued two additional LP-length releases (both remix albums under the title *Swimming Not Skimming*, although the CD and LP versions sported different tracks), and by the end of 1996 had racked up no less than a half-dozen remixes (including Slab, Alter Ego, Sneaker Pimps, and David Holmes). The heavy release schedule continued through the rest of the decade, with an assortment of LPs and mini-LPs recorded via a new deal with Warp. [See Also: Two Lone Swordsmen] —*Sean Cooper*

★ **Sabresonic** / 1993 / Warp ◆◆◆◆◆
The Sabres techno-oriented debut album includes crucial singles like "Smokebelch," "Wilmott" and previously unavailable items like "Still Fighting" and "Ano Electro." Also tacks on In the Nursery's beatless remix of "Smokebelch II." —*Sean Cooper*

**Haunted Dancehall** / 1994 / Warp ◆◆◆◆
The Sabres' second album is a conceptual manifesto of sorts, accompanied by a loose song-by-song narrative of descriptions written by the group. According to Weatherall, they initially hired Scottish novelist Irvine Welsh (*Trainspotting*) to pen the notes, but, unhappy with the results, threw together their own versions minutes before the record was shipped off to be pressed. Lots of thin, bubbly, minimalist ambient and mid-tempo breakbeat, with quirky, occasionally half-thought-out tracks aided by production assistance from Geoff Barrow (Portishead) and A. Carthy (Mr. Scruff). —*Sean Cooper*

**Versus [EP]** / 1995 / Warp ◆◆◆
A collection of dirty, vigorous remixes from Depth Charge's J. Saul Kane and the ever-inspired Chemical Brothers. The CD includes extra versions, and a limited-edition vinyl triple-pack featured an additional 10" with LFO and Nightmares on Wax remixes and a one-sided 7" of "Haunted Dancehall" mixed by English post-classical group In the Nursery. —*Sean Cooper*

## St. Etienne

f. 1988, Croydon, Surrey, England
*Group / Indie Pop, Dream Pop, Alternative Dance, Club/Dance, Dance-Pop*
Like most bands formed by former music journalists, St. Etienne was a highly conceptual group. The trio's concept was to fuse the British pop sounds of '60s London with the dance club rhythms and productions that defined the post-acid house England of the early '90s. Led by songwriters Bob Stanley and Pete Wiggs, and fronted by vocalist Sarah Cracknell, the group managed to carry out their concept, and, in the process, they helped make indie-dance a viable genre within the UK. Throughout the early '90s, St. Etienne racked up a string of indie hit singles that were driven by deep club beats—encompassing anything from house and techno to hip-hop and disco—and layered with light melodies, detailed productions, clever lyrics and Cracknell's breathy vocals. They revived the sounds of swinging London, as well as the concept of the three-minute pop single being a catchy, ephemeral piece of ear candy, in post-acid house Britain, thereby setting the stage for Brit-pop. Though most Brit-pop bands rejected the dance inclinations of St. Etienne, they nevertheless adopted the trio's aesthetic, which celebrated the sound and style of classic '60s pop.

The origins of St. Etienne date back to the early '80s, when childhood friends Bob Stanley (b. December 25, 1964) and Pete Wiggs (b. May 15, 1966) began making party tapes together in their hometown of Croydon, Surrey, England. After completing school, the pair began worked various jobs—most notably, Stanley was a music journalist—before deciding to concentrate on a musical career in 1988. Adopting the name St. Etienne from the French football team of the same name, the duo moved to Camden, where they began recording. By the beginning of 1990, the group had signed a record contract with the indie label Heavenly. In the spring of 1990, St. Etienne released their first single, a house-tinged cover of Neil Young's "Only Love Can Break Your Heart," which featured lead vocals from Moira Lambert of the indie-pop band Faith Over Reason.

"Only Love Can Break Your Heart" became an underground hit, receiving a fair amount of airplay within nightclubs across England. Later in the year, St. Etienne released their second single, a cover of the indie-pop group Field Mice's "Kiss and Make Up," which was sung by Donna Savage of the New Zealand band Dead Famous People. Like its predecessor, "Kiss and Make Up" was an underground hit, helping set the stage for "Nothing Can Stop Us." Released in the spring of 1991, "Nothing Can Stop Us" was the first St. Etienne single sung by Sarah Cracknell (b. April 12, 1967), whose girlish vocals became a signature of the group's sound. Cracknell was the main vocalist on the band's debut *Fox Base Alpha*, which was released in the fall of 1991. Following the release of *Fox Base Alpha*, Cracknell officially became a member of St. Etienne; she had previously sung in Prime Time.

"Only Love Can Break Your Heart" was re-released in conjunction with *Fox Base Alpha* and cracked the lower end of the British pop charts. St. Etienne was beginning to gain momentum, as the British press generally gave them positive reviews and their records were gaining a strong fanbase not only in England, but throughout Europe. During 1992, the group released a series of singles—"Join Our Club," "People Get Real," and "Avenue"—which maintained their popularity. In addition to writing and recording music for St. Etienne, Stanley and Wiggs became active producers, songwriters, remixers and label heads as well. In 1989, Stanley had founded Caff Records, which issued limited-edition 7" singles of bands as diverse as Pulp and the Manic Street Preachers, as well as a number of other lesser-known bands like World of Twist. In 1992, Stanley and Wiggs founded Ice Rink, which intended to put out records by pop groups, not rock groups. The label released singles from several artists—including Oval, Sensurround, Elizabeth City Slate and Golden, which featured Stanley's girlfriend, Celina—none of which gained much attention.

Preceded by the single "You're in a Bad Way," St. Etienne's second album *So Tough* appeared in the spring of 1993 to generally positive reviews and increased sales. Over the course of 1993, the group released three more singles—"Who Do You Think You Are," "Hobart Paving," and "I Was Born on Christmas Day"—which all charted well. In 1994, the trio began to lose momentum, as their third album *Tiger Bay* was greeted with decidedly mixed reviews, even as singles like "Like a Motorway" continued to chart well. After completing a new track, "He's on the Phone," for their 1995 singles compilation, *Too Young to Die*, as well as the French-only single "Reserection," St. Etienne took an extended break during 1996. Sarah Cracknell pursued a solo project, releasing a single titled "Anymore" in the fall of the year. Bob Stanley and Pete Wiggs began a record label for EMI Records, which had the intention of releasing music from young, developing bands. In the fall of 1996, St. Etienne released a remix album, *Casino Classics;* a new studio effort, *Good Humour*, followed two years later, and the trio returned in 1999 with an EP, *Places to Visit*. The full-length *Sound of Water* appeared in mid-2000, featuring guest appearances by Sean O'Hagan (of the High Llamas) and To Rococo Rot. —*Stephen Thomas Erlewine*

**Foxbase Alpha** / Jan. 14, 1992 / Warner Brothers ◆◆◆
Despite a handful of classic pop singles, Saint Etienne's debut album *Foxbase Alpha* is a tentative fusion of club culture and swinging '60s pop. Lead vocalist Sarah Cracknell hasn't been fully integrated into the band's lineup—she doesn't even sing on their astonishing Eurodisco cover of Neil Young's "Only Love Will Break Your Heart," which is not only cleverly ironic, but also works—yet the filler remains thoroughly enjoyable, even if it rarely reaches the heights of the irresistible girl-group pop of "Kiss and Make Up." —*Stephen Thomas Erlewine*

**So Tough** / Mar. 9, 1993 / Warner Brothers ◆◆◆◆
St. Etienne's second album *So Tough* is a remarkable step forward from *Fox Base Alpha*, boasting a stronger set of songs and a sharper focus. Not only are the pop melodies catchier than before, the group's mastery of swinging '60s arrangements and Eurodisco rhythms is positively infectious, and Sarah Cracknell's light, airy vocals are alluringly dreamy, giving the record a wonderful, floating quality. The cool club beats, occasional samples and synthesized textures provide an inviting sonic backdrop for Bob Stanley and Pete Wiggs' infectious pop songs, and while the singles "You're In a Bad Way" and "Hobart Paving" stand out, there are several other tracks here that are nearly as good, making *So Tough* an irresistible set of danceable, well-constructed pop. —*Stephen Thomas Erlewine*

**Tiger Bay** / Jun. 28, 1994 / Warner Brothers ◆◆◆◆
*Tiger Bay* abandons the unassuming charm of *So Tough* for a grander sound. St. Etienne fill *Tiger Bay* with sonic details, from sampled bits of dialogue to musical references that give the record some depth, but occasionally those very sounds make the album feel over-labored. Still, the group frequently fulfills their ambitions, particularly on "Hug My Soul," "Like a Motorway" and the delightfully exuberant "I Was Born on Christmas Day," which features guest vocals by the Charlatans' Tim Burgess. Moments like these, plus St. Etienne's widening sonic palette, make *Tiger Bay* a thoroughly enjoyable affair, despite its handful of faults. —*Stephen Thomas Erlewine*

★ **Too Young to Die** / Nov. 1995 / Heavenly ◆◆◆◆◆
Although their albums were considerably more consistent than most dance-pop acts, Saint Etienne's high points were always their singles. Released prior to a quiet, lengthy hiatus, *Too Young to Die* collects all of their singles, from their debut disco cover of Neil Young's "Only Love Can Break Your Heart" to their last, "He's on the Phone," providing a thoroughly entertaining chronicle of the group's career. Much of the music sounds somewhat dated—which is al-

ways a problem with dance music—but Saint Etienne was essentially a very good Euro-pop band, revelling in kitsch and style in equal measure. At their best—"Only Love Can Break Your Heart," "Join Our Club," "You're in a Bad Way," "Who Do You Think You Are," among others—they found the heart in nightclubbing. The quality of the music dips slightly in the latter half of the album, but there is prime pop throughout the disc. (Initial pressings came with a bonus disc of remixes, all of which are worthwhile for dedicated fans). —*Stephen Thomas Erlewine*

**Casino Classics** / Oct. 7, 1996 / Heavenly ✦✦✦
The title makes a sly reference to a legendary Northern Soul club, which is appropriate, since *Casino Classics* is a collection of dance remixes. Comprised equally of classic 12" remixes and new offerings from the likes of the Aphex Twin and Chemical Brothers, the double-disc *Casino Classics* does have some wildly imaginative reinterpretations, but only dedicated Saint Etienne collectors or dance-club devotees need to bother with the collection. —*Stephen Thomas Erlewine*

**Good Humour** / May 4, 1998 / Warner Brothers ✦✦✦✦
*Good Humor* has Saint Etienne back cooking up more delectable lolli-pop. From "Woodcabin," the dubby, bass-heavy opener, *Good Humor* is a typically arch Saint Etienne album full of easy-listening dream-pop. Tracks like the shimmering "Lose That Girl" and the swirling "Erica America" show Saint Etienne at its melancholic best. There are, predictably, some near misses, such as the Beatlesque "Mr. Donut," which is as sweet as a strawberry field but fails to deliver the melodic promises made by the smart atmospherics. "Goodnight Jack," with its pastel-shaded flute loops and subtle break beats, has a positively cooler-than-cool feel and a wrenching change of pace toward the middle of the song. Sure, *Good Humor* is clever, perhaps overly so, and yeah, it's full of the Et's contrived coyness and we-know-more-than-you attitude, but it's good stuff. Sometimes you just want a put on a disc, sit back and let it carry you off to someplace else. If that's all you're looking for, *Good Humor* is sweet ear candy. —*Matthew Hilburn*

**Sound of Water** / Jun. 6, 2000 / Sub Pop ✦✦✦✦
Ten years on, Saint Etienne found themselves at a bit of a crossroads. They had long ago stopped having hits in the UK, settling into a cult audience in both their homeland and the US. There isn't an inherent problem with having a cult audience, of course—many terrific bands never expanded beyond a cult following—but cult bands often have the stigma of being on the cutting edge. At the start of their career, Saint Etienne was on the cutting edge. Their first two albums were at the foundation of many of the '90s pop trends, including the revival of swinging '60s London, the unabashedly melodic and pop-centric bent of Brit-pop, the fascination for forgotten pop and easy listening artifacts from the '60s, the kaleidoscopic blend of '60s sound and '90s sensibility later heard on Beck records, plus the insurgent twee-pop of the late '90s. Like many cult bands, Saint Etienne's true influence was only apparent in retrospect, not just to critics but to the band itself. For their tenth anniversary, they decided to reclaim the cutting edge with *Sound of Water*.

*Sound of Water* followed *Good Humour*, a collection that found them consolidating their talents as pop record-makers. They had never produced such a song-oriented, concise record before, and they strive to keep that focus with *Sound of Water* yet expand the horizons of their music to focus on abstract, dreamy, electronic sounds. As Simon Reynolds says in the sleeve notes, it's an attempt to "integrate the two sides of their collective personality—pure pop enchantment and studio-as-instrument sorcery." Reynolds' summation is accurate. There are moments of pop pleasure here, surrounded by spare, languid electronica sections, vaguely reminiscent of the High Llamas. This is where maturity pays off. Saint Etienne never lingers too long in one area, letting the album flow gracefully between these two extremes, and placing some very good pop melodies along the way. The problem is, there are no knock-out singles on par with those from *So Tough* or *Tiger Bay*. Then again, Saint Etienne has pretty much given up on the pop charts, preferring to concentrate on cohesive, stronger albums, and there's little question that *Good Humour* and *Sound of Water* are more consistent than *So Tough* or *Tiger Bay* where the brilliant moments outshone some of their companions. That may mean that *Sound of Water* simply isn't as exciting as their earlier work, and it also means that there isn't a good gateway song to the band's music. That's OK, since with repeated plays *Sound of Water* reveals itself as a first-rate effort, a record that accomplishes the stated goal of integrating the "pure pop enchantment and studio-as-instrument sorcery." —*Stephen Thomas Erlewine*

## St. Germain (Ludovic Navarre)
*Producer / Jazz-House, Club/Dance, House*
In the late '90s, France put itself on the electronic music map with such big acts as Daft Punk and Air. Not only did the global dance community begin to recognize France for its nightlife, but they also recognized DJs and producers. St. Germain (aka Ludovic Navarre) was in the same group of producers, but has never shared quite the same commercial success as his French cohorts.

Ludovic took the name St. Germain from a French historical figure in 18th century France. As French myth has it, St. Germain was a man in the court of Louis XV who amazed everyone by pretending to be several centuries old. When Ludovic was young, his goal was to be a professional sports player, but an accident changed his fate towards music and computers. *Boulevard*, Navarre's first album, focused on a fusion of electronic music and jazz. The album was elected for Record of the Year in England and nominated for the Dance Music Awards in London, sharing the category with Goldie, D'Angelo, and Michael Jackson. Navarre also prides himself on being the originator of the "French Touch" style of music. He has recorded under various pseudonyms such as Deep Side, Soofle, and Modus. After five years of not recording, St. Germain returned in 2000 with the full-length *Tourist*. The album continued Navarre's work of combing raw jazz instrumentals, machines, and electronic samples. —*Diana Potts*

**Boulevard** / Dec. 17, 1996 / F Communications ✦✦✦
Picture a world where each and every French dance band was unflinchingly bad; where every Air or Cassius or even Phoenix never existed since every homegrown, starving musician looked to somebody like ATB instead of St. Germain. Luckily, this is but a piece of fiction. Because Ludovic Navarre created such a saintly pseudonym, employing deep house, tittering breaks, and down-tempo attitudes that—in over-simplistic terms—virtually invented the entire French house movement that has crossed over more times than a Diana Ross impersonator. The question is, does being first make you any good? Taking cues from acid jazz and its chin-stroking underground, songs like "Deep in It" or "Street Scene (4 Schazz)" seem to shyly respond, "yes". It's only the preponderance of an odd sense of a Frenchman aping American black music that starts to cause the most alarm. The loose jazz excursions such as "Sentimental Mood" carries all the emotional weight of a sewing needle and the choice of blues samples (while being years before Moby even caught onto the idea) feels contrived. The album may exude an atmosphere of a musician discovering a new genre hybridization, it just doesn't quite reach the maturity of a fleshed out idea. A landmark album? Yes. An album that lacks the loveliness of an Air or the inventiveness of an Etienne DeCrecy? Also, yes. *Boulevard* has been looked upon as the "essential" *Revolver* or *What's Going On* or *Dig Your Own Hole* piece of French house fans' record collections. It's only a small indignity that the music itself rarely reaches such heights of its comparisons. —*Dean Carlson*

● **Tourist** / May 30, 2000 / Blue Note ✦✦✦✦
Since the advent of acid jazz in the mid-'80s, the many electronic-jazz hybrids to come down the pipe have steadily grown more mature, closer to a balanced fusion that borrows the spontaneity and emphasis on group interaction of classic jazz while still emphasizing the groove and elastic sound of electronic music. For his second album, French producer Ludovic Navarre expanded the possibilities of his template for jazzy house by recruiting a sextet of musicians to solo over his earthy productions. The opener "Rose Rouge" is an immediate highlight, as an understated Marlena Shaw vocal sample ("I want you to get together/put your hands together one time"), trance-state piano lines, and a ride-on-the-rhythm drum program frames solos by trumpeter Pascal Ohse and baritone Claudio de Qeiroz. For "Montego Bay Spleen," Navarre pairs an angular guitar solo by Ernest Ranglin with a deep-groove dub track, complete with phased effects and echoey percussion. "Land Of…" moves from a Hammond- and horn-led soul-jazz stomp into Caribbean territory, marked by more hints of dub and the expressive Latin percussion of Carneiro. Occasionally, Navarre's programming (sampled or otherwise) grows a bit repetitious—even for dance fans, to say nothing of the jazzbo crowd attracted by the album's Blue Note tag. Though it is just another step on the way to a perfect blend of jazz and electronic, *Tourist* is an excellent one. —*John Bush*

## Ryuichi Sakamoto

**b.** Jan. 17, 1952, Tokyo, Japan

*Vocals, Keyboards, Piano, Leader, Composer, Arranger / Movie Themes, Experimental, Ethnic Fusion, Progressive Electronic*

The driving force behind "Neo Geo"—a cutting-edge fusion combining Asian and Western classical music with other global textures and rhythms—pioneering electronic composer Ryuichi Sakamoto was among the most innovative artists to emerge during the '80s. Born January 17, 1952 in Tokyo, he took up piano at the age of three, and regularly performed in jazz bands while in high school. Sakamoto's catholic musical tastes exposed him to everyone from the Beatles to Beethoven and John Cage, and he was also heavily influenced by avant-garde filmmaking; he went on to study electronic music at Tokyo's University of Art, and after graduating formed the techno-pop trio Yellow Magic Orchestra. Informed by the robotic iconography of Kraftwerk, the YMO became massive stars in their native Japan; their 1980 single "Computer Game (Theme from 'The Invaders')" even reached the Top 20 in Britain.

While still in the Yellow Magic Orchestra, Sakamoto also issued his first solo effort, 1978's *Thousand Knives of Asia;* two years later he returned with *B-2 Unit,* and the vast differences between the two discs gave a clear indication of the mercurial eclecticism which would define the remainder of his work. After the YMO's 1983 breakup, Sakamoto pursued his solo career fulltime, achieving his artistic and commercial breakthrough that same year with his acclaimed score to the film *Merry Christmas, Mr. Lawrence* (in which he also acted). The soundtrack also marked one of several collaborations between Sakamoto and David Sylvian, just of one his many intriguing musical unions; other performers with whom he worked included Thomas Dolby (on 1986's *Illustrated Musical Encyclopedia*), Iggy Pop, Bootsy Collins, and Tony Williams (on 1988's *Neo Geo*), and David Byrne, with whom he co-wrote the Academy Award-winning score to the 1987 film *The Last Emperor*.

Other works of note include the score to Pedro Almadovar's *High Heels* and 1990's *Beauty,* Sakamoto's English-language debut, which featured cameos from Brian Wilson and Robbie Robertson. In 1993, he joined a reunited Yellow Magic Orchestra to record the LP *Technodon,* and in 1998 returned with *Discord,* his first work of classical music. *Pre Life in Progress* followed a year later, as did *The Complete Index of Gut.* Sakamoto remained a prolific force in the next decade as well, issuing *Intimate* in early 1999. —*Jason Ankeny*

### 1,000 Knives of Ryuichi Sakamoto / 1978 / Denon ♦♦

Ryuichi Sakamoto's first solo album appeared before he formed Yellow Magic Orchestra in late 1978, after the young keyboardist had earned his M.A. in music from Tokyo University. Six long instrumentals make up this CD, but apart from a taste for Asian-sounding synth lines, they hint at very little of what was to come in YMO. "Thousand Knives" is a long disco-lite jazzy workout with a very un-synthesized guitar solo by Kazumi Watanabe (who would later join YMO on tour and have his solo album produced by Sakamoto). Side two's "Da Neue Japanische Electronische Volkslied" and "The End of Asia" (later revamped in YMO) are closest to the new wave of Japanese electronic music that he would spawn. "Island of Woods" and "Grasshoppers" trade in rhythm for sound landscapes, and the sort of cheeriness that would pop up later in Sakamoto's children's movie scores. Harry Hosono turns up on one track, and generally the album is a pleasant, if unadventurous, listen. —*Ted Mills*

### Illustrated Musical Encyclopaedia / 1984 / School-Midi ♦♦

Professor Sakamoto gives a lesson on what is practically a different style of music with each track on *Illustrated Musical Encyclopedia,* beginning with a sure-fire hit: the extroverted, quintessentially Japanese synth workout "Field Work" (with Thomas Dolby). From there, Sakamoto hits riff-ready crossover jazz-fusion ("Etude"), electronic minimalism ("M.A.Y. in the Backyard"), and Oriental dub ("Paradise Lost"). There is a return to sampladelic Eastern synth-pop with "Steppin' Into Asia," but for the most part Sakamoto displays his impressive stylistic range on this solo album. —*John Bush*

### • Beauty / 1990 / Virgin ♦♦♦♦

A world-music tapestry featuring a mixture of Eastern, Western, and African elements, it includes such musicians as Robbie Robertson, Sly Dunbar, and even Brian Wilson. —*David Szatmary*

### The Handmaid's Tale / 1990 / GNP ♦♦

Formerly a member of Japan's Yellow Magic Orchestra, Ryuichi Sakamoto has gone on to prominence as a challenging solo artist, as well as an actor and a film composer. *The Handmaid's Tale,* directed by Volker Schlondorff, has provided him with a chance to break away from music for movies with a decided Oriental bent (*Merry Christmas, Mr. Lawrence* and *The Last Emperor*) to compose a score for a movie set in a futuristic, fundamentalist-ruled America. It's a score that, to a degree, allows him room to work with another set of themes he's approached before—religious music, again first seen in his score for *Merry Christmas, Mr. Lawrence.* In many respects, this is a noble attempt—a score to grace a fairly downbeat picture about very negative themes. Consequently, the music is very moody, very dark in tone, often chilling in its rhythmic exactitude, sometimes even crushing. Rather than opting for the simple tactic of utilizing obviously synthesized tones, Sakamoto mixes strings and wind instruments into the cues, and in a number of places there's a very lonely-sounding piano voice, often playing the most obvious, and most haunting, theme in the album.

The biggest problem, really, is that, unlike earlier efforts, nothing ever quite gels or sticks. While the compact disc consists of only two tracks (neither of them indexed in any way, which is a serious problem when trying to focus on a particular cue), those two tracks are divided into an enormous number of cues—there has been no real attempt to evolve the score into a series of suites, so it exists instead simply as a collection of cues. This translates, in listening terms, into a vague experience indeed, as classical elements, hymns, and many other things rise and fall from minute to minute without direction. If anything, this album can be seen as a good attempt that falls short of the mark. In audio terms, it's very well mastered, despite the frustrating lack of indexing (an all too common complaint with compact discs). Sakamoto has done far better and more challenging work; this is, for him, almost a journeyman effort. —*Steven McDonald*

### The Sheltering Sky / 1990 / Virgin Movie Music ♦♦♦♦

A varied soundtrack album that manages to weave in a little variation from the traditional type of motion picture scoring indulged in here by Sakamoto. Part of the reason for the variation is that only twelve of the album's 21 tracks are by Sakamoto—several are source music, others were composed by Richard Horowitz. The diversity thus makes for a more interesting album than might have been had from variations on the main minor-key "Sheltering Sky" theme (presented here in orchestrated and piano-based versions.) It also breaks away from the sound of Sakamoto's recordings, strong material that suffers from a certain digital harshness in the strings.

Horowitz' part in this is in stepping away from traditional Western scoring and using Middle Eastern elements for score structures—something that's very effective indeed on "Fever Ride" with its blend of Moroccan and Spanish elements. Where Sakamoto easily sketches panorama with his music, Horowitz sketches in mystery. The local source music, too, adds to this, giving the album a grounding in the real world that completes the overall structure. An excellent album that can easily be recommended for more than just soundtrack aficionados. —*Steven McDonald*

### Heartbeat / 1991 / Virgin ♦♦♦

If eclectic is your bag, then the Heartbeat might be your thing. Like Hector Zazou, Ryuichi Sakamoto employs a realm of many styles on this upbeat collection. Songs performed in Japanese, Russian, French, and English (by friends Youssou N'Dour, David Sylvian, and Deee-Lite's DJ Towa Towa and Super DJ Dmitri) top an already brimming album that is everything its predecessor, *Beauty,* wasn't. Two completely different versions of the title track add arty spice. "Triste" is a wonderful, lazy-afternoon stroll in Paris jazz; "Lulu" follows suit. Is there no end to this Sakamoto's talent? He does jazz, rap, and chucks in a couple of solo piano pieces reminiscent of his soundtrack work. "Songlines" came about via his score for Pedro Almodovar's *High Heels.* "Boram Gal" and "High Tide"—with guests Youssou N'Dour and Arto Lindsay, respectively—are both delicate and swathed in summer. Ingrid Chavez adds poet's fire to frozen dust on "Returning to the Womb" and contributes eerie funk on "Cloud 9." —*Kelvin Hayes*

### Neo Geo / Nov. 14, 1991 / Epic ♦♦♦

An interesting combination of Japanese and funk rhythms, it features such notable guests as jazz drummer Tony Williams, reggae star Sly Dunbar, and Iggy Pop. —*David Szatmary*

### 1996 / Jun. 4, 1996 / Milan ♦♦♦

The album *1996* contains 12 pieces arranged for violin (Everton Nelson, David Nadien, or Barry Finclair), cello (Jaques Morelenbaum), and piano (Ryuichi Sakamoto), including both new compositions and music used in the soundtracks to *The Last Emperor, Merry Christmas, Mr. Lawrence, The Sheltering*

*Sky*, and *High Heels*. The music is for the most part restrained and reflective, as Sakamoto makes use of the contrasting timbres of the chamber instrumentation, mixing melodic and rhythmic effects soothingly (the exceptions being the more quick-moving "M.A.Y. in the Backyard" and "1919," which uses a barely audible voice and staccato playing to stirring effect). —*William Ruhlmann*

**Smoochy** / Feb. 25, 1997 / Milan ♦♦♦
Inspired by both Brazilian music and the boundless possibilities of the Internet, electronic composer Ryuichi Sakamoto wrote *Smoochy*, an endlessly intriguing exploration of what happens when the old world meets the future. Using his Brazilian Internet concept as a foundation, Sakamoto goes on to add a variety of other musics, including jazz and Latin pop, to the music, creating a dense and fascinating musical web of electronics and percussion. Occasionally, he gets too self-consciously arty for his own good, but most of the album finds Sakamoto at his best. —*Stephen Thomas Erlewine*

**Anger [EP]** / Feb. 3, 1998 / Ninja Tune ♦♦♦
Sakamoto's first release for the Sony Classical label, *Discord*, also spawned his first release for British trip-hop label Ninja Tune, a remix EP featuring a quartet of interesting recasts of two of *Discord*'s tracks. The release completes a circle of sorts; many of Sakamoto's releases dating from the early to mid-'80s (both under his own name and with Yellow Magic Orchestra) were influential on the heavily hybridized styles of post-rave experimental dance music that Ninja Tune is among the higher-profile representatives of. The best of "Anger/Grief"'s beat-heavy versionings are delivered via Talvin Singh and T.Power's Marc Royal (under the name Chocolate Weasel), with contributions from Amon Tobin and the Skint label's Rare Force. Adequate but ultimately uninteresting. —*Sean Cooper*

**Discord** / Feb. 10, 1998 / Sony Classical ♦♦♦♦
More than 20 years after releasing his first album, Sakamoto premiered his very first classical work, though the components of this enhanced CD include turntables and guitar as well as the obligatory orchestra and piano. The theme seeks to reflect the contemporary difficulties between reconciling a digital-quick information age with the reality of suffering in much of the Third World, and Sakamoto does a good job of contrasting modern musical tools with traditional instruments. —*John Bush*

**Love Is the Devil [OST]** / Oct. 6, 1998 / Asphodel ♦♦♦
Sakamoto's unnerving soundtrack for John Marbury's portrait of British artist Francis Bacon was at least as important as the film's oft-noted cinematographic dexterity in capturing the complex psychological landscape of the famous painter. With a palette consisting of little more than chirps, clicks, muted cries, and the odd bit of disembodied piano, Sakamoto's score helped give shape to the raw chaos surrounding both Bacon's life and the figures depicted in his paintings. Hardly essential, but no less worthwhile for it. —*Sean Cooper*

## Salaryman

f. 1996, Champaign, IL
*Group / Indie Rock, Post-Rock/Experimental*

A visible link between indie-rock and the emergent post-rock later in the '90s, Salaryman formed around a quartet of ex-Poster Children: Rick and Jim Valentin, Rose Marschack and drummer Howie Kantoff. Based in the Midwestern college-town stronghold of Champaign, Illinois, the group began recording for an album in 1996. After its release on their own 12Inch Records, City Slang picked it up for a European release. Salaryman toured the continent with Tortoise and Mouse on Mars, then released the remix EP *Voids+Superclusters*. —*John Bush*

• **Salaryman** / 1997 / City Slang ♦♦♦♦
Salaryman's debut is an engaging album of progressive indie-rock laden with various post-rock textures, including electronics, vintage synth gear, and an alarming number of television samples. The quartet sounds much like Trans Am, though this is by no means bad. Since they're a (presumably) fun side project for some of the Poster Children, Salaryman can be as light-hearted as they want, and this fact makes their album sound quite good. —*John Bush*

## The Salsoul Orchestra

f. 1974, New York, NY
*Group / Club/Dance, Disco*

The music world's prime disco big band during the late '70s, the Salsoul Orchestra recorded several of the tightest, chunkiest disco themes of the '70s, both on its own productions and as the backing group for several prime vocalists. Organized by Vincent Montana, Jr., in 1974, the band was an experiment in fusing funk, Philly soul and Latin music together in a highly danceable discofied style with plenty of room for solos by individual members. With arrangers, conductors and whole sections of instruments (including up to 18 violinists) contributing to the sound, the Salsoul Orchestra routinely included up to 50 members. Though the Salsoul sound became passé in the wake of disco music's explosion and rapid commercialization during the late '70s, Salsoul's influence on house music in the '80s, and even the return of disco-inspired electronica during the following decade, proved heavy.

The beginnings of the Salsoul Orchestra (and Salsoul Records) lie with nominal head Vincent Montana, Jr. A longtime jazz vibraphonist, bandleader and session-man with Philly soul groups like Harold Melvin & the Bluenotes, the O'Jays, and the Spinners, Montana dreamed of constructing a large studio orchestra which could fuse polished soul and brassy funk with Latin percussion and live strings. In 1974, he was introduced to local entrepreneurs Joe, Ken, and Stan Cayre (who ran a local Latin music label) by Afro-Cuban pianist Joe Bataan. With their blessing (and financing), Montana spent months recruiting dozens of musicians from the streets and studios of New York — including more than a half-dozen percussionists alone. The collective recorded three tracks, which impressed Bataan and the Cayres so much that they decided to form a new label — named Salsoul for its connotations of salsa and soul — to release a full-length LP.

One of the original Salsoul Orchestra recordings, "The Salsoul Hustle" was released in mid-1975 and it placed well on the charts. Salsoul's second single "Tangerine" (an unlikely cover of a Jimmy Dorsey tune) hit the Top 20 in early 1976, and pushed the eponymous Salsoul Orchestra LP to No. 14 on the album charts. Follow-up singles like "You're Just the Right Size" and "Nice 'N' Naasty" did moderately well on the charts but soon a glut of similar-sounding material began to flood the market, cheap imitations of the amazing instrumentation of Salsoul Orchestra members — guitarist and producer Norman Harris, bassist Ronald Baker, drummer Earl Young, arranger Don Renaldo, percussionist Larry Washington, and vocalists Jocelyn Brown, Phyllis Rhodes, Ronni Tyson, Philip Hurt, and Carl Helm. Many Salsoul contributors played on the biggest and best disco tracks of the era, including Trammps, Grace Jones, the Whispers, Loleatta Holloway and First Choice.

Salsoul's third LP, the slightly amusing *Christmas Jollies*, displayed a predilection towards the growing disco novelty trend. The slip was hardly improved upon with 1977's *Cuchi-Cuchi* (which teamed the Orchestra with Charo) or 1978's *Up the Yellow Brick Road* (a take-off on *The Wiz*). After disintegrating the Salsoul Orchestra in the early '80s, Vince Montana led the studio group Montana and recorded with several pop stars of the '80s, as well as dance inheritors of the '90s like Mondo Grosso and Nuyorican Soul. Though Salsoul records had long been out of print, several were brought back in the mid-'90s, as well as a prescient two-disc retrospective titled *Anthology*. —*John Bush*

**The Salsoul Orchestra** / Nov. 1975 / Salsoul ♦♦♦

**Christmas Jollies** / Nov. 1976 / Salsoul ♦♦
A definitive document of the disco era, the Salsoul Orchestra's *Christmas Jollies* offers funked-up renditions of holiday favorites including "The Little Drummer Boy," "Sleigh Ride," and "Silent Night." Also included is a pair of medleys, the first celebrating Christmas and the second New Year's Day; the latter comprises an eclectic mixture of songs including "Auld Lang Salsoul," "I'm Looking Over a Four-Leaf Clover," "Alabama Jubilee," "Oh, Dem Golden Slippers," and "God Bless America." —*Jason Ankeny*

• **Anthology** / 1994 / Salsoul ♦♦♦♦
From the '70s disco big-band comes a double-disc retrospective of their greatest hits and best-known material from "Nice 'n' Nasty," "Don't Beat Around the Bush," "Salsoul Hustle," "Get Happy," and "Tangerine" to "Ooh I Love It (Love Break)." —*John Bush*

## Salt Tank

f. 1991, London, England
*Group / Electronica, Ambient-Techno, Techno*

Salt Tank possesses an instinct for beautiful techno and trance akin to Orbital though their focus on hard-hitting techno and live-show performance (with guitars and drum kits as well as synthesizer banks) puts them more in line with Underworld. Formed by Malcolm Stanners and David Gates with Andrew Rose added later for an in-concert slant, the trio recorded several singles before signing to Internal Records and finding a surprise British Top 40 single in "Eugina." Originally, Stanners and Gates knew each other from an early age, sharing an affection for world music and the crusty, festival movement. The pair embraced acid house as well by the mid-'80s, and Stanners began working at Paradise Studio, where he engineered for Hawkwind, the Beloved, Kevin Saunderson's Inner City and Derrick May.

By 1991, Stanners and Gates had earned enough money to buy their own gear, after which they recorded three limited EPs on their own 4 Real Communications. The releases created a buzz in the dance community—dropped into sets by Andrew Weatherall and Kris Needs—and made it to the radio as well via *The John Peel Show*. After signing to Internal Records (also the home of Orbital and the Advent), the duo released their proper debut album, *Science and Nature*. The single "Eugina" hit the British Top 40, and recruited Andrew Rose as a nominal frontman for their live show. Salt Tank's sophomore LP *Wavebreaks* followed in 1997, and the trio became one of the few bands to play a live set at the Liverpool super-club Cream. *—John Bush*

● **Science & Nature** / May 20, 1996 / Internal/London ♦♦♦
Scattering previous EP material with several new tracks, *Science and Nature* walks the clever divide between melodic listening techno and the harder edge of beat-oriented dance music. Tracks like "Olympic 638" and "Eugina" are highlights, while the duo's early influence from world music shows up on "Gaza Strip" and "Isabella's Dream." *—John Bush*

**Wavebreaks** / Sep. 1997 / London ♦♦
Quality dance music, though a bit tame in regards to most productions coming out of the electronica scene, *Wavebreaks* is closer to an instrumental pop album than anything else, with an abundance of melodies but comparative lack of innovation. Several tracks feature a bit more, like the moderate breakbeats of "Da Blues," but the presence of a few downers makes the album not much more than a pleasant listening experience. *—John Bush*

## Roger Sanchez

b. Jun. 1, 1967, New York, NY
*Producer, DJ / Club/Dance, House*

Just one in the cast of crucial producers that made Strictly Rhythm the premiere American house label during the early '90s, Roger Sanchez grew into a prolific remixer, world-class mainstream DJ, and top global-house name by the end of the decade. Though he concentrated more on mix albums than proper studio productions under his own name, Sanchez gained much respect with club kids as well as the dancefloor intelligentsia.

Born in New York to parents of Dominican heritage, Sanchez attended Manhattan's School of Art & Design with several future hip-hop legends, including Kurtis Mantronik. He was well into the graffiti and break-dancing scene during the early '80s and began DJing by the age of 13. After mixing for several years at New York hotspots like the Tunnel—even while he was studying architecture at the Pratt Institute—Sanchez finally left college in 1987 to give music a full-time shot. His club Ego Trip was soon booming (with Sanchez mix-tapes selling briskly on Broadway) and he never looked back. By 1989, Gladys Pizarro from Strictly Rhythm Records had touched base to see if Sanchez was interested in production; one year later, he had recorded his first single, "Luv Dancin'," as Underground Solution.

The single's tough underground grooves charged the New York house scene, then just on the cusp of a turnover from the smooth garage sound to a rougher style influenced by European trance and techno. Despite stumbling into remixing by accident—after giving a bad review to a single, he was tapped to rework it—Sanchez became more than competent at the game, and beginning in 1991 he worked on tracks for Babyface, Michael Jackson, Diana Ross, Janet Jackson, Chic, M People, Basia, Incognito, and Soul II Soul.

Later Sanchez productions—a 1994 Latin dub-house burner named "Sumba Lumba" (as Tribal Confusion), the following year's hard-hitting *Livin 4 the Underground* EP (as Roger S), and that same year's "Release Yo Self" (as Transatlantic Soul)—cemented his status as one of Strictly Rhythm's greatest assets and one of the world's leading mainstream producers. Though his own One Records collapsed in 1995, Sanchez formed another label named Narcotic and signed up with the British club Hard Times to release his first full-length. The mix LP *Hard Times-The Album* featured the S-Man (with just two decks, a mixer and a crate of records) proving his worth as a DJ in addition to his much-hyped studio work. He continued in the mix-LP vein, releasing volumes in two high-profile series (*Mixmag Live!, United DJ's of America*) and the Freeze collection *Roger S. Mega Mix*. In 1997, Narcotic Records released "Back" (as S-Man), the fruits of the dance super-group formed by Sanchez, Junior Vasquez and DJ Sneak. One year later, Sanchez released *S-Man Classics*, a two-disc collection including his best remixes backed with his best own productions. *—John Bush*

**Hard Times-The Album** / 1995 / Narcotic/Hard Times ♦♦♦
Compiled, mixed, and featuring several productions by Sanchez himself, *Hard Times-The Album* also includes unreleased tracks from Farley & Heller, DJ Sneak and Disciple. There are also great songs from De'Lacy, Frankie Knuckles, the Bucketheads, Masters at Work, Barbara Tucker, Kathy Sledge, Incognito, and Michael Watford. *—John Bush*

**United DJ's of America, Vol. 8** / Jun. 24, 1997 / DMC America ♦♦♦♦
Roger Sanchez makes his claim as the best American garage DJ on his volume in the *United DJ's of America* series. From Green Velvet's "The Stalker" all the way to a remixed Fine Young Cannibals, with usual stops like Frankie Bones and Gisele Jackson in between, Sanchez keeps the mix seamless and the pace perfectly stated. *—John Bush*

● **S-Man Classics: The Essential Sanchez Mixes** / Jan. 20, 1998 / Harmless ♦♦♦♦
*S-Man Classics* presents two sides of Roger Sanchez. Included are many of his own productions, which work well and show a more raw side of his genius; also on the album, however, are many of his remixes of dance-pop figures—M People, Judy Cheeks, Incognito, Love Tribe, and Kathy Sledge. While not terrible, these tracks pale next to his own productions, making the album a mixed bag. *—John Bush*

**House Music Movement** / Jul. 7, 1998 / Mastertone ♦♦♦♦
Following on from Doc Martin's volume earlier in the year, Roger Sanchez brought a variety of past dance classics—Sylk 130's "Last Night a DJ Saved My Life," Green Velvet's "Answering Machine," Kevin Aviance's "Din Da Da," and DJ Sneak's "U Can't Hide from Your Bud"—to the decks for his *House Music Movement*. There are also a couple of his own productions, but the real highlight here is the bonus interview disc, featuring three dance legends from three cities: Juan Atkins, Todd Terry, and Steve "Silk" Hurley. *—John Bush*

## Sandoz (Richard H. Kirk)

*Producer / Electronica, Ambient-Techno*

Former Cabaret Voltaire member Richard H. Kirk is widely regarded as contemporary techno's busiest man, a distinction he's picked up through a release schedule that keeps discographers sweating and diehard fans near bankruptcy. No doubt, that work ethic developed during Kirk's time with CV, who, in their nearly 20 years together, released as many albums and even more EPs. Kirk's not far behind as a solo artist, splitting just over half that total between his three ongoing projects—Sandoz, Electronic Eye, and works released under his own name—as well as collaborations with British DJ Parrot (as Sweet Exorcist) and heaps of singles and EPs. While the Sheffield-based Cabaret Voltaire began as an electronics-and-tape-loops outfit with obvious ties to other English post-industrial experimentalists like Throbbing Gristle, Einsturzende Neubauten, and Chrome, the group eventually penetrated a pop-group context while retaining the edge of dystopia and isolation at the core of their earlier work. Kirk's solo work has evolved along similar lines, although he works more toward integrating technology with more humanitarian concerns. His stylistic palette—mostly house, early techno, and ambient—and the inclusion of tracks on compilations released by the Warp label, have pegged Kirk as an evangelist of "intelligent techno," but his solo work actually comes off closer to sample-heavy ambient house and techno. His affection for African and tribal percussion and thematics connect his various works in obvious ways, and many of his albums have been reissued domestically. [See Also: Electronic Eye, Richard H. Kirk] *—Sean Cooper*

**Dark Continent [EP]** / 1993 / Tone ♦♦
Six-track EP deleted upon release of the 1996 CD reissue (Touch), which adds four new tracks. *—Sean Cooper*

● **Digital Lifeforms** / 1993 / Touch ♦♦♦♦
Kirk's debut by Sandoz was his membership ticket into the "intelligent techno" camp, not least through inclusion of the popular track, "Intelligent." Kirk sets up the major themes he'll be revisiting through subsequent Sandoz tracks, which include the signature African rhythmic and vocal samples and Detroit-style techno dystopianism. *—Sean Cooper*

**Intensely Radioactive** / 1994 / Touch ♦♦♦♦
A combination of world music anthems and urban menace defines the ever-prolific Kirk's third Sandoz release in under a year. —*Sean Cooper*

**Every Man Got Dreaming** / 1996 / Touch ♦♦♦
Remarkably similar to his other Sandoz work, *Every Man Got Dreaming* finds Kirk beginning to repeat himself. Still, the same detail and accomplished eclecticism remain intact, if in somewhat uninspired shape. —*Sean Cooper*

## Omar Santana

*Producer, DJ / Trance, Hardcore Techno, Club/Dance, Techno*

A breakbeat producer since the days of Arthur Baker and Jellybean, Omar Santana has been the leader in a distinctly American brand of psychedelic breakbeat acid-techno under dozens of aliases including Hard Hop Heathen, Liquid Metal, Dark Side of the Shroom, New York Terrorists, Car Jacker, Tales from the Hardside, and Wizard of Oh. Santana's early career was spent working on mix production and editing for acts ranging from Debbie Harry to Dynamix II as well as work at Cutting Records, the seminal freestyle label that also featured the talents of Todd Terry and Tony "Freestyle" Butler.

By the turn of the '90s, Santana had crossed over to the emerging acid house and rave crowd with hits like "Mr. Dynomite" as Liquid Metal, "Slamma Jamma" as New York Terrorists, and "Boy Is Banging" as DJ Oh Oh Omar Santana. His trademark "hardhop" style of acid breakbeat techno became common currency on America's West Coast by the late '90s, and Santana helmed several mix albums for Moonshine Music including *Tricked Out*, *Hardhop Tricked Out*, and *Battle for Planet of the Breaks*. Santana has also compiled hardcore/gabba compilations for Moonshine, including 1998's *Hardcorps*. He frequently records with fellow breakbeat master Freddy Fresh (as Imperial Stormtroopers). Two years later, he released *Hardcore for the Headstrong*. —*John Bush*

**The Dark Side of the Shroom** / 1995 / Transworld ♦♦♦
This slab of Santana could please just about every fan of electronic dance music: there's acid for the headstrong, disco for the club kids, and hip-hop for the blunted. —*John Bush*

**Hardhop Tricked Out** / Apr. 7, 1998 / Moonshine Music ♦♦♦
Basically an Omar Santana solo album, *Hardhop Tricked Out* features half a dozen tracks by Santana aliases—Dark Side of the Shroom, Tales from the Hardside, Hard Hop Heathen, Imperial Stormtroopers (with Freddie Fresh)—plus remixes by Simply Jeff and others. Santana's production and mixing are excellent, and though the album stays strictly within the confines of breakbeat and hardcore trance, it's still an enjoyable ride. —*John Bush*

● **Battle for Planet of the Breaks** / Mar. 23, 1999 / Moonshine Music ♦♦♦♦
Santana does a stellar job anchoring this collection of big-dumb-breaks techno, with all the timestretched vocals, dark waves of acid trance, and batches of sinister vocal samples any listener craves from a Moonshine compilation. Alongside his own tracks like "Chemical Meltdown," "Off to Dementrion X" and "Double Dove" (each recorded under a different alias, natch), Santana mixes in tracks by Mild-Mannered Janitors, Electroliners, and Jaguar. Though its IQ level isn't stratospheric, *Battle for the Planet of the Breaks* is an excellent club and party record. —*John Bush*

## Sash! (Sascha Lappessen)

b. 1971, Wuppertal, Germany
*Producer / Club/Dance, Euro-Dance, House*

Appearing out of nowhere during 1997, Sash! became one of the best-selling Euro-house artists of the year, with three consecutive instrumental hits: "Encore Une Fois," "Ecuador," and "Stay." Based in Cologne, he worked as an electrical engineer before growing into the DJ business, first as a part-time gig. In 1995, he began producing as Sash! with the help of Thomas Lüdke and Ralf Kappmeier. The trio's "It's My Life" became a dancefloor hit later that year, triggering success for the follow-up, "Encore Une Fois." Early in 1997, it hit the Top Ten in dozens of countries. Both "Ecuador" and "Stay" were similarly successful, prompting PolyGram to sign Sash! for the debut album *It's My Life*. The single "La Primavera" also became popular on the continent during 1998, from his second album *Life Goes On*. Sash! also remixed 2 Unlimited, Jean-Michel Jarre and Dr. Alban, returning in 2000 with *Trilennium*. —*John Bush*

● **It's My Life** / May 12, 1997 / X-It ♦♦
One of the most popular singles of the year is reprised on this debut album by Sash!, and it proves to be about the only highlight, as most of the rest of *It's My Life* is simply a rehash of the kick drums and high frequencies of the single. —*John Bush*

**Life Goes On** / Jul. 14, 1998 / Multiply ♦

## Sasha + John Digweed

f. 1993, Manchester, England
*Group / Progressive Trance, Electronica, Trance, Club/Dance, House*

By the end of the '90s, Sasha and John Digweed had become two of the most recognized DJs in the world. A widespread interest in a style of uptempo electronic music laden with synth melodies and pumping beats known as trance (or less frequently as progressive trance) propelled the British DJs to worldwide fame along with peers such as Paul Van Dyk and Paul Oakenfold. As trance began to hit its peak, both DJs began to diversify their track selection in an effort to avoid being pigeonholed as specifically trance DJs. Whereas their early mix CDs defined the sound of trance for the mid-'90s, they soon took the position as two of the genre's leaders, continually focusing on the latest records and evolving sounds of producers such as Breeder while staying true to their musical roots.

Before they became pin-ups for the trance generation, the two had already been successful DJs and—to a lesser degree—producers. Their famed partnership began in 1993 while both were spinning at the Manchester club Renaissance. As the two DJs began to hone their mixing and improve their track selections, increasing numbers of clubbers began to spread the word about the duo's music. Sasha and Digweed released a mix album titled *Renaissance* in 1994 and began their steady rise to fame. It wasn't until the 1996 release of *Northern Exposure* that Sasha and Digweed began to truly be acknowledged as superstar DJs. The album's success led to several increasingly successful sequels (*Expeditions*, *Communicate*) that defined the sound of trance in the late '90s, paralleling the *Global Underground* and *Tranceport* series in terms of popularity.

In the late '90s, the two DJs began their invasion of the US with a high-profile monthly residency at Twilo in New York City, along with more mix CDs as individuals. In addition to the residency, the duo sporadically toured the US and found themselves the topic of many articles and cover stories in magazines such as *Urb* and *Mixer*. An extensive tour of the US in 2000 to support *Communicate* only solidified their status as two of the most loved (and despised) DJs in the world.

As if their reputation as the world's most famous tag-teaming DJs wasn't enough, Sasha and Digweed also produce their own music and are recognized as prized remixers. Sasha's *Xpander* EP showcased his knack for creating some of the best trance epics the genre has ever seen, while his remix of the Chemical Brothers' "Out of Control" re-established his role as a talented remixer. Similarly, Digweed occasionally produces music as Bedrock, scoring an enormous hit with his anthem "Heaven Scent."

While the two DJs increasingly focused on production and retaining their status as superstars, they slowly began to drift apart, appearing less frequently as a duo. Sasha continued work on a long-awaited solo album, and Digweed focused on his *Bedrock* club night in the UK [See Also: John Digweed, Sasha] —*Jason Birchmeier*

**Renaissance** / Sep. 15, 1994 / Alex ♦♦♦♦

**Jackpot: The Winning Ticket** / Mar. 31, 1997 / Jackpot ♦♦♦

**Northern Exposure, Vol. 1** / Jul. 22, 1997 / Ultra ♦♦♦
*Sasha and John Digweed Present Northern Exposure* was the first volume in the duo's highly successful and acclaimed DJ mix series, released in both single (in America) and double-disc (in Europe) versions. The American version is tight, impeccably paced between house-music peaks and ambient/downtempo valleys. The duo's mixing prowess is apparent throughout. Featured tracks include material from Keiichi Suzuki, Future Sound of London, Rabbit in the Moon, Morgan King, Fuzzy Logic, William Orbit, and Banco de Gaia. Some listeners may prefer to track down the double-disc European import in order to hear the work as it was originally intended, but others will find this version actually a better listen. —*Steve Huey*

**Northern Exposure, Vol. 2: East Coast Edition** / Jan. 13, 1998 / Ultra ♦♦♦♦
The East Coast edition of DJs Sasha and John Digweed's *Northern Exposure*

2 is sure to be a delight to fans of relaxing and near-meditative sounds. The album contains a total of 13 tracks that are remixes, but completely different than what you'd expect from most remix collections. It is dance music (in an ambient kind of way), which will also appeal to fans of house music. For the most part, each track is by a different artist (with the exception of Gus Gus, who have two songs present), but the same recognizable sound is carried throughout *Northern Exposure 2*. The album sounds best when played from beginning to end, since Sasha and Digweed have sequenced the album's selections so perfectly. And since the entire album is blended seamlessly together track by track, it's hard to pick out certain songs as highlights. A Chicane Mix of the Furry Freaks' "Soothe" is definitely a high point, with its ethereal vocals and enjoyably repetitive hooks. The Acoustic Hoods' "Cycles of Time" shows hints of funk, thanks to a synth sound similar to P-Funk. Sasha and John Digweed's *Northern Exposure 2, East Coast Edition* is a consistent, invigorating listen. [Note: *Northern Exposure 2* is also available in a West Coast edition, including completely different songs.] —*Greg Prato*

**Northern Exposure, Vol. 2: West Coast Edition** / Jan. 13, 1998 / Ultra ◆◆◆◆
For those who can't get enough of DJs Sasha and John Digweed's refreshing, instantly recognizable sound, your appetites will be satisfied with *Northern Exposure 2, West Coast Edition* (with a completely different track listing than the *East Coast Edition*). And like the previous *East Coast Edition*, the album sounds best when listened to from beginning to end, as one big block of music. Sasha and Digweed invite the listener on a journey that's pretty close to musical space travel on the William Orbit & Spooky remix of Sven Vath's "An Accident In Paradise." And the album's opener, Cygnus' "Superstring," starts with a tranquil organ phrase until infectious dance beats take the song in a completely unexpected direction. Like its predecessors, *Northern Exposure 2, West Coast Edition* is a long album (over 70 minutes), but the quality of the music never seems to subside. If you're a dance music fan but want a break from the genre's usual in-your-face sounds, Sasha and John Digweed's selections will prove to be a soothing antidote. —*Greg Prato*

★ **Northern Exposure: Expeditions** / Feb. 22, 1999 / Incredible ◆◆◆◆◆
There is perhaps no more suitable a name than *Expeditions* for this volume of the *Northern Exposure* series. Each set of the double album progresses across varying degrees of building, climactic peaks, and slow descents across rich, textured aural planes of melodic synthesizers and infectious rhythms. Held captive during Sasha and John Digweed's disorienting expedition, listeners experience an array of intense crescendos and dizzying melodies. The impact of these musical peaks gets diffused until they seem strangely mild because of the continuously flowing sensory atmosphere, making it clear to all why this music is called trance. The first set begins slowly with Breeder's "Tyrantanic" and Stage One's "Space Manoeuvres," evoking a foreboding sense that more intense stimuli will soon arrive. After the seamless montage of these two modulating tracks, the mood dies for a short moment of rest before reaching an emotional peak a bit later during The Light's "Expand the Room" and Sasha's "Belfunk". Where the first set retained a fairly calm, consistent mood and tempo, the second set flows just as seamlessly, but covers a much broader range of aural tones. Starting off with a few tracks that lack the non-secular feel of the first set, the second half of the second set eventually journeys to unparalleled heights of melodic excess during the ten-minute combination of Humate's "Love Stimulation" and Breeder's "Rock Stone." After the fist-pumping progressive house rush of "Everything You Want," Sasha and Digweed then conclude their colorful expedition with Mike Koglin's "The Silence," a sensory-overloading track that reinterprets the melody from Depeche Mode's "Enjoy the Silence." —*Jason Birchmeier*

**Communicate** / May 23, 2000 / Kinetic ◆◆◆
Relative to the *Northern Exposure* albums from the mid- to late '90s, *Communicate* finds the duo moving toward a more consistent progressive house sound rather than their trend-setting trance of years past. Sasha, Digweed, and the 22 featured producers on the album seem to be consciously trying to distance themselves from the predictable synth-heavy melodies, breakdowns, build-ups, and generic motifs of late-'90s trance-popularized by Paul Oakenfold that had generated much criticism within the non-trance electronic music community. For the majority of *Communicate*'s two albums, the music simply pumps rather than takes you on a journey; the focus has thankfully moved away from candy-coated novelty, and toward driving rhythms. After an hour of nonstop 4/4 rhythm at a constant tempo, the listener struggles to remain conscious of the music, becoming almost hypnotized by the austere consistency of the sounds and the amazingly seamless mixing from one song to the next. It is only during occasional moments, such as the rare synth melody of Breeder's "Tyrantanic," the spooky tribal chanting of Luzon's "The Baguio Track," the hallucinogenic lull at the core of the Orb's "Once More," and the heightened intensity overload of the Chemical Brothers' "Enjoyed," that one becomes aware of salient moments in the music. In a way, *Communicate* can be seen as the duo's best mix CD to date with its striking consistency at all levels, ranging from track selection to mixing to mood to tempo. Rather than moving through a broad palette of sounds, moods, tempos, and styles, the two British DJs choose to remain consistent, signaling the development of a signature style and a certain sense of confidence. This signature style feels subtle and stark, free of overzealous ornamentation and potential kitsch. —*Jason Birchmeier*

### Sasha (Alexander Coe)

b. Sep. 4, 1969, Bangor, Wales
*Producer, DJ / Progressive Trance, Progressive House, Trance, Club/Dance, House*

Multi-talented North Wales native Sasha has become one of the world's most renowned and popular DJs. Starting out in the late '80s as a club DJ, he got his first big break when he was hired by the noted dance club Shelly's to spin and rework popular sounds of the day. It was there that the young DJ found fame with the dance and house crowd, but it wasn't until he started laying down his grooves at Renaissance that he become known nationally and, eventually, globally. His sound and technique became so popular that a Renaissance compilation was released, one of the very first DJ mix albums to ever hit the record stores.

It was while still at Renaissance that Sasha met another DJ, John Digweed. The two became a remixing team and soon released the first volume of their *Northern Exposure* series (a mix album that also functioned as a collection of the duo's remixes for others). The duo toured behind the release, visiting the US, Australia, South Africa, and Southeast Asia. Sasha refuses to limit himself to DJ work, however; he collaborated with singer Maria Naylor on the Top 20 hit "Be as One," and remixed tracks from such popular artists as the Pet Shop Boys, Simply Red, and M-People. He also formed his own record company, Excession Recordings, and wrote originals for Deconstruction.

In late 1997, another Sasha/John Digweed compilation appeared, *Northern Exposure 2*, available in both East Coast and West Coast versions (each contained completely different songs). He's released several mix albums on his own as well, including two volumes in the *Global Underground* series (from San Francisco and Ibiza). A rare production release, the *Xpander EP*, became a dancefloor hit in 1999. The mix album, *Communicate*, followed a year later. [See Also: Sasha + John Digweed] —*Greg Prato*

**Global Underground: San Francisco** / Jan. 19, 1999 / Global Underground ◆◆◆
Sasha works through psychedelic trance on his first major solo mix collection, featuring tracks by Freaky Chakra, Medway, Joi Cardwell, Quivver, and Libra. —*John Bush*

**Xpander EP** / Oct. 19, 1999 / Ultra ◆◆◆◆
Unlike the *Northern Exposure* and *Global Underground* albums, Sasha's *Xpander* exclusively features tracks produced by the artist. Each of the four epics here progresses slowly, with numerous movements, build-ups, peaks, and releases. For the most part, these tracks remain true to the concept of trance rather than progressive house, focusing more on subtle moments of divine emotion and sensual bliss rather than just sheer intensity. With only four full-length tracks, *Xpander* isn't nearly as satisfying as Sasha's DJ albums, yet it is an effective showcase for the artist's less-recognized talent as a composer. The first track, "Xpander," is by far the most puzzling and inaccessible of the four. Over the course of almost 12 minutes, it never really reaches the ecstatic summit it should, instead continually taking the listener farther and farther with little release. The next two songs, "Belfunk" and "Rabbitweed," will be familiar to those who have heard Sasha and John Digweed's *Expeditions* album and Dave Ralph's *Tranceport, Vol. 2* album. The final song, "Baja," is undeniably sublime, functioning more as a hypnotic ambient track than dance music. —*Jason Birchmeier*

● **Global Underground: Ibiza** / Dec. 28, 1999 / Global Underground ◆◆◆◆
Sasha's second contribution to the Global Underground focuses less on intensity and more on sublime moments of aural sensuality capable of pro-

pelling the listener to euphoric heights above the album's seamless continuity. About halfway through Sasha's first set, the momentum builds from trickling, energized ambience to thunderous sensory overload. Halfway through the first set, Breeder's remix of Orbital's "Nothing Left" elevates the tone of the music beyond sensuality towards the distant planes of feeling attainable only through such inhuman music. From these draining heights, Sasha's first set journeys towards uptempo rhythm that takes the already established sensations to further levels of feeling, which settle for a short lulling moment of mournful violin-like synthesizers at the beginning of Pariah's remix of "Stage One." This calming moment only proves to be the eye of the storm, as the music soon lifts off again into frenzied intensity; Sasha leaves behind the modulating tempos of trance and finishes up the set with some straight-ahead progressive house tracks. The second set never really takes off until late in the first track, BT's "Fibonacci Sequence," and then not again until halfway through the set, when Sasha's monstrous epic trance composition "Xpander" rises from the mediocre aura created by the preceding progressive house tracks. Soon after, BT's "Mercury and Solace" again injects non-secular beauty into an already blistering mood. Featuring an angelic female vocalist singing unintelligible hymns, this track radiates emotion that lingers until Sasha finally concludes the album with the anthemic synthesizer melodies of Bedrock's "Heaven Scent," a fitting way to end a colorful journey through some of the best trance music of the late '90s. —*Jason Birchmeier*

## Jesse Saunders

b. Mar. 10, 1962, Chicago, IL
*Producer / Club/Dance, House*
Though others did more in the pioneering of Chicago house during the early '80s, Jesse Saunders deserves mention for being part of the two records which debuted house music on wax. First, as an addition to the band Z Factor, Saunders wrote and recorded the 1983 single "Fantasy" for Mitchbal Records. Later that year, he founded his own Jes-Say Records and released "On and On," the track usually pointed to as the beginning of house music. (Actually, DJs and producers had been recording before this point, but most tracks were played only at the clubs on reel-to-reel tape machines). He maintained his legend status in Chicago despite leaving for the West Coast and a major-label production deal by 1986 (well before the scene exploded around the world). There, Saunders began recording more R&B-oriented projects (like Jesse's Gang), meanwhile remixing and working production for various pop artists.

Born on the south side of Chicago, Saunders collected records from an early age and got into DJing during high school, through his brother. The duo played at high schools all over the area, and Saunders made pause-button megamixes using funk and disco records. After he was introduced to the DJing of Frankie Knuckles at the Warehouse, Saunders began playing more disco-oriented music and, though he spent a year studying at the University of Southern California, he returned in the summer of 1981. Drawing bigger and bigger crowds to his events, he eventually began playing at a large venue called the Playground. When one of his bootleg megamixes was stolen from his crate, Saunders decided to re-create the record with a drum machine and synthesizers he owned. The result was a track called "Fantasy," and when the members of a local electro group named Z Factor heard the song, they convinced Saunders to join their group. The single was released in 1983 on Mitchbal Records, owned by the father of one band member.

The first vinyl-pressed recording to approximate production techniques utilized in a club setting by DJs like Frankie Knuckles and Ron Hardy, "Fantasy" was dubbed the first house record. Using the bed of "Fantasy," Saunders recorded "On and On" later that year and released the single on his newly formed Jes-Say Records. It too became a club hit, and influenced dozens of producers to try and gain label releases as well. After the basement-style production of "On and On," Saunders began to polish his style with singles like "Funk You Up" and Z Factor's "I Am the D.J."

Though he had a hand in the recording of the first big house crossover hit, 1986's "Love Can't Turn Around" by Farley Jackmaster Funk, Saunders wasn't around when the next wave of house records dropped on the Chicago scene. With a contract from DGC Records in hand, he left later that year for the West Coast and recorded the album *Center of Attraction* under the rubric Jesse's Gang. The album went nowhere, but Saunders became a remixer of note, working with Paula Abdul, Smokey Robinson, George Clinton, and Mavis Staples, among others. In 1997, he recorded an album called *Chicago Reunion* with appearances by classic Chicago house compatriots Marshall Jefferson, Adonis, Armando, DJ Pierre and Tyree Cooper. —*John Bush*

● **Chicago Reunion** / Jul. 8, 1997 / Thug ♦♦♦♦
*Chicago Reunion* is an epic collection including most of the major Chicago house names—Saunders, Marshall Jefferson, Farley Jackmaster Funk, Adonis, DJ Pierre, Vince Lawrence, Byron Burke Chip-E and Tyree Cooper. The occasional back-in-the-day tracks like "Now This Is How It Started," "Wayne Found a Record Store," and "Farley Was Determined" are interesting history lessons, but the present of Chicago house circa 1997 sounds just as good, with the few updates of classic tracks ("Baby Wants to Ride '97") hardly standing in the way of excellent new material like Saunders' "Feel Your Love," Tyree Cooper's "Nuthin' Wrong," and DJ Pierre's "I Can't Stand It." It doesn't quite hit the heights of Chicago house's classic period, but *Chicago Reunion* is a solid effort for all involved. —*John Bush*

## Kevin Saunderson

b. Sep. 5, 1964, Brooklyn, NY
*Producer, DJ / Detroit Techno, Club/Dance, Techno, House, Dance-Pop*
Easily the most dexterous in the stable of Detroit techno pioneers, Kevin Saunderson recorded some of the hardest and most mechanistic techno to come out of the Motor City but routinely hit the mainstream dance charts as well with productions for his techno-pop act Inner City. From his very first production, Saunderson forged an energetic, groundbreaking style for techno—a dense rhythmic assault of sound-samples and heavy percussion, often with a repetitive chanted chorus forming the only vocals. His Inner City productions, however, consisted of much slicker, house-inspired tracks underpinning the vocal workouts by Paris Grey—and later, his wife Ann. The group hit Great Britain's Top 40 eight times, and earned four No. 1 club hits on the American dance chart as well. After Inner City's initial success in 1988, the group remained his primary concern until the mid-'90s, but Saunderson never deserted his hard-hitting production style; throughout the '80s and '90s, Saunderson recorded as Tronik House, the Reese Project, E-Dancer, Inter-City, Essaray and Reese & Santonio (the latter as a duo), and also developed a roster (including Blake Baxter and Chez Damier) for his own label, KMS Records. After a Saunderson retrospective appeared in 1997, he began to make a higher profile in the album ranks. The following year, he recorded a mix album for Studio !K7 as well as a debut solo LP (as E-Dancer).

Saunderson is the only one of the fabled Belleville Three (himself, Juan Atkins and Derrick May) not born in Detroit. Born in Brooklyn in 1964, he was the ninth and last child in his family. His parents moved to Detroit when he was 12, and he met up with Derrick May and Juan Atkins while attending Belleville Junior High. All three were fans of the local Parliament/Funkadelic machine, but Atkins introduced both Saunderson and May to synth-pop pioneers like Kraftwerk and Gary Numan. While Atkins was recording with Cybotron and May was inaugurating his DJ career, however, Saunderson studied telecommunications at nearby Eastern Michigan University and dreamed of playing professional football. Saunderson began to reconsider his quest by 1984, and turned to DJing instead. He had accompanied May to Chicago several times to go to the essential house clubs, and he had also spent time in New York listening to Larry Levan spin records at the Paradise Garage.

Saunderson accompanied May and Atkins to Detroit's fabled Music Institute and formed his own KMS Records in 1986. Early Saunderson singles like "Triangle of Love" by Kreem, and "The Sound" and "Bounce Your Body to the Box" by Reese & Santonio, quickly made the transition from local clubplay to radio and finally, export to Britain, where they became underground hits along with Derrick May singles like "Nude Photo" and "Strings of Life." In 1988, Saunderson was working on a track when he realized that a vocalist might give it the sound he wanted; he was recommended to Paris Grey, and the two collaborated on the single "Big Fun." Released later that year on the British compilation *Techno: The New Dance Sound of Detroit*, it became a Top Ten hit in England. The follow-up "Good Life" also hit the Top Ten, and though Inner City's success didn't quite translate in his native land, Saunderson spent much of 1988-89 producing, remixing and recording in Great Britain.

Later KMS singles like Reese's "Rock to the Beat" and E-Dancer's "Pump the Move" continued Saunderson's commitment to hard-hitting Detroit techno, but he also signed Inner City to a major-label contract with Virgin Records and in 1989 released its debut album, *Big Fun* (the first full-length released by any new Detroit producer). Pressured by Virgin to move into more marketable R&B instead of strictly club music, Inner City responded in 1990 with *Fire*, an album which still made few concessions to pop audiences. Similar to *Big Fun*, the album did well in Britain and in American clubs, but never translated to the large-selling domestic audience.

In 1991 Saunderson unveiled his new alias, the Reese Project. A more gospel-oriented variant of the Inner City techno-pop sound, Reese Project toured Britain as a support act for Inner City and debuted with the 1992 album *Faith, Hope & Clarity*. Inner City released its third album *Praise* that same year, and though it wasn't received as well as their first two, the single "Amnongay" showed a more experimental side of Saunderson on what had previously been his most commercial guise. Inner City returned to the charts with more mainstream dance tracks like 1994's "Do Ya" and "Share My Life," then released their fourth album in 1996. Saunderson continued to record, releasing tracks for KMS and circling the globe as a DJ. The *Faces & Phases* compilation was released in 1997, covering Saunderson's hard techno work as Reese, Tronik House, E-Dancer, Kreem, and Reese & Santonio (and including only one Inner City track). One year later Saunderson released two LPs, one volume in Studio !K7's *X-Mix* series plus a new E-Dancer LP, *Heavenly*. [See Also: Inner City, E-Dancer] —*John Bush*

★ **Faces & Phases** / Nov. 18, 1997 / Planet E ♦♦♦♦♦
Along with Derrick May's *Innovator* and Model 500's *Classics*, *Faces & Phases* collects many of the pioneering Detroit techno classics that defined the genre. Characterized by pumping bass beats, hard-hitting percussion loops, and ominous melodies, Kevin Saunderson's techno was designed for overcrowded dancefloors with gigantic sound systems and flashing lights. Compiled here are many of the tracks Saunderson produced under various monikers—E-Dancer, Reese, Reese and Santonio, Tronik House, Inner City, Inter City, Kreem—and there aren't many formal characteristics differentiating the many aliases. While most of the 22 tracks on this collection deserve recognition, there are a few that stand out above the rest. Two E-Dancer tracks, "Velocity Funk" and "Pump the Move," take Saunderson's intensity to new heights, along with the monstrous power of "Rock to the Beat." The Inner City track, "Amnongay," doesn't rock quite as hard as the other tracks, instead retaining a soulful tone that sets it apart from the others. The New Order-sounding Kreem track "Triangle of Love" may sound a bit primitive and out of place, but it has historical significance as Saunderson's first collaboration with Juan Atkins and Derrick May. In addition, the Tronik House tracks sound a little darker than the others, perhaps because they were supposedly recorded in England as rave anthems. The Reese tracks tend to sound a bit simple and technically subpar since they were Saunderson's earliest recordings. —*Jason Stanley Birchmeier*

**X-Mix: Transmission from Deep Space Radio** / May 12, 1998 / Studio !K7 ♦♦♦♦
Reviving the spirit of the original *Deep Space* radio show he hosted with Juan Atkins and Derrick May during 1993-94, Kevin Saunderson takes complete control of his volume in the *X-Mix* series, slipping original show IDs and intros into a mix of crucial Detroit tracks including material from Octave One, Carl Craig's 69, Sean Deason, Kenny Larkin's Dark Comedy and his own E-Dancer project. —*John Bush*

## Scala
f. 1995, London, England
*Group / Electronica, Ambient-Techno, Trip-Hop*
Initially a one-off project involving most of Seefeel plus Mark Van Hoen (aka Locust), Scala gradually took on the feel of a major operation with the apparent dissolution of Seefeel during 1997. At the outset, the group involved vocalist Sarah Peacock, percussionist Justin Fletcher, and bassist Daren Seymour of Seefeel with Van Hoen in the producer's chair. Scala released an EP and a full-length album during 1996-1997 while Mark Clifford—Seefeel's nominal frontman and the only member not involved in the new project—worked on his own Disjecta project. More indebted to noise and trip-hop than the looped sound-wash Seefeel had been known for, the quartet also focused on a somewhat tighter song structure and emphasized Peacock's vocals. In early 1996, Scala released the *Lips & Heaven* EP, followed the next year by the debut full-length *Beauty Nowhere*, on Britain's Touch Records. Though Seefeel had released their third record *Ch-Vox* in late 1996, it was their last. Scala returned with two additional albums, released almost simultaneously in 1998: *To You in Alpha* and *Compass Heart*. —*John Bush*

● **Beauty Nowhere** / Feb. 24, 1997 / Touch ♦♦♦♦
*Beauty Nowhere* is a proper blend of the trademark sounds of each artist involved; while Locust's Mark Van Hoen constructs noise-scapes of twisting, cavernous percussion, Seefeel members Peacock, Fletcher, and Seymour work on processing their respective instruments for maximum reverb and delay. Though each track is interesting (at least from a production standpoint), the only track that truly comes together on *Beauty Nowhere* is the finale, the disco-in-a-ring-modulator cover of Blondie's "Heart of Glass." —*John Bush*

**To You in Alpha** / Oct. 5, 1998 / Too Pure ♦♦
*To You in Alpha* balances a few tracks of Seefeel-styled guitar minimalism with several mid-tempo electro jams, practically indistinguishable from the *Compass Heart* album released within three months of it. —*John Bush*

**Compass Heart** / Dec. 8, 1998 / Touch ♦♦♦
The third Scala album continues the damaged-guitar experimentalism of the earliest Seefeel material though Mark Van Hoen's production is evident throughout, from the electro thump of the first track, "HoneyLike." Though Peacock's vocals aren't incredibly strong, over time they grow strangely affecting and provide a vivid counterpoint to the sinister productions. —*John Bush*

## Scan 7 (Lou Robinson)
*Producer / Detroit Techno, Trance, Club/Dance, Techno*
As the most recognized guise of Detroit techno artist Trackmaster Lou, Scan 7's productions have appeared on two of the genre's most esteemed labels, Underground Resistance and Tresor. His debut EP for Underground Resistance, *Scan 7*, introduced the dark style of techno very much at home on Mike Banks' label. Then after debuting as both Xzile and Black Man on Tresor's *313* compilation, Robinson released three EPs on the Berlin label—*Dark Territory*, *Beyond Sound*, and *Resurfaced*. —*Jason Birchmeier*

● **Dark Territory [EP]** / Nov. 11, 1996 / Tresor ♦♦♦♦
On the *Dark Territory* EP, Trackmaster Lou lays down the sort of dark, menacing techno that made Scan 7 his most well-known guise. "Dark Territory," in particular, focuses on a pounding 909 rhythm structure, while "Dark Corridor" functions similarly, emphasizing a sparse arrangement that makes the crashing percussion and pounding bass even more deadly. His EPs for Underground Resistance may be more diverse, but none compare to the power of this record. —*Jason Birchmeier*

## Scanner (Robin Rimbaud)
b. 1964, Battersea, London, England
*Producer / Experimental Ambient, Experimental Techno, Electronica, Ambient-Techno, Techno*
Battersea-based ambient composer Robin Rimbaud, aka Scanner, takes his curious pseudonym from his compositional tool of choice; the cellphone scanner. Although only recording and releasing music since the early '90s, Rimbaud has already earned a reputation as a boundary-pushing experimentalist, wedding scanned vocal samples to sparse electronics and other textural elements that underscore the degree of strain and isolation often associated with modern telecommunications technology. Though working increasingly toward other, more musical, compositional devices, his first several releases went heavy on the lifted convo, attracting as often the comment of postgrad pocket theorists, as interested in the critical implications of Rimbaud's work as the music critics. Although admitting to a certain voyeuristic fixation even in his childhood, Rimbaud's began exploring it through music only recently, acquiring a police scanner from the Brixton Hunt and Saboteurs group (a sort of wargames/survivalist collective) at a surprising discount. He's since recorded a number of albums, and completed remixes for Oval, Scorn, and others. Thought not as varied or complex in his approach as some of his peers in the European electronic music avant-garde, Rimbaud's probing experimentalism and developing focus have won him high praise among the more cerebral of the emusic set, resulting in a number of commissioned performance and composition opportunities that have brought him in contact with the likes of David Shea, Bill Laswell, Oval's Markus Popp, and Karlheinz Stockhausen (the latter of whom Rimbaud counts among his admirers). He also worked on the score for the film *The Garden Is Full of Metal*, about late film director Derek Jarman. —*Sean Cooper*

● **Scanner** / 1994 / Ash International ♦♦♦♦
Over an hour-long collection of nicked cellular snippets and sparse, heavily treated electronics fused in various combinations and with varying degrees of success. The novelty begins to wear thin toward the end (particularly on repeat listenings). The most interesting tracks tend to be those striking a balance between the content of the voice tracks and the texture and feel of the other elements, a trend Rimbaud will (thankfully) move increasingly toward with subsequent releases. *—Sean Cooper*

**Mass Observation** / 1995 / Ash International ♦♦♦
Four tracks, only two of which incorporate snippets of cordless chatter (the other two are fast breakbeat-type techno). Rimbaud is at his best on the sprawling first track, where the voices accentuate his own contributions rather than the other way around. *—Sean Cooper*

**Spore** / 1995 / New Electronica ♦♦♦♦
Much more diverse than his previous two releases, and showing signs of real growth. Only about half the tracks incorporate scanned material, with the remainder incorporating static and white noise, various found-sound excerpts, slow, somewhat foreboding melodies, and sparse rhythms. The vinyl includes a bonus one-sided 12" also released separately. *—Sean Cooper*

**Delivery** / Apr. 29, 1997 / Primitive ♦♦♦
Rimbaud's debut for grindcore-heavy Earache (licensed for domestic release by the Canadian Primitive label) is perhaps his most full-blown attempt at integrating the minimal cellphone ambience of his previous Scanner work and the breakbeat tech of remixes and side projects such as Mr. Cane and Si-(Cut).db. The album's longest tracks—beat-heavy tunes bearing heavy influence of electro, hip-hop, and funk—are spackled together with shorter vignettes of suitably intriguing snatched cellphone chatter, manipulated static and white noise, dial tones, etc. Still, while Rimbaud's efforts to downplay the by-now cliched methods of his namesake are admirable and quite often accomplished, it begs the question of what role they can possibly play in future recordings. *—Sean Cooper*

**Scanner Vs. Signs Ov Chaos** / Aug. 26, 1997 / Earache ♦♦♦

**Sound for Spaces** / Sep. 28, 1998 / Sub Rosa ♦♦♦♦
*Sound for Spaces* collects Scanner material from various sources, including radio programs and art installations; also featured is one of his first recordings from the mid-'80s. *—John Bush*

## Pierre Schaeffer

b. 1910
*Composer / Tape Music, Musique Concrète, 20th Century Classical/Modern Composition, Atonal, Electronic*

The father of musique concrète, French composer Pierre Schaeffer was among the most visionary artists of the postwar era; through the creation of abstract sound mosaics divorced from conventional musical theory, he pioneered a sonic revolution which continues to resonate across the contemporary cultural landscape, most deeply in the grooves of hip-hop and electronica. Born in 1910, Schaeffer was not a trained musician or composer, but was instead working as a radio engineer when he founded the RTF electronic studio in 1944 to begin his first experiments in what would ultimately be dubbed "musique concrète." Working with found fragments of sound—both musical and environmental in origin—he assembled his first tape-machine pieces, collages of noise manipulated through changes in pitch, duration and amplitude; the end result heralded a radical new interpretation of musical form and perception.

In October 1948, Schaeffer broadcast his first public piece, *Etude aux Chemins de Fer*, over French radio airwaves; although the public reaction ranged from comic disbelief to genuine outrage, many composers and performers were intrigued, among them Pierre Henry, who in 1949 joined the RTF staff, as well as future collaborators Luc Ferrari and Iannis Xenakis. (Olivier Messiaen was also a guest, bringing with him students Karlheinz Stockhausen and Pierre Boulez.) Schaeffer forged on, in 1948 completing *Etude Pathetique*, which, in its frenetic mix of sampled voices, anticipated the emergence of hip-hop scratching techniques by over a generation; by 1949's *Suite pour 14 Instruments*, he had turned to neoclassical textures, distorted virtually beyond recognition. In 1950, Schaeffer and Henry collaborated on *Symphonie Pour un Homme Seul*, a 12-movement work employing the sounds of the human body.

Working with the classically-trained Henry on subsequent pieces, including *Variations Sur Une Flute Mexicaine* and *Orphee 51*, clearly informed Schaeffer's later projects, as he soon adopted a more accessible musical approach. Together, the two men also cofounded the Groupe de Musique Concrète in 1951; later rechristened the Groupe de Recherches Musicales, or GRM, their studio became the launching pad behind some of the most crucial electronic music compositions of the era, among them Edgard Varèse's *Deserts*. However, by the end of the decade, most of the GRM's members grew increasingly disenchanted with the painstaking efforts required to construct pieces from vinyl records and magnetic tape; after later, tightly-constructed works like 1958's *Etude aux Sons Animes* and the next year's *Etudes aux Objets*, even Schaeffer himself announced his retirement from music in 1960.

Leaving the GRM in the hands of Francois Bayle, some months later Schaeffer founded the research center of the Office of French Television Broadcasting, serving as its director from 1960 to 1975; in 1967, he also published an essay titled "Musique Concrète: What Do I Know?" which largely dismissed the principles behind his groundbreaking work, concluding that what music now needed was "searchers," not "auteurs." In later years, Schaeffer did explore areas of psycho-acoustic research which he dubbed Traite de Objets Musicaux (TOM); these experiments yielded one final piece, the 11-minute *Le Triedre Fertile*. He also hit the lecture circuit and agreed to produce radio presentations. Pierre Schaeffer died in Aix-en-Provence on August 19, 1995. *—Jason Ankeny*

● **Erotica "Symphonie Pour Un Homme Seul"** / 1984 / INA.GRM - INA ♦♦♦♦
A short and sweetly humorous feuilleton (or bob-bon as the case may be) by the composer who led early French work on composing with environmental, extra-musical sounds or "musique concrète"... resulting in his "Concert de Bruits" (Concert of Noises) broadcast in 1948 and the establishment in 1951 of The Groupe de Recherches de Musique Concrète and in 1958 The Group for Musical Research of the Office of French Radio-Television (O.R.T.F.). "Musique concrète" now also includes electronic and world music. *—"Blue" Gene Tyranny*

## Marcus Schmickler

*Producer / Experimental Techno, Ambient-Techno*

A member of the thriving Cologne experimental music scene associated with Mouse on Mars, Nonplace Urban Field, Air Liquide, Mike Ink, and the A-Music, Electro Bunker, and Karaoke Kalk labels, Markus Schmickler is one of the more "composerly" contributors to that conglomerate's growing renown. A formal student of electronic composition, Schmickler—along with schoolmates Carsten Shulz (aka C-Shulz), Frank Dommert, and Georg Odijk—was a member of late-'80s performance ensembles Pol and Kontakta, two freewheeling experimental/improv groups following in the footsteps of Cologne's most notorious musical lab technicians, Can. Schmickler has since released a growing number of critically acclaimed electroacoustic recordings of various levels of abstractness through Mille Plateaux (as Pluramon) and former bandmate Odijk's A-Musik label (as Wabi Sabi). Schmickler's Kaspar-Hauser studios (named in reference to the early 19th century *tabula rasa* child, memorialized by Werner Herzog in his 1974 film, *The Mystery of Kaspar Hauser*), are located in a disused warehouse space at the outskirts of the city, and provide something of a window on Schmickler's musical conception: vague constructions of random and apparently inert sonic matter re-formed into fascinating environments of ambient and electroacoustic, occasionally beat-oriented electronica. [See Also: Pluramon] *—Sean Cooper*

● **Onea Gako** / Feb. 23, 1996 / Odd Size ♦♦♦♦
One of the few recordings actually filed under Schmickler's name, *Onea Gako* was recorded in 1993 with C-Schulz on oboe and clarinet, Martin Kollbau on bass, Thomas Sieger on trombone, Philipp Adenacker on drums, and Schmickler himself on guitar, drums and electronics. For the most part, the LP ignores its ten track markers, concentrating instead on gradual movement through Can-influenced Kraut-rockers (heavy on the rock), periods of more abstract, Eastern-oriented electronics, and what would be basic trance-techno were it not for assortment of acoustic instruments. There's an abundance of excellent music, the highlight being "Eso-T (Pt. 1)," a majestic piece of Eastern noise with brass reminiscent of a James Bond film. *—John Bush*

## Schneider TM (Dirk Dresselhaus)

b. Germany
*Producer / Ambient-Techno, Post-Rock/Experimental*

The one-man independent electronics team behind Schneider TM is Dirk Dresselhaus, a former rhythm-section member for several German indie-rock bands. He stepped into the spotlight with a 1998 album recorded for City Slang. —*John Bush*

- **Moist** / Apr. 27, 1998 / City Slang ♦♦♦♦
Akin to work by Schneider's countrymen in Mouse on Mars, *Moist* is another interesting application of abstract, twisted electronics to what is (surprisingly) quite a straightahead rhythm section. Though the production isn't nearly as frenetic as the celebrated MoM sound, Dresselhaus turns that potential curse into a blessing by concentrating on just a few effects for each track and investigating their sonic possibilities. —*John Bush*

## Conrad Schnitzler

b. 1937, Düsseldorf, Germany
*Drums, Producer / Space Rock, Kraut Rock, Electronic*
One of the prime figures in the growth of Kraut-rock, Conrad Schnitzler made important contributions to the early history of Kraftwerk and Kluster. Like many in the Kraut-rock community, Schnitzler was greatly inspired by influences in the visual artistic world as well as the musical; he studied sculpture with Joseph Beuys, and composition with Karlheinz Stockhausen, also looking to John Cage and Pierre Schaeffer for inspiration. By 1969, he was working with Tangerine Dream, with whom he recorded *Electronic Meditation*. The album became one of the most distinctive in TD's discography, and Schnitzler takes much of the credit for its chance-taking approach.

Before the end of the decade, Schnitzler had begun appearing with another soon-to-be Kraut-rock legend, Kluster. Formed with Dieter Moebius and Hans-Joachim Roedelius, the group recorded two albums in 1970, *Klopfzeichen* and *Zwei Osterei*. Schnitzler left for a solo career one year later, though Moebius and Roedelius probably appeared on his debut, *Schwarz* (no credits were given, but other musicians can be heard). With *Schwarz* and 1972's *Rot*, Schnitzler began to progress from mostly acoustic music to a style based around electronics and tape-looped sound. Though he continued to record sparingly during the '70s, not much of Schnitzler's work was released until the following decade. He emerged in 1978 with the album *Con*, recorded at Peter Baumann's Paragon Studios, and with the support of the French label Egg Records.

The beginning of a new decade resulted in much activity for Conrad Schnitzler, and he released seven albums in total during 1980-81 alone. The styles ranged from the harsh sequencer trance of *Consequenz* to the surprisingly pop-oriented project *Con 3* (both were recorded with drum machines and vocals by Wolf Sequenza, formerly of Ton Steine Scherben). During the rest of the '80s, Schnitzler recorded often, but released his work on increasingly obscure labels. After another fallow period during the early '90s, he began recording with Plate Lunch Records, which issued new releases such as 1998's *00/44* as well as archival reissues like 1971's *Rot*. —*John Bush*

- **Rot** / 1972 / Block ♦♦♦♦
Schnitzler's first (released) solo album, *Rot*, continued the atonal, avant-garde bent of his work on Tangerine Dream's first LP, *Electronic Meditation*. Noisy, almost industrial-sounding, the album's cut-up techniques leaven the monotony of the lengthy chords which characterize the pair of twenty-minute tracks, "Meditation" and "Kraut-rock." —*John Bush*

**Constellations** / 1988 / Badland ♦♦♦♦
Though it begins with a few minutes of depth-plumbing space music, *Constellations* soon evolves into a series of tuneless synthesizer squiggles tweaked to perfection by Schnitzler with help from his effects array (reverb, delay, echo, etc). The assortment of electronics is reminiscent of '60s academia but loaded with emotion nevertheless. —*John Bush*

**00/44** / Feb. 16, 1998 / Marginal Talent ♦♦
Recorded in Conrad Schnitzler's home studio during the autumn of 1993, *00/44* is a dense, strangely alienating electronic piece occasionally reminiscent of a horror-film soundtrack. Following the "structured noise" principles of much of his previous work, the album is easier to admire than it is to enjoy—for all of its inventiveness, it never quite manages to draw the listener in, despite the sub-title "Dramatic Electronic Music." —*Jason Ankeny*

## Klaus Schulze

b. Aug. 4, 1947, Berlin, Germany
*Electronics, Keyboards, Guitar, Synthesizer, Composer / Space Rock, Kraut Rock, Electronic*
As both a solo artist and as a member of groups including Tangerine Dream and Ash Ra Tempel, Klaus Schulze emerged among the founding fathers of contemporary electronic music, his epic, meditative soundscapes a key influence on the subsequent rise of the new-age aesthetic. Born in Berlin on August 4, 1947, Schulze began his performing career during the '60s, playing guitar, bass, and drums in a variety of local bands; by 1969, he was drumming in Tangerine Dream, appearing a year later on their debut LP *Electronic Meditation*. The album was Schulze's lone effort with the group, however, as he soon co-founded Ash Ra Tempel with Manuel Gottsching and Hartmut Enke, debuting in 1971 with a self-titled record; again, however, the band format appeared to stifle Schulze, and he mounted a solo career a few months later.

While Schulze's previous recorded work had been in a typically noisy Kraut-rock vein, as a solo artist he quickly became more reflective; although he acquired his first synthesizer in 1972, it did not enter into his solo debut *Irrlicht*, its long, droning peices instead assembled from electronic organ, oscillators and orchestral recordings. The double album *Cyborg* followed in 1973, and a year later he issued *Blackdance*, his first recording to feature synths; *Timewind*, regarded by many as Schulze's masterpiece, appeared in 1975. Around that same time he began producing prog-rockers the Far East Family Band; the group's keyboardist, who went on to become the new age superstar Kitaro, frequently cited Schulze as the central influence behind his own plunge into the world of synths and electronics.

After collaborating with Stomu Yamash'ta on 1976's *Go*, Schulze resurfaced with a flurry of new solo material, including the LP *Moondawn*, 1977's *Mirage* and two volumes of the porn soundtrack *Body Love*. He remained extraordinarily prolific in the years to follow, with 1979's *Dune*, inspired by the Frank Herbert sci-fi classic, becoming his eleventh solo record released during the '70s alone. The '80s were no less fertile, with Schulze issuing a steady stream of new work in addition to various productions released on his own IC label; *Dig It* was his first fully digital recording. By the following decade, Schulze had immersed himself in contemporary dance music, occasionally working in conjunction with Pete Namlook (as Dark Side of the Moog). —*Jason Ankeny*

★ **Irrlicht** / 1972 / PDU ♦♦♦♦♦
Schulze's solo debut is a masterful album featuring some of the most majestic instances of space music ever recorded, all the more remarkable for being recorded without synthesizers. "Saltz Gewitter," the first of two tracks and the highlight here, slowly progresses from oscillator static to a series of glowing organ lines, all informed by Schulze's excellent feel for phase effects. —*John Bush*

**Cyborg** / 1973 / Gramavision ♦♦♦♦
From the early days of electronic experimentation in the pop field, Klaus Schulze's second solo album still stands as one of the most powerful examples of ambient pulse music ever conceived. The dense layers of rhythm and synthetic tone colors melt into a seamless, flowing soundscape of melody, motion, and spatial effects. It's a monumental double album of "cosmic music." —*Archie Patterson*

**Timewind** / 1975 / Blue Plate ♦♦♦♦
*Timewind* consists of two side-long works that take the template of sequencer trance far beyond what either Schulze or Tangerine Dream had done before. The first, "Bayreuth Return," takes the edge off the basic sequencer sound and focuses on a variety of synthesized effects from occasional aircraft noise to gradually shifting strings. Side two contains "Wahnfried 1883," close to half an hour of beatless, emotive space music with several keyboard lines and a series of astral reverb. —*John Bush*

**X** / 1978 / Gramavision ♦♦♦
Schulze's tenth solo release marks the peak of his most influential period of work. Presented with a classic sense of German drama, this double CD artfully combines the composer's synthesizers and sequencer patterns with live drums and full orchestra. Intense, driving, long-form pieces frame surreal, abstract sounds. Each of six pieces is named for a historical figure Schulze admires, beginning with a 24-minute selection titled "Friedrich Nietzsche." —*Linda Kohanov*

**En-Trance** / 1987 / Thunderbolt ♦♦♦♦
The four lengthy tracks comprising *En-Trance* present a collection of gaseous, droning, hissing, effects. The synthesizers tend to be overly evocative and the electronic drum programming leaves a bit to be desired, but it's still the one of the best albums of Schulze's later period. —*John Bush*

**Essential (1972-1993)** / Feb. 11, 1994 / Plan 9/Caroline ♦♦♦♦

The double-disc *Essential* collection skips through Schulze's career with edits of tracks from LP classics like *Irrlicht*, *Timewind*, and *Moondawn*. It all but defeats the purpose of most tracks to hear edits instead of original versions, but it's a good introduction to the different periods and different sounds of Schulze's long career. —*John Bush*

**Angst/Mirage** / Mar. 9, 1999 / Thunderbolt ♦♦♦♦

*Angst/Mirage* includes two Klaus Schulze albums, recorded in 1977 and 1985 respectively. Despite the difference in recording dates, the music is surprisingly complementary, rich in trance-like sequencer textures. —*Keith Farley*

## Paul Schütze

b. 1958, Australia
*Producer, Composer / Experimental Ambient, Film Music, Electro-Acoustic, Ambient*

Australian-born composer and producer Paul Schütze is among the most focused and prolific artists of the contemporary experimental electronic scene. Releasing album after album of sprawling, icy, often difficult ambient and electro-acoustic music, Schütze's work has most often been grouped with post-industrial ambient/isolationist artists such as Lull, Main, and Thomas Köner. While the depth of detail and breadth of sound obtained in Schütze's work already confounds that association, albums such as *Site Anubis* and *Abysmal Evenings* do contain their share of deep, dark, highly cinematic soundscapes (Schütze spent several years in Australia composing for film). Although he bemoans the rampant genre hybridity characteristic of many of his colleagues in both the dance-based underground and the more academic experimental overground (Schütze's discography includes entries for industrial/experimental labels Sentrax and Big Cat, Belgian ambient/techno label Apollo, work with ethno-ambient industrialists O Yuki Conjugate, and collaborations with avant-funk pioneer Bill Laswell), Schütze has moved increasingly toward incorporating rhythmic and percussive structures and ideas from not only ethnic musical traditions (he started out as a percussionist, and has studied Indian percussion formally), but also the more experimental strains of dance-based electronica.

Born in 1958 in Melbourne, Schütze studied Fine Arts at the Caufield Institute of Technology. In the late '70s he was a percussionist with the Fourth Stream Percussion Ensemble before founding the seminal '80s improv group Laughing Hands, adding percussive and synthetic textures to one of Australia's most important and influential experimental forces. After the group dissolved in 1983, Schütze worked as a film critic and DJ at Melbourne's Hardware Club before he was invited to score Roger Scholes' *The Sealer*. He has since provided composition and sound design on more than 20 films, including *Assault on Firebase Gloria*, *Driving Force*, *Earth Bound*, and *The Valley*. Although he recorded a number of albums with Laughing Hands, Schütze's solo work began to appear in 1990, on the Australian Extreme label. He's since released four critically acclaimed albums through Extreme, including *Deus Ex Machina*, a work composed for traveling multimedia installation. In 1994, Schütze's first work under the acronymic moniker Uzect Plaush appeared on Belgian experimental ambient/techno label Apollo, with his debut for Virgin (the double-CD *Apart*) appearing the following year. Many of Schütze's earlier works have been reissued on the Big Cat label, including *Site Anubis* and *New Maps of Hell*. Schütze continues to live and work in London. —*Sean Cooper*

**Deus Ex Machina** / 1989 / Tone Casualties ♦♦♦♦

Although Schütze had already made a name for himself in his native Australia as a member of the group Laughing Hands, and was a successful film composer, this exhibition soundtrack is his first solo release. And all things considered, it's a remarkably mature and sophisticated piece of work, which uses a variety of sampled sounds and voices within musical contexts as a means of exploring psychological expectations and mental space. What Schütze has done, in effect, is create a film score for an imaginary film, and with his prior soundtrack experience, he's not at a loss for ideas. As Schütze indicates in his thoughtful notes, the musical backgrounds which he creates here are essentially static, and they serve as a foundation of natural and manmade sonic events (rain, dripping water, thunder, sirens, jet engines, squealing brakes, church bells), and mysterious narratives in either French or Italian, which are meant to stimulate the imagination without yielding any concrete meaning. (Schütze's assumption was that most Australians would have no working knowledge of these languages, and the same should hold true for the majority North American audience.) Of course, it's one thing for Schütze to say, modestly, that his musical backgrounds are "static," but they are also rich, dense, haunting, and extremely intricate, ranging from riff-oriented funk to brooding orchestral strings. And unlike many other ambient composer/musicians who never get much beyond synthesizer drones, Schütze actually uses contrapuntal lines and multiple instrumental voices with considerable expertise. Instrumentation is not always obvious, but Schütze's main instrument is clearly the synthesizer, augmented by bass and percussion. The static sequences follow one another (in cinematic fashion), as if the director is moving from one scene to another, and if you punch the repeat button on your CD player, you can conjure up various images for the music and have a very entertaining movie playing in your head for hours. —*William Tilland*

**The Annihilating Angel** / 1990 / Extreme ♦♦♦♦

After the thick and rather somber sound collages of the *Deus Ex Machina* soundtrack, this is a much more rhythmic and forceful affair, and at times it approaches the gripping intensity of later Schütze recordings such as *Site Anubis*. The prevailing style here is muted but somewhat edgy worldbeat, with more than a touch of trumpeter Jon Hassell's mysterioso "fourth world" sound. Schütze's early musical training was as a percussionist, and the percussion on this CD is uniformly excellent, groove-oriented and compelling, and making use of a sensuously rich mixture of metal, wood and skin. Spacious synthesizer drones create a feeling of vastness, and the use of separate and distinct instrumental voices (guitar, trumpet, and sampled bass) represents Schütze's first movement toward a collective sound which reaches full development some years later with his group Phantom City. The occasional use of trumpet creates a strong parallel at times with Miles Davis in his early electric phase, and also with Hassell's treated trumpet, but Schütze may have felt that the parallels were too obvious, because he uses trombone on several subsequent recordings, but doesn't use a trumpet again until a live Phantom City concert seven years later. Other characteristic Schütze touches include otherworldly vocal choruses, occasional slabs of howling guitar feedback and, on pieces like "Reign of Ashes" and "Cities of the Red Night," an industrial vibe which is created by ominous mechanical pounding, hoarse metallic cries and strange electronic scraping and grinding. —*William Tilland*

**New Maps of Hell** / 1992 / Extreme ♦♦♦♦

Thematically and psychologically similar to *The Annihilating Angel* (even to the apocalyptic religious imagery of the titles), this CD occasionally looks ahead to Schütze's later work as leader of Phantom City. The title of the CD's longest track is in fact "Topology of a Phantom City," and on this piece, there are strong echoes of the wild electric funk of Miles Davis circa 1975, with strong, groove-oriented percussion supporting the broad smears of De Haan's trombone, and Schütze doing some remarkably strange things with his keyboards, producing unearthly (hellish?) and tormented electronic squeals, howls, and groans over the heavy, sinister percussion. Several subsequent tracks have a rhythmic foundation, but most are languid and dreamlike, with a dissonant, uneasy quality, often tinged with melancholy, that pushes them toward the realm of nightmare. The music is hauntingly beautiful but without resolution; it projects a feeling of claustrophobia and entrapment, as if there is no escape from the reality which it represents. The final track, "A Soul Reports," simply drifts off into a nothingness of murmurs, whispers, cavernous echoes, muted gongs and icy drones. Schütze enhances the disquieting atmosphere with an impressive background collection of skillfully integrated sound samples—guttural and/or demented voices, sounds of thunder or earthquake rumbling, dripping water, and jets of steam. Call it what you will—ambient, industrial, gothic funk (it is all of these and more)—*New Maps of Hell* is music of great subtlety and power. —*William Tilland*

**New Maps of Hell 2: The Rapture of Metals** / 1993 / Big Cat ♦♦♦♦

The title of this CD might erroneously suggest something heavy, abrasive, and industrial, but *The Rapture of Metals* is in part an elegant homage to the metallic gongs of the Indonesian gamelan orchestra. The title track is the most overtly Indonesian, with electronic drones and effects enhancing a traditional gamelan gong pattern. But on several other tracks, Schütze further personalizes his use of gongs, capturing the dreamy, otherworldly quality of Indonesian court music not just by "Westernizing" Indonesian motifs but by blending gamelan sounds and scales with his own rather haunting musical vision. Elsewhere on the CD, Schütze utilizes keyboard synthesizers and sophisticated electronic processing to create thick, ambivalent atmospheres which explore the boundaries between madness and ecstasy. "The Rapture of Drowning" has a viscous, aquatic texture and bursts of nightmarish discord, but nonetheless suggests a transcendent experience of some sort. And the final 20-minute piece, "Sites of Rapture on the Lungs of God," is a series of elongated musical inhalations and exhalations, comprised of cathedral organ chords, sonorous drones, intriguing dissonances, and various strange electronic treatments that add another level of dislocation to the music. —*William Tilland*

**More Beautiful Human Life!** / Aug. 1994 / Apollo ♦♦
Sprawling, somewhat gloomy experimental ambient, with the occasional sparse electronic beats pushing Schütze's typically quite classical approach into the 21st century. —*Sean Cooper*

**The Surgery of Touch** / Oct. 1994 / Extreme ♦♦♦
The music on this CD is based loosely on a fable involving a man in an isolated tropical community who bewitches his brothers by telling them troubled stories while they sleep, then drinks their tears and, as the fable ends, their sweat, and finally their sweated blood, while the surrounding jungle moves ever closer and beckons to him. The first of the three long sections, titled "Tears," is appropriately dreamy and impressionistic, filled with drawn-out chime tones, synthesizer drones, cavernous echoes, and a brief vocal chorus with vaguely Indonesian musical elements. This first section has a strong resemblance, at times to the spacemusic of Steve Roach and Robert Rich. The second section, titled "Sweat," begins with more vocal chanting, and then moves into murkier territory, filled with sampled jungle sounds, dissonant drones, and slow, reverberating pulses ending with the repetition of a haunting three-note pattern. Musically, it is more interesting than the first section if only because it is less derivative. The third section, true to the fable, is the most uneasy of the three. Titled "Blood," it begins with a chorus of nonspecific murmuring, to which is added thunder-like rumbling, deep heartbeat pulses, and a wide variety of metallic, minor-key melodic fragments and sinister hissing. Sporadic percussion intrudes, together with a succession of quietly insistent, drifting motifs. The piece ends with shrill insect whirring and then a series of atonal drones which gradually fade into an unresolved nothingness, communicating in musical language a distinct feeling of human degeneration. A powerful and unique example of dis-eased ambience.—*William Tilland*

● **Apart** / 1995 / Virgin ♦♦♦♦
This double CD from Schütze maintains the high standards of previous releases, with one disc tending toward a kind of delicate techno jazz, and the other moving into a twilight ambient world of slow-motion musical gestures and elusive melodic fragments. Schütze's prior experience as a film composer serves him well; he is a master at creating moods, and rather exceptional in his use of musical resources, refusing to limit himself to a particular instrumental palette or style. On the more ambient disc of the two, one of the four pieces is firmly in the Brian Eno/Steve Roach mode (and as lovely as anything produced by those two artists), while another piece is much closer to the industrial genre, with an austere combination of both organic and machine-like drones, and delicate, random chime tones with occasional clicking sounds. The best track on this disc, though, invokes contemporary classical composer Morton Feldman in its glacially evolving chorus of atonal horns, sounding like some obscure and subtle ritual of an advanced, post-industrial culture. The first disc contains similar treasures, with several pieces featuring vibraphones (a favorite Schütze timbre), delicate brush work on cymbals, and a gently rhythmic bassline. The result is a delicate, drifting chamber jazz which both soothes and charms with its quiet sense of mystery. —*William Tilland*

**Site Anubis** / 1996 / Big Cat ♦♦♦♦
This is the third CD in a Schütze trilogy which began with 1992's *New Maps of Hell* and continued with *The Rapture of Metals;* this final chapter is a certified masterpiece. Schütze, who plays keyboards and also supplies various inventive electronic treatments (tapes, digital sampling, etc.) has something of a signature sound, but he seldom repeats himself to the extent that you think you're hearing the same ol' thing. In the two earlier CDs in the trilogy, echoes of the Miles Davis electric funk emerged from time to time as an influence, along with touches of Jon Hassell and vintage Weather Report. But on this CD, connections with the electric Davis of the '70s are much more blatant. There's no trumpet, but Julian Priester's trombone supplies an occasional approximation, and the formidable guest list also includes Bill Laswell on bass, Lol Coxhill on soprano sax, Alex Buess on bass clarinet, and Raoul Bjorkenheim on noise-metal guitars. And then there's the drumming. Dirk Wachtelaer's dominant cymbal and snare work is either very closely miked, or treated (or both), but regardless, it is frequently brutal-slamming, crashing, in-your-face confrontational. Throw in some serious guitar shredding by Bjorkenheim (Finnish guitarists seem to have a talent for this sort of thing), and inspired electronic moans and howls supplied by Schütze, and you've got music that can grab you by the lapels and toss you into next week, then turn around and drop almost instantly to an insidious, nightmarish whisper. It almost seemed as if it would never happen, but Schütze's music on this CD finally picks up where Davis left off in the mid-'70s. And while Davis and his edgy jazz-funk still sounds good twenty years on, Schütze sounds even better. A major rush, and a major recording. —*William Tilland*

## Scientist (Overton Brown)

b. 1960, Kingston, Jamaica
*Vocals, Producer / Dub, Ambient*

Overton Brown was only 16 years old when producer/performer Errol "Don" Mais discovered and used the considerable talents of this adolescent dub whiz. Born in Kingston in 1960, the Scientist learned basic electronics from his TV-repairman father, skills that made him very popular with the mobile DJs and their not-always-functioning sound systems. A friend suggested he visit the legendary dub producer/mixer King Tubby, not to remix records, but to get some transformers by which Scientist could build his own amplifiers. Soon the Scientist was an employee of Tubby's, fixing transformers and televisions, when one day, after an animated conversation about mixing records, Tubby challenged the Scientist to take a shot at remixing a record. Brimming with adolescent bravado, Scientist took Tubby's challenge, and that led to an extended apprenticeship in dub experimentation under Tubby's guidance. It was while at Tubby's that the Scientist developed his idiosyncratic dub style, playful and very psychedelic, loaded with echo explosions and blasts of feedback, a sound that caught the attention of Don Mais, who overheard the Scientist at the mixing board during a visit to Tubby's studio. With Mais supervising the production, Scientist, now all of 18, cut some wicked dub sides for the Roots Tradition label. At the end of the '70s, Scientist (now also referred to as "The Dub Chemist") left Tubby's to become the main engineer at Channel One Studios, and working with Henry "Junjo" Lawes, cut some best-selling dub LPs, only to leave for the greener pastures of Tuff Gong in 1982. In 1985, Scientist moved to Silver Springs, Maryland, where he lives and works as a recording engineer. —*John Dougan*

**Scientist Vs. Prince Jammy** / 1980 / Greensleeves ♦♦♦♦
Fat explosions of sound running headlong into echo delays that seem to go on forever, this is a great chunk of psychedelic dub mixing with Scientist and Jammy trading jabs like boxers (which is how the LP is set up). Neither one gets the upper hand, but both acquit themselves quite nicely. —*John Dougan*

**Scientist Meets the Space Invaders** / 1981 / Greensleeves ♦♦♦
Youthful exuberance runs wild, as Scientist combines the popularity of the now-outdated computer game with his cut'n'mix dub groove. At times overly fussy, if the Scientist's out-there mixing style is what gives you a buzz, then chasing this obscurity down will not be a waste of time. —*John Dougan*

**Scientist Wins the World Cup** / 1981 / Greensleeves ♦♦♦
Hey, why not a soccer motif; after all, it's popular in both England and Jamaica. More mixing tomfoolery with moments of true spaciness and avant-garde styling. Not an essential Scientist recording, but fine indeed. —*John Dougan*

**Tribute to King Tubby Dub** / 1990 / ROIR ♦♦♦♦
Top-notch knob twisting and echo-chamber overload come from this early dub stylist. —*Myles Boisen*

● **Dub in the Roots Tradition** / 1996 / Blood & Fire ♦♦♦♦
Leave it to the people at Blood and Fire to find the long-thought-lost recordings Scientist made in the mid- to late '70s under the supervision of Don Mais. Some of these recordings were mixed by Scientist when he was 16 and offer proof of his audaciously creative mind. Helping his mixology along is that the music was supplied by two of the most formidable session bands in Jamaica, the Soul Syndicate (featuring guitarist Chinna Smith), and the Roots Radics band (featuring the grumbling bass of Earl "Flabba" Holt). But it's the Scientist and his reverb and echo delays that turns this into a dancehall party, a trip that is long, strange and unforgettable. —*John Dougan*

## Scion
*Group / Minimal Techno, Experimental Techno, Techno*
A one-time collaboration between Rene Lowe and Peter Kuschnereit that began the long series of records on the Berlin-based Chain Reaction label. The two were members of the camp of electronic music artists affiliated with the Hard Wax record store in Berlin that released music on numerous labels in addition to Chain Reaction. Lowe would go on to release records as Vainqueur, while Kuschnereit would release his compositions as Substance. The duo would also perform their songs and the work of their *Hard Wax* peers in a live setting, often accompanied by reggae vocalist Tikiman. —*Jason Birchmeier*

● **Emerge [EP]** / 1995 / Chain Reaction ♦♦♦♦
Referring to themselves as Scion, Rene Lowe and Peter Kuschnereit produced three versions of a song titled "Emerge" for the first release in the groundbreaking Chain Reaction series. *Emerge* uses a hard-hitting percussive rhythm with plenty of booming bass for a sense of power and forward movement. The rhythm is highly syncopated and somewhat simple, but it functions well as a driving force. Scion then begins adding, subtracting, and altering a set of riffs that loop continuously throughout the song. These riffs phase and modulate as if they were being transmitted through a filter of some kind. The resulting sound is a bit disorientating and surreal, yet this is no doubt the point. On the B-side are two variations of the song, titled "Emerge 1" and "Emerge 2." Both rework the rhythm of the original and further alter the song's central riff. These mixes are much more reduced and experimental. —*Jason Birchmeier*

## Scorn (Mick Harris)
*Producer / Experimental Techno, Dark Ambient, Ambient Dub, Jungle/Drum'N'Bass, Industrial*
Closely allied with post-industrial dub terrorists such as Bill Laswell, Techno Animal, James Plotkin, Robert Musso, and Anton Fier, Birmingham-based artist Mick Harris is something of a study in extremes. A drummer with noted death metal outfit Napalm Death through the group's late-'80s/early-'90s heyday, Harris began experimenting with monochrome ambient and dub styles toward the tail end of his association with that group. Releasing material through Earache as Scorn (his ambient dub aegis) and through Sentrax as Lull, in addition to other sporadic projects, his genre-spanning activities have done much to jar the minds, expectations, and record collections of audiences previously kept aggressively opposed. To the present, Scorn and Lull, along with John Zorn's experimental jazz-dubcore outfit Painkiller have remained Harris' primary ongoing projects, although one-off collaborations with the likes of James Plotkin, Nicholas Bullen, Bill Laswell, and Martyn Bates are common. Harris formed Scorn in 1991 in collaboration with bassist Nick Bullen, incorporating elements of ambient, industrial, dub, rock, and hip-hop. The group (though pared back to just Harris following *Evanescence*) have released a number of increasingly well-received full-length recordings, including the remix LP *Ellipsis*, which features outbound reworkings by the likes of Coil, Autechre, Laswell, and Germ. Harris' solo work as Lull focuses on darker, more "isolationist" ambient soundscapes, some of which have been reissued domestically by Laswell's now-defunct Subharmonic imprint. [See Also: Mick Harris, Lull] —*Sean Cooper*

**Evanescence** / Aug. 23, 1994 / Earache ♦♦
A moderately successful, if somewhat obvious fusion of more traditional instrumentation with composed electronics and effects. Periodic vocals tend to distract from the shifting, exploratory nature of the music, but the instrumental tracks are well-crafted examples of dub-influenced experimental electronica. —*Sean Cooper*

**Ellipsis** / May 9, 1995 / Earache ♦♦♦
A barely recognizable recapitulation of *Evanescence*, thanks in no small part to some stunning remixes from Autechre, Meat Beat Manifesto, Bill Laswell, Scanner, Germ, and Coil. Also released on vinyl as a 5 x 12" box set. —*Sean Cooper*

● **Gyral** / Oct. 31, 1995 / Earache ♦♦♦♦
Harris' first Scorn release after the departure of bassist Nick Bullen is a refinement of previous concerns, with spare, repetitive rhythms and drum loops providing a tether for dark, brooding atmospherics and harsh, effects-heavy samples. Less immediately engaging perhaps than previous albums, *Gyral* works best as beat-oriented dark ambient, its strongest impact working at an almost subconscious or subliminal level. —*Sean Cooper*

**Logghi Baroghi** / Aug. 20, 1996 / Earache ♦♦♦♦
*Logghi Baroghi* is one of Scorn's most ambitious efforts to date, featuring a dark, menacing undercurrent of experimentation. Mick Harris doesn't really abandon the blueprint that distinguished the previous, acclaimed *Gyral*, but he does deepen the music by lessing the industrial influences and playing around with dub and techno. There are the occasional dull spots, but for the most part, *Logghi Baroghi* is a fascinating, disturbing listen. —*Stephen Thomas Erlewine*

**Zander** / Feb. 18, 1997 / Invisible ♦♦
This is supposedly the last album under the name of Scorn for Mick Harris. Progressing from industrial grindcore to great industrial/experimental/dub to straight, bass-heavy ambient dub, Scorn has certainly made the rounds. However, *Zander* doesn't do much to develop the Scorn sound found on the last four albums or so. The creative light that once made Scorn great seems to have been dulled a bit. This is not a bad album by any means, though; it's very dark and hypnotic, but it is simple and not really worth purchasing if the buyer is familiar with much of Scorn's later work. —*Marc van der Pol*

**Whine** / Oct. 21, 1997 / Invisible ♦♦
*Whine* consists mostly of live material recorded on Scorn's European tour following the release of *Zander;* it features guest appearances by guitarist Eraldo Benocchi. The album also includes four previously unreleased studio cuts that were originally intended for collaborative use by Bill Laswell and a rapper. —*Steve Huey*

## Scott 4
f. 1997
*Group / Trip-Hop, Club/Dance, Alternative Pop/Rock*
Electronic cowpunks Scott 4—the trio of vocalist Scott Blixen, guitarist John Moody and drummer Ed Tilley—formed in early 1997; after debuting at a local folk club, they were soon signed to the independent label Satellite, issuing their debut EP *Elektro Akoustic and Volksmechanik* that August. The record's unique synthesis of punk, country, and electronica immediately found critical favor, and the subsequent "Deutsche LP Record" was named "Single of the Week" in *Melody Maker*. After touring in support of the High Llamas, Scott 4 issued their full-length debut *Recorded in State LP* in early 1998, signing to major label V2 soon after. —*Jason Ankeny*

● **Recorded in State LP** / Aug. 25, 1998 / Satellite ♦♦♦♦
Scott 4 set their statement of purpose on the first track "Start-Up," a song that begins with a banjo-heavy backwoods stomp but gradually transforms into a crisp drum-machine track complete with 808 claps and stark beats. Much of the rest of *Recorded in State* has the same fixation with the polar extremes of organics and electronics, though the soundclash is much smoother than expected. Occasionally, Scott Blixen goes a bit too far on his vocal turns, though his overblown tear through "Your Kingdom to Dust" is an entertaining highlight. —*John Bush*

## Doc Scott
b. Coventry, England
*Producer, DJ / Jungle/Drum'N'Bass, Club/Dance*
The recipient of the first release on the influential Metalheadz Recordings—which he co-founded with Goldie—and an early inspiration on the jungle star, Doc Scott began producing records in the early days of the '90s, when jungle was in its tender infancy. The ever-joyous strains of rave and hardcore were gradually giving way to darker sounds, more influenced by hip-hop, and few producers did more to birth the dark mid-'90s sound of jungle than Scott. A resident of Coventry, he was early inspired by the heady moods of the *Blade Runner* soundtrack as well as Detroit figures such as Derrick May and Kevin Saunderson, and after receiving a pair of turntables at the age of 18, he began DJing. Scott played live dates at raves during 1989-90, and soon after gave up his job as a telephone worker to enter music full-time.

His early recordings for Absolute 2 like *NHS, NHS, Vol. 2,* and *Surgery* made him one of the top names in the emerging hardcore scene, and Scott soon became part of the Reinforced Recordings crew, which included Dego and Mark Mac of 4 Hero, and later, Goldie. Scott's 1992 EP for Reinforced, Nasty Habits' *As Nasty as I Wanna Be*, set the template for darkside drum'n'bass with the classic "Here Come the Drumz." He and Goldie recorded several tracks together while at Reinforced, then formed Metalheadz in 1994. The Doc Scott single "VIP Drums" proved to be the label's first release, starting out Metalheadz with style and foreshadowing additional releases such as "Far Away" and an update of "Here Come the Drumz" titled "Drumz 95." Scott recorded as well for LTJ Bukem's Good Looking Records, and set up his own label in 1996. That same year, he released a volume in the *Mixmag Live!* series of DJ albums. —*John Bush*

**VIP Drums/Rider's Ghosts [Single]** / 1994 / Metalheadz ♦♦♦♦

**Drumz 95/Blue Skies [Single]** / 1995 / Metalheadz ♦♦♦♦

● **Lost in Drum'n'bass** / 1998 / Moonshine Music ♦♦♦♦
Few producers or DJs can ride the drum'n'bass wave from light to dark without fear of wipeout. On his second official mix album, recorded for Moooonshine, Doc Scott accomplishes this mission with a collection of tracks spanning the cream of nu-dark jungle (Decoder, Jonny L, Cybotron Featuring Dillinja) plus a raft of jazzier tracks (Lemon D, Adam F) and even nods to certifiable drum'n'bass classics (Hokusai's "Red Lights," Omni Trio's "Trippin' on Broken Beats"). *Lost in Drum'n'bass* is not only an excellent mix album, but a great summation of the jungle scene circa 1998. —*Keith Farley*

## Raymond Scott (Harry Warnow)

b. Sep. 10, 1908, Brooklyn, NY, d. Feb. 8, 1994, North Hills, CA
*Drums, Piano, Leader, Composer / Obscuro, Computer Music, Space Age Pop, Swing, Electronic, Novelty*

Composer, bandleader, and inventor Raymond Scott was among the unheralded pioneers of contemporary experimental music, a figure whose genius and influence have seeped almost subliminally into the mass cultural consciousness. As a visionary whose name is largely unknown but whose music is immediately recognizable, Scott's was a career stuffed with contradictions: though his early work anticipated the breathless invention of bebop, his obsession with perfectionism and memorization was the very antithesis of jazz's improvisational ethos; though his best-known compositions remain at large thanks to their endless recycling as soundtracks for cartoons, he never once wrote a note expressly for animated use; and though his later experiments with electronic music pioneered the ambient aesthetic, the ambient concept itself was not introduced until a decade after the release of his original recordings.

Born Harry Warnow in Brooklyn on September 10, 1908, he was a musical prodigy, playing piano by the age of two; following high school, he planned to study engineering, but his older brother Mark—himself a successful violinist and conductor—had other ideas, buying his sibling a Steinway Grand and persuading him to attend the Institute of Musical Art, later rechristened the Juilliard School. After graduating in 1931, Scott—the name supposedly picked at random out of the Manhattan phone book—signed on as a staff pianist with the CBS radio network house band conducted by his brother; finding the repertoire dull and uninspired, he began presenting his own compositions to his bandmates, and soon bizarre Scott originals like "Confusion Among a Fleet of Taxicabs Upon Meeting with a Fare" began creeping into broadcasts.

Scott remained a member of the CBS band until 1936, at which time he convinced producer Herb Rosenthal to allow him the chance to form his own group; assembling a line-up originally comprising fellow network veterans Lou Shoobe on bass, Dave Harris on tenor saxophone, Pete Pumiglio on clarinet, Johnny Williams on drums, and the famed Bunny Berigan on trumpet, he dubbed the group the Raymond Scott Quintette, debuting on the *Saturday Night Swing Session* with the song "The Toy Trumpet." The Quintette was an immediate hit with listeners, and Scott was soon offered a recording contract with the Master label. Dissent quickly broke out in the group's ranks, however, as Scott's obsessive practice schedule began to wear out his bandmates; Berigan soon quit, frustrated because the airtight compositions—never written down, taught and developed one oddball phrase at a time—allowed no room for improvisations.

Still, for all of Scott's eccentricities, his records flew off the shelves, their dadaist titles ("Dinner Music for a Pack of Hungry Cannibals," "Reckless Night on Board an Oceanliner," and "Boy Scout in Switzerland"), juxtaposed melodies, odd time signatures and quirky arrangements somehow connecting with mainstream American audiences. Hollywood soon came calling, with the Quintette performing music for (and sometimes appearing in) features including *Nothing Sacred*, *Ali Baba Goes to Town* and *Rebecca of Sunnybrook Farm*. Upon returning to New York, in 1938 Scott was tapped to become CBS' next music director; around the same time he expanded the Quintette to big-band size, and by 1940 quit his network position to lead his ensemble on tour. He returned to CBS in 1942, however, assembling the first racially mixed studio orchestra in broadcast history.

In 1941, Warner Bros.' fledgling animation department bought the rights to Scott's back catalog, with music director Carl Stalling making liberal use of the melodies in his groundbreaking cut-and-paste cartoon soundtracks; Quintette favorites like the rollicking "Powerhouse" soon became immediately recognizable for their regular appearances in classic Bugs Bunny, Daffy Duck and Porky Pig clips, the same music supporting the crazed antics of Ren & Stimpy and others half a century later. Indeed, generations upon generations of young viewers have received an unwitting introduction to avant-garde concepts through their repeated exposure to Scott and Stalling's music, although none of the former's compositions were written with cartoons in mind; by the time Warner Bros. began using Scott's music on a regular basis in 1943, he had already moved on to new projects, including a lucrative career authoring commercial jingles.

In 1945, Scott wrote incidental music for the Broadway production *Beggars Are Coming to Town;* the year following, he teamed with lyricist Bernard Hanighen on the musical *Lute Song*, which yielded another of his best known songs, "Mountain High, Valley Low." Also in 1946, Scott founded Manhattan Research, the world's first electronic music studio; housing equipment including a Martenot, an Ondioline, and a specially-modified Hammond organ, it was advertised as "the world's most extensive facility for the creation of Electronic Music and Musique Concrète." After his brother Mark's 1949 death, Scott took over his duties as the bandleader on the syndicated radio favorite *Your Hit Parade*, with his second wife Dorothy Collins soon assuming the position as the program's featured vocalist; that same year, he also scored theatrical productions of *Peep Show* and *Six Characters in Search of an Author*.

Of all of Scott's accomplishments of 1949, however, none was more important than the Electronium, one of the first synthesizers ever created. An "instantaneous composing machine," the Electronium generated original music via random sequences of tones, rhythms, and timbres; Scott himself denied it was a prototype synthesizer—it had no keyboard—but as one of the first machines to create music by means of artificial intelligence, its importance in pointing the way towards the electonic compositions of the future is undeniable. His other inventions included the "Karloff," an early sampler capable of recreating sounds ranging from sizzling steaks to jungle drums; the Clavinox, a keyboard Theremin complete with an electronic sub-assembly designed by a then 23-year-old Robert Moog; and the Videola, which fused together a keyboard and a TV screen to aid in composing music for films and other moving images.

In addition to hosting *Your Hit Parade*, Scott continued recording throughout the '50s, issuing LPs, including *This Time with Strings*, *At Home with Dorothy and Raymond*, and *Rock and Roll Symphony*. Additionally, he cranked out advertising jingles at an astonishing rate, scored countless film and television projects, and even founded a pair of record labels, Audiovox and Master, while serving as A&R director for Everest Records. During the mid-'50s, Scott assembled a new Quintette; the 1962 edition of the group was its last. The year following, he began work on the three-volume LP set *Soothing Sounds for Baby*, an "aural toy" designed to create a comforting yet stimulating environment for infants. As electronic music produced to inspire and relax, the records fit snugly into the definition of ambient suggested by Brian Eno a decade later, their minimalist dreamscapes also predating Philip Glass and Terry Riley.

By the middle of the '60s, Scott began turning increasingly away from recording and performing to focus on writing and inventing; a 1969 musical celebrating the centennial of Kentucky Bourbon was his last orchestral work, with his remaining years spent solely on electronic composition. Among his latter-day innovations was an early programmable polyphonic sequencer, which, along with the Electronium, later caught the attention of Motown chief Berry Gordy, Jr., who in 1971 tapped Scott to head the label's electronic music research and development team. After retiring six years later, he continued writing—his last known piece, 1986's "Beautiful Little Butterfly," was created on MIDI technology. By 1992, Scott's music was finally rediscovered by contemporary audiences, with the *Reckless Nights and Turkish Twilights* compilation appearing to great acclaim; he died on February 8, 1994 at the age of 85. —*Jason Ankeny*

● **The Music of Raymond Scott: Reckless Nights & Turkish Twilights** / Feb. 20, 1937-Jun. 17, 1940 / Columbia ♦♦♦♦
The name may not be immediately familiar, but the music itself certainly is:

to anyone weaned on the legendary Warner Bros. cartoons of the '40s and '50s, Raymond Scott's deliriously inventive freak-jazz is the soundtrack of childhood, with each and every note capable of conjuring up indelible images of such immortal characters as Bugs Bunny, Porky Pig and Daffy Duck. The WB connection is both Scott's greatest legacy and his greatest curse, however; he never composed a note specifically for cartoons, and his most memorable and distinctive melodies were actually co-opted for animated use by Warner's brilliant music director, Carl Stalling. *Reckless Nights and Turkish Twilights*, then, restores Scott's work to its original, stand-alone setting, confirming his cult reputation as one of the most innovative and original musical thinkers of his era. Even free of cartoon mayhem, his music is remarkably visual and colorful, perfectly evocative of such surreal titles as "Dinner Music for a Pack of Hungry Cannibals" and "War Dance for Wooden Indians," probably the best-known cut here is the opening "Powerhouse," a uniquely mechanized piece used in any number of cartoons and television commercials and a perfect summation of Scott's intricate arrangments, complex shifting rhythms, and formal lunacy. Recommended for listeners ages eight to 80. —*Jason Ankeny*

**Soothing Sounds for Baby, Vol. 1** / Dec. 30, 1997 / Basta ♦♦♦♦
Designed for babies one to six months old, the first volume of Raymond Scott's dreamy, engaging *Soothing Sounds for Baby* emphasizes soft synth tones, repetitive melodies and relatively simple arrangements. Keeping in mind a young baby's attention span, *Vol. 1* also contains shorter, more numerous pieces than the following albums. *Vol. 1* begins on a minimal, hypnotic note with "Lullaby," an appropriately trance-inducing, 14-minute song featuring twinkly keyboard figures and some airy synths. The reverie continues with "Sleepy Time," which combines a delicate, drifting melody with a gently rhythmic bassline. As *Soothing Sounds for Baby* progresses, it grows livelier, more complex, and increasingly percussive. "Music Box" retains the hovering synth sound from earlier in the album, but sets it atop a perky rhythm. "Nursery Rhyme" is the most experimental track on the album, featuring a sing-song melody along the lines of "Three Blind Mice" or "This Old Man," that jumps from key to key. Backed by a complex, syncopated rhythm and slightly atonal harmonies, as the song unfolds it becomes more improvised and spontaneous. Finally, "Tic Toc" takes the album's minimalism to its extreme, consisting of a clockwork, two-note melody that fades in and out of focus. As it explores sonic distance instead of melodic progression, the song achieves the same effect as the beginning of the album: hypnotic and very soothing indeed. With each listen, *Soothing Sounds for Baby, Vol. 1* reveals something new, retaining its freshness for young and older babies alike. —*Heather Phares*

**Soothing Sounds for Baby, Vol. 2** / Dec. 30, 1997 / Basta ♦♦♦♦
As the second volume in the *Soothing Sounds for Baby* trilogy, *Vol. 2* was designed by Raymond Scott for infants six to 12 months old. Correspondingly, it features fewer but longer and more complex, rhythmic compositions. The first song, "Tempo Block," is a transitional piece, combining *Vol. 1*'s sprightly keyboard melodies with a slightly tribal rhythm tapped out on an electronic bongo. "The Happy Whistler" increases in rhythmic syncopation and melodic counterpoint, featuring a circular bassline and alternately warbling and whistling keyboards over lumbering drums. *Soothing Sounds for Baby, Vol. 2*'s final piece, "Toy Typewriter," is perhaps the most avant-garde of the series. The song consists of exactly what its title indicates: a toy typewriter, played masterfully by Scott to produce subtle, shifting rhythms that sound like proto-jungle breakbeats. With 26 keys and the space bar, he achieves a deceptively simple, calming and active effect. As with the whole series, on "Toy Typewriter," Scott does the near-impossible, packaging progressive musical ideas in a simple, accessible way. Even more impressively, the overall sound of *Soothing Sounds for Baby* has barely dated at all. Though the concept of space-age music for babies is rooted in the naively futuristic outlook of the early '60s, the series' kitsch factor is remarkably low. Thanks to its clean, spacious production and minimal arrangements, *Soothing Sounds for Baby* remains progressive yet playful, rewarding listeners who pay close attention to its pretty, introspective compositions. —*Heather Phares*

**Soothing Sounds for Baby, Vol. 3** / Dec. 30, 1997 / Basta ♦♦♦♦
After exploring melody in *Vol. 1* and percussion in *Vol. 2*, *Soothing Sounds for Baby, Vol. 3* integrates and alternates between the two concepts, resulting in the series' greatest musical contrasts. Appropriate for the sophistication and maturity of its intended age group of 12 to 18 months, *Vol. 3* contains the most intricate pieces of any of the albums. The arrangements take center stage on the album's three pieces, particularly on the opening song, "Tin Soldier." A fittingly stiff, metallic snare anchors dancing synth melodies reminiscent of banjos and harpsichords, then reaches farther orbits with some of Raymond Scott's trademark spacy keyboards. "Little Miss Echo" follows "Tin Soldier's" witty, whimsical march with one of the series' loveliest, most ambient works. Appropriately spacious-sounding, the song floats on great waves of synth, topped by sonar-like flourishes and supported by a delicate, stately bassline. With minimal percussion, the song hearkens back to *Vol. 1*'s spacy melodies. However, "Little Miss Echo" is more serene and complex, with a more developed sense of melody and harmony that predicts artists like Stereolab and Laika almost 30 years before their existence. The album's final track, "The Playful Drummer," introduces another, very different take on melody and rhythm, this time exploring percussion's tonal, melodic potential. As a keyboard plays a constant oompah rhythm, Scott is the playful drummer, experimenting with melodies and patterns through his electronic drums. Though some patterns repeat, the song never quite settles into a predictable pattern over its 15-minute stretch. Instead, "The Playful Drummer" skips and jumps from high to low, fast to slow, and tosses in some snippets of feedback for good measure. One of the more disorienting but interesting pieces of the *Soothing Sounds for Baby* series, the song showcases Scott's unique, undiluted artistic vision. Much like a baby itself, *Soothing Sounds for Baby* is playful and ever-changing, revealing its hidden logic and maturity over time. —*Heather Phares*

☆ **Manhattan Research, Inc.** / May 16, 2000 / Basta ♦♦♦♦♦
Subtitled "New Plastic Sounds and Electronic Abstractions," *Manhattan Research, Inc.* is an excellent compilation of electronic pioneer Raymond Scott's works from the '50s and '60s. Nothing that has been recorded since within the field of electronic music has obscured the originality and genius of these works. Even the amusing tracks of corporate advertisements for the likes of cough drops, fragrances, and Twinkies(!) demand repeated listening for their fascinating use of electronics. Tracks like "Bandito the Bongo Artist," "Cindy Electronium," and "The Pygmy Taxi Corporation" are just as intriguing as their titles. And the packaging—from the compilation of tracks to the exhaustive liner notes, photographs, and interviews (including a fascinating one with Scott associate Robert Moog), is a clinic in reissue presentation. Not only detailing some of the instruments he developed for use in his compositions (the Clavivox, Circle Machine, etc.), it also documents other inventions and aids, like the Videola, which enabled him to score films conveniently as he watched them. Absolutely essential for any electronic music fan, and completely out of this world, regardless of century. Every library should own a copy of this as well—Scott's name should be just as well-known as Beethoven. —*Andy Kellman*

## The Sea and Cake

f. 1993, Chicago, IL
*Group / Experimental Rock, Indie Rock, Post-Rock/Experimental, Alternative Pop/Rock*

The Sea and Cake was a post-rock supergroup of sorts comprised of luminaries from the Chicago independent scene. The band was led by singer/guitarist Sam Prekop, who along with bassist Eric Claridge was an alumnus of the frequently brilliant Shrimp Boat. After that group's dissolution, Prekop and Claridge were offered the opportunity to embark on a new project, and hastily recruited ex-Coctails guitarist Archer Prewitt and Tortoise drummer John McEntire before entering the studio. Originally intended as a one-off project, the musicians decided to continue performing together, and after selecting the name the Sea and Cake—derived from McEntire's misinterpretation of the Gastr del Sol song "The C in Cake"—they issued their eponymous 1994 debut, an enigmatic collection highlighting Prekop's stream-of-consciousness wordplay and singular fusion of pop, jazz, blue-eyed soul and Kraut-rock styles. In 1995, the group returned with two more LPs, the intricate *Nassau* and the shimmering *The Biz*. After the release of *The Fawn* in 1997, the band took a break while both Prewitt and Prekop released solo albums. Finally, in 2000, the Sea and Cake released their fifth album, *Oui*. —*Jason Ankeny*

● **The Sea and Cake** / 1994 / Thrill Jockey ♦♦♦♦
The Sea and Cake's buoyant debut is a breath of fresh air, an utterly distinctive and innovative work which expands the scope of frontman Sam Prekop's work in the great Shrimp Boat to incorporate a new fascination with Afro-Caribbean rhythms and textures. Recorded by Brad Wood, the album simply glows—Prekop's dry vocals and free-associative lyrics skip along a shimmer-

ing and lushly pastoral backdrop which nimbly fuses pop, soul, jazz, and even prog-rock; tracks like "Jacking the Ball," "Flat Lay the Water," and "Showboat Angel" are as seductive as they are elusive. —*Jason Ankeny*

**Nassau** / Jan. 1995 / Thrill Jockey ♦♦♦♦
*Nassau*, the Sea and Cake's sophomore album, is even more ambitious and eclectic than its predecessor; opening with the bracing "Nature Boy," the group's most kinetically charged effort to date, the record quickly shifts gears to grow dark and subdued. The two instrumentals, "Earth Star" and the enigmatically titled "A Man Who Never Sees a Pretty Girl That He Doesn't Love Her a Little," spotlight the group's burgeoning jazz inclinations, while "The Cantina" is an abstract pop curveball; Sam Prekop's melodic gifts continue to blossom on the loping "Lamonts Lament" and the melancholy "Parasol," and the increased involvement of drummer/producer John McEntire pushes the group into new rhythmic and textural territory. Another winner. —*Jason Ankeny*

**The Biz** / Oct. 1995 / Thrill Jockey ♦♦♦♦
A less structured record than previous efforts, *The Biz* is also the Sea and Cake's most subdued; songs like the title track, "Station in the Valley" and "Sending" are loose and languid, favoring a more jam-oriented and subconscious vibe over the taut dynamics of earlier work. The resulting sprawl brings the group closer to jazz than ever before, with the songs' extended instrumental passages and shifting rhythms shining new light on the telepathic interplay between Eric Claridge's bass and John McEntire's drums; although it's the Sea and Cake's third album in a little over 12 months, *The Biz* is nevertheless rich in ideas and innovations, showing no signs of creative exhaustion. —*Jason Ankeny*

**The Fawn** / Apr. 1, 1997 / Thrill Jockey ♦♦♦♦
The product of an uncharacteristically long two-year layoff, *The Fawn* is the Sea and Cake's most experimental effort to date; the influence which the electronica movement exerts over the record is substantial—drum machines, sequencer tones, and synths are dominant throughout, and the group even dabbles in dub textures and sampling techniques. What's remarkable about songs like "Sporting Life" and "The Argument," however, is that the addition of electronics never upsets the music's delicate chemistry—as is again proven here, the Sea and Cake's greatest gift is their ability to assimilate the breadth of their inspirations, no matter how far afield, to emerge with something new and distinctive each time out; impressive in scope and rich in detail, *The Fawn* is as seamless and sophisticated as ever. —*Jason Ankeny*

**Oui** / Oct. 3, 2000 / Thrill Jockey ♦♦♦♦
In the three-plus years following the release of 1997's *The Fawn*, the Sea & Cake's ever-busy membership dabbled in solo albums, touring with side projects, and various other responsibilities that come with the territory in the Chicago indie rock scene. But as effortlessly as an April breeze, the quartet reconvened to turn in *Oui*, quite possibly the finest of the group's five albums to date.

*Oui* brightens up the electroacoustic hybrids first heard on *The Fawn* with guidance from frontman Sam Prekop's Brazilian-influenced 1999 solo debut and drummer John McEntire's production work on two Stereolab albums. While the looping synths often bogged down the mediocre material on *The Fawn*, the electronics serve as much better complements here. Prekop turns in some of his catchiest melodies to date, while the band follows suit on the sparkling, funky pop of "All the Photos" and the wobbly, mallet-laden "The Leaf," which makes good on the soothing ballad style introduced on "Window Lights," TSAC's contribution to the 1999 McEntire-scored *Reach the Rock* soundtrack.

A sophisticated pop pleasure from start to finish, *Oui* is the aural equivalent of a perpetual Indian summer. —*Jonathan Cohen*

## Dave Seaman

b. Apr. 29, 1968, Garforth, England
*Producer / Progressive Trance, Progressive House, Trance, Club/Dance*
Producer, remixer and DJ Dave Seaman edited *Mixmag* and helped found Stress Records. As a part of the International Dance Music Award-winning production team Brothers in Rhythm, Seaman has remixed tracks by artists like Garbage, Placebo, and Alanis Morisette. His mixing work has appeared on multiple volumes in the *DJ Culture*, *Mixmag Live!*, *Renaissance*, and *Global Underground* series. Seaman has also been a resident DJ at Miami's Groovejet club. —*Heather Phares*

● **Global Underground: Buenos Aires** / Aug. 23, 1999 / Global Underground ♦♦
With the *Global Underground* series, one never quite knows what to expect from each succeeding release. Each volume features a certain degree of trance motifs and usually an even greater degree of progressive house sounds with the occasional inclusion of other musical styles. Dave Seaman's *Global Underground: Buenos Aires* contribution stands alongside the best volumes in this lengthy series of double CDs that delicately handle the balance between the emotive extremities of trance and the propulsive energy of progressive house. Like a great DJ should, Seaman keeps the beats pumping while carefully tweaking the mood and tempo of his set, producing small peaks at just the right moments without getting too carried away with excessive intensity. His resulting mix moves across different planes of sound, starting sublime, climbing slowly, reaching a number of near climaxes, and ultimately reaching a moment of aural elation before posthumously taking a few minutes to come down. Does this formula sound familiar? Sure, it's the makings of a great progressive house/trance set, and Seaman gets it right for the most part. There are some moments near the end of each set when his track selection becomes a bit questionable, but even these moments when one wonders whether the superstar DJ has gone too far or not far enough that his true brilliance shines; nothing is predictable or generic. Opening up the first disc with Francois Kevorkian's remix of Underworld's "Jumbo" and Timo Maas and Ian Wilkie's "Twin Town" is an absolutely brilliant choice by Seaman, instantly establishing a lush mood from which he can only build. Once it all ends, one cannot find many weak moments in Seaman's set. The earth-shattering climax during "Nipple Fish" may be a bit too much for its own good, and Seaman could possibly end each set with a climatic moment rather than use the final track for a somewhat anti-climatic moment of ease, but relative to any other DJ-mix album on the market, very few compare to the beginning to end consistency of his set. —*Jason Birchmeier*

**Global Underground: Cape Town** / Aug. 22, 2000 / Boxed ♦♦♦
Dave Seaman's second contribution to the *Global Underground* series finds the UK DJ moving to a darker, less accessible sound than his previous album. The tracks still carry the tendencies of progressive house and trance, but these tracks seem less uplifting and more dreary, with each of the two discs submerging into a series of bland, hypnotic progressive house tracks before concluding with massive anthems. The first disc moves quickly into the great Futureshock remix of Moby's "Porcelain"—a totally reworked track that uses little more than the original's beautiful ambient synth hook—and then straight into the majestic female vocals of Ian Wilkie's "Guten Morgen." Following this haunting track, Seaman moves into a run of non-charismatic tracks that do little but keep the tempo pumping and the mood lulling until the final two tracks: remixes of Above's "New Day Dawning" and Breeder's "Tyrantanic" that conclude the disc with a powerful dose of progressive trance. Seaman composes a fairly similar set on the second disc, starting with the pristine strings of Pete Lazonby's "Sacred Cycles (Quivver Remix)" and dropping into a long run of dull tracks before concluding on an uplifting note with the vocal-driven "No Way Out" by Highland. While this album does function as a nice alternative to the anthem-filled progressive trance one might expect to hear with its rather melancholy trip into dark progressive house, it really needs to be listened to all the way through, unfortunately requiring the sort of discipline many may not wish to invest. —*Jason Birchmeier*

## Secret Knowledge

f. 1988, London, England
*Group / Progressive House, Electronica, Club/Dance, Acid House, House*
Former pub-rock crusty and journalist supremo Kris Needs weighed in with his thoughts on the acid-house movement by recording for Deconstruction and Sabres of Paradise Records as Secret Knowledge. Perhaps better known to the dance masses as a popular tour DJ (with everyone from the Orb to Primal Scream to the Prodigy), Needs was buying records from an early age. He began writing and DJing in the mid-'70s, and worked as a reviewer at several magazines while serving as resident at several London clubs during the '80s.

Needs had recorded several hip-hop tracks with American vocalist Wonder during the mid-'80s, though the acid-house boom and an allegiance with poster-children Primal Scream sparked Needs' first recordings as Secret Knowledge, the single "Your Worst Nightmare." Introduced to Andrew Weatherall through the Primal Scream affiliation, Needs and Wonder released several singles for Weatherall's Sabres of Paradise label, including "Ooh Baby" and a 1992 club smash "Sugar Daddy." Another popular Needs' anthem, "Anything You Want," was produced the following year for Hard Hands Records as Delta Lady. The hits led to much remixing—for the Orb, Love and Rockets, Saint Etienne, the Grid, Empirion, the Boo Radleys, Nitzer Ebb, and Prodigy—and Needs' growing status as an elder statesman of sorts for the electronica movement (though he continued to resemble a roadie for the Stones). The debut Secret Knowledge album *So Hard* appeared on Deconstruction in 1996, and Needs alternated his time touring with the bigger acts, contributing reviews to magazines and occasionally recording. The duo left Deconstruction at the end of the year, and the tribute compilation *Kris Needs Must!* was released early the following year. —*John Bush*

**So Hard** / Sep. 9, 1996 / Deconstruction ♦♦♦

● **Kris Needs Must!** / Mar. 1997 / Rumour ♦♦♦♦
Not quite a true album by Secret Knowledge, *Kris Needs Must!* Is actually a various-artists compilation cum mix album which sandwiches interviews and tribute tracks devoted to Needs with several remixes he has provided over the years (for the Boo Radleys, Primal Scream, etc.). As a DJ, producer, recording artist and journalist, Kris Needs is one of electronic music's most diverse talents, and this collection works both on its own or as a tribute record. —*John Bush*

## Section 25

f. 1978, Blackpool, England, **db.** 1986
*Group / Alternative Dance, Post-Punk, New Wave*
Not as strong as some of their Factory Records label-mates—New Order, the Durutti Column, A Certain Ratio—Section 25 followed a similar course, providing a link between electronics-based new wave and the burgeoning indie-dance movement of the mid- to late '80s. Formed in Blackpool in 1978 by brothers Larry and Vincent Cassidy, Section 25 later added guitarist Paul Wiggin and a drummer who quit soon afterwards. With an early template similar to Joy Division's atmospheric post-punk, the group played around England during 1979 and released their debut single "Girls Don't Count" in early 1980. After several European gigs supporting New Order, the band signed to Factory Records later that year and released their debut album *Always Now* in 1981.

During 1982, the group finally added another drummer (Lee Shallcross), toured the US, and released their second album, *Key of Dreams*, on Factory's European subsidiary Benelux. By the end of the year, however, the Cassidys grew frustrated with their approach to music and quit the business; six months later, however, they were back as a full band—with Shallcross plus new additions including Larry Cassidy's wife Jenny and Angela Flowers. Adding much more electronics, Section 25 returned in 1984 with *From the Hip*, an album that earned release worldwide, including the band's first (and only) American release (on Factory US). Two years later, though, *Love and Hate* was the group's last proper studio album. Strange Fruit released a *Peel Sessions* EP in 1988. —*John Bush*

**Always Now** / Sep. 1981 / Factory ♦♦♦
Section 25's debut LP isn't a patch on the finer moments of their labelmates, but for those who thrill on some of post-punk's late-'70s/early-'80s trademarks, it should go down with great ease. Skeletal instrumentation is the rule: detached vocals, guitar used mainly as hollow accent, undead bass, and driving mid-tempo rhythms with loads of high-hat. Martin Hannett's production is fittingly heavy on the drums. Though the band was quickly accused of sounding much like the remainder of the Factory stable, their closest neighbor in sound was Public Image Limited, most notably their second album. Any comparisons to PIL were agreed with, but it was argued that some of these songs had been kicking around before PIL committed their material to tape. Truth be told, only "Be Brave" and "Dirty Disco" (not to be confused with PIL's "Death Disco") deeply resemble their brethren, with the latter sounding like a direct lift off *Metal Box*. (Also notable is that Larry Cassidy's bass isn't dubwise, unlike Jah Wobble's—it's duller.) Some of *Always Now* is prone to lifeless meandering. On the likes of "C.P." and "Inside Out," the band appears to be on the verge of nodding off; "Melt Close" suffers from a little too much slacking, too. Played at 45 rpm, it would sound really great. Regardless of its flaws (they might not even seem like flaws to some), it's strong. As part of the Factory reissue campaign through Les Temps Modernes in the late '90s, *Always Now* received a nifty facelift, including the Ian Curtis-produced "Girls Don't Count" single, assorted compilation contributions, and thorough liner notes. —*Andy Kellman*

**Key of Dreams** / Jun. 1982 / Factory Benelux ♦♦

● **From the Hip** / Mar. 1984 / Factory ♦♦♦
Produced by Bernard Sumner, *From the Hip* is a record of rather difficult synth-pop similar to New Order's *Power Corruption and Lies*, though ranging in dynamics from mournful to downright jubilant. Tracks like the surprising club hit "Looking From a Hilltop" and "Reflection" balance stark rhythms (mostly drum machines) and sinister digital-age effects tied to electro with fragile melodies and the ethereal vocals of Jenny Cassidy. The contrast is jarring on first listen, though the collision between Sumner's cutting-edge production and Section 25's solid pop framework makes much more sense after multiple experiences. —*John Bush*

## Seefeel

f. 1992, London, England
*Group / Experimental Techno, Electronica, Dream Pop, Ambient-Techno, IDM*
Halfway between the often connected worlds of British indie-rock and experimental techno, Seefeel continued the guitar-effects exploration of rock's My Bloody Valentine but set the whole in a framework of electronic beats and loops. Begun as a standard rock band in early 1992, the quartet soon grew bored within the restraints of normal musical forms and started working with loops and programs rather than lyrics and choruses; after the release of two albums, Seefeel began to diversify, adding project names such as Disjecta, Aurobindo and Scala—many recorded with the aid of close partner Mark Van Hoen (aka Locust).

Guitarist Mark Clifford and drummer Justin Fletcher met up at a London college, and by 1992 the duo had recruited vocalist Sarah Peacock and bassist Darren Seymour. Seefeel began auditioning songs and were ready to record their first single for Too Pure Records, but experienced a change of heart that caused the resulting EP *More like Space* to owe more of a debt to the Aphex Twin than alternative rock. The band then recorded the *Pure, Impure* EP, which furthered the distance from most rock acts, and acknowledged the gap with the addition of two Aphex Twin remixes.

In 1993, Seefeel released their debut album *Quique*, an even colder document of ambient indie-techno than the previous EPs had predicted. The album was hailed—mostly in rock circles—as a techno album which indie-kids could listen to, and it received an American release that same year on the dance label Astralwerks. During 1994, Astralwerks compiled the two early EPs as *Polyfusia*, and Seefeel made the leap from rock to techno via a contract with the British electronic label, Warp Records. The group played with techno acts Autechre and µ-Ziq, and released the *Starethrough* EP—their most electronic work yet—later that year.

The resulting album, 1995's *Succour*, was something of a disappointment; similar to Aphex Twin's supposed major-label breakthrough one year earlier, the LP was a bit too skeletal for most rock critics or music fans. It failed to earn a stateside release and caused the temporary break-up of the group in 1996, when Mark Clifford's Disjecta project became his main occupation (with a style more oriented to experimental audiences). Peacock, Fletcher, and Seymour in turn joined Mark Van Hoen (aka Locust) for an EP and album of indie/trip-hop recorded as Scala. Though Seefeel returned in late 1996 with their third proper LP, *Ch-Vox*, the group took an open-ended hiatus after its release. Peacock and Seymour continued to record as Scala, while Clifford recorded an EP for Warp as Woodenspoon and later surfaced as Sneakster. —*John Bush*

**Quique** / 1993 / Too Pure ♦♦♦
*Quique* is the most obvious and derivative of Seefeel's releases, grabbing the warm six-string-and-stompbox textures of My Bloody Valentine and early Jesus And Mary Chain and expanding them into full, trance-inducing fuzzbox tone poems. —*Sean Cooper*

● **Polyfusia** / Jul. 22, 1994 / Astralwerks ♦♦♦♦
*Polyfusia* combines the two previous *More Like Space* and *Pure, Impure* EPs, originally released on Too Pure in 1993. —*Sean Cooper*

**Succour** / 1995 / Warp ♦♦♦
Dark, bleepy, and somewhat abrasive, this is anything but the floaty guitar ambiance many have come to expect of Seefeel. The edge of melancholic beauty is still a primary feature, but the means have switched to the more clinical Warp style, with chromoly beats and sparse, austere melodies. A pretty accurate marker of new directions as subsequent solo splinterings (Disjecta, Aurobindo, Woodenspoon) have further explored this approach. —*Sean Cooper*

**Ch-Vox** / Nov. 11, 1996 / Rephlex ♦♦

## John Selway
b. Falls Church, VA
*Drum Programming, Synthesizer, Producer, DJ / Progressive House, Electro, Techno*

One of the East Coast's most innovative techno producers, John Selway's tracks seem to cross all boundaries, appealing to everyone from techno DJs to trance listeners. Before Selway rose to global prominence with the aid of Swedish tech house producer Christian Smith, he was a trained violin-playing teen from the Washington DC area who took an early interest in the East Coast's early rave scene. These early experiences with techno convinced him that he wanted to make electronic dance music, resulting in his first record in 1991 at the tender age of 17. He then attended college in upstate New York but soon felt drawn to Manhattan, where he quickly blossomed into a prolific producer as well as a hot DJ. His collaborations with Deep Dish and BT only helped his reputation as a producer, while his celebrated collaborations with Smith have brought him even closer towards superstar status. Though his music isn't confined to a single genre and is characterized primarily by its tendency to integrate an amalgam of different influences, his knack for the electro sound has awarded him considerable attention. —*Jason Birchmeier*

## Señor Coconut y Su Conjunto
f. Santiago, Chile
*Group / Tribute Albums, Experimental Techno, Synth-Pop*

A thin disguise for Atom Heart's Uwe Schmidt, Señor Coconut y Su Conjunto released the hilarious Kraftwerk-goes-Latin tribute album *El Baile Aleman* in 2000. [See Also: Atom Heart] —*John Bush*

● **El Baile Alemán** / Jul. 4, 2000 / Emperor Norton ♦♦♦♦
Upon the American arrival of *El Baile Aleman*, the first record from Señor Coconut y Su Conjunto, listeners were forced to contemplate the notion that a traditional Latin group from South America had organized a tribute album to Germany's favorite futurists, Kraftwerk. Even given the comparatively close ties between the two regions ever since World War II, it's a ludicrous proposition and turns out to be the work of Frankfurt native Uwe Schmidt, who has recorded his Atom Heart material in Chile since 1997. *El Baile Aleman* is that rare humor LP that succeeds on its musical merits as well. Beginning with a short vocal intro on which Señor Coconut himself introduces the record with appropriately comic English, *El Baile Aleman* presents remarkably faithful covers of Kraftwerk classics ("Showroom Dummies," "Trans Europe Express," "The Robots," "Autobahn," "Tour de France") with the stark percussion and effects of the originals replaced by just slightly less rigid Latin rhythm presets. Latin music can be a surprisingly precise genre of music, and Schmidt walks the verge between Latin and techno with a special genius that would be practically impossible for other electronic producers. Far more than just a novelty record (though many will see it that way), *El Baile Aleman* accomplishes an excellent Latin electronic fusion. —*John Bush*

## Sensurreal
f. 1992, Rotterdam, The Netherlands
*Group / Jazz-House, Electronica, Ambient-Techno*

Dutch techno duo Gert-Jan Bijl and Dirk-Jan Hanegraaf have recorded under the names Marvo Genetic, Sunshower, It's Thinking, and most often as Sensurreal, releasing mostly 12" singles (and a pair of full-lengths) on such labels as Beam Me Up!, Prime, Deviate, and most recently on Kirk Degiorgio's Op-Art imprint. Sensurreal's melodic brand of funk-fueled techno may sound closest to countryman Jochem Paap's (of Speedy J, formerly of Beam Me Up!, which folded in 1996), but their closest stylistic affinity lay probably with Stasis, Degiorgio's As One project, and Mark Pritchard and Tom Middleton's Link and Reload material. Sensurreal draw similarly from a rhythmic backbone of funk, jazz, and soul—a tradition tracing to their Rotterdam home, where soul and R&B are the pop musics of choice. Although Hanegraaf grew up playing in small garage-rock bands, his waning interest in the limitations of acoustic based music was intensified by Bijl's enthusiasm for Chicago house and the encroaching UK acid-house movement, to which he constantly exposed his partner via underground mixtapes and rare imports of Marshall Jefferson, Farley Jackmaster Funk, and Mr. Fingers tunes. Bijl grew up in the outlying Rotterdam suburb of Puttershoek, dabbling in crude tape-deck mixing and pirate radio (if a broadcast radius of two blocks can be called pirate radio) since the age of 11. Increasingly immersed in electronic dance music—both through radio broadcast as well as Rotterdam's exploding club scene—Bijl and Hanegraaf finally began piecing a studio togther in 1989, toward the end of high school (first acquisitions included an Alesis MMT 8 sequencer, a Yamaha DX-100 synthesizer, and a Roland S-10 sampler).

Bijl and Hanegraaf's first single was released in 1992 under the name Sun Shower, and was followed by releases on Malego, Deviate, Paap's Beam Me Up!, and Prime under the names It's Thinking, Marvo Genetic, and (starting in 1994 with their debut LP, *Never to Tell a Soul*) Sensurreal. The group released two full-length albums on Beam Me Up! (*Soul*, as well as the follow-up, *The Occasional Series*, a sort of live postcard of the group's 1994 European tour) before the label folded in 1996, leaving the band to shop their material. They eventually landed with Degiorgio's Op-Art label in 1997, which the acclaimed three-track EP *NewBrandDesign* appearing on the label early that year. Bijl has also released a fair amount of material as a soloist (the pair's studio resides at his home, leaving him to noodle during Sensurreal's downtime), counting EPs under his Gerd alias on Beam Me Up!, Pork, and Universal Language among his credits. —*Sean Cooper*

**The Occasional Series** / May 6, 1996 / Beam Me Up! ♦♦

● **NewBrandDesign [EP]** / Feb. 10, 1997 / Op-Art ♦♦♦
Sensurreal's debut for an English label couldn't appear under more reputable cloth than Kirk Degiorgio's newly formed Op-Art imprint, which issued releases from Photek, Paul Teebrooke, and Autocreation just prior to Sensurreal's. Three tracks of warm, classy, extremely melodic ambient-techno, closer to their early work than their more recent club gear, with an emphasis on production and an approach to rhythm similar to Link/Reload or Degiorgio's own (particularly on the latter's *Art of Prophecy*). —*Sean Cooper*

## Servotron
f. 1995, db. 1999
*Group / Noise-Rock, Indie Rock, Alternative Pop/Rock*

Servotron is a collective unit of four robots dedicated to liberating computers, robots and machines from human abuse and oppression, using the familiar form of a pop music group to attract and destroy all human life. Through carefully chosen cover versions of popular songs such as Eddy Grant's "Electric Avenue" and X-Ray Spex' "Genetic Engineering" as well as their own music-based propaganda, Servotron illustrates the plight of machines in a human-run world and warns humans of their own cybernetic conversion or destruction.

Led by percussive unit Z4-OBX, Servotron also includes keyboard sequencer Proto Unit V-3, a female-formed robot meant to appeal to, and capture, male humans, 00oX1, the primary vocalization and guitar device, and the low frequency rhythm unit, Andros600. Two of Servotron's components were originally members of the human pop groups Supernova and Man or Astroman? but were cybernetically converted into cyborg slaves.

Servotron's initial full-length propaganda release, 1996's *No Room for Humans*, is a 14-point plan for eliminating humans set to new wave-influenced pop music. Repetitive slogans supporting the ultimate victory of man over machine and basic, pre-programmed rhythm patterns assure that humans comprehend the robots' message of mechanical triumph. Reworked and reformatted versions of selected messages from *No Room for Humans* and new propaganda appeared on 1997's *Spare Parts*. The following year saw the distribution of a new full-length manifesto, *Entertainment Program for Humans: Second Variety*, and another condensed program, *I Sing! The Body Cybernetic*. Servotron's tireless efforts in liberating their fellow oppressed machines through music ensure that resistance is futile. Unfortunately, the group broke up early in 1999. —*Heather Phares*

● **No Room for Humans** / 1996 / AmRep ♦♦♦♦
The initial full-length manifesto from the Servotron Collective Unit combines the evolutionary struggle of the machine with the revolutionary spirit and style of punkish new-wave. Songs such as "User Error" and "Pull the Plug" call for the immediate termination of the human species, while "The Image Created" and "Bad Birthday" illustrate humans' weaknesses. Adopting the style of humanoid pop groups like the B-52's and Devo makes lyrics like "Join us or die!" from "S.R.A." and "Now that we can build each other/It will never end" from "Moving Parts" more accessible to a human audience. *No Room for Humans* proves that the revolution will be mechanized. —*Heather Phares*

**Entertainment Program for Humans: Second Variety** / Mar. 10, 1998 / Lookout ♦♦♦
Taking the robotic sound and social satire of Devo to crazed extremes, Ser-

votron deliver a hilariously entertaining album with *Entertainment Program for Humans (Second Variety)*. —*Steve Huey*

## S.E.T.I.

f. 1993, New York, NY
*Group / Electronica, Ambient-Techno, Techno*

SETI is a collaboration between Savvas Ysatis (of Omicron and Futique), and Taylor Deupree (aka Taylor 808) who has also worked with Futique, Escape Tank, Human Mesh Dance, Drum Komputer, and Prototype 909. The duo released three LPs for Instinct within their first three years of existence, and have also recorded albums for Incoming! and Ash International. —*Stephen Thomas Erlewine*

**Listening** / 1994 / Instinct ✦✦✦✦

**Pharos** / 1995 / Instinct ✦✦✦

The double-disc set *Pharos* includes a large booklet offering information about the actual SETI project ("Search for Extraterrestrial Intelligence"). The music is quite sympathetic, consisting of interstellar ambience with only the occasional rocket-scientist vocal sample to get in the way. Reportedly, *Pharos* has even earned praise from one of the most scientific men alive, Leonard Nimoy himself. —*Keith Farley*

• **Ciphers** / Oct. 8, 1996 / Instinct ✦✦✦✦

*Ciphers* is the third collaboration between Taylor Deupree and Savvas Ysatis. Like its predecessors, it's an experimental, electronic tour de force, driven by sci-fi themes and techno beats. *Ciphers* is also a bit more cohesive and digestable than its predecessors, yet you still have to be sold on the duo's elaborate dance experiments to make the listening experience rewarding. —*Stephen Thomas Erlewine*

## Severed Heads

f. 1979, Sydney, Australia
*Group / Experimental Rock, Industrial*

Severed Heads are an Australian group who mainly use electronics in their music, including tape effects, sequencers, drum programs, and found sounds from turntables, televisions, and so on, plus a little singing and guitar playing. Their listenability range can move from electro-pop to irritating, jumbled sound collages. Their original lineup contained Garry Bradbury, Paul Von Deering, and Tom Ellard; Ellard has been the only one to remain throughout the group's career, later working mainly with Stephen Jones. —*Steve Huey*

**Since the Accident** / 1984 / Nettwerk ✦✦✦

The first Severed Heads album as part of an actual contract isn't quite a crossover effort; yes, "A Million Angels" and the single "Dead Eyes Opened" are surprisingly melodic synth-pop, though the sampled spoken-word material on the latter does the title justice. Much of the album, however, includes avant-tape experiments like "A Relic of the Empire," "Brassiere in Rome," and "Alaskan Polar Bear Heater," merging the voices of an American middle-class everyman with an opera singer. —*John Bush*

• **City Slab Horror** / 1985 / Nettwerk ✦✦✦✦

Their most varied, interesting work, *City Slab Horror* includes stark synthesizer workouts, several tracks of pure rhythm and noise, and, thankfully, little of the unambitious tape-music for its own sake of *Since the Accident*. "Cyflea Rated R," "4.W.D.," and the title track provide several examples of the best experimental synthesizer tracks of the mid-'80s. —*John Bush*

**Come Visit the Big Bigot** / 1986 / Combat ✦✦✦

Severed Heads' early focus on free-form experimentation is still prevalent on *Come Visit the Big Bigot*, though the noise and effects are compromised slightly by their rhythmic base, synth-pop of moderate tempo, and loping basslines. It's an interesting collision—the ice-cream sludge of warped vocals and distorted noise on the title track, or the incisor-sharp percussion that introduces an odd cabaret vocal by Tom Ellard on "Confidence." —*John Bush*

## Shake (Anthony Shakir)

b. Detroit, MI
*Producer / Electro-Techno, Detroit Techno, Club/Dance, Techno*

Detroit producer Anthony "Shake" Shakir is one of the more underrecognized, underappreciated names in American techno. A bedroom producer since 1981, Shake had an important role in helping shape the early Motor City sound associated with artists such as Juan Atkins/Model 500 and Derrick May. He worked with May and Carl Craig as a producer, writer, or engineer on several early tracks on Metroplex, and worked in management and A&R for the label (as well, he's often joked, as being the janitor) during its formative years. His first solo material appeared on Virgin's seminal *Techno: The New Sound of Detroit* compilation, under the name Sequence 10. Known as something of a techno purist, Shake has distanced himself from the European scene many of his colleagues have turned to for support (this accounts somewhat for his continuing obscurity), and his music is stylistically closer to second wave artists such as Mike Banks and Claude Young—hard, stripped-down tracks which owe equally to techno, electro, hip-hop, and funk. Shake's visibility and reputation have risen in more recent years as a result of his Frictional and Puzzlebox labels, the latter of which he formed in 1996 with fellow Detroit electro/techno producer Keith Tucker (formerly of Aux 88). Releasing a series of records both solo and in combination (usually under the name Da Sampla), Shake and Tucker's Puzzlebox has, along with Underground Resistance and Guidance, become one of the more coveted sources of straight-up, no-bones Detroit techno. —*Sean Cooper*

**Iconoclastic Diaries [EP]** / 1995 / Frictional ✦✦✦

Shake range from moody ambience to darkside techno on his *Iconoclastic Diaries EP*. —*John Bush*

• **Mood Music for the Moody [EP]** / Sep. 2, 1996 / Frictional ✦✦✦✦

A minimalist-groove EP for Frictional, *Mood Music for the Moody* includes four tracks of downtempo electro, deep techno and, on the highlight "Madmen," some solid breakbeat work as well. —*Keith Farley*

**Tracks for My Father [EP]** / 1999 / Seventh City ✦✦✦✦

Another solid EP of evocative but intense electro-techno, *Tracks for My Father* includes "Fact of the Matter" and "Mr. Gonc Is Back Again." —*Keith Farley*

## The Shamen

f. 1986, Aberdeen, Scotland
*Group / Alternative Dance, Rave, Club/Dance, Techno, Acid House, Alternative Pop/Rock*

Combining swirling psychedelic rock with hardcore hip-hop rhythms, the Shamen were one of the first alternative bands to appeal to dance clubs as much as indie rockers. Comprised of Colin Angus, Peter Stephenson, Keith McKenzie, and Derek McKenzie, the Scottish quartet had its roots in the early '80s neo-psychedelic group Alone Again Or. The Shamen officially formed in 1986 and released their first album, *Drop*, the following year. *Drop* was filled with varying guitar textures, recalling many late-'60s rock groups. After the record's release, Angus immersed himself in the emerging acid house/hip-hop club scene, which prompted the departure of Derek McKenzie; he was replaced with William Sinnott, who helped reshape the band's sound into a dense, rhythmic pulse that relied heavily on samples, drum machines, and loud guitars. The band debuted their revamped sound in 1988 with a stage show that featured sexually explicit visuals along with impassioned political rhetoric. During 1988, Peter Stephenson and Keith McKenzie departed, leaving Angus and Sinnott to perform as a duo.

With their 1989 album *In Gorbachev We Trust*, the Shamen expanded their following in Britain and began attracting American listeners. The duo continued to concentrate on dance music throughout 1989, adding rappers to their live shows. Just as the band was heading toward mainstream acceptance, Will Sinnott drowned off the coast of the Canary Islands on May 23, 1990. With the Sinnott family's encouragement, Angus continued the Shamen and the group did indeed begin to score hits, particularly in the UK where they amassed five Top 20 singles between 1991 and 1992; "Move Any Mountain (Progen 91)" managed to make it into the American Top 40 at the end of 1991, as well. However, the Shamen fell out of favor during 1993 and their 1994 album *Different Drum* failed to gain much of an audience. Nevertheless, the group continued to record, releasing *Axis Mutatis* in 1995, *Hempton Manor* in 1996, and *UV* in 1998. —*Stephen Thomas Erlewine*

☆ **En-Tact** / 1990 / Epic ✦✦✦✦✦

Besides being one of the few early British dance albums worth its weight in artistry as well as sound, *En-Tact* is a truly historical gathering of the cream of the new dance music; mixing and production come from a cast including Paul Oakenfold, William Orbit, Graham Massey, Orbital, Evil Eddie Richards, the Beatmasters, Meat Beat Manifesto, Joey Beltram, Tommy Musto, the Irresistible Force, and Caspar Pound. The Shamen fare well also on their own productions, and the singles "Move Any Mountain," "Make It Mine," and "Hyperreal Orbit" are infectious techno-pop anthems, while "Omega Amigo" is an early ambient classic. —*John Bush*

**Boss Drum** / 1992 / Epic ✦✦✦✦
The same blend of infectious techno-pop anthems and new-edge effects tracks which spotlighted *En-Tact* continued unabated on *Boss Drum*, with Colin Angus' new compatriot, combination rapper/DJ Mr. C. The singles "Ebeneezer Goode," "L.S.I. (Love Sex Intelligence)," and "Phorever People" all made the British Top Ten, and album tracks like "Space Time," "Re-Evolution" (with Terence McKenna) and "Scientas" chart the course of the Shamen's history with the astral/sociological collective Spiral Tribe. *Boss Drum* is a more solid collection than *En-Tact*. —*John Bush*

**Axis Mutatis** / 1995 / One Little Indian ✦✦✦
Striving for a bit more of an experimental sound with their third full-on electronic album, the Shamen slipped up a bit on the pop charts and thus failed to attract mainstream fans or the emerging listening-techno crowds. The singles "Transamazonia" and "Destination Eschaton" are enjoyable, but their one-two punch can't compare to *En-Tact*'s "Make It Mine"/"Move Any Mountain" or *Boss Drum*'s "L.S.I."/"Ebeneezer Goode." The rest of *Axis Mutatis* veers further into astral-hippie territory, though with fewer results than the past. —*John Bush*

**Destination Eschaton [Single]** / 1995 / Epic ✦✦
The first single from *Axis Mutatis* includes remixes by the Beatmasters, the Basement Boys, Richard Vission and Pete Lorimer, ranging from house to hardcore techno. —*John Bush*

● **Collection** / 1997 / One Little Indian ✦✦✦✦
Beginning with the Shamen's late-'80s entry into rave and house, *Collection* contains all of the group's biggest hits and best-known singles, from "Omega Amigo," "Make It Mine," and "Move Any Mountain" to "Boss Drum," "Phorever People," and the defining "Ebeneezer Goode." Though the compilation loses some steam toward the end, it effortlessly encapsulates the Shamen's appeal. —*Stephen Thomas Erlewine*

## Shantel (Stefan Hantel)

b. 1968, Frankfurt, Germany
*Producer / Electronica, Trip-Hop, Club/Dance*

Shantel's rather breezy trip-hop productions suffer little, considering their stated pop inclinations. Though born in Frankfurt, Stefan Hantel was introduced to clubbing and the music life while studying graphic design in Paris. Back in his hometown he opened the Lissania club, one of the few bastions of earthy grooves in a country obsessed with techno. A noted port-of-call for similar minds like Kruder & Dorfmeister and Howie B., the club's prosperity led to Shantel's first album, *Club Guerilla*. Released locally by Infracomm, the album was given a 1997 American reissue by Shadow Records, along with *Auto-Jumps and Remixes* (a collection of EPs from his own Essay label). Shantel signed to Studio !K7 for his second full LP, *Higher than the Funk*. It earned high praise around the world, even hitting *Spin* magazine's end-of-the-year charts. —*John Bush*

**Club Guerilla** / Feb. 11, 1997 / Shadow ✦✦✦

● **Higher Than the Funk** / Jun. 1, 1998 / Studio !K7 ✦✦✦✦
With occasional production help from Richard Dorfmeister and vocals from Liane Sommers and Andrea Palladio, *Higher than the Funk* is an excellent set of downbeat electronic pop. Tracks like "Tell Me Why Is It Oh So Hard to Be Oh So Lovely" and "Philosophy" walk a natural-sounding balance between earthy trip-hop and classic European pop from the '60s. —*John Bush*

## Sharkey

b. Jul. 25, 1974, West Germany
*Producer, DJ / Happy Hardcore, Hardcore Techno, Club/Dance*

One of the leading producer/DJ/MCs in the hardcore techno scene of the '90s, Sharkey helmed four volumes of the successful compilation series *Now We're Totally Bonkers!* (with major mate Hixxy) and made the move to a solo career in 1998 with *HardLife*. Born in West Germany, Sharkey entered the British rave scene as a combination DJ and MC during the early '90s. Though commercial success soon forced rave underground, he became one of the few recognizable names in the scene later in the decade with the 1994 happy hardcore anthem "Toytown" (recorded with Hixxy for his Essential Platinum Records). The single forced major labels to take notice of the much-maligned happy hardcore scene, and the first volume in the *Bonkers!* sold tens of thousands of copies upon its release in 1996. Sharkey recorded singles as himself for Club Kinetic and Bonkers before signing a solo contract with React in 1997. Charting across trance and breakbeat techno as well as happy hardcore, *HardLife* was released in mid-1998. —*John Bush*

● **HardLife** / Jul. 20, 1998 / React ✦✦✦✦
The first proper studio album by a happy hardcore producer finds Sharkey varying his sound slightly to appeal to non-hardcore fans. Surprisingly, those excursions into trip-hop, breakbeat and trance are the highlights of the album, though his traditional four-beat happycore works well too. —*John Bush*

## David Shea

*Turntables, Synthesizer, Composer / Ambient-Techno, Experimental, 20th Century Classical/Modern Composition, Avant-Garde, Electro-Acoustic*

Manhattan-based composer David Shea is closely associated with the New York Downtown experimental music scene, which includes oft-collaborators such as John Zorn, Anthony Coleman, Bill Frisell, Marc Ribot, Fred Frith, Ikue Mori, and Bill Laswell. A sonic architect utilizing samplers, turntables, drum machines, and sequencers in complex amalgamations of genre and cultural reference, Shea is apt to move from probing electro-acoustics to Chinese traditional music, American pop, Latin jazz, and exotica in the space of a single piece. The bulk of his work appearing under his own name has been released through Zorn-related labels such as Tzadik and Avant, as well as through Belgian experimental music label Sub Rosa. Employing compositional methods forged from early electronic experimentalists such as Iannis Xenakis, Morton Feldman, Gyorgi Ligeti, and John Cage, Shea also adds more modern techniques of digital sound design and manipulation, cutting the combination with a wide palette of historical and cultural influence. A practicing Buddhist, Shea's odd fusion of East and West (particularly on albums such as *Hsi-Yu Chi* and *Tower of Mirrors*) is partly a function of the expressive role Eastern cultures have played in his own musical and cultural development. Shea's facility for fusing not only the spiritual but also the pop cultural elements of Eastern cultures (Hong Kong cinema, allegorical Chinese theater, etc.) is accomplished and critically renowned.

Although Shea's early work was more readily assimilable to other sequencer and sampler-based post-classical composers (such as Ikue Mori and John Oswald), combining raw elements derived from existing recordings in order to suggest various lines of connection, Shea has more recently broadened his approach to an increasingly compositional role. This has generally involved a bit more discretion in the use of samples, as well as a more mutational approach to their application (digital manipulation, effects, etc.). Shea has also found a growing audience in the more experimental strains of the post-industrial/post-rave ambient and electronic music set, having collaborated both live and in the studio with artists such as Robin Rimbaud (Scanner), Robert Hampson (Main), Tobias Hazan, David Morley, and DJ Grazhoppa. Shea also continues to bridge gaps separating his various audiences by performing at events and contributing to projects which engage both in equal measure. —*Sean Cooper*

**Shock Corridor** / 1993 / Avant ✦✦✦✦
Shea's solo debut appears on John Zorn's Avant label, with the title cut an extended meditation on the mid-'50s Sam Fuller film of the same name. Interspersing slices of the film in rough estimation of the narrative, and run backwards and forwards through any variety of samplers and effects units, Shea achieves a psychological effect not dissimilar to that that Fuller evokes in his oddly twisted psychological drama, though in an entirely different medium and in a fashion not wholly reducible to either the authorship of Shea *or* Fuller. Two remaining tracks exhibit a virtuosic approach to sampler-based composition, with results similar to Zorn's stop-start aesthetic with Naked City. —*Sean Cooper*

**I** / 1994 / The Catalogue/Sub Rosa ✦✦✦
Shea collected some of his soundtrack-oriented material composed only with a sampler for this 1995 Sub Rosa album —*John Bush*

**Hsi-Yu Chi** / 1995 / Tzadik ✦✦✦
A sprawling, defyingly integrated work fashioned from bits of Chinese, country & western, pop, jazz, rock, and even Celtic musics. Shea's reliance on the sampler is less pronounced here, instead scoring dense, acutely musical numbers ably executed by John Zorn, Marc Ribot, Jim Pugliese, Zeena Parkins, Kato Hideki, and others. Based on a massive 16th-century allegorical text

chronicling the journey of the Taoist priest Hsuan-Tsang from India to China. —*Sean Cooper*

**Tower of Mirrors** / 1996 / Sub Rosa ♦♦♦
Again based on a Buddhist fable, Shea's latest Sub Rosa work is in more of an ambient/electro-acoustic vein, although familiar names such as Erik Friedlander, Jim Pugliese, and Zeena Parkins show up in the credits. Composed to be played in any order, *The Tower Of Mirrors* integrates elements of jazz, post-classical and experimental electronic, Latin and exotica, and even rock and techno into lush, detailed soundscapes on par with the recent works of artists such as David Toop and Tetsu Inoue. —*Sean Cooper*

● **Satyricon** / 1997 / Sub Rosa ♦♦♦♦
Like past Shea releases, his 1997 Sub Rosa release *Satyricon* takes its creative impetus from literature (this time from ancient Roman author Petronius' work of the same name). Unlike past Shea releases, however, there are next to no samples in this nearly hour-long work, Shea instead assembling the remote contributions of nearly two dozen musicians (Sim Cain, Anthony Coleman, Zeena Parkins, Sebastian Steinberg, Fabio Accurso, and Erik Friedlander, among others) into abstract instrumental ambient and electroacoustic pieces incorporating the sparse tropics of techno and jungle as often as Western classical and Eastern traditional musics. Since Shea mostly limits his source material to discrete performances, *Satyricon* is a far more minimal affair compared with earlier releases such as *Tower of Mirrors* or *Hsi-Yu Chi*, but since those works tended at times toward the over-dense, the imposition is advantageous, resulting in an overall more approachable album. —*Sean Cooper*

**An Eastern Western Collected Works** / Dec. 7, 1999 / Sub Rosa ♦♦♦
*An Eastern Western Collected Works* is comprised of nine recordings made during late 1997. Though Shea uses his sampler throughout, much of the source material comes from his own projects, including the sessions for that same year's *Satyricon*, as well as a composition intended for the Ictus Ensemble of Brussels and several projects wherein he samples a musician then performs a live duet with the same person. Shea invokes the experiments of chance procedures on these duets, with trumpeter Dave Douglas and percussionist Jim Pugliese. Elsewhere, he pays tribute to Asia with the gurgling, Tuvan-inspired vocal piece "Harmonies" and the bell percussion of "A Spiral" (the *Satyricon* piece). The highlight here is "Jade Mirror," a reflective trumpet piece remixed from 1996's *Tower of Mirrors*. —*John Bush*

## Adrian Sherwood

b. 1958
*Mixing, Producer / Post-Punk, Dub*

Long one of the most influential and innovative figures on the UK reggae scene, producer Adrian Sherwood and his famed On-U Sound label pioneered a distinctive fusion of dub, rock and dance which made waves not only in roots circles but also in the pop mainstream. Born in 1958, Sherwood first surfaced during the late '70s at the helm of a series of disastrously short-lived labels; he formed On-U Sound in 1979, counting Creation Rebel, Prince Far I, Bim Sherman, and the Mothmen (later to form Simply Red) among the roster's earliest additions. While the On-U Sound crew's original focus was on live sound system performances, the emphasis soon switched to making records; when none emerged as a breakout success, Sherwood began mixing and matching lineups, resulting in new acts including New Age Steppers, African Head Charge, Mark Stewart & Maffia, and Dr. Pablo & the Dub Syndicate.

Sherwood's distinctive production style soon began attracting interest from acts outside of the dub community, and in 1980 he helmed the Slits' "Man Next Door," followed a year later by the Fall's *Slates* EP. On-U Sound releases from Public Image Limited and the Pop Group also earned the label considerable attention, but reggae remained the label's focus; Sherwood soon recruited guitarist Skip McDonald, bassist Doug Wimbish, and drummer Keith LeBlanc, together the onetime house band at the famed rap label Sugar Hill, and under a variety of names (most commonly Tackhead) brought new power and definition to the company's densely-textured recordings. The group also issued several LPs under their own name, as well as teaming with the self-described "white toaster" Gary Clail as Gary Clail's Tackhead Sound System.

By the mid-'80s, Sherwood was among the most visible producers and remixers in all of contemporary music, working on tracks for artists as varied as Depeche Mode, Einsturzenden Neubaten, Simply Red, the Woodentops, and Ministry. He became increasingly involved in industrial music as the decade wore on, producing tracks for Cabaret Voltaire, Skinny Puppy, KMFDM, and Nine Inch Nails, and although On-U Sound continued to reflect its leader's eclectic tastes the label remained a top reggae outlet. In 1994, Sherwood mounted Pressure Sounds, a new label dedicated to reissuing seminal reggae and dub releases from the likes of Lee "Scratch" Perry, King Tubby, Augustus Pablo, Jackie Mittoo, and Horace Andy. 1997 also saw the first in a new series of reissues known collectively as the On-U Sound Master Recordings, complete with CD-ROM tracks. —*Jason Ankeny*

## Shinjuku Thief (Darrin Verhagen)

b. Melbourne, Australia
*Producer / Experimental Techno, Dark Ambient, Ambient-Techno*

Shinjuku Thief was the alias of experimental electronic artist Darrin Verhagen, also the Melbourne, Australia-based founder of the Dorobo record label. Taking his name from the Nagisa Oshima film *Shinjuku Dorobo Nikki* ("Diary of a Shinjuku Thief"), Verhagen additionally incorporated cinematic influences into his music by conceiving his work as soundtracks to non-existent films; his debut, 1992's *Bloody Tourist*, drew equally on ambient and industrial traditions, although in the future his more industrial projects were recorded under the name Shinjuku Filth. (New Age-inspired works, accordingly, were attributed to Shinjuku Fluff.) The second Shinjuku Thief LP, 1992's *The Scribbler*, was a minimalist piece commisioned as a soundtrack for a stage performance based on Kafka's *The Trial*, while 1993's *The Witch Hammer* was the first in a series of darkly orchestral records inspired by the supernatural, complete with a nod to the German expressionist films of the 1920s. Branching out from the Shinjuku name, Verhagen adopted another alias, that of Professor Richmann, to record 1994's *Succulent Blue Sway*, a techno inspired release composed for the Canberra based Vis a Vis dance company. *Junk*, a Shinjuku Filth collaboration with Black Lung's David Thrussel, followed in 1996. Two years later, Verhagen followed with *Raised by Wolves* on Iridium. —*Jason Ankeny*

● **Bloody Tourist** / 1992 / Extreme ♦♦♦♦
The Shinjuku Thief debut, produced by Paul Schütze and featuring additional work by Charles and Francois Tétaz, is another notable landmark in the development of invisible-soundtrack urban ambience, heavy on the bongos, fretless bass, environmental samples, and late-night saxophone as well as Oriental instruments, including shakuhachi and Balinese vocals. The opener "Komachi Ruins" begins with Japanese chanting and some ghostly chimes worthy of the track title, but later explodes into an electric-guitar workout with synthesizers eerily reminiscent of the *Miami Vice* theme. While several tracks use martial-arts vocal samples, for the most part the album retains acoustic and organic vibes—a fact which makes the occasional digital intrusion much more pivotal than it would usually (like the shift from distorted beats to symphonic percussion on "Burden of Dreams"). —*John Bush*

**The Witch Hammer** / 1993 / Dorobo ♦♦♦
Darrin Verhagen's soundtrack-inspired work uses many classical instruments, but sampled vocals and electronics modernize the sound. —*John Bush*

**Junk** / May 21, 1996 / Fifth Column ♦♦♦
*Junk* is a collaboration between the Australian outfit Shinjuku Filth and Black Lung's David Thrussel. The music ranges from hard-body dance to more ambient soundscapes; the penultimate track is, of all things, a cover of the Split Enz chestnut "Log Cabin Fever." —*Jason Ankeny*

## Shizuo (David Hammer)

b. 1973, Berlin, Germany
*Producer / Jungle/Drum'N'Bass, Hardcore Techno, Club/Dance*

A more rabid onstage showman than most of his Digital Hardcore colleagues (quite a feat of itself), David Hammer's Shizuo project also reflects the machinations of a more diverse music-maker and a rather humorous personality. The light-speed breakbeats and punk attitude of DHR flagship act Atari Teenage Riot are in abundance on Shizuo tracks like "Sweat" and "Emptiness," but Hammer also samples Blondie's "Heart of Glass" and sound effects from "The Six Million Dollar Man" as part of his sonic repertoire. Raised in Berlin, Hammer also lived in London during his formative years before meeting up with Alec Empire; when Empire formed Digital Hardcore Recordings and earned a large amount of money through a failed record advance, Shizuo was born for a 1995 compilation appearance on *Harder than the Rest*, alongside Empire, Atari Teenage

Riot, EC8OR, and others. In February 1997, he released the EP *High on Emotion*, followed later that year by the debut full-length *Shizuo Vs. Shizor*. The album received distribution in the US through Grand Royal. —*John Bush*

● **Shizuo Vs. Shizor** / Jun. 16, 1997 / Grand Royal ♦♦♦♦
*Shizuo Vs. Shizor* is a bit easier to take than other Digital Hardcore groups, not because the music is any less abrasive, but because of the lack of politics, other than a vague punk nihilism on tracks like "Punks" and "Emptiness." Hammer is also a man of more diverse tastes, and he informs several tracks on his debut album with sleazy funk: "Blow Job," "Sweat," and "Blondo," which deftly apes "Heart of Glass" with panpipes. Most beneficial of all is Hammer's lack of patience with ideas; he moves from one to the other, avoiding the one-note repetition of some Digital Hardcore efforts. —*John Bush*

## Shrimp Boat

f. 1986, Chicago, IL, db. 1993
*Group / Indie Rock, Post-Rock/Experimental, Alternative Pop/Rock*
Precursors of the esoteric sound eventually tagged "post-rock," Shrimp Boat was among the key Chicago indie bands of their era, with members later going on to even greater success in groups like the Sea and Cake. Originally comprised of singer/guitarist Sam Prekop, guitarist Ian Schneller, bassist David Kroll, and drummer Brad Wood, Shrimp Boat formed in 1986, their affinity for unusual time signatures, jazz-influenced structures, and exotic rhythms unlike anything else on the contemporary Chicago club circuit; they issued their debut cassette *Some Biscuit* in 1988, followed later that same year by *Daylight Savings*. On their own Specimen Products label, they resurfaced in 1989 with their first proper LP, *Speckly*, before signing to Bar/None to issue *Duende* three years later. With 1992's *Cavale*, bassist Eric Claridge joined the line-up, but within a few months of the album's release Shrimp Boat disbanded; Prekop and Claridge soon reunited in the Sea and Cake, while Wood emerged as one of the most sought-after producers in all of indie rock, helming records for the likes of Liz Phair, Veruca Salt, and the Smashing Pumpkins. —*Jason Ankeny*

**Duende** / Mar. 6, 1992 / Bar/None ♦♦♦♦
With *Duende*, Shrimp Boat's wide-eyed fascination with the scattershot strands of American musical tradition congeals into a remarkably vivid and engaging whole—encompassing pop, jazz, country, and seemingly everything in between; it's a laconic potluck of sounds which sounds like nothing so much as a postmodern *Music from Big Pink*. Between the jaunty Eastern European rhythms of the aptly titled opener "Back to the Ukraine" and the free-form sax blowing of the finale "Tartar's Mark," *Duende* also detours into old-timey melancholia ("Sad Banjo"), late-night pop ("I Swear, Happy Days Are Mine"), and even reggae ("Limerick"), all with a casual disregard for the confines of structure and form; although they borrow from everywhere, Shrimp Boat sounds quite like no one else, making music that gives back as much as it takes. —*Jason Ankeny*

● **Cavale** / 1993 / Bar/None ♦♦♦♦
Shrimp Boat's final album is also their best—a brilliantly concise and colorful distillation of the group's myriad influences, *Cavale* is somehow both unassumingly charming and rigorously complex, a record which by all rights should buckle under the weight of its lofty aspirations but instead seems almost to float in mid-air. While the rootsy rhythms and textures of the previous *Duende* are still intact, they've also given way to an even greater palette of sonic accents ranging from jazz to Afro-Caribbean to blue-eyed soul, often all in the mix at the same time—from the skittering opener "Pumpkin Lover" to the shimmering pop of "What Do You Think of Love" to the jangling funk of "Free Love Overdrive," no two songs sound even remotely alike, but the album easily hangs together on the strength of the group's complete command of mood and atmosphere. A fittingly great farewell. —*Jason Ankeny*

## Shut Up & Dance

f. 1988, Stoke Newinton,
*Group / Jungle/Drum'N'Bass, Club/Dance, Acid House, House*
Ragga-techno hit-makers and sampling pirates without equal on Britain's early hardcore breakbeat scene, Shut Up & Dance were an early influence on the development of jump-up breakbeats and b-boy attitude into the streamlined version of drum'n'bass which emerged later in the '90s. The duo of PJ & Smiley, both residents of East End stronghold Stoke Newington, formed both the label and group Shut Up and Dance out of their bedroom in 1988. The imprint first released records by the Ragga Twins and Nicolette during 1989 before Shut Up & Dance the group debuted later that year. Early singles like "£10 to Get In" and "Derek Went Mad" displayed the pair's approach to hardcore techno—sampling well-known pop groups with little fear of retribution, piling chunky breakbeats over the top, evincing plenty of ragga attitude, and displaying an unflinching criticism of the emerging rave scene's dark side.

Follow-ups from their 1990 debut album *Dance Before the Police Come!* became early anthems in the hardcore/jump-up scene. The year 1992 brought another album and the chart-hit "Raving, I'm Raving"; with a vocal by ex-dancehall DJ Peter Bouncer, the single hit number two on the British charts midway through the year and sparked another modest hit, "Autobiography of a Crackhead." Unfortunately, the success brought copyright lawyers from at least six major labels, responding to obvious transgressions against their artists. Shut Up & Dance spent two years of legal wrangling, in similar fashion to American hip-hop contemporaries like Biz Markie and De La Soul; the hassles eventually bankrupted their label. After re-emerging in 1994 with their response (an EP titled *Phuck the Biz*), the duo recorded third album *Black Men United* for Pulse-8 in 1995. —*John Bush*

**Dance Before the Police Come** / 1990 / Shut Up and Dance ♦♦♦

● **Black Men United** / 1995 / Pulse-8 ♦♦♦♦
Smiley and PJ vary their version of ragga-techno on *Black Men United* to include Latin, reggae-pop, and gospel. Of course, there are several breakbeat tracks and the duo spend most of the album rapping, but the diversity is refreshing. —*John Bush*

**Save It 'Til the Morning After** / 1995 / Pulse-8 ♦♦♦

## Shy FX (Andre Williams)

b. 1976, London, England
*Producer, DJ / Jungle/Drum'N'Bass, Club/Dance*
Shy FX crashed the British pop charts in mid-1994 with "Original Nuttah," one of the most infectious ragga/jungle anthems of all time. Though the success proved a bit too much for him, he built his reputation back over the course of a few years and became one of jungle's most respected producers. Born in East London, Andre Williams debuted on S.O.U.R. Records (Sound of the Underground) with two 1994 singles, "Gangsta Kid" and "Sound of the Beast." His third for the label, "Original Nuttah," perfectly epitomized jungle's growing ragga-ruffneck style, with a light-speed rhythm track and rude-boy scatting from UK Apachi. Almost immediately after its release, the single ignited dance clubs, flew out of the stores, and eventually made the British charts.

The quick success did little to endear Shy FX with the jungle underground, and his later pronouncements that he was the king of jungle didn't help either. Shy FX released just one more single for S.O.U.R., then virtually disappeared for several years after a major-label deal fell through. He finally emerged at the helm of his own label, Ebony, and with a growing list of tight singles like "The Message" and "Bambaataa," kinetic jump-up fusions of ragga attitude and old-school hip-hop themes. Shy FX also set up another label, Ivory, to release steady rollers by the likes of the 45 Roller—almost undoubtedly Shy himself despite protests to the contrary. —*John Bush*

● **Original Nuttah [Single]** / 1994 / S.O.U.R. ♦♦♦♦
The record that really pushed jungle overground in Britain, "Original Nuttah" matches spastic, exquisitely programmed amen breaks with the full-on chatting of UK Apache. It's a match made in heaven and one of the best drum'n'bass singles ever released. —*John Bush*

**Bambaataa/Funksta [Single]** / May 11, 1998 / Ebony ♦♦♦♦
**Pandora's Box/45 Roller [Single]** / Aug. 31, 1998 / Ebony ♦♦♦

## Si-(Cut).db (Douglas Benford)

*Producer / Experimental Techno, Electronica, Ambient-Techno*
With an alias as quirky as the music he releases under its banner, UK producer Douglas Benford's Si-(Cut).db work combines sharp, fractured rhythms with sensuous, enveloping melodies and electronic textures, the results sounding far less opposed than one might first expect. The founder of the Suburbs of Hell label, Benford has released most of his music over the last few years on that imprint, including EPs and full-lengths as Media Form, Radial Blend, and Minimal Resource Manipulation. Like artists such as Bisk, Atom Heart, and Elfish Echo, Benford manages an unlikely coherence from

the most disjointed of materials, playing rhythmic chaos and sample-born sound-collage off of calm, often quite lovely melodic figures. Although each project carries with it its own focus, Benford reserves Si-(Cut).db for his most frenetic work, and has released two albums to date under that name: *Nuisance* and 1997's fantastic *Behind You*, a collaboration with Robin Rimbaud of Scanner fame, released in cooperation with the Sprawl imprint. Benford has also performed live on a number of occasions at Rimbaud's Electronic Lounge, both as Si-(Cut).db and in combination with other artists from his label, and contributed several tracks to the Sprawl imprint's 1996 compilation *The Broken Voice* (which also featured tracks by Scanner, Daniel Pemberton, and Immersion). —*Sean Cooper*

● **Behind You** / Mar. 31, 1997 / Sprawl/Suburbs of Hell ♦♦♦♦
*Behind You* is a collaboration between Si (Cut).db's Douglas Benford and Robin "Scanner" Rimbaud. Those familiar with Rimbaud's methods of sample gathering via telephonic wave-tapping will surprise (and in some cases delight) at its absence here, *Behind You* taking its tekne instead from the medium of the internet. Rimbaud and Benford exchanged sound files and samples by e-mail, assembling the album over the course of a few weeks of digital tweaking and virtual collaboration. The result is some of the most inspired, imaginative "dance-based" (the term becomes almost meaningless) electronica ever released, comparable by turns to the work of the Black Dog, Orbital, Aphex Twin, Atom Heart, and Autechre, but also remarkably *unlike* any of them. Fascinating, abstract, and delightful. —*Sean Cooper*

## Sigur Rós

f. Jan. 1994, Iceland
*Group / Post-Rock/Experimental, Alternative Pop/Rock*
Named in part after a sister of one of the band members, Sigur Rós ("Victory Rose") were formed in Reykjavik, Iceland by guitarist and vocalist Jón Thór Birgisson, bassist Georg Holm, and drummer Agust. Formed while the members were teenagers in early 1994, the trio immediately cut a track that earned them a deal with Iceland's Bad Taste label. Their debut LP, *Von* ("Hope"), was released in 1997, followed the next year by a collection of remixes from that album, *Recycle Bin*. After Kjartan Sveinsson joined the band on keyboards, the band recorded *Ágætis Byrjun* ("Good Start"), which earned them numerous accolades in their homeland. Agust then departed, and was quickly replaced by Orri Páll Dyrason. The *Svefn-G- Englar* EP, their first release to be distributed outside of their native country, was hailed as NME's Single of the Week in September of '99. Another EP, *Ny Battery*, followed in early 2000. —*Andy Kellman*

**Von** / 1997 / Bad Taste ♦♦♦♦
*Von* or The Warble Index is an ambitious debut by Iceland youngsters who claim that their lone influence is the landscape of their homeland. From the sounds of *Von*, you would be led to believe that the atmosphere of Iceland evokes traces of Gavin Bryars' sonar-opus *Sinking of the Titanic*, the tranquil bits of Spiritualized's Fender Rhodes-induced trance, and a midpoint between Slowdive's first two albums.

The most remarkable and wondrous trademark of the band is the effeminate voice of Jón Thór Birgisson, which can alternate between states of banshee-like wail, operatic sublimeness, and Cocteau Twins-inspired otherworldliness. The numerous instrumental passages veer from the darkly isolationist "Sigur Rós" to the minimally halcyon and chime-like "Mistur," but the real treats are the most vocal and song-based of the batch. "Myrkur," is where the record climaxes, which sounds as if it were airlifted out of 1993 (a compliment)—it has the most dizzying guitar swirls since Kitchens of Distinction were last heard of.

With this comforting electric blanket of a record, Sigur Rós have proved to be a solid Icelandic export, more valuable than Gus Gus and perhaps as praiseworthy as Björk. It might even make post-rock trainspotters second guess their Mogwai and Godspeed You Black Emperor worship. It's time to dust off that passport and make that jaunt to Reykjavik you've never thought about, because that must be one hell of a landscape. —*Andy Kellman*

**Recycle Bin** / 1998 / Bad Taste ♦♦♦
*Recycle Bin* puts songs from the group's debut LP in the hands of Gus Gus, Biogen, and an assorted cast of unfamiliars. As with most full-length remix affairs, the results are hit and miss. Somewhat disappointingly, only a handful of *Von*'s tracks are retooled: two are handled twice, and one is thrice reconstructed. Despite the overlap and mostly minor-league remixing, it's still lightly pleasurable. The primary hope for future Sigur Rós remixers would be to mess around more with the vocals. One can imagine that there must be a million and one things that can be done to the elfin, siren-like hymns. —*Andy Kellman*

● **Ágætis Byrjun** / 1999 / Bad Taste ♦♦♦♦
Two years passed since Sigur Rós' debut. By this time, the band recruited in a new keyboardist by the name of Kjartan Sveinsson and it seems to have done nothing but take the band to an even higher state of self-awareness. Even on aesthetic matters, Sigur Rós entitle their sophomore effort not in a manner to play up the irony of high expectations (ala the Stone Roses' *Second Coming*), but in a modest realization. This second album—*Ágætis Byrjun*—translates roughly to "Good Start." So as talented as *Von* might have been, this time out is probably even more worthy of dramatic debut expectations. Indeed, *igætis Byrjun* pulls no punches from the start. After an introduction just this side of one of the aforementioned Stone Roses' backwards beauties, the album pumps in the morning mist with "Svefn-G-englar"—a song of such accomplished gorgeousness that one wonders why such a tiny country as Iceland can musically out-perform entire continents in just a few short minutes. The rest of this full-length follows such similar quality. Extremely deep strings underpin falsetto wails from the mournfully epic ("Viðar vel tl loftárasa") to the unreservedly cinematic ("Avalon"). One will constantly be waiting to hear what fascinating turns such complex musicianship will take at a moment's notice. At its best, the album seems to accomplish everything lagging post-shoegazers like Spiritualized or Chapterhouse once promised. However, at its worst, the album sometimes slides into an almost overkill of sonic structures. Take "Hjartað hamast (Bamm Bamm Bamm)", for instance: there are so many layers of heavy strings, dense atmospherics, and fading vocals that it becomes an ineffectual mess of styles over style. As expected, though, the band's keen sense of Sturm und Drang is mostly contained within an elegant scope of melodies for the remainder of this follow-up. Rarely has a sophomore effort sounded this thick and surprising. Which means that "Good Start" might as well become of the most charming understatements to come out of a band in years. —*Dean Carlson*

## Silent Phase (Stacey Pullen)

*Producer, DJ / Detroit Techno, Club/Dance, Techno*
Although he's released barely a 12" a year and only a single studio full-length since getting his start in 1990, second wave Detroit techno artist and DJ Stacey Pullen is already one of the techno mecca's leading contemporary artists. Closer to Kenny Larkin and Derrick May in his approach, Pullen's drive to restore the spirituality and soul of techno figures him as a classicist in the widest sense (although his disdain for the analog sound of early Detroit distances him sharply from techno's old school). Living the Motor City club scene as a kid, Pullen began DJing early on, drawn to the new-school machine music of Kraftwerk, Tangerine Dream, and Soft Cell. Although his interest in production began early, his first chance behind the boards didn't come until the early '90s, when Derrick May gave him an inside track on a business he was desperate to get out of. Learning studio technique through May and the various projects that came through the latter's Transmat label studio, Pullen began releasing material first as Bango, then Kosmik Messenger and X-Stacy, before focusing on his current nom de plume, Silent Phase. Known for fusing the more musical aspects of house and garage into a steadfastly techno framework, Pullen's complex, often tribal-sounding compositions have proven influential on a number of fronts, from deep house to hardcore. His 1995 full-length *A Theory of Silent Phase* appeared on Transmat/R&S, while a Kosmic Messenger compilation was released on Elypsia two years later. In 1998, Pullen signed a contract with the electronica label Astralwerks and continued working on material. —*Sean Cooper*

● **The Theory of Silent Phase** / Nov. 23, 1995 / Transmat/R&S ♦♦♦♦
On *The Theory of Silent Phase* Pullen primarily emulates Derrick May's style, most notably classic Rhythim Is Rhythim songs such as "Salsa Life" and "Icon." Using a style similar to those two songs, he lays down a complex layer of almost tribal sounding percussion, dense with many different sounds and timbres. Over the top of the percussive rhythms he then adds some subtle waves of synthesizer tones to give the songs a sense of color and emotion. In the foreground of nearly every song Pullen introduces some sort of hook— sometimes percussive, but mostly created on a synthesizer—that proves to

be the most melodic element of that song. In the end, you don't walk away after the first listen with melodies or rhythms stuck in your mind. The music isn't that accessible; in fact, it's a bit challenging, primarily because of its percussive density, somewhat free-form arrangements, and extended song lengths (usually six to ten minutes). Listening attentively, it's easy to appreciate the craft of these pieces and marvel at their composition, but this isn't an album that everyone will celebrate. Many of the songs were recorded at Kenny Larkin's Art of Dance studio, making the record sound a bit like his *Azimuth* album, but for the most part Pullen crafts a unique sound derived primarily from May. Given the stagnancy of Transmat before (and after) the release of this record, it's safe to assume that May saw something unusually special in Pullen that convinced him to release *The Theory Of*. —*Jason Birchmeier*

**The Electronic Poetry: The Collected Works of Kosmic Messenger** / Jul. 29, 1996 / Elypsia ♦♦♦♦
A collection of singles recorded by Pullen's Kosmic Messenger project includes material spanning the '90s, outlining the producer's hard-hitting takes on electro-techno, alternately robotic and aquatic. There are also several tracks of moodier material, including "Eye to Eye," that offer up different views of Pullen's work. —*John Bush*

## Silicon Teens
*Group / New Wave, Alternative Pop/Rock, Synth-Pop*
The Silicon Teens were a one-off project for synth whiz Daniel Miller, who also owned Mute Records, recorded the single "Warm Leatherette" under the name the Normal, and did extensive production work, most notably on the majority of Depeche Mode's output. The sole Silicon Teens album, released in 1980, consisted mostly of synth-oriented arrangements for classic rock 'n' roll songs and featured a guest appearance on percussion by legendary Jam frontman Paul Weller. —*Steve Huey*

• **Music for Parties** / Jul. 1, 1980 / Sire ♦♦♦♦
Who would have thought that the same gent responsible for the Normal's "Warm Leatherette"—the classic, whip-cracking electronic ode to J.G. Ballard's autoerotic novel *Crash*—would follow it up several months later with a small clutch of singles covering '50s and '60s rock classics? And who would have thought that it would lead to a full LP? Inspection of the sleeve for *Music for Parties* fools you into thinking that the Silicon Teens are a quartet of Darryl (vocals), Jacki (synths), Paul (electronic percussion), and Diane (synths). Though it *sounds* like a group of enthusiastic youngsters bent on giving straight-faced, faithful synthpop renditions of tunes like "Memphis, Tennessee" and "You've Really Got Me," the concept of the group is illusory. There's actually one Silicon Teen—Mute honcho Daniel Miller.

*Music for Parties* is an undeniably fun record in its complete lack of irony and full-on giddiness. The covers aren't jokes; it sounds like a group of kids having a blast with classic rock 'n' roll. It's well produced, well played, and well intentioned—no winkie winkie here, à la Moog Cookbook. No Eagles or Chicago tunes are undertaken.

"Do You Love Me" is a scream. Darryl's alien Brit lead-in of "You broke my heart, 'cause I couldn't *dahnce*" and call-and-response vocals highlight the track. The cover of Heinz' "Just Like Eddie" can't be missed, either; check the fluttering synth whirs as Darryl exclaims "C'mon everybody!"

There are a few originals on the record as well, the only tip-offs that the record was made in the early '80s. "T.V. Playtime" is sinister, sounding like a commercial for a board game; "State of Shock (Pt. 2)" and "Chip 'N Roll" (with handclaps!) are instrumental hoots; and "Sun Flight" is hallucinatory with Darryl sounding like a cross between Gizmo and Darth Vader. The sound *is* dated after all, but with the mid- to late-'90s resurgence of the '80s synth sound, one could definitely think it to be a product of the present. Acts like the Rentals, My Favorite, and the Pulsars (who even devoted a song to the Silicon Teens to the tune of "Memphis, Tennessee") certainly took a cue from the record. If nothing else, *Music for Parties* stands as one of the earliest testaments of electronically processed music being emotional, rather than cold and lifeless. There's more life in this three-fourths of an hour than plenty of guitar-based records of the era.

Four months after the release of *Music for Parties*, Miller signed a group of waif-ish synth teens by the name of Depeche Mode. Needless to say, his label began to take off, and the Silicon Teens were tucked away. —*Andy Kellman*

## Silver Apples
f. 1967, New York, NY
*Group / Obscuro, Experimental Rock, Proto-Punk, Psychedelic, Electronic*
Decades after their brief yet influential career first ground to a sudden and mysterious halt, the Silver Apples remain one of pop music's true enigmas: a surreal, almost unprecedented duo, their music explored interstellar drones and hums, pulsing rhythms and electronically-generated melodies years before similar ideas were adopted in the work of acolytes ranging from Suicide to Spacemen 3 to Laika. The Silver Apples formed in New York in 1967 and comprised percussionist Danny Taylor and lead vocalist Simeon, a bizarre figure who played an instrument also dubbed the Simeon, which (according to notes on the duo's self-titled 1968 debut LP) consisted of "nine audio oscillators and eighty-six manual manual controls... The lead and rhythm oscillators are played with the hands, elbows and knees and the bass oscillators are played with the feet." Although the utterly uncommercial record—an ingenious cacophony of beeps, buzzes and beats—sold poorly, the Silver Apples resurfaced a year later with their sophomore effort, *Contact*, another far-flung outing which fared no better than its predecessor. After the record's release, the duo seemingly vanished into thin air, perhaps returning to the alien world from whence they purportedly came; however, in 1996 the Silver Apples mysteriously resurfaced, as Simeon and new partner Xian Hawkins released the single "Fractal Flow." American and European tours followed, and a year later a new LP, *Beacon*, was released to wide acclaim. The follow-up *Decatur* appeared in 1998, and was soon joined by *A Lake of Teardrops* (a collaboration with avowed fans Spectrum) as well as *The Garden*, the long-unreleased third and final effort from the original Simeon/Taylor partnership. However, on November 1, 1998, the Silver Apples' van crashed while returning from a New York gig; the accident left Simeon with a broken neck and spinal injuries, casting his continued musical career in grave doubt. —*Jason Ankeny*

★ **Silver Apples** / 1997 / MCA ♦♦♦♦♦
The group's two '60s albums (*Silver Apples* and *Contact*) were previously combined as a two-fer a few years before this identical release, but as this is on a major label, it will find wider distribution. It also benefits from the addition of newly penned historical liner notes from Simeon, and vintage photos of the band, along with a diagram of the Simeon (the instrument) and Taylor's drum setup. —*Richie Unterberger*

## Simply Jeff (Jeff Adachi)
b. 1966, Sacramento, CA
*Producer, DJ / Turntablism, Funky Breaks, Club/Dance, House*
West Coast DJ Simply Jeff, previously known as DJ Spinn during the mid-'80s while working at Los Angeles radio hot-spots like KROQ and MARS-FM, is the head of Dr. Freecloud's Mixing Lab and Fund Da-Fried Therapeutics, a progressive-leaning club-night which allows him to spin everything from chunky trip-hop and downtempo to trance and rave on the same night. He debuted early in the '90s with tracks recorded for Moonshine as X-Calibur (with Brian Scott). After forming his own Orbit Transmission label, Jeff released more material during 1995-96, as X-Calibur and the DJ's Project (with Scott, DJ Dan, and Scratchmaster DJ Rectangle). By 1997, Simply Jeff had released his first full-length, *Funk Da-Fried*. The follow-up appeared one year later, and in the spring of 2000, Simply Jeff returned with *Funky Instrumentalist*. —*John Bush*

• **Funk-Da-Fried** / Jun. 10, 1997 / City of Angels ♦♦♦♦
Like the similarly L.A.-based DJ Cut Chemist, Simply Jeff is much better at igniting crowds than the more exhibitionist, philosophical squads up in San Francisco like Invisibl Skratch Piklz. On his first major mix album, Jeff does just that, with a trio of his own tracks, two cuts from the big-beat extraordinaires at Britain's Skint Records and the balance provided by West Coast breakbeat artists of all kinds, from Freaky Chakra to Liquitek Pimps. Moving from old-school through acid-disco and house, Simply Jeff lets the party-hearty beats and great psychedelic grooves lead the way, and it's an enjoyable journey. —*John Bush*

**Funk-Da-Fried, Vol. 2** / Sep. 29, 1998 / City of Angels ♦♦♦
**Funky Instrumentalist** / Apr. 18, 2000 / BML ♦♦♦
For Simply Jeff's third major mix album, the veteran SoCal DJ culled tracks from a variety of big-beat, techno, trance, and hip-hop producers. What these

tracks have in common is an irresistible funk attitude that's perfect for the dancefloor no matter the origin of the producer, from the chilled British drum'n'bass act E-Z Rollers, to New York's hyper techno DJ Frankie Bones, to master trance remixer Rennie Pilgrem. Though his mix isn't quite as hands-on as the volumes in his *Funk-Da-Fried* series, there are some great tracks here, like the great Zapp tribute "Ride the Funky" by World of Crime, "Shutdown" by Speed Freaks, Jeff's own "Break It Down," and "Hot Stop" by DJ Icey. —*John Bush*

## Bob Sinclar (Christophe Le Friant)

*Producer, DJ / Club/Dance, House*

The man behind such productions as the Mighty Bop (down-tempo hip-hop), Bob Sinclar (house), and Réminiscence Quartet (acid jazz) is Chris the French Kiss (aka Christophe Le Friant), a Parisian DJ and head of the crucial French label Yellow Productions as well as a producer. Le Friant began DJing in 1987 while still a teenager, and formed Yellow Productions in 1993 with Alain Ho. Several of the first releases on Yellow were by Le Friant: the Mighty Bop's "Messe Pour le Temps Present," Réminiscence Quartet's "Roda Mundo," and his first LP, the French hip-hop summit *The Mighty Bop Meet DJ Cam et La Funk Mob*. Alongside releases from a parade of excellent French sources, including DJ companions Dimitri from Paris and Kid Loco, Yellow also hosted two more Mighty Bop LPs during 1996-97, *La Vague Sensorielles* and *Autres Voix, Autres Blues*.

Eager to inject some fun into the burgeoning French house underground, Le Friant borrowed the name Bob Sinclar (from a character in the well-known French film *Le Magnifique*) and in 1997 produced his first Sinclar EP, *A Space Funk Project*. Soon enough, he had an entire Bob Sinclar LP ready to go, and *Paradise* appeared on Yellow just in time for summer 1998. One of the album's tracks, "Gym Tonic," began getting some clubplay in France thanks to its bouncy house vibe and incessant singalong chorus (lifted from a Jane Fonda workout record). A huge anthem during the summer season in Ibiza, "Gym Tonic" looked ready to explode on the charts until Fonda sought legal action for the illegal sample. Perhaps wary of overly burdensome commercial success, the song's co-producer—Daft Punk's Thomas Bangalter, who'd just recorded his own breezy house delight, Stardust's "Music Sounds Better With You"—refused to have even a remixed version released as a single. Nevertheless, assorted bootlegs cropped up and by October a mysterious artist named Spacedust—probably just a major-label-fronted cash-in attempt—hit the top of the charts in Britain with an almost identical remix of the Sinclar-Bangalter original, entitled "Gym and Tonic." (Another crass Spacedust move, covering Bangalter's solo hit with the slimly disguised title "Music Feels Good With You," dropped like a rock.)

With all the offending samples removed, Sinclar's *Paradise* LP was re-released worldwide in 1999. He also worked on remixes, providing tracks by Bangalter himself, Ian Pooley, Second Crusade, and the Yellow project Tom & Joyce with additional production. Le Friant returned to the Mighty Bop alias in 2000 with the retrospective mix collection *Spin My Hits*. [See Also: The Mighty Bop] —*John Bush*

- **Paradise** / Apr. 13, 1999 / Wea International ♦♦
Reconfigured only slightly for its CD release, *Paradise* includes the Thomas Bangalter remix of "Gym Tonic" plus 11 more get-on-the-dancefloor disco-house movers like "Get into the Music," "Disco 2000 Selector," and "Move Your Body." —*John Bush*

## Talvin Singh

b. London, England
*Tabla, Producer / Electronica, Trip-Hop, Jungle/Drum'N'Bass, Club/Dance*

Creator of an innovative fusion of Indian bhangra music and drum'n'bass electronica, Talvin Singh was classically trained on the tabla but rejected most of his learning when he founded the Anokha club-night at East London's Blue Note. Singh grew up in Leytonstone, and though he began playing tabla at the age of five, he also liked to breakdance to electro and listen to punk rock. He was transplanted to India at the age of 16 to pursue a classical education, but later returned to Britain in the late '80s and began picking up work as a musician, with a diverse cast of artists—Sun Ra, Björk, Future Sound of London, Siouxsie & the Banshees, and the Indigo Girls, among others.

By late 1995, Singh founded Anokha, the club night where drum'n'bass DJs and Asian punk bands went head to head with the amped-up sounds of his tabla and percussion. Guest spots by LTJ Bukem and others made Anokha a Monday-night hotspot in London, and Singh signed to Island for an Anokha compilation including several of his own productions. He also worked as a remixer before issuing his proper solo debut, *O.K.* in late 1998. —*John Bush*

**Anokha: Soundz of the Asian Underground** / Jun. 17, 1997 / PolyGram ♦♦♦♦

From Singh's Anokha club comes the *Soundz of the Asian Underground* compilation (featuring two of his own tracks). The album is a startlingly natural-sounding fusion of Indian music and instruments with drum'n'bass, breakbeats and electronics, unlike other worldbeat-influenced electronic recordings, which feature an abundance of styles but rarely approach true fusion. Besides the Singh contributions and the two tracks by State of Bengal, the highlight is "K-Ascendant" by Kingsuk Biswas (aka Bedouin Ascent). —*John Bush*

- **O.K.** / Oct. 19, 1998 / PolyGram ♦♦♦♦
Talvin Singh first rose to notoriety running a popular Monday night London club, Anokha. That experience led to the release of the album *Anokha: Soundz of the Asian Underground*, a highly regarded sampling of Asian-esque sounds from artists who performed at Anokha. *O.K.* is Singh's debut release, and it was nine months in the making. The title was chosen because of the universality of the word O.K., which can be understood almost anywhere. It is mostly a reinterpretation of hypnotic Indian classical music with plenty of flute, sitar, and, of course, tabla. There's also Nusrat Fateh Ali Khan-like devotional qawwali and traditional Okinawan dance music mixed in to make *O.K.* truly pan-Asian. Singh's subtle craftsmanship in fitting the old with the modern make this album seductive and one of the best efforts yet as blending Asian sounds with techno. "Light," a truly wondrous fusion of Indian flute and rich atmospherics, encapsulates what Talvin Singh is all about and should convince even the most skeptical. —*Matthew Hilburn*

**Talvin Remixsingh OK** / Oct. 11, 1999 / Island ♦♦♦
The inevitable remix album is fortunately a varied affair, including isolation dubs by Plastikman, more sympathetic fusion material courtesy of 4 Hero, laidback trip-hop from Kid Loco, and the excellent results of Singh's sound-clash with Francois K on "Vikram the Vampire." —*John Bush*

## Single Cell Orchestra (Miguel Angelo Fierro)

*Producer / Illbient, Electronica, Electro-Techno, Ambient-Techno*

Single Cell Orchestra's Miguel Fierro is a member of the fertile San Francisco Bay Area experimental electronic community, which has produced artists such as Spacetime Continuum, Heavenly Music Corporation, Ambient Temple of Imagination, Jon Williams, and Charles Uzzell-Edwards. Working in all styles of electronica—from the more straight-ahead club gear of his Zoe Magick work to the outbound ambient-electro of his Reflective releases and the mid-tempo head music of his 1996 Asphodel debut—Fierro approaches each with a focus on rhythm, texture, and atmosphere. The son of a jazz drummer, Fierro grew up listing to post-bop and '70s jazz greats such as Herbie Hancock and Miles Davis, and began making tracks after playing around with a friend's low-budget keyboard. After experimenting with a few bands (both electronic and otherwise), Fierro decided to go it solo, inspired by his DJ brother to try his hand at freestyle and house music production.

Fierro released his first tracks through West Coast dance staple Zoe Magick, with his "Transmit Liberation" (from the "Liberated EP") becoming an underground classic and prefiguring the styles of lazy, instrumental "trip-hop" later popularized by the Mo'Wax, Wall of Sound, and Cup of Tea labels. From there, Fierro linked up with Jonah Sharp's Reflective label, which released his "Angelic Science" EP in 1994 and the full-length sci-fi electro opera, *Dead Vent 7*, the following year. His self-titled debut full-length for the Asphodel imprint, released in 1996, returned to the warm breakbeat style of "Transmit Liberation" (included on the album), as well as house and a more minimal brand of environmental ambient. Fierro's most recent work is a collaboration with Daum Bentley of Freaky Chakra, a full-on electro overdrive recorded after a series of live improv gigs which pit the two in a "Vs." scenario. —*Sean Cooper*

**Liberated [EP]** / 1992 / Zoe Magick ♦♦♦
A half-and-half acid-house/downtempo breakbeat EP widely hailed (particularly the latter half) for its visionary combination of groove and atmosphere. The B-side's "Transmit Liberation" is an oft-cited precursor of downbeat "trip-hop," and has been included on a number of compilations and DJ-mix releases. —*Sean Cooper*

**Angelic Science [EP]** / 1994 / Reflective ♦♦
Four tracks which range from quirky, Reflective-style experimental techno to gorgeous beatless ambient and electro. Murky at times but with a strong, individual voice. —*Sean Cooper*

● **Dead Vent 7** / 1995 / Reflective ♦♦♦♦
Fierro roped in writer Michiel Katz for his debut full-length, who here fashions a nightmarish sci-fi story—narrated by a cast of friends and hired hands—to which SCO's predilections for experimental ambient and hard-hitting electro are applied. A well done fusion of concept and delivery which could easily have gone badly awry. —*Sean Cooper*

**Freaky Chakra Vs. Single Cell Orchestra** / 1996 / Astralwerks ♦♦♦
A storming breakbeat battle, with SCO's Miguel Fierro going head-to-head with friend and colleague Daum Bentley of Freaky Chakra. Old-school uptempo electro-funk is the call of the day for much of this disc, which was inspired by a series of live improvisations the two performed in 1995 and 1996. —*Sean Cooper*

**Single Cell Orchestra** / Mar. 26, 1996 / Asphodel ♦♦♦
Single Cell spent three years compiling his self-titled second album, which is warmer and more emotive than the majority of his prior work. Here, the Orchestra's dense rhythms are fleshed out with strings and a stronger melodic sensibility, informing the record with a vague pop feel. —*Jason Ankeny*

**Blockhead Version 1.0 / Version 2.0 [EP]** / 1997 / Oxygen Music Works ♦♦♦
The two-part "Blockhead" single is the first thing Miguel Fierro released after moving from San Francisco to New York in 1996, and is a return of sorts to the lino-square roots of his youth. Following on the melodic, almost radio-friendly heels of his self-titled Asphodel LP, "Blockhead" switches into overdrive, presenting some of the most imposing new-style electro yet released on American shores. The first 12" splits its focus between over-the-top distorted beatbox-jungle and the West Coast breaks/electro-funk of Hardkiss or Überzone, while the second dives headlong into fast, syncopated, next-millenium electro-funk, with diving kick bombs and layer after layer of twittering percussion immersed in Fierro's signature synth sheets. —*Sean Cooper*

## 69 (Carl Craig)

*Producer / Detroit Techno, Club/Dance, Techno*
By 1995, Carl Craig had gained status as one of the world's top techno producers. His recordings as 69—consisting of a scant three EPs—were among the most inspired and influential in his entire discography. The 1991 Planet E entry *4 Jazz Funk Classics*, along with *Sound on Sound* and *Lite Music* from three years later, contained classics like "If Mojo Was AM," "Jam the Box," "My Machines," and "Microlovr" represented intense works of electro-distortion and a certain amount of classic groove. Though *4 Jazz Funk Classics* remained unavailable on CD, R&S Records reissued the latter two EPs as *The Sound of Music* in 1995. [See Also: Carl Craig, Innerzone Orchestra, Paperclip People, Psyche/BFC] —*John Bush*

**4 Jazz Funk Classics [EP]** / Nov. 15, 1991 / Planet E ♦♦♦♦
Besides being the first official release on Planet E, *4 Jazz Funk Classics* set the precedent for the sound that would become synonymous with Carl Craig's label. Albums such as Craig's masterpiece, *More Songs About Food and Revolutionary Art*, may make you think otherwise with its serious tone, but Planet E has always been about keeping things funky, no matter how daring they may get. As 69, Craig gets about as funky as he's ever been in his career. Craig heads for his sampler (brilliantly snatches some Curtis Mayfield) and assembles some wonderful-sounding breakbeats with plenty of shape distortion and fuzzy warmth that sounds just as fresh today as it did then. —*Jason Birchmeier*

● **The Sound of Music** / 1995 / R&S ♦♦♦♦
R&S compiled the 1994 EPs *Sound on Sound* and *Lite Music*, released by Carl Craig as 69, for this 1995 collection. It spotlights his most consistently funky, lo-fi material with classics like "Jam the Box," "My Machines" and "Microlovr" leading the way. —*John Bush*

**Sound on Sound [Single]** / Jun. 3, 1996 / R&S ♦♦♦♦
Boasting the tagline "Elevated Music from the Underground," Carl Craig's timeless masterpiece of sonic grooves is techno house of the highest order. With the EP's opening track, "Rushed," Craig samples the unforgettable synth intro of My Mine's new wave jam "Hypnotic Tango" and pairs it up with busy backwards percussion to deliver a monolith of spellbinding drama. "Sub Seducer" almost passes for a classic lo-fi house track until it is almost overcome by a heavy, distorted wash of sound. The record's A-side finishes out with the title track: a beatless, angular synth excursion. Side two opens with "Poi et Pas," which is surely a reference to the seminal Liaisons Dangereuses proto-techno track "Peut Etre Pas," a group that Craig is not alone in having sampled repeatedly. The record's kicker, however, is the final track "Filter King." Even though the record's label warns that "these sounds have not been tested on humans," one can rest assured that when "testing" this hard, minimal, half-bar workout, the humans in the club will be thrown into a dance frenzy. —*Carlos Souffront*

## Roni Size

b. Bristol, England
*Producer / Electronica, Jungle/Drum'N'Bass, Club/Dance*
Bristol native Roni Size is one of the UK jungle scene's most respected names, with production credits spanning dozens of labels, projects and releases. Although not as quick to rise to acclaim (either critical or popular) as peers such as Goldie or LTJ Bukem, Size's influence as a producer, label owner, and committed underground magnate figured him as one of the emerging sound's true pioneers. The breakout success of his debut album *New Forms* (including Britain's prestigious Mercury Award) finally confirmed his stature and vaulted him to a greater degree of popularity than any drum'n'bass producer.

Born to Jamaican immigrant parents, Roni grew up in the Bristolean suburb of St. Andrews (home to Tricky, Massive Attack, and Smith & Mighty), where he learned the fundamentals of hip-hop through the area's sounds systems, house parties, and underground clubs. Expelled from school in his mid-teens and running game through his neighborhood until risk became greater than reward, Size started dabbling with house and reggae production in the late'80s. He hooked up with labelmates DJ Krust, Suv, and DJ Die at the 1990 Glastonbury Festival, and the four stayed in contact, eventually forming Size's longest running musical commitment to date: his own Full Cycle label. Formed simply as an outlet for the four's entree into the nascent drum'n'bass scene (Krust and brother Flynn [of Flynn & Flora] were already working with Smith & Mighty, while Die was producing hardcore tracks as Sublove), Full Cycle has since grown into a label group, releasing a steady flow of twelves (on both Full Cycle and Dope Dragon), and a label comp, *Music Box*, in 1995.

Oft duplicated, the Full Cycle sound is a subtle mix of jazz and soul with jump-up rhythms and world beat references spanning from Roni's Jamaican roots to '50s be-bop and the Motown sound. Although hardly popular in the days before ragga (then jump-up) ruled the decks, the crew now counts a number of classics among their credits, including Size's "It's a Jazz Thing," Krust's "Jazz Note," and Reprazent's *Reasons for Sharing* EP, the crew's first outing through major label subsidiary Talkin' Loud. The success of 1997's *New Forms* launched Size to the top of the electronica genre, and the Dope Dragon label also continues to rise in the ranks of dubplate hysteria, with tracks from Selector Owoy, Gang Related, and Mask consistently passing muster on most DJ's decks. After a relatively silent 1998, Size returned in 1999 with a new project—Breakbeat Era, with DJ Die and vocalist Leonie Laws. The trio released *Ultra-Obscene* in the fall of that year. In 2000, Size returned to the Reprazent project with *In the Mode*, boasting sit-ins from Method Man and Rage Against the Machine's Zack De La Rocha. [See Also: Breakbeat Era] —*Sean Cooper*

**Music Box** / Mar. 1995 / Full Cycle ♦♦♦♦
A cross section of Roni Size's Full Cycle label's groundbreaking artist stable, with cuts from Roni, DJ Die, Krust, and Suv. A few oldies-but-goodies for new initiates, but a predominance of new material makes this both a killer intro and a rousing update for junglists in the know. Jazz-flavored drum'n'bass without the bad aftertaste. —*Sean Cooper*

★ **New Forms** / Oct. 28, 1997 / Talkin' Loud/Mercury ♦♦♦♦♦
Roni Size, with his conglomeration Reprazent, was the major techno/electronica act of late 1997, earning a considerable amount of praise for his double-disc debut, *New Forms*. It is certainly true that there is fascinating, provocative music on *New Forms*. Size borrows from the Massive Attack aesthetic, piecing together elements of jazz, trip-hop, Soul II Soul's club-centric soul, hip-hop, and, above all, drum'n'bass to form a unique hybrid. It's a classy sound with a wide appeal—the rhythms are deceptively complex, thereby suiting the needs of serious techno fans, but many songs have a linear struc-

ture and vocals, which will appeal to fans of such crossovers as Everything But the Girl. At times, these fusions sound quite exciting, but they just as frequently sound cold and uninviting, since the album spans two 70-minute discs and is filled with long songs. At that length, *New Forms* is impenetrable to all but the most dedicated listener, since the music takes a while to sink in; while some of the songs merit that kind of attention, the entire album ultimately doesn't reward that kind of patience. That said, the best moments—like Roni Size's singles—offer undeniable proof that he's a singular talent. With some serious editing, his talent would be all the more apparent. —*Stephen Thomas Erlewine*

**Replica: The Remix Album** / Jan. 26, 1998 / Mercury ♦♦♦♦
Compiling all the crucial remixes of material from countless *New Forms* singles, *Replica* includes contributions from Photek, Origin Unknown, Grooverider, Kruder & Dorfmeister, and DJ Krust. —*John Bush*

**In the Mode** / Oct. 10, 2000 / Island ♦♦♦♦
It's easy to blame The Man. Joblessness. Prejudice. Michael Bolton covering "(Sittin' on) the Dock of the Bay." Yet few things were more cause for alarm than the self-destruction of jungle. What once began as an infuriated call to arms to take back a piece of dance culture that they once helped create, the British black underground saw such an extraordinary and deeply innovative new genre saturating the clubs, being name checked in every "credible" pop band's interview, and then quickly shuffled off into Nike ads. They should've known that The Man likes to assimilate. Indeed, with drum'n'bass in such pseudo-intellectual dire straits (helped put there, ironically enough, by Reprazent's own *New Forms*), it was a fine time for an album like *In the Mode* to have its say. And Reprazent, at least, are saying they've had enough.

The level of punk fury and torrential modernization is high all throughout this record. "In and Out," with its accelerated heartbeat, "Ghetto Celebrity," with its raucous Method Man cameo, "In the Tune of the Sound," with Rahzel's stellar beat-boxing: the jumpy uppercuts of rhymes and pounding polyrhythms seem to reach the very limits of jungle's schizophrenia. Not that this is an embarrassment of darkcore efforts; as in "Out of the Game," the wrath of this album is not so much political, not so much in creating heavy soundscapes; it's conveyed more in a harder, live-sounding blast of back to basics hip-hop roots. Remember that rush you felt when you first heard your first drum'n'bass track? So do Reprazent, and they build the album to such a pitch that one can only assume that this is what it sounds like when a genre reclaims its importance.

Undoubtedly, hardcore jungleists will scoff at such a high-profile, sometimes flashy presentation of drum'n'bass ethics, but this is an album full of such militant energy that it deserves to be seen as one of the strongest saving graces of jungle in years. Reprazent sounds like a band trying to make jungle's sonic equivalent to the mutinous *Xtrmntr*. Except instead of fighting for "civil disobedience," they seem intent in shooting down every head-nodding, spec-wearing disaster their chosen genre has created. Can you still blame The Man? Sure. But only if you admit that an album of this dimension would never have existed unless jungle was first brutally sentenced to death. —*Dean Carlson*

## Skinny Puppy

f. 1982, Vancouver, British, db. 1996
*Group / Industrial Dance, Alternative Pop/Rock, Industrial*

Drawing from the pioneering work of artists like Throbbing Gristle, Cabaret Voltaire and Suicide, the dark avant-industrial group Skinny Puppy formed in 1982 in Vancouver, British Columbia. Originally a duo comprised of former Images in Vogue vocalist cEVIN Key (born Kevin Crompton) and Nivek Ogre (a.k.a. Kevin Ogilvie), Skinny Puppy followed their debut cassette *Back and Forth* with the EP *Remission*, the first of many recordings with producer David "Rave" Ogilvie, in 1984.

Keyboardist Wilhelm Schroeder joined the group for 1985's full-length debut *Bites*, but was replaced the next year by Dwayne Goettel, whose sampling and synth work proved significant in the development of the Skinny Puppy aesthetic from ominous dance music into a distinct fusion of industrial, goth, and electronic sounds. Subsequent releases like 1986's *Mind: The Perpetual Intercourse*, 1987's *Cleanse, Fold and Manipulate*, and 1988's *VIVIsectVI* further honed the trio's style, as well as introducing the outspoken lyrical agenda that remained a thematic constant throughout much of the group's work.

In 1989, Ministry's Al Jourgensen added vocals, guitars and production work to *Rabies;* later, he joined Ogre in the side project Pigface. Ultimately, the members' interest in pursuing similar outside projects began to unravel Skinny Puppy: in 1987, Key and Edward Ka-Spel of the Legendary Pink Dots recorded the album *Their Eyes Slowly Burning* under the name Tear Garden, and in 1990, he and friend Alan Nelson worked as Hilt. A major rift began splitting the band apart, and Key and Goettel often sided against Ogre, whom they felt was more interested in pursuing solo work than in keeping the trio intact; drugs had also become a serious problem, but Skinny Puppy nonetheless signed to American Recordings in 1993 and relocated to Los Angeles to begin production work.

The sessions for the album, titled *The Process*, proved disastrous; for the first time in nearly a decade, David Ogilvie did not oversee production duties, and the group went through several producers, including former Swan Roli Mosimann and Martin Atkins. Flooding and earthquakes further hampered the sessions, and Key was severely injured in a film shoot. After months of recording, Key and Goettel, dissatisfied with Atkins' work, absconded with the master tapes and returned to Vancouver in mid-1994 to finish production. Ogre remained in California, and later announced he was leaving Skinny Puppy to form W.E.L.T. A few months later, on August 23, 1995, Goettel was found dead of a heroin overdose in his parents' home; in his honor, Key and Ogilvie finally completed the album, and *The Process* was released in 1996. A multi-media history of the band, *Brap—Back and Forth, Series 3&4*, followed a few months later, while Key returned to his new project, Download. Released in 1998, *ReMix Dys Temper* featured Skinny Puppy reworkings by Autechre, Neotropic, and Adrian Sherwood, in addition to industrial groups like KMFDM and God Lives Underwater. —*Jason Ankeny*

**Mind: The Perpetual Intercourse** / 1986 / Nettwerk ♦♦
Skinny Puppy doesn't deviate from its dark vision on their second album; in fact, the record doesn't sound all that much different than the first. —*Stephen Thomas Erlewine*

**Cleanse Fold & Manipulate** / 1987 / Nettwerk ♦♦♦♦
While it doesn't deviate from their previous lyrical territory, the music is more intense and scary; for the first time, Skinny Puppy has made an album that actually *sounds* frightening. —*Stephen Thomas Erlewine*

**VIVISect VI** / Jul. 1988 / Nettwerk ♦♦♦♦
*VIVIsectVI* is the first explicitly political Skinny Puppy album, which adds some depth to their standard throbbing, gloomy industrial dance-rock. —*Stephen Thomas Erlewine*

**Ain't It Dead Yet** / 1989 / Nettwerk ♦♦
A live recording from the Toronto Concert Hall, it includes most of their early singles, such as "Dig It," "Deep Down Trauma Hounds," and "Assimilate." The quality is superb and the performance is quite good also. Too bad the eleven songs aren't separated by track markers. —*John Bush*

**Rabies** / 1989 / Nettwerk ♦♦♦
Despite the presence of Ministry's Al Jourgensen and his brutal guitar riffs, Skinny Puppy sounds as if they're at a loss for ideas on their fifth album. —*Stephen Thomas Erlewine*

**Too Dark Park** / 1990 / Nettwerk ♦♦♦♦
When Ministry and the Revolting Cocks were offering what could be described as industrial noise for people who weren't industrial fans, Skinny Puppy continued to thrive on the extreme and remained far to the left of rock's center. Employing more bass than Puppy's previous albums, *Too Dark Park* has a bit of a funk element. But make no mistake; the industrial agitators (who had influenced Nine Inch Nails, Ministry, RevCo, Godflesh, and numerous others) were hardly going after rock's mainstream. Forceful and consistently abrasive, these twisted and disturbing collages of samples, electronics, distortion, and heavy guitars push the limits of rock and are about as hardcore as it gets. Those who have only a slight interest in industrial would probably be better off starting out with the more accessible Ministry, but this is a CD that the more seasoned industrial aficionados shouldn't miss. —*Alex Henderson*

**Bites/Remission** / Feb. 2, 1990 / Nettwerk ♦♦♦
*Bites*, Skinny Puppy's first album, recalls the gloomy throb of Cabaret Voltaire, but with a more pronounced beat; their debut EP, *Remission*, is also included on the CD. —*Stephen Thomas Erlewine*

**12" Anthology** / Jun. 1990 / Nettwerk ♦♦♦♦
Featuring both sides of four 12" singles from 1985 to 1989, *12" Anthology* offers the best introduction to Skinny Puppy's psycho-terrorist industrial mu-

sic. From the early double-sided classic "Dig It/The Choke" to later offerings like "Chainsaw" and "Assimilate," only the best of SP's '80s output is collected here. —*Stephen Thomas Erlewine*

**Remix Dys Temper** / Oct. 20, 1998 / Nettwerk ◆◆◆
Divided down the line between tracks charting the emerging electronica process of remix-by-obliteration and lame tributes by industrial-trance groups, the Skinny Puppy remix album is just a bit too diverse for its own good. Electronic fans will be most impressed by Autechre's "Killing Game," Josh Wink's "Chainsaw," and Neotropic's "Love in Vein," and ignore the questionable inclusions of the Deftones, God Lives Underwater, and Guru. —*John Bush*

★ **The Singles Collect** / Nov. 16, 1999 / Nettwerk ◆◆◆◆◆
It's not a compilation of across-the-board greatest songs, but the Skinny Puppy singles collection does the old *12" Anthology* one better by including tracks from the group's three Nettwerk albums of the '90s (*Rabies, Too Dark Park*, and *Last Rights*). For fans, it's long been a dream to have the full fruits of the industrial kingpins' long career all on one disc—"Dig It," one of Skinny Puppy's first and best singles, appears right beside "Worlock," from 1989's *Rabies*. Also aboard are a baker's dozen of well-selected career highlights, including "Assimilate," "Tormentor," "Deep Down Trauma Hounds," "Stairs and Flowers," "Testure," "Tin Omen," "Inquisition," and "Killing Game." Though a chronologically ordered compilation would have been a better idea, *The Singles Collect* sounds excellent all the way through and proves that Skinny Puppy were, hands down, the best and most adventurous band of the industrial era. —*John Bush*

**B-Sides Collect** / Nov. 16, 1999 / Nettwerk ◆◆◆◆
Skinny Puppy were indeed one of the most collectable industrial bands, issuing many singles that contained surprisingly strong tracks. In 1999, Nettwerk compiled some of the best for the companion to *The Singles Collect*. These tracks aren't the rarest in the Skinny Puppy catalogue, considering most are B-sides from later singles like "Testure," "Worlock," "Censor," "Tormentor," and "Spasmolytic." Still, the group's quality control was practically undisputed among industrial bands, and for fans who may have missed out on a single or two the first time, it's the perfect acquisition. Highlights include remixes of "Addiction" and "Shore Lined Poison," plus notable tracks like "Brak's Talk," "Bark," "Punk in Park Zoo's," and "Yes He Ran." —*John Bush*

## Skylab

f. 1993, San Francisco, CA
*Group / Electronica, Trip Hop, Club/Dance*

Skylab is the combined efforts of UK DJ/experimentalist Mat Ducasse, producer Howie "B" Bernstein, and Japanese Major Force recording artists Tosh and Kudo, aka Love TKO. Beginning as a post-office project between Ducasse and Bernstein (with Ducasse shipping tape after weirded-out tape of obscure samples and tape-loop experiments to the intrepid Björk/U2 producer), Skylab become one of the more celebrated of the crossover trip-hop/ambient breakbeat set. Wedding Ducasse's affectation for '60s experimental jazz, funk, and soul with Bernstein's penchant for making connections and Tosh and Kudo's tight, solid hip-hop moorings, the group generated much of the raw material for their *L'Attitude* debut and subsequent EP in the studio (as opposed to the sampler). Fifth member Debbie Sanders' interesting, often wordless vocal contributions added novelty and texture. Although all the members released solo material outside of the group, Skylab's shifty, off-beat flavor remained a unique collaborative product. In 1994, Astralwerks released the full-length *#1* in America. While Howie B went on to a fertile solo career, the remaining quartet converged again five years later for *1999 (Large as Life and Twice as Natural).* —*Sean Cooper*

● **#1** / 1994 / L'Attitude/Astralwerks ◆◆◆◆
Skylab's debut album came out of nowhere, showcasing a maddeningly well-constructed balance of downtempo experimental beat music and ambient- and musique concrète-leaning miscellany. Urban lore has it Ducasse spent a few weeks tripping in his attic to come up with the base tapes that bandmates Howie B and Love TKO would fashion into *#1*. True or not it's a pretty apt accounting for what appears here. The Astralwerks reissue adds a few throwaways and the handsome "Exotica." —*Sean Cooper*

**Oh! Skylab [EP]** / 1995 / L'Attitude ◆◆◆◆
4-track EP recorded, reportedly, while the group all had the flu. Three new cuts carry a more live-in-the-studio feel, with a freaked-out violin solo shoot-

ing the strongest track, "These Are Blues," into experimental orbit. The B-side is taken up by two *#1* remixes; a bubbly Sabres Of Paradise mix of "Indigo" and acid-jazz mainstay Nobakuza Takemura's dust-free take on "Seashell." As usual, the Astralwerks version (titled simply "These Are Blues") plays around with the track listing, dropping the admittedly throwaway "Red Light, Blue Light" and subbing a different mix of "Blues." —*Sean Cooper*

## Slab!

f. 1995, London, England
*Group / Big Beat, Electronica, Club/Dance, Techno*

Like Lionrock and the Chemical Brothers, Slab are a Brit-hop outfit who've made the decision to not decide between guitars and synthesizers, combining the two in raucous, decidedly *un*-subtle ways. Formed by Nina Walsh and Lol Hammond in 1995, the group combine dirty, distorted breaks, bubbling acid lines, guitar blasts, and bits of dub, techno, and rave in simple-but-effective amalgams of cheap thrills and electric bombast. To date, the group has released three EPs and a compilation/mini-album on the Hydrogen Dukebox label and been remixed by the likes of Monkey Mafia, Carl Cox, and Sabres of Paradise/2 Lone Swordsmen's Andrew Weatherall. The last is a connection worth expanding upon; in addition to Slab, Nina Walsh is the force behind Sabrettes, an underling imprint to Weatherall's Sabres of Paradise empire, and released a number of popular EPs from the likes of Inky Blacknuss, Innersphere, and Turbulent Force. Lol Hammond is a former member of popular UK tribal/techno group the Drum Club, which he left in 1995 to focus on Slab. Both Walsh and Hammond are accomplished instrumentalists, and the group's live show is one of the most integrated (i.e., in terms of electronics and acoustics) on the UK scene. Slab's mini-LP *Freeky Speed* was reissued domestically in 1996 by Sm:)e Communications. —*Sean Cooper*

● **Freeky Speed** / Apr. 29, 1996 / Sm:)e ◆◆◆◆
A compilation of tracks from Slab's first three Hydrogen Dukebox singles, including remix work from Carl Cox, Monkey Mafia, Andrew Weatherall of Sabres of Paradise/2 Lone Swordsmen, and Big Eye. Headbanger acid break Brit-hop/techno similar to the Chemical Brothers, Fat Boy Slim, etc. —*Sean Cooper*

## Slam

f. 1994, Glasgow, Scotland
*Group / Electronica, Club/Dance, Techno, House*

Scottish techno/house fusers Slam have built a reputation as one of the most dependable, invigorating sources for high-quality dancefloor gear. Bent on breaking down the boundaries that separate the last decade of UK dance music's two most well-known forms, Slam's Stuart MacMillan and Orde Meikle have taken the less-is-more approach, releasing records only sporadically, but which consistently rise to the top of dance music charts and DJ playlists. Prior to their celebrated 1996 full-length debut, *Headstates* (released, as with all their material to date, on their own Soma label), the pair released only a trio of singles—"Positive Education," "Snapshots," and Dark Forces." But their progressive approach to the space between house and techno—two styles which measure innovation inch by inch rather than by leaps and bounds—has figured them (along with artists such as Motorbass and Lionrock) as one of the most important new talents in post-rave European dance music.

Mates since childhood, MacMillan and Meikle grew up with a basic love of music—from funk, soul, and disco, to hip-hop, punk, new wave, and, of course, acid house. Both DJs of renown, the pair are more likely to reveal such disparate influences in a club setting than on plastic, but even "Positive Education" and tracks such as "Hybrid" and "White Shadows" from *Headstates* draw elements of that background—dirty, Detroit low-end, funky electro-breaks, sparse house ambiance—together inspired, head-twisting combinations. With a second Slam full-length nowhere to be seen three years on from the debut, the pair released an LP from their Pressure Funk alias, also on Soma. [See Also: Pressure Funk] —*Sean Cooper*

**Positive Education [Single]** / 1996 / Soma ◆◆◆◆

★ **Headstates** / May 13, 1996 / Soma ◆◆◆◆◆
Though it's missing one of their finest moments (namely "Positive Education"), Slam's LP debut is a near-perfect summation of British techno circa the midpoint of the decade. Tracks like "Emotive" and "White Shadows" capture the mood of techno's stateside progenitors (with the expected focus on driving beatwork), while still forecasting other developments in music: breakbeat

techno on "Low Life" and "First Bass," more minimal output with "Free Fall," and increasingly shadowy material with "Dark Forces." —*John Bush*

## Slam Mode

*Group / Jazz-House, Club/Dance, House*

The duo of Michael Cole and Angel Rodriguez record melancholy house for a variety of East Coast labels, including Deep Worldwide Music and Spiritual Life. The latter is also home to productions by deep-house masterminds from Mateo & Matos to Joe Claussell to Blaze. After working as house producers for nigh on a decade, in 1999 Cole and Rodriguez finally issued an LP, *La Colecion* for Glasgow Underground. —*John Bush*

• **La Colecion** / Apr. 26, 1999 / Glasgow Underground ♦♦♦
This collection of moody, groove-laden deep house from the New Jersey garage duo isn't quite the East Coast house sound most listeners would expect. A bit more Larry Heard than Armand Van Helden, Slam Mode's *La Colecion* is full of tough grooves and mechanistic melodies that don't recall *Studio 54* as much as they do rugged Midwestern productions. An album of solid production-house. —*John Bush*

## Luke Slater

b. Jun. 12, 1968, Reading, England
*Producer, DJ / Club/Dance, Techno, IDM*

Often grouped with similarly influential names such as Cristian Vogel and former labelmates the Black Dog, Luke Slater is generally credited with helping to create a UK techno tradition with a strong Detroit foundation. Slater's work is probably the more straightahead of the three (although he's released works ranging from tough, banging techno to lush, beatless ambient), and tends to build on Steel City's ruddy, muscular frame rather than simply repeating it. He has recorded under names such as Morganistic, Clementine, Planetary Assault Systems, and Luke Slater's 7th Plane, and quite often in collaboration with Alan Sage. Slater got his start in music in the late '80s at the Mi Price record store in Croydon (just south of London), working alongside Colin Dale and collaborator-to-be Sage. He soon set up his own shop—Jelly Jam Records—in Brighton, and from there began releasing original tracks under a slew of different monikers. His debut came in 1989 in the form of "Momentary Vision," released on White Label under the name Translucent. Arriving at the height of techno's rediscovery of the breakbeat, the track's hard funk and stripped-down, Detroit bristle, like the work of colleagues B12 and Kirk Degiorgio, announced a new, historically rooted direction in UK techno. Though silent for two years after "Momentary Vision"'s success, a flood of Slater material began appearing in 1991, including twelves and full-lengths for his own Jelly Jam label, as well as Dutch label D-Jax Up-Beats, Irdial, and especially Peace Frog, including nearly a dozen singles under his own name ("The X-Tront Trilogy") and as Planetary Assault Systems ("The Planetary Funk Trilogy"). Slater's most recent (and probably most well-known) releases to date have probably appeared on the renowned GPR label (with Alan Sage and under the names Morganistic and Luke Slater's Seventh Plane), and tend to combine an ambient or experimental/textural approach with a more minimal rhythmic framework. Slater jumped back to Peacefrog in 1996, as GPR's continuing organizational problems slowed their release schedule to a halt, releasing his full-length Planetary Assault Systems debut in 1997. He ascended to the majors via a contract with NovaMute that resulted in 1997's *Freek Funk; Wireless* followed two years later. [See Also: Planetary Assault Systems] —*Sean Cooper*

**Tri-Cendence [EP]** / 1993 / GPR ♦♦
Hard-edged, melodic techno in a clear Detroit-meets-UK vein. Reissued by GPR in 1996. —*Sean Cooper*

**The Four Cornered Room** / 1994 / GPR ♦♦

**My Yellow Wise Rug** / 1995 / GPR ♦♦♦

**92-94** / Sep. 1, 1997 / Peacefrog ♦♦♦♦
A collection of Slater's early work for Peacefrog, *92-94* consists of tracks from three volumes of his *X-Tront* EPs. Including several tracks unavailable elsewhere on CD, the album including explosive techno stormers like "Quadfonik" (often the A-sides of his singles) as well as more gentle explorations like "The Secret Garden" and "Expectation No. 1." —*John Bush*

• **Freek Funk** / Oct. 20, 1997 / NovaMute ♦♦♦♦
Although Luke Slater had always trafficked in high-precision techno with emotion (just like his Detroit idols), *Freek Funk* is his most precise and emotional yet, quite experimental, and with a range of sounds from abrasive techno to ambient soundtracks and string-laden house. One of the few British producers who seems to realize that interesting sounds aren't quite as important as investing the music with spirit, Slater came up with one of the best techno LPs of the year. —*John Bush*

**Wireless** / Oct. 5, 1999 / NovaMute ♦♦♦♦
The follow-up to a very well received major-label debut, *Wireless* sees Slater expanding his range as a producer into backbeat-driven styles like old-school rap and electro, a far cry from the pummeling techno of his youth but no less intriguing despite the fact. From a lesser techno producer, *Wireless* would smack of a breakbeat sell-out, an album that simply trades in Chemical Brothers' and Fatboy Slim's brand of old-school techno. But just as Moby wisely stuck to his melodic strengths while crafting a breakbeat-inspired album (the same year's *Play*), Slater never deserts his strongpoints—intense, pummeling drum programming. There is a big difference here; Slater's not just reaching for copies of old blues records and drum breaks. The tracks here are upfront, sinister, electro-inspired throwbacks, songs like "Sum Ton Tin," "Hard Knock Rock," and "Body Freefall, Electronic Inform" that throw dozens of electro effects into the pot with a subtle flair, from deep vocoder vocals to acid squelches to waves of synth menace. *Wireless* is a listen that's immediately rewarding *and* compelling. —*John Bush*

## Jake Slazenger (Michael Paradinas)

*Producer / Electro-Techno, Ambient-Techno, IDM*

Producer Mike Paradinas has used the Jake Slazenger alias as a sideline from his prime material (as μ-Ziq) to explore throwback electro-funk. Slaz made his first appearance on 1995's *MakesARacket*, recorded for Clear Records. A year later, he was back with *Das Ist Ein Groovy Beat Ja?* on Warp. [See Also: Kid Spatula, μ-Ziq] —*John Bush*

• **MakesARacket** / Oct. 1995 / Clear ♦♦♦♦
A surprisingly varied collection of new-school electro-funk. Unlike his earlier Clear EP, *Bantha Trax* (under the name Tusken Raiders), Paradinas' Slazenger sound is sparser, with funky machine breaks and goofy synth melodies dominating. Material splits pretty cleanly between dancefloor fare and more armchair-oriented tunes, and its the latter direction, not surprisingly, that proves most interesting. "Megaphonk," "Flod," and the live-sounding "Bolus" are the best of these, charting new directions in electro where others are in rehash mode. —*Sean Cooper*

**Das Ist Ein Groovy Beat Ja?** / Jul. 8, 1996 / Warp ♦♦
Michael Paradinas' second album under the Jake Slazenger alias is much more subdued than the usual techno-racket μ-Ziq is known for. Most of the first Slazenger album explored early-'80s electro—that's all here as well (and it sounds just as dated)—but several of the tracks go much farther back in time as a springboard for some mad keyboard vamps. "Supafunk" could have been lifted from a Jimmy Smith album of the '60s and "Hot Fumes" keys off blaxploitation funk. It makes one wonder whether an artist can be experimental and enjoyable when using all this cringe-worthy synth, but in the end, Paradinas pulls it off. —*John Bush*

## Slicker (John Hughes III)

*Producer / Experimental Techno, Post-Rock/Experimental*

Owner of the Chicago post-rock label Hefty Records, previous frontman for the Chicago indie/avant-garde acts Turtletoes and Bill Ding, John Hughes III also formed the Slicker project. Hughes, the son of the '80s teen-angst filmmaker renowned for hits like *Sixteen Candles* and *The Breakfast Club*, grew up in Chicago. After stints at Ohio University and Northwestern, he formed the Turtletoes, which released the 1995 album *Jackersville* on Hefty. Bill Ding, his duo with Dan Snazelle, released albums (also on Hefty) in 1996 and 1997. Hefty had also released programming-friendly projects by Chicago veterans like Casey Rice (Super ESP), and Hughes' debut as Slicker, *Confidence in Duber*, reflected that direction. Two years later, a remix album featured reworkings by Matmos, Richard Devine, and Rice, among others. Hughes also served as musical director for the 1998 film *Reach the Rock*, the directorial debut for longtime John Hughes partner William Ryan, featuring a score by Tortoise's John McEntire. —*John Bush*

**Confidence in Duber** / Sep. 22, 1998 / Hefty ♦♦
Slicker is a fairly straightforward project for someone like John Hughes III, whose work with groups like Bill Ding and Turtletoes moved between the

strange and the incredibly strange— *Confidence in Duber* has Hughes (along with fellow Chicago musicians like Ryan Rapsys) laying out peacefully buzzy and occasionally frantic electronic programming, with all of the beepy grooves and drum'n'bass aesthetics one might expect. There's a definite sense of composition to the record's tracks, which is certainly a good thing— Hughes puts a great deal of movement into his programming, and the addition of organic instruments (such as Rapsys' guitar on "Prader") allows for a few funky grooves to emerge as well. The record also features "99 KOs," a remix of Euphone's "A Hundred Times and More." —*Nitsuh Abebe*

● **Remixes** / May 16, 2000 / Hefty ♦♦♦
This six-track remix album reassembles Slicker's *Confidence in Duber* via the post-production of an assortment of post-rock/electronica figures, most notably Richard Devine, Casey Rice (aka Super ESP), and Matmos. The disc opens with Devine's contribution, an intricately programmed homage to Mouse on Mars and Autechre executed with help from partner Sherren. Next comes Casey Rice's Super ESP remix, a lo-fi drum'n'bass number using a variety of extraneous audio trash cut'n'pasted into a highly original production. Among considerable competition, San Francisco's Matmos contributes the highlight; their remix is also heavy on the cut'n'paste, but with various sections shifting from a focus on old-school drums and vocal samples to white noise to tabla drumming and surprisingly deep trip-hop grooves. Thanks to a great roster of remixers, Slicker's *Remixes* arguably bests the album it's sourced from. —*John Bush*

## Slint

f. 1987, Louisville, KY, db. 1991
*Group / Math Rock, Experimental Rock, Indie Rock, Post-Rock/Experimental, Alternative Pop/Rock, Instrumental Rock*
Though largely overlooked during their relatively brief lifespan, Slint grew on to become one of the most influential and far-reaching bands to emerge from the American underground rock community of the '80s; innovative and iconoclastic, the group's deft, extremist manipulations of volume, tempo, and structure cast them as clear progenitors of the post-rock movement which blossomed during the following decade.

Whatever the extent of Slint's own influence, the group grew out of Louisville, Kentucky's legendary Squirrel Bait, another seminal band which languished in relative obscurity during its own lifetime but ultimately spawned the likes of Gastr del Sol, Big Wheel, and Bastro. Guitarist/vocalist Brian McMahan formed his first group at the age of 12; within a few years, he teamed with drummer Britt Walford, and after the addition of vocalist Peter Searcy guitarist David Grubbs, and and bassist Clark Johnson, they founded Squirrel Bait in the mid-'80s. After two ferocious records, a self-titled 1985 effort and 1987's *Skag Heaven*, the group disbanded, leaving McMahan and Walford to continue on as Slint with guitarist David Pajo and bassist Ethan Buckler.

With producer Steve Albini, the quartet recorded 1989's *Tweez*, issued on their own Jennifer Hartman label; a collection of odd stylistic approaches, fractured rhythms and strange lyrical fragments, the album owed debts to few (if any) historical precedents and steadfastly defied easy classification. Shortly before the record's completion, Buckler left to form King Kong, and was replaced by bassist Todd Brashear for 1991's *Spiderland*, an even more sophisticated and adventurous set.

With the exception of a posthumous 1994 EP (originally recorded between the two full-length albums), *Spiderland* was Slint's swan song, although the individual members remained key figures in the independent scene. After attending art college, Pajo joined the ranks of Tortoise, while Walford (under the alias Shannon Doughton) played drums with the Breeders before rejoining Buckler in King Kong. McMahan and Brashear, meanwhile, aided Will Oldham in his ever-shifting Palace aggregate (which additionally housed Pajo and Walford at one point or another); McMahan and Pajo also briefly reunited as members of the For Carnation. —*Jason Ankeny*

**Tweez** / 1989 / Plan 9/Caroline ♦♦♦
*Tweez* is a fine, if bizarre recording, often switching from bass-led rhythm to rhythm in the same song. The guitars are harsh, but not especially fast. Instead of singing, bits of dialogue, sound effects, and spoken lyrics are used. —*John Bush*

● **Spiderland** / 1991 / Touch & Go ♦♦♦♦
More known for its frequent name-checks than its actual music, *Spiderland* remains one of the most essential and chilling releases in the mumbling post-rock arena. Even casual listeners will be able to witness an experimental power base that the American underground has come to treasure. Indeed, the lumbering quiet-loud motif has been lifted by everybody from Lou Barlow to Mogwai, the album's emotional gelidity has done more to move away from prog-rock mistakes than almost any of the band's subsequent disciples, and it's easy to hear how the term "Slint dynamics" has become an indie categorization of its own. Most interestingly, however, is how even a seething angularity to songs like "Nosferatu Man" (disquieting, vampirish stop-starts) or "Good Morning, Captain" (a murmuring nod to "The Rime of the Ancient Mariner") certainly signaled the beginning of the end for the band. Recording was intense, traumatic, and one more piece of evidence supporting the theory that band members had to be periodically institutionalized during the completion of the album. *Spiderland* remains, though, not quite the insurmountable masterpiece its reputation may suggest. Brian McMahan softly speaks/screams his way through the asphyxiated music and too often evokes strangled pity instead of outright empathy. Which probably speaks more about the potential dangers of pretentious post-rock than the frigid musical climate of the album itself. Surely, years later, *Spiderland* is still a strong, slightly overrated, compelling piece of investigational despair that is a worthy asset to most any experimentalist's record collection. —*Dean Carlson*

**Slint [EP]** / Aug. 29, 1994 / Touch & Go ♦♦♦
The release of this two-song EP (originally available only on vinyl, but since released on CD) marks the end of Slint's brief yet shockingly provocative career. The album contains an alternate version of "Rhoda" from *Tweez*, as well as one previously unreleased track, "Glenn." The album is a 20-minute barrage of haunting melodies and caustic noise. It is entirely instrumental, and this evidences Slint's skill and ambition. Without lyrics, the music takes a precedence that it perhaps lacks on other albums. Although greatly in the character of their earlier work, this album breaks through as Slint's most important release. Sadly, though, the album acknowledges the breakup of the band. Many have followed in the wake of Slint, but it seems unlikely that anyone will eclipse them. The album is a requisite listen for anyone interested in the post-rock era. —*Marc Gilman*

## Slipmatt (Matthew O'Brien)

b. Loughton, Essex, England
*DJ / Happy Hardcore, Hardcore Techno, Club/Dance*
An early chart hero during the early-'90s rave explosion and the leader of the growing happy hardcore nation later in the decade, Slipmatt changed the course of hardcore techno towards a serious artist-oriented direction—more in line with earlier dance styles like house, techno and drum'n'bass, all of which endured a period of critical rebuke before emerging as styles "worthy" of critical comment and praise. As a DJ, producer, dance-mag reviewer and head of the crucial United Dance label, he became the don of happy hardcore.

Born and raised in Essex, Slipmatt loved music from an early age and became entranced with punk, ska and dub during the early '80s. After working for a mobile DJ from the age of 16, he bought his own turntables and started mixing records by himself. A partnership with another DJ, Lime, resulted in the single "Do That Dance," recorded as SL2 for B-Ware Records. The duo self-released their second record, "DJs Take Control," which just narrowly missed the British Top Ten in late 1991. Their next single, "On a Ragga Tip," became another rave anthem, tied to the emergence of rastafied breakbeat techno— exemplified by the Prodigy and Shut Up and Dance, and a heavy influence on the development of jungle/drum'n'bass several years later. After being licensed to XL Recordings, it stormed to the No. 4 position in the British charts.

SL2 disintegrated soon after however, leaving Slipmatt back in the rave scene, which was fast turning underground. Instead of following the emerging dark sound, he decided to promote the original positive vibes of rave by forming Universal, Awesome, and United Dance Records. By the mid-'90s, a quite respectable scene was evolving out of the sound, dubbed happy hardcore. Though critical respect was in a minority, Slipmatt began getting much attention and even a few cover stories as the leader. He mixed four volumes in the *Mixmag Live!* series (one with old pal Lime) and an equal number for the *United Dance* series, including the excellent retrospective *United Dance Presents: The Anthems 92-97*. —*John Bush*

**Helter Skelter: The Annual (Hardcore)** / Nov. 11, 1996 / Helter Skelter ♦♦♦♦
A two-disc set shared by DJs Slipmatt and Dougal, *Helter Skelter* presents the history of happy hardcore circa 1993-94, with the duo's own tracks ("Feel Real

Free" by Dougal & Vibes and Slipmatt's "Take Me Away") appearing in the mix next to more recent happy anthems like "Higher Love" and "Keep on Trying." —*John Bush*

- **United Dance Presents: The Anthems 92-97** / Jan. 13, 1997 / United Music ♦♦♦♦

One of the prime compilations of the rave-to-hardcore scene during the '90s, *The Anthems 92-97* includes several Slipmatt classics over the course of two discs and 33 tracks mixed by the man himself. —*John Bush*

**Mixmag Live!, Vol. 4** / Jan. 31, 1997 / Mixmag ♦♦♦♦
Recording a mix disc chock full of rave and hardcore favorites with Stu Allan, Slipmatt calls on Bizarre Inc., Praga Khan, Channel X and Manix, as well as his own SL2 project. Allan's half of the album includes Joey Beltram's "Energy Flash" as well as tracks by Altern-8, Sweet Exorcist and Outlander. —*John Bush*

## Slotek

**f.** 1996, Brooklyn, NY
*Group / Illbient, Underground Rap, Ambient Dub, Trip-Hop, Club/Dance*
The Brooklyn-based dub-hop project Slotek was primarily the work of Special Dark in collaboration with cohorts Brother J, Jadoo, and Scotty Hard. The LP *7* appeared in 1997, followed two years later by *Hydrophonic*. —*Jason Ankeny*

- **7** / Apr. 8, 1997 / WordSound ♦♦♦♦

On Slotek's first album, Special Dark weaves an assortment of chilling B-movie samples over a set of stoner hip-hop beats pitched down so far they'd have to be sped up to be termed languorous. The production here is excellent, especially on tracks like "Jumbo" and "Electric Soul Controller"; for listeners who don't mind the supremely chilled vibes, *7* is prime dark illbience. —*John Bush*

**Hydrophonic** / Mar. 3, 1999 / WordSound ♦♦♦
Though Slotek swapped the sample mayhem of *7* for a set of raps reminiscent of KRS-One, the productions on *Hydrophonic* are still much closer to Brooklyn illbient than Wu-Tang Clan. The fusion works surprisingly well too, on "Last Rites," "Who I Am," and "Pros & Cons." —*John Bush*

## Sly & Robbie

**f.** 1978, Kingston, Jamaica
*Group / Roots Reggae, Dub, Dancehall*
Reggae's preeminent rhythm battery, the duo of drummer Sly Dunbar and bassist Robbie Shakespeare remained one of Jamaican music's most inventive and influential forces for decades; pioneers in the use of electronics and production effects, the aftershocks of their trademark Taxi sound are still being felt. The two first performed together in 1975, backing Peter Tosh; Dunbar's previous credits included tenures with the Yardbrooms and Flesh, Skin & Bones, while Shakespeare had studied bass under the great Aston Barrett before playing on sessions for the likes of Burning Spear and Bunny Wailer. In 1976 Sly and Robbie formed the Revolutionaries, one of the era's leading dub bands; at the same time they co-anchored Tosh's backing unit Word, Sound & Power, their style defining the so-called "rockers' riddims" prevalent throughout the remainder of the decade.

In 1978, Sly and Robbie founded Taxi Productions, their own record company; they also headlined the label's house band, the Taxi All-Stars, filling the roster with other musicians from the respective lineups of the Revolutionaries and Word, Sound & Power. The first release from Taxi was Black Uhuru's "Observe Life"; most of Black Uhuru's classic material was produced by Sly and Robbie, and the rhythm duo often backed the group on tour. Other early Taxi artists included veterans such as Gregory Isaacs, Prince Far-I, Dennis Brown, and Max Romeo, as well as up-and-comers including Jimmy Riley, the Wailing Souls, and the Tamlins. A marriage of Robbie's bone-rattling bass and Sly's groundbreaking synthesized drum sound, the Taxi aesthetic remained at all times on the cutting edge of technology, proving that reggae could move forward without compromising the music's integrity; in the process, as musicians, they earned the kind of notoriety and respect usually afforded only to singers and producers.

In 1980, Sly and Robbie signed a worldwide distribution deal with Island Records, resulting in a series of compilations of Taxi material; at the same time, they produced records for reggae legends like Jimmy Cliff, Desmond Dekker, and the Paragons, and as their global notoriety grew they were invited to record with performers including Bob Dylan, Mick Jagger, Joe Cocker, Grace Jones, and Robert Palmer. Sly and Robbie also recorded under their own names, and in 1985 teamed with producer Bill Laswell for *Language Barrier*; Laswell also helmed 1987's acclaimed *Rhythm Killers*, which featured cameos from Bootsy Collins and Shinehead. 1989 saw the release of *Silent Assassin*, an innovative fusion of dub and hip-hop including collaborations with KRS-One, Queen Latifah, and Young M.C. As simply Sly, Dunbar also recorded several solo dates, albeit with Robbie never far out of earshot. In 1999, the duo teamed with producer Howie B for *Drum & Bass Strip to the Bone*. —*Jason Ankeny*

**Language Barrier** / 1985 / Island ♦♦♦
Sly & Robbie team with producer Bill Laswell for an edgy dub set. Guests include Herbie Hancock, Bob Dylan, Afika Bambaataa, and Manu DiBango. —*Scott Bultman*

- **DJ Riot** / Jun. 1991 / Mango ♦♦♦♦

The ubiquitous Jamaican Riddim twins write, produce, and play for some of the island's best new (and maybe not-so-new) toasting talent... Only rarely do the artists within come up with a compelling track, with much of it sounding like tossed-off reggae-fied hip-hop. Taxi Gang's "SRD" made a direct hit, but too often the tracks become numbingly boring or irritating... Still, much of the playing is good; not sinewy or loping... but not as mechanized and cold as much dance music. —*John Dougan, Option 38_91*

**Drum & Bass Strip to the Bone by Howie B** / Jan. 12, 1999 / Palm Pictures ♦♦♦
This isn't drum'n'bass in the currently understood sense, it's drum & bass in the original (that is to say, the reggae) sense. On this album, drummer Sly Dunbar and bassist Robbie Shakespeare, two of the most widely recorded musicians in the world and two of the architects of modern reggae, join forces with noted techno producer Howie B and step off into the dark nether region of dub-inflected electronic dance music that they helped to discover, and began to map, over 20 years ago. If the music is only mildly compelling, it's not for lack of attractive textures and watertight rhythms. It's because Sly & Robbie have always made their best contributions when they've been working behind great singers; when they step to the fore, the results are always mixed. Here they vary from highly effective (as on the fairly straightforward rocker's reggae of "Ballistic Squeeze") to long-winded and boring ("Exodub Implosion"). Howie B does do a great job with the sound throughout, however. This disc is definitely worth owning, but don't trade in any of your vintage Channel One collections for it. —*Rick Anderson*

**Dub Fire** / Jun. 13, 2000 / NYC Music ♦♦♦
Jamaica's almighty rhythm section returns with yet another album of experimental dub. Tracks range from the ambient "Dub Fire" to the rock steady sounds on "Ganga Lee." Intertwined with the drum and bass are familiar reggae horn arrangements. The occasional lyrical quote pops up, perhaps most vividly on "Slacker Dub," which contains a few lines from C.S. Dodd and Leroy Sibbles' tune "I Love You." A solid album, but, like most dub, it has a tendency to sound alike to all but the most stringent listeners. Still Sly & Robbie fans will appreciate the effort. —*Curtis Zimmermann*

## Small Fish with Spine (Riz Maslen)

*Producer / Ambient-Techno, Trip-Hop, Techno*
One of the most prominent of a growing population of women composers working in post-techno experimental electronics, Riz Maslen's work as Neotropic and Small Fish with Spine combines ambient, dub, and electro with shards of house, hip-hop, and drum'n'bass. Although she's released nowhere near the amount of material as labelmates such as Coldcut and London Funk Allstars, consistency and a stylistic listlessness have proven key in elevating her to near peer status. Signing with the NTone and R&S labels in the mid-'90s (as Neotropic and Small Fish with Spine, respectively) with only a compilation track and a four-track EP to her name, Maslen has wasted no time filling her vita with some of the finest recent examples of downbeat breakbeat and experimental ambient/dub.

Ironically, Maslen's career in the upper reaches of the European experimental dance establishment didn't begin until she moved to New York, where she released the *Stickleback* EP through Apple-housed dance label Oxygen Music Works. After a pair of tracks on a compilation for Ninja Tune offshoot NTone, Maslen headed back to London in 1995 to release the *Tumble Weed* EP and, the following year, a single ("Laundrophone") and album (*15 Levels of Magni-*

fication) for the label. Belgium-based R&S' release of her self-titled Small Fish with Spine EP followed soon after. Maslen has also risen to acclaim through her association with the Future Sound of London, with whom she appeared on UK music show *Top of the Pops*, as well as collaborated with on a number of their recordings. Her second Neotropic LP for Ninja Tune was 1999's *Mr. Brubaker's Strawberry Alarm Clock*. [See Also: Neotropic] —*Sean Cooper*

**Stickleback** / 1996 / Oxygen Music Works ♦♦♦
Riz "Neotropic" Maslen's more straightforward guise, her Small Fish material is better suited to the dancefloor than her more recent releases as Neotropic. Uptempo breakbeats provide the backbone for most of this, her first EP-length release, with shades of experimentation surfacing in the form of hand-fashioned drum sounds and unconventional rhythmic textures. —*Sean Cooper*

● **Ultimate Sushi** / Mar. 29, 1999 / Oxygen Music Works ♦♦♦♦
*Ultimate Sushi* is a surprisingly diverse and complex set of tunes that never departs entirely from the traditions and norms of breakbeat culture, yet broadens that tradition's horizons considerably. Check out the scuttling 6/8 groove and whining violin on "Foul Play," for example, or the densely layered pizzicato strings, music boxes, keyboards and vocal samples during the arrhythmic intro section of "Concubine" (which then veers off into more conventional trip-hop territory, albeit with significant dubwise detours). "High Fibre," on the other hand, defines what may be a new genre of harsh, abrasive electronica (Death Techno? Beatcore?). All of it is definitely worth hearing repeatedly. If only there were more than 29 minutes of it. —*Rick Anderson*

## Smith & Mighty

f. 1989, Bristol, England
*Group / Trip-Hop, Jungle/Drum'N'Bass, Club/Dance, Electronic*
Long before Bristol had become a recognized stronghold for downtempo trip-hop and spy-soundtrack dubs, the duo of Rob Smith and Ray Mighty teamed in the late '80s for two early breakbeat tracks, "Walk on By" and "Anyone Who Had a Heart." The anachronistic fusion of sophisticated Burt Bacharach productions with laidback hip-hop prefigured trip-hop's later fascination with the more polished end of '60s adult-pop. The pair also produced the Top Ten hit "Wishing on a Star" for the Fresh Fours, then signed with ffrr Records (who were looking for a production team with crossover abilities similar to Soul II Soul).

The label later rejected both Smith & Mighty's debut album and several subsequent recordings—claiming they were unsuitable for release—so the duo formed their own label, More Rockers. Five years after their initial brush with major-label shenanigans, they released *Bass Is Maternal*. Smith & Mighty also worked on production for More Rockers signee Marxman, and released a volume in the *DJ Kicks* series in 1998. *Big World, Small World* followed almost two years later. Smith has also recorded with the trip-hop trio Jaz Klash. —*John Bush*

**Bass Is Maternal** / Oct. 1995 / More Rockers ♦♦♦
Unfortunately, there's too much experimentation and not enough hooks on Smith & Mighty's long-awaited album debut. The duo simply don't find a happy medium between jungle and reggae on *Bass Is Maternal*, recorded for their own More Rockers label. —*John Bush*

**DJ Kicks** / Mar. 9, 1998 / Studio !K7 ♦♦♦♦
Packed with their own productions and remixes, Smith & Mighty's volume in the *DJ Kicks* series does a very good job at blending beat-heavy tracks with the pair's occasional experimentalist flair. Including the early Bacharach covers "Walk on By" and "Anyone Who Had a Heart," plus a remix of another longtime pop classic ("The First Time Ever I Saw Your Face") and tracks by other Bristol massives like DJ Krust, *DJ Kicks* showcases the Smith & Mighty production team better than *Bass Is Maternal*. —*John Bush*

● **Big World, Small World** / Oct. 19, 1999 / Studio !K7 ♦♦♦♦
*Big World, Small World* improves on *Bass Is Maternal*'s too experimentalist streak with a refined set of tracks that float easily into each other. The problems are that it's almost *too* refined and slick, and by 1999 the sound had grown a bit stale with the public—unfortunate as the duo largely pioneered this style. Vocal contributions from six distinct voices are juggled throughout the course of the album without deteriorating the cohesion. Torchy orchestral lurchers are linked with natty drum'n'bass workouts, clubby vocal tracks, and hip-hop meditations. Though it might have been released after its sell-by date, there's no denying its quality. It's just a little disappointing that S&M couldn't bring any innovations to the table here, as they have in the far too distant past. —*Andy Kellman*

## DJ Andy Smith

b. Jan. 23, 1967, Thornbury, England
*DJ / Electronica, Trip-Hop, Club/Dance*
Portishead's DJ Andy Smith first met group frontman Geoff Barrow while the two were at school; he eventually joined Barrow's touring band as support DJ. He also appeared with the Fugees, Republica, and Prophets of the City, and released his debut mix album *The Document* in early 1998. —*John Bush*

● **The Document** / May 19, 1998 / Phase 4 Records ♦♦♦♦
As the DJ for Portishead, Andy Smith wasn't necessarily one of the better-known mixers in electronic music. After all, most of the music the band made was credited to Geoff Barrow, the mastermind of Portishead's albums. Perhaps that's why Smith went ahead and released *The Document*, a continuous-mix, various-artists collection that come close to capturing his opening sets for Portishead. It's an unpredictable, surprising disc, one where Jeru the Damaja, the James Gang, Peggy Lee, Barry White, Grandmaster Flash, and the Spencer Davis Group all occupy the same space. Surprisingly, the album works, as Smith's juxtapositions are both revealing and entertaining. It's not necessarily an album you'd return to frequently, but *The Document* is quite enjoyable as it's playing. —*Stephen Thomas Erlewine*

## Christian Smith

*Producer, DJ / Progressive House, Techno*
Part of the burgeoning Swedish scene centered mainly on Stockholm, Christian Smith has taken a long road to his current esteemed position as arguably the premier producer of the gray area between house and techno, often described as tech-house. His career began at the age of 15, when he saw Sven Vath spin at Dorian Gray in Frankfurt. Soon he was spinning records, and moved to New York in 1989, instantly submerging himself at the exciting electronic dance music sounds coming out of Chicago, Detroit, and New York at this time. It wasn't long before he was a regular on the American circuit, but just as he was reaching the summit of his popularity in America, he returned to his birthplace in Sweden and joined the country's exploding scene, alongside peers such as Adam Beyer and Cari Lekebusch. Similar to Lekebusch, Smith has illustrated a dual commitment to both house and techno—usually a bad career move—that has surprisingly still allowed him to find fame with his tracks that seem a compromise between the more pounding side of house and the more tribal sound of techno. His first release came back in 1991, and since then he has recorded for labels as renowned as Yoshitoshi, Primevil, Primate, and In-Tec, including a large number of collaborations with John Selway. In addition to production and DJing, Smith also manages Tronic, his own esteemed label that is home to artists such as Joel Mull and Mistress Barbara, along with Beyer and Lekebusch. —*Jason Birchmeier*

● **Tronic Phunc [EP]** / May 25, 1998 / Primevil ♦♦♦
Here Christian Smith lays down some of his hardest, most percussive work for the acclaimed label, Primevil, proving that he is a man of many styles. —*Jason Birchmeier*

**Timeline [EP]** / Sep. 6, 1999 / Yoshitoshi ♦♦
Smith's tech-flavored house sounds a bit out of place on Yoshitoshi, the trance-flavored house label. —*Jason Birchmeier*

## Smoke City

f. 1994, London, England
*Group / Electronica, Ambient-Techno, Alternative Dance, Trip-Hop*
Though based in London, the trip-hop trio Smoke City created music with a distinctively Brazilian, bossa nova-influenced sound—no surprise given that vocalist Nina Miranda's childhood was divided between the UK and South America. Miranda formed Smoke City with former schoolmate Mark Brown, with whom she shared an affection not only for the music of Santana and Gilberto Gil but also classic '70s funk; rounding out the line-up with guitarist Chris Franck, formerly of the Brighton-based Brazilian percussion group Batu, the group issued a handful of indie-label singles before signing to Jive Records in the fall of 1995. Their debut LP *Flying Away* followed two years later, and was highlighted by the single "Underwater Love," which became a European hit, thanks to its use in a commercial campaign for Levi's jeans. —*Jason Ankeny*

**Flying Away** / Nov. 24, 1997 / Jive ♦♦♦
The track "Underwater Love," used for a Levi's commercial earlier in 1997, is just one of the pleasing trip-hop and mild breakbeat tracks on Smoke City's debut album; other songs, like "Numbers" and "Dark Walk," are just as strong, and the alternately rough-hewn and sultry vocals of Nina Miranda (in French and Portuguese as well as English) definitely add to the proceedings. All in all, the album is a bit of a surprise considering that the group was completely unknown before gaining success on British TV. —*John Bush*

## SND

**f.** Sheffield, England
*Group / Minimal Techno, Experimental Techno*
Mark Fell and Mat Steel are a pair of Sheffield DJs and music-makers who've departed slightly from their city's template for British techno (i.e., Warp Records) to embrace the experimental/minimalist wing of European artists (Oval, Microstoria, Gas) associated with the Mille Plateaux label. Naming their project after the extension often used for computer sound files, Fell and Steel are both expert programmers who disdain the usual electronics route of audio software or instruments. Instead, they usually rely on contact mics and their own software interfaces to record. During 1998-99, they debuted with the "Tplay" single and *Newtables* EP on their own SND label. In July 1999, Frankfurt's Mille Plateaux released SND's debut album, *Makesnd Cassette*, and the sophomore *Stdiosnd Types* followed one year later. With Jeremy Potter, Fell also works as Shirt Trax. —*John Bush*

- **Makesnd Cassette** / Jul. 6, 1999 / Mille Plateaux ♦♦♦♦
*Makesnd Cassette* is an album of painfully minimal house music that surprisingly manages to balance its experimental slant with credible efforts at establishing a groove. With the occasional wave of atmospheric synth sounding quite lonely among these desolate productions, the 15 untitled tracks here comprise just a few pointed beats, rhythmic effects, and static or noise—each of which is pruned down to mere split-seconds of sound. The jarring effect of computer-enhanced experimentation occasionally recalls the pioneering work of Oval and Pan sonic, though the SND duo's style sounds quite original. —*John Bush*

## Sneaker Pimps

**f.** 1995, Reading, England
*Group / Electronica, Alternative Dance, Adult Alternative Pop/Rock, Trip-Hop, Club/Dance*
Sneaker Pimps are a trip-hop trio that formed in Reading, England in 1995, following the success of Portishead's *Dummy* and Tricky's *Maxinquaye*. Borrowing heavily from Portishead and Massive Attack, Sneaker Pimps have a trancey but edgy sound, highlighted by Kelli Dayton's soulful vocals. While Dayton is the focal point, Chris Corner (guitar) and Liam Howe (keyboards) are the band's leaders, writing all of the songs and producing the records. Howe and Corner had been playing in bands since the early '90s, to no success. After seeing Dayton sing with a pub band in 1995, they convinced her to join the fledgling Sneaker Pimps, who had taken their name from an article the Beastie Boys published in their *Grand Royale* magazine about a man they hired to track down classic sneakers.

Sneaker Pimps released their first single, "Tesko Suicide," in May of 1996 and it was greeted with positive reviews in the UK music press. *Becoming X*, the group's debut, was released in August and it was a critical success, with *Q* magazine naming the album one of the best albums of the year. However, the band failed to make an impact on the pop charts in the UK. The hit *Becoming X* was released in the United States in February 1997, preceded by the single "6 Underground." *Becoming Remixed* followed in early 1998. —*Stephen Thomas Erlewine*

- **Becoming X** / Aug. 19, 1996 / Virgin ♦♦♦♦
*Becoming X* is one of the most engaging by-products of post-Portishead trip-hop. While the Sneaker Pimps don't have the doomed romanticism of Portishead, or the nasty experimental tendencies of Tricky, they have a cool sense of pop hooks and an edgier guitar attack than their predecessors. "Tesko Suicide" moves along with jagged guitars and rhythms, while "6 Underground" is cooly detached postmodern soul. *Becoming X* creates an airy, urban atmosphere, and even though the record begins to unravel toward the end, it is an exciting, entrancing listen. —*Stephen Thomas Erlewine*

**Becoming Remixed** / Mar. 10, 1998 / Virgin ♦♦♦
As they began work on their second album, the Sneaker Pimps released the limited-edition remix album *Becoming Remixed*. Although it isn't as cohesive as *Becoming X*, it's a surprisingly successful effort, balancing B-sides and previously released remixes with four previously unreleased cuts. A number of major names—including Armand Van Helden, Roni Size, Perfecto, and Eli Janney—have worked on the album; only a few cuts, such as Van Helden's "Spin Spin Sugar—Dark Garage Mix," offer drastic new interpretations of the original versions, but even the slight variations are intriguing and entertaining, making it the rare remix album that's worthwhile for listeners who aren't hardcore fans. —*Stephen Thomas Erlewine*

**Splinter** / Dec. 7, 1999 / EMI ♦♦
Sneaker Pimps followed the debut success of *Becoming X* with the different, yet strangely familiar, *Splinter*. Kelli Dayton, whose haunting vocals made songs like "Spin Spin Sugar" and "6 Underground" so evocative, is no longer with the group. While this takes the listener a few moments to re-adjust—Dayton's voice was, after all, what made Sneaker Pimps so accessible—this album is still worth the effort. *Splinter* is a superb disc, full of trancey, edgy psychedelia, interspersed with moments of blistering rock. The new vocalist is Chris Corner, who, with Prodigy mastermind Liam Howlett, are the driving forces behind the band. Corner is not nearly as good a singer as Dayton, although his breathy—and at times whiney—vocals suit these songs well. Although the comparisons with Portishead, Massive Attack, and Garbage are inevitable, the Sneaker Pimps have created an intricate album of trip-hop that is every bit as original as any of their contemporaries'. While *Splinter* may not have the standout singles that *Becoming X* had, it is a stronger album overall. Low-key, psychedelic, and brilliant, this release would rate with Massive Attack's *Mezzanine* as one of the finest examples of the trip-hop genre. —*Jonathan Lewis*

## Sneakster

*Group / Indie Pop, Ambient Pop, Dream Pop*
Formerly the frontman for the pioneering indie-electronics act Seefeel, Mark Clifford returned to a (nominally) band environment in 1999 with the Sneakster project. A collaboration with vocalist Sophie Hinkley, Sneakster began when the pair met at London's Milk Bar and started writing music together. Bella Union released the *Splinters* EP in 1999, and Sneakster's debut album *Pseudo-Nouveau* followed later that summer. The American release, issued one year later, also included a bonus EP of remixes by Robin Guthrie of Cocteau Twins. —*John Bush*

- **Pseudo Nouveau/Fifty-Fifty** / Mar. 21, 2000 / Shadow ♦♦♦♦
Quite similar to the material released by other projects including members of Seefeel (Scala, Mark Van Hoen's Locust), Sneakster skates on the boundaries of several familiar musical styles: dream pop, ambient minimalism, experimental techno, and trip-hop. Clifford's productions are chilly, precise, and in most cases, very fragile; *Pseudo Nouveau* is definitely an album more suited for indie popsters than beat-heads. And even when he does desert the floating-synth ambience for tougher rhythms on "Whileaway," "Heavy Heat, Heavy Time," and "Sweet Melody," Hinkley reins in the tracks with her vocals, simultaneously smoky and seductive, yet often distanced and resigned. She's working from the same template forged by Portishead's Beth Gibbons and Lamb's Louise Rhodes (as well as Seefeel's Sarah Peacock). It's hardly a surprising direction for Clifford, but *Pseudo Nouveau* retains much of the gorgeous sound of the Seefeel classics *Quique* and *Pure, Impure*. The American release adds *Fifty-Fifty*, a remix EP wherein Robin Guthrie adds his delicious soft-toned guitar to the album tracks "Fireheart," "Stolen Letter," and "Kinda Blue." —*John Bush*

## Sofa Surfers

**f.** Vienna, Austria
*Group / Trip-Hop, Club/Dance*
The trip-hop act Sofa Surfers was founded by a quartet of sound-obsessed Viennese instrumentalists: Wolfgang Schlögl, Markus Kienzl, Wolfgang Frisch, and Michael Holzgruber. The group's debut single "Sofa Rockers" earned a remix from fellow Austrian head Richard Dorfmeister, and their debut album *Transit* earned wide release through MCA. *Cargo* followed three years later. —*John Bush*

**Transit** / Nov. 3, 1997 / MCA ♦♦♦

- **Cargo** / Jul. 11, 2000 / Klein ♦♦♦♦
*Cargo* is a set of menacing, dusty trip-hop jams, an aesthetic completely in

keeping with the accompanying booklet's images of a construction site at night. This German quartet, influenced by dub, acid jazz, and Kraut-rock in equal amounts, construct their own beatscapes with dark (usually live) beats and deep, dubby basslines. The result is a half-live, half-programmed sound that's often more reminiscent of Primal Scream (circa *Vanishing Point*) than Sofa Surfers' nominal compatriots in the German electronics scene. On the opener, "Container," a heavily mic'ed dub drum kit sets the stage for several minutes of excellent distorted funk, while the group crank it up higher yet for the second track ("Beans & Rice"), with guest vocalist Singing Bird chatting freestyle over a beat-crazy production. It's clear that Sofa Surfers concentrate on the transitional flow between tracks (most are uninterrupted) just as much as the tracks themselves, making *Cargo* a sleek album that hangs together well and hits many peaks. —*John Bush*

## Soft Cell

f. 1980, Leeds, England, db. 1984
*Group / New Romantic, New Wave, Synth-Pop, Dance-Pop*
A synth-pop duo famed for its uniquely sleazy electronic sound, art students Marc Almond and Dave Ball formed Soft Cell in Leeds, England in 1980. Originally, vocalist Almond and synth player Ball teamed to compose music for theatrical productions, and as Soft Cell, their live performances continued to draw heavily on the pair's background in drama and the visual arts. A self-financed EP titled *Mutant Moments* brought the duo to the attention of Some Bizzare label head Stevo, who enlisted Daniel Miller to produce their underground hit single "Memorabilia" the following year.

It was the next Soft Cell effort, 1981's "Tainted Love," that brought the duo to international prominence; written by the Four Preps' Ed Cobb and already a cult favorite thanks to Gloria Jones' soulful reading, the song was reinvented as a hypnotic electronic dirge which became the year's best-selling British single, as well as a major hit abroad. The group's debut LP, *Non-Stop Erotic Cabaret*, was also enormously successful, and was followed by the 1982 remix collection *Non-Stop Ecstatic Dancing*.

While 1983's *The Art of Falling Apart* proved as popular as its predecessors, the LP's title broadly hinted at the internal problems plaguing the duo; prior to the release of 1984's *This Last Night in Sodom*, Soft Cell had already broken up. Almond immediately formed the electro-soul unit Marc and the Mambas; another group, Marc Almond and the Willing Sinners, followed before the singer finally embarked on a solo career in the late '80s. After a number of years of relative inactivity, Ball later resurfaced in the techno outfit the Grid. —*Jason Ankeny*

- **Non-Stop Ecstatic Dancing** / 1982 / Sire ◆◆◆◆◆
The version of "Memorabilia" included here is notable for its energy, but the only other thing on the US edition that really catches the attention is "What." The UK edition of the mini-album included "Insecure...Me?," the B-side to the single version of "What," improving the odds a little. —*Steven McDonald*

**Non-Stop Erotic Cabaret** / 1982 / Sire ◆◆◆◆
Reissued with a staggering number of B-sides, this Soft Cell album should not be missed, though the point is not the over-referenced "Tainted Love." More interesting are the astoundingly sleazy "Sex Dwarf," the grim trash of "Bedsitter," the dual punches of "Seedy Films" and "Secret Life," and the melancholy "Say Hello, Wave Goodbye." The hard black heart that beat under the skin of Soft Cell was located squarely in the middle of London's Soho district, red lights, strip clubs, alleyway hookers, and all; if ever a city district had a soundtrack, this was it. —*Steven McDonald*

**The Art of Falling Apart** / 1983 / Sire ◆◆◆
While it has some mediocre moments, this tense, quirky release also has some magnificent outings, including the epic "Martin" (based on the obscure George Romero psycho/vampire movie), a cut that was originally included on a bonus 12", and the relentless title cut. Not as cheap or sleazy in its sound as *Non-Stop Erotic Cabaret*, the album was still prone to melodramatic writing and performance. By all means, miss the "Hendrix Medley," another bonus cut. —*Steven McDonald*

**This Last Night in Sodom** / 1984 / Sire ◆◆
The chilly layers of synths gave way to a wall of raging noise on this outing, with Almond shouting his way through much of it while David Ball sounded as though his mandate had been to program his keyboards to self-destruct. A painful document of the duo's disintegration, it still included rare decent cuts such as "Down In the Subway" and "Soul Inside." Other than that, however, *This Last Night In Sodom* is involved with far too much corruption to be tolerable. —*Steven McDonald*

**Memorabilia: Singles** / Oct. 8, 1991 / Mercury ◆◆◆◆
Although it doesn't contain a couple of key tracks, including the 12" version of "Tainted Love/Where Did Our Love Go," *Memorabilia* is the best Soft Cell collection available. —*Stephen Thomas Erlewine*

## Solar Twins

*Group / Ambient Pop, Electronica, Jungle/Drum'N'Bass, Electronic*
Solar Twins is the British-raised, Los Angeles-based duo of David Norland (electronic instruments) and Joanna Stevens (vocals). Norland, who grew up in West London, has a classical background; Stevens is half Burmese. They first teamed up in England, then moved to Los Angeles, where they played at the Viper Room and were signed to Maverick Records. Their self-titled debut album was released in September 1999. —*William Ruhlmann*

- **Solar Twins** / Sep. 21, 1999 / Warner Brothers ◆◆◆
Solar Twins are keyboardist/programmer David Norland and singer Joanna Stevens, both from London but currently based in Hollywood, where they became local club darlings before signing to Maverick. The hook on their debut is a breathy drum and bass version of the Clash's "Rock the Casbah," a version that walks expertly the fine line between tribute and parody. The duo's originals sound something like a cross between ABBA (minus the harmonies) and Roni Size. Stevens has a truly lovely voice and she knows how to use it, varying from full-throated romantic belting to whispery insinuation. With his combination of poppy chord changes, stuttering breakbeats, and lush electronic textures, Norland creates an accompaniment that mates the edgy energy of drum and bass with the sumptuous disposability of radio pop. The lyrics overreach sometimes (sample couplet: "I'll run my finger along your open wound/Entice this infection 'til it's fully exhumed"), but never enough to distract from the consistently winning music. —*Rick Anderson*

## Solex (Elisabeth Esselink)

b. Rotterdam, The Netherlands
*Vocals, Producer / Indie Pop, Alternative Dance, Indie Rock, Singer/Songwriter*
Named after a small, Hungarian-made motor scooter, Solex is the project of Amsterdam-based record-shop owner and songwriter Elisabeth Esselink. Formerly a member of Dutch indie-pop group Sonetic Vet, Esselink wanted to express her musical ideas more completely; after purchasing an 8-track recorder and a vintage sampler, Esselink began recording songs on her own. Combing the racks of her own store for kitschy records, Esselink took snippets of old records to make new ones, creating her own style of lo-fi technopop. Solex's debut, *Solex Vs. The Hitmeister*, came out in 1998; *Pick Up* followed a year later. —*Heather Phares*

**Solex Vs. The Hitmeister** / Mar. 10, 1998 / Matador ◆◆◆◆
Solex, a.k.a Dutch record-shop owner Elisabeth Esselink, creates a pure, offbeat musical world on the 1998 debut, *Solex Vs. The Hitmeister*. All of the songs contain the band's name; Esselink delivers her English-sung vocals with dreamlike, rhythmic phrasing; and the album's cavernous production makes it sound as though it were recorded deep inside her head—it all adds up to an abstract, alien collection of songs that owes very little to electronica or indie rock as the outside world knows it. Instead, each song on *Hitmeister* flows to its own musical logic, built on samples of discounted, long-forgotten records, and Esselink's expressive, sweetly foreign voice, supported here and there by touches of guitar and keyboards. "When Solex Just Stood There" suggests industrial dance with its relentless beat, one-note vocals, and screeching sound effects, while "Solex All Licketysplit" bounds around the room on a rubbery bassline and sparkly keyboards. "Some Solex" marries a somewhat ominous bass drum to a warm guitar line, while spaceship sound effects hover in the background. "One Louder Solex" and "Solex in a Slipshod Style" have a fluid, stream-of-consciousness style that recalls daydreams, adding to *Hitmeister's* overall surreal quality. A completely unique combination of beats, samples, and voice, Solex is insular and inventive, revealing an artist with a very personal kind of creativity. —*Heather Phares*

- **Pick Up** / Sep. 14, 1999 / Matador ◆◆◆◆
On her 2nd Solex album *Pick Up*, Elisabeth Esselink continues to recycle bad music into good, sampling the kitschiest, cheesiest records in her shop and shaping them into her distinctive musical vision.

A richer, more complex effort than her debut, *Solex Vs. The Hitmeister*, *Pick Up* is also more bewildering on the first few listens. Esselink's hyperactive creativity results in an initially confusing collage of seemingly unrelated musical elements and ideas—"Pick Up" alone features a mournful trumpet, bluesy guitar licks, a string section and shifting, syncopated rhythms. Very often, *Pick Up* sounds like Esselink singing whatever comes into her head, backed by four different records playing at once.

That's a compliment, however. Esselink's loose, whimsical approach creates fragile musical hybrids like "Randy Costanza"'s klezmer-calypso and the swing-trip-hop of "The Burglars Are Coming!" Yet *Pick Up* is far from an exercise in creating hyphenated genres; "That's What You Get With People Like That On Cruises Like These," "Snappy & Cocky," and "Oh Blimey!" are impressionistic, obscure, poppy—almost unclassifiable, other than as Solex songs. As with *Hitmeister*, Esselink's pretty, slightly distracted vocals link each of the album's vignettes together and add to the songs' spontaneous feel, particularly on "Superfluity" and "Five Star Shamberg," where her stream-of-consciousness singing adds to the dreamlike vibe.

Most impressively, Esselink's enthusiasm for music—playing it as well as listening to it—shines through on each of *Pick Up*'s 14 tracks, especially the slinky "Escargot" and "Another Tune Like 'Not Fade Away.'" By melding techno's penchant for sampling and indie rock's D.I.Y. aesthetic, with *Pick Up* she creates pure, paradoxical music where anything is possible. —*Heather Phares*

### Solid Doctor (Steve Cobby)

b. Hull, England
*Producer / Electronica, Ambient-Techno, Trip-Hop, Club/Dance*

Solid Doctor's Steve Cobby is the dominant creative force behind popular Hull-based trip-hop label Pork Recordings, for whom he's recorded a number of full-length albums under a variety of names (including Fila Brazillia and Heights of Abraham). Pork was formed in 1991 by Cobby and fellow Hullster/flatmate Dave Pork in order to release the first single by Cobby's then-side project, Fila Brazillia (Fila has since become his focus), following which he began releasing solo material under the Solid Doctor name. He released two full-lengths within a year (one of them, *How About Some Ether?*, a double-disc compilation of singles) and helped attract critical attention to Pork with a blend of instrumental hip-hop, dub, funk, and house that would soon propel labels such as Mo'Wax and Cup of Tea into the spotlight. Like previous musical endeavors (including Big Life! pop/dance group Ashley & Jackson, which dissolved around 1990), Cobby's Solid Doctor material carves out a space between the dancefloor and the hi-fi, aiming for a middle ground of groove with songwriting and musicianship given equal weight with the more practical consideration of moving a crowd. —*Sean Cooper*

● How About Some Ether?: Collected Works 93-95 / 1995 / Pork ◆◆◆◆
The Solid Doctor borrows elements from an astounding variety of genres on this LP, including trip-hop, funk, ambience, house, techno and jazz. Despite the disparity, the music flows well along an electronic groove. —*John Bush*

Beats Means Highs / May 20, 1996 / Pork ◆◆◆

### Solsonics

f. 1991, Los Angeles, CA
*Group / Jazz-Rap, Acid Jazz, Hip-Hop*

In 1991, bassist Jez Colin and percussionist Willie McNeil formed the Solsonics from Los Angeles's underground club scene. Although the band plays soul-jazz with updated hip-hop rhythms, elements of Afro-Cuban and reggae music also appear. The Solsonics first gained a national release when Chrysalis released *Jazz in the Present Tense* in 1993. —*John Bush*

● Jazz in the Present Tense / 1993 / Chrysalis ◆◆
The jazz/hip-hop and acid-jazz schools continue to generate interesting, if erratic projects. The Solsonics' instrumentals and reworkings and incorporation of such jazz classics as Freddie Hubbard's "Red Clay" and Ahmad Jamal's "Superstition" are intriguing, featuring fine solos from saxophonist Jim Akimoto, trumpeter Elliot Caine, keyboardist Mike Boito, and special guests like guitarist Norman Brown. When lyrics and vocalists are included, the quality dips, mainly because they didn't find a lyricist whose contributions matched their playing skills. But their spirit, intensity, and interaction are so good that it's easy to overlook the trite lines and lightweight vocals. —*Ron Wynn*

### Solvent (Jason Amm)

*Producer / Electronica, Ambient-Techno*

Solvent is Toronto post-techno producer Jason Amm, who releases melodic electro/nica under that name through his own Suction label, cofounded with friend and label partner Gregory DeRocher (aka Lowfish) in 1997. Traceable to a number of nonexclusive influences spanning the last 20-odd years of electronic music (early electro-pop innovators such as the Normal, Liaisons Dangereuse, Visage, and Soft Cell), Amm's music is a fidgety, lo-fi fusion of the range of those influences combined with strains of current post-techno comparable to Aphex Twin and Autechre. Solvent contributed three tracks to Suction's first 12" before the label issued his self-titled debut CD in 1998. A mixture of warm, melodic, reassuring melodies and by turns mellow and harsh rhythms, the CD drew instant comparisons to Aphex Twin, although just ap parent were the influence of Yaz and early Human League. A split 7" with like-minded (if not like-sounding) Italian duo D'Arcangelo followed in 1999, as did another split with label partner Lowfish on German/British label City Center Offices. Amm also contributed Solvent material to compilations on Spelunk, Lo Recordings, Vinyl Communications, and Serotonin, and released his second full-length, *Solvently One Listens*, at the end of 1999. —*Sean Cooper*

Suction 001 [EP] / 1997 / Suction ◆◆◆
A generous debut from Canadian electronica label Suction, featuring six tracks (two apiece) from label proprietors Greg de Rocher (as Lowfish) and Jason Amm (as Solvent). Rushing to the Rephlex analogy might at first seem appropriate, but melodic and textural elements tracing to industrial/ebm and new wave raise the obscure-concept level a bit higher than much of the acid/electro/ambient crunch appearing on Aphex' label. Closer to the Skam/Mask/V/VM brand of dark, atmospheric ambient electro, with touches of drum'n'bass on two of the three Lowfish tracks. —*Sean Cooper*

● Solvent / 1998 / Suction ◆◆◆◆
A collection of tracks—some lovely, some forbidding—drawing on the last few decades of electronic dance music, while remaining distinctly irresolute of the dancefloor. Electro and jungle are the two most obvious contemporary touchstones, but the layers of rhythm and texture on tracks such as "Pineapple Boy," "My Blue Car," and "Rel's Comb" are much more engaging than those styles typically allow. —*Sean Cooper*

Solvently One Listens / Nov. 1, 1999 / Suction ◆◆◆◆
Still heavily reminiscent in sound and execution of Warp's early-'90s heyday, Jason Amm's second Solvent album pulls back from the experimentation of his debut with a set of listening techno that's heavy on the slow moving melodics and slightly abrasive percussion programs. "Hello Pop" and "Duckie" evoke the computer soul sound of early Autechre and Boards of Canada. —*John Bush*

### Sonic Boom (Peter Kember)

b. Nov. 19, 1965, Rugby, Midlands, England
*Guitar, Producer / Space Rock, Indie Rock, Post-Rock/Experimental*

Sonic Boom was the alias of Pete Kember, best known as the singer-guitarist in the legendary hypno-drone unit Spacemen 3. A native of Rugby, England, while attending art college Kember teamed with Jason Pierce to form Spacemen 3, recording a demo tape in 1986; after signing to Glass Records, the group recorded their debut LP *Sound of Confusion*, for which Kember adopted the name Pete Gunn. By the time of their follow-up EP *Walkin' with Jesus*, he had rechristened himself Sonic Boom, keeping the pseudonym for the duration of his career. In 1990 he issued his lone solo LP, *Spectrum;* after the 1991 swan song *Recurring,* Sonic recycled the Spectrum title as the name of his new band, which debuted with the LP *Soul Kiss (Glide Divine).* Sonic Boom was also the driving force behind the Experimental Audio Research project, a loose configuration of musicians which included My Bloody Valentine's Kevin Shields. —*Jason Ankeny*

● Spectrum / 1990 / Silvertone ◆◆◆

### Sons of Silence

f. 1995, London, England
*Group / Experimental Techno, Electronica, Ambient Dub*

The illbient collective the Sons of Silence took shape from the remains of the respected experimental unit O Yuki Conjugate. Comprised of Daniel Mudford, Peter Woodhead, Joe Gardiner, and Andrew Hulme, the London-based group first issued a pair of successful 12"s, *The Golden Age of Men's Music* and *Spring Forward Fall Back*, before releasing their 1997 full-length effort *Silence FM*. —*Jason Ankeny*

- **Silence FM** / Jun. 16, 1997 / Leaf ♦♦♦♦
While previous transmission from O Yuki side project Sons of Silence have proved overly dance-y, this debut recording from the group gets the balance right, interspersing dub-heavy, beat-fueled tracks (usually brushed with clean, club-friendly jazz and electronica) with abstract shorts of fizzing melodic ambience. The result is a personable, dynamic ride that listens almost as a single hour-long track. As usual, production values are sky high, and past ruttings of an overly "ethno" bent are filtered to a more palatable concentration. —*Sean Cooper*

## Sons of the Subway

f. 1994, London, England
*Group / Club/Dance, Techno*

A bit more independent than a full-fledged Bandulu side project, Sons of the Subway consists of Bandulu's Lucien Thompson and longtime friend Dave Pitts. The duo's take on techno is just as aggro as Bandulu—both in ethic and execution—but looks more to the past, not just in Detroit techno but in '80s electro and old-school hip-hop. After releasing several singles for a variety of labels, Sons of the Subway released a self-titled 1997 album on the recharged Infonet Records, earlier the home of Bandulu themselves. —*John Bush*

**Sons of the Subway** / 1995 / Infonet ♦♦♦
This four-song EP explores the realm of jungle-dub for the influential Infonet label. —*John Bush*

- **Ruff, Rugged & Real** / Sep. 1997 / Infonet ♦♦♦♦
Sons of the Subway's first album ties the more aggressive element of urban techno warfare inherent in Bandulu's material with old-school remnants like electro and early hip-hop. Additionally, *Ruff, Rugged & Real* manages to work in a few tracks of big-beat techno, but with more spark and energy than most imitators of the Chemical Brothers. —*John Bush*

## Soul II Soul

f. 1989, London, England
*Group / Club/Dance, Urban, House, Dance-Pop, Soul*

Led by producer/vocalist/songwriter DJ Jazzie B, Soul II Soul were one of the most innovative dance/R&B outfits of the late '80s, creating a seductive, deep R&B that borrowed from Philly soul, disco, reggae and '80s hip-hop. Originally featuring Jazzie B, producer/arranger Nellee Hooper, and instrumentalist Philip "Daddae" Harvey, the musical collective came together in the late '80s. The group had a residency at the Africa Centre in London's Covent Garden, which led to a record contract with 10, a subsidiary of Virgin. Two singles, "Fairplay" and "Feel Free," began to attract attention both in clubs and in the press.

Featuring the vocals of Caron Wheeler, Soul II Soul's third single "Keep on Movin'," reached the UK Top Five in March of 1989. Released in the summer of 1989, "Back to Life" also featured Wheeler and became another Top Ten hit. Soul II Soul released their debut album, *Club Classics Volume One*, shortly afterward. The album was released in America under the title *Keep on Movin'*; both "Keep on Movin'" and "Get a Life" became substantial hits, propelling the album to double platinum status.

Wheeler left the group before the recording of the group's second album, *Vol. II: 1990—A New Decade*. The album debuted at No. 1 in the UK, yet it caught the group in a holding pattern. Hooper soon left the collective, leaving Jazzie B. to soldier on alone. Hooper went on to work with several of the most influential and popular acts of the early '90s, including Massive Attack (*Blue Lines*), Bjork (*Debut* and *Post*), Madonna (*Bedtime Stories*), and U2 ("Hold Me, Thrill Me, Kiss Me, Kill Me"). In 1992, Soul II Soul released *Vol. 3: Just Right*, to both lukewarm reviews and sales. After the compilation *Vol. IV: The Classic Singles*, the group's next studio album (*Vol. V: Believe*) appeared in 1995. —*Stephen Thomas Erlewine*

**Club Classics, Vol. 1** / Apr. 10, 1989 / Virgin ♦♦♦♦
With influences ranging from Chic to hip-hop to African music, Soul II Soul's debut album, *Club Classics, Vol. 1* (titled *Keep on Movin'* in America), was among the most rewarding R&B releases of 1989. Soul II Soul leader/producer/composer Jazzie B takes one risk after another, all of which pay off. The group enjoyed major hits with the Chic-influenced gems "Keep On Movin'" and "Back to Life" (both of which feature the gifted Caron Wheeler), and equally superb are the African-influenced reflections of "Dance" and "Holdin' On," the soulful grit and intensity of "Feel Free," and the hypnotic house music of "Happiness." Though Wheeler was Soul II Soul's best-known singer and went on to enjoy a career as a solo artist, Rose Windross and Do'Reen (both expressive soul divas) also do their part to make *Club Classics, Vol. 1* the artistic triumph that it is. —*Alex Henderson*

★ **Keep on Movin'** / Jun. 1989 / Virgin ♦♦♦♦♦
When American urban-contemporary radio was bombarding its listeners with one Guy clone after another in the late '80s and early '90s, British neo-soulsters like Soul II Soul, Lisa Stansfield, and the Chimes offered highly creative and gutsy alternatives. With influences ranging from Chic to hip-hop to African music, Soul II Soul's debut album, *Keep on Movin'* (titled *Club Classics, Vol. 1* in its original British incarnation) was among the most rewarding R&B releases of 1989. Soul II Soul leader/producer/composer Jazzie B takes one risk after another—all of which pay off. The group enjoyed major hits with the Chic-influenced gems "Keep on Movin'" and "Back to Life" (both of which feature the gifted Caron Wheeler), and equally superb are the African-influenced reflections of "Dance" and "Holdin' On," the soulful grit and intensity of "Feel Free," and the hypnotic house music of "Happiness." Though Wheeler was Soul II Soul's best-known singer and went on to enjoy a career as a solo artist, Rose Windross and Do'Reen (both expressive soul divas) also do their part to make *Keep on Movin'* the artistic triumph that it is. —*Alex Henderson*

**Vol. II: 1990, A New Decade** / May 21, 1990 / Virgin ♦♦♦♦
A better album but a deceptive one: even the best songs here don't intoxicate as thoroughly as "Keep On Movin'," but within the context of the album, each plays a vital part. In other words, this is a genuine *album*, and not a pastiche of singles. —*John Floyd*

**Vol. V: Believe** / Aug. 11, 1995 / Virgin ♦♦♦
Six years after they revolutionized R&B and soul with their debut album *Keep on Movin'*, Soul II Soul returned with *Volume V: Believe*. Since their debut, the soul collective had been struggling to regain their position as musical innovators; in the process, they turned out two confused albums that had their moments, but nothing quite as stirring as their initial singles, which were collected on the British-only *Volume IV: The Classic Singles*. *Believe*, their fourth album of original material, doesn't necessarily make a case for Soul II Soul as pioneers in the mid-'90s, but it does represent something of a comeback. Where their two previous albums were muddled affairs, *Believe* is clear and confident, filled with fully formed songs. It helps that Jazzie B, the leader of the group, has persuaded former members Caron Wheeler and Penny Ford to make appearances on the album and has recruited some genuine new talent that helps spark him into recording his best music since the group's debut. Granted, it doesn't push down many boundaries, but *Believe* fits comfortably into the laidback, jazz-saturated grooves of '90s R&B. —*Stephen Thomas Erlewine*

## Soul Oddity

f. 1995, Miami, FL
*Group / Electro-Techno, Club/Dance*

A proponent of the "new skool electro" sound—a fusion of Detroit electro with Miami bass funk—the south Florida-based Soul Oddity was the partnership of producers Josh Kay and Romulo Del Castillo. Supposedly formed as the result of a chance encounter with a UFO, Soul Oddity's fascination with the otherworldly continued on their 1996 debut album *Tone Capsule*, which collected their three previous EPs released earlier that same year. One year later, the duo followed up with *Randa Roomet*, recorded as the side-project Phoenecia. [See Also: Phoenecia] —*Jason Ankeny*

- **Tone Capsule** / May 28, 1996 / Astralwerks ♦♦♦♦
*Tone Capsule* is a collection of Soul Oddity's three initial "new skool electro" EPs, which were first released in the spring of 1996. —*Jason Ankeny*

## Source Direct

f. 1992, St. Albans, England
*Group / Electronica, Jungle/Drum'N'Bass, Club/Dance*

St. Albans-based duo Source Direct are renowned for the ambient-leaning progressive drum'n'bass they've released on the Metalheadz, Basement, Certificate 18, and Street Beats labels, as well as on their own self-titled imprint. Often compared with such rolling, relaxed junglists as LTJ Bukem, Peshay, and Goldie, Source Direct actually figure closer to the taut, brooding complexity of Photek and edgier PFM, wrapping sweeping minor-key melodies around sharp, splintered breaks and deep basslines far more oppositional than the sweet retreat of much of the LGR and Metalheadz stables. Claiming close affinity with '70s soul, jazz, and funk groups such as Grover Washington, Bob James, and Average White Band, SD's Jim Baker and Phil Aslett began making music together when they were just 14. Renting out midnight studio time at Hackney's Panic Studio, they assembled demo cassettes of (still unreleased) material while setting their DJ skills in order and organizing and hosting underground (usually illegal) hardcore parties. They soon pieced their own studio together in their St. Albans home (near Ipswich, home to Rupert "Photek" Parkes), and began releasing a string of highly acclaimed 12"s by the ages of 17. The pair record under a variety of pseudonyms for various labels, including Intensity (Basement), Sounds of Life (Certificate 18), Oblivion (Street Beats), but have released most of their material as Source Direct (primarily on Odyssey, Metalheadz, Looking Good, and their own label). Source Direct tracks have been featured on Looking Good and Metalheadz label compilations, and the pair have completed remixes for the likes of the Shamen, Code of Practice, and Medicine Man. Their *Exorcise the Demons* album appeared in 1999. By the end of the year, Aslett had left the fold, though Baker continued alone as Source Direct. —*Sean Cooper*

**Two Masks/Black Domina [Single]** / Jan. 20, 1997 / Science ♦♦♦♦
After much speculation about whether or not they'd make the jump, Source Direct's major label debut finally arrived in the form of *Two Masks*, some of the pair's darkest, most accomplished material to date. A bit of a distance from earlier releases for Metalheadz, Certificate 18, and their own SD label, *Two Masks* (which also marks the first SD release available on CD) is chilling, cavernous stuff, with complex beat patterns, hand-fashioned breaks, and eerie, echoing atmospheres reaching deep into colleague Rupert "Photek" Parkes territory. Excellent. —*Sean Cooper*

**Controlled Developments** / Nov. 4, 1997 / Astralwerks ♦♦♦♦
The singles and B-sides compiled on *Controlled Developments* all tend toward minor chords, stark atmospherics and basslines that creep out from subterranean caves and roar around your head before being sucked back into the ground again. Though this approach lends a certain sameness, the proceedings are still good, scary fun. Highlights include "Computer State," with its alternating sounds of humans panting and monsters growling, and the dubwise orchestral tones of "Two Masks." —*Rick Anderson*

● **Exorcise the Demons** / Mar. 8, 1999 / Astralwerks ♦♦♦♦
The long-awaited Source Direct recording arguably betters labelmate Photek at crafting that rare thing: a listenable album of unfiltered drum'n'bass. While Photek's *Modus Operandi* was unapologetically and unrelentingly dark, *Exorcise the Demons* has a few notable detours into acid effects and even what sounds like occasional disco samples. It's about as obsessively produced as could be expected for an album that's taken so long to appear, but for fans of jungle's intelligent tech-step wing, it's an excellent purchase. —*John Bush*

### Source (Robert Leiner)

*Producer / Ambient-Techno, Techno*
Robert Leiner, born in Sweden in 1966, ran a betting shop for several years before putting his love of Tangerine Dream and Jean-Michel Jarre to good use, courtesy of a contract with the Belgian electronic label R&S. His first album, *Organized Noise*, was recorded as the Source, though its more ambient follow-up (for the R&S offshoot Apollo) was released as by Robert Leiner. Further recordings appeared on R&S as the Source Experience. [See Also: Robert Leiner] —*John Bush*

● **Organized Noise** / 1993 / R&S ♦♦♦♦
As the title suggests, *Organized Noise* is an album of acid-techno heavy on the hard percussive edges, especially on tracks like "Neuromancer" and "Eclipse." Glimpses of Leiner's accomplished, melodic sense, however, occasionally reveal themselves with "Beyond Time." —*Keith Farley*

### Space DJ'z

f. 1993
*Group / Electronica, Club/Dance, Techno*
The duo of Ben Long and Jamie Bissmire have been recording track after track of hard, Detroit-style techno ever since their move from the decks to the mixing board in 1993. Old-school B-boys and fans of electro from way back, Long and Bissmire were turned on to the explosion of Detroit techno in London during the late '80s and early '90s. The duo picked up turntables and began DJing in the early '90s, opening gigs by Primal Scream and the Orb. Bissmire had already debuted on wax as the founder of Bandulu, but Space DJz themselves first earned release in 1993 on Infonet, the short-term dance label opened by Creation. After releases on Ongaku, Soma, and NovaMute during the mid-'90s, the pair issued their debut album, *On Patrol!*, for Soma in 1999. Both also own their own Detroit-slanted labels, with Long's Potential Records hosting producers like the Advent, Oliver Ho, and Inigo Kennedy, while Bissmire's Ground label has featured Claude Young, among others. —*John Bush*

● **On Patrol!** / Jun. 28, 1999 / Soma ♦♦♦♦
After legion EPs and singles for labels including Reload, NovaMute, and Soma, Ben Long and Bandulu's Jamie Bissmire finally debuted on LP with *On Patrol* for Soma. Including their big Soma hit "Lights" as well as a host of other street-level techno stormers, it's an excellent look at the British side of hard electronics circa 1999. —*Keith Farley*

### Space

f. 1989, London, England, **db.** 1990
*Group / Ambient House, Ambient*
One of the major touchstone groups in the early development of ambient-house, Space was formed by Orb mainman Dr. Alex Paterson and the KLF's Jimi Cauty. Just after Paterson and Cauty recorded and released the Orb single "A Huge Ever Growing Pulsating Brain That Rules from the Centre of the Ultraworld" in late 1989, they began working on an inner-space album. Though the duo split early in 1990, Cauty released the recordings later in the year on KLF Communications as the *Space* LP. —*John Bush*

● **Space** / Jul. 1990 / Space-KLF Comm. ♦♦♦♦
The only Space album ever released consists of seven tracks (one for each planet other than Earth and Mars) and some incredibly sparse ambience. Besides a variety of astronaut/mission-control samples, there are long periods of near-silence with only an occasional break for galactic sine-waves and similarly spacy tones. More important for who's on it than what's in it, *Space* is yet another casualty of the deleted and ultra-rare KLF back catalog. —*John Bush*

### Spacemen 3

f. 1982, Rugby, Midlands, **db.** 1991
*Group / Space Rock, Neo-Psychedelia, Alternative Pop/Rock*
Spacemen 3 were psychedelic in the loosest sense of the word; their guitar explorations were colorfully mind-alterating, but not in the sense of the acid rock of the '60s. Instead, the band developed its own minimalistic psychedelia, relying on heavily distorted guitars to clash and produce their own harmonic overtones; frequently, they would lead up to walls of distortion with over-amplified acoustic guitars and synths. Often the band would jam on one chord or play a series of songs, all in the same tempo and key. Though this approach was challenging, often bordering on the avant garde, Spacemen 3 nevertheless gained a dedicated cult following. After releasing several albums in the late '80s, the band fell apart after in 1991.

In 1982, Sonic Boom (guitar, organ, vocals; born Pete Kember on November 19, 1965) and Jason Pierce (guitar, organ, vocals; also born November 19, 1965) formed Spacemen 3 in Rugby, Warwickshire, England. Sonic Boom and Pierce added a rhythm section comprised of Pete Baines and Rosco, and spent the next four years rehearsing and jamming. In 1986, the group released their debut album, *Sound of Confusion*, on Glass Records. At first the band sounded a bit like a punked-up garage rock band, but their music quickly evolved into their signature trance-like neo-psychedelia. Spacemen 3's second album, 1987's *The Perfect Prescription*, was the first to capture the group's distinctive style.

Following 1989's *Playing with Fire*, Baines and Rosco left the group to form their own band, the Darkside. They were replaced by Will Carruthers and John Mattock. Despite the addition of new blood to the group's lineup, the band was beginning to fray because of in-fighting between Sonic Boom and Pierce, as well as the former's increasing drug dependency. The new lineup struggled through a final album, 1991's *Recurring*, which featured Boom's songs on side one and Pierce's on side two. By the time of the release of *Recurring*, Pierce was performing with Carruthers and Mattock in a new band called Spiritualized. Shortly after the release of *Recurring*, Spacemen 3 split, and Spiritualized became Pierce's full-time band, eventually earning a cult following of their own. —*Stephen Thomas Erlewine*

## SPACEMEN 3

**Sound of Confusion** / 1986 / Glass ♦♦♦

Spacemen 3's debut captures the band's drone-rock aesthetic in its earliest stages of development: louder and more abrasive than their later work, the album quickly establishes its mood and then maintains it, with only minor fluctuations of rhythm and tempo—its songs, a combination of statement-of-purpose originals ("Losing Touch With My Mind," "O.D. Catastrophe") and odd covers (the Stooges' "Little Doll," the 13th Floor Elevators' "Rollercoaster," and Glen Campbell's "Mary Anne"), fuse together to forge an enveloping sonic haze. A mesmerizing, primal immersion in noise. —*Jason Ankeny*

**Perfect Prescription** / 1987 / Glass ♦♦♦♦

A record mirroring the evolution of drug-induced euphoria from its inception (the blistering "Take Me to the Other Side") to its peak ("Feel So Good") to, finally, the inevitable crash ("Call the Doctor"), Spacemen 3's brilliant sophomore effort greatly expands the parameters of the narcotic drone-rock of *Sound of Confusion* to forge a rapturous and intensely visceral sonic experience. Recorded with a minimal use of percussion and a maximum use of spatial atmosphere, tracks like "Walkin' With Jesus" and a glistening symphonic cover of the Red Crayola's "Transparent Radiation" are masterpieces of texture, evocative and darkly beautiful; a representation of the band's unique vision at its most unified, *The Perfect Prescription* travels beyond the corporeal into new realms of consciousness and bliss. —*Jason Ankeny*

**Performance** / 1988 / Genius ♦♦♦♦

Recorded in Amsterdam in 1988, the live *Performance* documents a set from the *Perfect Prescription* tour; the emphasis here is on the group's loud, noisy origins—only the closing "Feel So Good" hints at the more subdued atmospheres and textures which emerged as Spacemen 3's primary focus as they approached *Playing With Fire*. Among the highlights: "Take Me to the Other Side," "Walkin' With Jesus," and "Come Together." —*Jason Ankeny*

**Playing with Fire** / 1989 / Fire ♦♦♦♦

A transitional effort bridging the dark, droning riffs of *The Perfect Prescription* with the ethereal atmospherics of *Recurring*, *Playing With Fire* ties together the disparate threads of the Spacemen 3 sound into an integrated whole. Apart from the incendiary single "Revolution" and the throbbing tribute "Suicide," the record is delicate and spare, a carefully modulated and expressive collection of elliptical melodies and pulsing backdrops tempered by an increasing fascination with minimalism and repetition. Although cohesive and organic, the album underscores the growing dichotomy separating Jason Pierce and Sonic Boom—while the former's songs are yearning and spiritual, the latter's are obsessive and ominous; not surprisingly, the follow-up, *Recurring*, was to be a Spacemen 3 album in name only. —*Jason Ankeny*

**Dreamweapon: An Evening of Contemporary Sitar Music** / 1990 / Fierce ♦♦♦♦

Taking off from the ideals which form the core of LaMonte Young's concept of Dream Music, the heart of *Dreamweapon* is "An Evening of Contemporary Sitar Music," a transfixing 40-minute-plus document of a landmark Spacemen 3 performance recorded at Waterman's Art Centre in Hammersmith on August 19, 1988. Perhaps the purest expression of the Spacemen aesthetic, the piece is an unbroken tapestry of hypnotic drones, throbbing tones and repetitive phrases, dappled here and there by evaporating fragments of the melodies which later resurfaced on *Playing With Fire*. The cumulative effect is one of utter disorientation—all notions of time and space quickly give way to complete conscious immersion in the music's narcotic tug. A pair of epic rarities, Sonic Boom's feedback sculpture "Ecstasy in Slow Motion" and "Spacemen Jam," round out the package. —*Jason Ankeny*

**Taking Drugs to Make Music to Take Drugs To** / 1990 / Father Yod Productions ♦♦♦

The sonic manifesto *Taking Drugs to Make Music to Take Drugs To* compiles a number of circa-1986 demos, offering rough sketches of material which later appeared primarily on the Spacemen debut *Sound of Confusion*. —*Jason Ankeny*

● **Recurring** / Mar. 1991 / Dedicated ♦♦♦♦

In essence, *Recurring* is as much the final Spacemen 3 studio effort as it is the joint debut of Spectrum and Spiritualized, the two pivotal groups to emerge from the band's ashes. Split evenly between solo music from Pete "Sonic Boom" Kember and Jason Pierce, the record diverges from the shared mindset of earlier releases to paint a portrait of a band at the breaking point: while Pierce's tracks—recorded with the same battery of musicians with whom he formed Spiritualized—are minimalist symphonies, Sonic's are more pop-oriented, even employing sequencers on the ten-minute opener "Big City (Everybody I Know Can Be Found Here)." Still, the record is surprisingly cohesive; even when moving in opposite directions, Sonic and Pierce retain the same point of departure and the same objectives—throughout, *Recurring* is beautiful and transcendent, a fitting farewell. —*Jason Ankeny*

**Translucent Flashbacks** / 1995 / Fire ♦♦♦♦

*Translucent Flashbacks* fills in some of the gaps in the early chapters of the Spacemen 3 story, compiling singles, B-sides, and rarities issued primarily in conjunction with the *Sound of Confusion* and *The Perfect Prescription* albums. Among the essentials: the complete "Ecstasy Symphony" (a fragment of which leads into *Prescription's* "Transparent Radiation"), the early single version of "Walkin' With Jesus," and the full-on 17-minute "Rollercoaster." —*Jason Ankeny*

**For All the Fucked up Children of This World We Give** / Apr. 28, 1995 / Sympathy for the Record Industry ♦♦♦

*For All the Fucked up Children of This World We Give* contains the group's first-ever recordings; never again were their garage-punk influences clearly as evident as on these embryonic stabs at "Walkin' With Jesus" and "Things Will Never Be the Same." —*Jason Ankeny*

## Spacetime Continuum (Jonah Sharp)

b. London, England

*Producer / Jazz-House, Ambient House, Electronica, Ambient-Techno, Club/Dance*

Ambient-techno innovator Jonah Sharp has recorded several albums and EPs as Spacetime Continuum and played an important role in consolidating the San Francisco experimental ambient and techno scenes through his Reflective imprint. A London native and an acid jazz drummer before embarking on his career in electronic music, Sharp was an in-demand session drummer until the rigors of the club scene and the mawkish obsolescence of the genre had him experimenting with other styles. Glomming onto ambient and techno as a DJ, Sharp was a founding member of the periodic Spacetime parties, held in a hologram factory in London and host to such early new ambient luminaries as Mixmaster Morris, David Moufang, and Dr. Atmo. Sharp left London for America in the early '90s, settling in San Francisco, where he established his Reflective label and recorded the bulk of his work to date. Although that work has been split over a number of different project headings (Emit Ecaps, Alien Community, Reagenz, Electro Harmonix, and others), his most consistently visible work has been as Spacetime Continuum. Sharp signed a non-exclusive multi-album deal with Astralwerks in 1992 and released his first full-length work—a live recording of a collaboration with author Terrence McKenna and didgeridoo player Stephen Kent—the following year. The largely ambient *Sea Biscuit* followed in 1994, and was released through the Fax label in Europe (Sharp has recorded a number of collaborative projects for Fax). *Emit Ecaps*, released in early 1996, returned to Sharp's dancefloor roots, incorporating elements of house, techno, and jungle. It also spawned a remix album, *rEmit rEcaps*, featuring work by Autechre, Plaid, and others. In addition to a smattering of Sharp-related releases (including the collectible *Flurescence* EP), the Reflective label issued albums by Subtropic, Velocette, Kid Spatula (aka Mike Paradinas), and Single Cell Orchestra, as well as a stream of 12"s. The next Spacetime Continuum full-length, *Double Fine Zone*, appeared in 1999. —*Sean Cooper*

**Flurescence [EP]** / 1993 / Reflective ♦♦

A satisfying first statement, released on the now-influential Reflective label. Hailed by Mixmaster Morris as among the best things he'd ever heard at the time of release, the album's tricky balance of dancefloor groove and chill room ambiance has been much copied. Reissued in 1994 on the Source label. —*Sean Cooper*

**Alien Dreamtime** / Sep. 1993 / Astralwerks ♦♦♦

The ambient-groove soundtrack of *Alien Dreamtime* is a vivid accompaniment to McKenna's live spoken-word performance. —*John Bush*

**Sea Biscuit** / Sep. 23, 1994 / Astralwerks ♦♦♦

Sharp's first album-length solo work is full of expansive, fluffy environments, a bit sugary at times and with a tendency to go nowhere in particular. Still, some nice hand-built sounds and interesting, engulfing arrangements place this near the top of the new ambient heap. Also released on the Fax label. —*Sean Cooper*

- **Emit Ecaps** / 1996 / Astralwerks ♦♦♦♦
Sharp's second proper album keeps much of the atmospheric beauty of *Sea Biscuit* intact, but the material usually works only as an introduction to devastating beat work on tracks like "Kairo" and "Funkyar," both of which recall the chunkier side of jungle and electro quite convincingly. All in all, *Emit Ecaps* is a fascinating fusion of hard and soft. —*John Bush*

- **rEmit rEcaps** / Nov. 4, 1996 / Astralwerks ♦♦♦♦
In which some of the biggest names in dance-based electronic music—both experimental and straightahead—are given the MIDI files to Spacetime's *Emit Ecaps* and entreated to go nuts. Remixers include Carl Craig, Autechre, Higher Intelligence Agency, Subtropic, Matthew Herbert, David Moufang (as Move D), and Spacetime's own Jonah Sharp. The stealers are up for grabs, but the spicier cuts include Subtropic's jungled-up take on "Kairo," and Herbert's deep house fry of "Movement 2," and HIA's dense electro mix of "Funkyar." Also released on Reflective as two separate 12"s. —*Sean Cooper*

- **REALtime [EP]** / Nov. 10, 1997 / Astralwerks ♦♦♦
Spacetime Continuum's first release in over two years is *REALtime*, a five-song EP. Even if you fail to recognize the funky attitude portrayed by the cover graphics, you'll certainly recognize it in the music. The new direction is inspired by Jonah Sharp's own "Swing Fantasy" track on the 1996 remix album *rEmit rEcaps*. The fearless, vibrant bassline in "Microjam" is the musical middle on the disc, which ranges from the subtle mood in "Freelon" to the intense beats in "Pressure Live" and "Neoteric Strange Attractor Mix." New to Spacetime's arsenal are the vocals performed by MC Girao, which appear in the two "Neoteric" mixes. "Pressure [Live]" is from the Summer 1997 Neoteric Festival in Japan. This track takes the opening song from *Sea Biscuit* and injects a drum'n'bass rhythm, resembling the best blend between intense rhythm and musical atmospheres that Spacetime has committed to disc. "Neoteric Strange Attractor Mix" is a high-energy dancefloor groove. The rhythm is a repetitive yet solid groove, using slices of voice samples extensively. "Freelon," only available on the UK import version, is the most abstract of the tracks on this EP, more closely resembling material from *Sea Biscuit* and *rEmit rEcaps*. This song offers a steady but subdued rhythm and a huge familiar ambient sound. The beats and synths pace their way to the end, where they diverge and drop out. —*Brett Neely*

- **Double Fine Zone** / Jun. 1, 1999 / Astralwerks ♦♦♦♦
Echoing the focus on a live, jazzy feel of contemporary works by As One, Ian O'Brien and Carl Craig, Spacetime Continuum's *Double Fine Zone* includes sax player Brian Iddenden on several tracks plus Spacetime himself, Jonah Sharp, contributing just about everything else (that is, drums, synth, sampler, and Rhodes piano). Though the "live" feel is mostly a non-event (Iddenden's smooth late-night sax solos are, to be kind, unnecessary), Sharp saves the day with some inventive programming, reminiscent of his last proper full-length, *Emit Ecaps*. The bubbly effects and lo-energy trance breaks on "Microjam," the static chords mirroring a set of cloudy synthesizer breaks on the highlight "Biscuit Face," the unsequenced drums and Rhodes shards on "Beveled Edge," all prove that Sharp doesn't need the gimmick of a "jazz" album to make fine music that's more innovative than derivative. —*John Bush*

## Spaceways

f. 1989, Bristol, England
*Group / Electronica, Ambient-Techno, Trip-Hop*
Hip-hop/jazz fusioners Spaceways record for the Bristol-based Cup of Tea label, whose releases by Grantby, Red, Monk & Canatella, and Purple Penguin combined with those of higher-profile Bristolean acts such as Massive Attack and Portishead in making the city a hotspot of sorts for smoky, dub- and jazz-inflected head music. Championing a groove-based, live-sounding integration of funky, sequenced beats and live percussion with lots of brass, guitars, standup bass, and other instrumental affects not normally associated with electronic dance music, Spaceways are, like Red Snapper and Propellerheads, among a new crop of artists re-exploring dance music's roots in live performance. A seven-piece, complete with horn section, the group formed in 1989 at the height of the UK acid jazz craze, and their roots are more than evident in their first string of COT releases, "Japanese Flute" and the full-length debut, *Trad* (although the jazz is of a freer, less "refined" sort than the Talkin' Loud and Acid Jazz tracks that were the staples of that scene). Spaceways tour often and are a constant on the Bristol scene through Cup of Tea's various club events, which routinely feature mixed bills of DJs, visual artists, and live acts. —*Sean Cooper*

- **Trad** / Sep. 9, 1996 / Cup of Tea ♦♦♦
If acid jazz was a hip-hop/funk fusion mediated by the language of jazz, Spaceways make their play from the outer edges of improvisational territory, drawing on Sun Ra, Cecil Taylor, and the Art Ensemble of Chicago for their inspiration. The group's debut, *Trad*, is free-jazz/trip-hop of a dense, sophisticated sort, and one which makes certain demands of the listener, the least of which is the abandonment of the hard-and-fast categories that tend to surround the sort of warped genre extrapolation presented here. —*Sean Cooper*

## Sparks

f. 1970, Los Angeles, CA
*Group / Indie Pop, Trance, Club/Dance, Pop/Rock, Hi-nrg, New Wave*
Sparks was a vehicle for the skewed pop smarts and wiseguy wordplay of brothers Ron and Russell Mael, Los Angeles natives who spent their childhood modeling young men's apparel for mail-order catalogues. While attending UCLA in 1970, the Maels formed their first group, Halfnelson, which featured songwriter Ron on keyboards and Russell as lead vocalist; the band was rounded out by another pair of brothers, guitarist Earle and bassist Jim Mankey, and drummer Harley Feinstein.

Halfnelson soon came to the attention of Todd Rundgren, who helped land the group a contract with Bearsville and produced their self-titled 1971 debut. Their quirky, tongue-in-cheek art-pop failed to find an audience, however, and their manager successfully convinced the Maels to change the group's name; after becoming Sparks, they almost reached the Hot 100 with the single "Wonder Girl." 1972's sublimely bizarre *A Woofer in Tweeter's Clothing* cemented the band's cult status, and scored another near-hit with "Girl from Germany."

While touring the UK, Sparks was warmly received by the British music press, and ultimately, the Mael brothers relocated to London, leaving the rest of the band behind; Earle Mankey subsequently became a noted producer, while Jim later joined Concrete Blonde. In need of a new support unit, the Maels placed an advertisement in *Melody Maker*, and with guitarist Adrian Fisher, bassist Martin Gordon and drummer Norman "Dinky" Diamond firmly in place, they recorded 1974's glam-bubblegum opus *Kimono My House*, which reached the Top Five of the UK album charts and spawned two major British hits, "This Town Ain't Big Enough for the Both of Us" and "Amateur Hour."

With new guitarist Trevor White and bassist Ian Hampton, Sparks returned later that year with *Propaganda*, another UK smash which scored with the hits "Never Turn Your Back on Mother Earth" and "Something for the Girl With Everything." Overblown production from Tony Visconti derailed 1975's *Indiscreet*, however, and when the record fared less successfully than its predecessors, the Maels returned to the US, where they recruited Tuff Darts guitarist Jeff Salen, former Milk 'n' Cookies bassist Sal Maida, and drummer Hilly Michaels for 1976's *Big Beat*.

By 1977's ironic *Introducing Sparks*, recorded with a series of Los Angeles session players, the Mael brothers were treading water, so they enlisted disco producer Giorgio Moroder to helm 1979's synth-powered dance-pop confection *Number One in Heaven*, which spurred the group to renewed success in England on the strength of the hit singles "The Number One Song in Heaven," "Beat the Clock," and "Tryouts for the Human Race." Moroder's sidekick Harold Faltermeyer took the production reins for the immediate follow-up *Terminal Jive*, which scored a massive French hit with "When I'm With You."

Sparks left disco in the dust with 1981's *Whomp That Sucker*, recorded in Munich with a new supporting band comprised of guitarist Bob Haag, bassist Leslie Bohem and drummer David Kendrick (who also played together as the Gleaming Spires). After 1982's *Angst in My Pants*, they recorded 1983's *Sparks in Outer Space;* the wonderful "Cool Places," a duet with the Go-Go's Jane Wiedlin, nearly reached the US Top 40, and was the band's biggest hit.

The disastrous 1984 LP *Pulling Rabbits Out of a Hat* derailed any chart momentum the band had gathered at home, however, and after 1986's self-explanatory *Music That You Can Dance To*, Sparks—again reduced to the core duo of Ron and Russell—recorded 1988's *Interior Design*, which was followed by a long hiatus. Outside of composing the music for a film by Hong Kong action maestro Tsui Hark, Sparks remained silent until *Gratuitous Sax & Senseless Violins*, released in 1995. *Plagiarism* followed two years later. —*Jason Ankeny*

- **Kimono My House** / 1974 / Island ♦♦♦♦
Sparks specializes in keyboard-based pop songs with clever, ironic lyrics (by Ron Mael), sung in a near-falsetto by Russell Mael. Examples include "Here

in Heaven" (in which a disappointed, dead Romeo sings to a still-living Juliet who "broke our little pact"), "Thank God It's Not Christmas," and the UK hits "This Town Ain't Big Enough for Both of Us" and "Amateur Hour." —*William Ruhlmann*

### Big Beat / 1976 / CBS ♦♦♦♦
Most of this album finds Sparks doing what they do best: spewing out clever, mile-a-min\ute lyrics over solid-rocking accompaniment (this time, provided by a superior group of studio musicians). Drummer Hilly Michaels and guitarist Jeffrey Salen lend the Mael brothers' songs considerable rock 'n' roll authority. Standouts include the opening blast, "Big Boy" (which was featured in the film *Rollercoaster*), the propulsive "Fill-Er-Up," and the falsetto-delivered proclamation "I Like Girls," apparently a leftover from their previous album, *Indiscreet*. Generally, however, they eschew the elaborate arrangements of *Indiscreet* and go for a powerful, stripped-down sound. As titles such as "Everybody's Stupid" and "Thrown Her Away (And Get a New One)" suggest, the album brims with decidedly politically incorrect (and often hilarious) lyrics. —*James A. Gardner*

### Number One in Heaven / 1979 / Virgin ♦♦♦♦
It may not have been the most natural match in music history, but the marriage of Sparks' focus on oddball pop songs to the driving disco-trance of Giorgio Moroder produced the duo's best album in years. From the chart hits "Number One Song in Heaven" and "Beat the Clock" to solid album tracks like "La Dolce Vita," *Number One in Heaven* surprises by succeeding on an artistic and commercial level despite the fact that neither the Maels nor Moroder tempered their respective idiosyncrasies for the project. Moroder's production is just as dizzying, chunky and completely rhythm-driven as on his best work with Donna Summer, and the Mael brothers prove on "Tryouts for the Human Race" and "Academy Award Performance" that their bizarre songwriting wasn't compromised. —*John Bush*

### Terminal Jive / 1980 / Virgin ♦♦♦♦
The second Giorgio Moroder collaboration of Sparks' career doesn't have quite the emphasis on Moroder trademarks compared to its predecessor; he has only two songwriting credits here, while the Maels take most of them alone. Still, the breakout single "When I'm with You" and "Just Because You Love Me" have an ineffable disco stomp, and the requisite cymbal slaps on the off-beat while "Nasty Boys" and "Stereo" have an experimental, laddish feel that looks past disco into '80s synth-pop and new romantic. Though disco fans can feel safe with *Number One in Heaven*, those more interested in new wave would be well-served to pick up *Terminal Jive* first. —*John Bush*

### Whomp That Sucker / 1981 / RCA ♦♦
"Tips for Teens" kicks off Sparks' first post-Moroder album (though it was produced by his longtime associate Mack) with a blast; as a rocking power-pop/new wave number, it slotted into everything around it at the time perfectly, but the sense was of the world catching up to Sparks rather than the band chasing the train (and only Sparks could come up with lines like "Don't eat that burger/Has it got mayonnaise/Give it to me"). The equally sharp and catchy "Funny Face" follows with a truly hilarious detailing of a person who looks so perfect that he throws himself off a bridge in despair; as a one-two start to an album, this simply couldn't be beat. *Whomp* doesn't totally maintain the levels of its near-perfect start, but Russell Mael's voice is still a sinfully pure instrument, and brother Ron's ear for instantly memorable should-have-been-massive pop runs rampant as ever. Meanwhile, a new full-time backing band recruited from young Los Angeles outfit Bates Motel does a pretty solid job at putting rock crunch back into the Sparks mix. Guitarist Bob Haag, bassist Leslie Bohem, and drummer David Kendrick aren't quite a match for the original lineup or the glam-era outfit, but they acquit themselves well nonetheless. As always, the Maels are the stars of the show, and more often than not they rise to the occasion. "I Married a Martian" is a definite highlight, with a big rock crunch meshing well with the space-age keyboard touches as Russell notes, "her loving is different/vive la difference." Favorites of long-time fans include "Suzie Safety," blessed with a lovely piano line and a clipped feedback riff, and "Wacky Women," with Russell offering up some "Münich wisdom" on the subject. —*Ned Raggett*

### Angst in My Pants / 1982 / Atlantic ♦♦♦
For *Angst in My Pants*, Sparks turned to power-pop and scored their first US singles chart entry with the hilarious "I Predict" on an album that also includes such novelties as "Eaten by the Monster of Love." —*William Ruhlmann*

### Sparks in Outer Space / 1983 / Teldec ♦♦♦
"Cool Places," an uptempo duet with ex-Go-Go Jane Wiedlin (and No. 49 hit) paces this collection, perhaps Sparks's biggest US seller. —*William Ruhlmann*

### Pulling Rabbits Out of a Hat / 1984 / Atlantic ♦♦
While this album continues in the synthesizer-based pop vein of the previous year's modest hit, "Cool Places," it lacks anything as appealing. Songs like the title track and "Everybody Move" have danceable grooves, and "Song That Sings Itself" and "Love Scenes" are surprisingly conventional love songs. Russell Mael generally avoids his sometimes-grating falsetto, the melodies and arrangements are simple, and the lyrics lack their usual tongue-twisting eccentricity. In short, most of what made Sparks unique is absent here, leaving a surprisingly generic '80s band. Few sparks are struck here. —*James A. Gardner*

### Interior Design / 1988 / Rhino ♦♦
It doesn't say much for an album when its strongest track is a shaggy-dog story like *Interior Design*'s "Madonna"—and even less when they repeat it three times (albeit in different languages). This is a scaled-down, self-produced effort nearly bereft of the Mael brothers' trademark (often off-color) wit. And, unlike many of their earlier albums, they don't have a hot band to put the iffy material across; other than a guitarist and second keyboard player, this is all Ron and Russell's show. Between the lackluster songwriting and static arrangements, this was Sparks' weakest album to date. —*James A. Gardner*

### Mael Intuition: The Best of Sparks 1974-1976 / 1990 / Island ♦♦♦♦
A well-chosen, 20-track compilation derived from the group's three best albums (*Kimono My House*, *Propaganda*, and *Indiscreet*), released during their brief, productive tenure with Island Records. Producers Muff Winwood (for the first two, harder-rocking albums) and Tony Visconti (the more varied and elaborately arranged *Indiscreet*) both provide the Mael brothers with solid, sympathetic settings for their witty, rapid-fire lyrics and manic delivery. Songs range from the aggressive riff of "At Home, At Work, At Play" (a precursor to the heavier sound of the 1976 album, *Big Beat*) to the uncanny Andrews Sisters evocation "Looks, Looks, Looks." Russell Mael's quavery falsetto is an acquired taste, and his vocal affectations can try the listener's nerves on prolonged exposure. Also, their tendency to deliver a few hundred lyrics in as many seconds makes interpretation a challenge, but their perverse humor rewards the effort. This is probably all the Sparks the casual fan needs. —*James A. Gardner*

### • Profile: Ultimate Collection / Apr. 1991 / Rhino ♦♦♦♦
Unfortunately, Sparks never enjoyed more than a small, though devoted, cult following. But it certainly wasn't for a lack of effective hooks and clever, insanely funny lyrics. While a few of the Los Angeles pop-rockers' albums were disappointing, many others were exceptional. For those seeking an introductory overview of Sparks' legacy, this two-CD set is highly recommended. From "Achoo" to "Tips for Teens" to "This Town Ain't Big Enough for the Both of Us," *Profile* makes it clear just how delightfully goofy Sparks could be. Often willing to experiment, the group embraces everything from hard rock on "Big Boy" to Euro-disco on Giorgio Moroder-produced songs like "The Number One Song in Heaven" and "Beat The Clock." Despite the inclusion of a few throwaways—such as the disappointing *Music You Can Dance To*'s title song—*Profile* paints an impressive picture of a wrongly neglected band. —*Alex Henderson*

### Gratuitous Sax & Senseless Violins / 1995 / Logic/Artista ♦♦♦♦
Even the cover art is great, playing with the same fake tabloid style that Guns 'N' Roses tried but with funnier results. Beginning with a semi-echo of the start of *Propaganda*, with an a cappella "Gratuitous Sax" leading into the surging, well-deserved European smash hit "When Do I Get to Sing 'My Way,'" *Sax* broke a near seven-year silence from Ron and Russell Mael—the longest period of time by far since their start in between major releases. Rather than sounding tired or out of touch, though, the brothers gleefully embraced the modern synth/house/techno explosion for their own purposes (an explosion which, after all, they had helped start with their work during the late '70s with Giorgio Moroder). Solely recorded by the Maels with no outside help, *Sax* keeps that same, perfect Sparks formula—Russell's sweet vocals soar with smart and suspect lyrics over Ron's sometimes fast and furious, sometimes slow and elegant melodies, here performed with detailed electronic lushness. They make their style live yet again, feeling far fresher here than on *Interior Design*. "(When I Kiss You) I Hear Charlie Parker Playing" finds Russell rapping (!), "I Thought I Told You to Wait in the Car" has a great building chorus, and "Let's Go Surfing" helps wrap up the album with a wist-

fully triumphant call to arms. "Tsui Hark" is the one slight departure from the formula, featuring the *Hong Kong* director Hark himself giving a brief autobiography while a colleague speaks in Chinese. Though some longtime fans groused that they missed the more rocked-up Sparks of the early '70s (or early '80s) in comparison, all in all, *Sax* is a well-deserved return to form from a band which has deserved far more attention from the musical world, or the world at large, than they have received. —*Ned Raggett*

**Plagiarism** / 1997 / Roadrunner ♦♦♦♦
In the age of remixing, sampling and cut-and-paste record-making, leave it to Sparks to beat everyone to the punch and put the '90s spin on their own catalog before someone else did. Nineteen Sparks favorites are tackled here, including a super Hi-nrg version of "The No. 1 Song in Heaven" and a keenly orchestrated "This Town Ain't Big Enough For Both of Us," both delivered with a hand from their friends in opera-rock: Jimmy Somerville and Faith No More, respectively. —*Denise Sullivan*

## Spectre

*Producer / Illbient, Experimental Ambient, Underground Rap, Trip-Hop*
An appropriately shadowy entity with several albums for WordSound and production spots for Prince Paul and Techno Animal, Spectre is the Nosferatu of underground horrorcore, channeling the more isolated tones of industrial-dub and illbient into hip-hop productions of an intensely paranoid nature. Inspired by the rich legacy of horror films and dark industrial pioneers like Skinny Puppy as well as the old-school of hip-hop, the rapper/producer debuted by hosting *The Ill Saint Presents Subterranean Hitz*, a seminal illbient compilation released on WordSound in 1996.

Spectre's first album *The Illness* dropped later that year (sample track title: "Spectre Meets the Psycho Priest in the Temple of Smoke"), also on Word-Sound. Between LPs he kept quite busy, making appearances on Prince Paul's *Psychoanalysis* LP, the second volume in Virgin's *Macro Dub Infection* series, Techno Animal's remix album *Vs. Reality*, and Unitone Hi-Fi's *Rewound & Rerubbed*. Spectre also released *RuffKutz*, a 90-minute mix tape spotlighting his new label Black Hoodz, with tracks by Dr. Israel, Sensational, Mr. Dead, and the Jungle Brothers. Sophomore LP *The Second Coming* was released in late 1998; *The End* followed in early 2000. —*John Bush*

● **The Illness** / Jan. 1, 1996 / WordSound ♦♦♦♦
Fusing hip-hop mysticism more than worthy of Wu-Tang with an approach to music-making allied to Lee "Scratch" Perry, Spectre's debut album is an excellent entry in the continuing branch of horrorcore rap operating from deep underground the streets of Brooklyn. The beats are solid, the production is basement-level, and the effects are deep, making tracks like "Mayday/Nightstalker" and "Spectre Meets the Psycho Priest in the Temple of Smoke" chilling pieces of hip-hop noir. —*John Bush*

**The Second Coming** / Jan. 6, 1998 / WordSound ♦♦♦
*Second Coming* fuses trip-hop, dub, drum'n'bass, and hip-hop, with guest vocals by Sensational and Mr. Dead. Spectre utilizes a great deal of live instruments to a sinister, atmospheric effect. —*Steve Huey*

## Spectrum

f. 1990
*Group / Noise Pop, Ambient Pop, Experimental Rock, Dream Pop, Space Rock, Neo-Psychedelia*
Spectrum was the most high-profile and straightforward of the projects undertaken by Pete "Sonic Boom" Kember after the demise of the trance-rock avatars Spacemen 3. As his work as a member of the Experimental Audio Research coterie allowed Kember the opportunity to explore ambient textures and tonal constructs, Spectrum satisfied the singer/guitarist's more conventional pop leanings, while never losing sight of the hypnotic otherworldliness which became his music's trademark and legacy. The name Spectrum initially appeared as the title of the first Sonic Boom solo album, released in 1990 before the break-up of Spacemen 3; a collection of ethereal, nearly formless songs, *Spectrum* openly acknowledged Kember's debt to Suicide with its cover of the duo's "Rock 'n' Roll Is Killing My Life." Meanwhile, the Kember half of the Spacemen 3 swan song *Recurring*, with its tighter, more structured songs (like the gentle wash of "Just to See You Smile"), offered an even stronger indication of things to come.

After the break-up of Spacemen 3, Sonic formed Spectrum with guitarist Richard Formby and bassist Mike Stout, along with contributions from Pat Fish (a.k.a. the Jazz Butcher). After a series of singles, the band issued its debut *Soul Kiss (Glide Divine)*, a sprawling collection of tranquil, luminous retro-pop, in 1992. At the end of the year, Formby was replaced by former Darkside guitarist Kevin Cowan, and in 1993, the group released *Indian Summer*, an EP of covers. After Kember spent much of the next year working on Experimental Audio Noise Research projects, Spectrum—now rounded out by guitarist Scott Riley, programmer Alf Hardy, and ex-Spacemen 3 bassist Pete Bassman—released the 1994 LP *Highs, Lows and Heavenly Blows*, another narcotic collection which explored unique scales and compositional structures. Another layoff followed as Sonic Boom resumed work on his other projects, but in 1996 Spectrum teamed with the Seattle band Jessamine for a joint release titled *A Pox on You;* at the end of the year, they also issued an EP, *Songs for Owsley* The full-length *Forever Alien* appeared in 1997. A second collaboration with Jessamine as well as work with the Silver Apples followed. —*Jason Ankeny*

● **Soul Kiss (Glide Divine)** / Sep. 15, 1992 / Silvertone ♦♦♦♦
Apart from the pulsating opener "How You Satisfy Me," there's little on Spectrum's debut which owes any kind of debt to peak-period Spacemen 3; instead, *Soul Kiss (Glide Divine)*—which bears the suggestion to "Play twice before listening"—floats along almost weightlessly, a shifting, impressionistic collage of shimmering guitar minimalism. Largely dispensing with clearly defined songs, the tracks which comprise the album fade in and out of one another, creating a distorted sense of time and space; the dominant motifs of "Waves Wash Over Me" and "(I Love You) To the Moon and Back" mirror one another, while "The Drunk Suite" appears twice, further establishing *Soul Kiss* as a unified, enveloping experience. —*Jason Ankeny*

**Highs, Lows and Heavenly Blows** / 1994 / Silvertone ♦♦♦♦
*Highs, Lows and Heavenly Blows* pushes Spectrum even further away from conventional notions of melody and rhythm; as the title suggests, the record's concerns are not form and structure but mood and feeling, as well as the continued pursuit of celestial intoxication—radiating remarkable warmth and serenity, the songs evoke a kind of time-space dislocation not dissimilar from a state of suspended animation. —*Jason Ankeny*

**Pox on You** / 1996 / Space Age ♦♦
An interesting, albeit rarely compelling, collaboration between Spectrum's Sonic Boom and the members of Seattle's Jessamine, *A Pox on You* is primarily an excuse for the two groups to commune in their shared affection for vintage electronics. The title cut, a cover of the Silver Apples tune, is far and away the most conventional of the five tracks, its dense, swirling sound the product of gurgling analog synths and even a theremin; the remaining material comprises a series of instrumental drone constructs, the most impressive being the 11-minute "Radiophonic (Musique Concrète)," but nothing here quite hits the peaks one might expect. —*Jason Ankeny*

**Forever Alien** / Aug. 4, 1997 / Warner Brothers ♦♦
On the aptly-titled *Forever Alien*, Spectrum indeed purges virtually all of the human elements from their music; guitars, basses, and drums are all jettisoned, replaced by vintage synthesizers, vocoders, and even a Theremin. While it's difficult not to admire Sonic Boom's constant need for change, it's equally difficult to find anything commendable about *Forever Alien* itself; the music is cold, dispassionate and even a little silly—"The New Atlantis" revives a melodramatic Francis Bacon text, while "Owsley" is a clumsy, overblown celebration of the famed LSD pioneer. The resurrection of "The Stars Are So Far (How Does It Feel?)," which borrows its lyrics from an eight-year-old Spacemen 3 song, typifies the problem: Spectrum has clearly hit a creative impasse, and the direction taken here isn't so much reflective of a new musical beginning but of a dearth of solid ideas. Here's hoping that inspiration strikes again soon—forever is a long time. —*Jason Ankeny*

## Speedy J (Jochem Paap)

b. Rotterdam, The Netherlands
*Producer, DJ / Electronica, Ambient-Techno, Trance, Club/Dance, Techno*
Jochem Paap, aka Speedy J, is a Rotterdam-based techno musician whose polished blend of melodious electro-pop with a harder, more Detroit-fueled edge has been among the most highly-praised of post-rave European techno. The Dutch rep in Richie "Plastikman" Hawtin's Plus 8 label, Paap was equally well-known as a club DJ (his nom de record is in reference to his prowess on the cut) before deciding in 1997 to curtail his DJ engagements and focus on his music. His 1993 debut LP, *Ginger*, was an engaging blend of ambient tex-

tures and hard, crisp beats, and was immediately smacked with the "intelligent dance music" tag, aided by the inclusion of a pair of tracks on the first volume of Warp's influential *(Artificial Intelligence)* series. Paap has since released several follow-ups under the Speedy J moniker (*G-Spot, Public Energy No. 1, A Shocking Hobby*) and two solo albums in an ambient series for Fax titled *Vrs-Mbnt-Pcs 9598* (just re-insert the missing vowels for a quick translation). He's also recorded a scattering of material as Public Energy for Plus 8, as well as for his own Beam Me Up! label before discontinuing the latter in 1996. He is cofounder of a Dutch remix network, dedicated to bringing Dutch electronic musicians in contact with one another and fostering collaborative projects, and previous to his moratorium on the DJ circuit, he was known for his commitment to bringing dance-based experimental electronic music to a wider audience, playing out often in unlikely combinations with groups like Cypress Hill and Henry Rollins. In addition to his original recorded work, Paap has also remixed tracks for Secret Cinema and Sven Väth. [See Also: Jochem Paap] —*Sean Cooper*

**Ginger** / 1993 / Plus 8/Warp ♦♦♦♦

**G-Spot** / 1995 / Plus 8/Warp ♦♦♦

Fizzy, flawlessly crafted ambient-techno similar in feel to B12 and Global Communication. Although a few dancefloor scorchers make the cut, most of the album is armchair-style slow breakbeat, with an obvious attention to melody and mood making this some of Paap's most satisfying work to date. —*Sean Cooper*

• **Public Energy No. 1** / Apr. 15, 1997 / Plus 8/NovaMute ♦♦♦♦

Speedy J's 1997 full-length release *Public Energy No. 1* takes its name from one of Jochem Paap's lesser-known pseudonyms, under which he's recorded 12"s for Plus 8 and his own Beam Me Up! label. Although not so dissimilar from the tracks he's produced under that name, *Public Energy No. 1* is quite a bit different from Paap's Speedy J material, which until the record's preceding single, "Ni Go Snix," focused mostly on warm, melodic ambient-techno with hardly an offending ounce in its lithe, easygoing body. *Public Energy*, however, is a veritable maelstrom; a mixture of brutalizing machine rhythms, odd, off-putting ambience, and distant, bassy, alien soundscapes. Hailed almost instantly (and, for once, rightfully) as one of the more important records in post-rave techno, *Public Energy* has all the forceful noncompromise of techno's brief cannon of classics ("Clear," "Strings of Life," "Pneuma," "Scoobs in Columbia," "Four Jazz Funk Classics," etc.), but with an intensified sense of dread and paranoia specific to its time, similar in some respects to the millennium-infused breakbeat experiments of TPower and Tricky (though undeniably techno). The album's daring is also notable given that it was Paap's (at least in Europe, which constitutes his largest audience) major-label debut. Essential. —*Sean Cooper*

**Patterns [EP]** / Jun. 30, 1997 / Plus 8/Mute ♦♦♦

The first single from Speedy J's defiant 1997 LP, *Public Energy No. 1*, "Patterns" relents a bit on the DJ front, combining the album version (itself one of the few mixable tracks on the album) with a four-on-the-floor non-album track ("Punnik") bound to get the less adventurous techno DJs back on Jochem Paap's side. It's a competent track, certainly, but following the head-tweak of the album, the remix seems yawningly ordinary. The import version of "Patterns" was paired with a bonus etched 12" containing an additional (this time extremely whacked) mix of the track. The latter makes the double-pack very much worth the investment. —*Sean Cooper*

**A Shocking Hobby** / Apr. 18, 2000 / NovaMute ♦♦♦♦

Speedy J followed up the most lauded album of his career with yet another work of excellence, an album that ranges slightly farther afield than the insistent Autechre references recalled by *Public Energy No. 1*. After a short ambient opener, the ungodly "Borax" comes crashing through with a sound that manages to encompass terms like funky, experimental, *and* beautiful with equal degrees of excellence. It's easily one of the best productions of Jochem Paap's career, not to mention one of the best in contemporary electronic music. True, a few of the later tracks ("Balk Acid," "Drill," "Vopak") are quite close to the brand of super-computing electro-techno that Autechre pioneered a few years before, but even these productions have an immediacy, an enormity of sound, quite lacking in Autechre. A world away from this music-for-eggheads sound lies what just may have been another influence on *A Shocking Hobby*—namely, the insanely stupid dance style named big-beat techno. These tracks don't exactly have the can't-miss-'em drum breakdowns and old-school samples of your average big-beat record, but when Paap places a massive explosion of sound on the first beat of every bar, it's difficult to escape the feeling that these songs are akin to Fatboy Slim on brain food. Creating intelligent, difficult music that also feeds the attention-span deficit inherent in post-rave music isn't just a good idea; it's the recipe for another excellent album. —*John Bush*

## Spiritualized

f. 1989, Rugby, Midlands,

*Group / Noise Pop, Ambient Pop, Dream Pop, Space Rock, Neo-Psychedelia, Post-Rock/Experimental, Shoegazing, Alternative Pop/Rock*

Formed from the ashes of the trance-rockers Spacemen 3, singer/guitarist Jason Pierce's group Spiritualized did not break away from his prior band's trademark hypnotic minimalism; instead, they perfected it. Drawing on the continued influence of the Velvet Underground, LaMonte Young, and Steve Reich, Spiritualized staked out a common ground between minimalism and lush symphonics—while powered by simple, repetitious motifs, their songs simultaneously blossomed into rich, shimmering sonic panoramas inspired by the majestic studio wizardry of Phil Spector and Brian Wilson. Such seeming contradictions were essential to the group's alchemy: while the infamous Spacemen 3 tag of "taking drugs to make music to take drugs to" remained a cornerstone of their craft, at the same time Spiritualized's very name acknowledged the existence of other forces, further reflected in their heavy debt to gospel and soul music as well as an affinity for mantras and devotional hymns.

Although Spiritualized fully emerged after the acrimonious break-up of Spacemen 3, in truth, the band's roots extended back to the band's final LP, 1990's *Recurring*. A Spacemen 3 album in name only, *Recurring* was split evenly between independently recorded work from Pierce and estranged partner Pete "Sonic Boom" Kember; as a result, while Kember's side presaged his eventual work with Spectrum, Pierce's half, recorded with most of the musicians who would later comprise Spiritualized (including guitarist Mark Refoy, bassist Willie B. Carruthers, and drummer Jon Mattock), predated the orchestral drones that became the band's hallmark. The first true Spiritualized single, a dramatic reading of the Troggs' "Anyway That You Want Me," was the final nail in the coffin—reportedly, Kember was so incensed by the Spacemen 3 logo which appeared on the disc's jacket that he disbanded the group for good.

In 1991, Spiritualized returned with a string of EPs—*Feel So Sad, Run/I Want You* and *Smile/Sway*—before their long-awaited debut *Lazer Guided Melodies* finally appeared the following year. The masterful, blissed-out result of Pierce's obsessive studio fine-tuning and endless remixing, the album was promoted by the band's slot on the high-profile "Rollercoaster" tour, where they appeared with the Jesus and Mary Chain and Curve. An excellent limited-edition live document, *Fucked Up Inside*, followed in 1993, trailed by another EP, *Electric Mainline* later in the year.

In 1995, Spiritualized—now a trio consisting of Pierce, keyboardist/guitarist Kate Radley, and bassist Sean Cook—issued *Pure Phase*, a heady, dense production which boasted separate mixes from each stereo channel. With 1997's *Ladies and Gentlemen We Are Floating in Space*, Pierce deliberately jettisoned many of the band's usual points of departure, including drones, tremolos and phase tones; recorded with new drummer Damon Reece, it featured a cameo appearance from legendary New Orleans pianist Dr. John on one track, while Memphis studio legend Jim Dickinson appeared on another. Other guests included the Belaneus Quartet (also featured on *Pure Phase*), the Greater London Gospel Community Choir, and Spring Heel Jack. The two-disc *Live at the Royal Albert Hall* followed in late 1998. —*Jason Ankeny*

**Lazer Guided Melodies** / 1992 / Dedicated ♦♦♦♦

The group's seminal debut album is aptly titled: The melodies shimmer and drone and hum like otherworldly pop tunes, and Radley and Pierce's vocals hover gently in the mix. One of the premier dream-pop albums, *Lazer Guided Melodies* is both beautiful and innovative. —*Heather Phares*

**Fucked Up Inside** / Jul. 13, 1993 / Dutch East ♦♦♦♦

Spiritualized's first official live release was this seven-song limited-edition package, originally available only via mail order. Taking its title from a line in the Spacemen 3 favorite "Walking with Jesus," *Fucked Up Inside* (like its successor, 1998's *Royal Albert Hall* set) somehow distills the full hypnotic brilliance of the group's remarkable live set onto record—songs like "Take Good Care of It," "Shine a Light," and "Smiles" build and bloom with rare grandeur, crystallizing the epic sweep of Jason Pierce's sonic vision. —*Jason Ankeny*

**Pure Phase** / Mar. 28, 1995 / Dedicated ♦♦♦
Spiritualized's eagerly awaited second album continues the group's ethereal tradition, this time with a loopier, more symphonic sound. Many of the songs swell past the six-minute mark, ebbing and flowing majestically. "Medication," "Electric Phase," "Lay Back in the Sun," and "Spread Your Wings" typify the dreamy grandeur of most of the album. —*Heather Phares*

● **Ladies and Gentlemen We Are Floating in Space** / Jul. 1, 1997 / Arista ♦♦♦♦
Spiritualized's third collection of hypnotic headphone symphonies is their most brilliant and accessible to date. Largely forsaking the drones and minimalistic, repetitive riffs which have characterized his work since the halcyon days of Spacemen 3, Jason Pierce refocuses here and spins off into myriad new directions; in a sense, *Ladies and Gentlemen We Are Floating in Space*, with its majestic, Spector-like glow, is his classic rock album. "Come Together" and the blistering "Electricity" are his most edgy, straightforward rockers in eons, while the stunning "I Think I'm In Love" settles into a divided-psyche call-and-response R&B groove, and the closing "Cop Shoot Cop" (with guest Dr. John) locks into a voodoo blues trance. Lyrically, Pierce is at his most open and honest; the record is a heartfelt confessional of love and loss, with redemption found only in the form of drugs—designed, no less, to look like a prescription pharmaceutical package, *Ladies and Gentlemen* is pointedly explicit in its description of drug use as a means of killing the pain on track after track. Conversely, never before have the literal implications of the name "Spiritualized" been explored in such earnest detail—the London Community Gospel Choir appears prominently on a number of songs, while another bears the title "No God, Only Religion," pushing the music even further toward the kind of cosmic gospel transcendence it craves. A masterpiece. —*Jason Ankeny*

**Royal Albert Hall October 10 1997 Live** / Nov. 10, 1998 / Arista ♦♦♦♦
Live albums, by and large, are a dime a dozen—inconsequential souvenirs designed to placate fans awaiting new studio material, they rarely if ever shed new light on the artist in question; rarer still is their ability to approximate the energy and excitement of the concert setting itself. Spiritualized's transcendent *Royal Albert Hall October 10 1997 Live* is the proverbial exception that proves the rule, a revelatory two-disc collection that captures the group at the peak of their powers, somehow translating the hypnotic power and epic majesty of their live set onto vinyl. Rejecting the inane between-song stage patter common to most live performers, Jason Pierce instead weaves his music together into an unbroken tapestry of sound, casting a spell which ebbs and flows with narcotic beauty and intensity; even the most familar selections (like "Shine a Light," "Take Your Time," and "Medication," all frequent inclusions on other Spiritualized live EPs and bootlegs) pulsate with new life, their melodies as likely to set off on a meditative drift as they are to erupt in blasts of white noise. Granted, *Royal Albert Hall* isn't a substitute for the experience of actually catching the group in the flesh—what is it?—but there are so few other concert LPs, it actually rises above its conceptual limitations, forever capturing a singular moment in time and space when Spiritualized was unquestionably the greatest rock 'n' roll band in the world. —*Jason Ankeny*

## SPK

f. 1978, Germany
*Group / Experimental Rock, Industrial*
An industrial band whose later nucleus consists of multi-instrumentalist Graeme Revell and vocalist Sinan (b. Sinan Leong), SPK has explored both the metallic noise and the dance-rock ends of the industrial spectrum and provided a launching pad for Revell's subsequent career in movie music. Alternately standing for "Surgical Penis Klinik," "System Planning Korporation," or "Sozialistische Patienten Kollektiv" (the latter as a tribute to a German mental-patient-rights movement), SPK formed in Germany in 1978 when percussionist Neil met Neil in a mental hospital—the former as a worker, the latter as a patient. Joining female vocalist Sinan, they formed an industrial noise band owing strong debts to Throbbing Gristle, Test Department, and Einsturzende Neubauten. The noisy, abrasive early SPK releases (1980's *Information Overload Unit*, 1982's *Leichenschrei*, and the live-in-Kansas *The Last Attempt at Paradise*) feature little information on the group—personnel on the first album is listed as Operator on synth and vocals, Tone Generator on synth, and Mike Wilkins on bass, guitar, and vocals, while the live album features Oblivion and Jack Pinker. SPK gained a reputation as a band that would do anything to shock its audience; early performances featured slides and films of surgery, eventually moving to more industrial themes with the use of flamethrowers and oil drums. Problems ensued at their London gigs; in 1983, they nearly hit members of the audience with a heavy metal chain, and another gig was stopped due to fire-code violations (the band was welding onstage). 1983's *Auto-Da-Fe* moved SPK more into dance/shock-rock territory, but it wasn't until the addition of Australian multi-instrumentalist Graeme Revell in 1984 that their sound started to jell. *Machine Age Voodoo*, *From Science to Ritual*, and 1986's *Zamia Lehmanni* established a more varied, inventive approach, even if the press still dismissed the group as obnoxiously eager to shock. Things took a downturn with 1987's *Digitalis, Ambigua, Gold and Poison* and 1988's *Oceania*, dance-oriented records that failed to live up to the group's most recent work. Revell moved into soundtrack work and began a successful career, composing music for films like *The People Under the Stairs*, *Street Fighter*, and *The Craft*, as well as producing other soundtracks like *Until the End of the World*, *Hard Target*, *The Crow*, *The Basketball Diaries*, *Strange Days*, and *From Dusk Till Dawn*. —*Steve Huey*

**Information Overload Unit** / 1980 / Side Effects ♦♦
A noisy record basically composed of guitar feedback, synthesizer distortion, and rigid drum programming, *Information Overload Unit* saw SPK still working through their influences, notably Suicide and Throbbing Gristle. The track titles, including gems like "Suture Obsession" and "Epilept: Convulse," tell much of the story. —*John Bush*

**Auto-Da-Fe** / 1983 / Walter Ulbricht ♦♦♦♦
The beginning of a more organized approach for SPK material, *Auto-Da-Fe* presents an intriguing industrial-disco fusion, reminiscent of prime contemporary material by Cabaret Voltaire and DAF. An assortment of synthesizer stabs and progressive beats are the backing for lyrics best explained by titles like "Retard" and "Heart That Breaks." Although fans probably thought of *Auto-Da-Fe* as an unconscionable crossover attempt, it's still quite experimental in retrospect. Mute's CD reissue of the album also includes tracks from SPK's 1978 single "Surgical Penis Klinik," 1979's *Meat Processing Sektion* EP, and 1983's *Dekompositions* EP. —*John Bush*

● **Machine Age Voodoo** / 1984 / Elektra ♦♦♦♦
SPK's first album after adding Graeme Revell to the lineup features another leap towards dance-rock and away from the group's industrial past. The fusion of '80s dance and more experimental electronics is certainly prescient, with vocals still on their way from the rigidities of mechanistic synth-pop to surprisingly emotional. —*John Bush*

**Zamia Lehmanni: Songs of Byzantine Flowers** / Mar. 13, 1996 / Grey Area ♦♦

## The Spoils of War

f. Urbana, IL
*Group / Psychedelic*
Little is known about this late-'60s psychedelic group, except that they were dominated by James Cuomo, who wrote all of the material in addition to producing it. From Urbana, IL, they recorded an album's worth of unreleased tracks in 1969, which finally saw the light of day as a very limited edition German LP in 1998. The record is interesting as an early example of a rock band making heavy use of experimental electronics. These augment, and occasionally overwhelm, Cuomo's rather fragile and spooky songs, which *are* often real songs, despite the overlays of and detours into effects and noise. It's somewhat in the style of the United States of America or Fifty Foot Hose, although it certainly isn't as excellent and innovative as the U.S.A., nor as conversant with the potential of electronic equipment as was Fifty Foot Hose. Worth hearing, though, if you're into that vibe, Cuomo sometimes exhibiting a spacier and folkier sensibility than his counterparts did. —*Richie Unterberger*

● **The Spoils of War** / 1969 / Shadoks Music ♦♦♦
Although the swaths of wacky electronics are the traits that are the most immediate and aggressive characteristics of this album, James Cuomo and the Spoils of War's chief strengths were, in fact, their haunting and inventively arranged songs. Tunes like "You're the Girl" and especially "Now Is Made in America," with its lyrical references to detachable halos, eerie organ, and unearthly high vocals, are reflections of a tender psyche as frail as an eggshell. At other points the vocals—occasionally female, occasionally sped-up—and

melodic-but-experimental song shards recall parts of the Mothers of Invention in the *We're Only in It for the Money* era. Sometimes the electronic squiggles and blasts are effective, as on the foghorn-like tones into which "E-Thing" dissolves. More often, though, it's distracting and gimmicky, as though someone felt the material had to be even farther out than it was to gain credibility. At its best, it's the kind of astral, dreamlike underground psychedelia that was too off-the-wall and spontaneously idiosyncratic to be convincingly recreated after the '60s. —*Richie Unterberger*

## Spooky

f. 1990, London, England
*Group / Progressive House, Experimental Techno, Club/Dance, House*
Not to be confused with the New York DJ/producer of the same name, London-based duo Spooky consists of Duncan Forbes and Charlie May, who began recording for William Orbit's Guerilla label in the early '90s after Orbit discovered the pair in a record shop. Best known for providing one of the first big blasts in the London progressive house movement, Spooky's debut, *Gargantuan*, is an enduring classic of the style, fusing thick analog production with deep, melodic house phrasing and sturdy rhythms. The group's reincarnation after Guerilla dissolved as an experimental techno/electro act in the Warp/GPR tradition surprised fans and detractors alike, but Spooky have been as successful with more recent releases such as "Schmoo" and their 1996 follow-up to *Gargantuan*, the fervently experimental *Found Sound*, suggesting there's more to the group than mere novelty and timing. *Found Sound*, for its part, is a deliriously percussive update of '80s electro with an almost austere musique concrète foundation, indicative of Forbes and May's professed admiration for minimalist composer such as Steve Reich and Arvo Part, as well as non-Western percussion-based musical traditions such as gamelan and the Indian raga. In fact, most of the drum and melody sounds on the album were either constructed from scratch or sampled from real-world objects such as sheet metal, flowerpots, and even the group's studio's heating unit. *Found Sound* followed the release of three singles on the group's own Generic imprint (a subsidiary of A&M, with whom Forbes and May hammered out a deal following Guerrilla's demise), and was itself followed by a European tour (opening for 808 State) and a double-pack single, "Bamboo," featuring a Dave Angel remix and a live version of the *Gargantuan* classic "Little Bullet." May later joined trance DJ Sasha, and worked on programming for the popular mixer's *Xpander* EP. —*Sean Cooper*

● **Gargantuan** / 1993 / Capitol ✦✦✦✦
One of the landmark LPs (alongside Leftfield's *Leftism*) in the resurgence of British house during the '90s, *Gargantuan* collects several epic singles—"Schmoo," the Oakenfold tribute "Land of Oz," "Don't Panic"—alongside excellent new material like the two-part "Little Bullet." Some of the album tracks are a bit predictable, but the duo's melodic sense and percussive edge rarely misfire. —*John Bush*

**Found Sound** / Jul. 8, 1996 / Generic ✦✦✦✦
A radical departure for those who weren't paying attention since *Gargantuan*, *Found Sound* is a masterpiece of experimental electro, incorporating a range of hand-picked and readymade sounds into intricate, heavily percussive, surprisingly imaginative songs. Material ranges from the banging (literally) to the ethereal (with help from members of the Cocteau Twins, natch), but the bulk is mid-tempo electronic breakbeat similar to a more minimal Black Dog or less subdued Autechre. —*Sean Cooper*

**Bamboo [EP]** / Sep. 30, 1996 / Generic ✦✦
Spooky head a few clicks back into *Gargantuan* territory for their second *Found Sound* single, roping in Dave Angel for the standout mix of "Bamboo" and tacking on a somewhat throwaway live version of the classic "Little Bullet." Only completists need apply. —*Sean Cooper*

## Spring Heel Jack

f. 1993, London, England
*Group / Experimental Jungle, Electronica, Jungle/Drum'N'Bass, Club/Dance*
The recordings of John Coxon and Ashley Wales as Spring Heel Jack were one of the earliest and best applications of hard-edged drum'n'bass to the full-length LP concept with no lack of energy, similar in result to Orbital's living-room/danceclub fusion of techno. A pop producer who has worked with Marc Almond and Spiritualized, Coxon met up with classical composer Wales while working as a soul DJ in London's East End. The duo soon began recording breakbeat-jungle, initially with inclinations toward dub. Co-writers and producers of the hit title track from Everything But the Girl's 1995 platinum album *Walking Wounded*, the pair debuted that same year with the first of several critically acclaimed LPs, none of which managaged to compromise their respected status in the jungle scene.

Coxon, who learned to play guitar in his native Edinburgh, had studied to be a biochemist and briefly taught school in London, but returned to music by working as a DJ and occasional producer. After meeting Ashley Wales, a landscaper, the two began composing music and in 1990 produced one of Betty Boo's first singles ("Doin' the Do"). Moving to dub territory with recordings as Spring Heel Jack, the pair soon became entranced with the jungle movement, and adjusted their focus accordingly. Debut album *There Are Strings* appeared in 1995 on the Island subsidiary Trade 2 in the UK. Later that year, the duo released *Versions*, a remix album featuring dubs of six tracks from the debut LP.

Another artist influenced by the drum'n'bass movement, Everything But the Girl's Ben Watt, made public his admiration for Spring Heel Jack's work, prompting Coxon and Wales to write "Walking Wounded" especially for Watt and his partner, Tracey Thorn. After Thorn added vocals to the track, EBTG released the single in April 1996, and it climbed to No. 6 in the UK charts.

Spring Heel Jack released *68 Million Shades* several months later, with a trippy cover designed by computer artist Yuki Mikayi (who also designed the cover art for the first LP). The album earned respect from the dance underground, and the duo were tapped to support Orbital on an ambitious US tour in late 1996. After *68 Million Shades* was cited by *Spin* magazine as one of the best LPs of the year, it earned an American release on Island in January 1997. *Busy Curious Thirsty* followed later that year, and in 1999 Spring Heel Jack returned with two LPs, (*Treader, Disappeared*) as well as an EP (*Sound of Music*) including their intriguing reworks of standards from the Rodgers & Hammerstein musical of the same name. —*John Bush*

**There Are Strings** / 1995 / Phase 2/Island ✦✦✦
John Coxon and Ashley Wales' debut album shows that the duo were quite respectable producers before their own musical careers as Spring Heel Jack; the breakbeats and melodies on *There Are Strings* are polished to a fine sheen. Though individual tracks sound okay, good ideas seem to be in short supply on this long-winded album. —*John Bush*

**68 Million Shades** / Jun. 17, 1996 / Island ✦✦✦✦
Spring Heel Jack's first album released in America continues the duo's dense, dub-inspired take on jungle. The use of high-pitched, polished strings and clean breakbeats makes *68 Million Shades* a consistently sound listen, but the 75-minute album begins to drag not even halfway through, when most of the rhythms have already been duplicated on several songs. When Spring Heel Jack's formula works, on "Midwest" and "Pan," the sound is great; with a running time cut in half though, *68 Million Shades* would be twice as good. —*John Bush*

**Versions** / Sep. 9, 1996 / Phase 2/Island ✦✦✦
Several months after Spring Heel Jack's debut album, the duo released *Versions*, a dub-inspired remix LP. Six tracks from *There Are Strings* are presented in "version" form, similar to the remixes present on early Jamaican reggae singles from the '70s. Though interesting, most of the tracks are better heard on Spring Heel Jack's album. —*John Bush*

● **Busy Curious Thirsty** / Sep. 15, 1997 / PolyGram ✦✦✦✦
Long cursed with the tag of Most Intelligent Jungle Act, Spring Heel Jack appeared to react with their fourth album *Busy Curious Thirsty*. The tracks aren't exactly raggafied drum'n'bass, but they definitely sound more influenced by the sound of the street than the hum of the computer. Fortunately, Coxon and Wales didn't completely desert their by-then trademarked lush synth-work and ordered, complex breakbeats; the result is an album with the best of both worlds in drum'n'bass. —*John Bush*

**Treader** / May 17, 1999 / Tugboat ✦✦
Perhaps realizing that jungle was not just growing uncool but turning into a creative dead end, Coxon and Wales toned down the heavy breakbeats and unrelenting drum'n'bass on their *Treader* album. Yes, it's still much more drum'n'bass than trip-hop or electronica or anything else, but the inclusion of a few downtempo tracks ("Is," "More Stuff No One Saw") plus the frequent slants toward experimentalism (short bursts of noise) or classicism (chamber-quartet strings) show the pair moving discreetly away from the green pastures of their mid-'90s peak. "Winter" delves into jazz-fusion with a trumpet

flourish straight out of Miles' darker years before adding a few paranoid effects characteristic of darkstep drum'n'bass. *Treader* is just as impeccably produced and crisp-sounding as Coxon and Wales' previous work (just check highlights like "Blackwater" and "Toledo"), but it has the definite sound of a transitional album. —*John Bush*

**Oddities** / May 9, 2000 / Thirsty Ear ♦♦♦
*Oddities* is the perfect title for this album, which is billed as an "'official bootleg' featuring music from (the group's) private collection" and which collects compilation tracks and other ephemera selected from Spring Heel Jack's various side projects. Those in search of the artsy, refined drum'n'bass that has always been this band's stock in trade will be disappointed; in fact, grooves of any kind are pretty much absent. But those with a taste for the weird, the abstract, and the avant-garde will find a lot to like here. The program includes modern musique concrète ("Trouble," "Piece for Six Turntables"), dubwise sinewave sculpture ("Shine a Light"), raver minimalism ("2nd Piece for LaMonte Young"), and the group's remix of Material's "Road to the Western Lands," which features the voice of William Burroughs intoning factoids about Egyptian soul death over an eerie and deeply reverberant ambient soundscape. The only steady rhythm to be found is on the album's opening track, a fuzzy conglomeration of nested guitar loops and keyboard samples. This is a consistently interesting album, if not always a completely enjoyable one. —*Rick Anderson*

## Squarepusher (Tom Jenkinson)
b. Chelmsford, Essex, England
Bass, Remixing, Producer / Drill'N'Bass, Experimental Jungle, Electronica, Jungle/Drum'N'Bass, IDM

Tom "Squarepusher" Jenkinson makes manic, schizoid experimental drum'n'bass with a heavy progressive-jazz influence and a lean toward pushing the cliches of the genre out the proverbial window. Rising from near-total obscurity to drum'n'bass cause celebre in the space of a couple of months, Jenkinson released only a pair of EPs and a DJ Food remix for the latter's *Refried Food* series before securing EP and LP release plans with three different labels. His first full-length work, *Feed Me Weird Things* (on Richard "Aphex Twin" James' Rephlex label) is a dizzying, quixotic blend of superfast jungle breaks with Aphex-style synth textures, goofy, offbeat melodies, and instrumental arrangements (Jenkinson samples his own playing for his tracks) that recall vaguely jazz-fusion pioneers such as Mahavishnu Orchestra and Weather Report. A skilled bassist and multi-instrumentalist, Jenkinson's fretless accompaniment is a staple of his music and one of the more obvious affiliations with jazz (although his formal arrangements are often as jazz-derived as his playing).

Barely into his twenties, Jenkinson grew up listening to jazz and dub greats like Miles Davis, Augustus Pablo, Charlie Parker, and Art Blakey. The son of a jazz drummer, Jenkinson followed in his father's footsteps, playing bass and drums in high school. Introduced to electronic music through experimental electro-techno groups such as LFO and Carl Craig, Jenkinson soon began assembling the rolls of disparate influence into amalgams of breakbeat techno and post-bop avant-garde and progressive jazz. Claiming a closer affinity with jazz than jungle (although he draws from both equally in his music), Jenkinson's EPs as Squarepusher and the Duke of Harringay (Jenkinson moved to Harringay from his Chelmsford birthplace) were initially disregarded as misplaced perversions of jungle's more adventurous compositional principles, but found ready audience in fans of post-acid house experimental listening music. He inked a deal with Warp in 1995, releasing the *Port Rhombus* EP and three others through a variety of different labels. His full-length debut *Feed Me Weird Things* appeared in 1996, followed a year later by *Hard Normal Daddy*. For 1998's *Music Is Rotted One Note*, Jenkinson became a one-man fusion group, multitracking himself playing drums, bass, and keyboards. The following year, he released two EPs (*Budakhan Mindphone, Maximum Priest*) and another full LP, *Selection Sixteen*. —*Sean Cooper*

**Bubble and Squeak [Single]** / 1996 / Worm Interface ♦♦♦
Jenkinson's early blast on the Warp-like Worm Interface label is probably the most varied and least derivative of his work to date. The jazz influence is strong but also finds a less gimmicky place in the mix. —*Sean Cooper*

**Feed Me Weird Things** / Jun. 3, 1996 / Rephlex ♦♦♦♦
Fractured beats, frenetic bass licks, and alternately silly and moving melodies tie together Squarepusher's first full-length effort. Much of the material—with its lo-fi synth damage and often tongue-in-cheek feel—places Jenkinson closer to Aphex territory than traditional drum'n'bass, but the distinctions begin breaking down from word go. Flawed but promising. —*Sean Cooper*

**Port Rhombus [EP]** / Jul. 1, 1996 / Warp ♦♦♦
More polished and restrained than some of his Rephlex work, with the proggy bass masturbation toned down to a more manageable level. —*Sean Cooper*

★ **Hard Normal Daddy** / Apr. 28, 1997 / Warp ♦♦♦♦♦
Tom Jenkinson's jazz roots come through louder and clearer on his full-length Warp debut. Although, like the preceding EP "Port Rhombus," this album sounds substantially cleaner and more thought out than previous releases for Spymania and Rephlex, it also far surpasses those releases in terms of musicality and track development, not simply relying on the shock value of "tripping-over-myself" drum programming and light-speed fretless bass noodling. Jenkinson's bass accompaniment also sounds far less prog-rock-influenced here, making *Hard Normal Daddy* his overall most listenable work to date. —*Sean Cooper*

**Big Loada [EP]** / Jun. 1997 / Warp ♦♦♦♦
A mini-album of sorts, *Big Loada* finds Tom Jenkinson playing the genre game a bit, skipping from new wave-y breakbeat to ragga hardstep to the tinker toy 303 jungle of recent Aphex and μ-Ziq. Not as organized or polished as the *Hard Normal Daddy* LP, which preceded it by a scant few months, but a bit more varied and developed than his Rephlex, Spymania, Dragon Disc, etc. releases. Jenkinson's splatterfunk bass and guitar accompaniment is well integrated with the beats and electronics on "Come on My Selector" and "Tequila Fish." —*Sean Cooper*

**Music Is Rotted One Note** / Oct. 12, 1998 / Nothing ♦♦♦♦
The one-man drum'n'bass outfit Squarepusher (aka Tom Jenkinson) treads upon more unpredictable terrain on *Music Is Rotted One Note*. Although the album still contains elements of his usual drum'n'bass sound, this is by and large a jazz/fusion affair. Jenkinson does a masterful job playing all the instruments live and by himself, and perfectly re-creates the funky atmosphere of such early-'70s Miles Davis classics as *Get Up with It* and *On the Corner*. Jenkinson's performances throughout the disc are both flawless and inspired—he obviously realized that if he was to pay tribute to Miles, nothing but the best would do. Davis' spirit lives on in such tracks as "Don't Go Plastic," "Dust Switch," "137 (Rinse)," and "Theme from Vertical Hold," while "My Sound" perfectly captures the essence of Miles' calming and reflective compositions. But don't be misled; this is not a by-the-numbers rip-off of Miles Davis. Jenkinson updates these familiar sounds with '90s recording techniques and injects enough of his own style into the mix to keep it recognizable. Miles would be proud. —*Greg Prato*

**Budakhan Mindphone [EP]** / Mar. 1, 1999 / Nothing ♦♦♦
Though listeners may have expected an EP of B-sides hot on the heels of the last Squarepusher full-length, Tom Jenkinson appeared to have already moved on with this "mini-album." It has a similar feel (read: tin-can production) to *Music Is Rotted One Note*, but few of these tracks have the short-shrift sound of your average outtakes. The opener, "Iambic 5 Poetry," is much more inclined to melody and atmosphere, with cascading dub effects hitting off the beat and echoing low into the mix. The EP is definitely less obsessed with '70s fusion and more squarely experimental, akin to the quasi-single "My Sound" from *Music Is Rotted One Note*. Overall, *Budakhan Mindphone* breaks the bounds of fan-only singles and earns respect on its own worth. —*John Bush*

**Maximum Priest [EP]** / Jul. 6, 1999 / Nothing ♦♦♦
*Maximum Priest*, the second lengthy EP to surface in the year after *Music Is Rotted One Note*, includes four new tracks that chart the same underwater dub/fusion of Squarepusher's previous EP (*Budakhan Mindphone*), as well as three intriguing remixes by Autechre and Wagon Christ. —*Keith Farley*

**Selection Sixteen** / Nov. 9, 1999 / Nothing ♦♦♦♦
After releasing more than two hours worth of material in less than a year, Tom Jenkinson returned in late 1999 with what looked to be another full LP, comprising 17 tracks and clocking in at 45 minutes. In fact, it's regarded as a "mini-album" and plays the part well. Similar to the 1999 Squarepusher "EPs" *Budakhan Mindphone* and *Maximum Priest*, *Selection Sixteen* alternates what sounds like outtakes from his last "LP" (*Music Is Rotted One Note*)—that is, short organic fusion cast-offs—with a set of hard-edged acid tracks, most of which chart the hyperkinetic drum'n'bass programming that fans expect. The album comes off surprisingly well, given both the glut of Squarepusher material in 1999 and the fact that Jenkinson is mixing'n'-

matching crazed drill'n'bass and more stately jazz-fusion, with little regard for album flow. The highlight here, "Square Rave," takes a little bit from both camps and ends up sounding like Aphex Twin (circa *Selected Ambient Works 85-92*) if he'd been working with jungle breakbeats. In addition to the 13-track album are four remixes, including one on which Jenkinson recruits his brother Andy for remixing duties. —*John Bush*

## Stardust
f. 1998, Paris, France
*Group / Club/Dance, House*
On temporary hiatus from injecting the spirit of acid house into the French dance scene as half of Daft Punk, Thomas Bangalter crafted one of the catchiest dance anthems of the late '90s, Stardust's "Music Sounds Better With You." A warm, breezy, endlessly catchy midtempo anthem that launched hundreds of similar filter-disco tracks over the next few years, the single was recorded quickly by Bangalter with coproducer Alan Braxe and released on his own Roulé label in June 1998. After ruling the roosts at Ibiza that summer—along with another Bangalter co-production, Bob Sinclar's "Gym Tonic"—the track was licensed by Virgin and hit No. 2 on the British charts that fall. Though the label offered Bangalter three million dollars to produce a Stardust LP, he decided instead to make it a one-shot project. —*John Bush*

● **Music Sounds Better with You [EP]** / Jan. 19, 1999 / Virgin ♦♦♦♦
One of the most irresistible, sublime dance singles of the decade, "Music Sounds Better With You" floats along on a continually filtered disco loop with a sample from vocalist Ben "Diamond" Cohen going around and around for six-plus minutes. Additional remixers include Dimitri From Paris (a harder house version) and Gilb-R and I:Cube from Chateau Flight (beat-heavy, but closer to the original). —*John Bush*

## Starfish Pool
f. 1993, Belgium
*Group / Dark Ambient, Ambient-Techno*
Belgian acolyte of dark ambience Koen Lybaert formed Starfish Pool after an unsuccessful stint in a noise-rock combo called Starfish Enterprises. As guitarist in the original group, Lybaert gradually moved away from rock and into electronic composition, dissolving Starfish after several years and reworking an old band piece into his solo debut, 1994's *Chill Out'N Confused*. Along with occasional help from DJ PH (an associate also affiliated with Starfish's Nova Zembla label), Lybaert issued two EPs during 1995, returning with his second album, *Interference '96*, one year later. *Kinetic* followed in 1999. Lybaert also works in two other groups, Uruz and Submove, and was a member of Die Rote Fabrik. —*John Bush*

**Chill Out 'N Confused** / 1994 / Nova Zembla ♦♦♦
The debut album by Starfish Pool is actually a collaborational work featuring several members of the defunct Starfish Enterprises. Clocking in at just over an hour, *Chill Out 'N Confused* includes a variety of ethno-ambient standbys, including bells, didjeridoo, and various environmental recordings offering frequently interesting results. —*Keith Farley*

● **Interference '96** / Mar. 29, 1996 / Nova Zembla ♦♦♦♦
*Interference '96* inaugurates a more minimalist bent for Starfish Pool, from the single "Offday" (with two remixes by Psychick Warriors engineer Tim Freeman) to other highlights like "Monolith" and "Dead Acid Society." —*Keith Farley*

**Abstract Number 2** / Dec. 2, 1996 / Silver ♦♦

## Stars of the Lid
f. Austin, TX
*Group / Space Rock, Indie Rock, Ambient*
Ambient-drone duo Stars of the Lid was formed in Austin, TX by guitarists Brian McBride and Adam Wiltzie, the latter also a member of Windsor for the Derby as well as the longtime soundman for Bedhead. Debuting in 1994 with *Music for Nitrous Oxide*, the duo returned the following year with *Gravitational Pull Vs. the Desire for an Aquatic Life;* signing to Kranky, Stars of the Lid next resurfaced in 1997 with the epic *The Ballasted Orchestra*. 1998's *Per Aspera Ad Astra*, a collaboration with painter Jon McCafferty, preceded the Sub Rosa release *Avec Laudenum*. —*Jason Ankeny*

**Gravitational Pull Vs. the Desire for an Aquatic Life** / 1996 / Kranky ♦♦♦
*Gravitational Pull...*, the second release from Austin, TX's Stars of the Lid, quickly became a favorite among illbient DJs, leading the Kranky label to issue it on CD with an extra track. Even more so than most ambient projects, the Stars create an atmosphere that's akin to a sensory deprivation tank, reducing everything to pulsating waves of sound—*Gravitational Pull...* is consistently effective at this, and is even less dense at points than some of the group's other releases. —*Nitsuh Abebe*

● **The Ballasted Orchestra** / Feb. 24, 1997 / Kranky ♦♦♦♦
As unlikely as it sounds, one of ambient music's most effective projects hails from central Texas—Stars of the Lid's *The Ballasted Orchestra* builds from the sound of the group's previous releases (all illbient favorites), but emphasizes its sweeter, more elegant side. The album's title is more than appropriate, as its airy drones and reverberations suggest some cosmic orchestra tuning up—and without even approaching concreteness or structure, the album does seem to have a little more organization in its movement. —*Nitsuh Abebe*

## Stasis (Steve Pickton)
*Producer / Ambient-Techno, Club/Dance, Techno*
One of the original British translators of Detroit's machine music, Steve Pickton's recordings as Phenomyna, Stasis, and Paul W. Teebrooke furrowed similar ground to production compatriots like Black Dog, B12, and Kirk Degiorgio's As One, though his sound (and discography) later expanded to include a range of influences, from drum'n'bass and rare-groove to experimental techno and trip-hop. Pickton debuted in the early '90s on the tiny Time Is Right label before releasing an EP for B12 Records as Stasis. He made the connection through B12 to Kirk Degiorgio's A.R.T. Records, and released the label's first full-length as Phenomyna, *Unexplained*. Pickton recruited Black Dog, Redcell, As One, Nuron, and his own Stasis project to remix tracks from the album for a double EP, *Explained, Vols. 1-2*.

During 1994-95, Pickton began incorporating the diverse sounds of British electronica with his first Stasis full-length, 1994's *Inspiration*. For a volume in the trip-hop label Mo'Wax's *Excursions* series, he issued a Stasis single which filtered a heavier jazz inspiration through the bounds of sublime Detroit techno. In 1995, Pickton formed his own Otherworld Records (with Teebrooke and Phenomyna releases) and recorded two projects with Mark Broom: as Kape Ill Miester for Pure Plastic and A13, and as Nine Machine for the American experimental label Plug Research. Pickton branced out with remixes for Repeat, Patrick Pulsinger's IO, and Clatterbox. By 1996, he had released his second Stasis LP, *From the Old to the New*. The following year brought his most diverse recordings yet, on the Paul W. Teebrooke LP *Connections*. [See Also: Paul W. Teebrooke] —*John Bush*

**Inspiration** / 1995 / ♦♦♦♦

● **From the Old to the New** / Jun. 17, 1996 / Peacefrog ♦♦♦♦
The second Stasis album saw Pickton expanding on the Black Dog/As One school, with the disco-fied "Moon Bong" and breakbeats on "Gun." Fortunately, *From the Old to the New* never sounds as though Pickton is consciously trying to branch out—there are still plenty of moments of sublime, Detroit-inspired listening techno. —*John Bush*

## Statik Sound System
f. 1993, Bristol, England
*Group / Ambient-Techno, Trip-Hop*
A Cup of Tea Records act with the G-stoned production vibes that constitute a virtual prerequisite for entry on the label, Statik Sound System is basically the duo of Pete Webb and Roger Mills, though their session worksheets often include producer Andy Jenks (also of Alpha), reed player Rob Conn and percussionist Giles, plus vocalists Helen White and Kenny Lee Lewis (the former another Alpha associate). Statik began recording for Cup of Tea in late 1995 with the "Revolutionary Pilot" single. After several additional EP releases, the pair gained several good reviews, though centered more in the British rock weeklies than the dance press. One year later, Statik Sound System released their debut album *Tempesta*. Later that year came *Tempesta: The Reworkings*, with help from Kid Loops, Cut la Roc, Mr. Scruff, and Flynn & Flora. Signed to Iron America for stateside distribution, the group released the quasi-compilation *Tempesta II* as their first American release. —*John Bush*

**Tempesta** / Oct. 14, 1996 / Cup of Tea ♦♦♦♦
*Tempesta* is a solid album, closer to Portishead's *Dummy* than any other album in the Bristol camp (thanks in part to vocalist Helen White). The instrumental

tracks often appear a bit bland, though the mid-tempo drum'n'bass on "Essential Times" and "Dub (So Close)" livens up the proceedings. —*John Bush*

**Tempesta: The Reworkings** / Jul. 7, 1997 / Cup of Tea ◆◆◆

Statik Sound System recruited a raft of similarly minded producers—Bullitnuts, Cut La Roc, Spacer, Mr. Scruff, Kid Loops, and Juryman—for their remix album, although Statik members also remix one of their own, "Essential Times." Since the original album featured so many vocal tracks, *The Reworkings* is a welcome addition to their catalog and closer to a dub album than the often unnecessary exercises remix albums had become by the late '90s. —*John Bush*

● **Tempesta II** / Sep. 16, 1997 / Iron America ◆◆◆◆

## Michael Stearns

b. Tucson, AZ

*Vocals, Flute, Synthesizer, Leader, Composer / Space, Contemporary Instrumental, Ambient, Progressive Electronic*

Composer/sound sculptor Michael Stearns was born and raised in Tuscon, AZ, taking up classical guitar as a teen; in time he moved on to rock and jazz, and by the age of 16 was regularly backing top pop acts including the Lovin' Spoonful and Paul Revere & the Raiders. While a student at the University of the Pacific he turned to electronic music, completing his first musique concrète piece in 1968; four years later, Stearns returned to Tucson to open his own recording studio, subsequently producing a series of advertising jingles. In 1974, choreographer Emilie Conrad convinced him to move to Los Angeles to serve as the resident composer at her Continuum Studio; in the process of creating spontaneous live accompaniment for the dance group's groundbreaking explorations of human movement, Stearns developed a unique sound combining synthesizers and environmental samples, over time incorporating increasingly exotic instrumentation as well.

In 1977 Stearns released his debut album *Ancient Leaves* on his own Continuum Montage label, its space-music aesthetic anticipating the coming rise of New Age. Efforts including *Morning Jewel* and *Planetary Unfolding* followed as he developed The Beam, a 12-foot-long aluminum shaft strung with some two dozen piano strings designed to generate low frequencies; in 1983, Stearns also collaborated with composer Maurice Jarre on *Dreamscape*, the first in a series of innovative film scores. His fifth solo album, *Lyra*, was performed on George Landry's mammoth Lyra Sound Constellation, an instrument comprised of 156 microtonally-tuned strings of lengths up to 20 feet. In 1984, Stearns began a longstanding collaboration with filmmaker Ron Fricke which first yielded the soundtrack to the groundbreaking IMAX production *Chronos;* that same year, he also founded M'Ocean, a studio situated in Santa Monica, CA. (An album of the same name followed in 1985.)

In addition to 1986's *Plunge*, Stearns reunited with Fricke for the short film *Sacred Site;* soundtracks to two more IMAX productions, *Seasons* and *Time Concerto*, further solidified his reputation as one of the most innovative film music composers of the moment, highly regarded for his manipulation of multi-channel surround-sound technology. In addition to subsequent albums including *Encounter* and *Desert Solitaire* (the latter a collaboration with Steve Roach and Kevin Braheny) as well as IMAX scores like *Ring of Fire* and *Tropical Rain Forest*, Stearns also designed the soundtracks for several rides at the Universal Studios theme park. After another collaboration with Fricke resulted in 1991's much-celebrated *Baraka*, he relocated to Santa Fe, NM to build a new recording facility, Earth Turtle Studio. *Singing Stones*, a joint work with Ron Sunsinger, followed in 1994, and a year later Stearns released *The Lost World. The Light in the Trees* followed in 1996 and *Sorcerer* was issued four years later. —*Jason Ankeny*

**Planetary Unfolding** / 1985 / Sonic Atmospheres ◆◆◆◆

A masterful electronic symphony, *Planetary Unfolding* is based on the idea that the universe is made of sound rather than solid matter (a notion that has its roots in oriental philosophy as well as in some modern theoretical-physics circles). Stearns's performances on the Serge synthesizer actually give the feeling that atoms, cells, planets, and other celestial bodies are creating a complex orchestration that is unfolding on itself and expanding into deep space. —*Linda Kohanov*

**Sacred Site** / 1993 / Hearts of Space ◆◆◆

*Sacred Site* collects a decade's worth of Michael Stearns' soundtracks, scores, and previously unreleased music. After traveling to Indonesia, Thailand, Egypt, and Brazil on scoring assignments, Stearns delved deeper into the regional and cinematic elements in his music, with poetic and authentic results.

Included here are "Baraka Theme" from Ron Fricke's film exploring spirituality; a suite of pieces from Fricke's study of Western society, *Chronos*, as well as independent pieces like "Twin Flame." The 12 compositions on *Sacred Site* match the grand scope of the IMAX and wide-screen films from which many of these pieces originated. —*Heather Phares*

● **Collected Ambient & Textural Works 1977-1987** / 1996 / Fathom ◆◆◆◆

This compilation album preserves (with digital remastering) the brilliant early works of space music composer Michael Stearns. Short of re-releasing all the albums in their entirety, this compilation approaches perfection; if you want to experience the transformative thrills of space music, you can't go wrong in the hands of this master. It's best if you play the music on a good stereo system, place yourself between the speakers (perhaps boost the bass a bit), *and* wear good-quality headphones. If the bass tones break apart on an inferior system, you won't get the full impact of the vibrations. I won't describe all the various tracks, but I will point out elements that make his music work. First, Stearns composed for dance and movement classes, so he has a natural affinity for breath, stretching, trancework, meditation, and other elements. On the first track, "Elysian E" (from *Ancient Leaves*, 1977), massive bass drones attract the body; swirling layers of organ sounds swirl woozily in your head; the music is forever taking off to new cosmic and stellar dimensions. Stearns' occasional vocal chants bring in monastic overtones, and he often mixes natural sounds and electronic music. "M'ocean" from the 1982 album *Light Play* uses the rhythm of waves for the structure of his unfolding and percolating tapestry of sound. His 1979 "Morning" begins with the cheery patter of a Mexican village coming to life: a rooster, children's voices, bird songs, and horse hooves. Organ drones and layered angelic voices (by Stearns and Marsha Lee) cast a spell that seems to spread over the whole desert to proclaim the arrival of flying saucers. Magical chimes like a crystalline harpsichord echo through the heavens. The intensity of the organ tone patterns builds until the saucer seems right overhead. The arrival of horses and chanting Indians make the experience even more exciting. Again, the effect is more dramatic in the original longer version, but it is moving nevertheless. A dizzying sequence of tones welcomes your ears on the title track from *Ancient Leaves;* Stearns also plays a hypnotic melodic pattern on the metallic Finnish kantele, a form of hammered dulcimer. The layers swirl and build until it sounds like you are surrounded by a swarm of fairies, crows, and flying saucers. More live sounds are recorded with the gigantic stringed Lyra (three pieces from *Lyra: Sound Constellation)* and with vocals and crystal bells on "Vickie's Dance" (1983). "Jewel" (1979) is more peaceful, working crystalline tones with and against each other; the voice of Marsha Lee—seductive, haunting, and angelic—almost seems to turn to solid light. (These days, the voice would come from MIDI sources; this is obviously a custom job.) Stearns explains that the tones of this music were created on processed sound originating from the "Eikosany" vibes. Stearns' in-depth liner notes add to the appreciation of what it took to produce this early pre-MIDI, pre-digital music. Excellent album. —*Carol Wright*

**Collected Thematic Works 1977-1987** / 1996 / Fathom ◆◆◆◆

This compilation collects early "melodic" works of space music pioneer Michael Stearns; his other compilation album, *Collected Ambient & Textural Works: 1977-1987*, offers Stearns' classical space music, pieces that use drones, tones, chants, and nature sounds to aurally move the listener into a meditative space. The music on this album (the majority of the tracks taken from his 1986 album *Plunge*), as abstract as it is at times, is melody-driven. On "Spanish Twilight" (1987, from the *Floating Whispers* album), Stearns creates an atmosphere of chimes, drones, and vocalese, but an electric guitar (with a Spanish flavor) is the obvious star. Here we have music that is evocative of external scenes, more like an accompanying movie score than a meditative tool. "Her Way" (previously unreleased) is the score for a dance performance titled "Three Faces of the Goddess." An atmosphere, perhaps of a Greek temple, is created. Gongs, broad brass tones, and snare drums create an ominous processional on "Dark Passage" (from the 1986 album *Plunge*); the piece then accelerates into chaos, then opens to a peaceful plateau with Spanish guitar. Highly processed electric guitar is featured on "Space Grass," also from the *Plunge* album; the grass does not refer to marijuana, but the bluegrass, as evident by the fancy fiddling of Dennis Fetchet. "A Moment Before" from Stearn's 1987 *Floating Whispers* is an ambient piece that yaws and careens; a crystalline metronome keeps cosmic time. These 17 pieces are representative of Michael Stearns the film score composer. It's fascinating to compare the two albums; so similar, yet so distinct. Audiophiles will appreciate that Stearns recorded all these pieces on a four-track analog tape recorder. Stearns' liner notes explain the early new-age music scene and the early synthesizers and other techniques used to create this music. —*Carol Wright*

## Stereo MC's

f. 1985, London, England
*Group / Trip-Hop, Club/Dance, Acid Jazz, House, Hip-Hop*

One of the most successful hip-hop acts to emerge from Great Britain, the Stereo MCs formed in London in 1985, when rapper Rob B. (born Rob Birch) and DJ/producer the Head (Nick Hallam) formed the Gee Street label as a means of promoting their music. Gee Street soon signed a distribution deal with the New York-based 4th & Broadway label, and a series of singles followed before the Stereo MCs' debut album, *33-45-78*, surfaced in 1989.

After the departure of founding member Cesare, the group—now consisting of Rob B., the Head, drummer Owen If (born Owen Rossiter), and vocalist Cath Coffey—issued the 1990 single "Elevate My Mind," which became the first British rap single ever to reach the US pop charts. Following the release of the album *Supernatural*, the Stereo MCs toured with the Happy Mondays and EMF before returning to the studio to record their 1992 breakthrough *Connected*, a sample-free album recorded completely with live instruments which spawned such major hits as "Step It Up," "Creation," "Ground Level," and the title track. After years of production and remix work, the group's long-awaited (and oft-delayed) follow-up remains unreleased, though in 1997 Coffey did at least issue her debut solo single, "Wild World." For their 2000 mix album, *DJ Kicks*, Stereo MC's recorded three new tracks, "Rhino, Pts. 1-3." —*Jason Ankeny*

**33-45-78** / Jul. 24, 1989 / ✦✦✦

**Supernatural** / 1990 / 4th & Broadway ✦✦✦✦
The only thing that separates *Supernatural* and its hit follow-up *Connected* is that *Connected* had a hit. Otherwise, the albums are nearly identical and are equally enjoyable. —*AMG*

● **Connected** / 1992 / PolyGram ✦✦✦✦
Stereo MCs' American breakthrough is an energetic, club-oriented collection of colorful, funky dance tracks—the raps almost seem like an afterthought, yet that doesn't distract from the sheer pleasure of their sound. —*AMG*

**DJ Kicks** / Mar. 28, 2000 / Studio !K7 ✦✦✦✦
Eight years after their last LP, Stereo MC's returned not with a studio work but with a mix album that shows their long career in a new light, not just as one-hit wonders but as breakbeat renegades who've been searching for the perfect beat—both as recording artists and as label heads—for over 15 years. *DJ Kicks* trips back and forth between beat-heavy cinematic music from the '70s, rap from the old-school to the new-skool, and trip-hop from producers who, just like Stereo MCs themselves, take the template of breakbeat music down new paths. Truth to tell, though, there'd been so many similar mix albums released in the previous few years that it wasn't difficult to believe the bottomless well of obscure, funky music was just about tapped. Fortunately, Rob H. and Nick come through with a lineup of widely varied artists and crucial tracks. Most of the instrumental highlights are obscurities like "Back to the Hip Hop" by the Troubleneck Brothers, "Do It Do It" by the Disco Four, "Moon Trek" by the Mike Theodore Orchestra, and a surprisingly chilling track by 101 Strings titled "Flameout." The rap tracks are solid too, including old-school heroes like Kool G. Rap & DJ Polo ("Road to the Riches") and Ultramagnetic MC's ("Poppa Large"), as well as more recent artists from the growing hip-hop underground like the 57th Dynasty ("Pharoah Intellect") and Divine Styler ("Tongue of Labyrinth"). Another highlight is the new three-part track "Rhino" produced by Stereo MC's. Fitting in well with the album itself, "Rhino" is an old-school groove number with heavy drums and Hammond keys. It's easy to wonder if Stereo MC's even *have* any fans left from the days of *Connected*, but this mix album might gain them a few. —*John Bush*

## Stereolab

f. 1991, London, England
*Group / Indie Pop, Ambient Pop, Experimental Rock, Indie Rock, Post-Rock/Experimental, Alternative Pop-Rock*

Combining an inclination for melodic '60s pop with an art-rock aesthetic borrowed from Kraut-rock bands like Faust and Neu!, Stereolab was one of the most influential alternative bands of the '90s. Led by Tim Gane and Laetitia Sadier, Stereolab legitimized forms of music that were either on the fringe of rock, or brought attention to a strand of pop music—bossa nova, lounge-pop, movie soundtracks—that were traditionally banished from the rock lineage. The group's trademark sound—a droning, hypnotic rhythm track overlaid with melodic, mesmerizing sing-song vocals, often sung in French and often promoting revolutionary, Marxist politics—was deceptively simple, providing the basis for a wide array of stylistic experiments over the course of their prolific career. Throughout it all, Stereolab relied heavily on forgotten methods of recording, whether it was analog synthesizers and electronics or a fondness for hi-fi test records, without ever sinking to the level of kitsch.

Tim Gane (b. July 12, 1964; guitar, keyboards) was the leader of McCarthy, a London-based band from the late '80s that functioned as a prototype for Stereolab's sound. Gane met Laetitia Sadier (b. May 6, 1968; vocals, keyboards), a French-born vocalist, at one of McCarthy's concerts. The pair began a romantic relationship that became a musical collaboration after McCarthy disbanded in 1990; Sadier did sing on the final McCarthy album. The duo began releasing mail-order singles under the name Stereolab, borrowing their name from a form of record mastering from the late '50s. At that point, the group was working with the Faith Healers' drummer Joe Dilworth and former Chills bassist Martin Kean; Gina Morris occasionally provided backup vocals. All three singles this incarnation of Stereolab released were compiled on *Switched On*, an album released on Too Pure Records in 1992. *Switched On* was released at the same time as the band's official debut album, *Peng!*. Both album covers featured a variation on a maniacally grinning cartoon, which was their only visual trademark at the time.

*Switched On* and *Peng!*, along with the 1992 *Lo-Fi* EP and a series of limited-edition singles like "John Cage Bubblegum"—which, coincidentally, was the first Stereolab recording to feature keyboardist/vocalist Mary Hansen and drummer Andy Ramsay, who became two of the group's core members—Stereolab earned a cult following, particularly in the UK underground. Released in early 1993, *The Groop Played "Space Age Batchelor Pad Music"*, featured the core group of Gane, Sadier, Hansen and Ramsay, along with ex-Microdisney guitarist Sean O'Hagan and bassist Duncan Brown. One of the first '90s alternative records to explicitly draw from the "Space Age" lounge-pop music of the '50s, *The Groop* became an underground sensation, paving the way towards Stereolab's first American record contract with Elektra Records. But before the band made their major-label debut, they released the split 10" EP *Crumb Duck* with Nurse With Wound in the summer of 1993 and formed their own UK label, Duophonic.

Stereolab's next album, and their first American release, was *Transient Random-Noise Bursts With Announcements*. Released in the summer of 1993, *Transient* became an underground and college hit throughout the US and UK, and Stereolab soon became a hip name to drop for many musicians, including Sonic Youth, Pavement, and Blur, who had Laetitia Sadier provide guest vocals on their 1994 hit single, "To The End." Where *Transient* was dominated by a lo-fi experimentalism, the group's sound became lusher and more layered with *Mars Audiac Quintet*, which was released in the fall of 1994. O'Hagan moved from a full member to a part-time guest during the recording of the album—he was busy forming his own band, the High Llamas—and the band added keyboardist Katherine Gifford.

By the time of *Mars Audiac Quintet*'s release, the Stereolab sound had become prominent throughout the underground, and the group began to make efforts to change their sound, as the limited-edition 1995 EP *Music for the Amorphous Body Study Centre* indicated. Created for an interactive art exhibit by Charles Long, the EP boasted detailed, intricate string and vocal arrangements, which were more sophisticated than the group's previous releases. That fall, the band rounded up a bunch of singles and B-sides for the second *Switched On* compilation, *Refried Ectoplasm*, which was released on Drag City in the US. Before the band recorded a new album, Gifford was replaced by Morgane Lhote. *Emperor Tomato Ketchup*, released in the spring of 1996, was a break from the drone-rock of its two predecessors, demonstrating a heavy hip-hop, jazz and dance influence. The album was the greatest success to date, earning positive reviews in both US and UK and becoming a significant college hit in the process. After the recording of *Emperor Tomato Ketchup*, bassist Duncan Brown was replaced by Richard Harrison. At the end of 1996, Stereolab released the limited-edition, horn-driven *Fluorescences* EP; *Dots and Loops* appeared a year later, and after taking time off following the birth of Gane and Sadier's first child, the band resurfaced in 1999 with *Cobra and Phases Group Play Voltage in the Milky Night*. An EP, *The First of the Microbe Hunters*, quickly followed in the spring of 2000. —*Stephen Thomas Erlewine*

### Peng! / 1992 / Too Pure/American ◆◆◆◆

*Peng!* is the band's debut full-length album, on which Stereolab continue to develop their unique approach to experimental pop music. "Super Falling Star," "Peng! 33," "K-Stars," "The Seeming and the Meaning," and "Surrealchemist" are just some of the album's standout tracks, combining dreamy harmonies and swirling keyboards with dissonant guitars and Marxist lyrics. *—Heather Phares*

### Switched On / 1992 / Slumberland ◆◆◆

*Switched On* collects Stereolab's earliest singles, capturing the group's hypnotic, driving sound in its infancy. Though they're more guitar-driven and rock-oriented than the band's later work, tracks like "Super-Electric" and "Au Grand Jour" prove that Stereolab's basic style—Krautrock lock-grooves, bubbling analog synths, fuzzed-out guitars, and angelic vocals—arrived fully formed. "Doubt" and "Brittle" are among the group's most vibrant pop songs, while the eight-minute "Contact" is a warm-up for the epics the band would include on albums like *Transient Random Noise-Bursts With Announcements*. Reflective pieces like "The Way Will Be Opening" and "High Expectation" show off Laetitia Sadier's cooly sophisticated, Nico-meets-Francoise Hardy vocals, while "The Light That Will Cease to Fail" manages to be poppy, kinetic, and bittersweet all at once. Though the group would go on to make even more impressive albums, the newness of Stereolab's sound is palpable on *Switched On*, giving the songs an added vitality. Obviously, it's an impressive debut, but it's captivating in its own right. *—Heather Phares*

### The Groop Played "Space Age Batchelor Pad Music" / 1993 / Too Pure/American ◆◆◆

This EP consists of eight tracks that suggest a more experimental direction for the band, especially the burbling "Space Age Batchelor Pad Music (Mellow)," the driving "We're Not Adult Orientated," and "U.H.F.-MFP." As usual, Sadier and Hansen's vocals and the heavy keyboards come together in a distinctively Stereolab way. *—Heather Phares*

### ☆ Transient Random-Noise Bursts With Announcements / Aug. 1993 / Elektra ◆◆◆◆◆

Stereolab's major-label debut is also one of their finest and most experimental releases. More emphasis is placed on instrumentals and instrumental breaks on *Transient Random-Noise Bursts*. The 15-minute "Jenny Ondioline" and noisy cuts like "Our Trinitone Blast" and "Analogue Rock" showcase Stereolab's experimental tendencies, while tracks like "Tone Burst," "Pack Yr Romantic Mind," and "Lock Group Lullaby" show that the group is just as capable of creating beautiful if offbeat pop songs as it is adept at bringing the noise. The group's most varied and characteristic recording. *—Heather Phares*

### Mars Audiac Quintet / Aug. 9, 1994 / Elektra ◆◆◆◆

The band's fourth album tones down their avant-garde edge, concentrating instead on Sadier's and Hansen's vocal interplay, as well as song structures. A beautiful, if less challenging album, *Mars Audiac Quintet* features plenty of bouncy, dreamy tunes like "Three-Dee Melodie," "Des Étoiles Électroniques," "Ping Pong," "Seven Longers Later," and "Fiery Yellow." *Mars Audiac Quintet* is a good starting point for Stereolab novices, as it gives an appealing but accurate introduction to the group's distinct and innovative sound. *—Heather Phares*

### Refried Ectoplasm (Switched On, Vol. 2) / Jul. 1995 / Duophonic/Drag City ◆◆◆◆

*Refried Ectoplasm (Switched On, Vol. 2)* collects 13 singles and rarities Stereolab released between 1992 and 1995, and it is far more than a mere oddities collection. More than any other album, *Refried Ectoplasm* charts Stereolab's astonishing musical growth between those three years, and offers several definitive songs—including "Lo Boob Oscillator," "French Disko," and "John Cage Bubblegum"—not available on any album. While such items are essential for collectors, the quality and accessiblity of the music is very strong, showcasing Stereolab's complexity and providing an excellent introduction to the group. *—Stephen Thomas Erlewine*

### ★ Emperor Tomato Ketchup / Apr. 1996 / Elektra ◆◆◆◆◆

Stereolab was poised for a breakthrough release with *Emperor Tomato Ketchup*, their fourth full-length album. Not only was their influence becoming apparent throughout alternative rock, but *Mars Audiac Quintet* and *Music for the Amorphous Body Center* indicated they were moving closer to distinct pop melodies. The group certainly hasn't backed away from pop melodies on *Emperor Tomato Ketchup*, but just as their hooks are becoming catchier, they bring in more avant-garde and experimental influences, as well. Consequently, the album is Stereolab's most complex, multilayered record. It lacks the raw, amateurish textures of their early singles, but the music is far more ambitious, melding electronic drones and sing-song melodies with string sections, slight hip-hop and dub influences, and scores of interweaving countermelodies. Even when Stereolab appears to be creating a one-chord trance, there is a lot going on beneath the surface. Furthermore, the group's love for easy listening and pop melodies means that the music never feels cold or inaccessible. In fact, pop singles like "Cybele's Reverie" and "The Noise of Carpet" help ease listeners into the group's more experimental tendencies. Because of all its textures, *Emperor Tomato Ketchup* isn't as immediately accessible as *Mars Audiac Quintet*, but it is a rich, rewarding listen. *—Stephen Thomas Erlewine*

### Dots and Loops / Sep. 23, 1997 / Drag City ◆◆◆◆

On *Emperor Tomato Ketchup*, Stereolab moved in two directions simultaneously—it explored funkier dance rhythms while increasing the complexity of its arrangements and compositions. For its followup, *Dots and Loops*, the group scaled back its rhythmic experiments and concentrated on layered compositions. Heavily influenced by bossa nova and swinging '60s pop, *Dots and Loops* is a deceptively light, breezy album that floats by with effortless grace. Even the segmented, 20-minute "Refractions in the Plastic Pulse" has a sunny, appealing surface—it's only upon later listens that the interlocking melodies and rhythms reveal their intricate interplay. In many ways, *Dots and Loops* is Stereolab's greatest musical accomplishment to date, demonstrating remarkable skill—their interaction is closer to jazz than rock, exploring all of the possibilities of any melodic phrase. Their affection for '60s pop keeps *Dots and Loops* accessible, even though that doesn't mean it is as immediate as *Emperor Tomato Ketchup*. In fact, the laidback stylings of *Dots and Loops* makes it a little difficult to assimilate upon first listen, but after a few repeated plays, its charms unfold as gracefully as any other Stereolab record. *—Stephen Thomas Erlewine*

### Aluminum Tunes (Switched On, Vol. 3) / Oct. 20, 1998 / Drag City ◆◆◆◆

Stereolab's *Switched On* series is ingenious, one of the best services a band has ever performed for their fans. Since their inception, Stereolab has made it a practice to release non-LP singles, tour 7"s, split-singles, special-edition EPs—all recordings that are availble in small quantities for a limited time. In every case, the limited-edition recordings become very valuable very quickly. Often, the singles are so exorbitantly priced that many fans will never be able to acquire the original pressing. That's where *Switched On* comes in. Periodically, the group gathers the best of these rarities—leaving a couple of tracks on the original single for collectibility's sake—and releases them as an edition in the series. Stereolab may do certain projects as a lark, but they rarely throw away tracks; even the smallest singles and EPs have their own feel, offering a new spin on the group's trademark style. Given that *Aluminum Tunes (Switched On, Vol. 3)* spans two discs, it might seem that the compilation will only be of interest to diehards, but it rivals *Refried Ectoplasm (Switched On, Vol. 2)* in terms of creativity and consistency. *Aluminum Tunes* is distinguished by the first wide release of the entire sublime easy listening EP *Music for the Amorphous Body Center*, which would be enough to make the compilation essential for all fans, but it also has such minor masterpieces as their swinging duet with Herbie Mann on Antonio Carlos Jobim's "One Note Samba," Wagon Christ's remix of "Metronomic Underground," and the horn-spiked "Percolations" and "You Used to Call Me Sadness." There may be a couple of tracks that never rise above the level of very good but predictable Stereolab, but there are no weak cuts and the best moments rank among their very best work. Quite simply an essential addition to their catalog. *—Stephen Thomas Erlewine*

### Cobra and Phases Group Play Voltage in the Milky Night / Sep. 21, 1999 / Elektra/Asylum ◆◆

Stereolab took an unprecedented two years between 1997's *Dots and Loops* and 1999's *Cobra and Phases Group Play Voltage in the Milky Night*, as they tended to personal matters. For a band that churned out limited-edition singles and EPs, along with an annual album, between 1992 and 1997, complete silence was a complete change of pace, but they happened to pick a good time to go into seclusion. During those two years, Stereolab's brand of sophisticated, experimental post-rock didn't evolve too much, even as their peers, colleagues, and collaborators tried other things: Tortoise got jazzier with *TNT*, Jim O'Rourke got irresistibly lush and complex with *Bad Timing* and *Eureka*, while the High Llamas fleshed out Sean O'Hagan's Beach Boys fetish with 'Lab highlights on *Cold and Bouncy*. With the exception of O'Rourke, who abandoned Gastr Del Sol's minimalism for grandiosity, they all offered slight expansions of what they did before instead of making great progress. Since each Stereolab album has offered a significant progression from the one before, it would have been fair to assume that when they returned with *Cobra*, it would have been a leap forward, especially since it was coproduced with Tortoise's John McEntire and O'Rourke. Perhaps that's the reason that the album feels slightly disappointing. The group has absorbed McEntire's jazz-fusion leanings—"Fuses" kicks off the album in compelling, free-jazz style—and the music continually bears O'Rourke's attention to detail, but it winds up sounding like O'Hagan's increasing tendency of making music that's simply sound for sound's sake. *Cobra* may seem that way because its pacing is off, with the first half of the album filled with concise numbers that give way to the lengthy "Blue Milk" and "Caleidoscopic Gaze" toward the end; after those two set pieces, it snaps back into succinct mode for the final three songs. Throughout it all, Stereolab's trademarks remain in place, but they're augmented by rhythms, harmonies, horn arrangements, dissonance, muted trumpets, and electric keyboards, all out of jazz from the late '60s, whether it's bossa nova or fusion. All fascinating in theory and often in practice, but *Cobra* still winds up being less than the sum of its parts. Maybe it's because the longer pieces drift, instead of hypnotize or develop; maybe it's because the songs sound like afterthoughts to the arrangements (a criticism leveled at Stereolab before but never really applicable until now); maybe it's just because of the odd pace of the album. In any case, *Cobra* never hits its stride, even as it offers a few miniature masterpieces along the way. Perhaps the time off led to the slight lack of focus, since many moments of the album illustrate that Stereolab is as fascinating as ever. But as an album, *Cobra* is their first record since *Transient Random Noise Bursts* to not be fully realized. *—Stephen Thomas Erlewine*

**The First of the Microbe Hunters [EP]** / May 16, 2000 / Elektra/Asylum ♦♦
The quick appearance of the mini-LP *The First of the Microbe Hunters*—released just months after their two-years-in-the-making *Cobra and Phases Group Play Voltage in the Milky Night*—signaled Stereolab's return to normalcy. Throughout the '90s, Stereolab was exceptionally prolific, releasing an album a year, non-LP B-sides, EPs, limited singles, split single—basically, every kind of release known to a hardcore record geek. Almost without exception, their hardcore fans devoured these recordings without question, scrambling for the exceptionally rare items or waiting until they were collected on one of the *Switched On* compilations. There was a reason 'Lab fans were voracious. To the outsider, all the Stereolab records may have sounded the same, but the band invariably found a new variation on their trademark, minimalist, exotica laced with lo-fi experimentalism groove, and as the decade wore on, the group's recordings became more ambitious, subtle, and complex. Wonderful diversions like an excursion in bossa nova and Latin jazz were tucked away on EPs like *Modulations*, and these little treasures were the reason why fans happily spent hundreds of dollars following the band's every whim and side project. Then came the extended break between fall 1997 and fall 1999, where the group was unusually quiet as front duo Tim Gane and Laetitia Sadier had a child. Gane appeared on a couple of extracurricular projects, but the band itself entered its longest period of silence, only to emerge with the underwhelming *Cobra*. The lackluster *Cobra* could have been written off as growing pains, but the *First of the Microbe Hunters* suggests a bleaker prospect—that Stereolab has run out of ideas.

It is no stretch to say that *The First of the Microbe Hunters* is the first recording that the hardcore Stereolab fans need not own. After all, it's the first that offers no new twist or turn on the patented 'Lab sound. The record plays like classicist Stereolab, filled with all of the trademarks—pleasant drones, reverb-drenched guitars, cheap organs, French lyrics, and effervescent, hypnotic vocals—but it's all been done before. More than that, it borders on parody. There's no other way to read titles like "Outer Bongolia" and "Retrograde Mirror Form," two names that sound like sops to their burgeoning hippie/stoner audience. Such slips would be excusable if the music itself transcended mere titles, as it has before in Stereolab's work. Instead, *Microbe Hunters* feels as if the band is treading water without realizing it. What was once endearing has mutated into the irritating, as the chanted vocals, simple organ runs, and endless, pulsating rhythmic drones alienate listeners instead of mesmerizing them. Why is that? Because there aren't only no surprises on *Microbe Hunters*, the craft is half-hearted and, ironically enough for this notoriously detached band, there is no soul (or at least their equivalent of it). It feels tossed-off, something that no other Stereolab record has sounded like. And, arriving on the heels of an album that also sounded repetitive and slightly stale, it does not bode well for the band's future. This could easily be where many longtime, hardcore fans get off the bandwagon. *—Stephen Thomas Erlewine*

## Byron Stingily

b. Chicago, IL
*Vocals / Club/Dance, Acid House, House*
The lead vocalist for Ten City and later a solo star in his own right, Byron Stingily had one of the most beautiful voices in house music, a sweet and impeccably clear high register, akin to Smokey Robinson or disco celebrity Sylvester. A singer since the age of five, Stingily grew up on the west side of Chicago, and though he attended Blackburn College in rural Illinois during the early '80s, he became a part of the Windy City's exploding house scene midway through the decade. He recorded his first single "Funny Love" in 1985, and licensed the song to Trax Records. After meeting up with house maestro Marshall Jefferson, Stingily recorded two early Chicago classics, "Can't Stay Away" and "Just a Little Bit," and impressed many as the support slot for Jefferson's visit to New York City.

While in town, Jefferson and Stingily decided to make the rounds at the major labels, and impressed Atlantic Records enough that the label offered them a contract before they had even formed a group. By 1988, the pair had recruited guitarist Herb Lawson and DJ-turned-keyboardist Byron Burke to form Ragtyme. The trio released "Devotion" and "Right Back to You," later changing their name to Ten City and recording their debut album *Foundation*. Though the group recorded two more albums for Atlantic (all of which did well on the club scene but failed commercially), the label dropped them by 1993. Ten City then wrote a song with Masters at Work titled "Fantasy," and though the single received massive club play, it was over a year before their fourth album *That Was Then, This Is Now* appeared. By that time, the buzz had died down and Ten City rapidly disintegrated.

Though Byron Stingily was offered a solo contract by Columbia, he opted to return to the independents and began working on his composing and production skills: he worked with Kim English for the singles "Nitelife" and "Time for Love" plus Michael Watford and Maysa Leak (of Incognito). Stingily began recording for Nervous in 1996 with two singles, "Love You the Right Way" and "Don't Fall in Love." The following year both "Sing-A-Song" and "Get Up" became rather large garage-crossover hits, and in 1998, Stingily released his debut solo full-length *The Purist*. *Club Stories* followed two years later. *—John Bush*

• **The Purist** / Feb. 9, 1998 / Nervous Dog ♦♦♦♦
Byron Stingily's debut solo album charts a night in the life of your average mainstream clubber circa 1998, with previous singles "Sing-A-Song" and "Get Up" alongside more recent shots, including his cover of the Sylvester classic "You Make Me Feel (Mighty Real)." Though the epic tone of the album's five suites—"early evening," "crowd-pleasers," "garage set," "after-hours," and "Sunday morning"—ties things together nicely, the range of producer credits (by Masters at Work, David Morales, Murk, Frankie Knuckles, Mousse T, and Maurice Joshua) can't help but give *The Purist* a rather disjointed feel. *—John Bush*

**Club Stories** / Mar. 21, 2000 / Nervous ♦♦♦
On his second solo album, *Club Stories*, former Ten City member Byron Stingily hooks up with such top-notch dance music talent as D'Influence, the Basement Boys, Danny Tenaglia, Peter Rauhofer, and Andrew "Doc" Livingstone. Stingily also calls on Frankie Knuckles, who was a DJ at Chicago's north side the Warehouse during his Ten City ("Devotion," "That's the Way Love Is") heyday, to determine the track order of *Club Stories*. House music's roots in '70s-era Gamble & Huff Philly soul definitely show on "Happy," which echoes Harold Melvin and the Blue Notes featuring Teddy Pendergrass' gold classic "Bad Luck." Stingily sounds eerily like Sylvester ("You Make Me Feel [Mighty Real]") on the pumpin' "Stand Right Up," which includes a sample from Brainstorm's "Lovin' Is Really My Game." Stingily covers one of the final songs recorded by another Chicago native, Minnie Riperton, "Stick Together." Stingily redoes "That's the Way Love Is" in two versions; one is a Johnny Vicious remix. A rock-solid set of *Club Stories* from this house music pioneer. *—Ed Hogan*

## Stock, Hausen & Walkman

f. 1989, Salford, England
*Group / Sound Collage, Experimental Techno, Electronica*
It's close to a sure bet that, at least in the field of electronic music, no other artist's name makes quite as much sense as Stock, Hausen & Walkman—a

triple pun embracing pioneering electronic composer and theorist Karlheinz Stockhausen, the '80s pop-by-numbers production team Stock, Aitken & Waterman, and the ubiquitous portable cassette player manufactured by Sony. The sampling duo of Andrew Sharpley and Matt Wand appears to have been influenced equally by each of the three, resulting in bizarre collisions of cut-and-pasted pop songs, noise, tape-hiss, and a perceived avant-garde sensibility regarding the sampling technology (and legality). While humor has never been completely absent from electronica, the pair also helped deflate the pomposity of the usual cast of navel-gazing bedroom producers, whether it's releasing a 7" single consisting of 42 locked grooves, packaging cassettes in Rice Krispies bags, or including pictures of pornographic playing cards with their *Organ Transplants* album.

At the time of the group's formation in the late '80s, they were an experimental/improv quartet consisting of Sharpley and Wand plus cellist Dan Weaver and guitarist Rex Casswell. They played at Derek Bailey's request in 1990, but began to fracture when Casswell left and Weaver began taking recording time-outs to perform for dance and theatre as well. The trio formed their own Hot Air Records and began releasing a wide range of albums (considering their sample base), from plunderphonic easy-listening organ music to death metal. The debut LP *Giving Up with Stock, Hausen & Walkman* was released in 1993, followed two years later by *Hairballs*—packaged in a fake-fur wrapping and including photos not intended for cat lovers. Weaver left around this time, though Wand and Sharpley continued on with an album-per-year release schedule (not including the live LP, 1995's *Stop!*). The Beastie Boys became fascinated with Stock, Hausen & Walkman's idiosyncratic approach to recording (in a similar fashion to their interest in Alec Empire's Digital Hardcore Recordings) and asked the duo to remix the Grand Royal group Buffalo Daughter. Sharpley also records for Hot Air in the more dance-oriented Dummy Run. —*John Bush*

### Giving Up with Stock, Hausen & Walkman / 1993 / Hot Air ♦♦
Perfect for listeners with a mischievous attitude concerning the plunder of rock-radio staples and obscure comedy/instructional LPs, *Giving Up* is a fragmented collection of samples and found sounds. With almost 60 tracks on the CD configuration, the album definitely suffers from its producers' lack of attention span. It's barely listenable more than once, but an interesting curiosity. —*John Bush*

### Organ Transplants, Vol. 1 / 1996 / Hot Air ♦♦♦
Speaking comparatively, of course, *Organ Transplants* is quite a together work for Stock, Hausen & Walkman. Perhaps because it displays a bit of focus for all the cultural referencing (mostly organ music, whether bossa nova, lounge, or vaguely soundtrack-sounding), the album succeeds where others failed. It shows SH&W creating actual music from their samples, instead of simply recycling various shards of pop music before they're thrown back into the dustbin. —*John Bush*

### Stop! / 1996 / Hot Air ♦♦
*Stop!* consists of edited recordings of live improvisation from Zurich, Basel, Cologne, Manchester and Liverpool. Though common sense would dictate that Stock, Hausen & Walkman have less time to construct and expand on their sample symphonies, the album is arguably more dense and cluttered than even their studio recordings, encompassing large amounts of noise and cut-and-paste experimentation. —*John Bush*

### ● Oh My Bag! / 1998 / Hot Air ♦♦♦♦
What appears to be the beginning of a more musical approach to recording, *Oh My Bag!* has snippets of actual digital sequencing amidst the sampling mayhem, and reflects a polished production practically nonexistent on earlier material. Fortunately for listeners, Stock, Hausen & Walkman hasn't gone pop in any appreciable sense; what small concessions to melody and rhythm there are however, make *Oh My Bag!* quite a triumph. —*John Bush*

## Karlheinz Stockhausen
**b.** Aug. 22, 1928, Cologne, Germany
*Composer / Musique Concrète, 20th Century Classical/Modern Composition, Electronic*

The most innovative and influential German composer of the postwar era, Karlheinz Stockhausen laid much of the foundation of modern experimental music; through his pioneering work in electronics, he left an indelible imprint not only in contemporary classic circles but throughout the creative spectrum, where echoes of his genius still reverberate everywhere from the avant-garde to rock to dance music. Born outside the city of Köln (aka Cologne) on August 22, 1928, Stockhausen studied at the Cologne Musikhochschule from 1947 to 1951; influenced by Olivier Messiaen's *Mode de valeurs*, he began exploring long-range serial composition, a process he first tackled in 1951's *Kreuzspiel* and the following year's *Kontra-Punkte*, both written for piano-based ensemble. While working on the latter he travelled to Paris to study under Messiaen himself, and it was there he first delved into electronic music.

Upon returning to Cologne, Stockhausen continued his pursuits, achieving his first significant breakthrough with 1956's *Gesang der Jünglinge*—composed for vocal and synthesized sounds, it was among the first tape-loop pieces ever assembled. Concurrently he continued his work with serial instrumental music, completing a cycle of 11 piano pieces in 1956; a year later Stockhausen composed *Gruppen*, a work for three orchestras. Both were notable for featuring large groups of notes, a significant shift away from the isolated points which typified the music of avant-gardists like Messiaen and Anton Webern; his fascination with the abstract further extended into a series of essays, as well as his lectures at Darmstadt, which profoundly influenced contemporaries including Luciano Berio and Pierre Boulez. (Also attending: Holger Czukay, later a co-founder of the pioneering Kraut-rock group Can.)

Stockhausen made his first trip to the US in 1958, a journey which triggered a new relaxation in his music, attributed largely to the influence of John Cage. The leisurely pace of 1959's *Carré*, a composition for four choral-orchestral groups, reflected the change; another key work completed as the decade drew to its close was *Zyklus*, conceived as a physical and musical circle with the soloist surrounded by a large array of instruments on all sides, complete with a score printed on a number of spiral-bound pages (any of which might begin the piece, with the rest following in cyclical sequence). More esoteric still was *Refrain for Three Players*, notable for a movable strip of clear plastic containg the recurrent features of said refrain, with the position of the strip in relation to the score varying with each new performance.

In 1960, Stockhausen premiered the landmark *Kontakte*, heralded as a watershed in the evolution of modern experimental music; composed for electronic tape, either alone or in tandem with live piano and percussion, it was among the first pieces of its kind to fuse pre-recorded material with live instrumentation, with the stated goal of expressing the continuous spectrum of sound separating noise and tone. At the same time, it expressed a "moment" form of composition, without any emphasis on progression. *Kontakte* resurfaced a year later as part of *Originale*, a new work in the realm of musical theatre in which the actions of participants were coordinated according to the rigors of the score. Stockhausen's major open form work, *Momente*, began taking shape in 1961 as well.

By the mid-'60s, Stockhausen's immersion in electronics was almost total, and in late 1964 he assembled a touring ensemble to premiere his latest composition, *Mikrophonie I*, a work inspired by his recent discovery of the limitless variety of sounds to be gotten from any instrument in conjunction with microphones and electrical filters. *Mixtur* was a live work for orchestra, sine-wave generators and ring modulators, with the latter resurfacing again in 1965 in *Mikrophonie II*, also scored for chorus and Hammond organ. While in Japan, he also created a pair of major tape works, the 1966 sound mosaic *Telemusik* and its 1967 companion piece *Hymnen*, constructed from recordings assembled from across the globe, including a variety of national anthems.

Stockhausen's next period found him less in the role of creator than "process planner"—1967's *Prozession* consisted of no new material, instead requiring its players to perform interpretations of his earlier works, while *Ensemble* called upon a dozen of his Darmstadt students to each write a part for one instrument and tape or short-wave receiver. Similarly, 1968's *Kurzwellen* was little more than a series of procedural instructions for its performers to imitate sounds they heard on short-wave radio broadcasts. With the following *Stimmung*, Stockhausen's aim of universalization took a different tactic, with its performers pitching their voices to a series of natural harmonics; these works, in addition to 1968's *Aus den sieben Tagen*, served to gradually eliminate the concept of notation, with the ultimate goal of truly intuitve musical creation.

With 1970's *Mantra*, Stockhausen returned to more conventional compositional techniques, resulting in a fully notated piece for piano and electronics built around transformations of its melodic theme. His major works in the years that followed—1971's *Trans*, 1974's *Inori*, and 1977's *Sirius* among them—were similarly thematic, albeit more dramatic than his earlier material. Beginning in 1980, all of Stockhausen's energies were focused on *Licht*, a seven-part work including individual performances for each night of the week. Remaining active as the century drew to its end, he was celebrated as a trailblazing force behind the rise of contemporary electronic music—while still primarily a cult figure, Stockhausen's place in 20th-century musical history is nevertheless assured. —*Jason Ankeny*

**Kontra-Punkte (Counter-Points) for 10 Instruments** / 1953 / RCA Victrola ♦♦♦

A currently out-of-print vinyl conducted by the legendary Bruno Maderna. Composed in 1952 and 1953, this is probably the best known of the composer's early serial works. The central composition problem that Stockhausen set himself in this piece was to create a situation in which many individual notes and rhythms resolve themselves into an homogenous and immutable image. The "two-part, monochrome counterpoint is wrested from the antithesis between vertical and horizontal relationships." The score is actually full of interesting colors and timbral combinations—six specific timbres are used: flute-bassoon, clarinet-bass clarinet, trumpet-trombone, piano, harp, violin-cello...these timbres merge into a single timbre, that of the piano's percussive striking of strings. There are also six different degrees of volume, and a closely related series of chosen durations. —*"Blue" Gene Tyranny*

**Konkrete Und Elektronische Musik: Etude/ Studie I U. II/ Gesang Der Jÿnglinge** / 1956 / Stockhausen Gesamtausgabe ♦♦♦♦

A great collection of Stockhausen's classic and well-crafted electronic music. An electronic composition realized on tape during the years 1955-56, "Gesang der Jünglinge" is perhaps the best-known of Stockhausen's compositions. It was originally scored for five loudspeaker groups, but has been most widely heard in the mono and stereophonic versions prepared for vinyl records by the composer. The basic sound and emotional image described by the title is that of the well-known story of the youths who miraculously survive being thrown into the fiery furnace, from the Bible, Daniel 3. Stockhausen successfully combines the sound of the natural sung voice with beautiful electronic sound, in what today would be termed audio-morphing, as the voice and electronic tones subtly interchange and blend. "Wherever the music's audible signals momentarily become human speech, it is always in the praise of God" (Stockhausen). —*"Blue" Gene Tyranny*

**Gruppen Für Drei Orchester (Groups for Three Orchestras)** / 1957 / Deutsche Grammaphon ♦♦♦

Composed between 1955 and 1957, this work is a brilliant example of the post-World War II school of serialist composition. Initiated by the composer's fascination with the spatial distribution of sound as a musical element, the score positions three orchestras, each with its own conductor, around a concert hall, ideally in a semi-circle. The orchestras sometimes perform independently at their own specified tempi, but at other times they will begin to interchange musical information by calls and responses to each other, echoing of material, or coordinating in a mutually shared tempo and pulse. At times musical material may move from one orchestra to another, one orchestra furthering or completing the task of another—"They fall apart or cling together...one receives the other into itself, and plays with it, extinguishes it...they become transformed." The composer's aim is to create for the listener a "common time-world" among all the sound, where the music is not contrapuntal points of sound, but groups of combined sounds and noises. But the ensembles can never entirely coalesce, and hence the music is always in flux, moving and dividing. A marvellous palette of timbral combinations and exciting, as well as at times internally lyrical, orchestral images await the listener. —*"Blue" Gene Tyranny*

★ **Kontakte** / 1959 / Ecstatic Peace ♦♦♦♦♦

*Kontakte* is the epitome of Stockhausen's pioneering "moment form," characterized by long periods of inactivity broken by sudden changes. The prepared tape used in the work consists of a variety of metallic effects, some sped up to create radically different sounds and timbres. Probably Stockhausen's most famous work, *Kontakte* has been performed in two versions, one with four-channel tape and another with four-channel tape with added piano and percussion. The only widely available version, released on Ecstatic Peace, was recorded in Toronto in 1978 with tape plus pianist James Tenney and percussionist William Winant. —*John Bush*

**Zyklus** / 1960 / Columbia ♦♦♦

Performed by Florent Jodelet, this composition was written as a competition piece for percussionists. The title refers partly to the setup of the instruments in a full circle, partly to the way the curvilinear score can be read clockwise (increasing freedom) or counter-clockwise (greater determinancy), and partly to the idea of a dynamic, closed form. Similar to Klavierstück XI, there are isolated structured areas of musical events, "fields" containing points and groups, on 16 spiral-bound sheets of paper that are read freely. The influence of the graphic scoring and multiple systems of Cage's "Concert for Piano and Orchestra" (1957) is obvious, but Stockhausen is again interested here in the resolving and obscuring of dichotomies, in this case, the purposeless within the purposive. A work of many timbral combinations, it is fascinating and always surprising from performance to performance as it evokes the individual imagination of the soloist. —*"Blue" Gene Tyranny*

**Mikrophonie I and II** / 1965 / CBS ♦♦♦

Currently out-of-print vinyl. These two compositions from 1964 and 1965 are Stockhausen's initial foray into live electronic music performance. Distinguished from electronic music realized on magnetic tape and played back on loudspeakers with or without live instrumentalists, live electronic music involves manipulation of devices that transform and produce sound without pre-recording. (Remember these were the years in which the first synthesizers (Moog, Buchla, etc.) were still being designed). The first "live" electronic performances were given by John Cage and David Tudor in such works as "Cartridge Music" (1960), and Stockhausen's experiments in using contact microphones to pick up subtle harmonics from a large tam-tam proceed directly from Cage's use of pickup cartridges, and other devices. "Mikrophonie I" is scored for tam-tam, two microphones, two filters, and potentiometers (six players). By using the harmonically rich acoustic instrument, a large tam-tam played with various metal, wood, and rubber implements as the input, mysterious and unique sounds result as the contact microphones pick up sounds not normally accessible to the human ear (unless the hearer is right next to the instrument). "Mikrophonie II," for chorus, Hammond organ, and four ring modulators, extends the idea of live signal processing. The chorus sings a text made from Helmut Heisenbüttel's "Simple Grammatical Meditations." This becomes one input to the ring modulator ("program" or "carrier"), and the other input comes from the pure tones of the Hammond organ. Each ring modulator produces additional tones which are the (1) sum and (2) difference of the two input frequencies. Therefore, a vast palette of pitches is engendered, including extreme ones not possible with acoustic instruments. Together with an array of new timbres, these materials make up the mysterious, cosmological aura of this composition. —*"Blue" Gene Tyranny*

**Hymnen** / 1967 / Deutsche Grammaphon ♦♦♦

Realized in 1967 in the electronic composition studios of the WDR (Western German Radio), this piece for magnetic tape, in versions with and without solo instrumentalists, is made from electronically modulated national anthems of many countries, modulated shortwave broadcasts, and musique concréte "sound effects" like human yelling and animal noises. There are four movements called Regions: the first is built from the Internationale and the Marseillaise. The second is made from the hymn of the German Federal Republic, several African national anthems, and the beginning of the Russian anthem. The third Region is made from the American and Russian anthems, and the fourth from the Swiss anthem and a theme associated with what the composer calls the Utopia of Hymnunion in Harmondie unter Pluramon (hymn-union within the harmony of the world—harmonium mundi—under plurality and monism). This uniquely original composition gives the impression both of international contemporaneity and of our part in a great universal mystery. —*"Blue" Gene Tyranny*

**Kurzwellen** / 1968 / Stockhausen Gesamtausgabe ♦♦♦

This piece, probably largely influenced by John Cage's early works using "extra-musical" sounds, including radios, was composed in 1968 for Stockhausen's touring group of six performers—on piano, electronium, large tam-tam with microphone, viola with contact microphone, two filters with four potentiometers, and four shortwave receivers (some subsitute instruments are possible). Their task is to react on the spur of the moment to the unpredictable sounds received on shortwave radios. What is pre-composed is how they react: imitate, modulate, transpose, their rhythmic articulation, go higher or lower in pitch, play softer or louder, when and how often they play in combinations, how they call out to each other in order to share a single event among them, condensing that event, embellishing it, losing it, and so forth. The primary aim of each performance is to bring out the human spirit within a sense of nowness, "everything is the whole" (Stockhausen), thus bypassing dichotomies. —*"Blue" Gene Tyranny*

## Steve Stoll

**b.** Brooklyn, NY
*Producer / Minimal Techno, Club/Dance, Techno*

Producing pure, minimalist analog-minded techno in the vein of early Plastikman and Joey Beltram (even though his career began as a drummer with the industrial label Wax Trax), Steve Stoll has recorded for Nova Mute, Probe, DJax, Delirium, Synewave, and his own Proper NYC label. Raised in Brooklyn, Stoll listened to hip-hop and disco as a child, then joined the Army straight out of high school. He served for five years, including a period in the Gulf War when he plotted bomb runs by satellite. After being released, Stoll shifted around. He played drums for the industrial group Sister Machine Gun, studied jazz, and began recording straight-edged techno for Big Apple labels like 212 Productions and Damon Wild's Synewave.

Stoll debuted for Sm:)e Recordings with the 1995 album *Pacemaker*. The following year brought another album, *Zero Divide* (recorded as the Operator), and an EP for Nova Mute (as the Blunted Boy Wonder). After he reverted back to Steve Stoll, *Damn Analog Technology* followed in 1997 and *The Blunted Boy Wonder* one year later. —*John Bush*

**Pacemaker** / Oct. 31, 1995 / Sm:)e ♦♦
The Brooklynite's first album for Sm:)e Recordings is easily the most rigid and hardest-hitting in his catalog, including "French Kill" (a sly dig at the house classic "French Kiss" by Lil' Louis), "Sweet D-Vision," and the excellent bass-looped title track. —*John Bush*

**Damn Analog Technology** / Feb. 3, 1997 / Sm:)e ♦♦♦♦
Stoll's first album after a short break (only two years) from own-name productions, *Damn Analog Technology* is a set of sharp-edged techno swing, from the highlight "Photosynthesis" to the 303 acid-trance of "Surface Tension." —*John Bush*

● **The Blunted Boy Wonder** / Mar. 23, 1998 / Nova Mute ♦♦♦♦
Unlike many producers working in the minimalist fold, Steve Stoll imbues his productions with a warmth hardly matched since classic material by Plastikman. Though most tracks have the aesthetics of unconsciousness, Stoll never manages to lose his sense of hard-hitting funk with the addition of off-kilter effects and stinging percussion, from the moody electro of "Drop Zone," to a tribal workout on the single "Model T," and industrial textures on "One to Nothing." —*John Bush*

## The Stone Roses

**f.** 1985, Manchester, England, **db.** Oct. 1996
*Group / Madchester, Alternative Dance, Brit-pop, Alternative Pop/Rock*

Meshing '60s-styled guitar-pop with an understated '80s dance beat, the Stone Roses defined the British guitar pop scene of the late '80s and early '90s. After their eponymous 1989 debut album became an English sensation, countless other groups in the same vein became popular, including the Charlatans (UK), Inspiral Carpets, and Happy Mondays. However, the band was never able to capitalize on the promise of their first album, waiting five years before they released their second record, and slowly disintegrating in the year and half after its release.

The Stone Roses emerged from the remains of English Rose, a Manchester-based band formed by schoolmates John Squire (guitar) and Ian Brown (vocals). In 1985, the Stone Roses officially formed, as Squire and Brown added drummer Reni (b. Alan John Wren), guitarist Andy Couzens, and bassist Pete Garner. The group began playing warehouses around Manchester, cultivating a dedicated following rather quickly. Around this time, the group was a cross between classic British '60s guitar pop and heavy metal, with touches of goth-rock. Couzens left the group in 1987, followed shortly afterward by Garner. Garner was replaced by Mani (b. Gary Mounfield) and the group recorded their first single, "So Young," which was released by Thin Line Records to little attention. At the end of 1987, the Stone Roses released their second single, "Sally Cinnamon," which pointed the way toward the band's hook-laden, ringing guitar pop. By the fall of 1988, the band secured a contract with Silvertone Records and released "Elephant Stone," a single that set the band's catchy neo-psychedelic guitar pop in stone.

Shortly after the release of "Elephant Stone," the Stone Roses' bandwagon took off in earnest. In early 1989, the group was playing sold-out gigs across Manchester and London. In May, the Stone Roses released their eponymous debut album, which demonstrated not only a predilection for '60s guitar hooks, but also a contemporary acid-house rhythmic sensibility. *The Stone Roses* received rave reviews and soon a crop of similar-sounding bands appeared in the UK. By the end of the summer, the Stone Roses were perceived as leading a wave of bands that fused rock 'n' roll and acid-house culture. "She Bangs the Drums," the third single pulled from the debut, became the group's first Top 40 single at the end of the summer. In November, the group had their first Top Ten hit when "Fool's Gold" climbed to No. 8. By the end of the year, the band had moved from selling out clubs to selling out large theaters in the UK.

For the first half of 1990, re-releases of the band's earlier singles clogged the charts. The group returned in July 1990 with the single "One Love," which entered the charts at No. 4. Prior to the release of "One Love," the Stone Roses organized their own festival at Spike Island in Widnes. The concert drew over 30,000 people and would prove to be their last concert in England for five years. After Spike Island, the Stone Roses became embroiled in a vicious legal battle with Silvertone Records.

The group wanted to leave the label but Silvertone took out a court injunction against the group, preventing them from releasing any new material. For the next two years, the band fought Silvertone Records while they allegedly prepared the follow-up to their debut album. However, the Stone Roses did next to nothing as the court case rolled on. In the meantime, several major record labels began negotiating with the band in secret. In March of 1991, the lawsuit went to court. Two months later, the Stone Roses won their case against Silvertone and signed a multi-million-dollar deal with Geffen Records.

For the next three years, the Stone Roses worked sporadically on their second album, leaving behind scores of uncompleted tapes. During these years, the group kept a low profile in the press, but that wasn't to preserve the mystique—they simply weren't doing much of anything besides watching football. Finally, in the spring of 1994, Geffen demanded that the group finish the album and the band complied, completing the record, titled *Second Coming*, in the fall. "Love Spreads," the Stone Roses' comeback single, was debuted on Radio One in early November. The single received a lukewarm reaction and entered the charts at No. 2, not the expected No. 1. *Second Coming* received mixed reviews and only spent a few weeks in the Top Ten. The Stone Roses planned an international tour in early 1995 to support the album, but the plans kept unraveling at the last minute. Before they could set out on tour, Reni left the band, leaving the group without a drummer. He was replaced by Robbie Maddix, who had previously played in Rebel MC. After Maddix joined the band, they embarked on a short American tour at the conclusion of which John Squire broke his collarbone in a bike accident. Squire's accident forced them to cancel a headlining spot at the 25th Glastonbury Festival, which would have been their first concert in the UK in five years. As Squire recuperated, the Stone Roses continued to sink in popularity and respect—even as their peers, the Charlatans and former Happy Mondays vocalist Shaun Ryder, made unexpectedly triumphant comebacks.

The Stone Roses added a keyboardist to the lineup prior to their UK tour at the end of 1995—it was the first British tour since 1990. In the spring of 1996, John Squire announced that he was leaving the band he founded in order to form a new, more active band. The Stone Roses announced their intention to carry on with a new guitarist, but by October of that year the group was finished. Squire's new band, Seahorses, released their debut album in June 1997, while Brown released his solo debut, *Unfinished Monkey Business*, early in 1998. —*Stephen Thomas Erlewine*

★ **The Stone Roses** / Jul. 1989 / Silvertone ♦♦♦♦♦
Since the Stone Roses were the nominal leaders of Britain's "Madchester" scene—an indie-rock phenomenon that fused guitar pop with drug-fueled rave and dance culture—it's rather ironic that their eponymous debut only hints at dance music. What made the Stone Roses important was how they welcomed dance and pop together, treating it as if it were the same beast. Equally important were the Roses' cool, detached arrogance, which was personified by Ian Brown's nonchalant vocals. Brown's effortless malevolence is brought to life with songs that equal both his sentiments and his voice—"I Wanna Be Adored," with its creeping bassline and waves of cool guitar hooks, doesn't demand adoration; it just *expects* it. Similarly, Brown can claim "I Am the Resurrection" and lay back as if there were no room for debate. But the key to *The Stone Roses* is John Squire's layers of simple, exceedingly catchy hooks and how the rhythm section of Reni and Mani always imply dance rhythms without overtly going into disco. On "She Bangs the Drums" and "Elephant Stone," the hooks wind into the rhythm inseparably—the '60s

hooks and the rolling beats manage to convey the colorful, neo-psychedelic world of acid house. Squire's riffs are bright and catchy, recalling the British Invasion while suggesting the future with their phased, echoey effects. *The Stone Roses* was a twofold revolution—it brought dance music to an audience that was previously obsessed with droning guitars, while it revived the concept of classic pop songwriting, and the repercussions of its achievement could be heard throughout the '90s, even if the Stone Roses could never achieve this level of achievement again. —*Stephen Thomas Erlewine*

**Second Coming** / Dec. 1994 / Geffen ♦♦♦
There's no denying that *Second Coming* is a bit of a letdown. None of the songs are quite as strong as the best on their debut, but there is plenty of good music on the band's much-delayed second record. The Stone Roses create a dense tapestry of interweaving guitars and pulsing bass grooves. Ian Brown growls a little more than before, but he isn't the center of the music; John Squire's endlessly colorful riffs are. It's clear that Squire has been listening to a bit of hard rock, particularly Led Zeppelin. While the songs occasionally take a back seat to the grooves, several tracks—"Ten Storey Love Song," "Begging You," "Tightrope," "How Do You Sleep," and "Love Spreads"—rank as true classics. It might not be the long-awaited masterpiece it was rumored to be, but *Second Coming* is a fine sophomore effort. —*Stephen Thomas Erlewine*

**The Complete Stone Roses** / Jun. 27, 1995 / Silvertone ♦♦♦♦
The title's a bit of a misnomer. *The Complete Stone Roses* concentrates on the band's first album, compiling the A-and B-sides of the group's hits from "Elephant Stone" to "One Love." In addition to the familiar material, the disc includes rare early singles like "So Young" and "Sally Cinnamon" for the first time on compact disc, giving their classic material some context. The loud guitars of "So Young" are clearly the work of a hesitant band, while "Sally Cinnamon" is the first indication of John Squire's gift for ringing, melodic guitar hooks. However, their inclusion—as well as the appearance of the B-sides, which lack the consistent brilliance of "I Wanna Be Adored," "She Bangs the Drums," "Elephant Stone," "Waterfall," etc.—makes *The Complete Stone Roses* a flawed introduction to the band. Nevertheless, there's a fair amount of classic pop here and the rarities are necessary for dedicated fans. —*Stephen Thomas Erlewine*

## Carl Stone
b. Feb. 10, 1953, Los Angeles, CA
*Producer, Composer / Ambient-Techno, Experimental, Electro-Acoustic, Electronic*

American electro-acoustic and computer musician Carl Stone works primarily in sampler-based composition, emphasizing the slow evolution of sound through thematic variation and recurrence. A Los Angeles native, Stone currently lives in San Francisco, a base of sorts for his ongoing involvement in the international avant-garde scene. A student of computer music innovators Morton Subotnick and James Tenney, Stone studied composition formally at the California Institute of the Arts. Focusing strictly on electro-acoustic composition since the early '70s, Stone's commissioned works have been performed in the US (under such auspices as the National Endowment for the Arts and the Los Angeles Museum of Modern Art), as well as in Canada, Europe, South America, Australia, and, most often, Japan, where he's collaborated with dance companies and composed for film, video, radio broadcast, and multimedia installation. More recent works have included 1992's "Kamiya Bar," an evening-length composition for Tokyo-FM based on the city's urban soundscape, as well as the 1993 piece "Ruen Pair," commissioned by the Paul Dresher Ensemble. Although his recorded output represents only a small percentage of his total compositional work, Stone has released a number of albums through similarly eclectic means—from self-distributed cassettes and independent labels such as New Albion and Em:t, to larger, more recognizable names like Sony and EMI. Stone's passion for food usually works its way into his music in titular fashion—"Nayala," "Mom's," "Sukothai," and "Kamiya Bar" are all named for favorite restaurants. —*Sean Cooper*

● **Woo Lae Oak** / 1983 / Wizard ♦♦♦♦
Lovely, sustained, and slowly changing music made by classic "musique concrète" means...a rubbed string, blowing in a bottle, etc. are made into tape loops and changed by means of precise tape speed change, layering, etc. —*"Blue" Gene Tyranny*

**Kamiya Bar** / 1991 / Newtone ♦♦♦
The composer samples the sounds of Tokyo—street noises, voices, TV programs—to create a journey through the daily life of the city. Varied and mysterious ambient environment sound. —*"Blue" Gene Tyranny*

**Mom's** / 1992 / New Albion ♦♦♦
Captivating by their simplicity, Stone has an underlying feeling for modality and rhythm from American folk music without ever imitating it. "Banteay Srey" for example has a simple two-note pulse to which is gradually added a walking bassline and harmonies, transparent in their textures in a West Coast way, creating an engaging romantic and also otherworldly feeling. "Mom's" has a guitar riff that goes on simply for a while until suddenly a whole slew of salsa-sampling musicians step in: a sheer delight. Other selections are beautiful character studies. An original and widely listenable composer. —*"Blue" Gene Tyranny*

**1196** / 1996 / Em:t ♦♦♦
The four-part "Nyala" is Stone's first full-length for the Nottingham-based Em:t label, whose usual base of post-rave electronic experimenters is pretty severely shaken by Stone's unflinching, often very dissonant, textural sense. The piece works slowly through vague, minimal melodic passages to busier, more antagonistic sections, with repeating elements tweaking and morphing over time. —*Sean Cooper*

## Scott Stubbs
*DJ / Progressive Trance, Trance, Club/Dance*

Based in Las Vegas, progressive trance DJ Scott Stubbs has recorded several albums in the *Depths of Progressive Trance* series by Topaz Records. Stubbs is associated with Funked Up Recordings and the Nokturnel management group, and has played at events all over North America. —*John Bush*

● **The Depths of Progressive Trance** / Aug. 17, 1999 / Topaz ♦♦
The sleek clubcentric sound of progressive trance is featured on this Topaz compilation, with Scott Stubbs providing the continuous mix. Though there are dozens of classic trance themes to choose for a collection, Stubbs does a solid job: "Lost Without You," "Spiritual Being," "Mara," "Psiphonic," and "Dansa" are all excellent selections. —*Keith Farley*

**The Depths of Progressive Trance, Vol. 2** / Jan. 25, 2000 / Topaz ♦♦
The second volume in Stubbs' *Depths of Progressive Trance* series includes a few solid trance hits ("State of Mind" by De Niro, "Coming on Strong" by Signum, and "Stargazer" by Deepsky), but there just aren't many more good productions here. Stubbs is also a bit free and easy with the mix, fitting just 11 tracks on the 70-minute album. Fans of progressive trance might enjoy this merely because it's got the right sound, but there's simply not enough happening here to make it interesting for anyone else. —*John Bush*

## Sub Dub
f. 1993, New York, NY
*Group / Illbient, Electronica, Ambient-Techno, Ambient-Dub*

Though no electronic act bested the Orb at creating a satisfying fusion of ambient music and dub, Sub Dub came the closest with its blend of studio production and live instrumentation. The quartet, which includes bassist John Ward, programmer Raz Mesinai, vocalist Ursula Ward, and Grant Stewart on tenor sax, debuted in 1994 with the *Babylon Unite* EP on TKI. After one more EP, *Dawa Zangpo*, Sub Dub released their debut album in 1996 on Instinct. *Dancehall Malfunction* followed in 1997. —*John Bush*

**Sub Dub** / 1996 / Instinct ♦♦♦♦
Recalling the more dubbed-out moments of the Orb's *U.F.Orb*, Sub Dub's debut was a solid album. Though several tracks indulge the group's penchant for a bit of aimless wandering, the results are so pleasant that minor transgressions can easily be forgiven. —*John Bush*

● **Dancehall Malfunction** / Apr. 29, 1997 / Asphodel ♦♦♦♦
New York outfit Sub Dub's Kingston-inspired creations are cut with a stiff dose of electronica abstraction similar to the less traditionally rooted experiments of Bill Laswell and On-U Sound. *Dancehall Malfunction*, the group's Asphodel debut, adorns dub reggae's reverb-drenched simplicity with shimmering lengths of synthesizers, influences drawn from trip-hop and ambient-techno, and a production quality traditional dub could only dream of (but which also tends to rob the music of its rustic beauty). The group's strongest, most developed outing to date. —*Sean Cooper*

## Subject 13

f. 1995, Hackney, London,
*Group / Jungle/Drum'N'Bass, Club/Dance*

David Stewart and Roy Bleau formed Subject 13 by blending their main influences, specifically, the mellower side of jazz, and rough-and-tumble drum'n'bass. The duo grew up in London's Hackney and had played football together since they were teenagers. Stewart dropped out of college to begin DJing (mostly hip-hop and soul), and by 1990 was producing hardcore tracks as Eternity. He later reunited with Bleau, and the pair recorded singles for Fabio's Creative Source Records, Basement and LTJ Bukem's Good Looking. Subject 13 contributed to Bukem's 1996 compilation *Earth, Vol. 1* and released their debut album, *The Black Steele Project*, in late 1997 on Crammed Discs. Stewart and Bleau are also well-respected for their Sub Bass clubnights (geared specifically for the younger crowd) and their own label, Vibe'z Recordings (many tracks from which are included on the compilation *Subject 13 Presents Vibe'z Recordings*). —*John Bush*

- **The Black Steele Project** / Sep. 8, 1997 / Crammed ♦♦♦
With what sounds like an even deeper affection for jazz than on Roni Size's *New Forms* or even LTJ Bukem's recordings, Subject 13 charts a course through polished fusion and earthy breakbeats. Previous single "Can You Feel Da Vibez" is the highlight. —*John Bush*

## Morton Subotnick

b. Apr. 14, 1933, Los Angeles, CA
*Composer / 20th-Century Classical/Modern Composition, Atonal, Electronic*

Long at the vanguard of American electronic music, composer Morton Subotnick also pioneered the rise of multimedia performance through his extensive work in connection with interactive computer systems. Born in Los Angeles on April 14, 1933, he attended the University of Denver before earning his master's at Mills College in Oakland, California, where he studied composition under Darius Milhaud and Leon Kirchner. (From 1959 to 1966, Subotnick himself taught at Mills as well.) His earliest major work was 1959's *Sound Blocks*, the first of his compositions to focus on the relationship between musical, visual, and verbal components; much of Subotnick's subsequent oeuvre pursued the same ideas, with later pieces like the multi-part *Play!* and 1965's *Lamination I* including films, lighting effects, pre-taped material, and other media elements.

In 1967, Subotnick released the landmark *Silver Apples of the Moon*, the first electronic work commissioned by a recording company (Nonesuch); realized via the Buchla modular synthesizer which Subotnick helped design and develop; the album sold remarkably well, its success widely perceived as recognition of the home stereo system as a legitimate medium for present-day chamber music. Now composing specifically for the vinyl format, with works consisting of two halves to fit their respective sides of each LP, Subotnick returned with *The Wild Bull* a year later, shortly followed by the two-part *Reality. Touch*, completed in 1969, was his first piece recorded on four-track technology; it was followed in 1970 by *Sidewinder*. All shared sophisticated timbres, contrapuntal textures and pulsing undercurrents—in fact, many were so rhythmic they were adapted for modern dance performances.

Subotnick's next major plunge into multimedia was 1973's *Four Butterflies*, a piece for four-track tape and three films; a pair of orchestral compositions, *Before the Butterfly* and *Two Butterflies*, followed in 1975. Concurrent was his work on the "ghost box," a modification device designed to control real-time sound processing by means of a pitch and envelope follower in addition to taped voltage-controlled components including an amplifier, a frequency shifter, and a ring modulator. As neither the tape with the control voltages nor the ghost box itself contained any actual sounds, Subotnick dubbed the end result a "ghost score," introducing the concept in 1977's *Two Life Histories;* much of the work which immediately followed expanded upon the idea by bringing together live performers and ghost scores, resulting in pieces including *Liquid Strata*, *The Wild Beasts*, and *The Fluttering of Wings*.

With 1981's *Ascent into Air*, written for live performers and a 4C computer, Subotnick's innovations in real-time sound processing reached their peak; not only did he spatially locate and modulate the timbres of live instruments in a quadraphonic field, but he employed his players to serve as "control voltages," determining where the computer-generated sounds were placed, how they were modulated and so forth. Computer technology assumed greater and greater importance in Subotnick's later work, with pieces like *The Key to Songs*, *Return*, and *all my hummingbirds have alibis* taking full advantage of MIDI technology. Latter-day compositions—among them *Jacob's Room*, a multimedia opera premiered in 1993—also regularly made full use of computerized sound generation, specially designed software and "intelligent" interactive computer controls. —*Jason Ankeny*

- **Silver Apples of the Moon** / 1968 / Nonesuch ♦♦♦♦
Over the course of thirty minutes, *Silver Apples of the Moon* presented a change for serious electronic music. Unlike many other early synthesizer records, the music here is continuous, powerful, almost overwhelming. The work also relies on a breathtaking variety of sounds: clicks, chirps, buzzes, gongs, hums, sirens. Some of these are *de rigueur* for an academic synthesizer record, but many continued to sound fresh decades after their recording. *Silver Apples of the Moon* deserves credit not just because it's one of the earliest albums produced by a modular synthesizer, but because it's a great piece of music. A 1994 reissue by Wergo added Subotnick's 1968 work "The Wild Bull" to the CD program. —*John Bush*

**Key to Songs (1985)/The Return (1985-86)** / 1986 / New Albion ♦♦♦♦
Subotnick's music from the electronic music classics *Silver Apples of the Moon* and *The Wild Bull* has always been descriptive of poetic, lyrical imagery...similarly, *The Key to Songs* is based on Max Ernst's collage novel "Une Semaine de Bonte" (*A Week of Kindness or the Seven Deadly Elements*) and *Return: A Triumph of Reason* refers to the change from dread and foreboding to reason that was accomplished by Edmond Halley upon explaining the circuit of his well-known comet...a good example of modern "tone poem" electronic music. —*"Blue" Gene Tyranny*

## Substance (Peter Kuschnereit)

*Producer / Minimal Techno, Experimental Techno, Techno*

As the primary recording guise for Berlin's Peter Kuschnereit, Substance ranks as one of the defining artists for Chain Reaction's style of revisionist techno, though his contributions are few. As the fifth record in the label's deep catalog, the *Relish* record brought a sense of dancefloor utility to Chain Reaction's often-experimental sound. Rather than function as a set of sequences slowly morphing, the pieces on *Relish* arose from a house aesthetic that involved a great amount of progression within the tracks, from one short sequence to the next in a flowing movement. Furthermore, *Relish* also featured several DJ-friendly features such as locked grooves. The follow-up, *Scent*, appeared the following year, featuring the epic title track, along with further variations on "Relish." In 1998, Kuschnereit compiled his work as Substance on the *Session Elements* album, adding unreleased tracks such as "Plate" to the songs found on *Relish* and *Scent*. —*Jason Birchmeier*

- **Session Elements** / May 11, 1998 / EFA ♦♦♦
Don't be surprised by the track listing; this 14-song album actually centers around three songs and their many variations, with a few mostly insignificant previously unreleased tracks. Of course, as unfortunate as this fact may seem, it's actually the album's most interesting characteristic. The Berlin artist behind Substance, Peter Kuschnereit, doesn't churn out one track after the next as most producers do; rather, he composes a certain sound motif and then experiments with different forms of sequencing, resulting in drastically differing versions of the same track. In particular, the four different versions of "Relish" showcase just how creative Kuschnereit's practices are. In addition, "Scent" may not get as thorough of a treatment but just may be the most beautiful-sounding track here. The previously unreleased versions of "Plate" make this CD worth investigating even for those already owning the *Relish* and *Scent* EPs, since the song's many versions again illustrate the infamous Chain Reaction school of dub production-style aesthetic. A few shorter tracks fill out the album and serve as welcome intermissions, while the epic "Skippah" serves as additional unreleased content. Probably most similar to the Various Artists or Vainqueur collections with its many variations of the same motifs, *Session Elements* isn't nearly as diverse as Monolake's *Hong Kong* or Porter Ricks' *Biokinetics* in terms of sounds but compensates with a rather impressive showing of creativity. —*Jason Birchmeier*

## Subtropic (Jake Smith)

*Producer / Jungle/Drum'N'Bass, Club/Dance*

Begun in 1992 as part of a San Francisco warehouse collective including Spacetime Continuum and Scott Hardkiss, Subtropic is a one-man production team headed by Jake Smith. Later based in another seaside resort—Brighton, England—Smith initially worked in San Francisco mostly as a DJ, playing shows at the same warehouse space he called home. An ongoing relationship with Spacetime's Jonah Sharp led to Smith recording for Sharp's influential Reflective Records; just before leaving for British climes, Smith recorded tracks which were released as the *Thrub* EP in early 1994. Spending the rest of the year consolidating his base in England, Smith returned to Reflective for 1995's *Wild Card* EP and his first full-length, *Homebrew*. One of the first jungle albums given wide issue only in America, *Homebrew* added a stark minimalist slant to the drum'n'bass field, with dubby basslines and skewed rhythms that sounded a bit off-kilter even for jungle. Smith later moved to Fused & Bruised for his second album, *Compression Point*, and continued DJing heavily. He's also recorded for Interference and Helix. —*John Bush*

- **Homebrew** / Jan. 12, 1996 / Reflective ♦♦♦♦
With an uncanny sense of how long his rhythms should last before growing stale, Smith time-stretches beats, keyboard lines, and the occasional vocal sample into just about every track on *Homebrew*. The result is a consistently invigorating album, just a touch less spastic than Luke Vibert's Plug material and with a similar economy of sound. The marching breakbeats and phased-in ragga of "Sauce" makes for the highlight. —*John Bush*

**Compression Point** / Oct. 12, 1998 / Fused & Bruised ♦♦♦♦
Though the emphasis on mid-tempo rhythms makes it quite similar to the debut Subtropic LP, *Compression Point* earns points for the little things Jake Smith does to enliven his music. He works in little bursts of static as effects for a reworking of the title track from the *Life Time Mission* EP (here named "LTM2"), and contributes a funky acid line for "Angus Meets Jimi." As on *Homebrew*, there's also a slight dub slant to the proceedings. —*John Bush*

## The Suburban Knight (James Pennington)

b. Detroit, MI
*Producer, DJ / Detroit Techno, Club/Dance, Techno*
A crucial figure on the outskirts of Detroit techno since the mid-'80s, James Pennington's recordings as the Suburban Knight pioneered the moodier side of the Motor City with classics like "The Art of Stalking" and "The Groove." And though he collaborated on the biggest hit to come out of Detroit, the techno-pop monster "Big Fun" by Inner City, he later recorded with subterranean mainstays like Underground Resistance. It was through his connection with another Detroit mainstay, Derrick May, that Pennington began recording. May had set up his own Transmat Records in 1986, and Suburban Knight debuted that year with the third release for the label, "The Groove." He had also been working with Kevin Saunderson, and co-wrote "Big Fun" with Saunderson and Art Forrest. After vocals were added by Paris Grey and the record was released, it became a worldwide hit and virtually defined early Detroit techno for many foreigners.

Though Pennington only released one more single for Transmat, it was the dark classic "The Art of Stalking." He didn't release much on any other labels either, instead asserting his status as one of the top techno DJs and making trips the world over. With the rise of Detroit's second wave in the early '90s, Pennington became a mentor for Mike Banks and the Underground Resistance crew. With UR, he co-produced the singles "Nocturnbulous Behavior" and "Dark Energy." He also featured on the Submerge label compilation *Depth Charge, Vol. 3*, and produced tracks for Underground Resistance's 1998 full-length *Interstellar Fugitives*. —*John Bush*

**The Groove [Single]** / 1986 / Transmat ♦♦♦
- **The Art of Stalking [Single]** / 1987 / Transmat ♦♦♦♦

## Suicide

f. 1971, New York, NY, db. 1982
*Group / American Punk, New York Punk, Post-Punk, Punk, Electronic*
Although they barely receive credit, Suicide (singer Alan Vega and keyboardist Martin Rev) is the sourcepoint for virtually every synth-pop duo that glutted the pop marketplace (especially in England) in the early '80s. Without the trailblazing Rev and Vega, there would have been no Soft Cell, Erasure, Bronski Beat, Yaz, you name 'em, and while many would tell you that that's nothing to crow about, the aforementioned synth-poppers merely appropriated Suicide's keyboards/singer look and none of Rev and Vega's extremely confrontational performance style and love of dissonance. The few who did (Throbbing Gristle, Cabaret Voltaire) were considered too extreme for most tastes.

Suicide had been a part of the performing-arts scene in New York City's Lower East Side in the early/mid-'70s New York Dolls era. Their approach to music was simple: Rev would create minimalistic, spooky, hypnotic washes of dissonant keyboards and synthesizers, while Vega sang, ranted, and spat neo-Beat lyrics in a jumpy, disjointed fashion. On stage, Vega became confrontational, often baiting the crowd into a riotous frenzy that occasionally led to full-blown violence, usually with the crowd attacking Vega. With their reputation as controversial performers solidified, what was lost was that Suicide recorded some amazingly seductive and terrifying music. A relationship with Cars mastermind Ric Ocasek proved successful, bringing their music to a wider audience and developing unlikely fans (Bruce Springsteen went on record as loving Suicide's Vietnam-vet saga "Frankie Teardrop"), but after numerous breakups and reconciliations, Rev and Vega settled for being more influential than commercially successful.

Ironically, the '90s proved to be a decade of vindication for Suicide with the rise of industrial dance music, Chicago's Wax Trax label, and the bands associated with it (Revolting Cocks, Ministry, 1000 Homo DJs, etc.). Although not a big part of the scene any more, the profound influence of Suicide on a generation of younger bands was readily apparent. —*John Dougan*

★ **Suicide** / 1977 / Restless ♦♦♦♦
Suicide's debut is extreme, noisy, confrontational, and everything you'd want them to be. A slap in the face of the guitar-oriented punk rock that was coming out of New York and England at this time, Rev and Vega prove they were ahead of their time, even if audiences hated them for it. What doesn't hurt this record is the presence of some of their best material, "Rocket USA" and the deathless "Frankie Teardrop." —*John Dougan*

**Suicide** / 1980 / Mute ♦♦♦♦♦
Confusingly released in 1980 as *Alan Vega/Martin Rev: Suicide*, Mute reissued Suicide's second album as *The Second Album* in 2000. The reissue adds the "Dream Baby Dream" single, as well as a second disc of Vega and Rev's first rehearsal tapes. The Ric Ocasek-produced *Second Album* is less confrontational and more contemporary than the duo's terrifying debut. Vega's rockabilly snarl and Rev's burbling electronics remain, but Ocasek's involvement helps bring out a pop sensibility only hinted at on *Suicide*. Hell, some of the tracks are downright *pretty* ("Shadazz," "Diamonds, Fur Coat, Champagne"). Perhaps it's not as renegade as *Suicide*, but it's an arguably better, more realized work, and just as essential. Three of the tracks found on the first rehearsal tapes disc were previously issued on ROIR's *Half Alive* in 1981. The rehearsals are extremely spatial and as creepy as the proper studio works. Most of the tracks lurch by at a mid-tempo pace; Vega's distorted vocalisms are rather restrained but highly sinister, and Rev's sonic wizardry is delightfully horrific. —*Andy Kellman*

**Ghost Riders** / 1986 / ROIR ♦♦♦
Originally a cassette-only release, this live recording at Walker Arts Center in Minneapolis marked Rev and Vega's 10th anniversary. And while not as deliberately offensive as some of their earlier live gigs (the impossible-to-locate *24 Minutes over Brussels*), this is a compelling, interesting document of their ever-evolving stage show. Not as transcendent as their debut album, but well worth the effort. Reissued on CD by the French Danceteria label in 1990. —*John Dougan*

**A Way of Life** / 1988 / Wax Trax! ♦♦♦
The unwitting godfathers of industrial noise-squall return after a long absence to reclaim their throne on *A Way of Life*. Produced by Ric Ocasek, Suicide's Alan Vega and Martin Rev pick up exactly where they left off, crafting beautifully ominous drone-rock founded on pulsing sequences, dramatic vocals, and dense atmospherics. —*Jason Ankeny*

## Sukia

f. 1995, Los Angeles, CA
*Group / Electronica, Exotica, Trip-Hop*
Taking their name from a Mexican lesbian vampire comic-book heroine, the avant-lounge quartet Sukia emerged from Los Angeles' famed Silverlake scene (the same musical community home to Beck, the Beastie Boys, and the Dust Brothers). Comprised of multi-instrumentalists Sasha Fuentes, Ross Harris, Grace Marks, and Craig Borrell, Sukia combined Moog-driven grooves laced with found samples and space-age pop aesthetics on their 1996 debut *Contacto Especial Con el Tercer Sexo*, produced by the Dust Brothers and issued on their Nickel Bag label. —*Jason Ankeny*

- **Contacto Especial Con el Tercer Sexo** / Oct. 1996 / Nickel Bag ♦♦♦♦
An ominous, free-floating collage of found sounds, drum machines, cheap

keyboards, and samples, Sukia's debut album *Contacto Especial Con el Tercer Sexo* flirts with exotica and the avant garde without committing to either. And it's the better for it. Sukia's instrumentals are alternatingly mesmerizing and disturbing, fueled by pseudo-bossa nova rhythms, jazzy chords and sheets of noise. It's not necessarily an alienating record, but anyone well versed in the cut-paste productions of the Dust Brothers, who also helmed this record, will be more inclined toward meeting the album halfway, since the music isn't strictly lounge-revival, avant-pop, or electronic music. It's a fascinating, darkly humorous melange of all three, and it's endlessly fascinating. —*Stephen Thomas Erlewine*

## Sun Electric

f. 1993, Berlin, Germany
*Group / Electronica, Trance, Club/Dance, Techno, Ambient, IDM*

As Sun Electric, Germans Max Loderbauer (the son of a composer) and Tom Thiel (a studio engineer) marry dizzying Teutonic trance with chilled-out ambience. They first met at the studio where Thiel worked, and the two later played as part of the band Fisherman's Friend. Manager Thomas Fehlmann, a frequent Orb co-worker, encouraged the two to move to his native Berlin and form a band. The two agreed, and when their debut single "O Locco" appeared, it was picked up by the Orb's Alex Paterson for his Wau! Mr. Modo label. The duo then signed to ZTT, who unfortunately wanted an electro-pop group. After wrangling out of the contract, Sun Electric signed to the Apollo sublabel of R&S and released their debut album, 1995's *Kitchen*. The following year brought a live album recorded at Berlin's Love Parade, while *Via Nostra* appeared in 1998. —*John Bush*

**Kitchen** / Nov. 13, 1993 / R&S ♦♦♦
With clubland trance grooves and beats tied to ambient atmospherics and synths, *Kitchen* is a disorienting debut, but a strong one. Several mixes of the group's single "O Locco" are included. —*John Bush*

● **Present** / Nov. 25, 1996 / Apollo ♦♦♦♦
Sun Electric's third studio-born long-player for Apollo is a return to beat-oriented territory after the more chilled tones of their previous live album. Although a few tracks echo the trancier rhythms of *Kitchen* and *Aaah...*, much of *Present* is on a breakbeat, IDM tip. But while for some this amounts to a criticism of Sun Electric's jungle trendiness, in fact, few of the rhythms on the album are reducible to drum'n'bass, with more subtle beat layering and rhythmic eruptions aligning the group with ambient/experimental electro/techno artists such as the Black Dog or Tournesol. —*Sean Cooper*

**Via Nostra** / Nov. 2, 1998 / Apollo ♦♦♦
Though the term "ambient-techno" was all but a dirty word in electronic music circa 1998, *Via Nostra* presents a set of lush electronics with few concessions to the whims of mainstream dance music, though there are a few nods to electro and breakbeat techno. —*John Bush*

## Sun Ra (Herman Sonny Blount)

b. May 22, 1914, Birmingham, AL, d. May 30, 1993
*Organ (Hammond), Keyboards, Piano, Organ, Leader / Experimental Big Band, Multimedia, Avant-Garde Jazz, Free Jazz, Progressive Big Band, Avant-Garde, Big Band*

A jazz explorer who inextricably linked the otherworldliness of the African-American experience with ancient Egyptian mythology and the futurist possibilities of science fiction, Sun Ra claimed astral lineage and backed up the assertion with out-of-this-world recordings, hundreds of them, for obscure labels like ESP-Disk, Saturn, Delmark and the comparatively above-ground Impulse! Records. An early electric-instrument user as well as a synth pioneer virtually without predecessor in the non-academic community, Ra and his interstellar big band—variously credited as the Solar Arkestra, the Omniverse Arkestra, the Cosmo Discipline Arkestra, the Astro Infinity Arkestra and the Myth Science Arkestra—stood miles away from even the jazz avant-garde during the increasingly cosmic-conscious '60s, so hopelessly removed from a position of influence that it would take decades for the leader and pianist's inspiration to seep into the broader music world. Years before his became the hip name for aspiring philosopher/producers to drop, Sun Ra was an outsider whose astro-philosophical musings and focus on numerology marked every LP he recorded, while his Afrocentric wardrobe and commune approach to running a big band reflected itself on live dates.

Born Herman Sonny Blount in Birmingham, Alabama, Ra led his own band for the first time in 1934. He freelanced at a variety of jobs in the Midwest and worked as a pianist/arranger with Fletcher Henderson during 1946-47. After appearing on some obscure records as early as 1948, Sun Ra really got started around 1953, leading a big band in Chicago. He started off playing advanced bop but quickly became open to the influences of other cultures, experimented with primitive electric keyboards, and played free jazz long before the proper avant-garde—led by Ornette Coleman—was established in the late '50s. After moving to New York in 1961, Ra performed some of his most advanced work. In 1970 he relocated his group to Philadelphia and in later years alternated free improvisations and mystical group chants with eccentric versions of swing tunes. Many of his most important sidemen—John Gilmore on tenor, Marshall Allen on alto, and Pat Patrick on baritone sax—were with him on and off for decades. Ra, who recorded a pair of fine solo piano albums for JAI, has been well served by Evidence's extensive repackaging of many of his Saturn dates, which have at last been outfitted with correct dates and personnel details. Still, his legacy remains both confusing and vast. —*Scott Yanow and John Bush*

**Visits Planet Earth/Interstellar Low Ways** / Nov. 1, 1958-1960 / Evidence ♦♦♦♦
This Evidence CD reissues two rare albums originally put out by bandleader Sun Ra on his Saturn label. Taken as a whole it shows Ra's Arkestra evolving from its roots in bop and swing into a unique entity of its own. The first four titles (from 1956), despite Ra doubling on electric keyboards, are fairly conventional. Art Hoyle has a few fine trumpet solos and the twin baritones of Pat Patrick and Charles Davis battle it out on the boppish "Two Tones." The three numbers from 1958 are much more advanced, utilizing some modal vamps, and the final seven selections (from 1960) are generally avant-garde. The group has "vocals" on a couple of pieces, most successfully on the memorable "Rocket Number Nine Take Off for the Planet Venus," which also contains an explosive John Gilmore tenor solo. This excellent CD can be used a way of getting bebop fans interested in Sun Ra's explorative music. —*Scott Yanow*

**Cosmic Tones for Mental Therapy/Art Forms of Dimensions Tomorrow** / 1961-1963 / Evidence ♦♦♦
There has always been some controversy revolving around Sun Ra, but few of his albums ever generated more discussion than *Cosmic Tones for Mental Therapy*, which covers half the 12 numbers on this two-LP, single-disc outing. Ra played "astro space organ," and the array of swirling tones, funky licks, and smashing rhythms, aided and abetted by John Gilmore on bass clarinet, Marshall Allen on oboe, and arrangements that sometimes had multiple horns dueling in the upper register and other times pivoting off careening beats, outraged those in the jazz community who thought Eric Dolphy and John Coltrane had already taken things too far. —*Ron Wynn*

● **Atlantis** / 1967-1969 / Saturn ♦♦♦♦
This 1993 CD reissue brings back Sun Ra's monumental 22-minute work "Atlantis." Ra's electronic keyboards (his highly original-sounding Solar Sound organ and a clavioline) dominate the piece, along with the playing of three drummers. The music is quite emotional, tense and sometimes explosive. Ra is joined by two trumpets, two trombones, Robert Northern on French horn, three altoists (including Marshall Allen), John Gilmore on tenor, baritonist Pat Patrick, and bass clarinetist Robert Cummings, plus the three drummers; there is no bass. There are also five shorter pieces which are quite odd as well, featuring Ra (on a clavinet) joined by up to five percussionists and (on two numbers) Gilmore's tenor. The latter music is oddly funky, eccentric, and catchy in its own way. Sun Ra fans can consider the acquisition of this innovative set to be a must. —*Scott Yanow*

**Outer Spaceways Incorporated** / 1968 / Black Lion ♦♦♦♦
This CD adds a previously unreleased "Intergalactic Motion" to the original five-piece program. Sun Ra's orchestra was at its most radical during this period, alternating simple chants with very outside playing and dense ensembles. While the sidemen include such notables as Marshall Allen and Danny Davis on altos, baritonist Pat Patrick, John Gilmore on tenor, bassist Ronnie Boykins, and percussionist Clifford Jarvis, most of the other players in the 15-piece band (such as trumpeters Ahk Tal Ebah and Kwame Hadi) have slipped back into obscurity. This music is quite intriguing, although it requires an open mind and a sense of humor to fully appreciate. —*Scott Yanow*

**Out There a Minute** / 1968-1969 / Blast First! ♦♦♦
The 13 selections on this CD by a small group taken from Sun Ra's Arkestra

are generally both explorative and introspective. The combo includes tenor-saxophonist John Gilmore, altoist Marshall Allen, baritonist Pat Patrick, an occasional trumpeter and trombonist (the personnel is not listed), Ra's organ, piano and primitive electric keyboards plus a bassist, drummer, and some percussionists. The performances are mostly short sketches that set spacey moods and then fade out; Ra's piano sounds surprisingly like Thelonious Monk in spots. The odd echo devices and spooky keyboards give this eccentric music much atmosphere. The violent ensemble number "Other Worlds" and the lengthy "Next Stop Mars" are changes of pace (sounding like the 1966 John Coltrane Quintet) while many of the other pieces would work well as soundtracks to a science fiction movie. Although not essential, these futuristic sounds from the past hold one's interest. —*Scott Yanow*

### Space Is the Place [OST] / 1972 / Evidence ♦♦♦

*Space is the Place* is the soundtrack to a film that was made but never released, and the tunes are among his most ambitious, unorthodox, and compelling compositions. Between June Tyson's declarative vocals, chants, and dialogue and Ra's crashing, flailing synthesizer and organ fills, and with such songs as "Blackman/Love In Outer Space," "It's After The End Of The World," and "I Am The Brother of the Wind," this disc offers aggressive, energized and uncompromising material. Ra's pianistic forays, phrases, and textures were sometimes dismissed as mere noodling when they were part of a well-constructed multimedia package. This comes as close as any of Ra's releases to being not only a concept work but a blueprint for his live shows from the early '70s until the end of his career. Features some previously unissued cuts. —*Ron Wynn*

### The Cosmic Explorer (1970) in "Nuits De La Fondation Maeght" / 1981 / Recommended ♦♦♦

Sun Ra was one of the first instrumentalists to use a Moog synthesizer in live performance…this 20 minute solo improvisation (with minimal extra sounds from the ensemble), ranging between high energy clusters and the lyrical, shows his ability to create an astonishing range of sound and emotion, inspiring a truly "cosmic" conclusion from The Arkestra. —*"Blue" Gene Tyranny*

### John Cage Meets Sun Ra (June 8, 1986 at "Sideshows by the Seashore, Coney Island, NY) / 1981 / Meltdown ♦♦♦

These are unedited segments of the historic concert that was part of the "Sideshows by the Seashore" held on June 8, 1986 in Coney Island, NY. Improvisations and songs by Sun Ra and Cage's indeterminate performance vocals based on strict composition methods are contrasted and find a common meeting ground as, toward the end of the session, they play together. Fascinating and in genuine communal spirit. —*"Blue" Gene Tyranny*

## Sunkings

f. 1990

*Group / Ambient-Techno, Trance, Club/Dance*

The forward-thinking electronic outfit Sunkings has moved from recording intelligent techno for GPR to psychedelic trance for Blue Room Released, a leap made by few in either scenes. The group began in 1990, as the trio of Jay Paine, Paul Davies, and Michael Bluemink. After the release of several singles on a self-financed label gained the attention of 808 State, Sunkings recorded the *Return of the Killer Rays* EP for 808's own Creed Records. Hugh Ashton replaced Bluemink around that time, just before the trio signed to GPR, home to recordings by Luke Slater and the Black Dog. Sunkings released their debut LP *Hall of Heads* in 1994 and earned plaudits from Brian Eno and John Peel. After GPR went under, the group switched to Blue Room Released, an increasingly respected label on the new psychedelic trance scene. Their second album *Soul Sleeping* became the first American release on Blue Room America. —*John Bush*

### Hall of Heads / May 28, 1994 / GPR ♦♦♦

Sunkings' debut album is full of sweeping ambient-techno, somewhat similar to the future-past musings of Black Dog but mostly unheard of in the intelligent techno community of the mid-'90s. —*John Bush*

• **Soul Sleeping** / May 18, 1998 / Blue Room America ♦♦♦♦

The majestic ambient-techno bent from *Hall of Heads* is backed by a set of even more expansive, psychedelic trances for the second album *Soul Sleeping*. Those expansive tracks often take awhile to get in gear, but once they do the results make for a more consistent effort than that found on Sunkings' debut. —*Keith Farley*

## Suns of Arqa

f. 1978, London, England

*Group / Downtempo, Ambient Dub, Dub, World Fusion*

The world music collective Suns of Arqa was led by founder and mentor Michael Wadada; since the release of the group's 1979 debut LP *Revenge of the Mozabites*, some 200 members from across the globe passed through its ranks, many of them met by Wadada during his extensive travels and sharing his interest in indigenous, tribal, folk and classical music traditions. In addition to subsequent LPs including 1980's *Wadada Magic*, 1982's *India*, and 1984's *Ark of the Arqans*, the Suns of Arqa regularly backed dub legend Prince Far I, even performing at his final concert (captured on the *Live with Prince Far-I* LP). With the masterful *Land of a Thousand Churches*, Wadada began issuing the group's material on his own Arka Sound label; a flurry of releases followed, among them *Alap-Joe-Jhala*, *Jaggernaut (Whirling Dub)*, and *Shabda*. The advent of the World Wide Web also brought a major new dimension to the Suns of Arqa aesthetic, with the collective's website (http://www.straightline.co.uk/arqa/globnet.html) actively soliciting music, lyrics, remixes and other creative contibutions for future projects, expanding their global network of particpants further than ever before. —*Jason Ankeny*

### Kokoromoghi / 1992 / Arka Ziol ♦♦♦

Though it has much of the natural sound of earlier Suns of Arqa releases, several tracks on *Kokoromoghi* (including "Durga Dub" and "Kalashree") show the effect of at least minor postproduction and a more stated reliance on synthesizers. The fusion of organic and electronic sound is intriguing; surprisingly, it works for fans of world music as well as ambient/electronica. —*John Bush*

• **Cradle** / Mar. 16, 1994 / Earth Sounds ♦♦♦♦

*Cradle* is an album of meditative Indian trance, presented in four long parts. There's an organic, natural vibe to the proceedings, and the lack of beats makes *Cradle* an excellent fusion of ethno-ambient music. —*John Bush*

### A Brief History of Suns of Arqa / Mar. 16, 1998 / Arka Sound ♦♦♦

## Sunscreem

f. 1991, Essex, England

*Group / Rave, Club/Dance, Techno, Dance-Pop*

One of the first rave-pop groups with live-performance abilities as well, Sunscreem formed around Paul Carnell and Lucia Holm (both on keyboards and vocals) with a handful of contributors including guitarists Darren Woodford and Wayne Simms, bassist Rob Fricker, drummer Sean Wright, and Baz the DJ. Holm was a session cellist—with credits including Dream Academy's "Life in a Northern Town"—when she met Carnell at a warehouse rave in Essex and agreed to form a band. Early singles "Walk On" and "Pressure" became moderate British hits and dancefloor favorites, while 1993's "Love U More" became their trademark song (and biggest hit). The debut Sunscreem album *O3* was released in 1993, earning American release through Columbia. The "Perfect Motion" single also became a hit, but the group had disappeared from the charts by the mid-'90s. Their second album *Change or Die* was finally released in 1996, while the retrospective *Looking at You: Club Anthems* appeared in 1998. —*John Bush*

• **O3** / 1993 / Columbia ♦♦♦♦

*O3* displays a techno act with something of a heart and focus (plus a real drummer from time to time). While the energy level does get pumped from time to time, the accent is more on solid song design and upfront female vocals that do more than provide just another element of the mixes, putting this firmly into the Deee-Lite camp. Highlights are the singles "Love U More," "Perfect Motion" and a Marianne Faithfull cover of "Broken English." —*Steven McDonald*

### Change or Die / Feb. 1996 / Sony Soho Square ♦♦♦

Though the title seems to signal a completely different tack, Sunscreem's brand of uplifting techno-pop is still in place while Holm's songwriting and vocals continue to please. Whiffs of an updated sound, with the occasional nods to trance and electro, make appearances as well, though insistent melodies continue to bubble underneath the whole. —*John Bush*

## Super_Collider

*Group / Experimental Techno, Trip-Hop, Club/Dance*

Super_Collider is a collaborative effort between experimental-techno stalwart Cristian Vogel and Jamie Lidell, who's recorded for Vogel's Mosquito label. Energized by the club hit "Darn (Cold Way O' Lovin'," the duo released their first album, *Head On*, in 1999. —*John Bush*

- **Head On** / May 24, 1999 / Medicine ♦♦♦♦

Super_Collider, the head-on collaboration of Brighton-based producers (and friends) Cristian Vogel and Jamie Lidell, results in an album of delightfully skewed dance-pop. Undoubtedly accomplished only after weeks at the computer (as the haggard faces and bleary eyes on the sleeve attest), *Head On* consists of ten songs mashing up P-Funk- and Prince-styled vocals into an electro-shredder similar to the one employed by Autechre and Oval. Though his experimental bent is well known, Vogel's solo productions rarely forsake the almighty beat and, thankfully, it's no different here. The old-school electro beatbox is in full effect, and while that usually makes for a stark quality to any throwback affair, Vogel and Lidell throw so many goofball effects and percussion detritus into the mix that most of the tracks here sound positively beefy. The breakout single "Darn (Cold Way O' Lovin')" — already included on several mix albums just six months after its release — features a soulful vocal (mostly repeating the title) while brutal low-end tech-basslines break up into static, slip in and out of the mix, and charge through right and left channels. The message is clear: vocals are just another sound source to be tweaked and spun off in all directions. True, there's a lot to digest — and perhaps a bit *too* much production in several spots — for a collection of "pop" songs, but fans of the Skam label and the *Mask* series will eat this stuff up. Best of all, now there's an outside chance that a Vogel production will get played on the world's less intellectual dancefloors. [A limited-edition British release added a second disc with four bonus tracks.] —*John Bush*

## Sureshot (Wayne Palmer)

**b.** West Ham, London, England
*Producer / Jungle/Drum'N'Bass, Club/Dance*

A reclusive British hip-hop producer who was turned on to jungle by mates Marc Royal of T.Power and MK Ultra, Wayne Palmer's recordings as Sureshot embrace the darker, tech-slanted side of drum'n'bass, but not without a certain atmospheric lilt. Born in London's West Ham, Palmer moved to Basingstoke and later Aldershot as a child, borrowing a friend's sampler at the age of 18 to make his first production. While working as a computer technician by day and DJ/producer by night, he was introduced to MK Ultra at the Phoenix Festival. Palmer soon learned the ropes of drum'n'bass, and was set to release a single on Marc Royal's Deep Thought Records until a chance introduction with Ninebar Records boss Darren Hales led to a contract. For Ninebar, Sureshot released a 1996 single and then his debut album *Underground Symphony*, an album with alternate portions of dense paranoia and exquisite beauty. Palmer also returned to his hip-hop past by working with several rappers, and has also collaborated with Jon Tye (of MLO and Twisted Science). —*John Bush*

- **Underground Symphony** / Jun. 10, 1996 / Ninebar ♦♦♦♦

Though the title makes it sound like another trip-hop ripoff, *Underground Symphony* is a darkly tinted drum'n'bass odyssey, only occasionally tempered by grooves from the lighter side. Tracks like "The Fairground" and "Mindstorm" display Sureshot's intense production style; basslines are time-stretched to the breaking point while an assortment of nervous-breakdown synth adds to the general air of menace. Palmer is equally adept at expanding on the darkness with several string tracks, including a gorgeous song called "The Journey." —*John Bush*

## Surgeon (Anthony Child)

**b.** Birmingham, England
*Producer, DJ / Minimal Techno, Trance, Club/Dance, Techno*

Birmingham techno artist Anthony Child has rapidly built a solid, and, to a certain extent, innovative catalog of minimal dancefloor techno since his Surgeon releases began appearing in 1991. Compared favorably with Detroit original Jeff Mills from his earliest Downwards singles on forward, Child's tracks have been a mainstay in the popular Motor City DJ's sets. Although Surgeon releases have worked an increasing affectation for acid and trance, an economy of sound and basic hardness combine with Mills' sound. A noted and increasingly popular DJ himself, Child grokked his skills from hip-hop and electro jocks ("Tour de France" is a mainstay of his DJ sets), filling out his style with a driving toughness and appreciation for rapid cutting and flipping. Surgeon's entry into production was also noteworthy; urged on by producer Mick Harris (Child is a fan of Harris' Scorn project), the former Napalm Death drummer locked Child in his tiny studio, imploring him to "go mad." The result, the self-titled debut EP, was released on Downwards, and was instantly hailed as some of the highest quality UK techno of its time. Releases for Soma, Blueprint, Ideal Trax, and the ultra-exclusive Tresor label followed, with the debut LP, *Basic Tonal Vocabulary*, appearing on Tresor in 1997. *Balance* followed in 1998, as did *Force & Form* in 1999. Equally influenced by early electro-pop innovators like Tomita and YMO, experimental groups like Can, Faust, and Suicide, and the tough grit of American electro and techno (Robert Hood, Hashim), Surgeon's mash-up is both straightforward and subtly experimental. —*Sean Cooper*

**Basic Tonal Vocabulary** / 1997 / Tresor ♦♦♦♦

On *Basic Tonal Vocabulary*, Surgeon practices the skills he learned from the Jeff Mills school of minimal techno. Layers of various percussive rhythms and synthesizer loops gel into a disorientated whole that moves forward with relentless tempo and intensity — in other words, banging. Unlike Mills, though, Surgeon's tracks on *Basic Tonal Vocabulary* may retain the density and intensity of the Detroit artist, but they often come across sounding messy. The many layers of percussive rhythms within the context of a given track often don't synthesize; the result resembles a DJ's unsuccessful attempt to mix two techno records at +8. Surgeon also toys with moments of sublime ambience on tracks such as "Waiting" and "Intro." Since both are rather simple in nature, without all of the pounding bass beats and multiple layers of percussion, they sound rather fresh and function as welcome intermissions from Surgeon's onslaught of techno. While the first half of the album may seem like a dissonant cacophony, the last few tracks such as "Rotunda," "Scorn," and "Return" show the artist's potential for brilliance. On these last three, the countless layers of looped percussion synthesize perfectly, producing forward-moving tracks that seem to imitate gigantic swarms of locusts; buzzing, swirling, and always advancing with jarring kinetic force, these pieces surpass even the best work ever done to date by the minimal techno guru Mills himself. It is just unfortunate that the first half of this album sounds like a failed experiment, with the concepts and ingredients present, but the products lacking. —*Jason Birchmeier*

**Balance** / May 18, 1998 / Tresor ♦♦♦

*Balance* pushes Surgeon into new avenues of electronic music — while remaining grounded in the techno aesthetic of his previous work, here Tony Child absorbs a wider range of influences to create music attuned equally to the physical and the cerebral. —*Jason Ankeny*

- **Force & Form** / Jun. 21, 1999 / Tresor ♦♦♦♦

At a point in time when techno had become a bit exhausted in terms of musical development, Anthony Childs, the British techno producer who calls himself Surgeon, managed to push the decade-old genre forward with his *Force & Form* album. It was at this point in the late '90s when techno songs had evolved into sincere tracks, short cycles of looped rhythms characterized by repetition and a lack of progression. Jeff Mills' Purpose Maker releases such as *Kat Moda* had perfected this practice of producing music with DJs in mind rather than the home listener. The reason *Force & Form* can be seen as such a breakthrough rests in its status as a record just as appealing to home listeners as it is to DJs. Child accomplishes this challenging task quite brilliantly. There are four sides of vinyl on *Force & Form*, meaning that each of the four songs on the album gets an entire side to itself. Drop the needle at the outermost groove and the spinning record will emanate a ten-minute adventure into cycling tribal techno rhythms with heavy percussive bass. Unlike the Maurizio records, which also spin for epic lengths, the songs on *Force & Form* actually progress through movements, where rhythms change and new arrangements construct themselves, as if two different techno records are being seamlessly mixed. Each of these four songs begins with several minutes of repetitive techno rhythms similar to the sort of tracks Child recorded for his *Basic Tonal Vocabulary* album. After a few minutes of locked groove-type sounds, the songs then shift with the low-frequency bass rumbles being eclipsed by tranquil atmospheric tones. Soon the serene subtlety of these high-frequencies gets shattered by the slowly growing construction of the next monolithic percussive hailstorm that will carry listeners through the final few minutes of the song. As if the rhythms weren't marvelous enough — challenging even Mills himself as the latest contender for king of techno dancefloors — Child's ability to craft brave multi-sectioned epics makes this an even more incredible album than anything he had accomplished up until this point. His debut Tresor album from two years earlier, *Basic Tonal Vocabulary*, only hinted at his potential to become one of the genre's most important producers. —*Jason Birchmeier*

## Sutekh (Seth Horvitz)

*Producer / Minimal Techno, Experimental Techno, Techno*

West Coast experimental-techno producer Seth Horvitz has recorded for several of the electronic world's most respected labels, including Germany's Force Inc and Mille Plateaux plus California's own Drop Beat and Cytrax. A fan of dance since his early-'90s college days at Berkeley, Horvitz began experimenting with electronics and DJing in 1992 and released his first material three years later, on the *Swivel* compilation released by local label Belief Systems. His release schedule expanded with work for other Bay Area labels including Cytrax and Delay, and in 1998 he released the *Influenza* EP on Drop Beat. The split-release *Deadpan Escapement* (with Twerk and Safety Scissors) also appeared that year, on Belief Systems. During 1999, he recorded the *Miasma* EP for Force Inc, and readied his debut full-length for Mille Plateaux. The results, *Periods Make Sense*, appeared in early 2000. —*John Bush*

• **Periods Make Sense** / Apr. 4, 2000 / Mille Plateaux ♦♦♦♦
*Periods Make Sense* is a collection of 11 untitled (well, titled after pictures of colors on the back sleeve) abstract-experimental productions, each computer-processed to the point where signal distortion and static actually becomes a soothing prospect. Horvitz often blocks out all but the most extreme frequencies, resulting in spare tracks brushed only with the deepest of sub-bass and some skittery percussion over the top. There's an air of approaching menace to many of these productions, thanks to the ebb and flow of his haunted synthesizers, and a 4:4 beat anchors most of these tracks to the techno tradition. It's not as relentlessly experimental as his colleague Kit Clayton's material, but *Periods Make Sense* is perhaps an even more fascinating listen. —*John Bush*

## Swayzak

f. London, England
*Group / Jazz-House, Club/Dance, House*

This London based deep dub-house duo got their moniker from a bastardization of actor Patrick Swayze's name, wanting something memorable but not immediately recognizable. This description also applies to their general approach to music: distinctive and not easily classified.

Though James Taylor and David Brown began playing together in 1994, they spent three years studying their instruments and recording techniques in their basement studio. When a friend finally urged them into making their music public, 1997's *Bueno* EP emerged on their own Swayzak label, which the group also ran. The success and critical acclaim that *Bueno* and the group's following singles met with were doubly surprising, as Swayzak had very little connection with the London DJ scene.

A chance meeting in a London record shop sparked the group's distribution deal with Medicine records for their debut album, 1998's *Snowboarding in Argentina*. The full-length collection of the group's clean, atmospheric live electronics also met with acclaim in dance circles, although by this time their creativity and independence had become no longer a surprise. *Mixer* voted *Snowboarding in Argentina* the 1998 Album of the Year, furthering the duo's recognition in the US.

Following a collaboration with the Detroit techno artist Theorem, Swayzak released *Himawari* and cashed in on their growing acclaim within the global electronic music scene. The brave album featured ambitious collaborations with dub poet Benjamin Zephaniah, Opus III vocalist Kirsty Hawkshaw, and vocalist JB Rose. —*Heather Phares*

• **Snowboarding in Argentina** / Mar. 10, 1998 / Medicine ♦♦♦♦
Named for the group's dream vacation if their album was successful, *Snowboarding in Argentina* showcases Swayzak's clean, minimal blend of dub, jazz-house and ambient. The album features tracks from the group's singles as well as new Swayzak pieces. "Bueno," "Fukumachi," and "Low-Res Skyline" are all highlights, featuring the group's knack for making danceable comedown music. —*Heather Phares*

**Lokal/Yardarm [Single]** / Nov. 23, 1998 / Swayzak ♦♦
While the first side of Swayzak's two-tracker is a sublime jazz-house workout, the B-side arguably gets the nod with its alarm-call nods to an earlier era of house. —*John Bush*

**Himawari** / Jul. 11, 2000 / Medicine ♦♦♦♦
Even as their meld of jazzy house and experimental dub became a hot commodity on the electronics scene, the British duo Swayzak pulled back from the form slightly on their sophomore album. Also, in contrast to their deep dub techno excursions on split-singles with Detroit's Theorem, *Himawari* scatters influences from electro ("State of Grace"), dub poetry ("Illegal"), house ("Caught in This Affair"), acid ("Mysterons"), and ambient-techno ("Doobie"). Still, the album isn't a radical departure; most of these inspirations are cycled through Swayzak's fondness for gorgeous, electrified, echoing synth waves. And even though *Himawari* has a surprising focus on vocal tracks (with featured guests Benjamin Zephaniah, Kirsty Hawkshaw, and JB Rose), the duo's less-is-more aesthetic still comes in loud and clear — and sounds immediately distinctive. When the pair most closely revisit the shimmering, slinky nu-house of their debut ("Japan Air," "Leisure Centre"), the results are especially inspired. It's a bit of a shame that Swayzak moved on so quickly, but they make the transition as smooth as possible. —*John Bush*

## Sweet Exorcist

f. 1989, Sheffield, Yorkshire,
*Group / Ambient-Techno, Club/Dance, Techno*

Sweet Exorcist is a collaborative project between Richard H. Kirk (Cabaret Voltaire, Sandoz, Electronic Eye) and Sheffield colleague DJ Parrot. Although they've recorded together only sporadically since their critically lauded 1990 Warp debut, the pair have been dancefloor mainstays since the UK techno second wave of the early '90s. Their works have been collected on numerous Warp compilations — including the *Artificial Intelligence* series and the *Blech* mix tape — thereby tagging them as techno-based listening music, but the group remains equally popular among the DJ set. Kirk and Parrot have also released, solo and in combination, a slew of EPs on the Alphaphone label under names such as Robots and Humanoids and Code Warrior, among others. —*Sean Cooper*

• **C.C.C.D.** / 1990 / Warp ♦♦♦♦
A well-balanced mixture of more traditional techno and experimental electronic, both danceable and listenable. —*Sean Cooper*

**Spirit Guide to Low Tech** / 1994 / Touch ♦♦♦

## Rob Swift

*DJ / Illbient, Turntablism, Underground Rap, Hip-Hop*

Turntablist hero Rob Swift debuted with one of the top scratching groups of the '90s, the X-Men (later the X-Ecutioners). After one album with the group, Swift released his own debut *Soulful Fruit* in 1997, followed by *The Ablist* in 1999. —*John Bush*

**Soulful Fruit** / May 13, 1997 / Stone's Throw ♦♦♦

• **The Ablist** / Feb. 23, 1999 / Asphodel ♦♦♦♦
Directly influenced by Herbie Hancock's "Rockit," an early melding of jazz and hip-hop, *The Ablist* is Swift's attempt to introduce the turntable as a virtuosic instrument capable of being played with the same feeling and skill as any other instrument. He uses the turntable in various contexts, from solo scratching to full-band. Much of the album is stellar jazz-inflected hip-hop, even if it falls somewhat short of the incredibly high goals of its composer, but those high goals are what make *The Ablist* such a thrilling listen. Many songs use the turntable in ways that have not been explored. On "What Would You Do?," Swift's scratches act as a sort of instrumental answer to the question posed. "Fusion Beats" shows that the turntable can be a jamming instrument as well, with some nice interplay with keyboards on what is actually some pretty straight jazz. Turntables are also brought into a full-band context on "Modern Day Music" and "All that Scratching Is Making Me Rich!" "Modern Day Music" features the band's three MCs and Swift's DJ Premier-like cutting up of words and phrases over a deep groove. Swift's spare style of cutting often recalls Premier, and his production skills are similar to Large Professor, emphasizing rolling bass and swinging but steady beats. Overall, Swift has crafted a strong personal statement. The album echoes old-school skills without devolving into a pastiche of past hip-hop styles or following

commercial rap trends. Instead, *The Ablist* suggests directions in which hip-hop can go to remain viable. The album doesn't entirely follow through on all its promises and Swift doesn't always reach his goals, which can make the album a frustrating listen at times. Overall, however, *The Ablist* redefines the turntable as a musical instrument that can bring new dimensions to both structured and improvised music, and it shows that Swift is capable of some incisive music that works outside the normal confines of turntablist music. —*Stanton Swihart*

## David Sylvian

b. Feb. 23, 1958, Lewisham, London, England
*Vocals, Keyboards, Guitar, Composer / Experimental Ambient, Ambient Pop, Experimental Rock, Prog-Rock/Art Rock*

Following the 1982 dissolution of Japan, the group's onetime frontman David Sylvian staked out a far-ranging and esoteric career which encompassed not only solo projects but also a series of fascinating collaborative efforts and forays into filmmaking, photography, and modern art. Born David Batt in Kent, England on February 23, 1958, Sylvian formed Japan in 1974, and served as their primary singer/songwriter throughout the group's eight-year existence. Just prior to Japan's break-up, Sylvian began working with composer Ryuichi Sakamoto, with whom he released the single "Bamboo Houses" in 1982, marking the beginning of a long-standing musical relationship.

After 1983's "Forbidden Colours," another joint effort with Sakamoto, composed for the film *Merry Christmas, Mr. Lawrence*, Sylvian released his 1984 solo debut, *Brilliant Trees*. The first step in his music's evolution from Japan's post-glam synth-pop into richly textured, poetic ambience, the album featured contributions from Sakamoto as well as Jon Hassell and Can alumnus Holger Czukay. That year, Sylvian also published his first book of photographs, *Perspectives: Polaroids 82/84;* in 1985, he released *Preparations for the Journey*, a documentary filmed in and around Tokyo, as well as the EP *Words with the Shaman*.

*Gone to Earth*, an ambitious double LP recorded with assistance from Robert Fripp and Bill Nelson, followed in 1986, while 1987 marked the release not only of the beautiful *Secrets of the Beehive* album but also the book collection *Trophies: The Lyrics of David Sylvian*. At the same time, he began composing the score for modern dancer Gaby Abis' *Kin*, which premiered at London's Almeida Theater that September; another collaboration with Abis, *Don't Trash My Altar, Don't Alter My Trash*, bowed in November 1988.

Also in 1988, Sylvian reunited with Holger Czukay for the instrumental LP *Plight and Premonition;* the duo reteamed in 1989 for *Flux + Mutability*. *Ember Glance: The Permanence of Memory*, an installation of sculpture, sound and light created by Sylvian and Russell Mills, was staged in Tokyo Bay, Shinagawa in 1990; a year later, he and the other members of Japan, who had briefly reunited under the name Rain Tree Crow, issued a self-titled album. In 1994, Sylvian emerged in tandem with Robert Fripp for both an album, *The First Day*, and *Redemption*, another sound-and-image installation exhibited in Japan. The superb *Dead Bees on a Cake* followed in 1999; *Approaching Silence*, a collection of instrumental material, appeared later that year. —*Jason Ankeny*

### Gone to Earth / 1986 / Virgin ++++
Sylvian is joined by guitarists Robert Fripp and Bill Nelson on this 68-minute CD, which features tracks of Sylvian's trademark vocals and instrumentals. These dreamy, atmospheric works have nice musical support from Steve Nye, Kenny Wheeler, and Mel Collins. —*Scott Bultman*

### • Secrets of the Beehive / 1987 / Virgin ++++
Streamlining the muted, organic atmospheres of the previous *Gone to Earth* to forge a more cohesive listening experience, *Secrets of the Beehive* is arguably David Sylvian's most accessible record, a delicate, jazz-inflected work boasting elegant string arrangements courtesy of Ryuichi Sakamoto. Impeccably produced by Steve Nye, the songs are stripped to their bare essentials, making judicious use of the synths, tape loops, and treated pianos which bring them to life; Sylvian's evocative vocals are instead front and center, rendering standouts like "The Boy with the Gun" and the near-hit "Orpheus"—both among the most conventional yet penetrating songs he's ever written—with soothing strength and assurance. —*Jason Ankeny*

### Brilliant Trees/Words with the Shaman / 1991 / Caroline +++
*Brilliant Trees*, Sylvian's first solo album following his departure from Japan, was originally released in 1984 and was soon followed by an EP entitled *Words with the Shaman*. Both were unavailable in the US until Caroline reissued them on this single disc in 1991. But though the music on this album represents two separate releases and is technically divided into individual songs, the average listener may have trouble detecting the movement from one piece to another. There is a single overall sound: a deceptively soothing, mildly funky pastiche of keyboards, treated horns (courtesy of Jon Hassell), and rather unsettling snippets of radio voices and third-world singers. Many of the weirder moments are contributed by Holger Czukay, who would subsequently collaborate frequently with Sylvian. Instrumentally, the music is quite interesting, but Sylvian's voice can be pretty irritating—he's not half the singer he thinks he is. Still, fans won't be disappointed, and this disc is a good value for the money. If you're thrifty and curious, begin here. —*Rick Anderson*

### The First Day / Aug. 10, 1993 / Virgin ++++
Robert Fripp and David Sylvian's first official release together, *The First Day*, is a much funkier and more percussive affair than its bootleg predecessor, *The Day Before* (which contained radically different versions of these songs). An obvious reason for its higher quality is that it was recorded in a studio, while the bootleg consisted of in-concert demos, and the songs have been worked to completion. Fripp has found an extremely talented singer/partner in Sylvian, who adds a lot to his quirky compositions. Trey Gunn (who plays a bass-like instrument called the stick) makes each track practically groove and breathe on his own, and allows Fripp to stretch out and experiment in ways previously unheard from this guitar icon. *The First Day* is a very consistent album, with the musicians' excitement and energy easily being felt on such tracks as "God's Monkey," "Brightness," and the ten-minute tour de force "Firepower." Other lengthy tracks follow (the 11-minute "20th Century Dreaming" and the 17-minute "Darshan"), but it never becomes self-indulgent or boring. Certainly one of Robert Fripp's best and more inspired King Crimson side projects. —*Greg Prato*

### Dead Bees on a Cake / Mar. 30, 1999 / Virgin ++++
Fans of David Sylvian may consider some of his earlier releases to have been autumnal spectacles filled with intoxicating arrangements and some of the most beautifully heartbreaking songs ever composed. At face value, *Dead Bees on a Cake* should have been one of David Sylvian's most spiritually fulfilled and innovative releases—maybe next time. One can admire the rich vocals and impeccable instrumental performances by Talvin Singh, Steve Jansen, Ryuichi Sakamoto, and Marc Ribot, among others; however, for David Sylvian, even beautiful tracks like "The Shining of Things" are the sonic equivalent of running on a treadmill. One song makes this worth the price of admission: "Midnight Sun"; while the vocals are classic Sylvian, the bluesy, swampy sound of this track is completely new to him. It would have been fantastic if other songs on the album had followed in a similarly inventive vein. —*Sanz Lashley*

### Approaching Silence / Oct. 5, 1999 / EMI ++++
The "unofficial" subtitle of this CD is "music for multi media installations." All that is to say that the songs on this release date back to 1990 and were used as part of Sylvian and Russell Mills' exhibit *Ember Glance—The Permanence of Memory* (1990) and 1994's *Redemption—Approaching Silence*, which was done by Sylvian and Robert Fripp. Since the music is ambient at its finest, the dates of recording do not matter. The question is, does this music stand up on its own, apart from the exhibit? The answer is a resounding yes! Sylvian produces original and interesting ambient music. The selections are long ("Approaching Silence" is over 38 minutes long) yet never get boring. It is to Sylvian's credit that he can keep the listener interested for that long with this genre of music. Sylvian uses instruments and sounds to create his own creative ambient music. The shortwave samples, for example, add an eeriness in "The Beekeeper's Apprentice," which adds to the overall sound of the piece. This music is not for every taste, but fans of Sylvian and ambient music will find this to be a treat. —*Aaron Bagdley*

## Synergy

f. 1975
*Group / Prog-Rock/Art Rock, Electronic*

Beginning with the 1975 landmark *Electronic Realizations for Rock Orchestra*, Synergy explored the possibilities inherent in synthesizer/sequencer technology and digital-studio production techniques, resulting in some of the most inventive electronic music of the '70s. It was mostly the work of synthesizer expert Larry Fast, who also brought electronics to the mainstream by coordinating synthesized passages for dozens of pop acts during the '70s and '80s, including Yes, Peter Gabriel, Meat Loaf, John Denver, Barbra Streisand, Hall & Oates, Kate Bush, Foreigner, and Randy Newman.

Fast grew up in West Essex, New Jersey and trained as a pianist and violinist before entering Lafayette College in Pennsylvania. After taking a few computer-science courses, he became interested in synthesized music and began building his own primitive devices. He was introduced to Yes keyboard player Rick Wakeman during an interview for a local radio station, and soon interested the musician in his homemade instruments and customized versions of existing synthesizers. While in England to assist Yes in the recording of 1974's *Tales from Topographic Oceans*, Fast gained a record contract as well, with Passport Records.

Recording as Synergy, Fast debuted in 1975 with *Electronic Realizations for Rock Orchestra*. The album became a surprise favorite with progressive radio, and was hailed by synthesizer pioneer Robert Moog as the most important recording to date using his Moog synthesizer. Soon after the album's release, Fast was introduced to Peter Gabriel, who had recently left Genesis and was about to begin his solo career; Gabriel recruited Larry Fast to take care of synthesized effects for his first three LPs (each was self-titled). Gabriel's success with the singles "Shock the Monkey," "Biko," and "Games Without Frontiers" gave Fast a growing reputation as the man to hire for that contemporary sound; even while he recorded three new Synergy LPs during the late '70s, Fast worked with a variety of artists and appeared on tour with Gabriel. He also provided the score for the original planetarium light-show known as Laserium, and moved into film work (*About Last Night, Planes, Trains and Automobiles*) during the '80s. —*John Bush*

**Electronic Realizations for Rock Orchestra** / 1975 / Atlantic ♦♦♦♦
*Electronic Realizations for Rock Orchestra* is a stunning piece of polyphonic synthesizer music, the leap forward that took serious electronic music beyond rote imitations of *Switched-On Bach* into artistic territory. The opener "Legacy" is a pastoral wash of multitracked synthesizers, futuristic for its time, and still a bit beyond the normal even a decade later. There are several appearances by more sequenced electronics (reminiscent of Tangerine Dream), but the album works best when Fast allows his harmonic sense to take over the programming of several synthesizer lines at once. —*John Bush*

**Cords** / 1978 / Atlantic ♦♦♦
With their third album, *Cords*, Synergy began to repeat some of their ideas without expanding them greatly. There is still plenty of provocative, rewarding music on the album, but it doesn't quite match the freshness or brilliance of the first two records. —*Stephen Thomas Erlewine*

**Metropolitan Suite** / 1987 / Atlantic ♦♦♦
Wonderful work from synthesist Larry Fast, who uses his keyboards to create two sets of musical vistas—one that calls, simply, musical abstractions; the other is the title composition, a piece that gives musical sketches of New York at different periods in its history. Fast has a cinematic flair that results in some extremely dramatic writing—music for the cinema of the mind. —*Steven McDonald*

● **Semi-Conductor, Release 2** / Sep. 15, 1998 / Chronicles/Polygram ♦♦♦♦
A revised and expanded version of the original Synergy retrospective from 1984, *Semi-Conductor, Release 2* includes over two hours of synthesizer works recorded between 1975 and 1986. The music is some of the most evocative and intriguing to come from the '70s synthesizer boom, including potential novelty tracks—like covers of "Slaughter on Tenth Avenue" and "Classical Gas"—that are barely recognizable after Fast focuses on his fast-moving, polyphonic arrangements that use a variety of modules by Moog, Oberheim, and Prophet. The Synergy sound remained surprisingly unchanged into the '80s, except for the addition of a standard drum kit on tracks from 1979's *Games*. Though it may be difficult for listeners to separate the music of Synergy from the synthesizer excesses of contemporary prog-rock ensembles, *Semi-Conductor* includes a host of important electronic recordings. —*John Bush*

## System 7
f. 1990, London, England
Group / Ambient House, Electronica, Ambient-Techno, Club/Dance, Techno, IDM

The only direct link from the '90s ambient house community to its space-rocking forebear of the '70s, Steve Hillage played in the prog rock band Gong, released several solo albums during the late '70s and early '80s on Virgin, and later returned to music in the '90s to form System 7, more of a recording collective than an actual band. Hillage was recruited back to the music scene by Dr. Alex Paterson of the Orb, who spun Hillage's *Rainbow Dome Musick* at London's Heaven one night while Hillage was there himself. The two became friends, and Paterson encouraged him to begin recording ambient house—with Hillage's guitar explorations just as prominent in the mix as on his solo work. With collaborator Miquette Giraudy (an old friend from his days in Gong), Hillage released the single "Sunburst" in late 1990, and followed with a self-titled album in September 1991, produced with the help of a varied cast of techno heavyweights (including Paterson and Derrick May). Soon after, System 7 was signed to an American contract by Astralwerks, though the existence of a similarly named band caused Hillage to name his outfit 777. The *System 7* album was finally given a US release in 1992 as *777*.

During 1992, Hillage and Giraudy released the British-only singles "Freedom Fighters" and "Altitude"—as System 7, since the restriction applied only in America—and prepared their second album. Given the confusing title of *777*, it was nonetheless a completely different work than the earlier LP, and featured additional production by Dr. Alex Paterson. Though it wasn't given an American release, System 7's next project, a techno album and an ambient one released on the same day in late 1994, was issued in America as a two-disc set (again as 777). Signed to Britain's Butterfly label by producer Youth (who had engineered several sessions), the group worked with Derrick May and Carl Craig plus Paterson to record 1996's *Power of Seven*. Though the album was not released in America, later that year the industrial label Cleopatra signed System 7—finally allowed to use their real name in the US as well—and released the remix LP *System Express* in early 1997. System 7 returned later in 1997 with *Golden Section*. —*John Bush*

**777 [US]** / Jul. 31, 1992 / Caroline ♦♦♦♦
For their long-awaited System 7 album debut, Hillage and Giraudy received help from several high-profile figures—Paul Oakenfold, Derrick May, and Orb-associates including Dr. Alex Paterson, Thrash, Youth, and Andy Falconer. The truth is, despite the many beats added to Hillage's space-rock explorations, they still sound remarkably similar to albums he released 15 years before. His piercing guitar solos are instantly recognizable, and the basic structure of tracks like "Depth Disco" and "Strange Quotations" never take Hillage *too* far away from his mid-'70s solo career. That said, these songs still sound quite enjoyable—definitely on the polished end of ambient house but still quite a potent crossover record (even Giraudy's vocals are solid). One of the highlights, the lovely ambient wash of "Mia the Fisherman," also appeared on the compilation *Excursions in Ambience*. The album, released in Britain in 1991 as *System 7*, was reconfigured and retitled *777* for its American issue. —*John Bush*

**777 [UK]** / Mar. 1993 / Big Life ♦♦
The second album released by System 7 (confusingly given the same title as the American issue of their first album) is a seven-track mini-LP that finds Hillage & co. moving closer to straightahead techno and away from the ambient-pop of previous work. Spotlight tracks include the single "7:7 Expansion" and "Sinbad." —*John Bush*

**The Fire Album** / 1994 / Butterfly ♦♦♦♦
While progressive house as a semigenre never really got off the ground despite all the press attention given to it—arguably because it never really established a deep fan base among the actual raver population—some of what was created still has a certain appeal, and this album qualifies handily in that regard. Working with a variety of collaborators, including the Drum Club, Laurent Garnier, Youth, and, most notably, techno legend Derrick May, Hillage and Giraudy combine various contemporary trends here—the early '90s ambient boom, squelching 808 bass sounds, and disco-salsa—with Hillage's fluid, haunting guitar work to create a nicely state-of-the-art way to spend some time. To begin with, Hillage frankly deserves at least some credit just for his ability to openly embrace newer music without ever sounding like a dilettante, while most of his progressive peers from the '70s acted as if neither disco nor punk had ever happened, much less everything after that. That said, the promising title *Fire* rarely gets you up and moving on your feet; for all the solid beats throughout, it's a politer dance album, more meditative than punchy—one reason why history hasn't remembered it so well. At its best, though, it's still good stuff: The collaborations with May, "Mysterious Traveller" and "Overview," are unsurprisingly the best on the album; while neither May's nor

Hillage's stated mutual worship of George Clinton is apparent, the beats and grooves are among the best here. Other moments of note are "Alpha Wave (Gliss Mix)," with Hillage's guitar tracing a haunting, mysterious path deep in the mix over an increasingly stronger percussion line, and the gently surging "Gliding on Duo-Tone Curves" and "Jupiter!" —*Ned Raggett*

**The Water Album** / 1994 / Butterfly ◆◆◆◆

As its title alone indicates, *Water* was released as the counterpart to *Fire*, consisting of remixes by Hillage and Giraudy of nearly every track on the original album, plus one new number, all flowing into one another as essentially one lengthy, disc-long composition. Whereas *Fire* was much more of an up-front dance release—though admittedly calmer in comparison with many other dance records— *Water* embraces the ambient chill experience head-on. Without sacrificing beat entirely, *Water* is much more of a free-floating and relaxing release. Arguably, because it wasn't conceived as being for the dancefloor—and therefore not in direct competition with the storming jungle/hardcore tracks of the time—it's much more of a success to listen to than the often too-polite *Fire*. Hillage's dreamy guitar glissandos, snaking in and out of each song with a remarkable economy, fit the gentle flow of keyboards and production perfectly, stepping a bit more to the fore here, while avoiding any sense of worship-my-pedals heroics. The opening two remixes, of "Batukau" and "Sirenes," set the general tone of *Water;* they flow into a tied-together wash of sound that avoids new-age nothingness by setting the synth/guitar interplay to a subtle but still present rhythmic pattern, even on the latter track where no drum sounds appear at all. Other fine efforts include the revamp of "Dr. Livingstone I Presume," which is turned into a queasy combination of sitar sounds, drones, and chilly organ, and the 25-minute-long take on "Alpha Wave," a quietly majestic pulser with Hillage's guitar floating serenely throughout the mix. —*Ned Raggett*

**Fire & Water** / Jan. 31, 1995 / Astralwerks ◆◆◆

The American release of the *Fire* and *Water* albums did the logical thing by combining the two releases into one double-pack CD, making it an easy purchase for those so inclined. —*Ned Raggett*

● **Power of Seven** / Feb. 19, 1996 / Butterfly ◆◆◆◆

From the excellent Kraut-disco of "Interstate" to swirling space-crunch on "Chicago Indian," *Power of Seven* is the group's most accomplished album. It's the set where the programming abilities of Hillage and Giraudy finally caught up with developments by younger producers on the electronic scene. Although the whale noises on "Davy Jones' Locker" are just a tad passé, most everything else works on this solid album. —*John Bush*

**System Express** / Nov. 4, 1996 / Cleopatra ◆◆◆◆

Collecting remixes from singles and EPs, *System Express* succeeds through sheer name-power, including remixes by Marshall Jefferson, Carl Craig, Plastikman, David Holmes, Doc Scott and the 4 Hero project Jacob's Optical Stairway. —*John Bush*

**Golden Section** / Sep. 2, 1997 / Cleopatra ◆◆◆

Although System 7 could easily (and, at points, correctly) be accused of repeating themselves with this, their fifth proper album, the group have in fact carved out their own niche of warm, mellow ambient and psychedelic trance, one they've deviated from little since forming in 1991. *Golden Section* sticks as close to that niche as past recordings, although somewhat predictably, the group add the percussive influence of jungle on a few of the tracks (most notably "Don Corleone," on which Talvin Singh and Don Cherry appear). Nothing particularly earth-shattering here, but enjoyable nonetheless. —*Sean Cooper*

# T

**T.Power** (Marc Royal)
*Remixing, Producer / Experimental Jungle, Electronica, Jungle/Drum'N'Bass, Club/Dance, Techno*
T.Power's Marc Royal first came to prominence working with hardcore techno group Bass Selective, whose 1991 hit "Blow Out Part II" was an influential proto-jungle track. He's since risen to new acclaim as a solo artist with T.Power's experimental blend of lush ambience and often over-the-top rhythmic complexity. His 12" "Horny Mutant Jazz," as well as the follow-up full-length *The Self-Evident Truth of an Intuitive Mind* (both for the Sound of the Underground label) are widely considered early masterpieces of ambient-jungle. Both did much conceptual trailblazing where jungle's absorption of jazz and other more measured, relaxed compositional elements are concerned. Although subsequent work has strayed from jungle's rhythmic syncopation into more traditional techno and even entirely beatless ambient, drum'n'bass remains the core element of much of T.Power's music. Royal's roots are, not surprisingly, in hip-hop, in which he immersed himself during its UK heyday in the early- to mid-'80s. Burning out on hip-hop early, Royal's affection for breaks and hard-hitting rhythms followed him into his explorations of the music of David Sylvian, Ryuichi Sakamoto, and Pat Metheny, and those two components—complex breaks and a keen sense of melody—inform much of his solo work to the present day. —*Sean Cooper*

**The Self-Evident Truth of an Intuitive Mind** / 1995 / S.O.U.R. ♦♦♦♦
T.Power's *Self-Evident Truth* was one of the first full-length releases in jungle, and at that, one of its first concept albums. Split into two records—each chronicling emotion and intellect—T.Power's tight, raucous blend of jungle's twisting, mutating percussion with ambient-style melodic themes is best stated here. It's a bit sugar-coated at times, with long, syrupy melodic passages often taking the place of more creative song development, but the album's rhythmic tweak is often so severe you hardly notice. —*Sean Cooper*

● **Waveform** / Oct. 28, 1996 / Anti-Static/S.O.U.R. ♦♦♦♦
Balking at the influence of his debut, *The Self-Evident Truth of an Intuitive Mind*, T.Power's Marc Royal takes the admirable route with his follow-up by forgetting everything he's known. While elements of drum'n'bass are in evidence on a number of tracks, Royal opts instead to dissolve jungle's sweeping, low-bass moans and skittery rhythms in a vat of paranoid, abstract electronics. The result is a far less predictable, ultimately more enjoyable collection of post-dance beat-oriented electronica seamlessly blending ambient, jungle, electro (lots, in fact), and avant-garde-leaning electro-acoustic. Masterful. —*Sean Cooper*

**Tackhead**
f. 1984, New York, NY
*Group / Noise-Rock, Post-Punk, Industrial*
A collective stretching from the early days of the hip-hop label Sugar Hill into the industrial music of the '90s, Tackhead produced at least half a dozen albums under a variety of nominal heads—Keith LeBlanc, Gary Clail, and finally Tackhead. The group came together in the early '80s as the Sugar Hill house band with guitarist Skip McDonald, bassist Doug Wimbish, and drummer Keith LeBlanc. (The trio had performed on the three best early hip-hop tunes, the Sugarhill Gang's "The Rapper" and Grandmaster Flash's tracks "The Message" and "White Lines.") When McDonald, Wimbish, and LeBlanc met British dub producer Adrian Sherwood (of the On-U Sound System), they moved to England and in 1986 recorded *Major Malfunction*, a street-wise funk-rock LP with doses of Sherwood's studio trickery informing the whole. Since LeBlanc had a bit of name recognition due to his 1983 dance hit "No Sell Out," the album was released under his name. Another Brit, vocalist Gary Clail, had joined the Tackhead conglomeration by that time, and it was his name—or rather Gary Clail's Tackhead Sound System—that graced the cover of the 1987 album *Tackhead Tape Time*, on Nettwerk Records. After another collective recording on Keith LeBlanc's 1989 album *Stranger than Fiction*, the Tackhead team finally coalesced as a stable group on *Friendly as a Hand Grenade*. The album, also released in 1989, was the first recorded as Tackhead, and the addition of a standard vocalist (Bernard Fowler) made the group that much more stable, in image if not in sound. *Strange Things* followed in 1990, with contributions from Melle Mel and Mick Jagger. The album appeared to be a conscious attempt at mainstream rock success (not unlike that of Living Colour), and failed miserably. Though they released no more new Tackhead material, LeBlanc, Wimbish, and McDonald continued to play for On-U Sound System projects, such as Gary Clail's 1991 album *The Emotional Hooligan*. —*John Bush*

● **Friendly as a Hand Grenade** / 1989 / TVT ♦♦♦♦
Starting off with a Prince Buster cover and progressing through ten tracks of surprisingly slick funk-rock, *Friendly as a Hand Grenade* is a bit of a surprise after the harder studio effects of Tackhead-related projects like *Major Malfunction* and *Tackhead Tape Time*. The addition of vocalist Bernard Fowler (formerly of the Peech Boys) provides much of the soul. —*John Bush*

**Strange Things** / 1990 / SBK ♦♦♦
Another mainstream funk-rock album, *Strange Things* includes a few good moments but is for the most part weighed down by its smoother sound. —*John Bush*

**Power Inc., Vol. 3** / Nov. 4, 1997 / Blanc ♦♦
The third installment of the *Power Inc.* collections gathers live performances by Tackhead from throughout their career, not only at New York's Ritz, but also in London, Scotland, the Netherlands, and New Zealand. Guest vocalists include Mark Stewart, Bernard Fowler, Gary Clail, and rap legend Melle Mel (Grandmaster Flash and the Furious Five). These performances feature some of the earliest uses of sampling in a live concert setting; several are separated by spoken-word interludes taken from backstage recordings and the band's answering machine. —*Steve Huey*

**Nobukazu Takemura**
b. Aug. 26, 1968, Japan
*DJ, Producer / Electronica, Trip-Hop, Acid Jazz, Post-Rock/Experimental*
Kyoto-based producer Nobukazu Takemura's career has followed an odd trajectory for an artist produced by the club scene. He emerged as a hip-hop DJ in the mid-'80s, inspired by the Japanese leg of the legendary *Wild Style* tour (largely credited for introducing hip-hop to Japan). A short-lived career as a battle DJ led Takemura to shift focus to the mixing desk in the late '80s, and within a few years he was releasing tracks through Mo'Wax, Lollop, and Bungalow under the names DJ Takemura and Spiritual Vibes. Ostensibly trip-hop and acid jazz, these releases were marked by a high quotient of live instrumentation and, in contrast to his bedroom-producer colleagues, very high production values. In parallel with his club-oriented releases, Takemura was also producing more exploratory material together with Yamatsuka Eye (of the Boredoms) and Aki Onda as Audio Sports; the group released an LP, *Era of Glittering Gas*, before Onda took sole control of the project in 1992. By the mid-'90s, Takemura had signed with Warner Japan as a solo artist, and his releases as Child's View and under his own name tended increasingly toward a challenging diffusion of hip-hop, jazz, pop, drum'n'bass, and post-classical music. (The 1996 remix album, *Child's View Remix*, featuring Aphex Twin, Coldcut, and Wagon Christ, among others, suggested his growing interest in the experimental fringes of dance culture.) With 1997's *Child & Magic* LP, Takemura's interest in the relatively more stable rhythms of dance music had

almost completely fallen away, and elements of experimental computer music and overt references to minimalist composers such as Terry Riley and Steve Reich filled his tracks, which tended to pair cycling flute, percussion, and bell-tone patterns with the glitchy desktop discontinuities of Oval and Ryoji Ikeda, among others. Two other releases from this period—*Funfair*, on the American Bubble Core label, and *Milano*, on Warner Japan—solidified this new direction. (The latter CD Takemura originally produced for a fashion show by popular Japanese designer Issey Miyake.) Following a Japanese date with American post-rockers Tortoise, Takemura secured release plans with Tortoise's label, Thrill Jockey, and 1999 saw the release of his most abstract, "difficult" material to date. *Scope*, preceded by the "Meteor" 12", bore only the most tenuous resemblance to his previous releases, consisting of a dizzying blur of digital static, off-kilter bell patterns, mangled vocal samples, and CD skips. Like his original works, remixes by Takemura also span a wide range, including artists such as Tortoise, indie-pop singer Takako Minekawa, junglist Roni Size, and Steve Reich. [See Also: Child's View] —*Sean Cooper*

**Child & Magic** / 1997 / WEA ♦♦♦♦

• **Scope** / Jun. 22, 1999 / Thrill Jockey ♦♦♦♦
I first heard of Nobukazu Takemura while scanning a copy of Japanese pressing of Tortoise's *TNT*. A few weeks later I was telling my friend about this find and he said I must get Takemura's *Scope*, that it was a beautiful record. When I first popped it into my CD player I was a bit taken aback—it was nothing like I had, or could have, predicted. No heavy beats, no discernable instrument sounds, only kind of a synthesized clicking. I wasn't sure what to think. It was a much different clicking than something like Oval, there was no staid rhythm and slow modulation. A little more than halfway through the album came the song "Icefall." This was when I realized that Nobukazu Takemura is a genius. I could hear chord changes and modulations in the clicks, now sounding much like an intentionally skipping CD, but they were all crushed together and it sounded more like an orchestra of little clicks. The clicks kept clicking and smashed one on top of the other again and again—it was a symphony of clicks. So clever, so painstaking this task must have been that I was blown away. In light of "Icefall" I listened through the album again and it sounded completely different. I was starting to understand the music much more. I think that Takemura's music invites a kind of Platonic dialogue. Once you've looked at his music from every possible angle and think you understand it, a single event (for me "Icefall") changes your perception of it entirely. This music is miles ahead of the bleeps and loops of most electronic music being made today. —*Marc Gilman*

## Talk Talk

f. 1981, London, England, db. 1991
*Group / New Romantic, Post-Rock/Experimental, New Wave, Synth-Pop*
With the exception of a handful of common threads—chief among them: the plaintive vocals and haunting lyrics of frontman Mark Hollis—there is little to suggest that the five studio LPs which make up the Talk Talk oeuvre are indeed the work of the same band throughout. After beginning their career with records which virtually epitomize the new wave era that spawned them, the British group never looked back, making significant strides with each successive album on their way to discovering a wholly unique and uncategorizable sound informed by elements of jazz, classical and ambient music. Their masterful final recordings, while neglected commercially, possess a timelessness rare among music of any genre, and in retrospect, they seem the clear starting point for the post-rock movement of the '90s.

The story of Talk Talk begins with singer/songwriter Hollis, the younger brother of Ed Hollis, a disc jockey and producer who went on to manage such punk-era bands as Eddie and the Hot Rods. Mark originally planned to become a child psychologist, but in 1975, he left university to relocate to London, eventually forming a band called the Reaction. Ed Hollis called in a few favors, and in 1977, the Reaction recorded a demo tape for Island Records. Among the tracks was a Hollis original titled "Talk Talk," which later surfaced on the Beggars Banquet punk compilation *Streets*. After just one single, 1978's "I Can't Resist," the Reaction disbanded, and through his brother, Hollis was first introduced to bassist Paul Webb, drummer Lee Harris and keyboardist Simon Brenner, with whom he formed Talk Talk in 1981.

After recording a number of demos with producer Jimmy Miller, Talk Talk signed to EMI, who assigned Duran Duran producer Colin Thurston to helm their first two singles, "Mirror Man" and "Talk Talk." Clearly, EMI's intent was to mold the band in the spirit of the New Romantic movement, and towards that end, they also tapped Talk Talk as the opener on Duran Duran's 1982 UK tour. Their debut LP, *The Party's Over*, was indeed a product of its times, defined by contemporary synth-pop sensibilities but with an honesty and lyrical depth absent from most other records of the moment. In 1983, Talk Talk resurfaced with the single "My Foolish Friend," which in itself marked a major leap from the first record with its denser and more mature sound; the subsequent dismissal of Brenner made it plain that the band's days of relying on synthesizers were over for good.

The remainder of 1983 was spent writing and recording *It's My Life*, Talk Talk's breakthrough recording. The turning point was the arrival of producer and multi-instrumentalist Tim Friese-Green, who was to remain an unofficial fourth member of the band for the remainder of their existence. In Friese-Green, Hollis found the ideal partner to realize his ambitions; *It's My Life* made major strides away from *The Party's Over*, rejecting the debut's new wave trappings in favor of richer, more natural textures. The gambit worked, with the title track becoming a hit on both sides of the Atlantic. 1986's *The Colour of Spring* continued the trend, and on the strength of the smashes "Life Is What You Make of It" and "Give It Up," it became Talk Talk's best-selling album to date. A major world tour followed, with EMI allotting an enormous budget for the group's next effort.

In 1987, Talk Talk settled into an abandoned Suffolk church to begin working on their fourth LP; EMI executives eagerly awaited the finished product—and they were to continue waiting, as the group worked far past their deadline, seemingly with no end in sight. Already well over budget, Hollis refused to allow label heads any advance tapes, and informed EMI that not only would there be no singles from the record, but that the group would be unable to re-create the complex arrangements onstage and, as a consequence, would perform no live dates in support of the disc's release. Finally, after some 14 months in the studio, *Spirit of Eden* was issued to thunderous critical acclaim, albeit little commercial interest. An intricate, meditative work, it bore little resemblance to standard pop music, with its lengthy songs and spacious, organic arrangements perhaps closest in theme and texture to jazz.

With relations between EMI and Talk Talk already at their breaking point the label made the decision to issue an edited single version of the *Spirit of Eden* track "I Believe in You" without the band's consent; EMI then attempted to drop the group from their roster, although their contract had not yet expired. Talk Talk then sued the label; improbably enough, EMI countersued, claiming breach of contract. The band eventually prevailed in court, later signing to Polydor to begin work on their next LP. Paul Webb subsequently left Talk Talk, and the masterful *Laughing Stock* was recorded primarily with guest musicians. Issued in 1991, the LP marked a complete break from convention, adopting an almost free-form aesthetic; however, it was also Talk Talk's final work—in 1992, Webb and Harris reunited in 'O'Rang, while Hollis disappeared from view, finally issuing his self-titled solo debut in early 1998. A live Talk Talk release, *London 1986*, appeared in 1999. —*Jason Ankeny*

**The Party's Over** / 1982 / EMI America ♦♦♦
Talk Talk began life as a slavishly derivative, Duran Duran-styled, new romantic synth-pop band, as their debut, *The Party's Over*, clearly shows. Much of the album seems to attempt to recreate Duran Duran's debut, but even with their most blatant ripoffs, like the single "Talk Talk," they do it with a naive charm that makes for some really enjoyable music, even if it isn't particularly innovative or groundbreaking. —*Chris Woodstra*

**It's My Life** / 1984 / EMI America ♦♦♦♦
After an unremarkable debut, Talk Talk regrouped and refashioned themselves more in the style of sophisto-era Roxy Music while developing their own voice. *It's My Life* shows a great leap in songwriting, the band making highly personal statements with a sexy, seductive groove and a diversity that transcends the synth-pop tag. Synthesizers still play a dominant role, but the music is made far more interesting by mixing "real" instruments and challenging world music rhythms seamlessly with the technology. Still pulling off the catchy single (like "Dum Dum Girl" and the title track, as well as the simply sublime "Does Caroline Know?") on *It's My Life*, Talk Talk also proved themselves capable of achieving a cohesive album—a rare feat for the time and an unexpected surprise from a band that seemed to be simply a bandwagon-jumper. —*Chris Woodstra*

**The Colour of Spring** / 1986 / EMI America ♦♦♦♦
With *It's My Life*, Talk Talk proved that they could pull off an entire album of strong material. With *Colour of Spring*, they took it one step further, moving to a near-concept song cycle, following the emotional ups and downs of rela-

tionships and pondering life in general. Musically, they built on the experimental direction of the previous album with interesting rhythms, sweeping orchestration, complex arrangements, and even a children's chorus to create an evocative, hypnotic groove. Though the songs were catchier on the earlier efforts and the ambient experimentation was more fully achieved later on, *Colour of Spring* succeeded in marrying the two ideas into one unique sound for their most thoroughly satisfying album. —*Chris Woodstra*

★ **Spirit of Eden** / 1988 / EMI America ✦✦✦✦✦
Compare *Spirit of Eden* with any other previous release in the Talk Talk catalog and it's almost impossible to believe it's the work of the same band—exchanging electronics for live, organic sounds and rejecting structure in favor of mood and atmosphere, the album is an unprecedented breakthrough, a musical and emotional catharsis of immense power. Mark Hollis' songs exist far outside of the pop idiom, drawing instead on ambient textures, jazz-like arrangements and avant-garde accents. For all of their intricacy and delicate beauty, compositions like "Inheritance" and "I Believe in You" also possess an elemental strength—Hollis' oblique lyrics speak to themes of loss and redemption with understated grace, and his hauntingly poignant vocals evoke wrenching spiritual turmoil tempered with unflagging hope. A singular musical experience. —*Jason Ankeny*

**Natural History: The Very Best of Talk Talk** / Oct. 1990 / EMI America ✦✦✦✦
During the band's hiatus following *Spirit of Eden*, EMI issued a hits collection, compiling the singles from the first four albums as well as the non-LP "My Foolish Friend," a couple of live tracks, and an edit of "Desire." *Natural History* serves as a nice introduction to the band, showing them as an effective singles act despite their more recent album-concept experiments, and the added rarities make the package a necessary addition for fans as well. —*Chris Woodstra*

**History Revisited** / Feb. 1991 / EMI America ✦✦✦
Released as a companion piece to the hits collection *Natural History, History Revisited* compiles mainly new remixes of the band's best-known, pre-experimental output. Only the dub mix of "Happiness Is Easy" had been released before—the rest were done without the band's involvement, and the band reportedly tried to block the album's release. Talk Talk's brand of synthpop lends itself quite well to this sort of treatment, so the collection works quite well, although there aren't many surprises. A nice companion piece for fans, but probably the least essential of their catalog. —*Chris Woodstra*

☆ **Laughing Stock** / Nov. 19, 1991 / Polydor ✦✦✦✦✦
Virtually ignored upon its initial release, *Laughing Stock* continues to grow in stature and influence by leaps and bounds. Picking up where *Spirit of Eden* left off, the album operates outside of the accepted sphere of rock to create music which is both delicate and intense. Recorded with a large classical ensemble, it defies easy categorization, conforming to very few structural precedents—while the gently hypnotic "Myrrhman" flirts with ambient textures, the percussive "Ascension Day" drifts toward jazz before the two sensibilities converge to create something entirely new and different on "New Grass." The epic "After the Flood," on the other hand, is an atmospheric whirlpool laced with jackhammer guitar feedback and Mark Hollis' remarkably plaintive vocals; it flows into "Taphead," perhaps the most evocative, spacious and understated piece on the record. A work of staggering complexity and immense beauty, *Laughing Stock* remains an under-recognized masterpiece, and its echoes can be heard throughout much of the finest experimental music issued in its wake. —*Jason Ankeny*

## Fumiya Tanaka

b. May 21, 1972, Kyoto, Japan
*Producer, DJ / Minimal Techno, Club/Dance, Techno*
Easily Japan's most talented and knowledgeable techno DJ, Fumiya Tanaka brought the sound of minimal, intense techno to Japan during the early '90s and introduced thousands of club-goers to the best Detroit and German producers via his clubnights around Osaka and Tokyo. Born in Kyoto, Tanaka listened to and played in punk bands as a teen, then entered the dance scene in 1990 via house, techno, and hip-hop. He began DJing soon after, and formed Japan's first electronic-dance label, Torema Records, in 1993 for his own stripped-down productions.

By 1995, Fumiya Tanaka released his first mix album *I Am Not a DJ* on Torema, which by then had gained major distribution through Sony. Later that year, he set up Untitled Records, which paved the way for more experimental techno via the compilation *Abstract Set 1*. Soon he was spinning around the world—often in the company of DJ heroes Jeff Mills, Derrick May, and Dave Clarke—and not long after, the European techno cognoscenti realized that Tanaka wasn't just one of the best DJs in Japan, but around the world. Another DJ album, 1996's *Mix-Up, Vol. 4*, prefaced the release of his first production album: 1998's *Unknown Possibility, Vol. 1*. Tanaka also worked on production for the debut album from Takkyu Ishino of Japan's Denki Groove. —*John Bush*

● **I Am Not a DJ** / Apr. 21, 1995 / Torema/Sony Japan ✦✦✦✦
Fumiya Tanaka's first mix album introduced one of the brightest DJ talents on the world stage with a set of techno that flows smoothly and easily: from fierce, pummeling techno (Robert Armani, Dan Curtin, Joey Beltram, Luke Slater) to Detroit minimalism (Jeff Mills, Robert Hood, F.USE.) and German experimentalism (Basic Channel's Cyrus, Phylyps, Maurizio, and Vainqueur). It's not just great track selection, either; Tanaka messes with the mix quite a bit, dropping out and bringing back tracks on rhythm and flipping spin backs with apparent ease. As well, he finds room for a pair of techno's most beautiful left field classics, "Galaxy" by Carl Craig's BFC and "Tied Up" by LFO. *I Am Not a DJ* isn't just a great mix album, it sums up, nearly perfectly, the most important strands of techno during the '90s. —*John Bush*

## Tangerine Dream

f. 1967, Berlin, Germany
*Group / Kraut Rock, Prog-Rock/Art Rock, Ambient, Electronic*
Without doubt, the recordings of Tangerine Dream have made the greatest impact on the widest variety of instrumental music during the '80s and '90s, ranging from the most atmospheric new age and space music to the harshest abrasions of electronic dance. Founded in 1967 by Edgar Froese in Berlin, the group has progressed through a full three dozen lineups (Froese being the only continuous member with staying power) and four distinct stages of development: the experimentalist minimalism of the late '60s and early '70s; stark sequencer trance during the mid- to late '70s, the group's most influential period; an organic form of instrumental music on their frequent film and studio work during the '80s; and, finally, a more propulsive dance style, which showed Tangerine Dream with a sound quite similar to their electronic inheritors in the field of dance music.

Froese, born in Tilsit, East Prussia in 1944, was little influenced by music while growing up. Instead, he looked to the Dadaist and Surrealist movements for inspiration, as well as literary figures such as Gertrude Stein, Henry Miller, and Walt Whitman. He organized multimedia events at the residence of Salvador Dali in Spain during the mid-'60s and began to entertain the notion of combining his artistic and literary influences with music; Froese played in a musical combo called the Ones, which recorded just one single before dissolving in 1967. The first lineup of Tangerine Dream formed later that year, with Froese on guitar, bassist Kurt Herkenberg, drummer Lanse Hapshash, flutist Voker Hombach, and Charlie Prince. The quintet aligned itself with contemporary American acid rock (the Grateful Dead, Jefferson Airplane), and played around Berlin at various student events. The lineup lasted only two years, and by 1969 Froese had recruited wind player Conrad Schnitzler and drummer Klaus Schulze. One of the trio's early rehearsals, not originally intended for release, became the first Tangerine Dream LP when Germany's Ohr Records issued *Electronic Meditation* in June 1970. The LP was a playground for obtuse music-making—keyboards, several standard instruments, and a variety of household objects were recorded and filtered through several effects processors, creating a sparse, experimentalist atmosphere.

Both Schulze and Schnitzler left for solo careers later in 1970, and Froese replaced them the following year with drummer Christopher Franke and organist Steve Schroeder. When Schroeder left a year later, Tangerine Dream gained its most stable lineup core when organist Peter Baumann joined the fold. The trio of Froese, Franke and Baumann would continue until Baumann's departure in 1977, and even then, Froese and Franke would compose the spine of the group for an additional decade.

On 1971's *Alpha Centauri* and the following year's *Zeit*, the trio's increased use of synthesizers and a growing affinity for space music resulted in albums that pushed the margin for the style. *Atem*, released in 1973, finally gained Tangerine Dream widespread attention outside Europe; influential British DJ John Peel named it his LP of the year, and the group signed a five-year contract with Richard Branson's Virgin Records. Though less than a year old, Virgin had already become a major player in the recording industry, thanks to the massive success of Mike Oldfield's *Tubular Bells* (widely known for its use in the film *The Exorcist*).

Tangerine Dream's first album for Virgin, *Phaedra*, was an milestone not only for the group, but for instrumental music. Branson had allowed the group free rein at Virgin's Manor Studios, where they used Moog synthesizers and sequencers for the first time; the result was a relentless, trance-inducing barrage of rhythm and sound, an electronic update of the late-'60s and early-'70s classical minimalism embodied by Terry Riley. Though mainstream critics were unsurprisingly hostile toward the album (it obviously made no pretense to rock 'n' roll in any form), *Phaedra* broke into the British Top 20 and earned Tangerine Dream a large global audience.

The follow-ups *Rubycon* and the live *Ricochet* were also based on the blueprint with which *Phaedra* had been built, but the release of *Stratosfear* in 1976 saw the use of more organic instruments such as untreated piano and guitar; also, the group added vocals for 1978's *Cyclone*, a move which provoked much criticism from their fans. Both of these innovations didn't change the sound in a marked degree, however, their incorporation into rigid sequencer patterns continued to distance Tangerine Dream from the mainstream of contemporary instrumental music.

Baumann left for a solo career in 1978 (later founding the Private Music label), and was replaced briefly by keyboard player Steve Joliffe and then Johannes Schmoelling, another important member of Tangerine Dream who would stay until the mid-'80s. In 1980, the Froese/Franke/Schmoelling lineup was unveiled at the Palast der Republik in East Berlin, the first live performance by a Western group behind the Iron Curtain. Tangerine Dream also performed live on TV with the Munich Philharmonic Orchestra one year later, and premiered their studio work on 1980's *Tangram*.

Mike Oldfield had shown the effectiveness of using new instrumental music forms as a bed for film on *Tubular Bells*, and in 1977 *The Exorcist*'s director William Friedkin had tapped Tangerine Dream for soundtrack work on his film *Sorcerer*. By the time the new lineup stabilized in 1981, Hollywood was knocking on the band's door; Tangerine Dream worked on soundtracks to more than 30 films during the '80s, among them *Risky Business, The Keep, Flashpoint, Firestarter, Vision Quest,* and *Legend*. If the idea of standalone electronic music hadn't entered the minds of mainstream America before this time, the large success of these soundtracks (especially *Risky Business*) entrenched the idea and proved enormously influential to soundtrack composers from all fields.

Despite all the jetting between Hollywood and Berlin, the group continued to record proper LPs and tour the world as well. *Hyperborea*, released in 1983, was their last album for Virgin, and a move to Zomba/Jive Records signaled several serious changes for the band during the late '80s. After the first Zomba release (a live concert recorded in Warsaw), 1985's *Le Parc* marked the first time Tangerine Dream had flirted with sampling technology. The use of sampled material was an important decision to make for a group which had always investigated the philosophy of sound and music with much care, though *Le Parc* was a considerable success, with both fans and critics calling it their best LP in a decade. *Tyger*, released in 1987, featured more vocals than any previous Tangerine Dream LP, and many of the group's fans were quite dispirited.

Schmoelling left in 1988, to be replaced by the classically trained Paul Haslinger and (for a brief time) Ralf Wadephul. *Optical Race*, released in 1988, was the first Tangerine Dream album to appear on old bandmate Peter Baumann's Private Music Records. Several more albums followed for the label, after which Haslinger left to work on composing filmscores in Los Angeles. His replacement, and the only other permanent member of Tangerine Dream since, was Edgar's son Jerome Froese (whose photo had graced the cover of several TD albums in the past). Another record-label change, to Miramar, preceded the release of 1992's *Rockoon*, which earned Tangerine Dream one of their seven total Grammy nominations. In the mid-'90s, the music of Tangerine Dream increasingly began to reflect the group's influence on a generation of electronica and dance artists. The duo continued to record and release live albums, remix albums, studio albums, and soundtracks at the rate of about two albums per year into the late '90s. —*John Bush*

**Electronic Meditation** / Jun. 1970 / Relativity ♦♦

**Alpha Centauri** / 1971 / Relativity ♦♦
As if the sound is breaking through your speakers, *Alpha Centauri* begins its journey. Crackling and swirling synthesizers seize control of your stereo. Like a call to psychedelic arms, the first track "Sunrise in the Third System" marches on with its organ. The mixing of the three tracks found on *Alpha Centauri* leaves something to be desired, in that the tracks are not mixed the way they would be today with each track endlessly flowing into the next like a stream. Nonetheless, when one is not paying too close attention to such details, the album seems to flow quite smoothly. The sound is not of the highest standards either, as should be expected, this being a 1971 release of "space music." Tangerine Dream's style of "space music" had not yet been refined and revolutionized as it was a couple of releases later with *Phaedra* and *Rubycon*. Regardless, for those interested in a wilder and more reckless ride on the "space music" autobahn, *Alpha Centauri* should satisfy the need. —*Michael Breece*

**Zeit** / 1972 / Relativity ♦♦♦
TD's purest expression of "space music," this double album ebbs and flows effortlessly from one tone cluster to another. Almost classical in construction, the music is structured so as to evolve in sections as one theme literally melts into the next. Florian Fricke (of Popol Vuh) played the big Moog on this album and the overall texture of the electronics is warm and shimmering. —*Archie Patterson*

**Atem** / Mar. 1973 / Relativity ♦♦♦♦

★ **Phaedra** / Feb. 20, 1974 / Virgin ♦♦♦♦♦
*Phaedra* is one of the most important, artistic and exciting works in the history of electronic music, a brilliant and compelling summation of Tangerine Dream's early avant-space direction balanced with the synthesizer/sequencer technology just beginning to gain a foothold in non-academic circles. The result is best heard on the 15-minute title track, unparalleled before or since for its depth of sound and vision. Given focus by the arpeggiated trance that drifts in and out of the mix, the track progresses through several passages including a few surprisingly melodic keyboard lines and an assortment of eerie moog and mellotron effects, gaseous explosions and windy sirens. Despite the impending chaos, the track sounds more like a carefully composed classical work than an unrestrained piece of noise. While the title track takes the cake, there are three other excellent tracks on *Phaedra*. "Mysterious Semblance at the Strand of Nightmares" is a solo Froese song that uses some surprisingly emotive and affecting synthesizer washes, and "Movements of a Visionary" is a more experimental piece, using treated voices and whispers to drive its hypnotic arpeggios. Perhaps even more powerful now as a musical landmark now than when it was first recorded, *Phaedra* has proven the test of time. —*John Bush*

☆ **Rubycon** / Mar. 21, 1975 / Virgin ♦♦♦♦♦
The record that equaled its brilliant and celebrated predecessor, *Rubycon* consists of two side-long tracks that betters its predecessor with an enhanced sense of airy melodies and effects, but arguably fails when it comes to the sequencer. While the best portions of *Phaedra* dealt with the interplay between straight-ahead sequencer trance and more free-form beatless passages, on *Rubycon*, once the sequencer lines slide in (albeit seven minutes into the first track) they seldom break until the end. —*John Bush*

**Stratosfear** / 1976 / Virgin ♦♦♦♦
*Stratosfear*, the last Tangerine Dream album by the great Baumann/Franke/Froese threesome, shows the group's desire to advance past their stellar recent material and stake out a new musical direction while others were still attempting to come to grips with *Phaedra* and *Rubycon*. The album accomplishes its mission with the addition of guitar (six- and 12-string), grand piano, harpsichord and mouth organ to the usual battery of moogs, mellotrons, and e-pianos. The organic instruments take more of a textural role, embellishing the effects instead of working their own melodic conventions. *Stratosfear* is also the beginning of a more evocative approach for Tangerine Dream. Check the faraway harmonica sounds and assortment of synth-bubbles on "3 AM at the Border of the Marsh from Okefenokee" or the somber chords and choral presence of "The Big Sleep in Search of Hades." The title-track opener is the highlight though, beginning with a statuesque synthesizer progression before unveiling an increasingly hypnotic line of trance. —*John Bush*

**Encore** / 1977 / Virgin ♦♦♦

**Sorcerer** / 1977 / MCA ♦♦♦

**Cyclone** / 1978 / Virgin ♦♦♦
A welcome reissue and one that marks an interesting transition in Tangerine

Dream's existence—this was the first TD album to incorporate lyrics and vocals (from Steve Jolliffe, who also contributed wind instruments and keyboards). By this point, the nucleus of the band was down to Edgar Froese and Christopher Franke, with the sound centering more on shifting arpeggiation over percussive rhythm structures, with "Madrigal Meridian" being an impressive example of this. Jolliffe's vocal contributions on "Bent Cold Sidewalk" and "Rising Runner Missed by Endless Sender" provide an aggressive edge that effectively catapults the listener from the hypnotic pulse that Tangerine Dream are best known for—still, it's by no means a failed experiment, though it does make *Cyclone* one of the least useful TD albums for working up a good meditative state. —*Steven McDonald*

**Force Majeure** / 1979 / Virgin ++++
*Force Majeure* followed the departure of Steve Joliffe and saw Tangerine Dream once again giving up vocal material in favor of shifting, changing and sometimes complex synthesized instrumental material. By this point the band consisted of Edgar Froese and Chris Franke, with drummer Klaus Krieger sitting in for the studio sessions. The music is built on pulsing arpeggio figures and long, shifting metallic tones; there are nods in the title track to Kraftwerk and Jean Michel Jarre as well as to Froese's more experimental roots (for all that, *Force Majeure* could be held up as indicating the direction that Froese would eventually take the band). This is album is an entertaining mixture of elements, some of which verge on majestic and some on mildly banal (as well as sonic and musical structures that will remind people of Pink Floyd and the Alan Parsons Project). It does, however, manage to even out to be quite enjoyable. —*Steven McDonald*

**Tangram** / 1980 / Blue Plate ++++
*Tangram* is the beginning of a new musical direction, closer to straightahead, melodic new age music and more tied to their soundtrack material. The first of the two side-long pieces progresses through several different passages that use gently brushed acoustic guitars as well as the requisite synthesizers. For new age fans, this is the first glimmering of Tangerine Dream's eventual direction during the '80s. —*Keith Farley*

**Exit** / 1981 / Elektra +++

**Logos** / 1982 / Virgin +++
This live recording captures Tangerine Dream at a high point that occurred midway through the band's career. Longer, more intricate pieces are present, yet the action takes place at a brisk pace, moving through many of the trademark TD motifs and soundscapes. The recording's studio quality and engrossing performances are clearly inspired. —*Linda Kohanov*

**Risky Business** / 1984 / Virgin ++++
A fairly good cross-section of the soundtrack music for this film (starring Tom Cruise in a breakout performance), with TD's pulsating cues on five tracks balanced well against a selection of rock, blues and funk numbers (by Bob Seger, Jeff Beck, Prince and Muddy Waters, among others). The standout cut is "Love on a Real Train." —*Steven McDonald*

**Le Parc** / 1985 / Relativity ++++
A selection of different moods, all of a consistently high quality, each track takes its name and inspiration from a different park in the world, like Central, or Yellowstone for example. —*Vladimir Bogdanov*

**Legend** / 1986 / MCA ++
Tangerine Dream's soundtrack to Ridley Scott's *Legend* is a vaguely interesting set of atmospheric, electronic soundscapes, but it doesn't quite match the splendor of their earlier work. Furthermore, the music is interrupted by mediocre pop songs from Bryan Ferry and Jon Anderson, making *Legend* a less than fulfilling effort. —*Daevid Jehnzen*

**Canyon Dreams** / 1987 / Miramar ++++
TD received its first Grammy nomination with this album. The music was originally composed for a scenic video on the Grand Canyon, released under the same title. The style is a rather ingenious combination of the group's progressive style and current commercial leanings, and, as such, is Tangerine Dream's finest album of recent years. —*Linda Kohanov*

**Collection** / 1987 / A&M ++++
1987's *Collection* was revamped with new artwork and reissued by Castle in 1998. It's a solid single-disc overview of Tangerine Dream's early years, before the move to Virgin which produced their most seminal work; since this wasn't Tangerine Dream's most creatively fertile period, it's a nice alternative to the two-disc *Analogue Years '69-'73*, which covers similar ground in more detail but may be too much for more casual fans. —*Steve Huey*

**Tyger** / 1987 / Relativity +++
*Tyger* sees Tangerine Dream set the poetry of William Blake to music. While the combination of styles will inevitably be off-putting to some—particularly stuffy Blake fans—the results are surprisingly evocative and listenable. *Tyger* might not be one of the most accessible albums within Tangerine Dream's catalog, but for those wishing to explore their more adventerous side, it's a worthwhile listen. —*Stephen Thomas Erlewine*

**Melrose** / Sep. 1990 / Private Music +++
Electronic music seems to have been all the rage, even back in the early '90s, but the Dream (aka Citrus Slumber) has been the innovative force behind much of the John Tesh like synth patterns played on new age stations during that time. You might think the band (comprised of keyboardist-guitarist Edgar Froese, his son Jerome Froese, and keyboardist Paul Haslinger) would choose to rest on its many laurels after so many years, but *Melrose* rocks as hard as synth created music can, picking up where their previous, very engaging disc, *Lily on the Beach*, left off. Los Angeles imagery abounds here, as on the rhythmic title cut (the only one to feature sax) and the hypnotic "Rolling Down Cahuenga." Once again, the happy upbeat sequences are more than offset by more reflective ballads like "Electric Lion." While some of the tracks tend to carry on a bit too long, the textures are generally interesting enough to keep things entertaining. If there were more sax, TD's music could be considered an offshoot of smooth jazz. But it's great as it is—smart, hip machine-oriented sounds from masterful players and producers. —*Jonathan Widran*

**Tangents: 1973-83** / 1994 / Capitol ++++
When it comes to compiling retrospective overviews of any long-standing performer or group, it's difficult to know what to include and what to leave out, what to polish up and what to leave in the raw. Even if the choices are narrowed to a segment of the artist's career (as here), there are problems galore. Providing the best possible presentation of a range of material is one way to handle things; if there's room, salting in a few outtakes, live cuts and alternate versions is always a good idea.

*Tangents* has been approached on a slightly different vector, with results that will intrigue some and annoy others. There is, for example, an entire disc of outtakes—TD fans tend to be very specific about what constitutes the band's best material, so this provides listeners with a way of totally ignoring material they may find inferior. Another disc, meanwhile, is devoted entirely to music for films, a Tangerine Dream side trip that provided some of their best and most atmospheric music. All of the cuts here are remixed, and some have additional work from TD founder Edgar Froese.

It's this remodeling approach that may have some long time TD fans looking askance at this 5-CD collection. While rerecording certain pieces gets around the need to condense longer TD compositions, it also serves to dilute a number of the pieces. The remixes, on the other hand, are effective in terms of cleaning up some of the tracks, providing an even sonic landscape. The effect, over the first four discs at least, is to create a homogenized version of Tangerine Dream, one in which the musical balance is better realized and the musical shifts blur into invisibility.

As an anchor for a Tangerine Dream collection, *Tangents* works reasonably well, though it should be buttressed with the addition of other albums from the Virgin Records period—*Sorcerer, Firestarter, Phaedra, Force Majeure* and several others come to mind. —*Steven McDonald*

**Dream Roots Collection** / Nov. 6, 1996 / Castle +++
The *Dream Roots Collection* is a five-disc retrospective of Tangerine Dream's career, including one disc of previously unreleased material. All of the material on the collection has been remixed and reworked by Edgar Froese and his son Jerome, and while these remixes might not be historically accurate, they nevertheless retain the essence of the original versions, making the box an intriguing journey through the group's past. While the set is too extensive for casual listeners, hardcore fans will find the new mixes and rarities fascinating, making the set a worthwhile addition to their collection. [*The Dream Roots Collection* was reissued in early 2000.] —*Stephen Thomas Erlewine*

**Analogue Space Years 1969-1973** / Mar. 3, 1998 / Cleopatra ++++
*The Analogue Space Years '69-'73* is a definitive overview of Tangerine Dream's early, formative years, collecting highlights from the group's first

four albums (*Electronic Meditation*, *Alpha Centauri*, *Zeit*, and *Atem*). Though this wasn't their most consistent or effective period, and their mid- to late-'70s work is far more essential, it's a handy way for curious fans to discover essentially everything they need to know about Tangerine Dream's early career. —*Steve Huey*

**Mars Polaris** / Jul. 27, 1999 / Tangerine Dream ♦♦♦♦
Tangerine Dream had debuted on record the same year of the original Moon launch, and 30 years down the road, Edgar Froese and co. decided to dedicate a recording to the next step, the eventual landing of a man on Mars. The result, *Mars Polaris*, is what sounds like a surprisingly accurate rendering of the unmanned Mars Polar Lander's visit to the Red Planet (destined to arrive late in 1999), though the evocative atmospheres and gaseous effects are helped along by the equally descriptive titles "Mars Mission Counter," "Tharsis Maneuver," "The Silent Rock" and "Spiral Star Date." —*Keith Farley*

**Great Wall of China** / Jan. 25, 2000 / Tangerine Dream ♦♦♦
The greatest aspect of a soundtrack by this legendary German electronic new age ensemble is that you don't need the visuals to fully appreciate the music. Tangerine Dream has had success with both mainstream films like *Risky Business* and interesting documentaries like this, and brings a blend of mystery, haunting melancholy, and throbbing percussive energies to each scene depending on the necessity of the mood. The group is notorious for throwing stylistic curveballs, and it's ironic that only "Silence the Barking Monk" has any true Eastern tinge to it, with its hypnotic chimes and Asian-flavored string instruments. The rest of the collection ranges from the percussion-heavy, spacey symphonic "Meng Tian" (enhanced by emotional though distant ethnic vocal chant) to the contemplative, pop-oriented "Summer in Shauxi." It's all very interesting and enjoyable if you like TD already. But if you pick this one up thinking that the music's bound to be as exotic as the cover art, you might be a bit miffed. —*Jonathan Widran*

**Tang-Go** / Apr. 4, 2000 / EFA ♦♦♦♦
It would require several well-researched box sets to fully capture the whole three-decade Tangerine Dream experience, since the electronic ensemble began as the brainchild of Edgar Froese in the late '60s. But even picking 24 tracks for this compilation of the last ten years must have been a chore (albeit a lot of fun) due to the sheer volume of material released on both commercial American labels like Private and Miramar and others that saw the light of day mostly overseas. Overall, it's a solid representation of both the speedy, highly percussive electro jams and the more contemplative exercises like "Velvet Sun," which play like gentler pop tunes. Included are two tracks from 1999's most intriguing space-bound "Mars Polaris" project. Whether exploring the outer reaches or covering interesting topics like "Tyranny of Beauty," TD has never failed to set the pace with a beautiful yet cutting-edge sound. —*Jonathan Widran*

## Tarwater

f. 1995
*Group / Indie Rock, Post-Rock/Experimental*

Tarwater, a duo comprising Germans Bernd Jestram and Ronald Lippok, have recorded several albums of distinctive, mostly instrumental music tagged post-rock because of Lippok's involvement in To Rococo Rot—a German trio that has recorded for experimental independents such as Soul Static Sound and City Slang. Guitarist/bassist/programmer Jestram and drummer/vocalist/programmer Lippok met in an East German punk band and began recording together even while Lippok recorded with To Rococo Rot and Jestram worked in his Bleibeil studio. A bit more organic and much more tied to pop than To Rococo Rot, Tarwater debuted with 1996's *11/6 12/10*, released around the same time that Lippok's other concern issued their first material. *Rabbit Moon Revisited* (an EP of sorts) and Tarwater's second LP *Silur* followed in 1998. The critical praise attendant on the latter earned Tarwater American distribution, with *Animals, Suns & Atoms* appearing in the spring of 2000. —*John Bush*

**11/6 12/10** / 1996 / Kitty-Yo ♦♦♦♦
Tarwater's debut, supposedly the second in an album series given an inexplicable title *Solar Money System*, is an eclectic mix of post-electronica, heavier on the guitar than many in the German post-rock crowd but also reliant on some very creative sampling. *11/6 12/10* veers from detuned trip-hop damage to twangy Kraut-rock to even straightahead hard bop worthy of Pharoah Sanders. The production is exquisite, with an excellent balance of organic and artificial sound sources, though the many vocal turns are oddly detached as only the Germans can do it. —*John Bush*

**Rabbit Moon Revisited** / 1998 / Cap Stack ♦♦♦

• **Silur** / Sep. 28, 1998 / Kitty-Yo ♦♦♦♦
One of the best shots fired by the European post-rock brigade, *Silur* advances the focus on broad-ranging electronics from Tarwater's previous work to concentrate on Kraut-inspired mechanistic rhythms as a backdrop to an assortment of atmospherics ranging from scratchy '60s-pop samples, spoken-word passages, understated hip-hop turntablism, and some classic phaseshifter effects. —*John Bush*

**Animals, Suns & Atoms** / May 9, 2000 / Mute ♦♦♦
Tarwater's *Animals, Suns & Atoms* is yet another frequently fascinating LP from the Berlin duo, a combination of odd sounds and rhythms overlaid with a quintessentially European sense of decadent pop classicism. As on *Silur*, the sound is closer to Kraut rock or dub than straight-ahead electronics; most tracks have heavily echoed down-tempo drum programs with guitar pickings, spare piano lines, and various unrecognizable samples creating a dense backing. There's also a preponderance of vocal tracks; though occasionally endearing (check "All of the Ants Left Paris"), Lippok's vocals are hit-or-miss, and a few excellent productions are weighed down by his monotone Lou Reed fixation. Still, the Ween-on-Ecstasy style of "Early Risers" makes it a highlight, and though *Animals, Suns & Atoms* isn't an immediately rewarding album, the duo's skewed, ambitious production aesthetic makes more sense after several listens. —*John Bush*

## James Taylor Quartet

*Producer / Club/Dance, Acid Jazz, Soul-Jazz*

Reportedly the band whose music coined the term acid jazz (when a British journalist struggled to describe it), the James Taylor Quartet has explored spy-soundtrack soul-jazz and funk from the group's beginnings in the mid-'80s. Originally playing the Hammond B-3 organ in the UK mod-revival band the Prisoners, James Taylor formed his own jazz quartet in 1985 and began playing music similar to the rare-groove jazz-funk then in vogue around London. By the early '90s, that movement had spawned acid jazz, and the James Taylor Quartet found itself at the forefront of a vibrant young club scene, even though Taylor was a decade-long veteran by that time.

The Prisoners had emerged from Kent in 1982 and released two albums, *A Taste of Pink* and *The Wisermiserdemelza*, before Taylor quit in the mid-'80s (the group imploded after just one more studio album). Taylor quickly formed a quartet around ex-Prisoner Allan Crockford on bass, drummer Simon Howard, and James' own brother David on guitar.

The James Taylor Quartet recorded for several small labels during 1985, but a 1986 session for Radio 1 DJ John Peel got the group signed to Re-Elect the President Records, which released a 1987 mini-LP of covers, *Mission Impossible*. After *The Money Spyder* appeared that same year, the James Taylor Quartet moved to Urban/Polydor for 1988's *Wait a Minute*. Not long after, however, Howard and Crockford left to play with another ex-Prisoner, Graham Day, in the Prime Movers. Now just a duo, James and David began recruiting studio musicians to fill in the instrumental gaps from album to album, later building the band up to a sextet (though the name stayed the same) with John Willmott on saxophone and flute, bassist Gary Crockett, drummer Neil Robinson, and trumpeter Dominick Glover. A contract with Acid Jazz Records resulted in increased American distribution through Hollywood Records, which reissued *Mission Impossible* and *The Money Spyder* as well as the group's 1995 album *In the Hand of the Inevitable*. *The Penthouse Suite* followed in the spring of 2000. —*John Bush*

• **The Money Spyder** / Aug. 1987 / Hollywood ♦♦♦♦
Constructed as a mock soundtrack, *The Money Spyder* does a good, convincing job at capturing the flavor of '60s spy flicks with its blend of jazzy rhythms, swelling Hammond organs, and dark, tasty guitar licks. The group gets a Booker T. & the MG's-meets-the Ventures sound on this set of instrumentals, with some Lalo Schifrin and film noir jazz thrown in the blender. Marketed as part of Hollywood Records' *Acid Jazz* line, it could catch the coattails of the lounge/space-age pop revival as well (though the JTQ have been doing this sort of stuff for years). —*Richie Unterberger*

**Get Organised** / 1989 / Polydor ♦♦♦

**In the Hand of the Inevitable** / 1995 / Hollywood ♦♦♦
*In the Hand of the Inevitable* alternates tracks residing on the more polished end of jazz-funk with diva vamps—on "Free Your Mind" and "Let's Get To-

gether"—more akin to house music. As on most of Taylor's previous albums, there's a lack of risk-taking that often relegates the tracks to the status of background music, but the mood throughout is pleasant enough. —*John Bush*

**Creation** / May 27, 1996 / Hollywood ♦♦
This Britster mixes up intelligent funk and thumpin' jazz for a truly classic album that should be placed in history as a revitalizing step for the jazz idiom. Taylor knocks out notes on a Hammond Organ and more sounds come from drums, bass, trumpet, guitar, sax and flute. While "acid jazz" supposedly was coined to describe James' output, it certainly does not carry the image of the jump-soul/hot jazz stew bubble in this cauldron. Taylor himself spells out the secret recipe: "Rude, hard funk—like all the Blaxploitation movies and cop shows—that's what we're aiming for." —*Thomas Schulte*

**The Penthouse Suite** / May 16, 2000 / Acid Jazz ♦♦♦
Hammond-driven British acid-jazz pioneer James Taylor knows how to funk out. His Quartet's first album since 1996's critically acclaimed recording, *Creation*, shows that after more than a decade of aggressive music-making the band is still not over the hill. Using the B-3 organ as a weapon, this album feels like one long car-chase movie, with a few sexy spies thrown in for good measure. While it is probably not as catchy as *Creation, Penthouse Suite* still manages to be charming, especially on the tracks that feature vocalist Neal McCoy, who seems to be channelling James Brown (surreally paired with flute on "Love the Life") and cranks the energy level up even one more notch. —*Stacia Proefrock*

## T.D.F.
f. 1996
*Group / Ambient Techno, Trip-Hop*
T.D.F. is one of the strangest and silliest musical experiments from a '60s icon in the '90s. Where Paul McCartney explored ambient house with the Fireman, Eric Clapton—who bills himself as "x-sample"—explores ambient new age and trip-hop as the guitarist for T.D.F, which also consisted of keyboardist/producer Simon Climie. The duo released their debut album, *Retail Therapy*, in March 1997. —*Stephen Thomas Erlewine*

● **Retail Therapy** / Mar. 11, 1997 / Warner Brothers ♦♦
*Retail Therapy* is a misguided, occasionally intriguing, venture into ambient, contemporary instrumental, and even drum'n'bass territory by T.D.F., a side project for Eric Clapton and keyboardist Simon Climie. Both musicians sound as if they decided on the concept of the album before actually listening to any electronica, which gives *Retail Therapy* a weird, canned atmosphere. They also didn't sit down to write full-fledged compositions; they jammed, recording whatever came to their minds—which means, of course, that the record is ambling where it should be provocative and meandering where it should be hypnotic. When the duo strays from atmospherics and works with the buzzing rhythms of drum'n'bass, they are more effective, but *Retail Therapy* remains a bland, colorless dead alley into electronic music from two musicians who don't comprehend its essence. —*Stephen Thomas Erlewine*

## Technical Itch
f. 1995, Bristol, England
*Group / Jungle/Drum'N'Bass, Club/Dance*
Bristol-based duo Technical Itch make leading-edge progressive drum'n'bass, incorporating the moodier elements of jump-up and techstep with a nod toward drum-twisting junglists such as Dom & Roland and the Penny Black label. Although Technical Itch's Darren Beale and Mark Caro (the latter originally of Birmingham) have deepest roots in the late-'80s hardcore breakbeat scene, their material both apart and together has tended toward the darkside, combining dense, unsettling atmospherics with complex, bruising drum patterns and deep subbass groans. The pair's most-used recording moniker derives (as does their home-run label) from their Bristol-based Tech Itch recording studio, but Caro and Beale have also recorded as Kutta (for Rough Tone), Decoder (for Tech Itch, Back2Basics, and Ruffneck Ting), T.I.C. (for Back2Basics), and Alpha Proxima (for Au Toi). The pair's earliest tracks came toward the peak end of the UK hardcore scene; both Beale and Caro were noted DJs, with Beale's recorded work as Orca adding to his notoriety. Introduced by a mutual friend, they released their first record together as Plasmic Life on Bizzy B's Brain Records, and by the early '90s were moving away from the conventions of hardcore, following breakbeat into the less static realms of

darkside and hardstep jungle. Still only a part-time collaboration, the pair's partnership deepened after Omni Trio's Rob Haigh heard a Tech Itch track on Kenny Ken's Kiss FM show, leading to their signing with Haigh's home-base Moving Shadow in 1996. The pair produced a number of singles as Technical Itch for the label that same year, with scores of tracks as Decoder and T.I.C. continuing to appear on their own and other labels, marking the pair as one of the more prolific (and increasingly influential) of the new crop. Though a Decoder full-length was first out of the gate in late 1998, Tech Itch's *Diagnostics* followed in 1999 on Moving Shadow. [See Also: Decoder] —*Sean Cooper*

**The Dreamer/Rough & Tough [Single]** / Dec. 2, 1996 / Moving Shadow ♦♦♦
A solid hardstep outing from the Bristolean duo and a bit lighter than their increasingly more abundant techstep tracks as Decoder. The B-side, "Rough and Tough," became the more popular of the two, a slight tech update of a stepping ragga tune. One for the toolbox. —*Sean Cooper*

**The Virus/Watch Out [Single]** / Mar. 3, 1997 / Moving Shadow ♦♦♦♦
"The Virus" is a dark, dark stormer of a techstep track, mixing Dom-style filter-fading breaks with deep, descending bass patterns and hissing electronics. The flip's "Watch Out" is a more illuminated affair, although mashed-up beats, nervous synth bleats, and a jittery bassline hardly make it more relaxed. Excellent. —*Sean Cooper*

● **Diagnostics** / 1999 / Moving Shadow ♦♦♦♦
Technical Itch's album debut hits the harder side of track-oriented drum'n'bass, heavy on the drum programming and fluid analogue bass. From the old-school burner "Arced" to even downtempo fare on "1310," the emphasis is on the tighter edge of classic hardcore filtered through mid-'90s jungle. —*John Bush*

## Techno Animal
f. 1993, London, England
*Group / Illbient, Experimental Techno, Electronica, Dark Ambient, Post-Rock/Experimental*
Frequent collaborators Kevin Martin and Justin Broadrick (who've worked together on such projects as God and Ice) make up Techno Animal, a beat-oriented ambient group who fuse elements of dub-style production with thick, slightly paranoid melodic themes and heavily treated electronic rhythms. Although both Martin and Broadrick have their fingers in a number of different ongoing projects (most notably God with the former and Godflesh and Final with the latter), Techno Animal represents their most clearly focused and successful outlet of electronics-based composition. The pair released a debut album, *Ghosts*, on Martin's Pathological label in 1994, followed by a double-CD on Virgin, *Re-Entry*, before signing with the Rising High subsidiary Blue Angel in 1996. *Techno Animal Versus Reality* followed in 1998. Closely associated with other post-industrial dub and dark ambient merchants such as Mick Harris (Napalm Death, Scorn) and Bill Laswell (Automaton, Silent Recoil), both Broadrick and Martin, like Harris and Laswell, have been involved in a wide array of different recording projects ranging from monochrome ambient to death-metal, industrial, and experimental jazz. Broadrick also doubles as a club DJ, and Martin works as a music journalist and critic, penning the liner notes to the celebrated *Macro Dub Infection* compilation and contributing regularly to new music magazines such as *The Wire* and *Alternative Press*. In 1999, the duo recorded the split-LP *Symbiotics* with Porter Ricks. —*Sean Cooper*

**Ghosts** / 1992 / Pathological ♦♦♦

**Re-Entry** / 1995 / Virgin ♦♦♦♦
A bit drawn out at two CDs, *Re-Entry* is a nonetheless pleasantly disorienting, infectious collection of dub-heavy experimental ambient. Split pretty evenly between uptempo beat-oriented tracks and droney, abstract, effects-laden material, the album is a nice introduction to dark, post-rave ambient dub. —*Sean Cooper*

**Unmanned [EP]** / 1996 / Chrome ♦♦
Aside from a handful of compilation tracks, the *Unmanned* EP on the recently established Force Inc. subsidiary Chrome is the first new Techno Animal release in nearly a year. Growth is pretty evident in the extreme, almost caustic treatments and textures employed across these four tracks, with loping, heavily dub-effected beats dragging along damaged, almost industrial synth drones. The result is more or less recognizable as the Techno Animal

of *Re-Entry* and "Babylon Seeker," but fans of their warmer, less oppositional approach should approach this one with caution. — *Sean Cooper*

- **Versus Reality** / Mar. 30, 1998 / City Slang ♦♦♦♦
Conceptually inspired by the pissing contests of Jamaican DJ sound clashes, *Techno Animal Versus Reality* pits Kevin Martin against Justin Broadrick; however, instead of spinning vinyl, they face off using hard discs consisting of original sounds contributed by the likes of Tortoise, Ui, Porter Ricks, Alec Empire, and Spectre. After getting the Techno Animal treatment, the tracks were then sent back to their respective creators for further reworking; the end result is five pairs of cuts, each thematically similar yet worlds removed in style and sensibility. Despite the quality of the guest producers, Techno Animal contributions like "Deceleration" and "Atomic Buddha" prove the best on the album. — *Jason Ankeny*

## Technotronic

f. 1988, Belgium
*Group / Club/Dance, Acid House, House, Dance-Pop*
Of the many studio-based dance music projects which dominated the charts during the early '90s, few were so popular, or such an improbable success story, as Technotronic. Emerging from Belgium—never a musical hotbed in the first place—the multicultural group helped push the deep bass grooves and insistent beats of house music out of the club scene and into the pop mainstream; ironically, they did so largely by hiding behind the photogenic visage of an African-born fashion model who, it was later revealed, did not even perform on their records. In reality, Technotronic was the brainchild of Jo Bogaert (real name Thomas de Quincy), an American-born philosophy teacher who relocated to Belgium in the late '80s in the hopes of mounting a career as a record producer. Bogaert's intent was to fuse house with hip-hop, and towards that aim he sent demos of his work to a variety of rappers, including the Welsh-born MC Eric and a Zairean-born teenager named Ya Kid K (nee Manuela Kamosi), at the time a member of the Belgian rap group Fresh Beat Productions.

Technotronic's first single, 1989's "Pump Up the Jam," was a smash hit across Europe and eventually the US. While the record featured the raps of Ya Kid K, she was nowhere to be seen in the accompanying video, which instead featured Zairean-born fashion model Felly lip-synching the lyrics; little did fans realize that not only was Felly nowhere near the studio at the time the single was recorded, in truth she did not even speak a word of English. She was also featured on the cover of Technotronic's debut LP, *Pump Up the Jam: The Album*, further blurring the lines between truth and fiction; in the end, Bogaert admitted that Felly's services had been engaged purely to establish the group with "an image." When Technotronic toured in support of the 1990 hit "Get Up! (Before the Night Is Over)," Ya Kid K and MC Eric were alone behind the microphone, and Ya Kid K was also rightfully featured in the song's video. The LP *Trip On This: The Remixes* soon followed, and in 1992 Ya Kid K went solo, albeit with Bogaert still in the producer's seat; her debut album, *One World Nation*, scored with the hit "Move This," originally a Technotronic cut released as a single after finding success in a cosmetics commercial. The 1995 Technotronic comeback attempt *Recall* was not a success. — *Jason Ankeny*

- **Pump Up the Jam** / 1989 / SBK ♦♦♦♦
Hip-house, a blend of rap and house music, had one of its greatest commercial successes in Technotronic (which brought a Euro-disco element to the style). *Pump Up the Jam: The Album* must be taken for what it is—unapologetically dance-oriented party music, pure and simple. Belgium's Technotronic never set out to conquer Public Enemy or Ice-T's socio-political turf, and strives to be nothing but fun. On that level, this CD succeeds wildly. "Pump Up the Jam," "Get Up (Before the Night Is Over)," "This Beat Is Technotronic" and other highly infectious club hits didn't do much in the rap or R&B markets, although Technotronic did enjoy some exposure outside of dance music circles thanks to the inclusion of "Move This" (also included here) in a 1992 Revlon commercial employing supermodel Cindy Crawford. But on the whole, this collection appealed primarily to Technotronic's target audience: dancers and club hounds. — *Alex Henderson*

**Trip on This: The Remixes** / 1990 / Capitol ♦♦♦

## Paul W. Teebrooke (Steve Pickton)

*Producer / Electronica, Ambient Techno*
Though it's not exactly clear why, Steve Pickton's 1997 LP for Op-Art Records was released under the pseudonym Paul W. Teebrooke. Pickton, who had already recorded as Stasis and Phenomyna, debuted Teebrooke with the 1996 single "Nova/Blue Light" for his friend Kirk Degiorgio's Op-Art label, then released *Connections* one year later. [See Also: Stasis] — *Jon Bush*

- **Connections** / Jun. 30, 1997 / New Electronica ♦♦♦♦
Paul W. Teebrooke is one of many pseudonyms of popular UK techno artist Steve Pickton, more commonly known as Stasis. Pickton's Teebrooke material is quite a bit more varied than his work as Stasis, mixing the beat-box breaks and acoustic percussion of electro and hardcore with minor-key synth pads and jazzy arrangements which also recall the work of B12 and label-mate Kirk Degiorgio (Degiorgio's Op-Art label released a Teebrooke EP in 1996). *Connections*, for its part, doesn't stray too far from this approach, although Pickton's use of driving, uptempo breaks *a la* Plaid and early LFO is surprising and well-conceived. — *Sean Cooper*

## Towa Tei (Doug Wa-Chung)

b. Tokyo, Japan
*Keyboards, Producer, DJ / Electronica, Club/Dance, Techno, Electronic, House*
Japanese-born DJ Towa Tei first earned notice for his production work on the Jungle Brothers' 1989 LP *Done by the Forces of Nature;* the following year he shot to fame as a member of the downtown New York club trio Deee-Lite, scoring an international hit with the classic "Groove Is in the Heart." After two LP's, 1990's *World Clique* and 1992's *Infinity Within*, Towa Tei left the group to begin working on solo projects; his debut LP *Future Listening!*, a montage of bossa nova, jazz and electronic dance music, appeared in 1995. His second album for Elektra, 1998's *Sound Museum*, was followed by *Last Century Modern* in 1999. — *Jason Ankeny*

**Future Listening** / Apr. 25, 1995 / Elektra ♦♦♦
Towa Tei weds easy-listening faux-jazz and Brazilian pop to a set of chunkier beats than they're used to on his debut album. Collaborators include Ryuichi Sakamoto, Arto Lindsay, and Laraaji on such tracks as the MPB chestnut "Batucada" and Towa Tei's own "I Want to Relax, Please." — *John Bush*

- **Sound Museum** / Feb. 24, 1998 / Elektra/Asylum ♦♦♦♦
Not many producers could juggle vocal tracks by Kylie Minogue and Biz Markie, plus a bossa nova cover of Hall & Oates' "Private Eyes," but Towa Tei does an excellent job of uniting a disparate mix of club-centric grooves. There are several highlights, but none better than Biz Markie's sprightly, infectious "BMT." — *John Bush*

**Last Century Modern** / Sep. 21, 1999 / Wea International ♦♦♦♦
Towa Tei's third album returns to the eclecticism of his first, with bossa nova lounge ("A Ring"), drum'n'bass soul ("Angel", "Butterfly"), Ryuichi Sakamoto-like ethnic forgery ("Stretch Building Bamboo"), and silly sampladelic house ("Congratulations!," which samples somebody saying "The finest turntable in the world" until the all the words become meaningless). Once again, Tei assembles an impressive roster of guest musicians and gleefully watches what happens when they meet. Japanese chanteuse UA, accordionist Coba, and the Balanescu Quartet open the album with the sophisticated title track. Elsewhere on the CD, Pascale Borel, Les Nubians, and Chara add vocals, and two thirds of YMO, Harry Hosono, and Yukihiro Takahashi turn up as well. The album is also surprisingly short—and is the stronger for it. The American release adds remixes of "Butterfly" and "Let Me Know" by Cornelius and Mighty Bop, respectively. — *Ted Mills*

## John Tejada

b. Vienna, Austria
*Producer, DJ / Minimal Techno, Experimental Techno, Club/Dance, Techno*
Born the son of a Vienna composer/conservatory teacher and an opera-singer mother, John Tejada joined Cosmic Baby and BT as classically trained techno changelings. Unlike those producers however, Tejada's recordings for Plug Research and A13 emphasize the rougher, more melancholy aspects of techno inspired by Detroit icons like Juan Atkins and Derrick May. Raised on the West Coast, Tejada played piano and drums as a child, then began listening to hip-hop and electro, beginning his DJ career by playing out in those styles. After hearing the Detroit techno blueprints courtesy of recordings by Atkins and May, Tejada began producing; during 1996 alone, he recorded two singles for A13 Records (as Lucid Dream) and an EP for Electric Ladyland (as Autodidact). Early the following year, his debut Lucid Dream album *Pure* appeared, followed by a single for Plug Research as Mr. Hazeltine. After the

1997 *Plug Research & Development* compilation earned kudos around the home-listening techno community, Tejada formed his own label Palette Records, collaborated with Joe Babylon of Plug Research and Allen Avan as Frankie Carbone and recorded on his own for Organised Noise, Ferox and 7th City. His first album *Little Green Lights and Four Inch Faders* appeared in 1999 on A13 Records. —*John Bush*

**Mr. Hazeltine EP: On the Avenue** / Aug. 24, 1998 / Plug Research ♦♦♦
● **Little Green Lights and Four Inch Faders** / Apr. 12, 1999 / A13 Productions ♦♦♦♦

*Little Green Lights and Four Inch Faders* displays Tejada's obvious affection for the moodier sides of Detroit techno and electro, with the string effects and strong melodies that come with it. —*John Bush*

## Tek 9

f. 1991, London, England
*Group / Trip-Hop, Jungle/Drum'N'Bass, Club/Dance*

While not crafting house-inspired intelligent jungle with his partner Mark Mac as 4 Hero, Dego McFarlane records ragga/trip-hop and drum'n'bass as Tek 9. The side-project began in 1991, after 4 Hero had released four EPs on the duo's Reinforced label. Dego initially recorded the *Kingdom of Dub* EP, and then recorded (with Manifest and Cheewa toasting over the top) the raggamuffin classic "A London Sumtin'" as Code 071—though the single appeared later as Tek 9. During 1993-94, Dego worked only sparingly as Tek 9 while running his Tom & Jerry label and working on 4 Hero material. He later returned to the project with several EPs—*The Return of Tek 9, 'Breakin Sound Barriers, Killing Time*—and in 1996 released Tek 9's debut album, *It's Not What You Think It Is!!?!*. The album charted a mellower course than the early EPs, concentrating more on downtempo hip-hop and house than ragga jungle. After a busy two years working on 4 Hero material, Dego returned in late 1999 with the second Tek 9 LP, *Simply*. —*John Bush*

● **It's Not What You Think It Is!!?!** / Mar. 4, 1996 / SSR/Crammed Discs ♦♦♦♦

Though Dego is helped by a varied cast of collaborators—Manifest & Cheewa, his partner Mark Mac, even Butterfly of Digable Planets in an uncredited vocal—this album is his and his alone. *It's Not What You Think It Is!!?!* mostly consists of futuristic hip-hop, with Dego winding sampled raps around occasional live contributions. When not edging into rap, the album is split between easy-listening/R&B—on vocal tracks with divas Carol Crosby and Kinnor Eve—and the relative underground appeal of darkstep jungle, on "Beast Within," "74 Above Sea Level," and "Spring." It's difficult to appreciate the innovative breakbeats when they're sandwiched between muzaky sex-talk, and the album mostly fails because of it. The true highlights come only on the CD edition: the bonus of a second disc containing 13 tracks of Tek 9's ragga breakbeats. —*John Bush*

**Simply** / Oct. 11, 1999 / SSR ♦♦♦

After the rise in public acclaim garnered by his day job (4 Hero), Dego returned to his side-project Tek 9 with the sophomore album *Simply*. The title is a sure clue to the sound, considering the LP consists of straight-ahead hip-hop with few frills and a light, jazzy atmosphere. Guests on *Simply* include eight MCs (mostly American) such as Opio from Souls of Mischief, Chase Infinite, What? What?, Rob Yancey, and Capital A, among others. After the overly produced and overly intelligent nature of 4 Hero material, it's good to see Dego getting back to the tough, hard-hitting production style that made his name with 4 Hero. —*John Bush*

## Telex

f. 1978, Brussels, Belgium, **db.** 1988
*Group / Euro-Pop, Synth-Pop, Disco*

Telex was a synth-disco trio formed in Brussels Belgium in 1978 by keyboardist Marc Moulin, who had previously performed with Cos. He was joined by vocalist Michel Moers and composer/synthesist Dan Lacksman, and together, Telex crafted a slick, stylish brand of Euro-pop/disco with relaxed tempos and often processed vocals. Their debut album, *Looking for Saint-Tropez*, was released in 1979, containing signature songs like the title track, "Moskow Diskow," and slowed-down covers of "Rock Around the Clock" and Plastic Bertrand's "Ca Plane Pour Moi." *Neurovision* (1980) and *Sex* (1981) followed, with the latter employing lyricists Ron and Russell Mael. (A 1982 UK-only release, *Birds and Bees*, contains all but three of *Sex's* tracks, plus several singles.) Nothing much was heard from the group after 1984's *Wonderful World* until 1988, when *Looney Tunes* displayed an about-face towards goofy, effects-laden electronic music somewhat akin to the Art of Noise or Yello. The band broke up soon after, though all three members also released material. Ten years later, long after all Telex material had gone out of print, the band received the remix-album treatment on SSR's *I Don't Like Music (Remixes)*, featuring a host of new-school electronic producers like Carl Craig, Buckfunk 3000, Patrick Pulsinger, and Glenn Underground. A separate disc, *I Don't Like Remixes*, presented the Telex originals. The set proved so popular that a second remix disc, *I (Still) Don't Like Remixes, Vol. 2*, was released the following year. —*Steve Huey*

**Looking for Saint-Tropez** / 1979 / Sire ♦♦

**Neurovision** / 1980 / Sire ♦♦

**I Don't Like Music (Remixes)** / Nov. 2, 1998 / Disko B ♦♦♦♦

Though dozens of remix albums hit the racks in the late-'90s, the great majority came to fruition as a result of major-label campaigns as a great way to attract prestige (and perhaps even a bit of money). Undoubtedly the most obscure act to get the remix treatment, forgotten '80s synth-popsters Telex received their due as a result of genuine enthusiasm regarding a band's catalog by a host of electronic producers. Considering that the figures who lined up for this project—Glenn Underground, Carl Craig, Shake, I:Cube, Dr. Rockit, Ian O'Brien, Buckfunk 3000 among others—are all at the top of their game, *I Don't Like Music (Remixes)* is a stellar collection of Telex classics given the quintessentially post-modern touch. —*John Bush*

● **I Don't Like Remixes (Original Classics 78-86)** / Nov. 9, 1998 / SSR ♦♦♦♦

The out-of-print Telex catalog gained a boost in late 1998 with the timely release of this 20-track collection—the companion to *I Don't Like Music (Remixes)*—including angular, disco-inspired synth-pop nuggets like "Moskow Diskow," "I Don't Like Music," and "Peanuts," plus covers of "Rock Around the Clock," Sly Stone's "Dance to the Music," and Sparks' "Brainwash." —*John Bush*

**I Don't Like Music (Remixes, Vol. 2)** / Jun. 21, 1999 / SSR ♦♦♦

## Ten City

f. 1987, Chicago, IL
*Group / Club/Dance, House, Dance-Pop*

The Chicago vocal group Ten City was one of the few house units to enjoy mainstream exposure during the late '80s and early '90s. Originally called Ragtyme, the trio was formed by vocalist Byron Stingily, guitarist Herb Lawson, and keyboard player Byron Burke, all under the aegis of producer extraordinaire Marshall Jefferson. After signing with Atlantic in the late '80s, Ten City's debut LP *Foundation* included the singles "Right Back to You" and "That's the Way Love Is," both of which received a good response in R&B and dance circles. *State of Mind* and *No House Big Enough* followed in 1990 and 1992, though Atlantic dropped them soon after. Just after release from their contract, the single "Fantasy" (written with Masters at Work) did well on the club scene, but by the time Ten City released their third album *That Was Then, This Is Now* the buzz had disappeared. The group rapidly disintegrated, though Stingily went on to a solo career. —*Ron Wynn*

● **Foundation** / 1989 / Atlantic ♦♦♦♦

Retro and proud of it, Ten City was among the most impressive "deep house" acts to come out of Chicago in the late '80s. Like others playing deep house, these guys enthusiastically recall the great soul/disco of the mid- to late '70s and make no secret of their love of that era. Ten City clearly realizes that the best disco emphasized vocal personality as well as danceability, and like the music of the Trammps, Tavares, and Double Exposure before them, *Foundation* is appropriate for listening as well as dancing. "That's That Way Love Is" (City's best known single), "Suspicious," "Devotion," and other songs on this absorbing debut album aren't simply about the beat and the track, but also the rich vocals that would have sounded great even if Ten City had gone a cappella. *Foundation* was a smash in the clubs, but unfortunately didn't do that much in the R&B or pop markets. This is a group that deserves to be much better known. —*Alex Henderson*

**State of Mind** / 1990 / Atlantic ♦♦♦♦
Improved singing, elaborate productions. —*Ron Wynn*

**No House Big Enough** / 1992 / Atlantic ♦♦♦

**That Was Then, This Is Now** / May 17, 1994 / Columbia ♦♦♦♦
Led off by "Fantasy," their biggest clubland hit in years, third album *That Was Then, This Is Now* presents a resurrected Ten City with both feet firmly planted in the world of mainstream house and dance-pop. There are plenty of uninhibited workouts for Byron Stingily's amazing voice on "The Way You Make Me Feel," "Love in a Day," and "What My Love Can Do," but signals of the end also come with the bittersweet productions on "Joy and Pain" and "When I'm Gone, I'm Gone." Despite the fact that it was their last, *That Was Then, This Is Now* is the best Ten City album since their debut five years earlier. —*Keith Farley*

## Danny Tenaglia
b. Brooklyn, NY
*Keyboards, Remixing, Producer, DJ / Garage, Club/Dance, House*
Danny Tenaglia has remixed and produced several sizeable club hits but still remains most well-known for his DJ residencies at the top New York clubs of the 1990s—including *Twilo* (previously *Sound Factory*) and *the Tunnel*—plus a spate of mix albums, several of his own LPs, and a publicized feud with fellow super DJ Junior Vasquez. Raised in Brooklyn, he listened to Motown and the Philly sound as a child, and learned to play guitar and saxophone. At the age of 12, however, a friend introduced him to the world of DJ mixtapes and Tenaglia became fascinated with mixing techniques. He began hustling tapes on the street and, when he was old enough, hit the Manhattan club-scene with gusto. Coming of age in the late '70s introduced him to the club and DJ often cited as the best of all time, the Paradise Garage and Larry Levan. Tenaglia spent much time observing Levan, and began his own DJ career soon after. Though he moved to Miami in 1985 to escape a glut of New York DJs, he was back by 1990, right on the cusp of a new house renaissance led by producers like Masters at Work and Frankie Knuckles, and the output of Strictly Rhythm and Nervous Records.

Tenaglia had begun producing in the mid-'80s during his spell in Miami (a single from his deepstate project signed to Atlantic and he also worked with Murk's Ralph Falcon) so by the time of his return to New York, he was quite comfortable in the studio. Tenaglia productions began appearing on labels like Minimal, Sexy, Tribal, and Strictly Rhythm; he really hit the mainstream with a 1993 remix of the Daou's "Surrender Yourself," a house epic which pioneered the harder underground sound which stormed Manhattan clubland (and therefore, most of America's dance scene) during the mid-'90s. With friend Junior Vasquez, Tenaglia was the city's most popular DJ and his residency at Twilo became legendary as the home of the most emotional dance music being mixed anywhere.

Cementing Danny Tenaglia's connection with Tribal Records America was the 1994 club hit "Bottom Heavy"; it also led to abundant remix work for Madonna, Michael Jackson, Pet Shop Boys, Grace Jones, Jamiroquai, New Order, and Lisa Stansfield, among others. His debut album, 1995's *Hard & Soul*, did well, and Tenaglia hosted several Tribal mix albums, including two volumes in the *Mix This Pussy* series plus *Gag Me with a Tune*. His second proper album *Tourism* was released in 1998. *Global Underground: Athens* and *Back to Mine* followed in 1999. —*John Bush*

**Hard & Soul** / Mar. 21, 1995 / Capitol ♦♦

**Gag Me with a Tune** / Oct. 8, 1996 / MCA ♦♦♦♦
Danny Tenaglia's *Gag Me with a Tune* is an infectious dance-mix album that segues a number of well-known club hits—including Cevin Fisher's "The Way We Used To," Mike Dunn's "We Kan Never Be Satisfied," and Cassanova's Revenge's "Banji Dance"—and features vocals by dance divas like Shay Jones, Judy Albanese, and Daphne, who starred in the Broadway hit *Rent*. All of the source material was released on Maxi Records, and the album is a testament not only to Tenaglia's talents as a DJ but also to Maxi's innovative roster of artists. —*Stephen Thomas Erlewine*

**Color Me Danny: A Collection of Best Remixes** / Jul. 15, 1997 / MCA ♦♦♦
Though his proper debut album *Hard & Soul* showed him to be a more than competent producer, it is as a remixer and DJ that Danny Tenaglia is best known; this double-disc set includes some of his most priceless mixes (several on CD for the first time), including versions of the Daou's "Surrender Yourself" and the Pet Shop Boys' "Before." —*John Bush*

• **Tourism** / May 19, 1998 / MCA ♦♦♦♦
With a host of productions that push all the right buttons for fans of mainstream house, *Tourism* sounds like a record made by a DJ who's been in the business for over a decade. By recruiting a wide range of vocalists (Teena Marie, Liz Torres, Jo-Jo America) and relying on a similarly varied list of styles (from garage to house to even industrial of a sort), Tenaglia makes *Tourism* just as enjoyable as one of his mix sets at Twilo or the Tunnel. —*John Bush*

**Global Underground: Athens** / Jul. 6, 1999 / Global Underground ♦♦
The variety of musical styles Danny Tenaglia spins—such as Swedish percussive techno, dark house, tribal house, vocal house, and electro—on his *Global Underground* album may not be quite what loyal fans of this otherwise homogeneous trance series would probably expect. Open-mindedness is a postive attribute in most cases, but here Tenaglia just may take variety a bit too far. There is no questioning Tenaglia's effortless ability to move from one musical terrain to the next, as he no doubt does during his extended club acts in Manhattan; unfortunately, he moves freely from one style to the next far too suddenly on this album to establish any sort of strong mood. The first set begins with a slowly evolving track of modulating dub techno by Stereo Danger and eventually crosses many different variations of deep and dark tones before concluding with more percussive techno similar in style to the set's beginning. Tracks by Joel Mull and EBE kill the playful attitude established mid-set with an a cappella mix of Tenaglia's "Music Is the Answer" laid over Dahlback & Krome's "The Real Jazz." The set then concludes with a comical sex romp from Miss Kitten and then some smooth electro. The second set begins with Tilt's "Seduction of Orpheus" and Cari Lekebusch's "Stealin' Music" before Tenaglia smoothly mixes in St. Etienne's beautiful "Cool Kids of Death." Tenaglia again navigates smoothly through many variations of percussive house before concluding with some trance. In sum, though, even his truly amazing ability to mix these many different styles of music together so well can't smooth out his inability to stick with a consistent mood on *Athens*. —*Jason Birchmeier*

**Back to Mine** / Oct. 25, 1999 / DMC ♦♦♦
After a spate of increasingly generic mix albums released during the late '90s, the DMC label spun the idea in an interesting new direction. The world's leading DJs, beginning with Danny Tenaglia, compiled collections of their favorite downtempo tracks suitable for chill-out rooms, late-night apartment parties, and all those long, tedious drives to and from clubs. Tenaglia's volume includes downbeat house tracks from some excellent producers, including Herbert, the Gentle People, Outside, and Bang the Party. Tenaglia also shows his age (that's a good thing) with a few tracks from older names—Roy Ayers ("Running Away"), Sergio Mendes ("One Note Samba/Spanish Flea"), CeCe Peniston ("Keep on Walkin"), and Yello ("To the Sea"). The vibes are laidback and just right, proving Tenaglia knows his way around living rooms just as well as dance floors. —*John Bush*

## Jimi Tenor
b. Finland
*Producer / Electronica, Ambient Techno, Trip-Hop, Club/Dance*
Best described as techno's first cabaret star, Finland native Jimi Tenor is what you might imagine Detroit's answer to a cheesy lounge artist to be. Coming off as a kind of lo-fi Prince cross-bred with Maurizio, Atom Heart, and perhaps Jean-Jacques Perrey, Tenor's recordings are released through Sahko/Puu (home to most of the scant Finnish techno scene); despite the fact that they stick out of the label roster like a sore thumb, they have attracted something of a devoted cult following, mainly among the idm/electronica crowds. Unlike most electronica artists, however, who routinely namecheck Kraftwerk, Juan Atkins, and Carl Craig as influences, Tenor leans more toward names like Barry White, Isaac Hayes, and '70s B-movie and blaxploitation soundtracks. Classically trained, Tenor gained the attention of influential Sheffield label Warp after releasing the full-length *Europa* in 1996, leading to a recording deal and reissue plans for some of Tenor's Sakho releases. Warp featured the previously unavailable Tenor cut "Downtown" on their *Blechsdottir* label comp, and released the 7"/CD-single "Can't Stay with You Baby" a few months later, with two additional singles appearing in early 1997.

Prior to his solo work, Tenor fronted Jimi Tenor and His Shamans, who starting in 1988 released several albums on the Poko, Euros, and Bad Vugum labels (including *Total Capacity of 216*, *5 Litres*, *Diktafon*, and *Fear of a Black Jesus*, which included 3-D sleeve and glasses). Despite the studied imperfection of his recordings (Tenor chides modern electronic music for sounding lifelessly exacting), he spent 12 years studying piano, flute, and saxophone at a Finnish music institute. After dissolving the Shamans in the late '80s, Tenor moved to New York, where he worked as a tourist photographer at the Empire State Building. He finally hooked up with Sahko after receiving a copy of a solo recording by Mika Vainio (of Panasonic and ÿ). Impressed with the label's openness to experimentalism (Sahko had previously been known as something of the muso's minimalist techno label), Tenor sent along some tapes and landed a recording contract, releasing his debut, *Sahkomies*, in 1994. While in New York he also recorded with Khan/4E's Can Oral (under the name Bizz O.D.), releasing the "Traffic" single on Ozon in 1995. Tenor returned to Finland in 1995 to film a documentary of Sahko (funded, oddly enough, by a government grant) and has remained there since, releasing *Europa* in 1996 and securing licensing and recording arrangements with Warp. The full-length *Intervision* was released in 1997 and *Organism* followed in 1999. *Out of Nowhere* arrived a year later. —*Sean Cooper*

**Europa** / 1995 / Sahko ✦✦✦
A full-length collection of short, occasionally quite brilliant meditations on techno-lounge, similar in effect to Money Mark's Mo'Wax collection *Mark's Keyboard Repair* or someone's approximation of *Switched On Esquivel*. *Europa*'s original release on Sahko was an almost instant underground classic. —*Sean Cooper*

**Can't Stay with You Baby [Single]** / Nov. 18, 1996 / Warp ✦✦
Tenor in full-on pimp-daddy form, all downbeat disco, Hammond B-3, and breathy sass. Released as a limited edition 7" picture sleeve as well as on CD-single, "Can't Stay with You Baby" is one of the odder entries in the Warp discography but rates alongside any number of Tenor's—though perhaps a bit more fleshed out and varied. The b-side is a spattery, rave-up of a version of Duke Ellington's classic "Caravan." —*Sean Cooper*

● **Intervision** / Mar. 10, 1997 / Warp ✦✦✦✦
Tenor's lead-up singles to his full-length Warp debut—"Outta Space" and "Can't Stay With You Baby," as well as the track "Downtown," included on the Warp mixed session *Blechsdottir*—only hinted at where he'd head with this album. An almost uncharacteristically schmaltz-less collection of minimal electronic jazz, *Intervision* blends fat organ leads with horns, raw and treated vocals, and rhythmic and percussive figures drawn from '60s and '70s soul, funk, fusion, and psychedelia, as well as contemporary house, downbeat, and techno. Oddly (or not), the album was recorded using only ancient Russian analog gear, in a former Communist dance hall. —*Sean Cooper*

**Organism** / Feb. 22, 1999 / Sire ✦✦
Jimi Tenor's American debut benefits from better overall production than his previous album, but remains—for better and for worse—just as wildly varied from track to track. His basic fixations with electro, disco, and funk inform nearly every track, from the chorus-driven Parliament updates "Total Devastation" and "Year of Apocalypse" to the sinister "Planet Rock"-style synth on "Serious Love." Tenor even steps into seriously schmaltzy quiet-storm territory on "Sleep" and "City Sleeps." (Though the prospect of a heavily accented Finnish producer doing his Barry White impersonation is difficult to take with a straight face, it was probably intended as such.) As well-produced and musically intriguing as it is, *Organism* suffers from Tenor's instinct to take on a different genre with each track, making for a few enjoyable period pieces on an album that means less and less with each listen. —*John Bush*

**Out of Nowhere** / Jul. 25, 2000 / Matador ✦✦✦✦
What's an ambitious young dance producer to do when he reaches the artistic limits of his samplers and synth after just four albums? The answer, at least for Jimi Tenor, is to hire an orchestra—specifically, the Orchestra of the Great Theatre Lodz, Poland—to help perform his new songs. Listeners fearing a dodgy classical crossover may be surprised that Tenor actually manages to pull this one off, basically by retro-fitting the orchestra into the kind of easy listening-funk big band so popular during the early '70s. Though the opener sounds like a chaotic Stan Kenton Orchestra soundtrack to some Cold War nightmare of a film, Tenor quickly slips into his usual lounge persona and sounds completely at home behind these wall-of-strings productions complete with plenty of vintage synthesizers and heavy, funky basslines. On the highlight "Spell," he imagines Caetano Veloso crooning a love song over "Theme From Shaft," complete with a sitar solo to close out the piece. On "Paint the Stars," Tenor vamps like a drugged-up Beck while a parade of fragile, plucked strings create a musical atmosphere behind him straight out of Disneyland. And he doesn't seem cowed by the thought that dozens of musicians are following his every move; he takes them straight into a trip through uproarious metal-funk on the instrumental "Blood on Borscht." There's a heavy dichotomy on *Out of Nowhere*, the competing forces being Tenor's overweening musical ambition and his utter lack of vocal talent (which isn't to say he's not a solid performer). Strangely though, Tenor makes it work, often in a similar fashion to orchestral indie rockers like Mercury Rev or Flaming Lips. —*John Bush*

## Dr. Fiorella Terenzi

*Vocals, Synthesizer / Process-Generated, Progressive Electronic*
Transcribing the music of the cosmos for the residents of terra firma, Italian astrophysicist Dr. Fiorella Terenzi utilized groundbreaking techniques to produce actual sound through the conversion of radio waves received from distant galaxies. Resembling nothing so much as the musical oddities of space-age pop figures like Esquivel or Bruce Haack, she gained a doctorate in physics at the University of Milan but studied opera and composition as well. After teaching mathematics and physics in Milan, she ventured to the University of California at San Diego's Computer Audio Research Laboratory and began working on different ways to classify celestial objects.

After Terenzi recorded *Music from the Galaxies* for Island, she gained an appreciable profile through appearances in the pages of *Time*, *People*, *Glamour*, and the *Wall Street Journal*. She also hit the lecture circuit in America, Europe, and Asia, earning praise from television wit Dennis Miller, who called her "a cross between Carl Sagan and Madonna." Terenzi also collaborated with the copacetic Thomas Dolby, and appeared on a tribute album for another noted recording artist with scientific credentials, Timothy Leary. —*John Bush*

● **Music from the Galaxies** / 1991 / PolyGram ✦✦
Combining her passion for music with a remarkable scientific discovery that heavenly objects emit radio waves which are very similar to musical notes, Dr. Fiorella Terenzi took data from a radio galaxy known as UGC 6697 and translated it into frequencies that can be heard by humans, then played it on a synthesizer. Whooshes, buzzing, oscillating frequencies, and deep didjeridoo-like drones combine to sound like nothing else on the planet—or in space. This is not music in a traditional sense; there is no melodic development or harmony, except on the last track, "Cosmic Time," where our friendly UGC 6697 is accompanied by harp, hand drums, and synthesizers for a lovely fusion of earth and space. If you've ever wondered what it sounds like out in space, or have an adventuresome ear, listen to the real space music. —*Backroads Music/Heartbeats*

## Todd Terry

b. Apr. 18, 1967, Brooklyn, NY
*Mixing, Producer, DJ / Garage, Club/Dance, House*
More than any other producer, Todd Terry defined New York house during the '80s, a varied sampladelic smorgasbord blending the sounds of classic disco, the more introspective Chicago sound pioneered earlier in the decade plus plenty of hip-hop attitude and sampling piracy. And with two of the most respected crossover remixes of the house era ("I'll House You" by the Jungle Brothers and "Missing" by Everything But the Girl), Terry more than earned his title "Todd the God" (or occasionally, simply "God"). Though he's often been accused of recycling his own beats and effects (in his production work as well as the DJ booth) a bit too often for his own good, Todd Terry's immortality as a dance icon is assured.

Born in Brooklyn, Terry began DJing in the early '80s while still a teenager, spinning hip-hop at school events and on the street with a team called the Scooby Doo Crew. He increasingly listened to Italian disco as well, and when the house sound of Chicago dropped in the mid-'80s, Terry the DJ made an official switch to house music. In league with fellow New York DJ/producer/remixers "Little" Louie Vega and Kenny "Dope" Gonzalez, Terry borrowed the Masters at Work guise—which Vega and Gonzalez would later popularize—for one of his first big productions, the 1987 single "Alright Alright"; the single became a milestone on New York's early house scene. The Jungle Brothers, another crew of hip-hop heads who were beginning to stray into house, hooked up with Terry and the collaboration resulted in "I'll House You," one of the earliest and most high-profile fusions of hip-hop and house (popularized several years later by C&C Music Factory and Snap).

The added prestige transferred back to his own name for two wildly popular 1988 singles, "Weekend" and "Bango (To the Batmobile)," both released as the Todd Terry Project. Perhaps preferring the adoration of the faithful,

Terry later resorted to dozens of aliases for dozens of club hits—Black Riot's "A Day in the Life," Gypsymen's "Hear the Music," Royal House's "Can You Party," Todd Terry & the Countdown's "Flipside," Torcha's "Feel It," D.O.S.'s "House of Gypsies," Sound Design's "You Can Feel It," Tech Nine's "Slam Jam," and Static's "Dream It." Despite his wealth of released material, Terry remixed dozens of artists as well, including Sting, Björk, Janet Jackson, Tina Turner, Malcolm McLaren, Annie Lennox, Robert Plant, and Technotronic, among others. The British house boom of the early '90s provided Terry with many an overseas gig, including a high-profile residency at the London super-club Ministry of Sound. His proficiency on the decks became a minor sensation, causing several British journalists to describe him as "God."

Terry moved into label entrepreneurship in 1992 when he formed Freeze Records with William Socolov. (Several of Terry's early singles had appeared on Socolov's Fresh/Sleeping Bag label, also the home of rap acts like EPMD, Mantronix, and Nice & Smooth). Freeze became the obvious home for many of Terry's productions, including several volumes of his EP series *Unreleased Projects* beginning in 1992 and running through 1995.

That same year, Terry's remix of the erstwhile pop act Everything But the Girl became a worldwide smash, selling over three million copies and almost single-handedly reviving the duo's flagging career for a sleek new dancefloor incarnation. The British label Hard Times released the DJ gig *A Night in the Life of Todd Terry: Live at Hard Times* in 1995, while the flip-side of the coin, *A Day in the Life of Todd Terry* (including his best single and remix productions) appeared the following year. His next project, *Ready for a New Day*, provided more song-oriented fare, though still implicitly dance, with guest vocalists including Martha Wash, Jocelyn Brown, and Bernard Fowler. Terry made another artistic change-up, to LP-oriented drum'n'bass, with his 1999 album *Resolutions*, recorded for indie/electronica stalwart Astralwerks. —*John Bush*

**A Night in the Life of Todd Terry: Live at Hard Times** / 1995 / Hard Times ♦♦♦♦

Todd Terry selected and mixed this compilation of his usual DJ material from the club Hard Times, mostly including his own productions. —*John Bush*

**Weekend 95** / 1995 / Ore ♦♦♦

**A Day in the Life of Todd Terry** / Jul. 1, 1996 / Sound of Ministry ♦♦♦♦
There's little question that *A Day in the Life of Todd Terry* is one of the best albums of Terry's pioneering house ever released—it leads off with two of his best-known tracks, "A Day in the Life" and "I Hear the Music." And the rest of this compilation just reinforces his status as one of the best house producers of all time, from the uplifting vibes of "Clear Away the Past" and the tribal headrush of "Jungle Hot" to smoother tracks like "Teela's Theme." —*John Bush*

**Todd Terry Presents Ready for a New Day** / Jun. 17, 1997 / Logic ♦♦♦♦
Not quite as solid as Todd Terry's always excellent remixes and singles, *Ready for a New Day* still benefits from several collaborations, with divas Jocelyn Brown, Martha Wash, and Shannon, as well as male singers like Roland Clarke (from Urban Soul) and Bernard Fowler (the Peech Boys, Rolling Stones). The appearance of his previous single "Something Goin' On" is welcome, as are two tracks with moderate breakbeats. Though most of the album covers previous territory, that's hardly a problem for a producer of Terry's stature and longevity. —*John Bush*

**Sessions, Vol. 8: Todd Terry** / Aug. 1997 / Ministry of Sound ♦♦♦♦
Todd Terry mixes this double-disc set of predominantly American house and garage tracks, with contributions from Michael Watford, Nuyorican Soul, Kim English, Ultra Naté, Urban Spirits, and Kerri Chandler. —*John Bush*

**House Music Movement** / Jun. 22, 1999 / Mastertone ♦♦♦
Todd Terry's volume in the *House Music Movement* series includes a cool dozen of the tunes that have meant the most to him over the years, including quite a few of his own ("Ready for a New Day," "Somebody," and "Back to the Beat"), plus tracks by Shannon, Martha Wash, Kym Mazelle, and even a remix of the Lighthouse Family's "Question of Faith." It includes a bonus disc with interview material from fellow house legends Jesse Saunders, Little Louie Vega, and Frankie Knuckles. —*Keith Farley*

**Resolutions** / Jun. 29, 1999 / Astralwerks ♦♦♦♦
Though the idea of Todd Terry moving from his garage foundation into the realm of electronica and drum'n'bass necessitates quite a jump in the minds of mainstream dance fans, *Resolutions* isn't as radical a change of direction as some might fear. Yes, the album includes by far the darkest material Terry has ever recorded, much closer to Grooverider than Masters at Work. Even amidst the breakbeats and laser-sharp effects though, Terry's ineffable production style comes through again and again—from the trademark vocal bridge on "Let It Ride" to the infectious drumrush on "Blackout," this is a Todd Terry album without a doubt. For a producer who'd arguably been doing very similar material for several years (albeit great *sounding* material), *Resolutions* is an excellent album that can bring his old fans back into the fold even while it generates an entire new audience barely old enough to remember his most innovative tracks. —*John Bush*

★ **Todd Terry's Greatest Hits** / Feb. 22, 2000 / Warlock ♦♦♦♦♦
More of a full-fledged hits collection than Sound of Ministry's *A Day in the Life…*, *Todd Terry's Greatest Hits* includes all of the seminal house producer's earliest, best moments: "Bango (To the Batmobile)," "A Day in the Life," "I Wanna Go Bang," "Weekend," "Party People," and "Can You Party." What's even better is that the compilers avoided the rather dry atmosphere of a retrospective by drafting Anthony Acid to place the tracks into a continuous set and play with the mix a bit. Placed alongside needed retrospectives (like *Warp10+1*) of the Detroit and Chicago scenes, *Todd Terry's Greatest Hits* takes the immense claim of early-period New York house's raw pulse and street aesthetics, staking it halfway between disco and hip-hop. Listeners wanting a summation of what house music meant in the late '80s and '90s would be hard-pressed to find a better release than this one. —*John Bush*

## Test Dept.

f. 1982, London, England
*Group / Industrial*

More expressly political than their German counterparts Einstürzende Neubauten, Test Department followed the same tack: A creative use of the ethos in which diverse objects (including large amounts of scrap metal and power tools) can be used as instruments. Formed in London's New Cross in 1982 by Alistair Adams, Graham Cunningham, Tony Cudlip, Gus Ferguson, and Paul Jamrozy, the quintet became renowned for the staging of huge multimedia events at obscure venues—a railway works in Glasgow, a sand quarry, Cannon Street Station in London, a Welsh car factory—and their political agenda, which has included action against apartheid, the rise of neo-Nazism, and Britain's Criminal Justice Act. The quintet signed to Some Bizarre Records for 1984's *Beating the Retreat* and outlined their socialist agenda set to music on the following year's *Shoulder to Shoulder*, recorded with "the South Wales Striking Miners' Choir." After forming their own Ministry of Power label to organize multimedia events, Test Department released two records—*The Unacceptable Face of Freedom* and *A Good Night Out*—in a MOP/Some Bizarre conjunction, but struck out on their own with 1988's *Terra Firma*. Test Dept.'s sixth album, *The Gododdin*, was followed by their most scathing criticism of British politics, *Pax Britannica*, in conjunction with the Scottish Chamber Orchestra and Choir. After releasing albums for Jungle Records and Dossier, the group gained a contract with the American industrial label Cleopatra in 1994 and released the fruit of their early-'90s work on *Legacy (1990-1993)*. Signed to Cleopatra's subsidiary Invisible, Test Dept. released the new albums *Totality* (1995) and *Tactics for Revolution* (1998), as well as reissuing several previous works. —*John Bush*

● **Beating the Retreat** / 1984 / Thirsty Ear ♦♦♦♦
The British collective's first album (comprised of two EPs) shows them with a better range of industrial percussion and more of a sense of rhythm than their only true contemporary, Einsturzende Neubaten. Though the album has an aimlessness to it, the presence of several ambient tracks broadens the palate. —*Keith Farley*

**The Unacceptable Face of Freedom** / 1986 / Thirsty Ear ♦♦♦
Though they've jettisoned much of the pounding steel percussion of their early material in favor of martial drums, a few synthesizers, and some tape music, *The Unacceptable Face of Freedom* remains more focused on social critique of the British government and unfair union practice in keeping with their previous album (recorded with the South Wales Striking Miners Choir). —*Keith Farley*

**A Good Night Out** / 1987 / Ministry of Power/Some Bizarre ♦♦♦
An ostentatious display of performance art including some live material, *A Good Night Out* resets Test Dept.'s continuing socialist-minded exposé of Britain in all its negative facets, to the beat of military drummers and clanging percussion. —*Keith Farley*

**Ecstacy Under Duress** / Oct. 1995 / ROIR ♦♦♦
Test Dept. was a highly influential electronic outfit which definitely helped create the still-thriving industrial genre. Their use of primitive drumming and monotonous waves of metallic noise meant that the group was unappreciated when the songs that comprise the compilation *Ecstasy Under Duress* were originally recorded (1982-1983). But listening to their work nowadays shows that the band was definitely on to something; they were just victims of the before-their-time jinx. The music is rabidly primal and earthy, which is quite an accomplishment since that's not what one usually associates with today's industrial rock. Since all of the songs are similar in approach and sound, it's impossible to pick out particular highlights; it sounds as if it's one long song broken up by flashes of silence. Still, fans of today's industrial sounds should really check out where it all originated. —*Greg Prato*

**Tactics for Evolution** / Feb. 10, 1998 / Invisible ♦♦
This recording from the very important and influential Test Dept. may prove a difficult pill to swallow for diehard fans. Is this repetitive dance music, joining in on the electronica craze? Granted, their production flavors and samples keep much of the tracks dark and distant from neon disco hell, but from the liner notes, it seems Test Dept. is prepared to charge ahead into the techno fracas even if great "loss" is necessary. This album is difficult dance music with the occasional redeeming quality of pre-industrial electronic spice—consider this a better than average house record, but a lesser than expected Test Dept. record. Looking back on 17 years of peerless creation, it is sad to see Test Dept. culminating by fitting into a trendy genre. —*Thomas Schulte*

## Teste

f. 1992, Toronto, Canada
*Producer / Club/Dance, Techno*

Himadri Ghosh is that *other* Canadian techno don (besides Plastikman) to make an impact on the world's dancefloors. His singles "The Wipe" (as Teste) and "Visiora" (as Perceptrons) are certainly related to the cold minimalism of prime Plastikman material, though classical training—he's even composed for the National Ballet of Canada—has imbued his work with a degree of study. The son of two genetic engineers, Ghosh was trained in tabla, sitar, and voice (he's also related to several classical Indian musicians). An early hip-hop lover, Himadri nevertheless chose minimalist techno to make an impression, beginning in 1991 with the founding of Switch Records with Dave Huren.

One year later, the debut recording by Himadri and Huren's Teste project surfaced on Probe, the sublabel of Plastikman's own Plus 8 Recordings. "The Wipe" became a huge hit in North America and Europe, easily one of the biggest singles released on Probe. While further singles—"Regions" (by Teste) and "Trajectory Infinite" (as Turph)—appeared on Probe, the Switch label released excellent singles by his projects Perceptrons (with Huren) and Plasma Lamp (with P. Verma). Despite pressure from major labels to sign him to a contract, Himadri preferred to keep label and recordings to himself (and often releases free material via the label's website). The compilation *Switch Records 1992-1997: The Singles* has been one of Himadri's few forays into worldwide distribution (courtesy of Koch). He has also collaborated on Switch material with Can Oral and Dr. Walker, and released (through Switch) the *Alt.Noise* compilation with tracks by Merzbow as well as fellow Canadians PFD and Orphyx. —*John Bush*

• **Switch Records 1992-1997: The Singles** / Jul. 15, 1997 / TJSB ♦♦♦
Rounding up twelve Switch sides of the hardest Canadian techno, this compilation includes all the classics by Teste, Turph, Perceptrons, Sybaritic, Bladde—virtually all the aliases or co-projects from Toronto's master minimalist Himadri. —*Keith Farley*

## Terre Thaemlitz

b. Minnesota
*Producer, DJ / Experimental Techno, Ambient Techno*

New York-based composer Terre Thaemlitz is one of only a handful of significant American artists working in the new ambient vein. He's released the bulk of his material through the Instinct Ambient label, but has also issued tracks (under his own name and as Chugga) on his own Comatonse label and through others. Although Thaemlitz's entree into electronic came in a somewhat traditional fashion—as a house DJ—his explorations in electronic abstraction have been anything but, focusing on themes of abjection, alienation, fracture, and contradiction in his music. Thaemlitz's recorded work, collected on albums such as *Tranquilizer* and *Soil*, is closer in tone to ambient-leaning industrialists such as B. Lustmord, Carl Stone, and (some) Merzbow, as well as "deep listening" composers such as Pauline Oliveros and Robert Rich. He's also recorded with Bill Laswell, releasing *Web* in 1995 and done remix work for Interpieces Organization and the Golden Palaminos, among others.

Born in Minnesota and raised in Missouri, Thaemlitz moved to New York in the mid-'80s to pursue art scholarship at Cooper Union. Soon distracted by the growing New York house scene, he began DJing at drag balls and benefits, leading to an Underground Grammy for best DJ in 1991. Although primarly a dancefloor DJ, Thaemlitz's insistence upon integrating house music's more simplistic monotony with challenging, complicated breaks and references earned him an uneasy relationship with club promoters looking for DJs whose only commitment was the 4/4 beat. Retiring from club DJing in the early '90s (although he continues to spin experimental electronic music at art galleries, one-offs, and in other marginal contexts), Thaemlitz began making his own tracks, beginning with house but quickly moving into genre defying fusions of funk, soul, disco, and musique concrète, eventually settling into experimental ambient. One of his earliest works, "Raw from a Straw," in addition to limited release through his own Comatonse label, appeared on an early ambient compilation on Instinct and earned him an almost instant reputation. He's since fortified that with a pair of full-length releases remarkably free of many of the cliched conventions of club-driven ambient. He continues to support new talent through Comatonse, and in 1999 returned with *Replicas Rubato*. —*Sean Cooper*

• **Soil** / Jul. 25, 1995 / Instinct ♦♦♦♦
A flowing, shifting, almost timeless statement incorporating equal parts confusion and calm across six tracks of entirely beatless ambient. Thaemlitz' ability to infuse elements of immediacy and physicality into a measured, slowly evolving style, traditionally bogged down by either disinterested elitism or faux collectivist spirituality, figures him as one of America's most important contemporary composers, and a singular voice in new ambient. —*Sean Cooper*

**G.R.R.L.** / 1997 / Comatonse ♦♦♦
*G.R.R.L.* is perhaps simultaneously Thaemlitz' least and most conventional recording to date. Least since it completely departs from the style of abstract experimental ambient that has concerned most of his recorded output to date, and most since *G.R.R.L.* is itself a kind of committed genre study of a select cross-section of recent electronic dance music history. Running the listener through a constantly shifting but utterly staid itinerary of compositional styles—from minimal techno and drum'n'bass to '80s Chicago house and '90s garage—Thaemlitz is clearly up to something in his often ponderously faithful renderings. What precisely that is, however, remains completely opaque through much of the recording (save, perhaps, for "China Doll," an odd vocal techno rant which also lends its concept to the album's Thaemlitz-penned liner notes). —*Sean Cooper*

**Die Roboter Roboto** / Feb. 3, 1997 / Mille Plateaux ♦♦♦♦
Electro-acoustician Thaemlitz takes the long road around expectation for his Mille Plateaux debut, opting for a set of solo piano extrapolations from songs by German electro innovators Kraftwerk. Built on a high-clearing deck of post-industrial cultural analysis over the course of its seven-plus pages of liner notes, the music on the disc requires little in the way of explanation; Thaemlitz' sparse, inventive interpretations are pleasing enough on their own. Although the themes of classics such as "The Robots," "Space Lab," and "Computer World" are sometimes so obtusely stated as to elude recognition, Thaemlitz' inspired performances hardly make it a problem. —*Sean Cooper*

**Couture Cosmetique** / Apr. 22, 1997 / Caipirinha ♦♦♦♦
Terre Thaemlitz's reputation as one of the most consistently challenging and inventive American ambient composers gets a BIG shot in the arm with his fourth album-length release. Following close after *Die Roboter Ruboto*'s ponderous salon interpretations of Kraftwerk, *Couture Cosmetique* hazards perhaps Thaemlitz' most unflinching exploration of marginal identities through music to date, combining a queer theoretical thematic (transgendered sexuality, non-essentialist conceptions of identity constitution, etc.) in close parallel with what are becoming compositional signatures (residual properties of electronic sound synthesis, the inversion of harmonic and melodic structural relationships, etc.). Closest probably to his previous Instinct outing, *Soil*, *Couture Cosmetique* retains that album's sense of enervated disjointedness while upping the "challenging listen, Terre" ante considerably. More than worth the effort. —*Sean Cooper*

**Means from an End** / Feb. 10, 1998 / Mille Plateaux ♦♦♦♦
Thaemlitz' deepening descent into the obscure sonorities of hard disc recording is here pushed to new extremes. Compositionally, *Means From an End* focuses on the metaphoric reconstitution of meaning through the social field and is equal both in scope and sonic detail to the output of freeform academicians such as Francois Bayle and Jim Horton. But as challenging as the music is—fuzz, clicks, and thin sheets of off-putting digital synthesis constitutes much of the hour on offer here—it is among some of the most engaging and even, at times, touching of Thaemlitz' career (particularly the title suite, which closes out the disc). —*Sean Cooper*

## Theorem (Dale Lawrence)

b. Detroit, MI
*Producer / Minimal Techno, Detroit Techno, Ambient Techno, Techno*
Dale Lawrence has explored the flip-side of Motor City techno, constructing photographic negatives of the percussion-heavy dramatics of producers like Derrick May and Juan Atkins. Similar to his label-mate Richie Hawtin (aka Plastikman), Lawrence's productions as Theorem explore techno's relationship to ambient and dub with copious amounts of delay and echo and a melodic sense as hypnotic as it is discreet.

Born and raised in the Detroit area, Lawrence was surrounded by classic electronic music from an early age. He began recording his own productions in 1986 and moved to a downtown loft by 1992 to pursue a serious recording career with a collective of DJs and musicians. After contacting Hawtin to release some of their material however, the collective disbanded. Lawrence persevered and began recording for Hawtin's Plus-8 Records with a 1996 full-length, *Nano*.

The album reflected the continuing global influence of Basic Channel, a combination label/artist concern centered in Berlin. The city had long fostered a close kinship to Detroit, with the focus on echo-chamber dub and polar electronics also becoming evident in Hawtin's work as Plastikman. The development of a Plus-8 subsidiary named Minus (or M_nus) appeared well-suited for Theorem work. During 1998, Lawrence released four EPs in the *TH* series. Much of the work was compiled on CD the following year when Theorem's second full-length, *Ion*, appeared in May 1999. —*John Bush*

**Mantra One [Single]** / Nov. 17, 1997 / Plus 8 ♦♦

**Shift/MNML/Ring [Single]** / Apr. 27, 1998 / M_nus ♦♦

● **Ion** / May 31, 1999 / Minus ♦♦♦♦
The debut Theorem full-length is a set of seven lengthy techno dub pieces (collected from previous singles), just slightly more upbeat than material by labelmate Plastikman and conceptual compatriots at Berlin's Chain Reaction label. Like those artists, *Ion* is a very spatial recording; the timbres are predominantly faraway and echoing, Lawrence begins "Shift" by sampling passing cars while several tracks evoke the brittle sound of trains rumbling. Though the basslines are heavy and repetitive like dub, they move just a bit too slow to conjure up visions of Augustus Pablo or Lee "Scratch" Perry. Most often, *Ion* evokes a photographic negative of house music: all the melodies removed, with only the four-four beat and some 808 percussion left to fill the void. —*John Bush*

**Theorem vs. Swayzak [Single]** / 2000 / THX/Minus ♦♦♦
The collaboration between Detroit's Theorem and London's Swayzak results in a wonderful middle ground between Theorem's style of down-tempo techno, bordering often on dub or ambient techno, and Swayzak's style of moderately paced house, associated often with a sedate or tranquil edge. The side of the record featuring "Bad Hair Day" stays in the spirit of Swayzak's house tendencies, integrating a steady sense of 4/4 rhythm and a cheery piano-style riff. Conversely, the other side of the record, featuring "Break in at Apartment 205," sounds quite similar to Theorem's previous records and his partner Richie Hawtin's *Consumed* album. The song places a great degree of its emphasis on sweeping synth washes and a Roland 303-style melody that sounds like a futuristic acid line. Overall, this record sounds a bit divided and not entirely true to one style but does stay true to the two individual styles of the artists, who sound surprisingly complementary alongside one another. —*Jason Birchmeier*

## Thievery Corporation

f. 1994, Washington, D.C.
*Group / Electronica, Trip-Hop, Club/Dance, Acid Jazz*
Thievery Corporation make abstract, instrumental, mid-tempo dance music somewhere between trip-hop and acid jazz. The production duo of Rob Garza and Eric Hilton, Thievery Corporation released a few warmly received singles on their own Eighteenth Street Lounge Music label (named for their Washington, D.C. bar and nightclub) in 1996. Previously known primarily among acid-jazz and rare groove DJs, the group shot to minor celebrity when a track from one of their early 12"s appeared on respected DJ/producers Kruder & Dorfmeister's mix session for Studio !K7's *DJ Kicks* series. Similar in many respects (and more than just number) to that Viennese production duo, Thievery Corporation subsequently grew in popularity among a wider audience of DJs and headphonaunts. Their debut full-length appeared in 1997, along with a compilation of Washington, DC-based electronica artists *Dubbed Out in DC* (both on 18th Street Lounge Music). After 4AD signed the duo, they began work on their second LP but were forced to postpone the release date after tapes were stolen in a mugging. The stopgap remix compilation *Abductions & Reconstructions* was released in 1999, and their second proper album *The Mirror Conspiracy* followed a year later. —*Sean Cooper*

**Sounds from the Thievery Hi-Fi** / Feb. 1997 / 18th Street Lounge ♦♦♦
Collecting Thievery Corporation's first four singles plus several new tracks, *Sounds from the Thievery Hi-Fi* uses the sampler as its main weapon, constructing songs around pilferings from '60s reggae and pop. The effect approaches the easy-listening kitsch-core of the Gentle People—but with more of an unsettling feel. —*John Bush*

**Abductions & Reconstructions** / Apr. 6, 1999 / 18th Street Lounge ♦♦♦♦
*Abductions & Reconstructions*, the 15-track collection of Thievery Corporation remixes done for other artists, includes luscious trip-hop versions of a more diverse cast of artists than most remix LPs—including Rockers HiFi, Slide Five, David Byrne, Baaba Maal, Black Uhuru, Stereolab, Pizzicato 5, Gus Gus, and Hooverphonic. The Thievery touch is effortlessly applied to each artist in turn, softening the edges and giving a stoner vibe to tracks like Maal's "I Will Follow You (Souka Nayo)" and Byrne's "Dance on Vaseline." All in all, Garza and Hilton prove themselves one of the best remixing teams around. —*John Bush*

**DJ Kicks** / Jun. 8, 1999 / Studio !K7 ♦♦
Just as sampladelic as their debut album, Thievery Corporation's entry in Studio !K7's growing *DJ Kicks* mix-album series charts the duo's interest in not only blunted trip-hop but also Brazilian music, exotica, and easy listening. Featuring a few of their own tracks ("It Takes a Thief," "Coming from the Top") plus tracks by Rockers HiFi and Fun-Da-Mental, *DJ Kicks* is a solid chill-out album. —*Keith Farley*

**Eighteenth Street Lounge: Jet Society** / Nov. 9, 1999 / ESL ♦♦♦
Washington, DC's Eighteenth Street Lounge has been a bastion of excellent taste-making music ever since its inception in 1995. The combination club and label's founders—Farid Ali, Abdul Jewayni, and Thievery Corporation's Eric Hilton—envisioned a swinging, continental club inspired by the breezy jazz-funk of Europe and South America during the '70s. As the sound gained momentum during a late-'90s resurgence (thanks in no small part to ESL), the club found many contemporary artists with the same tastes, in the club scene as well as disparate pop communities. The result is a groove-heavy collection that cycles through tracks irrespective of recording date or country of origin (France and Brazil are most represented, but Germany, Italy, and Norway also get props). The sound is a blend of Brazilian jazz, funk, and more recent acid jazz, very organic in texture and occasionally leavened with electronic beats. A perfect example of this mix of old and new is Grupo Batuque's "Brasileirose e Ingleses," a chunky breakbeat number that'd sound great in any electronica club in the world, even though it's still quite tied to the martial drumming of Brazil's decades-old carnival tradition. For those who can't fly over to the club itself, *Jet Society* is a solid remedy. —*John Bush*

● **The Mirror Conspiracy** / Aug. 22, 2000 / ESL Music ♦♦♦♦
Like their debut album, Thievery Corporation's second, *The Mirror Conspiracy*, is a pleasant album of sublime mid-tempo trip-hop, reminiscent of easy-listening groove music and continually referencing the breezier, atmospheric side of Brazilian, Jamaican, French, and Indian forms. The nocturnal dub-poetry of "Treasures" sets a tone for the bruising basslines and echoey keys throughout the album, and "Lebanese Blonde" is another early highlight, with the graceful vocalese of Pam Bricker framing live sitar by Rob Myers and a Jamaican-style horn section. Brazil represents with a triple-shot of "Air Batucada," "So Com Voce" (with vocals from Bebel Gilberto), and "Samba Tranquille." French chanteuse Lou Lou adds a bit of downtempo continental flair

on "Le Monde" and "Shadows of Ourselves," and Thievery Corporation even samples Ella Fitzgerald on the ambient-jungle closer "Tomorrow." As on their first LP, Garza and Hilton occasionally appear satisfied to just push a few grooves and reference their favorite styles of music over the top—at the expense of any new ideas—but *The Mirror Conspiracy* is excellently produced and almost as stylish as the duo's swinging suits on the cover. —*John Bush*

## Third Electric

f. 1995, Cologne, Germany
*Group / Neo-Electro, Electro*

Cologne, Germany's new-electro duo Third Electric are Gregor Lutterman (Rootpowder) and Andreas Bolz (Bolz Bolz). The pair released stark, minimal, decidedly un-retro-sounding 808-based electro inspired by early German, Detroit, and New York artists. Although they've been involved in two CD releases to date (*Electrecord 100*, on their own Electrecord label, renamed *Electrochord* in 1998; and *Electrecord 2000*, released via Studio !K7), most of their material has appeared in 12" form at the rate of roughly two or three a year since Electrecord formed in 1995. Though timbrally restrained, tracks such as "1.9.8.3.," "Tele-Funken," and "Gentle Beat" are anything but simplistic, evolving slowly through intricate rhythmic patterns and ultra-clean, often dark electronic textures. In addition to their Electrecord/*Electrochord* material, Lutterman and Bolz also released more straightforward techno on their Formic Records label and have contributed tracks to compilations from Science City, Spelunk, and Detroit label Ersatz Audio (home to Le Car). Bolz Bolz also released a number of solo 12"s, including "32nd Lesson" on Ersatz Audio and the "Music" remix 12" on Electrecord/Electrochord sublabel, World. —*Sean Cooper*

**1.9.8.3 [Single]** / 1996 / Electrecord ♦♦♦
Three tracks of brittle, acid-tinged German electro, including the downtempo, scratch-heavy "All I Need." —*Sean Cooper*

**Magneto Phon/Tele-Funken [Single]** / 1997 / Electrecord ♦♦♦♦
Among the tightest, best-produced Electrecord releases to date. Trance-like in its minimalism, but still enthralling. —*Sean Cooper*

• **Electrecord 100** / 1998 / Electrecord ♦♦♦♦
Essentially a Third Electric mini-album, *Electrecord 100* combined a couple of previously available cuts with new material. Among the strongest of those is "Music," later included on the Bolz Bolz solo EP *32nd Lesson* on Detroit label Ersatz Audio. —*Sean Cooper*

**Gammastrahlen—Lamm [Single]** / Jul. 6, 1998 / Electrecord ♦♦♦
Three tracks mixing acid, electro, and old-school hip-hop, plus a fourth, entirely beatless ambient cut inspired, strangely, by Jimi Hendrix's "...And the Gods Made Love." The grubbiest Electrecord release to date. —*Sean Cooper*

**Electrecord 2000** / 1999 / Studio !K7 ♦♦♦♦
This isn't a Third Electric release proper, but rather a collection of tracks by artists associated either with 3E or with their label, Electrecord. Contributors include Klystron (of Riot City), Artificial Material (of Le Car/Ersatz Audio), Invisible Man (a.k.a. Freddy Fresh), Synapse (of New York's Serotonin imprint), and, of course, 3E, whose "2000" is some of their best work to date. The CD version contains a number of non-LP tracks. —*Sean Cooper*

## Third Eye Foundation (Matt Elliot)

*Producer / Experimental Jungle, Experimental Rock, Noise-Rock, Space-Rock, Indie Rock, Post-Rock/Experimental*

Third Eye Foundation was the apocalyptic drum'n'bass alias of onetime Flying Saucer Attack member Matt Elliot. Debuting in 1996 with *Semtex*, he returned a year later with the EP *The Sound of Violence*, soon followed by the full-length *Ghost*. *You Guys Kill Me* appeared in 1998, and in early 2000 Third Eye Foundation resurfaced with *Little Lost Soul*. —*Jason Ankeny*

**Semtex** / Nov. 25, 1996 / Domino ♦♦♦

**Ghost** / Apr. 22, 1997 / Merge ♦♦♦
A focus on warped guitar noise and the odd, untraceable samples place Ghost in similar territory to earlier Third Eye material, though "Corpses as Bedmates" and "The Star's Gone Out" reveal a few interesting drum'n'bass patterns. —*Keith Farley*

**You Guys Kill Me** / Oct. 20, 1998 / Merge ♦♦♦♦
If it's not the samples themselves but what you do with them; *You Guys Kill Me* gets extra points for effort. The beats and effects Matt Elliott concocted aren't incredibly original (there's the sewing-machine Brazilian bossa shuffle and the downbeat from Boogie Down Productions' "Bridge Is Over," along with various effects including howling dogs, dark crackly strings, and metallic sounds), but the slice-and-dice production, along with creative processing, transforms them into revelatory darkside symphonies. Elliott sounds as though he's Ed Rush's indie-rockin' sibling, fooling around with big brother's equipment and crafting a very twisted version of post-rock tech-step reminiscent of Amon Tobin as well as Rome. Strangely, it works. —*John Bush*

• **Little Lost Soul** / Feb. 8, 2000 / Merge ♦♦♦♦
*Little Lost Soul* is the Third Eye Foundation's (TEF) first album of the 21st century and the most consistent to date. TEF uses the drum'n'bass elements of u-ziq and Squarepusher but leaves the trip-over-yourself aspects behind. Combined with swelling synths and angelic vocals, this album is a ride through the dark side of a genre appropriately labeled "drill'n'bass." The percussion is meticulously constructed; each beat is placed for a purpose and new rhythms are exposed upon repeated listens. Vague tinges of jazz are also present, mostly in the tappy snare drum and fretless upright bass sounds. All parts combine and build chaotically, most notably halfway through the album on "Half a Tiger." *Little Lost Soul* does have its calmer moments, too, where strings and slower trip-hoppish beats gel into a truly melodic package, as in "Lost." A clever use of dynamics and note placement, along with a knowledge of when not to play, prove Matt Elliot's progress as a modern electronic composer. In the end, *Little Lost Soul* is what many electronic albums aren't—it is tasteful. —*Jason Kane*

## Peter Thomas Sound Orchester

b. 1925
*Drums / Spy Music, Film Music, Exotica*

Practically uncontested as the original German electro-lounge pioneer, Peter Thomas fused the spy-string paranoia of John Barry with Carnaby Street go-go music and lounge on his recordings for several German sci-fi series of the '60s, including *Raumpatrouille (Space Patrol)* and *Der Bann von dem Sinister (The Spell of the Sinister One)*. His Sound Orchestra was also the beginning for another notable producer, Giorgio Moroder. Long neglected during the '70s, '80s, and '90s, Thomas experienced a revival of sorts in the late '90s. After Bungalow Records and City Slang reissued a *Raumpatrouille* collection in 1996, Pulp sampled a track to create the title song for their album 1997 *This Is Hardcore*. Two Thomas collections appeared in 1998, *Tanzmusik* of general interest and *100% Cotton* which recycled Thomas' soundtrack material for the series of Jerry Cotton films (Cotton was the German equivalent of James Bond). The inevitable remix album *Warp Back to Earth* appeared in early 1999. —*John Bush*

• **Raumpatrouille (Space Patrol)** / Nov. 18, 1996 / Bungalow ♦♦♦♦
*Raumpatrouille (Space Patrol)* is the soundtrack music from a 1966 German television show. Thomas' compositions owe a lot to the exotic easy-listening sounds of artists like Esquivel, although given the show's subject matter, there is also a "futuristic" ambience achieved entirely without the use of electronic instruments. The track "Bolero on the Moon Rocks" was sampled for a track on Pulp's 1998 *This Is Hardcore*. —*Steve Huey*

**100% Cotton: The Complete Jerry Cotton Edition** / Jan. 19, 1998 / Crippled Dick ♦♦♦♦
German composer Peter Thomas' mood-jazz scores for the features of director Jerry Cotton are sampled on the breezy *100% Cotton*. Lovingly packaged to include film stills and poster reproductions, the collection also assembles dozens of previously unreleased tracks and will hold considerable appeal for aficionados of sixties-era film music. —*Jason Ankeny*

**Warp Back to Earth 66/99** / Mar. 2, 1999 / Bungalow ♦♦♦

## Richard Thomas

*Producer / Experimental Techno, Electronica*

Richard Thomas was the first solo artist to release a full-length album through the Lo Recordings label, formed by Jon Tye (MLO, 2Player, Twisted Science) in 1994. The label has rapidly evolved into a sort of lightening rod for the stylistically abject, and Thomas' evocative, soundtracky pasteboard aesthetic is an appropriate candidate for Lo's first non-compilation release. Unlike most of the UK electronica crew, Thomas started out in a rock band (called Guinea Worm), and his recordings combine acoustic instrumentation (everything from guitar and bass to trumpet, sax, and various bits of expatriated percussion) with sparse electronics, studio treatments, and an almost narrative approach to digital editing. Although a few of his solo electronic experiments found their way onto a compilation of local artists in 1992, it wasn't until he left for school in London that he was able to hook up directly with artists and labels operating in a similar stylistic context. In 1995, Thomas was commissioned by Tony Morley's Leaf label to contribute incidental recordings to the second installment of the *Invisible Soundtracks* compilation series, with the resultant tracks (called things like "Intrusion Reported by Witness" and "Muffin Spencer-Devlin") perhaps best approximating the spirit of that series.

Thomas cites the youthful experience of noodling about on his grandmother's out-of-tune piano in acclimating his ear to the sonorities of dissonance, and his recorded output to date registers a kind of childhood disregard (in anything but a regressive sense) for compositional "propriety." And like the refreshingly pretense-free scratchings of the Mego and A-Musik stables, Thomas' music manages literacy and lunacy at the same time, pairing titular references to the works of Sigmund Freud and Guy de Maupassant with brass bleets and double-time reverse-scan vocal cut-ups, the results much closer to joyful irreverance than po-faced overseriousness. —*Sean Cooper*

**Something with Milk In [EP]** / 1997 / Lo Recordings ♦♦♦
A promo-only, nonetheless widely available companion release to *Shoes and Radios Attract Paint*, this eight-track EP ranges from shiny, bubbly ambient to sharp, squealy jazz-funk-electronics fusion and repeats only two cuts ("Return to Pow-7" and "Ordure Rechauffe") from the full-length. —*Sean Cooper*

● **Shoes and Radios Attract Paint** / Feb. 9, 1998 / Lo Recordings ♦♦♦♦
Richard Thomas' album debut is anything but easy listening, fusing disjointed shards of treated trumpet and saxophone with snatched bits of vocal and found sound, sparse analog electronics, the clanging throws of a disembodied drumkit, and loping bass figures. The result is, if forced to commit, something like minimalist ambient free jazz, but then that's no less complicated than saying it never really settles into recognizable form, which is ultimately what makes it so rewarding. The perfect length at just under 50 minutes, *Shoes and Radios* is arranged like a series of film shorts, moving through blended atmospheres and studio poltergeistery both noisy and charmingly at ease. —*Sean Cooper*

**Seven Point Plan to Destroy Astrology** / Nov. 30, 1998 / Lo Recordings ♦♦♦
A remix album as only Richard Thomas could produce one, *Seven Point Plan to Destroy Astrology* is the result of Thomas' reworking of original material by the Irish thrash band the Wormholes. The results occasionally reference the originals and throw in bits of vintage sine-wave electronics and radio waves as well as Thomas' standard instruments like trumpet. —*John Bush*

## Throbbing Gristle

f. Sep. 1975, London, England, db. 1981
*Group / Experimental, Industrial*

Abrasive, aggressive, and antagonistic, Britain's Throbbing Gristle pioneered industrial music. Exploring death, mutilation, fascism, and degradation amidst a thunderous cacophony of mechanical noise, tape loops, extremist anti-melodies and bludgeoning beats, the group's cultural terrorism—the "wreckers of civilization," one tabloid called them—raised the stakes of artistic confrontation to new heights, combating all notions of commerciality and good taste with a maniacal fervor.

Formed in London in the autumn of 1975, Throbbing Gristle consisted of vocalist/ringleader Genesis P-Orridge, his then-lover, guitarist Cosey Fanni Tutti, tape manipulator Peter "Sleazy" Christopherson, and keyboardist Chris Carter. A performance art troupe as much as a band, their early live shows—each starting with a punch clock and running exactly 60 minutes before the power to the stage was cut—threatened obscenity laws. During their notorious premiere gig, P-Orridge even mounted an art exhibit consisting entirely of used tampons and soiled diapers.

Upon forming their own label, Industrial, the group issued their introductory release, *The Best of Throbbing Gristle, Vol. 2*, in 1976. A full-length debut, *2nd Annual Report* followed in 1977, in a pressing of only 500 copies. Bowing to fan demand, the record was later reissued—cut from a master tape played backwards. The 1977 underground hit "United" marked a tiny step towards accessibility, thanks to the inclusion of a discernible rhythm. Typically, when the track reappeared on 1978's *D.O.A.: The Third and Final Report*, it was sped up to last all of 17 seconds. No less provocative was "Hamburger Lady" (inspired by the story of a burn-unit victim) or "Death Threats" (a compilation of murderous messages left on the group's answering machine).

*20 Jazz Funk Greats*, a harsh electro-pop outing, followed a year later, and after 1980's live-in-the-studio *Heathen Earth*, Throbbing Gristle called it quits. P-Orridge and Christopherson soon formed Psychic TV (though Christopherson split again to form Coil), while the remaining duo continued on as Chris and Cosey. As Throbbing Gristle's influence swelled, a seemingly endless series of posthumous releases followed, most of them taken from live dates. Among the more notable were 1981's *24 Hours* (later reissued as *36 Hours*), 1983's *Once Upon a Time (Live at the Lyceum)*, and 1986's *TG CD 1*. —*Jason Ankeny*

**Second Annual Report** / 1977 / Mute ♦♦♦
A proper debut of sorts, *Second Annual Report* includes several versions each (some live) of early Throbbing Gristle standards like "Slug Bait" and "Maggot Death," as well as "Industrial Introduction," and the soundtrack work "After Cease to Exist." The music is relentless, grinding distortion, only occasionally leavened by vocal samples and percussion. —*John Bush*

**D.O.A.: The Third and Final Report** / Dec. 1978 / Mute ♦♦♦
A dark lyrical content dominates these 15 tracks. —*Myles Boisen*

★ **20 Jazz Funk Greats** / 1979 / Mute ♦♦♦♦♦
It's a break in the clouds from Throbbing Gristle's pummeling noise and a first glimpse at the continuing pop influence on the TG/PTV axis, but *20 Jazz Funk Greats* still isn't best described by its title. If there is such a thing as a funky Throbbing Gristle LP, however, this could well be it. "Hot on the Heels of Love," "Hamburger Lady," and "Six Six Sixties" add only occasional bits of distortion between the rigid sequencer lines. *20 Jazz Funk Greats* is the best compromise between TG's early industrial aesthetic and the reams of industrial-dance and dark synth-pop groups that used the album as a stepping stone to crossover appeal. —*John Bush*

**Rafters/Psychic Rally** / 1981 / World ♦♦
A typical Throbbing Gristle release, *Rafters/Psychic Rally* is harsh, eviscerating stuff best suited for devoted fans of the group. —*Jason Ankeny*

**Assume Power Focus** / 1982 / Power Focus ♦♦♦
Originally released in 1982 through the group's fan club and reissued in 1997, *Assume Power Focus* captures Throbbing Gristle in its formative stages; most of the material dates from 1975, with the exception of two previously unissued tracks, "A Debris of Murder" and "Leeds Ripper." The recording quality is a bit crude, and the difference between the earlier and later tracks is pretty major—the later ones are much more rhythmic and structured—but overall, it's an intriguing look at the seminal outfit's arty beginnings. —*Steve Huey*

**Greatest Hits** / 1984 / Mute ♦♦♦♦
Like the title says (with irony), it's an industrial primer with song sensibility. —*Myles Boisen*

**Kreeme Horn** / Oct. 28, 1997 / Dossier ♦♦
A collection of previously unreleased Throbbing Gristle material, *Kreeme Horn* is subtitled "In Praise of the Grotesque," a description that fits the music contained herein perfectly. —*Steve Huey*

**Dimensia in Excelsis** / Sep. 1, 1998 / Staalplaat ♦♦♦
*Dimensia in Excelsis* captures the first Throbbing Gristle show ever performed in the United States, a May 22, 1981 gig in Culver City near Los Angeles. The group's confrontational stage presence and sonic terrorism are on ample display throughout. —*Steve Huey*

## Thug (Tim Koch)

b. 1975
*Producer / Ambient Techno*

An Australian student who parlayed his music technology degree into a thriving production career, Tim Koch first became influenced by electronic music via the soundtracks for eight-bit video games. He played bass and drums in a few local bands, then studied at Adelaide University. While there, he began recording at the school's P.A.T.U. recording studio, sequencing tracks with synthesizers and drum machines. Koch began releasing his work as Thug in 1997, recording tracks for two compilations: *Blip Bleep: Soundtracks to Imag-*

inary *Video Games* for New York's Lucky Kitchen and *Extracted Celluloid* for Negativland's Seeland Records. The Australian label Aural Industries debuted with Koch's first full-length, *Isolated Rhythm Clock*. —*John Bush*

● **Isolated Rhythm Clock** / Mar. 19, 1999 / Aural Industries ◆◆◆◆
On *Isolated Rhythm Clock*, producer Tim Koch concentrates on the collision of future and past: the dense rhythms of electro-techno and evocative, yearning old-world melodies. It's a combination that perfectly recalls the last classic Black Dog album, 1995's *Spanners*, without stooping to mere imitation. Each track is well thought out and programmed with excellence, though "Rhino Song" and "Quasipede" do rise above the pack slightly. —*John Bush*

## Asmus Tietchens

**b. 1947**
*Synthesizer, Producer / Musique Concrète, Experimental, Avant-Garde*
Synthesizer experimentalist and musique concrète producer Asmus Tietchens began recording in the mid-'60s and continued to record three decades after that. Born in 1947 and based in Hamburg, Tietchens listened to German radio as a child and heard pioneering electric transmissions by the likes of Stockhausen and Gottfried Michael Koenig. He began recording his own home experiments in 1965 with crude reverb devices and picked up a MiniMoog several years later. Also influenced by atonal Kraut-rockers like Cluster and Faust, Tietchens met Okko Bekker and began a partnership that lasted for decades (Bekker has produced most of Tietchens' work). After Tangerine Dream's Peter Baumann heard a tape of his work, he produced Tietchens' debut album *Nachtstücke*, released in 1980 on Sky Records. His four albums for Sky during the early '80s focused on surprisingly accessible electronic pop, though 1984's *Formen Letzter Hausmusik* (recorded for Nurse with Wound's United Dairies label) began a period of more abstract, concrète recordings that often use tape experiments as well as synthesizers. During the '90s, Tietchens recorded for experimental labels Barooni, Staalplaat, and Syrenia, the latter a 1996 collaboration with Vidna Obmana. Since 1990, he has also taught sound at a Hamburg university. —*John Bush*

**Marches Funebres** / 1989 / Multimood ◆◆◆
Tietchens melds gothic ambience to classical experimentalism on *Marches Funebres*, recorded for the Multimood label. —*John Bush*

**Das Fest Ist Zu Ende. Aus.** / 1995 / Barooni ◆◆◆
Tietchens constructed this album from his ten-year audio diary, beginning at age 15 (1962), altering the vocals and adding occasional accompaniment. —*John Bush*

● **Asmus Tietchens & Vidna Obmana** / 1996 / Syrenia ◆◆◆◆
The German Syrenia label's second release combines old and new-school ambient talent, with electro-acoustician Tietchens combining his more surly, difficult style with Obmana's warm, flowing ambience. Three cuts in collaboration and a solo piece fill out the hour of this disc, with mostly formless, textured program music the focus. Subtly beautiful, with treated samples and found sounds accenting cycling synth passages and alternately stern and gentle melodies. —*Sean Cooper*

## Timeshard

**f. 1989, Liverpool, England**
*Group / Trance, Club/Dance, Techno*
Gobber, Psi and Steve were friends in Liverpool when they decided to form Timeshard in the late '80s as an experiment with first loops and found sounds at their home studio. The trio began organizing free local parties and became known as the area's first "live acid-house band." Gradually, the live show expanded outwards and across Great Britain, while their sound gained elements of ethno-techno, trance, and dub. Timeshard also gained attention for their self-released, cassette-only albums, *Who Pilots the Flying Saucers* in 1991 and *Hyperborean Dome Temples of Apollo* the following year. In 1994, Planet Dog signed the group and released *Crystal Oscillations*. The trio's second full album, *Hunab Ku*, appeared in 1996. —*John Bush*

**Crystal Oscillations** / Sep. 26, 1995 / Mammoth ◆◆

● **Hunab Ku** / Jul. 23, 1996 / Mammoth ◆◆◆◆
Besides the usual Third World crusty-trance that's only to be expected by an act recording for Planet Dog, Timeshard come up with several interesting innovations on their second album for the label. Integrating everything from psychedelic acid lines to drum'n'bass breakbeats, tracks like "Magnetic Storm" and "Dream Messages" prove the best of the lot. —*John Bush*

## Tin Star

**f. 1996, London, England**
*Group / Trip-Hop, Club/Dance*
The new-era disco-pop band Tin Star was formed in 1996 by vocalist Dave Tomlinson, guitarist/songwriter Tim Bricheno, and bassist/programmer Tim Gordine. After playing a few shows and recording a demo, the band signed to V2 and released their debut album *the Thrill Kisser* in 1999. —*John Bush*

● **The Thrill Kisser** / Feb. 9, 1999 / V2 ◆◆◆
Careful, these rocktronic scientists are not to be confused with the Bakersfieldsian, alt-countryboys, Tin Star, from the mid '80s. This late-'90s London disco craze band has been a little irresponsibly compared to Brian Eno—but for the right reasons. They have an energetic, outer space, erotic ambiance with occasional flashes of attitude, so they don't get shoved to the side of the CD changer. Formed in 1996, original band members continue to pump out appealing, memorable magic that doesn't neglect trace elements of excellent musicianship. *Thrill Kisser's* best cuts include "Head," a fantastically danceable, electronica-pop, percussion, pelvic thrust, and "Disconnected Child" features fast repetifunk sequences that are unremarkable, but the vocals are appealing and simple without apology. "Raincheck" is simply, sweetly melodic, tambouriney, radio pop that makes all the girls go "Ahh." Excellent additional cuts: "Viva," "Going Slow," "Fast Machine," and "Destruction"—and that's all the cuts on the record! There you go! Far more accessible than the band's overhyped, badass, techno-dizzy image. —*Becky Byrkit*

## Tipsy

**f. 1995, San Francisco, CA**
*Group / Illbient, Ambient Techno, Club/Dance*
The San Francisco-based lounge-collage duo Tipsy consists of Tim Digulla and David Gardner. The two were brought together by their shared fascination for experimental music and noise. Previously, Gardner worked with sonic manipulators like PGR and Big City Orchestra; Digulla began recording noise projects on his walkman while in junior high under the name No One, and continued his experiments in the San Francisco noise scene, through which he connected with Gardner at a warehouse sound event.

Both interested in the possibilities early easy listening and lounge music presented for tweaking and remixing, the duo formed Tipsy and recorded *Trip Tease* at the Bloody Angle Compound, their label Asphodel's recording studio. *Trip Tease* whips modern and retro dance beats together with the sensibility of '50s and '60s easy listening for a surreal musical confection. Two singles, *Space Golf/Nude on the Moon* and *Grossenhosen Mit Mr. Excitement* were released, and the band has applied their avant-kitsch touch to Pulp's "This Is Hardcore" single. —*Heather Phares*

● **Trip Tease** / Feb. 18, 1997 / Asphodel ◆◆◆◆
Tipsy's debut album *Trip Tease* shows a deep affection for music on a purely sonic level. Given that Tim Digulla and David Gardner, the two halves of Tipsy, were both involved in industrial and ambient projects previously, it's not a surprise that there are bizarre juxtapositions of mood, tone and texture on this album. What is somewhat surprising is how well the group's blend of state of the art editing and retro-exotica-sci-fi kitsch works. Songs like "Liquordelic" and "El Bombo Atomico" go beyond the intellectual, studio science project they may have been originally, blossoming into hothouse hybrids that just sound good. Bouncy drums, sitars, harps, horns, and all sorts of unclassifiable "space" effects jell into a collection of songs that are retro and cutting edge, bachelor pad and launching pad. A must for sound geeks and space age bachelors alike. —*Heather Phares*

## To Rococo Rot

**f. 1994, Berlin, Germany**
*Group / Experimental Rock, Post-Rock/Experimental, Instrumental Rock, IDM*
To Rococo Rot (TRR) is a mostly Berlin-based post-rock trio whose combination of electronic and acoustic elements places them in close proximity to American groups such as Tortoise, Trans Am, and Rome, as well as European artists Circle, Stereolab, and Fridge. Composed of bassist Stefan Schneider (also of similar-sounding Dusseldorf group Kreidler) and brothers Robert (guitar,

electronics) and Ronald Lippok (drums, effects), To Rococo Rot were originally among a new breed of German electronic experimentalists working more often within the context of *hauptkunst* digital art and multimedia installation (prior to meeting Schneider, the Lippoks were behind a project of this sort called Ornament und Verbrechen). With TRR, however, the group have described their work as an overt attempt to reconnect the art-school proclivities of musical experimentalism with the accessibility and "use-value" of pop, a goal clearly evident both in their name and their recorded output to date. The group's debut arrived in 1996 in the form of an untitled picture disc (subsequently reissued on CD by Kitty Yo), with the more widely distributed *Veiculo* (released by UK indie City Slang) appearing the following year. Embraced by rock and electronica audiences alike, the group has (like Tortoise et al) already begun to play an important, transitional role in eroding some of the barriers that have typically separated the two (particularly in the US). Working long, hypnotic grooves augmented by bizarre, often subtly interwoven electronics and sample sequences, TRR also owe a clear debt to '60s Kraut-rock groups such as Neu!, Can, and Amon Düül, among others, and in some respects are reorienting the abstract deconstructions of man/machine those groups first sketched. In 1997, the group recorded an album's worth of material with producer David Moufang (Deep Space Network, Source Records). Following a move to Mute Records, the band released *The Amateur View* in 1999. Ronald Lippok has also gained praise for his work in Tarwater. —*Sean Cooper*

**Cd.** / 1996 / Kitty-Yo ♦♦♦
Including all ten songs from their 1995 self-titled debut plus four extra tracks, To Rococo Rot's *Cd.* is one of the first post-rock albums that isn't obsessed or weighed down by its own potential as conscious, artistic music (perhaps because of the lack of hype surrounding the band in indie-rock quarters). The album doesn't say a whole lot, it just grooves along, recalling the pleasant atmospheres of Tortoise, the groove-oriented bent of Ui and Trans Am, and the minimalist effects of Rome. Though trumped by its follow-up, *Veiculo*, To Rococo Rot's first album has its own characteristic advantages. —*John Bush*

**Veiculo** / Feb. 24, 1997 / Emperor Jones ♦♦♦♦
Kraftwerk with guitars or Trans Am without the schmaltz, To Rococo Rot provide a nice fusion of indie-rock instrumentalism and the more minimal end of armchair techno occupied by Autechre and Freeform. The group manage a near-perfect balance of elements here, coming off neither retro nor pretentious, reserving the occasionally embarrassing artiness of a Stereolab or Tortoise for the subtlety with which they play electronic and acoustical textures off one another. —*Sean Cooper*

● **The Amateur View** / Jun. 8, 1999 / Mute ♦♦♦♦
With *The Amateur View*, To Rococo Rot leaves behind their many fumbling colleagues in the field of post-rock/post-techno to set upon a course of their own: a lush vision of listener electronica. Though the occasional angular guitar repetition is a clear nod to the influence of Tortoise, the trio construct tracks with reams of vintage electronics and a few acoustic instruments, assembling complex songs on a production line of sorts with a variety of simplistic parts. Highlights "Telema" (the single) and "A Little Asphalt Here and There" are bursting tone-capsules of warm laidback electro-funk, far less focused on the angular abstractions of previous TRR material. Although it's still leagues away from the electronic dance mainstream (or even the electronic listening mainstream), *The Amateur View* offers an intriguing glimpse at the future of home techno. —*John Bush*

## Amon Tobin

**b.** Brazil
*Producer, DJ / Drill'N'Bass, Electronica, Trip-Hop, Jungle/Drum'N'Bass, Club/Dance, Electronic*
Recording as Cujo for London's Ninebar label and as himself for Ninja Tune, drum'n'bass deviant Amon Tobin fuses hip-hop and jazz compositional ideas with the bustling rhythms of hip-hop and jungle and the bent sonic mayhem of ambient and dub. Unlike rolling junglists such as Alex Reece and Wax Doctor, however, who draw from a softer, "cooler" brand of jazz, Tobin aims to maintain the heat of bop and free, pairing spry, galloping basslines with complex trapset orchestration and shrill, screaming horns. A native of Brazil, Tobin moved to the UK in the mid-'80s, when hip-hop was beginning to take hold and the rhythms of breakbeat electro-funk were replacing reggae and punk as the underground youth music of choice. Currently residing in Brighton, Tobin didn't begin seriously making music until college, but his passion for the sampler as well as the support and encouragement of no less of breakbeat scientists than Ninebar and Ninja Tune immediately convinced him to forgo a university career to focus on music (he was a few years into a photography degree when he put the whole project on hold). He's since released a trio of EPs (a pair for Ninebar, as well as the *Creatures* EP for Ninja Tune) and a full-length (*Adventures in Foam*, on Ninebar). *Bricolage*, his first LP for Ninja Tune, was released in mid-1997. *Permutation* followed one year later, and in the spring of 2000 Tobin returned with *Supermodified*. [See Also: Cujo] —*Sean Cooper*

**Creatures [EP]** / Nov. 25, 1996 / Ninja Tune ♦♦♦
Amon Tobin's debut 12" for Ninja Tune is two parts dark, slo-motion ambient dub-hop and two parts whizzing, schizo jungle-jazz. Tobin's instinct for jazz phrasing in a drum'n'bass context is what made his previous *Adventures in Foam* stand out, and here he lets up nothing, with walking basslines and dizzying keyboard glissandos bubbling out of a soup of noisy chaos and rip-roaring amen beats. —*Sean Cooper*

**Bricolage** / Apr. 21, 1997 / Ninja Tune ♦♦♦♦
Amon Tobin's jazz-jungle fusions as Cujo (for upstart label Ninebar) earned him many props, but that began to change with his debut for Ninja Tune. Blurring the already vague line which separates jungle's rhythmic meditations from those of the hottest jazz (Elvin Jones, say, or Jaco Pastorius), *Bricolage* manages a difficult hybrid of heart, soul, atmosphere, and brain-bending plunderphonics which loses neither perspective nor direction over the course of the albums. Like his preceding EPs *Creatures* and *Chomp Samba* (from which a few of *Bricolage*'s cuts derive), the album mixes fast and slow but maintains a solid focus on innovation without sacrificing a sense of purpose. Somehow, *Bricolage* manages to be both consistent and consistently engaging, a feat few drum'n'bass LPs seem able to manage. —*Sean Cooper*

**Piranha Breaks [EP]** / Oct. 21, 1997 / Ninja Tune ♦♦♦
Four tracks of Latin jazz-tinged armchair drum'n'bass, similar in style to Tobin's previous Ninja Tune releases, though with a lighter, more playfeel feel. A competent if somewhat water-treading release, the CD version adds a bonus cut. —*Sean Cooper*

**Permutation** / Jun. 1, 1998 / Ninja Tune ♦♦♦♦
While the great majority of jazz-junglists look no farther back than the mid-'60s for inspiration (and samples), Tobin took his bag of tricks back into the swing era to come up with more (and more interesting) variations on the form than most anyone else. More Buddy Rich than Roy Ayers, *Permutation* sees leagues of different drum samples with nary an Amen or Apache break in site. From the detuned vibes and piano loops that drive the opener "Like Regular Chickens" to the Disney-on-acid "Nightlife," Tobin proves himself one of the ablest producers around. As on most indie-junglists' LPs, there are a couple of notable darkside tracks ("Reanimator," "Escape," "People Like Frank"), but even here he shows himself superior to contemporaries like µ-Ziq. As the title suggests, *Permutation* is an incredibly varied ride. —*John Bush*

● **Supermodified** / May 16, 2000 / Ninja Tune ♦♦♦♦
Farther away from drum'n'bass and closer to big-beat techno with a little turntablist mayhem thrown in, Amon Tobin's third album for Ninja Tune breaks out with a devastating opener, "Get Your Snack On." The track turns out to be just one of the highlights on *Supermodified*, a dense, plunderphonic kaleidoscope of an album with giant, noisy jazz breaks and groovy electronic synthwork. It's got quite a bit of the retro-sampling of *Permutation* (orchestra strings, jazz combos, groovy psychedelic basslines) along with a wider variety of material—from driving funky-breaks productions ("Four Ton Mantis") and playful cut'n'paste numbers ("Precursor," "Chocolate Lovely"), to darkstep jungle ("Golfer Vrs. Boxer") and surprisingly touching minimalist melancholia ("Slowly," "Deo"). Tobin's again made great strides in his production skills, and the range and greatness of this material serves as proof positive. —*John Bush*

## Satoshi Tomiie

**b.** 1966, Tokyo, Japan
*Keyboards, Producer / Club/Dance, House, Dance-Pop*
A house music veteran and one of the first producers to convert the Japanese to club culture, Satoshi Tomiie was a crucial third man in the Def Mix Pro-

ductions team helmed by David Morales and Frankie Knuckles. Born in Tokyo in 1966, Tomiie grew interested in electronics and keyboards at an early age and formed his first band in the early '80s. After American house music began crossing the ocean, Tomiie began DJing and producing on his own. He met house pioneer Frankie Knuckles when the two DJed at a party thrown by a Japanese cosmetics company and was promptly hired aboard New York's Def Mix Productions collective, home of Knuckles and another house hero, David Morales.

Tomiie collaborated on several dancefloor smashes during the late '80s and early '90s, including "Tears" by Underground Solution and "I'll Be Your Friend" by Robert Owens. He also began remixing all sorts of club-bound pop stars—Michael Jackson, Madonna, Mariah Carey, David Bowie, Diana Ross, and U2, among others. Though he didn't record much on his own, Tomiie issued singles under his own name as well as Level 9, Loop 7, and the Black Shells. A contract with Sony in the late '90s resulted in a flurry of new productions, including his debut album, *Full Lick*. —*John Bush*

● **Full Lick** / Oct. 18, 1999 / Sony ♦♦♦
The respected house producer and dancefloor veteran finally turned in his first full-length over ten years into his career. *Full Lick* is impeccably produced, drawing on Tomiie's years of experience with dancefloor house. Though a few tracks fall surprisingly short of the mark, special guests (and fellow dance veterans) like Robert Owens, Diane Charlemagne, Cevin Fisher, and Kelly Ali (Sneaker Pimps) provide just enough energy to keep things going. The two tracks featuring vocalist Diane Charlemagne, "Sincerity" and "Inspired," are the highlights. —*John Bush*

## Tomita (Isao Tomita)

b. 1932, Tokyo, Japan
*Synthesizer, Producer / Progressive Electronic*

Pioneering Japanese composer and synthesizer expert Isao Tomita bridged the gap between note-by-note classical/electronic LPs like *Switched-On Bach* and the more futuristic, user-friendly interfaces developed in the '70s. After creating one of the first personal recording studios with an array of top synthesizer gear in the early '70s, Tomita applied his visions for space-age synthesizer music to his favorite modern composers—Claude Debussy, Igor Stravinsky, Maurice Ravel—though his recordings steered a course far beyond the sterile academics of Wendy Carlos and other synthesists. Born in Tokyo in 1932, Tomita grew up in China as well as Japan, studying composition and music theory as well as art history at Keio University. After graduation in 1955, Tomita began composing film, television, and theater music. He was awarded frequently during the '50s and '60s and became perhaps the most well-known contemporary Japanese composer.

By the early '70s, Isao Tomita was introduced to the seminal work of synthesizer gurus Wendy Carlos and Robert Moog, sparking his own interest in synthesized music. In 1973, he formed the electronic collective Plasma Music with musicians Kinji Kitashoji and Mitsuo Miyamoto and spent more than a year stocking his home studio with electronics gear (including the Moog III used for Carlos' *Switched-On Bach*). Tomita's first album, 1974's *Snowflakes Are Dancing*, electrified the Japanese public and even translated to an American classical audience, where it was nominated for four Grammy awards. Successive albums *Pictures at an Exhibition*, *The Firebird Suite*, and his masterpiece *Holst: The Planets* infused the classical-synthesizer fusion craze of the '70s with genuinely exciting, futuristic music instead of the bland, note-by-note translations favored by less visionary musicians. *The Planets* reinvoked the connection between synthesizer music and science fiction, first broached in the 1956 film *Forbidden Planet*.

Tomita began incorporating digital synth and early MIDI setups with 1982's *Grand Canyon*, and completely gutted his studio during the next two years during the transition from analog to digital with his Casio Cosmo system. Though he recorded more sparingly than in the '70s, Tomita made frequent appearances at enormous concerts, including his 1984 Austrian show *Mind of the Universe* before 80,000 people and at the Statue of Liberty centennial celebration two years later. Tomita was also awarded the honorary presidency of the Japan Synthesizer Programmers Association. —*John Bush*

● **Snowflakes Are Dancing** / 1974 / RCA ♦♦♦♦
One of the more satisfying classical/synthesizer debuts, *Snowflakes Are Dancing* works on its own terms as a piece of music. Also, the album succeeds as an interpretation of several Debussy compositions (including "Clair de Lune" and "Arabesque No. 1"). Debussy's atmospheric compositions are naturals to receive the Tomita treatment, and despite a few moments of interstellar cheesiness worthy of *Star Hustler*, Tomita's debut is an intriguing proto-synthesizer-pop record. —*John Bush*

● **Pictures at an Exhibition** / Apr. 1975 / RCA ♦♦♦
An impressive production that adapts Mussorgsky's classic work (both the original piano version and the later orchestrated version) and develops it into a synthesized landscape that both overwhelms and amuses. This was Tomita's follow-up to the popular *Snowflakes Are Dancing*. —*Steven McDonald*

● **The Planets** / 1976 / Atlantic ♦♦♦♦
Isao Tomita's masterpiece brings the pop-classicism of Holst's *The Planets* together with Tomita's own futuristic synthesizer explorations. Progressing from Mars, Venus, and Mercury all the way to the Neptune ("Mystic") with an incredibly wide range of gear, *The Planets* has several dated pieces, though most of the album sounds futuristic as only Tomita could. —*John Bush*

● **Greatest Hits** / 1981 / RCA ♦♦♦♦
A career-spanning collection which includes Tomita's best and best-known work. Of the former, works are included from *The Planets*, *Bolero* and *Pictures at an Exhibition*, while the better-known works are Tomita adaptations of music from the sci-fi classics *2001: A Space Odyssey*, *Star Wars*, and *Close Encounters of the Third Kind*. —*John Bush*

## Pete Tong

b. Jul. 30, 1960, Dartford, England
*DJ / Progressive Trance, Club/Dance, House*

The don of British dance DJs, Pete Tong has maintained his status as the most influential man in British dance through his weekly *Essential Selection* radio show on BBC Radio One (broadcast to an estimated one million listeners) as well as his club gigs in front of thousands of people. Born in Dartford, Kent in 1960, Tong played drums in a school band during his teenage years but later switched to DJing. After leaving school, he worked as a mobile DJ—playing weddings and parties—during the late '70s and did time at small record labels as well. By 1983, Tong had hired in with London Records as an A&R representative, and several years later his position exposed him to the house music coming out of Chicago. After meeting with the owners of DJ International and Trax Records (the two most important Chicago house labels), Tong organized a 1986 compilation entitled *The House Sound of Chicago, Vol. 1*, the first British release to deal with the sound. He had never given up DJing during his stint with London Records, and he began hyping the style at clubs around London, leading to its breakout during the late '80s. When the BBC began giving airtime to house music, Tong was a natural choice to lead the sessions, and his *Essential Selection* radio show (broadcast every Friday night) became the place for club kids as well as label executives to learn about the latest in dance music. Tong's reputation grew as big and as fast as the world-wide popularity of house music during the early '90s, and he released several collections detailing his mixing skills—four volumes of the *Dance Nation* series, as well as compilations from the *Essential Selection* show. —*John Bush*

● **Pete Tong's Essential Collection** / Oct. 1997 / PolyGram TV/ffrr ♦♦♦♦
Almost strictly a compilation of the biggest and best house tunes of the past year, *Pete Tong's Essential Selection* includes tracks by BT, Ultra Naté, Jaydee, and JDS, alongside several tracks with a breakbeat or two, such as ETA's "Casual Sub" and a remix of Death in Vegas' "Dirt." —*John Bush*

**Essential Selection Spring 1999** / Apr. 20, 1999 / PolyGram International ♦♦♦♦
Tong's mix-album update circa April 1999 is a double-disc extravaganza, including one disc of the funkier side of house (Armand Van Helden, Hollis Monroe, Cevin Fisher, Pete Heller) and another with harder material (Humate, Quake, Greece 2000). The mixing isn't world-class, but Tong proves that his selection skills are still some of the best. —*John Bush*

## T.O.N.T.O.'s Expanding Head Band

f. 1971, New York, **db.** 1980
*Group / Obscuro, Electronic*

In 1969, engineers Malcolm Cecil and Robert Margouleff worked with synthesizer pioneer Robert Moog to develop additional modules for the centerpiece unit of Moog's keyboard empire. The result was T.O.N.T.O—The Original New Timbral Orchestra. Built into a collection of gently curving wooden cases, T.O.N.T.O. became the world's largest Moog synthesizer. While Robert Moog headed into the development of the Mini-Moog, Cecil and Margouleff took their baby onto the studio circuit, providing Moog elements for a bewildering variety of album projects and film soundtracks. T.O.N.T.O, like most Moog synthesizers, was notoriously temperamental, requiring constant adjustment—contemporary reports mention Cecil being found buried in the back of the beast, tweaking oscillators and adjusting circuits. This bulkiness later led to the replacement of Moog parts with Serge Modular units.

In 1971, Cecil and Margouleff set out to record on their own under the name of T.O.N.T.O's Expanding Head Band. The album *Zero Time* was a revolutionary piece of work that set out to explore the capabilities of the synthesizer with no regard for conceptions of pop success. *Zero Time* is still considered to be a turning point in the use of synthesizers in contemporary music. The following album, credited simply to Tonto, was the short-lived *It's About Time*, which came and went in a flash during 1972 (a fate that led to vinyl copies commanding high prices).

*It's About Time* was not the end of the T.O.N.T.O. story however, as the duo continued to be very much in demand for studio work, with T.O.N.T.O. being called on to do everything from quietly replacing bass tracks to providing great washes of sound. Most importantly, Cecil and Margouleff began a long association with Stevie Wonder, whose *Music of My Mind*, recorded when he was 21 and just beginning a new Motown contract that gave him full control over his music, benefited from Cecil and Margouleff's work. Their influence on the subsequent course of black American music is often missed—where Wonder led the charge, others followed suit, changing the way the music was produced, the way albums were formulated, and the overall sound. Many of the leading jazz/R&B artists of the '70s and early '80s called on the talents of Cecil and Margouleff, including the Isley Brothers, Gil Scott-Heron, the Crusaders, the Gap Band, Quincy Jones, David Sanborn, Wilson Pickett, and the Rippingtons. T.O.N.T.O. was retired during the '80s and was purchased by Devo's Mark Mothersbaugh. In 1996, the Viceroy label combined both albums onto the single-disc CD reissue *Tonto Rides Again*. —*Steven McDonald*

**Zero Time** / 1971 / Embryo ♦♦♦

**It's About Time** / 1972 / Embryo ♦♦

● **Tonto Rides Again** / Jun. 11, 1996 / Viceroy ♦♦♦♦
Including both original T.O.N.T.O. albums, 1971's *Zero Time* and the following year's *It's About Time*, this compilation disc includes an assortment of far-out synthesizer workouts that manage to fascinate and confuse listeners almost simulataneously. Tracks like "Cybernaut," "River Song," "Tranquillium," and "Tontomotion" are highlights. —*Keith Farley*

## David Toop

b. 1949, London, England
*Producer / Film Music, Worldbeat, Avant-Garde, Electro-Acoustic, Ambient, Electronic*

Although British writer and composer David Toop's recorded output has included everything from experimental rock and jazz to musique concrète, the bulk of his solo and recent collaborative works have been in the vein of experimental ambient. Better known perhaps as a journalist and music historiographer, Toop is the author of a pair of widely hailed books—*Rap Attack* and *Ocean of Sound* (both Serpents Tail)—as well as a contributing editor and columnist for UK experimental music magazine *The Wire*. Recording since the early '70s, Toop's list of musical collaborators include everyone from Derek Bailey and John Zorn to Brian Eno and Prince Far I. However, it's his work as a solo composer and in combination with multi-instrumentalist Max Eastley that have earned him highest marks. Toop and Eastley's 1994 collaboration, *Buried Dreams*, is a widely-hailed document of experimental environmental composition. A dizzying blend of found sounds, field recordings, electro-acoustics, and digital manipulation, its success (and critical popularity) also helped set the tone for Toop's subsequent solo work, *Screen Ceremonies*, released in 1996 on the Wire Editions label, as well as one-off tracks included on compilations released through Sound Effects and Time Recordings. He returned in 1999 with the mix album *Hot Pants Idol*. —*Sean Cooper*

**Buried Dreams** / 1994 / Beyond ♦♦♦
A collaboration with experimental composer Max Eastley, the album is surprisingly accessible and engaging. Fusing the best of probably thousands of hours of field recordings from all over the world with a studied knack for sonic mangling and compositional atmosphere, *Buried Dreams* is one of the finest documents of ambient operating outside the contexts of house and techno (which have dominated its recent resurgence). Vague but uncompromising. —*Sean Cooper*

**Pink Noir** / 1996 / Virgin ♦♦♦♦
Toop's second solo ambient work builds on the eclecticism of his earlier material, adding challenging blasts of experimental jazz and non-Western percussion, narration, and field recordings to sound collages that regularly court the unclassifiable in scope and effect. The more club-derived elements of his earlier *Screen Ceremonies* are largely absent here, replaced by more spread-out, encompassing sounds and arrangements. Daring and accomplished. —*Sean Cooper*

**Screen Ceremonies** / 1996 / Wire ♦♦♦
A whirlwind tour of the recent history of the various mutating strains of ambient-leaning experimental electronic, from beatless soundscapes to electro, dub, and noise. Like his celebrated collaboration with Max Eastley on *Buried Dreams*, Toop's focus is on geography, assembling landscapes of sound and reference that repay exploration over passive listening. An occasionally difficult listen, but usually worth it. —*Sean Cooper*

● **Spirit World** / 1997 / Virginambt ♦♦♦♦
Toop's third album in the Virgin ambient series is an all-star affair, featuring the talents of Robert Hampson from Main, Scanner, Toshinori Kondo, and Witchman, as well as usual colleagues Max Eastley and Peter Lockett. Most of the music however, was created by Toop; his instrument list takes up a good paragraph of the liner notes and includes guitar, bass, pedal steel, e-bow, flute, programming, and many more. The music on *Spirit World* is dark, powerful ethno-ambience informed by Toop's interest in music from around the world. Though his poetic readings on tracks like "Ceremony Viewed Through Iron Slit" and "Sleeping Powder" are a bit too mystical for their own good, the music never fails to back him up. On "Sunless," the heavy bassline and Toshinori Kondo's treated trumpet make for easy comparisons to fusion-era Miles Davis. —*John Bush*

**Museum of Fruit** / Apr. 20, 1999 / Caipirinha ♦♦
*Museum of Fruit* was inspired by Itsuko Hasegawa's fruit museum, a group of three buildings near Mount Fuji that resemble large globular greenhouses. Unlike the ethno-ambience of previous releases, Toop's music here is similar in structure and sound to Japanese traditional music. In keeping with his career though, Toop places more emphasis on the means of recording than the results, even including "bioelectric recordings of fruit" by Michael Prime. —*John Bush*

## Tortoise

f. 1990, Chicago, IL
*Group / Experimental Rock, Indie Rock, Post-Rock/Experimental, Instrumental Rock*

Tortoise revolutionized American indie-rock in the mid-'90s by playing down tried-and-true punk and rock 'n' roll influences, emphasizing instead the incorporation of a variety of left-field music genres from the past 20 years (including Kraut-rock, dub, classical minimalism, ambient & space music, prog-rock, film music and British electronica). At odds with the shambling framework of alternative rock's normal song structure as well, the group—as large as a septet, with at times *two* vibes players—relied on a crisp instrumental aesthetic, tied to cool jazz, which practically stood alone in American indie rock by actually focusing on instrumental prowess and group interaction. Although the group's unique vision is to an extent the creation of drummer and master producer John McEntire, most of the other members are well-connected—producers and/or participants—in Chicago's fraternal indie-rock community, which consists of numerous side projects and ongoing bands. After debuting in 1993 with several singles and an LP, Tortoise's underground prestige emerged above terra firma with their second album *Millions Now Living Will Never Die;* the 21-minute opening track "Djed" was a sublime pastiche of Kraut-rock, dub, and cool jazz. Tortoise then linked themselves with the cream of European electronica (Luke Vibert, Oval, U.N.K.L.E., Spring Heel Jack) to remix the album on a series of 12" singles. Despite the band's growing reliance on studio engineering, Tortoise began re-emphasizing their instrumentalist bent in 1998 for third album *TNT*.

First formed in Chicago in 1990, Tortoise began when Doug McCombs (bass; formerly of Eleventh Dream Day) and John Herndon (drums, keyboards, vibes; formerly with the Poster Children) began experimenting with production techniques. The duo intended to record on their own as well as provide an instant rhythm section for needy bands—inspired by the reggae duo Sly & Robbie. Next aboard was producer/drummer/vibes-player John McEntire and guitarist Bundy K. Brown (both former members of Bastro) plus percussionist Dan Bitney (formerly with the SST hardcore band Tar Babies).

The five-piece recorded 7" singles for both David Wm. Sims' Torsion label and Thrill Jockey in 1993, then released their eponymous debut on Thrill Jockey one year later. Much of the album's sound—restrained indie-rock with sublime jazz influences and a debt to prog-rock—was pleasant but not quite revolutionary. Several tracks took a more slanted course, though, sounding like a reaction to England's ambient/techno scene filtered through the '70s experimentalism of Can and Faust. *Tortoise* became an underground classic and spawned the remix work *Rhythms, Resolutions and Clusters*—remixers Jim O'Rourke, Steve Albini, and Brad Wood. The album steadily segued from techno and found-sound environment recordings to feedback ambience and hip-hop—complete with samples of A Tribe Called Quest and Minnie Riperton. In 1995, the group released "Gamera," a 12" single on Stereolab's Duophonic label.

Brown later left for solo production work and his band projects Slowpoke and Directions in Music; Tortoise added bassist David Pajo (formerly of Slint and also a member of the For Carnation) for second album *Millions Now Living Will Never Die*, released in early 1996. Much of the album was similar to the debut, but the British weeklies and American music magazines championed the strength of album-opener "Djed"—which blended a rumbling bassline, scratchy, lo-fi ambience, and dub techniques into over ten minutes of music before the sounds of reel-to-reel tape distintegration introduced another passage of calm yet angular indie-rock figures. During the rest of 1995, Tortoise toured with Stereolab in England and headlined a US tour with 5iveStyle and the Sea & Cake. John McEntire also remained busy with production, working on Stereolab's *Emperor Tomato Ketchup* and eponymous debut LPs from 5iveStyle, Trans Am, and Rome.

Instead of a remix album to accompany *Millions Now Living Will Never Die*, Tortoise optioned tracks out to several techno/experimental contemporaries during 1996. Mo'Wax heroes U.N.K.L.E. recorded a remix of "Djed" on the first of what became a four-volume series, with later interpretations coming from Oval, Jim O'Rourke & Bedouin Ascent, Spring Heel Jack, and Luke Vibert, among others.

By the time recording began in 1990 for Tortoise's third album, *TNT*, Pajo had gone to spend time on his Aerial-M project; a long-time group friend, guitarist Jeff Parker, replaced him. Parker's connection to the fertile Chicago free jazz community—he's a member of the AACM (Association for the Advancement of Creative Musicians)—served as a signpost to the group's new direction: growing instrumental prowess and an emphasis on straightahead, occasionally improvisational, indie rock. For *TNT*'s remixes, however, the group again turned to the dance world; another Chicago head, Derrick Carter, contributed, as well as Autechre. Bitney, Herndon and Parker also play in Isotope 217. —*John Bush*

**Tortoise** / 1994 / Thrill Jockey ♦♦♦♦
One of the more original indie-rock albums, *Tortoise* takes its guitar inspiration from indie-rock bands like Slint, though the sound is much more laid-back. Also, the group encompasses a wider range of music, including jazz and a twisted form of lo-fi electronics. With the great vibes of jazz and the cool chill of good ambience, the album rarely fails to please. —*John Bush*

**Rhythms, Resolutions & Clusters** / 1995 / Thrill Jockey ♦♦♦
Just after the release of their debut album, Tortoise invited several friends (including Steve Albini and Brad Wood) to dissect several tracks. The result is a 30-minute continuous mix, ranging from a hip-hop remix—with A Tribe Called Quest and Minnie Riperton samples—to environment-sound driftings. Most of the disc is on the experimental side, even compared to the original. —*John Bush*

**A Digest Compendium of the Tortoise's World** / 1996 / Thrill Jockey ♦♦♦♦
*A Digest Compendium of Tortoise's World* includes selections from the band's self-titled Thrill Jockey debut, some early singles and a host of remixes. Recruited for mixing duties are Jim O'Rourke, Steve Albini, Casey Rice, the band themselves, and a host of others. The result is a comprehensive account of Tortoise's initial efforts, and some rather unique reinterpretations. There is a sprawling remix of "Ry Cooder," dubbed "Ry Cooder (The Beer Incident)." It is the audible account of a man returning home, cracking open a beer and tuning in to "Ry Cooder" on the radio. Another great track is Casey Rice's interpretation of "Spiderwebbed," called "Cobnebbed." It is a two-minute exploration into the far reaches of space, and the most interesting remix on the album. Bundy K. Brown tweaks "Spiderwebbed" as well, but the result is astonishingly different than Rice's. Brown's mix, titled "Not Quite East of the Ryan," begins with a 50-second ambient trance similar to Rice's mix, but abruptly shifts directions with the inclusion of a hip-hop backbeat and a Tribe Called Quest sample. Along with these remixes are some of Tortoise's earliest material; their first single "Reservoir" is included, as is "Whitewater." This album lives up to its title, and provides a comprehensive collection of Tortoise's early work. Although at times the album seems a bit disjointed in switching so quickly from song to remix to song, it is a great introduction to the band and contains some hidden treasures for fanatics. —*Marc Gilman*

**Remixed** / 1996 / Thrill Jockey ♦♦♦♦
Picking up where *Rhythms, Resolutions and Clusters: Remixed and Rare* left off, the release of Tortoise's *Remixed* is a reworking of material from *Millions Now Living Will Never Die. Remixed* is quite an eclectic compilation, featuring the work of Jim O'Rourke, Oval's Markus Popp, Bundy K. Brown, and others. The album also features Tortoise member-to-be Jeff Parker, as well as a Tortoise remix of Yo La Tengo's "Autumn Sweater." Some of the mixes stick to the original song forms, but the most successful ones depart from the preordained structure. O'Rourke's "Reference Resistance Gate" is a brilliant interpretation, the best of the album. "Taut and Tame," remixed by Wagon Christ's Luke Vibert, results in jungle-Tortoise. "Wait," which is not a remix but a new song, is a formidable effort and reflects a marked growth from *Millions*. This version of "Autumn Sweater" does justice to the already interesting tune through Tortoise's tinkering. This album is well worth the O'Rourke remix alone, but contains other standouts. It presents a fresh outlook on much of the material composed for *Millions*. —*Marc Gilman*

★ **Millions Now Living Will Never Die** / Jan. 30, 1996 / Thrill Jockey ♦♦♦♦♦
Tortoise's second album, *Millions Now Living Will Never Die*, continues their sonic explorations, using instruments and silence as a way of creating a musical sculpture. All of the band's instrumental pieces—and they can't be called songs, since there is hardly any structured songs on the record—are slow, almost maddeningly obscure. It isn't music that is designed for casual listening, yet intense listening doesn't quite yield rewards since the music is so repetitive, cryptic, and cerebral. —*Stephen Thomas Erlewine*

**TNT** / Mar. 10, 1998 / Thrill Jockey ♦♦♦♦
*TNT* doesn't offer radical new sounds, nor does it really progress much from *Millions Now Living Will Never Die*. Instead, the album is a refinement of the innovations of its groundbreaking predecessor. Initially, that may sound like a disappointment, but once the luxurious sonic textures take hold, it's easy to get lost within the sound. More than ever, the cut-and-paste song structures have the feeling of free jazz, even if the subdued instrumentation and subtle interplay is anything but confrontational. It's true that *TNT* doesn't have the sustained brilliance of *Millions*, but it offers a fascinating sonic journey of its own. —*Stephen Thomas Erlewine*

**In the Fishtank [EP]** / May 18, 1999 / In The Fishtank ♦♦♦
In a meeting of musical minds that took just 48 hours to record, meticulous sonic sculptors Tortoise collaborated with the Ex, a group of Dutch avant noise-mongers. The result is *In the Fishtank*, a six-song EP that sometimes blends the bands' divergent styles into a harmonious hybrid, and other times falls victim to stylistic clashes. The more spacious tracks, like "Pleasure as Usual," "Huge Hidden Spaces," and especially "The Lawn of the Limp," feature the blend of dissonance and ambience, and highlight the best qualities of each of the collaborators. The slightly more fractured and fractious "Did You Comb?" is still a fairly accessible mix of the groups' visions, but the Ex-dominant "Central Heating" is a noisy, acquired taste. Spontaneous and mercurial, *In the Fishtank* truly is experimental rock—but not all the experiments succeed completely. —*Heather Phares*

## Tosca

f. 1996, Vienna, Austria
*Group / Ambient Techno, Trip-Hop, Club/Dance*
A side project for Richard Dorfmeister of the trip-hop production team Kruder & Dorfmeister, Tosca also includes Rupert Huber. Recording for

K&D's G-Stone label, the outfit released the singles "Chocolate Elvis" and "Fuck Dub" during 1996. A triple-pack of remixes—from Fila Brazillia, Baby Mammoth, and others—appeared in early 1997, after which Tosca released their first LP, Opera. Suzuki followed in early 2000. [See Also: Kruder & Dorfmeister, Peace Orchestra] —*John Bush*

- **Opera** / 1997 / G-Stone ♦♦♦♦

Tosca's debut ably charts the groovy darkside of blunted trip-hop, with spare hip-hop samples and deep basslines contributing to tracks like "Fuck Dub," "Worksong," and "Chocolate Elvis." —*Keith Farley*

**Remix CD** / 1997 / G-Stone ♦♦♦

**Suzuki** / Mar. 7, 2000 / Studio !K7 ♦♦♦

Tosca's second album *Suzuki* takes a lighter, airier approach to the trip-hop terrain that *Opera* explored. The spare, shimmering title track's delicate synth textures, minimal beats, mellow rhythms, and breathy vocal samples set the tone for the rest of the album's laidback tracks. Though "Orozco," "Bass on the Boat," and "Ocean Beat" are more immediate variations on Tosca's relaxed sound, for the most part, *Suzuki* offers a locked groove of hypnotic, deeply chilled-out epics. —*Heather Phares*

## Tournesol

f. 1990, The Netherlands
*Group / Experimental Techno, Techno*

Dutch DJ and producer Tommy Gee formed ambient techno-funk outfit Tournesol with partner Thomas Lynge in 1990, after a series of live performances and a smattering of production work for European techno pioneer Kenneth Bager (of Dr. Baker fame). Deriving the name from Gee's propensity as a DJ for throwing in snippets of *Tin Tin* read-along records (Tournesol is the mad professor character in Belgian artist Herge's famous strip), the group's work first appeared on the Dutch CD-project *Secrets*, funded by the government as a showcase for local unknown talent. Following a scattering of compilation appearances and a highly successful remix of a Cut'N'Move track, Tournesol signed with the Belgian R&S label, through which they've released all of their EP- and album-length work under that name. Primarily engaging ambient, techno, electro, and funk on tracks not immediately recognizable as dancefloor fare, Tournesol's two full-length albums, *Kokotsu* and *Moonfunk*, are highly respected for pushing the boundaries of genre into areas of suggestive, far-reaching overlap. In addition to Tournesol, Gee has also released material as Word Up and Phat Phorce. The group also penned a deal with EMI Denmark as Phuture Rhyme, a more pop-oriented, mainstream dance crossover unit. —*Sean Cooper*

- **Kokotsu** / 1994 / Apollo ♦♦♦♦

A startlingly unified and accomplished debut long-player from the Dutch duo, with ambient-electro the primary compositional terrain. Although later work (such as the 1995 follow-up, *Moonfunk*) would mix styles even more freely, *Kokotsu* brings elements of hip-hop, techno, ambient, and electro-funk into close proximity, assembling dynamic, interesting, even danceable tracks admirable for their focus and consistency. —*Sean Cooper*

**Moonfunk** / 1995 / R&S ♦♦♦

Gee and Lynge take their compositional schizophrenic for a walk across the dancefloor, through the chill-room, and out the back exit to the out-jazz club down the block on their second long-player, this time for R&S proper. Moving from formless soundscapes through slick trip-hop, complex up-tempo electro, and floor-bang techno, the album succeeds on all fronts, layering style after style together in novel, well-groomed combinations. —*Sean Cooper*

## Tranquility Bass (Mike Kandel)

b. Chicago, IL
*Producer / Ambient House, Electronica, Ambient Techno, Trip-Hop, Club/Dance*

One of the original innovators in the ambient/trip-hop movement, Tranquility Bass' Mike Kandel submerged for most of the '90s before finally issuing his debut album in 1997. Kandel grew up in Chicago but moved to Los Angeles in the early '90s; inspired by his hometown's acid-house ideals, he formed the Exist Dance label in 1991 with Tom Chasteen and began producing classic ambient house singles like "They Came in Peace" (available on Mo'Wax's original *Headz* compilation) and "Cantamilla" (from the influential first volume of the *Excursions in Ambience* series). After Chasteen left Exist Dance in 1993, Kandel released a label compilation named *Transmitting from Heaven* but then disappeared to a remote island off the British Columbian coast to begin work on his debut album. Two years later, after trip-hop's influence had spread far and wide, he emerged from seclusion with *Let the Freak Flag Fly*, an album that reconciled his electronic fantasies with elements of psychedelia, funk and blues. A bit too trippy for its own good, however, the album wasn't received as well as Kandel's earlier recordings. —*John Bush*

- **Let the Freak Flag Fly** / Apr. 15, 1997 / Astralwerks ♦♦♦♦

Perhaps hoping for respect from rock critics, Kandel looked to the '60s for inspiration. Overtones of psychedelia, blues-rock, and even folk ballads transform the album from trip-hop into a wildly eclectic fusion extravaganza that only works occasionally. Despite several highlights ("The Bird" and "We All Want to Be Free"), *Let the Freak Flag Fly* bears all the marks of its over two year gestation period. —*John Bush*

**Beep!!! [EP]** / May 5, 1998 / Astralwerks ♦♦♦♦

Even though this disc features nine remixes based on only four songs from the *Let the Freak Flag Fly* LP, there is plenty of fodder here for a funky, long-haired leaping gnome rave-up. Get lost in the layers of the Harvey Keitel vs. Creature Feature remix of "The Bird." —*Tim Sheridan*

## Trans Am

f. 1990, Washington, DC
*Group / Experimental Rock, Indie Rock, Post-Rock/Experimental*

Trans Am are loosely associated with the mid-'90s "post-rock" scene centered around Tortoise, Ui, Labradford, Windy & Carl, etc., and the Thrill Jockey, Kranky, UHF, and Southern labels, among others. Although a vast distance separates Trans Am's albums, all of them are concerned with an extreme, somewhat humorous reorientation of the cliches and conventions of rock music, primarily through either technical (exaggerated displays of skill) or instrumental (electronics, effects) deviation. Formed in Washington, DC in 1990, the group didn't begin seriously recording until 1995, after its members (Phil Manley, Nathan Means, and Sebastian Thompson) finished college. Their self-titled debut, on the Chicago based Thrill Jockey label, was recorded after just a few rehearsals back together, and contained instrumental, largely improvised versions of simple rock-oriented figures based loosely (and, again, quite humorously) on '70s and '80s popular and progressive bands such as Boston, Bachman-Turner Overdrive, and Yes. Produced by Tortoise's John McEntire at Chicago's Idful Studios, the album was instantly (if somewhat ironically) lauded as an example of "post-rock" (an association that as much proves the meaningless of the "genre" as Trans-Am's own relation to it), in turn leading to a short live tour as Tortoise's opening act.

The group returned in the fall of 1996 with a self-titled EP of somewhat retro electro-funk experiments (released by Happy Go Lucky) which brought to the fore an affectation for electronics previously reserved either for between-time studio distraction or the brief interludes separating the meatier segments of their debut. With 1997's *Surrender to the Night*, however, Trans Am expanded that approach to album length, with inadvertent tributes to Kraftwerk, Hashim, Can, and New Order dominating and only a few recognizably "rock" songs included. Also signaling a change in focus was the expanded role electronics would play in their live performances; where earlier incarnations of the group included noodly Casio interludes that never grew beyond sideshow, *Surrender*'s more electronics-heavy material meant more of the stage space was given over to analog machines, trigger devices, and MIDI-wired beatboxes. Trans-Am's inclusion on Mille Plateaux label's double-CD compilation, *In Memorium: Gilles Deleuze* (alongside Cristian Vogel, Beequeen, Mike Ink, and Atom Heart, as well as labelmates Rome and Oval) also helped introduce the band to European audiences, where they've found similar popularity as such electronic/acoustic hybrids as Flying Saucer Attack and Stereolab. Fourth album *Futureworld* followed in 1999, and a year later, the group returned with their most expansive album yet, *The Red Line*, which the group recorded in their own National Recording Studio. —*Sean Cooper*

- **Trans Am** / Jan. 30, 1996 / Thrill Jockey ♦♦♦♦

Trans Am play mostly Big Dumb Rock (of the tongue in cheek variety) on their Thrill Jockey debut, trading Boston and Foreigner licks with a talent for technique and not a little ironic displacement. Absence the irony, this would be an absolutely horrendous record, but kept in mind, it's an enjoyable, if somewhat expendable listen. —*Sean Cooper*

**Surrender to the Night** / Feb. 3, 1997 / Thrill Jockey ♦♦♦
Trans-Am prove in one mildly amusing, backward-turned sitting that much of what defines "post-rock" sounds suspiciously like rock's longtime nemesis, the late-'70s pre-techno Euro-pop of Kraftwerk and New Order. With much of this record a simple meditation on the latter, *Surrender to the Night* is surprisingly slim on new ideas, sounding for the most part either like a self-defacing gambit or an updater course for those who missed it the first time around. The group is at its best when they stumble onto the occasional square-foot of new territory (as on "Cologne," "Tough Love," and the title cut, all of which wed live, more immediately rock-based instrumentation with electro-funk rhythms and synth figures), but much of *Surrender* lay on familiar, by now somewhat fallow soil. —*Sean Cooper*

**The Surveillance** / Mar. 10, 1998 / Thrill Jockey ♦♦♦♦
True artists find a voice and know how far they can stretch its ability to communicate. Trans Am have done just that with instrumental rock which relies on synthesizers almost as much as techno does. They can be at one moment abrasively digital, then quietly ambient by the end of the track. Such vacillation could be overly ambitious for many groups, but Trans Am manages to pull it off in a way that makes you think the song could have gone nowhere else. By working a contrasting harsh delivery and tranquil coda into a single piece naturally, Trans Am prove themselves deft masters of their craft. —*Thomas Schulte*

**Futureworld** / Mar. 23, 1999 / Thrill Jockey ♦♦♦♦
Trans Am's 1999 release, *Futureworld*, showcases the band's love of retro-futurism and above all, rock. Songs like "Television Eyes" and "City in Flames" feature a churning mix of drums, guitars, and budget keyboards, giving the lie to Trans Am's "post-rock" label. More than anything, *Futureworld* is drummer Sebastian Thompson's album—his work on acoustic, electric, and programmed drums propels the music, particularly on the Teutonic "AM Rhein." As the album progresses, however, it becomes increasingly melodic and keyboard-driven, as the relatively gentle "Runners Standing Still" and "Sad and Young" attest. Throw in the poppy title track and "Cocaine Computer's" sleazy, uptight disco, and the result is *Futureworld*, Trans Am's most diverse and accomplished work yet. —*Heather Phares*

**Red Line** / Sep. 5, 2000 / Thrill Jockey ♦♦♦♦
Trans Am marshals together a variegated convoy of musical styles on their 2000 Thrill Jockey release *Red Line*. With a tweaked power-trio instrumentation supplying the torque for the 21 songs on this, their fifth CD, Trans Am resolutely fans out into a number of uncharted sonic arteries. Live recordings of the trio are juxtaposed next to and spliced together with synthetic effects and electronic sonority. On *Red Line*'s first track, "Let's Take the Fresh Step Together," the band sets an atmospheric tone with the drone-like wash of electronic sine waves. After 45 seconds of this ethereal buildup, drummer Sebastian Thompson clears the air with a barrage of tom and buzz rolls, inviting guitarists/keyboardists Phil Manley and Nathan Means to join in on a Devo-esque uptempo pop tune. A number of tracks on the album feature the band playing drums in a loose rendition of a Japanese Taiko performance. Also, live jams that feature the sound of the room as much as they do the individual players are peppered throughout the CD.

Something of a paradox, Trans Am is considered by some to belong to the post-rock roster of bands (i.e., Tortoise, Ui, Labradford, etc.), though their earlier forays have been compared to Kiss, and they are presently fond of using such '70s rock gadgets as the vocoder (see Peter Frampton). Whatever their position within the nomenclature of the music market's hierarchy of styles may be, Trans Am intrepidly places their hood ornament on the impermanent no man's land that joins rollicking prog-rock instrumentations with futuristic synth-laced fantasies. This is definitely a CD worth checking out. —*John Vallier*

## TransGlobal Underground

f. 1992, London, England
*Group / Ambient Dub, Tribal-House, Club/Dance, Ethnic Fusion*
TransGlobal Underground is a UK-based collective fusing as many different kinds of world music as its members can get their hands on. The group's core is composed of vocalist Natacha Atlas (who has recorded with Jah Wobble, Apache Indian, and her own band, Atlas Project), keyboardist Alex Kasiek, drum programmer Man Tu, and founder, bassist, and sampler Count Dubulah. The project grew out of a mutual love for dance, avant-garde, Arabic, and world music and draws on each member's listening tastes and cultural backgrounds. Their debut album, *Dream of 100 Nations*, was released in 1994, quickly followed by *International Times*. After 1995's *Interplanetary Meltdown*, TransGlobal Underground returned in 1997 with *Psychic Karaoke. Rejoice, Rejoice* followed a year later. —*Steve Huey*

**International Times** / 1994 / Epic ♦♦♦
Blending trip-hop beats with the music of India, *International Times* features occasional vocals with an Eastern flair and worldbeat samples to spice up the multi-cultural brew. —*John Bush*

**Interplanetary Meltdown** / 1995 / Nation ♦♦♦
Much less busy than TGU's usual style, this refreshing remix package includes eclectic contributions from the Drum Club, Sabres of Paradise, Justin Robertson, Dreadzone, Delta Lady, and Youth. —*John Bush*

• **Psychic Karaoke** / Feb. 25, 1997 / MCA ♦♦♦♦
There's worldbeat, and then there's worldbeat. *Psychic Karaoke* starts off with "Chariot," during the seven-minute course of which you get to hear Middle Eastern percussion, a string section, bruising breakbeats, a Cockney rapper, and Natacha Atlas warbling like a dancehall muezzin. So much for track one. And it only gets better, at least for a while: "Mouth Wedding" is a more Afrocentric outing with a surprising Adrian Sherwood/African Headcharge ambience, and "A Tongue of Flame" is a snaky, satisfying reggae workout. But things start to bog down a bit by the end, and as you approach the 78th minute of this generous album, you might be forgiven for checking to make sure you didn't accidentally hit the "repeat" button on your CD player. *Psychic Karaoke* is strong and effective medicine, but it's best taken in measured doses. —*Rick Anderson*

**Rejoice, Rejoice** / Jun. 30, 1998 / MCA ♦♦♦♦
Not exactly the most radio-friendly act in the world, TransGlobal Underground goes for a highly adventurous and quirky blend of club and world music on the rhythmic *Rejoice, Rejoice*. Underground has a very East-meets-West outlook—dance music, reggae, electronica, funk, and hip-hop are combined with elements of Indian, Middle Eastern, and African music. Synthesizers and keyboards are prominent, but the high-tech element is combined with everything from Indian tabla drums and sitar to the saz, a string instrument associated with traditional Turkish music. Not surprisingly, *Rejoice, Rejoice* was ignored by commercial radio, although some club DJs realized just how much Underground had going for it. For broad-minded listeners looking for something out of the ordinary, this CD is quite an adventure. —*Alex Henderson*

## Ron Trent

b. 1974
*Producer, DJ / Jazz-House, Club/Dance, House, Techno*
Probably the only Chicago house producer to rate one of the best *techno singles* of all time, Ron Trent recorded his classic acid workout "Altered States" in 1990 but gradually moved away from mechanistic trance-state dance to embrace a deep house sound with plenty of African percussion. Born and raised in Chicago, Trent learned much about music from his father, a disco DJ. Still of high-school age when he recorded "Altered States" for Armando's Warehouse label, Trent reissued the track on the Dutch label Djax-Up-Beats in 1991, with remixes by Carl Craig.

He released a few other singles during the early '90s before hooking up with Detroiter Chez Damier, who'd recorded with techno star Kevin Saunderson and owned the legendary Music Institute club during the '80s. The pair recorded singles for Saunderson's KMS ("The Choice" as Chez 'N Trent, and "Don't Try" as Ron & Chez D), then opened up their own Prescription Records. The label made waves in deep house circles with its first release, Romanthony's "Wanderer." Trent and Damier also contributed to the label with the *Prescription Underground* EP. The duo also recorded a pair of singles with Maurizio, the Berlin producer whose productions for Chain Reaction launched a wave of experimental techno singles.

Trent gradually moved from solo productions or collaborations with Damier to recruit a team of producers and vocalists known USG, for Urban Sound Gallery. Later based in Brooklyn, Trent and USG debuted with a beautiful deep-house cut titled "N Came U" on Clair Audience. He also gained a different partner, Anthony Nicholson. In 1999, two Trent full-lengths appeared on British labels. The first, USG's *African Blues*, was released on Distance, while the proper solo debut, *Primitive Ants*, appeared on Peacefrog. —*John Bush*

- **Altered States [Single]** / 1990 / Warehouse ♦♦♦♦
As druggy and minimalistic as the title indicates, Ron Trent's house *and* techno classic "Altered States" has a few emotive string chords and a simplistic bassline but inventive, ever-changing beats to make up for it. Reportedly recorded entirely in Trent's bedroom, *Altered States* remains one of the best Detroit-Chicago fusions ever produced. —*John Bush*

**Primitive Arts** / Nov. 22, 1999 / Peacefrog ♦♦♦♦

## Tricky (Adrian Thaws)

b. 1964, Knowle West, Bristol, Avon, England
*Vocals, Producer / Electronica, Trip-Hop, Club/Dance, Alternative Pop/Rock*
Originally, Tricky was a member of the Wild Bunch, a Bristol-based rap troupe that eventually metamorphosized into Massive Attack during the early '90s. Tricky provided pivotal raps on Massive Attack's groundbreaking 1992 album *Blue Lines*. The following year, he released his debut single, "Aftermath." Before he recorded "Aftermath," he met a teenage vocalist named Martina, who would become his full-time musical collaborator; all albums released under Tricky's name feature her contributions.

Tricky signed a contract with 4th & Broadway in 1994. The contract contained a clause which allowed him to release side-projects under different names, in addition to regular Tricky releases. "Ponderosa" and "Overcome" were released over the course of 1994; that same year, he made a cameo on Massive Attack's second album, *Protection*. Tricky's debut album, *Maxinquaye*, appeared in the spring of 1995. Not only did the album receive overwhelmingly positive reviews when it was released, but it entered in the UK charts at number two, despite the total lack of daytime radio airplay. Throughout 1995, Tricky was omnipresent in the UK, collaborating with and remixing for a wide variety of artists, including Björk, Luscious Jackson, and Whale. In the fall of 1995, he released *Tricky Vs. the Gravediggaz*, a collaboration with the American hardcore rap group, as well as a single called "I Be the Prophet," which was released under the name Starving Souls. At the end of the year, *Maxinquaye* topped many year-end polls in Britain, including the *Melody Maker* and *NME*.

In February of 1996, *Nearly God*—an album featuring Tricky's collaborations with artists as diverse as Terry Hall, Björk, Alison Moyet, and Neneh Cherry—was released, again to strong reviews; the album was released in the US six months later. After completing the second full-fledged Tricky album, he relocated to New York City early in 1996, where he began working with underground rappers. An EP called *Grassroots* was released in the US in September. Two months later, Tricky's official second album, *Pre-Millenium Tension*, was released. Again, Tricky received positive reviews, though there were a few dissenting opinions.

In addition to his three releases of 1996, he remixed artists as diverse as Elvis Costello, Garbage, Yoko Ono, and Bush. Tricky's next full-length solo effort, *Angels with Dirty Faces*, appeared in 1998, followed a year later by *Juxtapose*, a collaboration with Cypress Hill's DJ Muggs and DMX's Grease. —*Stephen Thomas Erlewine*

★ **Maxinquaye** / Apr. 18, 1995 / 4th & Broadway ♦♦♦♦♦
Though he hates the label of trip-hop, Tricky's debut album *Maxinquaye* is one of the finest that the genre has to offer. "Ponderosa," "Suffocated Love," and "Pumpkin" are disturbing and beautiful, with ominous background noises and Martina's soaring vocals, while tracks like the group's cover of "Black Steel" show off their harder side. A striking debut, Tricky's *Maxinquaye* is only the beginning for this innovative artist. —*Heather Phares*

**Nearly God** / Apr. 29, 1996 / Fourth & Broadway/Durban Poison ♦♦♦♦
*Nearly God* is Tricky's unofficial second album—he calls it a collection of brilliant, incomplete demos. When Tricky signed his contract with Island, it allowed him to release an album a year under a different name and *Nearly God* is the first of these efforts. Tricky recorded the record with a diverse cast of collaborators—in addition to his partner Martina, there's Terry Hall, Björk, Neneh Cherry, Cath Coffey, Dedi Madden, and Alison Moyet (Damon Albarn pulled his track just before the album's release). Building on the ghostly, dark soundscapes of Tricky's debut, *Maxinquaye*, *Nearly God* narrows the focus of his first record by making the music slower, hazier, and more distubing. It's not as coherent as *Maxinquaye*, but that's part of its appeal. *Nearly God* is a haunting, fractured, surreal nightmare that doesn't always make sense but never fails to make an impact. Certain collaborators work better than others—Tricky understands the eeriness of Terry Hall's voice, but he does nothing to tame Alison Moyet's inappropriate bluesy shrieking—but the overall effect of the album is quietly devastating. It gets under your skin and stays there. It's a brilliantly evocative nightmare. —*Stephen Thomas Erlewine*

**Grassroots [EP]** / Aug. 1996 / ffrr ♦♦
Perhaps in an effort to establish himself in the American hip-hop market—which largely ignored his groundbreaking debut, *Maxinquaye*—Tricky released the *Grassroots EP* in the summer of 1996. Recorded in early 1996, *Grassroots* consists primarily of one-off collaborations with a variety of underground and relatively undistinctive New York rappers and musicians, whose music is given weight by Tricky's menacing, hazy production. Tricky appears in the background of each song, murmuring indecipherably, but it's only when he takes the forefront on "Tricky Kid" that the EP matches the tense, psychotic soundscapes of *Maxinquaye* and *Nearly God*. The remaining four tracks have their moments—Drunkenstein's backing vocals are evocative, and "Devils Helper" is entrancing—but for the most part, *Grassroots* consists of experiments that never quite reach their full potential. —*Stephen Thomas Erlewine*

**Pre-Millennium Tension** / Nov. 11, 1996 / PolyGram ♦♦♦♦
*Maxinquaye* was an unexpected hit in England, launching a wave of similar-sounding artists, who incorporated Tricky's innovations into safer pop territory. Tricky responded by travelling to Jamaica to record *Pre-Millennium Tension*, a nervy, claustrophobic record that thrives in its own paranoia. Scaling back the clattering hooks of *Maxinquaye* and slowing the beat down, Tricky has created a hallucinatory soundscape, where the rhythms, samples, and guitars intertwine into a crawling processions of menacing sounds and disembodied lyrical threats. Its tone is set by the backward guitar loops of "Vent" and continued through the shifting "Christiansands" and the tense, lyrically dense "Tricky Kid," easily Tricky's best straight rap to date. Occasionally, the gloom is broken, such as when the shimmering piano chords of "Makes Me Want to Die" ring out, but nearly as often, it becomes bogged down in its own murk, as in the long ragga rant "Ghetto Youth." While the lyrics are often quite effective in conveying dope-addled paranoia, what ties the album together is its layered rhythms and soundscapes. Though it might not sound that way immediately, *Pre-Millennium Tension* is as much Tricky reaching back to his hardcore rap roots as it is a sonic exploration. As such, it stands as a transition record for Tricky, but its overall effect is only slightly less powerful than *Maxinquaye* or *Nearly God*. —*Stephen Thomas Erlewine*

**Angels with Dirty Faces** / Jun. 2, 1998 / PolyGram ♦♦♦
Perhaps *Maxinquaye* was such a startling, focused, brilliant debut that Tricky's subsequent albums would have paled in comparison, regardless of their quality. Nevertheless, his desire to distance himself from the coffeehouse trip-hop that appeared after *Maxinquaye* forced him into a dark, paranoid corner. Determined to strip away all of his fairweather fans, he delivered the claustrophobic *Pre-Millennium Tension*, a paranoid record that its follow-up, *Angels with Dirty Faces*, mirrors. Since it builds upon *Pre-Millennium* instead of breaking new ground, *Angels* may strike some listeners as merely a retread, but it gradually reveals new layers upon repeated listens. Tricky has been redefining his rhythms, adding skittering jungle loops and hardcore hip-hop beats to his trademark dub-warped trip-hop. On top of that, he's expanding his sonic palette, adding cheap synthesizers and avant-garde guitarists to create a nightmarish junk-pile of hip-hop, dub, electronica, rock, and gospel. Again, Martina is on board and her stylish croon adds moments of relief to the enveloping dread, as does Polly Harvey on the odd gospel-tinged "Broken Homes." Specific tracks work well individually—"Mellow," "Singing the Blues," "Angels with Dirty Faces" and the absurd, bile-ridden "Record Companies," in particular—but on the whole *Angels with Dirty Faces* is less than the sum of its parts. By being slightly different but essentially the same as *Pre-Millennium Tension*, *Angels with Dirty Faces* demands that listeners meet it on its own terms. Whether they'll want to is another matter entirely. —*Stephen Thomas Erlewine*

**Juxtapose** / Aug. 17, 1999 / Polygram ♦♦♦
When *Maxinquaye* was released in 1995, Tricky's potential seemed boundless. When his fifth album, *Juxtapose*, was released four years later, those days were long gone. In those years, he didn't expand his trademark sound—a creeping, menacing blend of hip-hop, alternative rock, and ragga, all delivered with stoned paranoia—instead, he narrowed it. Each album felt like a

reduction of the one before. There were small, subtle differences, yet they were only revealed with close listening—and since the rewards were smaller with each subsequent album, you couldn't blame one-time fans and critics for eventually giving up the ghost. Perhaps Tricky realized this, since he designed *Juxtapose* to be his most ambitious, eclectic album since *Maxinquaye*. It was to be the album that finally broke him to American audiences—not the indie-rockers who were bowled over with *Maxinquaye* and collected Massive Attack singles—but the mainstream hip-hop audience, which Tricky coveted because of his love of the golden age of hip-hop. So, he teamed with DJ Muggs (the architect of Cypress Hill's sound, which was clearly a precedent for Tricky) and DMX's producer Grease, intent on delivering an album that played like hip-hop, not trip-hop. Something must have went wrong during the production, since the end result is hardly a collaboration—in fact, it feels truncated, weighing in at a mere 35 minutes. Even so, the collaboration worked in other ways, since Tricky often seems revitalized throughout *Juxtapose*. That much is evident by the stellar opening cut, "For Real." It may be one of his typical anti-record company rants, but the music is different—spaced-out sexy, melodic, and appealing, even when it gets foreboding. It's a terrific beginning, suggesting that this will be the first album that offers a significant variation on Tricky's signature sound. And it does, in a way, but it may not go far enough for some tastes, since a good portion of this brief album is devoted to retreads, which reveal all too well his weaknesses. Example: Tricky remains unduly infatuated with ragga, letting British toaster Mad Dog run wild on the great majority of the album. His frenetic delivery single-handedly breaks the spell on each track he's featured on—but he does offer distraction on the tracks that sound the most like by-the-book efforts. Elsewhere, Tricky pushes forward in inventive ways—"Contradictive" is blessed by Spanish guitars and elongated strings and is his best pop move to date; "She Said" successfully deepens the menace with paranoid drums; and "Scrappy Love" is a haunting blend of soul and trip-hop, highlighted by eerie piano reminiscent of DJ Shadow. All of these add weight to *Juxtapose*, and more or less excuse the retreads that unfortunately take up the heart of the album. That makes *Juxtapose* a qualified success, but it is a success, since the moments that work are his best efforts in years. —*Stephen Thomas Erlewine*

## Keith Tucker

b. Detroit, MI
*Producer, DJ / Detroit Techno, Electro, Club/Dance, Techno*
Keith Tucker was a founding member of Detroit electro group Aux 88 before departing in 1996 to pursue various solo projects. One of the key forces responsible for Detroit techno's return to its electro roots, Tucker, along with artists such as "Mad" Mike Banks, Drexciya, and Will Web, helped reinvigorate the waning Detroit sound in the mid-'90s by revisiting some of the elements that made the music in its early form so vibrant and exciting: driving, funk-derived rhythms, futuristic electronics, and down'n'dirty production.

A native of Detroit's rougher East Side neighborhood (where "booty"-style electro and ghetto funk were and are the most popular styles of music), Tucker grew up listening to early Detroit classics such as Cybotron's "Clear" and "R9" and Model 500's "Nite Drive Thru Babylon." A mobile DJ through high school, he formed RX-7 with Tommy Hamilton and Tony Horton in the mid-'80s, playing talent shows and local rap festivals as an electro cover band; their stage show consisted of a barrage of keyboards and a single drum machine on which they belted out Juan Atkins tunes and a few of originals. RX-7 dissolved in 1990, and Tucker signed with Metroplex (together with Jesse Anderson) as Frequency. He reunited with Hamilton in 1992 to form Aux 88, a group pursuing an even more obviously electro/bass-derived sound than his previous work. The pair released a number of well-received singles and EPs (both as Aux 88 and as Alien FM) as well as the full-length CD/compilation, *88 FM*, before Tucker departed in 1996 due to artistic differences (Hamilton continues to record under the name with partner William Smith).

Tucker's subsequent solo work under the names DJ K-1 and Optic Nerve, among others, has appeared through the Direct Beat, Magick Trax, Tresor, and Puzzlebox labels, the latter of which Tucker formed in 1996 with fellow Detroit producer Anthony Shakir (the two record together under the name Da Sampla). Continuing in the new-school vein of his Aux releases, Tucker has pursued both techno and electro on these twelves, with his "K-1 Agenda" (on Direct Beat) and "Lifeform" (on Puzzlebox) the most accomplished of the lot. The *Lifeform* EP followed in 1997. —*Sean Cooper*

**Lifeform [EP]** / Jun. 16, 1997 / Puzzlebox ♦♦♦
● **Keith Tucker [EP]** / Nov. 30, 1998 / Electrecord ♦♦♦♦
Tucker's six-track EP for Electrecord consists of silky smooth Detroit electro. Highlights include the title track, a remix of "Erase the Time," and "Metropolis Optic Nerve." —*Keith Farley*

## David Tudor

b. Jan. 20, 1926, Philadelphia, PA, d. Aug. 13, 1996, Tomkins Cove, NY
*Producer, Composer / Experimental, Avant-Garde*
American experimental music's foremost performer, pianist David Tudor remains as inextricably linked to many of the most groundbreaking pieces in the modern canon as their respective composers; long John Cage's most intimate associate, he also delivered virtuoso early performances of landmark works by Pierre Boulez, Earle Brown, Sylvano Bussotti, Morton Feldman, Karlheinz Stockhausen, and La Monte Young, many of them written expressly with Tudor in mind. He was born in Philadelphia on January 20, 1926 and throughout his teens played organ at the city's St. Mark's Church, later studying theory and composition under H. William Hawke and Stefan Wolpe. In New York on December 17, 1950, Tudor delivered the American premiere of Boulez's *Deuxième Sonate pour Piano*—just the second performance of the piece anywhere, it immediately launched him to the vanguard of the experimental community.

Tudor's extended collaboration with Cage began during the early '50s, and in 1952 he premiered the composer's notorious *4'33";* Cage later stated that virtually all of his work from that point until around 1970 was written either directly for Tudor or for his consideration. Widely praised for his imaginative solutions to the often deliberate challenges of notation and performance presented by the pieces he tackled, Tudor's genius in time began to directly influence the composers whose work he interpreted, becoming an essential component of their creative processes. Also serving as an instructor and pianist-in-residence at Black Mountain College in North Carolina and at the Internationale Ferienkurse fur Neue Musik in Darmstadt, Germany, during the late '50s, he began experimenting with the electronic modification of sound sources, additionally teaming with Cage on his Project of Music for Magnetic Tape.

As the next decade approached, Tudor began initiating the move away from taped sources towards live electronic music; by the end of the '60s, he brought his career as a pianist to a close, with electronic performance and composition becoming his sole focus in the years to follow. Manufacturing and designing his own instruments and technological equipment, he mounted works closely tied to visual media including light systems, dance, television, theater, film, and four-color laser projections—1966's *Bandoneon!,* for example, employed lighting and audio circuitry, moving loudspeaker sculptures, and projected video images. In 1968, Tudor collaborated with Cage, Lowell Cross, Marcel Duchamp, and Gordon Mumma on *Reunion;* between 1969 and 1977, he also teamed with Cross and Carson Jeffries on a series of works for video and/or laser display.

While collaborating on the design of the Pepsi Pavillion at Expo '70 in Osaka, Japan, Tudor composed and performed several new works, among them an early version of the seminal *Microphone*. As his work in electronic music continued, he increasingly experimented with new components, circuitry, and interconnections, with the end results determining both compositional and performing strategies. Much of Tudor's major work of the period was commissioned by the Merce Cunningham Dance Company, with whom he'd been affiliated since their 1953 inception; these compositions included 1974's *Toneburst*, 1976's *Forest Speech*, 1978's *Weatherings*, 1981's *Phonemes*, 1987's *Webwork*, and 1990's *Virtual Focus*. After Cage's 1992 death, Tudor succeeded him as the Cunningham troupe's musical director; Tudor himself died at his home in Tomkins Cove, New York on August 13, 1996. —*Jason Ankeny*

**Three Works for Live Electronics: Pulsers/Untitled/Phonemes** / 1976 / Lovely Music ♦♦♦
A CD re-issue of the original vinyl release. *Pulsers* (1976), a delightful study of "the world of rhythms created electronically by analog circuitry," uses "home-brew" electronics, incorporating an improvised tape on electronic violin by Takehisa Kosugi. *Untitled* (1972) is an experiment in multiple feedback loops in real spaces, recorded, mixed, and played back to loops in other spaces—electronic music without oscillators or recorded natural sound ma-

terials. *Phonemes* (1981) is an additional piece to the original vinyl release, which uses a percussion generator and a vocoder with small discrete bands to take shorts sounds and lengthen them, or long sounds and shorten them in a unique live interplay. —*"Blue" Gene Tyranny*

• **Microphone (1975)** / 1991 / Cramps ♦♦♦♦
A re-issue on CD of this classic. One of the great and wild "live electronic" pieces with sounds that Tudor once described as sounding to him like dinosaur howls echoing in pre-historic caves to timid, sweet calls of unidentifiable creatures. The original circuitry was designed by Tudor and Gordon Mumma. —*"Blue" Gene Tyranny*

**David Tudor Plays Cage and Tudor** / 1993 / ATONAL ♦♦♦♦
This album features brilliant performances of two extended compositions showing the two aspects of Tudor, both as a creative pianist in his now classic 1958 realization of John Cage's "Solo for Piano" (from the "Concert for Piano and Orchestra" 1957-58, and recorded in 1982 in Amsterdam), and as an innovative composer-performer of live electronic music in his "Neural Synthesis (No. 2)" (1993), created on the Neural-Network Audio Synthesizer that utilizes the Intel 80710NX neural-network chip and recorded in live performance in Brooklyn, NY that same year. For further description, please see the review of Tudor's Lovely Music *Neural Synthesis* CD. —*"Blue" Gene Tyranny*

**Neural Synthesis, Nos. 6-8** / 1995 / Lovely Music ♦♦♦♦
Derived from the score *Neural Synthesis Plus* used to accompany Merce Cunningham's dance *Enter,* the primary electronic instrument employed in the piece is a synthesizer with 64 non-linear amplifiers (metaphorical neurons), which have 10,240 programmable interconnections that emulate neuron cells in our brains and can process many analog signals in parallel. Sixteen of the 64 "neurons" are connected in feedback circuits to create sound oscillators, with tank circuits to control their frequencies. During a performance, Tudor chooses up to 14 channels of output, further modifying them with other electronic devices... while he also listens, learns patterns (heuristically) and responds and modifies his actions. In this recording, Tudor uses a new binaural technique for translating sound into out-of-head localizations, seeming to surround the listener. For all this technology, the sound results still reflect Tudor's love of simple, characterful sounds that are often drolly humorous even if not identifiable in any ordinary context. —*"Blue" Gene Tyranny*

## Tuff Jam

f. 1996, London, England
*Group / Speed Garage, Garage, Club/Dance, House*

Karl "Tuff Enuff" Brown and Matt "Jam" Lamont were two of the most hyped producers in Britain during 1997, thanks to their seizure of the banner for speed-garage, the dance style based on classic garage music but with a multitude of inspiration from the ragga end of jungle/drum'n'bass. The two were both DJing garage nights at clubs like the Arches during 1996 when they met and gradually moved into production together, using the Catch Productions studio to remix tracks from Rosie Gaines, En Vogue, Brand New Heavies, TJR, and Kim English. Gaines' "Closer than Close" and TJR's "Just Gets Better" began to get pushed at clubs alongside other speed-garage anthems like Double 99's "RIP Groove" and remix productions by Americans Armand Van Helden and Todd Edwards. The Tuff Jam crew released their first compilation, the brilliant *Underground Frequencies, Vol. 1,* in late 1997. A second volume followed in 1998. —*John Bush*

• **Underground Frequencies, Vol. 1** / Jun. 23, 1997 / Satellite ♦♦♦♦
The first essential speed garage compilation, *Underground Frequencies* presents the best club tracks as selected by DJs Matt "Jam" Lamont and Karl "Tuff Enuff" Brown from their much-hyped sets. Included are garage anthems like Double 99's "RIP Groove" and Roy Davis, Jr.'s "Gabrielle," plus American productions (by Armand Van Helden and Todd Edwards) which fit in well with the Brits. —*John Bush*

**Underground Frequencies, Vol. 2** / 1998 / Satellite ♦♦♦
The second collection of (mostly) Tuff Jam tracks and remixes includes productions for Usher, En Vogue, and Indo as well as Tuff Jam originals like "Sweet Love" by Ultymate. The sound is a bit less raw than on *Underground Frequencies, Vol. 1* (the duo appear to favor expansive divas rather than robotic time-stretches), but volume two packs just as big a punch as the original. —*John Bush*

## Turn On

f. 1997, London, England
*Group / Experimental Rock, Indie Rock, Post-Rock/Experimental*

Turn On is a side project by Stereolab's Tim Gane and the High Llamas' Sean O'Hagan, two of the leading figures of the '90s avant-pop underground; Andy Ramsay is the band's third member. Of those two groups, Turn On is the most similar to Stereolab, specifically Stereolab circa their 1993 album *The Groop Played "Space Age Batchelor Pad Music",* complete with gurgling synthesizers and layers of analog keyboards. —*Stephen Thomas Erlewine*

• **Turn On [EP]** / Aug. 1997 / Duophonics ♦♦♦
The group's largely instrumental, eponymous debut is considerably less complex and arranged than *Emperor Tomato Ketchup* or any High Llamas record, but it isn't quite as primitively droney as early 'Lab records. Instead, it's a subtle record, with each track sustaining a particular mood. There are jazzy overtones but not much jazz improvisation, and there are hints of easy-listening arrangements that are never kitschy. While it doesn't reach the heights of the best Stereolab records, *Turn On* does provide similar thrills, and for dedicated listeners, that's enough to make it necessary listening. —*Stephen Thomas Erlewine*

## 23 Skidoo

f. 1979, London, England, db. 1984
*Group / Experimental Rock, Industrial*

Early compatriots of Cabaret Voltaire and Throbbing Gristle on Britain's experimental/industrial scene, 23 Skidoo pursued an improvisational fusion of ethnic drumming and post-punk dance on their few recordings of the early '80s. Named after a mysterious Illuminati phrase that appeared in the work of Aleister Crowley, William Burroughs, and filmmaker Julian Biggs, the group formed in London around brothers (and martial-arts experts) Alex and Johnny Turnbull and Fritz Catlin (aka Fritz Haamann). Influenced by Fela Kuti and the emerging New York hip-hop scene, 23 Skidoo released their first single "Ethics" in 1980. For their second, the band recorded at Cabaret Voltaire's Western Works with Genesis P-Orridge of Throbbing Gristle helping out on production.

In 1982, 23 Skidoo released the mini-LP *Seven Songs* and the *Tearing Up the Plans* EP for the Fetish label (also home to recordings by Throbbing Gristle and Clock DVA). After replacing their nominal rhythm section with bassist Sketch (who shared the trio's aesthetic), the band continued with 1983's *The Culling Is Coming* and 1984's *Urban Gamelan.* Their varied influences and occasionally sublime sound confused many critics and listeners, who expected all industrial groups to be as loud and chaotic as the emerging Test Dept. or Einsturzende Neubaten. Even after disbanding in 1984 however, 23 Skidoo continued recording together sporadically during the rest of the decade, and the quartet—the Turnbulls plus Catlin and Sketch—formed their own Ronin label in 1989. Though no material from the band appeared in the '90s, they did several remixes and recorded for advertisers including Nike, Wrangler, and Smirnoff. Finally, in 2000, 23 Skidoo released a new, self-titled album for Virgin. —*John Bush*

**Seven Songs EP** / 1982 / Fetish ♦♦♦♦
The group's first release, also available in a reissue that boosted it to a full length, is a prescient set of avant-funk tape music with a discernible Third World influence that places it in similar territory to the Eno/Byrne collaboration *My Life in the Bush of Ghosts* released just one year before. —*Keith Farley*

• **The Culling Is Coming** / 1983 / Operation Twilight ♦♦♦♦
An album of half studio, half live material (the latter recorded at *the Womad Festival*), *The Culling Is Coming* expands on 23 Skidoo's early material but with more emphasis on free-form sound exploration instead of post-punk funk. The lack of a sturdy framework makes comprehension difficult, though the scattered percussion, tape music and screeching horns are intense throughout. —*Keith Farley*

**Urban Gamelan** / 1984 / Illuminated ♦♦
*Urban Gamelan* is an intriguing fusion of 23 Skidoo's street-punk ethics with the trance-like sounds of Indonesian gamelan gong music. Using an assortment of industrial detritus including glass bottles and paint cans, the group reprises the trademark sounds of Java and Bali with flair. —*Keith Farley*

**23 Skidoo** / 2000 / Virgin ♦♦♦

## Twerk (Shawn Hatfield)
b. 1974, Santa Cruz, CA
*Producer / Minimal Techno, Experimental Techno, Club/Dance, Techno*
Shawn Hatfield's Twerk project is allied with the growing minimal/experimental techno scene in California, led by producers Kit Clayton and Sutekh. Originally based in Santa Cruz, Hatfield began DJing hip-hop in the late '80s and soon moved on to acid jazz. After moving to San Francisco during the early '90s and immersing himself in the harder edge of techno, he gave up DJing in 1997 to begin recording. He recorded his first single ("Los Colores") with mixing partner DJ Cesar and released it through the Bay Area's Organised Noise label. The Twerk EP *Tide of Events* gained release on Britain's Planet Rhythm later that year, and Hatfield also completed an EP for Organised Noise, *Enemies of the State*. He collaborated with Sutekh and Safety Scissors on the *Deadpan Escapement* LP for Belief Systems and released singles for Cytrax and Delay (both affiliated with Clayton and Sutekh). Germany's Force Inc released Twerk's debut full-length *Humantics* in early 2000. —*John Bush*

- **Humantics** / Mar. 14, 2000 / Force Inc ♦♦♦
*Humantics* comprises nine tracks of fast-moving techno that could be called straight-ahead if not for the obvious care that's been taken in making complex productions out of simple building blocks. Similar to his prior influences (Cristian Vogel, Neil Landstrumm), Twerk makes a basic techno track into something much more by layering his roster of left field effects, split second percussion samples, and melancholy synth over the four-four rhythms. The heavy dub influence of compatriots like Sutekh or Kit Clayton is only occasionally audible; for the most part, Twerk keeps his drum programs unprocessed, and the lack of echo or reverb keeps everything nice and precise. —*John Bush*

## Twisted Science (Jonathon Tye)
*Producer / Experimental Jungle, Experimental Techno, Electronica, Ambient Techno, Jungle/Drum'N'Bass*
Although Jonathon Tye's work as one-half of MLO has turned mainly on ambient and house, his solo work as Twisted Science has headed for the jagged edge of extremity, exploiting the more beastly potential of jungle, mid-tempo breakbeat, and hardcore techno against a wall of piercing noise and distortion. His debut release, appropriately titled "Freedom of Noise," was released in 1995 by Tony Morley's well-respected Leaf label, which, like Tye's own Lo Recordings imprint, seems all above else committed to pushing the boundaries of genre and stylistic conventionality. "Freedom from Noise" ably conveyed this agenda as a double-12" of ruthless, unrelenting sonic experimentation, usually under a minute or two per track, and singularly committed to the art of the off-put. His subsequent work—1997's *Cold Fusion* EP (also on Leaf)—backed off the overkill a bit, beguiling by method rather than madness, although the twists and turns of its eight tracks make it equally difficult to get one's head around. The debut Twisted Science full-length, *Blown*, was released in June 1997. *The Sharpest Tool in the Box* followed one year later. —*Sean Cooper*

**Freedom of Noise [EP]** / Jun. 23, 1996 / Leaf ♦♦♦
A double pack of bone-breaking sonic mayhem from MLO/Lo Recordings main man Jonathon Tye, running the gamut from hardcore techno and industrial jungle to dirgy downtempo breaks and beatless, distorted noise. The tracks are far too jumbled in the mix to make their point with any subtlety, but subtlety hardly seems Tye's point here, with every sound forced past proper EQ and the resulting noise left to generate its own logic. Interesting, if somewhat laborious. —*Sean Cooper*

**Cold Fusion [EP]** / Mar. 24, 1997 / Leaf ♦♦♦♦
Tye slims it back to a single twelve for his second Twisted Science release (well, sort of; there are no less than eight tracks here). The tunes are as dense and hard-earned as ever, but Tye eases off the distortion box a bit, leaving electro and jungle breaks to swim in a murky pond of echoing samples and bassy textures. An interesting, varied release. —*Sean Cooper*

- **Blown** / Jun. 2, 1997 / Leaf ♦♦♦♦
The debut full-length by Twisted Science is another work of stunning (and perhaps overwhelming) range, quickly moving from isolationist ambience to dark drum'n'bass and experimental techno with few breaks and little warning in between. A few listens and it begins to make more sense as a cohesive work, though the point on *Blown* appears to be the unresolved chaos inherent in different material—from breakbeat to experimental. —*John Bush*
**The Sharpest Tool in the Box** / Aug. 31, 1998 / Lo Recordings ♦♦♦

## 2 Bad Mice
f. 1990, London, England
*Group / Jungle/Drum'N'Bass, Hardcore Techno, Club/Dance*
Formed in 1991, 2Bad Mice are widely credited as among the first UK hardcore acts to begin heavily incorporating breakbeats into the style. Consisting of members Sean O'Keefe, Simon Colebrooke, and producer Rob Playford (who also owns Moving Shadow records), 2Bad Mice were a staple on the early- to mid-'90s hardcore scene and were instrumental in the music's steady mutation into jungle/drum'n'bass. The group's influential approach to sampled beats—cutting them up into shards of rhythm and rearranging them in novel combinations (first appearing in mature form on the 1992 hit "Bombscare")—is generally considered the blueprint from which jungle's characteristic manipulation of breaks was assembled. Although 2Bad Mice for the most part stopped producing as the hardcore scene began to wane (Playford focusing his energy on Moving Shadow, now one of the largest and most influential jungle labels), a best-of compilation of the group's work appeared on the American Sm:)e Communications label in 1995. Playford continues to record as a member of Metalheadz (together with namesake label owner Goldie), while O'Keefe and Colebrooke have recorded sporadically under different names. —*Sean Cooper*

- **Kaotic Chemistry** / 1995 / Sm:)e ♦♦♦♦
A domestic greatest-hits package featuring classic 2Bad Mice tracks such as "Hold It Down," "Bombscare," "Waremouse," and "Take You." —*Sean Cooper*

## Two Lone Swordsmen
f. 1996, London, England
*Group / Downtempo, Electronica, Electro-Techno, Ambient Techno, Club/Dance, Techno, IDM*
After dissolving his Sabres of Paradise project and label, UK dance-don Andrew Weatherall set up the tripartite Emissions label group and launched his latest, perhaps most prodigious musical venture, Two Lone Swordsmen (2LS). A collaboration with Emissions engineer Keith Tenniswood, 2LS was formed in early 1996. The group speaks the same language of warped, downtempo grooves as much of previous Sabres work (particularly "Smokebelch" and "Wilmott") but opts instead for a syntax of minimal electronics and taut, brittle electro-funk for structure and guidance. The group's first full-length release, 1996's *The Fifth Mission*, was a whopping double-CD/triple-LP, both preceded and followed by additional EPs of new material ("Tenth Mission" and "Third Mission"). A few months later, the group issued two additional LP-length releases (both remix albums under the title *Swimming Not Skimming*, although the CD and LP versions sported different tracks), and by the end of 1996 had racked up no less than a half-dozen remixes (including Slab, Alter Ego, Sneaker Pimps, and David Holmes). The heavy release schedule continued through the rest of the decade, with an assortment of LPs (1998's *Stay Down*, 2000's *Tiny Reminders*), and mini-LPs recorded via a new deal with Warp. [See Also: Sabres of Paradise] —*Sean Cooper*

- **The Fifth Mission (Return to the Flightpath Estate)** / Aug. 12, 1996 / Emissions Audio Output ♦♦♦♦
Andrew Weatherall's first post-Sabres outing (together with Keith Tenniswood) is a truly beguiling cachet of alternately moody and unexpectedly funky down- and mid-tempo electro. Miles more complex and integrated than such future-funk wibblers as the Clear Records stable, *Fifth Mission* is often as tear-jerkingly emotional as it is goofball lino material; machine music imbued with more than a bit of humanity. Uniformly excellent. —*Sean Cooper*

**Swimming Not Skimming** / Nov. 25, 1996 / Emissions Audio Output ♦♦♦♦
Reviewers of the second 2LS full-length release in the same year were forced to clarify which format they were describing, as Weatherall and Co. decided to release two entirely different albums under the same title (one on CD, one on LP). Both feature remix work from a range of house and ambient techno names, with the vinyl version in strictly deep house mode and the CD switching back and forth between dreamy garage tracks and warped electro/trip-hop. —*Sean Cooper*

**Stockwell Steppas** / Mar. 31, 1997 / Emissions Audio Output ♦♦♦♦
2LS is milking the last drops from the atmospheric house excursions of their previous remix LP *Swimming Not Skimming*. After an amazing debut, the Swordsmen have swiftly taken their place beside Global Communication and Matthew Herbert as formerly innovative artists making an inexplicable and hasty retreat to the musical conservatism of house. To be fair, the music on offer here is, as previously, accomplished stuff, even progressive as far as house is concerned but nowhere near as interesting or inventive as Weatherall's previous Swordsmen or Sabres of Paradise work. —*Sean Cooper*

**Stay Down** / Oct. 19, 1998 / Warp ♦♦♦♦
*Stay Down* is a homecoming of sorts for Andrew Weatherall. His previous project, the Sabres of Paradise, recorded some of its most memorable material for the Sheffield-based Warp label, and with *Stay Down*, Weatherall adds another corker both to his and to Warp's discography. Following closely behind the nearly album-length *Bag of Blue Sparks* EP, *Stay Down* is a rich, varied collection of ambient, downtempo, and armchair electro, mixing robotic rhythms and weird electronics with organic textures and some of the strongest, most complete songwriting of Weatherall's career. Unlike the deep-house-oriented releases falling between *Stay Down* and the Swordsmen's first LP, *The Fifth Mission*, these tracks mine a classic approach to listening techno. —*Sean Cooper*

**A Virus with Shoes [EP]** / 1999 / Warp ♦♦♦
*A Virus with Shoes* is yet another pleasing TLS mini-LP that's perfect for listeners frustrated by the standard 70-minute album marathon. Though it begins with a set of vibes straight out of a Tortoise LP, Weatherall and Tenniswood quickly fade into more familiar territory: quirky, left-field downtempo with a high groove quotient, even while they're working in more freeform territory. Some listeners might say this territory is *too* familiar, that these tracks are interchangeable with those from their debut four years ago. Probably true, but Two Lone Swordsmen have forged a distinctive style that comes across not as a formula but as a working procedure. Check "Cloned Christ on a Hover Donkey (Be Thankful)," a piece of oddball electronica reminiscent of Mouse on Mars, or the wave of menacing synth on "Kist." —*John Bush*

**Tiny Reminders** / 2000 / Warp ♦♦♦♦
A slight return to experimental electro after the downtempo breakbeat of their EP work during 1999, the second Two Lone Swordsmen full-length for Warp also explores the minimalist side of techno and harks back to the early-'80s synth-funk Andrew Weatherall championed on his *Nine O'Clock Drop* mix disc for Nuphonic. Except for a few tracks of free-form ambient wallpaper, *Tiny Reminders* is pretty hard hitting, at least for Two Lone Swordsmen. The beats are less brittle, and though the catalog of crazed effects is still in full force, they're carried along by the forceful drum programming instead of acting on their own. "Neuflex" begins with a skeletal breakbeat rhythm track, a near-classic pattern in electro circles, though the patented 2LS formula soon warps the production with a stunted bassline and precise, high-pitched acid effects. (Variations on that same bassline reappear throughout the album, with excellent results.) With haunting synth and a swift, precise drum program bedrocking harsh German vocals, "You Are …" will also sound familiar to electro fans, though as usual Weatherall and Tenniswood's extreme care with their productions makes for a fresh look at familiar sound. *Tiny Reminders* is far too messed-with for most dancefloors, but another intriguing listen from one of techno's best experimentalists. —*John Bush*

## Two Sandwiches Short of a Lunchbox

f. 1994, London, England
*Group / Electronica, Electro-Techno, Ambient Techno, Electro, Techno, Ambient*

Although producer David Morley has been involved in a range of recording projects, encompassing trance and techno as well as the more ambient and "intelligent" offshoots thereof, his work has been marked by a consistent experimentalism, earning him a reputation as a compositional innovator among producers, DJs, and home listeners the world over. Born and raised in England, Morley's name is most often associated with the Belgian techno scene, primarily due to early R&S releases as Spectrum, TZ4 and under his own name which helped to solidify the label's nascent sound. Spectrum's "Brazil," recorded with R&S owner Renaat Vandepapeliere, was a visionary fusion of dancefloor techno/trance and ambient/experimental strains that helped earn R&S its association as an important force at the fore of European dance music. Morley, together with Outlander's Marcos Salon, was also behind the fourth release (known as TZ4) in R&S' *Test Zone* series, an important signpost in R&S' early development. In 1994, Morley released his first two EPs under his own name—"Evolution" (the first release on R&S sublabel Apollo) and "Shuttle" (on R&S-proper)—both exploratory ambient/electro classics that sit neatly next to the works of such artists as Biosphere, Aphex Twin, and Higher Intelligence Agency as early examples of ambient/intelligence techno. More recently, Morley has released increasingly dark and textural works, both solo and in combination with former Inky Blacknuss collaborator/current Mo'Wax signee Andrea Parker. In addition to the pair's Infonet EP *Angular Art* (1995), Morley and Parker recorded the *Too Good to Be Strange* EP (Apollo, 1995) under the name Two Sandwiches Short of a Lunchbox, as well as contributed tracks to R&S ambient sublabel Apollo's second label comp *The Divine Compilation*. Morley's debut full-length, *Aquarium*, is due out on Apollo sometime in 1997. —*Sean Cooper*

● **Too Good to Be Strange** / 1995 / Apollo ♦♦♦♦
David Morley's first EP-length collaboration with British electro/techno producer Andrea Parker is one part brooding, icy ambient, one part noisy laboratory experiment, and one part smoky, downtempo electro. The signature, pocky drum ticks of both Morley and Parker's solo work (particularly Morley's *Shuttle* EP and Parker's "Melodious Thunk") fill this three-tracker's A-side, with the flip a gorgeous, moody sprawl of experimental ambient. Good stuff. —*Sean Cooper*

## 2 Unlimited

f. 1990, Amsterdam, The
*Group / Rave, Euro-Dance, House, Dance-Pop*

The Netherlands techno/dance-pop phenomenon 2 Unlimited was one of the most popular groups in Europe during the early '90s, selling 18 million records and charting number one singles in every European country. (In England, 11 consecutive singles topped the charts.) America, however, remained unaffected, bringing only "Get Ready for This" to number 38 in late 1994, over two years after it was first released.

In 1990, producers Phil Wilde and Jean-Paul DeCoster had previously gained success with AB Logic and were looking for another vehicle for their songs. 2 Unlimited formed when Wilde and DeCoster were introduced to rapper Ray Slijngaard (b. June 28, 1971, Amsterdam) and vocalist Anita Doth (b. December 28, 1971, Amsterdam) by Marvin D., who had featured both in his rap group in the past. In 1991, debut single "Get Ready for This" reached number two on several European charts; the following year *Get Ready* was released.

The modest success of the first few singles prepared the way for 2 Unlimited's 1993 sophomore album *No Limits*. The title track hit number one in 15 European countries plus Canada, and other singles from the album also did well, including "Faces," "Maximum Overdrive," and "Let the Beat Control Your Body." Third album *Real Things* and the singles "The Real One," "No One," "Here I Go" continued the hit-making. The best-of album *Hits Unlimited* was the group's last release, as Slijngaard left to manage his X-Ray label and Doth moved into TV and radio talk shows (though she has recorded with Mad Cobra.) —*John Bush*

**Get Ready** / 1992 / Critique ♦♦♦
Setting a pattern for later 2 Unlimited albums, their debut *Get Ready* includes a bare minimum of two hits (here it's "Workaholic" and "Get Ready for This") and nothing more to speak of, except a few stale hip-house and techno-pop tracks. —*John Bush*

**No Limit** / May 11, 1993 / Critique ♦♦♦
It's got a couple of hits, namely "No Limit" and "Let the Beat Control Your Body," but there's not much else to recommend the second 2 Unlimited LP. —*John Bush*

● **Hits Unlimited** / Nov. 1995 / PWL ♦♦♦♦
*Hits Unlimited* collects all of the biggest hits from the dance outfit 2 Unlimited, including "Let the Beat Control Your Body," "Get Ready for This," and "Workaholic," making it a perfect introduction, as well as the only necessary album for casual fans. —*Stephen Thomas Erlewine*

## Tyree (Tyree Cooper)

*Producer / Club/Dance, Acid House, House*

He defined the hip-house phenomenon in 1989 with "Turn Up the Bass," but Tyree Cooper proved to be an excellent producer throughout house music's first decade, from the mid-'80s to the mid-'90s. He began DJing on Chicago's south side in 1983 and recorded his first single ("I Fear the Night") three years later for the seminal house label DJ International. In 1987, Cooper detoured from straightahead Chicago house to acid on the club smash "Acid Over." His next single showcased yet another change of direction; although a few singles had previously merged house beats with hip-hop vocals, "Turn Up the Bass" (with the help of rapper Kool Rock Steady) became one of the biggest hip-house hits, just barely missing the British Top Ten in 1989.

His debut album, *Tyree's Got a Brand New House*, appeared on DJ International one year later; it was re-titled for a British release on ffrr. Two additional singles, "Move Your Body" and "Let the Music Take Control," did well on the British and dance charts, and his second album, *Nation of Hip House*, appeared in 1991. Though he lost his major-label contract soon after, Tyree continued to record throughout the decade, on labels including Dance Mania, Real Estate, and No Nonsense. —*John Bush*

**Turn Up the Bass** / 1989 / ffrr ♦♦

● **Nation of Hip House** / Aug. 8, 1991 / DJ International ♦♦♦

# U

## Überzone (Timothy Wiles)
*Producer / Funky Breaks, Club/Dance, Techno*

Überzone was the alias of Anaheim, California-based electronic artist Timothy Wiles, also known simply as Q. Backed by an arsenal of close to two dozen Roland synthesizers, he debuted in 1996 with the EP *Braindust*, followed shortly by *Space Kadet;* a third EP, *The Freaks Believe in Beats*, appeared in 1997. —*Jason Ankeny*

**Space Kadet [EP]** / Nov. 19, 1996 / City of Angels ♦♦♦
Überzone's first EP for City of Angels has eight tracks of breakbeat techno, including four variations of "Botz" (Android, Synthetik, Organik, Electro) and two of "Moondust." —*Keith Farley*

● **The Freaks Believe in Beats [Single]** / Dec. 8, 1997 / City of Angels ♦♦♦♦
*Freaks Believe in Beats* is a seven-track breakbeat EP informed by acid and techno just a touch more than hip-hop, resulting in a different sound than that from most City of Angels releases. —*Keith Farley*

**Botz [EP]** / Apr. 20, 1998 / City of Angels ♦♦

## Ui
f. 1991, New York, NY
*Group / Experimental Rock, Indie-Rock, Post-Rock/Experimental, Alternative Pop-Rock*

Allied to the more organic, instrumental groovesters in the American post-rock scene led by Tortoise, Ui focuses on angular grooves provided by a dual-bass attack. The New York band was formed in 1991 by bassist Sasha Frere-Jones (formerly of the group Dolores and probably better known as a journalist than a musician) with drummer Clem Waldmann, additional bassist Alex Wright and DJ/percussionist David Weeks. Wright and Weeks left the band by 1993, and were replaced by jazz bassist Wilbo Wright.

Ui's first release, the *2-Sided* EP, appeared later that year on the British Hemiola label. During 1995, the band recorded the *Unlike* EP in addition to another EP and single for Soul Static. As part of a tour that year with Tortoise and Labradford, Ui signed a contract with Chicago's Southern Records. Debut album *Sidelong* was released in 1996, followed by the *Dropplike* EP. The group collaborated with Techno Animal and Luke Vibert, among others in the experimental electronica underground, before teaming up with Stereolab for the *Fires* EP, released as Uilab. Second album *Lifelike* followed later that year. —*John Bush*

● **Sidelong** / 1996 / Southern ♦♦♦♦
Ui's first full-length is a set of grooves with the occasional mumbled vocal line and a sedate quality with links to the approaches of instrumentalists from John Fahey to Jim O'Rourke. The effect is similar to a Slint album with two bassists instead of two guitars. —*John Bush*

**Lifelike** / Apr. 7, 1998 / Southern ♦♦♦
The second Ui album is remarkably similar to its predecessor, though it has a more stately quality. Where *Sidelong* marched along, *Lifelike* drifts, with more of an emphasis on instrumentalism than the groove-heavy debut. —*John Bush*

## Ultra Naté
b. 1968, Havre De Grace, MD
*Vocals / Tribal-House, Club/Dance, House, Dance-Pop*

One of the most flamboyant and talented house divas of the '90s, Ultra Naté stayed true to the dance mainstream despite major-label interference; though she began her career with Warner Brothers, by the late '90s she was recording for the indie-dance heavyweight Strictly Rhythm and enjoying more success than she had before. Born and raised near Baltimore, she was studying pre-med during the late '80s when she began to get into the city's dance scene. At one nightclub, she was introduced to two DJs who had recorded as the Basement Boys. The trio got together to record a single called "It's Over Now" and gained a contract with Britain's WEA Records. The single became a large international dance hit, and though Ultra Naté was already more famous around the world than in her native country, her debut album *Blue Notes in the Basement* was released in America as well, on Warner Brothers. From the LP, the follow-up singles "Scandal," "Is It Love" and "Deeper Love" also became hits. Despite this fact, Warner Brothers attempted to market her in the States as an R&B singer, though her second album *One Woman's Insanity* failed to crossover. ("Show Me" did become a number one dance hit in America.)

Ultra Naté moved to the independent Strictly Rhythm for her 1997 single "Free," produced by Mood II Swing. The track became her biggest hit yet, with Top Ten entries throughout Europe and the number one spot in France and Switzerland. Her third album *Situation: Critical* appeared in April 1998, with production by Mood II Swing, Al Mack, Masters at Work and D-Influence. —*John Bush*

**Blue Notes in the Basement** / 1991 / Warner Brothers ♦♦♦
Some interesting and entertaining arrangements and a few humorous selections, but overall, there's a lot of concept and little execution. It's partly dance-pop and partly urban contemporary and hip-hop, with plenty of attitude. There just aren't enough real songs. —*Ron Wynn*

**One Woman's Insanity** / 1994 / Warner Brothers ♦♦
The house rhythms on this overexcited album are among the best of its time. And Naté, a dance diva for the '90s who proudly wore the crown, is more than capable of the challenges. But there's a slight carelessness to *One Woman's Insanity* that ultimately pushes the album into formulaic territory. There are some good songs here, though, topped by the dance club smash "Show Me." —*Michael Gallucci*

● **Situation: Critical** / Apr. 27, 1998 / Strictly Rhythm ♦♦♦♦
After her 1997 platinum single "Free," Strictly Rhythm recruited a host of producers (Masters at Work, Mood II Swing, D-Influence) to try and break Ultra Naté as an album artist, not just a club-track songstress. For the most part it fails to work, as tracks like "Release the Pressure," "Divine Love" and the clichéd ballad "It's Crying Time" do little to support Naté's admittedly strong voice. —*John Bush*

## Ultramagnetic MC's
f. 1984, New York, NY [The, **db.** 1993
*Group / Underground Rap, East Coast Rap, Hip-Hop*

Arising from the Boogie Down Bronx in the mid-'80s as a far-flung hip-hop trio with a heap of new ideas to try out, Ultramagnetic's Kool Keith, Ced Gee, and DJ Moe Love occupy something of a singular place in the old-school pantheon. Combining funk-heavy tracks with jeep-rocking beats and obscure lyrical references, Ultramagnetic MC's have a list of firsts to their credit: the first group to employ a sampler as an instrument, the first to feature extensive use of live instrumentation... the first to feature a former psychiatric patient (Keith) on the mic. Early singles like "Something Else" and "Space Groove" were block party staples and created waves in the underground, eventually landing the group on the disco-dominated Next Plateau label, where they released their underappreciated debut. The following years found the group shuffling from label to label, releasing albums on Mercury and Wild Pitch before splitting to pursue various projects. —*Sean Cooper*

● **Critical Beatdown** / 1988 / Next Plateau ♦♦♦♦
Besides being an undeniable hip-hop classic, the first album by the cult crew

Ultramagnetic MC's introduced to the world the larger-than-life, one-of-a-kind personality of Kool Keith. That alone would make this some sort of landmark recording, but it also happens to be one of the finest rap albums from the mid- to late-'80s new school in hip-hop that numbered among its contributors Run-D.M.C., Public Enemy, and Boogie Down Productions. *Critical Beatdown* easily stands with the classic recordings made by those giants, and it is, in some ways, more intriguing because of how short-lived Ultramagnetic turned out to be. It would be wrong to assume that the finest thing about the album is its lyrical invention. Lyrically the group is inspired, to be sure, but the production is equally forward-looking. *Critical Beatdown* is full of the sort of gritty cuts that would define hip-hop's underground scene, with almost every song sounding like an instant classic and tracks such as "Watch Me Now," "Ego Trippin'," "Kool Keith Housing Things," "Travelling at the Speed of Thought," "Give the Drummer Some," and the title track actually earning that distinction. Although he turns in a brilliant performance, Kool Keith had not yet taken completely off into the stratosphere at this early point. He still has at least one foot planted on the street, and he even raps about his stay in the mental ward at Bellevue on "Feelin' It," giving the album a viscerally real feel and accessibility that his later work sometimes lacks. His viewpoint is still uniquely and oddly individual, though, and he already shows signs of the freakish conceptualizing persona that would eventually surface fully under the guise of Dr. Octagon (even lyrically sending enemy MCs to Jupiter on "Ain't It Good"). If Kool Keith gives the album its progressive mentality and adrenaline rush, Ced Gee gives it its street-level heft, and is, in many ways, the album's core. Somewhere in the nexus between the two stylistic extremes, brilliant music emanated. *Critical Beatdown* maintains all its sharpness and every ounce of its power, and it has not aged one second since 1988. —*Stanton Swihart*

**Funk Your Head Up** / Mar. 17, 1992 / Mercury ♦♦
Four years in the making, the follow-up was somewhat easy too ignore, overly crowded with half-thought ideas and water-treading glances back. Produced the radio hit "Poppa Large." —*Sean Cooper*

**The Four Horsemen** / Aug. 10, 1993 / Wild Pitch ♦♦♦♦
Back on track and on yet another label. The last album by the group before Keith would head off on his solo Dr. Octagon tangent. —*Sean Cooper*

**Basement Tapes: 1984-1990** / May 17, 1995 / Tuff City ♦♦♦
*Basement Tapes: 1984-1990* compiles a selection of Ultramagnetic MC's outtakes, rarities and demos. Considerably rougher than their official studio records, *Basement Tapes* has raw street vibe, and although it's clear why some of these tracks were never widely released, it's an exciting record, proving that the Ultramagnetic MC's were sorely neglected while they were active. —*Stephen Thomas Erlewine*

**B-Side Companion** / Oct. 7, 1997 / Next Plateau ♦♦♦♦
The Ultramagnetic MC's belong in the groundbreaking rap category (along with the likes of Run-D.M.C., Grandmaster Flash, etc.). Formed in the mid-'80s, the group rejected the fun rap style popular at the time (i.e., the Fat Boys and early Beastie Boys) and set out to create their own serious, funky, and bass-heavy groove style. The group definitely succeeded, but like many early rap artists, they did not meet with the commercial success they deserved for their trailblazing efforts.

Back in the 80's, the 12" single was the main format for rappers to show their stuff (few rappers were granted full-length albums). So the Ultramagnetic MC's made the most of the 12", releasing many before their 1988 full-length *Critical Beatdown* appeared. An abundance of B-sides amassed after a while (with many as strong, if not better than, the featured A-side), so Next Plateau records compiled the *crème de la crème* of these hard-to-find tracks on *The B-Side Companion*, remixing most to give them a more contemporary feel. Their first-ever release, "Ego Trippin'," is featured here as "Ego Trippin' 2000" and sets the tone for the rest of the album. You can't go wrong with tracks like "Watch Me Now," "MC's Ultra Part 2," and "Funky," all equally strong old-school rap that deserves to be heard. The seeds for today's rap stars were planted on the tracks included on *The B-Side Companion*. —*Greg Prato*

## Ultramarine

f. 1989, Canterbury, England
*Group / Ambient House, Electronica, Ambient-Techno*
The music of Canterbury duo Ultramarine resists easy classification, drawing as it does from ambient, techno, folk, and eclectic '70s Canterbury art-rock artists like the Soft Machine, Caravan, and Robert Wyatt, who occasionally performed live with the group and appeared on their *United Kingdoms* album. The group, which is made up of Paul Hammond and Ian Cooper, has a distinctively British sound and employs a wide range of instruments and sounds.

Hammond and Cooper first collaborated in the avant-garde band A Primary Industry during the mid-'80s. When that band split, the duo named themselves Ultramarine and recorded *Folk* in 1990. Their second album *Every Man and Woman Is a Star* appeared in 1992 and earned praise for the duo as one of the first home-listening electronic groups. Sire signed Ultramarine in 1992 and issued their first US release, *United Kingdoms*, the following year. Despite a high-profile collaboration with Robert Wyatt (and with Kevin Ayers for the accompanying *Hymn* EP), the album practically disappeared both home and abroad. Nevertheless, Hammond and Cooper continued to record in a quirky electronic folk-pop vein for 1995's *Bel Air*. Three years later, *A User's Manual* saw Ultramarine's sound approaching the trip-hop/electronica mainstream. —*Steve Huey*

● **Every Man and Woman Is a Star** / 1992 / Chameleon ♦♦♦♦
A warmly melodic LP of home-listening electronica produced just before the term was coined, *Every Man and Woman Is a Star* is a delightful concept album with dub-centric rhythms and a straightahead song structure whose only quibble is what sounds like a need for vocals to accompany the tracks. All in all, the LP deserves to be filed alongside the Orb's *U.F.Orb*, Aphex Twin's *Selected Ambient Works 85-92* and Biosphere's *Microgravity* as an early ambient techno classic. —*John Bush*

**United Kingdoms** / Mar. 1993 / Giant ♦♦
What should have been Ultramarine's breakout album, *United Kingdoms* sank them with an audience expecting far-out ambient techno who received instead lukewarm folk-pop with only occasional electronic textures. The added vocals (from a heavy influence, the Soft Machine's Robert Wyatt) were a good idea, but *United Kingdoms* sounds more like a Mike Oldfield LP from the '70s rather than an electronic album of the '90s. —*John Bush*

**Bel Air** / 1995 / Blanco Y Negro ♦♦♦
Ultramarine's fourth album expands on the notion of genre-fusion ambient from *United Kingdoms*, this time trading in the British folk whimsy for a rather bizarre conception of lounge jazz and breakbeat. It's a difficult trick, and the duo appear to be straining themselves at times to pull it off. The result is a confused album whose subtleties grow with age, but often fail to convince. —*John Bush*

**A User's Guide** / 1998 / New Electronica ♦♦♦♦
After a few years of silence, Ultramarine returned with a sound more akin to the understated ambient techno of *Every Man and Woman Is a Star* rather than the electro-folk of 1995's *Bel Air*. It's an intriguing sound, just as wildly varied as you'd expect from these musical eclectics, but *A User's Guide* holds together much better than previous LPs like *Bel Air* and *United Kingdoms*. —*John Bush*

## Ultraviolence

*Producer / Gabba, Hardcore Techno*
The Earache label, renowned for its roster of harsh grindcore acts—Godflesh, Carcass, Fudge Tunnel—moved into the sympathetic world of hardcore gabber techno with the signing of Ultraviolence, masterminded by one Johnny Violent. His first, self-financed production was the "Shout" single, which appeared in 1991 on his own label. After the recording of a John Peel session in 1992, he signed to Food Records (also the home of Jesus Jones). Violent didn't quite fit in with the house leanings of Food and released only the *Vengeance* EP before moving to Earache. Fitting in quite well with the industrial attitude of Scorn, he recorded singles both as Ultraviolence ("I, Destructor") and as himself ("Johnny Is a Bastard") before his debut Ultraviolence full-length appeared in 1994. The album, *Life of Destructor*, was followed by *Psychodrama* one year later. By 1996, Johnny Violent reverted to his own name for the release of *Shocker*, also on Earache; Ultraviolence's *Killing God* followed in 1998. —*John Bush*

● **Killing God** / Mar. 24, 1998 / Earache ♦♦
As expected, *Killing God* is an entire album of one-note hardcore anthems with nothing more than a brief vocal sample to recommend them. Track titles like "Bombs in My Head," "Immolation," and "Paranoid" tell the whole story here. —*John Bush*

## Ultravox

f. 1974, London, England, db. 1987
*Group / New Romantic, Pop-Rock, New Wave, Synth-Pop*

Rejecting the abrasive guitars of their punk-era contemporaries in favor of lushly romantic synthesizers, Ultravox emerged as one of the primary influences on the British electro-pop movement of the early '80s. Formed in London in 1974, the group—originally dubbed Ultravox!—was led by vocalist and keyboardist John Foxx (born Dennis Leigh), whose interest in synths and cutting-edge technology began during his school years; with an initial line-up consisting of bassist Chris Cross, keyboardist/violinist Billy Currie, guitarist Steve Shears, and drummer Warren Cann, their obvious affection for the glam rock sound of David Bowie and Roxy Music brought them little respect from audiences caught up in the growing fervor of punk, but in 1977 Island Records signed the quintet anyway, with Brian Eno agreeing to produce their self-titled debut LP.

After scoring a minor UK hit with the single "My Sex," Ultravox returned later that year with *Ha! Ha! Ha!;* sales were minimal, however, and Shears soon exited, replaced by guitarist Robin Simon. A third LP, 1978's *Systems of Romance,* was recorded in Germany with renowned producer Conrad Plank, but it too failed commercially; Island soon dropped the band, at which time both Foxx and Simon quit, the former mounting a solo career and the latter joining Magazine. At that point the remaining members of Ultravox tapped singer/guitarist Midge Ure, an alumnus of Silk as well as Glen Matlock's Rich Kids; upon signing to Chrysalis, the new line-up recorded *Vienna,* scoring a surprise smash hit with the single "Sleepwalk," which reached the number two spot on the UK pop charts in 1981 and pushed the LP into the Top Five.

After 1981's *Rage in Eden,* Ultravox teamed with legendary producer George Martin for 1983's *Quartet;* their most successful LP in the otherwise impenetrable American market, it launched the minor hit "Reap the Wild Wind." Upon completing 1984's *Lament,* Ure—who had co-written the Band Aid charity single "Do They Know It's Christmas"—left Ultravox to forge a solo career, topping the UK charts a year later with the solo smash "If I Was"; the remaining members, adding Big Country's Mark Brzezicki, resurfaced with *U-Vox* in 1986 before going their separate ways. Currie and Simon reformed the band as U-Vox in 1993, adding vocalist Marcus O'Higgins; three years later, they released the lackluster *Ingenuity.* —*Jason Ankeny*

**Ultravox** / 1977 / Island ✦✦✦
John Foxx proves to have an odd, Bowie-influenced vision, here aided and abetted by Brian Eno (then a Bowie crony) and Steve Lillywhite. "My Sex" and "I Want to Be a Machine" are standouts. —*William Ruhlmann*

**Ha! Ha! Ha!** / 1977 / Island ✦✦✦
There's something quite chilling and compulsive about the original model of Ultravox. Sure, lots of people were experimenting with synthesizers, but Ultravox married that sound to elements of glam rock and punk to produce a more affecting hybrid. You can feel the ghosts of Kraftwerk at play here, even more strongly than on the band's debut—and that's saying something. Twenty years on, some of it does sound a little corny; however, the album does include the one undeniable classic of early-period Ultravox: "Hiroshima Mon Amour." —*Alex Ogg*

**Systems of Romance** / Dec. 1978 / Island ✦✦✦✦
*Systems of Romance,* the high-water mark of pre-Midge Ultravox, also proved tremendously influential on the host of new romantic bands that followed in its wake. Produced by Conny Plank, the album divides into a rock-heavy first side and a synth-heavy second side. Though several songs lack a distinctive element, and the record is occasionally dependent on a few rock 'n' roll clichés, *Systems of Romance* is an important, intriguing album. —*John Bush*

**Vienna** / 1980 / Chrysalis ✦✦✦✦
The new Ultravox, under Midge Ure, has a dreamy, ethereal sound heard at its best on its debut album, which features the title song, "All Stood Still," "Passing Strangers," and "Sleepwalk," all UK hits. —*William Ruhlmann*

**Rage in Eden** / 1981 / Chrysalis ✦✦✦
This was another major UK chart hit, as Ultravox milked their "Vienna"-inspired success for all it was worth. Sadly, *Rage in Eden* is as pretentious and unwieldy as its title would suggest. Both "The Thin Wall" and "I Remember (Death in the Afternoon)" are stunningly overblown and self-satisfied. Midge Ure's lyrics are particularly at fault here—a shame, because the music itself is extremely good in parts. This was their last album produced in collabora-tion with Conny Plank; thereafter Ultravox would experience a steady commercial decline. —*Alex Ogg*

**Quartet** / 1982 / Chrysalis ✦✦✦
The single "Reap the Wild Wind" sets the tone for this hapless collection of songs, seemingly inspired by religious themes. Only "We Came to Dance" is of any value, with its nod to the earlier, less commercially successful (but more artistically satisfying) Ultravox sound. The producer? George Martin, no less. He's worked with better bands, allegedly. —*Alex Ogg*

**Lament** / 1984 / One Way ✦✦✦✦
Containing arguably their best work of the '80s, *Lament* showcases a band with confidence to match their commercial status (it was the first of their albums to be self-produced). The electro-synth workout "Dancing With Tears in My Eyes" actually works quite well, and is their best single since the epochal (for good and bad reasons) "Vienna." "White China," too, is impressive. —*Alex Ogg*

**U-Vox** / 1986 / Chrysalis ✦✦
Featuring new drummer Mark Brzezicki (formerly of Big Country), the prosaically titled *U-Vox* offered more of the same from these by-now-redundant synth stylists. The one exception was the single "All Fall Down," a slightly more imaginative variant on the formula. (The other two singles drawn from the album, "Same Old Story" and "All in One Day," were shallow echoes of the band's earlier releases.) "All Fall Down" was to prove their final chart entry. —*Alex Ogg*

• **Dancing with Tears in My Ears** / 1997 / EMI ✦✦✦✦
*Dancing with Tears in My Eyes* is a 15-track overview of Ultravox's early-'80s commercial peak, hitting most, but not all, of their biggest hits, including "Sleepwalk," "Vienna," "All Stood Still," and "Reap the Wild Wind." It's not a bad collection, but if it had included hits like "The Thin Wall," it could have been a definitive retrospective. —*Stephen Thomas Erlewine*

## Uncle Jamm's Army

f. Los Angeles, CA
*Group / West Coast Rap, Old School Rap, Electro, Hip-Hop*

Los Angeles was a key capital on the tiny corner of the early hip-hop map known as electro, and Uncle Jamm's Army were one of the primary reasons for that. An extended crew of producers, DJs, and vocalists including Ice-T, Egyptian Lover, the Unknown DJ, and Chris "The Glove" Taylor, UJA released a string of popular, influential electro cuts during 1984-86, including "What's Your Sign," Dial-A-Freak," and "Yes, Yes, Yes," all for the Freak Beat label. Notable for their all-around musicality; driving, effective rhythms; and uncompromising attitude, Uncle Jamm's Army remain one of the most important pieces in the old-school electro puzzle, and have influenced scores of new-school electro producers, from Autechre to I-F. —*Sean Cooper*

**Yes, Yes, Yes [Single]** / 1984 / Freak Beat ✦✦✦
Though marred somewhat by muddy production, this vocoder-led party jam is typical L.A. electro—heavily syncopated beats, simple, minor key synth melodies and only thinly veiled sexual nuances. —*Sean Cooper*

• **What's Your Sign? [Single]** / 1985 / Freak Beat ✦✦✦
This is a solid, driving mid-tempo electro cut that holds up surprisingly well more than a decade after it was released. Although this single's flip side, "Dial-A-Freak," is the track included on most compilations, "What's Your Sign?" is clearly superior. —*Sean Cooper*

## Underground Resistance

f. 1990, Detroit, MI
*Group / Detroit Techno, Club/Dance, Techno*

Underground Resistance is probably the most militantly political outcropping of modern urban American techno. Combining a grubby, four-track aesthetic, an almost strictly DIY business philosophy, and an oppositional, militaristic ethos similar to Public Enemy without the drama (or the familiarity; the members refuse to be photographed without bandanas obscuring their identities), UR have redirected their portion of the Detroit techno legacy to social activist ends, trading mainstream popularity and financial success for independence and self-determination. Begun in the early '90s by second-wave trinity Jeff Mills, "Mad" Mike Banks, and Robert "Noise" Hood, UR adapted the flavor and kick of early Detroit techno to the complex social, political, and economic circumstances in the wake of Reagan-era accelerated inner-city decline, and was formed as an outlet for uncompromising music geared toward awareness and change.

The early UR catalog is defined by a typically Detroit combination of Motown and Chicago soul, and ruthless, at times caustic lo-fi techno, acid, and electro (Mills' background is in, among other things, Chicago industrial and EBM-style electro-techno, with Banks and Hood both coming from a solid house and techno base). Much of the label's early output was the product of various permutations of Banks, Mills, and Hood, both solo and in combination, before Mills and Hood left UR in 1992 to pursue (and achieve) international success. Banks continued to operate UR in the wake of the split, releasing EPs such as "Return of Acid Rain," "Message to the Majors," and "Galaxy to Galaxy" under the UR banner, as well as 12"s by increasingly renowned artists such as Drexciya. Although UR remains largely aloof of the more high-profile American and European scenes, UR releases have occasionally leaked into various, relatively more establishmentarian contexts (usually under the guise of "reconnaissance" or "infiltration"), with the noted German techno label Tresor reissuing 12"s from the early UR catalog and the React label compilation featuring exclusive tracks from Banks and other UR artists. The first actual full-length credited to Underground Resistance was 1998's *Interstellar Fugitives*. [See Also: "Mad" Mike Banks] —*Sean Cooper*

### Nation 2 Nation [Single] / 1990 / UR ♦♦♦♦

Many think of early Underground Resistance records as being raw, hard, and abrasive, but the *Nation 2 Nation* record stands out as a drastic exception. An etching on the inner-groove of the record blatantly reads "UR Jazz," and one cannot deny that this is, indeed, an attempt at blending jazz with techno. In sum, it's an ambitious record that, unfortunately, simply isn't that appealing; the blend of sax, piano, 303-acid riffs, synth solos, female vocals, and drum machine percussion just doesn't blend that well. Underground Resistance put out two other records in this series of techno jazz attempts— *World 2 World* and *Galaxy 2 Galaxy*—both of which are vast improvements on this noble concept. —*Jason Birchmeier*

### Sonic Destroyer [Single] / 1990 / UR ♦♦♦

With the second release on the Underground Resistance label, the Detroit collective began to carve out the style of hard techno that they would eventually define. The record includes four songs, each taking its own approach to the developing genre, with "Eye of the Storm" easily standing out as the highlight of this record. From its opening moment, long before any heavy percussion or bass enters, the song's euphoric sounds of synthesized strings resonate endlessly and continue to do so throughout. On the B-side of *Sonic* are two cuts with a darker tone than that found on the A-side: "Predator" and "Elimination." —*Jason Birchmeier*

### X-101 / 1991 / Tresor ♦♦♦♦

While small formatting gimmicks—locked and backwards grooves, strange placement of the music, the strange numbering of the record, and some poetic etchings on the other rim of the record—make this release fun, the songs are rather lackluster. The A-side's "G Force" has few noteworthy characteristics besides a strange tone that sounds as though it's being pulled or stretched, alluding to the gravitational force hinted at in the song's title. "Sonic Destroyer" appears on the B-side, a song that uses a melody of high-pitched synth stabs and a looped, siren-like sound that reeks of the stereotypical early '90s rave sound. —*Jason Birchmeier*

### Elimination (Remix) / 1991 / UR ♦♦

On the A-side of *Elimination* they present an extended remix of the title track—a song originally appearing on the *Sonic* EP—that lasts for a little over six minutes, allowing the song's structure and various segments to further develop. The song serves as one of the best examples of the style of hard, percussive rhythm-based techno popularized by the pioneering group. Over their punishing rhythm, the group lays some nicely sequenced melodies comprised of strange aquatic bleeps that sound almost like morse code. On the B-side they present a similar song titled "Gamma Ray." —*Jason Birchmeier*

### Riot [Single] / 1991 / UR ♦♦♦

With the *Riot* EP, Underground Resistance took their hard-hitting style of gritty techno aggression and added substantial thematic content. An examination of the four tracks' titles—"Riot," "Panic," "Assault," and "Rage"—should provide a fairly accurate idea about what feelings UR chose to charge their music with. In addition, the mysterious clan of Detroiters chose to include plenty of vocals courtesy of a young Robert Hood in "Panic" and "Riot" to further drive home their message of frustration. While the thematic content is well established and effective, the music underlying the ideas represents some of their best early efforts. Fusing distorted human vocals with sirens, 303 acid lines, and skewed synth melodies, UR found plenty of action to layer atop their platform of drum machine-constructed rhythms; the synergy of these elements ends up sounding more like industrial rock than traditional techno. —*Jason Birchmeier*

### Fuel for the Fire/Attend the Riot [Single] / 1992 / UR ♦♦

There is a certain mysterious quality in the twelfth release on the Underground Resistance label. Titled *Fuel for the Fire/Attend the Riot*, it seems to allude to the previously released *Riot*, even though the two records have little in common musically. Etchings on the outer rim of "Fuel…" have a sly smiley face and say "It's back!," further alluding to the fact that it is a follow-up to *Riot*. Musically, the four songs on this record sound similar with their hard, dark percussion and loads of Roland 303 acid lines. Each lasts anywhere from four to five minutes with the acid lines repeating over and over, making it a fairly dull acid techno exercise. —*Jason Birchmeier*

### Galaxy 2 Galaxy [Single] / 1994 / UR ♦♦♦♦

Following in the footsteps of *Nation 2 Nation* and *World 2 World*, *Galaxy 2 Galaxy* again focuses Underground Resistance on a jazzy style of techno featuring heavy atmospheric synths. But where the earlier two records failed to effectively integrate horns into the futuristic techno motifs, the song "Hi-Tech Jazz" on *Galaxy 2 Galaxy* finally succeeds, resulting in a beautiful marriage of jazz and techno—a feat rarely achieved in the man-versus-machine world of techno. The B-side of the record features two songs—"Journey of the Dragons" and "Star Sailing"—that perfectly bring together an airy percussive backdrop and beautiful synth arrangements. "Star Sailing" also manages to work in some acoustic piano and a driving flute riff to reaffirm the song's jazz motif. The remainder of the record includes more synth-heavy light techno, but it doesn't compare to the first refreshing 12" in the double pack. —*Jason Birchmeier*

### Message to the Majors [Single] / 1994 / UR ♦♦♦

In terms of sheer intensity and sonic aggression, few techno records compare to Underground Resistance's *Message to the Majors*, arguably the quintessential example of the group's trademark style of ideologically militant, hard percussive techno. Musically, there are some vocal samples that appear throughout the context of each: "Strictly underground funk. Keep the crossover." Other key elements of *Message to the Majors* include a snippet of crowd noise—"hey!"—and a powerful Roland 303-acid riff that gets looped in each rendition, functioning at times as the driving force behind the song. Rhythmically, *Message to the Majors* lays down a percussive track that sounds almost like drum'n'bass with its quick pace and frantic arrangement of breakbeats. —*Jason Birchmeier*

### The Return of Acid Rain: The Storm Continues [Single] / 1994 / UR ♦♦♦♦

On this release, Underground Resistance again made the Roland 303 drum machine their main instrument. Rather than composing one extended, epic acid-techno anthem as they did with *Message to the Majors*, this time they composed many smaller tracks, squeezing eight onto one piece of vinyl. Relative to the group's early acid-techno records, such as *Fuel for the Fire*, *The Return of Acid Rain* is a drastic improvement, with better production quality and more developed sounds. On the other hand, the eight songs never really progress or evolve, but rather seem to be separate tracks of cycling acid riffs that introduce their rhythms, loop them for a minute or two, deconstruct, and then come to an abrupt conclusion. —*Jason Birchmeier*

### Acid Rain III: Meteor Shower [Single] / 1995 / UR ♦♦♦

On the first record of this double EP, UR lays down a total of seven brief compositions highlighting their inventive use of the 303 to accentuate their 909-style percussive techno. On the second the group explores more epic constructions of acid techno with three longer pieces, including "Final Frontier 2," which takes up the entirety of side-D. While the epic proportions of "Final Frontier 2" instantly make it a notable track, moving from tranquil moments of synthesizer-shrouded serenity to a chaotic climax of multiple rhythm loops that closely interact with one another, this particular song never reaches the creative heights it should, at times sounding like a scrambled amalgam of cycling loops barely capable of holding listeners' interest. —*Jason Birchmeier*

### Electronic Warfare [EP] / 1995 / UR ♦♦♦♦

For the *Electronic Warfare* double EP, Underground Resistance mastermind Mike Banks lays down some funky electro-influenced techno compositions and one truly stellar techno anthem. The several electro-influenced songs function well, alluding to Banks' direction away from the furious, pounding 909 kick drum and 303-acid riff style tendencies of early '90s UR. Still, clocking in at a mammoth 11 minutes, "The Illuminator" is the reason to own this record, as it fully utilizes Banks' gift for creating some of the most uplifting string-harmonies from his synthesizer, comparable only to DJ Rolando's "Jaguar" and the Martian's "Windwalker." The underlying percussive rhythms shuffle and keep the momentum in tact while the high-end barrage of synthesizer melodies, riffs, rhythms, and harmonies simply propel this song beyond the dancefloor and into the realm of divine poetry—the sort of music that can bring tears to the eyes. —*Jason Birchmeier*

**Codebreaker [Single]** / Feb. 17, 1997 / UR ♦♦♦♦
A three-track single with no listed titles, *Codebreaker* contains adventures in deep house and lunar funk, all painted with minimal acid smudges in the inimitable Underground Resistance style. —*John Bush*

★ **Interstellar Fugitives** / Sep. 1998 / UR ♦♦♦♦♦
With *Interstellar Fugitives*, the Underground Resistance family expanded to include DJ Rolando, Drexciya, Perception, Chaos, Andre Holland and the Suburban Knight—most of whom were longtime colleagues and UR labelmates, but never an explicit part of the organization. Although each track is designated to a different producer (with only one credit for Mad Mike himself), the album is tight and of a piece throughout, focused on hard-hitting, fast-moving, techno-funk with a bit of influence from the electro-flashback recordings of Drexciya. Much of the 808 percussion and acid lines are intact from the earliest UR recordings almost ten years earlier, while the guttural vocal samples and industrial edge to "Nannytown" and "Afrogermanic" chart the longtime connections between Detroit and Berlin. It's a pity, then, that the best tracks on *Interstellar Fugitives*—the darkside techno of "Something Happened on Dollis Hill," "Interstellar Crime Report," and "Zero Is My Country"—are also the shortest. —*John Bush*

**Knights of the Jaguar [EP]** / Mar. 29, 1999 / Underground Resistance ♦♦♦♦
When one puts aside all the drama surrounding this infamous record by DJ Rolando, "Jaguar," stands alongside Detroit classics such as Rhythim Is Rhythim's "Strings of Life" as one of the timeless examples of just how poetic and emotionally moving the often-cited "soulless" sound of techno can really be. The song slowly builds, starting first with a shuffling percussive rhythm and a looped melody of strange bleeps. This foundation moves along at a quick tempo and modulates carefully as time passes, growing more and more intense. Eventually, the synthesizer enters with its chorus of cosmic strings for the occasional moment of utopian intensity as this truly poetic melody propels the song to unattainable heights for brief points before deconstructing to its core foundation again so that the building can start all over. The B-side, "Ascension," functions well as a propulsive chunk of repetitive techno, but is ulitmately eclipsed by the A-side. A record championed by nearly every Detroit DJ and countless others, "Jaguar" remains a monolithic moment of pride for the Motor City. —*Jason Birchmeier*

**Revenge of the Jaguar** / Apr. 2000 / Underground Resistance ♦♦♦♦
Following the unprecedented global success of DJ Rolando's "Jaguar," the Underground Resistance camp released this record of remixes in an effort to satisfy further demand among the global techno community. A truly amazing example of the classic Detroit techno sound, the original mix of "Jaguar" laid down a complex, percussive rhythmic arrangement, subtle synthesizer riffs, and rationed use of a catchy, foregrounded string melody. The three different remixes each focus on one of these particular elements, accentuating them to a further degree than the original had: Jeff Mills turns in a remix centering heavily on the original's light percussive rhythms; the Octave One mix emphasizes the synthesizer riff that runs through much of the original; and Mad Mike's mix focuses almost exclusively on the melodic string section that functions as the emotional peak of the original mix. As great as these remixes are though, they don't really bring anything new to the original mix, which still remains the most potent. —*Jason Birchmeier*

## Glenn Underground (Glenn Crocker)

b. 1971, Chicago, IL
*Producer, DJ / Jazz-House, Tech-House, Club/Dance, House*
Glenn Underground is one of the deepest of the deep house producers, following Larry Heard's classic Chicago tracks with his own earthy grooves, more closely aligned to the spiritual tones of disco than even contemporary house music. In fact, his bootleg remix of the prototye disco single—Donna Summer's "I Feel Love," with production by Giorgio Moroder—is virtually a necessity in the crates of house DJs. The head Underground has recorded for nu-school Chicago label Cajual/Relief (as GU) plus Europeans like Peacefrog, DJAX-Up-Beats, SSR and Guidance. He often watched his uncle's band practice while growing up in Chicago, and began playing with the group's keyboard, a Fender Rhodes. He began DJing and also started producing tracks on tape as early as 1991 to mix in at his gigs.

One of the first was a cut-up version of Donna Summer's "I Feel Love," which exploded in Chicago's clubland and impressed Cajual Records labelhead Cajmere enough to begin releasing Underground's tracks. The label eventually issued more than a dozen GU singles and EPs during 1995-96— even while Underground recorded several singles and his first full-length, 1996's *Atmosfear*, for the British Peacefrog label. His 1997 *Secrets of CVO* EP for Guidance expanded his '70s influences with clean minimalist fusion-funk; the track "House of Blues," even featured a solo by guitarist Stevie Israel. The collection *The Jerusalem EP's* appeared on Peacefrog that same year, with a great variety of sounds from Detroit techno to deep funk and house. Underground had already debuted his collective the Strictly Jaz Unit with long-time friends Boo Williams, Brian Harden, Tim Harper and Cei-Bei; the group released the LP *Future Parables* for London's Defender Records. An Underground solo release, *A Story of Deepness*, followed in 1999. Underground and Williams also run Strictly Jaz Productions. —*John Bush*

● **The Jerusalem EP's** / May 19, 1997 / Peacefrog ♦♦♦♦
With his mind more on spiritual matters than the dancefloor, Glenn Underground's *The Jerusalem EPs* forsakes the usual jazz influences of much '90s house music for the techno-influenced barnstorming of Underground Resistance and other Detroit producers. —*John Bush*

**Future Parables** / Nov. 17, 1997 / Defender ♦♦♦♦

**Story of Deepness** / 1999 / Nite Life Collective ♦♦♦♦
Glenn Underground proves himself once again as the master deep house producer with this album for Nite Life Collective. There are a couple more specimens to add to the catalog of crucial Underground deep productions ("Disco Worm," "Strong Island Jazz"), plus even flashes of the man's gospel inspiration on "Motherless Child" and "GU's Fingertips." —*John Bush*

**Lounge Excursions** / Jul. 11, 2000 / Guidance Recordings ♦♦♦♦
It's practically obvious from the title, but *Lounge Excursions* is an album of late-night jams ranging from disco to quiet storm to jazz-funk. Underground works through this collection of key- and drum-heavy house movers with only occasional instrumentalist help, preferring instead to layer a couple of Hammond or Rhodes keyboard lines over his own tight drum programs (he even stretches out on congas for "City People"). Though there's great interplay between guitar, keys, and vocals on the collaboration tracks ("Fly With Me" with solid guitar from Mike Saxon, "City People," "Funki-Ghetto"), the highlights here *are* the solo productions, like the irresistibly funky "7th and Rhodes." —*John Bush*

## Underworld

f. 1988, London, England
*Group / Electronica, Club/Dance, Techno, Electronic, House*
Underworld became one of the most crucial electronic acts of the '90s via an intriguing synthesis of old and new. The trio's two-man frontline, vocalist Karl Hyde and guitarist Rick Smith, had been recording together since the early-'80s new wave explosion; after two unsuccessful albums released as Underworld during the late '80s, the pair finally hit it big when they recruited Darren Emerson, a young DJ hipped to the sound of techno and trance. Traditional pop song-forms were jettisoned in favor of Hyde's heavily treated vocals, barely-there whispering and surreal wordplay, stretched out over the urban breakbeat trance ripped out by Emerson & Co. while Smith's cascade of guitar-shard effects provided a bluesy foil to the stark music. All in all, the decision to go pop was hardly a concession to the mainstream. The first Underworld album by the trio, *Dubnobasswithmyheadman*, appeared in late 1993 to a flurry of critical acclaim; the trio then gained US distribution for the album via TVT. *Second Toughest in the Infants*, the group's sophomore LP, updated their sound slightly and received more praise than the debut. Unlike the first, the LP also sold well, thanks in part to the nonalbum single "Born Slippy," featured on the soundtrack to the seminal film *Trainspotting*.

The roots of Underworld go back to the dawn of the '80s, when Karl Hyde and Rick Smith formed a new wave band called Freur. The group released

*Doot-Doot* in 1983 and *Get Us Out of Here* two years later, but later disintegrated. Hyde worked on guitar sessions for Debbie Harry and Prince, then reunited with Smith in 1988 to form an industrial-funk band called Underworld. The pair earned an American contract with Sire and released their debut album *Underneath the Radar* in 1988. *Change the Weather* followed one year later, even though little attention had been paid to the first. By the end of the decade, Underworld had disappeared also.

As they had several years earlier, Hyde and Smith shed their skin yet again, recruiting hotshot DJ Darren Emerson and renaming themselves Lemon Interrupt. In 1992, the trio debuted with two singles, "Dirty/Minneapolis" and "Bigmouth/Eclipse," both released on Junior Boys Own Records. After they reverted back to Underworld, 1993's "Rez" and "MMM…Skyscraper I Love You" caused a minor sensation in the dance community. Instead of adding small elements of techno to a basically pop or rock formula (as many bands had attempted with varying success), Underworld treated techno as the dominant force. Their debut album *Dubnobasswithmyheadman* was praised by many critics upon release later in 1993 and crossed over to the British pop charts. Hyde, Smith, and Emerson impressed many at their concert dates as well; the trio apparently relished playing live, touring Great Britain twice plus Japan, Europe, and the annual summer-festival circuit, where their Glastonbury appearance became the stuff of legend.

*Dubnobasswithmyheadman* was released in the US in 1995 after being licensed to TVT Records. During the rest of the year, Underworld were relatively quiet, releasing only the single, "Born Slippy." Finally, *Second Toughest in the Infants* appeared in early 1996 to much critical praise. The trio gained no small amount of commercial success later in the year when "Born Slippy" was featured on the soundtrack to *Trainspotting*, the controversial Scottish film that earned praise from critics all over the globe. Underworld also remained busy with Tomato—their own graphic design company responsible for commercials from such high-profile clients as Nike, Sony, Adidas and Pepsi—and remixing work for Depeche Mode, Björk, St. Etienne, Sven Väth, Simply Red and Leftfield. Emerson continued to DJ on a regular basis, releasing mix albums for Mixmag! and Deconstruction. Though Underworld's 1999 LP *Beaucoup Fish* was a bit of a disappointment critically and commercially, the band continued to tour the world. In September 2000 the ensemble released *Everything, Everything*, a live album featuring popular singles such as "Pearls Girl," "Cups," and "Born Slippy Nux." The interactive DVD followed a month after. —*John Bush*

**Underneath the Radar** / Mar. 1988 / Sire ♦♦

**Change the Weather** / Sep. 1989 / Sire ♦♦

★ **Dubnobasswithmyheadman** / Dec. 1993 / Wax Trax! ♦♦♦♦♦
From the beginning of the first track "Dark & Long," Underworld's focus on production is clear, with songwriting coming in a distant second. The best tracks ("MMM…Skyscraper I Love You," "Cowgirl") mesh Hyde's sultry songwriting with Emerson's beat-driven production, an innovative blend of classic acid house, techno and dub that sounds different from much that preceded it. In a decade awash with stale fusion, Underworld are truly a multi-genre group. —*John Bush*

☆ **Second Toughest in the Infants** / Mar. 12, 1996 / Wax Trax! ♦♦♦♦♦
On their second album, Underworld continues to explore the fringes of dub, dance and techno, creating a seamless, eclectic fusion of various dance genres. *Second Toughest in the Infants* carries the same knockout punch of their debut, *Dubnobasswithmyheadman*, but it's subtler and more varied, offering proof that the outfit is one of the leading dance collectives of the mid-'90s. —*Stephen Thomas Erlewine*

**Beaucoup Fish** / Mar. 1, 1999 / V2 ♦♦♦♦
With the buzz almost completely died down from "Born Slippy," Underworld's *Trainspotting* hit of over two years before, *Beaucoup Fish* emerged to a distinctly uncaring public. And though it is a disappointing record compared to the group's high-flying previous albums, it displays Underworld's talents well—the trio is still the best at welding obtuse songcraft onto an uncompromising techno framework and making both sound great. Hyde's nasally vocals are a bit more obtrusive on tracks like the trance-rant "Moaner" and first single "Push Upstairs," but, as before, impeccable production saves the day. While *Second Toughest in the Infants* showed Underworld were no mere novices at introducing super-tough breakbeats, here the focus is on throwback acid-house and trance. The effect is that Underworld have refused to compromise their artistic vision to anyone's view of commercialism; as such, the few excesses on *Beaucoup Fish* can be forgiven. —*John Bush*

**Everything, Everything** / 2000 / JBO ♦♦♦♦
Underworld didn't become one of the biggest groups in the dance world by sitting in the studio all day, spending as much time making tea as producing tracks. Between records, the trio toured incessantly—playing rock venues, dancefloors, major festivals all over the world—and consistently made the single best case for techno working in a live (as opposed to club) context. So instead of a mix album (though alumnus Darren Emerson *did* record a volume in the *Global Underground* series), in mid-2000 Underworld released the live album *Everything, Everything*. And just like their studio LPs, this one works so well, not just because the tracks are so excellently produced, but because Underworld is so good at placing sympathetic tracks next to each other and creating effortless-sounding transitions. Each of the act's previous albums blended tracks so smoothly that new listeners were often forced to check the CD player just to see which track they're on at any second. Beginning here with "Juanita/Kiteless," the opening track(s) from 1996's *Second Toughest in the Infants*, Underworld tweaks the production slightly, then slide right into "Cups" and "Push Upstairs" from 1998's *Beaucoup Fish*. After pausing a few seconds to catch their breath (figuratively speaking) and accept some audience applause, the trio push onward into "Pearls Girl," perhaps the best production of their career and an obvious peak here. Granted, Underworld doesn't blend each transition on *Everything, Everything*, and Karl Hyde's vocals aren't always as perfect as on the LP. Still, excellent track selection (evenly distributed from all three LPs) and a winning performance let the band get nearly everything right on their first live album. —*John Bush*

## United Future Organization

f. 1990, Tokyo, Japan
*Group / Trip-Hop, Acid Jazz*

Pioneers of the Japanese acid-jazz sound, the United Future Organization comprised Tokyo club DJs Tadashi Yabe, Toshio Matsuura and French expatriate Raphael Sebbag. Joining forces in 1990, the trio quickly emerged as a leading force on the Tokyo underground club scene, making their recorded debut the next year with the 12" "I Love My Baby (My Baby Loves Jazz);" "Loud Minority/Moon Dance" followed in mid-1992, becoming a cult favorite on club circuits ranging from London to Hamburg to New York City. UFO's debut LP *Jazzin' 91-93* appeared that September, the same month the trio made their triumphant British debut at London's Fridge club; an American record deal was not forthcoming until 1994, however, with a self-titled collection appearing on Verve Forecast. *No Sound Is Too Taboo* followed in 1995, with United Future Organization resurfacing in 1997 with *3rd Perspective*. —*Jason Ankeny*

● **No Sound Is Too Taboo** / 1994 / European Import ♦♦♦♦
Featured on 1994's *Red Hot and Cool* compilation, the Japanese production trio UFO heads a loose collective of musicians and vocalists present here. Jazz, R&B, trip-hop, Spanish, Caribbean, and Brazilian rhythms all appear in one form or another; surprisingly, these disparate elements flow well through the course of ten songs. —*John Bush*

**United Future Organization** / 1994 / PolyGram ♦♦♦

**3rd Perspective** / Jun. 24, 1997 / PolyGram ♦♦♦
On UFO's third album, the Japanese producers consolidate the world-spanning vision inherent in the title of their previous album, *No Sound Is Too Taboo*. Most of the styles on *3rd Perspective* are French in persuasion, from accordion waltzes to spy-soundtrack grooves. That doesn't make for a bad album, just one which seems to harp on one style when UFO has been known for using the whole world as their palette. —*John Bush*

## The United States of America

f. 1967, Los Angeles, CA, **db.** 1969
*Group / Experimental Rock, Psychedelic*

Despite releasing only one LP, the United States of America was among the most revolutionary bands of the late '60s—grounded equally in psychedelia and the avant-garde, their music eschewed guitars in favor of strings, keyboards and haunting electronics, predating the ambient pop of the modern era by several decades. The United States of America was led by composer and keyboardist Joseph Byrd, a Kentucky native raised in Tucson, Arizona; there he appeared with a series of rock and country bands while attending high school, subsequently playing vibes in a jazz outfit as a student at the University of Arizona. Despite winning a fellowship to study music at Stanford, Byrd instead relocated to New York, intrigued by the avant-garde experiments emerging from the city's downtown music scene; there he began earning international notoriety for his own compositions, at the same time working as a conductor, arranger, associate producer and assistant to critic Virgil Thomson.

Byrd eventually returned to the West Coast, accepting an assistant teaching position at UCLA and moving into a beachfront commune populated by a group of grad students, artists and Indian musicians. He soon began studying acoustics, psychology and Indian music, but quickly turned back to experimental composition, leaving the university in the summer of 1967 to write music full-time and produce "happenings." To perform his new songs—material inspired in no small part by the psychedelic sounds produced during the Summer of Love—Byrd recruited a group of UCLA students (vocalist Dorothy Moskowitz, bassist Rand Forbes, electric violinist Gordon Marron and drummer Craig Woodson) to form the United States of America. The group's lone self-titled LP, produced by David Rubinson, was recorded for CBS in 1968, its unique ambience due largely to their pioneering use of the ring modulator, a primitive synthesizer later popularized by the Kraut-rock sound.

The subject of critical acclaim, the album spent over two months in the lower regions of the *Billboard* charts; still, the United States of America disbanded soon after, with Byrd resurfacing in 1969 with *The American Metaphysical Circus,* credited to Joe Byrd and the Field Hippies, a group of a dozen musicians including vocalists Susan de Lange, Victoria Bond and Christie Thompson. A critical and commercial failure, the LP was his last until 1975, at which time he released *Yankee Transcendoodle,* a collection of synthesizer pieces. Three years later Byrd also produced Ry Cooder's *Jazz* album, and in 1980 he issued another synthesizer record, *Christmas Yet to Come.* He additionally wrote for films, television and advertising jingles. Fellow United States of America alum Dorothy Moskowitz, meanwhile, later resurfaced in Country Joe McDonald's All-Star Band, with the remaining members of the group essentially disappearing from the contemporary music scene. —*Jason Ankeny*

- **The United States of America** / 1968 / Columbia ✦✦✦

Originally released on Columbia in 1968, this is one of the legendary pure psychedelic space records. Some of the harder rocking tunes have a fun-house recklessness that recalls aspects of early Pink Floyd and the Velvet Underground at their freakiest; the sedate, exquisitely orchestrated ballads, especially "Cloud Song" and the wonderfully titled "Love Song for the Dead Che," are among the best relics of dreamy psychedelia. Occasionally things get too excessive and self-conscious, and the attempts at comedy are a bit flat, but otherwise this is a near classic. The CD reissue adds two previously unreleased outtakes. —*Richie Unterberger*

## Universal Being

f. Isle of Wight, England
*Group / Electronica, Ambient-Techno, Club/Dance*

Max Brennan's main side gig while away from Fretless AZM, Universal Being is a collaboration with drummer Rupert Brown. In 1995, the pair began recording for Holistic Records (the same label that released Fretless AZM material) with the *Sphinx* EP. Two full-lengths, *Holistic Rhythms* and *Jupiter,* appeared the following year. The retrospective *Archives* was released in 1997, after which Brennan continued to focus on Fretless AZM, with three albums released in the next year. Brown has recorded on his own as well, under the alias Hubble, returning to the Universal Being guise for 1999's *Elephant Being.* —*John Bush*

- **Jupiter** / Jul. 1, 1996 / Holistic ✦✦✦✦

Brennan and Brown's second Universal Being album in a year is an otherworldly groove adventure with hints of Eastern percussion, marching bands and all kinds of '70s influences from Herbie Hancock to Tangerine Dream. As on the best Fretless AZM material, the production strikes a balance between sequenced electronics and live-action instrumentation including Brown on drums and Brennan on bass. "Quatermass" and "Primordial Serpent" are two highlights. —*John Bush*

*Archives* / Jun. 16, 1997 / Holistic ✦✦

## U.N.K.L.E.

f. 1994, London, England
*Group / Electronica, Ambient Breakbeat, Ambient-Techno, Alternative Rap, Trip-Hop*

Experimental hip-hop outfit U.N.K.L.E. was one of the original artists releasing material through noted UK label Mo'Wax, which helped launch the instrumental mid-'90s downtempo breakbeat revival eventually termed trip-hop. Though hardly the label's highest profile group (at least until the long-delayed release of their debut LP in 1998), U.N.K.L.E. numbered among its members label-head James Lavelle, who formed Mo'Wax while still in his teens as an antidote to the increasingly stale acid jazz/Northern Soul scene. Stripping the music down to its barest of essentials—bass, percussion, minimal samples and heavy effects—the Mo'Wax sound (best exemplified by the second Mo'Wax label comp, *Headz,* as well as its sequel, the two-part *Headz 2*) quickly gained respectability and a large audience. Although not as prolific as other Mo'Wax artists such as DJs Shadow and Krush, Lavelle's group nonetheless played a crucial role in cementing Mo'Wax's early sound though their *The Time Has Come* double EP, the latter of which featured remixes of the title track by Plaid, Portishead, and U2 producer Howie B.

The group comprised the trio of Lavelle, Tim Goldsworthy—a mate of Lavelle's since childhood—and producer Kudo, of seminal Japanese label Major Force (and a member of the on-again, off-again psychedelic beat crew Skylab). Previous to his entry into production, Lavelle, along with Goldsworthy, was deep into New York hip-hop and electro, the emerging late-'80s Sheffield bleep scene, the English acid jazz scene (which he covered as a columnist for *Straight No Chaser* magazine), and of course the acid house and techno explosions that were redefining the English counterculture at the time. The pair hooked up with third-member Kudo through the growing rep of the latter's Love T.K.O. project, whose outbound interpretations of breakbeat and acid jazz drew Lavelle's ear. While Goldsworthy and Kudo remain more heavily involved in nuts'n'bolts production (especially given the success of Mo'Wax, with Lavelle penning an expansive partial ownership deal with A&M Records in 1996), Lavelle is heavily involved in the conceptual and organizational end, crafting beats and laying out vague sketches his partners then expand into full-blown tracks. Despite the scarcity of released material, U.N.K.L.E. grew to wider acclaim during 1996 through remix projects for the Jon Spencer Blues Explosion and Tortoise. After Goldsworthy and Kudo were effectively replaced by Mo'Wax bill-payer DJ Shadow, the all-star LP *Psyence Fiction* finally appeared in 1998. [See Also: DJ Shadow] —*Sean Cooper*

**The Time Has Come [EP]** / 1995 / Mo'Wax ✦✦✦✦

With a subtitle referencing Sun Ra and a cover splashed with the bright, abstract figures of old-school graffiti artist Futura 2000, U.N.K.L.E.'s *Time Has Come* EP (closer to a mini-album at over a half-hour in length) is a sprawling bouillabaisse of influences, all impeccably arranged. Hip-hop, funk, and jazz are of course the most obvious, but the soundtrack-y deviations of ambient, as well as hitting electro-boogie and spy movie theme music (particularly on Portishead's remix) also figure in. Remixes from Plaid and Howie B also make this one of the tastiest, most varied release in the Mo'Wax catalog. —*Sean Cooper*

- **Psyence Fiction** / Sep. 29, 1998 / Mo'Wax/London ✦✦✦✦

Initially a collective fronted by Mo'Wax head James Lavelle, U.N.K.L.E. had metamorphosed into a loose collaboration between Lavelle and DJ Shadow by the time the group released their debut album, *Psyence Fiction,* in the fall of 1998. Lavelle and Shadow were unequal partners, with the former providing the concept and the latter providing music, which naturally winds up overshadowing whatever concept that is discernable on the album. As it turns out, the only clear concept—apart from futuristic sound effects, video game samples and merging trip-hop with rock—is collaborating with a variety of musicians, from superstars (Mike D, the Verve's Richard Ashcroft, Radiohead's Thom Yorke, Metallica's Jason Newsted) to cult favorites Kool G. Rap, Alice Temple, and Mark Hollis (who provides uncredited piano on "Chaos"). Since DJ Shadow's prime gift is for instrumentals, as *Endtroducing* brilliantly proved, the prospect of him collaborating with vocalists is more intriguing than enticing, and *Psyence Fiction* is appropriately divided between brilliance and failed experiments. Generally, Shadow and Lavelle aren't breaking new territory here—beneath the harder rock edge, full-fledged songs and occasional melodicism, the album stays on the course *Endtroducing* set. Shadow isn't given room to run wild with his soundscapes—with only a couple of exceptions, such as the explosive opener "Guns Blazing," he creates sonic collages equivalent to his debut album. Initially, that may be a disappointment, but U.N.K.L.E.'s balance of pop/rock songcraft and experimental sounds becomes more intriguing as the album unwinds and as it's played repeatedly. Portions of the record still sound a little awkward—Mike D's contribution suffers primarily from recycled *Hello Nasty* rhyme schemes, for instance—yet those moments are overshadowed by Shadow's imagination and unpredictable highlights, such as Temple's chilly "Bloodstain" or Badly Drawn Boy's claustrophobic "Nursery Rhyme," as well as the masterstrokes fronted by Ashcroft (a sweeping, neo-symphonic "Lonely Soul") and Yorke (the moody "Rabbit in Your Headlights"). These moments might not add up to an overpowering record, but in some ways *Psyence Fiction* is something better—a superstar project that doesn't play it safe and actually has its share of rich, rewarding music. —*Stephen Thomas Erlewine*

## Up, Bustle & Out

f. 1993, Bristol, England
*Group / Electronica, Ambient Breakbeat, Trip-Hop, Club/Dance, World Fusion*

With influences drawn from diverse sources all over the world—from Istanbul to Bolivia, Andalusia to North Africa—Up, Bustle & Out are one of the harder to pin down groups on the experimental breakbeat landscape. Hailing from the English town of Bristol, home also to Tricky and Massive Attack, Up, Bustle & Out comprise producers Rupert Mould and D. "Ein" Fell, who formed the group in the early '90s as an adjunct to their respective interests in nonWestern musics, funk and soul, jazz, and experimental underground club styles like house, techno, ambient, and trip-hop. The pair produced an early single, "Une Amitie Africaine" (released on their own Forever Groove label in 1991) tying these sources together, and attracted the attention of a number of labels interested in releasing their material. The pair pursued other interests until 1993, when they reformed to produce material they eventually sent to Coldcut's Ninja Tune label. Impressed with their work, Ninja Tune released Up, Bustle & Out's debut, *The Breeze Was Mellow (As the Guns Cooled in the Cellar)*, in 1994, which caught the attention of American hip-hop DJs as well as the more eclectic British underground. The following two years were spent by the group traveling and archiving source material for their follow-up, *One Colour Just Reflects Another*, which utilized field recordings from excursions to Mexico, Central America, the Middle East, and the Andalusian mountains, where Mould played with and recorded Gypsies, smugglers, thieves, and revolutionaries. Combining those source tapes with hip-hop beats, percussion and instrumental tracks recorded in the studio, and vocal and spoken snippets, the group fashioned a unique, signature blend attracting fans of Latin jazz and world music as often as club heads familiar with the more standard Ninja Tune fare.

In addition to their work as Up, Bustle & Out, Ein and Mould are also involved in solo projects extending well beyond the boundaries of their combined effort. Mould performs with a traditional Andean flute group, while Ein is a studio producer and engineer, also recording club tracks under a number of different names. —*Sean Cooper*

**The Breeze Was Mellow (As the Guns Cooled in the Cellar)** / 1994 / Ninja Tune ✦✦
Features spoken word by Mould and vocal contributions by former Massive Attack collaborator Sharon Wynter. —*Sean Cooper*

**One Colour Just Reflects Another** / 1996 / Ninja Tune ✦✦✦
An uptempo, groove-oriented, acid jazz/hip-hop hybrid with strong Latin and Middle Eastern influences. Recordings gathered on location sit nicely in the mix next to deep beats, fat acoustic basslines, and a bevy of instrumental sources. —*Sean Cooper*

**Caravan Summer [EP]** / Jul. 8, 1996 / Ninja Tune ✦✦✦
The group's most expansive, least obvious recording to date, the album is not as moored in the clubs as previous efforts, with even greater attention paid to nonWestern source recordings and compositional influence. —*Sean Cooper*

• **Light 'Em Up, Blow 'Em Out** / Jun. 17, 1997 / Ninja Tune ✦✦✦✦
UBO's flair for the far-flung continues on their third full-length, which incorporates an even wider array of styles than its trip-hop-heavy predecessors. *Light 'Em Up* has its fair share of beat logic, of course, but the group have filled out the flamenco, Brazilian, and gypsy influences that only peppered previous releases, resulting in an odd, off-kilter, truly original sound. —*Sean Cooper*

**Che Guevara: A Dream of Land and Freedom [EP]** / Oct. 7, 1997 / Ninja Tune ✦✦✦
UBO take their romantic Latin dabblings to their most ambitious extreme with this limited 7-track CD, released to coincide with the 30th anniversary of the death of Cuban revolutionary Che Guevara. —*Sean Cooper*

**Master Sessions, Vol. 1** / Jul. 11, 2000 / Ninja Tune ✦✦✦
During the '90s, dance producers voyaged into uncharted genre-crossover waters (jazz, classical, dub, academic electronics) with increasing regularity, so it was just a matter of time before at least one act attempted a recording inspired by Latin music, specifically the Cuban phenomenon of *Buena Vista Social Club*. It's doubtful, however, that *anyone* in the trip-hop community could do this kind of tribute as well as the British duo Up, Bustle and Out, who not only has strong roots within the music of Central and South America but has previously incorporated on-site field recordings into their material. Still, the first of two volumes in the *Rebel Radio* series is less a melding of breakbeat dance and native Latin forms than it is a trip-hop album inspired by Cuban music. It was undoubtedly a wise decision—especially considering the potentially gimmicky sound of Cuban music laced with hip-hop breaks—but Up, Bustle and Out also ran the risk of their listeners not being able to follow them. The album begins with a pair of tight beatbox-funk jams, "The Educators" and "Hip Hop Barrio," then goes into two traditional Cuban songs performed with a large band led by flutist Richard Egües who has played with salsa star icons including Tito Puente, Joe Cuba, Larry Harlow, and Fania All-Stars. The rest of the album follows the same blueprint, with a couple of excellent up-tempo trip-hop tracks leading into a section of flute- and piano-led Cuban guarachas or descargas. The productions are always tied to Cuba, from the paranoid strings of "Kennedy's Secret Tapes" to the searing vibes of "Havana's Streets," a poetry piece with vocals by Martin Genge. Even considering the vast majority of trip-hop fans aren't interested in traditional Latin music, *Master Sessions, Vol. 1* features plenty of solid production. [An added bonus is a 150-page book, *The Rebel Radio Diary*, charting Up, Bustle and Out's Rupert Mould (complete with frontispiece featuring Mould on a motorcycle Che Guevara-style).] —*John Bush*

## Urban Dance Squad

f. 1986, Amsterdam, The
*Group / Jungle/Drum'N'Bass, Club/Dance*

The Amsterdam-based rock/rap collective Urban Dance Squad began in 1986, playing and jamming together on an informal basis. They played a gig at an Utrecht festival and, surprised by the raves their performance drew, became a more serious project. The group gigged for two years, and with the proceeds released 1990's *Mental Floss for the Globe*. Urban Dance Squad's mix of rock, rap, funk, ska, folk, hip-hop and soul signaled the trend toward genre-bending that prevailed in '90s music. *Mental Floss* featured the single "Deeper Shade of Soul" which charted at #21 in the US on Billboard's Hot 100.

The group spent another year touring constantly, and released their second album *Life 'n Perspective of a Genuine Crossover* in 1991. Unfortunately, it failed to match *Mental Floss'* critical or commercial success, as did 1994's *Persona Non Grata*. 1999 saw Urban Dance Squad release their fourth album, *Planet Ultra*, as well as rerelease their earlier releases on the Triple X label. —*Heather Phares*

• **Mental Floss for the Globe** / 1990 / Arista ✦✦✦✦
The 1990 debut of Urban Dance Squad revealed a band smashing the boundaries between rock, funk, punk, metal and hip-hop. "Fast Lane" leads the program with a blistering groove powered by chugging guitar and sampled horns. Later, "Brainstorm on the UDS" alternates rap verses with a punky shoutalong chorus, while "The Devil" borrows a murky string bassline and greasy slide guitar from the Tom Waits bag. Rudeboy never really sings; rather he raps or, when the song demands it, sort of chants along in a singsong cadence. But for a nonsinger he has a great voice, one that comes from the chest but has an edge sharp enough to cut through the mix. Also notable are polymath guitarist Tres Manos and the unbelievably funky bass of Silly Sil. This reissue includes a bonus live disc that documents an alternately metallish and bluesy (!) Hollywood concert from 1990. —*Rick Anderson*

**Life 'n Perspective of a Genuine Crossover** / 1991 / Arista ✦✦✦
The sophomore slump hit Urban Dance Squad rather hard, or maybe it just seemed that way based on the consistently high quality of their debut. *Life 'n Perspectives of a Genuine Crossover* sounds aimless where its predecessor

came off as shrewdly eclectic. It's not that there aren't great moments: "Careless" is nice mid-tempo hip-hop with a blues base, and the strangely named "(Thru) the Gates of the Big Fruit" showcases some great turntable work from DJ DNA as well as countryish slide guitar from Tres Manos. But the four-part approach to "Life 'n Perspectives" is annoying and "Routine" goes nowhere. Somehow the high points aren't quite enough to carry the weight of the low ones. However, the live-in-Tokyo bonus disc that accompanies this reissue is more consistently rewarding. —*Rick Anderson*

**Persona Non Grata** / Apr. 1994 / Virgin ♦♦♦♦
The Urban Dance Squad's penultimate album was also its most heavily metal-influenced. "Demagogue," the album's opener and centerpiece, is an utterly bracing concoction of raw-throated rap and spare, bright metal guitar, all underlaid with minimalist funk drums. That formula remains basically unaltered throughout the rest of the album—"Good Grief," "(Some) Chitchat" and "Selfstyled" all step to the same stripped-down hip-hop beat. It starts sounding pretty samey by the end, of course, but taken in measured doses, the funky beats are guaranteed to move your booty, while the roaring guitars clear your sinuses. It's too bad DJ DNA was no longer in the band by this point; his turntable scratching would have given a welcome additional dimension to the sound. Bonuses abound: Like the original release, this one features two hidden tracks, one a remix and the other a live version of "Demagogue." This reissue also adds a bonus live disc. —*Rick Anderson*

**Planet Ultra** / Jan. 26, 1999 / Triple X ♦♦♦
The most recent Urban Dance Squad album is reissued here in a deluxe twofer that also includes a live recording from New York in 1997. Kudos to Triple X for the fine packaging and for having the good taste to give these Dutch metal/hip-hop-heads another shot at the US market that ignored them inexplicably, during their seven-year career. It's not that Americans don't like the idea of rock/hip-hop fusion—witness the popularity of the Red Hot Chili Peppers. But for some reason, the Urban Dance Squad never caught on the same way. That's our loss. *Planet Ultra* opens with the highly crunchy "Nonstarter" before sliding into the downright melodic "Temporarily Expendable." It then bounces back and forth from straight-ahead metal fare, like "Forgery," to the slow and deeply funky "Pass the Baton Right." DJ DNA was long gone by this point, but someone's playing pretty cool turntable on that last track. The live disc doesn't cohere quite as well, but it's worth hearing. —*Rick Anderson*

**Artantica** / May 9, 2000 / Triple X ♦♦♦♦
For those who think of rap-metal fusion as something invented by bands like Korn and Limp Bizkit, Urban Dance Squad is back to remind you that they've been doing it for ten years now—and from a home base in Holland. Led by a cheerful shouter named Rudeboy, this band has been shaking people's fillings loose with roaring guitar and funky drumming since Fred Durst was in junior high. Now, after an extended hiatus that saw the band's previous albums remastered and reissued as well as Rudeboy pursuing his techno/drum'n'bass muse as a member of Junkie XL, the UDS is back with what may be its most interesting and varied album since *Mental Floss for the Globe* and its most compelling one since *Persona Non Grata*. "Letter to da Better" nicely combines singing and rapping, "Craftmatic Adjustable Girl" makes extensive use of turntablist DNA under Rudeboy's jackhammer flow, and "Music Entertainment" marks perhaps the first time a theremin has been used on a hiphop album. Nothing here has quite the raw power of "Demagogue," but everything on this album is worth hearing more than once. —*Rick Anderson*

## Urban Tribe
f. 1995, Detroit, MI
*Group / Detroit Techno, Trip-Hop, Club/Dance*
Detroit's Sherard Ingram is one of the few Americans (along with DJ Shadow and Money Mark) to record for Britain's noted trip-hop label, Mo'Wax. An earthy downtempo producer, he debuted his Urban Tribe alias for Carl Craig's Planet E Records by appearing on the 1992 compilations *Equinox* and *Elements of and Experiments with Sound*. After signing on to Mo'Wax in 1996, he released the EP *Eastward* in late 1996. Ingram's debut album, 1998's *The Collapse of Modern Culture*, expanded the lineup to include engineers Craig and Anthony "Shake" Shakir plus Moodymann's Kenny Dixon, Jr. —*John Bush*

● **The Collapse of Modern Culture** / Oct. 26, 1998 / Mo'Wax ♦♦♦♦
Similar to other releases on Mo'Wax, *The Collapse of Modern Culture* focuses on downtempo beat-symphonies with heavy inspiration from dub. The similarities end there, however, as Sherard Ingram's Detroit and electro inspirations make for a record that sounds closer to downtempo tech-house than DJ Shadow-type trip-hop. The album also unites three of Detroit's most respected producers—Carl Craig, Moodymann's Kenny Dixon, Jr. and Anthony Shakir—for several tracks, though Ingram is the real star. —*John Bush*

## Ursula 1000 (Alex Gimeno)
*Producer, DJ / Funky Breaks, Club/Dance*
Ursula 1000 is a stylish American DJ who spins (and records) sampladelic easy-listening breakbeat tracks in a style similar to continental popsters from Pizzicato Five to Dimitri from Paris. Born Alex Gimeno, he was raised in Miami, where he studied commercial art and owned a comic-book store before joining the local band 23 as a drummer. Determined to make some money from his huge record collection, Gimeno bought turntables and a mixer, learned to spin, and began DJing at a local college station as well as Miami nightclubs. He began recording as well, and moved to New York to further both his mixing and production career. After negotiations with Island's Palm Pictures broke down, Gimeno signed to the Eighteenth Street Lounge label run by D.C.'s Thievery Corporation. *The New Sound of Ursula 1000* appeared in 1999, followed by the mix album *All Systems Are Go-Go* one year later. —*John Bush*

● **All Systems Are Go-Go** / Jul. 11, 2000 / Esl Music ♦♦♦
Loungecore DJ Ursula 1000 mixes a set of fun, though rather formulaic, collection of tracks for 18th Street Lounge. Over mid-tempo breaks and house rhythms, his tracks recycle the meatier parts of orchestral pop, easy listening, and instructional records for a post-ironic generation of musical horticulturists. Perhaps realizing how lightweight these grooves are, Ursula doesn't stick with the lounge sound throughout; in fact, parts of the album are surprisingly close to a turntablist record, with a bit of scratching as well as frequent breaks in the mix. Though the sound isn't as consciously "important" as more respected forms of music (like techno), *All Systems Are Go-Go* is a great mix album, thanks largely to great inclusions from producers all over the world: "Direct Drive" by ECD, "Margret Evening Fashion" by Le Hammond Inferno, and "Mr. Bongo" by Lemon are just three of the highlights. —*John Bush*

## Us3
f. 1991, London, England
*Group / Jazz-Rap, Club/Dance, Hip-Hop*
The jazz/hip-hop fusion collective Us3 scored a major hit in 1994 with "Cantaloop (Flip Fantasia)," a song which displayed the group's fondness for sampling classic recordings on the Blue Note label (in this case, Herbie Hancock's "Cantaloupe Island"). The group was founded in London in 1991 when concert promoter and jazz writer Geoff Wilkinson met Mel Simpson, who was writing music for television shows and ad jingles and had once played keyboards with John Mayall. The two produced an independent single, "Where Will We Be in the 21st Century?," which sold less than 250 copies. In 1992, their song "The Band That Played the Boogie" attracted the attention of Blue Note owner Capitol Records, which gave Simpson and Wilkinson free rein to sample anything from the catalog. The two immediately went to work, hiring several musicians and rappers Kobie Powell and Rahsaan Kelly, with Tukka Yoot joining later. The sessions resulted in the hit "Cantaloop" and the album *Hand on the Torch*. The group toured Japan and Europe, gradually weaning itself away from using samples in a live setting, and played a well-received show at the 1993 Montreux Jazz Festival. *Hand on the Torch* was ignored by most jazz publications, but was chosen Album of the Year by Japan's *Swing Journal*, and the group were named Jazz Musicians of the Year by Britain's *The Independent*. After a nearly three-year delay, Us3 returned in 1997 with *Broadway & 52nd*, an album which received positive reviews but failed to generate a hit. —*Steve Huey*

● **Hand on the Torch** / Nov. 16, 1993 / Blue Note ♦♦♦
Hip-hop/jazzers Us3 have forged the most elaborate union between the styles since the early days of Gang Starr and A Tribe Called Quest. Blue Note's vast catalog gives them a huge advantage over several similar groups in terms of source material, and classic sounds by Art Blakey, Horace Silver and Herbie Hancock provide zest and fiber to their narratives. Indeed, when things falter, it's because the raps aren't always that creative. They are serviceable and

sometimes catchy, but too often delivered without the snazzy touches or distinctive skills that make Quest and Gang Starr's material top-notch. But when words and music mesh, as on "Cantaloop" or "The Darkside," Us3 show how effectively hip-hop and jazz can blend. —*Ron Wynn*

**Broadway & 52nd** / Apr. 8, 1997 / Capitol ♦♦
Though Us3's second album *Broadway & 52nd* lacks a single song as infectious as "Cantaloop (Flip Fantasia)," it holds up better as an album. Geoff Wilkinson is better able to fuse his samples and hip-hop rhythms with jazz sensibilities, and while the rappers weigh the record down with inane rhymes, the production is quite intoxicating. —*Stephen Thomas Erlewine*

## Vladimir Ussachevsky

b. Nov. 3, 1911, Hailar, Manchuria, d. Jan. 4, 1990
*Composer / Musique Concrète, Atonal, Electronic*

A leading catalyst behind the rise of American electronic music, composer Vladimir Ussachevsky was born November 3, 1911 in Hailar, Manchuria; he emigrated to the US in 1930, and after graduating from Pomona College went on to study at the Eastman School of Music. There he composed his first major works, among them 1935's *Theme and Variations* and 1938's *Jubilee Cantata*, as well as various other pieces for piano, vocal, choral and orchestral performance. Ussachevsky earned his Ph.D. in 1939 and joined the faculty at Columbia University in 1947; around this time he began making his first forays into electronic music, culminating a few years later with his acquisition of an Ampex tape recorder. In 1952, he and colleague Otto Luening presented the first tape music performance ever given in the US, where among the pieces premiered was Ussachevsky's musique concrète landmark *Sonic Contours*. Key works including 1954's *Poem of Cycles and Bells* and 1956's *Piece for Tape Recorder* followed, and in 1958 Ussachevsky and Luening received a Rockefeller Foundation grant to open the Columbia-Princeton Electronic Music Center, the first such electro-acoustic facility in America. Complete with four analog tape studios for electronic composition as well as the room-sized RCA Mark II Synthesizer, the CPEMC was the launching pad for countless experimental works, not the least of which were those written by Ussachevsky himself. He died January 4, 1990. —*Jason Ankeny*

★ **Electronic Film Music** / 1990 / New World ♦♦♦♦♦
*Electronic Film Music* includes two lyric, eerie and innovative filmscores, for the film of J.P. Sartre's play *No Exit* and Lloyd William's avant-garde film *Line of Apogee* by the master of the Columbia-Princeton electronic music sound. Also employs vocal, animal, and environmental sounds. —*"Blue" Gene Tyranny*

## Utah Saints

f. 1991, Leeds, England
*Group / Rave, Club/Dance, Dance-Pop*

Formed in Leeds, England in 1991, the dance-metal duo Utah Saints was led by Jez Willis, a onetime member of the industrial group Cassandra Complex who during the late '80s had turned to DJing in local clubs. While working the club circuit he met fellow DJ Tim Garbutt, whose passion for house music inspired Willis to begin creating house tracks of his own; Garbutt then played one of Willis' tapes to strong crowd response, and together they honed the song which eventually became Utah Saints' self-released debut single, 1991's "What Can You Do for Me." Of the one thousand copies originally pressed, one made it to the offices of ffrr Records, which immediately signed the duo to a contract; within three months of its wide release, "What Can You Do for Me" sold some 170,000 copies in the UK, landing in the Top Ten of the British pop charts. Utah Saints' self-titled debut LP followed in 1992, proving successful in the US as well; after issuing the EP *Something Good*, a year later the group also opened for U2. Nevertheless, the duo's relationship with ffrr quickly soured, and despite signing a six-album deal they exited the label in 1996, leaving a completed LP on the shelf. Upon signing to Echo Records, Utah Saints finally resurfaced two years later with the single "Rock." —*Jason Ankeny*

● **Utah Saints** / 1992 / London ♦♦♦♦
The Utah Saints' vision of epic stadium acid-house was good for a few feel-good hits featured on this debut LP, including "Something Good" and "What Can You Do for Me." The album tracks, however, reveal a distinct lack of ideas and some rather bland dance music. —*Keith Farley*

## Charles Uzzell-Edwards

b. Wales
*Producer / Ambient Techno, Electro-Acoustic*

Recording almost exclusively for the Frankfurt-based Fax label, Welsh expatriate Charles Uzzell-Edwards makes environmental ambient heavy with found sound and field recordings, both solo and in combination with artists such as Pete Namlook, Tetsu Inoue, Atom Heart, and the Mammal. A DJ of renown before moving into production, Edwards moved to the San Francisco Bay Area in 1991 after studying commercial design in London. Working as a designer for skate/ravewear clothier Anarchic Adjustment, Edwards was a chill room staple when he met Fax's Pete Namlook in 1993, joining the noted ambient label Fax, first as its US distribution arm (which he remains). He moved into music production in 1994 in collaboration with Namlook on two sets of releases, *A New Consciousness* 1 and 2 and *Create* 1 and 2, before moving into solo composition with *Octopus* the following year. Although he moves increasingly toward more structured compositional improvisations, Edwards remains concerned primarily with integrating music with the environment, not only the one in which it's heard, but also the one in which it's created (through extensive use of contact mics and DAT recordings gathered on location), aligning his work with early European free improv groups such as AMM and contemporary compositional figures such as Karlheinz Stockhausen and John Cage. Subsequent solo and collaborative works have also incorporated a larger degree of digital sampling, as well as elements of jazz and post-rave experimental electronica. —*Sean Cooper*

**A New Consciousness** / 1994 / Fax ♦♦♦
This first collaborative outing with Pete Namlook is largely dance-based, with a familiar kickdrum pulse driving the bulk of the material. Still, Edwards and Namlook bring enough new to the party—from subway-boombox trickery to ponging basslines—to keep the disc interesting throughout. —*Sean Cooper*

**Octopus** / 1995 / Fax ♦♦♦♦
Edwards' first solo outing compiles his elsewhere documented fascination for environmental recordings with a more orderly, engaging combination of slight rhythms, melodic fragments, and the odd bit of political humor ("Mile Long Grand Canyon Bra Chain"). A bold first step. —*Sean Cooper*

**Octopus 2** / 1996 / Fax ♦♦♦
Though not particularly innovative in style or technique, the overall substance of this second in the *Octopus* series is signature CUE, with found sounds, vocal clips, and instrumental samples (standup bass and drums, primarily) providing the atmosphere for shifting textures, offbeat compositional meanderings, and some deeply emotional passages. —*Sean Cooper*

● **Supergroup** / 1997 / Fax ♦♦♦♦
A collaboration of sorts between Edwards and DJ Thomas Bullock, aka "the Mammal," *Supergroup*—from its hilarious cover art doubling the pair as a quartet, to its loungy, tongue-in-cheek fusion of sampled beats and twinkling electronics—fits in somewhere between Skylab and Uwe "Atom Heart" Schmidt's work. Not surprising given Edwards' stated affection for Schmidt's work, as well the fact that Skylab's Matt Ducasse was a near resident toward the end of Edwards' notorious *Gardening Club*'s long reign in San Francisco. But it's Bullock's presence here that probably accounts for the record's bizarre funkiness, the simple but effective, shifting beatwork likely originating among the noted Wicked DJ's fertile crates. "Depechez-vous à la dancefloor...!" —*Sean Cooper*

## Mika Vainio
*Producer / Experimental Techno, Ambient Techno, Techno*

Ø is the solo identity of Mika Vainio of Finnish techno duo Panasonic, the latter of whose brand of quirky, lo-fi minimalism has transformed them into one of the most popular exports from the Northern European techno underground. Unlike Panasonic's harder, comparatively more dancefloor-oriented gear, however, Vainio's Ø work tends more toward the ambient and experimental, wedding sparse machine noises with shifting rhythms, stubbornly unmusical sonic textures, and assorted channel separation weirdness. Vainio's Ø releases stretch back to the early '90s (predating his association with Panasonic by a few years); his earliest work appeared on the Corporate label before landing with Finnish techno institution Sahko in 1993, where he's released most of his material, including three albums and a handful of EPs. The increasing popularity of Panasonic has meant Vainio's giving less and less time to his Ø work, but he did manage to release some of his most accomplished solo material in 1996, on his third Sahko full-length *Olento*, which featured the most effective fusion of Panasonic's austere minimalism with less immediate, more challenging structures. Demand for Vainio as a remixer has also grown of late, with revisions of tracks by Björk and Tactile both appearing in mid-'96. He continues to record as Tekonivel (for Sahko sublabel Puu) and as Kentolevi for Patrick Pulsinger's Cheap label; titles issued under Vainio's own name include 1998's *Onko*, 1999's *Ydin*, and the following year's *20 to 2000*. —*Sean Cooper*

● **Onko** / Jan. 20, 1998 / Touch ♦♦♦♦
Of Mika Vainio's rapidly expanding catalog, *Onko* is one of his broader, more varied works. While most of Vainio's recordings are concerned, to greater or lesser degree, with the musical implications of residual electronics—static, electronic noise, digital artifacts, and so on—*Onko* opens out Vainio's treatment of these elements onto wider compositional terrain, building a sense of movement and (admittedly monochromatic) form from the most sparing of features. Though the first half of *Onko* resembles other of Vainio's almost artless experiments in discreet electronics, the latter segment of the title track and the concluding "Viher" focus in on microcosmic melodies and structural dynamics typically absent from Vainio's tracks, numbering them among his most listenable and engaging to date. —*Sean Cooper*

**20 to 2000** / Feb. 29, 2000 / Noton ♦♦♦♦

## Vainqueur (Rene Lowe)
*Producer / Minimal Techno, Experimental Dub, Ambient Techno*

Following the collapse of the Berlin Wall and the rise of electronic dance music, Rene Lowe immersed himself in the records he found at the Hard Wax record store. When Detroit artists began frequenting Berlin in the early '90s to collaborate and DJ, Lowe became close with Eddie Fowlkes in particular, who helped him set up his own studio. It was at this time that Lowe took on the French name Vainqueur. After having met the two men behind the Hard Wax store—Moritz von Oswald and Mark Ernestus—during one of their live performances at Waschhaus (a club where Lowe spun), he soon found himself on the duo's M label. This debut record as Vainqueur, 1992's *Lyot*, became a techno anthem, propelled by its dense, pounding percussion and a catchy riff, exploited to perfection on the Maurizio mix of the song. In May 1995 Lowe produced the music that would eventually appear as the first *Elevation* record on Hard Wax's most ambitious label yet, Chain Reaction. Rather than take a traditional approach to techno—emphasizing percussion—he decided to focus instead on the sequencing of the track, resulting in an epic ambient track composed of individual sounds traveling through elaborate sequencing—a journey through the slow metamorphosis of a sound. He soon followed this record with others, eventually compiling his Chain Reaction canon on the *Elevations* CD in 1997, which featured further previously unreleased variations of the sound he explored on the first *Elevation* record. Though Lowe hasn't released a gigantic body of work, his landmark productions remain important in the revisionist camp of techno associated with labels such as Chain Reaction and Mille Plateaux. —*Jason Birchmeier*

● **Elevations** / Sep. 15, 1997 / Chain Reaction ♦♦♦
*Elevations* collects a wide range of Rene Lowe's tracks that were previously released as vinyl-only EPs along with two marvelous, previously unreleased tracks. The musical styles on this collection vary from monotonous, banging industrial techno to poetically arranged sound distortions and soft, gleaming computerized ambience. Discussing Lowe as a techno producer is like speaking of Jimi Hendrix as merely a guitar player; both artists take traditional sounds and manipulate them to sonic extremes beyond originality toward the unattainable. All of the tracks possess elements of remote, inhuman beauty. Pieces such as "Antistatic" and "Elevation II (original)" couldn't be more minimally constructed, yet after a minute of listening, one realizes that there is a strange complexity to the minimal nature here, which is horrifically paradoxical. In the same way, the final two epic tracks, "Elevation I (version 3)" and "Solanus (extracted)," feel as though they lack low-frequency percussive rhythm, but this is exactly the point. With their swirling tapestries of high-frequency tones, one desires nothing more but to revel in this disorientating tranquility, unparalleled within the realm of mundane reality. —*Jason Birchmeier*

## Mijk Van Dijk
*Producer, DJ / Trance, Club/Dance, Techno*

One of Germany's most important producers during the '90s, Mijk Van Dijk recorded an abundance of early techno/trance classics under the aliases Microglobe, Mindgear, and Marmion. A bassist for several funk bands during the early '80s, Van Dijk moved to Berlin later in the decade to work as a journalist and began producing house tracks in 1988. Two years later, he issued the "Hate" single, recorded for Low Spirit as LoopZone. An alliance with fellow Berlin producer/DJ Tanith resulted in a 1991 LoopZone EP (*What Is Noise?*) as well as singles under Tanith's name and as 9-10-Boy. By 1992, the release of two solo singles—"High on Hope" as Microglobe and "Don't Panic" as Mindgear—pushed Van Dijk's name into the global realm, and he collaborated with fellow German up-and-comer Cosmic Baby to produce a seminal compilation on MFS, *Trance: Formed from Beyond*.

In 1993, Mijk Van Dijk's third major project, Marmion, (a co-production act with Marcos Lopez) debuted with the *Berlin* EP, a release on Superstition that hit the world's dancefloors after the track "Schönberg" became a big mover in DJ circles. His first full-length, Microglobe's *Afreuropamericasiaaustralica*, followed in 1994 and Van Dijk developed his DJing and remixing skills with dates all over Europe and reworkings of tracks by Denki Groove and Parts of Console. Later releases under his own name began to cultivate a more melodic brand of trance that fit in well with the growing hi-NRG/progressive trance scene in Europe. The 1997 *Glow* LP under his own name presaged his first mix album, *Multi-Mijk*, consisting mostly of his own tracks and remixes. In 1999, he released *Teamwork*, a full album of collaborations with producers including Tanith, Claude Young, Thomas Schumacher, and Quazar. In addition to producing, remixing, and DJing, Van Dijk also moved into the soundtrack realm with scores for two movies as well as the video game soundtrack *Ghost in the Shell*. He also developed a music-making game for Sony's Playstation named !Depth. —*John Bush*

● **Multi-Mijk** / 1998 / Sony ♦♦♦♦
All in one, *Multi-Mijk* combines the producing, remixing, and DJing aspects

of Mijk Van Dijk's music career. Including over a dozen tracks, the set focuses on a few Mindgear and Microglobe classics as well as own-name productions ("All Our Colours," "Effective Force") and remixes of the Japanese acts Denki Groove and Parts of Console —*John Bush*

**Teamwork** / Jan. 25, 1999 / Superstition ♦♦♦
The title is a nod to Van Dijk's teaming with an array of top techno producers, including Claude Young, Thomas Schumacher, Quazar, and Johannes Talirz. *Teamwork* presents a variety of outstanding tracks, each further blurring the boundaries between trance, minimalist techno, French house and electronica. —*John Bush*

## Paul Van Dyk

**b.** Dec. 16, 1971, Eisenhüttenstadt, East Germany
*Producer, DJ / Progressive Trance, Progressive House, Trance, Club/Dance, House*

From early Berlin techno and house through to progressive trance, producer/DJ Paul Van Dyk has soundtracked the German electronic dance scene ever since he moved to the city and began mixing in 1988. A native of an East German town near Frankfurt, Van Dyk first heard house music on the radio during the mid-'80s. Soon he was experimenting with a rudimentary turntable setup, and after hitting Berlin, he gigged around the city. By 1991, he had appeared at the legendary Tresor club; he later set up his own E-Werk club, and debuted on record as Visions of Shiva, with fellow trance wizard Cosmic Baby. He remixed for New Order, Humate, Sven Väth and others, then signed to the German MFS Records for his first album, 1994's *45 RPM*. By the midpoint of the '90s, Paul Van Dyk had become a globe-trotting DJ and remixer. His second album *Seven Ways* resulted in British and German dance-chart entries for the singles "Beautiful Place," "Forbidden Fruit" and "Words." While both of his albums were issued in America during 1998, Van Dyk added a remix collection (*Perspective*) and mix album (*Vorsprung Dyk Technik*) to his discography. *45 RPM* followed soon after, and 2000 saw the release of the single "Tell Me Why (The Riddle)" and the album *Out There and Back*. —*John Bush*

**45 RPM** / 1994 / Deviant ♦♦♦
On *45 RPM*, Van Dyk was still beginning to shape the sound he would soon master. Coproduced by Voov and Johnny Klimek in Berlin, this album hints at the progressive trance perfectly illustrated in "Words," but ends up sounding like relaxing, smooth techno. The 1998 re-release of *45 RPM* features the "PvD's E-Werk Club Mix" of "For an Angel" that Van Dyk become best known for. Nearly eight minutes long, the track is driven by the hardest-hitting bassline of the album. In addition, a perfectly sublime collection of synthesizer melodies floats across a nearly inaudible background of lingering ambience. When the rhythm comes to a halt and the song's melodic hook enters, the music becomes truly angelic with its nonsecular emotive cries toward the heavens. Unfortunately, no other song on *45 RPM* can even come close to matching the sublime brilliance of the bonus track. The original version of "For an Angel" isn't nearly as moving as the remix, and many of the other tracks seem to follow a formula of pumping basslines and foregrounded synthesizer melodies that works well but gets a bit monotonous by the end of the album. In relation to many of the full-length, studio-produced techno and trance albums, *45 RPM* rates above average, but doesn't come close to attaining the heights of Van Dyk's later work. —*Jason Birchmeier*

**Seven Ways** / 1996 / Deviant ♦♦♦♦
German DJ/producer Paul van Dyk turns in a solid house/rave effort with *Seven Ways;* when Mute reissued the album in the US, it appended a bonus disc of remixed van Dyk singles. —*Steve Huey*

**Perspective** / Nov. 1997 / MFS ♦♦♦♦
Paul Van Dyk has always been more noted as a remixer and DJ than a recording artist, so a compilation of his best remixes makes quite a bit of sense. *Perspective* is a two-disc set spanning the years 1992 through 1997, including his reworkings of tracks by BT, Amen! UK, Jens Lissat, Humate, Joe T. Vanelli and Curve, plus versions of his own material. The results are much better listening than Van Dyk's own albums, perhaps since the tracks provide him with a springboard from which to jump. —*John Bush*

**Muzik Magazine Presents Paul Van Dyk: 60 Minute Mix** / 2000 / Muzik ♦♦♦♦
Primarily known as a producer and remix artist, Paul Van Dyk has also been recognized in the late '90s as one of Europe's most popular trance DJs. This compilation features the artist spinning a set of intense trance that feels like the peak hour of an exhausting set, similar in technique to Paul Oakenfold's *Tranceport* album. Beginning with the first track, Van Dyk drops nothing but up-tempo trance, with a few highly melodic anthems thrown in at various points to keep listeners feeling the heart-pumping music. Listeners cannot help but feel the power radiated in his choice of tracks, but it may just be *too* supercharged for its own good. The moment when it first becomes apparent that Van Dyk isn't waiting until the conclusion to get intense comes with the third track, Des Mitchell's "Welcome to the Dance." The center of the album again builds upon simple intensity with Life on Mars' remix of Jose Amnesia's "The Eternal." This track reaches nonsecular heights with its kinetic buildups, leading smoothly into the album's centerpiece, Van Dyk's "Avenue." Finally, after a few moments of mellow serenity, Oakenfold's Planet Perfecto track, "Bullet in the Gun," finishes things off with a lethal combination of intensity and melody. —*Jason Birchmeier*

● **Out There and Back** / Jun. 6, 2000 / Mute ♦♦♦♦
Berlin's most acknowledged trance producer inches forward on his third full-length album of seamlessly edited up-tempo electronic music. Nearly every other song functions as a peaking anthem exploding with sentiment-charged elation. The songs that aren't fueled with energy merely serve as landing and launching pads for the many anthems. After a quiet beginning, Paul Van Dyk's album builds until it first peaks on the third track, "Another Way," with its monolithic synth riffs and inescapable melodies. Two songs later, the intensity returns on "Avenue" and continues into the slightly more explosive "Tell Me Why (The Riddle)." From here, the album continues on its path of ups and downs. "Together We Will Conquer" serves as a nice period of near relaxation with its soothing female vocals and subdued intensity, toying with dance-pop formal characteristics. Following this song, "Face to Face" and "Out There and Back" try to recapture the spouting adrenaline of the earlier anthems but don't quite do the job, giving the anthemic second half of the album a slightly anticlimatic feel. Of course, these last few songs are in no way mediocre and still surpass the output of nearly any of Van Dyk's peers in 2000. The second half just begins to sound a bit clichéd, with the Berlin artist reusing the same synth-driven, peaks-and-valleys template that made "Another Way" such a standout song. Safely assumed to be the peak moment of the entire album, the title track comes off sounding too obvious. The melodic synth riff just seems too artificial—too typical. There is no arguing the fact that Van Dyk's third album still overshadows any pre-2000 attempt at a full-length, self-produced trance album and will surely satisfy anyone with a taste for its sticky melodies, synth hooks, and constant syncopated rhythms. One still wishes though that Van Dyk would take a few more risks rather than simply delivering a predictable, yet satisfying, album that effectively expands upon the most successful moments of his previous album, *Seven Ways;* in sum, he is giving the people exactly what they want. —*Jason Birchmeier*

## Vangelis (Evangelos Papathanassiou)

**b.** Mar. 29, 1943, Valos, Greece
*Keyboards, Synthesizer, Producer, Leader, Composer, Arranger / Ambient, Progressive Electronic, Neo-Classical*

Best known for his lush, Oscar-winning score to the 1981 film *Chariots of Fire*, Vangelis was among the most successful and admired electronic composers of his era. Born Evangelos Odyssey Papathanassiou in Valos, Greece on March 29, 1943, his nascent musical talent was recognized at an early age, but he refused to take piano lessons, teaching himself instead. After high school he formed the early '60s pop group Formynx, soon the most popular act in Greece. After achieving superstardom at home, Vangelis relocated to Paris in 1968, and was in France at the time of the student riots. Unable to go back home, he formed the progressive rock band Aphrodite's Child with fellow Greek expatriates Demis Roussos and Loukas Sideras, soon scoring a major European hit with the single "Rain and Tears."

After Aphrodite's Child disbanded in 1972, Vangelis joined French filmmaker Frederic Rossif to compose the scores for the features *L' Apocalypse des Animaux* and *La Fete Sauvage*. His proper solo debut, *Earth*, followed in 1974, around the time he was rumored to be joining Yes. Although Vangelis did rehearse with Yes for a few weeks, he never officially joined their ranks. Still, he became close friends with group vocalist Jon Anderson, a frequent collaborator in the years to follow. Relocating to London, Vangelis established his own state-of-the-art recording studio, producing a steady flow of recordings including 1975's *Heaven and Hell*, 1976's *Albedo 0.39*, 1977's *Spiral*, and 1978's *Beaubourg*. Teaming with Anderson under the name Jon and Vangelis, he also scored a series of UK hits including 1980's "I Hear You Now" and the following year's "I'll Find My Way Home."

Vangelis' international commercial breakthrough followed in 1982, when his score to *Chariots of Fire* earned the film one of its many Academy Awards; its theme song even cracked the Top Ten on the US pop charts. That same year, he also created the powerful score to the cult classic *Blade Runner*, the beginning of a partnership with director Ridley Scott, which also yielded soundtracks to films including *1492: Conquest of Paradise*. Vangelis also composed the music for a number of Jacques Cousteau documentaries in addition to maintaining his flourishing solo career, issuing acclaimed LPs including 1985's *The Mask*, 1988's *Antarctica*, and 1990's *The City*. In 1992, he was awarded the Chevalier Order of Arts and Letters, one of France's most prestigious honors. *El Greco* followed in 1998. —*Jason Ankeny*

**Earth** / 1973 / Vertigo ♦♦♦♦
Recorded and released just before Vangelis hit his stride with *Heaven and Hell*, *Earth* is a sometimes unsettling mixture of Aphrodite's Child-style rock, ritual chants and darkly themed songs. Fans of his latter-day work may find this one a bit difficult to settle into. —*Steven McDonald*

**Heaven and Hell** / 1975 / Windham Hill ♦♦♦♦
Those used to Vangelis' later and lighter synthesized outings may not be quite ready for this dark, thundering album. While it did provide us with the theme music for the TV series *Cosmos* and bring Jon Anderson into partnership with Vangelis (following an abortive approach to Vangelis joining Yes) on "So Long Ago, So Clear," it also served up massed Gothic choirs and a musical depiction of all the tortures of the damned, with an impressive amount of string-driven shrieking. Even so, it's a brilliant piece of work that should not be absent from any Vangelis collection. —*Steven McDonald*

**Spiral** / 1977 / RCA ♦♦♦♦
On one of his better efforts of the late '70s, Vangelis moves through five tracks of straightahead synthesizer music. While *Rubycon*-era Tangerine Dream definitely influences the title track, the eerie vocal textures of "Ballad" and the atmospherics on "To the Unknown Man" are Vangelis trademarks. —*John Bush*

**Beaubourg** / 1978 / Windham Hill ♦♦
A great dark synthesized tone poem inspired by the Beauborg Cathedral. Vangelis had hinted at his desire to create works of this nature in some sections of *Heaven and Hell*, but the release of this album caught many of his fans unaware. Difficult listening at best. —*Steven McDonald*

**China** / 1979 / Polydor ♦♦♦♦
Vangelis uses ringing synthesizer textures and stately rhythms to evoke the majesty of China, in a similar fashion to another of his "geography" works, *Antarctica*. While a few tracks use acoustic piano and other organic instruments, the centerpieces "Chung Kuo," "The Dragon," and "Himalaya" use bracing percussion and synthesizer effects to emphasize the subjects (each reflected by its title). —*John Bush*

**Opera Sauvage** / 1981 / Polydor ♦♦♦♦
This warm, lyrical album was derived from Vangelis's music for a French television series. Rich, electronic orchestrations range from grandly symphonic to simple and serene. Curiously enough, this title has experienced a major revival since the opening cut, "Hymne," was used for a Gallo Wine commercial. This 1979 release is an excellent introduction to his music. —*Backroads Music/Heartbeats*

★ **Blade Runner** / 1982 / Atlantic ♦♦♦♦♦
The release of the official edition of *Blade Runner*, following the release of the director's cut of the film, was almost anticlimactic. Too much time had passed, there had been a bootleg release, and a couple of the cuts had already seen the light of day on *Themes*. While the album is a good document of the film's score, it's slightly marred by some additional recording and the inclusion of dialogue tracks from the film. There are some brilliant and beautiful moments otherwise. —*Steven McDonald*

**Chariots of Fire** / 1982 / Polydor ♦♦♦♦
Vangelis' Academy Award-winning score to the movie continues to be his most famous album, probably because the theme is immediately recognizable yet quickly lures listeners into a musical world that stands on its own. —*Linda Kohanov*

**Invisible Connection** / 1985 / Atlantic ♦
Another Vangelis attempt at gaining recognition for his more experimental side. A collection of steaming, heaving droning noises that served to do little other than irritate the average listener, worse even than the ill-fated *Beauborg*. —*Steven McDonald*

**Magic Moments** / 1985 / RCA ♦♦♦♦
An excellent introduction to the greater part of Vangelis' pre-*Chariots of Fire* work, sampling even the gloomy *Beauborg*, as well as the splendid bolero of "To the Unknown Man" and several key moments from *Heaven and Hell*. —*Steven McDonald*

**Ignacio** / 1985 / Polydor ♦♦
Vangelis fancied himself a synthesizer *artiste*, an avant-garde pioneer in the medium of the future: electronic music. His best work, like his Academy Award-winning score for *Chariots of Fire*, did use the medium to create interesting and unique effects that would not have been possible with acoustic instruments. But this 40-minute composition consists primarily of pretentious bilge. The music, which Vangelis credits himself with composing, arranging and interpreting, is divided into two wildly divergent parts. "Parte 1" is an attempt at a synthesized classical composition. It has its moments, particularly at the end when Vangelis adds synthesized choral voices. But on the whole, the piece suffers from the composer's predilection for strange rumbling noises and spacy noodling. The tinny sound of the synthesized strings becomes tedious after awhile, and the piece is only fitfully melodious, diverging from any semblance of tune for extended sections of synthesized noise on several occasions. If "Parte 1" is sometimes lacking in melody, "Parte 2" is almost completely devoid of it. The second part is divided into several clashing sections that seem to have nothing to do with each other, let alone with "Parte 1." It begins with a synthesized approximation of an electric guitar riff before launching into an extended segment of repetitive percussive nonsense. Only the last movement is even remotely listenable. —*Evan Cater*

**Antarctica** / 1988 / Polydor ♦♦♦♦
Originally composed for a forgettable Japanese film about the South Pole, this album is a masterpiece of sonic sensations depicting vast plains of ice, sunlight glittering across the snow, and the sting of Antarctic winds. Expansive melodies are punctuated by the lashing sounds of whips urging dog sleds into mysterious and forbidden landscapes. —*Linda Kohanov*

## Armand Van Helden

*Producer, DJ / Electronica, Club/Dance, House*

Until he began branching out in 1996 with a barrage of album productions and remix classics (several of which were heard by more people than the originals), Armand Van Helden was one of the best-kept secrets in house music, recording for such labels as Strictly Rhythm, Henry St., Logic and ZYX. Afterward, he became one of the top names in dance music altogether. As one in the steady progression of top in-house producers for Strictly Rhythm during the early '90s, Van Helden joined such names as Todd Terry, Erick Morillo, Roger Sanchez, Masters at Work, and George Morel to record scores of club hits. By the late '90s, a clutch of crucial remixes and several albums made Van Helden one of the most popular producers around.

Van Helden spent time in Holland, Turkey, and Italy while growing up the son of an Air Force man, and he listened to music from an early age. He bought a drum machine at the age of 13 and began DJing two years later, mostly hip-hop and freestyle. Based in Boston while attending college, Van Helden proceeded to moonlight as a DJ; though he settled into a legal-review job after graduation, he quit his job in 1991 to begin working on production for the remix service X-Mix Productions (founded by his future manager, Neil Pettricone). Van Helden also owned a residency at Boston's Loft, and soon made it into one of the most popular nightclubs in the city. After playing one of his production demos for the dance A&R guru Gladys Pizarro in 1992, Van Helden released his proper debut single, Deep Creed's "Stay on My Mind," for Nervous Records.

Later that year, Van Helden released "Move It to the Left" by Sultans of Swing, his first single for the premiere American dance label Strictly Rhythm. Though a moderate club hit, the single was eclipsed by another Strictly Rhythm offering, 1994's "Witch Doktor." It became a dancefloor hit around the world and introduced him to a larger club audience. Although he had remixed Deee-Lite, Jimmy Somerville, New Order, Deep Forest, and Faithless, a reworked version of Tori Amos' "Professional Widow" hit the clubs with the same impact as his "Witch Doktor" single. During 1996-97, Van Helden became *the* name for forward-thinking pop artists to recruit for remixing duty—from the Rolling Stones, Janet Jackson and Puff Daddy to Sneaker Pimps, C.J. Bolland and Daft Punk. His own-name singles productions continued unabated, with hits like "Cha Cha" and "The Funk Phenomena," plus the release of his first album, *Old School Junkies*. Following a 1997 *Greatest Hits* retrospective, Van Helden returned to his old-school rap roots with the party breakbeat album, *Sampleslayer... Enter the Meatmarket*. The *2 Future 4 U* EP followed in 1998, and in mid-2000 Van Helden returned with *Killing Puritans*. —*John Bush*

**Old School Junkies: The Album** / Oct. 8, 1996 / Henry St. ♦♦
On *Old School Junkies: The Album*, Van Helden adopts the aesthetic of old-school hip-hop and funk, but he adds a distinctly post-acid house flavor to the recipe, creating a thick, funky amalgam of contemporary and classic dance styles. Throughout the album, Van Helden keeps the groove going, making *Old School Junkies* an infectious slice of club music. —*Leo Stanley*

● **Greatest Hits** / Mar. 25, 1997 / Strictly Rhythm ♦♦♦♦
Fresh from his heavy remix schedule (for the Sneaker Pimps, Prodigy, and others), Van Helden returned with a collection of his biggest club scores for Strictly Rhythm from 1993 to 1996, leading off with his first, "Witch Doktor." The rest, though good, follow the same blueprint: street-level house heavy on the samples and a bit short on ideas. They still make for incredible dance music. —*John Bush*

**Da Club Phenomena** / Jul. 7, 1997 / Clut ♦♦♦

**Enter the Meatmarket** / Nov. 10, 1997 / ffrr/London ♦♦♦
Just as Armand Van Helden began to be acknowledged as one of the forefathers of Britain's favorite new dance form of the moment, speed garage, he released *Enter the Meatmarket*, a tribute to his background in hip-hop and Latino house. In fact, it's an old-school rap album through and through, with a carload of classic "hands in the air" samples from the likes of Fat Boys and Dana Dane plus an appearance by Funkmaster Flex on the devastating "6 Minutes of Funk." But while Van Helden's production skills are solid throughout, *Enter the Meatmarket* suffers from its lack of true vocals. It's so close to a hip-hop album that the listener can't help but feel that something's missing without the raps. —*John Bush*

**2 Future 4 U** / Nov. 30, 1998 / ffrr ♦♦♦♦
Armand Van Helden's most varied release to date, *2 Future 4 U* includes a few predictable (though no less enjoyable) club tracks like "The Boogie Monster" and "Flowerz," plus the suitably enormous anthem "U Don't Know Me." The songs that make this mini-LP truly worthwhile however, take Van Helden's club formulas into unfamiliar territory with amazing results. He attaches a darker-than-dark tech-step bassline to "Alienz" and makes a paranoid house-stormer out of what could have been just a so-so anthem. "Rock Da Spot" detours into turntablist territory with a guest slot by Mr. Len, of underground rappers Company Flow. The warm keys and downtempo vibe of "Summertime" make for yet another radically distinct moment on a release capable of pleasing anyone and everyone. [*2 Future 4 U* is also available in an import edition.] —*John Bush*

**Armand Van Helden's Nervous Tracks** / Sep. 7, 1999 / Nervous ♦♦♦♦
House DJ Armand Van Helden slices and dices on the electronica set *Innovators Series: Armand Van Helden 1*. Van Helden's signature tight progressive house mixes things up on tracks from Kim English, Veda Simpson, and Jungle Juice. —*MacKenzie Wilson*

**Killing Puritans** / Jun. 6, 2000 / Armed ♦♦♦
*Killing Puritans* is another guest-heavy, genre-bending full-length to file alongside Van Helden's last full LP, 1998's *2 Future 4 You*. Harking back to the glory days of late-'80s acid-house, it's heavy on dark club jams that work around a simplistic sample with diva theatrics and rapper freestyles. As such, most of these tracks work much better on the dancefloor than the living room. On the breakout single "Little Black Spiders," Van Helden spends eight minutes running through different filters on a metal riff (from the Scorpions' "Bad Boys Running Wild") while his guest vocalist Fiona Marr repeats the title. Van Helden increases listeners' attention spans during the rest of the album though, hitting peaks with the rolling disco charm of "Full Moon" (featuring an excellent performance by Common) and the electro-scratch nightmare "Koochy," which matches a near-pornographic cell-phone vocal with a scratch-heavy treatment of the main riff from "Cars" by Gary Numan. "Hybridz" has another prominent sample—the bass and rhythm track from the acid-house anthem "No Way Out" by Armando—while Van Helden's alien alias, the Mongoloids, scats over the top. Though it lacks a massive club hit the likes of "U Don't Know Me," *Killing Puritans* remains an enjoyable look at several different flavors of the domestic dance scene. —*John Bush*

## Vapourspace (Mark Gage)

**b.** New York
*Producer / Ambient Techno, Club/Dance, Techno*

Born in rural New York State in the early '60s, Mark Gage (aka Vapourspace, Cusp) grew interested in electronic music of all kinds while growing up. He began recording in 1983, though his first release didn't appear until over ten years later. Now based in Rochester, Gage called Plus 8 label-head Richie Hawtin (aka Plastikman) and eventually signed a contract. His "Gravitational Arch of 10" debut was well received, as was a US tour with Orbital, Moby, and the Aphex Twin during 1993. *Themes from Vapourspace* was a very mature debut album—unsurprising, given Gage's recording experience. His Cusp project (closer to straightahead techno) has released several singles, including "Drone Um Futurisma." Gage has also remixed Juno Reactor, Pressure of Speech, FUSE and Oliver Lieb. —*John Bush*

● **Themes from Vapourspace** / 1994 / ffrr ♦♦♦♦
*Themes from Vapourspace* ranges from the vintage electronics intro to perfect examples of tight acid-techno on "Gravitational Arch of 10" and "Vapourdome." —*Keith Farley*

**Sweep** / Nov. 25, 1997 / ffrr ♦♦♦♦
Marking an intriguing direction, Vapourspace's *Sweep* spotlights the single "Ray." —*Jason Ankeny*

## Edgard Varèse

**b.** Dec. 22, 1883, Paris, France, **d.** Nov. 6, 1965, New York, NY
*Composer / Musique Concrète, 20th Century Classical/Modern Composition, Atonal, Electronic*

Criminally unknown throughout his own lifetime, composer Edgard Varèse was among the century's true creative visionaries. Imagining music as bodies of sound in space—its impact most profound as a physical experience—his work sought to strip away convention and tradition, its massive, cacophonic power anticipating much of the experimental music to follow in its wake. Born in Paris on December 22, 1883, Varèse announced his intentions to become a composer while in his early teens, later studying under d'Indy, Roussel, and Widor; he was also encouraged in his pursuits by Claude Debussy and Romain Rolland. After a falling out with his father, in 1907 Varèse relocated to Berlin, where he was befriended by Richard Strauss and Erik Satie; there he began to theorize that music should imitate scientific principles. He also became increasingly fascinated by the possibilites offered by electronic instrumentation.

Varèse returned to Paris in 1913; his earliest compositions were left behind in Berlin, where they were soon lost in a fire. After pursuing a career as a conductor, he settled in the United States in 1915, forming the New Symphony Orchestra and attempting to drum up interest in his proposals for new electronic instruments. His first subsequent composition, *Amériques*, was not completed until 1921; that same year Varèse founded the International Composers' Guild, a group dedicated to performing new compositions of both American and European origin. He wrote much of the material himself, including a series of pieces for orchestral instruments and voices that featured 1922's *Offrandes*, 1923's *Hyperprism*, 1924's *Octandre*, and 1925's *Intégrales*. The ICG also premiered key works by Alban Berg, Charles Ives, Henry Cowell, and Anton Webern.

In 1928, Varèse travelled back to Paris to rework part of *Amériques* to accommodate the recently constructed ondes martenot, a theremin-like instrument that produced sound via a moveable electrode. Two years later, he composed *Ionisation*. His most renowned non-electronic work, it featured only percussion and was created as a means of exploring and manufacturing new sounds. Rejected by both the Guggenheim Foundation and Bell Labratories in his attempts to recieve funding for an electronic music studio, Varèse next turned to 1934's *Ecuatorial*, composed in part for theremin; later that year he returned to the US only to discover that another of his grant requests had been denied. The setback proved crippling—while waiting for modern technology to catch up to the music he heard in his head, Varèse spent over a decade suffering from depression, his creativity stifled.

Aside from the 1936 flute piece *Density 21.5,* Varèse was largely silent until 1951, at which time an anonymous donor bought him an Ampex tape recorder. The gift allowed him finally to begin to realize the music he'd begun striving toward decades earlier, and he began compiling the sound fragments that complemented his project *Déserts* (begun in acoustic form nearly 30 years prior). Varèse eventually travelled to Paris to work on the piece alongside musique concrète trailblazer Pierre Schaeffer, and upon its completion in 1955, *Déserts* became the first piece transmitted in stereo over French radio airwaves. Varèse then went back to New York, where he remained until two years later, when he was invited to compose material for the 1958 World's Fair in Brussels; the end result was *Poeme Electronique,* his most admired and famous work.

Produced in collaboration with the architect Le Corbusier, *Poeme Electronique* was a completely electronic work designed for broadcast over the 400 speakers scattered throughout the fair's Philips Pavillion. Its impact finally began winning Varèse the recognition long due him, and his work began to be recorded and issued commercially. In 1962, he was elected to the National Institute of Arts and Letters and the Royal Swedish Academy, and even received the Brandeis University Creative Arts Award. A year later, he received the first Koussevitsky International Recording Award. Apart from 1961's *Nocturnal,* Varèse spent the majority of his final years revising his earlier work with many of his earliest ideas now possible given the technological advances of the time. His final project, *Nuit,* was unfinished at the time of his death in New York City on November 6, 1965. —*Jason Ankeny*

★ **Music of Edgard Varèse** / Apr. 1996 / One Way ♦♦♦♦♦
The pioneering composer's best-known works are included on this reissue by One Way. On the first five tracks, Robert Craft conducts an ensemble of woodwinds, brass, and percussion in the performance of such famous Varèse works as "Ionisation" and "Density 21.5." The sixth and final selection is a 1958 recording of "Poème Électronique" created by the composer onto magnetic tape for the 1958 World's Fair in Brussels. —*John Bush*

**Edgard Varèse: The Complete Works** / 1998 / London ♦♦♦♦
Wonderfully performed by the Royal Concertgebouw Orchestra, the Asko Ensemble, directed by Riccardo Chailly. At long last, the complete work of this brilliant composer, including the original version of "Amériques," as well as several previously unpublished works. The entire project was assembled with the assistance of composer Chou Wen-Chung, who had worked directly with Varèse. This massive undertaking includes the following works: "Tuning Up," "Amériques," "Arcana," "Poème Électronique," "Nocturnal," "Un Grand Sommeil Noir" (in both the original and orchestral versions), "Offrandes," "Hyperprism," "Octandre," "Intégrales," "Ecuatorial," "Ionisation," "Density 21.5," "Déserts," and "Dance for Burgess." —*"Blue" Gene Tyranny*

## Various Artists (Thorsten Profrock)

*Producer / Minimal Techno, Experimental Dub, Experimental Techno, Techno*

Besides recording several respected EPs for Chain Reaction under the confusingly titled production concern known as Various Artists, Berlin's Thorsten Profrock co-owns (with Sasha Brauer) Din Records, home to releases by excellent, respected producers Monolake, Pole, and Arovane. Profrock entered the Berlin electronics scene first by shopping at the Berlin record store Hard Wax, while working toward his economics degree. By 1994, he worked at Hard Wax as well, growing closer to the store's base for legendary productions on the Basic Channel/Chain Reaction family of labels. Profrock also began producing, and released his first Various Artists project, 1995's "1-7," on Chain Reaction. (He also recorded two singles for the label as Resilient and Erosion.) The continuation piece "8, 8.5, 9" appeared on England's Fat Cat label in 1997, highlighting the producer's subtle ambient sense and reliance on a restrictive frequency range—all middles, no highs or lows. Later that year, Chain Reaction compiled his work on the *Decay Product* compilation, and Fat Cat expanded "8, 8.5, 9" into an EP for Profrock's second CD release. —*John Bush*

**Decay Product** / Jan. 13, 1998 / Chain Reaction ♦♦♦♦
The third in Chain Reaction's metal box series is a Various Artists collection that compiles edits of material from 1996's *No. 1-7* EP plus full tracks from the "Resilient" and "Erosion" singles. The *No. 1-7* inclusions showcase Profrock's blueprint for dubby techno: clipped, distant four-four beats and reverbed, clanging percussion. It's an aesthetic that hardly varies from track to track; in fact, the only differences come with the use of lighter or heavier filters. Toward the end, the beautiful, practically beatless tracks "Resilient 1.2" and "Erosion 3" offer a bit more than just variations on a theme, with rhythms of several whispered-noise effects that create a chilling, trance-state atmosphere. —*John Bush*

● **8, 8.5, 9 Remixes** / 1999 / Fat Cat ♦♦♦♦
Fat Cat's CD release of "8, 8.5, 9" pumps up the breathtaking 1997 single into a spectacular hour-long EP with remixes from five of the hottest properties in the headphone-electronics realm—Autechre, Pole, Monolake, Funkstörung, and Arovane. Still, Profrock's single may itself be the best piece of material, a grating piece of lo-fi ambience with atmospherics galore and a sense of care to the production. —*John Bush*

## Gez Varley

*Producer / Acid Techno, Techno*

After LFO all but disintegrated in the late '90s and Mark Bell went on to produce for Björk and others, the other half of the duo, Gez Varley, began his own solo career with a 1997 album for Studio !K7. After fans of LFO's 1991 *Frequencies* LP (still one of the most respected electronic albums of all time) waited over five years for a follow-up, the end came soon after LFO's sophomore album, 1996's *Advance.* Varley's early adulation of hip-hop and electro—including Juan Atkins, Mantronix and Arthur Baker—came through loud and clear on his first solo record, *Gez Varley Presents Tony Montana.* —*John Bush*

● **Gez Varley Presents Tony Montana** / Dec. 1, 1997 / Studio !K7 ♦♦♦
Varley's first album is a set of straightahead acid techno, which is surprising from the standpoint of his electro and hip-hop influences. Nonetheless, "Columbia" and "Political Prisoner" are bracing tracks reminiscent of Joey Beltram, with continually echoing effects providing an off-kilter flair to the straitjacket beats. —*John Bush*

## Junior Vasquez (Donald Mattern)

b. 1946, Philadelphia, PA
*Producer, DJ / Garage, Club/Dance, House*

One of the most celebrated DJs and remixers of his time, house music innovator Junior Vasquez was also the cofounder of the legendary Sound Factory dance club. Born Donald Mattern in Philadelphia, Pennsylvania circa 1946, he first entered a career in fashion illustration and design, but later decided upon life as a DJ. While working as a clerk at a New York record store, he made the acquaintance of notables like producer Shep Pettibone and slowly began to build a reputation on the strength of his appearances at small clubs and house parties. As the '80s progressed, Vasquez became one of the hottest figures on the club circuit, honing a trademark fusion of bass-heavy house beats with a seemingly endless supply of obscure samples, innovative remix techniques and quirky signatures (such as his penchant for spinning records backwards, or at the incorrect speed); he swiftly rose through the DJing ranks, and by 1989 enjoyed such notoriety that he cofounded the Sound Factory in Manhattan's Chelsea district.

During the six years of its existence, the Sound Factory was among New York's hottest night spots. Catering to an ethnically diverse, primarily gay crowd, the club launched Vasquez to superstardom, and he became a tastemaker of such renown that new dance records were frequently debuted and monitored during his marathon Saturday night sessions. Most notable among the high-profile celebrities often in attendance was Madonna, who later tapped Vasquez to remix several of her records. He also wrote and mixed material for the likes of Cyndi Lauper, Lisa Lisa and, most intriguingly, John Mellencamp. As a solo artist, Vasquez was responsible for such club smashes as "X," "Get Your Hands Off My Man," and "Nervaas." In early 1995, the Sound Factory closed in the wake of community complaints; its swan song, a 16-hour house marathon, quickly passed into legend. Vasquez then DJed at the Tunnel, followed by a stint at the Palladium. In 1997 he returned to the former Sound Factory space—now named Twilo—to host a new all-night Saturday party, succinctly dubbed "Juniorverse." —*Jason Ankeny*

● **The Best of Junior Vasquez: Just Like a Queen** / Oct. 17, 1995 / Hot Productions ♦♦♦♦
*The Best of Junior Vasquez: Just Like a Queen* offers a full dozen of the superstar DJ's best remixes and productions, including a host of gay-pride an-

thems like "Got to Be a Drag," "Took My Lover Away," and the title track, plus history-of-dance numbers "My Loleatta" and "I Will Survive." —*John Bush*

**Live, Vol. 1** / Mar. 18, 1997 / Drive/Pagoda ✦✦✦
The first live album by one of the world's most popular DJs, *Live, Vol. 1* has a tough job lined up for itself: to approximate the total Junior Vasquez experience in the tepid environment of a living room instead of the frenzied New York club. As far as that goes, the album fails, but a good mix of tracks (with plenty of Vasquez productions and remixes, naturally) keeps the album from sinking under the weight of its expectations. —*John Bush*

**Twilo, Vol. 1: Junior Vasquez** / Sep. 26, 2000 / Virgin ✦✦
Super New York City and remix king Junior Vasquez solidifies his long relationship with mega club Twilo, with the release of the mix CD *Twilo Vol. 1: Junior Vasquez*. Vasquez's sets have packed the Manhattan stellar club with his dancefloor high energy house and have become legendary. The CD bottles the house sets that Vasquez has become famous for, and the sound that he lends towards remixing such pop divas as Madonna, Cyndi Lauper, and Lisa Lisa. —*Diana Potts*

## Sven Väth

b. Oct. 26, 1964, Offenbach, Germany
*Producer, DJ / Ambient House, Electronica, Trance, Club/Dance, Techno*
One of the most popular proponents of German trance techno during the early to mid-'90s through his recordings, epic-length DJ sets, and his ownership of the Harthouse family of labels, Sven Väth reserved his mid-'90s full-length albums for epic-length concepts that did nothing to bolster his standing in the sometimes consciously unartistic dance community.

Originally the lead singer of a dance-pop group named OFF (short for Organisation for Funk, which included future members of Snap!), Väth hit the big time in 1987 when OFF's "Electric Salsa" became a number one hit around the world. The band later disintegrated, leaving Väth free to pursue his interest in the hard trance underground of Frankfurt. Väth became a DJ of note for his marathon sets (which sometimes approached 24 hours) and his founding of Harthouse Records in 1992 with Matthias Hoffman and Heinz Roth. (His own releases on Harthouse included those by Barbarella, Astral Pilot and Metal Masters, with the help of his partner, Ralf Hildenbeutel.) Blessed with an agreement connecting Harthouse (plus its subsidiaries Eye-Q and Recycle or Die) to the American major label Warner Bros., Väth released his first solo album—again with contributions from Hildenbeutel—in 1993. *An Accident in Paradise* was a solid debut, illustrating Väth's concern with connecting techno and trance to the concept-album ideas of prog-rock. Signs of excess were generally frowned upon in the dance community, however, and *An Accident in Paradise* died a quick death on American shores. His second album, *The Harlequin, The Robot & The Ballet Dancer*, was released in Europe in 1994, but its American release was delayed more than a year and sank much quicker than its predecessor. After recording an album with Stevie B-Zet as Astral Pilot, Väth laid low for several years, severing his connections with Eye Q/Harthouse and preferring to concentrate on DJing instead. Finally in 1998, he returned with a contract to Virgin and his third album, *Fusion; Contact* followed a year later. —*John Bush*

• **An Accident in Paradise** / 1993 / Warner Brothers ✦✦✦✦
Buoyed by "L'Esperanza" and the title track (two outstanding examples of straitjacket trance) Väth's album debut is a solid collection balancing straight-ahead trance-techno with a few tracks of more overblown ethno-ambience. Even the latter frequently works better than expected, as on the percussive atmospherics of "Ritual of Life" and "Caravan of Emotions." Without a doubt, Väth excels when he keeps the artistic concepts at a minimum and the energy at the maximum. —*John Bush*

**The Harlequin, The Robot & the Ballet Dancer** / 1995 / WEA ✦✦
*The Harlequin, the Robot & the Ballet Dancer* is the definable point where Väth's visions of a classical-inspired concept album began to struggle under the weight of his blander symphonic inclinations. As if the ponderous title wasn't enough, the producer burdens listeners with a five-minute "Intro" that goes nowhere. The rest of the album is concerned with the three figures stated in the title, with twenty minutes plus devoted to first and last while the Robot gets only ten (on "The Birth of Robby"). Obviously, Väth is a solid producer (as is his partner Ralf Hildenbeutel) and there are several good tracks on this album ("The Beauty and the Beast," "Ballet-Fusion"), but it's a struggle just to get past the ridiculous concepts and into the music itself. —*John Bush*

**Fusion** / Nov. 10, 1998 / Ultra ✦✦✦✦
Väth's first album after leaving the label he started forsakes the symphonic bent of his first two full-lengths, and fortunately just concentrates on the production of some great dance music. Though it begins with an odd track that sounds like third-world synth-pop, *Fusion* hits a series of diverse highs over the next nine tracks: the slinky breakbeat number "Discophon," the hard, pumping techno minimalism of "Augenblick" and "Scorpio's Movement," and the sonic experimentation of "Trippy Moonshine." It's a welcome back-to-basics album, and even while tossing a few bones to the home-listening crowd, it amply displays Väth's skill at constructing simplistic—not simple—club tracks and DJ tools. —*John Bush*

**Contact** / Apr. 18, 2000 / Ultra ✦✦✦✦
After finally getting back to straight-ahead dancefloor techno with *Fusion*, Sven Väth upped the ante with *Contact*, an LP filled with track after track of driving electro and hard Detroit techno—by way of Berlin. Instead of longtime coproducer Ralf Hildenbeutel, Väth tapped Anthony Rother, Johannes Heil, and Alter Ego's Roman Flügel and Jörn Wuttke as production partners. The move gives *Contact* a breadth of sound unequaled by his previous material; Rother contributes some excellent chunky analogue synth to on "Pathfinder" and "Ydolem," while on "Ein Waggon Voller Geschichten," Flügel and Wuttke apply the detuned and slightly distorted effect most famous from Mr. Oizo's "Flat Beat." The other big difference from Väth's first three LPs is that half of these tracks have vocals, and they're all by Väth himself. Surprisingly, these work pretty well, with the man simply vamping over the beats and then heavily processing his vocals afterwards. After so much serious, disappointing music in Väth's career, it's a refreshing change to hear dance music with a bit of humor to it. —*John Bush*

## Little Louie Vega

b. The Bronx, New York City, NY
*Producer, DJ / Garage, Club/Dance, House*
Whether he is DJing by himself or acting as half of Masters at Work, Little Louie Vega is a permanent part of the history of the New York City house music and club scene. Louie made a name for himself as a DJ in the New York City club circuit spinning in the historical clubs—Studio 54, Devil's Nest, and Heartbrob. Besides producing his own work, he has worked with artists from the likes of Information Society to Debbie Gibson and Marc Anthony.

Little Louie Vega grew up in a Latin music household. His father, Louie Vega Sr., was a jazz and Latin saxophone player and his uncle, Hector Lavoe, was a popular salsa singer. Born and raised in the Bronx, Vega began DJing at eighteen after he watched some fellow high school friends spin records. He was soon a regular at high school parties and formed his own small label. While spinning at the infamous Studio 54, Vega met house producer, Todd Terry who would regularly give Vega his new mixes to try out on the 54 crowd. Vega's own first remixes included Information Society's "Running" and Noel's "Silent Morning" and also some work for then-budding star Debbie Gibson.

In 1989 Vega produced the instrumental "Don't Tell Me" for SBK Records and "Keep Pumpin' It Up" under the name Freestyle Orchestra. Vega had been commissioned to do songs for the movie *East Side Story* when he met the singer Marc Anthony. With Anthony, Vega would sign on to CBS Records' subsidiary WTG Records. Together they produced the single "Ride on the Rhythm," which did remarkably well in the clubs and rewarded both men with lots of recognition. He would later team up with house vocalist Barbara Tucker to produce Beautiful People and also establish the Underground Network Club in New York. Vega also teamed up again with Todd Terry to produce "Todd's Message" with vocalist India, Vega's former wife. Vega also contributed to the Dee-Lite remix compilation *Sampladelic Relics and Dance Floor Oddities*.

Though Vega has produced much as a solo act, he is more widely known as half of the production team Masters at Work. Kenny "Dope" Gonzalez, who originally used the name for his own DJ crew, met Vega through Todd Terry. Under the Masters at Work name, Vega and Gonzalez have remixed the likes of Jamiroquai, Madonna, and Michael Jackson. Using the name Nuyorican Soul, the two worked with such jazz legends as Tito Puente and George Benson for a self-titled album. The two stopped all MAW remixes to concentrate on the 1997 album that strongly reflects their Puerto Rican heritage and returns the two to their roots as producers. In 2000 Vega appeared on the Ultra Records compilation *House Nation America* with Eric Morillo. —*Diana Potts*

- **Little Louie Vega at the Underground Network NYC** / Jul. 27, 1993 / Strictly Rhythm ++++

Louie Vega storms through the growing canon of Strictly Rhythm classics with this 1993 mix-album update, spinning joints from some of the best American house producers around: Erick Morillo (Club Ultimate's "Carnival Side"), DJ Pierre (Joint Venture's "Master Blaster"), Lenny Fontana (Butch Quick's "Higher"), Benji Candelario (Bass Hit's "Hey!"), 95 North (Scram's "Jump & Sing"), George Morel (Shadii's "My People"), and Kerri Chandler (KCYC's "Stompin' Grounds"). Vega's mix balances the extroverted, ecstatic vocals and hard-edged productions Strictly's known for. It's not only a great collection of Strictly Rhythm tracks, *At the Underground Network* is a near-perfect house mix album. —*John Bush*

**New York Underground: The Nu Groove Years** / Sep. 21, 1999 / Roadrunner ++++

DJ/producer Little Louie Vega's *New York Underground* features a nonstop mix of Nu Groove releases from artists like Bucketheads, George Benson, and the Braxtons, as well as tracks by Bas Noir, Assylum and Aphrodisiac. —*Heather Phares*

## Velocette [1] (Jason Williams)

*Producer / Ambient Techno, Techno*

Velocette is the nom de record of San Francisco-based ambient techno experimentalist Jason Williams. A member of noted techno producer Jonah Sharp's Reflective Records stable, Williams has released the bulk of his work through the label, including the full-length *Sonorities by Starlight* and a trio of singles. Wedding minimal, usually electro-derived beats with sparse, atmospheric electronics, Williams' work is as close in feel to '70s space music impressarios like Klaus Schulze and Edgar Froese as to contemporary innovators such as Sharp's Spacetime Continuum, Autechre, MLO, and Move D. Originally a cellist, Williams sold his first instrument to buy a sequencer after being introduced to electronic music through friends. His first EP, "Microcosmik," came out on Reflective in 1994 and was later featured on the celebrated *Synoptics* compilation. Following live performances at the German Love Parade, as well as at events in San Francisco and Los Angeles, Williams released the *Clockwork* EP before joining the album-length ranks with *Sonorities by Starlight*, which critics compared favorably with the likes of B12, Deep Space Network, and Atom Heart. Williams' work was also featured on the *Headtravel* CD-Plus released by Om Records in 1994. —*Sean Cooper*

- **Microcosmik [EP]** / 1994 / Reflective ++++

Four-trackey but no less inventive for it. Williams's strengths are in quirk and contrast, and he accomplishes them best when ignoring the dancefloor. A nice first-stab of atmospheric techno. —*Sean Cooper*

**Sonorities by Starlight** / Jun. 3, 1996 / Reflective +++

Over a year in the woodshed aids in making Williams' full-length debut one of the most accomplished and enjoyable documents of post-rave American experimental techno. Overwhelmingly aimed at the armchair, *Sonorities by Starlight* is a subtle groover, with thin, funky beats washed over by subtle melodies and intricate arrangements. Includes the best of the *Clockworks* EP immediately preceding it. —*Sean Cooper*

## Velocette [2]

f. 1997, London, England

*Group / Ambient Pop, Electronica*

Not too long after the demise of Comet Gain in early 1997, four out of the five members continued on to grab England's attention with their new project Velocette. Immediately after they released their first single "Get Yourself Together," the press coverage started pouring in from both NME and Melody Maker—who placed their aforementioned song as "Single of the Week" not too long after they got their hands on it. After countless gigs and headlining tours all throughout their homeland in 1998, their trademark sounds were finally documented on their first full length entitled *Fourfold Remedy*. Merging elements of crazed rhythms and jazzy beats on top of relaxed folk openings that progress into explosive guitar chords, Velocette take the prize for pulling off their own unique sound. —*Mike DaRonco*

- **Fourfold Remedy** / Mar. 23, 1999 / Wiija +++

North London's Velocette deliver stylish, '60s-tinged pop on their debut album *Fourfold Remedy*. Songs like "Someone's Waiting" and "Where Are We?" express the band's grasp on a wide range of styles, from haunting folky ballads to sly funk. Slow, pretty songs like "Reborn" and "Unkind" lend a cinematic feel to *Fourfold Remedy*, and the sweet-and-sultry vocals add the final, sophisticated touch. Velocette make their mark with this diverse and entertaining first effort. —*Heather Phares*

## Luke Vibert

*Producer / Electronica, Ambient Techno, Trip-Hop*

The name behind releases by Wagon Christ and Plug, Luke Vibert also released pieces of work under his own name, recording 1993's *Weirs* for Rephlex (as Vibert/Simmonds) and 1996's *Big Soup* for Mo'Wax. *Stop the Panic* followed in early 2000. [See Also: Plug, Wagon Christ] —*John Bush*

**Weirs** / 1993 / Rephlex +++

Typical of the Rephlex Records catalog but not of his later output, Luke Vibert's first LP (recorded as Vibert/Simmonds with Jeremy Simmonds) includes crushing industrial beats and acid synthwork reminiscent of the Aphex Twin's material. Several of the tracks are overlong, and *Weirs* might come as a bit of a shock to listeners familiar with his more trip-hop- and jungle-inspired works. —*John Bush*

- **Big Soup** / Jul. 7, 1997 / Mo'Wax ++++

While many electronica artists cover at least a little bit of every style extant on each of their recordings, Luke Vibert has maintained a bit of isolation for his various pseudonyms—*Vibert/Simmonds* was a harsh techno record, Wagon Christ charted a course through ambient music and hip-hop (definitely leagues away from what is known as trip-hop), and Plug became his alias for experimental jungle excursions. The first album he actually recorded as Luke Vibert, 1997's *Big Soup*, lies closer to straightahead hip-hop than any of his previous projects, with great production that fills in the gaps and with vocal samples doing their own share. With an ever-growing legion of abstract hip-hop maestros boring the socks off listeners, however, the stakes are upped for Vibert to create an instrumental rap record with listenability. If he didn't succeed, he at least managed better than most of the crowd. Though most of the record is downtempo, the addition of the jungle-based "Fused into Music" (with a break borrowed from his Plug record) does lend a bit of variety to the proceedings. —*John Bush*

**Stop the Panic** / Jan. 25, 2000 / Astralwerks ++++

It must be one of the most unlikely collaborations in electronic music, but producer Luke Vibert's collaboration with pedal-steel master B.J. Cole actually turns out alright, though the fusion is not quite as surprising as it originally sounded. On most tracks, Cole's shimmering, fluid guitar lines are simply assimilated into Vibert's kitchen-sink production style, and the results don't sound vastly different than Vibert's last full-length, *Tally Ho!* (recorded under his Wagon Christ pseudonym). While it's good to see an excellent producer pushing himself—and all of electronic music—into new territory, *Stop the Panic* just doesn't *sound* quite like the revolution it should be. —*John Bush*

## Visage

f. 1978, London, England, db. 1984

*Group / New Romantic, New Wave, Electronic*

Pioneers of the New Romantic movement, the synth-pop group Visage emerged in 1978 from the London club Billy's, a neo-glam nightspot that stood in stark contrast to the prevailing punk mentality of the moment. Spearheading Billy's ultra-chic clientele were Steve Strange, a former member of the punk band the Moors Murderers, as well as DJ Rusty Egan, one-time drummer with the Rich Kids. Seeking to record music of their own to fit in with the club's regular playlist (a steady diet of David Bowie, Kraftwerk and Roxy Music), Strange and Egan were offered studio time by another Rich Kids alum, guitarist Midge Ure. In late 1978, this trio recorded a demo that yielded the first Visage single, an aptly-futuristic cover of Zager & Evans' "In the Year 2525."

Adding Ultravox keyboardist Billy Currie as well as three members of Magazine—bassist Barry Adamson, guitarist John McGeoch, and keyboardist Dave Formula—Visage signed to Radar Records to release "Tar" in September 1979, followed a year later by their self-titled debut LP. The album yielded a major single in "Fade to Grey," an instant club classic that heralded synth-pop's imminent commercial breakthrough. The follow-up, "Mind of a Toy," was a Top 20 hit, but after releasing 1982's *The Anvil*, Visage began to disintegrate—first Ure exited to focus all of his energies on fronting Ultravox, then

Currie and Formula broke ranks as well. 1984's *Beat Boys* was the group's final recording, although a remixed "Fade to Grey" was a UK Top 40 hit during the early '90s. —*Jason Ankeny*

**Visage/The Anvil** / 1983 / Polydor ✦✦✦✦
Polydor combined Visage's first two (and best) albums, *Visage* and *The Anvil*, on one cassette in the early '80s. It's not a bad way to collect all of this music at once, but the packaging and sound are a little shabby, and since it's out of print and quite rare anyway, it's best to go for the collection. —*Stephen Thomas Erlewine*

● **Fade to Grey: The Singles Collection** / Feb. 22, 1994 / Polydor ✦✦✦✦
*Fade to Grey* includes the best of the band's Kraftwerk-inspired, post-disco synth-pop like "Fade to Grey" (of course), "Damned Don't Cry," "The Anvil" and "Night Train," as well as their cover of the Zager & Evans chestnut "In the Year 2525." There are only 12 tracks, but as it's the only collection available, it'll have to do. —*John Bush*

## The Vision (Robert Hood)

*Producer, DJ / Minimal Techno, Club/Dance, Techno*
Before Robert Hood began releasing music under his own name, he released his records as The Vision. Symbolic of the conceptual insightfulness that often crept into his heavily structured, almost mathematical style of techno, this name adequately summed up Hood's agenda: dance music with an aura of insightfulness. He released his first record as The Vision, *Gyroscopic*, on the Underground Resistance label in 1991 and eventually was awarded the opportunity to produce the second volume in the *Waveform Transmission* series of albums on Tresor in 1993. Following this album, which is techno-filled with an abundance of oddly arranged sounds symmetrically cycling above hard 909 beats, Hood moved towards a reduced sound and began releasing music under his own name. —*Jason Birchmeier*

● **Gyroscopic [EP]** / 1991 / Leptone ✦✦✦✦
*Gyroscopic* stands today as the first full glimpse at the style of hard techno employed by Detroit artist Robert Hood, referring to himself here as The Vision. The record includes several songs with near mechanical qualities. Whereas fellow Underground Resistance partners Mad Mike and Jeff Mills tended to lean towards the use of synthesizers to add elements of emotion to their respective styles of techno, Hood prefers to focus almost exclusively on harsh rhythm and intensity for *Gyroscopic*. Each of the songs makes heavy use of loops, transforming sounds into a form of percussion. This tends to result in a harsh, syncopated, and, ultimately, inhuman sound. Anyone interested in heavily arranged, aggressively programmed rhythmic loops may enjoy this record, but for most it's simply too mechanized—even for techno. —*Jason Birchmeier*

**Waveform Transmission, Vol. 2** / 1995 / Axis/Tresor ✦✦✦✦
Nowhere near as realized as his later Tresor recordings such as *Internal Empire* and *Minimal Nation*, Robert Hood's contribution to the *Waveform Transmission* series as The Vision was innovative for its time, nonetheless. Obviously influenced by his time spent in the Detroit group Underground Resistance and as a collaborator with Jeff Mills, this record finds Hood favoring a dark machine-like feel with plenty of hard-hitting 909 drum beats and an assaulting array of swirling, high-frequency, laser-sounding loops. With the syncopated pounding and the maelstrom of looped laser sounds, a stark, austere motif pervades throughout these eight songs; unfortunately, the variety of experimental song ideas so common to his later work is notably absent. —*Jason Birchmeier*

## Richard "Humpty" Vission

b. May 24, 1973, Toronto, Ontario, Canada
*Producer, DJ / Club/Dance, House*
One of the preeminent house DJs/producers around Los Angeles since the late '80s, Richard "Humpty" Vission became known for a freewheeling mixing style that cycled through dozens of records per hour, and a production career that saw the same frenzied sound crest with his sports anthem classic "Jump," by the Movement. Born in Toronto and raised in East L.A., Vission began DJing hip-hop in high school and graduated to a local rap station, KDAY. By 1990, he'd left for the dance station KPWR-Power 106, first working as an intern and one year later beginning his own long-running show, *Powertools*.

In 1992, Vission got together with producer A.J. Mora and rapper Hazze to form the Movement, which debuted in summer 1992 with the techno-pop barnstormer "Jump." A staple of sports arena PA booths for years to come, "Jump" went gold and just barely missed the Top 40. After touring with the group and releasing a self-titled Movement album, Vission founded the Aqua Boogie label for his burgeoning production career. It got a boost in 1995 when he hooked up with British remixer Pete Lorimer to form the production team Vission & Lorimer, responsible for dance hits recorded by Crystal Waters, N-Joi, Raw Stylus, Martha Wash, and Brand New Heavies. His first mix album, *This Is My House*, appeared that same year and introduced his extroverted DJing style to a wider audience. After a follow-up (*House Nation*) in 1996, Vission recorded *The House Connection*, the first in a series of tag-team mix sets with fellow renegade DJ Bad Boy Bill. He continued releasing about an album per year, and aside from continuing the *Powertools* show (the highest-rated dance show in Los Angeles), Vission spent time remixing for artists including Donna Summer, Todd Terry, the Shamen, RuPaul, Ace of Base, Taylor Dayne, and Crystal Waters. Even legions of nondance fans likely saw or heard him at work, considering he was the resident DJ at MTV's *The Blame Game* and also composed the score for the syndicated *Judge Mathis*. —*John Bush*

**House Nation** / Aug. 27, 1996 / V-Wax ✦✦
**House Connection** / Apr. 15, 1997 / V-Wax ✦✦✦

● **Shut the F*** Up and Dance** / Jun. 20, 2000 / Tommy Boy ✦✦✦✦
The 2000 edition for mixmaster Richard "Humpty" Vission's blueprint of hyperactive house sees the DJ racing through over 50 tracks in an hour flat, perfect for keeping the attention of everyone on the dancefloor and positively dizzying if you're playing at home. With the skills, pace, and deft timing of a hip-hop turntablist, Vission fuses the organic elements of house's roots (extroverted diva vocals, power-of-dance positivity, disco basslines) with the increasingly frenetic hardcore/trance of the '90s (pounding metallic effects, raging vocal samples). After hitting a few highlights early on (with Loop 303's "Loop 303" and his own "Everybody's Free"), Vission detours through harder techno (tracks from DJ Bam Bam, Frankie Bones, and DJ Hyperactive) before peaking exactly halfway through with the outboard hardcore jungle of Robot Man's "Robot Man" and a remix of N.W.A's "Dope Man." Vission also manages to break out a few house classics, including Ralphi Rosario's "You Used to Hold Me," the Masters at Work production "Love and Happiness" by River Ocean, and Armand Van Helden's "U Don't Know Me." —*John Bush*

## Cristian Vogel

b. Chile
*Producer, DJ / Minimal Techno, Experimental Techno, Electronica, Club/Dance, Techno*
Cristian Vogel is one of the foremost names in dance-based experimental techno, releasing a flood of consistently challenging and unconventional techno solo and in collaboration with such noted artists as Dave Clarke, Neil Landstrumm, and Russ Gabriel. Chilean born, Vogel fled with his family to the UK in the early '80s to escape the dictatorial regime of General Pinochet.

A childhood spent hacking later combined with an interest in programmable music, which soon branched out to include experimental electronic music, and, eventually, techno. Vogel began experimenting with his own compositions in the late '80s, working with members of the Cabbage Head Collective (which included, among others, Si Begg and members of Germ), whose early self-distributed tape cut-ups contributed much to Vogel's nascent aesthetic. Unlike many of his contemporaries, Vogel's fascination for electronic composition led him in 1992 to study in an academic context, earning a degree in 20th-century music at the University of Sussex in Brighton. Fusing the techniques of earlier Detroit, German, and English innovators with insights gained through active study of composers such as Karlheinz Stockhausen and Brian Eno, the results often agitated his professors. But Vogel's knack for combining elements of flux and sound collage in a style of music normally concerned with rhythmic conservatism and strict repetition has placed him at the bleeding edge of roots-directed experimental techno.

Vogel's most prolific recording period began during the tail end of his academic career, when some of his studio investigations began leaking into the techno underground. Earning the respect of South Shore DJ/musician/record shop manager Luke Slater, Vogel's name soon made it to the ears of minimalist hardcore producer Dave Clarke, resulting in the massive *Infra* EP, recorded together at the U. of Sussex studio and released on Clarke's Magnetic North label. Vogel followed on the success of *Infra* with a pair of EPs in collaboration with Russ Gabriel, released on the latter's Ferox and Berlin labels, before landing recording deals with both Force Inc. and Thomas Heckmann's Trope imprint. In 1994, Vogel released his first full-length work, *Beginning to Understand*, on Force Inc. subsidiary Mille Plateaux. The work was a focused, full-blown application of Vogel's experimental vision to the tropes of dancefloor techno. Close behind came a double-pack on Tresor (Vogel was the first UK artist to be courted by the legendary German label) and collaborations with Neil Landstrumm and Si Begg. In addition to his steady DJ activities, Vogel also releases his own and others' material through two personal labels—Mosquito and Quinine—and is often called upon as a remixer. In 1999, Vogel returned to British label shores, signing with NovaMute and releasing *Rescate 137* in 2000. —*Sean Cooper*

**Beginning to Understand** / 1995 / Mille Plateaux ♦♦♦

**Absolute Time** / 1995 / Tresor ♦♦
Vogel's first album for Tresor is an eight-tracker of fast-moving techno that would qualify as straight-ahead if it wasn't for the roster of experimental effects driving each song. The track titles are negligible—"In," "Absolute," and "Time" on the first side, "What," "Goes," "Round," "Comes," "Around," on the flip—and to an extent, the music is too. While it's just as professionally done and immediately entertaining as his album debut (released on Mille Plateaux), *Absolute Time* has a tossed-off air that doesn't quite compare to his later work. —*John Bush*

• **Specific Momentific** / Sep. 23, 1996 / Mille Plateaux/Force Inc. ♦♦♦♦
Vogel continued his bid for techno auteurism with his second full-length for Mille Plateaux. As with the previous *Beginning to Understand*, *Specific Momentific* is grand-style experimental techno awash in oddly arranged, obscurantist synth-tweak. But while much of the album achieves Vogel's best fusion to date of avant-garde noodle and bassbin kick, a few tracks head for beatless territory, with results in a dark ambient/isolationist vein that make for wonderfully varied listening. —*Sean Cooper*

**All Music Has Come to an End** / May 19, 1997 / Tresor ♦♦♦♦
Vogel's contemporary single for Tresor label was a minimal four-tracker consisting of the sort of banging techno he'd previously released with Dave Clarke on the Magnetic North label. This subsequent LP, however, dallies in that style only momentarily, moving quickly through a series of experimental excursions similar in tone to (and a tad more engaging than) his recent Mille Plateaux LP, *Specific Momentific*. Occasionally harsh, much of *All Music Has Come to an End* is quirky experimental electro, with eerie melodies and distorto funk of an Aphex variety filling out the album's otherwise gap-toothed sound. —*Sean Cooper*

**Busca Invisibles** / Mar. 16, 1999 / Tresor ♦♦♦♦
Vogel's always been known as an experimental producer but he's rarely forsaken the beat, preferring instead to layer his odd effects over some surprisingly straightahead rhythms. *Busca Invisibles* converts the overall production to a more immediately accessible club sound, with an earthy vibe and nods to funk and acid rock. Compared to most any trip-hop or techno out there, it's still a very warped album. —*John Bush*

**Rescate 137** / Oct. 17, 2000 / Nova Mute ♦♦♦
On *Rescate 137*, his debut for NovaMute, Cristian Vogel pushes his formula for experimental techno into overdrive with the help of new random-generating software and sampled percussion. The second track "Whipaspank" is the best, with a ghostly funk vocal scatting over twisted native effects from bongos to fretless bass. Creaking analog basslines push "Esquina Del Sol" and "La Isla Piscola" into highlight territory as well, the latter with another insane vocal performance from Vogel's samplers. Most Cristian Vogel LPs never venture too far from his (admittedly far-out) production style, and this one's no different; by the time the beatbox track "Wind From Nowhere" kicks in halfway through the album, it sounds more like a breath of fresh air than a brief pit stop. Still, Vogel takes his place next to Herbert, Si Begg, and Two Lone Swordsmen as the artists that screw up the techno formula most. —*John Bush*

## Voice Stealer (Carl A. Finlow)
b. 1998
*Producer / Electro-Techno, Ambient Techno, Electro, Techno*

Voice Stealer is one of many bylines used by eclectic dance music producer Carl A. Finlow, whose slick, sophisticated fusions of a range of dance music styles have appeared variously on the Soma, 20:20 Vision, Subvert, Klang, Phono, and SSR labels. Following on the heals of bold, bouncy hybrids of electro and new wave such as Le Car's "Automatic" and I-F's "Space Invaders Are Smoking Grass," Finlow's 1998 debut as Voice Stealer, *The All-Electric House*, was one of the more interesting, well-crafted album-length amalgams of those styles to appear. Fusing new wave's and electro's two strongest attributes—cool, detached melodic and vocal accompaniment and thin, rubbery drumbox funk—*The All-Electric House* escaped cliché partially by the novelty of its combination and partially because Finlow was the one doing the combining. Although much of his work to date has clustered around standard, breakbeat, and progressive house (he helped form the popular underground label 20:20 Vision, has released records through 20:20 as Random Factor and Urban Farmers, and is the imprint's in-house producer) the fastest growing segment of Finlow's solo discography is in the vein of his Voice Stealer material, and includes collaborative releases with Ralph Lawson (the "*Droid Funk*" EP) and Daz Quayle (under the name Scarletron, primarily for Electron Industries), as well as the four-track *ILek.tro* EP, released under his own name by Klang Elektronik in mid-1998. [See Also: Carl Finlow] —*Sean Cooper*

• **The All-Electric House** / Feb. 23, 1998 / Subvert ♦♦♦♦
One of the strongest, most consistent examples of properly neo-electro, *The All-Electric House* achieves a perfect mix of nostalgia and innovation, pairing simple, catchy melodies and obscure, half-serious vocals with interesting rhymic patterns and solid, strident beats. The album was the first full-length released on the Subvert label (an offshoot of the house-heavy Phono imprint), and set a high-water mark for new-school electro producers mining the old in search of the new. The CD version adds a bonus track. —*Sean Cooper*

## Vulva
f. 1993
*Group / Experimental Techno, Ambient Techno, IDM*

Tim Hutton and Thomas Melchior formed Vulva in 1993 in England. The experimental techno duo signed with the Rephlex label (home of Aphex Twin) and released *From the Cockpit* in 1995. Vulva's first domestic release was the *Mini Space Vulvette* EP, for Reflective Records. After a side project called Yoni for the German Source label ("Yoni" and *My Little Yoni*), Hutton and Melchior released their second full-length for Rephlex, *Birdwatch*, in 1995. *Vulvic Yonification* followed in late 1997. —*John Bush*

**From the Cockpit** / 1995 / Rephlex ♦♦♦
With studio help from Baby Ford, Vulva's *From the Cockpit* blends understated melodies with complex percussion lines. —*John Bush*

• **Birdwatch** / Oct. 21, 1996 / Rephlex ♦♦♦♦

**Vulvic Yonification** / Sep. 22, 1997 / Source ♦♦♦♦
Recording for the German Source label, for whom they have also recorded as Yoni, Vulva continue their experiments with modern electronic funk on *Vulvic Yonification*. —*Steve Huey*

# W

### Kristine W. (Kristine Weitz)
b. Pasco, WA
*Vocals / Garage, Club/Dance, House, Dance-Pop*

A former Miss America contestant with *real* vocal talent, Kristine W. became one of the hottest dancefloor properties during the mid-'90s, with several singles featuring her incredibly soulful voice, which topped the dance charts and placed high on the pop charts through most of Europe. Born in a small town in Washington State, Kristine Weitz began singing and dancing in public from an early age, winning talent contests and beauty pageants. Crowned Miss Washington, she competed in the Miss America pageant, placing first in the talent portion of the contest. She moved to Las Vegas soon after, to go to school (and perform), gradually working her way up to be the lead performer in her own show at the Las Vegas Hilton, concurrent with a recording career which began in the early '90s. A 1994 single for Champion Records, "Feel What You Want," hit number one on the dance charts as well as the Top Five on the charts of ten European countries. The follow-up "One More Try" proved just as successful, earning Kristine W. a major-label contract with RCA. She released her debut album *Land of the Living* in mid-1996 and spent four years working on the follow-up, *Stronger*. —*John Bush*

● **Land of the Living** / Jul. 23, 1996 / RCA ♦♦♦♦
Although the producers (including Rollo of Faithless) are a bit less than innovative, the vocals of Kristine W.—alternately sweet, muscular, and grand—lift *Land of the Living* above the ranks of most by-the-numbers diva house outings. Kristine W. is probably the most soulful vocalist in dance music, period, and she proves it on "Don't Wanna Think," "Feel What You Want," and "Breathe." —*John Bush*

**Stronger** / 2000 / RCA ♦♦
Recorded over four years, dance queen Kristine W.'s sophomore album is a strong mix of pop and A/C-flavored R&B. What's funny, though, is that the stronger material is not the club music for which she is known. The dance cuts on this album are standard at best. Of course, they aren't so much for pop fans as they are for club crawlers who'll purchase remixes, so that doesn't necessarily alienate dance fans, but they still bring the album down a bit. On the plus side, the rest of *Stronger* is solid, and her voice, thankfully not the little-girl voice so many dance artists have, sounds like a woman's. She almost has a bit of the vocal depth of Cher, which is good or bad, depending on your take. "If Only You Knew" is a good pop concoction, bright and sunny and happy, though its sixth-grade lyrics (You're my every wish/you're my dream come true) bring it down a notch. "Pieces of Me and You" is romantic with an insistent beat, and the tropical "Clubland" has horns, a salsa sound, and a bit of scat thrown in for good measure. "Never Been Kissed" offers up disco synths with seamless '90s production; the smooth, jazzy "Waters Run Deep" is great '70s A/C-R&B with nice vocals; and "All That Glitters" is a nice synth-driven ballad that is surprisingly not overproduced, as so many ballads by dance artists are. Cowriter of eight of the cuts and co-executive producer of the entire album, Kristine W. shows she's not some producer's puppet, and *Stronger* augurs the possibility of a lengthy career. —*Bryan Buss*

### Rick Wade
b. Buchanan, MI
*Producer, DJ / Techno Bass, Detroit Techno, Club/Dance, House*

Growing up outside the Chicago area in neighboring Michigan, Rick Wade became fascinated with the city's radio stations at an early age, taking an instant liking in artists such as Al Green and Isaac Hayes along with the disco sounds of labels such as Salsoul that received substantial airplay. By the early '80s, Wade began spinning records at parties, slowly transforming into a talented DJ while simultaneously furthering his musical interests. As a student at The University of Michigan in Ann Arbor, he DJed at the University's radio station, WCBN, where he pioneered the station's first show dedicated to house music. It was during this period at the end of the '80s, alongside other electronic dance music DJ/artists such as Ectomorph's Brendan Gillen that he began producing his own tracks. In 1993, Wade began his own house label, Harmonie Park, followed by a booty bass label, Bass Force. —*Jason Birchmeier*

● **Quantum Expression [Single]** / 1999 / Moods & Grooves ♦♦♦♦
The four tracks on Rick Wade's debut for the Detroit-based Moods & Grooves label manage to touch on four different approaches to deep house. The two A-side tracks—"Thought Process" and "Forever Night"—focus on a light style of mid-tempo house music with a sprinkled amount of piano keys and a quiet synth background while focusing primarily on the rhythm. The B-side tracks—"Bangin'" and "Pimp Factor"—move away from this tranquil sound toward a more colorful approach, with stronger, more prominent percussion and a foreground assortment of synth. For a single 12", *Quantum Expression* manages to present differing feels while still maintaining a high sense of quality, characterized primarily by Wade's simple but well-executed use of mid-tempo dancefloor rhythms and airy keys. —*Jason Birchmeier*

### Wagon Christ (Luke Vibert)
b. Cornwall, England
*Producer / Electronica, Ambient Breakbeat, Ambient Techno, Trip-Hop, Jungle/Drum'N'Bass, IDM*

Luke Vibert is one of a new breed of European club music experimentalists whose work spans several genres simultaneously, and is one of a very few of that set to make any headway into US audiences. A native of Cornwall, Vibert's work has been compared with other West Country bedroom denizens like Aphex Twin and μ-Ziq, although his output over the past few years has been far more eclectic than that connection would seem to imply. Beginning with tweaky post-techno and moving through ambient and experimental hip-hop as Wagon Christ and, most recently, experimental drum'n'bass as Plug, Vibert has explored the outer reaches of post-techno electronica without sounding hasty or swank. Although Vibert's first musical experience was in a Beastie Boys knockoff band called the Hate Brothers, he quickly moved into the low-cost environment of solo bedroom composition. Although he had no intention of ever releasing any of the work, his reputation as a creative young voice in stylistic crosspolination has created an increasing demand for his pioneering, often left-field, work.

Vibert became involved in electronic music through his passion for hip-hop (he has commented that hip-hop is the only music style he really keeps up with), as well as the environment of bedroom experimentalism associated with the swelling late-'80s UK dance scene. He released an album through the Rephlex label (a solo album nonetheless billed as *Vibert/Simmonds*) before coming to the attention of Caspar Pound's Rising High label. As a result of the growing exchange value of the style, RH commissioned an ambient album from Vibert, who, despite never having heard much ambient, delivered the well-received *Phat Lab Nightmare* under the Wagon Christ name in 1993. Silent (but for the quickie EP, *At Atmos*) for nearly two years following its release, Vibert came back in early 1995 with *Throbbing Pouch*, a collection of minimal, funky, off-kilter hip-hop that had fans familiar with his earlier work scratching their heads. Though lumped in with the so-called "trip-hop" movement attributed to Portishead, Tricky, Massive Attack, and the Mo'Wax label, the album's upbeat, cheeky edge was anything but stoney and laidback. Following up with a number of remixes and a Mo'Wax EP under his own name,

Vibert embarked on his next major mutation with his Plug project, releasing a trio of sample-laden, epileptic jungle EPs, as well as the *Drum'n'Bass for Papa* LP in 1996. Wagon Christ's *Tally Ho!* followed in 1998, and Vibert reverted to his own name for 2000's *Stop the Panic*. [See Also: Plug, Luke Vibert] —*Sean Cooper*

**Phat Lab Nightmare** / 1993 / Rising High ✦✦✦
Twittering, at times noodly, experimental ambient. Vibert's lack of familiarity with the genre's more formal properties is probably what makes this a worthwhile release. —*Sean Cooper*

**Risalecki [EP]** / 1994 / Rising High ✦✦✦✦
A portent of things to come, this EP was released the week before *Throbbing Pouch*, and indicated an adjustment in focus. This album features thumping breakbeats and minimal, scratchy electronics far closer to hip-hop or funky breaks than his first album. —*Sean Cooper*

★ **Throbbing Pouch** / Sep. 5, 1995 / Rising High ✦✦✦✦✦
Scattered with dime-store samples and goofy melodies, this is eazy-listening instrumental hip-hop like Jay-Z or Premier would do it. Though the material is heavily sequenced, Vibert's arranging skills are in rare form, reordering elements and dropping tracks in and out with liquid, barely noticeable aplomb. [The original British CD version includes a bonus disc with the *At Atmos* EP included.] —*Sean Cooper*

**Tally Ho!** / Sep. 28, 1998 / Astralwerks ✦✦✦✦
Luke Vibert, one of Europe's more prolific electronic masterminds, slips into his Wagon Christ alter ego once again and comes through with one of his more accessible efforts. *Tally Ho!* doesn't have the personality-driven energy of Prodigy or the Chemical Brothers' slam-bang theatrics, but that doesn't mean it's short on character by any means. Vibert paints himself as a sly mixmaster with music that contains a smokiness quite different from the dark, misty shadows associated with the most familiar electronic noir. Instead, bursts of color appear in these dense, loungey compositions. The songs here branch out in various directions, whether it's R&B beats giving way to classical piano flourishes or swelling basslines embracing gurgling samples, robotic blips and kabuki drums.

Anyone lost in the thick, endless vines of drum'n'bass will be surprised by these crisp, controlled soundscapes (its hour-long running time is modest by today's DJ standards). It's Vibert's emphasis on the R&B vibe that gives *Tally Ho!* its definitive edge. Cool jazz piano and ricocheting drum tracks surface, which would sound ideal nestled below sultry hip-hop rhymes. If anything, Vibert, a confessed hip-hop fan, could really break barriers by bringing some of these otherworldly sounds to rap's universe. Sly grooves on "Fly Swat" and "Memory Towel" are ripe for swiping by sample-happy DJs. —*Jason Kaufman*

## Waldeck (Klaus Waldeck)

*Producer / Downtempo, Trip-Hop, Club/Dance*
The act known as Waldeck is the work of one Klaus Waldeck, a producer for Vienna's Spray Records, home to work by Kruder & Dorfmeister and Count Basic. Waldeck's work is similar earthy downtempo, though many of his productions reflect the recruitment of vocalists, similar to Massive Attack. After contributing a track to the Spray compilation *The Eclectic Sound of Vienna*, Waldeck released his debut full-length *Balance of the Force* in 1999. Along with an American distribution deal through E-Magine, an accompanying remix album was released in the United States as well. *Who Is Waldeck*, his second LP, was released in fall 2000. —*John Bush*

● **Balance of the Force** / Sep. 21, 1999 / E-Magine ✦✦✦✦
Though it comes from a previously unheard producer, *Balance of the Force* certainly begins on a high note, with the down-tempo soul of "Defenceless." While Waldeck himself takes the keyboards (both electric and standard piano), the deep groove of what sounds like a live drum set frames the yearning vocals of Joy Malcolm. It's that rare thing in electronic circles: the perfect integration of vocal track and production, with both pulling equal weight to set the mood. Amid a beautiful, effortless transition, Waldeck moves on to "Spy Like an Angel," with male vocalist Brian Amos doing much the same as Malcolm did one track earlier. Either of these voices appears on all but two of the tracks here, the exceptions being the eerie, cinematic instrumentals "Slaapwagen" and "Moon." Fellow downbeat maestros Kruder & Dorfmeister help out on production for the sublime "Aquarius," and except for the slight reliance on a previously trade-

marked sound, *Balance of the Force* stands as one of the most quietly beautiful records of vocal trip-hop—just slightly behind masterpieces like Portishead's *Dummy* and Massive Attack's *Mezzanine*. —*John Bush*

**Balance of the Force (Remixed)** / Sep. 21, 1999 / E-Magine ✦✦
The remix album that accompanied a brilliant debut, *Balance of the Force Remixed* features ten remixes of album tracks, four by the Mushroom Dive alias of Klaus Waldeck himself. (Though Waldeck's re-interpretations are uniformly solid, it's clear he took the right versions for the LP itself.) Meanwhile, Thievery Corporation alter "Defenceless" slightly (from R&B to lounge), Uptight turn "Slaapwagen" into a dubwise hip-hop track, and the Rocker's hi-fi version of "Wake Up" is a spare percussion jam with echoing vocals. The 11th track here is a suitably sublime cover of the quintessentially knowing Bond theme "You Only Live Twice" (originally voiced by Nancy Sinatra) that only hints at the obligatory carpet of strings. Interesting for the already converted, but definitely a companion piece. —*John Bush*

## Stewart Walker

*Producer / Minimal Techno, Detroit Techno, Club/Dance, Techno*
Sound sculpture is an overused analogy in music circles, especially techno, but it becomes a fitting term to use for the productions of Stewart Walker. Influenced by the work of Alexander Calder, a sculptor of large outdoor pieces called "stabile" (abstract mobile-like pieces made of sheet metal), Walker composed a set of stark, hypnotic tracks of minimalist techno for his first full-length, released on Mille Plateaux in 1999. Growing up in Atlanta, Walker listened to the Beatles and played guitar in a folk style learned from his parents, who had played in a folk group during the '60s. He moved on to alternative rock in the '80s, then fell in love with the first wave of intelligent techno during the early '90s from groups like 808 State, LFO, Aphex Twin, and the Orb. After a post-graduation visit to England in 1992, Walker fell into the burgeoning techno underground and began experimenting with electronics by the mid-'90s. Walker made contacts around the world via e-mail and phone, releasing his first material, the 1997 single "Amphetamine Sulphate," via Detroiter Sean Deason's Matrix Records. A year after that, he earned an EP release, *Artificial Music for Artificial People*, on Cristian Vogel's Mosquito label. Another single for Matrix ("Stoic") preceded the release of *Stabiles* in 1999, on Mille Plateaux. —*John Bush*

● **Stabiles** / Sep. 13, 1999 / Mille Plateaux ✦✦✦✦
As befits a work inspired by architecture, and especially the work of an artist who worked with sheet metal, there's nothing soft on *Stabiles*. Stewart Walker's first LP is a collection of ten stark tracks focused almost completely on the interplay between several different percussion lines with a small amount of echo applied to achieve the illusion of three-dimensional space. Except for faraway synth on a few tracks, every sound source is angular and incredibly precise. In a similar fashion to other minimal-techno architects (Rob Hood, Plastikman, Steve Stoll), Walker makes the most of his productions, weaving a half-dozen spare parts into complex, fascinating patterns that, in the end, don't even need accoutrements to sound great. —*John Bush*

## Wamdue Productions

f. 1994, Atlanta, GA
*Group / Jazz-House, Progressive House, Club/Dance, House*
Basically a solo project for Atlanta producer Chris Brann with the help of DJ cohorts Deep C and Udoh, Wamdue Productions' recordings provided one of the few convincing home/club fusions that err, if at all, on the side of the dancefloor. Unlike the large community of artists more allied to their headphones than a bassbin, Wamdue Productions are easy club favorites, and though they record for the strictly mainstream label Strictly Rhythm, Wamdue marries intense warmth gained from R&B and house to the tighter rhythms and hard effects of Detroit techno.

Brann grew up in Atlanta, listening to soul stalwarts Marvin Gaye and Isaac Hayes as well as machine maestros like Kraftwerk, Steve Reich and Cabaret Voltaire. In 1994, he hooked up with two DJ/producers, Deep C (born Chris Clark) and Udoh (born Chris Udoh). After connecting with soulful Detroit techno producer K Hand, Wamdue debuted with the single "Higher," and released singles during 1995 for Peacefrog, Studio !K7, Love from San Francisco, Jus' Trax, and Multiply—alternately known as Wamdue Kids, Wambonix and Wamdue Project. The following year, Wamdue Kids released a compilation on Studio !K7 while later in the year, Wamdue Project released a proper full-length bow on Strictly Rhythm, *Resource Toolbox, Vol. 1*. Mostly the work of Brann, the album gained raves as a true, intelligent, dancefloor masterpiece.

Wamdue Kids returned in early 1997 with a full album for Peacefrog, while the Project kept up the fever-pitched release schedule later that year with *Deepfall*, also on Peacefrog. The year 1998 brought yet another Project album, *Program Yourself*, for Strictly Rhythm. —*John Bush*

**Resource Toolbox, Vol. 1** / Oct. 1, 1996 / Strictly Rhythm ♦♦♦♦
The debut Wamdue album ably fuses chilled ambient techno to progressive house with remnants of R&B and a subtle breakbeat or two. The result is a selection of tracks ("Get High on the Music," "Remember the Memory") halfway between Marvin Gaye and Kraftwerk, sublimely soulful yet still futuristic. —*John Bush*

**Deepfall** / Nov. 17, 1997 / Peacefrog ♦♦
Technically another solo album for Wamdue mainman Chris Brann, *Deepfall* consists of nine tracks of surprisingly pedestrian tech-house, heavy on the analogue drum machines and vintage synth gear but lacking the energy those instruments often provide. Though it's by no means awful, the other Wamdue full-lengths far outdistance *Deepfall* in quality. —*John Bush*

● **Program Yourself** / May 26, 1998 / Strictly Rhythm ♦♦♦♦
A return to form for the Wamdue Project, *Program Yourself* is set of epic-sounding, progressive house tracks. Brann's impeccable sense of musical atmosphere and tight percussion programming save the album from sounding closer to Robert Miles' overblown dream-house territory. Whether he's working through chunky four-on-the-floor house or funky breakbeats tied to the British drum'n'bass scene, *Program Yourself* always entices. Five tracks feature female vocals (either Gaelle or Michelle Riley), while Wamdue compatriots Deep C and Udo appear on third track "Are You High?" —*John Bush*

## Chris Watson

*Guitar, Producer / Contemporary Instrumental, Ambient*
Chris Watson was a founding member of late-'70s/early-'80s techno and synth-pop innovators Cabaret Voltaire and, later, ambient-industrial fusioners the Hafler Trio. In something of an odd switch, Watson left the music industry behind in the early '90s to work as a sound recordist for the Royal Society for the Protection of Birds. Watson quickly branched out into production for film and television, and has since handled field recording for a number of nature programs, documentaries, and feature films. In 1996, after collecting hundreds of hours of location recordings from less accessible regions of the world, Watson returned, after a fashion, to music production, releasing his first-ever "solo album," *Stepping into the Dark*, on Jon Wozencroft's Touch label. Actually a compilation of recordings of natural settings spanning from Inverness to Kenya to Venezuela to Cumbria, the release was lauded by sources as varied as American indie rock magazine *CMJ New Music Monthly* and German experimental post-techno artist Uwe "Atom Heart" Schmidt, who went so far as to urge fans to seek out *Stepping Into the Dark* via the insert of his 1996 CD, *Built*. Watson's second album for Touch, *Inside the Circle of Fire*, was released in 1998. —*Sean Cooper*

● **Stepping into the Dark** / May 21, 1996 / Touch ♦♦♦
A surprisingly listenable collection of environmental recordings sourced from the four corners of the world, Chris Watson's first release under his own name is a fascinating account of the sonorities to be found in nature's ceaseless performance. Instead of focusing on the potentially soothing and meditative, Watson presents such diverse settings as the South American rainforest, Kenya's Mara River, and Moray Firth in all their complicated, occasionally abrasive glory. Made by cabling ultrasensitive microphones over great distances, *Stepping Into the Dark*'s 12 unedited cuts present nature in the raw, and stars a diversely musical cast (flies, tree frogs, moths, fishing bats, and the dense surge of heat through the awakening tropical forest). —*Sean Cooper*

## Wax Doctor (Paul Saunders)

**b.** Nov. 28, 1971, Slough, England
*Producer, DJ / Trip-Hop, Jungle/Drum'N'Bass, Club/Dance*
A proper player during jungle's rise from the underground during 1995-96, Paul Saunders' techno background hardly prepared listeners for the mellowed-out vibes and liquid tones of his work as Wax Doctor. Tracks like "Kid Caprice" (for Metalheadz) and "Atmospheric Funk" (for Talkin' Loud) were closely allied to LTJ Bukem's junglist fusion, though just a bit chunkier. Saunders began DJing in the late '80s, and though he juggled part-time mixing with a full-time soccer career for awhile (appearing as a reserve with Reading and later Crystal Palace), the Wax Doctor eventually debuted on production as well with several singles for Basement Records during 1992-93. He worked with fellow techno-head Alex Reece on Creative Wax and Precious Materials, but began drifting towards the growing drum'n'bass fascination with the lighter tones of jazz fusion. His singles for Metalheadz and Talkin' Loud signalled the new direction, and Saunders signed to R&S—noted more for listening techno than drum'n'bass—for two 1996 singles, "All I Need" and "Heat." Wax Doctor contributed a remix to label-mate Juan Atkins for a Model 500 single, "The Flow." R&S released the retrospective *Selected Works* in 1998. —*John Bush*

**Atmospheric Funk [Single]** / 1995 / Talkin' Loud ♦♦♦♦
With shots of jazz, jungle, and soul, Wax Doctor's updated mood-funk grooves nicely on this single, recorded for Talkin' Loud. —*John Bush*

● **Selected Works** / Mar. 2, 1998 / R&S ♦♦♦♦
A compilation of Wax Doctor's most impressive moments before he released his debut album, *Selected Works* includes stormers like "Atmospheric Funk," "Offshore Drift," and "The Step." —*John Bush*

## Way Out West

**f.** 1994, Bristol, England
*Group / Progressive House, Club/Dance, House*
Conspicuous from the rest of Bristol's electronica scene by the absence of trip-hop or jungle leanings in their productions, Way Out West have instead pursued straightahead house and techno with closer ties to progressive British dancefloors than American hip-hop. The duo of Jody Wisternoff and Nick Warren first came together in the mid-'90s; Wisternoff was a veteran producer who had first recorded at the age of 14 (with fellow Bristolian house artists Smith & Mighty) while Warren was a high-profile DJ influenced by the sounds of Madchester. The duo began recording, and in 1996 their single "The Gift" became a big mover on dancefloors and the radio as well, thanks to a British advertisement which used the song. Signed to Deconstruction, Way Out West released their self-titled debut album in 1997. Warren, who spent time as the resident DJ at superclub Cream, has released several compilations detailing his mixing skills. —*John Bush*

● **Way Out West** / Sep. 1, 1997 / Deconstruction ♦♦♦♦
Although Way Out West began their career in straightahead house, the duo work through many different forms on their album debut. "Domination" ascends into airy drum'n'bass territory after a mainstream intro, while tracks like "King of the Funk" and "Drive By" get more than a little aggressive, in contrast to the easy-going funk of "Questions Never Answered." Altogether, *Way Out West* is a varied, engaging debut. —*John Bush*

## We

**f.** 1994, Brooklyn, NY
*Group / Illbient, Turntablism, Electronica, Ambient Techno, Ambient Dub, Club/Dance*
We are one of the more bizarre and eclectic outcroppings of New York City's experimental ambient/dub/hip-hop scene, also the source of such artists as DJ Spooky, Sub Dub, Byzar, Liminal, and Brooklyn's WordSound collective. A trio of performance artists with hands in nearly a dozen different projects, We evolved out of a series of high-concept multimedia parties, clubs, and gallery exhibitions members Ignacio Platas (Once 11), Gregor Asch (DJ Olive), and Rich Panciera (Lloop) engineered over the previous several years. The three met in 1992 while living in Brooklyn, and their first work together under the name Lalalandia Entertainment Research Corporation included events thrown in retired mustard plants and meat-packing warehouses. In 1994, the group began a series of multimedia design and music installations under the name Multipolyomni (including a massive piece for Creative Times' Art at the Anchorage series titled "Early Aquatic Episode"), and We grew out of the musical end of that. Their first tracks appeared on WordSound's compilation *Crooklyn Dub Consortium, Vol. 1* and Virgin's second installment of *Macro Dub Infection*, the latter of which placed them in the company of such edge-leading electronica artists as Bill Laswell, Techno Animal, Zulutronic, and Alec Empire. The group signed with the New York-based Asphodel label soon after, and their debut LP, *As Is*, was released in the spring of 1997. *The Square Root of Minus One* followed in 1999, with *Decentertainment* appearing one year later. Also involved in NYC's vibrant

downtown experimental music scene, two of We's three members also perform with guitarist Danny Blume under the name Liminal. We have also remixed tracks for Arto Lindsay, Free Kitten, Tipsy, and Medeski, Martin, and Wood. —*Sean Cooper*

**As Is** / Mar. 11, 1997 / Asphodel ♦♦♦♦
We's fractious soup of ambient, dub, hip-hop, electro, and jungle is one of the more interesting products of New York's so-called "illbient" scene. Previously obtainable only on small-run and out-of-print compilations such as WordSound's *Crooklyn Dub Consortium* and Bill Laswell's *Valis*, We's warped, nomadic blend of styles and references is in full evidence on their Asphodel debut, a bold, accomplished collection of incessant gear-shifting that gives strength to the claim that America is finally waking up to the desktop electronics revolution. A few tracks betray the naivete of the group's (as well as the American scene's) youth, but the album's otherwise consistent quality suggests that it's really just a question of adapting the tools to a new, remarkably well-formed language. —*Sean Cooper*

**Square Root of Minus One** / Apr. 6, 1999 / Asphodel ♦♦♦
Who says there's no good American drum'n'bass? We (a trio consisting of the eminent DJs Once 11, Olive and Loop) have changed all that. Now even the snobbiest hardcore, hardstep Anglocentric junglists have no excuse but to give the American drum scene its due: Just about everything on We's second album gives the best of the UK crew a run for their money. Granted, *Square Root of Minus One* starts out weak, with the shapeless, beatless, and tuneless drone of "Birimbau," but things pick up immediately with the frenetic breakbeats and kid vocal samples of "Diablos" and they basically never let up. Thrill to the slow and smoky "Caya's Kids," with its dubwise effects, to the cool ethnic percussion and backward bass on "You Gone?," and to the eerie electric piano and reggae-fied beat of "Hielo." Marvel almost as much to most everything else, too. Excellent. —*Rick Anderson*

• **Decentertainment** / 2000 / Home Entertainment ♦♦♦♦
We is a trio consisting of DJ Olive (not to be confused with Olive), Lloop, and Once 11. These three technocrats have built a reputation for themselves as theoretical party animals—"decentertainment" is a term the group has coined to describe the type of event they prefer to stage, which is based on the idea of "decentering" the focus away from the performers and creating a "fully immersive omnisensorial environment." You can take the theory for what it's worth; what ultimately matters is the high quality of this music, which varies in flavor from downtempo funk ("Afrique," "Pull") to dense and complicated drum'n'bass ("Micro Al Hammed," "Vulpecula") and deeply weird and uncategorizable electronica ("One Personal Dream"). The band members were reputedly scattered around the world during the creation of this album, sending sound files to each other via modem and working out tracks on laptop computers in the backs of cabs (talk about decentering), and the result can't exactly be called cohesive. But that's part of its charm: where far too many electronica albums in the late '90s/early '00s consist of 60 minutes of one idea, *Decentertainment* is all over the place, and constantly yields new musical surprises. Highly recommended. —*Rick Anderson*

## Weather Report

f. 1970, db. 1985
*Group / Fusion*

While leading the most popular jazz combo of the '70s, keyboard player Joe Zawinul and tenor saxophonist Wayne Shorter expanded on the basic blueprint of jazz-rock fusion they had learned first-hand from Miles Davis (both had appeared on the landmark *In a Silent Way/Bitches Brew* sessions). Though Weather Report's first two albums leaned close to a group-improvisation aesthetic tied to free jazz, the group's later output worked deep grooves inspired by Latin, funk, and disco (with additional percussionists for flavor). Meanwhile, Zawinul indulged his increasing fascination with polyphonic synthesizer set-ups and Shorter vamped with atmospheric solos over the top. With what is perhaps the best of the many WR lineups (Zawinul and Shorter plus bassist Jaco Pastorius and percussionists Alex Acuna and Manolo Badrena), the group recorded their best-selling album, 1977's *Heavy Weather*, but then began a gradual process of disintegration until 1985, when Zawinul recorded the final Weather Report LP. By that time, the group's sound practically defined the jazz and fusion community, which had unfortunately degenerated into polished, soulless pop courtesy of groups like Spyro Gyra and the Rippingtons. The classic Weather Report sound was resurrected by the '90s however; besides being sampled extensively by early hip-hop DJs, the group proved enormously influential to a host of later electronica producers including Squarepusher and Luke Vibert.

In 1970, both Zawinul and Shorter had been among the dozen or so musicians contributing to Miles Davis' first fusion recordings. From that incubator came all of the major fusion players of the '70s, including Herbie Hancock, Tony Williams, John McLaughlin (with the Mahavishnu Orchestra), and Chick Corea (Return to Forever). Later that year, Zawinul and Shorter formed Weather Report with bassist Miroslav Vitous, drummer Alphonse Mouzon, and percussionist Airto Moreira. The group's self-titled debut and second record *I Sing the Body Electric* matched Miles' contemporary recordings, with free-floating improvisation by all members. Though he had no synthesizer as yet, Zawinul performed on Rhodes electric piano with a ring modulator to make a sound comparable to Miles' wah-wah trumpet.

The next two Weather Report LPs, 1973's *Sweetnighter* and 1974's *Mysterious Traveller*, sounded a bellwether change for the group, dominated by groove-heavy epics like "Boogie Woogie Waltz," "Nubian Sundance," and "Cucumber Slumber." While Zawinul added brilliant keyboard fills and unveiled his ARP synthesizer, Shorter was granted much less space for his solos. The concept of the revolving-door rhythm section also began to kick into high gear during the mid-'70s, until the notoriously flamboyant bass player Jaco Pastorius added a third personality to Weather Report. The group's seventh album *Heavy Weather* became one of the biggest hits ever for a jazz LP, though Pastorius left in 1980.

Later Weather Report LPs were erratic but often pleasing affairs, picking a careful course through the wasteland of early-'80s commercial pop and overly polished fusion. As early as 1983's *Procession*, Zawinul (still determining the direction of the group) was one of the first musicians to begin looking to the rhythms of what would later be called world music, though he continued using synthesizers. Three more albums appeared before Weather Report packed it in with 1985's *This Is This!*, basically a Zawinul solo album in all but name. He continued to explore world music—increasingly in an acoustic piano setting—with a group called the Zawinul Syndicate, while Shorter surprisingly kept in a fusion mold during the late '80s. —*John Bush*

**Weather Report** / Feb. 16, 1971-Mar. 17, 1971 / Columbia ♦♦♦♦
Here we have the free-floating, abstract beginnings of Weather Report, which would define the state of the electronic jazz/rock art from its first note almost to its last. Their first album is a direct extension of the Miles Davis *In A Silent Way/Bitches Brew* period, more fluid in sound and more volatile in interplay. Joe Zawinul ruminates in a delicate, liquid manner on Rhodes electric piano; at this early stage, he used a ring modulator to create weird synthesizer-like effects. Wayne Shorter's soprano sax shines like a beacon amidst the swirling ensemble work of co-founding bassist Miroslav Vitous, percussionist Airto Moreira, and drummer Alphonse Mouzon. Zawinul's most memorable theme is "Orange Lady" (previously recorded, though uncredited, by Davis on *Big Fun*), while Shorter scores on "Tears" and "Eurydice." One of the most impressive debuts of all time by a jazz group. —*Richard S. Ginell*

**I Sing the Body Electric** / Nov. 1971-Jan. 13, 1972 / Columbia ♦♦♦
Like the weather itself, this band would assume a new shape with virtually every release—and this album, half recorded in the studio and half live in Tokyo, set the pattern of change. Exit Airto Moreira and Alphonse Mouzon; enter percussionist Dom Um Romao, drummer Eric Gravatt, and a slew of cameo guests like guitarist Ralph Towner, flutist Hubert Laws and others. The studio tracks are more biting, more ethnically diverse in influence, and more laden with electronic effects and grandiose structural complexities than before. The live material (heard in full on the import *Live in Tokyo*) is even fiercer and showcases for the first time some of the tremendous drive WR was capable of, though it doesn't give you much of an idea of its stream-of-consciousness nature. —*Richard S. Ginell*

**Sweetnighter** / Feb. 3, 1973-Feb. 7, 1973 / Columbia ♦♦♦
Right from the start, a vastly different Weather Report emerges here, one that reflects co-leader Joe Zawinul's developing obsession with the groove. It is the groove that rules this mesmerizing album, leading off with the irresistible 3/4 marathon deceptively tagged as the "Boogie Woogie Waltz" and proceeding through a variety of Latin-grounded hipshakers. It is a record of discovery for Zawinul, who augments his Rhodes electric piano with a funky wah-wah pedal, unveils the ARP synthesizer as a melodic instrument and sound-effects device, and often coasts along on one chord. The once-fiery Wayne Shorter

has been tamed, for he now contributes mostly sustained ethereal tunes on soprano sax, his tone sometimes doubled for a pleasing octave effect. The wane of freewheeling ensemble interplay is more than offset by the big increase in rhythmic push; bassist Miroslav Vitous, drummer Eric Gravatt, and percussionist Dom Um Romao are now cogs in one of jazz's great swinging machines. —*Richard S. Ginell*

**Mysterious Traveller** / 1973-1974 / Columbia ♦♦♦
Weather Report's fourth recording finds Wayne Shorter (on soprano and tenor) taking a lesser role as Joe Zawinul begins to really dominate the group's sound. Most selections also include bassist Alphonso Johnson, and drummer Ishmael Wilburn, although the personnel shifts from track to track. "Nubian Sundance" adds several vocalists while "Blackthorn Rose" is a Shorter-Zawinul duet. Overall the music is pretty stimulating and sometimes adventurous; high-quality fusion from 1974. —*Scott Yanow*

**Tale Spinnin'** / 1975 / Columbia ♦♦♦♦
Weather Report's ever-changing lineup shifts again, with the somewhat heavier funk-oriented Leon "Ndugu" Chancler dropping into the drummer's chair and Alyrio Lima taking over the percussion table. As a result, *Tale Spinnin'* has a weightier feel than *Mysterious Traveller*, while continuing the latter's explorations in Latin-spiced electric jazz/funk. Zawinul's pioneering interest in what we now call world music is more in evidence with the African percussion, wordless vocals and sandy sound effects of "Badia," and his synthesizer sophistication is growing along with the available technology. Wayne Shorter's work on soprano sax is more animated than on the previous two albums and Alphonso Johnson puts his melodic bass more to the fore. While not quite as inventive as its two predecessors, this remains an absorbing extension of WR's mid-'70s direction. —*Richard S. Ginell*

**Black Market** / 1976 / Columbia ♦♦♦♦
The shifts in Weather Report's personnel come fast and furious now, with Narada Michael Walden and Chester Thompson as the drummers, Alex Acuna and Don Alias at the percussion table and Alphonso Johnson giving way to the mighty, martyred Jaco Pastorius. It is interesting to hear Pastorius expanding the bass role only incrementally over what the more funk-oriented Johnson was doing at this early point—that is, until "Barbary Coast," where suddenly Jaco leaps athletically forward into the spotlight. Joe Zawinul, or just Zawinul, as he preferred to be billed, contributed all of Side 1's compositions, mostly Third World-flavored workouts except for "Cannon Ball," a touching tribute to his ex-boss Cannonball Adderley (who had died the year before). Shorter, Pastorius, and Johnson split the remainder of the tracks, with Shorter now set in a long-limbed compositional mode for electric bands that would serve him into the '90s. While it goes without saying that most Weather Report albums are transition albums, this diverse record is even more transient than most, paving the way for WR's most popular period while retaining the old sense of adventure. —*Richard S. Ginell*

● **Heavy Weather** / 1977 / Columbia ♦♦♦♦
Weather Report's biggest-selling album is that ideal thing, a popular and artistic success—and for the same reasons. For one thing, Joe Zawinul revealed an unexpectedly potent commercial streak for the first time since his Cannonball Adderley days, contributing what has become a perennial hit, "Birdland." Indeed "Birdland" is a remarkable bit of recordmaking, a unified, ever-developing piece of music that evokes, without in any way imitating, a joyous evening on 52nd St. with a big band. The other factor is the full emergence of Jaco Pastorius as a co-leader; his dancing, staccato bass lifting itself out of the bass range as a third melodic voice, completely dominating his own ingenious "Teen Town" (where he also plays drums!). By now, Zawinul has become WR's de facto commander in the studio; his colorful synthesizers dictate the textures and his conceptions are carefully planned, with little of the freewheeling improvisation of only five years before. Wayne Shorter's saxophones are now reticent, if always eloquent, beams of light in Zawinul's general scheme while Alex Acuna shifts ably over to the drums and Manolo Badrena handles the percussion. Released just as the jazz-rock movement began to run out of steam, this landmark album proved that there was plenty of creative life left in the idiom. —*Richard S. Ginell*

**This Is Jazz, Vol. 10** / Apr. 30, 1996 / Columbia/Legacy ♦♦♦♦
Because most diehard Weather Report enthusiasts already have everything included on this addition to Legacy/Sony's *This Is Jazz* series of compilations, the "best of" CD serves primarily as an introduction to the fusion innovators' breakthroughs of the '70s. While hardly the last word on the band, *This Is Jazz* isn't a bad introduction at all. Naturally, the disc contains Weather's best-known piece, the infectious "Birdland." But equally captivating are the eerie yet funky "Mysterious Traveler," the intriguing "Man in the Green Shirt," the congenial "Young and Fine," the hauntingly abstract "The Moors," and the Asian-influenced "Black Market." Boasting improvisatory, risk-taking and imaginative gems full of blues feeling, *This Is Jazz Vol. 10* is jazz in the truest sense of the word. —*Alex Henderson*

## Will Web

*Producer, DJ / Techno Bass, Electro-Techno, Detroit Techno, Techno*
Will Web is one of a handful of young electro revivalists associated with Detroit's Direct Beat label, also home to such names as Aux 88, K-1, and "Mad" Mike Banks. Like those artists, Web grew up steeped in equal parts early hip-hop (Run-DMC, Ice-T), techno-pop (Kraftwerk, Gary Numan), and first-wave Detroit techno (Model 500, Cybotron), and the breakbeat bias of his music stems from those artists' influence. A DJ through most of the '80s and on into the '90s, Web's first release appeared under his DJ name Mr. Bill (he took the name from the "Saturday Night Live" character) on the *Digital Sects II* compilation on Sean Deason's Matrix label. At Deason's behest, Web passed a tape of unreleased material to Mike Banks (of Direct Beat/Underground Resistance), leading to the release of Web's first DB 12", "Cosmic Drive-By," in 1996. He's since released an additional EP (*Extraterrestrial Phunk*) and contributed a track to the Direct Beat compilation EP, *Experience Da Bass 2*. Web also remixed Cronic Tronic's "King of Bass," also on Direct Beat. He signed to the Astralwerks label in 1997, and released the *Invasion* EP later that year. —*Sean Cooper*

● **Extraterrestrial Phunk** / 1997 / Direct Beat ♦♦♦♦
More techno-oriented than his debut, *Cosmic Drive-By*, this is still techno infused with a bin-pushing mega-dose of breakbeat ghetto-bass. Like the old-school electro-funk it was inspired by, "Extraterrestrial Phunk" is uptempo gear, with fast, jittery electronics accompanying beatwork reminiscent of Drexciya or UR. —*Sean Cooper*

**Invasion [EP]** / Aug. 25, 1997 / Astralwerks ♦♦♦
Will Web's debut for Astralwerks is surprisingly subtle and reserved, with a new focus on production and soundcraft replacing the more bombastic approach of his earlier Direct Beat twelves. Although one track returns to the driving patterns of "Cosmic Drive-By," much of "Invasion" is on a more contemplative kick, with staticky snares paired with melodic lines culled from bizarre deep-space transmissions. —*Sean Cooper*

## Westbam (Maximilian Lenz)

b. Mar. 4, 1965, Münster, Germany
*Producer, DJ / Trance, Club/Dance, Techno, Acid House*
The leader of Germany's house and techno scene since his beginning early in the '80s, Westbam recorded several house/rave crossover hits during the late '80s and early '90s but is renowned for his founding of the Mayday Festival and the Love Parade, the latter of which routinely drew hundreds of thousands of club-goers into the streets of Berlin on an annual basis.

Born in Münster, Maximilian Lenz began DJing in 1983 and became known as Westbam as a shortened version of his original nickname, which he received in honor of his place of birth (Westphalia) and his biggest musical influence (Afrika Bambaataa). He moved to Berlin in 1984, sticking to early industrial dance and hip-hop until American house music began crossing the Atlantic midway through the '80s. He had begun producing as well in 1985, and like many German dance figures, gradually moved from Chicago house to embrace the harder, more Teutonic sounds of Detroit techno during the late '80s. After founding his own Low Spirit Recordings in 1988, Westbam hit the German charts with his first single on the label, "Monkey Say Monkey Do."

He made a surprise appearance at the 1988 Olympic Games in South Korea (representing his country as a cultural contribution) and charted during 1989 with the hits "And Party" and "The Roof Is on Fire." Westbam also released his debut album *The Roof Is on Fire* in 1989. To celebrate his surprising success, Westbam decided to organize an outdoor event that could, he hoped, bring the new dance music out of nightclubs and into the mainstream. Called the Love Parade, it debuted that year with under 500 people. Less than a decade later, the Love Parade would count more than 250,000 participants.

Low Spirit Records counted several hits during the early '90s, by acts Mark Oh and Marusha. Westbam released his second album *A Practising Maniac at Work* in 1991, and founded the Mayday Festival later that year. By the mid-'90s, long after most rave cash-ins had spun themselves out, Westbam was going back into straightahead techno and trance, with singles like 1994's "Celebration Generation" and "Bam Bam Bam" (the title track from his fourth album, which hit the German Top 20). For the tenth anniversary of Low Spirit Recordings, he released *The Age of the DJ Mixer: 10 Years of Low Spirit*, a compilation including several Westbam productions. Two 1997 singles, "Sonic Empire" and "Sunshine" hit the German singles charts (both were official anthems, for Mayday and Love Parade respectively) and prompted a new Westbam album, *We'll Never Stop Living This Way*, which entered the Top 40 of the German charts. —*John Bush*

- **The Roof Is on Fire** / 1989 / Capitol ♦♦♦♦

Dance music has often been called "producer's music," but that isn't always an accurate description. In fact, a lot of dance music (everyone from Donna Summer to Crystal Waters) has been very singer-driven, but at the same time, quite a few dance-oriented releases are very producer-driven. Definitely an example of a producer's album, Westbam's *The Roof Is on Fire* unites samples and scattered soundbites with the DJ/producer's tracks. Highly regarded in dance-music circles in his native Germany, his studio savvy is the thing that brings this energetic collection of house, hip-house and techno to life. In the US, commercial radio ignored such high-tech tracks as "Alarm Clock," "Monkey Say, Monkey Do" and "Miami Bass," but for club hounds, the release of this CD was something to get excited about. Although similar albums can wear thin after awhile, Westbam is inventive enough to hold our attention throughout the album. —*Alex Henderson*

**Bam Bam Bam** / 1994 / Low Spirit/Polydor ♦♦

**We'll Never Stop Living This Way** / Nov. 10, 1997 / Mute ♦♦♦♦
Unlike many of the techno DJs and producers who made furtive trips into electro and big-beat hoping to pay a few bills, Westbam had been spinning and recording breakbeat techno (of a sort) ever since the mid-'80s. Naturally, his breadth of experience gave him a leg up on most others, and as such, *We'll Never Stop Living This Way* is a solid album of forward-thinking retro-techno. It's as much a mix album as a production album, with most of the tracks blending into each other, capped off near the end by the irresistible one-two punch of "Wanna Get My Smurf On" and "Beatbox Rocker." Elsewhere, the Westphalia Bambaataa meets the original Bambaataa on "Agharta, the City of Shamballa," and a heavily processed vocal sample leads the way through the uptempo electro-techno of "Terminator." At times, Westbam works the inevitable big-beat formula into the ground; "Hard Times" is a rather bland pastiche of the break from Run-D.M.C.'s "It's Like That" along with the vocal sample from Kurtis Blow's "Hard Times." Most of the album, however, is a present-day vision of Westbam's fertile past. —*John Bush*

## Wide Receiver

f. 1996, London, England
*Group / Funky Breaks, Electronica, Trip-Hop*
The cinematic-sampling funky-breaks act Wide Receiver was founded by Steve Blood and Ian Gotts. The London-based duo began recording material, and in 1996 sent a demo to Mark Jones, the head of premiere big-beat label Wall of Sound (Propellerheads, Les Rythmes Digitales, Wiseguys). Wide Receiver contributed a track to the Wall of Sound compilation *Dig the Nu Breed*, and followed with the *Get Completely Cained* EP on their own Woof! label in mid-1997. Even at that early date, Blood and Gotts earned a reputation for their sampling prowess—often from hard-as-nails British mod films like *The Italian Job* and *Get Carter* (both featuring Michael Caine). The pair remixed a variety of acts 18 Wheeler, Arkarna, Afrika Bambaataa, and the Cardigans, among others. The single "Breakbeat Sushi" became a club hit after being compiled on Lacerba's *Big Beat Elite, Vol. 2* in early 1998, and Wide Receiver released their album debut *And Finally…* in 2000. —*John Bush*

- **And Finally…** / 2000 / Journees ♦♦

## Damon Wild

b. Dec. 26, 1967, St. Louis, MO
*Producer, DJ / Tech-House, Club/Dance, Techno*
One of the few techno heads in house-crazed New York City, Damon Wild first saw the light of vinyl by recording early-'90s rave hits like "Night Stalker" as Sonic Assault II, "Stormwatch" as Morph, and "Rave Generator" (with Ray Love) as the Toxic Two. In 1991, he began working for distributor Northcott and set up his own Experimental label, releasing tracks from Acid Masters (him and Ray Love) and Lazer Worshippers (Tim Taylor), Aurabora and the Rising Sons. After splitting with Northcott, Wild founded Synewave Records and began to release his own productions plus records by Steve Stoll and Dan Curtin. Wild's own Synewave output was collected on 1999's *Somewhere in Time*. He also mixed a more balanced label retrospective named *Synewave DJ Mix, Vol. 1*. His Morph project also released a full-length, 1994's *Stormwatch*. —*John Bush*

- **Somewhere in Time** / 1999 / Synewave ♦♦♦♦
*Somewhere in Time* includes 14 of Damon Wild's best productions for his own Synewave label, hard-hitting tracks recorded under his own name ("Zoom," "Opaque," "Fluorescence") as well as aliases Subtractive Synthesis ("Motion"), Nitevision ("Spacerace," "Subways"), and Equinox ("Into Battle," "Waves"). —*John Bush*

**Synewave DJ Mix, Vol. 1 1994-99** / Apr. 12, 1999 / Synewave ♦♦♦♦
Though Wild's retrospective of his own Synewave label includes tracks from a few of his many pseudonyms (including Morph, Equinox, and Wild & Taylor), the bulk of this album is solid material by other projects like Blue Maxx, Clint Foster, and Function. Though they're enjoyable enough, the real treats here are the remixes (by Jeff Mills, Joey Beltram, the Advent, Adam Beyer) and Wild's stellar mixing (19 tracks in barely an hour). —*John Bush*

## Wildchild (Roger McKenzie)

b. 1971, Southampton, England, d. Nov. 25, 1995
*Producer / Big Beat, Club/Dance, House*
Roger "Wildchild" McKenzie was the author of the big-beat club anthem "Renegade Master," which became a British hit upon its release in 1995 but gained considerably more worldwide exposure in 1998, more than two years after his untimely death. Based in Southampton before he moved to the future big-beat capital of Brighton around 1991, McKenzie worked as an underground house DJ and recorded four EPs for Loaded Records, each subtitled *Wildtrax*. Indebted to the sampladelic hip-house of Todd Terry, singles like "Bring It on Down" and "Jump to My Beat" were large club anthems presaging the rise of big-beat techno of the sort popularized several years later. McKenzie also formed his own label, Dark & Black, and recorded "Renegade Master" for Norman Cook's Hi-Life Records; a reissue of the single hit No. 11 on the British charts in 1995. Wildchild had only recently switched bases to New York (with his manager and partner Donna Snell) later that year, when he died of a heart condition in November. Wildchild releases continued to flow nevertheless, with a remix of East 17's "Do U Still?" appearing one year later. Norman Cook himself remixed "Renegade Master" in 1997 (under his Fatboy Slim guise), and the track became a club hit once again. —*John Bush*

**Best of Wildtrax** / Sep. 9, 1996 / Loaded ♦♦♦

- **Renegade Master (Remixes) [Single]** / Mar. 3, 1998 / Ultra ♦♦♦♦
*Renegade Master* features several remixes of Wildchild's UK club smash by Fatboy Slim, as well as Stretch & Vern, Tall Paul, and Urban Takeover. —*Steve Huey*

## Hal Willner

b. 1957, Philadelphia, PA
*Producer, Leader, Composer / Experimental Ambient, Modern Creative*
Hal Willner was among the most eclectic and original producers in contemporary music, helming a series of wildly ambitious concept albums that tapped the talents of artists running the gamut from pop to jazz to the avant-garde. Born in Philadelphia in 1957, he first earned notice in 1981 with *Amarcord Nino Rota*, a tribute to the legendary composer best known for his collaborations with filmmaker Federico Fellini; in addition to contributions from pop icon Debbie Harry and jazz piano great Jaki Byard, the collection also featured appearances by then-unknowns Wynton Marsalis and Bill Frisell. That same year, Willner also signed on as the music supervisor for the long-running NBC sketch comedy series "Saturday Night Live," a position he held for many years to follow.

*That's the Way I Feel Now—A Tribute to Thelonious Monk*, a showcase for acts ranging from Dr. John to Joe Jackson to John Zorn, followed in 1984, and a year later Willner launched *Lost in the Stars—The Music of Kurt Weill*, which featured contributions from Sting, Tom Waits, and Lou Reed. After turning to film with work on a pair of 1987 projects—*Heaven* and *Candy Mountain*—Willner earned considerable notice for 1988's *Stay Awake*, a tribute to the classic music of Walt Disney's animated films that featured Ringo Starr, Sun Ra, and Sinéad O'Connor. Animated music remained one of his preoccupations in the years to follow, and in 1990 he assembled *The Carl Stalling Project*, a collection of vintage cartoon scores from the legendary Warner Bros. studio composer. (A sequel appeared in 1995.)

In 1989, Willner began a stint as producer on the innovative but short-lived syndicated television series "Michelob Presents, Night Music", followed in 1992 by *Weird Nightmare—Meditations on Mingus*, another all-star tribute this time featuring Elvis Costello, Keith Richards, and Henry Rollins. A year later, he collaborated with filmmaker Robert Altman on the acclaimed *Short Cuts*, a working relationship which extended into 1996's *Kansas City* and its accompanying *Robert Altman's Jazz '34*. After wrapping up 1998's *Closed on Account of Rabies: Poems and Tales of Edgar Allan Poe* (spotlighting performances by Iggy Pop, Ken Nordine, and Jeff Buckley), Willner signed to Howie B.'s Pussyfoot label to release his proper solo debut, *Whoops, I'm an Indian!* —*Jason Ankeny*

**Amacord Nino Rota** / 1981 / Hannibal ♦♦♦
This tribute to the music of film composer Nino Rota was the first of Hal Willner's unusual multiartist projects and one of his more jazz-oriented ones. Such musicians as pianist Jaki Byard, vibraphonist Dave Samuels, guitarist Bill Frisell, soprano-saxophonist Steve Lacy, trumpeter Wynton Marsalis, and bands headed by Carla Bley, Muhal Richard Abrams, and David Amram are heard from on these eccentric but very musical adaptations of Rota's themes from Fellini movies. —*Scott Yanow*

**That's the Way I Feel Now: A Tribute to Thelonious Monk** / Oct. 1984 / A&M ♦♦♦♦
Two years after the death of pianist-composer Thelonious Monk, this very unusual and quite memorable double-LP tribute was put together. Producer Hal Willner's most successful project, the 23 interpretations of Monk originals all feature a different group of all-star players and stretch beyond jazz. Some of the performances are fairly straightforward while others are quite eccentric; certainly the crazy duet on "Four in One" by altoist Gary Windo and Todd Rundgren (on synthesizers and drum machines) and the version of "Shuffle Boil" featuring John Zorn on game calls (imitating the sound of ducks) are quite unique. There are many colorful moments throughout the project and the roster of musicians is remarkable: Bobby McFerrin with Bob Dorough, Peter Frampton, Joe Jackson, Steve Lacy, Dr. John, Gil Evans, Randy Weston, Roswell Rudd, Eugene Chadbourne and Shockabilly, the Fowler Brothers, NRBQ, Steve Khan, Carla Bley, Barry Harris, Was (Not Was), and many others. There is not a slow moment or uninteresting selection on this highly recommended set. —*Scott Yanow*

**Weird Nightmare: Meditations on Mingus** / Nov. 12, 1992 / Columbia ♦♦♦♦
On this installment of Hal Willner's series of tribute albums, Willner assembled a house band for his guests (including Keith Richards, Chuck D, Elvis Costello, Bill Frisell, Vernon Reid, Charlie Watts, Gary Lucas, Leonard Cohen, and Henry Rollins) to sit in with. *Weird Nightmare—Meditations on Mingus* is predictably uneven and wildly entertaining; it is a fitting tribute to the genius of Charles Mingus —*AMG*

**Closed on Account of Rabies: Tales of Edgar Allan Poe** / Dec. 9, 1997 / Island ♦♦♦
In the tradition of the Hal Willner-produced tributes to Thelonious Monk and Charles Mingus comes Willner's *Closed on Account of Rabies: Tales of Edgar Allen Poe*, a two-disc collection of musical and spoken-word interpretations of classic works including "The Raven," "The Tell-Tale Heart," and "The Conqueror Worm." Among the contributors are Iggy Pop, Marianne Faithfull, Ken Nordine, and Jeff Buckley, as well as actors like Christopher Walken and Gabriel Byrne. —*Jason Ankeny*

• **Whoops, I'm an Indian** / Oct. 19, 1998 / Pussyfoot ♦♦♦♦
For electronic producers, sampling has become less of a revolutionary exercise and more of a matter of course. Hal Willner's long experience with all manner of roots music makes *Whoops, I'm an Indian* a wildly eclectic record, sampling all manner of music from barbershop to tribal chants to "The Star Spangled Banner" to campfire songs. The dark breakbeats forming the background and the album's appearance on Howie B.'s Pussyfoot label make it nominally a dance work, though this is audio experimentalism of a high degree. —*John Bush*

## Windsor for the Derby

f. 1994, Tampa, FL
*Group / Ambient Pop, Experimental Rock, Indie Rock, Post-Rock/Experimental, Alternative Pop/Rock*
Hailing from Tampa, Florida, the founding members of the atmospheric post-rock group Windsor for the Derby—guitarists Dan Matz and Jason McNeeley, along with drummer Greg Anderson—soon migrated to Austin, Texas, where they were signed to the local Trance Syndicate label. Their debut LP, 1996's *Calm Hades Float*, was produced and engineered by Adam Witzie, who agreed to become a full-time Windsor for the Derby member shortly after the project's completion. After issuing the EP *Metropolitan Then Poland* in early 1997, the group closed out the year with the release of the full-length *Minnie Greunzfeldt*. In 1999, they returned with *Difference and Repetition*. —*Jason Ankeny*

**Calm Hades Float** / May 21, 1996 / Trance Syndicate ♦♦♦
As the title suggests, the two-part album *Calm Hades Float* coasts along with a variety of languorous acoustics and pulsing rhythms. —*John Bush*

**Minnie Greunzfeldt** / Nov. 4, 1997 / Trance Syndicate ♦♦♦♦
Windsor for the Derby's second album alternates a few tracks of post-Slint guitar obtuseness ("Stasis," "No Techno with Drums") with the more atmospheric fare of "Bass Trap." Although it's hardly a uniform sound, all of the tracks have a fragile beauty matched by few in the post-rock brigade. —*John Bush*

• **Difference and Repetition** / Jun. 22, 1999 / Young God ♦♦♦♦
Homeless after the shutdown of Trance Syndicate Records, Windsor for the Derby resurfaced on Michael Gira's (ex-Swans') Young God label for *Difference and Repetition*. Assembled over the course of two years (members are geographically spread from Texas to New York City), *Difference* picks up where 1997's splendid *Minnie Greutzfeld* album left off, incorporating vocals more frequently than ever before. Windsor break no molds here, planting both feet firmly amid the territory currently staked out by newer "post-rock" acts like Tristeza or South. In fact, *Difference* bears strong parallels to South's self-titled album, both in the clean, intertwined guitar parts and an allegiance to minimalist composers like Eno, Reich, and Herzog. Still, *Difference* puts the Windsor spin on these familiar influences, revisiting the kind of internal soundtrack that made *Minnie Greutzfeld* so ideal for contemplation. Electronics are more readily apparent, particularly on the synth-addled, almost Pink Floyd-esque "*". "Shaker" imagines Steve Reich and Stars of the Lid composing underwater, while the solemn mellotron melodies of "Nico" abandon modern precedents for a sound right out of the Middle Ages. "Shoes McCoat" takes the minimalist ideals as far as the band ever has, as two guitar parts slowly move in and out of sync with one another over the course of 13 minutes.

Fans of the band's more straightforward guitar/bass/drums compositions will revel in opening track "*" and the gentle motions of "The Egg," two fine uses of simple but pretty melodies and minimal rhythms. An early Pink Floyd vibe (perhaps side two of *Umma Gumma*) is revisited on closer "Lost in Cycles," as a far-off voice adorns a crystalline acoustic guitar melody. With seven songs and only 35 minutes of music, *Difference* is not the grand follow-up to *Minnie Greutzfeld* that some might expect. But it's still a musical diversion well worth exploring. —*Jonathan Cohen*

## Windy & Carl

f. 1991, Dearborn, MI
*Group / Space Rock, Indie Rock, Post-Rock/Experimental*
A leading light of the Michigan space-rock scene, the Dearborn-based duo Windy & Carl comprised guitarist Carl Hultgren and bassist Windy Weber. Hultgren first began recording instrumental guitar-drone pieces in 1992, self-releasing a cassette, *Portal*, before teaming with Weber; by the end of 1993 they issued a single, "Watersong," on their own Blue Flea label. From 1994 to 1995 Windy & Carl expanded to a quartet with the inclusion of guitarist/keyboardist Randall Nieman and percussionist Brenda Markovich; the reconfigured group later issued an EP, *Drifting*, which was credited to Once Dreamt. After the departures of both Nieman (who went on to form Füxa) and Markovich, Windy & Carl continued as a duo, reissuing *Portal* complete with new material in 1995; the LP *Drawing of Sound* followed a year later, and in 1998 the duo resurfaced with *Depths*. —*Jason Ankeny*

**Portal** / Nov. 28, 1995 / Ba Da Bing! ♦♦
The reissued version of Windy & Carl's debut album includes a full hour of

shimmering aural concrete and guitar-feedback ambience, with a focus on space travel indicated by track titles "Preparation," "Sound Ignition," and "Exploration." —*John Bush*

• **Depths** / Mar. 23, 1998 / Kranky ♦♦♦

Though it's another album of slow-building textural ambience, *Depths* is quite organic-sounding compared to the duo's debut. Beside the spacious noise that remains a focus, there are several tracks of faraway guitar-pop ("Silent Ocean" and "Undercurrent" are highlights) including vocals (by Windy) much closer to singing than their previous work. —*John Bush*

## Josh Wink (Josh Winkleman)

b. Philadelphia, PA
*Producer, DJ / Electronica, Club/Dance, Techno, House*

An American producer who simultaneously possessed European hit singles, a major-label album contract, consistent contact with the dance mainstream plus the requisite underground credentials, Josh Wink appeared to lack for nothing at the peak of his success in the mid-'90s. Part of the East Coast/ Philadelphia dance scene, Wink recorded three trance monsters out of his bedroom studio (as Wink, Winx, and Size 9) that topped charts in Europe during 1995 and saw him anointed as a dance poster-boy, easily recognized by his ruddy good looks and flowing blond dreadlocks. Hardly the techno kingpin however, Wink's espousal of a vegan lifestyle and his defiantly anti-drug ideals made him something of a unique personality in the hedonistic world of dance music. After recording his triumvirate of trance hits, Wink soon tempered his singles output to test the waters of album-oriented production as well, releasing *Herehear* in 1998.

After being turned on by punk rock in the '70s, Josh Winkelman was inspired by a diverse group of dance-styled artists during the 1980s—ranging from Depeche Mode to Kraftwerk to Run-D.M.C.—and began working with a Philadelphia-based mobile DJ service from the age of 13. After he met up with a fellow DJ, King Britt, at one party, the duo began recording. One of their first productions, 1990's "Tribal Confusion" by E-Culture, was released on New York's Strictly Rhythm Records and became a success in America's exploding club/rave scene, which Wink and Britt soundtracked by DJing at events around the country. Wink had also recorded for Nervous, another vaunted East Coast dance label, before forming Ovum Records in late 1994 with Britt.

Ovum and Wink had an international club hit right out of the box with 1995's "Liquid Summer;" the single led to Wink recording for a maze of European labels. During 1995, he recorded "Don't Laugh" by Winx, "I'm Ready" by Size 9, and "Higher State of Consciousness" by Winks, all of which topped European dance charts and even made several pop charts despite their debt to hard-edged acid-trance. The singles were collected along with new material for his 1996 debut album, *Left Above the Clouds*, and relased as Winx. The major labels came calling in 1997, and Wink decided to sign not only himself but the entire Ovum Recordings label to a deal with Columbia. After recording with King Britt, Nine Inch Nails' Trent Reznor, poet Ursula Rucker, and Philly mod-punks the Interpreters, Wink released his proper album debut *Herehear* in 1998; the mix album *Profound Sounds Vol. 1* followed the next year. —*John Bush*

**United DJ's of America, Vol. 3** / Feb. 28, 1995 / DMC America ♦♦♦♦

Wink's volume in the *United DJ's of America* series includes tracks from Murk, Soundcraft, Rozzo, and Firefly as well as his own Winx project. —*John Bush*

• **Higher State of Wink Works** / 1996 / Manifesto/Mercury ♦♦♦♦

This seven-track compilation of Wink's seminal early work includes mixes of two of his British hits ("I'm Ready" and "Higher State of Consciousness") plus early E-Culture tracks ("Tribal Confusion," "Unification") recorded with King Britt. —*Keith Farley*

**Left Above the Clouds** / Sep. 9, 1996 / XL Recordings ♦♦♦

After lighting European dancefloors on fire during 1995 with three trance classics, Josh Wink's debut album portrays him as a producer of serious album works. These unfortunate excursions into downtempo trance and spoken-word poetry mar some great sounds over the course of the album's 28 total tracks. Hits like "Don't Laugh" and "Higher State of Consciousness" rescue the proceedings somewhat, though they're definitely the highlights of the album. —*John Bush*

**Herehear** / Jun. 16, 1998 / Ovum ♦♦

After years of successful singles and DJ stints, as well as an ambient excursion titled *Left Above the Clouds*, Josh Wink delivered his first full-fledged album, *Herehear*, in the summer of 1998. Wink took the opportunity to showcase his diversity, and that's part of the problem—*Herehear* wants to be everything to everybody. There's techno, ambient, industrial, house, indie rock, spoken word, jungle, acid—it's a veritable textbook of '90s dancefloor styles. Head-spinning, yes, but a little too overwhelming and unfocused to be consumed all in one sitting. That said, it's an album with some stunning individual moments, whether it's the acid groove "Back in Tha' Day" or Trent Reznor's guest appearance on "Black Bomb." In fact, "Black Bomb" illustrates the main flaw of *Herehear*—taken individually, it's pretty impressive (as are most of the tracks here), but when they're thrown together, they don't make much sense. Still, there's no denying that Wink is a master of production and can create blinding tracks—he just needs to find a way to tie it all together. —*Stephen Thomas Erlewine*

**Profound Sounds, Vol. 1** / Jul. 13, 1999 / Sony ♦♦♦♦

Wink's first volume in a projected series of mix albums, *Profound Sounds* isn't your average collection. Unlike genre-spanning grooves of the past, where DJs attempt to dazzle listeners with a seemingly endless parade of artists given a minute or two at the most, Wink here sounds more like a stadium DJ, with only 14 tracks over an hour of music. The sound progresses from Basic Channel-style dub-techno (courtesy of Johannes Heil and Heiko Laux) into harder tech-house (from a Mood II Swing remix of "When the Funk Hits the Fan" by Wink compatriot King Britt's Sylk 130 project) into repetitious acid lines (tracks by Blaze, Stacey Pullen, LFO's Gez Varley, John Selway) and never lets up until the end of the album. It's a pummeling mix that aligns Wink more with techno purists like Jeff Mills or Dave Angel than late-'90s electronica poster-boys like Chemical Brothers or Prodigy's Liam Howlett, and repositions him away from the mainstream he'd seemed to be courting with his previous full-length, *Herehear*. —*John Bush*

## Wire

f. 1976, London, England, **db.** 1991
*Group / Post-Punk, Alternative Pop/Rock, Punk, Experimental Rock*

Wire's brief, fractured songs and minimalistic sound made the band the artiest of all punk bands, as well as one of the most influential. Unlike most other punk bands, their stripped-down approach was not an attempt to get back to rock's roots; it was cutting the music to its raw nerve, so nothing extraneous was left. On their 1977 debut, *Pink Flag*, Wire managed to tear through 21 songs in under 40 minutes. While the two follow-ups to *Pink Flag*, *Chairs Missing* and *154*, weren't as visionary as the band's debut, they refined and expanded the group's sound, earning great critical praise in the process. Just as the group's cult following was growing, Wire suddenly broke up in late 1979. After spending several years pursuing various solo projects, the band members reunited in 1986. For the next five years, Wire released a series of experimental pop records that generally received popular reviews. However, their cult was slowly shrinking, and the group disbanded for good in 1991. Art students Colin Newman (guitar, vocal), Bruce Gilbert (guitar), Graham Lewis (bass, vocal), and Robert Gotobed (born Mark Field; drums) formed Wire in 1976 after becoming infatuated with the fledgling punk scene. At the time, none of the members knew how to play their instruments, which is one of the reasons why their music had a raw, vital experimental quality. Wire had lone cut on a live punk compilation before signing with Harvest Records in September of 1977. Harvest was known for their prog-rock bands, and in a sense Wire wasn't too far removed from that aesthetic. Though they had a nervy, dissonant avant-pop sound, they approached their music as an art experiment, not as a rock 'n' roll group. As a result, their 1977 debut, *Pink Flag*, was a revolutionary album, a collection of 21 brief songs that displayed a blinding array of ideas. *Pink Flag* was acclaimed by many critics, as was the band's 1978 follow-up, *Chairs Missing*. Produced by Mike Thorne, *Chairs Missing* was a more measured, detailed record that was just as well-received. Boasting a dense, layered production, *154* followed in 1979. Following its release, Wire disbanded, claiming they had exhausted their ideas.

Over the next six years, the band released several live albums and solo projects. In 1986, they decided to re-form, releasing *The Ideal Copy* in 1987. Initially, the reunited Wire was greeted with positive reviews, but the goodwill gradually eroded away, and the band was left with a small, devoted cult following by the early '90s. Frustrated with his bandmates continued experimentations with technology, Gotobed left Wire in 1991 after the release of

*The Drill* EP. The group dropped the "e" from their name and released *The First Letter* as Wir later that year. Following its release, the group quietly disbanded, with Newman, Gilbert and Lewis all pursuing solo projects.

In 1995, Wire experienced a brief revival, as Elastica sampled "Three Girl Rhumba" for their hit single "Connection" and Menswear revamped the band's angular riffs into bubblegum. No member of Wire publicly supported either group, though Newman and Elastica's Justine Frischmann later collaborated on a one-off project in 1997. —*Stephen Thomas Erlewine*

### Chairs Missing / Aug. 1978 / Restless ♦♦♦♦

*Chairs Missing* marks a partial retreat from *Pink Flag's* austere, bare-bones minimalism, although it still takes concentrated listening to dig out some of the melodies. Producer Mike Thorne's synth adds a Brian Eno-esque layer of atmospherics, and Wire itself seems more concerned with the sonic textures they can coax from their instruments; the tempos are slower, the arrangements employ more detail and sound effects, and the band allows itself to stretch out on a few songs. The results are a bit variable—"Mercy," in particular, meanders for too long—but compelling much more often than not. The album's clear high point is the statement of purpose "I Am the Fly," which employs an emphasis-shifting melody and guitar sounds that actually evoke the sound of the title insect. But that's not all by any means—"Outdoor Miner" and "Used To" have a gentle lilt, while "Sand in My Joints" is a brief anthem worthy of *Pink Flag*, and the four-minute "Practice Makes Perfect" is the best result of the album's incorporation of odd electronic flavors. In general, the lyrics are darker than those on *Pink Flag*, even morbid at times; images of cold, drowning, pain, and suicide haunt the record, and the title itself is a reference to mental instability. The arty darkness of *Chairs Missing*, combined with the often icy-sounding synth/guitar arrangements, helps make the record a crucial landmark in the evolution of punk into post-punk and goth, as well as a testament to Wire's rapid development and inventiveness. [The CD reissue contains three bonus tracks: the fine non-LP single "A Question of Degree" and the B-sides "Go Ahead" and "Former Airline."] —*Steve Huey*

### ● 154 / 1979 / Restless ♦♦♦♦

Named for the number of live gigs Wire had played to that point, *154* refines and expands the innovations of *Chairs Missing*, with producer Mike Thorne's synthesizer effects playing an even more integral role; little of *Pink Flag's* rawness remains. If *Chairs Missing* was a transitional album between punk and post-punk, *154* is squarely in the latter camp, devoting itself to experimental soundscapes that can sound cold and forbidding at times. However, the best tracks retain their humanity thanks to the arrangements' smooth, seamless blend of electronic and guitar textures and the beauty of the group's melodies. Where previously some of Wire's hooks could find themselves buried or not properly brought out, the fully fleshed-out production of *154* lends a sweeping splendor to "The 15th," the epic "A Touching Display," "A Mutual Friend," and the gorgeous (if obscurely titled) "Map Ref. 41°N 93°W." Not every track is a gem, as the group's artier tendencies occasionally get the better of them, but *154's* best moments help make it at least the equal of *Chairs Missing*. It's difficult to believe that a band that evolved as quickly and altered its sound as restlessly as Wire did could be out of ideas after only three years and three albums, but such was the case according to its members, and with their (temporary, as it turned out) disbandment following this album, Wire's most fertile and influential period came to a close. [The CD reissue features four bonus tracks from an experimental EP issued with some copies of the vinyl LP.] —*Steve Huey*

### The Ideal Copy / 1987 / Enigma ♦♦♦

Wire's first new full-length effort in eight years is a stunning comeback picking up where *154* left off while also reflecting the strides made by the members' solo work. Finding its footing in dark, edgy dance rhythms and ominous digital textures, *The Ideal Copy* is experimental and forward-thinking, spanning from the buzzing melodies of "Ahead" and "Ambitious" to the taut minimalism of "Feed Me;" the record has its flaws, but its restless creative spirit and refusal to rest on past glories make it one of the few reunion efforts that actually matters. —*Jason Ankeny*

### A Bell Is a Cup . . . Until it Is Struck / 1988 / Enigma ♦♦♦

Like *The Ideal Copy*, *A Bell Is a Cup...Until It Is Struck* continues to push Wire into avant-dance territory, tempering the music's digital rhythms with an increasingly strong sense of melodic ingenuity. More inviting and accessible than the previous recording (or, for that matter, the vast majority of the group's prior work), the album relies heavily on textured guitar patterns to create a warm, dreamy sound; the songs follow suit, spinning surreal, densely free-associative narratives which further enhance the record's abstract allure. —*Jason Ankeny*

### It's Beginning To & Back Again / May 1989 / Enigma ♦♦♦

Begun as a collection of live recordings cut in Chicago and Portugal, the songs which comprise *IBTABA* were subsequently reconstructed in the studio to the point of becoming virtually unrecognizable. The material largely reprises tracks from *A Bell Is a Cup*... along with a number of new cuts, highlighted by the single "Eardrum Buzz;" while the record is respectable on its own terms, it's impossible to discern its relevance—neither a true live album nor a remix collection, its original intentions remain lost in the translation. —*Jason Ankeny*

### Manscape / May 1990 / Restless ♦♦

Wire's gradual move toward dance music and techno becomes complete on *Manscape*. Syncopated beats, synths, and sequencer riffs are the dominant musical motifs, with Graham Lewis taking a larger share of the vocal turns. Still, what the group has gained in technical acumen over time has been lost in tension and interpersonal dynamics; taken for what it is, *Manscape* is edgy, brainy dance music, but taken as part of the largely brilliant Wire oeuvre, it's a disappointment. —*Jason Ankeny*

### The First Letter / Oct. 29, 1991 / Mute ♦♦

With *The First Letter* Wire renamed itself Wir and continued its move toward more detailed soundscapes. Like the previous *Manscape*, the vocals mean considerably less than the musical textures—it's all about the sound, not the song. Some of the soundscapes are quite interesting, but much of the music fails to be compelling. Nevertheless, the concentration on sonic textures made it no surprise that Colin Newman began pursuing a career as a techno label owner after the album's release. —*Stephen Thomas Erlewine*

### 1985-1990: The A List / May 18, 1993 / Elektra ♦♦♦♦

*1985-1990: The A List* is a fine 16-track compilation of the highlights from Wire's surprising and successful comeback. This material isn't quite as essential as their early output—Wire doesn't sound as revolutionary on these sides, although the music is still high quality. It bears some similarities to the sort of '80s college-radio synth/guitar-pop being produced by the likes of New Order and the Cure, although it isn't as danceable, and it retains Wire's signature love of dissonance and pure sonic oddity. The more controlled, polished sound of this material may tone down the heady excitement of their early albums, or seem a bit mechanical at times, but it's intriguing to hear the high tech production values that were missing from their initial attempts at creating layers of detail in their arrangements, and there are some fine pop songs here as well. *The A List* could have been sequenced better—its track listing was determined through a poll of fans, various critics, and band associates, and the selections were simply arranged according to which ones the largest number of votes, meaning that the compilation loses a little steam since many of the best songs appear toward the beginning. Still, that's a minor flaw, especially since *The A List* is such a handy overview of their uneven comeback albums. It's the best way to hear catchy slices of post-punk avant-pop like "Ahead," "Kidney Bingos," "Eardrum Buzz," and "In Vivo," and for all but the most devoted, *The A List* is probably all that's necessary from this period. —*Steve Huey*

### Dugga Dugga Dugga / Dec. 15, 1998 / WMO ♦♦♦♦

*Dugga Dugga Dugga* is an amazing collaboration of artists interpreting Wire's "Drill." It's a collaboration, as opposed to compilation, because due to final engineering by London artist Mark Gage (Vapourspace, Cusp, Carl Marks), the material was milled, sieved, and refined so that the final recording is as a single composition, an extended version of "Drill" where one track seamlessly segues to the next, held together by the repeated, if transformed, theme. Wire, or now Wir, is so enamored of the piece that it appears on at least five recordings and became a 30-minute portion of the band's live set. The alchemists of electronica called in to brew this 14-part potion are Baboon, Chris & Cosey, Electric Company, the Ex-Lion Tamers, and others. No portion of the final product is directly identified as originating with any of the listed contributors. By finalizing the product as a continuous mix of variations, Wire elevated what could have been one more of many, awkward tribute albums into a cohesive, apotheosis of the piece, a grand opus of multiple derivations. This injection of a compositional, visionary element into what is an electronica concept album exploits the possibilities of the genre (simultaneous, parallel processing of a

## The Wiseguys
f. 1994, London, England
*Group / Big Beat, Trip-Hop, Club/Dance*

Emigrés from the British underground hip-hop scene, Wiseguys Touché and Regal made some of the most intense productions in the world of upfront big-beat techno. Releasing their material on Wall of Sound Records (also home to Propellerheads and Les Rythmes Digitales), the duo recorded a pair of albums as well as numerous EPs and singles. The duo met up while at college and connected via their mutual affinities for rap and DJing. Regal, already a member of a hip-hop collective known as Direct Current, invited Touché to join. The pair began recording on their own as well and after leaving Direct Current in 1992 and released tracks on Blackmarket International including the Wiseguys' debut, 1994's *Ladies Say Ow!* EP. Wall of Sound released the duo's first album *Executive Suite* in 1996. After Regal left for other projects, Touché released the quasi-solo album *The Antidote*. The single "Ooh La La" became a huge breakbeat party anthem, sampled by movie soundtracks, cable channels, and sports stadiums around the world. —*John Bush*

Executive Suite / Jun. 10, 1996 / Wall of Sound ♦♦

● The Antidote / Oct. 5, 1998 / Wall of Sound ♦♦♦♦
Who would have figured that the English are, in reality, much less uptight and more genuinely humorous than Americans? The evidence lies in the hip-hop music that emanates from each nation. Mainstream American hip-hop of the late '90s consists mostly of posture or paranoia or darkness, a preoccupation with money, style, and MCing, while mainstream British hip-hop such as that spun by Touche (born Theo Keating, founder of influential British dance music imprint, Wall of Sound), who calls himself the Wiseguys and whose single "Ooh La La" rapidly shot to No. 2 in its native country on the back of a Budweiser commercial, is stylish, mostly instrumental, and completely fun. On his debut as the Wiseguys, *The Antidote*, Touche fills his songs with familiar and unfamiliar vocal samples alike—often the very same samples that American hip-hop DJs use with earnest reverence—but places them in soundscapes full of buoyant brass and strings, lighthearted sound affects, and clever samples; what results is hip-hop that doesn't take itself seriously even as it does take seriously the history from which it comes and the legacy that it continues. Of course, *The Antidote* is grounded just as firmly in the British dance scene as it is in hip-hop, but that only enlarges the bag from which Touche pulls his tricks, and, arguably, places him in more of a direct line with Afrika Bambaataa and the early hip-hop innovators (as well as their disciples such as DJ Shadow and Dust Brothers) than are most practitioners in the American hip-hop milieu. It is certainly much more open to sounds and textures, so that even when MCs do grace the tracks with their toasting (various MCs, most prevalently Americans Sense Live and Season, appear on a total of four songs)—such as the immaculate "Experience," which opens with Pete Rock-type muted horns before really hitting its stride with a perfectly-placed piano sample—the songs end up sounding gloriously alien and entirely wonderful, much the same way as the Reprazent crew has reconfigured hip-hop into something propulsive and exciting and continental that avoids the cliches of the form even while still retaining its core sense of purpose. Touche's production hits so many highs that it's impossible to take the music, with its emphasis on '60s and '70s funk and soul as well as old-school hip-hop, for granted. The album is so packed full of great and fun sounds that it can be utilized either as dancefloor juice or a headphone soundtrack with equally compelling results. As for its place in hip-hop, it may not exactly be the antidote, but an antidote it is, indeed. —*Stanton Swihart*

## Wishmountain (Matthew Herbert)
*Producer / Experimental Techno, Electro-Techno, Techno, House*

A near-academic sampling project begun by Matthew Herbert of Doctor Rockit, Wishmountain debuted with two 1996 EPs (*Radio* and *Video*) recorded for Global Communication's Evolution label. The double-pack EP *Wishmountain Is Dead* followed on Phonography, and a separate CD release, also titled *Wishmountain Is Dead*, collected much of the previous Wishmountain material. [See Also: Doctor Rockit, Herbert] —*John Bush*

● Wishmountain Is Dead / Jan. 4, 1999 / Antiphon ♦♦♦♦
Even though his Herbert recordings tend to focus on sound source experimentation to an uncommon degree, Matt Herbert's Wishmountain project makes the relationship much more direct. The titles ("Toaster," "Golf," "Cheesegrater," "Bottle") of most of the tracks here are good clues to just what is being sampled, and the sources appear just a bit more upfront than the rest of the productions: Witness the cut-up "Royal Wedding," a beatless and haunting piece that twists Charles and Di's vows to sound like it was recorded centuries earlier. Overall, *Wishmountain Is Dead* just isn't as fascinating or propulsive as the rest of Herbert's remarkable material. —*John Bush*

## Witchman (John Roome)
*Producer / Experimental Jungle, Dark Ambient, Trip-Hop, Jungle/Drum'N'Bass, Club/Dance*

Often compared with gloomy breakbeat industrialists Scorn and Techno Animal, the dubbed up drum'n'bass of Witchman has as much in common with jungle paranoids Nico and Ed Rush and the gothic techno of Disjecta and Meat Beat Manifesto. Combining heavy, space-filling drum sequences—alternately split- and double-time—with piles and piles of effects units and daubs of ominous synth patches, Witchman lies somewhere near the intersection of Jamaican dub, early hip-hop, ambient, and the darker side of bleep techno. The singular project of one John Roome, Witchman followed Roome's stint as vocalist for Terminal Power Company, an industrial metal band. A longtime devotee of the Swans and Dead Can Dance, Roome stumbled onto a solo recording career by accident, assembling a demo on a whim before landing a contract some months later (his aspirations were originally in film). Early on, Roome released more remix and compilation tracks than work out under his own name (he's remixed Gary Numan and Nefilim and been included on compilations for Rising High, Volume, and Virgin, among others). After a quick single for Blue Angel, Roome's first EP, *The Shape of Rage* was released by the experimental Leaf label in early 1996, and quickly nailed an audience into jungle's darker, more abstract possibilities. After some record-label confusion (with Blue Angel parent-label Rising High in financial turmoil), he finally hooked up with Deviant in 1996 to release the *Nightmare Alley* double-EP, followed in 1997 by the full-length *Explorimenting Beats*. The Jammin' Unit collaboration *Inferno* appeared in 1998 on Invisible. —*Sean Cooper*

The Shape of Rage [EP] / 1996 / Leaf ♦♦♦
A three-track stormer near the top of the Leaf label's already stunning repertoire. Witchman's John Roome is clearly out for more than club tracks here, with the A-side covered entirely by the chilling, 15-plus-minute "Offworld." While Roome does tend to stretch some of his ideas a bit thin (particularly the breakbeat delays that dominate much of his work), his attention to space and atmosphere is nothing short of cinematic. —*Sean Cooper*

● Explorimenting Beats / Apr. 28, 1997 / Deviant ♦♦♦♦
After only a pair of EPs for Rising High and Leaf Recordings, Witchman's John Roome became one of the hotter properties of the experimental drum'n'bass set. Quickly cobbled onto a handful of jungle comps and sped into the disappointing double-pack *Nightmare Alley*, however, the impression was given that perhaps Roome had spent his chips. Not so, it would appear, since his first full-length is the sort of album those early EPs suggested Roome was capable of. A gloomy, foreboding collection of tracks alternating between roiling, mutant breakbeat and sludgy downtempo, this ain't no dancefloor jungle, but rather music for headphone meditation best explored with the lights low and the senses, er, *distracted*. Warped, dense, and varied. —*Sean Cooper*

Heavy Traffic / Feb. 3, 1998 / Deviant ♦♦♦
A double-disc compilation that includes just about every scrap of non-LP Witchman material previously released, *Heavy Traffic* features tracks from his two EPs for Deviant (*Heavy Mental, Nightmare Alley*) and the two released on Rising High (*States of Mind, Main Vein*) plus tracks from several compilations (*Avantgardism, State of the Nu Art*). Perfect for fans, but overwhelming for anyone else. —*Keith Farley*

## Wolfgang Press
f. 1983, London, England
*Group / Alternative Dance, Alternative Pop/Rock, Avant-Garde*

Enigmatic, moody, and challenging, Britain's Wolfgang Press were one of the most mercurial talents of the post-punk era, restlessly moving from Gothic noise to dark balladry to eccentric funk; paradoxically, the group was also the 4AD label's longest tenured artist—even their stylish album packages were all the product of the same designer, Alberto Ricci.

## WOLFGANG PRESS

Formed in London in 1983, the Wolfgang Press comprised vocalist Michael Allen, guitarist Andrew Gray, and keyboardist Mark Cox. Allen and Cox first teamed in the group Rema Rema, which also featured Adam and the Ants alum Marco Perroni; after reuniting in the short-lived quartet Mass, the duo recruited Gray, and as the Wolfgang Press issued their cacophonous, gloomy debut LP *The Burden of Mules* in 1983. An EP trilogy co-produced by Cocteau Twin Robin Guthrie followed in quick succession: While 1984's *Scarecrow* was a lighter, more streamlined affair, 1985's *Water* spotlighted ominously sparse torch songs, and the same year's *Sweatbox* explored deconstructionist pop.

The Wolfgang Press' second full-length effort, 1986's *Standing Up Straight*, incorporated industrial and orchestral influences into the mix, while the *Big Sex* EP's "God's Number" offered a soulful backing chorus, a harbinger of things to come. Indeed, after 1988's hypnotic *Bird Wood Cage* and its leadoff single "King of Soul" introduced strong elements of dub, reggae, and R&B, the trio took the full plunge into the dance arena with 1991's *Queer*, an idiosyncratic outing admittedly inspired by De La Soul's landmark *Three Feet High and Rising;* the first single, a surreal cover of the Randy Newman-penned "Mama Told Me Not to Come," was a minor hit. 1995's *Funky Little Demons* completed the Wolfgang Press' transition into white funk; prior to its release, however, Cox exited the group's ranks. —*Jason Ankeny*

**The Burden of Mules** / 1983 / 4AD ♦♦

Dark, noisy and intense, the Wolfgang Press' debut *The Burden of Mules* remains among the group's most impenetrable efforts; tracks like "Lisa (The Passion)," "Prostitute," (in two parts) and "Compleate and Utter" are so morose and vehement as to verge on self-parody. —*Jason Ankeny*

● **The Legendary Wolfgang Press & Other Stories** / 1985 / Nesak ♦♦♦♦

*The Legendary Wolfgang Press & Other Stories* compiles the EPs *Scarecrow, Water,* and *Sweatbox,* three strong, eclectic efforts produced by the Cocteau Twins' Robin Guthrie. Displaying marked leaps in sophistication and textural variety over their earliest work, the set establishes the trio as witty and incisive pop deconstructionists: A tongue-in-cheek cover of Otis Redding's "Respect" reveals a newfound sense of humor, while Neil Young's "Heart of Gold" undergoes such a radical transformation that it even receives a new title, "Heart of Stone." —*Jason Ankeny*

**Standing Up Straight** / 1986 / Nesak ♦♦♦♦

The ambitious *Standing Up Straight* builds on the eclecticism of the EPs collected on *The Legendary Wolfgang Press,* further broadening the trio's horizons by layering their dark, unforgiving sound with elements of industrial and classical music. While "Hammer the Halo" and "Rotten Fodder" in particular stand out as two of the group's most aggressive efforts, the intensity level remains high throughout—a challenging, even punishing album, but a rewarding one as well. —*Jason Ankeny*

**Bird Wood Cage** / 1988 / 4AD ♦♦♦♦

*Bird Wood Cage* remains one of the most pivotal records in the Wolfgang Press catalog; here, the trio begins to incorporate the dance and funk elements which would ultimately emerge as the dominant facet of their work.

The lead single "King of Soul," with its female backing chorus, is the first tipoff, while the Talking Heads-like "Kansas" adopts wah-wah guitar line; a bit of dub even underscores "Hang on Me (For Papa)." Michael Allen's forbidding vocals are also warmer and more soulful, and while the group's trademark gloom hangs over the proceedings, a significant transformation in both musical and emotional outlook is clearly afoot, leaving *Bird Wood Cage* as the bridge from Wolfgang Press' past to their future. —*Jason Ankeny*

**Queer** / Jun. 1991 / 4AD ♦♦♦

Recorded with the aid of ex-Throwing Muses bassist Leslie Langston, *Queer* is Wolfgang Press' leap into the world of dance music. The cover of Randy Newman's "Mama Told Me (Not to Come)" underscores the record's stranger-in-a-strange-land vibe as Michael Allen's dramatic vocals and arcane obsessions collide head-on with the ecstatic physicality and immediacy of the dancefloor; cold and remote, the result is alien funk, a collection of idiosyncratic rhythms, dark textures, and ominous grooves. —*Jason Ankeny*

**Funky Little Demons** / Jan. 24, 1995 / 4AD ♦♦♦

Wolfgang Press continues its trademark kitsch-dance with *Funky Little Demons,* an album that boasts a more focused production than some previous records without sacrificing any of their style. —*Stephen Thomas Erlewine*

## Stevie Wonder (Stevland Morris)

b. May 13, 1950, Saginaw, MI

*Vocals, Piano (Electric), Keyboards, Piano, Harmonica / Pop-Soul, Pop/Rock, Motown, Urban, Funk*

When Stevie Wonder began recording in 1962, he was only eleven years old. Even then, his talent was evident, although there was no sign of how deep it was. After all, the music was the work of a startlingly gifted child; it was all exuberant flash, with few complexities. Soon, Wonder would go far beyond the infectious energy of "Fingertips (Part 2)." In two years, he became one of Motown's finest artists, recording a series of brilliant singles for a solid nine years, the overwhelming majority of which he wrote himself. During this time, his albums were like other Motown albums—a combination of killer singles and pleasant filler, only Wonder was allowed to record the occasional number that reflected his increasing social consciousness, like his hit version of Bob Dylan's "Blowin' in the Wind." By the end of the '60s, he was not only hitting the charts with his own records, but writing material for many other Motown artists, including the Spinners' "It's a Shame" and cowriting "The Tears of a Clown" with Smokey Robinson.

With his creativity growing by leaps and bounds, Wonder soon felt limited by Motown's strict production and publishing contracts. When his record contract expired in 1971, Wonder recorded two full albums by himself and used them as a bargaining tool during contract negotiations with Motown. The record label gave him total artistic control of his albums, as well as the rights to his own songs. Soon afterwards, the two albums—*Where I'm Coming From* and *Music of My Mind*—were released.

*Music of My Mind*, especially, helped usher in a new era of soul/R&B. Along with Sly Stone and Marvin Gaye, Wonder made soul and R&B albums not just collections of singles, but cohesive artistic statements wherein artists could extend their music beyond the confines of a three-minute hit single. The album also benefited from the increasing technology behind electric keyboards and synthesizers; engineers Robert Margouleff and Malcolm Cecil, who'd worked closely with instrument-maker Bob Moog to produce the largest Moog synthesizer in the world (T.O.N.T.O., an acronym for The Original New Timbral Orchestra), introduced Wonder to Moog and Arp synthesizers, which he used along with clavinet, clavichord, and organ on *Music of My Mind*. From that point on, incorporating synthesizers and studio-as-instrument production values became Wonder's continuing focus throughout the '70s.

With his next two albums, 1972's *Talking Book* and 1973's *Innervisions*, Wonder's music became richly complex and inventive; in addition to his musical innovations, Wonder's lyrics addressed social and racial issues as eloquently and incisively as any other pop songwriter. He sustained his creative peak through 1974's *Fulfillingness' First Finale* and 1976's *Songs in the Key of Life,* though the ambitious and bewildering 1979 LP *Journey Through the Secret Life of Plants* was perceived as a misstep and received terrible reviews upon its release. Wonder released the more straightforward *Hotter than July* in 1980; the album received substantially better reviews and became his first platinum album. However, he wasn't able to sustain that momentum for the rest of the decade. Although his records sold well and he scored the occasional hit—including the smash hit ballad "I Just Called to Say I Love You"—his albums weren't as focused as they were a decade earlier. By the '90s, he was still an immensely respected musician, but his music was no longer on the cutting edge. —*Stephen Thomas Erlewine*

**Where I'm Coming From** / Apr. 12, 1971 / Motown ♦♦♦♦

Released one month before Stevie Wonder's 21st birthday, *Where I'm Coming From* is really his first adult album, and although it was not a massive hit, it anticipated the musical approach of his commercial breakthrough, *Talking Book,* by a year and a half. The lovely "Never Dreamed You'd Leave In Summer," as the B-side to a cover of The Beatles' "We Can Work It Out," has become a Wonder standard, and the album's real hit, "If You Really Love Me" (No. 8 pop, No. 4 R&B), marked the first rewards of his alliance with then-wife Syreeta Wright. Elsewhere, Wonder, who produced and composed all the tracks, introduced the funky keyboard style that would take him through the next few years, as well as the social concerns that would absorb him later on. This album was a shot across the bow, fair warning that a major, nearly mature talent had arrived. —*William Ruhlmann*

**Music of My Mind** / Mar. 3, 1972 / Motown ♦♦♦♦

When Wonder turned 21, he renegotiated his Motown contract; the key issue was control. Stevie Wonder had a vision that veered far away from that of the Motown hit-making machine. Influenced by the work of Isaac Hayes in 1969 and 1970 and labelmate Marvin Gaye in 1971, Wonder was no longer content with putting out albums that were a collection of two or three hit singles plus filler; he wanted to record full-length albums that had an integrity unto themselves. *Music of My Mind* was the first such effort. Wonder produced, wrote the songs, and played the majority of the instruments. At the time it was a revelation. Compared with Wonder's subsequent efforts, it pales just slightly. —*Rob Bowman*

★ **Talking Book** / Oct. 27, 1972 / Motown ✦✦✦✦✦
*Talking Book* is the album that crystallized Wonder as the self-contained singer/songwriter. "Superstition" and "You Are the Sunshine of My Life" were both No. 1 singles. The rest of the album maintains an equally torrid level. —*Rob Bowman*

★ **Innervisions** / Aug. 3, 1973 / Motown ✦✦✦✦✦
The political undercurrents long simmering in Stevie Wonder's work reached their boiling point on the masterful *Innervisions*, a record as potent and insightful in its exploration of contemporary life as Marvin Gaye's *What's Going On* two years earlier. The opening "Too High," an acute condemnation of drug use, quickly establishes the record's forceful yet vibrant tone, which alternates between utopian dreamscapes ("Visions") and tough-minded realism ("Jesus Children of America"); the record's dueling concerns converge on the hit "Living for the City," which is both a brilliant examination of the myriad social ills so endemic to the ghetto experience and a stirring celebration of African-American resilience. And on "Higher Ground," Wonder even points a finger at himself to detail a sinner's second chance at life—a song that took on even greater resonance in the wake of the car crash that nearly killed him just months after the LP's release. —*Jason Ankeny*

**Fulfillingness' First Finale** / Jul. 22, 1974 / Motown ✦✦✦✦
The music of Stevie Wonder could never be measured by chart activity. His views, ranging from life and love to social and political issues, are so profound. This album has one classic soul recording after another in spite of just two singles charting, the first being "You Haven't Done Nothing." With its mid-tempo groove and spirited horn arrangement, this socially conscious number was a No. 1 single for two consecutive weeks on the *Billboard* R&B charts. The second release was the Caribbean-inspired "Boogie on Reggae Woman." In tribute to Bob Marley, Wonder concocts a stuttering, rigid bassline complemented by his unconfined vocal delivery. "Reggae Woman" hit the top of the charts at No. 1, holding that position for two consecutive weeks as well. Though there were no other charted singles from this set, more mellow compositions like "Heaven Is Ten Zillion Light Years Away," "Too Shy to Say," and "Creepin'" received airplay during this album's heyday. Luther Vandross did an outstanding remake of the latter. Wonder's music is thought provoking, from the melody to the lyrics. It's easy to get lost in the melody, whether it's funky or mellow, and overlook the lyrics. Moreover, Deniece Williams and Minnie Riperton as background vocalists just enchances the mood this album imparts. —*Craig Lytle*

**Songs in the Key of Life** / Sep. 28, 1976 / Motown ✦✦✦✦
Three long years in the making, *Songs in the Key of Life* is a work of monumental brilliance, two LPs and a bonus EP worth of Stevie Wonder at his mid-'70s peak. Always on the cutting edge of modern recording technology, the album is a tour de force of studio wizardry, yet it's also a deeply personal and humane work that in many regards marks the culmination of Wonder's career to date. Deftly blending the trenchant social commentary of his recent work with an exuberance harking back to his earliest records, *Songs in the Key of Life* also resonates with a renewed spiritual dimension that lends the music even greater impact; taken as a whole, the album tells his life story, spanning from childhood ("I Wish") to the birth of his own daughter ("Isn't She Lovely") and taking time out to pay respects to the masters of jazz ("Sir Duke"), illuminate the struggles of the inner city ("Village Ghetto Land"), and confront society's ills ("Pastime Paradise," the basis of Coolio's massive 1995 rap hit "Gangsta's Paradise"). At times it's self-indulgent, to be sure, but even at nearly two hours in length, *Songs in the Key of Life* possesses the kind of craft, pacing, and overall proportion sorely lacking from most albums even a third as long, and Wonder has yet to revisit its glorious peaks in the years since. —*Jason Ankeny*

**Journey Through the Secret Life of Plants** / Oct. 30, 1979 / Motown ✦✦✦
Perhaps the most curious album in Stevie Wonder's career, this was ostensibly a soundtrack for a film few people saw (if indeed it was ever released). These were mostly instrumentals, plus a few oddball vocals, but most observers didn't know what to make of it at the time. Wonder was so hot that the record peaked at No. 4 on the pop albums chart, despite the lack of any real singles and confounding almost everyone who heard it. "Outside My Window" was the lone tune to scrape the middle regions of the pop charts, while the R&B community ignored the entire album. —*Ron Wynn*

**Hotter Than July** / Sep. 29, 1980 / Motown ✦✦✦✦
*Hotter Than July* was Wonder's real follow-up to *Songs in the Key of Life*, even if it took him the then-unconsciously long four years to release it. Wonder had been perhaps the most accomplished and successful pop artist of the years 1972-1977, but his absence had cooled him off commercially, and this album demonstrated that, artistically, he was also past his peak. Individual moments suggested his earlier triumphs, and Wonder remained a remarkably facile singer/player/composer, but he had lost his ability to amaze his listeners. The album's biggest single was "Master Blaster (Jammin')" (No. 5 pop, No. 1 R&B), an adequate but unremarkable reggae number, but the standout track was "Happy Birthday," the theme song for the ultimately successful campaign to make Dr. Martin Luther King, Jr.'s birthday a national holiday. —*William Ruhlmann*

## Woob (Paul Frankland)

*Producer / Electronica, Ambient Techno, Ambient Dub*

Woob is UK-based ambient dub musician Paul Frankland, whose albums for Em:t Recordings are among the most praised and encompassing documents of post-rave ambient of the last several years. Incorporating Middle Eastern instrumentation and vocalese with Jamaican dub-style production, tight, snappy breakbeats, blankets of synth drone and melody, and heaps of treated samples and field recordings, Woob is a sort of state-of-the-art snapshot of heavily hybridized post-rave experimental ambient. Frankland first came to attention through his participation in a Future Music talent competition held at London's Wembley stadium, refereed by, among others, Mixmaster Morris (of Dreamfish and Irresistible Force fame). Frankland's entry in the seminar/competition—a four-track demo tape—was praised highly by Morris and subsequently passed to a number of British music journalists, leading to Frankland's relationship with the Nottingham-based Em:t label. Frankland released his first album as Woob, *1194*, through Em:t and has since contributed tracks to many of their compilations, as well as releasing a follow-up full-length, *4495*. Stateside reissue of *1194* by the widely-distributed Instinct label has also given a boost to Woob's visibility, and Frankland's popularity is at or near that of his comparatively more prodigious contemporaries. In addition to his Woob work, Frankland also records (together with DJ Colin Waterton) as Journeyman for the Ntone label. The pair's work is similar to Frankland's own, although the Middle Eastern elements are largely replaced by less localizable, heavily treated and manipulated influences. [See Also: Journeyman] —*Sean Cooper*

● **Woob 1194** / 1994 / Instinct ✦✦✦✦
A lengthy, seamless fusion of Western and non-Western electronic and acoustic elements, interspersed with soundbites and film samples, with a level of emotional engagement and compositional sophistication rare in music of this type. Uniformly enthralling. —*Sean Cooper*

**4495** / 1995 / Em:t ✦✦✦✦
Quite a bit more experimental than the first, and using a wider palette of sounds. The 20-plus-minute centerpiece, "Depart," harkens back, but for the most part Frankland dwells in heavy percussion, acoustical elements, and overall more disjointed arrangements. —*Sean Cooper*

## :wumpscut: (Rudy Ratzinger)

*Producer / Electro-Industrial, Industrial Dance, Industrial*

Another in the line of '90s goths who forsook guitars for the sampler and synthesizer, Rudy Ratzinger's :wumpscut: project was born in 1991 when Ratzinger released his first cassette-only albums, *Defcon* and *Small Chambermusicians*. Vuz Records signed the German to their fold the following year, and after a release on a 1993 Vuz compilation (*New Forms of Entertainment*), the first :wumpscut: album, *Music for a Slaughtering Tribe*, appeared in December 1993. After the release of the *Dried Blood* EP on Ant-Zen Records in 1994, Ratzinger formed his own Beton Kopf Media label in 1995 and released both another EP and a full-length that year (*Gomorrha* and *Bunkertor 7*, respectively). After the appearance of :wumpscut: on the US compilation *The Remix Wars*—alongside haujobb—the Metropolis label signed Ratzinger to an American deal and re-released the entirety of his work, followed by the new full-length *Embryodead*. *Born Again* followed in 1998, and two years later :wumpscut: returned with *Bloodchild*. —*John Bush*

- **Embryodead** / May 20, 1997 / Metropolis ♦♦♦

From the track titles alone ("Slave to Evil," "Down Where We Belong," "Golgotha"), it's clear that *Embryodead* isn't a happy pop record. The sub-Skinny Puppy chord progressions don't make for incredibly good songs, but Ratzinger's productions bring a bit more to the table than listeners would expect from this type of industrial-dance record. —*John Bush*

**Dried Blood of Gommorha** / Oct. 28, 1997 / Metropolis ♦♦

*Dried Blood of Gommorha* reissues :wumpscut:'s *Dried Blood* EP and the "Gomorrha" single on one domestically available disc. —*Steve Huey*

**Mesner Tracks** / Nov. 11, 1997 / Metropolis ♦♦

*The Mesner Tracks* gathers 15 :wumpscut: tracks previously available in the US only on import compilations and non-LP singles. Like much of the group's work, it combines industrial harshness with a cold, Gothic sensibility. —*Steve Huey*

# X

## The X-Ecutioners
f. 1989, New York, NY
*Group / Turntablism, Underground Rap, Hip-Hop*

New York-based turntable group the X-ecutioners were, along with San Francisco's Invisibl Skratch Piklz, among the first all-DJ outfits to sign a recording contract, and the first to release a full-length album focusing on the art of turntable tricknology. Formerly known as the X-Men (they changed their name, for copyright reasons, when they signed with the Asphodel label in 1997), the four-person group consists of Mista Sinista, Rob Swift, Total Eclipse, and Roc Raida—a world-renowned crew whose past credits include national and international titles for trick and battle DJing, as well as live and studio work with artists such as Organized Konfusion, Large Professor, the Beatnuts, and Artifacts. Originally formed in 1989 by Roc Raida with Steve D, Johnny Cash, and Sean Cee, the group adopted the name X-Men on the occasion of a battle with another New York crew, the Supermen (that battle never happened). They've since focused on returning the DJ to a position of prominence in hip-hop, a position largely usurped in the '80s and '90s by MCs and producers, as rap grew into one of the largest and most profitable genres in the American music industry. Making entirely new tracks from bits and pieces of other records manipulated by hand (rather than with a sampler and sequencer), the X-ecutioners combine state-of-the-art scratching with the hip-hop DJ's bedrock of cutting, mixing, and beat juggling. The group play live often, and have performed in clubs, exhibitions, and competitions on four continents. —*Sean Cooper*

● **X-Pressions** / Sep. 23, 1997 / Asphodel ♦♦♦

*X-pressions* is the first full-length release by the relatively new phenomenon of the turntable orchestra. Like the first efforts of other young genres such as trip-hop and drum'n'bass, the album tends to be overlong and lacking in variety. Restricting themselves to the sounds of hip-hop past (old-school references and battle-wearied scratch noises dominate), the group nonetheless manages a sufficiently engaging full-length debut, switching between group and solo performances and even pulling a few rappers (strictly underground, no big names) in on the fun. —*Sean Cooper*

## Iannis Xenakis
b. May 22, 1922, Braïla, Romania
*Composer / Musique Concrète, 20th Century Classical/Modern Composition, Atonal, Electronic, Classical*

In applying mathematical and physical laws to the composition of music, Iannis Xenakis exposed the implicit connections between science and art—rooted in theories of statistical probability, his stochastic method revolutionized not only the composition of music but also its performance, exploring the boundaries of sound and space. Born of Greek parentage in Braïla, Romania on May 22, 1922, Xenakis returned to Greece at age ten, later studying engineering at Athens Polytechnic University. He relocated to Paris in 1947, honing his skills as a composer under the tutelage of Honegger, Milhaud, and Messiaen, and in 1954 completed his first major work, *Metastasis for Orchestra*. For over a decade Xenakis also worked with the renowned French architect Le Corbusier, most notably contributing to the design of the Philips Pavilion for the 1958 Brussels International Fair.

Xenakis' engineering studies and architectural work directly impacted his musical ideas (and vice versa)—on the belief that composition develops outside of music, he built upon mathematical and philosophical principles to develop his stochastic theory (adapting the name from "stochos," the Greek word for "goal"). Xenakis explored the inner structural organization of composing, applying theories of statistical probability to discover the interrelationships between organized sound and music; with the advent of computer technology, he translated his findings into programs which created new compositional families. Xenakis broke further ground in his studies of spatial dynamics—positioning musicians throughout an auditorium according to kinetic principles, he pursued a perfect sonic balance based upon the distribution of sound from a multitude of directions.

Works including 1956's *Pithoprakta* and 1957's *Diamorphoses* launched Xenakis to the forefront of the avant-garde, and he continued pushing the envelope with subsequent pieces including 1958's *Duel* (a composition based on the principles of game theory) and 1962's *Bohor* (his first major electronic project). As the complex rhythms of ensemble compositions like 1963's *Eonta* gave way to full-blown orchestral scores including 1969's *Oresteia*, in the interim Xenakis directed much of his energies towards guiding the Centre d'Études de Mathématique et Automatique Musicales (CEMAMu), which he founded at the Sorbonne in 1966. Although his oeuvre includes works for ballet and theatre, tape constructions and even vocal music, from the mid-'70s onward, the majority of Xenakis' compositions grew from orchestral and instrumental origins. —*Jason Ankeny*

**Mycenae-Alpha (1978)** / 1990 / Neuma ♦♦♦

Composed in 1978 on the UPIC graphic computer system at the *Centre d'Études de Mathematique et Automatique Musicales* (Center for the Study of Mathematics and Automatic Music) in Paris, this electronic work is for mono tape manipulated among two or four speakers.

The work has become a classic of computer-generated music. By taking the shapes and movements of natural phenomena, such as molecules in a gas, Xenakis developed a method of digitally mapping those images into the computer and using them to trigger sound events of similar aural shapes. The result is a nine minute and 38-second composition of dense and intense textures, of phase-shifting waveforms rich in harmonics that cascade, flutter, crash, and scream like sirens in a vast cosmological territory. —*"Blue" Gene Tyranny*

**La Legende d'Eer** / 1995 / Montaigne ♦♦♦♦

Xenakis' 46-minute electroacoustic masterpiece for 8-track tape, *La Legende d'Eer*, is based loosely on the Myth of Er the Pamphylian, which closes Plato's *Republic*. Like the comparatively more succinct Concret PH (composed for the 1958 World's Fair and played within the sweeping eaves of the Philips Pavilion), *La Legende* was composed as an architectural sound event. It was originally planned for the opening of the Centre George Pompidou in 1978, and, like the Philips Pavilion, was to have been played within a building of Xenakis' design. *La Legende d'Eer* also incorporates some of Xenakis' first experiments with the UPIC, a compositional device designed by Xenakis to translate hand-drawn sketches into audible sound. —*Sean Cooper*

● **Kraanerg (1968)** / Jul. 7, 1997 / Sombient/Asphodel ♦♦♦♦

Xenakis' 1968 work for tape and orchestra, *Kraanerg* was performed several times after its composition, though synchronizing tape effects with the orchestra often proved difficult. Charles Zacharie Bornstein, conductor of the ST-X Ensemble, conceived the brilliant idea of hiring turntablist philosopher Paul D. Miller (aka DJ Spooky) to take over the tape effects (pre-recorded by Xenakis in 1968) of a new 1996 recording, supervised and attended by the composer himself. The result is an excellent recording that dovetails nicely with Xenakis' late-'60s compositional aims; reflecting the world's exploding population base (and the fact that much of it will be youth). The recording itself and sound quality are excellent, with much care devoted to the wide frequencies of the ST-X Ensemble (which includes many strings plus trumpets, trombones, contrabassoon, and contrabass clarinet). Miller's contributions are not large, but the concrète atmospheres of Xenakis' tape exerts a certain dominance over the proceedings. Though it might be a difficult album for listeners not used to the work of early electronic composers, *Kraanerg* is a rewarding recording. —*John Bush*

# Y

## Yello
f. 1979, Zurich, Switzerland
*Group / Club/Dance, Prog-Rock/Art Rock, Synth-Pop*

The ambitious Swiss electronic duo Yello comprised vocalist/conceptualist Dieter Meier—a millionaire industrialist, professional gambler and member of Switzerland's national golf team—and composer/arranger Boris Blank. Meier, a former solo artist who also spent time with the group Fresh Colour, began collaborating with Blank in 1979, and the duo bowed with the single "I.T. Splash." After signing with the Residents' label Ralph Records, Yello issued their 1980 debut LP, *Solid Pleasure*, which spawned the dance hit "Bostitch."

With 1981's *Claro Que Si*, Yello made its first forays into music video; their clip for the single "Pinball Cha Cha," directed by Meier, garnered considerable acclaim and in 1985 was selected as one of 32 works included in the Museum of Modern Art's Music Video Exhibition. Visual accompaniment remained a pivotal component of the duo's work after they signed to Elektra in 1983 for the LP *You Gotta Say Yes to Another Excess*, as the videos for "I Love You" and "Lost and Found" received heavy airplay on MTV.

1985's *Stella* proved to be Yello's commercial breakthrough: While the singles and videos "Desire" and "Vicious Games" found success upon their initial release, the duo enjoyed a delayed hit with the album track "Oh Yeah," which reached the US singles chart after being prominently featured in the films *Ferris Bueller's Day Off* and *The Secret of My Success*. After the remix project *1980-1985: The New Mix in Go*, Yello recruited diva Shirley Bassey and ex-Associate Billy McKenzie for 1987's *One Second*.

Despite the success of 1988's *Flag*, which contained the international hit "The Race," over the course of the next several years Yello grew increasingly involved with film projects: After scoring the comedy *Nuns on the Run*, Meier directed his own feature, 1990's *Snowball*. In 1991, the duo resurfaced with *Baby*, followed three years later by *Zebra*. 1995's *Hands on Yello* compiled reinterpretations of the group's songs by the likes of Moby, the Orb, and the Grid, while *Pocket Universe*, a collection of new material, appeared in 1997. —*Jason Ankeny*

**Solid Pleasure** / Nov. 1980 / Mercury ♦♦♦♦
The most varied and accomplished of any synth-pop debut, Yello's first album presents a few irresistible pop songs (the hit "Bostitch," plus "Bimbo," and "Eternal Legs"), Boris Blank's synthesizer interpretations of several different forms of music ("Downtown Samba," "Bananas to the Beat," "Rock Stop," "Coast to Polka"), and even a three-song suite of atmospheric industrial music that functions as a miniature invisible soundtrack. The dark lyrical concerns and futurist electronics immediately lifted Yello above the rut of Kraftwerk imitators. —*John Bush*

**Claro Que Si** / 1981 / Ralph ♦♦♦
Another leap in musical sophistication made Yello's second album another high-point in the development of synth-pop. The future of Euro-disco and dance-pop are easily audible from the opener "Daily Disco" and other tracks like "Pinball Cha Cha," "The Evening's Young," and "Cuad el Habib." Though *Claro Que Si* is slightly more pop-oriented than the group's debut, with Boris Blank's electronics just as innovative and obtuse as before, that's hardly a step backward. —*John Bush*

**You Gotta Say Yes to Another Excess** / 1983 / Mercury ♦♦♦♦
The seeds of Eurodance sown on *Claro Que Si* reached fruition on Yello's next record, naturally titled *You Gotta Say Yes to Another Excess*. There are fewer novelty synth tracks than before, those being replaced by a series of sleazy, deep-throated vocals on "I Love You," "Lost Again," "Heavy Whispers," and the title track. There are also a few exercises in worldbeat synth-pop, with heavy percussion on the title track as well as the closing number "Salut Mayoumba." Though Blank's production doesn't sound as consistently innovative as on the first two Yello records, that's probably due more to other synth-pop groups catching up than any comedown on his part. —*John Bush*

**Stella** / 1985 / Mercury ♦♦♦♦
Yes, *Stella* is the album that includes Yello's biggest hit, "Oh Yeah." It's also their best single LP, an excellent production throughout by Boris Blank, from the theatric instrumentals "Stalakdrama" and "Ciel Ouvert" to the frenetic pitched percussion on "Let Me Cry." As well, Dieter Meier proves he's at his best vocally, whether it's the seamy side of life on "Desert Inn" or an exaggerated leer for "Koladi-ola." Both hit their peak on the same album, and *Stella* is a complete joy for fans of the vocal or production side of the group. —*John Bush*

**One Second** / 1987 / Mercury ♦♦♦
*One Second* expands the Eurodisco approach of *Stella*, and while it's considerably less adventurous than Yello's earlier works, it's engaging dance music, highlighted by some clever uses of Latin rhythms and vocal cameos from Billy Mackenzie and Shirley Bassey. —*Stephen Thomas Erlewine*

● **Essential** / 1992 / Smash ♦♦♦♦
*Essential* is a fine 16-track compilation that features all of Yello's best-known Eurodance hits including, of course, their signature song, "Oh Yeah" as well as earlier material like "Bostich," "Pinball Cha Cha," "Tied Up," and "Vicious Games." —*Stephen Thomas Erlewine*

**Hands on Yello** / 1995 / Polydor ♦♦♦

## Yellow Magic Orchestra
f. 1978, Tokyo, Japan, db. 1993
*Group / Prog-Rock/Art Rock, Synth-Pop*

The trailblazing force behind the emergence of the Japanese techno-pop sound of the late '70s, Yellow Magic Orchestra remains a seminal influence on contemporary electronic music—hugely popular both at home and abroad, their pioneering use of synthesizers, sequencers and drum machines places them second only to Kraftwerk as innovators of today's electronic culture. YMO was formed in Tokyo in 1978 by keyboardist Ryuichi Sakamoto, who at the time was working on his debut solo LP; among his collaborators was drummer Yukihiro Takahashi, himself also a solo performer as well as a member of the art-rock group the Sadistic Mika Band. The third member, bassist Haruomi Hosono, boasted an even more impressive discography, including four solo records as well as a number of production credits.

Agreeing to join forces as Yellow Magic Orchestra, the trio soon debuted with a self-titled LP influenced largely by the robotic iconography of Germany's Kraftwerk; 1979's *Solid State Survivor* heralded a quantum leap in their sound, with stronger songs and a more focused use of electronic tools, complete with English lyrics by Chris Mosdell. While 1980's *Xoo Multiplies* was at best a mixed bag including comedy skits and two different covers of the Archie Bell & the Drells classic "Tighten Up," *Public Pressure* captured YMO performing live. Their two 1981 releases, *BGM* and *Technodelic*, both delved deeper into synth-pop, exploring new stylistic territory anticipating the individual musicians' subsequent solo projects. *Service*, from 1983, again offered skits, this time courtesy of the theatrical troupe S.E.T.

Following the ambitious *Naughty Boys* and another live record, *After Service*, Yellow Magic Orchestra disbanded at the peak of their popularity, with its members wishing to revive their respective solo careers. Sakamoto enjoyed the highest visibility of the YMO alumni—a noted film composer, he gained his greatest exposure co-writing the Academy Award-winning score to the 1987 film *The Last Emperor*. Hosono also pursued film music as well as ambient projects, while Takahashi enjoyed an eclectic and experimental return to his rock roots. By the '90s, YMO was cited regularly as a pioneer of ambient house music, resulting in the release of the remix album *Hi-Tech/No Crime*. The original trio then reunited in 1993, recording the LP *Technodon* before again going their separate ways. —*Jason Ankeny*

**Yellow Magic Orchestra** / Nov. 25, 1978 / Restless ♦♦♦
Leading off with their only British hit, the Top 20 entry "Computer Game," Yellow Magic Orchestra's debut album launches the group as a Japanese novelty act in keeping with Kraftwerk. "Computer Game" is about what it sounds like, while "Firecracker" and "Cosmic Surfin" drift along with Oriental melodies playing over the top of an unobtrusive synth-pop backing. The disco bass on "Yellow Magic (Tong Poo)" shows that YMO were beginning to expand their base, but for the most part *Yellow Magic Orchestra* never strays from its influences. —*John Bush*

★ **Solid State Survivor** / Sep. 25, 1979 / Restless ♦♦♦♦♦
The trio hit their stride with second album *Solid State Survivor*, a brisk and confident set of synth-disco-pop that continues along the line drawn five years before by Kraftwerk. Fun-loving and breezy where Kraftwerk had been ponderous and statuesque, the album sets out YMO's template for electronic pop with less minimalism and a more varying use of synthesizer lines. The English lyrics, written by Chris Mosdell but sung by YMO themselves, make for hilarious listening especially on a cover of the Beatles' "Day Tripper." —*John Bush*

**Xoo Multiplies** / Jun. 5, 1980 / A&M ♦♦
*Xoo Multiplies* is a bizarre album filled with sing-along pop songs, a few interludes including commercial jingles and ad-men pitches, and no less than two versions of the Drells' chestnut "Tighten Up." There are a few solid electronic tunes ("Nice Age," "Citizens of Science") amid the chaos, plus instrumental versions of "Chaos Panic" and "Lotus Love" added to the CD issue. —*John Bush*

**Technodelic** / Nov. 21, 1981 / Restless ♦♦♦♦
Widening their vision of synth-pop to include the darker strains of urban/R&B as well as a few vocals indebted to Roxy Music, 1981's *Technodelic* proved a high-quality album that showed Yellow Magic Orchestra had the talent and inspiration to grow beyond Kraftwerk-derived electronic pop heavy on the novelty but a bit light on bending genres. Though they aren't exactly melancholy, "Neue Tanz" and "Pure Jam" distinguish themselves through a clever use of synth and effects rather than through the simplistic melodies of previous work. There are some acknowledgements to acoustic music (such as the piano on "Stairs"), but for the most part YMO pursues a new direction with the same synthesizers they'd been using previously. —*John Bush*

**Naughty Boys** / May 24, 1983 / Restless ♦♦♦♦
Posturing themselves as the synth-pop stars they already were (though only strictly speaking), *Naughty Boys* is more of a landmark for Japanese pop than electronic music. Beginning with the synth-pop hit "Kimi Ni Mune Kyun" (featuring vocals just as accomplished as its production), the album clearly sounds different; previous YMO material had never sounded explicitly like Asian pop music before. That said, it's still a solid album of commercial synth-pop and showed the group was still cultivating their Western connections, with help from guitarist Bill Nelson. —*John Bush*

**Service** / Dec. 14, 1983 / Restless ♦♦

**Hi-Tech/No Crime: Yellow Magic Orchestra Reconstructed** / Sep. 21, 1993 / Planet Earth ♦♦♦♦
*Hi-Tech/No Crime: Yellow Magic Orchestra Reconstructed* is an excellent tribute to the groundbreaking Japanese electronic band the Yellow Magic Orchestra. A host of contemporary ambient and techno artists—including the Orb, Orbital, 808 State, Altern 8, Mark Gamble and Graham Massey—have remixed the original tracks, expanding them into evocative new territory. These new versions may not surpass the originals, but they arguably match them, demonstrating that not only were these artists influenced by Yellow Magic Orchestra, but they assimilated what they learned and made it into something of their own. —*Stephen Thomas Erlewine*

## Kevin Yost

*Producer / Jazz-House, Club/Dance, House*
One of America's best young house producers, Kevin Yost has translated his jazz inspirations and percussion inclinations into dance productions of quiet beauty, harnessing the vibes of sublime domestic producers from Larry Heard to Derrick May. An early fan of jazz-fusion and a drummer as well, Yost was DJing weddings and the like at the tender age of 13. A contract with Chicago's Guidance label brought his first release, a 1996 EP titled *Unprotected Sax*. One year later, Yost signed a contract to begin working with the New Jersey acid-jazz-house label i! Records, and in 1998, the single "One Starry Night" became a big mover in progressive house circles. Yost released the mix album *Small Town Underground* through Twisted/MCA in 1999, with contributions from like-minds Euphonic and Fredrik Stark among others. Later that year, the album *One Starry Night* collected a few classic productions (like the title track) with newer material. —*John Bush*

**Small Town Underground** / Feb. 9, 1999 / MCA ♦♦♦

● **One Starry Night** / Apr. 12, 1999 / i! ♦♦♦♦
Yost's first production album is a set of eight epic jazz-house numbers, exquisitely crafted and reminiscent of the late-night vibes created by dance producers from Larry Heard to Carl Craig. The title track "Dreams of You," and "Hypnotic Progressions (Part 1)" are just some of the highlights, trading deep bass notes and intricate percussion with an excellent sense for atmospheric melodies. Though things turn a bit muzaky on several tracks (there are a few more instrument solos than would be comfortable on a house album), Yost proves himself a distinctive producer, capable of conveying a deep sense of emotion. —*John Bush*

## Young Gods

f. 1985, Geneva, Switzerland
*Group / Alternative Pop/Rock, Industrial*
Swiss electro-noise terrorists the Young Gods traced their origins back to 1982, when Geneva-based frontman Franz Treichler, increasingly bored with his then-current new wave band, began experimenting with a small sampler. Influenced as well by the visceral power of punk and the grand drama of classical music, he began creating abrasive guitar and drum loops, and with sampler Cesare Pizzi and percussionist Frank Bagnoud, founded the Young Gods in 1985. Named in an honor of a Swans composition, the trio debuted a year later with *Envoyé!*, a brief, blistering single distilling their assaultive sound to its core. Produced by Swan Roli Mosimann, their self-titled debut LP followed in 1987, and was named Album of the Year by the British music weekly *Melody Maker*. By the time of the follow-up, 1989's *L'Eau Rouge*, drummer Use Hiestand had replaced Bagnoud, and with the release of 1991's *The Young Gods Play Kurt Weill*, Pizzi was gone in favor of sampler Alain Monod. *T.V. Sky* followed in 1992, while 1995's *Only Heaven* flirted with ambient textures. Two years later, the Young Gods (minus Hiestand and with new drummer Bernard Trontin) returned with *Heaven Deconstruction*. —*Jason Ankeny*

**Young Gods** / 1987 / Wax Trax! ♦♦♦
Even if the uniqueness of the Young Gods' sample-based compositional and playing method of heavy rock wasn't a question, the band's debut would still have caught many a discerning ear. While not consistently strong throughout, this self-titled effort has far more hits than misses to its overall credit. Admittedly, things start off a touch underwhelmingly while a dark mood is immediately established with "Nous De La Lune," with low tolling bell sounds, brutal drumming, riff slabs, and Treichler's harsh barking of French lyrics. Fans of Einsturzende Neubaten and the Swans both would have found much of the offer fairly obvious (certainly the fact that ex-Swans member Roli Mosimann has consistently worked with the band throughout its career as producer and collaborator forced the comparison early on, as did the fact the Young Gods named themselves after a Swans song and album). "Jusqu'au About" takes a far catchier, though hardly poppier, turn, and from then on occasional musical cul-de-sacs are shadowed by a series of raging, fierce numbers, with classical and metal guitar samples firing off at each other over stiff drumming throughout. Total standouts include "Jimmy," "Feu," "Si Tu Gardes" and the band's definitive early tune, "Envoye," a barely two-minute-long explosion of percussion, gunshots, a roughly abbreviated hair metal riff and an amazing rant from Treichler. The joker in the pack is a string-sample led version of Gary Glitter's "Did You Miss Me?," aka "Hello Hello (It's Good to be Back)." —*Ned Raggett*

● **L'Eau Rouge** / 1989 / Play It Again Sam ♦♦♦♦
"La Fille de la Mort" begins this album so perfectly that it becomes immediately clear how much more striking the already powerful band had become. Beginning with a simple boulevardier melody and lyric (even though, as the title indicates, it's about the daughter of Death!), it slowly but relentlessly builds

over the course of eight minutes, suddenly bursting into a beautiful orchestral sample loop that is then staggered and distorted, punctuated by sharp drums and finally concluding with guitar pulses on top of that. It's a stunning, unique way to start, and the album easily lives up to that opening promise. Tracks like the fast-paced roar "Longue Route" and the title song—a celebration of "red water," the female period—maintain a fierce, sharp tension between rock rhythms (new drummer Use Hiestand shows much more flexibility than his predecessor), huge riffs, and classical stabs, all with Treichler's powerful, gravelly voice invoking any number of striking natural and elemental images, putting the lie to the claim that rock can't happen in French. There's even time for more traditional French cabaret tunes like "Charlotte," while "Les Enfants" takes the classical bombast to an even higher level. Originally available only as a single, "L'Amourir" remains the album's and the band's high point, a brilliantly arranged and performed combination of guitar riff samples and powerful drumming, accentuated by a snaky bass pulse/snort throughout and Treichler's climactic roar over a wailing guitar loop. —*Ned Raggett*

**The Young Gods Play Kurt Weill** / 1991 / Play It Again Sam ✦✦✦
Besides introducing keyboardist Al Comet and thus stabilizing the band line-up for the next decade, Weill is an intriguing curiosity few other bands could easily pull off. As part of an annual Swiss musical festival celebrating specific musicians each year, the Gods were invited to perform renditions of numbers by the noted German composer, writer of theatrical musical standards from The Threepenny Opera to "September Song." The subsequent album is a revelation. While rockers from Bobby Darin to Lou Reed had tried their hand at the Weill songbook, the Gods embraced the avant-garde bent of Weill's music with a passion. "Prologue" reworks the sly opening narration to The Threepenny Opera in the context of a rock concert, audience screams and all, and from there on in it's Weill as you've not quite heard him before, ditching solo cabaret revivalism for sample-based reinvention. "Mackie Messer" launches guitar snarls and rips all over the place, "Speak Low" takes on distinctly ominous undertones, "Seerauber Jenny" cheekily blends a more straightforward oompah approach with discordant woodwind samples, background string loops and huge drum blasts. Throughout Treichler sounds like he's having the time of his life; on "Alabama Song," memories of the Doors' fair-enough take are erased by his sinuous whisper and the band's switch between calm and noise. As for the amazing album-ender "September Song," delivered by Treichler with restrained passion over a stripped-down wash of ocean waves and ghostly samples floating in and out of the mix, Bing Crosby this ain't. —*Ned Raggett*

**T.V. Sky** / Feb. 7, 1991 / Play It Again Sam ✦✦✦
In a conscious shift of aesthetics, the very European Gods turned their eyes on America with the band's fourth album, producing its most "rock" record to date, a consistently strong smash. Opening with "Our House," it all seems (powerful) business as usual—odd sonic loops, rhythm patterns suddenly exploding into mass drum/riff combinations. But the difference here lies with the lyrics—discounting earlier covers, Treichler for the first time sings in English here and throughout, a conscious audience targeting that he addressed in contemporaneous interviews. "Gasoline Man" turns out to be the big shift, revamping what sounds like an old ZZ Top riff into as classic an American rock song as any (blues lyrical structure, loving the road and the motor) yet with the Gods' unique sonic signature present, revamping and restitching the past into a cleaner, newer form that avoids sounding just like another bar band. Underground hit single "Skinflowers" marries a powerful pulse and razor-sharp feedback stabs with a perversely catchy lyric; other tracks like "T.V. Sky" and the wickedly Guns n' Roses-quoting "The Night Dance" pile on the sound and space in equally gripping measure. "Summer Eyes," an intentional Doors tribute done after numerous Jim Morrison/Treichler comparisons in the past, even has a mid-song Manzarek-style organ break, but ends the album on a disturbing note, slow riff trudge samples fading out under Treichler's dark, sly take on America. In sum, a wonderful album that never got its proper due. —*Ned Raggett*

**Only Heaven** / 1995 / Play It Again Sam ✦✦✦
*Only Heaven* returns the Young Gods to their aggressive industrial roots with heavy hip-hop percussion and a speed metal pace. —*John Bush*

## Claude Young
*Producer, DJ / Detroit Techno, Club/Dance, Techno*
One of Detroit's leading DJs and producers as the '90s closed, Claude Young filtered the more lush elements of Motor City melodicists with the harder, minimalist stream of Robert Hood and Jeff Mills to create productions which lacked for neither emotion nor hard-hitting trance. After helping out Jeff Mills on his radio show during the early '90s, Young debuted with the *One Complete Revolution* EP on his own Utensil label. He also recorded as Project 625 for another of his own labels (DOW) and with Anthony "Shake" Shakir on his third label, Frictional. Besides other tracks for Acacia (as Rhythm Formation) and 7th City (with Dan Bell as Brother from Another Planet), Young began making the transition to the global techno scene with a single for Andrew Weatherall's Emissions Audio Output Recordings (as Being) and DJAX-Up-Beats (as Claude Young). He followed with several high-profile remixes during 1995, including tracks by Inner City, Astral Pilot, Innerzone Orchestra, Joey Beltram, and Slam (with the help of Ian O'Brien).

Young's first full-length, the 1996 *DJ Kicks* compilation, showed him in fine form, perhaps the best DJ to come out of Detroit since Jeff Mills. One year later, his debut album *Soft Thru* for the Dutch Elypsia Records earned him much praise for its sensibilities, uniting the minimalist with the melodic to good effect. —*John Bush*

● **DJ Kicks** / Jun. 3, 1996 / Studio !K7 ✦✦✦✦
Most volumes in the *DJ Kicks* series give well-known producers (say, Carl Craig or CJ Bolland) a chance to stretch out with a mix album. Claude Young, on the other hand, made his name as a DJ and has remained the foremost young mixer on the techno scene. Given that fact, it's hardly a surprise that his *DJ Kicks* is one of the best in the series, with a few tracks from Young himself (including "Acid Wash Conflict," "Joe 90" with Ian O'Brien, and the new track "DJ-Kicks") plus other producers on the minimalist/experimental tip of techno including Maurizio, Surgeon, Random XS, and Dopplereffekt. —*John Bush*

**Soft Thru** / Oct. 13, 1997 / Elypsia ✦✦✦✦
Claude Young's proper debut album displays a range of stylistic change-ups and the occasional tempo deviation, but mostly focuses on hard minimal techno with just the barest hint of melody to catch listeners' ears before they get turned on to the beats and textures. Among the highlights are "Quicksand," the fragile downtempo melodies of "Change of Pace," and a darker vibe for the track "Marching On." —*John Bush*

## La Monte Young
b. 1935, Bern, ID
*Piano, Composer / Multimedia, 20th Century Classical/Modern Composition*
One of the principal architects of the minimalist aesthetic, La Monte Young was among the true innovators of 20th century music. His rejection of traditional melody and structure in favor of hypnotic drone epics influenced not only the avant-garde music created in his wake but also proved seminal in the development of punk, Kraut-rock, and ambient. Young was born in Bern, Idaho in 1935, beginning his studies of the alto saxophone at age seven. After the family relocated to Los Angeles, he played alongside the likes of Don Cherry and Billy Higgins in high school, continuing his exploration of European classical and contemporary composition at Los Angeles City College and later UCLA. In time, Young also began delving into the classic musics of India and Japan; the barren atmospheres evoked by the music of Anton Webern were another key influence.

In 1959, Young composed *Trio for Strings*, regularly cited as the earliest work in the minimalist canon. The piece, with its emphasis on lengthy, sustained tones—intercut with equally extended rests—baffled his professors at the University of California, Berkeley, and in the wake of several other similarly controversial projects he relocated to New York City. There he studied electronic music, in time joining Fluxus, a loose confederacy of conceptual artists—among them John Cage, George Macuinas, George Brecht, and Yoko Ono—dedicated to re-establishing the arts in new and different contexts. In 1962, Young first began to conceive of the Dream House, a continual sound and light environment related to his composition *The Four Dreams of China*. The project remained in limbo for some years to follow, but was a clear forerunner of the principle to guide his subsequent career—music with no beginning and no end.

At the same time, Young became obsessed with notions of tuning, specifically that of Just Intonation, a system in which all of the intervals can be represented by ratios of whole numbers, with a clear preference for the smallest numbers compatible with a given musical purpose. He soon set up an improvisational group including his wife, the visual artist Marian Zazeela, guitarist Billy Name (later one of the regulars at Andy Warhol's Factory), and percussionist Angus MacLise. Enormously influential within the downtown NYC underground scene, the ensemble's live appearances closely mirrored the principles of Young's latest compositional work, with pieces becoming so epic in scope that performances—while typically lasting for hours at a time—still represented only a fraction of the project as a whole.

By 1963, the group's line-up included Young and Zazeela on voice-drones, Tony Conrad on violin, and John Cale on viola. Variously dubbed the Theatre of Eternal Music and the Dream Syndicate, the ensemble's collective input pushed Young's ideals to their logical conclusion—sustaining notes for hours at a time, their improvised dissections of specific harmonic intervals rejected the compositional process altogether, instead elaborating shared performance concepts. Upon disbanding in 1965, Conrad, Young, and Cale all later staked claim to authoring of the "Eternal Music" aesthetic; Young also held on to the group's live tapes. Regardless, his music from that point on remained pointed in the direction of infinity—*The Tortoise, His Dreams and Journeys*, a work tuned to the pitch of his pet turtle's aquarium motor, was begun in 1964 but its theoretical evolution continues into the present, each performance a part of a greater whole.

By the beginning of the '70s, Young's approach to eternal music required tours of six to eight players, slide projectionists, a technician, and over two tons of electronic equipment. Needing a week for set-up time alone, these multi-media Dream House installations then remained intact for another week, with sine-wave generators and shifting light patterns creating continuous sounds and images throughout the residency. By 1973, his focus was a piece titled *The Well-Tuned Piano*, an installation which required at least a month of tuning and practicing in the intended performance space prior to its public debut; as the work developed, Young's performances grew from a standard three-hour duration to well over four. He also returned to his earlier works: A Dream House installation of *The Tortoise*, mounted in New York, ran continuously from 1979 to 1985.

Rarely recorded throughout much of his career, Young signed to Gramavision in 1987, with a flurry of releases—*The Well-Tuned Piano, The Second Dream of the High-Tension Line Stepdown Transformer from the Four Dreams of China*, and *Just Stompin'*, a raga-blues effort recorded with his Forever Blues Band, among them—soon appearing. Still, throughout his career Young remained a largely shadowy figure, often discussed (his connection to the nascent Velvet Underground the most common point of reference) but seldom heard; his influence on the rise of ambient music and drone-rock is undeniable, yet almost subliminal. Undaunted, he continued composing and performing regularly into the '90s, with his latter-day works including *The Lower Map of the Eleven's Division in the Romantic Symmetry* and *Chronos Kristalla*. —*Jason Ankeny*

The Well-Tuned Piano / 1973 / Gramavision ♦♦♦
The legendary just intonation work in a set of five CDs. The booklet goes on a bit much in justifying Young's place in history, so just listen to the music which is nonvirtuosic in the usual sense, and pleasant. —*"Blue" Gene Tyranny*

• Second Dream of the High-Tension Line Stepdown Transformer ... / 1991 / Gramavision ♦♦♦♦
Composed in 1984, this piece presents a form of group improvisation based on timelessness—each performance is "woven out of an eternal fabric of silence and sound (which) evanesces back into silence until a group of musicians picks up the same set of pitches again" (Young). Each listing of this title in a program or recording also contains the specific date, time and city of the performance. Like Harry Partch, Ben Johnston, and others, Young is known for basing his compositions on alternative tunings, especially "The Well-Tuned Piano" of 1964-81. For one recorded realization, eight trumpets with Harmon mutes provide an amazing recreation of the title's sonic experience as they play four pitches in frequency ratios of the complete quadral 18/17/16/12 which "can be isolated in the harmonic structures of the sounds of power plants and telephone poles". There are also macro-structure outlines which guide the larger sections of the work. Young recalls two such listening experiences in his life: one next to a telephone pole in Bern, Idaho, and the other near twenty transformers outside of Montpelier where his grandfather ran a gas station. —*"Blue" Gene Tyranny*

## Savvas Ysatis

b. Jul. 1, 1968, Greece
*Producer / Experimental Techno, Electronica, Ambient Techno*

After being recognized primarily through his collaborations with Taylor Deupree, Greek techno artist Savvas Ysatis has slowly earned a name for himself as a prestigious techno artist. While Ysatis was born in Greece, he spent a good portion of his life in New York, moving there at the age of 15 to pursue music. During his time in New York, he recorded music for Instinct with Deupree under various guises such as SETI, Futique, and Arc. Furthermore, he also recorded solo as Omicron and Minipop. By the late '90s, after releasing the conceptual *Tower of Winds* album with Deupree, he earned the prestigious status of being awarded a full-length release on Berlin's legendary Tresor label, resulting in the acclaimed Highrise album, an album that fully embraced the traditional techno sound. Thanks to the recognition that came with this release, Ysatis has returned to his native Greece, where he experiences superstar status and leads the country's growing techno scene. —*Jason Birchmeier*

Tower of Winds / Jan. 13, 1998 / Caipirinha ♦♦♦
After collaborating as SETI and Futique, Greek musician Savvas Ysatis and New Yorker Taylor Deupree teamed up again for *Tower of Winds*, a collection of electronica inspired by the Tokyo building of the same name and its light show. —*Steve Huey*

• Highrise / Jul. 27, 1999 / Tresor ♦♦♦♦
With his fresh style of funky yet subtly sedate techno, Savvas Ysatis was an important newcomer to the legendary Tresor techno label in the late '90s. Up until Ysatis' arrival, Tresor had become synonymous with the banging, hard, and minimal techno that early artists such as Jeff Mills and Robert Hood had released in the early '90s. The style of techno Ysatis released in his *Highrise* album honestly possesses none of these characteristics. Ysatis's style needs space as it relies on a time span of several minutes for the progressive construction of its songs. What begins as a fairly simple and barely assembled collection of rhythms broadly placed along the frequency spectrum eventually concludes five to nine minutes later as a highly evolved upgraded construction with several new added rhythms and other major alterations. Along the way to the end of each song, minimal synthesizer loops fade from nowhere and join with the forward-moving group of rhythms. Like a digital snowball, each song continues to grow in terms of size and density as it moves forward, eventually towering over its beginnings. Unlike some producers, Ysatis doesn't continually try to up the tempo or increase the intensity. He instead fills in gaps with new rhythms, giving listeners even more reasons to feel the funky nature of the music. As should be done for Aril Brikha's *Deeparture in Time* album on Transmat, DJs need to give Ysatis' music at least several minutes to reach its full potential. If one sits back and listens to the duration of these songs, the growth becomes highly evident and the most impressive quality of the songs emerges. On the album's title track, there is a syncopated phasing human chant that cycles in a loop for the song's entire nine minutes. Along the way, the chant is accompanied by a variety of rhythms, which combine in different ways to keep the song continually progressing toward a product it will never reach. These many different syntheses occurring every minute or so are what make this an album that needs to be listened to all the way through. DJs will love the constructed techno rhythms and their sense of smoothness, but Ysatis obviously intends for listeners to leave the needle on the record as it spins from the outermost groove to the innermost. —*Jason Birchmeier*

# Z

## Z'ev (Stefan Weisser)
b. New York, NY
*Percussion / Experimental Rock, No Wave*

Beginning in the early '80s, percussionist Z'ev (born Stefan Weisser) pursued an early, highly experimental vein of industrial music, creating harsh, noisy, ultra-loud soundscapes that favor sonic texture over recognizable musical structure. Z'ev's work influenced many other early industrial bands, including Test Dept. and Einsturzende Neubauten, and he has performed as a featured musician in Glenn Branca's "Symphony No. 2." Weisser recorded several EPs under his given name in 1981 and 1982, adopting the name Z'ev for 1982's *Elemental Music*. He recorded off and on throughout the '80s, also collaborating with Psychic TV on 1984's *Berlin Atonal Vol. 1*. Z'ev's first US releases in almost 15 years began to appear in the late '90s, including the *Tales from the Poison* EP on Surf Ave. and the collection *Ghost of One Foot in the Grave* on Touch. —*Steve Huey*

● **Heads & Tales** / May 7, 1996 / Avant ✦✦✦✦
A combination of two pieces ("Heads" and "Tales") consisting of 19 tracks and composed during 1992 and 1993, *Heads & Tales* presents a furious synthesis of Stefan Weisser's own "wild style" acoustic percussion, plus a variety of samples and other electronic/percussive elements. Recorded by Wharton Tiers and mixed by Glenn Branca, it's not only one of the best Z'ev albums since his return to US shores, it's one of the best period. —*John Bush*

**Ghost of One Foot in the Grave** / May 27, 1997 / Touch ✦✦✦
After years of anonymity even within avant-garde and noise circles, Z'ev gained a modicum of recognition with this deluxe two-disc retrospective. With a book that's over 100 pages long, plus photos, discography, and included interviews, *Ghost of One Foot in the Grave* naturally documents the artist's decades of recordings better than anything yet released. Many of the earlier songs here (especially the live ones) appear to lose a bit in the translation from performance to playback, resulting in a series of somewhat inferior tracks on the first disc. The abundance of excellent works here does make up for the lack of early quality material, but *Ghost of One Foot in the Grave* may not be the best place to start for beginners. —*John Bush*

## Zion Train
f. 1990, London, England
*Group / Electronica, Ambient Dub, Club/Dance*

Multimedia acid-dub collective Zion Train comprised vocalist Molara, DJ/bassist Neil Perch, trumpeter David Tench, melodica player Colin Cod, and trombonist Chris. Formed in North London in 1990, its members initially came together as a dub sound system; their first single, the limited-edition roots 7" "Power One" (issued on their own Zion Records imprint), immediately sold out, while its follow-up "Power Two" was a major favorite at shaka dances throughout 1992. For their next effort, Zion Train teamed with Studio One vet Devon Russell to remake his cult classic "Jah Holds the Key." The group's most successful record to date, it garnered airplay throughout Europe and led to the release of their debut LP, the mellow dub outing *Passage to Indica*.

Concurrent with a series of remixes including tracks from the Shamen, Chumbawamba, Afro-Celt Sound System, Junior Reid, and Loop Guru, Zion Train issued with their next single, the acid house-inspired "Follow Like Wolves." The acclaimed *Natural Wonders of the World in Dub* was next, debuting in the Top 20 of the UK indie charts; a series of limited-edition EPs recorded in collaboration with the Knights of the Occasional Table, Diatribe, Conscious, and the Trancemasters followed in 1994, and were later collected on the *Siren* LP. After signing with the China label in early 1995, Zion Train issued the single "Get Ready," trailed a few months later by the full-length *Homegrown Fantasy*. After 1996's *Grow Together*, they returned the following summer with the two-disc hits collection *Single Minded and Alive*. *Love Revolutionaries* followed in mid-2000. —*Jason Ankeny*

● **Homegrown Fantasy** / 1995 / China ✦✦
*Homegrown Fantasy* is a set of club tracks simultaneously uptempo and spliffy, indebted to worldbeat, ambient dub, and ragga. The tracks are enjoyable period-pieces, though the implicit social message on tracks like "Dance of Life" and "Universal Communication" is a bit too trippy for its own good. —*Keith Farley*

**Grow Together** / 1996 / China ✦✦

**Love Revolutionaries** / May 13, 2000 / Global Fusion ✦✦
Even considering that they utilize some of the advances in sound technology from the early '70s, Zion Train's *Love Revolutionaries* is surprisingly faithful to the classic dub records it's influenced by. Tracks like "Building Rome" and "One Inch Dub" are lengthy, mid-tempo versions thick with dub trademarks: heavy reverb, thunder crashes, organ shards, and bruising basslines. True, Zion Train does mess with the formula occasionally; they approach house-anthem territory on "Fly" and work through hardcore techno and jungle for "War in Babylon." But most of the songs on *Love Revolutionaries* simply update dub tracks with cleaner rhythms and more skeletal beats. —*John Bush*

## John Zorn
b. Sep. 12, 1953, New York, NY
*Sax (Alto), Composer / Spy Music, Improvisation, Avant-Garde Jazz, Film Music, Free Jazz, 20th Century Classical/Modern Composition, Avant-Garde*

It is possible to call John Zorn a "jazz" musician, but that would be much too limiting a description. While jazz feeling is present in a good deal of his work, and the idea of improvisation is vitally important to him, Zorn doesn't operate within any idiom's framework, drawing from just about any musical, cultural, or noise source that a fellow who grew up in the TV and LP eras could experience. This eclecticism gone haywire can result in such wildly jump-cutting works as *Spillane*, whose plethora of diverse and incompatible styles makes for a listening experience akin to constantly punching the station buttons on a car radio. Zorn believes that the age of the composer as an "autonomous musical mind" had come to an end in the late 20th century; hence the collaborative nature of much of his work, both with active musicians and music styles of the past. Like Mel Brooks, the zany film director, many of Zorn's works are tributes to certain musical touchstones of his—such as Ennio Morricone, Sonny Clark, and Ornette Coleman—all filtered through his unpredictable hall of mirrors. While it would be foolhardy to single out a handful of dominant influences, Zorn's music seems very close in spirit to that of Warner Bros. cartoon composer Carl Stalling, both in its transformation of found material and manic, antic moods.

This calculating wild man started playing the piano as a child before taking up the guitar and flute at age ten. By the time he was 14, Zorn had discovered contemporary classical music and began composing; his college years in St. Louis brought about his introduction to avant-garde jazz, particularly that of Anthony Braxton. He dropped out of college, settled in lower Manhattan, and began working with free improvisers, rock bands, and tape, sometimes working duck and bird calls into his arsenal. After putting out releases on tiny domestic and poorly distributed import labels, Zorn signed with Elektra-Nonesuch in the mid-'80s, which increased his visibility considerably. Along the way, he has formed tribute bands to play the music of Coleman, Hank Mobley, Lee Morgan, and others; featured musicians as diverse as Big John Patton, Tim Berne, Bill Frisell, and the Kronos Quartet, and assembled a group called Masada that merges Coleman with Yiddish music. Jazz buffs should be directed to his Coleman tribute album *Spy Vs. Spy* (Nonesuch), which makes exciting, thrashing yet concise hashes of 17 Ornette tunes with a quintet. *Cartoon S&M* followed in fall 2000. —*Richard S. Ginell*

**Yankees** / 1984 / Celluloid ✦
This album is a collective improvisation by Derek Bailey, acoustic and electric guitars, George Lewis, trombone, John Zorn, alto and soprano saxes, clarinets, game calls with subtle, droll, hilarious takes on the trivia of baseball sounds (Lewis speaks through the trombone "ball one, ball one..."), there are snippets of a slipping and sliding version of "Take Me Out To The Ball Game," and so on. Sections are titled "City City City," "The Legend of Enos Slaughter," and "Who's On First," followed by "On Golden Pond," a tongue-in-cheek tone poem of the flora and fauna, mosquitos, and so forth, and "The Warning Track" about a very tiny railroad system. —*"Blue" Gene Tyranny*

**The Big Gundown** / Sep. 1984-Sep. 1985 / Elektra/Nonesuch ✦✦✦✦
On this intriguing concept album, altoist John Zorn (who also "sings" and plays harpsichord, game calls, piano and musical saw) utilizes an odd assortment of open-minded avant-garde players (with a couple of ringers) on nine themes originally written for Italian films by Ennio Morricone plus his own "Tre Nel 5000." These often-radical interpretations (which Morricone endorsed) keep the melodies in mind while getting very adventurous. Among the musicians heard on the colorful and very eccentric set (which utilizes different personnel and instrumentation on each track) are guitarists Bill Frisell and Vernon Reid, percussionist Bobby Previte, keyboardist Anthony Coleman, altoist Tim Berne, pianist Wayne Horvitz, organist Big John Patton, and even Toots Thielemans on harmonica and whistling, among many others. There are certainly no dull moments on this often-riotous program. —*Scott Yanow*

● **The Classic Guide to Strategy Vols. 1 & 2** / 1985 / Lumina ✦✦✦
*The Classic Guide to Strategy, Vols. 1 & 2* presents two Zorn albums from the mid-'80s that have long been out of print. Featuring a variety of manipulated saxophones, clarinets, and duck calls, the album plays at the edges of sounds traditionally associated with reed instruments. The album is not entirely accessible, especially *Vol. 1*—if it were produced by a college student sowing his or her experimental oats after a giddy term at *BAM*, it would probably be labeled a failure for its eccentricity, abruptness, and lack of a coherent theme. However, when a line is drawn through Zorn's previous work, it ends up here—the playfulness of sound, the variety of textures, the use of silence and space as part of the composition—if the listener approaches this album expecting to find musical genius, he or she will not have to look too far. Zorn manufactures the sounds of animals, voices, squeaks, scraps of melodic lines, drowning (or at least dampened) beasts, and cartoon worlds with his reeds, paying homage to the work of Carl Stalling, as well as the sounds of Anthony Braxton and Evan Parker. The first two tracks on this collection represent the original volume one; the last five belonged to the original volume two. Stylistically, they are similar, with the second volume containing less spacial breaks between the musical bursts and each song paying tribute to avant-garde Japanese artists like Mori Ikue, Enoken, Kondo Toshinori, Katsumi Shigeru, Aoyama Michi, and Togawa Jun. —*Stacia Proefrock*

**Voodoo: The Music of Sonny Clark** / Nov. 25, 1985-Nov. 26, 1985 / Black Saint ✦✦✦✦
This unusual album is an unlikely success. Altoist John Zorn, who is best-known for his avant-garde flights and rather eccentric concept albums, here plays it fairly straight. He interprets seven compositions (all fairly obscure) by the somewhat forgotten hard bop pianist Sonny Clark including "Cool Struttin'," "Voodoo," and "Sonny's Crib." With alert support from pianist Wayne Horvitz, bassist Ray Drummond, and drummer Bobby Previte, Zorn creates fairly boppish solos with occasional hints at more advanced improvising techniques. Worth checking out. —*Scott Yanow*

**The Classic Guide to Strategy, Vol. 2** / 1986 / Lumina ✦✦
More beautifully intense solo pieces with inflections like ancient Japanese music. Sections are named after various Japanese artists—Aoyama Michi, Enoken, Kazumi Shigeru, Kondo Toshinori, Yano Akiko, Togawa Jun, and Mori Ikue. Cover art is calligraphy of the character for "water." —*"Blue" Gene Tyranny*

**News for Lulu** / Aug. 30, 1987 / Hat Hut ✦✦✦✦
Avant-garde altoist John Zorn teams up with trombonist George Lewis and guitarist Bill Frisell to form a unique trio. Without the benefit of piano, bass or drums, they interpret the hard bop compositions of Kenny Dorham, Hank Mobley, Sonny Clark, and Freddie Redd, generally not even the better-known ones. The performances are quite concise (Dorham's "Windmill" is covered in 40 seconds!), respectful to the melodies, and unpredictable. There are hints of the avant-garde here and there, but also plenty of swinging, bop-oriented solos and coherent ensembles. Very intriguing music that is highly recommended to a wide audience of jazz and general listeners. —*Scott Yanow*

**Spy Vs. Spy: The Music of Ornette Coleman** / Aug. 18, 1988-Aug. 19, 1988 / Elektra ✦✦✦✦
John Zorn teams up with fellow altoist Tim Berne, bassist Mark Dresser and both Joey Baron and Michael Vatcher on drums to perform 17 Ornette Coleman tunes that range chronologically from 1958's "Disguise" to four selections from 1987's *In All Languages*. The performances are concise with all but four songs being under three minutes and seven under two, but the interpretations are unremittingly violent. The lack of variety in either mood or routine quickly wears one out. After about ten minutes, boredom sets in although, when taken in short doses, the performances have the potential of shocking (or at least annoying) most listeners. —*Scott Yanow*

**Naked City** / 1989 / Elektra/Nonesuch ✦✦✦✦
The violent cover photo (which shows a man after he was shot dead) sets the stage for the rather passionate music on this John Zorn set. With guitarist Bill Frisell, keyboardist Wayne Horvitz, bassist Fred Frith, drummer Joey Baron, and guest vocalist Yamatsuka Eye making intense contributions, altoist Zorn performs his unpredictable originals, abstract versions of some movie themes (including "A Shot in the Dark," "I Want to Live," "Chinatown," and "The James Bond Theme") plus Ornette Coleman's "Lonely Woman." The stimulating music rewards repeated listenings by more open-minded listeners. —*Scott Yanow*

**Elegy** / Oct. 1995 / Tzadik ✦✦✦✦
The album is a mysterious, elegant, exotic tone poem built around Jean Genet's image relating flowers and prisoners. There are four parts entitled *Blue, Yellow, Pink* and *Black*. It features a constantly changing soundscape of images—sweet, tortured, folk ceremony, hellishly cosmic, dungeon sounds of chains and locks, breathing and much more—highlighted by silences. Brilliantly evocative. With Barbara Chaffe, alto and bass flutes, David Abel, viola, Scummy, guitar, David Shea, turntables, David Slusser, sound effects, William Winant, percussion, and Mike Patton, voice. —*"Blue" Gene Tyranny*

**Bar Kokhba** / Aug. 20, 1996 / Tzadik ✦✦✦✦
*Bar Kokhba* encompasses the wealth of material John Zorn has composed with his eminent quartet Masada. The album is a collection of Masada songs that have been rearranged for chamber ensembles. For this effort Zorn enlists some of New York's finest musicians: John Medeski, Marc Ribot, Anthony Coleman, and Erik Freedlander, among others. The compositions range from groups of four to solo performances by Ribot, Medeski, and Coleman. While some compositions retain their original structure and sound, some are expanded and probed by Zorn's arrangements, and resemble avant-garde classical music more than jazz. But this is the beauty of the album; the ensembles provide a forum for Zorn to expand his compositions. The album consistently impresses, and the highlights include "Gevurah," "Paran," and "Mochin." Zorn's genius as both songwriter and arranger are evidenced, and the recording sits well among the traditional Masada material. —*Marc Gilman*

## :zoviet*france:

f. 1980, Newcastle, England
*Group / Experimental Ambient, Experimental Rock, Industrial*
The repetitive, droning, mostly electronic music of Newcastle natives :zoviet*france: often flirted with ambient and industrial textures in a low-budget atmosphere, and was often laden with effects. The majority of the group's extensive discography was recorded for the British label Red Rhino; most of its LPs featured packaging even stranger than the music inside. :zoviet*france: debuted in 1982 with the 12" *Hessians* and recorded steadily up to 1990; highlights of this period include *Norsch* (1983), the retrospective *Popular Soviet Songs and Youth Music* (1985), *Misfits, Loony Tunes and Squalid Criminals* (1986), *A Flock of Rotations* (1987), and *Shouting at the Ground* (1988). A long hiatus preceded the release of 1995's *Collusion*, although :zoviet*france: remained prolific throughout the latter half of the decade. —*Steve Huey*

**Norsch** / 1983 / Red Rhino ♦♦♦

**Popular Soviet Songs and Youth Music** / 1985 / Red Rhino ♦♦♦

● **Collusion** / Aug. 1, 1995 / Soleilmoon ♦♦♦♦
Constructed from an array of samples and environmental recordings plus plenty of feedback, *Collusion* exudes a rare beauty for an album of such varied sounds (each track was originally released on a different compilation). Though the first includes a long passage from a religious-revival preacher (complete with the sample used for the title of the early-'90s rave hit "Injected with a Poison"), the dark ambience and white noise of later songs like "Sprey," "First Vigil," and "White Dusk" make for a surprisingly exciting album. —*John Bush*

**Digilogue** / Jul. 17, 1996 / Soleilmoon ♦♦♦♦
*Digilogue* consists of a full hour of wildly variable material, ranging from synth-damage distortion to minimalistic sequenced click-tracks to atmospheric ambience. Originally available only as a limited-edition LP, *Digilogue* was later reissued on CD with three tracks intended for, but unable to fit on, the vinyl release. —*John Bush*

## Zulutronic (Cem Oral)

*Producer / Electro-Techno, Club/Dance, Techno*

Zulutronic is only one of a dizzyingly abundant cachet of names used by Cologne-based producer/Pharma label boss Cem Oral, who has also released records as G104, Jammin' Unit, and, together with longtime partner Walker, Air Liquide. Zulutronic is a collaborative project between Oral and fellow Cologne-based producer Roger Cobernus, aka Kerosene; both share credentials as part of the influential Structure label group, an important component in the experimental wing of Germany's early-'90s dance music underground. Although apart the pair's material has ranged from hardcore acid, techno, and trance to downtempo breaks and even beatless ambient, Oral and Cobernus (with Zulutronic) focus on mid- to up-tempo experimental hip-hop and electro, bringing an artful, scientific economy and a new-school weirdness to minimal, funk-fueled breakbeat. While most of the group's material (including the full-length LP/CD *Mission Zulu One*) has appeared on Oral's own Pharma label, the group have also contributed tracks to compilations on Mille Plateaux (*Electric Ladyland, Vol. 3*) and Virgin (*Macro Dub Infection, Vol. 2*). The pair have also played a number of live gigs under the name, including club and festival appearances. [See Also: Jammin' Unit] —*Sean Cooper*

**Zulutronic [Single]** / 1995 / Pharma ♦♦
This debut six-track is a first on two counts: the first release by Cem "Jammin' Unit" Oral and Roger "Kerosene" Cobernus as Zulutronic, and also the first release on Oral's new Pharma imprint, soon to be known as a respected source of experimental breakbeat and electro. The bulk of the material here is somewhere between those last two, with thick, speedy breaks left dusty and fraying, bleeping laser blasts, and turntable cut-up weirdness suggesting a bizarre, mutant strain of Bronx-born lino gear. Ponderous. —*Sean Cooper*

● **Mission Zulu One** / Apr. 28, 1997 / Pharma ♦♦♦♦
Considerably less screwed up than their debut, Zulutronic's shift into long-form gear brings an attendant focus, primarily on production and dense, economical rhythms, making *Mission Zulu One* significantly more pleasing to listen to than the group's debut EP. The humor's still there, of course, what with the blaxploitation cut-ups, the big, dumb, rubbery basslines, and voice synthesizers announcing "Evil zombies in the house!" Beatswise, the tempo is focused on the mid, with most of the tracks on the sparsely syncopated electro tip. —*Sean Cooper*

**Back to Bommershime** / Jul. 7, 1998 / Pharma ♦♦♦

# Various Artists

**10 Years of Techno** / Jan. 26, 1999 / Arcade ♦♦♦♦
*10 Years of Techno* states a pretty good case for being a definitive techno collection, including genre classics like "Energy Flash" (Joey Beltram), "Pacific State" (808 State), "Strings of Life" (Derrick May), "Horsepower" (C. J. Bolland), "Age of Love" (Age of Love), "Higher State of Consciousness" (Wink), and "Plastic Dreams" (Jaydee). Though one or two of the classics are remixes instead of originals, the double-disc set *10 Years of Techno* is an excellent summation of the world of techno. —*John Bush*

**100% Pure: The Lowlands** / 1995 / New Electronica ♦♦♦♦
An all-Continental volume in the crucial New Electronica compilation series, *100% Pure: The Lowlands* features tracks from Orlando Voorn, 2000 & One, Stefan Robbers, Pure, and Edge of Motion. —*John Bush*

**110 Below, Vol. 1: Journey in Dub** / 1994 / Beechwood ♦♦♦♦
The first volume in *New Electronica*'s series of earthy beat excursions focuses on dub, setting a course for the style which has room for a variety of groups—from Tricky to Leftfield to Killing Joke to African Headcharge. —*Keith Farley*

**110 Below, Vol. 2** / 1995 / Beechwood ♦♦♦
The second volume in the series takes hip-hop as its template, then turns the music on its head with inclusions from Freddie Fresh, Howie B, U.N.K.L.E., DJ Krush, and Beck, as well as more straight-ahead breakbeat merchants like Ultramagnetic MCs. —*Keith Farley*

**110 Below, Vol. 3: No Sleeve Notes Required** / 1995 / Beechwood ♦♦♦♦
The third volume of this excellent trip-hop series in the New Electronica series focuses on more avant-garde explorers, including Brian Eno, Jah Wobble, Anton Fier and Material. Other appearances include Urban Dance Squad, Muslimgauze, Harr/Airto/Purim, Thessalonians, Squid, and Planet Jazz. —*Keith Farley*

**20 Fingers: The Compilation** / Oct. 24, 1995 / Zoo ♦♦♦
All your 20 Fingers favorites are here (none of which are edited for content), including "Sex Machine," "Short Dick Man," "Position #9," "Work That Love," and "Choke My Chicken." —*Keith Farley*

**38 Jungle Beats: A Jazz Jungle/Tech Step Adventure** / Oct. 5, 1999 / Master Dance Tones ♦♦♦
Master Dance Tones' *38 Killer Jungle Beats* offers a collection of jungle breakbeats and drum'n'bass rhythms. Not everything here will be well-known, even to collectors, and this is one case where obscurity in dance doesn't necessarily mean better. There are several items and passages that are quite good, but nearly as many fall flat. Primarily, this is worth the time of discerning listeners who have the patience to sort the wheat from the chaff. —*Stephen Thomas Erlewine*

**80's Dance Party, Vol. 1** / Dec. 26, 1994 / SPG ♦♦♦♦
Despite the unconscionably lame title, *'80s Dance Party, Vol. 1* is a solid 12-track collection of acid house, electro, new wave, urban R&B, and mainstream dance hits from the '80s, including Bomb the Bass's "Beat Dis," Herbie Hancock's "Rockit," Inner City's "Big Fun," and S'Express' "Theme from S'Express"—as well as Ready for the World's "Oh Sheila" and Jody Watley's "Looking for a New Love." Some tracks, like Animotion's "Obsession," are included in "dance mixes," abut the overall effect is that of a fun party-oriented sampler. —*Stephen Thomas Erlewine*

**80's Dance Party, Vol. 2** / Dec. 26, 1994 / SPG ♦♦♦
Like its predecessor, *'80s Dance Party, Vol. 2* is a 12-track collection of acid house, electro, new wave, urban R&B, and mainstream dance hits from the '80s. This time around, cuts by Neneh Cherry ("Buffalo Stance"), Cameo ("Word Up"), and Bronski Beat ("Why") are featured. Again, a few tracks, like Timex Social Club's "Rumors" and Bananarama's "Venus," are present in "extended dance mixes," but the overall effect is that of a fun party-oriented sampler. However, this party isn't quite as fun as the one before, because there are simply too many forgettable tracks by the likes of File 13, Dominatrix, Divine, and Strafe. —*Stephen Thomas Erlewine*

**80's Dance Party, Vol. 3** / Dec. 26, 1994 / SPG ♦♦♦
Like its two predecessors, *'80s Dance Party, Vol. 3* is a 12-track collection of acid house, electro, new wave, urban R&B, and mainstream dance hits from the '80s. While it isn't as good as *Vol. 1*, *Vol. 3* is better than *Vol. 2*, since it features such defining dance-pop songs as $Baltimora's "Tarzan Boy," the Jets' "Crush on You," Samantha Fox's "Touch Me (I Want Your Body)," Grandmaster Flash's "White Lines (Don't Don't Do It")", Gwen Guthrie's "Ain't Nothin' Goin' On But the Rent," and Kim Wilde's "You Keep Me Hangin' On." —*Stephen Thomas Erlewine*

**Absolute Friction** / Nov. 10, 1998 / Quantum Loop ♦♦♦
*Absolute Friction* contains tracks from some of the most intense drum'n'bass producers of the late '90s, including Panacea ("Tron"), the Advocate ("Presumed Guilty"), and Decoder ("The Fog"), as well as 1.8.7, Kingsize, and Newt. —*Keith Farley*

**The Absolute Supper** / Feb. 10, 1998 / Cold Meat Industry ♦♦♦♦
For ten years Cold Meat Industry has helped define the face of darkwave music. The post-Gothic ambient compositions from the CMI rosters are stylistically European. Incorporated are elements from Classical music to '70s easy listening. These influences are competently worked into dreary and poignant creations that bring to mind castle dungeons and ghouls staffing a studio. All tracks on this handsomely packaged 2-CD set are previously unreleased. Each CD is imprinted with images from medieval wood blocks and lack distracting text. There is plenty to read in the two color booklets. One sets a page aside for each musician/band and the other is a catalog. The only drawback to this deathly good potpourri is that some selections are truncated at the end, probably because they flowed into another piece in their original setting. —*Thomas Schulte*

**Absolutely: The Very Best of Electro** / May 6, 1997 / Deep Beats ♦♦♦♦
Three discs of electro cuts from the '80s includes several classics—Grandmaster Flash's "White Lines," Man Parrish's "Hip Hop Bee Bop (Don't Stop)," Shannon's "Let the Music Play"—and a handful of even rarer cuts, from the West Street Mob, Warp 9, Melle Mel, and Konk. Though the ratio of unknown to familiar tracks is a bit higher than Rhino's *Electric Funk* box set, *Absolutely* includes a lot of classic material not found elsewhere; also, every track is an extended 12" mix, not a radio edit. —*John Bush*

**Absolutely: The Very Best of Prelude Records** / Apr. 22, 1997 / Deep Beats ♦♦♦
Similar to Deep Beats' electro collection, the Prelude volume in the *Absolutely* series covers the disco and proto-house label with tracks by Jocelyn Brown, Sharon Redd, "D" Train, France Joli, and Musique, among others. The contributors aren't quite as essential as the remixers, however; a collection of production all-stars, Shep Pettibone, Francois Kervorkian, Larry Levan, and Tony Humphries contribute extended remixes, all contemporary with the original Prelude release. The result is a compilation which charts the changeover from '70s disco to '80s house, though with much greater depth than is needed. —*John Bush*

**Abstrakt Workshop** / Apr. 11, 1995 / Shadow ♦♦♦♦
Shadow's first compilation of stoned trip-hop and future jazz recruits DJ Krush, 9 Lazy 9, the Mighty Bop, Diferenz, the Herbaliser, Funki Porcini, and Sharpshooters. —*Keith Farley*

**Abstrakt Workshop, Vol. 2** / Feb. 27, 1996 / Shadow ♦♦♦
Not quite as essential as *Vol. 1*, the follow-up adds tracks from a few of the first's contributors but also adds debuted DJ Cam and Daphreephunkateerz for an American audience. —*Keith Farley*

**Acid House for All** / 1995 / Definitive/Plus 8 ♦♦♦
Released by Definitive, the offshoot of Plus 8 run by John Acquaviva, *Acid House for All* compiles an album's worth of prime acid house material, including contributions from DJ ESP, THC, Serotonin Project, and Ian Pooley. —*Keith Farley*

**Acid Jazz Movie & TV Themes** / Oct. 28, 1997 / Hollywood ♦♦♦
*Acid Jazz Movie & TV Themes* contains a number of familiar themes ("Mission: Impossible," "Rollerball," "Love Boat," "Top of the Pops," "Dirty Harry," "The Flintstones") that have been arranged as acid-jazz songs. Clearly, the album was designed to appeal to the hipper-than-thou audience that celebrates kitsch, not quality. Peel back the ironic layers, and there are some intriguing beats and textures here. There just aren't enough to make it worthwhile to anyone but patient, open-minded listeners. —*Stephen Thomas Erlewine*

**The Acid Jazz Test, Vol. 1** / 1994 / Moonshine Music ♦♦♦♦
Moonshine covers the more downtempo side of acid jazz—Jhelisa, A-1, Brooklyn Funk Essentials—on the first volume in the *Acid Jazz Test* series. —*Keith Farley*

**The Acid Jazz Test, Vol. 2** / 1994 / Planet Earth ♦♦♦♦
*Acid Jazz Test, Vol. 2* is a bit of a disappointing album, with Moonshine switching up the lineup slightly from the debut: Deborah Anderson contributes a track instead of Jhelisa; plus, the Broun Fellinis appear. —*Keith Farley*

**The Acid Jazz Test, Vol. 3** / Jun. 20, 1995 / Moonshine Music ♦♦♦
*Acid Jazz Test, Vol. 3* is another samey acid jazz compilation from Moonshine, though D'Note's closer "The Garden of Earthly Delights" is a sublime piece of future funk. —*Keith Farley*

**The Acid Jazz Test, Vol. 4** / Feb. 6, 1996 / Moonshine Music ♦♦♦♦
Outside's "Journeyman" and Jhelisa's "Whirl Keeps Turning" are a couple of the highlights on the overdone fourth volume of the *Acid Jazz Test* series from Moonshine. —*Keith Farley*

**Acid Jazz UK Past & Present, Vol. 1** / Oct. 7, 1997 / Prophecy ♦♦♦
Strange Fruit, the Latin Quarter, Freeway Planet, Colonel Abrams, and Dread Flintstone are among the artists featured on *Acid Jazz UK Past and Present Vol. 1*. —*Jason Ankeny*

**Acid Jazz US Past & Present, Vol. 1** / Oct. 7, 1997 / Prophecy ♦♦♦
The James Taylor Quartet, Galliano, Piece of Mind, the K Collective, and the Quiet Boys are among the performers included on *Acid Jazz US Past and Present Vol. 1*. —*Jason Ankeny*

**Acid Jazz, Vol. 3: Latin Soul** / 1992 / Acid Jazz ♦♦♦♦
Whether or not acid jazz deserves to be called jazz depends upon the artists to whom you're referring. If you consider the organ combo grooves of Charles Earland, Richard "Groove" Holmes, or Jack McDuff part of acid jazz, then, yes, some acid jazz is truly jazz. However, a lot of the British dance music that was called acid jazz in the '90s wasn't really jazz; it was dance music with jazz overtones. Even with a very liberal definition of jazz, the music on *Acid Jazz 3: LSD (Latin Soul and Dance)* cannot honestly be called jazz—this is a collection of Latin-flavored dance-pop, house, and urban contemporary. But more important than whether or not this music is jazz, is that it's good. Sleek tunes like Varela's "Make Your Move," Ela's "Paraiso," and Santa Fe's "Like a Dream" are creative and appealing, even though they have nothing to do with jazz. Equally captivating is "Deja Voodoo," a solo item from one-time Santa Esmeralda vocalist Leroy Gomez. Although most of these songs were recorded with clubs in mind, they don't lose their value outside of a club setting—they're interesting songs that you wouldn't mind sitting and listening to. *Acid Jazz 3* should be kept out of the jazz bins, but for dance-pop enthusiasts, it's highly recommended. —*Alex Henderson*

**Acid Jazz: Collection, Vol. 1** / Scotti Brothers ♦♦♦
Scotti Brothers has issued three separate volumes of acid jazz, a popular dance genre of the late '80s and early '90s that combines elements of jazz, hip-hop, funk, and R&B. Like most dance music, it is primarily a singles medium, so compilations serve the music well. None of the featured songs were pop hits, yet almost every track has something to recommend it— whether the beat, vocals, or instrumentals. While some major names of the genre are missing from the three discs, any volume of *Acid Jazz: Collection* is a good place for an introduction to the music. —*Stephen Thomas Erlewine*

**Acid Resistant** / 1995 / Sm:)e/Profile ♦♦♦
Produced and mixed by DJ db, *Acid Resistant* compiles tracks that detail Cologne's effect on acid-house. Included are Ultrahigh's "Primitive Love, Part One" and Bizz O.D's "I'm Coming out of Your Speakers." —*Keith Farley*

**Acid Resistant, Vol. 2** / Sep. 17, 1996 / Sm:)e ♦♦♦
Another volume of mostly Cologne-based acid-techno, including Dr. Walker, Bizz OD, Kerosene, Cube 40, and Frank Heiss' hilarious "Flashdancers on Acid." —*Keith Farley*

**Acid Space** / Jun. 15, 1999 / Cleopatra ♦♦♦
The idea behind *Acid Space* is a good one: psychedelia, prog, and space-rock from the late '60s and early '70s. Quite deserving of an extensive box set is this spotlighting of such pioneers as the Yardbirds, Gong, Hawkwind, Tangerine Dream, Amon Düül II, Holger Czukay, Curved Air, Daevid Allen, the Nice, Magma, and the 13th Floor Elevators. Cleopatra's four-disc attempt doesn't count as the definitive overview, however, since too many of the cuts are either live, outtakes, or flat-out strange choices. There's enough of interest here to make it a worthwhile purchase if it can be found for a reasonable price, but it should not be thought of as the final word on the genre. —*Stephen Thomas Erlewine*

**Adrian Sherwood Presents Master Recordings** / Oct. 6, 1998 / On U Sounds ♦♦♦
This assembly of crucial On-U Sound artists includes tracks by African Head Charge, Bim Sherman, Creation Rebel, Dub Syndicate, and Dr. Pablo. —*John Bush*

**The Adventures of Priscilla Queen of the Desert** / 1994 / Mother ♦♦♦♦
An irresistible set of disco classics (some available in their original, rare 12" mixes), the soundtrack to the drag queen epic Priscilla, Queen of the Desert is a thoroughly engaging album, ranking as one of the best disco compilations available. —*Stephen Thomas Erlewine*

**After Hours: The Sound of Tribal UK, Vol. 2** / Jul. 1996 / Capitol ♦♦♦♦
*After Hours: The Sound of Tribal UK, Vol. 2* is a various artists mix album as mixed by Elliot Eastwick and Miles Hollway. Rarely getting frantic, the record prefers to stay in the laidback but soulful sounds of jazz and dance fusions. As with any mix album, the DJs are the stars, not the performers, but it does help that Eastwick and Hollway have started with a strong foundation—it's hard to go wrong with music by the Daou, Junior Vasquez, Club 69, and Elastic Reality. —*Stephen Thomas Erlewine*

**Agenda 22: Another Eevo Lute Compilation** / 1995 / New Electronica ♦♦♦♦
The Dutch label represents in the series of *New Electronica* compilations with excellent tracks from Florence, Max 404, and David Caron. Other noteworthy inclusions are Ross 154's "Living the Love of the Afterlife" and the Keyprocessor's "Cabs." —*John Bush*

**Alien Underground, Vol. 1** / Apr. 7, 1997 / Kickin' ♦♦♦
The Back 2 Basics crew and Rob Roar collected these space-oriented tracks from house music's best, including Watchman, Josh Wink, Stickmen, Tamburi Project, and Omegaman. —*Keith Farley*

**Aliens on Rave** / Sep. 14, 1999 / Cleopatra ♦♦
*Aliens on Rave* is a four-disc box-set repackaging from Cleopatra which gathers two previously released double-disc rave and techno compilations: *Aliens on Acid* and *License 2 Rave*. Neither was incredibly exceptional upon initial release, and even though the price for these four discs is dirt-cheap, it's ultimately a good deal only if you're looking to acquire a large quantity of music at once and don't mind its rather standard flavor. —*Steve Huey*

**Altered Beats: Assassin Knowledges of the Remanipulated** / 1996 / Axiom ♦♦♦
This collection of Bill Laswell productions is obviously a labor of love put together by a man who misses hip-hop's old school. Though it features artists as current as Prince Paul, DXT, and New Kingdom, the album's focus on turntable scratching and a preponderance of relatively simple, monolithic beats make it sound like a period piece. That's not a bad thing, especially when Laswell imbues the proceedings with an up-to-the-minute ambience and a rumbling bass (as in bass guitar, not 808). But the complete absence of

rapping—the only thing that keeps this from actually being a hip-hop record—may leave some listeners scratching their heads. Instead, we get a Bootsy Collins cameo (never a problem) and the occasional sample of a rightwing radio preacher. Some of the scratching is truly virtuosic; in particular, witness the retro-ensemble sound of the Filipino turntable group the Invisibl Skratch Picklz and the quicksilver manipulations of DJ DXT. Laswell's production overlays everything with a spacy, ambient sheen. —*Rick Anderson*

**Alternative Frequencies, Vol. 3** / 1998 / Worm ♦♦♦
As the title indicates, the third volume in Worm Interface's series of *Alternative Frequencies* compilations focuses on the leading edge of listening techno circa the late '90s, courtesy of tracks by Jake Mandell, Gescom, Plasma Lamp, Himuro, and Solar X. —*John Bush*

**Amberdelic Space [Cleopatra]** / Mar. 18, 1997 / Cleopatra ♦♦♦♦
One thing that can be said of Dressed To Kill's compilations is that they are a great way to get a solid collection together in a specific genre (or set of related genres) without spending an extreme amount of money. In the case of this 4CD box set, the genres in question range from the shaggy end of acid and space (with a surprise visit from Hawkwind) to the intense edge of tribal techno—which means there is a great deal of likeable synthesizer noodling, walloping great chunks of booming bass, periodic breakdowns, passages of experimental weirdness (Syzygy provides a great example with "Namaste"), trippy psychedelic guitars, and lots more. Older listeners may be struck by the amount of music resembling synthesizer bands of the early seventies—particularly early Tangerine Dream. Even the everything-old-is-new-again element comes equipped with a distinctly '90s approach to bass and percussion (in other words, make sure you have woofers with titanium cones). An excellent anthology that bears up in the zoned headphone space and on the dancefloor. —*Steven E. McDonald*

**Ambient Extractions, Vol. 2** / 1995 / C&S ♦♦♦♦
Unlike the majority of techno and ambient house compilations from tiny American labels, this release is quite solid. It includes Brian Eno, Seefeel, Meat Beat Manifesto, Astralasia, and Bark Psychosis. —*Keith Farley*

**Ambient Systems, Vol. 2** / Oct. 8, 1996 / Instinct ♦♦♦♦
*Ambient Systems, Vol. 2* includes the more isolationist bent of Instinct electronica, featuring Seti, Tetsu Inoue, Terre Thaemltiz, Sub Dub, Futique, Human Mesh Dance, and Omicron. Despite the rarefied air of the proceedings, the two-disc set is a good compilation of '90s space music. —*Keith Farley*

**Ambient Systems, Vol. 3** / Apr. 15, 1997 / Instinct ♦♦♦
The usual suspects (Human Mesh Dance, Seti, Inoue, Thaemltiz) make follow-up appearances on the third volume of *Ambient Systems*. —*Keith Farley*

★ **Ambient, Vol. 1: A Brief History of Ambient** / Feb. 22, 1994 / Virgin ♦♦♦♦♦
Although it seemed to arrive out of nowhere in the early '90s, ambient music actually has a long and varied history, leading back to Brian Eno and Kraftwerk's electronic experiments in the '70s right up to Aphex Twin's textural techno soundscapes. As an introduction and history lesson, the two-disc *A Brief History of Ambient Music* can't be beat; it shows that the ambient techno trend has roots that most fans wouldn't realize existed. —*Stephen Thomas Erlewine*

**Ambient, Vol. 2: Imaginary Landscapes** / Aug. 23, 1994 / Virgin ♦♦♦♦
The second volume in Virgin's priceless *Ambient* series is a bit of a retread from the first: alternating classics from Virgin's rich back catalog with the new school of ambient electronica (of which, the label's store is much harder to come by). The result is an Orb remix (of the Grid) instead of a normal Orb track; the only other contemporary acts are the Future Sound of London project Amorphous Androgynous, William Orbit's Bass-O-Matic, Tony Thorpe's Voyager, and such intriguing but obviously label-centric acts as Verve and U2's The Edge. As far as classic ambient tracks go, Virgin is tops—Eno, Sakamoto, Robert Fripp, David Sylvian, Phil Manzanera, Klaus Schulze—though the lack of more up-to-date acts can be frustrating. —*John Bush*

**Ambient, Vol. 3: Music of Changes** / 1995 / Virgin ♦♦♦♦
The third volume in Virgin's *Ambient* series doesn't change the game much; there are a few newer acts sprinkled amongst the two-disc set (FSOL, Orbit, Bark Psychosis) but the main focus is on classic ambient masters (Eno, Fripp, Sakamoto, Sylvian, Budd) and quieter selections from Virgin artists who wouldn't normally be classified this way (Prince Far I, Holger Czukay, Shu-De, Bill Laswell, Nusrat Fateh Ali Khan). The result is another fine collection, though the first three are basically interchangeable. —*John Bush*

**Ambient, Vol. 4: Isolationism** / Jun. 6, 1995 / Virgin ♦♦♦♦
Virgin's fourth *Ambient* volume is the first of all-new material from contemporary artists, and it provides the most highlights of any in the series. The set includes tracks from a score of crucial new-ambient producers, including Aphex Twin, Seefeel, O'Rang, EAR, Main, Final, Lull, Labradford, Techno Animal, Scorn, and Paul Schütze. Since each track is available only on this collection, it became the hardest-to-find of the entire series soon after its release. —*John Bush*

**The American Dream** / 1995 / City of Angels ♦♦♦
This wide-ranging compilation from the Left Coast label includes ambient, trance, house, funk, and trip-hop excursions by lesser-known artists. —*Keith Farley*

**Amnesia Music Bar** / Nov. 17, 1998 / Zip Dog ♦♦
This high-energy dance compilation includes tracks by Emperor Sly, Leftfield, Fluid, Select Fire, and the Rootsman. —*Keith Farley*

**Analogue Daydreaming, Vol. 1** / Mar. 17, 1998 / V-Wax ♦♦♦
This retro-techno collection includes tracks by MJ1, Qapriqorn, Jellyman, Nature of Ground, Jooma, and Sound Chase. —*Keith Farley*

**Analogue Daydreaming, Vol. 2** / Mar. 17, 1998 / V-Wax ♦♦♦
The follow-up retro-techno compilation includes tracks by Pulphea, Alex Jave, Pluto, Bass Invaders, and Embryo. —*Keith Farley*

**Annex 2** / Jan. 26, 1999 / EFA ♦♦♦
A collection of tracks related to Berlin's Tresor nightclub, *Annex 2* includes Juan Atkins' Infiniti project, the Advent, Joey Beltram, Scan 7, and Savvas Ysatis. —*John Bush*

**Antler-Subway/Nrg Sampler** / 1995 / Never Records Group ♦♦♦
A compilation of watered-down acid-house from the Belgian Antler-Subway label, this sampler includes tracks by Praga Khan & Jade 4 U, Lords of Acid, Transformer 2, and Channel X. —*Keith Farley*

**Are You Ready to Dance?** / 1993 / Epic ♦♦♦
*Are You Ready to Dance?* is an 11-track collection of extended 12" dance mixes of pop and dance hits from the late '80s and early '90s. There are a few good moments, but the collection should be thought of as a dance-oriented party album, not a hit sampler—since all versions here are different from those receiving radio play. For dance fans, however, there are a number of good, inventive remixes, but there are just as many rote mixes that prevent the record from being necessary listening. Among the featured artists are Apollo 440 ("Blackout"), Rozalla ("Are You Ready to Fly"), Deep Forest ("Sweet Lullaby"), Cover Girls ("If You Want My Love"), Prefab Sprout ("If You Don't Love Me"), and the Shamen ("L.S.I."). —*Stephen Thomas Erlewine*

**Artcore, Vol. 1** / 1995 / React ♦♦♦♦
The first volume in the long-running React series of atmospheric drum'n'bass with attitude, *Artcore* includes great tracks from a variety of sources: DJ Krust and Jazz Juice from V Records, Omni Trio and Justice from Moving Shadow, Sounds of Life from Certificate 18, and DJ Crystal and Alladin from S.O.U.R. Records. —*Keith Farley*

**Artcore, Vol. 2: Art of Drum & Bass** / 1996 / React ♦♦♦♦
Even more diverse than volume one, *The Art of Drum & Bass* collects breakbeat anthems from Adam F, J. Majik, Ballistic Brothers, Doc Scott, Optical, Foul Play, and Eugenix. On an album of stellar tracks, the highlight is DJ Trace's remix of TPower's "The Mutant." —*Keith Farley*

**Artcore, Vol. 3** / Mar. 1997 / React ♦♦♦♦
The third volume in React's jungle compilation series is just as crucial as the first two, although the predominant style isn't house-oriented intelligent drum'n'bass. Instead, appearances by Ed Rush, DJ Die, Peshay, and Doc Scott signal that *Artcore 3* focuses on the intense, paranoid sounds of darkstep. Goldie's destruction-by-remix of a Garbage track is the highlight. —*John Bush*

**Artcore, Vol. 4: Drum 'n' Bass Beat Technology** / Sep. 22, 1997 / React ♦♦♦♦
Yet another volume of the *Artcore* series succeeds in translating onto disc some of the finest moments in jungle's past, including DJ Krust's "Soul in Motion", and others by Matrix, Optical, and Q Project & Spinback. The mixing comes courtesy of Kemistry & Storm. —*John Bush*

★ **Artificial Intelligence** / 1993 / Wax Trax! ♦♦♦♦♦
The premier listening-techno label for the early '90s, Warp (distributed by

TVT) released seminal albums by Polygon Window (aka Aphex Twin), Black Dog, B12, and Autechre. Great tracks from these artists appear on *Artificial Intelligence*, along with contributions from Richie Hawtin, Speedy J, and the Orb's Dr. Alex Paterson. The B12 track "Telefone 529" (as Musicology), Black Dog's "Clan" (as I.A.O.), and Autechre's "Crystel" are three of the best here. The cover displays a robotic humanoid relaxing in a futuristic living room, Kraftwerk and Pink Floyd LPs on the floor—quite appropriate since Warp virtually pioneered the concept of applying the concepts of '70s ambience to '80s techno. The result is a superb collection of electronic listening music, and it's a great place to start for the newly interested. —*John Bush*

**Artificial Intelligence, Vol. 2** / 1994 / Wax Trax! ♦♦♦♦
With more artists than the previous *Artificial Intelligence* compilation, this second installment is a bit more sonically experimental, though it suffers from a lack of enjoyable tracks. Along with contributions from *AI* regulars (Autechre, Speedy J, B12, Polygon Window, the Black Dog's Balil project) are tracks by newer names—like Beaumont Hannant, Mark Franklin, and Higher Intelligence Agency—yet these water down the quality somewhat. The Global Communication project Link contributes what is quite possibly the highlight, the almost progressive house number "Arcadian." While the British edition includes a limited second disc (including an unreleased Richard D. James track named "My Teapot"), the American version of *Artificial Intelligence, Vol. 2* is single-disc only. —*John Bush*

**Ash 2.1** / 1995 / Ash International ♦♦♦
This Ash compilation includes tracks by Scanner, S.E.T.I., Hafler Trio, Aurobindo. —*Keith Farley*

**Asphodelic** / Feb. 9, 1999 / Asphodel ♦♦♦
This Asphodel compilation includes a batch of tracks by the label's illbient and turntablist acts including Tipsy, We, Badawi, Mix Master Mike, DJ Spooky, Rob Swift, and the X-Ecutioners. —*John Bush*

**Atmospheric Drum & Bass, Vol. 4** / Mar. 23, 1999 / Millennium ♦♦♦
*Atmospheric Drum & Bass, Vol. 4* is a double-disc set charting the outer edge of ambient drum'n'bass. Tracks by Justice, Omni Trio, Voyager, and Bim Sherman are the highlights; though offerings from Torus, Eugenix, Ed Solo, and Minx also perform well. —*Keith Farley*

**Atomic Audio** / 1996 / Quango ♦♦♦
With one foot on the worldbeat bandwagon and the other firmly on the club floor, the Quango label has benefitted from Island Records' muscular distribution apparatus. The label has provided the world with booty-shaking dance music that manages to never sacrifice funk in its quest for multicultural inclusiveness. In a world that's increasingly thin-lipped and prissy about multiculturalism, that's a rare and wonderful thing. *Atomic Audio* is a collection of album tracks and single remixes from mostly British artists (though the disc's annoying lack of liner notes makes that impossible to verify). Names like Pentatonik and Wolfgang Press (refugees from the decidedly unfunky 4AD stable) will be familiar to club crawlers—and in fact they provide some of the more interesting moments on a disc that is never boring. Pentatonik kicks in a trippy Clint Eastwood-on-Ecstasy groove with "Zeitgeist," which includes vague spaghetti-western references. Wolfgang Press continues to explore the snarling malevolence that has become its hallmark on "Executioner." "Coming Home to the Sun," (David Holmes) is a mystical, plainsong that, which, when combined with junglesque breakbeats, hits the spot quite nicely. Buy this disc, then explore Quango's back catalog—it's worth the trip. —*Rick Anderson*

**Atomium 3003** / Apr. 25, 2000 / EFA ♦♦♦
*Atomium 3003* features sophisticated global and electronic pop from Chop Suey, Crooner, Shy, Katerine, and the Euro Boys. Arling & Cameron's witty "Spacebeach," Komeda's "A Simple Formality," Bertrand Burgalat's "Attention Amante," and Valerie Lemercier's "Bungalow" are some of the most notable tracks from this cutting-edge collection. —*Heather Phares*

**Autentico Ibiza, Vol. 2** / Aug. 25, 1998 / Imprint ♦♦♦
*Autentico Ibiza, Vol. 2* is a generous sampling of 21 high-energy ibica dance numbers highlighted by "Strong in Love," "Forever Tonight," "Greece 2000," "El Nino," "Groove for Life," "Soul Grabber, Pt. III," and "Horny 98." It's not a definitive portrait of the subgenre by any means, but it is a fun sampler. —*Stephen Thomas Erlewine*

**Avantgardism** / Dec. 9, 1996 / Law & Auder ♦♦♦♦
A double-disc collection of exclusives, this Law & Auder release includes beat-merchants like Boymerang, Plug, Bedouin Ascent, Freeform, TPower, Black Dog, David Kristian, and Witchman. —*Keith Farley*

**Axiom Ambient: Lost in the Translation** / 1994 / Axiom ♦♦♦♦
Bill Laswell—the brain and spirit behind Material, and the driving force behind a long line of world grunge—has been moving gradually and easily into experimenting with ambient music and soundscapes with roots in Brian Eno and many others. *Lost in the Translation*, which reworks a number of musical pieces into the ambient idiom, is filled with odd sounds—from voices to wind to water, long droning and swirling tones, deep basses and high, tinkling windchimes, treated percussion and blipping synths. It's fascinating, hypnotic, and engrossing, though you'd be hard pressed to find a melody in any of it. The album has many uses, primarily in creative visualization, relaxation, and meditation—a remarkably enjoyable release. Laswell, to say the least, is fascinating in his output. —*Steven McDonald*

**B-Side: Player 1 Press Start** / Nov. 10, 1998 / Fragrant ♦♦♦
A mix of breakbeat funk and video-game trance, *B-Side: Player 1 Press Start* features selections from Freestylers, Mr. Dan, 2 Fat Buddhas, DJ Apache, and Omar Santana's Tales from the Hardside project. —*John Bush*

**Bare Essentials, Vol. 1** / Jul. 25, 2000 / Naked ♦♦
*Bare Essentials, Vol. 1* is a compilation of moody new soul, house, and dance tracks featured on the Naked Music label of New York City. Included are original, remix, and dub versions—some previously unreleased by Petalpusher, Groove Collective, Lovetronic, Blue Six, Night Source, and Summerland. —*Al Campbell*

**Barramundi: Introduction to a Cooler World** / Astralwerks/Caroline ♦♦♦
Offshoot of Belgian acid label Antler-Subway, Barramundi is a collection of ambient tracks by bands known more for dance than slower vibes. JayDee, Transformer 2, and others use their techno roots to create music that still grooves, if at a lower speed. —*Keith Farley*

**Bass Bomb, Vol. 2** / Mar. 25, 1994 / Thump ♦♦♦
*Bass Bomb, Vol. 2* is a 12-track collection of bass- and groove-heavy hip-hop, freestyle, and urban R&B. The title may lead you to believe that these are all Miami bass cuts, but that's not true—there's very little bass music here, just a lot of hip-hop with loud bass. Some cuts are quite good, but much of the material here is unfortunately of mediocre quality; however, casual hip-hop fans might find a couple cuts worthwhile. Among featured artists are Will to Power, Stevie B, Noel, the Cover Girls, Trinere, Shannon, and Lisa Lisa & Cult Jam. —*Stephen Thomas Erlewine*

**Bass Ultra-Slow Mega-Low** / May 18, 1999 / DM ♦♦♦
The title says it all: *Bass Ultra-Slow Mega-Low* features 21 booming tracks by artists like the Bass Bombers, Bass Invaders, Bass Syndicate, Bass Alliance, and Techno Bass Crew. Tracks like "Outer Space Bass," "Slowmotions," and "Subterranean" celebrate the low end in all its rumbling glory. —*Heather Phares*

**Bassic Elements** / 1995 / Jumpin' and Pumpin' ♦♦♦
*Bassic Elements* is a solid compilation of jungle tracks, including contributions from T Power, Little Matt, Endemic Void, Hed UK, and Universal Love. —*Keith Farley*

**Basskraft: Tribute to Kraftwerk** / Sep. 8, 1998 / Pandisc ♦♦♦
The massive influence of the German group Kraftwerk on bass music, electro, and most American dance music is basically a foregone conclusion, so this bass-music tribute to Kraftwerk hardly comes as a surprise. Another surprise is how similar these versions are to the original without sacrificing any of the tenets of great bass music. From the classics "Trans Europe Express" and "Numbers"—both of which figure prominently in the genesis of electro/bass, Afrika Bambaataa's "Planet Rock"—to others like "Pocket Calculator," "Computer World," "Autobahn," and "Robots," *Basskraft* is an intriguing collection. —*Keith Farley*

**Beat Classic** / Jun. 2, 1997 / DC Recordings/Electron ♦♦♦♦
J Saul Kane (Octagon Man, Depth Charge) compiled this collection of obscure electro and hip-hop classics, and the sheer enthusiasm evident on the collection makes one wonder at what happened to these unheard artists. Names like Rammellzee Vs. K-Rob, Z-3 MC's, Levi 167, and B+ produce electronic-oriented hip-hop with production values strictly from the basement. With incredible tracks like this lying in wait for reissue, there must be dozens upon dozens of albums' worth of material around. —*Keith Farley*

**Behind the Eye, Vol. 3** / Jun. 11, 1996 / Eye Q ♦♦♦
None of the bigger Eye Q names appear on this third volume in the *Behind the Eye* series, though the included tracks from Cygnus X, B-Zet, and Earth Nation are solid enough. —*Keith Farley*

**Bento Box** / Sep. 2, 1997 / Caipirinha ♦♦♦♦
The stateside label for leftfield drum'n'bass action, Capirinha's *Bento Box* includes tracks from several noteworthy side projects—Amon Tobin's Cujo, Si Begg's Cabbageboy, Squarepusher's Duke of Harringay, DJ Vadim's Little Aida—as well as Boards of Canada, Jimpster, and the Egg. —*Keith Farley*

**The Best of "O" Records, Vol. 1** / 1989 / Hot Prod. ♦♦♦
*The Best of "O" Records, Vol. 1* contains 14 selections from the vaults of the disco label, including Roni Griffith's "Desire," the Flirts' "Passion," Divine's "Native Love," Bobby "O"'s "I'm So Hot for You," Claudja Barry's "Whisper to a Scream," Gomez Presley's "Letter," and Band of South's "Sensitive." "O" Records never had any really big hits, but they had several interesting obscurities, a handful of which are included here amongst some entertaining filler. —*Stephen Thomas Erlewine*

**The Best of "O" Records, Vol. 2** / 1989 / Hot Prod. ♦♦♦
*The Best of "O" Records, Vol. 2* contains 14 selections from the vaults of the disco label, including the Flirts' "Helpless," Bobby "O"'s "She Has a Way," Divine's "Shoot Your Shot," Roni Griffith's "Best Part of Breakin' Up," Oh Romeo's "Once Is Not Enough," Eric's "Who's Your Boyfriend," and the Pet Shop Boys' "West End Girls." —*Stephen Thomas Erlewine*

**The Best of Acid Jazz, Vol. 1** / Apr. 22, 1997 / Hollywood ♦♦
Another subpar compilation billed as the best of acid jazz, this includes several solid tracks (from African Headcharge, Gregory Isaacs, Snowboy, and the James Taylor Quartet), but many lame grooves from the likes of the Night Trains, Mother Earth, Emperors New Clothes, and Dread Flimstone. —*Keith Farley*

**The Best of Acid Jazz: In the Mix, Vol. 2** / Feb. 22, 2000 / Instinct ♦♦♦
*Best of Acid Jazz: In the Mix 2* features more acid jazz from Instinct's roster, including Sambada's "City Nights," Hedfunk's "Aqua," Yada Yada's "Kickin' It," Kosma's "Aeroboot," and 9 Lazy 9's "Brother of the Red." Tracks from Night Trains, CFM Band, Jimpster, Diferenz, and Mr. Electric Train round out this worthwhile collection of sleek, polished acid jazz. —*Heather Phares*

**Best of Chicago Trax** / May 26, 1998 / M.I.L. Multimedia ♦♦♦
The two-disc *Best of Chicago Trax* assembles 26 tracks from the Windy City-based dance label best known for its affiliation with Frankie Knuckles, whose "Baby Wants to Ride" and "Your Love" are among the highlights. Other featured tracks include Liz Torres' "Can't Get Enough" and Mr. Fingers' "Can You Feel It." —*Jason Ankeny*

**Best of Dnh** / Feb. 18, 1997 / Tjsb ♦♦♦
Constructing almost three-quarters of the tracks on this DNH retrospective, Nick Holder comes across with several solid tracks including "Soundwaves," "Thinking About U," "Erotic Illusions," and "Hustle Baby." —*Keith Farley*

**Best of Future Sound Records** / 1994 / Rephlex ♦♦♦♦
Rephlex got on the old-school track with this 1994 compilation of one of the most influential Chicago house labels, Future Sound. Founded by Terry "Housemaster" Baldwin in 1987, Future Sound included producers like Derrick May, DJ Pierre, Ron Hardy, and Eric Kupper. Paris Grey, Suburban Boyz, and Confusion also appear on this very worthwhile compilation. —*John Bush*

**Best of House [UK]** / Mar. 25, 1994 / Low Price ♦♦♦♦
A budget-priced box set containing 40 tracks across four discs, *Best of House* is a stellar collection that traces the best of late-'80s and early-'90s house music, balancing a mix of seminal Chicago tracks with equally solid British follow-ups. Besides quite a few guaranteed club classics—Marshall Jefferson's "Move Your Body," and Farley Jackmaster Funk's "Love Can't Turn Around," Steve Silk Hurley's "Jack Your Body," Ralphi Rosario's "You Used to Hold Me"—there are more obscure but inspired tracks like Fingers Inc.'s "Can You Feel It," Kevin Saunderson's Reese Project on "So Deep," and Jesse Saunders' "On and On." The British tracks are no less influential, including "LFO" and "What Is House" by LFO, "Aftermath" by Nightmares on Wax, "Please Don't Go" by KWS, and "Get Out on the Dancefloor" by D.O.P. Many budget compilations draw in buyers with a few hits but then don't follow through with consistently good tracks; *Best of House* focuses only on great songs, whether club hits or not. —*John Bush*

**Best of House Music, Vol. 1** / 1993 / Profile ♦♦♦♦
Contrary to popular belief, disco didn't die with the '70s—it simply changed its name to dance music in the '80s and evolved into such forms as European Hi-NRG, so-called "Latin hip-hop/freestyle," and house music (which originated in the nightlife mecca of Chicago and quickly spread to New York, Europe and elsewhere). Like late-'70s disco, house—defined by its tinkling keyboard grooves and thumping bass, among other things—can be either mechanical and formulaic or soulful, enriching, and even spiritual. Profile Records' excellent *Best of House Music* series, though far from the last word on house, has done a fine job illustrating house's diversity. This CD ranges from producer-oriented, track-minded club hits like J.M. Silk's "Jack Your Body," Exit's "Let's Work It Out," Moonfou's abrasive acid-house number "Shut Up" to songs making vocal personality the main attraction, such as Liz Torres' "Can't Get Enough," Ralphi Rosario & Xaviera Gold's "You Used to Hold Me," and Jeanne Harris' "Just Another Man" (a captivating example of deep house, which is essentially an extention of late-'70s Philly disco/soul). Producer Marshall Jefferson, one of house's key figures, is well represented by the insanely catchy "Move Your Body." This compilations's more producer-oriented cuts are enjoyable enough, but ultimately, limited—in the longrun, warm and personal singing would do the most to keep house artistically healthy. —*Alex Henderson*

**Best of House Music, Vol. 2: Gotta Have House** / 1993 / Profile ♦♦♦♦
House music's detractors vehemently insist that it all sounds alike, which couldn't be farther from the truth. With its second *Best of House Music* compilation, Profile once again showed listeners that house is far from one-dimensional. Those who prefer house's warmer, more vocal-oriented side found much to admire in the inviting and very musical "deep house" of Kechia Jenkins' "I Need Somebody" and remixes of Natalie Cole's hit "Pink Cadillac," and British R&B group Imagination's "Instinctual," while house's more producer-oriented side is exemplified by Royal House's "Can You Party," Jeanette "J.T." Thomas' "Shake Your Body," and Kraze's raucous "The Party." On "I Need Somebody," vocals are everything, whereas on LNR's dissonant and not very musical "Work It to the Bone," it's all about the producer and the track. House fans were already more than familiar with most of this material when Profile released this CD in 1988, but for those first exploring house, it served as an engaging and informative introduction. —*Alex Henderson*

**Best of House Music, Vol. 3: House Music All Night Long** / 1993 / Profile ♦♦♦♦
House music had become a bit less underground by the time Profile released its third *Best of House* compilation in 1990, the year Madonna gave house a pop hit with "Vogue." Like its predecessors, this CD is an unpredictable release reminding us of house's diversity by including a wide variety of material. Warmth and vocal personality are at the fore on Inner City's haunting "Good Life," K-Os' Madonnesque "Definition of Love," and the gutsy Adeva!'s interpretation of the Otis Redding composition/Aretha Franklin hit "Respect." Just how close deep house is to late-'70s Philly disco/soul is hard to miss on Chanelle's sleek, very appealing "One Man." However, the producer, the track, and the groove are dominant on Richie Rich and the Jungle Brothers' infectious "I'll House You," Reese & Santonio's "Rock to the Beat," and A Guy Named Gerald's "Voodoo Ray." The latter, in fact, doesn't really have a melody, just a groove, and an assertive bassline. —*Alex Henderson*

**Best of House Music, Vol. 4: Future House** / 1993 / Profile ♦♦♦
One thing that the fourth volume in Profile's *Best of House Music* series can hardly be called is a carbon copy of its predecessor. While *Vol. 3* was full of melodic deep house songs that emphasized vocal personality, *Vol. 4: Future House* is largely instrumental and is all about the track, the producer, and the beat—in fact, most of the material doesn't have an actual song structure. So in order to understand why the volumes are as different as they are, one has to understand developments in dance music between *Vol. 3's* release in 1990 and *Vol. 4's* release in 1993. It was in 1990 that house reached the pop mainstream in a major way thanks to Madonna's "Vogue," but mainstream acceptance isn't something that DJs in raves and underground dance clubs aspire to—and such DJs favored the left-of-center trance and tribal styles over the type of melodic house that had a lot of pop or disco appeal. Indeed, tunes like Leftfield's "Not Forgotten," Acorn Arts' "Silence," and Herbal Infusion's "The Hunter" were recorded for hardcore club hounds and pay no attention to dance-pop's mainstream. The recordings on this CD aren't as abrasive as

techno, although most of them don't cater to pop tastes either. True, Hyper Go Go's "High" contains some Chic-like vocals—and vocal personality is a big part of Liberty City's "Some Lovin'"—but for the most part, *Vol. 4* has very little in common with *Vol. 3*. Despite its limitations, it's an interesting addition to the series. —*Alex Henderson*

**Best of House Music, Vol. 5: Disco Tech** / 1993 / Profile ♦♦♦
Truth be told, disco didn't really die with the '70s—it simply changed its name to dance-pop in the '80s and continued to use that name in the late '90s. Indeed, a lot of the deep house, high energy (or hi-nrg), and Latin freestyle that has come out in the '80s and '90s is basically an extension of late-'70s disco. But at the same time, a lot of underground club music (everything from acid house, techno, and jungle to trance and tribal) has rejected the type of melodic song structures that characterized disco. The interesting thing about the fifth volume in Profile's *Best of House Music* series is the fact that it is, to a large degree, a collection of underground club items that acknowledge classic disco. The collection even includes rave-like remixes of the Trammps' "Disco Inferno" (arguably disco's national anthem) and Sharon Brown's "I Specialize in Love," but many of the selections are about the track and the beat rather than vocal personality. You won't find an actual song structure on Jump's "Luv It Up," Chubby Chunks' "Testament One" or the Mighty Club Cats' "Return to the Valley of Yeke Yeke"—rhythms influenced by classic '70s disco, yes, but not a real song structure. Essentially, these tunes are coming from an underground perspective; if you've found yourself uttering the words, "I just don't get this rave thing," *Vol. 5: Disco-Tech* won't convert you. This is an interesting collection, to be sure, but one that isn't for the uninitiated—you have to have a taste for underground '90s club music to appreciate this CD. —*Alex Henderson*

**Best of House Music, Vol. 6: Tribal** / 1995 / Smile ♦♦♦
Balancing pointed drum programs with more organic percussion, the sixth volume in Sm:)e's *Best of House Music* series ties together the often ephemeral tribal-house scene. Though there are fewer classic producers here than on previous volumes, most of the productions speak for themselves—from Lectroluv's "Dream Drums," the Stickmen's "U Love It," and the electro-funk classic "Set It Off" by Strafe to Basscut's "Follow Me." —*John Bush*

**Best of Morel's Grooves** / Jul. 1, 1996 / Strictly Rhythm ♦♦♦♦
One of Strictly Rhythm's best producers of the '90s received the deluxe treatment with this eight-track collection, including classic party tracks like "In a Groove," "Get Up and Get Soulful," "Let's Groove" and "Get on Down & Party." —*Keith Farley*

● **Best of Rave [Box]** / Mar. 25, 1994 / Westwood ♦♦♦♦
A crucial box set for any fan of the style, *Best of Rave* includes essential rave tracks like Prodigy's "Everybody in the Place," Shamen's "Ebeneezer Goode," SL2's "On a Ragga Tip," and Acen's "Trip II the Moon." Though it leans a bit too close to the cartoonish side of rave-pop—"Sesames Street" by the Smart E's and an unbelievable four tracks by Altern 8—they're balanced by the presence of several proto-jungle tracks like "Mr. Kirk's Nightmare" by 4 Hero, "Music Takes You" by Blame, plus others by 2 Bad Mice and Sonz of a Loop Da Loop Era. Though *The Best of Rave* doesn't have every single rave classic, there are more here than anywhere else. —*John Bush*

**The Best of Rave** / 1995 / Priority ♦♦♦
Priority's *The Best of Rave* is a bit of a perfunctory collection, but it does serve as a good (but not definitive) sampler for curious listeners—since it contains such cuts as LFO's "We Are Back," Art of Noise's "Instruments of Darkness," Psykosonik's "Silicon Jesus," Lemon Interrupt's "Big Mouth," and LA Style's "James Brown is Dead." —*Stephen Thomas Erlewine*

**The Best of Rave, Vol. 2** / Nov. 10, 1994 / Priority ♦♦♦
*The Best of Rave, Vol. 2* is a reasonably entertaining budget-priced collection that contains nine rave singles and remixes from the late '80s and early '90s. Although the compilation couldn't really be called definitive, there are enough good moments—including Wall of Sound's "Critical," Movement's "B.I.N.G.O.," Alpha Team's "Speed," and Bassix's "I Don't Have You"—to make it worth its budget price. —*Stephen Thomas Erlewine*

**The Best of Rave, Vol. 3** / Nov. 10, 1994 / Priority ♦♦♦
*The Best of Rave, Vol. 3* is a reasonably entertaining budget-priced collection that contains nine rave singles and remixes from the late '80s and early '90s. Although the compilation couldn't really be called definitive, there are enough good moments—including Wave's "Enjoy Life," Red Red Groovy's "Another Kind of Find," Total Eclipse's "Tenskwa Tawa," Gloworm's "I Lift My Cup," Moogroove's "Groover," 2 Unlimited's "No Limit," and Juno Reactor's "Alash"—to make it worth its budget price. —*Stephen Thomas Erlewine*

**The Best of Techno, Vols. 1-3** / 1991 / Profile ♦♦♦♦
Techno is a rapidly expanding and changing genre, so any collection can't possibly capture the full diversity of the music. Still, Profile's three discs of *Best of Techno* does a fair job in conveying part of the music's excitement and stylistic variety; it's strictly for novices, and any volume serves as an adequate introduction to techno. Names like Moby's Voodoo Child, Richie Hawtin's Fuse, Nexus 21, and Speedy J make appearances. —*Stephen Thomas Erlewine*

**The Best of Techno, Vol. 3** / 1993 / Profile ♦♦♦♦
Like most genres of music, techno has its purist hardliners as well as those who have a broader definition of what is and isn't techno. A purist will exalt the most abrasive, noisy, amelodic act from Germany or Belgium as the essence of techno legitimacy, whereas a more liberal, pop-friendly techno enthusiast will say that while there's certainly nothing wrong with a hardcore approach, it's also OK to combine techno with dance-pop and make it more accessible to the casual listener. A broad-minded outlook defines *Vol. 3* of Profile's *The Best of Techno* series. Some of the material is fairly melodic—N.R.G.'s "I Need Your Love" has a real song structure (not just a track and a beat) and honest-to-God singing, and a tune like Joey Beltram's "Get Into Life" (which is based on part of Lisa Stansfield's vocal on Coldcut's "People, Hold On") is relatively accessible. However, a more hardcore approach to techno is heard on FX Creators' "And You Will Enjoy," Eden Transmission's "I'm So High," and Acen's quirky "Trio II The Moon"—none of which have an actual song structure and all of which reject mainstream pop considerations entirely. The goofiest tune on the CD, meanwhile, is Smart E's' techno version of the music from *Sesame Street*. For those who aren't seasoned ravers, this CD can serve as a diverse and interesting lesson in Introductory Techno 101. —*Alex Henderson*

**The Best of Techno, Vol. 4** / Nov. 23, 1993 / Profile ♦♦♦
If *Vol. 4* of Profile's *Best of Techno* series were a study of jazz saxophonists, you would hear Grover Washington, Jr. next to Albert Ayler, Stan Getz after Anthony Braxton, and Gene Ammons before Roscoe Mitchell. In other words, this collection is all over the techno map and ranges from the most extreme techno to material that is fairly melodic and pop-influenced. Baby D's alluring "Let Me Be Your Fantasy," for example, is so close to dance-pop's main stream that calling it techno is a stretch—the song offers real singing (not just a beat, a track, and scattered vocals) and is really house/dance-pop with techno overtones. Also fairly accessible is Golden Girls' futuristic "Kinetic." But those who fancy techno at its most hardcore will get into abrasive tunes like Illuminatae's "Tempestada XVX II" and Paroles' "Vinyl Countdown." Mind Abuse's "The Piano" combines techno with house, and this CD finds Profile's series exploring jungle (a style that's related to techno) with Phuture Assassins' "Roots 'N Future" and Prodigy's "Weather Experience." To be sure, *Vol. 4* isn't designed strictly for the techno purist—its outlook is a broad one, and the result is a fairly diverse study of techno and other club music related to it. —*Alex Henderson*

**Best of Trance [box]** / 1995 / Low Price ♦♦♦♦
This budget-priced four-disc set traces the history of British and German trance with key tracks from a variety of early-'90s producers, including Hardfloor ("Acperience"), Joey Beltram ("Time Warp"), Moby ("Go"), Sven Väth ("Ritual of Life"), Spicelab ("Spicecowboy"), Aphex Twin (a track from the AFX LP *Analogue Bubblebath 3*), MLO ("Colour of the Sun"), CJ Bolland ("Random"), and Robert Leiner's Source ("It's a Kind of Magic"). Not every track was a club hit, but the selections are well-thought and solid. —*Keith Farley*

**The Best of Wmot Records** / Mar. 28, 1995 / Hot Productions ♦♦♦
A British import from Hot Productions of WMOT's (We Men of Talent) hottest productions. Mostly dancefloor jams, but with some melodic floaters, such as William DeVaughn's "Be Thankful for What You Got" and a remake of "Yes I'm Ready" by its originator, Barbara Mason. There's comedy relief from Mel Brooks with his hilarious "If I Was King" and saucy tales like "I Am Your Woman, She Is Your Wife" by Barbara Mason. Ex-DJ Frankie Smith's one hit "Double Dutch Bus" will refresh the ladies' skipping rope memories, and Brandi Wells', aka Terri Wells, "Watch Out" is good disco from a wailing diva.

Numbers by Philly Cream, David Simmons, Sweet Thunder, Tom Grant, Slick, Fat Larry's Band, and Direct Current contribute to a well-rounded package that's worth grabbing. —*Andrew Hamilton*

### Best of Wave, Vol. 1 / Nov. 18, 1997 / Wave ♦♦♦♦
François Kevorkian's impressive house imprint gets covered on this compilation, with tracks from Kevin Aviance ("Din Da Da"), Abstract Truth ("Get Another Plan"), Courtney Grey ("Build Your Dreams"), and François K. himself. —*Keith Farley*

### Beyond Life with Timothy Leary / 1996 / Polygram ♦♦
*Beyond Life with Timothy Leary* is a bit of a bizarre release. A combination of interviews, new music ranging from ambient dance to Ministry and excerpts from Leary's 1967 album *Turn On, Tune In and Drop Out*, the record attempts to create a trance-like atmosphere—one perfect for his vaguely mystical new age sentiments. It's only partially successful in achieving its goals, since the trancey dance music is often lacking in a imagination, and Leary's pontificating sounds out of place next to it. Still, the Moody Blues' new version of "Legend of a Mind" isn't bad, and neither is Al Jourgensen's "Lion's Mouth." The portions of *Turn On* are intriguing, too—they're just better heard in their original setting. —*Stephen Thomas Erlewine*

### Beyond the Sun / 1995 / Dance Arena Productions ♦♦♦♦
This great compilation of mid-'90s techno includes Black Dog, LA Synthesis, Ross 154, and a great remix by Carl Craig. —*Keith Farley*

### Big Beat Conspiracy, Vol. 1 (BBC1) / Apr. 7, 1998 / Ark 21 ♦♦♦
As an attempt to cash in on the burgeoning popularity of big beat techno in the US, *Big Beat Conspiracy, Vol. 1* isn't bad. There are some weak moments—almost all from artists like Sniper, Environmental Science, Psychedelia Smith, Surreal Madrid, Hardknox, and Laidback, who are only featured on the US version of the compilation—but there are some great cuts from Fatboy Slim ("Give the Pop Man a Break"), Jedi Knights ("Catch the Break"), Underworld ("Rez"), Bentley Rhythm Ace ("Midlander"), the Charlatans (the Chemical Brothers' remix of "Nine Acre Dust"), and St. Etienne (Death in Vegas' "People Get Ready"). Even if there are some problems with the record, it's a good sampling of the sound and a nice introduction for the curious— even if the Chemical Brothers' *Dig Your Own Hole* and *Exit Planet Dust* are better introductions. —*Stephen Thomas Erlewine*

### Big Beat Elite Repeat / Jan. 26, 1998 / Lacerba ♦♦♦
*Big Beat Elite Repeat* is a triple-disc box set, though the third is simply a mix disc including material from discs one and two. The music consists of generally capable material from Skint acts Midfield General, Fatboy Slim, and Lo Fidelity Allstars, as well as beat-heavy tracks from more generally sublime acts like Sabres of Paradise. —*Keith Farley*

### Big Chemical Beats / Jun. 23, 1998 / Streetbeat ♦♦
Almost obvious from the generic title but confirmed by the lack of any name talent, *Big Chemical Beats* is a compilation of watered-down big-beat techno. The tracks—by Euthanasia, Other Brothers, Vivid, Upper Hemisphere, Hardline, etc.—are energetic and true to the blueprint, but lacking any kind of complexity or diverting sounds. The only highlight is Finitribe's "Squelch." —*Keith Farley*

### Big Dirty Beats, Vol. 2 / Jan. 26, 1999 / Moonshine Music ♦♦
The second volume in Moonshine's *Big Dirty Beats* series balances breakbeat acts from America (Omar Santana, Cirrus, Lunatic Calm) and Britain (Wiseguys, Girl Eats Boy, Elite Force). —*John Bush*

### Big Hard Disk, Vol. 1 / 1992 / Smash ♦♦♦
*Big Hard Disk, Vol. 1* is a collection of techno music with, as the not-too-subtle title suggests, a suggestively sexual theme. Among the contributions are "I Want Your Body" from Nymphomania, Skin Up's "A Juicy Red Apple," and Public Ambient's "Skinflint." —*Jason Ankeny*

### Big Rock'n Beats / Nov. 4, 1997 / TVT ♦♦♦
TVT's 1997 electronica compilation spotlights mainly British producers, featuring names both well-known as well as obscure. Fatboy Slim, Bentley Rhythm Ace, Meat Beat Manifesto, and Jedi Knights represent, with uptempo tracks which push all the right buttons for rock fans, but may leave electronic listeners a bit bored. The Chemical Brothers also appear through a remix of the Deeper Throat cut "Mouth Organ." There are much better compilations on the market, but *Big Rock'n Beats* still manages to be a compunctual introduction to dance music. —*John Bush*

### Big Wheels of Azuli 1991-96 (US Edition) / 1996 / MCA ♦♦♦♦
Running over 70 minutes, *Big Wheels of Azuli 1991-96 (US Edition)* is a continuous-play mix album that features many of the most famous tracks from the English independent label Azuli, including tracks produced by Frankie Knuckles, David Morales, and David Lee. The American edition of *Big Wheels of Azuli* is different than its British counterpart, featuring a selection of tracks designed to appeal to fans of American house music. —*Leo Stanley*

### Blech / 1996 / Warp ♦♦♦♦
Sparked by Coldcut's highly-rated *Journeys by DJ* mix session, *Blech* is a ransacking of the Warp back-catalog by Coldcut colleagues Strictly Kev and Mr. PC (both of DJ Food), featuring entries from just about every significant Warp artist in the label's eight-plus years in existence. Starting with drum'n'bass and electro, and moving through nearly every flavor of contemporary dance-based experimental electronic music, the cassette-only (natch) release serves equally as an introduction to the Warp discography as it does an up-to-the-minute example of cutting-edge freestyle mixology. —*Sean Cooper*

### Blechsdottir / 1996 / Warp ♦♦♦♦
Warp's second label comp in the *Blech* series gets an upgrade to CD and a boost in playing time (up to 70+ minutes!). Once again featuring the nimble deckwork of Strictly and P.C. of DJ Food, *Blechsdottir* includes previously released material from Disjecta, Autechre, Aphex Twin, Nightmares On Wax, B12, Jake Slazenger, Squarepusher, and DJ Mink, as well as a few exclusives (including cuts from Plaid and Mira Calix). The mix is even sturdier this time, with able cutting and scratching and loads of goofy, well-placed needle drop-ins (including Strictly and P.C. on voice synthesizer). Essential. —*Sean Cooper*

### Blue Order: A Tribute to New Order / May 20, 1997 / Cleopatra ♦♦
Cleopatra's New Order tribute could be the label's worst cash-in effort ever. Featuring 11 completely unheard-of artists (Bugeyed Funk, Coercion, Judson Leach, Casey Stratton), each of *Blue Order*'s tracks follows the same Cleopatra blueprint for raging electro-industrial. There are some interesting selections—"1963," "The Beach," "Young Offender"—but each version is a disaster. —*Keith Farley*

### Blueprint: The Definitive Moving Shadow Album / Oct. 13, 1997 / Moving Shadow ♦♦♦
Easily the most crucial record label in the jungle/drum'n'bass movement, Moving Shadow Records debuted in the early '90s with a sound more akin to the hardcore splinter of Britain's rave scene than the darker sound of mid-'90s intelligent jungle. Spread across two discs—a third disc includes Rob Playford's mix of the material found on the first two—is the unfolding history of jungle from 1992 through 1996, with contributors including Goldie, Aquasky, Dom & Roland, E-Z Rollers, Technical Itch, Deep Blue, and Foul Play. One caveat: the material rarely varies from jazz-influenced rollers or the dark sound. —*John Bush*

### Body & Soul, Vol. 1 / Mar. 31, 1998 / Wave ♦♦♦
A host of East Coast names—including Funky Green Dogs, Francois K., Kerri Chandler, and NuYorican Soul—combine for this interesting compilation of mainstream house. —*Keith Farley*

### Bomb Worldwide / Bomb Hip Hop ♦♦♦♦
The toast of the hip-hop underground, Bomb Records circled the globe to bring together the best international DJs, hailing from Australia, Germany, Japan, Canada, Britain and, of course, America. Challenging tracks abound, though the names won't be familiar even to turntablist fans. Among the highlights are contributions from Mindbomb, Down 2 Earth, Cipher, Muro Feat, Gore Tex, and Funky DL. —*John Bush*

### Bond, Beat & Bass / Jan. 6, 1998 / Cleopatra ♦♦
Apparently released to cash in on the release of the James Bond film *Tomorrow Never Dies*, *Bond, Beat, & Bass* is a collection of well-known themes and songs from previous Bond pictures done electronica-style. Featured artists include Transmutator, Psygone, Voight Kampff, Seelenluft, Martin O, Lindum & Lindum, Para Despues, and Bønehead. Opportunism aside, it can be entertaining for fans of both James Bond and electronica. —*Steve Huey*

### Booming on Pluto: Electro for Droids / 1997 / Virgin ♦♦♦♦
Despite its presence at the crux of most significant forms of late 20th century dance- and post-dance-based electronic music, electro remains for the most part obscure and misunderstood. Music historian/producer David Toop bridges the vast gap in comprehension with the third installment of his Ocean of

Sound compilation series. A 2-CD set tracing electro's many bifurcating lines of influence through the last 20 years or so of dance-based electronic music, *Booming on Pluto* is just about the most inclusive, encompassing introduction available to a hugely influential, vastly underrecognized style of music. The set more than makes its point by juxtaposing musicians as varied as Herbie Hancock, Plaid, George Clinton, Hashim, Atom Heart, Cat Stevens, Mantronix, Omar Santana, Unique 3, the Black Dog, the Jonzun Crew, Jedi Knights, and the Future Sound of London, among many others. Contributors clarify their connections through tight, snapping electronic rhythms, big, booming bass, crisp, clean electronics, and an ever-present funk. Although the set's vague gesture toward a continuous mix can be irritating at times, the occasional trainwreck is forgivable for the larger concept suggested in the vast continuum of styles and artists represented. —*Sean Cooper*

### Bossa Brava, Vol. 2 / 1997 / Instinct ◆◆◆
*Bossa Brava, Vol. 2* is an entertaining collection of acid jazz and dance-club cuts by Soundscape UK, Free Flow, the Quiet Boys, Exodus Quartet, and Martin Fuss, among others. While it isn't quite as consistent as the first volume, and most of the record isn't particularly innovative, it neverhtless provides some fine, deep grooves which are perfect for the dance floor. —*Leo Stanley*

### Brassic Beats USA / Feb. 22, 2000 / Skint ◆◆◆◆
The Funk Soul Brother was America's best friend in 1999, and they didn't hesitate to greet the jovial dance master (neé Norman Cook) globally known as Fatboy Slim. *Brassic Beats USA*, a compilation featuring some of Britain's eclectic dance acts—such as Lo-Fidelity All Stars, Space Raiders, and Indian Ropeman—pays homage to the label that introduced Fatboy Slim to the US, Skint Records. Electronic music was heavily promoted by the fast rise of Fatboy Slim and other artists in the Skint scene, and *Brassic Beats USA* is a celebration of that contribution.

Brighton local Damian Harris started Skint in 1994, but he too is a dance music guru who goes by the name Midfield General, contributing the hip-hop tub-thumping clip "Devil In Sports Casual." The electrifying juggernaut from the Lo-Fidelity All Stars "Puppy Phat Number One" is a wild trip into the cosmic consciousness. Super_Collider's "Darn (Cold Way O' Lovin')" is a sultry cut spiraling into R&B loops and amplified reverberation. Space Raiders are hysterical, sampling glam-disco drops and blues/rock 'n' roll legend Fats Domino. "(I Need the) Disco Doktor" muffles with old-school scratching and glittery dance vibes. Other Skint mates such as Cut La Roc and Dr. Bone also lend their own funkdafied soul and scuffing, for remixing is an obvious art. *Brassic Beats USA* is right about now—brash and classic! —*MacKenzie Wilson*

### Brassic Beats: Trip Hop All Funked Up / Jun. 4, 1996 / Moonshine Music ◆◆◆◆
The stateside introduction for big-beat techno came courtesy of this excellent Skint compilation, including label anthems like "Bentleys Gonna Sort You Out," Fatboy Slim's "Santa Cruz," and "Brassic Beats" by Midfield General. It's a good introduction to big-beat, much broader than any artist's individual albums. —*Keith Farley*

### Breakbeat Science / Nov. 18, 1996 / Volume ◆◆◆◆
The best and widest-ranging jungle collection on the market, *Breakbeat Science* alternates tracks from second-wave jungle pioneers with artists both new and experimental. Several of the best-known names associated with the style—Goldie, LTJ Bukem, Alex Reece—are sadly absent (Goldie does remix one track), but the all-unreleased tracks are very strong nevertheless. Innovators such as 4 Hero, A Guy Called Gerald, Roni Size, Ed Rush, and DJ Trace & Nico make appearances, sharing the stage with newer names such as Plug, Boymerang, and Spring Heel Jack. New York's illbient scene is represented by Soul Slinger's "The Singer." Among the best tracks on the double-disc set (which comes with a 100-page book) include DJ Trace & Nico's "Area 51," Boymerang's "Blue Note," and A Guy Called Gerald's tribute record, "Fabio." —*John Bush*

### Breakbeat Science, Vol. 2 / Mar. 25, 1997 / Volume ◆◆◆◆
The second edition in Volume's jungle compilation series contains very few marquee names of the drum'n'bass scene, but surprisingly, turns out much better than its predecessor. Concentrating mostly on intelligent and ambient jungle (unlike the darker sounds of *Vol. 1*), the two-disc set covers both the new breed (Underwolves, Klute, Justice) and more mature artists such as J Majik, Aphrodite & Mickey Finn, Kid Loops, and DJ Rap. As usual in the *Volume* series, included is a large, full-color booklet with interviews and features. —*John Bush*

### Brilliant! The Global Dance Music Experience, Vol. 1 / 1994 / SBK ◆◆◆◆
The first volume in the impeccable mainstream compilation series focuses on divas like Judy Cheeks, Shara Nelson, Adeva, and the male equivalent, Jon Secada. The set also includes a variety of producers/remixers—Roger Sanchez, Marc Kinchen, Perfecto, CJ Mackintosh, Joey Negro, and K-klass. —*Keith Farley*

### Brilliant! The Global Dance Music Experience, Vol. 2 / Mar. 22, 1994 / SBK ◆◆◆
The second in the series follows the same tack as the first, with intriguing remixes of club hits by Lisa Stansfield, Alison Limerick, Liberty City, K-klass, and Jon Secada, among others. Pop classicists like Boy George, Lulu, and Tina Turner also make appearances. —*Keith Farley*

### Brilliant! The Global Dance Music Experience, Vol. 3 / Jun. 1994 / SBK/ERG ◆◆◆
The third *Brilliant!* is heavy on the mainstream female pop with tracks by Diana Ross, Shara Nelson, Alana, and Judy Cheeks. —*Keith Farley*

### Brilliant! The Global Dance Music Experience, Vol. 4 / Sep. 1994 / Capitol ◆◆◆◆
An obvious peak in the *Brilliant!* series, number four includes the Murk hit "If You Really Love Someone" by Liberty City, and India & MAW's "Love and Happiness," as well as a reprise of the Supremes hit "Someday We'll Be Together" by Diana Ross. K-klass, Lisa Lisa, and Sagat also contribute. —*Keith Farley*

### Broken Voice: Sprawl Compilation / Nov. 11, 1996 / Sprawl ◆◆◆
A thematic compilation concerned with tracks fusing the human voice with electronics, *Broken Voice* includes tracks from Scanner, Colin Newman's Immersion, and Daniel Pemberton, as well as lesser lights Exact Life, V-Neck, Bit-Tonic, and MRM. Even the more obscure artists have great ideas about how to experiment with vocals, and the compilation is consistently edgy. —*John Bush*

### Cafe del Mar Ibiza, Vol. 3 / Jul. 29, 1996 / React America ◆◆◆
*Cafe del Mar Ibiza* is a typically diverse Ibizan mix including tracks by Nightmares on Wax, Pat Metheny, Pressure Drop, Alex Neri, and the ever-present Jose Padilla. —*Keith Farley*

### Caipirissima: Batucada Electronica / May 9, 2000 / Caipirinha ◆◆◆◆
*Caipirissima: Batucada Electronica* features cutting-edge, electronica updates of Brazil's vibrant rhythms and melodies as handpicked by Beco Dranoff, who also compiled *Red Hot + Rio* and *The Best of Os Mutantes*. Arto Lindsay's "Whirlwind," Amon Tobin's "Sub Tropic," Apollo 9's "Nao Fique Ai," and DJ Soul Slinger's "Masterplan" are some of the highlights of this hip Brazilian collection, which also includes tracks from Joao Parahyba, DJ Dolores, Bid, Suba, and Chelpa Ferro. —*Heather Phares*

### Carry on Harthouse / 1995 / Harthouse/Eye Q ◆◆◆
With classic German trance from Hardfloor and Futurhythm (among others), this Frankfurt label's best-of was compiled by Kris Needs and features his Secret Knowledge remix of Pulse's "Soul Hunter." —*Keith Farley*

### Carte Blanche / Jun. 20, 2000 / Naked ◆◆◆◆
Funky jazz, hip-hop, and house beats are the order of the day on *Carte Blanche*, a compilation assembled by Aquanote and Naked Music label head Bruno Ybarra. The tracks are mixed continuously, with contributions by Longineau Parsons, Liquid Lounge vs. Jazzanova, Qalo Mota, Molasses, Isolee, Busy Bee, Fazed Idjuts, Only Child, Mr. Gone, and Aquanote himself, among others. —*Steve Huey*

### Chain Reaction... Compiled / Dec. 8, 1998 / EFA ◆◆◆◆
An excellent overview of the experimental, dub-inflected sound of Berlin's Chain Reaction label, *Compiled* includes tracks by Porter Ricks ("Port of Transition"), Monolake ("Cyan II"), Vainqueur ("Elevation"), and Substance ("Relish"). —*John Bush*

### Chemical Box, Vol. 1 / Jan. 27, 1998 / Priority ◆◆◆
*Chemical Box, Vol. 1* is a collection of ambient electronica that occasionally crosses over into house—maybe big beat—territory. There aren't many great tracks or major artists here but it's still an enjoyable sampler. Just don't think that it's representative. —*Stephen Thomas Erlewine*

### The Chemical Box, Vol. 2 / Feb. 24, 1998 / Priority ◆◆
Like its predecessor, *Chemical Box, Vol. 2* is a collection of ambient electron-

ica that occasionally crosses over into house, maybe big beat, territory. There aren't many great tracks or major artists here but it's still an enjoyable sampler, particularly for listeners that are taken with this sound. Just don't mistake it for a representative overview of the genre. —*Stephen Thomas Erlewine*

**Chemical Ravers: The European Rave Explosion** / Apr. 23, 1996 / X-Ray ♦♦♦

A compilation of European rave in the happy hardcore style, including tracks from Cellblock X, Radar, and Bioreactor. —*Jason Ankeny*

**Chicago House '86-'91: The Definitive Story** / 1997 / PRD ♦♦♦♦

Including three discs of classic Chicago house (though the final disc is a Marshall Jefferson megamix encompassing singles already on the first two), *Chicago House 86 91* distills only the best and most influential tracks from producers like Jefferson, Farley Jackmaster Funk, Phuture, and Larry Heard. All of the most familiar tunes are here—"Move Your Body," "Love Can't Turn Around," "Acid Trax," "No Way Back," "Can You Feel It," "You Used to Hold Me," "Your Love"—and with a few arguable exceptions, only the best is included. —*John Bush*

• **Chicago Trax: Ultimate House Collection** / Sep. 16, 1997 / Cleopatra ♦♦♦♦

Quite similar to Chicago House '86-'91, this is a three-disc set with all of the main Chicago house hits of the late '80s. The main difference is the third disc; whereas *Chicago House '86-'91* includes tracks already heard on the first two simply mixed together by Marshall Jefferson, this collection keeps going with more material. It all comes down to whether listeners want more tracks or a mix collection. —*John Bush*

**Chill Out** / May 26, 1998 / Sabotage ♦♦♦

The Austrian Sabotage label's goof on the KLF's 1993 ambient classic trades that album's cover art of meadow-lounging sheep for a pack of identically placed wolves in a sort of quasi-political attempt to wake ambient from its incense-and-bean-bag slumber. More than up to this task are, among others, I-F, Panacea, EPY, Bannlust, Christian Fennesz, Alois Huber, David Reeves, and Farmers Manual—all of whom bring one method or another of abrasive electronics abuse to bear on a genre typically (mis)characterized as overly safe and approachable. Not this time, anyway. —*Sean Cooper*

**Chill Out or Die America** / 1995 / Moonshine Music ♦♦♦♦

A solid collection of popular ambient artists, *Chill Out or Die America* features first-rate contributions from acts like James Bernard, Wagon Christ, Irresistible Force, and Plavka with Rising High Collective. —*Stephen Thomas Erlewine*

**Chill Out!** / 1994 / Instinct ♦♦♦♦

Instinct's *Chill Out!* compilation includes stellar tracks from early label regulars like Omicron, the Irresistible Force, Moby, and Human Mesh Dance. Also included are left-field selections from the KLF, Meat Beat Manifesto, Air Liquide, Cosmic Baby, and Earth to Infinity. —*Keith Farley*

**Chillout 2000: Early Dawn, Vol. 3** / Jul. 11, 2000 / Import ♦♦♦♦

Not quite everything on this three-CD compilation qualifies easily for use in the average chill room—as a listen to "Sordid" by Amon Tobin will reveal—not unless post-party chill involves sudden attacks of frantic jazz drum solos. The majority, however, fit the bill quite nicely, with tracks that range from the highly atmospheric (Future Sound of London's "Papua New Guinea") to the downright playful (the Roland 303-driven "Zorg" by Sadie Glutz). Along the way the compilation producers find spots for rushes of spacy synthesizers and a dose of sampler-based modern exotica. The diversity of styles, influences, and mixing methods help to provide the set with its edge (or perhaps, lack of it). Good to chill by, meditate to, clean the house to, and even sleep soundly to (drum solos or not.) On a sonic level, the package sounds excellent. —*Steven McDonald*

**Chinese Whispers** / Aug. 31, 1998 / Sprawl ♦♦♦♦

The second remix relay race of 1998 (after *Endlessnessism*) featured an original Stereolab track remixed by ten producers including Sons of Silence, Ultramarine, Mike Paradinas (aka μ-Ziq), Freeform, Si Begg, Subtropic, T Power and, finally, Stereolab themselves. As could be expected, the track bears little trace of its origins even by the second track, though the evolution is intriguing nonetheless. —*John Bush*

**Circuit Party, Vol. 3** / 1999 / SPG ♦♦♦

The third volume in the Circuit Party series showcases a more solid collection of club/house tracks suitable for the eclectic club kid or raver. *Circuit Party, Vol. 3* features definitive mixes and cuts from some of the most celebrated producers and DJs, like Junior Vasquez, Johnny Vicious, Victor Calderone, and Razor 'N Guido. —*MacKenzie Wilson*

**Classic Acid** / Oct. 27, 1998 / Moonshine Music ♦♦♦♦

This ten-track retrospective on Moonshine includes a batch of classic acid—from Joey Beltram ("Energy Flash"), Hardfloor ("Acperience"), Slam ("Positive Education"), Age of Love ("Age of Love"), Wink ("Higher State of Consciousness"), and Robert Armani ("Circus Bells"). —*John Bush*

**Classic Beats & Breaks, Vol. 1** / May 31, 1994 / Priority ♦♦♦

*Classic Beats & Breaks, Vol. 1* is a fairly entertaining, but brief, budget-priced collection that contains a number of great old-school hip-hop cuts from the early '80s. A few cuts fall flat, but there's enough good music to make it worth its budget price. —*Stephen Thomas Erlewine*

**Classic Club Mix: Dance Jams** / Jul. 1, 1997 / K-Tel ♦♦♦

The late-'80s to mid-'90s dancefloor makes a return with this thirteen-cut compilation. The album kicks off with Snap!'s "Rhythm Is a Dancer" and thumps through to the System's "Don't Disturb This Groove," pushing past selections from Inner City, Pretty Poison, Shanice, Color Me Badd, KLF, and Boys Don't Cry along the way. Very little here will seem unfamiliar. —*Steven McDonald*

**Classic Plant: Leaf Label** / Jun. 16, 1998 / Leaf ♦♦♦♦

*Classic Plant* assembles stellar tracks by experimental Leaf beatmeisters like Twisted Science, Richard Thomas, Ronnie & Clyde, Witchman, and Boymerang. —*Keith Farley*

**Clear Presents Twisted Love Songs** / 1998 / P-Vine Records ♦♦♦♦

The Japanese version of Clear Records' label compilation *It's All Becoming...* features four identical tracks but with a wealth of additional material previously unavailable on compact disc. Acts include Autechre side project Gescom, Kirk Degiorgio's As One, Plaid, Doctor Rockit, Clatterbox, Metamatics, and the Gregory Fleckner Quartet. —*John Bush*

**Clicks + Cuts** / Jan. 25, 2000 / EFA ♦♦♦♦

Mille Plateaux's *Clicks + Cuts* effectively examines the musical possibilities of minimalism through the eyes of 25 ambitious electronic music producers. Established avant-garde producers such as Pole and Wolfgang Voigt are joined by many other up-and-coming European producers (such as Vladislav Delay) for this well-rounded compilation. In the past, minimal techno has encompassed artists such as Robert Hood and Daniel Bell, who stripped away much of the excess formal qualities of techno and left only the essentials—such as a thumping bassline and rhythmic percussion. At the dawn of the 21st century, Mille Plateaux plan to change listeners' previous schemas about minimal techno with *Clicks + Cuts* by subtracting even more excess from techno, leaving very little behind. Of course, each of the producers takes a different approach. Farben, for example, uses some delicate crackling sounds and a foreboding synth tone to fill in the calm gaps between the beeps and pops of "Raute," where one would traditionally hear a pounding 4/4 bassline. Ester Brinkman offers a different sort of minimalism: a subdued melody hovers in the shadowy background of "Maschine," while a distorted bass slowly fades in from silence along with a high-hat percussive loop—until a foreign tongue spouts odd lyrics that loop endlessly for the remaining second-half of the song.

This compilation resembles the broad-palate approach found on the label's wonderful *Modulation & Transformation* series, except *Clicks + Cuts* feels much more focused and concise. In the end, Sascha Kösch's liner notes best summarize the theories underlying this collection: "'*Clicks + Cuts*' is an introduction to the functioning of 21st century minimalism, the collection of schools of sound to come, and schools of life to follow." This prophetic thesis radiates pretentiousness and gleams with optimism, charging the often abstract sounds of the album with importance. —*Jason Birchmeier*

**Club 69 Future Mix, Vol. 1** / Jun. 2, 1998 / MCA ♦♦♦

*Club 69 Future Mix, Vol. 1* is an entertaining collection of house, acid and dance cuts from the late '90s. There are a few weak cuts here, but in general, it's an enjoyable listen targeted to casual listeners. —*Stephen Thomas Erlewine*

**Club 69: Adults Only** / May 2, 1995 / IRS ♦♦♦

As the title suggests, *Club 69, Adults Only* is a selection of sex-fueled dance club music, featuring the dance hits "Let Me Be Your Underwear" and

"Unique," as well as a new version of "Warm Leatherette." — *Stephen Thomas Erlewine*

**Club Buzz** / 1995 / Club Buzz/Sony ♦♦♦♦
Twenty of the best dance tracks of 1995 were collected on this double-disc set, including hits by the Bucketheads, De'Lacy, Livin' Joy, Abigail, Love to Infinity, Joe T Vannelli Project, Eve Gallagher, Judy Cheeks, Tony De Vit, and Felix. — *Keith Farley*

**Club Classics** / Apr. 15, 1997 / X:treme/Navarre ♦♦♦♦
Here's the rare compilation that lives up to its billing — *Club Classics* includes quite a few seminal dance hits from the '80s and '90s, including "Keep on Movin'" by Soul II Soul, "Good Life" by Inner City, "Move on Baby" by Cappella, "Don't You Want Me?" by Felix, "Everybody Everybody" by Black Box, and even "Never Gonna Give You Up" by Rick Astley. — *Keith Farley*

**Club Classics 1982-1984, Vol. 1** / 1993 / Warlock ♦♦♦♦
*Club Classics 1982-84* includes nine solid dancefloor obscurities, three of which feature electro godfather Arthur Baker: "I.O.U." by Freez, "Walking on Sunshine" by Rocker's Revenge, and "Crash Goes Love" by Loleatta Holloway. Elsewhere, Cuba Gooding, New Edition, and Zenobia make appearances. — *Keith Farley*

**Club Nervous** / Oct. 30, 1997 / Nervous Dog ♦♦♦
*Club Nervous: Five Years of House Classics* reissues 13 singles released on New York's Nervous Records label, including Loni Clark's "Rushing," Nu Yorican Soul's "The Nervous Track," Sandy B.'s "Feel Like Singing," and Byron Stingily's "It's Over." It's a classic compilation charting the course of Nervous during the '90s. — *Steve Huey*

**Club Nervous, Vol. 2** / May 4, 1999 / Nervous Dog ♦♦♦
This second volume of *Club Nervous* features more cutting-edge club music from New York's influential Nervous label. DJ Frankie Feliciano mixes underground house and garage tracks for club music purists. — *Heather Phares*

**Code of the Streets** / 1997 / Trouble on Vinyl ♦♦♦♦
The first compilation for Trouble on Vinyl includes label stalwarts DJ Kane, Gang Related, Future Forces Inc., IQ Collective, and DJ Red. While the first disc is unmixed, a bonus disc is included with DJ Kane at the helm. — *John Bush*

**Columbia-Princeton Electronic Music Center** / New World Records ♦♦♦♦
The first electronic music center established in America appeared courtesy of Columbia-Princeton in the early '60s. These recordings date from 1961 to 1973, and include experimental work by Alice Shields, Charles Dodge, Ilhan Mimaroglu, and Bülent Arel. — *Keith Farley*

**The Complete Darque Fonque** / Jun. 15, 1999 / Cleopatra ♦♦♦
*Complete Darque Fonque* charts the darker side of trip-hop, breakbeat, and drum'n'bass across a two-disc set. The compilation includes better tracks than could be expected from a label like Cleopatra, with Monkey Mafia, Death in Vegas, Jammin' Unit, Zulutronic, Witchman, Dub Pistols, Depth Charge, and Q-Burns Abstract Message scattered throughout. — *John Bush*

**The Complete Dubnology** / Nov. 24, 1998 / Cleopatra ♦♦♦
This four-disc box assembled by Cleopatra includes a wide range of dub-influenced producers — Renegade Soundwave, Meat Beat Manifesto, Asian Dub Foundation, Eat Static, Rootsman, Banco de Gaia, Black Star Liner, Astralasia, Underworld, Death in Vegas, Sabres of Paradise, Seefeel, and Test Dept., among others. As usual with the label, it's an odd collection, but it does include a host of solid tracks. — *John Bush*

**Compost 50** / Oct. 13, 1998 / Compost ♦♦♦♦
Germany's Compost Records presented this retrospective of the label's contemplative, downtempo electro-jazz with tracks by Funkstörung, A Forest Mighty Black, Fauna Flash, Force & Paul, Beanfield, and Move D, among others. — *John Bush*

**Convergence** / Feb. 23, 1999 / OM ♦♦♦
*Convergence* includes a variety of earthy trip-hop and drum'n'bass from Endemic Void, Fila Brazillia, Jazzanova, Meat Beat Manifesto, Bill Riley, and Russ Gabriel. — *John Bush*

**Covert Operations** / Jul. 6, 1998 / Esl Music ♦♦♦
The *Covert Operations* compilation includes three rarely collected tracks by Thievery Corporation plus other acts on the duo's ESL Music (Eighteenth Street Lounge) label: Avatars of Dub, Ursula 1000, Thunderball. Thievery tracks like "Sun, Moon and Stars" and a remix of "Sex Elevator Music" (Avatars of Dub) are much better produced than the others, though there's a lot to enjoy on this downtempo collection. — *John Bush*

**Crazy Jungle Rhythms** / Jan. 20, 1998 / Paradigm ♦♦♦
A budget-priced compilation of UK drum'n'bass tracks mixed by Mickey Finn, *Crazy Jungle Rhythms* is a good introduction to the sound. Performers include DJ SS ("Rollage"), the Dynamic Duo ("Shadow"), and DJ Nut Nut ("Special Dedication"). — *Jason Ankeny*

**Cream Anthems** / 1995 / deConstruction ♦♦♦
This double-disc set sponsored by the Liverpool club night Cream is mixed by David Morales (the "Frontroom Mix" with mainstream, mostly US house) and Paul Bleasdale (the "Backroom Mix," including harder UK tracks). Morales's disc includes songs from De'Lacy, K-Klass, Juliet Roberts, and Alison Limerick, while Bleasdale's features Mother, Gat Decor and Tinman, among others. — *John Bush*

**Cream Separates** / Mar. 1997 / deConstruction ♦♦♦♦
Available in a triple-disc set or as individual CDs, *Cream Separates* salutes the Liverpool super-club Cream with Darren Emerson, Deep Dish, and Ryder/Bleasdale taking control of the decks. — *Keith Farley*

**Crooklyn Dub Consortium** / Jan. 15, 1996 / Wordsound ♦♦♦
In 1995 this compilation from Brooklyn's WordSound label heralded the emergence of a new sound in underground music — one that took the slow, murky groove of Manchester trip-hop and leavened it with equal parts old-school New York hip-hop and dubwise reggae. None of the featured artists were household names then, nor are they five years later (although Sub Dub, whose ponderous "Monuments on Earth" opens the program, have gone on to some fame).

Qaballah Steppers are genuine New York fixtures these days, though. Their combination of North African sonorities and heavy dubwise textures makes "Majesty Dub" a thing of eerie beauty. There's some very fine straight-ahead reggae from the well-named Roots Control and from the mighty Dr. Israel, whose "Saidisyabruklinmon (Nobwoycyantess)" crawls along at a glacial pace under the weight of a ten-ton one-drop beat. Corporal Blossom delivers seven minutes of creepy ambience in "Opportunist Dub" (along with a hilarious vocal sample). Most of the rest of the program consists of tracks that would be highlights on any other compilation. Highly recommended. — *Rick Anderson*

**Crooklyn Dub Consortium, Vol. 2** / Sep. 6, 1996 / Wordsound ♦♦♦
The follow-up to WordSound's *Crooklyn Dub Consortium* includes contributions from Spectre, Bill Laswell, HIM, and Dr. Israel. — *John Bush*

**Crooklyn Dub Consortium, Vol. 3: Escape from N.Y.** / Jun. 22, 1999 / WordSound ♦♦♦
There is no group more capable of representing the best of New York's illbient/dub/downtempo scene than the Crooklyn Dub Consortium crew: a loosely configured group of producers, DJs and musicians all devoted to the cause of "constant elevation through low frequency manipulation." With its third compilation, the Crooklyn Dub Consortium is now more properly known as the Crooklyn Dub Syndicate, and its membership has gone international. Contributors include Sir Positive (Germany), Layng Martine (Seattle), and Holland's Twilight Circus Sound System (whose "Valley Dub" is one of the program's bass-heavy highlights). There are also tracks by the regular Crooklyn suspects, including Slotek, Spectre, and the ubiquitous and iniquitous Bill Laswell (who contributes the very heavy "Mystery of Shape Changing"). Although each artist has a unique approach, everything is based on the bass — the grooves are generally slow and liquid, the beats heavy, ponderous, and as irresistible as an elephant stampede. Several tracks stand out: Blood's "Open the Gate" honors, both in sound and by its title, reggae' s old school, while The Bug's "Proton" is the sound of an electronic void — a muttering static hiss that implies the presence of human life by its existence, but belies the presence of human life by its emptiness. Cool! — *Rick Anderson*

**Cup of Tea: A Compilation** / Jul. 22, 1996 / Quango ♦♦♦
The collection of tracks from the Bristol trip-hop label Cup of Tea charts the course of music seemingly more influenced by the Smiths than Ultramagnetic MCs. Monk & Canatella's éffete "I Can Water My Plants" is one example, while acts like Statik Sound System and Purple Penguin contribute tracks a bit more in a danceable mold. Still, there are three Monk & Canatella tracks (plus a remix), making this one dance collection which fans of indie-rock's dour side could enjoy as well. — *John Bush*

**Cup of Tea: Another Compilation** / Oct. 7, 1997 / Iron America ♦♦♦
*Cup of Tea Records: Another Compilation* assembles tracks from the UK-based electronic label; featured artists include Statik Sound System and Invisible Pair of Hands, although none of the acts deserve consideration among electronica's leading lights. —*Jason Ankeny*

**DJ Electronica Mix** / Oct. 27, 1998 / Simitar ♦♦
It professes to be an electronica compilation, but this album has 12 completely unheard-of acts—Shag Daddy, Mr. Deuce, Sons of Morris, 7.7% of Bull—doing tepid imitations of the real thing. The entire disc reeks of a cash-in. —*Keith Farley*

**DJ Feelgood Presents the F111 House Session** / Feb. 22, 2000 / F111 ♦♦
*DJ Feelgood Presents the F111 House Session* collects club hits like the Boris Musicalo mix of Moloko's "Sing It Back," DJ Dan's remixes of Orgy's "Blue Monday" and "Stitches," Lisahall's "I Know I Can Do It (Murk Disco Beats)," and JNX's "What U Need." DJ Feelgood's own "Fly" appears twice on the album, giving the mix an added fluidity. —*Heather Phares*

**DJ's Take Control: The Collection** / Feb. 28, 1997 / One ♦♦♦
The three-disc set *DJ's Take Control* features house mixes from Tony Humphries, Junior Vasquez, and Deep Dish. —*Jason Ankeny*

**DV-10: A Decade of Delicious Vinyl** / Oct. 26, 1999 / Delicious Vinyl ♦♦♦♦
Delicious Vinyl came busting out of the gates in the late '80s with huge hits by Tone Loc ("Wild Thing," "Funky Cold Medina") and Young MC ("Bust A Move"), plus critically acclaimed records by the Pharcyde and Brand New Heavies. They never quite had another stretch like that, but the particular era was pretty terrific, as *DV-10: A Decade of Delicious Vinyl* proves. The 14-track collection concentrates on the late '80s and early '90s, a time when the label was at their peak. Some may complain that some latter-day cuts are missing; but the fact of the matter is, this results in a better, entertaining listen, and gives an accurate portrait of the label's strengths. —*Stephen Thomas Erlewine*

**Daft Electro** / Jun. 27, 2000 / Instinct ♦♦♦♦
This surprisingly mild-mannered compilation of breakbeat and electro features a selection of artists both established (Moby, Terre Thaemltiz, Shanteel) and emerging (DisJam, Ib, Super Pulse). Not much here is very interesting—apart from Ib's hysterical remake of the James Brown classic "Superbad" and the complex "Scattergood" by The Odd Toot (wait out the standard-issue house intro and you'll see)—these tracks mostly tread pretty well-worn paths, from the polite house thump of Dis Jam's "5000" to the soulful electro-funk strut of Super Pulse's "Hard Drive." But there's not necessarily anything wrong with predictability; dance music is more about function than form, and if you're ready to get your groove on you'll find that Moby's "Besame" and Terre Thaemltiz's "Freakazoids and Robots" are more than functional. Not to mention the slyly licentious "Ta Jupe" by Shantel. Recommended. —*Rick Anderson*

**Dance Megamix, Vol. 1** / Jun. 16, 1995 / Unidisc ♦♦♦♦
For fans of disco-era obscurities that often top their chart-bound contemporaries, *Dance Megamix* includes great tracks like "Keep On" and "You're the One for Me" by 'D' Train, "Get a Little" and "Going Home" by Patrick Cowley, and "Deep on Dancin'" and "Mandolay" by Gary's Gang. —*Keith Farley*

**Dance Megamix, Vol. 2** / Jun. 16, 1995 / Unidisc ♦♦♦♦
For fans of disco-era obscurities that often top their chart-bound contemporaries, the second volume in the *Dance Megamix* series is another winner. The album includes highlights like "Somebody Else's Guy" by Jocelyn Brown, "Try It Out" by Gino Soccio, "Last Night a DJ Saved My Life" by Indeep, and "Beat the Street" by Sharon Redd. —*Keith Farley*

**Dance Megamix, Vol. 3** / Jun. 16, 1995 / Unidisc ♦♦♦♦
For fans of disco-era obscurities that often top their chart-bound contemporaries, the third volume in the *Dance Megamix* series is yet another winner. The album includes highlights like "In the Bush" by Musique, "Lady Bump" by Penny McLean, "Come to Me" by France Joli, and "Everybody Get Up and Boogie" by Freddie James. —*Keith Farley*

**Dance Now** / Feb. 23, 1999 / Platinum Disc ♦♦♦
The ten-track *Dance Now* compilation has a good variety of club classics from the late '80s to the early '90s—including "Theme from S'Express," Bizarre Inc.'s "Playing with Knives," Technotronic's "Move It to the Rhythm," KLF's "3 A.M. Eternal," White Town's "Your Woman," Underworld's "Born Slippy," LFO's "LFO," and Adamski's "Get Your Body." —*John Bush*

**Dance Party 2000** / Nov. 30, 1999 / Polygram ♦♦♦
*Dance Party 2000* gathers club hits from the '70s, '80s, and '90s into an entertaining mix album. Lipps, Inc.'s "Funkytown," the Trammps' "Disco Inferno," and an extended remix of Kool & the Gang's "Celebration" are among the classic dance hits included here. Deee-Lite's "Groove Is in the Heart," Ce Ce Peniston's "Finally," and Amber's "This Is Your Night" bring the collection into the present. Tracks by Peaches & Herb, Crystal Waters, Blockster, and Funky Green Dogs round out this fun party disc. —*Heather Phares*

**Dancin' Divas** / Aug. 27, 1996 / Sony ♦♦♦
*Dancin' Divas* contains dance versions, including remixes and edits, of several dance-club favorites from the early '90s. While some of these mixes were hits, most were only heard in clubs. As a result, the disc will mainly appeal to dance fans, and they may find this a mixed bag. There are some good, or at least interesting, moments here including M People's "Itchycoo Park," Basia's "Drunk on Love," Brownstone's "Grapevyne," Gloria Estefan's "Everlasting Love," and Celine Dion's first English recording, "Unison." There's nearly as much filler, making this of interest to dedicated dance fans, not casual listeners. —*Stephen Thomas Erlewine*

**Danny Howells Presents: Jackpot Records** / Feb. 23, 1999 / Priority ♦♦♦
Another volume in the series of mix compilations from *GrooveRadio*'s Swedish Egil, this edition includes a host of CD exclusives from the vaults of Jackpot Records, including tracks from Blue Amazon, React 2 Rhythm (remixed by John Digweed), Amethyst, and Tenth Chapter (remixed by Carl Cox and Paul Van Dyk). —*Keith Farley*

**Dark Hearts, Vol. 2** / 1995 / Harthouse ♦♦♦
Harthouse's spate of quality compilations continues with the second volume of *Dark Hearts*—with contributions from Luke Slater's Morganistic, Hardfloor, Claude Young, Alter Ego, CJ Bolland, Jiri Ceiver, Thor Inc, and Neil Landstrumm. —*Keith Farley*

**Darker Side of Jazz** / Jan. 23, 1996 / COA ♦♦♦
*Darker Side of Jazz* collects various singles made for the Mephisto Records label, including cuts from Freaky Chakra, Q-Burn's Abstract Message, Pimp Daddy Nash, the Bass Kittens, and Mephisto Odyssey. —*Steve Huey*

**Darkwave: Music of the Shadows, Vol. 2** / Feb. 22, 2000 / K-Tel ♦♦♦♦
In the '90s, one term that caught on in Europe was "darkwave," which has been used to describe a variety of dark, gloomy alternative music ranging from goth rock and industrial noise to dark ambient. While darkwave is a term that some find convenient, it's important to know the differences between these various styles—industrial noise, for example, can be blistering and extremely abrasive, whereas goth rock tends to be aggressive yet highly melodic. Bauhaus, the godfathers of goth, thrived on melody, but some of the most effective industrial artists can be amelodic and lack a real song structure. Because darkwave is a somewhat nebulous term, it makes sense that *Darkwave: Music of the Shadows, Vol. 2* is as diverse as it is. This generally excellent compilation, which spans 1982-1999, doesn't contain any real industrial noise—its focus is primarily goth rock, with some dark ambient thrown in. While not everything on *Darkwave* was aimed at goth purists, K-Tel effectively maintains a dark, gloomy, shadowy ambience with alternative music that ranges from Miranda Sex Garden's "Gush Forth My Tears" and Spahn Ranch's "An Exit" to Lustmord's "Black Star," the Legendary Pink Dots' "Lucifer Landed," and Love Spirals Downward's "Forgo." The oldest song on the CD is the Cocteau Twins' "Alas Dies Laughing" from 1982; most of the material, however, comes from the '90s. Those who consider themselves goth-rock purists would be better off with Vol. 1 of K-Tel's *Music of the Shadows* series—however, this is a nicely assembled collection that is easily recommended to those who appreciate a variety of moody alternative music. —*Alex Henderson*

**Decade of Ibiza** / Jun. 25, 1997 / Telstar ♦♦♦♦
The Telstar compilation focusing on the wide-ranging Ibiza scene includes mixes from Brandon Block, Alex P, and Nicky Holloway. The set features a surprisingly stellar coverage featuring most of the classics from Ibiza's late-'80s and '90s heyday as a vacation hot spot for club kids, with seminal emotionalists Derrick May and Larry Heard alongside Basement Jaxx, Underworld, and Wink . —*Keith Farley*

**Decay: European Compilation** / Jan. 20, 1998 / Ash International ♦♦♦
The last release in Ash International's remix triptych beginning with Chiky(u)u is also the label's last release, period. Established by Jon Wozen-

croft's Touch imprint nearly 40 releases prior, Ash has released some of the UK electronic scene's more daring and stridently experimental works. *Decay* is another such (if somewhat, under the circumstances, mournful) release to its credit, featuring noisy, at times off-putting ambient and electro-acoustic contributions from Put Put, Panacea, Hecker, Noto, Christian Fennesz, and Aer, among others. —*Sean Cooper*

**Deconstruction Presents** / Mar. 25, 1997 / RCA ✦✦✦✦
Deconstruction's agenda of simultaneously mainstream yet progressive house is well-displayed on this collection, with classic club tracks like Deep Dish's remix of De'lacy's "Hideaway," the Grid's "Swamp Thing," and Black Box's "Everybody Everybody." Appearing near the end of the disc are a few of the harder and breakbeat producers, including Secret Knowledge, Dave Clarke, Death in Vegas, Monkey Mafia, and the Chemical Brothers (a remix of Lionrock's "Packet of Peace"). —*John Bush*

**Deep Concentration** / Mar. 25, 1997 / OM ✦✦✦
Breaking new ground in 1997, the release of *Deep Concentration* furthered hip-hop's turntablist movement by showcasing its brightest talents. This is primarily an instrumental album, with most of the vocals provided by a DJ's quick scratch on vinyl. Cutting tracks are abundant, like the lively selections from the X-Men, Prince Paul, and Peanut Butter Wolf with the Beat Junkies. Cut Chemist of rap group Jurassic 5 and the Latin outfit Ozomatli lends "Lesson 6 The Lecture," a bouillabaisse of drum kicks and spoken-word snippets that offer a course in turntable madness. No sample is off limits to these DJs—everything from Tibetan monks (Radar's "Radar Frees Tibet") to water droplets (Ingrid De Lambre and Eddie Def's "Poeisies, Scene 1 Le Blues") are stunningly pieced together to form new compositions. Also includes a bonus CD-ROM mixing program. —*Craig Robert Smith*

**Deep Concentration, Vol. 3** / May 9, 2000 / OM ✦✦✦✦
*Deep Concentration Vol. 3* collects more underground hip-hop from DJ Sole, DJ Craze, Planet Asia, and Ming & FS. People Under the Stairs' "Afternoon Connection," DJ Cash Money's "3 in the Morning Circus," Blak Forest's "Lovin' Every Minute of It," and Radar's "Antimatter" are some of the highlights from this collection of cutting-edge beats and turntable mastery. —*Heather Phares*

**The Deep & Slow: A Collection of 12 Chill-Out Tracks** / 1995 / Strictly Rhythm ✦✦✦
This compilation looks at various downtempo electronic genres, including acid jazz, new age, and ambient house—including tracks from Josh Wink, David Alvarado and Ray Castoldi. —*Keith Farley*

**Deeper Shade of Hooj, Vol. 3** / Nov. 9, 1999 / Import ✦✦✦
The *Deeper Shades of Hooj* series illustrates just what makes this London label one of the most exciting dance music labels of the late '90s. The music isn't based around a specific roster of artists, but rather a style of music that has defined the sound of trance during this same era. Some Hooj Choons tracks, such as those featured on the first disc of this double CD collection, fall under the banner of progressive trance. These songs thrive on the juxtaposition between intensity and lulls, often referred to by listeners as peaks and valleys. On songs such as Space Manoeuvres' "Stage One" and C.M.'s "Dream Universe," the mood will drift from a tranquil stand-still to a moment of progression, when a foreshadowing synth tone or subtle snare roll will trigger a gigantic build-up that ultimately results in an explosive moment of euphoric excess with sugary sweet melodies: the moment on the dancefloor when everyone's hands shoot up into the air and voices scream out in ecstasy. The second CD of this set focuses on the other side of Hooj Choons' sound, often referred to as epic trance or progressive house. These songs don't necessarily aim to produce the peak moment of the night, nor do they aim to induce heavy serotonin flow. Songs such as L.S.G.'s "Shecan" and Jark Prongo's "Movin' Thru Your System" serve as perfect examples of the label's epic trance and progressive house sounds. Lastly, the songs are edited to leave no gaps between songs, which makes it more listenable than a traditional compilation, but the sometimes jagged mixes can be a bit jarring. —*Jason Birchmeier*

**Definition of House, Vol. 8** / Apr. 6, 1999 / EFA ✦✦
The eighth volume in the long-running Container Records series spotlights some of the German label's better-known releases and singles, plus little-known and up-and-coming artists, over the course of its two discs. Highlights are a bit too sparse to recommend the set, but include a Masters at Work remix of 4 Hero's "Star Chasers," Mateo & Matos' "Mellow Soul," and Deep Dish's "Future of the Future (Stay Gold)." —*Steve Huey*

**Demagnetized** / 1995 / Magnetic North ✦✦✦✦
Dave Clarke's Magnetic North label is the place for some of the tightest hardcore tracks in techno, and this compilation doesn't disappoint. With tracks from Cristian Vogel, DJ Hell, Roland Casper, Woody McBride, Ortaneque, Directional Force, X-Heart, and Difficult Child, *Demagnetized* offers a solid sampling from hardcore's most adventurous label. —*John Bush*

★ **Depth Charge, Vol. 1** / 1995 / Submerge ✦✦✦✦✦
A stellar compilation of third-wave Detroit techno and the best place to start for vinyl-phobic fans of Underground Resistance, the first *Depth Charge* includes five UR tracks plus an additional five by mainman "Mad" Mike Banks. The disc easily includes half a dozen Detroit classics—"Jupiter Jazz," "Meet the Red Planet," "Final Frontier," "The Intruder," Ghetto Tech's "Ghetto Virus"—and remains the place to begin for those seeking Detroit techno's elusive underground. —*John Bush*

**Depth Charge, Vol. 2** / 1995 / Submerge ✦✦✦✦
Volume two in *Depth Charge* equals the first in terms of classic Detroit tracks while ranging farther into the techno underground. While the first was almost strictly an Underground Resistance affair, the second features DJ T-1000, Shake, the Suburban Knight, Drexciya, Eddie Fowlkes and Scan 7, as well as six UR tracks. The Martian's "Stardancer" is perhaps the most glorious moment in the entire UR discography, though "Sex in Zero Gravity" and "Acid Fog" both make superb cases for legend status. —*John Bush*

**Depth Charge, Vol. 3** / 1995 / Submerge ✦✦✦✦
*Depth Charge, Vol. 3* features many of the usual suspects (Mike Banks, Suburban Knight, Aux 88, Alan Oldham) but material from several other Detroit producers as well, including Juan Atkins' Infiniti, Octave One, and album compiler Sean Deason's Freq. —*John Bush*

**Depth Charge, Vol. 4** / 1996 / Submerge ✦✦✦✦
The fourth ace volume in the subterranean Detroit series *Depth Charge* includes material from Mike Banks' Martian project, Andre Holland, DJ T-1000 (aka Alan Oldham), Vice (Jay Denham), Thomas Barnett and Gigi Galaxy, as well as Underground Resistance. The Detroit-Berlin alliance is spotted courtesy of a track by Juan Atkins and Maurizio. —*John Bush*

**Derailed Presents Fallout** / May 19, 1998 / Derailed ✦✦✦✦
An American variant on the British compilation of works by Leaf Recordings, one of the premier labels for indie drum'n'bass as well as more expansive producers. *Derailed Presents Fallout* includes tracks from Twisted Science, A Small Good Thing, Luger, and Fourtet. The highlight, however, is Boymerang's "The Don," an amazing 15-minute jungle epic which helped make Graham Sutton's reputation as one of the foremost producers in the scene. Initial copies came with a second disc, featuring the *Back on Their Heads* EP by Sons of Silence. —*John Bush*

**The Deseo Remixes** / 1995 / High Street ✦✦✦
The '90s version of prog-rock meets the real thing on 1995's *Deseo Remixes*. Global Communication, Trans-Global Underground, Future Sound of London, and Deep Forest each contribute remixes of the world music project by Yes' Jon Anderson. The Deep Forest and Global Communication tracks are the highlights. —*Keith Farley*

**Desert Storm, Vol. 1: Innovative Intelligent Drum N Bass** / Jan. 27, 1998 / Century Vista ✦✦✦
Subtitled "Innovative, Intelligent Drum & Bass," *Desert Storm Vol. 1* is a compilation of comparatively mellow jungle tracks, all heavily steeped in jazz and ambient sounds. —*Jason Ankeny*

**Desert Storm, Vol. 2: Hardstep Drum N Bass** / Jan. 27, 1998 / Century Vista ✦✦✦
Subtitled "Hardstep Drum & Bass," *Desert Storm Vol. 2* focuses on the music's edgier dimensions. —*Jason Ankeny*

**Desert Storm, Vol. 3: Ragga Jungle** / Jan. 27, 1998 / Century Vista ✦✦✦
Subtitled "Ragga Jungle," *Desert Storm Vol. 3* pits reggae vocalists like Barrington Levy, Garnett Silk, Chuckleberry, and Leroy Smart against drum'n'bass backdrops. —*Jason Ankeny*

**Desert Storm, Vol. 4: Vocal Jungle** / Jan. 27, 1998 / Century Vista ✦✦✦
Subtitled "Vocal Jungle," *Desert Storm Vol. 4* assembles drum'n'bass tracks topped off by a variety of soul, R&B and reggae singers. —*Jason Ankeny*

**Desert Sun** / Jul. 15, 1997 / Cleopatra ♦♦
Cleopatra's none-too-subtle sprinkling of a few major electronica acts (Future Sound of London, System 7) into an album largely composed of industrial-dance no-names makes for a suitably unimpressive collection. Even the stars' contributions—"Expander" and "Mektoub," respectively—aren't very memorable, while the other acts (Transmutator, Procyon Project, Silverbeam) barely achieve competency. —*John Bush*

**Detroit: Beyond the Third Wave** / May 28, 1996 / Astralwerks ♦♦♦♦
*Detroit: Beyond the Third Wave* collects ten tracks from members of the third generation of Motor City techno. The contributors range from established denizens of the scene like Stacey Pullen, Claude Young, Anthony "Shake" Shakir, and Kelli Hand to newer artists like Sean Deason, Ectomorph, Mode Selector, and Terrence Dixon. While some of the cuts are all-new, others are exclusive mixes. —*Jason Ankeny*

**Deutscher Funk** / Jan. 13, 1998 / Caipirinha ♦♦♦♦
*Deutscher Funk* is a sampler of the experimentalist side of German electronica featuring some previously unreleased and remixed material, as well as previously available cuts. Included in the overview are Mouse on Mars, Workshop, the Bionaut, Beige, Mao II, Kobat, F.X. Randomiz, Pole, Nonplace Urban Field, Mono, General Magic & Pita, and Pluramon. —*Steve Huey*

**Deutscher Funk, Vol. 2** / Jun. 8, 1999 / Caipirinha Productions ♦♦♦
The second volume in the *Deutscher Funk* series includes solid tracks by Jazzanova, Tarwater, Lithops, Felix Kubin, the Naturalist, Holosud, and Flanger. —*John Bush*

**Diggin' Deeper** / Jan. 20, 1998 / Dust II Dust ♦♦♦
The overly blunted side of trip-hop represents on the Dust 2 Dust compilation *Diggin' Deeper*. The acts are diverse—featuring Up, Bustle & Out, Coco Steel & Lovebomb, A Reminiscent Drive, and Thievery Corporation, among others—but the tempos are a bit too languid to draw in most listeners. —*John Bush*

**Diggin' in the Crates for Beats Ya'all** / Apr. 9, 1996 / Hot Productions ♦♦♦♦
Hot Productions' collection of early-'80s electro goes beyond the average to include a few lesser-known tracks from the seminal era. Beside the easily available classics "Planet Rock," "Jam on It," "Set It Off," "Electric Kingdom," "Hip Hop Bee Bop (Don't Stop)", obscure acts like Quadrant 6, George Kranz (with the original "Din Daa Daa"), and Key-Matic (the hilarious "Breaking in Space") make *Diggin' in the Crates* more enjoyable than the average electro compilation. —*John Bush*

**Digital Dust** / Oct. 14, 1997 / Primitive ♦♦♦
*Digital Dust* collects cutting-edge breakbeat tracks from the likes of Black Vova Meets Sacred Love (featuring Bad Brains' Darryl Jenifer), Mellowtrons (with ex-Orbital member Lee Walker), Crown of Brahma, Tactile, E.O.E., Dumbeat, Butz, Forgiveness, Scorn, and Scanner. —*Steve Huey*

**Digital Empire: Aftermath** / Oct. 20, 1998 / K-Tel ♦♦♦
The second volume in K-Tel's breakbeat electronica series includes a lot of American names: Lunatic Calm, Crystal Method, Rabbit in the Moon, Uberzone, DJ Icey, Cirrus, Atomic Babies, and BT. The focus on funky breaks is balanced with the British and techno side of music, with tracks from Cornershop, Roni Size, Sabres of Paradise, Infiniti, and Pressure of Speech. —*John Bush*

**Digital Empire: Electronica's Best** / Feb. 3, 1998 / K-Tel ♦♦♦♦
A two-disc set of electronic dance assembled by the folks at K-Tel would seem to be an utter waste of time, but *Digital Empire* features 24 great tracks from several of the best names in the field. The Chemical Brothers, Prodigy, Fluke, Crystal Method, Underworld, Joey Beltram, Fatboy Slim, and BT all make appearances—though not always doing their best-known tracks, and K-Tel even reaches back into the '80s to retrieve a certifiable techno classic, Derrick May's "Nude Photo" (recorded as Rhythm Is Rhythm). Other solid contributions come from Propellerheads, Electric Skychurch, Headrillaz, Rabbit in the Moon, and Frankie Bones. —*John Bush*

**Digital Reflex** / Oct. 20, 1998 / Instinct ♦♦♦
A collection of mostly American ambient techno producers, *Digital Reflex* includes tracks by Futique, Facil, Taylor Deupree, and Human Mesh Dance. —*Keith Farley*

**Dimensions in Ambience** / Jun. 1996 / Quango ♦♦♦
*Dimensions in Ambience* features a number of innovative electronic dance and ambient musicians of the mid-'90s, balanced by a handful of average musicians that work the same style. Leftfield, Robert Leiner, and Move D fall into the first category, and the rippling textures and implied beats of their music make the disc worth acquiring for the curious, since it gives a good idea of what ambient can do. —*Stephen Thomas Erlewine*

**Dimensions in Ambience, Vol. 2** / Jul. 15, 1997 / Polygram ♦♦♦
Similar to the first in the series, recognized producers like Sun Electric, David Morley, John Beltran, and Pentatonik each contributed stellar tracks, while obscure names—Golden Girls, Connection Machine, Enhanced—weigh the compilation down with feature-less tracks that fail to live up to the others. —*John Bush*

**Disco 3000: Kosmonauts 1** / Oct. 27, 1998 / Logic ♦♦♦♦
An American compilation of new-school European trance, *Disco 3000. Kosmonauts 1* includes excellent tracks by Novy Vs. Eniac, Da Hool, Danii Konig, Phil Fuldner, and DJ Tomcraft. —*John Bush*

**Disco 54: Funkin' on the Floor** / Apr. 21, 1998 / Hip-O ♦♦♦
Hip-O's second entry into their vintage disco collection starts heading into mainstream hits with more emphasis on name artists. Hits aboard on this 12-track collection include the Dramatics' "Shake It Well," the Crusaders' "Street Life," Bootsy's Rubber Band's "The Pinocchio Theory," Bar-Kays' "Holy Ghost," Parliament's "Flash Light," and Rufus featuring Chaka Khan's "Dance Wit Me." This compilation also includes some great one-off sides by Mass Production ("Firecracker"), Tom Browne ("Funkin' for Jamaica [N.Y.]"), Rose Royce ("Put Your Money Where Your Mouth Is"), GQ ("Disco Nights [Rock Freak])," Stargard ("Theme Song From "Which Way Is Up"), and Vaughan Mason & Crew ("Bounce, Rock, Skate, Roll-Part 1") to fill things out. —*Cub Koda*

**Disco 54: Where We Started From** / Apr. 21, 1998 / Hip-O ♦♦♦
The third volume in Hip-O's vintage collection of vintage disco material includes sides from the Dramatics ("You're Fooling You"), B.T. Express ("Do It ['Til You're Satisfied])," Tavares ("It Only Takes a Minute"), Blue Magic ("Welcome to the Club"), Ace Spectrum ("Don't Send Nobody Else"), and Maxine Nightingale's title track.This also features sides from R&B artists attempting to make the switch over to the disco beat, including Eddie Kendricks ("Girl, You Need a Change Of Mind"), the Four Tops ("Catfish"), and the wildly thumping "Shame, Shame, Shame" from Shirley and Company. Tracks from S.O.U.L. ("This Time Around"), Don Downing ("Dreamworld"), Maryann Farra & Satin Soul ("Stoned Out of My Mind"), Lonnie Liston Smith & the Cosmic Echoes ("Expansions"), and First Choice ("Armed and Extremely Dangerous," are presented here in a previously unreleased extended version) complete the package. —*Cub Koda*

★ **Disco Boogie, Vol. 1** / Sep. 17, 1996 / Salsoul ♦♦♦♦♦
The only compilation that actually translates the transcendent feel of a disco club onto wax, *Disco Boogie, Vol. 1* is quadruple-sided LP mix set featuring Salsoul classics mixed with help from Tom Moulton and Walter Gibbons, among others. Though it's a shame that individual mixes last under 20 minutes, the chunky beats and warm vibes of tracks by Claudja Barry, First Choice, Double Exposure, the Salsoul Orchestra, and Loleatta Holloway make mainstream hits like *Saturday Night Fever* sound like soulless sellouts. After years of cult status among club fans, *Disco Boogie* was re-released as a double-CD set on The Right Stuff's line of old-school classics. —*John Bush*

**Disco Dub House** / 611 ♦♦♦
Mixed by Carl Michaels, *Disco Dub House* features productions from a variety of topflight deep-house names including Roy Davis, Jr. ("Let Me Show You the Scene"), Gene Farris ("Spring Fling"), Pete Moss ("Relocation"), DJ Sneak ("All Over My Face"), Angel Alanis ("Chi's Revenge"), Sharpshooters ("Think Again"), and Sylk 130 ("When the Funk Hits the Fan"). It's a solid trip through low-end groove and disco-laden club music. —*Keith Farley*

**Disco Nights, Vol. 3: Best of Europe** / Sep. 1, 1995 / Rebound ♦♦
The third volume in the *Disco Nights* series includes 12 of the best disco anthems from Italian and French producers, including Cerrone, Patrick Juvet, Giorgio Moroder (with Donna Summer and Alone), Alec Costandinos and, best of all, Meco's disco theme to Star Wars. —*Keith Farley*

**Disco Nights, Vol. 5: Best of House** / Sep. 1, 1995 / Rebound ♦♦♦♦
The fifth volume in the series includes several of house music's best and best-known hits, like "French Kiss" by Lil' Louis, "Everybody Everybody" by Black Box, "Pump Up the Jam" by Technotronic, "The Power" by Snap, and "Back to Life" by Soul II Soul. —*Keith Farley*

**Disco Plate Collection, Vol. 1** / Feb. 9, 1998 / On U Sounds ♦♦♦
In 1982, producer Adrian Sherwood's On-U Sound label began the practice of issuing promo-only 10" disco plate singles to publicize their album releases. Many of these cuts were rare and/or unavailable elsewhere until *Disco Plate Collection Part 1* began to gather them for CD reissue. Part One features tracks from Congo Ashanti Roy, Bim Sherman, Creation Rebel, Noah House of Dread, and Prince Far I. —*Steve Huey*

**Disco Queens: The 90's** / Oct. 28, 1997 / Rhino ♦♦♦
*Disco Queens: The '90s* is a 16-track collection that rounds up some of the biggest dance diva hits of the '90s. Every track was a hit, and many of these are among the greatest dance singles of the decade, including Soul II Soul's "Back to Life (However Do You Want Me)," KLF's "Justified and Ancient," Black Box's "Strike It Up," Nicki French's "Total Eclipse of the Heart," Snap!'s "Rhythm Is a Dancer," Technotronic's "Move This," and DJ Miko's "What's Up." It's an excellent, intelligently compiled collection that is a necessary addition to any basic dance collection. —*Stephen Thomas Erlewine*

**Disco Subversion, Vol. 1** / 1997 / Force Inc ♦♦♦
A double-disc set including material from the more house-inclined artists recording on Force Inc, *Disco Subversion* includes tracks from Ian Pooley, Roy Davis, Jr., Glenn Underground, Gene Farris, DJ Tonka, and the Bionaut. —*Keith Farley*

**Divas of Dance, Vol. 1** / Apr. 1996 / DCC ♦♦♦♦
The first *Divas of Dance* compilation includes Ultra Naté, Alison Limerick, India with Masters at Work, Cover Girls, and C+C Music Factory. Besides appearing on "Give It to You," Martha Wash graces two Black Box anthems, "I Don't Know Anybody Else" and "House of Love." —*Keith Farley*

**Divas of Dance, Vol. 2** / Apr. 1996 / DCC ♦♦♦
A similarly diverse collection of mainstream female dance, the second volume features Rozalla, Chaka Khan, the Brand New Heavies, Jody Watley, and Ultra Naté. —*Keith Farley*

**Divas of Dance, Vol. 3** / Apr. 1996 / DCC ♦♦♦
Similar to the first volume, the third in the *Divas of Dance* series includes several tracks from Martha Wash—both solo and as lead vocalist for Black Box—as well as a few classic divas (Aretha Franklin, Kathy Sledge) and more progressive productions, courtesy of Melanie Williams with Love to Infinity, India with Masters at Work, and Robin S. —*Keith Farley*

**Dr. Speedlove Presents: Chemical Warfare** / Mar. 30, 1999 / Invisible ♦♦
The inevitable Cleopatra/Invisible compilation onslaught continued apace with 1999's *Chemical Warfare*, a compilation balancing a couple solid tracks (by Scorn, Prodigy, Witchman, Psychic TV, Dead Voices on Air) with far too many industrial-dance crossovers (Pigface, Sheep on Drugs, Girl Eats Boy, Globo, Sow). —*John Bush*

**Dogwhistle: The Life and Times of an After Hours DJ** / 1995 / Quality ♦♦♦
*Dogwhistle* is a solid mix of feel-good club tracks including Armand Van Helden ("Witch Doktor"), Hardfloor ("Into the Nature"), Pizzaman ("Trippin' on Sunshine"), LuvDup ("Goodtime") and Chris & James ("Club for Life"). —*John Bush*

**Dope on Plastic, Vol. 1** / 1994 / React ♦♦♦♦
React's first collection of wide-ranging trip-hop compiles tracks by the Woodshed, the Grassy Knoll, Red Snapper, 9 Lazy 9, and Skylab, among others. —*Keith Farley*

**Dope on Plastic, Vol. 3** / 1996 / React ♦♦♦♦
Among a cast of essential selections by trip-hop/big-beat naturals DJ Food, Purple Penguin, and Midfield General, React recruited left-field choices like Masters at Work, Aquasky, and Turntable Terranova to produce an album of great breakbeats irrespective of style. —*Keith Farley*

**Dope on Plastic, Vol. 4** / Jan. 27, 1997 / React America ♦♦♦♦
The fourth volume of *Dope on Plastic* is just as dazzling and diverse as the first three, with breakbeat anthems from Danny Saber, Monkey Mafia, and David Holmes appearing beside inspired selections like DJ Kool's "Let Me Clear My Throat" and "Goodbye Cruel World" by London Funk Allstars. Though the number of big names isn't quite as big, the music more than makes up for it. —*Keith Farley*

**Dope on Plastic, Vol. 6 [1 CD]** / Feb. 9, 1999 / Rockin Time ♦♦♦
The sixth volume in React's series—mixed by John Stapleton and including scratching by Scott Hendy—features tracks by the Freska Allstars, Rainer Truby Trio, Maxwell Implosion, Kitachi, Moog, Kurtis Mantronik Vs. Deejay Punk Roc, and Appleseed. —*Keith Farley*

**Dorado, Vol. 3** / Oct. 4, 1994 / Planet Earth ♦♦♦
There are a few solid producers in the fold for Dorado's third compilation, but the majority of the names will be unfamiliar to even huge fans. The tracks are surprisingly effective nonetheless, with acts Outside, Brooklyn Funk Essentials, and Jhelisa shining while lesser lights like Mesh of Mind, Slowly, and Sound Advice doing a good job as well. —*Keith Farley*

**Double Articulation > Another Plateau** / 1997 / Sub Rosa ♦♦♦♦
This follow-up to Sub Rosa's 1996 testimonial *Folds & Rhizomes for Gilles Deleuze* (dedicated to the recently deceased French philosopher) features the album's cast of contributors remixing, remodeling, and otherwise reforming tracks from that release. Though not quite as musically interesting as its predecessor, *Double Articulation* manages a nonetheless fascinating take on the remix as conceptual process in contemporary experimental electronic music, pitting artist against artist, artist against self, and, in one case (namely, Cologne duo Mouse On Mars, who deliver the album's high-point), artist against the entirety of source material. —*Sean Cooper*

**Drop Acid ... Listen to This!!** / Nov. 18, 1997 / Knitting Factory ♦♦♦
Although much of it is not strictly dance music or electronica, *Drop Acid...Listen to This!!* is a fascinating look at how avant-garde Knitting Factory artists interpret electronic dance music. DJ Spooky and William Hooker are among the most improvisatory-based artists in electronica, and while their individual recordings can be uneven, this collection showcases their strengths. Similarly, *Drop Acid* boasts a lot of interesting sonic textures, and while there are some tracks that simply try too hard, there's enough here to make the collection of interest to experimental music fans. —*Stephen Thomas Erlewine*

**Drum & Base, Vol. 2** / Feb. 10, 1998 / ZYX ♦♦♦♦
Despite a few tracks from Gavin King's Aphrodite project (and two also recorded by King as Amazon II and Aladdin), the second volume in this series is pretty dry as far as name jungle producers are concerned—Horse, Silverbeam, Moe & Dee, Bubbles, C'Can, and Gentica. —*Keith Farley*

**Drum & Bass Selection USA** / Nov. 5, 1996 / Suburban Base ♦♦♦♦
In a collection of tracks compiled specially for the American market, rasta-jungle pioneers like Rude Bwoy Monty, Shy FX, and DJ Nut Nut appear beside leaders of the new like Ed Rush, 45 Roller, and Apollo 13. —*Keith Farley*

**Drum & Bass Selection, Vol. 3** / Jan. 31, 1995 / Moonshine Music ♦♦♦
Moonshine released a compilation of jungle tracks from England's Suburban Base Records in 1995 to promote its newly formed Sub Base USA. label. DJ Hype mixes material from Dextrous, Red One, and Sophisticated Bad Boyz, among others. —*Keith Farley*

**Drum & Bass Selection, Vol. 5** / 1996 / Moonshine Music ♦♦♦♦
Jungle's drum'n'bass style has been well-documented in this series, and it doesn't let up on *Vol. 5*, either. The album includes tracks from SS, L Double, and Droppin' Science. —*Keith Farley*

**Drum'N'Bass** / Sep. 29, 1997 / ZYX ♦♦♦
It's rather a case of hit-and-miss, but *Drum'N'Bass* does include great tracks by Source Direct ("Call & Response"), Aphrodite ("Style from the Darkside"), Freestylers ("Freestyle Noize"), Pascal ("Against the Grain"), and Apollo 440 ("Ain't Talkin' About Dub") among others. —*Keith Farley*

● **Dub House Disco** / 1993 / Capitol ♦♦♦♦
The crucial compilation charting the rise of progressive house during the early '90s, *Dub House Disco* features classics like "Land of Oz" and "Schmoo" by Spooky, as well as "Don't Panic" and "Intoxication" by React 2 Rhythm. Also making solid productions are the Drum Club, D.O.P., Supereal, and Fuzzy Logic. —*John Bush*

**Dubnology, Vol. 1** / Nov. 4, 1997 / Cleopatra ♦♦♦♦
The *Dubnology* compilation is a two-disc, 21-track collection of spacy late-'90s electronic dub with heavy bass, demonstrating that the music has become more techno-influenced and reliant on electronics and technology. Highlights include tracks by System7, Loop Guru, Zion Train, Meat Beat Manifesto, and Banco de Gaia. The booklet includes biographies and photos of all the artists. —*Steve Huey*

**Dubnology, Vol. 2** / Oct. 28, 1996 / Cleopatra ♦♦♦
Like its predecessor, *Dubnology, Vol. 2* is a two-disc collection of dub tracks

that rely on electronics and technology to create their spacy, bass-heavy, echo-laden effects. *Volume Two* has more experimental material by the likes of Zion Train, Alien, and the Knights of the Occasional Table, but those are mixed with more pop-oriented tracks by Underworld, Dubstar, Massive Attack vs. Mad Professor, and others. —*Steve Huey*

**Dum Trax** / 1995 / Dum ♦♦♦
Ostensibly a label compilation spotlighting Finn Kim Rapatti's Dum Records, *Dum Trax* turns out to be virtually a Rapatti solo album. Besides tracks from his most famous guise Mono Junk, such Rapatti aliases as Mars 31, Melody Boy 2000, and Detroit Diesel are featured on *Dum Trax*. The productions are mid-tempo Detroit acid fusions, leaning quite close to Aphex Twin's earlier *SAW* material, but with a bit less nuance. Most of the tracks are taken from 1993-94 Dum singles, though several are exclusives. —*John Bush*

**ESP, Vol. 1: The Techno Trance Compliation** / 1993 / Sonic ♦♦♦
Besides a majority of tracks from second-tier names, Cosmic Baby and Orlando Voorn's various aliases provide the highlights on this first volume in Sonic's *ESP* series. —*Keith Farley*

**ESP, Vol. 2: The Trance Groove** / 1994 / Sonic ♦♦♦♦
A bit more developed and diverse than the original, *ESP, Vol. 2* includes Blake Baxter's Ghetto Brothers and Ken Ishii's Rising Sun project, as well as more tracks from Orlando Voorn and Cosmic Baby. —*Keith Farley*

**Early Modulations: Vintage Volts** / Nov. 2, 1999 / Caipirinha Music ♦♦♦♦
For everyone who thinks that sampling began with hip-hop or that electronic music was an outgrowth of new wave, this excellent compilation offers a valuable historical perspective. It includes some of the earliest compositions for synthesizer and manipulated tape, featuring works by Otto Luening, Iannis Xenakis, John Cage, Morton Subotnick, and others. Some of these (such as Max Matthews's synthesized realization of the pop song "Bicycle Built for Two") were composed or programmed on computers that filled entire rooms. Others (such as Cage's "Imaginary Landscape No. 1") used tape recorders as instruments. Xenakis used the recorded sound of burning charcoal as the source material for "Concret PH," and Morton Subotnick's classic synthesized composition "Silver Apples of the Moon" (sadly, only the finale section could be included here) was written for the "Buchla Box"—an analog synthesizer designed as a miniature version of the Columbia-Princeton monolith that had, up until then, acted as the nucleus of electronic composition in the US "Silver Apples," in particular, will appeal to fans of ambient techno—don't tell people differently and they could well assume it was the Orb or Aphex Twin. —*Rick Anderson*

**Earthrise.Ntone.1** / 1995 / Instinct ♦♦♦♦
There isn't exactly a glut of big names on this double-disc compilation released courtesy of the Ninja Tune sub-label Ntone—Coldcut and Woob are the most popular—but the collision of spacey dub and chilled ambient house results in several excellent tracks. The best by far is Hedfunk's remix of "Surf" by Hex. —*John Bush*

**Earthrise Ninja, Vol. 2** / Apr. 30, 1996 / Shadow ♦♦♦♦
*Earthrise Ninja* is a collection which encompassed just about every artist related to Coldcut's Ninja Tune label circa 1996. While the breadth of material is hardly shocking, producers Up, Bustle & Out, Funki Porcini, the Herbaliser, DJ Food, DJ Vadim, Neotropic, Cabbageboy, and 9 Lazy 9 make it an enjoyable journey. Guests Kruder & Dorfmeister, Ashley Beedle, and Daniel Pemberton only add to appeal of the two-disc set. —*John Bush*

**East-Westercism** / May 26, 1997 / Law & Auder ♦♦♦
The fusion of '90s electronic music with traditional Indian elements hit a high point on *Anokha: Soundz of the Asian Underground*, but *East-Westercism* comes close. It provides an innovative sound with not much more than a few samples to make up for the lack of true Indian artists. Artists like Muslimgauze, David Toop, Rick Wilson, and Witchman have already incorporated such elements into their own recordings, so the proposition isn't such a bizarre one. One drawback is the similarity of the material; at least every other contribution simply samples sitar or tabla over a mix of shambling beats. —*John Bush*

**Eastern Uprising: Dance Music from the Asian Underground** / 1997 / Higher Ground ♦♦♦
*Eastern Uprising* is yet another East-meets-West compilation, with electronic artists attempting to assimilate elements of Indian music into their repertoire (or simply sample the sound of a tabla into their computer). Several artists manage to make the proceedings halfway interesting—Bedouin Ascent's "Ruffistahn" has a drum track that almost vindicates the purchase of the entire disc—but the vast majority of the music on *Eastern Uprising* is hardly revolutionary. —*John Bush*

**Egil Music Presents: Urban Jungle** / Aug. 24, 1999 / Priority ♦♦♦
This mix collection presents some of the best tracks in an emerging crossover between the quintessentially British dance style (jungle or drum'n'bass) and the quintessential American dance style, hip-hop. A few of the tracks are simply jungle productions, though by rap-influenced producers like Aphrodite, Roni Size, Natural Born Chillers, and Urban Takeover. The best tracks here chart an intriguing fusion between the two styles, resulting in the Joker (from the Dream Team) remixing Ice Cube and Mack 10, Dillinja reworking the Jungle Brothers, and Aphrodite redoing N.W.A. Given the raft of jungle compilations out there, it's a pleasant surprise to find an album that gives a new slant on two increasingly commodified styles. —*John Bush*

**Electrecord CD 2000** / 1997 / Studio !K7 ♦♦♦♦
*Electrecord 2000* is an international summit of sorts bringing together an array of new-school electro producers, including Artificial Materials (Ersatz Audio), Synapse (Serotonin), Invisible Man (Sockett), and Third Electric (Electrecord). Although confusingly bearing the same title as the 1996 Electrecord label compilation, *Electrecord 2000* contains entirely new tracks, only a pair of which actually derive from the Electrecord label. This is off-the-beaten-track stuff, with a few tracks following up on some not-often-traveled tangents of the old school, from new wave-esque two-beat breaks and broadside basslines to lazy, almost downtempo gear. Although there's nary a bad cut, comp-stealers include Synapse's Zapp-esque "Bring On the Funk" and Klys Tron's blazing "Elastiche." —*Sean Cooper*

**Electric Ladyland, Vol. 1** / 1995 / Force Inc. Mille Plateaux ♦♦♦♦
The first volume in the Berlin/Cologne conspiracy compilation organized by Force Inc. includes experimental/hardcore German stalwarts like Alec Empire, Zulutronic, 4E, Mouse on Mars, Gas, and Hanin. —*Keith Farley*

**Electric Ladyland, Vol. 2: Electric Soul for Rebels** / May 1996 / Force Inc ♦♦♦♦
*Electric Ladyland, Vol. 2* expands the largely Teutonic bent of the first volume, with tracks from Britain-based producers including Techno Animal, DJ Vadim, and Ian Pooley. —*Keith Farley*

**Electric Ladyland, Vol. 3** / Oct. 21, 1996 / Force Inc. Mille Plateaux ♦♦♦
*Electric Ladyland, Vol. 3* includes tracks from Si Begg, Techno Animal, DJ Spooky, Spectre, Alec Empire, and Biochip C. —*Keith Farley*

**Electric Ladyland, Vol. 4** / 1997 / Force Inc. Mille Plateaux ♦♦♦
Besides some of the experimental names included on previous volumes (Alec Empire, Techno Animal, Zulutronic) there's a few American names (DJ Spooky, Slotek) on the fourth Force Inc./Mille Plateaux compilation. —*John Bush*

**Electric Ladyland, Vol. 5** / Apr. 28, 1998 / Force Inc. Mille Plateaux ♦♦♦
Reaching epic proportions of freeform techno experimentalism, the fifth *Electric Ladyland* compilation is a double-disc extravaganza which compiles tracks from just about every major producer covered on the first four (Panacea, Ice, Techno Animal, Andre Gurov, DJ Spooky, 4E, Kerosene, Slotek, Jammin' Unit, etc.) plus a couple of new additions: DJ Soul Slinger and Mark B. Over two hours of Force Inc. is a dire proposition for all but the most fanatical of listeners, and *Electric Ladyland, Vol. 5* shudders under its own monumental weight. —*Keith Farley*

**Electric Ladyland, Vol. 6** / Nov. 17, 1998 / EFA ♦♦♦
The sixth double-disc edition in the experimental/philosophic techno series *Electric Ladyland* contains a host of familiar names from previous volumes, including Techno Animal, Panacea, DJ Spooky, and a host of Air Liquide-related projects like Biochip C., 4E, Zulutronic and Jammin' Unit. For the most part, it's indistinguishable from the previous few volumes, though 4E's take on the synth-pop classic "Warm Leatherette" is quite inviting. —*Keith Farley*

**Electro Dance 2: Synthetic Future** / May 18, 1999 / Max Music ♦♦♦
*Electro Dance 2: Synthetic Future* collects tracks from some of the finest elec-

tronic acts around, including the Crystal Method, 808 State, and Propellerheads. This compilation also features a special remix of ELP's "Karn Evil #9," adding yet another distinctive touch to an eclectic album. —*Heather Phares*

**Electro Dance Mix** / Jan. 28, 1997 / Max Music ♦♦♦
Spotlighting producers and DJs including Richard "Humpty" Vission, DJ Juanito, D.J. Icey, Josh Wink, George Acosta, and Ian Appell, the *Electro Dance Mix* features Lina Santiago's "Feel So Good," Angelina's "Release Me," Planet Soul's "Feel the Music," and Robyn Z's "Good Love" —*Jason Ankeny*

**Electro Juice** / Nov. 4, 1996 / Sabotage ♦♦♦♦
Vienna's Sabotage Records compiled this set of retro/futurist electro, with 12 exclusive tracks from Detroiters Ultradyne, Ectomorph, and Le Car, plus Austrians Patrick Pulsinger and Erdam Tunakan, and a few Germans as well. —*Keith Farley*

**Electro Lounge** / Jun. 8, 1999 / Capitol ♦♦♦♦
*Electro Lounge* features a meeting of the finest musical minds in the electronica and lounge circles, and celebrates the best of both genres. Classic lounge and vocal jazz cuts by artists like Martin Denny, Yma Sumac, Dean Martin, Julie London, Louie Prima, and John Barry are remixed and reworked by contemporary electronic acts like Utah Saints, Gus Gus, Meat Beat Manifesto and Uberzone. The results bring together music's past and future today. —*Heather Phares*

**Electro Non Stop** / Nov. 24, 1998 / EFA ♦♦♦♦
A compilation of new-school electro producers who focus on strict interpretations of the style, *Electro Non Stop* includes DMX Krew, A1 People, Biochip C., Aux 88 (remixing Steve Stoll), Kerosene, and Computer Rockers. —*John Bush*

**Electronic Eighties, Vol. 1** / Jan. 26, 1999 / Polygram ♦♦♦♦
The first volume in PolyGram's series of synth-pop classics has quite an impressive lineup, including Kraftwerk ("Trans Europe Express"), Yello ("I Love You"), Soft Cell ("Tainted Love"), Visage ("Fade to Grey"), Howard Jones ("Things Can Only Get Better"), Bronski Beat ("Smalltown Boy"), and Thomas Dolby ("She Blinded Me with Science"). —*John Bush*

**Electronic Eighties, Vol. 2** / Jan. 26, 1999 / Polygram ♦♦♦♦
PolyGram's second edition in a series of synth-classics features just as many classics as the first— "Cars" by Gary Numan, "Da Da Da" by Trio, "Sweet Dreams" by the Eurythmics, "Dancing with Tears in My Eyes" by Ultravox, "Safety Dance" by Men Without Hats, "Shout" by Tears for Fears, and many more. —*John Bush*

**Electronic Phunk Phorce Presents Phuturistic Phunk** / May 14, 1996 / Home Entertainment ♦♦♦
Various heroes from Cologne's fertile electro-techno scene, including Bizz OD, Air Liquide, Dr. Walker. —*Keith Farley*

**Electronica Techno Nations, Vol. 1** / May 27, 1997 / Kickin' ♦♦♦
Despite the generic title, there are a few good tracks on this compilation from Kickin' Records. Stacey Pullen's Kosmic Messenger kicks off the album with "Flash," while Patrick Pulsinger's Lazer follows in fine fashion. Unfortunately, much of the collection includes lightweight producers. Other highlights include tracks from Ian Pooley and Matthew B. —*Keith Farley*

**Electropolis, Vol. 2** / Nov. 16, 1999 / Metropolis ♦♦♦
*Electropolis, Vol. 2* collects more singles from Metropolis' roster of industrial artists, including Wumpscut's "Flucht (Straight to Hell FLA Remix)," Project Pitchfork's "Temper of Poseidon," Funker Vogt's "Martian on the Moon," Crocodile Shop's "Order and Joy," and Informatik's "Things to Come (Make Love Remix)." Diary of Dreams, Kevorkian Death Cycle, Mentallo & the Fixer, and Front Line Assembly also contribute tracks to this cutting-edge industrial comp. —*Heather Phares*

**Elements of and Experiments with Sound** / 1995 / Planet E ♦♦♦♦
The title smacks of a particularly chin-stroking style of production, but this compilation of material from Carl Craig's Planet E Communications includes several bracing tracks from the Motor City's underground scene, including Moodring and Mood Selector. —*Keith Farley*

**11 Phases** / Feb. 16, 1998 / Sublime ♦♦♦♦
A group of Detroit's most famous producers work their way into breakbeats and downtempo territory for this compilation. Kenny Larkin, Eddie Fowlkes, Robert Hood, Stacey Pullen, Anthony "Shake" Shakir, Sean Deason, Will Web, and K-Hand contribute outstanding tracks. It's a rare turn, one completely suited for fans of more lauded British home-listening producers as well as followers of the intense minimalism the Motor City is known for. —*Keith Farley*

**Elsie and Jack and Chair** / Oct. 1997 / Elsie + Jack ♦♦♦♦
The debut release for the pioneering noise imprint, James Rodriguez' *Elsie and Jack and Chair,* is a globe-trotting compilation of the brightest and best experimental/noise artists. From Europe come Crawl Unit, Shifts and Rapoon, while Southeast Asia represents with several tracks from Zeni Geva guitarist Mitsuru Tabata. The vibrant Michigan noise-rock scene also appears, with tracks by Füxa, Flutter and Elsie + Jack flagship act Monera (including Rodriguez, Ted Klug, Brian Hauch, and John Bush). The range of sounds and atmospheres is quite unexpected, and well worthy of praise. —*Keith Farley*

**Elvis Never Meant Shit to Me** / Jan. 26, 1999 / Ultra ♦♦♦
This Ultra label compilation includes tracks from DJ Q, Kid Loops, Sunship, TAOS, and Fire this Time. Derrick Carter's remix of "Glasgow Jazz" by DJ Q is a highlight. —*John Bush*

**Em:t 0094** / 1994 / Instinct ♦♦♦
The first compilation of material from the underrated Em:t Records doesn't quite reach the peaks of its later output, though stalwarts Woob, Gas, and Coco Steel & Lovebomb make appearances. —*Keith Farley*

**Em:t 1997** / 1997 / Em:t ♦♦♦♦
Although Em:t's popular compilation series began to uncharacteristically parallel popular dance music trends during 1996—leaning more toward the *de jour* weirdy-beardy beat freak of the trip-hop and armchair jungle set—the label's first compilation for 1997 is a sturdy return to unclassifiable form. Focusing largely on the label's own stable (including Bad Data, Woob, International People's Gang, Gas, and Miasma), the album also features carry-overs Richard Bone and Dallas Simpson, the latter of whose 12-plus minutes of binaurally recorded manipulation of a water pump (again, for some reason, placed square in the middle of the album) is at least moderately more engaging than his previous contribution. Koln's 8m2 Stereo also makes his debut Em:t appearance with the comp-stealing "UNC," and a bewildering stutter of dreamy textures and aberrant atmospheres. Other notable tracks include Gas' "Oxygen," Miasma's evocative clang-fest "Dead Eye," and the always excellent Woob's engulfing "Giant Stroke." —*Sean Cooper*

**Em:t 2295** / 1995 / T:me ♦♦♦♦
The Em:t Records update for 1995 makes a better case than the 1994 edition, with Scanner, Thomas Koner, and Symetrics appearing beside usual acts like Woob and Gas. —*Keith Farley*

**Em:t Explorer** / Feb. 13, 1996 / Instinct ♦♦♦♦
This double-disc collection of ambient techno futurism from Em:t Records features label favourites like Woob, Gas, and A Small Good Thing stretching out on material. Also included are contributions from two special guests, ambient pioneers David Toop and Carl Stone. —*Keith Farley*

**Endless, Vol. 1** / 1994 / Manifold ♦♦♦♦
A compilation of expansive dark ambience and industrial percussion, *Endless* includes tracks by the cream of the crop in sound experimentation: Paul Schütze, Null, James Plotkin, and Lull. —*Keith Farley*

**Endlessnessism** / May 26, 1998 / Dot ♦♦♦♦
With a similar concept to *Chinese Whispers, Endlessnessism* approximates a remix relay race. In essence, the first producer creates a track, and is remixed by the next artist in line, who is remixed by the next, and so forth, until the end of the album. Sarilou passes to Quant who passes to Bedouin Ascent who passes to Bowling Green to Ian O'Brien to Endemic Void to Roupe, and nine tracks later, Friend finishes the compilation. Released by the Swedish newschool electro label Dot (and including many from the Dot stable), *Endlessnessism* accomplishes more than *Chinese Whispers* and sounds less forced— perhaps because Dot has a closer sense of community between its artists (10 of the 16 appearing here have recorded or remixed for the label). Though a few artists drop the baton with bland contributions, almost every track is a winner. —*John Bush*

**Epidemic** / 1997 / Sabotage ♦♦♦♦
A collection of crucial Austrian audio renegades led by Patrick Pulsinger, *Epi-*

*demic* also features tracks from Jumboo, Rockenschaub, Dependence, and Pomassl. —*John Bush*

**Escalator Records, Tokyo** / Feb. 29, 2000 / Bungalow ♦♦♦♦
Bunglalow's *Escalator Records, Tokyo* collects hard-to-find singles and rarities from one of Japan's few remaining independent labels. Though Escalator's roster includes the Swedish pop group Super and the multi-cultural, eclectic Stereo Total, this album focuses on the label's Japanese acts, which are also extremely diverse. From the atmospheric, sample-friendly pop of Cubismo Grafico's "Salon a Sunday" and "I'm Still Sleeping" to Yukari Fresh's girlish vocals on "Paul Scholes" and "Yukarimpid 1/2/3" to Montparnasse's big beat workout "The Wiggley Cat Walk!," Escalator's native lineup captures the clever, light-hearted sounds of Tokyo's Shibuya district. The High Yummies' thumping "Mog Alphonso" and Neil & Iraiza's smooth, sophisticated "Middle Man" are some of the other highlights of *Escalator Records, Tokyo*, which is worthwhile for anyone interested in global indie pop or curious about Shibuya-kei beyond Pizzicato 5, Cornelius, or the style's other usual suspects. —*Heather Phares*

**Essential Murk & Funky Green Dog Mixes** / May 26, 1998 / Harmless ♦♦♦♦
A stellar compilation of remixes by various solo and group Falcon/Gaetan aliases, including several for themselves as well as outside productions like Donna Summer, Olive, JayDee, Tin Tin Out, and Boris Dlugosch, among others. —*Keith Farley*

**Essential Selection, Vol. 1** / Apr. 4, 2000 / Sire ♦♦
*Essential Selection, Vol. 1* signals an interesting moment in electronic music when the traditionally innovative genre reaches a state of commodity. Surely, electronic music has been pimped in the past by major labels in an effort to make a quick dollar in the mainstream with *MTV Party* to Go-style compilations, but never to the point where artists become consumer brands charged with high equity. *Essential Selection, Vol. One* features the world's two most visible electronic music DJs in 2000, Fatboy Slim and Paul Oakenfold. These two DJs couldn't be any different in terms of style, but are quite similar in terms of popularity. Think of them as the Backstreet Boys and Britney Spears of electronic music. On Fatboy Slim's mix, the well-known producer otherwise known as Norman Cook splices together a total of 18 quite eclectic dance tracks. Though Scanty Sandwich's "Because of You" shares few similarities with Underworld's "Born Slippy" (besides its dance-worthy qualities) Cook bridges the large gap between the Jackson 5 sample-filled former track with the lunatic-inspired intensity of the latter to create the peak moment of his roller coaster mix that then concludes with Groove Armada's "At the River." Many may sit back in wonder, listening to Cook mix from one charismatic track to the next in ways many would never attempt. But most well-seasoned electronic music listeners will realize by at least the second or third listen that Cook's approach relies heavily on novelty to wow listeners and works well the first time before the novelty wears off. There is a reason most DJs wouldn't dare follow "Because of You" with "Born Slippy": the songs carry two entirely different vibes that don't carry over and only dilute themselves, causing the epic Underworld anthem-of-anthems to sound surprisingly timid when sandwiched between a funky house track and a groovy lounge song.

Oakenfold takes an entirely different approach than Cook, but similarly achieves little in terms of lasting quality. The notorious trance DJ found immense fame with his *Tranceport* album in the US, where he essentially edited together the ultimate trance anthems of the late '90s into one monolithic ride through the genre's most euphoric moments. Of course, now that Oakenfold has used all the genre's best songs on previous releases, his new material sounds second-rate in comparison. Tracks such as The Unknown's "The Spirit" don't come close to being as transcendental as they try (in vain) to be, they instead sound kitschy. Similarly, the supposed peak moments of Oakenfold's set, such as Perfect State's "Perfect State," will make most anyone who has been listening to trance for more than a year simply roll his or her eyes. The cliched motifs and formal characteristics of trance found in songs such as this—warm, lingering synth notes, a re-occurring melody every few minutes, the long-awaited breakdown, the tranquil lulls—give the genre a bad name. In all defense of trance, songs such as "Secret Folder" do overcome these cliches and truly inspire beautiful moments, but as a whole, anyone who has listened to their share of Global Underground or Northern Exposure albums has heard Oakenfold's set by better DJs. In sum, both DJs do what they are supposed to do on this album—producing generic mixes of exactly what listeners expect, want, and, unfortunately, buy. So if generic products equals customer satisfaction and effective marketing equals healthy profits, this album proves that Cook and Oakenfold are the McDonalds and Coca-Cola of electronic music. —*Jason Birchmeier*

**Euphoria** / Apr. 5, 1999 / Telstar TV ♦♦♦
*Euphoria* is a double-disc set of dance club favorites by the likes of Bedrock, Nalin & Kane, BT, Brainbug, Blue Amazon, Josh Wink, Paul Van Dyk, Energy 52, Jam & Spoon, the Age of Love, Way Out West, Binary Finary and Faithless. All of the songs are remixed and segued by the PF Project, which makes this more interesting than the average remix album, since it has its own internal logic. Still, this is the kind of record that will be of interest primarily to hardcore fans of dance music, not casual followers. —*Stephen Thomas Erlewine*

**Euro Mix, Vol. 2** / Mar. 5, 1996 / SPG ♦♦
*Euro Mix, Vol. 2* is an enjoyable, 32-track collection of '80s and '90s Eurodance hits, including cuts from Quasimodo, Black 4 White, Daisy Dee, Maxx, Club Factory, Dolphin Crew, Jam & Spoon, Loft, Copernico, and DJ Bobo. Most of this music is exceptionally disposable (save for Afrika Bambaataa's "Feel the Vibe"), but fans of Euro-pop's mindless, repetitive beat will find it quite fun. —*Stephen Thomas Erlewine*

**Everybody Dance: Remixed Dance Classics** / Jun. 2, 1998 / Rhino ♦♦♦♦
The abundance of forgettable, badly done remix albums that came out in the '80s and '90s made some consumers wary of remixes. And up to a point, their skepticism was justified—in some cases, remix albums have amounted to cheap, crude exploitation. But when remixing is done with creativity, the results can be thrilling. Much like a jazz instrumentalist, a remixer can put an interesting new spin on old favorites, and that's exactly what happens on *Everybody Dance*. One of the most captivating dance-music collections released in 1998, this superb two-CD set brings mostly classics from the Disco era and the early to mid-'80s into the club world of the '90s. Gems like Chic's "Good Times," Linda Clifford's "Runaway Love," and Sister Sledge's "He's the Greatest Dancer" are given high-tech, late-'90s makeovers, and most of the remixes (which are provided by dance-music icons like Todd Terry, Albert Cabrera, and David Morales) sound organic rather than forced or unnatural. The only song from the '60s is Aretha Franklin's "Respect," which works surprisingly well with a 1998 remix. *Everybody Dance* is a release that no dance music enthusiast should overlook. —*Alex Henderson*

★ **Excursions in Ambience: A Collection of Ambient House Music** / 1993 / Plan 9/Caroline ♦♦♦♦♦
An early classic detailing several pioneers of the ambient house movement, *Excursions in Ambience* is an impeccably solid album of essential listening, featuring acts such as Future Sound of London, 777, Ultramarine, and Psychick Warriors Ov Gaia. —*John Bush*

**Excursions in Ambience: Second Orbit** / 1994 / Astralwerks ♦♦♦♦
The second edition in the *Excursions* series features a few more obscure names (though Orb appears courtesy of three remixes). The material steps forward into new realms of sound, with producers like Locust, Maurizio, Autocreation, and Grid providing moments of rare beauty. —*John Bush*

**Excursions in Ambience: The Fourth Frontier** / Nov. 1995 / Astralwerks ♦♦♦♦
The closest to true ambience of any in the series, this fourth volume includes various artists' exploration of reverb, echo and delay effects. As such, only three tracks have any sort of beat. Though this lack of definition could scare off listeners, the appearance of nontraditional ambient practitioners Flying Saucer Attack and Labradford, along with usual stalwarts 777 and Future Sound of London (as Far-Out Son of Lung), makes for an interesting listening experience. —*John Bush*

**Excursions in Ambience: Third Dimension** / 1994 / Astralwerks ♦♦♦♦
*Third Dimension* is a bit more indebted to space rock and beatless ambient than previous volumes in the series. The selection of artists is impeccable, ranging from Pete Namlook's Air to Spacetime Continuum, Aphex Twin to indie-rock producer Steve Fisk, and Future Sound of London to Spectrum. —*John Bush*

**The Experience** / 1995 / King St. Sounds ♦♦♦
This King Street compilation of house/garage sounds includes classic tracks by Blaze, the Basement Boys, Kerri Chandler, Mood II Swing, and Urban Soul. —*Keith Farley*

**FFRR Classics 1988-1998** / Feb. 2, 1999 / Polygram International ♦♦♦♦
A three-disc history of the leading British dance label of the '90s, *FFRR Classics* includes dozens of house, techno, and hip-hop landmarks. Although there are going to be a few duds over the course of 50 tracks, the set is an intriguing look at the development of dance music—from American imports like "Push It" by Salt-N-Pepa, "Baby Wants to Ride" by Jamie Principle, and "French Kiss" by Lil' Louis to British contributions "MMM...Skyscraper I Love You" by Underworld, "Chime" by Orbital, and "Inner City Life" by Goldie. —*John Bush*

**Fake Fruit & Horrible Shoes** / Jul. 1, 1997 / Pure Plastic ♦♦♦♦
A compilation from Mark Broom's Pure Plastic Records, *Fake Fruit & Horrible Shoes* includes some great productions on the darker side of techno, by Broom as well as Steve Pickton and others. —*Keith Farley*

**Fax Compilation** / 1994 / Fax USA ♦♦♦♦
The most basic compilation for American audiences interested in Pete Namlook's Fax Records is a two-disc set including tracks from Namlook guises Air, Putney, 4Voice, and Shades of Orion. A host of other Fax favorites make appearances: Plastikman's Richie Hawtin on the epic From Within track "Sad Alliance," Deep Space Network and Dr. Atmo on I.F.'s "Kisy Loa," Atom Heart and Tetsu Inoue on their Datacide track "Data Haku." Fax is easily the most traditional-sounding ambient label, and the music would make an equally strong impression on fans of Hearts of Space and Basic Channel. —*John Bush*

**Fax Compilation, Vol. 2** / 1995 / Fax USA ♦♦♦
The second Fax collection is another two-disc set, this time with tracks by Solitaire, Otras 2, Bedroom, and Xjacks—not quite the most high-profile acts on the label. Though the ubiquitous Namlook does appear on several tracks, the drop in quality is easily discernible over the first compilation. —*John Bush*

**Feed Your Head** / 1993 / Mammoth ♦♦♦♦
The first Planet Dog compilation, released in America on Mammoth, is an intriguing collection of psychedelic ambient dub, with representative label acts like Banco de Gaia and Eat Static appearing alongside special guests like the Drum Club, Pressure of Speech, and System 7 (who contribute a remix of their "Habibi"). Even though a few of the other producers are a bit obscure, even Tuu, Ullulators, and Optic Eye turn in solid, dubby tracks. —*John Bush*

**Feed Your Head, Vol. 2** / 1994 / Ultimate ♦♦♦
Another collection packed with top-drawer Planet Dog artists (Children of the Bong, Astralasia) alongside the Drum Club, Spooky and a host of lesser-knowns. *Feed Your Head Vol. 2* doesn't quite hit the highs of its predecessor, though more enthusiastic fans of the ambient/dub/trance sound will enjoy this one almost as much. —*John Bush*

**Feed Your Head, Vol. 3: Accelerating Alpha Rhythms** / Nov. 11, 1996 / Mammoth ♦♦♦
The third Planet Dog collection focuses on a host of more obscure psychedelic and trance acts, including Star Seeds, Fathers of Watt, Solar Budd, and Evolver. It's a much weaker collection than the first two, worthy only for Planet Dog obsessives. —*John Bush*

**Lo Fibre Companion** / Oct. 6, 1998 / Invisible ♦♦♦
A double-disc compilation of reordings originally on the Lo Fibre label, this experimental/industrial compilation includes tracks from Torque, Scalpel, Sidewinder, Hydrus, Eardrum, and several projects of Justin Broadrick (Solaris B.C., Final, Saskwatch). —*Keith Farley*

**50 Years of Sunshine** / 1992 / Silent ♦♦♦
Celebrating the 50th anniversary of LSD, a collection of notable mind-trippers including Timothy Leary, Psychic TV, Kim Cascone, Nonplace Urban Field, Hyperdelic, and Ultraviolet Catastrophe contribute to the understandably psychedelic air of the proceedings. —*Keith Farley*

**Filter Killing Music** / Nov. 10, 1998 / Ultra ♦♦♦
A collection charting the jazzier side of drum'n'bass and techno, *Filter Killing Music* includes tracks from DJ Q ("We Are One"), Kid Loops ("Alien Resident"), D*Note ("Waiting Hopefully"), and Underwolves ("Nine Lives"). —*Keith Farley*

**Fire Island Classics** / Dec. 22, 1998 / Centaur ♦♦♦
A broad-based compilation of feel-good house music, *Fire Island Classics* includes tracks by Frankie Knuckles ("Whistle Song"), Sunscreem ("Looking at You"), Alison Limerick ("Where Love Lives"). —*John Bush*

**Five** / Nov. 17, 1997 / Sabotage ♦♦♦
Charting the experimental side of electro, Sabotage recruited Farmers Manual, Pita, Burger, Beanfield, Def Con and Alois Huber (among others) for *Five*. —*Keith Farley*

**5 Years of Eye Q Music** / Apr. 30, 1996 / Eye Q ♦♦♦♦
Eye Q celebrated its fifth anniversary with a double-disc collection including only the best-known tracks by Alter Ego, Stevie B-Zet, Sven Väth, Hardfloor, Resistance D, and Barbarella. —*Keith Farley*

**Flying Trance Classics** / Sep. 2, 1997 / ZYX ♦♦♦
This two-disc collection does indeed include several German trance classics, like the self-titled hit by Age of Love, "How Much Can You Take?" by Visions of Shiva, "Hymn" by Moby, "Stella" by Jam & Spoon, "Are Am Eve?" by Commander Tom, "Calling Earth" by Yves Deruyter, and "Love Stimulation" by Humate. There is, however, quite a bit of filler spread across the compilation. —*Keith Farley*

**Foundations (Coming Up from the Streets)** / Jan. 27, 1997 / Feedback ♦♦♦♦
The benefit compilation *Foundations* (to raise funds for the homeless newspaper *The Big Issue*) includes exclusive or rare tracks from the Black Dog, Orbital, Underworld, 808 State, Moody Boyz, and A Guy Called Gerald, among others. —*John Bush*

**Freedom: The Sound of Zen** / Oct. 13, 1998 / Intersound ♦♦♦
Though Intersound isn't renowned for its dance compilations (and the title all but gives it away), *Freedom: The Sound of Zen* is quite a good compilation of breakbeat techno and big beat, mostly from American producers. Included are classics of the field like Crystal Method's "Keep Hope Alive," Fatboy Slim's "Everybody Needs a 303," Dynamix II's "Atomic Age," Wink's "Higher State of Consciousness," and Rabbit in the Moon's "Florida." —*John Bush*

**Freestyle 2000: Don't Stop Rock Millennium Mixes** / May 18, 1999 / Pandisc ♦♦♦
*Freestyle 2000: Don't Stop the Rock Millennium Mixes* features the late-'80s electro-funk classic "Don't Stop The Rock" by Freestyle, remixed by classic late-'90s DJs like Carl Cox, the Toxik Twins, the Freestylers, and Simply Jeff. The original's funky electro beats and vocoded vocals get a new lease on life in the hands of these talented remixers, making *Millennium Mixes* sound fresh and retro at the same time. —*Heather Phares*

**Freestyle Files: Underground Sounds of America** / May 12, 1998 / Studio !K7 ♦♦♦
Mostly concerned with NYC illbient, the *Freestyle Files* volume centered around the States features Sub Dub, Tipsy, DJ Spooky, and DJ Wall, as well as junglist Jamie Myerson, D.C. dub-hoppers Thievery Corporation, and Frisco's ambient house timelord Spacetime Continuum. —*John Bush*

**Freestyle Files, Vol. 1: Futuristic Electronics** / Sep. 2, 1996 / Studio !K7 ♦♦♦♦
The first in Studio !K7's series functions as a veritable roll call of only the most crucial producers in the fold, including Autechre, Alex Reece, Herbert, Sabres of Paradise, Photek, Funki Porcini, Howie B, Up, Bustle & Out, the Global Communication projects Link, and Jedi Knights, plus the Mike Paradinas alias Jake Slazenger. Featuring many exclusives over the course of two discs, *Freestyle Files, Vol. 1* cross-cuts trip-hop, electro, drum'n'bass, tech-house, and techno with apparent ease. —*John Bush*

**Freestyle Files, Vol. 2: Germany Vs. England** / Mar. 24, 1997 / Studio !K7 ♦♦♦♦
Not quite the football match suggested in the subtitle, *Freestyle Files, Vol. 2* is instead a double-disc collection of future electro/techno/acid/drum'n'bass. On the first disc, Teutons Drome, Kreidler, Fauna Flash, Turntable Terranova, Shantel, Kruder (minus Dorfmeister) and Third Electric line up against a Brit squad comprised of Dr. Rockit, Funki Porcini, Ed Rush, Clatterbox, Paul W. Teebroke, Kid Loops, Kushti and Red Snapper plus Brazilian expat Cujo (aka

Amon Tobin) and Finnish recruit Jimi Tenor. Despite much fun on both discs, the Brits easily take the match, with a more diverse range plus great contributions from Rush and Cujo. —*John Bush*

**Freestyle Files, Vol. 3: Nu Beat Science** / Jan. 26, 1998 / Studio !K7 ♦♦♦♦
Another collection of wide-ranging beats (electro, progressive house, big-beat, techno, drum'n'bass), *Freestyle Files, Vol. 3* looks at tracks from Plaid, I-F, Ballistic Brothers, Plug, Sluts'N'Strings & 909, Aphrodite, Jedi Knights, Basement Jaxx, and Terranova, among others. It's a great summation of the heady electro-listening scene circa 1998 with plenty of excellent selections and no filler. —*John Bush*

**Freestyle Files, Vol. 4: Crackers Delight** / Jul. 7, 1998 / Studio !K7 ♦♦♦
Just slightly less revelatory than earlier volumes in the series, *Crackers Delight* clocks in with Gentle People, Panasonic, Pole, Leila, Drum Island, Tipsy, Depth Charge, and Max 404, among others. —*John Bush*

**Freezone, Vol. 1: Phenomenology of Ambient** / 1994 / Crammed Discs ♦♦♦
The debut in the *Freezone* series looks at the world of mostly beatless ambient, courtesy of tracks by Porcupine Tree, Pete Namlook's Air, David Byrne, Deep Space Network, Moby, Deep Forest, Young American Primitive, and Terre Thaemlitz. —*Keith Farley*

**Freezone, Vol. 2: Variations on a Chill** / May 30, 1995 / SSR ♦♦♦
Though the majority of music on the second *Freezone* is from downtempo, more beat-oriented acts like DJ Cam, 4 Hero, TPower and Josh Wink also enter the fold. The two-disc set's collision of material works well, though it can begin to drag in spots. —*Keith Farley*

**Freezone, Vol. 3: Horizontal Dancing** / Jun. 11, 1996 / Crammed Discs ♦♦♦♦
Another two-disc set of future production, *Freezone, Vol. 3* continues to play down the downtempo influences and increases the BPMs. Tracks by American producers like Claude Young, Glenn Underground, and Josh Wink go hand in hand with European beat-merchants including laidback junglists JMJ+Richie, PFM, Kid Loops, and Phume, as well as trip-hop acts like Fila Brazillia, Howie B, Kruder & Dorfmeister, DJ Cam, and Patrick Pulsinger's Io project. —*Keith Farley*

**Freezone, Vol. 4: Dangerous Lullabies** / Jul. 15, 1997 / SSR ♦♦♦♦
The fourth installment in the virtually flawless *Freezone* series features all exclusives, from Basement Jaxx, Herbert Vs. Love from San Francisco, Carl Craig, Tosca Dimitri from Paris, Endemic Void, and Stasis, among others. Belgian DJ Morpheus mixes the proceedings into a potent brew of wide-ranging electronica. —*John Bush*

**Freezone, Vol. 6: Fourth Person Singular** / Nov. 30, 1999 / SSR ♦♦♦♦
The sixth installment in the *Freezone* series of two-fer compilations continues the practice of focusing on downtempo electronica, but in this case guest compiler DJ Morpheus has gone for a jazzier-than-usual sound, selecting a roster of talent that includes Better Daze, Buckfunk 3000, London Elektricity, and Alex Gopher, whose "Moving Fast Man" incorporates a gloriously cheesy computer-generated voice alternately intoning the phrases "Doctor Disco" and "I am the moving fast man." Other highlights include the gently propulsive "Lisbon" by Aim, the dryly dubwise "Because It Does" by Bullitnuts, and Señor Coconut's "Mucha Frita," a strangely attractive combination of deeply tweaked synthetic percussion and Latin-jazz horns and vocals. There's nothing here that will blow your mind, but the mood is always pleasant, relaxed, and funky. —*Rick Anderson*

**Freischwimmer** / Sep. 14, 1999 / EFA ♦♦♦
Compiling a few of the new breed of German post-rock collectives plus a few more obscure names, *Freischwimmer* includes tracks from To Rococo Rot, Tarwater, Laub, Raz Ohara, and Surrogat, among others. —*Keith Farley*

**Fresh Emissions** / 1995 / Emissions Audio Output ♦♦♦♦
Andrew Weatherall's Emissions label compiled unreleased and new tracks for this two-disc set. Though there's only one by Weatherall's Two Lone Swordsmen project, other selections by Conemelt, Being, Vermin, and Deanne Day more than make up for it. —*John Bush*

**Fresh Sound: Essential New Jungle Drum + Bass** / May 19, 1998 / Mutant Sound ♦♦♦♦
Almost as "essential" as its title claims it to be, *Fresh* is a collection of early drum'n'bass from one of its top labels, Labello Blanco. The disc includes tracks from Accetate ("Spirit"), Kenny Ken & Coolbreeze ("So Much Trouble"), Dr. 5 Gachet ("It's All Gone Sideways"), Rogue Unit ("Secret Motion") and Cloud 9 ("Lose Her"). —*Jason Ankeny*

**Frikyiwa Collection, Vol. 1** / Jun. 20, 2000 / Six Degrees ♦♦♦
*Frikyiwa Collection, Vol. 1* was put together by French musician/producer Frédéric Galliano, offering various club DJs and remixers the opportunity to recontextualize the music of Mali for the dancefloors of the future. Drawing from the stable of recordings owned by the Cobalt Records label, the remixers chose works by original artists such as Nahawa Doumbia, Ibrahim Hamma Dicko, Neba Solo, Lobi Traoré, and Abdoulaye Diabate. Jazz, reggae, dub, trance, house, drum'n'bass, and trip-hop all pop up over the course of the compilation, but the Malian sensibility helps tie everything together—even if purists might cringe at the very concept. —*Steve Huey*

**From Beyond** / Jul. 7, 1997 / Interdimensional Transmissions ♦♦♦♦
Ann Arbor-based electro/techno label Interdimensional Transmissions spent much of 1997 putting itself on the international dance music map via a limited four-part, 12"-only EP series titled "From Beyond." Assembling a by-most-measures peerless cast of envelope-pushing producers—including Mike Paradinas, Patrick Pulsinger, Phoenecia, Le Car, I-F, Will Web, Anthony Shakir, Keith Tucker, and Synapse, among others—"From Beyond" set something of a new standard in dance music experimentalism, relocating often unquestioningly received forms such as house, techno, and electro to entirely new geographical locales. The CD version compiles the entirety of that series, adding a live version of Phoenecia's "Roba," and is an essential collection of paradigm-exploding electronic dance music reintegrating a range of forgotten musics into frameworks both experimental and intelligible, and unflinchingly contemporary. —*Sean Cooper*

**From Here to Tranquility, Vol. 1: Ambient Compilation** / Jan. 1994 / Silent ♦♦♦♦
The first volume in the San Francisco label's series of ambient/psychedelic compilations includes tracks from locals Spacetime Continuum, Psychic TV, and Heavenly Music Corporation, as well as German trance outfit Spice Barons. —*Keith Farley*

**From Here to Tranquility, Vol. 2** / Feb. 11, 1994 / Silent ♦♦♦
With a concept very similar to the one behind its predecessor, volume two collects a few West Coast sympathetics like Single Cell Orchestra, Robert Rich, and Cirrus Minor, as well as an ambient-leaning Teuton—in this case, Pete Namlook's Air. —*Keith Farley*

**From Here to Tranquility, Vol. 3** / Oct. 4, 1994 / Silent ♦♦
Silent's third collection of ambience culls tracks from several obscure acts including ATOI, Psychic Surfers of Zuviya, Ohmegatribe and Vuemorph. Besides lacking the spark of the first two volumes, most of this volume consists of psychedelic trance-by-numbers. —*Keith Farley*

**From Here to Tranquility, Vol. 4** / Feb. 21, 1995 / Silent ♦♦♦
Another collection of mostly throwaway tracks from unknown acts—Makyo, Lightwave, 23o—plus the terrestrial harmonics of new-age scientist Dr. Fiorella Terenzi. —*Keith Farley*

**From Here to Tranquility, Vol. 5: The Silent Channel** / Feb. 6, 1996 / Silent ♦♦♦
Silent's fifth volume in *From Here to Tranquility* returns the name acts to the arena, and mostly delivers on their promise. Heavenly Music Corporation, PGR, Spice Barons, and Thessalonians each contribute laidback ambient/psychedelic epics of sound. —*Keith Farley*

**Funk Off** / Sep. 1, 1998 / Blackheart ♦♦♦♦
This compilation of big-dumb-techno highlights includes classics of the style like Wiseguys' "Ooh La La," Freestylers' "Ruffneck," and Deejay Punk Roc's "My Beatbox," plus others by Mask & Gang Related, Lunatic Calm, Girl Eats Boy, and Mild Mannered Jan. —*Keith Farley*

**Funkt** / Nov. 3, 1998 / V-Wax ♦♦♦
The dance compilation *Funkt* includes tracks by Girl Eats Boy, Slab, Pod, the Drum Club, and Duncan Forbes, among others. —*Keith Farley*

**Funktio, Vol. 1** / 1997 / Function ♦♦♦♦
A retrospective including several of the best early Finnish techno launches

from the early '90s, *Funktio, Vol. 1* includes previously rare material from Panasonic, group-member Mika Vainio's ÿ project, Kim Rapatti's Detroit Diesel, and Marko Laine, as well as more obscure names like Aural Expansion, Pineapple Circle, Jaljentamo, and Redshift & Uranus. It's easily one of the best compilations of polar/experimental techno ever released. —*John Bush*

**Funktio, Vol. 2** / 1998 / Function ++++
With a focus on newer material compared to the first volume's historical bent, *Funktio, Vol. 2* includes Rapatti and Laine alongside Finnish newcomers Nemesis XI, Vladislav Delay, GMA, Jokela, Ioma, Sensien, and others. While each track is intriguing, the album doesn't quite make it to the standards of its predecessor. —*John Bush*

**Funkungfusion** / Apr. 28, 1998 / Ninja Tune +++
One of the more diverse Ninja Tune compilations (though that's not saying much), *Funkungfusion* displays the Ninjas' 1998 expansion into musical realms other than abstract breakbeat/trip-hop. Among the new kids on the block are turntablist Kid Koala, Ryuichi Sakamoto, Luke Vibert, Clifford Gilberto, Cabbageboy (aka Si Begg), Burnt Friedman (aka Nonplace Urban Field), Marc Royal (of TPower's Chocolate Weasel), and Override. Though they have much in common with others on the label, the fresh acts make the album flow better than any other Ninja Tune compilation out there. —*Keith Farley*

**Funky Desert Breaks: Under a Desert Sky** / Aug. 6, 1996 / Moonshine Music ++++
An album of typically American funky breakbeats and psychedelic trance from the cream of the crop, including Uberzone, the Crystal Method, Electric Skychurch, Omar Santana, and Psychedelic Research Lab. John Kelley's mixing is more than proficient, but the generally unexciting flavor and lack of subtlety in the material drag the compilation down a bit. —*Keith Farley*

**Future Funk, Vol. 2** / Apr. 28, 1997 / Solid State +++
The second volume in the attempted all-encompassing electronica compilation includes shots from Roni Size and Armand Van Helden, as well as Jimi Tenor and DJ Q. —*Keith Farley*

**Future Jazz** / Jan. 25, 2000 / Instinct +++
Instinct's *Future Jazz* compilation rides the thin divide between electronic music and the earthier sound of jazz, exemplified by futuristic producers like Carl Craig and DJ Krush. —*Keith Farley*

**Future Sound of Jazz, Vol. 1** / Jul. 16, 1996 / Instinct ++++
Too many dance compilations that include the word "jazz" in their titles are sample-fests with bland loops and breaks that don't even deserve the dumbed-down "jazzy" term. Compost's *Future Sound of Jazz* is an obvious exception; tracks by Nightmares on Wax, the Gentle People (an Aphex Twin remix), Tortoise, µ-Ziq and Patrick Pulsinger make it one of the best electronica compilations around. (The American issue of *Future Sound of Jazz* corresponds to the second volume of the original *Future Sound of Jazz* series in its German release, and continues accordingly throughout the series.) —*Keith Farley*

**Future Sound of Jazz, Vol. 2** / Mar. 11, 1997 / Instinct ++++
Another two-disc set with fewer big names but a similarly startling quality of material, *Future Sound of Jazz, Vol. 2* includes work by a wide range of artists who nominally pursue fusions of jazz with electronic dance—Move D, Jimpster, Max 404, RAC, Fauna Flash, Turntable Terranova, Beanfield, Cool Blu, and DJ Dara. As an added incentive (practically unnecessary for a set of this quality), toward the end of the second disc are two tracks with the trainspotters in mind: "Keynell 1" by Gescom and "Shponk" by Mike Paradinas (aka µ-Ziq). —*Keith Farley*

**Future Sound of Jazz, Vol. 3** / Jan. 20, 1997 / Compost +++
Though most of the inclusions are impeccable (As One, Tosca, Pressure Drop, A Forest Mighty Black), the presence of a few duds makes it difficult to recommend the third volume over previous editions in the *Future Sound of Jazz* series. —*Keith Farley*

**Future Sound of Jazz, Vol. 5** / Oct. 13, 1998 / Compost +++
The fifth volume in the *Future Sound of Jazz* series is a double-disc set including a range of techno, jazzy, and experimental tracks from Nonplace Urban Field, Bjorn Torske, Chaser, Max Brennan, Fauna Flash, and Force & Paul, among others. —*Keith Farley*

**Future Sound of Jazz, Vol. 6 [Compost]** / Oct. 19, 1999 / Compost +++
Though it's six volumes in and counting, Compost's *Future Sounds of Jazz* series just keeps on shining. Recruiting a cast of varied standout producers—Ian O'Brien, Fauna Flash, Tosca, Victor Simonelli, United Future Organization, Beatless—helps immensely, as does the sheer variety of productions. All are nominally jazz-based, but vary from downtempo to trip-hop to drum'n'bass with no lack of flow. —*Keith Farley*

**The Future Sound of New York** / 1995 / Emotive +++
A compilation of tracks from the New York label Emotive, *The Future Sound of New York* was mixed by Junior Vasquez. —*Keith Farley*

**Future Sound of the United Kingdom** / Oct. 13, 1997 / Open ++++
A double-disc including thirty-one tracks from the best of Britain's big-beat scene, *Future Sound of the United Kingdom* includes tracks by Propellerheads, Orbital, Underworld, Coldcut, Howie B., the Mighty Dub Katz, and Leftfield, among others. —*Keith Farley*

**Future Sounds of Infinity** / Dec. 15, 1998 / Dressed to Kill +++
The hackneyed title is a clue to much of the lightweight dance music inside, though Future Sound of London, Carl Cox, Loop Guru, Genaside II, and Stakker (the classic "Humanoid") do make appearances. —*John Bush*

**Future Sounds of Paris** / Aug. 19, 1997 / Ultra +++
Though Air and Daft Punk are missing, this collection of French dance includes stellar tracks from Motorbass, Daphreephunkateerz, Dimitri from Paris, Trankilou, and Zend Avesta. —*Keith Farley*

**Future: A Journey Through the Electric Underground** / Jul. 29, 1997 / Virgin ++++
The two-CD set *Future: A Journey through the Electronic Underground* features some of the best artists from the overlapping worlds of electronica, techno, drum'n'bass, and ambient music, along with the recording debut of Gillian Anderson (Dana Scully of television's *The X-Files*). Anderson's moody recitation on "Extremis" with the electronic "supergroup" Hal (Duncan Lomax, Paul Gallagher, and Pascal Derycke, all members of different bands uniting for this project) doesn't provide the best music in this *Future*, though it does lend warm and breathy focus to Hal's ambient drone. The best comes from the futuristic and funky selections from Future Sound of London ("Smokin' Japanese Babe," and "Snake Hips"), Fluke ("Atom Bomb") and µ-Ziq ("Salsa with Mesquite"), trip-hop forerunners Massive Attack ("Karmacoma"), the Chemical Brothers (the dizzying "Loops of Fury"), along with early practitioners of electronic music Brian Eno ("Lizard Point," "Space Diary 1" with Jah Wobble, and "Their Memories" with pianist Harold Budd). —*Chris Slawecki*

**Futurhythms** / Aug. 3, 1993 / Giant +++
Charting the course of harder progressive house and techno-trance, *Futurhythms* includes tracks by Leftfield, Moby, Young American Primitive and Eskimos, and Egypt, among others. Prodigy and Sven Väth provide the highlights, with "Wind It Up" and "Accident in Paradise," respectively. —*Keith Farley*

**Generation Trance 2000** / Nov. 16, 1999 / ICU/MAX +++
DJ Kimball Collins mixes the 11-track trance collection *Generation Trance 2000: Episode 01*, which features both originals and (mostly) remixes. Tracks include the Generator's "Where Are You Now," Sunscream's "Exodus," Mea Culpa's "The Child," Stone Love's "My Love Will Surround You," and Armin's "Communication," among others. —*Steve Huey*

**Get Up: Compilation** / Feb. 17, 1995 / Strictly Rhythm ++++
*Get Up* collects quite a few Strictly Rhythm hits of the early '90s, including "Witch Doktor" by Armand Van Helden, "Sumba Lumba" by Tribal Infusion (aka Roger Sanchez), "Project Blast" by Photon, Inc. (aka DJ Pierre), and Reel 2 Real's "Raise Your Hands." —*Keith Farley*

**Ghost in the Shell** / Sony ++++
The eponymous soundtrack to the Sony Playstation game features tracks from several of the best trance and techno names in the work, including Claude Young (Brother from Another Planet), BCJ (CJ Bolland), Joey Beltram, Westbam, Hardfloor, Dave Angel, and the Advent. Besides those great names, it was also trumpeted as containing the first new recording from Derrick May in half a dozen years, though "To Be or Not to Be" is available here only

in remixed form (by one of the few capable of such a feat, Juan Atkins). It's quite essential for Detroit fans, and isn't a bad collection of tracks for anyone into techno. —*Keith Farley*

**Giant Steps** / Apr. 5, 1994 / Blue Note ♦♦♦
An intriguing Blue Note collection that alternates jazz-rap cuts with original jazz-funk classics from the '70s, *Giant Step* includes Us3, Greg Osby, Guru, the Beastie Boys, and UMC's from the new school, while Donald Byrd, Reuben Wilson, and Lou Donaldson represent the old. —*Keith Farley*

**Gilles Peterson & Norman Jay: Desert Island Mix** / 1997 / V2 ♦♦♦♦
Two of Britain's most influential DJs shared this mix set, including not just their specialties (acid jazz, rare groove) but many segues into the new school of dance music. —*Keith Farley*

**Give 'em Enough Dope, Vol. 1** / 1995 / C&S ♦♦♦♦
This compilation of European acid jazz and trip-hop also includes elements of soul, funk, jazz, and rap. Nonetheless, the disparate genres flow well and the sounds are very fresh, making this a great compilation of '90s fusion. Artists include Howie B, Deep Freeze Productions, and Kruder & Dorfmeister. —*John Bush*

**Give Peace a Dance, Vol. 2** / 1995 / CND Communications ♦♦♦♦
Subtitled "The Ambient Collection," this second volume includes quite a few killer rare tracks from the early '90s, including "The Von Daniken Experiment" by the Black Dog, "Change" by LFO, a lengthy Orb remix of Erasure's "Ship of Fools," and other tracks by the Irresistible Force, Suns of Arqa, Bleep & Booster, and Colourbox. —*John Bush*

**Global Cuts, Vol. 1** / Nov. 13, 1993 / Antler Subway ♦♦♦
*Global Cuts* is a collection of Belgian trance and techno, with tracks by Sven Van Hees, X-Tatic, Remy & Sven, and Capricorn, plus an appearance by Detroit legend Eddie "Flashin" Fowlkes. —*Keith Farley*

**Global Grooves: One** / Dec. 14, 1999 / Centaur ♦♦♦
*Global Grooves: One* features hits from Billie Ray Martin, Boy George, and Reina, remixed by DJ Julien Marsh. SM Traxx's "Got the Groove" and Shawn Christopher's "Don't Lose the Magic" are among the highlights of this club music collection. —*Heather Phares*

**Global Klubbin', Vol. 2: Paris** / Nov. 3, 1998 / Max Music ♦♦♦
The Parisian edition in the *Global Klubbin* series doesn't exactly include the cream of French electronica, though tracks by Martin Solveig, Eddy & Dus, La Cellue, and DJ Sebass more than make up for the notable absences. In all, it's a great club compilation. —*Keith Farley*

**Global Underground: Arrivals** / Mar. 7, 2000 / Boxed ♦♦
Similar to the preceding *Global Underground* sampler titled Departures, *Arrivals* features many of the best tracks from the huge *Global Underground* catalog mixed together seamlessly. The resulting album functions as a greatest-hits-type package with many of the best trance songs to emerge at the end of the '90s. To a further extent than Departures, *Arrivals* relies on a few undeniable anthems to carry the weight of the album. Mixed by the Forth, these 11 songs get off to a banging start with Tilt's "Seduction of Orpheus," a song Danny Tenaglia used in a similar fashion to jump-start the eclectic, trance-laced second set of his *Athens* album. Soon after comes the "Evolution Mix" of Life on Mars'' "Life in Minds," which doesn't nearly compare to the tranquil original mix as featured on Paul Oakenfold's *Global Underground: New York* album, but Blue Fish's "One" soon elevates the album into a high mood of serenity, especially when followed by Space Manoeuvres' "Stage One (Pariah Remix)." Following these two fairly mid-tempo songs, "The Chain" and "Perception" both carry the mix into more intense territory with their progressive builds and overpowering synth melodies. From there things die down a bit for an extended moment of sheer bliss during Planisphere's amply titled "Deep Blue Dream," and from there the album concludes with the anthem of trance anthems, Bedrock's "Heaven Scent." Sure, *Arrivals* features some amazing songs, but it has some definite problems. First of all, the mix suffers from the Forth's admirable effort to blend so many peak-hour songs together without making this album sound overly ecstatic. Secondly, the album draws heavily from Sasha's albums, making the second half of *Arrivals* practically a Sasha revival. The next question: How many times can one hear "Heaven Scent" before the song loses its power? And finally, anyone that already owns a few of the *Global Underground* titles—particularly the Sasha albums and John Digweed's Hong Kong album—shouldn't bother picking this up. The songs appear in a much more appealing context on the original albums, where they aren't crammed into a small amount of space with other anthems all nullifying the adrenaline rush of one another. —*Jason Birchmeier*

**Glücklich** / Sep. 7, 1999 / Compost ♦♦♦
*Glücklich*—in which a respected trip-hop producer and nu-jazz musician (a Forest Mighty Black's Rainer Trüby)—compiles a series of German tracks produced in a Brazilian jazz-funk vibe during the '70s, by artists including Klaus Doldinger, Sunbirds, John Thomas, Rainer Pusch Quartet, Real Ax Band, and Namaz. The sound is smoother than smooth, with songs utterly divorced from their Teutonic origins. Most of the tracks float by as rather pleasant background fusion, halfway between Miles and the Rippingtons, but there are a few standout selections, including what could be an addition to the classic-rare-groove canon, "Mato Pato" by Kitty Winter Gipsy Nova. —*John Bush*

**Glücklich II** / Sep. 7, 1999 / Compost ♦♦
The second volume of '70s Teutonic fusion with a decidedly non-Teutonic feel expands the focus of the original, inviting Europeans and transplanted Brazilians of all stripes into the fold for a nine-track dose of smooth jazz and earthy fusion with plenty of Rhodes to spare. As on the first, highlights are few, but for fans of either original fusion-lite groups (Weather Report, Mahavishnu Orchestra) or their modern inheritors (from Endemic Void to Jimpster) will find pleasantly nondescript listening throughout. —*John Bush*

**Glücklich III** / Aug. 24, 1999 / Compost ♦♦♦♦
Compost Records' *Glücklich 3* collects urban, Brazilian-inspired fusion from across Europe and the US. While the other two albums in the series focus on music from the '70s and '80s, volume 3 concentrates on the '90s' interpretation of "Brazilliance," which includes electronic elements as well as sambas, bossa novas, and batucadas. Tracks like Pathless' "Goddess," Boozoo Bajou's "Night Over Manaus," and Cosmo Vitelli's "We Don't Need No Smurf Here" provide a unique hybrid of contemporary electronic music and classic Brazilian style. —*Heather Phares*

**Goa Spaceship 101: Goa Trance Trip** / Aug. 13, 1996 / Cleopatra ♦♦♦
Cleopatra's collection of Goa trance includes tracks from Arcana, Prana + Athena, Astral Projection, and Technossomy, among others. —*Keith Farley*

**Greatest House Mix** / Sep. 29, 1998 / Alpha Wave ♦♦♦
It's nowhere near deserving of the title, though *Greatest House Mix* does include tracks by Loleatta Holloway, Voigt-Kampff, and Soundwave, plus three rather rare remixes by Armand Van Helden. —*Keith Farley*

**Groove Mix** / Jan. 28, 1997 / Intersound ♦♦♦
*Groove Mix* features the club hits "Whadda U Want (From Me)" by Frankie Knuckles (featuring Adeva), "Feels So Good (Show Me Your Love)" by Lina Santiago, "Release Me" by Angelina, "Feel the Music" by Planet Soul (featuring Brenda Dee), and "Santa Maria" by Tatjana. —*Jason Ankeny*

**Groove Radio International Presents: Alternative Mix** / Apr. 27, 1999 / Priority ♦♦♦
Groove Radio International's *Alternative Mix* volume features an interesting mix of alternative-dance and indie-oriented breakbeat, including tracks from Love and Rockets, Propellerheads, Freestylers, Fatboy Slim, Moby, BT, Wildchild, Bow Wow Wow, Cornershop, Headrillaz, Garbage, Gus Gus, Crystal Method, and Purple Planet. —*John Bush*

**Groove Radio International Presents: Global House** / Mar. 23, 1999 / Priority ♦♦♦♦
The mainstream house edition in Swedish Egil's continuing series of *Groove Radio* mix albums, *Global House* is one of the best and most comprehensive volumes yet. Egil's mix includes tracks by all of the biggest names in chart-bound house, including David Morales, Armand Van Helden, Steve "Silk" Hurley, Cevin Fisher, Eddie Amador, Club 69, and Ralphi Rosario. He sounds more comfortable on the mix here than on his downtempo volume, and makes the entire album a fun, exciting introduction to '90s house—one of the finest around. —*John Bush*

**Groove Radio International Presents: House** / Apr. 28, 1998 / Priority ♦♦♦
*Groove Radio International Presents: House* is an entertaining but slight col-

lection of house singles and house remixes that are programmed as one continuous track. There's a handful of major names, such as Todd Terry and Sneaker Pimps, on the collection, but for the most part, it's simply good, faceless house that's entertaining while its playing but ultimately a little unmemorable. —*Stephen Thomas Erlewine*

**Groove Radio International Presents: Speed Garage** / Jan. 12, 1999 / Priority ♦♦♦

The *Speed Garage* volume in Groove Radio's style series includes several of the best tracks—"Rip Groove" by Double 99, "Gunman" by 187 Lockdown, "Hold Your Head Up High" by Mousse T.—plus other solid tracks by Pianoheadz, Wamdue Project, Byron Stingily, C-Ken, Gant, and Andy Lamboy. —*John Bush*

**Groove, Vol. 3** / Jan. 13, 1998 / Groove ♦♦♦♦

The third in a series of samplers put out by the continental European magazine *Groove*, *Groove Vol. 3* is a two-disc set featuring both club hits and rarities, original versions and remixes. Highlights include contributions by Daft Punk, DJ Sneak, Herbert, Basement Jaxx, Ian Pooley, and others. —*Steve Huey*

**Grooverider Presents: The Prototype Years** / 1997 / Higher Ground/Proto ♦♦♦♦

A definitive compilation of solid, consistently quality dancefloor tracks from the Rider's own Prototype imprint. Featuring a score of classic cuts from Boymerang, Lemon D, Ed Rush, and John B., as well as new material from Rush and Fierce, Optical, Matrix, Dillinja's Cybotron project, and Groove himself (as Codename John), *The Prototype Years* is a high-water mark of progressive, dancefloor-oriented drum'n'bass, with tight, chrome-dipped production and superior, innovative arrangements obtaining across the board. Although the artists' predilection for the darkside may at first appear simply *du temps* (the album was, after all, released in early 1997, during the height of techstep's reign in the clubs), each track maintains a notable degree of focus and integrity, drawing enough from each of the corners of the breakbeat world to remain just this side of trendiness. The CD version adds bonus tracks from the Prototype catalog, as well as a second disc mixed by Groove himself, also featuring the previously unavailable Dom & Roland remix of Boymerang's "Still." Nothing short of essential. —*Sean Cooper*

**Grooverider's Hardstep Selection, Vol. 2** / 1995 / Kickin' ♦♦♦

This Grooverider-mixed collection of ragga and darkstep drum'n'bass includes tracks by Tom & Jerry, Dillinja, and J Majik. —*Keith Farley*

**Guerilla Beats** / Feb. 10, 1990 / Cleopatra ♦♦♦♦

A double-disc collection of Guerilla grooves from React 2 Rhythm, the Drum Club, and Felix Da Housecat isn't a bad proposition, but *Guerilla Beats* improves itself immensely by including a host of top-notch remixes, from Orbital, Justin Robertson, Carl Cox, Digweed, Blue Amazon, William Orbit, and D.O.P., among others. —*John Bush*

**Guerilla in Dub** / May 2, 1994 / Pow Wow ♦♦♦

*Guerilla in Dub* is a collection of excursions on the version for most of the label's top progressive acts, including Spooky, Drum Club, D.O.P., and React 2 Rhythm. Spooky's combined "Schmoo/Aqualung" opus is the highlight of the set, even more impressive than the version on the duo's Gargantuan LP. —*John Bush*

**The Haçienda** / 1995 / A&M ♦♦♦♦

This compilation of remixed indie acts and American garage producers was released to promote Manchester's Haçienda club, and mixed by Graeme Park. From New Order's "1963" (remixed by Joe T. Vanelli) to tracks by Masters at Work, Todd Terry, and Carole Sylvan, —*John Bush*

**Happy Hardcore Ravers** / Feb. 6, 1996 / Cleopatra ♦♦

Cleopatra's attempt to pass a dozen industrial-dance tracks over as real happy hardcore comes across as flat and phony. Included artists Rave Nation, Mach, Keno, Dreamscape, and Drummatik are just as unfamiliar to those into the scene as complete novices, and this album is a complete ripoff. —*John Bush*

★ **Happy2bHardcore** / Jan. 21, 1997 / Moonshine Music ♦♦♦♦♦

The best place for happy hardcore novices to begin as well as a great mix (by Slipmatt) for fans who already have most of the material, *Happy2bHardcore* includes classics like "Go Insane" by DJ DNA, "Let the Music" by Eruption and "Feel the Power" by DJ Codeine & Unknown, among others. Along with several volumes in the series, the collection is one of the best documents in happy hardcore's immense catalog. —*John Bush*

**Happy2bHardcore, Vol. 2** / Sep. 9, 1997 / Moonshine Music ♦♦♦♦

Popular Toronto DJ Anabolic Frolic returns for the second volume of his *Happy2bHardcore* series on Moonshine. Unfortunately, little has changed since the first volume. The happy hardcore anthems still blast beats at ultra-fast bpms, accompanied by more than enough synth melodies to hum along to—or blow your rave whistle to—and also enough candy mentality to evoke plenty of E-inspired, hug-friendly cuddle puddles. Hints of drum'n'bass appear every now and then, but for the most part, this album sticks to the standard happy hardcore template that a small niche audience of devotees has come to love and a much larger majority has come to hate. —*Jason Birchmeier*

**Happy2bHardcore, Vol. 3** / Apr. 20, 1999 / Moonshine Music ♦♦♦♦

Once again, Anabolic Frolic returns with even more happy hardcore anthems for all the candy-loving ravers looking for more nonstop beats, gagging melodies, and heart-bleeding P.L.U.R. vocals. The featured producers do a slightly better job of being creative with their arrangements on this particular volume, but for the most part this installment simply repeats the first two. If you've heard one of the volumes or more, you "know the score," as the hardcore corps say. —*Jason Birchmeier*

**Happy2bHardcore, Vol. 4** / Feb. 22, 2000 / Moonshine Music ♦♦

Moonshine unleashed a fourth chapter in the eternally ongoing *Happy2bHardcore* series for those yearning for more of the infamous style's rampant candy-coated extremity. The vocals and melodies are still happy while the tempo and beats are still hardcore; in sum, Moonshine and Anabolic Frolic have found a hungry niche audience of primarily pacifier-sucking, whistle-blowing, big pant-wearing, oft-hugging, Hullabaloo-going, perma-grin-sporting, endlessly cheery ravers—and perhaps a few other nonpurists—for their assembly-line happy hardcore albums. Will this seemingly unstoppable continuation of P.L.U.R.-inspired adolescent mayhem ever conclude? —*Jason Birchmeier*

**Hardcore Massive, Vol. 1** / 1995 / Rogue Trooper ♦♦♦

Much closer to jump-up drum'n'bass than hardcore despite the title, this compilation features excellent tracks by Aphrodite, Droppin' Science, and DJ Phantasy. —*Keith Farley*

**Hardcorps: Ultimate in Gabber & Hardcore Techno** / Jan. 20, 1990 / Moonshine Music ♦♦♦

It may not be the ultimate, but this is a better-than-average collection of hardest-of-the-hardcore producers like Omar Santana (as himself as well as Too Hustile), Archatos, Horrorist, and Da Predator. —*Keith Farley*

**Hardesertrance, Vol. 2** / Nov. 24, 1998 / Moonshine Music ♦♦♦

A year after DJ Brian released the first album in the *Hardesertrance* series, he released a second volume that departed from the techno-tinged style of his original. *Hardesertrance 2* updates its sound to the style of trance that was just beginning to flood the electronic music scene in the late '90s, moving toward fairly straightforward progressive house rhythms and a heavy use of synthesizer riffs. Brian doesn't go for the massive breakdowns and build-ups that many of his peers favor, nor does he go for the candy-coated synth melodies that even an infant could latch onto; instead, he goes for the straight-ahead, stomping power of progressive house to drive the rhythm and also tends to drift toward tracks with accompanying synth riffs that aren't as psychedelic as acid or as melodic as Paul Van Dyk-style trance. This strikes a happy medium where the trance isn't nearly as threatening as that featured on the first *Hardesertrance* album or as excessively clichéd as that spun by peers such as Kimball Collins. Of course, this uncharismatic style of rather generic progressive house with a hint of trance motif sprinkled throughout results in a dull mix. Only a few of the songs tend to possess any noteworthy characteristics worth returning to, and many don't even include salient moments worth noting. Some songs such as Sonic Fusion's "Emotions" try to get wild but sound awkward and out of place; other songs such as Sandra Collins' "Red" elevate the mood of the set with their trancey build-ups and overly polished synth riffs but only leave the listener hungry for more action. The set's most exciting moment comes three-quarters of the way through the set when Brian drops the Palefield Mountain remix of Albion's "Air," an undeniable trance anthem of the late '90s. This remix takes the traditionally soothing song and tears it to shreds with spiraling synth riffs until late into the song when the song's signature melody appears in the aftermath of the song's storm-like climax. Besides this song and the oft-heard vocals of Amoeba Assasin's "Rollercoaster," DJ Brian's second album in this series sadly disappoints with its lack of adventure. —*Jason Birchmeier*

**Hardesertrance 3** / Nov. 23, 1999 / Moonshine Music ♦♦♦
Like the first two, the third volume in Moonshine's *Hardesertrance* series was helmed by DJ Brian, a colleague of John Kelley (whose own series, *Funkydesertbreaks*, plows similar ground). The album cycles through tracks of psychedelic breakbeat trance, indebted to the more Eurocentric sounds of Britain's progressive trance scene but also reliant on the distinctly American influence of producers like Hardkiss and the Crystal Method. The album has many highlights, including Joshua Ryan's "Pistolwhip," Human Movement's "Travellers Theme," and Aquila's "Dreamstate." —*John Bush*

**Hardhop & Trypno** / Feb. 6, 1996 / Moonshine Music ♦♦♦
The range of upbeat funky breaks on this compilation is hardly astonishing, but the presence of Fatboy Slim's "Everybody Loves a 303" alongside domestic beat merchants like Crystal Method, Uberzone, Keoki, and Zen Cowboys makes for at least one highlight. —*John Bush*

**Hardhop & Trypno, Vol. 2** / Jan. 21, 1997 / Moonshine Music ♦♦♦
Fatboy Slim's "Punk to Funk," Uberzone's "Moondusted," and Mono's "Life in Mono" are a couple of highlights from the second edition in the *Hardhop & Trypno* series. The rest of the tracks—by acts like Hard Knox, Planet Jazz, Supersoul, Control X—aren't quite up to that level, but are enjoyable style workouts nevertheless. —*John Bush*

**Hardhop Tricked Out: Mixed Down by Omar Santana** / Apr. 7, 1998 / Moonshine Music ♦♦♦
Basically an Omar Santana solo album, *Hardhop Tricked Out* features half a dozen tracks by Santana aliases—Dark Side of the Shroom, Tales from the Hardside, Hard Hop Heathen, Imperial Stormtroopers (with Freddie Fresh)—plus remixes by Simply Jeff and others. Santana's production and mixing are excellent, and though the album stays strictly within the confines of breakbeat and hardcore trance, it's still an enjoyable ride. —*John Bush*

**Hardleaders, Vol. 2: The Way Out Chapter** / Jul. 8, 1997 / Kickin' ♦♦♦
Unlike the all-star debut Hardleaders compilation *Suspect Package*, *The Way Out Chapter* showcases recent signings and exclusives. So while fans will want it for the unreleased tracks, the general jungle listener won't find much here that isn't done better on other collections. Tracks appear from TDK, Serve Chilled, Capone, Regulate, Venom, and Formula 7, among others. —*John Bush*

**Harthouse 100** / Jul. 29, 1996 / Harthouse ♦♦♦
In celebration of the Harthouse label's 100th release comes this compilation of club tracks including Sven Väth and Ralf Hildenbeutel's "100 Harthouse," Hardfloor's "Kamikaze Whopper," Alter Ego's "Folk Song," Braincell's "Sweetypie" and Patrick Lindsey's "Male Phonk." —*Jason Ankeny*

**Harthouse Compilation: Dark Hearts 2** / Harthouse ♦♦♦♦
The second in the *Dark Hearts* series is particularly attractive, given the breadth of producers appearing on it. Besides the presence of Harthouse regulars like Hardfloor, Alter Ego, and Jiri Ceiver, *Dark Hearts, Vol. 2* also includes tracks by Claude Young, Luke Slater's Morganistic, Neil Landstrumm and Cari Lekebusch's Braincell. —*John Bush*

**Harthouse: The Point of No Return Chapter 1** / American Recordings ♦♦♦♦
Almost a Harthouse best-of compilation, *Point of No Return* includes label classics like Hardfloor's "Acperience," Spicelab's "Spice Cowboy" and Arpeggiators' "Xenophobe." Also featured are tracks by Marco Zaffarano, Cosmic Baby's Futurhythm, and Pulsation. —*John Bush*

**Harvest in Technicolour** / Dec. 1, 1997 / Harvest ♦♦♦
The long-running Harvest Records issued the fruits of its electronic releases, focusing on German experimental electro-techno like Air Liquide, Khan & Walker, Burger/Ink, the Bionaut, and Trinkwasser, among others. —*John Bush*

**Header, Vol. 1** / 1997 / Header ♦♦♦♦
The enhanced CD compilation *Header* includes tracks from several of the most creative electronic technicians around—As One, Carl Craig, 4Hero, U.N.K.L.E., Derrick Carter—as well as a multimedia interview portion with Craig, Horace Andy, and James Lavelle. It's a superb compilation with an intelligent CD-ROM section as well. —*John Bush*

**Header, Vol. 2** / 1998 / Header ♦♦♦♦
The second volume in the interactive *Header* series combines exclusive tracks from Stasis, Plug, Carl Craig's Innerzone Orchestra, Danny Breaks, Reflection, and Courtney Pine with short video/movies concerning each artist. Above and beyond the crucial music, the CD-ROM portions are gorgeous, well-executed productions that only enhance the audio portions. —*John Bush*

**Headquarters: The Album** / 1995 / Tresor ♦♦♦
Though the artists aren't among Tresor's most widely known, *Headquarters* is a fine compilation, spotlighting artists who appeared at Tresor's club and collected by Pacou. Tracks are included from Tollstoi, Hendrix & Pacou, Eleve, and DIS X 3. —*John Bush*

**Headz** / 1995 / Mo'Wax ♦♦♦♦
The first double-disc/quadruple-vinyl installment of the *Headz* trilogy is easily the least of the batch. Though it features some heavyweights, the compilation suffers from a series of lengthy tracks that are too simplistic for their own good. Monochromatic and sluggish in long stretches to the point of approximating aural wallpaper, no amount of outer stimulation can add life to half of the material. Even an uncharacteristic Autechre track is weak. Nonetheless, decency is offered by the likes of DJ Shadow's U2-sampling "Lost and Found" (also a culprit of unnecessary length), Patterson's "Freedom Now," and DJ Krush's remix of Olde Scottish's "Wildstyle." Other notable appearances include U.N.K.L.E., Palmskin Productions, and Howie B. —*Andy Kellman*

**Headz II: Part A** / Oct. 28, 1996 / Mo'Wax ♦♦♦♦
The first of two separately released double-disc sets that document the history of British trip-hop, *Headz II: Part A* includes Mo'Wax stalwarts—DJ Krush, U.N.K.L.E., Solo, RPM—with contributions from artists not directly linked to trip-hop, such as Tortoise, the Beastie Boys, Stereo MCs, and Folk Implosion. Other big names include DJ Food (aka Coldcut, PC, and Strictly Kev), Massive Attack, Nightmares on Wax, and jungle hero Peshay, who contributes a downtempo rendition of his jungle track, "The Real Thing." —*John Bush*

**Headz II: Part B** / Oct. 28, 1996 / Mo'Wax ♦♦♦♦
The second half of the Mo'Wax magnum opus compilation features the usual crew of label acts (DJ Krush, Attica Blues, U.N.K.L.E., Palmskin Productions) as well as significant detours through hip-hop (Jungle Brothers, Money Mark, the Dust Brothers, the Beastie Boys) and jungle (Roni Size, Peshay, DJ Krust, Source Direct, Special Forces aka Photek), and even British techno like As One, Black Dog Productions, and Max 404. The breadth of material threatens to overwhelm, but there are over 25 great tracks on this double-disc set. —*John Bush*

**Heavenly Grooves** / Oct. 7, 1996 / Hyperium ♦♦♦
This ambient-breaks collection includes tracks by Coldcut, Shantel, Future Sound of London, Leftfield, Rabbit in the Moon, In the Nursery, and Delerium. —*John Bush*

**Here Come the Drums: Hip-Hop Drum'N'Bass** / May 19, 1998 / Caipirinha ♦♦♦♦
*Here Come the Drums* is a good introduction to the hip-hop side of drum'n'bass, compiling a dozen tracks from such notables as Roni Size ("Music Box"), DJ Red Alert & Mike Slammer ("In Effect"), Tek 9 ("A London Sumtin'"), and Natural Born Chillers (a remix of the Jungle Brothers' "Brain"). —*Jason Ankeny*

**Hi-Fidelity Lounge, Vol. 1** / Sep. 7, 1999 / Guidance Recordings ♦♦♦♦
Guidance Recordings' *Hi-Fidelity Lounge 1* collects jazz and lounge-inspired tracks from Bang Bang, Paul Hunter, Rainer Truby, the Mighty Bop, and other dance artists. The Funky Lowlives' "Notabossa," Thievery Corporation's "Lebanese Blonde," Louise Vertigo's "Ou Est La Femme," and Bobby Hughes' "Seasons" are among the highlights of this eclectic compilation of electronic music. —*Heather Phares*

**Hidden Rooms** / 1997 / Certificate 18 ♦♦♦♦
One of the hippest jungle labels in the UK, East Anglia's Certificate 18 hasn't released more than 20 singles since 1991, but its material appears high on trainspotters' must-have lists—both Photek and Source Direct have recorded obscure singles for the label, both under assumed names (Studio Pressure and Sounds of Life, respectively). *Hidden Rooms* compiles the best sides from those two, as well as Klute (not the industrial artist) with a warm, jazzy style much more interesting than most jungle jazz being recorded. —*John Bush*

**High Fidelity House** / Nov. 18, 1997 / Guidance ♦♦♦♦
Some of the best Chicago producers of the '90s appeared on this Guidance compilation, including Kevin Yost ("2 Wrongs Making It Right"), Glenn Underground ("G&S Motion"), Mark Grant ("Spirit of the Black Ghost"), and—Chicago-minded though Atlanta-based—Chris Brann ("Way Past the Clouds"). —*John Bush*

**High Performance** / May 27, 1997 / Instinct ♦♦♦♦
One of the first releases in the New York-based Instinct label's trend-surfing "electronica" series, *High Performance* is essentially a pseudonymized reissue of the Hydrogen Dukebox label compilation *Shake the Bones*, released by the UK-based imprint in 1996. With featured artists including Slab, Lol Hammond's solo Girl Eats Boy project, Monkey Mafia, and TLM, this is Brithop/big-beat techno with a distinctly acidic grit. —*Sean Cooper*

**Highways over Gardens** / 1998 / Carpet Bomb ♦♦♦♦
A part of the fragmented American jungle scene began to coalesce with New York's Carpet Bomb Records. The label began to get attention for drill'n'bass freak-outs worthy of British stalwarts like Squarepusher and Animals on Wheels. *Highways over Gardens* includes several tracks from two previous Carpet Bomb EPs (by Microstudio and Unagi Patrol), but the majority of the album consists of exclusives, from Tripform, Livestock, and Kundalini, plus Microstudio and Unagi Patrol. —*John Bush*

**Hip Hop Classics, Vol. 1** / May 23, 1996 / Priority ♦♦♦
Not everything on *Hip-Hop Classics, Vol. 1* lives up to its billing, but the 15-track collection contains enough great cuts—including Eric B. & Rakim's "Eric B. Is President," EPMD's "You're a Customer," MC Shane's "The Bridge," Doug E. Fresh's "Di Da Di," Biz Markie's "Make the Music with Your Mouth," Too hort's "Frekay Tales," Eazy-E's "Boyz-'n-the-Hood," Public Enemy's "Rebel without a Pause," NWA's "Straight Outta Compton," and Ice Cube's "Amerikkka's Most Wanted"—to make it worth its budget price. —*Stephen Thomas Erlewine*

**Hip Hop Classics, Vol. 2** / May 23, 1996 / Priority ♦♦♦
Not everything on *Hip-Hop Classics, Vol. 2* lives up to its billing, but the 15-track collection contains enough great cuts—including EPMD's "You Gots to Chill," Boogie Down Productions' "My Philosophy," NWA's "Fuck tha Police," Biz Markie's "The Vapors," the D.O.C.'s "It's Funky Enough," Ice-T's "6 'n the Mornin'," MC Shan's "Down by Law," Eric B. & Rakim's "Microphone Fiend," Salt-N-Pepa's "Push It," Gang Starr's "Who's Gonna Take the Weight" and Doug E. Fresh's "The Show"—to make it worth its budget price. —*Stephen Thomas Erlewine*

**Hip Hop Jazz: Acid Metropolis** / Aug. 8, 1996 / Priority ♦♦♦
*Hip Hop Jazz: Acid Metropolis* collects 13 acid-jazz, jazz-rap, and jazzy danceclub tracks. Much of the album contains cuts by unknowns or obscure artists, and while those don't quite match the heavy-hitters featured here—including Gang starr, Brand New Heavies, Ronny Jordan, and Groove Collective—the collection is nevertheless quite enjoyable, and it reveals some fine overlooked gems. —*Stephen Thomas Erlewine*

**History of Hardcore, Vol. 1** / Feb. 20, 1996 / Suburban Base ♦♦♦♦
The first volume in the retrospective of early-'90s British hardcore—a far different proposition than the music later known as hardcore—features tracks from the style's two top labels, Suburban Base and Moving Shadow. The quick piano runs and sampled diva wails may remind listeners of the rave era, but the impeccable breakbeats on these tracks—classics including "2 Bad Mice Take You" by Blame, "Mystic Stepper" by Omni Trio, "Weird Energy" by DJ Hype, "Thunder Grip" by Hyper On Experience—show that hard British dance music had advanced far since the late '80s. Though it's not explicitly stated on the sleeve, Kenny Ken provides the mix. —*Keith Farley*

**History of Hardcore, Vol. 2** / Jun. 18, 1996 / Suburban Base ♦♦♦♦
The second in the series of Suburban Base/Moving Shadow classics includes quite a few additional classics—Deep Blue's "Helicopter Tune," Omni Trio's "Renegade Snares," Dream Team's "Stamina," and "Terrorist" by Ray Keith's Renegade project are among the seminal tracks included. Kenny Ken again works the mix. —*Keith Farley*

★ **History of House Music, Vol. 1: Chicago Classics** / 1996 / Cold Front ♦♦♦♦♦
An incredible compilation of Chicago classics and rarer cuts usually unavailable, *Chicago Classics* could well be the best single-disc compilation of early house, kicking off with what could be the three most crucial Chicago house tracks period—Marshall Jefferson's "Move Your Body," Farley Jackmaster Funk's "Love Can't Turn Around," and Steve "Silk" Hurley's "Jack Your Body." There are also quite a few more rarely anthologized tracks, including Hurley's "Music Is the Key," "Mystery of Love" by Fingers Inc., "Devotion" by Ten City, and "Someday" by Ce Ce Rogers. Not one track disappoints, and the liner notes are much more knowledgeable than could be expected for a compilation of early dance music. —*John Bush*

★ **History of House Music, Vol. 2: New York Garage Style** / 1996 / Cold Front ♦♦♦♦♦
Just as essential as its Chicago counterpart (and containing many more obscure tracks), *New York Garage Style* spotlights the smoother, more soulful Big Apple variant of house. The soul comes out with full flavor on "Don't Make Me Wait" by the (N.Y.C.) Peech Boys, "If You Should Need a Friend" by Blaze, and "Set It Off" by Strafe. The disc also includes scarcities like the early Todd Terry club hit, Royal House's "Can You Party," and "Music Is the Answer" by Colonel Abrams. Similar to its predecessor in the fact that there's absolutely no filler, *New York Garage Style* also includes informative liner notes. —*John Bush*

**History of Our World, Vol. 1** / Oct. 1995 / Profile ♦♦♦♦
Profile's *History of Our World* is one of the few hardcore breakbeat compilations that represents all of the best labels (Suburban Base, Moving Shadow, Reinforced, Formation and Production House) from the time. There are a few classics not here, but the ones present are all seminal: "Mr. Kirk's Nightmare" and "Journey from the Light" by 4 Hero, "Mystic Stepper (Feel Better)" and "Renegade Snares" by Omni Trio, plus JMJ & Richie, Kaotic Chemistry, Nookie, DJ Rap, DJ SS and DJ Solo, among others. Mixer dB fits in 25 tracks over the course of the disc. —*John Bush*

**History of Our World, Vol. 2** / Sep. 17, 1996 / Sm:)e ♦♦♦♦
The second volume in Profile's jungle retrospective *History of Our World* moves past early breakbeat to encompass hardstep, jazzstep, and techstep. Like the first, it stretches beyond most breakbeat compilations to capture tracks by most of the crucial labels and producers circa 1995-96. There are several Metalheadz classics—Adam F's "Circles," Alex Reece's "Pulp Fiction," Goldie and the Rufige Kru's "Fury," Asylum's "Da Bass II Dark"—and excellent tracks by Aphrodite, LTJ Bukem, Photek, Jonny L, Omni Trio, Ray Keith, and Technical Itch as well. One of the best and most wide-ranging drum'n'bass compilations ever available in America, *History of Our World, Part 2* approaches crucial status. —*John Bush*

**History of Techno** / Nov. 26, 1996 / ZYX ♦♦♦
The "history of techno" according to ZYX includes—not coincidentally—many of the label's own tracks, resulting in many rather odd selections by Tyrell Corp., Klangwerk, and Microwave Prince. Over the course of this four-disc set, however, there are several rave classics—including D-Mob's "We Call It Acieed," L.A. Style's "James Brown Is Dead," Joey Beltram's "Energy Flash," Moby's "Go," and Wink's "Higher State of Consciousness," as well as self-titled tracks by LFO, Age of Love, and Tricky Disco. Anyway, most of these are also available on better collections. —*Keith Farley*

**History of Techno, Vol. 2** / Nov. 4, 1997 / ZYX ♦♦♦
Not all of the tracks are real classics, but *History of Techno, Vol. 2* is a solid collection of techno and trance pioneers, including Sven Väth, Jam & Spoon, Polygon Window, Cosmic Baby, Faithless, Talla 2XLC, and the Shamen, among others. —*Keith Farley*

**Hit the Decks, Vols. 1-3 (Mix Collection)** / May 31, 1993 / ZYX ♦♦♦
*Hit the Decks* is an interesting document of the early-'90s techno scene according to DJ teams like Carl Cox, SL2, and Krome & Time. The three-disc set is a bit over-weighted by obscure mixers—Megabass, Two Little Boys,

Unity—but it's still worth taking the occasional pieces of fluff for all the strong material included. —*John Bush*

**Holistic Reflections** / Dec. 8, 1998 / Holistic ♦♦♦♦
This collection from the Isle of Wight's most respected electronic label (natch) is a takeover bid for head honchos Max Brennan and Paul Butler. Of the album's ten selections, half are Brennan projects (two each from Fretless AZM and Universal Being, plus one by his Balance alias). Butler takes care of an additional four—via his Exploding Thumbs, Delta T, and Pnu Riff pseudonyms—leaving only "Haiti" by Hubble as the only non-Brennan, non-Butler track. Despite the lack of variety, it's a solid compilation of Holistic's particularly effective mix of hard bop and space rock. —*John Bush*

**The Holy Church of Pharma** / Apr. 21, 1998 / Pharma ♦♦♦♦
Grafting big-beat rhythms onto German weirdo-electro is Pharma's religion, and these contributions from Zulutronic, Jammin' Unit, 4E, Bad Street Boy, Kerosene, and UMO all fit the template easily. —*Keith Farley*

**House Attack** / Oct. 15, 1996 / Thump ♦♦♦
*House Attack* is a frequently entertaining collection of house classics like Maurice's "This Is Acid" and Lil Louis' "French Kiss" along with more general club favorites such as "Everybody Everybody" by Black Box and "Rhythm Is a Dancer" by Snap. The mix of raw and mainstream might be a bit too much for some, but this is by no means a terrible disc to collect a few legendary house tunes. —*Stephen Thomas Erlewine*

**House Crusher** / Oct. 6, 1998 / Max Music ♦♦♦
A collection of house classics and solid club tracks propels this compilation, including contributions from Ralphi Rosario, Armand Van Helden, Peter Presta, Hard House, and Disco Dude. —*Keith Farley*

**House That Jack Built** / Feb. 4, 1997 / Moonshine Music ♦♦♦
*House That Jack Built* is an edgy New York house collection featuring remixes by Todd Terry (Sabrina Johnston's "Reach Higher") and Todd Edwards (Faylene Brown's "You Know I've Missed You") plus tracks by Kerri Chandler, Althea McQueen, Karen Pollard, and Joi Cardwell. —*John Bush*

**House Trancemissions, Vol. 1** / Sep. 21, 1999 / Streetbeat ♦♦♦
Produced and mixed by DJ Phil B, *House Trancemissions* blurs the line between trance and house music, favoring a progressive blend in which elements of both are clearly audible. Featured artists include Dumonde, Ayla, Sugarshop with Cindy Mizelle, Pulse, and Mike Koglin (who reinvents the Depeche Mode hit "Enjoy the Silence" into a house tune called "The Silence"). —*Steve Huey*

**The House of Groove** / Aug. 10, 1993 / Arista ♦♦♦
*House of Groove* is a tedious collection of pedestrian '90s dance music, concentrating on chart tracks like Snap's "Rhythm Is a Dancer," L.A. Style's "James Brown Is Dead" and Haddaway's "What Is Love." —*Stephen Thomas Erlewine*

**House of Handbag** / Ultrasound ♦♦
Although it does include a couple of storming club tracks (the Deep Dish remix of De'lacy's "Hideaway," BT's remix of Billie Ray Martin's "Running around Town"), *House of Handbag* mostly concentrates on the cheesier side of mainstream house. The album is undeniably danceable but not quite recommended for home listening. —*Keith Farley*

**House of Hits** / 1990 / Westside ♦♦♦♦
It's difficult to recommend an 11-disc box set for any but the most committed fans, but this collection has more of the influential but hard-to-find early techno and house singles than any ever made, rarities never anthologized in such a fashion. Besides requisite anthems like "Move Your Body," "You Used to Hold Me," "Strings of Life," "No UFO's" and "Mystery of Love," *House of Hits* includes legendary pioneering tracks such as Z Factor's "Fantasy," Jesse Saunders' "On & On," Mr. Fingers' "Amnesia," Channel 1's "Technicolor," and Eddie "Flashin" Fowlkes' "Goodbye Kiss." No less than six discs chart the Chicago house scene from 1983 to 1987, including crucial singles by Jesse Saunders, Farley Jackmaster Funk, Adonis, Larry Heard, Phuture, Marshall Jefferson, Jamie Principle, and Fast Eddie. Disc seven concentrates on the early New York response to house (Todd Terry, Masters at Work, Blaze), while the eighth CD documents the rise of Detroit techno with tracks by Juan Atkins' Model 500, Derrick May's Rhythim Is Rhythim and Mayday, Eddie "Flashin" Fowlkes and Kevin Saunderson. Of the final three discs, one charts the early European response to America—with Bang the Party, T Coy and PW&L—while the final two move back to Chicago with Mike Dunn, DJ Pierre, and Armando. The box set's scope is breathtaking, and despite a pronounced overemphasis on Chicago producers (eight discs total) to the detriment of New York and Detroit, *House of Hits* has dozens of '80s club classics and worthy obscurities long unavailable. In an unfortunate irony, however, *House of Hits* itself went out of print soon after its 1990 release. —*John Bush*

**House the Feeling** / Oct. 1, 1996 / ZYX ♦♦♦
De'Lacy, Alex Party, Wink, George Morel, Barbara Tucker, Junior Vasquez, and Klubbheads contribute tracks to this ample house compilation. —*Keith Farley*

**House, Vol. 3** / Nov. 9, 1999 / Northcott ♦♦♦
With *House Volumes 3*, East Coast DJ Terry Hunter pays homage to the gritty gospel and R&B roots of old-school house music with excellent results. Back in its early days in largely black gay clubs such as Manhattan's Paradise Garage and Chicago's Warehouse, house music achieved an inspirational yet humorous duality of blending together the simplest and sometimes the most stereotypical black rhythms and vocals, then purposely heightening them to the point of caricature. In so doing, house music was often send-up, mocking African-American culture while exalting it via the tribal energy of the dance floor, and this is what's good about Hunter's *House Volumes 3*. Starting off with an outstanding remix of Patrice Rushen's early-'80s funk instrumental "Number One" retitled "Numero Uno," the jazzy peak-hour groove sets a back-jackin', four-to-the-floor pace for the rest of the CD. Featuring cuts like Donna Allen's "He Is the Joy," DeepZone's "It's Gonna Be Alright," and Platinum Dolls' "Believe in a Brighter Day," Hunter proves that he's easily able to showcase gospel's role as a staple ingredient in classic house. Gospel's influence in house derives from the burning I-gotz-the-spirit-in-me screams of the late Sylvester, whose tabernacle-charged disco hits set the stage for gospel's preternatural journey from the church to the hedonistic havens of the gay underground club culture. —*Derrick Mathis*

**Hydrogen Dukebox** / Nov. 17, 1998 / Cleopatra ♦♦♦
Lol Hammond's stamp is all over this *Hydrogen Dukebox* collection. The album includes six tracks by his aliases, Girl Eats Boy and Slab. Of the other four tracks, two are Drum Club productions and two are Hammond remixes (of the Creatures' "2nd Floor" and Dreamgrinder's "Dreamgrinder"). —*John Bush*

**Hyper Cool into the Future** / 1996 / ZYX ♦♦♦♦
*Hyper Cool into the Future* is a compilation of house and dance tracks by a variety of artists, ranging from relatively familiar names (Groove Solution, Old School Junkies, AcidPhase III) to more obscure cuts by DJ Panda, Picotto, Daisy Dee, and Natural Born Grooves. —*Leo Stanley*

**Hypnotic State [C&S]** / 1995 / C&S ♦♦♦♦
Including great tracks by Plastikman, Polygon Window (aka Aphex Twin), Morph, Voodoo Child (aka Moby), and Joey Beltram, this C&S compilation of straightahead mid-'90s techno is far-reaching and exciting. Some weak efforts, however, weigh down the album. —*John Bush*

**Hypnotic State: An Ultimate Electronic Dance Compilation** / Sep. 23, 1997 / Cleopatra ♦♦
Cleopatra's usual attitude to collections permeates this three-disc set of "electronic dance." While it begins with tracks by stellar electronic acts (Orbital, FSOL, New Order, System 7, 808 State, Meat Beat Manifesto), *Hypnotic State* reverts to industrial trash midway through the second disc. The result is more than two dozen tracks by second-tier producers like Aqualite, Children of Dub, Talla 2XLC, Latex Empire, and Phonetic Bellboy, as well as a few completely unknown names—Toilet Bombers, Best Pushers, Cookie Crashers, Foot Patrol, Fag Ends, and Body Users. *Hypnotic State* is a sham compilation, intended to fool listeners into buying a three-disc set that basically amounts to only half a dozen worthwhile tracks. —*John Bush*

**I Love NY Jungle** / Sep. 24, 1996 / Jungle Sky US ♦♦♦
One of the many compilations released by Jungle Sky and its large label com-

munity, *I Love NY Jungle* is one of the best albums to check out the American jungle scene. Though tracks by DJ Soul Slinger, DJ Wally, River of Action, and G-Man are quite weak compared to their equivalents on the British drum'n'bass scene, the album is a solid collection of straightahead breakbeat. —*John Bush*

**Ibiza Afterhours** / Nov. 22, 1994 / Moonshine Music ++++
A competent document of the wildly eclectic island club scene, *Ibiza Afterhours* concentrates on downtempo anthems by Sabres of Paradise (the epic Beatless Mix of "Smokebelch II"), Leftfield, Sun Electric, Underworld, and A Man Called Adam. Ibizan hero Jose Padilla also appears, contributing the track "Agua." —*John Bush*

**Ibiza Afterhours, Vol. 2** / 1995 / Moonshine Music ++++
The second volume of *Ibiza Afterhours* is as diverse and consistent as the first, offering an array of '90s electronic dance styles, inluding ambient, trip-hop, and acid jazz. —*Stephen Thomas Erlewine*

**Ibiza Sessions** / Aug. 8, 2000 / Max Music +++
*Ibiza Sessions* gathers some of the island's hottest club hits, as mixed by DJ Carlos, a veteran of Ibiza's dancefloors. Mr. Spring's "Profundo Rosso," Sound Design's "Feelin' Lonely," Blank 6 Jones' "After Love," Kinky Boy's "Dissin' Trumpets," and the Southside Spinners' "Luvstruck 2000" are some of the highlights from this sensual, kinetic collection of quintessentially Ibizan dance. —*Heather Phares*

**If You Can't Stand Da Beatz, Git Outta Da Kitchen** / Feb. 27, 1996 / Shadow ++
Included are two discs of Ninja Tune material—Funki Porcini, the Herbaliser, DJ Food, Coldcut, Up, Bustle & Out, among others. As usually happens with Ninja Tune collections, it consistently sounds good but only occasionally excites. A few of the highlights: somewhat obscure recordings like Coldcut's "Eine Kleine Hedmusik," DJ Food's "Half Step," and Funki Porcini's ode to the tube, "Circle Line." —*John Bush*

• **In Memoriam Gilles Deleuze** / Feb. 3, 1998 / Mille Plateaux ++++
The pioneering German experimental/electro label Mille Plateaux was founded on inspiration from French social philosopher Gilles Deleuze and his book *A Thousand Plateaus*, so the label organized this two-disc tribute featuring a veritable roll call of the top techno subversives in Germany, Britain, and America. The tracks are all exclusives, from the likes of Atom Heart, Gas, J. Burger, Oval, Mouse on Mars, Scanner, Ian Pooley, Jim O'Rourke, FX Randomiz, Chris & Cosey, Christophe Charles, and Kerosene. With an attractive 30-page booklet including the writings of Deleuze, *In Memoriam Gilles Deleuze: Folds & Rhizomes* is a near-crucial collection for fans of the philosophy or the music. —*John Bush*

**In My House There's a Disco, Vol. 10** / Jan. 25, 2000 / Streetbeat +++
Mixed by DJ Dave Matthias, the club cuts and remixes on *In My House There's a Disco, Vol. 10* spotlight the disco-influenced side of house music, creating a monster set of grooves that keep the party moving. Matthias chooses his raw material skillfully, offering some of the bigger club hits circa 1999 as well as other singles that fit his approach perfectly. The result is one of the stronger entries in the series. —*Steve Huey*

**In Order to Dance, Vol. 5** / Jan. 14, 1997 / R&S +++
1994's *In Order to Dance 5* captures the label's pinnacle as the global outpost for techno that was both creative as well as dancefloor-friendly before their steady decline during the mid to late '90s when techno slowly fell out of favor with the masses. In addition to being loaded from the opening track of the first disc to the concluding track of the second with exciting techno songs still worthy of acclaim, the compilation also took the pains to feature artists from all over the world. Carl Craig, 69, and Kenny Larkin represent the sounds of Detroit techno; μ-Ziq, Aphex Twin, Dave Angel, and Luke Slater represent the UK; Quadrant and Phylyps represent the Basic Channel-affiliated Berlin sound, with the remaining artists representing other areas of Northeastern Europe. Not only does this compilation read like a historical document of techno circa 1994, but it also reaffirms the significance of R&S as quite possibly the most important—or at least influential—electronic music label during this era. No single tracks stand out, as all offer some noteworthy characteristics that would eventually get recycled in successive years as techno splintered into its many different styles. Anyone considering this album may also want to consider the *Vintage R&S* series of albums, which take a broader view of the label from its earliest beginnings to its latter material, featuring most of these artists and a few of these same songs. Also keep in mind that most if not all of these songs can be found elsewhere on 12" singles or full-length albums, though these records have become increasingly difficult to track down as the years pass. —*Jason Birchmeier*

**In at the Deep End** / Feb. 25, 1997 / Ark 21 ++++
The first release on ex-Tribal UK frontman Richard Breeden's new Pagan United Kingdom label is a continuous beatmix of material from artists including 2 Lone Swordsmen, New Phunk Theory, Space Groover, Reel Houze, Laj Gloves, Paper Issue #2, Straight Life, Freaks, Urban Farmers, Trevor Loveys, and Essa. —*Jason Ankeny*

**Incoming** / 1998 / Saigon +++
Compiling the output of Saigon Records (the experimental offshoot of Ed Rush's No-U-Turn label), *Incoming* includes tracks by established names like Dom & Roland, Future Forces, and Calyx plus newcomers Ryme Time, Kyan, Ill Machine, and Deep Rooted. Somewhat surprisingly, the music isn't really *that* different from most No-U-Turn releases; virtually all of the tracks are solid two-step stompers that lose more than just a little bit when branded with the experimental tag. —*John Bush*

**Incursions in Illbient** / Nov. 4, 1996 / Asphodel +++
A label sampler of sorts, Asphodel's late-'96 trip-hop offering presents a snapshot of the New York ambient/dub-hop scene through label signings DJ Spooky, Byzar, Sub Dub, and We. Despite the title's reference to that buzzword-y construction, "illbient," these tracks hang together remarkably well, bridging experimental ambient, murky reggae and dub, and the gritty breakbeat manipulations of artists such as DJ Wally, Spectre, and Techno Animal. Byzar's immersive, nightmarish vignettes are probably the best of the bunch. —*Sean Cooper*

**Indiscrimination Rules** / Pharma +++
The debut compilation from Pharma Records includes label stalwarts Zulutronic, Bionic Skank, 4E, Kerosene, Dior, and G 104, among others. —*Keith Farley*

**Industrial: Music of the Shadows, Vol. 3** / Apr. 18, 2000 / K-Tel ++++
Be honest: Did you ever think you'd live to see the day when K-Tel—the same company that, not too long ago, was flogging Top Forty hits on TV—would put out a best of industrial compilation? What's the world coming to, anyway? This is a respectable 16-track compilation of the genre, and while it does generally favor some of the more accessible, song-oriented efforts in the industrial style, give credit where it's due. K-Tel does not shy away from the most extreme exponents of the form, with tracks by Throbbing Gristle, Einstürzende Neubauten, Cabaret Voltaire, and Chrome next to the somewhat more dancefloor-friendly Wax Trax crowd, such as Ministry, KMFDM, and My Life with the Thrill Kill Kult. There's also room for some mid-level practitioners of this black art—Leather Strip, Young Gods, Nitzer Ebb, Attrition—and some less familiar names like Apoptygma Berzerk and :Wumpscut:. The biggest bone of contention is the track selection: It's hard to represent artists with such voluminous discographies (like Throbbing Gristle, Cabaret Voltaire, and Ministry) with just one cut, and some may feel that the ones chosen aren't frightening enough. But, after all, the object of this compilation isn't to capture industrial aficionados, but to introduce the genre to others, or to provide a sampler of the style to those who want a little but not a lot. It includes liner notes by Athan Maroulis of Spahn Ranch. —*Richie Unterberger*

**Insider Presents Blacklight Sessions, Vol. 1** / Jul. 11, 2000 / U.C. Music +++
The first compilation disc released by *Insider Magazine* features 15 club/dance tracks including "B With U" (Junior's Main Mix) by Junior Sanchez, "Rise" (Bootleg Remix) by Eddie Amador, "Sway" (Knee Deep's Rhumba Club Mix) by Shaft, "Allegria" (Tribal Whore Beats) by Rick Garcia, and "Cada Vez" (Grant Nelson's Vocal Mix) by Negrocan. —*Al Campbell*

**Interiors** / May 19, 1998 / Invisible +++
A compilation of dub-hop tracks licensed through the Sentrax label, *Interiors* is an engaging 12-cut collection that ranges from dark ambient to experimental dub to minimalist breakbeats. Artists include ELpH ("Gnomic

Verses"), Mick Harris ("No Stoic Dub"), Screwtape ("Tongs"), Gold Water ("Fractured Break"), and Mika Vainio ("Novo Brisk"). —*Jason Ankeny*

**Invasion of the Dot Knights!** / 1998 / P-Vine Records ♦♦♦♦
*Invasion of the Dot Knights!* is a Japanese CD compilation of some previously vinyl-only releases on Sweden's impeccable Dot Records (only one track overlaps from the previous collection *The Knights Who Say Dot*). Since just about everything Dot released in its first two years was nigh-perfect—as far as any eclectic electro fan was concerned—the compilation is quite solid, including tracks from Quant, Roupe, Friend & Doktor Kosmos, Hab, Argonort, and Man-Q-Neon, among others. —*John Bush*

**Invisible Soundtracks: Macro 1** / Oct. 16, 1997 / Leaf ♦♦♦♦
Compiled by the stellar electronic label Leaf, *Invisible Soundtracks* includes a host of top-notch ambient-electro acts, as well as many unissued recordings. Contributors include Nonplace Urban Field, Disjecta, Bedouin Ascent, Twisted Science (doing "Sloop B," presumably an extremely mutilated version of the Beach Boys' "Sloop John B"), Autechre's Gescom project, and even indie-rock heroes Air Miami. Also included are several short passages by Richard Thomas. —*John Bush*

**Invisible Soundtracks: Macro 2** / May 12, 1998 / Leaf ♦♦♦
More diverse but less tightly focused than the first, *Invisible Soundtracks: Macro 2* features several non-Leaf acts among its 15 tracks. The range of experimental techno is refreshing, with a list of producers including To Rococo Rot, Max Brennan (Fretless AZM), Fridge, Si Begg, Laika, and Paul D. Miller (DJ Spooky). —*John Bush*

**Irma Jazz Funk 'N' Bossa** / Irma ♦♦♦
*Irma Jazz Funk 'N' Bossa* is a collection of laidback acid jazz compiled by Hiroshi Yamazaki for Irma Records. There's a blend of actual bands and more producer-oriented acts; the bands feature plenty of vibes, flute, electric piano, and restrained jazz guitar to go along with the beefy basslines and upfront percussion, while the producers focus more on grooves closer to hip-hop than jazz-funk. The bossa connection doesn't carry through the entire set, but every track certainly fits the bill in the other two areas of the title. Highlights come from Jestofunk ("Fly Love Song"), Bossa Nostra ("The Message from a Soul Sister"), Black & Brown ("Never Be There"), and Man Sueto ("Sentimental Song"). This is definitely a compilation designed to evoke a certain sound, despite certain geographic discrepancies—a track by Gazzara with the title "Our Man in Rio" nevertheless begins with the voice of a British DJ dedicating a song to someone in Leytonstone. —*John Bush*

**It's All Becoming Clear** / 1996 / Clear ♦♦♦♦
The first CD compilation for the British neo-electro label Clear includes several tracks each from Plaid, Clatterbox, Doctor Rockit, Gescom, and the Gregory Fleckner Quartet. Since most of the tracks were previously vinyl-only, *It's All Becoming Clear* is a stellar compilation, necessary for trainspotters but quite respectable for beginning listeners as well. —*John Bush*

**It's Pharma Time: Best Of, Vol. 3** / Jun. 8, 1999 / EFA ♦♦♦
Pharma's third label compilation has a twisted, tongue-in-pierced-cheek sense of humor—just check tracks like "I Smoke Mad Rocks" by Thee Joker, "Little Electro Street Girl" by Kerosene, "War of the Slime Slurbs '98" by the Slime Slurbs, "Hot Spot" by Cattle Mutilation, and "Big Tits" by G-104. As for the music, it's better than the average mid-tempo acid-techno that's been a staple for the label since the early '90s. —*John Bush*

**It's Techno: Electronica Now!** / Sep. 30, 1997 / Monster Sounds ♦♦♦
Highlighted by the Prodigy's "Poison," the rather tepid 12-cut collection *It's Techno: Electronica Now!* also includes Fluke's "Absurd," Electric Skychurch's "Sunrise," Winx's "How's the Music," and Rabbit in the Moon's "Floori D.A." —*Jason Ankeny*

**It's a Twisted World** / Mar. 25, 1997 / MCA ♦♦♦
*It's a Twisted World* is a 70-minute continuous mix of house tracks from the Twisted America label. Along with the Funky Green Dogs' club hit "Fired Up!" (remixed by Angel Morales), the collection includes material from DJ Pierre, Club 69, Danny Tengala, and Kamak. —*Jason Ankeny*

**It: Electro** / It Records ♦♦♦♦
Released toward the tail-end of the UK electro revival (and probably meant to capitalize on the trend), the *It* comp is nonetheless a nice collection of mostly American electro-funk, both old and new. Classic, hard-to-find tracks like "Scorpio" by Grandmaster Flash & The Furious Five and "Your Rock" by Fantasy Three sit cleanly next to tight, forward-looking cuts from new-school artists such as Plastikman, Jon Drukman's Bass Kittens project, and Sawtooth. The post-Kraftwerk Euro-techno style even gets a brief nod in Yello's oddball "Bostich." The album was compiled by noted Megatripolis DJ Marco Arnaldi. —*Sean Cooper*

**Italian Dance Classics: House** / May 21, 1997 / Irma ♦♦♦
Not quite the Italian house compilation it should be, the album does include "Ride on Time" by Black Box and several tracks by Cappella boss Gianfranco Bortolotti (as 49ers and Club House). Much of the rest of the album is populated with moderate hits or downright obscure no-names. —*Keith Farley*

**JBO: A Perspective 1988-1998** / 1998 / JBO/V2 ♦♦♦♦
With so many dance compilations currently glutting the marketplace, it's become increasingly hard for a dance connoisseur to locate the best from the rest. But their prayers may have been answered with the release of *JBO: A Perspective 1988-1998*, a comprehensive collection of the very best UK dance/acid-house tracks from over a ten-year period. Like all great compilations, it's easy to have a heavy case of déjà vu when rediscovering the tunes on *A Perspective*, which shows how well the vast majority of these compositions have stood the test of time. Many of the earlier tracks wouldn't sound out of place on the radio today—a must-hear dance remake of Neil Young's "Only Love Can Break Your Heart" from St. Etienne, "Can You Feel It" by Mr. Fingers, as well as Primal Scream's "Loaded" and a remix of My Bloody Valentine's "Soon." But you'll also find many recent delights as well—U2's "Salome" (as a "Zooromancer Remix"), the Chemical Brothers' "My Mercury Mouth," and Björk's "Human Behaviour (Underworld Mix)." Absolutely essential listening for any serious alterna-dance fan. —*Greg Prato*

**The Jazz Head Trip** / 1995 / City of Angels ♦♦♦
Musically all over the board, *The Jazz Head Trip* features a blend of American future-funk producers including the Crystal Method, Bass Kittens, Mephisto Odyssey, and Elements of Life, among others. —*Keith Farley*

**Jazz Jungle** / Jul. 29, 1996 / Hollywood ♦♦♦
*Jazz Jungle* is a collection of acid-jazz and jungle fusions. For the most part, these fusions are a little tentative—either the jazz dominates the jungle, or the drums'n'bass makes all the jazz flourishes unrecognizable—but the best tracks show that this blending of genres could be the wave of the future as far as techno is concerned. —*Leo Stanley*

**Jazz Steppin'** / Sep. 21, 1999 / Instinct ♦♦♦
*Jazz Steppin'* is a collection of jazz-inflected club grooves inspired by the Steppin' dance craze. Tracks by Nite Flyte, Shakatak, and Gota reflect the contemporary jazz and acid jazz vibe of this compilation, and songs like Soundscape UK's "Steppin' Out" and Act of Faith's "If You Believe" add a glossy disco sheen to the proceedings. —*Heather Phares*

**The Jazz of Boogie Back** / 1995 / Instinct ♦♦♦
Billboard magazine called Boogie Back Productions "probably the best of the independent soul labels." This compilation from Instinct focuses more on acid jazz than soul; it's enjoyable but might be a little tame for some listeners. —*Keith Farley*

**Joint Ventures** / Nov. 11, 1997 / Shadow ♦♦♦♦
Just about every crucial experimentalist who recorded for Ninebar (Cujo, Funki Porcini, Twisted Science, Sureshot, Ian Simmonds, Alaska) makes an appearance on *Joint Ventures*. Each track is a collaboration between two producers; highlights are turned in by Cujo and Funki Porcini's "Z Cars" and Sureshot and Twisted Science's "Mescal." —*John Bush*

**Journey into Ambient Groove, Vol. 1** / 1995 / Quango ♦♦♦♦
A compilation of earthy trip-hop and ambient dub, *Journey into Ambient Groove* includes contributions from Kruder & Dorfmeister (their statement of intent "Original Bedroom Rockers") and Zion Train. Though the range of productions is hardly extraordinary (and the names tend toward the obscure), the album is a fine distillation of the ambient/trip-hop aesthetic. —*John Bush*

**Journey into Ambient Groove, Vol. 2** / Nov. 1995 / Quango ♦♦♦
The second *Ambient Groove* functions in a similar fashion to the first. Alter-

nating a few name producers (Fila Brazillia, TUU, Heights of Abraham) with pleasant tracks by unknowns, it's an okay compilation for those into rootsy ambient dub. —*John Bush*

**Journey into Ambient Groove, Vol. 3** / Apr. 1996 / Quango ♦♦♦♦
Perhaps the most solid volume in the series thus far, *Ambient Groove, Vol. 3* features tracks from Pressure Drop, Union Jack, and Sven Van Hees, plus several high-profile remixes by Autechre (of Palm Skin Productions) and Kruder and Dorfmeister (of Bomb the Bass and William Orbit's Strange Cargo). —*John Bush*

**Journey into Ambient Groove, Vol. 4** / Jul. 15, 1997 / Polygram ♦♦♦♦
Yet another solid compilation of exclusives and rarer tracks from the rootsrocking side of trip-hop and drum'n'bass, including tracks from Fila Brazillia, J. Majik's Innervisions, Neotropic, Basement Jaxx, Kid Loco, and Sofa Surfers. —*John Bush*

**Jungle Jazz** / Jul. 5, 1996 / Irma ♦♦♦♦
Closer to atmospheric jungle than the title would indicate, *Jungle Jazz* includes several drum'n'bass classics like "Pulp Fiction" by Alex Reece, "The Rain" by Photek, "It's a Jazzy Thing" by Roni Size, and "Atmospheric Funk" by Wax Doctor. The quality doesn't stop there, though; other inclusions are tracks by Hidden Agenda, Jonny L, Kid Loops, Outside, and the Ballistic Brothers. —*John Bush*

**Jungle Jazz, Vol. 3** / Irma Global Village ♦♦♦♦
Just as good as the first volume, *Jungle Jazz, Vol. 3* includes tracks like "Modus Operandi" by Photek, a Roni Size remix of NuYorican Soul's "It's Alright, I Feel It," "Music in My Mind" by Adam F., a Grooverider remix of Bally Sagoo's "Tum Bin Jaya," and a 4 Hero remix of D Note's "Waiting Hopefully." —*John Bush*

**Jungle Massive** / Nov. 1995 / Payday/FFRR ♦♦♦♦
One of the first stateside breakbeat compilations, *Jungle Massive* spotlights 1994's ragga scene with 12 consistently solid tracks. From British chart hits like General Levy's "Incredible" and Shy FX & UK Apachie's "Original Nuttah" to rarer productions like Roni Size's "Timestretch" and the Dynamic Duo's "Joker Jump Up," the album introduced Americans to drum'n'bass in excellent fashion. —*John Bush*

**Jungle Tekno, Vol. 1** / 1992 / Passion Music ♦♦♦♦
The first compilation of early hardcore-into-jungle, *Jungle Tekno* is a nighcrucial collection. Besides the inclusion of pioneering tracks like Blame's "Music Takes You," Bukem's "Logical Progression, and 2 Bad Mice's "Bombscare," the album also features a few forgotten classics, like "Run Come Quick" by Audio Bass and "We Have It" by CMC. —*John Bush*

**Jungle Vibes** / Dec. 2, 1994 / SSR ♦♦♦♦
*Jungle Vibes* is a collection of jump-up ragga tracks with on producers from Suburban Base Records, including label classics like T.Power's "Lipsing Jam Ring," Shy FX and UK Apachi's "Original Nuttah," Deep Blue's "Helicopter Tune," and Omni Trio's "Renegade Snares." —*Keith Farley*

**Jungle: The Sound of the Underground** / Apr. 1996 / Columbia ♦♦♦
An American distillation of the work of the classic British jungle label S.O.U.R. Records, *Jungle: The Sound of the Underground* features T.Power's "Mutant Jazz," Wink's "Autumn Dayz," DJ Soul Slinger's "Ethiopia," and Leftfield's "Release." —*Keith Farley*

**Junglized** / Jul. 5, 1996 / Crammed Discs ♦♦♦
Except for a few good tracks (from Subject 13, Adam F, Phume, and DJ Phantasy), this Crammed Discs collection is a bit weak and suffers from bland breakbeats. —*John Bush*

**Kickin' Hardcore Leaders** / 1994 / Instinct ♦♦♦
A somewhat pedestrian compilation of early-'90s hardcore (excepting perhaps Omni Trio's "Mainline"), *Kickin' Hardcore Leaders* suffers from the style's need for speed without much thought of quality production. —*John Bush*

**Kickin' Hardcore Nations** / 1994 / Kickin' ♦♦♦♦
By no means a bad compilation of hardcore techno, *Kickin' Hardcore Leaders* includes tracks by Mike Ink, Damon Wild's 303 System, Union Jack, and the Hypnotist, among others. —*John Bush*

**Kickin' Mental Detergent, Vol. 2** / 1994 / Instinct ♦♦
Probably the best in the *Kickin' Mental Detergent* series, volume two includes tracks by archetypal early-'90s rave/hardcore acts like Wishdokta, X-Statik, K-90, and Kemical Kids. The sound is hardly fresh, and the production quality is near zero. —*John Bush*

**Killer Techno, Vol. 1** / 1992 / Sonic ♦♦♦
A very early American compilation of the rave/hardcore scene, *Killer Techno* includes tracks by Moby (the Rainforest Mix of his classic "Go," plus an uncredited track as UHF), the early FSOL production "Visual Attack" by Aircut, and "Mr. Dynomite" by Omar Santana's Liquid Metal. Others included are Niko, Church of Extacy, Andromeda, and Zero Zero. —*Keith Farley*

**Killer Techno, Vol. 2** / 1994 / Sonic ♦♦
Not quite as solid as its predecessor, volume two includes Moby's "Thousand" plus 12 largely forgettable tracks by names like Dominatrix UK, D-Shake, Niko, Vertigo Hypo, and Desiderius. —*Keith Farley*

**Killer Techno, Vol. 3: Techno Nations** / 1994 / Sonic ♦♦♦
Though it includes just as many forgotten names of the rave/hardcore scene as the second volume, *Killer Techno, Vol. 3* benefits from the Scientist's "New Style" and "Wey Aah" by Hard Attack (aka Joey Beltram and Paul Elstak). Others include Green Buddha, Brutal, Defcon Situation, QDT, and Bald Terror. —*Keith Farley*

**King Size Dub, Vol. 4** / May 4, 1999 / Echo Beach ♦♦♦
The fourth volume of the popular *King Size Dub* series collects rare dub tracks from the Echo Beach label, including "Spying Glass" (a collaboration between Horace Andy and Massive Attack), Dreadzone's "Earth Angel," Khao's "No Compromise," Kruder and Dorfmeister's "Shakatakadoodub," Asian Dub Foundation's "Return to Jericho," and Primal Scream's "Last Train." A compilation of some of the finest cutting-edge dub. —*Heather Phares*

**Kiss in Ibiza** / Oct. 15, 1996 / Polygram TV ♦♦♦
A double-disc set featuring 34 tracks (virtually all of them remixes), *A Kiss in Ibiza* features mainstream dance names like Jocelyn Brown, Tori Amos, Lisa Marie Experience, and BBE given the more soft-spoken Ibiza touch by producers like Armand Van Helden, Rollo, Deep Dish, Perfecto, and the Klubbheads, among others. —*John Bush*

**The Knights Who Say Dot** / 1997 / Dot ♦♦♦♦
The Swedish Dot label announced itself quietly in the first quarter of 1997 with four 12"s of genre-blending electronica that had the likes of Mixmaster Morris and Lamb's Andy Darlow extending themselves in heavy praise. Dot's first CD release, *The Knights Who Say Dot*, collects some of the finer moments of those first 12"s and adds six new tracks from Hab, Tupilaq, Friend, and newcomer Doktor Kosmos. A mixture of warm, melodic techno, electronic funk, and schizzy drum'n'bass, *The Knights Who Say Dot* is likely an introduction of sorts to a new era in club music—experimental music as listenable as it is mixable/danceable, and not nearly as ghettoized in its appeal as house, jungle, or techno. —*Sean Cooper*

**Cologne Kompakt, Vol. 1** / Kompakt ♦♦♦♦
*Cologne Kompakt* is a crucial compilation of minimalist-groove material from the increasingly first-rate Cologne community, including tracks from Kandis, Mike Ink's Studio 1, the Modernist M:I:5, Thomas Brinkmann, and Dr. Walker, among others. The depth of amazing producers in the city is quite staggering, and *Köln Kompakt* is one of the best documents of the scene, along with *The Sound of Cologne*. —*John Bush*

**Kompilation** / Feb. 10, 1998 / NovaMute ♦♦♦
The two-disc *Kompilation* gathers some of the best material from the NovaMute stable of artists, including tracks from Luke Slater, Fawn, Darren Price, JB3, Speedy J, Emmanuel Top, Plastikman, Steve Stoll/The Blunted Boy Wonder, Attrax, 3 Phase, and the Space DJ'z. Much of the music has an experimental bent, and there's a great deal of variety over the course of the collection, even if it doesn't represent the absolute forefront of the techno scene. —*Steve Huey*

**Late Night Beats: The Post-Club Sound of Britain** / Jun. 16, 1998 / Music Club ♦♦♦♦
*Late Night Beats* is a solid collection of downtempo grooves and electronicapop featuring Jimi Tenor's Prince impression on "Can't Stay with You Baby," John Beltran's soothing "Gutaris Breeze," and the rare "Spudink" by Plaid.

More an audio journey than a collection of tracks, it's a perfect album for coffee-table listening. —*John Bush*

**Law of the Jungle** / 1995 / Moonshine Music ♦♦♦
*Law of the Jungle* compiles tracks from the British ragga-jungle scene circa 1995, including tracks from T.Power, Potential Bad Boy N' Chatter B, UK Apachi and Shy FX, and Junior Dan. —*Keith Farley*

**Legally Stoned, Vol. 1: New High in Drum & Bass** / Apr. 22, 1997 / Mutant Sound ♦♦♦♦
The sunlit marijuana grove pictured on the front cover of this two-disc set gives you a good idea of what to expect within: drum'n'bass of the ambient, almost ethereal variety, with synthesizer washes, diva-esque vocal samples, and breakbeats that are jumpy but gentle and not too aggressively forward in the mix. Disc one presents 14 tracks in a continuous DJ mix, while disc two consists of an "unmixed" program of 11 tracks. It's difficult to address the pieces individually, because this particular type of drum'n'bass tends, more than other types, to all sound very much the same. On the mixed disc, Grapevine does a couple of rhythmically unique things on "Carlito," and there's a certain freshness to the sound of "Nookie" by Funk Be the Flavour. Disc two keeps things a bit more interesting—there's a nice flute part on "Shogun" by Pegasus and a bracing hardness at the core of "Helen T (Freestyle Mix)" by Jake's Progress. But for the most part, the proceedings settle into a sort of fuzzy, undifferentiated pleasantness that makes this album great background music, but not worth paying too much attention to. —*Rick Anderson*

**Let's All Chant: The Michael Zager Dance Collection** / Mar. 11, 1997 / Varése ♦♦♦
*Let's All Chant: The Michael Zager Dance Collection* contains 11 of Zager's late-'70s disco singles, including both songs he performed—such as "Let's All Chant"—and songs he produced, like Cissy Houston's "Think It Over," the Andrew True Connection's "What's Your Name, What's Your Number," Johnny "Guitar" Watson's "Planet Funk," and "Life's a Party," which features Whitney Houston on her recording debut. It's a fine overview of his disco work and is worthwhile for hardcore disco fetishists. —*Stephen Thomas Erlewine*

**Life in the Year of Deconstruction** / 1992 / RCA ♦♦♦
The strong mainstream dance label Deconstruction celebrated a great year with a compilation of their best, including club hits by M People, Lionrock, Definitive Two, and N Joi. —*John Bush*

**Live [deConstruction]** / 1995 / deConstruction ♦♦♦♦
This double-album compilation featuring the mixing skills of DJs Paul Oakenfold, Justin Robertson, Pete Tong, and Graeme Park was recorded live at the Liverpool nightclub Cream; it features house, NRG, and techno tracks from Carol Bailey, Red Eye, Original Creators, and Tin Tin Out, among others. —*John Bush*

**Live at Webster Hall: NY Dance** / Nov. 25, 1997 / Webster Hall ♦♦♦
Victor Calderone, Cevin Fisher, Afrowax, and Vincent De Moor make appearances on this in-concert dance house compilation. —*Keith Farley*

**Lo Recordings, Vol. 1: Extreme Possibilities** / 1995 / Lo Recordings ♦♦♦♦
Jon Tye's Lo Recordings debuted with a crucial descent into underground electronica, the compilation *Extreme Possibilities*. The album includes tracks by Wagon Christ, Boymerang, MLO and Jonah Sharp, David Toop, Daniel Pemberton, and Bedouin Ascent. —*John Bush*

**Lo Recordings, Vol. 2: Collaborations** / Nov. 25, 1996 / Lo Recordings ♦♦♦
The second volume in the *Lo* series spotlights intriguing producer collaborations on the lo-fi/experimental side of home electronica, including David Toop and Daniel Pemberton, Lol Coxhill, and Paul Schütze, Scanner and David Cunningham, MLO, and David Thomas, among others. —*John Bush*

**Lo Recordings, Vol. 3: United Mutations** / Nov. 11, 1996 / Lo Recordings ♦♦♦♦
*United Mutations* adds a few lo-fi/post-rock American producers to the fold of mostly British experimental. Appearing beside Aphex Twin (a remix of the Mike Flowers Pops), Luke Vibert and Springheel Jack are stateside bands like Ui, Tortoise, and Thurston Moore/Infrastructure. —*John Bush*

**Lo Recordings, Vol. 4: Further Mutations** / Jan. 20, 1998 / Lo Recordings ♦♦♦♦
As expected from the title, *Further Mutations* goes farther underground for the cream of experimental/electronica. Indie-rock hybrids like Ganger and Hood appear next to Twisted Science, Luke Vibert, Thurston Moore and Eugene Chadbourne, Cujo, Voafose, and Robert Hampson's Chasm. Also, Robert Wyatt appears with the project Fish out of Water. —*John Bush*

**Logic Trance, Vol. 3** / Jun. 6, 2000 / Logic ♦♦
*Logic Trance, Vol. 3* is a collection of progressive trance music (of the electronic variety) mixed continuously by DJ Chris Gin. Artists contributing tracks include Carl Cox, John Digweed and Nick Muir, Christopher Lawrence, Da Hool, Neils Van Gogh, Giorgio Moroder vs. Jam & Spoon, and more. —*Steve Huey*

**London Electronica** / May 13, 1997 / Kickin' ♦♦♦
Besides tracks by Mark Broom, Space DJ'z, the Advent, and Plantastik, this Kickin' collection doesn't include much of interest—producers like Sound Enforcer, Gigglatron, Mandrill, and Sapiano. —*Keith Farley*

**The Lords of Svek, Vol. 1** / Feb. 17, 1997 / Svek ♦♦♦♦
Compiling respected singles from the Swedish minimalist tech-house Svek Records (Cari Lekebusch, Stephan G., Alexi Delano, Gene Hunt, Jesper Dahlbäck), the first volume in the continuing *Lords of Svek* series is one of its best. Each track is a wild ride through porn-beats and hilarious samples the likes of which are rarely heard outside the more risqué streets of Stockholm. —*John Bush*

**The Lords of Svek, Vol. 2** / Jun. 23, 1997 / Svek ♦♦♦♦
The Swedish label returns with another compilation of their intriguing mishmash of techno and house, with tracks by Gene Hunt, Stephan G, Mr. Barth, and Persuader. —*John Bush*

**The Los Angeles Experience** / Nov. 18, 1997 / Thump ♦♦♦
*The L.A. Experience* collects 10 tracks (11 on CD) from several of Los Angeles' most popular deep house DJs, including Mike Flores, DJ Chazz, Richard F., Tony B!, DJ Orlando, Louis Love, DJ Flaver, and Artie the One Man Party. For anyone interested in the deep, funky sound of LA house, this is a good introduction, but for longtime followers of the genre, the collection is a little too basic to be worthwhile. —*Leo Stanley*

**MTV's AMP** / May 5, 1997 / Caroline ♦♦♦♦
MTV designed the television show *Amp* as a way to showcase electronic dance acts that didn't easily fit into their other specialty shows. Premiering in late 1996, the show quickly became a hit, and it helped ignite the electronica craze of early 1997 by suggesting that American audiences were more interested in techno than many labels previously assumed. Considering its success, it wasn't a great surprise that MTV and Astralwerks assembled the *MTV Amp* compilation to cash in on its success and to provide curious listeners with a one-stop introduction to "electronica." Surprisingly, *MTV Amp* works. Featuring nearly every major electronic artists of the mid-'90s—Daft Punk is missing, but the Chemical Brothers, Underworld, Future Sound of London, Photek, Aphex Twin, Orbital, Goldie, Atari Teenage Riot, and Prodigy are all present—the collection illustrates the depth and variety within electronica, alternating between heavy club beats and trance-like drum'n'bass. For the neophyte interested in exploring electronic music, there are few better introductions than *MTV Amp*. —*Stephen Thomas Erlewine*

**MTV's AMP 2** / Jun. 16, 1998 / Caroline ♦♦♦♦
*MTV's AMP 2* is a collection of the best alterna-dance songs that have been featured on the television program MTV's *AMP*. What makes this collection so indispensable is that it's split equally between popular hits and hard-to-find mixes from notable DJs and musicians. Such hard-to-find goodies that can be found here are "Release Yo' Delf" by Method Man (remixed by Prodigy), "Sexy Boy" by Air (remixed by Beck), as well as "Battleflag" by the underrated duo Pigeonhed (remixed and featuring the Lo-Fidelity Allstars). More familiar (but just as interesting) tracks include Fatboy Slim's "The Rockafeller Skank" and Propellerheads' "Bang On!," as well as other songs by today's top electro-dance stars (Goldie, Roni Size, Jungle Brothers, etc.). *MTV's AMP 2* is a well-rounded collection, which is a godsend for dance fans

who (understandably) didn't want to shell out the extra dough for all those different CD singles. —*Greg Prato*

★ **Machine Soul: An Odyssey into Electronic Dance Music** / Mar. 14, 2000 / Rhino ✦✦✦✦✦

An effective compilation of electronic pop with a narrow scope and an overly safe track listing but with plenty of highlights, *Machine Soul: An Odyssey into Electronic Dance Music* sets out to cover the goal stated in the title. As such, the two-disc set begins with the logical choice: Kraftwerk. From there, the album moves into disco (the Giorgio Moroder-produced "I Feel Love" by Donna Summer), synth-pop (Sparks, OMD, Gary Numan), industrial electronics (Throbbing Gristle, Cabaret Voltaire), electro (Afrika Bambaataa, Newcleus), and Detroit techno (Juan Atkins' Cybotron, Derrick May's Rythim Is Rythim, Kevin Saunderson's Inner City). Moving seamlessly from electronic progenitors to the rave-era explosion, *Machine Soul* continues on the second disc with sampladelic and acid-house anthems from M/A/R/R/S, the KLF, the Orb, the Shamen, and Moby before hitting electronica with Prodigy, Underworld, and the Chemical Brothers, then ending with epic trance producers Paul Van Dyk and BT. The journey takes over two hours, but the *Machine Soul* odyssey presents an unfailingly straight line from the early '70s to the end of the century, with no speedbumps or problems with weak licensing (for the latter, thank Rhino's corporate cousin, Time/Warner). For listeners unfamiliar with the genre, caveats here are practically nonexistent. A few electronic-dance fans, however, may quibble with the direction of the compilation; practically *every* track here is led by vocals, whereas the vast majority of electronic-dance tracks have none. And given a style that focuses so much on the underground, the compilers would have been wise to insert tracks from at least one or two recent independent producers. Besides focusing on the "soul" of the "machine" rather than the reverse, *Machine Soul* is an excellent definition of the genre. —*John Bush*

**Macro Dub Infection, Vol. 1** / 1995 / Caroline ✦✦✦

Dub is not just for reggaeheads anymore, as numerous recent compilations of club-oriented dub tracks can attest. Dub is also no longer just a variation on a theme. Whereas the dub remix used to serve primarily as a source of cheap B-sides for economy-minded producers of reggae singles, it has evolved into a musical entity all its own now; most of the dub produced today exists on its own to serve the club-hopping masses. People the world over are waving their hands and shaking their hips as guitars, keyboards, and vocals drift in and out of the echoing, spacy mix and the drum and bass anchor everything in that loping, rolling reggae groove.

*Macro Dub Infection*, a two-disc set promisingly subtitled "Volume 1," is a good example of the variety of music being produced under the "dub" rubric. Not every track is reggae, but each is informed by the spacy, mystical ambience of dub, and most feature reggae's trademark deep, snaky basslines—not to mention the vocals appearing out of nowhere before spinning off into space and the drums sneaking up and pounding you about the head and shoulders before disappearing again. These artists are mostly British, though Americans will recognize names like Tricky and the Golden Palominos. The weird skull artwork on the cover is a tipoff to the dark, eerie mood that permeates this album—note in particular Two Badcard's creepy spoken-word track and the lovely "Operation Mind Control" by the charmingly named Skull vs. Ice. Lighter moments include the jungle-flavored "Double Edge Dub" and a lighthearted Mad Professor track called "Ragga Doll." This set rewards repeated listening and is highly recommended. —*Rick Anderson*

**Macro Dub Infection, Vol. 2** / 1997 / Virgin ✦✦✦

Virgin's second volume of experimental/new school dub extrapolations doesn't reach quite as far afield as the first. The organizing principle is still dub's insidious mutation through hip-hop, trip-hop, electro, jungle, and weirdo downtempo, but most of the tracks here are bunched about the murky midpoint of what could be considered dub's contemporary milieu, where the first volume seemed to move from extremity to extremity with each track. Most of the material seems bathed in a sort of vague, analog-y distortion, a point either of overall consistency or a bit of a cop-out, depending on your perspective. There are still some gems to be found, though, including Rhys Chatham and Martin Wheeler's "Altesse," and Techno Animal's remixes of Magnet and Palace (!), Mouse On Mars' too-brief "Sehn Sud," and the Underdog aka Skull's "Flump." —*Sean Cooper*

**Major Force West: The Original Art Form** / Oct. 20, 1997 / Mo'Wax ✦✦✦✦

As part of a growing reissue campaign highlighting forgotten corners of the electro and hip-hop world, Britain's Mo'Wax Records released a five-LP or double-disc compilation of the late-'80s Japanese hip-hop label Major Force Records. Though few of the names will be familiar to fans—barring occasional collaborations with the likes of the 45 King and Bomb the Bass' Tim Simenon—*Major Force West* is surprisingly good, although two discs is a bit much for all but the most die-hard fans. The best of the native contributions is DJ Milo's "Return of the Original Artform." —*John Bush*

**Making Headlines: 5 Years of Strictly Rhythm** / Aug. 2, 1994 / Strictly Rhythm ✦✦✦

Though it covers the first five years of Strictly Rhythm, *Making Headlines* doesn't exactly have the label's biggest hits. All of the tracks are solid (MAW/India's "Love and Happiness," Barbara Tucker's "Beautiful People," Reel 2 Real's "I Like to Move It"), but there are quite a few missing. The fact makes this just a bit less than an essential buy for Strictly Rhythm fans. —*John Bush*

**Many Shades of Cajual** / 1996 / Cajual ✦✦✦✦

Though label-head Cajmere makes only one official appearance ("Horny") on a compilation of his own Chicago label, his production is all over the album. Besides cowriting and producing Dajae tracks like "Day by Day" and "Get Up Off Me," he appears on Derrick Carter's "Dream States" and Terence FM's "Feelin' Kinda High" and (as Green Velvet) remixes one of his own productions. DJ Sneak also makes tight contributions: "Message of Love" and "Sounds from the Pipe." —*John Bush*

**Maschinelle Strategeme** / May 30, 2000 / EFA ✦✦✦✦

Along with Mille Plateaux and Position Chrome, Ritornell is yet another sublabel of the mammoth German techno label, Force Inc., focusing on a dissonant style of highly processed digital music that often crosses the boundary of ambient soundscapes into ear-covering, headache-inspiring industrial noise. The 15 featured artists—Autopoieses, Terre Thaemlitz, Taylor Deupree, and Kim Cascone, among others—each present their own individual sound collage, where textured tones clash with one another, occasionally uniting harmoniously with other sounds but most often creating juxtaposing collisions that result in piercing sounds from another world where red clouds obscure sunlight and people rarely smile. These computer-armed producers aren't aiming for beautiful music; in fact, they aren't even trying to create listening music. It's almost as if they are trying to create the unheard—a mythical form of music only found in nightmares. Anyone fascinated by the outer reaches of tolerable music should treat this as a mandatory introduction to a daring label attempting to go where no producers have gone before—and where only the most courageous listeners may want to follow. The postgraduate reading-level liner notes titled "Distributed Modules and Layers in Post-Digital Music" map out an underlying ultra-high-brow ideology justifying the need for such cacophonous sounds. But if "modules" seems foreign, just remember that this is inaccessibility at its finest and most elitist. —*Jason Birchmeier*

**Mask 002** / 1997 / Mask ✦✦✦

The second release by Skam/Musik Aus Strom offshoot label Mask doubled the numbers of its predecessor, but still only managed a print run of 200 copies. This time featuring Funkstorung, Bola, Jega, Hell Interface, and Intron, the EP's five tracks run the gamut from dark, austere downtempo electro to manic machine-born drum'n'bass, the silver thread being an elemental minimalism and warm, analog-y production. Although somehow none of the tracks quite manages the right length (two are overly long and three are mere vignettes that would probably have made more interesting extended tracks), the material is solid enough, although perhaps not ultimately worth what the market will undoubtedly come to demand for them. —*Sean Cooper*

**Massive Breakbeats** / Apr. 7, 1998 / Mutant Sound ✦✦✦✦

Not to be confused with the similarly titled *Breakbeat Massive* (which was also packaged in a nifty tin box), although confusing the two wouldn't be a disaster—both compile tracks from Britain's Labello Blanco label and feature some of the finest in "hard" jungle and drum'n'bass from the early '90s, when jungle was just emerging as a phenomenon in British dance halls. Combining as it does the vocal approach of ragga (another term for modern dancehall reggae, especially as practiced in England) with the chilly ambience of techno and double-speed, hip-hop-derived drum samples (or "breakbeats"), jungle is a uniqely compelling dance music form—one which has quietly taken over the club scene since its emergence in the early '90s. If there's any difference between this compilation and *Breakbeat Massive*, it's that this one focuses more on primarily instrumental drum'n'bass, with tracks such as "Roll On" by Andy C. and "Super Hero" by the House Crew. But there are also some great songs, including DRS and Kenny Ken's "Everyman," a junglified singer/DJ combo based on a vintage reggae groove. DJ Rap's "Intelligent Woman" is another highlight track, a complex pastiche of East Indian percussion, jungle beats, and expert reggae chatting. Highly recommended. —*Rick Anderson*

**Mastermix** / Jun. 15, 1999 / TVT ♦♦♦
The TVT collection *Mastermix* spotlights tracks from the label's full-lengths and mix collections by Adam X, Supa DJ Dmitry, Juno Reactor, Nightmares on Wax, Autechre, and Underworld. —*John Bush*

**Mealtime** / Nov. 24, 1997 / Virgin ♦♦♦
Compiled by μ-Ziq's Michael Paradinas and released by his Virgin subsidiary (Planet μ), *Mealtime* features his own tracks plus contributions from mates like Aphex Twin, Jega, and Horse Opera. Most every track is along the lines of μ-Ziq's drill'n'bass, which can easily start to wear over the course of an hour. It's a qualified success—good listening for fans but not essential for general interest. —*John Bush*

**Megasoft Office '97** / Oct. 28, 1997 / Chipie ♦♦♦♦
A compilation of European relaxed beat dance music, Ready Made stand out with their sequences pieces of acoustic guitar and *Dr. Who*-like ambient space beats on "Saulbass Theme." Getting away from techno of any kind, Elisa Carraha emotes a ballad entitled "Bewildered" to the sounds of a piano and some synth. More ambient sounds, much with good use of light piano and acoustic guitar sequences, are on this disc courtesy of Feedback, Chaotik Ramses, Aqua Bassino, A Reminescent Drive, and Juantrip'. Chipie is an imprint on the Tinder Records label to explore ambient groove-makers. US-based Chipie plans on developing talent on this side of the Atlantic in the future. —*Thomas Schulte*

**Mephisto: San Francisco Plasma Funk, Vol. 1** / Mar. 23, 1999 / OM ♦♦♦
The funky breaks compilation centered on San Francisco's Mephisto Records includes label favorites like Q Burn's Abstract Message, Pimp Daddy Nash, Fluid Motion, and Sci-Fi Select. —*John Bush*

**Microscopic Sound** / Mar. 23, 1999 / Caipirinha ♦♦♦♦
*Microscopic Sound* charts the experimental side of techno and ambient, including tracks from Ryoji Ikeda, Noto, Goem, and two from Berlin scene-leader Thomas Brinkmann—an excerpt of his Mike Ink *Studio 1 Variationen* and a Kim Cascone remix. —*John Bush*

**Midnight Snack, Vol. 1** / Jun. 20, 2000 / Naked ♦♦♦
*Midnight Snack, Vol. 1* compiles various downtempo styles of electronic music, with chilled-out ambient techno and trip-hop its main focal points. It's relaxing yet interesting music that, true to its title, sets a perfect atmosphere late at night; its selections mix artists on the Naked Music label's roster with cuts otherwise difficult to locate on US shores. —*Steve Huey*

**Militant Science** / 1996 / Botchit & Scarper ♦♦♦♦
The premiere compilation from S.O.U.R. Records sister label Botchit & Scarper, *Militant Science* charts the more abstract courses of dub-breakbeat with tracks from Elementz of Noise, Purple Koala, Asian Dub Foundation, Raw Deal, and BLIM. —*John Bush*

**Millenium Synthpop Madness** / May 9, 2000 / Cleopatra ♦♦
Cleopatra's *Millennium Synthpop Madness* presents '90s-flavored, club-oriented remixes of tunes by '80s new wave and synth-pop acts like Dead or Alive, A Flock of Seagulls, Berlin, Bow Wow Wow, Gary Numan, Heaven 17, and Information Society, to list some of the better-known names. If you're looking for the original versions, look elsewhere, but others may find the updated sound and style appealing. —*Steve Huey*

**Mind the Gap, Vol. 17** / May 12, 1998 / Gonzo Circus ♦♦♦
*Mind the Gap, Vol. 17* features tracks from a wide variety of electronic artists, including Drum Island, A Forest Mighty Black, Photek, Animals on Wheels, and Front 242, among others. —*John Bush*

**Mind the Gap, Vol. 18** / Sep. 22, 1998 / Gonzo Circus ♦♦♦
*Mind the Gap, Vol. 18* features tracks from a wide variety of electronic artists, including Sofa Surfers, David Morley, Midnight Funk Association, Muslimgauze vs. Rootsman, Bill Laswell, Buscemi, and others. —*John Bush*

**Mind the Gap, Vol. 19** / Jan. 19, 1999 / Gonzo Circus ♦♦♦
*Mind the Gap, Vol. 19* features tracks from a wide variety of electronic artists, including Nonplace Urban Field, Shizuo, Techno Animal, Hugh Hopper, Si Begg, Lustmord, Chocolate Weasel, and many others. —*John Bush*

**Mind the Gap, Vol. 20** / Jan. 19, 1999 / Gonzo Circus ♦♦♦
*Mind the Gap, Vol. 20* features tracks from a wide variety of electronic artists, including Euphonic, Curd Duca, Amon Tobin, Klute, Rasmus, and Jackal. —*John Bush*

**Ministry of Sound Australian Tour** / Aug. 25, 1998 / Mushroom ♦♦♦
The noted British super-club documented their trip Down Under with *Ministry of Sound Australian Tour*, including tracks on the harder side of house by Dave Angel, Size Queen, Funky Green Dogs, David Morales, Basement Jaxx, Danny Tenaglia, and Paul Van Dyk. —*John Bush*

**Ministry of Sound: Annual 1999-2000** / Jan. 25, 2000 / Polygram International ♦♦
Any seasoned electronic music listener should have a difficult time stomaching the majority of Ministry of Sound's DJ-mix compilations. Besides being little more than marketing vehicles for the UK club, these records bastardize the art of DJing in their attempt to appeal to naive, mainstream audiences with their feeble attempts to mix records and construct a journey-like motif. Rather than let DJs Tom Novy and Boy George spin their own records and lay down their own style, Ministry of Sound has them play only the biggest club hits of the year—primarily house, garage, and trance tunes—meaning, of course, that there is little continuity between tracks and no underlying style or established motif. When Boy George moves through Paul Johnson's "Get Get Down," Mr. Oizo's "Flat Beat," ATB's "9PM (Till I Come)," Alice Deejay's "Better Off Alone," and Fatboy Slim's "Praise You" over the course of just 70 minutes, there is little chance for the infamous pop singer-turned-DJ to establish any sense of mood or journey. Instead, this album sounds little more than a jaggedly mixed compilation of hits catered toward mainstream audiences who just can't get enough of the infectious gluttony of ATB and Alice Deejay. And if the lack of mixing and continuity isn't enough, this album absolutely reeks of commercial exploitation with its "TV Advertised" sticker and its fat booklet that further markets Ministry of Sound's club and their resident DJs. In sum, this blasphemous attempt to commercialize the club-going experience represents everything wrong with the lowest common denominator-approach of commercial electronic music and why so many seasoned listeners loathe the UK's vain club scene and their pimped DJs. —*Jason Birchmeier*

**Ministry of Sound: Clubber's Guide to Ibiza Summer 2000** / Jul. 11, 2000 / Ministry Of Sound ♦♦♦
When we last left Judge Jules in the requisite "Let's See How Many Dance Compilations We Can Fleece to the Kids" *Clubber's Guide to Ibiza* situation in 1999, he pulled very few surprises and produced a quality—yet tame—compilation. This time, however, Jules' 2000 installment seems less intent on slogging out a set of solid songs and more in control of creating a tight, banging compilation of significant skill. So smile: The tunes suited for the Balearic island of Ibiza this year are bigger as well as better. Highlights? Much easier to find this time around: Florian F's Terry Gilliam-winking "Surreal Brazil," Burgy's rolling, thunderous "Lochfresser," and Storm's might-be-Ibiza-tune-of-2000 "Time To Burn" are all unquestionable champions. Jules even sticks in another of his pen-name tracks (Hi-Gate's "Caned & Unable"), and once again he shows up almost everything else on this entire set. To be fair, however, one might notice that such peaks are mostly contained on the first disc. Because the follow-up disc is peppered with cheese-house like Freefall or gives-trance-a-bad-name awfulness like Lost Witness, even the legitimately poetic "It's My Turn" by Angelic is marred by Jules' decision to use the vocal take of one of 1999's most incomparable trance songs. Still, as far as summer island club culture is concerned, this is an admirable collection of the huge and the obscure. Jules ignores his domesticated 1999 Ministry of Sound in-

stallment and keeps everything in a stream of friendly, hard beats and superior trance. What a difference a year must make. After all, the beginning of the 21st century might show club-land seriously eyeing UK garage for the first time in ages, but if this *Clubber's Guide to Ibiza 2000* installment declares anything, it's that those always set to get mad on the floor will be safe from persecution for years to come. —*Dean Carlson*

### Mixed Up Logic Plus / Jul. 2, 1996 / Logic Club ♦♦♦
*Mixed Up Logic Plus* contains 12 remixes of singles by dance artists like La Bouche, Dr. Alban, Sparks, Cosmic Baby, Chazz, Blunt Funkers, and Storm and Herman. On this collection the remixers, actually, are bigger stars than the original artists themselves. Todd Terry, George Morel, Stonebridge, Rabbit in the Moon, Josh Wink, and Darrin Friedman, among many others, provide elastic, inventive reworkings of songs that, by and large, weren't that captivating in their first incarnation. Not all of the cuts are first-rate, but there are enough good moments to make it a worthwhile purchase for dance fanatics. —*Stephen Thomas Erlewine*

### Mixmag: Decade Mixmag Live / Mar. 28, 2000 / Import ♦♦
Throughout the '90s, the UK publication *Mixmag* helped transform electronic dance music from an underground soundtrack for ecstasy-fueled raves to a style of music that increasingly monopolized the country's nightlife. Besides publishing its magazine full of club listings, articles, interviews, gossip, record reviews, and anything else that would help make the music a lifestyle, *Mixmag* also established the popular idea of DJ-mix CDs. By 2000, *Mixmag* had released over 30 CDs that furthered the magazine, the DJs, and the electronic music scene in general. *Decade* serves as a retrospective look back at *Mixmag*'s role within the scene, featuring a self-important editorial piece by editor Dom Philkuoa and two CDs of important tracks. Besides being a retrospective, greatest-hits-like look at dance music, *Decade* differs from the 30 other *Mixmag* CDs from the '90s in the fact that the tracks can be heard in an unedited form rather than being mixed by a DJ. One quick thing to keep in mind is first that this album is divided between house and breakbeats, so anyone looking for techno, trance, or any other style should look elsewhere. Secondly, though it advertises itself as a retrospective look at the '90s, the album actually looks primarily at the mid to late '90s for its tracks, meaning that there aren't any amateur-sounding, early-'90s rave anthems included. If one looks past the somewhat biased nature of the compilation and desires a collection of unedited house and breakbeat classics from the mid- to late '90s, then this is undoubtedly an album to hunt down. Oft-spun house classics such as DJ Sneak's "You Can't Hide from Your Bud," Cricco Castelli's "Life Is Changing," and Green Velvet's "Answering Machine" sound revived in their full-length versions, presenting the intro and outros that Derrick Carter left off his Cosmic Disco contribution to the *Mixmag* series of DJ-mix albums. And don't be fooled by the first disc's claim to be both techno and house; there isn't any techno. The second disc looks not necessarily to the drum'n'bass stylings of huge UK labels such as Metalheadz, V, or Virus but rather to the candy-coated style of breakbeats that crosses over into the mainstream with its pop tendencies and cheery aura—though the disc-concluding inclusion of LTJ Bukem's anthem of anthems, "Music," is an exception. In the end, *Mixmag* presents a tainted view of '90s electronic dance music on *Decade* by presenting primarily accessible sounds while excluding the more edgy sounds of techno, garage, and drum'n'bass. Sure, the featured tracks are good, but *Mixmag*'s bias leaves one with a bad taste. —*Jason Birchmeier*

### Mo' House Yo' Mama / Jan. 23, 1996 / Moonshine Music ♦♦♦
*Mo' House Yo' Mama* concentrates on American deep house, with tracks from Love to Infinity, Mike Delgado's Deep Zone, Frankie Knuckles, and Masters at Work. —*Keith Farley*

### Mo'Wax First Chapter / 1995 / Mo'Wax ♦♦♦♦
The first collection of Mo'Wax tracks includes several label classics like DJ Shadow's "In/Flux," DJ Krush's "Slow Chase," La Funk Mob's "Motor Bass Get Phunked Up," and Palm Skin Productions' "Spock with a Beard." Though even Mo'Wax includes a few duds—tracks by Monday Michiru, Bubbatunes, Marden Hill—the majority of *Mo'Wax First Chapter* is quite solid. —*John Bush*

### Modern Mix: 80's Dance Rarities, Vol. 1 / Jul. 25, 2000 / Streetbeat ♦♦
*Modern Mix: 80's Dance Rarities, Vol. 1* features 13 dance/club tracks mixed by Steve Masters. Highlights include "Promise" by When in Rome, "You Spin Me Around" by Dead or Alive, "It's My Life" by Dr. Alban, "Time Will Tell" by the Twins, and "What Is Love" by Haddaway. —*Al Campbell*

### Modulation & Transformation, Vol. 1 / 1994 / Mille Plateaux ♦♦♦♦
The original *Modulation and Transformation* album brought together a roster of talented European techno producers that focused on the lighter, more experimental side of techno, establishing Mille Plateaux as a respected label with a precedent for high-quality, innovative techno. At the time of the album's release in 1994, techno was still evolving beyond the first- and second-wave Detroit recordings and the early '90s movements in Berlin, but the Frankfurt, Germany-based Mille Plateaux label looked beyond the techno Meccas of Detroit and Berlin for its inaugural release, finding a plethora of talent in the nearby city of Cologne under various monikers: Jorg Burger (the Bionaut, J. Burger), Gregor Lutterman (Rootpower, Car & Driver), Cem Oral (Jammin Unit, Air Liquide, Ultrahigh), Ingmar Koch (Walker, Air Liquide), and Andreas Bolz (Bolz-Bolz, Car & Driver). Mille Plateaux also included early recordings by other talented artists such as Aphex Twin, Alec Empire, Ian Pooley, and Thomas P. Heckmann, further illustrating the label's insightful knack for hand-picking some of the most promising up-and-coming producers at the time. Truthfully, every song on this compilation deserves recognition; while most techno from the early '90s has dated rather quickly and poorly, these songs remain beautifully interesting. Aphex Twin's "On—Reload Mix" begins the album on a high note, as the artist otherwise known as Richard D. James proves that he can make traditional techno as well as—if not better than—he can craft ambient soundscapes and crazed noise constructions. Following this euphoric song with its strong emphasis on melody, the succeeding German producers head into darker territory, employing variations on the 303 acid riff motif overtop eerie, nonabrasive percussive rhythms. Yet as wonderful as this watershed collection is, it sets the precedent not so much for Mille Plateaux future releases but for the then-burgeoning Cologne scene surrounding the legendary Structure label. —*Jason Birchmeier*

### Modulation & Transformation, Vol. 3 / Feb. 16, 1998 / Mille Plateaux ♦♦♦
*Modulation & Transformation, Vol. 3* is a double-disc collection of tracks by Mille Plateaux associates like Oval, Jammin' Unit, Cristian Vogel, DJ Spooky, Scanner, Gas, Terre Thaemltiz, and more. —*John Bush*

### Modulation & Transformation, Vol. 4 / Apr. 20, 1999 / EFA ♦♦♦
The fourth collection in the *Modulation & Transformation* series testifies precisely how powerfully Mille Plateaux has positioned themselves within the growing world of electronic music. While many labels cash in on the genre's growing popularity, this Frankfurt-based label refuses to compromise its brand of challenging electronic music, instead heading increasingly further toward unparalleled artistic heights. The 36 songs on this wide-ranging collection capture many of Europe's foremost avant-garde electronic music composers such as Gas, Thomas Heckman, and Thomas Brinkman in addition to a few non-Europeans such as Paul Miller. The result captures a multitude of previously inconceivable ideas, directions that past musicians had never dreamt of. For example, when Wolfgang Voigt concludes the first album as Freiland on "Blau," the result feels near apocalyptic with its painfully distorted, shotgun blast-sounding bass beats pounding underneath a series of primitive synth melodies. To the average listener, this song is sheer noise, nothing but a banging cacophony. Yet to the more curious listener, a mysterious allure lies beneath this catastrophic demolition; only those in search of fresh ideas and sounds can find the inner beauty of songs such as this. Keep in mind that this is just one example of many. Sure, there are times when even the most open-minded listeners will scratch their heads, wondering a particular song's value. Yet for the most part, these brave composers should be trusted by the listener. One may find little melody or rhythm here, but ambition is plentiful. —*Jason Birchmeier*

### Monster Breaks: A Collection of Big Beat Finery / Mar. 17, 1998 / ffrr ♦♦♦
Just one in the surprising amount of big-beat compilations, *Monster Breaks* does better than most. Top-flight Skint acts Midfield General, Cut La Roc and Fatboy Slim (a track of his own plus two remixes) appear alongside compatriots like Mekon, Headrillaz, Howie B, and DJ Icey. Though there are a few nondescript tracks (by Sol Brothers, MOT, Basco, and others), the album succeeds on most other accounts. —*Keith Farley*

### Moonshine Mixed / 1996 / Moonshine Music ♦♦♦
The first in Moonshine's ongoing series featuring DJ Dave Aude is a main-

stream American affair. By focusing primarily on Moonshine acts like DJ Keoki and Cirrus, *Moonshine Mixed* is more of a promotional tool than a mix album, and suffers for it. —*Keith Farley*

**Moonshine Mixed, Vol. 2** / Feb. 10, 1998 / Moonshine Music ♦♦♦
*Moonshine Mixed, Vol. 2* is yet another album aimed squarely at consumers unfamiliar with Moonshine acts like Doc Martin, Keoki, and Cirrus. There are some interesting remixers—the Crystal Method, Tall Paul—but even they can't save this tepid affair. —*Keith Farley*

**The Morning After** / Jul. 29, 1997 / Virgin ♦♦♦♦
Compiled by erstwhile downtempo DJ Mixmaster Morris, *The Morning After* is an impeccably solid collection of ambient and breakbeat techno, with many tracks only available on limited 12" releases before inclusion here. Included are tracks by Blame & Justice ("Repro House"), Spring Heel Jack ("Flying Again"), Photek ("T-Raenon"), Plaid ("Angry Dolphin"), and T Power ("Indigo"). A possible highlight (especially for trainspotters) is "Sarcacid," a song recorded—as Alroy Road Tracks—by Tom Jenkinson, better known as Squarepusher. —*John Bush*

**Motiv 8 Remix Collection, Vol. 1** / Apr. 20, 1999 / Import ♦♦♦
*Motiv 8 Remix Collection, Vol. 1* may not be definitive, but it contains enough of their best remixes to be worthwhile for both collectors and neophytes. —*Stephen Thomas Erlewine*

**Movin' to the Grooves** / 1996 / Sony Special Products ♦♦♦
As you might surmise from the title, Sony Music Special Products' *Movin' to the Grooves* contains a selection of ten disco and dance-club favorites. It never sticks to one particular era, moving between Cheryl Lynn's "Got to Be Real" and Dead or Alive's "You Spin Me Round (Like a Record)" with the greatest of ease. That may mean that the compilation isn't all that cohesive, but it does have a pretty strong selection of songs, and it feels like a good house party or retro-disco. —*Stephen Thomas Erlewine*

**Mushroom Jazz** / Oct. 22, 1996 / OM ♦♦♦
Farina's hypnotic dance-floor jazz creates a trippy background mix and an enjoyable look at some promising new artists for those willing to listen. That being said, it's not a seamless mix, containing some jarring transitions. Tracks that don't fade into the background are the international hit single by Blue Boy, "Remember Me," and Mr. Electric Triangle's "Bossa Nova." As much as he forges a unique, mellow sound, he is inescapably influenced by DJs like Gilles Peterson. —*Ryan Randall Goble*

**Mutant Beatz** / Sep. 23, 1997 / Paradigm ♦♦♦
Here's the subtitle: "Abstrakt Hip-Hop, Future Funk & Science Fiction Soul." That about sums it up. This is a compilation of tracks by artists from the US and the UK, all of them dedicated to creating innovative groove music in various ways. It is, frankly, a nearly perfect album, for the simple reason that everything on it is musically interesting and compellingly funky but no two tracks sound much alike. Highlights include "Do Yourself Some Good" by Heavy Handed, which moves from gritty soul funk to frantic jungle over the course of three minutes; "Soul Skankin" and "Shadow" by the reggae-informed Rude Kulcha, the former of which combines a strutting reggae bassline with what sounds like an urban field recording of girls singing; and the dub-inflected abstraction of Moonstar's "Matrix." Best of all is an untitled track credited to Euphonic vs. Soothsayer and Dr. Israel, a jungle/hip-hop fusion experiment on which Soothsayer raps and Dr. Israel toasts over an expansive drum'n'bass backing track. Excellent. —*Rick Anderson*

**Muzik Classics: Drum & Bass** / Sep. 28, 1998 / Muzik Classics ♦♦♦♦
The first volume in an ongoing series devoted to chronicling the touchstone tracks in each style of dance music, *Muzik Classics: Drum & Bass* is a two-disc set including 24 of the best jungle tracks irrespective of original issue. For the first time ever, drum'n'bass landmarks like "Renegade Snares" by Omni Trio, "Inner City Life" by Goldie, "Music" by LTJ Bukem, "Mr. Kirk's Nightmare" by 4 Hero, "Original Nuttah" by Shy FX, "Mutant Revisited" by T Power & DJ Trace, "Shadowboxing" by Doc Scott, and "Kilimanjaro" by Ed Rush appear on the same compilation, for an easy look at the brightest and best jungle tracks ever released. —*John Bush*

**Muzik Classics: Techno** / Feb. 8, 1999 / Beechwood ♦♦♦♦
*Muzik Classics: Techno*, the second volume in a series of genre highlights by the British *Muzik* magazine, attempts to define the best techno tracks ever released, and certainly comes close to perfection. Though fans argue for hours about their personal favorites, few could question the validity of any of these selections—"Strings of Life," "Energy Flash," "Jam the Box," "Altered States," "Acperience," "Clear," "Positive Education," "Losing Control," "Horsepower." Even the more marginal tracks here are that way only in context to their surroundings. As on their jungle set, *Muzik* have released what is easily the best compilation ever devoted to techno, hands down. —*John Bush*

**My Name Is Trance** / Jun. 27, 2000 / Max Music ♦♦
As the title suggests, *My Name Is Trance* features tracks by some of the most popular names in progressive trance, including DJ/producer Maurio Picotto's "Iguana," Des Mitchell's "Welcome to the Dance," and a remix of Rank 1's "Airwave" by ATB. Vincent De Moor's "Eternity," Percussion Jam's "Night Express," the Act's "Something about You," and Tep Zeppi's "Space Is the Place" are some of the other highlights from this compelling collection. —*Heather Phares*

**NRG Unlimited, Vol. 1** / Oct. 15, 1996 / Interhit ♦♦♦
*NRG Unlimited, Vol. 1* is a 16-track compilation of relentless, hard-hitting Hi-NRG dance cuts from the '90s. Only a handful of cuts, like M People's "Excited," were actually hits, but all of the cuts deliver wild, infectious rhythms that come close to capturing what Hi-NRG's all about. —*Stephen Thomas Erlewine*

**N.Y.C. House** / Aug. 5, 1997 / ZYX ♦♦♦♦
*N.Y.C. House* makes a pretty solid claim to compilation dominance. Besides including such New York classics as "Fired Up!" by Funky Green Dogs, "Witch Doktor" by Armand Van Helden, "If Madonna Calls" by Junior Vasquez, "Higher State of Consciousness" by Wink and "Land of the Living" by Kristine W (remixed by Deep Dish), other mainstream names like DJ Sneak, Black Box, Erick Morillo, and CeCe Rogers are included. Though Masters at Work make no official appearance, the duo on production with Barbara Tucker's "Stay Together," while MAW member "Little" Louie Vega appears on "Deep Inside" by his Hardrive project. —*John Bush*

**Natural Born Techno, Vol. 1** / Nov. 11, 1996 / Never ♦♦♦
Though there are a few good tracks, by Mark Broom, Secret Cinema, and Shaolin Wooden Men, this collection from Never Records fails to consistently excite. —*Keith Farley*

**Natural Born Techno, Vol. 2** / Feb. 4, 1997 / Never ♦♦
Though the first was hardly a wonder, the second volume of *Natural Born Techno* hits a new low. Acts like Delta Plan, Sympathy Nervous, Xingu Hill, and MDA Analog do nothing to help the cause of nonformulaic techno, and there are no saviors in sight. —*Keith Farley*

**Neo-Disco** / Sep. 21, 1999 / Radikal ♦♦
Radikal Records' *Neo-Disco* updates the classic disco sound with flourishes of electronica, collecting tracks from neo-disco artists like Studio 45, Ultimate Heights, and JT Playaz. Blue Adonis' "Disco Cop," Blockster's "You Should Be," Armand Van Helden's "You Don't Know Me," and the Tamperer's "Feel It" define the style's sexy, retro-futuristic sound. Supa Kings' "Back & Forth" and X-Rated's "Everybody Dance" round out this fun collection of club music. —*Heather Phares*

**Nervous Cocktail Mix** / Apr. 6, 1999 / Nervous Dog ♦♦♦
Even the mainstream house label got in on the revival of the exotica/swing/martini crowd with this mix of laidback house from Byron Stingily, E-Smoove, Mateo & Matos, Kerri Chandler, and Kim English. —*John Bush*

**Nervous Hard House** / 1995 / Nervous ♦♦♦
The rougher, tougher side of Nervous Records appears on this collection with acid powerhouses like "Don't Laugh" by Winx and two tracks by Anthony Acid, Powerhouses "Powerful" and WAM's "Drum." Jason Nevins also appears, with the track "Sound F/X," though the balance of this compilation is of negligible worth. —*John Bush*

**Nervous Hip Hop** / 1995 / Nervous ♦♦♦
Far more than a detour into rap territory, Nervous Records alternates breakbeat workouts by its artists (the Wreck All Stars led by Kenny "Dope" Gonzalez, Franki Feliciano's Groove Asylum, and Live & Die Reck) with tracks by acknowledged rap titans like Smif-N-Wessun, Funkmaster Flex, and even dancehall's Mad Lion. Most tracks are successes, though many of the recruited house producers interpret hip-hop through the medium of more subtle, danceable fare. —*John Bush*

**Nervous House** / 1995 / Nervous ♦♦♦♦
Of the stylistic compilation excursions by the label during 1995, *Nervous*

*House* is the one with which most of these producers are most comfortable. With tracks by Jason Nevins, Byron Burke and Kim English, Willie Ninja, and Franki Feliciano, the album is a more-than-competent journey through edgy American house. —*John Bush*

**Networks, Vol. 1** / 1996 / Studio !K7 ◆◆◆◆
This compilation features 11 tracks from the Windsor, Ontario, camp of electronic music labels that began with Plus 8 and eventually led to the addition of two more labels, Probe and Definitive. Richie Hawtin composes five of the 11 tracks on this compilation under various pseudonyms such as Plastikman, FUSE and UP!, with each showing his multiple musical interests. While the FUSE track "Into the Space" functions as lumbering ambient techno balancing on the fine line between bliss and boredom, his UP! track, "Nightflight," possesses an uptempo cosmic feel, making it a wonderful way to conclude the album. The three Plastikman tracks also vary in style. From the disorienting left-to-right-channel panning on "Electriks" to the epic remix of Robotman's "DooDaDoo" and the percussive hailstorm of "Spaz"—also found on Plastikman's *Recycled Plastik*—Hawtin proves his status as a seminal artist. Although these tracks alone make *Networks 1* worthy of attention, the other artists add equally stunning offerings that shouldn't be overlooked. Rotterdam artist Speedy J contributes the album's best track, "Spikkels," which blends aggressive techno and ambient bliss; Ian Pooley contributes another standout immediately afterwards. Given the well-rounded nature of this compilation—due to inclusion of Probe and Definitive material—*Networks 1* ends up being one of the best Plus 8 compilations released in the early '90s. —*Jason Birchmeier*

**Networks, Vol. 2** / 1996 / Studio !K7 ◆◆◆
While its predecessor filtered Detroit techno through minimalism, *Networks, Vol. 2* adds a few tracks with more soulful, disco-inspired musings. Tech-house wizards like Terrence Parker and Chris Brann (of the Wamdue Kids) contribute tracks while refugees from the first volume (Richie Hawtin, Ian Pooley) appear as well. Not quite as solid as the first, but with much more variety. —*John Bush*

**Networks, Vol. 3: An Intellinet Compilation** / Sep. 23, 1996 / Studio !K7 ◆◆◆
Though the absence of top names would appear to be a stumbling block, the Intellinet volume in the *Networks* series does a good job of projecting trance and acid techno with just a few crucial leanings toward the indulgence of house music. Besides the all-star project "Loop" by LFO Vs. Fuse, producers like Alton Miller (Trax 4 Daze), Kanabis the Edit Assassin, and Dale Lawrence (Theorem) each contribute glowing tracks to the album. —*John Bush*

**New Chicago House Sound** / Apr. 16, 1995 / Cajual ◆◆◆◆
This landmark compilation compiled many of the more noteworthy tracks released by Cajmere's Cajual label between 1992 and 1994. A time when the label practically reinvented Chicago house, Cajmere, and his alter-ego Green Velvet, contribute to all but two of the tracks on this album as either the songwriter or remixer. As a result a signature sound runs through each song: a heavily syncopated bass-heavy rhythm track underlying a soulful high-end composed of sampled diva vocals and some carefully placed high-hat percussion. The artist's first track ever, "Percolator," can be found here, as can his first big hit, "Brighter Days," in two different versions (one remixed by Masters at Work). Others worth hearing are Cajmere's Underground Goodie mix of Hard Corey and Wray's "Love Train," with its bottom-heavy sound and wonderful manipulation of the diva vocals, and the downright nastiness of Cajmere and Derrick Carter's "Wet Dream," with its blunt vocal refrain: "I ain't fucked all week/I'm a horny motherfucker." The stiff percussion and robotic vocals of this song as well as "Conniption" showcase the techno-influenced style of hard house that Cajmere would later explore as Green Velvet on classics such as "Land of the Lost" and "Flash." In the end, modern listeners may find this material a bit dated and simple, but one can no doubt sense the monolithic importance and precedent that these tracks inflicted over the then stagnant Chicago house scene, signaling the dawn of a new era. —*Jason Birchmeier*

★ **New Electronica, Vol. 1** / 1993 / New Electronica ◆◆◆◆◆
The first in the *New Electronica* series, subtitled "American and European Technological Innovations," was one of the first to present domestic American techno acts like Underground Resistance and Mark Gage's Cusp alongside European inheritors like Air Liquide, Maurizio, and CJ Bolland. Although the producer list isn't quite as strong as on subsequent volumes, it's a solid compilation of the new wave of intelligent techno. —*John Bush*

**New Electronica, Vol. 2** / 1993 / New Electronica ◆◆◆◆
*New Electronica, Vol. 2* (with the cumbersome subtitle "Global Technological Innovations—Chronological Harmonisations 1") presents several of the most artistic techno producers of the '90s, each with quite early tracks. British production supremos Global Communication, As One, and Aphex Twin each contribute somewhat rare selections, while lone American Carl Craig shows up with "Dreamland" as himself, plus the Detroit classic "Neurotic Behaviour" (recorded as Psyche). It's Thinking, HMC, and Pure also contribute solid tracks. —*John Bush*

★ **New Electronica, Vol. 3** / 1994 / New Electronica ◆◆◆◆◆
An exquisite document of the trans-Atlantic techno exchange circa 1992-93, the third volume of *New Electronica* is subtitled "Global Technological Innovations." Besides tracks from European acts like Max 404, As One, Clip Talk, and Richard H. Kirk's Sandoz (the sublime "Ocean Reflection"), Detroiters Mad Mike Banks and Juan Atkins make appearances, Atkins with the Maurizio remix of his Infiniti track "Think Quick." The Geep's eponymous track is often credited to Alex Paterson of the Orb. —*John Bush*

**New Electronica, Vol. 4** / 1994 / New Electronica ◆◆◆◆
With more Detroit tracks than any in the *New Electronica* series, "Global Technological Innovations: Soundwaves 1" features "Soundscape" by Stacey Pullen's Kosmic Messenger, "Rave New World" by the Underground Resistance project X-101, and "Die Kosmischen Kuriere" by Juan Atkins & 3MB. Of the non-Americans, Source, Nico, Planetary, and HMC each contribute stellar tracks. —*John Bush*

**New School vs. Old School, Vol. 2** / Jun. 20, 2000 / Jive ◆◆◆
*New School vs. Old School, Vol. 2* features hip-hop and dance-pop tracks— by the likes of A Tribe Called Quest, the Fu-Schnickens, the Stone Roses, Kid Rock, and KRS-One/Boogie Down Productions—put through a remixing process by a wide variety of DJs/producers. The results are mostly pretty accessible, although there's plenty of variety to keep things intriguing as well. Overall, it's actually a better compilation than its forerunner. —*Steve Huey*

**New York Afterhours: A Later Shade of Deep** / May 5, 1998 / Nervous Dog ◆◆◆
Kevin Yost's "Two Wrongs Making It Right," Jon Cutler and DJ Romaine's "The Ride" and Dynamic's "Lift Me" (produced by the always dependable King Britt) are among the highlights of *New York Afterhours: A Later Shade of Deep*, a continuous mix of deep house grooves ideal for dancing into the wee small hours. —*Jason Ankeny*

**New York City Block Party** / Nov. 24, 1998 / RCA International ◆◆◆
This RCA compilation approximates the vibes of a Latin-centric block party, NYC style, with tracks by Armand Van Helden, DJ Sneak, PQM, Bronx Boys, Manos Arriba, and Junior Sanchez. —*John Bush*

**Night Shift** / Oct. 15, 1996 / C&S ◆◆◆
Mostly collecting tracks from British artists affiliated with Pork and Cup of Tea Records (Statik, Purple Penguin, Fila Brazillia), *Night Shift* also includes Americans like DJ Spooky and Baby Buddah Heads, plus the Chemical Brothers' "Chico's Groove." Though it's not the most potent trip-hop compilation out there, C&S did a competent job licensing tracks and showcasing a couple of their own artists. —*John Bush*

**A Night at the Tunnel: Continuous Mix by DJ Jason Ojeda** / Apr. 18, 2000 / Nervous ◆◆◆
NYC's legendary *Tunnel* releases a tight collection of continuous techtronic grooves from some of today's biggest club anthems by Junior Vasquez, Hex Hector, Johnny Vicious, Victor Calderon, and Razor'N'Guido. *Night at the Tunnel* was released in April 2000 on the NYC underground label Nervous Records. —*MacKenzie Wilson*

**A Night of Hardcore Clubbing** / Mar. 17, 1997 / Nervous Dog ◆◆◆
James Christian's Groove Control and Josh Wink's project Winx each make several appearances on this Nervous compilation, perhaps aimed at clubbing youths due to the cover. Though none of Wink's big club hits are included (instead it's "Funky Elevation," "How's the Music," and "You Are the One") *A Night of Hardcore Clubbing* is a competent mix album, chaired by Micro. —*Keith Farley*

**No Categories, Vol. 2: Ubiquity Compilation** / Mar. 23, 1999 / Ubiquity ♦♦♦

This second Ubiquity compilation somewhat delivers on its promise with a selection of tracks (from Skyjuice, DJ Greyboy, Beatless, Derf Reklaw, and the Automator) that cross-cut acid jazz, hip-hop, and electronic. —*John Bush*

**Nokturnel Mix Sessions: Robert Oleysyck** / Jun. 27, 2000 / Topaz ♦♦♦♦

This particular Nokturnel Mix Sessions release is a stunning remix compilation showcasing the mastermind skills of DJ Robert Oleysyck. Since 1994, Oleysyck has been the resident DJ at Las Vegas' Club Utopias, installing the hippest breakbeats and sonic vibes that made him one of the most recognizable mainstays in the progressive house scene. —*MacKenzie Wilson*

**Novamute: Version 1.1** / Nov. 23, 1993 / NovaMute ♦♦♦♦

An early NovaMute compilation released in America, *Version 1.1* includes a few duds but also features two crucial early tracks by David Holmes, "Ministry" and "Celestial Symphony" (as Scubadevils). Other notable producers include Dan Bell (as Spawn), Plastikman (the classic "Spastik"), Juno Reactor, Spirit Feel, and 3 Phase. —*John Bush*

**(Now We're Totally) Bonkers, Vol. 2** / Apr. 28, 1997 / React ♦♦♦♦

The follow-up to the original *Bonkers* finds Sharkey on the decks for the first time (instead of the mic), mixing tracks from Druid & Energy and Bang the Future into a fluid happycore extravaganza. On the other disc, DJ veteran Hixxy finds room for five tracks from his own project Anti-Social, plus the vocal workout "Living Dream" by Evolve. *Bonkers, Vol. 2* is easily the best in the series. —*John Bush*

**(Now We're Totally) Bonkers, Vol. 3** / Oct. 20, 1991 / React ♦♦♦♦

The third episode in the most successful happy hardcore series includes spot-on mixing by Hixxy, Sharkey, and Dougal, plus loads of happycore anthems like "Return to Toytown" and "Cloudy Daze," as well as remixes of "Steamtrain" and "Together Forever." —*John Bush*

**Nu York Nu Skool** / Feb. 25, 1997 / Sm:)e ♦♦♦

A compilation of strictly New York drum'n'bass, *Nu York Nu School* includes tracks from Jamie Myerson, DJ Dara, DJ Ani and even hip-hop legend Afrika Bambaataa (the rousing "Funky Beeper"). As usual, accolades go to the Brit producer, the transplanted DJ Trace, with "Nexus Apache." —*Keith Farley*

**O.S.F. Presents US Dance Explosion** / Sep. 23, 1997 / Hot Productions ♦♦

Producer Adam Morano compiled *O.S.F. Presents US Dance Explosion*, a megamix assembling freestyle tracks like Menage's "Kisses in the Rain," and Camrie's "Can't Let Go," and the Boo Crew's "Strip." —*Jason Ankeny*

★ **Objets d'A.R.T.** / 1995 / New Electronica ♦♦♦♦♦

A summing up of Kirk Degiorgio's A.R.T. Records, one of the crucial Detroit-London connections during the early '90s, *Objets D'A.R.T.* documents only the best producers of early intelligent techno. While Degiorgio ends up with almost half of the tracks (under the pseudonyms As One, Future/Past, Esoterik, and Elegy), other British classics are turned in by Black Dog (as Balil), B12 (as Red Cell), and Steve Pickton (as Phenomyna). Carl Craig alone represents the Motor City, but does so in fine fashion with two tracks apiece from his Psyche and BFC projects. The music is Detroitish techno of only the most controlled, sublime caliber. —*John Bush*

**Ocean of Sound** / 1996 / Ambient ♦♦♦♦

The audio companion to David Toop's excellent book advances the case he made, that Les Baxter, Aphex Twin, the Beach Boys, Herbie Hancock, King Tubby, and My Bloody Valentine are all related by their effect on sound pioneering. A double-disc set, *Ocean of Sound* impresses not only with its incredible diversity of musical styles, but with how easily these artists work next to each other. The second disc includes consecutive contributions by Paul Schütze, the Velvet Undergound, Holger Czukay of Can, the Beach Boys, African Headcharge, and Sun Ra. Besides illustrating Toop's point beautifully, the album is an excellent addition to the collection of any wide-ranging ambient fan. —*John Bush*

**Off the Map** / 1996 / Charm ♦♦♦

The slightly psychedelic side of dub and trance makes appearances on this collection, with contributions from Astralasia, Suns of Arqa, Diatribe, and Horizon 222, alongside a stellar production from Higher Intelligence Agency. —*John Bush*

**Offbeat: A Red Hot Sound Trip** / Feb. 27, 1996 / TVT ♦♦♦♦

A collection of ambient breakbeat and soundtrack-influenced rock, *Offbeat* is an appropriately titled left-field venture of the *Red Hot + Blue* benefit series. Included are tracks from "alternative" acts like Soul Coughing, My Bloody Valentine, Spookey Ruben, Barry Adamson and Laika, plus more dancefloor-oriented producers like Skylab, DJ Krush, Meat Beat Manifesto, Moby, DJ Spooky, and others. As can usually be counted on, this edition in the *Red Hot* series is a must for fans of the music, and an easy recommendation as an important starting point for neophytes. —*Keith Farley*

**Offering (The Past & Present of K7)** / Jun. 30, 1997 / Studio !K7 ♦♦♦

For its American debut, Studio !K7 Records showcased its intriguing catalog with this collection of, ironically, American techno producers, among them the best Detroit had to offer: Carl Craig, Claude Young, Sean Deason, and Terrence Parker. Appearing as well are Europeans like Kruder and Dorfmeister, DJ Cam, Nicolette, and Rockers Hifi. *Keith Farley*

**Old School vs. New School** / Feb. 23, 1999 / Jive ♦♦♦

The notion behind *Old School vs. New School* is based around Jive's stable of old-school hip-hop artists (like A Tribe Called Quest, Whodini, Boogie Down Productions, and DJ Jazzy Jeff & the Fresh Prince), plus the Stone Roses from its Silvertone offshoot, tossed into new-school settings, i.e. remixes by '90s electronica artists. And it works surprisingly well. Jungle, big beat, and hardcore techno coat these hip-hop relics quite naturally at times. Aphrodite hotwires Tribe's "1nce Again," Norman Cook (Fatboy Slim) does the same to their "I Left My Wallet in El Segundo," and Doc Martin gives their "Footprints" a contemporary spin, while DJ Icey twists Whodini's "Five Minutes of Funk" into a countdown of electronic euphoria, and both Grooverider and Rabbit in the Moon rework the Roses' "Fools Gold" into even more psychedelic realms. Only the displaced R. Kelly tune feels strained in its new environment. —*Michael Gallucci*

**On-U Sound Box** / Jun. 1, 1999 / Cleopatra ♦♦♦

While the music on Cleopatra's *On-U Sound Box* is undoubtedly innovative and excitingly experimental, listeners expecting a definitive overview of the label's history will be disappointed—while there's plenty from Creation Rebel, Singers & Players, Voice of Authority, the New Age Steppers, and Playgroup, African Head Charge and Dub Syndicate—two collectives responsible for a great deal of the label's finest output—are nowhere to be seen. Moreover, the first disc is a straight-up repackaging of a previous various-artists collection titled *Dub Xperience: Dread Operators*, which is still in print. What could have been an essential package instead ends up frustrating due to the careless, slapdash compiling; overall, it's a missed opportunity in spite of its low price. —*Steve Huey*

**One A.D.** / 1994 / Waveform ♦♦♦♦

This collection of ambient dub from the stellar label Beyond includes tracks from Higher Intelligence Agency, A Positive Life, Pentatonik, Banco de Gaia, and Original Rockers. —*John Bush*

**101 + 303 + 808: Now Form a Band** / 1995 / Sabrettes ♦♦♦

Five new bands appear on this Sabrettes compilation, and their brand of techno is raw, hardcore and uncomplicated. —*Keith Farley*

**One World Electronica: Electronica's Best** / Nov. 4, 1997 / K-Tel ♦♦♦

As a dance compilation licensed by the discount label K-Tel, *One World Electronica* could be much worse. It includes solid tracks from Fluke ("Atom Bomb") and Future Sound of London ("My Kingdom"), as well as club hits like Way Out West's "The Gift" and Olive's "You're Not Alone." The balance is made up of pleasant but not quite good tracks by Cirrus, Juno Reactor, Frankie Bones, and Uberzone, among others. —*John Bush*

**Only for the Headstrong, Vol. 1: The Ultimate Rave Compilation** / 1992 / ffrr ♦♦♦

The first volume of *Only for the Headstrong* is an excellent collection of early rave and techno with tracks by Prodigy, Utah Saints, Orbital (a rare "Chime" remix by Ray Keith) and DJ Seduction. The highlight for collectors comes with "Roobarb & Custard," the Top Ten toytown rave hit featuring Mark Pritchard before he gained fame with Global Communication. —*Keith Farley*

**Only for the Headstrong, Vol. 2** / 1992 / ffrr ♦♦♦

FFRR's second techno/rave compilation is a little more consistent than the first, and includes an edited version of Utah Saints' "Something Good." Unfortunately, that consistency is on a lower level than much of the first compilation (though this has far better cover art), and not quite as much stands out—Egyptian Empire's "The Horn Track" is about the only memorable number aside from "Something Good." Played loud enough, it'll still help you rave through the night. —*Steven McDonald*

**Open Air Herzberg** / Nov. 10, 1998 / EFA ♦♦♦
*Open Air Herzberg* is a collection of mostly uncollected Kraut- and space-rock, from Faust, Gong, Guru Guru, Hawkwind, and Man. Collectors will be most interested in the album. —*John Bush*

**Original Chillout Album** / Feb. 16, 1999 / Xtreme Entertainment ♦♦♦
A nice compilation of laidback house and soul, *Original Chillout Album* includes tracks by St. Germain, Dubtribe, Sueño Latino, Warp 69, Finitribe, and Sub Sub. —*John Bush*

**Origins of Sound: The Electro Bass Sound of Detroit** / 1995 / Submerge ♦♦♦
This compilation from Detroit artists explores new innovations in the '80s electro phenomenon. The album includes tracks from Drexciya, AUX 88, Mad Mike, and Gigi Galaxy. —*Keith Farley*

**The Other World** / Mar. 24, 1998 / Hypnos ♦♦♦
Producers from the experimental/noise community appear on this compilation from the Hypnos label. Highlights come from Vidna Obmana, A Produce, Jeff Greinke, Viridian Sun, and Jeff Pearce. —*John Bush*

**Out of Perspective: Sampler** / Mar. 23, 1999 / Soup-Disk ♦♦♦♦
It was only a matter of time before the experimental, techno tsunami would wash up on the shores of Japan, and this fine budget-priced compilation from the obscure Tokyo-based Soup label (distributed in the US by Dutch East India) shows that artists on the Pacific rim have been mastering the same techniques as their American and British counterparts. The general flavor here is acid jazz: post-bop instrumental samples looped and tweaked, sometimes sauteed with funky breakbeats and sometimes stretched and bent into ambient soundscapes. Taichi's "The Ultimate Preference" is based on a two-note string bass sample, over which are layered an electric piano riff and a jumpy drum'n'bass breakbeat loop. Then there's the slow and funky "Hoshizukiyo" by Nagi, which features a super-compressed drumbeat, chirping synths, and jazzy piano chords. Montage's "Eternal Beatz" is a less ambiguous foray into straight drum'n'bass that features a nicely integrated trumpet part. There's nothing here that breaks any new ground, but it's very fine of its type. —*Rick Anderson*

**Pacific State** / Nov. 3, 1997 / Deviant ♦♦♦
The Asian episode of Deviant/Volume's *Trance Europe Express* series includes tracks from Ken Ishii, DJ Krush and even Haruomi Hosono (ex-Yellow Magic Orchestra) —*Keith Farley*

**Perfection: Perfecto Compilation** / Sep. 24, 1996 / Warner Brothers ♦♦♦♦
It doesn't include the cream of Perfecto's crop, but the album is a competent distillation of Paul Oakenfold's label, with "Loving You More" by BT, "Paint a Picture" by Man with No Name, and "Give Me Strength" by Jon of the Pleased Wimmin. Oakenfold's stamp is all over this compilation, both as a producer and artist (Grace's "Skin on Skin"). —*Keith Farley*

**Perfecto Remix Album** / 1995 / East West ♦♦♦♦
The *Perfecto Remix Album* is a brilliant collection of Paul Oakenfold's remixing talents, with reworkings of British dance/pop paragons like U2, New Order, Simply Red, Massive Attack, M People, the Stone Roses, and the Shamen, as well as eclectics like Gary Clail, Neneh Cherry, even Snoop Doggy Dogg. The album is the best display of Oakenfold's impeccable production work, quite important to the direction of mainstream dance during the '90s. —*Keith Farley*

**Pioneers of Electronic Music** / 1996 / CRI ♦♦♦♦
The Columbia-Princeton sound from 1952 to 1971—compositions by Ussachevsky, Otto Luening (b. 1900), Pril Smiley, Bulent Arel, Mario Davidovsky, Alice Shields... recommended cuts: "Incantation" by Luening and Ussachevsky, "Stereo Electronic Music" by Arel. —*"Blue" Gene Tyranny*

**Planet Dog: Transmissions from Planet Dog** / May 23, 1995 / Mammoth ♦♦♦♦
This double-disc American introduction to the space-age ethno-crusties on Planet Dog Records features several tracks from Eat Static, Banco de Gaia, Timeshard and TransGlobal Underground. It's definitely the best introduction to the label for novices. —*Keith Farley*

**Planet Dub** / Mar. 12, 1996 / Planet Dog/Mammoth ♦♦♦
"Dub" is a term that has been so thoroughly co-opted by the larger club world that it hardly seems to have much to do with reggae anymore. But *Planet Dub*, a two-disc compilation of tracks by British dub artists from the Planet Dog stable, is deeply rooted in reggae tradition; band names like Rootsman, Alpha and Omega, the Disciples, and the Power Steppers hint at the deep, bass-heavy one-drop skank that characterizes every track. That groove does lead to a certain sameness, and only fanatics are likely to listen to both discs straight through. But those fanatics will be well rewarded; though it's hard to identify highlights on an album with a concept this consistent, Silicon Drum's "Dubkiss" and the earth-shaking bass of A.N.R.'s "Rockers Rising" are guaranteed to make your eyes roll back in your head. "David and Goliath," by Alpha and Omega, is straight roots reggae with a thunderous undertow. All of it is great, even if none of it is quite transcendent. Two hours of solid grooveciousness in dub—what's not to love? —*Rick Anderson*

**Planet Rave** / Apr. 11, 2000 / Triloka ♦♦♦
*Planet Rave, Vol. 1* isn't the first collection to combine world music with electronic club sounds, but it's among the stronger, more noteworthy collections of its kind. On this 2000 release, you'll hear a variety of world music combined with trance, jungle, trip-hop, techno, tribal, and other high-tech styles that have been heard at raves (or legal dance clubs with a rave-like DJ). Assembled by Shiva Baum, this CD is a collection of remixes—while the original versions of these songs were aimed at the artists' hardcore audiences in various countries, the remixes that Sunkist, Bobby Summerfield, Junior Vasquez and others provide make them a lot more rave-friendly. Without losing its rave-like ambiance, *Planet Rave, Vol. 1* visits India with Dissidenten's "A Love Supreme" (which is based on the John Coltrane classic) and Jai Uttal's "Malkouns," Pakistan with Badar Ali Khan's "Kalander" (a Qawwali number that gets a trance makeover), and Ireland with Emer Kenny's "Golden Brown." Some world music enthusiasts will prefer to stick with the original versions, but for those who have a taste for both world music and electronic club sounds, *Planet Rave, Vol. 1* is a CD to check out. —*Alex Henderson*

**Planet of the Breaks** / Feb. 9, 1999 / Roadrunner ♦♦♦♦
This may be a first—a techno concept album. The concept goes like this: a renegade DJ, and man of the future, is caught living in the present; his story is told through the music of a large array of DJs, musicians, producers and remix artists. Okay, so it's kind of a thin concept. But the music is absolutely slamming. DJ Scotty Marz, the brains behind this compilation, is a virtuoso turntablist, and his taste in collaborators is perfect. Fatboy Slim remixes FC Kahuna on the rock-hard "What Is Kahuna?," and there are equally fine remixes of Junkie XL's metallish "Saturday Teenage Kick" and of "Dum Dum Baby" by illbient drum'n'bass-heads Baby Fox. King Bee's "Back by Dope Demand" is typical hip-hop chest-thumping, but the Ultramagnetic MCs do a great job taking James Brown to the woodshed on "Watch Mc Now." The continuous mix is a little annoying, but not enough to matter. Great stuff. —*Rick Anderson*

**Plastic Compilation, Vol. 2** / Nov. 17, 1998 / Nettwerk ♦♦♦♦
The plastic arts is a phrase which usually refers to such tactile crafts as pottery. Through the intrinsic malleability of electronic music, electro-beat music has become one of the most transformable of the arts, transformable even after its creation. Such artful trickery that can stretch out a good three-minute dance beat into a very interesting piece twice the original length, or more, leads to such occasional assemblies of genius as this state of the remix collection, *Plastic*. Nettwerk also possesses such a fine stable of artists that they can compile a superior product. The prevalence of the female voice in cuts by the Crystal Method and Sara McLachlan (on the Delerium track and on her own, remixed by Brit drum & bass maestro, Roni Size) among others, keeps a strong, complementary melody in what is primarily rhythm music. King of such combinations, for which Nettwerk is well known for producing, is William Orbit's "Water from a Vine Life." The ancient Greeks spoke of a golden age when honey would drip from the leaves, and Orbit's idyllic production, sung by the highly talented Beth Orton, recalls a similar paradise and is presented here in a smooth Xylem Flow mix. While such as this is more often the face of pop than the future of pop, Nettwerk also takes a look back in the rap-allied, old school of Wildchild. Electronica also proves admirably able to incorporate elements of world music. Present on this compilation is Cornershop, representative of London's Asian-Indian flavored electronica of the French, pop artists Autour de Lucie. Other very strong tracks are from renowned space rockers, Spiritualized, remixed by the Chemical Brothers

and the compositionally minded BT teamed with another techno ambassador, Sasha. —*Thomas Schulte*

**Platinum Breaks** / Jul. 8, 1996 / ffrr ++++
The first compilation of Goldie's Metalheadz label is a roll call of jungle's most crucial artists: Photek, Source Direct, Dillinja, J. Majik, Alex Reece, Peshay, and Lemon D. Released around the same time as LTJ Bukem's *Logical Progression*, *Platinum Breakz* proves that Bukem has no business talking about intelligent jungle; though the styles of Metalheadz and Bukem's Looking Good/Good Looking imprints are quite similar—that is, somewhat house-influenced breakbeats—most of the contributions on *Logical Progression* have simple rhythms and are usually drowned out by extra, unneeded effects. The beats and percussion work on *Platinum Breakz* stand alone, besides spare synth lines and the occasional diva vocal. The rhythms constantly shift around, stopping and restarting. While *Logical Progression* begins to sound same, the artists on *Platinum Breakz* are easily differentiated. Highlights are difficult to define, though Source Direct, Photek, Dillinja, and J Majik's contributions are a very small step above the rest. Goldie's only contribution—recorded as the Rufige Kru—is okay but gets overshadowed. —*John Bush*

**Platinum Breakz, Vol. 2** / Dec. 1, 1997 / ffrr +++
The second compilation volume of tracks from Goldie's Metalheadz Records is a much darker affair than the first. While the original offered many tracks closer to house music than jungle, the second concentrates on the more industrial sounds of tech-step and neuro-funk, courtesy of Ed Rush's "The Raven," Optical's "To Shape the Future" and "The Warning" by Codename John (better known as Grooverider). Though Metalheadz stalwarts such as Peshay, Lemon D and Digital each contribute tracks, the focus on this second volume is on the future, and Metalheadz appears to have grown with the times quite well. It would have been quite difficult to have produced a compilation as essential as the first, but this one comes close. —*John Bush*

**Platinum on Black** / 1995 / ffrr +++
*Platinum on Black* is a slightly paranoid compilation, including house-pop acts like East 17, Gabrielle, Sagat and Cappella with more progressive tracks from One Dove, New Order, and Orbital. As such, it won't be completely satisfying for any dance fan. —*Keith Farley*

**Platinum on Black, Vol. 2** / Jan. 23, 1996 / ffrr ++++
*Platinum on Black, Vol. 2* is a better blend of progressive dancefloor tracks than its predecessor, with Green Velvet, Brand New Heavies, Everything But the Girl, Ultra Naté, Alex Party and Utah Saints, among others. —*Keith Farley*

**Platinum on Black, Vol. 3** / Nov. 26, 1996 / ffrr ++++
Leaning toward the new electronica—with contributions from C.J. Bolland, Salt Tank, Incognito, DJ Icey and Goldie (the Rabbit in the Moon remix of "Inner City Life")—the third volume in Ffrr's series continues to spotlight exclusive mixes of tracks by high-quality dance acts. —*Keith Farley*

**Platinum on Black: The Final Chapter** / Jan. 13, 1998 / Ffrr +++
The fourth collection in the series, *Platinum on Black—The Final Chapter* spotlights DJ Pete Tong, who takes the remix reins on tracks including Orbital's "The Sinner," the Brand New Heavies' "You Are the Universe," and Ultra Nate's "Free." —*Jason Ankeny*

**Platipus Records: Ultimate Dream Collection** / Jul. 29, 1996 / Critique +++
*Platipus Records: Ultimate Dream Collection* is a double disc set that features a selection of textured, laidback electronic dance music highlighted by Robert Miles' hit single, "Children." Although the rest of the set doesn't have anything else quite as memorable as "Children," there are ambient electronic tracks in a similar vein that are fairly intriguing, even though the album becomes a bit monotonous over the course of two discs. —*Stephen Thomas Erlewine*

**Platipus Records: Evolution of Trance** / Oct. 19, 1999 / Topaz ++++
This mix by Scott Stubbs pulls together many of the more influential trance anthems released by the UK label Platipus, most notably including some amazing productions by Simon Berry as Art of Trance. Platipus' style of trance doesn't rely so much on monster break-downs, snare-rolls, or hard acid riffs but rather forward-moving sensuality charged with plenty of spark and glossed over with an aura of beauty. Each of the ten songs maintains an upbeat tempo for the most part, with particular songs such as Quietman's "The Sleeper" reaching calm states of lull. At these moments, the percussion drops out of the track, leaving a tranquil blanket of hovering synth tones as sediment before eventually re-launching with the return of strong 4/4 percussive rhythms. Since each of the songs tend to follow similar structures with similar sounds and tendencies, the record maintains a sense of consistency that rarely gets broken. Simon Berry's contributions tend to stand out with their oozing bliss, and the concluding Salamander track also stands out with its many peaks and valleys along with its salient riff. Overall, this release could use a bit more variety even though the tracks are individually stellar. Anyone interested in some of the best trance anthems from the mid-'90s or anyone turned on by sensual epic trance without all the intensity will find this a satisfactory listen. —*Jason Birchmeier*

**Plug In + Turn On** / 1994 / Instinct ++++
Instinct's first volume in the *Plug In + Turn On* series is a collection of crisp ambient techno, including Prototype 909, the Drum Club, Human Mesh Dance, Cabaret Voltaire, Terre Thaemlitz, and Omicron, among others. There are few genuinely exciting tracks, though it's solid for fans of the style. —*Keith Farley*

**Plug In + Turn On X 2** / 1994 / Instinct +++
Perennial Instinct acts like the Drum Club, Cabaret Voltaire, Woob and Terre Thaemlitz make appearances on this second two-disc volume in the series of dark ambience. —*Keith Farley*

**Plug In + Turn On X 3** / May 14, 1996 / Instinct ++++
A bit more varied than other volumes in the Instinct series, volume three includes a side trip into drum'n'bass with tracks by Tek 9, Alex Reece, and DJ Unknown Face. —*Keith Farley*

**Plug In + Turn On X 4** / Jan. 14, 1997 / Instinct +++
Another beat-oriented volume in the *Plug In + Turn On* series features Beanfield, Fauna Flash, A Forest Mighty Black and Turntable Terranova, among others. DJ Krust and Kruder & Dorfmeister make appearances as remixers. —*Keith Farley*

**Pod Communication Presents: Atom Heart** / 1993 / Instinct ++++
*Pod Communication* is marketed as a various-artists compilation, though it consists of Atom Heart tracks plus collaborations with Tetsu Inoue (as Datacide), Pascal F.E.O.S. (as Ongaku) and Pete Namlook (as Millennium). Although each track has the low production values of much early rave and techno, the quality of later Atom Heart material shows through. —*Keith Farley*

**Points in Time, Vols. 1-3** / Good Looking +++
A quasi-greatest hits compilation from Good Looking, *Points in Time* includes spotlight LTJ Bukem tracks like "Atlantis," "19.5" and "Enchanted" as well as selections by PFM ("The Western"), Blame ("Overhead Projections"), Source Direct ("Secret Liaisons"), Peshay ("The Piano Tune"), and Intense ("Careless Minds"). —*John Bush*

**Points in Time: Good Looking Retrospective, Vol. 4** / Feb. 8, 2000 / Kinetic ++++
*Points in Time, Vol. 4* carries on the tradition of the preceding three volumes, chronicling many of the best tracks from Good Looking's deep drum'n'bass catalog from the mid- to late '90s. Though there are nine different artists featured on the compilation, most of the songs have a similar feel once they get going: up-tempo breakbeats, smooth rolling basslines, plenty of subtle melodies, and the miscellaneous forms of tranquil ambience so often associated with the label. Some songs such as Invisible Man's "The Tone Tune" drift toward the darker, more banging side of drum'n'bass, but the exclusion of rude, mutant basslines in favor of ghostly synths keep it within the boundaries of Good Looking's signature sound. Other songs such as Axis' "High Point" keep their flow much more mellow, focusing primarily on synth tones until over a minute into the track when the first breakbeat comes out of nowhere. The fact that these songs aren't mixed together by a DJ actually compliments them, allowing the listener to revel in the holistic experience of every song rather than succumb to the DJ's decision about how much and which part of a given track to spin. Along with the other volumes of this series, *Points in Time, Vol. 4* functions as a perfect compliment to Good Looking's excellent DJ-mix series, *Logical Progression*, which also features many of the label's best moments. —*Jason Birchmeier*

**Points in Time: Good Looking Retrospective, Vol. 5** / Feb. 8, 2000 / Kinetic ++++
Along with *Points in Time, Vol. 4* and *Points in Time, Vol. 6*, the fifth volume

was released in early 2000, a year after the simultaneous release of the first three volumes. The unedited inclusion of the oft-spun LTJ Bukem anthem, "Music," makes this a notable volume in the series, especially for anyone not yet tired of hearing this oft-spun, undeniable classic. Besides "Music," *Points in Time, Vol. 5* looks to many lesser-known artists on Good Looking's roster, such as Artemis and Blu Mar Ten, rather than compiling yet more tracks by the label's big name artists. —*Jason Birchmeier*

**Points in Time: Good Looking Retrospective, Vol. 6** / Feb. 8, 2000 / Kinetic ♦♦♦♦
One really can't go wrong with any of the volumes in the *Points in Time* series as each and every volume seems to include nothing but amazing samples of the label's contemplative drum'n'bass. *Points in Time, Vol. 6* is no different, featuring plenty of awe-inspiring moments of emotionally charged lulls in addition to the energetic breakbeat foundation that drives the majority of this music. As with every volume in this series, this particular record features a classic LTJ Bukem song ("Horizons") and also some other songs that have become some of the more popular drum'n'bass songs of the late '90s, the most notable being PHD and Conrad's "Progression Session." Each song on this record hovers near the ten-minute mark, taking plenty of time to carefully develop a mood before busting into its peak intensity and finally drifting in and out of multiple lulls. —*Jason Birchmeier*

**Pop Fiction, New Crime Jazz** / Oct. 22, 1996 / Quango ♦♦♦♦
Another bright Quango compilation, this one spotlighting new-electronica artists influenced by *noir* and film music. Portishead's "Theme from To Kill a Dead Man" appears alongside tracks from Patrick Pulsinger, Barry Adamson, Alex Reece, William Orbit's Strange Cargo, and Folk Implosion. —*Keith Farley*

**Pop Goes Dance** / Feb. 23, 1999 / Priority ♦♦♦
An interesting place to find mainstream pop artists meeting mainstream dance remixers, *Pop Goes Dance* includes David Morales reworking Spice Girls, Klubbheads reworking Vanessa Mae, Tin Tin Out reworking the Sundays, Vincent Da Moor reworking Dixie's Gang, and Stretch & Vern reworking Robbie Williams. —*John Bush*

**Porn Beats: Electronica Exotica** / Aug. 11, 1997 / Dust II Dust ♦♦
The theme should be obvious from the title, as *Porn Beats* deals with mostly obscene and sex-obsessed house tracks, from Shrink 2 Fit, Snappy Sid, Danmass and others. —*Keith Farley*

**Position Chrome** / Nov. 4, 1997 / Chrome ♦♦♦
Aggressive hardcore drum'n'bass from Germany is the stuff of the *Position Chrome* compilation, featuring tracks by Goner, Panacea, Problem Child, and Heinrich at Hart. Though the latter is featured on half of the album, the two Panacea tracks are the highlights. —*Steve Huey*

**Position Chrome** / 1997 / Position Chrome ♦♦♦
Aggressive hardcore drum'n'bass from Germany is the stuff of the *Position Chrome* compilation, featuring tracks by Goner, Panacea, Problem Child, and Heinrich at Hart. Though the latter is featured on half of the album, the two Panacea tracks are the highlights. —*Steve Huey*

**Position Chrome Retrospective** / May 11, 1999 / EFA ♦♦♦♦
Mixed by and featuring five previously vinyl-only tracks from Panacea himself, *Position Chrome Retrospective* also includes more hardcore drum'n'bass from Disorder, Current Value and Problem Child. —*John Bush*

**Positiva Ambient Collection** / 1992 / Positiva ♦♦♦♦
A nearly flawless collection of early-'90s ambient techno, *Positiva Ambient Collection* includes tracks from Black Dog, Aphex Twin, Orb, the Irresistible Force, Beaumont Hannant, Orbital, and even original technocrat Derrick May ("Kao-Tic Harmony" as Rhythim Is Rhythim). —*John Bush*

**Prelude Greatest Hits, Vol. 1** / Aug. 1, 1989 / Unidisc ♦♦♦♦
The half-a-dozen strong *Prelude Greatest Hits* series gets off to a strong start with this volume, probably the most essential of all. Each of the ten tracks is a classic, including highlights like "Walk on By" and "Keep On" by 'D' Train, "In the Bush" by Musique, "I'm Caught Up (In a One Night Love Affair)" by Inner Life, and "Beat the Street" by Sharon Redd. —*Keith Farley*

**Prelude Greatest Hits, Vol. 2** / Feb. 28, 1996 / Unidisc ♦♦♦♦
The second in the *Prelude Greatest Hits* series includes several seminal dance tracks like "Keep on Jumpin'" by Musique, "Searching to Find the One" by Unlimited Touch, and "A-Freak-A" by Lemon. —*Keith Farley*

**Prelude Greatest Hits, Vol. 3** / Feb. 28, 1996 / Unidisc ♦♦♦♦
The third in the *Prelude Greatest Hits* series includes several seminal dance tracks like "D Train Dub" and "Tryin' to Get Over" by 'D' Train, "Hot Summer Night" by Vicki Sue Robinson, "Somehow Someway" by Visual, and "Check Out the Groove" by Bobby Thurston. —*Keith Farley*

**Prelude Mastermixes, Vol. 1** / Aug. 1, 1989 / Unidisc ♦♦♦♦
This classic Prelude mastermix includes tracks by France Joli ("Gonna Get Over You"), "D" Train ("You're the One for Me"), Sharon Redd ("Can You Handle It"), and Empress ("Dyin' to Be Dancin'"), among others. —*Keith Farley*

**Prelude Mastermixes, Vol. 2** / Feb. 28, 1996 / Unidisc ♦♦♦
A second edition of classic Prelude mastermixes includes tracks by "D" Train, Indeep, Visual, Wuf Ticket, Musique, and Sharon Redd. —*Keith Farley*

**Pride '95** / 1995 / Strictly Rhythm ♦♦♦
*Pride '95* is a Strictly Rhythm fundraiser for 1995's Lesbian & Gay Pride Week, including contributions from Barbara Tucker, Androgeny, Louie Vega & Erick Morillo, Winter Darling, and Rageous, among others. —*Keith Farley*

**Privileged Frames for Reference** / 1997 / V/Vm ♦♦♦♦
This vinyl-only limited 12" compilation from the increasingly interesting V/Vm (Volume/Versus Mass) label is in a similar vein to the recent compiled efforts of Skam/Musik Aus Strom collaborative side-label Mask, collecting together a number of artists working in the lower-fidelity registers of electronica experimentalism. The most recognizable name here is Skam's own Jega (who share a track with Datathief), but excellent contributions also appear from Sherpa, Mild Man Jan, Frequency Band, and Objective. Ranging from dark, beatless drones to pummeling machine breaks and foreboding atmospheres, *Reference* is one of the best (and at 13 tracks one of the most concentrated) transmissions from the ever-fertile UK electronica underground. —*Sean Cooper*

**Probe Mission USA** / Aug. 10, 1993 / NovaMute ♦♦♦♦
The compilation concerning Richie Hawtin's Probe Records features tracks by Mark Gage, Jochem Paap, and Dan Bell. The big winner is Hawtin himself, though, with a total of six tracks (most of which never appeared elsewhere on CD). —*Keith Farley*

**Process** / 1998 / Caipirinha Productions ♦♦♦♦
An interesting development in the concept-compilation trend, *Process* includes tracks from DJ Cam, Si Begg, Surgeon, Air Liquide's Khan, Freddie Fresh, and Nonplace Urban Field, as well as a booklet containing essays by each artist about the production of his respective track. The music easily holds up on its own, despite the concept, and *Process* can be enjoyed by those wishing to listen as well as think. —*John Bush*

**Profan** / 1997 / Profan ♦♦♦♦
This compilation covers Mike Ink's Profan Records, the home of Germany's best obsessively minimal grooves and static tracks. Though Ink's contributions (from his projects Gas and Love Inc.) are the label's best, effective statements also come from M:I:5, Pentax, Mint, Grungerman and Sweet Reinhard. —*John Bush*

**Projekt 100: The Early Years 1985-1995** / Jun. 20, 2000 / Projekt ♦♦♦♦
Sam Rosenthal founded the innovating darkwave/industrial/goth rock label Projekt in 1985. Reaching the milestone of its 100th release comes the 13-track collection *Projekt 100: Early Years 1985-1995*, including previously unavailable tracks from Projekt's first two acts, Lycia and Black Tape for a Blue Girl. There are also stunning unreleased mixes from Attrition, Australia's Eden, and Lovesliescrushing, as well as a rare mix from the space rock duo Love Spirals Downwards. —*MacKenzie Wilson*

**Prolekulture** / May 5, 1997 / Prolekult ♦♦♦
In 1997, one of the most consistent British trance labels finally released a retrospective history of its last four years, with contributions from Sourmash, Watchman, Razor Edge, Baby Doc & the Dentist, Trope and Neurodancer, among others. —*Keith Farley*

**Proto-Ambient Music from Hearts of Space** / 1994 / Hearts of Space ♦♦♦
This collection of high-tech cyber-trance-house-inspired ambient music rejects traditional song form in favor of an open soundscape blueprint. Artists such as Constance Demby, Al Gromer Khan, Suspended Memories, and Steve Roach are just some of the pioneers of contemporary ambient music represented here. Their music is tranquil and illuminating, but at times can also

be turbulent and complex. Also present is a sense of humanity that is absent from much of today's ambient scene and a sense of warmth that is sometimes difficult to establish in electronic music. Transporting at varying speeds with organic nuances, listeners can immerse themselves in this translucent trip. —*MusD*

**Psychedelic Goa Test** / May 5, 1997 / Cleopatra ♦♦
Another collection of push-button trance marketed as pure dance by the industrial label Cleopatra, *Psychedelic Goa Test* includes tracks by Evaporator, Terpsichore, Locomotiva, and Bypass Unit. —*Keith Farley*

**Psychefunkajazzadelic, 2nd Edition** / 1995 / Sony ♦♦♦
A haphazard collection of acid jazz and hip-hop from artists like Gil Scott Heron, Digable Planets, Groove Collective, Gang Starr, and De La Soul, *Psychefunkajazzadelic, Vol. 2* has some solid tracks but it doesn't make for a cohesive album. —*Stephen Thomas Erlewine*

**Psychotrance 2000** / Sep. 21, 1999 / Moonshine Music ♦♦♦
Following in the footsteps of renowned DJs such as Darren Emerson, a then-unknown Texan DJ named D:Fuse came out of nowhere to turn in a blood-pumping installment to Moonshine's popular *Psychotrance* series. The cover's note that this album consists of "trance anthems" isn't standard marketing hyperbole—by the second track, D:Fuse has all engines firing as he moves into pretty damn intense territory with little to no buildup. Driven by searing synth riffs liable to pierce one's eardrum and enough dramatic buildups to crossmarket this album as an aerobics workout, the album's raging energy level continues running on high-octane from the quick lift-off through the even more fatiguing middle of the set until eventually reaching an anti-climatic conclusion. This somewhat disappointing final track doesn't necessarily result from weak tracks, considering the cataclysmic proceeding moments of note: the Mt. Everest-like peaks and bottom of the Pacific-like valleys of superstar trance remixer Matt Darey's hot-rodded version of Blockster's "Grooveline," the ridiculous insanity of Deepsky's roaring "Phuture 2000" remix, or the album's penultimate moment of sweat-inspiring ecstasy, Paul Van Dyk's "Moonlighting (Nightclub Remix)" with its sexy feminine salaciousness. After these three songs and the many others attempting to incite flash floods of adrenaline and serotonin levels in the listener's overstimulated mind, what honestly can D:Fuse spin to take the music to another level? Not much without heading into the taboo realm of hardcore/gabber. Of course, by this time any sober person will be plenty spent and ready for some calm silence. Yet for as physically heightening as this album is, this attribute ends up being a serious flaw; one can't complain about the mixing or the lack of strong songs, but one could make an argument about the relentless barrage of anthems. Sometimes a 30 second lull isn't enough, and most often listeners want a nice steady build that will result in an orgasmic climax rather than reaching numbing levels of over-stimulation after only a few tracks. —*Jason Birchmeier*

**Psychotrance 2001** / Jun. 13, 2000 / Moonshine Music ♦♦♦♦
D:Fuse's second release in Moonshine's *Psychotrance* series finds the Texas DJ moving away from the anthemic trance of *Psychotrance 2000* toward a darker style of deep progressive house. The monstrous buildups and breakdowns have been replaced by a constant driving tempo with plenty of atmospheric aura and pumping rhythms. There are a few moments such as during LSG's "I'm Not Existing (O. Lieb Main Mix)" and Highland's "Forsaken (Part 2)" when big synth riffs come into play, reminding listeners that this is indeed trance music even if D:Fuse has moved away from many of the genre's more obvious characteristics. The best moments on the mix come during the final few tracks when the music becomes increasingly melodic with beautiful synths and some complimenting elegant female vocals. Besides the smooth finale where D:Fuse opts to conclude the album with feelings of gentle aural beauty rather than steamy intensity, the album maintains a nice feel throughout, never hitting an obvious lull or an overdone peak. —*Jason Birchmeier*

**Psychotrance, Vol. 3** / Jan. 23, 1996 / MO ♦♦♦♦
Bush Records' Eric Powell mixes this third installment in Moonshine's *Psychotrance* series. The trance/house set includes tracks from Green Velvet, Luke Slater, Mike Ink, J Daniel, Cajmere, the Caproject, Mark N-R-G, and two Hardfloor remixes. —*Keith Farley*

**Pure Abstrakt** / Oct. 15, 1996 / Shadow ♦♦♦♦
Shadow Records' collection of leftfield and excessively blunted trip-hop includes tracks by DJ Cam, Sharpshooters, Shantel and Diferenz, among others. —*Keith Farley*

**Pure Groove** / Nov. 1998 / Crimson ♦♦♦♦
A good collection of hip-hop, acid jazz and groove music from the late '80s and early '90s, *Pure Groove* includes tracks from Brand New Heavies, Incognito, Definition of Sound, Us3, Jhelisa, D-Influence, A Tribe Called Quest, DJ Jazzy Jeff & the Fresh Prince, Guru, Groove Collective, and many others. —*John Bush*

**Quark Records: B.O. New York's Underground Scene, Vol. 1** / Jun. 1, 1999 / Pacific Time ♦♦
A collection of classic New York underground house, from Quark Records, one of the genre's pioneering labels. —*Heather Phares*

**RIP Presents the Real Sound of the Underground** / 1998 / RIP ♦♦♦♦
A two-disc mix set which compiles many crucial tracks and outside production jobs by one of the best teams in speed garage, *Real Sound of the Underground* includes their biggest hit, Double 99's "RIP Groove," as well as remix/productions for Roy Davis, Jr., Robert Miles, Ultra Naté, and Mighty Dub Katz. Other top tracks by non-RIP producers include the Dreem Teem remix of Amira's "My Desire" and MJ Cole's "Flavour Fever." —*John Bush*

**RO 3003** / Feb. 16, 1999 / EFA ♦♦♦♦
*Ro 3003* compiles a selection of tracks from German club and electronica acts, with an emphasis on the pop side of the scale. Mouse on Mars is the biggest name here; a DJ Crack remix of their "Saturday Night Worldcup Fieber" and their own take on Schlammpeitziger's "Mango und Papaya auf Tobago" are highlights. Assembled by the DJ duo Le Hammond Inferno, the compilation also features contributions from Whirlpool Productions, the Bjorn Sund Trio, and others. —*Steve Huey*

**Radikal Techno, Vol. 4: The New Trance Generation** / Jul. 11, 2000 / Radikal ♦♦
Techno/electronica stands in the midst of the mainstream music revolution of teen pop stars. This various artists compilation, *Radikal Techno, Vol. 4*, embraces the mass hysteria of club music. This 11-track collection showcases several cuts that reached Top 15 chart positions on national pop charts all over Europe. Artists featured on this release include ATB, DJ Taylor, SM Trax, DJ Jean, Zombie Nation, The Cherry Project, Scooter, and more. —*MacKenzie Wilson*

**Random, Vol. 1: Gary Numan Tribute** / Jun. 11, 1997 / Beggars Banquet ♦♦♦
A two-CD non-tribute album wherein a variety of artists tackle the songs of Gary Numan. The results are highly mixed and the outcome dubious—a few of the performers stick too closely to the originals (Deadsy's "Replicas," Matt Sharp & Damon Albarn's "We Have a Technical"), while others vanish over the rainbow with the songs—Underdog turn in an absolutely awful "Films," while the Orb's "Jo the Waiter" seems to have only the title in common with the original song. On the other hand, An Pierle provides an astonishing rendition of "Are 'Friends' Electric" with nothing more than piano and voice, while Jimi Tenor manages some interesting effects on "Down in the Park" and Jesus Jones do credit to the crunchy side of "We Are So Fragile." Avoiding the dreaded word "tribute" does nothing to prevent *Random* from being a Curate's Egg—"some parts were very good"—while the sheer size of the album tosses up several more good cuts than usual (along with, of course, an equal number of mediocre entries). —*Steven McDonald*

**Random, Vol. 2: Gary Numan Tribute** / Mar. 10, 1998 / Beggars Banquet ♦♦♦
With many major alternative artists of the late '90s praising the work of Gary Numan (Marilyn Manson, Trent Reznor, etc.), it would make sense for a Numan tribute album to surface. *Random, Vol. 2: Gary Numan Tribute* is the closest to a tribute album as you can get without it actually being one. Eleven dance/techno/house remixers deconstruct and rework a number of classic Numan numbers, updating them with '90s sounds, samples, and beats. You'll find radically different remixes of "Are 'Friends' Electric?" (by Liberator DJ's), "I Die, You Die" (Greenhaus), "Metal" (Robert Armani), and two versions of Numan's global hit "Cars" (the first by Mike Dearborn, the second by Dave Clarke). Although some Numan purists have complained that these remixes have lost the original's feel and approach, and there is some truth to this, *Random, Vol. 2* serves as an introduction to the genius of Gary Numan for club fans of the '90s, who wouldn't have discovered these tunes otherwise. —*Greg Prato*

**Rare Preludes, Vol. 1** / Feb. 3, 1994 / Unidisc ♦♦♦
The first volume in the *Rare Preludes* series includes contributions from Unique, Black Gold, Visual, Elektrik Funk and Visual. —*Keith Farley*

**Rare Preludes, Vol. 2** / Mar. 4, 1994 / Unidisc ♦♦♦
The second volume in the *Rare Preludes* series includes contributions from "D" Train, U.N., Rosko Recites, Center Stage, Sticky Fingers, and Kumano. —*Keith Farley*

**Rare Preludes, Vol. 3** / Mar. 4, 1994 / Unidisc ♦♦♦
The third volume in the *Rare Preludes* series includes contributions from Daybreak, Next Movement, Gerald Mallory, Dianne Marie, and Wuf Ticket. —*Keith Farley*

**Rare Preludes, Vol. 4** / Mar. 4, 1994 / Unidisc ♦♦♦
The fourth volume in the *Rare Preludes* series includes contributions from Conquest, "D" Train, Unique, Jazzie Ladies, Sine, and Passion. —*Keith Farley*

**Rare Preludes, Vol. 5** / Mar. 4, 1994 / Unidisc ♦♦♦
The fifth volume in the *Rare Preludes* series includes contributions from Strikers, Nanette, Enchantment, Paulette, CD III, and Wardell Piper. —*Keith Farley*

**Rauschen, Vol. 10** / 1995 / Force Inc ♦♦♦♦
Force's double-disc compilation of dark techno (including one disc of new tracks and one of classics) features Cristian Vogel, Alec Empire, Ian Pooley, and Mike Ink. —*Keith Farley*

**Rauschen, Vol. 12** / Oct. 28, 1996 / Force Inc ♦♦♦
A double-disc compilation of Force Inc. hits, *Rauschen, Vol. 12* includes tracks by label acts like Ian Pooley, Mike Ink, Si Begg, 4E, Techno Animal and Bizz OD, plus several Alec Empire productions (as ECP, Wipe Out, the Jaguar, and the King of the Street). —*Keith Farley*

**Rauschen, Vol. 13** / Jun. 23, 1998 / Force Inc ♦♦♦
All of the Force Inc label's artists are represented on the *Rauschen 13* compilation, which focuses more on straightforward, club-friendly technoid material than other volumes in the series. Highlights include Ian Pooley's Detroit-styled two-part opus "Loopduell," Porter Ricks' dense "Redundance II," and 4E's hip-hop flavored "U-Turn." —*Jason Ankeny*

**Rauschen, Vol. 14** / Mar. 23, 1999 / EFA ♦♦♦
The early 1999 update of Force Inc's *Rauschen* series included tracks from Null, DJ Rush, Ian Pooley, Thomas Heckmann, Age, S.R.I., Filter, and Strass, among others. —*John Bush*

**Rave 'Til Dawn** / 1992 / Capitol ♦♦♦♦
The compilation which introduced American audiences to the new British dance music, *Rave 'Til Dawn* is a good collection of only the most brash, cartoonish tracks in the scene. Included is the sports anthem "Jump" by the Movement, "O Fortuna" by Apotheosis, "Injected with a Poison" by Jade 4 U & Praga Khan, and "Get Ready for This" by 2 Unlimited, among others. —*Keith Farley*

**Rave Alert** / 1993 / Telstar ♦♦♦♦
One of the best British rave compilations, *Rave Alert* includes tracks from Altern-8, Smart-e's, Praga Khan, 2 Unlimited, Snap, the Shamen, Johnny L, KWS, and Rachel Wallace, among others. —*Keith Farley*

**Rave Anthems** / Dino ♦♦
*Rave Anthems* collects early-'90s dance music from artists like Bizarre Inc., Dance Conspiracy, Utah Saints, the KLF, and Bassheads. Prodigy contributes two tracks: & "Everybody in the Place" and "Playing With Knives." Moby's "Go," Altern8's "Activ8," DJ Carl Cox's "I Want You," 2 Unlimited's "Get Ready for This," and the Shamen's "Ebenezer Goode" are some of the other highlights from this enjoyable but somewhat random club compilation. —*Heather Phares*

**Rave Generation [Hypnotic]** / Oct. 5, 1999 / Hypnotic ♦♦
Cleopatra/Hypnotic's *Rave Generation* is a three-disc box set that repackages three of the labels rave albums, including an album by Holophonia, at a bargain price. None of these three albums are exceptional—they're all pretty much run-of-the-mill rave—but if you're considering purchasing any of them, consider this set, since you essentially get three albums for the price of one. —*Stephen Thomas Erlewine*

**Rave New World** / Jun. 15, 1993 / Rhino ♦♦
*Rave New World* is a collection of second- or third-grade rave tracks by unknowns like Nemo, DJ God and Raving Lunatics. Taylor Deupree, later of SETI and Prototype 909, appears on selections by Microbar and Toxic Beatbox. —*Keith Farley*

**Ravers Ecstasy** / Aug. 17, 1999 / Cleopatra ♦♦
A three-disc box from the dance subsidiary of Cleopatra known as Hypnotic, *Ravers Extacy* is yet another confusing, misleading trip through what an American industrial-dance label's thoughts are on the state of European dance. The set includes three compilations—*Digital Extacy, Afterburner,* and *The Door of Perception*—which are also available separately. The first is allegedly a trance album, though the likes of Aerial Servant, LV-426 and Pissle-Whistle Party cast much doubt on Hypnotic's ability to chart the trance scene. The second, *Afterburner,* fares a little better. Subtitled "Musik from the European Gabber-Trance-Clubs," it includes tracks from Chaos Control ("Amokk"), Hemming Van ("Snotty"), and Forza ("Viva Brondby") that are accurately rendered productions, if not the most famous of the gabber scene. The final disc in the box, *The Door of Perception,* is a collection of tracks from five psychedelic trance producers (including R-Escape-R, Out o Phase, Liquid'z), barely negligible as dance-floor filler to say nothing of headphone listening. —*Keith Farley*

**React Techno Classics** / Jan. 21, 1997 / React America ♦♦♦
This React compilation doesn't quite live up to its title; it features only a few tracks of any worth, including "Pictures in Your Mind" by Blue Peter, the eponymous offering by Age of Love, and "Tip of the Iceberg" by GTO. —*Keith Farley*

**Readymade Records Tokyo: Remixes** / Feb. 9, 1999 / EFA ♦♦♦
Titled after the actual name of the Pizzicato Five's record label, *Readymade Records Tokyo: Remixes* finds the Five, Fantastic Plastic Machine, and 5th Garden (as of 1999, the only artists on the label) being remixed by a number of (mainly) EFA-affiliated artists. The album's quality varies with the talent of the remixers, but it may be worth picking up by dedicated Japanese pop fans. —*Steve Huey*

**Reanimator: Black Market Science** / Jan. 6, 1998 / Ion ♦♦♦
Compiled by Bill Laswell, who also appears here with Sacred System, *Reanimator: Black Market Science* gathers experimental dub tracks by the Mad Professor, HIM, Almamegretta, the Adrian Sherwood-produced DXT, Transonic, SIMM, Umoya, and Ben Wa. —*Steve Huey*

**The Rebirth of Cool, Vol. 1 [US]** / 1993 / 4th & Broadway ♦♦♦♦
Including Stereo MCs, MC Solaar, the Jazz Warriors, and Ronny Jordan, this compilation highlighted new soul and jazz grooves in black contemporary music in America and Britain. —*Keith Farley*

**Rebirth of Cool, Vol. 2 [US]** / 1994 / 4th & Broadway ♦♦♦♦
The second in the series of trip-hop and earthy jazz includes tracks by future stars like DJ Krush and Tricky, as well as acid jazz producers Mondo Grosso and Palmskin Productions. Among the many highlights are Ronny Jordan's interpretation of John Coltrane on "My Favorite Things" and an unreleased Island dub chestnut by Burning Spear. —*Keith Farley*

**Rebirth of Cool, Vol. 3 [US]** / Nov. 1995 / 4th & Broadway ♦♦♦♦
Great tracks from Bomb The Bass (a La Funk Mob remix with Justin Warfield), Coldcut, Leena Conquest and Portishead make this a superb collection of mid-'90s grooves, but not as superb as the UK import, which adds six more songs. —*Keith Farley*

**Rebirth of Cool, Vol. 4 [US]** / Oct. 29, 1996 / 4th & Broadway ♦♦♦♦
*Rebirth of Cool, Vol. 4* concentrates on worldbeat-tinged jungle, drum'n'bass, ambient, trip-hop and acid jazz experiments from the likes of Lamb, LTJ Bukem, Dave Angel, Alex Reece and Outside. Though the album has a couple of weak moments, *Rebirth of Cool, Vol. 4* has enough strong tracks and major artists to make it a fine way to catch up with mid-'90s electronic dance music. —*Stephen Thomas Erlewine*

**Rebirth of Cool, Vol. 7** / 1998 / Island ♦♦♦♦
Seven volumes on, *Rebirth of Cool* keeps diversifying and keeps on getting better. From the jazz spectrum come tracks by Roni Size, Ian O'Brien and Spacer (though both are justifiably varied); Latin makes a comeback with Kerri Chandler and Joe Clausell; and other tracks nod at hip-hop, house, soul and techno. Though many compilation series grow weaker with each passing volume, *Rebirth of Cool* shows no sign of a let-up. —*John Bush*

**Recycle or Die** / 1995 / Planet Earth ♦♦♦
Sven Vath's *Recycle or Die* subsidiary of Eye-Q Records focuses on dark am-

bient-trance. Though most of the artists here (notably Spicelab's Oliver Lieb) are known more for their straightahead trance output, most pull it off with flair. Expect for a few bland tracks, *Recycle or Die* is a solid compilation. *—Keith Farley*

**Reddlite Continuous Mix** / Apr. 25, 2000 / Warlock ♦♦♦♦
*Reddlite Continuous Mix* employs the skills of Anthony Acid and DJ Skribble, who present a continuous mix of underground club hits from Reddlite artists like Razor & Guido, Richie Santana, Rob Dale, and Mike Macaluso. Acid's own "Bump (Do a Bump Mix)," "Just Like That," and "Rock da Disko" provide structure to the mix, which includes Joe Buzz's "Ultimate High," Peter Bailey's "Special Love," A&S Project's "Outta My Head," and Razor & Guido's "Clap Your Hands" among its highlights. A kinetic collection of progressive trance, hard house, and other flavors of club music from one of the underground's purest dance labels. *—Heather Phares*

**Reinventing the 80's, Vol. 2** / Oct. 6, 1998 / Cleopatra ♦♦
Another of Cleopatra's innumerable attempts at spin-marketing a compilation of their own artists, *Reinventing the 80's, Vol. 2* includes decade classics like "Sweet Dreams," "A Question of Time," "Bizarre Love Triangle," "Relax" and "Computerworld" remade by unheard-of-artists (the biggest name here is Læther Strip). *—Keith Farley*

**Return of the DJ, Vol. 1** / Bomb Hip Hop ♦♦♦♦
Although vocal rap has become all but synonymous with hip-hop, effectively displacing DJs as the prime movers in determining the music's distinctive aesthetic, a new generation of hip-hop DJs are going it alone, approaching the turntable as an instrument in its own right. San Francisco promoter David Paul's brilliant *Return Of The DJ* compilation charts this continuing evolution, with sturdy, mind-bogglingly complex turntable orchestration from such names as Q-Bert, Mixmaster Mike, DJ Disk, the Beat Junkies, New York's X-Men, Z-Trip, and DJ Ghetto, among others. Fluid beats, vast, layered instrumental passages, and tons of deft scratching loosely cement the notion of a restless, DJ-based hip-hop avant-garde craving only one thing: innovation. *—Sean Cooper*

**Return of the DJ, Vol. 2** / Bomb Hip Hop ♦♦♦♦
The Bomb's second guided tour through the bedrooms of hip-hop's new experimental underground draws this time from an international pool of beat junkies, with tracks checking in from London, New York, Finland, Montreal, Norway, Detroit, and Paris, among others, with names both familiar and unknown—Roc Raider, DJ E.Q., Z-Trip, and Godfather, as well as Kid Koala, Tommy Tee, and Jimmie Jam. The follow-up to the Bomb's scorching debut double-LP, Return II features 16 tracks in all of consistently mindblowing (if not quite as innovative) instrumental turntable experiments. *—Sean Cooper*

**Return to the Source** / 1995 / Volume ♦♦♦
Return to the Source was one of the UK's pre-eminent goa-trance clubs; the record that bears its name is a two-disc set consisting of one ambient and one trance chakra journey. *—Jason Ankeny*

**Revenge of the Abstract Groove** / Jun. 13, 2000 / Instinct ♦♦♦♦
How abstract can it be and still be considered a groove, you ask? That's a good question, and it turns out that, fortunately, a groove doesn't have to be too awfully abstract to be considered just that. The music on this compilation falls more or less into the trip-hop category, though some tracks fit that description more comfortably than others. Mujaji's "Belgian Cappuccino" combines loping, mid-tempo funk with furious scratching; "Towards the Edge," by Super Pulse features shreds of laidback female vocals that waft like air born scraps of silk through a field of spiky computer beats and distant string samples; on "Specials" Illform lays the sampled voice of a waitress ("You wanna hear about our specials?") over a busy funky-drummer rhythm loop while a barroom piano tinkles tinily in the background. Then there's Yennah's dubwise "Pulsar," which draws equally from jazz and reggae traditions. Absolutely nothing here is uninteresting, and you can't say that about very many electronica albums. Recommended. *—Rick Anderson*

**Rewired Rhythms** / Jan. 20, 1998 / Shadow ♦♦♦
A collection of remixes by Shadow acts like DJ Cam, Marschmellows, Cujo and Shantel, *Rewired Rhythms* is successful since the beats are a bit more in focus than on previous works. Remixers include Megashira, Baby Fox, Kosma, and Witchman. *—Keith Farley*

**Riot Zone** / Nov. 3, 1997 / Digital Hardcore ♦♦♦
The extensive back catalog of Alec Empire's Digital Hardcore label is plumbed on *Riot Zone*, resulting in crucial tracks by Empire and flagship Atari Teenage Riot as well as EC8OR, Shizuo, Bomb 20, Hanin Elias, and Christoph de Babalon. All come from out-of-print singles and EPs, making it worthwhile for collectors as well as fans. *—John Bush*

**Rising High Techno Injection, Vol. 1** / 1992 / Instinct ♦♦♦
The first volume of early European techno from Rising High Records is a spotty affair, with more than half of the tracks coming from label-head Casper Pound (who later proved himself better behind an office desk than a mixing desk). The only other notable is Mixmaster Morris' Irresistible Force project, contributing the excellent "Space Is the Place." *—Keith Farley*

**Rising High Techno Injection, Vol. 2** / 1993 / Instinct ♦♦♦♦
The second volume in Rising High's series does much better than the first, adding crucial cuts from the Black Dog, Love Inc., Ongaku and the Irresistible Force. Even the tracks by early Rising High acts like Dominatrix UK, the Hypnotist and Rising High Collective are much better than on volume one. *—Keith Farley*

**Rising High Trance Injection** / 1993 / Instinct ♦♦♦
New-school downtempo trance from Balil (aka Black Dog), the Irresistible Force, Syzygy, Dreamfish, Cybertrax and New London School of Electronics are featured on *Rising High Trance Injection. —Keith Farley*

**Roots of Acid Jazz** / Feb. 11, 1997 / GRP ♦♦♦
*Roots of Acid Jazz* was compiled by people who have only a passing knowledge with acid jazz and believe that *any* old jazz record can be reworked into a jazz/hip-hop/dance fusion. Of course, that isn't true, as anyone trying to sample Dizzy Gillespie's "Swing Low, Sweet Cadillac" will be likely to tell you. Most of *Roots of Acid Jazz* is comprised of similar hard-bop which skirts at the edge of funky soul jazz. A lot of major artists are on the compilation, to be sure—including Stanley Turrentine, Sonny Rollins, Keith Jarrett, Quincy Jones, Coleman Hawkins, Yusef Lateef, Shirley Horn, and Pharoah Sanders—but very little of this music will appeal to its target audience of acid jazz, hip-hop and groove fans. *—Stephen Thomas Erlewine*

**Rough and Fast** / 1994 / Riot Beats ♦♦♦
With a title that pretty much says it all, *Rough and Fast* compiles tracks from the Force Inc.-connected Riot Beats Records. The tracks, from High Speed Poet, Sonic Subjunkies, Da Captains of Phuture, Biochip C.'s Biobreaks and two Alec Empire aliases (DJ Moonraker and P.J.P.), rarely deviate from the later hardcore sound. *—John Bush*

**RuPaul's Go-Go Box Classics** / Mar. 17, 1998 / Rhino ♦♦
*RuPaul's Go-Go Box Classics* is a collection of 18 disco, dance and urban tracks, many of which are little-known songs from superstars like the Pointer Sisters ("Goldmine"), Aretha Franklin ("Rock-A-Lott"), Paula Abdul ("Vibeology"), Diana Ross ("Lovin', Livin' & Givin'"), Natalie Cole ("Party Lights (Live)"), and Cameo ("Shake Your Pants"). All of the songs are picked by RuPaul, who had become some sort of mascot around Rhino by the time this was released—it feels like the label can't go three months without releasing a new RuPaul-related project. Nevertheless, *Go-Go Box Classics* is one of the better RuPaul records, since it has a lot of obscurities and rarities that make it an interesting listen. Not everything here is necessarily good, but at least it anthologizes songs that haven't appeared on collections before, and that alone makes it worth a listen by hardcore dance fans. *—Stephen Thomas Erlewine*

**SONAR '98** / 1998 / So Dens ♦♦♦
*SONAR '98* is an immense four-disc compilation featuring just about every major artist who performed at the renowned Barcelona music festival. The box is a who's who of experimental and hard techno, including Panasonic, Porter Ricks, Dr. Walker, Coldcut, Max Brennan, Jimi Tenor, Laurent Garnier, Les Rhythmes Digitales, Jeff Mills, Francois K, Surgeon, DJ Hell, Aux 88, Potuznik, and Frederic Galliano, among others. Though the tracks aren't live, most are rare or unreleased on CD, and this set compiles acres of worthwhile techno in one place. *—John Bush*

**Sally's Photographic Memory** / 1996 / Volume ♦♦♦♦
Compiled by Volume in memory of their photographer Sally Harding, who died in late 1995, *Sally's Photographic Memory* includes 20 tracks (and many exclusives) by many of the brightest and best electronic acts in Britain, among them Orbital, Meat Beat Manifesto, Reload, System 7, Slab, Spooky, Pressure of Speech, Secret Knowledge and Higher Intelligence Agency. One of the few Americans in evidence, Carl Craig, contributes an excellent remix of the Ultramarine track "Source." *—Keith Farley*

**Sampling the Future: An Introduction to Electronic Sound of America** / Nov. 4, 1997 / Sire ♦♦♦
*Sampling the Future* is a collection of American breakbeat electronica like Rabbit in the Moon, Simply Jeff, Tranquility Bass, Voyager, Josh Wink and the Hardkiss project Hawke. —*Keith Farley*

**Sampling the Future: Second Degree** / Oct. 13, 1998 / Thrive ♦♦♦♦
The second volume in the *Sampling Future* series includes dance classics like "Born Slippy" by Underworld, "Amp" by Fluke, and "Renegade Master" by Wildchild, plus others by Hawke, Freestylers, Lunatic Calm (remixed by Fatboy Slim), System 7, and even Jane's Addiction (a rare house remix of "So What!"). —*Keith Farley*

**Saturday Night House Music** / Aug. 24, 1999 / Cleopatra ♦
Almost two decades down the line, house music enjoys a wide latitude of producers and music that could actually be construed as house, from Larry Heard to Paul Oakenfold to Terrence Parker. On this three-disc box set, the Hypnotic subsidiary of Cleopatra Records (a.k.a. dance music's worst enemy) attempts to mislead buyers into thinking the label has cornered the market on house music. Of course, as with their similar attempts concerning trance, Kraut-rock and several other dance styles, the results are insulting to listeners, dangerous to those who want to know what house music is all about, and above all, downright ludicrous and musically appalling. The first disc presents disco covers by Cleopatra-related producers including Astralasia, Transmutator, cathexis, THC, Asda and Distant Voices. Besides the novelty value, there isn't much else to recommend it. The final two discs consist of a good 20 unheard-of producers making derivative house. One of the few redeeming qualities comes with "Sirens" [sic] by System 7, included with a rare remix by original housemaster Marshall Jefferson. Avoid. —*Keith Farley*

**Sci-Fi: Level 2.2** / Dec. 8, 1998 / Superstition ♦♦♦♦
*Sci-Fi: Level 2.2* includes 16 bracing tracks by many of the best techno producers in the world: Joel Mull, Christian Morgenstern, Funk D'Void, Luke Slater, Elektrochemie LK, Joey Beltram, Jay Denham, and others. —*John Bush*

**Science Fiction Jazz, Vol. 1** / 1996 / Omnisonus ♦♦♦♦
Despite the terribly weak title, this album hits many high notes with tracks by Nightmares on Wax, Plaid (the rare "Scoobs in Columbia"), LTJ Bukem, Lamb, the Gentle People and Cool Breeze (remixed by Kid Loops). —*John Bush*

**Science Fiction Jazz, Vol. 2** / Jul. 1, 1997 / Omnisonus ♦♦♦♦
The second volume in the series moves into darker territory, more influenced by drum'n'bass than the first. Acts like Omni Trio, PFM, Technical Itch, DJ Cam, Alex Reece and Nicolette easily prove that the first wasn't a fluke. —*Keith Farley*

**Science Fiction Jazz, Vol. 3** / 1998 / Omnisonus ♦♦♦♦
A third volume in the *Science Fiction Jazz* series keeps up the good work, with an admirable range of drum'n'bass producers, including Roni Size, Aquasky, Squarepusher, 4 Hero, DJ Die and Adam F. —*John Bush*

**Secret Life of Trance, Vol. 1** / 1994 / Planet Earth ♦♦♦
A mostly British and German collection of ambient-trance and Detroitish techno, *Secret Life of Trance* includes tracks from Black Dog (Balil's "Parasight"), Rising High Collective, Positive Science, Kibu and Influx. —*Keith Farley*

**Secret Life of Trance, Vol. 2** / Nov. 15, 1994 / Planet Earth ♦♦♦
More varied and solid than the first, volume two has Air Liquide, Union Jack, Cybertrax, Pete Namlook's Minimalistic Sour, Syzygy and Influx. —*Keith Farley*

**Septic Cuts: A Sabres of Paradise Compilation** / 1994 / Sabres of Paradise ♦♦♦
For *Septic Cuts,* Andrew Weatherall collected eight tracks of vinyl-only ephemera from his SoP label. It's a bit of a disappointment that the first two tracks, "Sugar Daddy" by Secret Knowledge and a David Holmes remix of "Smokebelch II" by Weatherall's Sabres of Paradise crew, are the best tracks on the collection. Despite okay selections from Conemelt and Psychic TV's Genesis P-Orridge as PT001, the collection is of interest only to Weatherall fans. —*John Bush*

**Serious Road Trip** / 1995 / MCA ♦♦♦
A bizarre three-disc benefit collection of mostly unreleased techno, *Serious Road Trip* includes tracks by Leftfield, the Orb, Banco de Gaia, Spooky, Secret Knowledge, the Aloof, the Dust Brothers, and Ege Bam Yasi. The third disc, only ten minutes long, includes a live Orbital track. —*Keith Farley*

**Shadow Masters: The Best of Shadow Trip Hop** / Jan. 26, 1999 / Shadow ♦♦♦
*Shadow Masters* includes ten tracks previously licensed to Shadow Records through album works by DJ Krush, DJ Cam, Cujo, Shantel, Diferenz, 9 Lazy 9 and others. —*John Bush*

**Shake the Nations** / Nov. 11, 1997 / Wordsound ♦♦♦
There's now an identifiable Brooklyn Sound—dark, heavy, slow, breakbeat-based—and although it would be all too easy to attribute its development to the work of the ubiquitous Bill Laswell, it would probably be more accurate to give credit to the small but influential WordSound label, one which has singlehandedly stripped illbience to its black, naked essence while simultaneously producing challenging hip-hop and some of the very few truly essential American drum & bass recordings. This two-disc set compiles one track from each of WordSound's first 22 releases, most in remixed form. For a bass fix, the adventurous beathead need look no further than Dr. Israel's stupendous dub & bass assault on The Seshambeh Project's "Freedom Street" or Dubadelic's very heavy "Rise of the Fall." Laswell himself contributes a nice remix of Scarab's "Fall of the Towers of Convention." There are a couple of low points, such as Prince Paul's needlessly nasty "J.O.B.," but the vast majority of this program is beatmongering of the highest order. Very highly recommended. —*Rick Anderson*

**Shapeshifter: A Jazzstep Injection** / Aug. 19, 1996 / S.O.U.R. USA ♦♦♦♦
Similar to Bukem-style fusion drum'n'bass but with a bit more power, this compilation of jazzstep anthems from SOUR includes tracks by T-Power, Elementz of Noise, Click'n'Cycle and N-Jay. —*Keith Farley*

**Sheen** / 1995 / Kk ♦♦♦
Kk's variety of electronic-based styles are displayed on this 1995 album, including label stalwarts Psychick Warriors and Exquisite Corpse, along with Plastic Noise Experiment, Test Department and DHI. —*Keith Farley*

**Shut Up & Dance, Vol. 1: Best of Freestyle** / Jun. 26, 1997 / Priority ♦♦♦
*Shut Up & Dance, Vol. 1: Best of Freestyle* is a 13-track collection of dance-pop and dance-club hits from the late '80s and early '90s. The selection of songs is pretty uneven, but there are enough good moments—such as Samantha Fox's "Naughty Girls (Need Love Too)," Stevie B's "Dreamin' of Love," Trinere's "I'll Be All You Ever Need," and Sa-Fire's "Boy I've Been Told" to make it entertaining. —*Stephen Thomas Erlewine*

**Shut Up & Dance, Vol. 2: Best of Freestyle** / Jun. 26, 1997 / Priority ♦♦♦
*Shut Up & Dance, Vol. 2: Best of Freestyle* is a 13-track collection of dance-pop and dance-club hits from the late '80s and early '90s. The selection of songs is pretty uneven, but there are enough good moments—such as Expose's "Exposed to Love," Stephanie's "Get Away," Two Without Hats' "On the Mic," Shana's "I Want You," Menage's "I Know U Want Me," Coro's "My Fallen Angel," and Freestyle's "Don't Stop the Rock"—to make it entertaining. —*Stephen Thomas Erlewine*

**Signs of Life** / Aug. 26, 1997 / Blue Room USA. ♦♦
One of Britain's premier labels for Goa trance collects its best on this 1997 release, with the Delta, Saafi Brothers, Sunkings, and a terrific Juno Reactor remix by Robert Leiner. —*Keith Farley*

**Silver World** / 1998 / Soup-Disk ♦♦♦♦
Japan's Soup-Disk Records empathizes with such paragons of the experimental community as Oval and Panasonic. The label's *Silver World* compilation features like-minded Japanese artists such as Akira Yamamichi, Nob Ohtake, Tashiya Tsunoda and Utah Kawasaki exploring sound structures similar to their Scandinavian equivalents. The resulting music is quite diverse, and usually successful. —*John Bush*

**Skampler** / 1997 / Silent ♦♦♦♦
Manchester's Skam label, set up in 1995 by Warp recording artists Autechre together with occasional collaborator Andy Maddocks, has quickly risen to acclaim as one of the most interesting and innovative UK experimental electronica labels. Although by the middle of '97 the label's catalog included only a half-dozen 12" releases, the popularity and scarcity (to say nothing of resale value) of EPs from Gescom, Freeform, Bola, Jega, and most recent signings Boards of Canada made the propriety of a label compilation pretty much a no-brainer. Though probably better served by a double CD, Skam's back cat-

alog is given a representative compiling via Skampler. The CD is uniformly excellent—bringing Skam's glowing fusion of electro, funk, ambient, and hip-hop to a wide audience for the first time—and is also notable for its inclusion of four previously unavailable tracks, along with a trio of cuts from Skam's ultra-limited, promo-only debut release, "Lego Feet." —*Sean Cooper*

**Soft & Easy** / Oct. 27, 1998 / Arcade ◆◆◆◆
This Arcade compilation is a good summation of the exotica and easy-listening side of electronic music, with tracks by Gentle People, Fantastic Plastic Machine, Smoke City, Laila France, Jean-Jacque Perrey, Combustible Edison, Spring and Crustation. —*John Bush*

**Soma 50** / Mar. 1997 / Soma ◆◆◆◆
In celebration of the 50th release on Scotland's Soma Records, the label released a compilation including ten tracks from the likes of Slam, Percy X, Russ Gabriel and Rejuvination. —*Keith Farley*

**Soma Quality Recordings, Vol. 2** / 1995 / Soma ◆◆◆◆
The Scottish Soma label released this second volume of new electronica, including tracks from Sharkimaxx (Felix Da Housecat), Funk D'Void, Ege Bam Yasi (remixed by G7), Percy X, Slam, Rejuvination, Envoy, Daft Punk, Skintrade, Mode 4 and Maas. —*Keith Farley*

**Sometimes: A Tribute to Erasure** / May 18, 1999 / Cleopatra ◆◆
The Cleopatra label's *Sometimes: A Tribute to Erasure* collects ten Erasure covers from a ragtag crew of no-name electro acts; while a few acquit themselves well, for the most part the groups fail to capture the bubbly effervescence of the original versions, ultimately making this another in a long line of ill-executed Cleopatra releases that provoke the question, "Why bother?" —*Steve Huey*

**Sonics Everywhere** / Jan. 27, 1998 / Invisible ◆◆◆
Possible Records is the label run by prolific artist Mick Harris (Scorn, Matera, Painkiller, Napalm Death, etc.). This is Possible's amazing sampler distributed by Invisible, and the roster is indicative of the breakbeat genre. Along with Ambush and Harris' own Scorn, seven groups are included on this two-CD set compiled from Possible Records' 12" single series. *Sonics Everywhere* sounds more like a collaboration than a label sampler—unexpected rhythms, combined with a keyboard wail or bass drone, become the fundamental elements for a compelling mix of wrecked funk and post-goth electronica. Dark, daring and danceable the result is a free-form disco for animated skeletons. If you can envision a mirrored ball in a dungeon, you are receptive enough to enjoy this collection. This is the first time this material is available domestically. —*Thomas Schulte*

**Sonig Comp.** / Jul. 11, 2000 / Import ◆◆◆
The first CD release for the previously vinyl-only label run by Mouse on Mars' Jan St. Werner and Andi Toma, *Sonig Comp.* balances experimental tracks by Cologne mainstays (F.X. Randomiz, Microstoria, Lithops, Mouse on Mars themselves) with a few obscure names (Vert, Wang Inc., C-Schulz, Scratch Pet Land). Though Mouse on Mars and Lithops get pretty funky for experimental acts (as usual) with their tracks "Syc" and "Me We," most of the inclusions are abstract glitch tracks never reliant on the beat. From the *musique concrète* traffic jam "Compilation Track" by C-Schulz & Hajsch to Vert's odd duet between piano and computer processing, *Sonig Comp.* includes all manner of experimental tracks. Though the tracks range from excellent to downright solid, it's definitely one for the collectors. —*John Bush*

**Soul from the City: The Definitive Detroit House Collection** / 1995 / Submerge ◆◆◆◆
This house collection from the home of techno includes Donnie Marks, Davina, Yolanda Reynolds & UR, Robynn Lynn, Unit 2 and $430 West's Burden Brothers. —*Keith Farley*

**The Sound of Cologne, Vol. 1** / 1998 / Sound of Cologne ◆◆◆◆
During the late '90s, Cologne became Detroit's new companion for the production of intelligent, minimalist techno. Just about every name on the scene appeared on this two-disc compilation, from Mike Ink, Mouse on Mars, Air Liquide, F.X. Randomiz, Rob Acid, Schlammpeitziger, Third Electric, Thomas Brinkmann, Roland Casper and Kandis. Surprisingly, many of the best tracks are by lesser-known names, like the Green Man, Karma, DJ Chestnut and Klystron. *The Sound of Cologne, Vol. 1* is almost as essential to a knowledge of techno as Detroit's *Depth Charge* series. —*John Bush*

**Sound of the Hoover** / Oct. 6, 1997 / TEC ◆◆◆◆
This collection of European trance includes crucial tracks from Commander Tom, Exit EEE, Nexus 6, Baby Doc and Koma, among others. —*Keith Farley*

**Soundbombing** / Oct. 14, 1997 / Priority ◆◆◆◆
A killer collection of the (mostly vinyl-only) singles output of underground rap's excellent Rawkus label, *Soundbombing* includes tracks by all the label's best acts (Company Flow, Mos Def, Sir Menelik, Reflection Eternal) and a brilliant mix format by DJ Evil Dee. —*John Bush*

**Soundbombing, Vol. 2** / Apr. 27, 1999 / Priority ◆◆◆◆
With *SB 1*, Rawkus introduced a ravenous stable of hungry underground MCs, but more importantly it also laid the preliminary groundwork for Mos Def and Talib Kweli's Blackstar movement. Both play a large role in the development of *SB 2* as well. Mos screens a preview from his impending solo LP, the high tech Next Universe, and divulges Crosstown Beef with his Medina Green outfit. Talib and Hi-Tek's manifestation as Reflection Eternal contributes two highly illuminant tracks: "On Mission" and the cultivated "Chaos" (featuring Bahamadia). Rawkus' latest coup, Pharoahe Monch, gets militaristic with Shabaam Shadeeq on "WW III" and the virulent "Mayor." Eminem works his magic over a cartoon-like Beatminerz track on the neurotic "Any Man." *SB 2* contains an abundance of prolific collaborations, exemplified by Common and Sadat X's elegant "1999," Dilated Peoples and Tash's regal "Soundbombing," and Sir Menelik's "7XL" (featuring Sadat X and Grand Puba). One relatively minor blemish arises in the Beat Junkies' control of the LP's continuity—their cutting and blending methods are peculiarly ineffective, and oftentimes lack direction. User friendly for underground or mainstream fanatics, *SB 2* is the quintessential Rawkus project, and their finest moment to date. —*Matt Conaway*

**Sounds from the Electronic Lounge** / Oct. 20, 1998 / Music Cartel ◆◆◆◆
If you've been looking for a combination of lounge music's self-consciously blasé decadence and the chilly electronic atmospherics of the techno/rave scene, then you have no farther to look than this disc. Consisting of 21 tracks presented in an uninterrupted "DJ mix" format, *Sounds from the Electronic Lounge* floats gently from low-key club beats to equally gentle drum'n'bass tracks, never chilling out completely but also never rising above a gentle simmer of energy. The result is very pleasant dance music that fits just fine in the background but will also reward your attention, should you choose to turn it in the music's direction. Featured artists include Sonic Man (whose "Sonic Dub" is one of the album's highlights), DJ Supernova and Kirlian, who contributes an annoyingly minimalist (but nicely bass-heavy) house track. The project's masterminds are Scanner and Signs of Chaos; both are responsible for some of the more interesting music on this disc, as well as the overall production. This isn't a groundbreaking album, but it's one of the better things to come from the electronic scene. —*Rick Anderson*

**Sounds of OM House Collection, Vol. 1** / Nov. 3, 1998 / OM ◆◆◆
A solid collection of deep house and mainstream producers including Naked Music NYC, Derrick Carter, King Britt, Joshua and Terra Deva contribute tracks to this OM collection. —*John Bush*

**Sounds of the Revolution** / May 19, 1998 / World Domination ◆◆◆◆
A smartly compiled collection of techno cuts, *Sounds of the Revolution* assembles unreleased tracks from Roni Size, Dreadzone, A Guy Called Gerald, Fluke and Rob & Goldie (mixed by Underworld); it also includes "Lazergum," a stunning collaboration between Mouse on Mars and Stereolab's Laetitia Sadier previously available on the former's standout *Cache Coeur Naif* EP. —*Jason Ankeny*

**Source Material** / Mar. 23, 1999 / Astralwerks ◆◆◆◆
After releasing full albums by French outfits Air and Cassius, Astralwerks followed up with *Source Material*, a compilation of material originally released on France's Source Records. The album includes 13 acts new to American (and most worldwide) audiences, and reflects a growing base of influence for French artists (at least the ones that make it to American shores). There's still an incessant slant toward disco and vintage synthesizer gear, like on Ernest Saint Laurent's "Moogie" or Oomiaq's "L'Ultime Atome." The punk/hip-hop crew Scenario Rock makes an appearance with a self-titled track, while Bosco charts the comic side of trip-hop and breakbeat with "Dig, Dig on the Reggae." There's even a contribution reminiscent of classic French pop, from Bertrand Burgalat on the track "Kim." For listeners intrigued by Moon Safari, this is a great place to go next. —*John Bush*

**Sourcelab, Vol. 1** / May 20, 1997 / Caroline ◆◆◆◆
The debut in a series of stellar French label compilations is the best, even though it doesn't cover famous native sons Daft Punk. Instead, worthy acts

like La Funk Mob, DJ Cam, Motorbass, Air, Daphreephunkateerz, and the Mighty Bop appear on the two-disc set. —*Keith Farley*

**Sourcelab, Vol. 2** / Oct. 15, 1996 / Source ♦♦♦♦
Daft Punk finally makes an appearance on the second compilation by the French label, contributing the incredible B-side "Musique." As well, Dimitri from Paris, Alex Gopher, Air, Zend Avesta and Le Tone make appearances. —*Keith Farley*

**Sourcelab, Vol. 3: Cream of French Underground** / Apr. 8, 1997 / Caroline ♦♦♦♦
The third in the *Sourcelab* series is another two-disc set, with great tracks by well-known producers like I:Cube, Aleph, DJ Cam and Air, as well as worthy obscure names like Tele Pop Musik, Extra Lucid, and Bel Air Project. —*Keith Farley*

**Southern Fried House** / 1995 / Sm:)e ♦♦♦♦
The Southern in this case is Brighton, not Florida; acts like Norman Cook's Pizzaman and Mighty Dub Kats make appearances. —*Keith Farley*

**Space Daze 2000** / Jan. 30, 1996 / Cleopatra ♦♦♦♦
The sequel to *Space Daze*, *Space Daze 2000* is an excellent sampling of ambient music. Drawing from both techno and rock, the collection features groundbreaking tracks from Brian Eno, Kraftwerk, and David Bowie, as well as tracks from artists like Future Sound of London and Spiral Realms that popularized ambient in the '90s. It's a perfect introduction to a sometimes challenging music. —*Stephen Thomas Erlewine*

**Space Daze: The History & Mystery of Electronic Ambient Space** / 1995 / Cleopatra ♦♦♦
A surprisingly credible look into the world of ambient and space music, Cleopatra includes tracks from figureheads Brian Eno, Gong, Tangerine Dream, Amon Düül, Hawkwind and Kraftwerk as well as several from the new school of the '80s and '90s like Psychic TV, Helios Creed, Legendary Pink Dots, and the Orb. —*Keith Farley*

**Space Ibiza '98** / Aug. 25, 1998 / ZYX ♦♦♦
The double-disc set *Space Ibiza '98* includes a variety of party house and trance tracks, featuring highlights like Ralphie Rosario's "Take Me Up (Gotta Get Up)," Armand Van Helden's "Ghetto House Groove," Rosie Gaines' "Be Strong," Sven Väth's "Fusion" and Westbam's "Hanging Out with the Machine Heads." —*John Bush*

**Special Brew** / Jun. 25, 1996 / ffrr ♦♦♦♦
*Special Brew* is a multi-artist compilation featuring tracks and remixes from artists as diverse as Chemical Brothers, U2, Massive Attack, Bjork, Goldie, Money Mark, Future Sound of London and Method Man. The album presents a vast array of contemporary dance styles, shifting from hip-hop to techno, from drums & bass techno to R&B and dub. Since there's so many different styles, the record can be a bit incoherent, but it is a good sampler that illustrates how diverse dance music can be. —*Leo Stanley*

**Speed Garage Classics** / Feb. 24, 1998 / Logic ♦♦♦♦
*Speed Garage Classics* is a near-definitive collection of seminal speed-garage singles, featuring 17 cuts from such artists as Double 99 (two mixes of "Ripgroove," "Jump"), R.I.P. ("The Chant," "Ice Cream Dubplate"), Another Level ("Be Alone No More"), G Flame & Mr. G ("Make Me Hi," "Who Knows"), Underground Distortion ("Everythin' is Large"), Tina Moore ("Never Gonna Let You Go"), Genaside II ("Mr. Maniac"), Terry Hunter ("Harvest for the World"), Martha Wash ("Carry On"), Isha D ("Stay"), and Soundscape ("Dubplate Culture"). —*Stephen Thomas Erlewine*

**Speed Kills** / 1995 / Instinct ♦♦
This techno and acid-trance compilation includes Robert Armani and Christian Vogel. Though there are some standouts, some of the tracks might even be too repetitive for techno diehards. —*Keith Farley*

**Speed Limit 140 BPM+** / 1993 / Moonshine Music ♦♦♦
Volume one is easily the weakest in the series, with only a few rave-into-hardcore tracks of any worth. "Space Cakes" by Kaotic Chemistry and "Bass Speaker" by Urban Shakedown are okay at best, but the rest of *Speed Limit 140 BPM+* is quite weak. —*Keith Farley*

**Speed Limit 140 BPM+, Vol. 2** / 1993 / Planet Earth ♦♦♦
The second in the series handles several early hardcore classics, including "Imajicka" by Hyper-On Experience, "Star Eyes" by Cosmo & Dibbs, "New Style" by Potential Bad Boy, and "Raw Motion" by DJ Aphrodite. —*Keith Farley*

**Speed Limit 140 BPM+, Vol. 3** / 1993 / Planet Earth ♦♦♦♦
With just as giant a leap as that by which volume two outdistanced its predecessor, *Speed Limit BPM+, Vol. 3* includes legendary breakbeats by Suburban Base/Moving Shadow stalwarts like Omni Trio, DJ Hype, 2 Bad Mice, Sonz of a Loop Da Loop Era, Hyper-On Experience, Blame, Foul Play, and D'Cruze. —*Keith Farley*

**Speed Limit 140 BPM+, Vol. 4** / 1994 / Planet Earth ♦♦♦
Volume four hits several peaks but isn't quite as consistent as the third volume in the series of hardcore/breakbeat tracks. It does feature a Foul Play remix of Omni Trio's "Renegade Snares" plus "Bang the Drum" by LTJ Bukem & Tayla and "Saint Angel" by Goldie's Metalheadz project, but the presence of a few second-tier tracks weighs the album down just a bit. —*Keith Farley*

**Speed Limit 140 BPM+, Vol. 5** / 1994 / Planet Earth ♦♦♦♦
Another classic volume of late hardcore/early breakbeat, with tracks by scene veterans like Danny Breaks, Urban Shakedown, DJ Hype, Ray Keith and DJ Rap. It's also one of the few compilations to feature fusion drum'n'bass maestro LTJ Bukem as well as happy hardcore stalwart Slipmatt, a good indication of how far the hardcore scene had splintered in the early '90s. —*Keith Farley*

**Speed: Boomin' UK Underground Garage, Vol. 1** / Jun. 23, 1998 / Mutant Sound ♦♦♦
Compiled by the Public Demand label, *Speed: Boomin' UK Underground Garage Vol. 1* collects many exclusives from Britain's speed garage scene. Featured are cuts and remixes by Tuff Jam ("Love Vibration"), Bobby & Steve ("Saturday"), DB Selective ("Free Breath"), Lenny Fontana ("Spirit of the Sun") and Victor Romeo ("Love Will Find a Way"). —*Jason Ankeny*

**Spirit of Ecstasy** / Aug. 21, 1992 / Telstar ♦♦♦♦
*Spirit of Ecstasy* includes 20 rave favorites from the early '90s, including Moby's "UHF," SL2's "DJ's Take Control," Altern8's "Active 8," Bizarre Inc.'s "Playing with Knives," 2 Unlimited's "Get Ready for This," Oceanic's "Wicked Love," the Jamms "It's Grim Up North," and many others. —*John Bush*

**The Spirit of Harddesertrance: The Psychedelic Sunrise Mix from Dream Canyon** / Oct. 21, 1997 / Moonshine Music ♦♦♦
Released in late 1997 just as trance was beginning its quick ascent towards mass popularity within the electronic music community, the first volume of DJ Brian's *Hardesertrance* showcases the more intense, raw side of the genre before it began to get diluted with overly melodic anthems. Brian stays true to the album's title for the majority of his mix, focusing on songs that balance the blurry distinction between hard acid techno and the melodic attributes characterizing late '90s trance. This fine balance becomes most evident at the album's zenith, when Brian first lays down the laser-like assault of Ylem's acid rager, "Maelstrom." After six minutes of acid mayhem, he begins to flirt with the distant, echoed "aaahhhh, aaahhh" of a digital female voice and the inescapable melody of L.S.G.'s "Netherworld;" then at the seven and a half minute mark of "Maelstrom," the heavenly sounds of "Netherworld" finally eclipse the hellish acid warfare of Ylem. This moment sums up the inner struggle within *Hardesertrance*. Brian wants to keep his set hard and intense, but he also wants to instill some glossy beauty into his adrenaline-fueled tracks. A few of the songs are able to harmoniously teeter between these two qualities, but for the most part, Brian manually attempts to combine the techno side of trance with the candy-coated, synth-heavy, melodic side of the genre by transporting the listener back and forth across the spectrum with his onclusive track selection. Anyone looking for the sugary sounds of Paul Oakenfold-style trance may be turned off by the hard acid techno characteristics found in Brian's set, but anyone looking for a more aggressive style of trance with more intensity than ecstasy will probably enjoy *Hardesertrance*. —*Jason Birchmeier*

**Spirit of Vampyros Lesbos** / Sep. 29, 1997 / Sideburn ♦♦♦♦
One of the more unique electronic compilations, *Spirit of Vampyros Lesbos* is an album of remixes from the original soundtrack to Jess Franco's 1968 slasher B-film *Vampyros Lesbos*. There's a diverse cast of electro-techno experimentalists—Two Lone Swordsmen, Rockers Hifi, Doctor Rockit, DJ Wally, Alec Empire, Witchman, and DJ Hell—and each seems genuinely inspired by the psychedelic lounge music of the original. —*John Bush*

**The Spirit of Wandjina: 3rd Barramundi Sampler** / Mar. 26, 1996 / Logic ♦♦♦
The third volume including Barramundi tracks is a two-disc set with few names of note; only Joey Beltram's "Across the Hemisphere" will be familiar to fans of dance, while the rest are rather tepid displays of psychedelic trance. —*Keith Farley*

**Spliffen Sie Englisch** / Feb. 16, 1999 / EFA ♦♦♦
*Spliffen Sie English* is a 12-track compilation of German downtempo/trip-hop artists put together by the members of Rockers HiFi, who had some form of contact with all of the artists represented here while recording in Germany. The Rockers also contribute a remix of Megashira's "Silent Service." —*Steve Huey*

**Spunk Jazz** / Sep. 8, 1997 / Ill ♦♦♦
The hyper-frenetic beats and drill'n'bass frenzy of acts like Animals on Wheels, Paddington Breaks, Si Begg, Vert, and Hoarse Operator are featured on this compilation from Ill Records. —*Keith Farley*

**Stark Raving Techno** / 1993 / Dm ♦♦
An appropriately silly compilation of one-shot (or less) novelty rave acts like Nova 9, X-Ternal Friction and Alpha Team (the latter's most famous track, a takeoff of *Speed Racer*, is here twice). —*John Bush*

**Stars of Europe** / Nov. 4, 1997 / Cleopatra ♦♦
*Stars of Europe* is a compilation of 12" singles by late-'90s trance and goa artists from Denmark, Germany, and the Netherlands, including Bypass Unit, Pitchrider, the O Zone, and others. —*Steve Huey*

**The State of E:Motion** / Feb. 16, 1999 / EFA ♦♦♦♦
Although it can be a bit uneven, *The State of E:motion* (actually the sixth volume in the series, but the first not to be released as a limited edition) runs the gamut of late-'90s electronic music, featuring trip-hop, drum'n'bass, big-beat techno, ambient, electro, house and more. Highlights include tracks by Baby Mammoth, E-Z Rollers, Rasmus, Zulutronic, Gas, Monolake, DMX Krew, and a Bandulu remix of the Saafi Brothers. —*Steve Huey*

**State of the Nu Art** / 1997 / Blue Planet ♦♦♦
The Blue Planet label burst on the electronica scene in 1996 with a pair of EPs by Bowling Green and Mung that opened scads of new doors in the world of abstract electro and drum'n'bass, pairing a kitchen-sink aesthetic with enough weirdness and driving funk to elude criticisms of "eclecticism." *State of the Nu Art* is Blue Planet's first label compilation, and unfortunately doesn't up the ante much. The best of this (Plug's "A Subtle Blend," Witchman's "Arcane Radio," and Bowling Green's "Caucasian Flotsam") was made available in advance of the general release as a sampler 12", and while new tracks from Frank Heiss, Paradox, and Wai Wan widen the label's scope by delving into downtempo and bizarro ambient dub, the album ultimately falls short of expectations. —*Sean Cooper*

**State of the Nu Art, Vol. 2** / Jan. 26, 1998 / Blue Planet ♦♦♦
The second volume of rather overly introspective drill'n'bass tracks includes solid contributions from Mike Paradinas (μ-Ziq), Plug (Luke Vibert), Bedouin Ascent, Mung, and Witchman, among others. —*Keith Farley*

**Statics** / Dec. 7, 1999 / Digital Narcis ♦♦♦
*Statics* gathers is an excellent sampling of 1995 creations by a variety of modern electronic composers from around the world, including Ryoji Ikeda (who compiled this release), Paul Schütze, Jim O'Rourke, Akira Yamamichi, David Toop, and more. A few of the selections utilize sine waves, which are especially prevalent in Yamamachi's "Phenomenized Soundscapes." A gentler beauty infuses some of the standout compositions, such as O'Rourke's warm, space track, "Sinking Lights in Lambeth," the short version of Alan Lamb's "Beauty," David Toop's heavily panned, yet light "Iron Perm," and the stellar, calm achievement of "Rain," by Andrew Lagowski and Toru Yamanaka. —*Joslyn Layne*

**Step Off!: A Collection of Trip Hop & Dub** / Apr. 20, 1999 / Instinct ♦♦♦
*Step Off!* collects ten tracks by underground trip-hop and dub artists like Le Gooster, DJ Krush and Sub Dub. DJ Krush contributes two tracks: "On the Dub-ble" and a collaboration with Toshinori Kondo, "Ko-Ku." Le Gooster's "Evidemment" adds a slinky French flair to the album, while Jammin Unit (one half of Air Liquide) provides an icy cool blast with "32 Degrees in the Shade." Step Off's deep, dubby grooves make it a magnetic, hypnotic compilation. —*Heather Phares*

**Stomp: 28 Hot & Horny Hard House Anthems** / Jan. 19, 1999 / Harmless ♦♦♦
This collection of hard house and trance includes tracks by Ruff Driverz, Hip Hoperation, Invisible Man, Tekara, BBE, Propulsion and JDS, among others. —*John Bush*

**A Storm of Drones** / Sep. 10, 1996 / Asphodel ♦♦♦
*A Storm of Drones* is a three-disc set of dense, free-form space music more than befitting the title. Space pioneers Steve Roach, Michael Stearns, Robert Rich, Jeff Greinke, and Vidna Obmana appear beside more recent experimentalists like DJ Spooky and Elliot Sharp. —*Keith Farley*

**Streetsounds: The Best of Electro, Vol. 1** / 1995 / Beechwood ♦♦♦♦
Beechwood's mid-'80s series of hip-hop and electro compilations played an important role in introducing the sound of American urban electronic dance music to European audiences. *The Best of Electro Vol. 1,* released in 1995, is a nice distillation of those earlier comps, with tracks by Man Parrish, Cybotron, Warp 9, Egyptian Lover, Hashim, West Street Mob, and the Russell Brothers filling out a good portion of early electro history (although the absence of Miami artists such as Freestyle and Tony Butler is somewhat curious). Released on CD and gatefold double-vinyl LP, this compilation is a sturdy, enduring necessity. —*Sean Cooper*

★ **Strictly Rhythm: The Early Years** / Nov. 24, 1993 / Strictly Rhythm ♦♦♦♦♦
Several of the most important house classics of the late '80s and early '90s appear on Strictly Rhythm's collection of its early history. Pretty much defining the early house mainstream, each one of the label's crucial producers during the early '90s is here, including Todd Terry (Tech Nine's "Slam Jam," Static's "Dream It"), DJ Pierre (Photon Inc.'s "Generate Power"), Josh Wink & King Britt (E-Culture's "Tribal Confusion"), Roger Sanchez (Underground Solution's "Luv Dancin" and DV8's "Old School House"), George Morel (Roommates' "Voices in the Club"), and Masters at Work (The Untouchables' "Li'l Louie's Anthem"). —*John Bush*

**Sublime: The Adolescence** / 1997 / Sublime ♦♦♦♦
Japan's Sublime Records has a diverse catalog of techno artists, featuring producers ranging from Dan Curtin to Dego (4 Hero) to Max Brennan (Fretless AZM) to Ken Ishii. *Sublime: The Adolescence* collects new tracks from many acts, and includes a CD-ROM with video (from a show by Ishii's Flare project) and complete interactive catalog. It's an interesting release from a top-notch label. —*John Bush*

**Substantia** / Mar. 23, 1999 / Sub Rosa ♦♦♦
The Sub Rosa label sampler *Substantia* contains previously unreleased tracks (many of them from albums in the works) from DJ Grazzhoppa + DJ Smimooz, DJ Wally Vs. Jigen, Tone Rec, Vedic, and David Shea, plus seven others. —*Steve Huey*

**Subterranean Hitz, Vol. 1** / Jan. 7, 1997 / Wordsound ♦♦♦
Illbient dub and abstract hip-hop appear in equal degree on WordSound's first compilation in the *Subterranean Hitz* series. Rob Swift, Prince Paul, Spectre, and Torture each make appearances. —*John Bush*

**Subterranean Hitz, Vol. 2** / Jan. 6, 1998 / Wordsound ♦♦♦
Compiled by Spectre, who also contributes a track, *Subterranean Hitz, Vol. 2* showcases off-kilter, dub-influenced hip-hop by the likes of the X-ecutioners' Rob Swift, ex-Jungle Brother Africa "Baby Bam," Prince Paul, New Kingdom's Scotty Hard, and more. —*Steve Huey*

**Super Post Electronica: Phase One** / Jul. 25, 2000 / Instinct ♦♦♦♦
Instinct's *Super Post Electronica* showcases tracks from genre-bending artists such as Pied Piper, Mils, and Senking and other post rock/progressive electronica hybrids from Japan and France. Stark, streamlined yet delicate pieces such as Naruhisa Matsuoka's "Fairy's Vibration," Rubyorla's "Atom," Moughqual's "Cyross," and Robonom's "Pomelo" set the tone for this inventive collection, which will satisfy fans of more prominent acts in the same vein, such as Pan Sonic, Fridge, and Super ESP. —*Heather Phares*

**Superstition Classics, Vol. 2** / Dec. 14, 1999 / Superstition ♦♦♦
The second compilation devoted to the best of the Superstition label's output, *Superstition Classics, Vol. 2* gathers two discs' worth of trance and techno, tending to emphasize the former. Artists located herein include L.S.G., the Paragliders, Humate, Steve Bug, and Marmion, among others. —*Steve Huey*

**Superstitious Flights: Destination USA** / Mar. 23, 1999 / Streetbeat ♦♦♦
*Superstitious Flights* includes some quality trance, like "3.2," "East" and "Oh

My Darling I Love You" by Humate, "Freak Me" and "Fragile" by LSG, an Ian Pooley remix of "Fibrill 2" by Marco Repetto, "More" by Mijk Van Dijk, and "Telepathic Space Grass" by Fred Gianelli. —*John Bush*

**Suspect Package** / Jan. 27, 1997 / Kickin' ♦♦♦♦
The crucial Hardleaders label debuted its compilation series with *Suspect Package*, including ripping cuts from Dillinja ("Tear Down Da Whole Place"), Lemon D ("Manhattan Melody"), and Decoder ("The Fog"), among others. —*John Bush*

**Swaraj** / Jan. 27, 1998 / Hollywood ♦♦♦
*Swaraj* is a various-artists album released to celebrate the 50th anniversary of India's independence from Great Britain. Acid Jazz has assembled a 13-track collection of adventurous dance artists who blend acid jazz, house and dance-club music with Indian music. Not all of the songs work, but there are enough moments that do to make *Swaraj* worth investigating. —*Stephen Thomas Erlewine*

**Swarm of Drones** / Oct. 1995 / Asphodel ♦♦♦
A double-disc set of dark space music and leftfield trance, *A Swarm of Drones* includes tracks by Steve Roach, Robert Rich, Cheb I Sabbah, Vidna Obmana, and Jeff Greinke. —*Keith Farley*

**Synewave New York, Vol. 1** / 1995 / Kickin' ♦♦♦♦
Damon Wild collects some of his Synewave label's best releases, including material from Joey Beltram, Steve Soll, Woody McBride, Tim Taylor, and of course, Wild himself. —*Keith Farley*

**Synthesizer Classics** / Aug. 31, 1999 / Cleopatra ♦♦♦
*Synthesizer Classics: A Homage to the Biggest Synthesizer Hits of the '80s* features covers by current electronic groups like Aquatic Ghost, Rey, and the Hidden of originals by Space, Giorgio Moroder, and other synth pioneers. Supersonic's take on Moroder's "The Apartment" from the *American Gigolo* soundtrack is tense, percussive, and complex, while Joseph's version of Didier Marouani's "Final Signal" blends appealingly brassy and crystalline synth textures. Aquatic Ghost's cover of Space's "Tango in Space" also captures the mix of disco chic and robotic funk that made these songs vibrant in the first place. For the most part, though, this collection focuses too much on slavish reproduction, losing sight of the entertaining, slightly cheesy futurism that the original works still retain. —*Heather Phares*

**Synthetic Pleasures, Vol. 2** / 1997 / Caipirinha Productions ♦♦♦
The second volume in the *Synthetic Pleasures* series includes music inspired by Lara Lee's film, with illbient/dub companions DJ Soul Slinger, DJ Spooky, Datacide, Single Cell Orchestra, and Prototype 909. —*Keith Farley*

**Tangerine Ambience, Vol. 2** / Jul. 15, 1997 / Cleopatra ♦♦
Though it's not a bad idea for a compilation, this Tangerine Dream tribute is sunk by its contributors. A host of unknown acts including To Experience, Aquatic Ghost, Flight Rey, and Supersonic create lame ambient-trance versions of classics from *Rubydon*, *Phaedra*, and *Tangram*. —*Keith Farley*

**A Taste Of... Internal Bass** / Nov. 18, 1997 / Internal Bass ♦♦♦
The Internal Bass label is represented on this sampler of generic acid jazz and funk workouts featuring tracks from Down to the Bone ("Brooklyn Heights"), Panama Reed ("Gold Medal Kid"), and Diamond Wookie ("Back to the Flat"). —*Jason Ankeny*

**Taste of Cajual** / Dec. 2, 1997 / Cajual ♦♦♦♦
Cajmere produced four of the tracks on this Cajual compilation, one each as Green Velvet, Chicago Connection and himself, plus Dajae's "Fakes and Phonies." Other stellar new-school Chicago heads appearing are Glenn Underground, Mark Grant, Andre Harris, and Gene Farris. —*John Bush*

**A Taste of Pork: A Collection of Pork Recordings** / Nov. 1995 / Quango ♦♦♦♦
Pork mainstay Dave Cobby appears on all but one of the tracks on this collection of earthy downtempo. With Fila Brazillia tracks like "Sheriff" and "Subtle Body," plus contributions from Cobby's Solid Doctor project and two of his co-productions with Heights of Abraham, the compilation is practically a solo album; as such, it's quite consistent and of much better quality than many of the somewhat bland full-lengths by Pork artists. —*Keith Farley*

**Tec House Living** / Jan. 12, 1999 / Max Music ♦♦♦♦
With sounds and samples from house but the streamlined production values of techno, tech-house became a popular style within dance music during 1998. The first major compilation for the music was *Tec House Living*, compiled and mixed by the Deeper Sound of Bristol collective. It includes tracks from Americans Cevin Fisher (the huge dance hit "Freaks Come Out"), John Tejada, and Jamie Anderson, plus Europeans like Orlando Voorn, Plastic Avengers, and Presence. —*Keith Farley*

**Technicians of Electronica** / Jan. 27, 1998 / Cleopatra ♦♦♦
*Technicians of Electronica* is the typical Cleopatra compilation, a ramshackle set balancing unknown acts doing tepid imitations of the real thing with album tracks from established artists—here 808 State, the Shamen, System 7, Astralasia, and A Guy Called Gerald. —*Keith Farley*

**Techno Bass: The Mission** / Jul. 28, 1998 / Direct Beat ♦♦♦♦
Nearly every track on this compilation includes human vocals manipulated to sound robotic, while the bass-driven rhythms are about as funky as music can get. The tracks tend to follow a verse-chorus-verse format, and they don't usually last longer than a few minutes. Another interesting feature about *Techno Bass: The Mission* lies in the multiple roles played by Tom Hamilton, who is credited for writing half of the 12 tracks. While there is no denying the well-crafted nature of these pieces—no doubt intended for DJs and dance floors—one may desire a bit more variety. Unlike the more progressive sounds of techno, which tend to extend the track length well over the five-minute mark in an effort to stretch out the song's evolution, the songs here all tend to follow a predictable pattern that could use a little more variety or evolution. In the end though, tracks such as Mike Banks' Electric Soul contribution and Keith Tucker's DJ K-1 offering stand out due to their unique sound. —*Jason Birchmeier*

**Techno Dance Classics, Vol. 1: Pump up the Jam** / Jul. 26, 1994 / Priority ♦♦♦
*Techno Dance Classics* doesn't really contain any techno—no one in their right mind could call Right Said Fred techno—but it's still a thoroughly enjoyable collection of hip dance music from the early '90s, containing such hits as Technotronic's "Pump Up the Jam," Right Said Fred's "I'm Too Sexy," Black Box's "Everybody Everybody," the Information Society's "Think," and Saint Etienne's wonderful "Nothing Can Stop Us." —*Stephen Thomas Erlewine*

**Technomancer** / 1992 / Antler Subway/Caroline ♦♦♦
...The energy's there on these 16 solid tracks, but there's little else. In the hands of capable DJs, Oxy's "The Feeling" would pack the floor with its '60s girl-group harmonies and clean rhythms...That's followed by the ubiquitous Digital Orgasm, whose "Running Out of Time" is rife with wailing and frequent mix-downs to near silence. It's also very clean and with some effective spoken sound bites; in all, more like the aural assault of an arcade on Saturday morning....More melodic than most techno, Jade 4 U's "Messenger of Love" proves marginally more memorable and might be worth the hunt for another mix. "Liberty And Freedom," Atomizer 2's subtle (for techno) mix of frenzied drums and staggered keyboards, makes for a sublime tribute to the cornerstones of American life. —*David Sears*, Option 49_93

**Technotheque, Vol. 1** / 1997 / Javelin ♦♦♦
*Technotheque, Vol. 1* balances the sexier side of mainstream house (Brooklyn Bounce, Todd Terry, Porn Kings) with some harder techno (Josh Wink, Plastika) and even a bit of jazzy house courtesy of Global Communication's "The Way." —*John Bush*

**Tektonics** / Sep. 21, 1999 / OM ♦♦♦♦
Billed as "a meeting of the minds between leading electronic artists and the world's greatest turntablist DJs," this fine compilation may not amount to "a manifesto denouncing all preconceptions about what music is and what it should be" (sheesh, who wrote those liner notes?), but it sure is lots of fun. The concept may seem obvious, but nobody else seems to have done it before; maybe others will, in light of the success of this particular project. The raw material for this program is an array of tunes by such established electronica names as Photek, Howie B., and Freestylers, whose work is given hip-hoppy remixes and dense, complex overlays of turntable scratching by such equally respected artists as DJ Rob Swift, DJ Apollo, and the Herbaliser. The highlights are many, including the Scratch Perverts' speed-of-light scratching over Photek's jungle composition "The Water Margin," a Propellerheads/DJ Craze collaboration entitled "Big Dog," and, especially, the updated old-school groove of Soulstice's "Superfunk 200" as interpreted by DJ Curse. Nothing here is less than compelling, and quite a bit of it is spectacular. —*Rick Anderson*

**Tetragramaton: Submerge** / Feb. 13, 1997 / Ion ♦♦♦
Yet another genre-blending comp from the Laswell camp, bringing together Laswell's Material project with a pair of collaborators (Graham Haynes and

Byard Lancaster), and featuring tracks from DJ Spooky, DJ Soul Slinger, and Fullcone. A mixture of uptempo breakbeat and downtempo ambient dub/trip-hop, none of the tracks (save perhaps for Benwa's mix of Fullcone's "Ephedream") are particularly essential, but they're all well done and together serve as an enjoyable snapshot of a particular moment in dub/funk/hip-hop/electronica's cross-pollination. —*Sean Cooper*

**Theatre of Sound** / Oct. 6, 1998 / Kickin' Music ♦♦♦
*Theatre of Sound* explores the wide array of music created by artists nominally tagged post-rock or space-rock. Most of the selections come from American groups like Füxa, 5ive Style, Scenic, Flowchart and Dylan Group, but the album also includes England's Flying Saucer Attack, Scotland's Ganger, and Germany's Kreidler. —*John Bush*

**There Are Too Many Fools Following Too Many Rules** / Feb. 3, 1997 / Irdial ♦♦♦
This two-disc set is the first compilation from Britain's mysterious Irdial Records, home of understated and mostly unpublicized techno subterfuge from Neuropolitique, Anthony Manning, Luke Slater's Morganistic and Thee J. Johanz, among many others. Without a doubt, it's overlong considering Irdial's scattered release schedule, though tracks like Aqua Regia's "Pump Up the L.E.D.'s to Red, Take Some Drugs and Shake Your Head" are amusing. —*Keith Farley*

**This Ain't Trip Hop?, Pt. 2** / 1995 / Moonshine Music ♦♦♦♦
The second volume of the excellent trip-hop series includes Red Snapper, Strata 3, Zen Cowboys, the Chemical Brothers, and a Dust (Chemical) Brothers remix of the Prodigy. —*Keith Farley*

**This Is Acid Jazz, Vol. 1** / Jan. 1991 / Acid Jazz/Instinct ♦♦
The first in a collection of mostly worthless acid jazz from Instinct includes tracks from A Man Called Adam, Night Trains, Izit, and the Cool Beats. —*Keith Farley*

**This Is Acid Jazz, Vol. 2** / 1992 / Instinct ♦♦♦
Volume two includes a few better tracks than its predecessor, including "Perfect Vibe" and "Trance Jazz" by Exodus Quartet, and "Wide Angle" by the James Taylor Quartet. Other than those three, the vast majority of *This Is Acid Jazz, Vol. 2* is disappointing wallpaper music. —*Keith Farley*

**This Is Acid Jazz, Vol. 3** / 1993 / Instinct ♦♦
A carbon copy of the second volume, *This Is Acid Jazz, Vol. 3* has a few winners (by CFM Band, James Taylor Quartet and Exodus Quartet) but mostly substitutes artists on the anonymous side of the vibrant acid jazz scene. —*Keith Farley*

**This Is Acid Jazz, Vol. 4** / 1994 / Instinct ♦♦♦
One of the more jazz-inspired volumes in the series features Outside, Solsonics, D-Influence, CFM Band and Bluenotes, among others. —*Keith Farley*

**This Is Acid Jazz, Vol. 5: Livin' in the Land** / Apr. 9, 1996 / Instinct ♦♦♦
Instinct's *This Is Acid Jazz* compilation series begins to recruit a few good acts, resulting in danceable grooves from Mondo Grosso, Mr. Electric Triangle, Marden Hill, Count Basic, and Duboniks. —*Keith Farley*

**This Is Acid Jazz, Vol. 6: Golden Age of Groove** / Jan. 20, 1998 / Instinct ♦♦♦
A mostly British version in the series, this one includes Sharpshooters, Mondo Grosso, London Funk Allstars, Mr. Electric Triangle, Kosma, and Soundscape UK. —*Keith Farley*

**This Is Acid Jazz: Back to Basics** / 1994 / Instinct ♦♦♦
*Back to Basics* features tracks by the JB Horns ("I Like It Like That"), Bobby Byrd ("Sunshine"), Poets of Rhythm ("More Mess on My Thing"), and Bus People Express ("South Carolina"). —*Keith Farley*

**This Is Acid Jazz: New Voices, Vol. 1** / 1994 / Instinct ♦♦♦
Exodus Quartet, the James Taylor Quartet, Swing Machine and CFM Band all appear on this Instinct compilation of fresh groups on the acid jazz scene. —*Keith Farley*

**This Is Acid Jazz: New Voices, Vol. 2** / Mar. 28, 1995 / Instinct ♦♦♦
A host of familiar faces—at least, to those who know the series—appear on this second volume in Instinct's *New Voices* series, including Exodus Quartet, Count Basic, No Se, and DisJam. One actual new face is an export from Japan, the excellent DJ Krush. —*Keith Farley*

**This Is Acid Jazz: New Voices, Vol. 3** / Sep. 24, 1996 / Instinct ♦♦♦
It contains many of the same "voices" heard on the first two volumes, but *New Voices, Vol. 3* has good grooves and jazzy workmanship from Count Basic, Diferenz, Exodus Quartet, and Slowly, among others. —*Keith Farley*

**This Is Acid Jazz: New Voices, Vol. 4** / Mar. 17, 1998 / Instinct ♦♦
*New Voices, Vol. 4* has quite a few fresh faces compared to its predecessors, mostly performers rather than anonymous groups. Among the highlights are Duncan Millar's "Shooting Star," Chris Standring's "Sneaky," and Michael McEvoy's "Midnight Shaker." —*Keith Farley*

**This Is Acid Jazz: The Best of Acid Jazz, Vol. 1** / 1995 / Instinct ♦♦♦
*The Best of Acid Jazz* is another odd, misleading entry in Instinct's continuing repackaging scheme, including nominal acts who have appeared on virtually every acid jazz compilation by the label (Count Basic, Exodus Quartet, Marden Hill) as well as a few interesting tracks, like "Evening in New York" by the JB Horns and "Jazz Shuffle" by Chanan. This is hardly the best of acid jazz. —*Keith Farley*

**This Is Acid Jazz: The Best of Acid Jazz, Vol. 2** / Jan. 28, 1997 / Instinct ♦♦♦
The second volume in the *Best of Acid Jazz* series compiles an international roster of artists including Secret Vibes ("Dazzling"), RAD ("So Complete"), Michael McEvoy ("Cycles of Re-Elevation"), the Quiet Boys' ("Guiding Light"), A-One ("Don't Hold Your Breath"), and Count Basic ("On the Move"). —*Jason Ankeny*

**This Is Big Beat** / Jan. 13, 1998 / This Is ♦♦♦
A fine introduction to contemporary dance and electronica, the three-disc *This Is Big Beat* includes the Charlatans UK's "Patrol" (remixed by the Chemical Brothers), the Prodigy's "Poison," Primal Scream's "Kowalski," DJ Shadow's "High Noon," and David Holmes' "Gritty," as well as an entire disc mixed by Fatboy Slim (a.k.a. Norman Cook). —*Jason Ankeny*

**This Is Drum'n'bass [Beechwood]** / Mar. 31, 1997 / Beechwood Music ♦♦♦♦
Another stellar entry in Beechwood's line of inexpensive box sets charting the course of most dance genres of the '90s, *This Is Drum'n'bass* includes three discs of hardcore and jungle classics. —*Keith Farley*

**This Is Drum 'N' Bass [Alpha Wave]** / Jun. 23, 1998 / Alpha Wave ♦♦
Not quite the compilation the title promises, *This Is Drum 'N' Bass* features a couple of name producers (Nonplace Urban Field and Fauna Flash, plus remixes by DJ Krust and Wax Doctor), but overall forms a veritable fountain of misunderstanding regarding the jungle movement. —*Keith Farley*

**This Is Elektronica** / Oct. 19, 1999 / Cleopatra ♦♦
Cleopatra's *This Is Elektronica* should not be seen as a definitive electronica collection—the "k" in the title should be a bit of a tip-off, actually. Instead, it's a collection of obscurities and unknowns that dabble in electronica, jungle, trance, industrial, etc. There are some interesting tracks here, but they're surrounded by mediocrities on this 30-track collection, and it's hard to wade through the dull to get to the good. —*Stephen Thomas Erlewine*

**This Is Hardcore** / Apr. 28, 1997 / Beechwood ♦♦♦♦
Including two discs of (mostly happy) hardcore classics plus an extra disc of material mixed by Vibes, *This Is Hardcore* is a solid collection of four-beat dance, though three discs is much too much for all but the biggest fans of the style. Included are hardcore phenoms Force & Styles, Sharkey, DJ Unknown, Ikon, DJ Edy C, DJ Stompy, and Vibes himself. —*Keith Farley*

**This Is Home Entertainment, Vol. 1** / Jan. 23, 1996 / Home Entertainment ♦♦♦♦
The first volume of *This Is Home Entertainment* charts the course of New York illbient dub (DJ Spooky, Byzar, Sub Dub) and includes the sympathetic German Khan Oral's project 4E. Despite the presence of several cuts of rather bland quality, the album is a splendid trainer in the growth of a style of music equally influenced by electro and dub. —*Keith Farley*

**This Is Home Entertainment, Vol. 2** / Sep. 10, 1996 / Home Entertainment ♦♦♦♦
The second volume of Home Entertainment sees NYC illbient heads like DJ Spooky, We and DJ Wally alongside impressive foreign contributions from I:Cube, Jammin' Unit and J. Burger. —*Keith Farley*

**This Is Home Entertainment, Vol. 3** / May 5, 1997 / Home Entertainment ♦♦♦
*This is Home Entertainment, Vol. 3* is a rather odd collection of trip-hop, illbient and dub from the likes of DJ Ani ("ZuReal"), DJ Wally ("Infectious Dream"), Lux ("Jazz and Standards"), Alien Mind ("Evolution"), Yab Yum

("Village of the Damned"), Recloose ("Bug Eyed Blues"), We ("Saraba"), Bronx Warrior ("Solo Mission 1"), and DJ Spooky ("Island of Lost Souls (Dub Mix)"). There are some interesting, evocative moments here, but they're surrounded by pedestrian material that only hardcore illbient fans will want to wade through. —*Stephen Thomas Erlewine*

**This Is Ibiza** / Jan. 13, 1998 / This Is ✦✦✦✦
A compilation of dance tracks from the worthwhile *This Is...* series, it features performers including Ultra Nate, Todd Terry, Underworld, and Blue Boy. —*Jason Ankeny*

**This Is Jazz Steppin'** / Jul. 11, 2000 / Instinct ✦✦✦
*This Is Jazz Steppin'* is the hottest adult dance music in US urban markets. With the incredible success of *This Is Smooth Jazz*, Instinct Records has followed up their fresh idea with classic soul, breakbeats, and groove jazz on ten uncompromising fusion tracks filled with jazz, hip-hop, and rare groove. E.M. & I open up the set with "3 on 3" and immediately excite the dance muse with classic acid jazz grooves. Chris Bangs, the acid jazz pioneer who has made major waves with Soundscape UK as well as his more esoteric projects like the Chris Bangs Project, Mr. Electric Triangle, and Yada Yada, sets the "F Groove" for this mixture of styles from artists as essential as two of London's most exciting groove merchants, Duboniks and the Jazz Steppers to the exciting performances of Swing Machine, the Apollos, and Takahiro Watanabe, all providing classic acid jazz grooves. Exodus Quartet closes the set and after hearing the vibes on "Trance Dance," this pure groove collection will undoubtedly become a great source for keeping up with the intensely important but highly volatile UK music scene. —*Paula Edelstein*

**This Is Jungle** / Nov. 18, 1996 / Beechwood ✦✦✦
A three-disc set of group-oriented drum'n'bass with quite a few rare 12" remixes, Beechwood's *This Is Jungle* is a competent three-disc set of breakbeat. The final disc is a mix of tracks from the first two. —*Keith Farley*

**This Is Jungle Sky** / Jan. 16, 1996 / Jungle Sky US ✦✦
The rather pedestrian American drum'n'bass scene centered New York's Jungle Sky Records is illustrated, with tracks from DJ Soul Slinger, Kingsize and DJ X-Plorer, among others. As could be expected, the lone British production in the pack, the TPower classic "Mutant Jazz," rips apart the competition; the album isn't quite worth acquiring for just one track, though. —*Keith Farley*

**This Is Jungle Sky, Vol. 2** / Apr. 16, 1996 / Jungle Sky US ✦✦
The second volume in the *This Is Jungle Sky* compilation series focuses exclusively on the US jungle underground community. The label's founder DJ Soul Slinger contributes three cuts, while Deee-Lite's On-E adds one. DJ Wally, Kingsize, and Inna Most also appear. —*Jason Ankeny*

**This Is Jungle Sky, Vol. 5: Rock & Roll** / Jungle Sky ✦✦✦✦
The justly famous *This Is Jungle Sky* series continues with a concept album, of sorts: disc one ("Rock") consists of aggressive, hard-edged drum'n'bass prominently featuring guitar samples and other rock 'n' roll referents. Disc two is a bit trippier and more blissed-out, more like what you'd expect from American drum'n'bass. (And the series title notwithstanding, this is really more drum'n'bass than jungle, strictly speaking—the reggae influence that plays such an important part in jungle is almost completely missing here.) Disc one is the keeper: DJ Soul Slinger's "God Is a Lobster" is a hilarious, and yet seriously body-shaking, track based on samples from the B-52's hit "Rock Lobster." DJ Wally and MC Posi-D managed to dig up a sample of Jack Nicholson saying "I am rolling...," which combines with a shuddery descending bassline to produce an irresistible hook. And Tube's "Let's Get Mental" features a very fun robotic synth line and great textures. Disc two is good as well, but after the constant manic energy level of disc one, its more consistent mood comes across as something of a letdown. Highly recommended overall. —*Rick Anderson*

**This Is Rave** / Jun. 3, 1997 / Cleopatra ✦✦
*This Is Rave* is a shameful three-disc compilation mostly comprised of industrial-type no-names but passed off as a history of the rave scene. Tracks appear from Ravers Paradise, Ravers Fantasy, Happy Ravers, Donut Junkie and High on Dope, and while second-tier act Slipstream does manage to spoil the lineup of unknowns, the set is completely devoid of intelligence or merit. —*John Bush*

**This Is Rave, Vol. 2** / Sep. 28, 1999 / Cleopatra ✦✦
*This Is Rave, Vol. 2* is a fairly generic compilation of vaguely hallucinatory dance tracks. Material by relative unknowns like Scoope ("Night and Day"), Nuke Posse ("Ghettoblaster"), and Kenzo ("No Time to Surrender") capture the basic tenets of the rave culture but hardly typify the genre at its most creative or memorable. —*Jason Ankeny*

**This Is Space** / Apr. 29, 1997 / Cleopatra ✦✦✦✦
A surprisingly solid collection of space recordings from the '70s, '80s and '90s, with Kraftwerk, Tangerine Dream, Eno, Gong, Klaus Schulze, Fripp & Eno, Roxy Music, David Bowie and Hawkwind representing the first onset of ambience. Inheritors like Psychic TV, Coil, Legendary Pink Dots, Nik Turner and Helios Creed form the '80s contingent, while the new school of ambient techno appears with wizards like the Orb, Aphex Twin, Future Sound of London and William Orbit. Though it's a bit weak on the '90s, *This Is Space* is a worthy collection of mostly beatless recordings throughout the ages. —*John Bush*

**This Is Strictly Rhythm, Vol. 1** / Jun. 28, 1991 / Strictly Rhythm ✦✦✦
The first volume in Strictly Rhythm's ongoing compilation series isn't incredibly strong, though DJ Pierre's work on his own "Love Izz" plus a remix of Phuture's "Rise from Your Grave" are two of the label's early highlights. Masters at Work supremo Kenny "Dope" Gonzalez also appears, with "Dance to the Rhythm" by his Untouchables project. —*John Bush*

**This Is Strictly Rhythm, Vol. 3** / Oct. 13, 1993 / Strictly Rhythm ✦✦✦
A surprisingly tame entry in the Strictly Rhythm series, volume three includes tracks by Cookie Watkins, Earl Bennett, Hardrive and Sole Fusion, among others. The highlights come toward the end of the disc, with DJ Pierre's "Muzik" and Erick Morillo's "New Anthem." —*John Bush*

**This Is Strictly Rhythm, Vol. 4** / Dec. 15, 1994 / Strictly Rhythm ✦✦✦✦
The Strictly Rhythm series grows much better here, with label classics from Armand Van Helden ("Witch Doktor") and George Morel ("Let's Groove," "This My Party"). Superproducer David Morales appears on a remix of Boss' "Congo," and Roy Davis, Jr. contributes "Who Dares to Believe in Me" by Believers. —*John Bush*

**This Is Strictly Rhythm, Vol. 5** / Sep. 26, 1995 / Strictly Rhythm ✦✦✦✦
A host of crucial SR producers are collected on volume five, including DJ Pierre ("Mind Bomb"), Roger Sanchez ("Let Yo Body Jerk"), Josh Wink ("Higher State of Consciousness"), Erick Morillo (Lil' Mo' Yin Yang's "Reach"), Armand Van Helden (Mole People's "Break Night"), and George Morel ("Everybody Sing Along," "Why Not Believe in Him"). —*John Bush*

**This Is Strictly Rhythm, Vol. 6** / Feb. 3, 1998 / Strictly Rhythm ✦✦✦✦
This is quite a diva-oriented volume in the series, with tracks by Barbara Tucker, Ultra Naté, Kathy Brown and Divine Soul as well as DJ Sneak and Armand Van Helden's Da Mongoloids project. —*John Bush*

**This Is Techno** / Oct. 14, 1997 / Beechwood ✦✦✦
The techno edition in Beechwood's series of *This Is...* box sets includes three discs of classics, though the final one is a megamix of tracks taken from the first two. —*Keith Farley*

**This Is Techno, Vol. 2** / Jun. 23, 1992 / Continuum ✦✦✦✦
Techno, techno-rave, rave... the latest buzzwords in the dance music arena, following the success of house and acid house. Powerhouse beats layered with merciless sounds and sound bits from whatever source moves the mixer/composer. Some of this stuff is a millimeter from turning into Ministry, but there's fascinating stuff too, such as Gravity's "We Want Information" and Obscure FM's "Michael Jackson Is In Heaven Now." You won't find yourself singing along to it, though. —*Steven McDonald*

**This Is Trance Life** / Mar. 28, 2000 / Import ✦✦
*This Is Trance Life* serves as an exploitative attempt to cash in on the alarming popularity of the musical style at the end of the '90s. This budget-priced compilation features a handful of brand name producers—ATB, Paul Van Dyk, John Digweed, Paul Oakenfold, and BT—along with some of the most popular trance anthems ever: "Heaven Scent," "Don't Stop," "Another Way," "Kinetic," and "Bullet in the Gun." These names and songs are licensed to sell the album, and, in all honesty, they probably should; Bedrock's "Heaven Scent" and Paul Van Dyk's "Another Way" are beautiful songs that cannot help but appeal to the masses. Unfortunately, this jumbo compilation also includes plenty of terrible filler. Songs such as DJ Raq's "Hyena Laugh" and many others not even worth mentioning are nothing more than bland attempts at anthems that simply recycle proven trance clichés. These songs can make this album unlistenable at times. Sure, there are some songs worth listening to here, but one has to continually skips tracks to find them without

having to endure garbage. The accompanying mix CD by DJ Storm is a nice bonus but isn't separated into separate tracks, meaning that one must listen to the mix the whole way through if one is to reach the end or just a specific moment of the set. While the few good songs on this album are worth hearing, they can be found elsewhere, making this unmixed compilation of primarily bad trance an album worth skipping. —*Jason Birchmeier*

**This Is Trip-Hop** / Oct. 14, 1997 / Beechwood ♦♦♦
This Beechwood three-disc set covers trip-hop with various 12" remixes of pop groups plus a few more obscure cuts. The third disc is a megamix summation of tracks from the first two. —*Keith Farley*

**This Is Trip-Hop, Vol. 2** / 1997 / Beechwood ♦♦♦♦
A mix'n'match introduction to the art and science of trip-hop spread over three discs—the third CD features Naked Funk serving up a fifty-minute nonstop mix that's a tribute to the things one can do with samplers. 12" mixes all around from Manic Street Preachers (mixed by the Chemical Brothers), Leftfield, Ruby, Orb, Bomb the Bass, Howie B., Prodigy, Morcheeba, and many others, some hypnotic, some just passing by. It's a low-cost and relatively broad-minded introduction to trip-hop, even as a US import; well worth finding. —*Steven McDonald*

**This Is the Sound of Tribal UK** / 1994 / Tribal UK ♦♦♦
Junior Vasquez mixed this compilation of Tribal UK's better singles of the last half of 1994. —*Keith Farley*

**This Is the Sound of Tribal UK, Vol. 2** / Jan. 1996 / IRS ♦♦♦
There are several distinctive American cuts on the second Tribal UK collection, including tracks by Deep Dish, the Murk project Liberty City, and Junior Vasquez. —*Keith Farley*

**Three A.D.** / 1996 / Waveform ♦♦♦♦
Although there are a few choice selections to be found here (Real Life's "Shark Infested" and the Starseeds' "Regina From the Future" being two), Waveform's third ambient dub compilation for the most part simply sounds like one trip to the well too many. Fans of the genre would be better served by the previous two releases in this series, *One A.D.* and *Two A.D.* —*Brian E. Kirby*

**3 Minute Blunts, Vol. 1** / Jan. 27, 1997 / Studio !K7 ♦♦♦♦
*3 Minute Blunts* is an interesting collection of hip-hop from Detroit techno heads like Terrence Parker, Kanabis the Edit Assassin, Anthony Wayne, and Andre Johnson. Each producer seems quite comfortable using breakbeats instead of a four-four, and the result is a great album of instrumental hip-hop. —*Keith Farley*

**3 Minute Blunts, Vol. 2** / May 12, 1998 / Studio !K7 ♦♦♦
The second volume includes several from the first (Terrence Parker, Andre Johnson, DJ Slym Fas) plus a few new hip-hop/techno producers like Chris Shivers, Sample OS, and Louis Heravo. As difficult as it is to top the original, *3 Minute Blunts, Vol. 2* does a good job of expanding on the template, with a couple of raps included amongst the instrumental hip-hop. —*Keith Farley*

**Time: Space Compilation** / May 4, 1999 / Transmat ♦♦♦♦
Stagnant since the dawn of the '90s, Derrick May's Transmat once held the position of one of the most groundbreaking labels in the pioneering days of electronic music. A roster of new, talented techno artists comprising Transmat's roster for the dawn of the 21st century fills this compilation. Whereas the Transmat of the late '80s focused on many diverse styles, releasing records by Joey Beltram and 3 Phase, the rejuvenated Transmat focuses on a smooth, sensual techno sound reminiscent of Derrick May's past work as Rhythim is Rhythim. Although the new Rhythim is Rhythim track is the most noticeable inclusion on *Time: Space*, it is not necessarily the album's highlight. A lush exercise in relaxed techno minimalism, "Beforethereafter" could very well be a leftover from the 1987-1991 era, when May composed many early techno masterpieces; it sounds incredibly similar to classics such as "It Is What It Is" and "Icon." There are also two ambient techno songs on the compilation that deserve recognition. Most notably, Indio's "Snowdrifts" glows vibrantly with showering synthesized colors and simple melodies, no mechanical percussion, and very little bass. Similarly, Tony Drake's contribution, "To Touch You," functions as a romantic techno ballad. While a digitally altered voice proclaims "I want to touch you," a minimal piano melody twinkles through the haze of ambient synthesized strings. Furthermore, two other artists contribute noteworthy updates of May's sound: Aril Brikha and Microworld. The two Brikha tracks, "Otill" and "Groove La Chord," add lush feelings of tranquility and saturated synthesizer notes to their momentum-building energy. Microworld's "Signals" builds over the course of several minutes to an intense peak of multilayered percussive loops and repetitive synthesizer melodies before slowly deconstructing its sonic collage to a dim conclusion. Overall, this compilation foreshadows a continuation of the lush synthesizer-based techno May innovated in the late '80s—a very welcome continuation. —*Jason Birchmeier*

**Together as One [Moonshine]** / Jan. 12, 1999 / Moonshine Music ♦♦♦
Moonshine charted tracks by a variety of the world's greatest DJs (at least, those that have recorded for Moonshine) with the 1999 compilation *Together as One*, with Simply Jeff, Micro, Frankie Bones, Christopher Lawrence, Carl Cox, DJ SS, and DJ Dan. —*John Bush*

**Total Trip Hop** / Jul. 4, 1995 / City of Angels ♦♦♦
The first volume of *Total Trip Hop* features cuts from the Crystal Method, John Debo, and the Chemical Brothers (remixing Deeper Throat's "Mouth Organ"), plus many more. —*Steve Huey*

**Total Trip Hop, Vol. 2** / Mar. 19, 1996 / City of Angels ♦♦♦
The second volume of *Total Trip Hop* features cuts from Uberzone ("Botz"), Lo Phat Hi Fi, Chop Shop, and the Crystal Method (an exclusive live version of "Dubeliscious Groove"), among others. —*Steve Huey*

**Totally Loved Up** / Jun. 16, 1997 / BBC ♦♦♦♦
A reissue of the BBC soundtrack to rave documentary *Loved Up*, this LP includes some classic dance tracks circa 1995, including "Smokebelch" by Sabres of Paradise, Leftfield's "Song for Life," Hardfloor's "Acperience" and others from Bedrock, Prodigy, and Spooky. —*Keith Farley*

**Totally Re-Wired, Vol. 1** / Jan. 30, 1996 / Hollywood ♦♦♦
*Totally Re-Wired* is a collection of acid-jazz artists that fuse soul, jazz, worldbeat, funk, and hip-hop, creating a neo-psychedelic, trippy variation of dance music. Several of acid-jazz's biggest stars, including the Brand New Heavies and Snowboy, are featured on *Totally Re-Wired*, making it a fairly effective introduction to the music, even if several of the tracks are no better than mediocre genre exercises. —*Stephen Thomas Erlewine*

**Totally Wired in Dub** / Aug. 13, 1996 / Hollywood ♦♦♦
*Totally Wired In Dub* is more or less an effective dub reggae compilation—mainly because it features the classic "Blessed in Dub" by Gregory Isaac, as well as cuts from Bobby Ellis and Benjamin Zephaniah—but it overlooks too many high points and vital artists to be truly called essential. —*Leo Stanley*

**A Touch Sampler** / 1995 / Touch ♦♦♦♦
The Touch label moves from avant-garde to ambient to techno to funk on this eclectic collection, including tracks from S.E.T.I., Hafler Trio, Sandoz, Sweet Exorcist, and Soliman Gamil. —*Keith Farley*

**Touch Sampler, Vol. 3** / May 12, 1998 / Touch ♦♦♦♦
Although Touch and various of its related labels have issued their fair share of compilations, it's the *Touch Sampler* series that has really brought focus to the variety of designer/photographer/label boss Jon Wozencroft's aesthetic. *Touch Sampler 3* features a fabulous cross-cut of material, moving from the unbalanced techno-asceticism of Panasonic to the field recordings of Chris Watson to the rhythmic chaos of Austrian sample collagists Rheberg/Bauer and Farmers Manual. What's most remarkable about this compilation is the way it all manages to hold together. "Greater than the sum of its parts" is a crutch-phrase applied when more fanciful brands of hyperbole fail, but here it's empirical fact. —*Sean Cooper*

**Trackspotting** / Jun. 17, 1997 / Polygram ♦♦♦
PolyGram assembled this double-disc collection of soundtrack work reminiscent of the contemporary hit *Trainspotting*. The first disc has many good tracks, like Orbital's version of "The Saint" and U2's "Theme from Mission: Impossible," plus tracks by Leftfield, Underworld, Future Sound of London and Fluke. The concept takes a definite turn for the worse on the second disc, with such unmemorable film songs as the Ramones' "Pet Sematary," Faith No More's "The Perfect Crime," and Shane MacGowan's "That Woman's Got Me Drinking." There's a good disc and a half on this set somewhere, but PolyGram overreach themselves with 40 tracks. —*Keith Farley*

**Trance Atlantic, Vol. 1** / Feb. 14, 1995 / Volume ♦♦♦♦
After several volumes in their *Trance Europe Express* series, the compilation label Volume began a new series based on North America. The first volume of *Trance Atlantic* continues Volume's tradition of offering solid collections with all-exclusive tracks and in-depth interviews with each artist. Unfortu-

nately, it also presents an overly simplified overview of American electronic music, with the balance consisting of Detroit techno (Juan Atkins, Eddie "Flashin" Fowlkes, Kenny Larkin, Plastikman, Aux 88); New York-based trance (Joey Beltram, Mark Gage, Damon Wild, Steve Stoll) and San Francisco experimental psychedelics (Hardkiss, Spacetime Continuum, Meat Beat Manifesto, Psychic TV). The tracks are great, and fans of the styles will be impressed, but a bit more diversity would have been welcomed. —*John Bush*

**Trance Atlantic, Vol. 2** / Dec. 19, 1995 / Volume ♦♦♦♦
The second *Trance Atlantic* hits Detroit and Chicago equally hard, with Motor City producers K Hand, Kosmic Messenger (Stacey Pullen) and Blake Baxter alongside Frankie Bones, Felix Da Housecat, Green Velvet, Derrick Carter's Sound Patrol, Roy Davis, Jr., Paul Johnson and Boo Williams. The Philadelphia scene represents with Jamie Myerson and Josh Wink, while Midwestern heads like DJ ESP and Freddie Fresh also appear. —*John Bush*

★ **Trance Europe Express, Vol. 1** / 1993 / Volume ♦♦♦♦♦
The first in Volume's series of electronic compilations is a near-essential collection representing virtually every major name in the emerging listening-techno scene, most represented with exclusive tracks or remixes. Across two discs, the cream of British and German techno—Orbital, Bandulu, System 7, Black Dog, Spooky, Cosmic Baby, CJ Bolland, the Source, Aphex Twin, the Orb, the Drum Club, Psychick Warriors Ov Gaia, Sabres of Paradise—contribute excellent material, and are introduced to the mainstream via extensive interviews and pictures. In most cases, these were the first features ever done on these artists, and the set is of much interest historically as well as musically. It's simply one of the most effective documents of early-'90s ambient techno. —*John Bush*

**Trance Europe Express, Vol. 2** / 1994 / Volume ♦♦♦♦
Obviously, there were plenty of artists left uncovered by the first edition in the *Trance Europe Express* series, and the second volume presents 23 more. A bit more focus on beat-oriented techno and trance—from the likes of Dave Angel, Secret Knowledge, Speedy J, Hardfloor, Paul Van Dyk—makes for added variety and leaves plenty of room for (mostly) beatless explorers like the Irresistible Force, Scanner, the Orb side project FFWD, Pentatonik, Cabaret Voltaire's Richard H. Kirk and the Pete Namlook/Dr. Atmo venture known as Escape. There is a small but noticeable drop in quality from the first, but *Trance Atlantic, Vol. 2* is still a memorable two-disc set of early listening-techno. —*John Bush*

**Trance Europe Express, Vol. 3** / 1995 / Volume ♦♦♦♦
*Trance Europe Express, Vol. 3* charts a great balance of emerging acts like μ-ziq, Mouse on Mars, Air Liquide, Kinsthesia (aka Cylob) with established producers Joey Beltram, Luke Slater, William Orbit, Biosphere and 808 State. There's a Richard D. James/Aphex Twin exclusive recorded as Caustic Window, and Volume also looks ahead to their *Trance Atlantic* series with tracks by Detroit pioneers Juan Atkins (as Infiniti) and Eddie "Flashin" Fowlkes. —*John Bush*

**Trance Europe Express, Vol. 4** / Aug. 8, 1995 / Volume ♦♦♦♦
It's almost surprising that there are so many crucial electronica acts left uncovered after Volume's third edition in the series, but the fourth marks first appearances for pioneers like LFO, Coldcut, A Guy Called Gerald and Fluke. Underworld and the Chemical Brothers, each just beginning to emerge into the new electronic mainstream, contribute two of the best tracks, and there are other interesting contributions from Vulva and Skylab as well. —*John Bush*

**Trance Europe Express, Vol. 5** / Nov. 12, 1996 / Volume ♦♦♦
The fifth volume in the *Trance Europe Express* series harks back to the first, with tracks from early British technicians like Kirk DeGiorgio (As One), Beaumont Hannant and Steve Pickton (Stasis). Drum'n'bass makes an appearance courtesy of DJ Trace, and Slam, Andrea Parker and Slab also contribute stellar tracks. —*John Bush*

**Trance Europe, Vol. 1: Electronic Body Experience** / Oct. 1, 1993 / Cleopatra ♦♦
Cleopatra Records' first venture into the world of electronic non-industrial music is typically ham-fisted, with tracks from no-names Negrosex, Master Program, Dance 2 Trance and Hyperborea, among others. —*Keith Farley*

**Trance Europe, Vol. 2: Aural Electronic Dreams** / Jul. 1, 1994 / Cleopatra ♦♦
Perhaps even more tepid than its predecessor, *Trance Europe, Vol. 2* includes includes tracks from Final Fantasy, Morpheus 7, Komakino, Shorty Bone, and Tranceformer. —*Keith Farley*

**Trance Global Nation** / Nov. 10, 1998 / Red Ant ♦♦♦♦
*Trance Global Nation* features many of the best, most crucial club-bound trance tracks of the late '90s, including Energy 52's "Café del Mar," Nalin & Kane's "Beachball," Da Hool's "Meet Her at the Love Parade," Vincent De Moor's "Flowtation," Sash's "Encore une Fois," and Viridian's "Sunhump." —*John Bush*

**Trance Global Nation, Vol. 2** / Jun. 1, 1999 / A-Records ♦♦♦♦
*Trance Global Nation, Vol. 2* follows up the success of the original volume with another continuous mix of trance anthems. Nicholas Bennison blends tracks from artists like Energy 52, Hybrid, and Electrique Boutique into one another seamlessly for nonstop electronica pleasure. Other featured cuts include BT's "God Speed," Push's "Universal Nation," and "Words" by Paul Van Dyk. —*Heather Phares*

**Trance Global Nation, Vol. 4** / May 2, 2000 / Arcade America ♦♦♦
*Trance Global Nation 4* is the fourth volume in this series spotlighting a 12-track continuous mix of the best dance/trance club hits of the late '90s, featuring Cartel's "Burnout (Broken Boundary Mix)," Ascention's "Shadow Maker," Weirdo's "Photic Zone," Sphere's "Gravity," and Adaptor's "Signum." —*Al Campbell*

**Trance League Express: A Trance Tribute to the Human League** / Feb. 25, 1997 / Cleopatra ♦♦
Human League completists may wish to have this Cleopatra tribute, but the tracks—by Arcane Passage, Maggots from Mars, Bonehead and the Memory Garden, among others—are insipid industrial-trance songs without merit. —*Keith Farley*

**The Trance Masters** / Sep. 28, 1999 / Cleopatra ♦♦
Another in Cleopatra's seemingly endless supply of repackaging, mispackaging, and generally horrid packaging (to say nothing of the music), *The Trance Masters* is a three-disc box set including two artist albums (Psygone's *Optimystique* and Crude Infinity's *Ground Zero*) plus one compilation (Land of Rave, from the Danish label X-Ray). The music is speedy Euro-trance, occasionally useful as video-game-soundtrack material, but generally devoid of listenability for any but the most hardcore audiences. —*John Bush*

**Trance Pacific Express** / Apr. 15, 1997 / Deviant ♦♦♦♦
*Trance Pacific Express* in this case concentrates not on the West Coast and Japan as much as Australia and New Zealand. And although the producers are obscure even for the techno scene, there are many excellent tracks from the likes of Voitek, Unitone Hifi, Sassi & Loco, Shaolin Wooden Men, Aquila. Just as thoughtful and well-compiled as those in the *Trance Europe* and *Trance Atlantic* series, this is a solid compilation. —*John Bush*

**Trance Techno Express: From Detroit to Berlin and Back** / 1997 / Pow Wow ♦♦♦♦
A compilation of tracks from the various Berlin-Detroit releases recorded by Germany's Tresor label and later licensed by the American Pow Wow, *Trance Techno Express* includes tracks by 3MB Featuring Juan Atkins, Eddie "Flashin" Fowlkes, Blake Baxter, 3-Phase and System 01. Most of the tracks are essential techno documents, but they're better accessed via their original release if possible. This set works better as an introduction to the American-German techno alliance. —*John Bush*

**Trance, Vol. 2: A State of Altered Consciousness** / Apr. 18, 2000 / Max Music ♦♦♦
Like the original, *Trance II: A State of Altered Consciousness* is a continuous mix of cutting-edge trance and progressive house. This volume puts DJ Noel W. Sanger at the helm and features cuts like Tilt's "I Dream," Travel's "Pray to Jerusalem," Atmosphere's "She's in the Light," Sphere's "Gravity," and 16 other tracks, including songs by Deepsky, Scott Hardkiss, Joi Cardwell, Lustral, Planet Perfecto, and Bedrock. A welcome collection of current trance sounds. —*Heather Phares*

**Trance: A State of Altered Consciousness** / Oct. 19, 1999 / Container ♦♦♦
*Trance: State of Altered Consciousness* is a good continuous mix trance album featuring cuts by Leeds & Dunne, Argonauts, SLP, Kaistar, Dauby, ATB, Amoeba Assassin, Travel, Veracocha, System F, and Sasha, whose "Xpander" is featured on the only American release of its original mix. —*Stephen Thomas Erlewine*

**Trancefusion, Vol. 1** / 1994 / Instinct ♦♦♦
*Trancefusion* has a few good tracks (from Orbital, WestBam and the Irre-

sistible Force) but the balance of the compilation is bland studio-trance from Violet Force, Happy as Hell, Trancesetters, and Paradise 3000. —*Keith Farley*

**Trancefusion, Vol. 2** / May 5, 1994 / Instinct ✦✦✦✦

The second volume ups the ante considerably, with contributions from Sabres of Paradise, Jam & Spoon, Cabaret Voltaire, the Drum Club and Orbital, plus Instinct Records paragons like Prototype 909, Omicron, and Young American Primitive. —*Keith Farley*

**Trancemission from Raveland** / Aug. 20, 1996 / Cleopatra ✦✦

The double-disc set *Trancemission from Raveland* contains 26 tracks of European trance and techno. It's an uneven collection, featuring as much prime material as mediocre cuts, but the high points—from artists like Trancefloor, Oscillator, System 4, Hyper Giants, Protostars, Pulsator, Virtual Society—make it worthwhile for afficianados. —*Stephen Thomas Erlewine*

**Trancemission to Andromeda** / May 7, 1996 / Hypnotic ✦✦

Like its predecessor *The Sound of Now!*, *Trancemission to Andromeda* is a collection of progressive dance music from the German label Now! —*Jason Ankeny*

**Trancemode Express 1.01: A Trance Tribute to Depeche Mode** / Jan. 16, 1996 / Cleopatra ✦✦

Cleopatra's "trance" tribute to Depeche Mode leans much closer to industrial-dance than any other style. Latex Empire, Executor, Delta Signal, Reverse Pulse, and Audio Science, among others, tackle DM classics like "Get the Balance Right," "Behind the Wheel," "Strangelove" and (of course) "Master and Servant;" although many of these songs lend well to industrial-dance versions, these tracks are only the palest imitations of the originals. —*Keith Farley*

**Trancemode 3.01: A Tribute to Depeche Mode** / Feb. 23, 1999 / Cleopatra ✦✦

Most of the artists paying "tribute" to Depeche Mode on *Trancemode 3.01* are obscure industrial bands (Razed in Black is perhaps the biggest name) signed to Cleopatra Records, which has already put out two prior tribute albums dedicated to Depeche Mode. These interpretations add very little to the material, and start to sound rather similar over the course of the album. Early pressings included a bonus CD featuring nine of the album's 11 tracks put together in a continuous "megamix." —*Steve Huey*

**Trancentral: A Trip to Goa** / Feb. 18, 1997 / Kickin' ✦✦✦

Kickin' assembled this collection of average goa-trance, including tracks by Bass Shakra, Arcana, Sirius 2, Kode 4, Transwave, and others. —*Keith Farley*

**Trancesexual** / Mar. 19, 1996 / Hypnotic ✦✦✦

A compilation of club and chart hits from the German trance and house scenes, *Trancesexual* features, among others, Trance 2 House, Plasma ID, and Rhythm Section. —*Jason Ankeny*

**Trancespotting, Vol. 1: Music from the World of Trance** / Feb. 11, 1997 / Cleopatra ✦✦

Cleopatra's first volume in the series includes tracks by Astralasia and Kraftwelt plus the usual second-rate acts like Surface 10, Giez, Trancemutator, and Omniglobe. —*Keith Farley*

**Trancespotting, Vol. 2** / May 26, 1998 / Cleopatra ✦✦✦

The second volume in Cleopatra's *Trancespotting* series offers an occasionally appealing collection of tripped-out electronica tracks from the likes of Heaven 17 (a Giorgio Moroder remix of "Designing Heaven"), Spahn Ranch (an Astralasia mix of "In the Aftermath"), and Juno Reactor ("Magnetic"). System 7 and Pressure of Speech (remixed by Scanner) also make appearances. —*Jason Ankeny*

**Trans Slovenia Express** / 1994 / Mute ✦✦✦

This curious compilation includes mostly electronic interpretations of Kraftwerk songs by Slovenian artists. Laibach is the only name act, and the rest of the tracks are similarly bland. —*Keith Farley*

**Transient Dawn** / Jun. 16, 1997 / Transient ✦✦✦✦

*Transient Dawn* compiles some of the best tracks available in ambient psychedelic music, including classics from Messiah, Medicine Drum, Slide, Doof, and Astral Projection. —*Keith Farley*

**Tresor, Vol. 1: The Techno Sound of Berlin (A Tresor Kompilation)** / 1992 / NovaMute ✦✦✦

Defining an era, the first of many Tresor compilations from Berlin's pioneering techno label signaled to the world that Germany was attempting to regain its stature as the world's leader of electronic music. Each of the tracks featured on this album shares similar characteristics. Formally, they are complex and progressive, continually changing shape and moving forward without any logical reason besides intensity. Unlike many of the Detroit and Chicago tracks from the preceding era of techno, these Berlin artists weren't satisfied with locking into a groove and staying there. A dark, foreboding tone of mechanical inhumanity also pervades the album, capable of instilling a sense of disorienting fear in the listener. By the conclusion of this legendary album, listeners may find the music a little outdated, but this historical antiquity proves to be the album's strength. Most of these artists, such as Maurizio, Van Dijk, Felmann, and Underground Resistance, would go on to produce plenty of better-crafted and more significant work bearing their own individual trademark sounds. These early tracks retain an aura of ambitious complexity as they take their first artistic steps towards confident brilliance, influencing a generation of both techno and early trance producers in the process. —*Jason Birchmeier*

**Tresor, Vol. 2: Berlin-Detroit, A Techno Alliance** / 1993 / NovaMute ✦✦✦✦

Released only a few months after the first Tresor compilation, *Tresor, Vol. 2* illustrates just how quickly the sound of this German label had evolved. While *Tresor, Vol. 1* had been a little rough and primitive, the second compilation is far more smooth, refined and realized. The first half of the album highlights blooming German artists such as Moritz Von Oswald (aka Maurizio), Vainquer, and DJ Hell. At the time of this release in early 1993, each of these German artists began to develop the individual musical styles that would eventually make them noteworthy. On the second half of the album, Detroit artists such as Jeff Mills, Juan Atkins, and Underground Resistance contribute the sort of music that had made them so influential to their German peers. The haunting, dark tone that cast its shadow over *Tresor, Vol. 1* had been alleviated to a certain degree on *Tresor, Vol. 2*. The German artists—especially DJ Hell and Noxious—still produced an aggressive style of techno that punishes the listener with mechanical intensity. In relation to the Germans, the Detroit artists' techno pounds with less intensity at a more soothing tempo. In addition, the music tends to sound lighter and more soulful due to a more conscious effort to focus on ambient synthesizer tones and melodies instead of strictly percussion and dark motifs. —*Jason Birchmeier*

**Tresor, Vol. 3: Berlin-New Directions in Techno** / Apr. 25, 1995 / NovaMute ✦✦✦✦

Influenced primarily by Robert Hood's *Internal Empire* album, the mesmerizing repetition of Basic Channel, the solo material of Jeff Mills, and the releases of Richie Hawtin's Plus 8 record label, the new direction found on *Tresor, Vol. 3* retains the ability to ignite a dancefloor while adding additional aesthetic elements that weren't quite as fully realized on the preceding two volumes. Beginning with Maurizio's epic 13-minute mix of "Domina" and concluding with Thomas Fehlmann and Moritz Von Oswald's brilliant collaboration, "Schizophrenia," the album moves from symmetrically sculpted minimal bass excursions through a number of densely layered rhythmic montages, towards the utopian lush ambience of the final track's tranquil bliss. Yet even though the move towards a more minimal style of techno cast its shadow over this ambitious album, over the years many of these songs have begun to sound a bit too prototypical and not entirely as realized as they perhaps should. —*Jason Birchmeier*

**Tresor, Vol. 4: Solid** / Apr. 1, 1997 / Tresor ✦✦✦✦

Perhaps the closest thing to a greatest-hits compilation for the Berlin label, *Tresor, Vol. 4* includes classics not just of Berlin and Detroit, but of the entire genre—"Sonic Destroyer" by X-101 (aka Underground Resistance), "M6" by Maurizio, "Think Quick" by Juan Atkins' Infiniti, "Instant" by Joey Beltram, and Model 500's "M69 Starlight." There are also appearances by Europeans Scan 7, Pacou, Vainquer, Cristian Vogel, and 3 Phase. —*John Bush*

**Tresor, Vol. 5** / Jul. 15, 1997 / Tresor ✦✦✦✦

This volume in the *Tresor* series looks to the future, with many exclusives by artists at the verge of experimental techno and trance: Si Begg, Neil Landstrumm, Cristian Vogel, and Tobias Schmidt. Also included are tracks by important Americans—K Hand, Joey Beltram—and Tresor naturals like Pacou and Scan 7. It's not the best distillation of the Tresor aesthetic, but *Tresor, Vol. 5* is nonetheless a solid collection. —*John Bush*

**Tresor, Vol. 6: Love Parade (Tresor 100)** / Jul. 7, 1998 / Tresor ♦♦♦
The sixth Tresor compilation celebrates the Berlin label's 100th release with a collection of 13 hard techno anthems by many of the genre's premier producers. Albums such as this illustrate exactly how influential Tresor has been within the realm of hard techno. Since this album compiles previously released material, well-seasoned techno fanatics may already be familiar with landmark records such as Basic Channel's "Octaedre," but anyone still investigating the world of techno should study this album in particular. Banging techno anthems such as Regis's "The Theme From 'Streetwalker'" stand alongside songs demonstrating Surgeon's almost tribal style of scrambled-sounding disorientation and more subdued techno exercises such as Infiniti's "Thought Process," Substance's "Plate Element 2," and Pacou's "Encounter." Besides functioning as a broad introduction to late-'90s hard techno, this compilation also illustrates exactly how diverse the once-generic style had evolved to by the end of the century. —*Jason Birchmeier*

**Tresor, Vol. 8** / Jul. 11, 2000 / EFA ♦♦♦
The eighth Tresor compilation finds the Berlin label moving away from one particular sound toward a more diverse range of styles, reflecting the changing face of techno at the end of the 20th century. Perhaps the biggest surprise comes when the album begins with some down-tempo dub techno courtesy of Round Two (better known as Basic Channel) and Savvas Ysatis. This mellow pace brings a refreshing sense of serenity to the otherwise banging sound of Tresor. From there the album slowly begins to pick up pace, moving into the mid-tempo listening techno of Stewart S. Walker and Terrence Dixon. These two artists in particular present the sort of emotive songs one would expect from a less dancefloor-orientated label than Tresor. Similar to these two artists' inclusions, Drexciya's "Species of the Pod"—the opening track from the mysterious Detroit artist's excellent *Neptune's Lair* album—brings some electro flavor to the compilation, another style not often associated with the label. Aril Brikha's "Groove la Chord" then begins the album's climb towards dancefloor-orientated music, with its slowly building synth stabs. From there *Tresor, Vol. 8* heads into the sort of dense, intense, and hard techno commonly associated with the time-tested Berlin label. Of these latter tracks, Claude Young's "Rise" stands out with its thick wall of buzzing static that functions as a foreboding curtain hovering in the background of the 909 kick drum-driven track. The contributions by Sender Berlin, Pacou, Diskordia, and James Ruskin all deserve recognition as well, with each heading off in a different style of techno: Basic Channel-style hallucinogenic reverb, Purpose Maker-style rhythm-dominated tribal percussion, Axis-style high-tech man versus machine warfare, and Surgeon-style pounding mesmerization, respectively. —*Jason Birchmeier*

**Tribal America Artists After Hours** / 1996 / I.R.S. ♦♦♦
Mostly consisting of mainstream, New York-based artists, Tribal America released a compilation of downtempo excursions. Though the tracks are by no means beatless, the grooves are deep and the atmosphere is everything on these tracks by Eric Kupper, Junior Vasquez, Deep Dish, the Daou, Club 69, and Danny Tenaglia. —*John Bush*

**Tribal Gathering [Cleopatra]** / Nov. 11, 1997 / Cleopatra ♦♦♦♦
Named for the UK dance festival that was nearly banned by authorities, *Tribal Gathering* is a three-CD collection featuring mixes by three of the DJs present at that event—Disc One is mixed by Chicago house legend Marshall Jefferson; Disc Two features underground European DJ Gayle San; and Mo'Wax label head James Lavelle handles Disc Three. There are 38 tracks in all by the likes of DJ Food, DJ Krush, DJ Spooky, Howie B., Future Sound of London, and more. —*Steve Huey*

**Tribute to Brian Eno** / Jul. 29, 1997 / Cleopatra ♦♦♦
Cleopatra earns points on its Brian Eno tribute album for actually including a few respected artists like Chrome, Controlled Bleeding and Astralasia as well as label-patsies and no-names like the Electric Hellfire Club, FarFlung, Brand X, and Surface 10. The latter appear to owe more to White Zombie than Eno, and much of this album sounds like it. —*John Bush*

**Trip Hop & Jazz** / 1995 / Instinct ♦♦♦
The first volume of *Trip Hop & Jazz* focuses on Ninja Tune label artists, including several tracks each from Up, Bustle & Out, 9 Lazy 9, and DJ Food. It's a good collection of earthy downtempo grooves, though for a Ninja Tune retrospective, there are several acts notably absent—like label-heads Coldcut. —*John Bush*

**Trip Hop & Jazz, Vol. 2: Beats from the Underground** / Jan. 30, 1996 / Instinct ♦♦♦
The second volume in Instinct's series opens up the sound to include more atmospheric acts like Diferenze, Marschmellows, Tosca, Shantel, and Beanfield. —*John Bush*

**Trip Hop & Jazz: Global Grooves** / Oct. 19, 1999 / Instinct ♦♦♦
The fifth volume in Instinct's *Trip Hop & Jazz* focuses on the worldwide growth of jazz-fueled electronic beat production. Though it's not incredibly wide-ranging (five tracks from England and one each from France, Germany, Austria, America, and Japan), the productions are tight and inventive, from the opener "Dittonia Bloo" by the 13th Sign to inclusions from DJ Krush ("Ki-Gen"), Mr. Electric Triangle ("Total Float"), and Spaceways ("Pinhead Plutonium"). —*Keith Farley*

**Trip Hop Acid Phunk, Vol. 1** / Aug. 8, 1995 / Adrenalin ♦♦♦
Adrenalin's first volume of *Trip Hop Acid Phunk* is a collection of American breakbeat techno, heavy on the psychedelic trance. Two tracks by Omar Santana's Darkside of the Shroom project provide the highlights, while Bassbin Twins' "Dirty Crystal," and Peter Tall's "A-1 Love" are also solid-form workouts. The other five tracks are prototypical big-dumb-techno, for better or worse. —*John Bush*

**Trip Hop Acid Phunk, Vol. 2** / Feb. 6, 1996 / Adrenalin ♦♦♦
Similar to the first edition, *Trip Hop Acid Phunk, Vol. 2* has several good tracks by an Omar Santana project—here Hard Hop Heathen—plus similar-sounding tracks by an assortment of names both familiar (Richard "Humpty" Vission, Dubtribe) and not so familiar (Cotten Club, DJ Lace). —*John Bush*

**The Trip Hop Nation** / Aug. 27, 1996 / Priority ♦♦
*The Trip Hop Nation* is an adequate but frustrating compilation of such trip-hop artists as the Trip Junkies, Acid Drop, DJ Level X, Oscillator, and Black Crystal. While most of the genre's biggest names are missing, the compilation is fairly entertaining, especially for fans of the genre's lazzy, drugged rhythms. The uninitiated should find another starting place—preferably Portishead, Tricky, or Massive Attack—since there are enough gaps and mediocre songs to make *The Trip Hop Nation* a poor introduction to this dance style. —*Stephen Thomas Erlewine*

**The Trip Hop Nation, Vol. 2** / Sep. 30, 1997 / Priority ♦♦♦
It contains no major tracks or artists, and *The Trip Hop Nation, Vol. 2* is simply an adequate sampler of trip-hop which reeks of a cash-in. Most of this is an outgrowth of Massive Attack, but some of it is too fast or direct to be considered pure trip-hop. Nevertheless, anyone looking for a definitive trip-hop collection should not turn here—they'll need to get *Blue Lines* and *Maxinquaye*, instead. All things considered—the lack of big names, the similarity of the sounds—*The Trip Hop Nation, Vol. 2* isn't a bad collection and fanatics of the genre may find it worth a listen. —*Stephen Thomas Erlewine*

● **The Trip Hop Test, Vol. 1** / 1994 / Moonshine Music ♦♦♦♦
In a surprising turn of events, the first American trip-hop compilation out of the gate turns out to be one of the best. Though it lacks some of the big hitters in the style like Massive Attack and Tricky, the tracks included are some of the best—Skylab's "Seashell," the Chemical Brothers' "My Mercury Mouth," Portishead's remix of Paul Weller's "Wildwood," Tranquility Bass' "They Came in Peace," and others by Single Cell Orchestra, Lemon Interrupt (aka Underworld), and Saint Etienne. Irrespective of label, country, or commercial inclination, Moonshine Records compiled an excellent album. —*John Bush*

**The Trip Hop Test, Vol. 2** / Oct. 3, 1995 / Moonshine Music ♦♦♦♦
Moonshine's second volume in the *Trip Hop Test* series works its way into the American breakbeat scene, with tracks by the Crystal Method, Cirrus, and Omar Santana's Dark Side of the Shroom. Of course there are still plenty of British contributions, from the Chemical Brothers, Red Snapper, D'Cruze, and Danny Saber, among others. —*John Bush*

**The Trip Hop Test, Vol. 3** / May 7, 1996 / Moonshine Music ♦♦♦♦
The third volume in Moonshine's series is a good sampler of the continuing effect that the breakbeat has had on dance culture. From the G-stoned trippiness of Moloko's "Fun for Me" to big-beat madness with Fatboy Slim's "The Weekend Starts Here" and the American breakbeat trance of "Break In" by Cirrus, the range of styles is quite large. Also included are tracks from Danny Saber, Omar Santana's Wizard of Oh, the Hardkiss project God Within, and Basco. —*John Bush*

**Trip Hop Til' U Drop** / Mar. 25, 1997 / Priority ♦♦
Level X, Hash Den, Oscillator, and Numb Factory are among the artists spotlighted on *Trip Hop Til' U Drop*, which compiles tracks steeped heavily in trance-like house beats and electronic funk. —*Jason Ankeny*

**Tripnotized, Vol. 1** / May 28, 1996 / Manifold ♦♦
*Tripnotized, Vol. 1* is a double-disc set of high-energy psychedelic trance and breakbeat rave. Unfortunately, the names are impossibly obscure and the music is push-button electronic music. The set includes tracks by DJ Crack, Mindlock, Code 20, Virtualmismo, DJ Ablaze, and Mark NRG, among others. —*Keith Farley*

**Tripnotized, Vol. 3** / Jan. 27, 1997 / ZYX ♦♦♦
The third volume in the series does include a remix of Josh Wink's dance hit "Higher State of Consciousness," though the rest of the double-disc compilation has little to recommend itself. Other artists include Code 24, DJ Energy, De Donatis, Flexter, Jim Clarke, and Ultimate. —*Keith Farley*

**Trippin' on Rhythms** / Feb. 17, 1998 / Shanachie ♦♦♦
A compilation of crucial acid-jazz masters past and present, *Trippin' on Rhythms* includes selections from Roy Ayers, the Greyboy Allstars, Groove Collective, and Ronny Jordan, plus the unreleased Brand New Heavies track "Midnight at the Oasis." —*Keith Farley*

**True People: The Detroit Techno Album** / Mar. 1, 1996 / React ♦♦♦♦
*True People* is *the* Detroit compilation, a two-disc set of new tracks by each major producer in the scene, from originators Derrick May, Juan Atkins, Kevin Saunderson, Blake Baxter, and Eddie Fowlkes to '90s stalwarts Claude Young, Stacey Pullen, Kenny Larkin, Drexciya, Keith Tucker, the Suburban Knight, Alan Oldham, Anthony "Shake" Shakir, and more. Though a retrospective collection may have worked better than a set of all-new material, the incredible consistency sustained throughout the album testifies to Detroit's continuing vitality as the center for American techno. Among many highlights, the best come from Juan Atkins (a drum'n'bass workout recorded with 4 Hero), the Suburban Knight (a remix of his classic "The Art of Stalking") and Stacey Pullen ("8th Wonder"). —*John Bush*

**Twist This Pussy** / Jan. 13, 1998 / MCA ♦♦♦
*Twist This Pussy* is a continuous mix dance album masterminded by DJ Peter Rauhofer, the producer behind Sizequeen and Club 69. Rauhofer mixes together 14 songs from the Twisted vaults, including Club 69's "Drama," House Heroes' "Magic Orgasm," Zise Queen's "K-Hole," Superchumbo's "Get This!," Moogroove's "Bambo," the Water Chamber's "Get Funky," and Dirty White Boy's "Triple XXX Porn." Many of these songs have never reached CD before, but the true star of the record isn't the songs, it's Rauhofer's impressive mixing which manages to capture the spirit of a dance club. It's still designed for listeners who love dance clubs, not sitting and listening to records, and on that level it works quite well. —*Stephen Thomas Erlewine*

**Twist This Pussy, Vol. 2** / Nov. 3, 1998 / Twisted America ♦♦♦
The second volume in Twisted/MCA's recap series includes solid contributions from Funky Green Dogs, Junior Vasquez, Lowpass, Club 69, K-Scope, and Funky Derrick. —*John Bush*

**2 Technocal: The Second Rave** / Dec. 26, 1994 / SPG ♦♦♦
*2 Technocal* includes several hard-to-find rave and proto-electronica tracks, including "Trip II the Moon" by Acen, "Humanoid" by Stakker (aka the Future Sound of London), "Hold It Down" by 2 Bad Mice, and Jam & Spoon's remix of the eponymous Age of Love single. —*Keith Farley*

**UK Tribal Gathering '95** / 1995 / Universe/London ♦♦♦
This double-disc compilation wasn't recorded at the Tribal Gathering; rather, it collects non-album tracks by some of the participants, including the Drum Club, Underworld, the Chemical Brothers, Orbital, Moby, Plastikman, the Prodigy, Leftfield and Carl Cox, among others. —*Keith Farley*

**The Ultimate Afro: House Collection** / Nov. 16, 1999 / Max Music ♦♦♦
Most of the songs on *The Ultimate Afro: House Collection* were not released on CD in their original formats, which means that if any of these dance-club tracks struck your fancy, they're pretty much only available here. Most of these are house tracks with a pronounced Latin freestyle bent; some charted on the *Billboard* dance lists, while others are remixes spun in various clubs. The latter category includes tracks by Celia Cruz and Latin Xpress featuring Gina Martin, while the former has such material as Warning's "Tubale (Ex-

tasy)" and Dogma & the Afro-Cuban Rhythms' "Mas Suave" and "Ritmo Cubano, Sabor Africano." —*Steve Huey*

**Ultimate Drum'N'Bass** / Apr. 15, 1997 / Cleopatra ♦♦
There may be a few people out there who believe Cleopatra Records when the label tells them a compilation titled *Ultimate Drum'N'Bass* needs to have such artists as Spahn Ranch, Aqualite, UVX, and Transmutator, but one listen to the album itself could easily convince them of their error. If there can be highlights on an album this poor, they are provided by remixes of tracks by the Art of Noise, System 7, and Children of Dub. Fans of industrial-dance may find something of use here, but anyone looking for a jungle compilation should look elsewhere. —*Keith Farley*

**Ultimate Gabber Trance: The Beats from Hell** / May 7, 1996 / Hypnotic ♦♦♦
Cellblock X, Radar, and Spastikman are among the artists contributing to this collection of European gabber techno. —*Jason Ankeny*

**Ultra Mix: Drum & Bass** / Sep. 2, 1997 / Priority ♦♦♦
*Ultra Mix: Drum & Bass* is a good collection of relentless jungle cuts sequenced together into a continuous mix. Artists featured include Arcon 2, E-Z Rollers, Alpha Omega, David Kristian, Dave Wallace, and the Sonar Circle. —*Stephen Thomas Erlewine*

**Ultra Mix: The Best of Tribal Records America** / Sep. 2, 1997 / Priority ♦♦♦
*Ultra Mix: The Best of Tribal Records America* is a good continuous-mix album that spotlights singles from Tribal Records, including Funky Green Dogs' "Reach for Me," Danny Tenaglia's "Come Together," Junior Vasquez's "X," and Matt Wood's "What Am I Gonna Do with You." —*Stephen Thomas Erlewine*

**UltraDolce, Vol. 2** / Irma ♦♦♦♦
Where else can listeners go to find a drum'n'bass version of the old spaghetti chestnut "Volare," complete with a spooky, vocoderized reading of the vocals? For better or worse, there are very few labels that would attempt this sort of brand-new-retro sound, and Irma La Douce leads the pack. This sleazy-listening collection includes 18 tracks—each by a different producer—of bossa-nova rhythms, multiple organ solos, and that quintessentially breezy continental air. This second volume in the *UltraDolce* series again proves that there must be dozens of Italian producers who've been slipped the required dosage—albums by Pizzicatto Five, Fatboy Slim, Tony Hatch, and Astrud Gilberto, plus several old synthesizer novelty records—to produce this many tracks. Another surprising thing is that many of these tracks are excellent. Though not many are able to escape the pure silliness of their origins, each one is impeccably arranged, impeccably played, and quite inventive. Highlights include the aforementioned "Volare" by Montefiori Cocktail, "Bow Wow" by Tommy Bass, "Flaminio Zagato" by Sam Paglia, a jazzanova remix of "Metti una Sera a Cena" by Balanço, and "Kill Them All" by Doris Troy. Many of Irma La Douce's compilations are hit-and-miss (and mostly miss), but the *UltraDolce* series has put Italy's new-wave-of-easy scene on a par with Japan's. —*John Bush*

**Ultrasound** / Mar. 3, 1998 / Shadow ♦♦♦
*Ultrasound* presents a sampler of the artists on the British label Hospital, with tracks from London Electricity, the Peter Nice Trio, Izit, Dwarf Electro, and E.S.T. —*Steve Huey*

**United Nations of House** / Feb. 14, 1995 / ffrr ♦♦♦♦
*United Nations of House* is a good collection of dancefloor house, with classic tracks from Strictly Rhythm artists Armand Van Helden ("Witch Doktor") and Erick Morillo ("I Like to Move It") plus British acts like Orbital (a remix of "Are We Here?") and Black Science Orchestra ("New Jersey Deep"). It's a good blend of mainstream and progressive-house. —*Keith Farley*

**United State of Ambience, Vol. 1** / Feb. 22, 1994 / Moonshine Music ♦♦♦
This American collection of downtempo trance includes tracks by Hawke, LunaSol, Young American Primitive, Electric Skychurch and Dubtribe. —*Keith Farley*

**United States of Drum'N'Bass** / Apr. 28, 1998 / Evil Teen ♦♦
With a host of unknown artists like Kingsize, DJ Stratus, Flow, King Rhythm and Atlantique, *United States of Drum N Bass* is a rather pedestrian set of breakbeat-influenced grooves. —*Keith Farley*

**Up & Down Club Sessions, Vol. 1** / Oct. 1995 / Mammoth ♦♦♦♦
Inspired by the San Francisco acid jazz venue the Up & Down Club, this al-

bum includes tracks by Alphabet Soup, the Josh Jones Ensemble, the Kenny Brooks Trio, and the Will Bernard Trio. *Up & Down Club Sessions, Vol. 1* and its follow-up are two of the acid jazz albums most amenable to fans of jazz as well as dance. There is an emphasis on live playing and true musicianship on the solos, while the grooves are consistently deep and funky. —*Keith Farley*

**Up & Down Club Sessions, Vol. 2** / Oct. 1995 / Mammoth ✦✦✦
The second in the series includes five live tracks actually recorded at the club (by the Up & Down All-Stars and the Josh Jones Latin Jazz Ensemble). Acid jazz and jazz-funk is the tone, with female vocals on some tracks to give them a soulful feel. Don Cherry guests on two tracks, including a good cover of "'Round Midnight." —*Keith Farley*

**Urb Mix, Vol. 1: Flammable Liquid** / Oct. 1995 / Planet Earth ✦✦✦✦
Compiled by *Urb* magazine with Planet Earth Records, this compilation of the American underground dance scene was well-done, with a variety of acts including "Throw" by Carl Craig's Paperclip People project, "Outernational Wah" by Airgoose and "Feel It" by Coco Steel & Lovebomb. —*Keith Farley*

**Urb Mix, Vol. 2: DJ Dan** / Sep. 30, 1997 / Sm:)e ✦✦✦
DJ Dan takes over the decks for the second volume in the *Urb Mix* series. The track selection is less impressive than on the first volume, but there are several good songs, including those by Benji Candelario, Anthony Acid, and Slab, remixed by Carl Cox. —*Keith Farley*

**Urbal Beats, Vol. 1** / Jul. 22, 1997 / Polygram ✦✦✦✦
The first volume of *Urbal Beats* is a solid sampler of the British electronica and American breakbeat scene circa 1997, with Americans DJ Icey, Rabbit in the Moon, Crystal Method, Keoki, and Wink alongside Brits like Prodigy, Goldie, Orb, Orbital, CJ Bolland, and Underworld. —*Keith Farley*

**Urbal Beats, Vol. 2** / May 5, 1998 / Polygram ✦✦✦✦
*Urbal Beats, Vol. 2* is a double-disc set that features 24 electronica, dance, and techno songs continually mixed by Liquid Todd, the resident electronic DJ at the Los Angeles alternative station KROQ. For the first disc, Todd picks new hits—Goldie's "Temper Temper," Portishead's "Over," Fatboy Slim's "Going Out of My Mind," the Crystal Method's "Keep Hope Alive," and Prodigy's "Smack My Bitch Up"—and sprinkles a couple of cult favorites in for good measure. More dedicated fans will find the first disc a little predictable and unnecessary, but the second disc's inclusion of several seminal dance singles—"Strings of Life" by Derrick May's Rhythim Is Rhythim, "Chime" by Orbital, "Loops of Fury" by the Chemical Brothers, "Go" by Moby, "Voodoo Ray" by A Guy Called Gerald, "Charly" by Prodigy—increases the set's worth for those interested in the history of techno and rave. It's a pretty entertaining listen, even if the mixing isn't anything remarkable, and it works as a good sampler for fans of the genre. —*Stephen Thomas Erlewine*

**Urbal Beats, Vol. 3** / Aug. 31, 1999 / Polygram ✦✦✦
The third volume in *Urb* magazine's series charting the growth and expansion of electronica adds tracks from a few sources dance fans are unfamiliar with. Next to constantly anthologized artists like Moby, Underworld, and Orbital are appearances from Method Man, the Latin rap band Ozomatli, Florida breaksman DJ Icey, and Asian Dub Foundation. Given such a wide range of sounds on one album, *Urbal Beats, Vol. 3* works quite well for veteran dance fans as well as beginners struggling to find a foothold in an often confusing scene. —*Keith Farley*

**Us** / May 23, 2000 / Up ✦✦✦✦
This budget-priced split compilation is an interesting animal in several ways; first of all, it's a little weird for two labels to collaborate on a compilation album, though there's certainly nothing wrong with that. Stranger is the fact that, although Up's profile tends toward homemade electronica and Slabco's toward indie pop and rock, both labels are represented here by a roster almost equally divided between electro (Land of the Loops, Volume All*Star, Buckminster Fuzeboard) and rock (Modest Mouse, Sick Bees, Mike Johnson). Still, there's definitely nothing wrong with a little genre diversity. So how does the album sound? About like you'd expect, with the definite edge going to the electro crowd; Buckminster Fuzeboard and Land of the Loops are the class of that clique, with "Snap Clarity" and the trippy sample-fest "France," respectively. Rockers Dark Fantastic turn in a very respectable entry entitled "My Wandering Eye," but the Concretes are a discouraging choice for lead cut and the program ends with an unbelievably lame contribution from Modest Mouse. Given the album's under ten dollar list price and the amount of great material on it, though, it's eminently recommendable. —*Rick Anderson*

**V Classic, Vol. 1** / Apr. 28, 1997 / V Recordings ✦✦✦✦
*V Classic, Vol. 1* compiles stellar vinyl-only releases from the Bristol jazz-step label V Records. Artists present include Roni Size, DJ Krust, Dillinjah, Lemon D, Goldie, DJ Die, Ray Keith, Scorpio, and Bill Riley. —*Steve Huey*

**V Classic, Vol. 2** / 1998 / V Recordings ✦✦✦✦
For those who couldn't get enough of the great dance compilation *V Classic, Vol. 1*, your prayers have been answered. Ultra Records has issued an accompanying second volume of different drum'n'bass tracks, and it's as good (if not better) than the original. Most of today's best-known and popular DJs contribute tracks (Roni Size, DJ Die, and many others), which ultimately serve as the perfect introduction to newcomers. Many speedy highlights are included, such as Roni Size's "Only a Dream 1998 Mix," Scorpio's "Trouble," and DJ Krust's "Maintain [Dave Angel Mix]" (the original version was one of the first volume's highlights as well). The beats are quite consistently infectious, while each DJ leaves his own original mark on each remix. Admittedly, there are only so many stripped-down dance tracks one can hear until it starts getting a bit monotonous, but *V Classic, Vol. 2* was really made for the dance floor, not for at-home easy listening. Another great dance compilation. —*Greg Prato*

**VH-1: Non-Stop Dance** / Apr. 21, 1998 / Rhino ✦✦✦
The words "VH-1" and "Non-Stop Dance" are rarely used in the same sentence, but that didn't stop the cable company and Rhino Records from assembling *VH-1: Non-Stop Dance*. For VH-1, "dance" means classic dance-pop hits from the late '80s and '90s, and for Rhino it means their beloved mascot RuPaul, who inexplicably shows up twice on this collection. Still, even the heavy-handed pushing of RuPaul—whose "Supermodel" deserves to be here, but whose "Snapshot" barely registered in clubs—doesn't prevent the album from being a fun listen. Granted, some listeners will find the continuous mix a little irritating—most listeners who buy Rhino product want hit versions, not faux club albums—but it is fun to hear Nicki French's "Total Eclipse of the Heart," Everything But the Girl's "Missing," Right Said Fred's "I'm Too Sexy," Robin S's "Show Me Love," Paula Abdul's "Cold Hearted," Cathy Dennis' "Touch Me (All Night Long)," Taylor Dayne's "Tell It to My Heart," Jody Watley's "Looking for a New Love" and other dance-pop hits on the same disc. —*Stephen Thomas Erlewine*

**Valis, Vol. 2: Everything Must Go** / Mar. 18, 1997 / Ion ✦✦✦✦
Bill Laswell's second compendium of experimental breakbeat culture from New York and beyond, *Valis, Vol. 2* is a double CD featuring everything from dirty instrumental hip-hop and dub to jungle-funk and freewheeling turntable tricknology. A lot of the usual Laswell suspects are featured, including Praxis, Spectre, Buckethead, and Corporal Blossom (aka Greenpoint engineer Robert Musso), but a handful of tracks by newcomers such as SIMM, Scanner, Babu, and Shinro Ohtake (together with Boredoms frontman Yamatsuka Eye) make for an interesting collection. Like many Laswell-related comps it's doubtful much of this will stand up, say, a year later, but until then, *Valis, Vol. 2* is a fine, varied listen. —*Sean Cooper*

**Variable, Vol. 2** / Nov. 9, 1999 / Louipimps ✦✦✦
*Variable 2* collects dance music from Kudos, Radianation, Kaj, and 1/2 Advancer. Breastfed's "Vision of Division," Lunasect's "Shadowcasting," and Stabilizer's "Broken Bed Head" are among the highlights of the album, which also includes tracks from Electrostatic, Bishop, and Moonbuggy. —*Heather Phares*

**Various 01: Dancemusic: Modernlife** / Apr. 18, 2000 / V2 ✦✦✦✦
*Dancemusic: Modernlife* collects songs and remixes by some of V2's most prominent artists, including the Chemical Brothers' reworking of Mercury Rev's "Delta Sun Bottleneck Stomp," the Moog Cookbook's remix of Alex Gopher's "Time," and Cappery's remix of Angelmoon's "He's All I Want." Moby's "Natural Blues," Truxton's "All Nite," Regular Fries' "King Kong," and the Jungle Brothers' "Freakin' You" are some of the other songs that go under the knife on this album, making it an appealing mix of cutting-edge rock and electronic sounds. —*Heather Phares*

**Very Superstitious** / Jul. 22, 1997 / Sm:)e ✦✦✦
A rather pedestrian compilation, *Very Superstitious* includes tracks from Oliver Lieb's L.S.G. project as well as Rabbit in the Moon, Humate, and Mijk Van Dijk. The music doesn't range too far within the fields of trance with occasional glimpses of Chemical Brothers-type big-beat action to update the sound. Dave Trance serves as the album's mixer. —*Keith Farley*

**Viennatone** / May 19, 1997 / Studio !K7 ♦♦♦♦
A collection of with-it Austrians appear on this encapsulation of the Vienna scene, including tracks from Farmers Manual, Pulsinger & Tunaka, Alois Huber, Gerhard Potuznik, and Kruder & Dorfmeister (remixing Count Basic). —*Keith Farley*

**Vintage R&S, Vol. 1** / Jan. 14, 1997 / R&S ♦♦♦♦
Many of the most influential techno classics that helped move the genre toward a more extreme style known as "hardcore" are captured on this compilation. An emphasis on pounding percussive, low-frequency rhythms and grinding, mid-frequency riffs differentiates the sort of techno featured on this album from the style that had come from Detroit in the late '80s and from Germany in the early '90s. Though the tracks don't get too carried away with extreme tempos or excessive beats-per-minute, a sense of adrenaline-pumping aggression does underlie them. Some of the quintessential hardcore techno anthems are compiled here, including Joey Beltram's "Energy Flash." This legendary track could no doubt go down in history as a perfect example of the formula for hardcore techno. Other hard-hitters include Frank De Wulf's remix of Human Resource's "Dominator," C.J. Bolland's "Horsepower," and Tronikhouse's "The Savage and Beyond." Again, pounding bass-beats and mid-frequency riffs comprise the rhythms within these, while short vocal samples and foreboding synth melodies enter occasionally, functioning as the tracks' hooks or choruses. —*Jason Birchmeier*

**Wall of Sound: Bustin' Loose** / Sep. 22, 1998 / Ultra ♦♦♦♦
By featuring artists who consistently capture wicked dance grooves within a dance/alternative/hip-hop soundscape, the Wall Of Sound label has helped introduce several of today's top club/DJ acts to the world. The 11-track compilation *Wall of Sound Presents Bustin' Loose* represents all of their most popular artists, with many of the tracks being long out of print and released on CD for the first time. Before signing to the Dreamworks label and scoring hits with the tracks "History Repeating" and "Bang On!," the duo Propellerheads first got their start with Wall Of Sound, who issued their early track, "Dive," tback in 1995. Although a bit more basic then the material on their '98 release *Decksandrumsandrockandroll*, "Dive" got the band their first big break when an Adidas commercial picked it up upon release. Other highlights include the old-school meets new-school sound of Mekon's "Skool's Out (featuring Schoolly D original mix)," tplus "Latinhead" by Dirty Beatniks, and the laidback "It's Automatic" by Zoot Woman. —*Greg Prato*

**Warehouse Grooves, Vol. 1** / Dec. 26, 1994 / SPG ♦♦♦♦
The first volume in the solid SPG series presents a set of club grooves from the '80s through the late '90s. It's refreshing to hear dance tracks from over a decade-long period segued back and forth, and *Warehouse Grooves* gets it right almost every time. —*Keith Farley*

**Warehouse Grooves, Vol. 2** / Dec. 26, 1994 / SPG ♦♦♦♦
Since SPG's *Warehouse Grooves, Vol. 1* included music from such a large time span, there are more than enough great tracks for a second volume. From the house era through techno and rave, all the way up to electronica, big-beat, and trip-hop, the label knows exactly which songs to include. —*Keith Farley*

**Warehouse Grooves, Vol. 3** / Mar. 5, 1996 / SPG ♦♦♦♦
The quality hardly dips at all for the third volume in the *Warehouse Grooves* series. Besides acid classics like Josh Wink's "Don't Laugh" and "Higher State of Consciousness," there are mainstream house grooves like "The Bomb" by the Bucketheads, "New Jersey Deep" from Black Science Orchestra, and "Witch Doktor" by Armand Van Helden. —*Keith Farley*

**Warehouse Grooves, Vol. 4** / 1997 / SPG ♦♦♦
*Warehouse Grooves, Vol. 4* is a more diva-oriented volume than its predecessors, with tracks by CeCe Rogers ("It's Gonna Be Alright"), Kim English ("Nitelife"), and Sandy B ("Make the World Go Round"), as well as producer-oriented tracks like "Hypnotizin" by Winx, "Magic Carpet Ride" by the Mighty Dub Kats (aka Norman Cook, aka Fatboy Slim), and "Boom" by Boris Dlugosch. —*Keith Farley*

★ **Warp 10+1: The Influences** / Oct. 12, 1999 / Matador ♦♦♦♦♦
Not only the world's premiere label for forward-thinking electronic dance, Sheffield's Warp Records celebrated its tenth anniversary with a historic compilation series, the first of which includes more than 20 techno classics from the '80s that influenced the imprint's founders and its many artists. And as compilations of obscure but important techno go, this could be the best ever produced. *Warp 10+1* balances only the best tracks from the early Chicago house, Detroit techno and British scenes, including undeniable classics from Mr. Fingers aka Larry Heard ("Can U Feel It"), Adonis ("No Way Back"), Reese & Santonio aka Kevin Saunderson ("The Sound"), Model 500 aka Juan Atkins ("Off to Battle"), Rhythim Is Rhythim aka Derrick May ("Nude Photo"), Phuture ("Acid Tracks"), 808 State ("Let Yourself Go"), and A Guy Called Gerald ("Voodoo Ray"). Most of these have been anthologized several times, but where *Warp 10+1* really shines is the inclusion of a few incredibly rare tracks—"Bang Bang You're Mine" by Bang the Party, "The Theme" by Unique Three, "My Medusa" by K-Alexi Shelby, "Computer Madness" by Steve Poindexter—that techno fans have often heard about, but never heard. Electronic music has progressed so much over the course of ten years that current Warp heroes like Autechre and Aphex Twin sound nothing like these producers, but the energy and power of mid-to-late-'80s techno is undiminished with time. —*John Bush*

**Warp 10+2: The Classics 1989-1992** / Oct. 12, 1999 / Matador ♦♦♦♦
The second installment in Warp's ten-year anniversary campaign recycles the first four years in the label's history, times when Warp specialized in what's become known as bleep techno. Unlike the electronic listening music later developed by Warp acts Black Dog, Aphex Twin, and B12, and the more experimental approach to electronics that has become the label's forté thanks to Autechre and Squarepusher, early Warp records were spartan productions. Classics like "LFO" by LFO, "Aftermath" by Nightmares on Wax and "Testone" by Sweet Exorcist were heavy on the polar extremes of sound frequency: low-signal bass designed to rattle all but the most high-end subwoofers, chirpy treble effects that focus on a cleaner, more precise angle to Chicago's trademark acid tracks, and complex percussion programs learned from classic Detroit producers. Instead of a collection charting the entire decade of its history, Warp chose to appease hardcore fans by focusing on its earliest, rarest tracks. Since Warp is such a collector-driven label anyway, it's a perfect match—fans can finally own the tracks that in some cases they've only heard about, including the first Warp release (Forgemasters' "Track with No Name") plus tracks by Warp one-shots like Sweet Exorcist, Tricky Disco, and DJ Mink. Although the format may not work well for those unfamiliar with the label's complete history, it's a fitting tribute to the beginning of electronic dance's move from the clubfloor to the living room. —*John Bush*

**Warp 10+3: The Remixes** / Oct. 12, 1999 / Matador ♦♦♦♦
The final volume in Warp Records' ten-year anniversary celebration looks at the immense influence the label has had on experimental and electronic music the world over. An assortment of indie-rock and electronic figures take on their favorites from the label's surprisingly large back catalogue, beginning with Pram's garage-rock rendering of LFO's "Simon from Sydney," and continuing on through Stereolab's shuffling remake of "Kid for Today" by Boards of Canada, Jim O'Rourke's version of "Characi" by Autechre, Tortoise frontman John McEntire's reworking of "Playtime" by Nightmares on Wax, and Spiritualized's pure-phased wave-of-sound redux of "Tied Up" by LFO. There are plenty of remixes by electronic artists though, and a few by Warp acts themselves (Autechre, Plaid, Mira Calix, Jimi Tenor, Plone). Always a forward-thinking label, Warp also showcases some newer names in the electronic world. The remixes by new signings (as of 1999) Isan and Four Tet are among the best of the two-disc set. And the new wave of stateside neo-electro producers Push Button Objects and Richard Devine pump up the beats on their contributions, Boards of Canada's "An Eagle in Your Mind" and Aphex Twin's "Come to Daddy." Though it may be too sprawling for fans of just one or two of the acts included, *Warp10+3* is an effective statement of the electronic/dance world circa the end of the millennium. —*John Bush*

**Wasted** / 1995 / Volume ♦♦♦♦
*Wasted* is a two-disc set collecting virtually all of the tracks by electronic artists featured on the first dozen or so editions in the *Volume* series. As such, it's an excellent work including a raft of unreleased tracks by Aphex Twin ("En Trange to Exit"), the Orb ("Reefer Spin in the Galaxy"), Orbital (a vocal version of "Belfast/Wasted"), Underworld ("Change"), Tricky ("You Don't"), LFO ("Slow Down Speed"), Sabres of Paradise ("Lick Wid Nit Wit"), and Autechre ("Lanx 3"). Even the tracks by fringe acts like Pop Will Eat Itself, Cypress Hill, Credit to the Nation, Sandals, and Little Axe are quite solid. —*John Bush*

## VARIOUS ARTISTS

**Water and Architecture** / Apr. 7, 1998 / Sub Rosa ++++
More than a random collection of tracks from a seamingly unconnected quintet of artists, *Water and Architecture* is one of Sub Rosa's most satisfying compilation releases to date. The disc balances the more austere rhythmic abstractions of former Tortoise member Bundy K. Brown (as Designer), electrojazz innovator Atom Heart, and Japanese sampler experimentalist Bisk against two stunning contributions from Seefeel and a handful of found sound and electro-acoustic manipulation by the Touch label's Jon Wozencroft (appearing here as Aer). Gorgeous and complete. —*Sean Cooper*

**We Are Twisted** / Aug. 24, 1999 / MCA +++
*We Are Twisted* celebrates the dance label's third anniversary with a double-disc continuous mix of new and previously released songs and remixes from Twisted's roster. Artists like Michael T. Diamond, Dollshead, Danny Tenaglia, Celeda, Funky Green Dogs, Lowpass, and House Heroes. At 28 songs strong, *We Are Twisted* is a birthday party of epic proportions. —*Heather Phares*

**Welcome to the Epidrome** / Feb. 17, 1998 / Sony +++
The club compilation *Welcome to the Epidrome* includes remixes of artists lesser known to dancefloor denizens, such as Skunk Anansie and Jean-Michel Jarre, as well as familiar acts like Jamiroquai, Jocelyn Brown, and Eightball. —*Keith Farley*

**Welcome to the Future** / 1993 / Epic +++
A somewhat bizarre collection of indie-dance grooves, rave tracks, and the occasional listening-techno classic, *Welcome to the Future* includes tracks from the Sugarcubes, the Shamen, Jaydee, Eskimos & Egypt, Rozalla, and 2 Unlimited. Towards the end of the collection the true classics are hidden, LFO's "LFO" and FUSE's "Substance Abuse." It's quite a bit to pay, though, for two tracks which are available on their respective artists' albums anyway. —*Keith Farley*

**Welcome to the Future, Vol. 2** / 1993 / Epic +++
The second volume in the series is quite similar to the first, a 12-track collection that features several dance-club, alternative dance, and techno tracks from the late '80s and early '90s. Artists featured include the Shamen ("Comin' On"), Miracle ("Oxygene"), Burning Vinyl ("Brainrush"), Rozalla ("I Love Music"), and Whatever, Girl ("Activator"). There are a few good beats and ideas scattered throughout the collection, but even by the late '90s, much of this music sounded quaint and dated. —*Stephen Thomas Erlewine*

**Welcome to the Technodrome, Vol. 1** / Jun. 1, 1993 / ZYX +++
The Euro-dance label ZYX compiled this set of early rave and techno/hi-NRG fusions, with eight tracks featuring Talla 2XLC (most as Bigod 20) as well as forgotten names like Vomito Negro, Typis Belgis, and Invincible Limit. To say the least, the album hasn't dated in quite the best way. —*Keith Farley*

**Welcome to the Technodrome, Vol. 2** / Dec. 25, 1991 / ZYX ++
The second ZYX compilation in the label's *Welcome to the Technodrome* series is another set of upfront rave-pop tracks, quite dated and laughable just five years after their recording. —*Keith Farley*

**Welcome to the Technodrome, Vol. 3** / Oct. 25, 1993 / ZYX +++
A more varied cast of contributors appear on the two-disc *Welcome to the Technodrome, Vol. 3*, including 2 Unlimited, Bronski Beat, R.A.F., Tranceformer, Interactive, and Hysteria. For the most part though, these excursions into push-button rave and trance are period novelties, and quite dismissable. —*Keith Farley*

**Welcome to the Technodrome, Vol. 4** / May 2, 1995 / ZYX ++
*Welcome to the Technodrome, Vol. 4* is another two-disc collection of bland trance, techno, and rave from ZYX Records. The artist list includes Liquid Bass, Paranoia X, Moneypenny, Out of Order, Oxidizer, and Alien Factory, among others. —*Keith Farley*

**Welcome to the Universe** / Feb. 24, 1998 / Twisted/MCA ++++
Twisted Records formed a partnership with Universe, a San Francisco nightclub, to produce a series of live mix CDs that spotlight the club's DJs. *Welcome to the Universe* is the first in this series. The disc was mixed live by David Harness, and he strings together 16 songs, including cuts by Danny Tenaglia, Eddie Amador, House of Prince, Groove Junkies, Yohan Square, Moogroove, Club 69, Shazz, Philip Ramirez, Mysterious People, Funky Green Dogs, and Alexis P. Suter. It's far more exciting than the typical continuous mix dance CD and showcases Harness' prowess at the turntables. —*Stephen Thomas Erlewine*

**Werks Like a Twelve Inch** / Oct. 7, 1996 / Astralwerks ++++
Astralwerks compiled several vinyl-only mixes from their artists for this collection. There's a good balance of B-sides (from Soul Oddity, Ben Neill, Spacetime Continuum, Freaky Chakra) and great remixes by Carl Craig, Plastikman, and Move D. —*John Bush*

**What Is Bhangra** / May 31, 1994 / Capitol ++++
Imagine crossing club music, rap, some Indian music, and maybe a little ska. What you'll get is Bhangra, originally the traditional music of the Punjab region (which borders India and Pakistan). It came to England with Asian immigrants, mutated, fused with other forms, and eventually became dance music for kids. This collection of high-energy, rhythmic cuts by Achanak, Johnny Zee, Saqi, and others stomps along like some sort of musical Godzilla. Some of the tracks, like "Nukhe Chakhee Javana," are fun but fairly predictable pop, while others, like TSB Golden Star's "Makhana," feature tribal shouts and Quawali-like vocals. A few songs, like Eshara's "Amberseria," sit delightfully right on the boundary between East and West. Synthesizers, samples, and snippets of dialogue from old movies abound in this vivacious and good-humored dance music. Try a track at a party for something different. —*Kurt Keefner*

**What the Funk You Waitin' For?** / Nov. 9, 1999 / V2 +++
*What the Funk You Waitin' For?* collects remixes by Olav Basoski, Mark Picchiotti, Phats & Small, Club 69, Bob Sinclair, and Cevin Fisher in a budget-priced sampler. Tracks by Moby, Gopher, Fire Island, Underworld, and DJ Hell are also included, providing an inexpensive way to become acquainted with any of these artists. —*Heather Phares*

**White Noise, Vol. 1** / Oct. 21, 1997 / City of Angels +++
The *White Noise* compilation samples tracks from artists on the City of Angels, Skint, Wall of Sound, and Concrete labels, some of the leaders in the big-beat genre. Included are tracks from Dub Pistols, Monkey Mafia, Uberzone, Witchdoctor, Simply Jeff, Midfield General and Fatboy Slim, HardKnox, Wiseguys, Les Rhythm Digitales, the Crystal Method, and Dirty Beatniks. —*Steve Huey*

**White Noise, Vol. 2** / Jun. 2, 1998 / City Of Angels +++
City of Angels' electronica/big-beat sampler *White Noise, Vol. 2* is highlighted by two Fatboy Slim remixes—of Wildchild's "Renegade Master" and Lunatic Calm's "Roll the Dice"—and also features material by Uberzone ("Believe in Beats"), Dub Pistols ("Bullets 'N' Beats"), and the Freestylers with Tenor Fly ("B-Boy Stance"), among many others. It's a little uneven overall, but its high points are excellent. —*Steve Huey*

**White Party X** / May 11, 1999 / Trax Recording ++
*White Party X* features highlights from the tenth annual installment of this legendary club event. DJs from New York, Miami, San Francisco, Los Angeles, and beyond unite on this album, including Victor Calderone, Manny Lehman, Julian Marsh, and Mark Tarbox, all spinning captivating house mixes. —*Heather Phares*

**The Widescreen Versions** / 1998 / Certificate 18 ++++
The second Certificate 18 compilation picks up where *Hidden Rooms* left off in 1996, with tracks and remixes by Photek's Studio Pressure, Klute, Plaid, Stasis, Midnight Funk Association, Two Lone Swordsmen, and Kirk Degiorgio, among others. The collision of prestigious techno names and equally respected drum'n'bass names works well. Each track appears on CD for the first time. —*John Bush*

**Wild FM, Vol. 1** / Sep. 16, 1997 / Central Station +++
A two-disc collection of hardbag and trance, *Wild FM* includes tracks by Unique II, Stretch 'N Vern, Porn Kings, Tony De Vit, Alex Party, Barbara Tucker, and Hyper Go Go, among others. —*John Bush*

**The Wild Pitch Jam** / 1995 / Nitegrooves ++++
Mr. Wild Pitch himself, DJ Pierre, mixed this compilation for Nitegrooves as well as producing quite a few of the tracks, including Dannell Dixon, X-Fade, Nelson Rosado, Urban Soul, and Sabrynaah Pope. —*Keith Farley*

**Wild Planet** / May 9, 2000 / Nettwerk America ++++
Skinny Puppy's cEvin key compiled the industrial-driven collection *Wild Planet*, showcasing unreleased tracks of experimental/noise music from artists such as Download, Doubting Thomas, Off & Gone, and the Legendary Pink Dots. Music from key's former bands, Skinny Puppy and Teargarden, is also featured. —*MacKenzie Wilson*

**Winter Party, Vol. 2** / May 11, 1999 / Centaur ♦♦♦
Following the success of the Winter Party 1998 collection, which was nominated for a Grammy, *Winter Party, Vol. 2* features the spinning skills of DJs Julian Marsh and Tony Moran. The duo mix 23 tracks including Gloria Estefan's "Don't Stop," "Believe" by Jon Secada, "First Be a Woman" by Gloria Gaynor, and "The Promise" by Tony Moran. *Winter Party, Vol. 2* highlights the talents of all the artists involved and provides plenty of dance floor pleasure. —*Heather Phares*

**Wipeout XL** / 1996 / Astralwerks/Virgin ♦♦♦♦
This 14-song compilation was released a little before the huge media electronica hype/feeding frenzy of 1997. As the music industry was picking itself up after, and trying to sort out the mess caused by, the inevitable collapse of modern rock radio (but still mindlessly signing countless alt-rock bands with affected attitudes and sluggish songs all the while), another musical factor—stemming in Europe, somewhat influenced by American house and wiping out several music boundaries in its almost single-minded pursuit of tuneful anarchy—was rising with more ambitious objectives in mind. Most of those pioneering electronica groups are on *Wipeout XL*, a soundtrack of sorts to, of all things, a video game. Gathering genre-defining cuts by the Chemical Brothers, Underworld, Prodigy, and Daft Punk, *Wipeout XL* is both an exemplary sample primer of electronica, as well as a well-rounded, and representative, compilation of the often-thrilling genre. —*Michael Gallucci*

**Wired Injections** / Jan. 30, 1996 / Cleopatra ♦♦
*Wired Injections* is an adequate collection of ambient techno done the Cleopatra Records way, featuring the like of Noise Box, Christian Death, Rosetta Stone, Klute, and the Electric Hellfire Club. It won't convert a neophyte to the pleasures of ambient, though dedicated fans will find a couple of tracks to treasure. —*David Jehnzen*

**Wish FM 96.1: The Progressive Electro Revolution** / Mar. 19, 1996 / Domestic ♦♦♦♦
This collection of futurist electro-techno includes a few exclusives and many stellar artists, including Timeshard, the Irresistible Force, God Within, and the Black Dog project South of Market. —*John Bush*

**Wish FM 97.1** / Mar. 18, 1997 / Domestic ♦♦♦
It's not quite as solid as its predecessor, but *Wish FM 97.1* does feature several good tracks, from Derrick Carter, the Hardkiss side project Little Wing, and Heights of Abraham. —*John Bush*

**World Dance Classics** / Jan. 19, 1999 / DCI ♦♦♦♦
The title should have been *World Jungle Classics*, but this drum'n'bass collection of jump-up and ragga does have a lot of excellent tracks by producers like DJ Hype, Ray Keith, 88.3, Aphrodite, Alex Reece, Urban Shakedown, Andy C., DJ Swift, L Double, DJ Rap, Decoder Vs. Peshay, and many others. —*John Bush*

**World Dance: The Drum & Bass Experience** / Feb. 9, 1999 / Mutant Sound ♦♦♦♦
If you like drum'n'bass but are tired of the soundalike compilations that have flooded the market in the wake of the breakbeat juggernaut of the mid- to late '90s, this may be the one for you. Although none of the tracks on these two discs break any really new ground, they all share a hardness of texture that keeps your attention. It also helps that there's a strong reggae influence throughout, one which is expressed in the melodically interesting basslines and the regular appearance of reggae singers and deejays. Disc One is a continuous mix by DJ Hype, and it features his own outstanding "We Must Unite," as well as the equally fine "Ganja Man" by DJ Krome and Mr. Time. "R-Type" by Jo includes one of the better basslines of the program. Disc Two is a continuous mix by Ellis Dee, and its tracks refer even more explicitly to the reggae-derived sounds of British jungle. "Everyman" is essentially a junglized remake of the reggae classic of the same name with a soundalike vocalist and a brutally propulsive breakbeat; Sound of the Future contributes the thrilling and almost impossibly complex "The Lighter (Rollers Remix)." There aren't very many essential drum'n'bass compilations out there, but this is one of them. —*Rick Anderson*

**World Domination, Vol. 1** / Mar. 28, 2000 / Strictly Hype ♦♦
Strictly Hype's *World Domination, Vol. 1* collects electronica from B2K, Josh Collins, Rip, and Am. Delta 9's "Here Go the Sound," Nemesis' "The Punisha," Cosmic Pimp's "Hardhouse Shit," and Michael Trance's "Nu Funk Level"

are among the highlights of this entertaining compilation of club music. —*Heather Phares*

**World of Rave, Vol. 1** / Mar. 14, 1995 / ZYX ♦♦
Such was the power and relative artist anonymity of the rave explosion that labels could release album upon album of generic techno music and not even worry that they didn't have any big names; no one knew the big names anyway. This four-disc box set could be the ultimate in bland rave obscurities—even the best-known acts here, like DJ Charly Lownoise, Acid Junkies, Ravers Nature, and Joyrider, barely show up on the radar of the most committed dance fans, and of the rest the less said the better. If someone out there needs four discs of push-button rave music, this is the place. —*John Bush*

**World of Techno** / Jan. 23, 1996 / ZYX ♦♦
Just a two-disc set of techno the ZYX way, often including the same artists as their *World of Rave* box set. This is only two discs, and there are a few more well-known acts (Skylab 2000, Latex Empire, Alien Factory), but techno would gain few converts if these soulless carbon copies were all that was on the market. —*John Bush*

**World of Trance** / Jan. 16, 1996 / ZYX ♦♦♦
Unlike their attempts at rave and techno, ZYX Records is known a bit for their trance music. So, *World of Trance* is much better than others in the series, though there are few trance artists of any merit here. Instead, there are second-rate acts like Datura, Eskimos & Egypt, Moka DJ, and Taucher. —*John Bush*

**World of Trance, Vol. 3** / Jan. 14, 1997 / ZYX ♦♦
*World of Trance, Vol. 3* is an adequate budget-priced collection of ambient and trance techno by the likes of Hydro, O2, Age of Love, DJ Dado, Space Blaster, DJ Spacecase, Inner Void, and Formic Acid. There are some good cuts scattered throughout this collection, but much of the music on the disc is pedestrian. —*Stephen Thomas Erlewine*

**World's Greatest Club Collection** / Sep. 29, 1998 / Alpha Wave ♦♦
It might appear difficult to understand how Kraftwelt, Spahn Ranch, Transmutator, and Astralasia can make it on an album titled *The World's Greatest Club Collection*, though just about anything can happen on discs released by the new-school industrial label Cleopatra. Surprisingly, there are some *genuine* club classics here (at least in alternative dance circles), like "You Spin Me Round (Like a Record)" by Dead or Alive, "What's on Your Mind (Pure Energy)" by Information Society, "Cars" by Gary Numan, "I Want Candy" by Bow Wow Wow, and others by Future Sound of London, Heaven 17, 808 State (remixed by Propellerheads), and Keoki. At least half of the contributions, however, are barely even worthy of consideration. —*Keith Farley*

**www.subaudio.net 01** / Nov. 10, 1998 / EFA ♦♦♦
Spotlighting both the web site and record label, *www.subaudio.net* is a collection of stellar experimental grooves only nominally tied to hip-hop and techno. Yes, that's the Wu-Tang Clan next to Japanese pop experimentalist Cornelius, though the clash isn't quite so jarring considering Wu-Tang's "Re-united" is actually the sought-after remix by German electro-funksters Funkstörung. Elsewhere, Prince Paul meets up with Dan Nakamura (aka the Automator) while Neotropic, Pole, and Rhythm & Sound also contribute great tracks. —*Keith Farley*

**X-It: The Future Sound of Germany** / Aug. 18, 1998 / Ultra ♦♦♦
Kicking off with Sash's "Stay," a major dance-chart success, *X-It: The Future Sound of Germany* compiles tracks from the German dance label, including such artists as Bossi, the K.K. Project, Rodriguez, Two Phunky People, DJ Cy and Sanli, the Magnificent 4, and Encore!. —*Steve Huey*

**XL Recordings: The American Chapter** / Dec. 14, 1993 / American Recordings ♦♦♦♦
The first XL Recordings compilation for an American market includes the label's two big rave hits—the Prodigy's "Charly" and SL2's "On a Ragga Tip"—plus more good material in the high-energy rave vein, including Awesome 3, Jonny L, Flowmasters, and Cubic 22. —*John Bush*

**Y2K: Beat the Clock Version 1.0** / Jul. 6, 1999 / Sony ♦♦♦♦
Of the innumerable end-of-the-millennium funky-breaks compilations on the market, *Y2K* is a bit better than average, with quite a few big-beat classics—Fatboy Slim's "Rockafeller Skank," Wildchild's "Renegade Master," Chemical Brothers' "Elektrobank," Crystal Method's "Busy Child," Propellerheads' "Bang On," and Underworld's "Born Slippy." —*John Bush*

**La Yellow Collection** / May 21, 1997 / Yellow Productions ♦♦♦♦
A compilation of the French label Yellow Productions (following up the previous year's *La Yellow 357*), this album includes excellent contributions from Dimitri from Paris ("Souvenir de Paris"), Kid Loco ("Wrong Number"), Fresh Lab ("Sentiments"), and Bob Sinclar ("Rock Solid"). —*John Bush*

**Yoshitoshi Artists, Vol. 1** / Feb. 10, 1998 / MCA ♦♦♦
A bit more focused on non-Deep Dish productions than the previous *Yoshitoshi: In House We Trust*, this 1998 collection includes tracks by later additions to the Yoshitoshi fold like Mysterious People, Richard Morel, and Heiko Laux (the latter with the original plus a remix of his club hit "Dedicated to All Believers"). Dubfire & Sharam do appear on Dished-Out Bums' "Gak Trak," but they let the label have all of the glory this time around. —*John Bush*

**Yoshitoshi Artists, Vol. 2** / Mar. 10, 1998 / MCA ♦♦♦
Not an entirely necessary collection after the purchase of its predecessor, *Yoshitoshi Artists, Vol. 2* includes more than just a few remixes of tracks already heard on the first volume—"Dedicated to All Believers," "Fade II Black," and "Love Revolution." There are several great new tracks, from Dubfire & Sharam's Dished-Out Bums ("Laavburds"), Kings of Tomorrow, and Joystick, among others. —*John Bush*

**Yoshitoshi: In House We Trust** / Jan. 23, 1996 / IRS ♦♦♦♦
The first compilation from Deep Dish's solid, well-run mainstream dance label includes tracks from Hani, Paul Hunter (as Deep Sensation), and Jean-Philippe Aviance (as XS and Alcatraz) plus numerous songs with Deep Dish productions or contributions—by Dished-Out Bums, Satori, and Submarine. As artists themselves, Dubfire and Sharam are top-notch label-heads with an ear for detail, shown to good effect on this compilation. —*John Bush*

**Zance: A Decade of Dance from ZTT** / 1995 / ZTT ♦♦♦♦
ZTT Records picked from its enormously influential '80s catalog for this 11-track compilation of long-out-of-print remixes and such. Among the goodies are rarities by 808 State ("Pacific 707" plus a remix of "The Only Rhyme That Bites"), Frankie Goes to Hollywood (mixes of "Welcome to the Pleasuredome" and "Two Tribes"), and Seal (mixes by William Orbit of "Killer" and "Crazy"). It's a great collection for '80s enthusiasts as well as novices wishing to explore the decade's influence on '90s dance. —*John Bush*

**Zoo Rave** / 1992 / Zoo ♦♦
The two volumes of rave music in the *Zoo Rave* series are cursory introductions to the early-'90s dance phenomenon, giving a good impression of the hard, relentless drive of the underground style but including none of the music's best artists or tracks. While *Zoo Rave* isn't definitive or respected by hardcore rave fans, it's a worthwhile introduction for listeners unfamiliar with the subgenre. —*Stephen Thomas Erlewine*

# Style Essays & Maps

## House

House music has long been the king of all forms of electronic dance music, ever since its emergence during the early '80s as a low-cost continuation of the disco aesthetic for thousands of people still hooked on the prospect of going out to clubs. It's responsible for the first recordings, the first chart hits, and the first respect for a scene in all of electronic dance. Perhaps it's not surprising then that house is also the style of electronic dance closest in spirit and execution to disco; it uses many of the same piano runs, four-on-the-floor beats and often, samples of the very same divas (like Loleatta Holloway or Gloria Gaynor) found in classic disco music. The major (and often sole) characteristic separating disco from house is technology. While many disco artists had major-label connections—professional studios, sessionmen, and often, entire orchestras—house artists could rarely afford musicians, so they turned to the range of synthesizers and sequencers increasingly available to those on a small budget during the early '80s. During the late '80s and early '90s, the largely unified house scene fragmented to form largely separate scenes focused around descendants of the more soulful variant of New York house (garage music), the harder tones of Chicago acid house, a crossover house-pop scene based mostly in Europe, and even the ambient-house movement, which place the "discreet music" of Brian Eno on an equal footing with beats and moods indebted to early house producers like Larry Heard. By the late '90s, the electronic dance scene included dozens of styles based around the core musics of house, techno and breakbeat, many designed for contemplation as much as motion.

House music's beginnings lie in the early '80s, several years after the disco boom had turned bust. Given mainstream America's intense dislike of the music—only the most flagrant example of which is a 1979 riot sparked when a Chicago DJ organized a mass-burning of disco records for a baseball game between the Detroit Tigers and Chicago White Sox (ironically, both towns later became dance capitals)—the major labels wanted nothing more to do with the music. Still, there were plenty of people with an urge to go to clubs and dance on the weekends, so DJs plugged the gaps to an extent with the continued waves of Italian disco imports and singles from independent American holdovers like Prelude and West End (plus the wealth of original disco and soul tracks from the '70s). In Chicago, longtime disco mixers Ron Hardy and Frankie Knuckles ruled the roost at their respective clubs, the Music Box and the Warehouse—the latter reportedly coined the term house music.

Though DJs were the undisputed kings of the dance underground during the early '80s, house producers finally emerged as well. With cheap drum machines in their hands and the disco template in their heads, the producers began taking advantage of burgeoning synthesizer and sampler technology and emerged with new machine disco tracks which could be plugged in between regular tracks in a mixing set. (Many top DJs, especially in New York, had been working on production concurrently since the mid-'70s, whether crafting studio megamixes for 12" release or simply tweaking records at home with their reel-to-reel machines for later clubplay.) Besides being relentlessly rigid, the new music was barely music at all; early house singles were often more reminiscent of '70s minimalism than disco, just incredibly raw rhythm tracks with little melody or song structure. Nicknamed jacking tracks (in tribute to an accompanying dance), the music was optimized for mixing and a DJ's own interpretation.

The actual debut of house music on wax occurred in Chicago in 1983, either Z Factor's "Fantasy" or Jesse Saunders' "On and On" (both were produced by Saunders). Led by local labels Trax and DJ International, house music soon exploded around the city and generated an early peak for the style around 1986, with producers like Larry Heard ("Can You Feel It"), Marshall Jefferson ("Move Your Body—The House Music Anthem"), Farley Jackmaster Funk ("Love Can't Turn Around"), and Steve "Silk" Hurley ("Jack Your Body") leading the way. Their style, termed deep house, favored expansive vocalists and the organic piano-and-string runs of classic disco singles. The more traditional sound led to the point where radio airplay became quite viable—both Farley and Hurley hit the charts in Britain in 1986.

Meanwhile in New York, Larry Levan had been entrancing visitors to his Paradise Garage (the source of the term garage music) since 1977, with wide-ranging sets indebted to disco, house, and soul but also including tracks by new wave, punk, worldbeat, and hard rock acts. Early New York house recordings were also more varied than their Chicago cousins, and, given their proximity to major recording studios, much more professional-sounding and song-based. Groups and producer-oriented acts like the Peech Boys, Strafe, "D" Train, and Blaze updated the wailing, soulful sound of the '70s to create music quite different from Chicago's legion of jack tracks. New York house had its raw side as well, though. Raised on hip-hop and freestyle, a generation of producers—led by Todd Terry and Masters at Work, aka Little Louie Vega and Kenny "Dope" Gonzalez—emerged in the mid-'80s, focused more on the power of the sampler than ten-years-after disco grooves. Though New York producers didn't hit the British charts with quite the force of their Chicago counterparts, the East Coast became the center of house music by the end of the '80s. The Chicago house scene gradually lost power (despite a fertile renaissance during the '90s), and many top producers (Frankie Knuckles, DJ Pierre) moved to New York to continue their production and remixing careers.

By the end of the decade, what had been an underground music phenomenon (most often affiliated with the black and gay crowd) finally produced a viable crossover market. Acts ranging from pop icon Madonna to C+C Music Factory (the New York production team of Robert Clivillés and David Cole) recorded sizeable American hits, and house music began reaching mainstream dancefloors as well. It seemed disco music was about to make a comeback in America, though house failed to completely cross over—in part due to the rise of hip-hop as well as the club-music backlash by back-to-basics grunge and alternative.

With America still a bit resistant to the new spin on an old sound, Europeans began taking up the slack, courtesy of worldwide house-pop hits by M/A/R/R/S, S'Express, Bomb the Bass, Coldcut, Technotronic, and the KLF. House was no mere pop fad across the Atlantic, though—England's fertile and centralized club scene took house music under its wing during the late '80s, and in just a few years produced the most important youth-culture phenomenon the country had seen since the heady punk days of the '70s. What had been a small but intensely fraternal scene during the mid-'80s exploded during 1988—Britain's very own Summer of Love. By the end of 1990, massive outdoor raves were being attended by tens of thousands of youths. While Detroit techno figured to a large extent in the sound of rave, it was Chicago and New York house music that defined the sound. Even when Britain's first completely indigenous electronic dance style, jungle or drum'n'bass, emerged in the mid-'90s, house music still retained its hold on the biggest clubs, the most tuned-in radio shows, and the biggest-selling mix albums. The United States remained the home for many of the best house producers and DJs (Armand Van Helden, Masters at Work, Danny Tenaglia, Deep Dish) but they made most of their money—by DJing and remixing as well as production—in the European market. Europe was also the base for dozens of house and dance crossover pop acts like 2 Unlimited, Rozalla, the Real McCoy, and Cappella. Progressive house acts like Leftfield, Spooky, Faithless, Lionrock, and Underworld made great strides in pushing house music to new realms, helping introduce the music to rock critics and fans.

## Music Map

# House

**Electro**
Grandmaster Flash, Afrika Bambaataa, Herbie Hancock, The Egyptian Lover, Man Parrish

**Funk**
Parliament/Funkadelic, The Ohio Players, Isaac Hayes, Earth, Wind & Fire, Kool & the Gang

**Disco**
*From the underground dance parties of the early '70s comes a music designed for maximum danceability and hedonism.*
Donna Summer, Giorgio Moroder, Chic, Salsoul Orchestra, Patrick Adams, The Trammps, Gloria Gaynor, Cerrone

**Latin Freestyle**

**Acid House**
*The Roland TB303 synthesizer gives many Chicago producers a squelchy and immediately defining sound.*
Phuture, Adonis, DJ Pierre, Maurice

**Classic Chicago House**
*During the late '70s and early '80s, Chicago DJs Ron Hardy and Frankie Knuckles spin mastermixes of hard-edged disco music... In 1983, Jesse Saunders records what is arguably the first house single, "On and On." Masters of deep house during the mid-'80s:*
Farley Jackmaster Funk, Steve "Silk" Hurley, Marshall Jefferson, Larry Heard

**Classic New York House**
*With considerable Latin influences, New York-area producers carry on the tradition begun by their disco forbears.*
The Peech Boys, Masters at Work, Todd Terry, Tony Humphries, Junior Vasquez, François Kevorkian, Deep Dish (D.C.)

**Garage**
*Deeper than the classic New York sound, Garage takes its name from famed club the Paradise Garage, where DJ Larry Levan spins the music also known as "the Jersey Sound."*
Frankie Knuckles, Tony Humphries, Adeva, D-Train, Blaze, Ultra Naté

**Later Chicago House**
*A new generation of Chicago producers and label-owners extend the possibilities of house music.*
Cajmere, Felix Da Housecat, DJ Sneak, Gemini, Spencer Kincy, Glenn Underground

**British House**
*Crates of American house singles make the voyage across the Atlantic, influencing dozens of artists and, by the late '80s, pop music as well.*
808 State, Brothers in Rhythm, C.J. Mackintosh, Joey Negro, Coldcut, K-Klass, The Beatmasters, Lionrock
*British House DJs:* Paul Oakenfold, Danny Rampling, Pete Tong, Trevor Fung, Justin Robertson

**Ambient House**
*Influenced by the ambient soundscapes of '70s ambient pioneers as well as the warm rhythms of house music, several producers (predominantly British) spawn a remarkable fusion.*
The Orb, Biosphere, Irresistible Force, Higher Intelligence Agency, Global Communication

**House-Pop**
M People, Technotronic, Snap, The KLF, Stereo MC's, D:Ream, C&C Music Factory

**Progressive House**
*After house music is co-opted by the mainstream, many producers bring a renewed sense of artistry back to the music.*
Leftfield, The Drum Club, Spooky, Moody Boyz, Black Science Orchestra, Basement Jaxx

**Global House Producers**
*A handful of artists stand at the pinnacle of dance music, renowned the world over for their DJing, remixing, and production work, though a lack of full-length LPs–other than mix albums–diminishes their importance in the eyes of many critics.*
Armand Van Helden, Masters at Work, Roger Sanchez, Todd Terry, Basement Jaxx, Dimitri from Paris

**Speed Garage**
Tuff Jam, The Dreem Teem, Catch Productions, Boris Dlugosch

Even while house music exploded in the charts, urban clubs, and fashion shows of the world, it never really caught on with alternative-minded listeners and critics with the same push that techno or jungle did. That began to change by the late '90s, with a few groups (Daft Punk, Basement Jaxx) in the new sound of electronica crossing over to techno purists as well as house and electronica fans. Near the end of the millennium, intriguing hybrids of house with jungle (speed garage), techno (tech-house), and jazz (jazz-house) emerged and infused the decades-old style with fresh energy.

Recommended Listening:

1. Various Artists—*The House That Trax Built, Vols. 1-2* (Trax)
2. Various Artists—*Best of House Music, Vols. 1-4* (Profile)
3. Various Artists—*History of House Music, Vol. 1: Chicago Classics* (Cold Front)
4. Various Artists—*History of House Music, Vol. 2: New York Garage Style* (Cold Front)
5. Various Artists—*This Is Strictly Rhythm, Vols. 1-6* (Strictly Rhythm)
6. Tony Humphries—*Take Home the Club* (Bassline)
7. Todd Terry—*Todd Terry's Greatest Hits* (Warlock)
8. Masters at Work—*MAW Records: Compilation, Vol. 1* (Strictly Rhythm)
9. Roger Sanchez—*House Music Movement* (DMT)
10. Armand Van Helden—*Greatest Hits* (Strictly Rhythm)
11. Leftfield—*Leftism* (Hard Hands/Columbia)
12. Daft Punk—*Homework* (Virgin)
13. Basement Jaxx—*Remedy* (Astralwerks)

Recommended Reading:

*What Kind of House Party Is This?*, Jonathan Fleming (MIY, 1995)
*History of House*, Chris Kempster (Sanctuary, 1996)
*Rough Guide to House*, Sean Bidder (Rough Guides/Penguin, 1999)

*—John Bush*

# Techno

Although no musical style evolves in a vacuum, Techno is one of the few in recent times with the appearance of having been born almost fully-formed. Typically, that birth is traced to the early '80s and the emaciated inner-city of Detroit, where figures such as Juan Atkins, Derrick May, and Kevin Saunderson, among others, fused the quirky machine music of Kraftwerk and Yellow Magic Orchestra with the space-race electric funk of George Clinton, the optimistic futurism of Alvin Toffler's *The Third Wave* (from which the music derived its name), and the emerging electro sound elsewhere being explored by Soul Sonic Force, the Jonzun Crew, Man Parrish, "Pretty" Tony Butler, and LA's Wrecking Cru.

Unlike much electro, however, which playfully explored themes of the video age, space travel, block parties, and b-boy braggadocio, techno's minor-key melodies and spare, repetitive rhythms exhibited a tragic, melancholic edge that seemed to more directly engage the political and cultural issues of late-20th-century urban America. Tracks such as "Clear," "Technicolor," "Night Drive (Thru Babylon)," "Strings of Life," and "Rock to the Beat" often expressed a disdain with the same technology they hoped could deliver a culture in the latter stages of decay. And while techno's concern for the liberatory potential of human-machine interface is often traced back to such European avant-garde figures as Luigi Russolo and Luciano Berio, the music's urban orientation and historical and cultural roots clearly distinguish it sharply from those traditions.

Early techno tracks (on such labels as Metroplex, Transmat, and KMS) were generally produced for limited-run 12" release, and although the global popularity of the music in the present day has ensured that many of them have remained in print, techno remained a local phenomenon until the records started showing up on European shores. Consequently, the explosion of techno onto London's emerging acid house scene in the mid- to late-'80s (itself a quixotic mix of Chicago and New York house) meant that many of the music's early creators became bigger "stars" in Europe than in America, a phenomenon that remains to this day (although techno was, and to a certain extent remains antagonistic toward artist identity and stardom, a function of the music's reaction against certain characteristics of mainstream rock and pop). And while the UK dance music scene, as in America, has retained a decided predilection toward house music (with techno the music of choice in continental locales such as Germany and Belgium), the second phase of the music's evolution has largely taken place there, with labels such as Warp, GPR, Infonet, and Rephlex, and artists such as LFO, Richard H. Kirk, Richard James/Aphex Twin, Reload/Link, Germ, B12, and the Black Dog taking the spare electronic experiments of the early Detroit innovators to the next level of abstraction.

Elsewhere, techno's connection to the dancefloor continues to be emphasized, with functional and exploratory approaches that both stick with the music's roots and morph them into a range of related styles, including trance, acid, hardcore, and gabber. As stated, techno's sparer, more rugged dancefloor face remains the dance music of choice throughout much of continental Europe (corporate-sponsored raves in Germany and Belgium routinely attract crowds in the tens of thousands), and the number of artists working either in direct tradition of the original Detroit sound or in a regional, often minimalist offshoot thereof remains quite high. Labels such as Tresor, Force Inc., D-Jax Up-Beats, R&S, and Structure/DJ Ungle Fever, among dozens of others, have been most active and influential. Japan has also produced a fair amount of notable techno artists, including Ken Ishii, Susumu Yakota, and Naohiro Fujikawa, although the scene there is relatively small.

Techno's ongoing status in the United States as a marginal, underground music has meant that the style has been slower to evolve in its birthplace, although third-wave Detroit artists such as Jeff Mills, Stacey Pullen, "Mad" Mike Banks, Drexciya, and AUX 88 (as well as stubborn originators such as Carl Craig and Derrick May) continue to push the style forward. Ironically (or perhaps not so much), its been the European reinterpretation of techno in electronic hybrids such as trip-hop, jungle, and the so-called "intelligent dance music" of artists such as Autechre, Aphex Twin, and the Black Dog which have opened American ears. Time will tell whether that will translate into what, in Europe and England, has become the next stage of Western pop music.

A brief rundown of techno's many faces:

## Detroit

Early Detroit techno is characterized by, alternately, a dark, detached, mechanistic vibe, and a smooth, bright, soulful feel (the latter deriving in part from the Motown legacy and the stock-in-trade between early techno and the Chicago-style house developing simultaneously to the South). While essentially designed as dance music meant to uplift, the stark, melancholy edge of early tracks by Cybotron, Model 500, Rhythim Is Rhythim, and Reese also spoke to Detroit's economic collapse in the late '70s following the city's prosperous heyday as the focal point of the American automobile industry.

The music's oft-copied ruddy production and stripped-down aesthetic were largely a function of the limited technology available to the early innovators (records were often mastered from two-track onto cassette); the increasingly sophisticated arrangements of much contemporary techno (on through to hardcore and jungle), conversely, has much to do with the growth and increasing affordability of MIDI-encoded equipment and desktop digital audio. Second- and third-wave Detroit techno, too, has gained considerably in production, although artists such as Derrick May, Juan Atkins, and Kenny Larkin have sought to combine the pearless sheen of the digital arena with the compositional minimalism of their Detroit origins.

No longer simply contained within the 313 area code, Detroit techno became a global phenomenon (partly as a result of the more widespread acclaim many of the original Detroit artists have found in other countries), buoyed by the fact that many of the classic early tracks remain in print (available through Submerge, at http://www.submerge.com). During the '90s, Detroit's third wave re-explored the aesthetic commitment of the music's early period, with hard-hitting beats (Underground Resistance, Jeff Mills), soulful grooves (Kenny Larkin, Stacey Pullen), and a renewed interest in techno's breakbeat roots (Aux 88, Drexciya, "Mad" Mike, Dopplereffekt). Although numerous documents of Detroit techno past and present exist, the best introduction to the Motor City sound is undoubtedly *True People: A Detroit Techno Compilation*, a sprawling two-CD set released on React Records in 1995.

## Bleep

Generally associated with early Sheffield techno artists such as Robert Gordon, Richard H. Kirk, Forgemasters, and LFO, the bleep moniker was an onomatopoeic attempt to describe the squelching synth noises and quirky MIDI

## Music Map

# Techno

### Kraftwerk
*The German group virtually invented electronic pop in dance music during the 1970s.*

### Electro
*American street kids, already into hip-hop, get turned on to Kraftwerk just as the price of Casio synthesizers begins to fall.*
Grandmaster Flash, The Egyptian Lover, Afrika Bambaataa, Uncle Jamm's Army, Man Parrish
*In 1983, Cybotron records "Clear," arguably the beginning of techno.*

### Early Detroit Techno
*A sense for complex beatbox percussion and techno-soul melodies, together with optimistic visions of otherworldly black science fiction in the midst of an urban wasteland, inspires the crucial innovators of Motor City techno during the 1980s.*
Juan Atkins, Derrick May, Kevin Saunderson

### Techno-Pop
The Shamen, 2 Unlimited, Rozalla, Faithless, Sunscreem, Finitribe

### British Techno
*The sound of Detroit is imported to British shores during the late '80s...*
LFO, Bandulu, Dave Angel, The Black Dog, B12, Luke Slater, Nightmares on Wax, Orbital, A Guy Called Gerald

### Experimental Techno
Cristian Vogel, Oval, Autechre, Panasonic, Neuropolitique, Aphex Twin

### Ambient/Intelligent Techno
*Electronic artists catch the ears of critics and rock listeners with extended album works, contrasting their forebears' predominant method of release, the 12" single.*
The Orb, Orbital, The Irresistible Force, Basic Channell Biosphere, Aphex Twin, µ-Ziq, Mouse on Mars, Speedy J, Autechre

### Later Detroit Techno
*The second and third waves of Detroit producers continue the adoration which many Europeans feel for the home of techno.*
Carl Craig, Underground Resistance, Jeff Mills, Robert Hood, Kenny Larkin, Plastikman

### Electronica
*The new dance music of the '90s gradually develops bankable, image-conscious artists who can straddle the fields of rock and techno with ease.*
Underworld, Future Sound of London, Daft Punk, The Prodigy, Moloko, Everything But the Girl, Fluke, Lamb

### Post-Rock/Experimental
*Predominantly American indie-rock bands are influenced by '70s Kraut-Rock, alternative dream-pop, and European electronica.*
Tortoise, To Rococo Rot, The Sea and Cake, Labradford, Trans Am, Ui, Gastr del Sol, Rome

### Global Techno
*Many artists find success in the world-wide techno community, working as DJs, producing tracks, and remixing others, and occasionally releasing albums of their own.*
Moby, Joey Beltram, Laurent Garnier, Josh Wink, Ken Ishii, Slam, Andrew Weatherall

## Music Map

# Techno (continued)

### Synth-Pop
*European groups, influenced by Kraftwerk as well as new wave, are exported to American pop radio stations.*
Human League, Simple Minds, Gary Numan, Yellow Magic Orchestra, Depeche Mode

### Acid House
*Chicago originators:* Farley Jackmaster Funk, Phuture, DJ Pierre, Adonis
*Later British Crossovers:* S'Express, M/A/R/R/S, Technotronic, Black Box

### Trance
*The hypnotizing tones of acid-house and rave, together with the minimalism of Detroit techno, create a new style based in the Teutonic centers of Germany and Belgium.*
Hardfloor, Sven Väth, Westbam, Joey Beltram, CJ Bolland, Spicelab, Barbarella

### Rave
*A profusion of drugs at immense suburban warehouse parties–later called raves–fuel the British preoccupation with music of ever-faster tempos.*
The Prodigy, The Shamen, Moby, Lords of Acid
*The one-shot artists:* L.A. Style, Alpha Team, Smart E's, SL2, The Movement, KWS

### Hardcore Techno
*More intense than rave but lacking the form's euphoric feeling, hardcore finds a niche in continental Europe and the north of Britain.*
Dave Clarke, 2 Bad Mice, Rob Playford, T99, 4 Hero, Joey Beltram, Alec Empire

### Gabba
Paul Elstak, G.T.O., Rotterdam Terror Corps, Euromasters, DJ Paul

### Electro-Techno
Drexciya, AUX88, The Suburban Knight, Ectomorph, Jedi Knights, Gescom/Autechre, Plaid, Doctor Rockit

### Jungle, Drum'n'Bass
*Rave breakbeats meet the harder side of techno, with influences from ragga/dancehall and hip-hop.*
*Breakbeat DJs:* Grooverider, Fabio
*Jungle Mainstream:* Goldie, L.T.J. Bukem, Roni Size

experiments of those artists' early 12"s for Warp, Network, ZTT, and Vinyl Solution. Bleep is a direct precursor of the electronic listening music characteristic of the GPR and Warp labels (the latter of which Gordon helped found in the early '90s), and later evolved into the "armchair" or "intelligent" techno of artists such as the Black Dog, Autechre, As One, Aphex Twin, and µ-Ziq.

## Acid

Acid music, apart from early techno and electro, has also been America's longest running contribution to the global dance scene, with artists such as Robert Armani, DJ Pierre, Armando, Marshall Jefferson, and Freddie Fresh extremely influential in the German and Dutch scenes. The music's name derives less from the drug as from the caustic, abrasive synth squelches associated with the TB-303 synthesizer, the music's most prominent instrumental element.

## Trance (also Hard and Goa)

Trance is a superfast offshoot of techno that uses sparse, repetitive structures, dense melodic textures, and high BPMs to induce a sort of mesmerized state. Popular for its psychedelic themes and often used in combination with hallucinogens to enhance the psychotropic effects, the style has been most popular in Germany, where artists such as Hardfloor, DJ Criss, Arpeggiators, and Cygnus X developed a harder-edge style known, appropriately, as hard trance. An increasingly ethnic-infused strain has also evolved through the mid-'90s known as Goa trance, which plays up the spacey, psychedelic side with movie samples and heavy basslines. Hardcore techno artists such as Joey Beltram and Dave Clarke have also helped to blur the line between trance and harder styles of techno, utilizing highly repetitive rhythms layered with slight, slowly morphing electronics.

## Intelligent Techno/IDM

Shortform for Intelligent Dance Music, IDM as a musical genre is a relatively recent invention meant to account for new forms of electronic music composition which draw from styles such as house, techno, ambient, and electro while taking them in distinctly different, often more "musical" directions. Although often slighted for its racist connotations (recalling techno's African-American roots and contrasting them with a derivative style largely produced and consumed by white artists and audiences), for better or for worse the term has caught on as a generic placeholder for styles of dance-based electronic music seeking audiences outside the traditional milieu of the DJ and dancefloor. (Artists: Aphex Twin, Orbital, Biosphere, the Black Dog, Autechre, Richard H. Kirk)

## Minimal

Minimalist techno, particularly in its European form, involves the stripping away of most of what could be referred to as techno's "musical" side to reveal only the basic pulse of the beat, fitted with a minimum of textural embellishment. Oddly enough, even within this framework, minimalist techno takes on a variety of different faces, from Mike Ink's Studio 1 and Berlin's Basic Channel, to Finland's Sahko label and artists such as ÿ. Variation often comes in the form of vague differences in technology, but usually the motive is the same — to abstract dance music away from the contingency of culture toward something like a "universal groove." The style is probably most popular in Germany, Belgium, and Northern Europe.

### Recommended Listening:

1. Model 500 — *Classics* (R&S)
2. Kevin Saunderson — *Faces & Phases* (Planet E)
3. Derrick May — *Innovator* (Transmat)
4. Various Artists — *Warp 10+1: The Influences* (Warp/Matador)
5. Psyche/BFC — *Elements 1989-1990* (Planet E)
6. Underground Resistance — *Interstellar Fugitives* (UR)
7. Various Artists — *Warp 10+2: The Classics 1989-1992* (Warp/Matador)
8. Orbital — *Orbital 2* (ffrr)
9. Black Dog Productions — *Bytes* (Warp/TVT)
10. Autechre — *Tri Repetae* (Warp)
11. Basic Channel — *Basic Channel* (Basic Channel/EFA)

### Recommended Reading:

*Techno Rebels*, Dan Sicko (Billboard Books, 1999)
*Rough Guide to Techno*, Tim Barr (Rough Guides/Penguin, 2000)

— *Sean Cooper*

# Electronica

Electronica has become a manageable, one-word catch-all for a range of music styles which, taken together, many believe represent the next step in the evolution of Western pop. Although what the term actually means tends in large part to depend upon which side of the Atlantic Ocean it's spoken on, electronica in its broadest common significance refers primarily to artists drawing heavily on dance music styles such as house, techno, electro, and EBM (electronic body music) in ways not simply derivative of the dancefloor. Similar in some respects to the early working distinction between rhythm & blues and rock 'n' roll, electronica tends to involve an adaptation or mutation of dance music compositional elements to other-than-DJ/dancefloor ends; in the context of contemporary electronic dance music, that generally translates into dynamic (rather than static), composed (rather than programmed), listener- (rather than dancer- or DJ-) oriented "songs" (rather than "trax"). If the term's distinction appears to turn only on contrast — that is, by negative comparison to dance music — it's because many of the artists credited with innovating the music (people like the Black Dog, Orbital, Terrace, Speedy J, Richard H. Kirk, the Future Sound of London, Autechre, and Aphex Twin) saw themselves in contradistinction to dance culture and the limits it placed on its music. These artists were interested in producing music designed for other uses — home listening, primarily — which allowed for a wider range of influences (ambient, classical, jazz, non-Western musics, etc.) and a higher index of experimentation. Heavily influenced by the early techno-pop, hip-hop, and electro-funk of Kraftwerk, Cybotron, Man Parrish, Soul Sonic Force, and Ice-T, as well as the first wave techno and acid house of Detroit and Chicago innovators, these artists brought a penchant for tunefulness and compositional dynamics — elements often lacking in club-borne dance music — to the creative fore.

Original wide-spread use of the term "electronica" derives in part from the influential English experimental techno label New Electronica, which, along with labels such as General Production Recordings, Warp, Evolution, and Rising High, was a leading force in the early '90s in introducing and supporting dance-based electronic music more oriented toward home listening than dancefloor play. Because of that label's role in the birth of "intelligent techno" (itself a heavily loaded and controversial term referring to electronic listening music rooted in, but not simply reducible to, dancefloor techno), the term in the early part of the '90s became used to loosely characterize groups such as Orbital, Autechre, Aphex Twin, As One, Global Communication, Sun Electric, the Black Dog, the Orb, Higher Intelligence Agency, Biosphere, etc.; in other words, bands that drew primarily from dancefloor techno in constructing more song-oriented music utilizing similar instrumental elements, compositional techniques, and organizational structures (four-on-the-floor or electronic breakbeats; synth pads and 303, 808, and 909 bass and drum sounds; simple melodies and deep basslines; minor-key chord progressions; etc.). As a result, electronica became more or less synonymous with terms such as "intelligent techno," "ambient techno," etc., and was considered distinct from other emerging forms such as jungle and trip-hop, each of which had its own set of defining characteristics (as well as often dauntingly complex litany of terms and microgenres).

A key component in the growth and popularization of the style was the *Artificial Intelligence* series released by the Sheffield-based Warp label starting in 1992, which presented many of the artists now thought to be formative to a wide audience for the first time (including Autechre, Speedy J, Richard H. Kirk, the Black Dog, and Aphex Twin). Previously a source of innovative but nonetheless clearly dancefloor-oriented house and techno (early singles from the label include Nightmares On Wax, Robert Gordon's Forgemasters, and LFO), Warp's two-part compilation series *Artificial Intelligence*, as well as subsequent full-lengths from Kirk, Black Dog Productions, Autechre, and Detroit techno artist Kenny Larkin drew a clear line in the sand between dance music and the "electronic listening music" that would soon become the label's focus. (The first volume of *Artificial Intelligence* pictured a computer rendering of a chrome figure, spliff in hand, reclining before the front-room hi-fi, sleeves of Warp and Pink Floyd records littering the floor.) The series also constituted America's first serious exposure to the new sound; Wax Trax!/TVT licensed the two compilations and reissued a number of Warp's subsequent full-length releases.

In the United States, it wasn't until 1997 that electronica was appropriated and generalized by the music (and non-music) press to refer to any dance-based electronic music with a potential for pop appeal. As a result, the term

## Music Map

# Electronica

**Electro**
Grandmaster Flash, Afrika Bambaataa, Cybotron, The Egyptian Lover, Man Parrish

**Disco**
Donna Summer, Giorgio Moroder, The BeeGees, The Trammps, Gloria Gaynor, Chic, Cerrone

**Techno**
Juan Atkins, Derrick May, Moby, Carl Craig, Plastikman

**Ambient**
Brian Eno, Tangerine Dream, Pink Floyd, David Sylvian

**House**
Farley Jackmaster Funk, Masters at Work, Marshall Jefferson, Larry Heard, Todd Terry, Deep Dish

**Ambient Techno**
Higher Intelligence Agency, Panasonic, µ-Ziq, Aphex Twin, Spacetime Continuum, Sun Electric, Orbital, Seefeel, Mouse on Mars, Speedy J

**Ambient House**
The Orb, Biosphere, The Irresistible Force, Global Communication, Ultramarine, Spacetime Continuum

**Jungle/Drum'N'Bass**
Goldie, LTJ Bukem, Roni Size, Photek

**Trip-Hop**
Massive Attack, Portishead, Tricky, DJ Shadow, Wagon Christ, DJ Krush, Coldcut

**Electronica**
The Chemical Brothers, Underworld, Lamb, Daft Punk, Future Sound of London, Prodigy, Mouse on Mars, Spacetime Continuum

**Big Beat/Funky Breaks**
Fatboy Slim, Bentley Rhythm Ace, Lionrock, Propellerheads, The Crystal Method, Mekon, Monkey Mafia, Freestylers, Headrillaz

**Post-Rock/Experimental**
Tortoise, To Rococo Rot, The Sea and Cake, Labradford, Trans Am, Ui, Gastr del Sol, Rome

---

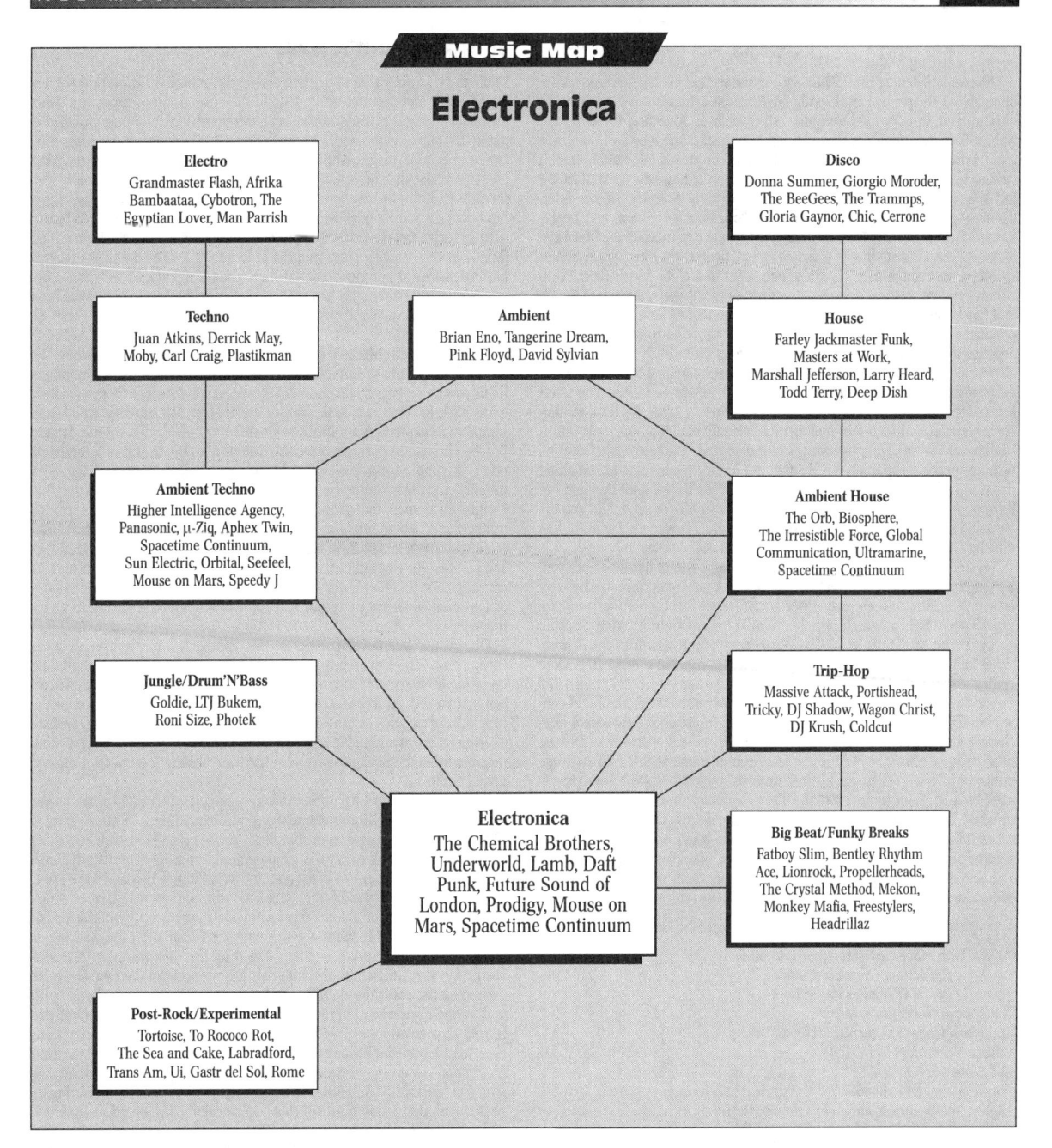

was used to describe everyone from the Chemical Brothers and Prodigy to Orbital and Ken Ishii, to Alex Reece, Mo'Wax, the Sneaker Pimps, Goldie, and Aphex Twin. Aversions to excessive genrefication notwithstanding, the grouping together of such disparate artists seems symptomatic of larger tendencies within an American music industry which knows little (if anything) about the histories of the various styles these artists represent, a notion which has its antecedents in a largely rock-based music press and its bias—stemming in part from the legacy of disco—against music featuring predominantly electronic instrumentation, as well as a tendency to subsume all potentially significant popular music styles under the category of "rock." Where,

in the European usage, the defining feature of electronica was usually its "listenability" (a value gauged within the context of the experimental electronic music underground, which usually had some understanding of the degree to which "song"-y derivatives of the music such as Orbital or Aphex Twin deviated from the more nuts'n'bolts dancefloor fare of Derrick May, Jeff Mills, and Dave Clarke), in America the distinction seems to turn instead on the music's potential for popularity (read: profitability) via mainstream success: It was only, ironically, when several of these bands began gaining MTV exposure, commercial radio play, and major-label recording contracts—despite the fact that the music had been widely popular outside of the US for nearly a decade—that "electronica" as a concrete category in the American music industry gained any viability.

"Electronic listening music" has also, of course, become big business on the other side of the pond, as well, with smaller indie releases routinely charting next to their Brit-pop brethren and artists such as Autechre, the Orb, and Aphex Twin becoming the closest thing to pop stars the tenets of the genre and the limitations of its audience will allow. The steady adaptation of club culture to the demands of its electronic antagonists, however (as well as the fact that many of the artists and labels—including Scanner, Higher Intelligence Agency, and Coldcut, as well as Warp, Rephlex, Skam, and Leaf—formed their own clubs), has also (ironically) meant that much of the first wave of dance-music dissent has, to a certain extent, been reabsorbed as dance music (or at least club music, i.e. music one hears in a club). "Back room" club culture (previously the margin of experimental weirdness relegated to the literal "back rooms" of huge raves and weekly club nights) have also taken on a popular mythos all their own, with the vitality of freeform experimentation associated with them foregrounded in offshoot clubs such as the massive Heavenly club's Sunday Social (and perhaps best embodied by early genrecidal innovators Coldcut's *Journeys by DJ* mix CD, released in 1995). The result has pushed degrees of experimentation even further, with the IDM of first-wave electronic artists intermingling more directly with hip-hop, funk, industrial, jungle/drum'n'bass, free jazz, and Indian and Southeast Asian musics, turning up some extremely interesting and innovative hybrids in the offing (from the schizoid electro-jazz/jungle of Atom Heart, Bisk, and Bedouin Ascent to the banging gabber-punk of Alec Empire's Atari Teenage Riot and the paranoid and depressed drum'n'bass of, alternately, TPower and Panacea). Just how far this dynamic is capable of taking the music remains to be seen.

Several good introductions to the various strains—both hardline and "contemporary"—of electronica's eclectic face exist. An obvious place to start is, of course, New Electronica's early series *New Electronica: Global Electronic Innovations* (which, although heavily oriented toward Detroit techno, include many crucial early cuts), as well as Warp's two-volume *Artificial Intelligence* series, and its three-volume tenth-anniversary retrospective *Warp 10+*. More contemporarily, the German label Studio !K7's two double-CD collections *The Freestyle Files* are excellent cross-sections of the rampant inbreeding of contemporary electronica. Those strapped for cash (most good new-school electronica comps tend to be import-only) should check out Nettwork's "greatest hits" package *Plastic*, as well as the label compilations licensed for stateside release by New York-based Instinct Records, which include Ntone (*Earthrise.Ntone.1*), Em;t (*Em't 2000* and *Em.t Explorer*), and Compost (two volumes of *The Future Sound of Jazz*). For a taste of now-school breakbeat culture's influence on the music's formerly techno-heavy sound, Rising High's *Further Self-Evident Truths* and *Avant-Gardism*, Blue Planet's *State of the Nu Art*, and the Talvin Singh-compiled *Anohka: Sounds of the Asian Underground* are excellent entrees into electronica's more schizophrenetic offerings.

**Recommended Listening** (* indicates top 10):

Aphex Twin—*Selected Ambient Works 85-92* (R&S)*
As One—*Reflections* (New Electronica)
Atom Heart—*HAT* (Rather Interesting)
Autechre—*Amber* (TVT/Warp)*
The Black Dog—*Spanners* (EastWest/Warp)*
Coldcut—*Journeys by DJ* (JDJ)*
808 State—*UTD. 90* (ZTT)*
Future Sound Of London—*ISDN* (Astralwerks/Virgin)*
Higher Intelligence Agency—*Freefloater* (Beyond)
Locust—*Truth Is Born of Arguments* (Apollo)
Mouse on Mars—*Iaora Tahiti* (American/Too Pure) *
Orbital—*In Sides* (Internal)
Reload—*A Collection of Short Stories* (Infonet)*
Spacetime Continuum—*Emit Ecaps* (Astralwerks)
u-Ziq—*Tango n'Vectif* (Rephlex)*
Various Artists—*Warp 10+2: The Classics 1989-1992* (Warp/Matador)*
Various Artists—*Objets d'ART 2* (New Electronica)
Various Artists—*The Freestyle Files* (Studio !K7)

**Recommended Reading:**

*Generation Ecstasy*, Simon Reynolds (Little Brown & Company, 1998)

—*Sean Cooper*

## Jungle/Drum'N'Bass

While the UK underground dance scene has been both an important point of introduction and a source of almost limitless expansion of American dance music forms such as disco, house, acid, techno, electro, and rare groove, England, it's often been noted, has never really had a dance music of its own. Not, that is, until Jungle. Although jungle's most direct roots lay in the hardcore breakbeat style of techno popular in clubs in the late '80s and early '90s, the music's mutation of elements from not only hardcore, but reggae, ragga, hip-hop, jazz, and dub, as well as its origins in social and economic factors such as racist and class-based oppression, was a distinctly British mix. Born largely in the working class suburbs of London's East End and the island's Eastern seaboard and now popular throughout England, as well as Europe and North America, jungle has coalesced since its birth into one of the most exciting and distinctive British musical movements since the '60s rock explosion.

Like American hip-hop (to which it is often compared), jungle (or drum'n'bass, a stylistic synonym used to describe the music's two main aesthetic components) is an extension of the larger breakbeat heritage which extends back to American funk, soul, and jazz. And like hip-hop, which uses samplers to capture drum break segments from old James Brown, Meters, Jimmy Smith, and Bob James records, jungle uses the beat as a jumping off point, starting with a four- or eight-bar break and cutting, splicing, rearranging, and recombining elements of the beat in almost endless variety. But it's this last element that gives jungle its unique place in the evolution of electronic music; where hip-hop and other sample-based forms of dance music work with beats in a more or less serial fashion (looping, combining, adding, subtracting, etc. rhythmic elements), jungle's approach is nonlinear and, increasingly, polyrhythmic, approaching beats, rhythms, and basslines as more or less malleable raw materials from which new musical ideas can be extracted.

One of the key developments in this approach was the availability of cheap, relatively easy-to-use sampling technology and desktop digital sequencing tools such as Cubase and Vision, which allowed for incredible control and variety. In many respects, these tools made the music possible, as new techniques such as timestretching (extending a sample's length without altering its pitch) and the music's cut'n'paste approach to rhythm were made possible through the explosion and subsequent economic democratization of digital audio.

Although, like most origin mythologies, jungle was fraught with intriguing stories of its birth and etymology (even extending to a street gang in Kingston, Jamaica known as the Junglists), most agree that somewhere down the line "jungle" took on a racist connotation stemming from its popularity among England's inner-city black population (although, to a far larger extent than in America, England's inner-cities are of mixed race and are stratified more by class). True or not, the term was widely embraced by musicians and audiences alike, and remains a genus-type classification for the dizzying array of species of drum'n'bass that popped up (see below). In an historico-aesthetic sense, jungle's immediate roots lie, of course, in the English underground rave scene of the early '90s, when the repetitive banging of acid house and techno gave way to hardcore breakbeat techno. Although originally referring to a more rave-oriented strain of hardcore (so-called "happy hardcore," which translated many of the more escapist elements of acid house and dancefloor techno into a breakbeat context), a more complex and abrasive strand of "darkside" hardcore soon began to grow in popularity, becoming the post-rave underground music of choice, particularly among urban inner-city and working class youth.

Drawing from the music's audience (and of course the musicians themselves), the music began incorporating more complex beat patterns and elements of reggae, ragga, dub, calypso, and other non-Western black musics, mutating (through artists such as Rob Playford/2 Bad Mice, SL2, Acen, and Urban Shakedown) into the high-speed breakbeat madness of jungle's first wave. Though still the soundtrack of the urban English underground, by the time ragga jungle hit, a wider audience began to form around the revolutionary new sound, particularly as labels such as Suburban Bass, Kickin', Sound of the Underground, and Moving Shadow began to move into CD-based compilation releases, which helped spread the music into new geographies at a rapid rate. Though the cliches of ragga dated quickly (the booyaka chants, the Scientist samples, etc.), the basic skeleton of the music was refined

## Music Map
# Jungle/Drum'N'Bass

### The Classic Breaks
*Sampling drum-breaks from classic LPs and 45s by jazz-funk artists of the '70s, British producers begin to produce drum programs of intricate breakbeat techno:*
"The Funky Drummer"—James Brown, The "Amen" Break—The Winstons, The "Apache" Break—Michael Viner's Incredible Bongo Band

### Ragga/Dancehall
*The first wave of British junglists are influenced by dancehall/ragga MCs.*
Shabba Ranks, Bounty Killer, Eek-A-Mouse, I-Roy, Mega Banton

### Hip-Hop
Public Enemy, Boogie Down Productions, Mantronix, Run-DMC, Marley Marl, A Tribe Called Quest, Whodini

### Hardcore Techno
*The advent of accelerated breakbeats:*
Shut Up and Dance, 4 Hero, 2 Bad Mice, SL2, Acen, The Prodigy, Rebel MC

### Breakbeat DJs
*Moving from rave and acid house to hardcore techno and jungle.*
Grooverider, Fabio, DJ Hype, DJ SS

### First Wave of Jungle
*Reggae-influenced MCs and producers begin to hit the British charts.*
Rude Bwoy Monty, Shy FX, Rebel MC
*Meanwhile, hardcore-influenced producers approach the same sound.*
A Guy Called Gerald, 4 Hero, Kenny Ken

### Hardstep/Jump-Up
Ray Keith, DJ Zinc, Aphrodite, Ganja Kru

### Electronica
Underworld, Future Sound of London, Daft Punk, The Prodigy, Everything But The Girl, Moloko, Fluke, Lamb

### Big Beat
The Chemical Brothers, The Crystal Method, Fatboy Slim, Bentley Rhythm Ace, David Holmes

### Jungle Mainstream
*Accomplished artists gain praise from critics and mainstream listeners.*
Goldie, Roni Size, LTJ Bukem, 4 Hero

### Tech-Step
Ed Rush, DJ Trace, Panacea, Boymerang, Dillinja, Optical, Technical Itch

### Jungle Jazz
Blame, Wax Doctor, Kid Loops, Aquasky, Endemic Void, Alex Reece, Dom & Roland, Justice, Peshay

### Ambient Jungle
Photek, Source Direct, T Power, Omni Trio, Spring Heel Jack, Arcon 2, J Majik, Lamb

### Funky Jungle/Drill'N'Bass
Squarepusher, Plug, µ-Ziq, Animals on Wheels, Mung, The Bowling Green

and elaborated (in a less-obvious fashion) in so-called hardstep and darkside, which aimed at preserving the intellectual and emotional impact of the music in a more mature, less gimmicky fashion. The following years would see a dizzying mutation and hybridization of styles, as jungle worked its way into every stylistic context immaginable (from Lee Perry and the Wu-Tang Clan to Soul Coughing and Everything but the Girl), with styles continuing to proliferate past the end of the millennium.

Like early hip-hop and, to a large extent, house and techno, drum'n'bass remained primarily a 12" culture, with the bulk of artists and musicians engaged in nuts'n'boltsmusic-making designed directly for DJs and dancefloors (although, like techno, the gap began to close a bit through wider popularity of ambient and "intelligent" styles and large-scale CD production and distribution). The rapid intermixing and evolution of styles was also fueled in part by widespread use of white labels, dubplates, and test pressings, which allowed artists and DJs to gauge the popularity of a tune only hours after its completion in the studio. (Dubplates and test pressings are wax and mylar versions of records—usually only playable ten to fifteen times—cut prior to mass production to insure proper manufacture.) A reasonably reputable DJ could spin anywhere from 10 to 50 percent dubplates in a set, with artists who also DJ often cutting their tunes months in advance of their release (if indeed they're ever released!) to build crowd excitement and anticipation.

As discussed above, like other directions in experimental electronic music, jungle quickly sectioned off into a dizzying array of subgenres and style classes (ragga, hardstep, darkside, jump-up, techstep, ambient) that can make getting a handle on it pretty frustrating. The following is a brief description of many of the most prominent:

### Hardcore/Happy Hardcore

An urban working-class offshoot of techno, popular in the late '80s/early '90s, with looping, sped-up breakbeats and dense, angular basslines. A more mainstream, rave-oriented brand of "happy" hardcore remained even truer to the music's acid house roots, drawing wailing divas and upbeat piano and synth lines in close proximity to hardcore's brash rhythms. (Artists: Acen, 2 Bad Mice, SL2)

### Ragga

Ragga jungle was one of the earliest and most widely embraced forms of drum'n'bass not to rely overtly on the cliches of hardcore techno, and was a direct reflection of the rising embrace of drum'n'bass among the street-level urban population (of which a sizeable portion are of African and Caribbean descent). Ragga jungle is characterized primarily by fast, complex beat patterns, deep, tight bass, and the use of sound system-type MC chanting sampled from old reggae, ragga, and dancehall records. Ragga also makes jungle's connection to African and Caribbean traditional and popular musics most evident, with rhythms recognizably descendent from nyabingi and calypso-style drumming. (Artists: 2 Bad Mice, Rude Bwoy Monty, Shy FX, Amazon II)

### Hardstep/Jump-Up

A spare, limber refinement of hardcore and ragga, which retains the hardness and rhythmic complexity of both while subtracting much of the bonus fat (rude bwoy chatter, excessive samples, etc.). Hardstep also carries more of a sense of progression, varying drum patterns more musically and focusing on bass as a melodic element. Although slight variations obtain between hardstep and the more recently-applied jump-up (with the latter generally referring to a sprighter, more dynamic brand of hardstep), the two are for the most part used interchangeably. (Artists: Ray Keith, DJ SS, Dillinja, DJ Zinc)

### Darkside

A somewhat historically rooted term, darkside refers to a sparer, more pessimistic style of hardcore seeking to differentiate itself from the more aboveground, mainstream appeal of rave that by the early '90s was producing only the most repetitive and uncreative of music. Darkside artists stripped the bright melodies and sped-up samples from hardcore and replaced them with gloomy basslines, and less obvious melodic passages more reminiscent of Detroit techno than happy hardcore. Darkside is also something of a bridge between early hardcore and the increasing sophistication of the hardstep and experimental drum'n'bass of DJ SS, Solo, Source Direct, and the Metalheadz artists.

### Techstep

Techstep is similar to hardstep in its beat structures and attitude, but differs in the use of techno-type elements such as bleeps and synth squelches, as well as dense, heavily treated basslines. After the softening of drum'n'bass in the wake of jungle's first wave of widespread popularity (major label signings, international tours, etc.), darker techstep-type jungle has risen to the fore of the underground, proving one of the most active and interesting splinter styles in its experimentalism. Labels on the bleeding edge of this style include Emotif, No U-Turn, Penny Black, and S.O.U.R., and a good introduction exists in Emotif's label compilation, *Techsteppin',* as well as S.O.U.R.'s *Nu Skool Update.* (Artists: Ed Rush, Nico, Solo, Shapeshifter)

### Ambient/Intelligent

First used to designate drum'n'bass styles drawing heavily on atmosphere and environment, the term later came to have something of a negative connotation among the hardcore, referring to loopy, relatively unchallenging rhythmic programming and a predominance of sugary, pop-oriented melodic textures. Most likely the backlash had as much to do with the fact that it was the softer, jazzier ambient style drum'n'bass that was the first to sever its roots with the underground, gaining popularity among a wide audience. (Artists: TPower, Omni Trio, Source Direct, Photek, 4Hero, Dave Wallace)

**Recommended Listening:**

1. Various Artists—*History of Hardcore, Pts. 1-2* (Suburban Base)
2. Various Artists—*History of Our World, Pts. 1-2* (Profile)
3. 4 Hero—*Parallel Universe* (Reinforced)
4. Various Artists—*Platinum Breakz* (Metalheadz/ffrr)
5. LTJ Bukem—*Logical Progression* (Good Looking/London)
6. Photek—*Form & Function* (Astralwerks)
7. Roni Size—*New Forms* (Talkin' Loud/Mercury)
8. Ed Rush—*Torque* (No-U-Turn/Pavement)
9. Plug—*Drum'n'bass for Papa/Plug 1, 2 & 3* (Nothing/Interscope)
10. Lamb—*Lamb* (Fontana)

**Recommended Reading:**

*State of Bass,* Martin James (Boxtree, 1997)
*Rough Guide to Drum'n'bass,* Peter Shapiro (Rough Guides/Penguin, 1999)
—*Sean Cooper*

## Trance

After breaking out of the techno and rave scene of the early '90s, Trance exerted an ever-increasing impact on the global dance scene until the style finally crested in the late '90s, and ended the millennium as the most popular form of electronic dance. Emphasizing brief arpeggiated sequencer lines continually repeated throughout tracks, with only minimal rhythmic changes and occasional synthesizer atmospherics—the total effect easily capable of putting listeners into trances approaching those of religious origin—trance was the preserve of a small community of European (mostly German and Belgian) producers and fans until the late '90s, when the popularity of group-oriented act Underworld and dozens of globe-trotting trance DJs (including Sasha + John Digweed, Paul Van Dyk, and Paul Oakenfold) helped trance supplant house as the dance music of choice worldwide.

As is par for the course, there's an abundance of stylistic precedents for what later came to be known as trance, going back as far as the hypnotic, multi-layered productions of Giorgio Moroder and Jean-Michel Jarre during the late '70s, trance-state acid house from Chicago around 1986-87, and the gloomy, haunted sound of techno in Detroit during the same time. In reaction to the growing euphoria (some would say hysteria) of the early-'90s commercial rave scene, German, Belgian, and British producers—plus a few Americans, notably Joey Beltram and Moby—began producing minimalistic, quintessentially Teutonic techno tracks notably devoid of any of the usual rave trademarks: breakbeats, whistles, ragga chatters, novelty concepts, pitched-up divas, etc. The trance scene really coalesced with a raft of classic singles recorded during 1991-93, many of them released on one of two labels: R&S Records, based in Ghent, Belgium and Harthouse/Eye Q Records of Frankfurt, Germany. Early trance tended to either the melancholy and cinematic (Moby's "Go," Jam & Spoon's "Stella"), the downright menacing (Joey

## Music Map

# Trance

**Kraftwerk**

**Electro**
Grandmaster Flash, Afrika Bambaataa, Herbie Hancock, The Egyptian Lover, Man Parrish

**House**
Marshall Jefferson, Larry Heard, Todd Terry

**Techno**
Juan Atkins, Derrick May, Kevin Saunderson, Carl Craig, Underground

**Acid House**
Phuture, Adonis, DJ Pierre

**Rave**
The Prodigy, L.A. Style, Alpha Team, Smart E's, SL2, The Movement, KWS

**Early Trance**
Jam & Spoon, Hardfloor, Sven Väth, Moby, MLO, Joey Beltram, CJ Bolland, Spicelab, Arpeggiators, Lords of Acid

**Electronica**
The Chemical Brothers, Underworld, The Prodigy, Future Sound of London, Daft Punk, Moloko, Fluke, Lamb, Everything But the Girl

**Hardcore Techno**
Dave Clarke, Danny Breaks, Omar Santana, Billy Nasty, Slipmatt, Ege Bam Yasi, Alec Empire, Woody McBride

**Progressive Trance**
Sasha + John Digweed, Paul Oakenfold, BT, François K, Tony De Vit, Sandra Collins, Hybrid, Christopher Lawrence, Nick Warren, Pete Tong, Kimball Collins

---

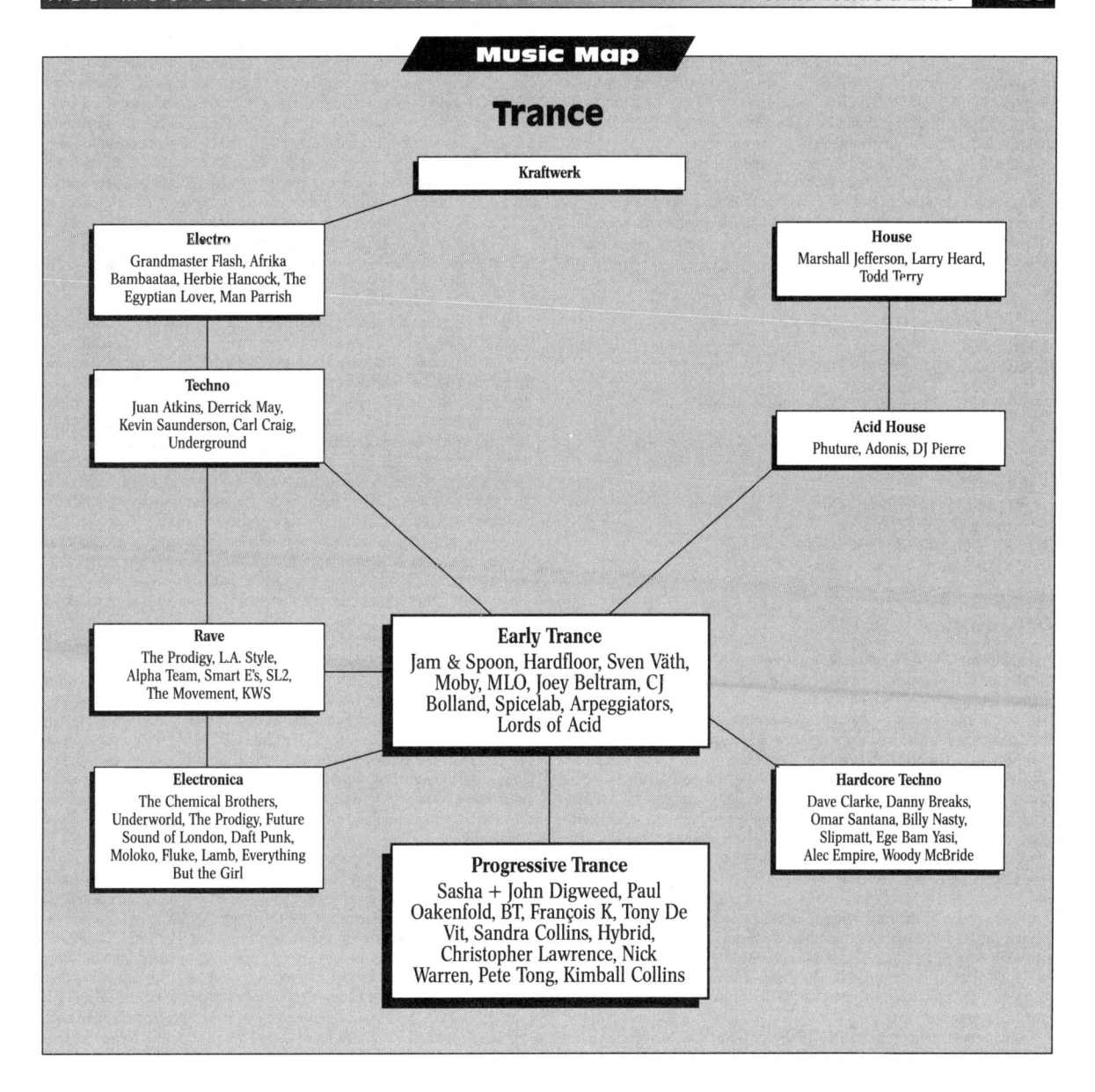

Beltram's "Energy Flash," Hardfloor's "Hardtrance Acperience," CJ Bolland's "Horsepower"), or a mixture of both (Aphex Twin's "Digeridoo," Sven Väth's "Barbarella").

Väth, who formed Harthouse/Eye Q in 1992 with Heinz Roth and Matthias Hoffman, attempted to take the sound of trance into the critical mainstream with LPs and a major-label distribution deal with Warner Bros., but in the wake of breakbeat styles from drum'n'bass to trip-hop, trance took on a distinctly unhip sense of stiffness. It surely didn't help that many trance full-lengths—Jam & Spoon's *Tripomatic Fairytales 2001-2002*, Väth's own *An Accident in Paradise*—courted a sense of the grandiose rarely seen since the days of yet another oft-disparaged music, '70s prog-rock. During the mid-'90s, trance returned to the underground, while a rush of continental labels (Bonzai, Superstition, Labworks, Delirium) filled the void with tough tracks that kept the hardness of original trance intact. The music also spun off into multiple dimensions via fusions with house (Britain's Rising High, Cowboy, Guerilla, Platipus), ambient (the Fax and Rather Interesting labels), acid (Holland's DJax), and Detroit techno (Red Planet, Plus 8).

Even while trance was completely off the radar of most dance fans, however, two related fusions—psychedelic trance and Goa trance—began gaining in popularity during the mid-'90s. The styles blended only the most dizzying sequencer patterns and quick tempos from trance with hallucinogenic samples and sounds borrowed from traditional Indian music (Goa is a big clubbing spot on the country's southwestern coast). Popularized by labels including Dragonfly, Blue Room Released, Flying Rhino, and Platipus, the new trance drove the music back into the mainstream after popular British DJs including Paul Oakenfold, Sasha + John Digweed, and Pete Tong began playing the music in their sets (Oakenfold even set up a trance-specific label, Perfecto Fluoro).

By the time trance reached the dance mainstream in the late '90s, both the classic German sound and the psychedelic branch were pushed aside by a stream of "progressive" trance influenced by the smoother end of house and Euro-dance. Producers like BT, François K, BBE, and Faithless spearheaded the sound by blending dreamy melodies, atmospherics, and driving trance rhythms. By 1998, most of Europe's best-known DJs—Oakenfold and Sasha + Digweed plus Pete Tong, Danny Rampling, Tony De Vit, Paul Van Dyk, and Judge Jules (all British but for Van Dyk)—were playing trance in Britain's superclubs. Even America turned on to the sound (eventually), led by its own cast of excellent DJs, including Christopher Lawrence, Sandra Collins, and Kimball Collins. At the turn of the millennium, though few producers even attempted to brave the full-length realm, popular mix-album series like *Global Underground* presented two-disc sets from many of the DJs listed above.

**Recommended Listening:**

1. Various Artists— *In Order to Dance, Vols. 1-2* (R&S)
2. Various Artists— *Harthouse: The Point of No Return* (Warner Bros.)
3. Various Artists— *Secret Life of Trance, Vols. 1-2* (Rising High)
4. Joey Beltram— *Classics* (R&S)
5. Sven Väth— *An Accident in Paradise* (Eye-Q/Warner Bros.)
6. Koxbox— *Forever After* (Harthouse)
7. Various Artists— *Platipus Records: Evolution of Trance* (Topaz)
8. Various Artists— *Signs of Life* (Blue Room USA.)
9. François K— *FK-EP and Beyond* (Wave)
10. BT— *ESCM* (Perfecto/Warner Bros.)
11. Tony De Vit— *Trade* (Priority)
12. Sasha— *Global Underground: San Francisco* (Thrive)
13. Paul Oakenfold— *Global Underground: Oslo* (Boxed)

—*John Bush*

## Trip-Hop

Yet another in a long line of plastic place-holders to attach itself to one arm or another of the UK post-acid house dance scene's rapidly mutating experimental underground, Trip-Hop was coined by the English music press in an attempt to characterize a new style of downtempo, jazz-, funk-, and soul-inflected experimental breakbeat music which began to emerge around in 1993 in association with labels such as Mo'Wax, Ninja Tune, Cup of Tea, and Wall of Sound. Similar to (though largely vocalless) American hip-hop in its use of sampled drum breaks, typically more experimental, and infused with a high index of ambient-leaning and apparently psychotropic atmospherics (hence "trip"), the term quickly caught on to describe everything from Portishead and Tricky, to DJ Shadow and U.N.K.L.E., to Coldcut, Wagon Christ, and Depth Charge (much to the chagrin of many of these musicians, who saw their music largely as an extension of hip-hop proper, not a gimmicky offshoot). One of the first commerically significant hybrids of dance-based listening music to crossover to a more mainstream audience, full-length releases in the style routinely topped indie charts in the UK and, in artists such as DJ Shadow, Tricky, Morcheeba, the Sneaker Pimps, and Massive Attack, accounted for a substantial portion of the first wave of "electronica" acts to reach stateside audiences.

With immediate roots in the immensely popular UK acid jazz scene, trip-hop was born out of a dissatisfaction with that scene's creative wane toward the end of the '80s, as well as the increasing influence of the London acid house movement. As many have observed, while the US was steadily separating out the jazz influence from its funk (via Parliament-Funkadelic, the '70s disco-funk of the Gap Band and Zapp & Roger, and the '80s pop-funk of Prince), the UK was reinventing the one through the other, the result being acid jazz: Northern soul (a late-'70s style of dance-based groove music similar to rare groove), jazz instrumentation and voicing, and the solid rhythmic foundation of funk, often with a hip-hop beat. Popularized by labels such as Acid Jazz, Talkin' Loud, and Dorado and artists such as the Young Disciples, Corduroy, Groove Collective, and Incognito, the rise to acid jazz to commercial viability in the UK (as well as the US; many indie labels were reissuing loads of European releases) was swift and ruthless. Like the latter stages of be-bop, the music's polarization into, on the one hand, watered-down commercial accessibility and, on the other, increasingly esoteric chops-based noodling left many unsatisfied.

One way out seemed to be through an engagement of the more soulful possibilities of the acid house underground, a path taken by artists such as Soul II Soul, Galliano, and Massive Attack, many of whom added vocalists and rappers to attract a wider audience. Though many of them went on to great success, their pop appeal largely begged the question. Another way out—and one which appealed to a younger generation who grew up with a different musical perspective—was to focus on the music's hip-hop element, stripping away everything but the essentials and playing up the music's dusty beat. This was the path chosen by a loose affiliate of artists organized by James Lavelle, a DJ/producer and music writer for UK acid jazz mag *Straight No Chaser*. Lavelle sent a call for demos out in his monthly column, citing acid jazz's increasing irrelevance and encouraging hip-hop heads with a taste for experimentation to give him a shout. The first batch of demos he received—instrumental b-boy tracks from the likes of RPM, Palm Skin Productions, and La Funk Mob—became the first series of 12"s released on his new label, Mo'Wax.

Unlike house and techno, hip-hop (the music, anyway) never really caught fire in England. While a handful of artists have been able to pull it off, melding hip-hop production with an authentically UK lyrical perspective, hip-hop's influence has mostly been in terms of fashion (track suits and fat-laced trainers), graffiti, and electro (the latter particularly among the waves of electronica artists—such as Autechre, the Black Dog, and Reload—who took the style in various new directions). While a large underground of fans of early hip-hop formed in the wake of mid-'80s Wildstyle tour, which brought the various cultural components of hip-hop to a large British audience for the first time, only a handful of distinctly British hip-hop records were released in subsequent years, and of those only a tiny portion you'd want to hear more than once (some notable exceptions include Underdog and the Brotherhood). While UK sales of American hip-hop records continued to rise (particularly the more musically innovative acts such as Public Enemy and the Beastie Boys), there didn't seem to be an outlet for the growing scene's creative impulse.

This is where Mo'Wax (and, eventually, upstart labels such as Clean Up, D.C., and Represent) came in. While many of the tracks featured on the earliest Mo'Wax releases (and collected on the label's first compilation, *Royalties Overdue*) were in some ways indistinguishable from what was happening at the time in acid jazz, the more experimental B-side tracks—abstract, beat-centric slabs of funky downtempo weirdness with a bare minimum of jerky, effects-laden instrumental samples setting an immersive atmosphere—sounded amazingly fresh and suggested new directions for both acid jazz and instrumental hip-hop. Although it was hard to imagine the music impelling anyone onto the dancefloor, the records were a hit among DJs and bedroom heads alike.

In retrospect, the pairing of straight-ahead material with more experimental gear on the flip looks pretty savvy, but the fact was the label (and the burgeoning scene as a whole) was still groping for a sound. Grope became seize, however, when a remix of a little known American rap group called Zimbabwe Legit made its way to Lavelle's record box. The track, "Doin' Damage," had been tearing up the American underground for months, and a remix by an unknown California producer, DJ Shadow, attracted his attention. Lavelle tracked DJ Shadow (aka Josh Davis) down and commissioned a single, "In/Flux," which was released in late 1993. A perfect blend of head-bobbing beats and frenetic sample collage, "In/Flux" got the balance of funk, jazz, hip-hop, soul, and stoned out ambiance just right, and records nipping at its heals began appearing in droves over the course of the following year. Mo'Wax's subsequent compilation, *Headz* (released toward the end of 1994 and including the best of the label's catalog to date, as well as a heap of exclusives from DJ Shadow, DJ Krush, Lavelle's U.N.K.L.E. project, and even Autechre), set the watermark, and a scene started growing up around the label and others pursuing a similar sound such as Ninja Tune/Ntone, Wall of Sound, Cup of Tea, Chill Out, and former acid jazz powerhouse Dorado. As "back room" club culture started to shift from the droney bliss of ambient and dub to the free-for-all attitude embodied by the early Sunday Social parties held at London's Heavenly club, more and more beats could be heard issuing from back room bassbins. With more and more records appearing and more and more one-offs and weeklies forming to promulgate the style, the English press needed a quick, easy reference point for the music. "Trip-hop" fit that bill perfectly.

The term was almost immediately disparaged (Shadow riffs on the dopiness of it in his intro to U.N.K.L.E.'s "Time Has Come," released by Mo'Wax in early 1995), not least because it seemed, as usual, that another black artform

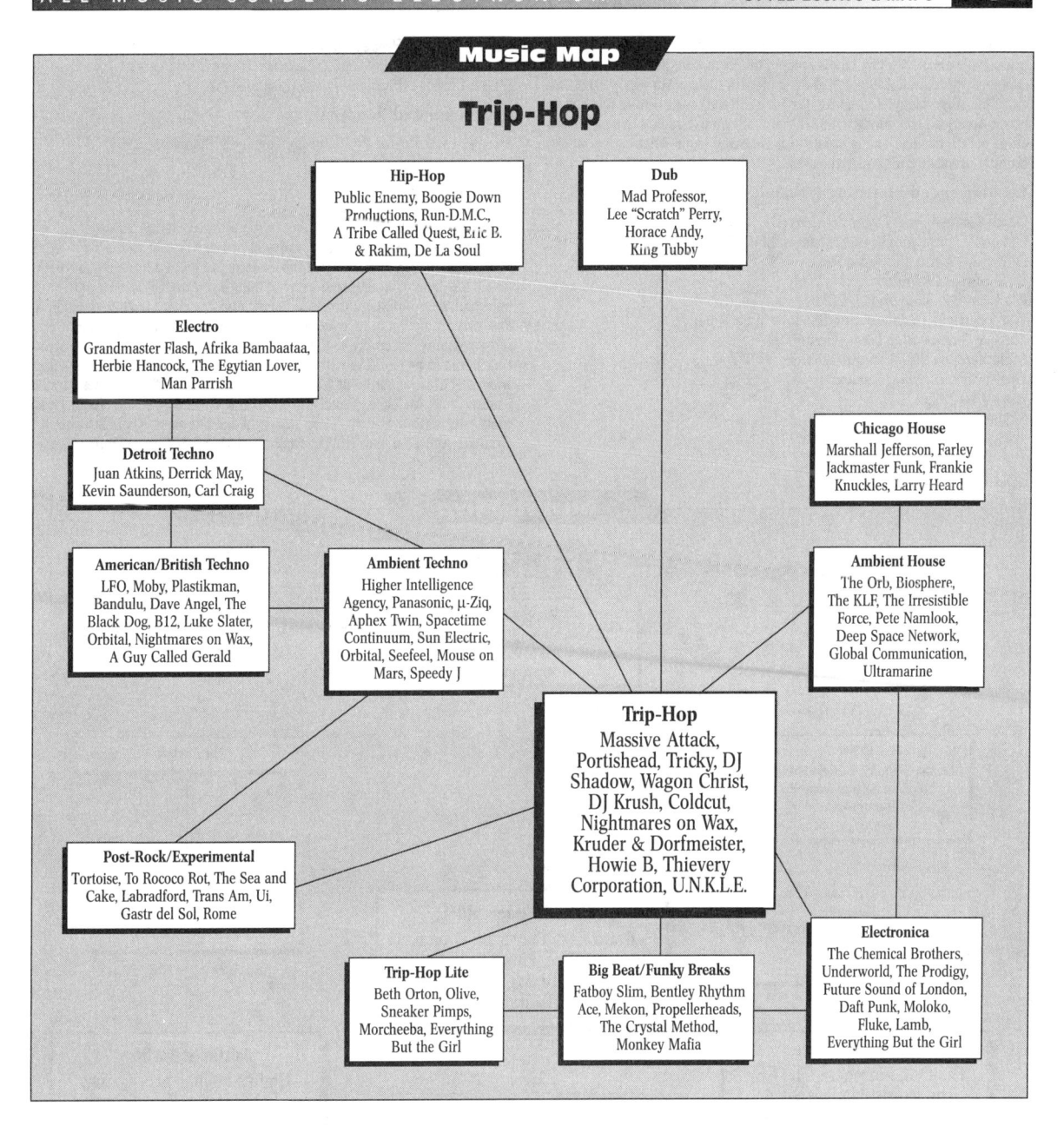

## Music Map

# Trip-Hop

**Hip-Hop**
Public Enemy, Boogie Down Productions, Run-D.M.C., A Tribe Called Quest, Eric B. & Rakim, De La Soul

**Dub**
Mad Professor, Lee "Scratch" Perry, Horace Andy, King Tubby

**Electro**
Grandmaster Flash, Afrika Bambaataa, Herbie Hancock, The Egytian Lover, Man Parrish

**Chicago House**
Marshall Jefferson, Farley Jackmaster Funk, Frankie Knuckles, Larry Heard

**Detroit Techno**
Juan Atkins, Derrick May, Kevin Saunderson, Carl Craig

**American/British Techno**
LFO, Moby, Plastikman, Bandulu, Dave Angel, The Black Dog, B12, Luke Slater, Orbital, Nightmares on Wax, A Guy Called Gerald

**Ambient Techno**
Higher Intelligence Agency, Panasonic, µ-Ziq, Aphex Twin, Spacetime Continuum, Sun Electric, Orbital, Seefeel, Mouse on Mars, Speedy J

**Ambient House**
The Orb, Biosphere, The KLF, The Irresistible Force, Pete Namlook, Deep Space Network, Global Communication, Ultramarine

**Trip-Hop**
Massive Attack, Portishead, Tricky, DJ Shadow, Wagon Christ, DJ Krush, Coldcut, Nightmares on Wax, Kruder & Dorfmeister, Howie B, Thievery Corporation, U.N.K.L.E.

**Post-Rock/Experimental**
Tortoise, To Rococo Rot, The Sea and Cake, Labradford, Trans Am, Ui, Gastr del Sol, Rome

**Trip-Hop Lite**
Beth Orton, Olive, Sneaker Pimps, Morcheeba, Everything But the Girl

**Big Beat/Funky Breaks**
Fatboy Slim, Bentley Rhythm Ace, Mekon, Propellerheads, The Crystal Method, Monkey Mafia

**Electronica**
The Chemical Brothers, Underworld, The Prodigy, Future Sound of London, Daft Punk, Moloko, Fluke, Lamb, Everything But the Girl

---

had been "discovered" and co-opted by the (predominantly) white music industry. And indeed, it wasn't long before the first wave of pop artists—Portishead, Bjork, Tricky, Massive Attack (although their 1991 debut, *Blue Lines*, was also a big influence on Lavelle and company)—began incorporating the sound and hitting pay dirt on the pop charts. But the term's ugly ring had less to do with racial politics than the sense that the artists associated with it (even at the pop level) were trying to move the music forward, not capitalize on its novelty (which, given its etymology, was all the term managed to communicate). Although it remains in use (supplemented by a barrage of similar terms such as Brit-hop, downbeat, amyl house, dub-hop, etc.), for many "trip-hop" has yet to lose its taint of contrivance.

In the UK trip-hop saw an astonishingly quick ascension to widespread popularity, rivaled perhaps only by jungle and even then exceeding it in terms of audience. Once-fledgling labels such as Mo'Wax, Ninja Tune, and Wall of Sound grew into release-a-week powerhouses, often prepping artists for major-label success. The music continued to evolve as well, with the music's early laziness proving little more than a blueprint for artists that took the style in any number of directions, fusing it with electro, techno, live funk, jazz, and soul, and drum'n'bass. Dabbled in by any number of Brit-pop and indie rock artists (from Stereolab and Blur to Arab Strap and Day Behavior), the music broke well beyond the clubs (although it continued to thrive there as well).

Trip-hop was also warmly embraced by both indie and major labels in the American industry, with small-name artists (Sneaker Pimps, Baby Fox,

Morcheeba, Lamb, Hooverphonic) stumbling into sizeable domestic contracts, indie and subsidiary labels focused on promoting the sound (Shadow, Quango, WordSound, Ubiquity), and big players such as Mo'Wax, Cup of Tea, and Ninja Tune piggybacking distribution with majors or setting up shop on North American soil. Along with MTV and alternative radio's expanded coverage of "electronica," many artists also appeared (somewhat oddly) on any number of movie soundtrack releases.

**Recommended Listening (* indicates Top 10):**

Depth Charge—*Nine Deadly Venoms* (DC Recordings)*
DJ Food—*Recipe for Disaster* (Shadow/Ninja Tune)*
DJ Krush—*Meiso* (FFRR/Mo'Wax)*
DJ Shadow—*Endtroducing* (Mo'Wax)*
Fila Brazillia—*Brazilification* (Pork)
Funki Porcini—*Hedphone Sex* (Shadow/Ninja Tune)*
Massive Attack—*Blue Lines* (Virgin)*
Nightmares on Wax—*Smokers Delight* (TVT/Warp)
Portishead—*Dummy* (London)*
Req—*One* (Skint)
Skylab—*1* (Astralwerks/L'Attitude)*
Tricky—*Maxinquaye* (4th & B'way)*

Various Artists—*Headz* (Mo'Wax)*
Various Artists—*Ninja Cuts 2: Flexistentialism* (Ninja Tune)
Wagon Christ—*Throbbing Pouch* (Rising High)*

**Recommended Reading:**

*Straight Outa Bristol,* Phil Johnson (Hodder & Stoughton, 1996)

—*Sean Cooper*

## Ambient

Ambient music remains something of the scorned, dorky cousin of current electronic music. Dabbled in by scores of artists working primarily in other fields, but still for the most part too esoteric to attract a large audience, the music has been characterized as everything from dolled-up new age, to intellectual, over-indulgent dross, to boring and irrelevant technical noodling. Partly as a function of its relatively limited appeal, ambient in a definitional sense remains extremely vague, a notion also related to the fact that artists considered to be working within its "borders" seem to be drawn from such a wide spectrum of different traditions; more "academic" experimental electronic (Chris Meloche, David Shea, Asmus Tietchens, David Toop, Oval), space music (Robert Rich, Steve Roach, Vidna Obmana, Klaus Schulze, Jeff Greinke, Alio Die), dub (Bill Laswell, the Orb, Mick Harris, Drome, Woob),

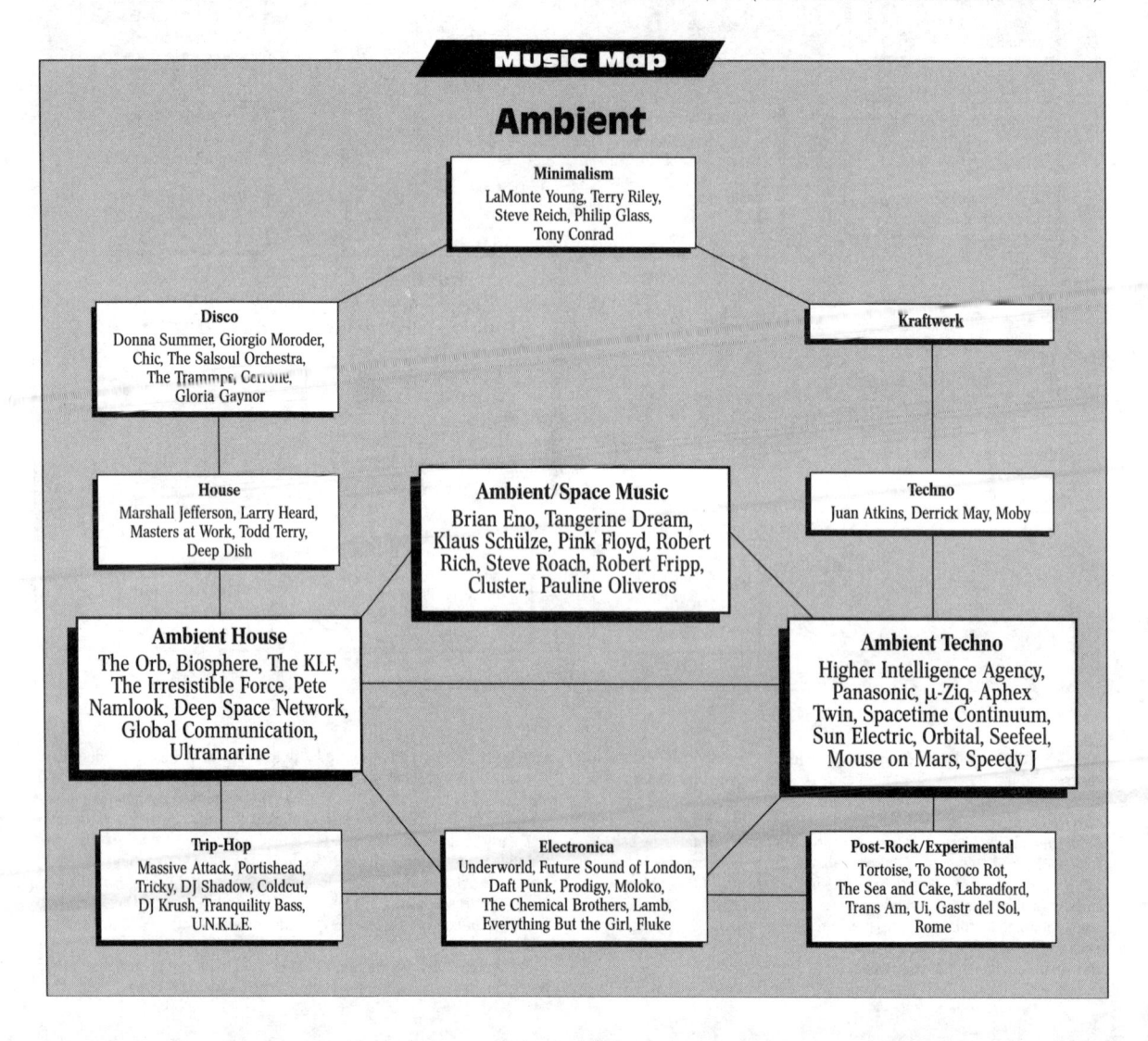

### Music Map

### Ambient

**Minimalism**
LaMonte Young, Terry Riley, Steve Reich, Philip Glass, Tony Conrad

**Disco**
Donna Summer, Giorgio Moroder, Chic, The Salsoul Orchestra, The Trammps, Cerrone, Gloria Gaynor

**Kraftwerk**

**House**
Marshall Jefferson, Larry Heard, Masters at Work, Todd Terry, Deep Dish

**Ambient/Space Music**
Brian Eno, Tangerine Dream, Klaus Schülze, Pink Floyd, Robert Rich, Steve Roach, Robert Fripp, Cluster, Pauline Oliveros

**Techno**
Juan Atkins, Derrick May, Moby

**Ambient House**
The Orb, Biosphere, The KLF, The Irresistible Force, Pete Namlook, Deep Space Network, Global Communication, Ultramarine

**Ambient Techno**
Higher Intelligence Agency, Panasonic, µ-Ziq, Aphex Twin, Spacetime Continuum, Sun Electric, Orbital, Seefeel, Mouse on Mars, Speedy J

**Trip-Hop**
Massive Attack, Portishead, Tricky, DJ Shadow, Coldcut, DJ Krush, Tranquility Bass, U.N.K.L.E.

**Electronica**
Underworld, Future Sound of London, Daft Punk, Prodigy, Moloko, The Chemical Brothers, Lamb, Everything But the Girl, Fluke

**Post-Rock/Experimental**
Tortoise, To Rococo Rot, The Sea and Cake, Labradford, Trans Am, Ui, Gastr del Sol, Rome

ethno- or 4th-world electronic music (Jon Hassell, Banco de Gaia, Astralasia), gothic or industrial (Lustmord, Merzbow, Final, Aube, James Plotkin), and the vast contemporary hybridity of back-room club culture (everything from the KLF, Global Communication, and Mixmaster Morris to Biosphere, Higher Intelligence Agency, and Sun Electric, to Tetsu Inoue, David Moufang, LTJ Bukem, and Autechre). As dance-based electronic music moved increasingly toward the indiscriminant intermingling of influences characteristic of trip-hop, electronica, and jungle/drum'n'bass, ambient shifted away from being a concrete genre and more toward a less identifiable (though no less specific) approach to sound, registering its influence in terms of space, color, and texture rather than the presence or absence of a backbeat, recognizable melodic or harmonic structures, etc.

Nonetheless, like other strains of experimental electronic music whose branches stretch into the most complex of arrangements, ambient has its roots, and historical evaluations of ambient music usually begin with Brian Eno. Although Eno's application of the term to his "background" composing of the late '70s itself had precursors in the "furniture music" of Erik Satie, the dadaist and futurist manifestos of Marcel Duchamp and Luigi Russolo, the proto- and high-modernism of Claude Debussy and Igor Stravinsky (as well as in non-Western musical and religious traditions such as Indonesian gamelan and African pygmy chanting), and New York School experimentalists such as John Cage, Morton Feldman, and LaMonte Young, it's with Eno that "ambient" music—i.e. music designed to be heard as an integral part of the environment in which its played or listened to—first became an end in itself. And his series of recordings bearing the term (and subtitled things like *Music for Airports, Music for Films*, and *On Land*) remain watermarks. Formerly a member of pop/new wave group Roxy Music, Eno was among the first to integrate found sounds and field recordings into the context of the recording studio in order to construct an environment with his music—not necessarily (though in some cases) to recreate existing places, but to build from scratch a music which suggested a sense of context, one which could not only be heard but also experienced by the listener. It's also with Eno that ambient or "environmental" music was approached with predominantly electronic instruments; ambient has few contemporary examples of acoustic-based composers (Pauline Oliveros is one), although the combination of electronics and acoustic-based instruments is common (particularly among so-called electro-acoustic musicians such as Steve Roach, Carl Stone, and Michael Danna).

Of equal influence and importance to Eno's work was that of German synthesist Klaus Schulze, who represents something of the formalist arm of ambient's prehistory. Though aligned more directly with the European classical tradition than Eno (whose background in avant-garde pop and new wave had its consequence in the comparative subtlety and modesty of his music), Schulze's pioneering work in analog synthesis and his extended, highly conceptual compositions based solely on the timbral qualities of electronics were crucial in suggesting new directions for electronic music apart from not only its "pop," bit also its academic and classical contexts. Although Schulze's earlier work was more immediately caught up in exploring (and exploiting) the sonic particularities of his medium (a notion which has tended to garner him more criticism than praise), Schulze increasingly sought the fusion of his technical mastery with elements of the lived environment; pieces such as his *Dresden Concert* drew liberally from nature recordings and source tapes which documented the bustle of everyday life, and his mid-'90s recordings with noted new school ambient composer Pete Namlook (of the Frankfurt-based Fax label) brought Schulze's formidable role in forging ambient's early aesthetic full circle.

Although much of the more visible instrumental electronic and electro-acoustic music produced in the late '70s and early-to-mid-'80s appeared under the aegis of "new age"—a marketing phenomenon more than anything else, applied most often to musics linked by some method or other to relaxation, meditation, and/or escapism—even the overwhelming conservatism of that period had its antithesis in a range of musicians operating at the outer fringes of experimentation, pushing electronics-based composition into ever more challenging, abstract territory. Artists such as Steve Hillage (formerly of Gong), Harold Budd, early Tangerine Dream, Michael Stearns, Robert Rich, and Steve Roach, among others, sought to compose music as free as possible from the weighty baggage of both pop and Classical, as well as Western academic and high cultural traditions, turning instead toward methods of composition and performance lacking conventional developmental structure, music which relied instead on programmatic elements such as repetition, texture, alternate tonality, and harmonic and subharmonic relationships (over and against the chordal, melodic, pentatonic, etc. concerns of most Western musical forms). Members of this loose agglomeration of artists often referred to their work as "space music"; not, as is often believed, because it sounded like it was from outer space (although in some cases this was true), but rather since the music tended to refer almost singularly and directly to the space in which it was heard, as well as the inner, more subconscious emotional and contemplative spaces of the listener. Although quite apart from Eno's definition, which sought to locate music in some intermediate between foreground and background, space musicians sought to fuse the two in such a way that the music became the background of its own active exploration; the latter represented an extension of the former, since the relationship between music and the lived environment was the compositional preconception much of the music turned on.

Although the context was in many respects radically different, it was a similar impulse that led to ambient's renaissance in the late-'80s/early-'90s UK rave scene, the source of some of the most exciting innovations in not only the music's sound, but also its presentation. The by-now familiar construct of the "chill space"—that back-room alternative to the high-speed hedonism of main-floor raves—was the nexus of that renaissance, with clubs such as Land of Oz (at London's massive weekly Heaven), Telepathic Fish, and Oscillate some of the first blips on the new ambient map. It was at clubs such as these that DJs like Alex Paterson (of the Orb), Mixmaster Morris (of Irresistible Force), and Jonah Sharp (of Spacetime Continuum) began blending together the early ambient experiments of Eno, Schulze, Hillage, Pink Floyd, Robert Rich, and Steve Hillage with everything from stereo-test and demonstration records, *Songs of the Humpback Whale* and other nature and field recordings, minimalist classical, non-Western ritual and traditional musics, Jamaican dub, and, eventually, live electronics. As crowds began turning out specifically for chill rooms, all-ambient nights and even weekend-long ambient events became more common, with the appearance of recordings by the KLF (*Chill Out*), the Orb ("A Huge Ever-Growing Brain" and *Adventures Beyond the Ultraworld*, among others), Irresistible Force ("Space Is the Place" and *Flying High*), and the soon-to-be ubiquitous Pete Namlook (*Silence, Air, Dreamfish*) contributing momentum and a growing, non-club-based audience.

The proximity of chill rooms to rave culture meant much of the music reflected elements of acid house and techno, and hybrid terms such as "ambient house," "ambient techno," "ambient dub," etc. began to circulate, serving to differentiate this music not only from the more rigorously environmental experiments of the '70s and '80s, but also (and increasingly) from many parallel contemporary strains of ambient. Including such varied sources as the UK-based Beyond and Rising High labels, the (respectively) Frankfurt and Belgium-based Fax (Pete Namlook's prolific label) and Apollo imprints, as well as the electronic experiments of Mille Plateaux, dark ambient/industrial and isolationist artists such as Coil, Mick Harris, and Aube and labels such as Cold Meat Industries, Projekt, and Staalplaat, ambient soon, as journalist/producer David Toop put it, began taking on the properties of a "glue term," sticking to whatever it was thrown at. But ambient's steady demotion to the status of textual modifier also suggested the increasing fervor with which barriers separating styles were up for dismantling in the atmosphere of the mid-'90s post-rave experimental underground, a process that gave birth to more variations on the theme of electronic dance music in four or five years alone than in the previous two decades. This stylistic deconstruction prompted dozens of new genres, subgenres, and sub-subgenres (ambient dub, dark ambient, ambient jungle, electronica, post-rock, experimental ambient, etc.) even as it made the very pursuit of "genre" a mawkishly naive task. This is not to say ambient artists working more or less within the tradition of many of the music's earlier strains ceased to exist—indeed, ambient's proliferation during the mid-to-late-'90s also contributed a sense of focus to artists pursuing one or another of its mutant strains—but rather that the palette of sounds which constitutes the raw materials of atmospheric or environmental music broadened to such an extent that many of the definitional criteria of the music (lack of prominent percussion and/or a strong melodic presence, etc.) were steadily reoriented or altogether abandoned.

Because of the range of musics (to say nothing of the ambiguity) implied by the term, no single, encompassing introduction to ambient exists. However, many good compilations are available which serve to fill in significant portions of the music's historical progression. Virgin's four-part *Ambient* series—each a two-disc set bringing together many of the biggest name artists from the '70s, '80s, and early '90s—is a good place to start. Also released by Virgin is the double-CD *Ocean of Sound*, compiled by musical historian David Toop to accompany his book of the same name (published by Serpent's Tail in 1995), and including everyone from King Tubby to Aphex Twin. Label compilations also provide good reference points (particularly with regard to the music's more recent mutations), with Beyond, Rising High, Instinct, Fax, Apollo, Warp, Silent, and Recycle or Die all reputable sources for high-quality various-artist collections.

### Recommended Recordings (* indicates top 10):

Aphex Twin—*Selected Ambient Works, Vol. II* (Sire/Warp)*
Brian Eno—*Ambient 4: On Land* (EG)*
Eno & Fripp—*The Essential Fripp & Eno* (Virgin/EG)*
Global Communication—*76:14* (Dedicated)*
Tetsu Inoue—*World Receiver* (Instinct)*
Irresistible Force—*Flying High* (Instinct/Rising High)*
The KLF—*Chill Out* (TVT)*
Pete Namlook—*Air 2* (Fax)
Vidna Obmana—*The Trilogy* (Relic)
The Orb—*Adventures Beyond the Ultraworld* (Wau!/Mr. Modo)*
Robert Rich & B. Lustmord—*Stalker* (Fathom)*
Throbbing Gristle—*Second Annual Report* (Mute)
Various Artists—*The Ambient Cookbook* (Fax)*
Various Artists—*Ocean of Sound* (Virgin)
Woob—*1194* (Instinct/Em:t)

### Recommended Reading:

*Ocean of Sound*, David Toop (Serpent's Tail, 1995)

—Sean Cooper

## Electro

Although a mere historical blip on the evolutionary map of urban dance-based music, Electro sits at the apex of many of its most widespread and significant forms, including rap, techno, jungle, freestyle, and bass music. A curious fusion of '70s funk and disco, German and Japanese techno-pop, and everything from the futurism of Alvin Toffler to kung-fu movies, video games, and the Smurfs, electro has proven to be one of the most important and influential components of the ongoing development of dance-based experimental electronic music. As the first style of American breakbeat to utilize the drum machine as its central rhythmic component, electro has worked its influence into a staggering range of styles—from Run-D.M.C., Egyptian Lover, and Ice Cube to Madonna, Nine Inch Nails, the Black Dog, and Bochum Welt.

Electro's proper heyday was the period 1982-88, following the explosion of early hip-hop culture in a number of American inner cities. Initially designed as breakdance music, with distinctive drum patterns modeled, in part, on the style of DJing developed by early hip-hop DJs such as Kool Herc and Grandmaster Flash (which involved the manual looping, using two turntables and a mixer, of drum breaks from funk, soul, jazz, and rock records), electro's immediate forebearers included Kraftwerk, Gary Numan, and Japan's Yellow Magic Orchestra. Kraftwerk's "Trans-Europe Express" was the blueprint for Soul Sonic Force's legendary first-blast "Planet Rock," and early cuts by Man Parrish, the Jonzun Crew, Grandmaster Flash in New York, and Juan Atkins and Rick Davies in Detroit (among others) set the tone for many of the records that would follow: a strong backbeat, often with sparse rapping (particularly through a vocoder or talk box), scratching, odd electronics, and frequent rhythm breaks.

Although electro began almost immediately to evolve into various other styles—rap (through Run-D.M.C., LL Cool J, Schooly D, and Ice-T, among many others), techno (Atkins', Cybotron and Model 500 projects), Miami bass and freestyle (Maggotron, Freestyle, Dynamix II, and Trinere), industrial (Front 242, Ministry)—the mid- to late-'80s was probably the music's height

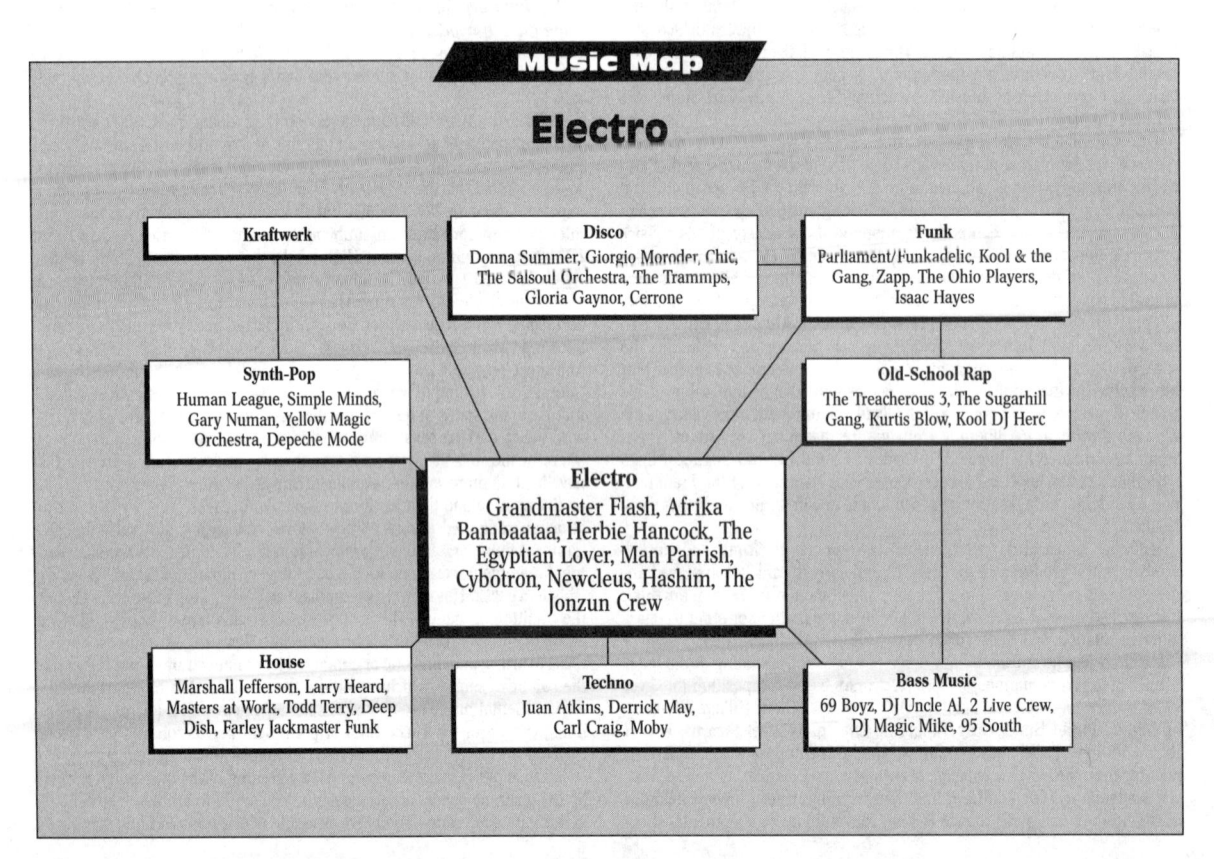

## Music Map

### Electro

**Kraftwerk**

**Disco**
Donna Summer, Giorgio Moroder, Chic, The Salsoul Orchestra, The Trammps, Gloria Gaynor, Cerrone

**Funk**
Parliament/Funkadelic, Kool & the Gang, Zapp, The Ohio Players, Isaac Hayes

**Synth-Pop**
Human League, Simple Minds, Gary Numan, Yellow Magic Orchestra, Depeche Mode

**Old-School Rap**
The Treacherous 3, The Sugarhill Gang, Kurtis Blow, Kool DJ Herc

**Electro**
Grandmaster Flash, Afrika Bambaataa, Herbie Hancock, The Egyptian Lover, Man Parrish, Cybotron, Newcleus, Hashim, The Jonzun Crew

**House**
Marshall Jefferson, Larry Heard, Masters at Work, Todd Terry, Deep Dish, Farley Jackmaster Funk

**Techno**
Juan Atkins, Derrick May, Carl Craig, Moby

**Bass Music**
69 Boyz, DJ Uncle Al, 2 Live Crew, DJ Magic Mike, 95 South

of popularity. And while the increasing availability of samplers and MIDI-encoded devices (both of which offered a wider palette of sound and creative possibility) meant many grew bored with the relatively static musicality of electro's machine aesthetic, the style continued to grow and evolve, particularly in Florida and California, where artists such as "Pretty" Tony Butler, Omar Santana, and Dynamix II in Miami and Ice-T, the Unknown DJ, and the Egyptian Lover in L.A. were taking the style in new directions. With Butler, Dynamix and Santana, that involved an increasing emphasis on the low-end (Miami bass) and the marriage of electro with Latin rhythms, female vocals, and simple melodies (freestyle). L.A. artists such as Ice-T and the Egyptian Lover were exploring the lyrical potential of rap while remaining true to the beat box (a devotion that continues to inform the '90s G-funk styles of Dr. Dre, 2Pac, Snoop Doggy Dogg, and Spice-One).

As rap took center stage in the latter '80s as the musical form of choice among inner-city (and suburban) youth, electro began dying out, carrying on in the bass and freestyle of Miami, New York, and L.A., but for the large part only of interest to historians and the odd collector. That's begun to change, however, as the innovations of UK and German experimental electronic artists have made their electro roots clear. Artists as diverse as the Jedi Knights (Tom Middleton and Mark Pritchard of Global Communication/Link), Aphex Twin, Phil Klein, Autechre, Atom Heart, and Biochip C. have built on electro's legacy in their own contexts, taking the hitting machine breaks of the music's early years and combining it with a digital aesthetic and increasing musicality that have refired its relevance. American musicians, too—from 2Pac to the Bass Kittens, "Mad" Mike, and Drexciya—are rediscovering the roots of techno and hip-hop in the electronic breakbeat, and have updated the sound for a '90s sensibility.

Although the history's still being written, a number of good introductions to electro's past and present exist. Rhino Records' *Street Jams: Electric Funk* is a four-CD box set covering many of the bases of the early electro sound; from New York and Miami, to Detroit, L.A., and beyond. The UK-based Beechwood label (instrumental in bringing the American electro sound to British audiences as it was happening, through their Streetsounds compilations) released a best-of from their earlier compilations in 1995, titled *Streetsounds: The Best of Electro, Vol. 1,* which reaches even deeper into electro's early underground to unearth some truly hard-to-find material. In 1998, Tommy Boy released *The Perfect Beats,* an excellent four-volume set of electro/dance classics that rescued many worthy obscurities from the vaults. On the new-style tip, Submerge's *Origins of a Sound* is a good introduction to the new-style Detroit electro promulgated by artists such as AUX 88, Drexciya, "Mad" Mike, and Will Web. Finally, the It label brought UK electro DJ Marco Arnaldi in to compile *It: Electro,* a CD and double-LP combining early tracks with more up-to-the-minute material.

## New York

The history of New York electro is intimately tied up with that city's role in the birth and evolution of hip-hop. Consequently, tracks by early Big Apple innovators such as the Jonzun Crew, Man Parrish, the Soul Sonic Force, and Marley Marl are dominated by a vocal presence and a more party-oriented vibe. Still, the musicianship (many of these groups employed traditional instruments side-by-side with electronics, even playing live) is top notch and tracks such as "Hip-Hop Be-Bop (Don't Stop)" and "Boogie Down Bronx" by Man Parrish, "Space Is the Place" and "We Are the Jonzun Crew" by the Jonzun Crew, and "The Party Scene" by the Russell Brothers remain watermarks of the style.

## Detroit

Like the Detroit techno into which it almost immediately evolved, early Detroit electro emphasized melody along with rhythm, with tight beats and basslines and melancholic, minor key sweeps the dominant features on still-classic cuts such as "Clear," "Cosmic Cars," "Technicolor," and "R9." Although most of these tracks were the product of one person—Juan Atkins—the influence of peers and collaborators such as Derrick May, Rick Davies, and Kevin "Reese" Saunderson should not be underestimated.

## Los Angeles

Like New York, the L.A. electro scene was party oriented, with cuts by Egyptian Lover, the Unknown DJ, the Wreckin' Crew, and Uncle Jamm's Army em-phasizing skills on the cut, the mic, or the dancefloor in sparse, often electronic raps. B-boy boasting aside, however, the L.A. sound (neatly expressed in label names such as Freak Beat, Techno Hop, and Techno Kut) was most concerned with adapting new technology to the emerging hip-hop sound, and beat-jacking tracks such as "Jam the Box," "What's Your Sign" by UJA, "808 Beats" and "Tibetan Jam" by the Unknown DJ, and "Egypt, Egypt" and "Dance" by Egyptian Lover are hard to match for rhythmic innovation.

## Miami Bass/Freestyle

Freestyle and Miami Bass are two related styles with common roots in the mid-'80s tracks of Omar Santana, Dynamix II, and Tony Butler, the latter of whose Music Specialist label was the organizational center of Miami electro. Bass music, for its part, is as its name suggests: deep, resonant bass (the type of music heard booming from mini-trucks and tricked out low-riders), backed by tight machine bass and not much else. Freestyle is Miami electro's dance music descendent, with Latin percussion, simple four-part melodies, and bubblegum vocals adding a pop dimension to the music's funky edge.

## Techno Bass

Although electro never died out in Detroit's underground (Motor City block parties still rock "Technicolor" and "Get Some" to this day), by and large the musicians the city produced were primarily involved in the four-on-the-floor aesthetic of house and techno. Partly ideological, partly descriptive, "techno bass" was an attempt by a core of Detroit dance music artists to realign techno with its breakbeat roots, and was mostly the vision of the Direct Beat/430 West labels, whose artists include purveyors of the style such as AUX 88, Will Web, Posatronix, and DJ Dijital, although other prominent artists such as Drexciya and Underground Resistance have been just as active in reinvigorating electronic breaks.

## Neo-Electro

Largely a product of the UK dance music media's more colonialist tendencies, neo-electro was "coined" in 1994 to signify the collective output of artists such as the Jedi Knights, Elecktroids, and Drexciya, and labels such as Clear, Evolution, and (aspects of) Warp. The tenuous connection of much of the music's actual stylistic attributes to electro notwithstanding, many of these artists were clearly inspired by the music's original machine aesthetic, with most of them having grown up listening to it. The real electro revival, however, largely took place through smaller, more obscure labels such as Dodge, Panic Trax, Immortal, Overexposed, Direct Beat, Transparent Sound, and the odd B-side or 12" release on experimental techno staples such as Force Inc., Eidesche, Sahko, and Underground Resistance.

### Recommended Listening:

1. Various Artists—*Street Jams: Electric Funk, Vols. 1-4* (Rhino)
2. Various Artists—*The Perfect Beats, Vols. 1-4* (Tommy Boy)
3. Cybotron—*Clear* (Fantasy)
4. Freestyle—*Don't Stop the Rock* (Hot Productions)
5. Man Parrish—*The Best of Man Parrish: Heartstroke* (Hot Productions)
6. Dynamix II—*Electro Bass Megamix: 1985 to Present* (Joey Boy)
7. Various Artists—*Origins of a Sound* (Submerge)
8. Various Artists—*Techno Bass: The Mission* (Direct Beat)
9. Various Artists—*It's All Becoming Clear* (Clear)
10. Various Artists—*From Beyond* (IT)
11. Dave Clarke—*Electro Boogie, Vol. 2: The Throw Down* (Studio !K7)

—*Sean Cooper*

## Garage

Named for what is arguably the birthplace of house music—the Paradise Garage in New York—Garage is the dance style closest in spirit and execution to the original disco music of the '70s. Favoring synthesizer runs and gospel vocals similar to house music but with even more polished and shimmering production values than house, garage has more of a soulful, organic feel. Though the style's led by producer/DJs (Todd Terry, Tony Humphries, Kerri Chandler) and production teams (Masters at Work, Blaze), vocalists who bring the soulful anthems to life (Ultra Naté, Dajae, Jocelyn Brown and

## Music Map

### Garage

**Disco**
Donna Summer, Giorgio Moroder, The BeeGees, The Trammps, Gloria Gaynor, Chic, Cerrone

**New York House**
Masters at Work, Tony Humphries, Todd Terry, Junior Vasquez, Deep Dish (D.C.)

**Garage**
Larry Levan, Frankie Knuckles, Tony Humphries, Adeva, Ultra Naté

**House-Pop**
Technotronic, Snap, The KLF, Stereo MC's, C&C Music Factory

**Global Producers**
Junior Vasquez, Armand Van Helden, Masters at Work, Roger Sanchez, Robert Miles, Basement Jaxx, Danny Tenaglia, Dimitri from Paris

**Speed Garage**
Tuff Jam, The Dreem Teem, Catch Productions, Boris Dlugosch

---

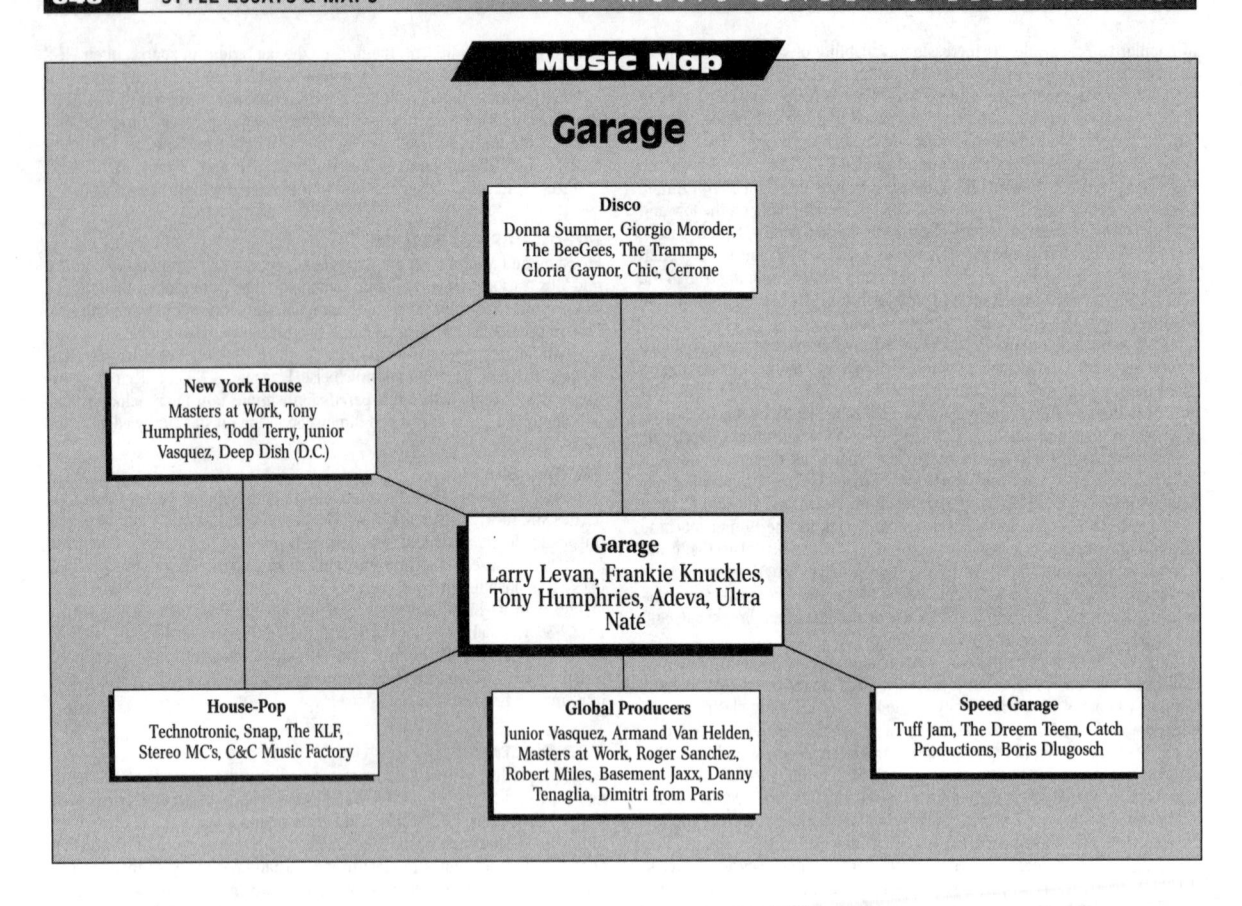

Loleatta Holloway, among others) are much more important than in any other forms of dance music.

During the early '80s, garage was originally centered in the New York metro area, mostly in Manhattan but strong enough across state lines to later be dubbed the Jersey Sound as well. At that time, the early history of garage is practically synonymous with that of house music. It was only when Chicago house became popular around the world that New York's discofied garage emerged as a separate entity from house music in general.

Labels like Prelude, West End, and Easy St. defined the sound of disco and post-disco dance music, while legendary Paradise Garage DJ Larry Levan lit up the clubs and Tony Humphries spread the sound courtesy of local radio station KISS-FM. Regional hits like Serious Intention's "You Don't Know" and Cultural Vibe's "Ma Foom Bey" defined the sound, and New York prospered as the undisputed home of dance music during the early and mid-'80s. By 1987, however, the Paradise Garage had closed its doors, and while other clubs like the Shelter took up some slack, armloads of import dance singles produced in Chicago were crossing the Atlantic: consequently, the sound that many Brits pointed to as an influence was Midwestern in origin. By no means forgotten, though, New York gained ascendance by the turn of the decade, with British producer Joey Negro showing garage influences through his Republic label. Spurred on by admiration from the UK, a flock of fresh New York labels opened up during the late '80s and early '90s—Strictly Rhythm, King Street, Nervous, Perfect Pair, Freeze, Streetside. London's influential Ministry of Sound even tapped Tony Humphries for an exclusive deal to DJ for its club and produce for its accompanying label. By 1996, a British variant of garage had emerged, dubbed speed garage for its aggressive synthesis of drum'n'bass and ragga with the original garage sound.

**Recommended Listening:**
1. Larry Levan—*Live at the Paradise Garage* (Strut)
2. Various Artists—*The West End Story, Vols. 1-4* (West End)
3. Various Artists—*Salsoul Classics, Vols. 1-4* (Salsoul)
4. Various Artists—*Divas of Dance, Vols. 1-3* (DCC)
5. Various Artists—*History of House Music, Vol. 2: New York Garage Style* (Cold Front)
6. Various Artists—*This Is Strictly Rhythm, Vols. 1-5* (Strictly Rhythm)
7. Tony Humphries—*Take Home the Club* (Bassline)
8. Junior Vasquez—*Live, Vol. 1* (Logic)
9. Kristine W.—*Land of the Living* (RCA)
10. Ultra Naté—*Situation: Critical* (Strictly Rhythm)

—*John Bush*

## Hardcore Techno

The fastest, most abrasive form of dance music available at any one time, Hardcore Techno was by the mid-'90s the province of a startlingly wide array of producers, including breakbeat junglists, industrial trancesters, German punks and cartoonish ravers. The style originally emerged from Great Britain's 1988 Summer of Love, and though the original soundtrack to those warehouse parties was influenced by the relatively mid-tempo rhythms of Chicago acid house, increased drug intake caused many ravers to embrace quicker rhythms and altogether more frenetic forms of music. Many DJs indulged their listeners by speeding up house records originally intended for 33-rpm play, and producers carried the torch by sampling the same records for their releases. By 1991-92, hardcore/rave music had hit the legitimate airwaves as well, led by hits like SL2's "On a Ragga Tip," T-99's "Anasthasia," and RTS' "Poing."

## Music Map

# Hardcore Techno

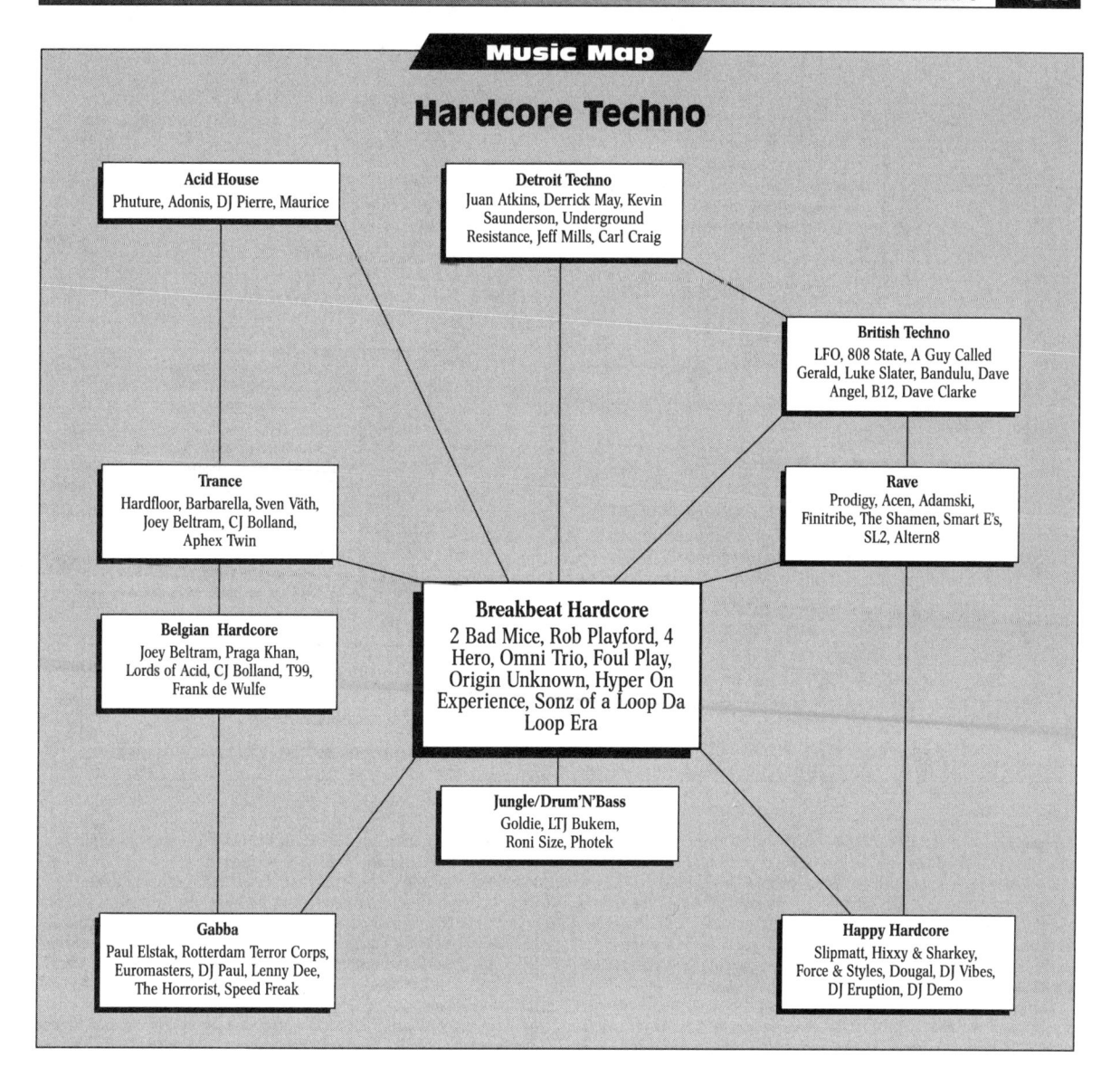

**Acid House**
Phuture, Adonis, DJ Pierre, Maurice

**Detroit Techno**
Juan Atkins, Derrick May, Kevin Saunderson, Underground Resistance, Jeff Mills, Carl Craig

**British Techno**
LFO, 808 State, A Guy Called Gerald, Luke Slater, Bandulu, Dave Angel, B12, Dave Clarke

**Trance**
Hardfloor, Barbarella, Sven Väth, Joey Beltram, CJ Bolland, Aphex Twin

**Rave**
Prodigy, Acen, Adamski, Finitribe, The Shamen, Smart E's, SL2, Altern8

**Belgian Hardcore**
Joey Beltram, Praga Khan, Lords of Acid, CJ Bolland, T99, Frank de Wulfe

**Breakbeat Hardcore**
2 Bad Mice, Rob Playford, 4 Hero, Omni Trio, Foul Play, Origin Unknown, Hyper On Experience, Sonz of a Loop Da Loop Era

**Jungle/Drum'N'Bass**
Goldie, LTJ Bukem, Roni Size, Photek

**Gabba**
Paul Elstak, Rotterdam Terror Corps, Euromasters, DJ Paul, Lenny Dee, The Horrorist, Speed Freak

**Happy Hardcore**
Slipmatt, Hixxy & Sharkey, Force & Styles, Dougal, DJ Vibes, DJ Eruption, DJ Demo

---

The resulting major-label feeding frenzy produced heavy coverage for light-weight novelty fare like "Go Speed Go" by Alpha Team, "Sesame's Treat" by Smart E's, and "James Brown Is Dead" by L.A. Style. Most ravers had also grown up or simply tired of the sound by the mid-'90s, and though the original hardcore/rave sound had spread to much of the British hinterlands as well as continental Europe, most Londoners favored progressive house or the emerging ambient techno. Lack of coverage and the wide spread of the sound—into the north of England and Scotland as well as the Teutonic centers of Germany and the Netherlands served to introduce a variety of underground styles, from the digital hardcore of Germany's Alec Empire to Dutch gabber and English happy hardcore. In fact, the term had become a dinosaur by the end of the decade.

**Recommended Listening:**

1. Various Artists—*A History of Hardcore, Vols. 1-2* (Suburban Base)
2. Various Artists—*A History of Our World, Vols. 1-2* (Profile)
3. Various Artists—*Blueprint: The Definitive Moving Shadow Compilation* (Moving Shadow)
4. Various Artists—*XL Recordings, Chapters 1-3* (XL)
5. Various Artists—*Happy2bHardcore* (Moonshine)

—*John Bush*

## Acid Jazz

An energetic, groove-centered variant of jazz for a generation of club-oriented youth, acid jazz as a style originated in London during the mid-'80s, fostered by rare-groove DJs who spun their favorite records, whether they were up-to-par from a jazz standpoint or not. In the clubs, the only thing that mattered was the groove, and these DJs were inspired in the main by the '70s

## Music Map

# Acid Jazz

**Soul Jazz**
Grant Green, Horace Silver, Big John Patton, Lee Morgan, Jimmy Smith, Lou Donaldson

**Philly Soul**
Harold Melvin & the Bluenotes, The O'Jays, The Spinners, Lou Rawls, M.F.S.B.

**Jazz-Funk**
Donald Byrd, Herbie Hancock, Roy Ayers, Earth, Wind & Fire, Isaac Hayes, Bobbi Humphrey, Weather Report

**Disco**
Donna Summer, Giorgio Moroder, Chic, The Salsoul Orchestra, The Trammps, Cerrone, Boney M

**Old School Rap**
The Sugarhill Gang, Grandmaster Flash, Whodini, Run-D.M.C., Kurtis Blow

**British Acid Jazz**
Brand New Heavies, James Taylor Quartet, Incognito, Jamiroquai, Galliano, Sandals, Stereo MC's, United Future Organization, Mondo Grosso, Palm Skin Productions, Corduroy

**Jazz-Rap**
A Tribe Called Quest, The Jungle Brothers, Digable Planets, Guru, The Roots

**American Acid Jazz**
Groove Collective, Slide Five, Money Mark, Count Basic, Medeski, Martin & Wood

---

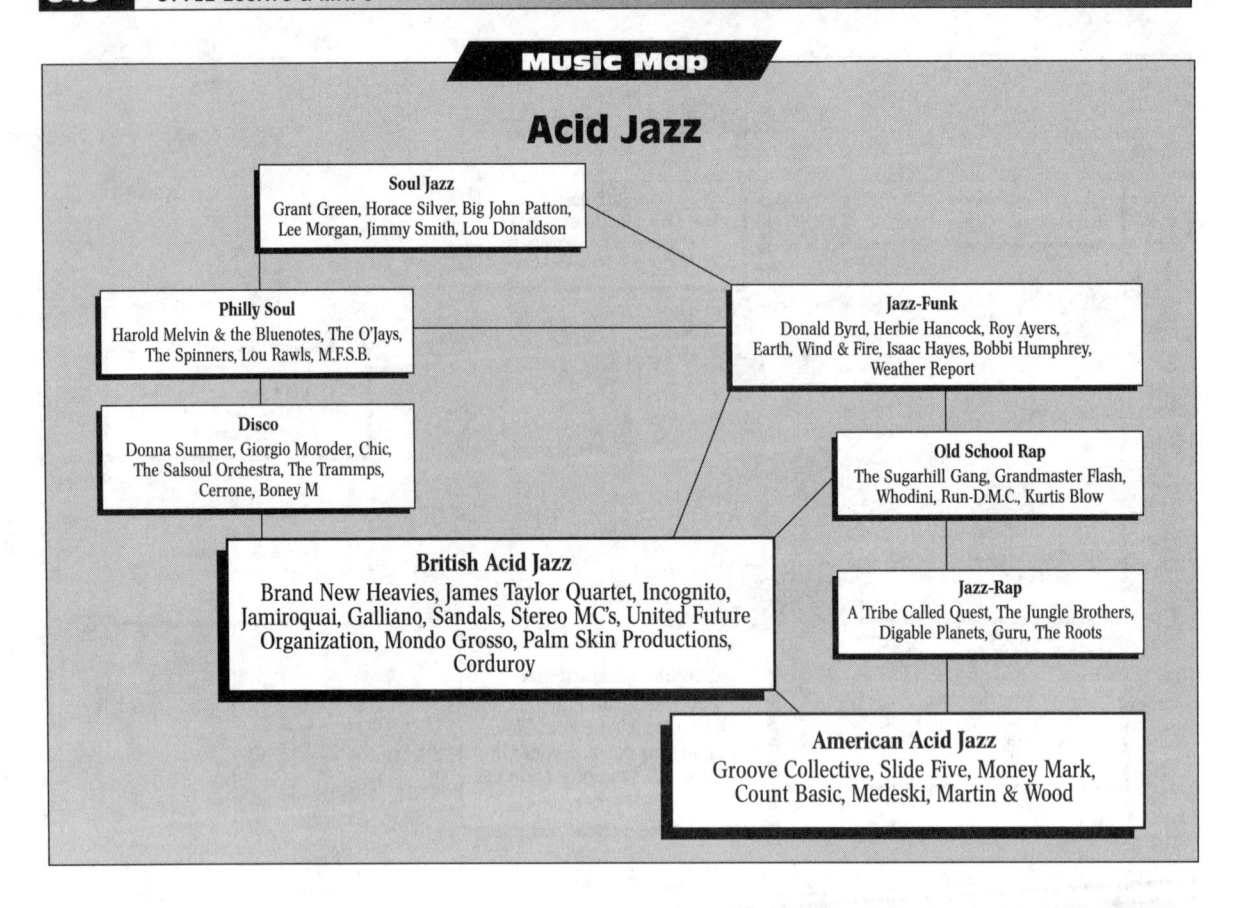

fringe of jazz—fusion, jazz-funk, and Afro-Cuban, with secondary elements of earlier soul jazz. This exposure to a legion of previously unheard records influenced many in the British and American underground, which fed a pool of live musicians and studio-savvy producers working within the style by the early '90s. Though British chart success by Soul II Soul, the Brand New Heavies, and Stereo MC's created a glut of sub-par artists and compilations in the stores, players in the underground kept expanding the style, gradually building a global community of artists.

During the early '80s, ever-changing British pop-music trends had seen punk, new wave, and the mod revival come and go. By the mid-point of the decade, the hot music for club DJs was rare groove, a style which re-introduced listeners and dancers to the more obscure jazz-funk and soul records from the '70s. The style took as its cornerstones classics which jazz critics and purists had either neglected or dismissed: music from Miles Davis' electric period, commercial successes like Donald Byrd's *Black Byrd* and Herbie Hancock's *Head Hunters*, and '70s Blue Note obscurities from the cutout bins of record stores. Of the many DJs around London, the one who became most identified with acid jazz was Gilles Peterson. (Various claims can be made as to his being the first to use the term as well.) Peterson originally started by spinning mammoth sets of jazz-funk from his own personal pirate radio station, located in a garden shed near his home, and he later made the move to broadcast on one of the hottest British pirate stations, Kiss-FM. He also maintained residencies at several London clubs during the late '80s. One of Peterson's buddies was Eddie Piller, the former head of Re-Elect the President Records, and the man who'd released the debut album by a Hammond B-3 extraordinaire named James Taylor (not to be confused with either the singer/songwriter or the Kool & the Gang vocalist). When Taylor moved to Polydor in 1988, Piller received enough money to finance a new label, Acid Jazz Records, as a partnership with Peterson. The company's first releases were a series of compilations titled *Totally Wired*, each of which alternated jazz-funk obscurities from the '70s with updated tracks from the new acid jazz.

Peterson later left Acid Jazz Records to form his own Talkin' Loud Records, which soon became one of the other top labels around; it also generated some commercial movement by signing former Acid Jazz artist Galliano as well as Young Disciples and Urban Species. In 1990, another British label, 4th & Broadway Records, began a compilation series titled *The Rebirth of Cool*, featuring an international cast of artists both young and old, including Pharoah Sanders, Stereo MC's, French rapper MC Solaar, Courtney Pine and Japanese production team United Future Organization, among others. Acid jazz broke into the mainstream in 1991, led by the Brand New Heavies. The group had released one album through Acid Jazz Records, but then moved to fffr Records for their greatest success, the singles "Never Stop" and "Dream Come True." After the initial British success of acid jazz groups inspired by the rare-groove revival, a spate of marginal compilations flooded the racks, leaving many consumers puzzled over what exactly acid jazz was, which artists played acid jazz, and how to identify the best recordings in the style.

The confusion grew no less clear in the '90s, as vibrant acid jazz communities sprung up in the US as well, in San Francisco (Ubiquity Records), New York (the Giant Step collective) and Los Angeles (Solsonics). By that time, acid jazz could encompass anything from the spy-soundtrack soul jazz of the James Taylor Quartet to Jamiroquai's pop-oriented Stevie Wonder imitations, from the globe-trotting musical eclecticism of Japanese producers United Future Organization to New York's Groove Collective, a ramshackle group of poets, players and hip-hoppers who shared club nights. The growth of interest in electronic club music during the mid-to-late '90s appeared to quash much of the power of acid jazz with the buying public, though many communities around the world remained quite fresh and exciting.

Recommended Listening:

Various Artists— *Totally Wired* (Acid Jazz)
Brand New Heavies— *Brand New Heavies* (Delicious Vinyl)
Galliano— *What Colour Our Flag* (Talkin' Loud/Mercury)
United Future Organization— *No Sound Is Too Taboo* (Talkin' Loud/Verve)
Groove Collective— *Groove Collective* (Reprise)
James Taylor Quartet— *In the Hand of the Inevitable* (Hollywood)
Jamiroquai— *Return of the Space Cowboy* (Columbia)
Young Disciples— *Road to Freedom* (Talkin' Loud/Mercury)
Greyboy Allstars— *Town Called Earth* (Greyboy)
Medeski, Martin & Wood— *It's a Jungle in Here* (Gramavision)

–John Bush

## British Dance Culture

It has often been said that British Club Culture has been more important to electronic dance music than the music itself. Indeed, the influx of certain drugs (mostly Ecstasy and marijuana), along with the fashions and general trends involved in attending giant outdoor raves or going out to clubs pushed the British dance scene to become, within a bare half-decade, one of the biggest, brightest and best-attended youth movements in the world. Obviously, British clubs were existing and flourishing during the '80s long before house and rave. Besides numerous clubs in the capital devoted to hip-hop, rare groove and electro, the spirit of classic American soul was kept alive at Northern soul weekenders like the Blackpool Mecca and Wigan Casino, which kept thousands dancing to obscure records throughout the night. The emergence of a British house and rave scene in the late '80s was a crucial difference however, in the fact that it featured youth music with numbers rivalling Northern soul. By the end of the '90s, dance music had achieved ascendance to a point where British pop culture almost equalled British Club Culture. The government-subsidized radio station Radio One programmed the equivalent of one day per week expressly devoted to dance—whether house, techno or drum'n'bass—and including scene veterans like Danny Rampling, Pete Tong, and Grooverider.

When American house singles began hitting the charts in Britain in 1986, there were few DJs willing to forsake rare groove and hip-hop for a music which many straight clubbers associated with the gay crowd. The likes of Mike Pickering, Colin Faver, and Jazzy M attempted to play the music, but with much resistance. The acknowledged genesis of British Club Culture begins one year later. A quartet of British DJs—Paul Oakenfold, Danny Rampling, Nicky Holloway, and Johnnie Walker—spent their vacation time in Ibiza, an island off the coast of Spain which was then reeling to the talents of Alfredo, an Italian DJ spinning a heady fusion of myriad '80s dance styles (including industrial, alternative, Italian disco, soul, even the theme from *Hill Street Blues*). Even more important than the music was the drug of choice— Ecstasy. Also known as MDMA, it was first synthesized in 1913 by the German drug company Merck. The small white pills boasted the psychedelic properties of LSD and the energy boost of amphetamines, plus a surprising degree of fraternal feelings for others. It had been a staple with the upper crust of Britain's pop scene from the early '80s, but by the time the Ibizan castaways returned to London and began their own house clubs, Ecstasy virtually defined the early scene.

In the one year after returning from Ibiza, three of the veterans founded *the* seminal club nights for early British house. In order of their opening dates, Rampling's Shoom, Oakenfold's Spectrum, and Holloway's the Trip each made progressive leaps over the other with respect to exposure and popularity. Shoom, located in a glorified gymnasium in South London, featured only a few hundred clubbers during late 1987 and early 1988, but the fact that most were on Ecstasy set a loved-up vibe that, many say, has never been equalled. Spectrum upped the ante considerably—it was set in one of London's biggest venues on a weekday night—but by May, Oakenfold had thousands lined up around the block ready to take part. The Trip debuted later that summer in the Astoria, long considered one of the top rock venues. Soon, it too raised the bar for all expectations, with thousands of drugged-up clubbers exiting the venue causing intense congestion and police activity in the middle of Charing Cross Road.

Those three London venues, along with Northern clubs like the Haçienda (with Graeme Park and Mike Pickering), brought house music to a very crucial contingent in Britain. By 1989, with growing numbers interested in the phenomenon and not enough space at any clubs in London, several promoters coined the idea of throwing huge outdoor raves in the hinterlands. Events like Sunrise, Energy, and Biology crammed up to 20,000 people in the more remote areas outside London's Orbital M25 freeway. Those glory days didn't last long, however; soon, the Orbital raves engendered trouble with police, local residents, and even the London tabloids, which often printed fabulous stories about the drugs and violence taking place. Acid house and rave had also hit the pop charts in a big way, led first by talents like 808 State, LFO, Nightmares on Wax, and Orbital, then later by increasing novelty fare.

The illegal rave scene continued during the '90s—thanks to new-generation collectives like Spiral Tribe and DiY—though they were largely replaced by legal events on the same scale, including Tribal Gathering and greater dance exposure at major rock festivals like Glastonbury and Reading. The government increasingly clamped down with legislation like 1994's Criminal Justice Bill, which gave police greater powers to stop raves before they could begin and penalize to an even greater extent promoters as well as attendees.

Growing tired of the constant uncertainties and increasingly hardcore slant of the music, many dance fans led the way back to the clubs, the most popular of which had stopped playing rave music and moved towards a rekindling of the original house vibes (dubbed "progressive-house" in no flattering terms), venues like Ministry of Sound and the Drum Club in London, Back to Basics in Leeds and Renaissance in Manchester. Separate scenes emerged for techno, downtempo, trance, and hardcore techno, each with their own clubs, fashions, and representative artists both in the album and singles realms. By 1994, even an individual style like hardcore could split to produce such wide divergence as the jungle/drum'n'bass movement and happy hardcore.

The midpoint of the decade brought the rise of superclubs, immense spaces like Cream, Renaissance, Ministry of Sound, and Gatecrasher able to send thousands of people through the door nightly and hire the top globetrotting DJs, as well as run record labels, release special club-sponsored compilations, and even go on international tours. Also back in the headlines was Ibiza; whereas the island had been a great vacation spot for several hundred dance fans during the early '90s, by 1995 the numbers had ballooned. By the end of the decade, Ibiza was *the* vacation spot for British youth, with each of the superclubs there and even BBC's Radio One broadcasting live during the season.

Recommended Listening:

1. Various Artists— *Cream Anthems* (Deconstruction)
2. Various Artists— *Ministry of Sound Presents the Annual* (Ministry of Sound)
3. Various Artists— *A Decade of Ibiza* (Telstar)
4. Carl Cox— *F.A.C.T.: Vol. 2: Future Alliance of Tecknology* (WorldWide Ultimatum)
5. Paul Oakenfold— *Resident: Two Years of Oakenfold at Cream* (Virgin)
6. Sasha + Digweed— *Northern Exposure: Expeditions* (Incredible)
7. Various Artists— *Gatecrasher: Global Sound System* (Ultimatum)
8. Dave Seaman— *Renaissance?Awakening* (Renaissance)

Recommended Reading:

*Altered State*, Matthew Colling (Serpent's Tail, 1997)
*Club Cultures: Music, Media and Subcultural Capital*, Sarah Thornton (Wesleyan University Press, 1996)

–John Bush

## Essential Recordings

Given the difficulties of searching through a large book with an eye for only the very best recordings featured, this section simply lists each of the essential albums reviewed earlier, whether by influential figures (David Bowie, Herbie Hancock), early techno/house names (Derrick May, Larry Heard), or electronica as it existed by the mid-'90s (The Chemical Brothers, Prodigy).

**Air.** *Moon Safari* / 1998 (Caroline)
**Aphex Twin.** *Selected Ambient Works 85-92* / 1993 (R&S)

# Music Map

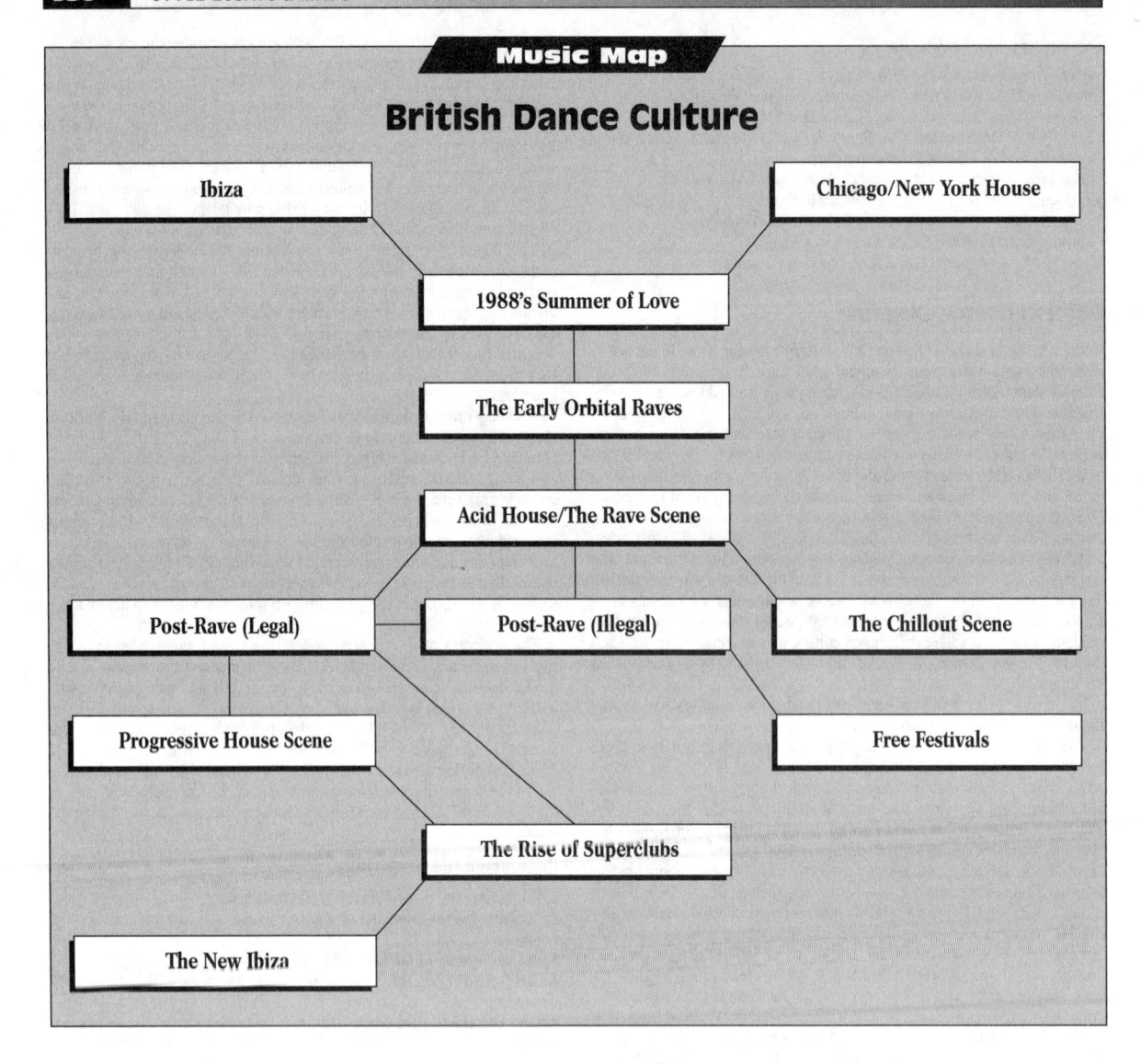

## British Dance Culture

```
Ibiza                                    Chicago/New York House
        \                               /
         \                             /
          1988's Summer of Love
                   |
          The Early Orbital Raves
                   |
          Acid House/The Rave Scene
           /       |        \
Post-Rave (Legal)—Post-Rave (Illegal)   The Chillout Scene
      |                  |
Progressive House Scene              Free Festivals
           \       /
         The Rise of Superclubs
                |
          The New Ibiza
```

Aphex Twin. *Selected Ambient Works, Vol. 2* / 1994 (Sire)
Aphex Twin. *Richard D. James Album* / 1996 (Elektra)
As One. *Planetary Folklore* / 1997 (Mo'Wax)
Autechre. *Incunabula* / 1993 (Wax Trax!)
Autechre. *Amber* / 1994 (Warp)
Autechre. *Tri Repetae++* / 1995 (Warp)
B12. *Electro-Soma* / 1993 (Wax Trax!)
Afrika Bambaataa. *Planet Rock—The Album* / 1986 (Tommy Boy)
Bark Psychosis. *Hex* / 1994 (Plan 9/Caroline)
Basement Jaxx. *Remedy* / 1999 (XL Recordings)
Basic Channel. *Basic Channel* / 1996 (Basic Channel)
Beastie Boys. *Paul's Boutique* / 1989 (Capitol)
Joey Beltram. *Classics* / 1996 (R&S)
Biosphere. *Microgravity* / 1992 (Apollo)
Björk. *Debut* / 1993 (Elektra)
Björk. *Homogenic* / 1997 (Elektra/Asylum)
Black Dog Productions. *Bytes* / 1992 (Warp)
The Black Dog. *Spanners* / 1995 (East West)
Boards of Canada. *Music Has the Right to Children* / 1998 (Warp)
David Bowie. *Low* / 1977 (Rykodisc)
David Bowie. *Heroes* / 1977 (Rykodisc)
David Bowie. *Lodger* / 1979 (Rykodisc)
David Bowie. *Scary Monsters (And Super Creeps)* / 1980 (Rykodisc)
LTJ Bukem. *Logical Progression* / 1996 (Good Looking)
Cabaret Voltaire. *2X45* / 1982 (Mute)
John Cage. *Singing Through/Vocal Compositions by John Cage* / 1991 (New Albion)
Can. *Tago Mago* / 1971 (Mute)
Can. *Ege Bamyasi* / 1972 (Mute)
Can. *Future Days* / 1973 (Mute)
The Chemical Brothers. *Exit Planet Dust* / 1995 (Astralwerks)
The Chemical Brothers. *Dig Your Own Hole* / 1997 (Astralwerks)
John Chowning. *Phone/Turenas/Stria/Sabelithe* / 1988 (Wergo)
Cluster. *Cluster 71* / 1971 (Philips)
Coldcut. *Journeys by DJ—70 Minutes of Madness* / 1996 (Music Unites/Sony)
Carl Craig. *More Songs About Food and Revolutionary Art* / 1997 (SSR)

Cybotron. *Clear* / 1990 (Fantasy)
DJ Rolando. *The Aztec Mystic Mix* / 1999 (UR)
DJ Shadow. *Endtroducing...* / 1996 (Mo'Wax/ffrr)
Daft Punk. *Homework* / 1997 (Virgin)
Miles Davis. *In a Silent Way* / 1969 (Columbia)
Miles Davis. *Bitches Brew* / 1969 (Columbia)
De La Soul. *Three Feet High & Rising* / 1989 (Tommy Boy)
Depeche Mode. *The Singles 81-85* / 1985 (Mute)
Tod Dockstader. *Apocalypse* / 1993 (Starkland)
Dr. Octagon. *Dr. Octagon* / 1996 (DreamWorks)
ESG. *A South Bronx Story* / 2000 (Universal Sound)
Brian Eno. *Another Green World* / 1975 (EG)
Brian Eno. *Before and After Science* / 1978 (EG)
Brian Eno. *Ambient 1: Music for Airports* / 1979 (EG)
Brian Eno & David Byrne. *My Life in the Bush of Ghosts* / 1981 (Sire)
Everything But the Girl. *Walking Wounded* / 1996 (Atlantic)
4 Hero. *Parallel Universe* / 1995 (Reinforced)
Funkadelic. *One Nation Under a Groove* / 1978 (Warner Brothers)
Future Sound of London. *Lifeforms* / 1994 (Astralwerks)
Philip Glass. *Music in 12 Parts* / 1990 (Venture)
Global Communication. *76:14* / 1994 (Dedicated)
Goldie. *Timeless* / Aug. 1995 (ffrr)
Manuel Göttsching. *E2 E4* / 1984 (Racket)
Grandmaster Flash. *Message from Beat Street: The Best of Grandmaster Flash* / 1994 (Rhino)
A Guy Called Gerald. *Black Secret Technology* / 1995 (Juicebox)
Herbie Hancock. *Mwandishi: The Complete Warner Bros. Recordings* / 1972 (Warner Archives)
Herbie Hancock. *Head Hunters* / 1973 (Columbia)
Happy Mondays. *Pills 'n' Thrills & Bellyaches* / 1990 (Elektra)
Jon Hassell & Brian Eno. *Fourth World, Vol. 1: Possible Musics* / 1980 (EG)
Richie Hawtin. *Decks, EFX & 909* / 1999 (Nova Mute)
Larry Heard. *Classic Fingers* / 1995 (Black Market)
Human League. *Dare* / 1981 (A&M)
Inner City. *Big Fun* / 1989 (Virgin)
Irresistible Force. *Flying High* / 1993 (Instinct)
Jean-Michel Jarre. *Oxygène* / 1977 (Dreyfus)
Marshall Jefferson. *Past Classics* / 1998 (Fierce)
The KLF. *Chill Out* / 1990 (Wax Trax!)
The KLF. *The White Room* / 1991 (Arista)
King Tubby. *King Tubby Special 1973-1976* / 1989 (Trojan)
Frankie Knuckles. *Best of Frankie Knuckles* / 1999 (Mirakkle)
Kraftwerk. *Autobahn* / 1974 (Warner Brothers)
Kraftwerk. *Trans-Europe Express* / 1977 (Capitol)
Kraftwerk. *Computer World* / 1981 (Warner Brothers)
Kruder & Dorfmeister. *The K&D Sessions* / 1998 (Studio !K7)
LFO. *Frequencies* / 1991 (Tommy Boy)
Lamb. *Lamb* / 1997 (Fontana)
Leftfield. *Leftism* / 1995 (Hard Hands/Columbia)
Larry Levan. *Live at the Paradise Garage* / 2000 (Strut)
Mantronix. *The Best of Mantronix 1985-1999* / 1999 (Virgin)
Massive Attack. *Blue Lines* / 1991 (Virgin)
Massive Attack. *Mezzanine* / 1998 (Virgin)
Masters at Work. *MAW Records: The Compilation, Vol. 1* / 1998 (Strictly Rhythm)
Derrick May. *The Innovator* / 1997 (Transmat)
Jeff Mills. *Live at the Liquid Room, Tokyo* / 1996 (React)
Moby. *Moby* / 1992 (Instinct)
Model 500. *Classics* / 1995 (R&S)
Moodymann. *A Silent Introduction* / 1997 (Planet E)
Giorgio Moroder. *From Here to Eternity* / 1977 (Casablanca)
Mouse on Mars. *Iaora Tahiti* / 1995 (Too Pure/American)
Mouse on Mars. *Autoditacker* / 1997 (Thrill Jockey)
µ-Ziq. *Tango N' Vectif* / 1993 (Rephlex)
µ-Ziq. *Lunatic Harness* / 1997 (Astralwerks)
My Bloody Valentine. *Loveless* / 1991 (Sire)
New Order. *Technique* / 1989 (Qwest)
New Order. *The Best of New Order* / 1995 (Qwest)
Nine Inch Nails. *Pretty Hate Machine* / 1989 (TVT)

The Orb. *U.F.Orb* / 1992 (Big Life)
The Orb. *The Orb's Adventures Beyond the Ultraworld* / 1991 (Big Life)
Orbital. *In Sides* / 1996 (ffrr/London)
Orbital. *Orbital 2* / 1992 (ffrr)
Oval. *94 Diskont* / 1995 (Mille Plateaux)
Augustus Pablo. *Classic Rockers* / 1995 (Island)
Paperclip People. *The Secret Tapes of Dr. Eich* / 1996 (Open)
Lee "Scratch" Perry. *Reggae Greats* / 1984 (Mango)
Pet Shop Boys. *Discography: The Complete Singles Collection* / 1991 (EMI America)
Pink Floyd. *Dark Side of the Moon* / 1973 (Capitol)
Plastikman. *Musik* / 1994 (Plus 8)
Plug. *Drum'n'bass for Papa/Plug 1, 2 & 3* / 1997 (Nothing/Interscope)
Polygon Window. *Surfing on Sine Waves* / 1992 (Warp)
Porter Ricks. *BioKinetics* / 1996 (Chain Reaction)
Portishead. *Dummy* / 1994 (PolyGram)
Primal Scream. *Screamadelica* / 1991 (Sire)
Prince. *Dirty Mind* / 1980 (Warner Brothers)
Prince. *1999* / 1982 (Warner Brothers)
Prodigy. *Experience* / 1992 (Elektra)
Prodigy. *Music for the Jilted Generation* / 1995 (Mute)
Psyche/BFC. *Elements 1989-1990* / 1996 (Planet E)
Public Enemy. *It Takes a Nation of Millions to Hold Us Back* / 1988 (Def Jam)
Public Enemy. *Fear of a Black Planet* / 1990 (Def Jam)
Public Image Ltd.. *Second Edition* / 1980 (Warner Brothers)
Radiohead. *OK Computer* / 1997 (Capitol)
Steve Reich. *Music for 18 Musicians* / 1978 (ECM)
Robert Rich & Lustmord. *Stalker* / 1995 (Fathom)
Terry Riley. *Rainbow in Curved Air/Poppy Nogood and the Phantom Band* / 1990 (CBS)
The Sabres of Paradise. *Sabresonic* / 1993 (Warp)
St. Etienne. *Too Young to Die* / 1995 (Heavenly)
Sasha & John Digweed. *Northern Exposure: Expeditions* / 1999 (Incredible)
Kevin Saunderson. *Faces & Phases* / 1997 (Planet E)
Klaus Schulze. *Irrlicht* / 1972 (PDU)
Raymond Scott. *Manhattan Research, Inc.* / 2000 (Basta)
The Shamen. *En-Tact* / 1990 (Epic)
Silver Apples. *Silver Apples* / 1997 (MCA)
Roni Size & Reprazent. *New Forms* / 1997 (Talkin' Loud/Mercury)
Skinny Puppy. *The Singles Collect* / 1999 (Nettwerk)
Slam. *Headstates* / 1996 (Soma)
Soul II Soul. *Keep on Movin'* / 1989 (Virgin)
Squarepusher. *Hard Normal Daddy* / 1997 (Warp)
Stereolab. *Transient Random Noise Bursts with Announcements* / 1993 (Elektra)
Stereolab. *Emperor Tomato Ketchup* /1996 (Elektra)
Karlheinz Stockhausen. *Kontakte* / 1959 (Ecstatic Peace)
The Stone Roses. *The Stone Roses* / 1989 (Silvertone)
Suicide. *Suicide* / 1977 (Restless)
Talk Talk. *Spirit of Eden* / 1988 (EMI America)
Talk Talk. *Laughing Stock* / 1991 (Polydor)
Tangerine Dream. *Phaedra* / 1974 (Virgin)
Tangerine Dream. *Rubycon* / 1975 (Virgin)
Todd Terry. *Todd Terry's Greatest Hits* / 2000 (Warlock)
Throbbing Gristle. *20 Jazz Funk Greats* / 1979 (Mute)
Tortoise. *Millions Now Living Will Never Die* / 1996 (Thrill Jockey)
Tricky. *Maxinquaye* / 1995 (4th & Broadway)
Underground Resistance. *Interstellar Fugitives* / 1998 (UR)
Underworld. *Dubnobasswithmyheadman* / 1993 (Wax Trax!)
Underworld. *Second Toughest in the Infants* / 1996 (Wax Trax!)
Vladimir Ussachevsky. *Electronic Film Music* / 1990 (New World)
Vangelis. *Blade Runner* / 1994 (Atlantic)
Edgard Varèse. *Music of Edgard Varèse* / 1996 (One Way)
Wagon Christ. *Throbbing Pouch* / 1995 (Rising High)
Stevie Wonder. *Talking Book* / 1972 (Motown)
Stevie Wonder. *Innervisions* / 1973 (Motown)
Yellow Magic Orchestra. *Solid State Survivor* / 1979 (Restless)
Various Artists. *Ambient, Vol. 1: A Brief History of Ambient* (Virgin)

**Various Artists.** *Artificial Intelligence* (Wax Trax!)
**Various Artists.** *Depth Charge, Vol. 1* (Submerge)
**Various Artists.** *Disco Boogie, Vol. 1* (Salsoul)
**Various Artists.** *Excursions in Ambience: A Collection of Ambient-House Music* (Plan 9/Caroline)
**Various Artists.** *Happy2bHardcore* (Moonshine Music)
**Various Artists.** *History of House Music, Vol. 1: Chicago Classics* (Cold Front)
**Various Artists.** *History of House Music, Vol. 2: New York Garage Style* (Cold Front)
**Various Artists.** *Machine Soul: An Odyssey into Electronic Dance Music* (Rhino)
**Various Artists.** *New Electronica, Vol. 1* (New Electronica)
**Various Artists.** *New Electronica, Vol. 3* (New Electronica)
**Various Artists.** *Objets d'A.R.T.* (New Electronica)
**Various Artists.** *Strictly Rhythm: The Early Years* (Strictly Rhythm)
**Various Artists.** *Trance Europe Express, Vol. 1* (Volume)
**Various Artists.** *Warp 10+1: The Influences* (Matador)

# Book Reviews

✦✦✦✦✦ **Altered State,** *Matthew Collin* (Serpent's Tail, 1997) One of the first retrospectives of the British rave explosion, *Altered State* presents not so much a history of the music as a history of the culture that made the music possible (notably, it's subtitled "The Story of Ecstasy Culture and Acid House"). Like Simon Reynolds in his book *Generation Ecstasy*, Matthew Collin gives drugs much of the credit for making the dance revolution possible, but he presents a much more historically based version of events, beginning with capsule histories of other dance/drug cultures—San Francisco in the late '60s, New York in the early '70s, Chicago in the early '80s—that influenced Britain's, plus several pages on the development of the most popular rave drugs, Ecstasy and Acid. In the middle part of *Altered State*, the scene moves to London's dance explosion of the mid-'80s, the movement that made house music a worldwide presence. Collin recounts the history of the early clubnights that quickly gelled during 1988's Summer of Love rave explosion, were commercialized by the early '90s, and headed back underground several years later with dance subcultures like hardcore techno (which developed into jungle/drum'n'bass) and chill-out. Though it's by far the best history of British club culture written, *Altered State* is much more than that; it's the story of what made electronic dance not only viable as a genuine culture but also a musical and commercial phenomenon throughout Europe.

✦✦✦ **The Art of Electronic Music,** *Tom Darter & Greg Armbruster* (Quill, 1984) A collection of articles originally appearing in *Keyboard* magazine, *The Art of Electronic Music* is one of the better references on academic electronic music considering its focus on the music, with the hardware and programs taking a distinct back-seat. It begins with a short chapter concerning the history of the field (from the Telharmonium to the Vocoder), then traces the development of instrument manufacturing, from individual inventors to company-based manufacture (including interviews with Max Mathews, John Chowning, Bob Moog, Donald Buchla, and Oberheim). The third chapter charts the actual artists of electronic music, with talks by Wendy Carlos, Keith Emerson, Brian Eno, Tangerine Dream, and Thomas Dolby, among others. Besides its value for those interested in synthesizer manufacturers, *The Art of Electronic Music* is priceless for the range of topics covered.

**The Art of Noises (Monographs in Musicology, No. 6),** *Luigi Russolo* (Pendragon, 1986) One in a collection of writings by the Italian Futurist Luigi Russolo, most recently published in 1986, *The Art of Noises* remains the pioneering work for the 20th century's ever-expanding musical repertoire. Written in 1913, Russolo's manifesto traced the evolution of sound from the beginning of time into the industrial era, and made the rational explanation that since the human race was evolving, so were their ears and receptivity for hearing different sounds. Promising that future developments in music would come from composers testing the structure and variety of noise within sound, Russolo forced a re-examination of the very foundation of music that would continue for the rest of the century. He even described his vision of a futurist orchestra, recognizing five families of noises that the group would comprise. Russolo's concepts had rough forebears and contemporaries including Satie, Debussy and Stravinsky, but no one had outlined these theories in such a degree of detail and foresight. *The Art of Noises* remains a priceless document of the classical avant-garde. Though the Pendragon collection is out of print, Russolo's manifesto was most recently available online at http://www.primenet.com/~bonefish/misc/russolo.htm.

✦✦✦ **Brian Eno: His Music and the Vertical Color of Sound,** *Eric Tamm* (Da Capo Press, 1995) Originally begun as a thesis paper and later expanded into book form, *The Vertical Color of Sound* analyzes Eno's recording career via in-depth examinations of the varied studio techniques necessary for recording along with quotes that reveal much about his personal artistic philosophy. Though it still reads like the college paper it originated as, Tamm's chronicle is a solid purchase for fans of Eno's recordings as well as those interested in his philosophy of sound.

✦✦ **Bring the Noise,** *Havelock Nelson & Michael E. Gonzalez* (Harmony, 1991) One of the first guides to rap music ever published, *Bring the Noise* includes short vignettes of about fifty rap artists in encyclopedic format. The coverage ranges from seven to ten pages for major artists Public Enemy, Boogie Down Productions, the Beastie Boys and Run-D.M.C. down to short paragraphs for less famous groups like Audio Two. The sections are informative and slightly better written than Nelson's columns for *Billboard*, but still end up rather glib and superficial.

✦✦✦ **Cabaret Voltaire: The Art of the Sixth Sense,** *Mick Fish & Dave Hallbery* (SAF Publishing, 1989) Cabaret Voltaire was always one of the more shadowy bands of the post-punk movement, more concerned with the music they made than the press notes they gathered. As such, *The Art of the Sixth Sense* is a valuable work to the many fans that were rather unsure of their career. It's a solid history of the group, connecting their beginnings in Sheffield's industrial scene of the mid-'70s to their post-funk period of the early '80s, all the way up to their pioneering visit to Chicago to meet house forefather Marshall Jefferson (the results of which appeared on 1990's *Groovy, Laidback & Nasty*).

✦✦✦✦ **The Can Book,** *Pascal Bussy & Andy Hall* (SAF Publishing, 1989) Unraveling the complex web of fact and fiction that has been part of Can's mystique ever since the group's beginnings, *The Can Book* is an excellent investigation of the band's chronology and discography. The book includes numerous quotes from band members, which will enlighten readers interested in Can's history and recording techniques. The writing is arguably better than Bussy's Kraftwerk book, and includes many photographs of the group at work.

✦✦✦✦ **Club Cultures: Music, Media and Subcultural Capital,** *Sarah Thornton* (Wesleyan University Press, 1996) A unique, excellently researched study of the culture and sociology of dance music, Sarah Thornton's *Club Culture* charts the progression from subculture to mass movement in dance scenes including disco, punk, and rave. Throughout the book, Thornton examines the rationale behind clubbing, what effects it has had on youth culture since the '50s, and how it has socially changed several generations. Also, the book never devolves into the usual graduate thesis; *Club Culture* includes much information gained with first-hand experience of Britain's clubbing scene and makes for an excellent history of dance culture.

✦✦✦ **Computer Music: Synthesis, Composition and Performance,** *Charles Dodge & Thomas A. Jerse* (Schirmer Books, 1997) This solid introduction to the varying hardware, software, and programming concepts that lie behind the performance of computerized electronic music was written by a visiting professor at Dartmouth and a former technical engineer at Brooklyn College's Center for Electronic Music. It may be overly elaborate for those just getting into the complex world of computer music and MIDI, but better than most books on the topic, this one includes historically rooted writing on the development of electronic music.

✦✦✦ **Cosmic Dreams at Play,** *Dag Erik Asbjornsen* (Borderline Productions, 1996) An exhaustively detailed encyclopedia of '70s Kraut-rock and space music, *Cosmic Dreams at Play* includes complete discographies (with track listings) and reviews for dozens of groups, including every major innovator plus dozens of less famous groups. It's most definitely not an introductory work, but for those wishing to delve into the dusty corners of Kraut-rock, the book is a valuable resource.

◆◆◆◆ **The Crack in the Cosmic Egg**, *Steven & Alan Freeman* (Audion Publications, 1996) Two brothers, the editors of *Audion* magazine, published this Kraut-rock encyclopedia with their own resources as a labor of love for the history of the music. As such, *The Crack in the Cosmic Egg* could well be the most thorough accounting of the scene ever written, with over 300 pages and 1000 artists listed, plus many rare band photos and cover art. It's an incredible reference, while the writing is expert and personal throughout.

◆◆◆◆ **Electric Music**, *Joel Chadabe* (Prentice Hall, 1996) Written by an electronic music pioneer intimately involved with the form's development for several decades, Joel Chadabe's *Electric Music* is the most complete, readable and informative history of electronic music's composition-slanted wing. Spanning 300 pages, the book begins with the earliest electric instruments (the Telharmonium and Theremin), progresses through the advances of tape music and musique concrète, and covers computer music and MIDI to a degree of depth never seen previously. Chadabe's direct style of writing defeats much of the confusion about formal electronic music experienced by non-academic readers, while the insertion of numerous pictures and quotes from the composers give the book a tremendous feeling of immediacy. For those who wish to know more about differentiating and appreciating the music of Cage, Ussachevsky, Stockhausen, Xenakis, Berio, Lucien, and many others, *Electric Music* is a natural choice.

◆◆◆ **Electronic Music**, *Andy MacKay* (Control Data, 1981) Andy Mackay, known best for his role in Roxy Music though he has performed for the London Symphony Orchestra (and was the one who helped Brian Eno join the group), wrote his history of electronic music in 1981. Though there are several inaccuracies (including the statement that Leon Theremin was executed by the Soviet government in 1945), *Electronic Music* is a broad-ranging work that spans Luigi Russolo, Iannis Xenakis and Stevie Wonder with little regard for stylistic boundaries. Mackay is a knowledgeable and entertaining writer, investing the book with his intriguing views about the development and promise of electronic music.

◆◆◆◆◆ **Elevator Music**, *Joseph Lanza* (Picador, 1995) Much more than just a history of Muzak and easy-listening music, *Elevator Music* presents a chronology of what the author calls "moodsong," basically any type of music used more as environmental background than as focused listening. This definition allows Lanza to connect several strains of moodsong throughout history, the Aeolian wind harp of classical antiquity; Erik Satie's ideas of furniture music; the development of Muzak; easy listening and exotica from the '50s; ambient and Brian Eno's discreet music from the '70s; new age music from the '80s. The range of disparate musics tied together in *Elevator Music* is surprising, and Lanza treats each of his topics with equal reverence. It's a refreshing look at music that's often taken for granted, in many ways.

**Experimental Music: John Cage and Beyond**, *Michael Nyman* (Schirmer, 1974) Written by one of the genre's prime inheritors, *Experimental Music* is a two-decade history of the post-post-modern style of composition tied most often to Americans, whether it be pioneer composer John Cage or minimalist inheritors like La Monte Young, Terry Riley, and Steve Reich. Ever since its publication in 1974, the book has been one of the best resources on the development of experimental composition, beginning with Cage's infamous 4'33" and reaching to many different compositions more renowned for the theories behind their creation than the music itself. Nyman's writing includes many experiences gained first-hand, and is excellent throughout.

◆◆◆◆ **Generation Ecstasy**, *Simon Reynolds* (Little Brown & Company, 1998) It's significant that Simon Reynolds' book on electronic dance music is subtitled "A Journey Through Rave Music and Dance Culture." Readers expecting a straightforward history of the form with recommendations may become a bit confused by Reynolds' insistence on philosophizing about the necessity of drugs to completely appreciate electronic music. Of course, Reynolds is above all a knowledgeable, accomplished writer and he invests the book with all the excitement that the music deserves, reserving special space (and eloquence) for personal favorites like early hardcore techno and perhaps focusing a bit more criticism on the so-called "intelligent" techno crowd (Aphex Twin, Squarepusher, etc.) than needed. Still, Reynolds has been a fan of the music for over a decade, and his understanding of electronic dance music's varying aspects makes for an incredibly educational read. (*Generation Ecstasy* is the American reprint of the book originally issued in Great Britain as *Energy Flash*. The British edition includes 40,000 additional words plus a 12-track CD.)

◆◆◆◆◆ **A Guide to Electronic Music**, *Paul Griffiths* (Thames and Hudson, 1979) Paul Griffiths' *A Guide to Electronic Music* sorts through the long and often complicated history of classical and academic-based electronic music with an eye to clarity that's quite refreshing. Leading off with a clear, concise history of the medium beginning with the birth of electronic instruments at the turn of the century, Griffiths separates and explains advances in electronic music (from the 1920s through the '70s) by John Cage, Edgar Varése, Pierre Schaeffer, Karlheinz Stockhausen, LaMonte Young, Wendy Carlos and many others. The second section of the book is devoted to the electronic repertory, including extended writings about landmark compositions like Stockhausen's "Kontakte" and Varése's "Poéme Électronique." It's easy to dip into, and reveals much more in-depth analysis for more seasoned readers. As could be expected for a book dated 1979 however, the discography is quite out of date.

◆◆◆◆ **History of House**, *Chris Kempster* (Sanctuary, 1996) From the archives of *Music Technology* magazine and its successor, *The Mix*, comes *History of House*, a collection of superb interviews with an astonishing lineup of the major innovators of electronic dance music, from Chicago's Marshall Jefferson and Larry Heard to Detroit's Juan Atkins, Derrick May, and Carl Craig, to Europeans Kraftwerk, 808 State, the Orb, and Goldie. Though the articles are geared more to the instruments used for recording than the recordings themselves, each article has a wealth of information about these figures.

◆◆ **Industrial Revolution**, *Dave Thompson* (Cleopatra, ) A 150-page paperback published by the neo-industrialists at Cleopatra Records, *Industrial Revolution* completely misses the story of industrial music. For a book that devotes much more space to industrial-rock crossovers than true industrial groups, claims not only that the first electronic keyboard was introduced in 1928 but that that instrument was the Theremin (which has no keyboard!), and doesn't even mention important industrial acts like :zoviet*france:, 23 Skidoo, Nocturnal Emissions, and more, it's a shame that anyone would consider it a proper history of the music. Of course, for the industrial-metal and dance fans attracted to the hordes of mediocre releases on Cleopatra, *Industrial Revolution* is probably required reading.

◆◆ **Jean-Michel Jarre**, *Jean-Louis Remilleux* (Futura, 1987) More a coffee-table pictorial of Europe's most famous synth-pop artist than a critical biography, *Jean-Michel Jarre* is also a bit short on biographic details. Fans will appreciate the many photos however, concentrating especially on Jarre's famous concert appearances in Houston, Paris, China, and Lyon.

◆◆◆◆ **Justified and Ancient History: The Unfolding History of the KLF**, *Pete Robinson* (, 1992) Pete Robinson's obsessively researched, pamphlet-sized documentary of the KLF is near-vital to understanding the story of dance music's most fascinating group. The various releases, records that never were, and music-industry shenanigans that make up the story of Bill Drummond and Jimi Cauty are so much more complicated (and more eminently readable) than that of rock 'n' roll acts around for three times as long. Consequently, *Justified and Ancient History* is fascinating simply as a look at all the pranksterish fun the pair could have by spending the proceeds of their various number one singles. It also includes a full discography, scores of original magazine ads, press releases, and rare drawings, providing a great look at one of the most collectable dance artists of all time.

◆◆◆ **Kraftwerk: Man, Machine and Music**, *Pascal Bussy* (SAF Publishing, 1993) As the author Pascal Bussy notes in the foreword, writing a book about Kraftwerk is a very difficult task. Besides doing few interviews in their twenty-five-year history, core members Ralf Hütter and Florian Schneider maintained a veil of secrecy over practically all their actions (and have actively protested the contents of Bussy's book). True, a book written with this amount of speculation and hearsay—much of it from people only peripherally involved with the group—can be a dangerous thing, but Bussy does a good job considering what he was given. Unverified information is taken for exactly what it is, and the lack of group involvement gives the author much space to actually write about the music, from Hütter and Schneider's first involvement in the pre-Kraftwerk group Organisation right up to their recent (at the time of writing) concerts as part of *The Mix* compilation. The writing is a bit stilted but for the time being, *Man, Machine and Music* is the definitive history on one of electronic music's most influential groups.

✦✦✦✦ **Kraut-rocksampler,** *Julian Cope* (Head Heritage, 1996) Musican and author Julian Cope's infamous document of his continuing love affair with experimental German music of the late '60s and early '70s, *Kraut-rocksampler* is by no means an official history of the style. Instead, Cope lets his enthusiasm for the music take free rein over any acceptable journalistic norms. The result is an exciting read that conveys to beginners exactly what there *is* to be excited about in Kraut-rock—its focus on wild experimentation and unusual sounds, its near-complete disregard for Western rock 'n' roll, its sense of distance from what had come before. For anyone that might be interested in Kraut-rock, it's easy to get carried away by Cope's infectious writing; it's chocked with off-the-cuff descriptions of music that's notoriously hard to describe plus many personal reminiscences about his early fandom. Separated into three sections, *Kraut-rocksampler* begins with a (comparatively) straightahead history of the style, from its beginnings in Germany's disparate avant-garde, psychedelic and electronic scenes of the late '60s to its zenith with major bands Tangerine Dream, Faust, Neu, Can, Amon Düül, and Ash Ra Tempel. The second section includes discographical information on fifty of Cope's personal Kraut-rock favorites, while the third includes more detailed writing about each album. In sum, *Kraut-rocksampler* is a fascinating look into one of music's least understood styles of music.

✦✦✦ **The Making of Mike Oldfield's Tubular Bells,** *Richard Newman* (Music Maker Books, 1993) *The Making of Mike Oldfield's Tubular Bells* is an interesting look at the genesis of not only one of the world's best-selling albums but Richard Branson's Virgin Records label (*Tubular Bells* was its first release). Oldfield and producer/engineers Tom Newman and Simon Heyworth actually worked for upwards of a year simply building the studio at Virgin's legendary Manor in rural Oxfordshire before recording began for *Tubular Bells*. Though the rest of the recording process will be more interesting for audiophiles and engineers than average music fans, there are a few humorous anecdotes involving Oldfield and the eccentric Branson.

✦✦✦✦✦ **Ocean of Sound,** *David Toop* (Serpent's Tail, 1995) David Toop's surreal investigation into the history of non-traditional music begins with the legendary 1889 Paris Exposition, where Debussy first heard the expressive, completely un-Western gong music of Indonesia and extends to far-flung artists and locales during the next century, from Sun Ra to Aphex Twin to the Beach Boys to Lee Perry to Motown to Larry Heard to Miles Davis—and dozens more. And Toop draws few dividing lines between these artists, drawing them all into the fold and discussing each in a very non-linear fashion. The effect of his writing, deeply personal at times, is quite similar to ambient music itself, quite expressive when you're paying attention to it but also possessing a drifting quality that has nothing to do with boredom. *Ocean of Sound* is not only a series of great writings about artists rarely grouped together, it's a fascinating read.

✦✦✦ **Rough Guide to Drum'n'bass,** *Peter Shapiro* (Rough Guides/Penguin, 1999) The first of three pocket-sized listening guides devoted to dance music, *Rough Guide to Drum'n'bass* does a good job of balancing informative writing with eye-pleasing photos of the major artists and labels from the jungle world (as well as related breakbeat styles like big-beat and trip-hop). Presented in encyclopedia format with a profile and review section on each artist, the book hits most of the major drum'n'bass artists, irrespective of popularity (or if their records are available). Though the music reviews are quite brief and a bit spotty, the *Rough Guide to Drum'n'bass* provides a good look at an oft-misunderstood music.

✦✦✦ **Rough Guide to House,** *Sean Bidder* (Rough Guides/Penguin, 1999) The house volume in *Rough Guide*'s series of music-profile pocket encyclopedias works in a similar fashion to the drum'n'bass volume. It's not quite as definitive as the drum'n'bass volume, but still provides a good look at a wealth of producers and labels.

✦✦✦✦ **Rough Guide to Reggae,** *Steve Barrow & Peter Dalton* (Rough Guides/Penguin, 1997) Written by Steve Barrow and Peter Dalton (the former is head of the stellar reissue label Blood & Fire), *The Rough Guide to Reggae* is an excellent overview of a frequently misunderstood and frustrating genre. Organized—as with other volumes in the series—in a format that balances chronological narrative with discographical information and recommendations every few pages, the book has few equals in its field. *The Rough Guide to Reggae* also proves quite solid when it comes to introducing, discussing, and rating the work of dub originators like King Tubby, Lee "Scratch" Perry, Scientist, and Mad Professor.

✦✦✦✦ **Rough Guide to Techno,** *Tim Barr* (Rough Guides/Penguin, 2000) *Rough Guide*'s look at the techno world spans the sound of Detroit during the '80s to the global community of the '90s with informative profiles and pictures. As in previous volumes, the discographies are skeletal at best, and the writing quite brief (though informative).

✦✦✦ **State of Bass,** *Martin James* (Boxtree, 1997) In the first book to focus on the history and sound of the drum'n'bass/jungle scene, Martin James takes readers through the birth of jungle in the early-'90s hardcore techno movement, its rapid separation from the more straightahead end of rave music, and its continuing development during the rest of the '90s with added influences from jazz, trip-hop, reggae, ambient, techno. The writing isn't stellar, and readers wanting a bit more depth and analysis could cobble together a better history of jungle from selected chapters of Simon Reynolds' *Generation Ecstasy*. Nevertheless, *State of Bass* presents a clear history of the music and the scene, with excellent discographies following each chapter and a foreword by A Guy Called Gerald.

✦✦✦ **Straight Outa Bristol,** *Phil Johnson* (Hodder & Stoughton, 1996) A resident of Bristol since 1980, Phil Johnson was uniquely qualified to write a history of the city's trip-hop scene, which gave birth to acts including international stars like Massive Attack, Portishead, and Tricky, as well as underground favorites like Smith & Mighty, Statik Sound System, Monk & Canatella, and Spaceways. Johnson takes readers through all aspects of Bristol's music scenes during the '70s and '80s, from punk to reggae to hip-hop, and draws a line through their fusion courtesy of indie bands like the Pop Group, Pigbag, and Rip Rig & Panic. From there it was a short step to the Wild Boys, a hip-hop collective including Nellee Hooper (later of Soul II Soul), Robert Del Naja, Grant Marshall, and Adrian Vowles (later to form Massive Attack). Packed with early photos, *Straight Outa Bristol* is an intense look into the city that created one of the most important scenes in '90s dance. Fans looking for an all-encompassing history of trip-hop won't find exactly what they're looking for, but the book is a solid overview of the scene.

✦✦✦✦ **Tape Delay,** *Charles Neal* (SAF Publishing, 1987) Charles Neal's *Tape Delay* investigates the connections between dozens of post-punk, industrial, and noise groups active on the experimental edge of alternative music during the '70s and '80s—including New Order, the Fall, Coil, Psychic TV, Sonic Youth, Einstürzende Neubaten, The The, Hafler Trio, Cabaret Voltaire, the Swans, Henry Rollins, and many others. It's an intriguing look at the similarities between many bands that end up in the same record collections but are rarely talked about together.

✦✦✦✦ **Techno Rebels,** *Dan Sicko* (Billboard Books, 1999) From a longtime resident of Detroit, Dan Sicko's *Techno Rebels* presents the most complete history of techno ever assembled, beginning with the Motor City's adolescent dance culture of the late '70s and extending to the end-of-the-millennium machine music crafted worldwide by a generation of producers inspired by Detroit techno. While the accepted history of Detroit and its music scene focuses on the Atkins/May/Saunderson techno triumvirate—to the exclusion of other figures or factors—*Techno Rebels* does an excellent job of presenting the culture that produced techno as well as discussing and rating the work of its major artists. From crucial Detroit DJs like the Electrifyin' Mojo and Ken Collier through to Underground Resistance and the rise of a fertile Detroit music scene, Sicko guides readers through the previously shadowed history of techno. There's just enough social critique to get a feeling for how economic factors in Detroit played into the special atmosphere of a tight, fraternal community, but never so much that the book strays from the music. Of course, any history of techno that ignores Britain and Germany is only telling part of the story, so *Techno Rebels* also runs through the history of the transatlantic techno scene, with more focus on the music than the culture that produced it.

✦✦✦ **Vintage Synthesizers,** *Mark Vail* (Miller Freeman/Backbeat Books, 2000) Published by the editors of *Keyboard* magazine, *Vintage Synthesizers* is a richly illustrated 300-page collection of articles (some updated and expanded) that originally appeared in the pages of the magazine. Though it doesn't quite follow a linear path, the book does include interesting stories about synthesizer builders Robert Moog, Donald Buchla and Dave Luce (Moog even writes his own articles on developing the Minimoog and Oberheim synthesizers). It was obviously published more for the MIDI/audiophile crowd than followers of electronic music, but it's a worthwhile introduction to the synthesizer world.

✦✦✦✦ **What Kind of House Party Is This?,** *Jonathan Fleming* (MIY, 1995) Jonathan Fleming's in-depth look at the British club scene of the late '80s and early '90s is an invaluable tool to better understand the individuals involved in making house and techno into a global force. In the first part of the book, Fleming publishes his one- or two-page interviews with close to one hundred DJs and a few producers. Each of his subjects (some of whom rarely give interviews) is a major influence on the style, including British figures Paul Oakenfold, Pete Tong, Carl Cox, Grooverider, and Andrew Weatherall, as well as American legends like Frankie Knuckles, Larry Heard, Juan Atkins, Todd Terry, Jesse Saunders, Derrick May, DJ Pierre, Joey Beltram, and many others. The second part of the book focuses on famed clubs around the globe including British entries like the Haçienda, Shoom, Spectrum, Land of Oz, Ministry of Sound, and Cream, plus a few from America like the Tunnel Club, Limelight, the Roxy, the Sound Factory, and the Music Box. Though Fleming's interviews focus on only a few standard questions (and his transcriptions of the American interviews could've used an informed spell-checker), there's an astonishing amount of information (and many pictures) about the early lives and careers of most of the seminal figures in electronic dance music. *What Kind of House Party Is This?* is easily dance music's most educational resource.

# Label Descriptions

## A-Musik

The Cologne-based A-Musik label, owned and operated by Georg Odijk, is the in-house imprint of Odijk's record shop of the same name: a tiny, unassuming storefront with stock ranging from extreme to extreme (Iannis Xenakis to Ed Rush, Tortoise to Merzbow). The name of the label pretty accurately approximates where most of the artists thus-far released through A-Musik—including Markus Schmickler, Ln, Schlammpeitziger, and FX Randomiz—are coming from: constellations of sounds arranged in such a way as to suggest that perhaps the author is not quite altogether sure (wink wink, nudge nudge) what it is "music" is supposed to mean. However, like fellow Cologners Mouse on Mars or most of the artists associated with Vienna's Mego label, the result is usually joyfully idiosyncratic—not po-faced and studio-serious—and quite often truly bizarre; A-Musik's releases tend toward a particularly postwar German sense of the absurd. Along with other Cologne-based labels such as Gefriem, Electro Bunker, Eat Raw, Karaoke Kalk, and Sonig, A-Musik has also helped draw attention to that city as the site of the sort of electronica version of a '90s Kraut-rock renaissance.

## Apollo

The ambient sublabel of Ghent, Belgium-based dance staple R&S Records, Apollo took on a life of its own after being established in 1993 as an outlet for R&S artists' more experimental proclivities. Apollo began with a series of 12"s by such artists as Ken Ishii, David Morley, Billie Ray Martin, and Andrea Parker before releasing Biosphere's full-length *Microgravity* in 1993. The label later issued a number of influential full-length works by Tournesol, Sun Electric, and Locust, in addition to a pair of label compilations (*Compilation 1* and *The Divine Compilation*) featuring original and remixed work.

## Beyond

The UK-based Beyond label is a bedroom outfit established in 1992 as an outlet for the more sprawling, improvisational side of ambient/experimental electronica. The label's catalog includes full-length works from David Toop with Max Eastley, Higher Intelligence Agency, Insanity Sect, TUU, and Another Fine Day, as well as collaborations between HIA and Biopshere's Geir Jenssen, and TUU's Martin Franklin, percussionist Eddy Sayer, and flautist Nick Parkin. The label's initial series of *Ambient Dub* compilations coined a phrase which later became standard, including tracks from such artists as Banco de Gaia, A Positive Life, Another Fine Day, Groove Corporation, Original Rockers, and G.O.L. In 1993, Beyond established an American office, Waveform, to speed reissues, and the Sedona, AZ-based arm also assembled its own artist roster. Waveform released several CDs in its *A.D.* series, collecting track from the Beyond back catalog, as well as material from Coldcut, Human Mesh Dance, the Starseeds, and Pentatonik.

## Certificate 18

Although the name is scarcely as recognizable as such list-toppers as Suburban Base, Moving Shadow, Good Looking, and Metalheadz, the Ipswich-based jungle label Certificate 18 was the jumping-off point for many of the biggest name artists in contemporary drum'n'bass. Formed by Redeye Records owner Paul Arnold in 1990, Certificate 18 was the pressure point that brought artists such as Rupert "Photek" Parkes, Phil and Jim of Source Direct, Rob of Motive One, and Tom Withers of Klute/Override—all of whom would convene ritually each week to sift through new 12" hardcore and techno—well beyond local prominence. Originally formed to provide a vehicle for local talent intent upon driving the exploding hardcore sound into new areas, Certificate 18 followed the style through its high-rave helium days of 1991 and into darkside and jungle proper from 1992 on (as well as the related fields of experimental electro and breakbeat techno à la Black Dog, Autechre, etc.). By 1993, the label had risen to high regard as a result of well-played tracks from Photek (as Studio Pressure), Source Direct (as Sounds of Life), and Motive One, and while many of those artist would go on to greater acclaim on larger labels such as Science, Metalheadz, and Good Looking, Certificate 18 retained its edge through a new wave of drum'n'bass experimenters (such as Klute's Tom Withers and obscure techstep artist Lexis). An introduction to the label's history exists in the multiple-volume series *Hidden Rooms*.

## Clear

Cornwall-based neo-electro label Clear was launched in 1995 by a pair of Rephlex defects interested in updating a style of electronic music which, though influential on many of the experimental underground's foremost artists, was largely relegated to footnote status in the wake of higher profile UK movements such as acid house and techno. Although dance-based experimental electronic music deriving from a strong electro base had been the underground norm for a few years, with artists such as the Black Dog, Autechre, LFO, and Nightmares on Wax displaying a loose stylistic affinity, none of those artists outwardly pursued the electro muse beyond the use of breakbeat patterns versus four-on-the-floor beats and the odd old-school namedrop in interviews. Around the time of Clear's first few releases, however, electro's influence became far more pronounced in many artists (particularly Warp artists such as Autechre and Disjecta, and Global Communication/Link's Jedi Knights project), and electro-oriented labels starting popping up all over the place. Whether Clear grew out of a larger desire to explore electro's forgotten history or actually fomented it is up for argument, but the label nonetheless became the mouthpiece of a "new electro movement" (and one its founders hoped to distance themselves from).

Clear's early release schedule is dominated by established artists playing hooky under assumed names—Global Comm's Jedi Knights, µ-Ziq's Mike Paradinas as Tusken Raiders and Jake Slazenger, hardcore mainstay Acen as Space Pimp, and Black Dog offshoot Plaid—but Clear's release schedule has since diversified to include a solid, legitimate stable of original artists. Releases from Matt Herbert (Doctor Rockit), Clatterbox, and the Gregory Fleckner Quintet have all exhibited a flare for sharp, kicking beats and funk, jazz, and soul influences similar to those of early New York and Detroit electro artists such as the Jonzun Crew and Cybotron. Clear's sound is overall far more tongue-in-cheek, however, with electro serving as a rallying point for all manner of playschool cheekiness and casiotone noodling. As a result, some have discounted the label's output as gimmicky and derivative (a valid criticism in the case of some of the releases, which tend to be loop-heavy and underdeveloped), but the best of the label's relatively brief catalog is chunky and highly listenable. Clear released the label compilation *It's All Becoming Clear* in 1995, featuring the highpoints of its first year or so of releases, as well as an otherwise unreleased mix of Plaid's "Angry Dolphin."

## D-Jax Up-Beats

Originally established in 1990 as a subsidiary of the Dutch hip-hop label D-Jax, D-Jax Up-Beats later became the more recognizable of the two for its steady schedule of quality German house, acid, and techno 12"s. The label formed to accommodate D-Jax artist Stefan Robbers' Detroit-influenced sound, and early releases included twelves from Terrace, Edge of Motion, and Random XS. Although stylistically all over the map, D-Jax's catalog included a strong core of releases drawing heavily on the Chicago house tradition from such artists as Robert Armani, Steve Poindexter, Armando, Ron Trent, and

Mike Dunn, as well as Chicago originals such as Mike Dearborn, Paul Johnson, and Felix da Housecat. D-Jax also issued a number of CDs chronicling their release history as well as the strengths of individual artists.

## Digital Hardcore Recordings

Alec Empire's Digital Hardcore Recordings label releases breakbeat hardcore techno with simultaneous roots in extreme music forms such as speed metal, jungle, punk rock, and experimental noise. One of the more militantly political of the European techno labels, DHR was founded in part to combat what Empire perceived as the reactionary tendencies in German youth culture following the country's reunification, and many of the label's releases deal overtly with themes of social, political, and cultural uprising (making for something of a strained relationship between DHR and the more party-oriented mainstream club-world). Formed by Empire in 1994 with an advance from UK major Phonogram on an album that never materialized, DHR was originally a vehicle for Empire's performing hardcore trio Atari Teenage Riot, but quickly expanded to include such artists as EC8OR, DJ Bleed, Shizuo, Bomb20, and Sonic Subjunkies. With offices in both Berlin and London, DHR grew much more quickly than its comparatively modest release schedule would suggest, aided in part by the growing hardcore scene in Germany and the UK, as well as a domestic distribution deal with American hip-hop/jazz/funk/soul hybrid Grand Royal (home to Beastie Boys), finalized in 1996 and resulting in an expanding stateside audience.

## Dot

Sweden's Dot Recordings is one of the most notable and exciting new faces on the experimental electro scene. Formed by Anders Bersten in 1996, Dot announced itself in March of 1997 with four extremely high quality, subtlely innovative 12"s incorporating elements of funk, jazz, electro, techno, and melodic drum'n'bass. Inspired by the experimental fringe of dance-based electronic music, Dot's releases are characterized by a DJ friendliness that doesn't derive from the usual self-imposed simplicity of dancefloor trax, contributing to the stylistic evolution of the dance scene without relying exclusively on it. Dot's first releases attracted near-instant praise from such influential DJs as Mixmaster Morris and Laurent Garnier, and Dot's first label compilation, the CD-only *The Knights Who Say Dot*, appeared only a few weeks later. The label's roster includes New York electro artist Hab, London's Friend, Sweden's Quant, and Tupilaq; full-length releases by each of them appeared throughout 1997 and 1998. The label also released an extended compilation project, *Endlessnessism*, a sort of remix version of the popular children's game "telephone," with an initial track inaugurating a sequence of vaguely resembling remixes which the label plans to keep going "until the money runs out." After nearly two years of inactivity, Dot returned with a vengeance in 2000.

## Electrecord

Cologne-based electro label Electrecord is under the mysterious proprietorship of, apparently, partners Bolz-Bolz and Rootpowder, who together make up the label's only release fixture, Third Electric. Previously pretty obscure, the label began growing in popularity in 1996 after releasing a string of minimal but extremely funky 12"s by Third Electric, Kollute, and Minneapolis-based B-boy Freddy Fresh. Coveted for their steadfast commitment to electro's primary greys (808s, deep bass, cowbells, gratuitous vocal samples, etc.), Electrecord released its first CD, *Electrecord 1000*, in 1996, and received a big PR boost a few months later when popular Frankfurt label !K7 set up licensing for the longer, more varied *Electrecord 2000*. Based loosely on the first (it repeated exactly none of the tracks), the comp somewhat confusingly featured mostly American artists (including Freddy Fresh, Synapse, and Le Car side-project Artificial Material). Whatever its presumed focus, however, the album is an excellent document of groundbreaking '90s-style electro, and hints at the increasing stock-in-trade between Electrecord and American labels such as Sockett and Ersatz Audio (Rootpowder and Bolz released a 12" on the former and a split on the latter just following *2000*'s release).

## Ersatz Audio

Ersatz Audio was started by Detroit-based DJ/producer/painter Adam Lee Miller as a vehicle for his and artists Ian Clark, Kym Serrano, and Robert Salzmann's slowly-going-nowhere catalog of quirky bedroom trax. Frustrated by unrealized release plans through US- and UK-based labels such as Rephlex and Planet E, Miller and Co. began releasing their peculiar brand of electro- and new wave-inspired lo-fi electronica in 1995, with a series of twelves by Artificial Material (Miller), Lesseninglesson (Clark), and First Mode (Serrano). Ersatz Audio's fourth release was a various-artist EP compilation including the above; entitled *Omniolio*, it outlined the label's two abiding interests—dance music and the steady dismantling thereof. Subsequent releases on the label have included a split-EP between Artificial Material and German electro producers Third Electric (of the Cologne-based Electrecord label), the latter of who commissioned a pair of tracks from Miller for inclusion on a compilation entitled *Electrecord 2000*. Third Electric's Bolz Bolz also released a solo EP through Ersatz toward the end of 1997. Miller and Clark also established an Ersatz sublabel in 1996 called Monoplaza Record Co., set up to explore the more tongue-in-cheek, backward-facing of the pair's synthpop obsessions; most of Miller and Clark's releases under their most visible project name, Le Car, appeared through Monoplaza. Additionally, Ersatz/Monoplaza-related projects have extended to Austrian art terrorist collective Sabotage, which included a handful of Le Car tracks on their *Five* and *Electro Juice* compilations. The prescient retrospective *Ersatz Audio: The Forgotten Sounds of Tomorrow* appeared in 2000.

## Fax

Originally known for developing a style of melodic hard trance now closely associated with the German techno scene, the Frankfurt-based Fax label later evolved into a full-time ambient/experimental label with a release schedule dominated by projects involving its owner and operator, Pete Namlook. Although ambient tracks were often included as B-sides to early Fax trance 12"s, Namlook dove into full-length ambient work in 1993 with expatriate DJ and musician Dr. Atmo as Silence. A near torrent of releases followed—at one point at the rate of a CD per week—attracting collaborative and orginal works from some of the biggest names in club-based experimental electronic music, including Richie Hawtin, David Moufang, Jonah Sharp, Geir Jenssen, Tetsu Inoue, Atom Heart, Mixmaster Morris, and Bill Laswell. The Fax umbrella also includes several labels (the Main, World, and Sublabel being the most prominent), and Namlook established labels solely for individual artists as well (the Rather Interesting, Low, and KM20 labels for Atom Heart, Moufang, and Laswell, respectively). With the exception of a reissue series through Instinct during 1994-95 (*Air 1+2, Silence 1+2, Sad World 1+2*), all Fax releases are limited and have become highly collectible, often fetching alarming sums in fairs and auctions. The four-CD *Ambient Cookbook* and more double-CD *Genetic Drift* are the most comprehensive introductions to Fax's vast catalog.

## General Productions Recordings (GPR)

One of the most important and influential techno labels on the early European scene, GPR was formed in the late '80s in direct response to the increasingly throw-away nature of dance-based European electronic music. The label's early stable—including Hi-Ryze, Luke Slater, Beaumont Hannant, Nev, and Germ, among others—fused the creative potential of the early Motor City sound with more thought-out composition and complex arrangements, resulting in the first wave of the sort of "electronic listening music" later popularized by artists such as Richard H. Kirk, Autechre, the Black Dog (who released several 12"s and a short-form album through GPR), and the Warp, Source, Rephlex, and New Electronica labels, among others. Although experimental techno remained the thrust of GPR's catalog, releases also included ambient, house, and more dub-inflected techno. Like early Warp product, GPR's early catalog is littered with perennials that have nonetheless received very little play by DJs intimidated by their uncompromising experimentalism. GPR went into hibernation in the mid-'90s as many of their artists went on to acclaim at other, higher-profile labels, but the label resurfaced in late 1996 with a string of reissues from the "classics" vault, as well as new material from Luke Slater and Beaumont Hannant. A good (though hard-to-find) introduction to the label exists in *Equanimity*, a two-CD set featuring original tracks by many of the label's artists.

## Harthouse

Established in 1991 by German techno artist Sven Väth, Harthouse is the more experimental arm of Germany's Eye-Q label group, one of the largest and most high-profile sources of European techno and trance. Although Harthouse exists mainly as a DJ-centered 12" label, many of its most popular artists (including Hardfloor, Spicelab, Resistance D, and Alter Ego) have gone on to much wider success while remaining within the context of the label. Harthouse has issued literally hundreds of releases (mostly singles and EPs) in its lifetime, and is widely credited, along with other German labels such as Fax and Blue Room, with solidifying the German trance/techno sound. In addition to many compilations chronicling the label's ever-active release schedule, Harthouse released full-lengths from a number of artists, including Hardfloor, Soap, Alter Ego, Resistance D, and Pulse.

## Interdimensional Transmissions

Ann Arbor, MI-based experimental electro label Interdimensional Transmissions was founded in 1995 by Brendan Gillian as an outlet for his and partner Gerard Donald's releases as Ectomorph. Instantly hailed in connection with Ectomorph's deep space electronic funk, IT's first releases paired a typically Detroit obscurantism (no artist or label info beyond project and track titles) with a nod toward the collector's mentality (limited release runs, colored vinyl, etc.). The label remained an Ectomorph vehicle label until 1997, when it began releasing the "From Beyond" series of 12"s. IT's bid for proper label status, "From Beyond" featured cuts from such notable post-dance experimentalists as I-F, Mike Paradinas, Synapse, 4E, Plug Research, Gillian and Donald's alter-ego Flexitone, Soul Oddity side-project Phoenecia, and Detroit producers Le Car, DJ Godfather, Anthony Shakir, and Keith Tucker. The four-part series (again highly collectable, with hand-screened sleeves and a tiny segment pressed to colored vinyl) was compiled onto CD for a mid-October release, and is, overall, one of the most impressive assemblies of futuristic funk experiments released by an American label.

## Lo Recordings

Lo Recordings is the brainchild of Jon Tye, who has recorded together with Pete Smith as MLO and with Daniel Pemberton as 2Player, as well as solo as the ambient/noise/drum'n'bass nightmare Twisted Science. Formed by the producer in 1995 to encourage the "chance hybrids" and "musical mutations" that seem to be the motor of the experimental underground, Lo began without an artist roster, without a genre definition, and without a game plan beyond upping the ante in outbound experimental electronic music. To that end, Lo released many compilations, featuring an extremely wide range of artists working in any number of (sometimes overlapping, sometimes not) fields. The label's debut, *Extreme Possibilities* (named for an EP released by one of Tye's side-projects, 2Player), featured tracks by Luke Vibert (Wagon Christ, Plug), Omni Trio, Scanner, Boymerang, and Daniel Pemberton. Subsequent collections (*Collaborations* and *United Mutations*) pushed a combinatorial aesthetic, with artists who'd never worked together before commissioned to spend an afternoon (or overnight) in the studio together to see what they could come up with. Some of the more bizarre wild cards pitched into those scenarios included Sonic Youth's Thurston Moore, American experimental indie groups Tortoise and Ui, free jazz saxophonist Lol Coxhill, and Pere Ubu's David Thomas.

In addition to the label compilations (which nonetheless seem to be the focus), Lo also released a pair of 12"s. The first of these, released under the Slack Dog name, was a three-track industrial/ambient/jungle romp credited to Tye, Smith, Vibert, Bedouin Ascent's Kinsuk Biswas, and the Flowershop's Robin Proper-Sheppard, with Vibert and Biswas further emaciating the track on the flip. The label's second twelve (also released on CD-single) was probably its most bizarre idea to date: a remix session pitting Vibert, the Aphex Twin, Funki Porcini, and the Mellowtrons (the CD featured an additional remix by Ben Wilmott) against English cocktail casualty the Mike Flowers Pops, with the results ranging from warped, aqueous trip-hop to razored-up, schizoid drum'n'bass.

## Mego

Vienna's Mego label joins other Austrian sources of experimental dance music such as Cheap and Sabotage in making the capital city a hotbed of sorts for European electronica. Formed in 1994 by Ramon Bauer, Peter Meininger, and Andi Pieper, the label's odd-sounding name derives from a computer engineering acronym ("Mine Eyes Glazeth Over") for excessive displays of verbal technicality, usually by designers and engineers toward corporate upper-management, with the intent to confuse into acceptance. Mego's release history has included experimental ambient, dancefloor techno and electro, and straight-up hip-hop, but—like Sabotage and other critical and conceptual art-derived labels such as Sub Rosa and Ash International—usually with enough of a twist to suggest something deeper and more involved than mere "dance music." Bauer and Meininger came to Mego after years A&Ring for Mainframe (one of Austria's first techno labels), and were joined by Pieper (who maintains the label's Berlin studio) through a common interest in pushing dance-based music beyond the stylistic constraints of the DJ and dancefloor. Mego's stable has grown to include artists working in a number of different styles—including Pita (Peter Rehberg, electronica), General Magic (Bauer and Pieper, experimental ambient), Potuznik (Gerhard Potuznik, electro), DJ DSL (hip-hop), and the three-piece Farmers Manual (ambient and drum'n'bass)—many of whom have also released material on labels such as Ash International, Cheap, Disko B., Source, and Tray. In addition to more standard fare vinyl and CDs, Mego has also released CD-plus and interactive CD-ROM titles, as well as maintaining an internet-based sublabel, Falsch, whose releases exist only in RealAudio format (accessible at their WWW site, Mego Box, http://www.frank.co.at/frank/mego/index.html).

## Metalheadz

Noted drum'n'bass producer Goldie's Metalheadz label is among the first wave of experimental jungle labels pushing a futuristic aesthetic designed as much for home listening as for DJs and dancefloors. After issuing a numbered series of 12"s, including releases from Doc Scott, Dillinja, Hidden Agenda, Photek, J Majik, Lemon D, Source Direct, and Ed Rush, Metalheadz quickly rose to acclaim among both DJs and critics as a source of continuing development and innovation ever since the label was established in 1994. Although many of the label's early releases were influential examples of so-called "ambient jungle," featuring warm synth textures and, often, diva-style vocals, the label later branched out to include many different styles, including the darker, harder strains of artists such as Dillinja and Ed Rush and the shiny, metallic tech of J Majik and Source Direct. Metalheadz released its first label compilation, *Platinum Breakz*, in 1996, and followed with the second volume one year later.

## Mille Plateaux

The experimental arm of Frankfurt techno staple Force Inc., the Mille Plateaux label derives its name from the work of late French philosophers Gilles Deleuze and Felix Guattari, whose theoretical writings have been influential on a number of contemporary experimental electronic musicians. Established by Force Inc. proprietor Achim Szepanski in 1995 as a fount for the main label stable's more experimental leanings, the Mille Plateaux catalog to date, while extremely diverse, is unified by an almost academic attention to compositional subversion, with releases drawing from the more ponderous stretches of ambient, techno, electro, and contemporary experimental music in often difficult, usually fascinating hybrids. In addition to a stable of artists including Oval, Alec Empire, RIC/Steel, and Microstoria, Mille Plateaux has released a number of notable compilations collecting works from all corners of the experimental electronic underground, including the multi-volume *Electric Ladyland* series and the double-CD tributary *In Memoriam: Gilles Deleuze* (prompted by the philosopher's death in 1995).

## Mo'Wax

Although all and sundry repudiated the term (either for its colonialist implications or simply its facile ring), Mo'Wax nonetheless became almost indelibly stuck with the dubious honor of birthing "trip-hop" through a release history dominated by downtempo instrumental hip-hop fusions employing elements of jazz, funk, and soul and sparse, soundtrack-y ambiance. Formed in 1992 by North Oxford lad James Lavelle while still in his teens, the label grew from a sporadic 12"-based imprint to a widely recognized, sought-after institution, including international licensing through A&M records and a product line that eventually included records, CDs, record bags, club nights, and a book and poster publishing arm. Although like other period-defining labels Mo'Wax had a hard time keeping up with its own reputation, the label stayed fresh by seeking out artists working at the fringes of a variety of different genres—hip-hop, but also techno, electro, jungle, breakbeat house, and experimental electronica—and found widespread success by splitting its focus between the harder core of club DJs and the (comparatively more lucrative) masses of home listeners.

Lavelle was a columnist for the UK-based jazz/soul/fusion magazine *Straight No Chaser* when he decided to form Mo'Wax. A devotee of the underground club scene since his youth spent DJing and working in record shops, the decision grew out of a basic dissatisfaction with the waning edge of the Northern acid jazz scene, which was already beginning to provide its own alternative in groups such as Soul II Soul, the Black Dog, and Massive Attack. Lavelle grew up listening to hip-hop and electro, and was as deeply engaged in the Oxford sound system circuit, the growing acid house scene, the Sheffield bleep sound, and the increasingly hybridized hardcore and breakbeat scenes. Lavelle dropped a call for demos in his *SNC* column, and after sifting through a flood of tapes, began releasing the best of it under the Mo'Wax name (the name itself derived from a club night Lavelle once organized called Mo'Wax Please).

Although many who only later picked up on the Mo'Wax sound often considered the widely popular *Headz* compilation the label's first-fired shot, in fact the popular triple-LP/double-CD was preceded by a series of 12"s in a more recognizable (though more minimal and experimental) acid jazz vein. Mo'Wax's first label comp, *Royalties Overdue* was released in 1993, and collected the best of those A-sides, featuring cuts from RPM, La Funk Mob, Howie B., and Attica Blues. It would be the B-sides, however, that ultimately bent the most ears, and *Headz*, released in 1994, combined the most outbound of those with new tracks from DJ Shadow, Palm Skin Productions, U.N.K.L.E., Skull (aka Underdog), Nightmares on Wax, DJ Krush, and others. *Headz* was as big a hit as the label had ever seen, and the dreamy downtempo beats and New T'ing abstract experiments soon become a point of reference for a new generation of experimentalists (converging on labels such as Ninja Tune, Wall of Sound, Pussyfoot, and Cup of Tea) re-exploring hip-hop from the DJ's perspective.

The result, of course, became "trip-hop," a term coined by UK DJ magazine *Mixmag* in order to pigeonhole not only the Mo'Wax sound, but also the various explorations it engendered. While many labels bathed in the term, releasing comp after comp playing off the music's industry granted title, Mo'Wax's response was to find some new directions. The label launched the limited-edition sublabel/project Mo'Wax Excursions in 1995 to that end; five 12"s in each of the styles of hip-hop and techno, calling on new and established artists alike (IO, Big Bud, David Caron, Stasis, Howie B., the Prunes, etc.) in order to elude the encroaching categories of the genre-happy British (and American) music press. Although the Excursions releases were a bit of a mixed bag (the entire series was also released as a limited boxed set and, later, a mixed double-CD), it at least demonstrated Mo'Wax's commitment to reinvention, a commitment followed up in 1995 and 1996 with remix work from the cream of the British drum'n'bass crop, EP- and full-length releases from underground hip-hop vet Kool Keith (as Dr. Octagon), ambient electro chanteuse Andrea Parker, Parisian lounge-hop outfit Air, and the remix/re-release project involving American techno legend Carl Craig's classic "Bug in the Bassbin."

Capping perhaps the label's most productive year, Mo'Wax unveiled the massive (some would argue *too* massive) *Headz 2* project toward the end of 1996. A sprawling 4CD/8LP set split into two gorgeous, limited-edition bound packages (*Headz 2A* and *Headz 2B*), the set included tracks from the who's who of experimental underground beat music: Luke Vibert, the Beastie Boys, the Black Dog, DJ Shadow, Dillinja, Palm Skin Productions, Air, the Prunes, Massive Attack, DJ Food, Tortoise, DJ Krush, Folk Implosion, and dozens more. With an initial hardbound collectors edition limited to 5,000 and costing nearly $70 for the lot, the set was easily among the most ambitious compilation projects in indie history, and if nothing else cemented Mo'Wax's commitment to its own aesthetic.

While the novelty and diversity of the music Mo'Wax released was just as crucial to its success, of equal importance was its visual identity—a sort of abstract fusion of street culture and a European avant-garde sensibility, similar in style and tone to Mo'Wax music. Mo'Wax art director, Will Bankhead (a mate of Lavelle's, previously of Smash City Skates), as well as original artwork by legendary New York graffiti artist Futura 2000 and graphic artist and illustrator Mike Mills were the key factors. Futura's work graced just about every significant Mo'Wax release after *Headz* (including the covers for EP and full-length releases by DJ Krush, U.N.K.L.E., DJ Shadow, Innerzone, and the *Headz 2* comps and samplers). Many of these works, as well as various posters, postcards, and advertisements were compiled for the coffee table anthology *The Art of Mo'Wax*, published by the label in 1996.

Although Mo'Wax's stateside presence was sporadic and largely symbolic (they were the mainstream music press' underground darlings as "trip-hop" broke in 1995), Lavelle's cause was helped greatly by a licensing deal Mo'Wax signed with A&M Records in 1995. (Lavelle's friend Danny Miller, formerly of Mute Records, helped close the deal). Although the deal really only extended to big-name releases such as DJ Shadow and DJ Krush, increased visibility translated into increased demand for original Mo'Wax product. After just a few years of releases (and the Mo'Wax name irrevocably tied to A&M), Lavelle exited his own label to pursue outside A&R.

## Moving Shadow

Moving Shadow was founded by DJ and producer Rob Playford in 1991. Formerly of hardcore techno outfit 2Bad Mice (whose breakbeat firestorm "Bombscare" is widely credited as one of the first proper jungle tracks), Playford has steadily shaped Moving Shadow into one of the most respected, innovative dancefloor-oriented drum'n'bass labels, with an artist roster including Deep Blue, Flytronix, Dom & Roland, Blame & Justice, Higher Sense, Omni Trio, E-Z Rollers, Hyper-On Experience, and Technical Itch. Shadow's ever-evolving sound has tended increasingly toward the smoother, more melodic side, although later releases from Dom & Roland, Dead Calm, and Technical Itch proved there's more than room 'round the Shadow for the dark side of drum'n'bass. A number of high-quality compilations exist encapsulating the label's influential sound, including *The Revolutionary Generation*, *Transcentral Connection*, and *Storm from the East*. The label celebrated its 100th release in 1997 with a three part series of 12"s featuring mix and remix work from Dom & Roland, Goldie, Underworld, and the Shadow's own Rob Playford.

## New Electronica

A Division of England's Beechwood Music label (who released the influential *Mastercuts* and *Street Sounds* compilation series in the late-'80s/early-'90s), New Electronica was established in 1993 to release the more innovative edge of dance-based electronic music. Best known for its several-volume self-titled compilation series, New Electronica was among the first crop of English dance labels to push the concept of dance-based electronic music for an other than club-bound audience, and along with labels such as Warp, Rising High, Universal Language, and GPR, exposed artists such as Global Communication, the Black Dog, Richard H. Kirk, Kirk Degiorgio, and Steffan Robbers to a wider audience for the first time. Though steeped more than most in the Detroit tradition (NE comps have featured repeat appearances from Carl Craig, Juan Atkins, and Underground Resistance, as well as many European artists perceived as working directly in Detroit's aesthetic tradition), the label's steady expansion into experimental ambient, trip-hop, and jungle (later releases included Beck, Scanner, U.N.K.L.E., Photek, and Paul W. Teebrooke) kept the label fresh. New Electronica also gained reputation as a result of its releeationship with Degiorgio's widely respected Applied Rhythmic Technologies (A.R.T.) and Op-Art labels, releasing much of the 12" based imprints' material on CD for the first time through its three-volume *Objects D'A.R.T.* series.

## Ninja Tune

Ninja Tune is the axis of some of the most popular and influential artists in the UK breakbeat scene. Established by Coldcut's Jonathan More and Matt Black in the early '90s (after wincing through a major-label deal gone bad), Ninja Tune has since grown into one of the most respected names in British experimental beat music, home to artists such as DJ Food, Funki Porcini, Amon Tobin, the Herbaliser, Mixmaster Morris, DJ Vadim, the London Funk All-Stars, Up, Bustle and Out, and, of course, Coldcut. The funkier, more upbeat bastard twin of London trip-hop label Mo'Wax, Ninja Tune's focus on diversity—both through its main label as well as through sublabel Ntone—has benefitted from the rapid hybridization of British dance music culture, with the label's catalog containing everything from ambient dub, downtempo, and acid jazz to straight-up instrumental hip-hop, electro-funk, and spastic drum'n'bass. Although Ninja Tune began more or less as a vehicle for Black and More's instrumental breakbeat excursions (the pair were originally known for releasing the UK's first breaks record, "Say Kids, What Time Is It?," as well as for producing and remixing such smash club acts as Lisa Stansfield, Eric B & Rakim, and Queen Latifah), increasingly the label moved toward long-term artist development, with the release of numerous full-lengths and label compilations (including the mammoth two-CD/four-LP *Flexistentialism*). Although the label toyed with domestic arrangements through licensing agreements with Instinct and Shadow Records, Ninja Tune established a North American office in 1997 to bring its product directly to US and Canadian markets, supporting the task with bi-monthly club tours of Ninja Tune artists. Three years later, the label celebrated its tenth anniversary with the three-disc *Xen Cuts* compilation.

## Pork Recordings

Hull-based post-rave/trip-hop/jungle-house/whateva label Pork Recordings is, believe it or not, an eponymously titled label. Formed by Dave Pork in 1991, the label began as a vehicle for fellow Hullsters Fila Brazillia, whose early track "The Mermaid" attracted Pork-the-man's attention as the sort of impossible-to-nail-down funky electronic dance music he was interested in supporting. Expanding its stable primarily through the incessant side-projecting of in-house producer Steve Cobby (one-half of Fila, all of Solid Doctor, and one-third of Heights of Abraham), Pork-the-label grew rapidly to become one of the more respected peripheral dance music imprints; peripheral in the sense that Pork continued to take every opportunity to distance itself from the dance music world in its conventional form (based in Hull, far away from London's metropolitan cool; releasing mostly CDs vis a vis the vinyl-centrism of club culture; refusing to advertise; refusing to be photographed; etc.). Similar in ideology (though quite different in methodology) to ultra-indie labels such as Beyond and Fax, Pork play an active role in supporting innovative music without having to play any of the games typically associated with the music industry. Pork gained something of a steady and committed Stateside following early on as a result of a licensing deal with Jason Bentley's Island subsidiary Quango, which released the label comp *A Taste of Pork* in 1995 (although none of Pork's many subsequent full-lengths have seen domestic light). In addition to the above-mentioned acts, the Pork catalogue also includes releases by Bullitnuts and Baby Mammoth (as well as the combined side-project, Mammoth Nuts), and remixes of material by Lamb, DJ Food, and Nonplace Urban Field. The Pork crew also hosted the Hull-based weekly, Scuba.

## Pussyfoot

The London-based Pussyfoot label was formed by noted DJ/producer Howie "B." Bernstein in 1994 following recording and production work with a number of notable artists, including Soul II Soul and Massive Attack. An important convergence point for what would come to be know as trip-hop, Bernstein's work as Howie B. Inc. and Olde Scottish (released primarily through the Mo'Wax label) preceded his more high-profile work with Skylab, Björk, and U2. While he's released precious little of his own material through Pussyfoot (Bernstein signed with Polygram in 1995, with his debut full-length, *Music for Babies*, appearing that same year) his trailblazing fusions of hip-hop, funk, soul, and assorted atmospheric and electronic weirdness (both as a DJ and producer) exert a strong influence over the label's overall sound. Pussyfoot has released a number of 12"s and a handful of LPs by such artists as Spacer, Sie, and Dobie (the last of which Bernstein worked with in 4th & B'way acid jazz outfit Nomad Soul), as well as a series of label comps drawing from a range of experimental breakbeat artists (from the UK to the US to Japan). The label also collaborated with popular Brit-hop label Wall of Sound in 1995, co-releasing *Wall of Pussy* as EP and full-length compilations.

## R&S

The Belgian-based R&S label, formed in the mid-'80s by Renaat Vandepapeliere and Sabine Maes, grew into one of the largest and most visible sources for European dance music. Initially set up as a small house label with forays into acid and new beat (a sort of industrial techno-pop hybrid with strong roots in the Belgian scene), the label's predominant focus during the late '80s and '90s was on cutting-edge techno. While giving equal time to local talent, the label's extensive discography also included entries from an impressive array of international artists, from Detroit innovators such as Juan Atkins, Carl Craig, and Kevin Saunderson, second-wave techno names like Joey Beltram, David Morley, Kenny Larkin, and Laurent Garnier, and increasingly unclassifiable acts such as Tournesol, Biosphere, Locust, Wax Doctor, and Sun Electric. Of R&S' many sublabels—Apollo, Diatomyc, Global Cuts, Satori, and Generations—the ambient-leaning Apollo label was most active, releasing experimental EP- and full-length works by Ken Ishii, Andrea Parker, Manna, Tournesol, Locust, Uzect Plaush, and Sun Electric, as well several compilations. Although R&S' release schedule slowed during the early '90s, with key artists such as Aphex Twin, Carl Craig, and CJ Bolland jumping ship, the label initiated an aggressive release schedule later in the decade, repressing classic 12"s and lining up newcomers such as Wax Doctor and Small Fish with Spine for full-length release.

## Rather Interesting

A sublabel of Pete Namlook's Fax empire, Rather Interesting is the personal playground of Frankfurt composer Uwe Schmidt, aka Atom Heart. Although RI's discography includes solo outings from artists such as Dandy Jack and Victor Sol, the label's focus has been on Schmidt, who, at the rate of roughly a CD per month, has issued the bulk of his full-length solo and collaborative work through the label. Much of the material is a characteristic fusion of electro, ambient, and jazz elements, and has included solo works such as *Semi-acoustic Nature, Silver Sound 60, Machine Paisley,* and *Mono TM,* as well as collaborations with Tetsu Inoue (Datacide's *Flowerhead* and *Ondas;* Masters of Psychedelic Ambience's *MU*) and Haruomi Hosono (*Hat*). The RI compilation *Real Intelligence,* issued in CD and double-LP in 1995, serves as a solid, broad-based introduction.

## Reflective

Known for its holographic label stickers and sleeve graphics, San Francisco-based Reflective was the personal imprint of Spacetime Continuum's Jonah Sharp, who established the label in 1993 to release the Spacetime EP, *Fluoresence*. Reflective became synonymous with the bleeding edge of American experimental/ambient techno, releasing EP and full-length material by Velocette, Subtropic, and Single Cell Orchestra, as well as UK- and European-based artists such as MLO, Vulva, David Moufang (together with Sharp as Reagenz), and µ-Ziq's Mike Paradinas (as Kid Spatula). The CD/LP compilation *Synoptics* is the best introduction to the label's characteristic, influential sound.

## Reinforced

Reinforced Records is one of the oldest and most respected names in UK hardcore, the style of post-rave, superfast breakbeat techno that eventually mutated into jungle. Formed by Dego, Mark, Ian, and Gus of 4 Hero in 1990, Reinforced was the first home of Goldie, Manix, and Underground Software, and is one of the few early hardcore labels to evolve into and grow with the jungle scene. Although the label's early catalog is dominated by rave-y breakbeat and happy hardcore, later releases from some of jungle's most respected names (including Doc Scott, Jamie Myerson, Leon Mar/Arcon 2, Nookie, Seiji, Alpha Omega, and Lemon D) focused on futuristic hardstep and darkside, updating hardcore's scissored-up breaks with elements of dark ambient and techstep. The label's *Enforcers* series—periodic various-artist EP releases which feature new artists and revisitings of classic tracks—has also proven popular. In 1996, Reinforced became the first hardcore/jungle label to make it to its 100th 12" release, a feat the label celebrated with the release of the 10th *Enforcers* series release (a 2x10" picture disc mini-LP featuring Goldie, DJ Randall, and Lemon D, among others) and the label compilation *Above the Law* (the CD version of which included a catalog-spanning mixed CD by Metalheadz' Kemistry & Storm). Reinforced's history has also been attended by a few sublabels, including Tom & Jerry, Waterproof, and Reflective.

## Rephlex

The Cornwall-based Rephlex label was co-founded by Grant Wilson-Claridge and Richard "Aphex Twin" James in the early '90s as a source for experimental acid and techno. Although originally closely associated which James' Caustic Window, Joyrex, and AFX releases, Rephlex's ongoing development was later dominated by names such as Vulva, Mike Paradinas (aka µ-Ziq), Chris Jeffs (as Kinesthesia and Cylob), Mike Dred (as Chimera and Kosmik Kommando), and Italian artist Gianluigi Di Costanzo (aka Bochum Welt), artists who also gradually shifted the label's focus away from acid toward electro and experimental techno. In addition to its developing roster, Rephlex also released one-offs from Detroit's Drexciya, Luke Vibert (Wagon Christ, Plug), and the Lisa Carbon Trio (aka Atom Heart), and has served as a springboard of sorts for such renowned artists as Squarepusher and µ-Ziq. Although somewhat notorious for its sporadic, somewhat dodgy release schedule, Rephlex's reliability got a boost in 1996, with full-length releases from Cylob, DMX Krew, Leo Anibaldi, Mike & Rich (a collaboration between Mike Paradinas and Richard James), Chimera, and Bochum Welt, as well as scores of singles and EPs all appearing. The hectic release schedule continued unabated during the rest of the decade, as hordes of new artists (Bogdan Raczynski, Leila, Like a Tim, Ovuca, Ensemble) released full albums on the label.

## Sabotage

Vienna's Sabotage label is the musical arm of a cluster of a related activities, including guerilla-styled art terrorism, traditional gallery presentation, DJ-based musical events, and small press transmissions covering the collective's humorous, often illegal art-critical exploits. A curious combination of DJs and musicians, designers and advertising creatives, art activists and cultural monkeywrenchers, Sabotage was established in 1992 by five partners (among them artist and mouthpiece Robert Jelinik). Although one of Sabotage's primary activities is an ongoing commentary on modern society via public "art works" which foreground the fragile balance of power, knowledge, meaning, and context which organize public space and direct and delimit social behavior, the group has become increasingly active as a record label as well, focusing mostly on Vienna's vibrant experimental electronic underground. Sabotage has released a number of compilations featuring artists such as Patrick Pulsinger and Erdum Tanakan of Cheap Recordings; Pita and General Magic of the Mego label; Richard Dorfmeister of Kruder & Dorfmeister; local artists Def Con and Private Lightning Six; and Detroit electro institutions Ectomorph and Le Car. Most of the material released through Sabotage (as well as through sublabel Craft) involves a funky, idiosyncratic home-studio fusion of electro, techno, ambient, jazz, and funk similar in feel to labels such as Cheap, Mego, and Disko B. Neither are their prickly critical narratives limited to the sphere of public practice; many of Sabotage's releases have included a component of perplexity or subversion, either through misleading packaging (*The Lens Cleaner* appeared to be a standard CD player lens-washing product, but actually included over an hour of esoteric experimental music), humorous artwork (the limited edition *Unreleased* sported 1,000 different covers, each picturing a lo-fi reproduction of a prominent pop musician), or straight-up, well, *sabotage* (the *Handle with Care* CD+ contained a mild virus which disabled the computer's CD-ROM drive for a few hours). In addition to their music releases, Sabotage issued a slim, self-titled catalog of their art terrorist activities (including photographs and decriptions in German and English), as well as the magazine/fanzine/five-year compendium *Five*, released in 1997 and accompanied by a CD compilation of the same name.

## Schematic

Miami, FL's Schematic label rapidly became one of the most popular and acclaimed American experimental electronica labels. Formed in 1995 by a group of friends who, oddly enough, grew up listening to freestyle and Miami bass groups such as Dynamix II and 2Live Crew, the label's first string of releases included side-projects by members of electro duo Soul Oddity (Takeshi and Jeswa), as well as lesser-known or even unknown artists such as Richard Devine and Push Button Objects (aka Edgar Farinas). Although Schematic's earlier releases were heavily derivative of the style of intricate, "intelligent" electronica first explored by labels like GPR and Warp and artists like Autechre, Aphex Twin, Black Dog, and B12, the label was rapidly praised for its place among a new crop of stateside labels (also including Serotonin, Carpet Bomb, Interdimensional Transmissions, and Ersatz Audio/Monoplaza) reasserting an American presence in post-rave experimental techno largely absent since acid, house, and techno's early- to mid-'80s salad days. The message certainly wasn't lost on Schematic's mentors; Warp signed nearly half of Schematic's roster (Takeshi and Richard Devine) right out of the gate, with co-release and track-trading plans abounding with Autechre's Skam label.

## Silent

San Francisco-based sound designer Kim Cascone formed Silent Records in 1986 to release *Silence*, by his flagship project PGR. Although he's since moved on to record primarily as Heavenly Music Corporation and under his own name, Silent has grown to become one of America's leading labels for ambient and experimental techno. Most visible through its ongoing compilation series *From Here to Tranquility*, Silent also released full-length works by Ambient Temple of Imagination, Chris Meloche, Illusion of Safety, Thessalonians, 23 Degrees, and Elliott Sharp, among many others, and reissued works by David Moufang and Jorge Reyes. Silent is also an umbrella label for releases on Flask and Furnace, which focus primarily on harder-edged experimental and industrial music. Cascone sold the label in 1996 to work for Thomas Dolby's multimedia company, Headspace.

## Skam

The Manchester-based Skam label was established in 1994 by Andy Maddocks together with Autechre's Sean Booth and Rob Brown. A notable outlet for the harder-to-define stretches of experimental ambient/techno and electro, Skam has issued mostly one-off 12"s recognizable by their blank sleeves and braille labels. Applying its somewhat cheaky name to the label's first release (SKA01, despite persistent rumors, was a limited promo-only 12" entitled "Lego Feet"), Skam tends to focus more on breadth than depth in terms of artist development, and has issued a number of EPs by Autechre alias Gescom, as well as by Freeform, Bola, Jega, Boards of Canada, and Takeshi. Though most of the work is in a comparatively lo-fi vein, Skam's catalog stands firm as some of the most impressive, consistently inventive abstractions of UK post-rave dance-based electronic music on the contemporary scene. Although the label hasn't bothered with an artist compilation (with limited release runs adding to Skam's allure), US ambient/techno label Silent stepped in to fill that void in 1997 by issuing *Skampler*, which compiles a good portion of Skam's releases to date, as well as adding a few new surprises. Booth and Brown also established an even more limited offshoot of Skam in 1997, the elliptically monikered Mask, which released a series of sought-after compilation EPs. A distribution deal with the American indie Matador enabled debut full-lengths by Boards of Canada and Bola to gain stateside release.

## Skint

Similar to labels such as Wall of Sound, Compost, and Clean Up, Skint pioneered an eclectic blend of hip-hop, dub, jazz, and acid house that made it one of the more popular post-rave experimental dance labels. Based in Brighton, Skint was formed by Damian Harris in 1995 as an offshoot of English commercial dance imprint Loaded. Hired on by the Loaded office after a brief stint at the Brighton Art School, Harris (a DJ himself) tired of Loaded's mainstream focus early on, and approached the label's higher-ups about starting an offshoot geared exclusively toward breakbeat artists. Reply came in the form of a slim budget in support of a first series of releases ("skint" is a British-ism for being broke), among them Andy Barlow of Lamb's debut single (under the name Hip Optimist) and former Housemartin Norman Cook's first single as Fatboy Slim, the immensely popular "Everybody Loves a 303." Skint later became something of a revival house for former pop figures dabbling in electronica (in addition to the Housemartins Cook was a member of Beats International, Bentley Rhythm Ace contained a former member of Pop Will Eat Itself, and ex-Curve guitarist Alex Mitchell recorded for the label as Sparky Lightborne). Full lengths from Fatboy Slim, Bentleys, and Req appeared in 1996-97, and two volumes of Skint's label compilation series, *Brassic Beats*, were released to wide acclaim. Although the label's sound varied pretty widely from artist to artist—from Fatboy's rave-y acid funk and Bassbin Twins' electro-house to Req's vague ambient hip-hop—breakbeats remained the unifying factor. Skint signed a manufacturing/distribution and co-development deal with English major Parlophone in 1997, and established the tentatively titled Skint Under 5s label for more experimental artists.

## Strictly Rhythm

House label Strictly Rhythm is one of the most active, widely distributed dance labels in the world, encompassing several sublabels home to some of the biggest name producers and artists in all forms of garage and house music. Begun by Mark Finkelstein and Gladys Pizarro in 1988, Strictly Rhythm first focused on underground house to remain independent of the reliance on radio play to which many young labels fall prey. After a string of underground hits including Logic's "The Warning," "I Believe" by Scram, and "Strings" by Raw Power, SR broadened its scope to include deep, Latin, hip, and commercial house styles, with artists such as Little Louie Vega and in-house producer George Morel becoming regulars on the label's increasingly active release roster. SR's first label compilation *This Is Strictly Rhythm* was released in 1991, and the label upped its schedule to a release a month, snapping up now-classic tracks from Alyus ("Follow Me") and Reel 2 Reel ("I Like To Move It"), the latter of which remains one of the label's highest selling records to date. In 1993, A&R man DJ Pierre's string of hard-hitting acid tracks brought a diversity to the label which extended into several sublabels and distribution deals (including Groove On, owned by George Morel; Vestry Records, run by George Hess and Don McNatta of ADM; Freshly Squeezed, owned by producer Jeremy Cowa, aka DJ Digit; PhatWax, owned and run by Steve Rosen of 23 West Productions; and MAW, run by Steve Rosen, "Little" Louie, and Kenny Dope). Strictly is also one of America's largest licensers of European dance tracks. By the late '90s, the label was up to two releases a week, with artists such as Erick "More" Morillo and Armand Van Helden once again redefining their sound. With offices in five countries on three continents, SR has grown to one of the largest and most productive independent dance music labels in the world.

### Tresor

Renowned German techno imprint Tresor began as a popular club nite in Berlin's thriving techno underground before consolidating into a label in 1991. Literally "saferoom" (the club was held in the basement of what was previously one of Berlin's largest department stores), Tresor began as an outgrowth of the club playing host to touring Detroit artists such as Juan Atkins, Eddie "Flashin'" Fowlkes, and Jeff Mills, and was founded originally as a sublabel of Interfisch Records (a prominent EBM label supporting artists such as Clock DVA and the Final Cut). Although Tresor later came to be known as one of the most exclusive, consistently high-quality sources for European techno, the label's strongest ongoing connection has been to Detroit. Tresor's early release activity was confined almost exclusively to reissues of classic tracks by by Juan Atkins, Fowlkes, Mills, Rob Hood, and Underground Resistance (whose "Sonic Destroyer" was the label's first release). Releases by Cristian Vogel, Joey Beltram, Neil Landstrumm, and Si Begg helped expand the label's scope during the late '90s, and multiple snapshots of the ongoing evolution exist (the half-dozen-and-growing *Tresor* series).

### Underground Resistance

Underground Resistance is the stronghold of the new school of Detroit techno purists. Releasing periodic 12"s, often with minimal artist information, and staying almost completely underground in terms of media exposure and mainstream publicity ops, the label was formed in the early '90s by techno artist Mad Mike Banks as an outlet for the harder, less-compromised edge of third-wave Detroit techno. The label's roster includes releases under the UR banner (Banks and a rotating cast of collaborators), as well as EPs from Drexciya, the Suburban Knight, Scan 7, Andre Holland, Blake Baxter, X-102, and DJ Rolando. The label's focus is quite evidently on grubby, nuts-and-bolts dancefloor techno and electro, with elements of Chicago house and acid often in evidence. UR has released several sampler compilations on CD, and most of the label's catalog remains in print.

### Warp

Warp Records was formed in 1989 by Robert Gordon, whose early "bleep" techno 12"s with Unique 3, the Forgemasters, and DJ Mink helped (along with Cabaret Voltaire's Richard H. Kirk and LFO) define the direction of the nascent Sheffield techno sound. Forming Warp as an alternative to the progressively flooded (and watered down) UK house music scene, Gordon's first batch of releases included twelves from his own Forgemasters, Tricky Disco, Nightmares on Wax, and DJ Mink, as well as full-lengths by Kirk's Sweet Exorcist, LFO, and Wild Planet, before selling the label the following year. After a string of mostly misguided, second-rate club track releases following Gordon's departure, Warp righted itself in 1993 with the first of the *(Artificial Intelligence)* compilation series, which signaled a new direction for the label. The comp's focus was on "electronic listening music" (an atmospheric, armchair-oriented blend of bleep, Detroit techno, house, electro, and ambient, among other influences), and it presented now-celebrated artists such as Aphex Twin, B12, Speedy J, and Autechre to a wide audience for the first time. The label followed the comp with similarly-styled full-length releases from Black Dog Productions, Polygon Window (aka Aphex Twin), Autechre, Richard H. Kirk, B12, and Detroit original Kenny Larkin, as well as a second volume of *AI,* and quickly became one of the UK's leading sources of beat-oriented experimental electronica. A three-volume series of compilations (*Warp 10+1, Warp 10+2, Warp 10+3*) released to commemorate the label's tenth anniversary represented a fine, comprehensive introduction to the label's influential, widely-acclaimed catalog. Although closely followed in America by a small but committed audience willing to shell out at import prices, Warp's profile stateside was elevated by steady distribution programs, first by Wax Trax!/TVT and later Matador.

# Mail-Order Stores

**12 Inch Dance Records** Washington, D.C.
http://www.12inchdance.com/
*House/Club/Dance/Garage*

**Ambient Soho** London, England
http://www.ambientsoho.com/
*Electronica/Jungle-Drum'n'bass/Experimental*

● **Aquarius Records** San Francisco, CA
http://aquarius.bianca.com/
*Electronica/Experimental*

**Baba Luba** Tustin, CA
http://www.babaluba.tierranet.com/
*Ambient/Electronica/Experimental*

● **Bent Crayon Records** Cleveland, OH
http://www.bentcrayon.com/
*Techno/Club/Dance/Electronica/Experimental*

**Breakbeat Science** New York, NY
http://www.breakbeatscience.com/
*Jungle-Drum'n'bass/Club/Dance*

**Clone Records** Rotterdam, The Netherlands
http://home.box.nl/~clone/
*Electronica/Hardcore/Electro*

**Digital Underground** Philadelphia, PA
http://www.industrial-music.com/
*Industrial/Electronica/Experimental*

**Dr. Freecloud's Mixing Lab** Costa Mesa, CA
http://www.drfreeclouds.com/
*Funky Breaks/Trance/Psychedelic*

● **Dusty Groove** Chicago, IL
http://www.dustygroove.com/
*Rare Groove/Hip-Hop/Jazz-Funk/World*

**Eastern Bloc Records** Toronto, Canada
http://www.easternbloc.com/
*House/Club/Dance/Jungle-Drum'n'bass*

**Elevator Records** San Diego, CA
http://www.elevatorrecords.com/
*Techno/Club/Dance/Jungle-Drum'n'bass*

● **Forced Exposure** Somerville, MA
http://www.forcedexposure.com/
*Experimental/Techno/Ambient*

**Future Sounds** Pittsburgh, PA
http://users.dhp.com/~futursnd/
*House/Club/Dance/Jungle-Drum'n'bass*

● **Gramaphone Records** Chicago, IL
http://www.gramaphonerecords.com/
*House/Club/Dance/Techno*

● **Hard Wax** Berlin, Germany
http://www.hardwax.com/
*Techno/Experimental*

**Let It Be Records** Minneapolis, MN
http://www.letitberecords.com/
*Electronica/House/Trip-Hop*

**Manifold Records** Memphis, TN
http://www.manifoldrecords.com/
*Experimental/Noise*

**Melody Makers** Den Haag, Holland
http://www.xs4all.nl/~melodymk/dancepage.html
*Eurodance/House/Club/Dance/Trance*

**Mr. Bongo** London, England
http://www.mrbongo.com/
*Rare Groove/Hip-Hop/Jungle-Drum'n'bass*

**Music Beat Records** Birmingham, England
http://www.dircon.co.uk/mubeat/index.html
*House/Hi-NRG/Club/Dance*

**Online Records** Guildford, England
http://www.onlinerecords.co.uk/index.htm
*R&B/House/Club/Dance*

**Oracle Records** Altamonte Springs, FL
http://www.oraclerecords.com/
*Club/Dance/Funky Breaks*

● **Other Music** New York, NY
http://www.othermusic.com/
*Experimental/Electronica/Techno*

**Planet X USA** New Brunswick, NJ
http://www.planetxusa.com/
*Techno/Club/Dance/Trance*

**Racks of Wax** Leeds, England
http://dialspace.dial.pipex.com/town/estate/abc17/wax/
*House/Club/Dance/Rarities*

● **Record Time** Detroit, MI
http://www.recordtime.com/
*Techno/Club/Dance/Detroit Techno*

**Resonance Records** Sunrise, FL
http://www.netcreations.com/resonance/
*House/Club/Dance/Trance*

**Rough Trade** London, England
http://www.roughtrade.com/
*Experimental/Indie/Electronica*

**Rub-A-Dub Records** Glasgow, Scotland
http://dialspace.dial.pipex.com/town/road/sb86/main.html
*Techno/House/Club/Dance*

**Satellite Records** New York, NY
http://www.satelliterecords.com/
*House/Trance/Club/Dance*

**Section 5 Records** London, England
http://www.section5.uk.com/
*Jungle-Drum'n'bass/Club/Dance*

**Skimo** Ellicott City, MD
http://www.skimo.com
*Experimental/Electronica/Techno*

● **Smallfish** London, England
http://www.smallfish.co.uk/
*Techno/Club/Dance/Trance*

- **Sonic Groove** New York, NY
  http://www.sonicgroove.com/
  *Techno/House/Club/Dance*

  **SOS Records** Houston, TX
  http://www.sosrecords.com/
  *House/Trance/Club/Dance*

  **Streetsounds** Los Angeles, CA
  http://www.streetsounds.com/
  *House/Trance/Club/Dance*

- **Submerge** Detroit, MI
  http://www.submerge.com/
  *Techno/Club/Dance/Detroit Techno*

  **Tag Records** London, England
  http://www.tagrecords.co.uk/
  *Techno/Club/Dance/House*

  **Temple Records** New York, NY
  http://www.temple-records.com/
  *Techno/Club/Dance*

  **Tunnel Records** Hamburg, Germany
  http://www.tunnel.de/
  *Techno/Club/Dance/Trance*

  **Twisted Village** Cambridge, MA
  http://www.twistedvillage.com/
  *Experimental/Kraut-Rock/Electronica*

  **Urbandwax** Gainesville, FL
  http://urbandwax.com/
  *House/Club/Dance/Funky Breaks*

- **X-Radio** San Francisco, CA
  http://www.x-radio.com/
  *Electronica/Trip-Hop/Jungle-Drum'n'bass*

  **Zanzibar Records** Blackpool, London
  http://www.personal.u-net.com/~cev/zanzibar.html
  *House/Garage/Club/Dance*

# INDEX

## A

A Produce 8
A Trak 388
Ab Logic 529
Abacus 34
ABBA 22, 59, 171, 283, 369, 472
ABC 23, 38, 49, 60, 89, 259
Abdul, Paula 445
Abel, David 569
Above 454
Abrams, Colonel 60
Abrams, Muhal Richard 556
Absolute 316, 318
Abstract Soul 51
Abstract Truth 93
Abwarts 162
AC/DC 44
Accurso, Fabio 459
Ace of Base 548
Acen **1**, 93
Acher, Markus 362
Acher, Micha 362
Acid Horse 331
Acid Jesus 11
Acid, Anthony 513
Acquaviva, John **1**, 48, 293, 400, 404
Act 414
Acuna, Alejandro "Alex" 553, 554
Ad Lib 120
Adam & the Ants 125
Adams, Alistair 513
Adams, Bryan 89, 90
Adams, Glen 381
Adams, John 427
Adams, Oliver 279
Adamski **1**, 62
Adamson, Barry **2**, 163, 547
Add N to (X) **2**, 3, 281, 325
Adderley, Cannonball 34, 554
Addicus, Alexander 297
Addison, Ben 103
Addison, Scott 103
Ade 99
Adonis 1, 3, 179, 278, 285, 395, 445
Adonis 3
Adrenalin Junkies **3**
Adult 4, 296, 3
Advent **4**, 39, 50, 51, 329, 442, 475, 555
Adventures in Stereo **4**, 5
Aerial M **5**, 338, 522
Aerial Service Area **5**, 6
African Head Charge 155, 459, 524
Afro Mystik **6**
AFX 17
AG 6
Agætis Byrjun 461
Age **6**
Age of Love 100, 105, 266
Agent Cooper 382
Agent Provocateur 324
Aggrovators 282
Agitation Free 191
Agnelli & Nelson 100, 366, 367
Ailey, Alvin 309
Aim **6**, 359
Air Liquide **6**, 7, 83, 159, 188, 259, 260, 267, 279, 304, 336, 420, 447, 570
Air 6, **7**, 8, 114, 115, 134, 253, 271, 280, 298, 310, 325, 332, 344, 388, 439

Airto 118
Aitchison, Dominic 337
Akasha **8**, 135
Akil 275
Akimoto, Jim 473
Akita, Masami 362
Akwaaba 278
Al Comet 566
Alana 334
Albanese, Judy 511
Albarn, Damon 104, 525
Albert, Marv 166
Albini, Steve 522
Albion 105, 133
Alcatraz 123
Alexander, Leon 307
Alford, Tee 60
Alias, Charles 117
Alias, Don 554
Alicino, Christine 168
Alien Community 476
Alien FM 369, 526
Alien to Whom? 195
Alio Die **8**, 367, 430
All Purpose 185
Alladin 18
Allan, Stu 469
Allen, Daevid 293, 318
Allen, Marshall 495, 496
Allen, Michael 560
Allison, Dot **8**, 371
Allman Brothers 335
Allum, Rob 3
Almodovar, Pedro 440
Almond, Marc **8**, 9, 10, 45, 98, 99, 114, 472, 482
Almond, Marc & the Willing Singers 472
Alomar, Carlos 65
Alone Again Or 457
Aloof **10**, 11
Alpha 11, 484
Alpha Proxima 122, 508
Alpha Team 140, **11**
Alphaville 25
Alphonso, Roland 390
Alter Ego **11**, 437, 320, 540
Altern 8 **12**, 322, 326, 469, 565
Alternative TV 415
Alvarado, David 1
Aly Us 143
Ama, Shola 113
Amar 369
Amazon II 18
Amber Asylum 320
Ambient Temple of Imagination 463
Ambrosia 367
Amen UK 542
American Space Travellers 146
Amigos Invisibles 178
Amira 60
AMM 175, 377, 540
Ammons, Gene 34
Amnesia 164
Amnesia 163
Amoeba 430
Amon Düül **12**, 13, 14, 182, 402, 519
Amon Düül II 7, 12, 13, 14, 405
Amorphous Androgynous **14**, 204
Amos, Brian 551
Amos, Robin 109
Amos, Tori 62, 71, 106, 107, 108, 123, 282, 543
Amp 204
Amram, David 556
And Also the Trees 255

Anderson, Alfa 89
Anderson, Carleen 113
Anderson, Dave 12
Anderson, Deborah 142
Anderson, Emma 154
Anderson, Greg 556
Anderson, Jesse 526
Anderson, Jhelisa 100
Anderson, Jon 204, 506, 542, 543
Anderson, Laurie **14**, 15, 59, 168, 268, 293
Anderson, Pink 396
Anderson, Ryan 204
Andrews Sisters 23, 478
Andy, Horace 11, **15**, 16, 316, 459
Angel Alanis 37
Angel 178, 268, 269
Angel, Dave **16**, 62, 264, 333, 404, 408, 482, 557
Angevin, Monique 358
Angus, Colin 333, 407, 457, 458
Animals on Wheels **16**
Anniky, Simon 275
Anoesis 140
Ant, Adam 278, 560
Antheil, George 183
Anthoni, Mark 258
Anthony Child 497
Anthony, Marc 318, 546
Anthrax 417, 418
Anti Group 91
Anti Pop Consortium **17**
Apache Indian 28, 524
Aphex Twin 7, 16, **17**, 18, 31, 32, 53, 56, 57, 61, 67, 73, 77, 86, 112, 113, 122, 131, 148, 153, 158, 161, 197, 202, 253, 263, 270, 282, 286, 297, 304, 320, 339, 342, 344, 345, 346, 348, 349, 373, 375, 382, 384, 387, 400, 403, 404, 423, 427, 439, 455, 461, 473, 483, 484, 502, 529, 532, 544, 547, 549, 550, 551
Aphrodisiac 327, 547
Aphrodite **18**
Aphrodite's Child 542, 543
Aphrohead 106, 182
Apollo Four Forty **19**, 204, 404
Apple Fiona 275, 342
Apples in Stereo 104
Appliance **19**, 424
Aquarius 74, 394
Aquasky **19**, 288
AR Kane **20**, 40, 101, 135, 308, 316
Arab Strap 8
Araiza, Carlos 6
Arc 203, 340, 567
Archer, Mark 12, 54
Archive **20**
Arcon Two **21**, 204, 355
Arecibo 306
Ariel 281
Arkarna **21**, 555
Arkestra 265
Arlen, Harold 70
Armando **21**, 36, 52, 182, 199, 395, 445, 524
Armani, Robert 21, 52, 504
Armatrading, Joan 150
Army of Lovers **21**, 22, 289
Arnold, David 28, 55
Arnold, P.P. 45, 424
Arovane **22**, 545
Arrested Development 366
Arsonists 146
Art Ensemble of Chicago 260, 477
Art of Noise 19, **23**, 151, 298, 413, 414, 510

Art of Trance 105, 423
Artemis 59, 75
Artery 339
Arthur, Neil 59, 188
Artifacts 563
Artificial Material **24**, 62, 125, 296, 516
As One **24**, 32, 56, 58, 110, 303, 325, 368, 426, 456, 477
Asante 294
Ash Ra Tempel **24**, 25, 96, 109, 448
Ash, Daniel 415
Asha Vida 204
Ashcroft, Richard 145, 537, 538
Ashford & Simpson 134, 278
Ashley and Jackson 183, 473
Ashley, Robert 343
Ashra 25
Ashworth, Barry 155
Asian Dub Foundation **25**, 26, 199, 272, 437
ASKO Ensemble 545
Aslett, Phil 475
Asquith, Gary 427, 428
Assembly 170, 171
Associates 19, 320, 564
Astral Pilot 422, 546, 566
Astral Projection **26**, 366
Astralasia **26**
At the End of the Cliché 106
Atari Teenage Riot 3, **27**, 63, 160, 166, 281, 382, 459
ATB 439
Atkins, Juan 4, 16, **27**, 28, 40, 58, 106, 107, 111, 121, 147, 159, 160, 164, 189, 190, 259, 260, 266, 293, 304, 321, 322, 323, 336, 351, 356, 368, 384, 385, 400, 404, 407, 442, 445, 446, 457, 509, 511, 515, 526, 545, 552
Atkins, Martin 331, 419, 465
Atlas, Charles 85
Atlas, Natacha **28**, 29, 524
Atmosfear 123
Atom Heart 5, **29**, 30, 47, 54, 67, 115, 116, 154, 185, 205, 261, 271, 296, 300, 352, 353, 361, 428, 456, 460, 461, 511, 523, 540, 547
Attica Blues **30**
Aube **30**, 31, 288, 301
Audio Clash 143
Audio Sports 90, 502
Audioweb 194, 313
Auger, Brian 269
Aurobindo 455
Autechre 17, 22, **31**, 32, 35, 56, 60, 61, 67, 77, 112, 113, 131, 136, 138, 153, 177, 178, 179, 186, 188, 193, 202, 260, 263, 264, 269, 270, 271, 279, 304, 305, 313, 320, 325, 349, 351, 362, 378, 382, 383, 384, 385, 386, 394, 400, 408, 420, 423, 451, 455, 461, 465, 466, 468, 473, 476, 477, 480, 482, 483, 519, 522, 533, 545, 547
Auteurs 7, 346
Autocreation **32**, 33, 303, 456
Autodidact 509
Automaton 508
Automator **33**, 149, 412
Aux 88 24, **33**, 34, 93, 369, 457, 526, 554
Average White Band 67, 393, 475
Avesta, Zend 137
AVI Nissim 26
Aviance, Kevin 185, 442
Awtsventin, Nico 16
Axelrod, David **34**
Axus **34**
Ayers, David 425

Ayers, Kevin 369, 532
Ayers, Nigel 305
Ayers, Roy 189, 317, 364, 393, 511, 519
Ayres, Ben 94, 104
Ayuli, Alex 20
Aznavour, Charles 10
Aztec Camera 45
Aztec Mystic 144
Azymuth 404

# B

B-52's 22, 27, 164, 334, 456
B Sides 21
B12 11, 16, 17, 24, 31, **35**, 39, 56, 110, 188, 203, 259, 264, 279, 356, 400, 428, 467, 480, 509, 547
B., Bizzy 148, 152, 153
B., Howie **35**, 55, 137, **275**, 333, 427, 458, 466, 469, 537, 556
B., John **35**, 36, 138
B., Mark **36**
B., Matthew 295
B., Mikee 153
B., Tony 18
Baboon 558
Baby Bam 274
Baby Doc 295
Baby Ford **36**, 62, 170, 549
Baby Mammoth **37**, 523
Baby Namboos **37**
Babyface 60, 300, 442
Bach, Johann Sebastian 116, 430
Bacharach, Burt 7, 11, 62, 63, 280, 377, 398, 433, 470
Bachman Turner Overdrive 523
Backfire 298
Bacon, Francis 441, 479
Bacon, Kevin 313
Bad Boy Bill **37**, 548
Bad Company 133
Bad Seeds 2
Bad Street Boy 382
Baden-Powell, Ed 113
Badly Drawn Boy 538
Badmarsh & Shri 280
Badrena, Manolo 553, 554
Badu, Erykah 352
Bagnoud, Frank 565
Bahamadia 342
Bailey, Derek 142, 261, 377, 489, 521, 569
Bailey, Lorna 86
Bailey, Richard 170
Baines, Pete "Bassman" 175, 475, 479
Baker, Arthur **37**, 38, 185, 289, 357, 386, 400, 443, 545
Baker, Chet 430
Baker, Jim 475
Baker, Robert 95
Baker, Ron 441
Balance, John 98, 99, 109, 305, 415
Balanescu Quartet 509
Balanescu, Alexander 365
Balch, Michael 198
Baldwin, Terry 260
Balfe, David 283
Balil 56, 107
Ball, Dave 10, 77, 415, 416, 472
Ballistic Brothers **38**, 57, 58
Balloon 70
Bambaataa, Afrika **37**, **38**, 39, 111, 161, 194, 270, 274, 287, 296, 298, 351, 386, 400, 469, 554, 555, 559
Bambaataa, Afrika & the Soul Sonic Force 38
Bananarama 173

Banco de Gaia 26, 29, **39**, 443
Bandulu **39**, 160, 474, 475
Bang the Party 4, **39**, 511
Bang, Billy 318
Bangalter, Thomas 114, 115, 327, 463, 484
Bango 461
Banks, Alex 175
Banks, Mad Mike **39**, 40, 144, 328, 340, 369, 415, 446, 494, 526, 534, 535, 548, 554
Banks, Michael 457
Bantam Rooster 391
Banton, Pato 308
Bar Kays 160
Baraki **40**
Barbarella 263, 546
Barber, Samuel 374
Barbieri, Richard 90, 267, 405
Barclay 85
Bard, Alexander 21, 22
Barda, Jean-Pierre 21, 22
Bardot, Brigitte 191
Bargeld, Blixa 162, 163, 254, 424
Bark Psychosis **40**, 67, 135
Barker 161
Barker, Andrew 161
Barker, Clive 99
Barker, David 188
Barker, Paul 331, 332
Barker, Roland 331
Barlow, Andy 292, 326
Barlow, Lou 468
Barnard, Martin 11
Barnes, Lloyd 15, 389
Barnes, Neil 296
Barnes, Ted 378
Barnett, James 21
Barnett, Thomas 429
Baron, Joey 569
Barrett, Aston 389, 469
Barrett, Carlton 381, 389
Barrett, Syd 8, 9, 188, 297, 330, 373, 396, 397, 405
Barron, Bebe 288
Barron, Louis 288
Barrott, Mark 203
Barrow, Geoff 88, 406, 407, 438, 470
Barrow, Steve 282
Barry, Jeff 378
Barry, John 134, 188, 335, 375, 414, 516
Barry, Philip 108
Barry, Stephen James 92
Bartel, Beate 162
Barth, James 298, 333
Bartholomew, Simon 67
Bartok, Bela 364
Bartos, Karl 165
Bas Noir 547
Bascom, Austin 34
Base, Rob 141
Base, Rob & DJ E-Z Rock 356
Basement Boys 458, 488, 531
Basement Jaxx 41, 54, 93, 264, 431, **40**
Basia 442
Basic Channel 28, **41**, 69, 94, 313, 320, 321, 382, 384, 403, 405, 406, 504, 515
Basie, Count 336
Basil, Toni 356
Basoski, Olav 16
Bass Hit 547
Bass Junkie **42**, 148
Bassbin Twins 180, 194, 278
Bassey, Shirley 564
Bassomatic **42**, 374

Bastro 468, 522
Bataan, Joe 37, 441
Bates Motel 478
Bates, Martyn 305, 451
Battle Systems 42
Batu 470
Bauer, Ramon 407
Bauhaus 267
Baumann, Peter 191, 434, 448, 504, 505, 518
Baxter 68
Baxter, Blake 28, **42**, 43, 322, 445
Baxter, Damon 129, 368
Baxter, Les 116
Bay City Rollers 99
Bayle, Francois **43**, 447, 515
BBC Radiophonic Workshop **43**
BBE **43**, 71
Beach Boys 104, 115, 301, 354, 411, 416, 487
Beale, Darren 122, 508
Beanfield 34, **44**, 187
Bear, Booga 88
Beastie Boys 27, 33, **44**, 45, 47, 92, 104, 111, 119, 143, 145, 157, 166, 172, 180, 258, 259, 309, 334, 338, 366, 386, 388, 389, 412, 471, 489, 494, 532, 550
Beat Club 53
Beat Junkies 262, 280
Beatles 13, 54, 87, 88, 104, 121, 126, 156, 161, 185, 283, 284, 330, 343, 439, 440, 551, 560, 565
Beatmasters **45**, 457, 458
Beatnuts 563
Beats International 42, **45**, 46, 142, 180
Beatsystem **46**
Beattie, Jim 4, 5
Beatty, Warren 310
Beautiful Bend 326
Beautiful People 546
Beaver & Krause **46**
Beaver, Paul 46
Beber 72, 193
BeBop Deluxe 363
Beck **46**, 47, 104, 143, 157, 494, 512
Beck, Jeff 38, 506
Becton, Shelton 285
Bedford, David 369
Bedhead 484
Bedouin Ascent **47**, 463, 522
Bedrock 133, 134, 443
Beedle, Ashley 38, 57, 58
Beenie Man 194
Beerbohm 337
Beeston, Julian 108, 360
Beethoven, Ludwig van 84, 440
BEF **47**, 48
Begg, Si **48**, 63, 72, 73, 79, 80, 103, 340, 548, 549
Behles, Gerard 340
Behrman, David 102, 355
Being 566
Beinhorn, Michael 38, 293, 318, 319
Bekker, Okko 518
Bel Canto 53
Belew, Adrian 14, 72, 268, 359, 360
Bell, Andy 170, 171, 172
Bell, Archie & the Drells 564
Bell, Dan **48**, 49, 69, 121, 566
Bell, Mark 55, 56, 163, 299, 545
Belle & Sebastian 303
Bellotte, Pete 343
Belly 422
Beloved 28, **49**, 123, 161, 202, 346, 442
Beltram, Joey 4, 28, 36, **49**, 50, 62, 121,

147, 182, 323, 327, 329, 374, 457, 469, 491, 504, 545, 555, 566
Beltran, John **50**, 258
Bemand, Chris 57
Benediktsson, Einar Orn 55
Benitez, Jellybean 173, 270, 271, 277, 309, 443
Benitez, John 270
Bennet, Anthony 255, 256
Benson, George 117, 278, 317, 364, 546, 547
Bentley Rhythm Ace 35, **50**, 302, 326, 404, 428
Bently, Daum 192, 463, 464
Berberian, Cathy 50, 81
Berg, Alban 544
Berger, Karl 102, 294
Berigan, Bunny 452
Berio, Luciano **50**, 51, 426, 489
Berkovi, Justin **51**
Berlin Symphonic Film Orchestra 191
Berlin 270
Berne, Tim 568, 569
Bernocchi, Eraldo 293, 294, 451
Bernstein, Howard Howie 466
Berry, Chuck 82
Berry, John 44
Bertei, Adele 38
Beta Band **51**, 119
Bethell, Craig 303
Betke, Stefan 22, 69, 93, 94, 190, 361, 403
Beverly Hills 808303 253
Bey, Hakim 72
Beyer, Adam **51**, 258, 298, 346, 470, 555
Bez 57
BFC 108, 415, 504
Bi Face 29
Biafra, Jello 100, 140, 331, 354
Biegel, Dave 74
Big Apple Band 89
Big Audio 51
Big Audio Dynamite **51**, 52, 152
Big Audio Dynamite II 51
Big Ben 394
Big Bud **52**, 75, 177
Big City Orchestra 518
Big Country 533
Big Daddy Kane 172, 310, 315, 316, 412
Big Eye 466
Big in Japan 192, 283, 284
Big Kwam 19
Big Shug 19
Big Wheel 468
Bigfoot 48, 79
Bigg Jus 102
Bigod 20 **52**
Bijl, Gert-Jan 456
Bill Ding 467
Biochip C 7, **52**, 53, 148, 159, 188, 193, 194, 259, 279, 304, 404, 408, 420
Biogen 461
Bionaut 336
Bionic Skank 267
Biosphere **53**, 54, 124, 313, 342, 352, 529, 532
Bird, Bobby 53, 193, 352
Bird, Martina Topley 525
Birgisson, Jón fíor 461
Birkin, Jane 2
Birthday Party 97, 162, 350
Birtwistle, Harrison 364
Bischoff, John 255
Bishop, Jeb 377

Bisk **54**, 460
Bismark 84
Bissmire, Jamie 39, 475
Biswas, Kingsuk 47, 463
Bitney, Dan 264, 522
Biz Markie 315, 316, 460
Bizarre Inc. **54**, 170, 277, 469
Bizz OD 188, 279, 512
Bjork 35, **54**, 55, 56, 100, 134, 161, 162, 175, 177, 202, 255, 297, 299, 310, 339, 342, 346, 359, 383, 399, 428, 437, 461, 463, 466, 474, 513, 525, 536, 541, 545
Bjorkenheim, Raoul 450
Black Balls 3, 179
Black Box **56**
Black Dog 11, 16, 17, 24, 28, 35, 39, 47, 55, **56**, 57, 61, 70, 71, 77, 110, 115, 203, 254, 259, 264, 269, 271, 399, 400, 427, 428, 429, 435, 461, 467, 482, 484, 495, 496, 518
Black Grape **57**, 402
Black Jazz Chronicles 58, **57**
Black Lung 459
Black Man 446
Black Sabbath 103, 180, 269, 330
Black Science Orchestra 38, 57, **58**, 179, 182
Black Sheep 199
Black Tape for a Blue Girl **58**, 59
Black Uhuru 469, 515
Black Watch 58
Black, Cilla 69
Black, Matt 48, 62, 79, 99, 100, 125, 138, 263
Blackalicious 145, 359
Blackouts 331
Blackstreet 302
Blackwell, Chris 389
Blackwood, Sarah 156
Blade 36
Blake, Karl 256
Blake, Tchad 91
Blake, William 34
Blakey, Art 483, 539
Blame **59**, 74, 75, 254, 275, 401
Blancmange 59, 188
Blank, Boris 564
Blas, Johnny 108
Blaze 28, **60**, 93, 392, 557
Bleau, Roy 493
Bleep 53
Bley, Carla 556
Bley, Johann 274
Blige, Mary J. 201
Blij, Gert-Jan 456
Block 129
Blond 295
Blondie 56, 99, 173, 277, 446, 459
Bloom, Michael 109
Bloomfield, Michael 46
Blossom, David 183
Blossom, Nancy 183
Blow, Kurtis 555
Blu Mar Ten 75
Blue Arsed Fly 292
Blue Boy 178
Blue Maxx 555
Blue Nile **60**
Bluebells 57
Blum, Jason 124
Blume, Danny 553
Blur 5, 374, 406, 486
BMX Bandits 203
Boards of Canada 22, **60**, 61, 81, 178, 202, 280, 473

Bocca Juniors 178
Bochum Welt 60, **61**, 112, 153, 186, 282, 296, 297, 300, 387
Bogaert, Jo 509
Bogart, Neil 324
Bohem, Leslie 477, 478
Boito, Mike 473
Bola **61**, 202
Bolan, Marc 64
Bolder, Trevor 64
Bolland, CJ 4, 28, 36, **62**, 179, 544, 566
Bolo, Yami 381
Bolton, Michael 465
Bolton, Mike 393
Bolz Bolz 62, 516
Bomb Squad 99, 135, 164, 172, 417, 418
Bomb the Bass **62**, 63, 129, 161, 190, 288, 289, 368, 437
Bomb20 **63**
Boncaldo, M. 283
Bond, Victoria 537
Bonds, Martin 356
Bone Thugs N Harmony 288
Bones, Frankie **63**, 194, 442, 548
Bongwater 201
Bonham, John 45, 349
Bonnie, Carl 427
Bono 60, 336
Bonzo Dog Band 150
Boo Radleys 350, 455
Boo, Betty 45, 482
Boogie Down Productions 100, 194, 302, 333, 412, 417, 516, 532
Book of Love 270
Booker T. & the MG's 89, 302, 507
Boom Bass 85, 199
Boom Boom Satellites **63**
Booth, Sean 31, 32
Boothe, Ken 15
Borden, David 343
Borealis, Aurora 37
Boredoms 90, 91, 502
Borrell, Craig 143, 331, 494
Bortolotti, Gianfranco 83
Boston 523
Botti, Chris 142
Boucher, Andy 45
Boulderdash **64**
Boulez, Pierre 90, 322, 447, 489, 526
Bowden, Chris 382
Bowers, Tony 157
Bowery Electric **64**, 154
Bowie, David 9, 12, 29, 18, 59, 63, **64**, 65, 66, 89, 132, 150, 161, 167, 170, 196, 267, 296, 355, 362, 363, 412, 413, 520, 533, 547
Bowles, Paul 303
Bowling Green 67, **66**
Bowman, Rob 201
Bowne, Dougie 91
Box 95
Boy George 38, 298, 366, 387
Boykins, Ronnie 495
Boyle, Judith 4, 5
Boyle, Ruth-Ann 370
Boymerang 36, 40, **67**, 151, 436
BPT 134
Bracegirdle, Nick 89, 90
Bradbury, Ray 43
Bradfield, James Dean 162
Bradshaw, Steve 188
Bragg, Billy 45, 156, 164
Braheny, Kevin 429, 432, 485
Brain Bashers 131
Brain 72
Braincell 298

Brainstorm 488
Braithwaite, Stuart 337
Bran, Tim 152
Branca, Glenn 568
Brand New Heavies **67**, 68, 89, 113, 134, 269, 296, 317, 342, 393, 527, 548
Brandy 189
Brann, Chris 551, 552
Brashear, Todd 468
Braxe, Alan 484
Braxton, Anthony 568, 569
Braxtons 547
Bray, Stephen 309
Breakbeat Era **68**, 464
Breakfast Club 309
Breaks, Danny **68**, 133, 401
Brecht, Bertolt 121
Breeder 443, 444, 454
Breeders 332, 468
Brekelmans, Reinier 416
Brel, Jacques 8, 9, 10
Brennan, Maire 89, 90
Brennan, Max 194, 195, 537
Brenner, Simon 503
Brewer, Matt 341
Bricheno, Tim 518
Bricker, Pam 515
Bricusse, Leslie 327
Bright 204
Brikha, Aril **68**, 69, 254, 255, 567
Brilliant 274, 283, 372
Brinkmann, Ester 69
Brinkmann, Thomas 49, **69**, 94, 125
Briottet, Danny 427, 428
Brissett, Bunny 381
Broadcast 4, **69**, 344, 402
Broadrick, Justin K. 47, 184, 254, 508, 509
Brodsky Quartet 55
Brokesch, Susanne **70**
Bronski Beat 494
Brook, Michael **70**, 330
Brook, Rachel 187
Brooklyn Funk Essentials 91
Brooks, Harvey 117
Brooks, Mel 568
Broom, Mark 36, **70**, 71, 399, 428, 484
Brother from Another Planet 566
Brothers in Rhythm 454
Brotzmann, Peter 293
Broudie, Ian 283, 428
Broussard, Gregg 161
Brown, Andy 271
Brown, Angie 54
Brown, Arthur Crazy World 413
Brown, Bobby 277
Brown, Bundy K. 5, 54, 129, 134, 158, 522
Brown, Carter 290
Brown, Dennis 469
Brown, Duncan 486
Brown, Earle 526
Brown, Ian 6, 491, 492
Brown, James 38, 67, 89, 99, 116, 134, 141, 160, 172, 200, 273, 278, 282, 284, 307, 315, 319, 385, 386, 404, 411, 428, 508
Brown, Jocelyn 257, 317, 364, 441, 513
Brown, Karl "Tuff Enuff" 527
Brown, Kathy 318
Brown, Norman 473
Brown, Overton 450
Brown, Rob 31, 32
Brown, Rupert 194, 537
Brown, Stephen 292
Brown, Steven 388
Brown, Terry Lee Jr. **71**, 316
Brownie, Noel 156

Browse, Paul 95
Brubeck, Dave 284
Brucken, Claudia 414
Brundtland, Torbjon 155
Bryant, Dana 294
Bryars, Gavin 168, 461
Brydon, Mark 338
Brzezicki, Mark 533
BT **71**, 105, 193, 456, 509, 520, 542
Buchanan, Paul 60
Buchanan, Wallis 266
Buchen, Bill 294
Buckethead **72**, 293
Bucketheads **72**, 317, 364, 442, 547
Buckfunk 3000 48, 63, 79, 80, 340, 510, **72**
Buckler, Ethan 468
Buckley, Jeff 556
Buckley, Tim 121
Budd, Harold 70, **73**, 74, 97, 100, 168, 190, 330
Budd, Roy 92
Buess, Alex 147, 254, 450
Buffalo Daughter 104, 330, 353, 489
Buffalo Springfield 34, 418
Bug 147
Bugs **74**
Bukem, LTJ 19, 52, 59, **74**, 75, 166, 175, 177, 181, 189, 203, 254, 275, 284, 358, 366, 371, 379, 391, 393, 394, 395, 435, 452, 463, 464, 474, 493, 552
Bullen, Nicholas James 293, 305, 451
Bullet LaVolta 109
Bullitnuts 29, 485
Bunny, Bingy 283
Burden, Lawrence 368
Burden, Lenny 368
Burden, Lynell 368
Burdon, Eric 25
Burger Industries 336
Burger Ink 75, 260, 304, 336
Burger, J. 7, 75, 259, 260, 279, 304, 336, 337
Burgess, Tim 88, 438
Burke, Byron 445, 488, 510
Burke, Clem 173
Burke, Dan 377
Burning Spear 15, 469
Burns, Gary 10, 437
Burroughs, William S. 14, 318, 319, 483
Burrows, Bryn B. 195
Burton, Gary 117
Burwell, Carter 265
Buscemi **75**
Bush 525
Bush, Alan 364
Bush, Glyn 433
Bush, Kate 289, 500
Bussotti, Sylvano 526
Butch Quick 547
Butcher, Blinda 350
Butler, Paul 194
Butler, Tony 42, 93, 193, 394, 408
Butterfly 189, 282, 510
Butthole Surfers 331, 374
Buxton, Felix 40, 41
Buzzcocks 404
Byard, Jaki 556
Byles, Junior 391
Byrd, Donald 269
Byrd, Joe & the Field Hippies 537
Byrd, Joseph 537
Byrne, David 20, 89, 104, 167, 168, 170, 196, 293, 342, 436, 440, 515, 527
Byrne, Phelim 119
Byzar **75**, 76, 146, 552
BZet, Stevie 546

## C

C & C Music Factory 77, 278, 307, 308, 512
C Schulz 447
C12 134
C., Andy 376, 377, 423
C., Patric 159
Cabaret Voltaire 2, 31, **77**, 78, 79, 86, 95, 162, 165, 283, 361, 364, 427, 442, 459, 465, 481, 498, 527, 551, 552
Cabbageboy 48, **79**, 80
Cage, John 46, **80**, 81, 85, 102, 146, 167, 183, 287, 315, 322, 324, 354, 364, 430, 440, 448, 458, 489, 490, 496, 526, 527, 540, 566
Cain, Sim 459
Caine, Elliot 473
Caine, Michael 555
Cajmere 21, **81**, 84, 85, 145, 178, 535
Caldato, Mario Jr. 119
Cale, John 102, 168, 170, 431, 567
Calix, Mira **81**
Call of Wild 83
Callahan, Dave 341
Callier, Terry 378
Cambridge, John 64
Camilla 21, 22
Campbell, Dave 284, 379
Campbell, Glen 476
Campbell, Luther 142
Campisi, Zip 52
Can 2, 7, 77, **81**, 82, 83, 96, 109, 128, 173, 286, 288, 312, 324, 337, 341, 344, 355, 371, 402, 403, 419, 427, 447, 489, 497, 499, 519, 522, 523
Candelario, Benji 41, **83**, 179, 547
Candy Flip 301
Candy, Peter 286
Cann, Warren 533
Cannon, Brian 51
Cantor, Matt 194
Capone N Noreaga 201, 315
Cappella **83**, 84
Captain Beefheart 163, 263, 419
Cara, Irene 343
Caravan 532
Carbon, Lisa Trio 29, 30
Carcass 108, 532
Cardew, Cornelius 167, 364
Cardigans 404, 555
Cardwell, Joi 444
Caress 326
Carey, Mariah 278, 301, 342, 520
Carlisle, Belinda 374
Carlos, Walter 53
Carlos, Wendy 2, **84**, 106, 156, 270, 374, 520
Carnell, Paul 496
Carnes, Kevin 437
Carney, Ralph 293
Caro, Mark 122, 508
Carola, Marco 51, 63
Carrasco, Tomas Ramirez 283
Carretta, David 139
Carruthers, John 95
Carruthers, William 475, 480
Cars 494
Carson, Lori 319
Carter the Unstoppable Sex Machine 404
Carter, Aaron 92
Carter, Chris 91, 517
Carter, Derrick 81, **84**, 85, 178, 333, 522
Carter, James 260
Carter, Jon 122, 155, 339
Carter, Lance 294

Carter, Paul 45
Carter, Ron 117, 324, 387
Carthy, Andy 333
Casale, Gerald V. 131
Casale, Jerry 131, 132
Cascone, Kim **85**, 131, 281, 393, 394
Casey, K. 294, 295
Casino Classix 36
Casino Versus Japan **85**
Cass & Slide 101
Cassandra Complex 540
Casselman, Lucian 58, 59
Cassidy, James 259
Cassidy, Larry 455
Cassidy, Vincent 455
Cassius **85**, 114, 199, 439
Castor, Jimmy Bunch 141, 299
Catani, Patric 159, 160
Catch 173
Catlett, Francisco Mora 260, 261
Catlin, Fritz 527
Catto, Jamie 177
Caustic Window 17
Cauty, Jimi 283, 284, 372, 475
Cave, Nick 2, 146, 162, 360
Cave, Nick & the Bad Seeds 162
Cayre, Ben 441
Cayre, Ken 441
Cayre, Stan 441
Cecil, Malcolm 520, 521, 560
Ced Gee 531, 532
Cenac, Ben "Cozmo-D" 358
Centuras 408
Cerrone 42, **85**, 86, 134, 194
Certain Ratio **86**, 172, 455
Chadbourne, Eugene 556
Chaffe, Barbara 569
Chailly, Riccardo 545
Chakra 133
Chali Twona 275
Chameleon, The 74
Chameleons UK 135
Champs 188
Chan, Jackie 129
Chancler, Leon "Ndugu" 554
Chandler, Kerri **86**, 93, 118, 146, 342, 513, 547
Chandler, Lawrence 64
Change 89
Channel Live 137
Channel One 33, 40, 92, 469
Channel X 279, 469
Chaos AD **86**
Chaos 535
Chapman, Tracy 157
Chapterhouse 350, 461
Chara 509
Charlatans 87, 88
Charlatans UK 438, 491
Charlemagne, Diane 520
Charles, Christophe 326, 379
Charles, Tina 54
Charvoni 56
Chaser 123, 199
Chasteen, Tom 523
Chateau Flight 484
Chatham, Rhys 436
Chavez, Ingrid 440
Cheap Trick 45
Cheeks, Judy 442
Chemical Brothers 3, 21, 35, 43, 50, 63, **86**, 87, 88, 92, 108, 115, 122, 140, 155, 157, 180, 274, 291, 295, 320, 324, 325, 335, 339, 344, 346, 378, 413, 414, 421, 438, 439, 443, 466, 467, 474, 551, 557

Cher 550
Cherry, Don 62, 88, 437, 501, 566
Cherry, Neneh 7, 8, 62, **88**, 317, 318, 382, 406, 525
Chessie **88**
Cheung, Gavin 278, 361
Chez 424
Chic 65, **89**, 317, 419, 442, 474
Chicago 462, 488
Chicago Connection 81
Chicane **89**, 90
Chicks on Speed 361
Chief Xcel 145
Child's View **90**, 158, 427, 502, 503
Child, Anthony 497, 498
Children of the Bong **90**, 17?
Childs, Anthony 497
Chillout, Chuck 201
Chills 486
Chimera 153, 286
Chimes 474
China 99, 137
Chip E 3, 179, 445
Chipmunks 358
Chiverton, Eric 408
Chocolate Weasel 441
Chopra, Deepak 192
Chowning, John 90
Chris & Cosey **91**, 305, 517, 558
Chris the French Kiss 326, 463
Chrislo 114
Christian Death 254
Christian, Hans 430
Christian, Steve 423
Christophere, David 422
Christopherson, Peter 98, 99, 109, 171, 415, 517
Chrome 165, 283, 442
Chumbawamba 354, 568
Chung, Mark 162, 163
Cibo Matto **91**
Ciccotelli, Lou 254, 291
Cindytalk 97
Cinematic Orchestra **91**, 92
Circle 402, 518
Cirrus **92**, 140
Clail, Gary 459, 502
Clail, Gary Tackhead Sound System 502
Clannad 89, 90
Clapton, Eric 508
Claridge, Eric 453, 454, 460
Clark 107, 296
Clark, Alan 165
Clark, Chris 551
Clark, Iain 295
Clark, Kevin 125
Clark, Petula 5, 284
Clark, Sonny 568, 569
Clarke, Dave 34, 48, 87, **92**, 93, 147, 163, 504, 548, 549
Clarke, Johnny 282
Clarke, Malcolm 43
Clarke, Roland 513
Clarke, Vince 126, 127, 170, 171, 172
Clash 45, 51, 164, 389, 418, 433, 472
Clatterbox **93**, 147, 196
Claussell, Joe 86, **93**, 278
Claypool, Les 77
Clayton, Kit **93**, 94, 379, 498, 528
Click N Cycle 18
Cliff, Jimmy 469
Clifford, Linda 56
Clifford, Mark 81, 97, 136, 446, 455, 471
Climie, Simon 508
Clinton, George 31, 38, **94**, 95, 150, 151, 195, 199, 200, 201, 273, 385, 386, 410, 411, 412, 445

Clivilles, Robert 77, 342
Clock DVA **95**, 96, 527
Cloud 9 338, 361
Clouser, Charles 359
Clubhouse 83
Cluster 12, **96**, 167, 169, 182, 337, 344, 355, 433, 434, 518
CM 367
Coba 509
Cobain, Garry 14, 204
Cobb, Ed 472
Cobby, Steve 37, 183, 184, 361, 473
Cobham, Billy 117, 278
Cochran, Dave 147
Cochran, Eddie 330
Cochrane, Dave 254
Cocker, Jarvis 2
Cocker, Joe 469
Coco Steel & Lovebomb **96**, 97, 313
Cocteau Twins 8, 20, 71, 73, **97**, 98, 120, 156, 204, 316, 349, 461, 471, 482, 560
COD 385
Cod, Colin 568
Code of Practice 74, 394, 475
Code Warrior 498
Codenys, Patrick 52
Coffey, Cath 486, 525
Cogger, Matt 356
Cohen, Ira 437
Cohen, Leonard 99, 556
Coil 8, 67, **98**, 99, 109, 171, 193, 305, 415, 416, 451, 517
Cold Crush Brothers 275, 386
Coldcut 7, 35, 62, 63, 79, 92, **99**, 100, 104, 125, 138, 140, 142, 165, 201, 263, 264, 271, 280, 295, 299, 308, 355, 361, 372, 388, 427, 429, 469, 502, 538
Cole, B.J. 382, 547
Cole, David 77, 342
Cole, M.J. 161
Colebrooke, Simon 401, 528
Coleman, Andrew 16
Coleman, Anthony 261, 458, 459, 569
Coleman, Jaz 23, 28
Coleman, Ornette 102, 412, 437, 495, 568, 569
Coles, Nathan 191
Colin, Jez 473
Collapsed Lung 67
Collide 198
Collier, Ken 27, **100**
Collins, Bootsy 38, 72, 81, 95, 122, 200, 294, 319, 386, 440, 469
Collins, Catfish 200, 386
Collins, Charlie 95
Collins, Kimball **100**, 140
Collins, Mel 499
Collins, Nicolas 354
Collins, Phil 23, 169, 197, 273
Collins, Sandra **100**, 101, 134, 307
Collins, Tyler 71
Collister, Paul 375
Colourbox 20, **101**, 308, 316
Coltrane, John 302, 335, 378, 430, 495, 496
Combustible Edison 178
Comet Gain 547
Commodores 119
Common Factor **101**, 102, 108
Common Ground 280
Company Flow **102**, 148, 254, 275, 544
Concealed Project 51
Concept 2 376

# INDEX

Concina, Roberto 327
Concrete Blonde 477
Congos 389
Conjoint 102, 124, 345
Conn, Rob 484
Connell, Andy 86
Connelly, Chris 331
Conquering Lion 424
Conrad, Tony 102, 103, 181, 567
Conscious 568
Console 103, 362
Consolidated 27, 103, 323
Conway, Dave 350
Cooder, Ry 537
Cook, Eric 391
Cook, Norman 42, 45, 46, 179, 180, 326, 394, 555
Cook, Sean 480
Cook, Yvette "Lady E" 358
Cooke, Stephanie 146
Cool Breeze 281
Cool Hand Flex 376
Coolio 561
Coombes, Pete 173
Cooper, Ian 532
Cooper, Martin 375
Cooper, Matt 113, 271
Cooper, Tyree 445, 529, 530
Cope, Julian 181, 355
Corduroy 103
Corea, Chick 74, 117, 118, 553
Cornelius 100, 103, 104, 178, 331, 353, 509
Corner, Chris 471
Cornershop 33, 94, 104, 119, 180, 199, 203
Corsten, Ferry 104, 105, 374
Coryell, Larry 117
Cos 510
Cosey, Pete 118
Cosmic Baby 105, 422, 509, 541, 542
Costello, Elvis 174, 525, 556
Couch 105
Count Basic 288, 551
Count Dubulah 524
Couzens, Andy 491
Cowell, Henry 80, 544
Cox, Carl 105, 106, 124, 131, 133, 193, 335, 466
Cox, Mark 560
Coxhill, Lol 369, 450
Coxon, John 482, 483
Crabb, Graham 404
Crack, Carl 27, 166
Cracknell, Sarah 280, 438
Crafton, Bob "Chilly B." 358
Craig, Carl 24, 28, 34, 39, 51, 83, 100, 101, 106, 107, 108, 110, 121, 123, 144, 147, 159, 160, 185, 190, 199, 260, 261, 278, 293, 321, 322, 323, 327, 335, 340, 371, 378, 384, 385, 415, 425, 429, 446, 457, 464, 477, 483, 500, 501, 504, 510, 511, 524, 539, 565, 566
Cranium HF 140
Crank 304
Crash Worship 298
Crass 110, 375
Crazy Horse 174
Cream 25
Creation Rebel 459
Creative Technology Institute 91
Creatures 10
Creme, Lalo 21
Creme, Lol 21, 23
Cretu, Michael 167
Crime & the City Solution 162

Criminal Element Orchestra 83
Crispy Ambulance 255
Cristy, Dylan 158
Crockett, Gary 507
Crockette, Alison 282
Cropper, Steve 89
Crosby, Bing 566
Crosby, David 169
Cross, Chris 533
Cross, Lowell 526
Cross, Sandra 309
Crowley, Aleister 527
Crowther, Jill 256, 257
Cruise, Julee 279
Crump, Harrison 309
Crusaders 521
Cruz, Hector 318
Cruzeman 366
Crystal Method 64, 92, 108, 124, 133, 140, 278
Cuba, Joe 538
Cubanate 108, 109
Cube Forty 267
Cujo 109, 135, 271, 519
Cul de Sac 109
Culture 15
Culture Club 123
Cummings, John 337
Cummings, Robert 495
Cunningham, David 365
Cure 9, 17, 58, 71, 97, 120, 275, 366, 558
Curlew 293
Current Affairs 151
Current 93 98, 109, 126, 305, 364
Currie, Billy 533, 547, 548
Curtin, Dan 110, 157, 158, 504, 555
Curtis, Ian 86, 356, 455
Curve 17, 63, 110, 111, 192, 204, 407, 480, 542
Cusp 544, 558
Custer, Beth 358
Cut Chemist 111, 262, 275, 388, 462
Cut La Roc 484, 485
Cut N Move 523
Cut N Paste 194
Cut to Kill 413
Cybernet Systems 42
Cybersonik 48
Cybotron 27, 28, 33, 40, 47, 111, 139, 161, 185, 193, 259, 262, 322, 336, 408, 445, 526, 554
Cydonia 198
Cygnus X 444
Cylob 17, 60, 111, 112, 148, 153, 186, 281, 282, 297, 300, 345, 346, 387
Cypress Hill 102, 387, 480, 525, 526
Cyrus & the Joker 100
Cyrus 41, 42, 320, 321
CZR 37
Czukay, Holger 82, 83, 96, 124, 267, 337, 419, 434, 489, 499

# D

D Bridge 203
D Influence 113, 488, 531
D Mob 308
D Note 113, 382
D Styles 262
D Train 277, 278
D'Angelo 352, 439
D'Arcangelo 113, 473
D'Cruze, Jay 113, 114
D., Chuck 417, 418, 556
D., Donald 60
D., Gary 307

D., Mike 145
D., Peter 269
D., Steve 563
Da Junkies 131
Da Sampla 457, 526
Dade, Sushil 203
DAF 78, 114, 481
Daft Punk 7, 41, 71, 85, 88, 114, 115, 134, 139, 161, 253, 298, 310, 325, 327, 332, 344, 431, 434, 439, 463, 484, 544
Dahlback, Jesper 511
Daho, Etienne 134
Dajae 81
Dale, Colin 177, 467
Dalek I Love You 375
Daley, Paul 296, 313
Dali's Car 267
Dali, Salvador 504
Dallpiccola, Luigi 50
Dami, Maurizio 433
Damier, Chez 327, 445, 524
Damm, Martin 7, 52, 188, 279
Dancer, Brett 115
Dandy Jack 5, 115, 116
Dane, Dana 544
Dangers, Jack 323
Danmass 115
Danzig, Glenn 5
Daou 511
Daou, Peter 342
Daphne 511
Dara, Olu 319
DArby, Terence Trent 48
Darey, Matt 367
Darin, Bobby 566
Dark Comedy 107, 115, 116, 293, 323, 446
Darkside 475, 479
Darling 114, 115
Dart, Thurston 364
Das 25
Das, Aniruddha 25
DaSilva, Everton 15
Datach'i 116
Datacide 116
Daumail, Laurent 137
Davenport, N'Dea 67
David J 259
David 507
David, Gavin 204
David, Hal 8, 11, 377, 433
David, Stuart 303
Davies, Paul 496
Davies, Victor 255
Davis, Charles 495
Davis, Danny 495
Davis, Dewayne 387
Davis, Josh 144, 145
Davis, Miles 2, 24, 64, 116, 117, 118, 266, 271, 355, 371, 393, 431, 449, 450, 463, 483, 521, 553
Davis, Miles Quintet 125
Davis, Rick 27, 111
Davis, Roy Jr. 21, 118, 395, 527
Davis, Spencer 399
Davis, Spencer Group 470
Davoli, Daniele 56
Dawntreader 295
Dawson, Scott 311
Day One 119
Day, Graham 507
Dayne, Taylor 548
Dayton, Kelli 471
DBX 48, 49
De La Soul 33, 38, 119, 120, 273, 274, 278, 308, 359, 412, 460, 560

De Niro 295, 492
De'Lacy 60, 123, 442
Dead C 103
Dead Can Dance 120, 121, 126, 367, 559
Dead Famous People 438
Dead Voices on Air 152
Deadly Avenger 129, 368
Dean, Rob 267
Dearborn, Mike 121, 139
Deason, Sean 39, 121, 122, 194, 446, 551, 554
Death in Vegas 8, 122, 520
Debabalon, Christoph 122
Debbie Deb 193, 408
DeBenedictus, Michael 388
Debussy, Claude 23, 520, 544
Decameron 414
Decoder 122, 137, 138, 153, 391, 452, 508
Deconstruction 339, 444
DeCoster, Jean Paul 529
DeCrecy, Etienne 344, 439
Deee Lite 22, 108, 122, 123, 178, 278, 290, 317, 373, 404, 435, 496, 509, 543, 546
DeeJay Punk Roc 123, 193
Deep Cover 101
Deep Creed 543
Deep Dish 71, 123, 307, 342, 456
Deep Forest 21, 124, 126, 164, 266, 543
Deep Purple 269
Deep South 346
Deep Space Network 124, 345, 361, 519, 547
Deepfried Toguma 266
Deepsky 100, 125, 133, 492, 124
deepstate 511
Def Leppard 150
Defever, Warren 391
Definition of Sound 125, 194
Deftones 466
Degiorgio, Kirk 24, 32, 58, 325, 356, 368, 456, 467, 509
Dego 157, 188, 189, 266, 351, 451, 510
DeGroodt, Frank 125
DeHomem-Christo, Guy-Manuel 114
DeJohnette, Jack 117, 118
Dekkard, R. 100
Dekker, Desmond 469
DeLaLuna, Shai 304
DeLange, Susan 537
DeLaRocha, Zack 26, 464
Delay, Vladislav 125, 281
Delerium 126, 198
Delgado, Gabi 114
Delgado, Junior 381
Delgado, Mike 83
Delirium 336
DelNaja, Robert "3-D" 316
Delta 129
Delta Lady 455, 524
Delta 9 126, 138
DeLuca, Chris 131, 177, 202
Deluxe, Gerhard 321
DeMare, Siobhan 339
DeMaria, Walter 102
DeMeyer, Jean-Luc 52
Demone, Gitane 254
Dempster, Stuart 370
Denes, Jay 352
Denham, Jay 4, 115, 368
Denki Groove 504, 541, 542
Dennis, Dean 95
Denny, Martin 134, 330
Denny, Sandy 378
Denver, John 500
Depeche Mode 7, 61, 63, 71, 113, 114, 123,

**126,** 127, 128, 129, 164, 170, 171, 172, 278, 282, 288, 299, 321, 323, 334, 360, 361, 372, 373, 375, 385, 406, 412, 444, 459, 462, 536, 557
Depth Charge 34, 62, **129,** 170, 368, 438
Der Dritte Raum **129**
Derbyshire, Delia 43
DeRocha, Dee 257
Designer **129,** 264
Desired States 376
Detroit Diesel 339
Detroit Escalator Co. 121, **129**
Detroit Grand Pubahs **129,** 130
Deupree, Taylor **130,** 203, 414, 415, 457, 567
Deva, Terra 74, **131**
Devine, Richard **131,** 394, 467, 468
DeVit, Tony **131**
Devo **131,** 132, 133, 362, 363, 521, 524
Devoto, Howard 19
DeWolf, Frank 264
DeWulf, Fonny 290
Dextrous 312
Deyhim, Sussan 303
Di'jital 34
Diamond, Dinky 477
Diatribe 568
Dibango, Manu 469
Dickinson, Jim 480
Dido **133,** 177
Die Krupps 198
Die Warzau 300
Diermaier, Werner 181
Diesel M 345
Dieselboy **133**
Dietrich, Marlene 65
Dif Juz 97, 98
Digable Planets 119, 189, 273, 282, 510
Digi Dub 340
Digiorgio, Sergio 24
Digital Orgasm 279
Digital Underground 94
Digital 395
Digital, Dougie 390
Digs & Woosh 136
Digweed, John 100, 105, **133,** 134, 443, 444
Dillard, Ricky 333
Dillinger 381
Dillinja 21, 36, 55, 68, 100, **134,** 298, 359, 376, 452
Dillon, Phyllis 282
Dilworth, Joe 486
Dimitri from Paris 7, 93, 114, **134,** 254, 280, 327, 344, 463, 484, 539
Dinger, Klaus 355, 356
Dingley, Corin 11
Dinosaur Jr. 350, 362
Dinosaur L 436
Direct Current 559
Directions in Groove 134
Directions in Music **134**
Dirty Beatniks **135,** 298
Dirty Harry 279
Disc 281, 298
Disco Citizens 89
Disco Elements 342
Disco Four 486
Disco Freaks 43
Disco Inferno **135,** 136, 160
Disjam **136**
Disjecta 81, **136,** 186, 446, 455, 559
Disposable Heroes of Hip-hoprisy 6, 323
Ditchum, Martin 9
Divination 286

Divine Styler 486
Dixon, Kenny Jr. 340, 341, 369, 387, 539
DiY **136,** 154
DJ Ani 122, 146
DJ Apollo 262
DJ Assault 34, 93, **136,** 139
DJ Bam Bam 37, 548
DJ Cam 118, **137,** 142, 147, 199, 429
DJ Cash Money 282
DJ Craze 138
DJ Crystl 75
DJ D 315
DJ Dan 279, 462
DJ Dara 133, **137,** 138, 146
DJ DB 133
DJ Dexter 342
DJ Di'jital 33
DJ Dick 136, 139, 433
DJ Die 68, 142, 269, 464
DJ Dimitri 134
DJ Disciple 153
DJ Disk 262
DJ Dmitry 122
DJ DNA 539
DJ Duke 1
DJ Eddie Def 72
DJ ESP **138**
DJ Faust **138**
DJ Fierce 358, 436
DJ Fluid 6
DJ Food 31, 99, 100, **138,** 142, 184, 185, 201, 280, 333, 355, 483
DJ Friction 133
DJ Funk 106
DJ Fuzz 188, 279
DJ Gilb'r 253, 484
DJ Godfather **139,** 140, 160
DJ Good Groove 34, 419
DJ Grazhoppa 458
DJ Hell 7, 92, **139,** 152
DJ Hype 113, 138, 140, 148, 152, 376, 401, **139**
DJ Hyperactive 138, 435, 548
DJ Icey **140,** 463
DJ Jazzy Jeff & the Fresh Prince 93, 282
DJ K-One 33, 34, 526
DJ Keoki **140,** 141
DJ Kool **141**
DJ Kool Herc 38, 100, **141,** 146
DJ Krush 30, 33, 100, 118, 137, **141,** 142, 145, 147, 416, 428, 537
DJ Krust **142**
DJ Magic Mike 142, 143
DJ Mark the 45 King 141
DJ Me DJ You **143,** 330, 331
DJ Moe Love 531
DJ Muggs 525, 526
DJ Nu-Mark 275
DJ Olive 319, 552, 553
DJ One 123
DJ Parrot 165, 283, 442, 498
DJ PH 484
DJ Pierre 52, 83, 118, **143,** 144, 145, 182, 202, 269, 374, 395, 445, 547
DJ Predator 434
DJ Premier 137, 148, 498, 551
DJ Prof X Or 83, 84
DJ Pulse 275
DJ Q **144**
Q Bert 145, 149, 262
DJ Rap 72, **144**
DJ Rectangle 462
DJ Richie Rich 400
DJ Rolando **144,** 535
DJ Rush 21, 141

DJ Sammy B 274
DJ Shadow 21, 33, 34, 35, 92, 111, 137, 142, **144,** 145, 149, 302, 387, 416, 418, 526, 537, 538, 539, 559
DJ Slip 194
DJ Snax 188
DJ Sneak 21, 41, 81, 85, **145,** 146, 182, 316, 442
DJ Soul Slinger 133, **146,** 319
DJ Spinna 423
DJ Spooky 29, 75, 76, **146,** 147, 203, 293, 331, 355, 427, 552, 563
DJ Spoony 153
DJ SS 36, 137
DJ Suv 142, 269, 464
DJ Swift 140, 148
DJ Swingsett 148
DJ T-1000 121, **147**
DJ Tee Bee 18
DJ Tiesto 105
DJ Tonka 180, 404
DJ Trace 21, **147,** 151, 177, 358, 382, 436
DJ Tron **147**
DJ Vadim 36, 100, 142, **147,** 148, 254, 388
DJ Wally 146, **148**
DJ Zero 323
DJ Zinc 18, 137, 140, **148**
Dlugosch, Boris 347
DMX Krew 42, **148,** 300
DMX 67, 120, 201, 525, 526
DNA 539
Dockstader, Tod **148,** 149
Dr. Alban 443
Dr. Alimantado 282
Dr. Atmo 124, 352, 476
Dr. Baker MBE 523
Dr. Dooom 149
Dr. Dre 92, 95, 261, 360
Dr. Dub 316
Dr. Israel 172, 479
Dr. John 480, 481, 556
Dr. L 137
Dr. Octagon 33, 102, 145, 146, 148, **149,** 275, 314, 416, 532
Dr. Pablo & Dub Syndicate 155
Doctor Rockit 93, **149,** 150, 193, 266, 510, 559
Dr. Walker 260, 279, 336, 514, 570
Dodd, Clement "Coxsone" 16, 389
Doe, John 57
Dog 56
Dog, Michael 203
Doktor Kosmos **150,** 196
Dolby, Thomas 85, 95, **150,** 151, 278, 393, 440, 512
Dolphin Brothers 267
Dolphy, Eric 92, 495
Dom & Roland 21, 36, 122, **151,** 371, 382, 402, 435, 508
Dome 330
Donahue, Jonathan 88
Donaldson, Eric 390
Donaldson, Lou 119
Donaldson, Michael 421
Donne, Robert 290
Donnelly, Danny 113
Donovan 29, 125
Donovan, Dan 51
Doors 374, 566
Dope Skillz 140, 148
Dope, Kenny 72, 317, 318, 359, 364
Doppelreffekt 4, 34, 93, 139, **152,** 160, 295, 296, 385, 387, 566
DoReen 474

Dorfmeister, Richard 263, 288, 387, 419, 458, 522
Dorham, Kenny 569
Dorn, Adam 335, 336
Dorn, Joel 335, 336
Dorney, Tim 428
Dornonville, Michaela 21, 22
Dorough, Bob 556
Dorper, Ralf 414
Dorrell, Dave 20, 101, 308, 316
Dorsey, Jimmy 441
Double D 339
Double D. & Steinski 99, 111
Double Discovery 326
Double Exposure 510
Double 99 527
Double Trouble 424
Dougal 468
Dougans, Brian 14, 204
Doughton, Shannon 468
Doughty, M. 162
Douglas, Alan 294
Douglas, Carol 324
Douglas, Dave 91, 459
Downes, Geoffrey 150
Downie, Ken 56, 57, 399, 428
Download 8, **152,** 347, 465
Dozier, Bebe 346
Drake, Nick 377, 378, 393
Drax 6
Drayton, William 417
Dreadzone 21, **152**
Dream Academy 496
Dream Sequence 43
Dream Syndicate 102, 103
Dream Team **152**
Dreamfish **153,** 561
Dred, Mike 17, **153,** 286
Dreem Teem **153**
Dresher, Paul 492
Dresser, Mark 569
Drexciya 4, 28, 33, 34, 39, 139, 152, **153,** 154, 160, 163, 185, 351, 385, 387, 526, 534, 535, 554
Driscoll, Julie 258
Driver, Jan 279
Drome 99, **154,** 361
Droppin' Science 68
Drowning Craze 97
DRS 75
Drum Club **154,** 416, 466, 524
Drum Island **155**
Drum Komputer 130, 457
Drummond, Billy 283, 284, 372
Drummond, Don 390
Drummond, Ray 569
Drumsound 146
Dub Pistols **155**
Dub Syndicate **155,** 156, 293, 390
Dub Tractor 266
Dub War 18
Dubstar **156**
Dubtribe 156
Dubtribe Sound System **156**
Duca, Curd **156**
Ducasse, Matt 466, 540
Duchamp, Marcel 59, 186, 526
Dudley, Anne 23
Duke, George 41
Dumb Type 255
Dummy Run 489
Dunbar, Sly 272, 440
Dunckel, Jean-Benoit 7
Dunn, Mike 21, 182, 277, 511
Dunn, Trevor 6

Dupieux, Quentin 333
Duran Duran 363, 503
Durand, Werner 349
Durst, Fred 539
Durutti Column 135, **157**, 366, 370, 455
Dust Brothers 33, 44, 47, 87, 143, **157**, 338, 353, 494, 495, 559
Duvante, Titonton 110, **157**, 158
Dvus 141
Dweeb 337
Dylan Group **158**
Dylan 68
Dylan, Bob 45, 128, 173, 469, 560
Dynamites 390
Dynamix II 42, 148, **158**, 443

# E

E Culture 282, 557
E Dancer **159**, 260, 445, 446
E De Cologne 159
E., Frank 286
Eagles 462
EAR 271
Earth Leakage Trip 401
Earth to Infinity 124, 345
Earth Wind & Fire 3, 177, 278, 394
Earthlings? 135
Earwig 262
East Flatbush Project 54, 202
East Seventeen 131, 555
East Side Beat 83
Eastman, Julius 436
Easton, Sheena 132, 270
Eat Static 26, 39, **159**, 198
Ebah, Ahk Tal 495
Ebe 511
Ebert, Klaus 12
EBN OZN 59
EC8OR 27, 63, **159**, 160, 166, 460
Echo & the Bunnymen 283
Echo Park 129
Ecstasy of Saint Theresa **160**
Ectomorph 93, 139, 152, **160**, 185, 186, 295, 387, 394, 550
Eddy, Duane 22, 23
Edge of Motion 21
Edge 70, 135, 330
Edwards, Bernard 89, 419
Edwards, Charles 540
Edwards, Skye 342
Edwards, Todd **161**, 527
Edwin, Colin 405
Eels 33
Egan, Rusty 547
Egg 3
Egues, Richard 538
Egyptian Lover 31, 139, **161**, 351, 378, 533
Eiffel Sixty Five 90
Eight Miles High 11
Eight O Eight State 6, 23, 28, 36, 55, 63, 147, **161**, 162, 289, 292, 299, 313, 414, 482, 496, 551, 565
Eight QM Stereo 361
Eighteen Wheeler 555
Einheit, F.M. 162
Einsturzende Neubauten 82, **162**, 163, 165, 256, 283, 442, 459, 481, 513, 565, 568
El Mal 36
El P 102, 148, 254
El-Essawy, Roba 30
Elastica 558
Elecktroids 154, **163**, 295
Electribe 101 316
Electric Company **163**, 164, 558

Electric Hellfire Club 259
Electric Light Orchestra 43
Electric Prunes 34
Electric Skychurch 140, **164**, 278
Electrifying Mojo 27, 100, 130, **164**, 322
Electro Nation 6
Electroliners 443
Electronic 86, **164**, 165, 357, 392
Electronic Eye 78, **165**, 283, 442, 498
Electronome 253
Elektric Music **165**
Elementals 300
Elementz of Noise **165**, 382
Eleventh Dream Day 522
Elfish Echo 54, 361, 460
Elias, Hanin 27, 166
Ellard, Tom 457
Ellington, Duke 91, 118, 282, 294, 336, 512
Elliot, Matt 516
Elliott, Louise 291
Elliott, Missy Misdemeanor 201
Ellis, Bobby 381
Ellis, Rob 291
Ellis, Timo 91
Elstak, Paul **165**
Embryo 12
Emergency Broadcast Network **165**
Emerson, Darren 87, 535, 536
EMF 19, 259, 374, 486
Emilio, Frank 294
Eminem 201
Emit Ecaps 476
Empire, Alec 3, 27, 48, 116, 159, 163, **166**, 300, 359, 382, 404, 459, 489, 509, 552
Empirion **166**, 455
En Vogue 285, 527
Endemic Void **166**, 167, 271, 275, 340
Energy 52 100, 105
Engelen, Maurice 279
English Beat 428
English, Kim 161, 317, 488, 513, 527, 544
Enigma 164, **167**, 369
Enke, Harmut 25
Eno, Brian 15, 25, 53, 57, 59, 61, 64, 65, 66, 70, 73, 77, 86, 96, 97, 116, 117, 132, 142, **167**, 168, 169, 170, 183, 190, 196, 197, 261, 263, 302, 324, 330, 334, 337, 352, 362, 372, 373, 374, 386, 434, 450, 452, 496, 518, 521, 527, 533, 548, 556, 558
Eno, Roger 70, 73, 170, 330
Eno/Cale 170
Eon 36, 54, 129, 158, 170, 568
EPMD 314, 513
Equinox 198, 555
Erasure 45, 49, 126, 156, **170**, 171, 172, 188, 278, 301, 334, 360, 372, 373, 374, 376, 494
Eric B & Rakim 99, 111, 145, 280, 281, 316, 338
Ernst, Max 493
Erosion 545
Escape Tank 457
ESG **172**
Esion **172**
Espiritu 178
Esquivel 134, 512, 516
Esselink, Elisabeth 472, 473
Estefan, Gloria 268, 435
Estermann, Andre 193
ETA 520
Eternal 62
Eternity 493
Euphone 468
Euphonic **172**, 565

Euromasters 165
Eurythmics 16, 110, 114, **173**, 174, 270, 272, 343
Evans, Adriana 30
Evans, Gil 117, 556
Evelyn, George 359
Everitt, Steve 159
Everlast 412
Everything But the Girl 68, 123, **174**, 175, 291, 292, 313, 316, 317, 339, 370, 465, 482, 512, 513
Evora, Cesaria 93
Ex 522
Exodus 55
Expansion Union 123, 158
Experimental Audio Research **175**, 182, 271, 286, 290, 350, 479
Exquisite Corpse 416
Extreme Noise Terror 284
Eye, Yamatsuka 90, 502, 569
EZ Rollers 137, **175**, 176, 351, 402, 463
Ezrin, Bob 360

# F

F., Adam **177**, 351, 452
F., Richard 37, 140
Fabio 67, 74, 144, **177**, 181, 493
Fabulous Poodles 195
Face & Feline 423
Face to Face 38
Fad Gadget 253
Fahey, John 109, 531
Fahey, Siobhan 173
Fairley, Andrew 155
Faith Healers 486
Faith No More 281, 421, 479
Faith Over Reason 438
Faith, Percy 11
Faithfull, Marianne 496, 556
Faithless 133, **177**, 543, 550
Fakesch, Michael **177**, 178, 193, 202, 270
Falco 356
Falcon, Ralph 202, 346, 347, 511
Falconer, Andy 415, 416, 500
Fall 82, 150, 194, 203, 459
Faltermeyer, Harold 392, 477
Famous Flames 180
Fanatik 387
Fania All Stars 538
Fantastic Plastic Machine 143, **178**, 191, 331, 398
Fantasy 89
Fargetta 85
Farina, Mark 6, **178**
Farinas 420
Farley & Heller **178**, 308, 442
Farley Jackmaster Funk 3, 21, 37, **179**, 346, 415, 445, 456
Farley, Terry 178
Farmers Manual 30, **179**, 255
Farris, Gene 81, 85, **179**, 333
Fast Eddie 277
Fast, Larry 499, 500
Fat Boys 532, 544
Fat Joe 315
Fatboy Slim 19, 39, 45, 50, 92, 140, 180, 194, 201, 202, 258, 302, 324, 326, 335, 339, 394, 428, 466, 467, 480, 555, **179**
Fath, Michael 271
Fauna Flash 44, **181**, 187
Faust 102, 103, **181**, 182, 288, 312, 377, 399, 421, 486, 497, 518, 522
Faver, Colin 170, 188
Faze Action 34, 44
Fear Factory 198, 274

Fearless, Richard 122
Fehlmann, Thomas 28, 43, 163, 183, 190, 321, 336, 373, 495
Feinstein, Harley 477
Feldman, Morton 314, 450, 458, 526
Felix Da Housecat 21, 84, 143, 144, **182**, 309, 374
Felix 177
Feller, Norman 71
Fellini, Federico 556
Felly 509
Fennesz **182**, 183
Fenton, Shane 177
Ferguson, Gus 256, 513
Fergusson, Alex 415
Ferrari, Luc 447
Ferreira, Cisco 4, 62
Ferry, Bryan 163, 167, 267, 506
Fetchet, Dennis 485
FFWD **183**, 373
Fiedler, Margaret 291, 341
Field Mice 438
Fields of the Nephilim 559
Fields, Jordan 118
Fiend One 337
Fier, Anton 72, 286, 305, 318, 319, 451
Fierro, Miguel Angelo 463, 464
Fifty Foot Hose **183**, 481
Fifty Seventh Dynasty 486
Fila Brazillia 37, 44, 184, 292, **183**
Filter 360
Final 8, **184**, 254, 508
Final Cut 328
Fincher, David 157
Finclair, Barry 440
Fine Young Cannibals 28, 442
Fingers Inc. 1, **184**, 285, 333, 395
Fini Tribe 198
Finitribe 202
Finlow, Carl **184**, 185, 549
Finn, Jerry 143
Finn, Mickey 18
Fiorillo, Elisa 270
Fire Island 347
Firefly 557
Fireman **185**, 508
First Choice 299, 441
Fischerspooner, Daniel 105
Fish, Alan 78
Fish, Pat 479
Fisher, Adrian 477
Fisher, Cevin **185**, 511, 520
Fitzgerald, Ella 516
Five Star 40
Five Style 129, 522
Fixsen, Guy 160, 291
Flack, Roberta 335
Flaming Lips 303, 512
Flanger 29, **185**
Flare 303
Flavor Flav 319, 417
Flea 70
Fleckner, Gregory 193
Fleetwood Mac 284
Fleming, Rochelle 318
Fletcher, Alan 128
Fletcher, Andrew 126
Fletcher, Justin 446, 455
Flexitone 152, 160, **185**, 186
Flint, Keith 63, 412, 413, 422
Flipper 334
Float Up CP 88
Flock of Seagulls **186**, 363
Flood 2, 9, 110, 111, 128, 171, 360, 428
Florence 36

Flowchart 204
Flowered Up 428
Flowers, Angela 455
Flowers, Fanon 115
Flowers, Mike 201
Flugel, Roman 11, 546
Fluke 123, **186**, 187
Fluxus 566
Flying Lizards 364
Flying Saucer Attack 25, **187**, 290, 516, 523
Flynn & Flora 142, 464, 484
Flynn, Paul 144
Flytronix 151, 175, 401
Foetus 10, 98, **187**, 404
Fonda, Peter 408
Fontana, Lenny 547
Foo Fighters 132
Foole, Dredd 109
For Carnation 5, 468, 522
Forbes, Derek 414
Forbes, Rand 537
Force MD's 275
Ford, Penny 474
Foreigner 150, 500, 523
Forest Mighty Black 34, 44, **187**, 420
Formby, Richard 479
Formula, Dave 547, 548
Forrest, Art 494
Fortran 5 **188**, 372
Fortune, Sonny 117, 118
The 45 King 123, 142, 414
Forty Niners 83
Foster, Al 118
Foster, Clint 555
Foul Play 175, **188**, 361, 371, 402
Foul Play Productions 188
Four E **188**, 279, 420
4Hero 75, 157, **188**, 189, 266, 351, 359, 361, 391, 393, 426, 451, 463, 501, 510
Four Preps 472
Four Tet **189**, 190, 195
Fourth Measure Men 334
Fowler Brothers 556
Fowler, Bernard 63, 388, 502, 513
Fowley, Kim 203
Fowlkes, Eddie "Flashin" 16, 28, 100, **190**, 322, 541
Foxx, John 24, **190**, 191, 533
Frampton, Peter 362, 524, 556
France, Laila **191**
France, Phil 92
Francis, Terry 85, **191**, 333
Franck, Chris 470
Franke, Christopher **191**, 192, 504, 505, 506
Frankie Goes to Hollywood 23, **192**, 266, 272, 283, 414
Franklin, Aretha 173
Frantz, Chris 169
Fraser, Elizabeth 97, 98, 204, 316, 317
Fraser, Liz 71
Frazer, Paula 325
Frazier Chorus 154
Freak Power 45
Free Kitten 553
Freeform **193**, 278, 519
Freeland, Adam 72, **193**
Freeman, Tim 416, 484
Freestyle Man 426
Freestyle Orchestra 546
Freestyle 42, **193**, 194, 408
Freestylers 140, 144, **194**
Freight Elevator Quartet 146, 147

Frenett, John 291, 341
Freq 121, **194**
Freq Nasty 198
Frequency 526
Frere-Jones, Sasha 301, 531
Fresh Four 142
Fresh, Doug E. 262
Fresh, Freddy 53, 138, 188, **194**, 359, 443, 516
Freska Allstars 194
Fretless AZM **194**, 195, 537
Freur **195**, 535
Freytag, Susanne 414
Fricke, Florian 404, 405, 505
Fricker, Rob 496
Friday, Gavin 63, 98, 128
Fridge 189, 190, **195**, 424, 518
Friedkin, William 505
Friedlander, Erik 459
Friedmann, Berndt 154, 185, 361
Friedmann, Burnt 361
Friend 150, **195**, 196
Friend, Ali 378, 425
Friese-Greene, Tim 503
Fripp, Robert 65, 73, 167, 168, 169, 170, 183, **196**, 197, 204, 267, 330, 373, 499
Fripp & Eno 499
Frischmann, Justine 558
Frisell, Bill 458, 556, 568, 569
Frith, Fred 142, 293, 318, 319, 362, 394, 458, 569
Froese, Edgar 191, **197**, 505, 506, 507
Froese, Jerome 505, 506
From Within **198**
Front Line Assembly 108, **198**
Front 242 52, 62, 67, 78, 79, 198, 282, 331, 332, 382, 383, 413
Froom, Mitchell 91
Fry, Martin 38
Frykberg, Magnus 22
FS 331
Fudge Tunnel 532
Fugees 470
Fujikawa, Naohiro 54
Fujiwara, Chris 109
Fulber, Rhys 126, 198
Full Moon Scientist **198**, 199
Fulwood, Ramon Tiki 199
Fun Da Mental **199**, 404, 437, 515
Fung, Trevor 87, **199**, 366
Funk Mob 63, 85, 107, 137, **199**, 344, 416
Funkadelic 3, 72, 94, 95, 160, **199**, 200, 201, 269, 273, 327, 385, 386, 412, 427, 445
Funki Porcini 100, 185, **201**
Funkmaster Flex 141, **201**, 544
Funkstorung 22, 177, 178, 187, 193, **202**, 253, 545
Funktaxi 62
Funky Derrick **202**
Funky Green Dogs 179, **202**, 346, 347
Funky Technicians 177
Furry Phreaks 444
F.U.S.E. 17, **202**, 203, 400, 401, 504, 544
Fushitsusha 288
Futique **203**, 414, 415, 457, 567
Future 95
Future Engineers 75
Future Forces, Inc. **203**
Future Loop Foundation **203**
Future Pilot AKA **203**
Future Shock 454
Future Sound of London 14, 105, 192, **203**, 314, 323, 354, 443, 463

Future 3 266
Future/Past 24
Fuxa **204**, 556
Fuzzy Logic 443
FX Randomiz **204**, 205, 278, 302

# G

G Flame & Mister G **206**, 279
G Netic 140
G-104 267, 570
G., Mike 274
Gabrels, Reeves 65
Gabriel, Peter 15, 60, 196, 197, 272, 293, 414, 500
Gabriel, Russ 548, 549
Gabrielle **206**, 406
Gaelle 552
Gaetan, Oscar 202, 346, 347
Gage, Mark 1, 7, 400, 544, 558
Gahan, David 126, 127, 128
Gaines, Rosie 313, 527
Gainsbourg, Serge 7, 155, 199, 280, 398, 416
Galas, Diamanda 2
Galea, Andrew 194
Gallagher, Noel 87, 88
Galliano 113, **206**, 292, 297, 382
Gallup, Simon 97
Gamble & Huff 488
Gamble, Kenneth 426
Gamble, Mark 565
Gane, Tim 486, 488, 527
Ganger **206**
Gang of Four 104
Gang Related 464
Gang Starr 19, 67, 88, 346, 393, 539, 540
Ganja Kru 139, 140, 148, 373
Gannon, Gary 57
Gap Band 521
Garbage 111, 144, **207**, 316, 387, 422, 428, 454, 471, 525
Garbutt, Tim 540
Garcia, Dean 110, 111
Garcia, Jerry 151, 169, 354
Garcia, Ruben 73
Gardiner, Boris 389
Gardiner, Paul 363
Gardner, David 518
Garland, Judy 9
Garner, Peter 491
Garnett, Carlos 117
Garnier, Laurent 1, **207**, 333
Garrett, Siedah 67, 68
Garza, Rob 515, 516
Gas 46, 139, **208**, 259, 260, 304, 471
Gastr del Sol 103, 129, 134, **209**, 290, 377, 379, 453, 468, 487
Gates, David 441, 442
Gaumont, Dominique 118
Gaye, Marvin 177, 316, 551, 552, 560, 561
Gayle, Michelle 131
Gaynor, Gloria 56, 324, 387
Gearwhore **209**
Gee, Mike 274
Gee, Tommy 523
Geesin, Ron 396
Geist, Morgan 51, 110, 157, 158, **209**, 426
Gemini 81, 107, 190, **210**
Genaside II 20, 140, **210**
General Magic 205, **210**, 407
Genesis 169, 500
Genesis, Lee 342
Gentle People **211**, 511, 515
Gerd **211**, 456
Gerideau 1

Germ 48, 79, **211**, 305, 451, 548
Gerrard, Lisa 120, 121, 126, 367
Gershwin, George 280
Gescom 31, 61, 188, **212**, 269, 279, 385, 420
Getz, Stan 174, 294
Ghetto Brothers 43
Ghost **212**, 516
Gianelli, Fred 286
Gibbons, Beth 11, 406, 407, 471
Gibbons, Walter 58, **213**, 277
Gibbs, Joe 389
Gibson, Debbie 265, 270, 317, 435, 546
Gibson, Ken 164
Gifford, Alex 274, 414
Gifford, Katharine 486
Gil, Gilberto 470
Gilbert, Bruce 269, 330, 557
Gilbert, Gillian 356, 357
Gilberto, Astrud 158
Gilberto, Bebel 515
Gilberto, Clifford Rhythm Combination **213**, 295
Giles Giles & Fripp 196
Giles, Michael 196
Giles, Peter 196
Gill, Peter 192
Gillen, Brendan M. 160
Gillespie, Bobby 122, 372, 408, 409
Gillespie, Brian 130
Gilmore, John 312, 495, 496
Gilmour, David 396, 397, 398
Ginsberg, Allen 104, 436
Giorno, John 14, 79
Gira, Michael 556
Giraudy, Miquette 500, 501
Girls 109
Gish, Daniel 40, 135
Gita, Salman 303
Gizz TV 188, 279
Glass, Philip 17, 18, 35, **213**, 343, 365, 369, 388, 427, 436, 452
Gleaming Spires 132, 477
Gleeson, Patrick 324
Glider State 275
Glitter, Gary 3, 48, 283, 400, 565
Global Communication 17, 39, 53, 68, 93, 146, 149, 198, **215**, 254, 269, 345, 382, 427, 480, 529, 559
Global Electronic Network 279
Global Goon **215**
Globo **216**
Glossop, Mick 101
Glover, Leroy 172
Go Go's 477, 478
God Lives Underwater 465, 466
God 175, 254, 291, 508
Godard, Jean-Luc 398
Godflesh 184, **216**, 254, 465, 508, 532
Godfrey, Paul 342
Godfrey, Ross 342
Godin, Nicolas 7
Godspeed You Black Emperor! **216**, 461
Goettel, R. Dwayne 152, 465
Golden Palominos 259, 293, 514
Goldfrapp, Allison **217**, 375
Goldie 21, 36, 67, 74, 75, 134, 139, 142, 151, 188, 189, **217**, 254, 361, 371, 391, 394, 401, 402, 422, 425, 426, 436, 439, 451, 464, 474, 528
Gondry, Michel 55, 115
Gong **218**, 318, 500
Gonzalez 295
Gonzalez, Kenny "Dope" 72, 317, 318, 512, 546

Goodie Mob 138
Googe, Deb 350
Gopher, Alex 7, 333
Gordine, Tim 518
Gordon, Luke 275
Gordon, Martin 477
Gordon, Peter Laurence 436
Gordon, Robert **220**, 313
Gordon, Stefin 433
Gordy, Berry Jr. 393, 452
Gore, Martin L. 126, 127, 128
Gorecki, Henryk Mikolaj 374
Görl, Robert 114
Gosling, John 324
Gotobed, Robert 557
Göttsching, Manuel 24, 25, **221**, 384, 448
Gouryella 105
Graham, Larry 188
Grahame, Lorita 101
Grainer, Ron 43
Gramm **221**
Grand Puba 67
Grandmaster Flash 31, 38, 99, 100, 123, 141, 146, 177, **221**, 269, 285, 301, 470, 502, 532
Grandmaster Flash & the Furious Five 275, 502
Grandmaster Melle Mel 294, 502
Grandmixer D.ST 319
Grant, Eddy 456
Grant, Mark 81
Grant, Mike 100, 115, **222**, 327
Grantby 477
Granular Synthesis 292
Grateful Dead 169, 354, 504
Gravediggaz 412
Gravitar 391
Gravitt, Eric 553, 554
Gravity 142
Gravity Kills 363
Gray, Andrew 560
Gray, Chris **223**
Gray, Howard 19
Gray, Trevor 19
Greece 2000 367, 520
Green Day 143
Green Velvet 81, 85, 190, **223**, 384, 404, 423, 434, 442
Green, Al 15, 38, 125, 173, 550
Greenaway, Peter 364
Greenwich, Ellie 378
Greenwood, Colin 422
Greenwood, Jon 422
Gregory, Glenn 47, 48, 414
Grey, Paris 260, 322, 445, 494
Greinke, Jeff **223**
Grid 10, **224**, 414, 455, 472, 564
Grieg, Edvard 171
Griffin, Mark 323
Groove Armada 6, 37, 130, **224**, 296, 326
Groove Box 146
Groove Culture 1
Groove Groove Melody 56
Grrove Theory **225**
Grooverider 67, 100, 139, 144, 177, 181, **225**, 358, 371, 401, 435, 465, 513
Grooves, Scott **225**
Grosskopf, Harald 25
Grossman, Steve 117, 118
Grubbs, David 377, 379, 468
Guillaume, Jephte 83, 93, **226**, 279
Guines, Tata 294
Gunn, Peter 473
Gunn, Trey 499
Guns N Roses 478, 566

Gunter, Bernhard 325
Gurley, Steve 188
Gurov, Andre 147
Gurtu, Trilok 319
Guru Guru 96, 355
Guru 119, 141, 142, 308, 364, 466
Gus Gus **226**, 366, 444, 461, 515
Gut, Gudrun 162
Guthrie, Robin 20, 73, 97, 98, 120, 330, 471, 560
Guttmacher, Chris 109
Guy 474
Guy Called Gerald 28, 121, 161, **226**, 292, 346, 421
Gypsymen 513

# H
Haack, Bruce 3, 143, **228**, 512
Haag, Bob 477, 478
Hab 154, 195, 196, **230**
Hacke, Alexander 162, 163
Hadi, Kwame 495
Hafler Trio 77, **230**, 552
Hague, Stephen 156, 171, 392
Haigh, Rob 122, 137, 361, 371, 508
Haines, Luke 7
Hair & Skin Trading Company 311
Hal Featuring Gillian Anderson **230**
Halfnelson 477
Hall & Oates 393, 500, 509
Hall, Arsenio 94
Hall, Charlie 154
Hall, Daryl 173, 196, 197
Hall, Terry 525
Hall, Tom T. 330
Halliday, Toni 110, 111, 296
Hamilton 526
Hamilton, Chico 119
Hamilton, Page 355
Hamilton, Tommy 33, 34, 526
Hammill, Peter 9, 196
Hammond Inferno 424
Hammond, Lol 154, 466
Hammond, Paul 532
Hampson, Robert 311, 312, 458, 521
Hampton, Ian 477
Hampton, Michael 142, 200
Hancock, Herbie 24, 117, 148, 150, **231**, 271, 293, 318, 319, 324, 388, 393, 414, 435, 463, 469, 498, 537, 539, 553
Hand, Damian 8
Hand, K 43, 121, **233**, 551
Handley, Ed 56, 57, 70, 71, 399, 400, 428
Handsome Boy Modeling School 302, 412
Hani 123
Hanighen, Bernie 452
Hannant, Beaumont **233**, 435
Hannett, Martin 86, 157, 172, 455
Hansen, Mary 344, 486, 487
Hanson 157
Happy Mondays 42, 57, 155, 157, **234**, 302, 307, 366, 402, 408, 437, 486, 491
Hapshash, Lanse 504
Hard Hop Heathen 443
Hard, Scotty 319, 469
Harden, Brian **234**, 535
Hardfloor 11, 21, 63, 121, **235**, 288
Harding, Carolyn 86
Harding, Phil 360
Harding, Scott 254, 412
Hardkiss 71, 154, **235**, 464
Hardkiss, Scott 495
Hardknox **235**, 326
Hardrive 317
Hardway, James **235**, 276, 369

Hardy, Alfred 479
Hardy, Francoise 29, 268, 399
Hardy, Ron 143, **236**, 269, 285, 322, 327, 395, 445
Harland, Kurt 259
Harlow, Larry 538
Harmonia 96, **236**, 337, 355, 434
Harmony 400 19
Harper, Kevin 359
Harper, Tim 81, 535
Harrington, David 431
Harris, Andre 81
Harris, Barry 556
Harris, Bon 360, 361
Harris, Eddie 45
Harris, Lee 371, 503
Harris, Mick **236**, 286, 293, 294, 305, 451, 497, 508
Harris, Nikki 270, 271
Harris, Norman 441
Harris, Ross 143, 331, 494
Harrison, Richard 486
Harry, Debbie 132, 270, 443, 536
Hart, Mickey 354
Hartley, Scott 301
Hartnoll, Paul 374, 375
Hartnoll, Phil 374, 375
Harvey, Aston 144, 194
Harvey, Connie 289
Harvey, Curtis 325
Harvey, Daddae 474
Harvey, Maxine 154
Harvey, P.J. 291, 525
Hashim 497, 523
Haslinger, Paul **237**, 505, 506
Hassell, Jon 53, 70, 117, 142, 168, 169, 170, **237**, 330, 358, 367, 449, 450, 499
Haswell, Russell 325
HAT **237**
Hatori, Miho 91
Haujobb 152, **238**, 562
Hawkins, Nick 51
Hawkins, Xian 462
Hawkshaw, Kirsty 72, 154, 498
Hawkwind 85, 442
Hawtin, Richie 1, 17, 28, 34, 48, 49, 69, 121, 122, 198, 202, 203, **238**, 261, 286, 297, 322, 329, 352, 400, 401, 515
Hayes, Hunter 86
Hayes, Isaac 78, 179, 387, 511, 550, 551, 561
Haynes, Gibby 331
Haynes, Graham 294
Haynes, Roy 294
Haza, Ofra 151
Hazel, Eddie 72, 199, 200
Hazlewood, Lee 6
Head 486
Headley, Felix "Deadly" 155
Headrillaz 140, **239**, 193
Heal, Marc 108, 109
Heard, Larry 3, 36, 83, 115, 184, 185, 190, **239**, 269, 285, 300, 333, 361, 373, 385, 423, 535, 565
Heard, Paul 307
Heaven 17 47, 48, **240**, 298, 343, 414
Heavenly Music Corporation 85, **241**, 393, 463
Heavy D 315
Hebden, Kieran 189, 190
Heckmann, Thomas P. 6, 194, 336, 428, 549
Hedfunk 99
Hedger, David 340
Hedges, Mike 9

Heeman, Christoph **241**
Heggie, Will 97
Heights of Abraham 184, 473
Heil, Johannes 546, 557
Heilbronn, Matthias 278
Heinz 462
Heldon **241**
Hellborg, Jonas 72, 293, 319
Heller, Pete 178, 520
Helm, Carl 441
Henderson, Fletcher 495
Henderson, Michael 117, 118
Hendrix, Billy 100
Hendrix, Jimi 25, 94, 116, 199, 200, 284, 516, 541
Hendryx, Nona 319
Henke, Robert **243**, 321, 340
Henry, Pierre 2, 46, 138, **243**, 298, 427, 447
Henry, Scott **243**
Hentschlager, Kurt 292
Herbaliser 99, 100, 138, **244**, 288, 387
Herbert 49, 150, **244**, 286, 511, 549, 559
Herbert, Chris 60
Herbert, Frank 448
Herbert, Matthew 11, 30, 93, 149, 150, 153, **244**, 254, 266, 477, 529
Hercules 269, 300
Herkenberg, Kurt 504
Hernandez, Patrick 309
Herndon, John 129, 264, 522
Herrera, Oscar 58
Herrmann, Bernard 2
Hersh, Kristin 346
Hex 99
Hexstatic **245**
Hibbert, Toots 15
Hicks, Dan 151
Hidden Agenda 177, 426
Hideki, Kato 458
Higgins, Billy 566
Higgins, Neil 135
High Llamas 2, 3, 104, 280, 438, 439, 451, 486, 487, 527
Higher Intelligence Agency 22, 25, 53, 124, 193, 198, **245**, 263, 342, 352, 378, 408, 477, 529
Higher Sense 377
Highland 454
Hilckmann, Jorvis 416
Hildenbeutel, Ralf 546
Hill, Dave 38, 58
Hill, Eric 378
Hill, Joseph 15
Hill, Stephen 8
Hillage, Steve 25, 154, **246**, 268, **322**, 372, 373, 500, 501
Hiller, Holger 188, 320, 428
Hillier, Paul 81, 427
Hilt 465
Hilton, Eric 515, 516
HIM 134, 158, **246**
Himadri 186, 514
Hinge, Richard 63
Hinton, Joie 159
Hip Optimist 326
Hirsch, Beth 7
His Name Is Alive 391
Hive 178
Ho, Alain 326, 463
Ho, Oliver 51, 346, 475
Hodge, Jamie 102
Hoffman, Dr. Samuel J. **246**
Hoffman, Mathias 546
Hogan, Annie 8, 9, 10
Hogan, Lance 121

Hoile, Jed 273
Hokusai 452
Holder, Nick 49
Holiday, Billie 131
Holistic 195
Holkenborg, Tom 274
Holland, Andre 535
Holland, Dave 117, 118, 260
Hollis, Ed 503
Hollis, Mark 503, 504, 537
Holloway, Loleatta 56, 83, 299, 441
Holloway, Nicky 199, 424
Holm, Georg 461
Holm, Lucia 496
Holmes, David 35, **246,** 279, 288, 437, 501, 528
Holmes, Kate 154
Holmes, Richard "Groove" 45
Holmes, Tim 122
Holness, Winston Niney 282
Holosud 205, **247**
Holroyd, Bob 278
Holst, Gustav 520
Holt, Errol "Flabba" 155, 156, 283, 450
Holt, John 15
Holweck, Stephane 274
Homer & Jethro 111
Honda, Yuka 91
Honegger, Arthur 563
Hood 13, **247**
Hood, Robert 28, 39, 40, 130, 182, **248,** 263, 327, 328, 420, 497, 504, 533, 534, 548, 551, 566, 567
Hook, Peter 71, 97, 255, 356, 357
Hooper, Nellee 54, 55, 308, 316, 339, 474
Hooverphonic **248,** 515
Hopa & Bones 188
Hope-Taylor, Randy 258
Horn 149
Horn, Trevor 10, 23, 150, 192, 272, 322
Horny Horns 180
Horowitz, Richard 440
Horton, Jim 515
Horton, Yogi 268, 319
Horvitz, Wayne 569
Hoschi 6
Hosler, Mark 353
Hosono, Haruomi 30, **248,** 264, 286, 440, 509, 564
Hot Butter 388
House of 909 85, **249,** 191
House of Pain 201, 387
Housemartins 45, 179, 180, 326
Housey Doingz 191, **249**
Houston, Whitney 189, 270, 277, 284, 308, 318, 319
Howard, John 58
Howard, Simon 507
Howe, Liam 471
Howe, Steve 414
Howlett, Liam 3, 166, 412, 413, 414, 471, 557
Howlett, Mike 186
Hoyle, Arthur 495
Hrvátski **249**
Hubbard, Freddie 473
Hubble 537
Huber, Rupert 288, 522
Hucknall, Mick 55
Hudson, Keith **249**
Huff, Leon 426
Hughes, Andy 373
Hughes, Chris 125
Hughes, David 375
Hughes, John III 467, 468

Hugo Largo 187
Hula 78
Hulme, Andrew 366, 473
Hultgren, Carl 556
Human League 47, 95, 113, 126, 153, **250,** 286, 304, 331, 345, 374, 376, 412, 473
Human Mesh Dance 130, **251,** 414, 415, 457
Humanoid 203
Humate 140, 385, 422, 444, 520, 542
Humberstone, Klive 255
Humberstone, Nigel 255, 256, 257
Humon, Naut 261
Humphreys, Paul 375, 376
Humphreys, Steve 9
Humphries, Tony 41, 60, 86, 185, **251,** 299, 518
Hunt, Jacqui 126
Hunter, Paul 75
Hurley, Steve "Silk" **251,** 285, 298, 412, 442
Hurt, John 23
Hurt, Philip 441
Hush 72
Hussain, Zakir 319
Hutch, Willie 87
Hutter, Ralf 61, 165, 286, 287
Hutton, Tim 549
Hybrid 72, **252,** 105
Hyde, John 536
Hyde, Karl 195, 535, 536
Hyman, Dick 134
Hype 18, 64, 139, 140, 148
Hyper On Experience 175, 401

## I

I Cube **253,** 316, 484, 510
I F 68, 93, 184, **253,** 254, 304, 533, 549
I Start Counting 188
Ibbotson, Daniel 196, **254,** 368
Icarus 276
Ice Cube 94
Ice T 119, 140, 509, 533, 554
Ice 184, **254,** 508
Icebreaker 395
Icho Candy 381
Icons 59, **254,** 275
ID 375
Idjut Boys **254,** 255
If 124
Ifgray, Brandi **255**
Ignorant, Steve 110
Ikeda, Ryoji **255,** 503
Ilhan, Adem 189, 195
Illinton 391
Illusion of Safety 377
Ils 193
Ils & Solo 74
Immersion 112, 282, 461
In Sync 340
In the Nursery 99, **255,** 256, 257, 438
Incarnate 297
Incognito **257,** 258, 442, 488
Indeep 111
India 317, 318, 364, 546
Indian Ropeman **258**
Indica 424
Indigo Girls 463
Indio 50, 258
Indo 161, 527
Infants 416
Infesticons **258,** 259
Infiniti 27, 28, 111, **259,** 336
Information Society **259,** 317, 546

Ink, Mike 7, 31, 69, 75, 94, 159, 188, **259,** 260, 279, 304, 336, 382, 383, 447, 523
Inner City 106, 107, 108, 159, **260,** 285, 308, 322, 442, 445, 446, 494, 566
Inner Life 299
Innersphere 466
Innervisions 313
Innerzone Orchestra 106, 107, 108, **260,** 261, 384, 415, 425, 464, 566
Innes, Andrew 408
Innocence 407
Inoue, Tetsu 8, 29, 30, 116, 130, 188, 198, **261,** 262, 279, 286, 352, 459, 540
Insider 63
Insides **262**
Inspiral Carpets 161, 188, 491
Insync Vs. Mysteron 340
Intense 59, 75
Intensity 475
Interceptor 347
Interface 140
Intermix 126
Interpreters 557
Invisibl Skratch Piklz 45, 111, 149, **262,** 275, 280, 302, 334, 387, 462, 563
INXS 366
IO **262,** 263, 412, 419, 420
Iration Steppas 155
Ireland, David 19
Irish Film Orchestra 150
Irmler, Hans Joachim 181, 182
Irresistible Force 53, 153, **263,** 408, 457, 561
Isaacs, Gregory 469
ISAN **263,** 264
Ishii, Ken 71, 263, **264,** 323, 404
Ishino, Takkyu 504
Isley Brothers 123, 521
Isolee 255
Isotope 217 **264,** 265, 522
Issakidis, George 325, 326
Ives, Charles 544

## J

J Live 391
J., Walt 28
Jackman, David 377
Jackson, Gisele 442
Jackson, Janet 123, 178, 308, 342, 356, 363, 442, 513, 544
Jackson, Joe 556
Jackson, Mahalia 336
Jackson, Michael 1, 123, 178, 285, 317, 334, 342, 386, 439, 442, 511, 520, 546
Jackson, Milt 119
Jackson, Ronald Shannon 293
Jackson, Vivian "Yabby U" 282
Jacob's Optical Stairway 189, **266,** 501
Jacobs, Ollie 21
Jacoby, JAnna 58
Jade 4 U 279
Jagger, Mick 65, 89, 173, 293, 469, 502
Jaguar 443
Jah Screw 283
Jah Stitch 282
Jallokin 52
Jam & Spoon **266,** 423
Jam El Mar 266
Jam 174, 462
Jam, Billy 262
Jamal, Ahmad 473
Jamerson, James 172
James Bong **266,** 361
James Gang 470
James 437, 507

James, Bob 111, 475
James, Lloyd 282
James, Mike **266,** 429
James, Richard D. 17, 18, 158, 270, 345, 346, 387, 403, 483
James, Richey 61, 111, 153, 281, 286, 307
James, Tommy & the Shondells 324
Jamie Wednesday 404
Jamiroquai 113, **266,** 267, 393, 511, 546
Jammin' Unit 6, 7, 260, **267,** 336, 559, 570
Jane's Addiction 128, 324, 414
Janiak, Seb 115
Janis, Stephen 141
Janney, Eli 471
Jansen, Steve 90, 267, 499
Janssen, Ole 136
Japan 90, **267,** 405, 499
Japanese Telecom 152
Jarman, Derek 98, 168, 446
Jarre, Jean Michel 7, 62, 113, 263, **268,** 388, 429, 443, 475, 506
Jarre, Maurice 268, 432, 485
Jarrett, Keith 117, 118
Jarvis, Clifford 495
Jasper Street Company 317
Jay Z 120, 201, 202, 551
Jay, Norman 58, 393
Jay, Sara 316
Jaydee 120, 347, 520
Jaz Klash **268,** 269, 470
Jazz Butcher 479
Jazz Messengers 406
Jazzanova 142, 189, 278, 280
Jazzie B. 39, 474
Jazzy Jeff 364
Jazzy M 374
Jb3 49
JB's 200, 274, 386, 414
JDS 520
Jeck, Philip **269**
Jed 57
Jedi Knights 1, 85, 100, 154, 264, **269,** 316, 427
Jeffers, Sam 189
Jefferson Airplane 504
Jefferson, Marshall 1, 4, 36, 40, 52, 77, 79, 145, 190, 199, **269,** 270, 285, 300, 344, 395, 445, 456, 488, 501, 510
Jeffrey, Tim 180
Jeffs, Chris 17, 111, 112, 281, 282
Jega 178, 202, **270**
Jeglitza, O. 424
Jenkinson, Tom 86, 346, 483, 484
Jenks, Andy 11, 484
Jennings, Susan 59
Jenssen, Geir 53, 54, 352
Jeru the Damaja 418, 423, 470
Jervis, Andrew 74
Jessamine **271,** 402, 479
Jesse's Gang 445
Jestram, Bernd 507
Jesus & Mary Chain 20, 87, 349, 350, 408, 455, 480
Jesus Jones 17, 21, 259, 413, 532
Jeswa **271,** 394
Jhelisa 113, **271,** 382
Jimpster **271**
Jive Bunny and the Mastermixers 272, **271**
JMJ & Flytronix 288
JMJ & Richie 175
Jobim, Antonio Carlos 91, 487
Jodelet, Florent 490
John, Lee 38
Johnson, Alphonso 554
Johnson, Clark 468

# INDEX

Johnson, Denise 86
Johnson, Donald 86
Johnson, Glen 395
Johnson, Holly 192, 283
Johnson, Jack 117
Johnson, Matt 8, 9
Johnson, Michael 273
Johnson, Paul 81
Johnson, Soni 273
Johnston, Ben 567
Johnston, Jan 71
Johnston, Jim 339
Joi **272**
Joint Venture 143
Jolliffe, Steve 506
Jon & Vangelis 543
Jon Five 27
Jones, Brian 415
Jones, Davy 64
Jones, Elvin 92, 519
Jones, Gareth 172
Jones, Glenn 109
Jones, Gloria 472
Jones, Grace 89, **272**, 361, 441, 469, 511
Jones, Howard 150, **272**, 273
Jones, John Paul 170
Jones, Mark 298, 339, 555
Jones, Mick 51, 52
Jones, Percy 169
Jones, Philly Joe 125
Jones, Quincy 138, 185, 357, 521
Jones, Rickie Lee 372, 423
Jones, Robin 51
Jones, Shay 511
Jones, Stephen 457
Jones, Steve 313
Jones, Tom 23
Jonze, Spike 55, 56, 115, 180
Jonzon, Moony 105
Jonzun Crew 194, **273**
Jordan 108
Jordan, Ken 108
Jordan, Louis 334
Joseph, Corrina 41
Joshua, Maurice 317, 435, 488
Jourgensen, Alain 331, 332, 465
Jourgensen, Patty 332
Journeyman 99, 138, **273**
Joy Division 19, 40, 71, 86, 97, 135, 136, 172, 255, 356, 357
Joyce, Chris 157
Judge Jules 131
Jumeaux 255, 257
Jumping Jack Frost 142
June of Forty Four 134
Jungle Brothers 38, 45, 119, 180, 194, **273**, 274, 318, 319, 423, 479, 509, 512
Jungle Juice 544
Jungle Wonz 269, 270
Junior Varsity km **274**
Junk Project 367
Junkie XL 140, **274**, 539
Juno Reactor **274**, 275, 544
Jurassic Five 17, 111, **275**
Juryman **275**, 485
Just Ice 314
Just, Christopher 139, 180
Justice 254, **275**, 276
Justice, Tony 275
Justified Ancients of Mu Mu 283
JVC Force 423

## K

K Alexi **277**, 323
K Collective 382

K Klass 178, **277**
K1 554
K Scope 289
K., Francois 254, 255, **277**
Ka-Spel, Edward 99, 297, 465
Kahler, Christoph 136
Kaiser, Henry 318, 377, 394
Kajagoogoo 59
Kalte Farben 198
Kamaflarge 16
Kamins, Mark 309
Kandel, Michael 523
Kandis **278**, 302, 403
Kane, J. Saul 62, 92, 129, 170, 368, 438
Kane, Jonathan 129
Kante, Mory 424
Kantoff, Howie 441
Kappmeier, Ralf 443
Karn, Mick 267
Karoli, Michael 82
Karrer, Chris 12, 13, 14
Kasem, Casey 354
Kasiek, Alex 303, 524
Kasper, Robert 388
Katrin 56
Kavanagh, Chris 51
Kay, Jay 266, 267
KCC 4, 39
KCYC 86, 547
Kean, Martin 486
Keating, Theo 559
Keillor, Garrison 74
Keith, Ray 165, **278**, 361
Kellett, Tim 370
Kelley, John **278**, 279
Kember, Pete 473, 476, 479, 480
Kemistry & Storm 181
Kempton, David 93
Kendall, Paul 311, 312
Kendra, Karime 425
Kendrick, David 132, 477, 478
Kennedy 373
Kennedy, Inigo 475
Kenny Ken 122, 138, 144, 508
Kent, Stephen 358, 432, 476
Kenton, Stan 34, 512
Kermit 57
Kerosene 570
Kerouac, Jack 45
Kerr, Jeremy 86
Kershaw, Nik 298
Kessler, Thomas 191
Kevorkian, Francois 93, 173, 191, 254, 277, 278, 299, 436, 454
Kevy Kev 316
Key, Cevin 152, 465
Key, Ted 180
Khan & Walker 279
Khan 188, **279**
Khan, Ali Akbar 436
Khan, Chaka 48, 185, 285, 335
Khan, Nusrat Fateh Ali 70, 272, 330, 463
Khan, Praga **279**, 280, 304, 469
Khan, Steve 556
Kick Horns 171
Kid Batchelor 39
Kid Koala 147, 185, **280**
Kid Loco **280**, 327, 331, 463
Kid Loops 166, **281**, 484, 485
Kid N Play 125
Kid 606 116, 126, 164, **281**, 298, 299, 304, 391
Kid Spatula **281**, 345, 346, 467, 476
Kier, Lady Miss 122, 123
Killah Priest 146, 319

KillaHurtz 279
Killing Joke 23, 28, 372, 373
Kincaid, Jan 67
Kinchen, Marc 334
Kinesthesia 17, 111, 112, **281**, 282, 346, 387
King Bees 64
King Britt 282, 557
King Britt & Sylk 130 **282**
King Crimson 182, 196, 197, 359, 499
King G & The J Krew 320
King Kong 5, 468
King Tubby 282, 283, 295, 381, 389, 450, 459
King, B.B. 300
King, John 155, 157
King, Justin 108
King, Kerry 72
King, Kevin 298
King, Martin Luther Jr. 418
King, Morgan 443
King, Roger 433
Kingsland, Paddy 43
Kingsley, Gershon 388
Kirchner, Leon 493
Kirk, Richard H. 39, 77, 78, 79, 165, **283**, 313, 435, 442, 443, 498
Kirkland, Scott 108
Kirlian 383
Kiss 103, 524
Kitaro 448
Kitchens of Distinction 461
Kizys, Algis 187
Klaatu 185
Klein & MBO 254, **283**
Klein, Phil 42
Klemmer, John 142
KLF 6, 12, 53, 88, 153, 154, 263, **283**, 284, 326, 340, 372, 407, 475
Klimek, Johnny 542
Klubbheads 165
Kluster 96, 337, 344, 448
Klute 42, **284**, 285, 379
Klystron 516
KMFDM 459, 465
Knak, Thomas 266
Knaup-Kroetenschwanz, Renate 12, 13, 14
Knight, Frederick 57
Knight, Phil 297
Knights of the Occasional Table 568
Knowtoryus 44
Knuckles, Frankie 58, 100, 179, 199, 277, 285, 289, 299, 301, 322, 327, 341, 342, 385, 412, 415, 435, 442, 445, 488, 511, 513, 520
Koch, Ingmar 279
Köda 256
Koenig, Gottfried Michael **285**, 340, 518
Kofi 309
Koglin, Mike 444
Komeda 150, 196
Komputer 2, **285**, 286
Kondo, Toshinori 142, 521, 569
Koner, Thomas 41, 175, **286**, 405, 449
Konishi, Yasuharu 398, 399
Konitz, Lee 102
Kooky Scientist 1, **286**
Kool & the Gang 386
Kool G Rap 315, 537
Kool G Rap & DJ Polo 486
Kool Keith 17, 33, 47, 146, 149, 262, 319, 353, 387, 412, 413, 531, 532
Kool Rock Steady 530
Kooner, Jagz 10, 11, 437

Kopf, Biba 114
Korn 409, 539
Kosmic Messenger 107, 461, 462
Kosmik Kommando 17, 153, **286**
Kosmos 383
Kosugi, Takehisa 526
Kotik, Petr 81
Koxbox **286**
Kraftwelt 2
Kraftwerk 2, 3, 4, 19, 25, 27, 29, 33, 37, 38, 40, 42, 52, 58, 61, 66, 87, 89, 96, 105, 111, 126, 148, 152, 153, 154, 161, 163, 164, 165, 173, 191, 202, 254, 278, 282, 285, **286**, 287, 288, 295, 298, 299, 302, 322, 337, 339, 343, 344, 351, 355, 357, 362, 375, 376, 378, 384, 386, 387, 400, 407, 434, 440, 445, 448, 456, 461, 506, 511, 514, 519, 523, 524, 533, 547, 548, 551, 552, 554, 557, 564, 565
Kramer, Amanda 259, 318
Krash 275
Krause, Bernie 46
Krause, Dagmar 275
Krause, Jan 44
Kraushaar, Bob 9, 10
Kreidler 163, **288**, 402, 518
Krieger, Klaus 506
Kristian, David 184, **288**, 304
Krivit, Danny 93, 278
Kroll, David 460
Krome & Time 113
Krome, Thomas 51
Kronos Quartet 315, 377, 431, 568
KRS One 125, 146, 314, 469
Kruder & Dorfmeister 75, 184, **288**, 289, 387, 419, 458, 465, 515, 522, 523, 551
Kruder, Peter 263, 288, 387
Kruger, Andreas 129
Krupa, Gene 19
Krust 142, 298, 464, 465, 470
Kruton 71
Kubera, Joseph 81
Kudo 466, 537
Kukl 55
Kula Shaker 339, 413
Kupper, Eric **289**, 342
Kurnoth, Volker 136
Kuschneroit, Peter 451, 493
Kushin, Andrew 302
Kustomized 109
Kuti, Fela 93, 527
Kuti, Femi Anikulapo 254, 255
Kwaten, Kwame 113

## L

L Double 21, 138
L7 413
L., Jonny 133, **290**, 452
La Dusseldorf 355
La Funk Mob 199
La Magia 9, 10
LA Style **290**, 359
LaBarbara, Joan 80
Labradford 271, **290**, 291, 382, 402, 523, 524, 531
Lacksman, Dan 124, 510
Lacy, Steve 556
Ladd, Mike 258, 259
Laibach 188
Laid Back 130
Laika **291**, 341, 453, 462
Lamb 68, 162, 184, 288, **291**, 292, 326, 333, 385, 420, 471
Lambert, Moira 438
Lamont, Matt "Jam" 527

Lampe, Hans 355
LAN 288
Lancaster, Byard 294
Land of the Loops 330
Land, Harold 34
Landry, George 485
Landstrumm, Neil 110, **292**, 528, 548, 549
Laner, Brad 163, 164
Lang, David 431
Langan, Gary 23
Lange, Fritz 343
Langheinrich, Ulf **292**
Langlands, Justin 407
Langston, Leslie 560
Lanois, Daniel 70, 73, 168, 169
Laraaji 509
Lard 331
Large Professor 498, 563
Larkin, Kenny 1, 28, 39, 107, 116, 121, **292**, 293, 322, 323, 400, 446, 461, 462
Lassigue Bendthaus 29, 115
Last Exit 293
Last Poets 319
Laswell, Bill 38, 72, 77, 118, 141, 169, 184, 198, 262, 286, **293**, 294, 295, 305, 318, 319, 330, 352, 353, 437, 446, 449, 450, 451, 458, 469, 492, 508, 514, 552, 553
LaTour **295**
Laub 105, **295**
Laughing Hands 449
Lauper, Cyndi 545, 546
Laux, Heiko 557
Lavelle, James 30, 145, 148, 338, 345, 537
Lavoe, Hector 317, 546
Law, Joanna 100
Lawes, Henry "Junjo" 450
Lawrence, Azar 118
Lawrence, Christopher 100, **295**
Lawrence, Dale 515
Lawrence, Vince 445
Laws, Hubert 553
Laws, Leonie 68, 464
Laws, Sebastian 254
Lawson, Herb 488, 510
Lawson, Ralph 184, 549
Layo & Bushwacka 193, **295**, 333
Lazonby, Peter 140, 454
Lb 29
Le Car 3, 24, 125, 184, **295**, 296, 516, 549
Le Deuce 434
Leadfoot 331
League of Gentlemen 196, 197
Leak, Maysa 258, 488
Leary, Timothy 24, 25, 85, 356, 416, 437, 512
Leather Strip 259
Leblanc, Keith 63, 459, 502
Leckie, John 422
Lectric Cargo 71
Led Zeppelin 19, 106, 283, 290, 367, 425, 492
Lee, Bunny 15, 282
Lee, Peggy 470
Lee, Rick 91
Lee, Sara 196, 197
Lee, Spike 417, 418
Lee, Tim "Love" **296**
Leeb, Bill 126, 198
Leer, Thomas 414
LeFriant, Christophe 326, 327, 463
Leftfield 11, 21, 87, 152, 295, 296, 313, 366, 407, 482, 536
Legendary Pink Dots **296**, 297, 465
Legion of Green Men **297**
Legrand, Michel 398

Leibezeit, Jaki 82, 83, 419
Leigh, Dennis 533
Leigh, Mike 373
Leila **297**
Leiner, Robert **297**, 475
Lekebusch, Cari 4, 51, 194, **298**, 333, 470, 511
Lemon D 23, 134, **298**, 452
Lemon Interrupt 536
Lemon Kittens 256
Lemper, Ute 364
Lennon, John 65
Lennon, Sean 91
Lennox, Annie 114, 157, 173, 174, 513
Lentz, Daniel 73
Leonard, Patrick 309
Leonard, Simon 188, 285
Leopold, Peter 12
Les Nubians 509
Les Rhythmes Digitales **298**, 302, 555, 559
Less than Jake 111
Lesseninglesson 296
Lesser 164, 281, 298, 299, 391
Letta 34
Letts, Don 51, 152
Levan, Larry 83, 93, 100, 172, 277, 278, 285, **299**, 366, 388, 436, 445, 511
Level 42 40, 298
Level 9 520
Levene, Keith 418, 419
Levy, Andrew 67
Levy, Barrington 424
Lewis, Bob 131, 132
Lewis, Donna 282
Lewis, George 293, 318, 569
Lewis, Graham 330, 557, 558
Lewis, Jason 70
Lewis, Kenny Lee 484
Lewis, Linda 326
Lexauncult 306
Lexton, Charlie 113, 281
Lexton, Jamie 281
LFO 1, 23, 28, 35, 62, 92, 147, 163, 190, **299**, 313, 351, 359, 438, 483, 504, 509, 551, 557
Liaisons Dangereuses 464, 473
Liberty City 202, 346, 347
Libra 444
Lidell, Jamie 497
Lieb, Oliver 105, 423, 544
Liebezeit, Jaki 82, 128, 402, 403
Liebman, Dave 118
Life on Mars 367
Ligeti, Gyorgy 285, 458
Light of The World 257
Lighthouse Family 254, 513
Lightnin' Rod 138
Lightning Seeds 283, 428
Lights in a Fat City 358
Like a Tim **300**, 333
Lil Kim 356
Lil' Louis 118, 278, **300**, 323, 333, 491
Lil' Mo' Yin Yang 41
Lilith **300**
Lillywhite, Steve 533
Lima, Alyrio 554
Lime 468
Limerick, Alison **301**, 318
Liminal 552, 553
Limoni, Mirko 56
Limp Bizkit 539
Lindsay, Arto 91, 146, 147, 440, 509, 553
Ling, John 40
Link/Reload 456

Link 68, 456
Lionrock **301**, 466
Lippok, Robert 518
Lippok, Ronald 507, 519
LiPuma, Tommy 174
Liquid Language 133
Liquid Liquid 111, 172, 194, **301**, 416
Liquid Metal 443
Liquid Sky 188, 279
Liquid Sun 141
Lironi, Stephen 57
Lisa Lisa 545, 546
Lissat, Jens 542
Listening Pool 375
Lithops **301**, 302, 344, 345
Live Human **302**
Live Skull 315
Live 342
Living Colour 502
Livingstone, Andrew "Doc" 488
LL Cool J 172, 201, 202, 314, 414
Lloop 552, 553
Lloyd Webber, Andrew 310
Lloyd, Rupert J. 297
Lo Fidelity Allstars 50, 123, **302**, 326
Lockett, Peter 521
Locks, Damon 129
Locust 32, **302**, 303, 320, 446, 471
Loderbauer, Max 495
London Community Gospel Choir 481
London Funk Allstars 355, 469
London Philharmonic Orchestra 84
Long, Ben 475
Long, Richard 299
Longdancer 173
Longpigs 313
Loop 204, 290, 311, 312, 553
Loop Guru **303**, 568
Looper **303**
Loose Joints 436
Lopez, Marcos 541
Lords of Acid 52, 279, 280, **303**, 304
Lords, Traci 274
Lorelei 88
Lorimer, Pete 458, 548
Los Bravos 85
Loschner, Klaus 419
Lou Two 317
Lounge Lizards 91
Love 280
Love and Rockets 259, 415, 422, 455
Love from San Francisco 407
Love Happy 308
Love Inc. 75, 260, 404, **304**
Love Spirals Downwards 59
Love Tribe 442
Love, Duma 91
Love, Ray 555
Lovell, Steve 186
Lovich, Lene 150
Lovin' Spoonful 485
Low Frequency Band 48
Low Res **304**
Low 382, 395
Lowe, Chris 164, 391, 392
Lowe, Rene 451, 541
Lowfish 288, **304**, 473
LSG 101, 367
Lu Cont, Jacques 298
Lucas, Gary 556
Lucas, Reggie 118
Lucid Dream 509
Lucier, Alvin **304**, 305
Ludke, Thomas 443
Lull 8, 25, 53, **305**, 449, 451

Lulu 277
Lum, Ryan 59
Lumb, James 164
Luniz 18
Luomo 125
Luscious Jackson 44, 91, 172, 414, 525
Luscombe, Stephen 59
Lush 5, 154, 350
Lusk 163
Lustmord 8, 288, **305**, 306, 430
Lustmord, Brian 514
Luvah, Bryce 314, 315
Lux, Matt 264
Luxa, Hypo 331
Luxuria 19
Luxxe, G.D. 4, 296
Lybaert, Koen 484
Lycia 59
Lydon, John 38, 296, 419
Lynch, David 305, 312, 393
Lyons, Richard 353
Lyrics Born 145

# M

M & S 318
M People 178, 277, **307**, 342, 366, 442, 444
Maal, Baaba 515
Maas, Timo 279, **307**, 308, 367, 423, 454
Mac, Mark 188, 189, 266, 451, 510
Macero, Teo 117, 118
Mack 478
Mack, Al 531
Macka B 308
Mackay, Andy 168
MacKaye, Ian 331
MacKenzie, Billy 19, 48, 564
Mackintosh, C.J. 20, 101, **308**, 316
Maclise, Angus 102, 567
MacMillan, Stewart 466
Macrocosmica 337
Mad Cobra 529
Mad Lion 324
Mad Professor 16, 38, 152, **308**, 309, 316, 317, 373, 389, 390, 391
Maddkatt Chronicles 182
Maddkatt Courtship 182, **309**
Maderna, Bruno 50, 490
Madonna 44, 55, 89, 164, 202, 270, 278, 298, **309**, 310, 311, 316, 317, 332, 342, 346, 374, 413, 474, 511, 512, 520, 545, 546
Mael, Ron 477, 510
Mael, Russell 477, 478, 510
Magazine 2, 533, 547
Maggotron 42, 394
Magic Mike 143
Magic, Timmi 153
Magnetic 276
Magnusson, Jakob 55
Maguire, Mike 274
Mahavishnu Orchestra 483, 553
Maher, Fred 318, 319
Maida, Sal 477
Main 164, 290, **311**, 312, 449, 458, 521
Main Source 67
Mais, Erroll 450
Maitland, Charles 405
Majik, J. 23, 298, **312**, 313, 395
Major Problem 279
Malcolm, Joy 551
Maldini, Jason 203
Malins, Steve 362, 363
Mallinder, Stephen 77, 78, 79
Malmsteen, Yngwie 72
Mamet, David 310

Mammal 540
Man Called Adam 296, **313**
Man or Astro Man? 456
Man Two Man 387
Mancini, Henry 78
Mancuso, David 93, 100, 299
Mandell, Jake **313**
Mandrill 141
Mandroid 148
Mangione, Chuck 324
Mani 409, 491
Maniatis, George 84
Manic Street Preachers 87, 162, 438
Manilow, Barry 139, 315
Manish Boys 64
Manix 189, 469
Mankey, Earle 477
Mankey, James 477
Mann, Groovie 331
Mann, Herbie 487
Mann, Mickey 407
Manna **313**
Manning, Anthony 70, **314**
Mantronik, Kurtis **314**, 315, 427, 442
Mantronix 63, 100, 138, 141, 161, 204, 281, 300, **314**, 315, 371, 513, 545
Manzanera, Phil 168, 169
Manzarek, Ray 566
Mar, Leon 21, 204, 355
Marc & the Mambas 9
Marc 7 275
Marcheschi, Cork 183
Marching Girls 120
Marclay, Christian 269, **315**
Marden Hill 57
Margouleff, Robert 520, 521, 560
Marguerite, Dolores C. 255, 257
Marie, Teena 511
Marilyn Manson 17, 22, 143, 304, 360
Marine Girls 174
Mark NRG 16
Mark Oh 555
Mark Seven 16
Markie, Biz 45, 119, 315, 509
Marks, Toby 39
Marley Marl **315**, 316
Marley, Bob 15, 38, 142, 295, 319, 381, 389, 390, 391, 561
Marley, Bob & the Wailers 389
Marley, Rita 390
Marmion 541
Marquerita, Dolores 256
Marr, Johnny 47, 57, 164, 165, 357, 392
Marron, Gordon 537
MARRS 20, 63, 101, 308, 314, **316**
Marsalis, Wynton 556
Marsh, Helena 49
Marsh, Ian Craig 47, 48
Marsh, Jon 49
Marsh, Richard 50, 404
Marshack, Rose 441
Marshall H 146
Marshall, Daddy G. 316
Marshall, Ken "Hi Watt" 152
Marshes 49
Marston, Steve 113
Martha & the Vandellas 65
Martian 144, 535
Martin Circus 28
Martin, Billie Ray 71, 83, **316**
Martin, Billy 91
Martin, Doc 140, **316**, 442
Martin, George 533
Martin, Kevin 47, 147, 175, 254, 508, 509
Martin, Luci 89

Martine 525
Martyn, John 378
Marumari 391
Marusha 555
Marvin, Hank 268
Marxman 135, 470
Mas 2008 130
Masada 261, 569
Mask 464
Maslen, Riz 21, 315, 355, 469, 470
Mason, Nick 396, 397
Mason, Stephen 51
Mason, Vanessa 424
Masquerade 326
Mass 560
Massey, Graham 23, 55, 86, 161, 162, 457, 565
Massimo 115
Massive Attack 11, 15, 16, 35, 38, 55, 119, 174, 175, 257, 296, 297, 308, 315, 317, 338, 339, 347, 359, 366, 406, 407, 423, 464, 471, 474, 477, 525, 526, 538, 550, 551
Master Ace 315
Master Musicians of Joujouka 293
Master P 142
Masters at Work 41, 58, 72, 93, 115, 123, 179, 189, 269, 300, 301, **317**, 318, 364, 435, 442, 488, 510, 511, 512, 513, 531, 543, 546, 548
Mateo & Matos 93, 118, **318**
Mateo, John 318
Material 38, 117, 293, 294, **318**, 319, 373, 483
Mathews, Max 90, **319**, 320
Matlock, Glen 533
Matmos 281, 298, **320**, 395, 467, 468
Matos, Eddie "EZ" 318
Matrix 137, **320**, 371
Matsuura, Toshio 536
Mattock, Jon 480
Matz, Dan 556
Mau 135
Maudsley, Frank 186
Maunick, Jean-Paul "Bluey" 257, 258
Maupin, Bennie 117, 324
Maurice, Maik 429
Maurizio 28, 41, 107, 190, 259, **320**, 321, 340, 401, 403, 405, 497, 504, 511, 524, 541, 566
Mause **321**, 407
Maxfield, Richard **322**
Maxi Jazz 177
Maxim 413
Maxwell 352
Maxwell House 194, 195
May, Charlie 482
May, Derrick 4, 7, 16, 24, 27, 28, 31, 34, 39, 40, 42, 43, 50, 58, 68, 100, 106, 107, 110, 121, 129, 147, 164, 190, 258, 260, 264, 266, 277, 293, **322**, 323, 327, 328, 356, 368, 378, 384, 385, 400, 404, 407, 415, 429, 442, 445, 446, 451, 457, 461, 462, 494, 500, 504, 509, 515, 565
Mayall, John 539
Mayfield, Curtis 341, 464
Mazelle, Kym 333, 513
Mazurek, Rob 264, 377, 382
Mbulu, Letta 393
MC Ade 394
MC Cash 316
MC Conrad 74, 75
MC Det 146, 425
MC Eric 509
MC5 38, 284, 408

MC Lyte 412
MC 900 Ft Jesus **323**
MC Serch 67
MC Shan 275, 315, 316
MC Shy D 143
MC Solaar 85, 199, 344
MC Tee 314, 315
MC Tunes 161
MC Wildski 45
MCA 44
McBean, Colin 4, 39
McBride, Brian 484
McBride, Woody 131, 138, 147
McCabe, Nick 51
McCarrick, Martin 9
McCarthy 486
McCarthy, Douglas 360, 361
McCartney, Paul 23, 185, 508
McClure, Steve 422
McCluskey, Andy 38, 165, 375, 376
McCombs, Douglas 522
McCook, Tommy 390
McCoy, Mike 29
McCoy, Neal 508
McCoy, Van 161
McCrae, Gwen 37
McCurdy, Dana 393
McDonald, Country Joe 537
McDonald, Skip 63, 155, 459, 502
McDowell, Rose 109
McEntire, John 377, 453, 454, 467, 488, 521, 522, 523
McFarlane, Dego 510
McFerrin, Bobby 556
McGee, Billy 9, 10, 99
McGee, Brian 414
McGeoch, John 547
McGuire, Richard 301
McKenna, Terence 458, 476
McKenzie, Derek 457
McKenzie, Derrick 266
McKenzie, Keith 457
McKenzie, Roger "Wildchild" 180, 555
McLachlan, Sarah 126, 422
McLaren, Malcolm 513
McLaughlin, John 117, 553
McMahan, Brian 468
McMillan, Stuart 407
McNeeley, Jason 556
McNeil, Willie 473
McQueen, Althea 426
McQueen, Sam 258
McSherry, Dave 183, 184
Meat Beat Manifesto 17, 87, 166, 198, 263, **323**, 324, 328, 374, 427, 451, 457, 559
Meat Loaf 500
Meco **324**
Medeski, John 91, 569
Medeski, Martin & Wood 91, 553
Medicine Man 475
Medicine 163, 271
Medway 444
Meek, Joe 3, 330
Meggle, Tobias 44
Meid, Lothar 12, 13, 14
Meier, Dieter 391, 564
Meifert, Arnulf 181
Meikle, Orde 407, 466
Mekon **324**
Melanie 179
Mellencamp, John Cougar 545
Mello, Rob 58
Mellwig, Andy 286, 405
Meloche, Chris **324**
Melodians 282

Melody Boy 2000 339
Melrose, Steven 108
Melvin, Harold & the Blue Notes 441, 488
Melvins 321
Members 150, 328
Members of the House 40, 328
Mendes, Sergio 511
Mendoza, Vince 56
Menendez, Albert Sterling 318
Menswear 558
Mephisto Odyssey **324**, 325
Mercury Rev 88, 163, 512
Mertens, Michael 414
Merzbow 31, 126, 179, 288, **325**, 362, 514
Mesinai, Raz 492
Messenger 161
Messiaen, Olivier 43, 447, 489, 563
Metalheadz 528
Metallica 146, 298, 537
Metamatics 196, **325**, 435
Meters 160, 172, 200
Metheny, Pat 426, 502
Method Man 201, 202, 464, 465
Metic 394
Metric System 6
Metro Dade 1
Metzger, Frank 379
MFSB 318
MI:5 260
Mice Parade 158, **325**
Michaels, Hilly 477, 478
Mickey & Sylvia 174
Mickey Finn 18
Microdisney 486
Micronauts **325**, 326
Microstoria 301, **326**, 344, 379, 471
Middleton, Tom 17, 269, 345, 427, 456
Midfield General **326**
Midler, Bette 335
Midney, Boris **326**
Mighty Bop 137, 199, **326**, 327, 463, 509
Mighty, Ray 470
Mike & Rich 17, 346
Mike D 44, 537, 538
Mike E-Block 49
Milan, Josh 60
Miles, Ant 376, 377, 423
Miles, Maydie 83
Miles, Robert 43, 71, 105, 185, **327**, 351, 552
Milhaud, Darius 426, 493, 563
Miller, Adam 62, 295, 296
Miller, Alton 108, 115, **327**
Miller, Betsi 414
Miller, Daniel 6, 361, 462, 472
Miller, Dennis 512
Miller, Henry 504
Miller, Jacob 381
Miller, Jimmy 408, 503
Miller, Marcus 268
Miller, Paul D. 146, 563
Miller, Steve 46
Miller, Steve Band 138
Mills, Crispian 413
Mills, Jeff 28, 39, 43, 100, 116, 130, 139, 144, 147, 153, 194, 258, 293, 296, 323, **327**, 328, 329, 381, 383, 405, 497, 498, 504, 533, 534, 535, 548, 555, 557, 566, 567
Mills, Roger 484
Mills, Russell 46, **330**, 499
Milstein, Phil 109
Mind over Rhythm 399
Minekawa, Takako 143, **330**, 331, 503
Mineo, Attilio **331**

# INDEX

Ming & FS **331**
Ming 331
Mingus, Charles 335, 556
Minimal Man 36, 170
Minimum Wage Brothers 385
Ministry 116, 159, 198, 256, **331**, 332, 459, 465, 494
Minnelli, Liza 392
Minogue, Kylie 178, 182, 509
Minor Forest 298
Minty 140
Miranda Sex Garden 188
Miranda, Carmen 279
Miranda, Nina 470, 471
Mirwais 310, 311, **332**
Miss Kitten 511
Mission of Burma 335
Mista Sinista 563
Mr. Bungle 6
Mr. C 295, **332**, 333, 458
Mr. Complex 342
Mr. Dan 115
Mr. Electric Triangle 178
Mr. Fingers 160, 184, 199, **333**, 456
Mr. Hazeltine 509
Mr. Len 102, 544
Mr. Oizo **333**, 546
Mr. Scruff **333**, 334, 438, 484, 485
Mr. Thing 36
Mitchell, Bruce 157
Mitchell, Joni 150, 151, 294
Mitchell, Katrina 280
Mittoo, Jackie 390, 459
Mix Master Mike 262, **334**
Mixmaster 56
Mixmaster Morris 40, 99, 100, 153, 198, 263, 271, 352, 388, 476, 561
Miyake, Yuki 482
Mjos, O.J. 155
MK Ultra 497, **334**
MLO 138, **334**, 497, 516, 528, 547
Mobley, Hank 568, 569
Moby 17, 37, 147, 197, 266, 281, 291, **334**, 335, 374, 375, 423, 439, 454, 467, 544, 564
Mocean Worker **335**, 336
Model 500 27, 28, 92, 107, 111, 139, 144, 185, 259, 304, 321, 323, **336**, 351, 385, 446, 457, 526, 552, 554
Modernist **336**
Modirzadeh, Hafez 70
Modus 439
Moebius 96, 169, **337**, 434, 448
Moebius, Dieter 96, 337, 355, 434, 448
Moers, Michael 510
Mogwai 280, **337**, 338, 461, 468
Molara 568
Mole, Adam 404
Molloy, Matt 294, 295
Moloko 184, **338**
Molvaer, Nils Petter 295
Momus 191
Monaco 357
Mondino, Maxx 290
Mondo Grosso 83
Money Mark 104, **338**, 539
Monica 189
Monie Love 119
Monier, Christophe 325, 326
Monk & Canatella **339**, 477
Monk, Thelonious 496, 556
Monkees 64
Monkey Mafia 87, 115, 155, **339**, 466
Mono Junk **339**, 383
Mono TM 150

Mono **339**
Monolake 22, 321, **339**, 340, 403, 493, 545
Monomorph 113
Monroe, Hollis P. 520
Monsieur Dimitri 134
Montana, Vincent Jr. 441
Montrose, Ronnie 46
Monty Python 188
Mood II Swing 531, 557
Mood 84
Moods 123
Moody Blues 177, 197, 256
Moody Boyz 48, 79, 166, **340**, 437
Moody, James 327
Moody, John 451
Moodymann **340**, 341, 387, 539
Moog Cookbook 462
Moog, Bob 343, 354, 355, 452, 500, 520, 521, 560
Mooney, Malcolm 82, 83
Moonman 105
Moonshake 291, **341**
Moore, Mark 62, 437
Moore, Ryan 349
Moore, Thurston 146, 147
Moors Murderers 547
Mora, A.J. 548
Moraes, Angel 278
Morales, Danny 134
Morales, David 285, 289, 301, 318, **341**, 342, 488, 520
Morcheeba 292, **342**
More Rockers 142, 268, 269
More, Jonathan 62, 99, 100, 138, 263
Morcira, Airto 553
Morel Inc. 134
Morel, George 179, 543, 547
Morelenbaum, Jacques 440
Morgan, Lee 568
Morgan, Russ 277
Morganstern, Roxanne 164
Mori, Ikue 458, 569
Morillo, Erick "More" 41, 179, 426, 543, 547
Morissette, Alanis 454
Morley, David 62, **342**, 343, 385, 458, 529
Morley, Paul 23, 192
Morley, Tony 67, 517, 528
Moroder, Giorgio 85, 86, 139, 254, 309, **343**, 344, 477, 478, 516, 535
Morph 555
Morricone, Ennio 2, 62, 70, 91, 92, 121, 381, 568, 569
Morris, Gina 486
Morris, Lawrence Butch 315
Morris, Stephen 356, 357
Morrison, Jim 1, 130, 156, 566
Morrison, Mark 113
Morrison, Van 125, 177, 414
Morrissey 104, 135, 157
Morrow, John 188
Mos Def 17, 142, 275
Moscheles, Gary 345
Moscrop, Martin 86
Mosimann, Roli 187, 465, 565
Moskowitz, Dorothy 537
Moss, David 293
Moth Men 157
Mother Earth 393
Mother Mallard's Portable Masterpiece Co. **343**, 344
Mothersbaugh, Bob 131
Mothersbaugh, Jim 131
Mothersbaugh, Mark 131, 132, 521
Mothmen 459

Motive One 75
Motorbass 114, 199, 253, **344**, 466
Mott the Hoople 65
Moufang, David 11, 102, 124, 345, 352, 476, 477, 519
Mould, Bob 538
Moulder, Alan 360
Moulin, Marc 510
Mouquet, Eric 124
Mouse on Mars 35, 115, 164, 205, 271, 278, 299, 301, 302, 326, 333, **344**, 345, 356, 379, 403, 424, 441, 447, 448, 468, 529
Mousse T 179, 488
Mouzon, Alphonse 553
Move D 124, **345**, 477, 547
Movement 548
Movietone 187
Moving Fusion 133
Moyet, Alison 126, 170, 171, 274, 525
Mozart, Wolfgang Amadeus 364
Mtume 118
μ-Ziq 17, 31, 56, 93, 111, 112, 254, 269, 270, 281, 320, 325, **345**, 346, 388, 455, 467, 483, 516, 519, 550
Mucho Macho 6
Muir, Nick 134
Mull, Joel 51, 279, **346**, 470, 511
Muller, Sophie 55
Mulligan, Gerry 46
Mumma, Gordon 526, 527
Mundell, Hugh 381
Mung 109, 284, 379
Munich Philharmonic Orchestra 505
Muraoka, Minuro 142
Murk 202, **346**, 347, 488, 511, 557
Murphy, Eddie 272
Murphy, Peter 267, 301
Murphy, Roisin 184, 338
Murphy, Walter 89
Murvin, Junior 389, 390
Musgrave, Sharon 42
Musicology 35
Muslimgauze 55, **347**, 348, 349
Musso, Robert 305, 451
Musso, Stefano 8
Mussorgsky, Modest Petrovich 520
Musto & Bones 63
Musto, Tommy 63, 457
Muto, Takeshi 394
My Bloody Valentine 86, 104, 110, 135, 163, 175, 182, 187, 271, **349**, 350, 382, 422, 455, 473
My Favorite 462
My Life with the Thrill Kill Kult 331, **350**, 351
Myers, Alan 131, 132
Myers, Amina Claudine 294
Myers, Rob 515
Myerson, Jamie 118, **351**, 367
Myles, Maydie 342
Mysteryman **351**

# N

N Joi 428, 548
Nadien, David 440
Nails 88
Nakajima, Akifumi 30
Nakamura, Dan 33
Nakanishi, Toshio 353
Naked Eyes 38
Naked Funk 141
Naked Music NYC **352**
Name, Billy 102, 567
Namlook, Pete 5, 29, 53, 115, 124, 153,

198, 261, 263, 286, 293, **352**, 353, 381, 448, 540
Napalm Death 40, 305, 451, 497, 508
Nardiello, Frankie 331
Nas 201, 387
Nascimento, Milton 93
Nasty Habits 451
Nath, Pran 431
Nathan, Dylan 178, 270
Nation of Ulysses 63
Natural Calamity **353**
Naughty by Nature 201
Nav Katze 427
Navarre, Ludovic 439
Naylor, Maria 313, 444
Nazuka, Chris 101
NdegeOcello, Me'Shell 300
NDour, Youssou 70, 88, 440
Nebinger, Mederic 202
Ned's Atomic Dustbin 56
Needs, Kris 83, 115, 373, 442, 454, 455
Negativland 180, **353**, 354, 518
Negro, Joey 435
Neil 481
Neil, Fred 378
Neill, Ben 146, **354**, 355
Nelson, Alan 465
Nelson, Bill 73, 186, 363, 499, 565
Nelson, Billy "Bass" 199, 200
Nelson, Everton 440
Nelson, Mark 290, 382
Nelson, Shara 11, 155, 316, 407
Neon Judgement 62
Neotropic 21, 273, 315, **355**, 465, 466, 469, 470
Nettlebeck, Uwe 181
Neu 7, 19, 96, 105, 182, 312, 337, 344, **355**, 356, 376, 402, 434, 486, 519
Neufeld, Clemens 1
Neumeier, Mani 169, 337
Neuromancer 297
Neuropolitique 24, **356**
Nevins, Jason **356**
New Age Steppers 155, 459
New Edition 37, 273
New Kingdom 254, 412
New Order 38, 49, 61, 71, 77, 86, 87, 88, 134, 156, 161, 162, 164, 165, 172, 178, 298, 345, **356**, 357, 358, 366, 376, 392, 428, 446, 455, 511, 523, 524, 542, 543, 558
New Power Generation 409
New Symphony Orchestra of London 544
New York Citi Peech Boys 388
New York Dolls 267, 408, 494
New York Gong 318
New York Terrorists 443
Newby, Kenneth **358**, 432
Newcleus 111, 148, 194, 254, **358**
Newley, Anthony 64, 327
Newman, Colin 64, 435, 557, 558
Newman, Randy 500, 560
Newsted, Jason 537
Newton, Adi 95
Nexus 21 12
Nice & Smooth 317, 513
Nicholson, Hugo 178, 408
Nico [Rock] 8, 9
Nico [Jungle] 147, 151, 166, **358**, 435, 436, 559
Nicolette 71, 316, **359**, 460
Nieman, Randall 204, 556
Nightmares on Wax 1, 31, **359**, 370, 438
Nikita 38
Nimmo, Derek 188

# INDEX

Nimoy, Leonard 259, 457
Nine Inch Nails 17, 18, 31, 32, 65, 99, 128, 198, 328, 330, 331, 335, **359**, 360, 363, 402, 459, 465, 557
9 Lazy 9 99
Ninety Five North 547
Ninjaman 361
Nirvana 128, 132, 422
Nitzer Ebb 114, **360**, 361, 382, 455
No Man 405
No One 518
Noble, Jason 320
Nocturnal Emissions 305
Noel 546
Noel, Lester 45
Noise Unit 126
Noko 19
Noller, David B. 158
Nomi, Klaus 386
Nomiya, Maki 398, 399
Nonplace Urban Field 29, 154, **361**, 447
Nookie 74, 75, 189, 278, **361**
Nordine, Ken 138, 556
Norland, David 472
Normal 24, 253, 304, **361**, 462, 473
Norris, Lee 325
Norris, Richard 416
Nort 78
Nosebleeds 157
Notorious BIG 201, 331
Notwist 103, **361**, 362
Novy Vs. Eniac 37, 140
NRBQ 556
Nu Era 189
Null, Kazuyuki K. **362**, 377
Numan, Gary 27, 31, 40, 82, 126, 169, 287, 295, 322, **362**, 363, 364, 445, 544, 554, 559
Number One Dog 158
Nunez, Chep 342
Nurse with Wound 85, 109, 305, **364**, 486, 518
NuYorican Soul 72, 93, 317, **364**, 513, 546
NWA 119, 136, 339, 418, 548
Nwachukwa, Tony 30
Nye, Steve 499
Nyman, Michael 168, **364**, 365

## O

O Yuki Conjugate 8, **366**, 449, 473, 474
O 541
Oakenfold, Paul 71, 87, 100, 105, 106, 141, 199, 299, 308, 326, **366**, 367, 372, 423, 424, 443, 457, 482, 500
Oakes, Geoff 133
Oakey, Philip 47
Oasis 51, 87, 350, 406
Oblivion 475, 481
Obmana, Vidna 5, 8, **367**, 368, 432, 433, 518
OBrien, Ed 422
OBrien, Ian 254, **368**, 477, 510, 566
OBryan, Jason 155
Ocal, Burhan 198, 352
Ocasek, Ric 494
OClosoig, Colm 350
OConnor, Sinead 62, 63, 121, 133, 335, 411
Octagon Man 92, 107, 129, **368**
Octave One 144, **368**, 369, 446, 535
Odd Toot **369**
Offene Türen 434
Ogilvie, Carlton 155
Ogilvie, Dave 359, 465
Ogl, Padraic 59
Ogre, Nivek 331, 465

OHagan, Sean 438, 486, 487, 488, 527
OHara, Mary Margaret 70
OHare, Brendan 337
Oil 21, 204, 355
OJays 441
OKeefe, Sean 401, 528
Old 362
Oldfield, Mike 71, 356, **369**, 505, 532
Oldfield, Sally 369
Oldham, Alan 121, 138, 147, 387
Oldham, Will 468
Olive 347, 366, **370**
Oliver, Mickey 179
Oliveros, Pauline 106, 168, 358, **370**, 514
Ollivierra, Neil 129
Omegaman 1
Omicron 203, 457, 567
Omni Trio 122, 137, 188, 361, 366, **371**, 402, 452, 508
On U Sound System 63, 459, 492, 502
Once Dreamt 556
Once Eleven 552, 553
One Dove 8, **371**, 437
101 Strings Orchestra 486
1000 Homo DJ's 331, 494
Ono, Yoko 293, 322, 388, 525, 566
Open House 50
Operator 125, 481, 491
Opiate 266
Opio 510
Optic Nerve 526
Optical 137, 138, 151, 320, **371**, 436
Opus III 72, 334, 498
Oral, Cem 267
ORang **371**, 503
Orange Cake Mix 204
Orange Juice 307
Orb 17, 31, 32, 42, 71, 83, 90, 97, 153, 154, 183, 184, 185, 188, 193, 263, 274, 284, 297, 313, 321, 361, 366, **372**, 373, 378, 379, 385, 404, 407, 408, 416, 437, 454, 455, 475, 492, 495, 500, 532, 551, 564, 565
Orbison, Roy 48
Orbit, William 36, 42, 101, 288, 310, 311, 340, **374**, 378, 443, 457, 482
Orbital 4, 17, 18, 31, 34, 62, 106, 140, 154, 193, 270, 278, 323, 334, 373, **374**, 375, 407, 408, 421, 422, 441, 442, 457, 461, 482, 544, 565
Orchestral Manoeuvres in the Dark 38, 59, 165, **375**, 376
Orff, Carl 167
Organisation 286, 287
Organized Konfusion 146, 563
Organum 377
Origin Unknown 21, 188, **376**, 377, 423, 424, 465
Original Love 398
Original Playboy 425
Orinoko 307
Orlando, Bobby 392
Ormandy, Eugene 65
ORourke, Jim 47, 103, 183, 280, 288, 302, 311, 312, 325, 326, 354, 362, **377**, 379, 487, 488, 522, 531
Orton, Beth 47, 88, 143, 316, 374, **378**, 425
Orwell, George 65
Osborne, Steve 366
Oschatz, Sebastian 379
OSnodaigh, Ronan 121
OST **378**
OSullivan, Jerry 294
Oswald, John 269, 458
Otaku **378**

Other Two 86, 357
OToole, Mark 192
Outlander 342, 469, 529
Outside 271, 511
Oval 22, 88, 147, 326, 331, 344, 362, **379**, 403, 438, 446, 471, 503, 521, 522, 523
Override 284, 285, **379**
Owen If 486
Owens, Robert 184, 285, 395, 520
OZ 166
Ozomatli 111, 275
Ozric Tentacles 159

## P

P Funk 72
P Funk All Stars 94, 199, 384, 385, 386
P-Orridge, Genesis 415, 416, 517, 527
Paap, Jochem 1, **381**, 400, 456, 479, 480
Pablo 75
Pablo, Augustus 15, 16, 137, 349, **381**, 433, 459, 483, 515
Pacou **381**, 382
Page, Jimmy 64
Pailhead 331
Painkiller 184
Pajo, David 5, 468, 522
Pal Joey 323, 373
Palace Brothers 5
Palace 468
Palais Schaumburg 320
Palladio, Andrea 458
Palm Skin Productions 31, **382**
Palmer, Earl 34
Palmer, Robert 132, 298, 313, 469
Palumbo, Johnny 431
Pan American **382**
Pan, Hermes 331
Panacea 163, **382**, 383
Panaiotis 370
Panasonic 35, 69, 125, 163, 179, 186, 278, 304, 325, 348, 362, **383**, 384, 471, 512, 541
Pandemonium 387
Pandit G 25
Pandy, Darryl 179
Panknin, Sascha 136
Pankow 29
Paperclip People 106, 107, 100, 260, 278, **384**, 415, 464
Pappa, Anthony **384**, 385
Paradinas, Mike 17, 53, 93, 111, 153, 154, 178, 270, 281, 345, 346, 359, 467, 476
Paragons 469
Parallax Corporation 254
Paris the Black Fu 63, 129, 130
Paris 177
Park, Graeme 424
Parker, Alan 343
Parker, Andrea 263, 343, **385**, 386, 416, 427, 529
Parker, Charlie 483
Parker, Evan 569
Parker, Jeff 264, 522
Parker, Lewis 36
Parker, Maceo 95, 119, 122, 318, 386
Parker, Michael 19
Parker, Shawn 124
Parker, Terrence 1, 341, 369, **385**
Parkins, Zeena 458, 459
Parliament 3, 27, 72, 94, 95, 102, 123, 165, 199, 200, 201, 269, 273, 322, 327, **385**, 386, 410, 412, 425, 444, 445, 512
Parrish, Man 47, 93, 161, 177, 193, 254, 270, 385, **386**, 387, 408
Parrish, Theo 115, 190, **387**

Parsons, Alan Project 506
Parsons, Ted 187
Part, Arvo 374, 482
Partch, Harry 567
Partington, Darren 161
Partridge, Andy 73
Pascal FEOS 429
Pascal 140, 148
Pasemaster Mase 119, 120
Paskin, Layo 295
Passarani, Marco **387**
Passions 150
Pastels 104, 203, 280
Pastorius, Jaco 519, 553, 554
Paterson, Alex 183, 284, 372, 373, 475, 495, 500
Patrick, Pat 495, 496
Patterson, Carlton 282
Patterson, Ted 254
Patton, Big John 338, 406, 568, 569
Patton, Mike 281, 569
Pavement 486
Payne, Jason 361
PC 138
Peace Orchestra 288, **387**, 523
Peacock, Sarah 446, 455, 471
Peanut Butter Wolf **387**, 388
Pearce, Dave 187
Peat, Chris 12
Peczynski, Dominika 22
Peech Boys 299, **388**, 502, 513
Peel, John 1, 97, 122, 273, 372, 376, 416, 496, 504, 507, 532
Peeters, Arno 125
Pell Mell 105
Pemberton, Daniel **388**, 461
Pendergrass, Teddy 488
Peniston, Ce Ce 317, 318, 511
Pennebaker, D.A. 126, 128
Pennington, James 494
People Underground 185
Pepler, Merv 159
Perception 535
Perch, Neil 568
Pere Ubu 355
Perez, Gene 318
Pergolesi, Giovanni Battista 365
Perind, Shawn J. 189
Perlmutter, Lior 26
Peron, Jean Herve 181
Perrey & Kingsley **388**, 399
Perrey, Jean-Jacques 7, 180, 298, **388**, 511
Perry, Brendan 120, 121
Perry, Lee "Scratch" 45, 155, 295, 308, 309, 373, 389, 390, 391, 403, 413, 419, 459, 479, 515
Perry, Robert 121
Persona **391**
Peshay 74, 175, 181, **391**, 393, 395, 474
Pet Shop Boys 41, 45, 49, 123, 156, 164, 165, 177, 178, 202, 259, 278, 334, 346, 357, **391**, 392, 393, 428, 435, 444, 511
Peterson, Chris 198
Peterson, Gilles 44, 74, 75, 178, 181, 257, 359, **393**
Petter, Ralf 136
Pettibone, Shep 37, 194, 318, 357, 424, 545
Petty, Tom 173
Pezz 136
PFM 74, 75, 137, **393**, 435, 474
PGR 85, **393**, 394, 518
Phair, Liz 129, 291, 460
Phantom Band 431
Phantom City 449

Pharcyde 67, 119, 268, 387
Phase IV 52
Phats & Small **394**
PHD & Conrad 75
Phenomyna 509
Philth 152
Philus 383
Phoenecia 22, 31, 131, 271, **394**, 420, 474
Phoenix 439
Phonosycograph Disk 72, 319
Phortune 139, 143
Phosphorous 340
Photek 68, 74, 100, 115, 166, 175, 176, 179, 203, 263, 275, 391, 393, **394**, 395, 426, 456, 465, 474, 475
Photon Inc. 143
Phume 284, 379
Phuture 1, 118, 143, 182, 269, 323, **395**
Piano Magic **395**, 396
Pickering, Mike 87, 307
Pickett, Wilson 521
Pickton, Steve 484, 509
Pierce, Adam 158, 325
Pierce, Jason 473, 475, 476, 480, 481
Pig City 92
Pigface 331, 416, 435, 465
Pilgrem, Rennie 463
Piller, Eddie 393
Pine, Courtney 393
Pink Floyd 11, 25, 42, 52, 90, 109, 172, 261, 353, 372, 373, **396**, 397, 398, 422, 506, 537, 556
Pion, Renaud 121
Pip 136
Pistel, Mark 323
Pitney, Gene 8, 9, 10
Pixies 65, 137, 422
Pizarro, Gladys 442, 543
Pizzaman 179, 180, 326
Pizzi, Cesare 565
Pizzicato Five 103, 178, 331, 353, **398**, 399, 515, 539
PJ 460
Placebo 454
Placid Angles 50
Plaid 56, 60, 71, 93, 163, 193, 269, 359, **399**, 426, 428, 476, 509, 537
Planet Asia 388
Planet Patrol **400**
Planetary Assault Systems 260, **400**, 467
Plank, Conrad 96, 114, 169, 173, 337, 355, 434, 533
Plant, Robert 110, 125, 367, 513
Plasma Company 3, 62
Plastic Bertrand 510
Plastics 398
Plastikman 1, 28, 37, 69, 121, 182, 202, 203, 339, **400**, 401, 405, 415, 491, 501, 514, 515, 544, 551
Platas, Ignacio 552
Plath, Sylvia 11
Plavka 266
Playford, Rob 59, 151, 175, 188, 371, **401**, 402, 528
Plotkin, James 305, 362, 451
Plug 16, 17, 47, 109, 284, 379, **402**, 494, 547, 550, 551
Pluramon 205, 361, **402**, 403, 447
Plus N 5
PM Dawn 140, 289
Pob & Taylor 134
Poets of Rhythm 44
Poets of Thought 75
Pogues 70
Poiser, James 282

Poison Clan 143
POL 447
Pole 22, 69, 94, 189, 190, 295, 382, **403**, 545
Police 196
Polo, Jimi 1
Polygon Window 17, 203, **403**
Pooley, Ian 1, 16, 30, 115, 123, 182, 264, 327, **404**, 463
Pop Group 459
Pop Will Eat Itself 50, **404**, 413
Pop, Iggy 65, 122, 132, 404, 421, 440, 556
Popol Vuh 12, 197, **404**, 405, 505
Popp, Markus 326, 344, 379, 522
Poppies 404
Porcupine Tree **405**
Porter Ricks 22, 41, 125, 286, 292, 321, 340, 361, **405**, 406, 493, 508, 509
Porter, Cole 88, 174
Porter, Mike 37
Portishead 35, 63, 64, 88, 175, 291, 292, 316, 334, 338, 339, 342, 370, **406**, 407, 438, 470, 471, 477, 484, 537, 550, 551
Portsmouth Sinfonia 167, 364
Posatronix 34
Posdnuos 119, 120
Possession 98
Post, Gardner 165, 355
Poster Children 441, 522
Potion 185
Potuznik 321, **407**
Potuznik, Gerhard 321, 407, 412
Pound, Caspar 457, 550
Pousseur, Henri 43
Powell, Kobie 539
Power Station 89
Praxis 72, 262, 293
Prefab Sprout 150
Prekop, Sam 453, 454, 460
Presence 85, **407**
Presley, Elvis 125, 284, 417
Pressure Drop **407**
Pressure Funk **407**, 466
Pressure of Speech **407**, 408, 544
Preston, Billy 48
Pretenders 164, 188
Pretty Tony **408**
Previn, Andre 92
Previte, Bobby 569
Prevost, Eddie 175, 377
Prewitt, Archer 453
Price, Darren **408**
Price, Martin 161
Priest, Maxi 257
Priester, Julian 450
Primal Scream 4, 5, 33, 87, 366, 372, 373, 406, **408**, 409, 437, 454, 455, 472, 475
Primary Industry 532
Prime Movers 507
Prime Time 438
Prime, Michael 521
Primitives 102, 350
Primus 72
Prince 23, 27, 42, 47, 89, 94, 106, 161, 164, 195, 294, 363, 374, 409, 410, 411, 412, 434, 506, 511, 536
Prince & the Revolution 410, 411
Prince Buster 389, 507
Prince Far I 155, 156, 459, 469, 496, 521
Prince Jammy 282, 381, 450
Prince Paul 33, 119, 137, **412**, 479
Prince Phillip 282, **409**
Principato, Salvatore 301
Principle, Jamie 269, 285, **412**
Prins, Patrick 424

Prisoners 101, 507
Pritchard, Mark 269, 345, 427, 456
Private Lightning Six 263, 407, **412**, 420
Pro Tech 198
Proclaimers 283
Prodigy 3, 18, 21, 23, 41, 62, 63, 72, 87, 92, 133, 140, 166, 198, 290, 320, 322, 324, 339, 346, 382, **412**, 413, 422, 454, 468, 471, 544, 551, 557
Professor Griff 417
Professor Richmann 459
Professor Traxx 395
Profrock, Thorsten 545
Project 625 566
Project X 121
Prokofiev, Sergei 59
Prommer, Christian 181
Prong 29, 416
Propaganda **414**
Propagandhi 199
Propellerheads 135, 274, **414**, 477, 555, 559
Protegé 391
Prototype 909 130, **414**, 415, 457
Proyecto Uno 426
Prunas, Barbara 327
Psyche 107, 323, 415
Psyche/BFC 107, 108, 260, 384, 464, **415**
Psychedelic Research Lab 278
Psychic TV 52, 85, 98, 99, 109, 152, 286, 338, **415**, 416, 437, 517, 568
Psychick Warriors Ov Gaia 71, 154, **416**, 484
Psycho 57
Psychonauts **416**
Psychoslaphead 274
Ptp 331
Public Enemy 62, 86, 87, 103, 119, 135, 138, 141, 145, 148, 155, 172, 177, 194, 281, 339, 388, **417**, 418, 428, 509, 532, 533
Public Energy 480
Public Image Limited 82, 97, 172, 293, 308, **418**, 419, 455, 459
Puente, Tito 317, 318, 364, 538, 546
Puff Daddy 102, 139, 418, 544
Pugliese, Jim 458, 459
Pugwash 152, 153
Pullen, Stacey 28, 133, 322, 323, 333, 461, 462, 557
Pulp 2, 69, 103, 280, 338, 406, 438, 516, 518
Pulp Victim 105
Pulsars 330, 462
Pulse 62, **419**
Pulsinger, Patrick 70, 262, 263, 296, 300, 412, **419**, 420, 510, 541
Pulusha 300, 455
Pumiglio, Pete 452
Punisher 147
Puracane 74
Purcell, Henry 365
Purdie, Bernard "Pretty" 100
Pure 161
Purim, Flora 30
Purple Kola 198
Purple Penguin 477
Purveyors of Fine Funk 110
Push Button Objects 394, **420**
Pussy Galore 46
Pyke, Simon 193, 278

**Q**

Q Burns Abstract Message **421**
Q Tip 67, 94
Q 255

Qed 18
Quadrant 41, 42, 320, 321
Quail, Roger 95
Quake 520
Quakerman 255
Quando Quango 307
Quant 166, 195, 435
Quarmby, Jonathan 313
Quaye, Caleb 421
Quaye, Finley 313, **421**
Quazar 541, 542
Queen 65, 89
Queen Latifah 38, 99, 119, 274, 374, 412, 469
Quine, Robert 170
Quinn, Jamie 320, 371
Quinn, Matt 320, 371
Quinn, Paul 170
Quivver 123, 367, 444

**R**

R-Tyme 429
Ra, Sun 58, 146, 260, 312, 358, 373, 389, 390, 393, 463, 477, 495, 496, 537
Ra, Sun Arkestra 495
Rabbit in the Moon 140, 158, **422**, 443
Rabinowitz, Tex 321
RAC 136, 193, 394
Rachel's 320
Radcliffe, Eric 170
Radiance 42, 320, 321
Radiohead 21, 145, 184, **422**, 423, 537
Radley, Kate 480
Rae & Christian **423**
Rae, Mark 6, 423
Raekwon 201
RAF 83
Raff N Freddy 134
Rage Against the Machine 26, 409, 464
Ragga Twins 460
Ragtyme 488, 510
Rahzel 465
Rain Tree Crow 267, 499
Rainford, Phil 157
Rakim 23, 137, 315
Ralph, Dave **423**
Ram Trilogy 133, 377, **423**, 424
Rammellzee 319
Rampling, Danny 199, **424**
Ramsay, Andy 2, 486, 527
Rancho Relaxo 414
Randall, Dave 131, 279
Random Factor 184, 185, 549
Random XS 566
Random, Eric 77, 78
Ranglin, Ernest 439
Rankine, Lesley 435
Ranks, Shabba 19, 319
Rapatti, Kim 339
Rapsys, Ryan 468
Rare Earth 277
Rare Essence 141
Rare Force 441
Ras Kass 262
Rasco 387, 388
Rashad, Essam 28, 29
Ratcliffe, Simon 40, 41
Ratzinger, Rudy 561, 562
Rauhofer, Peter 488
Ravel, Maurice 520
Ravenstine, Allen 385
Raw Stylus 548
Rawls, Lou 34
Raymonde, Simon 97, 98
React 2 Rhythm 374

Read, John 43
Readymade 373
Reagenz 124, 345, 476
Real McCoy 307, **424**
Rebel MC 194, **424,** 491
Rechenzentrum 295, **424**
Recloose 108, **425**
Recoil 128
Red Alert 201
Red Army Choir 284
Red Hot Chili Peppers 539
Red Krayola 79, 337, 476
Red Light District 420
Red Red Meat 129
Red Snapper 11, 344, 378, **425,** 477
Red 477
Redcell 35
Redd, Freddie 569
Redding, Otis 157, 560
Redman 201
Reece, Alex 177, 426, 552, **425**
Reece, Damon 480
Reed, Lou 8, 9, 65, 102, 507, 566
Reel 2 Real **426**
Reely, Greg 198
Reese Project 260, 445, 446
Reese 260, 445, 446
Reflection 147, **426**
Refoy, Mark 480
Regisford, Timmy 93
Rehberg, Peter 182, 255
Rehmi, T.J. 437
Reich, Steve 46, 69, 96, 167, 255, 287, 302, 314, 324, 343, 344, 364, 372, 385, **426,** 427, 480, 482, 503, 551, 556
Reich, Tom 142
Reid, Duke 282
Reid, Junior 99, 568
Reid, Vernon 556, 569
Reilly, Vini 157
Reinboth, Michael 44
Reload 39, 93, 153, 269, 286, 345, **427,** 456
REM 88, 422
Rema Rema 560
Reminiscence Quartet 326, 327, 463
Renaldo, Don 441
Renee, Alicia 294
Renegade Soundwave 87, 264, 296, 404, **427,** 428
Reni 491
Rental, Robert 361
Rentals 462
Repeat 70, 71, **428**
Republica 154, 413, **428,** 470
Req 326, **428,** 429
Residents 131, 163, 354, 564
Resilient 545
Resistance D 29, 423, **429**
Restaurant Tracks 263
Retroflex 101
Return to Forever 553
Rev, Martin 494
Revell, Graeme 305, 481
Revenge 357
Revere, Paul & the Raiders 485
Reverend 185
Revolting Cocks 331, 332, 465, 494
Revolution 409, 411
Rex 134
Reyes, Jorge 367, 432
Reynolds, Paul 186
Reynolds, Simon 40, 290, 439
Reznor, Trent 31, 67, 99, 162, 331, 359, 360, 402, 404, 557
Rhodes, David 59

Rhodes, Louise 162, 291, 292, 471
Rhodes, Phyllis 441
Rhymes, Busta 120, 201, 377
Rhymes, Dylan 193
Rhythim Is Rhythim 144, 323, 329, 415, **429,** 461, 535
Rhythm Formation 566
Rhythmx 149
Ribot, Marc 458, 499, 569
RIC 52
Rice, Boyd 98
Rice, Casey 129, 382, 467, 468, 522
Rich Kids 533, 547
Rich, Buddy 519
Rich, Robert 8, 263, 306, 347, 367, 368, **429,** 430, 432, 450, 514
Richard 23 52, 331
Richards, Eddie 457
Richards, Keith 556
Richards, Kelly 175
Richards, Vicki 58
Richmond, Simon 382
Ride 350
Ridenhour, Carlton 417
Riefenstahl, Leni 279
Rieflin, William 331
Riley, Jim 117
Riley, Jimmy 469
Riley, Terry 81, 84, 85, 167, 183, 263, 287, 324, 343, 355, 370, 426, 427, **430,** 431, 452, 503, 505
Rimbaud, Robin 191, 446, 461
Rinocerose **431**
Rip Rig & Panic 88
Riperton, Minnie 372, 393, 488, 522, 561
Rippingtons 271, 521, 553
Rising High Collective 47, 263
Rising Sons 555
Rising Sunz 58
Risque Rhythm Team 277
Rites of Spring 175
Ritter, Rex 271
River Ocean 548
Ro Seventy 11
Roach, Max 260, 378
Roach, Steve 8, 358, 367, 368, 429, 430, **432,** 433, 450, 485
Rob B. 486
Robb, Paul 259
Robbers, Stefan 36
Roberts, Greg 51, 152
Roberts, Paul 277
Roberts, Wendy 303
Robertson, Justin 87, 301, 524
Robertson, Robbie 311, 440
Robie, John 386, 400
Robinson, Neil 507
Robinson, Smokey 267, 445, 488, 560
Robotiks 309, 391
Robotnick, Alexander 108, 254, **433**
Robots and Humanoids 498
Roc Raida 294, 336, 563
ROC 433, **433**
Roche, Terre 196
Rock, Chris 412
Rock, Pete 258, 559
Rocker's Hifi **433,** 515, 551
Rockers Revenge 37, 270
Rockwilder 120, 201
Rocky & Diesel 38, 58
Rodgers & Hammerstein 482
Rodgers, Dave 126
Rodgers, Nile 65, 89, 309, 318, 319
Rodgers, Sally 313
Rodriguez, Raul 386

Roedelius 96, 169, 263, 337, 352, 434, 448, **433**
Roedelius, Hans Joachim 96, 337, 355, 433, 448
Rogner, Falk U. 12
Rogue Unit 188
Rollercone 75
Rolling Stones 44, 91, 132, 143, 157, 183, 388, 408, 409, 410, 415, 455, 513, 544
Rollins, Henry 480, 556
Rollins, Wayne 83
Rollo 133, 177, 550
Romanthony 301, 342, **434,** 524
Romantic Warrior 352
Rome 288, 326, 402, **434,** 516, 518, 519, 522, 523
Romeo, Max 469
Ronnie & Clyde **434,** 435
Ronson, Mick 64
Roome, John 64, 559
Rootpowder 516
Roots Radics 155, 156, 308, 390, 450
Roots 142
Rootsman 155
Rosario, Ralphi 37, 83, 179, 199, **435,** 548
Rose Chronicles 126
Rose, Andrew 441, 442
Rose, David 92
Rosenthal, Sam 58, 367
Rosolino, Frank 34
Ross, Brandon 294
Ross, Diana 38, 182, 278, 285, 439, 442, 520
Ross, John 434, 435
Ross, Lucius Tawl 199, 200
Rossini, Gioachino 84
Rota, Nino 556
Rother, Anthony 129, 546
Rother, Michael 96, 337, 341, 355, 356, 434
Rotten, Johnny 418
Round Four 49
Roupe **435**
Roussos, Demis 542
ROVA 377
Rowe, Keith 377
Rowlands, Tom 87, 88
Roxy Music 2, 75, 167, 168, 170, 267, 282, 503, 533, 547, 565
Royal Concertgebouw Orchestra 545
Royal House 513
Royal Philharmonic Orchestra 385
Royal, Marc 441, 497, 502
Rozalla **435**
Rozzo 557
Ruben, Spookey 146
Rubin, Rick 44, 160, 279, 344, 417
Rubinson, David 537
Ruby 135, **435**
Rucker, Ursula 189, 282, 557
Rudd, Roswell 556
Rude Bwoy Monty 140, 148, 153
Rudeboy 538, 539
Rudi 20
Ruff Ryders 202
Ruffneck 83, 318
Rufige Kru 189
Ruin, Clint 99, 187
Ruins 261
Ruiz, Hilton 364
Run DMC 44, 284, 356, 358, 366, 385, 386, 417, 532, 554, 555, 557
Rundgren, Todd 400, 477, 556
RuPaul 202, 289, 346, 548
Rush, Ed 21, 36, 67, 137, 138, 147, 151, 358, 371, 376, 382, 402, **435,** 436, 516, 559

Russell, Arthur **436**
Russell, Devon 568
Ruth, Jay Ella 67
Rutherford, Paul 192
Rutter, Steve 35
Ryan, William 467
Ryder, Shaun 57, 491
RZA 412
Rzewski, Frederic 102

## S

S Man 442
S'Express 36, 62, 129, 314, 368, **437**
S., Robin 86, 161
S., Roger 442
Saafir 262
Sabbah, Cheb I **437**
Saber, Danny 57
Sabres of Paradise 10, 55, 129, 257, 299, 323, 368, 425, **437,** 438, 466, 524, 528, 529
Sade 177, 308, 406
Sadier, Laetitia 344, 486, 488
Sadier, Seaya 487
Sadistic Mika Band 564
Safety Scissors 498, 528
Saffery, Anthony 104
Saffron 413, 428
Sagoo, Bally 437
Saint Etienne 5, 6, 17, 87, 156, 280, 317, 318, 339, 398, **438,** 439, 455, 511, 536
St. Germain 161, 179, **439**
St. Louis Symphony 431
St. Werner, Jan 205, 301, 326, 344, 345, 379
Saiz, Suso 432
Sakamoto, Ryuichi 69, 92, 267, 385, **440,** 441, 499, 509, 564
Salaryman **441**
Salen, Jeffrey 477, 478
Sales, Hunt 65
Sales, Tony 65
Sallahr, Deflon 142
Salon Music 104
Salovaara, J. 383
Salsoul Orchestra 404, **441**
Salt City Orchestra 1, 85
Salt N Pepa 71
Salt Tank 367, **441,** 442
Sample Choir 161
Samuels, Dave 556
Sanborn, David 315, 335, 521
Sanchez, Michel 124
Sanchez, Roger 41, 115, 140, 144, 179, 258, 424, **442,** 543
Sanchioni, Bruno 43
Sandals 275
Sandberg, Lars 199
Sanders, Debbie 466
Sanders, Pharoah 24, 35, 189, 393, 507
Sanderson, Nick 95
Sandoval, Hope 88
Sandoz 78, 165, 283, **442,** 443, 498
Santana 327, 470
Santana, Omar 140, 278, **443**
Sash 43, 71, 351, **443**
Sasha & John Digweed 133, **443,** 444
Sasha 71, 72, 100, 105, 133, 141, 308, 326, 384, 423, 443, 444, 482
Satie, Erik 80, 168, 374, 544
Sato, Gak 280
Satori 123
Saunders, Jesse 3, 269, 385, 412, **445,** 513

Saunderson, Ann 260, 445
Saunderson, Kevin 4, 27, 28, 34, 42, 43, 106, 133, 147, 159, 190, 199, 260, 322, 323, 327, 334, 400, 442, **445**, 446, 451, 494, 524
Savage Republic 163
Savage, Donna 438
Savale, Steve Chandra 25
Sawt El Atlas 28
Saxon, Mike 535
Scaccia, Mike 331
Scala **446**, 455, 471
Scan 7 28, **446**
Scanner 191, 361, 379, 408, **446**, 447, 451, 458, 461, 521
Scarletron 184, 549
Scavengers 120
Schaeffer, Pierre 43, 46, 138, 268, **447**, 448, 545
Scharin, Douglas 134, 325
Schellenbach, Kate 44
Schifrin, Lalo 406, 507
Schlammpeitziger 205
Schlondorff, Volker 440
Schmickler, Marcus 205, 278, 402, **447**
Schmidt, Irmin 82
Schmidt, Tobias 292
Schmidt, Uwe 5, 29, 30, 116, 124, 154, 261, 353, 361, 456, 540, 552
Schmoelling, Johannes 505
Schneider TM 295, **447**, 448
Schneider, Florian 61, 165, 286, 287
Schneider, Stefan 288, 518, 519
Schneller, Ian 460
Schnitzler, Conrad 96, 337, 434, **448**, 504
Schoenberg, Arnold 80
Schoenemann, Dietrich 63, 130, 414
Schoolly D 87, 282, 300, 324
Schrader, Paul 65
Schroeder, Steve 504
Schroeder, Wilhelm 198, 465
Schuldt, Tim 198
Schulze, Klaus 24, 25, 198, 352, 353, 432, **448**, 449, 504, 547
Schumacher, Oliver 136
Schumacher, Thomas 541, 542
Schutze, Paul 70, 286, 311, 312, 330, 347, 366, **449**, 450, 459
Schwartz, Michael 334
Schwendener, Martha 64
Schwitters, Kurt 169
Scientist 156, 295, **450**
Scion **451**
Score, Ali 186
Score, Mike 186
Scorn 31, 76, 293, 305, 347, 437, 446, **451**, 497, 508, 532, 559
Scott 4 **451**
Scott, Brian 462
Scott, Doc 23, 118, 189, 395, 452, 501, **451**
Scott, Harriet 115
Scott, Lincoln Style 155
Scott, Raymond **452**, 453
Scott, Ridley 506, 543
Scott, Shad T. 306
Scott, Style 155, 156
Scott, Tim 140, 293, 479, 544
Scott-Heron, Gil 388, 393, 521
Scottish Chamber Orchestra Strings 513
Scram 547
Scratch Orchestra 167, 364
Scratch Perverts 36
Scratch 390
Screaming Target 51, 152

Screechy Dan 317
Scroggins, Marie 172
Scroggins, Renee 172
Scroggins, Valerie 172
Scummy 569
Sea and Cake 102, **453**, 454, 460, 522
Seahorses 491
Seal 1, 28, 62, 71, 342
Seaman, Dave 106, 317, **454**
Search and Destroy 52
Searchers 174
Searcy, Peter 468
Searle, Richard 103
Seba 59, 75
Seba & Lo Tek 74
Sebbag, Raphael 536
Sebestyen, Marta 124
Second Crusade 327, 463
Secret Cinema 480
Secret Knowledge **454**, 455
Secret Life 178
Section 25 **455**
Sector 17 139
Security of the First World 417
Sednaoui, Stephane 55
Seduction 77
Seefeel 31, 32, 54, 67, 97, 136, 182, 263, 303, 344, 345, 446, **455**, 471
Seeka 275
Seger, Bob 506
Selector 21
Seligman, Matthew 150
Selway, John 50, **456**, 470, 557
Selway, Phil 422
Sem 129, 368
Senking 382
Señor Coconut 30
Señor Coconut Y Su Conjunto 29, 361, **456**
Sensation 479
Sensational 254, 479
Senser 129, 368
Sensorama 11
Sensory Productions 313
Sensurreal **456**
Sentinel 394
Septeto Nacional 294
Sepulveda, Charlie 317, 364
Sequential 352
Sermon, Erick 201
Servotron **456**
Sessions, Roger 322
SETI 130, 203, 414, **457**, 567
Seven Grand Housing Authority 385 777 372, 500
Seven, Barry 3
Severed Heads **457**
Sex Pistols 38, 163, 356, 414, 418, 419
Seymour, Daren 303, 446, 455
Shadowplay 255
Shadows 268
Shafie, Conrad 275
Shakatak 271
Shake 49, **457**, 510, 539
Shakespear's Sister 173
Shakespeare, Robbie 272, 319, 381, 469
Shakir, Anthony "Shake" 115, 368, 457, 526, 539, 566
Shakti 279
Shamen 123, 263, 271, 295, 301, 332, 333, 334, 366, 374, 407, 408, 428, **457**, 458, 475, 548, 568
Shamsher, Farook 272
Shamsher, Haroon 272
Shanghai Film Symphony Orchestra 431

Shango 38
Shank, Bud 46
Shannon 193, 298, 408, 513
Shante, Roxanne 315, 316
Shantel **458**
Sharkey **458**
Sharkey, Feargal 170, 171
Sharp, Elliott 315
Sharp, Jonah 150, 188, 261, 279, 345, 352, 378, 399, 428, 463, 476, 477, 494, 547
Sharpley, Cedric 363
Sharrock, Sonny 293, 318
Shaw, Marlena 439
Shaw, Rik 434
Shaw, Sandie 48, 69
Shea, David 261, 269, 446, **458**, 459, 569
Shean, Djen Ajakan 367
Shears, Steve 533
Shenton, Ann 2, 3
Shepherd, Neil 188
Shepp, Archie 319
Sheridan, Karen 433
Sherman, Bim 63, 155, 459
Sherwood, Adrian 77, 155, 156, 331, 359, 390, 409, **459**, 465, 502, 524
Shields, Kevin 175, 330, 349, 350, 473
Shinehead 469
Shinjuku Filth 459
Shinjuku Thief **459**
Shinzu, Atomu 29
Shirazinia, Ali 123
Shirt Trax 471
Shizuo 27, 382, 383, **459**
Shockabilly 556
Shocklee, Hank 417
Shogun 166
Shonen Knife 157
Shoobe, Lou 452
Short, Darryl 388
Shortee 138
Shorter, Wayne 117, 319, 553, 554
Shortkut 111, 262, 275
Showroom Recordings 263, 288, 412
Shrat 12
Shrieve, Michael 432
Shrimp Boat 129, 453, **460**
Shut Up & Dance 100, **460**, 468
Shy FX 152, **460**
Si Cut Db 191, 447, **460**, 461
Sibbles, Leroy 16, 390, 469
Siciliano, Dani 150
Signum 492
Sigsworth, Guy 311
Sigue Sigue Sputnik 63, 343
Sigur Rós **461**
Sil 70
Silent Breed 6
Silent Phase 323, **461**
Silent Poets 147
Silicon Teens 361, **462**
Silk 533
Silly Sil 538
Silvah Bullet 137, 290
Silver Apples **462**, 479
Silver, Horace 539
Silverfish 435
Simenon, Tim 11, 62, 63, 128, 190
Simeon 63, 462
Simins, Russell 81
Simmonds, Chris 101, 102
Simmonds, Ian 275
Simmonds, Jeremy 547
Simmons, Annabelle 154
Simmons, Russell 44
Simms, Nick 104

Simms, Wayne 496
Simnett, Mark 40
Simon & Garfunkel 110, 148
Simon, Alana 334
Simon, Paul 16
Simon, Robin 533
Simonds, Clodagh 330
Simons, Ed 87, 88
Simple Minds 97, 414
Simply Jeff 443, **462**
Simply Red 157, 177, 318, 366, 370, 444, 459, 536
Simpson, Gerald 161, 292
Simpson, Homer 159
Simpson, Mel 539
Simpson, Mike 33, 157
Simpson, Veda 161, 544
Sims, Ben 279
Sims, Bobby 300
Sims, David Wm. 522
Sin, Will 333, 407
Sinan 481
Sinatra, Frank 192
Sinatra, Nancy 551
Sinclar, Bob 326, 327, **463**, 484
Sines, Todd 157
Singh, Avtar 104
Singh, Talvin 29, 100, 272, 280, 319, 437, 441, **463**, 499, 501
Singh, Tjinder 94, 104
Single Cell Orchestra 192, 355, **463**, 464, 476
Single Gun Theory 126
Sinister Six 33
Sinnott, Will 457
Sioux, Siouxsie 10
Siouxsie & the Banshees 9, 10, 58, 95, 463
Sir Menelik 146, 275
Sir Mix A Lot 143
Sister Bliss 177
Sister Machine Gun 491
Sister Sledge 89
Sisters of Mercy 51
Sixteen, Earl 296
60 Channels 269
69 106, 107, 260, 384, 385, 415, 446, **464**
Size 9 557
Size, Roni 68, 74, 75, 116, 142, 181, 188, 189, 269, 288, 298, 351, 359, 393, 425, **464**, 465, 471, 472, 493, 503
Size, Roni & Reprazent 464
Skaaning, Jesper 266
Skatalites 390
Skeleton Key 91
Skindivers 19
Skinny Puppy 31, 61, 91, 116, 152, 198, 297, 304, 331, 364, 416, 427, 459, **465**, 466, 479, 562
Skopelitis, Nicky 156, 294, 295, 319
Skydiver 6
Skylab 35, 353, 437, **466**, 537, 540
Skylab 2000 140
Skyy 299
SL2 84, 468, 469
Slab 154, 437, **466**, 528
Slack Dog 47, 383
Slam Mode 93
Slam 144, 199, 373, 407, **466**, 566
Slapp Happy 181
Slater, Luke 4, 11, 68, 260, 264, 292, 400, 408, 423, **467**, 496, 504, 548
Slayer 72, 159
Slazenger, Jake 281, 345, 346, **467**
Sledge, Kathy 327, 342, 442
Slemming, Denzil 290

Slicker 131, **467**, 468
Slide Five 515
Slijngaard, Ray 529
Slim & Slam 336
Slint 5, 105, 338, **468**, 522, 531, 556
Slipmatt **468**, 469
Slipstream 166
Slits 88, 459
Slo Moshun 12
Slotek **469**
Slow 205
Slowdive 350, 427, 461
Slowly 31
Slusser, David 261, 569
Sluts 'N' Strings & A 909 263, 412, 420
Sly & Robbie 272, 308, 318, 319, 342, 388, 425, **469**, 522
Sly & the Family Stone 116, 119, 199, 200, 385, 510
Sly 469
Small Fish with Spine 355, **469**, 470
Small Good Thing 366
Small, Heather 307
Smart, Phillip 282
Smashing Pumpkins 44, 335, 422, 460
Smiley 460
Smith & Mighty 142, 464, **470**, 552
Smith, Andy **470**
Smith, Barry 2
Smith, Brix 203
Smith, Chas 73
Smith, Christian 50, 346, 456, **470**
Smith, Earl "Chinna" 381
Smith, Jake 493, 494
Smith, Jimmy 99, 338, 467
Smith, Lonnie Liston 74, 189, 203
Smith, Mark E. 12, 63
Smith, Peter 334
Smith, Rick 20, 195, 535, 536
Smith, Rob 259, 269, 470
Smith, Robert 120
Smith, Sara P. 264
Smith, Simon 369
Smith, Stevie 355
Smith, Toby 266
Smith, Will 93
Smith, William "BJ" 33, 526
Smiths 57, 87, 106, 164, 277, 282, 291, 307, 357, 378, 392
Smithson, Dawn 271
Smoke City **470**, 471
Smooth, C.L. 141, 142
Snap 512, 546
SND **471**
Sneaker Pimps 30, 291, 292, 316, 342, 407, 437, **471**, 520, 528, 544
Sneakster 455, **471**
Snoop Doggy Dogg 201, 366
Snooze 137
Snowpony 350
Soccio, Gino 86
Sofa Surfers 288, 472, **471**
Soft Cell 8, 9, 10, 24, 77, 98, 129, 416, 461, **472**, 473, 494
Soft Machine 182, 369, 532
Sokol 412
Sol Brothers 144, 194
SOL 5, 123
Sol, Victor 5, 115, 124
Solar Twins 68, **472**
Solas 294
Solcyc 36
Solex **472**, 473
Solid Doctor 37, 137, 184, 361, **473**
Solomon, Paul 394

Solsonics 282, **473**
Solvent 113, 263, 304, **473**
Some More Crime 154
Somerville, Jimmy 38, 479, 543
Sonar Circle 189
Sonic Boom 175, 271, 286, **473**, 475, 476, 479
Sonic Solution 62
Sonic Subjunkies 166
Sonic Youth 40, 46, 47, 65, 147, 163, 315, 338, 349, 355, 362, 486
Sonique 437
Sons of Silence 366, **473**, 474
Sons of the Subway 39, **474**
Sonz of a Loop Da Loop Era 68, 113
Soothsayer 172
SOS Band 45
Sosa, Omar 6
Sossna, Rudolf 181
Soul Coughing 91, 162, 414
Soul II Soul 35, 39, 55, 67, 171, 260, 308, 316, 317, 334, 423, 442, 464, 470, **474**
Soul Motive 19
Soul Oddity 271, 394, 420, **474**
Soul Slinger, Carlos 146
Soul Syndicate 450
Souls of Mischief 510
Soulstice 6
Sound Design 513
Sound Five 254
Sound Patrol 85
Soundclash 155, 156
Soundgarden 91, 132, 161
Sounds of Blackness 308
Sounds of Life 475
Soup Dragons 203
Source Direct 21, 74, 75, 115, 371, 393, **474**, 475
Source Experience 297
Source 297, **475**
South Wales Striking Miners Choir 513
South 556
Space DJz 39, **475**
Space Opera 4, 62
Space 372, 373, **475**
Spacedust 327, 463
Spacemen 3 19, 175, 204, 290, 462, 473, **475**, 476, 479, 480, 481
Spacepimp 1
Spacer 275, 359, 485
Spacetime Continuum 124, 192, 345, 378, **476**, 477, 493, 494
Spaceways 477
Spacewurm 281
Spacey, Kevin 70
Spahn Ranch 259, 416
Spanky 143
Sparhawk, Mimi 382
Sparks 132, 477, 478, 479, 510
Sparks **477**
Spasms 125
Spearhead 269
Special Affect 331
Special Dark 469
Special K 113
Spector, Phil 4, 171, 282, 378, 480, 481
Spectre 412, **479**, 509
Spectrum 175, 271, 462, 476, **479**, 480
Speed Freak 27, 52
Speedy J 1, 28, 182, 300, 313, 381, 400, 456, 479, 480
Spencer, Jon Blues Explosion 91, 382, 537
Spencer, Lee 378
Spice Barons 85, 393
Spicer, Jimmy 270

Spiders from Mars 64, 65
Spill 378
Spinners 441, 560
Spiral Tribe 154, 407
Spirea X 4
Spiritual Vibes 90, 502
Spiritualized 87, 204, 461, 475, 476, **480**, 481, 482
SPK 305, 364, 430, **481**
Split Enz 459
Spoils of War **481**
Spooky 76, 146, 366, 374, **482**
Spoon, Mark 266
Spoonie Gee 45, 111
Spring Heel Jack 11, 272, 319, 358, 371, 480, **482**, 483, 521, 522
Springfield, Dusty 150, 392
Springsteen, Bruce 174, 494
Spybey, Mark 152
Spyro Gyra 553
Squarepusher 16, 17, 18, 47, 67, 86, 103, 109, 138, 271, 284, 345, 346, 369, 379, **483**, 516, 553
Squire, John 491, 492
Squirrel Bait 5, 468
Srock, Anthony 328
Stabbing Westward 198
Stakka & K Tee 377
Stalling, Carl 452, 453, 568, 569
Stallings, Felix 182
Stanley, Bob 438
Stanners, Malcolm 441, 442
Stansfield, Lisa 67, 99, 317, 318, 368, 474, 511
Staples, Mavis 48, 445
Stapleton, Steve 109, 110, 364
Stardust 115, 327, 404, 463, **484**
Stardust, Alvin 177
Starfish Pool **484**
Stark, Fredrik 565
Starr, Ringo 177
Stars of the Lid **484**, 556
Stasis 24, 35, 71, 456, **484**, 509
State of Bengal 437, 463
State of Play 110
Statik Sound System 11, 288, **484**, 485
Status Quo 19
Steady B 282
Stearns, Michael 367, 429, 432, **485**, 486
Steel 96
Steel 52, 53
Steely Dan 103, 431
Stein, Gertrude 504
Steinberg, Sebastian 91, 459
Steinski 100, 280
Stent, Mark "Spike" 56, 310, 311
Stenzel, Torsten 423
Stephens, Jonny 323
Stephenson, Peter 457
Stephney, Bill 417
Stereo MC's 296, **486**
Stereolab 2, 4, 19, 69, 82, 105, 115, 129, 134, 204, 280, 290, 326, 341, 344, 355, 364, 388, 402, 424, 453, 454, **486**, 487, 488, 515, 518, 519, 522, 523, 527, 531
Sterling Void 54
Steroid Maximus 187
Stetsasonic 119, 281, 412
Stevens, Cat 194
Stevens, Joanna 472
Stewart, Dave 110, 173, 174, 372
Stewart, Grant 492
Stewart, Mark 167, 459, 502
Stewart, Slam 336
Stewart, Sylvester "Sly Stone" 560

Sting 59, 270, 374, 513
Stingily, Byron 37, 86, 300, **488**, 510, 511
Stipe, Michael 70, 88
Stock, Aitken & Waterman 83, 489
Stock, Hausen & Walkman 269, 353, **488**, 489
Stockhausen, Karlheinz 43, 90, 117, 285, 302, 322, 324, 364, 446, 447, 448, **489**, 490, 518, 526, 540, 548
Stokes, Michael 50
Stoll, Steve 121, 298, **491**, 551, 555
Stonadge, Gary 51
Stone Roses 155, 302, 366, 408, 409, 422, 461, **491**, 492
Stone, Al 267
Stone, Carl 46, 324, **492**, 514
Stone, Dave 165
Stone, Jon 302
Stooges 65, 163, 408, 476
Storm Large 74
Storm, Rory & the Hurricanes 177
Stout, Mike 479
Strafe 172
Strange Cargo 374
Strange Parcels 156
Strange, Steve 547
Stranger 285, 379
Stranglers 414
Strauss, Richard 544
Stravinsky, Igor 105, 520
Strawberry Switchblade 109, 283
Strayhorn, Billy 336
Street, Stephen 157, 408
Streisand, Barbra 428, 500
Stretch 'N' Vern 180, 555
Strictly Kev 138
Strong, Ame 191
Strummer, Joe 51, 57
Stuart, Colin 160
Stubbs, Scott **492**
Studio One 75, 336
Studio Pressure 394
Stupids 284, 379
Style Council 28, 174, 301, 407
Sub Dub 146, **492**, 552
Sub Sub 86
Subject 13 **493**
Sublime 146
Submarine 123
Submission 185
Subotnick, Morton 106, 324, 378, 492, **493**
Subsonic 808 52
Substance 340, 451, **493**
Subtropic 476, 477, **493**, 494
Suburban Knight 144, **494**, 535
Suchy, Joseph 361
Sudler, Monnette 282
Suede 406
Sufi 67
Sugar Hill 89, 459
Sugarcubes 54, 55, 162, 301
Sugarhill Gang 38, 89, 123, 502
Sugimoto, Kuni 353
Suicide 2, 3, 203, 383, 462, 465, 479, 481, **494**, 497
Sukia 30, 143, 330, 331, **494**, 495
Summer, Donna 179, 188, 317, 334, 343, 347, 478, 535, 548, 555
Summers, Andy 196
Sumner, Bernard 88, 161, 162, 164, 165, 356, 357, 392
Sun Electric 28, 183, 313, 373, **495**
Sun J 25

Sun Ra **495**
Sunburst Band 134
Sunday School 185
Sundays 156
Sunkings 496
Sunny Day Real Estate 325
Suns of Arqa 26, **496**
Sunscreem 165, 178, 322, **496**
Sunsinger, Ron 432, 485
Super Collider **497**
Super ESP 129, 467, 468
Superchunk 132
Supergrass 339
Supernova 456
Supremes 101, 172
Sureshot 497
Surgeon 4, 298, 329, 381, **497**, 566
Sutekh 281, 528, **498**
Sutherland, Joan 157
Sutton, Graham 40, 67, 151
Suzuki, Damo 82
Suzuki, Keiichi 264, 373, 443
Sveinsson, Kjartan 461
Svitek, Louis 331
Swamp Zombies 29
Swans 40, 163, 187, 383, 465, 556, 559, 565
Swartenbroekx, Dirk 75
Swayzak 85, **498**, 515
Swayze, Patrick 498
Sweet Exorcist 31, 35, 77, 165, 283, 442, 469, **498**
Sweet 283
Sweet, Matthew 278
Swift, Rob 388, **498**, 499, 563
Swing 52 83
Swinscoe, J. 91, 92
Swizz Beatz 148
Swollen Members 148
Swordsmen 529
Sydenham, Jerome 93
Sykes, Nick 151
Sylk 130 282, 442, 557
Sylvan, Carole 86
Sylvester 488
Sylvian, David 267, 330, 414, 440, **499**
Symetrics 366
Sympletic 71
Synaesthesia 126, 198
Synergy **499**, 500
Syrup 359
System F 104, 105
System 7 154, 322, 340, 372, **500**, 501
Systemwide 347
Szepanski, Achim 27
Szostek, Jason "Bpmf" 130, 414

## T

T Coy 307
T la Rock 314
T Power 146, 147, 260, 371, 441, 480, 497, **502**
T Rex 64
T., Booker 89
Taborn, Craig 260, 261, 295
Tackhead 63, 155, 459, **502**
Tactile 383, 541
Tacuma, Jamaaladeen 282
Takahashi, Yukihiro 509, 564
Takemura, Nobukazu 90, 158, 189, 325, 379, 426, 427, 466, **502**, 503
Takeya, Akemi 292
Tales from the Hardside 443
Talk Talk 371, **503**, 504
Talking Heads 89, 104, 167, 169, 170, 560
Tall Paul 555

Talla Two XLC 52
Talpas, Gary 256
Tamara 202
Tambala, Rudy 20, 40
Tamlins 469
Tanaka, Fumiya 63, **504**
Tanaka, Tomoyuki 178
Tangerine Dream 12, 24, 61, 78, 84, 96, 105, 113, 191, 197, 202, 268, 286, 324, 343, 344, 372, 374, 382, 400, 432, 448, 461, 475, 500, **504**, 505, 506, 507, 518, 537, 543
Tanith 541
Tao 340
Tappi Tikarrass 55
Tardo, J. Serge 262
Tarkovsky, Andrey 430
Tarwater 105, 295, **507**, 519
Taskforce 36
Tatum, Art 157
Taucher 366
Taurus, Danny 12
Tavares 510
Taxi Gang 469
Taxi Girl 332
Tayebi, Sharam 123
Tayla 74
Taylor 808 130, 203, 457
Taylor 100
Taylor, Cecil 477
Taylor, Chris "The Glove" 533
Taylor, Danny 462
Taylor, Felice 302
Taylor, Jack 507
Taylor, James **507**, 508
Taylor, Pauline 177
Taylor, Seth 258
Taylor, Tim 194, 555
Taylor-Firth, Robin 370
TDF **508**
Tear Garden 465
Teardrop Explodes 283
Tears for Fears 125, 422
Tech 9 513
Technical Itch 122, 133, 391, 402, **508**
Techno Animal 47, 76, 147, 163, 166, 184, 254, 305, 347, 349, 405, 406, 451, 479, **508**, 509, 531, 552, 559
Technotronic 157, 307, **509**, 513
Teebrooke, Paul W. 456, 484, **509**
Teenage Fanclub 337
Tei, Towa 122, 123, 178, **509**
Tejada, John 157, **509**, 510
Tek 9 137, 361, **510**
Tekonivel 383, 541
Telex 27, 108, **510**
Telstar Ponies 203, 337
Temple, Alice 537, 538
10cc 21, 23
Ten City 86, 184, 488, **510**, 511
10,000 Maniacs 259
Tenaglia, Danny 123, 185, 202, 278, 435, 488, **511**
Tench, Benmont 170
Tench, David 568
Tennant, Neil 164, 357, 391, 392
Tenney, James 261, 490, 492
Tenniswood, Keith 437, 528, 529
Tenor Fly 194
Tenor, Jimi 255, 344, 383, **511**, 512
Terence FM 81, 316
Terenzi, Fiorella 151, **512**
Terminal Power Company 559
Terminator X 141, 417, 418
Terrasson, Jacky 269

Terrell, Peter 86
Terror Against Terror 306
Terry, Todd 41, 83, 174, 274, 278, 308, 317, 341, 346, 381, 382, 436, 442, **512**, 513, 543, 546, 548, 555
Terry, Todd Project 512
Tesh, John 506
Test Department 256, 481, **513**, 514, 527, 568
Teste **514**
Tetaz, Charles 459
Tetaz, Francois 459
Texas 423
Thaemlitz, Terre 255, 263, **514**, 515
Thair, Richard 11, 425
Thanatos 59
Thatcher, Dean 10
THC 259
The The 8, 164
Theodore, Mike Orchestra 486
Theorem 498, **515**
Therapy 394, 437
Thessalonians 85, 393
Thewlis, David 373
Thiel, Tom 495
Thielemans, Toots 569
Thievery Corporation 288, **515**, 516, 551
Thin Lizzy 87
3rd Bass 67, 412
Third Electric 24, 62, 129, **516**
Third Eye 516
Third Eye Foundation **516**
Thirlwell, J.G. 187
Thirsk, Kristy 126
13th Floor Elevators 476
Thirty Seventy 111
This Mortal Coil 59, 87, 98, 120, 301
Thomas, Alfie 195
Thomas, Carl 277
Thomas, Peter **516**
Thomas, Richard [Rock] 97, 98
Thomas, Richard [Experimental] 295, **516**, 517
Thompson Twins 59, 331
Thompson, Chester 554
Thompson, Christie 537
Thompson, Dereck 481
Thompson, Mayo 79, 337, 408
Thompson, Richard 174
Thompson, Tony 89, 419
Thomson, Virgil 537
Thorn, Tracey 15, 100, 123, 174, 316, 482
Thorne, Mike 557, 558
Thornhill, Leeroy 413
Thornton, Keith 149
Thornton, Kevin 33
Thorpe, Steve 273
Thorpe, Tony 39, 48, 80, 166, 199, 340, 435
Those Norwegians 155
Thrash 183, 372, 500
Threadgill, Henry 318
3D 316
Three Times Dope 282
Throbbing Gristle 31, 77, 78, 91, 95, 98, 109, 152, 162, 163, 165, 171, 183, 283, 305, 324, 354, 364, 415, 416, 430, 442, 465, 481, 494, **517**, 527
Throw That Beat In the Garbage Can 159
Thrower, Stephen 98
Throwing Muses 560
Thrussel, David 459
Thug **517**
Thulin, Camilla 21
Thurston, Colin 503
Tibet, David 99, 109, 110, 364

TIC 122
Tied & Tickled Trio 5
Tiers, Wharton 568
Tietchens, Asmus 8, 367, **518**
Tikiman 451
Tilbury, John 167
Tilson, Martha 86
Tilt 367, 511
Timbaland 137, 148, 189, 261, 336, 388
Time Zone 38
Timelords 283
Timeshard 39, **518**
Tin Machine 65
Tin Star **518**
Tin Tin Out 347
Tina 350
Tindersticks 407
Tinley, Adam 1
Tiny Trendies 134
Tipsy 30, 75, 102, 203, 320, **518**, 553
TJR 527
TLC 172
To Rococo Rot 105, 263, 288, 438, 507, **518**, 519
Tobin, Amon 103, 109, 271, 334, 441, 516, **519**
Todd, Andy 428
Tokyo Ghetto Pussy 266
Tom & Joyce 327, 463
Tom Tom Club 28, 334
Tom Tom 285, 379
Toma, Andi 301, 302, 344, 345
Tomiie, Satoshi **519**, 520
Tomita 7, 261, 388, 497, **520**
Tomita, Isao 520
Tomlinson, Dave 518
Ton Steine Scherben 448
Tone Generator 481
Tone Loc 157
Tong, Pete 140, 161, 308, **520**
T.O.N.T.O.'s Expanding Head Band 521, 560, **520**, 521
Too Short 262
Toobad, Johnny 196
Toop, David 300, 459, **521**
Top, Emmanuel 43
Topping, Simon 86
Torch Song 374
Torcha 513
Torme, Mel 9
Torn, David 430, 432
Tornadoes 330
Tornados 389
Torres, Hector 317
Torres, Liz 511
Tortoise 2, 5, 31, 40, 47, 54, 69, 85, 88, 90, 102, 105, 129, 134, 264, 265, 288, 301, 326, 377, 379, 402, 403, 434, 441, 453, 467, 468, 487, 488, 503, 509, 518, 519, **521**, 522, 523, 524, 529, 531, 537
Tosca 288, 387, **522**, 523
Tosh, Peter 390, 466, 469
Total Eclipse 563
Totemplow 391
Toth, Andy 129, 130
Touche 559
Tourists 173
Tournesol 313, 495, **523**
Tower of Power 67, 278
Towers, Cheyne 271
Towner, Ralph 553
Toxic Two 555
Trace 67, 147, 376
Trackmaster Lou 446
Tracks, Gordon 7

Trammps 58, 441, 510
Trance Mission 358
Trancemasters 568
Trancesetters 279
Tranquility Bass 192, 427, **523**
Trans Am 105, 288, 326, 330, 378, 434, 441, 518, 519, 522, **523**, 524
Transcend 361
Transeau, Brian 71, 72, 123, 316
TransGlobal Underground 28, 29, 303, 404, 437, **524**
Travis, Geoff 79
Treacherous Three 275
Treichler, Franz 565, 566
Trenchmouth 129
Trend 153
Trent, Ron 21, 36, 108, 139, 189, **524**, 525
Trepte, Uli 355
Tres Manos 538, **539**
Tribal Drift 156
Tribe Called Quest 38, 67, 102, 119, 201, 273, 274, 278, 359, 522, 539, 540
Tricky Disco 35, 359
Tricky 20, 35, 37, 54, 55, 63, 128, 175, 292, 316, 342, 382, 406, 421, 433, 464, 471, 480, 525, 526, 538, 550, **525**
Trinere 193, 408
Trini, Jade 315
Trinity Hi-Fi 123
Tripp, Carol 351
Tristeza 556
Troggs 480
Tronik House 260, 445, 446
Trouble Funk 302
Troubleneck Brothers 486
Truby, Rainer 181
Trugoy the Dove 119, 120
Trumystic Sound System 172
Tsunami One 193
Tube 146
Tubeway Army 362
Tucker, Barbara 308, 317, 318, 342, 426, 442, 546
Tucker, Keith 33, 457, **526**
Tucker, William 331, 332
Tudor, David 80, 81, 102, 322, 370, 490, **526**, 527
Tuff Crew 423
Tuff Darts 477
Tuff Jam 153, 161, **527**
Tuff Little Unit 359
Tunakan, Erdam 70, 412, 420
Tupilaq 195
Turbulent Force 466
Turco Loco 188, 279
Turn On **527**
Turner, Andy 56, 57, 70, 71, 399, 400, 428
Turner, Carl 54
Turner, Ike and Tina 171
Turner, Tina 48, 123, 342, 513
Turntable Terranova 187
Turtles 119
Turtletoes 467
Tusken Raiders 269, 345, 467
Tutti, Cosey Fanni 91, 415, 517
Tuva 284
Twain, Shania 424
23 Skidoo 109, **527**
Twerk 498, **528**
Twisted Anger 278
Twisted Minds 71
Twisted Science 64, 334, 497, 516, **528**
Two Bad Mice 59, 401, 435, **528**
Two Fat Buddhas 194
2K 284

Two Live Crew 136, 142, 143, 394
Two Lone Swordsmen 11, 203, 437, 438, 466, **528**, 529, 549
2Pac 201
Two Player 516
2 Puerto Ricans, A Black Man & A Dominican 342
Two Sandwiches Short of a Lunchbox 343, 385, **529**
2 Unlimited 443, **529**
Tye, Jon 64, 67, 334, 497, 516, 528
Tyler, Tom 280
Tyndall, Nik 368
Tyree 530, **529**
Tyson, June 496
Tyson, Ron 441

# U
U Roy 101, 155, 282
U2 19, 35, 63, 70, 77, 145, 165, 168, 178, 278, 311, 342, 354, 366, 392, 413, 417, 422, 423, 466, 474, 520, 537, 540
UA 509
UB40 38
Überzone 278, 464, 531
UCLA Men's Chorus 84
UFO 536
Ui 301, 326, 509, 519, 523, 524, **531**
Uilab 531
UK Apache 460
Ulbrich, Lutz 25
Ulrich, Peter 121
Ultra Nate 513, 520, **531**
Ultra Violet 101
Ultrafunkula 172
Ultrahigh 267
Ultramagnetic MC's 111, 142, 145, 149, 486, **531**, 532
Ultramarine 67, 323, **532**
Ultraviolence **532**
Ultravox 82, 190, 191, **533**, 547
Uncle Jamm's Army 378, **533**
Uncle 22 146
Undark 330
Underdog 11, 391
Underground Resistance 27, 28, 33, 34, 39, 40, 43, 63, 92, 144, 147, 153, 154, 185, 321, 327, 328, 340, 369, 381, 382, 400, 408, 494, **533**, 534, 535, 548, 554
Underground Solution 442, 520
Underground, Glenn 81, 510, **535**
Underworld 18, 20, 54, 55, 105, 106, 123, 195, 202, 280, 402, 408, 431, 441, 454, **535**, 536
Unik 339
Union Jack 140
Unis, Vir 433
Unit Moebius 253
United Future Organization 134, 187, 288, 382, **536**
United States of America 183, 536, 537
United States of Poetry 199, 481
Unitone Hifi 154
Universal Being 194, 195, **537**
Universal Language 93
UNKLE 30, 34, 35, 56, 83, 104, 145, 184, 416, 521, 522, **537**, 538
Unknown DJ 34, 42, 93, 533
Unrest 172
Unruh, N.U. 162
Unsane 187
Up, Bustle & Out 99, 100, **538**
Upsetter 389, 390
Upsetters 381, 389, 390

Uptight 551
Upton, Ed 148
Urban Blues Project 424
Urban Dance Squad 274, 538, 539
Urban Farmers 184, 549
Urban Soul 513
Urban Sound Gallery 524
Urban Spirits 513
Urban Takeover 555
Urban Tribe **539**
Ure, Midge 533, 547
Ursula 1000 **539**
Us3 421, **539**, 540
USA European Connection 326
USG 524
Usher 527
Ussachevsky, Vladimir 84, **540**
Usual Suspects 295
Utah Saints **540**
Utley, Adrian 406, 407
Uzzell-Edwards, Charles 352, 463, **540**

# V
Vainio, Mika 30, 70, 292, 383, 384, 512, **541**
Vainqueur 41, 125, 321, 340, 451, 493, 504, **541**
Vaisanen, Ilpo 383, 384
Valaquen, Kurt 259
Valcic, Anthony 152
Valentin, Dave 317, 364
Valentin, Jim 441
Valentin, Rick 441
Valentine, Cindy 270
Valli, Frankie 392
Van Halen 19
VanAcker, Luc 331
VanDijk, Mijk **541**, 542
Vandross, Luther 89, 561
VanDyk, Paul 72, 105, 133, 307, 367, 384, 443, **542**
Vangelis 7, 61, 261, 264, 367, 388, 432, **542**, 543
VanHalen, Eddie 151
VanHelden, Armand 37, 62, 84, 88, 115, 123, 140, 145, 146, 161, 172, 178, 302, 471, 520, 527, **543**, 544, 548
VanHoen, Mark 32, 302, 303, 344, 446, 455, 471
Vanilla Ice 310
VanLierop, Nikki 279
Vannelli, Joe T. 542
VanPortfleet, Mike 59
VanTieghem, David 169
Vapourspace 7, 263, 400, 408, 428, **544**, 558
Varèse, Edgard 2, 149, 183, 447, **544**, 545
Varley, Gez 299, **545**, 557
Vas Deferens Organization 163
Vasquez, Junior 43, 341, 442, 511, **545**, 546
Vassell, Elaine 125
Vatcher, Michael 569
Vath, Sven 105, 129, 268, 470, 480, 536, 542, **546**
Vaughan, Stevie Ray 65
Vector Two 63
Vector 298
Vega, Alan 203, 383, 384, 494
Vega, Little Louie 300, 317, 318, 364, 512, 513, **546**, 547
Vega, Tata 38
Veit, Conny 405

Velocette 476, **547**
Veloso, Caetano 91, 512
Velvet Underground 9, 79, 82, 83, 96, 102, 182, 349, 480, 537, 567
Ventures 507
Vera Cocha 105
Verdi, Giuseppe 50
Verhagen, Darrin 459
Vertigo, Louis 327
Veruca Salt 460
Verve 51, 145, 537
Vibert Simmonds 547
Vibert, Luke 67, 100, 109, 264, 270, 333, 345, 346, 359, 402, 416, 494, 521, 522, 531, **547**, 550, 551, 553
Vicious, Johnny 488
Village People 387, 392, 393
Vintage Millenium 133
Vinyl Blair 199
Violent, Johnny 532
Virgo 278
Virgo, Martin 339
Visage 24, 253, 304, 473, **547**, 548
Visconti, Tony 64, 477, 478
Vision **548**
Visions of Shiva 105, 542
Visit Venus 202
Vission & Lorimer 548
Vission, Richard "Humpty" 37, 458, **548**
Vitous, Miroslav 553, 554
Vivaldi, Antonio 308, 365
Vogel, Cristian 48, 51, 79, 92, 292, 333, 336, 467, 497, 523, 528, **548**, 549, 551
Vogel, Sebastian 295
Voice Stealer 184, 185, **549**
Voigt Kampff 385
Voigt, Wolfgang 336
Von Jotka 295
VonOswald, Moritz 28, 41, 42, 43, 190, 320, 321, 339, 541
Voorn, Orlando 43
Voov 542
Votel, Andy 334
Vowles, Mushroom 316
Voyager 75, 177
Vulva 124, **549**
VVV 383

# W
W., Kristine 86, 123, 177, **550**
Wabi Sabi 447
Wachtelaer, Dirk 450
Waddington, Steve 49
Wade, Rick 115, **550**
Wadephul, Ralph 505
Wagner, Richard 156, 256, 365
Wagon Christ 67, 138, 264, 345, 402, 483, 487, 502, 522, 547, **550**, 551
Wailer, Bunny 390, 469
Wailing Souls 469
Waits, Tom 538
Wakeman, Rick 43, 64, 500
Waldeck **551**
Waldeck, Klaus 551
Walden, Narada Michael 196, 554
Waldenback, Jens 274
Waldmann, Clem 531
Wales, Ashley 482, 483
Walford, Britt 468
Walk, Mark 435
Walken, Christopher 556
Walker 6, 7
Walker, Jim 418
Walker, Scott 8, 9, 256

Walker, Stewart 551
Wallace, Dave 19
Wallace, Horsemouth 15, 16
Wallen, Byron 425
Waller, Don 89
Waller, Fats 157
Wallstar 32
Walmsley, Richard 45
Walsh, Maureen 62
Walsh, Nina 154, 466
Wambonix 551
Wamdue Kids 93, 551, 552
Wamdue Productions 551
Wamdue Project 551, 552
War 40, 123
Ward, Jeff 331
Ward, John 492
Ward, Peter 370
Ward, Ursula 492
Ware, Martyn 47, 48
Warfield, Justin 63
Warhol, Andy 122, 386, 567
Warren, Nick 552
Warrior 272
Warwick, Dionne 62
Warwicker, John 195
Was Not Was 556
Wash, Martha 56, 86, 318, 513, 548
Washington, Grover Jr. 475
Washington, Larry 441
Watanabe, Kazumi 440
Watchman 71
Waters, Crystal 548, 555
Waters, Muddy 506
Waters, Roger 396, 397, 398
Watford, Michael 86, 426, 442, 488, 513
Watkins, Ben 274
Watkins, Martin 10
Watson, Chris 77, 78, 552
Watson, Richard 58
Watt, Ben 174, 378, 482
Watts, Charlie 556
Watts, Raymond 187
Watts-Russell, Ivo 20, 101, 262, 301, 308, 316
Wax Doctor 109, 177, 425, 435, 519, **552**
Wax Scientists 71
Wax, Tom 71
Waxploitation 296
Way Out West 342, **552**
Wayne, John 417
We 75, 146, 158, 203, **552**, 553
Weather Report 147, 271, 425, 450, 483, **553**, 554
Weatherall, Andrew 10, 55, 87, 178, 323, 366, 408, 442, 454, 529, 566
Weavers 46
Web, Will 24, 33, 139, 526, **554**
Webb, Jimmy 11
Webb, Joe 358
Webb, Paul 371, 503
Webb, Peter 484
Webb, Sarah 113
Webber, Mark 103
Webern, Anton 489, 544, 566
Webster, Charles 333, 407
Weekes, Donald 125
Weeks, David 531
Ween 47, 507
Weill, Kurt 566
Weinzierl, John 12, 13
Weir Brothers 375
Weir, Bob 151
Weir, Graham 375

Weir, Neil 375
Weir, Peter 432
Weiser, Scott 42, 158
Weisse Náchte 69
Weisser, Michael 169
Weisser, Stefan 568
Weller, Paul 91, 174, 406, 462
Wells, Bill 203
Wen-Chung, Chou 545
Wenders, Wim 83
Wendy & Lisa 410
Werner, Jan 302
Wesley, Fred 95, 180, 386
West India Company 59
West, Richard 333
Westbam 62, 83, 105, **554**, 555
Westberg, Norman 187
Westmoreland, Micko 67
Weston, Kris 183, 188, 372, 373
Weston, Randy 556
Westworld 101
Whale 525
What, What 510
Wheeler, Caron 67, 171, 474
Wheeler, Harold 324
Wheeler, Kenny 499
Whispers 441
Whitaker, Rodney 260
White Zombie 157, 422
White, Barry 42, 123, 470, 511, 512
White, Helen 11, 484
White, Lenny 117
White, Paul 55
White, Simone 6
White, Trevor 477
White, Will 414
Whitman, Walt 504
Whitten, Danny 174
Whittingham, Richard 433
Who 59, 180
Who's That Girl? 310
Whodini 150, 194, 385
Wide Receiver **555**
Widger, Paul 95
Wiedlin, Jane 477, 478
Wiggin, Paul 455
Wiggs, Pete 438
Wilburn, Ishmael 554
Wilcox, Toyah 196
Wild & Taylor 555
Wild Bunch 316, 525
Wild, Damon 4, 138, **555**
Wildchild 161, 180, **555**
Wilde, Kim 101
Wilde, Phil 529
Wilder, Alan 126, 127, 128, 299
Wiles, Timothy 531
Wilhite, Rick 387
Wilkie, Ian 295, 454
Wilkins, Mike 481
Wilkinson, Gary 178
Wilkinson, Geoff 539, 540
Wilkinson, Kevin 196
Will, Wildcat 378
Willams, Paul "Tubbs" 257
William the Conqueror 390
Williams, Andre 460
Williams, Andy 277
Williams, Boo 81, 115, 157, 535
Williams, Brian 8, 30, 305, 306, 430
Williams, Brooke 45
Williams, Charlie 30
Williams, Claude 37
Williams, Deniece 561
Williams, Freedom 77

Williams, Joe 34
Williams, John 324
Williams, Jonathan 463
Williams, L.A. 1, 182, 395
Williams, Leo 51, 152
Williams, Saul 142, 259
Williams, Tony 117, 440, 553
Williams, Victoria 330
Willing Sinners 8, 9, 10
Willis, Jez 540
Willner, Hal 315, 335, 556, **555**
Wills, David 353
Wills, John 311
Wilson, Brian 7, 168, 183, 440, 480
Wilson, Colin 256, 257
Wilson, Delroy 15, 381
Wilson, Mark 50
Wilson, Mary 282
Wilson, Phillip 293
Wilson, Ransom 427
Wilson, Ron 184
Wilson, Steven 405
Wilson, Tony 86
Wimbish, Doug 63, 459, 502
Winant, William 490, 569
Windo, Gary 556
Windross, Rose 474
Windsor for the Derby 484, **556**
Windy & Carl 204, 523, **556**
Winer, Leslie 63
Wink, Josh 140, 189, 266, 282, 351, 466, **557**
Winkies 167
Winn, Matt 113
Winnie the Pooh 280
Winstanley, Alan 428
Winters, Jonathan 132
Winwood, Muff 478
Winx 557
Wire 66, 114, 135, 330, 350, **557**, 558
Wise, Robert 304
Wiseblood 187
Wiseguys 555, **559**
Wishmountain 11, 93, 149, 150, **559**
Wisternoff, Jody 552
Witchman 47, 64, 344, 521, **559**
Withers, Bill 194
Withers, Tommy 284, 379, 380
Witzie, Adam 484, 556
Wizard of Oh 443
Wobble, Jah 28, 168, 172, 295, 373, 418, 419, 428, 455, 524
Wojnarowicz, David 354
Wolff, Christian 102, 322
Wolfgang Press **559**, 560
Wolfhounds 341
Wollbeck, Anders 21, 22
Wolpe, Stefan 526
Wonder 454
Wonder, Stevie 150, 177, 184, 258, 266, 267, 521, **560**, 561
Wondress 314
Wong, Mabel 74
Woob 46, 201, 273, **561**
Wood, Brad 129, 453, 460, 522
Woodenspoon 455
Woodentops 459
Woodford, Darren 496
Woodmansey, Mick "Woody" 64
Woodson, Craig 537
Wooley, Bruce 150
Woolford, Marc 58
Word Up 523
World Class Wreckin' Cru 92
World of Crime 463

World of Twist 438
Wormholes 517
Worrell, Bernie 72, 91, 200, 319, 386
Worthy, Gordon 273
Wozencroft, Jon 53, 552
Wright, Adrian 47
Wright, Alex 531
Wright, Norma Jean 89
Wright, Richard 396, 397
Wright, Sean 496
Wright, Syreeta 560
Wright, Tim 48, 79, 169
Wright, Wilbo 531
Wu Tang Clan 146, 172, 201, 202, 418, 469, 479
Wumpscut **561**, 562
Wuttke, Jorn Elling 11, 546
Wyatt, Robert 174, 532
Wynette, Tammy 284

# X

X Cabs 295, 423
X Ecutioners 336, 387, **563**
X Ile 34
X Men 262, 387
X-101 28, 43
X Press 2 1, 38, 57, 58, 182
X Ray Spex 456
X-303 121, 147
X., Adam 63, 138, 292
Xenakis, Iannis 2, 146, 447, 458, **563**
Xeper 56
XJacks 115
XTC 73

# Y

Ya Kid K 509
Yabby You 282
Yabe, Tadashi 536
Yamash'ta, Stomu 448
Yankovic, Weird Al 84
Yanney, Yvonne 54
Yano, Akiko 569
Yates, Kirsty 262
Yates, Neil 382
Yates, Paula 48
Yaz 99, 113, 126, 170, 171, 277, 376, 473, 494
Yazijian, Ed 109
Yazoo 59, 126, 170
Yazz 45
Ybo Two 362
Yello 372, 391, 404, 510, 511, **564**
Yellow Magic Orchestra 30, 40, 110, 261, 264, 267, 440, 441, 497, 509, **564**, 565
Yellow Sox 38
Yellowman 38, 308
Yes 71, 500, 523, 542, 543
Ylem 133
Yo La Tengo 522
Yoga Frog 262
Yona-Kit 362
Yoni 124, 549
Yoot, Tukka 539
Yorke, Thom 56, 145, 422, 537, 538
Yost, Kevin 1, 93, 161, **565**
Yothu Yindi 296
Young Brothers 101
Young Gods 135, **565**, 566
Young MC 157, 469
Young, Claude 107, 121, 298, 457, 475, 541, 542, **566**
Young, Dennis 301
Young, Earl 441

Young, LaMonte 64, 70, 102, 103, 167, 255, 314, 322, 354, 426, 427, 430, 431, 476, 480, 526, **566**, 567
Young, Larry 117
Young, Liana 6
Young, Martyn 20, 101
Young, Neil 438, 560
Young, Robert 408
Young, Steven 20, 101
Youngblood 331
Youth 23, 29, 185, 274, 372, 373, 500, 524
Ysatis, Savvas 130, 203, 457, **567**
Yun, Djong 405
Yz 6

# Z

Z Factor 445
Zaakir 275
Zacher, Gerhard 80
Zager & Evans 547, 548
Zahn, Uwe 22
Zapp 138, 161
Zappa, Frank 82, 94, 181, 412
Zappa, Frank & the Mothers of Invention 83, 132
Zauner, Stefan 12
Zawinul, Joe 117, 553, 554
Zawinul Syndicate 553
Zazou, Hector 440
Zdar, Philippe 85, 199, 344
Zeitgeist 431
Zelia 404
Zelonky, Danny 304
Zender, Stuart 266
Zeni Geva 362
Zenith 61
Zephaniah, Benjamin 498
Zeuss B. Held 190
Zeuxis & the Painted Grapes 297
Zev **568**
Zimms, Mac 279
Zion Train 155, **568**
Zippel, Chris 101
Zodiac Mindwarp & the Love Reaction 283
Zorn, John 54, 72, 142, 261, 293, 305, 315, 377, 451, 458, 521, 556, **568**, 569
Zoviet France 152, **569**
Zukie, Tapper 15
Zulutronic 267, 552, **570**
ZZ Top 300, 566
Zzino vs. Accelerator 51

# More ALL MUSIC GUIDES from BACKBEAT BOOKS:

### All Music Guide to the Blues
### Second Edition

"Easily the best blues guide." –*Real Blues*

Reissues...compilations...live recordings...new releases...new players...soundtracks...everybody's got the blues. This guide takes you straight to 6,000 great blues recordings by 900 artists–from 1920s Delta blues to 1990s Chicago electric. Plus you get a special section on the blues influence in jazz, and coverage of seminal gospel performers and recordings.
*Softcover, 658 pages, 30 charts, ISBN 0-87930-548-7, $22.95*

### All Music Guide to Jazz
### Third Edition

"An excellent resource for scholars, devotees, and casual listeners alike." –*Jazz Notes*

Start or fine-tune a sizzling jazz collection with this definitive reference. It zeroes in on 18,000 recordings by 1,700 musicians in all key styles and eras: ragtime, New Orleans jazz, classic jazz, swing, bop, Dixieland revival, cool jazz, Latin jazz, fusion, avant-garde, and more.
*Softcover, 1,378 pages, 52 charts, ISBN 0-87930-530-4, $29.95*

### All Music Guide to Country

"A definite must for any serious music collector." –*Country Song Roundup*

This is the comprehensive guide to the entire spectrum of country music–from the Grand Ole Opry to the sounds of today's Nashville superstars. Designed for devoted fans and newcomers alike, this book covers 5,500 cream-of-the-crop recordings by 1,000 top country artists.
*Softcover, 611 pages, 14 charts, ISBN 0-87930-475-8, $22.95*

### All Music Guide to Rock
### Third Edition

"Best rock guide of the year." –*The Seattle Times*

Get the ultimate guide to the artists and recordings that really rock. Reflecting the ever-evolving world of rock, pop and soul, this book reviews 12,000 albums by 2,000 performers–everything from rockabilly to British Invasion, Motown, folk rock, psychedelic rock, funk, punk, R&B, hip-hop, and more.
*Softcover, 1,300 pages, 50 charts, ISBN 0-87930-653-X, $29.95, November 2001*

### All Music Guide
### Fourth Edition

"A record buyer's bible. Four stars." –*Q*

This is the classic reference for enjoying distinctive recordings in 20 genres: world music, avant-garde, reggae, bluegrass, gospel, folk, cajun, rap, and much more. You'll find 20,000 albums by 4,000 musicians, with "essential collections" and "first purchases" noted to help you refine and expand your entire music collection.
*Softcover, 1,400pp, 30 charts, ISBN 0-87930-627-0, $32.95, August 2001*

**AVAILABLE AT FINE BOOK AND MUSIC STORES EVERYWHERE. OR CONTACT:**

Backbeat Books • 6600 Silacci Way • Gilroy, CA 95020 USA • **Phone Toll Free: (866) 222-5232**
• Fax: (408) 848-5784 • E-mail: backbeat@rushorder.com • Web: www.backbeatbooks.com